AWAKEN TO A DREAM

Joy Esterby, Editor
Amanda D'Wynter, Associate Editor

THE INTERNATIONAL LIBRARY OF POETRY

Awaken to a Dream

ISBN 1-57553-181-X

Printing and Binding by
BPC Wheatons Ltd, Exeter, UK

Editor's Note

The line separating truth and fiction is often a fine one. This is why humans are constantly motivated to test the definition of reality. What happens to our souls after death? Is life as we know it reality? Or are we actually living a dream? And what about the everyday mysteries of life? Do flowers feel pain? What do animals think? The poets within *Awaken to a Dream* seek to awaken our minds and our senses to reality as they perceive it.

Peter Linden's "Once When in Autumn" (p. 193) relates the persona's experience of becoming one with the world and thus learning what he believes to be "the truth". Linden creates original hyphenated words to compose an eloquent collection of sensory experiences which lead to his great revelation. The first two lines of the poem clearly demonstrate Linden's originality:

> *Once, when in my new eyes, I caught the rainbow*
> *And sucked it in whole-hungered, marrow-deep.*

The phrase "when in my new eyes" suggests that the persona is observing autumn as if for the first time. Linden cleverly arranges words in such a way as to allow his readers to see autumn in a different light as well. The hyphenated words "whole-hungered" and "marrow-deep" lend an increased intensity to the experience of seeing a rainbow. Figuratively speaking, the persona swallows every last morsel of this awe-inspiring occurrence, down to its very "marrow".

As the poem continues, the reader follows the persona on his journey, each stanza representing a stage in his pilgrimage to "the truth". Linden begins each stanza with the word "once", suggesting how fleeting the moments of clear revelation are throughout a lifetime. In the third stanza, the persona comes in contact with the awesome reality of death:

> *Once, when in the heartbreak of a year, I climbed the mist*
> *With eyes shroud-hung in funeral weeds of change,*
> *The milk-wet surface lipped and drowned the tottering sun;*
> *And on the sleep-wound hill I knew*
> *My clay was Adam-found.*

Nature mirrors the persona's emotions: the mist is a shroud; ugly weeds overtake the landscape; the "tottering" sun has drowned. The persona sadly realizes his own mortality; that, like the Biblical Adam, he is made from clay and shall return to dust when he dies.

Yet, by realising the transience of his flesh, in the last stanza the persona is able to release his spirit into the world and thus achieve union with it:

> *My cockle-frame dissolved and flew the reel of leaf-turned force;*
> *Alone, incorporeal, I touched the truth.*
> *I was the world.*

The cockle-frame represents the boundaries around the persona's heart and soul. As it dissolves, his soul can swirl like the leaves in the wind, and he can truly transcend all human limits. Peter Linden essentially creates a masterpiece of language and form to convey a powerfully intense feeling of freedom.

Douglas Dunker also considers the human condition in his poem "A Kind of Consolation" (p. 495). Dunker contends that humans are constantly looking for happiness, or a "kind of consolation", amidst the pain of living. He compares this with the example of nature:

> How unlike the solitary bee
> feasting on copious cornucopias
> and the heavy scent of honeysuckle,
> We try to pick out one specimen
> from a dense cloud of insects,

While the bee is flitting from flower to flower enjoying the feast of nectar it gets from each one, humans often search for the specific things in life which they believe will make them happy or bring enjoyment. Specific things, however, are much more difficult to find. For instance, how do you pick out "one solo song amid / the senseless sea gulls' clamour"?

In the second stanza, Dunker educates us as to how humans are saved despite their fruitless searching:

> But somewhere in the crude ingredients
> there lingers yet some love and loveliness,
> a curtain of remembered kindness,
>
> . . . .
> and somehow, somewhere, sometimes
> our little anger is humbled by the thunder
> and a quietness, a kind of consolation
> eases into the secret space behind the pain.

There are little things which happen every day--a hug from a friend, the opening of a rosebud, the purr of a cat--that can bring us great enjoyment if we allow them, or at least ease the discontent we may feel in our lives.

In "A Sonnet to Kieselguhr" (p. 466), John Spooner addresses one such pain in life-- the pain of deceit. Using the form of a classic Shakespearean sonnet, Spooner paints a disturbing portrait of the mining industry:

> When rising throats forgo the unforseen
> Take all their cares to call the rusting claw,
> For journeys may be cautious or obscene,
> And fancy fires create the blemished law.

The "rising throats" are caused by the inhalation of mining dust, yet the miners must "call the rusting claw", or take up their tools and move forward with their work, despite the constant danger of black lung or cave-ins. Their work provides fuel for the "fancy fires" of the rich; therefore, the law does not protect the working class miners or halt their unsafe working conditions. The mining industry has become a "symbol" in the world now, complete with its own songs and legends:

> *What shall deny the symbol's comely rest?*
> *Though fitter lays bemuse and never dread,*
> *Their wily ones recant the royal jest.*

Thankfully, the mining industry's health standards are no longer as they were in the past, yet we are still reminded of the deceitful nature of the industry through the songs that speak of the "royal jest". Spooner ends his verse with a lesson for us to learn from the miners:

> *Give heed to he who draws the ample guise!*
> *It merits not the waking feast of lies.*

Spooner writes a polished piece using an economy of words, and his concise language effectively creates a riddle for the reader to unravel. Not coincidentally, Spooner is showing that the truth behind the mining industry was also a puzzle to be solved.

Audrey West's "Pica in a Western Jamaican Woman" (p. 558) is a study into the truth about human ancestry and its importance. "Pica" is defined as a mental disorder which causes the craving for non-food items. On the surface the persona has this unfortunate condition; it makes her "gnaw" on her daughter's "miniature soapstone rabbit". By opening the poem with this bizarre image, West immediately grabs the reader's attention. Then she considers the mystery of this unusual craving:

> *Why the urge? How long possessed?*
> *What prehistoric desires*
> *link with ancestors, dust to dust?*

As the poem continues, West surmises that perhaps all humans have inside them the desire to be a part of their ancestry and their homeland:

> *Going towards Eastbourne in the train*
> *the sight of a chalk cliff face*
> *stirred up longing*
> *like for chocolate or sex*
> *for living or for dying*
>
> *Like all these things*
> *I could do without*
> *my piece of soil*
> *but I will always want*

The persona refers to her "piece of soil" as something for which she longs. In the context of the mental disorder, the reader can picture the persona physically eating the chalk of a cliff and the soil of the earth; this makes the metaphorical image more clear. The persona feels the universal desire to "consume" her ancestry, her roots, so that it becomes a part of her in a real sense.

There are other poems featured within this anthology which you will not want to miss: "The Old Year Passes" (p. 586) by Edward Denyer Cox, "Cueva De La Pileta" (p. 536) by Linda Terry, and D. A. Hipwell's "Snow Garden" (P. 471). In fact, there are too many excellent poems to name in the space I have. All poets whose work is contained within the pages of *Awaken to a Dream* should be proud of their accomplishments.

I would like to say a special thanks to those who have made *Awaken to a Dream* possible. The editors, assistant editors, graphic designers, and customer service representatives have all brought their talents to bear on this project and I sincerely appreciate their assistance.

Joy L. Esterby
Editor

Featured Poetry

"Who Knows"

"Sitting here in my sheltered seclusion hiding
from life and all its confusion; I contemplate
all I can't emulate in not succumbing to the
conformity of life's social apathy."
"As time rolls on just like a ball, I wonder
if I'm here at all; or just a speck upon a
wall, a pebble on a beach; a blade of grass,
or even the bottom of a glass - suppressed in
darkness till it's lifted, thrown to break or even tilted."
"You tell me, I'd like to know if I'm not
really a drop of snow on a flower's petal, or
just the molecule in a metal; in another world
that I don't know, wandering about unromantic for
who is to say what is not problematic when a
tormented soul is so tragic...

Edward Crawford

The Teacher

The teacher has a grumpy look
with a solid face and a bristle eye
which turns towards my desk.
I gulp!
Then she said to me,
"Stop talking, girl, and sit down in your seat."
"But I have to borrow a pen."
Now the teacher's steaming red and what do I do?
I look at Miss Maple who just walked in the door.
The place goes silent.
I bend to sit but miss the chair
and hurt my bum.
"I want my mum", I scream.
She says, "Don't be silly, girl."
I grab for the table and pull myself up.
I reach for the pen,
I've got it!
"Now I'm alright, Miss."

Joanna Thompson

Moon Mood

The moon has a mood tonight my lady.
Afraid to venture forth.
It hides itself in heavenly state
behind a gathering cloud.
Nor will it meet tonight our rendezvous.
A tryst to keep it steals away awhile.
Behind that shroud of silent cloud.
Transparent not in deep or word.
It mingles with that fleecy herd.
Come we must keep our trust,
Let not like flowers in the dust, die for want of rain.
That moon will again in heavenly splendour reign.
And like into the darkest hour,
Restore the light again.

E. V. Walkden

The Silken Billows

Ever westward, ever free, as she glides upon the sea
past the peaks of ice and snow, watch the Silken Billows blow.

And she glides just like a dove, the only woman we can love,
there's a dragon on her bow, watch the Silken Billows blow.

She stands ready now for war.   She can never shed a tear, will
we live? I do not know, watch the Silken Billows blow.

Soon the truth will be revealed, forty axe men with their shield,
but our fear we will not show, watch the Silken Billows blow.

Hear the lonely raven cry for those brave men who'll soon die,
for the sword will lay them low, watch the Silken Billows blow.

In my dreams I heard her sing we'd have Harald for our king,
but to him we shall not bow, watch the Silken Billows blow.

Ever westward to stay free, our old homeland we'll ne'er see,
to a new land we must go to watch those Silken Billows blow.

Ron Greer

Morning Light

Ripples of water
glistening in the morning light,
the weeping willow dips
as a soft breeze came
embracing every bud
with a magic spell of light,
cold is the earth,
after winters night.
All seems asleep
until silver turns to gold
and the sun embraces are no longer cold,
the snowdrop hangs her head
in slender pride,
the buttercups soon will open wide
and stay awake until the day is done
then fold their silken petals one by one
there is no power on earth
to stop this miracle we see
that is how it is and will always be.

Betty Thomson

Marloes

Patterns wrought upon the sands
By wind-driven, white flecked waves;
Bald headlands, green atop, dun red below,
Stand fast against th'unceasing wear
Of water, time and winds.

Bright shadows sprint across the scene,
Lighting here on jumbled rocks
And there on sparkling secret pools.
What unseen treasures lie within their depths?

Feathered fliers float o'er all,
Wheeling, soaring, diving,
Winning movement from the winds;
Their strident calls are all that breaks
The silence, deep yet peaceful.

Human print nor sign intrudes
Upon the Marloes Sands.

John Bambrook

The One

You are;
The one I cherish and always will
The one I need, my dream to fulfil
The one to share my whole life through
The one to say I love you too
The one to come to when the day is done
The one to laugh with and to cry
The one to listen and not question why
The one true love a lifetime brings
The one true friend to my mind, springs
The one person on earth there's no-one above
The one perfect partner I give my love
The one and only yes it's true
The one, The only, I love you.

Denis McDermott

The Viking 793

The long boats came so long ago,
With dragon like ships they did row.
Up estuaries they would make their route.
Only to pillage, and scourge and loot.
So there they stood, so good they feel,
Seven feet tall, and wrists like steel,
They worship their Gods, Odin and Thor.
Only to help them with their war,
Fear ran through the village ward.
How could they fight these men of Norse.
Yet once they had settled in their stake.
Good and generous men they would make.
But now, have gone these Viking men.
Now only to find remains of them.

C. Pentelow

"For Sale"

What life was cherished within their walls?
No grand staircase here, or pillared halls.
Crumbling masonry and rotting boards.
Bent shoulders and lowered heads
Has this home enclosed?

Patient, determined grimaces,
Pink-wrinkled babies,
Firm-brown limbs and
White-veiled-radiance
Once passed here.
Summer brought oppressive, stifling heat
But winter cosy firelight embraces.

Roses patterning the bulging walls,
Low, painted architraves, boarded doors.
Black-leaded grates once shone with pride.
Cobwebby casements low and small
(All) once wrought with muscle and sweat
Silently waiting fateful destruction by man's noisy, steel
invention.

Frances L. Fleet

My Antique Tea Pot

I have a little tea pot and I cherish it with glee
It belonged to my mother long before I came to be.
She saw it in a window when she was only ten.
And the price they wanted for it was 6 old pence back then.

Six pence was too high a price for her to pay you know.
All she had was two pence! For the rest where would she go?
So halfpennies were gathered up from friends and family.
And so she bought her treasure and brought it home for all to see.

That's almost ninety years ago and my mother has long since died.
But I love to tell this story and remember her with pride.

Mary Brady

Look Into Your Soul

You can't predict a lifetime of futures mystery,
It is set out like a giant book and takes its places in history.
No matter what unhappiness you stumble on in life,
There will be much brighter things to remove the pain and strife.
As you end another chapter - so another begins,
A door will always open as the light behind you dims.
Sometimes you have to sacrifice a possession or a friend.
But greater strength you will acquire for the beginning not the end.
With this strength and hopeful heart a new era is begun.
And don't forget, for battles lost there are battles to be won.
Decisions are not easy, do you follow your heart or head?
You must choose what is being born, not what is already dead.
You know your tears will fall again, like dew drops from a rose,
But for every rose that is watered down a bigger one soon grows.
Remember what is said to you - a fragile heart is bad.
And when you find an inner strength love will not be so sad.
So when the battle's over and victory is won,
Stand up and be counted, for you are the cherished one.

Kim Louise Thomas

Sammy Snail

This little verse is to tell the tale
Of a little creature called Sammy Snail
His head was round and his tail slim
Wherever he went his house went with him

It was lovely in his garden glade
He liked it best in the damp shade
Beneath some stone or maybe a tile
He certainly could live there in style

If it should rain or even hail
He could withdraw into his shell
He's lucky of course and never does grouse
Because wherever he goes he takes his house.

R. H. Stephens

To Flo

Green was the grass where the sun shone down,
Golden its rays - and cheering.
Verdant too was the leafy crown
Of the tree in the earthy clearing.

Purple and mauve, the shrubs in bowers
Proffered their treasures fine.
I thought: if wealth is in plants and flowers,
It is mine, that wealth, all mine...

Gone were the colours when nightfall came,
Its darkness my garden hiding.
From border to border it seemed the same,
Only the gloom abiding.

Seeing naught else, I looked at my heart
And found it began to shine.
I thought: Of course, for it's something apart:
It is thine, that heart, all thine!

Peter S. A. Cooper

Memories

I stare at her picture and try to remember the sound of her
voice, her smile, her laugh.
I smile, as the memories come flooding back.
I see her sitting in her chair, holding out her arms for a cuddle
as I've just arrived home from school.
She enquires on my day.
I kneel by her chair and tell her all the funny events that have
happened.
Her face lights up with laughter,
I look down and see we're holding hands.
Then suddenly the phone rings and I hit reality with a bump.
I stare at the picture and no longer just see an image frozen in time,
I now see the person I loved, the person I miss.
I now remember my Nan.

Cathryn Panks

'A Highland Journey'

Cloudy skies and waters calm bathe the sleepy dawn,
As busy wheels and changing reels excite the early morn,
A morn without concrete mould to obscure the well set scene,
Where mountain air and nature's sound does kiss the lazy stream
Faster, faster the new age speeds on the country's more
     gentle breast
Where babes and kids and adults too witness the old and
     new's unrest,
The old with firm identities, the new with brash ideas,
The old steeped in centuries, the new engulfed in fears.
'Animals in a field' cried a wayward well fed child
As if eternity's triumphs past were discovered as anew.
Briefly, slowly, rendezvous are made at stages on the way,
And maybe by chance, there is, to glimpse yesterday, mourn
     today,
New scenes unfold as nature's slight of hand does play
Some kind of magical mystical move to give four seasons in a day.
Suddenly the nest, a whisper travels and welcomes do abound,
And as they subside, images reside without a trace or sound.

David J. Will

My Creek Boy

My creek boy
My little boy
My big boy
My man.
We are what we are just for each other
Stay with me always, my man and my lover.
My creek boy, my man.
You are as eternal an the trees that you plant,
As the seeds that you sow.
As the tides come and go.
You will always be there
My creek boy, my man.

Mary Parrish

Homeland

Beneath the wolds, the valley unfolds,
Revealing rich countryside,
The fields and the hedgerow, the gardens and homes
Where country people reside.

Every tree is the home of some little creature,
Every hole is a haven, for a rabbit or mole,
Every pathway delights the country rambler,
Every hedge provides shelter from the winter's cold.

The streams and the springs trickle down from the hillside
To the valley and winding river below,
This is the home of the swans and their cygnets
The moorhens and ducks watching little ones grow.

High up in the sky, the hawk is hovering,
Keenly watching for movement below,
Down in the pasture or corn crop,
Growing in stretches, and row upon row.

The cuckoo has been here and whistled his tune,
Now, we look, for the bright glowworm in June,
In the lovely valley beneath the Wolds,
Which truly the heart of the country enfolds.

N. M. Walker

Death Of A Cowboy

They came like thunder in the night
Hooves pounding the ground
Thudding with the fright
Of a thousand stampeding horses
But only ten men rode with the wind and rain
to bring the fateful news that
Ben had disappeared into the darkness

The horses snorted and stamped
impatiently awaiting their stables
tired from the night ride
after the long flight through terror filled canyons
forest, desert and finally the shallow creek
just beyond the edge of town

Morning light came without the dawn chorus
The town melted slowly into the daylight hours
The people floated past the sheriff's office;
No-one could bring themselves to look inside

Ben's horse came home today; alone
There was blood on the saddle

Lesley Lock

The Solitary Piper

A solitary piper in a lonely valley stands
An eerie sound emerging from the bagpipes in his hands
It echoes round that valley and away the music goes
As a piper pipes his tribute in the only way he knows.

A solitary piper in the hellish trenches plays
As battle follows battle and the hours grow into days
Weary soldiers in these foreign fields leap up and charge the foe
Bewitched by the melody that follows where they go.

A solitary piper plays as countless have before
Though around him lie the bodies of the men who'll rise no more
Yet still he marches at the fore playing with all his might
Armed only with his pipes he is the first to reach the fight.

A solitary piper on a lonely hilltop stands
An eerie sound emerging from the bagpipes in his hands
And all around him shadows dance, called by his age old tune
To do its bidding once again by the light of the ghostly moon.

What tribute is more fitting to the men who'll rise no more
Than the wailing of the bagpipes that led them into war?
Tears have washed away the blood and yet the scar remains
Highlighted forever in the piper's eerie strains.

Camilla Fraser

Weather Worn

It's Ecstasy!
This life that be,
well, at least today, it is for me.
Definitely not due to the material riches of the lottery.

For today the weighted dark cloud
edged away subtle, letting in a warm ray,
momentarily shifting that they shroud,
for the little pale buds to come out to sway.

It will not after all bury me, this foggy wet melancholy,
that torturously infests degree by degree
what in my possession is a minute sense of purificatory.
No, no, it cannot choke me inevitably.

Even if it be for a precious short spell
the lumination cleared the vision of a damp hell,
to focus on the beauty about a previously closed shell.

A. Coad

What Is Love?

No documents nor vow guarantees it
Not available on prescription
No good and honest witch supplies a potion of it
No shop sells a pound of it or even an ounce of it.
Not gathered in any meadow.
We can't see it. We can't touch it. We can only feel it.

It's like a will-o'-the-wisp
It just happens, in its own time, at its own bidding.
It's layer-upon-layer of wishes and kisses and promises and dreams.
It needs a guardian angel to protect it
and a sage to guide us.
Love can slip and slither from our grasp.
Careful! Clasp tenderly.

When in love, beware!
Temptations lurk everywhere.
Could you bear the pain of falling from grace?
Desire flounders and drifts away
True love cuts deep into the heart.
Hearts bleed, they don't shed tears.

Mary B. Brown

Autumn Woods

A hint of fog in the air,
A sudden chill on the breath of the wind,
The gleam of the sun's dying rays
Through the canopy of the trees.
The sudden hurry and scurry, and the glimpse of
    bronze fur in the tree tops:
Berries glowing red and orange like warning lights,
And nuts clustering thickly in the hedgerows.
A faint elusive scent of bracken,
And the smoke from a distant bonfire
Twisting and writhing against the purple haze.
The sound of the stream rippling
Between the shaded banks,
And the blur of wings as the kingfisher
Darts and swoops and disappears.
The peace and beauty of an Autumn evening
Before the night of Winter.

Edith N. Kellow

Untitled

The air conditioning groaning away,
Fighting the heat of another sweltering day.
The breeze blows often, though not cool enough.
The birds in the sky fly aimlessly above.
It's peaceful it's quiet, the view is serene,
Oh how cool it must be, in the mountains above.
The groaning is now a welcoming buzz,
Enough to send you to sleep, and dreams of mountains aloft.
Oh for the cool of a mountain resort,
Though swap it for this? No, I think not.

Fiona Middleton

The Tree

She was my friend in idealistic youth
And cradled in her arms I'd often lie
Watching the summer breeze play in her hair.
It made no difference what each new day brought,
Sorrow or joy, she always understood,
Was always there with outstretched arms that waved
A greeting as I hurried to her side.
One day she spoke these words I marked them well,
"I am eternal, as are all things fair,
A spirit being nothing can destroy,
Lean now on me and when the pangs of life strike,
Come, and I will soothe your heart and pain".
I stroked her smooth, grey face and I believed.
Later in time and burdened with the years
Her words came back through mists of memory,
I took my tears to her, only to find
A stump - left by some reckless, wanton blade.

G. R. Keith

Remember

Together we sit, yet each one alone,
Strangers who love and laughter have known.
Once we were carefree, young and gay,
When did shadows come, our dreams slip away?
What of our child, our pride, our joy?
God's wonderful gift, our baby boy.
Born out of love we both knew,
In the years we shared, all too few.
If I hold out my hand will you remember all this,
Turn to me, not with a sigh, but a kiss?

Ann Metcalfe

Moon Glow

O lovely moon high in the sky
Explain to me who you are and why
You grant us your gentle gracious light
Asking nothing in return for your might.

The twinkling stars stay by your side,
Are you their father figure, a gentle guide?
Do you ever look down on us in pity, puzzled how
We ever got into the muddle we are in now.

Whilst gazing down on us folk, what do you see,
Trouble, strife, sickness and misery?
All fault is ours - we are all to blame -
Each one of us should hang down our heads for shame.

Some folk will look up and see a bright new moon.
At least you are called that as of you they croon.
Love and romance, love forever true,
A blue moon, a silvery moon, yet always it is you.

O moon someday we will learn to be true,
Forever and always - just like you.
To shine out brightly and show that we care,
Sprinkle our light for others to share.

Maureen Connelly

Alice Through An Empty Glass

Life can be kind yet often cruel,
my feeling conflict, an emotional duel
are things true? Is life what it seems?
Or am I lost like Alice? Dancing through dreams.

Sometimes love, sometimes hate!
Should life be planned? Or left to fate?
Was I here today? Or am I someone I dreamed?
"Curiouser and curiouser" Alice screamed!

They say "Do Not Lie", is the truth any better?
Or merely words, held together letter by letter.
Why am I here? Do I have a choice?
Do you feel my words? Or just hear my voice?
No need for this conflict?
No point feeling sad! As the cat said to Alice,
"We all must be mad".

D. J. Jovetic

In My Mind

In the colour of a song's flight,
I fall into my suffocating night.
I appeal for what will never be.
I weep for love that never came to me.
I cry out for unknown caresses that died
Without fruition. Fictions of me. I lied.
To keep my truth I lived too long alone.
Alone, my hope screamed, fading to a moan.
I never found the love I believed in.
I put all my faith in dreams. For that sin
I loveless lie, in false embraces.
Tears chain me down with their traces,
Over my cheeks. Rips me apart.
My dark loneliness mirrors my heart.
I shall never feel, never know
The truth of love. Let it all go.
All I have left are the final songs,
Dying away. Who can belong
In my world, live in my nation?
I live in a torment of my creation.

Jackie Lowy

Best Day Of The Week

Saturday morning pictures
Were the highlight of our week
We always had a sixpence
To secure our favourite seat.

Settled at last and comfy
Our group at last would sing
The chorus on the big screen
Which rose our adrenalin.

"We like to laugh and have our sing song
Such a happy crowd are we
We're all pals together
We're members of the A.B.C."

Watching "Hi Ho Silver"
"Batman and his Batmobile"
Cartoon characters featured
To us it seemed so real.

We loved our Saturday mornings
Only a child would understand
What those two hours meant to us
For we lived in wonderland.

C. E. Giles

Kingdom Of Mist

Misty morning
Conifers bathed in dew
Tall, majestic, emerald kings in a fairyland
Their shadows cast to mark supremacy
Wood pigeons call
Caretakers of the trees in royal chant
All is well
Flapping wings, like toy-land gunfire through the silence
From tree to tree, for sovereign and servant
Survival begins a new day
Gossamer cobwebs sprinkled with dewdrops
Diamonds glistening in the pale morning sun
As sun and mist fight for command
Silken drapes, designed by tiny creature architects
Guardians to the palace jewels
Enticing with deadly intent
Sun conquers mist
Magic fades
Emerald kings give up their crowns
To await the coming of another dawn

Patricia A. Maubec

6

Suicide

In a lonely place of desolation.
By a misty field, at the murky dawn of The Last Day,
stood an armed guardian of the last men left alive.
Believers only in all that can be seen and touched
and therefor is.
"Who goes there?" Said the soldier.
"Nobody." Was the calm reply.
"Where are you going?" Asked the soldier.
"Nowhere." Was the calm reply.
"I know you." Said the soldier.
"Yes."
"Are you friend, or foe?"
Both.
"Don't come any closer, or I must shoot,
don't come any closer!"
"What is your name?" Said the soldier, as he fired his gun.
"God."
Said the man, as he died.

Bridget Thomas

My Love For Princess

You are my little friend, Princess, since you came to stay last year
The charity knew I'd give you a life that's always free from fear
Your needs are easy to deal with and of love you have my share
I'm so pleased you let me hold you in my arms of tender care.

I wonder what went through your mind as the bond between us grew
You look at me with trusting eyes, so round and azure blue
You really are a lovely cat as you are standing there
As first I comb and then I brush your fine silky white hair.

When I pull string across the floor, on the end of it you pounce
I throw small sponge balls up the stairs and you chase them
    as they bounce
I am amused when you mark time upon my thighs and lap
Then you look so contented as you curl up for a nap.

When I feel your head is rubbing against my legs and feet
I know you're trying to tell me you want something to eat
In winter time you often sleep upon my bed at night
Every time you lie beside me you keep me warm all right

You prowl around the garden and walk indoors with lots of grace
You show me love and affection by licking my hands and face
Your purring as I stroke you is a splendid sound to hear
I hope that our friendship will extend for many a year.

Rodney Dean

The Right To Die

What could be more ethical than to allow free choice,
A person may be dying, but they've a sound mind and a voice,
Should it really come into account, the fact it may be murder.
Or are they just going to suffer with their lives prolonged
    much further.
Where is the moral reasoning in extending their pain as they cry,
When an end will come with no hope found, they whither
    away and die,
I can never comprehend how justice takes its toll,
When all but the person suffering, take that feeble life in control.

Sally L. Woods

Faded Girl

When I saw him for the first time,
My heart skipped a beat.
He was no longer that silly little boy always playing practical
Jokes on everyone.
The smile that could kill
Those eyes you could melt in
I'd hope he would look over
And flash me a smile that would make my heart beat ten
Times faster
I seem not to exist to him
I'm just that faded girl in the back round
Maybe someday he will notice me
Before it's too late!

Nicola Legassick

Invitation To Visit A Friend

A gorgeous lunch was already laid.
We sat down to eat, all of which we enjoyed.
Our friend took us walk some letters to deliver
We had to tread carefully, the road was like a river

Looking through the window thee rain has come to stay
April is truly over and we'll soon be into May
We need lots of sunshine, everywhere is drenched
Tramping through the fields it's squelsh, squelsh, squelsh

We went to church this morning, a good sermon we heard
And rushed home quickly to get the dinner prepared
Today it is five, and so southport we went
And called at the farm shop with good intent

Caulies and carrots were bought, they were scarce,
Surprised and pleased, it was easy on the purse
I have a freezer and must stock it well
For any visitors, or when I am unwell,

Then the meals are ready, no worries for me
I just take things out, ready prepared you see
We arrived in southport a little later on
And soured through the shops and onto the prom

L. Govan

The Sea

What fascination the sea has for me,
Its arms stretch wide as far as can be!
The toils the troubles the fears it shall keep,
For the sea is silent, and the secrets are deep.
The sea is a friend, the sea is a foe, one day
It will take me as deep as it goes.
Goodbye to sorrow, no more tomorrow,
So there is the end, the end of all strife
The end of all time, a nothing a life.
The sea is the king the master of all
Once in the sea, there's nowhere to fall...

Joan Barrett

Silences

In life it's the simple things that matter.
The walking with you. The shouting at the dog.
The sometimes talking. The sometimes not.
In the silence the river oblivious to you and me.
Reflected on its grey shiny hide the trees, and sentinel herons
Guarding who knows what, who cares what!

The sky, off white, hides the sun and time till weary,
We turn into the cold blue of evening and home
Where in the warm the cold peels off and leaves us there.
And in the quiet between words, you listened to our time ticking by
And I, to the somnolent Paris dreaming in his lair.

The summer evenings are warm and blue and the
Silences less friendly, and I can't and don't see you,
When unawares you reach out and into me and
Twist me round and round.

George W. Douglas

The Death Of Our English Elms

And as our elms begin to die
With scarred branches reaching to the sky,
Just standing there, as though betrayed
As upon our fires their logs we laid:
And leaving gaps in roadside hedge,
With loss shelter at forest edge -
Their summer beauty, we'll no longer see,
So sadly missed, by bird and bee:
And now, as we walk our country lanes
Their limbs stretching up - like weathering veins,
English elms - hearts are bled
By a mysterious bug that we dread,
And as I watch them at their end
It was as though I'd lost a friend.....

Brian Ducker

Decade Of Gold

My Golden Girl you are to me
The summer and the Spring
Would I were your constant love I'd sing
My world would burst to song
Of love the whole day long
Your Golden face with shining eyes

Would every day light up the skies
Love me love you I do adore
Without your love I am so poor
Your love I know will yet respond
My Golden Girl with shining eyes
Please Please evermore for me
    Light up the skies.

The Honourable Percival E. Pyke

The Pain In Dunblane

The pain we all feel is universal,
The words we utter offer no condolence,
I can find no meaning,
I have no understanding
How innocents can be so brutally slain,
Fresh young flowers cut short from their bloom.

My heart feels numb,
My mind is blank, such is my grief.
But I cannot compare my pain to that of a parent,
Desolation, shock and utter disbelief,
I shake my head,
of how this act came to be.

Fear not of this pain,
For it is God we turn to,
To answer our questions,
And unburden our hearts.
For it is he who will guide us in our time of need,
And help us understand
Through the power of time why this came to be.

Vipula Bist

It Is Gone

It has gone now
Everything is over
An eternity of limbo
After the end but before the beginning
Now is the time of peaceful forgetfulness
But a lifetime of remembrance
Hopes for the future
And longings for the past
This is time
But in this there is no time present

S. Gordon

The Note

I feel my life drawing to a close
I'll lie in wait but not in pose
The suicide note it lies near
I hope I've made myself very clear
Yours is not to reason why
'Twas my decision to want to die
The lands that I have left behind
Can't be better than the new I'll find
I know I take a chance on torment
but the previous land in which I was sent
I did not mix or make a match
I must have come from a very poor batch
For those of you that tried so hard
To keep my ace the winning card
Thanks for persevering so long
but now it's time I must be gone
Sorry for bowing out at this stage
but the internal me is full of rage
promise me this the path you take
is not the one that I've had to make.

Josie Anderson

The Lasting Lesson

The world is full of laughter, of joys and love untold.
God made this world of wonder and gave it to His fold.
But something happened to this beauty; it's gone just like our
    laughter.
If we should ever get it back, let's answer what comes after.

Vain promises, what use are they, if they're kept for just a day?
For wars are not won if the peace does not stay.
All the horrors of war were not meant by our Creator;
We started off with Paradise, but the evils came on later.

For there are none so blind as those who will not see
And there are none so helpless as those who are not free;
If men are to dig in mines, in the bowels of the earth,
Let us show them honour, and pay them what they're worth.

Let us keep our children, the flowers that are our sons;
Give them now our pledge to keep, relieve them of their guns.
Let's keep our post-war promises; gain peace instead of strife;
For to keep our freedom is to keep our life.

Fascism is the evil, their treachery and lies;
This first we must destroy, there is no compromise.
When our children learn their lesson, with history as their tutor,
There is no good live Fascist if the world's to have a future.

Mildred Frey-Michaels

Lady Of The Night

Night-time basks in the moon's elegance
as she dances through the sky
In her flowing negligé she's a temptress
many say.
Shades of white and that of grey
hints of silver interlayed
giving colour to her face, adding to her
simple grace.
She is the keeper of the night
Sending hope to sleepers' sight.
In their dreams she spins her web
leading them to worlds untread.
Ageless youth she does possess
but it would never rule her head
Darkness is her shining knight
who does fill her with delight.
Always tender but will fight
if a suitor set its might
on his lady of the night.

Amanda Elphick

One Act Play In Seven Scenes

Curled in the fleshly womb
lay this drama's lead actor

Folded in babyhood
he drank the warm milk of love

Through village street and hills
the small child ran rejoicingly

Nazareth and home could not contain the urgent boy
Jerusalem - the temple court - became the stage for the next scene

Now through all Palestine
the Man taught and brought healing life and hope

But then the climax came -
with stark cross and darkened sky and wounded hands
outstretched
and words of pain and love

Some applauded, others wept
but when the last scene came, the curtain was not drawn
but opened wide, from heaven to earth, so all could see that
Light -
pouring forth from His great act
to illuminate the world

Deirdre Daniel-Baker

Memories Of Jesmond Vale

In a little grey stoned mill house,
in a place called Jesmond Vale
'Twas there I was born, therein lies a tale
There I learned to walk and talk and paddle in the burn.
Progress it seems has ended the dream to retire in the dale.
   To-day I am a gran, old and worn, I'd
give my all to wander round the burn
hoppings there was, stotty cakes, toffee apples,
pears, willicks, galore.
All for a halfpenny a time, down by the shore
   A great big family, the valers were
Uncle and Aunts, the bairns had by the score.
Granddad's and grandma's, there were a few
which were which, and who's were who
the bairns of village, never knew,
great times, we had in the green pool
fields. Picnic's, and dancing with our parents indeed
To share in our fun, and pleasure was great
nothing, can ever compare, life in the village then
with to days Match Box Estate.
   Emily L. Ellison

The Grandparents

Today, again I paid another visit,
and again could I see the consequences
that time had etched upon their faces.
Those three over-eighty year olds,
My grandparents and grandma's sister,
Great Auntie Doris who lives there now.
The slow routine of their days
upsets me. Always in their chairs
of an afternoon, they take the same ones
all the time.
The visitors are never many but never enough.
Time hangs. The lock ticks and recriminations
for lack of visits increase in my mind.
News of the family? What has been going on?
Is mummy coming tomorrow? How could I know
all those things?
My young life bears no resemblance to theirs
yet I know, deep down, one day, it could be me
relying on a grandchild, a little kiss,
a word of comfort, a small deed one.
   Anne Wheeler

The Lollipop Lady

There once was a Lollipop Lady
Helping children to cross the road
Some walked quite nice and behaved themselves
But others acted like toads.

On some sunny mornings
Some mothers stop by for a chat
Some tell of all their troubles
and the men talk of this and that.

Some holidays are long ones
and some mothers think that they are a pain
But when at last they are all over
There are tears because it is all back to school again.

Wet days are a problem,
standing in the rain
All she can dream of home
or watch the water running down the drains.

But when the day is over
and she puts her stick away
All she really wants to do is
say Hip Hip Hooray!
   D. Sheasby

The Pipes Of Pan

Oh foolish man, do you believe
That life's whole purpose you can cheat?
And love - the string of life deceive
Yet still declare the world is sweet?

Can you not hear the pipes of Pan?
The song of Aphrodite still?
And know it was of love she sang
And not of fleshy seed to spill.

When on the battle ground you stand
And call upon the Gods above
Is it for lusty flesh you ask -
Or for the strength of those you love?

Poor silly flower - What do you think
Your petals are - dropped one by one.
It is the whole bloom, proud and true
That rises to the morning sun.

And when your empty world is strewn,
This breast and that, from womb to womb,
You will not hear the pipes of Pan
For life is dead. Oh foolish man.
   Priscilla Greville

The Laggan

Oh my homeland how I love thee
And my thoughts are oft times there.
With heavenly skies clear blue above me
And bird song always fills the air.

I wish I could be there once more
To stroll on Machrihanish Bay,
Golden sunshine steeps the shore
And washes all my cares away.

Before me, as my memory flies,
I see again that fertile plain,
And listen to the curlew's cries,
And feel the warm soft summer rain.

Behind Drumlemble, where once I played,
There stands a heather covered ben.
The Laggan's splendour below displayed,
A stream gurgles through old Rhudal's glen.

More loyal folk you ne'er will find,
None truer, and with kindly hearts,
Sadly, I left them all behind
And set my sights on foreign parts.
   Liz MacSporran

The Raging Seas

The rolling waves roll unto me
as I sit upon the shore.
They speak to me of distant winds
that violently swirl to fore.

For this great sea that breathes so quiet
has a temperament so wild.
It rages up and spits its venom
falls back and dies so mild.

The bubbling froth with pebbles fired
comes roaring unto me.
It tells me of the wicked things
this horrendous looking sea.

The tales it tells as it beats the rocks
the whispers of its crime.
It has no guilty complex as it's
forgotten in our time.

Beware the raging sea, I say
you don't trust what's got depth.
It will spit its venom with ferocity
and take away your breath.
   J. P. Thorpe

S. Africa 1954

From tawny Arab on the northern shore,
Through tall Masai of torrid heights
And Bushmen of the equators zone,
To bronzed and bravest Zulus
of the south
This is their land alone.

Yet man from all the parts has sought
its lure. For three hundred years or more
They've settled on this azure shore.
Whose is it then?
The tawny brown or black or white
None can say who has the right.

It is the African alone who laughs
The deep-bellied warmth or disarming smile.
The white has fear at heart,
So anger's fanned throughout the land,
The dark embittered, the white distraught
Would it were otherwise!
This land I love will never be
In my life-time a Paradise.

Isobel M. Smith

"In The Beauty Of Holiness"

I could hardly believe my ears as I silently listened in dismay,
"The church is only a building", I've heard some people say.
Nothing could be further from the truth,
as I honestly believe that Christians have the proof.
It is the House of God, a sanctuary for the humble heart,
a place of prayer and love, and consolation when loved ones depart.
"Where else on earth could you find such a friend"?
Our Lord is always there when needed, faithful to the end.
The sweet whispers of His Holy name floating on the air,
are like the sounds of heavenly music, beautiful beyond compare.
The infinite wisdom of God's mercy is truly unsurpassed,
as justice and mercy will be freely given, if you ask!
It is not to be taken for granted and not without cost,
as sometimes the chances we have rejected are the blessings
    we have lost.
Remembering all the now departed, who gladly laboured
    without earthly reward,
To build a Holy Temple which was worthy of our Lord.
We love to sing of the place oh God, wherein Thine honour dwells.
The eternal joy of Thine abode, all earthly joy excels.
When we meet Him face to face, in the heavenly skies,
visions of Gods glory, reflecting radiant Holiness, descending
    from His eyes.

Diana Forgan

"Mum"

I stand at the window thinking of you
I look up to the sky all shiny and blue
I say to myself why dear Lord why
And then I remember that tear in your eye

The best friend that I ever had
The day that you left I was ever so sad
We knew you were ill, they all tried in vain,
But now my dear mum you're without any pain

I know that you're up there looking at me
My Dad and sisters and all at number three
With you in God's house up there in the sky
I still ask my God just tell my why

A kinder wee lady you could never meet
When she greeted her friend's in our towns main street
She on top of the hill now looking down on us
How I wish I could see you on our local bus

The memories you gave me, I remember so well
The good times we had were ever so swell
So if you can hear me in the sky so blue
Remember dear Mum I'll always love you

Iain Morrison

Untitled

He hadn't known the line of time
Would show his life in detail.
Everything for ever shown
And nothing ever deleted.
His every move, his every word,
His actions, his ideas,
Which showed the thoughts
That made the acts,
So nothing could be secret.

And everyone since time began
Was watching without comment.
He hid his head and crouched and screamed,
So shamed by their forgiveness.

Gerry Ackerman

A Life Goes Around In Circles

Sailing through life is not as easy as it
Sounds, we have our ups and we have our downs,
One day is good, another bad,
One day happy, another sad.
It does not matter, if we are rich or Poor.

We are born so bright eyed and new, we start
To grow and admire the views.
Once we have finished with milk, we start
To eat solids, some food is nice, some taste
Horrid, as we begin to grow, teeth start to show.
We start school one day, try to learn all
Sorts of strange things, then we yearn for the holidays.

Teenagers now, we think we know best.
We go to parties, dances, and shows,
We have a yearning for fashionable clothes.
We want to change the style of our hair,
Maybe a colour streaked here and there.

Life goes around in circles it never
Seems to stop, until we know nothing again,
We know no happiness, we know no pain.

Gwen Leahy

Twins

We have has this bond before we were born
And it's gone on and on
through play, laughter and tears
work, love and all our fears

Now I am old and on my own
That special magic is there
I know that I am not alone
For that bond of love is there

No-one understands the love we share
No-one understands the love that is there
It's special and magic in its own way
And it's only twins that can share

You will wonder how I know
And you will always say Ah' No
But I have that special love within
Why' of course I am a twin

Anna Lillian Locker

Untitled

Reach for a hand when you are weary.
Have faith in your heart and smile
For troubles that seem such a burden
Are made lighter, when you stop and think for a while.
Just take a good look around you
Thank God you are safe and well.
Your blessings may only be small ones.
But better than living in hell.
Today in the world that we live in
You will find a much faster pace,
But stop and remember the good times,
Walk tall with a smile on your face.

Miriam I. Lloyd

Untitled

I seem to see things clearly now
What once was dark is turned to gold
Come with me on a journey then
To once, to now, and what may yet unfold.

We've come this far, the journey's on
Time to think of things gone by
We toddled, walked, then ran and ran
Our dreams could see the sky.

The present came in sombre guise
Of thwarted dreams and sightless eyes
Of memories lost and secrets told
Of loves once new and now grown old.

The future then must hold the key
To light our way, to make us bold
I seem to see things clearly now
What once was dark is turned to gold.

Terry Green

United Together!

Eric they kicked you whilst you was down,
Boy did you show them when you took the crown
Provoked by Symmons a very evil man,
Your retaliation, received a harsh eight Month ban
October 1st eventually judgement day came,
From that day on "King Eric" shall reign,
To Many "The Godfather" to you a best friend,
Alex Ferguson stood by you, from beginning to end,
For no-one nor nothing, Eric in you he never gave up,
You then repaid him with the 1996 F-A-Cup,
5 Minutes to go, Eric you produced that match winning goal
"The Godfather's" actions and face said it all,
Together you raised that F-A-Cup with such pride
To end as it started with you two side by side,
"United Together" Alex and Eric you sure showed them all
You two will remain "The Kings" in the history of Ball.

Nicola Woodrup

Heaven

As I sit on the edge of my heaven to be,
    As I watch the water flow by,
I can hear the wind in the trees around me,
    And the call of the birds as they fly.
I sit on the edge of this magical place -
    This is my heaven revealed.
Spiders webs, with rain like lace,
    And all my thoughts concealed.
But as I sit here I begin to think,
    There's just one thing that's wrong:
    I need someone to share this with,
    To make it more than just a myth.
    You provide that missing link,
Wherever you are: That's where I belong.

Charlotte C. Reeve

Alice

Alice is tucked away in bed,
Bedtime story and prayers are said,
She opened one eye and there behold,
A beautiful fairy dressed in gold.

A fairy so dainty and full of delight,
Alice just gazed at this wonderful sight,
"But why are you here"? Alice did say,
"I've never seen you before today".

The Fairy replied "I've come because you're so good,
In helping your mummy each day as you should,
I'll grant you a wish, and I hope it comes true",
Then away went the Fairy in the night so blue.

Then Alice just wished with all her might,
With eyes fixed firm on the Fairy's flight,
But Alice just wished that she could say,
That I'll always be happy, as I am today.

Irene Firman

Dreams Of My Lifetime

I long for the good things in my life to be
The love of a woman full of trust and honesty
To a world where the media don't cover another bloody war
Innocent people dying.   What the hell for?

An end to corruption, to greed and to lies
Where hospital budgets decide whether a man lives or he dies
The demise of dictatorships, regimes and alike
To a place where a person may speak freely in a mike.

The bringing together of man, woman and child
A stop to the slaughter of our animals in the wild
A place were we care for our young and our old
Not leaving them to die outside in the cold.

Everyone's right for a roof above their heads
Not living in squats, doorways or back street sheds
A chance for people to work and earn a wage
Not to rely on welfare handouts until they're dying in old age.

These are the things that matter most to me
Which hopefully in my lifetime I hope to see
As I hope and I pray that one day these wishes come true
For a world full of peace, kindness, and love is long overdue.

Paul Bache

Death!

You were once here
But not any more,
You lie silent and still
All alone.
No one cares any more,
First they brought you flowers
But now you're covered in weeds.
You're neglected,
Nothing but a shadow of a memory.
Someone who it was vowed never to be forgotten,
But you were forgotten, for a while.
Here you lie in this vast open space,
Full of others,
Who have been lost and forgotten for years.
But there is one, one who still remembers,
One who still cares.
Although they have forgotten, where you are and what you were.
Your memory still haunts them, every day you're there.
You give them the courage to go on the strength to survive.

Louise Morris-Didcote

Till Death Do Us Part

I'm dying of a broken heart
It's gradually splitting in two
Our love was once a work of art
but to save it there's nothing I can do.

He told me it was over
Not too long ago
I asked if there was someone else
all he said was no

When I asked him for a reason
Why he was saying goodbye
He told me that I made it sound
like an act of treason.

He said he didn't love me
He never really did
He told me to stop crying
that I was acting like a kid.

So now my heart has broken,
It's time for me to die
I hope he feels guilty.
even though he won't cry.

Kerri Barr

Thoughts

Thoughts running, whirling and flying through my head,
I want to know where they come from, but in everything I'd read,
No answer can I find for the thoughts that fill my mind,
And dreams busy in my head at night, also no reason for can I find,

Good thoughts, bad thoughts,
Kind thoughts, cruel thoughts,

Everyone original to me,
Thoughts will not the same be,
As spouse, lover, father, brother,
Sister, cousin, aunt, or mother,

Why do I think as I do?
Why do you think the way you do too?
Rows and debates many anxious states,
Can cause trouble even although we are mates,

Negative thoughts, positive thoughts,
Self destructive thoughts, constructive thoughts,

Do these thoughts come to us via spirit of the past?
How much are we influenced by memories that last?
Everything that happens to us reflects the thoughts we had,
So if everyday you watch your thoughts then in your future
    you'll be glad.

Christine Kijko

At Sundown

The eventide was closing, the sun had gone to rest,
A nightingale was singing in the park,
And I sat here simply wondering where all the years had gone,
The memories kept flooding through the dark.

Happy school days came before me, with many cherished friends,
Quite a number of them perished in the war,
Without a chance of proving what kind of men they'd be,
Their lives were taken, like the closing of a door.

My teen years were through torrid times, praying for the peace,
Which arrived, and then I met my wife,
After many years together, children's children on the scene,
We have shared so many facets of this life.

We have shared the times of sorrow, pain, and hardship,
There were times of joy, sweet happiness, and bliss,
Good friends, sincere and true, have always been there,
And are among the many loved ones we would miss.

I pray that those who gave their lives for others,
Have shared with me this span of life, sublime,
For when it comes for me to meet my maker,
I will gladly go to join them for all time.

Frank W. Collins

To An Autistic Child

Ethereal butterfly child,
Laughing in your world,
Unreachably beautiful, restless brown eyes
Like hummingbirds.
Almost fairy-child, so often scared; vulnerable,
Dancing with invisible shadows,
Shouting pleasure at a life
Which you don't understand, can't really understand you,
Only love and protect you,
And enjoy the vibrance of this little blonde fellow.
His intangible soul
Throws out gossamer threads of joy to us,
Frail world of a shared moment;
Makes us ache to reach you -
But we're lucky to know you,
Little being,
We are ignorant and cannot understand,
But know enough to love.

Lucie Guilbert

Old Shoe

Moulded to the skin, flexible with movement.
Age shown with creases, by turned up leather.
Old, protective layer - dusted and battered.
Tread after tread,
Relentless.

Mud-flecked and travelled, along concreted paths.
Shapeless, it sags - unsupported cover.
Rain-splattered, hail-pounded, snow-embordered,
    sun-bleached.
Tread after tread,
Relentless.

Faithful, re-heeled, braving the worst.
Polish-layered - mud-caked once more.
Veteran shoe, scuffed with decrepitude,
Tread after tread,
Relentless.

Kirsty Dickson

Alone (At Midnight)

Greeted, a cycle, the powerful night sky,
As a silent disturbance sounds a far distance cry,
Absorbing the vastness viewed above, and beyond,
I balance the existence for that which is longed.

Reflecting my conquests, the events time create,
Like the footsteps, diminishing, a homeward migrate,
The car alarm, ten seconds, an intrusion to fright!,
Then return does the silence, the power of the night.

The question is ultimate, I address to the black,
Tell me the answer, how to gain what I lack,
Will it be given, or for me, must I take,
Or maybe I'll join you up in the dark lake.

Your offer is strong, a utopia of the mind,
Gaining a destiny, a personalized mankind,
My thoughts materialized, my feelings dictate,
Freedom and comfort, the dissolution of hate.

Oh! I've dreamed deep with feelings sought to show,
Reality storms through, laughter heard below,
I must return to find happiness, I can't drift away,
For this night will dissolve, repeats, bring the day.

Murrough O'Brien

For Michael

  We argued tonight
  In the maelstrom of bedtime
But now my king of Leggo sits in striped pyjamas
As the evening sun warms the blueness of his room
  Melting the anger
  Into pools of quiet, grey light.

  When the shouting has sunk
  Under the weight of his duvet
And his need for love has overcome his self-assertion
He will reach for me and pull my head down beside his
  Until the only smack we hear
  Is the soft, safe sound
  Of his thumb
  Searching for
  Sleep.

Janet Sellars

Untitled

Thank you for treasured memories
of your care, in bygone days,
For services you have rendered
and for the wisdom of your ways.

Always, revered by your saviour
gained respect from the nation too
may the Gods forever, grant you their forever
so the wish of my heart for you.

Mabel Nindheys

"Oh Sh—!"

Little bird up in your nest
is that where you go to rest,
high up in the stable roof
keeping away from every hoof?
There is one thing I'd like to ask,
I don't think it would be a major task,
but when you come down to steal the grain
do you think you could refrain
from doing 'things' on the stable door,
it would be much better on the floor
as every time it seems to land
exactly where I put my hand
to open up that stable door
to shovel other 'things' off the floor.

Jackie George

Parting At Evening

And coming up the road we sensed the sea
For the fog was settling in; and we
Saw the windows and street lights blear
Like widows' thoughts from year to year.
We'd kept this dog-watch quiet, discreet;
Now, only the sea's miasma
Breathed in the street.

The tired old gas-light
Observed two backs grow smaller in the night,
One up, one down the way
And muttered foolishly
As those who pray.

A. G. Owen

In The End

I will bend to a child, but not to adults
In the end they will recognize faults
Give them lots of tender, loving care
In the end they will learn to share
Give them love, be a guide
In the end they will abide
Treat them harsh you make a rod
In the end, then they will be a sod
Being a parent can be very wearying
In the end they must be caring
What's this about? I hear you scorn!
In the end, brain will beat brawn
Now it's time for me to stop
In the end, we come out on top

L. J. Rayner

Father Figure

With passing time comes a greater distance
between what was and now is.
Your touch fades with my minds resistance
to the torture and frustration
as my imagination fails me.

Littered photographs capture your being
Fragmented shards of your wholeness.
So still, so silent your voice unrepresented
no resonant laughter nor reassuring breathe.
A moment, a time space, I look without seeing
your wholeness.

Shrouded in your clothes is the scent of your living,
your outer shell, I stroke and hold tight.
With desperate disappointment, eyes open, comprehending,
they hang limply and lifeless without your fullness.

Gathering the evidence of your lifetime,
I sculpt an artificial (but comforting) new you,
personalities in pictures, sensations in clothing,
its failings are stark
but I have no substitute.

Annaliese Tilley

Baby Love

A baby is a precious gift
For you to cherish and love
You watch it grow and guide it
with help from God above
But one thing often overlooked
is how your baby sleeps
You don't just put it in its cot
and tell it to count sheep
There are some rules which you should follow
To give you peace of mind
Keep baby warm but not too hot
and lay it on its side
If you do these things I've said
Your baby will sleep sound in bed
And you will say before you burst
That baby's safety must come first

Margaret Preou

Cold Wind

How windy it is to-day,
Enough to blow whiskers of cats-away,
The clothes on washing lines dance together,
Holding hands all in a shiver,
Doing high-kicks, trying the splits,
While crispy leaves behind you leap,
Running as if they had feet,
So cold weepy eyes and icy cheeks,
Set the sound of chattering teeth,
On black-tar road in snowy poker-dots,
When chores are done there's doggy trots,
Home seems far, in cold winds,
Now by the fire, the warmth it brings,
Even puppy dogs tail to singe,
Echoing hear the sound of cold wind,
While on the cheerful hearth the kettle sings.

Joan McAvoy

Life A Nothing Poem Nothing

The blackest of black,
The darkest shade of black.
Silence, uncontrollable silence,
Maddening to the untrained ear.
The only sight is no sight,
Comfort isn't it?
Discomfort is.
The only truths told are dark lies.
Home is unknown, sunken into a pool of lost hope.
Trust, thrown aside by my blank, black mind.
The mind a pit of discomfort.
Thought and worries whirl and spin,
Looming, waiting,
To take comfort and overpower you.
The maddening squabbles of thought wind down the body
As a clockwork toy.
Sleep is conscious, yet unconscious knowing today is over.
Tomorrow is nothing again, nothing.
The place is dark and shall lie with me always
Until I am nothing .... on one tomorrow.

Louise Wrightson

Fading Dreams

I have walked and climbed for many years,
Up winding paths, and heights I feared.
The trunks of trees majestically standing there,
The sight I have yet, too ever compare.

But now that the years have gone past,
And I look up at the weeded paths,
The old trunks of the trees with roots snarling bare
O how I hate to stand and stare.
But now I will keep in my mind and heart
Of those faded dreams, I will never part.

Mary C. Roberts

Sunset

In the golden rays of the setting sun
As the day God gave us is nearly done
We should thank Him, He's simply the best
He gives us our work, He gives us our rest
All the wondrous things we see
The misty mountains the endless sea.
These little things, that mean, so much
All come from him and his magic touch
Every good thing we all share
He puts all our emotions there
This life for us all to enjoy
He gives to every girl and boy
There's nothing He has missed out
God is love without a doubt
So as we watch the sun go down
Don't start tomorrow with a frown
Live your life one day at a time
Because tomorrow may never be thine

Eva Wilkinson

Joe Peabody The Rabbit

Mr. Joe Peabody went to the Zoo,
And met an elephant, and kangaroo
A lion nearby, roared: "What have we here?"
"With such a short fluffy tail, and long
droopy ears?" But Joe; he likes carrots,
and none could be found, though he searched
and he sniffed, as he wandered around.
Then a nice little girl, with saucer like eyes,
said: "Come home with me Joe; I've got a
surprise. I've plenty of carrots, would you
like two or three? If you like, you could
even have dinner, with me". Then Joe;
twitched his nose, and then he replied:
"What's your name, little girl"?
"It's Jean, she sighed."

John Kynaston

Innocence

I was four in the war.
"Which war?" she said
A bright-eyed child who looks like me.
I heard the noise of the coal as I covered my head.
"What sort of coal?" the little girl said.
"It was noisy coal", I smiled to her.
"It was my mother's invention
The love of prevention
To pretend and protect."
I was four in the war.
We walked to the shops
To queue for an egg.
With eyes so round, "one egg", she said.
We dived in the hedge, my mother and me.
As the plane screamed low
To drop its load
Splattering bullets into the road.
I was four in the War.
Eyes like mine looked back at me certain and sure
It was a long time ago I was four in the war.

Erica Ann Quarterman

Why?

Why do people kill? Why do people die?
Why do people hate each other?
Why do people lie?
Why do people rob? Why do people hurt?
Why does everyone treat each other like a piece of dirt?
Why don't they love and care for their family and friends,
and be loyal and true?
Why don't they be honest?
They just don't have a clue.
Will this world ever be happy and sincere?
Or will we live forever in a life of fear?

Hayley Morris

Dads Must Wait Or The Perils Of Fathers Lending Money To Daughters

Dads have got pots of money, with pockets like a bottomless pit
So when daughters are broke and need a loan, they always
   give them a bit.
"I'll pay you back next month" daughters say, "I'll be in credit then"
And dads just sigh and hand it out, knowing they've been
   suckered again!

Now dads are wise old creatures who've heard all the sob
   stories before
And sure enough, just as they thought, no cheque pops
   through the door.
But dads don't mind too much because they know it is their fate
That if they want their money back, they're going to have to wait!

Then dads get the phone call - it's the daughter on the line
"I'm really sorry - I didn't forget - but may I have more time?"
"Or can I pay you over two months, my accounts in a terrible state"
And dads agree because they are dads and yet again they wait!

Now daughters love their dads and don't mean to be rotten
But when they see some gorgeous clothes, the debt just gets
   forgotten!
So, before you lose your patience and start to get irate,
Here's the cheque, which goes to prove
That everything comes to dads who wait!

Z. Gerrard

Memories Of Youth

When I was young, and free from care.
When every day dawned fair and sweet.
I had no thoughts of growing old.
Or of sorrows I might meet,
In my youthful days, life seemed so bright
I did not fear the darkest night.
Or dread the moaning mournful breeze.
Shaking the branches of the trees
As I went loving, laughing dancing,
Unaware that time was passing
On and on I sped light hearted
But time flies by an winged feet
And suddenly I know
My span of life is shorter now
I have not far to go,
Now I can only sit and dream
Of all the things that might have been
Only memories now remain,
Youth will not pass my way again.

D. Lindsay

Another World

I am here, safe and well,
In a place far better than there.
Everything is pure and innocent,
Nothing can frighten you here.

Do not fear from my health,
Just drink to it.
Do not worry for yourself,
I am taking care of you.

You know I am here,
You can sense it,
And yet I am up there too.
I can be everywhere.

My soul is up here with me
My spirit is down there with you.
I will be with you until we meet again,
until then, my love will be forever true.

I know you will never forget me,
and I know you will worry some,
but never be concerned for me,
I am in a world far better than this one.

Sarah Wood-Heath

"Messenger Of Spring"

Let that which is pure stay pure, do not spoil
let it be:
Cloaked in dewy mantle before the morning sun,
Whose warming fingers lift the shade beneath a head so young.

This thing of beauty, this jewel neath the hedgerow crown
With leafless arms and buds in winter shroud
Strives to raise its breeze blown head
To tell the world that nature's not abed

Let foot nor blade this gem destroy to lay a furrow straight.
Lay on and bend a path around this messenger of spring
To later grow, and sway, and colour shout when
nature has her fling

Do not spoil, let it be — for me.

Hugh Jones

First Born

Oh! What a wonderful sight to behold.
This tiny life, worth so much more than gold.
What happiness! What joy!
To hold my beautiful baby boy.

The dark shadows have been driven away,
On this magnificent sunny day.
The past has fled, gone for good
Chased away by the arrival of this new blood.

Perfect fingers and tiny toes,
Skin as velvet as the petals on a rose
Eyes, like the blue of the sky
Full of trust when he gazes into mine

Take him for granted? No, this I could never do.
Sweet little boy I longed for you
You are amazing and you're mine
Forever and ever till the end of time.

Rachel Dickson

In Praise Of The Dawn

Dawn's scarlet fingers stroked away the night,
Unveiling yet another virgin day.
A waning moon ran down the sky in fright,
To hide, before the sun burned her away.
The unborn buds lay sleeping in the ground
Beneath a quilt of gold-encrusted snow.
I listened, but I heard not any sound-
Save for the breathing of the earth below.
Night's frozen tears lay sparkling on the grass,
And gold and silver threads adorned the trees.
I couldn't let this beauteous moment pass
Without a prayer whispered through the breeze.
O Lord, you spun in gold a wondrous scene-
Made me a day where once the night had been.

Anne P. Robbins

All Alone

The passing sound of a car makes me feel I'm not alone
But the distant bark and humming birds remind me of my
home sweet home.
It's a strange and different world for me. A sight I've always
hoped to see. But now I'm here, feeling the things I've always feared.
I take a long deep breath and begin to walk
As snow falls down like dusts of chalk
I watch each flake hit the ground and wish to hear
a different sound.
I ask the birds to make me fly
But a whistling sound was their reply
I felt afraid, so began to run,
my face is cold, my hands are numb.
I beg the clouds, please where am I?
Fall to the ground, and start to cry.

I miss my home. My home sweet home,
someone please just take me home.

Rosie Sarkis

Untitled

Can anything last of a friendship
When one of the couple is gone
Though acres and oceans divide them
Is it madness to try and hold on
To a memory, a faith and a yearning
Though the waters of time run between
To wash out the spark that's still burning
In a heart that is still seventeen
Is it merely a lifetime's illusion
That friendship can live through the years
Can weather the hazards of fortune
Alike amid laughter and tears
If I thought that you'd love me a little
And remember me still to the end
I'd give you my heart for a keepsake
For the honour of calling you - Friend.

Winifred Knight

Antagony

The passionate cold kisses my cheeks
Yet I feel no affection
A frosty blanket covers my feet
Yet I feel no warmth,
No warmth.
Peppered air stings my eyes
Yet I do not sneeze at the cold
Immaculate tears drown my sighs
Yet my soul is not cleansed,
Not cleansed.
Darkened globules tarnished my delinquent blood
Yet my heart was once untainted
Mother nature protected my maturing bud
Yet now she antagonizes,
Antagonizes,
Antagonizes.
She antagonizes.

Sabrina Barlow

Untitled

Oceans apart,
Day after day,
And I slowly go insane.
I hear your voice,
On the line,
But it doesn't stop the pain.
The pain builds up strong inside,
Than of the day before.
The ache will be stronger tomorrow,
As my heart continues to call out loud for your love.
But like today and yesterday,
Tomorrow will be just the same,
You'll never hear my crying,
My bleeding heart,
You'll never know its pain.

Shilpa Amin

Belief The Thief

We hear of religious freedom
A good thing in our world today
We have the freedom and of the press
Of man's full freedom also no less
But yet we see and with some distress
That religion can, does, sadly divide
Mankind deeply
Wars! Indeed, cruelty, greed, all stem from
Religious beliefs then we read
Yet! One God we have, one world, one saviour
One hope of heaven, alone, in Christ the saviour
Yet! In freedom man does choose to worship who?
And what then favour, to be true?
Is it true peace, and neighbourly love?
Is it love towards God, he in heaven above?
Is "Good" the outcome, or the word, at all?

Margaret Lightbody

Love

Love is just a little word.
Meaning so much to those who care.
Everyone needs to be told
From the very young, to the old.

Like a ripple on the sea.
It will flow forever through eternity
The breeze swept gently through the trees
As children's laughter fills the air,
Of knowing that their parents care.

The smile on the faces of people you meet
Send you light hearted, down the street,
Through sunshine and rain, and days of pain
Let our love show
Then we will gain more than we know.

Gives us oh Lord this gift of love
To strengthen us on our way.
So that when the storms do come.
We will be able to say.
Thank you God for this wonderful day.

K. MacCreanor

The Journey

Visualizing and floating
Among the azure blue sky,
And the brilliant white clouds,
Would be a dream;
A dream that can be fulfilled.

The feeling of going higher,
Makes me leave my troubles behind,
And my smile becomes wider.
I want to reach out and touch
The cotton-wool clouds,
And feel the breeze rush into my face.

As I approach the land of humanity,
The daily troubles become present within me.
My smile begins to fade,
As I loss touch with the clouds and the sky.

It's a beautiful experience;
An experience that should be treasured for life.
A beautiful journey;
A journey that will not be forgotten.

Tracey Dawkins

"My Home"

Home is where you find it, you fill it with your love,
Then you take good care of it, with water and soap suds,
Sometimes it's quite noisy, with the contents you have installed
But on the other hand it's peaceful, when you tired and weary,
And it does not matter where you go, you cannot get back too soon,
Because of all you have, longs for you to come back home.

Edna Matkin

Alien Self

I remember you.
Like an alien for so long,
but every now and then I catch a glimpse of you,
to remind me of years gone;

Was it painful that for you, she had no room.
With renewed strength you are forcing your way back into sight,
but have you considered how she will cope?
Have you considered her plight?

At odds, you appear to me now,
but nothing can stop your drive.
You found it painful not to exist in her life,
but now alongside you, she will have to survive;

I know you.
I can no longer hide from our being one,
but I wish I didn't have to face you,
as you remind me of the years to come.

K. N. Toyne

SPECIAL PEOPLE

Friends are very special people
They help you out in times of need,
They're there to help you when you fall
They never fail to hear your call

I have friends old and wise,
Stretched across the world so far
They've been truly tried, a long long time,
If I should need them,
They'll be there.

Friends and time go hand in hand,
Truly tried, friends are rare,
Special people.

Moira Kirkland

Emotion

A ruler must control his emotions and protect his Nation.
A ruler's actions are judged by his Nation.
The Nation emulates from their ruler's actions, thus, control
your emotions and protect your Nation.

W. Hull

Devils Dance, Gods Kiss

Did you dance with me under the ground
In devils hands I was found
I was tempted by the rising dead
Then kissed by God as I bled

He whispered softly in my ear
you've sinned my child, but have no fear
Tempting evil maybe
Strike them back and set them free

Emma Perrott

Where The Pegasus' Roam

I could never say for certain,
just where the pegasus' roam.
But if at night you search the sky,
you may see the pegasus' fly.

Once they are up very, very high,
through the clouds in the clear night sky
I believe they are in their own little world,
where nothing else can enter and nothing else can see.

The hills would not be green nor brown,
the storms of our world would never be there.
Instead the hills would be purple with blue
and never a storm could chill the air.

The little ones would play in the streams by noon,
and the stallions would fly through the sky by the moon.
Before the break of dawn they'd return,
and they all would rest beside the burn.

You could not see them in winter time,
they would be far away,
but on May day they would return,
and once again you could seen them play.

Donna Gregory

Cold Comfort

Shuffling slowly through silent sleet,
the clouded sky veils far stars.
Ebon gust in the distant street, but
light reveals its wrapper scars
and city crispy leaves in doorway,
bitter blows hoar spiteful breath,
whispers in chilling tone, 'go home,'
I'll rouge your cheeks and bite your neck.
So turning back, via faint stretched shadows
and asking ears to numb the frost,
I cleared the litter from the doorway
and paused to thank my cardboard box.

Noel Davies

'All Is Not Lost'

Oh! Just look, at our Yorkshire weather, so cold, so damp with
   a touch of frost.
The ground is slippy with icy patches, the damps set in but
   All Is Not Lost.
It won't be long before Spring is upon us, and the lambs all
   jumping in the air.
Then comes along Summer, that makes us feel younger, so
   care-free, happy without a care,
Then Autumn comes and before you know it, you're reaching
   out again, for woollies and thick socks.
It seems a blink of an eye, then winters back on us, another
   year Older, but All Is Not Lost.
I would not leave Yorkshire, whatever the weather, with its
   cold, damp, and a touch of frost.
I'm alive, and that's all that matters, I can't grumble, and health,
   Not too bad, for this Yorkshire lass.
So whatever the weather, with seasons in regions, Yorkshire's
   lucky, just to have that Wintry Frost.
And whenever I'm down, tired, and weary, I remember the seasons,
   then say, "Oh Well, All Is Not Lost"

   Mary Shaw-Taylor

The Day Of Love

The sun on my face would be ne'er so sweet,
as a Kiss from this girl if perchance we should meet.
With fire in my heart and love in my soul,
I know if she held me my life, would be whole.

She tears at my heart when my eyes drink her beauty,
she tears at my soul when I listen with duty,
I long to belong to her soul with my soul,
but yet dare not step forward because of my goal.

When thunder and lightning do meet and collide.
When forces of nature affect earthly tide,
there you will find me my dream held in heart,
with all my love on my lips to impart.

Tell me sweet father, I'll wait for the day,
oh how I would dance if her love came my way,
but hold ye my heart, be still and just pray
for valentines here, yet 'tis only one day!

   Alan Dodd

Tribute To Mr. Mojo Risin

Are you Jimbo? The person who trembled
like a sinner in your sacrifices;
Giving away lavish personally crafted
Bits of your-self?
To attempt to stand by your opinions which
Were instantly glued to your imageries.
In those days you couldn't get away with saying words.
Something that sparkled away inside
interested us, instantly, for that sparkle,
For were instantly a victim who had
to convince us before the head-hunters.
They knew you were - the real prophet
Among blindness, deafness, a genuine
Article strode forward: Whose only weakness
Was to practice what you preached
Anything less is a cop-out, it was your fate;
being realistically akin to prophets
of old, thank you for gesturing to the other side
Please don't chase the clouds pagodas.

   K. Smith

Jerusalem

Jerusalem, O Jerusalem, where is thy peace deserved?
With such rich past that must be yet preserved.
The strife so caused through ignorance and greed
That men have wrought regardless to their creed.

Jerusalem, O Jerusalem, what future is in store?
Will foes unite, and vow in faith against a fruitless war?
Were this to be and harmony restored,
The world will cheer and all then rest their sword.

   Ken Harris

A Cat We Had

In the surgery
came the time to say goodbye
to an old friend on my lap whose luminescent eyes,
pain filled and knowing, were aligned with mine.
In the market we had bought the kitten for a pound
because he was so ordinary and black.
He had grown with us in common need and in affection,
a working symbiosis with the family. This I recalled as
the vet softly explained the speed and dignity of the process.
I stroked the plain black ordinary neck, and he forgive me with
a purr.

Driving to depleted home, hoping
for simple traffic, conscious of nearby black furry form receding;
conscious of lively feline images spinning
away from earth at high velocity, carrying with them
a twelve year aliquot of life;
conscious of palate ache, strained tear ducts, hoping
for rapid grief attenuation, I wondered
whether I had loved the cat, or whether
I just loved myself.

   B. G. Curtis

September Four

Amongst the locals, gather the locals
laughing, joking, drinking, smoking
you enter there
and they slightly stare
imagine the deathly glare
amongst the beer is silent fear
amongst the spirits, gather the spirits
of violence past
of chairs thrown and innocents glassed
of pent-up anger and frustrated hate
of last September four
when they closed up late and bolted the door
amongst these public places, gather those with little tact and
social graces
they will fight no questions asked
the one still standing will be the one to die last
no mercy and no regret
if you come in you deserve what you get
we don't want you coming in alone
bring your wife, a first-aid kit, and a stanley knife.

   Gavin Owen

"Meditation Days"

Nothing now of the restless rush of spring time.
Nothing now of the searing summer blaze,
Not yet a while the bitter blast of winter,
This is autumn....these are contemplation days;
Days for drifting, both morning and evening,
Mist-meandering along hedgerow and field,
Marvelling at the never-failing harvest
That sun and rain from dark earth yield;
To savour slowly the ripeness of the season,
To let the juice run sweet into the mouth,
Watching birds whirling, wheeling, and waiting
To take their long uncharted journey south;
A time for musing, a time for reflecting,
To be still, becalmed in purpling haze,
Tread softly now, softly September,
This is Autumn....these are meditation days

   Brenda Clare

Ceasefire

Have you no pity, compassion or guilt,
You would destroy everything that's been built
Just to play a political game,
Proves to everyone your principles are lame,
What principles are these? The begging question,
Murderous treachery killing your ambition
Associate most with your weakening cause?
You may laugh in my face,
But the world despises yours.

   Duncan Peter Woodhead

Untitled

The tears will flow as it should be
If you need a shoulder remember me
Love is a feeling that will never flee from your heart
But after the tears comes a brand new start.
And stop to remember all the poor souls
Who have never known the kind of love
That comes from being part of someone
And knowing you will never be alone again.
When the darkness is over and life reappears
Love will still be there, but no longer the fears
Have pity on those that skim over the top
Of life's deepest feelings and never stop
You will see the freedom that comes from within,
After tears have been shed
Contentment therein.

Linda Rhodes

Butterfly

Trapped in time
The silken strands of mystery
Envelop, and protect me in my infancy.
The web of life is fragile and uncertain
Swaying with every gust of strong emotion,
Then the metamorphosis, and I am free
From my incarceration, and wing above
My former self with joy and love.
The world is mine.

Edward Carlton

The Coming Of Spring

It's spring again! I hear folks say
The tiny lambs are gambolling in their play
Not straying too far from mother ewe
Who chews the grass, head down and far away.

The daffodils are here again
With their dainty yellow heads a-bobbing
As the gentle breezes fan their stems
And set their brilliant trumpets nodding.

Down in the garden the birds take wing
Each fledgling venturing from its nest, to try
To reach the nearest green leafed bough
From thence up to the glorious blue sky.

But how do I know it is spring?
I see the tiny rabbits on the land
Each year, this time, they all appear
As if by magic! The waving of a wand.

They sit in groups along the verge
That runs beside the dual carriage way
May God protect and keep them safe,
And not allow them on the killing road to stray.

V. Holmes

A Summer's Day

The first hint is a bright rising summer sunshine,
And in it lies the barest of swiftly clearing mist;
As the light grows a cock crows and myriad insects fly,
While gradually the air warms as if with promise kissed!

Come midday, life seems to say - "'Tis time to rest awhile",
Tools laid by, a cool drink, and somewhere to lie down,
A shady nook, a good book, and let the world go by!
And later, evening breezes steal to cool the fevered crown.

When day is done and sinks the sun and time for sleep is come
Take a last walk round outside in the soft night air;
Stars gleam steady, huge moon ready to welcome us to rest,
While owls dine, mosquitoes whine, and our pillow's waiting there.

A rare day this, a touch of bliss, to lock in memory's store,
To live again when tempests roar and wind cuts to the bone,
When trees creak and seem to speak of memories they too share
Of basking sun and gentle breeze and insects' drowsy drone!

Ken Whitten

Untitled

You brought me sorrow you brought me joy
But I realize now you were only a boy.
You never grew up, you were never a man
I was only a woman fitting in with your plan

You used me my love I was only a toy
When you took my love it was only a ploy
You lied and you cheated used me time and again
You didn't care when you caused me such pain

You can't hurt me now I have nothing to give
I just carry on pretending to live
I'm only a shell my love feels unreal
And you don't even know just how I feel.

Tho' I don't love you now I cant ever leave
Because of the magical spell that you weave
It can't be love I know that now
But I married you dear and I made a vow

To stay with you husband till death do us part
I'll give my obedience but never my heart
There's a part of me that I'll always save
And that part of me I will take to my grave

Joan Hartland

Untitled

I see your face in every moonbeam
I see your eyes in every star
The touch of your lips I seek
In the wind on my cheek
As you smile at me from afar

I love the nights, 'tis then with me you speak
Tantalizing, in the night you play hide and seek
I see your face, there, now it has gone
To peep again elsewhere and on and on
'Tis a game you play when we are alone
To reassure that always you will be my own

To hold you now I know that cannot be
The world you're in as yet I cannot see
In course of time, not for me to judge
We'll meet again, the wait I'll not begrudge
For in the night I see your face, your eyes, your smile
You whisper in the breeze: soon, just wait awhile.

James H. Brandon

My Granny

My Granny is the best,
She always takes her daily rest,
My Granny's nice and kind, she loses things sometimes.
But then she looks and finds,
All the things she's lost,
Like money and a couple of jars of honey,
The honey goes off,
But she doesn't mind,
As long as it doesn't have the smell behind.

My Granny's the best,
She always takes her daily rest,
Reading her books,
Or looking at her antique gold hooks,
She's had them for years.
They must be worth something,
But my Granny would not part with her hooks,
Not even if they gave her a hundred books,
That's my Granny she's the best,
And after all she still has her daily rest.

Emma Smith

The Mouse

Scampering, scuttling at incredible speed,
Faster than the wink of an eye.
Out on the patio swiftly you dash,
Your minute furry body is gone in a flash.

The seed for the birds
You are craftily stealing.
Your big ears for danger
Are constantly listening.
Oh, tiny mouse in your world of survival,
At least in our garden, you have very few rivals.

Something about you to me did occur,
Something only another mouse would know.
As you streak past in a furry blur,
Are you a him,
Or a her?

Freda Jones

The Rabbit

The Rabbit stirs and wakes at dawn's first light.
He rises, stretches, twists and stands upright.
Washing his forepaws he expertly grooms his fur complete,
All over his body, long ears and strong hind feet.

He stretches again and in two hops is out of his manger.
He stops: watching, and listening for signs of danger.
Sniffing the fresh, raw hoar-frost on the morning air,
He feels the first rays of sun on his satin grey fur.

His ears are like periscopes, twisting and turning every way.
To north, south, east and west he appraises the day.
Listening intently to the birds' dawn chorus,
The Rabbit, aware and alert sits back on his haunches.

His nose forever twitching absorbs the morning smell,
His whiskers sensing everything - the day bodes well!
He preens himself again covering his silk fur -
When cleaning and grooming is over, he rests content and austere.

And so there he sits handsome and regal,
Absorbing all around, his eyes sharp as an eagle.
The new day is here, its beauty has come
And the Rabbit is waiting and ready to have fun!

Peter M. Maguire

Through Netted Curtains

Through netted curtains
I heard you fall,
I heard you scream
And your children cry,
I put money into the charity envelope
Believing, I had done my bit.

Through netted curtains
I watched you hang your head,
As you pulled the shopping,
And pushed the children.
I watched your children plead that daddy would not come home tonight,
And I gossiped with my friend, stating what a tragedy.

Through netted curtains,
I saw the police arrive
After I had heard you fall for the second time.
I saw your children, wrapped in towels
Being carried to an ambulance,
Alive, but lifeless.

Through netted curtains, I saw the body bag,
Through netted curtains my tears fell.

Claire Thomas

November Landscape

The dowager's brown brow is stained with silver
Her brittle fingers stark against the shroud
And her grey soldiers scour the empty trenches
Where Mercury's steel beacons stride the sky.

Sally O'Sullivan

Untitled

As I became a blushing bride then children came along,
the years flew past so quickly
"mother you're always wrong".
I'd like to watch the weepy films
not boxing, golf or war
I never get to please myself
to soothe my inner core.

As I became a pensioner, false teeth, glasses stick
fumbling, stumbling aching, slow,
hurry up, move along be quick.
"You have to go to hospital,
you can no longer live alone,
you've no choice you're not capable
it's a residential home".

As my life force dwindles, I have a smile upon my face,
I want to be cremated dressed in white and lace.
My hymns and prayers are chosen
It's all written in my will.
And for the first time ever -
It's my choice, I can be still.

Chris Barnes

Guinevere

How can a name be an evening breeze,
A chime of temple bells.
How can it dance upon the tongue like
An ocean's gentle swells.

And how can a name bring to mind the
Fragrance of a rose, to caress my aching
Senses with slumber's soft repose.

How can a name be a seraph's song,
An angel's offered prayer to fill the
Silence of my soul,
The name that's 'Guinevere.'

Jim Glen

Upon Southampton Docks

Twelve months done
My country sends me off to war
Defending our soil against a Junta state
Who are calling the Falkland Islands' fate.
But few had heard of such isles before
The Argies muscled in.

So it is
Upon Southampton Docks I meekly stand.
With Navy new kit bag and case
Emotions searching for a proper face
And a head full of thoughts of what I could
Be sailing to.

Alone within
And for all the world, a token 'Jack'.
A minute statistic of Britain's force
Drafted to a ship bound for that southern course.
Not knowing when I was coming back,
Or if at all.

Michael Jones

Escape

Escape from the world that let you down,
Escape from the people that were never around.
Escape from the life you knew before,
Escape from the ever closing door.
Escape from sadness, sorrow and tears,
Escape from bitterness and nerve wrenching fears.

Escape to the future where everything's new,
Escape to a world where there's a born again you.
Escape to a place where you can dance in the sun,
Escape to a vision of happiness and fun.
Escape to a feeling satisfaction can bring,
Escape to a world with a new and fresh understanding.

Kaye Louise Johnson

Reflections

Trees and leaves and trunks and barks
Empty benches in the park
Nature has done wondrous things
Skies and seas and living things
If you look around yourself
You will find it's true to say
It is best to be alive sharing love from far and wide
Look upon a new born babe see how tiny are his hands
And his lips and nose and eyes but gigantic is his heart
He has love enough for you he will help you to get through
If you're ever in despair just look at a baby's face
It will tell you all is fair in this world we live today
You'll accept life with its actors with its clowns and its disasters
You will see there still is freedom there is love and life and wisdom
If we crave for innocence the world will be a happier place
If you ever need to know what is right and what is wrong
Have a look within yourself and an answer you should get.

Sylvia Ellen Mifsud

"Recession"

The factory stands, gaunt and tall,
Walls blackened and decaying.
It looks out of sightless eyes,
To a desolate landscape of despair.

It once had a great heart,
Men laughed and joked,
The white-hot molten steel
Ran like a river,
Now it's all dead.

Outside, men pass by, eyes averted,
Memories of past days.
Heavy back-breaking jobs,
Proud and strong and great camaraderie.

The rain comes,
Dripping down the walls
Like tears,
Washing away the despair and sorrow.
A new era begins, The heart starts to beat,
Breathing new Life,
Into that once proud factory gaunt and tall.

H. M. Fergusson

Motorway Travel

Why do we pile onto motorways
with congested traffic and road work delays?

It's all in an effort to get there quicker,
but when all's said and done, we only bicker.

Travelling doggedly in straight lines,
exceeding the speed limit, but dodging the fines.

We follow the juggernauts mile after mile
and kid ourselves we're travelling in style.

Boringly watching the cars up front,
praying to avoid a possible shunt.

Why do we pile onto the motorway
when over the hill, not far away

there are quaint little villages, basking in sun.
Some of the scenes are second to none.

Picturesque cottages with roofs to thatch,
beautiful settings so difficult to match.

Cats on the window sills, snoozing in peace,
roses round doorways, white and cerise.

Lovely old Inns with great atmosphere .....
Let's bring back the travel of Yesteryear.

Beryl Stone

And Go To Sleep

Those who claim that euthanasia is bad
Are probably the ones who've never had
To watch over a loved one, suffering the agonizing pain,
Of an incurable illness, enduring the strain.

Losing their battle, their dignity, their pride,
While those near and dear sit at their side,
Praying for each breath to be their last,
Trying hard to remember happier days past.

When quality of life is no longer there
And relatives and friends who deeply care
Are left feeling helpless, inadequate and despairing
Of the heartache each one of them is sharing.

When hope for the future is all but a dream,
Surely then, it must only seem
Kinder, less selfish and more humane
To put them to rest and remember them sane.

Why then, I ask, isn't it legal or right
To simply and painlessly end the plight
Of the sufferer, the carers, their families too?
Euthanasia holds the key for me and for you.

Amanda Couchman

To Believe

She was more than just your aunt
You were more than just a friend
To go through it all,
To the unpleasant end,
When the time came, she passed on,
You found the strength to carry on,
Even though at the time it didn't seem right,
That someone so young was
guided into God's bright light.
Now she's in a better place and
You'll never forget her face, for
the memories you have,
Won't be forgotten or taken away
But will stay with you until
your dying day.

Joanna Davies

New Life

Delving into the dark, drear, distant past
I shuddered, fearing frantically
What long-buried memories might surface:
Lying, lurking, lusting for re-discovery.
Painful past life-experiences now rising
Scars from the dark grey mass within.
One by one they rise in agonizing recollection
Turning grey to white
Light shining where darkness reigned.
From below ground spring colourful flowers
Of understanding, forgiveness, peace.
New hope, new life.

Anne Donockley

The Bridge

Love is the bridge which eases the pain
Of death, whether by illness or war,
Accident or old age. Know
That love endures, forms a bridge
Between the worlds, this and the next.
Thoughts may be shared, memories too;
Realise a presence beside you,
Perhaps a familiar perfume.
Weep not, grieve not for yourself;
Rejoice that your loved one is safe,
Free as a bird in a new body of light,
Able to hear all thoughts, kind or not,
Able to love maybe more than before.
Let love be the bridge which eases the pain.

Diana Myers

A Babe In Arms

A smile, a memory, a held-back tear,
The moment arrives, all parents fear,
A child, no more - becomes a man,
Suddenly, "No you can't, becomes "I can!"
The weaning, feeding, shaping, moulding,
Smacking, praising, laughing, scolding,
Disappear, and show again,
in Kodacolour ways,
The photo-album's all we have,
to remind us, of forgotten days,
Have 18 years really passed,
has our son reached voting age,
Have days of school and cricket field,
given way to earning wage,
Must we really cut the 'cord',
is innocence no more,
Can this nation take him from us,
and send him, proudly, into war.

    P. T. Janion

Thoughts

There was a tear so very near,
as I walked alone along Broad Beach;
for I did not have far to reach within my brain,
to remember once again the happy energetic ways
we spent our Summer holidays.
Sometimes, when I close my eyes,
why then, to my great surprise,
I can so clearly picture things
that happened - and the pleasure sings
within my heart; but, of course, it cannot last,
for they are recollections of the past
that so quickly seem to have gone away,
although, at times, to me it's yesterday.

And so, I do not know how much more time
that I still have upon the earth,
but I hope that this small rhyme
will bring back to you the fun, the mirth,
the happy memories of what we did together
and that those little joys will stay with you for ever.

    D. Proffitt

To A Candle

A prayer to God ascends on smoky wings.
Two lovers, eyes aflame with matching fire
sit, in its light, aglow in their desire.
It stands, a mourner, at the bier of kings;
whilst birthday children giggle at the puff
of cake-spiced breath, extinguishing the years.
Across the lane, a lonely widow peers
at visions of her life when full enough,

From cave to castle it has been our guide
and o'er the eons always at our side.
It compensates, consoles when all else halts.
A peaceful constant undemanding friend
with gentle face on which we still depend
whilst slowly shedding tears at all our faults.

    Ronald A. Pargeter

Searching

Today I sit upon the silent common,
And wonder if God floats by upon those soft clouds,
Staring down into the heat of time.
But when the clouds are gone
The quiet wind washes on,
The light continues to shine,
The flowers still dance with the butterflies.
And then a cloud swims into view,
The sun is hidden and it is cold,
As I realise that
The answer is the searching.

    Richard Reid

Otherwise Known As...

Why did it happen? Why to my sister?
It all went so fast, oh how I miss her.

She was my twin, the person I could trust,
I wish for so many things, and one to clear away the dust.

She used to be so funny, the centre of attention,
Harri was her best friend,
Though there's lots more I could mention!

I don't know whether she can hear me,
I don't know whether she can see me,
But I know one thing for sure, there will always be a "we"

We went everywhere together, we were never apart,
Without her I'm lost, all the memories in my heart.

But my Nicky will be back, you wait and see,
When all the sorrow is over, and Nicky and I will be a we!"

Just because she can't walk or talk, it doesn't mean I don't care,
Our lives will start again, and all the good times we'll share!

But I still don't know why, and I still don't know how,
I wish she could do all the things we do,
And be with me always and now!

    Clare Reynolds

The Healing Hand

A child's tears, what stills them?
A mother's hand held out in love,
A child's fears what quells them?
A mother's hand held out from above.

In hospital bed we lie morose,
Covered with silent thoughts and fears,
Approaching the bed, the messenger,
Is all now well, can we banish those tears?

A hand held out to grasp our own
Is a message the world understands,
It's the soft healing touch of flesh to flesh,
Claiming friendship in its demands!

It's a divine thing, the loving touch,
To often we dismiss it,
We strive to show our abundant strength
It's a folly to be submissive.

In all of this, we have lost the way,
Who would wish to know humility?
Can we find the healing hand again?
It offers the world its ability!

    Joan Miller

Untitled

He put me behind the driving wheel
And told me to make it go
I listened to all instructions
And set to work just so.

I tested the brake and put it in gear
And low and behold it rolled
But goodness me, what do I do next
How was I being so bold.

Make it go faster, keep up the revs
Before you change the gear
That's right, now change it back again
He says to me, oh dear.

Which is the footbrake, which is the clutch
Cricky, how does it stop
I need many hands of an Octopus
It's caught me on the hop.

Anyone got any feet for sale
I could do with some more of these too
My brains never worked so hard before
But I'll sort it out. That's true.

    Joan Vincent

Pharisees All

He was there again today.
Sitting huddled in the biting wind,
His hat at his side on the flags.
"Something for the homeless," he muttered.

"Put it back in your purse, love.
He'll only spend it on booze or drugs."
Kindly protective of me, the old lady?
Or coldly contemptuous of him at my feet?
In the warmth of affinity I paused for thought -
Does it really go on drink or drugs?
How can I tell? I shall be very annoyed if it does.

But I must get on and go home out of this icy wind,
Back to my fire, my tea and the telly,
Or perhaps a good book and the treats I've just —
— "only spend it on booze or drugs"?
  I dropped the coin in his hat.   .

Irene Holden

Hypothermia

Winter has laid bare the barren wastes within my heart.
I am alone and discontent with my existence.
There is a time for all, but this is not mine.
My temperature drops and the thoughts in my mind are stifled.
I see a bridge to greener pastures that I must walk over.
It is a bitter end to a happier beginning.

Maureen Ferguson

Untitled

Don't stray away from home
And hasten not your steps;
You have become so ugly and so old;
Weak is your heart and muddled is your mind,
The people that you meet may not be kind.

Don't look around or stare;
Keep your mouth closed in order to survive,
Hold to yourself all thoughts.
People who stop to listen deem you a bore,
A miserable wretch and even more.

Don't waste your time composing
Verses much out of fashion;
But write instead long tales sexual and cheap.
What you have missed in youth you'll miss it still;
If you have never lived you'll never will.

Paul J. Mifsud

The Sky

Has ever one wrote of the sky
That super gorgeousness on high,
From grey to pearly white it fades
And shimmers forth in blue cascades.

Then, with a radiancy divine
A mottled splash of crimson wine
Appears and spreads its heady charm
Like a crimson gash on an outflung arm.

With purpose bent on harming all
Come stormy clouds - the blackest wall,
Which sweep the sky from keel to stern
And harsh with fury wreck and burn.

But gradually the clouds pass by
And leave a rain-drenched glistening sky,
The azure blues and turquoise bright
Are bathed in iridescent light.

Then suddenly out of the blue
Appears a rainbow strong and true
And heaven opens 'fore our eyes
To greet the glory of the skies.

M. Cashmore

Untitled

The view from my window is pleasing to the eye.
A broad and shallow valley reaches out to touch the sky.
Nature's brush has painted, every shade of green.
On quilted fields and hedgerows, a truly restful scene.
To the right, a tree clad hill, crowned in leafy glory.
On eastern edge the poplar line tells its windswept story.
Leisurely the sheep do crop the daylight hours away.
Whilst tiny lambs, in frisking rush, racing games do play.
A flash of white, a rabbit's tail, it quickly hides from sight.
When on high the buzzard flies, in striking graceful flight.
Straight and true the furrows, in the rich dark soil.
Tractors do the heavy work, and men long hours do toil.
Sea gulls whirl, scream, and fight, to glean the pickings there,
And calling birds, with their song, do find a mate to pair.
Rounded oak, sparkling birch, sweet smelling fronded larches.
Nesting sights highly prized, offer up their branches.
The tranquil sight, moonlight belies, serenity out there.
For fox will hunt, and owl must feed, little creatures do beware.
Out for food, the secret world of night life comes unfolded.
For patient watcher in the dark, vigil is rewarded.

D. J. Walsh

Arrest

I try to piece together the moments I forget
The more I think about it no nearer do I get.
I want to make more solid the fragmentation in my mind
And put the trauma and the stress so very far behind.
It's such a strange old feeling to know that for some time—
how long?
I was not alive on earth, but was dead and so was gone.
How long did it last? What did they do? Whatever did they say?
What exactly went on while I was so far away?
I need to get things sorted out and settled in my mind,
I need to come to terms with life—and death, so peace I'll find.
I know I'll never rest until I get things sorted out
I want to make it very clear and leave no room for doubt,
No doubt at all within my mind of all events occurred
And then continue with my life feeling undeterred.

Barbara P. Timmins

Nightmare

In pin-dropping quiet, and small-hours black
I awake in fearful dread,
Though bedclothes warm my ice cold back
Chilly images fill my head

Once more I am at that same stark place
Where phantoms all screech and swirl,
And in the form of a screaming face,
The terrored look of a girl

Shadowed by a structure high above
She fights for her every breath,
Beneath cruel hands of an erstwhile love
Who now strangles her to death

Then I see on that remembered ridge
The clear outline of 'The Murder Bridge'

P. G. Jones

Space

Up beside the shiny stars,
There's nine planets such as Mars,
Radio controlled robots roaming around,
Astronauts bouncing off the ground.

Deep craters and U.F.O'S,
Mysterious creatures with one hundred toes,
It's dark up there, with little light,
All you see is the colour white.

Space is a place I'd like to see,
As long someone comes with me,
I'd love to go there someday soon,
In a rocket passed the moon.

Leanne Allan

'A Jewel In Winter'

The darkening billowed clouds roll ever eastwards
Touching, now and then, a hump-backed hill
Whose windswept crown of winter branches seem
To draw the grey and clinging mist until
The hill seems cloaked in grey as if a God lay
Smoking his great ethereal pipe atop the green-clad mound
This mist of silence dripping, crawling down
To deaden more staccato sound.

And then, as if a mighty Angel's chorus sings
The sun bursts through an unsuspecting fissure in the clouds
And, slashing down, floods the withered leaves and furrowed
    fields
With gold to give a glimpse through winter's shortening shrouds.

The gulls, disturbed by warmth, then leave their pecking in the
    rich brown sod
To soar with graceful flap and glide
Up, up forever smaller now, 'til hung as micro points of light
Against a blackened screen, daytime stars with the God of all
    creation
By their side.

Alfred William Harwood

Vagrant R.I.P.

Smashed in the road the vagrant lay
Injured, expected to die
Hit by a cat on a foggy night.
And there's no-one to care or to cry.

Hanging on to life by a slender thread.
Helped by machines and drips
But no-one to sit beside him,
And moisten those poor parched lips.

Death holds his hand now, and beckons to him,
To wander the roads no more,
And there's no-one who cares to detain him.
No-one whose heart is sore

A last look back down the lonely life
Of a vagrant with-out a home
Then he closes his eyes with a weary sigh.
Never again to roam.

There's no-one to claim that poor broken man.
No-one to say him a prayer.
No-one to weep at his grave side
No-one to give it a care

Greta E. Dye

Elegy

The rain fell softly on her face
    Mingling with silent tears
That could not wash away the pain
    Or hurt of wasted years.

She'd come to see him laid to rest
    His tortured soul set free;
"Such a fine man, my dear? They said
    As she stood beneath the tree.

They'd known, but had not known the man
    Whose secrets she had kept,
Her friendly public face had smiled
    Whilst heart and soul had wept.

"Oh! Thank you for your kindly words"
    She said. Soft fell the rain -
"Dearest Lord, send down a deluge
    To wash away the pain!"

She cried and now, she'd died with him
    Her battered spirit spent -
She turned and slowly walked away;
    The secrets with her went.

Mollie Williams

One Day When My Work Is Done

One day when my work is done
I'll go to where my wishes begun
Among the life and light of a tree
It's hard to explain but it's me
I'll be as slender as a willow band
And bear the love of life in my hands
Clad in white and green in my hair
If you look twice I'm not there
Yet dancing in the golden sun
I feel my colours start to run
It seems the hands of life are so unfair
And with a sigh of the wind I'm not there.

Julie Webster

A Hunter's Moon

The huntress pauses on the grassy knoll
Green eyes gleaming in black-furred poll
Plumed tail waving in menacing motion
The huntress is come to cause destruction

The moon rides high in the cool clear night
Lighting the path for our huntress's sight
Gleaming and sailing in a sea called the sky
Unknowing ally up there on high

Silently forward the huntress glides
Quietly so that no victim hides
Lit by the moon they have no notion
That there in the shadows their fate awaits them

A pounce, a scream, then all is quiet
The moon sails on, she heard no riot
And the huntress pausing on the grassy knoll
Looks round once, then moves swiftly on

Helen Foley

Life As A Tree

Can you imagine a person standing as tall as a tree,
With arms outstretched like branches, protecting entirely.
With young saplings beneath starting life, in a world that is
    not always fair,
Its branches so positioned to give light to give warmth to give care.
To shield from all the winds and torrents of storm,
The leaves fall on young shoots, to protect and keep warm.
But as the saplings grow either twisted or straight,
The tree does not know how they'll grow, in what trait.
Now as the tree ages, showing scars from its past,
It gives way to the young, for their futures are cast.
Will they grow tall and straight as can be,
Or will they be destroyed by strong winds from the sea.
Will they bear blossoms, and fruit of their worth,
With strong roots firmly fixed deep down in the earth.
A lot we could learn from the life of a tree,
Young saplings the children, the tree you or me.

Anne Seymour

Old Man's Lament

My eyes are full of hills
that lower to the grooved earth.

Crow and willowherb swoop and
    tumble and tread.

The harvest is early my love.
The barns are full my love.

On the last day
I carry you up to your death-bed.

Your eyes are full of hills
and the laughing girl I courted.

You lived each day amidst
the voices of children.

Knowing you
and growing through life with you
has been the greatest gift a man could have.

A. E. Ward

Clarity Of Conscience

A clear conscience harbours no harm,
  It Loves perfectly;
Even when wronged,
  It finds a way to Love and Forgive;
When wounded,
  It finds a way to console;
There's no guile, or bitterness in it,
  All it does is Love;
For in Love,
  there is a perfection of strength,
In love, is the power to Live;
For a clear conscience, is a Loving heart,
And a loving heart, has no foe, for all foes, become friends,
When a clear conscience vibrates;
Throw off your guile, O son of man, and put on a Loving heart;
For in Love, is health, perfect health;
In love, is the fullness of your being;
Clear your conscience, O son of man, and
Let Love reign and shine in every heart;
That we may all live, and shine, out of a clear conscience.

Ayoade Olaoluwa Ayotade

Dear Dad

The fact that you have gone from us, still does not ring true,
Now we are left wondering, just what we shall do.
The tears have flowed and we all know, that there will be more yet,
How you bore your suffering we never will forget.
You fought on like a lion Dad, your faith so strong and true,
I know that God in heaven, has opened the gates for you.
You left us many wondrous things that money couldn't buy,
And to the last, dear Dad, we saw the love light in your eye.
We know you're still beside us Dad, in everything we do,
Walk in God's good sunshine now, that's what we want for you.
You did not want to leave your love, our Mother sweet and kind,
But God gave you your last call, you had to leave her behind.
We will take good care of her and help her through her sorrow,
Knowing, she'll smile again for us, until she joins you on some
  tomorrow,
So rest in peace our Father dear, you've played your part on earth.
We your children love you, as you did us, from birth.

Carol Ann Donnelly

I Cannot Find The Words

I cannot find the words, I wish that I knew how
To tell to you at deep of night, the way that I feel now.
When I'm no longer with you I know the things to say,
Like I'll spread my hands beneath your feet,
I'll give you the month of May.
I'd sing to you a ballad that no-one's ever heard.
Yet you ask me do I love you, and I cannot find a word.

Each day I find new things to say, I tell you in my mind.
I write you songs and verses of the free and subtle kind.
I give you all my silken words like glow-worms in my head,
Then you take my hand and smile to me, and not a word is said.

I would tell you that I love you, would make the stars your crown,
Would take your smile and light up the whole of London Town.
You whisper the sweet hours that glide away the night.
I lead you thro' the ways of love, till early morning's light.
But with dawn thro' the window, and the chorus of the birds,
Your bright eyes ask a question, and I cannot find the words.

Desmond M. Sheahan

Tranquillity

Ever so slowly creeps the dark and evening,
And the treetops sway from side to side.
With the sky that hides the dark blue heavens,
God let me there abide.

The leaves begin to shower me
Like snow from the dark, dark clouds,
And the stars look down to see
The glory that God enshrouds.

J. V. A. Collins

Towards The End Of The 20th Century

Living with fear, living with sneer,
A vicious way of life.
Repression and hate seem to dominate,
Life in triumphant style.

I awake in morning, and miss the chirping birds.
Their abodes are broken, children stolen,
To appease the profiteers hunt.

State is a factory, privileged notoriety, keep their valour above.
Rich is richer, poor, poorer, so goes the order,
I fabric and style.

Out of work, hastens graveyard,
Killeth the spirit in a wasted career.
Welfare state, an empty shade, kindles no hope nor light.
Glory is dethroned, life forlorn, quest in vain for pursuit of
  direction.

Nothing is wrong, nothing is right, the attitude seems permissive
  kind.
Downhill road, sound and up-roar, fill the life's cup full.
Mind quivers, wind murmurs,
A lantern dimly burns in my parlour.
My heart is heavy, bleeds in agony,
Longs for stormy weathers.

Dakshina Ranjan Deb

From The Heart

I wish this pain would go away, it never ending seems.
I'm drowning in such sadness, of how it could have been.
My son, Oh how I love him, was born for me to care.
With washing, dressing and feeding and not, for others to stare.
Educational statements, fighting for his rights.
Stress and worry all the time, many sleepless nights.
Walking is a problem, special shoes on feet.
Tiredness and tears, he finds it hard to speak.
Lots of operations, and hospital appointments too.
Speech and physiotherapy, I have to cope, could you?
Medicines and physio, at home the norm to give.
He's my special boy, with the strongest will to live.
Heart disease and epilepsy, learning disability too.
Dyspraxia, asthma and blood disorder, what's a mum to do?
You learn to live, to carry on, to cope and say your prayers.
To be grateful for his love, and see through all the despair.
What he needs, is lots of love, and confidence restored.
Encouragement, not criticism, nor overlooked, ignored!
The sun comes out, when I see him smile, and laughter fills the air.
I hope and pray for God's kind help, a friend who's always there.

Ruth Elizabeth Westhoff

Life Is What You Make It

Too many people spend most of their time
Complaining the world is unpleasant, unkind.
If only they could stop, look and see
The world is as good as they want it to be.

Life and the world seemed right against me,
Because I'd been hurt so. I just couldn't see.
I would always feel sorrow, it didn't seem fair.
Bad luck and misfortune, I sure had my share.

Then one fresh spring morning, I looked all around.
The birds they were singing, a glorious sound.
There was dew on the green grass, the sun it did shine
The world seemed to greet me. I felt peace of mind.

God gave to his people many wonderful things:
The beauty of winter, the splendour of spring.
He gave us a world where we could all take
a part, to help those who badly still walked in the dark.

So stop your complaining, the world is just fine.
It is just that some people still remain blind.
I hope that one day, they will find just like me,
The world is a good place, just stop, look and see.

G. E. R. Evans

My Daughter

Oh my little girl you're growing up so fast,
I wish the years could stand then this precious time would last.

Just now I am the centre of your world
But I'm afraid this won't always be,
You'll soon be meeting others that will mean more to you than me

You have such a lot to learn of life,
Some lessons will be hard
I hope you'll always turn to me when life and times get hard.

I love you so my little one
Perhaps one day you'll see,
What happiness and oh such pleasure you have brought to me.

Susan Lomas Fletcher

Evening In Winter

Slumbering days of winter
Lazy smoke curling from chimneys
Where jackdaws nested in the
Hectic days of spring and summer.

Birds seek shelter along the hedgerow
While above us the crows gather blackly
To weave patterns in the fading light
Before heading off to their roosting place.

A winter sunset flushes the sky
While chilled air creeps damply round us
We are glad to see the lamplit window
As we walk up the familiar path.

Now we will thaw by the log fire
Drink strong tea and feast on warm scones
While Julia tells tales of winters long ago
And the last ray of light gives way to a velvet darkness.

Wendy Kelly

The Inward Eye

I can see an Autumn
Changing colours round a grave,
In falling leaves and grasses overgrown,
While the flowers in the vase turn to stain upon the glass
And the Moss fills in the name upon
The stone.

And I can see a Winter
In a carpet on the ground,
In broken cobwebs tangled in the breeze,
While the sleeping forms below, in shrouded mounds of snow,
Lie peaceful in the shadows of
The trees.

And I can see a Springtime
In blossoms on the bough,
In flowered earth that wakens from the spree,
And the Daffodils that wave, yellow patterns on the grave
And all that comes to life again
But me.

Ray Maslin

Our Silver Wedding

To celebrate this illustrious do
I've composed a line or two
To welcome you, from far and near
Family and friends all gathered here
To say, thanks for the presents, we appreciate
Marking our silver wedding date
I'd like to thank Margaret and Jan for the cake
I'm always far too busy to bake
These twenty-five years have flown by fast
Who was it said "it'll never last"
So what is the secret, there is one I'm told
It's not leaving your partner out in the cold
By caring, and sharing all dreams will unfold
With the hope that the silver, one day will be gold

Andrea Housley

Quiet Times

I close the door to my mind, and leave the
world to its own salvation.
For I, a mere mortal, have little effect on
this great planet on which I revolve.
A silken cocoon I wind around my thoughts,
keeping them locked inside my head.
Slowly the healing takes place, as I drift along.
Forces beyond my comprehension take me in
their arms, and rock away the strains of this worldly life.
Oh the peace and bliss of these quiet times.

Slowly like a snail emerging from its shell
Earthly commitments pull me back.
I hope that death is like my quiet times.
But until my life is over, I shall not know.

Shirley Jowett

Memories

In the autumn of my life the fallen leaves
Of all my summers surround me, lying at my feet.
As I kick them around their rustling stirs in me
Memories of the glory that once they were.

As I bring them all together in one great pile
There to remain in one corner, half forgotten
Their very presence betrayed by every breeze
To stir in me once more thoughts of yesteryear.

Maybe, as the winter of my life brings darkness
The leaves may not be seen as once they were.
But, for now, the leaves remain in all their glory
There to be stirred and the memories recalled.

William Eyre

How To Get The Genie Back In The Bottle

Loud, lewd, lawless, licentious
Renegade role models ruling T.V.
Youngsters agog, aghast and aquiver
Wait on the outcome, whatever it be.
Will murdering moron and bullying bounder
Get his come-uppance? He should, shouldn't he?
But that would be boring, bland and expected.
No kinky quirk or twist in the tail.
Show something different, no matter how evil!
Morals and good now must never prevail.
Who cares a jot if the young are degenerate?
The bottom line is - that ratings don't fail.
Children were good on the whole and attentive
Back in the fifties - seems aeons ago.
'Permissive' T.V. and 'progressive' inspectors
Frowned on our children behaving - "Oh, no!"
"Let them run round, introduce self-expression."
"Quiet is out! 'On the go' is the thing."
"Make things exciting." Who said - hyperactive?!?
We reap what we sow - now crime's in full swing!

Kathleen Blades

"A Heartfelt Sadness"

Simplify the message, take time to look.
Feel what's in the heart, that's the good.
Release, break free, nothing to carry, no burden.
Let others break the ice, caring and sharing.

Happiness and fun, different meanings
To bring a smile, bear in mind, remember.
Each and every one is different, makes a world.
Emotions tie them together, what a gift.

Innocent faces, bringing joy, little children.
Born into this world, a joy, all the same.
Unison, a powerful conclusion, not hard, easy.

Music, variety, feet tapping, inner gladness
Fold the pleats, make a bow, elastic.
Signing the message, love, no hatred.
Gold and silver, just words, better phrases.

Emily Burnett

25

Fen

My name is Fen I am a little cat
  F is for friendly which I am
  E is for energy I've got that
  N is for naughty some say so
Inquisitive of course - lots of places to go.

Born in March I come with the Spring
I'm sure my coat was meant to be black
But I'm flecked with gold from nose to tail and permanent too!
How did it happen? I'm told high lights were in fashion
For which my maker must have had a passion.

When I was tiny I couldn't keep still
Lots to see and do, and so I will
Neighbours to meet and test them out
Their reactions to my frolics and pranks
One threatened handcuffs! No thanks!

I've settled down now that I'm three
I'm a "Pat Cat" so let me sit on your knee
People have so much stress
Stroke me gently - it soothes both you and me
Thanks for your patience - I love your caress

Myrtle E. Holmes

Amaranth Caudatus

Seeds are sown in April and May,
the Sun just beginning to proudly shine.
Roots become firm, friendships strong,
and everyone looks forward to Summertime.
Life and loves are fresh and free,
the air filled with youth, passion and laughter...
But Autumn comes, and we become wise,
and the air is filled with disaster.
In September, the crimson shards of the flowers bloom,
and our hearts break beyond believing.
Like tears the petals flow, as Love Lies Bleeding.

Sigrid Marceau

Time Denied

I read another book today,
what's new in that, I hear you say
well, this one was different.

I've read of love, of war and peace,
variety of subjects never cease,
to amaze me.

There's adventure stories biographies too
books of poems, make mend, and do,
all there waiting just for you
if you have the time.

But in the book that I've just read
time was denied most folk,
they're dead.
Killed in the Holocaust.

Hilda Atchison

Cowslips (Progress)

When I was young I well recall
A sight my eyes did please
Where myriads of cowslips bloomed
And swayed there in the breeze

My friends and I would make our way
Across the field each day
Then go to school through nature's yield
And laugh and sing and play

I've often yearned to see again
Those cowslips in the spring
So I returned to that same place
To do that very thing

Instead of flowers what I saw
Just made me want to cry
They've built a motor way instead
And let the cowslips die

Leonora Steele

Old Age

Cataract eyes opened, wearily surveying,
peeled wallpaper and carpets fraying.
Transparent curtains, permitting the light,
to emphasize the old fellows plight.
Reflecting on a life once full of bliss,
he glances down, 'have I come to this'?

Bladder so weak, joints that won't bend,
hip operation that refuses to mend.
Beloved wife departed, callers abating,
going down fast on life's credit rating.
Saturated pyjamas newly amiss,
he cranes his neck, 'have I come to this'?

Tries to reach down, clean up the mess,
but can't bend his back, knees even less.
Get back in bed, put up with the smell,
cough a bit more and wait for death's bell.
A single tear shows his diagnosis,
his head hangs low, 'I have come to this'.

Christopher Brough

"Marry Me," He Wrote 3,000 Years Ago

Could this dream I dared to dream
Come true? Or am I deceived,
By Shu, the God of air, who paints
Pictures of water in deserts
To make the unreal seem real, then fades
Them, like morning-mists, to nothingness.

Let me live my life by your side
My own star of "bright appearing."
Become my wedded wife, my flower
Of heaven! Share your future with mine;
Our desires and starlit dreams combine, so
They spread out before us in silver light.

O you - whom I promise to worship
With my love for all this life of ours
In endless time, awake or asleep,
O my love - most beautiful of all!
Before I let "my heart go forth in haste,"
How long must I wait for you to answer?

Colette Thomson

Untitled

Transcend this beauty so unreal
Preside amongst us and stay a while
Confide in your presence only I can
yet my eyes cannot see past man's clinging veil

Imagine you, I try but to no avail;
Despise myself do I when others see you in detail
Praise I render to you, seeking deliverance for me
So descend down on us and eternally leave us true to you

Your treasure that lights our minds is lost in progress, caverns
And your seeds of life no longer blossom and bloom
The ethereal orb that laces the sky, dries bleeding veins
And churning seas leap to swallow the lighting moon

With clipped wings, the angelic doves fly no more
The tongues of honest men slip all the while and say no more
Trapped my soul finds no solace in this sea of pain
Breached is our faith, so come with and save our fate.

Amish Patel

Killing Time

With the sharpest of swords I slayed the night.
Buried it in an old sack and tied it tight.
There it joins yesterday.
Last week,
Last month.
Last year.
If tomorrow you come to me,
Then tomorrow has nothing to fear.

Duncan J. McNeill

Pen-y-groes Hill

Once I ran up Pen-y-groes hill with hair a'flying and dancing feet,
Roses and honeysuckle filled the air with their cloying
perfume heavy and sweet.
The world was wrapped in soft golden light, time held my
hand as we danced along,
No dark clouds then - to turn bright daylight to dark night
For there my love stood waiting.

Now the winds blow rough and chill and I walk slowly up
Pen-y-groes Hill,
Skeleton fingers reach for the sky grasping at clouds as they
sidle by overhead.
Would that I had grasped at love, followed my heart to where
it lead.
The mountains seem so bare and cold they look to me more
worn and old than time himself,
He and I walk side by side, as friends, hoping soon to see my
love return.

Years have passed o'er Pen-y-groes Hill, the roses and
honeysuckle long long gone,
Tall grasses wave their lacy fronds where once the golden
kingcups grew.
Nature trespassed over all the ground, the trees themselves
are tightly bound
By creepers of a darker hue.
My feet are clumsy as I climb the hill no longer now, is time
my friend,
For he found my love on foreign soil where crimson poppies
bloom and I
Am left to mourn alone the love I failed to grasp and hold.

Maggie Pryce Jones

This Is The Hand

This is the hand that picked the flowers,
And got very wet in the showers.
This is the hand that climbed the tree,
And it surely bothered me.

This is the hand that dressed me,
And is sure to impress me.
This is the hand that built a big wall,
And is sure to see a big waterfall.

This is the hand that went on a plane,
And it has not got a name.
This is the hand that pulled down the blind,
And is easy to find.

This is the hand that went for a walk,
And came back with a flower stalk.
This is the hand that rode the horse,
And made it pause.
This is my hand, he's my best friend.

Sarah Louise French

To Be Still

Just sit, come sit with me and
look around you, observe, marvel,
absorb your surroundings, yourself, your existence,
please, not later, now.
The sink overflows, leave it, watch it,
The water lapping so very gently,
listen, hear it, believe it, but don't touch it, please don't.
See how clear it is, so beautifully transparent,
did you notice that before?
The way it sparkles,
reflecting the sunlight; a prism,
So many colours so little time.
Help, The floor, it's wet.
Leave it, wonder at the wetness,
the way the water trickles, a thin glassy trail
like an icicle, but wonderfully different.
Oh it drips! round smooth beads
Perfect, like the puddle on the floor.
Deep now, an untouchable well
and look, you are drowning in its stillness.

Anna Richey

University Bound

The air is full of excitement
The house has become a 'tip,'
Your child is leaving home, to go
On this his biggest trip.

He's passed exams. He's got his place
It's what he wants to do,
A big adventure, start to life
And all great pastures new.

Don't shed a tear, or fuss too much,
However you may feel,
Your thoughts, ambitions, plans and hopes
Are packaged in this deal.

"Good Luck," (he'll need it in the world)
May all his wants come true
May he be proud of all he does
And we'll be happy too.

Margaret Canton

Nana

Tragedy has followed you throughout your life,
Your mother died young and your gran raised you,
You married young, had your family and nursed your
   dying gran,
You didn't have to but, you wanted to,
Your husband took ill and you nursed him until his death,
You didn't have to but, you wanted to,
Your family grew and tragedy struck again,
Your son's young wife was dying,
You gave up your job and flew to their side,
You didn't have to but, you wanted to,
Two young children needed your help, the youngest was only four,
You raised them as your own,
You didn't have to but, you wanted to,
I am that youngest child and now that you are ill
I want you to know I will always be here for you,
I don't have to but, I want to.

Karin Martin

Life's Reign

Darkness reigns, supreme in might,
its mantle cast o'er deepest night,
a covering shroud to hide the skies
as nature steeped in slumber lies.

The reigning darkness of the night,
gives place to dawn and morning light,
and light to day, and sunshine - glare
with natures glory everywhere.

A few short hours that pass away
soon ends the reign of that short day,
the sunlight fades, its glory bright
is hid again by darkest night.

So life is as the daylight fair
a few short years of life to share,
an allotted span, threescore and ten
and yet not always given to man.

A life that blooms and blossoms gay
soon passes into yesterday
man died, forgotten, life's scarce begun
remembered only by what he has done.

H. G. Inglis

Spring

Summer is getting closer.
Planes are in the sky.
Ring-a-ring of roses the little children cry
I run through the meadow with grass so green
Now I'm off to have a big ice-cream
Grass needs mowing that's what I'm
going to do have a nice day with
love from me... to... you.

Lisa Roe

Sea Storm

She's in a ferocious and dangerous mood, this changeable madam
so calm and so cool - satanical spirits possess all her force
she lashes, she gashes she rears like a horse. Superbly
hypnotic she rants and she raves, her frothiest petticoat
proudly displayed - her burning desire is to reclaim the land,
she surges still further with lean outstretched hands.

She flings and she tosses the rocks with no effort - to her
they are peppercorns, light as a feather, her refuse is
spattered - she cares not on whom - impassable highways are
    littered and strewn.

The house is in darkness, the candle is lit - the rafters
above, almost airborne, are split - at the mercy of demons
intent to destroy, the long night approaches with deafening cries.

Aboard an old sea vessel tattered and torn is my body
transported through this night of storm, its creaks and its
groans serve to torment my soul as hellfire and damnation is
    raging 'till dawn.

I pray for the morning when all will be calm 'though I know
I will witness destruction and harm - her venom exhausted,
contrite and serene, this madame, so winsome, this treacherous
    queen.

C. J. Horrocks

Moonlight

The scarlet of sunset had faded,
The splendour of evening was o'er,
And cool night had gently descended
On valley and forest and moor.

Then slowly above the horizon
The moon in her fullness did rise,
Embracing the land in her mystical light.
Tinting the clouds in the skies.

A breeze stirred the trees in the forest.
Their leaves seemed to dance with delight,
Like silvery-clad ballerinas
On the moon lightened stage of the night.

Down through the meadow, a brooklet ran singing,
Reflecting the moon's pallid sheen;
Ran, singing its song to the valley and forest,
Of the magical sights it had seen.

Yes! A magical landscape of beauty and wonder,
No mortal e'er witnessed more lovely a sight,
What painter could capture with his brush on a canvass
That cascade of silver...on the velvet of night.

Robert James Ovell

Reflections

With beguiling finger the river beckons.
Its sight and sounds untie the knots
of my mind and carries me on its way
passed mountain gorge and tree-ferned banks
ever downwards as it continues to the sea.
Flowing unmindfully alongside
the industrial noise of the steelworks,
it majestically moves at night
below a blasted sky of red.
Gulls screech and fly this river, calling
to it to merge with the source,
which gave it birth in heavy clouds.
With wonder children are heard with
distinctive voices in play
from a remembered time of flood and laughter
and of warm, long summer nights talking
by the riverside.

Now so many of my voices are silenced,
yet still the river flows, beckoning
to unite my beginning with my end.

Mairwen Morgan

Laburnum

Colour of the intellect:
Feathered fronds dance in splendid disarray.
Fading now, but nonetheless remarkable.
When was your metamorphosis?
Those dark December days when all was still?
A dust of snow perhaps?
Yet poisonous your fruit became;
Your lovely yellowness concealed.
Bitter black seeds enclosed in brittle finger pods.

Trefoils now your renaissance herald,
And all is light and bright again -
Breathtaking your early summer show.
Inspiration for the intellect.

Sheila McGoran

Light Of Life

From the darkness of night, we see the dawn
And on the horizon, there's a shimmering sun
'Tis the break of day and the darkness gone
Bringing the light and the warmth to everyone.

A new day begins with the doves on the wing
With this light of life that comes from above
Our tasks to perform, and happiness bring
As we spend our time in work, play and love.

This daylight is timed and we watch the sun
As it slowly bridges the vast sky of blue
Then shadows appear and the sunlight is done
It's time to rest, as all the doves do.

This light of life, as right from the start
Begins once again with the sun and the dawn
And the doves come again, as they flutter and dart
And we wake again, as a new day is born.

With this light from the sun, day after day
We prepare for our time, while still here on earth
And we live all our lives, as well as we may
With this light of life, as God meant from birth.

Leo J. Martin

A Son Named Matthew

I carried you inside me for nine tiring and morning
sickness months.
My body fit for bursting, and full of stretch marks
and lumps.
Then came your arrival a happy time for all.
We named you Matthew meaning gift from God.
Now some birthday's later God help us all.

Margaret Dawson

To A Friend

I'm sorry to say you are one of they
That keep your brain in your pocket
When your money runs out your brain shouts
Fill me up fill me up any way to the top

So your brain in your pocket starts to rocket
With ways of getting cash it can be very rash
People get hurt some get trampled into the dirt
To you it does not matter as long as your grey matter
Gets what it wants

So in future if you wouldn't mind
Keep your brain in your head like I do with mine
I work hard for the money I get
And do not want a silly twit coming along and taking it

So take your brain out of your pocket
And put it in the right socket.
If you do not take it out of your pocket
And put it back in its right socket

Then eventually there will grow a hole
And through it will roll
The brain lost for ever

James L. G. Kent

School Holidays In The Welsh Valleys

How we looked forward with delight, counting every day and
   night.
No School, no homework to be done, just Holidays and
   having fun.
To Grandma's house, where we could stay, enjoying every
   lovely day.
In memory I see them still, the rows of houses against the hill.

Small and terraced, joined as one, shaded by the hills from sun.
White washed doorsteps, all same size, net shrouded windows
   like blinked eyes
The Ty Bach in the backyard fell, and oft a pigeon loft as well,
And if you came down in the night, you could not see without
   a light.

In the best room, for all to see, an Aspidistra like a tree.
Its leaves were polished every day, this hallowed room was
   not for play.
In the fireplace, standing guard, two china dogs, with eyes so hard,
Which seemed to watch you as you go, and even in the dark
   would glow.

In the hall, with stately tock, against the wall, grandfather clock,
Marking out, with sombre chime, the passing of our pleasure time.
Bath night was one to best recall, tin bath brought in from
   outside wall.
How we giggled, splashed and played, when towels on the
   floor were laid.

In the day in the clear fresh air, we climbed the mountain
   without care.
How we loved to climb the heights, to look down at all the
   town's best sights.
The people looked so small below, hurrying hither, to and fro.
While we, so full of childish glee, romped through the heather,
   feeling free.

   Gwyneth Pritchard

Blow On Gayle My Love, Blow On

I watched you grow into a child, your nature was so meek and
mild, your eyes were of the deepest blue, your skin was such a
lovely hue, your smile lit up your pretty face, you learnt to tie
your own shoe lace, your hair was think, straight and blond,
your legs were muscular and strong, a little girl so loving and
sweet, who had the daintiest pair of feet, I wonder why you
had to go? My heart will never really know.
Heavenly Father up above, please protect our Gayle we loved,
give her all the love you can, while you hold her tiny hand, as
you guide her to your home, never leave her all alone, shine
upon her night and day, give her plenty time to play, hold her
gently to your chest, give her plenty time to rest, let the gale
in her keep blowing, to remind us of the girl we knew, who now
lives up there with you. Blow on Gayle my love, blow on.

   Faith Gilbert

Edwin

"Here lieth Edwin James Murray"
And here sits young Elspeth,
Her hair pinned beneath her clean cotton cap,
Her blue skirt billowing on fine white linen, edged with spun lace.
She ponders in her simple way about life and love
And pulls idly on the hedge mustard growing wild about the grave.
She pictures Edwin toiling in the field
With tools that make the hands blister but the heart strong.
She sees his gleaming muscles, moist below the beating sun,
And his uncombed hair, restless, wanton.
He was big was Edwin,
A man of men, made mightier by his arduous work,
Yet as gentle as the lambs that added to his spring-time tasks.
"He liked yellow," she muses,
Twirling the small yellow flowers in her fingers
And pulling the deep lobed leaves from the stem.
She sighs, in the sultry air of the June day
And leans against the stone that speaks of life not death.
Then, startled by a call,
She again takes up her own binding chores.

   Kathy Leach

Morning In The Meadows

Butterflies fluttering gently in the air,
From flower to flower they move,
Their wings like velvet,
The flowers bow their heads as on the petals
These gentle creatures rest,
Delicate colours and designs I see with these eyes,
Like fabric so delicate to the touch
as fine and soft as thistledown,
As though kissing by the painters brush.

Who creates something so gentle,
Something so delightful as this.

The birds who greet the morning,
With their happy tune,
Their plumage so colourful,
As they fly around looking for fun.

The smell of the perfume in the meadow,
Of the delicate flowers I see,
Is this where inspiration is born,
Or is it the dew on the grass,
Forming cobwebs on the bushes in the early dawn.

   Evelyn Wood

"Reflection"

"Mortal life is but a fragment.
Use every precious moment to the full.
Seek, strive, but never yield.
Each passing day, accomplish something new.
Learn of others and be thankful.
There is so little time.
Temptations may beset thee
Fear not, but to thyself be true.
Mortal love may beckon thee,
Fulfilment bring thee joy or rue.
But, 'tis a passing human feeling,
And wondrous sights await
For those who seek, have eyes to see.
The ache of beauty, pain and sadness
Will one day be shed,
And awe-ful in its immensity
The veiléd future, un-veiléd be
And you shall see - not in a glass darkly,
But, as we ourselves are seen - and seeing understand."

   Renée Arlett Lawson

The Emigrant's Dream

For years, I dreamed my dreams
Of a thousand different schemes
How I could sail away from England's shore
To a land across the sea
Where every man is free
And the only thing that's missing are the poor.
I saw many different lands
Trod on countless foreign sands
Until, at last I reached my goal so far away
Now I've found that promised land
Yes, I had it in my hands
It was England.
And I'm coming home to stay.

   Ronald Edwards

Skeleton

And the wind blows through the empty heart.
Gone all proud trappings, down to soft dust
Where pride lies level, sidling lust
Now idle as its neighbour sloth; no part
To play for avarice, when envy is dead
At last; nowhere for wrath to be fed,
Gluttony to feast. Defrauded by death
No longer deadly, sins fled with the breath.
And the wind blows through the empty heart

   Eric Chapman

Senses

Our senses essentially tell us
our feelings, scents, touch, taste and sound.
The tempo of life is forever
in minds and hearts eternally bound.

Thunder, lightning - elemental drama,
the roar of the sea and the waves on the shore,
the salty tang of the spray on our faces
and the small voice of man can be heard no more.

To hug and love and to kiss our loved ones,
a handclasp from a friend can mean so much,
a little help, a shoulder to cry on
with the offered hand and the gentle touch.

Feelings can run high and low
hopes and fears on our hearts do play
love, hate, sadness and pleasure,
all have their moments in our day.

The sixth sense is somewhat obscure to me
a strange foreboding that grips the heart,
the future! A sighting of what might be,
transient, fleeting, only to depart.

Rosalie H. Randle

Hand of Darkness

The hand of darkness silently
veils our eyes so we can't see
and blind to nature's purity
we allow a crude insanity
To dominate our lives too readily.

A veil of darkness ensnares the truth
so light and love are rare to perceive
and if one should strive to voice alarm
It seems it is truth that will shatter the calm.

So speeding trucks demand more space
as money feeds the human race
with darkness and dumb tolerance
shall one more tree fall from grace
and dictate the weather's latest pace.

And what if a bomb costing much more
Explodes too near our silent shore
Should we praise the torch of deadly skill
Or shun the villainous blackened will
perhaps forevermore.

Velma Ferguson

Simply Enchanting

I focus on a feather floating on a whispering breeze
And marvel at the rasping sound of the heavy bumble bees
The earthworm tumbling in the soil
The draught from a ladybird's wings
So delicate - so magical, those simple earthly things

Louvaine Atkin

January 1996 "The Queerest Wee Beastie"

Stonin high up oan a Scottish moor,
The smoke fae the city I was trying tae cure,
Cause a' the work had been a michty strain,
Trumendous pressure oan ma brain,
Then oot the blue de ye ken wit I saw,
The queerest wee beastie runnin awa,
Wi fur like straw an legs like twigs,
An a massive snout like yae see oan pigs,
People hid telt me aboot the haggis afare,
I thought it wis lies but doubt nae mare,
I went tae that place many times since then,
But never did I see the haggis again,
I'll always mind that feert look oan his face,
Nae wonder he had hid fae the human race.

Brian Rooney

Loneliness

The Window is cracked and murky. Outside it's cold, dank
    and miserable.
In front is a blazing fire, with flames flickering, dancing,
    as the warmth swirls around the room.
The light is dim but comfortable.
Eyes still search outside for hope, trust, desire, a chance for
    happiness.
Taken away, snatched from the arms, not caring, pain, tears, hurt.
It stays like a stone hand wrapped against a warm heart,
Pulling, tugging, tearing the life, love, wishes, dreams,
    leaving only nightmares, suffering, loneliness.

Sue McIntyre

Untitled

In darkened shadows, there I stand
a frightened soul from distant land
and watch in light of moon approach
a lady in a wondrous coach.
This lady fair with sparkling eyes,
Far from my trembling touch she lies;
her beaming smile in dead of night
puts stars and moon to shameful flight.
My heart it shakes and sighs, I sway
as weakened legs at last give way.
I struggle fiercely with my fears,
my blood it boils, my eyes stream tears
of need, frustration, love, desire
what would I give to have this fire
that burns in me course through her breast!
I must act now, I cannot rest!
The coach moves on, too late, I fail,
panicked I rise, a love torn male.
Then, on the street, I find a note
as dawn breaks I read what she wrote...to me.

Igor A. Ledochowski

Migrating To Warmth

Mice will soon be hibernating
In warm burrows.
Graceful leaves falling
Russets, golds and ochres
All on the carpeted ground.
The trees are gaining colour
In the frosty sky;
North winds blow
'Gainst our frozen faces.

Time to store our food
Over the long hard winter.

Wrapping ourselves up as we play outside
And heating our homes and beds.
Rosy cheeks as we walk
Making dragon breaths.
Time for change,
Here is autumn.

Kevin Hoffin

Another 'If'

If you can make your bed
    when all around are leaving theirs,
If you can cook a meal
    when all your friends are eating out,
If you can wash and iron clothes
    and ignore the launderette just down the road,
If you can soothe a fevered brow and clean up vomit
    instead of calling the doctor,
If you can make order out of chaos, confusion and mess
    and still remain calm,
If you can rock the baby and vacuum at the same time
    without relying on your mother,
Then, you will not only be a man my son, but a husband
    and father too.

Joan Hunter-Brown

Wheels

Baby buggies and prams, trolley buses and trams
The motors that deliver our meals
Ploughs and tractors, steam driven saws
Where would they be, without wheels.

Motor cycles and bikes, machines that dig dykes
Each has its own special appeal
Engines that fight fires, police black Maria's
All of them rely on the wheel.

Wagons and carts, clocks moveable parts
A serious thought, here reveals
That locomotives and trains, helicopters and planes
Would not get very far, without wheels.

Taxis and cars, spaceships to the stars
The spurs that a cowboys horse feels
Pumps and windmills, dentistry drills
Not one can operate, without wheels.

Ships on high seas, trolleys for teas
Roller skates, and fairground mobiles
A lorry, a van, most inventions of man
Where would they be, without wheels.

Aubrey Pickess

The City

To the station - To the City - they hasten on their way,
Expensive suits and garish ties hide their natural colour - grey,
The bankers and accountants and lawyers by the score,
The secretaries and clerks and dealers from the 'Floor'.

It's Seven in the morning - there's plenty to be done.
A rushed "Hello" to colleagues - and then we'll start the fun,
The "Footsie's" looking shaky, But the "Dow's" shot through the roof,
The Market boom goes on and on - the "Nikkei's" living proof!

Switches pressed to 'on' - Screens flicker into life.
See what state the Market's in - before they ring the wife,
July Futures in "Exco" are looking a good bet,
Perhaps we'll Buy tomorrow - certainly not quite yet.

Prawn salad sandwich at the desk - Eleven Thirty - Lunch,
Sell a 'Put' and buy a 'Call' - purely on a hunch,
The afternoon gets busy - A 'Merger's ' to be had,
The 'phones, they don't stop ringing, the Market's going Mad!'

Thank God that's over - Four Thirty - Time for us to go,
"Well see you in the Boozer" and let a few pints flow
Five Thirty - To the station, and back to suburban life,
Is it really worth it? - This City wheel of strife.

S. J. Peters

Space

After 76 voyages around the sun, I am ready
to assert that space is not inert.
The world through space does not go.
Space carries the world to and fro.
It is the conveyer of our sphere. Be of
good cheer. The truth at last is here.
Let it be said "Gravity is dead." "Newton
was mad." "The people have been had."
God can make a tree - but not gravity.
With smooth effortless grace the super fluid
called space carries our world apace.
We pay no heed to our 20 miles per
second speed because super fluid engineering
at Nature's best makes perpetual
motion seem like rest. With hot stars
and our sun burning and churning,
space is alive and pulsating with energy electrified.
  In a whirlpool of space our world
plays its part 93 million miles away
from the sun's boiling bubbling heart.

David Martin

Laughter

She gave her tinkling beady laugh
His, like a base bell, from his belly came,
The others laughed with shades of in-between
Some wildly joyous, some by contrast, tame.

Few made no sound but from their eyes
Like sun that peeps from clouded skies
Came twinkling laughter, with lines drawn fine
Around the eyes, a happy sign.

Laughter led to song and song to dance,
One a guitarist, one a trumpet player
Made music for dancing and for song
Folks brought their gifts of mirth from far and near.

Even daisies in haphazard lines
Danced with golden headed celandines,
And late birds, humming, stopped to sing.
Gay laughter is a wondrous thing.

Florence Otterburn

Luck Of Three Sisters

One night during the 1939 to 1946 war,
My two sisters and myself decided
To attend a local whist-drive, which we did.
When 24 hands of whist had been played,
The person running the whist drive called
For the top ladies scores, then the gents.
When the ladies' winners names were called for first,
My two sisters and myself were
The top three winners 1st, 2nd and 3rd ladies' prizes.
Leaving only the booby prize for someone else
The next morning on opening the daily paper
We read, Great Britain had won a section of the war.
Was it a coincidence our name being spelt the same way?

Mary G. A. Britain

Buttercups

When I was three or was it four
The year forty-three or forty-four
My dad came home from war
I remember it vividly
We went for a walk in a meadow in Leicestershire
The buttercups came over my head
Now the buttercups are all dead
And so is my dad
No longer do flowers grow with such profusion
This only leads to my confusion
Do buttercups no longer grow so tall
Or was I just so very small

Sheila Taylor

June Evenings

June evenings - when daylight lingers long,
  And the world is still,
When a chorus of birds sing evensong
  In the woods, on the hill.

When not even a whisper shakes the trees
  And the flowers are asleep
And the clover is sought by wandering bees
  As dim stars peep
  In the western sky.
The muffled cooings of pigeons arise
  Distant and low,
And a velvety softness touches the sky
  From the new moon's glow,
  And the bats dart by.

June - when sweet-smelling blossoms scent the night,
  And the days are long,
When the world is filled with drowsy delight
  And nothing seems wrong.

Joan Letts

Untitled

Does anyone want some more turkey?
Or gammon? It's all for today.
A sausage with bacon, or stuffing?
Now don't let me throw it away.

Who'd like some more crunchy potatoes?
I didn't dish up very much.
I'm sure you'd all like second helpings,
But the dish is quite hot, so don't touch!

I'll get the green beans and the carrots,
And the sprouts and the parsnips as well.
And then there are peas and the cauliflower cheese,
You might want some more - who can tell?

I'm just bringing in some more gravy,
Two dishes - they're not very deep.
Now eat up and then we'll have pudding
Oh dear - you've all fallen asleep!

M. Doig

The Truth

Your words have been spoken, sincerity high,
Can they be believed, or is it a lie?
Or rather a lie, untruth to be told,
You're getting in deep now, how long can you hold?

Another is needed to justify the last,
Lost in confusion, distortion of facts.
But oh ho you've changed now - I nearly forgot,
Just verbally inaccurate, lies they are not.

Well is there a difference? You hope there will be,
Or is that another lie given to me?
Nonentity and worthless, I'm trapped by your guilt
My life on the line - you'd lie to the hilt.

Expect me to live my life through your eyes,
The gap slowly widens with the web of your lies,
Deserving the truth and to trust what is said,
To flee from the fiction that grows in your head.

Dorothy Dudgeon

Untitled

There is no future
There is no past
For Jesus love us from first to last
He gives us guidance when we are lost.
And offers courage from off the cross

The story of Jesus is known to many
It's known to yourself and known to your enemy

Trust in Jesus from above
And from His kingdom he'll give you love
A love so true that will not waver
Ask, the Lord and if that favour is so sound
He'll grant your wish - and you've been found.

Lawrence Hughes

Farewell To A Friend

I am grateful to have had a friend,
Who values my company as I value theirs.
Someone who I can always depend
Upon to exchange views on everyday cares.

Life has many wonderful gifts,
Friendship being most precious,
So, when we reluctantly drift
Apart, let fond memories sustain us.

I hope that through the rest of my life
I shall make friends anew,
Building on the firm foundation
Of the friendship I once knew.

C. Whittaker

Visitors

The answer is yes, when your best friend says, we'll be down
   your end soon, can we stay a few days?
You look around the lounge, and the decor looks drab, so a tin
   of white gloss and a paint brush you grab.
It starts to improve I hasten to say, but the wallpaper needed
   a change anyway.
The room looks tremendous, so clean and so bright, but the
   dining room now is a terrible sight.
We had to do this, and the kitchen and bedrooms, and though
   it looks good, we are dead from the paint fumes.
Now the house is pristine and the visitors have come, we feel
   far too shattered to join in the fun.
Let this be a lesson to all of like mind, let your guests come
   and stay, and just take what they find.

Margaret Juanita Roberts

"Love"

There is this lad I know
I met him only a few months ago
he is tall with dark hair and dark eyes
who likes steak and kidney pies
I fell in love with him only last week
I think he's sexy and really neat,
kissing him would be bliss
just a chance to get one little kiss.
I've never felt this way before
he moves my heart with such galore,
an arrow was shot straight to my heart
and I want to be by his side and not apart.
Does he like me?
Only he knows
how can I tell him that my love for him
grows,
please help me to figure it out
because I can't say what love's all about.

Covette Scamp

Whose Fault?

Bog cold body on a bog cold night
No longer able to put up a fight
Or struggle for freedom from hands that claw,
And maul, and probe, where nobody saw
A thing, or heard a sound -
Not down there where there's no-one around.

"She shouldn't have been there", that's what you say,
"Of course she'll become a victim to prey".
Close your ears to the darkness, turn your back on the fear,
It doesn't happen if you can't hear.

Her death was silent, her life was to show
The price to be paid for daring to go
Alone in the shadows where night-terrors roam -
"If you want to be safe, you should stay at home!".
Your truth's an illusion; You haven't a clue!
And you'd soon change your mind if it happened to you!

Sian Kelly-Scott

She Takes The Floor

She takes the floor one more time; she takes the floor
for the last time; but the last time will last
me a lifetime like diamonds that shine with a
speck of gold, so much glamour, so much soul
She takes the floor one more time; she takes the
floor for the last time;
she's the queen of the cadburary;
she makes her name; she earns her fame; she
takes the floor one more time; she takes the floor
for the last time; what a marvellous, a practical
way to end it, standing ovation, flowers
from little children; she takes the floor one more
time; she takes the floor for the last time;
but the last time will last me a lifetime.

Clifton Tobin

Back In Time

As I passed the highways and byways
I started reminiscing about my school days
Children churning against the vicious winds
Hearts beating fast, ringing into the darkness
The glow of the skin, like a diamond in the sun
The delighting of the eyes, how grand it was to be a child

Now I'm an old man sitting in my recliner
White beard full of words from long ago
My ragged fingers from days long past
I'd forgotten how beautiful the countryside was
It really, really is

Storms now gathering momentum
Skies black which seem like birds' wings
Don't ever scurry away, enjoy the rich juicy smell
From our land and seas
Don't worry about time, this may be all gone
Yes, in a thousand years from now

Lena Hilton

"The Old Oak Tree"

I remember this Oak tree in our local park
With its contorted branches, and vast rugged bark
It was like an old friend, the kind you can trust
To climb its full height I felt that I must

But I never went further than a branch that was there
All curved to sit like a cosy armchair
I'd talk to the tree, say "I like you so much"
Then its leaves gently rustled, like an answer, as such

In a world of my own, I would sit there and dream
Pretend I was Princess, fine lady or queen
Imagine adventures in far distant lands
In a mansion I'd live, richly furnished and grand

The leaves then would whisper, "It's time to go home
The riches are there, you don't have to roam
To all those who love you, a Princess you'll be
And the grandeur of nature, is to all given free"

Joan Miller

Where Is Spring?

The wind teased, gusting from the east
A greedy monster in the cherry tree, enjoying a feast.
Soft petals danced, snow fairies on the wing.
Fluttered to the shadowed lawn below.

I mourned their passing, heard a bird sing.
Sad tears of rain fell on the pink carpet.
I listened, and the bird song echoed, plaintive.
Where is spring?

Irene Paddock

The Beach By Night

The sun goes down across the beach,
The sea gulls are coming in.
Most of the land is deserted,
The light is very dim.
But jumping over the sand castles, chasing crabs away,
Playing with the seaweed and prowling along the bay,
Ready to catch a fish or two,
Hiding there so small,
Then pouncing on the black and red fish,
Becoming so big and tall,
Stands a beautiful black and white cat
So tall, so big, so proud.
He starts to roll on his back
And purr so very loud.
Then the beach is silent,
The sun begins to shine,
Wake up everybody,
It is morning time.

Elizabeth Simpson

'Goldie'

When he was first brought home
he was very small and cute
his hair was a golden blonde look
and he had lovely velvet ears!
He would bite and nibble at a rubber bone
and his little sharp teeth used to bring me close to tears

He used to play in the 'toy box'
and used to tear at clothes and socks
he used to stumble and fall
when he tried to stand up tall!

His golden hair and bright eyes
his little paws
and neat little jaws
his squeaky bark and whimpering cries

But now he's rather elderly
his golden hair has turned almost white
he cries and barks to get out at night
we've had him nearly fifteen years
and he's still got those lovely velvet ears!

Linda Sweetland

Gratitude - From A Guide

The Boer War had ended and a famous General said
'Now that the war is over what do we do instead?'
The boys who once had helped him - he put them into groups
He taught them how to fish and stalk
And formed the Boy Scout troops
The Scouts were busy all the time - there was so much to do
They went to camp and learned to climb.
The Movement grew and grew
The girls thought they would like to join. 'No no' the General said
But in the end he said they could - and so they formed the Guides
Not only Guides by Rosebuds too - the Brownies and the Rangers
The Movement grew and grew and friendship came from strangers
And now there are Young Leaders to carry on from there
And of course the Trefoil Guild to go from year to year
The General was of course "B. P." to whom we must say 'Thanks'
For allowing us so long ago to join the Boy Scout ranks
To Lady Baden-Powell as well who was always at his side
She gave her all to Guiding. Our beloved world Chief Guide
They gave us happiness and joy - they gave us so much more
The most important things of all.
Our Promise and our Law.

Anne Purves

If He Walked Back

Drifts of trampled instants fell
mutely as sand threads in a glass.
They lived between extremes, playing
ring-a-rosy games around a shut box
full of dullness.

Her baffled fascination became a force of habit,
but there was no feeling in his touch;
and she couldn't love the empty air.

In their distant haze of strawberry
evenings, her love drained him;
but she couldn't turn him off.
Her forgotten memories sought remembrance
in his paper promises;
whilst she dreamed on, writing if he walked
back lyrics,
in her leather bound desk diary.

Chris Senior

Helford River

The mist coils upward to the ghost of the sun.
A cloud pink-tinged, but all is silent;
Still sleeps the world.
A bird's first plaintive cry blurring the edge of dawn
Then daylight comes and Heaven is revealed.
It's a watercolour morning.

Yvonne Stirling

Trapped Within Sins

A little older for more wiser
With ever breath I learn just a little more
There's no use trying, I'm no saint
I've seen the sinners and I've been there before
I cannot wash away the sins
Too much darkness behind these eyes
I want so much to be free from it all
But within my soul I can't break the cries.
No escaping the reasons of past
All my future will now be lost
For all that I used to be, and I was
I will, now forever pay the cost.
Flashes of the days that used to be
Now and then they appear.
But now all I see is what now will be
And all falling from grace will be a tear.

Samantha Searle

A Silent Prayer

For baby Jake, who's sadly missed.
A short poem, that's blessed and kissed.
All though you never breathed the air.
The love around you, made you rare.
As each year passes by, my love,
We watch over you from above.
I know you're being well looked after.
And hope your day's are full of laughter.
Each rose that blooms each and every summer,
Means there will always's be another.
Where ever you are, be at peace.
Our love for you will never cease.
So sleep on my little one,
As you rest under the warm, warm, sun.

Susan Pasifull

Sudden Death

You left without warning,
You were here, then gone.
My mind became numb,
I only realized with next day's dawning.

No time for recriminations,
No time for explanations,
You went,
Your life spent.

Years later I look back,
I have survived,
I am at peace with myself,
What if you had not died?

J. E. Twelvetree

Yesterday's Tomorrow

Beside me, there was you.
Twisted and torn by shattered dreams,
Knowing that it was only a matter of time.
Forget? It's not so easy,
The truth won't be swallowed.
But why?
When there could have been another way.
We would have found another day, together.
Instead I bear the pain,
The sadness and the sorrow.
Your ghost is my company
But also my dear friend.
Your death is my enemy
Torturing my mind,
Destroying my sanity.
Suicide kills,
I never needed proof.
Just you.

Jayne Massey

What A Smile Can Do

I smiled softly to relieve the anger that was within me
The tears were flowing down my cheeks
I tried to wipe the falling tears and the more I wiped them, the more
they came out
I even tried to hide my face that nobody could see me
Then, Suddenly
Something happened deep from inside of me
Something is telling me. . .
Hush my daughter do not worry... It will soon be over

E. Burnett

A New Me

Today is the beginning of the rest of my life
Today I stop worrying about trouble and strife,
Today I start living my life to the full
No time to be boring and stuffy and dull,
All strong emotions I'll try to repress
I'll grab a new life and begin to redress,
I wont fritter my precious time away
Or dwell on the things of past yesterdays,
I'll welcome the new dawn with arms open wide
And shake off this depression and heaviness inside,
I'll just take my chance, I'll survive and be strong
For what is true happiness but one moment long,
So I'll share all I have let my heart run free
Today's a new beginning, a new start - a new me.

Vera Veronica Adams

Ode To The Human Mother

At lilac time she went to stay
With fragrance of the month of May
She left me with a heavy heart
That she and I should have to part.

Another year has come and gone
Through grief and pain the sun has shone
The gap she left was wild and wide
Her memory shall firm abide.

Though tears are less, I miss her still
At times like this my thoughts do fill
With scenes and echoes of the past
That only sunny hours should last

She saw me through life's thick and thin
Until she knew that I could win
I owe to her as to no other
My grateful heart the dearest mother

And when each year the spring returns
The warmer glow within me burns
Then I will upward lift my eyes
To see her in God's clear blue skies.

Norma Anne MacArthur

Images Of An Indian Summer

It is over a month since home we did fly
To the green, green grass and the dark grey sky
I have unpacked my suitcase and Indian drums
Now I sit at a table and twiddle my thumbs
I look out of school windows at kids in the yard
I'm trying to work, but it all seems so hard
People have said that I look like a rake
But my hair is not bleached; the tan is no fake
The food was quite strange, and the poverty hell
Cities were noisy, with a terrible smell
I remember the smiles of people I saw
The very warm welcome and wide open door
Most of all I remember the Indian sun
And travelling the country and having great fun

It has been said before, by people who roam
But it really is true: There's no place like home

Tom Davis

Sunday Evening Inactivity

Toys, still and lifeless.
A well-used box of treasures
And beyond
A line of bricks
Arranged with loving care.
When again will they come to life?
Where are the minds that give them
Movement?
In slumber, regaining strength and imagination.
So tomorrow it will be
Before inanimate becomes again
Animate
And stirred at the touch of lively fingers.

Alan Bushnell

This Thing

Sweet as sugar.	Bitter as tears.
Salty as the sea.	Bloody as the sunset.
Cool as a breeze.	Grey as clouds.
Dense as fog.	Sharp as a blade.
Fast as a horse.	Loud like thunder.
Exciting like a race.	Unpredictable as a storm.
Destructive like a quake.	Mad as a hatter.
Aromatic like a rose.	Long and winding like the Nile.
Hard as a rock.	Passionate as music.
Mind-blowing like drugs.	Funny like Norman Wisdom.
Sad like Othello.	Tragic like Gone with the Wind.
Beautiful as a model.	Thumping like a heart.
Varying like a show.	Hot as the sun.
This is just one thing:	Life!

Maryam Yahyavi

I Like Noise

I like noise.
The crash of the waves, the blast of a rocket.
The sizzle of bacon.
The swish of the sea crashing on the rocks.
The beep of a horn, the bang of a hammer.
The moo of a cow.
The roar of a lion locked in its cage.
The rap of a cane, the scream of a girl.
The bark of a dog as it scratches the door.
The boom of a drum.
All of that makes the brain boil.
The chime of a clock, the creak of a door.
The gush of water.
The gurgle of children at a neighbouring door.
All of these sounds make me laugh.
I like noise.

Ryan McGarrie

No Time

Why is everyone so busy?
Rushing, rushing everywhere.
No time to greet the neighbours,
Not a minute can they spare
To stop and think for once of others
The homeless - unemployed,
The hungry and the broken-hearted,
Suffering and the soul-destroyed.
How much time would it take,
To think about the others,
The sick, the lonely and the sad,
Broken families, childless mothers,
War torn countries, soldiers, prisoners,
Battered children, those in fear,
No time to think of all these people
To hesitate, to shed a tear.
Let's pray to God for just a moment,
He gave us love to share.
The list is endless, of the needy.
So is time:- It's always there.

P. Buchanan

The Path Of Reason

The path of reason asks a deadly toll;
The drudge of occupation summons me.
Yet to be bold, and to be truly free,
A man must walk alone and keep his soul.

The purity of excellence is gone,
Destroyed by obsolescent deference,
And in its place the world gives preference
To liars and the filth they feed upon.

Betrayed by plagiary, truth overthrown,
Perfection bows and imperfection sands.
The hourglass shatters; drifting with the sands.
Forgotten words of men yield up their crown.

We lost without a care our greatest art:
We sold to avarice our mortal heart.

Jamie Liddell

Untitled

I have contemplated time and time again,
why have I been subdued to all this pain,
from people whom I have befriended,
in which now the friendship has sadly ended.

Why is it so that I'm trapped in this cage,
playing the lead role on the stage.
Lying and cheating is all part of the act,
so that I myself can stay intact.

With only books on the shelf for me to read,
that hold all the knowledge in which I feed.
I've read my past, now I read my future,
to find the question without an answer.

Heidi Warren

Belgium (Christmas 1944)

He was a priest; and for a moment's time
We stood - then walked across the devastated place.
He clasped his hands together in despair.
Looked at the dead and the bewildered dying.
And in God's Holy name blessed them.
And those that could, answered
     When he said, "What is your name?"
And some lived long enough to say "Amen",
When he, the priest, absolved them from their sins.
I walked away and lit a cigarette, looked at the sky
Saw clouds serene and free.
     Watched this priest to whom names meant so much;
     As if he was an auditor for God
Making a tally for the eternal book.
Nearby a bitch in whelp,
Too tired to flee this busy place of death.
     Whimpered in pain.
I knelt beside her, fondled her weary head.
"What is your name?" I said
And held her close to me, and wept.

D. C. Deacon

A Girls View Of The: Big Wide World!

Look at me what do you see?
Do you see a girl beautiful and free?
Now, time has past and I've grown to know,
How people are mean in this world with some, it shows,
All people seem to care about is sex and money
But why? I wanna know Mummy.
Prejudice and hate white people will never know.
As well as Blacks, Indians and Latinos.
We are the people of the world.
Why don't we stick together?
We've done damage to the world that'll live forever.
This is our world mother-nature, this is our mess.
The price we can never repay for our carelessness.
This is our world God, look at how many things have gone wrong.
These problems will go on and on...
This is the big wide world Mummy where I'll have to go.
Do I really want to? I'll never really know.

Andreya Triana

Persistence

Singly at first, then in batches
The plants burst through the grass,
Broad bladed leaves, the eye first catches
And quickly now they do amass.

Tall tubular stems with heavy buds
Now dominate this ever growing scene,
In road-side verges, fields and woods
It seems that every where they're seen

Now the buds burst into flowers
Wild flowers, among which, this is a beacon
That in persistence, above all others towers,
And who's tenacity, never seems to weaken.

A sea of yellow that covers everywhere
Blooming strongly, until petals fall, and change
To rounded puff-balls, that "melt" on the air,
And widely over the land they range,

Spreading seeds to further ensure
The future of this wild flower, a scion,
That seems for ever will endure,
That stubborn, tenacious, prolific, timeless dandelion!

R. A. George

Beyond

When all the world is done, my love, and stars resume their sleep,
When there is no more space to fill and no more time to keep,
When there is no more darkness and the light has died away,
When there is no tomorrow, as there was no yesterday,
When nothing is infinity with you and I above,
The void devoid of shape and sound shall hold and sing my love.

When memory is forgotten and forgetfulness is done,
When cold and warm have met at last within the silent sun,
When all the poems reach their end and all pens lie asleep,
When there is no more cause to laugh nor any need to weep,
When all the universe has gone away with all of time,
There shall at last be space enough to hold my love in rhyme.

When all things that may come to pass are past and cannot be,
When there is nothing left to know and none are there to see,
When there is no more meaning, for all things are at an end,
When there is no reality and no place to pretend,
When we shall meet at last, my love, as I have always known,
We shall be as in all of time and never be alone.

Donald H. McAllister

Illusion Of Love

We say our love is a shining light.
Hold me tight...
   Follow the light,
Love me tonight...
   Follow the light,
Love me forever...
   Follow the light.
In our loves profusion we saw no illusion.
We followed that light into the night.

Aileen McGowan

Our Earth And Our Heritage

P Pollution spoils, industrial oils.
O Our earth so precious filled with life
L Living life a wonderful thing
L Lust filled greed, destroys our needs
U The only ones to play your part, give thought,
   Give heart to our future
   Our beautiful earth, given us in trust.
T Time to care, time to share in hopes and
   Dreams, of life unspoiled.
I In animals we can learn, they do not spoil
   Their habitat, so why do we?
O Oxygen given by trees, yet we kill them.
N Now we must leave something behind when
   We leave, then let it be our beautiful earth.

Rachael Phillips

Tranquillity

I wish I could see the sun so bright,
So warm and inviting and free.
Cascading down and spreading around,
making everything warm as can be.

Then for the sky so blue "Oh", so blue,
not a cloud to be seen anywhere.
Then as for the sea what a colour to be,
it shimmers and shines like a star.

The sand is so white, so fine and so smooth,
Just like salt when you hold in your hand.
The palm trees so tall and their leaves wave so free,
As the wind takes a breath in the heat.

What a place to go when the need is some peace,
All you will hear is the sea,
Splashing at rocks as it flows up the sand,
"Tranquillity it surely must be."

Linda Hilton

The Wind

Trees swaying to the same rhythm,
   as if beating time to a well known concerto.
Leaves blowing around, whipping up and down,
   carelessly landing on cars or passers-by alike,
      seeming to have no worry about what will become of them.
Will they end their days in somebody's dustbin?
Or, will they just stay on mother earth and rot into compost
   to form new life?
   WHAT DOES THIS?
We see what it does, but not what it looks like.
We hear where it goes, but not what it sounds like.
It blows through our hair and into our faces,
   but we'll never know just where it comes from.
It's that invisible force that can, maybe, cause carnage,
   it's the blow that can make a small fire less harmless.
But we all need it sometimes to clear out the mind.
It's nature's way of helping us believe without the seeing.
We all know it's out there, but nobody will ever see it,
   it's the mysterious, unstoppable wind.

Melanie Mannering

Dream Pony

There are nights when I am lying in bed,
comes a noise that makes me lift up my head.
Up to the curtains I have to reach
and pull them back to reveal a beach.
I know this is another night,
I'll see my Dream Pony in the moonlight.

My pale white pony I see at last,
running on the sand so fast, so fast.
Long white tail and mane flowing,
beautiful and wild in the moonlight glowing.
Tall and sturdy it does stand,
in the dark blue sea beside the sand.

At this moment on its back I should be,
splashing and crashing through the waves of the sea.
But in my heart I know all's not as it seems,
I know all I see is just a dream.
Oh why does it all disappear and leave no trail,
Oh why, oh why can't my Dream Pony be real?

Fionnuala Tohill

The Cleaning Lassie From Kinglassie

Although it was ten years to this day, there was
a young lass called kay.

Who decided to start on a cleaning lark to earn
a fair day's pay.

But when she recalls back the years, all the blood
and the sweat and the tears,
she sighs with a huff and gives it a puff roll on
another ten years.

Andrew Collins

Shall I

Shall I stand by and see you sorrow, yet not say for you I
  sorrow too?
Shall I walk by and say, "tomorrow I shall come to comfort you?"
Shall I not shed a tear today for all your tears shed
  yesterday?
Shall I instead just turn my head, or even turn away?
Shall I pretend that I care not and leave you shed your
  tears alone?
Shall I unbend? For that is what my heart insists; the
  heart you know is yours to own.
Oh, my love! How I hurt for you and for the pain I know you feel.
For I more than most, know the love you had for that poor
  dead man was real.

R. Davidson

The Crutch

I am a crutch,
I am picked up when you're too weak to go.
I am a crutch,
Oh so much loved when strength in you is low.
I am a crutch
I get picked up when things are going wrong,
I'm leant on very heavily, I'm leant on for so long.
But when the power's back in you,
There's so much that you want to do,
And now this crutch that's made of wood,
Stops you from doing things you could
Without it, so it cannot stay,
And so you throw your crutch away.
I am a crutch,
Discarded now, I lie here truly broken.
I am a crutch,
Not needed now, no looks, no words are spoken.
When you were down the priceless value that you saw in me,
Is now forgotten, in the past, you're out, you're free, you're free!

Sharron Phillips

"Our Journey"

Where do we go as we slip away
Over the rainbow or a crest of a wave,
Enter a treasure of a cave
With jewels a glistening all arrayed.
Fly on a cloud taking us where we will,
Or maybe we skip on a moss padded hill.
Whatever our path we know for sure
The warmth and the peace would endless endure.
Family and friends who have paved the way,
Would beckon us home for a heavenly stay.

P. Jocelyn Pascoe

'So Wonderful'

Isn't it wonderful to sit by the sea,
With the people you love for company,
Isn't it wonderful, having nothing to do,
Just sitting and looking at the sky so blue,

No pressure from others to move from your rest,
Just watching the birds flying down from their nest,
With a sign of contentment you relax in your chair,
Feel the warmth of the sun, and breathe lots of fresh air.

Walking amongst dandelions on a green velvet hill,
The colours of nature are more than a thrill,
More time to enjoy 'Gods Beauty' on earth,
It's His way of showing us what we are worth.

Prime time to think now, and ponder the past,
And look to the future, and not move very fast,
Enjoying our life now in a much better way,
With wide open spaces for us every day.

Smiles of contentment we wear on our faces,
As we jump in the car and visit new places,
Life has been good and there's lots more to see,
Then coming back home to a nice cup of tea.

Joan Yvonne Matthews

Our Neighbours

What can one say of Colin and Brenda
That young couple so loving and tender
For twenty-five years they have been together
Surviving all life's matrimonial weather
Two sons have bought them so much pleasure
And that black cat for added measure
As they jog life's weary road
They always help with another's load
From petite Brenda a kindly word
Yes, we've heard it from a little bird
And Colin's advice is always ready
To help the failing going steady
So let's hope as the years roll by
That they reach that diamond in the sky.

Harold Percivall

The Witches Brew

To start off with, a bat
Hairy spiders to add to that
Erm...a couple of tails from a rat

Wriggly worms all chopped up with spice
I don't think this brew is going to
Taste very nice
Croaking frogs hoping to be set free
Howling wolves their tongue's taken by me
Eggs from an eagle, beat them twice
Succulent eyeballs mix them with rice

Blood thirsty vampire trying to bite my arm
Rude little hedgehog giving me a snarl
Exciting, this is going to be
What I need now is a child to drink it for me

Joyti Salhan

Untitled

Crisp was the air - Sunday morning walk,
Remembering the past, the future only talk.

Six-o'clock train to return me to hell.
I looked at the sunset: Of a change I could tell.
The feeling inside a hate of the past.
I had to go south; this time it would last.

I threw in my job, I packed up my gear,
I hit the road - no longer in fear.
My future is mine to do what I will.
Free of their society, to live as I feel.

I sing to the moon, the clouds of mist,
Night of the pure. The loved to be kissed.
The strands of my mind blow clear in the wind;
Sea lapping shore. Past memories dimmed.

Clear is the moment as I look in your eyes.
There's no double meaning; we're telling no lies.
I walk to the dawn. You walk by my side,
Arms 'round each other. We've nothing to hide.

R. B. Keach

The Flag Of Peace

I wish the flag of peace would wave
  Imagine all the people it would save
I wish the world was a better place
  And no one cared about your race
What does it matter if you're young or old
  Neither should be left in the cold
I hate the thought of death and war
  My life and family being no more
War is ugly there is no need
  To stop war is a great deed
Hunting is cruel not kind
  A better sport hunters need to find
Many wars have been before
  Don't you see we need no more
Our lives are not for lease
  So please wave the flag of peace

Kathryn I. Geddes

Quarter Moon Tide

Here on the beach as the sun disappears,
Perched on drift wood, alone with my fears.

I watched as the ocean begins to unfold,
Its strength and its beauty, both timid and bold.

Sorrow I've felt and lessons I've learnt
There's no turning back, once the bridge has been burned.

A wave crashes down and darkened the sand,
Like the ocean is reaching, to me with its hand.

The mast of a boat, tries to turn in the breeze,
But the sea whips it back, with the greatest of ease.

There's no stronger force than a quarter moon tide,
Except maybe love, or possibly pride.

Clouds start together, the water turns grey,
Night is approaching engulfing the day.

Away in the distance a bell starts to ring,
The wind becomes bitter, my face starts to sting.

The sun paints the sky a shimmering red,
Autumn is leaving,... winter ahead.

David Tinsley

A Step Above

You may have thought your loved one gone.
And miss them oh so much,
To you it's such a lonely time
Your life's gone out of touch.

But be assured they're not that far
away from us you know.
Its just a step above the sun
In warmth and love they grow.

Their light's still here, and oh so strong
Their light shines far and wide
It may seem far away to us.
It's just the other side.

So keep your faith for life goes on,
Above the clouds into the sun.
And there is spirit all around.
Not just up there but on the ground.

They are but just a breath away
And with each one of us each day.
So don't be sad, we are not far,
But just above, with all our love.

Janet Bentley

Age Of Hope

If I could escape this time, an age of hope for me I'd find.
Be quick to get there, slow to leave. A place where no one
could deceive, nor tell a lie, nor bend the fact. With truth and
innocence intact, be slow to anger, quick to learn. A place like
this is all I yearn.

But from my time I can't escape. The hatred, violence, death
and rape, where darkness reigns, where evil wins, and all must
suffer for its sins; where human monsters seek to prey on
fellow man for fun and play, releasing pain and sorrow free.
Who made this loathsome world for me?

And for the children I despair, as some will die while others
dare to live their lives as best they can - corrupted, caught,
then tried, then damned to be as humans always will and live
to fight, destroy, and kill; be slow to think, yet quick to die.
My world is hopeless, tell me why?

Why must this earth revolve on fear? Why must we feel fear's
grasp so near? Why are we quick to seek revenge, but all too
slow to be as friends? Do I have answers? No, not I. And so,
my friends, you now know why if I could just escape this time,
an age of hope for all I'd find.

Allan Stark

Tomorrow

In thoughts of tomorrow, hidden, unseen,
The dreams of yesterday, tomorrow's dream,
Clouds of the morning, ascending to me,
All aspects of sunshine, in my heart to see,
Forget that which is gone, linger no more,
Becoming the shadow, where once stood the door,
Knocking to enter, but cannot come in,
Where once stood yesterday, that which cannot begin,
For eternally gone, tomorrow may care,
A dream is a dream, if you really dare,
Then what will I do, when yesterday's gone,
I'll live for tomorrow, that's how I begun.

Carol Roberts

'The Golf Club'

Oh, the days I spend at the Golf Club,
in my declining years of catering.
Yes, the days were long, the work
hard, but, all so worth while,
in those lovely surroundings,
no two days were the same, but,
all lovely, on the fairways and the greens
come sun, wind or rain, the deer
wandered round, their coats so velvety
atlas ever! Then, one wondrous
evening, in the setting sun, I can
see it now. All those years ago, two
stags fought, for the lady of their love!

Pamela Gilmour

Coming Close

If Einstein's right and we are bound to nearly always
live alone, separated in our experience from all others
by the time it takes the light to pass between us.
If we can never see another as he is but only as he was,
never be as we are seen to be, so long as we are cleft
by space from him.
If we are really isolated as we stand alone in time, then
perhaps our only sanctuary from solitude is when
we touch, as in bed together; two locked instantaneous beings
vibrating, reacting as one whole; the only true communication.
A recapitulation of our early contact through the breast.

Arthur Crisp

Good News

I took some flowers for my grandparents today
And as I was near, for my father and brother by the way
Whilst I was there I cut the grass
And talked of things of which had passed.
There's a sheltered spot by an ivy wall,
A cherry tree with branches tall.
I said it was with heavy heart
Their sudden leaving - tore me apart.
They listened well, with not a word,
All I could hear was a singing bird.
I went to the cemetery again today
To tell them - my daughters baby is on the way.

Maureen Gibson

Inspired Idea

I sit all alone, racking my brain.
The same dull ideas are coming again.
To get the right thoughts, it takes concentration.
The right atmosphere and imagination.
Waiting and waiting for a rhyme that's just right.
I'm thinking of topics, well into the night.
And suddenly a rush and ideas swirl round.
Possibilities spring up for the theme that I've found.
An idea has arrived and I'm no longer tired.
Put a pen to paper, once more I'm inspired.

Julia Wilkinson

Postponed Shopping

Lady, do not avert your eyes
in disgust, as you pass.
Once I too rushed about,
Christmas shopping top priority.
Clutching bags to my chest,
as I now clutch my bottle.

Do not steer you children by me,
as you would by a pool of vomit.
I once too had a child,
shielding him my pleasure.
Holding his hand in mine,
as I now hold my bottle.

I did not choose to be addicted - I am.
But right now I choose to feed it.
God help me to stop and fight,
To live my life again,
To hold you close to my heart,
To cast away my bottle.

Mary Keaveney

"And The Tide Never Came Back In Again"

I just stood there calmly on the edge of the shore.
The last wave tickled my feet.
I didn't know then, I wish I had done
That never again would we meet.

And the tide never came back in again.
For the rest of time there was no sea.
So I sat and I wondered where it could have gone
But inspiration fell short of me.

Each day I went out to where I'd seen the tide go
But there was blackness and silence, it was dry.
For although I had wished, my beach the sea missed.
A gap left between land and the sky.

And the tide never came back in again
Even though to the beach we all crept.
The distance remained bare
Just a grey mass of sand.
A wasteland, isolated, windswept.

Thomas Ward

Don't Wait

If I had some advice to give then surely it would be, to say the
things you really feel, on that you must agree. Don't put off
till tomorrow what could be said today, if you want to say "I
love you" then do it, don't delay. For a lifetime you know is
not that long though you think so when you're young, as you
grow older you know that's not true and that's why when you
lose someone you really love, it brings it home to you. So I
urge you once again. Treasure the people you love, don't
feel silly, embarrassed or stupid, just give them a great big hug.

Lisa Griffiths

Lying Together

Lying together in this half light,
Suspended between morning and night.
Rapturous love carries us away,
Souls, minds, bodies emotionally claimed.

What we possess nothing can replace,
Let us never refuse an embrace.
For precious hearts will only break,
If forsakened by a devoted mate.

And if time were to take us now,
Our love so strong would defy death.
For we feel the power within,
That others have yet to detect.

Lying together but now in Sunrays,
Praising our bodies once again.
Make me safe with the strength of your smile
The warmth of the sun adorns our desire.

C. Bradshaw

Invisible Me

'I could do that,' I heard myself say,
The eyes stared right through me, the head turned away,
'I know I can do it, I'm sure that I could',
The eyes turned to marble, the head turned to wood.

'Ladies and gentlemen, I've something to say,
It's awfully important, please listen, I pray,
I'm going to tell you - I really insist',
Nobody heard me - I didn't exist.

Queuing at the counter caused my poor feet to burn,
At last I had reached it - it must be my turn,
'Hello there! Excuse me! It's my turn, I think',
The girl looked straight through me at a woman in pink!

The heavy glass door swung back in my face,
'Sorry', I mumbled to the now empty space,
Collisions, collisions, why should they care,
No one could see me, I just wasn't there!

It's possible that sometimes I must share my views,
There's bound to be times when I'm first in the queues,
But there's one thing for certain, they don't want to see
Anything resembling the invisible me!

Liz Harvey

Greek Islands

Bathed in sun, islands of our dreams,
How beautiful they are, or so it seems,
How can I tell you my pain, my suffering,
I am only a poor donkey, who needs care and loving.

Ride me if you will, I'll take you there,
But do you stop to think, and do you even care,
The day is hot, the ride a steep one,
The weight I carry is not for a weak one.

For you only memories of laughter and pleasure,
Things to look back on, things to treasure,
But what about me, the poor little donkey,
For me only suffering beyond anyone's measure.

Next time your dream of your idyllic island,
Think about me, in a far distant harsh land,
No-one can change things, save only you,
You know what to say, you know what to do.

Make your voice heard, wherever you are,
Someone will listen, no-matter how far,
Help me to live the life I deserve,
And speak for those who haven't the nerve.

Janet Burton

Loss

Yesterday I felled your lovely fir
I did not weep. The time had come
The tree had long outgrown its place
The felling needed to be done.

You pulled a seedling from the bedrock
Long ago when you were small
Brought it proudly home, planted it
In your special patch beside the kitchen wall.

Carefully cherished, among Love-in-a-mist
Pansies, radishes and marigold
It flourished, grew as you grew
Beautifully, straight and tall.

It put down penetrating roots
Through the gladness of your childhood
Cloaking the house in pungent green
As you soared to self reliant manhood.

It wound itself about my heart
In all its spreading loveliness
But when you left it had to go
It too outgrew appropriateness.

M. P. Dickinson

Who Am I

Who am I, please tell me, who I am
I use to be someone worthwhile
With style and charisma
A kind of action man
Then fate stepped in and became cruel to me
I lost all my worldly goods
Including my family.
Over the years I tried to think positive
Tried to gain myself respect.
But as I trudge along life's
Weary path.
I lost hold and so became a nervous.
Wreck.
Who Am I please tell me I beg of you
Because if it wasn't for the grace
of God.
When you look at me
The vision you see
Could so easily have been you.

Patrick Fahy

Somewhere

There is no sunshine, only rain
Can't talk and can't explain
Despair, confusion, hidden pain.
Inventions cannot stem the flood.
You're weak, abandoned - just no good.

Something's wrong - nothing right
And surely as the dusk descends at night
Dark clouds envelope all that's bright.
You try to sleep, you cringe and hide
There's no escape - too deep inside.

Some would tend you for a while
Offer comfort, perhaps a smile
But they're not you - how can they be?
They have their own complexity.

Change is certain in this life
Bringing joy and causing strife
So cling onto this but slender rope.
After the storm there's always hope.

A beautiful rainbow as your guide
Together you can change the tide.

B. J. Charlton

Removal Day

"Removal Van" stood in the road:
Curious, a neighbour's Pussy crept....
The van drove off with well-packed load,
In which the cat curled up and slept.

At last the van came to a stop
About two hundred miles away.
Puss stirred, jumped out with eager hop
And found - her world had gone away.

Back home her owner, much dismayed,
Searched, called her name, then advertised.
"She's stolen, dead, or simply strayed?"
Her end could only be surmised.

Far off some found her lost, discussed -
"Whose is this cat none seems to claim?"
They took her in and won her trust,
Gave her a home and chose a name.

All thought and talked, but never found
What happened on removal day.
Confused, the cat sensed all around
The world she'd known had gone astray.

S. C. Hemming-Clark

My Friend

Three months ago my best friend died.
As I laid him to rest, oh how I cried,
And as the tears rolled down my face,
I whispered no one else will take your place.
Oh how I wish you could come back again,
And take away this endless pain.
Without you my world is empty and cold,
My ginger Sam, so big and bold.
You'd bring in a friend, what a surprise,
And look at me with those big green eyes,
Always willing to share your dinner
With someone looking a little thinner.
You never hissed or even spat,
Such a gentle loving cat.
Sammy darling, when you departed
You left a mum broken-hearted.
A stone cat now marks your grave,
In memory of one who was so brave.
Dear God, on you I now depend,
To please take care of my special friend.

Hazel Grant

At The Bottom Of The Garden

You would think that with all the "words of wisdom", fiction and
non-fiction written, draughted and eventually published (not to
mention The Bible and Shakespeare), dare one mention such
names and titles in the same breath, not forgetting "Thank
God for the Poets" and beautiful music that we have, and so
on... that one would tire from it all?
What is further down the road for us? Around the distancing corner?
The seasons happening regardless of us mere mortals?
With society as it is? Stressed and more stresses...
And yet, let me tell you about a girl who lived in the bottom
of a garden, who had no shoes!
On reflecting on her childhood, now as an elderly lady,
still living in that same house, at the bottom of the garden,
she laughs to herself, recalling a moment when on such an
occasion she put upon her feet a pair of slippers and fell to the
bottom of the stairs.
After picking herself up, she promptly opened the front door
and flung the slippers into the garden.
The feeling of sheer indulgence beneath her toes, the morning dew?
You can still be free, she would say out loud, you still can be free?

Melanie Ruth Paxford

Reflections

An old soldier in pensive mood,
In his fireside chair he sits and broods.
Looks into the flames and there so clear
Sees faces of old comrades dear.

Can fifty years have passed away.
It seems like only yesterday.
When young men, we were all together
In sunshine, rain and wintry weather.

Six months in Italy's winter line
We spent a damned frustrating time.
The Sangro River wild in spate,
And many a colleague met his fate.

Dougie Sherlock springs to mind
While on patrol he struck a mine.
Just like the snowflakes on the Sangro River.
A moment white, then gone forever.

Yes, Dougie Lad, you done your bit,
We missed your Liverpudlian wit.
For you, and all those others dear
Unashamedly I shed a tear.

T. Cunningham

Silence

Silence fell,
After the clamour of voices raised,
After the volley of gunfire blazed,
After the music —— discordant, crazed.
A flick of the button —— and blissful calm
As silence fell.

Silence grew
With darkening shadows around the place,
With unexplained absence of loving face,
With yesterday's ghosts haunting every space.
Alien thoughts spawning awful fears
As silence grew.

Silence reigned
When Nature's passion raged no more,
When daily struggle of Life was o'er,
When dimmed the light and closed the door.
The World at rest —— serene, benign
As silence reigned.

J. Harding

Promise

What better place to study paradox, than by the mill stream weir?
Wise Iris flag the path, only flat-faced Lilies stare.
A brilliant light illumines seeds floating on the breeze.
White collared doves croon of love shaded by the trees.

The promise of a gentle summer whispers through the grass.
As greedy trout snatch Hawthorn flies, ceaseless water chatters by.
To the rhythm of the searching bees a brace of magpies dance;
Nature will have its sway - our couple steal a knowing glance.

Why the need for more convention when such warmth and
happiness they know:
Like rose-webbed trellis by the wall, will vows assist security
to grow?
Yes, they judge, this summer both are ready to commit to
Church and Law.
Following the season's cycle, the river of tradition flows once more.

Valerie Langrish

Call Of The Sea

With sand in my shoes and head in the clouds
My body is bathed in the sun
I feast my eyes on romantic blue skies
The call of the sea has begun.

The air is as fresh as the morning dew
And breezes caress me at will
I'm as free as the wind in the willows
Or a kite flying high o'er the hill.

The crest of the waves are like pure driven snow
As they rush in to 'plenish the shore
The glistening sea casts a spell over me
I'm bewitched and drawn to its lure.

With my eyes upon the horizon
Still I hear the call of the sea
One day I'll sail to the land of my dreams
Where my spirit will e'er be free.

Phyllis R. Harvey

Man

I remember June.
Not because of my birthday,
But because Nan used to come down,
It was school Holidays.
Yes, I envied my friends having fun,
I did to, with my Nan.
I like the guessing game.
Do you want Tea, Nan?
Yes it is a lovely day outside,
Nan's not with us now, or is she?
Dad sits in the chair with Nan's beady eyes
No teeth, saying "What-Ah"?
I think she is, Don't you?

Zoe Marie Putman

Mannequins

The immediate, raw and sharp
Insects minds, buzz and match their form
They pass and shake,
Are real are not diffuse.
But as I travel and
Greet, encounter the minds of men,
I need more colours, more shades
than the palette provides.

Vague and indistinct
Infinitely complex though,
The order there is masked.
The mathematics crumbles as
Not geometric but gordion
The thoughts combine and
Muddle.

The minds trail their shells
They float, pulse, some metres
Behind
As grinning bodies jerk
And manic forms are empty.

Jonathan Stefani

Look At...

Look in the street, see children play
Look in the church, see vicars pray
Look in a mortuary, bodies lay
Look in the eyes and know what to say

Look at the rivers and say what you see
Look at the bride and her husband to be
Look at the forest and name all the trees
Look in the mirror and see what is me

Look at the dead and know when to cry
Look at the living and know when to lie
Look at the old man who knows when to die
Look at the poor boy whom seems a bit shy

Look at the archer who loads up his bow
Look at the showman who puts on his show
Look at the road lights now saying go
Look at the scientist to learn what he knows

Look at the pool player chalking his cue
Look at the pilot the distance he flew
Look at the band that was then called The Who
Look at us both and see just me and you.

Stephen J. Craddock

Lawrence Weston - Can We Survive

Lawrence Weston used to be the ideal place for the family.
As children we played for hours and hours in stretches of
woodland amidst the wild flowers. From high on the hills we'd
look over to Wales, then we'd run through the fields and hide
in the dells. I was a small child when my family moved here -
fifty years later I'm living in fear. Now when I wake to the
sound of birds singing, I wonder what terror this new day is
bringing. There's no longer peace on this run-down estate,
where a 'lost generation' is governed by hate. Where violence is
raging and drug dealing rife, no hope for the future what price
for a life? To see mothers weeping saddens my heart. Fami-
lies once strong are now torn apart. Sons and daughters high
as a kite on illegal substances 'shipped' in the night. Small
children screaming "Mummy's not well", they don't understand
that she's living in 'hell'. Caught in the web of deceit and
suspicion, frightened to speak for fear of admission. Even the
doctors can't cope any more, we're looking for miracles, not
just a cure. They are doing their best, what more can we ask,
the dealers have made it a gigantic task. I pray that one day
we'll come up with the answer to rid Lawrence Weston of this
deadly 'cancer'. To drag our community up from its knees will
take trust and commitment. Don't abandon us...please.

Doreen Robinson

Alone With My Thoughts

As I lie in bed on this chilly night,
My vision is blurred, even though there is light.
I have been ordered to open my eyes and see;
Only now, am I facing up to reality.
The truth is harsh, my future looks bleak.
Happiness is now pointless to seek.

The country I have lived in for so long,
Has done me good, and nothing wrong.
This beautiful island is my home,
And far from it I do not wish to roam.
They tell me that it is now time to move on,
and that the good times are over, gone.

Everything I know, my way of living
Will be wiped out, I'll have to start from the beginning.
I'll have to leave my childhood friends behind,
Oh why is fate so unkind?
I had it all, can't you see?
And now it is to be taken away from me.
Will the pain, the tears ever end?
Will the broken heart ever mend?

Tanya Poturicich

A Grain Of Faith

Can men cry peace or hell, on earth,
When men have slain the prince of peace?
Human reason could define a total contradiction.
Though wisdom divine, a very real prediction.

How many times must the cock crow?
Must I deny that I'm really awake?
Must I rise in the dark, live and die,
In the dark, and deny that my
Soul is at stake?

How often must I doubt?
Must I shout at the sky, day and night?
Demand to see with my eyes
What has been seen with the eyes,
A vision of heavenly light!

The treasure, buried on this earthy field,
With risen glory has revealed truth!
Life and salvation for all is found
On this sacred, hallowed ground.
Lord, have mercy for those whose fate
Is to find the truth, too late.

Denis O'Neill

Happily Sad

Peacefully, quietly sitting here.
Amongst the crowds, full of Christmas cheer.
The tree looks majestic, all decked out in gold.
Bells jingle softly. Stories being told.

In the hearth, a fire. People gathered round.
Piano keys tinkling. What a wonderful sound.
Families laugh together. Children play and fight.
Snow falls softly in the dead of the night.

It's past 12 o'clock now, no longer Christmas eve.
People open presents. Give and receive.
The guests are now leaving. Tracks in the snow.
Just one more quiet drink and then I must go.

Stephen A. Edgington

Untitled

We are slimming our way to happiness
forgetful of our health,
Sun and love and high days make
our only wealth,
We need lots of fun and laughter to help
us on our way,
For on this lovely planet we are all
so proud to stay.

Sarah Cochrane

Wonderland

Headrush as it seeps into the veins,
Electric tissues are alive inside
Adrenaline pumping through the brain,
The mind is king of the country.

The moist palate becomes a dry desert,
Mirages of the mind play tricks
The painful reality of a sandpaper mouth
Stops concentration until the liquid cures.

Surrounded by others you are alone
Music coincides with the pumping heart.
Rhythm is lost causing panic, everything stops,
Until your feet come back from Wonderland.

Music stops but the mind dances on.
No sleep for Alice, her clock has stopped.
Time is a matter for the sane world,
For now, sanity is a dreamland away.

Like jumping jacks the eyes will not sleep.
The pattern on the wall becomes a friend
Nothing left but to drink her coffee,
And let her mind indulge in the ticking of the clock.

Ceri Welsh

Success

I come from nowhere
But I'm going somewhere
It's time that I should start to believe
I have no money
Just a suitcase full of dreams
That's all I'm taking with me
    Show me the road to success
    I want to be the best
    I want to be seen
    Riding round in limousines
    And be better than the rest.

Gary Harlington

The Goodship

Southern winds of long ago, had picked up seeds with which to grow a hundred trees of pine and oak, shading valley in leafy cloak.

Now, the trees are gone, every one. The ground is bare and feel the sun. Twelve men took them, with which to make to the greatest ship, to cause a wake.

The greatest ship they could conceive, the greatest sails, where the wind will breath. The greatest oars for the warrior braves, the most beautiful figurehead to crest the waves.

An immense crowd to the beach did the flock to watch the ship glide form the dock. A heralded icon it was to be, winning battles out to sea.

For many a year, through many a mile, this ship had skimmed and sculled with style. Fast on voyage to far and distant land. Oh yes, these days were grand.

So widespread was her fame, every sailor knew her name. But, after sunshine came the rain, as other ships began again.

Newer fleets, taller of mast. Small, strong, lean and fast The old "Goodship" was easily past, like a singer, about to sing her last.

As quickly as she had appeared from her golden course the "Goodship" veered. Now. Time itself had planted seed. Whose fruits made "Goodship's" timber bleed.

With younger vessels she could not complete. All ingenious. All elite. Memories of the day she was made, as if a sunset, began to fade.

Resting alone, down on the ocean floor. After neglect gripped her sails and tore. Returned to the earth, from where she came, maybe one day she'll be bourne again.

Oliver Anderson

Laugh Mother My Mother

Have you heard the wind laugh behind a fleeing storm?
Its piercing, shrieking, whistling, collapsing battle-worn?

Have you heard the sun laugh as it bursts in on the day,
Splitting up the night sky, chasing blues away?

Now, have you felt a tremor and the silence in its wake,
A mumbling and a rumbling earth begin to quake?

Or have you heard the ripple of a gently ebbing tide
As it smooths away from pebbles, life's flotsam in its stride?

Then you have heard my mother laugh in all her varied ways,
As she copes with joys and hardships and the treasures of her days.

And you'll know whatever happens, be it happiness or sorrow
Just as the wind has done; earth, sea and sun
She'll laugh again tomorrow.

Jan Blow

The Mirror Of Eternity

Playing with the Sun and the Moon
thus having the Universe in my hand.
Not until now and yet so soon,
I realize the nature of Man.

Sun and Earth inseparable one,
eternity Stars shining bright.
The search is finished, Questions? None!
Everything is fine and right.

From the beautiful Morning of beginningless Time,
we drank the Wisdom nectar as Wine,
we drifted away like waves in the Sky,
always United not you and I.

Jette Lauritsen

"The Carpet Of Life"

Life is like a silken carpet woven into a pattern,
Intricate as gossamer lace.
Then the threads in time decay just as man himself.
Some are weak, some just rot, some are trodden on.
But God will help to mend those threads,
If we seek for his help.
Those that rot just turn to dust, weak ones given strength.
Tread on some and you will find, they just spring up again.
Life's carpet is a beauty if we treat it with respect.
To love and care and tolerate, trueness be our aim,
Lets patch the holes with silken threads,
Of colours fast and true.
Let's work just like the spider with thread and weave so fine.
That God will smile upon this earth,
As we try and try again,
Invisible mending can take place if we only count to ten.

Doreen Scott

To Hell With It All...

The laugh echoes through the church.
Those blessed worshippers raise bowed heads, frowning,
but the cavernous tombs' tricks send only shadows
to be withered and burnt under God's reproachful eye.

Gleefully floating with the mist and the silence
around the moss and the earth and the trunks of trees;
giants that stretch up into darkness, gone even before
the branches spread, the laugh dances through the forest.

Spiralling and weaving in and out of the silver buildings
of ancient metropolis's; whooping with the unabashed
exhilaration of speed, daring too close to each glass barrier,
above the smog, with the clouds and the birds, the laugh
mocks the city.

Technology blurs by, all nature melds into one with the speed
of the passing. Man and animal look up, and it's gone.
Only a fiery trail branded into the blue above
and the faint echoes, the wailing vestiges, of the last laugh remain.

M. L. Lewis

Down Redcote

I remember in childhood, a winding walk,
And fields where poppies grew,
The soft air filled with bird's talk,
And sky of summer blue.

We set off down the 'Lantern Hole'
Its real name Redcote Lane;
And oh the joy of poppy fields,
Then home for tea again.

A toll was on the Halfpenny Bridge,
King buttercups grew wild,
Brown rabbits played along the ridge,
The tiptoed breeze blew mild.

With nearby Kirkstall Abbey there,
No journey since has seemed so grand,
A gently flowing River Aire,
And poppy carpet on the land.

To take that walk again today,
Would break my heart in two,
To see the Power Station
In the fields where poppies grew.

Kathleen Rudd

My Mum-In-Law

Toads and newts and fish eye stew,
Mixing in the cauldron is a very special brew,
Black cat, pointy hat, wart on nose,
Green nails, orange hair, oil black clothes.

Broomstick in the corner, raven on a perch,
People in the village, cowering in the church,
Spider in a cobweb, strung across the door,
Bats in the attic and slime on the floor.

Spell book at the ready, page open wide
I'm the one who's worried,
She's the mother of the bride!

Ray Wicks

The Bride

Hush, I think I hear a car arrive to bring the flowers for the
    happy bride
For the wedding day planned so many months ago
At last has arrived with the sun as well
All brides dream of their wedding day with a dress so white as
    driven snow
And flowers all scented in a big bouquet
The day at last, yes had arrived, but oh God where was the bride
As up in her room we went to look around for just one clue
To find out if she had left some words as to which way she
    had gone you see
The bird had flown
But no not her, not even one single word to tell
So let her go to hell.

Ruth Blackbuon-Evans

Taboo

So it's happened, what can you do?
Your parent's treat you like something scraped
off their shoe
The neighbours treat you as if you're in exile
Some daren't even give you a smile
People whisper behind your back
You know they think it's because you are black
Colour, creed, religion and race
Have nothing to do with the state of your face
All it is, is a sicko with a warped mind
Who gets pleasure out of an attack of this kind
Whatever way the jury find this man
You are still left to carry the can
Your life is just a ruin
And it is all his doing
But what can you do
Because rape is strictly taboo

Melanie Service

Footprints In The Snow

Footprints in the snow
Leading to a destination
Someone's footprints in the snow
Made without hesitation
Footprints in the snow marking out a route once walked
Someone's footprints in the snow
Where once a group just stood and talked
Footprints in the snow winding trail like railway track
Someone's footprints in the snow
Crissing, crossing, forth and back
Footprints in the snow now disturbed by many others
Someone's footprints in the snow
With those of our younger brothers
Footprints in the snow pointing to an iced construction
Someone's footprints in the snow
Leaving from snowman's destruction
Footprints in the snow disappearing in the thaw
Someone's footprints in the snow
Once were there but now no more

Kevin Matless

The Streets To Nowhere

The street lights come on, another night is here.
The homeless and hungry look for a place, they see no fear.
Where they've come from no-one knows, they've lost all respect and most of their clothes.
What they would give to feel sheets on their toes, a proper bed and tomorrow who knows.
The young ones in the subways try to sing and play, hoping for a few pennies today.
As we pass a penny we toss, after all we don't really care, they are not our lot.
They are someone, ma, pa, daughter or son and given a home they'd feel they had won.
But the rain starts to fall and the night is so cold,
Tomorrow will be better, I'm sure they've been told.
They come out of the clubs and there's only stars in the sky.
In the distance a dog howls and a young baby cries.
So while we in bed all cosy and warm,
Remember there's more homeless today being born.

Caroline Gill

Tears Of Loneliness

Oh! my child, my child; what has become of thee?
When I see you, a porcupine I see.
When I reach out to touch you, I feel pain.
When I speak, you hear; but in hibernation you remain

Oh! my child, my child; for years now I've been brokenhearted
Ever since the day that Eden's children ate, and we were parted
I beg you please, my child; wake up, and look, and see
When I made you, I didn't make a porcupine, I made another me!

Oh! my child, my child; I'm crying, shedding many tears
Please relieve me of this agony of all these many years
All you have to do it leave those prickly spines behind
And turn into the mini-me that I first had in mind

Oh! my child, my child; please listen to my anguished cry
And come back now before another morning passes by
I'm your broken-hearted father, who's feeling so alone
So please my child, make the effort to come home

Tibor Zoltan Vitai

Untitled

The children play while far away, the trenches fill with father's blood
And eyes turn black when frightened boys grin rotting smiles in the mud.
The daffodils are blooming now in England. Side by side they sway.
But poppy fields hold bleeding dreams in a blood soaked country far away.

Forgive me, noble England for the fear I feel inside.
Forgive me for my shamed relief when other soldiers die.

Alice McCornell

My Daughter

You were a dream, my darling, a vision yet unseen,
Conjured by loving fantasy, in mind and tender murmuring,
Starry youth, Life and hopes—a translucent bubble.

Beside my heart I carried you, a dream coming to life.
Precious, longed for and so loved, God's blessed miracle for us in store,
Maturing youth. Complete in faith—the bubble rises.

Carried to highest ecstasy on the wings and gentle breeze,
Upsurged as orchestral music, glorious as a swift flying bird to the loftiest place,
Our idyllic life complete. You were born—the bubble flew high.

Dancing along in warm sunshine, fanned by the soft English air,
Together we made joy and laughter—talked overall, baby, then girlish fears and hopes.
Always close together, sadness had drawn us as one.
Supreme happiness—never taken for granted.
The bubble having faltered for a while, rose high again in thankfulness.

Insidiously and ominously as the branches of cancer growth,
Life is threatened, all is dark and cold.
Our dreams, our hopes and ideals, mean nothing now to you.
Rejected, humiliated, betrayed, destroyed—thrown to one side,
The bubble BURSTS—and suddenly—I feel very, very old.

M. Maguire

A Woman Alone

Lots of people pass you by
they will never know, the tears you cry
As you wonder round, all alone
The shops, the market, or just at home
Friends are few and money tight
What will you do with yourself tonight?
The TV's on but you don't really listen
Just sat alone in your own little prison
Go out, get an interest, is all people say
They just don't understand, and try as you may
You're stuck in a rut there's no way out
You can't go alone, you want to shout
People all stare if you walk in a pub
There's worse to come if you go to a club
So you stay at home, with nothing to do
there has to be more to your life than this
To be loved and held and given a kiss
By someone who cares, and knows how you feel
Who'll always be there, to make your life real.

Pat A. Ridgway

Love And Tears

Adults and children in hospital under care
Babies and toddlers it hardly seems fair
Relatives and family try to show no fear
But when alone our eyes fill with tears.

Breathing is low and pulses beat slowly
No movement is seen in the beds of the patients
Row upon row of silent white faces
Lay upon beds with crisp white pillow cases.

Machines do the work while our loved ones rest
Our thoughts are with them as they are the best
We pray for a miracle with a silent prayer
Please look after our cherished while in your care.

We remember the good times, your touch, smile and kiss
Happiness and laughter, you will be truly missed
My darling, my precious, I love you so
I am begging you, so please do not go.

The feeling is strong as my eyes drip tears
Your time is coming and it's very near
A small smile you give, then a little sigh
And I know in my heart that you said goodbye.

J. Baker

Apple-Wood Fire

I could not say what images were there:
I had no paper nor a pen at hand
To write the words for you to understand.
In the fire's heart trace labyrinthine ways,
Deep secret grottoes and the sudden flare,
And recollect those other autumn days
When fruit was gathered in the golden air.

Tomorrow's ash shall mulch tomorrow's tree,
In hope new-planted, healthy, lichen-free.
Another harvest on a golden day?
In the fire's heart, breathing the incense air,
What images were there I could not say.

G. E. M. Tamlin

My Autumn Child

October Morn when she was born
With hair like Autumn gossamer that shines in
Misty hedgerows - touched by sunsets
So small, so gentle all her life. She blossomed
Slowly. Embracing life tentatively, courageously
And successfully at her own pace.

She frowned, she smiled, she laughed
Through cornflower eyes set in white silk.
As seasons changed she developed.
The impatient Spring
The lazy Summer
Sometimes touched by Winter tears.

Her life experience will mould her well if
Concern and love emanate from her thoughts
And she learns from life why that was wrong for her.
And stores the good things in life
Like seasons gifts grow and die, and if
Nurtured, only the best will burst forth in Spring.

Gwen Owen

Isles Of Scilly

Entry is guarded by the towering "Bishop",
whose mitre is a helicopter platform
to ease the changeover for light housekeepers.
Then come scattered rocks with clustered birds:
A crowd of cormorants like a union meeting,
or solitary ones with outstretched wings
like statues. Camouflaged on other rocks
enormous seals lay basking, hardly seen
until they lumbered down into the sea.
Others pop up their heads as though in greeting,
delighting all the watchers in the boats.
The Isles themselves present a varied programme:
Tropical Tresco gardens, near-white sands,
curious stone formations, and the bulb-fields,
miniature plots protected by high hedges
of flowering evergreens, and everywhere
rare garden flowers dotting the lanes like weeds:
Blue Agapanthus and tall Jersey lilies,
whilst rarely out of sight was deep blue sea,
and bonus of warm sun though long past summer.

Katherine Brown

English Countryside

The singing birds, a gentle breeze,
Pleasantly whistling through the trees
A nervous rabbit, a leaping hare,
New born ponies with caring mares.
Last Autumn leaves,
Lying brown and dry,
A bunch of daffodils grows nearby,
A clump of primroses among the nettles,
Small white daisies with pink tipped petals.
A place to rest, freedom to roam,
The ideal holiday away from home.
A place to walk, a place to hide,
The beautiful English Countryside

Les Paxford

The Cliff Top

Drowsily dreaming the hours away.
Sunshine a soaking as now I lay on my back,
    eyes closed to it all;
The laughter of children, the gulls as they call
Gliding, white as pure swansdown, on breeze,
Like a sigh,
Reach across the still water as blue as the sky.

The low hum of voices drift up from the beach,
As I lie on the cliff top, well out of reach
Of the swarms and the masses who come every day
To build sand pies, and sunbathe;
I'm glad I'm away from the swimmers
And paddlers and trays-of-tea tribe;
The water wings and air beds that go out with
    the tide;

I'm glad I'm alone where there's only just me,
Where the breeze and my dreams drift over the sea,
Where the sun seems hotter and the wind doesn't blow,
Just high on the cliff top that only I know.

Shirley Arnold

Redeeming Features

It slipped away so slowly, we never missed its passing
People changed, ideals, respects and love went out of fashion
Arrogance, vanity, greed concerned with wealth amassing
Forgotten in the rush, man's finest virtue lost - compassion

This human sickness, needless, wanton, mindless slaughter
As our world spins around, and pieces fall away
Skins stolen, used to adorn the rich man's daughter
Whilst the bombs rain down, and the mad men play

What is the point of conflict, no prize at the end of the fight
Deciding to take a precious life, who to die, who to live
How to know the answers, are we wrong, are we right?
These tormented decisions we never had the right to give

Is it man's compassion that saves the ape or whale
So far removed from commerce, hoarding, covetous, misers dreams
Or the loving care a nurse bestows, upon the ill, the frail
She sees the golden sunsets, walks the silver moonlit scenes

Gentle people, sitting mellowed in their twilight years
Remember life when trust and honour were more than words
Now anger seethes, impatience, hostility, all have fears
And people's lives are stamped, manipulated, caged like birds

T. R. Bates

Where Will You Be?

Where will you be, when the summer has gone,
And the birds have no song to sing.
When the sun no longer shines in the sky,
And the harvest is all gathered in.

Where will you be, when the days grow cold,
And the wind blows the clouds in the sky.
When the flowers fade and lose their blooms,
And the leaves on the trees fall and die.

Where will you be, when the frosty nights come,
And the children are wrapped from the chill.
When the snow flurries fall and make everything white,
And icicles hang from the sill.

Where will you be, when the trees are in bud,
And the lambs skip about in the grass.
When the crocus appear from under the ground,
A sign that spring's here at last.

Now summer is here, and the flowers they bloom,
The sun burns so bright in the sky.
The birds all sing their songs from the trees,
Together we watch, you and I.

Deborah Brown

Ode To Greyfriars Bobby

Greyfriars Bobby, you lay near his graveside.
Lay by his grave when they laid him to sleep.
You were his friend and he was your dear master.
As nighttime came through churchyard gates you'd creep.
And nose on paws you waited in the darkness,
Keeping at bay, bad spirits from his side.
Your faithfulness to your only master,
Made you the great City of Edinburgh's pride.

For fourteen years, you lay near his graveside.
Good folk around would feed you day by day.
In daylight hours you wandered through the city.
As darkness fell, by him you came to stay.
Fourteen long years, your nightly vigil keeping,
'Til came the day that you had waited for.
Your body died, you went again to meet him,
To be beside your master dear forevermore.

Anne E. Abbott

No Man's Land

The eerie silence of no man's land hangs heavy with unshed tears.
And rotting smells of lifeless flesh fills the air with untold fears
Bullets and bombs exchange as the raging war goes on,
Kindred spirits all together, into battle united as one.
Either side of no man's land, a gathering of boys and men,
All fighting for their freedom, never knowing where or when.
But for these poor souls who've fought and died,
Upon their faces see their honour, see their pride.
For them the war is in the distant past.
No more suffering, no more pain.
In no man's land they've found peace at last.

Linda Ewan

Winter

Winter, I see the trees all bare
The leaves have gone, I know not where,
The birds are here more often now
It's Winter.

Fields are all gathered and looking grey
Snow is due, or so they say
It's Winter.

Nights are shorter, mornings dark,
Wrap up well when in the Park,
It's Winter.

Robins here, that's made my day
All is not lost, and so I say
Be happy, be happy, happy and gay
For when it's over, Spring's on its way,
and Winter has gone, gone far away.

C. H. Acton

The Host Man

Kicked down a door.
Her face, vanity varnish.
A case of friendly fire?
The long arm of the law, reaches out.
Pulls me in.
The desk sergeant charges and free meals are provided.
Amazed enforcers stare at my streaky bacon skin,
patterned by my loose capped tooth that I hadn't
handed in.
The surgeon sighs. He's seen it all before.
He tells me I'm ingenious. I give a little grin.
A uniformly large policeman. Blue coat, grey skin;
asks me. 'Can you find your way home?'
Smiling and pointing with bloody fingers, he reads
my forehead.
it says, 'Lost Man!'

Gareth Hopkins

Love Will Survive

We live in a world of love, hate and sorrow,
Our lives are short and unfulfilled by one thing, called time.
With every tick of the clock our lives get that much shorter.
Each day we live is slightly varied, yet very much the same.
We sleep, we eat, work and drink, there is only one thing in
    life we can really share, that's our love for one another.
You hold my hand, you kiss my lips, you press your body
    close to mine and all our worries disappear.
For that short time we spend together, makes this life of ours
    worthwhile.
The toils of life that tie us down, your life and mine, get
    knocked about like two corks in a stormy sea.
We may be pulled apart, but the bonds of love tie us closer
    together.
This love of ours can never die, as long as we love one
    another from our hearts.
Even time itself cannot sever the bonds of love we have for
    one another.
So treasure this heart, as I do yours, and our love will last
    longer than forever.

Peter Walter Nelson

Sand

When He calls; tell Him I'm out.
Somewhere; anywhere; nowhere.
Loving the love and hating the hate.

Like sand in between soft cockles
The juicy flesh
Swallowed in a second.
Sand.
Stuck.
Stubborn.
In the awkward gaps you
Never forget.

He loves.
Swirling, twirling, unfathomable depths.
Offers an armband to everyone.
Stretch; for the solid from the spirit.
And yet some,
the small, the weak,
Plummet through seething waters
To find their flesh burst, with sand.

Angharad Philpott

Stages

Life on this earth is but one stage,
As of a book 'tis only one page,
When our mortal flesh fades away,
To another world, in the universe we stay.

Move to different worlds to make perfection,
Guided by a great power in this direction,
And when this great power has done his work,
No more evil or corruption does ever lurk.

No earthly logic in this stage we now dwell,
It is now a heaven there is no hell,
Where absolute goodness there is wrought,
Where no wickedness is done or thought.

This is the paradise of which we dreamed,
This is the ultimate when all redeemed,
This is the end of all that is wrong,
This is the stage we've waited for so long.

These thoughts of mine, I'll always believe,
These thoughts of mine may have a curious weave,
But thought is infinite, cannot be defined,
Woven mysteriously through the mind.

F. Simpson

The Path

How lovely are the colours
On the surface down below.
The blues, the grey, the white and brown,
And a warm red rusty glow
Of rotted pine tree needles
Blown down so long ago.
Pieces of slate, some yellow stones
And multi-coloured sunken rocks.
Between them, all green grasses,
Yellow lichen, and red moss.
Along the sides pink rhododendron,
Above, a bird's sweet song.
Where is this place?
It's just a little woodland path
We often walk along!

Patricia E. Smith

The Meaning Of Love

Why do people fall in love
No one will ever know the strong attachment that one feels
Could sometimes feel unreal
It's a pain in the heart when two are apart
It's the ecstasy of sharing and caring
When love is divine, it's a power rather like a shrine
Nobody will ever know till one tends to show
What they truly know when they both feel aglow
So keep love alive, it's a power inside
That no one will ever deny
Love is most powerful
It is supreme
It's for humans who only have a dream
It's a longing so rare that no other can share
So love till the end of all life
And maybe someday when we kneel down and pray
We'll thank God
That our love came to stay.

Alice Raine

Second Chance

To me you are so precious, I know that's true,
You are as precious as the sunshine and the morning dew,
When we're apart I'm helpless, like a bird with a broken wing,
Together my world is complete, there's joy in everything.

This love came unbidden, though special and so good,
We are bound together forever. If only we could?
We cannot wreck our children's lives and cause them to fear,
The loss of their parents love. The ones they hold so dear.

We are just like children too, happy as turtle doves,
Young in heart, enjoying life, just being in love,
Who knows what the future holds, troubles we will share,
With you beside me all is well, knowing that you care.

G. Parratt

The Leaving

As I walked through a lonely graveyard
its past was quiet plainly to see
for its history was carved on its tombstones
for all the living to see

I stood by its tall morbid yew trees
that overshadowed its lonely mounds
and shuddered at the rustling breezes
that created such a lonely sound

As I passed by a grave in which an old woman lay
an old man stood quietly in sorrow
The mourners were praying for the corpse in the grave
For whom there wasn't any tomorrow

I gave him my shoulder as his tears fell to the ground
and I tried to console him as he stood there alone
but his voice was so sad as he uttered these words
O God, now there is no one at home

T. H. Power

And You Were Gone

On that foggy November day
We had a kiss and you drove away
You were not going very far
In your small and smart red car
It was only to the village shop
And you were not going to buy a lot
I only needed a packet of rice
But as you were always so very nice
You said you'd go, it would not take long
And as I waved Goodbye, you were gone
Time went past, half an hour or more
Feeling anxious, I waited at the door
Suddenly I heard a distant sound
Sirens wailing, my head spun round
Thoughts racing through my head
My heart feeling as heavy as lead
I lost you my Darling that November morn
But by Christmas, our son was born
He brought me joy, but I felt so sad
For I would have to be both His Mum and Dad

M. R. Whale

It's Okay To Dream

Have you ever wished that you were a bird,
That could fly on high, and see the world,
And at the paradise of Heaven take a peak,
And in awe, your freedom from earth seek.

Have you ever wished for the moon and stars,
To touch the sun, or land on Mars,
Have you ever wished to live in the sea,
To swim with the dolphins, and forever there be!?!

Have you ever wished to fall in love,
And know it true in the eyes of God above,
To never have a hurt or a scar,
To know that your friend and lover will never be far!

Have you ever wished that friends did not die,
But took a holiday, way up in the sky,
And came back to tell us of the unknown,
And never again be left alone!

My friend, it's okay to dream,
No matter how outrageous they may seem.
But if you do not dream; then they'll never come true
And you'll never find the genuine you!!!!

Geraldine Hyland

Autumn Leaves

Autumn, in her golden splendour
Makes my heart leap with joy!
Colours! Brilliant orange, yellow, and tender
Pinks. The dancing leaves, that sometimes clutter and annoy,
Flutter away, upon a tempest tossed.
They whizz and whirl then float to earth;
To be trampled and scuffed and lost!
Lost? Not really! Blankets, at spring's birth,
The lifeline and protector of winter's foetus!
Oh, what lessons nature has to teach us!

Joan Bevan

Movement

The wind blew the branches
Of the willow tree from side to side
To the floor, gracefully the leaves glide
On the soft green grass they land,

The melody of the leaves rustling
Up in the branches of that tree
How they sway so delicately
Really does enchant me

The movement of everything that I see
Whether it runs, walks, crawls, soars
Or trips clumsily, is like a type of magic
That is not found easily.

Laura Thomas

Good Manners

Being mannerly is not hard; it's much easier than being rude
After a while it becomes habitual; it also makes you feel good
It opens up new avenues and your circle of friends starts to grow
We all feel a bit down at times and need cheering up to give
us that glow

A kind word can sometimes work wonders; often this is all
that's required
It makes you feel wanted and part of the scene; you no longer
feel tired
You have a new lease of life and raring to go; all it took was a
kind word
The Bible says it is better to give than to receive; it's not so absurd

The way the world is at present it's badly needing more
kindness and love
If we all do our bit, everyone will benefit with a little help from
above
There is love and understanding in us all; it's just a matter of
letting it out
Sharing it with others can only be good; let there be no
mistrust or doubt

When the time comes to meet our Maker, we will feel we've
done some good
It's rewarding if your kindness and patience helps someone in
a bad mood
Surely no matter how busy a day you have there will be a little
time to spare
To help others not so fortunate; let them know that someone
does care

James Wilson

Postcard To Mum And Dad From The Mountains

Well! Mum and Dad, we're here at last,
You can't drive down these roads too fast,
We've got no light, no fire, no telly,
I think I'm now a lump of jelly!

There's plenty of birds, no people in sight,
There's rocks, and more rocks, and it's Dark at night,
They've killed me off, without a doubt,
I haven't even strength to shout!
My feet, my legs, my back as well,
I think I've left them there, in Hell!

Lorraine Harrison

A Poet In The Landscape

Who is around to so ably disperse the wealth of the beauty in
the Universe?
Of streams and fountains and blue rugged mountains,
Of fields and hedges, of moorlands with sedges?
Who else could set it
In Word and Song?

Who else could write of summer's delight,
Of long winter shadows and land snowy white,
Of the songbird on wing, or the bee with its sting,
Of reflections on lake, the cry of the tern,
The chirp of the cricket, the ripple of burn,
In Word and Song?

Just who would encapture the turbulent seas,
The soft sighing wind and murmuring breeze,
Fairy-like gossamer and dewdrops which glisten?
Here is the music for those who would listen, and lovingly
embrace it
In Word and Song.

The eye of the poet forever beholds the passage which nature
each season unfolds,
Who gently describes by stanzaic means, the wonder of earth
and changing scenes.
Thus, it's enshrined for all and forever, In Word and Song.

Percy J. Davidge

Questions

How do we know what went on in the past?
How can we know the future?
How do we find out about pain and fear?
Who will be there, to ask?

What can we do to relieve our sorrow?
How can we show it to the world?
Should we worry if love is not around?
Who will be here tomorrow?

Why do questions keep appearing?
Why do they go on to torment us?
Should the news tell us about wars and crimes?
Or is it the questions they are creating?

This is the story of life,
That no-body can explain for us,
We have looked to the past for answers,
While we wait for the future to arrive.

Angela Henderson

The North Sea

It was in a bleak November
That day I can remember,
The wind did blow
The sea was rough,
Two men went forw'd
And they were tough,
They bounced and bounced
From side to side,
That's what they got
For all their pride,
The mate in pain
The chippie too,
The mattresses red
Where this blood soaked through,
In a helicopter the doctor came
But hopes to save them were all in vain,
I was there I seen it
I swear the North sea did not mean it.

John O'Donnell

My Diary

My diary tells me the secrets,
that I have just told it.
I go back day by day,
and read it bit by bit.

It doesn't give me advice,
and never laughs at what I say.
I tell it all my problems,
that I think won't go away.

So when my diary's ended,
at the end of the year.
I look at all the wrong things I've done,
and wipe my slate clear.

Lesley Nicolson

A Schoolboy's Lament

I'm not a genius, and yet I do try,
At my studies I aim to do well,
I don't always seem to, although I do mean to.
For who wants to be a dumbbell.
I'm a bit of a joker, and do like a laugh,
I was never a serious chap,
But the teachers don't always appreciate me,
That's why I'm blowing the gaff.
They just don't understand, that I'm bubbling inside,
I'm alive, I feel happy each day,
But there's always someone who'll flatten me down,
And chase all my pleasure away,
It's sad you'll agree, that a fellow like me,
Who tries hard, and though he may jest,
Can't always be clever, yet makes the endeavour,
I really am doing my best.

Audrey Peters

Birthday Calendar, Life's Progress

At one day old my life has begun
At one year old it seemed such fun.
And at two years old it seemed just great
While at three years old I could swing on the gate
Four years old life wasn't so bad
But at five years old I felt quite sad "school days were here"
Then at six years old I felt real brave
And at seven years old life was a rave
Then I was eight and life was just fine
One more year and I'd be nine
And so on to ten my own friends and then
To eleven oh life was just heaven
So to the magic age of twelve
And a future of mystery to dig and delve
Thirteen - fourteen saw me courting
The love of my schoolgirl dreams
While fifteen, sixteen, seventeen and eighteen
Were days of hilarious screams
And so on to nineteen and to twenty also twenty one
My childhood has passed also my teens now my purpose in
life has begun

Irene Dixon

Leaving So Lonely

I watched you, while you were sleeping;
And tended your every need
And kept your words for safe keeping
Although, they've made me bleed.
I kissed you, so softly, yet you did not know
You whispered my name in your sleep
You shivered, amidst the moonlight's glow
And held me, as though to keep.
I wept as I finally left you;
Although you did not hear
You slept so silent, as I left you;
As I trembled, with every tear.
You'll quickly fill your hurried arms
Whilst I shall hold thin air
One day, your own prisoner to your charms
Though I was waiting there,
I awoke, when you kissed me
And lived amongst your hold
But died, the day I left you
In our world, which seems so cold.

Amanda Druce

Lines On An Artist's Death

When the smart machines came
You mastered them with ease
And put by pens and brushes
For the artless mouse.
But then the smart men came
With sharp eyes for main chances
Yet blind to worth and quality,
Able only to paint you into your corner.
Maybe, feeling the chill draught,
Thinking years on half pay
Just too much too soon,
Seeing the pension people
Tot you up as worth more dead,
You simply took a hard decision
For your family's sake.
I wish you'd known how much
You would be missed.
But you have shown us
Just how cold and evil
This whole empire is.

George Stuart Macgregor

In The Hands Of The Thrower

Snakes and ladders, the game of life we all participate,
The die being the judge and the players just the bait,
All trying to ascend to the rung at the top,
Until the slithery snake hisses its tongue and then the
big drop,

This scaly serpent only a hurdle in the pathway
to a better thing,
Just another problem that can be conquered by
giving the die a fling,

Believe in the magic and give it your best shot,
Whether the outcome is prosperous or not,
Keep in mind there is no big stake prizes if you win,
And this so called 'losing', well it's not a sin,
Aim of the game - have a laugh and enjoy,
We're all waiting on the board for our turn of this
life like toy.

Lisa Riddell

Solitary Silence

Standing alone in the cold midst of silence
In the town where the traffic should be
But here on my own stands me
Suddenly, almost out of nowhere
Comes a passer-by
He stops, looks round and gives a tired sigh
Then he walks on, leaving me all alone, and thoughtful
I am left to stare at, the chilling shadows of skeletal trees
Whose treetops gently sway in the winter breeze
Come to a standstill, I am left on my own, and thoughtful
A light gust of wind taps at my face
I tremble at its cold and icy embrace
It disappears leaving me all alone, and thoughtful
I wonder if in this usually busy street
That solitary silence is all that I will meet
And so I try to escape but I can't
And I am left in silence.

Fiona Mahon

Endurance

The old tree that I climbed as a child,
Its sturdy boughs supporting me.
A name engraved before my time.
The wound partially healed over, so I cannot see
What manifestation was made.
Lovers long ago, telling their secrets to the tree?
Did they lie in its shade making promises
Of endurance and eternity?

Did you smile, having heard it often before:
Secret assignations, saying one day they'd be free
From restrictions and rules that kept them apart.
Did you give shelter when one came alone in misery?
Did the sap weep from your wound when they spoke
Of betrayal and the pain that seemed to be
Inconsolable. You have seen many pass, yet still you remain.
When I return to dust will you remember me?

Judina G. Smit

Little Sophie

I don't know you
But how I miss you
I don't know the pain you have been through
But how it hurts to be without you

The world aches feeling your absence
My inner pain growing with vengeance
So pretty and tender in your innocence
You look upon this cruel universe with no revenge

Your spirit and soul clear in the midst
Protecting all our little boys and girls
Next to God you are in pearls
Your Divine so pure rest in peace

Andeea Mauree

Missing A Brother

Here one minute, and the next minute gone
Life can be cruel, our feelings so strong
Mystery lies just around each corner
Heart felt pain, I am the mourner

My mind in a turmoil, I am in distress
I've just lost a loved one that shone out from the rest
I need to be quiet to think for a while
How will I carry-on, how will I get by

My family around me, but not the one I want to see
In a room full of people, but feeling lonely
I keep turning and looking my eyes full of tears
I reminisce all them golden years

His clothes just lie there as still as death itself
I think of the good times, when he had good health
But heart ache and pain drove him out to this world
The reason depression, sent his mind in a twirl

J. Ball

A Thought

If there was a God
Would he allow all the suffering in this world?
Would he allow the evil of man.
The evil of money,
To destroy our world?
Would he allow our trees to be taken away,
Our oceans to be polluted,
Or our animals to become extinct?
Would he allow the suffering of our people?
Or the level of hatred that caused disasters,
Disasters such as the holocaust?
Would he allow the fascists, the racists to be in control?
Would he allow the madness, the violence, the bad?
Would he allow the wars, the fear, the terror people face?
Would he allow the suffering of children, of women, of us all?
You see, I don't think he would.
Yet, it's happening, all this is happening.
So, it makes you think doesn't it?
If there really is a God!

Emma Cole

Lecture Number Nine

Books on books read
Octave after octave played and heard
Wood carved marble cut
Paint on canvas brushed on sold or not sold
Love letters with a red ribbon wrapped and stored
All this yet knowing
Absolutely nothing still
'Til a fine-kiss-goodnight
Is passionately placed on pink lips
And in that moment it seems that
All knowledge is revealed

Basia Palka

"Day" Dream

To Doris Day - A Sonnet

Fair songstress! When first your silvery strains
Caressed my ears and so bewitched my mind,
I was o'erjoyed, while listening, to find
How purest pleasure pulséd through my veins.
Your silky, sunshine tones, in sweet refrains,
Soaring lark-like, 'roused my youthful passion,
Set me yearning to behold the fashion,
The form, which such a velvet voice contains.

I looked: And saw a celluloid Goddess,
A filmy Venus with a siren's voice,
Blue-eyed, freck-faced, crownéd with flaxen tress.
O chanting charmer! By my own free choice
Your Ulysses am I, imprisoned fast,
Within the 'witching, warbling spell you cast.

Peter Mahony

As Love Slips Away

Tranquil silence, the hateful hurtful howling silence.
Unmade beds and unmade meals, toys discarded never to be reclaimed.
The abstract symphony of love and child,
is replaced by a solemn paean of rustling trees and creaking floors.
I explore my new world, every step recounting their final farewell.
Each silent burst of pain trying to exorcise the dark vulture of
despair, whose beating wings enshroud her unsuspecting prey,
to gorge on the pathetic remains of reckless hope.

The cold blade of dawn cuts my open eyes to make me face
another day.
Bare black trees encircled by crying crows
stand stark against the white winter sky of my life.
I stand like a sentinel and look to the south, awaiting the return
of my flock, but they will never return or be unchanged.

I hold their image in my hand,
and view with eyes that embrace their unchanging souls,
my life as frozen as their smiles.
Guilt and confusion run down my cheek and splatters on their faces.
I distort and drown their lives with stupidity and selfishness,
but paradise is never found until it's lost.
But it's the price I must pay, as love slips away.

Colin Lainson

Remembering

When you are gone I shall remember
The warm clasp of your strong brown hand
Helping me to stand,
The way you turned your head and smiled,
The sound of your firm tread upon the path
I shall not be alone - for-
Half of you will with me stay
And half of me you'll take away-
Thus shall we always be as one.
And when the evening lamp is lit
In your armchair I shall sit,
And then unlock our treasure chest of memories
Sharing once more these days we walked side by side,
or sat in silent companionship-
How wise you were my love to say
"Let us live each day"
I shall remember - and remembering - carry
our warm and happy springs
Thro' to our Decembers.

Lottie S. Butcher

Vienna

I see an open space,
A field of green or a long stretch of beach and I think of her,
Of galloping, lost in my own world,
The sound of her thudding hooves filling my ears.
The breeze is pleasant on my face and I feel free.

But when I open my eyes I know I have been dreaming,
For her days are over.
 "Learn to let go" they say
Why should I, she was taken away too soon.

It seems like no-one cares,
Or feels her loss as I do.
I am alone.

I watch as the world speeds by
But I do nothing. I am a spectator.
My life is happening without me
Because I am trapped by her memory.

"Face the facts" they say

"Fact" I say.

"DEATH"

I need a hug!

L. J. Sparks

The Fleeting Shadows

In solitude they lie in wait, the disciples of
the devil's gate.
   Like demonic moles they burrow deep and wake
you from a restful sleep.
   With bated breath you look around, but the
fleeting shadows cannot be found.
   Ever watchful, ever near, scrambling thoughts
and instilling fear.
   Clawing at your very soul, in reflective minds
they take their hold.
   How many times have you felt their touch,
heard a whisper, sensed their look.
   From deep inside a troubled mind, the snakes
of depression they slither in slime.
   Constant companions from birth to death, but when
you think that they have left, and all is right with
the World once more...
   The Fleeting Shadows come to call.

C. D. Harris

'Friendship'

'Friendship' is a wonderful thing, everlasting through the year.
Warming us in Winter's cold, something very dear.
When Spring was just beginning, some seeds fell on stony ground.
But others took root and prospered, while Summer roared around.

Hot and sultry this may not be, rampant, nor raging, nor fierce.
It's free for the likes of you and me, the heart and soul to pierce.
Summer nurtures seedlings strong, as the sun arks across the sky.
Warmly watching, butterflies flirt, playfully dancing by.

'Friendship' is a wonderful thing, everlasting through the years.
Something to reflect upon when Autumn leaves appear.

And late in late December, before the new year becomes of age,
I can review the final chapter and the setting of the stage.
And remember all the parties of bygone New Year Eves,
because 'Friendship' is a wonderful thing, something in which
   to believe.

David John George

Mournings Past

The darkened skies are turning red.
Above the misty grey
The ghosts and fears of past now dead
I cherish this new day

But memories can be reborn.
Not cast away for good by dawn.
The past and present can't be torn
Apart for I feel need to mourn.

Now day by day the pain retreats
To an army of fond memories
Of times we shared of life's small treats
Of what my dearest meant to me
Now I must tread the path alone.
Your hopes for me are now my own.
For all our lives are but a loan
From he who sits upon the throne

Damian Hurley

Gardening Man Observed

I saw him there hard at it stooping
Among the tulips, dead-heading the flowers,
Fanatically engaged body and soul
In that one single task.

Thin brown hands reached out and cut
Debris for the compost heap
Intent to render to the earth
Goodness spent and recreated.

The faded figure in the sun
Bowed in dedication to the soil
Worshipped like any anchorite
Though moving on a wider ground.

Derryan Paul

A Little Child Cries In The Night

Is it dreaming a nightmare, that gives it a fright?
Can it be the wind rushing by in the night
Brushing the tree against the window pane
Along with the driving rain.

A light goes on, a parent has stirred
Woken by the crying child which, was heard
Then with muffled steps along the landing
To the child which needs attending.

With words of comfort and of love
As from an angel up above,
The crying which has now subsided
The child snuggles down as if in hiding
A final kiss upon the head, the parent pads on back to bed.
Silence again returns to the house
A parent never needs to grouse.

Even in the cold morning light
We may never know what woke the child in the night.

Ian Martin Lawrence

Clock Rule

The Upstairs clock sits by my bed
And whispers in my ear.
"With a soft tick-tock-tick
I'll lull you to sleep
Till sunrise, never fear".

The Kitchen clock is a busy little clock
That shouts each passing minute.
"Tick-tock-tick-tock-tick-tock-tick-tock
In your race against time,
I'll win it".

In the dining room stands the Granddaughter clock
With a pendulum long and slow.
She solemnly ticks
And solemnly tocks
My life away, — blow by blow.

The Sitting Room clock is my favourite clock
Its tick can scarcely be heard
My life is my own
To do as I wish
And nobody utters a word!

Heather J. Lightowler

Mr. X

The word got around, Mr. X had died
On a wet and windy night.
Tom, Dick and Harry weren't sure how he went
But it was a sorry plight.
Tom said he died in his sleep
But then I might be wrong
No said Dick it wasn't that way
He was watching "Going for a Song"
Harry wasn't sure which way it was
But he was willing to bet
It was at the bar Mr. X had gone
Having his final 'wet'

Now listen hear Tom, Dick and Harry as well
This is Mr. X writing these words
I hope to go on for a few more years
Before I'm up there with the birds
Thank you all for having me dead
Well before my time
It's a lovely feeling coming back from the grave
To write my resurrected rhyme!

F. A. Copp

Sunrise

Let my body blow to the four winds,
I need it no more, though it served me well,
The mantle of my spirit I leave behind,
The whitened ashes of my discarded shell.

Flowers bloom where my fallen atoms lie,
And trees grow strong from fragments of my bones,
All that's manifest must die, but the spirit enters
    timeless zones.

Upon my strewn form many feet will tread,
Singing birds pluck worms from nourished earth,
Bursting life emerges from the dead,
For learning souls to take new birth.

My eyes have gone, the speech no more,
Desires still flicker on the earthly plane,
But the questing spirit seeks the far flung shore,
So that I need not be born again.

Keith Goodall

Woman By The Sea

Time on an idling beach kept at bay
sand shoals crazy pebble paved shouldered by sweeping waves
gaunt rocks spying from shadows
age notched crevices wrinkled and tear dried
space staring back at a woman
wide liberty of the horizon broken loose from her perspective
of plummeting days and detachment
gulls reeling drunk with zest
gleeful in the gusty blowing from the sea
stooping she watches inward
swooping they hurl off death
and jostling with the breathy air
snatch at messages winging invisible
splayed from the spray of sand and wave
grazed by wing-beating power
glazed the woman hunts in the past
catapulted the truth from the sea/sky line
falls short of her lost thoughts
and dives shuddering in cold depths
rocketing on course to earth's core

Maureen Hanrahan

The Ocean World

Heads or tails
Sharks or Whales
They're all in the ocean world

From the electric eel to the swimming seal
Or hammer heads and ocean beds
They're all in the ocean world

So as you can see
Big or small it does not matter at all
Because they all live in the ocean world.

Ronan McConville

Reality

Have you once, ever considered reality?
Ever considered happiness, joy, shame, pity?
The scope of the planets, the structure of stars?
Ever thought of a soul's journey from Earth to Mars?
Ever questioned the concept of man's space travel?
Or maybe, a God's anger at how men dabble?
Ever considered the concept of one's true self?
The choice between material and emotional wealth?
Ever thought about ageing, wrinkles and white hair?
Ever considered destiny and what is out there?

I once began to consider reality.
Then slit my wrists.
Believe they said "shame" and "pity".
So now I know, and understand "planets" and "stars".
Believe me, reality exists only from jars.

Liz Griffiths

"The Coal Miner"

Down there in the very depths of mother earth herself he
inched slowly ever forward below the oceans shelf. On
bended knees he inched along, he hacked, he picked, he'd
trace, a never ending pattern on the black coal face. In the
inky blackness, the shadows and the gloom, he was a living
human being in a coal black tomb. Sunbeams couldn't
penetrate, moonbeams, nor a star, no light ever entered there,
no door to leave ajar. Shoulders grazed and bleeding from an
overhead beam, following the treasure of the black coal seam.
Murky, dirty water sometimes up to his chest, bones stiff and
frozen longing for a rest. Crawling on his hands and knees on
a road three feet high, no room to flex his aching muscles with
a long, loud, sigh. Grazes on his shoulders, cuts upon his
hands would heal and forever leave, deep blue bands. Like a
fire-fly glowing in a velvet night, the welcome flicker from
another miners light, the acrid smell off the carbide lamp, the
ever present danger of feared fire-damp. Down there on his
hands and knees did he ever pray? Did he ever wonder if he'd
see the light of day?

Katherine MacIntyre

Untitled

At the end of dim October month they came,
Boy and girl, to stay in a cottage by the sea.
Apart, stood to watch polythene drizzle
Sizzle in the seaweed on the oily shore
And grasped the sand's reluctant quest.

Too real, too real, the implication of the time
Recalled in the ache of thudding hearts
To the grey-green mirror of the sea.

Lips moistened by dark, drifting spray,
Buffeted by malevolent currents of air
They turned once more indoors, to find
Only the gleaming axe by the vacuous fireplace
But looked without success for coal.

Too soon, too soon, his lashing, frantic storms
Battered down their hard-earned peace
And washed the plaster from the walls

Out there, an antique pleasure craft, up and down,
Giddy megaphone blasting at the coast.
Here, a crusty shutter banged brick unceasing
And from the chimney the smoke of blood.

Alan Leroy Colman

The Changeling

Who am I now, I wonder?
I've leapt again whilst sleeping, if it the sleeping;
My essence progressively transcends, in nature with my keeping:
For I am a Changeling.

I've lived far beyond my given time,
Adapting to new forms, as new forms arrive,
Prolonging my soul, prolonging my goal to survive:
For I am a Changeling:

A myriad of stars have been my slaves,
Each star a life, each life I took,
To fill a page in my eternal book:
For I am a Changeling.

Today I woke, new wonder!,
A sentient male my new disguise, to view the world
through human eyes,
Perchance to spring my next surprise:
For I am a Changeling.

Through this incarnation, I'll promote my generation;
Procreate within its kind and leave a seed of mine behind,
To maybe steal another mind:
For I am a Changeling.

Stephen Peters

Friendship

Friendship is a mysterious thing,
Much happiness it can bring.
Special friendships always last,
Even when youthful days have past.
Caring friends will be forever,
In awkward situations they will stay together.
A real friend is always there,
To offer help, sincere and fair.
A kind friend will make a sacrifice,
And will give honest advice.
Through the good times a friendship goes,
Even in the bad times a relationship grows.
You find the perfect friend through pure fate,
Although a friendship is often broken with hate.
To lose a friend is more than a pity,
But a true friend will be there for eternity.

Rebecca Darlington

Untitled

Mother you gave me birth. And breath
    also a childhood. I'll never forget
you nurtured, cradled, cuddled me
    and also helped with my family.

You're remembered in mind, body, and soul
    and the Lord taking you. Has taken its toll
I have to be strong now, to take care of my own
    otherwise like me they'll feel all alone.

Thank's for the memories we shared together
    forget you I'll not, I promise you never
But life must go on. and I must be strong
    for other's who need me, dear mother.

May angel's watch over you day. And night
    and the Blessed Lord's arms, cradle you tight
Because you are still and will always be
    The only mother in this world for me.

J. E. Hill

Untitled

Have you just found you've a talent
You once didn't know that you had?
Have you found something new you can do?
It could be a gift from our Father above
A way that He wants to use you.

Tell someone - a friend - all about it
It helps if together you pray.
If you're not able to use it at once
Keep it fast in your mind don't ignore it
If you do it might go away

And if it's from God
It's a million to one
He'll want you to use it some day.

Peggy C.

Always And Forever

I love you very dearly,
Just like I always should.
I'll help you when you need it,
You know I always would.
Sometimes I may have hurt you,
It may have seemed I did not care.
But always and forever,
For you I will be there.
Through good times and through bad times,
In sunshine and in rain.
I'll smile when you are happy,
I'll share your every pain.
My love for you is strong now,
And from deep within my heart.
We may not always be together,
But we'll never be apart.

Pamela M. Kerr

Over The Hill

I stare at the painting.
The road winds upwards and over the hill.
There's a cottage with flowers and a wooden gate,
A wood runs alongside.
Slowly my gaze follows the path upwards to
The top of the hill.
To the top of the picture where it stops.
What is on the other side; eyes closed I visualize,
Mind flying to that summit and yes over it.
What is on the other side?
The path winds slowly down through more woodland to a lake;
I am soaring; a small island in the lake becomes a dot,
Higher and higher until the very earth disappears
And I am God.
Man's limits are unrestricted.
All is in the mind and it is omnipotent,
Goodbye dogma, goodbye restriction,
Life is mind and mind is might.

J. C. Smith

"The Dark"

Are you, afraid of the dark?
I am too, it left its mark
The past, is it something that haunts you too
What can you do, when you're afraid of the dark.

To cure, this fear of the dark
I can't go on, I can't go back
I'm trapped a prisoner in my own mind
can I break free or is the dark my destiny

Cold memories frozen in time, etched on my mind
something I've tried to forget
I thought it would pass with the years, taking my fears
out of the dark and into the light.

I must believe in myself, rise above this hell
conquer the demons within
There's always tomorrow like there was always today
what else can I hope to do but pray

That I, I won't always be afraid
of the night and the dark of today
I am lost will it forever be so
tell me do you know, the way out of the dark.

James Wood

My Church Street Memories

When I was a kid in the forties, ours was the best street around,
The church was at the very top; its bells made a wonderful sound.
You could imagine the clock face smiling, in the middle of the tower,
While in bed late at night it would strike away the hours.

I was born next door to mi grandparents who kept saddle back pigs.
They also kept a black cockerel who'd always chase us kids.
I collected tatie peelings and would go from door to door.
I got half a penny for half a bucket, a penny if I got more.

At times we got small taties, which granddad would boil for the pigs.
Us kids would say, treat day, we'd always sneak one us kids.
They smelt lovely in the copper at the top of the yard.
You had to watch for the cockerel, like a dog always on guard.

Our travis school a few doors away with Miss Naylor and Gaff Hirst.
You got codliver oil in the morning, boy did that put on a thirst.
I saved all mi half pennies and pennies, to spend in Mrs.
Townend's shop.
And after the mornings of codliver oil, first in for her ginger pop.

I loved her sugar dummies, then the spitfires came on the scene.
Rationing on Kylie and Lollys, our faces lost their beam.
Our coupons were 2 ozs and a quarter, and lettered E and D.
But along with mi girlhood memories, this was the best, for me.

Shirley Ann Quinn

Storyteller/Lindworm

His voices - he has many and faces besides
drop from ordinary speech to hypnotic cadence,
softening consonants, ululating vowels in river-running gurgles,
brushing softly the clayed banks of memory,
washing bare roots that snag surrender to the mainstream pull.

"I am the firstborn,
A bride for me before a bride for thee".

Seven skins shed thrice washed purified purged
by dip and dive of sound spinning down to mud depths
plunging to sky filtered leaf and frond patterning existence
shadowing pasts and back lighting futures
in a millpond limbo where
mossed logs make green snakes and fire smokes
a contrived magic for my camera.

Still the story casts its spell
binding reason, moving the heart's eye to scan
dark monsters of a deep unknown
world contained
in a tale.
Carol Byrne Jones

A Facile Fence Between Humorous Friends

But please I; in greater pain than he, for who is present?

Interjections displease and are your vulgarity,
At once on guard;
You're vulgarity I in turn intern with facetious clarity,
Unsheathe your epigrammatic epee he parries. To match your
Freudian foil? Ridicule I: Touche.

Blase! He parodies (Bon mot; our shared forte).
Facetious interjections are juvenile and rude. "Juvenal!";
Was not satire rudimentary, I quip in deserved riposte.
Such swarded scintillation: A brilliant guard.
Reflecting a (wise) crack to the heart for wise it was.
Draw I, my edge so sharp and keen as I, at his expense,
And for his jocular vein I lunge: To spill his wit.

But why to play our joust of classic puns and jests, quid pro quo?
For with double entendre I do strike, and strike (in vein) I do.

Now I cover my malevolent badinage for fear of dangerous farce,
Mock not masters, however flash your repartee.
For I cut, many facetious friends, with jokes. Who suffered
dearth of laughs, and also life.
Robert Eales

"Problem Drinking"

The tears have gone...dried up?...Cried so much...
Nothing left...only emptiness.
Cried for you...lied for you,
Feel like, I have died for you.
lived your life...been your wife,
What's left? Nothing?...Emptiness?
Felt pain lived again! Happy and sane!...But then...
Tears fall like rain...feel insane, once again.
No security
Poison liquid?...Imprisons me.
So much loneliness...where are you?
Clock watching again...to you, I am true
One again pain...smoke like a chain
Security in a fag...what a laugh!
I want your touch...need you so much...
you need...
Poison liquid..dull's your brain leaves you insane.
The heartache will be yours, you left with nothing,
only...
Poison Liquid
Eve Clare

Can You Exist?

Your voice energy ideas are gone to
somewhere beyond our sphere.
We all exist and grow, doing things that
we first shared together.
The younger faces wear shadows, that were
never there before.
And often my heart will send pain to
my very core!
Your going left many damaged dreams,
hearts and days so changed by this cruel deed.
Can you exist without the love borne
by these children of pure joy.
How sad to see this great spirit of joy
and love laid to waste.
Your family without its head
without the lead it should have had.
Laurie Hobley

Spring

As I stand on the hill, looking down on the scene,
All around me seems merry and gay,
The bright coloured flowed keep up through the green,
of the fields, in Hyperion's bright ray.

The frost and the snow have melted away,
And the birds have returned to their nest.
The woods are resounding with song all the day.
Till at e'en the sun sinks in the west.

The bright little insects are busy from morn,
'mid the flowers and the grass now so green.
The tender young violets hide from the storms,
In nooks by man's eye rarely seen.

The sun now peeps out from the dark cloud,
Which hid it while cold reigned supreme,
Now Phoebus, wrapped up in his fine golden shroud,
O'er the wide path of blue drives his team.
Helen Reid

Shorn Lamb

Black pools pitifully stare
At the sad spectacle
Heavy-laden from his thankless wheelchair.
Wincing at his shuffled body,
Oblivious to the damned watching
Plump cheeks rubefy into ripe apples
And lucky lips nervously twitching,
Turning into thin strips.

Fretted faces forever focus
Upon this shunned wretch;
Labelled since infancy,
Mimicked by mankind.

Dreaming of Abraham's bosom;
Longing to escape his living death.
Sadie Lunn

The Old Man And The Blind Woman

He guided her onto the bus
as carefully as if she were bone China.
"Here's a little wee step, dear"
dressed in baggy clothes, time lining his weather worn face,
love shone through his words.
The old woman's white cane tap tap tapped in gentle unison
to the voice of her beloved,
guiding her onto a bus she'll never see
to sit on a seat whose poison graffiti
she cannot gaze at, and wonder why 'Jay is a plonker'
or 'MUFC Rule,' and the old man doesn't mention it.
The bus passes by weary buildings as oblivious to her
as she is to them.
The old man stays at her side, speaking in a gentle voice,
creating for her a steady rock
in a swirling sea of noises.
Darren Warlow

54

Memories

Will you come for a walk with me dear,
For a trip down memory lane,
Where I told you that I loved you,
and you said you felt the same,
Shall we look for the old oak tree dear,
Where you promised you'd be mine, and
Under the boughs, we made our vows,
and you placed your hand in mine,
Lets walk by the banks of the rippling stream,
Where we picked primroses fair they
looked oh so beautiful entwined in your
long brown hair.
Alas, we're old and grey now, but I love
you just the same, so please will you
come for a walk with me, just a trip
down memory lane

E. M. Saywell

Sheep! Oh Sheep!

Sheep! Oh sheep! Where'er you stray,
You act the same just every day.
You stare at me with vacant face,
Which culminates in such frantic race;
I feel uncertain what to do,
You appear to say, "Who are you?"
Although I strive not to offend,
Your plaintiff voices loud you rend,
You start to scatter wildly,
'Though I approach you kindly;
You view me as some intruding beast;
So unkind! To say the least.
But when I scan the human race,
Do we not bear a similar face?
When we think we are so clever
Our thoughts and aims are but trite endeavour.
So do not scorn the silly sheep,
In their short life, the more they reap.

J. M. Hayes

Homage To War

On that dreadful winters night
When most soldiers were curled up out of sight,
I saw at my post the most terrifying scene.
Which I declare was of no earthly been.
From the shrouds of enveloping mist I saw,
To my horror and my awe,
War and death walk hand in hand.
Across the dreary vicinity of no man's land.
And with every step they took across that accursed mud,
The land began to bubble up and froth with blood.
And with it, it did take many a youth
Who stood for peace, justice, and truth.

Rebecca Allott

Korean Dawn

Grey dawn appears
and heralds the sunrise.
The shapes of broken houses
show dark against the lightening sky.
From the rubble of blasted villages
shrouded forms of people rise
to search for loved ones
in the light of the greyish dawn.
Bomb blasted and derelict
the streets lie in ruinous array
with rescue parties struggling
in the first pale rays of sun.
Improvised stretchers move
back and forth and back again
as the injured are recovered and
the dead laid out in rows.
Day comes and with it
the village throbs with the will of life
and people build anew.

Keith F. Thomson

'The Flag'

Put simply: the flag on the flag pole was dying.
It was there to be seen; no point in denying that gone were
its days of unfurling and flying.

The silk - all in tatters, and colours once regal of blue, red
and gold portraying an eagle - majestic and strong; now pale,
as a sea gull.

But a breeze out of nowhere causes insecure flapping, then a
gust has the aged cloth streaming and slapping on flagpole
which now is in danger of snapping.

The Eagle, unfettered, is once more seen winging in Summer blue
sky, where its call, loudly ringing, joins in with the wild
wind's unstructured singing.

The resuscitation is short, one last cry, then the eagle folds
wings thus ceasing to fly whilst the flag, now deflated, goes
limp with a sigh.

The Wind has escaped, through ragged holes seeping but we see
no more cause for sadness or weeping; the flag is not dying
it is merely sleeping.

Janet Morgan

Wilting Love

Love is like a flower
Growing more each day
Until it is a blooming passion
And I love you in every way.

Now the flower is wilting
Our passionate love going away
My world is now shattered
I still need you to stay.

Come spring the flower will bloom again
My memories of you are still clear
Deep down you know I still care for you
And that feeling won't ever disappear.

That flower didn't blossom
But I've found somebody new
I care for him very much
He'll never take the place of you.

V. C. Ingram

Beside Me

Deep in the darkest watches of the night,
When the world's in slumber and men dream
And the ghost-white owl takes flight
In silence, save for a haunting scream,
I can hear you breathing, smell your hair,
See the rise and fall of your breast, there
Beside me.

I lie still as death, not daring to touch
The beauty of your sleep-enveloped skin
Lest the shock of contact prove too much
And my lovely vision evaporates within
The palm of my trembling hand. Then I see:
The spirit of your love will always be
Beside me.

Miles Hedley

Children

To hold a child is a wonderful thing,
To love a child is rewarding,
To take a child by the hand is to step
  into a wonderland,
To take that step is a reward for both.
To take one's own child by the hand is a
  magical feeling,
To take one's grandchildren by the hand
  is magical and unbelievable,
To have a child's love and trust gives one
  a feeling of exaltation.

Patricia Jane Richmond

The Child Within

No longer must you hide away
I have a place for you to stay
Side by side we'll face it all
We'll grow in strength and stand up tall
I know your story well you see
For I was you and you were me

No-one else will really know
What shame or guilt you dared not show
You were to those so unaware
A child at play without a care
Such innocence was easy prey
He set the stage and wrote the play

You saw no danger, felt no fear
No shouts of warning did you hear
And so quite willingly you fell
In with the plans he laid so well
Your world could never be the same
As his silent victim you became
> *J. P. Mitchell*

Breathe

Weary, he sits, wizened like a plant
Deprived of sunlight, curling at the edges.
Photosynthesis? Nothing can be done
His roots are dry
He seeks no sun.

Outside he frowns, cursing the world,
Lazy and lonely and sucking in death.
Inhaling infection, a cavity of smoke
I am engulfed
I make him choke.

Inside he weeps, self pity and pain
Cavity clogged and membrane maimed.
Respiration? No lungs - no life.
Lack of oxygen
Cuts like a knife.

Slower I pulse, defying diffusion
I suck through the windpipe, gasping for air
Deterioration, like a rasp rubbing bark
Slowly I deflate.
All is dark.
> *Kirstin Elsby*

Thoughts Of Home

I thought last night of my home town
And all that it means to me.
Of loved ones, far away, yonder,
With thoughts that are dear to me.

I thought of the River Leven,
Where chestnuts great overhang,
The path that leads to the garden,
Where my heart so often sang.

I thought of lanes that I'd travelled
Dear country - second to none!
The hills standing guard around it,
The becks flowing gently on.

Loved Cleveland! There's no place the same!
Dear home - we're fighting for you.
When his strife is ended and over
Sweet home, I'll come back to you.

We fight - for peace everlasting
Safe surety - come to our shore!
Freedom. that really is freedom,
We treasure; come, stay evermore!
> *John S. West*

'Racism'

The deadly plague that sweeps the land,
And on its side many people stand,
It causes anger, hate and pain,
These things it has, racism is its name.

Its grasping claws stretch from man to man,
It has formed the ku klux klan,
It causes fear, humiliation and shame,
How can we stop it? Racism is its name.

What consequences hold by the colour of skin,
To be hounded down, to feel like a sin,
And on all this what do we have to blame?
The answer is simple, racism is its name.

"Leave Britain to whites" graffiti cries,
Tears of sorrow well in eyes,
Water will spread but blood will stain,
Our souls have no colour, racism is its name.
> *Melanie Smith*

A Wedding Poem

A beginning, a seed, a tiny flower,
A shaft of daylight, in the early hour,
Fresh eyes pierce through the morning dew,
Eager to start the day anew,
Birds sing from high above,
Stirrings of life, stirrings of love.

Like fruits upon a laden tree,
And plants now in full flower,
Like streams, now rivers, that flow free,
And the sun that has full power,
Man's hopes and dreams are kept alight,
Whilst strength of life and love burn bright.

The partnership of time and tide,
The moon and stars watchful, protecting,
Lighting the way, no need to hide,
Through rough seas, directing.
The partnership of man and wife,
A partnership of love and life.
> *Roger Compton*

Heartbreak

My heart is broken, bleeding and torn
Crying and aching like the gash from a thorn.
My tears are like raindrops
Silver and sad
Dripping with heartache from the love that we had.
My eyes they are glistening
Like pools full of dew,
Inside me I loved you -
But I doubt if you knew.
> *Mandy Mitchell*

Dreams Of Suspense

An unreal word, under the thick blanket misconduct hath sewn.
Royal dreams of orange nights are grown, yet die.
The history of the world lay in a doomed anthology
Waiting to be burnt with revived mythology.
This is a new world, with new ideas,
Mad dogs weep timeless spheres.
Scientific mind are shaping the ever closer future that
doesn't look good
Not for the cult, the optimist nor the gods with the
dark hoods.
An unborn creation is swimming in time, in time with
peace
A brand new world padded with the saviours fleece.
A brand new world is forming on the horizon of
the bleak dreams, dying.
A brand new world to end the shame of crying.
> *John Harris*

Ide Hill, Ken October 1992

Autumn's rainbow rapture unfolds its symphony
As trees yield quiescently
To winter's promiscuous charm.
Bruised greens; but hopeful, higher suffering
Enflames with yellow, orange and red
Of ecstatic maturity.

Then dark clamour of clouds across the Weald
Dampens the fuller notes of autumn -
Heralding winter's more churlish grasp
Into a long, deep, funereal sleep,
Under a cold, white winding sheet.

Retiring leaves frolic; finally falling
To brown earth's consummate, mute embrace.

But suddenly, when sparkling frost
And glistening morning mist
Subdue a sterner cry-
The heart's fast-forward sigh,
The gentle touch of spring.

Robert G. Bringloe

Moonlight

Delights to peep and gaze there on,
To listen to whispers woebegone.

The clouds gather towards the shining God.
All that can be heard is the mourning of the descending darkness.
The wind at its peak, the trees swaying free,
The light being spread to bring glaze and glee.

A blanket of white is now conjured, on this vast and dauntless night.
Shadows of death are now repelling, and fogs of doom retrace,
Whilst the evil atmosphere lies dormant, ready to embrace.

As the early hours of the dawn commence,
And the stars all fade away,
The magic from the moonlit sky
Entices us to pray.

Seek your dreams,
And hold your heart,
Today is the full moon
And tomorrow is the start.

Arif Nedjat

Untitled

So on the canvas for years and years
While the tympanum assails my closing ears,
Venetian flesh, eyes, nose and mind green
To maturing seventy, purple notes seen, soon, all too soon.

Visualize, auralise, multitudes to size
Analyse, moralize, this and that way whys
Violins, saxophones, pencils and telephones
Conversations, observations in graphic tones. Soon, all too soon.
Lines splash but blotches are drawn, sing 'Ah'
On the scale light to dark with blue from afar,
Week day, holiday, holy day and Sunday
Colour and sound on the merry-go-round play, soon, all too soon.

The brush drawing low notes from keys,
Then silence and white and it flees.
The purple envelope attacks, decays with slow release,
Blue thirds like distant mist, tritones in sharp focus cease,
soon, all too soon.

Ancient and modern and 'fine' 'da capo'
To begin is to end so 'morendo', 'morendo'.
Bald brush, bald bow, bald pate, all white
All colours, all sounds, on the merry-go-round take flight, soon,
the end, all too soon.

E. W. M.

Elegy

Will ever she walk in the woods again
Or climb the downs,
Where the wind makes rivers in her hair
And scatters the words on her lips?
Will the sunlight fade the light in her eyes
And time tangle the days at her feet,
Or the morning frost whiten the warmth of her breath
And curl in her finger tips?
Will ever she watch where the swift cloud flies
Or hear the slow footsteps of death,
That shuffle her thoughts and smother the hours
As the mist enfolds, as the daylight dips,
As the tears are trapped in the silent flowers?
Will I be there?

Mary Gordon

Over The Wall

In the trenches the smell is vile, climbing over the bodies in a pile,
Sending out the fearful command, he could feel the desperate
   chill of death's hand.
He was pushing over the wall, as the Sergeant Major began to call,
The bullet sent a frantic wail, the poor man's heart began to fail.
The fraying uniform was died blood red, the screaming man
   held his head,
His legs began to shiver with pain, as he tried to fight on in
   the pouring rain.

Stumbling over the mud-drenched land, he could feel the chill
   of death's great hand,
As another bullet hit the half dead man, he had totally ruined
   the battle plan.
Dropping down pouring with blood, he collapsed face first in
   the mud,
His heart let out a final flutter, as the half dead man began to
   mutter.

"Mary forgive me for not coming back, my train has finally
   crashed off the track."
Silence followed quickly behind, as England lost a budding mind.

Sarah Cuthill

Now Nothing Can Save Us

When partners turn their backs upon,
The love that they once knew,
broken binds and empty souls are all that come to view.
One lover takes the cynic look on life after rejection,
and insecurity is the producer of deception
Then gestures come with guarantees,
that hearts will break no more,
they instead grow old and lose their faith,
and love is frail and poor.
Then gallant knights draw back their swords,
to face redundancy,
and spirits starts to weaken and fade in agony.
Trust is nigh the world is dark,
our hearts have now betrayed us,
we've lost the battle and the war,
and now nothing can save us.

Charlotte Sowden

The Common

Around the common the children play,
The street lights emit a warm autumn glow,
The only fright, some ghostly spectre, or playful fist,
The Catholic Comprehensive
Is swathed in mist:
High above is a blue silver dome,
And gold are the lights, that twinkle from home.
The big bad wolves though fancy or love may move,
Are in their dens, ablaze with light
And it's left to the owls to hoot good night.

Oswald Stuart Harforth

Death

How can I love you in a place I don't know
how can I see you when I'm rotting down below,
Will I remember your smiling face
your wit, your love, your style, your grace,
How can it be paradise when you're not there
a world without you would make my heart tear,
Death will snatch me away from my life with you
and take me to a place which is strange and new,
Forgetful? No, your face would never leave my mind
but I could never touch you, hold you, or hear
your voice so kind.

I may return as the whistle in the breeze
the glistening dew or the wind in the trees,
But still I could not touch you, or tell you how much I care
everyone else could but me, that's not fair,
Life is so delicate, you can lose it just like that
and now I will never see you again and I cannot cope with that,
Death has stopped my love forever.
        Claire Furnell

My Kaleidoscope

Blue are the soaring skies,
That are full of birds at sunrise,

Green are the gleaming grasses,
That grow in the mountain passes.

Purple are the vivid violets,
That nestle in the Scottish Islets.

Pink are the blossoms of the cherry tree,
That flower in spring for all to see.

Brown are the autumn leaves,
That flutter and fall in the swirling breeze.

Yellow are the sparkling sands,
That drift across the desert lands,

Turquoise are the shining seas,
That roar towards the harbour quays.

Gold are the rays of the setting sea,
That leaves you when the day is done.

Orange are the fire's flickering flames,
That dance and prance in their games.

Silver are the shimmering stars,
That shine upon us from afar.
        Heather L. Francis

Untitled

When the waves have weathered the storm,
And the sea is calm and tranquil,
When the rain ends,
And the sun comes out,
Everything is bright and beautiful.
Nature is a rare gift to us all,
Each day,
Unwrapping our appreciation for its
Animals,
Great and small.
Love is another of life's little
Treasures.
Taking it for granted would be a
Mistake,
Because it's something very precious.
To live and to breathe,
How glorious it is,
To share and to learn,
In this kingdom of his.
        Barry John Evans

Birth Of A Poet

I see a multitude acclaim a gallant son
Laughing, crying - here's the prize he's won.
I see a mother lay her babe to rest
Mirrored in her eyes the love light blest.
Beyond the hill I see the sun-god set
And leave a symphony of trees in silhouette.

Inner murmurings rise and swell
Demanding exit through the pen
And in my brain surge fragments, phrases
Which suppressed, unconquered rise again.

To translate with power, with words of fire
The stirrings of my soul;
To compose with skill, in fitting form -
Creation in control.
To mould each thought that craved expression
Quick unit of the whole;
And make that whole a living, throbbing poem -
Here is my task defined - herein my goal.
        Cyril E. Lee

'To Dad'

Now sadly mum has passed away, no longer here to see this day,
But I'm sure she'd like to join with me in wishing you happy anniversary,
40 years spent side by side since that day she was your bride,
the love we feel keeps her here and fills the void inside we fear.

One day we'll surely meet again, we know not how, we know not when,
Until that day we have to try to make the most of time going by,
We have our lives we've got to live with lots of pleasures yet to give
Let's look ahead to pastures new and see tomorrow's brighter hue.

This tragic loss has made us sad, but don't forget the good times had,
We laughed, we played, we argued some, alas just now we feel just
numb, if mum could talk I'm sure she would, tell us to stop this
sombre mood, tell us to wipe our tears and smile, get on with
our lives now, not in a while,

Life's too short to sit and mope, let's have fun, let's have hope,
Tomorrow brings me know not what, let's make the most of time
we've got, we all have faults, we all have flaws, but mum was like
a perfect rose, always there to help and advise, healing hearts
and easing cries

No better wife could you have chose, the best of all, no other's
close, you picked the girl who had it all, smart and chic and on
the ball, forty years you had with mum, lots of joy and lots of fun,
Best wishes on your ruby anniversary from all the family
including me.
        Heather Dunbar

Life

The winds of change come blowing in as
The days go passing by,
Our lives move on out of our control with
No help from you or I,
We are mere bystanders travelling a long
The corridors of life,
Some days peacefully moving on, some days
Full of strife,
Our lives drift slowly like the waves upon
The shore,
Lapping at the sands of time for yesterdays
No more,
The future beckons us forward, not knowing
What tomorrow will bring,
It could be troubled or it could be freedom
Like the bird upon the wing,
Whatever life has in the store we should treat
Each day as our last,
Our memories are made up of our future, present
And past.
        Lesley Jarvis

Do Not Believe

Do not believe in roads without an end.
All roads run out: the worst of agony
Is transient, a broken life can mend,
The stab of loss is numbed in memory.

Do not believe you walk on the last road,
Or that this night will never see the day.
In Auschwitz where the tides of Death once flowed,
Silence returned. Hell become yesterday.

Pain is our fate, but not this present pain:
Time like a wind above the flowing grass
Will blow, and everything will pass -
Sorrow as readily as happiness.

The years are like a furnace that will burn
This grief to ash, this fear to nothingness;
And we shall know normality again:
For Hell shall fail, and silence shall return.

Geoffrey Hoffman

Images Of Inward Feeling

Catch myself inwards on top of self-controlled bottle.
On metal names of cornered hills I cried hampered motto.
Many ties can reach no flames and time to time clock round
    and round,
Their fired wrenched out eyes, fly past the banner running
    from the ground.
Sigh and byes treat one who begs, grand games of laughter
    and sin,
Why not fight and drive the world, taking everything in.
Waves of light stream out in creases the military man far riding strong.
Skies of pink flow deep in valleys, on paths that lie beyond.
Floating on water urging to swim preoccupied from weather
beaten hand
Conduit on harbour high surface, spiking journeys to release
    the sands.
Stripes of blue fly together with flags, stars of silver shine
    with shape,
Aching light pursue the frail wooden soles captured on tape.
Taste climbs smoky skins, framed heart beats circles through,
Panic motion rain down in rhyme defying sound cupped in twos.
Spinning like textured shells, find plucked fruit of cream,
Spiralling twists fall helplessly on giant pendulum of frayed
    squeezed dreams.
Plummeting pauses ask, "On what grounds are these?"
Pray for freedom on bended knee.
Higher they climb, slower they go, dusty roads are not
appealing
Eventually stop to quench the scene of images of inward
feeling.

Richard Stickler

The Daring Mice

Sitting together by the old hearth fire
Gran and granddad would never tire
Recalling things of days gone by
Memories bringing tears to their eye.
Happiness and sorrow, shared through the years
Lovely to watch these two old dears
The warmth of the logs, an occasional kiss
Quietly sharing, the evening bliss
When three little mice boldly appeared
Scampering around, bright eyed, long eared
Granddad grabbed the poker, but was too slow
The mice had gone before he could strike a blow
Later that night, undressed, half asleep
Gran felt a nibble, scratching of feet
"There's something up in my night gown,"
She scrambled up with a frown
Grabbing the intruder, squeezing it tight
It was one of the mice, but it was dead on sight
It must have run up her skirt when granddad let fling
Gran squeezed it so hard it died the poor thing.

A. F. Childs

"Elixia"

If music be the food of love, play on 'tis said
And I would breakfast mainly upon bread,
Cereals too, an egg now and then
The product of an organic her.
Lunchtime, nyeoita and cheese would suffice,
Maybe something involving nice.
My evening meal would be a cooked one.
Takes more preparation so maybe less fun

How do I've equate music with love?
The way to a man's heart is through his stomach 'tis said;
So come my little turtle dove;
Lashings of food, including bread.
Turkey especially for holidays high.
There's nothing nicer than a home made pie.
Brush up my dear, your culinary art.
That's the way to your loved one's heart!

Peter J. Rumble

Love

As the music that stems from a violin,
springs from the original tree.
So it is with me,
I cannot leave this world, I'm entwined with it.
As a tree's roots entwine with the earth
as the wind wraps around the sea
as eye connects me to the moon, and
as my body lovingly embraces the sun's rays
as my being once flowed
From the dust that fashioned me,
now returns back to my creator.
So in death as the wondrous clay entombs me
I await the next stage of my journeying
to many more of your promised delights.

Constance Fahey

Yesterday Dross

Childhood memories, we all have a few,
But do we want to share them with you?
Catharsis you'd say, well probably so,
Maybe, maybe not, I really don't know,

Remembering, digging, sifting the past,
What would it achieve myself I ask?
Events and emotions hidden from sight,
What good would it do to now start to write?

Achieve inner peace, put ghosts at bay,
By writing it down to me you'd say,
But digging takes longer the older one gets,
And time goes so quickly so let's forget let's,

Ripples it's true from the past to the present,
Can flood our consciousness, sometimes unpleasant,

But who wants to deal with yesterday's dross?
The fragile emotions of someone's old cross,
No, let's keep the lid on and poke them back down,
Let's keep what we've got and we'll all be fine.

Patricia Clark

Old Lovers

Last night, I slept with an old lover. Oh, nothing
special - just a moment's plain joining to fill,
momentarily, the searing space within.

With all my mind, I longed for perfect connection-
for the fizz and dazzle of mind in mind, spirit in
spirit and flesh in flesh. But somehow I missed you.

So instead of participants in the lush golden-edged
after-harmony, we were left cheated-stumbling and
sore. Embarrassed by our joint despair,

You left before morning with polite words floundering
for expression and escape. And in your going,
I found only brief heady sorrow and emptiness.

Anne L. Brooke

Heaven's Gates

Take him to a place where he feels no pain
Pull him out from the crowd to somewhere it doesn't rain.
Days go by like a train.
Growing more social aware each day
The world is burning can't you see it
Turning round and round each day.
Send him to a place where he feels no pain,
Take him to a place where the clouds can't reach
That place called Heaven's Gates.

Yet again another stranger stares and frowns
At the dying man in the corner
As I watched him pass him by,
I thought to myself
What has this dying man to gain?
So take him to place where he feels no pain.
Send him to a place where the clouds can't reach
That place called Heaven's Gates.

Karen McPhilemy

Mother!

The pain and sorrow in your eyes,
i can see even though you try to hide,
your aching pain and all your sorrow,
are filled with all your tomorrow's,
you lost a love that won't come back,
and you wish that yesterday were here,
for if you could have another chance,
to look back for another glance,
at the face you'll never see,
of the little boy who'll never be;
you carried him for six whole months,
just to have a bundle of joy,
to be your life throughout your day's,
and see him grow and watch him play,
but heaven is where he'll wait for you,
he'll play with the harp's — and angles too!
don't be sad for me my mother,
for it was meant to be like this,
so don't be sad for me, as I am near,
to watch over you, so let there be not a tear.

Rosanna Ledwold

Tears

Tears of joy, tears of sorrow,
Tears of mirth, tears of woe,
Tears of pain, tears of sadness,
Tears are ready for to flow.

Tears from babies in their cradles,
And from children in their play.
Tears of childbirth from their mothers,
Tears of heartbreak every day.

Tears of anguish from the parents
For a child who's gone astray,
Tears of memories of loved ones
Who have gone so far away.

There will be tears, and tears, and tears
Shed throughout each day and night,
But the precious love of Jesus
Shows through all to make things bright.

A. E. Harris

Omission

Do not betray that moment,
Fate decrees is yours,
Great silence waits for comment,
You dare not give it pause.

The trembling heart may render dumb,
That word you should have sense to name,
And thereby cheat life's natural sum,
To reap that dying called self blame.

Christopher Dale

A Trip To The Seaside

Rising, with the waves,
I watched the boat bobbing,
The smaller waves supporting and guiding.
Shrieking cries from birds,
fighting for discarded fish.
Salt stinging the eyes of passers,
walking their educated dogs.
Sewage sneaking into the sea,
abandoned by its owners.
Waves battling against the walls,
for their rightful place.
The sun falling, leaving pools,
with its spiteful glare.
Odd boots missed by their
ignorant owners.
Still the boat is defended by its rival.

Emma Lloyd

Vision

I have seen the mushroom clouds devastating cities fine,
as rockets fly to free men's souls before their time.
While riding high upon the dark, dark clouds,
the Apocalyptic horsemen plunder laughing loud.
Killing unborn babies and our children free,
as the universal Mother weeps in the darkness of eternity.

A planet void I can see no light,
men hide in burrows deep within the earth hidden from
the horsemen's sight.
As death dust settles on our global sphere,
killing all her beauty Armageddon draws near.
Mortally wounded Mother earth shall be,
by evil hordes who's bear shall main the eagle free.
Then men will enter a darker age, darker than eternity.

R. J. Rylance

The Hairdressers

The air was thick with heat and spray.
The young girl said, "Please come this way".
I settled in a swivel chair
and there was left to sit and stare.
My ageing tresses stared at me,
they were not what they used to be,
gold and sparkling round my head,
now tinged with grey and rather dead.
"Please shampoo Madam", said this voice
and suddenly I had no choice,
led to the slaughter like a lamb
I really did feel such a ham.
The hair was washed and I was tossed
back to the swivel chair.
Ronald approached and I was coached
on difficulties with hair.
Then lightning precision
reduced my trailing locks,
took away my indecision
like meat on the chopping block.

Gina Peirson

Flu

Our family has the flu
Except Mummy and me
And I'm just as miserable as can be
Nobody knows I'm here at all
Mummy's at everyone's beck and call
Up the stairs goes the patients' brew
Mummy gasps, "Later I'll see to you"
And my throat is getting hot and dry
If I were a girl I bet I'd cry
But I'd better dash to the bathroom quick
My tummy's gone funny, I want to be sick
Mummy's feet running, a welcome sound
for the bathroom's going round and round
At last I'm safe in my own warm bed
And Mummy is fussing me up instead

Margaret Duffield

The War That Stopped The World

The sun arose that day, over scenes of devastation;
From horizon to horizon the weary battleground unfurled;
Trails of dusty carnage: wails of lamentation:
All day, we watched the waging
Of the war that stopped the world.

Then slowly twilight fell that day,
But no stars came out to guide us:
No moon shone in the darkness
And the nightmare was complete
When - in thunderclaps of blinding light -
The great Mushroom clouds engulfed the night
Raining the obscene death, on all beneath.

"The last day is nigh!" the warlords cry,
Dug deep in fallout shelters yet deafened by the din.
"The last day is nigh and we are alive!"...
...Mocking echoes...
   ...Make no reply...
   June Lamb

A Poem To You Son

I wonder whether love's just a dream
Or just a phrase to make you scream
To love as one or as a team it all depends on what you've seen
Love's not so very clean sometimes it's fun, but often mean
How often true these words I speak, there like a winter cold
and bleak
For some love is full of fun, for others it's just full of woe
Alas for me I often know, back home with sorrows I will go
Once a teenager, I let life go it passed me by without a sigh
I drank, I smoked, I met a guy
Now I sit, I moan, I cry,
A baby in a cot have I, no exams, no job, no money, no guy
It's funny how things just fly right by off into the yonder
without saying goodbye
To learn a lesson is what I've done, but all my love goes to
my darling son
Someone to love and call my own to guarantee I'm never alone
The only person in my life to love me true just like you do
Someday there may be someone willing to love me just as
much as you
Until that day I will remain so proud, so quiet, and so unwilling,
For to let a man have his evil ways, will reduce me back to my
foolish ways.
   Rosemarie Pitcher

Moods

When I'm feeling nervous,
I start to bite my nails.
Especially at Lanimers
With all the gulps and wails!

When I feel lazy,
I won't do anything.
The computer, I will not play,
I don't even try to sing!

Boredom is another mood,
Where there is nothing to do,
People are outside playing,
I wish I was playing too!

Feeling frightened is the worst of all,
When you hear eerie sounds,
It makes your skin crawl!!

When I go to Motherwell games,
I always feel excited.
We won 2-0 at Pittodrie,
I came home quite delighted!!
   Kristopher Jack

Hope

The sun shines, a warm glowing ball in the sky,
melting the frost on the lawn from way up on high.
Wish it were as easy to melt the ice in my heart,
The ice which has lodged there since we've been apart.

I've had fun, and I've giggled, and I've laughed till I cried,
But nothing and no-one can help from outside.

They say it takes time and that time is the healer,
But how can they know for they know not the dealer
Who dealt me the hand that wrenched the warmth from inside me
and replaced that perfect pink feeling with a finger so icy.

It took only seconds to change laughter to tears
To destroy what had been growing inside me for years.

Then, out of nowhere, he crept into my heart,
And that finger of ice he slowly shredded it apart,
Allowing the flame of hope to grow warmer and stronger,
And melting all within - an iceberg no longer.
   Pat Salisbury-Ridley

Mistress Autumn

As if by magic she arrives,
To brighten up our hum drum lives,
Red and gold, bronze and brown,
The fluttering leaves come drifting down.

Strewing a carpet full of light
It truly is a glowing sight,
Strolling on the rustling leaves
We marvel at this spell she weaves.

Her subjects wave their leafy arms
As this queen of colour works her charms
In city great and village small
Every year she thrills us all.

Before the dawn of winter drear
This magic mistress does appear
She paints our world with tender love,
taught from the Master from above.
   Rosaleen McCafferty

Beautiful Aged

Her wrinkled skin is like ruffled silk,
she moves slowly like a creeping dawn,
Wisps of smoke curl around her head,
like an intricate web of silver threads.
She passes by the window and I see her time-weathered face,
So many pictures lie in her memory,
covered by the dust of an ageing mind,
occasionally disturbed by a faded photograph,
commemorating her long life.
Her eyes, blue as the ocean,
glitter like the treasures that hide behind them.
She is beautiful,
like an ancient temple, full of immeasurable riches,
carved into a time old hill,
forever beautiful. Aged.
   Katherine Duff

The Circle Of Love

I lost you a long time ago to a place that
was no part of my world.

With pains of hunger and pains of sorrow
causing the neglect that my body receives.

I struggled and I prayed to break down the
barrier that held me so far from you.

My loss of appetite and loss of energy are
all the symptoms that needed to be seen.

When you come to me and hold me tight it
feels that everything will be alright.

So as one day disappears into the next the
circle begin again.
   Nicola Joy

"Happiness"

If everything was happiness, the world would be in joy,
And all the people smiling, whether they girl or boy.
No matter where they come from, no matter what their race,
as long as they stay smiling, they keep a happy face.

Happiness means laughter, which all of us must share,
For if we did not show our laughter, nothing would be there.
If the world stays happy, then all will be okay,
But if it turns to sadness, we all will have to pay.

So let us all be happy, and enjoy this lovely feeling,
For if we miss out happiness, who knows what we are dealing.
When you feel the sadness, slowly creeping in,
Just relax and let yourself chuck it in the bin.

Remember always where you go, to give a nice big smile,
'cause smiles mean you are happy, and they stretch out a mile.
Remember laughter in your dreams, don't let them fade away,
And always show your happiness, each and every day...

Donna Hawkins

Shady Days

As autumn leaves crackle
and summer ends its time
Burnt amber colour comes beaming through
With red or golden wine

Dreamy days and fireside scenes
with the gentle pleasures of life
Unhurried times with all its rivals
Take away our worry and strife

Release your passions gear up ambitions
for wintry days ahead
The year matures the day withdraws
And trees are all but dead

The snowflakes fall and rivers freeze
And mountains turn so bleak
The Robin sings still full of life
When the wind of fury speaks

Alicia Devereaux

Connections

People are the pieces of a dancing jigsaw
Moving in and out, pictures of our lives;
Fitting snugly or not matching,
Forced together tight-embraced,
The wrong piece in the wrong place.

The pictures form, break-up and reform
Colours, shapes, patterns like sun through stained-glass
Windows painting the cold, grey stone.

Chance brings the pieces to proximity, but
Who paints the picture?
Chance is the sister of Chaos,
Jumbled forms and clashing colours
The motifs on her trailing skirts.

Ann Rushbrooke

A Friend

When I first saw the look in your bright eyes,
Your golden hair gleaming in the sunshine,
The truth not known. Your face hiding the lies,
The painful truth was yours to know, not mine.

Your nature was kind but often unsure.
You often stood out with your face so proud,
I did not know the pain that you endured,
Protected by your happy leaps and bounds.

The fateful day that something was so wrong,
You tossed and turned, your eyes now told the truth,
My broken heart told me your life was done.
At first I was uncertain, I now had proof.

The illness overcame you with such force,
My dog is dead. Epilepsy the cause.

Joe Payne

Before The Truth

What reason is there here in thought,
What measure of wisdom, do we fall upon.
My thoughts they change, like green to
Blue, like green to blue.
What waste of thought, I say to you.
What faded hopes? What dreams of rust
I find that I no longer trust, I want
to, but seem to find that all my hopes
are left behind.
If I could tell, if I could trust just
one soul, indeed I must, they are
never there those people who you
thought were near and dear to you.
I find my heart is in my hands
it falls as if on shifting sands,
it never breaks, but stumbles on
to climb once more my dreams upon.
How small I feel, how last in thought,
It seems I cannot now be taught,
No wise man is at hand you see, for I am lost, oh woe is me.

Pamella Saunders

Summer, 'At Last'

Fresh as the swelling grapevines
I wrapped me in summer's shawl
Merry to part from winter's chill
Singing, with sweet bird's call,
Locked in the arms of romance
Lips tingling with grape, and thirst
Locking outside bleak winter, such joys, I feel fit to burst!...

'Burst' like the buds that blossom
Free as the birds on high, my hopes are constant strumming
A melody to the sky,........

Ah! Don't you just love the mornings?
And, don't you just love the night?
For he lies who never loved dawnings
That cast off drear winter's bite,.....
I look at the crisp grass swaying, my senses breathe fresh
sweet air,
Buds bloom, and the hens are laying,
Now I feel I have, 'not one care',
I'm not 'mad' I've not; lost my senses;
In fact, I have just begun, to cast off
The cold defenses, to welcome the new day's sun....

Kathleen A. Millington

"Poor Old Thing!"

Life was hard when I was young, my elders wouldn't let me speak.
I could be seen, but not my knees; and often told I'd too much cheek.
To tell the truth, but never tales, meant resorting to a truth in halves.
To say no to seconds when taken out, whilst my tiny little
belly starves.
"I'll give you a penny when I get a ha' penny," so I ran the
neighbours errands free.
Whilst sixpence was the money earned by her daughter just
as old as me.
I thought I was an ugly child - squinty eyes is what they said;
Mouth too wide and nose too long, something like a horses head.
Never praised, one's head would swell, compliments the
devil's tools.
A look in the mirror was for the vain, to consider looks was
just for fools.
Cuddles were just for tiny tots. A hug was something never
shared.
A smack, you took that in your stride, it didn't mean that no
one cared.
Few sweets, no toys, holidays nil. Often told to watch your
tongue.
The war was going great guns too; yes life was hard when I
was young.

Yes life was hard when I was young. It has such a familiar ring.
It wasn't good - Oh! Dearie Me. You poor old thing!!

Joan Howard

Watch The Fire Hear The Fire

Watch the flames as they curl and twist
Around the blackened walls
Watch them climb with a fiery will
Till a burnt our cinder falls
Watch the cinder glow a while
Till it loses all desire
And lies there just a charcoaled lump
A cast out from the fire.

Hear the flames as they sizzle and crack
Between the glowing coal
Hear them as they throw their sparks
Up the darkened chimney hole
Hear the fire shout its power
Till it starts to lose its cry
As the flames begin to dwindle
For the fire too must die.

Maureen Tarrant

Feelings

Oh dear what will we do, we've been told the illness is terminal
Our thoughts are so fumbled with fears anew, there's not much hope,
Just each other to hang on to.

He tries to fight with all he might he's being so brave
Telling of all his wishes when the time comes
The little ones told Granddad's going to heaven
He's so sad at not seeing them grow.

At home now his wishes are met, to have love all around
When he's finally put in the ground.

My darling gone now, what will I do he was my life for so long
I feel broken in two, I cry and I cry but feel no better,
Every day more anguish a birthday a letter
So many memories over the years, but all I have now is tears,
I can't be consoled they say this is normal "They say time heals"
How much time nobody knows?
When death comes to me, I will feel not afraid,
My loved one and me will be together eternally.

Marie E. Rumsey

Knighton-On-Teme

In Tenbury Wells in Worcestershire
there is a parish my brother and I hold dear.
Knighton-on-Teme,
a part of the country that is a dream.
When we were young we roamed the shady
wood with a sea of bluebells nodding in the glen
OH! Happy days I wish we could live again.
We were both christened in beautiful
St Michaels church,
In the vestry a jackdaw used to perch.
What he was doing in there we never found out,
The chair was empty, the cardinal was not about.
But that jackdaw made us laugh,
Hopping all over the cassocks.
We never felt down or blue,
Nan lived in tiny "Glen cottage," we did too.
Oh! Happy days I wish we could live again
Now forever dear locked in my heart they will remain.

Gwenneth Donnelly

The Blinkered Winker

Does a one eyed man blink
or does he wink
I suppose he must do both
Would you recognize a one eyed winker
and would you really care
The pure frustration of the one eyed man
as blinking is taken for flirtatious winking
The dismal disillusion as winks are rejected
and he doesn't get from the girls what he blinking well
expected

John S. Chapman

Memories My Brother

When you were born
I was there...
You eyes so brown
You hair so fair

You went to school
I was there
You were 5 years old
Without a care

You soon left school
I was there
Finding a job
A big nightmare

So you joined the army
I wasn't there
You went abroad
Without a care

Then troublesome times, family and wife
You became mixed up said with life

We drifted apart, it's hard to bear
You left this world and I wasn't there...

June Brown

Gentle Giant

Each day at dawn you would be ready to start work on the land,
You have your harness fitted and are led to the field by hand,
Then you are the hitched up to the plough and off you go,
The pace is nice and steady, not too fast, not too slow,
After turning the soil you hear the seagulls and crows cry in delight,
As you have brought the things which they eat to the surface
    and in sight.

After a while you have a rest and something to eat,
As you find it tiring being most of the time on your feet,
Then you plough the rest of the field in the heat haze,
Then you are taken back to the farm and left to graze,
Then at the end of the day you are taken back to the stable,
Tomorrow you will be out again working the way you do, as
    you are able.

People who see you are in awe of your size and power,
Perhaps there will come a time when again above us you will tower,
The oil will not last forever, as we all know,
You just stay around, please don't ever go.

Raymond Hutchinson

A Fool's Thorn

And now that he lusts for her touch,
Her thought she burns in his soul...
He seeks only her pleasure,
And no crime is ever too foul...
And yet so many days they have passed,
Since the last time he looked in her eyes...
And such feelings he felt in his glance
How his emotions could ever have disguised -
    The way he felt about her.
And still hand in hand with ignorance,
He's with neglect in his heart...
To deprive himself of such love that he felt,
Such a fool he was from the start.

And now that so many years have passed,
He stood still feeling the thorn in his side...
For the torment of his wrong doing and the bitterness inside,
    He can blame no other.
So never can his feelings end with thought of sweet emotion.
For that never-ending pain, His constant devotion...
    'Love is in the whispering winds'.

James W. McMenemy

Untitled

Creeping shadows along the wall
Ghostly whispers down the hall
A creaking stair when no one's there
A sudden chill in the midnight air.

Grey wraiths drifting over the moor
Icy mists veiling a cold grey moon
A blasted oak where once a gibbet stood
A creaking shadow, flurry of wings
A hollow laugh from who knows where.

Shadows leaping on a nursery wall
Ghouls and goblins at the witches' ball
Creaking footsteps cross the floor
What's that tapping at the door?
The moon shines bright on the window pane
Oh how I wish it was morning again.

D. Nealis

The Maze

Dense bushes planted out and set in fine array,
placed so as to be a maze to help you at your play.

So, gaily as you enter, you hope that you will find the
way into the centre, those outside to leave behind.

Come each day, and hide away amongst those bushes
in the maze, a maze so like your mind, where in
getting to its centre are encountered twists and turns
just like the inside of your brain.

Daily come inside the maze of all those thoughts
that dwell inside your head.

And, having been there at the centre, find your
way outside the maze; remembering where you've
been, all twists and turns unwinded, and if
you can do all this, then live each day, your life
away, uncluttered and unhindered.

Philip Trevor Williams

Autumn Awareness (All On A Tankersley Lane)

I stroll along the lane with scarce a thought inside my head;
My feet scuff fallen leaves; they're brown and shrivelled, very dead.
I gaze with vacant stare upon a world all misty grey,
Then realize that Summer's gone, and Autumn's come to stay.

I peer then, into hedgerows, through the rosie hips and haws;
A squirrel in a tree is piling nuts for winter stores.
A spider spins a cobweb like a finely silk cartwheel,
Defenceless flies he hopes to snare to make his midday meal.

That weedy, purple willow-herb coughs seeds all o'er the place.
They make me feel like Neptune when they settle on my face.
An ash tree, careless, drops her keys upon the fading grass.
I pick them up; I shake them, when along the path I pass.

Around the floor are scattered shiny conkers, russet round.
They burst their green pods open when they clatter to the ground.
Amongst them hops a robin, puffing out his breast of red;
He wings towards a nearby wall - and cocks a cheeky head.

A farmer on a tractor is combining golden corn.
He reaps a rich ripe harvest on this bleak October morn.
As I watch him I reflect upon just what life might have been,
Had Autumn never come and this had stayed the Summer scene.

Dorothy Frederick Hitchman

Sunset

God for our pleasure, has painted the skies
  With colours so lovely to still the eyes
He used the wind to weave the red.
With pink, yellow, and orange fed.
His canvas is vast of grey and blue,
To show the colours of lovely hue
This wonderful artist, then blows them away,
And thrills us again the next windy day.

Kathleen Carle

The Human Voice

The power of the human voice, as
"Subject Matter" it gave me great choice.
'Twas a "Human Voice" which commanded
The "Roman Legions" when conquered
They this our land and a "Human Voice"
Ordered "The Crucifixion" of Jesus in a
  manner quite offhand!!
A human voice decided on the fate of
victims in the hell of any "Death Camp"
But this is only one side of the power of the "Human Voice"
For "The Lady With The Lamp's" gentle murmur was
many a soldier's dying choice.
A "Human Voice" raised in song has lifted many a weary load,
and even cheered the poor work-worn slaves
as they struggled with bales of cotton on a never-ending road!
The "Human Voice" is God's greatest gift to the human race"
If only use it to help the world to be a better place
So let "The World Leaders" use the power of "Speech"
To bring peace, freedom from hunger
and disease within every nation's reach.

Flora Divers

Nature's Picture Book

To sit in peaceful solitude, beneath a roof of blue
Never-ending marvels, of every shape and hue
The countryside's a photograph, from Mother Nature's Album
She sits relaxed and turns each page at random
Revealing all her wonders, if you take the time to look
You'll see that everything has beauty, in her never ending book.

Each blade of grass, a creative work of art
Birds outclassing melodies of the great Mozart
So many colours, decorating God's Earth
Seemingly to celebrate each new creature's birth
Wild flowers with their delicate perfume
A tapestry of beauty, woven on Nature's secret loom.

Gentle fragile Butterflies to enchant the very soul
The smallest of God's creatures seem to play a role
For a first night performance in a famous play
Laid out before you, you don't even have to play
Nothing's too important, to prevent you looking in
Passing by without a glance, would be a mortal sin.

Patricia Kelly

Upon A Summer's Day

A gold and crimson horizon forming
  another fleeting day's morn is dawning.

White are the peaks of mountains upwardly streaking
  almost to a point the blue ceiling breaking.

Fast do they flow rivers icy, fresh and cold
  onwards to deep seas that roll and fold.

A blue and white horizon changing
  as midday begins its fading.
The grass fresh but dry within a short day
  and men have toiled to gather bales of sweet hay.

The herds and the flocks undisturbed they graze
  not they concerned for a spacious cool shade.

A deep blue and gold horizon forming
  as the night shades the evening.

A trees soiled roots damp and unclean
  as yet they remain vast but unseen.

And with time the suns last gleaming giving
  thought to the night that I was dreaming.

Steven Brian Jones

Loved From Afar

You did not know, how could you tell, you would not see that far,
That a man sat at a table, or watching from a bar;

Could pick you out with one quick look and see his dreams unfold,
But with all his cowardly dignity he must put these on hold;

For he knows that your lovely face and body made to love,
Must fly free with serenity as graceful as the dove;

So he must stand with doleful look and ever painful thirst,
For something that can never be and a heart about to burst;

If it were ever possible to keep your heart ajar,
Please spare a thought for the wretched man who loves you
from afar.

H. J. Baker

Untitled

We trim the tree and hang the tinsel
Blow up balloons and bake the cakes
Wind is blowing snow is falling
Squeals of joy the children make
Hustle, bustle, preparations
Wrapping presents for relations
Hang the stockings, children to bed
Silently waiting for someone in red
Dreaming of presents they hope he will leave
On this another Christmas Eve.

Lynn Johnson

Untitled

One day I saw a bird in flight
It looked so peaceful,
Such a lovely sight.
I spread my arms and ran so fast,
That I feel myself take off at last.
I swooped and dived and drifted there,
The wind made my eyes run and it blew
in my hair.
I felt so big looking down,
At children from Stanley in the playground.
I saw the quad and the trail and the slide,
And the bridge and the tunnel where
people hide.
Then as I swooped down at such a high
speed,
I saw a lady with a dog on a lead.
I could not stop, the ground got so near,
When I felt a great bang on my head
And realized I had fallen - out of my bed!

Frederick A. Winton

Sacred

You look at me, enchanted moon,
as if I may somehow understand
what wish I make in your sight.
I know it cannot be far, or too soon,
your shining is clear, casting a glow,
warming the heart that struggles inside.
Disturbing thoughts thus are strewn,
dismembered, dispatched away, deep away,
no longer have they the power to fight, to fright.
Your presence is welcomed like comfort,
this nothing feels humble, lost in your wakening,
yet I have expected and now you do show.
You yawn with wide gape, arise to the darkness,
you are brightness faced by blackness, that softens,
a cast that soothes, healing the wounds;
I dread the dawn when they may bleed again.
What will you send to inhabit the space?
Lost childhood innocence, love in return?
Perhaps nothing, therefore thus I shall stay,
until purpose beyond meaning finds me someday.

Saskia Van Barneveld

Death Of A Moth

Incapable of flying
With wings clamped,
thin legs like unstable spokes
reeling within the wheel of lamp-light
on to-night's table,
this moth is dying.

Flat on its back now
the pattern of the cloth
etched in its transparent, treasonous wings;
a thing among things more brutally dead,
for two legs, stretched
in perpendicular pose,
like feelers will still reach out
for inscrutable reasons.

Mien V. D. Veere

Our School Trip

Tension rose, excitement grew
No one spoke as it came into view
Every child was filled with elation
As the train pulled into the station
We'd waited for weeks for our school trip
Not put a foot wrong, not made a slip
Now the day's dawned, and we are off
All scrubbed and clean, dressed like a toff
All round the city for a good look
Down by the river a picnic we took
Oh what a time was had by us all
Too soon it was over, time for roll call
Tired and weary back home to our beds
The thrill of the day still in our heads

S. E. McMillan

In Love

You're suddenly miles away, on an island of your own
at first you wonder what's happening a world you've never known.
Sad and happy and you don't know why
one minute smiling the next you cry
no concentration can be found
your feet don't seem to touch the ground.
What's this change I have in me,
does anyone else look and see.
Thinking - what is on my mind
what door has opened what will I find.
Where is he/she now what are they doing
remembering a wonderful day we had then reviewing
the situation, the eyes, the smile, I can't sleep
oh know I'm in love, I want to weep.

Pat Sadler

Thoughts In A Chinese Restaurant

Over prawns,
I saw the bracelet crease of skin
Where your palm and wrist unite;
I watched in awe as comely fingers
Snapped spare ribs with eager might.

I gazed, transfixed,
As you stabbed defenceless shredded beef:
Your scant sleeve rose with every reach,
Revealing to my longing gaze,
A forearm textured like a peach.

Sipping tea,
I knew at once that 'neath that sleeve
There lay, concealed, an elbow fair:
Within which crook a close embrace
Might thrill the heart, or crush it there.

And now I dream,
That I might fold away that silk;
And wonder at your arm - and, bolder
In farther hope, might gently stoop,
And softly touch and kiss your shoulder.

Alan Lindsay

The Rose

The rose on the hill stands tall and proud
In its struggling quest to survive
And through many years witness battle and tears
It's a wonder that it is still alive
This dying earth we have helped to destroy
With jealousy, power and greed
War torn country's rubble all around
And more hungry mouths to feed
When does it stop, will we ever have peace?
Mad governments deciding our fate
The rich get richer, poor get poorer
Our hearts keep filling with hate
One day in the future in the final war
When man no longer exists
And the horrors of war fall into the past
With nobody shaking their fists
One little object not affected at all
Untouched by the mushroom clouds
Is the rose on the hill there since time began
And it's still standing tall and proud.

Vanessa Ealand

The Yearning Years

She awoke one sunny morning and thought of him once more,
And the longing started over - the pacing of the floor,
And the memory of how he'd said he oft walked on the shore,
To clear away his sadness and feel complete once more.
Before her thoughts had clarity
She was driving to the coast,
Just to catch a glimpse of him her one thought uppermost,
And so, when 80 miles had passed she walked along the sand,
And prayed that he'd be waiting and he would hold her hand,
But a thousand strangers faces met her searching stare,
Her mumbled aching whisperings
Lost on the salty air,
So after many sandy hours,
With long low sobs she turned,
And realized that now at last,
A lesson she had learned.
A teenage love, so intense then,
With all its fire and pain,
Was for that time, and certainly,
Can never come again.

Subi

Victims

Suppressed is the smile on the sombre face
Of the child, who casts its eyes out
From a cold, lamp lit dormitory window
Dry, are the tears of innocence,
From the young mother, heartbroken
By the say so, of a so called social work carer.
Just one more statistic.
In a world with no conscience.
Where we live each day,
In the hands of officialdom.
Sleep easy... and stone faced.

Kenneth A. Nisbet

A New Arrival

September fourteenth. A red letter day
Andrew James, our new baby, has come here to stay
Mum and dad are so proud of their wee baby boy
Brother Stephen is glad, and jumping with joy
Both the grandmothers with faces abeam
Gaze down on the babe, in their own special dream
Remembering days, that don't seem far away
When they looked at their own, on their special day
God bless this new baby, so helpless and small
May your future be happy and life long and full
May blessings aplenty. Be yours all the way
Is the wish of us all on this wonderful day

D. Barley

Fury

She knew the Daemon that lurked within.
She saw through such feeble skin,
And brought to bare the darkest night;
With no sanctuary to be found in dreams,
Where memories as serpents bite.

It's the killing time - the Daemon said,
It's time to die.
But who sheds tears and who will cry?
Perhaps my Guardian Angel,
For as Satan fell ruined, so too have I.

To the stars I see Hell,
And her eyes:
My Hades.
From my last glimpse - my fall from grace,
God hath suffered me naught his searing gaze.

She unleashed the Daemon;
The serpents;
Her eyes.
It's the killing time - the Daemon said,
It's time at last to die.

Christopher Ellis

The Many Shades Of Yellow

In July, the Esala blossoms droop in bridal veil clusters
    from the boughs of the trees,
Their citron cups so fragile, yet protective
    of the dormant life within.

Underfoot, the gleam of chrome, of orpiments and lemon,
Taway, creamy, dushed with dew, humble flora
    raise their heads, radiant with bloom.

A flash of purest sunshine ray, an oriole wings past,
Dropping notes of liquid gold to match his sick array.

The forest roads to search the shrines are rimed with
    ochre dust, and set with bricks of umber,
    shards of tan, gamboge, brouge and rust.

Glints of gold on arm and ear of pilgrims in transition.
Not striving to outshine the sun, but seeking revelation.

Dusk - and clay wick lamps are lit in temples by the faithful.
Their watchful faces lit by flames
    fed with aureate oil.

The clergy in their soffroa sobes, with modest downcast glance.
In guest of truth within this sphere.
Heroic in serenity, in spiritual advance.

Faith J. Simpson-Ratnayake

The Rain

My life is black and empty,
I am alone,
I am no one and no one cares about me,
As I stand in my empty prison looking out at the night,
I am quite alone,
All is silent,
The dark clouds scurrying across the sky
Reflect my loneliness and desolation,
The church clock strikes three,
As the metallic sounds drift across the valley,
There is a roll of thunder,
As I watch, a swallow swoops from its nest,
I am not alone,
As the first drops of rain fall, I begin to smile,
I run out into the rain and feel the cooling drops on my face,
I remember as a child skipping among the bluebells
The raindrops falling on my face like a sparkling fountain,
In that instant my life changed
I am not alone,
I am part of this wondrous universe.

Jill Garrett

66

Jesus

An elephant are you to me, you walk with slow purpose.
A gentle giant of love.
Going about your business with the minimum of fuss.
You only look down on your children to make them look above.

Like a tiny ant, so small and yet so strong.
You carry enormous weight on your back.
All for the love of your family, the distance you travel is so long.
And even when you tire, you never once look back.

A chameleon are you, blending in to the environment.
Hidden to some you cannot be seen, like a super sleuth.
It matters not your colour, only your judgement.
Like your tongue it never fails because you speak the truth.

Like an unconquered mountain you stand so tall.
Not with pride but with a love so high.
There's an air about you, a wind that seems to call.
It's cold at the top, but the ice melts with the warmth from
your eye

You are a lighthouse calling to those who are lost.
In the darkness of a raging storm.
To the fishermen who follow your light there is no cost.
Only the gain of salvation because to you giving is the norm.

Lee Devlin

"Living In Dreams"

It's not easy to get over first love
Never quite time to make a goodbye
Like watching a train leave a station
If your heart is still living a lie.

Making the next move is harder
Life's struggle is much more unkind
Trying for new love means trouble
If you feel like you're losing your mind

Being adrift in a spaceship of aliens
is a preferable action by far
Than trying to trace lost emotions
When you don't really know who you are.

Life looks like a costly idea
And maybe not all that it seems
But existing is just bitter tears
When first love is holding your dreams

We never get over first love
Getting tough with our feelings is wise
For how can we meet a next love
With sweet fondest memory clouding our eyes?

Ann Horsfield

"Meet The Family"

There's Ma and Pa and uncle Ned,
Who always wears his boots in bed,
And Grannie's running bootleg liquor,
And making up to a city slicker.

My Grandpa on my Pappy's side,
Was hung by the neck until he died,
A widow woman he wanted to wed,
So he got her husband - and shot him dead.

Now cousin Joe from Tyler County,
Was gonna earn a living collecting bounty,
This idea of his'n tho' kinda turned sour,
'Cos you're paid by results and not by the hour.

My Pa's younger brother was a 'Jackleg Preacher',
Started paying court to a Sunday School teacher,
He ate some food cooked by her alone,
If you go by the church - you can see his stone.

I hope now you've heard what I've got to tell,
You'll come on a visit with us a spell,
We'll give you 'chitlins' 'midlins' 'souse' and 'pone',
One way or another - you'll never go home.

Ralph Leslie Harris

"A Countryside Sight"

I love the countryside beautiful and bright
When morning dawns a radiant sight
I see a rabbit scurrying around
Squirrels in their treetops are found.
Flowers lift their weary heads
Splashed with colours blues golds and reds,
Like the patterns of an artists brush
Then silently you'll whisper, oh hush!
I hear the trickle of a way by stream
And little fish in the water gleam.
Further down the meadow the lambs bleat,
Corn and wheat stand in the meadows tall and neat.
At night flowers with drowsy heads
Once more asleep in their soily beds,
Comes night time when the sky is red,
And every one's asleep in their bed.
The stars twinkle in the heavens on high
Till morning comes again on nigh,
Of all the countryside I've been
These are the many wonders I've seen.

S. Bellas

Too Much To Ask?

Is it too much to ask to blow the clouds away,
And let the thickest ice melt in the newborn sun?
To lift the night's darkness with fresh light of the day?
To let all four seasons unite and merge in one?

Oh, yes, eternal spring could have been ours to share,
But you've forsaken it and lost our paradise,
The seeds that had sprouted in our soul's sunlit glare
Turned to dead autumn leaves under the gloomy skies.

The pleasure of giving is more than the taking,
And yet, I only had this one gift to impart:
Not some precious jewels of an artist's making,
But love and tenderness of just one human heart.

If only once again our estranged eyes could meet,
And in one single glance our faces drop their mask,
Let our fading hearts give that one more louder beat...
Or is it, is it really so very much to ask?

John Sadler

My Gemini Cat

Stealthily prowling beneath midnight skies,
With the fire of the jungle aglow in his eyes,
Perfectly poised for a fast, fateful spring -
Can this be the same playful, kittenish thing
That - purring contentedly - on my lap lies?

Audrey Ellis Matthews

Parent-hood Despair!

You try and help, what for, to get slapped in the face,
for interfering, or fussing,
you're pushing the child too much! She won't get on.
Ok! Shut up, mind your own business, harder said
than done.
Sadness creeps in, eyes start to smart

'Why shouldn't I help!' you're just an interfering old
parent, who doesn't know left from right.
Grandparents, Oh leave the child alone! she's a good
child trying hard, but who does all the hard work.
The nosy old interfering parent.

OK! I will sit back, let them get on with it then,
see where they get, but deep down inside the
hurt is still there, nobody understands,
just back biting and arguing, I love my child very much.

Perhaps it doesn't show, instead anger, worry,
and despair. I didn't think parent-hood
would be all roses, like a marriage, but it's
damned hard work.

J. M. Cripps

Knowledge

School was never meant for me,
A lone wolf not wanting the company.
Longing for darkness or a light of my own
Not the brightness Knowledge has shown
To men who seek but never find
The knowledge needed to save mankind.
Some wish to own it or image it yet stay a man.
They never will, they never can,
For Knowledge like time races faster
Never diminishing, growing vaster.
School is the evil which leads you to the race
Forcing you to follow to join the chase.
But unlike life it has no end
The small earthly time we spend
Uncovering more of its bright light
Could never manage to unveil its sight
For it should blind us to a darkened pen
And we would start the race again.

Lorraine S. Crighton

The Bonfire

The smoking cloud hung suspended on the early morning air
Writhing, twirling and twisting.
Portraying ghostly figures consumed by some deep despair.
Writhing, twirling and twisting.

The spectres floated before me, some gruesome, some wild
 and some fair.
Approaching, nearing then withdrawing.
Wreathed in translucent garments with trailing gossamer hair.
Approaching, nearing then withdrawing.

The wind was behind them as they sped upon their misty way
Without seeing or hearing or speaking.
They hastened ever upwards, upon the earth they dared not stay
Without seeing or hearing or speaking.

Some were voluptuous maidens, some old men with long grey hair
Ever stirring, never pausing.
The pageant of phantoms kept moving into the cool morning air
Ever stirring, never pausing.

The bonfire had burned itself out, the phantoms had made
 their last dash.
No flaming, no burning or smoking
And all that remained of their passing was a mound of
 smouldering ash.
No flaming, no burning or smoking.

D. M. Fisher

Granny Smith - Sweet Apple Of My Eye

I've fallen in love with a granny; of whom I'm very proud.
She's a little hard of hearing; so I have to shout out loud.
She talks to herself, always laughing; and gives me tea and cakes
And the lid of the teapot rattles; when Granny gets the shakes.

I pretend I've not seen and call her "Me Queen" and tell her
 of my love,
So she smoothest down her apron blushing, and says "Good
 Heavens above"
Sometimes I clean her window; making faces through the panes
Chop wood and light the fire and fetch coal when it rains.
I often give her a cuddle and hold her in my arms
And tell her she's a wonderful woman; and how I'm a slave
 to her charms.

She has on old bentwood armchair where she sits to pray her beads
Praying with great devotion: Asking God for other's needs.
Sometimes she looks in the mirror and sees her careworn face
But I only see her soul's image - full of piety, love and grace.
I'll always love my Granny: who paved the way for me
And led me on to heaven with cakes and cups of tea
One day she told me frankly, that she's in love with me!

D. J. Walter

The Tramp

There you sit in the bus shelter with tangled hair
All pride gone
With unseeing eyes you stare
A bottle of whisky your only comfort
It dulls the pain of memories past
As you slip into oblivion at last
What happened; I wonder
Did you lose all those you held dear?!
No one left to love and care
Perhaps your family were killed in the war
Or they did not want you anymore
As you sit there, your clothes dirty and torn
They look at you with eyes of scorn
And cross the road to pass you by
What do they care if you cry
Your sorrow they cannot share
They do not understand your life was too much to bear

A. D. Macey

A Bosnian Tale

The last night in Mostar,
You could smell the fear.
The skyline cracked then faded,
An all to familiar atmosphere
Despair excels through the day,
Then darkness brings its ghost
The coldness feels like an unwelcomed shock,
These things remembered most.

Our media turned its interest into a show,
Bosnian nightmares, a dollar a go.
United nations training ground.
No love nor mercy to be found.
If everyone I know can forget so quick,
Then why does it still make me feel so sick.
Explain yourselves.
Don't shelve your love,
For even one death,
Is already enough.

E. J. A. MacKinnon

Unrequited

He drew a circle that shut me out, but love and I had wit to win.
I drew a circle and then I took him in.

So Scientist claim they know only what love does, that love
properly applied could virtually empty our asylums, our
prisons, our hospitals.
To love my life through labour is to be intimate with life's
inmost secret. I grew up the day I had my first real laugh at
myself, although I wanted a soul so full of joy that life's
withering storms would not destroy.

Come what may hold my love. Though men should rend my heart.
I will not let him embitter or harden it. That I may win by
tenderness and conquer by forgiveness.
And now I see things not as they are, But As I Am.

Orla White

The Rose Window

The Lord really spoke through that beautiful window,
As the shafts of light shone through the panes,
As the choir boys sang in the stalls below
A number of their numerous refrains.

The stillness of God and peace that He brings,
Touched a small part of my innermost being,
That our heavenly Father's the King of all Kings,
I could feel my heart positively agreeing.

The magnificent colours and the amazing light,
The sense of security the Lord can bring,
Reminded me of the Lord's power and might
As we dwell in the shadow of His wings.

Clare Whitfield

Decisions

Mark Anthony in Ceasar's praise
Came forth with that resounding phrase
"The evil that men do", he said
"Lives after them" now they are dead

How much more evil can we stand
What does this world of ours demand
That men should once again be free
To carry out their destiny

When men of conscience take the strain
To rid the world of all its pain
And new parameters are set
We might just win and save it yet

Let's hope our children and theirs too
Can face the world with hope anew
Pursuing fruitful lives at last
With ne'er a thought of pollution passed.

"Propwash".
Brian Berry

"Step Toe"

You've heard "my old man's a dustman"
Well my cousins one better you see
He'd always collected scrap for fun
Then a dealer he decided to be

He used to be called a scrap merchant
When he first started out in the trade
Although he's still called step toe
He seems to have gone up a grade

His granny use to say "Hey lad"
It's time you gave up all that
And settled down to a proper job
Stop messing with all that scrap

But if she were here now to see him
She would be proud and give thanks
He now lives in a mansion
And has money in the bank

So take notice of this true story
Where there's muck there's money it seems
And if you're not afraid to work hard
There can be money in dreams.
S. Gartside

Silent Prayer

I flew above as you stole my eggs,
And stripped me of my kind.
I flew above with pumping panic,
As confusion filled my mind.

I landed on a stony shore,
My wings were heavy and shaken,
Darkness came and morning lifted,
My chicks would never waken.

It's hard to fly, when you're broken-hearted
And eyes are wet and swollen.
To share my peace, with earth and man
When all your love's been stolen.

How full, this emptiness to bear,
Of silence in the tree.
The darkened flowers have hung their heads,
To show their love for me.

It's not my nature, to threaten man.
To me, he bears his grudge,
For man one day will meet his match,
When God becomes his judge.
Duncan M. MacNicol

Spring

I love a spring. Morning back home in dear
England, when the sun. Climbs up behind the
oak trees, it's watery. Rays catch the glint
of pond waters, and lightens the lilies
in to a display.
    When the bluebells and primroses
all say "Good Morning" to the thrush and the
swallows as they wing their way by.
    Where the new on the grass reminds
me of diamonds. And the proud old elm trees
reach up to the sky.
    No where else is there such a spring
morning, with white fluffy clouds scurrying by.
    No how I wish once again I could see
that spring morning, before time. Like the
clouds go hurrying by.
    Joan Morris

The Raid

Now the last flight is over
And the last of all who will return have
    struggled back
To tell their tales of fighter and of flak.
The fierce flowering fire, and wrenching
    wreaking blast.
The tension of the long run up to bomb
The sudden short attack, the gasp of pain
The coughing engine, and the lurching plane
The sickening silence on the intercom.

But there are moments which remain concealed.
Unlit by any bright heroic glow
Deep in the heart, convention sealed
Such moments must the raiding airman know
Who knows the undeniable, unrevealed
Terror and sorrow in the flames below.
    Thomas J. Atherton

Snowsong

Show me shards of shadow
That climb the wandering lonely cloud of
Swiftly silent silver
Drifting long the velvet-throated night.
Shallow shining ships
That cruise the streamlined windway down of
Softly sighing snowflakes
Falling from the breathy dark-eyed sky.
The sculptured ice embrace
Of star-spun silent space.
    Rosy Adams

On The Outside

People come in different sizes,
Just like clothes and shoes,
Some are big, young and small,
Others are fat, and slim or tall.
People come in different shapes,
Just like books and stamps,
Some are short, round and old,
Others are hairy, chubby or bald.
People come in different grades,
Just like tests and results,
Some are common, posh or famous,
Others are rich, poor or homeless.
People come in different colours,
Just like meat and ink,
Some are black, brown or white,
Others are dark, a mix or light.
On the outside people are different,
Just like clocks and cakes,
Some get teased so they hide,
But before you tease them,
Check out what they're really like inside.
    Katherine Davis

An Outing

In the shade and the cool of an old Beech tree
Where the sun pokes its light through the branches at me
I sit and I watch as the world passes by
Like the fluffy white clouds in the clear blue sky

The grass in the meadow sways in the warm breeze
As Daisies and Clover play host to the bees
A Dragon Fly dips over waters so still
But no water wheel turns in the broken down mill

The silence is broken by songs of a Thrush
As a field mouse goes passed, but he's in no rush
There's no need for haste on this beautiful day
So he stops, looks and listens then goes on his way

The friendly faced Scarecrow in tattered old clothes
With his big Turnip head and his red Carrot nose
Guards over his field, which he never leaves
Against Pigeons and Rooks and such other thieves

Now my day in the country is very near over
As I make my way back through the sweet scented Clover
To the city I'll go if I catch the last train
But I won't leave it so long 'till I come back again

Edwin Grace

Many Pathways To God

'In God we trust', a God of loving care,
Who with so many other faiths we share,
No sect or group should claim exclusive right
Are we not equal in His holy sight?

In worshipping the great Creator God
Varied are the ways used, and pathways trod,
Many are the names by which God is known
As the world's millions claim Him as their own!

With such passions rife between the nations
And discord spoiling the whole creation,
More tolerance to others should be our aim
If commitment to God is what we claim.

If God is love as Christians claim and say
We should accept that there are other ways
In which to worship God, and so find peace
Within ourselves, and then let quarrels cease.

How can we dare to say God will condemn
All of the other faiths that did not stem
From Bible stories that we know and love,
Judgement of that must rest with God above.

George V. Goodchild

Untitled

Hello missus; how are you today?
Fine thank you, how goes it your way?
Not so good you know; no work.
Happens like this not every day.
Yesterday it was all planed.
Work today he had said.
Comes rain, there is a delay.
End the day; with no pay.
Have you a friend or two.
Who needs a handy-man.
Cleaning, Gardening, repairing.
Any thing will do
I will asked and let you know
No promises you know
In slow-motion he mounts his bike
rattles down the lane
amongst the pouring rain
Though my thoughts I wondered
Time spent resting, debating not wondering, pondering
In slowing down he might slowly let go.

Beverley Hutchinson

The Seas Of Life

Seas can be gentle, they can be strong, form massive waves or just amble along. Enfolded within are wonders galore some we can see but always there's more. Fish of all colour, each shape, every size, all so unusual cannot believe eyes. Strange little creatures hide in each cleft, some we may know of but not all the rest. Lying on sea bed are parts of a boat, once a fine galleon when it was afloat. Chest holding treasure trapped under spar, contents once seen but now never are. In many places lie folk who have drowned, entombed below, they may never be found. Bright patterned shells shine in the sun, lobsters and crabs hide behind some. Oysters shell open showing milky white pearl. Which one day adorn neck of young girl. Fishes swim round in search of prey, in undersea world throughout night and day. Seaweed grows thicker than plants on the land, as if marine forests to go there was planned. Buffeting water crash over rock, wind picks it up, then lets it drop. How puny we humans beside all of these, how strong the God who created the seas. Marvels of nature on both land and sea, wonders of God in his great majesty. We all know well, what is right or wrong, as we know seas both gentle and strong. So our ship can flounder break on the sea floor, unless we steer true to the heavenly shore.

Barbara Goode

A Friend In Need

Growing up together in the early years
sharing the laughter, sharing the tears
I loved thinking of what we did
When you and I, were just a kid
Many emotions we often shared
It was nice to have a friend who cared
Our days together meant so much
It's sad we no longer keep in touch
Now different people with different lives
Certain things you sacrificed
You're so different now it's such a shame
Stress and worry we could blame
I wasn't needed in your life anymore
There's so much you were looking for
You threw my help and friendship away
In search of happiness, that might come your way
I guess I filled in, the gap in between
While you were searching for your dream
The love and warmth I felt for you
Has gone with the friendship, I once knew.

Dawn Connaire Warner

Thoughts

Down by the river wandered I
Gaily the rippling water flowed by
A warm summer sun adorned the sky
How lucky I am, thought I, thought I

Tall trees swayed gently, a breeze caught my hair
Wild flowers in abundance seemed everywhere
I breathed in their fragrance, looked up to the sky
How lucky I am, thought I, thought I

Birds they sang sweetly, their song filled the air
Bright coloured butterflies fluttered here and there
Bees softly humming a low lullaby
How lucky I am, thought I, thought I

I gazed all around me to take in the sight
When a flock of wild geese passed, their wings in full flight
How long I had been there one just cannot say
But peace and tranquillity were mine that day

As I turned to leave and make my goodbye
How lucky I am, thought I, thought I
So oft I think of that special day
When the cares of the world just flitted away

J. Mortimer

Echoes Of Love

Above the fields the smoke of autumn rise
In windless columns to the darkening sky.
With deep serenity I hold in view
The misty purple of the watching hills,
Companions of my solitary years.
How far away the infant green of spring,
When leaf by leaf new life is being born!
It calls to memory the distant days
Of early manhood, and a treasured time
Of friends and girls and fragrant new desires,
And in especial, one immortal hour.
There was a girl whose name is past recall,
Whose very face is shadowed in my mind,
Whose gentle voice was beautiful as flutes.
And yet with diamond sharpness I am sure
That once upon a very special time
We stood apart in shy bewilderment,
Searching to find a heart, to find a life,
Hand touching hand in half-uncertain love,
Silent against a frosty night of stars.

Robin MacLean

The Death Of A Dear One

Burning its sulphur glow the candle stood,
Surrounded in its pocket by witchcraft ages;
Devils dancing, jeering, laughing -
No pity, no sorrow.
I watched it from the dark corner and counted
The times it bowed to me -
So few in what seemed eternity,
And my broken soul felt every slow moving second as it passed.

The light flicked momentarily: Distracted me,
And for a moment we were back in time.
The trees were singing and the birds stood still,
The sky was green with envy.
Then the devastation fell like hell.
The emptiness and futile gap
Split like a gulf before my dulled senses
And my brow became yet a little more intricate.
I had no breath in my body to speak.
I had no will in my mind to speak.
But scream. No scream.
No breath. No strength.

Tina M. Bell

Adrift By The Fireside

To the glowing embers, quite close
I sit dreaming, images forming
In black and ruddy glow.
Who can know
The fleeting fancies which cross my mind
And free me of that tedious burden time?
Who feels that warm contentment
In which I bathe in contemplative confinement?
Now I hear a lark whose peaceful songs,
Contrast from wicked worldly wrongs.
Now a sliding ship, gliding over a slippery sea
Through an ocean of delightful solitude
Slips, free, free, free.
And now a fall, a resounding crash,
And on the hearth I see an isolated force,
Advancing, leaving a trail of burning brown,
And now the red is black, and the black is grey
And all I see is fire, coal and ash.
Torn from exotic enchantment of fantasy's varied way,
I'm back to cruel reality, to stay.

Roderick Croskin

Gone

The time is gone, flown past our faces,
Yet what is done to fill empty spaces?
Tried to make some right, correct the wrong.
But has it worked? we've tried so long
To forget the past, and live for today,
Make a life for ourselves, how we've had to pay.

As the room silenced and people stood
to say goodbye, for now and for ever.
Tears rolled down cheeks, watched him go
To say, if forgotten, not now, never.

A hard decision, for man to make,
But as was said, for all our sakes.
He loved to live, now life is over,
Go back to our own, and to discover.

Life is full of meaning
Live for the moment of the day,
Not in the past or future.
For in a second it could be taken away.

Anneke de Jong

Just Believe

When things aren't going quite to plan,
And everything's gone wrong,
when you just don't have the strength to stand,
And the day goes on and on.

Or when you feel tired and worn,
And you think no one's on your side,
When maybe your friendship has been torn,
And you've no one in whom to confide.

Then this is the time to remember,
That you can't get up and leave,
You have to stay and see it through,
You have to try and believe.

Believe in what you think is right,
Believe in who you are,
As long as you don't give up your fight,
Then you'll shine like the brightest star.

So when things aren't going quite to plan,
And everything's gone wrong,
If you believe in yourself as much as you can,
Then you'll have the strength to go on.

Kerry Taylor

Oh Mountain

Who put you there Oh mountain?
    Who made you stand so tall?
I gaze at you in wonder,
    For you do me enthral.
I always loved you as a child,
    And still do, even when you're wild,
Or calm, or mantled in a shawl of white;
    You bring to me so much delight.
So many gave away their lives
    To reach your peak,
Did not survive, but would they
    Do it all again if given chance,
I'm sure they would;
    For what you give is something
One cannot explain.
    It's more than joy, or love or pain.
It's like you're reaching for the sky,
    Nearer to Him, who is on high.
Maybe that's why I lean to you;
    To guide me to whatever's true.

C. Carr

The Little Man Who Sits All Alone In An Office That Only He Would....

Somewhere here, in this concrete nightmare,
  a little man shuffles and prods his way through
  a life that is not meant for him;
  not made for a nervous timid little man with
  tiny hands and a fractured smile,
  and a terrible emptiness there in his eyes.

But shuffle he does, and gets no reward
  for the pain he endures and the names he is called.

Somewhere else, perhaps, is an empty space
  that would amply be filled by our little man,
  and a world that exists just for people like him;
    a place (finally) where they all would fit in.

Nicholas Gibbs

Jitsu Blues

Oh, them Jitsu Blues,
The sanseis make you sweat and toil,
Then tell you, 'You've failed',
Get beaten and Smacked!,
Oh!, you get kicked 'n' wacked,
And what's it worth?

You put in nine hours of practice a week,
Just to be told you can't obtain the belt you
seek,
So I sing the blues today,
To mourn all the blood that's run away,
I sorrowfully think (and it puts me down),
I won't never ever make it to Brown,
The only colour I see is Blue Baby!
Oh!, those Jitsu Blues invade me!

Giles Brown

Why?

Why did you have to go, my love, why did you have to die
Why did you have to go, my love, and leave me here to cry
Why did you have to go away and leave me here alone
Why did you have to go away leaving me to cry on my own

The kids watch every caller who comes knocking at the door
And I have to sit and tell them why you won't come home any more
Why did it have to happen leaving me by myself
Why did it have to happen - me, once more on the shelf

We married very late in life and the kids came along so quick
And now I have this dreadful strife, I now have wounds to lick
Pick up and go on, they say, and wish for happiness
Once more you will find a way - I hope
Good night, my love
God bless.

Carolin H. Coward

The Eleventh Day

Away up in the Northland, in Scotia's high mountains.
A lone piper he played a lament for the brave.
The heart-breaking music which echoed through valleys.
It echoed through mountains, o'er rivers and streams.

The Flowers of Scotland, the Bluebells and Thistles,
They all bent their heads, and dropped tears like the dew.
The great Golden Eagles, who soar in the heavens,
Flew down to their nests and not kill like they do.

The wildest of creatures who hunt in the forests
Lay down and sobbed on that fateful day.
In the light of the gloaming, the mountains were silent.
The whole world was in mourning, as the sad tune was played.

Millions of people all died for nothing.
Never a foot was gained either way.
Surely a lesson for stupid world leaders.
These are the ones who should have been in the fray.

John Burns Murphy

(Place Of Rest) Cemeteries

I stand here among the dead, reading tombstones above their heads.
Once you were very much alive and well, walked on this Earth
  with all its smells.

Felt the wind within your hair, and sweet song of birds
  singing high in the air.

On your stone I read your name, but never seen your sweet,
  sweet face.

Your birthday I know, and when you died, but still never send
  a card.

On your stone is written 'Gone But Never Forgotten', but safe
  in God's arms in heaven.

To the sweet girl I've never met, rest in peace and God bless.

Donald Richardson

The Apple Tree

The apple tree
Spread its wide branches to the sun;
Each sleeping bud stirred in its bed of green;
And presently
Came frothing blossoms one by one,
Which falling, shed pink snow upon the scene.

The blossoms fall,
And now she spread her branches proudly
As rosy apples wink from every bough;
Then like a pall
Snow decks her, and the winds howl loudly
Alone and bare she stands deserted now.

But spring will come,
And once again she'll waken
And like the sleeping beauty of old legendry,
Her sleeping done,
Her finery she's taken,
And clothed in beauty is the apple tree.

E. P. Wilkinson

Quietus

Best china then. A perilous dawn
An anxious world surprised,
The captain is coming to supper.
I am commanded to attend
Come haze or hurricane.

In a valley soft and wild
Where grow the slender grasses of long years,
I would gather mushrooms and bilberry
I would clothe myself in garments fine
And scan the horizon for omens and premonitions.

Let the boom of darkness swing,
I am commanded to attend, and no more to dream
Dreams ponderous with possibilities.
I sense the changing winds and harried clouds -
Never more my navigation by the stars.

Sandwiches like semaphores,
Low-lit joists and tepid baccarat,
Splices and turbines, all in readiness,
And the triceratops of the Dawn has raised its head east
Among bushy clouds subpoenaed for a feast.

Andree Gibson

Centenary

Cradled by a church, challenged by a cross,
Entered for life's marathon, meeting gain and loss.
New replaces old, but eternal values stand,
Time waits for memory, and gently holds her hand.
Eternity draws closer with the passing of the years,
Newborn generations wake to laughter, and to tears.
A man from Galilee still draws men to their knees,
Rich are the host, who hear God's laughter in the breeze,
Youth holds the promise, the hope of future years.

M. E. Nicol

Just To Walk

When you set off you feel so tense,
And nothing seems to make much sense.
You see much more if you just walk
All by yourself, no-one to talk.

The pompon of a Thistle high
Attracts the dainty Damsel Fly.
The shimmering, dancing Dragonfly
Sees breathless joggers passing by.

There's Ladies' Bedstraw as I pass,
Two Toads go scrambling through the Grass.
Insects buzz round Ivy flowers
Making most of daylight hours.

To walk beneath the scented Limes
Is peace itself in hurried times.
When you return, a slower pace,
Jumbled thoughts slot into place.

R. J. Dowsing

Tomorrow's Harvest

Leaves, tumbling past my window in the cool twilight,
Light of life; gone their discontent,
Arrayed in Summer, coloured mossy bright,
To Autumn blown and trod, distorted, rent.

Those Summer leaves that rustle to the winds shrill call,
Or gentle breeze that plays through leafy boughs,
On balmy evenings, wandering 'mid trees majestic, tall,
To whisper Winter's gone, the time is now.

Then Winter blusters on its spike-trod pathway,
The trees stand dead and black against the sky,
A few stray leaves still circle on the sidewalks,
Blown by shrill Winter, brown and cracked and dry.

Then suddenly it's spring, a time of waking,
Those sticky buds begin to break again,
A sign of spirit through the bleak tree breaking,
Forget those days of Winter's hidden pain.

So must we look ahead to all Life's Seasons,
Relinquishing the lessons that it shares,
And try to come to terms with all its reasons,
To separate Life's Harvest from its tares.

Doris M. Jackson

My Swim

"I'm happy in the water, that's where I like to be
Swimming here, swimming there, from pain it sets me free.

I'm happy in the water, sometimes I'd like to be a fish,
But someone said "You'll be swallowed up,"
So perhaps that's not a sensible wish.

I'm happy in the water, swimming on my back,
As I move my legs at every stroke, no freedom do I lack,
Then I lunge my body to left, then right
The movement makes me feel so light!

The breast stroke next I try,
I swim on my left side, then turn to my right,
Giving relief to arms and legs,
But especially my arthritic thigh!

Time to leave the water, I swim the steps to reach
One by one I slowly climb, but the pain makes me want to screech!!
I sway a little, limp a little, on the way the cubicle to dress
But as I reflect upon my swim I feel invigorated
Body and mind it does impress!!

I'm happy in the water, that's where I long to be, I speak those
words with joy and truth because from pain I feel so free.

Phyllis M. G. White

The Old Windmill

Was it so long ago? The mill
Had busy sails a'turning on its hill,
The laden horse-cart climbing stony track,
The wiry miller, heavy sack on back,
Millstones rumbling, fantail slowly turning,
Bakehouse chimney smoke, gently curling,
Sails a'creaking, farmers chatting,
Children laughing, cats a'ratting,
The mill was alive.

Now stands the mill, in deep and sad decay,
The walls are broken, more and more each day.
The sails have fallen, the cap's collapsed inside,
The beams are rotten, the door is open wide,
The once white fence is now a dirty brown,
The chimney's gone, the bakehouse falling down.
Gone the mill cats,
Now there are mill bats.
The mill is dead.

Frederick Atkins

Dreaming Realities

Walking alone in the realm of dreams
Among spiritual, human and alien beings
Can this be a place betwixt life and death
Perhaps it's a world to be seen here on earth

All through my life I have learned and perceived
What elders have taught me, I've heard and believed
My eyes are wide open and still I can't see
All the wonderful worlds that are waiting for me

Some people feel cheated and seek out the truth
While others spend life-times destroying the proof
If the average man knew of his power within
He'd learn of the worlds upon worlds to live in

I know now that my dreams are in a world which is here
To be entered without any feeling of fear
So onward I journey in this universe of dreams
With the knowledge that my life is not quite what it seems

David Aird

Enlistment

I can't imagine why I ever went to war,
I saw posters of the enemy and just wanted to settle the score.
The war was glorified, the dangers were unknown,
I didn't realize what could happen to me far from the safety of
my home.

I wanted a uniform I could show to my mum,
With a brightly polished bayonet and a shiny silver gun.

When I came home on that cold winter's day,
I found my girl had gone away.
There would have been less for her to see,
For my right leg now stopped just below the knee.

One arm missing, uniform torn,
Oh, why had I enlisted on that frightful morn?
I look back now and think of my life,
If I had stayed home, I would have had a wife.

Lucinda Highley

The Result

The result comes today - but no word.
Tomorrow? But nothing is heard.
Wednesday, and grief overwhelms her,
Today we heard Mum has Cancer.
But she has a faith that's strong and true
And my own will help her come through.
Every word and every cry I will heed,
I will be there wherever she's in need.
No tasks too great or too small,
I will be there to do it all.
I will be the sunshine that melts her pain,
Until the winter's gone and spring comes again.

Roslyn Harris

73

Wheatfield

A liquid, glazed, green pelt swayed silkily.
The softly hushed close-breathing fur rose
then fell, again...and again
covering the ground with sighing undulations.

In the arctic moment, ripples and waves are transfixed,
sculptured.....still.....
like a motion-picture's breakdown
or a T.V. sponsor's frozen smile.....

Regular, even, spring-fresh groomings
have polished a sleek equestrian sheen
glowing with health
its surface reflecting life's bright source.

But,
as the seasons pass
there's a midas change to the mirror glass
Until,
blazing with life's captured light
passed on its burning heart
to man.

J. Baron

Unhappy Child

Giving affection, receiving rejection,
Behave badly and jump to attention,
Children bullied, deprived of love,
Craving attention and given a shove.

A violent background, a discontented child,
Not talking to others, quiet and mild,
Or adverse to home pressures, totally wild,
The emotional disturbances, unhappy child,

Put down and always wrong,
Goes the common verse of the song,
No matter how hard they try,
Forever wondering and asking why.

Sandra Russell

The Enemy

For years I played intricate music with ease
Recitals and sing-songs my family to please
My stiffened fingers are now challenged to fight
Tired eyes prefer dull days to bright
Attempting fine crotchet, more a favour than choice
The hook had its own mind in spite of my voice!
Embroidered pictures seem to gaze at me
All that care and patience, now a memory
Threading a needle is quite a thrill
I clatter the crockery, drop things, have a spill
Spelling often faulty, from top of the class
Memory failing on names I have to a "pass"
We take for granted the assets of our prime
Regardless of the relentless passing enemy, -time.-

M. Wall

Holding Hands

So many sad things in my life have occurred,
That I used to wonder if God ever heard.
My prayers that my life might improve and get better,
Then along he came like that longed for letter!
He came with a smile and his great big hug.
That enfolded and warmed like a thick, soft rug.
Along with the hug came his holding of hands,
As we walked through the streets, or across the sands.
It made me feel loved, and terribly safe.
It supported my soul and restored my faith,
That I could be happy, and my life could be fun,
Like coming out of the darkness, back into the sun.
And now that no more his hand can I hold,
It makes me feel sad and ever so cold.
But I notice when I'm walking along with the girls
A hand around mine can often be curled.
Giving me strength, but taking it too,
For that's what the holding hands can do.

Alison Wood

Questa My Guide

Dear Questa, you are my closest friend, always beside me no
matter where,
You cannot talk but yet you bring me comfort in the silence
we share,
For me there is no day or night, but I have no pity for myself,
but pride,
Pride in you because you keep me safe as we walk together
side by side.
I think back the years and wonder how I felt before you
became my eyes,
How did I manage I ask myself, but I do not remember, nor do
I really try,
You have my trust and you are my treasure, I am happy you
are in my life,
For seven years we have shared so much and still I rely on
you to be my guide.
'Tis said that a dog is the best friend of man, how little some
people know,
For you have brought new meaning into my life, albeit I am a
mere woman no longer alone,
You are without fault and throughout our time together, you
have worked hard,
Because you were entrusted with my life, you became my eyes,
my friend of the dark.

Margaret Carr

Open Heart Surgery (Intensive Care Unit)

Voices! Voices calling from afar
I can't think of who they are
Ah! they are louder now what is it they say
"Wake up, Bernard, it's a lovely day."
Am I asleep then, I wonder why
my eyes won't open even though I try
"Come now, Bernard, it's time to wake"
Those voices again, this time they shake
me gently and caress my brow
My eyes flick open, don't ask me how
And then the pain, the awful pain
deep in my chest time and again
What have they done, what is wrong
then recollection comes over strong
Panic, fear, I begin to dread - am I still alive or am I dead
My eyes focus weakly on a face
and I feel my pulse begin to race
I am alive! Oh thank you God:
the face looks at me and gives a knowing nod.
I feel myself drifting off to sleep, all my questions will have to keep.

Bernard Elwell

The Golden Years

I miss him when the daffodils bloom
And when the leaves doth fall
I miss him when I enter a room
And never hear his call.

I love him now as I did then
As we happily strode the aisle
My sweet memories of him when
He gave me that special smile.

The love through fifty golden years
With a beautiful family of three
Mixed with laughter and many tears
Never wanting to be free.

If I could hold his hand, stroke his face
And feel his gentle touch
The world would be a brighter place
For I miss him so much.

My silent prayers, my silent tears
Reaching out on a desolate whim
Knowing through all my lonely fears
That I still love, and miss him.

Mavis Heel

Untitled

Your kiss so soft, so warm and sweet,
Awakes my sleeping heart, each time we meet.

If people pass, I do not see them go,
You're here with me, and this is all I know.
'Though sound of birds, and scent of flowers
Are noticed in the empty hours,
What do I care, within your loving arms,
If any other thing on Earth has any charms?
All day I beg the hours to fly
'Till we're together, you and I, for just a little while.
And then I wish the night away,
Impatient for the coming day, when once
   again, I'll see you smile.
Then, full of love, so fresh and new,
My sleeping heart awakens, just for you.

Dorothy Dodds

The Last Goodbye

Imprints of touch cling to a moment of time as it hangs
motionless, scattering the mind like a raging fire searching
for relief... waiting, wanting night till dawn, breathing
shallow breath to still the heart.

Distance eternal within walls of restriction, reminders as
eyes meltdown to the very core... a calm caress that
warms the soul as it resist the inevitable.

Sorrow drawing together the fibers of strength from deepest
recesses enclosed in ones own private despair.

Drops of tears held captive, now drowns the prisoner held by
chains of emotion, as he himself awaits the executioners
'Glory' hour... in the words,
Goodbye, my love, goodbye.

Elizabeth-Ann Harse

Get Going

Have you ever tried your skill
At riding on a clacker mill
Or played upon the ooslum pipe
While eating half a pound of tripe?
Surely you have hidden in the kale
While quaffing half a pint of ale
Or dangled on the garden gate
With your neighbour's sister Kate?
Have you never had a bit of fun
Picking currants from a bun
Or languished on a cold collation
While waiting at the railway station?
Has no one ever mentioned this before
Or shown you the secret inner door?
Get going friend and tempt your fate
There's still a chance, it's not too late

John Hickmott

Lost In A Distant Thought

An aged figure looked back from the mirror:
The years had drown away all fragments of smile.
The thought of living once, now became a travesty;
For this stranger had once lived in this world.

An echo of past love faintly whispered,
An existence that even reality doubted occurred;
But if it wasn't for these vague images,
The loneliness would be filled with utter emptiness.

Sunshine celebrates, and thus cruelty taunts me,
A day of beauty is more painful than hurt.
How I long for ugliness to smother me,
To protect me from memories which once were so real.

I exist alone with nothing but pictures: therefore I am alone,
For these pictures have left and now love elsewhere.
I am a prisoner of a distant world,
A world, alas, that stopped breathing long ago.

D. H. Williams

War Child

War child, I'm sorry for the past,
And what happens still today,
I'm sorry it ended in tragedy,
And how it ends for those who got away.

War child, I'm sorry for the way you lived,
That you prayed for the hell to stop,
That you stood at the edge of a bottomless pit,
And we just let you drop.

War child, I except my share of the blame,
And I'm sorry for the part I played,
I'm sorry that now you can never see peace,
And that you lie in an early grave.

War child, please forgive us for what we have done,
Forget cease fire that came and went,
Forget you lived in Godless times,
Forget no miracles were sent.

War child, I wish, where ever you are,
Eternal sleep is nightmare free,
I hope where you are is full of true peace,
And a better place to be.

Gemma Williams

Moving House

Mummy smacked us today, my brother sister and me
She's never done that in company before
She's as lonely as we three.
Perhaps she misses the long white walls,
The mess she used to clean
The chair she would sit on
Gaze through the window and dream.

I think she longs for the ocean
Where we all went down to play
Catching crabs and splashing around
What a lovely, lovely day.

Soon we are moving from here
To a big old house to stay.
Then mummy can clean up the mess
And we'll all be happy again

We hope you'll come to visit
When you're passing by our way
We'll welcome you with laughter,
love and make you want to stay.

Pauline Wint

Jurassic Recording

In days when central heating was a rarity
And double-glazers hadn't yet been born
When there was far more cold about than charity
I'd wake up shivering in some winter's dawn

And see outside the trees blank bare and sere -
Grey road and houses, dismal as the tomb,
Curtained with dingy lace, perhaps, or bare,
And skimpy yards where no flower'd ever bloom

But once it chanced the window's dreary view
Was blotted out by pools of purest white
As if some stranger, silent as the dew,
Had done some busy brushwork in the night

And as I looked I saw another land -
Ferns, forests, pines that reached immensities,
Deep pools where serpents sleeked along the strand,
And spiky lizards thundered through the trees

My blood ran warm to greet the fertile earth -
White turned to green, petals to scarlet red;
This was before the human race had birth
Oh, sweet recall of paradise long dead

Elsie Karbacz

Heavy Breathing

Self-doubt-what a terrible thing to have
I know you can't help it
It was born inside of me too
Hide it and have confidence
Then leave there with a smile
Take in his eyes as he takes in your control
Sent wide over the table
But who's to know?
Illegal charms it was closer to you
Will the horrors object?
So what it they do
Live life to the full
Cross my palm with silver
See your fortune and die
Lost in a world of endless rapture

Yes-I am happy
For once the negative freak is joyed
All will be revealed by this time tomorrow
Do you think I'm crazy
Or is that an idea of my own?

Sarah Seaton

"My Friend"

A little boy was standing as if he couldn't care,
A dimple in his cheek and hair that was so fair
Down his face there rolled a tear from big and sad blue eyes,
There was no sunshine in his life - just dark and cloudy skies.

I said, "Oh little boy why do you stand and cry?"
He just looked up at me and gave a great big sigh.
"There must be something wrong which makes you oh so sad;
If you could talk things over I'm sure it's not so bad."

I seemed to gain his confidence he looked at me quite coy,
My heart went out to this ten-year-old wee boy,
"You see", he said "Mister," at last he wants to talk,
"I used to have a friend and every day we'd walk."

"Now I am left so lonely and always on my own,
Why did my friend have to go and leave me all alone?
One day we were playing and I was full of joy,
The next day I was so miserable - a sad, sad boy."

"I went to bed last night and said a little prayer,
Because my friend took ill - and for her I did care,
I didn't want to lose my friend, I always called her Molly,
You see my friend, so faithful, was a little Border Collie."

Sheila Irvine Fraser Wann

Royal Windsor

Royal Windsor - town on the Thames,
Where streets and houses recall historic names,
Nestled below the Castle walls.
Where the presents meets up with the past,
And a pavement clock no shadows casts.

Royal Castle - gem of present and past,
Massive and strongly built to last,
Founded more than thousand years ago,
Home to many Kings and Queens,
And at its feet the Thames still streams.

Royal Windsor - gardens and parks,
Admired by trav'lers from near and afar,
Pride and joy of the nation,
Where the Kings and Knights once hunted for game,
Today families stroll down leafy lanes.

Royal Windsor - Castle, River, Park and Town,
A famous place, imposing and renown,
Loved by young and old alike,
Where old harmoniously blends with the new,
And if you care to listen, the stones will talk to you.

Elfriede A. Winter

Feelings

A world waits and I smile in the darkness of my mind.
Through the black waters I travel with slow and measured steps.
Shoals of depression float past me and
Schools of love and hate battle in the swaying mists.
A sublime renaissance flowers within me and dances to the surface,
Breaking the floe that roofs me.
Underneath I see; I sense; I feel.
Darling Death greets me at blackened and twisted gates,
Inviting me from beneath his soft robes;
Blanketing; enveloping.
The pale light shimmers into existence;
I cry a tear; one for every experience I shared with someone.
His moods once matched the colours of my bleeding heart
Which lies exposed; naked for everyone to see my suffering.
They swoop in - Carrion birds to the nearly dead flesh of pain.
You wake me from my hellish nightmare,
Gentle kisses showering my face like summer rain.
You grab my hand and I'm freed from anguish.
You pull me from suffocating madness into a thousand dazzling
Realities. I thank you.

Jo Boulton

People

There are emotions and thoughts and feelings
That change as people grow.
There are good ones and bad ones and silly ones,
That make people we love and know.

There are smiles and tears and anger
That we show our feelings by.
When we smile it means we are happy,
When we're sad we start to cry.

We laugh if we find something funny,
Like if someone falls over in the snow.
And if someone gets annoyed with us,
We too get annoyed as you know.

Also, people like us can write poems,
That make us sad, make us happy or plead;
Like prayers, songs or sayings
That we can sing, pray or read.

We can also write poems
About things that we've done, thought or said,
And one of these you can find right here;
It's the one that you have just read!

Melissa Paddick

"A New Baby"

A birth of a baby
Is such a joy
If it's a girl or if it's a boy
They may be hard work
And cost quite a bit of money
But that is the child
You carried in your tummy
For nine months long
You feed them lots and keep them warm
While they grow and then they're born
You can keep them safe
And help them grow
Some days you may feel tired
And some days low.
But they will give you so many happy days
Watching their achievements
And giving them praise
You will be there for each other
Each and every day
But being a parent must grow harder in every way.

Tracy Stoffell

My Daughter's Big Day

It's here at last your big day
you will soon be a bride
Today you'll leave the church
With your husband by your side
just reminiscing, looking back
As I stand in the pew
The time has flown so quickly
Where have the years gone to?
I turn to see my little girl
Came walking up the aisle
Leaning on her father's arm
Her face with a beaming smile
Her eyes are filled with tenderness, and mine are filled with tears
As I look back on childhood days,
And then to teenage years
We've had so many lovely times, we've shared so many things
Thought, ambitious dreams, desires
And now I have to let you go, and hope that you soar on wings
My thoughts are in a whirl
This lovely radiant woman to still my little girl

R. Stewart

Rizzio And Queen Mary

His hand awakes the silken strings
    To strange, enchanting harmonies;
Yet in his ears there only sings
    The sweeter music of her sighs.

The walls are hung with the bright blaze
    Of rare and costly tapestries;
And yet the minstrel can but gaze
    In wonder on her moist, brown eyes.

His tales of tragic love unfold,
    Of Lancelot and Guinevere,
Of fated Tristan and Isolde;
    Yet all their agony is here.

In the perfection of her form
    Is all of loveliness contained.
His heart shares too their fiery storm
    Beneath a carefree mask restrained.

In ecstasy beside her feet
    He sits, a slave devoid of cares,
Until the moment exquisite
    Is crushed by footsteps on the stairs...

Gil White

Friendship

There are many things quite valuable in the world today,
But none so priceless as a friend, sincere in every way.
Without friends we are lonely, and we become so sad.
But a true friend ever near always keeps us glad.

It takes all kinds to make a world, at least that's what they say
But every person needs a friend, as they wander down life's way
The young, the old, the poor, the rich, no matter what they be
They cannot do without a friend, the same as you and me.

What a happy place this world would be, if we were full of love
A warm feeling in our hearts, just like the sun above
The wars and strikes of bitter hate, would all come to an end
And everybody that we meet, would greet us as a friend

So why not start making friends, you can start right here today
For no matter where we are, we have our parts to play
Just be humble, for snobbishness will only cramp your style,
To having a pleasant chat, or giving a cheery smile.

Make up your mind that you're the one, who really could do good
Try to make someone happy, because I know you could.
Just look around and lend a hand, and see what you can do.
Someday, someone may need a friend; that someone may be you.

Thomas M. Adam

Autumn

The coloured leaves are falling all around
My hedgehog friend seems to have gone to ground.
On starlit nights I've watched his little clockwork legs
Scurrying across the lawn,
Hurrying homeward, before the pearly summer dawn.

The air is moist, warm, unseasonal,
Some days the world is chilled,
The early evening darkness with the scents of bonfire filled.

Folk already frowning in despair, mourning summer's passing
Worrying what the months ahead will bring
In spite of all their fears, one thing is certain,
If there were no Autumn, how could there be Spring?

Joan Simpson

The Butterfly

Oh tiny egg, hiding under some obscure leaf.
Your life, as such, is destined to be brief.
Some mighty sunbeam will awaken your tomorrow.
I pray for you no breathings of some future sorrow.

As you emerge into your crawling state,
I hope no bird is waiting to decry your fate.
Oh hairy, ravenous and pretty thing,
Rash would he be who touched your gentle sting.

As you devour each tender, appetizing leaf,
Let no busy mother bird make your life end in grief!
Then fat, and full, in silk you wrap your form.
And wait, in sunshine. Silent. Warm.

Your chrysalis - quite ugly to behold!
But soon, one day, your beauty will unfold.
Your skin will crack and damp wings stretch. Unfurled
Your welcome loveliness will cheer a waiting world.

Helen Buller

The Reluctant Hero

Grandfather fought for the Empire a hell of a time ago.
Dad marched off to settle with Hitler, I know he told me so.
Korea seemed a good idea, unless you died with the best.
Falklands gave us back our pride, and a hero put to the test.

This time I'll have to go, if the fuel runs out too soon.
Sadam has called a Jehad under the flag of the Crescent Moon.
He thinks he's right, we know we're right, oil has to flow.
If it wasn't oil and money, would we really want to know.

Am I fighting for my country, or the pipe line on the ground.
Will I really give a damn when the noises of battle sound.
Will I come home on a battle ship or in rustling body bag.
Does my mother really want a neatly folded British flag.

If my country calls me, and I really think it might.
Then I'll join the army briskly and off I'll go to fight.
But I hope it doesn't happen because my life has just begun.
And I haven't seen the world yet, I haven't had my fun.

Penelope Broady

Out Of Sorts

Vacant eyes hound my steps,
subtle smiles mock my fragile facade,
bemused, forlorn, I stand apart,
in the Silence, in the Dark.

To Life's music I am deaf,
to Nature's beauty I am blind;
what is this ringing in my head,
the green man's shadow which I see?

These days shall pass, I have no doubt,
your tender notes shall kiss my cheek
and re-awake my spirit, mirth.

But just for now
please let me be -
I feel, I fear, I sense and see,
the World has turned its back on me.

Lynn-Marie Cody

Winter's Chill

'Tis strangely still - yet do I hear a soughing in the hills?
The ground is hard, yet muddy yesterday.
A long-dry leaf a-trembles at my feet,
And Robin's feathers ruffle daintily.

The logs I've gathered pile upon the hearth,
Yet do I hear a booming in the flue?
I see the branches swaying on the breeze,
And ponder on the traumas they go through.

Were I but young these things would go unseen,
But I am old - have learned of Nature's whims.
How many storms have come on gentle breeze,
On stillness, stealth, from careless, sulky schemes?

But I've got the logs, and coal lies in the hod,
I think of cheer and warmth and cosy days -
But spare a thought for those who're not well-shod,
And shudders chill my soul and taint my ways.

The clear blue sky already turns to grey -
And do I spy a snowflake, pure and still?
Can I hear a distant door slam shut -
Have others felt the stealthy Spectre's chill?

Frances Alder

Life

I lost my love so long ago
When I chose another,
I bade my mother's words you see,
In order to cause less bother,
But she was not always right
And I did him such a wrong,
I should have done as I wished
And heard my own heart's song!
We stayed good friends through many years
Although we rarely met,
We kept in touch the usual ways,
Although our lives were set.
But around the corner of each day
Events are hard to foresee,
The tapestry of life is played
Upon us all - you and me.
And now my loves both old and new,
Have left me with a dream.
The memories of my younger days,
The pain, the joy, the might have been!

Irene Welch

Life Will Be Better When I'm Older...

You look through your wardrobe for things to wear,
Throwing them out if they're torn,
But the clothes I have; the ones I wear,
Are the only ones I've worn,

You go to school with all your books,
With lots of things to learn,
But what I have and I want,
Are things for which I yearn.

For what I want, and what I have,
Are totally different things,
I have no choice but to take in,
Whatever my life brings,

I sometimes sit and wonder,
What will happen when I'm older,
Will people sit and stare at me,
Or give me the cold shoulder,

I'd like to see the future,
Predict what is to be,
Will people still be suffering,
Throughout the world like me

Charlotte Brewer

Beyond Lilleyveil

What wonders are lurking here, beneath the scrub,
In this silently brooding, midday bush?
Sprawling under summer's white lot sky,
It's shimmering silence so intense
That it clamours upon the inner ear
Like the insistent bell that warned of coming siege;
Heavy with it's pungent drowsy scents,
Silent yes, but never still;
For though no bird wings beat the air above,
And no song arises from those sleepy throats,
Yet down below, upon the sandy, littered floor,
A myriad life forms go their busy ways;
Intent upon their tasks; each a part,
A fraction of that wondrous whole,
Whose knowledge of its ceaseless, ever changing self,
Depends on all those tiny, finite parts,
Expressions of its immortality.

Bet Simmons

No Time No Time

There's no time for you and me
No time to bake the bread for tea
No time to witness babies first step
No time until we are out of debt.

No time to check the neighbours need
No time to hear the church bells heed
No time to hear the cuckoo's song
No time to see the blue bells throng.

No time to picnic on the beach
Or watch the children play, only time
To work long hours for another dreary day.

No time to go fishing on a summers day,
No time to watch the sunset in its gold array.
No time to notice that time has passed you by,
No time! No time! No time!

Rita Rea

Dunblane

The children walked happily to school
Thinking nothing would happen at all

It was just a normal happy day
Where they could talk and read and play

Until the gunman came along
Knowing what he was doing was wrong

So when you drive along in your cars
Spare a thought and look at the stars

Because this is where the children have gone
Turned to angels singing songs

Abolish guns, we don't need them here
So children can live without any fear

This has caused our island so much pain
There must never be another Dunblane.

Tikki Baker-Keeping

Ode To A Dead Swan

Virgin white wings outstretched, imploring
Shocking, gaping, ravaged breast
Mauled by the predator, ripped and desecrated
Dragged unheard from the mute swans nest

My anger screams at this mutilation
Beauty spoiled in the broken reeds
Cruel nature, cold, unheeding
Turns her face from the evil deed

What beast has killed here, raw, unfeeling
The cygnets pain in this violent way
I turn away, my footsteps heavy
This death has marred the brightening day

Josephine Bernier

Is It Time To Leave?

It started out so good, life seemed so fine,
In all the sophisticated places, we would sit and dine.
Now that has all gone now, there's nothing left
To say, we just go on pretending, from day to day.

Where do we go from here? Do we call
It off? Are we just pretending that
Friendship is enough?
In all the years I've known you,
I thought we had it made, all the riches
In the world your love I would not trade.

Did habits die hard as the saying goes,
The child that you gave me, means more
To me than you will ever know.
I look into her eyes; she has such
A pretty face, blond curly hair that
Cheery stare, that no one can replace.

Margaret McNicholas

Untitled

Onward, Onward, he had to go
Where he was bound he did not know.
The Love he'd left lay in slumber deep,
Her dreams of him, were for her to keep.
His heart was hers she knew that well,
His soul in turmoil, wrapped in Hell.
She saw him winging through the night
Believing his need to leave was right.
Onward, Onward he had to go
Where he was bound, she could not know.
In visions on waking she found his form.
His body enclosed her, slender and warm,
His kiss was gentle, then hard and slow,
The musk of need only Lovers know.
He fell away and she slumbered on,
To realize in Time, He was gone - gone.
Onward, Onward, He had to go
Where he was bound, She would never know.

Carol Abrams

'Landscape'

The landscape lay before me, clouded in a hushly mist,
Birdcalls woke the silence, heralding the dawn,
I felt so insignificant, in surveying what I saw,
The majesty of nature left me feeling in such awe.
As I looked, the sunlight dispersed those clouded mists,
I really felt a part of me - join in with natures
plan, and thank the good creator, for in his
land, I stand.
The majesty and splendour are ours to have
and hold. If only we can treasure what
we see before us unfold.

Kathleen M. Tupper

Just A Moment

Words said in anger, without thought
Spoken in haste, while distraught
Then silence, like a cloud lingers
Trembling lips, twitching fingers
Gradually tempers cool down
Smiles appear, where there was a frown
Eyes meet across a room
Heart beat like a thunderous boom
The tension is eased by a flickering smile
We seemed like enemies for just a while.

No word was spoken, he came to my side
The anger now gone like the ebbing tide
Our fingers meet, like a magnet draws
Our bodies close, breath takes a pause
Forgotten the reason for our row
Forgotten the anger, no tension now
Our hearts warm again like a fire's ember
Forgotten our hate, just our love to remember.

Dory Bond

The Letter

Dear God, mummy went away today,
Dad says to visit with you,
And although she's been so very ill,
You'll make her well and quiet new.
I asked if she would come back soon,
He said she wasn't allowed,
But she'd watch over me forever,
And that I'm to make her so proud
So if she's staying with you up in heaven.
Please bear these few things in your mind,
That she gets really cross if you're naughty,
But mostly she's loving and kind.
Please tell her how much that I love her,
And I miss her since she went away,
I'll try hard to look after daddy,
We both talk to her picture each day.
Please God, look after my mummy,
Keep her safe while she is with you,
Until some day in the future.
When I come to visit you too.

Christine Morris

While The Slithy Snake Sleeps

These resurrected fandangle styles of spyglass,
I adjust awhile, slithering to and fro cross face, so I
can catch a glimpse of place, the cobbles beseemed nice
and good - dust rood beyond to reach I must - as message by
some lad there local - come to me the for flung yokel -
Christmas day they may come to call it - at present
so many names an awl it came and saw us
Mother dear, father from town here local, too, I fear, he still
drunkard, you're lost, jaded, - though portraits of
both, not faded,
    Come many wait to see you, J. C. how
very best it must to be you.

A. G'art'on

Flowers And Chocolates

Flowers, chocolates, happiness, trust,
Her favourite scent and lots of lust.
Arguments, apologies a diamond ring,
They're happily wed like queen and king.
Nine months later the child is born,
And everything turns to be like corn.
Wavy and wobbly and crying and tired,
A second mother seems best to be hired.
Mother and daughter plan a trip to the mall,
As little one needs her first things for school.
Next comes periods and boyfriends and bras,
Soon she'll be complaining her friends all have cars.

Lauren Mackay

'I'm In Solitude'

I'm in solitude, no friend to talk to me.
I'm in solitude, no family to care for,
No-one to care for me.

Here I am again, lying all alone.
The night is dark and long, this floor is cold and hard.

The noises above bring back the memories.
A life I've left behind echoing through my mind.

I hear the cars go by, but I'm left paralysed.
Anyway I've got nowhere to go, no-one to go and see.

How I wish I had a purpose, some motivation in my soul.
My bottle is empty now, and I've got no goal.

If only I could find a way, someone to help me out,
And make tomorrow a better day.
But I'm in solitude!

I'm in solitude, no friend to talk to me.
I'm in solitude, no family to care for.
No-one to care for me.

Matthew Graham

Untitled

I hate writing, yet it's the only way. Everything gets down
To earth when you try to keep it. Every thought, every feeling
Just loses its magic when you say to yourself:
"That's good, I have to keep it."
The brain starts looking for a piece of paper and a pen,
Energy goes wasted while you move your body.
The connection is lost,
The sequence is being raped. You start writing. You
Begin from the first thought which was never meant to be written
And you go on.
As you go on new thoughts find their way and come alive on
the paper,
But these are different, these are bound to reality, these are made
To be written.

They might sound logical and revolutionary, but they just
carry you away.
They distract you from your first-born thought, the one that made
You start writing. When you finish, the result seems nice, sometimes
Even successful, but you realize, unless you already knew, that this
Was not what you wanted!
You pray for a recorder of thoughts and dreams.

On the other hand, maybe we are lucky in a sort of way
We are still in touch with reality.

Ioannis Kleanthidis

Untitled

The leaves shook gently in the summer breeze.
The owls hooted mournfully from their perch in
the eaves.
The old barn creaks with impending doom,
as if it knew, it would have to come down to
make more room.

Yes, that great invention the motorway,
is slowly taking shape to the farmers dismay.
No more exploring through the woods on a hot
summers day,
No more childish voices shouting out "what did
you say?"

Instead of wild colourful flowers growing
amongst the trees.
Men with hard hats will be seen poking and
prying with forms and deeds.

Nature should be allowed to keep her green and
lush fields.
Instead of miles and miles of dirt splattered
wheels.

Cath Wild

Teachers

Deep in the dark murky depths of the school,
Lies a monster to shame any demon or ghoul.
In the horrid music room does it lurk.
Setting painful demonic homework.

In case the answer is unable to reach ya',
The topic of my poem is called a teacher.
Not just any old Sir or Miss.
This one teaches us English.

It sits its victims down in seats made of plastic,
And tells us of punctuation and things just as drastic.
Shakespeare, riddles, verbs and how to use a noun,
Inspire the whole class to want to leave town.

It makes us read books and other types of torture,
Once you've been teachered there's nothing to cure ya'.
They make you eat toxins and drink cyanide,
When it comes to lunch time, I advise you to hide.

I feel there is one thing that I have to say,
I hate to admit it but the lessons do pay.
If my brain had been left to erode,
I would not have been able to construct this ode.

Nathan Busby

Someone Special

Someone special is a person you care for
Someone special is a person you're prepared to give your life for
A person you love and that person loves you
A person who will shelter your love within heart too

A person who will feel lonely when you go away
A person who hurtful words will never say
A person who will share your sorrows
A person who will be there for you today and tomorrow

A person whose smile shines like the sun
A person who will guarantee you fun
A person whose love will capture your soul
A person who will help you reach your goal

A person you can't imagine life without
A person you'll give your life for no doubt
A very special person this poems about!

Jasvinder Singh Dhillon

Blame To Year 1996 From Sumerian Obelisk

On a stroke of crying air....I leave my voice.
I light a fire of memory.....I read monody verse on what is left.
I join their branches, which have not die yet....
I look from a hidden balcony on all the dead.

No thunder, no cloud...no water flowing... no hope...no door
will open without me.... I called myself... where's happiness, o
oh....o ...oh night where's happiness... where's peace.
What on earth will guide me... but I covered my face with my
palm... A crumbled loaf of bread will buy my people...

In the morning when I was passing by... I saw a handkerchiefs
wave carrying my name. I know for certain that the Euphrates
water had busted its banks... I gave my secret to.... To the
sailors of my imagination.... I kept repeating to myself... I said
peace upon... Peace upon.... myself overflowing with wounds.
Peace... I searched deep into my heart... Until midnight...and
talked to my heart. Whenever a trembling of breeze... or
threaten suspicion.

With agony I will drop the dagger of the universe on my
guitar and say loud "Why us.?" Why distribute our clothes
among so many?....Why cut away the plaits of our dream....?
And entering into blind discussion... Where is the peace on
earth, with people?....where is happiness? Are the Iraqi
children sacrificed and slaughtered for sin they never did
commit?

Tajia Al-Baghdadi

The Last Soldier

On the 11th of November
Eleven A.M.
We all remember
The brave Contemptible men

Silence has broken
Heads fall bowed
2 minutes have started
The gun blast is loud

One man alone
Too frail to walk
Stands still in remembrance
Refuses to talk

The last of his troop the army is gone
His time will come the memorial goes on

The guns fire again Edward Harding looks up
Remembering his friends the tear drops, drop

War is bad.
Many men are dead
We all remember them
The poppy is Red.

Christopher Byers

Broken Images

Everything to live for,
The world at your feet,
But your dreams evaporate in the summer heat,
Your future is there hiding in the sun,
Confusion blinds you, where do you run,
The future's still there; it's not too late,
In cold winter your fate will be clear,
Those summer blues will disappear.

Christopher Butler

Domestic Violence

A cry in the night, again there is a fight,
the neighbours hear with fear,
as the beatings get louder towards their ear,
He hits her once, he hits her twice, the vicious
monster that beats his wife.
To call the police is a waste of time, for when it
comes to domestic affairs, they don't even care.
The police can not be trusted for they are a fool,
for turning a blind eye to what is so cruel.
The pain in her eyes, the tears of her face,
to call him a husband is a disgrace.
For a woman is frightened in her own home,
for he causes a violent and abusive life,
this vicious monster does not deserve a wife.
This monster can not be called a man from the one above,
for a real man knows how wrong it is to hit a woman he loves.

Neda Parastar

The Butterfly

If I was like a Butterfly,
I'd sit in peace and sigh.
The breeze would flutter by with time
and life pass briefly by.

Amidst the Gardens I might be,
Bloom to bloom serenely gliding.
Where flowers amass, you'd find me,
from calling scents there'd be no hiding.

I'd rest majestic on a hill
and see the world in peace and splendour.
My heart could only long for life
and love so warm and tender.

Of war and hate, I would be blind,
while in a meadow I would lie.
For in my world of Innocence,
I would slowly fade and die.

Florence May Richardson

Pointless Killing

Soldiers crouching, soldiers crawling,
Soldiers shooting, soldiers falling,
Winners leaping, losers crying,
Winners living, losers dying.

Soldiers eat, the food's disgusting,
But it's either that or nothing,
Men still hungry, men still looking,
Nothing left, there's nothing cooking.

Down the trenches, soldiers writing,
Guided by the candle lighting,
Writing to their sisters, brothers,
Aunties, uncles, fathers, mothers.

Soldiers stretching, soldiers yawning,
Welcome to another morning,
Some aren't moving, but instead,
They're lying still, they're lying dead.

"Come on boys, take up positions,
Set to work, you know your missions".
Bored of all this mournful drilling,
Soldiers start the pointless killing!

Michael Smith

To A Much Loved Nun

Once through a garden beautiful
where the flowers were all in bloom
came a lady, graceful and gentle
As a bell chimed the hour of noon.
Her eyes were steadfastly gazing
at the sky so blue and clear
and her lips were moving in Prayer
as she said "my God I thank thee, for sending me here.
I came from Thee to this world,
As the answer to on oft said prayer
And so I came here to thank Thee
for the life which thou hast spared
O Lord I pray thee to help me
to be loving, faithful, and true
and only to do in this world
as thou wouldst have me do,
just to be kind to others
And lend a loving hand
To smooth rough roads for weary feet,
And to carry out God's plan
so the Mother's Prayer was answered, by the babe they
dearly loved
So they called her forever,
Dorothea, The Gift of God.

Doris M. Pass

Waste

Babes, innocent -
With eyes not yet able to see-
Don't know they have arrived in a world
Fixated with BSE.

Their mothers, with their warm moist tongues,
Lick their pains of birth away
And suckle - safe, secure and close
Their calves upon the hay.

Worried farmers - betwixt scientists
And politicians toss the blame,
But at whoever's foot the fault must fall
The end is still the same.

At 10 days old they're dragged away,
Their bleating cries - no use,
To a bitter death
For the sins of man
And his animal abuse.

Anna J. Browning

Seasons Of Life

Springtime of the seasons, means
the starting of our birth - our own
Earthly existence, on this our "Mother Earth."
Years pass on quickly by, into the
Summer of the seasons - where we marry
in haste, for lots and lots of reasons.
Where we raise a family, and build a
lovely home, so that when the seasons
change, we will not be on our own.

Autumn time ascends, with the
leaves, that fall around - and our
children now depart, to a more fertile ground.
As we look out of the window, on this
our eventide - we two, are now but one, as one of us had died.
The final season comes, of winter,
frost and cold, and we are left so desolate, and yet so very old.

Yet, we have the memories of life throughout the years -
the struggle and survival, that only 'Love' endears.
It's time to say farewell, to this our earthly home -
as the seasons will remain, as we depart Alone.

B. T. Stoner

Night

A veil of darkness covers the Earth.
The night has come.
I fear the night.

I cannot sleep, my mind thinks strange of the night,
still and quiet.

I am alone, no one to talk with, no one to tell
my inner most fears.

Moonlight streams across my bedroom,
I see strange figures dance on the wall.
What are these figures, who are they, what are they.
My mind screams, my body violently trembles,
God help me.

Moonlight dispatched by the night to terrorise me.
Tears fill my eyes, the pain of fear, the smell of fear,
I feel I cannot go on.

I rise go to my window look into the heavens,
piercing white lights flicker on and off, some people
say they are heavenly bodies, some people say
they are the dwelling place of God.
I fear they are the eyes of the damned souls of hell.

I cry, I pray for the souls in hell.

I pray night will pass, the sun will rise,
the souls of hell will have their freedom.

Please please God wake me from this
dark and hideous world we call a nightmare.

Pat O'Hara

Season To Season

Russet and brown leaves fall like dry paper
to moulder in the wet grass.
Brown spikes stand where once bright flowers bloomed
Their glorious colours gone.
Memories of hot sunny days when butterflies on gossamer wings
Settled on the perfumed heads of roses - where now
are the bees that once hummed round
blue heads of sweet lavender?
Gone are the yellow and orange hues of
golden summer days
Now blackened leaves touched by cruel frost
show dreary winter is here.
A glimpse of green bravely pushing through
the dark cold earth
Heralding the birth of future spring and
the delicate white of snow drops.
Winter will pass and once more the
blossom will open on the tree
And welcome Summer again.

Kathleen Doris Callow

Death's Dream

'Tis a shame that such young men
Fall as fodder, before they should wake.
Such realization becomes heady blows;
More than mere life is at stake.

They've lined the field forever;
One falls as another takes place.
Wide eyed in death's clammy grasp:
Clutching sky in saving grace.

What good are coffers in death;
When arrows plumed skyward point;
Past agony spent - in bloody rent:
Limbs asunder - ripped from joint.

Life is but a dream, dear men:
Its price is high for you to take.
Lest you fall - by sword or pen:
Best you fall - before you awake.

Brett Chaney

He Who Comes When I Have Prayed

I'm screaming at myself for the hatred that I feel
Killing all my thoughts until nothing seems quite real
Scared to hope and scared to love
Scared to fly where angels dream above
Fighting against the feeling that no one seems to care.
Lying in the darkness I sense his presence there
He who holds the golden key
I pray to come and rescue me
Teach me to walk into the light
Dry my tears and hold me tight
Please understand that I am afraid
He who comes when I have prayed

Yvonne Sclater

Animal Holocaust

At the nativity you were there,
In wonderment you stood to stare,
At a beautiful baby nestled in straw
Who was born to keep the world in awe.
Long, long ago. -

Of course you would eat what you were given,
We all accept food as manna from heaven,
In some Eastern lands you are thin but Holy
We kept you fat, we made you poorly,
A modern mistake?

Your rich creamy milk we are now told to skim
Yet we thanked this for healthy body and limb
Do what we are told a dream or a whim -
"All creatures great and small", not part of a hymn
What should we believe!

Wherever you grazed and gazed we'd shout "Shoo" -
Accept and laugh at the phrase - "silly moo"
Can we ever lament and say 'sorry' to you!
Beautiful bovine, forgive us - please do,
You die, we sigh, we cry -

Eleanor Stephenson

Chips And Me

Mr. Chips claimed a "Heinzs" mixture
Named after the lead in my favourite picture
Long white hair, intelligent face
Slim neat body, of infinite grace
Dear little dog, trusting and true.
We're going a'rabbiting me and you
We're going a'rabbiting you and I
Under the oak that lingers by
The five barred gate the cows go through
Past three elms and an evergreen yew
Through the fields our footsteps bound
Where maybe a rabbit is to be found
Burrowing its way through distant ground
Waving in the breeze like an unfurled sail
All I can see of Chips is his tail
The rest of his body is down a hole
No longer white but black as coal!
But nary a rabbit was to be found
And now our steps are homeward bound
Chips and Me

Gardyne Richmond

Graveyard

Bluebells, daisies, buttercups, and speedwell
Grow upon the mounds
Under which the dead rest.

If ever I am asked
To justify my life
I shall point to
The bluebells, daisies, buttercups, and speedwell.

Jack Newland

"Traffic Jam"

Imprisoned in their ferrous shells
The puce commuters stare
O'er banks around the Hedgehogs' Field
At tents erected there -
Whilst taking supermarket harvest home.

Behind each foamy plastic seat
Lurk cartons packed so neat
As tubes and cubes of coloured wares
Declaring all constituents
Like some malign experiments.

In the field beyond the hedge
the hopeful growers illustrate
That "Onward Peas, Kerr's Pink nor Cos"
Needs no monosodiumglutamate
In or out of Harvest Home!

But more than hedge divides the shell from tented field
Rather an Age and mode of living
Which have changed beyond recall
E'en as taking has replaced giving,
Thus Nostalgia shows at Harvest Home!

Peter Bacon

'Emmy'

Attention seeking all the time
Mischievous through and through
Tormenting us all day and night is all you seem to do
You are such a pretty thing
Well, you have a pedigree!
And everyone that meets you definitely agree
Chocolate ears and chocolate nose
Your eyes a shade of green
Fur so soft and silky, best I've ever seen
You purr at almost everything
And sleep between each meal
I think I'd like to be a cat
Seems such a purr-fect deal!

Tracey D. Whalley

Mother Nature

If you were mother nature
We would have a peaceful future
The birds would be singing every day
The animals in the land would always play.
In the human race there would be no war
Because each other they would adore,
You are like a breath of fresh air,
For everything you really do care
If everyone was like you
I don't know what I'd do.
You are the aching in my heart.
I hope that we are never apart.
With these words that are so true
The world would say I thank you.

Martin Hughes

Then There Came Love

Once there was the loneliness;
No purpose to my days.
I lived and breathed, but my soul was dead
Unfulfilled in so many ways

Then there came love.

Love brought a reason for living,
The birds had a much sweeter song.
The sun and the moon in their brilliance
Seemed happy that I should belong.

My heart filled with love and compassion,
My days full of laughter and fun,
I had someone to watch and to care for,
To share with, 'till my life was done.

When there came love.

Rosemary Christie

Symphony

When I'm alone and we are long apart
There is no solace for my hungry heart.
Hungry for you and sunkiss'd heathered hills
'Til unfulfillment all my passion kills.

The wind-blown leaves dance in the evening air;
Where once I felt, I feel no symphony there.
The scent of rainy roses offers sweet surprise,
And yet there is no hope when I lift up my eyes —
Only the scudding clouds across the storm-swept sky.
Only the nearing night, only the falling rain - and only I.

I cannot weep when most I feel despair;
I dare not dream to find no comfort there.
Where now is happiness and where is truth?
Why must we waste like this the transient years of youth?

Yet could I cry, those tears would free my heart,
And I could see once more the beauty
Which is part of me forever - when you return
I'll weep until I feel again
The symphony of the trees, the roses and the rain.

Joan M. Crowther

Peace

The fields of poppies bright and gay
The souls beneath rot and decay
The ones who died shall ever stay in mind
Someday I pray those who remain
Will learn how to be kind
Alas the passing of time has taught no lesson
For all around is death and depression
My prayer for all is a world wherein
The faults of man can be less grim
Religion can be met with kind respect
And the fields of poppies we never forget

Christine Ferguson

Kernow

Gleaming gorse;
Tormented retreating trees.
The white uncalled-for hills.
Paintbox pools, remember nothing; know nothing!
Ruined chimney spikes the sky.
Memorial or condemnation?
No men, no work.
A lark sings.

Across the hill white angels stand.
In ranks they wait, and turn and turn.
Sing sad memorial songs,
Laments of wind and need.

Jacquie Perkin

'Surreal Reality'

I'm sitting visaging my perfect
World in a domain of

Fury, anger, isolated hatred
Plagues my distant real world in

Masses and masses
Of people flock to breathe a now poisoned air which is

Asphyxiating children
Lie alone in pools of possessive obese oil they are

Lying still
Cats chase only the surrealists rats in small shrinking

Brains
Are eroding within once perfect bodies and negative natures
and then it is all

Slowly stopping
The atmospherical weathering the planets crash
on elliptical orbits while

The earth stops.

Jolene Roos

Love Beats With Jesus

I heard the choral voices and the beating of the heart
Love beats with Jesus, it was a glorious impart
At Alpha class we learned from Bible readings
The ways and hows to carry on our teachings
harmony to our lives by the grace of God we bring
Power of inspiration and peace through the Lord our king
When we are sick or weary, our God he understands
Love beats out the miracles of those healing hands
All peoples as they go, the Lord wants them to know
Listen to your intonation shared by all denominations
Knowing that special feeling together with you in prayer
gentle precious moments with your loving care
Bells ringing out a musical medley
heart beats of Jesus the living God who fed me
Holy Spirit give us strength and hope as we believe
Fulfil in body and mind our understanding of God receive
Strengthened by our fellowship, not much room for doubt
Joining hands with Jesus whose love is beating out
Privilege of gifts, a blessing beyond compare
king of all creation, a forever love affair

Marjorie Stainer

Soulmates

Your brief presence
Opened a world I once knew
Do you remember our ascension?
Our journeys through distant lands
Strange bodies entwined
With familiar souls.
How we laughed at ourselves far below,
Writhing, probing, searching for something
Which cannot be contained.
You left me desolate
When you favoured another world,
But I refuse to weep,
For we will dance again,
Amidst the elements
And laugh at strange bodies down below.

Sharon Gay

The North Sea Tiger

Waving goodbye to his wife and his child,
The North Sea tiger, looks so gentle and mild.
Two weeks at home and two weeks away,
A fortnight's leave is too short for play.

Never mind, darling, it won't be long,
Think of us and please be strong.
I worry about you, but you already know that,
You hear it in my voice when you phone for a chat.

The two weeks are up, at the airport I stand,
Waiting so patiently for your plane to land.
I can imagine you working in hard hat and boots
And remember your pet name for me...

Melanie Thomson

Just You

Just to have you near me
it's like a physical breeze
seem's like a wave rolling from the sea.
    Close enough,
yet so far away,
a shiver you send me all through the day.
    Rushing feelings wash over me
keeping me knowing that it's with you I want to be.
Drifting around my soul-mate I've found.
    You're like a sunny ray
beaming down on a mountain top
on a beautiful summers day.
    A deep breath held inside
my body feels so alive.
    You make me feel so happy
I never new it was possible for someone to do
I'm so glad I found you.

Nicola Hughes

Sonnet In Gratitude For A Pot Of Chutney

At night I ate my solitary meal-
Culled with what duress from the butcher, grim,
By flick of eye, not whiplash, aimed at him.
Mutton or beef in never ending reel!
Cushioned that night in hard-won pommes-de-terre,
So lately hidden in some dark recess
And cajoled thence by wit or smooth address,
I felt that this, indeed, was frugal fare.
But then came chutney of ambrosial breed
Gifted from Heaven, or a secret hoard,
To grace the plate and decorate the board,
Made as exacting palate had decreed -
Pleasantly spiced yet not a whit too hot.
I kiss the cunning hand that stirred the pot!

Grace A. Clarke

The Whisper

I heard just a whisper,
Saw no face for darkness was total.
The voice had no pain or passion,
Not even a shadow of happiness or sorrow.
That voice troubled me for it had
A ring of compassion.
Within its calmness it portrayed
A wonderful feeling of beauty and tranquillity.
Then the voice began to take me back in time
And said to me without emotion:
"You are lost, Let me take you into tomorrow,
For that is the joy to come".
We started to talk and I began to understand
What yesterday meant and the time I had wasted.
I began to hope that the voice would not leave me.
But without a farewell and only a last comment:
"You don't need me, but I will return",
It was gone.

D. S. Dullaert

Living In Hope

One day I wrote a poem that I thought was very good,
So I sent it to a publisher, as anybody would,
He wrote back and he thanked me, said he liked my work,
And could I write more of the same, or was it just a quirk?

And so I sat down once again, with pen and pad in hand,
And wrote another poem, which was really rather grand.
It seemed to me the greatest thing that I had ever written,
And so I sent it off to him, knowing he'd be smitten.

Alas, he didn't like it, which made me feel quite sad;
"Too flowery and involved," he said,
"And all the Rhymes are bad",
He thanked me for my efforts, but said I must agree,
That writing verse was something that appears to be beyond me.

Win M. Webster

The Goal

Score a goal! Score the goal!
Martin's Dad began to pray,
After all this time,
Please God, make it his day.

Stricken by ailment, he lay abed,
Thoughts in tandem with his boy,
So willing him on with all his strength,
Nothing this day, to mar their joy.

As the minutes ticked by,
Martin, on the wing flew on,
Passing one foe after another,
The Keeper in sight, so he struck, Hurrah! One up.

As the life ebbed out of Martin's Dad,
Gladly he too reflected on the life he'd had,
The result was good, to make his goal is all he asked,
Propinquity was very clear.

Frank Dearnley

The Sky Is Empty

Pale, mournful soul, he shuffled forth.
Confused, beholden.

The wet, dark, unfamiliar sky appeared as empty
As a broken mind, its secrets leached,
Attracting instant empathy
But that his voice had said; "Seek no solutions there."
Why not? Who knows!
Soon, wretchedness and sorrow ruled,
Covertly wild, no longer hard suppressed within
The woven fabric set to guide his hand.

Official transportation whisked him eerily away.
To where? He does not now recall.
Apathetic emptiness.
Whilst far afield, stark Institution's walls had
Frowned aggrievedly, barred windows dripping
Tears of regret, as if they too distinguished
Right from wrong
And so became as sorrowful as he.

Now he has sinned and killed, true to-
He knows not what.

D. J. Kay

The Swan

Oh! Beautiful swan, you fill me with delight,
When I see your mighty wings in flight,
Gliding with grace over a bright-blue lake,
Leaving gentle ripples in your wake.

When you are flying high in the sky,
You stir my emotions, I don't know why,
I'm sure the strange, peculiar noise you make,
Is so I'll look up, and from my reverie awake.

You sail by with a proud and arrogant air,
As if to say 'Look at me, you may stare,
Am I not beautiful, a fine and lovely bird,
The best of which you've ever seen and heard?'

I agree, and so, I'll give you some bread,
You disdainfully turn your elegant head,
There is a glimmer in your eye,
As you go majestically by.

Yet I seem to recognize,
The message in your daunting eyes,
I know you love me, my plumage I'll preen,
You'll remember me always, a royal queen?

I. Greenall

Hope

Long ago or so it seems
I had a mirage of dreams
The air was clean, the water blue
And the earth was warm where flowers grew.

The sun shone warmly in the sky
And long summer days went passing by
Everyone was nice and kind
No nasty things to blow your mind.

I thought this life would last forever
That everyone could live together
In peace harmony and tranquillity
Sadly this was not to be.

A change occurred which took its toll
And gave mankind a different roll.
But still there are things that give me pleasure
A baby's smile you cannot measure.

A kind word from the one you love
The morning light on the wing of a dove
A freshly mown lawn has a scent of its own
These are all pleasures we can condone.

Valerie Cresswell Hogg

Daughter

It's a girl.
Rejoicing and celebrating has begun.
You had a tiny life form, a tiny human being
in your arms.
Tiny hands and feet, wave around, and her little voice cries.
You have a daughter, before you
and will have for the rest of your life.
That voice you heard in the dawn of May
will call you for the rest of your life
That little girl will grow and need your
support, guidance and trust.
From her you will gain
love, troubles, worries and a life time of memories
She is the gem in your life
and you will protect her, but consider her feelings
As she grows she will need independence
You must help her and understand her.
Eventually you will have to let go
But you will always have your little girl.
Your Daughter.

Laura Smith

Love Conquers All

I came I saw I conquered not
an alien lot they were
a rather peculiar melting pot
of folks from here and there

(We had arrived unsynchronized
you were loved and I despised
I hoped and prayed that you would stay
        you moved away)

But stay I did since rather madly
I fell in love with you
the fire burning fiercely sadly
failed to inflame you too

(You'd smiled and known me there and then
the worlds I'd lost and tried to find again
you had perceived so quick so true
        I hated you)

Yet here we are 'midst many trials
give me your hand and trust in me
Delays indeed are not Denials
forgive me LOVE for doubting Thee

Carmen Lambert

Belsen

A grey place with grey thoughts.
Grey, with stone and silence
that's all the mind accepts.

Mounds with meaningless numbers
and small slabs with the legend
"One unknown dead".

Nothing moves inside the walls,
save for the wind and the people,
all else is dying in the field of the dead.

A coach arrives outside, with laughing, shouting people,
they look invincible as they march down the path together,
but the grey silence will swallow them all.

Noise without, silence within,
the grey stone touches them all.
Everyone whispers in the field of the dead.

Walking on slabs of grey,
through silent trees and fields of brown
you'll always see a mound or a single slab of stone.

Fire destroyed the physical shape,
but you won't forget the meaning,
for the spirits of the 30,000 still live on.

M. H. Hunter

Love Hurts

Wrenched heart strings tear apart
Like the blush of red flesh on an operating table.

Hurt spills like the softest waterfall.
And salty tears flood the naked eyes.

How love pains, how love hurts
When hearts are broken apart.

Daksha Patel

Great Britain? The Forgotten Ones

Living on a pension
Unnecessary tension,
Money's all spent,
Can't pay the rent.
Bills are coming in,
Your head's in a spin,
Which way do you turn
When you're too old to earn.
"Can you raise our pension up?"
"You'll be lucky, no such luck!"
Really fancy a nice juicy steak?
Only got bangers, give us a break!
Feeling cold, hand's numb and blue,
Can't be helped, a coat will have to do.
Hungry again, can't get fed,
Guess you'd better go to bed.
Feeling ill, need a hip repair,
Will you get help, no, they don't care.
Government won't help, we are just a chore,
What about us, we fought your bloody war!

S. L. Discombe

Untitled

Come now my love and talk with me
Come tell me all that troubles you
Let out those spirits, dark and drear
Which cloud your thoughts and make you sad.
Come close to one who holds you dear
Feel free to vent your woes and fears
Fear not that I will fail to know
That deep inside you wish no hurt
It is far better for your mind and soul
To let those frightful spirits go
You must not let them harbour there
For they're the ones that cause you harm
Come lean on me and let my strength
Go out to you and give you calm
Let one who loves and cares for you
Help make those burdens disappear.

C. R. E. Peirce

Portrait

I'd love to paint your picture Lord,
Devote intricate detail to you,
Your eyes, so bright and loving
Too magnificent for any hue.
Linear, prominent features,
Golden tumbling hair,
Palatable colours - which to use -
Pigments beyond compare.
Those gentle hands, bone structure long
Transparent washes fade,
No colour can portray your power
However delicately laid.
Strong, graceful neck - so quick to turn
Helping others in distress,
What colour can portray movement
On an artist's blank canvas?
No colour can depict pure love,
That's why my saviour dear,
Your portrait remains in my heart,
Just love for you - that's clear.

Rebecca Anne Harvey

A Highland Dream

So clear is the picture as I dream,
The charm and beauty of this land,
The lochs so long and mountains high,
So picturesque against the sky.
There on the hillside sheep are seen,
With shepherds dog alert and keen,
Thistle and bluebell here and there,
and purple heather everywhere.
The sun that sets behind hill and brae,
On which many a traveller plods his way,
To see the sights of Skye and Kyle,
Making his way on the Road to the Isles.
'Tis glad to know that I have seen,
and glad to know that I have been,
To see those glorious sights once more,
and knocked upon a certain door.

A. F. Turner

Christmas

C is for the Christ child born midnight Christmas Eve.
H is for the Happiness that we all receive.
R is for Rejoicing as we celebrate his birth,
I is for the Infant who brought joy to the earth.
S is for the Smile on his face as in his mothers arms he lay,
T is for the Thoughts of love on that special day.
M is for the Manger where the baby lay his head
A is for the Animals who shared his lowly shed.
S is for the Saviour who wanted no fuss,
This is what Christmas should really mean to us
Love and understanding in this world today
For a better place to live in, is what we ought to pray

Joyce Steele

Firstborn

Where have the years gone, O my son,
Since your life, too soon begun,
Hung by a thread? Your tiny form -
An incubator keeping you warm.

Minute nails; soft, crumpled ears;
The miracle of real salt tears.
From God's garden, the perfect rose,
Kept alive by tube and hose.

Your eyes were blue then; skin so pale,
Almost transparent, like a veil.
I prayed you'd have the strength to fight.
At last they said, "He'll be all right"!

It was a very special day
When you, my son, came home to stay.
And then the years passed, rushing by -
Gone in the blinking of an eye.

But you and I were always friends
Through teething, school and teenage trends.
Now, speaking as your proudest fan,
I introduce my son, the man.

Margaret Edwards

Just Try It

When you are feeling lonely, and don't know what to do,
Just have a glass of guineas, this will pull you through;
The loneliness will go, and you will feel on top,
Maybe go on drinking, because you just can't stop.

Friends will come and join, maybe strangers too,
Then when your money is all gone whatever will you do;
Smash your glass and bottle cause a hell of a fight,
Then along come police, to lock you up for night,

When morning comes you wonder how you got there,
And on being told, never again you swear,
your head, aches badly, your brain won't work,
Definitely, in future, yes guineas, you try to shirk.

M. Evans

86

Time's Fading Memories

The passing of time is a merciful blessing
as life's pages turn in an ever changing scene some looking back
Appear widely smoother in kind and taste.
Than if they had been today.
This negative of sorrow or joy
leaves a faded print on life material
and some entirely blotted out,
as if they never had been in my experiences.

If bang of sorrow there had been,
passing time dried fleire tears
If joy there was now mildly blind
for emotions cannot be stirred by memories of yesterday.

They lay asleep in there passed.
It is today I am awake,
I drink life
I fill my mind
These are fierce living fires
in my conscious of today.
for strident time effacer passing thoughts
in to forgetful bliss as new ones to live.

H. Dearlove

The Attic - The Place That Time Forgot

The attic brings to me bygone days.
Those hazy, crazy days.
Lost amidst the dust and shadows,
such happiness.

I love myself in memories of former bliss.
Entranced my fingers wander as I reminisce.
Over leather bound classics, tarnished by age,
And toys long forgotten
From my frolicsome days.

There stands the rocking hose,
after many a year.
Still grand and resplendent
A toy greatly revered.

I cast my eyes about the place
and a smile of descends upon my face.
A knowing smile of knowledge gained
that the child in me's still here today.

Ceasing to be in suspended time,
The place time forget,
adheres to my time.

Amanda Nwanosike

Myosotis

When eyes blue as for-get-me-nots
For-get-me-yet and know-me-not,
A vacant stare suspiciously questions
my motive, mind and mood

And thinks me more than somewhat rude
To claim a knowledge she would dispute
That I had toyed with forbidden fruit
Did I say I had? Not I! Not I!
To bring up things long since dead
Needs more than a knowledge of your bed...

You placed me way out beyond the pall
Of wearisome, and now have no recall
Of what I was or what I am
Forget me not eyes
Know me not lies

Have you known so many men?
Favoured in the savoured sanctum
You've forgotten me whose only crime
I refused you once...the second time...

Thomas D. Reynolds

To Die Without Dying

Old in age, wise in years,
Life for me holds no fears,
For I have learnt,
That death will come when it will come.

For be not told of my death,
Before my body is laid to rest,
A man should not die of age,
Before the body gives up the ghost.

To live man must grow, otherwise he will
stagnate,
To stagnate is to give up on life,
To give up on life is to die inside.

A. C. Gillie

Untitled

the way through the wood
to the point where we meet
is fraught with bluebells, and the
crushed songs of bird-high rustling leaves
that raise to brambles around the heart you keep
intact and lonely.

blind to the snares and heart-sharp thorns
I see the luscious fruits that lie without my grasp,
moved by long and tender sun-brown fingers;
fashioned by energy
and showered with morning light
the fruits, like my thoughts, fill and swell
only to fade and fall.

Light to dark.
Seed to earth.
My love seeks consolation.

Julia Elliott

Anger Within

Anger boils up within for injustice
Pain surges through those who are ill
Caution is born within us
Anxiety causes torment
For the brain that is never still
Heartbreak for those who are homeless
Through addiction, not sought
Picked up through years of hunger
Laced with violence and fear
Heads of State promises, put aside for political greed
Forgetting those who placed them there
Forsaking social needs
Real heroes are forgotten
Those who give their time and lives to others
We are dazzled with fantasy,
Stars with a talent for their own egos
We have all lost sight of human needs
Tolerance, misunderstanding, wanting to be liked
For loving is not easy, it has to be nurtured
Brought gently to those who need it most
Lets try and subside the anguish

Ellen O'Neill

Passion

Moonlit swirls, dark velvety sounds
Lover's thrills, warm hearts pound
Temperatures high, two bodies making love
Touching the sky, the essence of above
Skin touching skin, a passionate affair
Hearts caressed deep within, souls naked and bare
The need of embrace, held tight by a kiss
Emotions unfaced, love affairs missed
Nighttime encounters, yearnings too deep
Romance and devotion, a lover fought to keep
The depth of a dream, the love of a heart
The emotionless passion of hearts ripped apart...

Emma Charlton

Flying Like A Bird

Flying like a bird, flying over the moon.
It is astounding to be able to fly.
If I was a bird, I would fly into the sunset with my group of friends.
And our beautiful colours would match in with the sunset.
As the sun rises, the waves are calm, not many sea gulls are out.
Fish are at the surface, flipping about.
Flying over the moon, flying over the sun.
If I had my own fantasy world I would be a bird, and my friends
   would too.
A wonderful bluebird with a stunning tail.
We would soar into the air, flashing off our wonderful colours,
Nip down and say hello to the robins.
Flying over the moon.
As we soar through the air we would tell each other about our
Thoughts.
Flying over the moon.
It's nearly dinner time now, my Mum will be calling me in soon.
So fly, little bluebird, fly away home,
I don't want to leave you out here all alone.
Goodbye, little bluebird, I hope I'll see you soon.
Goodbye, goodbye, little bluebird, I'll see you soon.
Maybe to-morrow. Flying over the moon.

   Penny-Louise Bolton

Love In An English Garden

Across the shining river the hills still carry snow
The wind is blowing from the north, yet you would hardly know
That winter was still present, something you would not guess
When strolling warm and sheltered in the lovely grounds of Ness

Down in the peaceful valley spring flowers face the sun
Where can you match this blossom yet the year has scarce begun
Soon blackbird, yaffle, chaffinch each will their love profess
Love in an English garden, this Eden known as Ness

Known widely for its Excellence of shrub of flower of tree
The finest teaching garden in the country it must be
Not only birds & insects their suit with fervour press
But many a maid when courted here has also answered yes!

Love in an English garden! What better place than here
Where sea and marsh and mountain and colour at each
viewpoint appear
Where perfume form colour are perfect, nothing less
For love in an English garden the choice is surely Ness

   F. J. Camenisch

The Village Green Fair

That longed for days at last come round
   with the village green a gay fairground.
Coconut shies and hoopla stalls
   and another one for rolling balls.

Galloping horses on the roundabout
   the gayest sight there is no doubt.
Swinging boats flying so high
   almost touching the summer sky.

The shooting gallery with a row of duck
   boys and girls their candy floss suck.
Gaudy prizes tucked under arms
   others light-headed with magical charms

Empty purses all money spent
   everyone hurrying homeward bent.
Next morning at the break of day
   all is packed and on its way.

Passing by the village green
   the fairground might have never been,
Except for the chatter of the night before
   and a whole twelve months to wait for more.

   Kathleen M. Eastes

I Need To Know

When I am old and helpless I know I'll be a chore.
The little things which brought me pleasure I can do no more.
The ironing, the hoovering, the washing of the pots,
   the weeding in the garden and the care of tiny tots.
I know I'll be a burden. The indignities I'll hate.
I don't wish to be a problem but I can't control my fate.
I know I'll be a nuisance, a source of discontent,
I can only pray you know that this was not meant.
All I ask is... as you pass my door upon the stair,
please pop your head around it and let me know you're there.
I know you will not understand why I need the landing light.
My confusion is strange to me and fills me with fright.
Of this there is no question. I know that you all care.
But please pop in and speak to me

   I Need To Know You're There.

   Stan Kaiser

Memories Of Duke

The stable draughty and dark stands fossilized in time.
Vibrant echoes of the ancient walls have gone
And the Ploughman with his horse have passed beyond this life.
Yet, I stand here, 'midst mulled memories of childhood;
I see Spring heralded by lengthening light and greening grass
A time when Duke was harnessed to drag the plough.
I see the barren, weathered earth of winter past re-worked
And each furrow reluctantly, roll upside down,
Covered by flopping, screeching, gulls offering raucous thanks.

Harrows break the stubborn earth but no cortège as before.
Tilth prepared, the farmer fills his glistening seedlip,
Straps the leather laces across his woollen-shirted chest
And with hobnailed boots he imprints the dusty ground;
Marking the earth for overlapping seeds cast from flailing hands.
Duke is called again to drag spiked harrows, one more time.
I see the shiny seeds slipping into the shallow drills
Before the roller comes to fill the air with a cacophony of sound;
As the rusty metal rasps and stones play mingling tunes.

   S. J. Evans

Faraway

She was a faraway look in her eyes,
She doesn't want to hurt anymore.
She won't listen 'cause it'll make her cry.
She'd invite you in but she's closed the door.

She was a faraway look in her eyes,
She tires of playing the same game.
She won't stop 'cause she's getting on by.
She'd call a truce but it's not the same.

She has a faraway look in her eyes,
She needs to break out fly free.
She won't smile 'cause her humour's run dry
She'd confess to you but first she's gotta face me.

   Maria Janjua

Out Of The Cold

The wind did blow,
The chill did glow...

Being a leaf in life's wind is a terrible thing
Receiving from it its cold, empty sting.
Being caught in its rain is a miserable hell,
The clouds gathered thick, needing someone to tell.
And then the downpour, you feel the drains overflow
You sense the water gush, but there's nowhere to go.
Being hit by its lightning can be very confusing
There's so much at once, uncontrolled, overwhelming
The thunder you hear sometimes can sound so convincing
But listen more carefully to your own considering

Yet the sun shines again, hope in ascension
This, surely, must have final mention.

And it has
And it can.

   Keith Speed

88

Omega

All things must end
Not as they began, but rather
With hatred and unkindness and regrettable words.

All things must die
Not reincarnate, but rather
Corrupt and decaying and damned from their creation.

K. Cromwell

Escape To Freedom

Far from the teeming rivers of mankind,
Whose seething waters flood but soon decline,
Far from the brief-lived empires of the mind,
I seek forever that eternal shrine.

Where gently blows the sea-washed scented breeze
And graceful gulls forever dive and soar,
Where summer skies reach down to azure seas,
And limpid tides lap softly on the shore.

Here let me rest upon the golden sands,
Steeped in the sun-warmed bosom of the earth
Where God and Nature clasp eternal hands,
And drink the sparkling nectar of rebirth.

Here lie the tranquil seas of ageless peace,
Whose muted voices whisper timeless dreams,
Here, Time's unending motions never cease,
Replenished from life's deep immortal streams.

Derek Dodds

"It's Caught Me"! (Old Age) Heading Unknown

Sometimes I think I'm sight unseen,
Fading into the background
Feeling as small as a tiny dust mite.
Nobody knows I'm around.

I'm not here, I'm not there only a speck in the sun.
Floating away from a dust ridden pavement.
To a place, where a spider spun.
Time passes in a thickening haze hands fluttering in the air.
Wandering, wondering, swaying, unsteady.
Looking the worse for wear.

Morning, up in a cold and, shivering shake!
Then sinking in sheets so deep.
Faltering missing a step, yet onwards
Must not go back to sleep!
Living the hours, the minutes, the seconds

Always longing for night.
Making a stumble out to the day yet still living out of sight
Out of mind and body away in brain, but-sane.
Slowly walking like a zombie.
Never knowing why the pain!

Alice Porteous

Observing The Moon

I watched the moon clouds disappear
   and cloud across the sky
Partial shadow and fragmented light of darkness...
And saw the oceans of wandering wisps
Maintain their maddening hue
   after the storm

Blacker than the darkest night
   and chill the crisp cool air
Amongst the iridescent light -
I'll met by moonlight was the cry

Penumbra - shadow met with light
   and once again the moon appeared
      from behind its shelter from the storm...
The infant from behind the shade
The world was being born
   or was it?

Louisa Soto Williams

Just You

It doesn't cost you anything
To smile and say 'Hello'
To listen for a minute
To another's tale of woe.

Or perhaps they're feeling happy
And have no-one else to tell
Have you thought they might be lonely
Withdrawn in their shell?

Perhaps they'd like a helping hand
But are too proud to ask
You too, can get such happiness
From such a little task.

Try to see the good - not bad
In others that you meet
Spread a little happiness
The whole world's at your feet.

You wake up tired - it's cold, it's wet
And you are feeling blue
Say "Thank you God, another day
I'll do my best for you

A. M. Hoad

The Gift Of Healing

Feel the healing warmth within
When she touches you upon your skin.
Little hands that work with him,
Jesus guides this human being.
Whether she works near or far
You will feel her glowing power.

Close your eyes and see the colours
Glowing like the little flowers.
See the visions, misty or clear
When she's near they're very real.
Hands being guided to your pain,
Whether it's physical or in your brain.

Her smile is like a breath of fresh air,
With sparkling eyes that show they care.
This little person, so full of love
Working with the power sent from above.
Her company, Oh it's such a pleasure,
yes she is our own little treasure.
It's you Gladis.

Dawn Keeble

'Abuse'

She laid there wondering,
Wondering why she had to do what she was made to
Why was she so weak?
Why was she afraid?
But as she grew older
She realized,
That life is a game,
And she is the toy.
That everyone has been playing with.

Sukjinder Kaur

Feeling Blue

I wouldn't do that if I were you,
because in my heart you make me blue,
mum came in and said to you,
don't make my heart so blue,
when I woke up in the morning,
I stretched my arms and I was yawning,
to see the sun shinning through,
I just thought of you,
my whole world came together,
as I knew we would be friends for ever...

Jodie Jefferies

The World Is Crying

I am not blind
I just fail to see
Do I miss great pleasures surrounding me?

I am not deaf
I choose not to hear
For ignorance lets no chance turn to fear.

I feel not trapped
Just nowhere to go
Without Day's Routine I would fail to know.

I am not alone
Just sometimes lonely
Who, in this world, can claim to know me?

I feel not ill
Yet I am dying
A predictable end, and no denying.

I am not sad
The world is crying
The land on fire, the sea now sighing.

Michelle Pollard

Lament Of A Sea Gull

In a nest on a flat roof, there is really living proof
of nature's marvellous wonders to behold.
There are baby sea gulls there, whose loving parents care,
And one baby sea gull's story may be told.

"I'm a sea gull, I'm a twin, and what a state I'm in,
'Cos I'm out here in all weathers, and I've only baby feathers,
And the wind is blowing cold, and I'm not very old, and I'm fed up!
We sometimes practice flying, and it's not for want of trying,
That my tiny wings won't take me into flight.
'Though I flap and flutter madly, I know I'm doing badly.
I can't seem to get this flying business right. And I'm fed up!

With mum and dad on guard, life really seems quite hard.
They watch us every moment of the day.
At night, when we're asleep, their vigil still they keep.
'Til I'm grown up, I'll never get away, and I'm fed up!
It will be for the best, if one day I leave this nest,
To discover what life has in store for me—
To strike out on my own, to conquer the unknown.
And then, one day, to find my destiny. Who's fed up? Not me".

Catherine R. Gamble

"This 'Anthill' Earth"

This in the scheme of things
Now run by cabbages, once by Kings.
This majestic marvel that makes no sense
Except in terms of omnipotence.
This microscopic morsel of microcosmic dust
Which, if left to men would surely rust,
This miracle manifest in black and white,
Shapes and sounds and colours bright.
This gift of mystery and awe
Found on some eternal shore.
This in the scheme of things, with mankind
Might only be a moment in the Maker's mind.

Jack Lowe

Incident

He was propped up near the 'Gramby Head' wall
Leaning against a figure small,
Blood on his face, his eyes were closed,
A large black bruise on his face unfolds.
He'd met with it all in a recent fight.
But the Vicar didn't go into the 'wrong or right'
Unperturbed by the passing throng,
She cradled his head and stroked with care
His forehead broad as she tended there
The ambulance came and took him away
With some relief and my heartfelt prayer.

Alma Paget

That Cool Breezy Night

I clearly remember that cool breezy night.
The wonderful moment that I held you tight.
Looking deep into those sunset eyes
I was in love I couldn't deny.
You gave me that feeling so good and new.
That told me clearly that I loved you
I wanted to hold you and never part
When you softly reached out and touched my heart.
But the day went by and we carried on.
And I can't figure out where we went wrong
Though I can't help but wonder where you are now.
Or where our love went but we lost it somehow.
I sit here so lonely bitter and sad
Thinking about the love that we had
Cause life seems so hard without you here
We really had something I think that was clear.
I treasure the memories of our sweet past.
And greatly regret our love didn't last.

Naomi Weaver

Self Destruct

Across the frozen wastes of time
A trail of blood is left behind
A way of life for men to see
Come on and kill the world with me

The dream of power which shatters peace
And shows in every new made wreath
The flowers of love will die this way
There will be nothing left to say

And when the world is left behind
A burned out ruin of the time
That other worlds may see that day
Some where mankind has gone astray

Norman Stirrat

Rise Up And Walk

"Did you hear the command of Jesus.
To the cripple, on his bed?"
"Thy sins are forgiven", hallelujah!
Then, "Rise up and walk", Jesus said.

The past, by his death, is forgiven,
Saved by grace, hear his challenge today.
Rise up, in the strength God has given,
And walk in his footprints, always.

"Go, work in my vineyard" be active,
There's a task that is waiting for you.
Put your hand to the plough, look not backward,
Daily grace will the master renew.

Rise, and walk, lest you sink in depression,
Rise and walk, lest you drift helplessly.
The valiant in heart heed the message.
"Fold your bed, claim my help, follow me".

Walk in love, walk in truth, follow Jesus,
Whom we know, "went about doing good."
Idle not, short the time, 'tis your duty,
Rise and walk, in the name of the Lord.

Eileen M. Darke

Let Down

When I needed you, you were there
You wrapped me up with love and care
You made me free you gave me hope
You gave me strength you helped me cope
Then you clicked your fingers and everything changed
Suddenly my life rearranged
And through the worry and despair
I reached for you but you weren't there
The strength, the love, the hope, all gone
But through the tears I must carry on
I have to accept I am all alone
You turned your back I am on my own.

Veronica Wilson

Untitled

How quaint the word
How quiet the wood
Where once the feet of great men stood
Beneath the burning amber sky
A dark and brooding figure stands
Surveys the distant rolling lands
And asks himself the question, why?

How stark the sky
How stern the stare
Of that lone person standing there
A remnant of a bygone age,
When man and nature lived as one
With trees and beasts, the wind, the sun,
His mind and heart are filled with rage.

How quaint, how quiet, how stark, how stern
When will the white man ever learn?
Dianne Chapman

Hidden Depths!

Oh!, thou dark satanic river,
That I gaze upon with awe.
What evil lies beneath that calm exterior
That thy wicked soul doth hide -
Ravaged by forces unseen,
Silently ebbing and flowing
Condemning me as I stroll along in anger
My mood as dark and brooding,
As the clouds looking down in fury
Like drawn curtains across my face.
Ripples slowly widening as they calm a soul
Tormented by hate!
A breast beating wild with passion,
And emotions hitherto unknown....
Freda Ringrose

Lightning

Black Sky, reflects my mood
In purgatory, I wait, my soul scarred by hate,
For this world.

Stuck. Unable to move. Statue-like.
I hear the thunder in the distance.
An angry voice, calling to me.
Warning me to return from where I came.

Silence. At last.
I wait for the lightning to come and purify my soul,
Heat, I feel it all around me like fire.
Static.
Finally it comes, I see it.
My eyes are opened to the truth.
God, the universe and I are one.
A brilliant flame.
And then we are no more.
Charlotte McCarthy

Spring Gorse

Heralded by velvet scent,
flooding the mind, hurling back the years
to closeted warmth of childhood.

Around the corner, a blanket of
deep yellow, too rich for spring,
too musky, seducing the senses.

The need to trap, possess the scent,
the heady opium, the golden promise,
packed, crushed into a bottle tight.

It never worked. The flowers wilted
pale, diluted, the scent not captured,
the angry child, frustrated, cross.

Above the shore, they are at home these jewels,
their scent untrapped, their gift the key
free to unravel thoughts and memories long forgotten.
Ann M. Bate

The Docks

Grey skies cover your ceiling
and the factory men work no more,
the sound of the trollies the heavy weight
lorries have all left since they closed
the docks down.

The ships that you clean do not come
here and the bells that you ring are all
gone, the porter the packer the candlestick -
maker have all left since they closed
the docks down.

The wind blows the rubbish all over
and the rats have a wonderful time,
it breaks my poor heart for the years
that I've lost now that they've closed
the docks down.

They said we were losing money but so was
everyone else, we could have competed but
the government cheated now that they've
closed the docks down brothers! Now that
they've closed the docks down.
Brian Trengove

I Thought For The Future

When I die as all must die
Think of me kindly and please don't cry
Think of the good times, the joys we knew
I've just gone on, I'll wait for you,

In the warm summer sun and the soft gentle rain
There's a bright world up yonder where we will all meet again
Then I'll be there beside you
To comfort and guide you
When all receive pardon
Together forever
In God's beautiful garden -
Henry Thomas Tanner

The Purple Heather

A refreshing sight the heighlands; O it warms the heart my friend,
Crianlarich tae, fort William, its beauty ne'er will end.
Mony's the time I've trevelled through sun an' winter snow;
An' aye dae I get a shiver when I come upon Glen Coe.

The Buachaille bids ye welcome an' guides the way ahead.
The Rannoch ken's its limits, your load it gladly sheds.
If the Sisters tak' yer fancy, think lang which ane tae court;
Mony a man's set out tae tame, an' mony a man's been hurt.

The Ridge is easy come an' go, and time is his great friend.
But the Eagle's seen men lose their stride, an' time for them did end.
The Pap is God's own marker; a farewell bid tae thee,
But ne'er forget the mighty Coe an' a' her history.

The fort awaits the weary man, ay William waits ahead;
Sweet village o' refreshment on blue Loch Linnhe's head.
Bide a while an' catch yer breath, tak' in the fine surroundings;
Enjoy the ale, the warm log hearth, an' a' the evening brings.

When the sun has kissed the Nevis, tak' yer stick an' say yer cheers
An' look t'wards Mallaig harbour, wi' the Skye Boat Song in yer ears.

The days an' nights will nag ye in the city through a' weather,
Until the day yer heart runs free, at first sight o' heighland heather.
Neil S. Findlay

In My Garden

There's lots of bees buzzing round my trees,
There's ants and they bite the plants.
A butterfly goes flying by.
There is a mouse in my Wendy house,
There's a bat flying past my cat,
My dog put a bone under a stone.
I kick my ball up the wall,
And we're having fun playing in the sun.
Laura Drain

Saturday Again

Bleary-eyed but wide awake,
it must be Saturday again.
The radio waves break the silence,
a bowl of porridge to keep out the cold.
Through the damp window I can see the fog,
creeping around like a lost relative.

My tennis partner is five minutes late,
but we know the courts will be deserted.
Isn't it strange how our lives revolve around events?
Dreaming, walking, eating, loving, working, playing.

It's so cold that our breath escapes like smoke.
Checking our footing, we adjust the net.
We really should buy some new tennis balls.
The only sounds are wayward golf shots and
the wonderful songs of passing birds.

After three sets we check the time.
Our chores for the day have been decided.
At home, the family stirs into a semblance of life.
Already I'm dreaming of next Saturday morning.

Robert Simpson

In The Garden

Are these creatures friends or foes?
I know the green fly loves the rose.
A slow worm glides among the peas,
Larvae of beetles kill the trees.
Rosy worms and grey ones too,
Come to the surface in the dew.
Robins relieve the ground of grubs,
Slugs hide among the foliage in tubs.
Wood pigeons decimate cabbage leaves,
House martins attack insects from the eaves.
Are they all due their spot on earth,
Or should mankind recognize their worth?

S. N. Rose

Just Before Dawn

In the darkest hour, just before the dawn,
When dreams are shattered, hearts are torn,
And weary, from the lack of sleep,
Think of promises, we will never keep.

Those hurtful words, were never meant,
Why must we let our anger vent?
In a perfect world, this would never be,
Hurting each other, needlessly.

As each hour drags by, sleep is still denied,
Then the break of day, lights the dark night skies.
Bird-song fills the air, the cheery sweet sound,
That brightens up the world around.

So rise with the sun, it's a brand new day,
Let each sunbeam chase the blues away.
Be as cheerful as the birds, that sing each morn,
'Till the next dark hour,...just before the dawn.

Christine E. Smith

The View From The Cliff

The ferocious roar of the angry sea,
The voice of the wind cries out in vain,
The face of the moon looks down to see
The silent mist rolling in again.

An eerie cry that turns me pale,
Excited voices start to shout,
A bright red stain round a dying whale,
The sound of a boat as it turns about.

The ferocious roar of the angry sea,
The voice of the wind calls out a name,
The view from the cliff is sickening me,
The moon is hiding his face in shame.

M. H. Carver

The Destiny

It was a soft and tender flower,
blooming in its own soil.
A whirlwind came
and lifted it from its roots.
The tender flimsy petals
struck an iron rod.
The rod clasped it in its embrace.
It hugged, kissed and
created a bondage of love.
The flower once again showed its radiance.
But alas! When autumn came,
the flower gradually withered.
The iron rod stood around
and watched it wither
though it wouldn't bend
it got rusted from within
and the stooping flower served it still,
looked upon it for tender care.
But it didn't budge,
making the meaningful scent of love meaningless...

Sarla Markandya

Christmas Verse

Little children singing carols,
Around the Christmas tree.
Their little smiling faces
Are a treat to see,
Bringing joy and happiness to you and me
On this joyful Christmas day.

Opening all their presents,
Books, games and toys.
Pulling the crackers, and
Making lots of noise.
Lovely things to eat,
For lucky girls and boys,
On this happy Christmas day.

When this happy joyful
Christmas day is done,
The time to say goodnight
Godbless has come.
Tired out from all their
Happiness and fun,
They climb the stairs to dreamland.

Vera McNamara

"War And Peace"

What's happening to this beautiful old world
With people fighting everywhere.
Men in uniform with flags unfurled,
March to war, they don't care.

People dying, children crying,
For everywhere the word is kill, kill, kill.
And all around the bodies are lying,
The graves of the innocent are massed on the hill.

The faces of evil, the faces of pity,
The young, the old, all must die.
Murder and destruction in every city,
Tortured bodies in heaps do lie.

Someday, I hope the sun will shine bright,
The fields will be green, instead of red.
People will love, and not have to fight.
And no starvation, all will be fed.

So let's all pray for this beautiful old world,
For love and kindness everywhere.
The banners of wisdom will be unfurled,
The people want peace, they do care.

John Y. Simms

Patch Work

A patchwork of houses,
A patchwork of daisies,
Piecing together
The pieces to fit an exact pattern.

From the air,
Or looking down from the top of a hill,
The roofs of the village
Jig-sawed together,
Small gardens between.
Sleepily sloping, following the slope of the hill,
The grey of the tiles, the grey of the sky.
A patchwork of clouds, shapes developed at random
Oppose the formality of the shapes of the roof tops.

Under the slates,
A patchwork of life
Following the pattern, a patchwork of years,
Birth, death, and the space between.
Pat Donoghue

In One's Own Image

In one's mums and dads one has no choice,
Nor in colour, creed nor speaking voice.
It's a pure gamble at one's birth where one's born upon this earth.
It may be in a palace grand or within a nomad band;
With silver spoon in country seat or wattle hut in scorching heat.

If born in a mansion, thank God for your lot
But don't go through life not caring a jot
For those born more lowly, of more humble stocks
Who travel through life overburdened with knocks.
If born in mud hut or cottage or stall
Grow up to be proud, grow up to be tall.
Don't envy the fellow who lives on the hill
Try hard to achieve and you also will.

In each tribe and each nation, each village and street,
Show respect for each other and love those you meet.
If we believe in one God, whatever he's called,
And if born in His image, He must be appalled,
At our relations with others and this cleansing nonsense, or even
perhaps when we sit on the fence.
South Africa now can amends make,
but Ireland, oh Ireland, how long will it take?
Charles Thompson

Creation

From love or lust
copulation to creation
girls or boys, we may have joys

Infants so small
lost sleep and all
they soon learn the call
crying and sighing
your attention they call
changed and fed, some wind ahead

In no time at all
you'll be up the wall
they'll roll and crawl
explore and discover, and so will mother
walks and falls, knocks and bruises
the improvers

A babe in arms
the cooing sounds
talking squawking
what lovely sounds
my love my bond, my family strong
William James Evans

Wake Up, Shake Up

My alarm goes off at seven o'clock,
I leap out of bed in a state of shock;
My heart is racing, my head is spinning,
Objects around me seem to be grinning.

The first thing I grab is my brush off my table,
Then run to the bathroom, by then I'm more stable,
I turn on the shower and brush through my hair,
If I'm in for too long, my dad shouts through Claire!

Back in my room I rush with my shirt,
To do up my buttons and zip up my skirt;
I throw on my jumper and do up my tie,
Sit down on my bed and heave a big sigh.

I race down the stairs to get something to eat,
I have a quick drink and feel rushed off my feet;
Then I'm out of the house and off on my way,
With the strangest feeling that it's Saturday...
C. Ferguson

New Year's Revolution

Now is the time for all good cheer
I don't feel like jumping from Southend Pier.
Grahame's won the lottery and is not a grouse
For he has gone and bought this house.

The staff are all working for him now
Even the one that's a silly cow.
Advance Housing and Support is no more
It Kings Enterprises and clean that floor.

We're still running out of semi skimmed milk
Toilet rolls, washer powder and that ilk.
When Grahame's in charge all will be well
Or everyone will see the schizophrenic from hell.

Happy new year and don't drink to much
No grabbing a man by the crutch.
1996 will fine and dandy
As long as there's still some money handy.
Grahame King

Dat

The fireplace burns alone tonight
The rug in front sits untouched
And the only whistling to be heard
is the sound of the birds in the trees.

There'll be no more shouting just to be heard
No more laughing to be shared
Just an emptiness
Both here in front of the fireplace
and here in my heart.
Jaime Evans

Graffiti

Neon words glow on decaying brick,
luminous letters marking territory defended with blades,
Gangland.
A valley of wire fences and burnt cars,
It's theirs, their own, no-one messes with them,
They sign their patch with pride.
An art of its own,
Concealing hidden meanings,
signs decipherable only to the chosen few,
They belong, an instant family governed by fear,
more discipline than at home,
And their anger grows,
their hate flourishes.

An innocent lamb who hasn't tasted their pain,
he'll pay.
An headmaster, the shepherd,
he'll pay.

And the neon letters drip with blood,
concealing the signature beneath.
Caryl Lewis

My Tail Of A Witch

It's time the black witch on my tail flew away,
She's ridden, I'm sure, since the start of my days.

She screams with delight at my run of bad luck.
She cries like a child when I pick myself up.

She's wild and abandoned and scares me to death.
I take a step forward and she grabs at my neck.

She's nasty and vicious with hate in her soul.
My destruction and contrition were always her goal.

Step forward, two steps back, I've followed this track.
I can't follow it again but she shouts at my back.

In circles you'll go for my weight will upset thee.
I'll slow you and blind you so you'll cry out for mercy."

Tormentors, accusers, stand up and be counted.
The witch on my tail is your friend, my denouncer.

She stands by your side through thick and through thin.
She opens the gates and so lets you all in.

I look to my maker, and perfect self beside me,
Please guide and protect me and this I beseech thee.

Let the black witch who rides on my tail go away.
She's been there I'm sure since the start of my days.

Gillian Chubb

My Friend

"Don't leave the lassie standing at the door son. Bring her in!"
"She won't come in Mum - she's shy!"
Bottom resting on kerb of tiled fireplace - elbows on knees -
chin on hands -
I listened... "Bairn - go and get the lassie and bring her in!"
Silently I rose, sauntered down the dark lobby, too small to
reach the light switch,
and, standing on the landing looking tall to me, I was only nine,
you see, was someone whom I knew at once was going to
always be... my friend!
I proffered a hand which she took and she came in.
I'm glad to say she married him and, day after day, took care of me.
Whenever she was there I'd be with child-like faith confident that
perpetually everlastingly she would be always be... my friend!
I was eleven and in a church watching a funeral people crying,
shouting in grief, where just two years before, a wedding took
place and everyone wore a smiling face, I was slowly losing
my child-like belief!
A baby boy was left behind. I could only consider God unkind
to have taken away from he and me my treasured good as gold
only twenty-six years old, one who now could only be
spiritually eternally my friend!

Mhairi Jarvis Brown

Words

Tell me not that all is lost
when thou knowest otherwise,
For does a heart not show its all
with words spoken through the eyes?
And is this life of such great beauty
not there for all to share?
Imagine, dear friend, what enlightenment
if we would but only dare.
So many worlds entwined in one,
each life to choose anew.
Yet hearts and minds stand still it seems
for all but a chosen few.
From whence these words come unto me
shall ever I be sure;
Perceiving all and knowing nothing;
so much and yet no more.
But still, dear friend, should life be easy,
then nothing would I feel,
And all that is and all that was
could never then be real.

Janet Desmares

Proserpina Ascendant

Alas! The dreaded time has come again.
I, Proserpine, must leave my realm and King,
Rise upwards where the mournful Ceres waits
To welcome back her daughter and the Spring.

But I am loathe to leave my kindly shade,
To suffer, mounting, surging powers of might,
To struggle through unyielding, frozen earth
Into a glaring world of blatant light.

I tire of this, my fated yearly doom,
The flowers that spring no matter where I tread,
The teeming leaves which burst their sealing bonds,
The ceaseless scream of birds about my head.

I long for golden ripening of the corn,
The gathering of sun-warmed, luscious fruits,
For then, my work is done, I can return
Here, to my treasured realm of peaceful roots.

The Underworld of Shade where I am Queen.
But now the Task awaits. I dare not stay.
Beloved home of shadows and of peace
Adieu! The time has come. I must away.

Geraldine Squires

Gone

Today my dreams have ended, today it's finally done.
I didn't really believe it, till you'd really gone.
How can I carry on, go out and face the world?
My mind's an empty space, my body bent and curled.
While all around the people smile
And laugh and live and love and cry.
I can't do that now. I wonder why?
I didn't think you meant so much, just thought you were a friend.
Now I know I miss you, the pain won't ever end.
I wish I could go with you, but that can never be.
You've got your own life and you'll never be with me.
You never knew how I felt, you never knew my pain.
Even though my heart is broken. I'd suffer it again.

L. Cotton

Rock Rock

Rock rock the cradle or the grave
Such joy heralds new life
Such hopes and expectations.

Rock rock the stretched hand to eternity
The young mother cradles the new life
Hers already in its prime.

Rock rock the old lady stares ahead
Why is this the never ending end
Oh! time so fleeting.....

Rock Rock 'tis the beginning and the end.

A. Scallan

A Dog's Life

I am a little yorkie, my coat is black and tan
And I am very happy with the way I am.
I have no problem with my weight, I never have to diet
They say I make a lot of noise, but really I am very quiet
We often have a game or two, before we start the day
Then my mistress says to me, it's time to put your toys away
Sometimes she gives me quite a smack,
Right across my bottom, just because I stand and yap
You see the dog next door, sits right up against the wall
And I know she's sitting there, although I'm only small
Sometimes I try to get to her, but I know that we would fight
For we met outside the house one day, and she gave me quite a fright
Cause she's thrice as big as me, and she pinned me to the ground
I don't like her very much, for she's quiet, and creeps around
Perhaps one day we will be friends, and learn to trust each other
But I'm afraid until that day, I'll have to run for cover

A. H. Shepherd

The Great Black Bird

There is a great black bird who lives near by,
At dusk I hear its pitiful cry.
A shriek that jars my very bones;
Not an angry cry nor a wistful moan.
And I'm sure its wail could wake the dead
But I don't have the courage to get out of bed.
Still I long to look and catch its eye,
And learn the reason for its mournful cry.
To touch its cold heart and ease the pain
And free the spirit to sing again.

As night falls so silent, this great black bird,
From deep within lets its soul be heard.
It splits the night with a wraithlike sound
That shatters the air from clouds to ground.
With every breath of life, 'til final gasp,
An unearthly scream that could be its last.
Oh tell me great black bird, what tragedy,
Has chained your heart to never be free?
So that thy fear can at last take flight,
And restore the peace to your great black night.

Adrian Harris

Some Golden Days

Many people dread, the thought of growing old,
It's an attitude of mind, at least that's what we're told,
We have the best of both worlds, as for as I can see,
Simply close our eyes, and travel where we'd like to be.

If we feel nostalgic, we can go back to our past,
We've had many happy days and we can make them last,
Bring them out of hiding, relive them now and then,
Once more enjoy their pleasure, then tuck them back again.

Time out with the children, to where we had most fun,
Watch them at their happiest, playing in the sun,
Lie on sun kissed beaches, enjoy the golden sands,
Glory in these moments, as time slips through our hands.

Not a day is wasted, that we must leave behind,
We can always find them, in the recess of our mind,
It only takes a moment, to travel many miles,
Back into a past, of laughter joy and smile.

No need for always looking back, we must look forward too,
Find new places we can go, and different things to do,
Go back to the future, make now memories to unfold,
Then you'll find as in the past, some days will be pure gold.

Helen Simm

Valediction

Farewell, my friend, knowing you has been brief
And as you leave, to turn that autumn leaf,
I wish you well, in whate'er you choose to do.
Where'er you may go, I hope your dreams come true.
I say most surely as you leave me now to go,
That you have truly been a joy to know.
So short and sweet has been this interlude,
Remembering you will rekindle a cheerful mood.
When my mind is a torment, and a trial,
Recalling your personality will make me smile.
Perchance your going now will make me weep,
But memories will return, to sow, and I shall reap
Your encouragement of indeterminable length;
To be happy in heart and soul, with borrowed strength.

Jennifer Wright

"The Heavenly Path"

You chose to let go of our comforting arms,
You chose to approach the sound of the Psalms,
No need to look back we are still here,
Your support and comfort for many a year.
But now you must go the last steps alone,
For the angels are waiting to take you home.

Eve Young

My Dad

My dad is a man who is gentle and kind.
A man who loves me so.
A man who helped to shape my life.
Guide me through bad times and give me advice.

I love my dad
He is so great
And so this poem
To him I dedicate.

Linda Miller

God's Last Laugh

Watching the clock
craving for the day it stops,
it ticks onward to its end, dripping the seconds down,
too late for sorrow, close enough for fear.

And God will have the last laugh.

Is this the moment you waited for
made us pray for?
The audience awaits with malice intent.

And God will laugh last.

You hear the doors closing.
I saw the light fading
gratefully I let you go.
I heard you say - remember
I screamed inside - forget

And God laughed last.

J. Geraghty

The Kingfisher

I search for the stream of beginnings, the river of summer.
To hurl myself, a leper, into its painfully cold clarity
To half drown in its truths
To have it surround me, to breathe it into me
So deeply, to fill my lungs to bursting point.
And if I should die of its cures
Then that is better than to live with our sickness...

Flashing, like a kingfisher diving
Through the rays of the sun between the trees.
Naked and charged, primal
Then, paddling like a child, wordless innocence.
And then, splash and holler for all my soul's worth.
Full of my own pure existence
In the stream of beginnings, no resistance to the waters...

And when all my years of pent up feelings are discharged
I shall sit beside it and realize, all that has passed.
Digest and integrate it into myself
Breath again my first breath, open again my first eyes
Show again my first face, feel the pureness from the inside out
My evolution towards pure light complete.

Nigel D. Potter

A New Mother's Contemplation
On Her First Born Child

What are these thoughts that rise in me
   In turmoil in my brain?
My mother lost when I was born,
   But now comes life again!
My life itself was dearly bought.
   The price - a mother's blessing.
Make me worthy of it Lord,
   A life of Grace caressing.
New life comes and new found hope,
   Another generation.
May I give of all I missed
   And rejoice in the sensation.
Thou art with me kindly soul,
   Though you gave your substance in my making
Let your spirit through me guide
   This new life of Grace awaking.

Desmond G. McMahon

Love Abandoned

Empty? Is that how I feel?
Yet there must be something to hurt this much.
Alone?
Indeed, but so many offer kind thoughts and love.
Do I feel scorned?
That cannot be,
After all, I know he loves me as much as I love he.

Worthless? Is that how I feel?
It seems the very meaning of life now has no meaning.
Crushed?
Indeed, my will and strength have lost their objective.
Do I feel futility?
There is some sense in that,
Like a daffodil that blooms only to weep.

Courageous? Is that how I feel?
Only if courage can return my heart.
Hopeful?
Dare I be?
To ever hold him in my arms again.

Linda King

Fear

The most dominant factor in the world today.
Fear of the dark, and fear in the day.
Burst pipes in winter, and thunder in summer.
Fear of Road Rage, but more of old age.
Fear to go out, but dread to stay in,
Fear of flying, but worse of dying.
Fear to grow fat, yet hate to be thin,
What shall we eat, there's fear of all food.
Don't eat it say they, it will do you no good.
But if we would read it, the Good Book says,
Fear Me and then, you will, have nothing else to fear.

E. Pursglove

Untitled

Ice bound slopes with peaks of snow,
Gentle streams begin to flow,
Gathering pace in springtime heat
Till river lets their pathways greet.
Touching, searching, channels new,
Washing, reaching pathways through.
Finding ways past bold rocks groaning,
Grumbling torrents bursting, moaning.
Rock sentries tall, guard plunging waters,
Lap and kiss high peaks, small daughters.
Now the river's on its way
With glee past tree the waters play.
Through night, through day, the river drives
Determined, forceful it arrives,
Carrying with it silt and soil,
Escarpment drops, the waters fall.
Orchestrating nature's sound,
With life these waters now abound.

E. Feingold

Seasons Of Love

Love is like the seasons
That changes with the time
It blossoms like the flowers in spring
Its beauty so sublime
It blooms like flowers in summer
As warmth comes shining through
It sheds all lonely thoughts and fears
As autumn leaves are few
It sparkles like the winter snow
So soft so white and pure
The years go by the seasons change
But one thing we are sure
That like the seasons our love will change
We'll have our smiles and tears
But with God's help our love will last
To share seasons for many years.

Christine Sinclair

'The Master Key'

A key to a puzzle may solve it,
unlocking the door of the mind
The key to a city brings honour
fame and fortune are not far behind.

Many keys are suited for various tasks
yet, one outshines all the rest
being the Key to the Kingdom of heaven
It's the one I would like to have best

I am not academically brilliant
I have no attributes to fame
as for wealth, it seems to avoid me
and only friends have heard of my name

I have one great consolation
whatever life holds for me here
If I strengthen my faith and live honestly
the key for the Kingdom is near.

Patricia Ashby

Human Evil

Dunblane was in mourning and flowing with tears,
That terrible taking of innocent dears,
For a devilish monster was free on that day,
To prey on young children at laughter and play,
What God made that monster?
Who gave him his birth?
Who fashioned his thinking?
Who brought him to Earth?
Was Satan his maker?
From Hell perhaps sent.
Spewed out of Hades with evil intent.
Faith trust and promise have crumbled apart,
There's ache in the stomach, there's pain in the heart.
But quell all your anger, and let your tears run,
No one can now hurt them, together they're one.
Their love is inside you from now till you die,
Be strong for those children, look up at the sky,
You'll see them all playing in warm summer sun,
Forever as children, in laughter and fun.

S. J. Jones

Join The Army!

War is glorious, war is great,
Get rid of your anger, get rid of your hate.
Join up and fight and do your bit,
You'll come out of it fighting fit.
Say bye to your family, but bring your friends,
Be in with the fashion, keep up with the trends.
Fight for your country, fight for what's right,
It's not at all likely that you'll loose your sight.
There's just as much risk from dying in your home,
As there is standing in a battle field, all alone.
In years to come, when war is done,
You can tell the rest, how we did our best.
You can tell your son how you fought and won.
Join up today, why delay?
War is glorious, war is great,
Don't sit and let others decide the country's fate.

Caroline Moyser

Untitled

Mid joy and tears we go through
life which holds for us much strife,
On we travel through thick and thin
Sometimes out sunshine brightens
    for days on end.
Helping us our lives to mend,
Then comes the storms out of the blue
Making life tough again for me and you.
But we're conquered before, and we will again
Seeing out sunshine wipe out life's rain.

S. V. Cooper

The Learning Process

I once was filled with information
And black was black and white was white.
For I was crammed with education
And I was sure that I was right.

I lived and learned that there could be
Some grey in black and tan in white
And everything that seemed to be
Was really not all wrong nor right.

But finally, time has made the cure.
The change was very slow.
The only thing of which I'm sure
Is all that I don't know.

Jean Bonjour

Party Love

You came from nowhere into my life
I didn't know you but you soon caused me strife.
One night at the disco you asked me to dance
I had things on my mind but not a romance.

We danced really close our arms round each other
I thought I loved you but I shouldn't have bothered.
When the song ended you seemed so sad
You kissed me and thanked me I was so glad.

We danced so many times our bodies entwined
"Together forever" was the phrase on my mind.
Even my friends said "You looked so good"
I really loved you I thought you understood.

At the end of the evening I left for home
But you said nothing and I left all alone.
From that night onwards you've ignored me
It now seems so obvious we weren't meant to be.

I don't understand why you led me on
And now you won't talk to me but I did nothing wrong.
Two years have passed we're talking once more
The past is a memory locked up behind a door.

Laura Hayes

Memories

As I sit beside the sea.
I think of things that are to me.
The joy, of love of family
My children so gloom up grains.
Their little babes safe in their hands.
I sit and dream of yesteryear.
And what it means to park with things so dear.
But life must stay as we grow old.
And cherish, those memories like gold.

J. M. Hayward

Roses In Heaven

This could be the hardest poem I'll ever have to write
Because I don't really understand
But I hope one day I might
When you moved to another place
In my heart you left a space
Now I'm left on thinking why?
Perhaps I don't feel I've said goodbye!
I know you're with our granddad
Whilst you're happy the close ones are feeling sad
I feel guilty for not knowing you better
Took you for granted that you'd be around forever
I'll carry others memories in my heart
I know for certain they'll never part
But if I can't believe in what you believed
If I can't do what you do
When my time comes will I still follow you?
If I could just know the answer
I'm sure to be relieved.

Sian Wynters

Looking Out

Days of gold and green
Running, running through fields of dream,
free, jumping the hedge to the leafy lane way,
Alone, unafraid, a happy child,
Reflected in a clear stream - myself
Carpets, luxury suites, dusty heat, videos
CD's, TV's games a hundred ways
to pass the time indoors,
A book the only escape.
A comfy cage,
There sits my grandchild
afraid to venture - looking out.

Jean Reynolds

Broken Dreams

A young girl looking out beyond,
Her dreams all written in the sky,
Her great ambition to fulfil,
she will really try.
Swotting studying dawn till dusk,
Going to college is a must,
Then from beyond a young man appeared,
Her heart beat so fast
Her eyes filled with tears.
The feelings she felt have now changed her plans,
For now all she dreams of is a wedding band.

So happy and content she will now wed,
No college will she now tread.
Her dreams are for looking
after her husband and family instead.

Maureen Jean Cogar

Opting Out

Let's fly until our wings fall, broken from our bodies.
Fly away from all the false wonders and little games that life throws
At our "expected to be" Selves.
Fly, and join the band that make melody of the universe,
That play a war like song and lead false warriors to their deaths
And so called cowards to avarice.

Life is simply a school that we enrolled ourselves in,
To play our parts as the earth's little elves
So shall we make our flight traject us beyond the stars,
Then into and beyond ourselves.

There are no fears, no tears.
No hate, no ghosts.
Simply the sensation and thrill of existence.
No memories of our once loathed and sad life
So lets slip away and fly and let the games pass us by.

Stephen G. Oakley

Blessings

I have seen the sea caress the sky
The leafy trees, with arms held high
Giving their praise to the "Maker of Things"
Whilst the song of the birds - 'Mid the flutter of wings'-
Made me offer a silent prayer for sight.
The joys to see - to hear - to touch
Are blessings we accept - do not think of much -
Yet without these gifts, we are but half alive
The zest for living is dimmed - yet we survive,
To laugh with others in joy
To be sad with them in sorrow -
To hope when life grows cold -
There may be a happier morrow -
These are among God's finest gifts
Far greater than wealth or gain -
For with His love and our faith in Him
We are so rich
And we are walking in sunshine not rain -

I. M. Burton

The Cross

When we look thoughtfully at the Cross,
is it only a piece of wood,
Does it maybe mean more and remind us
what Jesus did was good.

A man completely without sin was put to death for us all,
Why do we hesitate to answer when we hear the Lord's call.

Take a moment and just try to imagine
the pain and suffering he went through,
Thorns on his head, nails through his hands and feet,
he endured all this for you.

Those of you out there who love him
will like me just want to cry,
This man gave up his life for us, he went to the Cross to die.

What gives us real joy is that he rose again forever to reign,
Let us always rejoice when we mention his wonderful name.

Jesus is only a prayer away from you today,
Surrender your life to him and forever with you
he promises to stay.

The Father loved us all so much that he sent for us his only son,
So remember the Victory on the cross that Jesus won.

Alistair Michie

Heart To Heart

Bracken and fern beneath his feet,
Gun is charged his prey to seek,
Unto his lair the hunter prone
Rifle eating against his bone.
Air so still - but summer hot
Blood soon to spill with a single shot,
His eye is fixed against his sight,
Knuckles bulge with grip so tight,
Then, into view, his trophy stood -
Darkened in colour, with antlered hood -
Face of beauty, but beauty sought
In a centuries old, bloodthirsty sport.
It lifts its head and their eyes do meet -
Like strangers across a silent street.
Beads of sweat run down his face
A crack of a shot! His heart does race.
Beast is silent and grass turns red,
Hunter triumphant with antlered head.
No guilt ridden expression (or remorse)
As carcass is dragged through the gorse.

Sean Boyle

The Treadmill Mouse

Arrogant man, what have you done?
Built a treadmill, and shut out the sun,
And now you run in your own great wheel,
Your frantic pace, a panic reveals,
There is no escape for the treadmill mouse,
As he runs, and runs, in his narrow house.

And man is caught in a web of his own,
He made it with skill and care,
His lines of thought, were clad with power,
And he is a prisoner there,
Akin to the mouse in his spinning wheel,
He goes, he knows not where.

The days, the months, the years go round,
And we are prisoners tightly bound,
By the rules we must follow to play the game,
That turns the wheel around,
Till time ordained has passed away,
Then freedom and joy will leap, like a flame,
From the mocking limits of life's grey game,
There will dawn a bright new day.

G. A. Gilfillan

Contemplative Listening

A space, a holy place; a hearth, a confession room.
Logs burning, green engulfed in yellow, blue and red.
Silence falls, whispering flames kiss and blush, and fade away.

Anyone listening? - soft womb walls.
Peaceful breathing - life-giving fluid.
Body resting - floating listless.
Anyone listening? - umbilical cord as yet uncut.

Silence embracing, smoke, grey not black!
Damp wood lyrics; hissing lullaby, warm, secure.

What did I do today? Will anyone believe me?
How did I feel today? Will anyone reject me?
Where were my thoughts today? Will anyone betray me?

'Where two or three are gathered in my name, there am I.'
Thoughts unfolding, nerves unwinding dreams unravelling.
Here I am! This is me! Help me to understand myself.

A space, a holy place; a hearth, a confession room.
Embers dying, absolution given without reserve.
Silence falls; acceptance is assured.

Let us pray! For darkness falls, and God awaits.

Philip N. Forker

Love

What is the meaning of this word,
That sends a shudder, when spoke or heard.
This word that makes us laugh and cry
The love we lose when people die.
It's all about caring and feeling for others.
Needing and wanting the loving from others.
Look at the stars so high in the sky,
The love that we have could not flash us by.
Aim for the highest and never give up.
And when you've found love don't ever slip up.

Melanie Louise Wilson

Nightmares

I hear her cry out at night,
She cries out in amongst pain and fright.
Her pillow and face stained with tears,
Her heart and mind filled with fears.
Her dreams are like those she had in the past,
But like the one tonight they never last.

It frightens me to know what's in her mind,
Why can't she leave the past behind?
Once again her eyes close,
From a familiar nightmare she already knows.

Natalie Wade

Untitled

The stars I see,
Are the people closest to me.
All and everyone glistens,
The life they once held shines out to me.
Every star was once a life's soul,
And every new-born has a soul of a dead star.
I know that life doesn't go on forever
Life makes us grieve for our loved ones.
Through the day they're dead,
But at night, when I look up at the sky...
Three stars shine out to me
And they become alive.
I know that their bodies have only died,
And their souls are still strongly alive
Deeply embedded in my heart.
When I can no longer see the stars
I will then know that their souls have been reborn,
Another one like them is reincarnated.
If only I knew the newly born
Then my life would be truly complete.

Kerry Goodman

The Evening Years

The Spring of youth has disappeared, evaporated in the years of time.
Lost innocence returns no more: We are not what we were before
transgression. Our inmost thoughts look back and ponder —
What are the things for which we yearn and pine?
Wounds of the soul, though healed, will ache;
The reddening scars remain and make confession.
Were things more lovely then, when we were young?
Were we more blessed because our strength endured?
Or were conceit and pride our hobby horse.
Thinking that what we thought was always best.
Come back to now; in these declining years
The light has dawned — we have matured.
Daily, nay hourly, we approach nearer and nearer to our
eternal rest.
But we are not alone: His presence is always near. He is our
peace of mind.
No need to hurry now but make our pace and meet each day
whate'er it brings.
The nights are sometimes restless, but even they, though
dark, are not unkind:
For in quietness it is a waiting time; we hear the flurry of
angels' wings.

Doreen Barwell

Homeless At Christmas

Christmas is coming, everyone is shopping.
Price tills are ticking, never stopping.
Homeless roaming, always begging.
Big bold turkeys in the oven.
Homeless not knowing from where the next meal's coming.

Christmas is coming; presents please.
Fill my stockings to the knees.
Chocolates and toffees all to eat.
Homeless are out and nowhere to sleep.
But out in the cold, their beds on the street.

Christmas night's upon us, all the shopping done.
The house is full of laughter and fun.
The children all waiting for Santa to come.
While for the homeless there isn't one.
No presents to open, no turkey to eat.
And for the homeless no Santa to meet.

So when you are eating your turkey,
Just think of one thing:
You are not homeless,
And you have everything.

Racheal Commons

Remember?

Try to remember if you can, the strident call of the muffin man.
Loud and harsh would sound his voice, "Who will buy my
muffins choice?"
Where is the milkman with his churn, who ladled milk into
your urn?
Where's the man with the turning stone, who all your kitchen
knives would hone?
Who would clear your junk for free, the rag and bone man -
it was he.
Where is the coalman with his sack of heavy coals upon his back?
Where is now the chimney sweep, who'd bring the soot down
in a heap?
Where too is the firewood man, his bundles drawn by horse
and van?
Where the days when horse and cart of life were once so great
a part?
Where's the bobby on the beat, who kept an eye on every street?
Why is the man no longer there, who'd sit and mend your
wicker chair?
No longer are such men at large, who never made a 'A call out
charge'.
Where are then all these men of yore, who brought a service
to your door?
Could it be they're still a'bed, or sadly all long gone, and dead?

Reginald G. Allen

Hope

Smile along life's highway,
Roam slowly down a by-way
Observing nature as you go along.
Be cheerful as you wander on.

Throughout days, months and years
Others have worries, doubts and fears,
An encouraging word to a passer-by
Will help them withhold that inept sigh.

There comes a time in life to be glad.
When they also smile at the lonely and sad.
For had they not trodden that same road?
Cheerfulness and encouragement had lightened their load.

So all who tread the path of life
Smile and encourage those who meet strife.
Remember those in North, South, East and West
Set an example for people to do their best.

If along these lines fellow citizens follow
Our world will have a brighter tomorrow.
Peace around the globe will reign
Wars will cease and life will be calm again.

Alicia Jean Bennett

'The Pity Of War'

What is the pity of war?
I hear people question.
How can you begin to explain
Such suffering, discomfort and tension?
It ruins lives you have tried to build
Harmless souls and minds are killed,
Loved ones have fled to fight for what?
The constant fear of being shot.
Minds are broken, bruised and damaged
Laughter and happiness are both savaged,
My life could end at any instant.
Can lives and hearts be mended?
When minds have been so twisted and bent.
Scornful memories prolong the agony
When in my head I still can see,
Scars that will never heal nor mend
From an unjustified war I was forced to attend.
When night would fall at the end of the day
My faith and hope grew as I closed my eyes
Bent my head and softly prayed.

Nicola Howe

Untitled

I woke early one misty summer morn and saw geese high in
the sky; the passion in my blood was slowly beginning to stir,
I got up and donned my black leathers ready to ride for sure -
the softness of them against my body was like a velvet skin.

I gathered my gloves and helmet and made towards the
garage, I opened the door, "There you are," I whispered softly
to the big 500; I wheeled her out and sat astride sometimes
there's an instinct to fly I touched the ignition she roared into
life we were away and on a high.

We thundered away in the early morning sun, wind on face
and doing a ton. There seemed no life as the beast hummed a
musical note travelling to beyond. I could see fields and trees
and feel sensations and warmth of the sun with a twist of the
throttle, I obliterated buildings to become a blur all in one.

The white lines on the road picked up speed and merged as
one as I went through the gears to reach top speed doing over
a ton. I came down the gears quickly with engine and brake to
slow and leaned in and out of bends like a slippery snake in tow.

The journey was long and yet it seemed to pass so fast, I needed
a drink as I made towards home at long last. We pulled up outside the
bike purring like a cat; survived, I switched her off all was
quiet like rebellion, it's the only thing that keeps you alive.

M. S. Charles

99

The Rainbow

Today I saw rainbow
That reached clear across the sky
Its colours so magnificent
It brought tears to my eyes
Tears of happiness I find hard to control
For as a child I was told
At the end of a rainbow
You will find a pot of gold
My life has been in turmoil
Since I was left alone
With no one to share my worries
Or my troubles to unload
In my prayers I asked the Lord
If He would send a sign
If He would help me in my hour of need
I would bide my time
So can you see why I am so happy
Carefree and gay
I saw a magnificent rainbow
In the sky today
Marjorie Percival

The Slave That Broke The Mould

We that dream of intangibles have the pull of kings
Yet not the burden of the plough!
Let me sow stellar seeds, and scatter them from
Their husks,
For I, earthbound, have more mettle for matter
To be mined from mind to weigh my worth.

Let them plant me in the ground for I'll sprout
Wings within cocoon...
I shall leave this land I love,
To soar above the mundane;
As an angel to return:
Then, when conscious candles flame snuffs out
They'll find my husk with spirit gone...
Words on wind to lash free their bond,
And slake the years of perennial fern:
They'll find my cry in cry of curlew:
My stoop in the swoop of the kestrel,
A sigh in the swelter of the sun,
And tears in the toil of the rain.
S. Vito Hind

Old News

Unemployment no jobs around, homeless people can be found,
Scratching for a living dare not be ill, cannot afford the
doctor's bill

Dad needs new glasses, and mum's in pain
Johney's got tooth ache, yet once again,
get two pennoth of jollop from the corner
shop, hoping that the pain will stop.

Private services on the road and rail
nothing runs for us, it's a sorry tale,
the gas is cut off, can't pay the rent, then
they ask on what your money's spent.

In the charity shops, for mum's new shoes.
Trousers for Johney, not a booze.
The cheapest cuts, bread and spam I wish that I could afford
some ham.

Let's hock Granddad's watch that he left for me.
At least then I can buy us tea.
Home's repossessed like the Rachman affair, tears and
sadness are everywhere
The nineteen thirty's were a dreadful time,
towns and streets are awash with crime. Pickpockets, muggers, what
can you say. It surely couldn't happen in this day. Nineteen
thirty's, kids out for kicks, no this happened in ninety-six.
K. Succamore

"The Hogarth Company"

38 ships of Addrossan
The seven seas kept crossing
But they never came back
They knew they had a job to do
To get those valuable cargoes through
So to hell with Hitler and to Germany too
They left their home ports knowingly
That those "U" boats waited patiently
But still they sailed on to their destiny
    Nothing could deter
    Those brave mariners
    Of the Hogarth company
38 ships of Addrossan
The seven seas kept crossing
But they never came back.
D. E. Barnes

My Friend

I had a friend, the best there was
I saw her every day
Sometimes we'd laugh and talk of many things
Some days not much to say

Through the years, as I grew up
She never let me down
I'd tell her all my troubles
She'd say, don't let it get you down

She never had a lot of wealth
But when by birthday came
There'd be a bunch of flowers
And a card that said my name.

Then one day she went away
With just a smile and sigh!
A friend like her. So good and true
I'd never find another
Because that friend I loved so much
Was my dearest Mother.
Kathy French

Nibs

I'm writing once again to be used at will
by Waterman, Parker or even quill.

To voice my opinion, to shock or amuse
I'll write to the Queen, got nothing to lose.

Scribble letters to The Times for what it's worth
get sued by the editor, it will cost me the earth.

Be careful not to swear or use the word phallic
amaze my admirers by writing in Italic.

Never become tiresome or ever bored
Remember that I'm mightier than the sword.

Last but not least to always be heard
for it's my place to have the last word.
Alexander Kovell

The Choirmaster

You have the means to interpret the notes and phrases
You dissect the chords and find the inner depth there.
Just what the composer set out to achieve, you trace,
And with baton you guide us through the maze in the air.

You touch all our lives and make the music live.
How can we thank you enough for your training?
You grind us down, mould us all and re-make us
Into one glorious sound, making our souls sing.

When task is completed and you have given your all,
And the choir and the audience have reached the sublime,
We can unwind and slip back into homely comforts,
Slowly to descend from the musical peaks we climb.
Linda R. Wilton

The Baptism

You lie so small and sweet so wrapt in love
and round your old friends meet so wrapt in
talk of old things you have yet to know.

Your own small world so vast and full of love
and mum and dad so proud and quietly knowing
old things you have yet to know.

Or do you confound us all by knowing all that
lies before
and all that has gone by.

We called you Jennifer Anne today
and gave our promise to the Lord that we
would keep you wrapt in love and teach you
old things you have yet to know.

Or do you confound us all by knowing that dear
Lord who kept you wrapt in love until
your birth
and who in coming years will teach you
old things you already know.

Maggie Sadler

Untitled

Please can you try to believe that I
know where my future lies.
There's no other place in time or space
That offers a greater prize.
The happiness I've found since you've been around
Couldn't be measured, you see
I never would break the vows I now make
Your love means too much to me
When you say you'll be mine our hearts will entwine
So nothing can cause us to part
You need never doubt nor worry about
The feelings were there from the start
A love this strong just can't be wrong
The tests have been hell to bear
But if we stick together loving each other
Our troubles always to share
I'm sure you will find I can ease your mind
and chase all your cares away
Starting a new life with me as your wife
So happy on our Wedding Day

Lynne Thomson

An Ode To A Caledonian Belle

In the early hours of the morning, before I rose from bed,
I looked on the face of my darling as she lay asleep at my side.
The radiance of an angel was on her head as it rested on the pillows.
Her eyes closed and her mind went to another world.
Sleep on, my sweetheart, you deserve the rest you get. I alone am
fortunate, for I alone can see your lovely eyes, as during the day the
world doesn't see them, for they are hidden behind heavy lenses.
If I leaned over and kissed your cheek, I'd only disturb your sleep.
I'd love to put my arms around and cradle you in my arms, or
wipe the hair from your brow. But alas in old Scotia we're still
too old fashioned to express our feelings, so sleep on my
bonnie Caledonian belle.
We've been through so much together, and weathered many
storms, but life would have been all the poorer if you'd not
been there to share it.
To me you're a lady of grace, full of goodness, and you have
a loving nature, and you always have time to listen to others.
When you awake in the morning, it'll never cross your mind,
of the time I took to gaze on your sleepy face, your greying
auburn hair, and bless you with admiration, and thoughts of
you that are dear to me.
Sleep on my princess you deserve the peace of this nice
warm bed of rest.

Peter Laird

The Power Of Fate

The power of fate, comes even if late.
The power of fate, is never too late.
It's like the power of love when,
It falls quite heavy at the gate.

At the time of fate, forgets the state.
All the plans on route make.
A moments distraction; a fatal attraction.
No preparation this inevitable exploration.

The power of fate; is sometimes content;
Fate knows the beginning of the moment.
That depth of emotions, no words can express.
Suddenly! A feeling of sharing and caring.

Fate, knows the door. Fate has the key.
Along each street, ship or boat on the quay.
Fate is an art, moving on a crowed street.
Then suddenly, a stranger greet;
An instant bond on meeting.

Yvonne Hazel

Shadows

Shadows dancing on your wall,
watch them as they rise and fall.
Rumbling, tumbling, splitting in two,
hovering right above you.
There's one, no two shadows 3 and 4,
laying across the bedroom floor,
and more sitting by the door,
you look out your window,
but nothings there,
it's a sign you'd better beware,
get back in bed pull the covers up high,
and go to sleep without a sigh.
As you drift you wonder why,
Shadows come from out the sky,
In your sleep you say good bye,
to the dancers from the sky,
there rumbling and tumbling
swaying to and throw,
but you know they'll never go.

Emma J. Grellier

Someone For Me

How I long for love, from a special one, who cares, one who
finds me beautiful and wants to make me theirs.

Someone, who finds I make their heart pound,
    so they hear it in their brain.
Someone, who finds me refreshing as the early morning rain.
Someone, who wants to take me away, and lavish me with love.
Someone, who thinks that I was sent from up above
Someone, who when he hears my voice, it lifts his dreary day.
Someone, who wants me in his arms to take the pain away.
If there is someone, who could see in me all these things,
Let me meet him tomorrow so then our life begins.

S. M. Walker

March 1944

He came to me in dreams, he was not dead
They all had lied, he must be still alive
They said he was shot in body and head
But I know that one day he will arrive

He came again sometimes, he never spoke
And then he was wounded - now on the mend
He would come, but where and when - then I woke
Again and again, no date in the end

Then the weeks went by, then the months went by
He still came but my dreams seemed less clear
Could my hopes and dreams be only a lie
And most I let go of one held so dear

The streets were full of joy and songs and cheer
"War was over" but no cheer could I hear

P. K. Brackley

Remembrance Parade

We marched today,
Not the way we used to march,
Not for us the fast drill pace,
Just a gentle walking step,
Because we're older, slower now.

Our tread today was firm enough,
Our minds recalled commands,
Right turn! Quick march! And stand at ease!
In other times, in other lands,
But today we still respond.

The parade was to remember
Our friends of long ago,
Who served with us and fought beside us,
But died as young men
And left us to grow old.

We won't last long,
Our time will come.
We'll leave you to remember us
As we remember friends who fell,
But we marched today.

Douglas MacDonell

Thomas

Thomas has got Down's, not that it really matters,
Some Down's are very clever, others "mad as hatters".

However much we grieve and cry the Down's won't go away,
So it's up to us to work hard now and help him on his way.

He may not be a 'brainbox', he may not make the grade.
It doesn't really matter it's just the way he's made.

Some days I really love him, some days he drives me wild,
You see he is no different from a so called "normal" child.

He may be "quite endearing" and his smile be "Oh so cute"
But will this be accepted at twenty in a suit?

Sometimes he is "amusing" but our laughs we must suppress,
You might not find it's funny when he's looking up your dress!!!

It's now we have to guide him and help him on his way,
To teach him what's accepted, what to do and what to say.

It's important for all children to learn what's wrong and right,
If Thomas is socially accepted then I think we've won the fight.

Thomas probably won't be a doctor or even an MP.
But if we help him reach his best, then that's alright by me!!

M. Eastwell

Presence

Inside the great cathedral, beneath its vaulted dome
In silent meditation I lingered, all alone.
My companions had departed, in pleasure-seeking mood,
But I had chosen to remain in peaceful solitude.
For me it was a brief from busy modern stress,
To contemplate this place, this church, its simple holiness.

How many souls, throughout the years, I mused in solemn thought
Had lived and loved and died here, and found the peace
    they sought?
My father too, so dearly loved, so lately gone from me,
Was he now part of that celestial company?
I missed him so, and mourned him, but tears are all in vain;
I knew that never ever would I see his like again.

Pausing to light a candle I watched the taper flare,
The thin smoke drifted upwards, lifting my silent prayer.
I recognized a well-loved voice, he whispered 'Do not grieve
for me, I could not bear the pain, it was time to leave.'
I turned, there was no one, but the tweed he used to wear
Had left its faint aroma, and I knew that he was there.

Joan Hollow

This World We Live In

I suppose those up in heaven, shouldn't really cuss,
But if they do, their reasons are, all because of us,
What an awful mess of things, we're making here on earth,
We, who have it in our charge, have no earthly worth,
Daily too, it doesn't improve, in fact it just gets worse,
And we, the ones who people it, are its biggest curse,
Everyone you care to turn, things which one were good,
Man has left his thumb print on, where he never should.
Our beautiful world, which once it was, truly was an Eden,
Until man with all his faults, chose to leave his seed on,
We are God's good creatures, the ones which he had made,
But when he watches what we do, he sees the price he paid,
No matter where you choose to look, the world's engaged in wars,
And when they've counted what they've won, all they'll find is sores,
Religion seems a reason for some to cause a fight,
And if we all were colour blind, we wouldn't know black from white,
What a world to live in, a world which could be good,
And but for man's great follies, it sure and truly would.

James Robinson

Evacuation

I went on a train to the country.
I waved goodbye to mum.
I saw things I'd never seen before.
It was great fun.
    - But I'd rather be with you.
If I was with you right at this moment,
I would think of the things that we'd do.
It is great fun here.
I like everything where I am.
    - But I'd rather be with you.
Mum, will you come soon please?
To see me and take me home.
I'd rather be with you mum.
That's what I'd like to do.
    - Hope to see you soon!

Helen Brockway

Dunblane

That time again
My stomach turns
The banging of the doors
The cries of mum were home - no more
No longer coats thrown on the floor
Books and toys now tidy in their drawers
I scream for this in my darkened void
Must I wait for my demise
Just to know the reason why

S. D. Robertson

Untitled

The purple lilac is in bloom.
Its fragrance fills my little room.
And rhododendrons, red and white
And pink, do bloom with all their might.
Laburnum clusters hanging down,
So pretty in their yellow gown.
And wallflower, growing row on row,
A scenting all the world below.
I could go on for hours and hours,
And tell you all about our flowers,
And shrubs and trees, and all the rest —
But very soon I must get dressed
To catch the train to boarding school,
Where work and play are all the rule.
But first, I must take one long look
At my dear home, for every nook
Is printed in my memory,
For times of stress, for me to see
And now I try to drink my fill,
A leaning on my window sill.

M. F. Lyburn

Why?

Why? Why? We hear this cry, over and over again
What has happened to this world that makes us feel despair
This world so big and beautiful it fills our hearts with pride
Then we hear of some evil deed, we shake our heads and sigh

We are all the creator's children, yellow black and white
What is the evil in this world, that causes pain and strife
It is not God nor Allah that makes one do these deeds
But mankind all by himself, to fulfil his selfish needs

No one was born selfish, nor one born with greed
Look into the children's eyes, there you will see the need
For love and gentle caring, for teaching and for trust
Put our arms around them, hold them to our breast

Look at one another in a different light
Stretch forth our arms in love and trust not with pain and strife
Listen to our inner selves each and everyone,
Then turn towards your neighbours, and become a child again

Margaret Ferns

Spring

Rejoice! With me, once more 'tis Spring,
With all its beauty, and birds that sing.
Wake up! It says, the winter is past,
With months of dreary waiting fast.

The bulbs come forth, and trees blossom out,
It makes you want to laugh and shout.
The earth that's looked so bare and cold,
Will wake up! In her white, blue and gold.

What's amiss with the fields and lanes,
They're all transformed, since December reigned.
The daisy awakes! Both bold and fair,
Green carpets she sees are everywhere.

No voice can tell, or fully explain,
The wonders of her beautiful reign,
It's beyond all compare, and leaves you dumb,
None can express it, and find their duty done!

Phyllis A. Jenkins

Uska

Uska you're a guide dog pup, you came
    to us a ball of fluff.
You grew so quick we were amazed we
    always gave you lots of praise.
With great big paws you ran about, elephant
    sounds came ringing out.
Your lovely face your floppy ears, brought
    lots of smiles and now some tears.

Guides your master on his way, keep him
    safe from harm.
Round the ladders over roads, just use your
    magic charm.
A partnership that is so strong a faithful
    friend in you.
A trust that no-one else can break, a love
    that is so true.

Margaret Currie

Looking For A Little Something

I hadn't even seen you, till I looked up,
Where high upon a shelf,
Elegant and appealing,
With your turquoise glaze,
Your size and shape
Revealing the beauty of your form,
I feel for you and like a lover
Lost in admiration
I knew I had found my little something
In the village antique shop.

S. Dallas

Dark Discontent

The world is all a'maying
    While fancy free I roam, as in the dreamy days of long ago;
When a child all free from care, I wandered midst these scenes
    Sunlit with wondrous beauties all aglow.

The river there a'winding like a band of silver sheen,
The leafy bough that overlaps its tide;
The water lily pushing up their petals scarcely seen
Through the maze of greeny leaf that round them glide.

The mountain towering high above, all purple green and gold,
Inset with many a white-washed cot and hall,
The brown cows dreamily browsing in the dead heat of noon tide
The azure blue that hovers overall.

The children gaily playing in the meadow by the farm,
The lambs that frisk so wildly o'er the lea.
The world seems all contentment to this dreary heart of mine,
Oh! To burst its chains of bondage and be free!

For my soul is seared with sorrow! That curse of every man
Dark discontent doth now my heart enfold.
Oh for the sweet contentment of my happy childhood day
I'd calmly barter all this life can hold!

J. A. Graham

When I Visit My Granny

When I visit my granny,
Soft dancing shadows
Play over her face gently
As the warm fire glows in the grate.

The scarf she's been knitting for a week,
Slowly grows at her feet
It probably stretches the length of the room now,
But never mind.

It's lovely to watch the scarf increase at her feet,
As she sits there, her eyes twinkling
Like the evening stars outside.

Soft and gentle she is,
Like waves lapping lovingly at the edge of the beach.
Just like the waves of time,
Etched upon her forehead.

Haesel Abbott

A Summer's Day

Summer's Day spent in a lazy way
A garden chair, flowers scent filling the air
A breeze to fan the heat of the sun
A bird song being sung on high
A satisfied person when day is done
To end with a contented sigh

Come Summer's night, with sky of deep blue
Of stars to fill with a silver hew
Sleep not easy to come, beds so often undone
Windows wide in hopes to catch the air
A Summer's day ends with a sigh of content
But Summer's night mostly sleepless spent

Doris B. Cook

The Gun Down The Lane

He was a nice little, neat little boy
And precious to his parents.
He made me weep, within, not openly,
For there he lay upon the neat, trimmed verge
Outside his peaceful home,
Fondling his toy machine-gun.
Lovingly making it chatter as he fired
At anything that moved, including me.
The sickening violence of the world
Rose up before me.
Once I too, in my childhood, had a pistol.
I meant no harm, he means no harm,
I know. Oh, little lad, grow up in peace,
I pray.

John E. Brigham

"The Coming Of Dawn"

So calm, and so dark, the still of the night,
Withholding its secrets, eluding the light,
A Teddy bear sleeps in the arms of a child,
The world is at peace, at least for a while.

The dreams of a nation, in its people asleep,
Their minds are a-racing, subconscious, and deep,
Farewell aspirations, at least for to-night,
Then cometh to-morrow, we continue the fight.

Flickering Stars are beginning to fade,
As the blackness is turning, to a much paler shade,
The light is appearing to force out the dark,
The world is awakening, to the sound of a lark.

Farewell to the night sky, farewell to the calm,
Awaken the people, the World in their Palm,
The Dawn is a-breaking, and gone is the night,
The Sun rays are brilliant, but will we see the light?

William T. Shenton

Farewell My Friend

I couldn't say goodbye my friend,
You quietly slipped away,
But you left behind a memory,
A memory that will always stay.

My friend the kindness you showed me,
You made life seem worthwhile,
Though you were ill yourself,
You always had a smile.

So farewell my friend for a little while,
That's all my heart can say,
Until the time we meet again,
Some place somewhere some day.

M. Ross

Tears From The Fountain

Remember Babylon, remember tide, I recall you cried
the night that I died.
Remember the date as I passed the gate, nine
rainbows, your small toes.
Remember me the one and he, queen of the waters,
stars, and sea.
Proud once we stood, yet aloft, now weather-beaten and
drawn off.
Thou'd weep but who's to keep thee now.
If only within me you'd trust, for certain I wouldn't let
thee rust.
Your eyes now closed once fired a glow, watered
fountains would'st out ye flow.
Lady then thou wer't as thou art yet, lest that all
thy children forget.
No tears from the fountains flow...

Ashley Kay

Inspiration

Inspiration is a rare gift given to few to atone,
In our destiny, we don't stand alone.

I understand fate differs
Many conclude this definition
"What's for us will not go by us"
Which to me is preposterous.

Can you grasp the vein?
It means perhaps you can do no wrong
The jigsaw will perhaps fall into place
Without attempting to solve the problem.

To predetermine the power of agency
Is not beyond human power or control
Spiritual guidance is specified.

One's lot or course of events
Is still to be transacted
Your destiny is in your own hands
What you make of it.

John Sneddon

The Ballet Of The Birds

In the high branches of the pussy-willow tree
the blue-tit waits.
She stares at the tomato-red nut-net swaying
in the breeze;
A swift flash of brilliant plumage suddenly
wings downwards
to cling to the net with purposeful, curved talons.
Great tit follows, adding slight weight to the swinging net;
Together
they perform - most delicately - a pas de deux.
On the ground sparrows and starlings peck nut chippings
as they fall.
Red-breasted robin, on thin, spindled shanks, is aloof
and stands shyly on the fringe of the group.
Ballet music
is borne on the air by the humming of bees.

Micklesfield

Ecstasy

Who cares that a girl lies dying
In a smooth white hospital bed,
Where she's lain since her eighteenth birthday?
She followed where you have led.

Why has that child come to this?
Why did she need to have 'fun'?
Why could she not find fulfilment in life,
In the stars and the moon and the sun?

How many people say they care?
How many think they do?
But how many people really care?
Do you? Can you? Will you?

Or will you simply turn away
And think "How very sad",
Until one day you're made to care
When the child is your own lad?

Valerie Sutton

The Camera

My world has been a camera, looking out at life
Recording now and filing prints; yes that is my wife
And that is son and that is dog, and yes that is my home
But what of heart and meaning, what stops the will to roam?
I speak of love and mystery; the central font of life.
Yet "All The World"; it lies here now, a feeling for my wife
A look, a smile, a glance, a thrill
Doors open now, no thorny hill
A vista wide and wonderful, a world as yet unseen
Two souls unite to pass this door; mysteries to wean
Hills to climb and skies to soar in
Wrongs to leave and love to bring in
What wonders these that now do pass;
what thrills and joys create to last
But what of past? And what of future?
What does it take to make us glad?
Oh irony! oh paradox! this was everything we had.
Life can be cruel, it can be hard; or Man can make it so
With fears and doubts and lust and greed and vision set too low
Or too high, it matters not; for both avoid the truth
That life and love and happiness is not some far off roof
But Here.

W. S. Charlton

The Falling Leaf

Gently she did leave go, taking to the air
and floating slowly down.
She thought a few last passing thoughts
of Spring and Life and Rest.
Regrets not one, her task well done
to rest at last - In Him.

David Creedon

An Awakening

This child, a flower, so open now,
so rich in splendour I should bow,
When freedom opens up its arms,
Caressing this sweet jewels charms,
Into another world it grows
And love like wine forever flows,
I wish to watch you as you sleep,
Your precious dreams your soul to keep.

This child, a flower, so open now,
The time has come to take a bow,
To all your dreams and your desires,
The glowing spark that lights the fires,
Your woolly mind a palace holds
That slowly unto me unfolds,
I wish to watch you as you sleep,
My precious dreams my soul to keep.

Anna Reeves

My Friend Eileen

Your caring ways, your love of life,
so brilliantly do unfold, a wondrous gift
of life success, of riches, still untold.
    For your riches are not gifts of
Gold, or Diamonds by the score,
your gifts are of the peace, and love, that
people admire you for.
    You spread around, where'er you go,
a stillness of tranquillity. A gentleness,
a quiet reserve.
But a loveliness beams out from within,
a soul so sweet and true.
God only knows why He sent us, a
wondrous, beautiful soul as you.

Kathleen Donohue

Untitled

It doesn't seem so long ago,
We held you in our arms,
Our precious baby girl,
Who blessed us with her charms.

Throughout the years, we watched you grow,
We shared your joys, your strifes,
Those memories are little jewels,
We'll treasure all our lives.

Your first few words, those shaky steps,
The temper tantrums too,
Those little bows, those dancing toes.
We were so proud of you.

And yet amidst your triumphs,
No moment can compare,
With the love and pride we felt today,
As we watched you kneel in prayer.

Our precious little angel,
No words can ever say,
How much it meant to share with you
Your first communion day.

Sharon McGeever

The First Day Of Spring

The grass around by knees
Danced in the gentle breeze.
The soaring birds seemed to sing
Rejoice! Rejoice! It is Spring.
The herons stood in the stream
With fish of all kinds, trout and grebe.
On the falls the salmon leapt,
And behind the reeds an otter crept.
When the moon came out and the sun went in
That was the end of the joyful din.
Home in the river bank the water rat lay.
What an end to a joyful day!

Richard Penketh

Untitled

His voice rang low in deep distress
Come quickly now - no time to dress
The old oak stairs creaked under strain
Stone floor shivered, only bolts remain
The worn, familiar joining path
Seemed strange and foreign in the dark.
The weight in my heart, so new to my plight
Put lead in my step as we sped through the night
With back door ajar, full light showing then
The stretcher descended with uniformed men
My mother lay quietly, her face turned away
Her body so still and no words I could say
The door closed behind them, my mother had gone
My aunts, brothers, sister and I were alone.

Jean Hatfield

The Lonely Hours

The evening gives way to the darkening night,
The door is closed and I am left within,
The curtained windows cloak the moon's soft light,
No voice disturbs the peace I fought to win.

The rooms are empty like the fresh-dug grave,
The phone is silent as I sit alone,
T.V. and Radio no answers gave
I speak to ghosts whose earthly days are gone.

To live alone in peace, was this my dream,
Was this the space on which my peace was based?
Silence and stillness now a nightmare seem,
In empty rooms like cells I am encased.

Day's minutes, like the birds, flew swiftly by,
I welcome sleep, when lonely hours are past,
Whose endless seconds tempt the soul to cry,
For sweeter hours, 'ere life's last die is cast.

As lonely hour succeeds each lonely hour,
The silence fences me more closely in,
No sound, no voice, alone in space I cower,
Silence I earned in thinking peace to win.

R. Taylor

Castlewellan

How many years have your walls known?
How many faces have your windows looked down upon?
As you have watched many generations of children
Playing on your lawns,
Have you shared in their youth and playfulness?
As their mothers have gazed upon them proudly,
Have you shared in their joy?

How many birds have started your day with their jubilant song,
And how many stars have gazed down upon you?
Who could count the dewdrops that have paused on your grass,
And who could count the sunsets
Which have illuminated your small world
With their crimson glory?

You seem to live in a time long gone,
For your splendour has remained untouched by passing years.
Now, as you're surrounded by this silent morning,
You seem almost serene.
Surely you were never as beautiful as you are now.
The present has enhanced the loveliness of the past.

Julie A. Magill

Voice Of The Elm

The voices I hear from far and from near
    the voices I hear are crying.
The words that I hear are crystal clear
    the words clearly say "we are dying".
A vision I see of a tall elm tree,
    sad vision - I see - of it lying.

W. Spalding

105

What Beef Scare!

My name is Alison Chee,
I eat beef for breakfast, lunch and tee,
BSE means nothing to me,
It's a load of old trollop,
In fact, it's codswollop,
You won't find it in my vocabulary!

My friends and family,
Think I'm risking my life, u see,
But, 'savour the flavour!'
And, 'thanks to John Major!'
For giving the stuff away free!

I'm feelin' all faint, oh gee!
I'm alright then the next I ain't!
Maybe I'm dehydrated?
I feel deflated, I know! It's an iron deficiency.

What a perfekt excuse for a snack!
Beaf's packed with iron by the stack!
I'll just pop to MacDonald's, and get a few Big Mac's,
Don't worry, I'll soon be back.

Elly Stevens

Home

I haven't heard a bird's song for ages,
I've seen them but I haven't heard them.
All I hear is the continuous drone, moan, rumble of traffic.

Cars conversing with each other,
interspersed with motorbikes roaring
and fire engines racing to flames which are soaring.
People walk by under my window
five floors down, but their voices are nearer.
Laughing, giggling and messing about,
teasing and shouting - the typical lout.

But there in the background the drone of the cars,
cold metal, impersonal, alone in a crowd.

Down at the round about, intricate dances,
white flashes, red stops, turning and pauses.
A dance much too complex to be recorded.
And I haven't heard a bird's song for ages
or heard a cat cry, or tapping of fingers on windows from trees,
nor lain in my bed watching shadows form pictures.
Seen the glow of the sun as it sets in the evening and the
smell of the dinner drifting up slowly. The voices and laughter
of my sister and mother and the love of my father,
 ever present but hidden.

Instead I see traffic, dead and impersonal
and a sea full of houses and lights.
A sea full of houses and lights.

Sarah Masters

True Love

I wake it's morning
I think to my self how lucky I am while I'm yawning
You wake we look into each others eyes
I wish it was last night so we would not have to say our
goodbyes
I get up and start to pack
But instantly you pull me back
We start to kiss and I wish it would last forever
Everyone knows we're meant to be together
You work abroad so you have to leave me
baby I love you please believe me
When you depart
It breaks my heart
A tear run's down my check
Although it's only for a week
When you get back I thank God above
because you my dear are my true love.

Gemma K. Lerner

Home With The Horses

I want to go home with the horses
To see them all comfy and fed,
And when the stars rise to their courses
I shall tuck them up safely in bed.

They can tell you their wants like a human,
If you'll listen with infinite care
While they whicker with simple acumen
And try to make hay of your hair.

I will go back with the horses
To see they don't stumble of fall;
I can use all the stable's resources
And sleep closely by lest they call.

There's the resonant voice of the hunter
And the musical neigh of the mare,
And the cob who so often sounds blunter
Is as soft at the core as he's rare.

When my own stars have outrun their courses
And I've touched on the rim of my days,
I shall rest for all time with my horses
In whichever Valhalla they graze.

Hazel M. Goddard

The Colour Of Love

The time together feeds the time apart,
From moment to moment
The cherishing is built and strengthened
In that wonderful realm of love

With its experiences and its needs,
Its articulation and its touch,
When love is given in a look
And received in the heart,

When love is felt by the touch
And experienced in the soul,
In all its variety and its beauty,
In all its differences and its demands;

Love remains love, graceful and joyous,
Always understanding, never demeaning,
Forever wanting to expand
To fulfil and be fulfilled,

To consume and be consumed,
The fieriness and the passion,
The gentleness and the lightness,
At once wild and innocent.

Naznin Hirji

The Battlefield

The banner, thrust into the ground at an angle like a broken lance,
Quietness, save for the birds encircling under scudding clouds.
The battle finished, broken men lie, motionless, no more to dance
Loved ones far away in distant lands unable to wrap their
resting shrouds.

This was a fight indeed, this was a most bloody day, man
against man.
Yeomen, woodmen, farmers, England's finest and fittest all
Wielding axe and lance, sword against sword, they fell and ran
This was a day the majestic and beloved longbow spoke for all.

The fallen lords lie entombed in dented armour, reflecting
sunlight now.
Horses lie still, condensation rising, the mix of morning dew
and warming sun.
Yesterday this field was home to grazing goat and cow.
Today the armies met and in a day a kingdom lost and won

Tomorrow will see the long and arduous journey home,
England for to crave.
The sick and wounded all. This day will not be soon forgot
To face the English Channel, pray Lord a peaceful sea for
warriors brave
And in the battlefield a rough hewn cross erected thus so
marks the spot

Ian Lees

Reverie

From church tow'rs Easter rings were rung,
Then Magdalen May Day singers sung
That Winter's pris'ner, Spring, was sprung.

Bare branches once with hoar-frost hung
Then carried blossom.
          Couples clung,
Wary of nettle stings among
Hedge-edged ditch once filled with dung.
(Though making hay not yet begun
Nor daisy chains together strung.)

The children's playground swings were swung
And babies back-pack slings were slung.
The naive tourist duly stung;
And cooling drinks a-tingled tongue
When publicans released the bung.

The village elders' hands were wrung
While youthful, joyous flings were flung.

    M. F. Kirby

The Old Man

At night he comes and lays him down,
A sad an shrunken world about him lies.
He cares not for the passing tread of town
Folk as they homeward go, as sounds
Of dusk dispel about the station rise.
For him the doorway is his bed, found
There for cold and doubtful sleep. No ties,
With no regrets in any heart, he is unbound
From all life holds too soon. No lies
For him more bitter than the truth. Around
His being spreads no waking joy to meet his eyes.
Yet once he was a little boy this sadness to confound,
He laughed and played with friends and tried
In happy places in the sun to find some mound
To build a wonder world of dreams and sighs,
Of joys his own, to share with others found.
While still alive what made him die?.
What darkness took away his sky?.

    Robin Guy

The Broken Hearts Mend

What hope can there be in tomorrow
When I can't even live for today
What's the point of planning a future
If my life is just slipping away
You taught me the meaning of dying
But I never quite learnt how to live
So yesterday's gone but not over
Some thing's you just don't forgive
I pray but prayers don't come easy
It's been hard since the day that you died
I know faith can keep me together
But faith without hope can soon slide
So here I'm left searching for answers
Your past caught me up in the end
And with feelings so slowly reviving
I wonder do broken hearts mend.

    Janice Bignall

Feelings Of The Elderly

An old woman sitting in her chair,
with nothing but the house all bare.
No-one to talk to, no-one to see,
only memories of times that have been.
The old woman feeling sad,
wondering if she is going mad.
The old woman, with nothing to do all day,
stares onto the wall, when her grandchildren want
to play.
One day, she will be gone,
with her family waiting for their time
to be alone.

    Anita Morris

The Highlands Of Scotland

Majestic nature, all around it lies,
With towering hills that reach up to the skies
Where Golden Eagles soar, with wings outspread,
Unfettered yet by manacles of dread.
Where secret burns still tumble into lochs,
A home to salmon, spawning 'neath the rocks
At journey's end, from oceans near and far,
Whence once they fled as princely salmon parr.
Where deep within a glen, a monarch stands,
His antler spread most regal in his lands
A'waiting, like some duellist of old
A young pretender, grown both strong and bold.
On distant moors, the grouse like phalanx rise
With whirring wings, their speed deceives the eye
Of predators, both men and birds of prey,
They swiftly weave then safely climb away.
All this the Highlands offer, yes, and more
Of joys, delights a'plenty held in store,
Their greatest treasure yet, a healing balm
Of peace, serenity, eternal calm.

    K. T. O'Connor-Mitchell

Recollections On An Old Friend's Fiftieth Birthday

When childhood airs blow soft with memories of our youth,
The dark mirrors of time reflecting images half seen,
I view, hindwards, those shadowed forms of people and of places.

The crouching figures, small when first remembered and uncouth,
With concentration of my mind begins to turn and preen
Their half-hid features: a light of recollection
Grows gold on round-turned childhood faces.

The red brick school stands high and square above our heads;
The sloping garden, paths paved with gravel, from the road below.
On our left, the wide iron fence, the field for play beyond.

Running with me, children come with eager, gathered treads
As learning comes from nature's play to help small spirits grow
To reading books: a simple explanation
Of that first touch of Education's wand.

Now we are grown: grandparents, parents; we know only how
The wand of youth gave way to Erudition's waste.
The dark limned glow of golden hindsight is best hidden now:
Else we perceive that race from dawn to final dark in all its haste.

    Nicholas Macy

Standing On The Bridge

Standing on the bridge,
Looking into the moonlit stream,
A stone causes ripples,
The moon shattered it seems,

Standing on the bridge,
Looking at the fragmented moon,
Glistening shards of light,
Becoming whole again soon,

Standing on the bridge,
Looking into her starry eyes,
Her three words cause ripples,
In the loneliness of your life.

Standing on the bridge,
Glaring at her wedding ring,
Your heart's a raging fire,
You want to kiss her but can't do a thing.

Standing on the bridge
Alone with your lonely life,
It seems that right from the start,
You've been playing with loaded dice.

    Robert Andrew Smith

Our Gordon (A Family Tribute)

Gordon, we love you and we know that you knew -
Part of us forever in all that we do
Till our paths meet again, straight and true,
Gordon, we love you, honest we do.

We'll take care of Carol, Colin and Diane,
As substitute for you, our brave Scotsman -
Why 'He' chose you so soon, we don't know
But our admiration for you will always show.

Gordon, look down from your cloud on high
As we look for you in that bright blue sky -
Maybe you have now met with your Dad
And, if so, our faces won't be so sad!!

We'll always remember your pipe playing skills
And each quiet moment that memory fulfils -
Gordon, in our hearts you will always be
Sharing our day-to-day lives triumphantly.

Margaret Rushby

The Little Puppy

The puppy was so cute and cuddly,
Sitting by the tree,
The presents, paper bits of rubbish,
Were all sitting there for him to see.
The people all shouting and laughing,
Excluding him from the fun,
Was this the beginning of his new life that had
just begun?

He started to see after a while, that he was not wanted.
So he started to prod and prance a little to see if
he could be spotted.
Then in a flash the door was opened,
And there was white stuff everywhere to be seen.
The puppy ran out;
Then came to a halt.
This was the best stuff he had ever seen.

Claire McCarthy

Litter Louts

Isn't it everybody's dream,
to walk a street that's really clean,
and swim a lake that's sparkling bright,
with no pollution there in sight?

Or wouldn't it be very good,
to save our waste so that we could
re-cycle it for further use,
this earth no longer to abuse?

So to this end, let us begin
to put our litter in a bin:
The aim of this there are no doubts,
to rid the world of litter louts.

Olive Armistead

Seasons Of Life

The sky is clearly blue in the Springtime of our lives,
as children days are endless, hopes are high.
The need for us to know, to find out how and why,
is wondrously reflected in the eagerness of eye.

In summer we are rushing headlong on our way,
no time to sit and wonder as long as needs are fed,
We grasp at every straw as if it were our last,
no thought about the future for now the colour's red.

The colour's rich and deep in the Autumn of our days,
experience has taught humility,
We fear onset of Winter, the river deep and wide,
remember Springtime's eager rushing sea.

And yet the tree in Winter, devoid of all its leaves,
stands in such stark beauty against a leaden sky,
its purpose is fulfilled, it's born the fruits of life,
its children look to Springtime with a yearning how and why?

Christine Lockton

Memories

Today is the first day of the rest of our lives,
So pick the past up and put it all away,
We can have so many happy tomorrows,
Living now, not lost in yesterday.

We all have different memories of how things used to be,
But know they'll never be that way again,
So we should move the past to the back of our minds,
Make way for future memories in our brain.

It's best to treat the past like an old coat,
That's been lying in the wardrobe for a while,
It's nice to try it on every now and again,
As fashion changes it's sure to make you smile.

And if it is a coat you're really fond of,
It will bring those memories flooding back to you,
You may feel a little sad you can't wear it anymore,
If you do, your friends may laugh at you.

So wrap it gently and store it in the attic,
When you feel nostalgic bring it down again,
Wrap it round you and feel warm in the memories,
Memories of times you'll never have again.

Aggie McGinty

The Mission?

Why is he here? Why did he come?
He was to his mother an only son

Risking his limbs, his life and all
going wherever, duty does call

Why he is here, he does not know
Those passing faces, friend or foe

Asking no questions, just doing his task
Resting and eating is all that he asks

As time goes by, he does not moan
Days passing by, his life on loan

Where does it lead, when will it end
Loss of life or maybe a friend

Soon he'll be home, his mother will cry
She'll hug him tightly, she thought he'd die

Tour is now over, back to barrack and squares
He may come back, but then, who cares

He's been used once as a pawn in the game
They don't know him, a number and name

In years to come he'll have no smile
For the time that he spent in the Emerald Isle.

S. J. Meah

"Memories Shared"

In the years of thoughts, as they come and go
I hope they leave a glow
of memories we shared.
Again and again to look
within the pages of this book
To recall the sweet past days
enjoyed in so many ways
To apply them to the present day
in the best of loving way
To derive some good ideas
for future years
To know just why
good memories never die
I adored every minute
each one of you within it.
Because of fun, love and care
we were able to share
the nicest thing in life:
'Friendships'.

Nicky Evans

On Retirement

Thinning hair, thickening waist,
All the things I've learned to hate.

Can't afford to have my hair done.
Talking hair styles was such fun.

How I miss the office chat,
Tiny scandals, happenings that

Reduced us all to helpless laughter,
Doing things we didn't oughta.

Company outings, late night meals,
Soon I'll be having meals on wheels.

But don't bring on the violins,
Life still has its outs and ins.

No more getting up at five,
To beat the traffic, half alive.

I've time to watch the birds and see
Them build their nests laboriously.

Time to watch the lunch time news,
Then lie back and have a snooze.

Neighbours' help through thin and thick,
After all, I think I'll stick.

Celia Andrew

Can You Understand

Alone in my world
Not exciting but bland,
For I'm living the past,
Do I alone understand
That the past's closed the door
On the future I long for?
Can you understand?

But what can I do?
Is there any way out?
Do I live for the day
Or do I map my life out?
Only one who is like me
Can through the maze of life guide me.
Can you understand?

Our vision of life,
It will seem much the same,
And our sorrowful hearts
Fill with similar pain.
And the future we'll fly to
From the day that I find you, can you understand?

Mathew Dike

No Future To See

When you first walked into my life
    It was such a mess,
Then you took me in your arms,
    and laid me down to rest.
The beating of my heart,
    matching the pounding in your chest.
I thought I belonged to you,
Maybe I was wrong.

I love you for a reason
This I know is true.
Whatever the reason
I really - haven't - a clue.
My heart fills up with gladness,
but my eyes sometimes shows sadness
not because I love you.
No this cannot be.
Perhaps it's the future, that I no longer see.
Life is like torture.
Where did it go wrong?

Angela Phair

Leaving Ipswich Behind

My the sun do wholly shine, our
Old dad used to say.
Let's catch the train to Felixstowe; we'll
Languish on the beach all day
If you prepare the sandwiches, cut cake
Enough for tea
Just grab the spades and buckets and
Off we'll go till three.
You know the next train is almost due
Come on, we've just got time
Each minute we spend standing here
Means less paddling in the brine!

All those joyful summery trips
In trains that seemed so magic - oh
No childhood memory can eclipse
Pa's sudden flights to Felixstowe.
Real happiness, that hardly cost,
Ineffable pleasure our days ascribed
Zigzagging along the railway track
Expressly on a seaside ride.

Molly Mainprize

Love

Love is black
It's deep and intimate
Secretive and moody
    Love is blind like the colour of night.

Amanda Carey

Birthright

No arable land is within their sight
Baron stretches, baked by the heat.
Flames of hope extinguished outright
Children wander, no shoes on tiny feet.

Meagre scraps are craved for survival,
degradation easily seen in the sharing
of such needed rations on arrival.
Unable to afford the luxury of caring.

I go to a tap to quench my thirst.
No gruelling days of dry, heat trails.
I have no necessity to feed my children first.
But this is what their life entails.

They bury dead as often as we drink tea.
From the minute a tiny foetus is uncurled.
What chance of sustaining life in this tragic reality?
My fortune was being born to a Western World.

Julie-Anne Henderson

High Tide

The waves at high tide roar in triumph.
Moved by an irresistible force they came
From the depth of the ocean
And the farthest shores of the globe,
Creeping along the beach, steadily moving upwards,
Whispering as they move, covering the rocks and the sands,
An irresistible army of waves stealthily up the beach
Where children are building sand castles
Decorated with pebbles and shells.
The waves push relentlessly on, driving at the sand castles,
Chasing the children before them
Until, at high tide, their whisper now a roar,
They pound the city walls.
But not for long: Moved by that same irresistible force
Shortly they will retreat back to the depth of the ocean
And the farthest shores of the globe
Leaving the pebbles a little smoother, the rocks a little bleaker,
The sands wiped clean of human prints,
Their roar again a whisper and their force spent.
Yet they are not defeated: They will be back.

Turid Houston

Loss of Loves One

My ship of love sailed into space
Leaving me bereft below
Orbiting in celestial grace
To a place I have yet to know.

How deep and hellish was the pit
That I was plunged into
Till my captain of love heard my cries up above
And sent the me a rock to cling to.

Oh how that rock did succour me
Thro' my despair and sorrow.
And taught me how to hope a gain
And live for each tomorrow.

C. M. S. Cumming

Untitled

Let us unknow the knowledge that was taken
From the tree so heavy laden
In the Garden of Eden.

Let us return to the man and the woman
Who wandered in that valley
Where shadows of light not death were cast.

What were their thoughts?
Their looks at one another?
How did they see
The things we see?

What did they know
That knowledge untaught them?
Can we by more knowledge
Ever know?

Philip Keeler

Footprints In The Sand

I walked along the shore leaving footprints in the sand -
  I marvelled at the wonders of God's almighty hand.
I looked back o'er my shoulder, my footprints were no more -
  I thought of all those other feet that had walked the sands before.

I looked up at the mountains, reaching high into the skies -
  Their beauty and their grandeur unfolding to my eyes.
Their colours ever changing, as they stood there proud and tall,
  I felt so insignificant-as if I wasn't there at all.

I stood high on the windy cliffs, and saw the oceans might-
  Such vastness overwhelmed me as I scanned its awesome sight.
I saw the golden sun descend, painting colours on the sea -
  I knew they would be ever there, for those who follow me.

I wandered through a country lane, amid flowers and barley tall -
  Butterflies and songbirds, God's creatures great and small.
Everything in harmony - just man, its only curse.
  Thank you Lord, for my split second, in your timeless universe.

Douglas A. Clarke

Cloud Nine

I must have died. Because,
I am sitting on cloud nine.
So white and soft, like cotton wool.
At night. The stars are shining bright.
They are company for me.
I see the moon looking down as though to say.
I am looking after you, and I wont let you fall,
through the day I have the sun I may go daft
and have some fun.
The sun, the moon, and stars, I think.
Is enough for anyone.
The alarms gone off oh! What a fright.
I am alive, not dead. I'm in my cosy bed.
So, when I really die. I'll go up to the sky.
Then sit on cloud nine.
That really will be mine.
And to see my friends
once again.

J. Jack

Untitled

Writing a villanelle like knitting grows
And grows until some form appears -
In out, two together - what next - who knows?

Like the knitter - the villaneller sews
New ideas, new pictures, new patterns.
Will they fit, full of wit, bit by bit, who knows?

Weft and weave, wool and words, in out, it goes
Like tapestry and patchwork bright
Form a carpet, or mosaic, who knows?

At least I've tried, and had some fun, God knows,
To put ideas like a kaleidoscope
Of dancing words in rows and rows and rows.

That give the music and the tune, who knows?
It all makes harmony I hope,
And like that bright dawn bird that crows and crows

This villanelle of wool and words now shows
The art of pen, needle when knit
Create a masterpiece that flows
In out, two together, what next, who knows?

Bridget Arscott

Untitled

Memory like an unbidden guest sits with me today
I wear a mantel woven by his hand
The yesteryears of youth and joy
Patterns of laughter love and tears
The legacy of my numerous years
A subtle guest is he
He is my friend
He is my strength
He is what is left of me.

Lilian Radcliffe

'O Jersey, Gem Of The Sea'

O Jersey, Gem of the Sea
Again you welcome me.
To wander the craggy shore
Bracken lined paths explore.
While, glistening down below
Sunlit coves aglow.
Azure waters crystal clear
Beckon to me, come in here.
Misty mornings, Seagulls cry,
Hear the fishing boats go by.
Warning voice of Corbiere
As ferries bustle past there.
Leafy lanes thro' fields of green
And pretty cows at leisure seen.
Walls of brown and golden hue
Sparkle with the morning dew.
Where the sun sets like a golden ball
And time doesn't seem to matter at all.
Please let me return to this island again
And rediscover the Jersey gem.

A. W. Peachey

Oil Spill

The South of Wales, the Sea Empress was bound,
Until it hit the rocks and ran aground.
Another disaster, worse than a drought,
Into the sea the oil spills out.
Fumes fill your lungs with every breath,
All around a sticky death.
Birds lay dead, all covered in slick,
Beaches are black, sludge is thick.
Rocks and plants admit defeat,
Fish are poisoned, unsafe to eat.
Just one explosion and the ocean would burn,
How much longer until we learn?

Janet Harris

The Neutered Iambus

I'd love to be a poet, but:
Composing verse can be a dreary curse;
I just don't have the time to work out rhyme,
And feel no sweeter botching up the metre;
Poetic discipline just makes my sense swim.

Yet having red the work of other modern "poets"
I ask myself: Why bother? Instead

I write a bit of fancy prose, suitably obscure,
Of course, song perhaps of love and passion,
Or conflict, blood and death, embracing
All the agonies our suffering souls endure,
Elegantly phrased in language that displays
The eloquence of a lucid mind, deeply versed
In human wisdom's venerable stores.

Then I dress it up a bit with ragged lines,
And capitals where capitals needn't go,
To make it look poetry ought to look,
The sort of things the pundits now acclaim: I find

I don't need iambs, trochees, rhymes and chimes
To get verse published in the Sunday Times.

Frank Littlewood

Fly Away

The stars have fallen,
The birds have flown,
And here I lay all alone,
I lay by my grave side
Stone, shattered and cold,
The moss grows over me
As I am unable to hold.
The moon glares above me,
With sorrow and scorn,
With death, my addiction
Depression, my throne.
I reach to the steeple,
To Gods awaiting arms
But they fail to catch me,
And I drown once more.
My tears ever burning
My chains deeper cuts,
My soul ripped away from me, as I scream in the dust.
I wait for a saviour my words never heard.
As the stone falls around me and the message still untold.

Katharine Anne Oram

Untitled

She takes you back in history, to country life and peasant.
When you meet, she always smiles. Her manner's very pleasant.
A natural wisdom's on her face.
She illustrates those bygone days
Of sowing corn, of oxen, plough and pheasant.

A coloured apron o'er her dress she wears in dirndl fashion;
A coloured scarf tied round her head. You never see her rushing.
Woollen stockings, hardwear shoes,
Walking stick; along she goes,
Greets - upon her cheeks a rosy blushing.

She needs these hours outside, she says. Indoors she feels stifled.
Due, she mentions casually, to the life she led
On a little farm with sheep and goats,
Pigs; and fields of wheat and oats,
Ducks and geese, and eggs to be collected.

Sunday mornings goes to church, to her religion true
(She radiates a calmness and a strength of character too.)
Then she's dressed up in her best,
No servile copy of the West!
In her style, with handbag and Sunday shoe.

Margaret Starck

The Deserted Garden

The garden wall is long and high, just right for soft black paws
To chase along, with tail erect, and sharpen strong white claws,
The sunshine plays on dappled leaves, a strong breeze stirs
the flowers,
Gently swaying, bright heads tossing, through the golden
sunlit hours
Fresh green grass on which to curl, and watch the birds in flight
Mystic shadows, patch of sun, a soft reflecting light
Lazily, with eyes half closed to stretch, and twitch an ear
Purr of pleasure, paws extended, whenever I drew near

But lonely is the garden, and empty the tall long wall,
No eager feet come running in answer to my call,
No soft black body, tightly curled behind the bush and hedge,
No golden eyes, and stand up ears upon the window ledge
No sitting on the gate post, to wait with proud disdain
The visit of a rival cat, and drive him off again.
Sometimes I think I see him, and feel he must be there.
But silently the garden waits, deserted, bleak and bare
And if I see a movement in the shadow of a tree
Could it be a small black ghost has come comfort me?

Irene Hustwait

The Newspaper Seller

I'm just an ole newspaper seller, I stand at me corner each day.
I stand there a-selling me papers, whatever the news, bright or grey.

I've stood there in all kinds of weather,
the snow, the heat an' the frost
I don't really mind, I quite like it, an' never a penny is lost.

I remember when quite young an' eager, I'd be a director some day
But somehow I never got started, well it don't seem to 'appen that way.

And though you wouldn't believe it, a nice little packet I've saved
Me kids 'ave all been educated, tho' me and the missus we slaved.

Still an' all we never minded, the papers 'ave been our 'ole life
I don't speak of course for me children,
I just mean for me and the wife.

Excuse me, the Rolls is approaching, he stops here mornings at nine
I nip up and give I'm 'is papers
And the smile that he gives me's just fine.

'Es some great big nob in the city, it's Sir 'ere and Sir there
For this lad, 'an my heart swells with pride
Fair to busting when he says, "See you home later, Dad"

V. Ray

Untitled

Early morning mist in my dreams,
of helicopters flying
and people dying.
Children standing over a marble stone,
with people's names they used to know.
A distant aunt holds their hand and wipes their tears away,
tells them of a promised land and takes them away.

Constantine Grivellis

Untitled

Just started school, much too young to die
And all of the nation is crying out 'why'
16 little angels, all so full of love
So tragically taken, to join God above
The nation now must take a stand
To restore some sanity to our land
What happened to our security
We can't walk the streets now, you and me
In Ireland it's happening every day
So come on IRA, throw your weapons away
Young children are watching, while parents are shot
At the end of it all, tell me what have you got
What happened to peaceful communication
The hatred and guns are destroying the nation
We must help to restore law and order again
And not let these young lives have been taken in vain

Marjorie Barker

Irregularity

Early summer smoke at roof-top time,
Shadowed by the crumbling orange viaduct,
And one solitary, rain heavy cloud.
The pang of a whiskey after-taste,
Just the essence of things not allowed
Contrasted with regular pink brick.
The coming and going of long days wasted
Or the broken Zippo, the flip lid
With its rhythmical tinny click, click, click.
Grass cuttings once poignant and erotic
Now only sludge, sickly sweet.
Another noxious herbal scent,
We've had too much of a good thing,
So soon the cloud shadow has to pass
Then we can lie in the grass.

Henry K. J. Mackley

Light Touch The Cover

The shelf sits full with collected books
Volumes, hardbacks, shiny cover jackets
Source of knowledge, pleasure and escape
Here one particular choice taken down
To handle with care a precious possession

Gaze first upon the smooth straight spine
My fingers glide light touch the cover
Ease open gently reveal its hidden secrets
Joy in the words and lines and pages
And soak in its moving spiritual content

You are another chosen book to me
I handle with care glides light my touch
No harm, no damage on you must fall
Preserve, protect, prolong your warm life
To gaze on, joy in and ease open gently

David Gale

The Golden Past

In the land of the sun
  Egypt has won
in all her glory of the past
has laid down her kings
and queens in their tombs
'O' king who lies in his tomb.
God gave him life but now in death
his heart, beat has stopped, and his blood turn cold
'O' king as you lie in your tomb
for over thousands of years
your past surrounds you
was it your queen? who laid you to rest
and is that? A tear on the ground which
has never dried for some unknown reason
from her sweet lovely eyes.

'O' King your life has gone, but now in death
which has your body but not your soul
so sleep your sweet dreams 'O' King for all
eternity and lie in peace forevermore.

Elizabeth McGhie

Books

Books, they come in all kinds.
Turn the pages and the stories unfold
The readers they behold.
Thick and thin
Let's hope the contents will win.
Some have lots of words
Others pictures of all kinds,
Stories for everyone
They really are terrific fun.
Instant appeal,
That makes the contents very real.
Memories that often linger long,
When our reading days are not so strong.
Books are there for all
To everyone's beck and call.

L. F. Williams

Looking Back

Now is not the time,
if there is ever a time,
for recrimination.
There is no point in pain,
no, not pain of heart or brain.
Why inflict on others that which we know hurts ourselves?
Let us try to say, 'Well that was then and this is now'.
Can we move forward, if not together, then at least in peace?
Let us agree to differ over the running of our separate lives.
Surely we can agree, if not in words at least in deed, and think,
everyone has a right to live and make mistakes.
If I did not stop to know you, I am sorry.
I did not always give myself a stopping space.
I was a me, a me in such a hurry.
Needing you in a way which you may not have understood.
Does this mean that one or other or both of us were stupid?
Or does it mean that, at the time, our pulses differed?
All I think I wanted was to love you.
What did you want from me?

Ann Lethbridge

Thoughts From Afar

As I sit here alone
  in the desert
The sky above is blue.
My thoughts are forever
  wandering,
but they wander back
  to you.
Although so far and yet so near,
That same moon shines above.
It brings back memories of home,
And those that you still love.
Across those burning deserts
where no trees, or green grass grow,
you see no signs of nature
or hear the streams that softly flow.
But I will return to England
the land I have grown to love and see again those green trees
with the cloudy skies above I will wake up at each day break
when the air is filled with dew and see old England's glory
a glory I once new.

D. G. Pearce

Commercial Debts

I have sussed them out, commercial bloodhounds!
Inextricably bonded in a belittling conspiracy
to seize my life - murderers!
Watch how stealthily they poison my body with
their chemical concoctions
And sicken me with atomic bombs.

To what extremes will they disillusion themselves
in "enhancing technology"?
For how long will they feed me with machine oil
and exact potatoes?
Should I surrender to their incessant excavating
and replenishing, leaving me scarred with blemishes?

No!
A day of regurgitation will come when I shall
spit out floods and drown their children!
I shall free my bowels of their dead, and make
them living ghosts among them!
Landslides will demolish their homes!
Their flesh, mortified with chronic diseases...
Somehow, they must be made to pay their accumulated debts.

Grace Kelly

Blood, Sweat And Tears

Are others any happier, or it is just a myth?
Would my life be any different, if I was known as Mrs. Smith?
I've come to the conclusion, with the passing of the years,
That life consists of three things, blood, sweat and tears.
The blood a symbol of the birth, the first stage has begun.
The lessons learned in childhood, as the blood begins to run.
Working for a living, so much you have to get.
You're young, strong and willing and you labour till you sweat.
The time it passes quickly, as you struggle through the years,
And encounter bitter sadness which will bring the flow of tears.

V. Reszczynski

Green Eyed Monster

There the monstrosity sat perched on the shelf
Taunting me. Tormenting my skull
Its green eye so very still
Red light by its side feeding the incongruous beast

I could almost hear the sound of silence
So dreadfully motionless
As my eyes transfixed on its sharp illuminated weaponry
Only movement from a playful cat.

Like in battle, I dare not lose sight of the enemy
For fear of being encroached; attacked unexpectedly
In a flash of light, body gashed
Little time for retaliation

So one becomes guarded and restrained
A solitaire of lonely existence
Staring at the colour of jealousy
The emerald
Symbolic of modern technology
Waiting....longing.... for thunder before lightening
The sound of a high pitched tone
From that confounded answer phone.

Karen Hodgson

Autumn

Crunchy leaves swirling and twirling down,
Owls swoop down to get their prey,
Nearly wintertime.
Keys fall from the sycamore tree.
Every bird is flying south,
Rabbits are hopping away to keep warm in their burrows,
Squirrels are collecting nuts.

David Martin

Loneliness

Patchy ceiling, bulb staring, balding walls, age sickened,
Bed, a raggy pyramid of darkened confused clothing
Receding lino, cracked, splintered, Submitting to wear and age
Table with wrinkling plastic, littered with the scars of use
And part covering of brittle browned newspapers with
    nobody's news
Stained cups, moulding dregs, witness to a million conversations
Twisted curling crusts, strewn and forgotten, victorious
Cold ashes strewn in a dying fireplace past all use and value
A man, prisoner of fate, almost still, but movement just
Paucity of hair, wretched, wrinkled face of a thousand stories
Slowing eyelids of sharpness deserted Figure of fading frailty,
Hands as fading rose petals, the colour of years, present
Thin fingers fatigued, fumbling, grasping, gripping fixtures
Patterned skin embroidered by a passing heat
Convicted of age, the pyramid of family now lost in the mist of time
Cast as seeds scattered by the winds of need ambition and
    independence
Years of devotion and care as a short summer melted into
    forgetfulness
Stepping into the quicksand of fleeting borrowed time
The levelling vulture, hovering, cutting the thinning string of
    existence
The storm of endeavour now past...Floating...peace...And...

Hugh Connolly

On 30 Years Married

You are not young and handsome -
    plain to see,
I love the way you cherish me.
You are not rich to give prodigiously,
I love the way you care for me.
You are not strong enough to make
    life trouble free.
I love the way you humour me.
You can not solve the problems yet to be,
I love the way you comfort me.
You always keep, protect me, tenderly,
I love the way you give your love to me.

Margaret Whitelaw

The Moon Still Shines

The sun still rises over Fuji Yama
The moon still shines on Singapore Bay
We walked hand in hand in Tangjong Pagar
I remember the moonlight on your lovely young face
But that was long, long ago and you are gone
I know not where
They came streaming down The Causeway
They took me to work on a railway bridge
They took you away from me
But I know not where
Tonight I walk once more in the moonlight in Tangjong Pagar
But I am alone
An old man with nothing but dreams
How I wish you were here to hold my hand
For the sun still rises over Fuji Yama
And the moon still shines on Singapore Bay
But you are gone and I know not where.

Robert Rockall-Brown

St Therese Of Lisieux

Wisdom of soul attained the 'little flower'
During a brief earthly span, measure not the years
    Of Therese, the strong Saint of God.
No sentimental image doth her life portray.
Her's the daily treadmill, the sorrows and the joys.
    A hidden life within the Carmel walls.
The simple gospel message, she lived it every day
    To love thy God and neighbour as thyself.
    She soared the heights of martyrdom,
    And shared with us those two abysses
    Self and almighty God.
Experienced every trial in an enlightened way,
    Inspired with apostolic zeal she sought
To convey the gospel message until the end of time,
    God loves each human soul,
Hers the 'little way' attainable by all,
Unfolding to the world the presence of the Lord.

M. L. Dawson

A Mother's Prayer For Her Baby

Your little face smiles up at me, like the sun from behind a cloud.
I rock you gently to and fro, my son, of whom I'm proud.
I dream about your future, that you'll grow big and strong
In a world that's free from sorrow,
A world where you'll belong.
I pray you will be happy, in health you will abound
With loving friends to be there, when I am not around.
I may not be here very long, the Lord has claim on me.
By His good grace, I'm merely lent
His will, so shall it be.
Whatever happens in your life, wherever you may go
There's something I must tell you
There's something you should know.
I'm glad that I gave birth to you, my darling babe, so sweet.
I love you very much my son,
My life is now complete.

Vera Kitson

Untitled

Place me near a well-loved tree,
Let summer sounds invade the air.
Send a breeze to touch my hair
And move the tall grass silently.

Scent the air with columbine,
Make all the woodlands rain-washed green.
Bring gay swallows on the scene
That I may taste life's rarest wine.

Leave me now, as evening brings
A faint red glow towards the west,
Night birds calling from their nest;
A lullaby for tired wings.

W. G. Saunders

The Cuckoo

O lazy bird of Spring.
Seldom these days, do we
see thee on the wing.
We hear thee though.
At early dawn.
Thy mocking call, unique of all.
In thy feathered world.
Foul weather does not put you off.
Your journey northwards to our Isle.
Your calls to make.
A home to find, of some smaller bird.
Your will.
This unkind act of selfishness, to dispossess.
No home to build of your own.
Yet you call to all, in that mocking tone.
Never fails to thrill.
Should our Spring be early or cold and late.
When we hear you call we know.
That spring is here, to start the year.
Lest we forget the date.

W. E. Speake

Early Morning

To see and hear the break of day,
To get a glimpse of the sun's first ray,
Listening to the bird's dawn song,
Seeing new-born lambs gambol along,
Watching the larks, high in the sky,
And other young birds learning to fly,
Observing a stag take a drink from the rill,
Inhaling the air, so pure and still,
Smelling the flowers as I walk along,
This is the time of day that I long.

D. H. Bott

Fate's Performance

On the sixth eve of June under a silvery moon
Fate appeared playing his favourite tune
but with more gusto than ever before
how the owls did screech, and the cats swore

The stars withdrew in dread of this night
at what the moon displayed in its light
All life did freeze with fear of the worse
those who did not, were already cursed

The scene was set, Fate was solo on stage
there he showed off his talents in rage
How the earth did weep under his stamping feet
as darkness watched closer, revenge he did reap

For this was the night he'd been waiting for
where he was the master, and his wish was the law
Not a living soul would dare dispute
his authority or actions, for he was the root
of the tree that governs the garden of tomorrow
with the strength to yield destruction and sorrow.

Rosemary Taylor

A Celebration

The land adorned with red and gold,
Buried in bronze (a silent death)
Scattered with ornaments untold
She yields but yellow evenings cold,
Blanched by bland, unblossoming breath.

Dewy-eyed she wakes, undreamed,
Bound by her to fall (darkening skies)
Laced with whispered white, beauty-streamed
She smiles, as yellow sunlight beamed,
Reflected in bewildered eyes.

Michael John Erian

Ashes To Ashes

Scatter my ashes on top of the hills,
And pour me out into the breeze.
If life has denied me exuberant thrills,
In death I will do as I please.

I may want to rest on the crest of a wave,
I might care to dance through the sky,
All of my life I have had to behave,
I shall do as I like when I die.

In this beautiful world, I'm sure that there are
Fine places my dust could be spread.
It is true when I say that I've never been far,
So I'll go where I choose when I'm dead.

And down in the wood I have seen the wind kiss
Spring blossoms with his wanton breath.
Cast some of me there, to experience bliss,
That I never knew this side of death.

Do this for the friend who had to conform.
You'll be sure of the joy that you bring
When you hurtle me into the eye of the storm...
And you hear every particle sing.

Joy Game

Whose Hands?

My mind is broke in two
One side fell into satins hands
The other hands belonged to you
I heard a whisper in one ear
It was a satin, he whispered "death is near"
You said something, it sounded clearer
You said "ignore him, your friends are nearer"
He whispered his message again
But louder now, then so did you
First a whisper, now a shout
Help me please I just want out,
I'm growing weaker, what will I do?
Will I fall into Satan's hands
Or the hands that belong to you

Lucy O. Neill

I Live Near...

I live near a school what a treat,
Children laughing, playing and dressed so neat.
I live near a school where graffiti rules,
Slogans sprayed and scrawled upon the walls, cans and papers scattered
(mob rule!)

I live near a park lovely and green,
People walk and family picnics are the scene.
I live near a park where after dark,
Mugger and pervert roam, druggies seek a fix, all looking for their own special kick.

I live near a city big beautiful and bright,
Hustle and bustle so full of life.
I live near a city changed with the times
Windows boarded and lots of sale signs, cardboard housing and squalor abounds.

Elizabeth Morgan

Through The Years

Love through the years.
Emotions overflowing into passion, sadness, laughter and
sometimes into tears.
Love, so completely,
organized, lined up neatly.
Love in disarray, abrasive, hurting, someone should pay.
Sometimes all these feelings in just one day.
There is no way you can ignore,
all your senses deep inside implore.
Heart to rule mind.
Two of a kind.
Love and longing runs through us like the names of the places
in seaside rock.
I dare anyone to cast a doubting look and mock,
of love through the years.

Sue M. Head

Dream Boy

Where are you dream boy
In my dream, in my church
Everywhere I search

You are always on my mind
But you are hard to find

I cry too much my tears always rush
Each passing day goes oh so slow
I seem to want to you more
It's you I cannot live without
That I am really sure

In my life there is no joy, no hope
without you, my darling, I could never cope

If you would ever come to this earth
Believe me, your heart I would nurse

They tell me, wake up
But I wouldn't give up

I know you would come
Take me and run
Fly away to another space
Far away from the human race

Christine Girges Abrahim

Dylan Thomas

I, in my darkbrown portered sloth,
Or ruminating in some redwining of the brain,
(Bibacious bibber forlorn I was at Laugharne)
Thought had I but had the pocket to imbibe,
Cognac, that burnished, nectared essence of a poem,
I might have been an even better scribe.

Deirdre Brander

Spring

The wind is blowing, the house it creeks
And snow has drifted by the gate,
Up in the Sky the moon so cold,
The clouds rush by no time to wait,
With winter here there's no denying
The wind and snow, the ice and rain
Will we see the sun again.
Then suddenly the slightest stir
Snow drops peeping every where,
Soon sap will rise, the leaves will grow
Forsythia very soon will glow
Spring is a whisper now so near
We see it happen every year
Each little bud is hiding there
We wait with wonder and with awe,
And see before us like a dream
The beauty that is life appear.

Paula Catherine Tripp

Madeline

Take me in your womb,
wrap me in your purple cloak.
The evergreen stretched its speckled arms
through the sheet of dusk and embraced
the desert moon.
Take me in your arms,
lead me to your cavern by the sea.
The waves of your hair
shall swamp my sodden head.
I will lap them up. Purr from my window.
Ancient one,
rise from your crimson slumber.
Offer me the pillow your dreams surround
and caress. I shall drown in that softness.
My head shall absorb the smoky visions
and we will join in the flight of the angels.
The eve of St. Agnes beckons
with a slender wave,
follows its path
to the seed where I repose.

Damien McCluskey

A "Little" Bit Of Heaven

My gorgeous roses here to see,
Some blushing pink, I think of thee...
Buzzing bees, all coloured too...
Dodge webs, fine - spun, still wet with dew;
Now, sun is warm; and perfumed air...
With birds in song...I'm pleased you're here;
...I've waited long, do stay a while,
These poems, just for you...in my own style,
All laid out for you to read;
I'll say a prayer, for all of this, indeed.
Here's a line seen in a dream,
For you, my love, in our own love scene;
And as you wait for me, I crave...
They'll grow these roses on our grave.

Bill Mitchell-Crinkley

Old Road

Winding across the lonely, windswept plain,
The Old Road, like a ribbon, soft and green,
Where only sheep and wandering kine are seen,
Now drenched with sunshine, now with driving rain.
At midnight, when the moon is riding high,
Pale Druids slowly pace the ancient way,
Or steel clad warriors of a bygone day
Retrace the age-old track that saw them die.
Then, as the dawn wind moves each blade and leaf,
Comes music seldom heard by mortal man,
The wistful piping of forsaken Pan,
The Old Road, only, shares his lonely grief.

R. A. A. Dawes

Hadleigh In November

Landscape retreats into nothing but distance.
Cobwebs hang heavy with dew.
Crystal-clear droplets like beads on a necklet.
Fog shrouds the castle from view.

Pigeon at rest in its oak tree perch morning,
Treetops nod gently, like reeds.
Muted the drone of a river boat's warning.
Sound, like the ebb-tide, recedes.

Rattling, a ghost train rolls by on the marshes.
Ghost ships pass close to the shore.
Calves, half asleep, graze the Down's Sally Army.
Kings ride in splendour of yore.

Just for a moment the retinue lingers.
Queens find their home of a kind.
Over your spine travel icy-damp fingers.
Footsteps - or hooves? In the mind.

Robert Hallmann

Voices On The Wind

I wonder, and by wondering set free
My puzzled mind from its ensnaring maze,
Are you, brave lark I hear but cannot see,
Some long-gone friend who tries to talk to me....
Long-gone companion of my boyhood days?

To draw attention to his presence there
It may be that as summer zephyrs deign
To send forth quiet balmy gusts of air,
His muted sighs and supplications stir
Minute tornados in a dusty lane.

And can it be that those who grieve and mourn
The passing of a loved one young and dear,
Can sense within the wimpling of a burn
Sensations that I feel... and oft return:
That voices span the void 'tween There and Here?

It may be that, communing thus with me,
Through Nature's voices' never-ending flow
He ventures not to solve Death's mysteries,
But only tries to put my mind at ease
With promises of brighter realms... who knows.

Jock Dalgleish

Wheels Of Confusion

Brightness, happiness and love,
on top and deep down everything fluttering like a dove,
then why do I feel like I need a shove?
And my senses have the sensation of wearing a glove?

Wedding bells have rung a peal,
a true love has been signed for with a kiss as a seal,
insecurities have had time to heal,
but life still has cards to deal.

I am now a proud wife,
who has plenty of fun and strife,
words are occasionally used which cut like a knife,
Reality "Jo" - this is life.

Why the confusion and turmoil?
Why do I wish to fling out and uncoil?
Why a smile as though hiding behind the shiny side of foil?
Why a wish to dig deep into the soil?

On thinking though it is nothing new,
Reality - it is not just confessing sat upright in a pew,
"Jo" - wipe away the dew,
I Am one of the lucky few.

Joanna Lewis

Night At Poltair

The long night is still, the patients are sleeping,
I sit at the table relaxed:
No sound breaks the silence, dear Cornwall is peaceful:
Not even quiet breathing distracts.

What cry do I hear o'er the countryside pleasant?
'Tis the full-throated sound of the fox:
As nearer it comes, the poor hungry creature
Seeks only the food for its cubs.

A scratch on the floor makes me startle and - lo -
A country mouse views me with calm:
Its eyes very bright are like pools of clear water;
And show neither fear nor alarm.

The light of the windows attracts the wild creature
He's brought the whole family along!
On the low window-sill they pause in their searching
For food from the hospital ground.

No longer my friend sits before me in wonder:
The family has broken the calm.
I am left with my thoughts of God's strange little creatures -
Bemused - and the night lingers on.

Mildred F. Long

The Soldier

The night is dark, the air is still, the earth is cold and damp
A lonesome soldier sheds his tears, as he looks around the camp
From the mangled bodies on the ground, came the cries of dying men
As in tortured pain and anguish, they willed their lives to end
This war has taken many lives, brave men have fought and died
What is it all in and of? The lonesome soldier cried
Through the bodies and the scattered limbs the soldier walks alone
The memories half forgotten, of distant lovers, friends, and home
From the stench of blood and debris came a shot, a stab of pain
The enemy had found his mark, this war's a stinking game.

Karen Brighty

The Rise And Fall Of Ecstasy

In a crowded club I was staring at the wall
When inside my head I heard voices call
Telling me I need a strawberry a dollar or dove
For the last time in my life I'm gonna feel love

I was rocking and wobbling about the dance floor
Looking for that geezer to get me some more
I was having palpitations that I just couldn't stop
Then my head arms and legs all started to flop

I had to find a seat I was having a bad turn
I could feel my vital organs starting to burn
All of a sudden I just fell to the floor
Then some stupid geezer shouts I'll get you some more

The stupid fool thought I was having a rush
He didn't realize my insides were mush
I was laid in a heap, people were gathering round
The disc jockey shouts there's another one down

Security came and tried to get me to my feet
They realized I was gone and threw me out in the street
I promise myself this is the very last time
But I know it's too late, my spirit's starting to climb

Chris Bartlett

"Families"

They can be a joy, also they can annoy,
Nobody's perfect so they say, that is true on any day,
But please keep in touch, don't wait until it's too late,
We all have our problems large or small,
Share them around don't be too proud,
There's a bright light behind each cloud.

Life is like a great big book open it
And have a look, sunshine yes and darkness too,
Lean on your family, they will pull you through,
Don't! Try and manage on your own,
We all like to be independent that's a good fault,
But need is great that's what we are taught.

Love one another is the text
Sometimes it's hard, but do your best.

Lal Hall

The Modern Man

I used to be so full of pride, I used to walk so tall,
I used to be a working man, I thought I had it all,
But now I am a modern man, that's what I'm told to think,
Dressed up in my apron, washing dishes in the sink,
No more earning wages, gone the future that was planned,
I'm drowning in the corruption, that festers in this land,
Fat cats with their fat wages, politicians who have lied,
Who will save the Modern Man, now the workers' rights have died?

As I switch on the Hoover, my thoughts drift to the past,
Thinking of old work mates, and the job that didn't last,
Images flash in my mind, the way working life had been,
Of laughter in the work place, now it's all a broken dream,
Because without prior warning, all our lives changed one day,
When I was told like all the rest, redundancy's on its way
I remember all the sad farewells, I recall grown men who cried,
Who will save the Modern Man, now the workers' rights have died?

Alan Van Rensburg

Life's Too Short

'The least that's said - the sooner mended' - words so wise and true.
Can time solve all our problems when we don't know what to do?
We can either make things happen or sit back and just accept,
We can reach out to a loved one - or sadly just reject,
We can clutch at straws forever hoping things will turn out right,
We can turn our backs on everything before we see the light.
But by then it may be too late, so blind we did not see.
The path that we have taken - was it really meant to be?
We could have clearly read the signs when we were so unsure,
Or was it that we did not care and chose to close each door -
Hoping time would solve the problem but by then we may regret -
That we did not say that kind word we had chosen to forget.
If we have turned our backs on those who care for you and me,
Then we have turned from those who gave us love and loyalty,
True friends are hard to come by, love is lost and gone,
But with hind-sight it may teach us to be wiser from now on.
We know that there's no going back, the future lies ahead -
Let's make the most of what we have - with wisdom now instead.
A little smile - a cuddle - a kind word would even do.
But don't forget, *'The least that's said - the sooner mended'* too.
Kate Chisholm

Nemesis Awaits

We were happy, you and me,
Together we had fun,
We laughed and danced, and life was great,
Beneath the summer sun.
Then winter came, and so did she,
I thought she was my friend,
But she struck pain into my heart,
And that took time to mend.
At first you two did not get on.
I was there to smooth the way,
A mistake, I know that now,
For dearly did I pay.
You and she may last for months,
May even stretch for years.
With head held high I smile at you,
And hide from you my tears.
I have felt the healing rays,
With love again my heart will leap,
My bitterness to pity turned....
For as ye sow - so shall ye reap.

Vanessa Stride

Thoughts On Keats' Death In Rome

On this foreign shore you lie
Frail youth, life too soon snatched away.
Healing summer sun came too late
To spin out your gossamer life span.

Skies are in mourning.
Cumulus clouds are descending
Darkening and cooling the blushing terracotta walls,
Lately radiating blessed heat,
Now blackening delicately wrought iron work
Transformed to impenetrable bars
Behind which you were trapped
To wither in Captivity.

Fly, sweet soul, and do not wait for night
And its awesome restrictions.
Your poet's words transcend you
And give you life everlasting.
Margaret M. Nivison

Untitled

The water flows down the stream.
To the most wondrous place you've ever seen.
The sound it makes is so heavenly.
And when I die there I'll be
My spirit will leave my body to burn.
Then I'll be scattered by the flowers and ferns
And this place we like to call is a peaceful flowing waterfall.
Karen Mills

Dunblane

Dunblane
Disaster-struck.
Distraught.
Dread deeds displayed.
Bereft of lives but newly began.
They walked so short a path.
Yet, each has stepped into our hearts today.

We send our thoughts, our prayers, our tears
For human hearts alone
Can never bear the anguish that you feel.
Believe us when we say
We grieve with you.
And draw on comfort stranger give.

We ask God's blessings on you
and your angels bright.
Sweet souls on high.
Catherine Hodges

Just Call Me Nanny

I'm only a Nan, going fast down hill,
I've given up the good life and I'm off the pill.
Grandchildren bellowing and blaring around me,
Interfering greatly with my sanity.
How I yearn for a simple life,
Far away and free from strife.
Surrounded by pets who don't answer back,
Just an old mud hut or a tumble down shack.
But no! I have to be here to answer any call,
Mum! Can you come round quick Billy's had a fall,
Lucy's dived off a chair and cracked her skull asunder,
How I wish I could change my telephone number!
I love them all really, they're pure solid gold,
But my oh my! They make me feel so old!
So I must carry on, and show very willing,
Let's hope up in Heaven I get Star Billing!

Daphne Poulter

Dandelions And Daisies

Yesterday the grass was green,
And nothing marred this 'scape of velvet sheen,
Each strip of moving evenly displayed,
Unblemished stretch, where only sunlight played.

This morning, as with magic wand,
The deep green shade, a liver hue has donned,
Specked over now, with white and brightest gold,
As dandelions and daisies fast unfold.

Gardeners scan with some dismay
Their velvet lawns - and nothing must delay
To rid this plot of such unwanted weeds,
So nature pleads, but man no longer heeds.

Whilst year by year as if to scorn,
The gold and white is scattered on the lawn,
That passers-by must surely gain some passers,
Contrary to the irate gardeners' measure.

Audrey Cleaver

I Live In Hope

I live in hope that this world will be at peace
no more fighting or killing, all wars cease
Destroy all bombs, weapon and gun
live life without fear
then we would all have won.

To treat and respect others as human beings
show courtesy to each others Gods in every religion.

I live in hope all people can love and help each other
Black white or any colour
the rich, poor, the sick and the healthy
all ages, races, no longer at war.

I live in hope I'm not alone in feeling this way
then maybe there really will be "Hope" one day.
H. Rands

Footsteps In The Snow

Arriving home one Christmas night
my eyes beheld a sacred sight,
footsteps frozen therein the snow
illuminated by the moonlight glow,
reminding me that earlier that day
friends gave greetings whilst passing this way.
So the proof was there for all to see
that their visit had been no fantasy,
and thereby lies a lesson for us to heed
that although the past soon fades away
it has already sown the seed
from which tomorrow emerges from yesterday.
For as those footsteps in the snow
only serve to go and show
that if we ourselves tread very carefully
we too may leave our own mark upon reality.

John A. Morris

Time

Time, it passes quickly by
Who can change it, not you or I.
Life can be gone with a blink of an eye,
So make the best while you are here
Before it's time to disappear
Back to the earth from where we came
Maybe to be born again
Seasons come and seasons go
What has man got to show
For his time upon the earth
War, crime, deprivation
What a legacy for the nation
Sow the seeds of love and peace
Then drugs, crime and violence will be on the decrease
So much pain, so much sorrow
Will it all change tomorrow?
Yesterday has been and gone
But tomorrow will hopefully follow on
Time, it passes quickly by
Who can change it, not you or I.

Yvonne Bowen

Anorexic Pouting

Honey primed and softly lilting... dancing petal
Pretty pouting, pouting pretty... cosmically tilting
Belly, belly, belly button... taut, taut, taut, tightening
Spiralling round the dry iced garden of forbidden desires.
Hunger strung, strong soul song sister
Warped to effect the so called affected
Lashed to style... elevated to fall
Swirling neurosis, subtle sideways glancing,
Criss crossing the crisis sector, spinning back to centre
Slender to the point to perpetual despair.
Mirror grooving, sliding the line, universally turning inside out
Arching, thrusting, aching not to be denied
Hollowed out by her lack of conviction
Forever, forever the haunted girl-woman-baby-child.

Matthew W. Jones

Palm On Paw

I remember when I was loved,
I had a hand with the softest touch,
It patted me and called me handsome.
When it was cold and my skin shook,
The hand's soft touch warmed me.
One dark night the hand went cold,
It did not touch me any more,
It did not touch me palm on paw.
A stranger's hand picked me up,
I found no comfort from it,
When I awoke I saw no warm hands,
I saw dark shoes, dark legs, dark hands,
Black clothed people holding a box above them,
My frail, wrinkled hand was never seen again.

Eleanor Gurney

The Border Hills

Snow in the high gullies,
The border hills give warning
Of belated Spring.
Cold the wind that stirs the daffodils
By the river bank.
A blue haze blankets the Moorfoots at dawn.

Come noon, and the scene has changed.
Sunlight picks out each slope,
In green, and brown, and gold.
By night, though slowly,
A hundred fires send smoke, like incense,
Heavenwards, in thankfulness.

Our country is like the hills -
A sleeping giant,
Waiting, longing to be roused to life
By the hand of God,
Could we but rest in Him,
Acknowledge that He made us
As part of His design.

Will Laird

Shadows

Evening shadows drift over the frosty land,
There within those who fear must hide,
For fear and shadows travel side by side
Constant, as the sea on sand,
Through the night like lovers hand in hand
Quietly, softly, at times must bide,
Fear always to the shadow tied
Stealth and cautions, nature can demand.
For those who choose to pay no heed,
Awaits the silent wing and piercing eye,
They the price must pay
Provide the hunter with his need,
As death, swoops silent from a cold grey sky,
Then just as silent, moves away.

Eddie Henigan

Computerized

Digital details composed by sound
Mozart and Bach control the mind;
A mind with disco variations, would soon astound
Her wondering what became of he,
Then he again what then of she.
The machine in need to depreciate the we
Could only answer perhaps?
To be or not to be.

The food the machine demands is not of love
Hard fax of science a neutered glove.
Each machine a tutored genius
Control'd by whom,
A touch of venus.
But that again would cause dispute.
The computer voice would stall
Then cry... refute.... refute.

Roy Hodges

The Mole

Exploring in a mine of coal
I met a furry little mole
Said I to him, "How do you find
Your way around, although you're blind?"

Said he to me, "I use my smell,
I use my little paws as well.
That is how I find my way,
Though I can't see the light of day".

He turned away and dug right down
Into the hard and dusty ground.
His little claws scraped at the soil,
Gone so soon he hardly toiled.

Elaine Carter

Pause For Thought

Pause for a second, perhaps even a minute,
An hour passes by - one is pushed to the limit.
Morning is soon gone and where is the beauty
No time to enjoy it you must do your duty.

You cannot appear to allow yourself pleasure,
Success and much wealth is the beacon of measure.
The sunset on water, the beauty of nature
Yet the human species is the busiest creature.

From noon until evening, travel over the land.
At work at the market a meal must be planned.
No time for your partner, your children or parents.
You must never relax, that is quite apparent.

For even at rest as you sleep in your bed,
Your mind rushes on, your accounts in the red.
The day's hardly started yet another week's gone.
Should you improve business, apply for a loan?

A month races by soon another year's past,
If you keep up this pace you surely won't last.
From youngster to adult it is an obvious fact
Life is not a rehearsal this is the final act!

Martha N. Selfridge

Too Dear

This isn't it- it's not the letter you are expecting from me,
And it's late
But I've been busy with the baby and everything...

I've thought about your offer and I do thank you for it,
But I can't...won't come to stay with you.
When things settle you can come here for a visit-like you used to,
Not now...not for some time,
There is still fighting here, not with guns, not in an organised way,
It's...lawless still. The people who hated have been buried
and replaced by others,
I know them now.

A lot of them are like me, people who never understood before,
I understood everything after I was dragged inside that truck.

You think I'm mad to stay here. I don't blame you for that, but
I don't think that I could be sane anywhere else now,
To the people around me here I'm a survivor...I'm lucky!
I need that- it does make a difference.

I know...I do know you're grieving for my mother,
I can't help everyone...so I have to help myself.
I'm sorry to hurt you...I'll write again soon xx

Joan Mackay

Untitled

Come Morpheus, woo this sodden shell
Seduce it from the brink of hell
The soul, released from jeopardy within
Will soar aloft - and all is well.

So Atlas, tremble neath the whip of vengeful Mars
The bloody earth shall rock upon your scars
Comus shall Perish! Circe shall reign supreme
And the dawn of nothing shall be witnessed by the stars

From the wilderness of death, there rang a cry
Echoing o'er the waste of Earth. And passing by
In gathering fury, blasted tight the door of life
With none to witness, save the brooding sky.

The mortal caprice of Cupid's play
Barbs not the arrow strong to slay
The Bird of Time, in quest of what?
The sorry pilgrims at the feet of clay

Oh! Tranquil heart in arrowed flight
Speeding beyond the beaded night
In urgent peace to kiss the dawn of time
Thus unify to effloresce the light.

G. E. J. Lawlor

Grief

This tired old world revolves in space, whilst history's clock
ticks on.
Not one turned missed; not one tick stopped, when one you
love has gone.
Life's busy rush seems hard to bear, when shrouded in our grief
We long to slow the pace of life to give our thoughts relief.
A favourite wine, a much loved tune, the jokes we used to share.
Friends rally round as best they can, to show us that they care,
But none can fill the empty void when two are cut to one.
God's actions seem a mystery, but still 'Thy Will Be Done!'
The veil of Death descends on all and guards its secrets well,
And whether we shall meet again, that, only God can tell.
But life goes on, and we must, too, though grim the task may be,
In hope our partners yet to join, to share eternity.
For sorrow never halted time nor stopped Earth in its track
And hard it is to start anew; still harder looking back.
This tired old world revolves in space, whilst history's clock
ticks on.
Not one turn missed; not one tick stopped, when one you
love has gone.

Richard J. Bradshaw

My Visit To The Beach

The soft blue waves crash with the sand,
People bathing with legs so tanned.
Punch and Judy draws in a crowd,
Boys and girls laugh very loud.

Seagulls fly past and cover the sky,
Searching for chips or remains of a pie.
The sweet smell of lotion fills the air,
For the risk of sunburn is treated with care.

Parents watch as children play.
Picking shells up on the way.
Straw hats and shades lie on the ground,
Buckets and spades are scattered around.

Toddlers paddle by the sea,
What a lovely picture from the quay.
It's time to go home now but I want to stay,
Still the thoughts and memories wont go away.

Sarah Horn

Rover, Where's Rover

Mummy there's a little girl in the water
And she looks just like me
And mummy I want to take her home
to tea
And Rover he won't let me
Naughty Rover

M. Sourbutts

Precious Memories

My love, my life, now he has gone
Throughout our marriage we became as one
I said my goodbyes with a heavy heart
A new life begins, where do I start?
With family and friends I'll get through
A widow now, I'll start anew
After all this time there is much sorrow
But who knows now, a new tomorrow
I am a person in my own right
So from now on I'll search for my light
Things to do and starts a new life
As an individual, not just your wife
Do I believe the words I say?
When I think of you darling every day
When you've been married nearly 40 years
You remember the laughter not the tears
I loved you my darling it always did show
I'm writing this now I want you to know
You taught me to love right up to the end
Now I have lost my love and best friend

Margaret Wardle

History

Through the swirling murk of a tombstone night,
From a forest light squinting distant,
Came the approach of figures, phantom-like
Stirring sharp his meditation on an open grave.

What past adventures did they who, unseen, speak?
Measured and measuring thoughts ambivalent
When glad eyes stared from dawn's crumpled sheets
Now, in that abyss of broken earth, rendered prelude.

A church bell tolls an hour unconscious to his gaze.
Caressed frigid by the damp kiss of Autumn's morbid step.
Raising a greasy bottle to lips inimical to thirst.
Drained listless, he lays himself in that perdition.

The dusky moon stares down on prone flesh
Stars glow admonishment ethereal to a dimmed mind's eye,
Which to cry aloud yearns but eternity forbids.
Incomprehensible mouth dumb, as bottle dribbles dregs to sludge.

Whose crime was it those night accusers found?
Harmony undetected, clarified in intellect's frail certitude?
That frosty corpse their soul melts prejudiced
Fearful of its reflection, they hug the dark for comfort.

David A. Russell

Divorce

Barbaric dreams squeeze your heart so cold,
Your inner feelings like a floating fire
Reach out and attack every twisted desire.
You awake from sleep like an empty shell,
No pain, no thoughts, I am in hell.
Yesterday I lived with emotion and life
Now I stare and scream at the silence,
No-one to hear me or watch me die,
The senses numb, but I need to be strong,
Other lives more important to shield from the wrong,
My pain of indifference shows only to them.
Inside I am melting like ice in a flame.
Hope is eternal my mentor did say -
To risk all again is a choice open to me;
Thank you I say, repairing my soul,
This love is different, it's making me whole
I know all these feelings are painful to me
So I give all I can and pray you be free,
I love you from within, no chains to your Soul
I give you me alone.

Les Shore

Jackdaw

Please can you tell me Mr. Jackdaw
Why you chortle, why you caw?
In your mouth you smoke a straw.

You make your bed in a Scarecrow's head
You rake about in old dustbins
And play fitba with two old tins.

You sit upon the stooks ungainly
With your head cocked so unmanely.

Why is your waistcoat oh so black
Or is it the devil who rides on your back?

You rake up stones for dead men's bones
You fix me with your glassy stare.

You hobble here, you hobble there
Then fly away into God's clear air.

You ride upon the winds that blow
You dark, satanic, beastly crow.

Alan Pow

Roses

Roses speak of love;
A gift that's given from heart to heart.
They speak of openness and vulnerability,
of beauty and hidden depth,
Of weakness, yet of inner strength,
of colour and of sweet aroma.
A gift of love;
Yet who knows how more splendid their
Heavenly counterpart will be;
They are indeed a touch of heaven,
Here on earth.

Ruth Noble

Fighting Anorexia

I ask,
    Who's that looking back from the mirror?
The haunted illusion sends more than a shiver,
NO, it's not 'me', I don't remember that face,
the smiles and the laughter have vanished, all trace.

Withdrawn, isolated and completely unaware,
a shattered appearance that now you must bear.
There's no remembrance of how, or of why?,
the daily destruction just passes you by.

Realization is only the start,
of a painful retrieval that begins with the heart.
Respecting yourself is essential to living,
without it, what can you to others be giving?.

I lost over a year, but have gained more than time,
It's not even important if this does not rhyme.
Conformity isn't a necessity to succeed on this earth,
more crucial to appreciate every single things worth.

Kerry Newman

Karol Ann

On a Thursday in September, 1977,
God gave us an angel, straight from heaven,
A beautiful daughter, we received in our care,
To love, and to nurture, and her life to share,
We welcomed her into our open arms,
She repaid us with all her love and charms,
A happy child she grew up to be,
And she gave us her love so willingly,
Eighteen years later, the years have flown by,
We now look at Karol, and then we sigh,
Our angel must soon spread her wings,
Tread new paths, try new things,
So please Lord, keep her safe and secure,
Throughout her future, and forevermore.

S. Bannister

Night Drivers Advice

At nights when it is dark so soon,
And we're without a light or moon,
We find that danger fills the air,
So please pedestrians do beware,
Some of you don't stop to think
And others take false steps to drink,
And we who drive by night don't know
From where you come or whence you go.

The toll of deaths is unsurpassed,
And when the night comes thick and fast
We've got to know and be prepared,
Remember those that have died and dared.
Life is so sweet and oh so good
It's not to be taken in useless blood,
So as you hurry home at night
Think of the drivers dismal plight.

Stick to the rules of the highway code
Be watchful of others on the road,
We want a decrease in deaths this year
So lets guard the life we hold so dear.

R. C. Ford

Christmas Time

Christmas upon us yet again,
Time for the lonely to feel the pain
The hustle and bustle of Christmas shopping
The people past without even stopping.
Stopping to give a thought to those
Whose Christmas time will only hold
Sadness with the feel of tears,
With thoughts of only yester-years.
If we can give at Christmas time,
Why can't we give all of the time?
There will always be those who need our help
Give time to them and forget yourself.
If each took a minute out of everyday
And stopped and listened to what they might say,—
Our world would live in a peaceful way.

S. Heys

Daystar Of Redemption

Daytime comes spreading rays of sun
Dispersing the clouds of night,
Like a bridge over white water rapids,
Searching for the child of night
To offer almond blossom and pink carnation
In modest confrontation.

Inner happiness forced to the surface
Unconsciously radiated to others,
By a contagious emotional aura,
Animated in the vivid hue of its creator.

The dark clouds of the night
Evaporate from sight
Replaced only by the ardour,
Emanated from the eye of heaven,
Within the hour of dawn.

Jane Hamill

The Telegram

Sunlight shines through the bright leaded glass
highlighting with starkness news at last.
My legs dead and heavy help my body descend
the steep, endless steps... I no longer pretend
that no news is good news. Brave hope now gone.
For that ominous brown envelope's contents are harm.

The day had begun like most had that year,
normality over, for now disappeared.
My heart hits my chest where it rhythmically beats.
My hand reaches out, recoils and retreats.
My head starts to throb as my eyes well with tears,
Knowingly I open and read what I'd feared...
'Lost In Action'
My eyes close, tears fall on the page...
'Presumed Dead'
My heart fills with anger and rage.
I clutch to my chest the news that I'd dreaded
remembering embraces forever ended.
I'd waited in hope from the first day he'd gone.
The war same day, was ended, we'd won!

Karen Crutchlow

World Rushes By

Watch the world as it rushes by,
Examine the reasons and wonder why?
Cast long dark shadows across the ground,
Be very careful - make no sound.

Ignore the love, forget the trust,
All that remains is worn away dust.
Hurting inside and trying to remain stable,
Whilst all you believed turns into some fable.

Empty the glass, leave it cold on the table,
Make sure that no way recovery is able.
Kiss him again, just one more final goodbye,
Then silently step out. As the world rushes by.

Niki Browne

"Think Of The Children That Was Silently Slain"

In the garden of the Lord our cries with Dunblane,
Oh how the cries of the children went through my mind,
By a man, that was useless to all "Mankind
Sadly the time passes away not forgetting that very sad day"
And we all sit and wonder as years pass away
All things were beautiful until that certain day"
Those lovely little children with lots of love to give
Were taken from this world without any motive
So lets all get together in a heart rendering way
And don't give in to evil think! Have your way"
The Lord will be with you wherever you go.
Running along like a river, that flows"
And at the end of this river. Who knows"
So try to keep your chin up and don't despair
If you think of the good times you're sure to get there"

Kenneth Stephenson

Teidi - Cool Lady Of Tenerife

Calm, aloof - she stands serene,
Quite effortless she steals the scene.

Countless numbers are her guests -
In jeans, or shorts - e'en tritty vests

She welcomes all with gentle smile,
Till - suddenly - the crowd seems vile!

Snow cap she dons, pulls down her veil,
Calls up the winds to blow their gale.

Her lovely face turns dark, and cold -
To visit then, few are so bold.

Yes - calm, aloof, she shows her pride,
True lady, she, with fire inside.

Anne Abbott

Untitled

The cold, sharp, crispness of the morning
In contrast, the warm hardness of my love
I watch you sleep.
Run my hand, across your cheek.
No movement.
I touch your arm.
You blink, smile,
Then back, to your unknown dreams.
I move closer, our bodies touch,
You sleep, but move yourself,
Allow me entry.
As I push, to feel loves warmth, you wake.
Draw me closer. Arms round my back.
Skin breaks, your nails dig deep.
With sighs of pleasure, we commit to love.
Bodies entwined, we lie naked,
Wearing only our love,
Bodies moving as if one.
Surge of passion, our love complete.
I kiss your lips, and watch your breath.

Paul Nolan

Lancaster Bomber

This lady of mine I can't forget, but that is no surprise,
I rest myself inside her womb as she points me to the skies.
The wind gives way to her shape and form to take her where
 she's bound
The throbbing sound of Merlins four lift her body from the ground.
She reaches out into the clouds, the grasses green below
Higher still over mountain peaks all glistening white with snow.
With arms outstretched she carries me to places far away,
to places that I fear to go lest I be there to stay
Her skin is scarred by weathers all from wind to hurricane.
The endless punishment she bears and suffers time and again.
My heartbeat hastens when I feel the flak rip through her breast,
Her smouldering body choking me, a burning in my chest.
But in my lady I feel secure, the battles all outside
Until her body is ripped apart in her I will abide.

J. R. Stokes

My Mother

My Mother worked hard her whole life through
To bring up us kids the best that she could do
She worked so hard, both night and day
To give us love and show us the way
She was not perfect, but need I say
I wouldn't have changed her in any way
She was always there for us every day
If we should slip and loose our way
She always had a real good ear
She even wiped away the tear
So full of love my mother was
A single thing I would not grudge
My childhood memories as I recall
In my eyes she always stood tall
I just wish she was here today
To help me and guide me on my way
But she is gone in piece to rest
But knowing that she did her best
And that means all the world to me
So she'll be in my heart for eternity

Lillie E. Sandham

Ignorance

Black, green, brown, white, blue I can wear any coloured coat
it doesn't bother you.
So why does my flesh colour cause such a commotion its
importance as minute as a drop in the ocean.
Uneasy silence, insensitive jokes hurtful comments, mindless
violence
what can be gained from acts so repulsive they leave me
feeling thoroughly convulsive.

Ethnic cleansing and holocaust just a murderous senseless
cull call, the reason is fear, it's the one to be held responsible.
Fear creator of the unsavoury, like fascism, racism, apartheid
and slavery.

Apartheid the instrument of ignorance used by fools to
prevent mankind's advance Segregation, separation surely
not in God's thoughts at the dawn of creation
Violence and hatred the ones to which you are betrothed.
Your message of evil passed on through generations, every-
one different from you to be despised and loathed.

Man's mountain of differences to high to scale, just too steep.
The cuts never heal properly, the wounds far too deep.
Our hatred for each other because of colour so pathetic, any
unification temporary unreal, unlasting, synthetic.

A world of racial harmony and equality a distant pipe dream,
that will never fit into the ignorants' crazy scheme.
But to this disease we must never yield, the fight must go on
continuing until we are all as one.

Kevin Costello

To A Rose

From bud to full blown
From countryside and town
We see your face fair, no garden to small
For you to grow tall,
Around cottage door and in hedgerows wild
In stately homes and hospitals tiled
Where 'ere you are with petals uncurled
Your message is love to a hurrying world.
Emblem of England and chosen by kings
Emblazoned at court and turned into rings
Plucked red and white to go to war
Beauty and perfume amid the gore.
Velvet beauty mid leaf and thorn
Rosebuds unfold like new baby born.
God created and loved by all
Scrambling over old grey wall,
Message of love 'tween sweethearts true
To shy to tell when love is new
All this and much more you bring to our earth
Queen of flowers - we salute your birth.

Olive Crombie

A Son's New Love

Parents hopes and dreams are such,
Their children will possess,
A sense of humour, joy and love,
Wrapped up in happiness.

Sometimes we know and feel their pain,
And share too, in their tears,
We can but try to understand,
And allay most of their fears.

Now when happiness at last shines through,
And most dark days are past,
Our hopes and dreams all realized,
Our Son has found love at last.

Those days of pain and tears now dimmed,
Though some may linger on,
Now the tears of joy once more,
A new life to build upon.

Someone to care, someone to share,
This new life you have found,
May all your future dreams unfold,
And every happiness abound.

Joy Oelmann

The Ill-Favoured People

If I must again encounter those ill-favoured people
Hanging about the alleyways of the city within,
Shall I walk by as if I do not know them,
Or offer recognition's sickly grin?

Must I continually endure their unpleasant attentions -
The ugly face, the clammy hand, the whining voice?
To give them the slip seems to be out of the question,
So I suppose I haven't any choice.

And yet I'm aware of their ever more censorious behaviour,
Their glances more reproachful, the curl of their lips more severe:
Among the crowds, perhaps, on the departure platform -
But no, I see their faces even here.

Perhaps in the cathedral they may not dare to molest me,
From the sanctuary itself the verger will turn them away:
Maybe a prayer would drown their insinuations?
Well, but I lack the hardihood to pray.

The fields of my own dear country are golden with the harvest:
Who will be the man to bring the harvest home?
Unfortunately I have other business to attend to,
Those people I know are waiting till I come.

J. C. G. Rouse

Now And Then

I am here, you are there, in mind no distance between
   Oceans apart but not in our hearts, only you can know what I mean
Why did I tell you? Why did you listen to my words so long ago?
   That sent you away - so far away, the world to right, did you?
   How will I know
No doubt you married, I did too - for safety a cowardly way out
   He was happy, children were two, special, they are - my
    salvation throughout
The abuse I received was my punishment I'm sure
   For the way I discarded your love - then shut the door
My legs defy me again and again, they have a will of their own
   Rest more the Doc. says, now and then do I smile
As I try to relax, memories come, soon I'm no longer alone
   I close my eyes, you are there, it dulls the pain for a while
Where have the years gone? My heart feels the same
   Weaker perhaps in medical terms, but stronger as I whisper your name
I love you now as I loved you then and know that again you'll find me
   In this world, the next or beyond to Eternity when finally
   your arms will bind me.

U. J. Preedy

She Came To Me In A Dream

She came to me in a dream,
the most beautiful lady I'd ever seen.
Attired in lace and silk,
Her face white and smooth as milk.
She sauntered majestically along the beach;
Offering her my hand, but I just couldn't reach.
Her hair as dark as the night,
Her eyes glowing bright,
Her body such a lovely sight,
Voluptuous and full of might.
The stars, way way above
Made her in the mood for love.
She whispered: "Come to me, Come to me"
to the sound of the wild sea.
We embraced, her lips met mine,
as sweet as crimson wine.
If this could last forever, it would be fine.
But I know she could never really be mine.
Because life is so cruel and mean,
I awoke to realise she had come to me in just a dream.

Steven Scappaticci

"The Gossip"

It isn't just the chatter or the idle natter,
But the aggravating things she tends to say.
About Mrs "This" and Mrs "That" and how she's got a scruffy cat
And "I bet she doesn't feed it every day".

About Uncle Claude and Auntie Maude, who often like to go abroad,
And "how they can afford it puzzles me"
About what they eat and what they wear, and "who would
want to live out there?
Especially taking all that family."

"And have you noticed Mrs Brown, who lives the other side
of town
Riding in her brand new limousine?
I've seen her shopping in her mules, but now she's won the
football pools
She wears the most outrageous clothes I've seen."

"And did you know that Mrs Rouse, who lives in that
enormous house
Is having an extension on the back?
How can she pay (I often say)
Especially now her husband's had the sack".

"That Mr Dobson (from the end) I hear he's got a fancy friend
And soon they'll be eloping to New York"
And then she whispers in my ear (so I'm the only one to hear)
"You'd better keep it quiet - neighbours' talk".

Janet Jones

April

April — and the laughing winds of spring
That send wash'd sheets a-flapping on the line
And shake the blackthorn boughs to fling
Petals like snow on shadowed turf beneath.

On laggard ash, no leaves unfurled,
A blackbird sings and sings again
His vibrant challenge to the world.
This spot, he says, is God's and mine.

The weaving swallows do not care
What song he sings. From deepest south
They've come to claim their share
Of happy long-remembered haunts.

Bright butterflies emerge from rest
To taste the lifting thrill of spring;
While humble bees seek where to nest
In mossy bank or mouse's hole.

Dry leaves stir on the woodland floor
Where the windflower nods to the shy primrose,
Saying it's time to open the door
To the rainbow hues of the waking year.

Peter Bell

A Mother's Love

There's nothing like a Mother's love,
It's steadfast, strong and true.
You cannot buy her precious gift,
She gives it free to you.

Turn to her in times of trouble,
In darkness and in sorrow.
For she'll try to give you good advice,
To brighten your tomorrow.

She's there for you through thick and thin,
In good times and in bad.
She'll try to lighten up your load,
When you are feeling sad.

She waits patiently to hear from you,
Where'er you feel the need.
She'll listen to your troubles,
And be a friend indeed.

Don't take her love for granted,
Don't treat her care with scorn.
For one day when you turn to her,
You'll find... that she is gone.

M. Muirhead

To My Unborn Child

O how I wish this child would arrive.
I wish to give her the love I feel inside.
She will be a child full of charm.
I long to hold her in my arms.
To hold her hands, to touch her toes
and to kiss her little button nose.
To gaze into the depths of those blue eyes.
For when they look upon you,
they look into your very soul.
And then she will know how I love her so.

D. Lampe

Rain

The rain is falling on the ground
I hear the rain swishing round
The sound it makes is pitter patter
The wind makes the dustbin lids fall and clatter

The rain is falling like pine needles and blossom off the trees
The rain is slanted in the breeze
When the rain hits the ground
It makes a light banging sound
When it hits the path it sways gently from side to side
The rain swishes in a puddle and the puddle is wide

Sarah Shepherdson

A Norfolk Storm

The storm builds and slowly the world starts to dance.
Wind blows, shouting, howling, fiercely piercing lance.
Beating, bashing, blasting, breaking nature's landscape,
Proudly displaying its mighty power, allowing no escape.

The snowstorm, now a blizzard, increases its rampage,
Strangling the countryside, with great anger and rage.
Roads lost beneath its swamping, beauteous white veil,
Enclosing, trapping, frightening, dangerous gale.

When will the wind-whipped snow cease its fight?
When will the fear tossed land ease, find light?
When will the calm beauty of nature return, give peace?
When will the earth settle, be still and turmoil cease?

Strong sunlight, calm floating clouds, silent breeze,
Melting snow, lanes now open, forgotten freeze.
The gentle calm, so good and kind, so serene,
Nature wears a gentle mantle, bright and clean.

Oh bitter battle, raging storm.
Blessed calm, strength reborn.
Fierce fighting, frozen fears.
Peace returned, no more tears.

Esme E. Wilson

View From A Train

Outside it was cold, but
Huddled cosily in my compartment
I watched the countryside scurry by
As the train plummeted onwards.

It moved its way through the towns and cities
And out once more into a land of fields and trees.
Ferns stood erect - turning their heads
As if to an unseen speaker.

Waterways rushed by,
Fields and fences blurred into one,
Soon the landscape became a green mass
Hurtling towards me.

Gradually the daylight diminished -
The train slowed -
Nearing its destination,
And - in the ghostly twilight -
It became a silver snake of light,
Slithering across the darkening land.

Lesley Gail Hickman

Destiny

Great is the mind that thinks for itself
Great is the love that I have in myself
Delicate is my heart that waits for your love
Pure is my soul that loves you and no one else.
Touched am I that I desire your lips
Yearn for your fingertips
I hunger for your soul
I ache for your whole
You come to me in whispers in the dark
Your passion I feel in the beating of your heart
I hear your call that never shall end
You to me are a lover and a friend
Great to me is the power of your love
That soars as high as the wings of a dove
As pure as love is I see it in you
For you to me are a love so new and true
I love you and through you I see only love
Together I know that we are to be.

Julie Robinson

Flying Lesson

I hover on the precarious ledge,
Wings flapping apprehensively,
Feathers ruffled in fear,
I flutter tentatively forwards....

\Plummeting,   Flying.
  Floundering,   Gliding freely,
    Squawking urgently,   Through the crystal expanse,
    Gripped by terror.   Soaring past forests,
                    And exhilarating ease,
  \I flap frantically,   With newly discovered grace
   As if treading water,   Cautious and uncertain,
    My tiny heart pounding, Then glide upwards,
   Until I regain composure...

Helen Pike

My Perfect Forest

I wander through an atmospheric forest,
Seeking something you only find in your imagination.
I close my eyes, I find some amazing colours,
A million miles from life.

I want it quick before life ends,
I close my eyes once more.
There it is again,
The fantastic sensation with brilliant light.

When I open my eyes it's all over,
I've seen fantastic colours
And now the forest's gone, and the colours with it.

Geraint Alan Irving

Our Future Home

Imagine our world, not a speck of green in sight;
Devoured by pollution, destroyed by mankind,
Some unlucky souls trapped on the planet, scrounging the
wastelands for food.
Rat and man on the same side, thinking only of survival.

Litter everywhere, even in the sea.
Oil polluting the oceans... all the fish have died.
Sea gull's snow white plumage now a black silk coat.
What once was beautiful, now wrecked by man.

No longer a continent left in one piece.
Nuclear wars saw to that, and the human race.
Radiation sweeping the planet, like a deadly gaze.
Carcases of man or animal hastily eaten without delay.

The sky dressed in a black mourning robe of darkness,
Bringing thoughts of eternal despair.
Parents telling children stories, beyond their wildest dreams.
Of people living in harmony, the times of Adam and Eve.

Sobbing, sniffing and crying, because of what we did today.
No hope in any mind, except the hope of dying.
Being relieved of this everlasting terror.
And going up to heaven, forever....

Raphael Gilbert

Our Future In The Stars

Twinkle, twinkle little star,
We know precisely where you are,
When Earth is poisoned by pollution,
You seem to offer a solution.

We will require a landing place,
Surrounded by an open space,
To store arms for our protection
Against your possible rejection.

Our Gods, in great diversity,
Guarantee to protect you from adversity
Whilst out genetic engineers
Will replace your ugly alien ears.

When Earth's resources are depleted,
And man's evacuation completed,
There, in a cave beside the sea,
You'll find some birds, two rabbits and me

Elsie Quick

My Daughter

My dearest, my darling, my lovely child.
My daughter so lovely, but not so mild.
A hurry you're in to grow up so fast.
You're letting your tender years drift past.
You're leggy and coltish with yet not much grace
Sometimes you're scruffy and look a disgrace
But, your beauty's all there, just peeping through
Just give it time, it will all come true
For you my daughter

Pearl Cloke

Untitled

I only see you once a week we live so far apart,
But no matter where you are you're always in my heart.
I talk to you every night and dream of you when I'm asleep,
I never had imagined I could fall in love so deep.
I sometimes read your letters when I'm alone at night in bed,
So that when I fall asleep sweet thoughts of you are in my head.
When you say you love me the feeling inside I can't explain,
It's like one day of sunshine after several weeks of rain.
It's unbelievable when we're together how fast the time does fly,
We're so engrossed in each other we don't notice the hours pass by.
To me you're like a nice cool breeze on a burning summer's day,
And when I tell you that I love you I mean each word I say.
I hope this love is forever and I pray that we never part,
But I want you to know whatever happens you'll always be
here in my heart.

Kate Brewster

Enchantment

In the garden at eventide
The path here winds the flowers beside
An arboured seat my need attends
How sweet the perfume that ascends

I breathe the sweetness, bless the day
My footsteps wandered along this way
A heaven sent blessing on earth today
Grand these moments bringing precious gain

My eyes just rest upon the leaves
See's layers of petals with velvety gleams
A beautiful rose nestles there
Defenceless, I gaze with enraptured stare

I feel a desire to have for mine
This beautiful bloom almost divine
The thorns make this a difficult task
Bravely I take within my grasp

Life so sweet - love divine
Know the sigh - feel the pine
Receive the scar - defeat the thorns
Grasp beauty, love above them all
Irma Humphries

Beachcomber

'Twas on a Sunday morning
I strolled 'long Bertha's beach,
In and out the penguins
With their little, orange feet.

Some were scurrying toward the shore
And others toward the sea.
While more of them stood very still
Just staring up at me.

Some flapped in pools left by the tide
Along the silver sand.
Whilst those of them that put to sea
Were tossed back on the land.

The sun was bright, the wind was sharp,
The breakers were a foamy white.
And for a time I felt refreshed
Just gazing at a simple sight.
Michael Francis O'Neill

I Used To Talk To The Moon

When I was a boy,
I used to talk to the Moon;
In the early evening of a cold, clear winter's day,
On my way home from school,
I'd tight-rope walk along a wall,
And tell him all I knew.

Now that I'm older,
The magic is gone,
I no longer talk to the Moon.
My eyes look down;
My head,
No longer amongst the stars.
P. M. Holloway

Sorted

For a few minutes she knows
What it's like to be an adult.
It's great.
She's given a pill to make it better,
"It's great, you're sorted."

She lies in a bed,
Tubes around her,
Her heart is being pumped for her by a machine.
Her memory fades into darkness,
She dies.

"It's great, you're sorted."
Patricia Rice

Somewhere

Maybe a bird, flying through the air
I know you're out there - somewhere
Clouds that move across the sky
Is that you passing by
In the oceans deep and wide
Or close by at my side
A sunset on a winters day
In everything, in every way
Upon the shore with the tide
With warm winds do you ride
Raindrops falling on my face
Are you there - sometime - some place
In the early morning dew
Can I see you
On a whispering breeze or still calm seas
Say you're there - somewhere - please.
C. Holcroft

Two Lost People

I know what hurts you so,
But do not be afraid.
You have known too much hurt - so have I.
I will try to heal it.
Do not spurn my help.
Through you, I help me!
Through me, you help you!
Let us try, tell me this - will you try?
Mostly we believe the same, feel the same, think the same.
Except you believe in just today,
I believe in every day.
I want to help you - do not be afraid.
I will not hurt you - only help you.
Together, we could find the way,
Not, perhaps to the very heights of heaven,
Though maybe we could,
But, perhaps from the depths of hell -
We could try, together.
Kathleen Camilla Garner

Granddaughter

My little girl you are now two
And Nanny thinks the world of you
With your pretty smile and blond-hair
There cannot be anyone to compare
I thought your brother had captured my heart
But when you arrived he only had part
The left is for him, the right is for you
And I love you both in all that you do
A beautiful girl by the name of Lian
Is even more beautiful than princess Diane
Have a wonderful birthday Nanny's girl
For in my oyster you're my beautiful pearl
Joan Van-Der-Kwast

The Willow's Comfort

The bright, warm golden days,
Slowly give way to cold dark winter clouds.
In despair, the weeping willow weeps for
A summer past, and long since forgotten.
Stirrings, uncommon upon the fallen leaves,
Denotes the dawning of the Christmas rush.
People like soldiers marching to and fro,
Treading heedlessly on precious memories,
Long since past and departed.
No one has time to wrap their arms,
And listen patiently of summers past.
The old, the sick, the homeless, the forgotten,
They have no one bustling in the leaves for them.
But as they weep upon the pure white snow,
Silently, the willow folds her arms around them.
A soft glowing knowledge enfolds them.
That Christmas will soon be over and beyond.
Until that time, contented, they stay, letting
The willow comfort them in the nest of her breast.
Karen Turner

'Mother Tongue'

My mother tongue
Is not my mother's tongue.
Our confabulation troubled
By our different song
We stare at one another
Failing to grasp
The empty borrowed words
Of our translated love
Deaf to each other's cry
My mother's tongue
Is not my mother tongue.
The warm air
Of her mysterious whispers
Kisses my face
Like the gentle breeze
Of a distant zephyr
Brushing
Over the surface of foreign lands

Ingrid Kerr

Rabindranath Tagore

The poems of a poet
in a strange and foreign tongue
and yet in translation
most melodious song.

Soft shades of mood and meaning
told with a quaint simplicity
delightfully expressing
the inexpressible for me.

A delicacy of description
which touches to the core
the eloquent vibrant verse
of Rabindranath Tagore.

Richard J. Matheson

End Of The Day

Silent now - he's coming
He'll soon be through the door
Silent now - stop running!
Pick those toys up off the floor

Will he hit us Mummy?
Will his mood be bad?
Why does he act so strangely?
He always makes us sad.

Hush now dears, he's here
Remember, try not to make a noise
Act naturally, no fear
Come on, tidy up those toys.

N. T. Campbell

Tinsel Time For Kittens

Oh! What a Christmas,
Oh! What a time,
He's opening the presents,
This kitten of mine.
He's into boxes,
That stood in rows,
Chasing the string,
And chewing the bows,
My Christmas tinsel,
Is tied up in knots.
He's pulled out my flowers,
And cares not a jot.
He helped with the chicken,
He's eaten the food.
The day is now over,
It's time for a snooze,
Good night...sleep tight,
I don't want to be rude,
But I can't stay awake,
So... snooze... snooze... snooze.

Denise A. Smith

An Azure Sky

I have a question for you,
said Kangaroo.

Who painted the sky
this azure blue?

It was I,
said Moo,
I thought you knew.

He's telling a lie,
said the Tsetse fly,
no Moo could fly
so high in the sky.

Then my oh my,
there was a to-do.

The Moo was challenged by Kangaroo,
who joined by friends of Tsetse too,
chased a poor deflated Moo,
with cries of Hi! A lie! A lie!
Yahoo, Yahoo, and Boo, Boo, Boo!

And this I declare,
is absolutely true.

L. Simcock-Daisy

Remembering Trevor James

I would have liked more time with him
To touch and hold and kiss,
To share with him, and give to him
The love he had to miss.

I would have liked to walk with him,
To talk, to laugh and sing,
To read a book, and play with him,
Watch birds upon the wing.

I would have liked to dance with him,
To watch him when asleep.
To see him grow, have pride in him,
Make promises, to keep.

I would have liked to tell him
How much there was to see.
Of all the hopes I had for him,
But it wasn't meant to be.

I couldn't touch, I couldn't hold,
I couldn't in my arms enfold.
I couldn't give him all my love.
He had to go to heaven above.

Doris Green

My Somerset

A County full of many delights
Valleys, wetlands, coast and hills.
Hamlets, Monuments and other sights
A Somerset that thrills.

The Beauty of a Country lane
Woodlands full of birdsong.
Foam on rocks from mighty main
Tranquillity for which I long.

Through heather on the highest moor
See huntsman after hounds.
Watching the sunrise from a tor,
Somerset knows no bounds.

Glorious gardens and their secret ways
Castles, Parks or a Stately Home.
My thoughts oft stray to bygone days
When in Somerset I roam.

I've been around to other lands
Travelled far and wide,
But Somerset is home for me
Where evermore I'll bide.

Caroline Russell

The Words Of Children

The words of children
Are mysterious.
Deep within
The dreams lie furled.

Unspeakable
Are the depths,
The dark pits of fear,
The snakes' eyes that lie there
Slowly gleaming,
To gobble them up
If they start screaming.

Yet, stars in flight
At Blackbird's calling,
Moth-kisses come;
Sunlight on grass
Arches in rainbows
Of joy too deep to drown,
Whispered only
In sleep
In the secret tongues of children.

Juliet Hopwood

Selfish Hearts

Mother and Father feel blue
cause you did what you wanted to do
You flew to the sun and the moon
and grew in the hot sand dunes

Today your dream came true
cause you did what you wanted to do
You live for the love of your life
and carry the pain like a knife

Today was the day you left us
cause you did what you wanted to do
You carry the burden forever
of knowing we weren't together

Today I'm sure you looked beautiful
cause you did what you wanted to do
You stood before God adoring
as the waves of the ocean came calling

Mother and Father feel blue
cause of what they did to you
You got what you wanted today
you don't need us no more, sail away

Rowena Tooms

The Plea Of The Tree

"Stop, stop!" said the tree,
as the workman got out his chainsaw,
"The World needs us for oxygen,
the animals a home, and more."

"Can't you see, if you fell me,
you'll suffocate the population,
famine, disease and poverty,
will sweep across the nation."

But the humble workman carries on,
with the task he has to do,
fell the tree, to make the space,
for a motorway to come through.

"It's only one more tree," he says.
"It means nothing to me,"
but if everybody thought like that,
where would our planet be?

Hayley Longster

Laughter

Laughter is a tonic-
It's better than any pill
And can really lift you
Even when you're ill

A joke, a funny story,
A simple little rhyme
Is all that's needed sometimes
Especially if they're mine!

People laughing at my work
Is the medicine for me
I'm then inspired to write more
It keeps me going you see

So, if you like this so far
My name's not hard to forget
One day, I might get lucky
I'll hit that "big time" yet!

Ruth Le-Vallois

Air

I am gliding on the wind
floating on its waves
I am reaching for the sky
and I have to fly so high.
The time..is quiet,
captured and held
- it is at this moment
there is a space...
a freedom..
a peace..
a being,..
A transition-
a change.

Justine Glenton

I Feel So Alone

Take my hand in yours Lord
and hold it very tight,
I feel so alone Lord
and life will not come right.

Now in a far off Country
away from scenes most dear,
none to share my troubles
and drive away my fear.

There are so many daily tasks
demands from those I love,
and I must deep on smiling
whilst mountains I must move.

So, put my hand in yours Lord
and hold it very tight,
let me rest upon your Strength
in long watches of the night.

Seek comfort in your presence
solution in my prayers,
and with my hand in yours Lord
I'll drive away my cares.

Peggy Netcott

Empty

Barren wasted womb,
Life-empty withering,
Natural mothering thwarted;

Grasping frantically.
Nothing!

Fear ever present now,
I dare not risk hope,
Life strangled;

Drowned in a torrent of
Red!

Carmel Brenan

Tightrope

Walking on a tightrope wire
Steps of atmosphere
Slips the line of destiny
Sweats a tear of fear

A screaming crowd looks high above
To see a dazzling dream
Movements thought so carefully
Through a spotlight beam

Inch by inch his skilful toes
Tread the danger vine
Balancing on life or death
Sees no danger sign

For destination's calling
What will be will be
Left a stand of security
Edging weightlessly

Walking on a tightrope high
To hear the great applause
To shiver as the lights go out
For only silence falls

Jeannette Anne Parker

The Forbidden Kiss

An innocent meeting,
A simple kiss,
A memory of warmth,
And a feeling of bliss,
A sense of loss,
From a sleepless night,
A wanting of something that's wrong,
But feels right.

Lee Eldridge

Untitled

"How beautiful!
The shimmering days of heat,
The sparkling sea,
The fluttering foam of grass,
The shaking tree."

"How beautiful!
The infinite stretch of sky,
The darting bird,
The unending calm of hills,
The clouds unstirred."

"But greater far:-
The simmering urge of man,
The restless soul;
The endless search in the night,
For the spirit's goal.

Phyllis Jones

The Heavens

I pause before I step inside,
    The night is crisp and cold.
Above my head the inky sky
    Is slotted through with gold.

'Tis no new sight, but hypnotised
    I let my lingering eyes
Drink in the perfect majesty,
    The glory of the skies.

I look for some familiar star
    Amongst the millions there,
My knowledge is so limited
    As still in awe I stare.

The birthplace of the universe
    Is there, and I perceive
Amidst such mighty splendour
    How could I not believe?

Florence Trew

A New Life

The wait has seemed forever,
Yet really time has flown
Since that first day they lay in love
And that small seed was sown.
Every week, and every month
Another subtle change
Clothes too tight, movements inside
A time to rearrange.

Soon the day will dawn, and then
A baby's gentle cry
Will echo in your hearts and
You will catch each others eye.
A special thought, all this is yours
Nothing can take away
This wondrous little baby girl
Who steals your hearts away.
How could you be so clever
To make this tiny perfect thing?
A special, living miracle
Such love this girl will bring!

V. Knight

"In Retrospect"

Married young in forty-one.
    In forty-three, our first son.
Second son, in forty-seven
    Another blessing as from heaven,
Our last son, in fifty four
    Decision time - no number four.

In fifty five, wife paralysed,
    Our lives would change,
We were advised.
    'For better, for worse'
Came into play
    We shape our lives,
From day to day.
    With God's blessing,
We have each other.
    My first girl-friend,
And still together.
    This was not chance,
'Twas meant to be.
    Our love will stay - eternally.

John Cole

Streams

Can't you see beyond these streams
I look at you inside my dreams
I'm so scared of what I'll face
I look around for you

Can you believe in all these things
Inside my head the bell still rings
It pulls me down towards the floor
I look around for you.

And in these times the lies begin
I can't believe I sucked you in
And now it pulls me to the floor
It will take all these things and more.

Can't even see beyond these streams
Of consciousness that puzzle me
And now I know what I have to face
I look around for you

And without wings the bee still stings
And without gain I still want things
So now I need them even more
And look around for you.

Simon Trelfa

The World Is Turning

The world is turning,
And you are moving.

The rivers are flowing,
And you are happy.

The procession is going by,
And making loud noises.

The drums are banging quickly,
And you are watching them.

The procession suddenly ends,
And you feel sad.

The rain has started,
And is beating like the drums.

The world is turning,
And you are moving.
On

Lewis Turek

Untitled

Who are these people
Where are they going
Along life's precious road
What are their thoughts
Where are their minds
Have they no fixed abode
That chap I see across the way
Does he care what goes on
He sits alone, mind wanders back
Maybe his dreams are gone.

Christine Cox

The Wind

The trees are silent
Tall and still.
Breeze and shadows
Stalk the wood,
Peacefulness abounds.

Flies and sunlight fill the air;
Water murmurs in the brook,
Magpies chatter,
Jays screech weirdly.
Silence reigns.

Wind is cooler;
Shadows spread,
Rain drops pierce the skin.
Overhead the clouds loom large,
Colour fades from everything.

Trees bend over,
Moan and writhe,
Twisting, seeking to escape.
Fiendish wind, howls through woodland,
Field and glade.

Keith Lewis Rawling

"October Leaves"

October held a party,
The leaves in thousands came.
Old hoary frost, he kissed them all,
And dressed them much the same.
Some wore gold and silver,
And some wore grey and brown,
The gentle wind it taxied them,
Until they reached the ground,
Soon party time was over,
They made a fast retreat,
And sad to say, their little stay,
Lay scattered at our feet,
Their noble work accomplished,
True beauty there was found,
They pass on now to greater things,
To fertilize the ground.

J. M. Forrest

Our School

There's just a pile of rubble
where our school once used to be,
And we are feeling very sad
My old school friends and me.
Cos' we remember teachers who
we're very strict, but fair.
Of being taught the right from
wrong, and knowing not to dare.
That once proud grey stone
building, majestic straight
and tall,
That overlooked a lovely park
Now isn't there at all,
So all you great and lesser
sons, who to that grand school came.
Remember all those happy times
Remember not the cane.

Norma A. Tweddle

"Matthew"

Midwife on her rounds
Five minutes to two.
Eight and a half pounds
Perfectly new
All dressed in blue
Grandson for me and you.

Life just beginning
Love so fulfilling.
Wide eyes searching
Cuddly toy or two
Grandson for me and you
"Matthew"

Maureen Linaker

Hallowe'en

Witches cackling, cauldrons rattling.
Ghosties howling, black cats yowling,
Makes you shake with fear.

Potions bubbling, darkness troubling,
Pumpkins flickering, witches bickering.
I feel that spooks are near.

Broomsticks flying, children crying.
Coffins creaking, rats a-squeaking.
I wish they'd disappear

Christel Watson

Still With Me

In the quiet bare room
I grew to hate
We waited.
Outside
White soled shoes
Shadow past.
A door opens and closes.

Below in the hot street
It is noiselessly busy,
I am surprised that it is lunch time.

You were soft,
Warm skin varnished with pain.
Your ice-blue eyes
Startlingly beautiful.
(The only colour I can remember
In that awful place.)
Empty as seashells,
Returning nothing.

I kissed you
As you left.

Elva Hayes

In Memory

Late May the sun shone,
Although I know I wished it,
Had poured you with rain
I'd kissed you good night
Said our silly little rhyme

Next morning,
A chill of sadness in the room
I thought you were asleep,
But bringing in the milk, I saw.

I saw blood pouring.
Not clotting.
Your face a deathly pale
I screamed,
Dad came running.

It was too late,
You'd gone and taken my
Childhood with you,
Alone in grief,
The three of us.
And we mourned, we mourned.

G. Sargeant

Childhood Days

Thoughts of childhood days
Ration books and tramways
Shuttle cocks and whipping tops
Sherbets dabs and lollipops
Crisps with little twist of salt
Each morning cod liver oil and malt
School write with ink and pen
Sounds of rag and bone men
Go to grandma's for tea
Day outing to the sea
Washing tubs and dolly pegs
Feed the hens, collect the eggs
Sugar in blue paper bags
Empire day, hang out the flags
Milkman with his horse and cart
Watching mirrors in the river dart
There's laughter and tears
When you remember the years

Della Jantschenko

Country Lane

Strolling down a country lane
Leaves falling from the trees like rain
That once were green but now are
brown
How they do come tumbling down
Oh the trees do seem so tall
Along the lane just like a wall
Round the bend the wind is keen
Through the trees I see a stream
By its side there is a mill
Ruined now - the sails are still
Now that autumn is in the air
The trees and country side seem bare.

Ruth Hodder

Where Am I Going?

Where am I going...
When will I arrive...
What makes me travel...
Will I survive...
Why am I moving...
Who chose this track...
Will I keep going...
Or will I turn back...
Is anyone with me...
Am I travelling light...
Or have I a burden
To carry this night?

D. E. Miller

Love

Love is not
irredeemable
or comforting
but a bright maybe
or a darkened cloud
meaning,
friendship,
compassion,
and hatred.
Love is a volcano
about to erupt
full of surprises
running through
your mind.
Love is the beating
of a drum getting
stronger,
louder
still slowly eating
away at my heart.

Emma Gawinowski

Real Love Is...

Love is when your eyes shine with
love,
and your feelings are as peaceful as
a dove.
Love is when your heart skips a beat,
and you feel your body in full heat.
Love is when you are low,
because the one you love, has
suffered a blow.
Love is when the one you love feels
your pain too,
that is when you know if your love
is true.
For when you feel all this,
you know around you, pure love is.

Jolene Hilliam

Sea Talk

Raging sea
Speak to me,
Tell me of your life;
Rant and roar
Upon the shore,
Vent your gathered strife.
Howl and rave
With pounding wave,
Spill your seething wrath;
Foam and boil
In swift recoil,
On your outward path.
Rise and fall
In backward crawl,
Steadily retreat;
Moan and sigh
With ebbing cry,
Your tidal run complete.

Janet Lowrie Brown

Sorry!

I am sorry for the pain
I'm sorry for the sadness in your heart
I'm sorry, because you were in love
I'm sorry that love has turned to pain
but the strongest pain of all
Is the pain of being sorry
sorry that I caused the pain
that caused you to hurt
but I am hurting more
with the guilt of being sorry

Elizabeth Barry

What Is Love

The sun is high
The sky is blue
Like a love
Between me and you

Times may be sad
They may be bad
But times may be fun
Like the burning sun

The times are the same
Like a burning flame
Times may grow cold
Or maybe old

But love will be there
As long as we care
Forever more
For always

Abigail May Owen

Romsey Abbey

Majestic monument,
Fine mother church,
Where centuries have
Hallowed sacred stones.
Mellifluous music
Issues forth -
Continuing choirs of
Unremembered nuns.
Mountbatten's bones and
Others of renown
Have found here
Rest from earthly turmoil;
Troubles left behind.
And here amid the beauty
With tranquillity -
'Neath Norman arches
Oratories ascend
For spiritual repose...
Of all who gather here
In transit - worship - prayer!

Z. M. Merriman

My Ghost

I saw a lady by my bed,
"I will not harm you, dear", she said,
Her face lit up by purple hue,
So serene, it was untrue.
My heart was beating a faster pace
I longed to touch her smiling face
She was clear in the pale moonlight
And came so close, it seemed alright
To reach and feel her silken gown.
But not to be. I lay back down
To wonder where that lady went,
Why she had come, with what intent,
The darkened room was all I saw,
My purple lady was no more.

Anne Schmidt

The Quest

Come, find me, friend,
Come, claim me now,
Before the long grey day is done,
Before cold winter comes.
I wear my solitude like a shield,
Come, seek me out, disarm me now,
Yes now, for even now is late,
The ebb tide fast recedes.
Some come, bold Conqueror of the night,
And take these brittle hands in yours,
Breathe soft upon these stony lips,
Gaze rapt into these sculptured eyes,
And win this so indifferent heart.

Molly Mettam

Polwheveral Reach

In such a place I could not speak
For leaf and lichen clothed the ground,
They sang in rich chromatic scales
And hung like fallen angels' veils.
My shoes depressed the rain-soaked moss
And led me to the creek's tide line,
All motion stopped and with it, time.

Peaceful, serene, the creek still lies
Beneath the circle of the hills,
Dun coloured mud, October sky,
The haunt of teal and goldeneye.
Shy whimbrel to dog otter calls,
A speech I cannot comprehend
In this my heart's retreat, tide's end.

Frances M. Searle

For The Otter

Wander wayward as the water
thro' the valley to the sea.
Mossy bank thy silken pillow
starlit sky thy canopy.

Run and tumble o'er the shillets;
chase the Salmon, catch the Eels.
'Fairy - windows midst the tree roots;
Oh! How pleasant freedom feels!

Winter snow has other play things,
frozen slides and fluffy falls.
When the wind bites lie ye snugly
safe within your holts stout walls.

Wander safely on forever
free from snare and hunting hounds.
Live in peace, o noble Otter,
living rich on nature's bounds.

A. Devenport

A First Class Dilemma

I saw upon my doormat clear
A letter from I soon guessed where
It was first class, which honoured me
But ne'er a postmark on it be

The stamp was sitting all alone
Remote and silent as a tomb
To marks of ink, no date at all
It looks so lonesome, beyond recall

It was as if it cried in vain
But utter silence from it came
It seemed to think it was to blame
Misbehaving above my name!

But now all day, it cries to me
To free it from its misery
"Boil the kettle make some steam
Release me quick before I scream."

K. Kundasamy

'Time-Blisters Of Sealed Perfume'

Yesterday up by the pond
I spied my lover sitting fond
Gazing at the healing water
Newly-scraped in every 1/4

'Pon the Onion-scented air
I then enquired what he'd done there?
He swore he'd touchèd no shallot
And frightened onions he had not.

Yet, (spurred by my reminder?) he
Dawn-pickled some, unknown to me
Lilac, pungent, slippery-small -
But *these* I hadn't smelt at all.

Andrea J. Lailey

Lonely Teardrop

I know we can't all live forever
and that someday we must die
but I didn't think it would be so hard
for me to say goodbye

I know that you'll forgive me
one day as time goes by
when you feel that lonely teardrop
fall from heaven where I cry

I know that you will miss me
for awhile or so it seems
but with every passing day you'll know
I'm there inside your dreams

I know that you'll remember me
with a smile upon your face
as you stand beneath our old oak tree
with a new love to take my place

I know that you will see me
here in heaven once you've died
but till then my love I'm up above
like an angel by your side.

Tina Pruden

Lost Happiness

Her charm has
become crude,

Like a tree that
has lost is blooms.

Her manners
are effected,
and she is lost.
And I, I am rekindling
memories of that lost happiness.

D. Nicoletti

Shepherd's Delight

Dusk blushes.
Vibrant crimson flames burn the sky.
Red devil seducing night.
Calm, cool sky ignites.

Glimpsing Mars.
Autumn scorching spring.   Dangerous!
Cherry pie. Strawberry tart.
Full lips. Beating heart.

Blood red wine;
Fragrant, tasting sweet as the rose.
Deep, passionate, inviting.
Desire heightening.

Dusk ages.
The velvet executioner
Buries day and gives birth to
The angelic moon.

Jacqui Fairley

Idle Thoughts From A Hospital Bed

Some with one limb,
    Some with none
Awaiting patiently
    Till all be over and done
Could turn me into a pacifist
    Saying "Drop that gun!"

Is there a promised time
    When war shall be no more,
And must we always stain our hands
    With other nations' gore,
Eternal Father, hear our prayer
    And save us 'ere we perish here

K. H. Rudolph

Try To Understand

It may be we're too hasty
To blame and to condemn
The works and ways which we observe
Among our fellowmen.

It's easy from the outside
To say what we would do
When we know only half the tale
And that half isn't true.

It is dangerous to make statements
For we know not what ensues
And we cannot judge another man
Unless we wear his shoes.

When faced with situations
Which doubtless do arise
It is better far we seek to help
And not to criticise.

For we all at sometime make mistakes
But how uplifting it can be
If someone tries to understand
And shows some sympathy.

John Osborne

God's Gift

The gift of life from God above
A precious gift blessed with love
We are all precious in his sight
He is our shepherd of the night
Within his shelter bright and clear
He keeps us safe from all we fear
He comforts us when we are sad
He protects us from all that's bad
He shines a light to guide our way
He hears our voice when we pray
The joys of life we shall fulfil
With his blessings of goodwill
The happiness we sought to find
He secures with peace of mind
His gift of those our lives we share
Are blessed with tender loving care
A staircase to heaven he has sent
The day after today he has lent
Our destinies shine from up above
Our yesterdays are blessed with love

Alison Felkin

Untitled

As I lie,
down to die.
I finally find,
my peace of mind.

May I rest in peace,
for eternity at least.
As I lie,
down to die.

I see myself,
upon my bed.
Then I realize,
that I am dead.

As I float,
far far away.
I hear a voice,
so calm so sweet say.

You are bad!
You are sad!
It's off to hell,
with you my lad.

Graham Joce

The Mirror Image

As I look in the mirror,
I see not myself,
But my self as seen
Through the eyes of the one
For whom my eyes search,
On whom, when found,
My eyes rest in wonder,
Haltingly tracing
Every line of his face,
Deciph'ring the changing
Expression of his eyes
And warming to his warmth
In shared laughter.

Ruth Caro Salzberger

I Came To Climb A Mountain

I came to climb a mountain
To be amongst the best,
To show that life's for living
And the body's there to test.

I came to climb a mountain
I'd something there to gain;
My body's weakness to expose
To tiredness and pain.

I came to climb a mountain
And now I'm back I know -
The body still bends to my will
And strength of mind can show.

I came to climb a mountain
A mountain of the mind;
The doubts and fears I've cast away
And peace in mind I find.

Geraldine Robinson

A Prayer For Peace

Fair winds blow me far across the sea.
To island green, to mountains high
and skies of blue.
Take my hand and walk with me
on Gods good earth
Open my eyes unto your wealth of
pastures new, where fishes fly and
birds on high spread out their wings
and cry of freedom.
Where flowers in abundance grow
and waves beat on the golden shores
where peace is not just another word
where love is free, for all to share
I'll walk with thee, and say a
prayer for peace on earth

Una Terelinck

Daylife

Surrounded by dawn light
With creatures awaking,
Precious new moments
The world is creating.

Infused with sunlight,
Propelled by its vigour;
The planet rolls onward
Constrained through its rigour.

Suffused by twilight,
With darkening neighbours;
Life acquiesces
And changes its labours.

Engulfed by blackness,
Infinity beckoning;
Nature continues
Beyond human reckoning.

David Berryman

Reflections Of Your Soul

Eyes are the windows to a man's soul,
Reflecting thoughts and feelings.
That deep, dark, inner hole,
A chamber of hidden meanings.

When your soul is sad and overflowing,
With emotion because of it all.
The eyes well up, mysteriously glowing,
And the tears, they fall.

The windows, as you look in,
Gradually open wide.
Revealing thoughts of ugly sin,
Another's darkside.

But when the eyes are shining bright
Reflecting rays of glorious gold.
It is that special inner light
Of beauty you behold.

Vickie Wheat

Soon Is Not Enough

So few times in life
thoughts and deeds combine,
kindling faith with hope.

We are all too brief.
Most go out untried -
strive to widen scope.

Soon is not enough.
Oh! Go sculpture time,
lest you sculpture cope.

Geoffrey Bennett

Life

Without you my life is a living
of knowing helplessness,

The yearning to be with you, to
feel your warmth through the touch
of your hand,

To caress, and with my lips
know the shadows of your face,

To kiss, and through my mouth
taste the beauty of your body,

To share your dreams, your tears,
your laughter, to be your life.

Madeleine M. Saunders

Nature's Cathedral

I heard a lovely choir of birds
So beautiful to hear
I seemed to understand their words
They told that God was near.
This church was built of stately trees
The roof of cloudless sky.
Old nature gave to me the keys
I could not ask her why?
The alter was a bank of flowers
Old nature's font was there
The windows were of leafy bowers
At atmosphere a prayer
The congregation was the flowers
The birds and rabbits too
This lovely scene I watched for hours
In nature cooling dew
The organ was a gentle stream
Its notes so sweet and clear
To me 'twas just a lovely dream
To tell that God was near

Moyra Wilding Rome

Living

Life is all bustle and hurry -
Full of cares trouble and worry.
Rushing and running for hours,
No time for sunshine and flowers.

Often we long for an island
Where tranquil rivers flow.
Away from the busy highway.
Away from the greed we sow.

Back to the grassy meadow where
Daisy and buttercup small
Lift heads to the golden sunshine
And smile, 'til the evening's fall.

Content with the patch there given
Push roots in the rich brown earth,
Making the best of the blessing,
Showing the world their true worth.

Elizabeth Searle

Elizabeth

Back in 1973
The good Lord he bestowed on me
A daughter.

There was none finer in the land
and as she grew she took my hand
My daughter

I tried to teach her right from wrong
and help all others as she passed along
My daughter

I loved her dearly with all my heart
Hoping that she and I would never part
My daughter

I knew that this could never be
a child is only lent you see
The cycle must begin again
with my daughter.

J. H. Grygoruk

One More Lesson

It was last summer when we met,
we laughed and talked of this and that.
And softly, through the winter too,
slow, but sure, our friendship grew.

Our feelings seemed to be the same,
in retrospect, 'twas all a game....
To you, a conquest to be made,
To me, a game I shouldn't have played.

So, there we were, our legs entwined,
your eager body joined with mine.....
then you recalled you were not free,
your guilt moved in, it couldn't be.

We pulled apart, I read your eyes,
and saw that it had all been lies.

Fredi Newton

Freedom

Locked inside this prison.
With no room to call my own.
I often dream of freedom.
When I can walk alone.

To come and go, just as I please.
To sit and watch the birds and bees.
Down at the seaside or in the park.
This is the dream locked in my heart.

To have a dream as nice as this.
And know this freedom.
I must resist.
Until the day I walk free.
And all my dreams turn to reality.

Brenda Wood

The Night Has Beauty

Softly walk the midnight hour,
creeping in to each shadowy bower.
With timid heart and bated breath,
for all is hidden in a misty vest.
Tangy whiff of autumned leaf fire,
careful now, glide past the mire.

Startling is the cry of the owl,
and other creatures on nightly prowl.
Above the moon in a silver shroud,
hides a while in a veil of cloud.
In hushed suspense quietly creep
into another world, just take a peep.

Hair bejewelled with glitter mist
like a laden web of beauty kissed.
The last on wing silently settled,
and the silver sea, moonlit speckled.
So tranquil is the night... so calm,
blotting out day with sweetest balm.

Dorothea Green

'Ghost In My Heart'

I search deep in this reflection
and I see eyes I've never seen before
I see a person I've never known before
I see loneliness written everywhere
and a heart that's in despair
a heart that's reaching for the skies
and crying out for that hand to hold
just yearning to re-live this memory
still holding onto my only dream
though I feel an emptiness inside
cause I'm alone with a ghost of you

As I'm looking out into the night
I see your face among the stars
I hear your voice echo in the wind
I feel your touch each time I sleep
I'm reaching out for you tonight
but I'm just fighting against time
trying to keep this memory alive
cause I'm alone with a ghost of you
a ghost of you in my heart tonight

Sharon Purcell

Love's Requiem

It's very strange how love can change
From perfect bliss to sordid strife;
How changing moods and attitudes
Can separate a man and wife.

See what a mess is wrought by stress
As mental pressures grow too strong;
And tranquillizers can't disguise
The fact that things are very wrong.

Then if by chance some new romance
Sweeps one or other off their feet,
They can't pretend the rift will mend -
The marriage breakdown is complete.

To curb the hate they separate
And try to live lives of their own.
For one, success; but bitterness
Constrains the other, lost and lone.

The last recourse is a divorce.
A judge unties the wedding knot.
The two loose ends aren't even friends
And where love bloomed, now love is not.

W. L. Tyson

Daffodil Time

My love died in daffodil time.
A lone thrush was singing.
All the earth was springing
But he could not stay.
Ahead just pain and sorrow,
No dignified tomorrow.
No words to say.
Better for him to leave.
I have to stay and grieve.
I cannot stop my weeping.
Wake in the early morning,
See lonely summer dawning.
There is no rest in sleeping.
The roses bloom tomorrow.
Will they deaden sorrow?
Will they soften pain?
They say time will relieve it.
I cannot quite believe it.
Shall I love daffodils again?

H. M. Liebeschuetz

To My Grandchildren

Will you walk with me down memory lane?
Would you care to hold my hand?
Shall we reminisce my childhood.
The castles built of sand.
The waves that tickled my small toes.
The ice creams, white, yet creamy.
The picnics, shared on our vast lawn
Those halcyon days, so dreamy!
When mother called us in from play,
Those days were all too short.
The "lucky bags" and bull's eye sweets.
With one half penny-they were bought.
'Twas safe to wander through the woods.
Our baskets, full of flowers.
We'd stop and pick ripe blackberries,
From heavy laden boughs
The mushrooms in the farmer's field,
As white as driven snow!
Yes! If I could turn the clocks back.
That's where I would love to go.

Betty Mai Challinor

A Lament For John Kennedy

Here on these treasured fields of ours.
With Hawthorn Hedge and wooded bowers
Where rich and poor alike may stray
There once more I wend my way
Across the meadow path well worn
In others footsteps ever onward borne
I come into the wood and grieve
With my beloved runnymede
The steps I climb and then a prayer
For the good man honoured there
The memory of him ever green.
In the heart of runnymede.

Elizabeth Starling

The Beginning

Oh little seed take root we pray,
For we have waited so long.
The soil is rich, the weather calm,
The birds are full of song.
Oh little seed stay firm and deep,
Take all the goodness spare.
For you will grow so big and strong
If you just linger there.
Oh little seed just grow and grow,
And let God give you life.
Allow us a chance to share our love,
A family, not just man and wife.

Alison Pisani

The Seasons

It's winter now and cold winds blow
and with them bring the ice and snow
The gardens look so bleak and bare
in spite of all your tender care.

But Spring will come and with it bring
the gift of life to everything
The buds will form upon the trees
and wave their branches in the breeze.

Then Summer comes in all its glory
and soon it is a different story
The flowers bloom, the trees abound
with fruit and colours all around.

And then it's Autumn, leaves will fall
the trees will need no help at all
To shed their leaves of red and gold
upon the ground now growing cold.

But everything must have its day
for we all know it's nature's way
The world revolves, we all depend
upon the seasons in the end.

Irene F. Mason

Dreams

The mind roams free,
a whole new world of questions.
Maybe answers
a chance to truly discover
a new dimension.
An escape from reality,
but maybe into an even more
terrifying realm.

Barbara Thomas

Here

Where I go none can see,
Deep down inside of me.
Where I go none can follow,
This place is mine for none to borrow.
Here is peace and solace,
Here is sanctuary from malice.
None come here deep inside,
In this place where I abide.
Reach me if you can,
None can enter, beast or man.
Only one spirit here, mine alone.
I alone sit on this throne.
From here I am in control,
Body, mind, heart and soul.
For here is me and I am here,
Here is a place only I can see,
When I die, here goes on;
   as me.

Hugh Adams

Past

Where have all our childhood,
our door games gone,
which made me
So very happy child.
Loving joyful,
the games we used
to share with our friends
where Skipping, Hopscotch,
rounders, marbles, cricket,
what time is it Mr. Wolf,
Farmer - farmer two
balls,
where we played for hours,
From sunset until night.
Which I have loving
memories of my
Childhood days.

Denise Doherty

Autumn

Golden Leaves are falling
why should we be sad
rather we're recalling
all the joys we've had

Round us like a glory
in the Autumn air
tell again the story
of a past so fair

Lift your hands to catch them
drifting from the trees
lift your heart to hold them
   Golden Memories.

D. M. Chamberlain

The River Is Dying

'Oh God' old river
You are dying
There should be life
On your bed there lying.

What has gone wrong
We all know the solution
We must put pay
To this terrible pollution.

For we know in our hearts
It has all gone wrong
But we must make again
This river strong

Because if we don't
It will take away
A part of our life
We could never repay.

Jeffery David Moyes

Pilgrimage To The Past

I pushed aside the bracken
From your lonely grave,
and peered at the tombstone
Blackened with age.
Long have I sought you,
I who bear your name.

I know you not - and yet
I am a part of you.
Your tinkling laugh
Or soft sweet smile?
A femininity that has small place
In this modern raucous while.

Dearest Jane - Great grandmother
Who died so young at twenty-four,
Said 'fair of face and gentle way',
What would you find in me - of you -
Were you but here
In this my day?

C. R. Parkin

The Kingfisher

The kingfisher darts upon the brook
I quickly glanced to take a look
but gone it is.
Like memories of forests by night
sunny days, so warm and so bright.
Like the echoes of a distant valley,
calling me, calling me.
We look to the future,
with eyes full of promises
but we won't be here,
only time will be there
we will be, like the kingfisher
within this song.
Just a flash of colour.
And we will be gone.

A. M. Lawrence

Love

"Draw back the clouds that I may feel
The sun upon my face -
The soft caress of comfort
And the warmth of its embrace

And like the sun you warm my heart
The clouds you blow away -
You've brought such happiness to me
To each and every day -

For when you're not beside me
You are here within my heart -
My thoughts are always with you
We are never far apart -

So thank you for you caring -
Your sharing, loving ways -
My love is yours forever
"Till the ending of our days"

Marie Hirst

Me

They try to mould me to their shape
Must stop it now before they take
Away my mind and personality
Or else I'll loose my sanity
Doctor, lawyer or ever nurse
I want to choose for better or worse
I'll be just what I want to be
See just what I want to see
Be myself both in and out
Just watch my whole world turn about
Leaving me as King of all
My thoughts and values growing tall
I'm different, I'm a miracle
A genuine faultless spectacle
Of truth, of hope and dignity
And all because of being me.

Kerry Jones

Absent

"I wonder where my daddy is?"
The little child said.
"It would be nice
If he could come
And read to me in bed."
"It would be nice
To take my head
And rest it on his knee.
To kiss my face
And wipe my tears
And say my prayers with me."
"My mummy came
Gave me a kiss
But how is she to know
I love them both
Not one alone
Oh! Why did daddy go?"

Violetta J. Ferguson

Flounder Man

Manipulate with eyes
Pretend to hate despise
Put him down so down when so far down
Putty pressed and soft
From eyes of man despair in hand
Then brings his mind aloft
Eyelids flicker so much quicker
Temptation work of art
Grace and beauty all at work
When hooked then will depart
The flounder man in every land
A fish from water gone
Captured by the angler
Unsound of woman song

R. P. Walker

"Round The Bend"

"How much further Gran?
Are we round the bend yet?"
"Oh, Gran's been there for ages
you just ask anyone she's met"
"Well, if you are there already
that means I am there as well,
but when did we go round it?
I've only seen this hill,
and a great big hill it is Gran
I don't know how you've made it,
let's see if there's a seat here,
bet you'd like to sit down a bit.
But Gran, what about this bend?
you said we'd be there after that,
now you say we're round it
and still, I don't know where we're at.
Never mind Gran, my dad told me
that you're sometimes in a muddle,
so 'til you're feeling better
we'll sit here and have a cuddle."

Pamela Wood

Desolate Glory

How beautiful was that summer
listening to the nearby stream.
Sometimes the call of the plover,
such was that summer of dreams.

Can they ever be forgotten
those men so close, and now slain?
The ache that this has begotten
recurring again and again.

In the heat of the battle
one calls, the other replies.
Each with his own task to grapple,
duty, not glory, the prize.

Does duty alone bring content?
With hindsight, it is plain
that both body and soul were rent
and cried out 'never again'.

Once more the same bright summer.
Listening not hearing the stream.
Muffled the call of the plover.
A different summer of dreams.

Collin West

Bosnia

Rich - brown,
the earth they till,
they turn and toss
and prod it still.

Their blood will seep
among the stones
their mothers weep
in empty homes.

And snow will come
- cover white
the graves they dig
for freedom's plight.

And from their burning
scorching earth
their hate will grow
and find rebirth.

Rich - brown,
the earth they till,
they turn and toss
and prod it still.

Caitriona Geraghty

In Memory Of Vota

Our Vota was a lovely dog,
Obedient and loving
A foxy face and bushy tail that
Made her more becoming.

When you came in the door her tail
Would start to wag with pleasure
We hope you have fond memories
Of the dog that you did treasure.

She's gone now, up to heaven
To a doggie paradise,
Where everything a doggie wants
Is plentiful and nice.

So do not grieve for Vota
Even though you are apart
But keep her in your mind
And even more so in your heart.

I. Newbury

Untitled

When she's happy the sky is blue
When she's sad it's a different hue
Her moods are like the changing sky
No one really can know why
When she smiles out comes the sun
Then life really is all fun
When she scowls just stay away
Disappear just for the day
Then when the sky is blue again
You know it's all not been in vain

A man is all a woman's not
Most times he's happy with his lot
His moods do not swing up and down
Seldom do you see him frown
He tends to take life each day
And copes with it in his own way
Of course at times he can be blue
But starts each day as if it's new
Forgets the worries that have gone
Starts again and carries on

Jean Ward

For Mam

My friend is gone,
So mourn with me,
For laughter lost.
No smiles to be
Bestowed with love,
For all to see.

My friend is gone.
Don't cry with me,
Your tears cannot atone.
And please, no sympathy
Though kindly meant.
I weep alone.

My friend is gone.
Come pray with me,
To place her in more loving arms
Where she is free
From pain and sorrow
And then I'll smile - tomorrow.

A. Long

Friends

Friends are like diamonds,
Precious and rare,
So please do take care of them,
And they will always be there,
Love them, and cherish them,
Until their life ends,
That is the best recipe
To make a good friend.

K. M. Mortimer

Useless

You're as useless
as a dead flower,
as a locked up tower,
as a sauce without its cup,
as a down without its up.

As useless
as a fire, without its heat,
as legs without their feet,
as a toilet without a flash,
as a glass that will not wash.

As useless
as a wrapper without a sweet,
as a cracker without a treat,
as a Christmas tree that won't light,
as a trouser that's too tight!

As useless
as a lock without a key,
as a gift that isn't free,
as an empty cup of tea,
That's right, you're as useless as me!!

Ruma Islam

Bulimia

You say you are depressed,
You act really stressed.
You slit your wrists,
and clench your fists.
It's hard to believe that you
make yourself sick,
You seem completely normal
and in love with Mick,
You always act happy,
But I know you're not,
You worry yourself quite a lot.
When I first met you I was
jealous 'cause you were so thin
But you think I'm lying
and won't take me in.

Lucy Hosking

The Tearful Heart

How long must the heart pine
For the love of thine?
Must it forever be denied?
Will nothing ever turn the tide?

Must its love fade away,
Like the hours of a summer day,
Its warmth turning to winter cold,
A feeble beat which once was bold?

Year after year goes by,
Slowly at first, then they fly.
A lingering hope, a shadow of the past.
Until it is still at last.

J. V. Ford

Loving You

Gentle skin caresses mine
Roaming hands that thrill
Hearts together beat in rhyme
Our cups of desire fill

Passioned lips that seek and find
Responsive passioned treat
Then our bodies one entwined
Will dance to loves own beat.

And when our cups shall overflow
We stay as one, us two
And sharing in the afterglow
We say "I love you"

Pat Casey

Untitled

Where are the one's life left behind,
Why were they treated so?
Are they still there, someone to find,
Or is the answer no?

Were they so evil, no-one cared,
Abandoned, with no thought?
Why were these outcasts - so declared,
Now helpless and so fraught?

The answers here are old enough,
'Tis nothing new or planned.
Types treated so, were often tough,
Their lives though, never grand.

The world that is, will never change,
Forever, some will suffer.
Be they of Animal or Human 'range,'
Will always find life tougher.

Of course, survivors will be found,
In one life or another,
However, truth is so profound,
'Tis left to nature's mother.

Ramon Clarke

In Praise Of The Isle Of Mull

Here, "nothing seems to matter,
That's the beauty..."
At least, that's part of it.
No stress, nor sense of pressure, nor
Of bounden duty,
Must be the heart of it.

Yet, greater than its tempo -
Shall we say - or,
At most, the lack of it,
The splendour of the sea and hills,
The night, the day,
Lie at the back of it.

Fairest of all the unspoilt isles,
As yet you stand -
(Is this the root of it?)
Fresh, as your first morning from
Your Maker's hand -
Aye! That's the truth of it.

Robert A. Hardwidge

Life

Sometimes we win,
Sometimes we lose
But we must cope.

In times of pain
In times of loss,
When we want to die
Somehow we survive.

And sometimes,
We may just drown.

In hardships, in stress,
When our hearts are broken
We feel we may not live,
But, we do.
It happens to all of us
At some point in our lives,
Whether it happens when
Young or old.

We may never get over it or if we do,
The feeling, the way,
Nothing will ever be the same again...

Merin Yilmaz

A Pleasant Room

A pleasant room,
A cosy fire,
Curtains, rich and full.

Colourful cushions
Scattered around.
Delicious fruit,
In a well loved bowl

Attractive ornaments,
Pretty lamps too
Creating soft light
Beautiful.

Magazines here,
A special book there.
Treasured pictures
Everywhere

Relaxing so,
In a comfortable chair
'Tis really a pleasure,
Just to be there.

Hilda Mason

The Night

The stars are out tonight
In a clear, beautiful sky.
Time seems to stand still
As I watch the night go by.
The moon is full and bright
With a magic of its own.
I feel so safe and peaceful
But strangely, not alone.
As I stare into space and wonder,
Something stirs within my soul
That connect all things to me
And I feel completely whole.

K. T. Blundell

Poppies

Windswept fields of bright red poppies
Silken petals disarrayed,
Dipping, swaying, join together
Dancing in a wild display.

Winds blow stronger, now the poppies
Move like soldiers on parade,
Columns marching into battle
Meet the challenge strong and brave.

Rising, falling mass of poppies
Hold steadfast, resist and fight,
Tearing winds abate, surrender,
Fragile triumph over might.

Tossing waves of bright red poppies
Heads held high in proud disdain,
Victors over winds of power,
They survive to dance again.

Pearl Hallett

Snowdrops

All is grey and gloomy,
November has come again;
Nothing to cheer the soul,
And everlasting rain.

December brings the snow;
A robin's breast glows red;
The light of Christmas gives us hope,
And spring lies just ahead.

January, and the gloom is lifting.
Our spirits rise, and not in vain;
Out of the dark and icy cold
Snowdrops have come again.

Sylvia Prevett

"Thousands Lose Jobs"

Dirt and money,
Hand in Hand,
Grime and grease,
Land from land.

That's that,
That's gone,
Seam too deep,
Price too steep.

Town up, town down,
Crime up, jobs down.

Dirt and money,
Hands on land,
Cuts and losses,
Bimbos and bosses.

It's time for change.

They all need labour,
Not benefit and a Super Saver.

Matthew Fairclough-Kay

The Cat To His Master

You killed my brothers, only me
You saved and drowned the other three.
For seven years we kept your house
And garden free of rat and mouse.
And now at last the old cat's gone,
I sit here, in her place, alone.
I curl my tail and fold my paws.
(The wind is howling out of doors,)
And for a little while I'll purr
And presently groom all my fur.
When spring returns I'll be out
Creeping, silent, about,
Hunting, among the grasses,
Any foolish beast that passes.
And as evening falls I'll sing
To the moon and to the spring,
To the object of my desire.
But tonight we'll have the fire,
Sit cosily together
And never mind the weather.

Margaret Wells

Goodbye

Say your words,
They are goodbye,
Say them again,
then you will fly,
up to heaven
you will go,
through the gates
and say hello.

Nicola Jane Bamford

Silent Friend

A castle of words
A room of silence
An air of stillness.

Soft, short whispers,
meaningless murmurs,
The flicking of pages.

A peaceful place,
A comforting quietness.

A reliable friend,
With all the answers.

Easy on the mind,
Soothing on the ears,
Staying in silence through the years.

Emma Clark

Shades Of Green

Shades of green, in every hue.
Brings great joy, to me, and you.
Heralding the months of spring.
Oh, what wondrous beauty, brings.
Beauty that is forever seen,
In the hues and shades of green.
As the months pass by we see
All the shades are there for we,
To enjoy in gentle tone
Through the windows of our home,
Or, in the spaces wide and free,
As the birds soar, so do we
At the beauty forever seen,
In the hues and shades of green.

E. Wild

Evening

Black boughs lace intricate designs
Against a pearly sky,
Like goblin etchings by some hand
Of cunning wizardry.
The blood-red circle of the sun
Below the dark earth's rim is hidden.
The shadows now grow long
And all small voices dim
While overhead the stars shine clear
In velvet blue impearled.
The silver moon sails there serene,
And stillness fills the world.

M. Thompson

Valley Of Doom

Sitting here looking at the moon
Shining down into the valley
The valley of doom
Where once people lived,
And children played
Down in the valley of doom.

It was said one day.
During a heavy storm.
A storm so cruel.
That swept down the valley
So swift and sure
It showed no mercy
For rich or poor.

When the waters went.
There was nothing left.
The ones that survived
Stood and looked with bated breath.
Down in the valley of doom.

Dave Pearson

'Evening'

A breeze blown in from an aged summer
That turned to autumn long ago
Stirs with fleeting presence
The tired lace hanging at
My window
Suddenly the air is charged
With an elusive scent of memory
And shadows cast by suns
Now faded
Slip back into the room
Dancing to a murmur
Of forgotten music

The corner chair seems occupied
I sense the whisper of my name
As if briefly
You'd returned

Peter Murray

My Teacher

Please give your teacher
Love and respect.
For, he sweats for your sake
And gives more than you expect.

He is a candle that lights
Your way to a future of your dream.
He is the architect, the guide
And the leader of the team.

His message matches
That of a prophet.
He works hard and glad
Without real profit.

His pleasure comes when
He sees you up and high.
Like a star or a moon
In the middle of the sky.

Please stand up and
Pay your teacher tribute.
And treat him with a
Gentle heavenly attitude.

M. A. Adlan

Unexpected Happiness

Forbidden fruits are nicer
    so I always think.
The pleasure is intense,
    the naughtiness complete.
The memories last forever
    if those times are past,
but you used your common sense
and made sure that they would last.

Nick Hayes

A Sonnet For A Special Friend

You will always be special to me,
Because you are very kind.
As long as you are happy.
I do not mind,
Who you are with,
Or what you do.
I just want you to know,
I will always care about you.
If somebody hurts you in anyway.
They will hurt me to.
Whenever we are together,
I am never sad or blue.
    I will be here if you need a friend,
    Until my life is through.

Jason Foulkes

Rowan

I am a dog o' high degree
I'm black, pure black in colour
My Mum bocht me, wi' pedigree
For an awfa' lot o' siller.
I sit and stay, and gi'e a paw
I'm really awfa' clever
And I never ever run awa',
Oh well then - hardly ever.
I seldom bark, well jut a bit
When strangers come tae visit
"But" says my Dad, "We should be glad,
That's no' a bad thing, is it?"
We have twa cats, I don't mind that,
No, really, I'm no' kiddin'
They baith like me, but I eat their tea
And Mum says that's forbidden
I love tae chase them now and then,
Big "Pepper" and wee "Sockies"
But my very favourite's up the den
Where Mum tak's me for "Walkies"

Elizabeth Mitchell

Another Forgotten Man

No-one is important,
But everyone wants to be,
Someone to be remembered,
Someone like you and me.

To do it they need their courage,
It's not easy to put out a light,
It almost makes it easy,
When they've gathered up their might.

The world's eyes are now upon you,
Are you happy now?
Your fate it all depends on
The man in the back row.

"Rise" the cleric bellows,
You rise for the last time,
At last the hype is over,
"Now fame at last is mine."

The years you longed are going,
Now no-one gives a dime,
For now you're forever inside,
Inside; doing time.

Clare Michael

Reverie

We need in life today
What ever people say
To recapture a sense of wonder
To probe the mysteries of life.

What is it that we could seek
That would make us halt and think
So much is beyond us
Because we're on the blink.

The mysteries we have been given
To wonder and reflect
We can never disentangle
For indeed we are inept.

There's something deep inside us
A longing to resolve
Which leaves us always groping
In such a humble way
To even find the reason
Why night must follow day.

Barbara Voss

Reality

I, realize
The beauty of creation.
The blue in the skies,
Heaven's countless bodies,
The gift of Paradise.

I, realize
Earth's fantastic magnitude,
The mountains high and low,
The foothills in their grandeur,
Man's state here below.

I, realize
Creatures small and mighty,
Things that creep and crawl,
Sea life a plenty,
Almighty made them all.

I, realize
Mysteries unfathomable,
Secrets strange and true,
Slowly, surely, revealable
In me and you.

Dennis R. DeSilva

I Can't Save The World

I didn't march for blacks
With Martin Luther King,
I didn't burn my bras
With unliberated women.

I didn't smash a window
For British suffragettes,
I didn't tear my clothes
Because of Grand his death.

But I buy a magazine
From people on the streets,
For I can't save the world
But it helps them make ends meet.

Jo Sutherland

Brother

I stand and gaze up to the sky,
No one knows but I know why,
You are the biggest one
That shines so bright,
I don't see you in the daytime
You only visit me at night
But you never really left me
You visit each day after another
But I'm so happy that I can say
I loved you
My big brother!

Dolores Y. Blease

Water Calm

Suspended from life's reality, I drift
    under Nature's spell,
on my path of liquid serenity that no
    spoken word can tell.
I meander along through the splendour
    of our English country side,
my transport a metallic wonder, being
    long and not very wide.
Relaxed in body, with peace of mind
    I tie her for the night,
the first of many nights to come, on
    this my holiday, so right!

Judith Bowles

The Tragedy At Dunblane

Off to school they go,
Primary 1, quick, not slow,
They go to the gym
With high expectation
Then - utter desolation
Throughout the nation.

To their parents we offer
Sympathy and prayer,
Entreaty and supplication.

Sister Dolores

That Day

That day he stepped into my life
That day it all began
That day he said, he would stay
Except, instead he ran

He promised we'd be together
He made me believe
I guess I fell for all his charm
Or was I just naive.

For since that day
My life has been
Lonely, full of tears
I doubt I'll trust another man
Throughout my living years.

Helen Lang

Our Contribution

(The thoughts of a retired
Play-group leader.)
We may not climb a mountain,
Or journey to the moon,
Or write a fine best-seller,
Compose a catchy tune.

To sing at Covent Garden
May never be our fate,
Nor yet create a masterpiece
For hanging in the Tate.

We may not win an Oscar
Or an Olympic prize,
On many a distant vista
We may not cast our eyes.

Maybe, one day, our children
When their pre-school tale is told
May rate our contribution
As worth much more than gold.

Betty M. Coles

My Ideal Beach

Smooth, soft, golden sand
Light blue sea.

Very hot weather
But a gentle breeze.

Lush green palm trees
Swaying in the restful wind.

The tropical birds rest so high
Near enough touching the sky.

A shiny hot tropical sun.
Colourful, beautiful fish.
beneath the translucent sea.

All this very beautiful to see
on my ideal beach.

Alana Colvin

The Twist In The Toil

I glide and slide from
sill to floor,
Ghostly, and marbled white.
Solitary, and unannounced,
Waiting for the night.

The unexpected visitor,
a welcome guest for me,
But once inside, my
friendly foe,
Fixated, still will be.

I am a friendly pussy-cat,
Replete, yet full of woe,
I didn't mean to eat him up
And yet he had to go.

Mary Thorn

Eve - Not So Sorely Tempted

The trauma in deeper living
    defies those good time girls
who will eat their cake with menace
    and disregard the pearls!

Of sweet love's bravest endeavours
    whereby we sacrifice;
all the dark getting and spending
    poor fools mistake for spice!

And growing old may bring unctious
    songs to rejuvenate
our hearts; at last content to see;
    one apple on each plate!

Patricia Howe

136

Lorraine

Lorraine is like a rose
She dresses in the best of clothes
her hair shines like silk
She does everyday work.

She is very careful with money
She is honest and polite
She works most of the daytime
and into the night

She will not be swayed in her beliefs
but some of her ways seem so brief
She goes to church on a Sunday
and if need be sometimes on Monday

She nurses her son.
All day and all night
and he to her is
her love and her light

To sum Lorraine up,
I would say of her:
She is always around
if you always need her.

Peter Morgan

The Time Between Times

When all things pass unnoticed,
The time between times,
Know that there is no forever,
And lets forget tomorrow,
As I caress your fair cheek,
And whisper in your ear,
With a gentle kiss of your lips,
And the smoothing of hands,
With the rustle of silk to the floor,
And the closing of eyes,
With your gentle affirmative voice,
Nothing is, anymore.

Howard Knowelden

I Want To Be With You

I want to be with you
Please hold me tight
Feel you next to me
All through the night.

Someone at last
Who likes me for me
And not want me to change
To what they want me to be

It's too late now
You've gone a different way
And darkness has fallen
Like clouds on my day.

I want you with me
Hold me close with no fear
I want to be with you
Always feeling you near.

Hannah M. McCormack

Twins

Twins are super, twins are special,
Twins are me and you.
Twins so very good together,
Because there's always two.
Two to share life's ups and downs,
Two to share life's sorrows.
Two who are as thick as thieves
For now and all tomorrows.
Two to share their inner feelings
For all the times ahead.
Two who'll always be together
Even when they're dead!

S. Mace

A Lonely Prisoner

At the county jail,
In the deepest darkest cell,
Sits a lonely prisoner,
Without a hope or dream,

Rain started falling,
Shrieks were heard from the streets,
The lonely prisoner all alone
Thought about what he'd done,

The pitter-pattering stopped,
The shrieks slowly faded,
The lonely prisoner tired and damp,
Regretful of the past,

The darkest night,
Silent but still,
The coldness doesn't chill him,
For there's warmth within his heart.

Lara Haworth

Times Past

Do you remember when we were young
And used to play out in the sun
No clouds appeared in our blue sky
We never used to wonder why

Such happy times those summer days
When fields were covered in heat haze
Butterflies fluttered over the corn
We were glad that we'd been born

How our laughter filled the air
Free from worry and from care
We'd run and frolic in the grass
Pity childhood doesn't last

Climbing trees fishing the stream
Now it seems just like a dream
But memories of yesterday
Still remain with me today

Remembering friends and the fun we had
Makes me feel so very glad
Although the years have quickly past
Our days in the sun will always last

Lesley J. Baker

Memories

Walking a long the woods in May
With the bluebells under your feet
Giving joy to the young in every way.
And to the old a memory treat

The carefree laughter
And tiny steps
of children where they play.
Makes smiling faces of older folk
And memories of another day

Barbara Hartshorn

Tragedy In Dunblane

How can one comprehend
The sad cruel end
Of future hope and joys:
Looking at the legacy, the toys.

Our emotions in turmoil
And thoughts in recoil;
Will media give mourners peace?
Or suffering gently release.

Oh, who can comfort gain?
We ask, and ask again;
The everlasting memories:
Young eyes looking up in smiles.

Arthur Speight

Fame

All the attention,
Caused by the public-eye,
Has got too much,
It's time to die.

Now all your pain,
Your fans will hold,
You killed yourself,
Your record went gold.

All the attention,
You hoped to lose,
Has caused you to make,
Headline news.

If you want easy fame,
Although it may cause sorrow,
Kill yourself today,
And be a legend tomorrow.

Sarah Kerr

Francesca

I wondered what made you smile,
I wondered what made you cry,
Yet all I really wanted,
Was to hold you for a while.

Gradually we came closer,
By flirting if you like,
Till my courage is strong enough,
To ask you for a date,
It was my surprise,
That with delight,
You said you couldn't wait.

I can't believe we are together.
Married; Man and Wife.
It's all I ever wanted,
To share love within my life.

Now our first baby's due,
The icing on the cake,
True love and happiness comes
To those prepared to wait.

M. Colwell

Love's New Dawn

A spark!
To set the world alight
Love in chinks...
Radiant, white.
Pure and glistening
Crystal clear,
Clean refreshing waters peer.
Gloomy slits of half closed eyes,
Unable are to recognize;
Wholesome thoughts, soothe the way.
Reflections of loves radiant rays.
Alabaster, marbled, smooth,
Elegance in ivory silk.
Rolled in silver, encased in milk.
Serenity - satin smiles imbue
Droplets - thread on strands into
Streams - bathed in candle light.
O loyal love,
Win the fight!

Cheryl Youngman

On Reading The Poems
In The Independent

I want to be deep,
deep as the ocean,
deep as the sea,
but only the ripples
leaving froth on the shore
are as shallow as me.

Brigit Barlow

Broken Winged Bird

One beautiful day,
in the dead of the night,
a broken winged bird,
took off in flight,

It sailed above roof tops,
a few feet from the ground,
chirping out loud,
not making a sound,

It flew a bit higher,
under the sea,
with nothing in sight,
it then hit a tree,

As it fell to the ground,
while floating in space,
it got there so fast,
but it wasn't a race,

So it starts at the end,
and stops at the start,
and lives life to the full,
as it's time to depart.

Patrick Killick

Look At The Moon My Son

Look at the moon my son and wish,
wish for all that is good.
I see its light upon your face
reflecting your innocence.
Your eyes are filled with wonder
of a World far away.
Look at the Moon my son and wish,
wish but do not tell.

Jackie Harvey

My Endless Darkness

I live in darkness
An endless one.
That causes no sadness,
And nothing, none.

I see no sun,
That might be true.
It makes no fun,
And no pain too.

Cause I have heart
That looses no hope.
And I can start
Each time I stop.

Mariam Nasser Al-Kaabi

Hooked

She laid her wares out with some care -
Aware that he was standing there
With moistened lips and greedy eyes -
Enticing him to patronize
Her titillating charms.

He gazed upon the luscious tart,
A fine, immoral work of art,
'Come-hither' oozing from each pore,
And felt desire within him gnaw;
He rubbed his sweating palms

His ample appetite well stirred
And conscience locked away unheard
Behind excuses old and lame,
He eased his ageing, portly frame
In through the open door.

She flashed him a beguiling smile
And, chatting pertly all the while,
Boxed up the luscious strawberry tart
That had seduced his hungry heart
And eager, drooling jaw!

Jane Edmond

The Beach

The other night I walked alone
Along the path beside the beach,
  I used to walk here long ago
And watch the tide, just out of reach.
  I used to sit and fantasize
Of things that never could have been,
  I used to nurse a broken heart,
While icy waves consumed my dream.
  These sands collected many tears,
The salty air would clear my head,
  But now, when I go back and cry,
I'm crying tears of joy instead.
  The other night the tide was in
And water splashed along the shore,
  And what was once, just out of reach
Is not so distant anymore.

E. M. Richardson

Picture, Picture On The Wall

As days go by
I think of you
As my dad, and best friend too
When I am low, I look at you
Your picture says it all for me
Your gentle eyes, and silver hair
The smile that says you really care
This poem I wrote is just for you
It's my way of saying, I love you too
I never said these words to you
So picture, picture on the wall
Keep me company, through Winter
Summer, Spring and Fall always.

Melba Pereira

Green Eyes

Looking to your green eyes
I discovered love
and there it was the happiness
all what I wished in this world!.
From your mouth words evaporated
as music to my ears,
the letters of my songs
and then I was in heaven
the earth under my feet was gone.

I am still up there
every time I see you around
forever will be like this
my mind and my heart
will not take you out!.

Theo Dutton

Love

The greatest love I've ever known
Is the love you gave to me.
The greatest love I've ever felt
Was there in my eyes
For the world to see.
You have lifted my heart
And filled it with joy
Till it dances and bubbles
Just like a child's toy.
... I hope that one day
You will feel as I do
And know of the love I feel for you,
Then together we'll go
To the land of romance
And together the world
We both will enhance
And all shall know
The joy of our love
And the world will live
With the peace of a dove.

B. Deacon

"Grief"

The dreams we had are
All tattered and torn,
Since that fateful day
I have felt so forlorn.

All I have now are memories
So beautiful and true,
Every minute of every day
My thoughts are all of you.

Although you suffered
You never complained,
And when God called you home
My heart cast no blame.

Your dignity and serenity
Shone through your pain,
You gave me the strength
To cope again and again.

So I'll say good-bye darling
Thanks for the privilege of your love,
Till we meet again in heaven above.

Sheila McCombe

Of Animal

Let us start a religion.
To win is to sin,
to pollute is to sin,
to learn is to sin.
To come here is to sin.
REPENT!
All the noble saints
kill themselves,
that, would be perfect.

Souls of the past dead.
They took and lived luxury.
WE suffer the consequence,
broken rule, unwritten law
of animal. Only survive,
create nothing but a home.
In my eye, in my teeth, in my cry,
in the way I move, there are no Gods
only madness,
question opened.

Iain Simpson

Emerging

Rabbit, warily,
Edgily it inches,
Extracting its bundle
Of habits and ticks.

Humbly, timidly
Snoops on its haunches,
Twitching its nostrils
Nosing down sniffs.

A fearful, fanatical
Anorak of acoustics -
Lappings of air pool
In those fibrillate ears.

Ruminates, palpitates,
A pelt of trapped nerves,
Emerging in worries,
Limping its sneaks.

Hesitates, ruminates,
A neurotic sprinter,
Crouched on its marks
In novelty slippers.

Paul Beasley

Who Are We?

Wondrous sights'n'sounds
A demanding world enriches
All souls, races and colour
The cultural experiences merge
Causing tension and death
Is it us?
Or are we a game of chess
For aliens above
If aliens are playing
It could explain racial black and white
If not!
Surly it is us
Who are we to judge?
We all could be pawns
Yet we all could be kings and queens
Maybe we are the aliens
And the things we destroys are our-
selves

B. Grime

Untitled

I whisper your name
On a cool summer's night,
My aching heart cry's in the dark
How could there ever be
Anyone like you.
Time dulls the pain,
And for a while
The memories cascade,
The mind - like a waterfall
Splashing down laughter,
Tears, smiles and pain
Only in my mind now
And the pictures I have
Bring me back all the joys of you
You, who were always there for me,
You, who judge but do not condemn,
You my lovely Jane,
My sister, my friend,
Rest in peace now my love
And one day I'll see you again.

Amanda Taunton

Rose

Towards the child
He reached and plucked
Her scarlet
Rose bud lips.

Peeling apart the flower
Revealing the heart,

He discarded.

Handing back the dried petals,
She wore them around her neck

Like a chain.

Time embedded them
Into her skin.

Paula Louise Fleet

November

November clad in gloomy grey
Goes drearily upon her way.
She loves dull colours people say.
But when the golden sun comes out
We are assailed by sudden doubt —
November turns her dress about.
Decked with sunbeams everywhere,
Twines crimson berries in her hair,
And makes herself exceedingly fair.

Muriel T. Dixon

Your Shadow

Have you seen your shadow
    Dancing and skipping?
Does it always follow
    Ev'rywhere you go?
When the sun shines brightly,
When the sky is blue:
You can always see your shadow
    Walking with you.

Can you catch your shadow
    Dancing and skipping?
Can you stop and shake it
    Firmly by the hand?
With rain clouds overhead,
Grey skies instead of blue:
You may find your shadow
Disappears from view - but -

Jesus is beside you
    waking or sleeping,
With you, like your shadow
    Ev'rywhere you go.

Marjorie Wheeler

Happy Days!!!

It's Monday again!
The long week ahead!
Last week's problems
are now this week's instead!

It's raining again!
It never stops!
It really is pouring,
I'll forget the shops!

More bills again!
They always come in!
No money for saving,
I'd better have a collection tin!

Weight's up again!
I really must slim.
Everything's bad for you.
Why does everyone else look so trim?

It's late again!
I must go to bed.
"Tomorrow is another day"
Maybe I'll be happier then instead?!!

Derek J. Day

Afterthoughts

The fire romantic fervour brings
And lovers feed their faith upon
Lends warmth to simple happenings -
But ashes when the flame has gone.

Surrounding our concupiscence
A pure and luminous starlight shone
So other-worldly, so intense -
The shadows stay: the lights have gone.

In fairyland we chanced to be
Titania and Oberon
Midsummer nights' fecundity -
But barren dawn now dreams have gone.

And every song my soul declared
Was answered with an antiphon
Such perfect melodies we shared -
But silence now the muse has gone.

And yet my life would seem replete
The days roll out, the years roll on
Grave issues for my time compete -
But to what end when you are gone?

Antony J. Goldman

"From The Kitchen Window"

The breath of earth rising from a
    hoar-topped hedge,
A giant beech offering arms of blazing
    copper to a clear blue sky.
A pale shy sun touching the lawns
    of white lace frost and opening
    windows of fresh green grass.
A shining morning of glorious colour
    so full of peaceful promise.
To stand and watch this brown earth
    waking is to drink beauty beyond
    thought.
How shall we use this new November
day?

Barbara Pounds

'First Lady'

It seemed too early for
The lady to go,
But then on reflection
Again, maybe no.
Sleep on serenely in
Heavenly glow,
While we keep our thoughts
Of you, Jackie, Jackie O.

Ernest Robert Thwaites

Last Red Apple

If I were the last red apple
In a basket of fruit,
I would make myself scarce
And not want to stand out.

But not being human
It would not know
That its bright red skin
Would be its downfall.

For a cricket ball
That would be fine,
When the fast bowler
Gives it that extra shine.

But for an apple
Being part of life's store,
It would not be aware
What it had been grown for.

So at the end of the day
It does not matter a lot,
Your time will come
Whether you're human or not.

Frank Dawson

Out Of Fear And Darkness

Children of the future,
walk into the light,
the present may look bleak
the future always bright.

Turn your back on hatred,
always look straight ahead
learn to respect your fellow man
to love, not hate, instead.

Turn, and face each other,
wipe away your tears,
touch each other on the cheek,
and banish hate and fear.

Now walk towards the distant light,
bring hope of peace to all,
make a promise to each other,
to work towards peace, not war.

Wendy L. Patrick

The "Quiet" Man

A smile, a nod, a friendly wave,
As he passes by every day,
On his way to tend the beast,
And toil the land.

A quiet man, thoughtful,
Kind and caring
To all creatures, great and small,
A quiet man, a shy man,
    Loved By All!

Mary Flower

Fate

No one knows what fate
Has in store for us.
For fate deals the cards.
Some of us are meant to be
Weak, and some of us strong.
Some are here for a short
Time, and others for a
Longer stay.
And no matter how hard some
People try, they just can't win,
And others have the Midas touch
And everything turns to gold.
For fate is the dealer,
And fate holds all the cards

Hilda Costello

As?

As the wind blows through the trees
As the sky becomes so blue,
As the animals roam in the free
As nature is allowed to be true.

As innocence becomes a virtue
As reality becomes a blur.
As freedom is only for a few
As it depends on whether you have fur.

As the greed of humans becomes greater
As each species becomes extinct,
As time grows later and later
As the need for that coat of mink.

As needs become stronger and stronger
As humans we are easily led,
As what right have we any longer
To go 'Bang, Bang, You're Dead'.

Kevin Watts

Greed

An erupting cascade of poison
Unchallenged, and moving with speed
Infecting all that it touches
A disease call Greed.

A desire fed by ambition
Unrelenting, while innocents plead
Inheriting others possessions
By a consuming Greed.

Countries wage war in defiance
The weak, scattered like seed
Carnage reigns unabated
Lives lost just for Greed

People in high positions
Ignoring populations in need
silently crushing resistance
With insatiable Greed

A growth spawned by man
Advancing, unchecked, take heed
The unwary have already fallen
Destroyed by Greed.

R. Wiggins

I Am Me

I am me,
Born, not of convention,
Born out of love,
Born from free flight,
I fight for my life,
I long for love,
I need to belong.
Just give me love,
And give me hope,
That I may have a place
In this wide open space,
That is life.

E. Anderson

Freedom

What is this thing called freedom
    There's not much left on earth
People fight each other.
    Just to prove their worth

If your skin is a different colour
    Or you come from another race
People try to move you
    To another place.

But freedom is not a gift of man
It's a gift of God above
And it's everybody's birthright
To walk free in the land they love

So if you live in a land
And the land you walk is free
Pray for others just like me
Where only bloodshed
    Sets you free.

Margaret Gregory

At The Bottom Of The Ocean

At the bottom
of the ocean
there are fish
There are wrecks

There are weeds
that bring you down

There are jelly-fish
that tickle
Me

The ocean is full
Of colour-full
Little fish
All different
Sharks

Martin Butterworth

Horrid World

All people gathered together
being awful to just one person
not knowing it'll hurt him forever.

He stands alone in the street
with no friends to meet
no one wants to know
so where should he go?

Should he run away
to die or to perish
why doesn't someone
want him to cherish?

All alone in a pale-coloured land
with no outstretched hand
the boy with the coloured skin,
there's really nothing wrong with him!

Jody Wright

Twenty-Five Of The Best

The years have sped so quicksteply,
We've waltzed along with you,
Holding hands so trustingly,
With every step danced true.

You've Rumba'ed past the happy days
And Samba'ed through the bad,
Rock and Rolled the nights away,
Jiving lady and her lad.

Pasa Doble and Tango done
Together side by side,
Prizes, cups and trophies won,
As round the floor you glide.

For your hard work and dedication,
Inspiring us to watch and learn,
Thank you both with great affection
And hope to see you back next term.

Muriel Turner

Inspiration

Whilst walking down beside the sea,
Taking in, the air so fresh.
I realized how much is free,
How much of life is left.

The sea laps on a sleepy shore,
Shells and pebbles dance.
Marble designs made by the surf,
Put you in a trance.

Hear, the jingle of the shale
As it heads, towards the sand,
Oh how blue the sea
How beautiful the land.

Seagull soaring high above as free,
As I do feel.
Gazing longingly at the sea,
To seek the next, live meal.
He soars up there so high,
A life alive against the sky,
How blue the sky so high, so clear
Not even a cloud, to cause us fear.

B. Bird

French Leaves

Dappled leaves of patterned sunlight
Danced across the dusty floor,
Earthy scents of early autumn
Drifted through the open door,
The wind sighed softly in the branches
Whispering secrets to the stone.
We stood together, silent,
While I made that place my own.
Now, many places later,
When the present proves unkind,
I turn to find you waiting
In the forest of my mind.

Lorraine Stark

'What Is Love'

Love is laughter, sometimes pain
Love is sunshine, after rain
Love is beautiful, love is fun
Love is happiness in the sun
Love is shining like a jewel
Love is hurting, sometimes cruel
Love surrounds us like a cloud
Love is magic, love is proud
Love burns brightly all around
Lifts our feet off the ground
Love is a gift let it win
Open your heart
And let love in.

Janice McLean

Untitled

We walked out every day
My Bobbin Beagle dog and I,
over fields or water ways,
wind or sunshine, rain or snow
made no difference, off we go.

The long and happy years we shared,
my bobbin beagle dog and I,
we kept each other fit and strong
and loved each other all along.

Now she's gone 'twas time to die
my bobbin beagle dog,
up to the heavens beyond the sky,
"I miss you so, my bob".

Linda Wilkes

Untitled

I dreamed your face
and almost knew the truth

A truth which sleep
will only half admit;

Then, hour by hour,
it took the day apart;

I dreamed your face
and almost knew the truth.

Sylvia King

Inevitable Consequences

The male was born early,
To choose a sandy beach;
At ebb tide came scorpy,
To live with old crabby.

A guest star, a lost man,
Within her heart sublime,
You will love her this time,
As you have paid the fine.

Once my star, my Island
My pristine ray profound;
With you now around,
My past I understand.

Goodbye to you who made,
My man his debt to pay;
I am now come to make,
His face brightened all day.

O true companion,
From thy realms O moon;
A crab and scorpion,
Best of all union.

J. A. Browne

Sea Gull

What does the sea gull see as he skims
across the waves?
Does he see the silver fish,
Or the hidden caves?
Seems his search is never-ending
soaring cliff face then descending.
A plaintive cry from time to time
then another rocky ledge to climb
a bit like life for you and me,
ever searching, never free,
but you know, as he glides by
he's got a twinkle in his eye
"You humans worry much too much
'bout life and money and the such
life's for living, soaring free,
so think of yourself
don't worry 'bout me".

Kenneth Millar Hold

The Shield

The sea
the icy cold sea
waves
lash against the rocks
the wind howls
ice flows through me
my hair
is torn by fangs
that blow surrounding me
my face is like marble
thread-like strands
tear from my face
they are blown in my eyes
your house
is distant
far away on the cliff top
where deep hollowed chairs sit
and cream teas await.

Pat Jones

At The Tomb Of The Unknown Soldier

In fancy I could see her
Beneath the echoing dome
Weeping for just one;
Is it you, is it you, my son?
Is my time of waiting past
And you're safe home at last?
Am I blest beyond any other,
Is it you, is it you, my son?
And countless voices murmured,
Mother! Mother!

Mary Victor

A Lovely Day

While gazing up into the sky
To hear again the lark's shrill cry
I see a bird upon the wing
Telling me again it's spring
Flowers with their lovely hue
Red and yellow, pink and blue
Or browsing on some park bench seat
With squirrels playing at my feet
Rabbits running all around
Making not the slightest sound
I think of God to whom I pray
And I thank him for this lovely day
Also his son whose life he gave
Upon a cross mankind to save
As homeward then I make my way
My step is light, my heart is gay
For I know I am not alone
God is with me on my journey home

W. Flitcroft

The Tip

I work at the local council yard.
Most people call it "The tip
mainly it's filled with rubbish.
Which people just tear and rip.

To me it's become a different place.
Full of lots of curious things.
Like bikes and lights and tables.
Who knows what tomorrow brings?

Sometimes I find a picture,
Which wouldn't cost much money
But looks good when it is rehung
In a home that is bright and sunny.
So remember when you
throw away things
To have them clean and neat
Because what you call rubbish
Could be someone else's treat!

S. Lucas

Music

Music is a gentle stream
    That washes souls
To conscious thought,
    Refreshing with a new
Awakening and
    Encouragement.
To learn of love
    And with it singing
In heart and mind,
    Pursue the ultimate
In happiness and truth
    With notes sublime.

Arthur Edward Morgan

Spider....

Spider on the ceiling,
Spider on the floor,
Spider in the cupboard,
Spider on the door.

Spider on the curtain,
Spider on the path,
Spider on the carpet,
Spider in the bath.

Spider, spider, everywhere,
Even on the chair,
They know they make me creepy,
It just isn't fair!

Simon F. Feather

Perfection

Perfection,
To perfect,
To be,
Geometric's, geology,
The birds,
The bees,
Reoccurring patterns,
The leaves,
The trees,
That hanging low,
In silence boughs,
To sunset glows,
Whose colours rouge,
Prism'd through a marbled pool,
For only lucky eye's to see,
Mirrored, stilled, reflective,
Perfect symmetry.

J. Fryatt

A 1940's Garden

Higher and higher the Hammock swings,
To Children it is Many Things.
As a Boat it tips them out.
They run away with a shout -
Climbing up the Old Fir Tree,
Tarzan, Jane and Boy, makes three.
Then as they dive inside the Tent,
With War-Cries now the peace is rent.
Hidden behind the Large Pear Tree,
Breath held. "Hope you can't see Me."
The unused swing rests peacefully.
The Children have all gone to Tea.
Abandoned Cycles lie forlorn,
Upon the now deserted lawn.
The Father now will have His Way,
Finished his Hard Working Day.
With his Woods he practised Bowls,
In the lawn were Special Holes-
"What a nuisance Tut Tut Tut"
"Damn I've missed another putt"

Elizabeth Ann Lee

Sez Anne?

Gilt-edged invitation,
Private view,
Prestigious location,
Favoured few.

Glamorous reception,
Champagne flute;
Artistic perception
Less acute.

Knowing cognoscenti
Patronise,
Reviewers aplenty
Criticize.

Well-dressed conversation
So divine;
Private consternation -
Philistine!

Lorna Carleton

A Morn In November

Soon see again
Our nation pause awhile—
And sombre stand
By Plinth and Plaque
Where Poppy wreaths array!

  A bugle call
  Sounds out o'er each and all—
  Who standing
  Ponder deep
  The tears and cost
  Be battles won
    Or battles lost!

And sounding still
Goes far and wide,
Bringing to where
  Each valiant died
A thought - a prayer!

Bill Rowan

Spring Poem

"Oh" spring you have come back again
My gardens turning green.

The little flowers are pushing up,
Its beauty to be seen.

The days are getting longer,
Birds now sing at last.

It's good to look and walk around,
Now winter it has hissed.

Peter Williamson

Impotence

Through ten thousand centuries
Successive tribes have striven
Unsuccessfully,
To civilize themselves;
So many twisted tongues
Have promised much
Yet ever failed.
The worldly word is war
In the name of peace;
The scanty glaze worn thin,
We glide towards
A fading future
On a stream of rhetoric.
History dies unheeded;
The ultimate solution,
Meek subservience
To political correctness
In a state of ruin.

John D. Warmingham

Scottish Poem

A fuff't and fuff'tma reekes a day
Roow the house and roon the tay
The win was willyart it blew the hay
A met a lassie wa' name was May

A was yeukin tae gee her a kiss
Then she kiss'd me she didna miss
We were twa joes fu o jo
She had a wean a wee wee boy

A hoast and hoast as a fuff't awa
She was ma hiney aluud her anna
Wi bith went hame tae her wee wean
Then tae her wither oon glasgae green

She was guid a guid willie lass
Wa loud me really true
Woo a fund a lass o ma awe
An ma lassie luves me the same

We were, daunk the rest o the night
Ma lassig luv'd me a luv'd her right
We bith got marri'd had a docher Anna
Noo we have a son aged twa

James Barclay Kane

The Gift Of Sight

To see the lovely sky of blue
With white and fluffy clouds,
To see the flowers in colour
Or faces of the crowds

To see a smile of pleasure
On the face of one you love
Or see a newborn baby
Sent from heaven above

The colours of the rainbow
Or foam upon the sea
A ship with sails a blowing
And fishermen on the quay

To see stars in the heavens
And a moon that's shining bright
Are things you take for granted
Each day and every night

But when you've lived in darkness
With just a memory
The gift of sight is precious
I was blind - but now I see.

Joy E. Ellis

Love Is

Always this longing
stemming deeply from within
which would send me to
the far corners of the world
seeking

and finding,
my love would rest
his head against my breast
be seemingly at peace
selflessly

to console me,
each of us knowing there is
no lasting peace or rest
that peace comes slow
and coming

hastens to go,
and even as I cling
to a restraining kiss
helpless, still I am drawn
towards the summoning abyss.

Louise Rogers

Take Time

Looking through the window
Watching the trees
Swaying very softly
In the cool summers breeze.

Flowers slowly opening
To greet the summers sun
People coming home
After a days work is done.

Do we really notice
And do we really care
About all the lovely gifts
God has put there.

Or are we too busy
Wishing our lives away
Planning on months ahead
Instead of living day by day.

Let us take life more slowly
And let the wonders all sink in
Let us make more time for loving
And a new world will begin.

G. S. Hughes

I Think Back..

I think back to the tragic days
We were lying in mud,
loaded with weapons and
covered in blood.

Lonely men in trenches,
Armed with knives,
look at pictures of their
children and wives.

A brave young soldier
stands up to fight.
only to be knocked down
by a bullet in flight.

For some it was all too much to bear,
I should know 'cause I was there.
And now the war had finally ended,
our lives and wounds might be mended.

And though in my heart I could
learn to forgive,
I'll never forget those days
as long as I live.

Louise Barson

Prees Heath

Walking the Heathland path in June,
Wild loveliness I there beheld,
No famous human artistry
But nature's living tapestry
Butterflies with wings of blue
Dance upon the purple hue.
Yellow gorse, its nectar sweet.
Welcomes the humming of the bees,
And silver birch, a graceful queen
Displays her summer dress of green.
A wild rose with blooms of pink
Delights the eye of passer by.
Varied hues of plant and tree
Blend in perfect harmony.
A symphony from larks in flight,
Seen outlined on a deep blue sky.
Some may own a painting rare,
But I declare that non compare.
The beauty that I see'th there,
When walking in the summer air.

M. L. Dawson

Love

If I could fly above the clouds,
To see the world below.
I'd like to see the fields of green,
and ocean shining blue.
With loving people no more war's.
Somewhere I'd like to go.
Happy faces no more fears,
Gentle thought's that's kind.
People rushing here and there,
No violence on their minds.
Tolerance and love surround.
Each to each his own.
A home a place somewhere to rest.
These thoughts are for mankind
So put these things in your minds eye.
And do what you must do.
To make the world a better place.
A brighter future too.

Norma Hewitt

The Twilight Years

I reach to touch the sunset
And the earth begins to retreat
I caress the stars in the heavens
While I treasure the stars at my feet

I feel I am fading slowly
Preparing to depart.
There is nothing I want to take with me
But the memories in my heart.

Always they are with me.
Good memories and bad.
And the sunshine of the joyful ones
Outshines the tears of the sad.

Lilian E. Fulker

Untitled

If I could like Mary
Sit at Jesus feet.
Look into this lovely face,
Hear his voice, so sweet.

If only I, like Mary,
Could be patient, calm and mild.
Untroubled by the daily toils,
Quiet in soul and mind.

Alas! I'm only Martha,
With all her troubled thoughts.
Ruffled, restless, harassed,
And many other faults.

But, dear Lord, I can take comfort,
You have love for simple folk.
So, old and poor and simple as I am.
Oh Please Love, and have need of me.

Katie Adams

Exploring

Come with me across the sea
To search for lands unknown,
Sailing on the seas so rough,
What a life so very tough.
Can we see new lands ahead?
Or is it just a cloud in the sky?
Days and days go by at sea
Following the stars by night,
Mountains and land, birds and beasts,
Will we ever sight the land again?
Will we ever reach our journey's end?
Will you come with me across the sea
To search for lands unknown?

Norma Dekanski

Attitude

There is an uneasiness
About the day
As if the breeze has stirred
itself from sleep
To pass my way
And leave behind an
Element of doubt in my mind

Constance Parry

I Will Never Cease To Love You

I will never cease to love you
I miss you more each day
The sunshine vanished from my life
The day you went away
It's a lonely life without you
Nothing is the same
All I have is memories
And your photo in a frame
So this is what it looks like
Now I'm all alone
You were my queen
Now I'm a king without a throne.

Ian Harber

Message To A Broken Heart

Poor young aching heart
why are you crying?
You lost your love
for a mistake you're denying.
But just remember
that time is a healer,
and soon you'll be once again....
A fiery-eyed dreamer.

Fiona Penza

To "My Dearest May"

You have always been my saviour,
  you will always be my guide
You will always be my anchor,
  In the ocean oh so wide.

Till the trees all lose their blossom,
  Till the flowers fade and die,
You will be with me forever,
  Till all the seas run dry.

Till all the seas run dry
  And the sun deserts the sky,
You will be with me forever
May, we never say goodbye.

You are the only one I've ever loved.
  You're the only one for me,
May you always be there by my side,
  Through all eternity.

  To have you there besides me,
Dear wherever I may roam
  It's nice to know you're always near
When I'm far away from home.

John Arbuckle

The Way I Feel

My dreams were crushed,
Nobody there, not anymore.

Silence greeted me,
Frowns and stares too.

A black cloud overhead,
No sun shone on me.

No more trust,
Not anymore

Suzie Laxton

In My Garden

From my back door,
I can see all the flowers watching me.
Pink ones, blue and yellow ones,
swaying in the gentle breeze,
as if to say 'Good Morning, you!'

Waiting for the sun to shine,
wasps and bees flying around,
taking pollen from the flowers.
Sparrows twittering in the trees,
taking seeds from the Butterfly Tree.

Peacocks and Admirals flying around,
some settle on the ground.
Then up and down and round they go,
and seem to say, 'you catch me and
I'll catch you.'
Just like children having fun,
they seem to be pleasing everyone.

E. Potter

Untitled

Did I come today to see
did I need to be confused
with grief and despair
and opening my heart
the hearty lies
of common emotion
to be wise
and after only love
disappears
can we come to be
despised and open
to suggestions of freer
days re-dress make
believe with tenderness
come to me someday.

Thomas McLoone

Mother

Catapulting out of bed
to spill the children
into a new day -
hair lathered into submission,
shirts escaping last minute
revision of belt and buckle,
feet knuckled into
double-knotted shoes -
sometimes I feel the proud
but wary ringmaster,
firing his unique cargo
of clown and elephant,
juggler and fire-eater
into an inscrutable crowd -
mantis-faced,
obliquely staring,
praying in the dark for pleasure ...
an appetite for failure
moistening its lips.

Maggie Goren

By The Waterfall

Beneath the cascading waterfall
I thought I heard a siren call
The cry that echoed off the stone
Made me feel I was not alone.

I shivered as I glanced around
To trace the source of every sound,
Yet all was still within my sight
As if life itself had taken flight.

And then my concentration broke
For it was only me who spoke
And so I turned my soul away
To face the dying of the day.

David Jonathan Pugh

Yesterday

A friend, a hope, a dream
Crumbled like the dust
beneath our feet.
No more than a memory,
of a time, a place
That never was, but is kept-
alive, never forgotten
Except by those, whose cowardice
overcoming that which so easily
changes
The mind, our world
Where all was right
and reality is not.
But all is gone
as distance tore it apart,
and we awoke, to an unforgiving world.

Fiona Irene Sinclair

What Is In A Teardrop?

What is in a teardrop?
That is what I'd like to know.
How can something so small
contain so much?
How can something so common
hold something so dear?
Each crystallised drop,
what does it contain?
Fear, distress, pain and hurt,
where does it all go?
The loosing of one small drop
can loose so much feeling
it's hard to believe.
What is in a teardrop
to make it matter so?

Louise Wright

The Unborn

Cocooned in soft misty light
Safe from all worldly woe
Feeding waking sleeping;
My days were ordered;
Nothing to do but grow;
Preparation for a journey;
Welcomed by warm loving arms
    at journeys end,
Feeding off soft flowing breasts.
Alas the journey won't take place;
I won't join the human race;
You can't feel my fear;
See the tears stain my face
    knowing I am rejected.
Yet someone hears my unborn cry
He'll come to fetch me by and by
With Him I know I'll gladly go;
Safe from worldly peril and woe
Into heavenly lasting light.

Mary T. Breslin

Lilies - Of - The - Valley

Exquisite bell flowers.
Cape'd in pale green.
Lift not their heads
To the sun to be seen.
They stand in the shade
And as you pass by.
Aware of the perfume
They hide from the eye.
Lilies-Of-The-Valley.
Small, dainty and neat
Perfection from God
And they grow at your feet.

Doreen White

Untitled

A cloak of grass like velvet,
flows down the mountain side,
Entwines amongst majestic trees,
Which stand for all of time,

A group of golden buttercups,
amongst the daisies dance,
To the sound of a Bumble Bee
Which hums and takes a chance,

A squirrel bronzed with sun light,
Drinks water made from dew,
Collects his food,
His winter store,
To eat when days are blue,

A Blackbird
In the tree tops high,
Sends forth,
His summer song,
All the joys of summer time
Tell all that winter gone.

Lisa Beckwith

Untitled

A child in a slum
Looked up from a street
As water cascaded around his feet
He longed for the sun
And a safe place to play
Away from tower blocks
All ugly and grey.

With the wind in her hair
And her toes in the sand
A child on a beach stood spellbound
Rounding the head land
A tall ship appeared
To carry her off to a mystery land

They met in their dreams
Held hands as they played
Danced our green hills
To a beckoning cross
Bathed in a rainbow
Far, far, away.

Peter Thames

The Soldiers' Christmas

Cease-fire has just started,
A soldiers laid down his gun,
For forty-eight hours only,
A soldier can join in the fun.

The noise of battle has ceased,
The soldiers have all left the field.
Everywhere seems now at peace,
The war now doesn't seem real.

When, oh when will man learn,
To stop and practice Gods law?
He didn't intend us to yearn,
For loved ones away in the war.

When will they stop this killing?
When will the soldier be free?
They're not really befilling,
What God intended to be.

Let the soldier cease-fire forever,
Let there be no more wars,
And let us all endeavour,
To uphold all of Gods laws.

Hilary Ann Torrens

Daughter

Oh daughter mine at last I see
From chains I wear you've broken
    free.
A woman now, just half my age,
Your face so fearless, full of rage
To change the world - rewrite the
    page
That told us how to act and be
Models of complicity.

Choices endless change your life,
Mistress, courtesan or wife?
No bonds of sweet gentility
Will bind you as they once did me.

So live your life and every day
Remember us who paved the way,
By love, and sacrifice and tears,
The freedom's yours - enjoy the years.

T. Butterworth

Tragedy

Two tearaways,
Trunk road,
Ton up,
Twenty tonner,
Twisting,
Turning,
Tyremarks,
Terror,
Torn torsos,
Terrible tragedy.

A. W. Forman

He Drinks To Forget... Life

He drinks to forget
he's committing slow
Suicide, but he'll carry
on because surely someone,
somewhere, will come along and
recognize his despair, his anguish.
Someone, somewhere will
surely show him the true meaning
of life. He'll drink to
forget that no one really
cares if he should
live or die. He drinks to
forget that wither sober
or drunk, he can't really handle life.
He drinks to forget,
the pain, the sadness,
the disasters, the mess,
Oh, the mess he's made of his life.
He drinks to forget...
He drinks to forget... Life.

Sonya Connor

After All

My main reason is to be loved
Cherished and respected
Kept warm away from danger
And to be infected,

By the love he gives to me.

I want to have gifts of pleasure
Love that blossoms flowers
Just us alone together
In caressing showers,

Of his love for me.

And now we are together
His love is left alone for me
I can say now I am contented,

And happy as I'll ever be.

T. Wood

Untitled

In silence now as silence will
I wish to see my true love still
Ah but alas for moments shared
I know for hours I must refrain
Until the embers of my love
Burst forth into a wondrous flame
I seek my love where'er she be
I seek to hold her with my hand
And for my love I'd die alone
And for my love I'd make my stand
Oh will you love come with me now
And stand on high above it all
And not be drawn to sorrows well
And not be tempted for to fall
I'll love you while the sun doth shine
Not stop 'ere the sun burn out
For you're the sweetness of my life
And oh my love there is no doubt
In silence now as silence will
I wish to hold my true love still.

P. M. Booth

Birds

Birds are beautiful,
Birds can fly, they fly all day
High up in the sky
Oh, why can't people fly
Birds sing to the tune of life
With tweets loud and clear
I love the sound in the sky.
Birds all colours, like grey and brown
Parrots bright and beautiful
Birds hop along the road
Ready for danger
Birds leap to the sky
When danger is near

Oh why can't people fly.

Alexa Phelps-Gardiner

Oil Slick

Silent, serpentine,
Captive of the restless tide,
At which whim, they turn they writhe.
From the bowels of hell they came,
They have not form,
Alone, they bear no blame.
Yet.....? Dark satanic fingers they,
Harbingers of death as yet untold.
The anxious shore, knowing waits,
To don its lacy veil of jet,
Like widow, so to mourn.

F. W. Brundrett

Untitled

A whistle it would seem
It crept down the hall
pointing at the figures
of scared and frightened fools

Many people sleep
only one lies awake
Thinking of that forest
and that wide and dirty lake.

A tall young lady with long
Swaying hair
with two million secrets she
Just can't share

So where should she wonder
where should she go
Nowhere... no-one will
ever know.

Shelley Tricker

Innocence

Innocence is something to behold,
Two small faces smiling in the cold.
All wrapped up in gloves and hat,
Watching a dog, chasing a cat.

You wish that they could always be,
Full of love and purity.
Never angry and never sad,
Always grateful for what they have.

You want their lives to be content,
Special, but simple, heaven sent.
No worries to cloud their little lives,
No one telling them vicious lies.

All their days full of fun,
Playing under the glorious sun.
Trying to climb a very big tree,
Running and laughing, forever free.

Dreams I know can never be,
Excepted in life's reality.
But surely no one needs to be told,
Innocence is something to behold.

Marilyn Charman

Going With The Flow

I'm hurtling down your river
not knowing what lies ahead
scared incase I hurt myself
don't worry, from the bank you said

Every now and then I cling to a rock
and look to the bank for an answer
there, until the force of the river
pulls me further on my journey.

How did I fall into this torrent
wondering where it will end
knowing that I must
ride the rapids and jump the falls
be blinded by the spray
though no life line will I take.

For with every twist and turn
and occasional calm
I know I must reach a wide open space
which I hope will take
these ripples from my face.

Ian Russell

Somehow

Today I am sad
Sad for no reason
The laughter of a child
in the Galleries
Cheered
temporarily.
Give me an outlet
Let me express
the slow metamorphoses
taking place.

A wife and a mother
But where
have I gone
Overshadowed
Hidden
by circumstance.
Is it safe to nurture
This revolutionary spirit
is it fair to expect them
to think about me.

Noeleen Charlesworth

Beyond The Veil

You left me when I least expected.
Our life together poised. Reflected.
Where are you now?
Through the mists that shroud and blur,
Quest and memories recur.
Where are you now?

Life and death in sharp relief.
Pain and sorrow compounding grief
Without you now.
Would the search had run its course,
Granting succour to remorse.
Without you now.

Here, a new dawn stands awaiting.
Love and eternity relating.
I see you now
High beyond the veiled curtain
All revealed; all is certain.
I see you now.

G. W. Girt

The Stone

The Salted sea
Has smoothed its jagged edges
To palms of hands
It has made it unique
It has a ceramic look.

Its oily feel
Its sad and unwanted face
A helpless mass trapped in loneliness
Never to communicate.

Put to one side
Never revealing itself
It bears no home
It is a loner
Something never understood.

Charles R. N. Powell

The Parting

It's time you stopped your work my love
It's time you stopped your play,
Someone has to see you now
He's calling by today.

No, don't dress up, he knows you well,
He'll gently take your hand
And lead you on wondrous walk
Into another land.

And as you go I'd give my all
To step out by your side,
But I must bide here still a while
To wait another tide.

So, dearest one, lift up your face
To kiss just once, and then
To hold your memory in my heart
Until we meet again.

William Edward Asprey

Help

Despair, dark and deep,
Bewildering, loosing reason,
Born of long frustrations and weakness.
Seeking, searching the innermost flaws
For pathways through the mind's maze
For light and laughter
To dim, extinguish, and silence.
Draining strength mustered,
Dreams and longings seek purpose
For another battle to emerge or drown.
Bleeding wounds the price of victory -
Insanity the cost of defeat.

Hazel Bowyer-Williams

Stand-In

The poets were not there
When Old George died
Heaving the rattling air
Between the gaps
And all turned to one gap
As George came
To his stop
After we had the three rumbling rockets
Drop
White as a dying engineer
His last words hiss
'That I should come
to this'
Ancient
Decrepit an ancient's home
Left over from some other war.

A. K. Claiden

Love Knows...

Love knows not good or bad,
But roams where the heart may lead,
True love cannot be controlled,
For it grows like a plant a seed,
But without this love in return,
This plant will wither and die,
And to me your love you don't send,
So surely this plant will die.

Richard Ball

Love Is...

Love is when
Two minds merge as one,
And all the worries
Of the world have gone.
When both hearts
Beat the same beat,
Pulsating together
Through body and heat.
This is the way I know to be true
This is how I know I love you.

Dean Homer

Flight Of Fancy

Bear me away on wings in flight,
Oh lovely morn so new and bright,
Through gentle haze and crystal dew
Where all is peace in sun and hue.
I'll linger there contented long
And hear the birds in morning song,
Then fly me where my fancy takes
To far off mountains, glen and lakes
And there may I its beauty reap
From morn till twilight brings me sleep
And line the fullness of my mind
With riches of the greatest kind.

Olivia F. Ash

Untitled

Oh Grandpa teach me how to play,
That well known game of Chess;
Where knights do play,
And bishops pray,
And queens in fancy dress
Protect their kings
And do the things
To save them from dismay.
No "checks" for them
Nor yet a "Mate".
For that indeed
Would seal their fate!

Gerald Tobert

Holding Back The Years

Don't hold back the years of bitterness
and tears. Bring it to the fore, where
joy and happiness can prevail. Your
dearest husband and precious son
would not want you to suffer so,
your heart has turned to ice like
the snow queens and needs to be
melted so tears can be shared.
Remember only the good times of years
gone by, not the sad ones.
Life is so very precious to dwell
on sadness still.
You have good friends to help you
through the heartache and tear times
That need to be shared
Your heart will be much lighter
and happier if you do this:
Live for the future; don't dwell
on the past.

S. Cohen

'The Christmas Swans'

The mist rose over the black
Enchanting Lake
To reveal two silhouetted
Lovers dancing under the
Glowing moon.

Slowly the mist clears
And the lake shimmers as
The lovers glide back and
forth.

Then they touch and caress
Each other's glances
With sparkling eyes only
For each other.

Oh what graceful beauty
Are the Christmas swans.

T. Hammond

The Doors Of Damnation

The doors, they opened slowly,
I walked into a hallway
of frightening images of myself,
Yet I could not turn away.
Wrinkled and distorted,
My life seemed at an end,
And the hall went on forever
Without a turn or bend.
The doors, they closed behind me,
I was trapped inside this leech,
The sun shone through the skylight
But this I could not reach.
I ran through this hallway
Hoping I was dreaming
But my gallery of images
Were staring back at me and screaming.
And running away from the past
That I had put myself in,
I found the end of my hallway,
A burning black coffin.

Elizabeth Lane

Tomorrow Will Soon Be Yesterday

Tomorrow will soon be yesterday
Time marches on, waits for no one.
For lovers, time passes quickly by,
We cannot wait, we may be too late
To realize our dearest dreams,
See fulfilment of precious schemes.
We must make the most of each chance
While we may.
Tomorrow will soon be yesterday.

Lawrence Burton

Alone

Sitting alone all by myself
Nowhere to go, nothing to do.
Oh why, oh why
Can't I be like you?

You have friends
Who will share your fears,
You have friends
To wipe away your tears

You don't sit
In school alone,
You don't dread
Having to go home

You have fun
And lot's of it too.
Oh why, oh why
Can't I be like you?

Judi Griffiths

The Kiss

I love the way our
Lips and bodies meet
The way you lift yours
Gently onto your toes
I kiss the tip
Of your nose...
Our moment of
Soul surrender
Our love
Slow and tender
Burning intensity
Emotions swells
And grows...
Twin sighs
As senses
Return to
Reality
Our Breath demands
We relinquish
The kiss

Jennifer Robinson

In Memory Of Dylan

No more muddy paws
  To push the door
  Or knock the picture on the wall

No soft paw to trace my face
No gentle nibble of my ear
Or nudge to calm a troubled tear

And by the fire an empty space
The clean washed floor no paws to trace

No more hiding in the flowers
  Chasing birds
  Dash in from showers

No one can fill your special ways
Only memories left of happier days

C. A. Pettet

When Will This War End?

Starvation and hunger,
People begin to wonder,
How long this war will last.
People dying and people crying,
Everybody trying,
To end this awful war.
Blood and guts
The putt, putt, putt of a machine gun
In the distance,
Bang, bang, bang
And the clang, clang, clang,
Comes the sound of bombs far away.
Will this war end some day?

Naomi Elliott

Old Age

They say that beauty is just skin deep
It's in the eye of the beholder
So when I look into the mirror I look
A damned sight older
My skin is slack I'm baggy eyed
I'm not a sight to see
So where on earth is all this beauty
It's certainly not in me
I've tried all cures the summer rain
Tested with a tan
At seventy four I must admit I'm just a
Withered old man.

W. Robinson

Untitled

On a Monday we pulled out the motor,
On Tuesday we gave it a clean,
On Wednesday and Thursday,
A crowd gathered by, and
Said, what a lovely machine!
On Friday we filled it with petrol;
Rubbed it all over with land,
On Saturday morning
It started to rain
So we bunged it back
Into the yard

G. E. Freeman

Nowhere = Now/Here

Rock pools, full of wonder,
seem a world apart,
self-contained, no solace
for an aching heart

Mirage in the desert -
will I never find
the substance not the shadow
for a hungry mind.

Sitting on the seashore
one idle sunny day,
the tide turned very softly
came creeping up my way.

The sea lay all around me,
no longer set apart.
The joy of all creation
not out, but in, my heart

W. R. West

The Sea

In childlike innocence
We gaze across the ocean
It speaks eternally
With its perpetual motion
And soothes our spirits
Though they soar
With restless fervour
On the shore
In its depths it holds
The secrets of all who
Cast their cares upon it
And as nature turns her tide
She diminishes
This distance what lies
Between us
Stretch your hand into the water
And let me feel your
Trembling fingers
Take delight in knowing
That in the water we unite

Lydia Meli

Unknown Presence

You can not see it,
Only feel it,
Shivers and chills
to give it away,
eerie sounds,
things that move
to make you believe
some things aloof,

The middle of the night,
when you're feeling down,
uneasy moments on your own,
slight chills will come,
unearthly sights,
frightened stiff but can not fight,

Beyond this life,
is something unknown,
some things happened,
something untold

Simone Blewer

Tribute To Science

Miracles only God can do
That's His provence we know that's true
No one walks on water today
But men can fly and do each day
Even outer space is in bounds
And mark what men can do with sounds
Pictures too flash around the world
Above our satellites are swirled

How many live today that would be dead
And neither are they still in bed
Some that could be blind see today
Hard of hearing know what you say
Constant change is so prolific
Maybe not all so terrific

But man is learning all the time
Some day he could end up real prime
He knows just what the problems are
Their cures though must be popular
So it's bye bye human nature
Then hello universal cure.

Harry C. Derx

Snow

Snow snow soft and white
Snow snow so calm and bright
Snow snow gently falling to the ground
Snow snow slowly piling up in a mound
Snow snow snow is nice
Snow snow gradually turning to ice.

Donna Holloway

Ajok (My Adopted Elephant)

Ajok is an elephant
As anyone can see,
Others may not like him.
But he means the world to me,
He lives out in Kenya,
With Daphne and her staff.
They've had some scary moments.
And a few to make them laugh.
He's fed on milk and greens.
And occasionally some rusks.
But that's for when he's fully grown
When he gets his tusks.
I'm saving hard to see him,
Though he lives so far away.
But you never know,
I might get there one day.

Anne Lewis

Children Of The World

Children of the world
of nations all around
Should all be filled with happiness
Should all be safe and sound
There should not be a time you see
For suffering and pain
As they are all God's children
When give his son in vain
Some children they are happy
Some children they are sad
For if the world was safer
It hick they would be glad
for some there is no food you see
For some there is to much
Why can't there be a unity
Why can't there be some trust
For children are the future
What ever come what may
So give them love and caring
To guide them on life's way

Linda Sheppard

Impressions Of A Winter's Estrange

The rippling tide ebbed slowly
From mud washed clean and free,
Welcoming the waders
Where river meets the sea.

The dunlins came, & plovers
With brilliant rhythmic flight -
Turnstone, redshank, godwit,
A thousand within sight.

On wet and shining sand
That mirrored winter's sky,
Were busy probing bills
And curlews fluting cry.

Then with the tide returning
And covering the shore
Away flew all the waders
To quiet roosts once more.

Marjorie M. Mackay

Spring

When the crocus starts to bloom
And the cuckoo gives its merry tune
When the sky above is blue
And everything starts anew
The birds start to build their nest
We throw off our winter vest
The daffodils start to appear
The sheep with their lambs so dear
Everything comes alive, with a zing
At the magical time called "spring".

Pam Newman

The Garden Of My Heart

Fond memories grow like flowers,
In the garden of my heart.
They intertwine, they bud and bloom,
of the memories you are a part.
The tulips and the daffodils,
They bloom in early spring
The Almond and the cherry trees.
Give homes to birds that sing,
The flowers in my garden,
start from seeds and then they grow.
Blossoming and smelling sweet,
as seasons come and go.
Of all my lovely flowers I know,
the nicest one of all,
must be the rose, sweet fragrance rare,
Rambling up the wall.

Rosalind Flower

147

Boston Manor

They should have called this station
'Addled Stop'
the air was but a panacea
with none save pigeons
on their quest
to say
yesyesyesyesyesyesyesyesyes

Then of varicose veins
of the lines of random Oaks
and genuflected grassland
have a hand in a seated train?
Germans and sport and business
papers perused on the way
to a party
would they to know of
Agripseudoscience
as a notice at Boston Manor
that said on feeding
grey flying warbling wobbly ones
nononononononononononononononono
Graham Ewens

O'Child Of Mine

O'child of mine, elusive dream
Sweetest face I've ever seen
Enquiring gaze to recognize
The love within my grateful eyes

Gift of life with time to spare
Born to grow, yet unaware
Let me teach you all good things
To marvel as the bird she wings

Watch the spider spin its web
Hear the ocean flow and ebb
Keep strength in adversity
Holding fast integrity

Go with luck when time to part
And let your love be from the heart
Follow where life dares to lead
Turn from envy, lust and greed

O'child of mine, elusive dream
I yearn for all you might have been
Never here, yet never gone
Forever in my thoughts live on
Maggie Moone

Full Moon At Seatown

She will be there in her full glory
Come this very night;
So suddenly she rose just now
Topping the brow of the hill.
Nightly clouds stream o'er her face;
Her face, now radiant
Shining brightly, as darkness descends
Around the green clad hill.
The hill, steeped in evening sunlight
So short a time ago,
Now rests in night repose; quietly
In the moon's serenity,
And so she guards us all,
Bids us to sleep:
As proudly with so great a majesty,
She rides the sky again.
High in the heavens; now over the sea
A double radiance her reflection brings
To those who from their window peep,
To see her glory yet once more.
Daphne R. Packham

Lament Of An Onion

I'm not a very pretty thing,
but at heart am stout and strong,
so I wonder why,
I make people cry,
I haven't done anything wrong.

I'm often used,
sometimes abused,
a cure for many ills,
with me around,
you have no ground,
for gulping down those pills.

So next time in your garden,
Listen to my plea,
Get to know your Onion
'cause I'm a V.I.P.
Barbara Trueman

My Special Bay

I awoke and there you were
I sat in my hospital bed
and gazed into your eyes
and you in mine

Sore all my pain
all my hurt
deep deep in my soul
only you could see

I new you were special
a face so young but a
soul so old I could see

My love is forever yours
and now you are four precious years
you cant read or speak of
how you fell

My son be patient with me
We have a long road to travel
Wait for me hold my hand
We will walk it together
dance and sing as only we do together

This is my gift to you, Ben
Maria Mynott

Dreams

Dreams are like pictures,
that flash before your eyes,
they dwell in your unconscious mind.

They can be of fact or fiction,
they can also be funny or frightening,
You can have dreams in the day or night

They can sometimes show you things,
you might want to keep,
within the hidden depths of your mind.
Melanie Bewick

Mother

When I was born, you protected me.
You washed my body.
You washed my hair,
And you washed my feet.
You gave me breakfast.
You gave me lunch,
And you gave me tea.
You gave me tea.
You gave me love.
You gave me life.
For me there was no other
I loved you with all my heart
For you were my dearest
Mother
F. W. Kent

Oh, I Love You So

The love that I possess is so real,
If only you could just feel,
My heart beating for you.

My love for you is so dear,
My love for you is so caring.
My love for you is so clear,
My love for you is so daring.

Oh, I love you so,
If you could only know,
That your heart is inside mine.

My love for you is so sure,
My love for you could never be wrong.
My love for you, no man could endure,
My love for you is so strong.

Your touch is so full of love,
Your swiftness is that of a dove.
You and I belong together,
I know that our love will last forever.
Elizabeth Davies

The Devil's Fold

A furnace glows in every wall
Where Nick the shepherd cools his nail.
They slowly rising out of hell
There snakes a teeny-weeny spell.
Goblins sighing, demons humming
While nick upon his harp is strumming,
Engaged in hectic preparation
For just one more initiation.
E. Fuller

Sea Through The Trees

There is the swish and surge of the sea
Through the trees today;
The unceasing sound of surf
Brushing the sand and the stones.
Above is the sea -
Here on the moss
The saplings swaying
Seem gigantic fronds of weed.
Greens and greys,
Yellows and browns,
Go on, on,
Deeper and deeper,
Rustling along this ocean bed
To the end
Where the sighing stays.

And there, across the hedge
Is the land,
Rainswept and grey.
Betty Swan

If Only

If I were a star,
In the velvet blue sky,
I'd try to shine the brightest of all,
Just to catch your eye.
If I were the moon,
And you lost on a foggy dark night,
I'd shine upon your pitch black path,
Lead you to safety with my light.
If I were a ray of sunshine,
Beaming down upon the land,
I wouldn't come to rest, until
I'd warmed the spot on which you stand
If I were a friend of Cupid,
And he said it were meant to be,
We'd aim and fire his arrows at you,
So you'd fall in love with me.
Katherine Price

Life

What is life?
Is this the dream,
And "the other world"
Life supreme?
What is the soul?
To which we cling,
Is it a myth
Or a precious thing?
What is the mind?
Is it of flesh,
Or chords that enmesh
This world of care.
What is the body?
Skin and bone
Moving clock-like
Is it alone?
Body, mind, soul,
Are we supreme?
Which is reality,
Which the dream?

Geraldine F. Lowe

Pretty Girl

Selling your life
For a line of white powder,
Cursed and blessed
By the way you look,
Knowledge and naivety
In the same package,
Too much too soon
But never enough.

Terence William Hughes

The Promise

Flaming June it is said
but autumn burns a truer fire
of leaping torches and sparks of red,
that brings to the heart a desire
to weep with each falling leaf
and the dew wet morning's heavy grief.

This fiery death needs no obituary,
or should cause the soul sad pain;
The cheery wave says "wait for me,
Anon I'll spring anew again".
And would we ever doubt the fact
that the Creator would break this pact?

Betty Vickeridge

The Friendly Touch

It doesn't matter who we are
or where we choose to live
Young or old and feeble
there's a lot that we can give

A smile now that works wonders
a hug well that's just fine
It means so much to others
It's our duty, yours and mine

To help when it is needed
and visit old and sick
Stop and hear their worries
don't ever take the mick

You'll find it most rewarding
a warmth you'll feel inside
one day you may be wanting
a door that's open wide

The moral to this story
is always take the time
To think of other people
do stop and talk a while

Joy Spickermann

Untitled

In the hues of the morning mists
Where blades of grass yawn and quiver
And skies send out their rays of light
Heralding the closure of the night

The owls shriek the night to dawn
As weary hedgehogs snuffle on
Into the hedgerows now to sleep
And darkness into morning creeps

Into oblivion the life unknown
Our senses dull our forms inert
We visit places all so strange
Tranquil turbulent all will range

In the hues of our earthly mists
Where life is just a thread of silk
That wavers in the winds of time
All waiting for the light sublime.

Jennifer A. Clark

Untitled

How lovely is our England
With its undulating land
The squirrels in the old oak tree
The weeping willows stand so free
We really love our dales and glens
The sun on which it all depends
Our flowers are our English pride
The bridle path the horses ride
Flowing rivers and grandeur lakes
What a lovely country this all makes
The kissing gates the cattle grids
The styles we have to climb
New morn hay and blue bell woods
And hedgerows all in line
The farmhouse and the cottages
Churches with their spires
All this ancient loveliness
The Englishman admires.

E. Groves

Suicide

Suicide, release,
Useless to resist.
Invincible depression
Calling me.
Indomitable darkness,
Darkness in every pore
Evermore.

Arthur Rice

Untitled

If life gets you down,
And you feel you can't cope,
Try to keep smiling,
Don't give up hope.
You may think you're hard done-by,
But I am sure it is true,
There is always someone
Worse off than you.
Don't envy or covet
Possessions or wealth,
More precious than these,
Self esteem, and good health.
Crying is useless.
Of self-pity beware
It is a futile emotion,
And gets you nowhere.
Share your problems with God,
He will show you the way,
All you have to do,
Is kneel down, and pray.

Audrey Norman

Untitled

With your warm arms around me
My fears will subside,
Through torment and hardship
You'll be my guide,
Oh stay with me Lord
Right to the end,
My Master, Redeemer
Healer and Friend

Olive Cooke

Heather Clad Hills

I hear the gentle rustle,
   and my weary heart it fills,
It's the rustle o' the heather,
   as the wind blows through the hills.

I hear the sound of bagpipes,
   and the blood leaps in my veins,
As I stroll amongst the heather,
   in the soft Autumnal rain.

The cottage on the hillside,
   with ivy, round the door,
The smell of baking bannocks,
   I'll remember, evermore.

A grey-haired lady by the gate,
   awaiting my return,
Those pictures in my memory,
   make my heart really yearn.

Soon, I'll be returning,
   to the land, where men are men,
And I'll roam among the heather
   of those Scottish hills again.

Evelyne A. McMaster

Journey Down A Cosmic Wormhole

The casement opened up,
he slithered down
through many-fingered veins
of branching time;
edging his way
through scattered hosts,
detritus
of forgotten pasts,
he reached a point of sweet regress,
of time without decay;
old age and childhood slipped away
to whorls beyond his birth,
while in their depths
he sensed
pre-embryonic being,
pure suspense,
the melody
of taut unmoving strings,
the last perfected void.

Frederic J. Jones

Dying All Alone

Dear, Anyone
I stare through the window
Jealous with pain,
Wishing my family,
Could be together again.
Seeing a family happy and glad,
My tears just fall, it makes me so sad.
Now that we've parted,
I will never be the same,
but as my life ends,
so will my pain.

From a lonely child.

Tanya Naylor

Untitled

When you think that I'm not listening
Or that I just don't care,
Perhaps I have forgotten you
Don't you know I'm everywhere?

From the heady days of summer
Through the days of dark despair,
If you know the place to look
You'll find me everywhere.

Of course it isn't easy
Life can be so hard to bear,
The only promise I can give is
I will be everywhere.

When time has eased the hurt and pain,
The warmth of Spring is in the air,
Be still and listen - in the peace
You'll hear me everywhere.

J. Grimwood

Untitled

Behold my Sacred Body
So painful, bruised and torn
Behold the crown upon my head
And the pain of every thorn

Behold my hands, such loving hands
That long to hold you near
Come see the nails, that you put there
Because of doubt and fear

Behold my feet that walked the path
Where I fell, beneath the load
And see, the suffering in my face
And the agony untold

Behold my heart so full of love
My heart so full of tears
For when I called, you answered me
With abuse and taunts and jeers

Behold your Lord, upon the cross
The cross, you made for me
Behold me in my dying
For I died, for love of thee

Sheila Halliday

"Answers"

You spoke.
You answered me.
Suddenly the world looked...
Inspired.
No regrets, but hope.
Anticipation, the future.
I will answer you...

Irene A. White

Untitled

It's May and gentle summer's near,
The birds all sing a ding a ding
But all around is drear
And it's as cold as anything.

The Ancients say that June was hot
In days they can remember
Of winters cold there were a lot
And snow came in December.

Now weatherman has got it wrong
Enough to send us to our graves
It rains and snows the summer long
And winter's full of heat waves.

Afraid there isn't any cure
All we can do us just endure.

Peta Tiley

Beauty Spot

Beauty in the eye of the beholder?
Come look over my shoulder
Look all around Abersoch Bay
Don't you wish here to stay?
When the crowds have gone away.
Snowdon in the evening light
What a lovely lovely sight!
With crescent moon in sky at night
Beauty spot, what does it mean?
From where I stand so much is seen
Cliffs. blue sea, and fields so green
Small, safe harbour on one side
Seals at play on rocks half-tide
Boats and yachts over waves ride
The only place for me to be
This beauty spot close to the sea

J. M. Taylor

Walking Alone

You were going you said to Chichester
to walk in the gardens
in the Cathedral grounds
and I thought of you there
walking alone
with your emptiness
and the loss that won't away
with your sorrow and grief
tangible
like a cloying marshmallow
that won't melt
stuck in your throat
or a sponge from under the salt sea
invading
weighing each breath
and I think of you
wondering why you here
alone
walking alone
in the evening sun.

Marcia Sayers

What Is Love?

To hold her in high esteem
To treat her with total respect
To wholly give her your trust
My friend, can this be love?

To forgive all her mistakes
To forget her unsavoury past
To ignore any character blemish
My friend, can this be love?

To buy her fresh scented flowers
To give her presents and gifts
To just show her that you care
My friend, can this be love?

To never fail to put her first
To surrender your own life
To save and enable her to live
My friend, that is true love

Glenn Fuller

Time

An ageless wonder
Lost
Never to be recaptured.
Mankind tries to defy its ferocity
Without success.
Everyone succumbs
At the finishing post.
Dust is all there is to show
For a life
Where toil and a wealth of experience
Once stood.

Peter D. Barrington

Sea Idyll

Great waves pounding,
Sea gulls sounding their plaintive cry.
Mats of seaweed
Flung over milk while carpets
And borne inward
To the long white sand,
Shadows of blue, and shadows of green
Angry grey and sunset gleam,
Great white horses prancing in anger,
Then softly falling, falling
And gently mewing
Into rippling waves
Along the soft white sand.

Caroline Isabel Clark

Different People

People are like chocolates in a box,
Old and young,
Hard and soft,
Different personalities,
Different views,
Different accents and
Different hues.
When you meet someone new,
Don't ever think they don't like you.
Don't judge people by their looks,
They are not covers of books.
Everyone's different and as you can see
No one is the same as me.

Heather D. Brierley

Telephone

Today's instrument of soft torture.
Enigmatic upon the table.
Then suddenly, surprisingly, it rings;
Summoning the unsuspecting
To emotions' wildest stage.
Welcome news it sometimes brings;
More oft hurt, the subtle stab,
Delivered direct into the ear.
Or the manipulator's web of deceit,
Woven round and round the head,
Till the final word echoes;
A bloodless blow.
Listening dramas played out alone.
No longer will I play;
My 'phone sits, shunned and silent;
I avoid it.
Knowing it can bring joys, but
More oft it sings a song of doom;
Is herald to misery and,
Reflection of itself, solitary gloom.

Sheila H. Marriott

We Can

We can't all be a Superman
Be handsome, bright or wealthy,
But with discipline and common sense
Keep minds and bodies healthy.

We can't all be a peacemaker
And sort out this World's fights,
But by example we can show
Our youngsters wrongs from rights.

We can't all nurse the sick and old
Or save species from extinction,
But we can care for those we love
Not seeking recognition.

So if we want a better World
Just think of one another
Not barring colour, creed or code
But treat him as a brother.

I. N. Parr

Dream

I follow on the track
  a pace behind
a beggar with a sack,
  witless and blind,
tossing on either side
  numberless seeds,
and sowing at each stride
  flowers or weeds.

I see them spring and shoot,
  each instant born;
berry and herb and fruit,
  thistle and thorn.

'What is your name?' I cry.
  'Whence come you here?'
Bleakly he makes reply
  in accents drear,
'I sow for sage and fool
  Blessing or Curse.
My name is Chance. I rule
  the Universe.

Edward Benbow

Our Garden Of Eden

A canopy of stars have we,
A sheet of silken sand,
A trove of corralled treasures
In a green and luscious land.

An ocean have we for a bath
Of waters clear and blue,
And every jewelled sunrise
Brings a dream of something new.

A "gamelan" to please our ear,
And palms to give us shade,
A fire to light the faces
Of the friends that we have made.

A moon to light our silvery path
When golden sunshine's gone,
Elixirs of exotic fruit
And fish to feast upon.

And when the final sunset
Has to stretch for many miles,
We'll always have our memories
Of paradise and smiles.

Joanna L. Lester-George

Heartbreaker

He likes to break your heart,
Into pieces which fall apart.
As it crumbles into tiny bits,
That's when it feels that nothing fits.
There's no-one else who loves you,
No-one left to help you through,
No-one standing by your side,
You want to run away and hide.
He's off with someone new,
He's gone and left you.
Two-timed you that's what he's done,
Don't worry you're not the only one.

He done it to me a long time ago,
I was his in between, his too and fro.
He took advantage of me,
But I was too blind to see.

He was playing a foolish game,
You think he's changed,
But he's still the same.

Sharon Mathieson

Mummy Doesn't Like It...

Mummy doesn't like it,
She likes it not at all;
I told her that I'd found it
Whilst looking for my ball.

  I don't think she believes me,
  Her face has gone all red.
  I think she's going to tell me off
  And send me straight to bed.

"But Mum, I couldn't leave it
Standing on its own.
It looked so lost and all forlorn
That I had to bring it home!"

  "I only tried to feed it grass,
  And not the sofa seats;
  It started them all by itself,
  Erm, 'scuse its muddy feet!?!"

Ooh, I do think I'm in trouble,
And I think it's pretty deep;
But this fuss is over nothing,
Coz after all it's just ONE sheep!

Rebecca Allen

Guts, A Pen And Passion

So you want to be a writer?
I hear you want to touch my soul
I'm told you feel you've got a gift,
A talent to behold.
So are your words in rhyme and verse?
Or are novels your creation?
Do you draw from life's experience?
Is misery your inspiration?
Are you candid in your narrative?
Do you give it to us straight?
Or are your tales pure fantasy?
Are dreams what you create?
So talk to me in chapters
And move me with your prose.
Let me think I know you.
Let me share your highs and lows.
But I've met so many like you
With guts, a pen and passion.
Romance and pain and guilt and hope
Each and every one a fashion.

Janet Bowen

The Fisherman

The fisherman stands alone
After everyone has gone home

With only his rod and fly
Silhouetted by the evening sky
The May flies hover and dance
The brown trout waiting to prance

Through his hardened eyes
He sees the big trout rise

Before the fly could land
He knew the trout played in his hand
The line went tight
'O boy', what a fight

Steaming runs and screaming reel
Vibrating rod, strong as steel

Wind singing with your line
Not a song! But a high pitched whine

The trout played into the net.
An evening he would not forget.

James Lively

Aurora Borealis

Sweet lady, divine temptress
Carefree child of mother earth
My breath your presence traps
My tongue your name delights
For you I wait to come to me
Each night I pray you show
At times when you I do not see
I fear you are forever gone
When, at last, you show yourself
Ethereal and gracefully serene
All of heaven you set afire
Your beauty there for me to see
My heart your essence fills
If mortal features you did bare
I know that you would smile
If a mortal sound you'd make
I know that you would sing
Oh what joy! To see you dance
Until, alas, once more we part
My sweet, sweet Aurora

Steven Jones

Snowflakes

Like ballerinas up on high
Snowflakes falling from the sky
Pirouetting to the ground
Falling fast they make no sound
All look so very nice
Those white and fluffy flakes of ice
Each one different as they fall
Like ballerinas at a ball
When the sun begins to beam
They melt into a sparkling stream
Giving life to plants and trees
Moistening the morning breeze
Evaporating from the ground
Into the sky, without a sound
Ready for Mother Nature's call
When once again as snowflakes fall.

Alan Chell

Fathers

Sometimes distant, sometimes near,
Brow once furrowed now is clear.
In that armour see a chink
Look within, all soft and pink.
A heart that's held in tiny hands,
Curly heads and wedding bands.
Look no more, too much revealed
Keep something secret and concealed.
But scratch that skin with hurtful deed
And see, like others, fathers bleed.

C. Boyce

A Humble Prayer

As I kneel in prayer
Hear my humble prayer
All I've come to ask "Lord"
That man becomes prepared.

Prepared to help each other.
As he go's along his way
In the way you taught us "Lord"
In a caring loving way.

As I kneel in prayer
Hear my humble prayer
For you give us so much "Lord"
In a caring loving way

In a caring loving way
Let there be peace
Peace between all nations "Lord"
No matter the colour or creed.
Amen

Jean Gibson

Envy

I know my brother
  who has never heard
Temple bells that tremble
  or seen an elephant herd
Who spends his leisure growing
  homeland bloom and tree
Into use and beauty
  is envying me.

I see my brother
  when the dusk begins
Turn into his driveway
  Into the arms of twins,
And while I wander
  down far trails and dim
And see the great world's wonders
  oh - how I envy him.

Joan Warde

A Journey

A dirty blue seat,
An overflowing ashtray,
A smell of people.

A man knows the guard,
They talk of diesel engines:
A slim woman reads.

We screech through stations,
Hardly a moment to think.
A journey by train.

Everything's the same:
Nameless names of faceless towns.
Sometimes, I wish we could go
Off the rails.

L. Thompson

Boats

Dark blue is the sea
Golden is the sand,
It flows along the river
With trees close at hand.

On goes the river
Down by the hill,
Along into the valley
Climbing to the mill.

Onward goes the river
To a little bay,
Filled with tiny boats
Bobbing around all day.

Felicity Edmead

Overlapping The Sea

Overlapping the sea is time,
like a wave too swift
for the eye to follow.
Yet as the sea plunges it
carries tales and the
sea is elusive with the
tales of time.
Time is one wave among
the many.
The sea cannot know time
or the wave, for in the sea
it dissolves.
It can only be seen
in motion, swift and
speeding to the shore.
The sea never knows
time as the wave,
in its foaming,
fleeting world.

Carolyn Frances Peck

Untitled

Man is gifted, man is clever,
  But not as clever as kidney beans.
It works this way, that man could never
  Find the manner, choose the means,
To feed on sunshine, like the beans.

So man, who'd starve out in the sun,
  Needs the food he so demeans.
The sunny lido he can shun,
  Abandon all his suntan dreams,
But eat his sun-grown wholesome
beans.

J. R. Pugh

Christmas Time

Christmas time will soon be here,
Cards will come from far and near,
Shopping, cooking, preparation,
Ready for the celebration.
Office parties, mistletoe,
People's faces all aglow,
Carol singing all around,
Listen to the tuneful sound,
Father Christmas comes at night,
Hopefully no-one in sight.
Christmas trees with pretty lights,
Come and see a lovely sight.
Exciting presents round the bottom,
Hope nobody is forgotten.
Turkey, stuffing, roast potatoes,
Oh how very fast the day goes.
Uncle breathing heavily,
Sleeping, dozing, watching telly.
Happy times without a doubt,
Yet, Who are we leaving out?

Margaret Challen

A Poem Of Love....

Love is a mystical,
So sacred and so sweet,
Love is a mystery,
So quiet and discrete.

Love is not visible,
though forever it lies.
Love is a friendship
which no other can despise.

Love is a barrier,
No being can break,
Love is a secret,
Which others cannot take.

Love is a destiny,
So real and remote,
Our heart and love,
We can devote.

Jadi Richardson

"Spring Is Coming"

Spring is coming
Love is looming
The thought of the alter
To wed someone's daughter
Spring is coming
Everything's greener
Makes the gardener so much keener
The thought of it all
More work I recall
Spring is coming
The evenings are lighter
Makes everyone feel that much brighter
When down comes the rain
Oh what a pain.

Winston Davies

Royal Babies

Every newborn babe is royal -
Son of Adam, son of God.
With a diadem imprinted
On its brow - 'of royal blood'.

Three Wise Men may not attend him
Newborn thing - a lamb - a king -
Child of Thomas, Richard, Harold.
People shout, rejoice and sing

He may hold the spark of genius:
She may rise to heady heights,-
A Carnegie, Einstein, Mozart,
All the glamour - name in lights.

They may prove the very leaders
That the world cries out to hear,
And together lead us forward
To a life more fit to bear.

Bear yourselves exultant, children.
You'll inherit wealth and fire.
Use them wisely in your future
Or Creation may expire.

Nita Nicholson

Got No Teeth

I am the baby, second in line,
I have an older brother,
And that's just fine, but,
I can't have a sandwich
Or a rasher of beef.
They just no smile at me knowingly
And say no! Got no teeth.
They pass around biscuits
Ice cream and sweets
Then smile at me knowingly
And say no! Got no teeth.
One day when I'm older
And mum is a gran
And sitting there knitting
And eating her bran
I'll get out the toffee
Nougat and beef
Then smile at her knowingly
And say no! Got no teeth.

Maggie Ledbury

Autumn

All the trees are very bare
Watch the leaves dance in the air
They fall to the ground all crisp
And brown,
Where they dissolve into the
ground,
The flowers have gone, that's not
true
They are hiding away from you.

Carol Ashley

Driving At Night

Driving at night, alone,
I see the pale moths
Flutter to death against my headlights,
Watch them whirl toward me
Like flakes of ash
Blown in a strong wind.

And I am like those moths,
Drawn from the darkness
Out of the safety of obscurity
Into the glare of you;
And I shall fall to death
Battered by your brightness.

Andrée Evans

Hibernation

Autumn now is truly here
The dark nights are drawing near
Leaves turning, red, brown and yellow
Only to fall, when the wind does bellow

The squirrel gets ready to hide
She gathers what's left behind
Frogs and fishes two by two
Hide away from me and you

Even the birds have flown away
As it's too cold for them to stay
Hedgehogs and tortoises go to sleep
As they burrow down, very deep

Now everything is sleeping sound
With frost and snow on the ground
And hopefully come next year
Each and everyone, will appear.

Maureen Hyam

Dark

The street was dark and lonely,
No footsteps could be heard,
You couldn't hear a pin drop,
You couldn't hear a bird.
A gun was shot in the distance,
I heard a cry out for help,
Everything went silent,
Then I heard a frail yelp.
A broad few footsteps,
Came running up the street,
The gun shot again.
There were six stomping feet.
The night had returned,
Hopeless mystery,
Although for some,
It was just pure misery.

Nicki Thornton

Untitled

Man walks out one misty evening
Man looks out one rainy night
Somehow wished he wasn't leaving
Wishes that the world was right
Man then hears a distant wailing
Man then cries a lonely tear
Somehow wished he didn't keep failing
Wishes he could forget his fear
Man looks up and sees the grey skies
Man feels the pressure of the storm
Somehow wished he hadn't told lies
Wishes that he hadn't been born

David Gorton

Thoughts

Why do I fear growing old.
To sit alone, no heat, just cold,
With just my memories of long ago,
We went out and fought the foe,
For freedom and for the young,
For all that
We have not won,
The common market runs our lives,
We have no say,
Just foreign jibes,
Why can't we have our country back,
Give foreign rule the sack,
We fought a war with guts and pride.
Give a thought to those who died.
Give us our pride and country back,
A good strong leader is what we lack,
This great land is all we've got.
Don't let us become a little dot.

D. Joyce

Alcohol

It begins when you're young,
It makes you grow old,
It can turn the most timid
into something quite bold.

Oh! the feeling it gives
As the first one glides down,
You're King of the castle-
You're wearing the crown.

You begin with just one,
But then you want more,
You're out of control-
You're paying a whore.

The days of the week
Now all the same
You walk with a stoop-
To hide from your shame.

Like so many before you
Whose cause is now lost,
You've taken the pleasure-
With no thought of the cost.

Ian E. Linsley

Becky's Haircut

Snip Snip Snip
And now my baby
Is a wee girl
Oh how I wish
He'd kept a curl
To put away
Some far off day
When old and grey
I'd look and say
My baby!

Geraldine Barton

Cricket At Night

Cricket at night
beneath the lights
before the shouting crowd
The shriek, the squeal
The fierce appeal
Alas, it's disallowed.

Cricket at night
the ball's in flight,
and every fieldsman tense.
Square leg and slips,
and coke and chips
and banners on the fence

A sudden shout,
"He's out, he's out!"
To all the crowd's delight,
caught in the deep,
who wants to sleep
when cricket's on at night.

Steven Payne

The Other Woman

You, in your newness
  burning the past
    with your flesh

And he, who was mine
  surrendering
    his conscience.

Time of his going
  a long-toothed year
    aching still

And I, the thorned rib
  stabbing his side
    constantly.

Mona Miller

Requiem To An Elm

Goodbye old tree
Goodbye old friend
The woodcutter's axe
Brought a speedy end
That axe cut deep
And down you fell
Never more in that place to dwell
It's not the same
Now you are not there
The field seems different, empty, bare.
No longer do you stand so tall
No longer looking down on all
No longer swaying in the breeze
That's left now to other trees.
No more sheltering
Under your leaves so green
Just memories now of what once had been
So goodbye old friend, goodbye old tree
In my mind you'll still grow
Eternally

Leslie Day

The Village Market

In a village market square,
The things you see, are very rare
The tinker with his pots and pans,
A stall with home-made jars of jam.

A scissor grinder, at his wheel
A horse, munching bran, for his meal
An artist with paintings bright,
A strong man, showing off his might.

Someone selling home-made sweets,
Another selling toys, for treats,
The farmer with his sheep to sell,
Over all rings the old church bell!

There is a stall, for cakes and pies,
Another with shirts and ties,
Plants and fruit, in great array,
All this you find, on market day.

Teresa Marsh

Our Planet

We are killing off our planet,
No-one seems to care,
We just go on poisoning the air,

We drop litter everywhere,
We don't seem to care,

It's our life we're ruining,
And the future races,
All those sweet innocent faces.

Liz Ireland

Tribute - Wedding Anniversary

The finest porcelain figurines
Are every collector's
Wildest dreams
As a pair
You are both unique
You make my collection complete.

The delicate rose.
Oh! wind
Don't blow so hard
I'm only a rose
You tend to discard
The oaks
The elms
They bend and sway
Please wind
Hear my plea.

James Brown

A Low Profile

When life is very daunting
I try to keep my end up,
And believe that help is given,
Through all the prayers I send up.
Frustration makes me sour,
And then I swear and growl,
But, at least, I feel it's better
Than to give up and to howl!
When my wheelchair hits a snag,
And small buttons are 'possessed',
Or I cannot reach a shelf,
Although I've done my best,
Then I think of Tony O.,
Bulgarian, so disabled,
No home, few friends, and yet
By character enabled
To maintain a way of living
In that impoverished state,
With so little to rejoice in,
And a questionable fate.

Elizabeth Brown

Valentine

V is for Vast
   The amount of beats in my heart
A is for Asking
   For our friendship to start,
L is for Long
   The hours, together we'll spend
E is for Excitement
   In my Heart which you'll mend,
N is for Nights
   Which will no longer be cold
T is for Tenderness
   We'll have even when old,
I is for Idle
   We will no longer be
N is for Natural
   For you to see me,
E is for Everything
   To have now and forever,
All I want is for us
To be always together.

Mary O'Donovan

To A Rose

How soft your petals are
   fragrant, sweet your scent
In colours wondrous to behold
   We know, you're heaven sent.

On the stems the thorn
   Yet did not Mary mourn,
To see the thorn cut deep
   As at her master's feet,
She knelt to weep.

O rose of velvet hue
   You are the flower of love
In gardens, many or few
   You stand in the morning dew,
Soft as the winged feathers
   Of a dove.

Joan Gentle

Untitled

Laugh and the world laughs with you
Cry and you cry alone.

It isn't the cough
that carries you off; it's the
coffin they carry you off in.

Joyce Bloomberg

"Poseurs"

Euphoric poseurs on a wave
Free but popularity's slave
Singing, dancing, sporting fashion
Exhibiting with crazy passion

Beautiful people who must impress
One upmanship without redress
Sexy smiles and sexy hips
Confident eyes and curling lips

Conditioned hair and shaking heads
Exaggerated walks for shapely legs
Phallic power of the latest car
The randy beat of the pop guitar

Modern paintings meaning nought
Defying explanations sought
Commercials which exceed the norm
Supposedly in acceptable form

Surely youth must have its fling
Apparently doing its own thing
But don't expect all who survey
To forget they had their day.

John Sanderson

A Lazy Man's Lament

Sometimes we do.
Sometimes we don't.
Sometimes we will.
Sometimes we wont.
Sometimes we do it in a wink.
Other times we stop to think.

Sometimes we do it right away.
Get it done without delay.
Sometimes we leave it for a while.
Add it to the mounting pile,
Leave it there to gather dust,
Saying that we really must
Get it done sometime today,
Or, possibly, next Saturday.
There really is so much to do
So, Saturday, we'll do that too
Or maybe Sunday would be best,
Though Sunday is the day of rest.
It might be Monday, after all
If we get it done at all???

Arthur Ronald Legg

Wild Cat - Mild Cat

Great green eyes glowing
Frisky tail fascinating
Wired whiskers twitching
   Cat on the prowl.

Shrouded eyes chinking
Throaty purr thrumming
Tapered tail twining
   Cat in a curl.

Francesca Beryl Leechman

Christmas Eve

Christmas tree and fairy lights,
What a sight to see,
Sitting round the fire side,
With all the family.

Chestnuts on the fire,
Brandy in your glass,
Children singing carols,
It's Christmas time at last.

Dinner's on the table,
Christmas Pudding's very hot.
Crackers ready to be pulled,
Thank the Lord for what we've got.

Julie Taylor

Stalking Love

You sent me the vase,
But not the love inside,
The flowers were missing,
The love you did hide.

You gave me your heart,
But without the love
It had all drifted,
Into heaven above.

Your hugs and no emotion,
Your arms loose by my side,
The vase of broken China,
Your love for me had died.

Whilst your love's in heaven,
My heart is lost in hell,
While you're seeking new love,
My heart's under a spell.

I thought our love was true love,
It seemed so good and real.
But in your eyes it must have looked
Like no big two-way deal!!

Bev Cammish

At Night

Moments tumble about
   my head.
Fragments of time
   escaping
from the future,
   to form
the mosaic of memory.

Inside each one
   you walk
in your sure footed way.

Your hair
   a mane of energy.
Your hips
   sing the songs of centuries.
Your softness,
   settles about me like a cloak.

I sleep;
   and
you follow me there.

Reg Kear

Lines...

Man is man and who
And what can be more? So...

Do you not feel for the dispossessed
Who may not even be born?
They cannot cry out against the carnage
We work on this land day after day.

Man is man and who
And what can be more? Though...

There are those of us who profess
A lingering sanity torn
'Tween the real and unreal of bondage
To subjective realities in our way.

Man is man and who
And what can be more? So...

Ours the task to clean up the mess
Time to call a peace shorn
Of all unnatural pretensions to wage
The essence of when and how to say.
Man is man and who
And what can be more? Right...

C. P. Ho

Departed Love

How dare you go and leave me here
When I loved you so well
There was no warning, no last word
And certainly no farewell.
But there are things too deep for words
That never fade from mind
Your laughing eyes, your innocence
And oh! you were so kind.
I feel you all around me
Especially on wintry nights
And I remember oh so clearly
How we loved by the firelight.
I close my eyes and see your face
I listen for your voice
To hold you close to me again
Would be my eternal choice.
But now I know you are at peace
I can live with it all
I think of you night and day
For Us there is no wall.

Moira Michie

Why Can't Girls Be Altar-Boys?

"Why can't girls be altar-boys?"
I asked me mam one day
"Why can't we stand beside the priest
To genuflect and pray?"

"Why can't I dress up like the rest
To help him say the mass?
My brothers look so good at it -
Why can't it be a lass?"

I'd love to ring the bells and stuff
And have them all watch me
I'd bow my head with such respect
They'd see the saint in me.

I want to light the incense
Or carry that big cross
And lead the way right down the aisle
In front of Father Ross.

"Why can't I Mam?" I nagged her
Her blue eyes looked at me
"Now, don't be such an eegit girl
Away and make the tea."

Mary Massey

Now Waiting

Somebody's waiting
For something to happen
Just waiting

Nothing happens
Still waiting

Thoughts
A lot of thoughts
It's all in the brain

Quietness
Going crazy

Still waiting

No harm done
Yet not harmless
To little done

Thinking about thoughts
Not a sound
To much light
The thoughts are dark

Waiting
For nothing to happen

Alasdair McNeill

Memories At Eighty

Kind memory its curtain draws
Across the pains of yore,
But dreams, unkindly scavengers,
Uncover them once more.

In these I am a boy once more
At undetermined schools,
Awaiting painful punishment
For breaking phantom rules.

Or I'm a raw recruit again,
On passing-out parade,
In terror's thrall because I have
Some fearful blunder made.

But fears that rise from memories
Of things I used to dread
Dissolve as I, now eighty, wake
And find myself in bed.

Awake in sweet relief I lie,
To find my dreams untrue;
For true it is, for all its pains,
Old age has comforts, too.

Donald D. Christie

An Ending

The eaves make shadows in a dark room,
Watching, waiting, anticipating,
Sometimes she knows me, remembers,
Eyes full of anxiety, fear.

The years count for nothing,
Memories, loves, hates,
I run in my mind, wanting an ending,
She smiles.

A bee buzzes in, alive, busy,
Then we are alone again,
Eyes not meeting, silence growing,
Rituals to go through, comforting.

The weekly flowers unseen,
The flowers of guilt and love,
Pointless gestures but necessary,
Flowers for show.

Fifty years and no words left,
The goodbye, promise of tomorrow,
The kiss so cold, run, run away,
An ending please.

Jane Mitham

Untitled

As the clock strikes midnight,
another day begins,
in winter there are snowflakes,
then blossom in the spring.
In summer all the flowers bloom,
in autumn fade and die,
the passing of the seasons,
as every year goes by.
From darkness through to daylight,
it always seems the same,
the world in which we live in
has hardly ever changed.
And then you came into my life
and filled it with great things,
but then you turned and walked away,
and shattered all my dreams.
So as the clock strikes midnight,
the day before has passed,
and all I have are memories,
of a love that didn't last.

A. D. Rose

Nature's Gift

I long to see a castle
On a mountain, by the sea.
I long to see a golden sun,
That sets my spirit free.
I long to see an ocean,
With water crystal clear.
I long to find true happiness
To know my saviour's near.
I long to see the moonlight
Beaming on the mountain
I long to see a garden
Surround a silver fountain.
And one day, in my heart I know,
I'll find my paradise.
For all my dreams, are natures gifts
And come without a price.

A. Simms

I Long To See

I long to see the flowers sweet
Lay in a carpet at my feet.
I long to see the clouds drift by
Across a bright and clear blue sky.
I long to see the summer rain
Flowing down a window pane.
I long to see a summer breeze
Rustling in the leafy trees.
I long to see a midnight star
Twinkling at me from afar.
I long to see a meadow in Spring
With baby lambs frolicking.
I long to see the face of another
The face of my Father and my Mother.
I long to see......
I long to see......

Linda Wroe

Evening

The downfire of the evening
And the dull thud of the gun
The abacus trained salesman
And the movement of the sun.

The journey which was fruitless
And the going which was tough
The actress who was stupid
And who couldn't get enough.

The award which was meaningless
Not glinting in the sun.
The water lost without further trace;
And the man with the golden gun.

The moorings at the beachy head
A rusty can comes to mind.
The anchor softly settling
And treasure hard to find.

The evening where you were restless
With the strange bump in the night.
The downfire of the day
And the upholding of the light.

Simon Maier

Untitled

I gaze aloft, at my world,
for he has seen fit to put me here,
to undergo a daily time, in
this place, is mine mine mine.
I thank the day, I thank the night
for what is wrong and what is right,
and for me I go from day to day
to live this life in my own way
that was yesterday.

George Henry Fish

Snow

The snow came gently in the night
Quietly it fell to earth
Turning the trees and bushes white.
The fields and hedges merged as one
Magically all bleakness gone.
I walked across the frozen ground
My footsteps making ne'er a sound.
The tracks I made were dark and deep
It seemed the world was fast asleep.
Falling flakes like thistledown
Added to winters wedding gown.
The sun came out and cast a glow
How wonderful to see pink snow.
Such beauty made me gaze in awe
Enraptured by the sight I saw.

Wendy P. P. Windle

The Everlasting Night Is Deep

The everlasting night is deep
　　And darkness stuns my eyes:
How can this questing spirit sleep
　　Girt round with mysteries?
Let mortal wits their silence keep
　　For God is only wise.

In all the arrogance of power
　　These tyrant Tamburlaines
Bestride the world, but in an hour
　　Their tinsel glory wanes
And withers like a wayside flower
　　And God alone remains.

The everlasting night is deep
　　And darkness sears my sight;
The mountain-ways of death are steep
　　And hard to scale aright:
Where eagles soar and vipers creep,
Where demons doubt and angels weep,
Let finite minds their vigil keep
　　For God is infinite.

Philip McNair

From A Soldier To His Girl Friend

Dancing in a rosy mist
Lovers ever to remain
We side step, hesitate, we kiss
Our dance, our champagne.

Dancing till you softly sigh
My love, my sleepy head
Is tired, then what do I do,
But carry you to bed
Then softly steal away
To wait outside
The dawning of another day
Then to open wide
Your door with morning tea

John Garrett

When I Discovered I Loved You

When I discovered I loved you
My heart missed a beat
When I discovered I loved you
I'm sure I went dark pink!
When I discovered I loved you
You rose to the top of my heart
When I discovered I loved you
You asked me to go out with you
When I discovered I loved you
We found we were the perfect couple
When I discovered I loved you
We found a love that lasts forever
When I discovered I loved you
I knew I really did.

Laura Pettigrew

Dreams

Dust my dreams with diamonds,
Cloak me in the purple night,
Slice the moon for stepping-stones,
Waltz me round the infinite.

Tempest, torrent, avalanche
Race me to the rings of fire,
Planets! Roll you up like marbles,
Sport with me until I tire.

Set a slumped and drowsy mountain
For a pillow for my head,
Smooth the corrugated ocean
For a mattress for my bed.

At first rising let my footsteps
Grave their unimmortal print
To some purpose and till night fall
Make me with that much content.

Charles B. Owen

Thoughts At The Sink

When I am standing at the sink
Of noble things I'd like to think,
But only mundane things instead
Fill my busy little head.

I think of meals I must prepare,
The family favourites year by year,
And formulate fantastic plans
While dealing with the pots and pans.

There's the washing I must do
And all the household shopping too!
And tradesmen calling with their wares
Just as I have gone up-stairs!

Maybe I worry without cause
About my daily household chores,
But it is of them I think
When I am standing at the sink.

John H. E. Rendall

Brothers

Brothers are all the same,
they call you a name.
When you get on their nerves.
They shout,
They say out,
I say no with a blow,
and cling onto something
like some clothing
say no with a blow.
Walk out with a shout,
and a bang of course!

Anne-Louise Jewell

Behind The Mask

What secrets kept within the heart,
Beneath a brave facade
What skeletons lie lurking.
Each given scant regard.

Whose soul can truly say,
No darkness hides within.
Who is purest white.
Without a trace of sin.

Which one of us can say with truth,
We harbour no ill will.
Are we honest when we say
We couldn't lie, or cheat, or kill.

So each of us must wear a mask.
And keep our dark side furled,
Hiding our ambivalence
From a hypocritical world

K. Tyler

Black Shadow

No one knows why,
But everyone's scared.
Not me
I know why.

Silent and deadly
Evil
Possessing your last breath.
Dragging your soul with it.

Ceasing your life,
Like the wave of a hand,
Touch of a devil.
Freezing the memories.

Terrifying the young,
Welcoming the old.
Black shadow.
No one knows why.

Fourentza Antoniou

Divorce

Divorce is such a messy thing,
It tears your heart apart.
Families suffer terribly
And that is just the start.
When parents get together,
The shouting just don't stop.
They argue over everything,
Even their old line prop!
How I wish that it were different
And they'd be best of friends,
So when they got together,
They could make amends.
The children haven't asked for this,
So please don't ignore us,
Be nice when you're together
And give us lots of fuss.
Loving isn't so very hard,
Just give us an hour or two
Of the happiness you once shared
And we'll be proud of you.

Dawn Croft

A Thought

Through our deepest illusions,
In darkness we lie,
Allowing feelings,
Desires,
and dreams pass us by.
Trapped in the knowledge
That one day will come,
When shadows
Uplifted,
with freedom, will run.

Lisa Chamberlain

Passing Away

If you ever knew the meaning
Of those bleak days,
Tearing us apart
Like a harsh blow.

Death's lovely voice was singing,
Her songs were like a lullaby.
But now it's too late for lying.
Her songs are dead music
Growing up inside me.

(A man is always too weak,
Sometimes too strong,
But he should never be told
What kind of dirt
He's made of.)

Inmaculada Medina Cuesta

Growing Up

I loved you from the start
I carried you
I nurtured you
When you fell down
I picked you up
Then you began to grow
Overnight, you changed
I wasn't needed, as much
You could manage, on your own
Your own views, opinions too
This was your life
Even though you had been part of mine
Now was the time, to let you go
You'll make mistakes, this I know
But you'll get by
You always do
I'll still be here, if you fall down
And if you'll let me
I'll pick you up.

Margaret Barker

Lunch Time

Faces, faces; I am surrounded
by an ambush of faces at the table.

Fragile as a bird, my aunt sits
at the head of the table.
Who would guess she is an
indomitable matriarch in the making?
(But they are afraid of her;
I can tell you - look at their faces).

My mother, pecked into order,
nods in anxious agreement
as Birdie lays down the law
with an elegant predatory claw.
As for my father, you'll see
the bewildered anger of a dog
whose tail is being pulled.

What can a clumsy dog do
to stop the subtle predations
of a bird that's never still?
A hulk of resentful silence, he sits,
and hate is phosphorescent in his eyes.

Rosanne Gomez

I Looked In The Lounge

A room filled with people
All sit there-alone
Each-with their memories.
The one thing - they own.
Stripped of their dignity.
Forced into sharing
The rest of their lives.
with others - uncaring.
Some lived their lives
For the welfare of others.
To be cast aside,
By sisters and brothers,
Families, friends. All
Too busy - elsewhere,
Pushed into homes.
No one seems to care.
Where is compassion?
In this 'throw away' world?
Where - alone - in the crowd.
Cries for love - are unheard?

Mary Eagle

Two Burials

On English grass and chalk you lie
Beneath a cloudless English sky,
A lark is singing high above,
This English world is what you love;
But I will lie on heather roots
And palest green of bracken shoots,
And I will hear a curlew cry
In drifting mist across the sky.
Your bones will grow a greener grass
And greener trees as time will pass,
But mine will grow a rowan tree
And twisted birches by the sea.

June Cooke

Acrostic

*To a Sweetheart on Going Overseas
with the British Forces, Early 1941*

Familiar joy, accustomed bliss
Enwrapped the concord of our days.
Life turned and we were plunged in this
Inordinately bitter phase.
Courage my love! We must abide
Inscrutably the present ill.
Though distance part or fortune chide
Yet time shall turn and bless us still

Norman E. Hannan

Mice

While we were asleep
the mice would peep
and run across the floor
Then out jumps the cat
with the black padded paw
there were no mice anymore

Holly R. Webb

Together There

I see you look
But you don't see
You listen, but
No longer hear
But still your beauty
That enchanted me
Has not changed
Through all the years
You're everything in life to me
A gift beyond compare
And when we reach eternity
I pray that you and I will be
    Together there

E. Hodgkins

The Sun

The sun awakes in the early morn,
After the dark and dewy night.
It is the wakening of the dawn
And the sky shines bright.

The eastern sky is gold
And red in the day so new.
The sun will melt the mistiness
And dry the morning dew.

Now the sun its rays will shine
Of warmth and light and cheer;
All through the hazy summer time,
Its glow forever near.

In the evening cool the sun dost lie
Round and red in the western sky.
Sinking slowly, dropping low.
The sky shines red again
With a golden glow.

Mary E. Ellis

Moments

Moments to walk in the quiet
Hand in hand.
Moments to ponder
Life's grains of sand.

Moments of sadness
Sat side by side
Moments for tears
Trying to hide.

Moments of joy
And also of pleasure.
Moments to bury
Like hidden treasure.

Moments of gladness
That you're ever near.
Moments of sureness
That your love is here.

A. J. Griffiths

Choices

Youth or Wisdom,
You have a choice,
Which shall it be,
In your head a voice,
Cries the choice is easy,
Wisdom is what you crave,
Alas here lies the twist,
With wisdom there is age,
Strength of youth is gone,
Torn from your life,
A book with no first page,
The rest makes no sense.
Youth or wisdom,
You have no choice.

Michele Heffey

The Ballad Of Alejandra

We kissed neath Banva's ancient sky
By amiable lake where lovers lie
To poetic words our senses fell
My sweet everlasting immortelle
Imprisoned to old myrrh's ancient youth
And to the embattled angelic multitude
Whose mystery inhabits the wind
There we two entangled lie
By amiable lake where lover sigh
With dragonfly seiche
And loves gay wandering cry.

Raymond Dinsmore

Snow Calmed

Too much snow.
One cannot get far.
It covers the car.
Ground collects flakes
At a billion per hour.
Not countable, No!!!

Oh slush! No!!
One cannot step dry.
We've no wellies, oh why?
The road is brown dirty.
Snow's white from the sky.
Oh, bring back clean snow!

Now hard ice!
One cannot help slip.
It gives you, "the pip!"
Let's stay indoors.
Make coffee to sip.
We'll cater for..?
Birds, squirrels, foxes...and mice?

Clive Robson

Soon You'll Be Gone

Why is it
That I can see you,
But can't see you.
Touch you,
But can't touch you.
Soon you'll be gone,
But I'll still have my dreams.

Claire Stenning

'Dancing'

Do you like dancing in the sunshine
upon the golden sand
I wouldn't mind dancing with you
I am the sunshine
you and I on the scorched sand.

Do you like dancing in the spring
with the cool air around you
flowers will dance just like I do
and I hear the blue-bells ring.

Do you like dancing in the winter
with wild winds upon you
the trees would dance
I would like to
but I can't come out in the winter.

Do you like dancing in the moonlight
the shadows dance just like I do
and my shadow will dance
forever with you.

Elaine N. Oskoui

Emotion

Everything we write
Is written with emotion,
Love, anger, hate,
Depression and devotion.
The various moods we feel
Are never really real
But begin and start
With the feelings of the heart.
So if you feel hate and anger
Try not to let it show
But change your mind
To a better kind
And alter your emotion
To that of love and true devotion.

Patrick Baron

Silhouettes

Dark, storm-filled skies,
Sun's rays penetrating,
A stark tree outlined,
On bleak, distant horizon.

Birds wing in formation,
'Cross setting sun's path,
Mixed faceless figures,
'Neath glare of street lamps.

Motionless owl on leafy bough,
Haloed in day's dimming glow,
Vision of wolf, eerily howling,
Contour projected on silvery moon.

Illuminating moonshine,
Highlighting through darkness,
Jagged shapes of branches,
Criss-crossing like fingers.

Hands casting pictures,
On brightly lit walls
Intensified with light,
All silhouettes of forms.

Janet Tinkler

Imagination

The moon it shines upon the banks
A faint and shimmering gleam
A pure white sparkle glitters on
The ever flowing stream
The stream it trickles on and on
Like a piece of silver lace
And after the moonlight
The stream has gone
Vanished, without a trace
An otter comes to make a dip
And bathe its silken skin
A rainbow trout swims swiftly by
And the otter reaches in
I open my eyes
The moon is bright
The ground is damp with moss
And all that's left is a blade of grass
And a stream that never was.

Nina Crane

Ave Atque Vale

Death, thou hast stood at my shoulder
too long. Now, I feel thee sleeping,
now, becomes thy menace bolder.
I'm ever in thy grasp, thou keep'st
thy hand on me. Now, almost kind,
again, thou send'st thy minion, pain,
to fire the furnace of the mind.
Our wills are interlocked again
like antlered stags before the hind.
To what end do I resist thee?
My broken weapon is my love
of life, its end a mystery.
Are you the hawk, am I the dove?
Will release come from that fell stoop
as in thy talons I am borne,
all life extinct, a shattered hoop
too proud for sorrow or to mourn,
with destiny I will have met.

Another life, another day.
Is that all you have to say?

Patrick Greenhous

Untitled

I had a little pussy cat
So very very cute,
One day it ran right through the gate,
And didn't stop to look
A motor car came down the lane
Just at that very minute —
And ended my poor pussy's life,
When it was just beginning.

F. Evans

Born Of Frustration

Born of frustration
Fruitful promises
Desired by many
But never seen

Fruitful promises
Laid down
Then snatched away
From under your nose

Desired by many
And many desires
Unseen wishes
Never fulfilled

But never seen
Are those thoughts
Which have been
Born of frustration

Kevin Grant

Untitled

Have you ever sat and pondered
on the things in life you've done,
things that you could alter
if you could have a re-run.
All that you remember
in your whole lifetime's range,
what is there you've regretted
what is there that you'd change?
Would you marry and have children,
would your preference be a career?
Maybe you'd like to travel
on oceans far and near.
Might you live in a mansion,
have more money than you need,
aspire to the Midas Touch
or would you think that greed?
Would you want the moon and stars
or wish for riches and fame
or would you be happy, just like me
to do the same things again?

M. Telford

Happy Retirement

Retired at last, a blissful sigh
Who could ask for anything more?
A life of leisure - freedom and time;
Roses round the door!

The years ahead have a rosy glow;
The things I now can do
Have a long lie in the morning
And a rest in the afternoon too!

But life has a way of behaving
In a strange and mysterious fashion;
The plans and the dreams I indulged in
Have dwindled with serious passion!

My children have given me babies
Grandchildren whom I adore;
Who else can look after the darlings
As the parents run out of the door!

So my dreams of leisure are over
Retired! I don't think so yet!
But I'd rather be loved and needed
And look at the pleasure I get.

P. A. Storie

"A Song For Deaf Ears"

I sit and watch you sitting there,
A world away from me,
And wonder if you're worrying
What the future is to be.

It started as a few small voices
Crying out in the dark alone,
Until they heard each other
Also joining in the song.

Not long before a trickle
Soon became a mighty flood
Of voices calling "Do Something
Before There's Not Time Enough."

Time to watch our children grow
And time to just grow old,
Are we really asking too much,
Or is our future closed?

How long until their time's run out,
Our loved ones out of reach,
Before the voices are all gone
And no one left to speak?

Christine Turnbull

Daydream

Alone she sat,
Upon the stair,
Her body was here,
But her mind was elsewhere.

She had no friends,
She was all alone,
The person that she'd talk to,
Couldn't be contacted by phone.

Nobody loved her,
Except the person in her head,
Only her parents understood her,
But her parents were dead.

She'd sit there and daydream,
About the life she use to know,
And the person in her head,
Until it was time to go.

Victoria May

Remembrance Day November 1995

Watching on the screen tonight,
Scarlet poppies fall.
Petals fluttered slowly down,
Colour of blood - so dark yet light.

Memories came flooding
Into my mind.
Of sirens wailing,
Of bombs falling,
Beds not slept in,
Shelter calling.

Can this be true?
Have fifty years passed?
Since I was young
With dreams that grew
And hopes filled the days
You never knew.

Eileen S. Kay

Poppies

Incredibly beautiful,
They charm the eye,
Amongst the corn,
Poppies, they don't last long,
Ephemeral,
They blaze against the sky,
Who put them there,
We know not,
God's hand at work,
They reflect his glory.

Linda Pullen

Moving House

One last look before we go
make sure that we've left nothing here
It's sad to see the empty rooms
they kept us cosy for some years
Have we forgotten anything?
This box needs tying up with string,
Now we've arrived lets have a break
My arms and legs are one big ache
where's the teapot? Where's the tea?
Oh dear my back is killing me
It's going to take a few hours more
before there's space on any floor
Lets leave the rest and go to bed.
I need some sleep to clear my head
Tomorrow maybe we'll start afresh
begin to tidy up this mess,
But after all the work and pain
I'm sure, I'll never move again.

Margaret Elizabeth Pay

Blonde In Bar

She's a blonde in bar
Where pretty girls are

Desperation to deliver shiver
Cold night air, window ajar

She's the best looker by far

She's a girl turning into woman
Last orders she takes
What a photograph she would make

She leaves her floor
I leave by the door
Will we come back
For repeat performance more

Jeffrey Coppin

Armageddon

The prophets say
The end is in sight
The time will come
When there's no day or night

The waters will flow
Without mercy or right
For most of the people
Pain and suffering will be their plight

There will be no seasons
As we know
Even in summer
We will see snow

The land of plenty
Will freeze over
And there be no more
White cliffs of Dover

So say your prayers
And fight with all your might
This world belongs to everyone
Not just the rich industrialites!

Nigel Bramwell

Nature's Way

A river runs through peaceful ground
Whispering waves the only sound
A home to many although unseen
This silent valley, evergreen

A dying tree, stark and bare
Birds come alone or in a pair
And see from here
All's far that's near

With solid stone and gentle moss
Guard the river before it's loss
For soon this scene will be forgot
What now is here, soon will not.

Shelagh Noble

Loneliness

How can you feel so lonely
Surrounded by people you love?
How can you feel so lost
When everything is known so well?
How can a heart be so empty
When filled with such emotions?

Is it possible to share
If there is no one to share with?
It is possible to be kind
If there's no one to be kind to?
Is it possible to love
If no one loves you?

Claire Sandercock

Catching Up With Dickie

One afternoon I caught up with Dickie
On our way home from school
And although woods were there
On either side,
His callipered legs
Were too slow,
So I saw the diarrhea yellow
Trickle down.

But like the woods
His seven-year-old smile was there,
And maybe,
Because no-one else was there
I did not deride
But smiled to his eyes
And thought of gold.

The woods are a long while down
But in my root dark mind
Dickie's ancient patient smile is there
To catch upon,
And beam vile nature blind.

P. Proud

Peace

In a far away land
Where no mortal may go,
Far higher than mountains
Covered in snow,
Lies sleeping a Queen
On a bed made of moss,
With features of beauty
And hair that is soft.
Her name is Peace
And mortals below,
Hold her in their power
Wherever she goes.
She will sleep for today,
She will sleep for tomorrow,
While creatures of long ago
Are mourning with sorrow.
For try as they may
She cannot be woken,
Until on the world, far below,
Love and Peace have been spoken.

Alison Ridgwell

Time Lost

All alone until this moment
Turned upon a lovers meeting
Charged by fate; now it seems
Years were wasted, separated
So alone
And not knowing.

Unhappy then the happiest hour,
Times of greatest joy most sad;
Lonely then in winter's shadow
Without her the summer nights
All alone
Still not knowing.

For there in all those yesterdays
Is left a lonely figure lost
In half-forgotten remembrances
With unwept tears he'll never shed.
But still to him will come the pain
Of knowing now the sadness then
And the longing and the losing
And the pity of it all.

R. C. Cornell

Gran'da Knows Pension Funds

Don't you go dabbling now
Like ducks and drakes in oil!
Odds favour insiders.
The wheeler-dealer hand
Of commerce, top-spinning
Our lives, our small monies
Fuel for its power-drive,
Writes-off traction-losses.

Shares tumble, factories
Shut their gates like buckteeth.
The wily few survive.
Anger heads home toothless
To mother and the kids.

Patrick Walsh

"Suicide"

What am I doing here I say
There's really nothing for me
Should I go or should I stay
If only you could see

The pain I feel deep inside
The torture I'm going through
The tablets! Should I hide
Don't know! Just feel blue

Made up my mind to take a few
It's the only way out for me
Can't take anymore I'm so blue
For there's nothing anymore you see

I lay down upon my bed
And think of what is to be
I place my hands beneath my head
And think of my destiny.

Maria Edwards

Creativity

Sometimes I sit and 'scribble' -
Sometimes I sit and write.
Does it really matter which,
If the rhymes are right?

Sometimes I cannot stop the flow
The words fall my pen.
At other times, though thinking hard
I'm stuck for words. And then-
The right thoughts are on paper.
Did I think them through?
Did I really write them down?
I must have done, it's true.

I wish I could write like Shakespeare,
Dickens, or Walter Scott.
On reflection - not a good idea -
They are gone, but I am not!!

I. Miller

Awake

Awake to find the morning light
softly brighten up my room

Awake to find another day
different from any other day

Awake to find another day
filled with life's little treasures

Awake to find another day
with joy, sadness, but with life

Awake to find another day
amidst the ones we love

Awake to find another day
has passed by so soon

To sleep, to rest, to dream
the joy to awake.

James McKay

Rubbish

The letter box just rattled,
   there's paper on the floor.
I really needn't bother to look,
   I've seen it all before.
Do you want a fitted bedroom?
   Or a deluxe kitchen plan?
Insurance, double glazing?
   A book club list to scan.

A catalogue of goods to buy,
   a Free Gift you can gain,
or perhaps a time share flat,
   far off in sunny Spain.

None of these I can afford,
   no prizes I shall win,
so I'll just go and pick them up,
   and put them in the bin.

P. Ludgrove

Joe

The old lady sits,
With eyes sad and dim.
What is she remembering
She's remembering him.
The love of her life
Has just passed away,
Like a candle that's snuffed
At the end of the day.
The carpet is worn,
The table is bare
What does it matter
She doesn't care.
With no one to turn to,
And no place to go.
just biding her time
Till she meets up with "Joe."

M. Colledge

Colour

   To-day
these sculptured shapes of colour
lie satin-smooth and shining
on the chopping board.
Voluptuous shapes of capsicum
sculptured to perfection.
Pools of flawless colour
in crimsons, yellow-golds and greens
   Too Vibrant
for a chopping board!
Return them to their woven basket
to blaze
among the darkly purple aubergines
for another day.

Pat Jenkins

Foolishness

What can she do that I cannot
Why do you speak to her and not me
When did our love die

What can she say that I cannot
Why do you look at her like that
When did our love die

What can she think that I cannot
Why do you believe her every word
When did our love die

What a fool I have been
Why did I yield to this
When my jealousy surged our loved died

What happened to her
Why has she gone now
When jealousy was hushed and now I know

Our love could never die

Jeanette Morgan

A Winter's Fantasy

Lingering mist like
Early morning dew on cobwebs
Snow with glaring sun
Beaming down.
Warm hearts like
Warm fires inside.
Cold fingers of frost
Boring into the body
Like in-built hatred.
Cold fingers
Brief dull daylight
Bare trees like witches fingers
Reaching up to the fading sunlight
Crispy mornings
Crunching along frozen
Blades of grass
Ice scrapers scraping frantically
At frozen screens making
Sounds like disembodied screams
Frozen ponds.

Caroline Ward

Time Goes On

I wonder how we know how long
it is until today has gone
and how long should tomorrow last
and when we can say it has past.

We all have noticed time slow down
but it just keeps going round and round
even though it seems so long
since the last past hour has gone.

Then often time it goes so fast
and things are very quickly past.
But time has only stayed the same;
this definitely is a crazy game.

Time is the ruler of all our lives
and no-matter what, you cannot hide.
Whatever we do, it's always there
just ticking along without a care.

Time is strange, it seems to me
that it is the only thing that's free.

Mark Pearson

Floral Messengers

When I began my nursing days
In nineteen thirty four
My life was so completely changed
From how it was before.

I was appalled by what I saw
The suffering; the pain!
I felt as though I'd never go
Inside a church again.

Night duty brought a calm retreat
From stress, in those small hours
Where in the sluice I saw and smelled
The scent of patients' flowers.

Exquisite beauty and design
Beyond range of mortal man
Heightened my sensitivity
To God's own perfect plan.

Their silent message come to me
Those floral rays of hope,
They gave me back my faith and so
I knew that I could cope.

L. Robinson

Life

Life is just a dream
Life is everyday
You sometimes play with life
So play it the right way.

Dream of the good and the bad
Just sleep and dream in the sky
Just note my word in your mind
That one day you'll have to say bye.

Enjoy your life and spend it
You really haven't got far
Get up and look in the mirror
And see just what you are.

Life could be dull
Life could be bright
If there's a darkness
There is a light.

So get the meanings out my words
And learn a little more
Listen to the sounds of life
Listen to lions roar.

Simrath Lally

Chris Riley

If you see the lightning flashing
As it zooms across the sky,
If you hear the thunder crashing
In the clouds away up high,
It's nothing to make you worry
Or to make your heart beat fast,
It's just the angels way of saying
That Chris Riley's home at last.
Oh there's a stomping and a yelling
And a banging of the drum,
And you can hear the trumpets playing
Loud and clear,
And a million happy voices
Are calling out and telling,
That Chris Riley's home at last
With loved ones dear.

Patricia Whittaker Copeman

No Man's Land

A child's face shattered,
The fear in it frozen,
Lay in the red snow,
Of a broken city.
Here,
Even the poppies
Did not venture,
Nor the mocking bird;
Into no man's land.

Their war of words,
Became the war of weapons,
But it was now,
The war of death:
And here;
Nobody had won.

Laura Foster

A Silhouette

In my dreams, I see you,
Like a silhouette you stand,
Under the moon light,
In the shadows of the trees,
I feel the tears, as I try to reach you
I wish to hold your hand,
So I wave and call your name,
To tell you, I still love you.
But like the moon,
Your soul out of reach
In my mind, like my dreams.
A silhouette you stand.

E. Templeton

"Bullied"

In a corner,
In a black room,
No help or love,
That's what it feels like.
Go to a grown up,
That's what they say,
What's the use,
Just ignore them,
That's what they say.

Pushed in a corner,
Called names and shouted at
It's a horrible feeling
To be bullied about

You're all on your own,
That's what you think.
No you're not,
Stand up,
Fight back,
Somebody wants to help.

Ceri Marie Morgan

Wild Rose Briar

Wild Rose, sweet summer briar,
Your presence sets my heart afire.
Palest pink, delicate frame,
No two shapes exactly the same.
On monstrous roadsides you survive
Determined to keep nature alive.
Midsummer days you are here to mark
Open at dawn, asleep by dark.
Cruel breezes may shake off your petal
On dewy grasses only to settle.
Then to hips and haws you become,
A reminder from whence you come.
Into autumn bright and shiny,
The life cycle of flowers so tiny.

Glenda J. Richardson

Autumn

I have seen the last leaves
Of autumn tumble down
To lie upon the ground
Awakening my grief.

And I have seen the wind
Sweeping through the silent trees
Gathering fallen leaves
Like a promise fulfilled.

William Brodrick

He's Not You

His words were your voice
His hands were your touch
His lips were your absent kisses

His lust was your love
His being was your ghost
His new hopes were your past histories.

Your joy was my fate
You destined my dreams
Your nightmares were my only sorrow.

Your love was my world
Your pleasure my life
You killed all my hopes of tomorrow

My love is your hate
My life is your fun
My dreams are there to entertain you

My mind is your toy
My life is your stage
My heart can no longer retain you.

Marie Houlton

Going Shopping

The shopping list
was long,
and the baby began
to pong.

As the church bell
gave a loud dong
the baby's face went
yellow.

As she ate the
last marshmallow
The baby was getting fat,
and I still need
to buy a new hat.

Elizabeth Cuzen

Time's Integrity

Time is the currency of energy
spent with diminishing return
on decaying matter until no longer
legal-tender;
rain drops, birds' song,
flower petals,
kind words, good deeds,
unacceptable as payment for debt
to creation,
lie in earth's vaults waiting
to be plundered.

Let the young lamb gambol, meanwhile,
secure in the moment of belonging
as individually it cries
and unerringly is heard and met
by its mother's voice.

Obsolescence is time's integrity,
for it steals only what is its own
to be made up, one day,
at the making up of jewels.

Angela Butler

The Rose

Already the slanting
rays of the sun
Are gilding a single white rose.
The russet lawn has gone
to sleep
And dreams of the summer
that was.

Just to be
is enough,
A cup of tea in my hand,
Outside myself.
At peace with myself.

Brit Elliott

Something To Treasure

Maybe now a different path
The special moment, over at last
Out in the open
Conscience clear
Where to from here?

A moment worth the written word
of which, cannot be spoken
Something to treasure
when it is awoken
Now for a while
the memory must rest
as a new life ahead
is put to the test.

Daryl Waring

The Stars Are Dark

There's a time when the
future looks bleak.

A very bad spot, you
have come to life's crossroads
of ups and down.
In such cases only your inner
voice will tell you right.
Be not dismayed. Go on
believer in your judgement

It's possible that what's
about to happen is God say.

Never be afraid to try
other ventures.

Chin up and God bless
There could be great, great
Times still ahead.

J. F. Jenkins

"Petals And Thorns"

The rose
Who's never been
Picked before,
Can't be cut;
She trembles
Like a thistle
All at once,
While asleep
In a flowerbed.

Her thorns
Would probably
Hurt you more
Than her shut
White petals
Would kiss you,
The romance
Hidden deep;
Wait a little bit...

Eve Catherine M. Wileczek

Don't Give Up

To work each day
As labour goes
We see happiness fade away
And to think only the future knows
The fortune that it might bring
(April 1996)

Liliana Shanbhag

When

When the hearts and minds of man,
Become as one, as we know they can,
When our want is less than need,
We can say goodbye to greed,

When we learn to look outwardly,
Then surely it must be,
That we give peace more than a chance,
And not give war a fleeting glance,

When our actions end all strife,
We can start a better life,
At least we'll be able to say,
At last man is on his way,

When we stop all hostility,
We can use the energy,
To benefit the human race,
And put mankind in his place,

When our ideals benefit all,
And none by the wayside can fall,
We'll take the steps to be free,
Then will be the time, you'll see.

S. Ford

People

People love, people hate
some are impatient, others wait
people are noisy, people are quiet
some like their food, others will diet
people study, people play
few will leave, some will stay
people walk, people run
some will work, some have fun
people are cruel, people are kind
some don't care, others mind
most are happy, some are sad
most are good, a few are bad
people are rich people are poor
few are satisfied, most want more
some are timid, others bold
the young are young, the old are old
most are cheerful, some will moan
some have others, others are alone
people laugh, people cry
people live until they die

Norma Simmons

I Am

I am vision, I am the dream,
I am sky, I am the stream,
I am sand, I am the sea,
I am peace, I am the tranquillity.

I am anger, I am the pain
I am thunder, I am the greed,
I am war and wanting to succeed.
I am!
What's in your heart.

Elaine D. J. Darlington

The Hand

The hand reached out to hold,
the dying life of old,
ebbing away with memories,
of birth of smiles of family's.

The curtain falling slowly,
deaths call takes the rich and lowly,
no hand to stop the night,
or quell the fear with light.

Hand holds hand with feeling,
the tear the prayer, the kneeling,
but the door of life closes,
and opens the garden of roses.

David E. Buck

A Mother's Thoughts

Don't weep for me, my loved ones
...when I am laid to rest
Just think of all the good times
they were of the very best
My life was full of gladness...
even sad times, true
But through all the ups and downs
I lived my life for you

Catherine Fisher

Untitled

Rain washed skies
Of blue and grey
...Demise of summer
Mirror of
A love now gone
Since you
Had it off
With the plumber

Peter Robert Matthews

Poetic Heritage

The star shines on. The poetic ray
Still glows in Scotia's heart today;
As bright is shone but yesterday
And will tomorrow.

Let critics scoff, let others keep
The dross for which they fondly sweep;
We know the poignant treasure deep
Is purest gold.

Emotion is the poet's key
Experience cannot borrowed be;
Posterity the beauty see
His heart the sorrow.

So once again the glasses raise
And to his portrait let us gaze;
And offer our unstinted praise
To Robert Burns.

M. W. Hebenton

Downhearted

In a perfect world free of crime
where violence does not exist,
in a perfect world void of evil
I hope one day to live.

In an ideal place full of hope
where goodwill rules the day,
in an ideal place peace is all
we strive to find the way.

In a vivid dream with eyes overt
where once I saw a sign,
in a vivid dream all hatred died
and allowed mankind to shine.

In reality brought down to earth
where dreams are torn apart,
In reality man's soul has died
and caused him to lose heart.

Colin Hughes

Jake The Bake

"Oh dear" said the Chicken,
    "this ovens too hot.
I think I am the one,
    that he's forgot."
A cry came from the sprouts,
    outside the winder.
"We are the ones,
    that he burnt to a cinder."
Up moaned the potatoes,
    with centres too hard.
"We cannot be mashed,
    so deep fry us in lard."
He is a poor cook,
    this young man we call Jake.
But into a super cook,
    him we will make.

P. E. Maskrey

Moving Hands

There was dignity on each face,
As they moved their hands with grace.
Laughter echoed around the room,
in their eyes there was no gloom.
I could only stand and stare,
watching their hands waving in the air.
The hands moved like leaves in flutter,
Yet, not one word did they utter.
Although these people could not hear.
The future for them held no fear.
As I saw their happy smile,
I gazed at them for a while.
Then from the room I did stumble
I felt very very humble.

B. E. Woodcock

Towards The End

Come sweet nighttime
Take me in your arms
Close my eyes
With your darkness
Let the light be cast away
From today

Let no sunshine
Fall upon my face
Let no light of any kind
Disturb me
Let no words or actions
Come from behind
And blind me
For I long too much
For the night
To touch me

Marco Grillanda

It's A Wonderful Life

God has given me the chance...
To see another spring
To work the soil; and plant the seeds
And watch what nature brings

God has let me live to see
The sun rise in the sky
To smell a newly-mown lawn; and watch
Another day go by

Every day's a bonus
Now I've reached that certain age
I don't desire material things
I'm way beyond that stage

The hustle and the bustle
Of life's well into my past
I can potter... or just ponder now
Contentment's mine... at last

Sandra Brewerton

Wine

I have drunk the wine of Spain
In the southern sun;
The red wine of La Mancha
In the noonday sun.
The sun lay low in the hills,
And the wine was done.

I have drunk the wine of Spain
By the gibbous moon;
The white wine of Rioja
By the waning moon.
The moon set in the mountains,
And the wine was done.

I have drunk the wine of life
In the morning sun;
The blood-red wine of life
In the afternoon.
Now the night approaches fast-
And the wine is done.

Frank Tisseman

Untitled

To find out something,
   you never knew.
To hold back the tears,
   of the one lost to you.
To remember the bad days,
   but never the good.
To hold back your anger,
   as you break down the wood.
To relight a fire,
   that's burned its last flame.
Like darkness so silent,
   like somebody's pain.

Louise Bracken

Mountaineering

I climb the heights
of self realization.
Yet - not scaling one
single inch of rock face.
My journey remains
within myself.

Facing no dangers,
surrounded by God's love
I am immune to evil forces.
My footsteps do not seek
the crevices and crags.

Soaring up high in
effortless flight and silent wonder
I find perfect peace.
With joyful heart
discover the mystery
that love surrounds me.

Brenda Morris

Black Wednesday

On a wintry weary Wednesday,
The sun doesn't seem to shine,
The bird doesn't sing a cheerful tune,
I feel like a thundery black cloud,
A seed trying to sprout,
A block of ice cold and numb,
A shabby cat in a dirty alley,
On a wintry weary Wednesday.

On a sun drained dreary Wednesday,
I feel like a sinking boat,
A broken wing upon a bird,
A drenched umbrella
With a snapped handle,
I feel like a drowning flee
Unable to hop,
A rusty bike
Falling apart
On a sun drained dreary Wednesday.

Sarah Taylor

Fairy Tale Dreams

I was only eight
I think that's what I was
I used to dream of castles
And flying off to Oz
I would be Rapunzel
With her long and flowing hair
I'd ride into the sunset
With my prince upon his mare
I would be the beauty
That never went to sleep
I would be Snow White
And I'd make that old witch weep
I'd have guessed the first time
Rumpelstiltskin's name
I'd be Cinderella
Except not quite as plain
I was only eight then
I think that's what I was
And 10 years further on
I still want to fly to Oz

Carol Quinn

"Sorry"

This man a putrid wretch of knots.
Whom limps amongst his fellow trees.
He is a lonely road of woes, and yet
forgotten, he's trampled; as he pleas.

This thing a storm exposed by doubt.
He hurts, used by moralities cause.
It is a wicked way to learn, and yet
excused, he's punished; for his flaws.

Ken McEwan

Memories Of Childhood

When I was child of long ago,
Remembering warmth and comfort.
Also remembering loving arms
And gentle touch.
With memories that meant so much.

The blue of the sky.
The green of the fields,
As I walked barefooted,
So Happy and Free.
To linger awhile by a running stream

I remember the buttercups yellow.
Daisies and bluebells
That grew in the meadow.
Getting up in the morning
So fresh with dew.
Eagerly looking for something new.

Remembering the winters of long ago,
Just to see the white carpet
Of brilliant white snow
Of when I was a child of long ago.

Nancy Rees

Untitled

Winter bares their autumn glory
And darkness fills the empty sky
Beginnings of a year's end story
For them to wait as time goes by

No glint of gold in sunlight passing
No sparkle now to take the eye
All splendour gone all clouds amassing
The wind of change their lullaby

With ever open boughs they stand
To catch each frosty fall
A winter scene so rare and grand
A picture to recall

But winter comes with every year
A season's end in sight
The elements they all must bear
This then be their naked plight

R. R. Glover

My Best Friend, Poppy

My best friend is my dog,
She is everything to me,
She is my baby, my life in every way,
But she is now in heaven
And I feel lonely every day.

She was always pleased to see me
I was lucky she was there
She would often bark on my return
Wag her tail and run around the lawn

But the feelings I now have
The pain I feel inside,
The churning of my stomach
Each time I realize.

I may begin to laugh a little
And try to feel quite good
But then I wonder why
And how I even could.

Amanda Bridle

Moonlight

Still, dark night, you frighten me,
until the moon steps out of her
dark vault, and lights my way.
Like some shy maid, she hides again;
my path grows dark, and how I
long for day.

Pamela Dewison

The Awakening

A new spring has come
And out of winter's icy whirlpool
Where confusion drowned
Revives a woman
Whose awakening brings
The sweet breath
Of a new beginning.

For she is as strong and as vibrant
As a bursting river
And she is proud
And eager to be one
With Nature's cycle.

Thus we must all grow
From bud to flower
For adulthood is rebirth
In itself
Not a child dying
For the child may live
In all of us.

Debbie Collier

Bonfire

The cold winds are blowing,
Little rosy cheeks are glowing.

Gleeful hands are clapping
Wet wood in the fire snapping.

Sausages are popping,
Small feet are hoping.

Catherine wheels are turning,
Watch the bonfire burning.

Crisp leaves are rustling,
Everybody's bustling.

See the falling guy,
Now say a sad goodbye.

Dorothy C. Vaughan

Sadness

Sadness is as black as death.
It tastes of salty tears
And smells of funeral flowers.
Sadness is the sound of weeping
In another room.

Rhiannan Hughes

Prejudice

Dear Sir,
You are prejudiced.
Don't you see the colourful flowers
In the garden of my heart?
Are you blind?
Are you colour blind?
You never say so.

G. G. Gench

Fern

You call me ferocious,
A 'devil dog', too,
But I'm loveable really,
Devoted and true.

A guard dog, a hunter,
A friend I can be,
And trusty along with it,
As you will see.

So next time you see me
Don't scream and run
'Cause under the devils'
A bundle of fun.

Alyson Hunter

Forgotten

The scar of my past love
Has left a painful ember
Upon my mind
I wish not to remember.

The loneliness, the emptiness,
Such a gaping hole.
A gash upon my heavenly self
A weakness of my soul.

So know not do I
Of the forgotten past
And the feelings
That have surpassed.

A crying child
A weeping being
Is it I
That I am seeing?

Lisa Jarman

Untitled

I have got an invalid husband
Who is sometimes very sick
I often wonder how I manage
With the money that comes in
I know we are not the only ones
Who have no ready cash
But how I dreamed about that cruise
but never mind, that's that.

Lucy Craig

Pangs Of Life

A father of one
He was my husband
It feels like today
It was way back in May.
A simple biopsy
Became a catastrophe
Took him away
From his family.
Each second, each minute,
Each hour a day.
I feel him with me
The pain I cannot bare.
You're away
In a dimension
Far far away.

Sahera Bhagoo

The Dark Pool

Twisting, turning
Burning
Set your soul on fire
See the dark face of a liar

Bend that precious little rule
Dark is the colour of despair
Not that the happy would care
Down at the dark pool

Twisting deadly viper
Listen to the song of the piper
As he plays in the band
Creeping hand in hand
Down to the dark pool

Swiftly he entices me
Never letting me be
Then he takes my soul away
Let the spirits down to lay
He steps only in the shadows
No glossy shining meadows
Down at the dark pool

Rachel Anderson

Untitled

How foolish of me to believe
That by flying to the other side
Of the globe I could forget you.
You, who had shared my life,
My work, my bed, my all
For nigh on fifty years
And whose death I mourned
(Mourned? Wept over more like)
As Indian summer turned
Inevitably to winter

I thought, and how wrong I was,
That New Zealand's glacial peaks,
Its bubbling thermal springs,
Its feeling of life eternal,
Would ease, perhaps banish
My lonely pain.

But alas, I found that the
Richer the experience
The more I needed to share it,
With you, of course, at my side

R. T. England

Looking Forward

I look forward to the spring time.
What a lovely time of year.
The hedges are all coming out
And birds sing laid and clear.

I look forward to the summer,
I love the sand and sea.
The laughter of the children
As they play so happily.

I look forward to the autumn days.
Though winters creeps up fast.
The dark nights have their beauty.
Though the days are overcast.

I look forward to my days with you.
No matter what the weather
So hand - in - hand we'll journey on,
As long as we're together.

Celia Marwood

Split Second Drama

Little legs racing
    long tail flailing
        head going side to side.
Pussy's not running
    rubber wheels stunned his brain,
        before he died.
I see this in seconds
    on the unlit road,
        my car lights show, pre-death.
A flick of the steering
    thank God for good gearing
        slow down and swerve
        like taking a curve.
I miss dying pussy
    no more can I do.
The car's straight once more.
    "Look back through the mirror".
        Poor pussy's quite still.

John Bragg

The Strain

Stalked still
The strain of gibbets way
The haunting lied a wilderness
Crying in the voice
Still loved
Still as
Born

Brian Whipp

A Winter's Night

The snow is falling hard outside
The ground is cold and white
Children tucked up in their beds
On this a winter's night

Icicles hanging from the gutters
Dangling from great heights
Everywhere is frozen
On this a winter's night

Logs are burning on the fire
Flames licking, glowing bright
The house is warm and cosy
On this a winter's night

And as I watch the snowflakes fall
So softly in my sight
Summer seems so far away
On this a winter's night

Pauline Twarog

Two Hatchet

Chiselled features, Roman nose,
    steely eyes, matted clothes.
Kiowa warrior, two hatchet, two blade,
    man of tools, hunter of great game.
Living off the buffalo,
    riding horses with long mane.
Manitou, great spirit,
    that way of life is gone.
Like cavemen gone forever,
    they still mark this earthly plane.
A full stop in history,
    a question mark in time.
Feeling close to nature
    at one with your environs.
We've so much to learn from you
Indian of the plains.

D. Hall

Spring In The Shires

May morning mist
Lit with shiny beams
Of warming yellow sunlight.
A shimmering sheen.
Bright cloudless day
As I look; far up, and away,
Sky clear blue, of cobalt hue,
And gentle breeze along the way.

Vista of valley and vale,
Old John in bracken and fern.
Deer, in Bradgate, rub soft bark.
New life of spring, the seasons turn.
Quorn and Charnwood, a canopy of green
Where intermittent icons are seen.
Nature in bloom, a budding display
Of Leicester, in the heartbeat,
Of May.

Brian Ward

Boredom

Boredom is life
It's dull and grey
Nothing is bright
Why are buildings brown,
They could be red.

Boredom is when you're alone
It is as if no one is your friend
Everyone has deserted you
You're in a cold world.

Boredom is people you don't like
But have to speak to
They talk about nothing.

Amanda Wardle

Who's There

I often wonder, are we alone?
On this small sphere, that we call home
And when at night, I gaze past Mars
To a multitude of twinkling stars
And knowing that they're like our sun
Possibly, there could be one
With planets, and conditions right
That could support some form of life

And if we ever conquer space
And meet these beings face to face
Will they be a single cell?
A sticky glutinous blob of gel

Perhaps they are a superior race
That travel regularly in space
They may have even landed here
Secretly, to cause no fear
And so dismayed at what they found
They very soon were homeward bound
And that is why we find no trace
Except for mysterious lights in space

Roy Willment

From The For'ard Deck

She lifts her prow to breast the swell
And plunges in the trough.
Her keel cuts water like a plough
And throws the billows off.

The foam fans out on either side,
But ere it tumbles o'er,
Another follows from the hull
To make the fine spray soar.

And as at rises to the light
The sun this prism plays,
With colours bright as in the sky,
A rainbow in the waves.

I stand aloft and proudly own
The air and sky and sea,
And feel how I am privileged
Of the elements to be.

Mary Stephenson Ellams

Soul Mates

Take me in your loving arms
And hold me close to you
Touch me with your healing hands
And say your love is true

You soothe away the cares of life
And my problems, they just flee,
With your selflessness and caring
You fulfil a need in me

Sometimes when life seems really hard
And I'm feeling sad and blue
When I need someone who really cares
That's when I think of you.

I know at times I'm difficult
But you handle me with care
You mean so very much to me
Because I know you're always there

Take me in your big strong arms
Chase the fear in me away
Make the sun come out again
And say you'll always stay

Jenny Whitehead

Golden Age

Are you searching for
a lost Golden Age
a place of ideal
perfection
of human equality and
freedom?
Are you tolerating
the sad picture
of this
horrible
apocalyptic
machine?
Spiritual values
of compassion and love
are marching to
victory;
follow their path
leading to life.

Michelle Giacomini

Light Impressions

The form of light
Its strength and beauty
Unstructured by the passing days
Retains the image
Once clear and focused
Now softened by the morning haze.

And as the moment
Clings - is captured
Trembling fingers hold the thought.
With gliding strokes
A wash of colour
Fleeting glimpses gently caught.

Once more the sated soul
Sighs softly
To ever ebb and flow it seems
The artist's curse
And blessings found
In brushes full of dreams.

Andrew Wood

Vasectomy

Needle and thread, scissors too,
This operation I must do.
I will give you just a little jab
It will make you drowsy and relax.

Just a little snip or two, is
All I'm really going to do.
Then stitch you up and tie the knot
Let's hope that this has done the job.
You will use some contraception
Until your tests come through.
When they do, you will give a cheer
For then you will know that
you are all clear.

June Jones

Ode To The Moon

Walking in the moonlight
    With the one I love.
Is so peaceful and so tranquil
    Like the flying of a dove.

Statues casting shadows
    Reflections on the lake.
Oh this calming, mellow night light
    No bulb could ever fake.

Sitting on a park bench
    So romantic so in love.
Underneath a moonlit sky
    A God send from above.

Andrew Warman

165

To Suzanne For Helen

Shall we all sit down and surrender
Because we've been hurt?
Or rendered inert?

Or gather round and visualize
Our final resting place?
And recognize the day?

Speak of former distant lovers
As though they meant less?
Than any other test?

Justify our final actions
As somehow quite bold?
Until the facts unfold?

Weep and cry and demonstrate
With stamping feet
One last great heartbeat

Or...meet someone quite suddenly
And feel the warmth again
Well...couldn't we my friend?

Ian Kellett

Violence

It seems there always will be wars
and violence of some kind.
Through the ages man has killed
and death, he's left behind.
The heartache and the sorrow
that victims have to bear
He shunned them all, without remorse
and left them weeping there.
Many years of blood shed
and the fighting still goes on,
Wives, may lose their husbands,
Mother's lose their sons,
Where does this fighting get us?
"We fight for peace," they say.
But still the wars continue
No peace on earth this day.
No peace on earth tomorrow
None, till nations can agree,
the world would be a better place,
if we live in harmony.

Beryl Palmer

Loving You

Hide away your hurt and pain,
Now's our chance to live again,
Though our lives were ripped apart,
We will rebuild our broken hearts.

My love for you just grows and grows.
The tears we shed fell on the rose,
The thorny rose of life subdued.
It's in the strength of loving you.

The wonder of the life we share,
The ups and downs, the hopes and fears.
We held it all and we came through
It's in the strength of loving you.

Lift your eyes above the storm,
New seeds of life, we are reborn.
The warmth and joy in all we do
It's in the strength of loving you.

Di Foulkes

Candle Is

A candle is like freedom,
  Like life, like earth,
It's like the sun with life,
  Like God.

Robert Beetham

The Good English Weather

Wouldn't you guess
it's happened again,
the sun has gone in
it's started to rain.

Quick, rush for the clothes
that are out on the line
should be dry now
they've been out some time.

Put on my raincoat
one step out of the door
well, wouldn't you guess
It's sunny once more.

Our good English weather
Never know what'll bring
a heat wave in winter,
a snowstorm in spring.

Kay Lowcock

Road Rage

Road rage, a frame of mind
Of the most aggressive kind
It is not surprising
When tempers are arising
That a heated moment
May end in lifetime torment
For some innocent road user
Could be an all time loser
Paying with his life
For one mindless act of strife
Road rage, seems to be
Today's reality.

Faith Mellor

Happiness

What tendrils hold within their grasp
The mastery of life and limb?
Oh beauteous world you do unfold
Your mysteries of life untold,
Repeating in their very mould
The lesson of the troubled soul,
Rejoicing as the clouds unfurl
Revealing warmth of sun within.

So is a life, with childlike grace
Self satisfaction first is all,
Until with facing hard the fact
That learning enters into all,
And hurt, frustration, fear and love
The greatest lessons to recall
When calm acceptance entering in
Brings peace and faith and happiness
To counteract whate'er befalls.

Evelyn May Berrisford

The Wind

The wind is very windy,
And also very strong,
The trees were all a bowing,
As I was pushed along,
They thought I was royalty
Waving their leaves at me
I'm sure I'd like the wind
If I were a tree.

The wind is very windy
It also blows a gale.
It whistles through the barn at night
Awakening the wise old owl
It's telling him that it's supper time
And the mice as well,
I'm sure I'd like the wind
If I were an owl.

John A. Holmes

Untitled

Fear
A crawling serpent
Biting into the heart of
Ignorance

Assuming
Faces of familiar love,
Hate habit, received wisdom,
Might even

Crouching
Inside the heart of darkness
Inside the heart
Fear of a handful of dust.

Olga Thomopoulou

A Golfer's Prayer

As I walk along life's fairways
Through the heather and the whin.
Avoiding all the hazards.
That try to love me in.

Through wind, rain, sleet and snow,
I battle on and on,
Until at last with great relief,
The ball drops in the hole.

I pray one day the sun will shine.
And my ball flies straight and true,
Until I say my last goodbye,
This I pray to you.

Reserve for me a place dear Lord.
In that clubhouse in the sky.
Where the handicaps are all the same.
And the tap is never dry.

Lindsay T. Brockie

The Starling

February morning,
Cold and grey
And steady rain falling,
When from my window I espied
Perched on the apex of a roof,
A starling, beak opening wide
Singing, singing.
Upwards his head was held,
As though through leaden cloud
His bright eyes could discern
The shining glory of the sun.
When sorrow dulls my heart and mind,
Lord, may I true solace find
Because I know, that though unseen,
With me Thou art
To comfort all the sorrow of my heart.

Daisy Neal

Caged Within

In this room,
animals are caged within their home.
In this house,
we're locked behind closed doors;
(and what we do is our business)

In this town,
we're trapped in by the gossip
step outside,
the gates of "normality"
and you become a freak.

Caged within,
the boundaries of the norms,
this is not
a free country anymore.
we're caged within our means.

Tara L. Huddless

His Early Years

On a great Monday morning
just before dawn
a cry is heard
a baby boy had been born

The next stage he's still small
all tiny and weak
all wait to hear
what first words he will speak

It's the beginning of school
for the rest of some years
he decides once again
to bring on the tears

But it isn't that bad after all
for he makes many friends
whilst he's learning at school

It's now time to leave
he has learnt what he can
it's time to start work
for he's now a young man

Lisa Philpott

My Friendly Wheelchair

I'm never alone
on my own
with my wheelchair!

Always there
taking care
in my wheelchair!

I'm alive
when I drive
in my wheelchair!

People hide
and move aside
from my wheelchair!

At top speed
all take heed
of my wheelchair!

Life's a ball
'cos after all
I've got my wheelchair!

Mark Leverton

"Fair Spring"

It rings of fair spring,
Every time the bloom and green,
Of winter chill and icy seal,
Sprout into a rebirth.
And you sing, Mercy, me,
A fresh melody, never sang.
It smells of sweet Opium
The delightful wave of your hair.
And you taste as pure as home.
A perfect welcome.

It rings of fair spring,
Every spring, every time you sing.
And you touch my heart
With the care in your eyes.
And you trill, Mercy, me,
Like a nightingale, never known.
The feel of gold around me,
And the wave of your warmth
As we brace to taste full summer.
A welcome bliss.

J. A. Brobbey

Refugees (Where Will They Go?)

See them walking down the street,
Heads bent, feeling weak,
Houses that once stood proud,
Now only debris and crater mounds,
"Where will they go?"

No one seems to care,
Trudging along in great despair,
Children weeping, moms entreating,
Moving in a trance,
"Where will they go?"

Food there is none,
Just drops of water and burning sun,
No shelter from the trees,
Blown away on a bombing breeze,
"Where will they go?"

Why do men of cruelty, envy, greed,
Resort to killing with such speed,
Not caring who they leave,
Homeless, hungry and in need,
"Where will they go?"

Iris Williams

Reflections

The moon has a special meaning to me
the moon to me is company.
Each lonely night I sit and watch
and dream of what I want so much.
That moon now knows my every thought
it knows each battle I have fought.
The moon will always lend an ear
when no one else is near to hear.
When all is calm and others sleep
the moon will watch me gently weep.
It gives me peace on tranquil nights
to pass my thoughts up to the heights.
This torch from God, this special glow
will always be my friend, I know.
One night I hope that I'll sit and see
the moon, with special company.
I hope and pray that night comes soon
when two of us will watch the moon.

Beverley Foulds

Doubt

There is a quiet softness,
a whisper, a breeze,
as I walk alone
surrounded by trees.
But, in my solitude,
My heart searches still,
to find the way to go
   that I will.

Lena Frances Pither

Love Trance

Across the room she looked at me,
Could this be the girl for me?
As I looked deeply into her eyes
I fell deeply into a love trance.
As soon as I could, I seized my chance.
To find we were both in the
same love trance.
We went outside and slowly
walked.
Under the deep black skies
Until we kissed and I lit the
stars
In her pale blue eyes.
Suddenly I realized
She was the one I had taken a
lifetime searching for!

Simon P. Lewis

Tempo

The sun
Melts into a hurricane
   of colours
And drops of stellar wind
Fall upon us

Us
Thousands and millions

Pause

A bed wet with perspiration
   Swallows in the desert
   Galleons and pirates
   in the barren sea
   Eternal thought and pangs

A baby has come off
   the womb
And runs in the cradle
Time already suffocates him
While the sun
Melts into a hurricane of colours
And drops of stellar wind fall upon us

Renato Ercoli

Nature's Garden

Rainbow gems crown the Earth
tiara fashioned with blossoms wild
beautifully styled, they lazily nod
while kissed by summer's roaming breeze
to tease the petals, pastel borne
worn by meadows and leafy dales
on trails of yellow and lilac-blue
with blushing pink and poppy red
pearls of dew coronet the head
of sleepy Mother Earth
her loveliness beguiles the morn
amidst the fields of cud and corn
festooned, each hill, as daisies spill
their milk of pretty petalled flowers
which never sours, yet drapes the days
in summer haze, on emerald down
each view, a humble sparrow's glance
with nature's dance of silvery shower
sprinkling drops on fragrant stems
of rainbow gems that crown the Earth.

Elizabeth Wilson

Time Doesn't Heal

When something hurts you
When the pain is for a time
Unbearable, and the words
Repeat, unending in your mind,
Your mind just blocks it out.

The repetitive sayings and names
The beatings and the bullyings
The endless circles of hate
These you never forget

If you are lucky they hide
In the shadows of your mind,
Waiting, until a phrase, or a word
No matter if in jest
Sends back the pain
In a flurry of fire
An explosion you cannot contain.

And then, if you are lucky
They hide, in the shadows
Of your mind...
Waiting, waiting, waiting.

Richard Cassidy

Still Small Voice

I'm born to a world of strife,
Where madness means more than life,
And daily destruction is rife,
And I'm helpless - I'm only a baby!

There's hunger and death all around,
With homes bombed into the ground,
"In the name of freedom" they sound.
But I suffer - I'm only a baby!

Lord of peace and sanity,
Speak to man's fighting vanity,
And bring some light to humanity
For me - for I'm only a baby!

Margaret M. Osoba

Turnstones

Flying low over the rippling waves,
Patterned wings against the sky,
dancing at the water's edge.

The crescent moon hangs suspended
in the darkening evening;
time to turn for home,
to follow the wheeling gulls
and the lowing cattle,
across the margin of the land,
to leave the sea
to the sky
and the sand.

Sue Brough

The Old Steam Train

Along the endless track
The old steam train went.
Huffing and puffing,
Roaming the country,
Until its time had come
When its steam ran out,
Its life work done,
Never to run again,
The old steam train.

Some people say life
Is like a steam train
Running along an endless track,
Huffing and puffing
Until their steam runs out,
Their life's work done,
Never to run again,
Like an old steam train.

Natasha Limoi

Dilemma

I slipped out between waves,
The morning and the evening,
As the water receded
On the inland falling laughter,
It was a drowning in life
Nobody saw me go

I have kept since then,
In all fairness,
To my expected ways,
Time out of number
I have told truths within a lie
And lied right up to the truth

My heart is fixed
It indites a good matter
It shoots blood in fountains
The redness crossing
Mine and others' eyes,
I live and I am dying
And I shine in life.

Roy Batt

Recognition

I did not know until I saw you
That October afternoon
On the steep path down
From the head to the heart
That you were the dark
But gentle presence
I have always felt

Margaret Morrell

Spoilt Child

I know a girl who isn't small
But doesn't seem to care at all
That all she ever does or says
Is in a myriad of ways
Mere simple, selfish, abstract praise
For her or for her
'Nouveau Craze.'
A robot puppet on an apron string
Without the guts to have a fling
Or laugh
In case it's not 'done thing.'
What a pain to be indoctrinated,
Self-obsessed, over-inflated,
Not to act on whim or fancy:
She's just a spoilt little Nancy!

K. L. Nellist

'The Blue Teardrop'

If forgotten...
If forgotten
In love
Don't worry
She smiles often
in life ...

As...

Between what we wish
and hope for
lies the sadness of
the blue teardrop
forever holding us to
a dream
that none of us, can
give share, or hope
to see the ending of...

So...
Smile at who you can
and remember
in that smile
there is everything.

Gerry McQuade

A Winter's Day

Grey winter weather
damp wet and cold,
mist that never rises
leaving bones and bodies cold.

Trees bare, and lonely
grass weighed down heavy with wet,
fallen leaves dark and dead like
lie lifeless on the path.

Sky leaden and dark and dreary,
just waiting to shed its load,
puddles lying still and dirty
in the wet and dismal road.

People with their heads down,
against the winter wind,
hurrying scurrying, every which way,
hurrying to go home out of winters way.

Annette Otter

And Now That I Am Old

And now that I am old.
A little frail and tired,
I think about those times of youth
When heart and soul were fired

To seek ambition's golden lure,
To conquer all the world,
But now I sit beside the fire
Wings clipped, and banners furled.

Then, I sought all the answers
To where? And why? And how?
Then, never satisfied, I prowled
Insatiable! But now -

I've settled in maturity
With answers so hard won.
I know, I know with surety,
The way this world should run!

And my philosophy of life
Is safe, and sure, unmoving,
With faith, and hope, but last of all,
And best of all, with loving.

Leila Pool

A Salmon's Life

In upper reaches I was born
One sunny day in the dawn
Felt the coolness of the stream
And wakened from my dream

Slowly drifted with the current
Quickly built into a torrent
Over the falls down to the sea
And other samlets join with me

Now the years have passed me by
Leave for home and with a sigh
Reached my river where life began
Fought the rip and strongly swam

Onward, upward forever higher
Shot the rapids like a flier
Getting weaker as time past
Reached my birthplace, at last

Looked around for waters still
Spawned my eggs on shale until
I close my eyes and with a sigh
My life forsake me and I die

P. T. MacWilliam

Disjointed

Globe of fire.
Black wolves,
Green eyes.
Red skies.
Empty hole.
Dead soil.
Hot rocks,
Cold stone.
Maniacal laughter,
Tortured screams.
Good Weeps,
Evil sings.
Charred hearts,
Burnt flesh,
Dripping skin.
Knotted veins,
Blood flows.
Molten soul.
No repose.
A faint suggestion of hooves.

C. R. Woolley

The Tramp

I saw him in an alley.
He looked so sad and lonely,
But familiar somehow.
I only saw a glimpse of him,
But I knew him by his eyes -
Those haunting eyes, so deep,
So blue. They see everything,
They peer into your soul and find
The secrets you have buried
Deep within your mind.
His face will haunt my dreams,
Tonight, every night,
Standing in the pathway,
The poor, circumstantial
Tramp.

Kareena McAloney

"What Is Grandmother"

What is a grandmother?
We ask ourselves
as the homemade jam
sits upon the shelves.

What is a grandmother?
What does she mean to thee?
As she kisses the graze
that's on our knee.

What is a grandmother?
As she dries our eyes.
We wonder what makes her
so very wise.

What is a grandmother?
What memories we share.
For us with our troubles
she was always there.

And now this day,
when death do us part.
She will never be gone
from deep in our hearts.

Denise Gouge

Dying Earth

Natural beauty once shone through,
from fresh spring flowers
to a fine morning dew.
Mother Earth was once so clean
the air so pure,
the grass so green.

Now we have pollution
and highly toxic waste.
Look at Mother Nature,
see her changing face.
Everything that has a life,
will have a natural death,
but are we forcing nature
to draw its final breath?

Wayne Curry

Mad Scientist

There was a mad young scientist
Who wanted to travel far
He wanted to explore the world
And beyond to the celestial stars

He tried to build a space ship
Out of his banged up Robin,
He finally got it off the ground
But the stupid thing kept stopping.

He finally got it going
And he travelled far and wide
'Till he ran out of petrol.
And crashed to earth and died

Angela Jones

A Mother's Day Prayer

Oh mother, dear mother,
If I had you here,
Since you answered Gods call,
All is so clear.
A gift is not all
I would give you that day
But a big hug and kiss
To go a long way.

Oh mother, dear mother,
I miss you so much,
But I'm happy to say
I'm not losing touch,
As along the long way,
I am cheered when I pray,
The joy of meeting you,
At the end of my stay.

E. T. Coyne

Rainbow

We chase you for the riches,
legend has it you provide.
An endless quest to find the place,
where hope and truth collide.

When the rain clouds part at last,
and the sun comes bursting through.
It's not the sun's rays we turn to face,
but to the archway drawn by you.

Alison Cray

My Pal

We wander through the hills and dales,
Through the valley and the vales
The woodland and the countryside.
We may call it the great divine.

We would pass through pastures green.
The countryside that looks serene.
My dog and I would wander far
Our only guide would be a star.

We would sit and take a break
And make a wish beside the lake.
My Bess and I will part not never
And she'll stay by me forever.

She is a faithful friend to me
And my pal she will always be.
Now she comes; I stroke her head
I know it's time to go to bed.

James S. Yeomans

The Locket

There it was;
It seemed to gleam
A golden locket
On a chain
And tucked inside
A lock of hair, so fair, a lock of hair
To conjure up
A vivid scene
Of life, romance,
And loves' young dream,
Perhaps its owner
Far away, another place.
Another day
Sweet evidence
Of what has been
A life fulfilled
To leave behind
A lock of hair
Once flowing free
To tantalize, with mystery.

Jean K. Gwilliam

Where Did We Go Wrong?

Distant traffic
Breaks the silence,
Distant memories
Break the peace.
Distant places
Break the journey,
Distant faces
Return home.

Eoin Ryan

Love

Our very existence depends on love
As do the flowers
And the stars above
Without love, there is no summer breeze
No pollen in the air
To make you sneeze
To show love you feel no pain
Nothing to lose
And everything to gain
Show love in everything you do
And be payed each tenfold
Buy this, I hope you knew.

Pam Newman

The Newcomers

We've got new neighbours at the back,
They don't speak!
They're always in and out,
but don't speak!
I see them come and go,
I don't speak!

I spy on them behind my curtain,
they bob inside their home - uncertain.

They're cautious - timid,
don't speak!
They've been so busy,
don't speak!

They're up at dawn and out all day,
they don't have time to rest or play!

They hardly stop,
They won't speak!
I love them both,
but don't speak!

Maybe I'll see the chicks - next week!!

Isabel Abbott

What Waste

In this room, so clean,
spiders dare not drop their thread
in fear of feathered broom.

Curtains, pleats inch perfect,
stand to attention, at windows
polished every day.

Flowered chintzes pristine clean,
a garden in this
sitting room

The carpet cleaned by
noisy motor.
Removes all trace
of human life.

Children, unloved, unclean,
have never known the kind
of loving care bestowed
upon this unfeeling room.
What waste.

E. M. Green

A Tear In Her Shadow

Dusk 'til dawn,
Night 'til morn
Her perfect stance is beauteous.
The physical idle
Of a thousand girls,
One fine object,
In a hate torn world.
Cameras flash,
Her smile beams bright...
But as I saw her in the light,
I caught a glimpse of her silhouette,
My deep fixation,
Held much regret.

I saw no tears fall from her eye,
But,
In her shadow I saw her cry.

Sara Hinch

New Beginning

You came into my life
    so Unexpectedly
Just like a breath of
Fresh-air bringing with you
Purpose and meaning into
    my life
I never would have thought
I could ever begin to love
again until I met you
You are now and always will
be the love of my life
And I will love you till
the end of
    Time.

Mark Peters

Walking

One day we went out walking
In the leafy bluebell wood.
We had no need for talking
The scenery was so good.

The birds above were singing
The sky was a deep, deep, blue.
The church bells started ringing
The bluebells joined in too.

Out came a rabbit hopping
Seemed to be performing a mime.
The dandelions started popping
Hoping to tell us the time.

One o'clock, two o'clock,
Three o'clock, four.
Five o'clock, six o'clock,
We have no time for more.

We have to leave our quiet wood
Back to the noise once more.
But then, again, we're feeling good
Behind our own front door.

Margaret Jones

Sunrise

Looking up over the clouds,
appears a small flood of light,
as people awake,
in the small houses below.

Animals lurking,
until sunrise
when they all go scampering away,
then I realize,
it's sunrise.

Emma Watkins

Untitled

The silence of an empty room
Can hold sounds, lovingly,
As though caressed
Till their release and they assume
The role of inner voices;
Memories at rest.

I enter, pause, and hear you say
Things half forgotten, beautifully,
The words possessed
Of thoughts which, garnered day by day,
Acclaim all round your presence
With which the room is blessed.

Geoffrey Nethercott

The City

I have viewed the moving crowd,
Of vehicles and limbs,
For mute is what this city is,
Save for the screaming horn.
A lonely town, without a soul,
Without a heart or mind.
Comfort's naught in word nor deed.
Can people believe they live?
Mine is a lesson truly learned:
Find solitude, one must:
But come alive, give of yourself,
To those surrounding close.

A. E. Weeden

Stonesfield

The white dense field
A rectangle of stone,
Is long enough
To pay its dues
To art and history.

It emanates tranquillity,
Admired in a minimal garden
Transposed to another key,
Another gateway to Liverpool.

Unveiling the autumn season
Where visitors stand and stare
Unsure of themselves,
But aware that behind
The silent monument to power
An oracle records unwritten signs
And taps into another road
Where we all could be.

Peter Corbett

Learning

Learning, yearning
Everyone concerning
Learning is forever
Yearning for that treasure
Memorizing, visualizing
Feeling a sense of tantalizing
Learning if a pleasure
Earning you cannot measure
Motivation, stimulation
Getting lots of admiration
Learning is not taxing
Helping to relaxing
Organizing, summarizing
Some of us computerizing
Learning is mind power
A new world to discover
Use it or lose it
If it's to be it's up to me

A. A. Durrant

The Sabbath Day

On a Sabbath Day some time ago
An incident took place,
'Tis recorded in the Holy Word
A lesson to our race.

When Jesus and His followers
Were passing through a field,
The lovely ears of ripened corn
Their hunger greatly revealed.

These followers of Christ our Lord
Plucked off some ears of corn
And chewed them with delight that day,
But others watched with scorn.

The pharisees who witnessed this
Had waited oh so long
So that they might accuse our Lord,
Point out to Him His wrong.

The answer Jesus gave to them
Again kept them at bay,
'The Sabbath Day was made for man,
Not man for the Sabbath Day.'

Alfred Clifford Heritage

Winter

Winter's here and now we see
this morning's frosted panes.
We look outside and at the snow
that's covering country lanes.

The trees that just the night before,
as we fell into bed,
Were dark and bare and not a leaf
when sinking sun was red.

Now covered with a mantle bright
of pure white virgin snow,
The morning sun reflected
with that pale and orange glow.

And Jack Frost has been busy
turning pearl-like drops of dew
Each jewelled branch and twiglet
now coated in frost anew.

The icicles that hang there
are a wonder on their own.
What glorious thing the winter
that God has given on loan.

Alan J. Vincent

Where Is Love?

Where is love?
Does it fall from skies above,
Is it underneath the Willow tree,
That I've been dreaming of?

Where is he?
Who I close my eyes to see,
Will I ever know the sweet "Hello"
That's meant for only me.

Who can say where he may hide,
Must I travel far and wide,
Till I am beside the someone who,
I can mean something to.
Where, where is love?

Every night I kneel and pray,
Let tomorrow be the day,
When I am beside the someone who,
I mean something to.
Where, where is love?

Sarah Pratten

Moving House

Moving house is quite a chore
You get in boxes by the score
Lifting dishes large
Ornaments too small in the hall
Memories that you hold dear
To the ones you leave behind
Are all remembered when you leave
That dusty old House behind

Ella Taylor

My Pocketful Of Sand

Our footprints in the sand,
Will soon be washed away
But, our memories will remain
In my pocketful of sand

Each grain will remind me
Of our love, each glance, each touch,
A love, that could never be
My memories to me, mean so much.
In my pocketful of sand.

We met in a far off land.
Your skin bronzed from the sun,
We loved, I laughed, and had such fun.
Then, I saw your wedding band,
Glistening, shining.
In my pocketful of sand.

Sylvia Hides

A Legend

Long ago in a wintry wood,
One November night,
A ghost appeared
In a golden hood
And a cloak of purest white.
Rising from the ground,
Without a sound
Mist encircling his veil,
A golden hood so richly crowned
Enclosing a face so pale,
As I reached for his hand,
Across this moon-shadowed land
Cool to the touch and opaque
He vanished without a trace
In the swirls of
The curving lake.

Emma J. Symonds

To Dad 1905-1988

I will not seek in graveyards
Or crematoriums grey,
I will not seek in churches,
For I know that's not the way.

No, I'll look for you in sunshine
And trees and fields of green,
In sunsets and in birdsong,
Beside a sparkling stream.

I will not seek in cities,
Midst crowds and noise and care,
Your heart is not in cities
And I know you won't be there.

No, I'll look for you in quiet ways,
In summer skies above,
In solitude, in music,
In kindness and in love.

I'll feel your presence near me
And I'll say a silent prayer,
Then I'll walk amongst the roses,
For I know I'll find you there.

J. Baldwin

Lincolnshire

If you come to Lincolnshire
For a stay, or a holiday do
Please visit all the country side
And you will never rue?
It beats the towns and cities
The smoke clouds and the smog.
Just take a good stout walking stick.
And your faithful pal your dog.
The people are so friendly.
With cups of tea and cheer.
Or if you prefer the pub
For a good old pint of beer.
And don't forget the dialect
To hear it, it is strange.
It makes you smile behind their backs
But it sounds nice for a change.

Mary Morton

Memories

Seven and a half years,
you came to stay,
and it only seems like yesterday,
sitting up on your hind legs that day
it was if you were saying,
"I'm here to stay"
I could almost see you smile,
and then
you'd bark and wag your tail,
and ask for biscuits once again,
you'd get your friend Flap,
and even my old friend, my cat.
Gone dear Skip,
though not out of mind,
because you will be in my memory
till the end of time.

Margaret Siddall

For Our Granddaughter Kirsty

You're Nannie and Granddad's little girl
And we love you very much
You are so very precious
And we always tell you so
You're like a little snowdrop
That pops up in the spring
You've made us very happy
Now all we do is sing

You're like a ray of sunshine
That comes into our home
Granddad says it's lovely
Seeing your little face
When he comes home
You're very special
And we thought you'd like to know
We love you very very much
More than you'll ever know

Marguerite Munsey

Travelling On

As through the vale of Death we go,
God grant we find it friend, not foe,
and should its course be swift or slow,
may we Thy Love within it know.

For some die young and some die old,
some die before their tales are told,
their flowers bloom, their buds unfold,
but All within Your hand You hold.

To loved one who are left behind,
give courage of a different kind,
with comfort to each heart and mind,
that they, in You, may solace find.

C. A. Lomas

Perfect Strangers

When perfect strangers meet
It could be on a walk, a busy street
Or on a bus,
An aeroplane.
Or a quiet port in sunny Spain.

Their time together
Can last or wither
Depending on their bond
If one's averse
The other'll reverse
And they may just correspond.

But to paint a living
Is as good as giving
The other fancy things.
The stars they travel
The sun does too
And the mocking-bird it sings.

Richard Gamble

On Loan

You were on loan to us for such a
    short short time
And yet you made us happy
    you loved and laughed and cried
You were so very very brave
    and yet so very young
In all the days and all the pain
    a smile for everyone
You were so very precious
    a rose amongst the thorns
And from the very first -
    the day that you were born
You brought joy love and laughter
    and lots and lots of fun
Your time is at an end now
    we had to say goodbye
Until we meet again one day
    in that playground in the sky

K. M. Manson

Down Memory Lane

Sundays used to be good fun,
Mostly, thanks to dear old mum,
Touring round the country side
Taking grandchildren for a ride.
I got to know all village parks
As my grandchildren were bright sparks.
Every local garden viewed.
Money spent was never rued.
Mother knew each flower by name,
Plants and bulbs we bought the same.
Sweet shops did a roaring trade.
Oh for a little peace I prayed.
Children sucking lollipops
It gave me time to have a nod
Wish I could relive those days
But my old mother passed away
Children now are mums and dads
Watching T.V. I feel sad.

E. M. Fairlie

Untitled

The love I have
in my heart for you
is greater than the
universe of love

How much I wish,
that you could see,
the love that is locked
in my heart, as you look up,
into the universe of love.

D. M. Spence

The Loneliness Of Old Age

The quiet gloom,
Slow darkening room,
The shadows thickly lie,
A shape is born in angular things
Footsteps hurrying by.

A ticking clock,
A clicking lock.
These are the things I hear
No human voice is here for me
No friendly person near.

This loneliness I now endure,
The quietness is grim
How come my world to be so still
Beloved music, just a hymn.

Must dream awhile
Must not mope
The dawn will come I know,
Until it does - as said - must dream,
At least the fire's aglow.
Dora Walker

The Most

We still recall the things gone by
The things that hurt the most
While drinking in the darkening sky
On visits to the coast.

While romance seeks you by the shore
To sweep you clean away
And leave you crying out for more
Of wondrous games to play.

And though the heart is often torn
When passions slowly rise
The way we laugh and dance and fawn
The foolish with the wise.

And to remember things once said
In times of love gone wrong
How a love so good is dead
So weak when once so strong.

So on returning to the sea
And beauty of the coast
Thoughts of love come back to me
The things that hurt the most.
Andrew Hearn

Care For A Friend

If your heart is young and light
You will often get a sight
Of people who are less well off
And have often had enough

Even though it may appear
There is little for them to fear
They may worry all the same
Their mind can play a serious game

Their problems may seem very bad
And they will seem oh so sad
Their life seems hopeless and so tough
By comparison to yours pretty rough

Try to help those is need
A kindly thought, a friendly deed
Give them a shoulder on which to cry
With your help they will get by

It's nice to know in days to come
By caring now you may have won
Pain and suffering at an end
With lots of help from a friend.
Michael R. C. Goss

A Cottage

A tiny thatched cottage
Down a quiet country lane,
An old fashioned garden
Refreshed by the rain.
A gate with a name on
A well by the path,
A cat and a dog
Asleep on the hearth.
And when you knock
The door opens wide,
A very warm welcome
Awaits you inside.
I've no wish for wealth,
I've no wish for fame,
But I would love a cottage,
Down a quiet country lane.
E. Martin

The Seasons' Maids

The dew is freshly laid,
Among the meadow's flowers,
Oh here comes the maid,
Of Spring and all the others.
The Summer maid will be coming soon,
Bright, beautiful, and full of bloom,
Next is the maid of greens and reds,
It's Autumn time! She's making beds,
Lots of different colours of leaves
You can see,
Lots for you,
And lots for me.
Last of all it's the Winter maid,
She covers the world with bright
White snow,
With a raise of a hand
Snowflakes come falling,
And everywhere you look,
They're all a'flow!
Andrea Roberts

'Echo'

She loves me. She loves me not.
I hear the childish voices cry
As blowing dandelion clocks
Across a cloudless summer sky.

Airily they float away.
Then down, to find a random plot.
But list! I hear the echo sigh,
She loves me. She loves me not.
T. Darling

Misunderstood

The misery of torment,
Persecution and the pain,
The cut of affliction,
To mutilate and maim.
Evolution, there inside me,
Nourished from my breast.
Nurtured and encouraged,
Inspired and impressed.
Every word I say now,
Is falsely misconstrued,
Was the tenderness we shared once,
Just a passing interlude?
I look into the mirror,
With question in my eyes.
Misgivings and confusion,
His aversion and despise.
I know that it's time now,
To smile and let you go,
But tell me, do you know son?
How I'll always love you so.
C. E. Baker

Heart's - Ease

I pass the cupboard in your room,
And am assailed by your perfume.

I see a shadow at the door,
And think, you are come home once more.

I turn towards you in the night,
But your bed lies bare, by moonlight.

I hear a foot fall on the stair,
And run to see if you are there.

I spy a figure on a bench,
A glimpse that gives my heart a wrench.

I hear a call, from the garden,
Sets me searching where you're hidden.

How your spirit pervades my heart!
Tender comfort while we're apart.

It's just a blink of Time's great eye,
Till we're together, you and I!
J. Hughes

Loved One

You never say when you are down,
Yet I can tell without a doubt,
from words and phrases that escape,
floating dully, round about.

Sighs and words that are out of tune,
a frown, a pause, that is not you.
A tone that lingers; you gently tread,
you just won't let the feeling through.

Would that you would let me see,
Would that you would soon reveal.
In time, you may light that light
and our friendship, softly seal.
Marie Barrett

Along The Lanes The Wye Valles

Along the lanes we wander
See two brown horses in a field.
Pick some grass and feed them,
could stay with them for hours.
You can see the trees in blossoms
The greenness of the fields.
A seat upon the mountain top
Looks down on the valley below
The river railway and the road
It's great to see the three
The picture of the hill tops,
Gosh! what a sight to see.
Yes God made all this possible
On earth down here below,
We really know he did this
Because he loved us so.
Enid Wilcox

Too Many

Too many ifs
Too many whens
Too many sorrys
And never agains.

Not enough love
Not enough sharing
Not enough giving
Not enough caring.

Too many promises
Too many lies
Far too many one more tries.

How many were there
Before I knew
That actions speak louder
Than promises do?
Maureen Natt

172

Seeds of Hope

Is it only a delusion
Of what things ought to be
Flower of my illusion
That you still care for me?

Or do I detect a change
A new exciting feeling,
The seeds of hope which so derange
Yet linger and are appealing?

Will they blossom into desire
As before if you remember?
The sweet bouquet of the fire
Rekindling from the embers.

Don't let foolish face or pride
Deny a feeling in your heart
If one day you might decide
Together is better than apart.

John Tynan

Words

Oh! How harsh,
Some words can be.
How hurtful, to the ear
They send one's heart pounding,
Bringing sadness and tears.

If only people would count ten,
Before abusive be.
Asking God to guide their tongue
To keep them from fits of jealousy.

This world would be more like heaven
All would be in harmony
No more heartbreaks or fears
For God's love would reign.
Through the years.

G. Davenport

Long Ago

In the valley birds were singing
On the hill, church bells ringing
Hushed was the Sabbath morn.
In the sky, clouds were breaking
In the field, new life awakening
Lo! A little ass was born.

In that country, long ago
Midst the cold and dreary snow
Broke another Sabbath dawn.
In the sky, angels singing
Joy and gladness they were bringing
Lo! A holy Babe was born.

Beast of burden, child of God
Both a weary way they trod
Each to service given,
Patient, kind, faithful true
Both a job of work to do.
Now rest in their own Heaven.

Toni Brinton

Revenant

In the deep and velvet dark of night
Through mists of memory
Into the transient world of dreams
You come again to me.
There for a few enchanted hours
You live for me, my love,
Until the silver-fingered dawn
Touches the sky above.
Waking, I lie with eyes still closed
To hold you yet a while,
And parting from you, seem to see
The shadow of your smile.

Margaret George

Tomorrow

If tomorrow comes too soon
Just remember I loved you all
nothing you did
just me
thoughts and pictures
and all people
all minds and heads
all faces and expressions
all bodies and movements
it's no good remembering
pointless
other things to get on with
just one less person
object, thing in your minds
memories
and then oblivion

Sabrina Sambrook

Nostalgia

War has come to our village
soon the sound of marching feet,
lorry loads of cheery soldiers
driving through our narrow streets.

Cockney slang assaults our ears
when lads from London town arrive,
we never saw their like before
such cheekiness and forceful drive.

Searchlights nightly probe the sky
enemy zepherlins soon appear,
gleaming silvery in the moonlight
filling us with deadly fear.

Our village sure has come alive
organizers soon appear,
entertainment for the troops
and suddenly they disappear.

Elsie Tindali

The Dreamer

He sleeps, yet he is wide awake;
His world is never seen.
He'll never tell of what he's done
Or of the places he has been.

He turns and calls to unknown friends
Or cowers from dangerous foe.
He smiles and cries and listens,
To whom we'll never know.

Every night he slips away
To a world all of his own,
A place that we can never reach
As we are fully grown.

But if he wakes and cries out loud,
We will always go to see
That he is safely back with us;
Besides he's only three!

Deborah Crew

What Is Here,
Will Never Really Be There!

The magical, but not.
Opens in a flame,
to what becomes a blur.
The picture of what could not,
will never become real.
As truth is not found,
all it's just a dream.
Like everything will leave,
to just appear again.
But next to be in darkness,
of what could be a sin.

Tasha Butler

Beyond The Glister

Why does a dew-drop glisten
And tinsel glitter on a tree?
Why does a moon ray gleam
And a star sparkle for all to see?

For this there is a reason,
Or so I have been told.
'Tis to remind us of greater treasure
Beyond the glister of greedy gold!

Miss Wendy Levett-Darling

Weights And Measures

Sixty minutes in every hour-
Until you go away.
Twenty four hours in every day-
Until you go away.
We flow together every night-
Until you go away.

When you go, there's a transformation;
Sixty minutes become a day,
Twenty four hours become a week.
Instead of inclination
There is frustration,
The heart is heavy and life is bleak.

Come back, so that life
Returns to its normal scale
Sixty minutes in every hour
Twenty four hours in every day.
The heart is light with jubilation,
Weights and measures
Back to true proportions.

Sheila B. Vickers

My Love, My Life

You are my only inspiration,
never seen, but always there.
I have not doubts,
only questions.

The more I find,
the more I believe.
So many hearts are touched by you,
I must be part of this great love.

Trying so hard to please,
sometimes not knowing how.
Trusting so much,
needing your guidance.

I seem to know so little,
things I can never understand.
Being content is easy,
for the certainty of your love is here.

Winifred O'Brien

The Golden Eye

Ankle deep in the receding tide
Sun on my back
I peer wide-eyed
Amongst the wrack
And the darting fry
For the ever elusive Golden Eye.
It's a new world that you look upon
Now you see it - then it Gone!
The mysterious glint
Of reflected light,
Like twinkling stars within the night,
Draws you - magnetic
Within its power,
to keep you out there
For more than an hour.
It's when you peer into those eyes,
That seems to hold you - Hypnotize
Until you reach out and drag
One more cockle into you bag.

David Talbot

A Doll For My True Love

A doll for my truelove
doled out in blue-green,
purple and gold.
'Tis so beautiful,
monocled, chronicled
and true.

Doreen Whitehouse

Memories of the War

Why cause pain and suffering?
Why promote grief and hurt?
Never ending human cries,
Civilisation becomes dirt.

Call for the death of peace,
All in the name of greed,
Innocent lives cast away,
And hatred plants its seed.

Enemies and friends are one,
Violence becomes their goal,
Shoot to kill, spare no life,
The guilt will drain your soul.

The deepest scars cannot be seen,
When the fighting is no more,
How does anyone ever forget,
The tragic memories of the WAR.

Miss Lindsay West

Just Another Mistake

In the darkness of the womb
the fetus throbs with life
which echoes in the mother's heart
as she signs on the crucial line.
It is as though the little being,
without a face or name,
knew its fate to be irrevocably sealed
before it ever could be free.
And as the probe enters its domain,
the cold steel arm of death,
advancing inexorably,
to suck its life away,
it throbs again.
One moment it lived,
a pulsing shapeless heartbeat;
the next it lay,
on a sterile surgical tray,
a lump of flesh,
warm, bloody,
and dead.

Cheryl Mary Xavier

Let's Pretend

For once,
Let's pretend
We are in love,
If not with each other
Then ourselves.
Let's pretend we are happy,
and nothing else matters,
except to be perfectly happy.
Let's pretend we are like children
and everything is a game,
Where we play all day,
without a care for tomorrow.
Let's pretend
We are lovers,
Where our passions
Run into each other,
Taking us to dizzy heights.
For once in our lives
If not for ourselves,
Then for love's own sake,
Let's pretend....

Jade Watkins

Sparrow's Song

Somewhere within the church,
a sparrow chirped:
A glorious, careless note
that multiplied itself
a thousand times
and filled the church with spring!

And though the organ plays,
the choir sings, the people pray;
I still can hear
the sparrow's song of joy,
eclipsing all, outdoing all
the voices raised in praise.

Somewhere within the church,
a sparrow chirped,
a paean for the spring
that lingers on
when priest and congregation
are both gone.

Sylvia Zammit

Beyond The Mountains Of Despair

So fair and talented you are
With spirit, grace and care;
You have the hope of Penelope,
As the great Alexander - you dare!

Although physical tribulations
Tried to impede your affairs;
With courage you stepped ahead
And confronted the raging "mer".

Look ahead and you will see,
Beyond th' misty mountains of despair,
The sun rising with such strength;
Look further! - What do you see?

You see hope, light and certainty,
You see vigour, youth and novelty;
Yonder is the end to all your troubles,
There's your reward above the sea.

So be hopeful, sanguine and endure
The unavoidable catastrophes;
Look!- with open arms someone awaits,
To lead you through to better pastures.

V. B. G. Verity

Nothing Really Matters

Slowly walking hand in hand
Family black with grief untold,
Heads hung low, their faces hid
Beneath a veil of lace and woe,
Bells swing slowly back and forth
So much fury in their toll,
For the soul that had departed
Memories cling from long ago,
Many people he had touched
Bodies, hearts, then let go.

Black shapes passed me two by two
Like shiny crows their heads hung low,
White flowers carried for the dead
Dropped petals for their weary tread,
Then from the family circle flung
Their arms up high to heaven above,
A small boy ran and took my hand
His big wet eyes spoke from his soul,
"No pasa nada madre mía
There's much for me before I go."

Frances Askew

Rich Indeed!

It's not the most expensive things,
That count in life, for me.
But the chorus of the birds at dawn.
The blueness of the sea.
The Glory of the sunset.
A Friend's kind word or smile.
The kettle whistling noisily,
As we pause to chat a while.
The presence of my family,
The pressure of a hand.
When things are going none too well,
You know they understand.
The sweet smell of a flower.
A special photograph.
To bring the memories back to you,
A tear, or else a laugh.
To know that I have done my best,
If I could help, I've tried.
For home, for family and friends,
With these, I'm satisfied!

Phyllis Frankish

The Happy Sound Of Slush

The dawn is icy, dark and cold,
The snow has fallen too,
It's covered all, I cannot see
The ice is hidden from my view,
I'll watch it

The slush is noisy, so I know
It is not icy here,
The drive is taken with great care
I cannot help but have some fear,
I'll watch it.

The drive is getting quieter now,

The slush is disappearing,
I fear the hidden ice below,
Engage low gear - slow - not so daring.
Must watch it.

Around the corner, there I spied
A car turned turtle on its side,
The driver - He had nearly died,
The ambulance was by his side.
He didn't watch it.

Judy McKechnie

An Ode To A King!

So tall so dark so handsome
That's how you seemed to be
A man so deep and dark as night
So full of mystery...

And yet your songs betrayed you
Well, they surely did to me
For in that voice I sometimes heard
Someone longing to be free!

Free of all the heartaches
All the sadness and despair
Free of all commitments
Free, to roam just anywhere

Still, one day you did find them
All these things you searched long for
The peace, the love, the happiness
Of this I'm very sure

So, though we loved and lost you
And bitter tears we shed
No greater force abound you
No finer King us led.

Y. A. Bolton

The Harbour Lights

Seven fluorescent lights were burning,
For across the silent water.
Two were calling, close together,
A pair that looked but did not see.

Did I catch a glisten there?
On a pebble on the beach.
The last of light, now it's all faded,
Gone forever from my sight.

Back on sea the boat is swaying,
Rocking cradle, magically,
Have to wait, the tide is changing.
So close and yet for now so far.

Do we ever get there really?
A place that we both know and love.
Will surface tension hold me, surely,
The short traversal to the light.

S. J. Powers

Not Wired Up

Interface teletex and cyber-space
Mobile phones, P.C's, vodaphones
Surfing the Internet to get netted?
Give me instead a real live smile
Free from traps of mechanical guile.

"It's good to talk" and walk slowly
Romantically thoughtfully
Along a river path
Where nature teaches
All we need to know....!

No motor-way aggro
No blasts from a blasting 'hi-fi'
From a speeding metal box
With a psycho at the wheel
Who is too far gone to care
For a world so woebegone.

For modest human power
Once built a mighty Parthenon!

Geoff Broady

My Son

Robes of White watching, waiting
Clasping hands, loving, caring
Words of comfort, cries of pain
Shared happiness to long remain

Anxious moments, watching, waiting
Sweetest sounds announce new life
Smiles and tears and wondrous joy
Welcome first-born baby boy

Over now the watching, waiting
One new life has just begun
May your days be long and happy
Dearest first-born baby son

Maureen Berry

Poetry

True poetry is spontaneous,
unpremeditated;
sudden as welcome tears
that purge a long-pent grief,
or unexpected laughter
lightening the lingering darkness
of sullen, frost-hard mornings.

It crystallizes forever
men's brief intimacy
with the immortal,
enshrining in words
the divinity of the moment,
storing the gift to perception
for the future's heritage.

Claudia Dick

Granddad Had A Garden

Granddad had a garden
With a narrow winding path,
And chickens at the bottom
That fed upon the grass.

There were apple trees,
Pear trees and peaches, galore
Sunflowers, wall flowers,
Rambler roses around the door.

Also in that garden
An old shed was granddad's joy.
With treasures he had hoarded.
When he was just a boy

Now granddad is no longer here.
And I am grown up too,
I will forever remember that garden,
And dear old granddad Lou.

R. M. Jefferis

Mary

And she was dark;
And fair
Beyond compare,
My Mary.
With beauty
Rooted deep
In empathy.
And symmetry,
My Mary.
And now her dark
Has turned to snow
A new third beauty
Starts to glow
From Mary.

Ron Hardwick

Euthanasia

I stare
I blink
I cannot talk
I twitch
I shake
I cannot walk
Will no-one stop and look at me
And end this pain and set me free.

I sit
I look
I cannot cry
I long
I hope
I want to die
Will no-one look across at me
And save me from this misery.

Sonia Griffiths

My Country Walk

To walk down a country lane,
Brings memories to the fore again.
To hear the sweet song of the thrush
And to see grass so green and lush,
To watch the river as it flows,
And feel the breeze that gently blows.
To smell the lovely new mown hay
To watch the happy lambs at play.
Far off, I hear a church bell ringing
Close by there is a black-bird singing,
High above is a hovering hawk,
All this in my country walk!
Oh, how I wish that I could stay
To watch the rabbits as they play,
Yet for all I might wish and yearn
To my home in the town I must return.

Lynda Wyatt

A Miner's Eulogy

A miners life is arduous
The perils real and true,
As any man who's underground
Will testify to you.

The comradeship's unrivalled,
No other job's the same,
For every man and boy I know
Feels pride in a miners name.

And when accidents do happen,
As we know they surely must,
That's when we all rely on
Each other's strength and trust.

For there's no braver band of men,
When danger rears its head,
For miners do not hesitate
Where others fear to tread.

And when each shift is over,
And we wend our weary way,
Towards the shaft and sunlight
We all give thanks and pray.

Terry Wood

Masquerade

Never have I been touched this way,
Inside you send me reeling,
Yet face to face detect no trace
Of how I'm really feeling.

Mistrust my words, beware my deeds,
My heart conceals a danger.
Beyond this safe, familiar front
There lurks a jealous stranger.

Deny the lie, betray the truth,
The private nights spent weeping.
It's living hell, I cannot tell
This secret that I'm keeping.

For life's a masquerade my friend,
There's much we all disguise.
You look at me, but fail to see
The need behind these eyes.

I'll don a mask, belie my love
And hide the tears I'm crying.
I'll wear it well; you'll never tell
That through the smile I'm dying.

Emma Cable

To Two Sleepyheads

Awake! Awake! The lark is up
And singing in the sky.
Awake! Awake! For breakfast time
Has long ago passed by.

Awake! And thrust the covers
From two small sleepy heads.
Awake! And leave the warm embrace
Of two small single beds.

The sun is at its zenith
And half the day is gone.
There's bustle on the highways,
Just look at all the throng!

Throw open all the curtains,
And throw the casements wide!
Let in the sunshine and fresh air,
There's none at all inside.

Take pleasure in each moment
Of every fleeting day,
For you do not yet understand
How soon they pass away.

Maurice H. Gould

Untitled

We must make time to stand and stare,
 We must make time to be aware
Of the beauty that is around
 And of the creatures that abound
But how long will they be around
 If no solution can be found
To man's inhuman acts of murder
 Both to creatures and much further
Man feels superior but what's he worth
 When he can't see the future's bleak
Because the World is getting weak
 Through atom blasts and acid rain
And creatures never seen again
 We must take time to stand and stare
And make them see and be aware
 That what we have upon this Earth
Is precious and has boundless worth
 Maybe if we strive to preserve it
We can feel that we do deserve it.

J. D. Holmes

"Naked Land"

Whilst the clouds bare their
Souls to God,
To release the ecstasy
Of utter misery

That lurks inside their bellies;
The land,
Turns to stone
And then to dust—

Till it is naked;
For the land
Cannot spring the fruits
Of life upon itself,

Unless the clouds that be
Shed their petal of tears,
And cover the nakedness
Of the land;

Oh clouds,
Sprinkle the air with your petals,
And let the land
Quench its thirst.

Aseem Verma

My Wish For Christmas

May the old that are so lonely,
Find company this day,
May the sick and all that suffer,
Make their pains all go away.

May the cold and homeless masses,
Find a warm and welcome bed,
And may there be no children,
Without a lap to lay their heads.

May the rich and greedy of this world,
Feel the greatest pangs of shame,
And give to those that need it,
Then they'll receive the same.

Warm glow that comes within you,
When right you know you've done,
Then God has made visit
To you, the loved one, his son.

May these wishes for this Christmas,
Not mean for just a day,
But go on and on forever,
For this wish I will pray.

Kathleen Brice

"Trees"

Trees everywhere from far and wide
so beautiful to see.
All different shapes and sizes,
And many shades of green,
They stretch their arms out to provide
Shade upon a sunny day

They lend themselves to little birds
To make their nests with pride
Somewhere for them to get away and hide
They stand so tall and elegant
Against the clear blue sky

Each one is very precious
They give us such a lot!
And if you hug a tree
You'll be filled with lifelong energy!
So, go on! Go hug a tree
And the stronger you will be.

Margaret Rose Edwards

Dreams

Sun, golden sands
Rippingly wares
children, bucket and spades
mums and dads dregging with
their hands

Dark clouds race across
The sun
Suddenly it comes
sheets of rain
An empty beach
Where once the castles
Proudly stood
Into the realms of times
Our memories fade away
Into the darkness of our mind

C. Cowell

Yellow

Yellow, a juicy succulent colour,
Mouth watering like lovely lemons,
Or delicious melons,
More powerful than the sun,
And better than fun.
Yellow, a colour,
Like sand and time,
Slips through your hands,
Like leaves to the ground.
Flowers gather round for winter,
Is around the corner,
Yellow dies,
Darkness covers the skies.

Tom Kellow

Threnody

So ere I die,
My final prayer;
That I may lie
Within the fearful sepulchre
Your mystery for my shroud;
Bound, all around,
With perfumed memories.

And 'gainst th'eternal cold,
That your sweet soul -
My soul's desire -
With me may rise
In one inseparable flame -
One mutual name -
From the funereal phoenix-fire.

Norman F. Price

It

Its eyes once glowed
Intense and bright.
Its skin once shone
Reflecting light.
Its gleaming teeth of
Polished chrome,
Invited me to drive it home.
I journeyed near I journeyed far,
With it (me in my motorcar).
Now sadly it's a pile of rust,
Gathering cobwebs rain
and dust.
Standing lonely in the street.
Awaiting kind scrap man.
To meet.
It really is unfitting end
for it, who was my favourite
friend.

Ben Herbert Brumel

The Thistle

I remember the thistle there,
You pointed on a small path,
Fresh air as if after a bath,
Carried early summer over there.
You showed me the flower,
Telling me the name quietly,
Sweet breeze passed gently by,
We wanted to stay longer,
But spoke fewer still,
Only the thistle swaying,
Swinging in that dreamy morning.

Tokiko Iwamoto

Untitled

Once a happy, joyful child,
Now a lonely heart inside.
Once you know but not for sure,
What is waiting behind the door.

Out of reality.
Into the world.
Heaven and Hell,
As my story's unfold.

Explain the traumas,
Explain the pain.
Why can't I be the same again,

Summer sun and winter rain.
All the seasons seem the same,
The darkness of the midnight light.
Confusion within,
Will it ever be?

Haylley Pittam

Untitled

The world is at war,
Wether it's people or their race,
There's bitterness and anger,
In every mile of space.

There's people killing people,
'Cause the colour of their skin,
Yet do they stop to think,
Of their devastated kin.

Theirs politics and rules.
That stop you in your tracks,
If you do not correspond,
You end up on the racks.

There's always innocent bloodshed,
Why does it have to be?
God is always blamed,
'Cause of us, you see.

Louise Hughes

Reason

Long is the path of reason
When wrong seems right to some
For they in blind abandon
Know nought of what is to come
When truth unfolding dawns

To tread the path of reason
Explaining other way's
To make a self sought mirror
Reflecting what the conscience say's
And enlightenment come

When you reach the pathway's end
And feel your conscience rest
Then will trouble disappear
Within; you are at your best
Be reasonable

Remember; the path of reason
If uncertainty is rife
Rein in, the instant need to get
To take, or want in life
If reasonable; it will happen

William F. Park

"An Apology"

I have lived a life that has been great
I've wandered near and far,
A sailor's life was my delight
for twenty years and more.
When the world was large and
full of fun I sailed the seven seas,
romance was always in the air
in every port encountered,
of all the girls that I did meet
each one was very special,
but now I'm wed and much in love
I wish to say I'm sorry
to any heart I may have broke
because of lust and passion,
I meant no harm to any lass
who lay beneath my spell
it was just my way of showing thanks
For the landfall and compassion.

Leslie Wallace

I Thought Of You

I thought of you this morning
As dawn began to break
Did you hear the birds sing
See the mist across the lake

I thought of you at lunch time
As the sun was at its high
Did you see the rainbow
When the clouds began to cry

I thought of you this evening
As the frost lay on the ground
Did you smell the bonfire
See the Catherine Wheels go round

I thought of you at midnight
When scared and all alone
Do you know I love you
I want you to come home.

Julie Rhyder

Haven (Dartmouth, Kingswear)

Oh! What a scene before my eyes,
Rolling hills and clear blue skies,
The light reflecting in a glade,
Dappled sunlight with the shade,
Mirrored on a tranquil sea,
A looking-glass there for me,
Amongst the fragrance of the flowers,
One could stay here for hours.

Elizabeth Jessica Jefford

Penny Dropped

The penny dropped the mind awoke,
And started knowing why.
It's easier for a human,
Not to think, just cry.

Does this do any real good!
Well yes it does in sorrow
That is, when we start to do,
Things for a brighter tomorrow.

Then the pennies really drop,
Yes things start taking shape.
Things are fixed inside our head,
Played back on our minds' tape.

For sorrow leads to compassion,
Which brings a focus clear.
Well has the penny really dropped?
Then make for people's cheer.

John Cowley

A Life So Short

That day we will remember
one we never shall forget
the call that came upon us
caused pain and much regret
what could we say who could we
blame, your life would never be
the same.
We really thought you'd make it.
You held on for so long. The accident
that killed you was very very wrong.
We visit your son and the memories
we have are now within him. His smile
his walk and even when we hear him
talk, the pain and sorrow remain
it will not lift your life to us
was such a gift.
We miss you so, was it really
your time to go I guess we'll
never know.

R. Slinger

Lost

My name is Groves,
I live on Earth,
A planet which,
For what it's worth,
Approximate,
Unto a star,
Not the largest,
One by far,
Somewhere up in,
The Milky Way,
Where's that you ask?
I cannot say.

Brian Groves

Three Little Boys

Run!
Fear, no hope, no dreams;
over spilling sun,
moist, smooth skin,
lifeless.

Looming shadows,
evil eyes,
pain, tears,
darkness.

The air, seas and mountains,
the sun, the stars, the moon,
belong to them.

Life, eternity,
earth, astral,
The Southern Cross above their grave.

Lis Rose

We Don't Understand

They were babies
Petals opening into
The flowers of life
Eager, happy, excited
As each new day dawned
So innocent of
Crime, drugs, and
Any harmful person
Such love for and from
Mummy, daddy, brothers,
And sisters
And now- Silence
Their happy voices
Are no more
One can never forget
The tragedy
Of those dear babies
On the threshold of life.

P. I. Eve

Morning Train

Hasten in the chill of morning
Unaware of scarlet dawning,
Pinstripe suits with pallid faces,
Robots glide with grim grimaces.
Skinny youths of doubtful gender,
Avon'd ladies tall and slender,
Toast in hand and coats undone,
Must not miss the eight-o-one.

Passed the paper boy in song,
On the station in the throng,
Now they hide behind the news,
Much too early for the views.
Children bound for school and culture
Pass the ticket clipping vulture.
Skirts that almost show the knickers,
Balding contemplating vicars.

All ride on the eight-o-one,
And home again when day is done.

Christine Wheeler

A Sonnet For Site Seers

Developing hills
of usable waste
obliterated
the sheer majesty
of soaring mountains.
Fumes from polluted
Long rivers of cars
were exchanged for air,
as they wound towards
man made oceans of
claustrophobic swamps
of supermarkets
with agoraphobic
channels of car parks.

Celia Heathwood

Untitled

I know at times it's hard to see,
exactly what you mean too me
but, as time passes I'm sure you know
of my love for you that's grown.

Full of respect I have for you
in every little thing you do
and as my lover you treat me well
to all my friends I do tell
of the love I feel for you
my feelings are sincerely true.

Tracy Hodson

177

Flowing Freely

To kill myself, to take my life.
Dying peacefully.
Choking the last breaths.
Cutting the soft skin.
Slicing the human meat.
Blood flowing freely.
So quickly, so quickly it's flowing.
Not long now, soon.
Soon I won't be.
No more waiting, no more pains.
No more thoughts and feelings.
Time and again.
At last it's time.
And the time is mine.
Mine to give.
Or mine to take.
I take.
I take my life.
And I give it away.

Sarah Jane Morris

Untitled

A tree is such a lovely thing
Re-Born again with every spring
Planted and grown for you and me
The poetic beauty of a tree
The whispered rustlings of its leaves
Brings sweet contentment to my ears
In lofty splendour there it stands
To Bless and Sanctify the land.
The Land that covers all the Earth
In which we Humans all give Birth
And from the land down to the sea
Goes on for all eternity
To see this beauty all un-furled
Uplifts our soul, in this wide world.
For which we Daily, Nightly pray
That it will never pass away
Through summer, autumn, winter, spring
The God made earth will ever sing
God Bless the Lord
For Everything

John Blair Brown

The Wish

I had a wish this afternoon,
That I could travel far,
To Hong-Kong, China and Japan,
And 'p'raps' Austral-i-ah.
I'd go by plane and then by boat
To see the wondrous things,
To Shanghai, Victoria and Tokyo
Taiwan and Alice Springs.
Then on to Hawaii, Barbados too,
Perhaps New York I'll see,
And up to Niagara to see the falls
A trip that has to be.
So now I'm on my way back home,
I've had a lovely time.
I wonder will it all come true?
Before I'm ninety-nine.

E. E. Davis

Teddy Bear

Teddy bear a child's wife,
Comforts me through growing life,
Problems solved and sorrow shared,
Teddy bear is always there,

My deepest thoughts in him confided
Button eyes just blink and stare,
His tattered mouth is frayed and worn,
To keep my secrets that he's sworn,
My dearest teddy bear...

Mark Andrew Sadler

The Eyes Have It

There are many different colours and so many different shapes
Every pair have their own language and some of them hearts will enslave
The eyes have it and no matter, whether black, brown, green or blue
Amber, hazel or albino, without them darkness will ensue.
Watch the eyes of a new mother as she cast them on her new infant
See the softness and protection that will change them in that instant.
There's the look of two young lovers gazing in each other's eyes
You see love, lust and great longing, they have found their paradise.
Notice the eyes of any youngster when they get their own new pet
See their wonderment of nature as they cuddle it to their chest.
Then they are the dreamy peepers, ever far in a world of their own
No matter what life throws at them, these misty eyes will still hang on.
Alas, there's eyes that's drowned with worry, deep and dark and in despair
And the world can't fail to notice when those eyes are filled with tears.
There's the ones that's filled with sorrow as they say their last goodbye
They know love's gone from their tomorrow and they mourn until they die.
Lastly now, there's the old sleepers, eyes so wise, knowing and dim
Who have looked upon a lifetime, but now resigned, calm peace within.
Yes, the eyes have it, each emotion reflects the mirror of one's soul
A most precious gift from Heaven, one cannot do without at all.

M. J. Ellerton

In The Dead Of Night

I stand alone on a winter's night, I often think in the dead of night
When all is quiet still and calm, when people sleep, and do no harm
I think about the times gone by, sometimes I laugh, sometimes I cry
I've reached the age where I think a lot, I think I am happy with my
lot, the trouble is mankind is not, it's hard to live amid these times
with war and such a lot of violent crimes, where people cheat and
steal and lie is this the future of mankind

R. A. A. Manwaring

Tribute To A Friend

The definition of a friend, is someone with a hand to lend.
She'll listen to your moans and groans, and when you're sick she always phones,
to see if you are feeling better, and sometimes even sends a letter.
She even says a little prayer, when you are feeling deep despair.
She puts up with your moody blues, even when you blow a fuse.
She doesn't seem to give a dam, she just accepts the way I am.
She doesn't frown, that's not her style, she does her best to make you smile.
She makes you laugh, she makes you cry, she doesn't really mean to pry.
She's just concerned, she really cares, and all your secret problems shares,
and never tells a living soul, to be a good friend, that's her goal.
And on that very special day, she thinks of an exciting way to make a day
you'll not forget, you'll always be deep in her debt.
One day she'll bring you in some flowers, and do all things within her powers,
to cheer you when you're feeling down, I think that she deserves a crown.
Good friends like you are hard to find, so stick around if you don't mind.
Of these qualities you've shown, there are not many that I own.
So from now on I'll try to be the kind of friend you are to me.

Pauline Fletcher

Mixed Blessings

My Dad is black, my Mum is white, why should that give you the right
To call me names and put me down, I'm just like you except I'm brown.
I have feelings too you see, it hurts when people say of me,
There she is half and half, and then they have a good old laugh
I may be half and half outside, but that only gives me pride.
I share two backgrounds of culture and race, I have a beautiful golden face,
my tastes are varied - peas and rice or fish and chips without any spice.
Reggae music I enjoy, I can dig a beat like any black boy.
But any music makes me dance and if I get just half a chance
I'll show you how I strut my stuff and you don't have to act so tough
We can dance together and have some fun, black and white, everyone.
We can live together as sisters and brothers, whatever the colour of our fathers and mothers.
We're all God's children underneath whatever our colour creed or belief.
He would want us to live as one and follow the example of his son.
Unselfish and caring to all mankind, if you do this you will surely find
that the colour of my skin won't matter to you, the person that I am will shine right through.
And when you become a friend to me you can say to the others "can't you see?
She has something, to say right out loud" and I will stand up tall and proud
"Now I have your attention at last I'd like to state I'm not half-caste.
When I was born God looked down and smiled at me his little mixed-race child"

A. Voce

The Zoo

Today I'm going to the zoo,
To see the lions and tigers too.
What I like most about coming here,
Is that the animals have nothing to fear.
Although they should all be free,
They are safer here, than from man you see.
Because when they are in the wild, and not the zoo,
Shoot them dead is what a hunter would do.
He will skin it and turn it into coat for his wife,
How can he take an innocent creature's life?
The hunter has no feelings, he just doesn't care,
Would he kill and skin his children?
No, he would not dare.
What have the lions and tigers ever done to him?
He deserves to be torn from limb to limb.

Gemma Reeman

To My Little Benji

Dear little dog with coat of black and gold.
You gave me love as much as my heart could hold.
We played with biscuits, had such fun,
Took happy walks in rain and sun.
Saw a cat! No fun in chasing that.
In the garden we would walk.
You explored the garden and listened to me talk.
We watched the television, I made the tea.
Then you nestled close to me.
You slept by my bed at night,
Making sure auntie was all right.
Then came the day we had to part.
Pain and sorrow filled my heart.
But I have hope, don't you see,
For I know that someday God will give you give back to me.

E. M. Burnett

Chainsaw Fins

Stateside,
Clapboard junction,
Small town avenue,
Behind pea-soup willow,
Back of fifty-two,
In the reeds on lake trim
We snagged lips on plain-tip cigarettes,
Drawing hard the heat,
Got drunk on pop's home brew.

No moon over cane-struts
When I slow-baked the bean;
And you did an eel run
oceanward, unspecified.

The sun a thirsty fry-on
a crow spit-turn flaps, beneath.
Sky is cirrus optimum
and I'm true to elver.
Trailing leftwards I see,
Feel you,
Chainsaw fins.

Katherine Jane Rawley

Lost Love

I wish I knew what to do
My feelings of love are still of you
Memories of your face are etched on my mind
I don't think I will find
Such a deep love again
If only it was as simple as catching a train
Wish I had the face of a clown
I could hide with ease not show my feelings of being down
You touched my life which I am glad
Hope in time not to feel so sad
Tomorrow is a new day
Things happen for a reason they say
It's very sad it could not last
I hope in time the pain will pass

Liz Warren

Goddess Of The Night

The neon lights, so pert and pretty
Illuminate the darkened city
A delirious drug-addict shuffles along in a
    traumatic trance
A blushing teenager steps out for the last dance
A railway traveller searches frantically for his ticket
He's just spent the day watching the cricket
The brooding genius surveys the wondrous skies
Two fervent lovers explode with gigantic sighs
Out in space enjoying this exotic sight
Sits the illustrious Nyx glorious Goddess of the night
As she muses alone just doing her duty
She can't help but envy Venus - the Goddess of beauty
A child of light, happiness and gaiety -
She's sure to wed a suitable deity
But as for poor Nyx she's got no reason to revel
She'll probably end up married to the Devil

Joseph Riley

To A Snowdrop

First to come of all the flowers,
Small fragile petal, graceful leaf.
You face February's freezing showers,
Feel frost and snow and ice, and breathe
Fierce east winds; from your frozen bed
You undaunted grow alone
Bravely hold up your snow white head
And bloom on stern earth's hardest throne.
You are steadfast and you stay-
Oh small witness tossed in the breeze-
To wave waning winter on his way,
Greet tiny blossoms, buds on trees,
And fading, herald everything
Fresh and green that comes with spring.

M. A. Duncan

The Gambler

He stood at the gambling table, blew on the dice in his hand,
His suit was shiny, his shoes were well worn
But he felt like a king of the land,
He'd won back all the money he'd lost that week
And more, oh yes much more, now he'd pay off his debts
And go back home laden with presents galore,
He stuffed his pockets with money, a smile upon his face,
Then he felt the "Sweet" in his pocket,
The tablet he'd planned to take, if he'd lost on this last gamble
The taste of death would have been his fate;
The thief came from the shadows, a club raised in his hand
He brought it down on the gamblers head
And he died without a sound,
The thief rifled through his pockets
Laughing loud with glee,
Then he came upon the "sweet",
Haa, you saved the last one for me.

N. Hughes

A Life Cut Short By War

A boy came with a telegram up to a cottage door,
My granddad didn't know then the sad
tidings that he bore.
It said that he had lost a son,
who lately went to war.

He had 3 others out in France, amongst
the battle scene. His wilf was only 22
It all seemed like a dream.

A carillon stands memorium
At boughborough's lovely park
My uncle's name a memory
of all those days so dark.

As the bells are ringing
upon the sunny days
we think about the soldiers lives
a dreadful price he pays.

Barton

A Tale of Two Mice

There once were two mice called Jimmy and Tim
Wherever Jimmy went Tim had already been
Tim went to the market, Tim went to the fair
As a matter of fact Tim had been everywhere

And then the day came when Jimmy said to Tim
I'm going somewhere you've never been
I'm going to visit my old grandma mouse
She lives in a cottage, a nice country house

We'll go to the market, we'll go to the fair
As a matter of fact we'll go everywhere
I'll tell of the city, I'll tell of the farm
I'll tell of the corn I cut with my own arm

I'll tell of the country, of all that I've seen
And of all of the places I've been you've not been
I'll go to Germany, to Spain and to France
I'll go to these places to sing and to dance

I will see foreign beauties to rival them all
I will travel the world spring, summer and fall
And during all this, where will you be
Why, you'll be right there, Tim, waiting for me!

Victoria Dawson

Untitled

Across the sands of time
I have waited for you.

Silent, still, breathless.
Watching your frantic flight.
Feeling your fear.
Hearing your tortured cries.

When you fell and were crushed,
I whispered quietly in your heart,
Words of Love and strength
Helping you to stand again,
And carrying you onward.

You continued to run,
Ever searching and hungering,
For that which eluded you.

I was always in you.
Your search was an illusive folly...
You only ran from that which could not be run from...

It WAS you.

Emrys Ashley

It's A Lovely Day...

I sit alone with my despair
My mind, my companion, is not quite there
I gaze ahead in vacant stares
And live the life for which no one cares

My life is empty, all enthusiasm gone
These are the words of my swan song

While you have striven blindly for your visions and schemes
I have been here among you, invisible it seems

I ask, who will remember me, when my life receives the final snub
When I am buried and grown over by shrub

But better that than my life's pain and suffering throughout
While you have expected and exacted its all, no doubt

Complex figures in darkness now dance before my eyes
Clearly they entice me to leave a world that I now despise

They make me reflect on many things
Showing the truth, or so it seems

That truth, now seen, I must prevail
To end all the sorrow and all the travail

It's a lovely day to die and I look forward to mortality
And with that, at last, to find life's long elusive tranquillity.

Jon Beckley

"The Person Inside"

When the darkness falls to the sky
Only then is when I want to cry
And it's my face, I hope no one will see
Because they won't know what happens to me
Sometimes, when I see him in the day
I often wish he would look my way
But from him. I will always hide
Too scared to show him the person inside
Sometimes, I ache so much
For him I long to touch
But, I know he and I will never be
My heart breaks for it won't be we
I will always be alone
Forever in my life on my own
All I ever wanted is for someone to care
But I know no one will ever be there

Shirley Ann Cole

Untitled

I have neglected, too long played fast and loose
With an already too elusive muse;
Left undisturbed those restless ghosts
That nightly stirred around my bed's foot.

Now, when the Desire conspires with the Will,
The Means deserts.
All my Deserts are mean,
Scant puns which do not even scan.

How I hate this puny pen!
Pouring out desire unlimited
Within the straits of straggling words and images
Without rhyme or rhythm.

Those hackneyed phrases of adolescent years!

And yet...
I still regret those nights,
Nights, when I was flung along the furthest furlong of my passion
To rape the stars,
Beget sonnets of an unconsummated love,
And the world sighed, lay on its side;
Became an Iambic Pentameter.

Jim Walton

Life's Treasures

Clear blue skies up above.
A newborn baby born out of love.
A carpet of bluebells inside a wood
The sun on your face feels so good.
A cascading waterfall, a breath taking sight.
A loved one to hold you so close in the night
A room full of flowers with their rich perfume
A peacock displaying its shimmering plume
A field of daffodils, like a cloak of gold.
All these are treasures in the heart to hold.

Irene Corin

The Haven

The red streaks of dawn fleck the sky,
Splashing pink, on the golden heads of the nodding daffodils.
Mist rises from the lake as the garden beckons me,
For another day's pleasured labour.
I wend my way to the lake side,
where a friendly robin calls to me from a golden yew.
His song echoes across the lake,
As does the sound of my fork against the stones in the soil.
Fish lazily rise to the surface of the lake like small rainbows,
The robin flies down for breakfast provided by my forking.
As I breath in the cool fresh air of early morning.
I relax, safe in the knowledge that I am in a
paradise of my own making.
This garden where I spend each day,
A haven from the noise and bustle of modern day living.
My favourite time of day, my favourite past-time.
Who could wish for more, than to spend their time in a garden.

R. Hoare

Conservation

There once was a beautiful forest,
With green grass all around,
But now it's all dead and uprooted,
And no wild life can be found.

No singing birds high in the sky,
No insects and voles, or rabbits down holes,
Just the noise of machines going by.

Make way for the roads, they say,
Because motors are here to stay,
But we must keep the earth, to encourage new birth,
The traffic will have to give way.

We must not despair, when we really do care,
For green things and nice fresh air,
We'll plant some new trees, and flowers for the bees,
Then with nature we really can share.

Then we'll finally say, at the end of the day,
We all did our best, when put to the test,
And conservation is here to stay.

Vera Langsford

I Heard A Rainbow In Your Head

I heard a rainbow in your head
sit down and taste a tear
your cheek is kissed by a falling brick
of joy that isn't here

You break a sleeping cloud in half
and then you sit there grinning
they're racing phantoms yet again
a strawberry is winning

You laugh into a paper-cup
it searches for a friend
lies dormant in an open grave
it isn't time to mend

I feel a colour pierce my mind
pollution is a trance
it shivers in an empty box of insignificance

Reality provokes a pain
a bird flies from a tree
I smile and feel a sense of right
an acquaintance, or just me?

Louise C. Allen

It Made A Difference

I didn't tell her that I loved her,
I didn't tell her I love her so,
I didn't say I loved her dearly,
And that made a difference.

I always felt so proud as
I saw her walking home,
How lovely she was, how elegant, how smart,
But I didn't tell her,
And that made a difference.

And so it looked all over,
To me it was the end.
I cried "Oh Lord Please Help me"
And someone answered
"You tell her that you love her"
And that will make a difference.

And now, I'm only waiting
For that voice to tell my love.
You tell him that you love him.
And that, would make a difference.
That would make a difference.

Fred Swindells

After Summer Has Gone

After summer has gone
and leaves are all falling
The berries we're picking
the blackie is calling
Calling so loudly, so lonely
so sweetly
The young have all flown,
the nest is so empty
If you sing you seem happy
after summer has gone.
A larder so full
and no one to share it
Is having all gold
and no where to spend it
So taste the good life when you're young
do not spare it
Then you will enjoy autumn
after summer has gone.

Patrick McCann

The Silver Man

This life I have, has been turned up side
down so many times that I feel so ashamed
that I am still alive today but for how long.
In this world there was someone I loved
and now disappears into the night once
again, I wish he could stay longer to say
goodbye but he has to fly away to
another world, off goes the silver man
flying high through the clouds every night.
Once the silver man said he loved me and
that we would be together for the rest of our lives,
shooting among the stars and
planets, but some how it didn't seem right
to leave this planet yet.
It made me shiver with fright that the
silver man was so violent to everyone else
but me of course, for there was only
love he felt for me and nothing could
ever change that for us.

Sarah Scarodimos

Creation

I love the earth I love the seas I love skies
so blue. I love the flowers, I love the trees
I love the birds too, I love the sun I love the
moon I love the stars that shine, but
most of all I love my god that made
the beautiful world, it's upside down but
what do I care, there's nothing wrong with
the world today it's the folks that's
living in it I love it

Elizabeth McAvoy

Southease Sussex

Walk uphill from the river,
Pull open the gate
Into the churchyard quiet and cold.
Consider the round tower,
Saxon stronghold
Ponder the gravestones,
Lichened and old
Then...
Gaze at the snowdrops
Unfurling the ground
In white and green
They move but gently
Away from the wind
Surrounding the church in tranquil calm.
"Centuries pass," they nod
"And we still scatter the grass."

Joy Roseveare

Flotsam

Pathetically he huddles on the seat,
  And all around
The swirling traffic fills the busy street
  With endless sound.

While passers-by allow an idle glance
  On him to fall -
The travesty of clothes, pick'd up by chance,
  Which are his all.

He heeds them not nor knows the endless roar,
  As, lost in dreams,
He sees again the purple heather'd moor
  And mountain streams.

Once more he hears the plover's mournful cry
  From heights above,
And gazes on the wild and storm-toss'd sky,
  He used to love.

Again the lonely moorland paths he takes
  'Neath summer's sun;
But when at last from memories he wakes
  His day is done.
  R. M. Shallard

Your Place....Your Peace

If there's one good place where you can stand
where laughter is your light,
Where thoughts of moments come to mind
Where pleasures are your sight.
Where peace can enter through your soul
and life is what you hear
Where skies hold winds to carry,
your emotions and your fear.
Where you can hold your head and laugh
with sunlight on your face
Where you can tread and know that here,
you'll never fall from grace.
Where you have seen the dancing waves
on waters running free
This one good place where you can stand,
Beside the precious sea.
  Fiona E. Rae

Poem By Thought

Summer's here at its best, no more baggy crinkled vests.
I played here in the cooling sea feeling happy being free.
Ice cream too sticky, too hot for tea,
Strawberry milkshake I prefer for me.
Six weeks holiday all for me, no more 'straight to bed after tea".
I close my eyes and fall to sleep, no more school timetable
I must keep.
Boys and girls and family noise, the golden sand they use for
Toys. 7.30 the sun still bright the beach soon empty to the night.
A beach ball floating in the sea, close to a hat that's reads
"Please kiss me".
The moon lights up the empty beach littered with the
Impressions of feet, now the gull's will come to eat. -
  C. Kirk

Drifting Homeward

Far away, far away, drifting on the oars,
Up above circling, the wild bird soars.
Far away, far away, drifting on the sea,
Wishing, wishing, my love was here with me.

Far away, far away ocean meets the sky,
High above, circling, see the Eagle fly.
Calm blue ocean, early morning dew,
Hoping, hoping, my love will still be true.

Far away, far away, winds will guide me home,
Waves lapping, swaying, on the gentle foam.
Distant shore approaching, through the haze I see
Standing on the shoreline, my love awaiting me..
  Carol Paterson

The Fisherman

The fisherman sits patiently in this boat.
Staring instantly at the bobbing float.
From early morn to approaching night
Silently urging the fish to bite.

From Monday to Friday the foundry's his life.
He works all day then it's home to the wife.
And when things get tough and the tension starts showing.
It's the thought of the weekend that keeps him going.

Come Saturday morning he's up before dawn
Not a thought in his head for mowing the lawn.
A quick kiss for the wife and he's off on his bike.
His thoughts on roach, perch or even a pike.

Neighbours smile and shake their
heads for they don't understand,
That strange breed of man,
That fanatic, the fisherman.
  Robert Broughton

A Symbol Of Peace

I look out into the inky night
And see a million candles burning bright
Behind every single candle is a child's smiling face
A child of every colour, nationality and race
The white candle burning is a symbol of peace, hope and love
The child too is a symbol of all the beauty from above

Look into the children's eyes, see their candles of peace
  burning bright
Speak to every one of those children; they'll tell you what's
  wrong and what's right
They'll tell you that animals shouldn't be killed anymore
They'll tell you that countries needn't be torn apart by war

They'll tell you it's time to put an end to agony and pain
They'll tell you not to think what you'll lose but what you
  stand to gain
So while ever there are children wrongs can always be turned
  to rights
And while ever there are children there'll always be candle lights.
  G. M. Percival

My Dad

It takes a noble mind, to keep a promise that is small
trifling bonds are soonest forgotten of them all.
Yet it is these little promises by sudden impulse made
often are the nicest that's been made.
That means a lot to someone happier for having heard
someone's waiting patiently who took you at your word.
  M. E. Worsley

The Hotel Called Heaven

There's a hotel called Heaven - I go to sometimes,
where the Angels - they serve me with kisses and rhymes.
They play me sweet music and show me fine books, and
paint me dream pictures, where everything looks -
like:

The Garden of Eden, with trees all around,
where grasses and flowers, and warm sunny showers,
make me lose track of hours,

And I can't understand how I ever got frightened or tired or sad,
for there's God in my heart, and it makes me feel glad.

Not the God of your Sundays,
nor morals, nor rules,
but the God of Life Loving Life,
God of lovers and fools,
God of Dreamers and Angels - of fields and of hope.

So on pillows innocence and bed sheets of bliss,
pick me some daisies, and give me a kiss.

For with all of my heart
I would never despair, if a room - Here - in heaven
with You, I could share.
  Jim Fleming

Snowdrops In The Garden

From winter's gloom and long dark days,
Snowdrops bloom and quietly raise
Gentle heads to herald in
All the beauties of the spring.

Earth, not ready to reveal
The golden glow of daffodil.
Hyacinths still so tightly curl
Await the moment to unfurl.

While bluebells sleep in woodland bowers,
And primrose dreams of sunlit hours.
The simple snowdrop is first to show
Its fragile bloom, though chill winds blow.

A promise that spring will surely come,
And nature's dress will yet become
A lovely robe for our delight;
From tender green and pristine white
To gold and primrose, azure blue
The world adorned in springtime hue.

Hilda Doble

Disproving Hypotheses?

Darwin had a theory;
There is no God!
Jesus would never rule,
With or without a rod.

Big bang and evolution,
Is what we believe;
It's all the truth,
We wouldn't deceive.

God was ignored,
By religions he founded.
Prophets were scarce
And apostles were grounded.

There were miracles and healings,
But they would soon disprove it.
We weren't concerned with that we saw,
But with the hope that we could remove it.

Evil finally got out of control,
But life after death would save the soul.
How about love and justice,
For eternal 'What' would we enroll?

Roland Hiller

Littered Lives

The swamped trenches are littered with bodies - desolate,
Trapped by the imposing stench of war,
Where the whistle is human law.

A bed among rotting corpses or a bath among fresh blood.

The gutted forms of courageous men, lifeless ever-more,
Have left behind their last known thought,
Like a white flag to the ditch side - caught.

A choice that for you is made and with it a place on the ground.

The much declared dignity and glory have sunk into the dirt.
In its place has risen the crashing sound of hell,
And the devils that are stopping us tell.

The fiendish hounds that bite our skin,
soon pierce our lives as well.

The staggering mortals, limbless and dying, tumble into the pit
-
They'd only ventured a head in distance,
But still that destroys their existence.

In a wrinkle of land - the Trench of Despair -
We are losing our lives for this Futile Affair.

Laura Hill

The Tramp

An elderly man sits in the Edinburgh streets,
Begging for money off the people he meets.
He is rudely ignored as people hurry on by,
Too ashamed to stop, to look him in the eye.

Through the dirt you can see, a saddened old man,
That is trying to survive just the best that he can.
His clothes are all torn, a blanket covers his legs,
He is homeless and hungry, to exist he just begs.

Through his hair and his beard, hides two weary blue eyes,
That shows hardship and loss as he fights to survive.
Maybe a man of importance that's ended up on the train,
Of societies cruelty, bitterness and pain.

You can take away his home, his money, the lot,
But leave his self respect, it's all that he's got.
So don't stop and judge him, a smile costs nothing from you,
One day the tramp that you see, could end up being you!

Samantha J. Kehoe

The Sea Of Humankind

People walking by, moving swiftly through each time,
In life, in space, with life's full gentle grace,
Sometimes full of smile, when they come face to face.
Yet through this same sea of life, when they do pass,
The gentle smile and love does seem to fade,
When they see, to their sadness and disgrace,
That same sweet face does not fit their race.

What matters if she is old? What matters if he is young?
Or indeed she is light and he is dark?
One is small and the other large?
When love, or fear, or desires seep through the veins,
The pain, the feelings alas, aren't they all the same?
Lets walk on, lets walk by, through this endless time,
when the journey we must make is but one,
Take each other by the hand, and ask not,
Who is what and which of race?

Anindita Lipner

Comparing Experiences - Love And Analysis

I had lain in the stone tomb
More than four days when his voice woke me,
When his tender touch melted my frozen blood ties.
Fronds of joy uncurled in the deep centre
And the quickening began.
Then the fish-cold skin cells flamed;
Life-affirming fingers uncramped the tense knots.
Muscles, toneless as dead snakes
Rippled in ecstasy. The throat bubbled in bird-song benediction
And the tiger of love was born.
Oh, Lazarus, this was not a rising of the dead only,
This was a second birth.

H. D. C. Pitts

Love's Thread

At last, at last love's thread has caught
And now it's landed where it ought
And tangled round some ladies old
Who try to do as they are told.
On looking up they saw a man
Who paused and chatted for a span.
Each one, they said: "A normal man".
And as each one his face did scan
He circled round her like a dove,
A dove descended from above.
Their faces now alight with joy
He kissed them like a friendly boy.
Oh what a difference love can make,
His kindness now is theirs to take
For sowing seeds which soon will root
And blossom into harvest shoots.
He'll be repaid a thousand fold
For helping to blot out the cold.

Mary Carr

Contentment

I met an old gentleman in the street,
It's true he was rather slow on his feet,
I thought life must surely be passing him by,
That was until I looked in his eye.

A sparkle of humour and yet so content,
To count his blessings to the fullest extent.
Every line on his face showed experience of life,
The joys, the happiness and even the strife.

He'd not had it easy of that I'm sure,
Yet each new day was another to store,
With his memories of life and there will be many,
Each one worth far more than a penny.

Perhaps we should all take a leaf from his book,
And at ourselves take a real careful look,
If he could sparkle with nothing to spare,
So happy and peaceful without even a care.

Then what are we doing always striving for more,
Oh where are we going, what's it all for?
We should all be happy with what we've got,
For peace and contentment can mean such a lot.

Irene J. Marriner

Peace At Last

Do I want to die?
just as the mad man before he leaps,
maybe not mad the most sane of us all,
he has got it right, unlike the rest.

To let him jump would be easier much quicker,
and as they pass, that's what they say.
But others who try to get him down off that bridge,
make it worse, much worse.

People talk but he can't hear what they say when they shout,
only want someone to tell him, they'll make it O.K,
And hold him, till it doesn't hurt when they shout anymore.

They just watch him fall, some laugh some cry,
but he knows as his body is being propelled
through the air and gravity is calling him to the
concrete coffin that lays below,
that it won't hurt when they shout anymore.

Liz Fisher

The Missing Millions

Fifty years ago the Nazis did invade,
This made the Jews very afraid.
Fear for us is in the head,
But fear for them meant millions dead.
The Nazis were horrible and cruel,
But they were living under Hitler's rule.
The Nazis aimed at the Jewish race,
One by one the Jews were defaced.
They were whipped,
They were stripped and the bodies left to burn,
But Hitler's stomach didn't even churn.
To write about fear for me is hard
I fear for the Jews as their hearts and lives are eternally
scarred.

Fiona Barbour

Learner Driver

The "L's" in the front and "L's" in the back;
The seat belt is on, and mirrors aglow;
So now I'm all fixed and ready to go;
I'm driving real well, there is nothing to fear
"Oh" my goodness, I'm in the wrong gear.

The driving instructor showed me the way
To handle a car and drive without fail;
He said I must do my very best
So that I might pass my driving test.

Sheila McKenna

The Magic Of Darkness

Grey clouds drifting over the dark shapes of the moors
A magical silence draped over misty landscapes
The meaningful cry of an eagle, its eyes darting back and forth
The grey-white moon, a break in the misty sky
Fog hanging low over villages and towns
Wind whistling through the bare branches of dark trees
A black cat, silently skulking through dark streets
The black shapes of houses, looming up on either side of narrow
Winding roads
The eerie hooting of an owl, its wings fluttering hesitantly
A creaking, disturbing sound from the graveyard
Maybe a tree settling, or the nearby church, or maybe....

Michelle Duffy

Trees In The Wind

I watch you growing: you're the image of me:
enduring the pain, of adversity:
Two trees in the wind: that's just how we are:
accepting our grief - as a battle scar:

All things are passing, so cling to this fact:
then as the wind threatens, you'll swiftly react,
by bending your boughs, whilst the force rages on
withstanding the strain, 'til the turmoil has gone:

There's always a reason! So don't feel bereft!
for God's rooting for you, on your right, and your left:
and there's me, just behind you, with the same kind intent:
uplifting and caring, whilst your branches are bent:

I'll stand with you gladly, in the wind and the rain:
so believe in God's plan, which to me is quite plain;
you'll sway and will bend, through the dark vale I've known;
'til you hear his soft whisper: "How well you have grown."

Patricia Mary Gross

The Girl

There is a girl who hurts inside,
She hides the pain because of her pride.
She loves you even though,
Time to time she feels like letting go.

She's so insecure when there's no one there,
Who loves her? What do they care?
Then when she's with you,
It seems alright,
there is no time to fuss or fight.
She knows it hurts what she does and says,
But believe me, she'll try and change her ways.

She is a poet, that poet is me,
Touch me, love me, and set me free.

Victoria Kean

Silent Thoughts

Our eyes meet every day,
Our bodies talk to one another,
Our books pass each other,
These silent sounds only we can hear individually.

I'm waiting for the day,
When all this will go away,
When we will speak to one another,
Before going our separate way.

I look forward to seeing you everyday,
Looking you straight in the eye as you pass me by,
And telling you how I feel,
I know you can hear me,
You know who you are so...

Don't fear those around us,
Don't fear what you feel,
Break your silent thoughts,
Say 'you come here' and,
Let our thoughts become actions for real.

Omer Ahmad

An Angel Came Down

An angel came down from heaven last week
And gently kissed her on the cheek
He lifted her away from pain
And stopped that poor tired old brain
He gently closed her eyes
And lifted her to paradise

She sits among the other saints
Gone are all the old complaints
She has gone to join the heavenly crew
Away from the likes of me and you
We miss her lots, of course we do
But she is watching me and you

So when you are feeling lost and low
Remember, there is a place to go
Remember mum, and all the fun
We as a family used to know
Time will heal the hurt
So they all keep saying
But, when she died she took a part
Of that old thing we call a heart.

Jenny Campling

Grandma's Poem

Grandparents we are proud to be,
Our darling boys, are, a joy to see,
Their presence, makes life worthwhile,
It lifts our hearts, to see their smile,
Their name for us, is super grans,
We're often around-lending a helping hand.
Granddad's thinning hair, goes through combing paces,
This routine, brings smiles, to their young faces,
They are well behaved boys, we must agree.
Daniel, Martyn, Linford-a total of three,
Who keep us young, and as fit as can be,
Stay good, and keep well boys.
For granddad and me!!

Eva Pickard

Gone Days Remember

What can each morning be, but Earth's new child?
And I, too, walk from darkness and from sleep,
young as this moment poured along the wild.
But years which I had thought were buried deep

Lift from the gravels. At my every stride,
gone days remember all the ways I came,
deep-housed in moments that had never died,
come from a year that, now, I cannot name.

The old slow skills of seasons change the scene;
but, like a camera, I hold time from flow,
walking once more where many years have been,
feeling the burn of their long afterglow.

William Granville Gay

Brand New Day

On my saddest day when hope ran out and life became unreal
I wandered through the lonely woods with a heavy heart to heal

I rested neath the willow and that was weeping too, perhaps it knew
how sad I was and what it had to do.

The fluffy catkin I recall laid softly on my hair
I sat there for a long long time in tears and silent prayer.
'Twas then my eyes felt heavy
and blissful sleep took o'er
I was at peace within myself and sorrow was no more

Was it the gentle breeze or something from afar that woke me up
in time to see the lovely shooting star
I looked up to the heaven's through the willows lovely gown
a myriad stars were shining ahead of a brand new dawn.

My heart floated up to heaven and slid down the milky way
I knew that I had made it at the start of a
  Brand New Day
Mary C. Willey

To Be The Best

Mask can finally crumble
Tears freely flow
Observation unlikely, besides tomorrow all evidence gone
Forgetting briefly her hand slides across her bed
Only the emptiness and the hollow warmth of a furry friend

A woman of independent means was her name
Conditioned masculine traits had ensured success
Loneliness? Well the constant bobby prize
Cry? She'd sooner fight
Bravado so much easier at breakfast time

Nobody there to refute her bluff
She sits up in bed and embraces her knees
Still the right balance has not been struck
Self-denial the winner again
Taken to extremes she cuts her nose to spite her face

Soldier on wriggle through
If the battle arose I know she'd fight
She's made of superhuman stuff (you know)
Funny how it all breaks down
When the lights are switched off...

Liz Shakespeare

Bitter And Sweet

We smiled we talked, we at that time connected.
We discovered a common ground, we acknowledged a
possible beginning of a shared life together.

I could not see beyond your smile height, and solid physique.
The thought of one day no longer responding to your touch,
was at that time unthinkable.

Just that one thought I expressed raised within you the
darkest deepest anger as never seen, and never felt before.
The physical blow received rocked, awakened me to what was
lying beneath your physical structure.

You showered onto me it seemed the anger and pain of years,
that I did not cause, yet still you felt at the moment to share
your pain by allowing me to feel your pain, not acknowledging
I did not ask for it.

As time moved on I was able to see where, and when your
field of pain began.
And as time moved on I was able to see I could not allow
myself to be your vent.

Having felt your pain and with memories of the love I had for
you, I leave you with these thoughts.

S. Edwards

Untitled

I am neither light nor darkness, creator nor destroyer,
Demon nor angel, beginning nor ending.
I am the link.
The forgotten abyss of infinite ideas
I am nature's blind truth.
I cry for rebirth as I watch the slow winding path of death
Evolve, revolve,
I am change
I am one,
I am none.
I am the divine knowledge of earth's splendour
I am the secret language of the Gods.
I am eternal
I am absolute
I look into the heart of man
I perceive his deepest fears, his wondrous dreams,
  Your enlightenment.
I hear the distant utterance of thy holy name,
  Your name (Man's word).
My power will enhance you — choose thy path.
Samantha L. Coldwell

I Am A Volcano

My restful body lies asleep-
I'm mud and magma in a heap.
I'm locked inside with an urge to be free,
When there's a ripple on the surface of the sea.

My top blows off, I start to rise
And in the air my ash hair flies.
My inner self erupts and covers the trees
And soon the magma reaches my knees.

More and more magma overflows,
Where it will stop, no one knows.
I let out a yawn, stretch my arms way up high,
As more magma flies in to the sky.

Now I'm finished, I'm out of stock
I've emptied myself of all this rock.
So slowly but slowly, down I lie,
And there I am left to peacefully die.

Corinne Nugent

The Flight

The Boeing soared above the clouds.
The angels surrounded it in their crowds.
"My God," said the pilot with serious face.
"Yes, my boy?" answered God, "This isn't your place.
You're flying too high, you should be lower.
You're not much of a pilot, you should drive a mower."

"You cheeky old God," the pilot replied.
"I'll send you to hell and you'll soon be fried,"
Answered God with a shrug and a twitch of the shoulders.
The Boeing flew on; the clouds looked like boulders.
God was angry and said, "I'll shoot you down.
I'll teach you a lesson, you stupid young clown."

Too late the pilot changed his mind.
He put the plane lower, the airport to find.
God sent down a bolt; the plane went reeling.
The passengers had a sinking feeling.
"Pilot Error", they said when reports came out.
"God's Will," said the insurers and had the last shout.

Denys Kendall

Untitled

I dreamed last night that I was running
through a field of hay.
It was in the early morning, when the
sun was heralding the day.
A blackbird singing to his mate.
Sat on a nearby tree
and little bobtail rabbits peered cautiously at me
before racing to their burrows to answer mothers call.
I saw lizards lying in the sun upon the mossy wall
and meadow sweet and roses wild scented the morning air
I was young and carefree, and all the world was fair
Then I awoke it was a dream, and yet it lingers on.
And even in my darkest hour I hear that blackbirds song.
It gives me hope that one day. my dream will just come true.
And I'll be running through a field
of hay - running just as I used to do.

Grace Bradley

Study In Pink (4): End Of A Legend

Lady Penelope, twenty years later,
Dumped by Jeff Tracy for being a lush,
Sat swilling champagne in the back of her Roller,
Slumped on the frayed, threadbare, faded pink plush.
The ancient Rolls Royce, with its two tail-lights blinking,
Gears grinding, its engine not purring but pinking,
Slowed and then stopped with a crunch and a creak,
A rattle, a clatter, an ominous squeak.
"Drive on, Parker." She slurred, her voice genteel but jaded.
And Parker replied, unperturbed undismayed,
As he shifted the Rolls into 'self-salvage' mode,
"FAB, Milady. Perhaps, one for the road?"

P. J. Kimber

Why - One So Young

He was so strong and tough,
Yet so loving and gentle too,
Young and so happy, never rough,
Helpful to all, thoughtful in all he would do.

He worked so long and hard, all day through,
In towns and villages, the whole country wide,
Roads and lanes foot paths too,
He made them all, for folks to ride.

Always fit, never ill, "I'm alright" he would say,
Then, came the day of his life long joy,
His son was born, it was a long long day,
So happy he as, so proud of that little boy.

The years rolled by, his son was his life,
The weather and work, took its toll,
Pain and torment caused so much strife,
Then the Lord thought of him, peace came to his soul.

Our son, so proud we were, gone?
So young he was, so gentle and kind,
Left behind his only son,
But peace and comfort, now he will find.

Raymond Westwood

Hope

Where the sun always shines and
There is no night, where the birds
Sing in tune with all their might
Where animals roam with a new burst of life
Where green grass and flowers
Adorn with delight, the pastures
And enclosures to be seen in sight
Where the new heaven and the new
Earth waits for those who belong
And through Jesus will enter a
New life forever.

N. Bell

Our World

We are not what we are in this world,
But it is what we are in our world,
Our world in which we love, are loved, can love.

It is our world which matters, our world who cares,
Matters not if we're wealthy, cares not if we're great,
But loves us for nothing, just for being ourselves.

So we must live in the world of our family
In the world of our friends, because
This is the world which really matters, the world which really cares.

Stephanie Jane Youngman

Alone At Last

In vivid dreams I was alone with you at last
We found ourselves in opulent place
With golden doors
Green marble floors
When the warm air unfurled itself around you
The ground trembled with delight
To feel your small feet
So intimate
Even birds flying by
Dipped their wings to salute you

People glimpsing you envied me
The privilege of my place at your side
When we were in loving stance
I remember you said
My touch was as light
As a butterfly's wings
When I kissed your long lashed eyes
You called me your dear one
Amid contented sighs

Patricia Maione

'Locked Inside My Heart'

'My heart is like an opera,
Singing out for your love,
Your love is like a prisoner,
Locked inside my heart.
It can't escape as I've thrown away the key,
Your love will be there for always and forever
And till the end of eternity.
Your love is like a golden shield,
Protecting me through my loneliness and pain,
Your love is warm yet soft,
Like the sun that shines upon my face.'

Tina Newbrook

Journeys

Sitting in trains, sitting in trains -
Crowded with people with somewhere to go -
People with faces, expressionless faces -
Listlessly swaying; yet with somewhere to go.
Is it the rhythm which cancels out laughter?
The hypnotic passing of overhead cables?
Rows of back gardens, a factory or two?
Trees endlessly dripping, fields sodden with rain?
Still the mute swaying of unseeing people -
Presumably people with somewhere to go -
Mindless and numbed, with an air of futility,
Can it be true that they've somewhere to go?
Change in the tempo, a gradual slowing,
The train approaches the point of arrival.
And, suddenly, the inertia changes to
An awareness of life, a readiness for departure.
These indeed are people with somewhere to go.

Joan Plewman

Coloured

A lonely Negro stablebuck,
his home a wooden shed.
His room well swept and tidy,
with just straw for a bed.

In his eyes there was a glitter,
an intensity just as gold.
His spectacles sparkled in the sun,
like a secret still untold.

Rubber boots, pairs of shoes, alarm clock
all had their place.
No mirror for to gaze upon,
that ageing wrinkled face.

His deep set eyes with stony stare,
his dry and tightened lips.
His bent and twisted body,
arose from over the hips.

By his side he kept a gun,
and the pain was drawing in.
Just a proud defenceless Negro,
the only difference being his skin.

Emma Toon

Do

Do you still look for me,
As I still look for you.
Do I still come into your thoughts,
As often as you do.
Do you turn every corner
To find me standing there;
Do you look into shop windows
And be totally unaware.
Do you believe you'll be there
To stay and always care.
Do you wish you could predict the future
And know what's in store there.

Deborah Robinson

Man's Destiny?

The search is on to explore "Space"
A second home for the human race?
So we can leave the mess we've made
Of air and sea and everglade.

Our abuse of this fair earth and land
Gives us no right to e'er expand
Our destructive ways to another world
Or into eternity we'll all be hurled.

So, if at last, Man gets to set
Its feet upon a new planet
Let's hope a lesson loud and clear
Will have been learned on this planet here

Or a different "BANG" will then be heard
But who will hear? None on this world!
Who'll witness it? Who will tell why
We've ruined our world and so must die.

Is this a cycle of our creation
Bird and beast and civilization
To start again in embryo
As life began aeons ago?

Madge Tompkins

Dear Granddad

My husband is a pipe smoker, as is his Father too,
His Grandfather smoked and looked quite lost without the
    pipe he knew.
I think a man who sits so easily, so comfortable with life..
...always smokes, he's a homely man, so satisfied, no strife.

He looked so calm did Granddad, a gaze so lost in thought,
His natural move to fill from pouch, a favourite tobacco sought.
He took his time to light his pipe, Vestas quite a few,
And when we thought of Grandfather, this sweet aroma grew.

A real man with a well-smoked pipe, a white moustache so stained,
His gnarled old hands that grew the veg' held pipe firmly,
    so soil ingrained.
Now Father's taken over, he's the old man that we meet,
But my Husband's not far behind him in smoking this Briar so sweet.

Lucy-May Bloxham

Praying Mantis

The motion-less predator of all,
The common praying mantis no less,
Awaits unsuspecting prey to call
Which results in ready meals I guess.
The mantis "sunbathes" through the day,
Holding its forelegs, a straightened pair
In a well-extended kind of way,
That shows the attitude of prayer,
Which bears out the name of all to share
The carnivorous praying mantis.

John Jarrett-Kerr

Summer Days

Summer days and the sun is shining
Children, running, laughing and tree climbing
The sound of laughter fills the air
Throughout the land there's not a care
Fresh mown grass and washing drying
In the distance a baby crying
Flowers swaying in the breeze
The pollens high I hear a sneeze
Summer evening and the sun's slowly dipping
Birds are singing and children and skipping
The smell of smoke from barbecues glowing
As sausages on the grill are going
Summer nights the temperature's dropping
The hustle and bustle is slowly stopping
People are heading for their bed
All tired and sore and lobster red.

Sylvia Fawcett

187

Being Homeless

No one to love me, no one to care, I watch the people who just
stop and stare.
I've got no belongings, no family or friends, no money or
shelter, only clothes that I rend.
Hungry and cold, left out in the rain, no hospital treatment - I
suffer in pain,
An old shop doorway is home for tonight, tomorrow-uncer-
tain, alone in my plight.

No job to go to, only money I find, on the floor with the rubbish,
I'm sure they don't mind.
Rushing to work with their money and car, if only they'd give
me even one chocolate bar.
My hair is dirty and so are my clothes, I'm starving and lonely,
"How far have I roamed?"
"The world is your oyster," the rich people say, "Get out and
work," is another old phrase.

If only they tried it- living like this, they'd soon miss their
lives, which were pleasant and blissful.
But I have no belongings- no car or t.v., what I wouldn't give,
just to drink some warm tea.
One kind person who stopped and smiled, offered their hand
and drove me some miles.
They gave me a drink, some food and a bed, some clothes and
a job, "Good Luck" they said.

I'm now one of you and so happy, you see, I look back at
someone who used to be me.
Now when I look at someone alone, with no luck, I offer my
hand and pick them back up.
It doesn't take much time or effort from you, it would mean
such a lot, and you'd feel happy, too.
That you'd given someone homeless a much needed chance,
and not just walked past, but made a difference at last.

Carol Spurway

A Child's Mind

An innocent mind of wonder, complete with hopes and dreams.
Laughter and amazement, all is what it seems.
Questions beyond answer, belief in all that's said.
Magic overflowing within a child's head.
His future lies before him, he wishes his life away,
with neither worries nor problems,
in his miniature world of play.
Will he be disillusioned with everything he'll do?
Will his dreams lose their grandeur
If he sees them coming true?
His childhood will fade away,
The sparkle turn to shade
but he'll remember always
the fantasies he made.

Lynn Kerr

Enter The Warfield

Front line dominion, richblood fleshmap daywatch confusion.
Welcome home the life-scarred patrol who
manage to trace the wobble of our domain in undemanding
petulance.
Mined, undefined and undermanned hives of buzzing metal
Undermine the terrified landscape that shifts
As if bullied by the battlelines and landmines
of our time hardened guns.
On the perimeter an iron scrapbook holds the line of
our campaign where even sleep will not surrender
The dripping ground that our shattered battalion
Occupies in defence of the realm.
Behind mental machine guns we all fall in
Weakened weekend warriors, home for tea
Then massacred by a child's firing squad.
Between the deadlock and the regimental outposts
Our shell shocked sentiments are carried off by
Stretcher bearers blinded by gas and shrapnel rent.
Camouflage, invisible uniformed - our unseen foe
Sweeps past our dug-out retreat as they cut
a swathe to victory through our hateful armistice of love

Bruce McRae

'Reflective Moments'

I stroll this path of memories
And enter a mood of reflective calm
Of days of sun, green grass and trees
And blue birds chirping with all their charm
'Twas here you taught me the art of fishing
A pastime so soothing to the soul
So tranquil and calm, the sun always glistening
And endless fields of buttercups of gold.
We'd sit there for hours awaiting a bite
But I'd never get bored, 'twas such a delight
Those happy days of my sweet childhood
Where are they now? They've gone for good
For here in the water my reflection is glistening
But next to mine there's something missing
These treasured memories are so sad
Yes, I truly miss him, my old dad
I visit you often, for I know you're hear
At our special place, I hold back a tear
I feel all around me, your presence so strong
The marble in the cemetery, in my heart is wrong

Barbara Newton

Challock Woods

Walking through the calm woods.
Leaves crackling twigs snapping.
The birds singing in the trees.
What a cool lovely breeze.

The sun looks like a buttercup in the air.
Beaming down upon my hair.
Ants gathering things on the ground
Ants' nests are all around.

I see the buds upon the trees.
In the summer they will be leaves
Bushes full of birds nests.
Birds sitting on their eggs.

The ground is full of pretty flowers,
They will be blooming for many hours.
Sculptures of snakes and bumble bees.
Almost hidden amongst the trees.

Moaning because my legs are aching.
My back feels as if it's breaking!
I leave the woods behind today.
And come again some other day.

Ami Longden

A Black Woman's Perception Of Life

My life is beauty, beauty is my life,
as a black woman, content with my life.
Living as best I can in a world of poverty and affliction,
at peace with myself and nature, although roasting in the heat
of discrimination.

Bated by the enemies who spit in my face,
taunt me, tease me, yet dignity shields me.
I won't be a victim, no, I won't turn back,
two feet on the ground, expression so cold, trying hard to
fight against attack.

I find it hard being equally treated,
shopping for clothes a constant pain.
Greeted by cold stares, my wealth being judged,
trying to get past the harsh, heavy, rain.

Memories are what keep me living,
listening to grandmothers reminiscence of the past.
Her time of ownership, under the hand of a notorious master,
who's resentment of my ancestors came first, not last.

I sit all alone eyes open wide, look up and see my face in the clouds.
Wherever I turn I'm reminded of my race, There will never be
anywhere for me to hide.
The fight of my forefathers for an equal status, has been past
now on to me.
I'll fight for my children, and my children's children, to be
born in a world of equality.

Yvonne Brown

Varieties Of Knowledge

I read a German sage who thought that reason
Hangs like a cobweb on the ancient walls
Of natural stone, and in its season
Catches the light, vibrates, and falls.

Another that the seed can comprehend
The sex and colour-coding of the flower,
The ranking of erected stamens, and to what end
The stigma gapes for the pollen's golden shower.

The egg contains the giggle or the hiss,
The squirm or leap; the gene does know
The colour of the eye, and who shall miss
All adult life, and feel the cancer grow.

Yet the mountain climber cried "It was so cold
I did not know that I was hurt, and so took hold".

Harold Sykes

The Fall To Death

I am feeling hot,
I feel the heat getting to me,
I step outside and suddenly the wind blows in my face.
I feel I'm going to fall,
I over balance,
I am too weak to keep myself upright.
As I fall I feel dizzy and strange.
Suddenly I feel the ground touch my head,
I can't take it anymore,
All my life passes by me,
All the times I have fallen,
All the times I felt weird,
All the times I struck out and hurt someone
or said something which offended someone's feelings.
All the times I lost friends through anger.
Now I just want to turn back time and take back what I've said
and done to other people.
But it's too late,
I know that now,
So I just fall asleep and never wake up again.

Rachel Allsopp

A Tribute To My Father

He is the kind of man everyone seeks,
He is the kind of man you love to meet,
Someone who is full of wisdom and wit,
Who would never think to scorn or hit,
A man so full of love and charm,
That's why he could never harm,
All the time he was on earth,
He made me feel the happiest time was my birth,
Even now he's not here,
To me he's still so dear,
I try to tell him every night,
God bless and I'm alright,
For me to have known this special someone,
Was a blessing from God and all that's unknown,
I give you my love and my heart,
For as long as it takes for us to be apart,
So if you don't mind, till we meet again,
If I keep asking, when, when, when.

Gillian Eyre

Loneliness

I sit alone and stare in space,
The tears roll down upon my face,
I wonder why I've reached that stage.
Then realise it is "my age".

I see a cripple going by.
With smiling lips and sparkling eyes,
a blind man with his tapping stick,
I think I know what he would pick,

So now I count my blessings too,
and with a smile I leave the rest to you!

E. Cochran

Red

As a river runs deep, like the mind of a lover.
As a fortune is told, there shall be no other.
As destiny has settled its place in the future
As a wise man once said, 'let fate be your tutor.
As the pressure is lifted your mind is then free.
Like the waves in the ocean you will come back to me.

The kindness of the dolphin.
The strength of the tree,
The colours of the sunset,
The pain in a tear.
All of these emotions, no man should fear.

A feeling which by many is just passed on by.
Yet in the simplest of minds there are still questions, why?

The last breath of freedom is finally drawn.
When your heart beats for two you are no longer alone.

Jennifer Teresa Knight

Jesus Took Me By The Hand

Once I was lost but now I'm found because
Jesus took me by the hand;

I heard Him say, I am the way the truth and the light
And I will take you through the harrows and care's of life;

I now have love: Trust: And faith and all
because Jesus took me by the hand;

He will guide me all my days and take me to
his promise land.

T. Taylor

'My Dad's House'

Flickering candle, trembling light,
Casting shadows through the night,
Dancing figures on the wall,
Outside? Wind bend trees so tall.

High on a hill, the old house stands,
Facing views of distant land,
A bush or two looms here and there,
Not much protection - seems unfair.

Oh strong wind, you see unending
Carrying twigs, and branches bending,
A sudden drop, then rage again,
Forcing leaves against the window pane.

But then that house was once our home,
Through raging storms, it would creak and groan,
We often think, how we miss it so,
Since we moved and wed all those years ago.

I. A. Chivers

My Baby Boy

I dedicate this to my baby boy,
so special to me, who brought me joy.
You are no longer with me, I wonder why,
but will never forget you, I'll never try.
I want you to know how much I care,
that one day I will be there.
Wishing you were born to be with me,
the wonderful life you were to be.
If only life was kind enough,
you could smile, you could laugh.
I'm sorry for the way things turned out,
so very sorry without a doubt.
I love you more than words can say,
no one will ever take that away.
If I could give you life I would,
for you to live, I wish I could.
My feelings for you are very strong.
I always wonder where I went wrong.
The time is here for you to know,
I will never leave you, I'll never go.

Emma Jane Fox

Alone

The place where I go when I've time to spare,
To sort things out, the things I don't like to share.
End of the garden to the great oak tree,
High up in its branches, there's no one there but me.
Perched upon my thinking seat,
The view extends for miles,
Children playing in the street,
With happy laughs and smiles.

But I'm all alone, no joy here for me,
Thoughts trapped in my mind, all longing to be free.
Problems in the world that I would give my life to solve,
Personal little things where I'm the only one involved.

It's time for me to go inside,
And leave my problems there,
Though worldly problems always ride,
There's more than me to care.

Bryony Chaplin

Untitled

Whisper my love upon my brow,
Sweet breeze within my hair,
   Of fiery steeds to burn my eyes,
Of love, of passions burning flame,
   Like silken threads upon the morning rise.
To fall, caress, low upon the wake.

For your breath, softly,
Is like the sweetest hush,
   An open touch upon my naked skin,
A gentle whisper of dim desire,
   Like a dream, half waking sin,
Embers beneath its resting fire.

I. A. Scott

Italy (I'll Truly Always Love You)

It was the summer when we met
I wasn't looking for love
but you just appeared...
I knew instantly that I wanted
to know you more.

Your smile captivated me
as you boarded the bus...
the sun shone brighter than ever
as you showed me the
radiant blue sea and I knew,
I knew that I had fallen in love (with Italy)

The months went by as we
shared good times...
the days I wished would never end
The nights just lasted forever...

Now I've said "goodbye" to Italy
the reality gone but the memories
are still very much alive.

Maybe one day I shall return to Italy
or maybe Italy will return to me...

Ally McCrae

Haunted Nights

Black cloaks of night smother white sheets of day
Vampire moon frowning evil rays
Darkness enters with misery, clocks have struck the twelve
Howling of the beast, blood frothing at the mouth
The scent of pure death that lingers all around
Listen to the sound of the screaming hearts that pound
From the zombies that appear in the blood ridden grounds
While human bones lay sleeping night times slowly
creeping away.
Blossom like a flower unfolded like a letter
Night time has turned into day.

Renee Dionne Busuttil

Picnic On Johnny's Hump

I used to have a little Dog,
Oscar was his name.
He always knew what time it was
When home from school I came.
I'd take him for a little walk,
To a place called "Johnny's Hump"
It wasn't an exciting place, just a grassy lump.
We'd take a picnic for our tea.
There'd be sandwiches, a boiled egg in its shell,
And if we were really lucky we'd have some cake as well.
I'd nibble at the sandwiches,
And give Oscar all the crumbs.
Then I'd roll the egg down the hill
And shout, "Oscar here it comes".
Oh how we had such lovely times,
It's very plain to see.
when picnicking on Johnny's Hump.
My little dog Oscar and me.

Julie Fisher

A Poem For Jasmine

I am writing on your drawing
   Your circular labyrinth of
childhood spokes
I am writing on your circular drawing
   to recapture again
the joy that filled my heart
As I beheld your angelic face
As I held your tiny hands in mine
   and with the yellow coloured crayon helped
you draw your circular spokes.
I am writing on your circular drawing
   to again dwell in nostalgia
   to imagine I hear you call, mum, mum, mum......
I am writing on your circular drawing
   to feel again warmth, contentment
   and to worry if these circular lines
   may tomorrow become legible
   numerals or alphabets.

Christie Belle

Concluded Weather

November - is grey, quiet and death like
natures clock seems to tick and not tock
everything is slowing, no sun is glowing
mother earth is tired, weary and wanting,

To rest, to sleep in cold December
but Christmas is coming, so remember
the holly, the ivy, red berries, white snow
it's only fooling us, you should know.

David Geddes

The Bundle Bag

'Tis Bundle Time - you can tell that!
For a skitterly skatterly little cat.
A kitten who can bundle back
This dreaded bundle bag attack.
Here it comes! Get the bundle bag!
Sideways skip; somersault to upside down;
Grasp, kick, bite and claw!
The bundle bag will return for more!
Wrestle, grapple, wriggle, jump,
This bundle bag is one big lump,
To tousle, grip and beat with glee.
Why is this bundle bag with me?
I am too busy to find that out,
Panting, flailing, turning - clout!
Phew! That's enough! I'm on my way,
I'll finish this another day.
Now as I quickly tiredly flag
I crawl inside my bundle bag.
There I curl up dreaming fast asleep -
Of bundle bags, that upon me creep!

D. R. Sharpe

The Great Divide

Turn on your T.V.,
The news is seldom good.
Do you ever listen,
Well, I say you should!

Sickness, disease, death...
An endless list of hurt.
The world's so full of pain,
I wish I could break the chain.

Now I flip the coin,
You see the other side,
Apathy and affluence I endure everyday.

People's petty problems
I have to grin and bare,
Does it really matter?
Should I have to care?

So now you can see, two worlds within one world,
But how can this be? When one side is rich and the other is poor!
Where is the wise man who can open the door
And break down the barriers that I so abhor!

Richard Hughes

My Stick And Trolley Villanelle

I find my spirits are kept quite jolly
After three strokes and disability
If I can travel far and wide with stick and trolley.

I'm carried on and off the planes, that's easy
And then if foreign climes will let me be
I find my spirits are kept quite jolly

I've been to Asia, Australia, and some of the EC
People are kind and helpful...mostly
If I can travel far and wide with stick and trolley

You might have an attitude problem when you look at me
Judging by what you see but usually
I find my spirits are kept quite jolly.

I've a high IQ, can articulate and see
You might ask yourself - how can this be?
If I can travel far and wide with stick and trolley

Don't judge with immediacy
I was struck down at forty three
I find my spirits are kept quite jolly
If I can travel far and wide with stick and trolley.

Susan Wilson

The Mermaid

I know a mermaid that lives in the sea, she used to walk on land.
She dances with the fishes, she used to hold my hand,
She swims with the dolphins, to keep bad at bay,
I've spoken to the mermaid, the things we used to say.

In a dream where emotions run wild and free,
I've married the mermaid in the deep blue sea,
Her flame red hair cascades in a crescendo of curls,
Her teeth as white as the mother of pearls.

A choir of angel fish sang to the songs of our hearts,
In a sea of silence that keeps us apart,
As the timeless sands slip away,
Only to be together, on our wedding day.

It was her day, as it was my night,
We danced away, the stars so bright,
Together in a time that holds no reason,
In a world that has no season

Now that I have to return to the shore,
And out of my slumber to greet the dawn,
Not a moment goes by, nor a tear shed,
That I will be with you, forever, in our sea bed.

Howard Thomas

To-day

To-day the sun is in the sky so bright,
There is no rain or cloud, but sun and light.
'Tis good to see the animals so free
The birds and all on earth are full of glee.

I walked the prom at crack of dawn so fair,
The wind it gently blew right through my hair.
"'Tis good to me alive and well" I said,
While forward on and on and on I sped.

The tide is out, the waves are calm, the sand
Is fine and loose and clear without a brand.
The cars are just about to drive away
Into the country-side, to spend the day.

With love, the sun the sea the earth the tide
All nature full of life in God abide.
The flowers full of bloom and sap and green
In gardens mown, the loveliest you've seen.

To-day is but a minute from the rest of time,
So why not live, and love, and play, and chime?
For death will come in just a while, and then
Our heaven forever we'll enjoy without sin

Bridie Mannion

Tipp-Ex

The atoms of tipp-ex were to be,
as they are this you will see.
Combined together they Join and split,
not worrying whether there is a hitch.
As a dotty inventor ground
Some pebbles, and also put in
some building scaffold.
Like a witch he put in a toad,
disgusting to look at but then he throwed
Scrunched up nails and left overs from tea,
what he hoped to make I cannot see.
But the last thing was the worst it really was, and now
I'll tell you that it was because.
Every other thing had been used, and at this point it was no cruise.
He put in banana flavoured ice-cream, ugh-and yuck,
"Eureka!" he shouted, "look at this muck.
It is the one that every person will use, because
Whenever something's written wrongly in ink the question brews.
'Have I written it wrong or do I really need specs?
But what they need is, Tipp-ex!'

Rekha Sandal

Joyce Knowles

Oh! I wish I was ten years old again,
To know Joyce Knowles as I knew her then.
To sit behind her desk in school,
Risk teacher's wrath by acting the fool!!

When lessons are over for the day,
And all my classmates choose to play,
I hear their shouts and derisive cries,
When I walk Joyce home and fantasise.

Escaping Red Indians attacking our wagon,
I slay twin-headed giants, and a fire-belching dragon;
For I am Sir Galahad and she's my princess;
Not really! I'm a boy, she's a girl, in a plain cotton dress.

Three score years have since passed, plus one or two,
Sweet memories are cherished of the girl I once knew,
War, death and oblivion were encountered en-route,
With a battered school photograph of a young lass so cute.

At the approach of self-pity and the depths of despair,
I rolled back the barriers with a lock of her hair,
The young girl in the photograph, in a wallet I carried,
Was the girl that I knew, and the girl that I married.

F. Ibbotson

Expression

A smile, a sigh, a release of emotion
Of pain, of joy or simple devotion
To see the light shine through the cloud
To feel the warmth of the sun enshroud

The burden of fear and worry are heavy
The price for living is a very high levy
To take it securely and handle with care
To ignore it with scorn, a serious dare

I have felt it and touched it too often I fear
My spirits have dropped so desperately near
The edge, as I've neared it, so sharp and so steep
But my Jesus was willing to give me my feet

I've returned yet again from the hurt and despair
Life's mystery surrounds which I fondle with care
I'll try once again to do but my best
Believing in truth that maybe I'm blest.

Colette Meleady

Pluck Me A Bud Of Rose

Pluck me a bud of rose, bright with a tear of dew;
Sing me a song, ever so sweet and true;
Show me a snowdrop's bell, carolling spring;
Lead where the autumn sun, rosily westering
Kindles the deep with fire. Let a lone star
Sparkle above the snow, tinsel of near and far.
Give me a tinkling stream, broidered in daffodil,
Beauty's whole treasure-store - I shall be asking still
For you to come with me into the walk of days,
Turning my young glad heart to a new deep praise.
I need my Queen. Then shall the whole array
Of loveliness, be it of night or day,
Here on the earth we walk, or in high heaven above
Be to my inmost self brightened through you, my love.

Fergus Macpherson

Touch Of An Artist's Hand

I'm lost in a picture, a beautiful sunset, a yellow red sky.
It rests upon the sea and the waves sparkle with the sunset
painted in the sky.
A touch of an artist's hand.

I see a lonely butterfly resting upon an open flower. Beautiful
wings are open and a pattern like a rainbow is painted upon its wings.
A soft touch of an artist's hand.

I see a clear waterfall pouring into a small lake. Children
playing in the heat of the day amongst the long grass swaying
to the timing of the breeze.
A beautiful touch of an artist's hand.

I see my self painted upon this earth. The whole picture speaks
a thousand words and my life is all part of it, and there is
meaning to the painting because I am there and I was created
by an artist's hand.

Kevin J. Phillips

Keepers Of Our Hearts

Who will be the keeper of our broken hearts
Who will take our pain on board
Be strong for us when they depart
And guide our lost and ravaged souls

Tell us how to bear this solemn pain
Tell us that we can survive
The sun will shine amidst our rain
And one day we may feel its warmth again

Our hearts are plundered, raped and torn apart
Our wounds are raw and weeping
Our dreams are gone now, forced apart
Our arms are empty and needing

He will be the guardian of our broken hearts
Draw from him the strength we sorely crave
He'll wipe our tortured tears and start
The healing process of another day

Gwen Dingwall

Whispering Wings

There was a whisper in the air,
a soft sound of silk.
Like stars, songs burst out,
as rested throats with passions shout.
Their bodies filled the budding branches,
tipping raindrops from their hold.
Glistening sun, reflecting rainbows,
warm air blows away the cold.
Insects reappear from nowhere,
butterflies flit in the blue.
Time has passed its merry hours,
old is teaching lessons new.
Squirrels dig beneath the compost,
blackening leaves around them strewn.
Sheep and lambs bleat in the pastures,
while long grass is neatly hewn.
"Here is spring then!" Flowers hail
and open out their petals pale.
They knew that it was there,
there was a whisper in the air.

A. Seed

My First Romance

We first met when you were Seven and I was Eight... Going
together we went hand in hand through the school gate...
From then on each and every day, it felt as though I was
floating on air... Knowing that you would always be there,
with Scarlet Ribbon in your hair. A wondrous thing in
remembering was our first embrace, when a page was torn
from time and space. From that very moment when you
touched my heart, my dreams had come true with you, one
so... Auburn and Fair, with Scarlet Ribbon in her hair... The
years were now beginning to pass, we went everywhere
together, a love that must and would... surely last... Through
the park we would roam, in Summer, and in winter till the trees...
turned bare... It was a thrill and heaven to be with you... The
girl with Scarlet Ribbon in her hair... The clouds of War were
now beginning to accumulate, my feelings alas I left too late...
Touching your hand, and you touched my heart, not realizing it
was time to part... 'Twas you I loved right from the start.

I had to go, you went away, I know not where, I lost my love
with Scarlet Ribbon in her... hair. All my life I will remember
knowing you, for now as I wander down our favourite lane...
In my solitude it seems I hear you call my name, and many a
time just now I wonder if you are there, for now it seems you
are constantly in my dreams, I see you with children on your
knee and around your chair, and smile as I see you tying
Scarlet Ribbon in their hair...

Douglas Ralph Bisset

True Love... Never Runs Smooth!

I met him on the platform of a number seven 'bus
He saved me, when someone gave me a shove
As he held me by the arm, he just radiated charm
And I knew instantly, I was in love

We both sat down together, discussed the awful weather
He was the most charismatic man I'd ever met
He wore an overcoat and a scarf around his throat
His eyes were turquoise blue and deeply set.

We reached the terminus, and alighted, both of us
He smiled, said 'Goodbye' then walked away
My heart gave a lurch when he went into the church
And I figured he had gone in there to pray.

Not a moment could be missed, I forgot my shopping list
And walked into the church to say a prayer
It was beautiful inside and I looked around with pride
But the man I followed in just wasn't there.

I read the daily lesson, maybe he was in confession
My heart was beating fast, then almost ceased
My loved one looked so grand with a candle in his hand
And I realized he was a Catholic Priest.

Olive Cason

Plea Of The Forest

Don't cut me down,
I've served you well,
My leafy arms beseech.
My roots are here amongst my kin,
The oaks, the ash, the beech.

Where will my friends the squirrels live,
When winter snow falls thick?
And where will robins build their nests
To hatch their little chicks?

My girth has thickened o'er the years,
My trunk is gnarled and old,
But I still have a purpose here
To shield the birds from cold.

My executions nearer now.
I hear the chainsaws sing.
Have pity please, don't cut me down,
I am a living thing.

Maureen Bevan Jones

"I Am What I Am!"

I have no brains or bones like you, and for decades gone
by and to come, I've been trodden on, drilled, holed, and
filled up again.
By daylight I can be "hot", Warm or cold, and in the morning
mist, while the Cuckoo calls his mate, the frog from the pond
leaps, around, but to me it makes no difference, for "I am
what I am",
Perhaps you may wonder having got this far, who are you, we
read about? but you know "I am, what I am".
So now you know the secret of life, for without her no one
would survive, the only one being left alive, would be me
and I know who I am, Mother earth of course.

A. W. Kendall

The Riverbank

What have you done, Man?
   That little silver fishes, marbled-eyed, float down the river
   in white soap shrouds, bent as tinfoil strips in toxic clouds.

Too soon the thin eggshells of bunting and warbler spill out
   their baby chicks to die,
No more sweet songs from reed beds, just a hurt cry.

What have you done, Man?
   Dead spawn wobbles with the movement of winds,
no frogs appear to jump in ecstasy from bank to bank and disappear.

What have you done, Man?
   watching a forest of skeleton trees whose arms heaven-raised
in beckoning thirst, swallowed acid rain in their soft green leaves.

Now the earth from the riverbank is rolling up like a carpet
   dirty and marred, as more putrid rain rips down the swirling river
      to stain the poor otter's graveyard.

Where the smell of decay of the spoiled riverbank is the scent
   of your ignorant labours -
What have you done, Man? What have you done?

Edna E. Smith

"A New Life"

The day I made my entrance the sun was shining bright
A beautiful September day I brought a special light
To the lives of my dad Alby and Carrie who's my mum
We hope it's the beginning of a life that's full of fun
I know they love me dearly and I will become a part
Of all their future hopes and dreams they keep within their hearts
I've come to share the dwelling - the house in which they live
And hope that in the future - my love back I will give
Sheba lives here also - a family friend is she
I hope she wags her tail with joy accepting little me
We know that friends and neighbours are happy I'm in town
Evelyn and Ted have sent a lucky silver crown
Just a little keepsake - a token of the day
That Margaret Elizabeth came in the world to stay.

Eve Cooper

Once When In The Autumn

Once, when in my new eyes, I caught the rainbow
And sucked it in whole-hungered, marrow-deep.
My blood spilled prism-rich and stained the mountain space
Which swelled and thundered in a million lights
Magnificent and brimmed.

Once, when in my autumn bed, I dreamed the taste
Of spike-tipped tans and ruthless slating greys,
Slashed feather-white with tumbled rock-foam lust;
I flung a challenge to the purpling sky
To share my dream.

Once, when in the heartbreak of a year, I climbed the mist
With eyes shroud-hung in funeral weeds of change,
The milk-wet surface lipped and drowned the tottering sun;
And on the sleep-wound hill I knew
My clay was Adam-found.

Once, when in the clawing wind, my soul streamed out
And fused its womb-kept form in cruel immensity,
My cockle-frame dissolved and flew the reel of leaf-turned force;
Alone, incorporeal, I touched the truth.
I was the world.

Peter Linden

Little Old Lady

The little old lady walking slowly up the street
A cheerful smile and greeting for everyone she'll meet.
Her bag is full of goodies, chosen with such care
Some for the old and some for the young; and of them to share.
Chocolates for the pretty girl and candies for her brother
Bananas for one neighbour and apples for another.
You would think she has no problems as she goes along life's way
But her heart is often anxious for what she sees and hears each day.
The world seems very different from the days when she was young
When children really played, and songs were really sung.
There was no television or computers or C.D's
People valued things like kindness and children tried to please.
It wasn't all "The good old days", some things were really poor
Young lives were lost through sickness and battles in the war.
But people held together, and did their very best to help
Thinking more about each other and less about themself.
So her head is full of memories, as she walks on up the street
A cheerful smile and greeting for everyone she'll meet.

Millicent Judson

To Care

It's nice to have someone you care about,
   As you go along life's way.
It's nice to have someone on whom you rely,
   And listens to what you say.

To give a smile when things look grey,
   To give a helping hand,
To show an interest in what they do,
   Can really make life seem grand.

If you send out love to friends,
   And let them know you care,
You will find it really comes back to you,
   And your problems you can share.

God gives love to everyone,
   So why not ask him and see,
He will listen to everything you say,
   And love my friends is free.

In this world there are people who care,
   And I would like to say this to you,
Think about people worse off than yourself,
   And the sun will come shining through.

Edna A. White

193

And So Beauty Rests...

Singing mournfully in choirboy tones,
the snow formed a blanket,
upon the open road.
Through the raging storm,
to the forest glades,
lies my love, my Sadie-Jane.
Deprived of his bow, cupid sighs,
"Silk hair so fine, but she'll not open her eyes."

Her face pale as snow, I reached to touch,
what solace I saw,
this pain's too much.
"My gold-tinted queen, oh, how we
planned to wed."
Never will I dry these tears I shed.
So I embraced her softly,
and wished "God bless,"
and lay a rose upon her chest.

Greg J. Simmons

"The Country Park"

The early morning is the time I love best
To get myself up and get myself dressed,
To go to the country park
five minutes from my home,
And walk with my dogs there,
And be all alone,
To enjoy the smells,
The sights and the sounds,
And gaze in awe,
At the beauty all around,
With the sheep in the meadow,
And the birds in the trees,
The sun over the Lough,
These sights, you really must see,
With a prayer in my heart,
I know I am not alone,
I know God is with me,
I am at peace - - - - -
Then I return home.

Erica Gordon

Breaking Free

Glittering eager atom of life, breaking free
From pupa-skin of soiled unlovely drape.
And realizes its innate destiny
Diversity of colour, beauty of shape.

Life gathered within, unfurls wings,
Borne upwards into freedom of buoyant air.
Fervent in ritual ecstasy to flowers clings
Plunging proboscis to suck the nectar there.

With sight and scent seeks its own kind,
Whirling, gliding in prolongation of flight.
To fill and be filled, back to back entwined.
Climax of day of butterfly, jewel-bright.

Idris Woodfield

Lament For Departed Youth

It has to be, I know. One cannot ream
The course of destiny nor halt awhile
The turning wheels of time. I've dreamed my dream
And though my heart is sad, I still can smile.
I've lived my hour, snatched from the turbulent seas
Of dread eternity. And though
The hopes of youth are gone, they somehow tease
The disillusionments of age. So
The toll of time that spells the end
Of what once was in years gone by,
Stays not the hour for those who wish to spend
Again their youth and age defy.

Bernard Wright

A Message From The Heart

Book's lay scattered around my room
very old books looking sad and worn.
New books with bright glossy covers.
Each book waiting to be read.

As I lay on my bed deep in thought.
Which book should I clasp in my hands
I was seeking a book with a message.
A passage to uplift me through the day.

As I quietly tossed on my bed.
Many thoughts came into my head.
There were red books, blue books old and dusty books
I chose an old book, worn and torn with age.

Carmen De La Torre

Snow Fall

As I look outside
The snow falls gently down.
Not a sound I will hear.
Where grey pavements once were,
Now a blanket of white.

As people walk past,
Footsteps I will see.
But just as fast as they appear
They will just disappear.
A snowball will swiftly pass the window.
And just as fast a small bundle of clothes,

Shall I venture outside and look up.
To see the magical site and snow falling onto my face
It will only take a couple of minutes,
And I will become a walking snowman.
But I am happy to just look outside.
As the light shall slowly dim.
And the snow will continue to fall.

Jordon Halstead

The End Of A Perfect Death

A perfect death brutally aside,
Expectant, turgid thought accepts its crippled due,
Then, gone is that ruddy, juvenile troubadour,
Soundly thrashed by a hollow-eyed, common place cadaver,
A wanderer to all ends that may be caught and devoured,
For its appetite abounds its shrivelled, mewling mother.

Perceive now its visage and know its vile purpose,
As it greedily grasps, a slick tailored harpy,
Goading the lost and blind towards unwanted paper baubles,
And knowing as it knows of callous, cursed necessity,
It burrows a dark and mortally hopeless expectancy.

Even now as a lank, listless child I gaze fearfully down,
And follow knowingly the bloody and damned life march,
Where furtive glances await chances where salvation may stray,
And I too stumble down as mercurial luck deserts me as a
    faithless comrade,
Whilst louder and harsher strikes the fearsome rhythm of time,
And as each beat falters, I taste a little of the last of my perfect
    death.

R. A. Moore

Ashes

From embers to ashes,
The fire in your soul has died
The desire your heart once held screams no more.
Will and life are strangers,
Hidden in the black abyss they call the truth.
Your life is not your own,
No meaning, no point.

Your brainwashed mind holds no key,
Its fortress lost by those who command its army
Suffocated by suppression,
Imprisoned by those who judged you,
Exit reality, enter madness

Francesca Riddell

The Cemetery

The sky dark and mournful,
The sun is gone from the sky,
The air left cold.
Clouds look down on the pitiful sight.
Sad thoughts linger and lost dreams die,
The murk of mist hangs in the shadow of Darkness.
Shining Crystal eyes leak,
Tears, like pools of sadness,
Drip,
And wet dark clothes.

Old stone crosses worn away by time,
Dust flies through the air,
Like fairies dancing in the wind,
knocking against them.
But no-one cares.
Life,
Like a maze of emotions,
all stops at one dead end.

Alison Gibbons

Stormbound

Behold! The night; dark and furious sight
in electric spasms flashing bright.
With angry beauty, elements fight,
and war; it's the clash of the Titans.
Cold, quick steel, oh! Frenzied kill,
Gone! All that's weak upon the hill.
Blood-like death reigns far around.
Bowed, broken, low, grasping the ground,
then drowned; to great destruction.
Shattered dreams; fearful awakenings made,
swords gleam in the sky with swift dazzling blades.
The firmament rent by a mad tirade,
on high, thundering clouds; huge giants slain.
Atmospheric insurrection.
Witness the tempest, raging overhead,
through howling winds to violence wed,
black shrouds eerily tinged vivid red.
Mourning heavens cry; enough!
Copious waters bled, on a vanquished wasteland.
Nature's resurrection.

Maria Therese Sharpe

"Written In Stone"

Lives sadly given dreams betrayed.
Promises broken, false words spoken
An ideal they died for - their souls we cry for
Two awful wars fought for what cause
A better life was the prize that was so easily denied
Too many widows have cried tears of sadness and pride.
Faces gaze out from old grey photographs
Red flowers bear witness round tall cenotaphs.
We should mourn so many young ones who never came home
Their sacred names now forever written in stone.

Peter Carr

Rain

On a rainy Autumn morning, we were waiting for a 'bus,
There weren't very many there, just the six of us,
Waiting at the bus stop, looking at the town,
Some had their brollies up, others had them down,
Each one wrapped up in their thoughts, or even felt the dread
Of the tasks that lay before them, (The one that lay ahead),
Of all the types of weather, which we are oft beset,
There's none, in this land of ours, that's worse than rain as yet,
It carries on its tapping sound, hastened by the wind,
And tries to find a little crack, it tries to get within,
It acts as though it's devilish, seems it has no bounds,
To get at you and also me, just like unleashed hounds,
Still never mind come spring, all the flowers will grow,
(Of course we'll have to wait awhile, for the rain to turn to snow),
Then we'll huddle round the fires, keeping out the cold,
Turn the heat up someone please, my bones are getting old.

S. Freeman, Sidimus The Scribe

Tears In August

It was all a long, long time ago
So long it's just a dim memory
Of warm August days, of exam fever.

Waking early, happiness smashed
By the sudden flop of an envelope behind the door.
A brown envelope, light-yet heavy with hopes
My future contained within its slim form

Later, bits of brown paper shredded on the floor
Me thinking 'I'm no good. Never will be.
It was true what those teachers said.
Butterfly, lazybones... rebel.'

But dad changed it all.
It's not the end of the world, lass', he said.
August's come round again and now dad's dead.
It's not the end of the world, I know.
But it just feels like it.

Liz Moody

My Pride And Joy

I had a little baby girl a gift from God above,
The most precious gift a mum can get, all through the gift of love
She weighed in at five pounds two, with lovely ash-blonde hair,
With great big eyes, the colour blue, she was so fresh and fair,
Deborah was her pretty name, it went with her pretty face,
She was so small and tiny but, she was full of grace.

Four years later I wanted a son to make my life complete,
To my surprise my task was done, when I saw him at my feet,
He weighed in at seven pounds eleven, big blue eyes, black curly hair,
When I saw him I thought I was in heaven,
I had been answered by a prayer,
Derek was the name I chose, he hardly slept at all,
He grew bigger by the day, he has grown so tall.

Now, that was sixteen years ago, my, how many years have flown,
Deborah is now a nice young lady, how quickly she has grown,
How I've learned to love my kids, my little girl and boy,
I just hope they love me too, they are———my pride and joy.

Frances Llewellyn

Untitled

Funny isn't it?
How we try each day to go our way.
Some thought for others - not a lot
Just enough to keep our plot in heaven.

Funny don't you think?
How all our lives are touched,
And tried, and sampled by another,
Each one trying to discover the door inside.

Funny, one must say, to discover
That others feel the same way too,
Don't you think that's true?
That they, like you, demand some justice, peace, protection.

Funny don't you think?
To seek perfection
When all around is always less so
Funny
Don't you think so?

Harriet Richards

Granddad

In loving memory of my Granddad
Who died some years ago.
A very special man to me and I told him so.
He cared for me so very well,
In times of good and bad,
He taught me how to read and write
So I am very glad.
We never used to fight at all,
We got on very well.
He really was a jolly man with happy thoughts as well.
But, what he ever thought about no-one could tell.

Elise Young

195

A Sense of Belonging

I have travelled far
but not in miles
and I have seen much
that the eye cannot perceive
I have stretched out my hands
and touched the sky
I have glimpsed the images of another world
and I have felt its happiness in my heart
but yet could not hold it for my own

I stand on a threshold
that moves at will
it is the doorway between the past and the future
and the promise of the other world
where greater horizons lie
and justice is a soul that endures forever

As my spirit, its narrow road
in a realm where few are kindred
I feel the greatest wish of mine
is a sense of belonging

C. Harrison

A Child Is Born

The contractions were coming thick and fast
As each one arrived she gave a gasp
Another started and she gripped my hand
I used a damp cloth to cool her down
She started to push and the head appeared
The excruciating pain drew a tear
I held her hand as tight as can be
Trying to draw the pain from her to me
I wanted to watch as the baby arrived
But at the time it didn't seem right
She had been through so much - it wouldn't be fair
It was a moment that both of us should share
With one last push it came into the world
And what a gift - a baby girl!
There was a sigh of relief as we heard the first cry
The three of us were about to unite
It's a wonderful feeling to create a life
Knowing there's love and care we can provide
We are parents together and we'll always ensure
She gets the best we can offer from the day she was born

D. R. J. Dallimore

The Hero

Five men spread, weapons drawn
Two men dead for the coming dawn.
Badge in the dust, law man no more
justice is coming through hells front door.

Pistols primed, eyes hawk keen
Senses alert, body whip lean
Pushed to the edge as a sword in a fire
Steps from the heat with a burning desire.

Bred as a winner, forged for the task
Reputation like thunder, speed lightning fast
There's no turning back and the glint in his eye
Shows a storm just beginning as dust starts to fly.

The shadows shrink back from the glare of each gun
As the snake strike timing flashes steel in the sun
One by one fates draw strings are tied
As man after man lays tested and tried.

Dusks cool breeze lifts follies reward
As payment to the Gods for the gift of their ward.
The distant sun sets as a haze on the plains
And the hero was gone in a whisper of reins.

Neil Gould

Time

Here, in the golden, musky after-time of love
Slow-slowly I unwind from your embrace
And raise my hazy, sleepy, dew-lashed eyes
To find them mirrored in the droplets on your face.

For a little while we'd stopped this spinning world
And stole space enough to cage relentless Time,
Then tried to pay the price with coiner's gold
But tomorrow's dreams were forfeit for our crime.

Revolving Earth, again, pays homage to the Sun
The mordant Moon and Stars stand still in space.
And Time? Uncaged and free no longer ours,
Slow-slowly Time wound back to its own place.

Thelma D. Taylor

Yesterday

Yesterday I fell in love for the first time
And my heart fell onto a cloud filled with roses
Yesterday I saw a blue sky
Delightful birds flying so high
And in my dreams I did sigh
And just last night she gave me her heart
And the sky was filled with bright stars
As we kissed our hate goodbye
Yesterday I fell in love for the first time
And in her eyes I knew she was mine
As the ocean sang her lullaby
As we waved this world goodbye
How could I ever forget yesterday
For yesterday was you and I
Yesterday till the day we die.

R. J. D. Baker

Written During An Attack

Three thirty-one in the morning

panic
nearly

My sickness from inside has arrived again

can't spell (nothing new there)
losing the ability to write
    sight has already betrayed me

if I cut off my little linger
will it stop

I am ugly to myself again
ugly in my slideshow of pain

My wrists my knuckles my finger-nails
are earthquakes of uncooperation

fight or give in
fight or give in to the tearing apart
that makes me once again
half a human

and I was sleeping feeling well

David Thorpe

Sweet This Dream

Silence, tangible substance
Balm on troubled minds
Soft and gentle quiet darkness
Takes you through labyrinths of time

You linger quietly on gentle shores
Or mountains swathed in misty cloud
Among the stars or valley green
The mind the transport from the crowd

Gentler now your thoughts as you
Are returned, to the reality's of life
To cope and not let the profanities through
Gentle silence, peace of mind, no strife

D. L. Wakeford

Memories Of Hills

The "shoe" walked over, as far as the "flush"
A stiff hilly climb, to me quiet a push!
Haversack over, one shoulder well filled!
Food to be eaten, o'erlooking those hills.

Now really upon those high mountain tops
Won't linger for long, this morning on stops!
Saw sunrise today, clearly on water
O'erlooking the lough at horse shoes corner!

Viewing black mountain, white mountain, divis.
Mount Gilbert, wolfhill, spread out to visit.
A wonderful splendour in purple and green,
Eating in lay by, o'erlooking the scene
Down through legoniel, and in through its parks,
A ramble for some, on way past saint marks.

William G. Whitcroft

Untitled

Consider this the face of love?
A mother gazing at her new born child,
Two children close entwined, snub noses, turned to watch a snail
a butterfly or other wonder of this world,
Two young ones, flushed with sighing breath and sweating
hands so tightly held that nothing
of this world around can come between;
Or can it be the face of love I see, in Christ,
eyes closed in pain with hands outstretched
as butterflies set out in some collectors drawer
with steel pins held fast,
a face begrimed with sweat and blood and tears
and yet so modelled that compassion gazes forth.
The impact, such disturbing view, consider this the face of love?

Terry Roberts

I Didn't Do It

I didn't spill Ribena, Mom, from my drinking cup,
It hasn't stained the carpet, Mom, the dog's just licked it up,
I didn't break that plate, Mom, it wasn't me at all,
It was on the table, Mom, and I just watched it fall,
I did not eat all the sweeties, Mom, it was Craig who ate the most,
I don't know who ate the rest, Mom, perhaps it was the ghost,
The mud on the towel, the mud in the sink,
It really wasn't me, Mom, who it was I just can't think,
You want to know who scratched your car? I'll help you if I can,
It certainly wasn't me, Mom, it must be the little green man,
I didn't break the window, Mom, I was over there as I recall,
Nope, it wasn't me, Mom, it must have been the ball,
Who pushed the little boy over? I didn't, I saw him trip,
There was another little boy here, but he's just flown off in
  that ship,
Why's the cat under the table, Mom, cowering shivering and pale,
I wanted to see if she had nine lives, so I swung her by the tail,
Water in the bathroom, Mom, it's more like a flood,
Sorry I can't help you, Mom, you know I'm always good.

Carol Ridgley

The Sea

The sun shone down on the vibrant blue sea,
images made on the waves cleverly.
The surf forming mouths that open and close,
as if whispering echoes to someone that knows.

The endless tide ebbs to and fro,
seemingly having nowhere to go.
Just backwards and forwards, forwards and back,
a gentle movement of taut and slack.

The sun dies and the winds start to blow
and the sea lashes in, to and fro,
smashing up stones on the cliff's edge bare,
ravishing rocks, the beach it will tear.

It soothes, it scares, and yet this deep sea
will always tempt and arouse in me
a sense of calm, of well-being inside,
those hidden depths of each new tide.

Jeanette Clinton

The Old Man

He sits on a bench within the park
with a twinkle in his eye
there's a smile on his face for the whole human race
as he watches the world go by.

His life has been really hard at times
he nearly did give in
but he found true love along the way
which gave him strength within.

His armour is bent and battered
he is bruised beyond compare
for he is a champion for good and right
and fights to make things fair.

He likes to help in many ways
you only have to ask
friendship the only price you pay
no matter what the task.

He is not an educated man
but he's lived life to the full
no matter what you think of him
his life has never been dull.

Nick Holden

The Golden Lion

The free spirit of the large cat.
The long straggly hair of the mane,
All knotted with the numerous fights for honour.
The powerful front legs,
The broad chest which hides a pounding heart.
The stealth of the body.
The roar of the voice.
The grip of the teeth.
The grooves of the claws.
All these make up the proud statue of the king of the pride.

The majestic golden lion.
So strong, powerful and protective, yet so very gentle.
Its body is like a flight of fancy when in hot pursuit of game.
It becomes a streak of lightning,
Hitting the ground every few seconds,
Throwing up clouds of dry dirt.
A quick turn and a sand storm appears.
A full stop.
The game is caught and the lion roars.
What a master! The gentle giant.

Muriel Murray

My Walk

I walk down the wooded Bridle Path
To see nature in full bloom, with its beautiful Summer dress,
Peace and tranquillity descends, I feel no urgency to dash
I hear Little rustles here and there, just to let me know my
  neighbours are there
Making nests or feeding their creations
or is it the intrusion of man they fear? And try to build their
  fences
My grandchildren scream with delight when a squirrel gives
  them a fright.
Aroma of damp wood, soil and weeds assault my senses
then tears fall, and I feel shame
I know around the world, children have died in vain and their
  country ruined

For what reason I ask myself, the question to me is hard to answer
It seems man has lost his way
violence and murder appears to be the order of the day
Yet in nature the colours I see, black and white, brown and
  black amongst the green - live in harmony
In that wooded bridle path. I pray for peace
Never to regress, just to cease
What will the violent men say to their children? Come the day
I have not left a wooded bridle path to play, but you have the
  ultimate supremacy

K. A. Burrows

Wheels Of Time

Wind driven sugar mills, hundreds of years old
Grind to a halt now, forgotten stories told
Remembered by the old folk as history turns its page
Underneath their shady spice and fruit trees bent with age.
The proud plantation houses still stand tall beneath the palms
The gentle Bajan people now sell fruit and soothing balms.

Tourism has come to their homeland island in the sun
And thirty-two old sugar mills have closed down one by one
No longer all the people in the fields on bended knee
Cutting cane with toil and sweat for all the family
The little children go to school in crisp clean uniform
Time is bringing changes as another world is born

Not for them the toil and labour of the ancient past
Life is changing rapidly, for some it comes too fast!
Don't lose your secret treasures, precious wonders of your race
Don't lose your hazy lazy days and slow Barbados pace
Rest a little longer under poinciana tree
And in my dreams I'll visit you, and you can sit with me.

   T. Perrins

The Dream I Dreamed

I dreamed a dream of a girl so fair,
With angelic features and flaxen hair,
A girl so pure, whose heart I sought;
A mythical figure, or so I thought.

In the warmth of an August night so still,
In the bustling cafe by the dwell of the hill.
I caught a glimpse of a creature rare.
With angelic features and flaxen hair.

My heart stopped beating, or so it seemed,
As I beheld the girl of the dream I'd dreamed.
Her eyes like pools of liquid blue,
Her lips as moist as the morning dew.

As I gazed in awe at the vision so real,
I cast a longing look in humble appeal.
Then my pounding heart leapt forth with joy.
For she smiled a smile, so shy and coy.

No burden now am I doomed to carry,
As I embrace the girl I am soon to marry.
I view the world without a care,
For I worship the girl with the flaxen hair.

   Malcolm Campbell

Bob

See him curled before the fire,
this fearless stalker of scraps of wool and tennis balls.
Half a foot of grey and white silk and a purr like a chainsaw
in oak.

See his first adventure in the wide world
with ever bolder forays into the Great Outdoors of the garden
all new to explore.

See him soar like a dolphin
to box the butterflies of the garden with frantic paws.

See his return from the dawn safari
presenting with awful pride his poor wee prey.

See him doze in the dog's bed, for goodness sake
throne by right of conquest to this fearsome slayer of rabbits
who still likes to give his mum a cuddle.

See him cold on the verge,
a brutal sacrifice to some callous lust for velocity
or just a wish to be two minutes early for a change.

See him now lie in his beloved garden,
unlike the hearts he captured
forever at peace.

   Duncan Kennedy

"Ode To Masada"

Within Herod's walls they stood steadfast
   now only a memory and deeds of the past
Hold all say the Zealots until we die
   then the Legions of Rome will surely know why
Stone catapults hurled at them by day and by night
   but stand fast as Jews with strength to fight
Of Ben Eleazor their staunch leader so brave
   urging them on in a battle to save-of three
Years struggle and no surrender at all
   In defying their might at the fortress wall
So come to this place and know of its fate
   and share in its glory however so late
Of Jewish resistance and history past,
   their bravery and faith forever to last
Though ye may travel in Israel's great land
   then never forget this most gallant band
Who said-we shall not age to tend our fields
   than to bear the brunt of the Roman shields
History will record the fight of the brave
   In that era of time with nothing to save.

   J. Kops

The Tempest

Stillness envelops an uneasy calm
In the atmosphere a sense of terror, alarm
Blue skies fade into a desolate grey
The sunlight's gone, for the storm it makes way

Like a tormented monster unleashed from a cage
Brings forth the tempest with incense rage
The taste of salt spray absorbs the air
As breakers dance together with incredible flair

Flashes of lightning illuminate a turbid sky
Whilst the thunder releases a harrowing cry
Age old cliffs beaten by deranged waves
Innocent victims plunge to watery graves

Gale force winds roar against lashing rain
Like a wild animal that nature refuses to tame
With anger and foam it does drool
Unpredictable, tempestuous and extremely cruel

Unexpectedly the picture is once again serene
Oblivious to the devastation that's just been
The gentle murmur of an unworried sea
The weather, a creature with dual personality

   Linda Handley-Wright

'Mother Of All'

A melee of clouds, with their black and grey faces,
Bring tears from the skies, whilst the winds do menace,
The sea, she is woken, her heart filled with rage,
At the growth of a storm, in our wondrous cage,
This Mother of all, feeds on the fear from above,
Raising wave after wave, like fists in gloves,
The rumbling crowd bares flashes of anger,
Unveiling a panoramic view to a sense of danger,
But to this mystical heroine, the forbearer of life,
It's a reoccurring battle, she's won day and night.

A squadron of gulls, sing to the tune of change,
And tranquillity plays to a percussion of waves,
She dances and breathes with the moon and the sun,
Her heart beats with life, from where we begun,
Yet, as we swim with our own admiration,
To this Mother of all, a mass of sensation,
We're blinded by arrogance, that weapon of mankind,
A perilous journey, to exploit what we find,
So go to her shores, where she whispers a story,
Of battles she fought, for love, not for glory.

   Stuart Stratton

God

When I was little, before I would
go to bed, I'd say a prayer.
Asking for your help to get me through
the good times, the bad times, the
happy and sad times.
    But then when you never came
through with a helping hand, I realized
you were a myth, a story from fairyland.
    Now that I'm older, I often wonder
if you're really made up, was it because
when I was little I was bad and
that was why you never lent me
a helping hand.
    But then I watch the news, and I
know I was right, if you really exist,
then why does everyone fight?
    You are a wonderful thing' so
it's said. So help us now! Before
we're all dead.

Danielle Baxter

Jigsaw Dreams

So, you want to be the best?
Top of the class, punctilious, precise
A cut above the rest.
A conscientious craftsman devoted to his cause,
Concerned with honour and integrity -
Not craving applause.
But market forces gather and darken your dream;
"Make more with less, at twice the speed" they scream.
Mountains of ply, oodles of glue,
Veneer covered mouldings with plastic too.
Reaching their objectives, you passed their test,
While sacrificing your standards on the altar of success.
You're one of the crowd, a high-flying star;
But are you the best? - Ponder awhile.

Marcus White

What Right?

What right have I, or any man, to end your noble life?
To fire the gun and throw the barb that cuts you like a knife;
What right have I to stand and watch your blood mix with the sea
And see you thrash and foam the waves in throes of agony?

What right have I to stalk and wait your final gasp of breath,
When all your crimson blood has flowed, and ebbed you
    to your death?
What right have I to deck your corpse and then to be a part
Of those who choose to butcher and flense you to your heart?

What right have I, or any man, to take you to the brink,
By pointless bloody massacre, and never even think?
What right to life do I possess, when finally I fail
To answer when my children ask, "Daddy, what's a whale"?

P. G. Doering

For Robert Medley

A royal flush of painters meet and kiss,
Squeezed out from silver tubes
On to a bright October morning palette.
A run of golden girls and watchful lads,
Bejewelled deadly queens in pairs -
Full house at Golders Green for Medley's obsequies.
The parking place for boys on bicycles is closed.

Mozart's music, Edmund Waller's verse,
A Charterhouse remembrance,
Auden's poem on their boyhood love
Delivered with true voice and comet eyes,
Amusing snapshots of his last two holidays abroad,
The homely tale of brushes bought the week he died:
A justly, quietly recollected life.

Relinquishing his daybed, going into night,
His friends about him, lilies at his feet,
Robert is as elegant in death as when alive.

Paul Vining

Julie

You speak my name
With long held syllables.
So sweet is your manner,
But yet, your words are not towards my ears...

I cringe, again.
How could you laugh and joke,
Am I not too precious to be pushed aside?

You turn and ask if anything is wrong.
I shake my head,
You shrug your shoulders,

And turn to laugh and joke once more.
With me? Not myself,
Just the name is the same.

Julie Kubiak

The World For Man

Alone in the Universe here are we,
Looked down on, by a God we cannot see,
The Earth turns on an axis, hidden from view,
A Sun that arises from darkness to renew,

Revolving; the good Earth follows a path,
That is constant, precise and certainly hath,
Been set in motion by a Great Hand,
Who moulded this world of sea and land,

Angels looked down and were the first,
To view the Earth and develop a thirst,
For the good things that had been created,
Lucifer's eye beheld; and felt cheated,

That was the beginning of passion and hate,
'Tis this, that keeps God's people at his gate,
The Almighty proceeded with his plan,
To create a place for His kind in Man,
Given the choice, Man decided to be,
Going his own way; and agents free.

Robert G. O'Cianaigh

Bliss

Oh for the joys of a summer day
When the cares of the world just drift away.
Stretched out in a chair beneath the trees,
Leaves rustling gently in the breeze.
Lying idly with nothing to do
But watch cottonwool clouds in a sky of blue.
A painted butterfly catches my eye.
I hear a bee hum as he buzzes by.
Two ring doves alight to bill and coo.
In the distant meadow I hear a cow "moo".
As my eyelids close, there's a change of scene.
The lawn becomes a sea of green
Which laps around the far off view
Of flower beds, pink and gold and blue.
Fragrant scents waft through the air
As I lie marooned in my lounging chair.
Drowsing on a day like this
Truly is the height of bliss!

Margaret Alston

Flower World

One flower died
The nearest flower cried.
The other side of the vase, just didn't care.
One other nearest flower knew,
But didn't bother.
It thought it was probably unworthy as life itself.
The blossoms suffered
And died before they grew.
In the other side of the vase,
More and more were dying.
The responsible ones said:
"It happened. Let's bury them."

Hejrae El-Habti

Aborigine

I Aborigine I,
I was, before -
We sailed, wailed, to our tree gods, rock gods,
Earth, wind, water gods
Hailed - the sun and the moon.
Rain scales encrusted our mops,
Dust trailed as we danced with our friends
The lithely spirits of the waves
And enticed them into our caves;
Our warm, dark, secret hidden caves.

They painted pictures, showed us patterns
To retain - the flame.
Warmth within as we fly,
Our arms entangled with the sky,
The drum beats urging us,
The hot earth bearing us.
We are not here, we are on high,
Dancing with the planets and the whole earth structure,
with the power of all, I.
I, Aborigine, I.

Hazel Heasley

"Days Of Yore"

If we could have lived in Victoria times,
Bric-a-brac on the mantle piece,
And a Westminster clock that chimes.
An iron clad cooking range centres the room,
A brass filled coal scuttle, a horse hair broom.
Scrubbed white top table, with chairs to match,
Corn doll in the window, made from straw thatch.
An umbrella, and "what-not" stand in the hall,
There's pictures of the royals nailed to the wall.

Shops with wrinkles, whelks, mussels and crabs,
Lobsters bright red, with white fish, and dabs.
Then down to the sea front, up to the stalls,
For lemonade, gobstoppers, and aniseed balls.
Stopping old "wallsey" pushing his trike,
For an ice cream cornet, - or, a three corner ice.
Girls in their cossies that went down to their knees,
With big floppy hats that blew off in a breeze.
Punch and judy show down on the sands,
Children screeching, laughing and clapping their hands,
Victorian times, we all thought would last,
Now remain days, forgotten, and past.

James Robert Young

Thoughts On Losing A Mother

I remember it well - the day I was told
That my mother was shortly to die.
How do you cope when faced with such news -
A hurt far too deep to just cry.

So I tried to be brave, for her sake and mine,
And now that some time has passed,
I'm able to write of the thoughts I had then,
And speak of my feelings at last:

Two years ago, I sat by your bed
And watched as your life ebbed away.
A sorrow so deep, and so hard to bear,
And so much I wanted to say.

Pressed close to your bed, your hand held in mine,
My eyes never leaving your face,
I whispered again of the times we had shared,
Aware of the widening space.

To put into words, the thoughts I had then,
Brings back once again all the pain.
My wish that the world could just melt away -
And leave me, unborn, once again.

A. Costen

Everlasting Fame

Swaying warming water gently surrounds me
Why am I here being held so firmly fast
It's so dark where am I
Is this situation going to last
Now there's something pushing, where am I to go
How long will this journey take, minutes. Hours I don't no
I hear gentle voices so very far away
If I go faster I may hear what they say
What am I to do, my eyes are tightly shut
This head of mine is being crushed, now it's very cold
I'm being wrapped in blankets someone holding me so close
Whispering words of comfort as I lay in loving arms
A soft voice called me Charlotte. Is this to be my name
It was nineteen hundred and eighty five
My everlasting fame.

Ann Allan

So Deaf, And Dumb

I can't hear a word that you speak
Or listen to the drums,
In your music,
From your system,
From your room,
'Cause that's all I know it as,
Your room.
Y' know, I don't hear people scream
That is when they're frightened, cause of the thunder outside.
But, I'm ok, I'm socially disabled remember.
Ha, my social disability, and, what was the other thing?
Noise pollution, ha!
They try to quieten that stuff, y'know, make it quieter
But I really know quiet, then maybe I don't
See, I don't know noise really either.
And don't think of trying to argue, no, don't!
'Cause I can't hear you anyway. And, I won't object to what you think
'Cause I don't know. How could I.
I don't understand. How would I, I wasn't told how to understand.
'Cause I couldn't hear them any way.

Claudia Stefania Contino

Qualification For Death

May children play, where bodies lay,
In dark cold solitude of winters plight.
Where no man mourns in cease of day,
With images of headstone chipped in full light.

Their hewed bodies placed under moist mounds,
In the corner that was once a dewy pasture.
And the grey leaves that are frozen to the grounds,
For the summer sun to no longer nurture.

Now corpses are strewn on roadside's edge,
With cold numb faces casting eyes.
And the living dead fall from buildings ledge,
I wonder, will there be anybody left to despise.

Now the youthful face in the photograph is gone,
Spoke and motioned on his very last breath.
The question I ask is, (and not before long),
"What is the qualification for death?"

Decklan Howard

Untitled

Thank you, our babe
for this most precious gift
that only you could give:
To hear and see and feel the world anew.

The evening birdsong in amazed brown eyes
The spider web between uncertain fingers
Poppy petals hiding little feet
The sharpness of the monkey puzzle tree yielding to the gentle touch
The scent of white lilac again and again and again
and the wondrous bee!
Indeed, indeed 'tis true, unless you become as little children
The kingdom of God will forever escape you

V. James

Untitled

Look into the eyes of a child, you'll see,
Loyalty, trust, curiosity.
Look into a man's, what will you find?
Jealousy, lust, body ruling the mind.
But out of the two which would you say,
Has the best chance in this world today?

The strong become weak then the weak appear strong,
Maybe that's where we are going wrong,
For when violence can appear out of the blue,
The truth will assume a different hue,
Yet wait, the values we leave behind,
Are still the best chance for the last of mankind.

So, when people stare, laugh and say,
You're asking for trouble if you trust today,
Remember the children and their trust in you,
Let them be the guides in the things you do.
For although it seems the world's going mad,
While children have their innocence it isn't all bad.

Elaine Contento

Life And Death Struggle

The sea wild and beautiful
White waves, open swell
Deep quiet habitat of mysterious creatures
Seabirds forage, seals bask
Bright neon schools swim beneath the dappled waters
Clusters of vivid corals
Sway in silent rhythm
The sea bed oozes life
And new life is born.

Thick black crude, raw sewage, toxic chemicals
carelessly spilt, dumped and tipped
Seabirds oiled, seals choke
Fish swim in the murky waters
soaking up the poison
Delicate plants wither
As the sea bed oozes silt
And nature struggles to survive

The sea once wild and beautiful
Coughs and splutters
As man pollutes its very life force.

Margaret Martin

Surreal Liverpool 1994

This blank cityscape holds me in its concrete arms.
My words slip away from the static Southern
speech you have taught me so well.

This is the town where I was born.
Framed black and grey reminds me
what it was all about: The Mersey thing.

But now all that's left behind are a pair of gates made
famous in some song by some Liverpool band years before.
I don't know what I expect to find here.

The Cavern, Mathew Street; it is over now.
"Four lads who shook the world," the epitaph reads.
The world needed more than love.

I'm a Merseysider. Proud. Sometimes stubborn (usually).
I look on in disbelief as your lips fall away
from mine. We stand back and wait.

But still I only see gates. Only gates, gates.
I've so many skeletons I can't close my closet;
I should buy a bigger one.

Phil Duffy

Untitled

The tax payers know it's not fair
　Nearly all MPs end up millionaires
The last PM let down and ditch
　Wrote a book that made her rich
We old UNS would like to see
the MPs live on money like the OAP
　I dare say one MP would try?
　All the bills and food to buy?
Give up your lifestyle for just a year
　live in a council flat without a beer
Don't forget the poll-tax did fail
　and put a few innocent people in jail
OAP's quality of life
Just ask a few of Britain's housewives
　Saying it could be made better
　Honest truth as I write this letter,
They don't get much that is free
Licence in Australia on TV you see
　British people will not let it rest
　All the sell off (will save NHS)

T. Blaney

A Poignant Phantasm

She's gone, My faithful friend of many years,
My dog, She's dead; I've exhausted all my tears.
Now, as I walk alone. A wraithlike form I see,
A shadow? A trick of light? It must be
A conjured image of a heart that grieves,
But the snap of twigs, The rustle of dead leaves,
As she runs ahead, down the woodland track,
Then stops, tongue lolling, eyes bright, looking back.
The illusion fades, forlorn, I sit and rest,
A questing cold nose on my hand is pressed,
I caress the silky head, the velvet ears,
A deja vu? A memory of other years?;
The warm weight of her head upon my knee,
I feel, But she is dead, How can that be?

Daphne White

Heroes Are They

The ghostly sound of marching men echoing down a lonely lane,
Their souls entwined leaving
Behind the blood red field of poppies in their wake,
For our sake all lost their day.
No monuments needed for heroes such as they
Their glory as they marched along the lonely road
Were the many kindnesses they bestowed.
Ordinary men from simple homes and work
And when duty called they didn't even shirk
But marched bravely on to war.
What debt we owe them all and never can repay
Except to remember they gave their tomorrows for our today.
And through the tears we see the poppies blossom where
once they trod
Their honourable sacrifice is a casting reminder of a living God.

M. Wiles

'The Single Mind'

Now I have drunk from water lit with gold,
This shining moment once allowed to me
Of single-minded calm- Aware at last,
That even here within, all thoughts can be
One swiftly healing stream of quiet delight
Gaining its power from a decisive will
Though fugitive in all I touch from now
The air this moment breathed is somewhere still.

The spirit, not confused, self-pitied, torn,
Wildly imploring for some man-made goal,
With energies splayed out in stagnant pools
Now flowing forward altogether whole.
Finding with joy, one point, one course, one sea,
As powerful waters of great rivers find
And forge their way by glorious consent
So the strong channel of a single mind.

Ann Boger

The Threshold

The sun looks in at break of day.
  Whirling grey scarves of mist away;
Gilded lace spills across the bed,
  Around my head.
"Whence came I?"
  I muse, "and why?"
Dogged by hurts that multiply
  Even as time crawls by.

Scenes from the early golden years,
Laughter and tears at childish fears;
Many-hued sights of splendour rare;
  I sometimes wonder, "Was I there?"
The halls are empty, the loved ones gone,
  Ghost voices fade into bournes forlorn;
  Hope lingers as I calmly await
    The shedding and the light.

    A. Jebaratnarajah

Old Oak Tree

Old oak tree
Standing so firm
What changes have you witnessed
In this land around you?

So many thoughts you could convey
If you had the means
History that could never be understood.

Your branches reaching to the sky beyond
Each gnarled twig has a story to tell.

With my walking away
you remain, so solid
My presence having been another chapter.

How many more will cling to your roots?
How many old oak tree?

    Catrina Court

"Devotion"

She is always waiting at the gate
Even when you get home late,
You never year her moan or whine
When you don't arrive on time.

She always sits by your armchair
Never tires of sitting there
She understands when you feel cross
She loves you, you're her boss

Walks with you are never a bore
The valleys and hills you both explore
She's happy running at your side
Going ahead to be your guide

Would you find a friend more true
One so loyal through and through
So trusting, so faithful, your mind I jog
Your very best friend - a devoted dog.

    J. Welstead

Suicide

Institutionalize me.
Make sure that I'm well fed.
Make sure that I have help getting my mind back on reality -
If it ever was.
Do you believe it that I still deserve it?

Aching body,
Restless, useless mind,
tired eyes-tired of life.
Hung and dangling: legs and arms
damage caused with intent to supply.

Poems and letters written by a self-confessed,
self-murderess.
Your mind turns to crime,
My mind turns to crying.

    Isla Railton

Springtime

Springtime arrives around us once more
As Mother Nature knocks again on our door
She casts her magical spell with a "hocus pocus"
Whilst rabbits appear with bright coloured crocus

The countryside now deep in glorious green
With clear blue skies and clouds unseen
Surrounded in warm sunshine to the cries of baby lamb
Makes picnics fun filled with fresh fruit and jam

Birds are a'singing, with the buzz of the bees
Strange pink cherry blossoms now cover the trees
What a joy to breathe in clean fresh air
With the smell of cut grass and flowers perfumed everywhere

On a sunlit evening walk in the park
Strolling along slowly as light turns to dark
Cricketers continue to battle, as adults stay laying
As dogs run loose as the children keep playing

A memorable spring day draws to a close
So remember your thoughts of this springtime prose
As humanity like summer is ready to take centre stage
Though the world still awaits to turn a new page

    Gary P. Davies

My Own Little Cherub

I call her my little cherub, each morning as I give her a kiss,
She has a loving personality and she fills the air with such bliss,
She'd say take care and God bless you, to every person she met,
She is so radiant and happy if you met her you'd never forget...
To me she was a nurse and doctor and a very good teacher too,
She'd give away her only possessions 'cause it was a good
    thing to do,
She believes in God and angels, but the church she doesn't attend,
She said if you can do a good turn just do it as you would do
  a friend
She treats all people with respect no matter what colour or race
She treats them as if they were family and tell you so to your face,
I've seen her give her last penny to someone who needed
    more than she did,
to children she always showed kindness and never the truth
    from them hid...
I'll love her for ever and ever, no matter what difficulties come,
I've always called her my own little cherub she's more than
that and some, she's disabled and confined to a wheel chair
and I would not have any other, you see she's the whole
world to me and will always be my most adorable mother.

    E. Stray

The Man On The Beach

I stood alone to look across the sea
When I felt a man standing next to me
I turned and looked into his face
His eyes went through me and off into space

I asked the man where he was from
He said from a land where everyone's gone
Then I saw a tear roll down his cheek
He wiped it away and continued to speak

Look at the water, the calm of the sea
Feel the cool wind, tell me what you see
I felt the wind, the waters started to stir
I saw the white horses leap into the air

Then I saw a young man walk onto the sands
He looked familiar as he held out his hands
Moving towards me intent I should see
A hole through each hand he was showing to me

Don't sacrifice yourself they'll not understand
With a gust from the wind he vanished from the sand
I turned to the man who had stood by my side
Standing alone I gazed at the tide

    Ian Stuart Purcell

Nightmare

He tried to awake
But was remorselessly held
In the dreaming night
Whose vaporous coasts
Revealed again dead faces
Paradoxically alive;
Some grimacing at their plight
Some loving in the dream light.
He struggled again
To reach the surface of his mind
But the night witch would not release him
Because she needed his kind.
He cried out to God in heaven.
Then she came
And bathed his streaming face.
'You must never dream like that again.'

D. A. Smyth

My Cats All Three

My cats all three a lovable mischievous trio they are.
Brought to me by owner going afar.
Every morning at eight bounty white and black
Pulls on the light switch
Above my bed and bumps my head.
Next goes Jenny daintily walking
Over the buttons on the teas made
Followed by trixie big and black
Who promptly hurries back
In case the funny noise is another cat.
They play the moggy games
With paper balls and pulling string.
Little furry presents they bring
And I do a rescue act
While they are face washing
On the mat by the flap,
And that's enough
About my cats all three.
It's time for tea.

Marguerite A. Auton

Madness

It sits there, swaying from side to side
Tormenting me
I hear its laughter and its cry
I see the fish wearing socks!
I stand in front of it trying to see beyond its solid form
It hums so slow so fast so silently
It makes me dizzy it makes me calm
So many forms and so many textures
It's thick liquid, oil like, it's a paper edge that cuts with no mercy
It's soft like petals, and harder than nails dropping on your head
Put it on your tongue, it's the taste you want it to be
From pink sherbet to earthworms
If it had a smell it would be two opposites
Like petrol and perfume
You control it yet can't
If it spoke to you could you cope?
Would it make sense to hear
Heebeegeebee the fish is singing
And the cans are dancing?
It's all in your head!!!

Jennie Short

After All A Dream

When I go back and find my Lily,
My true love Lily of the valley
Dream, dream together; The quiet
Night was mine and yours alone, my Lily,
of my own true love.

Dawn was breaking as I was left-
Alone how I love to be just as
I am as joy will never end,
My Lily.

R. E. Bilson

Untitled

Love Letters
Words may fumble but letters never lie.
Stories of love and tales of passion they write.
To set a flame a heart and fill it with delight
No wonder then - a postman is a girl's best friend.

Togetherness Is Bliss
Eyes on eyes, senses alert
Glowing in the company of the beloved, all ready to flirt
Verbal communication that thrills the heart
Promise of tomorrow, till death do us part.

The First Touch
The joy and the warmth of hand-in-tender-hand.
The flush of desire and a feeling so grand
The charm of fingers held entwined
Until the embrace becomes an exciting eternity in time.

The Waltz Of Passion
When the hearts beat as one, two souls sigh together
When love triumphs at last, and nothing else matters.
Except the sound of your voice and the music in your name.

Farzana Siddique

Black And White

If God had made the world in black and white,
We'd have no problem telling wrong from right.
It would be a simple case of all the time.
Watching the dividing line.

But God chose to use many different hues,
So the world is red and yellow, green and blue,
And it's not so easy to decide
If green belongs to black or white.

But come, these colours are inviting,
And they make the world far, for more exciting,
It would be an insult to our sense of sight,
If the world were only black and white.

And anyway it's much more fun to try-
To figure out which colours what and why,,
For man will always find a cause to fight,
And we do insist that black is white.

Aoidin ni Shiochain

Untitled

Our thoughts are like arrows, so slim and so long,
They fly ever onwards, like wings of a song,
Some find their objectives, so clear and so true,
But others just wander, and ne'er leave a clue.
Some of them fall by the barren wayside,
And this is so sad for their message has died.
If we score a "bull's eye" just now and again,
We feel we have lessened the anguish and pain.
So aim for the centre and you will then find
You may give many pleasures and much peace of mind.

Nesta Maud Carter

Sanctuary

Raita memories of an Asian town
solitary moments awaiting the door
are closed but not forgotten.
Time.
I shrug the past a faded coat
and kick the leaves of expectation
from around my transient base.
I advance with uncertain step
obsequious dust blows from my hair.
I grow.
My ghosts become friends, indelible shadows,
historians to feelings laid to rest.
I turn my back to face the sun
and step into the warmth of sweet
anticipation.

Paul Dooley

Lost On The Beach

Waves drop like dead all around,
Crashing screams making no sound.
Bloodwet feet on looking down,
Tears of feelings dying, drowned.

Mesmerized by midnight's tide,
You can be seen with arms stretched wide.
Damned departure of one who lied,
Awakened with destiny at my side.

Buried to my neck in this sandpit hell,
Condemned to love at each ring of the bell.
My pennies never reached the bottom of the well,
So I'll just sit here a few more hours, and yell.

As nighttime crawls beneath final curtain,
I cannot say what will happen for certain.
Lipstick smudges removed with submersion,
Memories flow away, too, with inertia.

Steely eyes with sunrise song,
The scars have healed, the feelings gone.
And everything said, has at last been done,
I can pick up my bags, for now I walk on.

Greg Ayles

Alone

It's a lonely life being on one's own.
No useless chat about this and that
Just me and me alone.

It's a lonely life with no one there to say
"And how are you, I'd like one too
Yes, it's been a lovely day."

The neighbours, they can be alright, "Come round," they
sometimes ask
But when it's done, it's home to one
And that's no easy task.

As in I go to an empty house which once was full of fun
No noise abounds, I hear no sounds
But things must still be done.

I know I ask some questions strange, like, "How do I find the
knack of cooking things the butcher brings"
But there's no answer back.

Yes it's lonely here with no one in your life
No talk today she's gone away
You see; I've lost my wife.

Anne Olds

Forgotten Workers

Sunlight spills across the valley,
Men from the village start to rally,
They all stand in neat little rows,
To go down the shaft to work below.

They mine coal in these eerie places,
All have determination on their faces
Cap, lamps, flashing to and fro
Then roof girder starts to bow

Miners stand and hold their breaths,
And pray to God to do the rest,
Miners running along railway tracks
Deputy's shouting don't look back,

Men are trapped some are dying
It won't be long before women are crying,
Rescuers stand in state of shock,
Mangled bodies among the rocks

But this has happened in the past,
So they won't be the first and nor the last

Mitchell Lough

Love Thy Neighbour

I have stood where dead men lay.
I have walked through the blood of children.
The death knell of thousands has thundered over my head,
The cry of babies has battered my ears.
I've watched as anger turned to hate...and then to fear.
I too have stamped on the struggling poppy.
There are too many begging arms, I look the other way.
But then the weary bullets wane,
Blank faces have forgotten the reasons why.
Hollow men climb out from the rubble, children peep through
peppered walls.
Words have failed. Guns have failed. What now?
Slowly two men face each other, no guns in their outstretched arms.
As they embrace, two faiths entwine.
They look into each other's eyes and a thousand words are
spoken by a thousand people,
The sky becomes bluer, the grass is greener
The sun shines on my hardened heart.
As one man holds the other he unites a nation.
I've seen no painting that can compare, nor flower that has
smelt so sweet,
There is no art that can capture such a beautiful sight
Of man in harmony with man.

Belinda Hastie

Lost Love At Mid Life

The hurt of love that lingers still,
So deep within my every mortal being,
He came, he left, three times or more,
How can I love within again.
To trust another, a long way off,
But found have I my freedom,
The worry gone, just loss, such deep tormented feelings,
I wonder is this freedom.
At mid life, crisis overwhelming, how can a woman start again,
Which path, which way, such great confusion,
Stepping cautiously on my own once more,
Wondering what life has in store.
Children growing, independent, some day soon will leave the nest,
My chance to start a new beginning,
As life throws up such uncertainty,
One moment "Oh what married bliss",
Then explosion and all this,
I'll tread along these unknown pathways,
Hoping soon all hurt will pass,
But can I ever trust again, or will I live my life in vain.

Barabara Goodbody

What More Can I Ask

As I walk across the gravel path they
see a new life beginning, I hear mother whisper, singing.
What more can I ask, as I walk along the gravel path.

Angels sing, love is around, gold and diamonds I see.
What more can I ask, as I walk along the gravel path.

Wedding bells ring, music is played lace white dress down the aisle.
What more can I ask, as I walk along the gravel path.

Now I see a new life beginning, as I see this child before me.
What more can I ask, now I know that she will walk along the
    gravel path.

The gravel path is nearly over, the end of my life has almost come,
as I sit here remembering.
What more can I ask, as we all walk along the gravel path.

I lay here a wondering how all the world
began, remembering my life along the uneven path.
What more can I ask, as I close my eyes I know I reached the
end of the gravel path.
I'm on my way to heaven, following the angels
song, I know my life along the gravel path has been great.
God, what more could I have asked, now I know I've finished
    that long gravel path.

Lia O'Kane

204

When Spring Returns

Through the twinkling grace of the suns reflection
the stream continues without cessation
its course meanders first left then right
past reeds and bushes it seemingly races
to reach its destination

Not long ago it appeared to stand still
under a coat of white it held the chill
of winters sleep, but now along its bank
the crocus peep their cheery heads
spring finally arrives, to awaken the earth

Everywhere you look there's new growth, new birth,
daffodils nod in the gentle breeze, first buds appear on twiggy trees
new chicks follow mum to the waters edge
on their first attempts they shiver and splutter
but they seem to inherently know how to swim, to fish

Children's squeals of pure delight, disturb the birds
who take off in fright,
but later return realizing they're in no danger
from chubby toes testing the water,
the suns reflection hides the truth,
but they care not, in the excitement of youth, in the spring of life
their own rivers flow, but where it will take them no one can know.

Yvonne Wilson

Loss

Now that you are gone, my love,
Life holds no joy for me,
The world seems dark and cheerless
My tears fall endlessly.

Never shall I know again
The clasp of your hands in mine,
Nor feel the touch of your warm red lips
As our eager mouths combine.

No more shall we lie together love
When the long tiring day is done,
Close and secure and loving
Two beings fused as one.

Nor shall I ever know again
The joy of love fulfilled,
For all that warmth and passion love
Forever now is stilled.

But I pray we'll meet again my love
Upon some heavenly shore,
When Death's kind hand has touched me too
And brought us close once more.

Winifred Norbury

For Love Or Money

I know there's your work,
   but can I carry on?
We rarely see each other,
   I try hard to be strong.

You say that you love me,
   I thought that it was true.
I was sure there was something there,
   special between me and you.

My loyal friends are here for me,
   When I need someone to listen,
but where are you to dry these tears,
   when upon my cheeks they glisten.

You say that you want the money,
   So that I don't have to pay,
but money cannot buy you love,
   Not this love anyway.

Maybe it's just the beginning
   Maybe it should be the end,
I will be there with you when you are around,
   And all my love I send.

Elizabeth May Bushnell

A Winter's Evening

When the night is new and full of dreams
That have yet to materialize
When folks are deep in slumberland
Their thoughts drift to the skies
To glorious winter evenings
Exclusively for love
Lit by rays of a bright cold moon
In lone sojourn above
Surrounded by a halo
Of ghostly mystic light
As if to try to warm the moon
In its clear cold might
The moon itself close guarded
By shyly twinkling stars
As if in humble worship
Of their master of the skies
I love these winter evenings
So quiet, with mystery filled
When I can dream that all my cares
And troubles have been stilled

Betty Allen

Life

I'm sitting at my desk, at the back of the classroom,
And everyone is shouting what?... Pardon?
My minds gone blank I've got too much work,
Numbers going round my head, I feel like such a jerk.
The last bell's rung and work's done for the day,
I'm going home, it's Friday... Celebrate?
Friday night-and no one has rung,
I'm sitting by the phone, while they're out having fun!
I guess I'm all alone again, and nothing's on T.V.
Even all the videos-seem too good for me!
You would think that by Saturday, I'd have scored myself a date,
But instead I'm reading shakespeare-what a wonderful life I hate!?

Pally Watts

Like-Unto-Me

Mirror, mirror on the wall,
Reflectory glances of shadows that fall,
Outlines of you and me,
Perfect images you see,
No false lines to deceive,
You see what you see and you must believe.

Cloned to perfection is the mirror's report,
No angled illusion, no tales to distort,
Nothing escapes its watchful eye,
A one optic centre on the world can spy,
No pain or emotion to cloud its decision,
Its only aim in life is perfect precision.

I gaze in the glass in splendid awe,
My eyes don't allow, they search for a flaw,
At length and at pain a mistake I find,
It haunts my being because it's part of my mind,
As I walk away and the light grows dimmer,
The show from the mirror is now just a glimmer.

Michael Toogood

Dunblane 1996

Flowers that were to be of the next generation
Plucked from life before a chance to blossom
No time to hide from a crazed gunman's weapon
They died where they lay; flowers no more.

No words or tears can express such sorrow
Such as was felt by all.

The weeks have passed but come what may
Nothing can erase that fateful day,
Forever etched on life's highway.

An eye for an eye, a tooth for a tooth is God's law.
That gunman has a lot to answer for.
We cannot say that it will never happen again,
The horror of Dunblane.

E. M. Barnes

Judy's Story

Pretty, Cute, Adorable - All waggy tail
Pretty, Nice, Affordable - Definitely female

Jeune de dix mois - No injections done
Irresponsible - Pretty, Cute, Adorable
Why do such a thing?

Jeune de douze mois - Unstoppable
Over friendly spotty dog
Made you suffer near to dead

Poor driver - beside himself. Deeply sorry - not his fault
Five days anguish, then sent home to mend

Left alone too long - Avant
Many nights adrift - Avant
Playful... unable; uninterested
Too selfish, uncaring to throw a ball

You learned how to play
Later when someone noticed
That you had no squeaky ball
Then life began,
ma chienne.

June Wightman

"For My Children"

"Put not your trust in princes, nor in any sons of man".
No, nor daughters too, nor any human thing.
What shall I tell you?
How shall I help you?
If I can.
Trust no-one? Nothing?
Keep yourselves unscathed, untouched, immaculate?
Keep clear from harm and hurt?
But then you'd be entombed,
Your mind, your heart, your soul
Wasted within you.
Trust everyone were better said,
And love and give.
Yet harm will come,
And hurt must come.
And love, my love
Can only watch
And suffer too.
And pray.

Cicely Ludlam

Day Dreamer

In my schoolroom fantasies abound,
My lesson's lost in vast surround.
My thoughts soar into outer space,
My spirit friends now take their place.

I see far from mountain peaks
Beauty that an artist seeks,
I hear music, magic to my ear
Those wondrous notes, so soft and clear.

I visit heaven of distance far
Where night is lit by a bright star,
My spirit friends, this haven graces
Where happiness dwells, sorrow, no traces.

I look down from phantom heights
I see bitterness, that causes fights,
Although on earth I live and muse
My spirit friends I cannot lose.

When down to earth, and puzzled stares
Aware now of those angry glares,
Cannot explain my happy venture,
To earthbound people, spirit adventure.

Dee Nelder

Reality

If you open your eyes,
You'll find you can see,
What others ignore -
Reality.

With people lying sick in bed,
Others are injured, may be dead.
This can't go on, it has to stop,
That's what we want, but still it's not.

Why do people make this happen,
Maybe, it's some sort of ugly pattern,
Soldiers with armour fighting at war,
Us the innocent are saying 'no more'.

War is our enemy, peace is our friend,
Why don't these people go make amends,
The earth is our life, our life is the earth,
Why spoil this beauty, look what it's worth.

One of these days, those people will pay,
Then it's their turn to say 'no way',
People are dying like a cloud of dust,
We just wait with no one to trust.

Maria Ferrara

Thoughts Of Life

As a child, my life was good,
The future too distant to consider,
At least - I thought it was!

The years at school were long and hard,
But I knew it would all be worthwhile,
At least - I thought it would!

Then came the times of falling in love,
My hopes, my dreams all coming true,
At least - I thought they would!

The wilderness years, oh, what went wrong?
No future for me - all hope gone,
At least - I thought it had!

I gave birth to my children,
They gave love and life to me,
Through them I became strong again,
And whatever the future holds,
I can face it with pride and dignity,
At least - I think I can.

Carolyn Witt

Ode To An Old Sleeping Bag

Hail to thee my feather-filled faithful friend! And must we say
    farewell?
It seems but yester-year you busted out,
All shiny new when I released you from your purchase plastic bag.

On many a freezing night you've held me
Warm in an encompassing embrace, all snugly in my tent.

Or some nights under slowly wheeling stars
I've peeped out from your softly hooded mouth,
The draw string tight about my face; and in
The morning hoar frost on your lower lip, my whitened frozen breath.

How often have I thrust you in your bag,
With numbing hand? Amazed that so much down
Should in so small a sack be stuffed.
At evening now, how jocund to be freed
And puffed you up to your full size again with your tremendous
    loft.

But you are old and She decrees that you must go and be replaced.
Your cover and your feathers may in the dump be tipped, but still
Your spirit lives and it will go to that great happy Campsite in
    the sky
To join old boots, old tents, old ice axes. A drop in the eternal
    ocean of our gathered mountain memories.

Jim Milledge

Face Of Justice

I saw you killing the prophets
and being sure their message was lost,
But you never suspected
My heart became its host.
On the night you destroyed the Caesar,
Triumph resided in your eyes;
Your whole existence awaited Great Rome's demise.
Rejoicing, you failed to see my coming Philippi;
Fatal battlefield, where your greed and treason lie.
And how stunned and shocked you looked,
When you learnt I'd hurled your swastikas down!
How appalled, when you heard the echo
Of your Wermacht boots forever drown!
I was the one who found you selling death of iron
To children starving, instead of life from food,
And it was me who unmasked
Your sinister face under a missioner's hood.
I saw your formidable power and watched your speedy pace,
But I also realized your failing:
You cannot recognize my face!

Helen Tsanikidou

"LOVE"

There is "Love" in every "Season",
Whatever they may bring,
There is "Love" in everyone's minds,
With the exchanging of "Gold Rings,"
But, the greatest "Love" of all
We can find within ourselves
Is the "Love" we give to others,
Without "Question", "Greed", or "Doubt",
For "Love" overcomes all obstacles,
Whether "Great" or "Small",
And the "Love" you have within your "Hearts",
Is the greatest "Gift" of all.

Sheila Salter Phillips

Paradise At Sunrise

The perfume of flowers fills the cool air,
As my heart truly lights up with a flare,
Busily, under the bright blue morning sky,
Roam squads of bees and a lone butterfly.

Dew-coated buds open for the honey bees,
As I feel refreshed, with joy and peace,
Even tiny insects begin their daily duty,
While I recline to admire Nature's beauty.

And on the petals little raindrops shine,
In front of this small house, that's mine,
Who can be the artificer than Almighty God,
Whose only divine tool is His magic rod!

Across the sky appears a colourful rainbow,
To make God's wonderful creations to glow,
I was always very eager to see Paradise,
But, I never knew I'd see it at sun-rise!

Deepak Jayavanth

Nanna Boyle's Poem

The time has come for my Nanna to go
She's suffering from cancer but doesn't yet know
The Doctors and Nurses all take a seat
To discuss the problem she thinks is her feet.

I know God calls for us one by one
And although we're scared, there's no place to run
But one day soon we'll all meet again
The place they call heaven where families remain.

So God if your listening Please here me out
Our candles are numbered till you blow them out
Me and my mum are one of a kind
So take us together to keep us bound.

Tricia Goulder

The Unwanted And The Wanted

Abandoned in a Builder's cold wheel-barrow:
Left in a damp basket at a Parson's door:
Hidden in a Hospital's soiled-linen chute:
Dumped in a lone, deserted, telephone booth:
Bartered for filthy lucre to make ends meet:
Strangled, to be rid of, for adulterous need:
Throttled dead, and smuggled in mother's bosom:
Pray, Who are these victims of crimes so gruesome?
Who are the perpetrators? Who are these rakes
Who victimize these little innocent babes?
Whose flesh and blood, and breath of life are so cheap?
Believe it or not; they're Mums, for whom we weep,
From whom should flow the "milk of human kindness";
In lieu whereof, swells the gall of wickedness!
In contrast, lonely hearts pine for motherhood,
And desolate couples yearn for parenthood.
Disillusioned Mums snatch from some Infant's Wards,
Or kidnap, to fill their void, against all odds!
The Unwanted child of one, transformed outright,
To another's endeared Angel of Delight!

Welch J. Balasingam

'Justice'

What is Truth?
Is it standing in the dock alone,
or pacing some old stone flagged floor
in the misty confines of the 'Moor'?
"I swear by Almighty God".
Is that the truth?
The 'Red Fox' talks of peace and war.
His truth is prostituted less or more
to skittle's in a wooden box,
whose truth lies in words that others say.
Truth is Justice!
But Justice is Vengeance.
She stands on the dead a common whore,
whose syphilitic eyes are bound in rag.
Whose sword drips quartered gore
and what is more,
Her scales smell of Billingsgate.

R. Pooley

Life

Life is something everyone is entitled to,
no one has the right to take it away.
Everyone should lead their own life,
believe what they want to believe,
be what they want to be.
So many lives are ruined by war,
   abuse and illness.
Every day someone's life ends,
and a new one begins.
Some people find life is too hard to bear,
others look forward to each new day.
Life can be long, but also short.
No one knows when they'll die,
or where they go when it all ends.
A lot of people believe in heaven,
but who can prove it's there?
You only find out when you get there,
but by then it's too late.

Holly C. Keeble

United?

I am I, and you are you,
And I am you, and you are me:
And thus shall it be, thus shall it be.

You think me, and I think you
Whenever we taste, or speak, or see:
And so shall it be, so shall it be.

The you that is me is the me that is us
Thus shall it be, and so shall it be,
And ever shall it be. Ever shall it be?

Noel Staines

Puppets Of Death

The dead are actors in a drama spent,
Their role played out
For better or for worse,
Cold-frozen now in an eternity
Of silence,
Mute victims of review and argument.
But in the hands of puppet-masters,
Us to whom the dead are close,
Like marionettes
Responsive to our strings of memory,
They, manipulated figures,
Live again,
Move, act and have their being
If we who love them
Pull them back
Into the theatre of our shared past lives,
In constant reenactment
Our dead still live,
For only silence casts into the final void.

Audrey E. Bradford

'The Secret Thing?'

I dreamt the hills and vales were cold and bleak,
Their furrowed ridges hard with frost, and bare.
Once sheltering hedges warmth themselves did seek.
Stark trees reached to the skies in their despair.

Then suddenly, a secret thing was there
That peered between the clouds and through the rain,
And whispering softly, as a joy to share
Awoke the trees to bud and spring again.

Come summer sunshine dress your poppies bright.
Sing summer lark as skyward you would greet.
To skim clear waters, dragonflies delight,
Shy butterfly will kiss the meadow sweet.

All autumn flowers of gold and bronze and red
Its golden leaves that rustle ankle deep
Have warmth enough to cheer, I will not dread
A world that surely will not die, but sleep.

L. M. Last

A Night In The Life Of The Moon

He is silent throughout the day
Strong and silent through the night
His nocturnal way of life indispensable
To all who live by night
Regal and majestic in his pure white gown
Attended by his many subjects
Sometimes half hidden by the infinite of his kingdom
Motionless he sits on his dark velvet chariot
He is silent in the superiority of his reign
A close friend to all insomniacs, and those who walk in the shadows
His beauty and independence - incomparable
To any other in the night
He is silent in his might
He is the night, he is the moon.

Jan Fairhurst

Evening

Oh, evening, how I love your fading mystery
The cooling air and birds still chirruping
The creatures of the night begin to play
And creeps a stillness o'er the closing day.

With pinetops silhouette on high
Like witches hats against a darkening sky
Some golden magic in the shadow lies
Caught for a space in time before it dies.

Yet leaves a yearning need unsatisfied.
We keep the mystic spell alive - inside.

Doreen Parkinson

How Green The Vale

How green the vale, in sombre expectancy, blue ridges
dominate the plains, and larks call the plough man, his
shears rupture the earth as plover answers back on silent
wing, she protests the springs intrusion.
On this silent hill I face the lowlands, to flush red roofs
and industrial confusion.
From this lofty height, the chiltern ridge awakes, and I tread
the solid earth I have known and loved.
See the cops set in the dell, tall slender firs stand firm
serene, for shadowing protected scenes, and I see the depth
and brilliance of the vale.
Rook and crow live here.
The Elms in sadness await the triumph of destruction, and
the rookery disappears in the echo of a thousand years,
The vale has witnessed, we do not see.
What know we of this place: Will we write the poetry of Cromwell:
Hampden. What say they of this life: Those who follow
Will they see the vale: The ridge will look down in secret splendour,
across the depth, to someone on the silent hill, looking out beyond
that we have seen, in sombre expectancy, the vale will be green.

Maurice James Saunders

Death

After the long winter wind, the cold frost
You came as the summer sun, the gentle breeze
The birds were singing softly in my garden,
you came and we held each other beneath
the old oak tree - we had the world to share -
a beautiful dream and death took our dream.
You were with me till the dawn and I saw
your shadow across the lawn.
The birds no longer sing for me, I share them
with the rest; you too are silent, but still I
hold you to my breast
cold in death, yet beating fast
Our love will stay through long nights and days,
The memory mine unseen, unheard
Farewell, my love; death is only as dawn
away for us

Pauline Day

Third Time Around

When I first met you, I was shy
And you loved another, and made me cry
But when you finally began to notice me
I was as happy as a girl can be...

When we finally got it together
Everybody said it would be forever
But my love for you began to stray
And I found myself pushing you away...

Not just the once, but twice altogether
But it won't happen again, oh no, never
A while ago I knew I still loved you
Deep inside my love is so true...

Now we're back together, again, at last
And all the deceit and hurt's in the past
This time we will stay together
This time it will be forever...

Charlene Musselwhite

Christmas Without You

The house is empty this Christmas because you have gone away
No decorations, no tree, no lights to celebrate this day
Remember how it used to be our home so warm and bright
But now no warmth or cheer to celebrate this night
Memories are all that I have now upon this Christmas Eve
The happiness the smiles that you have had to leave
So as future Christmas's come and go my thoughts will be of thee
And of the Christmas's long ago that can no longer be

B. E. Pointer

I Was In Love... But Never Again

I was in love, but never again,
My first love left me with a pain before the wound,
I had to stand from afar and watch my love,
Fall in love with another girl,

Now I cry all alone - no love is warm,
"He's" gone from reality - but not from my memory,

I needed to be loved, I still had needs and wants,
Then one day; He appeared, so unlike my love of before,
And as time elapsed - innocence was lost along with my youth,

Yet something was wrong, I sensed our love was all one sided,
And in time this man's falsehood struck home,
He didn't love me!!!... He just wanted all he could get,
I became his second hand rose...for a wife he kept;

The first love I had was true - now no love have I or want too,
For that love is gone...
Now adultery is my revenge - for an emotion called love,
I run a mock of it... For in my experience; it is totally
A myth.
Rachel Smith

Untitled

Sometimes light like fleeting clouds, oft heavy as the clay,
Thro' long dark lanes, short sunny paths, laughing when we may,
Treading footsteps long imprinted on this well worn way
    Because we live.

Glancing back regretfully but ever moving on
Knowing that what's past is lost and is forever gone,
Knowing too we had no choice, nought we could have done
We had to live.

Remembering hours of happiness now makes the saddest day,
Memories sting that are of joys since passed away,
Yet cheerfully recalling clouds along the way
    That we have lived.

Now it seems that nothing could transcend the world we know,
Moon and stars, trees and flowers, sunsets radiant glow
Then peace for us? beauty beyond all this? could it be so?
    When we don't live.

But no! methinks when life is gone there'll be no other land
Could we ask for more than this? another world demand
Great God! I shall not ask for more, could I but understand
    Why I have lived
    Isabel Pengelly

"Unless"

Canopies green reach to the sky
    parrots, quetzal and tanager fly.
The sun burns fierce upon the land
    forest too soon turns into sand.

The green fades fast, the earth laid bare,
    under man's hand without a care,
he strips the land, its soul in pain;
    with tarmac roads, no need for rain.

Man rips and cuts, he tears and slashes,
    Thick forests burn with ugly gashes.
Trees groan in pain—fall with no rain.
    man lives for destruction, are we insane?

The Earth laid bare, its heart is aching,
    no rain, salt seas, the crust in baking.
No time to think, just do the deed,
    the trees have gone—don't plant more seed?

Bones lay around bleached by the sun,
    creatures now from man, they run,
The soil erodes the land in dying.
    Unless we change—too late for crying!
    Ray Fitzgerald

"You Helped Me Remember How To Smile"

I felt banished from the world, locked
away in my strife, then along you came
to open up my dead life.
When I was in the shadows, you bought
me into the light. You were always there
for me, from morning through until night.
Every tear I cried, was filled with despair.
You comforted me, and gave me your care.
The troubles I carried were heavy, but
always, you kept my mind steady.
Life was unbearable, but you pushed me
through each day. Without you, I never
would have found the right way.
My life had fallen, I felt dead for
awhile, but then you helped me
remember how to smile.
    Hayley Julia Williams

Dream Pillow

The tell-tale moan - he woke- distraught
Came in at half past two
The wicked queen, a nasty piece,
Has she ever frightened you?
Through howl and cry and well-sucked thumb
The call came loud, unclear:
I want an ice cream, need it now
To chase away dark fear.

A calming cuddle, sobbing stops
Then feel returning lull
Back into bed, lay down his head
As up slow Thomas pulls;
But no! What's wrong? The pillow?
Upside down it seems:
The other side is dry and cool
Just right for a nice dream!
    Will Smith

The Dream Of The Snowflake

See a gentle snowflake; catch it in your hand
Find yourself a dream before you see it land
Walk a burning tightrope or swim a sea so blue
Sit and smile with lions; there's so much you can do

Meet a princess with a crown of daisies in her hair
Enjoy the warmth of the sun when you're going nowhere
Look into heaven, smile and wave to someone you once knew
Just let yourself dream; that's all you have to do

Fly like a bird, like an ocean skimmed by a stone
Open your eyes to trouble and see that you don't stand alone
Atlantis sleeps, waiting for you to come and reawake
Look inside, there's so many dreams that can be made

The snowflake's dream was to stand alone as ice
And kiss every flame that it could entice
Then he quickly turned to water and he was done
And you wake and find your dream and the snowflake have gone
    James Paul Burns

The Office

Monday through Friday all day long
The phones and the fax keep on and on.
Brokers, solicitors and applicants too
Together with branches, scream "What can you do?"
Chase up the references, we must have on offer.
Completion is set for the day after tomorrow.
Pink files are stacked from floor to the ceiling,
Everyone 'urgent' it sends our heads reeling.
We spend so much time just trying to placate,
There isn't a chance for 'notepad' to up-date.
so please, lend a land and phone after one.
Give us a chance to get some work done.
Now if it's urgent and the fax won't suffice
Then give us a call, but remember, 'be nice'
    J. A. Stacey

209

Infertility

Infertility, God what a word
hardly ever spoken, hardly ever heard
it's one of those things you'll have to accept
no children to bear, just tears to be wept.

I am no different, just unable to be
a much loved mother, a child for me.
Many tears, heartache and pain
hospitals and treatment, can be such a strain

Keep trying, never give up
a child to bear, a child to love
don't stay silent, speak the word,
to do nothing about it would be absurd.

You are not alone, don't sit and hide
ask for help, speak out and say
children born into this world today
let me be chosen to have one by my side.

Infertility is just a word
it should be spoken, we should be heard
we have been given the chance to be
the proudest parents on earth you'll see.

Helen Oliver

My Special Tin

Gazing at the contents I keep in my special tin,
Holding all the memories that are safely kept within.
Thoughts of children playing at a party just for you
Laughing playing games, as children love to do.

Blowing out the candles as they sing the birthday song.
Opening the gifts your friends have brought along.
This was what I'd wished for more than anything I know,
Just to have you with us and watch you slowly grow.

As I carefully write a message on your birthday card,
I come back to reality, it always seems so hard.
'Wishing a happy birthday to a special boy who's eight'
I read the card once more walking slowly through the gate.

Smiling at myself, in my mind I see you wave
I place the card gently with the flowers on your grave.
Yet soon to return to take it home again,
To keep it with the others, in my special tin.

Bernadette Charlton

The Everlasting Dream

He steps lightly, superbly into the sweetness of yester-year,
The elegant chin upon lace ruffles, the eyes without a fear.
How gallant my master looks, the throughout each day;
The velvet, lace brocade, the greying hair ne'er gone astray.
Take heart from the tranquillity, the gentleness of days gone by,
See as always the gondolas, let them not even try
To repeat the wondrous past,
When one was happy, no cloud overcast.
If one believes in dignity, forever it will stay;
Dear dreamer, dream your sweetest dream, that
lasts throughout each day.

Vera Simm

Visions

With my eyes I see many things that life brings
I see the stars in the dark blue sky.
Sunsets of deep pink and red,
The slow falling leaves of autumn,
Changing of the seasons as I live with them
My eyes take the pictures that last forever
So precious are these eyes of mine
I see beauty within others that no other eyes can see
I hope that before I pass on, my eyes will
See a few generations, see with their eyes
The beautiful things I have seen

Angela Lock

Continual Event.....

Speak to you again when your halo has fallen.
Your words are lesser now and bring no comfort here.
Like death when you said you loved another.
How I survived your affairs, each one like an earthquake.
Who are you to bring such pain. A mere man father to my children.
Unmeetness gone now can't pick up the phone.
Won't bring myself to make that call, honeyed words enthral!

I could not trust my love again or look into your eyes.
Rattlesnakes tails flickering with all your lies.
You set out to acquire what you said you lacked,
Your women changed by the week and now you want me back.
You have taken all my young life, and left me middle-aged.
I'll take the love you say is for me, with me to my grave.
This is no rehearsal of life's dreams. You betrayed the vows
And now my life's adventure becomes a shield around me true.
Not a sword I used to hold, trying to get close to you.
Life on my own I'll watch you roam
Seen Divorce though Starting life anew.....

Margaret Murray

Visions

I saw visions from a hill,
All alone as I stood still,
The silver stars in the sky twinkled and sparkled,
Like small fairies on gossamer wings,
Fluttering with merry glee.

The moon was oh so still,
Reminded me of Grandpapa,
It seemed to wane and say
Grandpapa in heaven he be.

The wind suddenly blew cold and chill,
I shivered on the hill,
Thought I saw old Father Time passing by,
Casting shadows before my eyes,
Like people I thought I recognized,
There they all were gliding down the hill.

Colours in the night sky seemed to glow with life,
So I take it all in my strife,
These visions long with me will stay.
As I say good night and kneel to pray.

Kathleen Gosling

Of Proliferating Exigency

Propaganda persists,
But it is despised,
Though we are affected by all it implies.
Stereotypical images conveyed
Results in prejudices overtly displayed.

Enforcing unity,
Whilst resentments arise,
Weakens the effectiveness
    of all who preside.
Without the will of society outside
Intervention is no more help than disguise.

When consolation is merely mockery -
Consolidation fails;
When unification is in jeopardy -
Separation excels.
While dissent only accents the feelings here voiced
The factions remain discordant;
Until all becomes one
Any difference that has begun
Will continue, though even more so.

Andrew Tolfree

Dark Shadows

Why am I down? I surely have no reason to feel these dark
shadows over my previously happy spirit, or to feel this deep
aching solitary loneliness inside which shows no remorse and
knows no limits.

I'm fortunate (or so I'm reminded by those who dare)
I'm 25, happily married with a climbing career.
So why instead of waking up smiling do I want
instead to pull the covers over my aching head and bury myself?

Why instead of seeing the generous patient love of a husband
do I see someone insensitive, unloving and uncaring?
Why do I dread and doubt my ability at work each day
and instead of sunshine and hope, see only shades of grey?

Had I a broken bone or known ailment I could,
at least gain sympathy of friends and doctors who could heal me.
But this illness I have is unseen, unspoken, intangible.
It is something only I can feel.

Or so I thought. I now glimpse sun breaking through from
behind the clouds.
There is a name for my pain-"Depression"-The suffering is no
longer just mine,
There are treatments for this darkness; prosac, supportive friends
and the other great known healer-"time".

Joan Pirie

Mojo Risin

He opened up with words of rhyme
He thought of dying all the time
The feeling from within his soul
Was benefiting all of rock and roll
The way he stood in those early days
The many strange and peculiar ways
The way he taunted all the fans
The drugs and drink leaving empty cans

His words were mystical and oh so deep
His drawings left untidily lying in a heap
He called himself the lizard king
Of him he used to sing
The doors were deep within his mind
No bells on them to ring

He spoke of Mojo Risin
Though I guess he never will
An anagram of his name
A message from Brazil
"What if I pretend to die", he said to all his friends
"It would give the group publicity and a life that never ends."

Lloyd Fortune

Andalusia

I was making my way on a high summers day, through the region
of Andalucia, not a cloud passing by in a blue infinite sky,
wish that I could reach so high.
The omnipresent prickly pear, the only thing that has no care,
and itself unlikely juxtaposed to a once red beautiful wilted rose.

The 'Guadalquiver' in Languorous flow, 'twixt banks of blood
red clay, the sun a copper ball of fire, a forlorn call
from a distant spire, dust choked sierra parched for rain,
a peasant aged from relentless strain, a hawk on the wing
flying high, ever watchful with his beady eye, a lizard
basking in the sun, a shadow falls, to late to run.

I come upon a village, the people all long gone, green
lichen staining the once white walls, abandoned to the sun.
Dark windows blindly staring, like the eyes of long dead
souls, melancholy invades my mind, and I'm touched by a
clinging cold.

So slowly the lazy, spinning earth, turns its back on
the fiery sun, and elongated shadows reach out for the
coolness to come, then darkness falls and hides from sight
the shadowy creatures of the night, cicadas calling their
mournful tune, darkness made lighter by a lucid moon.

R. C. White

Mischief Maker

Miserable indeed are the words from your mouth.
Make belief, is the dream for your future.
Mischief making be your daily occupation.
While deceit is always your comforting words.

Be the ages of the past your guiding light.
Or has wisdom forgotten the way to your ear?
Idle thoughts and sorrowful bliss, seems
to have frozen the tear drops from your crying eyes.

Your ignorance must have given birth to your hate.
Which must have given birth to your wickedness
You wilfully adopted war, and your only interest
is destruction, which breeds darkness and danger.

You have no light or protection from your ignorance
Why is it that these matters has for so long to you
been uncertain? It is your forgetfulness, that makes
it possible for things to be repeated.

True wisdom is the essence of obedience,
A good teacher is a wise teacher, but you
let darkness cloud your watchful eyes,
And so silence your tongue, you mischief maker.

F. Robertson

Threshold Of A Dream

Standing on the threshold of a dream,
A fragile opening in the vast, infinite vaults of sleep.
A flawless crystal portal,
Glittering as though the very stars had been melded and
beaten into a symmetrical sculpture of absolute perfection,
Each intricate detail replicated a million times.
Solid? Liquid? Gas? Who knows....? Who cares...?
Surrounded by a blazing corona of sparkling fire.
It opens yet remains closed.
Is infinite but still resolutely finite.
Universal, but small enough to hold in your palm.
Inside millions upon millions of paths unfold,
Each separate, an individual,
But irrevocably woven together in a tapestry so complete as
to be incomparable to all others.
Each route built with eldritch stone and mortar,
Held in place by an unseen bond.
Each stretching away to an impossible distance.
Each an ethereal road of wind,
Paved with liquid moonlight and dusted with new-born stars.
Not all the finest metals the earth could yield could even come
to this beauteous structure.
Impelled forwards I know no more as my mind spirals away
into its shining blue depths.

Jonathon Plant

Midnight Waves

Soft fresh fallen snow white.
Pure sunny days full of light.
Livid fresh paint
gentle swirling fleece
ink anointing on paper
everything that my hands can soil. All white.

Who am I brown?
What am I, black.

Dirty, dust, filthy, both brown and black
Danger, fear rising out of black,
Like the magic which for some turns tragic,
like the shadow of a cat which crossed my path.
I'm brown, I'm black. Which is right?

I should be white, I want to be white!
But: The beauty of Laila,
    the divinity of Kali Mata,
    the blessings from the grey clouds.

And what if: White eclipses the black,
    like the day conceals the night,
    a horizon beneath my sight.

Esfandyar Khan

211

A Cold Feeling

Hell hath no fury
Like a body robbed of warmth.
Five months into this year and still no sun!
These cold, cold winds
And frosts at night
Nipping new formed buds
And bringing on the aches and pains
In old and young alike.
How long before this winter goes away
Is it here to stay?
Or must I seek a sunnier clime?
If that is so
I must go now
Before my limbs are locked for ever
Too stiff to climb the steps
To reach that kite -
The bird that's going to fly
Me to the sun.

Barbara McGannan

Wheelchair Bound

I shut my eyes
and I dreamt I was sailing the ocean blue,
I shut my eyes
and I dreamt I was travelling along with you!
I shut my eyes
and I dreamt I was back in my walking days.
I shut my eyes
and I dreamt I was no longer in a maze.
I shut my eyes
and dreamt I was running and dancing too,
I shut my eyes
and dream... if only I could be like you!

Hilda Batten

Blencathra

Watching, waiting, early morning,
Checked equipment, all prepared,
Looking onwards, looking upwards,
Adrenaline flowing, anticipating.

Boot by boot, by boulder, by burn,
Happily participating,
Trudging onwards, trudging upwards,
Nervously resting - Scales Tarn reaching.

The edge ominously standing,
Trepidation in surveying,
Hauling onwards, hauling upwards,
Foot by hand, hand by foot.

Friendly bantering, helping, urging,
Cajoling, heaving, pulling, sweating,
Always onwards, always upwards,
Muscles protesting, sharply terrifying.

Deeply breathing concentration,
Ever onwards, ever upwards,
Summit attaining jubilation.-
Sharp Edge conquered.

Peggy Grey

Despair

A world of poverty, violence and crime,
Getting poorer and harder all the time.
Love and friendliness fading away,
Not looking forward to another day.

Days drifting by so long and slow,
Years of toiling and nothing to show.
Children I bore, now grown up and gone,
All alone, wondering where I went wrong.

The clock on the mantle still ticking and chiming,
My heart slowly beating, bleeding and pining.
When did life become so bad?
It's always been that way, how sad.

Rita Metcalfe

The Crucifixion On Good Friday

A disorderly crowd staggered up the hill
People were jostling to be in at the kill
They cared not what the results would be
Taking the life of our Lord, so cruelly.

The Cross was heavy, and He was so weak.
Yet the guards would allow no one to speak
Just more beatings with lash and whip.
But when, at last, He did fail, and trip,
One stalwart heart pushed forward and the Cross he bore
Sharing the load of those shoulders, so bruised and sore.

At last the rabble reached the hill crest,
Soldiers stripped off His clothes, baring His breast,
Crammed a crown of thorns on His head, amid laughter,
Over which the world has wept ever after,
Hammered nails through His hands and feet to the Cross.
Unaware this would be the world's greatest loss.

They hoisted Him high, and called Him an outcast,
A soldier cut His side and His blood flowed fast.
And when, at last, He did succumb,
His faithful friends were left...numb!

Vera Coaton

The Candle's Burning Out

When I look around
I see not life but death;
When I breathe
I breathe not air but selfishness;
When I listen
I hear not nature but cries for help;
When I die
I feel relief not anguish;
When I speak
I speak of holes in the sky not nature's child;
The world is a stranger to many,
But to me it is my second mother.

Adam Russell

His Return

When Jesus comes back again
Shall we, His people, be ready?
This poor and sorrowing world has such need
That can only be righted by Him.

He loved us once — He loves us still
And He wants us to love Him,
So let us tear down the chains and any strings
Which are not attached to Him,

Come, Lord Jesus in your glory
Come and set this world free.
Take away pain, suffering and strife,
Come and rule in your majesty.

We come before You now, repentant for
what we have done,
Sorry for words we have said that were not
a witness for You,
We must improve before it's too late,
Come Lord Jesus, on You we wait.

Moira Fisken

My Final Ode

All my life I was searching,
For what I never found.
It had no face, nor colour, nor form
But I almost felt it, like an oncoming storm
It was sometimes all around me,
Yet never quite there at all.
From some people I tried to take it,
But they weren't ready and I was too small.
Please pray that my soul has now found it,
And my earthly disquiet is at rest.
Please pray that my spirit's contented.
I'm sorry, I gave it my best.

Jennifer Ellis

New Light

Lying looking at the stars tonight.
I opened my heart and let in a new light,
I saw then, I needed to be love
I can't hold us to the past, that had just walked out.

I had to lose this feeling of soft silent grieving
And never shed that lonely tear of memories of love that was
so dear.

But recalling all the moments,
All the cards and all the photos

This new light dimmed,
How could I think this?
Is this a sin?

He does not want her, he wants me
But this mist is too thick, he cannot see,
I will wait for him, and he'll come running
And I will give him back, all my loving.

Until the day, that new light will never shine
And the memories of the old light
will always be mine

Diane Thomson

The Buttercup Field

The buttercups danced with a yellow sheen,
In waves of molten gold,
A more wonderful sight, I never have seen,
O'er the ground as they rippled and rolled.

They lifted my spirits, this sunshine day
Splashed against a sky of blue,
I gazed, then reluctantly went on my way.
In my eye I carried their hue.

I took out my pencil and drew them with car,
Worked with my colours as well,
But nothing I did, could ever compare.
With those flowers in their golden dell.

I then took my camera, with the sun at its height,
And caught them for all to see.
But, although the field was a beautiful sight,
Their glory was not there for me.

Then I lay on my bed, and saw them once more,
As I started to meditate.,
And slowly their beauty arose as before.
The vision was just as great.

Ursula Male

Memory Of A Friend

You are a friend from old a pal bursting with life.
I remember your haze of frankness
My good friend so sleep that long sleep.

Always there when I wanted a beer
You boasted of breath, body and wealth
My good friend so sleep that long sleep

You always showed off paying for affection
through gallons of beer and wine,
Tall as a statue and as proud
My good friend so sleep that long sleep.

Never were you to shy for fun and verse
With echoes of your laughter hanging in every corner of the pub
My good friend so sleep that long sleep.

These were the days of truth for you with memories held
through the mists of time
My good friend so sleep that long sleep.

Then I see you there still laughing at the bar
Boasting with shadows moving in elaborate forms of smoke.
My good friend so sleep that long sleep.

Will you remember me this way, my dear friend
When it is my turn to sleep that long sleep.

James Stewart

The Orb

A glint of light caught my eye,
a reflection of sunlight.
It looked magical, a small sphere,
an orb, each point equidistant
from its centre.

There it lay on a small cone of sand
left as the waves receded.
How many times had it tumbled,
Up and down the beach?
Washed by the waves, embraced in their water,
then abandoned.

A miniature fortune-teller's globe,
Glass, with bubbles of air, frozen within,
Slight tints of green, gold, violet and blue.
It lay on the palm of my hand,
Shadow circles radiating from it,
each with a centre of yellow light.

What is this magical thing?
Surely it is more than a boy's lost marble?

Janet Chaffey

Longing

Why do I live within four walls
When all around the air is free?
Cabin'd, cribbed, confined and bored
My dreams are of the sea.
The gulls are calling, calling, calling,
Calling me away.
The ebb-tide draining from the mud flat whispers
"Come with me - why stay?"
The grey-green seas beyond the bar
Driven by wind and tide,
Make their challenge loud and clear
"Who will with us ride"?
They tell their tales of sunlit seas
They will not be denied.
Oh! Man must reap where he has sown
I know to bitter cost;
And I must go and that right soon
Or I am lost.

David Bird

Untitled

Dearest Lord believe me when I say I care
About the needless dying and the countries in despair,
About the way we spoil the earth and mar our lovely land,
The way pollution kills the sea and stains the golden sand.
I cannot do much physically about the world's sad plight,
Just hope that all the powers to be will start to put things right,
But one thing I can do, each day, is come to you in prayer,
And ask your help in showing that everyone should care,
We all must mend our ways right now and show what we are worth,
All life's so very precious in our brief time on earth.

M. E. Y. Malkin

Weeping Willow

The lazy summer sun coats your leaves,
Wearily you hang,
Lightly sweeping in the warm summer's air,
Peacefully alone.

Your colleagues stretch towards their height.
Do your feathered branches exhaust you so,
That you must weep into the ground?
Constantly spreading night beneath you,
Sharing the gloom of your unhappiness.

Solitary mourner.
The perished past leaves you ghostly,
Silently swaying.

Poor weeping willow,
Will your sadness be everlasting?

Ellie Hardcastle

A Countryside Walk

We followed the arrows on our Countryside Walk,
As we wandered along all we did was talk,
In the depths of the country we suddenly saw,
The arrows of direction were sadly no more.

Which way do we go to left or to right?
Was the question to our plight,
We decided a left it would have to be,
As in the distance a farm we could see.

We arrived at the farm and knocked on their door,
For help to find our home once more,
'Ah me beauties can you see,
The track over there is the one for thee,
Follow it down both left and to right,
There you'll see the road in sight'.

So off we went down the long winding track,
Following his directions we were on our way back,
Down paths, past fields we wandered along,
To get to the road we should've been on,
As time got on we eventually got near,
At last! We knew our way from here.

Tanya Morant

Evil

What is it?... Can you see it?... Can you hear it?
   What's going on in me? What thoughts are they?
   Do I know about it?
      It's here...it's there....it's everywhere.

It's watching us with its cold dark eyes, with the red tints of greed.
   Waiting, waiting, watching watching...
      Hoping for the wrong move,
         To change day into night, smiling with adoring trouble,
            Always whispering...giving ideas
               Ready to ruin life's joy....

It's breathing over us, down our backs,
   You can feel it...but don't dare say a word...
      It's grinning!...Life's misery!...God's misery!...
         It can't be stopped, for it's human nature.
            Growing in the book of life.
               It's blinded us, it's blocked out the light.

But!.....
   Man struggles,
      Struggles for mercy....

Andrea S. Curran

A Silver Tear

Oblivious by the power of vanity
we are unconscious to the world,
while embraced by ourselves...

You can tell by the lines on his face
you can tell he's been crying, yet you walk on, never look back.

All you hear is him sighing.
Don't stop. Carry on regardless.
His silent screams are unheard.
His soul is weary from the work of endless waiting.

The ignorance of ourselves is but an inner
tempest of blind hostility...
When the dusk advanced rapidly,
and long shadows were cast across the city,
he sat quietly in the corner of an alleyway.
Beside him lay a torn cloth and for that he was grateful.

The night grew colder and the snow fell silently.
He closed his eyes, and awoke in a Kingdom of Silver cloud.

They found that December morning lying in the snow
On his face was a slight smile,
and on his cheek lay a frozen silver tear.

Aisling Corristine

Hannah

Your friends and colleagues asked me to say
A few kind words on your birthday
For many years your task has been
To keep the B.P. complex clean
From half past seven till after four
Cathy gives you more and more
When you arrive at seven thirty
The place is at its usual dirty
You polish desks and buff the floors
You clean the tables and dust the doors
Your buffing is the best we've seen
No one can match your brilliant sheen
A visit to greenridge caused a hitch
When you crossed swords with some old witch
She asked could you work in the garden
You said to her I beg your pardon
I'm here to clean your rooms and showers
And not to tend your bloody flowers
A happy birthday and our best wishes
Now hurry home and do your dishes

J. A. McKay

The Hills

I must go back to the hills again
To the lofty peaks and the sky,
And all I want is my walking boots
And my day-sac on my back,
The winding path, the grey stone
The heather, dry and springy,
And the lark's trill and the burn's song
And a heart that's light and free.

The grassy bank, the mossy cove
Where I can lay my head
And watch the eagle soaring o'er
Its outcrop grey and bare,
And when I reach my goal at last
With the wind's sough and the sun's glare
I'll view with lightening ease again,
In silence and in happiness
The scene around my feet.

Dorothy Currie

Where Nobody Goes

There's a place on earth where nobody goes,
an eerie corner of the globe.
In this corner lies a tomb,
a now silent reminder of what's to come?
Men do come here! in their special suits,
With masks and gloves and padded boots.
To keep an eye on man's achievement,
a monster, which now deals out bereavement.
This tomb of ours, this deadly creation,
has filled the skies with radiation.
Children are dying, parents, too,
but do any of us know just what to do.
The tomb is awake deep inside,
its concrete shell built to hide.
The horror which has befallen those,
in that corner of the world, where nobody goes
CHERNOBYL.

Stuart Bassett

A Memo

A Memo is a letter son that some can write so well,
Others think and ponder which is maybe just as well
Others like your Daddy Son do the best they can
Because they know that if they don't, that some, smart Alex can,
So listen to my story Son, and think as best you can
I know your Daddy isn't bright, but he does the best he can.
The moral of my story Son, is think before you speak
And when I write a memo it is your brains I will seek.

   A loving and not so brainy Dad.

G. J. Ford

Norwegian Flashbacks

In mist filled dales amid the craggy tops,
where island hillocks float on sea of cloud,
unfathomed lakes now glisten blue
beneath the summer sky - and gushing, rushing
turquoise rivers leave the glaciers above
which fell from clouds unfathomed years ago.

Between the blood-red dawn and sunset skies
which paint their rosebud bloom on winter hills,
the long-loved sun in azure shines, brightening
the snow-white glow; white jewels glisten by lamplight
cheerful on the drifts, feather light the flakes
fall faster now. Gleefully the skiers
wax their skis against tomorrow's run.

It's crisp. It's soft. Beware the ice below,
which lies in wait for unsuspecting soles.
Fresh snow on old ice does not grip-then flip!
those soles are in the air, and laughter rings
as on the feathery fullness flat I fall.
I gaze at the eternal blue and dream
I'm gazing from astride a fleecy cloud.

Diane Bennett

Thou And I

You come into my soul - is this blinding light
  Really You?
Like swallows plunging into noon-day heat
I drown in God yet perish not.
Nor does His fire extinguish me,
I gaze at Him in awe - and still I live.
He lends me flames for self-consumption
My heart is a Burning Bush!
We commune through the eloquence of His silent heart beat
  and mine
  echoing...
His eye contains the universe.
With His eyes - I see my own face, unseen before,
and to my own Self I stand revealed
  and feel compelled to Follow Him.
He sheds my tears and wears my kisses,
plays me into music...
Through me He loves the world.
I die in Him and live to love
as I learn that Eternity is Now.

Margaret Joy Philippou

Forbidden Love

There was a darkness to the air
And a coldness to the breeze
This is what I remembered
When you brought me to my knees.

You turned my life upside down
inside out and back to front
Leaving me soulless and empty
With my heart to take the brunt.

But now I have battled through the pain
To see the sunshine instead of rain
You tell me you want me back
But I am scared I'm going to crack
Through the strain, of loving you again.

You were all I lived for at one time in my life and in my mind
But times and lives have changed and another heart you must find.

Because I have battled through the pain
To see sunshine instead of rain
I can never come back to you
No matter what you say or do
as you would drive me insane, if you left me again.

John W. Thomson

When The Bell Tolls

When the bell tolls and the night rolls in
When the light fades and the dreams begin
With your eyes closed, your arms fold,
and tightly hold in.

And you breathe slow and your mind shows
Reflections....

In the darkness of the hours that slowly pass you by
you see yourself just as you are
within your own mind's eye;
and if you hold so tenderly - protect yourself till dawning
you'll find that you can rise and face the coming of the morning
And light will break, and you will wake and catch the morning star;
Leaving just the memories of the dreams that took you far -
Far above and far away and farther away still
You know that nights are only mornings, waiting for your
daytime will -

The will to rise and face it all again,
The will to rise and fight,
The will to try just once again,
To get the whole thing right!

D. C. Oldham

A Friend

A good friend
Is a precious blend.

A friend is one with a happy face,
Making the world a better place.
One who is there over the years,
Sharing with you your joy and fears.
She'll be there through thick and thin,
Never committing a deadly sin.
One who helps you see the light,
Making your life a great delight.
A good friend is found in few,
Helping with anything that you do.
Whatever a friend comes out to say,
You can never take the wrong way.
What they say is never untrue,
You can trust them, just them and you.

Friends like these,
Leave you with fond and loving memories.
Have a friend!
They will stay with you to the end.

Gemma Fossett

My Son

Only a mother through her eyes,
See where her baby's beauty lies.
His first sweet smile, his clutching hand;
His face serene in slumber land.

He say's 'Da-da' you proudly boast;
Then with the weeks you find a host
Of other words he tried to say.....
Stumbling in his baby way.

Freshly bathed, hair soft brushed,
Happy laughter now is hushed.
His toys lie scattered and dejected;
A golliwog that he selected
Is lying in ungainly pose.........
Against ten pink and tiny toes.

It isn't long since you were born, little man so soft and warm.
But, time will pass and you will grow
As waters through the bridges flow.

But whate'er you do and where'er you go,
Something you will always know your mummy loves and thinks of you;
Will cherish you your whole life through.

Pamela Bridle

215

Wasted Tears

My sorrow is my past.
Childhood memories of guilt, quiet tears.
Those countless years of pain.
The ache the heart can't take.
No one really knows.
Those wasted years.

It was so right. It was so wrong.
That lovers had come and gone, wondering
What was never to become.
What I could have had, but lost.
Cherished moments.
Forbidden trust.
Those wasted years.

She's always flying never landing
Unsettled yet demanding
No time to spare one's feeling's
Discard with no meaning
Angry screams with no sound.
Yet so profound.
Those wasted years.

Morag Hill

Living Words

We drown words with ceaseless chatter.
Soaked with conversation
We splash each other on the shores of speech.
Dripping with weighty talk
We try to wring out a waterlogged meaning.

But somewhere, among the cascading sentences,
Words have a life of their own, and emerge,
Crystal clear to dry out in the sun.

Maybe we shall shut up long enough
To hear what they say!

J. H. Baker

Good Time Town

We came and went away that day
In blue red bars while drinking away
we laughed and joked at what we saw
the respectable sex shops, the lifeless whore
yet still quiet moments stole the joy
and each in others eyes saw cold surprise
we came to the Good Time Town that day and took a part of it away

Patrick R. Phillips

"Irrelevant"

Through nights laden with atrocities
The child looked up with innocent eyes,
The days encumbered by irrelevance
The mouth spoken with unwanted lies.

The good times hated for what they have become
The bad times accepted for what they have done,
The world, a place of spoken mime
Philosophies are but only rhyme.

Imagery is blocked and all truth hides
Lies have fun on the fairground ride,
Anger is spoken, a feast to the dead
Another mark, another shoe, another tread.

Silence cuts through me like a chainsaw to a limb
Darkness hides secrets known only to those within,
Knowledge escapes me as I wonder why
Maybe in the end I will tortured and fried.

Tonight could be the worst in all my mortal hours
For I have lost all will and imagery powers,
I am gullible and weak and want to sleep
My outlook if any looks lonely and bleak.

Paul Scott Taylor

Lupus - Who Are You

The last day of the year, my diary's complete, I
turn a few pages and what do I meet? A day
of sorrow and pain and despair - "Oh please", my
heart cries, "doesn't anyone care?"
   Another day looms and what do I see -
words of compassion - my heart is carefree.
   I keep looking back - it wasn't all bad,
a mixture I see of the sad and its glad.
   Most days were sunshine, just some of them rain,
it wasn't all heartache and pleas made in vain.
   I see I fought back, my ladies need me -
I'm a contract you see and I have to be free
to listen and help in the best way I can,
so please keep on calling, I am what I am.
   My ear is yours, my lips are sealed, your
problems and troubles are never revealed.
   So please don't despair, I really do care -
we need each other - companions and friends,
fighting together whatever fate sends.

Etheldra Margaret Bishop

Granny And Her Cottage

I remember granny's buttoned boots, her long black skirt
Covered by an apron, also her striped shirt
The rag rug by the hearth, the black leaded grate
For the visitor, a special cup saucer and plate
Thinly cut bread, real butter to eat
The wicker basket chair her favourite seat
A paraffin lamp on the table giving light
Cheering the room on a dark winters night
A candle to show the way upstairs
The cellar below so cold and bare

A. Myers

Neither, Neither...

By my innocent eyes I see a world of temptation,
Through my crystal gaze I sense an unseen destination,
And through caresses of this distant universe,
I'm slid away and taken, to live its life coerced.

You take me to this outer plain, you take me to its core,
And silently throughout we sail to wonder at its law,
Past the keeper of dimensions to the keeper of the key,
I feel I'm leaving everywhere when I journey into me.

Flashes of your life fill fantastical dreams,
I slip into their night as I leave reality,
Behind the passage of my eyes there rests the secret hidden,
Within its shrouds of perfect lies, the truth inside is written...

Rachael Grey

The Reality Of Robin Hood

Robin Hood and his merry fellas
Enjoyed to raid posh people's cellars
And why do you think they were all so merry?
They were always pickled in Xmas sherry!
Now, this fat geezer named Friar Tuck
Really enjoyed a good long suck
Upon his bottle of jolly juice,
His "Holy Spirit" which turned him puce!
And then there's Little John of course.
He couldn't tell a rabbit from a horse.
His girlfriend left him... you know why?
Well think, what does his name imply?
Maid Marian? She couldn't lose.
She just loved Robin for his booze,
And then went back to Sheriff N.
Who was her husband number ten!
"Meat macrame" was his trade,
"Knotting Ham" was very well paid!
So now I'll leave you with this note...
Never trust a man in a Lincoln green coat!

Joanna C. Harston

Mother

Sitting by the hospital bed
holding my mother's hand
I sit there worried sick
fiddling with her wedding band.
Then the nurse came
my eyes filled with tears
as for my dear mother passed away,
"My Mother" who looked after me,
through my childhood years.
I was very distressed by this news
I suppose you could say I was feeling the blues.
I never got chance to tell my mother,
"How much I loved her so",
and now she's gone to that world above,
I guess she'll never know.

Karen L. Rust

A Lonely Man

The room is cold and lonely,
the chair so dank and bare.
I've suffered life's endeavour,
but no-one seems to care.

In weak despair I close my eyes,
voiceless calls I make.
My weary mind is troubled.
No more can this man take.

From first to last I loved her,
so full of natures vibes.
Our life-long chord is broken,
just like the rushing tide.

My sentimental flute plays on,
a tune filled full of pleasure.
It entertains me for a while,
surrounded by my treasures.

Each man should learn that life is short,
but filled with red not timbers.
Those burning fires that filled my heart,
are now just dying embers.

D. A. L. James

A Prayer

Stay gentle spirit just for a while
Let our hearts beat innocent of guile
Bring us mildness of airs from distant skies
And keep from our lips the language of lies
May our eyes meet together without the cold stare

As children again with never a care
Give to our footsteps the light touch of dance
Let us fecklessly leave all entirely to chance
Trusting lack of resistance is the guide
To the isle of happiness somewhere inside.
If gentle spirit I cry for the moon
Let me drowse one summer afternoon
Till fret and disquiet leave on the breath
Then shall I know you are not Death.

A. L. Phillips

Shadows Fled

A twisting vice, where pressure builds,
Brothers' scars and conscience cries,
Explosive spite, a target, a knife,
Consequential remorse with thought and pain,
An open window, where light shines in,
And shadows flee, no target, just resigned questions.

Shadows stalk by the window's edge,
Hope condenses on the window, and fiery light spreads,
Until with trust, the light spreads forth,
Shadows fled and broken vice,
A sad acceptance of all that is,
And gladness that the shadows fled.

Ralph Baldwin

Friends

Life is a highway,
    On it, our future blends,
And as we face each new day,
    We feel rich, when we have friends.

Friends are folk we like to greet,
    As we travel along life's way
And we know, when our friends we meet,
    We will share a happy day.

Friends always stand by you,
    When the skies are grey,
But in their company, the skies turn to blue,
    And your troubles, are chased away.

Friends do give you pleasure,
    They make you feel happy and gay,
And we share memories we treasure,
    As we sit and chat each day.

We all do have a special friend,
    With whom we spend more time each day,
And we hope that friendship will never end,
    As we journey on our way.

N. Queate

Poetry And A Journey

There comes a time,
When a journey has passed the start but not yet the end,
When poetry can be seen as an apparition of the young,
For words may console the mind,
But show no reason as to where life shall lead,
Sonnets may tempt our heart,
And stanzas may rub the soul,
But they show little guidance in the world we know,

Poetry is a phase of expression,
Of searching and of discovery,
A time to shape the mind and of others who may follow,
Then the point is reached where life begins and all else ends,
It is then we feel a frustrated soul,
For responsibility becomes stronger than passion,
And we begin to leave the phase of growth,
And enter into the world of wealth,
Where money numbs the brain and blinds the sight.

Paula Roche

Untitled

I wandered far away, beyond the rim
Of the horizon that had imprisoned me
In the false glory of a city life.
A track between the corn fields lured me on
Alone amid the seas of shimmering oats.
The path was strewn with flowers of brightest hue.
Poppies of scarlet fire and purple vetch,
And lady's bedstraw, yellow as the sun,
Embroidered on the borders of the cloth
That summer's hand had spread across the fields
The peace I sought filled the great bowl of sky
And overflowed into the distant blue
Of the far plains that lay below the hills.
No breath of wind disturbed the trembling air
Which seemed a veil that could be drawn aside
To show the ultimate peace in the heart of things

Dora Lewis

Love Heart

A heart is a symbol of love,
It has a deep sensation of affection,
It feels and cares about the things it adores,
Its emotions are strong, but can be broken,
It has fear, it has sorrow,
But it does have joy,
It loves to love a person,
But hopes for the love in return.

Gemma Russell

What Cracks You Up?

Crack in the ice when I'm skating - no dice.
Crack in my lips, with vinegar on chips - not nice.
Crack in my armour, revealing the pain from a bastard but was
he a charmer!
Crack in the pavement - not to be trod on
Crack in my confidence - I'll just have to plod on.

Crack in the sod of the earth in a drought.
Crack in an alibi - catching me out.
Crack in my face like a smug Cheshire cat.
Crack in my book where the corner's turned down
(to remind me of where I was at.)

Crack in the back of a workman's blue jeans
Crack in the wall where asbestos might lurk
Cracking the codes in my PC at work
Crack in my mirror - years of bad luck.

Crack in my glass and the wine oozes out
Crack goes a whip, or the sails of a ship, or the hip of a lady
who's old
Crack in an apple revealing the pips, but...
Crack in our kids is DEATH.

Wendy Gaynair

Life Today

This plastic throw-away world
 Man polluting the air and sea
The taking of the heritage of our children
 And possible denial, by you and me
Destroying the rain forests and natural beauty
 Created by mother nature herself
The cruelty of man with factory farming
 And for what? To create this wealth.
What a wondrous place this planet of ours
 What a wondrous place indeed
But destruction, killing and willing,
 Who was it that planted the seed?

 P. Lesk

For Your Dad

He was such a gentle man, thoughtful, loving and kind,
Special men like him are very hard to find.
He loved the women in his life in his own special way,
His smile will always be with you, forever and a day.
I know you'll always be so very, very glad,
That God chose him to be your lovely, loving Dad.
From a distance he'll be watching you with tender
 loving care,
We're thinking of him at this time and you in your
 despair.
Be strong and stick together, try to stand the pain,
Because someday, sometime, somewhere you'll all be
 together again.

 Christine Linden

Peace

What if there was peace?
No war, everyone loving each other.
The world would be a wonderful place
No more innocent lives being taken away
May be peace will come one day.
Bombs go off, children injured by gun shots
If peace came to earth to the world this would mean a lot.
Pain and devastation, it's becoming worse
For the countries who have suffered war feel that
They have been cursed.
It's us, the human race, who causes this devastation
And it will continue as long as there are
Nuclear weapons, greed and hatred.
We want peace, it's everything we all wish
We pray that one day this will be accomplished
So I ask myself once again - what if
There was peace and no more pain.

 Michelle Hoskins

Feeling The Loss

When someone so dear passes away,
There is usually little that one finds to say,
They send their condolences, flowers and wreaths,
But no one can stop that deep feeling of grief.

The sadness and pain is felt for a while,
But fighting the tears you force a smile,
The service is over and Bill's laid to rest,
Now you know for a time you won't be at your best.

Though sad it may be to loose him so soon,
He's there in the stars and the sky and the moon,
Looking down he's sending you strength and love,
For ever and ever from up above.

 Amanda Rose Jackson

Scarlet

Scarlet's in love, so intense that it hurts.
She longs to hold him. Someone else got there first.
Scarlet must wait, tears on her face,
She knows and accepts she must take second place.
He has a life to live of his own,
She is excluded and feels all alone.
Maybe tomorrow she'll see him again.
He'll hold her and kiss her and ease all the pain.
Her life's full of maybes, of wishes, and dreams
Is love to elude her? That's how it seems.
Scarlet's in love, it may be just for a while,
Though it fills her with sadness, she tries so hard to smile.

 Carol Wilson

Jaffa

You spent your nights in Spanish rain,
Crying tears of golden water,
Like the pocketed chin of a young lad,
You are dotted with clamouring pinheads.

Moistness, like the dank walls of
Abandoned cottages, engulfs you
And your womb of half moon shaped faces,
Conversing with brain shaped clouds.

Your temple of skin unfolds and reveals,
A rugby team discussing half-time tactics,
A cluster of swelling tonsils,
You are naked before my eyes.

A liquid balloon explodes, on the tongue,
Like the lungs of a drowned man,
A deflating football smelling of pine,
Roaring fires, snow and tiredness.

 John Honour

The River

As a child I was always attracted to the river,
Everyday it seemed to get bigger.
I often sailed a toy boat,
For the current of the river kept it afloat.

Sometimes I would make a fishing rod and line,
With a stick and a bent nail and twine.
Only thing wrong there seemed to be less fish swimming about,
So for me it was going to be hard to land a trout.

In summer I would do without my wellington boots.
Much fun was to be had when paddling in bare foot.
My friends and I held contests every week,
Throwing stones and making big splashes is what we did seek.

The water in the river was dirty I was often told,
But a child like me was too bold.
If the water kept on flowing through I thought,
Then dirty water would run on by and not be caught.

Now that I have grown and other rivers I have seen,
I compare them to the one I played in right up to my teens.
The lure of the water must have been the attraction.
Nowadays other children are getting the same satisfaction.

 Biddy McAuley

Petal Promises

Petals, the promises fall from lover's lips
"I love you, I will always love you"
Looking upwards into light, airy blossom decked trees,
Fountain foaming flowers,
Myriad blooms that conjure wedding
thoughts in cloud bursts of confetti.

The blossom tree, caught by the breeze
Sets petals twirling down in gossamer
gusts to fall with unbearable
clatter like white china plates
on quarried floor.

Sharp shards of shattered promises
pierce painfully depths of soul.
At length when shock has hardened into resignation,
Sweep up the broken promises
With quiet deliberation.

Heather Adams

The Pain Of Love

As daylight breaks the dark-night, calm,
I, safe in semi-slumber lie.
Enfolded in his manly arms
As pale light bathes the morning sky.

With the passing of the dawn,
My blissful dream's cruelly broken.
Our faces now with anguish drawn,
As harsh and angry words are spoken.

Noon; and now the sun is bright.
To daily chores I must comply.
While tears of anguish blur my sight,
I live my life a contented lie.

My suffering grows as day draws on;
When still he is not returning.
With fears that he is this time gone,
My body for his touch is yearning.

From above the dark descending.
The daylight fleeting as a dove,
As still within my heart, unending,
Remains the persistent ache of love.

Rachel Sandham

'Awakening'

Looking from my window I can see my garden, where
    For many months, when cold and dark, the flower beds lay bare.
But now that spring has come at last, with sunshine, light and rain
    The earth is showing signs of growth and has come to life again.

It seems to me as if, one day, there is no life at all
    Then in the twinkling of an eye, the plants are straight and tall.
They bring us so much pleasure, flow'rs yellow, pink and white
    With blossoms bursting in the day, and resting through the night.

It's wonderful how nature always seem to know what's best.
    In summer, winter, spring or fall, she never takes a rest
I never cease to be amazed at the wonders that I see
    When looking from my window - oh, want joy it gives to me.

Sheila Blacker

Closing Time

Light and colour make idiot of my senses;
Familiar outlines benignly do become;
A blurring softness saturates my soul
And plays havoc with my reason.
So dim the lights - but slowly -
And let me sink within myself.

But now the world is grey, the sun has lost its glow;
I've lost my way - I know not where to go.
Endless is the night, the dawn it never comes:
No future fills my sight; the present merely numbs.

Roger Lees

Untitled

Death is a creature that lives in your soul,
It eats from inside you, leaving you cold.
When you suffer your family dies,
A segment of their heart is killed,
The segment that you once filled.

At the end of your life your heart is like an empty box,
It is not cleared of the life you once lived.
Your troubles, loves, memories, pains and feelings,
Are wiped from your now useless body,
They are stored away in your friends and family's cares,
Until another depressing day.

Your body is left and your soul lives in heaven,
You live in the luxury of life up above.
You watch over your family and smile at happy moments,
You're glad that they still hold the memory and live on,
You're glad that they still hold the memory.

Erica Turner

"Speechless"

Born into the land of the living. Our freedom ride.
Naked, with no means to hide.
Speechless discovery that I can see.
360 degrees all round me, found! My community.
Every degree, every change, every turn.
Expose so varied experiences, so much to learn.
All life's ups and downs, overwhelmed by the gun the bomb
and the crown. The joys, gems and pleasures are all to be found.
Where do you go? Where do they go? Why do they go?
Once sunshine, now snow, then rain,
from Tim Buck to Australia, London, Boston and back again.
Every degree a change, every bad can't be neutralized by a plane.
Lost, betwixt and between immigration, sickness, sadness and a
troubled sense. The reapers justice overrules both pope and queen.
This earthly chaos, every turn through degree,
A new state of mind found as souls run aground on a disturbed sea.
Please! Please! Peace! Why do you illude all that can see.
Eyes closed, spin round and round, petition disorientation
And awaken fore sight or first sight of this land, direction to begin.
Close your eyes and begin within this land, begin! Begin! Begin!
After all it's only talkin'.

Kenneth Leddy

Freedom Of The Universe

We were born free in this universe,
Without the threat of war and curse,
    And yet every inch of ground,
    Man has grabbed and called his pound,
Even the sea is no longer free,
Like a colony of ants,
    Man is spreading his wings,
    Fighting taking over the beauty of things,
Why can't we live naturally?
Think of the world, not as ours,
    But being there for us to share,
    Take away arms to reduce the fighting,
Let this be the first sighting.

Enid Bowerman

Life....

Like a cloud of electrons in a pot-pourri of molecules.
Pointlessly circling, spiralling, decaying
In chemicals flowing, swirling and reacting
Releasing memories, thoughts, feelings and actions.
Into a mass of humanity; endlessly pursuing
Power and position; on a globe that is circling
A ball of gas; spinning slowly in the arms of a spiral
Ponderously swirling
In a circle of emptiness.
Endlessly rotating, churning and spinning
Lost madly in its giddy spell. Pointlessly
Jostling, fighting each other, why?
To be the first to go round in circles,
Like a cloud of....

W. J. Rennie

Keep Smiling

Keep smiling, keep laughing, keep hoping.
Each one has a problem to solve,
with each problem we learn a lesson.
So sit down and thank the Lord.
He gave us life, love and blessings,
To solve every problem he sends,
So hope for the best and stop moping.
Keep smiling, keep laughing keep hoping.

W. M. Innes-Hall

Safely Grazing

Silky day. Soothing sheep. Fells are dreaming.
The mirror of the tarn holds summer sky.
But grim, ungentle traffic far below
Destroys this cradling calm of green and blue.
Lorries scream. From maiming motor ways
Noise splits the mind with schizophrenic rage,
Life fed into a carburetor.
Torn limbs go bleeding to the slab.

Here munching sheep are safer than they know.
Their world is grass,
Their woolly nerves are grass.
They nibble peacefully upon the fells,
Their simple world defined.
Until swift abattoir controls their end
Their little lives
Move happily on grass.

Muriel Long

Time

Time is a most mysterious thing,
All sorts of changes it can bring
It passes so quickly when not expected to,
And other times goes slowly to frustrate you.

Time can cure each little worry,
Although memories don't vanish in a hurry
It is true that no precious moment can last,
As the present always becomes the past.

Everything you have now may look clear,
But when years pass it will not be here
To each person and thing, time does change,
And the future it does arrange.

Record today's events in your mind,
As no memory should be left behind.

Elaine Ede

The Jumbo Jet

I'm flying high in a 747,
With engines roaring on in heaven.
The Captain tells how fast we are
at five fifty miles an hour.

The stewardesses feed us well,
Up so high we can hardly tell.
We think we could be on the ground,
Having lunch in a sun-drenched town.

On and On we fly non-stop
until we reach our landing spot.
The Captain says, "We are coming down,
very soon we'll reach the ground".

We hear the wheels lock down and latch.
And soon the ground they touch and snatch.
We rumble on until we stop...
then taxi to our berthing spot.

The doors are flung open wide,
The stairway comes up to the side.
We thank the crew and disembark.
Then turn and look at the Wondrous Aircraft.

L. S. Harrison

A Snowflake

Over the quiet reaches of my soul you move
And cast such spells
That Tara's Harp rings clear about my dreams
And the music of the glens comes drifting
From the fringes of the past.
Time itself is frozen still,
A snowflake in your hair.

Your singing sweet as the thrushes song
That coaxes me from sleep.
Your laughter a silver bell
That echoes down the corridors of my mind.
Carefully you thread about my fears
Easing the pain, collecting the tears
Touching a cord, breathing a word
Anxious in your loving.

Patrick King

Dark Realisation

A life is ending-
Bright thoughts left isolated on the others side of life,
All senses wallowing in darkness
Like a grieving widow weeping for her lost light.

Dark shadows loom
Down on a closing door,
Hidden deep in a field of gloom,
No glow can be seen, no warmth can be felt,
Too bright is this source of darkness.

Gone is the source of life,
No longer providing the light.
Mother Earth's seedlings have wilted
No longer can hope bloom.

Many shoulders hold the blame,
But like a sulky criminal
They shy away
From the dark realisation-
No longer in this world can we stay.

Julie Barrett

One Day On The Way To The Theatre

Anxiety deafens me to other patients in the ward
Sounds of hospital routines recede to the furthest corners.
A self-imposed isolation conquers trepidation.
An antiseptic warmth creeps slowly over me; pains in my side diminish.
Around me, the soft clatter of caring and the murmurs of nurses,
Inject me with sleep....
Instantly, the curtain opens to an insistent calling of my name.
The ward sister, and two men in green attend my bed.
A fresh feeling of well-being makes me spurn offers of help
And I crawl like a tentative tortoise to the trolley.
I am flat on my back and helpless; my world assumes new limits.
The stretcher swishes smoothly from the ward; the cold air of the
corridors cools my face as, like a spent Michelangelo, I watch
pristine ceilings slide by. The porters prattle hospitably until we
stop beside double swing doors. I am at the junction awaiting
the green light, feeling too well to go on, too ill to go back.
From a door ahead comes a nurse dressed like a Dervish.
She greets me with a smile and tender words;
She takes my hand and we whirl into oblivion...

Barry Jacobs

Compassions

A slave of the impurity lies heavy on my heart.
My soul searches desperately for salvation.
A caring, sharing touch of a hand,
Penetrates through darkness, reaches out and hugs
the forgotten soul.
Silently a loving smile glows to warm the unloved heart.
The darkness weakens to rays of light, carpeted
with buds of love.
Marvelled in a tender glimpse of God's glories.

Jenifer Ellen Austin

My Beloved

Do not ever cross the road
So not to speak of my beloved
Where I am, he is.
So it has always been
Since I was seventeen

When war clouds drifted 'cross the sky
He went away to far beyond.
I fastened on a star.
And as I looked, I knew
He would be gazing at it too

When the clouds cleared
Giving way to peace
A truly glorious life we shared
Now he has gone away
I wish upon a star
I'll follow soon.

It is. It was. It will ever be
As we in life, loved the other each
There is no doubting this
Where I am, he is nothing can alter this

Dolly Harmer

Mind

Be still oh tired mind of mine.
No time to wonder what's in store
Be still, oh aching heart of mine
No time to long for what's gone before.

Cope only with the here and now.
Rely on God, to show you how.

Be still oh flowing eyes of mine.
No time for weeping salty tears
Be still self-pitying soul of mine
No time to deal with dreads and fears.

Care only for this man, who is your life
Who's mind has gone, no longer knowing you are his wife

Hold tight my hand, dear husband of mine.
For today we must make, the most of time.

Mary Rothera

Silent Tears

Loneliness sits in the empty chair,
Coldly, where warmth and love have been.
Sad eyes look once, then look away,
Look inward, now, to memories serene.
Reliving happy times within that love,
Feeling the warmth that surges at a touch.
Eyes that held dreams, and tenderness,
Hold nothing now, where once they held so
much.

H. Mackay

Hospitalized

We are at the wrong end of the line,
A shambling kaleidoscope of changing forms;
Self-contained capsules of pain and hope,
Trusting that all will be well.

We discuss our situation
Listening to the others with a far away look;
Thinking only of our own plight,
Which no other can match.

If we are young,
With infinite faith in the healer's art,
We absorb the confident air,
Alive with belief in the future.
But middle age, which so often brings
Not wisdom but regret,
Is a searchlight picking out human frailty,
Lighting up the brash certainty of youth
Which with one blow fascinates and appalls.

T. G. Herridge

Words

I have so many words going around in my head,
So many words that have got to be said,
Words that will tell you what you mean to me,
Words that will tell you where I want to be.
Words of such passion, my heart seems to break,
Words that are yours, if only you'll take.
Words of your nearness when we are together,
Words of the void when this nearness we severe.
Words of blue eyes, and a softness of skin,
So many words, I just can't begin.
Word that will tell you what I think of you,
So many words that can never come true.
Words, Words, I could tell you all day,
But these words when you're near me,
I just cannot say.

K. C. Gerrish

The Samuel My Husband

In the lonely silence of the night
Soul reaches out to soul to seek its own
And somewhere through the swirling mists of time
A love immortal joins again as one

When in your deep despair and did you not know
The one who loves you, knew you long ago
Stood by your side to cherish and amend
And echoing your prayers did comfort you

My love, my dearest love, you could not stay
The years swiftly passed, now you are gone
The music that we made will never end
Enchantment was the singers not the song

Monica Scarlett

Memories

Everyone loved you
And we thought the world of you;
To Dad you were his right and left hands,
For me you showed the way.

Your patience it was admirable,
Your smile - it said it all;
You always knew just what to say
And brightened many people's days.

A wife, mother, sister and friend,
Your caring nature enveloped all -
Not forgetting the animals and countryside
You grew up with and adored.

Now you've been taken from us,
In such a cruel and untimely way -
We'll take a leaf out of your book -
Be brave and look to future days.

But words alone cannot express
How much you meant to us;
And now the world seems incomplete
But you'll never die in our hearts.

Cathryn Rawsthorne

His Garden

In this garden our dad loved so much.
The flowers he grew, with his tender touch.
He loved the birds, and all the flowers
That started in spring, amid April showers.
On a bright sunny day, he would whistle a tune.
To his favourite flowers, on his birthday in June.
We lost him to God, on his birthday one year.
And when it comes round, we shed a tear,
But the Lord sends him down, from above.
To still tend his blooms, that he did love.
Although we lost him, we know he's around.
He's in our garden, tending the ground.
He shows us through flowers, not to be sad.
He proved his worth, our wonderful dad.

C. J. Barber

Bridge Lover

You say nothing, and I have never touched you,
At night and in the mist I cannot even see you,
But you are there,
Underneath this steel and air,
Underneath the world that comes and goes
Hurrying to work or to the shops before they close,
That may on a warm day pause to admire you from afar
But does not see that you are
Worth stopping for still when cold and grey,
When you mock your admirers and turn them away:
What remains then is worth more than summer,
More than the sunlight that shines on blue water,
It is a flowing in a single direction
At an unchanging pace, without hesitation
Towards the open sky where the trees end
Beyond our parting place at the river's bend
Where you half turn and say goodbye to me,
On to other lovers of bridges, and to the sea.

Alan Watt

A Stalled Ox

After the eventide, the eclipse of
Love, I move apart in a sea-girt realm,
Bounded by walls of silence at all points
Of the heart; a lotus land, a quasi
Life end where still-born hopes have tunnelled down
Steeps of hauteur to the swift-enclosing
Of all being; I will go unseeing
Into the barren court and when night comes,
Lift a be-jewelled chalice toward an
Infinite space...I feel the teeth of the
Sea-winds that snarl, hounded and night driven,
The waters unfolding on desolate
Shores; I talk into the passion of sounds
Where all things touch and are involved in life
And nothing moves toward a final phase.

Margret Phillips

The Firemen

They get the call, another shout,
What ever the job, they turnout,
From putting out fires in a rubbish bin,
Answering hoax calls, it's a sin,
Thoughtless people, who haven't a clue,
The risk they put these men through,
They fight fires, not counting the cost,
That even their lives, may be lost.
Persons reported, when this is the call,
The look on their faces, say it all,
When people die, they feel the pain,
But life, goes on again.
Jobs can vary from crashed car or train,
Even the crashing of a plane,
Bomb alerts, these men are near,
Never showing signs of fear.
These men are of a different mould.
Truly worth their weight in gold.

B. Powell

To A Snail...

Oh, little one with shell so neat
I'm glad that you have got no feet;
You glide along with the greatest ease -
But keep away from my lettuce, please!
I did not put them there for you,
So think of that as you slide through.
But I'm soft-hearted, so I might
Allow you just one little bite;
And then at last when you're in bed,
I'll know that you have been well-fed.
But there's one way you can make amends -
Just please don't *ever* tell your friends!

Jill Hasan

Untitled

Tell me where does the river flow.
Where does it come from, Where does it go
From beginning unto the end.
Along the way you gather friends.
Seeing life an every turn.
From new experiences we learn
Learn to love and laugh and hate.
Of which one will be your fate.
Will you love your river ride.
With another by your side.
Or will you laugh at everyday.
With new friends along your way.
Or will your water run too deep
The tide of change and hate to keep.
So keep your river running high
Hatred burning in the sky.
Then at last you meet the sea.
And peace forever there will be.

Susan Anne Kelley

The Lovers

Black velvet were the heavens
A billion stars unread
Each star a flashing mystery
Of meanings to be read.
Communion of the lovers
Translation of diamond-like specks
As reflects from eyes and pearls of teeth
In the silence of forgotten wrecks.
Spirit sought out spirit
For emotions to be synchronized
And, wondrously, in the haunting light,
Two tremulous were harmonized.
Indifferent to the night air sharp
Unaware of the unchristened dawn
Only, each, one with the other
The lovers and the dawn.

Lloyd Girling

Today

Remember yesterday, with its joy and pain,
and the changes you would make if you had your time again.

Remember yesterday, too late to cry
over all the opportunities you let slip by.

Dream about tomorrow, relieve your care,
go on, and build those castles in the air.

Dream about tomorrow, raise a smile.
Why not dream of 'Utopia' once in a while?

But Live Today. Reach out and find
how best today you can serve mankind.

But Live Today, this very minute.
Yesterday's gone, tomorrow comes not, there's only this minute,
so Live, Live in it.

William K. Allingham

Amazon Village

Stilted village sleeping on the shore
Above a brown and slowly moving stream
Fishing dugouts coming home before
The sudden darkness falls, and lanterns gleam.

Rice fields shining with a brilliant green
Along the mud flats out below the banks.
Palm-nut, pawpaw, breadfruit, plantain, bean,
The gardens brush each house's russet flanks.

Listening to the jungle's beating heart,
Let not your culture ever be undone
By the newer gods, fast destroying all.
Ten thousand years of living as a part
Of something greater than mankind alone.
Magic such as this go not beyond recall.

Michael Bradford

Darkest Hours

I can't see the sun in my eyes
　but horrible shadows of the hell.
I can't see the light in my world
　just darkness is what I know.

No word can express my desolation!
Nobody imagines how I feel now!
It's like a stone hanging over my soul!

I wake up every single morning
without apparent reason to live,
but... something... makes me... stay.

Is this the cross to bear in my life?
Maybe I should say 'I love you'
　but to whom is the question with no answer.

I remember when I was happy
　kissing once a boy.
But now I couldn't do it again.

I have sweet memories
　of that lost paradise.
And I feel unable to love anymore,
　as one time I did.

　Celia Franco Royo

Royal Engineers A Satpers O'de

There's the remnants of an orchard
its trees blasted out of line
There's a slit trench and a dug out
I somehow thought were mine
Yesterday many comrades fell
In a God forsaken terrain
To myself I said a silent prayer for those that still remained
So crawling along with bayonet, probing for the mines
My mate alongside laying tapes we lost all sense of time
The shattered blasted sight of Caen
Who can ever forget that carnage
I can still hear the hoarse cry above the din
bring a... stretcher not a bandage
Then the sergeant gave the order for a mine detector change
That order wasn't headed the 88's had found their range
A corporal called. Hey sapper! It's getting dark and late
But would you kindly give a hand to bury my old mate
From landing on the beach and up to then
Somehow I hid my fears but hearing that simple request
Could I hell suppress the tears.

　T. Jackson

Our Family

Draw back the shutters and peek inside
there to see comfort and joy our place to hide.
From the days of grey life tends to bring
with love and laughter, they become the yellow of spring.
A place to heal, a place to mend
where lips are sealed and an ear to lend.
As a unit, tall, against the world we will stand
subtract even one, our defeat is at hand.
Beneath a golden sun, or a silver moon
our every hour won't be in tune.
But we will disagree in harmony
as we face the fate that is our destiny.
Work and play, no day will pass minus any
friends plus acquaintances we will have many.
Betray each other, never, not for one or many reasons
even as in time we duplicate the seasons.
We are as one body from birth to death
its heart and soul its very breath.
Knowing now where its pulse begins, please let us be
draw close the shutters, on us "together", a Family.

　Megan Connors

Beech House

Inside this house, one winter's day,
a tiny baby born, just lay
inside her cot, mum watching over,
love in her eyes, straightening the cover.

Inside this house where joy and tears,
Become the memories of the years.
A woman she has now become,
Marries a man and leaves this home.

To this house she often goes,
sharing with Dad her joys and woes.
She tends to his needs, love in her heart,
Knowing for sure that they must part.

Back to this house that once was home,
She wanders around from room to room.
Echoing sounds of memories past,
Knowing this visit will be her last.

Outside this house she raises her eyes,
Whispers a silent prayer to the skies.
To the people she loves, beyond her reach,
Who lived in this house, known as Beech.

　C. J. Mace

Can Anyone Answer Me?

What is a family?
Can anyone tell me?
Is it a place of love and happiness?
Can anyone answer me?

I ask,
Why is my family unhappy, violence and full of hate?
Why do my mother and father argue constantly?
Is it my fault?
Do I deserve this?
Can I ever have a smile?
Can I ever be happy?
And, will my tears go away?

No one answers.

　F. Uddin

A Seashell

The sea brushed up against my feet,
And washed away the ice cold sleet,
The rain was hard the sea was rough,
You would think by now I had had enough.

I sit and stare all night long,
And wait for the birds early morning song,
I watch the night slowly pass by,
And see the sun rise up high.

My hollow body, gently weeps,
As the sea dies down and goes to sleep.

　Lydia Jane Hunt

"Fragrant Memories"

Roses, Roses all the way!
　That is Heaven, so they say.

But lovely, perfect Floribunda,
　Make me reminisce and wonder,

How fragrant, over-blown Cabbage-roses,
　Made me forget girlish poses;

And - scented old Tea-roses by the Tennis-court,
　Lured my mind away from sport.

Sweet-smelling primroses on the mossy ledge,
　The perfume of Honeysuckle, rampant in the hedge.

These I remember, with affection,
　They were not grown for perfection;

But just grew and spread in their own sweet way,
　And have lived in my memory for many's a day.

　Mary Agnes Elliott

The Home Of Love

As the storm tossed ship in the Harbour lies,
as the homing bird to its warm nest flies,
as the rain drenched rose to the sun above,
Thus do I turn to you my love.
As one grain of sand from the vast sea shore
Nestles close to the heart of the oyster's core
There forming a pearl so precious and rare-
Look to your heart dear and find me there
That grain of sand is small to compare
With the love I know that you and I share
and as in the oyster the pearl grows and thrives
So will our love dear for the rest of our lives

Rosemary Coleshill

Not Yet

I'm now retired - medically,
But I'm not washed out - not yet,
There's lots of life in front of me,
So I'll not despair - not yet.

There are things to do and folks to meet,
No, I won't give up - not yet,
There are places to go, old friends to see,
I'm not really down - not yet.

My backs real bad, my legs are too,
But I'm not bedridden - not yet,
I've got plastic eyes, rheumatic bones,
And, no, I'm not dead - yet

But let's be positive about all this,
The world is there, for me,
So I'll laugh and sing and live for life,
Well, I've not reached 63———Not Yet.

C. A. Richardson

Night Sky

With no beginning and no end
Just simple softness of the air
No cuttings, nor trimmings
For the wide embrace of our limitations
Eternity immortalized
Showing our belief in God

It is nothing but everything
Defying life, ignoring death
Always close, always receding
The whispered blackness taunts our senses
Shot with light, from life begotten stars
Their power wrapt in the cladding dark,
As they extinguish
We will have it happen too

Always black, sometimes red or blue
Endless as cruelty, transverse as love
I stare into the night's mystery...
And yelp - I've shook hands with a thistle

Natalie Westwood

"Perfect World"

When peace is unconditional
And there is no threat of any war
When people are so, so happy
And everybody on earths no longer poor

When each of our countries prospers as one another
Then every being on this planet deserves
to be called our Brother
When morning still brings those birds
up in the trees
And the summer months bring
the buzzing of the bees

Ocean will remain deep
sky will still be blue

Cause that's my perfect world
right here with you.

D. P. Gooch

Shepherd's Song

For their surface stuff they're valued:
    What's it clothe?
Only I may get to know them.
To the hillside trails I show them.
But, the greater heights to scale, you'd
    Say I'm loathe.

Grasses grow on the sleek hillside,
    None on peak.
I, these woolly charges leading,
Keep them, nervous-flocking, feeding.
They who'd travel the high trails guide
    Loftier seek.

So, while here, I'm watch a-keeping
    For that guide.
And, I fancy, moment's nearing:
One's soon coming, leads to shearing
Over lost trails! Ah, such stripping!
    Ah, such pride!

Keith Jefferies

Evacuation

Escape on the lines of silent relief,
away from the bombs of city grief.
Look down on the station platform of children's disbelief.
See the Mother with sad eyes,
conceals her feelings behind a cheerful disguise.
Up and down she gently strokes her Son's cheek,
holds back the tears, finds it so hard to speak,
has to turn away for a while,
then stoops down low, gives a comforting smile.
In a soft voice she whispers in his ear,
be brave my boy, have no fear.
A goodbye kiss, and emotional touch,
followed by these words,
"Mummy loves you so very much"
Must I go, he says with hesitation,
as the train rumbles in for evacuation.
"All aboard" is the final command,
as the carriages roll out, with waving hands.
White clouds of steam slowly begins to rise,
all alone on the platform is a Mother with sad eyes.

John Holloway

A Mother's Reflection On Life

The birth of our children was wondrous to me
The lives we had made so precious to see
With love and devotion and care through the years
The joy and the laughter the heartache and tears
Sometimes I wonder if I'd do it again
The toil, the anguish, the hard work and pain
Then I think of my children how quickly they'd grown
Now wonderful parents with babes of their own
Of course it was worth it for now I can see
The gathering at Christmas all started with me

Edith Kierce

Untitled

"The past of youth tugs on, still more
    of family, friends that float on visions -
        but no more.

Why saddened for these distant chimes which leave
    an ever sense of loneliness -
        for present family is ever near.

Perhaps, our thoughts, a sense of guilt invades,
    making the loneliness even more -
        attempts to find a foothold true - to hear
            again the voices, new.

Visits made to bygone places -
    at first seem real, alas no faces,
        no voice or call but silent breezes
            evade a long lost place.

B. E. Smith

Escapism

I can surf among the clouds, or grow wings so I can fly,
I can run my fingers freely through the oceans of the sky.
I can do 100 million things without people asking why.

I can talk to any animal, and they can talk to me,
I can bask on sun-baked islands, if that's where I want to be
I can see through women's clothing, if that's what I want to see.

I can clench in my fist unclenchable things that seem so far away,
Be the rich and powerful man, who always gets his way,
Say all the forgotten things I've always wanted to say.

I can feel safe, embrace a sanctuary that life's frailties cannot touch,
Stand firm without humility, walk without a crutch,
Live on the side, of reality where I cannot ask too much.

I can relive a million memories, but much better than before,
Indulge forbidden fantasies, knock upon the Devil's door,
Spin the shining mirrored ball and dance across the floor.

These things I do when I'm asleep, nature's rules I freely break,
Drink the cup of righteousness, or eat the Devil's cake.
Weave desire with imagination, and what a tapestry you make,
And when you drink upon its splendour, who needs to be awake?

Morgan Jones

The Sky Hunters

Looking down on fields and meadows
throwing forth their woven shadows,
see their reflections on rivers and oceans
flying by filled with emotions.

Who do they follow, where do they go,
what do they hide - no one will know.
Through all the seasons and endless time
will keep their secrets all so sublime.

Chased by the winds and all of their kins
sometimes get blamed for a thousand of sins;
they like to play just like a child,
their notions and motions often wilder than mild.

They look for adventure and never can rest,
they sigh and laugh always looking their best;
their colours delight us, from so far away
and sometimes send rainbows to crown our day.
Their size is immense, their pattern bizarre,
we can dream of them wherever we are.

Julie A. E. Reusemann

The Delian Lions

Two thousand years you guard and observe
with head poised high your God in view
looking, keeping your vigil anew
for dawning, the morning your task unfurls.

This way and that your eyes regard
the sanctuary of Apollo King;
long-backed, trim-ribbed, your haunches would spring
to the slightest thing that disturbs your mirage.

Archaic, in stone from a neighbouring isle
that sparkles and glints a myriad of ways;
can they be seen, the ancient race,
whose hands prepared these creatures wild.

Each character brave, a warden in whom
a life is entrusted: story yet true
from the wise men of old in history's dew
telling to-day of the love in your home.

So dazzling a sea surrounds your lair;
Spirit of Light with your fair and manly form
touch our hearts for to breathe your air
is to know no care.

E. M. Woolley

"Young Victim Of War"

He looked up in vain,
A little child sheltering his small face from the sharp
fragments of mortar.
His tiny hands raw and grazen from the exposure to the
bitter winter.
Oh what a sight!
How helpless can we feel for such a defenceless individual?
His world rocking fiercely around him, upsetting his niche.
How can insensitivity compare to the hurt and disillusion
of this child?
In the violent moments of war we often forget those
who see, feel the most and remember all... children!
Their eyes follow us with their haunted gazes,
pleading, praying.
Pity for such a tragic cause
Pity... too late... another young generation lost!

Sharoon Hosanoo

Towards Thee

Many a sail has been unfurled
Towards an unchartered sea
And man's hopes thereby curtailed
Before his dreams fulfilled to be

Courses have been schemed o'er
Till lights, their glow grows dim
Casts shadows across hands, their deftness slower,
And tiredness spreads to each limb.

Each man toward his goal must strive
Through storm and fire, lest less of a man unto himself must be
For no pleasure will he ever derive
Until his landfall he perceive.

Such a man am I,
My joy, still yet within my reach
I steer my course towards thee
'Ere twilight draws nigh.

W. Hughes

God's Precious Gift Of Life - A Baby

Gorgeous eyes a-peeping from the sheets,
Darling baby, innocent and sweet,
Captivating hearts with tenderness,
Enchanting all with your pure loveliness.
A few months old, this tiny baby boy,
For Mum and Dad their own dear pride and joy;
Precious gift of life from God above,
This babe was given to cherish and to love.
Dear little one, your family love you so,
Nurturing, caring for you as you grow;
Your cute small face is such an inspiration,
That beaming smile evoking adoration.
The gurgles, chuckles, show us your affection,
Your infant ways, endearing, sheer perfection:
The softest skin and hair, your purity,
Such perfectness and true naivety.
Oh baby, you give out much love to all.
So joyous, gentle, soft, you're beautiful.

Pamela Smith

The Sailor, Coming Home

And now thoughts turn to other things,
of coming home and door bell rings
the happy voices greeting back the man
perhaps a tear or two but quickly gone
as excitement wanes and lovely things to each and everyone

Then, with the children safe and fast asleep
in knowledge that for a short time at least
their Dad is home,
He'll turn unto his wife
and all the lonely days and nights will fall away,
as they rejoice their love without the words
that seemed so necessary on the day.
And all is well

M. Dunn

The Clown

And does the clown cry too?
Grotesque and ugly tears
Washing strange rivulets down his strange white face?
And what of the crowd then -
Do they laugh still more at this strange parody of grief
Or does unease set in
Or just one heart feel sorrow too,
More poignant still because it comes in such a strange form.
And what of me then?
A clown in another form
Trying not to bow my head to sorrow or loss,
To make a joke - to smile -
And hearing people say
"She's strong - she doesn't feel these things"
While inside me the tears burn
And sear their bitter tracks
And I long for a loving arm and an understanding heart
To help me bear my burden,
But there is no one -
O God! Could I but love thee more!
Peg Allen

These Things I Love

These things I love; life's little things,
Each tiny bird that gaily sings;

The wind softly sighing among the trees,
Fragrance of flowers wafted on the breeze;

Reflection clear in placid lakes,
the gentle fall of white snowflakes;

The musical murmuring of a brook
the simple delight of reading a book.

A rainbow shining in the sky
fleecy white cloud lets floating by;

Roses, violets and sweet Jessamine,
the soulful strains of a violin

A windy day is sheer delight,
a full moon sailing through the night.

The soaring lark, incessantly singing.
Sabbath bells calling, urgently ringing.

April with her sunny showers.
Misty September's golden hours;

Wild rabbits scurrying across the lea.
The melancholy moaning of the sea.

The harvest moon, the golden corn,
the reaper's song at early morn;

The urge to work when there's work to be done
And the joy of rest when the day is done.

Companionship along life's way,
a quiet chat to close the day-

These things I love, for each one brings
The simple joy of little things.
Ena M. Tate

My Lady Love

My lady walks the pale-moon night,
Bathed in fairy magic light.
With skin so fair, and gossamer hair,
She beguiles the souls of those who dare.

My Lady soothes my fevered brow,
With silken touch, she knows just how.
Forever in her presence charmed,
I feel no fear, my senses calmed.

My Lady knows the deepest me,
She sees such things, and yet to be.
My soul laid bare, to her I bow,
And each day new, my love avow.
Kathryn Craven

Untitled

I enjoy being a Granny, and I don't feel all that old.
Although my hair is going grey, at least, that's what I'm told.

Grey hair is honourable, or so they say,
I'll not use dye to make believe it's black,
When I know it's not, I'll be happy and content
With what I've got.

Yes, I enjoy being a Granny, and when I go to stay,
My lap is full of books and games, which we begin to play.

We're busy all the live, long day,
And when they are in bed,
I sit and think what fun we had.
Bath time frolics, good night kisses,
All the things a person misses,
Through not being a Granny.

November 5th was Freyja's birthday, what fun we had to be sure,
Firework's, a bonfire, cake with marzipan, guy and more.

Potatoes in their jackets, sausages on sticks.
Park in made by a very good friend,
We didn't really want it to end.

What fun being a Granny!
Dorothy Rigby

Imagine

Looking out across the land
the concrete jungle, somebody planned
no green trees or garden's in flower
life's so cruel in my ivory tower

I long to see fields of green
to see cows and sheep
like those from films on my TV screen

The wind on my face
the rain on my skin
to run barefoot through sand and sea
and feel for once that I am free

But since mankind has walked the land
they've have destroyed all they can
now my children can only imagine
what once was a land where dreams could happen

I tell them stories and show them pictures
of places I've been and animals I've seen
This was from when I was a lad
before war broke out and life became sad
Lynn Court

A Killer Among Us

Drugs are a killer we hold in our hand,
Spread by the loneliness sweeping through our land,
Praying on the poor people and the rich one's too,
Praying on those poor lost soul's with nothing else to do,

Weakening our bodies, destroying our minds,
Killing our spirits and anything else they find,
Stealing our memories, tearing us apart,
Making us forget the feeling in our heart.

Replacing the memories, the one's that they stole,
With nothing but emptiness, a living black hole.
Taking a hundred times more than they could ever give.
Until they are the only reason you have left to live,

Once you know them well it's hard to say goodbye
But if you do not leave them you'll be theirs until you die.
Drugs are like a well and the lights are dim.
You can't get out until you admit you're in.

They won't let you go you'll have to break free.
But if you stand against their grasp then stand beside me.
You don't have to do it for me or for you.
Do it for the sake of our children and our children's children too.
Mark Sword

The Tide Of Life

When the volcano erupts, the anger bursts.
The strength within the towering mountain
Comes in a rush of powerful emotion.
The surface is broken, but the heart is alive.
Torrents of red, hot feeling flow down the steep sides of life.

Purity begins, like a glacier rising from the pale, blue depths of
   the sea.
Love cannot hold the pressure within the lake of fortune.
Like a surging waterfall, hysteria rises,
Then falls, crashing against the cold harshness of stone hearts.

The relief of relinquished love
Is like the light, refreshing rain, falling, falling.
Far from home the sun sets,
A shimmer of deep red feeling, then lost forever.
Darkness comes, like a glove on a pale, white hand.
The earth, in its weakness, is covered.

The sun rises for the first time, never to fall in
The quiet stillness of the early hours.
When death is near, be content, like a graceful, white dove,
Launching into freedom for eternity.
Rest well, for the tide of life has turned.
    Fiona Wynne-Parker

A Sixth Sense...

Sparrows dart, wings blurring,
from one bush to another -

Revelling in speed and secrecy,
as they disappear from sight.

Seagulls call:
Call, call, call-call-

Boasting of strength and freedom
in the open space of beach and sky.

Butterflies spin around each other -
wing-tips caressing in the warm air

Dancing and playing
in fluttering courtship.

The solitary pine-tree, after rain,
wrapped in its sweet-sharp smell

Evokes a childhood memory,
a distant place of peace and well-being.

I catch a snow-flake on my tongue-
the crystal and the taste together melt.

Thus the senses melt the barriers between
the inner world and the outer world.
    Ian Pirie

The Awakening

There on the shores of desolation
The bloodless things shift listlessly
And slowly turn to stare
With eyes that cannot see,
While all around is devastation
And life endures - to die.
As deep within the mantle of the orb
Are damped the fires sublime
Quenched by the remorseless march
Of unfathomable time.

But wait -
For on those shores
Some other stirs,
Not warped by awful age
Nor withered at its birth,
But rising like the Phoenix from the dust
To kindle hope anew
That all is not yet lost,
That some new life exists
On planet Earth.
    Peter Newell

Elvis

He stands no more, in suit of white
He no longer plays his guitar
No more concerts, in the night
No more shining superstar.

The world will never be the same.
No-one can take his place.
All our hearts are filled with pain.
Tears on everyone's face.

He was the king, the superstar
A legend he will be become.
His songs were heard near and far
He was the greatest one.

Although he is no longer here
His music will live on
His memory will always be dear
Long after we have gone.

Now heaven has gained, what we have lost,
And now we can see quite clearly
His fame was too high a cost
And Elvis paid it dearly.
    P. A. Page

Happy Birthday Mummy.....

Upon a chilly Spring day in April, a special child was given life,
To a very happy husband and a proud and loving wife...
They named her Sweet Georgina and were sure that as time wore on,
that with her beauty, love and understanding, they knew that
   she would be strong...

She is an exceptional lady, five children she did bear,
And upon that time a decision was made, her love, her life to share...
This Lady radiates compassion, an understanding for all to see...
For she's given so much to others, and given so much to me...

Now another chapter unfolds for her, a grandmother she has
   now become,
what lucky children to share her life and love, great times have
   just begun...
She has always been there for her children, she has never
   turned us away
Through all the trouble that we have shared, there is only one
   thing I can say...

That I love you Dearest Mummy, you simply are the best,
Mother and friend I could ever want, a cut above the rest...
So to a warm and happy Birthday, lets raise a glass and sing
to wish you joy and happiness for all the years to bring.
    Samantha Carson

Parting Of Lips

Why can't people smile?
Their faces hang like
pictures on a bent nail.
Drooping down towards the ground,
if only they would smile,
they then would look so
meek and mild.

Their frowns would go,
their faces glow
eyes sparkle, big white teeth would show.
It seems we're forgetting how to smile.
Like seems to be just a scowl,
people shout, people swear
depressing news fills our air.

If only we could have a day
where everyone would smile,
I'm sure we would feel the benefits.
Would that really be so vile?
So go on, smile!!!
    Ann Ryan

Sonnet For Deborah

Petite and sweet was she, and so fair
I watched her walking away, walking there
She turned and with a smile acknowledged my singing
"Nice song" she said, and that got me smiling
As she walked on I thought to myself, "go for it"
For I knew if I didn't I'd somehow regret
So I ran after her and asked her her name
She readily told me and I did the same
So we got talking as I walked with her awhile
And I liked the way how she made me smile
"Every time we say goodbye" was, she said,
One of her favourite songs, and in my head
I silently gave a resounding hurrah!
Happy to know that my singing pleased Deborah

Vivian Anglin

Nothing Left In The Till

Down in the valley they took him for a ride,
then talked to each other - because he had died.
But there in the valley, he had heard what was said;
who laughed to himself, being pronounced dead.

There with their prayers - they laid him to rest,
shovelling all that earth, deep on his chest.
But there in the churchyard, he stood in the row,
throwing invincibly, a handful on himself below.

Now draw back the curtains, and let in the light;
for he is not buried down there tonight.
Sound off a fanfare before bringing in his will,
and let us see how much he has left in the till.

Down in the valley, they left him lonely and sad;
gathering together now - to share what he had.
But there in their finality, he studied each face.
Recalling favourites who had come last in each race.

Arthur S. Battey

'Single Room'

In a single room I spent the night;
A single room without a bed;
Alone I spent the night;
This little room and me;
Without a mouse in sight;
The squeaky floor boards and me;

I feel the joy but cannot sing;
The words are here without a ring;
Alone my thought and me, in this room;
A car gone by, it's rather odd;
One I ought to have seen;
And yet darkness is here and there;

My soul is at rest and at its best;
Rest, best for how long, eh;
As darkness come upon me;
But tomorrow the birds will sing and the sun will shine in
    celebration of a new day;
Knowing that my eyes will open once again;
Alone my thought and me;

Earlan Peters

Spring

Spring cracked like crystal glass
As through a mirror I did pass
Like golden myrods of the sun.
Floating on the breeze.

Cascading crystals formed a screen.
Rose coloured red vision I do see.
Of Goddess dancing in the sun.

Between the field no green and gold.
Did I softly strove toward the sun.
Soft perfume of flowers filled my heart.
As I drank the sweet nectar.
And drifted in endless dream.

R. E. Clifton

Death

There's one thing I'm certain of,
One day I'll die and meet the Lord above,
Why do so many people fear this,
Because death is so natural, more natural than a kiss,
Is it because people don't know what they'll be,
Because to me death is a way out,
It's a place where love and peace is all about.

Why is it people seem to cry when they find out it's their time to die,
Because death is full of beauty and heaven is a place where
    I long to be,
I look forward to the day when at last, I shall pass away,
And my body be laid to rest for to enter heaven surely there's
    no test.

But to kill yourselves is wrong,
You shouldn't stop singing before the end of a song,
To take your life is a crime,
Because everyone will die when it's their time,
With death you shouldn't interfere,
Because your punishment could be severe,
And then you will have to dwell,
For the rest of eternity, in that place called hell.

Danny Martin

Untitled

Of dreams not new that burn so bright,
I'll dream my favourite dreams tonight;
a peaceful life, good health, good times
with sleepy eyes, 'till clocks will chime.
Life is good and today's just begun,
my dreams last night of love and fun
will start my day with good intent,
remembering that life is Heaven sent.
Hard work and toil all my life,
now appreciated with little strife,
each day is new and full of hope
to enjoy to the full and not just cope.
The garden, the home and love all round
brings nothing but smiles and ne'er a frown,
I've worked and dreamt, but now today
I'll live my dreams in every way.
So per chance to dream so free;
not only in slumber, but in reality,
Life is to live to the full each day
in nothing but happiness in every way.
I've earned the right, I've worked all hours,
It's my turn now to enjoy my flowers;
whatever I want, I'll do with glee
alas my life now belongs to me!

Jan P. Clifford

Fast Food

On the great Arterial road
stood an inn of ancient mode
The Travellers Rest served pie and chips
with laughter and with merry quips
now it lies closed and still
there is a new road down the hill

The mighty motor way lies below
catching the traffic's ebb and flow
The vehicles tumble and race awry
to get to where by when and why?
Where are we going are we late?
it is a most important date.

A motor way cafe all hustle and bustle
serves fast food with vim and muscle
no one notices who is there
others like Zombies stop and stare
A very long way from the Travellers Rest
with thoughts exchanged and views expressed

What will the next century bring?
perhaps it's fast food on the wing!

H. Penry

228

Town And Country Boy

Walking in the country
About ten miles from town.
Where the air is pure and healthy
And no particles float down.
Rooks and pigeons in the fields
Rummaging for things to eat
A hawk is hovering gracefully
Swoops on a mouse - gathering fresh meat
The rabbits run freely along hedgerows
Squirrels gather their nuts
The birds are singing all in tune
And cows in the distant bellows
Yes, it's peaceful in the country
When autumn leaves start to fall
Then the still and quiet is broken
When a pheasant attracts his mate, with his all familiar call
Yes the country is a colourful place
When the leaves are all colours of brown
But when the snow starts to fall
I would rather be in town

Paul Everall

Man Almost Not A Man

Immersed in the bustle of the noisy world
the man almost not a man,
because he carries an infusion of poverty,
walks dragging his world,
his head melted by alcohol
or sitting at the underground exit
with his head plumped between his knees,
his dog at his side sleeps, waits,
nothing wakes him,
not even the sounds of the coins people throw.

Nobody claims him because nobody knows him,
he doesn't vote because he can't claim state help,
he doesn't claim state help because he doesn't have a home,
he doesn't have home because he can't pay the rent,
he doesn't pay rent because he doesn't have a job,

A third world in a first!
Hunger outside the bank,
fresh water in the sea.

Again the man by the bank
to drown himself in the soil's sea.

Antonio Jumbo

Fisherman

Your laugh and beauty
was beyond compare
your eyes like beautiful jewels
did not need to stare.

Into the eyes of love
of a poor fisherman
he would have given you a gentle life.

Full of promises and hope
his catch each day
would bring pearls from the shore
to adorn your beautiful throat.

His song at sea of love so true
would have been carried by seagulls
to be heard only by you.

The stars at night would be plucked
to make a comb for your long hair.

You would not even consider his love, when you would
fare far finer with the local sirs.

Their jewels and furs would adorn your beauty
Your heart not soothed by the fisherman.

Deirdre O'Sullivan

Thanks But No Thanks

I wouldn't hold a burning ember
Nor stroke a dog that bites
I don't invite a burglar to tea
Or walk the streets at night

I wouldn't jump off London Bridge
Or lie on a railway track
I don't drink from a bottle marked poison
So why would I want you back?!

Nicola M. Stott

My Journey Through Life

As a baby I had no worries, just had thoughts of pleasure,
And pleasure was comfort and food and fun,
As a youth I had no worries, just concern of leisure,
And leisure was sport and girls and sun.

As a man I had worries, worries of everything.
And everything was work and family dependency,
At middle age I had worries of what each day would bring,
And they would bring teenage kids and redundancy,

But now I am an O. A. P. and every day's a pleasure,
No worries now have I of death, no need to hurry,
Every day's a bonus, which I take at my leisure,
And leisure is no fear of death, now I've no need to worry,

When young men scorn my balding head, and leap around
with vigour,
I need no comb, nor brush, nor gel, no need to preen,
With no effort, I too was young and cut a dashing figure,
That I've done, that I've seen, and there I've been.

Charlie Boy Smith

Life

Life's but a drop in the ocean of time
from the time we are formed to the time we die
from the time it begins to the time it ends
like a drop from a tap to where and the distance it has to fall
into a pail or onto the ground
if into a pail we use it for many many reasons and purposes

Like rain falls in dry or wet seasons
if it falls on the ground, it may run away and be wasted
many of us are like this in our life of haste
like water it's some-thing we all take for granted

We are all but little drops in life's ocean
We must all take time and feel life's emotion
it's only, when like there's no water in the tap or we may feel ill
that we stop and realize how precious and delicate life is still

Doreen Aldous

Between Two Worlds

Between two worlds, today, I stand,
A woman, not totally feminine, nor, on the other hand
more masculine than my forebears
You see, this was unplanned for me
this freedom I have gained, yet am unprepared for
The culmination of the work of others
whose needs projected into today's world,
leaving me in part behind, in my mind
wanting to accept the change
which, though strange, seemed ordained.

Between two world's I now can choose a role, which one?
Lest I abuse the choice should I challenge every man,
Once seen as my peer, to prove my adequacy my dear?
Show supremacy, perspicacity, logicality and,
in expression of the total emancipated demand
Somehow lose the tenderness, warmth, strength and
almost revered dominance to which I am accustomed
in my role of woman, and deny the sense of purpose of man
so that he becomes not one with me, for I'll be free,
whilst he becomes a wanderer.

Christine A. Grant

Alone

If you're alone with nowhere to go
You think you are hopeless, 'cos
people say so
Everyone keeps picking on you
And you keep wondering what you
will do
Everything goes wrong, nothing goes right
And it could destroy you if you don't
hold on tight
No-one will listen, no-one will care
The stress is just getting too hard to
bear
They say life goes on, but it's not
always true
When someone's as unhappy, as unhappy
as you

Emma-Jane Welsh

Monument

They say that grief will fade, that time will creep
In and around softening and will wear
The jagged edges of a keen despair
To mellow smoothness and will lull asleep
Longing of heart, that sorrow does not keep
Its essence but diffuses through the years
Losing its bitter poignancy, that tears
Are transient and heart wounds heal though deep.

But lest with grief should fade remembrance too
And so be lost the rapture of a day
Of joy transcendent, or lest interests new
Rising in season crowd old thoughts away -
Here is a little monument to you
And all those hazy dreams of yesterday.

Elsie Tether

Loneliness

I hear a laugh but I can't join in.
I see the joy in other peoples eyes,
but I can't copy it.
It's as though I'm in a jar.
I can look, but when I reach out,
I am cut off by the cold, unfeeling
glass.
Somebody laughs in pure joy.
I reach out to catch it,
as the sound flutters towards me,
to share the warmth.
But as I reach out, it falls
and shatters, on the cold, hard floor.
People look into my eyes, and shudder,
as they see the misery and loneliness in them.
They can't understand.
They hurry away to their friends on the·
Sunny side of the room,
leaving me in the shadows.

Helen Easson

"The Big Hoose"

Mary rose at five.
The sun was rising high in the sky.
Coal to be placed on the fires.
Dust in the drawing room, dust in the parlour.
The white starched apron that was a must.
The never ending tasks that drained her fast.
From kitchen maid to parlour maid, cook and footmen too!
It was understood within their class, that this was their place
without any questions asked.
After all to work in "The Big Hoose" was such an honour for
any Scottish lass.
And tomorrow is Sunday an afternoon off, to stroll down the
Promenade and forget one's lot!

Maria Schneider

Retirement

A Lady of Leisure - who's kidding who,
I can always find plenty to do,
The floors to sweep, the beds to make,
How much more for goodness sake?

Now it's time for elevenses,
I seem to be all at sixes and sevens,
Goodness me, I've a cake to bake,
Did I put the salt in for goodness sake?

Then there's the washing and ironing too,
Why is there always so much to do,
My working life was done with ease,
Then I only had my boss to please.

But when the ground is covered with snow,
And winter is here and strong winds do blow,
It certainly gives me the greatest of pleasure,
To say I'm glad I'm a Lady of Leisure.

Elsie A. Musto

Thoughts On A May Evening

How pleasant the evening; the westering sun
Has lengthened the shadows that lie;
Completing his journey that first was begun
When morning was new in the sky.

Though aged,the apple-tree bears on its bough,
Its blossom as sweet as before,
And verdant the grasses around it grow now
As ever they have done of yore.

The ash-tree, reluctant to open its leaves,
Will soon be as green as the rest.
The swallow lies warm, where the sheltering eaves
Afforded a place for her nest.

The ewes with their lambs, in the fold of the hill
Have gathered, while slowly the light
Is fading to dusk, as the breezes fall still
And day is o'ertaken by night.

How blest is the coming of evening that falls
Like a coverlet soft on the day;
How blest are the thoughts of the heart that recalls
How providence orders its way.

Dora Tebbutt

"A Mother's Memories"

When I think of my "son" I have oft times cried, a finer "son"
would be hard to find.

For 19 years our pride and joy, a happy, smiling, very kind
boy. As a policeman always did his best, and gained com-
mendation with the rest.

This was for bravery, and I'm so proud "Peter" stood out from
the usual crowd. Six feet tall, a handsome lad, platinum hair,
blue eyes, like his dad.

Duke of Edinburgh's silver and gold he achieved, "Peter"
could always take the lead. Then fate stepped in, and took
him away. We can't find a reason to this day.

And yet another bitter blow, fate took his Dad, 'cos he needed
him so. Now I think of the blessings I have and see, a
wonderful daughter

Kind to me; "Jill" misses Peter, but doesn't say and spends
her time to brighten my day; she phones a lot, and takes me out.

Her children keep me happy, there's no doubt. Grandchildren
and great grandchildren are such a treasure,

And all I need to give me pleasure. When they're around I
smile once more, and find I need them, more at my door.

So I think of my "Peter" so dear to my heart, and I smile again,
as my memories start.

Jean Margaret Walker

Music

The first sound of music we often remember,
Is our Mother's lullaby, sung soft and tender

Later, we would sing our Nursery Rhyme,
Our first lessons in music, and how to keep time

At School our musical efforts were endured by the Teacher,
Disharmonious sounds of the tambourine and triangle, being
    the general feature

What bliss to be chosen for the School Choir,
Especially when placed in a Group, where the highest note
    one could acquire

Our Music Teacher, often with pained expression,
Eventually brought harmony, through a well rehearsed lesson

The piano would stop, and a strident voice, with anguish, yell,
Someone's not in tune! Begin again! I want this to sound like
    a bell!

On to the wonders of Motzart, Beethoven and Bach,
Helping us appreciate and love even the simple, sweet sound
    of the lark

For we now know, that all sweet sounds of harmony,
Bring joy to our hearts, as was meant to be
    Maureen Annette Norman

The Pictures (Memories)

As I sit here, now quite old,
My video is made of gold:

Betty Grable, Alice Faye
I could watch their films all day
For watching them I always find
Much contentment, peace of mind.

Betty Grable, Alice Faye
I could watch their films all day
Don Ameche, John Payne, and Tyrone Power,
Wiling away many an hour.

Going to the pictures
that was "the life" for me,
Sitting there a'dreaming
not thinking of my tea

Oh for Betty Grable
with my "Sister by my side"
going into Uxbridge
on that "Special Trolley Bus Ride"
    B. H. Claring-Bould

Sunset Morn

The retiring sun dipping slowly
In the western sky, sinking over the Isles
With a serene peacefulness all round
Wide spreading beauty in rainbow glories.
Stretching spanning, a vast distance through the skies
Seen by romantic roving eye far over distant miles.
As you divinely divert along your descending path.
In the evening at the end of each sunny day.
Farewell-finale a fiery fling a glowing ray.
Reflected on and over calm waters of loch and sea.
Dispatched a beauty of colour disturbed not tranquillity
Your last lost wink, across, to hills of heathery blue
A vibrant change from goldens to pink your hue.
Spellbound, strayed a world of silvery silent slumber
Graced by the cold icy moon.
Crystal clear the sky with twinkling star.
Yawning, yielding to retire from night shift
On daylight to the returning rising sun soon.
For in the scottish eastern sky is dawning
A brilliant, fresh-tartan morning.
    Yvonne Fraser

Clown

The face of a clown,
Is a happy one.
At least that's what he shows the world.
He's just pretending,
And defending.
The sadness that's inside.
So he acts it out upon the stage,
Until the show is over.
When he can be himself again,
And let the teardrops fall
And when you turn to look at him,
He's not a clown at all.
    S. McLeod

To Margaret

There is a girl I dearly love,
There's laughter in her eyes.
She's constant as the stars above,
That shine in the evening skies.
I'd walk with her, down a winding lane,
In a country far away.
And pledge with her, nor pledge in vain,
At the closing of the day.

We'd stroll along, in perfect bliss,
By the flowering country side,
And maybe share, a tender kiss,
In the flush of eventide.

Then under heaven's majestic dome,
Star spangled, dimly-light,
Both hand-in-hand, to that dear, dear, home,
We'd walk, through the still night.
    Henry Turner Staines

I Want To Be With You

When I saw you for the very first time,
I knew that I wanted you to be mine.
You triggered something inside of me,
That no one has ever done,
So baby I now know that you are the one.
Your eyes are so warm and gentle,
And your smile melts my heart,
I just want us to be together
And never, ever part.
I see you in my day dream,
I see you in the night,
Cos baby, my dreams are something that I would never fight.
When I close my eyes I see your face
And you come and take me to a place
Where it's just you and me and the stars above.
In the darkness of the night,
My love for you burns oh so bright,
So take my hand my luv
And you will see,
That I will love you eternally.
    Amanda Franklin

Agelessness

Relentlessly the wheels of time roll on
Creaking, grinding around a dying sun,
Floating in the gaping sea of space
Where shine the silent stars of hope and faith.
The soft caress of whispering winds
With Spirit's touch - destroy the lie,
Declare the fact - man cannot die.

Basking in the noontide of his glory,
Untouched by time's deceptive clock,
Unconcerned by matter's earthbound story
Lives the self as yet unfound.

This prison here forever cannot be,
It is a dream from which man must awake
To grasp the truth that sets him free:-
The ageless consciousness of Love.
    Brenda Jean Wilson

Misted Dreams

Wondering around, in a space, in my mind,
Is this the love, I've been waiting to find?
So the waiting is over and love is at one,
With the world at my fingertips, my life has begun!

As I walk through the mists, in the sands of time,
The heart you'll hear beating, is sure to be mine!
But when the mists clear and you come into sight,
I'll run to you lovingly and hold you real tight.

Makeshift love and some broken hearts,
Are not part of our love, because we'll never part.
The dreams and the promises, all broken in two,
Not our dreams and promises, because they will come true!

We sit on the hill and watch the sunrise,
And I tell you, I love you, as you look in my eyes.
There's no one around, all alone at last,
As nighttime and daytime, slowly go past.

We will get married, with kids sure to follow,
I'm not dreaming to much, I just have hope for tomorrow!
Well that is all, that I have to say,
If you like what I said, then tell me you love me, today!

Michael Spellar

"Tributes Of Love"

A reminder of how much you meant to me,
Your picture I carry for all to see.
From time to time I gaze into space
Amongst the clouds to find your face.
No one I know will ever replace
The vacant seat you left in haste.
One day in time I will know
Why my dearest love was chosen to go,
For not always can you find someone like you,
So loving, loyal and caring too.
It has become clear that you are near,
for when on my own, I'm not alone.
I know you've not gone very far,
only into God's Garden with the door ajar,
No one will ever fill the space,
or sit at the table you once graced.
My love for you will always remain;
My "tribute", your picture in my heart I have framed.

Selena De'Beer

Dark Young Man

He always loves bilberrying
Even 30 years on with white hair now
I wonder if it's because of me
And that magic day we went to get some
When I wore his too big flying jacket

Does he ever think of that when he goes now
And gets two or three pounds for his new wife.
That hot day we only got two
Rattling around in our jam jar.

Collette Thomas

Our Walk In The Dales

Once more into the dales we go.
We've been there in the rain and snow.
In the spring and summer too.
When the sky is oh so blue.

The church bell rings to greet the day
As by the stream we make our way
Walkers pass and give a smile.
Some will even chat awhile

Through meadows green to the swinging bridge
As bird calls sound across the ridge
So wearily we make our way
To end another perfect day.

Jean Stevenson

Finals Or Future Imperfect...

Winnowed was I
On the age old altar of education.
Stoked hot-house bloom, wearied with words,
And my roots wriggled, but settled,
So thus am I now:
A sipher to regurgitate,
A sacred vessel in sacrificial sub-fuse
To save what you weep might be lost.
And you strain me on the racks
Of lines to be filled,
A mosaic of my mind and theirs
And you clutch me just to empty me out
For my sell-by date is beckoning
As cracks appear in the three years prescribed enthusiasm
For in seven days the thoughts are spilt.
You grade your work
And mark my inadequacy,
Never thinking what your years have fashioned;
The tattered vestiges of a Romantic's nightmare,
The dawn of reality sears my sight.

Sally Carruthers

Green Pastures

Dear Reader have you ever thought
of a beautiful summer scene
where animals graze so peacefully
in their own pastures green.

There may also be a spinney
that shares a scented breeze,
where cloven feet may frolic
or shade beneath the trees.

The Romans even built a wall
on the north sides of these lands,
because alas, to protect such grass
from those cruel unhappy bands.

Where lovers walk with two hands clasped
because they are in love
to hear the cries of kitty wakes
beneath those skies above.

M. Pinder

Summer's Here

The sun is shining warm and yellow
The wind is blowing cool and mellow
I see that visitors have come to tea
We have three Blue tits feeding in the tree,
The Birds we love to watch
They come to feed here quite a lot
Robins, Sparrows, Blackbirds, Thrush
They always seem to be in a rush
Flying here, flying there, sometimes I do despair
We have one visitor which is rare
It is a Woodpecker I do declare,
When winter comes and all is white
We always leave them some food to bite
But for now, Summer is here,
So make the most of the Birds this year
And be a host All Through The Year.

Maureen Metcalfe

A Secret Kept

A secret to keep hidden inside
She sits alone with thoughts that hide.
No one can break through the harden silence.
For all revealed would cause inner violence.
All curled up in a mind of confusion
The secret is full of great oppression.
Blinded through the tears of pain
They fall to the ground like a shower of rain.
Innocence broken from the look of regret
This is where love and hate finally met.
Adolescence cannot cope with the thought
But trapped in between worlds she is caught.

Lynette Dunn

232

Beauty

The sun drenched face encased in gold,
The glowing meadows to behold.
The sunlight piercing through the old grey barn
Unfold wonders, far beyond charm.

The foaming, raging, swelling sea,
Enforcing the law, beyond reprieve.
Dashing and lashing, engulfing the land,
Undoubtedly master, so firm, so grand.

A gentle breeze, a mighty blow,
Cooling the air, stampeding—the foe,
Floating gently way on high,
Biting, storming - the wind laughs and cries.

C. A. McTurk

My Love

Love,
When I am with you my love
Your love surrounds me totally.
Like I'm laying on a bed of rose petals,
Like I'm floating naked on a soft breeze.
It's a dream.
For my love I know you would fight,
I know you would die,
Would give up your worldly possessions,
To love and to cherish,
To honour and obey.

The dream is real.
Your kisses are a soft breeze,
Your skin is made of rose petals.
You surround me totally
When I am with you,
My love.

Rebecca Tona

Mother Sea

Unchecked and mighty, magnificent but ruthless,
She dashes against our shores.
Her sons are undaunted, adventurous and countless, they clamour
to her by scores. Many a man feels the call within his heart,
The day will come when he'll depart.
She carries you far to distant lands,
where her blue beauty is bordered by golden sands.
But then perhaps when you are far from shore,
she'll turn upon you with a maddening roar,
to bear and lash you in her wrath
and engulf you in her foaming froth.
Then in alliance with the wind and rain
she'll come upon you in a hurricane.
In merciless fury she dashes and raves,
taking many fine ships beneath her waves.
But then she will calm and be gentle once more
and refrain from threshing upon the shore.
While in bosom, the unexplored deep, many brave sons lay
fast asleep. She called and claimed these sons of hers
and above them now.. she sighs.. and murmurs.

Stan Hyde

The Cynic

The world is a cold and merciless place
It gives you dreams then breaks them in space
The world befriends you then laughs in your face.
So charming, so damning, this human race.

The chains of the world blind tightly round me
The chains of world that claims it is free
One arm declaiming whilst bent on one knee
Is that what world freedom is meant to be?

Remember the time when truth won the day?
Remember the time when peace ruled the fray?
We fail to remember that which doth lay
In our dreams of the future, not in today.

Menna Poole

Pigeons At The British Museum

Dark edges of sloping stone, distinct and separate,
  Toned by time and weather to a hue
So indefinite as to lose their hardness
  Against a northern sky of solid blue.
Those small and rounded bodies on the cornice
  Are pigeons resting, peaceful in the sun.
So motionless and neutral that they might be
  A part of carving, blending in as one.
Midst boles of stone perpetual shade lies deeply.
  Below the steps some birds are seeking food.
To them the building seems but as a mere rock
  Conveniently pierced to raise their brood.
The heavy roll of traffic in the main street
  Concerns them not, they let it go on by.
The struggle of earning money does not touch them,
  Nor minds researching facts in pages dry.
There are idols in the galleries carved by ancients.
  The doves flew round the temples then as now.
We think, and labour on with toil unceasing.
  They live in sunlight, being is enow.

H. Keith Atkinson

Day After Day After Day

Looking through the window
At the same unchanging view.
I sit and watch for hours on end,
Well! I've nothing else to do.
I'd like to go down to the shops,
If someone could take me there.
Be nice if I got visitors,
With tea and cake to share.

Well blow me down, there's Mr. Smith,
With a brand new walking frame.
I bet he's off to see old Bert,
They love a good card game.

Now is it Sunday? Or is it Monday?
The days are all the same,
Let me think... the home help,
When was it she last came?.

Well I've fed the birds with some fat
They come here every day.
So I'll watch the kids come home from school
Now I remember it's Monday... or is it Tuesday?

Irene Burgess

The Man

He sits in his chair with a glass in his hand, the radio plays
tunes from some old time band
He's searching for reasons in the corners of his mind,
And his thoughts are forever of you.

He rocks his chair gently and closes his eyes, but he just can't
remember, as hard as he tries, he knows true love is a thing
hard to find, and his thoughts are forever of you.

The sun filters weakly through the gathering cloud, the man
starts to whisper, thinking aloud, his mind wanders off on a
new train of thought, but still remains ever with you.
With a trembling hand, he raises his glass, he knows this
moment is too good to last: A break from the loneliness,
sadness had brought and his thoughts are forever of you.

The lightening flashes, the thunder rolls, the room grows dim
as darkness falls, he turns on the light - the room is so bare,
and his thoughts are forever of you.
He looks at his watch, he's been sitting for hours,
he thinks of the grave, surrounded with flowers,
he cries out your name, though he knows you're not there,
and his thoughts are forever of you.

Gloria Kitchener

Untitled

To smell the air so fresh and clean and see the leaves so red
and green,
Shimmering in the summer sky and hear a Lark sing way on high
This is a special place.

The rustle of the leaves above give comfort to a nesting Dove
while down below young rabbits play watched by their mother
in case they stray And Bluebells like a carpet grow all in this
special place I know.

A Roe Deer now shows his face then swiftly off with style and grace
And just beyond a babbling stream young Otters playing, dance
and gleam in and out the stream they go all in this special
place I know.

Now the heat of the mid day sun stills all of nature one by one
And anyone who looks can see there's peace here and tranquillity
God watches both the meek and low all in this special place I know.

When care and heartache get too much and no one else is
there to touch
I close my eyes and off I go to this enchanted place I know.

Audrey Sollitt

Alien

I am an alien in outerspace,
I live on Mars, like a lonely bird.
I'm the only one left of my kind.
If I die then there'll be no more of us,
But nobody cares.
Perhaps they don't even know I exist.
I've tried communicating with other planets,
Like Saturn, Jupiter, and Earth,
But nobody listens, nobody cares.
I cannot travel, for I have no transport.
I cannot fly, for I have no wings.
I'm lonely.
Is anybody out there?
I beg you to save me from this endless prison of sad, dull,
loneliness.
I would climb a mountain,
Swim a sea,
Anything to know happiness.
But nobody listens, nobody cares,
If I live or die.

Emma Read

My Painted Picture

The sandy seashore, empty and wet,
Covered in shells, and the shimmering sun fades in the waves,
The cliff tops clashing together with stones,
Making a beautiful noise, that nobody knows.

Watching in silence, and my mind a glow,
Waiting to grow up, there's so much I don't know,
The wind in my ears, the shiver in my smile,
One more movement in my life, has turned another dial.

Feeling free and peaceful, against the crashing waves,
Indented foot prints in the sand, fading away,
Rocks and seaweed, together like a knife and fork,
A tranquil moment, somewhere to spend each precious day.

The sun has gone down, the days passing by, like the waves
on the sand,
Looking down on myself, innocent and young,
Not a care in the world, just happiness and love,
A reflection in the mirror, a sight so young.

Walking into the world, so fearful,
A stepping stone to climb over, a wave to jump,
The day is closing in, the moon is full,
My life is a destiny may I live like the waves, and never stop going.

Emma Hedley

Anonymous Fliers

I see the men with whom I flew
Laughing they pass the golden gate
Sharing their yarns with those they knew
Accepting their strange fate.

No more they'll crash into the clouds
Nor dodge the flak of those hot guns
Nor roar above astonished crowds
Nor shoot the line about their chums.

Yes they have gone who flew so well
Who fought and brought their squadron fame
Who wrote no story as they fell
And died without a name.

John Hodds

Vera

She looked so good, I was pleased to say.
See you tomorrow, is that okay?
We'd talked quite a lot... so much to say,
See you tomorrow, is that okay?

Hot lunch in hand, to her house I go,
Opened the door, "are you okay?
I saw her then, sitting just so;
Head tilted sideways, nothing to say.

She looked at peace, I was pleased to say.
There is no tomorrow... is that okay?
For her it was good, she'd wished it this way.
For me, filled with sorrow, what more can I say?

Joan Neyland

Northern Truckler

Northern Truckler I'm watching thee
From indoor occupations flee
Like bird of song on wing so free
No bars or chains detaining thee

Northern Trucker, no fixed abode
Residence for you, the road
No responsibilities bestowed
Forever dodging life's overload.

Northern Trucker run away
Live hand to mouth come what may
No consequence to face today
But they'll all catch up with you one day.

Northern Trucker fight the fight
With trusty steed and armour bright
Point thy self north and give all full flight
For the Northern Truckers home tonight.

Paul Hoffman

A Slice Of Bacon

I know a pig who's very fat.
But he is very smart at that
He had all the A levels you know
And Oxford University he'd go.
But he didn't know his reason for life
He went through so much strife
To find out why he was here
And people say that is queer.
It suddenly dawned to him one day.
God he went through such dismay
He knew why he was on Earth
The pig felt like such a smurf.
These farmers have really darked it
Because they're taking me to market
I wish I lived in the Middle East then I wouldn't be a feast
I would live until I die in a dirty piggy stye.
A slice of bacon I will be.
If I don't sort out Farmer Bee
So the next day piggy did, he ate Farmer Bee whose first name's Sid.
He said I like eating men it's fun I think I'll eat another one.

Jonathan Wright

234

"Arguments"

Arguments cause chaos, you fight with your mum
and your dad,
You can never say anything right, it always has to be wrong.

Inside, you feel that you want to just rage out,
Just let the anger go free,
You want to just pack your bags, move, get away from
everything,
Everyone has arguments,
Why!
It doesn't solve anything, it doesn't do anything.
To me, arguments, they're worth nothing!

Ruth Mack

The New Town

Tall thin chimneys, with blackened hats
Point the way to cloudy skies
Faceless buildings, mangy cats
Around about, a new town lies.

Living boxes, variously made
To suit the pocket and the grade
Of worker, who will live therein
And strive to keep it "like new pin".

Near at hand, the old town lives
Its timbered houses, spic and span.
The church, with gracious pointed spire gives
Succour to the worried mind of man.

The cuckoo came into the nest
It wasn't at the bird's behest
But now it's grown from fledgling state
There doesn't seem that much to hate.

John Harris

"Shadows"

We walked the sun-shine her and I
   Played the swings and slid on slides.
Precious days that fluttered by -
   Soft - like languid butterflies.

We heard the wind songs her and I
   and watched the surf tossed to the sky.
Shared secrets with the wild blown flowers
   Content together hour after hour.

Slow and soft a distant drum
   was warning of the death to come.
We raced the wind - heart in hand
   Young legs pounding silver sand.

It stole her from me in my sleep
   a timeless - mystic - gentle thief
took the dandelion days of youth.
   My heart bears fingerprints of proof.

But every summer now and then
   I hear its echo - and once again
We walk the sun-shine her and I
   Content to let youth softly die.

Wendy Carter

A Summer Day

Blazing sun, a clear blue sky,
We walked the Fire Hills, scorched and dry,
We shared our sorrows, spoke our fears
Of lonely days through the coming years.

His arms were warm, his kiss was sweet
As we sat together on a country seat -
Age forgotten in that brief hour
Affection blossomed like a desert flower.

As a desert flower it bloomed to die
After a tender moment under a summer sky.

Marjorie Mellor

Abandoned

As he was born his first bridge was crossed
Propelled from the womb to the light.
And having survived the awful shock
he lies cocooned, helpless, no sight!

It is cold and damp and cheerless
Lying here in a lonely place
What did he do wrong he wonders
Was his colour so hard to face?

But wait, he feels gentle hands lifting
And cuddling him close to their breast
Could it be that someone does love him?
He hears them say "Yes, he's the best"!

So with warm milk, warm clothes and loving
He senses the care that he's given
Pray that his mother comes for him
Not to miss one more hour - she's forgiven!

Jo Parsonson

Call On Me

When the sky is dark and grey
and troubles seem to come your way -
call on me.

When life is hard and full of fear
and eyes can only fill with tears -
call on me.

When your hearts are full of woe
and you have no place to go -
call on me.

My arms are always open wide,
just ask and you shall come inside.
I have so much for you to share
if you would only give yourself completely to my care.

Call on me, and I will be your Father, Counsel, Friend.
I shall stay beside you, even to the end.

Joyce Foale

Happiness

A little way along the road just on the right,
there is a winding lane; it's very steep and narrow,
right down till you reach the sea.

Just on the bend you will find a cottage bright and gay,
the windows shine, curtains all colours of the rainbow
brightness all around.

The sound of little voices of little ones at play,
Oh! Happy happy people with laughter sweet and true,
let's hope that you will always find,
as you travel your life through,
happiness and laughter, wherever you may go.

Joan Munt

Childhood Recollection

How I'd wish I was young again,
And wade down that puddled lane.
Cold autumn wind then chilled me still,
Those hardy boys that laughed at will.

Red sore little knocking knees,
Found comfort beneath the conker trees.
Tug and pull, shove and clamber,
Did the kids amongst the golden amber.

Then all too soon for those, not I,
Their voices fell and their spirits died.
And towards the great grey building stood,
We walked assembled, head to foot.

Nearer we herald the ragstone walls,
That mounted one by one that great old school.
And every thoughts of my childhood pain,
How I'd still wished I was young again.

Abby Claudette Winter

The Journey To Emmaus

He walked beside them on the road,
Yet who he was they did not know,
Their grief was like a heavy load,
Their hearts were full of doubt and woe.
And as along the road they walked,
He spoke of what the prophets said
And yet they wondered as he talked,
If they might find Christ was not dead.

They pressed Him, "Teacher come and dine."
But as they watched him break the bread,
It brought to mind the bread and wine:
That Supper, No! Christ was not dead!

The Saviour walks beside us still,
His presence guides us on our ways,
In Eucharist our lives fulfil
For Christ is with us all our days.

Back to Jerusalem with joy
Where each his urgent story gives:
Let prayer and praise our tongues employ
For Christ who died now ever lives!

Mary Hoyal

The Storm

The air was very humid, the sky had turned quiet grey,
Thunder rolled in the distance, I had
To hide away, my hands were feeling very moist my
Head began to throb,
My stomach felt a mass of knots I had begun to sob.
By now the storm was overhead, my fear I couldn't hide,
Dear Lord I prayed take the storm away,
Oh please dear Lord I cried,
The storm raged on the rain poured
Down I needed my bible near
A passage was running through my
Head a passage I held so dear
And lo I am with you always I
Knew I wasn't alone I felt his dear arms round me enfold
As when he comes to take me home
And he was there to assure me that
I would come to no harm
for he was Lord of the universe and I was one of his own
The fear of the storm subside and I was filled with peace
The love of the Lord was with me and I was now at ease.

Joan Kingston

Untitled

I beg of you, I plead with you, do not let them die;
The little calves, the little lambs - in a horrible! horrible! way.
Dragged by a leg to the slaughter house; hung by a leg - throat cut;
    blood pouring to the floor.
Helpless, innocent, blood - still pouring - - - fear in the eyes;
    looking, crying - - -
Is there more!! It is a long, cruel, wicked, barbaric thing, this ending.

Baby calves stand in small crates; five months agony; liquid fed.
No solid food; cannot move or lie down, just barely able to
    move the head;
Travelled for miles - - - no food, water, or fun - - -
We cross the sea to another Hell! It is - - - a crucified one;
Mother; where is she, Oh! Is there no mercy! Not even for her - - -
What have we done to Man; waiting, wondering, not well
now, still alone.

Compassion, compassion - - - was not found on the cross;
Forgive them; for they know not what they do - - -
Man does know what he does; he does what he does.
Compassion, compassion, for all kinds of Animals of the Ark.
It is in my dream; and held truly, deeply, in my heart.

Whatever those of you decide, on your conscience is blood
forever spilt.
In this world of destruction guilt and cruelty;
Man, all animals feel, fear, smell blood - - - give them back respect
and their dignity. Vanity they know not; they cannot speak,
cry help!! I care for them - - -
with freedom, and Mother Nature's wisdom.

Josephine Stewart

'Stephen'

The friendship blossomed, it took a short time,
The plans were made, your lives to entwine,
The wedding day came full of joy and hope,
Amid tears and laughter you knew you would cope.

As you settled down, you were akin to the task,
Honeymoon and wedding, seem long is the past.
Secure in the knowledge your future complete,
To tackle the problems, you knew you would meet.

How cruel were the fates on that sunny June day.
No chance our farewells to you to convey,
The tragic lose so hard to bare,
Stephen you went, oh how we cared.

That quizzical smile, sometimes put to the test,
The inquiring mind, now still, now at rest.
To meet again in the fullness of time.
When we all make that journey cross the great divide.

Briar Thatch

Mother Earth

Recycle everything that's the trend,
No rules to follow or to bend.
Don't fell trees just for wood,
Surely we are fooling ourselves,
That we are actually doing some good.

Over-population is no real problem,
Construct new homes to house them.
Build it yesterday finish it tomorrow,
It is then we come to realize,
The true cost and sorrow.

Ignorance means we ask not why,
If this is an inexhaustible supply.
Just slash and burn,
And what was once green and prosperous,
Into desolation we turn.

For it is with much ignorance and haste,
We rid ourselves of such potentially lethal waste.
Then it is sad to see Mother Earth,
Your most intelligent children,
Know not your true worth.

Dean Colcombe

A Child's Rejection Of His Father,
When He Worked Away From Home

Our bonding should be such, that nobody could ever destroy;
Hitherto, I know you reject me wrongfully and unknowingly,
But I love you, help you and watch you growing up rapidly.
Heaven feels heavenly holding you in my arms, my little boy.

Looking at you, your sunny disposition beckons an adoring hoy,
Notwithstanding this extraordinary virtuosity, your occasional kiss
And cuddle, showers me with a sense of overwhelming life's bliss.
Heaven feels heavenly holding you in my arms, my little boy.

Your wordings endow beauteous punctuation, your little mind employ;
'Tis like a sing-song that floods my tears, my ears never stop buzzing:
Yet, in the garden of my heart you are my sweet petal blooming.
Heaven feels heavenly holding you in my arms, my little boy.

Call my personal story: imaginary instinct or an idyllic play-ploy,
Do not let me suffer too much as I can't take it anymore, my child.
In your formative years, your plays, your intuition I adore are mild,
Heaven feels heavenly holding you in my arms, my little boy.

Ere duty calls, if in the celestial labyrinth I see a flickering stars envoy,
Wishing you the joys, I shall request the Planetary Maker, however,
To halt the Night and Earth from its odyssey, so we can play forever.
Heaven feels heavenly holding you in my arms, my little boy.

A. Boojawon

Disillusion

I feel death approaching, I know the end is near
So I wait feeling cheated, or is it simply fear
Fear of no more tomorrows, no Sundays full of rain
No walking in the countryside, or travelling on a train
Perhaps I'm just a burden, nothing but a pest
So the good Lord has decided that I must be put to rest
But my mind is still quite active, though my body's long been dead
So I dream of days that used to be, while lying on my bed
There isn't any future, no more need to carry on
So I'll have to say my last goodbyes, and then I will be gone
And does it really matter, that I've ever been around
Will anybody miss me when I'm deep beneath the ground
For I've left no great invention, no discovery of life
Just a lot of painful memories, of trouble, grief and strife
And if I had the chance to live forever in good health
surrounded by the ones I love, sheltered by great wealth
I'd have to say I've done my time, let others have a try
And maybe they'll get more from life, before they too will die.

John H. Oliver

If In Oblivion

If in oblivion I serve you best
There let me rest.
No thought of me live on
The moment I am gone;
Or let the sea
Your lethe be
To purge me from your memory.

But, should it be you cannot so forget,
And suffer no regret,
Still let my image be confined
To the inmost chamber of your mind
Where you still happily
May think of me.

Alwyn Trubshaw

A Way Of Seeing

My Welsh Dresser, in mahogany and oak, so sturdy stands.
The result of so much workmanship by so many hands.
The foresters and lumbermen and transporters for the wood;
And designers through the ages to evolve a shape so good:
Tall, with 3 shelves, a top and 2 cupboards under it;
To occupy so little space, in a small room to fit.

The carpenters and polishers with creative craft then come,
An added patina a century of cleaning hands have done,
The china it displays another crowd of workmen made;
Clay diggers, potters, painters, and others of many a trade.
When I survey my home, a pageant of workers pass before my eyes,
My thoughts go out in gratitude for all these human lives.

We are so absorbed with the business of life,
In a world where there is so much trouble and strife,
We only see the outward form that meets our gaze
And fail to probe the depths of what that sight portrays.
To ponder on these thoughts, a new dimension to my home I see;
An inward vision of past and present, enlarging life for me.

Mabel H. Ellis

The Stranger

He draws you slowly deeper, deeper, deeper,
through mist and time, 'til all sense is lost,
Pulled into a tunnel of irrational thought
Where the distant beam of reason grows ever smaller.

Darker, dimmer, the folds of his cloak encompass all.
All becomes an enigma.
Amidst confusion he becomes a lone soulmate,
One to be idolised without question.

You and me, the only reality
Converse a while; hypnotic persistence,
until with the tenderest grip
He leads you to madness.

Lisa Hayman

Getting Used To

It's been awhile since he died
I thought I was ok
I'd pushed it to the back of my mind
But as I walk past the graveyard gates
the pain comes rushing back
along with the quilt that tore my soul apart
we were close
But I hadn't seen him in awhile
I couldn't stand the thought of him slipping away
the colour in his cheeks
his voice...
I wanted to remember the man who told me stories as
a child,
tears swell in my eyes
the lump in my throat is back
as I leave daisies in the grave
the pain runs through my eyes and down my cheeks
I close my eyes and whisper "I love you"
He's before me now
smiling that smile

Sheila Bell

Tears

I've just heard the news,
Mum came in and told me,
It doesn't hit me straight away,
I feel confused and upset, what's happened?
Mum has puffy eyes and a tissue in her hand,
I feel the lump in my throat,
My eyes are stinging so I squeeze my lids shut
to take away the pain,
As I open them everything I see is a blur,
Like a painting when you spill water over it,
I feel the cold wet tears trickling down my cheeks,
Mum hugs me,
It is like when you are little and you fall over and
graze your knee,
Mum always hugged me then, now this is more important,
This is a lot harder to cope with,
The feeling isn't the same as when you used to fall over
and graze your knee,
The feeling is like someone has just ripped a part of you away,
I cry and cry.

Catherine Barker

The Pigeon

Grey cap;
iridescent lavender and sea-green mantle;
coat and wings of grey and white.

Greyhound of the skies.
Mercurial messenger from battlefields.
Unpaid entertainer of Trafalgar Square.
Glutton of our garden plots.

Loved and loathed in equal measure,
our beautiful English pigeon.

Suzanne Kyrle-Pope

The Blue Mover

Sweet blue moving through the air.
Soft click of shoes and tawny-honey hair.
Wonder where your mind is going, too.
Sweet smile me all the waking hours:
It's clear you have magic powers.
Soft click on shoes, blue by blue,
Making live art happen as you move.
Just a look would ease my pain;
A smile would free my troubles.
Please include me in your plan.
Being is believing;
You inspire,
You inspire,
You inspire.

Michael Fottrell

Hobo

Homeless and solitary, a man alone
  knows every highway and knows every stone,
Shelter he needs from the winters cold blast
  and maybe some whisky inside his flask.

He ask's for nothing, he has no wealth
  no comfort's, I pray he has his health,
From dawn to dusk he's out on the road
  he's travelling light he carries no load.

His possessions are few, this very wise man
  just a rucksack along with the old billy can,
Night fall and it's time to rest his head
  moon and stars for a blanket, earth for a bed.

His lonely life we don't understand
  no one to love him, or hold his hand,
He may feel down, but his head's held high
  the road is his buddy, his love is the sky.

He wants your help, he needs no pity
  the country lanes call him, but never the city,
Like animal, and bird his spirit roams free
  but the life of a hobo is not for me.

   Christine Farquhar

The Turning Tide

Away, away from the sandy shore
The ocean beckons the waves once more,
Leaving boats in the harbour proud and grand
Lying lonely on the dampened sand.

Seagulls crying "come back, come back"
As the waves retreat like wolves in a pack,
Children left playing in the pools and streams
Rebuilding the castles they've seen in their dreams.

The harbour wall stands remote and bored
Awaiting the fishermen with their hoard,
While the waves turn their back on the Ocean's roar
And long for the peace of the harbour and shore.

As the waves creep under the boats so still
Slowly the harbour begins to fill,
While the impatient ocean so vast and so wide
Waits once again for the Turning Tide.

   Rosemary Perry

Music

Recorders and flutes, lovely and sweet,
Violins and harps streaming out sounds
Soft as my hair.
Piano and organ playing high and low.
Clarinet and Piccolo as high as the wailing wind.
Trumpet and horns with the in different notes
Sometimes high,
Sometimes low,
Cymbals harshly vibrating,
Triangles gently tingling the air.
The timpani...
With that big drum..
Bang!
  Bang!!
   Bang!!!

   Claire Platts

Who?

She sits alone.
Who is she? What is she?
She is alive.
She cannot understand her physical being,
made up of genes and cells.
She cannot understand her emotions
and feelings.
Who is she? What is she?
Who cares?
She does.

   Tracey Stone

Abandoned

Left alone,
Where the freezing waves of doom
Come crashing slowly in
To set the stony beach awash.
Your only hope the rambling pathway
Through the sandy dunes.
From there I saw your trembling frame
Crouched beside a rock.
I knelt to stroke your dull and matted fur,
Wet from thunderous, salt-sea spray.
Your eyes beseeched.
I held you close for warmth.
No one saw us as we left for home.

   Gail Farrell

Mixed Media

Round the bed the curtains gently fall
Circling at last the would of him and me,
Sharing a love so known but not till now expressed
Laying bare a life times tragedy,
But as the breathing gently stops
  I see that little smile,
With anguished tears I pull the curtain wide,
He's already with another
  On the other side

   Mary Rose

My Boy, Sanjay

I found a photograph of you today!
There you stand all of twelve weeks old, head cocked
Slightly to one side, ears and eyes alert
Ready to take the whole world on as long
As we tackle it together, and I
Stretch my hand out to you where you lie now,
Fourteen years old today, beside my feet.

Still alert my faintest touch, you look
At me, to speak to me of days long gone
When many, many canine friends and you
Spent happy carefree hours chasing sticks and
Each other, in Lady Dixon's Park, round
And round what seemed to you, the big wide world
Revolving with each season as it came.

I turn again to the photograph and
To you. I'll shortly take another snap
And place it with the first. Looking at it
Some day for removed I fervently hope,
When the storm of love's first wild grief has passed,
I'll see the total you, my boy, and smile.

   J. C. Nelson

Day Dreamer

I have a dream,
I suppose everyone has a dream
But how many have a dream like mine,
Answer: None.

Oh, I have fantasies just like everyone else,
  And they're perfectly normal,
But this dream like I said before
  Is not ordinary
In fact it is far from it!

While others are dreaming of
far off places
ambitions
the ones they love
heck, even shopping
-for those that really have no imagination,
I'm lying in bed dreaming of...
No, I wouldn't tell you,
You're not ready yet
For the horrors that lurk inside my mind!

   Nokomis Curtis

After A Phone Call

How sweet the sound that bid my heart rejoice;
'Twas no surprise that I should hear your voice.
For e'en before you spoke, I knew that you were there.
The words that flowed, and your sweet laughter,
like the rippling of a brook through forest glade,
did but confirm your thoughts which I already knew.
For such, by now, is our affinity,
that distance, such as man would try define,
can never come between or hold us separate;
Where'er I go, or wheresoe'er you are,
this space is impotent to keep our souls apart.
Our spirits are not two, but one,
inseparably intermingled and entwined,
and shall fore'er remain until the end of time.

Arthur Barraclough

"Joy"

My heart is pounding, as I stand by the door
She's yelling and screaming, I can't stand much more
It's been going on hours, people in, people out
If it doesn't stop soon it shall be I who will shout.
Please, some one help her, take away the pain
It's so hard to listen, it's driving me insane.

Sh! What did I hear? I swear it's a cry
Everything is quiet, the minutes tick by.
The door pushes open, the nurse rushed out
Congratulations she yells, as she dashed about.

Is mother well, is the baby alright
When can I see them, I've been here all night.
As I enter the room to an emotional scene
Mother and father look so proud and serene
The joy that I feel I cannot describe
My darling new grandchild, has just arrived.

Beryl Franks

Bangles Gold In Dust

The golden mass sand and stone
Surreal to the end
A metallic shimmer crashing sea
A distant sun amongst the heavens
An ageing forecast set in ruin.

Twisting like twine
All its greenery stands tall
The lapping up of rain cupped its leaf
As feeble feet plod through
And gain their daily delicacy.

Deep in all glory it's the glint of hope
Buried, shelled, the riches found
Bangles gold in dust
Gold, pure gold, this precious treasure sold
This time for me inside I gleam
Riches lustre polished from rust
My beautiful escapade
Bangles gold in dust.

Heather McGowan

Inner City Decay

An old man sits on a crumbling wall,
His worldly goods in a carrier bag,
Ask him what his name is, he only mumbles.
His clothes are torn, his hair is matted,
Ask him where he comes from, he only mumbles.
His body is twisted, his spirit broken,
Ask him where he lives, he only mumbles.
He tries to stand, but his legs are stiff,
he picks up his bag, but his grip is weak,
Ask him his address, he only mumbles,
He staggers home, his back is bent,
I follow him there, now I know his address,
    Box number two,
    Cardboard City,
    London, W1A.

Brenda Hammersley

The Price Of Life

In the twilight of his years, sitting in a dim lit room
He contemplates his future and what appears to be his doom.
He's passed his biblical age of three score years and ten
And wonders how his end will be, and even more so when.

For he's been told by medics and his only kith and kin
That his maladies have come from his own accursed sin
In living life too high and much too much to his delight
That now he has to pay and this is now his plight.

His inner organs now are pickled through much excessive drink
And passed womanizing has brought him to very near the brink
Of life's sweet savour that he once scorned so very much
So now it seems he'll have to pay, and heavily for such.

Such liberties of life he took without a second thought
Now it seems that life at any price just can't be bought
Like other things he's always had the cash to buy
Now it's near the end for him and it seems his time is nigh.

For now it's left him in such awful agonizing pain
It's his end to life, that he treated with such disdain.
So take heed from this all those who go this way
That for some things in life, you always have to pay.

Gerard Oxley

The Daisy Chain

Through the grass and daisies white
Tiny feet are tripping light
As they flit from blade to blade
From shadow, sun and into shade.
The child is dressed in palest blue
With silver bows upon each shoe,
And the locks of gold about her head
Are braided up with ribbons red.
When she comes to the ancient gate
She sits down to wait and wait.
To wait and wait for her 'Granny B'
Who slowly comes with the picnic tea.
She helps unpack the royal spread
Of ham and buns and currant bread.
With pearl-like teeth she then doth eat
Until she finds herself replete.
She gathers then the daisies white
To make a chain of beauty bright,
And all about her Granny's curls
The chain she twists and turns and twirls.

Barbara J. Brockbank

After The Love Goes

After the love goes
You say things you didn't mean to say
As the skies turn distant from sunshine into grey

After the love goes
Emptiness suddenly strikes
Never forgetting your times together, never forgetting his
hates and likes

After the love goes
It's hard to carry on
To listen to the radio, when you know you'll hear your song

It's hard to read those stories
Of lovers all the same
Knowing that in any page turn, you're bound to see his name

But after the love goes
Love turns to sisterly care
And no matter how hard you fight it, his thoughts will always
be there.

So after the love goes
Remember all that you can
For one day you'll fall in love
With another unforgettable man.

Katie Boyman

239

A Tiger In The Sun

A lazy beast,
Made angry by human imagination,
Squinting in the brassy sunlight,
His breath fiery,
His body supple,
He melts into the long, quivering grass,
Crouching,
Pouncing,
And then - Silence,
He is lazy again,
Peaceful,
The sun beating down upon his golden back,
A tolerant magnificent beast indeed.

Anna-Marie Bray

Take The Night Away

Stepping stone upon a slippery floor
You took the meaning out of ineptitude
And hardened life's renewal to the core,
My callousness destroyed, leaving nothing crude.

Neon blazing amidst the ivory of conversation,
Shining pearls of a now-forgotten wisdom,
Was this my old love's solitary station?
Or maybe the ridicule of a lover, seldom?

Total indefatigable hammering of souls
Locked into a spaceless mind-enhancing reconstruction,
Like a novice at the birth of foals,
Alone, swallowing the carnage of life's creation.

It was easy to dream of eternity,
Numerous hidden population wanting to stay;
Even now, after a decade, I bear no enmity.
Just take the Night away.

Karl Baecher

Reflections In A Wineglass

A cafe small, a Summer's day,
So long ago, so far away,
'Twas there that we met, we shared our wine,
One glass between her lips and mine,
Where conjuring visions to enthral,
She made me a life where love was all.

In cafe small, that Summer's day,
Long long ago, far far away,
Ah what a world of sun we spied,
Within that glass there, side by side,
And oh how we laughed, we kissed, we planned,
The happiest pair in all the land!

I go back now the years have flown,
Alas, the glass I hold alone;
I lift it to phantom lips and mine,
To call back again those days divine;
Slowly I sip to bid them stay,
Then put down the glass - and come away.

Seymour Porter-Bryant

Shadows

It is they who are with you at every step,
It is they who are beside you at every moment,
It is they who are never willing to lend a hand or to give
friendly advice,
It is they who have been with you your whole life,
It is they you do not know.

They are dark,
Never able to reveal any secrets,
They are close to you, yet still distant,
They cannot tell the truth, or even tell lies,
They know everything about you,
But are never able to reveal anything to you about themselves,
They are your closest friends, that you do not know.

Cara Jones

Untitled

In a quiet little corner, in a field of hay,
Two little creatures were chatting one day,
Said one to the other, "isn't it funny,
That I am a rabbit, and you're just a bunny.
My father owns all that you can see,
Your father has nothing, you're not as good as me",

The poor little bunny felt really sad,
Then he thought to himself,
"But he's not his dad",
If I work hard, and develop my gifts,
That will give my career quite a lift,
I will work far too hard to have any bad habits,
And then, who knows, one day, I could be...
A rabbit.

C. E. McGinnity

Cherished Memories Of Love

How busy is life, with husband, family, and home
Too busy at first, to consider ending alone
Too late to recapture the laughter and tears,
The time gone so quickly, with passing of years
How easy it all seemed right from the start,
From falling in love, and giving your heart.
The children arrived, then growing so fast
Nurtured, then married, and leaving at last.
So now we were back from whence we had started.
Little knowing how short a time till we parted.
We made plans for things we would do
Was as well at that stage, that we never knew
Or realised, shortly we would run out of luck
From the moment that terrible illness struck.
How busy was life with husband, family, and home.
And I never considered, I would end it alone.

M. Kearley

A Meadow Concert

How bright the sun shines on this beautiful morn
A heavenly presence appears to be born.
The air is so still not a cloud in the sky
Not a million diamonds could my feeling buy.

As the dew soaks my shoes I have a limit to walk
But that does not hamper the birds constant talk.
While they greet one another to start a new day
Unaware of church goers as they pass by this way.

The sun beams pierce through a gap in the tree
To catch coloured breast while wings flutter free.
In a magical moment the meadows alive
What a glorious feeling penetrates my inside.

O please go on I don't want you to stop
But in the midst of the bird song I regret I forgot.
The variety artist and the bird with her brood
Must pull down the curtain to go looking for food.

The baton strikes down as the sun leaves the east
Scurrying birds change the scenery and the fledglings now feast.
No time for an encore it just cannot be
What a joy to remember and it was all given free.

Eric Sharrod

In Memory Of My Love

Love can it be defined
No. Though this love was mine.
For in my heart this love was born.
Each morning was a joy to meet the dawn.

To find my love beside me
Each night was bliss
Because we were together

Now all has gone.
For when I was not ready
One fine day
The weaver came, and stole my love away.

M. E. Warren

My Diary

This dusty old tome is home
To my earliest thoughts and memories,
The people I've been and the places I've seen,
Recordings of hoarded ambitions and dreams.

My angular father and literary mother
Reside beside my friends and foes,
Sketches of trenches from history class,
Regular corners and rhythmical flows.

Tracing the spaces between the lines
In assumed moods through a borrowed view:
Library guides to the keeping of records
Were, if returned, too long overdue.

From the very depths of my binding mind,
A margin for error in every preference;
The place I'll be buried is marked by its bearing,
My life is planned out here for future reference.

Adam Barnard

A Summer Evening

Dusk.
A slight breeze ruffles the pear blossom,
A sweet scent fills the air,
And then... a blackbird sings.
The trilling notes ripple through the dusk
With heart-rending beauty,
Touching chords of memory
Of other evenings in yesteryear.
On and on the throbbing melody soars,
Plucking the heart strings,
Filling the soul with its loveliness.
Twilight falls.
The stars begin to twinkle
In the velvet backdrop of the sky.
A hush descends -
And at last the blackbird sleeps.

Irene Way

Spring

See now, the suckling life, to earth's warm bosom cling,
It's Spring, the air is rife, Joyous in everything.

Look how the young shoots cleave their way through mossy loam,
and sparrows mating weave, a cradle for their home.

On bough the bursting green, clothes all the countryside,
and crocuses are seen, in all their golden pride.

The row, discordant din, of life reborn, astir.
All nature enter in, acclaim the new born year.

I vow, no livelier sight, could greet my eager eyes,
than dawn distilling light, unveiling spring's surprise.

Norman D. Paterson

Leaves

The leaves turn brown and gold
Their youth has gone they are growing old
The wind it blows so cruel and loud
They leave their boughs and flutter to the ground
The winter soon will come
and leaves there will be none
The trees stripped oh so bare
It just doesn't seem fair
But then the spring in all her glory
Time for celebration surely
All trees in bud bursting to get out
It makes one feel they want to laugh and shout
The leaves appear in all their splendour
Young and fresh and very tender
they dress the tree in her coat of green.
The prettiest picture you've ever seen.
The summer comes it doesn't last
We'll lose the leaves when it's gone past.

K. L. Wellington

Time

Time races by, all ages to the eye.
Proud youth, consumed with doddering age.
Fire quenched, with its flaming rage
Fond love's embracing passion,
Wanes from mighty oak to minute atom.

Sleep is past, within a trice,
Work deducts its awful slice.
Why are we here for trouble or strife?
Or, prelude, to some other 'life'?

There is no future and no past,
Only the 'now' on which we last.
The silicon chip for all it's worth
Cannot the dreadful future hold.
Time can never be retold.

Can mortals dare to show they care
For passing life with time's sharp knife?
Perhaps the 'spaceman' in the sky,
Or Mephistopheles with evil eye,
Will tell us when we 'die'?

John Shefford

Fashion Folly

Where do we go from here?
Somewhere we've been before!
When skirts were short and trousers wide
Bouffant hair was much admired;
Fashion experts oft' predict
The fashions we should follow;
But do they ever spare a thought
For you, for me for morrow;
For if we're tall or thin or fat
Do we look right in this or that;
Can we wear our hair up high
or platform shoes that reach the sky;
We never seem to satisfy
Our never ending yearning;
For wardrobes full of fashion 'musts'
that long since saw an airing;
When will we learn to be ourselves
to be what life intended;
To live for now for you and me
To be once more contented

Barbara M. Tinsley

Late Springtime

They bloomed this year so slowly.
In chilly winds and darkened days.
Nature continues unimpeded by climatic vagaries.
Strange to see flowers and blossoms amidst odd flakes
Of snow - a feeling of time and temperature out of sync.
Man, in his narrow unthinking way, may have helped
To create this change I think.

Geraldine Smithes

Seasons Of Life

Spring of life is to be born
Amidst the flowers as fresh as dawn
You grow and grow then learn to walk
Your teeth appear, you start to talk

Summer comes for you to play
A part in life from day to day
Laughter and sunshine are the thing
As this may be your natural fling

Autumn then rears up its head
A time of life you need not dread
For you have memories of the years
Of happiness, sunshine, joy and tears

Winter follows with it cold
You think that you are growing old
Then offspring of your children say
'Grandma, grandpa, are you coming out to play?'

A. G. Avery

Depression

You think you've got it beaten, then it rears its head again
You're worthless, useless, life means only loneliness and pain.
There's nothing friends can do to help - the feeling is inside
It gnaws away incessantly and will not be denied.
"A waste of space, a waste of time, that's all you are" it cried
"You even failed to kill yourself - you needed cyanide!"
You think you've got it smothered, this awful inner voice
But sometimes something sets it off - an unexpected choice,
or you hesitate, uncertain, with confusion in your mind.
This gives it chance to gather strength, and sneaking up behind,
it makes you doubt your sanity, start reaching for the pills,
but fear of further failure stops you - something in you kills
the urge to end it all for nothing. Things were getting better 'til
you dropped your guard, forgot intentions, never let old
feelings fillyour waking hours. Stay in control - your life is
yours to waste or lose. That inner voice can still be strangled -
you have got the right to choose.

Rosalyn Nancarrow

Want

His wife, her stomach distended in pain,
For the want of a handful of life giving grain.
From the misery of hunger, there could never be rest,
For the baby that sucked at her shrivelled up breast
In the innocent depths of its liquid brown eyes,
That in the heat of the day had been ravaged by flies
The light of life flickered and finally died,
And a wandering hyena mockingly cried.
He laid down the body on hot barren sand,
With a sense of injustice, he could not understand
Betrayed by rich nations, in whom he'd put his trust
And his wife's silent tears soaked into the dust.
As they gazed at the bundle, their object of love,
A jet curved a path in the heavens above.
On his emaciated shoulder, he cradled her head,
Before the dawn of tomorrow, they too would be dead
From a town in the distance, came a transistorized tune,
And another dark cloud, passed over the moon.

J. D. Rowland

Hell And Heaven

Where do people go I wonder,
up above or right down under?
When their souls are laid to rest.
And their past duty to God is put to the test.
Is there any where, any place at all,
Or just a black hole where we jump and fall?
Do we have another life as a soul?
Maybe as a horses new born foal,
Or do we lie and just rot away,
If we've sinned go to hell and pay.
Only those who've been in touch,
Will know if we've a ghostly hand to clutch.
To lead us down the path of death,
And stop and breathe our very last breath.

Helen Watson

Fragmented Girl

She didn't sit, she didn't stand, whilst pressing
    the blood icicle further into her hand.
She merely sighed and flashed her eyes towards
    the sky
She moved silently but in haste, her heart thumping
    to mirror her pace.
She licked her lips as if to taste the scent of life
    that inspired her race.
She danced upon the lily-pads that lead her way.
Passing the old man the same time each day.
He nodded his head in that curious way.
Suggesting a reverence knowing she'd obey,
And reaching the spot of her destination,
    turning back with the utmost hesitation,
Snatching a deep breath to fuel her race
She bowed to her heart's wishes as the ice gave way.

Veronique Astwood

My Mother - Ruby

Oh how I miss my mother so
The one who gave so much love to me
She was always there when times were bad
To give me love and hold my hand
What fond memories I have of her
That lovely face her smile so bright
Mother - where have you gone
When you were ill I cared for you
With the love you gave to me
How I wished I could take your pain
To make you laugh again
But sadly that was not to be
You're now in heaven where the angels sing
I know for sure you will be joining in
You always loved to sing a tune
When you were well and out of pain
Rest in peace my beloved friend
We will have that sing song
When we meet again
Oh how I miss my mother so.

Joan Hewitt

Rush Hour

Frantic noise, indifferent silence,
Busy world. We sit and stare.
Furtive glances,
Sideways snatches of someone else's sphere.
Jostled together in solitary confinement,
We're surrounded, alone. No space to breathe
Not daring to breathe.
The unnatural beat of a foreign tongue resounds,
Unrestrained, untrained,
Unaware of British reserve.
We want to look
To feast on every inch of someone else.
Silently admiring,
Critical. Jealous. Proud.
Hungry eyes, wide.
Vacant minds, churning.

In this hive of inactivity
Not a word is uttered.
We are hushed by our own creation
Hurtling noisily through the bowels of the earth.

Victoria Lyall

A Man Apart

I do not ask to live in a mansion,
    Nor yet wear a crown made of gold.
But a loving man who can understand
    My needs as I slowly grow old.

Someone to share the woes and strife
    That temper each new day.
And hold my hand when I feel downcast
    To keep me lively and gay.

A man who will show me compassion,
    When I'm irritable, sick and distraught.
A man who will be my companion,
    My pilot, my guide and escort.

A man who is honest and loving,
    Not just for the things that I own.
But loves me because I'm a woman,
    For myself and myself alone.

I have no desire to be famous,
    I've no wish to own treasures untold.
But a man apart, with a loving heart,
    And a face that's a joy to behold.

David Livingstone

Picnic In The Dark

Taking Time, tick tock.
Summer wine, maybe hock.
Fill your glass, take a snap-shot in the dark.

Milky Way, Magic Moon.
Spring May, Summer June.
Twinkling stars, far track in an astronomic arc.

Snatch a swim, scream and shout.
God it's cold, let's get out.
What next? Hot sex in the bushes in the park.

Morning dawn ends the night,
Give a yawn, now it's light.
Hamper bare, let's share the singing of the lark.

Richard Hill

The English Oak

The oak, oh the English oak,
How beautiful you stand out, among the nest,
No matter what time of year it is.
   you please me best,
Your bough stands out, and stretches above
   the silver birch.
From trunk to tip you are paramount
   in natural topiary.
Black, Brown, Bark cracked with age.
You look around and see all the young
   sapling oak you've made.
And then when Autumn comes, or fall,
You have your dormant sleep
And dream of spring

Tom Wilkinson

My Sutherland

My Sutherland I miss you, my dear highland home,
Land of my youth I far from you roam,
Your steep rocky mountains and silvery shore,
In my heart now I yearn to return there once more.

Where bracken and heather grow close to the sea,
And red deer and eagle live wildly and free,
Where the lone glens are shrouded in soft highland rain,
My Sutherland I long to return there again.

In memory I stand where oft as a lad,
I stood with the folk of my own native land,
And I dream of that country where I long to be,
My Sutherland, your beauty is calling to me.

The hills of my childhood I no longer see,
But one day I hope it is back there I'll be,
If I had a wish, with a wave of a wand,
It's to be back again in my dear Sutherland.

Alister H. Thomson

Mad Cow Disease Money Sleaze

No more brain.
No more time for the insane.
As the sign of the times,
Concedes and declines.
Because the cup that runs over,
To keep you sober.
Is now empty.
And the offal obese in you belly.
Is overweight.
So for you there is no immortality,
face your fate.
As the mad cow disease,
Starts to increase.
Just for the brainless,
And the heartless.
For it is a politician you have to please,
Just for their infected cancer greed, for
the money sleaze.

John David Margetson

Dreams, Ideals And Auguries

In childhood I dreamed of wide horizons, rolling plains
And I yearn for a life, full fine and free

In childhood I dreamed of rings
Rings within rings within rings
Like ripples left in the wake of a pebble cast into a pool
And I yearn for perfection in all things
Each ring is my entier, a thing as complete as it can be
Entiers within entiers, the full series of rings is my Eldorado
In childhood I dreamed of an enchanted land it is my Eldorado

In boyhood I dreamed of a lovely girl
She is the Queen of Eldorado

In childhood again I dreamed another dream
Is it just the wind or is it.... danger?
It's faint and faraway — why is it so sinister?
There is a fearful intuition of impending doom
What was it I saw?
It's all so long ago and faraway I cannot quite remember
Was it just the wind or was it danger?

Last night I dreamed again or is it lost repining I saw
   again my golden girl and could there be a reconciling?

Maurice Hemmant

The River Biss

Rarely afforded a second glance, often mistaken for a stream,
Yet an abundance of wildlife compliments its flow; the heron
   and kingfishers dream.
In places inches make up its depth, further on three feet,
Trim up the banks fenced off from the cows it's quaint and neat.
Winding its way through meadows and towns, passing
   unnoticed to some.

Adorned with teazles and willow trees, to me, it never looks glum.

Forever aware of its rarely spoilt path, I wander alone
   with the hounds.
For the moment at least enjoying the freedom, peacefully
   knowing no bounds.
Sat on the bank, an uncommon sight, an angler playing his skill.
The odd bites that come are often missed, the eventual fish a thrill.

Easily forgotten are life's problems and stresses,
Surrounded by teazles and proud standing rushes.

The fences and hedgerows still standing, nature's habitat
   housing cure.
Allowing the rabbits good breeding, a meal on its own for sure.
With the shouting of partridge and pheasant ever posed
   to take on the wing,
On the river, the coot and the mallard, you'll never hear these
   birds sing.
A river to cherish and look after for our children to walk and love.
A gift to appreciate, not squander, till we pass to the life above.

Will Davies

"Memories Of A Big Family Country Childhood"

Sometimes I yearn, just once to go
To that old brick house we used to know
Walk the loaning's stony ground
Where there was beauty all around
To hear my fathers voice, see my mothers gentle smile
I'd walk that loaning a million mile
The sound of my brothers and sisters at play
The joy of togetherness at the close of the day
The wonderful smell of new baked bread
Such comfort we had in our old brass bed
The swoop of the night owl, its haunting cry
Watch a lark soar high the summer sky
These thoughts that flow along the rivers of my memory
Why do they mean so much to me?
Or is this yearning for a time
When we were innocent and young
And our world, was fine
Will I ever be free from these feelings for then?
Sadly, the hands of time don't turn back again

Jeanette Stephen

The Union

The union is my shepherd
I shall not want,
It maketh me to lie down on the job.

It leadeth me besides the still factories,
It restoreth my insurance benefit.
Yea though I walk though
the shadow of decreased productivity.

I will fear no recrimination
For the Union is with me.
It prepareth a work committee for me,
In the presence of my employers
It anointh my hands with pay rises.
My bank balance runneth over,
Surely hire purchases payments,
and union dues shall follow
all the days of my life.

And I shall dwell in a
council house forever
And shop stewards
comfort me.

Clementina McAllister

Phasianum Colchicus

How fares this country squire?
Is he just a mini clown on stilts?
How suggestive in his head when he flounces!
It brings to mind cockaded knights astride their chargers.
So no ordinary being this, for sure!
With pride is he clad right bonnily
In a myriad of kilt-like colours.
He is a creature of beauty, of grace, innocence and peace;
No single soul has he ever harmed
In vain this royal laird would stem his fate;
The murderous focus of the sportsman's gun,
Though the veriest prince among game birds,
He is vulgarly termed "The Pheasant."

Gordon S. Cowie

Remember

He stands at the cenotaph, his face crumpled and cold
Life isn't easy when you grow old
He thinks of his comrades who never came home
Then he feels guilty for having a moan

He stands in the rain with his head slightly bowed
Hardly noticing the rest of the crowd
The war never ended for him on that day
It's been on his mind but he'll never say
He hopes they all just rest in peace, he always will remember
Every month of every year, not only in November
And when he grows too weak to go the young must take his place
We didn't share the pain he hides but you see it in his face
So we must also take the time, there's a date we must remember
To help to turn his pain to pride, it's the eleventh day of
November

Mary Wilkinson

A House Wife's Dream

I've always wanted to go to YORK,
But all I do is talk, talk, talk,
About going to York
I dream of lofty spires and cobbled streets,
Old world inns where the locals meet,
With weathered eyes they sit and stare,
At hordes of tourists everywhere,
Ghosts stalk. Ulph's Horn may be heard on a breathless night,
While Guy Fawkes passes flying his kite.
Dick Turpin thunders by for kicks,
Could it be him or was it swift Nicks?
I search in the library to find out more,
Much better this than household chores.
A flick through the brochures for the quickest way,
And my dreams are released as I book for my stay.

Gladys M. Mitchell

The Fox

The fox is out on his travels tonight.
Did you see it in your headlights?
With its beautiful brush and head held high,
A magnificent animal this one cannot deny.
Is it out hunting just for its own food,
Or has it to feed a hungry young brood
Of cubs it has left behind in its lair
Wondering what's on tonight's bill of fare.
Perhaps if they are lucky it will be a hen
That someone has forgotten to shut in its pen.
Or maybe a rabbit or even a lamb.
A fox has no scruples, it will take what it can.
It can also be naughty, be not happy with one
And kill more than it needs, it seems, just for fun.
So it may be beautiful, but to say the least
It's not every persons most favourite beast.
But it's not only the fox that takes more than it needs.
Look at us humans with our various greeds.
There are so many who take anything they can
With little regard for their fellow man.

R. H. Barge

Fair October Day

Subtle and sweet, this breath of morning air
Recalls our bright, cold mornings, long ago.
Beneath a sky diffused with coloured mist
The short, pale grass, bold in the morning sun,
Newly defrosted, now awaits my tread.
As the day lengthens, and the spiky grass
Brightens to green again, this pallid sky
Changes in colour to a deeper blue:
No drifting, trailing gauze
Obscures its azure beauty from my sight.
The angled line of roof-tops climbs the hill,
In solid, slate-dark shapes.
Shadows of chimneys, finely drawn,
Lie, in their differing patterns, on each roof.
If frost should come again tonight, my tread
Will bruise and darken the crisp morning grass;
Colours, diminished by their coat of ice,
Will seek renewal from the modest sun;
And these sweet, subtle scents recall a love
That brightened autumn mornings, long ago.

Noele Mackness

The Allotment

Black earth, enriched with compost and loam,
Old kitchen waste, smelly product of home,
Fertilizer, lime, with phosphate and dung,
Attacking with glee, throat, nostril and lung.

Poring o'er catalogues, illustrating seed
Artfully tempting your desperate need
To go one better than t'other bloke's plot,
By selecting what you think is best of the lot.

Carefully sowing when weather's just right,
Got to make sure there's no frost at night.
Covering with net to foil hungry birds
With youngsters to feed - oblivious to words.

Tending the young plants and chopping down weeds
That spring up - remorselessly choking your seeds.
Watering the roots when it's so hot and dry,
Recalling the days you were still young and spry.

Then comes the autumn, you're ready to drop,
But looking with pride at a wonderful crop,
Your wrinkled old face breaking into a smile
and you say to yourself - "By God, it's worthwhile!"

George Baker

The Garden Gate

How special was the garden gate,
I used to swing on it at eight.
And then I'd lean on it and chat
With schoolgirl friends, of this and that.
Then came the war, and helter-skelter
Through the gate, to the air raid shelter.
Then called up for the A.T.S.
A radar plotter, homesick? Yes.
But home for leave, my gate still there.
I opened it, with gentle care,
And stood awhile, my hand on latch.
Just thinking thoughts, no gift could match.
But years ahead, the modern man
Decrees the age of 'open plan'.
And I for one, deplore the fate
Of the cosy, comforting, garden gate.

Norah Beamer

Broken Dreams

On the ninth of February at seven pm, the peace was broken
by political men.
Playing dangerous games with innocent lives, bombing
Canary Wharf without compromise.

Almost eighteen months without terrorist fears, shattered by a
device that still rings in our ears.
We pray for the people caught up in the blast, thinking those
horrors were locked in the past.

The peace we shared though waters apart, gave hope to our
children and a peaceful new start.
But now the torment raises its head once again, giving
heartache, misery, and agonizing pain.

Think firstly of life not political gains, just sit down and
talk and unravel those chains.
Please restore peace and love of mankind, leave the pride and
self gains of your parties behind.

Kenneth R. Griffiths

The Glade

Here where the grass is cool and sweet beneath my hand
And overhanging branches of the trees
Form a shaded bower where I can sit and dream
Here I find peace.

Here resting quietly by the stream
Where sparkling tumbling waters never cease
This playful cascade over mossy stones,
Here I find peace.

And here, where golden shafts of sunlight
With touch as gentle as a fairy wand release
The hidden beauty all around this glade,
Here I find peace.

Doris L. Gates

A Mountain Stream

A few drops of water, a few lumps of stone.
Some fragments of moss and a wisp of fern.
The glint of the moonlight, a murmur, the tone
Of fairy bells ringing in early morn.

The pureness of innocence, the coldness of snow,
The thin air of hilltops where high winds blow.
Transparent shallows and deep little pools
Reflecting the heavens in varying hues.

The freshness of spring in its newborn youth,
The rich tints of Autumn, the colour of Truth.
The brightness of sunshine, the sweet breath of May,
The sparkle of jewels in watery spray.

Ripples of laughter and gurgles of mirth,
The lightest and brightest of sweet mother Earth.
God brought them together - a Fairy's Dream
He from them made - A Mountain Stream.

J. D. S.

I Know You Are With Me

I still feel you
I wake up to put my arms round you
You're not there
My life is hollow,
My body is bare,
Without you, I have no soul
I keep thinking
You are going to walk through the door.
Flash back
Saying goodbye to you was so hard
Oh! My darling, I can't bear not having you
With me.
I love you
I know you are with me, I feel you
My body goes cold, then warm,
As if you are trying to hold me again
I say "Hello"
Hoping you will speak,
Looking at your photo,
All I can do is weep.

Justina Payne

Forever Eleven

A great man has died today
He won't come back he's gone away
Cooper was the peoples king
The wizard, the maestro on the wing
His silky skills for all to see
That perfect pass he used to make
The great free kick he liked to take
Super Coop we'll remember you

Forever eleven forever blue
For Motherwell and Bankies too
In Scotland's shirt he played with grace
At Hampden Park in foreign place
One of Scotland's greatest sons
The talented one from Hamilton

Just in his prime at thirty nine
No more to grace the grassy stage
Destined to live on in history page
He wore the golden boot, a great left foot
The legend lives on in all our hearts
Rest in peace Davy, rest in peace

Pete Rennie

My Little Yoda

My little Yoda he's so sweet
With his fluffy body and his tiny feet
He's a ball of fur with such personality
I'm sure in fact he takes after me

He loves to jump, hide and run
My little Yoda, he's such fun
He knows just when it's time to play
But not when it's time to go away

He comes out to play quite late at night
If you're not used to him, he'll give you a fright
As he races round and round he goes
He keeps quite fit and me on my toes

He likes to chew almost everything
From cables to wallpaper and even rings
He loves to bath in his dust
To watch him bathe is an absolute must

He rolls and twists and makes a mess
But that doesn't matter 'cause he's the best
The best pet that there could be
But Yoda I'm afraid belongs to me

Joanne Albone

A Memory...

Remembering you...
Sitting here all alone, I think of you,
Knowing I'll probably never see you again,
Crying as I try to remember your face,
Crying as I see nothing but a vivid picture,
Oh why can't you be here?
Oh why can't you be here with me?

Will I see you again?
Maybe I'll see you again,
But not for a long while,
For now I'll have to settle for a
Vivid memory of you,
Reading your letters,
Remembering your face.

How long?
Thinking of the happy times we
Spent together, but now they're gone,
I sit there wondering,
Wondering for how long,
It'll be before I set eyes on your face again.

Emily Hastings

Kindred Spirits

Although she still wears mortal clothes,
The spirit within is still joined
By lifelong laughter, joy and love,
Sadly his mortal garb was loaned.

That spirit floats within the mist,
Is carried along on birds wings,
Knowing it was so truly blessed
With such true love and earthly things.

Funny stories still told somewhere,
That dry humour still carried on,
The mortal outer is not here
But the kindred spirits are one.

Margaret Hemmings

Tomorrow

I'm going home tomorrow for I really should not be,
here in this place for aged folk, that term just can't mean me.
How can they say I'm fragile, that alone I cannot cope?
I'm going home tomorrow, or at least that's what I hope.
Have they the right to put me here? I really don't feel old,
They say I'm hyper - something, - that my body's growing cold.
But I've a house, my dog, my cat are waiting there for me.
I'm going home tomorrow, if I ever find my key.
I know I don't remember when I last had owt to eat.
And sometimes when I look down I see odd shoes on my feet.
But I have lived a long life, and there's knowledge I can share,
So, I'm going home tomorrow, if, someone will take me there.

Caroline Turner

Lindisfarne (The Holy Island)

Is an island still an island, if not surrounded by sea?
For twice a day with causeway bare, you're not what you
  pretend to be.
When battered by the North Sea Storms, you sit there patiently,
As you have in ages past, wrapped in your own mystery,
And in the sun, when people come to your ruined Priory,
All are calmed, eased of heart, soothed by your serenity,
O Lindisfarne, O Holy Isle, seat of Christianity,
From where did spring, in greatest part, all faith and hope and charity,
The tidal watery arm that steals about you surreptitiously,
Is your captor and your saviour, you accept both placidly,
But do you wait for ebb of tide that anyone might see
Your uncloaked path across the sand, your naked availability,
Or do you wait for the waters' flow and your enforc-ed privacy,
The causeway drowned by the North Sea waves and the Isle
  by tranquillity.

S. Y. D. Ashton

"We're Never Apart"

No words of compassion, good will or intent
Can comfort the heart that is broken, or rent,
On the death of that being, from the heavens
Was sent, my dearly beloved mother

She went away on a hot summers day,
To her eternal home in the sky.
And when I first saw, my beloved was no more,
Tears began to well in my eye.

I touched her and kissed her,
And told her I loved her,
My eyes overflowing with tears.
I then said how lucky,
I was to have had her,
These long past 48 years

For I know in my heart
"we're never apart,"
My dearly beloved mother and me.
And when my time comes,
In some future year,
Her dearly loved face, I shall see.

Victor Stanwyck

The Other Land

What is it all about?
Where do we go?
The questions humans want to know,
The emptiness of minds,
The soulless bodies.
Bursting through cotton wool like shapes
Trying to grab a pure white gate.
Is it pain?
Or is it a feeling?
Is it the body in need for healing?
Your old life has now turned new,
With familiar faces welcoming you,
To a land of good fortune and with peace
Your chains have broken, you've now been released,
The only thing that's missing is you
But you can join us one day soon,
Don't be frightened, try and be brave
for we are not wanted any longer as slaves.
Mankind captured and stole our needs,
In this new land there is no greed.

Caroline Blankley

Lunar, Lunar

Lunar, lunar shining bright, pearl of the heavens,
jewel of the night. Cool and serene has you dangle in space,
a luminous glow lights up the place.
Enchainment and mystery come forth from thee,
magic and wisdom seem to set you free.

Lunar, lunar you stand out from the rest,
a radiant light filled with zest.
I gaze at you in total wonder,
the wind gets up and it starts to thunder.
Some fleeting clouds go sailing by,
but you just beam and light up the sky.

Lunar, lunar sparkling white, warm my heart but chill the night.
Lower and lower you'll sink in the sky,
soon I'll have to say goodbye.
You will set and the sun will rise,
the dawn will come and your memory dies.

Lunar, lunar come again, come and stir the hearts of men.
Patron of lovers you seem to be, keep on shining, smile on me.
The night has passed and you've gone away,
and here comes the break of day.

Sheila O'Donovan

A Fishy Tale

Fish as healers,
River of fish as faith doctors.
They suck out wounds.
That's their food.
Give them bread,
After a bite they die.

Nature so useful for humankind?
We destroy it.

Have we no conscience.

Fish as healers,
make me feel so helpless,
As they congregate round wounds
And suck it well.

Even tiresome mother might be healed.
I wonder if they can go deep into the brain?

A toast to you, nature.
Here's looking at you kid.

Fatma Durmush

Dream

I long to see the day
Everything bathed in a golden ray,
Moulted the rags to be in a silky suit
The day troubles give up their hot pursuit.

I tirelessly long that it be soon
So I caress an angel under the smiling moon,
From green gardens Nightingale playing melodious tunes
That day I would deny having scavenged the bins.

I long to see the blessed day
When I would playfully tickle my baby,
Telling him of my bitter past,
That's the day I would define life on the street.

Now, come day come if you be there
The chestless policeman to stop chasing me like a bear
Quick day I long to shave his beard,
That day I would teach him to behave.

Maxwell Mutami

The Sixteen Angels

Sixteen little children, never to laugh, or smile again.
Sixteen beautiful children, the angels of Dunblane.
Each one their parents pride and joy,
A beautiful cherished daughter, or a handsome boisterous boy.
Each little life taken, by a maniac, with a gun.
Because nobody in authority listened, not one, not one.

This tragedy has shocked the nation,
People from every walk, and station,
Everyone united in one grief.
Shock, horror, disbelief.

Dear little children, with all your lives ahead.
Mum and dad can no longer, tuck you safely up in bed,
But they also have private memories, to think of again and again,
And the nation will never forget, the sixteen angels of Dunblane.

Maureen Arnold

Never Forgotten

I was two at the time, everything seemed fine.
My mum came home, voice lowered a tone.
She left the room, face covered in gloom,
My dad followed, I could hear him swallow.
I listened at the door, my parents both swore.
My sister came to me, and held me tightly.
My parents came out, Linda asked 'What's this about?'
'Your brother has gone, I should have known all along,
He'll be with you in spirit, I can't believe that's it,
The 5 years of pain, and him taken in vain.'
Linda started to cry, and I didn't know why.
As the weeks went on, I realized he was gone.
I see his face every day, memories that will never fade away.

Elaine P. Fennell

A Prayer For Summer

Today you want to give me the world - make sure nothing
    ever hurts me
You say all the things that mean so much, to make me try again
I let you in, I want to believe ... my will is weak when my heart
    cries out
So I put away the pain of yesterday

Then my heart is in your hands again, my faltering hope fed
    by the warmth of your touch
My love is real but it's also blind
Against all odds, I pray that your dream is mine
That this time you've made up your mind

But tomorrow you change and the distance returns
Your words are harsh, your warmth has gone
Have you forgotten so quickly the promises you gave, the
words that stole my heart again?
Your betrayal cuts deep, Winter returns

So I ask for the truth - what is in your heart and your mind?
But you back away, tell me to go or stay
The choice is mine, no preference either way
My anger burns as my love is spurned

And yet somehow I still remember, the Summer of our love
Those precious days come back to haunt me - and plead with
    me to stay
So set me free or feed the fire that burns so low
I care so much if you stay or go

Karen Lesley Nield

Gloriana Lying Grey

"...Richmond Palace...where in 1603 Elizabeth I died on a great
pile of cushions, fading slowly like a spent fire, Gloriana until
she lay grey." D. Piper- Companion Guide to London

Cushions - a soft pyre of stuffs
Immeasurably rich in hue;
Brocades draped in triumphant carelessness,
Taffetas and silks,
Royal tapestries glowing in sunset ripeness,
Piled in the deepening gloom
Of Richmond Palace's great room.

On silent feet the felted servants go
To form the proclamation of eclipse
And quite alone atop this velvet catafalque
The failing queen peers for her empire
In last mortal scrutiny.

The day dies in a leap of flame
To burnish all the cords and tassels where she lies,
So kindling fire from jewels at her throat
And circling her hair and on the hand
That moves with dignity in one last gesture of command.

Thus through her doom she passes down
To unborn generations in a blaze of legend-
An immortal moon.

David K. Kennedy

'When Love Was Sweet'

Time and tides don't wait for me,
they move too fast from ecstasy
to emptiness... a broken shell,
where, within, two hearts did dwell.
Two hearts? Complete, as one they beat.
Now we are apart there is no warmth
no glowing embers... from that fire that I remember.
There was a time when we were one,
wrapped and warm, the world did scorn.
We had no need of external things,
we were complete with what love brings.
There was a place, it was our corner
of our world, there was no measure
for it was timeless and complete.
For thee and me, when love was sweet.

H. V. Dunkley

That Stained-Glass Window

His loin-cloth girded his weary limbs,
As from that rugged cross he hung.
His sentinels faithful unto death;
Martha - and the Virgin Mary.

I walked the aisle of that empty church,
Towards that stained-glass window.
Tinted in the blood of christ
Now forgotten in a world of lingo.

Absorbing its beauty I scanned its walls,
Plaques - further sacrifices - revealing
Those missing millions - 1914-'18
And then again - '39-'45.

I believe God is like an auctioneer.
He has already made you a bid.
It is now left for you to consider.
Isn't it time you rose your hand - and accepted?

Cyril C. Evans

My Granddad Is A Hippie

My granddad is a hippie - that's what they all say.
My granddad is a hippie who got lost along the way.
He's got all Dyllan's records and he swears by L.S.D.
My granddad is a hippie - but he means the world to me.

He wears his kaftan and his beads with the pride that they deserve,
He's banned so many bombs and things it must get on his nerves.
His centre parted hair hangs so grey and limp and sparse
And he reckons politicians all should bend and kiss his...as
For peace and love he is a dedicated freak,
You'd think the marriage vows were obsolete to hear him speak.

I suppose the day will come when he will leave this mortal slant
And smoke 'pot' all day with Angels and teach them how to chant.
He'll put a fuzz-box on his harp and top of the bill will be St. Pete
And the Heaven Club will be members only for the celestial elite.

My granddad is a hippie - that's what they all say.
My granddad is a hippie who got lost along the way.
He's got all the Beatles records - say's he'll leave them all to me.
My granddad is a hippie but he means the world to me.

B. M. Goss

The Little Rabbit!

Watch the little rabbit
Running fast and free.
Oh little rabbit, how I wish I were thee.
But bars they do surround me
And light I see no more
Except the light I see in you
As you travel through fields afar.

Come little rabbit, tell me what you see,
On your journey back and forth to me.
The grass is soft and green, upon your tiny paws
The hills, the trees, the soft green leaves
    look wondrous where you are.
The sun shining down on your silky white fur.
Oh why little rabbit is the world so unfair?

Debra Fisher

Think!!

If only we could sit a while
And ponder all we do,
Then maybe we could help our friends,
And lots of others too.
A touch, a glance, a cheery smile,
A, Can I help you for awhile,
It takes no time to think of others
They are all our sisters and brothers.
A helping hand, is all it takes,
We all sometimes make mistakes,
No one's perfect they never are
Just lend a hand and you will be a "star"

Sonia Gadeke

Pan Pipes

Down the Country Lane I wander,
    Lost in dreams of Countries far away
Where music, dance and happy song
    Echo and re-echo all day long.
Listen! Do I hear a far distant sound?
    In this country it is rarely found.
Suddenly I am transported to Peru -
    Surely it's the Pan Pipes so hauntingly true.

As the sound becomes more clear
    I watch a Gypsy caravan drawing near.
From within I hear a wondrous sound
    Echoing and re-echoing all around.

The caravan travels on its way
    As the pipes continued still to play -
Their sound grows fainter, then fades away
    I shall never forget that country lane -
Their sound reverberates through my brain

    God bless those who continue to play
Those uplifting Pan Pipes day after day.

Dorothy I. Harvey

In Confinement

On that resting day of the week
Sick was I and bed-ridden aloof
And to and fro the mind loomed afar
Pondering and craving for fitness

Just then all hell broke loose
Kicked ajar the room door to reveal
Sauntered in some tense duo like bullies
Looking for me and no one else to blame

The law at my throat in earnest
Away whisked for grilling and drilling
With remarks that seemed threatening,
Pushed into a quagmire of a cell

Reeking with foul air and smelly
The cell was all padded with junks
Hot and sweltering, the pent-up tears
Coursed down the pensive face in bondage

Seemingly the handiwork of no-gooders
Their jealousy imbided with complex
Did make their spirits subdued in disdain
On that resting day of the week to remember.

Nicholas Alex Bamidele

The Fields Of Heaven

Only the soaring lark above me in the summer sky,
Its tender, lilting song around me as I climb.
So steep this hilly field, it almost seems to touch -
Even as sea and sand unite, without a space -
Empyrean realms with their broad sweep into infinity.
If only I had height and strength enough, I'd draw it down,
That burnished, glowing, cloudless, timeless, lark-filled sky,
Which surely must be Heaven. For I have often dreamed
That somewhere are untrodden fields which, from the wood's dark edge,
Stretch boundless, cool, and sweet, far, far beyond
The limit of all sight. They are folded about the sky,
Cloaked in Eternity. And there forever sings the lark,
Full-throated blackbird, thrush's oft-repeated notes,
The robin's haunting song. Into the wood's dark pool
Cascading waterfalls fling their bright diamonds down
Over cold mossy stones, a thousand glittering jewels.
On those Elysian fields, I'd walk alone,
Then sleep a little, dream a little, lying quietly,
My eyes turned, first, to day-time-burnished, evening-azure sky -
And, last, on star-emblazoned night - until I see no more.

Elizabeth Ryeburn-Gilchrist

248

Untitled

I thought of you today.
My mind was transported, a thousand miles
From bleak surroundings;
To a world of my own.
Slowly invading the empty chasm
Which is me.
Unfolding my mind, unravelling the darkness,
Reveals the beautiful thoughts, hidden within an inner world.
Infinite mass,
Contained within my soul.
You may reach in.
But you may not receive.
For you touch my soul.
I can feel your very being, close to my own.
The searing pain tears through my heart.
Because I love you.
Tears fill my eyes.
Because I love you.

Erica Lay

Shortcut

If there was a spine that I could grab,
Find a pulse and measure it.
I should be like them.
Break a code (or shatter the enigma)
and find the secrets of the form.
There will be a link to them.
Rows of them over all the lands,
Endless corridors,
Infiltrating every home.
There's a silent humiliation as I try again
To discover the key to open a path for me.
Another failure and I will go back to
Studying the designs, the new formats;
The diction, the prose, imagery and themes.
Read them and weep or read them and pause,
Wondering,
But never breaking the code.

John-Paul Harold

The Journey

Holiday weekend, must rest the brain,
Go for a journey, travel by train,
Relax the body, time to unwind,
Eyes still working, feeling the mind,
Fast changing vista, each blink of eye,
Different small town, go flying by,
Buildings now red brick, not Yorkshire stone,
Beginning to feel, a long way from home,
Speeding through farmland, feeling serene,
Countryside's perfect, wearing spring green,
Into a tunnel, momentary black,
Out into sunshine, dream back on track,
Looking through window, now comes in view,
Soft rolling hillsides, track travels through.
Holiday journeys, train takes the strain,
Time to return to, real life again.

Brenda Vallow

Time

The room is dark, the fire burns with such a lovely glow.
All is quiet, clock ticks on, time goes so fast you know.
So much to do, the room to clean, then dinner, bathe, get dressed.
The hair to curl, put make-up on, then off to work I'm pressed.

Before I start to dash about and organize these things,
I like to sit to dream awhile, watching the mood it brings.
Pictures of health, and happiness, peace, friendship, love and joy.
Of things the heart will whisper low, not cares the world employs.

Time hurries on, I have to draw the curtains once again.
The sky is nearly darkest blue, the sun has lost its flame.
But, in the dusk shines one bright star to light the world to sleep.
The herald of another night, till time and daylight creep.

Mary P. Carrell

(Written before getting ready for an evening performance.)

A Small Creature

There is a small creature, who lives here in God's house
His name is Oscar, a little brown mouse,
He has a wife and a family of four.
He lives by the radiator, next to the door,
Don't come looking for him on a Monday night,
It's the families night out, not a whisker in sight,
It's those bells in the belfry, what a noise they make,
Just make the whole church just shiver and shake,
Just loves weddings and wedding rings.
But not very often he hears a choir sing.
He loves christingle with candles so bright.
With little faces beaming in a circle of light,
But, his favourite time throughout the years,
Has been the harvest festivals, all those apples and pears,
What has happened he wonders, to the harvest bread,
Was always a nice meal before going to bed,
So if you see Oscar here today,
Don't shoo him away, just let him stay,
This is his home, here in God's hose,
He's one of God's creatures, this little brown mouse.

June Lucas

"The Dilemma Of Love"

So near to happiness complete,
    Like reaching for a star,
With you my only love so sweet,
    So near and yet so far.

We've traced the rainbows through the rain
    So oft in times gone by,
But now the final thrusting pain
    Could sever every tie.

We'll live a life of 'Might have been's'
    As time rolls wearily on,
Sometimes as others beam - we'll smile
    With hearts of leaden stone.

The pain will ease to just a weight
    That deadens every joy,
As in the hands of cruel fate
    We break as an old toy.

It has not happened yet, of course,
    And it need never be,
If we unlock the love at source,
    For love's life's only key.

Geo S. Noble

Midnight Is Here

Hatred and lawlessness
fill the earth all around
The darkness spreads,
fears rule the heart of all mankind,
in every place.
Is there no hope?
Listen - look!
Beyond the sordid scenes of earth,
which pass away.
The love that came in infant form
has grown to kingly stature
He rules the earth and heaven
The distant sound of the return
is just beyond the hill
The beat of softly moving wings
is in the air so still
A joy beyond imagining will come to all
who left their hearts to him in love
The Lord of Love, Bridegroom lo, he comes.

O. L. Vasey

Noel

November's grey and cloudy days are done,
The mists and tints of autumn long since gone,
The leafless trees stand gaunt against the sky,
The short dark days of winter looming nigh.

But then to cast the cloak of gloom away
The Advent and the joys of Christmas Day,
The time for love, and grateful hearts to fill
With generous thoughts, forgiveness and goodwill.

With praise and thanks we shed a humble tear
For blessings granted through the passing year,
Mindful of those afflicted and in need,
We pray that from their troubles they'll be freed,

The old year gaily dies and with the morn
Are hopeful expectations newly born,
Fresh promises and vows to mend our ways,
What matter if they only last for days?

Reginald E. Miles

Shock

She felt a sudden tightness in her chest.
Her limbs refused to move at her behest.
Her lungs would not respond to inhalation.
Her heart was in a state of febrilation.
Her head was spinning like a drunken top.
The noises in her ears just wouldn't stop.
There was a frightening numbness in her spine.
She found she couldn't walk a steady line.
Her body trembled, and her mouth was dry.
But suddenly she just began to cry.
And then, still reeling from her awful trauma,
She thought "How best to break the news to Norma?"—
Her friend, with whom she worked down at the pottery:
They'd won the jackpot in the National Lottery!

Ken Waite

Scars

We're not very old when our first scar appears
When we've grazed our knee and shed our tears.
And it's often the first of many

We pick it a bit and it bleeds again.
It opens the wound and causes us pain
And we learn our lesson, or do we?

As we grow older they're different scars.
Caused by thoughtless actions or hurtful words
Many times without intention.

And once again we have to learn
To leave them alone or else they'll burn
Deep into our personality

If you have scars that are causing you pain
Then leave them alone, don't look again.
And they'll heal over beautifully.

Freda Bradwell

York Minster

It stands so magnificent.
So high, so wide,
It seems it surely touches the sky.
They come in there millions.
To visit this place.
And stand to wonders
At it's size, and grace.
They gave entrenched.
At the window of the rose.
Which stood defiant when behold.
Lightening struck like a dagged from the sky.
and tongues of flame left on light
York Minster on fire "oh no" they cry.
Restored majestic, still she stands
She reigns supreme through out and land.
Glory to God and all mankind.

P. Barrett

Through The Itchens And Worthies

Walking on the roadside verge
  By which the River Itchen flows
Large leaf gunnera, growing in patches
Have grown very close to the river and seem to merge.

The Itchen flows by Old Alresford
  And down to Itchen Stoke.
The home of brown and speckled trout;
  Close by, the homes of country folk.

Various fish sport and splash
  For the low and daring fly.
We stroll on to The Worthies
  Where once, long ago, a King walked by.

Dressed in peasant clothes
  To claim his crown and throne.
This man had courage, and what it takes
  To make a city his own.

The King, whose temporary home
  Was wattle, daub, and wooden stakes.
He was the King whom the city had waited for
  It was Alfred, the King who had burnt the cakes.

Roland Orridge

The Book Of Life

In the night a baby cries, a mother holds her son.
The book of life is opened, a new page has begun.
Years go by since that cry, many pages read;
The man lies back, eyes half closed and pictures in his head,
Of memories and experiences stamped on every page.
He turns them back to read the past with patience of old age.
He thinks of camp fires in the dark, games that children play;
Throwing snowballs in the park on a winter's day.
Playing rugby for his team and that winning try;
There, for just a moment, the boy was ten foot high.
He thinks of girl friends he has loved and rambling on the fells;
Dropping pebbles for a laugh down many wishing wells.
He starts another Chapter in his book of life,
And sees a wedding in a church, the bride becomes his wife.
Then turns another page and hears a baby cry
And sees the Miracle of birth performed before his eyes.
In the Final Chapter he's listening to a choir,
And asking God for guidance in his darkest hour.
Now the book is read - the last page has been turned.
His name is entered in the book a place he truly earned..

Annie Campbell

The Rocking Chair

In the corner stood the chair,
Old and worn and very bare,
Cushions torn but sewn across
Blending the roses with the moss.

Great Grandma was the first to rest
When she was young and at her best,
Grandma was the next to claim that seat
To rest, perhaps the time of death to cheat.

Mother was young and in her prime
To take her rest - she hadn't time,
Life was so full of things to do
For him and us - a set of two.

Would she really have to share
Her evenings with that rocking chair?
So one day, with brave intent —
Then thought its space was heaven sent.

So in the corner out of sight,
Not in anger put, but — fright.

Frank Williams

Untitled

A waterfall maybe beautiful
And so might be a red sky
But something more beautiful
is the friendship made up of you and I.

The heart to heart conversations
About the way we feel
And the way we stick together
means we care a great deal.

But the most important thing of all
Is the way we forgive and forget
The most special day of my life
was the day that you and I met.

So remember, no matter how big or small
embarrassing hard or true
I'm always here if you need to talk
I'm here to listen to you.

Lindsay-Laura

The Hospice Room

There you were, lying still,
Oh you've been so very ill,
Your braveness touched all our hearts,
Then the day came, for us to part,
We sat around your Hospice bed,
Where you laid your weary head,
Waiting for those final words,
"I'm sorry, but your Husband's dead",
But in that room, it must be said,
The feeling of peace, it filled our heads,
Our tears were flowing, as mum stroked your brow,
Singing, "beautiful brown eyes", don't leave me now,
And then the angels came from above,
To take you to the heaven above,
And though we know your pain is gone,
We'll miss you 'til our days are done.

Barbara CarolMoss

Bess — The Faithful Collie

Bess, the farm Collie, so faithful and bold,
returned home alone through the wet and the cold;
she'd left with Old Ben only minutes before,
now her whines and her barking brought Meg to the door.

Bess tugged at Meg's sleeve and led her away
across the dark yard to where Old Ben lay;
while feeding the lambs he'd slipped in the wet;
no-one would have known but for his faithful pet.

Bess stayed by Ben's side while Meg ran to the phone;
the ambulance came and then Old Ben was gone.
Bess trotted along with her mistress Meg;
on reaching the house-door she limped on one leg.

On seeing her limp Meg examined her pet,
and found a deep gash on her foot; and yet
while tending Old Ben where he'd fallen and lain,
the faithful old dog had 'forgot' her own pain.

Dave R. Brothwell

Autumn

Dew lands on the grass on an autumn morning
Brown dead leaves on the trees are falling
Farmers sowing seeds of corn
All this happens on an autumn morn

Gales and rain come from the sky
Sunday dinners and apple pie
Conker fights and shiny smiles
Autumn mist stretches on for miles

Prickly thorns and scratchy hedges
Climbing for fruit on branchy ledges
The damp grey weather and mist still lingers
Purple tongues and messy fingers

Thomas Clayton

Secret Symphony

Moonbeams dance a minuet
on shimmering silvan lake:
Graceful shadows silhouette
etched in pearl opaque:
Minuet changes to a waltz
then in turn, into a reel:

Faeries join the merry dance
entwined with moonbeams
they leap and prance:
'Til merry-go-round of swirling light
touches woodland glades of night,
Transforming all into dingles bright!

La lune bows out with some regret,
as moonbeams resume their minuet:
Allowing lumiere's golden gown
to usher dawn in donned with glittering crown:
Filmy gossamer wand re-awakens earth
reviving fresh sunbeams inspiring rebirth!

Sunlight filters through forests green,
As morn's prism'd cloak o'erspills fond scene:

Christina Angelique

Untitled

"Now you'll have the time for leisure
    Time for holidays, time for pleasure,
Time for all the hobbies you always wished to do
    Time for all the little jobs in house and garden too"

The words were said with confidence
    By family, friends and work mates
But no one had anticipated
    That days would fly at such rates

How did I find the time? You muse
    To go to work at all
Where have the days and hours gone
    In retirement's promised call?

The house repairs are still undone
    The garden must have grown!
The hobbies still a "good idea"
    But only that? I own.
No one said my age would count
    When not so hale and hearty.
I can't do all the things I want.
    One should retire at forty!

Audrey Foy

The Leprechaun

I came upon a music shop in town the other day
I'd never noticed it before, although it's on my way.
There, within its window, was a violin old and worn,
the bow was bent and tattered - its case was chipped and torn.

I felt a strong compulsion to open up the door.
There were cobwebs on the ceiling and dirt upon the floor.
Suddenly sweet music began to fill that room,
Dancers whirled around me, light banishing the gloom.

Then as the darkness faded, I found to my surprise,
A little man dressed all in green, appeared before my eyes.
The fiddle from the window, was tucked beneath his chin,
He played a lovely melody, it touched me deep within.

I bought that magic instrument and took it home with pride,
I couldn't find that shop again, no matter how I tried.
But sometimes when I'm lonely, I take it from the shelf;
The bow starts gliding on the strings, it seems to play itself.

Then once again that sweet refrain falls soft upon my ears.
Those ghostly arms enclose me and take away my fears.
No-one knows my secret, the way I dance till dawn,
or how I bought the old violin and met the leprechaun.

Evelyn Gladstone

Moments Of Reflection

For e'er have I the urge to write,
　Though none but I these words may see;
Within, feel I a strange delight,
　Relaxation it giveth me.

Still, at times I'm wont to ponder
　O'er the past with some regret,
Not through acts of reckless squander,
　Nor of things I failed to get.

'Tis just could I again relive
　Such portion of my earthly time,
When friends unselfishly did give
　Their trust and love, so, so sublime.

But memory can revert the past,
　To be the present happy days,
For even time shall truth outlast,
　So live again, our yesterdays.

How great a gift gave God to man,-
　Man's inability to see
The future of His worldly plan,
　The ignorance of his destiny.
Doris Coffey

Deceived

I gave you my life.
I believed your lies.
I felt special and loved.
I was a fool.

Once you filled me with happiness.
Once you brought me gifts and flowers.
Once you promised to love and care for me.
Once I was in love.

Slowly the mist cleared.
Slowly doubt crept in.
Slowly the truth appeared.
Slowly my love died.

Alas I realized to late.
Alas you have taken all I had.
Alas my soul has died.
Alas I am now an empty shell.
Susan Mitchell

'Yesterday's Thoughts'

Life's become an empty box:
Nothing comes, nothing goes,
Crazy crazy, just let it ride
Hot or cold, lots of time.

All I have a world of fire,
Light or dark never there.
Dreaming dreams of long ago
No tenure in any place.

Smiling means get on with life
Perplex communicate inside exists;
Good or bad feels just the same,
Come out, I say, get on with living.

Anguish objection ever close,
Memories telling who you are,
Was it left or maybe right,
Climb aboard, no rest along that way.

Where is home? "Here," I heard myself say.
Soul still lost floating on the edge of gloom,
Ever close the witching hour to come,
Fire and brimstone all around, is this the end?
Jon Aspinall

The Sinking Ship

Two hours of boring conversation
My ears are bleeding
If I should scream
You'd die a thousand deaths
Hit the depths of depression and fade away

More that tears like a sea of waves
You drown yourself in words
It's so absurd
It's a sinking ship
And the tide is high
Robert J. McManus

The Forge

Dark and dusty, but kindled flame,
Lights the way to the iron game,
Bellows puffing, crackling coals,
Orange embers, burning soles.

Tongs withdraw the metal rod,
From the furnace under the hod,
Laid across the anvils steel,
Hammer brings it down at heel.

Bending shaping horseshoe style,
Shoes to last many a mile,
Holding hoof between his knees,
Smithy fits the shoe with ease.

The nails are through, the task is done,
Another steed is free to run,
Put on more coal, the fire is low,
But before the next, he takes a blow.
Julian Holroyd

Winter

Clouds race across the graying sky
Summer has said a graceful good-bye
Winds blow hard, they descend with force
And just as quickly alter course
Leaves are snatched and flutter down
On the cold, hard, frosty ground
Familiar surroundings are now unkind
Blues, greens, left far behind
Drizzle and fog engulf and surround
The warmth of the sun unable to touch the ground
Stark and naked willowy trees stretch high
In an effort to reach the sky
Ghostly apparitions they appear to be
As winter turns its key.
Helen Williams

Waiting For Godot

Eating breakfast
Reading the mail
And listening to radio four
Glancing at heaven
Feeding the birds
Making calls
Reading the paper
Glancing at heaven
Eating lunch
Meeting a friend
Choosing flowers
Glancing at heaven
Working on the computer
Lighting candles
Drinking cool water
Eating dinner
Watching a film
Doing my homework
Brushing my teeth.
At night I always leave the curtains open, lest that pass
Me by, against which I was guarding.
D. A. Dowse

Land Of Inspiration

Inspired by your beauty I write about you
Threatened by your charm
I'm devoted to you
And when I walk within your soul
My heart beats in time with yours
A barren land for a barren man
And beauty within your shores
Your arms enfold me
And greet me with a shallow light
Consumed by a love for thee
Such a wonderful and envious sight
But one day all this will be gone
And where will I walk and where will I go
Into your heart and through your soul
Until a cold wind doth blow

Raymond Spybey

Rainbow Of Tears

Don't cry my dear, if the sky is grey
and the pain inside is so hard to bear
You cry the tears that fill your eyes
When you recall the words that were but lies

Do not be sad, if the light is dim
And there's no sign to show you the way
The memories hurt when the night is deep
And you long for a hand to caress you to sleep

There's always a gleam in the darkest hour
And a refreshing drop in the middle of a storm
Don't only smile to hide your sorrow
But share the moment of now and tomorrow

If at times the storm is too long to pass
Feel my support from wherever you are
Peace will find you as you forget your fears
And you'll see above the rainbow of your tears

M. Catalano

Searching The Sea

Through the void, drifting eyes are blind,
Rain becoming what we are not,
Immortal, unbroken net sweeping sleep
Under darkness and the roots of rocks.

All we hear and see is the storm
Unfolding on the waters, engulfing lives,
We wait, the boats are out, we try
Praying is not for us

The freezing rain turns our tears away,
When the ocean breathes, we feel it
As deep as their sunken souls,
Wherever the tide takes them.

Our fatigue haunts us, we are only
The lost on lands, one shone bound wave;
Let the darkness seep with the tears
Continued within distance.

Roderick Petrie

No Laurels

As writer of court odes
Poet laureate she never will be.
Worthy of laurels as eloquent poet
No poetry judge ever judge her to be.

Worthy of extinction?
The reader indubitably may claim
This poet presents herself worthily
For contemporary notoriety or fame.

If she had been a man
Would these years of neglect have been her own?
That is the question this whole work poses,
International now, but English grown.

Mildred Bateman

The Passing Of A Centenarian

This is not my room, that's not my bed.
These were the kind of things she said.
She does not know the living now.
But speaks only of the dead.

Her parents, brothers, sisters
Dear friends who have passed away.
She calls them out by name
And says they have come today.

Is it the angels? Or the spirits of the dead
Who hover round her bed
She is happy in their company; as she lies
I cannot see them, I am blinded by my eyes.

Through the long night, I keep awake and pray
Will God's call come before the dawn?
Or will she see another day?
Her long life slowly ebbs away.

The rattle in her chest, it's like a thunder now.
I wipe her brow and comfort her as only love knows how,
Goodbye, my dear, my mother, the greatest friend I've had
Come back again and take me when I am going to God.

Bridget Breen

Prospect Omega

In my third eye unfolds the scene,
is as I dream within a dream.
A dream of a heart-shaped sun.
Red it is, blood red, all brilliant and rising,
ascending so far then stopping abrupt.
For having come thus far the red sun can go no farther,
and will not therefore set in the heavens where surely
it must truly belong.
So the sun waits, as if for reprieve, and as it waits
it aches, aches for a time to come, to move on and
fulfil a hope of destiny.
The now faintly glowing heart-shaped sun breaks and
bleeds into the vault of the sky. Its wondrous
hue brings magical colour to the worlds below and
the sun says, "if only". For the sake of creation,
"If only, if only".
All yesterdays, today, a tomorrow perhaps.
"If only, if only, if only."
Then, as with the last day, the sun fades, alas, and
sadly dies.

Robert Connor

Lament Of A Fishing Widow

I am his Fishing Widow, he's been out day and night since
the season started, waiting patiently for a bite. He takes his
green umbrella and his fishing stool with numerous rods to
choose from, considers it mellow and cool. He is a fishing
fanatic, talks tactics, tips and fish. He could be more romantic,
I can always wish! I have been invited to join him, to watch
the float bob, down and up, to sit beneath the green umbrella,
sipping coffee from his cup. To share a cheese and pickle
sandwich, to enjoy the tension of the sport, to catch carp, and
tench, and bream to marvel at what's caught. He gets himself
excited, when a fish pulls at the line, reels it in, it's taken the
bate, but damn no fish this time. Then there are the maggots
that crawl and slide across the floor, the pinks, the reds, the
yellows and bronzed, all for them and more... the fish think it's
their birthday, with breakfast, dinner and tea, three meals a
day, they swim and they play, holds no interest for me. How
can this be exiting? Catching slippery fish from a pond, the
amount of time he spends just, waiting, he'd do better with a
wand By the time I've moaned about it, the season is all over
and He'll put away the tackle and the oversized pull-over, so I
sit alone, twiddling my thumbs, waiting for the sport to end,
but it's "I've caught a Big-un," that drives me round the bend.

Linn Jeynes

Remembered Youth

Oh! But I was young-then!
Grasses long and green.
Summer days, moonlight-nights,
Yes-that is how it seemed.
Laughing, singing, dancing, ere my work was done-
Oh! but I was young then,
and life it was such fun.
I dreamed my dreams in those days of youth,
I thrilled at the touch of a hand.
I found delight in a stolen kiss,
My world was a wonderland.
The fire and madness now are
gone, all the dreams have flown.
But I am very thankful for
the years I've known
As the chill of winter does
round my heart entwine
Always I'll remember
The youth that once was mine.

D. Scarratt

Ectopic Pregnancy

I think about you all the time
My little precious baby of mine
You're close to my heart and that's my shrine

Your little precious life was part of mine
You had to go you came too soon
You weren't implanted in my womb

But I know you're smiling down from the
Heaven's above - my precious, precious little love
I know we will be re-united again
My precious little baby of mine

I hold your hand each day and night
Even though you're not in sight
God please watch over my little baby's
Soul please let me have her back
That's my ultimate goal

Tanya Stephen

Childhood Memories

As I sit by the window quiet and full of thought,
I dream of all the things I knew, things I had been taught.
I believed in fairies when I was just a lass,
Although I could not see them, yes they were there upon the grass.
I used to make their little wands and leave them in the trees,
I imagined the smile upon each face, I knew they would be pleased.
I believed in Father Christmas, a really kind old man,
I imagined his great toy shop where he lived in Happy Land.
I knew he wanted it to snow as he went along his way.
He'd skim along the house tops, his attitude so gay.
Rudolph was his favourite or so it has been said,
I wouldn't know, I was asleep in my little bed.
Alas now I am old and grey, there's one thing I love to see,
It's the smile upon a child's face at the sight of the Christmas Tree.

Violet Trodd

Dear God

God give me strength to greet each day
And be happy by the way,
To count my blessings and be glad
That things are not quite as bad
As they used to be of yester-year.

God give me grace that I can cheer
And make happy the ones I am near,
If I can make people glad and smile
They will linger just for a while
And want my company another day.

God give me power that I can prove
It's not mountains I want to move,
But behind my closed doors there will be,
Plenty of love for company,
This is my prayer, please grant it to me.

Mavis Shaw

My Life

When I was a toddler around two or three
My Mother lifted me up and sat me on her knee
She told me I was adopted, my Mother couldn't cope
And I was the daughter they'd prayed for and hoped

The years went by and it didn't bother me
The parents God had given me were special you see
But when I had my daughter I couldn't understand
How anyone could give up a child on this land

I searched for my birth certificate and was surprised to see
I was adopted in the same town which was unusual to me
I felt really guilty going behind my parents' backs
So I ended the search and covered my tracks

Four years later my second child was born
My Mother had died, my emotions were torn
I had to dig further to find out about my birth Mother
But no one prepared me for what I uncovered.

She had died eleven years ago but that was not all
Strangled and murdered and left in the hall
My whole world was shattered it cut like a knife
But I learned just to live with it, get on with my life.

H. Malloch

The Joy Of Spring

Awake from your slumbers, arise to the dawn
For spring has come, and a new day is born
Farewell to the cold of winter now done
Feel joy in your heart, the dark days are gone

List to the lark as it soars to the sky
The cuckoos loud call from the woods nearby
And close from the hedgerow in blossoming bush
The sweet trilling song of blackbird and thrush

Hear the sighs and whispers of the gentle breeze
As it playfully blows through the now leafy trees
Lift up your heart, for the time is now here
When earth wakens up, new life to appear

The sweet scent of flowers now waft through the air
As they flaunt all their colours so gaudy and fair
Bees busily flit from one to another
Their nectar to sip, their pollen to gather

Awake from your slumbers and greet a new day
When worries and heartaches can all melt away
Look, smell and feel and let your heart sing
For at last it is with us, come herald the spring

Olive Woodhouse

A Prayer For Today

When you down and feeling cross,
When you wonder, Who is boss?
When life rolls by, a ton an hour.
Give me time... to look at a flower.

It's rush awake and in a tear,
Hurry up and down the stair,
Out the door, look and see.
Oh, give me time... to gaze at a tree.

In the car and on the road,
Traffic snarling, vans unload,
Jamming entrance. Where to turn?
Give me time... and let me learn.

Learn to stare and learn to look,
Take account of God's good book,
There's more to life than this mad pace.
Oh, give me time... for my human race.

Out of work and into shop,
Ever moving jump, skip, hop.
Teach me to exert a greater will
And give myself time... to just be still.

Janet Swales

My Homeland

England, my homeland is the place for me.
Over the years I've travelled far over land and sea,
Living in far off places I thought I'd never, ever, see.
Exotic Singapore, bustling Kuala Lumpur in Malaysia, and
  mysterious
Muscat, Sultanate of Oman in the Middle East, dreams turned
  into reality.
How lucky I've been, and are, to have travelled in ships
  and aeroplanes so far.
Meeting interesting people, and making such good friends in
  so many wonderful lands.
But always homesick for England, my homeland.
Back home in England, everything so wonderfully green, my
  wanderings just like a beautiful dream.
Now my travelling done, and here I am very content at home.
There's no place to beat it, as from my garden seat sit,
And observe the blue sky above, the birds flying around, and
  the beautiful flowers abound.
I shall always remember, my wonderful and interesting past,
But the pleasure is so sweet, to be back in England at long last,
I'm so very proud of England, my homeland.

D. O'Brien

God

I can change water, from water to wine
Perhaps that's not surprising because I am divine
I am the father of thunder, lightning and typhoons
I gave proud Jupiter her numerous moons
I made all the planets, including red Mars,
It was me who made Sirius, the brightest of stars
Sometimes, when I get the intention
I take a trip to an outer dimension
Beyond time and space, to where the souls of the dead do dwell
In the spirit world of Heaven and Hell
Now that I have told you all this, you'll probably think it quite odd
But no doubt you'll understand when I tell you I am God.

Joseph Riley

Silver Wedding

We are entering together the September of our years
Looking back to memories of laughter and of tears
We've faced the days together, the problems and the pain
Given the chance I have no doubt I'd do it all again.

We know that love's a gamble, who knows how it will end
To make it work each has to be both partner and a friend
We've made mistakes but tried so hard; that's plain for all to see
So "Come grow old along with me, the best is yet to be"

We'll look toward tomorrow, whatever it may bring
Our lives have reached their Autumn, but pretend that it is Spring
Now at our Silver Wedding the happiest of times
I tell the world with love and pride—the best of men is mine.

Virginia Susan Evans

Flowers In The Skies

Fluttering her lashes, Miss Peacock shyly hides her eyes,
But that painted lady is no Camberwell beauty, that's for sure.
The gatekeeper ignores her as he sits by the wall and gazes
Across the heath, by the speckled wood, white in the evening mist,
To the meadow, brown now, after the long hot summer.

While admirals strut in uniforms of white and red
And the grizzled skipper sails over the mazarine blue,
Towards the clouded yellow on the horizon,
The emperor, in purple attire, surveys his empire from on high,
Though it is true to say, he is not really the monarch.

Fire and brimstone as the sun goes down.
Soon, there is no fire, just a swiftly disappearing orange tip,
Leaving colours of tortoise shell sheen,
Like a poor man's aurora borealis.

Now all is still, but with the marbled white of morning,
The world will delight, once more, with those gems on the wing,
Those flowers in the skies... butterflies.

David Kellard

"A Day In The Garden"

Dawn's new light is heralding a glorious summer's day;
Birds, their chorus swelling, sing to greet the sun's first ray;
Flow'rs of every hue, shaking glossy, dewy leaves,
Lift their faces to the sun, nodding briefly to the breeze.

Delphiniums, majestic spikes of clearest, brightest blue
Mingle happily with foxgloves, holly hocks and cornflowers too;
Furled rosebuds open fragrantly, bright poppies dance with grace,
Responding to the warmth of midday sun upon each face.

Jasmine and honeysuckle, tendrils delicately entwined,
Create heady fragrance, spilling over striking columbine,
Lavender and rosemary, sweet peas, pinks and thyme
Add to the perfumed cocktail, aromatically sublime.

Seeds fall, as petals drop, upon the soil to propagate;
Birds sing their evensong to tell the world the hour is late.
Warm evening breezes ripple floral heads closed up to rest,
As red-flamed sky reflects a glorious sunset in the west.

Jacqueline Banks

"Emit At 0700"

Tick Tock,
No standing still,
Nothing begins but something will.
Urging,
Pressing,
Pressure peaks,
It chases us;
Days turn to weeks.

There lies a possible theory;
But theory in lying sleeps soundly through it.
Transcending puddles of seasoned quartet,
See sunburnt buds burst from Bach,
As one leaps to beat its pace,
Motion's drugs seduce universe sweetly.

So End what sense never started;
Over strange pebbles let heads decide,
Brain - blistering confusion is conclusive;
Too much tension takes up Time.

Louise A. Millward

A Toast On Her Majesty's 70th Birthday

You've worn the Cloak of Monarchy,
As Painter has Portrayed,
With Beauty, Grace, and Dignity,
A Wondrous Queen so made.

Queen Mary was your Guide in Youth,
King George - your Father - too,
I know that were They here Today
They'd be so Proud of You.

Now William, Young Fair Handsome Prince,
His Father's Child first born,
Prepares to follow Kingship Ways
In this Millennium's Dawn.

No 'Media Hype' affects our Trust,
No Sceptic's Words alarm,
We simply raise a Glass and say
"A Happy Birthday, Ma'am!"

Irene Birch

Childhood

You stole my childhood and I didn't know;
I preserved my innocence and held my peace.
You stole my joy, my childish, carefree joy
And I let you, in my ignorance and fear.
I walked my path alone, not seeing the grass beneath my feet
And only now I see it's been mown down.
Cropped short and prickly to my touch.
And burnt by sun and scorched by fire
And dead within its shell of life.

Alison McVea

Summer And A Victorian Garden

The sun was hot, and as I lay
and looked deep into summer,
the blue, blue sky, I thought,
was the deepest blue I had ever seen.

Then everything changed,
as a girl returns home after many years,
the sky became a softer blue.
Once again she sees her Victorian Garden.

In my garden overgrown and wild, half forgotten,
I loved it then, a squirrel and doves, wild daffodils,
that is what I saw there,
amongst the long grass in spring.

Later, came summer with tumbling sweet peas,
of mauve, of pink, of lemon and cream.
An old tree, a sea of leaves,
sighing with the wind.

Margaret M. McCallum

The Old Steel Town

He lay in his bed and gazed at the lights,
Which flashed and glimmered throughout the night.
When morning came with dawn's early light,
He heard the twitter of birds after the long hard night.

The noise and clamour of the works had ceased.
All was quiet and the world at peace.
The morning shift came on at six.
He loved the daily roar and mighty din.

But now a deathly hush had settled on the town.
Gone the clatter and banging of the works.
Gone were the sounds of the night and day.
Vanished the works that had been their mainstay.

No longer the noise of clattering clogs.
No longer the barking of a score of dogs.
All was neglected, all hope gone.
Perhaps something would happen to revive the place,
Bring new life and give it a happier face.

Joan Neeves

Spring

Out there, I hear a Robin Sing,
The lark above, heralds the spring.
As snowdrop bows her head to rest,
The Blackbirds start to shape their nest.
Though bitter winds, still keep on Blowing.
The soft green grass, will soon want mowing.
And, every lovely Daffodil,
Starts to show its yellow frill.
Buds are blooming on the Bough,
Hazel Catkins hang down low,
The Hazy Sun comes peeping through,
To warm the earth, and change the view.
Hearts are happy, let us sing.
Welcome! Welcome to the spring.

Queenie Hipperson

Man Destroying Our World

Precious is this life that we have been given
And when our time comes it's either hell or heaven
But somewhere along the line they got it wrong
Heaven could be here where all our creatures belong

Life could be magic without a second glance
If only our world could be given a second chance
Yes at times I wonder why they created mankind
But now I realize why, it seems to leave hell behind

Love is so marvellous a precious and wonderful gift
Like sailing across the oceans and towards land slowly drift
But they trampled and destroyed nearly every living thing
Yes just think of it, no fish no trees and not even one bird left
to sing

Ronald M. Fry

Silence?

Oh, The Peace and quiet and the stillness
of night.
Children asleep, Engines quiet at the
end of daylight.
Owls emerge to find food for their
young
Most birds roost quietly, not singing
their song
Snuggle down quickly the winds going
to blow
Windows will rattle, the Sand man will
show
Animals scurrying; mice and the like
To undergrowth havens, hedges and dyke
And the wind will whistle to its own
special tune
Branches will dance to the night or the moon
So snuggle down quickly get to sleep
right away
Then you can dream your dreams, till night turns to day.

Christine Coles

Just Two Minutes

The morning rises, oh Lord above,
To cast, once more, its shadow of death upon us.
Do we, the servants of our country, have to lay down our lives
in such a way, so that freedom, gained at so heavy a price, can
be tossed aside in years to come, by the youth of tomorrow.
Whose sin is not remembering, brings us such sad sorrow.
The sadness of our plight. In that yesteryear of hell and horror.
The deeds we did were for their future, not ours.
For our future was but determined.
To end our lives in ghastly sights, to suffer and to bleed.
Remember, please, for just two minutes
Of our deeds, our misery, our deaths.
Your freedom, this day, did not come lightly.
My generation, did all but few, give up their life, just for you.
Remember, remember, that eleventh day of November.
For just two minutes.
We ask not much, that you your thoughts gather, so to remember
us all and the sacrifice we made for you and your future.
Your silence, we know, will come to us. Our thoughts will merge.
Our generations, for just two minutes, will join as one, the
void of years gone by will once more be bridged by the youth
of yesterday and of this day.
So on that day that comes but once a year, that day when
nations mourn their dead,
just stand awhile, for just two minutes, and think of our glory,
our deeds, and our death.

I. R. Martin

"The Soul Of England"

"If we're to get the England back
That Churchill used to see, we need
To value, land like gold, and farm
With care, and ancient husbandry;

The time has come to make a stand
Against the biggest crime—
They're spoiling all the best of
England's "green," that's yours and mine;

"Creating wealth for just a few,'whilst
Others have "no living" attitudes have
Changed to "take, take, take," and
Sadly now, they're not "to giving;"

When all Traditional Crafts have gone,
And no one works the land—
And Bosworth field and Nasby
Can't record the battle scenes—
I wonder then, if people all, will march
With hand in hand, and try to save
The "Soul of England", that could
End up just in dreams.

Geoffrey Pearson

October After Noon

A last worm spell, unsettled season.
Holding winter back for just a little while.
She comes and goes till winter moves
in with ice snow and
left his trees on hard frozen ground.

Then tired old winter eyes look
heavenward though youth bled from
them. By cold winter past
just sleep till summer comes at last.

Margaret Dewar

Fifty Years On

Fifty years on '95 will be known for, 50 years on since we were
   at war.
People celebrating, parties in the street
smiles and salutations as old friends meet.
But should we celebrate when so many lost their lives?
So many orphaned children, so many saddened wives.
Yes we must remember the valour and the pain
of those young men who went to war and ne'er came home again.
whether in the navy the army or the Raf
and the thousands lost on D. Day because of some-ones 'gaff'.
No, I don't hold with celebrating deep within my heart
but I still say thank you every day to those who took a part
in the six year bloody battle to keep Great Britain free
Yes we must remember, because they died for you and me.

Yvonne King

Love And Love Again

I didn't know - I couldn't tell
How could I - It never happened to me
But then it did - One proud day back in seventy.
Times like that - it seems are few -
But it happened again in seventy-two

First one love then another
Born a sister then her brother, love and love again real love -
Everlasting - it's in the blood, precious gifts given to me -
gifts from heaven for all to see, makes me proud to think what
we've all been through and what we've got. I've known some
people as times gone by - some I've grown to love, but not
love and love again - They're part of my blood. They've been
my arrows - me their bow - And when you've got it you just
know and watch it feel it grow and grow, and I know -

Love and love will be forever - Could it end? No not ever
They will have me 'till the end - and why?'
'Cause they are my best friends.

Love and love again - Real joy
Real love - Part of my blood
My Girl - My Boy.

R. Read

Celebration

As we entered the room
Our eyes were led
By the dark red drapes
Of the olden bed
And the carved chest
Rich as the night
On which candles arrayed
Yielded soft, soft light.

Ancient walls held ancient tales
But gazing at each other
All time was stilled
As we saw, only one another.
A magical time, a mystical time
The sweeter for, oh so long, anticipation
And eyes held forever
In the sweetest embrace
In an ancient room
In an ancient place.

Sandy I'Anson

The Lake

In the quietness of the forest green
Lies the lake with rippling waters seen.
Bathing the rocks and stones alike, leaving
perches free, for the birds' delight.
Fish swim happily, in the waters dark and deep,
Hiding from the prey which they don't wish to meet.
Ducks sun themselves on the lakeside,
waiting for bread to be thrown from the side.

Above high mountains look from lofty peaks,
casting dark shadows on the lake beneath.
Trees with leafy branches bend, caressing the
dark waters in the forest glen.
The traveller stops to stand and stare,
admiring creation in its beauty there.
Time is short, and it's time to go
back to the town with all its woe.

Hazel Wilson

Memories

Those Happy Days and Cherished moments we have known.
That Casual Meeting, Friendship, and the love that has grown.
Those first hours together, that have long passed.
Those Vows of undying Love, that will forever last.
Those secluded spots we visit, where hand in hand we walk.
Moments, when we, So much in Love, have no need to talk.
That time when the piece of Heather you bent to pluck.
and turned to me with love, and said, May it forever bring us luck.
Those little things, that to me mean such a lot.
Those Memories, that will never be forgot.
As the sands of time keep flowing through the Years,
We stand together and recall moments of Laughter, Smiles, and Tears,
Our hopes, our Faith, and our Loving Trust,
Such things as these can never fail, Decay, or rust.
To you my Darling, I will forever be true.
Why my Darling, because "I Love You".

To Jan with all my Love.

J. V. Appleton

River Lambourne

Clear sparkling water threads its way through Berkshire's chalky downs.
With each curve a question mark and silence filled with sounds.
Deceptive stillness surfacing the busy life beneath.
A whole world of activity surrounds each floating leaf.
The smoothness wrinkled by fall of apples from a tree,
From whose branch comes clearly an echoing shree.
Beyond the stream the clumps of primrose cling to mossy banks.
Ignored by passing mallards with their acrobatic pranks.
Swift running water causes them to paddle very fast,
Till they pass the towering fir trees and the shadows that they cast.
Overhead, wood pigeons look down with wistful eye
Upon the swimming winged ones - for they can only fly
Joined by the blue tit, the blackbird and the sparrow,
Above the flowing water they fly fast as any arrow.
Crystal clear the river passes by my garden wall
And I am overwhelmed by the beauty of it all.

Patricia Elvira Lawrence

Of Winter

Winter, Winter, why do you only offer
bleak dark days,
With wind and rain and forever cloud,
Is this really the only way?
Your miserable face causes nothing but gloom,
Your mornings resemble a cold, black, tomb.

The trees without leaves stand uncomplaining,
how much more of you is remaining?
We long for Spring and see you gone,
It seems you always stay too long.
Why do you linger more each year?
Is it me growing older, perhaps that's my fear,
Or is it just the continuous cold,
that really makes me feel so old.

Denis Railton

Avarice

Sticky and the Cave-man going off to work,
one dressed like a space-man, the other like a berk.
Hands deep in their pockets, sucking on the weed,
cadging off their work mates, showing off their greed.

Sticky and the Cave-man loading up the boot,
taking all the work home, keeping all the loot.
Going down the market, buying all the gear,
going down the boozer, drinking all the beer.

Sticky and the Cave-man crawling to the man,
sliming up the work place as only snails can.
Acting like a lap dog, acting like a sheep,
following the leader even in their sleep.

Sticky and the Cave-man selfish to the end,
taking home the scratch cards hoping to offend.
poking in their noses, being what they're not,
speaking lots of bullsh**, talking Tommy-rot.

Sticky and the Cave-man ruining the job,
stealing all the profits, setting out to rob.
Lessening the work load, being double-faced,
making men redundant, closing down the place.

Robert Lines

Bodily Function

In his bath Johnny lay stewing,
the largest fart his lower half brewing.

His tummy moaned and gave loads of grief,
but Johnny just sat awaiting relief.

He wiggled, he squirmed, assumed the position,
half moon to the left was the decision.

So there he sat, his lower half loaded.
When out of the blue his bottom Exploded!!!

The water leapt up, the bath was no more,
like forty nights of rain it covered the floor.

Across the floor and off down the stair,
when his mother saw the mess she ran in despair.

She ran to the bathroom, her arms and legs flinging,
but Johnny just sat, in the bath he was grinning.

Darren James Mason

Untitled

Some people are happy of which I am
because I am the father of baby Sam.
Your Mother who is Carol that part is true
But she's a b**** keeping me from you
Although we're apart never fear all will turn
out by the end of the year
We'll see each other every other day
Until you're older and have your say
To stay with her or to stay with me
It will be your choice for all to see
So from the beginning of your time
Your mother said you weren't mine
But this I knew was a lie, cross my heart
and hope to die
So when you read this in your later years
this is my promise with all my tears
I loved you from day one.

Gary Pratley

The Village Green Fair

That longed for days at last come round
    with the village green a gay fairground.
Coconut shies and hoopla stalls
    and another one for rolling balls.

Galloping horses on the roundabout
    the gayest sight there is no doubt.
Swinging boats flying so high
    almost touching the summer sky.

The shooting gallery with a row of duck
    boys and girls their candy floss suck.
Gaudy prizes tucked under arms
    others light-headed with magical charms

Empty purses all money spent
    everyone hurrying homeward bent.
Next morning at the break of day
    all is packed and on its way.

Passing by the village green
    the fairground might have never been,
Except for the chatter of the night before
    and a whole twelve months to wait for more.

Kathleen M. Eastes

Chat Up Lines

The Barman
Called me over
Nice legs
Nice ass
He said.
I wanted
Pearls of wisdom
Astound me
With your wit
Knock me over
With a word
Tell me something
I don't know.
For your opening line
You chose anatomy
And became
Invisible to me.

Barbara Boyer

The Ploughman

I be a ploughman. I goes steady and straight.
I keeps going all day, from early till late.
They've taken me 'orse, and I drives a tractor now.
But, it ain't the same. I've lost a lifetime's know how.
I sits up in me cab all day and, me feet don't ache no more.
But, what I was proud of, me skill in me work, it's now a *** bore.
I don't hear the birds. I don't feel the wind. No warmth of the sun
On me back and, nothing out there for company. That's where I miss
Old Jack. You could always tell what Jack felt like. Watch out if he laid his ears.
But, a tractor gets all spiteful like and, crashes through the gears.
When I've done enough to fill the day, I leaves the tractor to stand.
I don't feed him, nor rub him down and, he'll never eat out of my hand.
I'll never hear him crunching oats, nor fork him down his hay.
I suppose it's progress of a sort but, it's a damned hard price to pay.
Me and me 'orse, we worked together, we made a happy team.
But, you get no sort of companionship, working with a machine.
But, 'orse or machine I does me best. It's the only way I know.
And, I hope they'll say when I am gone. Well, he kept a good straight row.

George Harcourt

The Candle

Tear-shaped flame, dancing as if suspended above a white wax pillar,
Alive, glowing brighter, bringing warmth into the cold darkness.

Comforting the woman in pain, as a new soul struggles for life,
Then the flame burning in thankfulness for the safe journey of
that soul.

Soon a light burning a bright and warm welcome,
As the soul is accepted into God's family in baptism.

The same flame though small and delicate, burns gaily on
The birthday cake. Burns again above the young bride and groom,
And again burning strongly to bring comfort to the sick and dying
In the winter of their lives,
And finally around our mortal remains,
When we leave this life.

It has accompanied us from the beginning and is still with us
At the end.
It may have flickered and dimmed as we journeyed through life
But now it shines brighter than before,
Bright as the new light that is almighty God.

Neil Doherty

Whispers

A whispered perception
A reconstructed apparent that renders me free
The whispers of a joyous conjurer
Guiding me, igniting my destiny
I gasp aloft a solemn being
Cast and moulded within the rhapsodies of time
Extradited from such I remain in touch
With the vision that is mine, pure, sublime
Distraction, abstraction, distraught in thought
I breathe incessantly to ignite the embers of my whispering world
Consider my mind as the womb of inspiration
So within a confinement I can nurture and protect
The prevalence of majesty and wonder, as is mine
The shining of this immortal coil will only be shuddered at
Through the eyes of those whose faith is compatible
With the merest glimmer of hope
Whispers become unified within the symmetrical images of faith
The conclusion is mine to draw, true whispers of belief that elate
Eradicate the whispers deep within my soul, a temperance
shall predominate.

Jane Boyce

Goodbye, Cambridge, My Lovely!

I pick up my bags with tears in my eyes,
Gently enough not to break her sweet night,
And throw a kiss instead of saying goodbye.
The lovely past first comes back to my mind:
Her grace stopped my pole on my first punting time.

In the summer flowers is her streaming hair,
With her green gown loose down to the fresh air,
And through many bridges rustle her white feet bare.
Proud swans deep lower their heads around her nearby,
While ducks keep silent and stop the wild cries.

In the strange land, some dogs barked at me here,
And even young drunks shouted at me there,
But calmed them down her pats light with much care.
Mad drivers slow down a lot in front of her gate,
And porters shut the doors much light and late.

Her beauty moves my heart and changes my mind,
But she was born to the Cam under the English sky,
Though I decide to win her hand through all my life.
I can't control myself, with tears in my eyes,
And cry out from my heart, my lovely, goodbye!

Wang Zhi-Jun

Decision

As the train rolls on by, I take in the scene,
Watching, yet dreaming of who I had been.
My life has no meaning, no niche yet been formed
But it begins to take shape now as night rolls into dawn.

A hand reaches out, beckons me through
Lights burning brightly, a dream coming true,
But as bells start to ring and I open my eyes
The clock says it's morning, my life says goodbye.

All that it takes is the will to go on,
But people give up, do no more, and are gone.
If you know it's important, the dream will unfold
Draw you in and, at once, there'll be love in your soul.

A part of your soul, of your heart and your mind
A deep sunken feeling you can't leave behind,
Then I'd realized my dream, what I had to do
And the shadows grew lighter, black became blue.

I know that I have to, I know that I must
To keep me alive, not crumbled to dust
for somewhere out there is the chance I must take
Make the choice, take the plunge, before it's too late.

Josie Bell

Friends

Right from the tender age of eleven,
Our friendship formed, a gift from heaven,
Through hardships, fun and adolescence,
Our bond just grew and grew,
We kept in touch throughout the years,
And shared our joys, and shared our tears,
Together, conquering all our fears,
And braving days to come,
And when were old, I know we'll be,
As close as ever, you and me,
And over cups of sweetened tea,
We'll chat of days gone past,
And even now, I'd like to say
Your visits brighten up my day,
I'd like to thank you for being my friend,
And in return I can lend,
A shoulder to cry on, an ear to bend, if ever you may need,
And whenever you are far from me
In my thoughts you'll always be
Just close your eyes and think of me, and I'll be there my friend.

Rhonay Terri Barter

Travelling By Bus

I travel by bus five days a week
Peace and quiet is all that I seek
But can you get it, no siree
It's the other passengers along with me

There are the ones who carry a pack on their back
They turn without thinking and you get a whack
Others with packages taking up a whole seat
When all you want is to rest your feet

Then there are some with feet stuck in the aisle
When you fall over they look up and smile
I've seen people caught in the automatic door
When the bus gives a jerk some end up on the floor

There are cans and rubbish all round your feet
The odd piece of gum stuck to the seat
The personal hi-fi - well that is a laugh
Some you can hear for a mile and a half

Yes, travelling by bus is fraught with danger
Your life's in the hands of a total stranger
I can see if I want to stay alive
I'll just have to try and learn to drive

M. Scott

Untitled

If you care about material things and not about life,
You have problems, like what to buy next, where shall we eat,
No thought of the old man in the street, or woman if it
comes to that.
they don't care they're not into all that
what gifts to buy friends, what car to have soon
To have no worries would be a boon.
A new house, a new fur coat, maybe diamond rings
The poor man in the street doesn't worry, he just sings,
As he wanders around, looking for help, somewhere to sleep.
People don't care they just walk past, and today,
Who knows, could be his last,
So if you care about material things, get off the
roundabouts and try the swings.
Care about life, especially of others, some have no-one,
No one at all, so try to understand why they fall,
They just need someone to care — that's all.

Betty Lancashire-Frain

Forget-Me-Not

When the day finally dawns and I'm no longer here
to laugh with you and hold you near,
you won't have to travel so far away
to find me ready, waiting to play.

Let your body or mind take you down to the sea,
wherever you turn, you'll always see me.
In the sparkling waves as they lap on the sand
gently caressing, I'm holding your hand.

Let the warm rays of sunlight soak into your skin
and my perpetual love will come flooding in,
in the gentle sea breeze as it brushes your ears
I'm whispering your name, calming your fears.

Turn your face to the wild and blustery wind
and I'll ruffle your hair until I find
a way to uplift your quivering chin
dry you briny tears, so your peace may begin.

So if the day finally dawns when you can't see me here
and the storm subsides but no rainbow appears
believe and find comfort that down by the sea, my spirit
lives on, happy, wild and free, waiting to help you feel closer to me.

Jacquie Crowther

The Sun Shines On

The sun's been shining through the day,
For the people, so that they,
Can all have fun down on the beach,
Summer no longer out of reach.

Sand in the sandwiches, wasps in the tea,
Surf of the waves, how warm the sea.
Playful cries while the wind goes by,
Not a cloud in the clear, blue sky.

The sky a glow of colours bright,
Just as day turns into night.
Smudged orange, purple and pink,
Blobs of blue, resembling ink.

Lights appear from the town,
The sun is slowly sinking down.
For the children it's time to go,
Beholding the glorious sunset glow.

Matthew Castagna

Untitled

The great divide ain't half so wide,
'Cos one day we'll meet, I know,
When the face of you faces the face of me,
and we smile.

D. J. Hargate

Words Of Comfort

How could you leave me when we were so close
My heart broken my best friend gone -
I still cry for you my heart is still broken
But God is love and you are still with me
And we walk and talk just as before
We laugh and I feel your warmth
Others may wonder what I'm smiling at
They may not understand
I pray for your soul and you pray for me
Every morning we meet at the garden in my mind
I can not yet pass through the gate
But we reach over and embrace
And smell the sweet roses that you grow
Then I return and as I turn you smile and wave
Sending me back to earthly work as you tell me
It is not my time and you turn back to your rose garden
Sending me back to my work feeling warm and comforted
Knowing you are still very much with me
All is well.

Wendy Anne Patel

Untitled

Look around us, the world a mess,
Pain, suffering, and distress.
I just want to stop it all,
In a world where people's minds are small.
The hurt is too much to bear,
And the peace keepers stand around and stare.
They say it's all a political war,
Sure. Tell that to widows, orphans, or
Turn a blind eye that what we do best
Or will we rise above the rest?
We hear the cries of refugees
Gunfire! Rings out, among the trees.
People run full of grief and strife,
Yes. They are running for their life.

Kenneth Johannesen

Midwinter View

I found I could not listen to the Brahms;
It reminded me of you and swept
my heart with tears for lost
companionship and lonely years.

But yet I listened, preferring
emotion to no emotion,
Watching silver buds of willow
gleam, sleek against the winter sky.

Maggi Watts

And She Waited...

And she waited, by the window,
   Dreaming dreams
   Of days gone by.
And she lived, as many seem to,
Passing time, before they die.

She had watched her children leave her,
   Dreaming dreams
   Of days to come.
But they never came to see her,
No time left, to visit Mum.

So she waited, by the window,
   Dreaming dreams
   That they were there.
But the past could not prepare her,
For the loneliness she'd bear.

When she died, there by the window,
   No more dreams
   Of what might be.
In her grave, they come to see her,
Bringing flowers, she'll never see.

Rossline O'Gara

260

Beliefs

As the sea tide's roar washes round the world
Sculpturing great rocks in new, bizarre shapes,
So does human thought constantly carve anew the rocks
Of our physical realities. It is the changing tides of
Our beliefs which forever sculpture the rocks of Being.
Once there was a destination to which man strove,
One reached only through the awesome gate of Death.
But now the tides of our Beliefs have swept away
The rocks of certainty and left the shifting sands of doubt
On which to build an earthly, faithless paradise.
Evolution, blind unknowing chance with no perception,
Is the reality and our journey to a destination,
Felt by the soul but never seen by eye, is
Crumbled away by the vast power of belief.
It gives us a today but no sunlit vision of tomorrow,
No vision of greatness, justice, hope or faith.
Little wonder men live badly when the greatest journey
Has been dissolved into illusion by the tides of thought.
The erosion of living is now complete and utter pointlessness
Is all.

Michael Brownbridge

Rest In Peace

The comradeship that then we knew
Was born of that day's strife
Friendship then which grew and grew
Stays with us through our life

Yes times were hard and grim and bare
In days both dark and grim
And now we know that with great care
Our help then came from Him

The one who bought with life's sweet joy
Our freedom with his giving
A love that now can never cloy
Through these our days of living

Was no more they had to toil
Laid to rest in God's good soil

John H. Allen

Tell Jesus

Tell Jesus when life's troubles grow too great for you to bear,
Go, lay them at the feet of Christ, and know that he will care.
Then tell him all those little things, which come to cloud your way,
The trials and perplexities which trouble you today.

Tell Jesus all there is to tell, about your daily needs,
About the dim uncertainties, through which your pathway leads,
About the cherished hopes, which lay, crushed lifeless, round
    your feet,
The broken dreams, your secret fears, and things left incomplete.

If you could know how tenderly he makes your needs his own,
You would not stand apart again, nor bear your grief alone,
You would not suffer needlessly, his strength will succour you,
And in life's bitterest darkest hours, his love will see you through.

John S. Rowley

My Beloved

My love for you is like a stream
that enters the water - rapids

At first the love flows gently
with each passing ripple

Gradually reaching the rapids where
the love grows fierce and out of control

Suddenly at the bottom of the water - rapids
a whirlpool is formed

Here my love for you just keeps
swirling round and round

Never reaching an end.

Wendy Taylor

A Lady For All Seasons

She's dressed in her new leafy green,
Majestic and regal - a queen.
In this Springtime attire, she'll stay for a while
Then quietly change almost unseen.

As Summer comes in, white flowers she'll bring
To gently perfume the air.
When the sun rides high and the weary pass by
A mantle of shade she'll fling.

Her Autumn gown will be glorious,
In gold, burnt-orange and grey.
Then she'll scatter in plenty the gifts of her bounty
Silk-smooth conkers, that children may play.

When Winter comes round, icy frost chills the ground
and clothes our Lady in white.
Now a sparkling queen,
All year she's been a lady to delight.

Joy Foster

Priorities

There's never a scum line around my bath
And hair in the sink is absurd
I never get finger marks all down the paint
And the glass of the mirror's not blurred
No-one ever comes in without wiping their feet
Or leaves a coat flung on a chair
If I'm listening to music I have peace and quiet
And that's because nobody's there
There's nobody now to leave plates in the sink
Or scoff the last cake I had planned
To keep for someone I hoped might drop in
Or "Stop playing tunes I can't stand!"
My children are gone to make their own lives
And oh how I wish I had known
That it isn't the coat or the bath or the noise
It's having your children at home
Priorities are the funniest things
And getting them straight's hard to do
But heed what I say and give all your love
Before it's too late - childhood's through

Betsy Wright

Wistful

I wander through the grass and flowers of summer glades
Where sunlight filters through the trees as daylight fades.
But everywhere, instead of flowers, it's you I see, your eyes,
Your smile, your very soul on every tree.

Your burning eyes, your laughing mouth, thick curling hair
A picture in my mind of you still there.
A certain sadness lingers on your smile each day
As though you think I'll fly away.
Or is it you, who soon may go,
And never know I love you so.

Shirley Shapers

Beauty

Beauty comes from within,
it's a feeling that warms the skin,
it's a rosy glow,
it's a face you know,
it's an inner grace,
it's pure silk lace,
it's a Heart of Gold,
Where thoughts unfold,
it's being kind to everyone,
And loving the world from when time began,
it's Blissfully Happy,
Never sad,
it smiles so openly it feels so glad,
to have the world within its grasp,
to please and praise and comfort too,
Let's Hope life's beauty is always with you.

Wendy Marie Welsford

261

Inside Out

Why is it, that people cannot accept people as they are,
Not like someone from a far away planet or star.
Black, White, Asian or African,
Jew, Muslim, Hindu or Christian,
Man, Woman, rich or poor,
People are people,
It's that simple
Just like a banana, not bought for its skin,
But for the fruit within.

Leanne Common

Devonshire Dumpling

How lucky I am to be born in Devon,
The breathtaking views makes one think of heaven.
Its spring, and the fields are vivid green,
Bluebells in the woods, a sight to be seen.

Tall hedges frame the winding lanes.
Sunlight sparkling on window panes.
Sheep and cows in fields so steep,
In the rushing river, salmon leap.

Quaint thatched cottages in village streets,
Church and pubs where people meet.
Sea gulls, following plough, the earth so red.
It's getting dimpsy, time for bed.

Honeysuckle scents the warm night air.
Foxes appearing from their lair.
Stars twinkling in a velvet sky,
Owls hooting in trees nearby.

Church clock striking the hour is late,
Call puss in, and shut the gate.
Gaze once more upon the tranquil scene
And realize how privileged I have been.

Peggy Moore

The Hermit's Shadow

He thought of God's beauty and saw mirror'd elves,
The shadow of Eden soft-cast in ourselves.
In hermit-craved silence in garret-lit prayer
He trod in bowed reverence, a rainbow-carved stair.
Beyond echoed midnight, the soul's shiver'd light
Words formed into wisdom and laboured delight.
Folklore of the ages, and life's garnered themes,
The child-froth of magic and learned men's dreams.
The faith of the muser in tune with fine art,
The whispers of angels in time with his heart.
Behind him the fairies grasped shadowy hems,
And touched his quiet mind with the rays of bright gems.
His love was a pathway of gold-glittered leaves,
And merit was humble like a carefully-stored sheaves.
Seraphic blessed verses with diligence sought,
Simplicity's rapture in fairy-blown thought.
Who dances in shadows within his own soul
Knows shades beyond sunset reflect beauty's goal.

Christopher Rothery

My Prayer

Heavenly father, hear our plea
We, thy children, call to thee
Guide us, teach us, lovingly
So we may turn our hearts to thee

Show us all the one true road
So those following must surely see
That though the way belong and rough
It's the one true road that leads to thee

So dear father, do not fail us
In our trials give us strength
So that one day we may be rewarded
And see, at last, your smiling face

Margaret MacDonald

Masked Secret

I've been sitting in my bedroom,
Thinking of your smile,
Hoping that I'd see you soon,
So I can talk to you for a while

I'd imagine what I'd say to you,
While you sit and listen,
Imagine things that we could do,
Now you don't want to be missing.

I will gently stroke your body,
Caress your rippling chest
Kiss you up and down
And fill you with all my sweet tenderness.

Feel our hearts beating,
As our lips meet,
It's not the central heating,
That's creating all the heat!

Daniella Blechner

My Prison Prayer

Please dear God, please, please, please listen,
Send me and all my love home from this prison,
If you could see my tormented eyes
Then you will know I always cry.

I try to hide my tears away,
Till all have gone, every-day,
I know I'm not out there any-more,
But one day God, I'll be out for sure.

Deep in my heart I miss them so,
And my, love for them, will never go,
I am all alone, but not at heart,
Because they were within me from the start

It's not the same, without them near,
But some-day soon, I will be there,
So please please God, if you will listen,
Send me home, from this dark prison.

A. Rogers

Mental Illness

The tears, like the thoughts, come unbidden, unwanted
welling up from the hidden depths beyond normal reach or ken.
Buried moments rise and burst on the surface of consciousness
as if being lived anew. Details which went unnoticed at the
happening live again, and having been resurrected the once
do not return to the depths but run riot, torment, mock
grow and at times completely overwhelm, threatening to
burst like pent up water behind a weakened dam
drowning here and now in its wake.

Reality becomes the then, no longer the now, the present
recedes to a dream-like haze - still there - but one step
removed, overtaken by the panic and pain of the past
struggling to surface in detail so fresh and minute
that it appears like a reshowing of a long archived
film, sounds, smells, thoughts all still present
and preserved in some unlabelled corner - freed to
appear unbidden, seemingly without reason or prompt
at their will not mine.

Pamela Odam

The Laburnum Tree

Exquisite are the fragile blooms,
That Grace the fair laburnum tree,
Doffing heads of Golden Plumes
Draping boughs with majesty.

Softly warn spring breezes sigh,
Gently rain drops patter round
Yet should one grieve that this should die?
When sunshine's scattered on the ground

E. Howarth

262

A Little Bit Of Nonsense

There it stayed for many days
Catching one's eye and in the sun's rays
It could not suit such an old lady
and yet one might when one's name is Sadie.

Made of cream mellowed straw
Must have caught many a man in awe
Passing the window every week
She could always take a peek.

Now let's see which way could it be worn
Tilted, on the side over the brow or straight on the crown.

Whichever way it must not be blown
Some ribbon upon it must be sewn.

Look how pretty it is bedecked in flowers
Not to be worn in showers
Shall she spend her savings
To quell her craving

Yes she'll have no conscience
To indulge in such a bit of nonsense.

V. J. Park

Untitled

Most people have got no idea
But you're a world famous superstar
And they laugh and sneer at you
And all the work you do
Why can't you reach them
Are their minds so closed?
I saw you at Wembley the other day
And you were at your best
I sang, I clapped, I cheered for you
I laughed at your sense of humour too
So why can't you reach them
Are their minds so closed?
I cry when you sing those lovely songs
You reach me with your passion
And the warmth within your heart.
The feelings wash over me and stab me like a dart
I understand why you can't reach them
They are so closed.

Michele Aylett

A Warning

I dreamt last night, the room was black.
Two yellow eyes were staring back.
And in those eyes, I thought I saw
My life as it had gone before,
When I awoke, and looked around.
The beast had gone, without a sound.
But then I knew what must be done.
The devil had sent, for me to see,
A demon who was once like me.

Lloyd Newton

Thoughts Of Loss

I smile, yet should enjoyment cross my path
threads of guilt cocoon my soul in wrath,
That I should dare this life to assuage
without your presence, to turn a better page.

I cry, I know that time will not heal, the
remaining tenancy of life destined to harass,
With languid thoughts unable to dispel the
realization that the suffering will not pass.

I pray, amid silent tears just for your touch
and manifold mercies that can never return.
Entreaties that will not give me what I want
but help me bear the pains that burn.

I know, as I drift across the vast oceans of
life, that you are still my mentor and guide.
You were my compass here on earth and
still my first-mate through the lonely tide.

G. Powell

Cat

She was called Cat, and at that, she was very good.
He had never met her, he consulted his pocket gazetteer.
Thumbing the track ball, he narrowed it down to a part of town,
In which the specialized software which he had had written
told him he would, if he could,
Find her who would be to him all that any might, if the code
was right.

The housing type was falling in value, though his expectations
notched up as the field narrowed.
Here was the house, the one was there, her with whom his life
he could share.
Mother answered, can I help you young man?
He stuttered and stammered, "I believe that you can".
I'm told through a friend that here lives a girl who might
possibly be suitable for me as a long term partner.

What makes you think that? She's a nice girl, our Cat.
Is that her name? How fireside can you get?
And yet I have not met her.
After an exchange of banter the child was brought forth.

I'm delighted to meet you, she held out a paw
complete with claws.

Wilburforce Hyde

Ring Out The New

The formation of wild geese
in the sky blue in its true
nature of colour
their white bellies showing
soaring towards the east

A compelling thought
like the quiver of a dart
pierced my wounded heart

Their flight is evidence
of the rhythm of life
since the world began

Heading to a new destination
what a sight to behold

Like a dance of hello - goodbye
I flew with them to their second home

And for once I wished that instead of them
it was me who would soar
above them - below them -
just to fly home
to me-

Waltraut-Paula Wandscher

My Shadow And "I"

My shadow and I are the closest of friends
The people I like "he" also befriends
Sometimes he's shorter, but often taller than me
Yet life without him, who knows where I'd be?

What I wear "he" wears, we're 'two of a kind',
Where I go 'he' goes. Never leaves me behind
It faced with a foe - he stays by my side
There are no secrets. Which from him I can hide.

We stick together through thick and through thin,
We have the same friends, also same 'next of kin'
Not always visible, but never outdone.
The sure way to see 'him' is out in the sun

He walks and runs at the same pace as me.
Nothing eludes him sees everything I see.
Our minds are in tune, our heart beats the same
we're Identical twins, with an Identical name.

If I fell in love my sweetheart I'd woo.
She may not know it, but he would come too
Whatever the outcome, we'd both have to share.
We have everything in common, we're truly a pair.

G. W. Dobson

263

Peace

The shrill, discordant screech of female voice,
The angry shriek of childish cruelty,
The jarring grind of traffic's madd'ning whirl
Had pierced and flung into a thousand bits
My very soul.
I yearned for Peace

Alone I strode to where the Orwell flowed,
A shim'ring mass beneath the glinting sun —
Just trees and birds and brownish fields fresh ploughed.
No sound save dancing leaf and tossing wave
And one bird's call.
I still sought Peace.

By Orwell's bank a lonely farm lay like
A child asleep; and as it slept, I felt
A little breeze caress its rugged fields.
Then suddenly it stirred and beckoned me
To share its calm.
I had met Peace.

M. W. Lee

Friendship

I have a friend, a special friend so dear to my heart.
I hope our friendship never ends, and that we never part.
She's always there to comfort me, and help in any way.
And listens to my moans and groans and everything I say.
She cheers me up when I feel down, and never does complain.
I feel sometimes without her help I'd surely go insane.
So I dedicate this ode to her, because to me she is the best.
And to have her as my special friend I know that I've been blessed.

B. Kiss

The Old Man

He sits there listening,
Expecting something or someone,
His eyes are narrowed.
His skin wrinkled by the passage of time.

It seems as if he's been there all his life.
Yet, in his eyes he is a young man again,
Laughing, running, playing with his children
A gleam of excitement dances in his eyes.

But now the dream is gone
No longer does he laugh,
No longer does he run or play.
He whispers the sweet words 'fare well.'

Adaobi Ifeachor

The Same Dull Haze

He awoke from his sleep in dull haze, the same dull haze that curses his every awakening. Will it be different today, he wonders. Will all that is lost be gained. Will all that is fire burn, the same painful memory. The same beautiful emotions, that once were love which are now the haunting aspect of his ever existence.

Which yanks him from his bed, pulling him into line, slapping reality in his face. He knows with a yawn and a stretch, that nothing has changed. The same dull haze.

He is dressed now for the day, in his modern day armour, which shields and protects him only from himself. He negotiates the stairs, still dark from absent light. He stops. He laughs. Love is light, days spent in her loving aura. Dark is joyful memories now painful with loss. He takes another step, he pauses. No, dark is love, night's so warm and cosy. Light is only distant memories of her joyful ways.

That so very near revelation, which would have been his foundation for the day. Crumbles and falls, back to reality, as he steps from the last tread. Nothing has changed. The same dull haze, the same dull haze.

Guy Scott Rogers

Gandalf

Who are they?
These guardians of the night,
The mysterious wanderers of the dark.
They come in many colours,
We hear them call, we see them fight.
At midnight, we can see them talk.
With gay abandon they perform,
Truly athletic feats,
Then snuggle up in front of the fire to keep warm.
Now you've guessed my riddle, they
Are pussy cats, of course.
They spring from the cupboards,
Climb up the stairs,
Cats can hide anywhere.
Sometimes they are kittens,
Often fully grown; they will love you to death, if
You give them a good home.
My cat's name was Gandalf, a
Pleasure and a treasure to me:
Full of fun, a joy to everyone.

I. P. Milne

First Day At A New School

I wonder if the other girls are feeling like this?
Tummy full of butterflies all trying to get out!
Some are talking loudly, but I only remember Miss-
And anyway, I could not talk a lumps stuck in my throat!

If Anthea were here today I know I'd be all right;
We always stuck together, but her family's moved again.
Fair and fun, and good at sport (a good friend in a fight!)
Hang on, there's one I seem to know, standing by the frame.

She goes to the same Brownies' group (I do remember that);
She's turned away and climbing up - gosh, that does look quite tricky!
I'll wander over nonchalantly and see if she will chat;
Anyway to miss the chance to climb would be a pity!

Put my satchel on the bench, but there's really not much in it:
Rubber, ruler, pencil box - oh, and my dinner money!
This is good, right to the top; I'm not frightened one bit!
Hello, are you new too? My legs are feeling funny!

There goes the bell, we'd better get down - we want some decent seats now.
Fancy that! We're the same height! (I am glad that I met her.)
Look, pull your beret round like this, I can show you how;
We had them at my last school! (Things are really getting better!)

Elizabeth E. Lovell

The Graveyard Watch

Nursing I love, I worked with speed, the hours were long but youth scorned fatigue, the only time of rebellion came - during the graveyard watch. From two to four, when death crept through the door, the patients turned, and muttered, and swore. The blood ran thin and you doubted your powers, the graveyard watch had the darkest hours.

It was only then, as we fought for a life - or gave souls ease from their final strife, That I shook my fists at whoever allowed the graveyard watch and its painful hours. I've stood in the cold with my cloak wrapped tight, shaken tears from my eyes, and demanded a sight of a glimmer, a reason, for suffering so - for the graveyard was a time of woe.

When children are small, it's the time they awake, for food, for comfort, so soothe and slake, The primeval fear that lies deep in their genes. The graveyard watch is a time of dreams. It is also a time when the mind is free, ideas can blossom, the eyes can see - as the dawn comes through, so the patterns evolve, in the graveyard watch you can problems solve.

So, during the years, I've been taught to use the hours in the night when sleep is refused. It's become a time I can call my own - in the graveyard watch I can be alone. I can write, and think, or read and learn, release the thoughts that swirl and churn beneath the surface beneath the surface that's shown to the world. The graveyard watch is my safety valve!

Rosemary Titterington

264

The Statesman

The Statesman stood rigidly, splendid and straight;
He looked at his watch - must be there by eight.
His audience waited in the quiet of the Hall,
Every word, every gesture they would wish to recall.

The Statesman emerged, so fine and so grand.
He must speak in a way they would all understand.
"My Lords, ladies and gentlemen" - he began with emotion,
His audience waited with love and devotion.

His gaze swept the Hall - so noble in manner.
No one could fail to stand 'neath his banner.
They all felt his power, the all-seeing eyes,
Who would not follow someone so wise?

Only then was his voice somehow lost in the mist,
For the notes he had brought were his wife's shopping-list -
'Lettuce, cucumber, a quarter of ham -
'Eggs and tomatoes, strawberry jam'.

The Statesman stood speechless, no words could he utter,
For what could he say about one pound of butter?
To his audience he turned, though with confidence shaken -
"Today I must talk of the price of our bacon."

Ronald J. Moore

My World

Time as always marches on relentlessly,
In our world, time takes on another dimension,
Each tender moment is precious and endearing.

Your hair is golden and reflects the sun, wild and untamed like
a free soul,
I long for your tender loving touch, the silkiness of your skin.

I get lost in those tender loving eyes, caring and deep, ever
thoughtful.
Your presence is always known, and never far away.
The joy and happiness I am beholden to that you create, with
each special moment.

My world is almost complete with the loving tenderness and
warmth you create,
That feeling of caring and need is ever present and shown,
Each day is new and ever rewarding,

Strength is not a measure of the body, but of the inner soul,
How immense you are......

Adam Gostling

A Fantasy

There she lay ... dead.
Wrapped in a veil of silence
Like the infinite depths
Of a peaceful sea.

Her frail form, which was once,
So lithe and so lissome...still
And enshrouded in pure white draperies
Like those of an angel.
Her fair white hands were clasped
On her bosom, which had once heaved
With all the joys of happy maidenhood
And there, lay a rose
It's pure petals so palely exquisite
Curving outwards like a holy spirit
Entering into the sacred veil of oblivion.
Her face so pale and wax-like in its deathly purity
Wax gilded over with a heavenly light
And her hair clung about her shoulders
In singlets of spun gold.
There she lay, and as I listened
I heard her voice singing, afar off,
Telling me to be patient and wait
Then, even as I listened, it faded
And sank, into the eternal peace from which it came.

Nora Crossley

Crux

Now! The three essential sprang,
Time, the wraith, the sequential thread,
Held Matter to pattern to Diversity's tread.
Fragments to atoms, frail dance steps then,
As energy mirrored, lensed, caught, lost and reran, lit
Chaos' spiked craw-yield, antimatter - theurgy split.
Gravity's ebb wielded a galactic sprawl, but
One jewel blue planet, bound in motion to Sol, saw
An intimacy of chemicals, a paradox withall, that
Decanted probability, here, in entropy's maw.
So Time, the sole interdict, set freedom local limits
That Matter in perpetuity would martyr itself as Life.
Spiral cables of codicils, a greater genetic dawn,
Ever tying into the future its more successful spawn.

Consider, quisling man, master of the Present,
See in this misunderstood gift, riddle in its mould,
That the Organiser, made impotent in
Fulfilment of freewill,
Millennia since and now and yet
    Waits....

Jill Prince

Bullied

Roar at me, whisper through me,
Don't isolate or overcrowd me.

I feel abandoned, insecure, crushed,
When I look over my shoulder,
I hear you snigger.

Desperately wanting to wake up,
From this cold, repulsive ordeal.
Through my tears, I can't breathe nor see.

I suffer from your inflicted burns.
Your glaring eyes,
And bitter words have struck a match.

Look at me; what have you done to me?

You manipulate my silence.
Imprison me, bind me,
Your hatred surrounds me.

Outside a concrete wall,
Inside I crumble.
When you laugh,
My heart goes down on its knees.

Bully, don't do this to me!

Guriqubal Pannu

Almatinsk Peak

Dry canyon ruins
lure wild steppe dogs up cruel mountain tracks;
stark peaks stay white into summer depths.
Storms swing back and forth,
a mood inconstancy is what they know.

Clouds void massive snows and turbulence
to brace the long forgotten green
of Tien Shan fir
and alpine treasure buried higher up
on till-littered surrounds
this peak, abraded to its pyramid shape
from scarred and jagged slopes.

An avalanche of rock spills down,
boulders dislodged by a rush
of flocks herded by a wolf
through choked crevices
to the mountain lakes and catchment quarries,
baring their sky-inflicted wounds.

All this, disguised by false spring sun
to take a life of youth and inexperience.

Julian de Wette

A Mother's Heart Is A Garden Of Love

A plaque which says this I was given on Mother's Day,
Also five bright flame red roses came my way,
There are five flowers planted in my garden of love,
They are precious gifts from my father above,
The strongest are called, mother of babes and mother of girls,
These two are my life's pearls
The third is growing shakily, it's mother of women it gets
    stronger every day,
But this one has had difficulties along the way,
The soil of my heart is arid and hard, sometimes I fear,
But it is watered and fed by laughter, dreams and tears
Which continues to be shared over the years,
The last two flowers, haven't yet grown,
But the seeds have been sown,
They are called, mother in law and grandmother,
These weeds will not be allowed to smother,
The master gardener from heaven tends them all,
As in prayer to him we call,
Our Lord knows the season for everything to flower,
And we must put our trust in his power

Nita Roskilly

Let Me Go

So let me go where the poppies grow
Like some blood red drops in the corn,
Or let me bide where the skylarks hide
When they've sung their song to the dawn.
Or let me stay where the mayflies play
In the reeds by the bubbling stream,
Or let me rest where the lapwing nest,
There I'll lay on the sward and dream.

I want no more of the city's roar
And the swarming throng in the street,
Or the putrid air you are breathing there
To the drum of a thousand feet.
I want to be where the air is free,
Of the song of birds take my share,
Where wild things live and nature will give
Of her secrets if I wait there.

A. R. Kerry

'The Wind At Night'

As I lie in bed at night under blanket and sheet,
I listen to the wind as it sweeps the street.

It brushes my window as it passes by,
leaving behind its weary sigh.

Somewhere a dog barks, the night is late,
because the wind has rattled the garden gate.

Like the voices of loved ones long since gone,
it whispers their memories and travels on.

It travels on like a thief in the night,
sweeping waste paper and leaves in flight.

It sweeps the fields and stirs the trees,
the lonely wind that no one sees.

It sweeps the roof tops, leaves fences torn
and fades away at the break of dawn.

Thomas Bell

Spell Of Love....

Love cannot be broken, it's a powerful magic between two people.
Love never dies and is never undone. Love can travel over
oceans and seas and you'll always have love in your heart.
You cannot live without love, love is eternal, lasting forever.
Love is special and should be cherished and not thrown away
like a piece of rubbish.
If you do that you have no soul you are heartless. You don't
belong in a world without love. Everybody should, if they don't
they are incomplete, you need love in your heart to be whole.
No one can take love away from you, and don't let them.
Love is for you to cherish.
Love is forever....

Kirsty Smith

Watching The News

I feel with my heart
I feel with my hands
I feel with my mind
I fear for mankind

My heart goes to those that are living in fear,
My hands hold their hands in vain effort to hear -
'Their cries'
My mind is in turmoil as wars still go on
What can I do, their lives are now gone

The world is a mess
I feel with my heart
We're losing our grip
I feel with my hands
God help us all
I feel with my mind
I fear for mankind

Barbara Casey

Farewell Old Home

You hold the secrets of forty years.
Our hopes our joys and our fears.
You've seen life given also taken.
Hopes fulfilled dreams forsaken.
The tears we've wept the sound of laughter.
The wishes for happiness ever after.
Seen a large family growing small.
Soon there'll be no one left at all.
For us who are gone will you sigh.
When through your rafters drifts a sad
Goodbye.

June Scrutton

Stony Heart

I am wicked and this I'm sure
you'll find out and tell me more
In my heart I'm no good
To do a good turn I never would
Lies and deceit and full of hate.
I'm mate of the devil and also a snake
Oh, why was I born for all to hate.

Not one good word does anyone say
I'm tired of it all I'll go away
How can I win, how can I love
The answer is with the one above
For this please tell me, HOW can I atone?
When you know I've only a heart of stone.

E. M. Cobb

Solitude

I have a new companion now, her name is loneliness,
she has no hand for me to hold, nor cheek for my caress,
yet she is ever there with me, constant by my side,
to keep reminding me of her, and mock tears I cannot hide.

Yet loneliness will sometimes bring, a friend called memory
and we walk the old familiar paths, that were so dear to me,
perhaps along a country lane, or by a bubbling stream
where we made our future plans, and shared each other's dream.

In thoughts I wander down the years, reliving once again
the happiness that we had known, the mind rejects the pain.
Strolling in the woodlands, filled with springtime flowers,
laughing, caught out in the rain, in sudden April showers.

Of those long summer evenings, days reluctant yet to go,
slowly turning into dusk, in the sunset afterglow.
The scent of honeysuckle, heavy on the warm night air,
a nightingale to charm us, as he sang his evening prayer.

How swiftly beat the wings of time, to bear the years away,
how soon all our tomorrows form, a part of yesterday
but life is not so empty now, clouds no longer fill the sky,
since Memory joined in company, with Loneliness... and I.

B. J. Pickett

A Passing Star

I dreamt I caught a passing star,
So beautiful and bright,
And for an eon of life's span
She lit the path down which I ran,
Then vanished in the night.

I dreamt we dwelt on sunny shores
And through the livelong day
We laughed and wandered, hand in hand,
Along an endless coral strand,
Then loved the night away.

I dreamt she came with open arms,
I woke with sudden start.
One moment deep in ecstasy,
the next in stark reality,
Oh disappointed heart!

For dreams aren't real and dreams soon pass
They vanish with the dawn,
And passing through the sleeping mind
On planes which, awake, one cannot find,
They leave the soul forlorn.

A. T. Brooke-Webb

Hope

Hope is in the sunrise and the touch of morning dew.
Hope is in the moonlight from the darkness shining through.
Hope is in the Springtime breaking forth from Winter rest.
Hope is in the birds song as they start to build their nests.
Hope is in the beauty of the flowers and the trees.
Hope is in the rainfall as it supplies creation's needs.

As we walk amongst God's world and see the beauty in these things,
Do we feel a need to know real hope and what to each it brings?
Hope of redemption, peace and love, of faith and eternal life;
Hope of a place in Heaven above far away from worldly strife.

Hope is in the giving of God's one and only Son
To be our Lord and Saviour - His Way is the only one.
Hope is through the cross on which our precious Lord was slain.
Hope is in His rising that each one may be born again.

So let's give thanks for God's love shown in the beauty of
this earth,
And in the giving of His Son Jesus Christ that we all might
have new birth.
Hope is there for everyone to see and to embrace,
And if we all take hold of it we'll come to know God's saving grace.

Martine L. Shelton

Going Home

Our stay is almost over
soon we fly away
now we start the packing.
The big stuff on its way
my pictures and the bedding
lots of china too
then of course the candlesticks
with my plates of blue
my stone hare's name is Georgie
he almost weighs a ton
then from the kitchen cupboard
down came the hot x bun
the cuckoo clock from off the wall
pots and pans galore lots and lots of photographs
the knocker from the door.
My little heart-shaped mirror
in its wooden frame, all my books and diaries
moving such a game; cartons now filled to the brim
'cept my ted, I'll carry him.
long ago was lost you see
in Troy City, Tennessee. Now it's time to say goodbye
back to England we will fly.

Amy Rome-Roberts

Life And Death Of A Gunfighter

Famous in the wild west, his guns made him the best,
Dressed somberly in black, tall and lean looking mean,
Conscious and aware of the next attack, sitting in a saloon alone,
Reputation exaggerated, nameless faces waiting to atone,
No longer able to enjoy,
Needing eyes in the back of his head, no words spoken,
Hands itching in anticipation,
Another shoot out about to happen
Some loud mouthed kid next with a bid, over!
Just another waste of life, knowing soon he'll be just a memory,
Carving a reputation across the nation,
Endless hours of tedium waiting for the time when he meets
Someone as fast, then to live forever in the past,
Not growing old with grace and dignity,
A legend for people to discuss,
He ponders why the fuss, finally his final bow,
Sweating from his furrowed brow, life ebbing slowly away,
This is judgement day, his speed gone,
Eyes closed lying dead in the hot noon sun,
Living and finally dying by the gun.

D. L. Redman

The Life Of A Rose

As I awake for the very first time, and I know my time is short.
Quickly I must remember, all the things that I've been taught.
Things around me are beautiful, some old and some new.
But I must sip something wet, my first taste of morning dew.
I wish that I could rest for a while, and through my burst skin peep,
But if I forget to unfold myself, I may fall back into sleep.
Things you will find very hard, mother nature said to me.
Try and you will succeed, and your life you shall see.
Push until your petals unfold leaving none of them bent.
Show the earth your soft red silk.
Which gives the fragrance of your scent.
I feel so very happy, and oh so very tall,
But soon the wind will be far too strong.
Parts of me will begin to fall,
Then no longer will I want to, through my burst skin peep.
So I will just float right back, way back into sleep.

Glenys Linda Reid

To My Dearest Husband

I was looking for a romantic card the other day
With words of love and kisses
To give to someone special, on this his Birthday.

But on finding this card it was hard to resist
To put down and give it a miss
So I'm sorry dear and please don't frown
That no romantic words are wrote down

For I love you still, have no need to fear
Even with the passing of another year
For birthdays come and birthdays go
It makes no difference to me you know

So my love I hope you will be
A little amused
And not take this card too literally.

Doreen Allwynn

Never Again

Never again to walk the hills together,
Never again to wander hand in hand.
Enjoying the sweet sea air, the smell of heather,
Or playing games with Lassie on the sands.
Never again to share your favourite music,
To look across the smile when you play "our song."
Never again to plan what we'll do tomorrow,
Or talk of the days gone by when we were young.
I can't believe you've left my side forever,
I can't come to terms with a life to be lived alone.
A day, a week, a year, but never to see
you again, seems too much to be borne.

Laura E. Gorst

I Believe

I believe in honesty,
In peace and love and harmony,
To defend what's mine,
And all that I love,
freedom of speech, and Asgard above,
In the dwarfs that lurk,
And the giants that spite,
And almighty Thor with all of his might.

With nature I give, and feel her pain,
In Freya's arms, I'm at peace again,
And in all I've heard, and all I've read,
My life is anew, like the eagle that flew,
Across the Rainbow Bridge,
Myself to myself, I give to you.

We see the pain, and teach to gain,
As I believe in you, I feel no shame,
With people so lost,
Their lives so downtrodden,
I teach through the wisdom,
Of you my friend Odin.

Joanna Fletcher

Stepping Stones

God has been my stepping stones through life,
    solid rock on which to place my feet
Barely visible in troubled waters, clearing with the calm,
    I reach out and the stones are there for me
So as I walk, along life's changing stream,
    from the safety of the banking I can see
Those pillars will be there, for me and him to share,
    whatever in my world there has to be.

Blanche Ali

If Only

If only all the wars could cease
And mankind learn to live in peace
If only there was no more crime
And one could say "What's mine is mine"
If only children could be good
And learn to do the things they should
If only greed was a thing of the past
And people learnt that love can last

If only the weather was always fine
And it only rained well after nine
If only we had money galore
And when it's gone just get some more
If only there was no disease
And illness never, if you please
If only the animals could be safe
And people spared all kinds of grief

If only I could cease to dream
Things might not be, quite all they seem.

Maureen Ann Baker

A Twilight Vision

Without a thought I slip into my silent slumber
And almost immediately I am representing myself
in that second world we all visit.
I am wrapped in wondrous fantasies,
Lost in a place where everything is as you want it to be.
No fighting, no killing, just peace and contentment.
It is a world truly unique,
It is a world where all problems and worries melt away.
Your mind, the creator during your slumber,
pieces together both that which is reality and that
which is illusion,
producing images no-one can steal from you.
Dreaming is a maze, where you get lost
but as you don't want to be found, you don't mind.

Kyra Chamberlain

Regret

The smoke drifts up from flickering fires
An echo of our sweet desires
And old men chew their pipes and dream
Of things that were, or might have been.

I loved you when my life was young
A virgin page without a stain
Now over decades I look back
And wish I had that time again.

In all the innocence of youth
I trampled on your gift of love
In ignorance I bruised the flower
And cast it down in life's crass mud.

Now as the years have passed away
And on this earth you no more tread
I wish that I had understood
And uttered words I should have said

If you look down upon me now
I hope that maybe you have seen
How I regret the way things were
And wish for things that might have been.

Kay G. Tucker

Ode To The Night

Recline thy head upon the earth
And to the stars give wondrous gaze,
A perfect dream could ne'er give birth
To such a mystic jewelled maze.
A dark rich pool of ebony
Splashed o'er with myriad diamonds bright
Allows thy heart and soul to see
The wondrous glory of the night.

Walter Mitchinson

Martin

I held you gently in my arms
Your eyes so tightly closed,
lying there so safe and calm
I kissed your tiny nose
A hundred plans, a thousand schemes, behind a million smiles.

I wondered what your dreams were?
And did you think of me
A football game with daddy
Or a bounce upon my knee
of Susie, or ice-cream, or even your balloons
Or staring through the window, just gazing at the moon

It's hard to find the words
To tell you how I feel
Are you an Angel Martin?
Or are you really real?

Ann Hedges

Walking Fastly Foxy

He walks fastly foxy, his haughty head up high,
His shiny shoes clatter on the pavement, as he walks on by,
The glowing street lamp stares at him, as he gives a sordid sigh,
A wanton woman looks him up and down, thinking my, oh, my!
I wildly wonder who he is and where he is going?
I wish he'd ask me directions, then I could show him,
What is his name? Where does he come from?
He looks so luscious. Do I look so lonesome?
He walks foxily faster and faster and further away,
I wish his lonely legs had stopped, I wish his dark deep eyes
    had strayed.
The wanton woman wildly wishes to share his sordid sigh tonight,
He's going, going, gone. Now out of sight.
My late date arrives, we walk hand in hand away,
Walking on to another night, walking on to another day.
We pass many people by in the street, who look us up and down,
Thinking, who are they? As we walk fastly foxy into the town.

Margaret-Elizabeth Strachan

World In Pieces

The hunger of the World astounds us because of the stark
photos and newsreels we are fed.
Greed and malice, which we apportion each other, are brought
about by circumstances, We create.
The fanatical, nay "Godly" try to teach us how to do things,
do we learn?
"It's not us" we said!
We allow the erosion of this earth, which cannot be forgiven,
but money shouts louder than us mate!

God in his wisdom looks down with pity as we gnaw at the
very essence of his creation.
Our charitable conscience makes us speak volumes on the
error of our ways, action - None!
Governments talk, express sorrow, waste time, talk more, sit
back and pray for inflation.
Taxes rise to compensate, green action costs more, while
fumes kill and maim, the "Rolls" hasn't yet gone.

Shall we weep for this sorry state of ours, blame it on others,
Japs, Yanks and Eurocrats.
Why can't we love each other without criticism, put aside our
different Gods, money and possessions.
Take all religions and mix them up, after all there is only one creator.
Should we sit back and let Governments waste time, how long
will it take for Them to learn the lessons.

Joan Lister

I See

I see
Brothers fighting against each other in war,
A mother fighting to save her young child's life.
I see
Houses destroyed by bombs,
Fish dying from nuclear testing.
I see
An old man lying on a park bench with a bottle in his hand,
Young children dying of starvation.
I see
Thousands of people flocking from their homes,
Children turning to prostitution after their family's let them
down.
I see
Teenagers committing suicide from confusion,
Good killed by evil.
I see
Our world being destroyed by greedy politicians.

Gemma Pugh

In Memoriam L.S.S.C.

Lizard Serpentine Stone Company

There is a feel of timelessness down here,
As if whatever was will ever be,
This sheltered vale, its few secluded homesteads,
And winding, tempting footpaths to the sea.

And yet, beside the rock-strewn beach, there stands
A monument to industry long gone,
Where serpentine was polished and refined
By craftsmen till it positively shone.

If you would see a sample of their skill
Then take the road to Landewednack church
Where proudly stands a dark-hued plinth which might
Irreverently be called the rector's perch.

A century ago the business thrived;
The veinèd stone was carved in shapes galore;
But economic troubles brought decline,
Until the workings ceased forevermore.

The building now stands silent and forlorn,
Its roof made safe, but entry still denied,
And we can trace where other buildings housed
Poltesco's trade in stone that long since died.

Colin T. Cooper

Mum

T is for all the thanks I'll give you.
H is for all the healing you've given me.
A is for all the affection you've provided.
N is for that times I've been naughty (sorry).
K is for all the kindness you've shared with me.

Y is for my yearning to see you everyday.
O is for outfits you've brought me.
U is for understanding my point of view.

V is for valuable which you are to me.
E is for the endless love I have for you.
R is for restoring my hope when it is gone.
Y is for your youthful look.

M is for being my mum.
U is for giving me your utmost attention.
C is for comforting me when I couldn't cope.
H is for all the hugs and kisses I'll give you today.

Alecia Richards

Untitled

I believe that God is not as we suppose.
I believe that no one really knows.
Man has a need to fill a space,
A creed to bring a state of grace
And give him an important place:
But who can claim to have the sight
And say "My Faith's the one that's right?"
And if some great and noble mind
Devised the world and all mankind,
Then what went wrong along the way
For evil seems to win the day?
The world is ruled by craft and greed
And seldom does the good succeed.
I feel that I can only try
To do my best and when I die,
Maybe then I'll learn the reason why!

M. Harlock

Seed Time And Harvest

On reaching a stile I rest for a while
And take in the scene below
The men in the fields are busy
The time has come to sow.

My thoughts are disturbed by the sound of the birds
Such a fuss, and such a show
The chase is on for survival, there's an urgency, nothing can wait
For all that abides in the country side
Are busily seeking to mate.

The fields in winter lie hard and cold, covered with ice and snow
The plough meets with resistance which makes the going slow
Somehow we too are like farmers, we too take a share of the plough
In weighing up our harvest, are we contented now?

I go on my way elated, trudging through grassland and weeds
And give thanks to the greatest farmer of all
Who first scattered these wonderful seeds.

E. M. Wooldridge

Memories Of Autumn

The Mackintosh hung limply on the hook across the hall,
With autumn sunshine lighting up the stairs,
A soft and gentle glow, enhanced by kitchen fires,
That dry the boots, stood neatly by in pairs.

Soft shades of leaves, through red and gold to brown,
That crunch and crackle, blown upon the breeze,
The garden rake, abandoned upon a frosted lawn,
And robin sings between the unclothed trees.

While wreaths of smoke rise and swirl, to mingle with the mist,
The blue-tits gather round the peanut feast,
Cold scents of winter, drift hazily, upon the morning air,
'Till glittering frosts announce the year's deceased

Carol Coleborn

Understanding

When you and I were in our youth
We often told the brutal truth
and ignored bright eyes full of pain
or teardrops falling as summer rain.

Soft pillows stifled night-time cries
and in the morn, as butterflies,
we'd fly towards a brighter light
and forget the terrors of the night.

Youthful dreams of bygone years
are sadly replaced by adult fears
then, slowly, trust within us dies
again soft pillows stifle the cries.

Gathering wisdom day by day
as adults we must choose our way
and let the wind scatter our fears
and allow the sun to dry our tears.

We can then, knowingly, share
in life's golden harvest, if we dare!
Caress precious moments of infinite pleasure,
understand friendship is a gift to treasure.

Margaret Parfitt

Rustic Thoughts

The sloping hills are now clad in mist
Until there dawns a new break of day.
Shades are no more where the sun has kissed
The scented hedgerows that pave the way
To the winding river's ceaseless flow,
Meandering through the meadow land
Where verdant banks of watercress grow.
The cattle grazing peacefully stand
Peering perchance at children nearby
Gathering posies of wild flowers.
The windblown trees above gently sigh
Church bells herald the silent hours
Of eventide's dusk before nightfall.
The nocturnal world begins to wake
The barn owl repeats its ghostly call
Can be heard across the moonlit lake.
And so my friend I've gladly written
This simple tale though short is finished
Of rural life in scenic Britain
Where the good earth has not diminished.

A. Denny

Untitled

Grab the day.
Don't say
That mountain in my way
I will climb tomorrow.
That field I need crop can another year lie fallow.
Strike in your piton now. Plough, and go forth and sow.
Grab the day.

Grab the day.
Don't say
That ocean I must cross I'll leave to another tide.
That objective which I seek for now in limbo can abide.
Cast off your ropes and sail, use breeze present lest you fail.
Give up on inactivity.
Grab the day.

It's been my fate.
In pursuance of my dream to ever watch and wait.
But you should grab the day.
For as life depends upon a heartbeat.
Then comes its absence if next moment, that pump should cease.
Then friend to grab, it is far too late.

A. J. Dalton

Kingfisher

I saw a kingfisher.
On that warm, soft summer afternoon.
A streak of blue; electric blue
Against the shining waters of the Dorset Stour,
The meadows dreaming round the quiet river banks.
A field of flax, misty blue, paled against the flight
Of that vivid rainbow flash, skimming
O'er the river's bright reflections. Trees, cows, clouds,
The tower of Winborne Minster, still and calm,
Complete the rural scene. In all that quiet beauty
I, now near my three score years and ten,
Never having had this joy before,
saw a kingfisher.

Pamela I. Bartlett

Laughing Times

No more this earth shall men Adar,
The chores to hasten to the silent call,
Nor woman to the kitchen flee to share,
That ever sounding bell of times to fall.
The cook is also crock at all the needs,
In passive times the crackles festival,
Sing the battle songs as swarms of feeds,
As pots and pans glow to light the table.
Then fishers of men evoke to do more;
Than chuckle again to lose ones overall,
to wives of next door to sing galore,
In all the world His voice to echo all.
To laugh and kiss the clover stone.
Or by decree enhance the jungle tone.

J. E. Richards

Victims

I am a Victim, I live all alone.
I am a victim when they steal all I own.
I am a victim asleep in my bed.
I am a victim, I wish I was dead.

I am a victim, I'm old and I'm frail.
I am a victim, my home is my jail.
I am a victim, my room is my cell,
I am a victim living in hell.

I am a victim, beaten and bruised.
I am a victim, I've been abused.
I am a victim, the court looks at me.
I am a victim, my tormentor walks free.

I am a victim, another statistic.
I am a victim of someone sadistic.
I am a victim, listen, for my sake.
I am a victim, how much more must I take?

Cris Ryan

Lusus Naturae

A day like any other day
Previous to this one;
Only this one will change my life
Forever!
All days change my life; but this one is inexorable,
Lacking all mercy; cruel, abusive in its insidious chill.
Long term illness is diagnosed and my animacy is joyless.
My innermost organs tighten in distressed panic
As outwardly I pledge to dispatch the lusus naturae;
This intruder,
This multiple sclerosis that, if I let it, will take away
Not only my dreams, my plans - but mostly my womanhood
and corrode family life.
God gave me the fortitude to face the inevitable future...
And now - thirty years from that fateful day,
Despite the horrors of those initial grievous prognostications,
I can smile and believe the pledge I outwardly made
Was worth all the tears I could have shed.

Rosemarie Evans-Hodge

A Tribute To Robbie Burns

If Robbie was alive today
I don't know what he would say
At the changes in the farming toil
They're even digging now for oil.

But not a horse to draw the plough
A mechanical monster does that now
The mousie never would of been seen
From the windscreen of this big machine

No wooden plough to turn the sod
But a big iron monster "oh my God"
The reek from it does nip your een
In Robbie's time the air was clean

The lassies tae have changed their style
Mascara'd een a dark we guile
Nae sack cloth dresser or hairy shirts
But high heeled sheen and mini skirts

Twa hunder years and mair have gone
Since first you wrote that immortal song
It's sung by all the world around
A lang syne is that happy sound

A. Howitt

Masquerade

Magnificent Ships go sailing by,
Disguised as clouds up in the sky,
Mountains peeked with cream white snow,
Billow softly as they flow.

What a joy to stand and stare,
To watch the castles in the air,
Some silver-lined and some tinged blue,
Fluffy, wispy, breezing through.

Silhouetted by the sun,
Buffalo clouds appear to run,
Then gathered round them like a shroud,
Come lots of full and fluffy clouds.

Pleasantly clouds gently stray,
Across the heavens day by day,
Oft' they disappear from view,
And leave the skies a starling blue.

As night falls, clouds congregate,
Clouds like to gather when it's late,
They fill the skies then the moon comes through,
Turning then a greyish hue.

Pamela J. Layzell

E=MC2

Bright sparks we enter into seeming reality
For how long we know not, nor ought of lives past.
So the why and the wherefore lying always in mystery
Why this family, this country, this body thus cast?

Reality deepens, egged on by life's passing
There go the teens, the struggle and the trials;
Prejudice comes with divisions and trauma
Varied experience shapes our journey and styles.

How haphazard life's twists and excursions
Loves and hates mingle on the fast moving track.
One day we stop - it may be retirement
What the gain, what the waste, looking critically back?

But wait, now we see that our sight has deceived us
Our fixed apparatus that shows us the hues
Translates the speed of approaching vibrations
Not really existing, these glorious views?

Beautiful tints in our band of energy
Intended for our participation.
But reality?

Brenda Sharp

Words

Words are heard and used by people everywhere,
Words beautifully sung, or solemnly said in prayer,
Words in encouragement, help to promote a job well done,
Words of arrogant self-praise, pleases only one,
Words of rage are strong, but kind words are of compassion,
Words of love to another, may well be laced with passion,
Words in a lovely letter, can show how much you care,
Words offensive, can hurt, and bring about despair,
Words are bad if they defend the breaking of rules,
Words of repentance, are not the words of fools,
Words that are honest, are so easy to say,
Words that are lies, haunt you all the way,
Words solely for gain, when every penny is measured,
Words thinking of others, yield bounties to be treasured,
Words that say "Thank You", fill all with good cheer,
Words which are omitted, may perpetuate drear,
Words can be difficult to friends, relatives or lovers,
Words in simple verse and meter,
    oft surpass all others......

Sid Robertson

Untitled

The years have left her helpless,
Aged lines upon her face,
With a mind that's filled with memories,
She but sit's and stares in space,

Is she to you a chore, a burden,
A number in your book,
Well if so, I plead reach deeper,
Take another look,

This lady who is hard work,
She's a person, just like you,
See deep inside her lonely eye's
That can tell a tale or two,

With concern as years pass by me,
The future brings a tear,
For will I be just a number,
A voice you never hear,

Please I beg, remember career,
This person you now see,
When I'm hard work and helpless,
Remember it's me!

Jacqueline Ann Amodio

Nature's Gifts

Early morning in the woodland
As the sun shines through the trees
Casting shadows dark and long
Birds' songs drift along the breeze
Sounding like a big massed choir
Rehearsing every note and song.

Shimmering leaves that shine like silver
Rustling and murmuring with glee
Seem to say to all below
Come to life and dance with me
Awaken all your little friends
A new day starts to say hello.

The ground below is like a carpet
Of flowers and twigs and leaves
Colours that all seem to mingle
Something only nature achieves
So come all you animals, birds and trees
Rejoice with the flowers in the cool, cool breeze.

V. Culley

Alone

When you are alone.
All, all alone,
No one to talk to,
No one to phone.
Silence all around.
Nothing, not a sound.
When you are alone.
All, all alone.

The washing is finished.
Dishes all done.
No mail has arrived.
A letter, not one.
I hear voices all around.
I try to block out the sound, because I'm alone.
All, all alone.

You see there's people all around me,
Family and friends.
But still I feel this loneliness.
I'm alone.
All, all alone.

Isla Isbister

The Waste Disposal Unit

Under the work top, sat on a chair,
Helen the waste disposal sits there,
her mouth is wide open, she lets out some squeals,
for Mum is above her, an orange she peels,
Mum scrapes out the plates, the left-over stew,
Helen chomps fast as she sits on her pew,
but that's not enough "Give me more please" she begs.
"Oh, very well" says Mum giving her the tea dregs,
this morning's bacon rind, yesterday's custard,
black forest gateau, a dollop of mustard.
Mummie's beef goulash, all lumpy and thick,
"Oh, goodness no, she's going to be sick,
we all stand right back, watch her and wait,
as she burps and she groans and brings back all she ate,
She's silent, then says "It's too good to waste"
And starts licking it up, claiming:
"It adds to the taste!"

Sarah Beech

Hostage

Trapped between two battling forces.
Witness to untold cruelty
Forced to fight for each side
Betrayed by both, nowhere to hide.
Words put into your mouth
Taken away for use as more positive ammo
Wanting to run, nowhere to go
No one listens, people seem blind,
Torn between both, just looking for a way out
Screaming, shouting, moved around
Hostage held, pain reaching
Tears slowly leak out.
Both fighting for the same thing
Yet a peaceful solution just far too much out of reach
Only one way to be free
    Divorce

Antony R. McCaw

The Cathedral

There was a beautiful cathedral that stood upon a hill,
And on that highest point therein she stood so calm and still.
Her walls were so impressive; the spires reached the sky
Her presence was compelling; you could not pass her by
She really was majestic in a soft and gentle way
But there was no mistaking that she ruled each day.
Once inside the large oak doors the peace and love was strong.
And somewhere in the distance was the sound of a song.
Maybe it was God's creation or maybe it was man's;
I only know I loved her the most in all the land.

Enid Deeprose

The Poet And The Actress

That meet, that first look of eyes
the poet and the Actress, inside it is love
nothing less and nothing more
love is gained in sentiments law

When your lips speak your brightest hour
my heart is inflamed, so sublime
so courageous, it is sweet Heaven
on a Theatre of love, the stage is set

Where the Flamingos dance in rhythm
the serenade of a classical love song
a poem of love, fantastic starts rotate
in sweet, sweet glory, you are supreme

A document of worth like a spear of gold
silver rain falls down upon you Madame
your courtly dress in midnight blue
sensitivity and so full of passion

Mighty Roman stars escalate and stain your white Mantle
Mighty Greek columns, Aphrodite's wand
in the ocean depths the Mermaids sing
they sing love to you, Oh yes they do

James S. Cameron

The Letter

Dear Mum, there are bullets flying all around,
And there are men getting shot every day,
To spend our next leave with our families,
Is what the lads all hope and pray.

Things here are far from comfortable,
There's always water in the trench,
We are not far from the First Aid post,
And the wind carries a terrible stench.

None of us get much sleep at night,
Taking turns on sentry guard,
The field rations are not very nice,
Being a soldier at the front, is hard.

Our Sergeant was wounded yesterday,
He was badly shot in the arm,
And he said when all this is over,
He'll return to the peace of his farm.

It's not long now, 'till our next leave is due,
I'll take you and Dad out, we'll have fun,
Well I've got to go, take my turn on guard,
All the best, see you soon, from your son.

D. A. Yarwood

The Kingdom Of Sad

Now I never knew of the kingdom of Sad, so foreign this domain to me. Our daughter had lived in a country of hope where always she wanted to be. There always she'd dream of a vision of fame, of a land just where pain is not known. With always the hope of a much fairer world; these flowers in her heart she had grown.

Why then did she die? Perhaps she had found that this life is so pointless and bad. And we that are left shall eternally roam this sorrowful kingdom of Sad. There is no escape from this land of the lost, no pity shall ever be found. Her words echo still 'Father grieve not for me' but I must so I now tread this ground.

I just cannot live in this dark dismal place, this sorrowful kingdom of Sad. For I must move on to the place she has gone where no more there are dreams to be had. So sad are the tears from a sad broken heart as they fall in this sad barren place. Here, I cannot stay while I still have the hope that one day I again see her face.

For the love that is ours for our dead darling girl, blooms not in the kingdom of Sad. Our love is now pain and our hope is despair, for the friendship of death we'd be glad. This friendship we seek as no solace is found in an alien land cold and mad. In death we are one and our shackles are left in the sorrowful kingdom of Sad.

David Hayward Saye

Living The Life Of Child Sexual Abuse

I feel a great loss, a part of me missing,
The child in me is gone,
The child is part of me I've never known,
The child was taken away the day he touched me in
   the wrong way, the sexual way,
I lost all my childhood, who would I have been
   if I had a normal upbringing
I missed the laughter of a child,
The innocent games I would have played,
The outside I can cope with, the stretch marks I
   can live with,
but not my insides, the fact he had entered me,
My body, the fact he had come inside me,
I'll never be able to live with, part of his body,
In mine, the dirt he releases,
the sweat dripping,
the noise he makes,
He knew what he was doing,
he enjoyed what he did,
   no one to turn to.

Amanda Byott

The Dream Of The Party Thief

Latterly we hold on tight;
So good to see you smile last night.
Somebody seemed to steal your name
And your prize from the party game.
Which later found us in the bin,
Both singing 'knock and I'll come in'.
And so it began with a whirr -
I asked you out, you spoke of her.
So span the penny in the air:
It smashed the light, which made you stare,
But all in vain, for in the dark
You could not see my lover's spark:
A spark which could ignite a room
If only it had time to bloom;
And, without means the fire to douse,
We'd singe our hair and burn the house.
No doubt you'd not forgive the bloom
Who lost your hair in that dark room.
But searching through the bin, you see
The prize, your name, the hair and me.

Emma-Louise Walker

The Village

The village was a small one, full of interest.
Everybody knew you, in working clothes or Sunday best.
There were cottages, an Inn, a church and farms.
A wood, further on, that held its charms.

Flowers in hedgerows and birds' nests too.
There were always plenty of things to do.
Every year it was the same,
In April the cuckoo came.

Lambs were skipping to and fro'
Before the farmer came to mow.
August arrived and the binder came out.
So did the rabbits causing a shout.

The leaves are changing colour now.
And fruit is hanging on the bough.
The Squirrel's seen collecting nuts.
Whilst ploughing's turned the field into ruts

The swallows all have gone away.
But other birds have come this way.
With snow-men now the children play.
And Santa Claus comes on his sleigh.

D. A. Littlewood

Untitled

And when the light is smooth against,
peach down and county cream or cupboards
of acid apple green.
Flooring vandyke, umber, dusty and warm.
If through eyes of mild dew do we perceive life,
as if a floating form with angled arms to gaze,
as if plutonium madness.
The gaze, onto the subtle orange and white
or the rigid blue and indigo.
If a window pane were crystal, geometrisized to engulf an image
of immense sadness, sharing science, parallel,
in unison, breathing for the germ of life,
seeking coherency with microscopic units, man made.
The myriad manifold elements of nature
and nearer we move.
To converse with a blade of grass. Ignition with meat.
Obscurity, but satiating evolution.
Abstraction floats and dwells alone amid reality,
in space abstraction pervades in peace amongst cosmos dominion.

Rod Wood

Requiescat In Pace

Tell me, little sprig of heather,
Bounding from your earthy bed,
Were your roots once warmly nurtured,
From the ageless ones who bled

On this boundless plain still blooming,
Purple shrouds for those who fell
Through sun-lit shafts, warm, golden, glowing,
Carpeting their road through hell.

Tell me poplars tall and slender,
Neath your parasols of green,
Did young hearts life's beat surrender,
For their world that might have been.

Did young eagles gasp their last breath,
For a life not satisfied,
Choked in anger, died in sorrow,
Their tomorrow, now denied.

Stones like sentinels, now guard them.
In their final resting place,
Tell me stones, do they lie easy
As upon our world they gaze.

Pat Farnell

The Storm

The cows stand still in the meadows lush
and slowly there spreads a deathly hush
even the birds in the trees are dumb
awaiting the storm that is to come
then comes the rain is a monstrous sheet
thunder crashing as dark storm clouds meet
lightening spreads across the leaden sky
to show the power of One on high
still peace at last and through golden haze
sun to dry the world for other days.

Minnie Maghie

Flight Of Fancy

Song of the morning, lift me up on feathered wing
Soar with me past floating, cotton clouds.
Drift with me while sunshine fills the earth with golden light.
Then pause - and rock me 'mongst the dancing boughs.

Break the silence with your love song.
Fill my heart with joyous sounds
Of an orchestra and chorus beating time,
As you stretch again and fly away
On journeys seeking out
All the messages that nature bids you find.
Lullaby of evening sweetly crooning as I rest,
While the sun casts shadows in the fading light,
Nestle softly as the moonbeams come to tuck me 'neath your wings
And stardust kisses gently say good night.

Hazel Valencia-Ramos

273

A Child Asleep

The look of serenity, innocence combined,
Curled up in that loving art,
A child asleep in a tumbled bed,
Is a sight to touch your heart.

Hair all rumpled, sheets untucked,
My child you loved so much,
Soft flesh, pink cheeks closed eyes,
Your simple life untouched.

How could that child you scold today,
That loving mass of emotion,
Enough to make you wake him up,
And plead for his devotion

Oh darling I do love you,
Please sleep safely to the morn.
And again your sweet day start afresh,
With my love for you adorn.

Heather Chandler

Obsession

As I see you across the street,
I want to run and kiss your feet.
I get so hot I need to scream,
I sprint and fly up to the stream.

I know exactly when you're near,
From afar I see you clear.
You fill my head with sweet sensation,
I put aside my hesitation.

It's oh so hard to live this life,
Wondering if I'll ever be your wife.
I'm hardly wise you're not even old,
We'll never get together or so it's told.

If I could be with you for just one day,
I know it would be perfect in every way.
You're not a sin in my confession,
You are my true and total obsession!

Caroline Lamb

God's Wonderful Things

God has made some wonderful things,
Like a little baby bird that sings.
The flowers with their smiling faces,
In all such wonderful places.
The trees that sway in the breeze,
Oh! What wonderful things are these.
The sun that lights your face in morning,
The moon that sets before it's dawning,
The rain that makes all things grow,
Oh! What a wonderful place to know.
God has made even you and me,
Oh! How special He really must be.

Nicole Louise Patterson

Christmas Time

We look out of our windows, and what do we see!
Snow drops from heaven covering the trees
Christmas is here, there is no doubt
Dreams of the future begin to sprout
Where are we going? What shall we do?
Another year over the next one is new
Then in come the children excited as ever
They go straight to their presents they are all very clever
Our hearts tend to melt as we sit by the tree
Christmas is for giving this we can see
Thoughts of our loved ones with whom Jesus is living
Thoughts of the poor maybe nothing was given
Those in a famine or in a war zone
Our children call out no stone unturned
So raise your glasses and salute them all
These angels of our time Santa Clause is in their hearts
This cannot be a crime...!

Adrian Norton

The Place Of A Season

The white cold frosts drape the landscape.
Like cool silks.

Grass upright stands.
Frozen against the winds of time.
Trees stark,
    too taut to move.
Dark against the jewels of winter.

The crisp fresh air.
Stinging the flesh.
Clearing the nostrils.

This is the cold exhilaration of time.
The place of a season,
cooling and resting the earth.

Clear starlit nights,
velvet heavens,
crystal moon.

Intoxication of nature.
In winters womb.........

Vivien Pfeiffer-Bowen

Third Generation

Born to this world before your time,
So tiny yet perfect, or velvet your skin,
Brown eyes to see an old face, whose
love for her third generation child,
forever holds sway. To hope that
the old one can stay for a while,
her mind so agile would show you the truth.
Your hospital bed in a land torn in two.
Of kin killing kin what do we tell you.
Soldiers, of which your father is one
watch over your cot with guns in their hands,
for Ireland the land of your birth
no colder place for an English baby on earth
The fears of the old one, they,
are not new, for hers are the fears
from wars one and two,
no third one wants she, for her
third generation so beloved as thee.
One small English baby if you could know how,
with the love of your old one, tell this sordid world how.

Valerie Gray

Christmas Time

*Dedicated to my Mum and Dad, for making
my childhood so very happy. Also Billy,
James, and Katie, may you always be happy
and content in everything you do.*

Christmas time is nearing,
Church bells we'll be hearing,
Celebrating of Christ's birth,
For all the people on this earth,
Presents wrapped from Santa Claus,
Everybody warm indoors,
Fun and laughter, games and toys.
Children making lots of noise,
Open fires burning bright,
Christmas trees all full of light,
Children's faces all aglow,
Sleigh bells ringing in the snow,
Christmas stockings gently hung,
Children's carols softly sung,
Looking out the window pane,
Christmas time is here again.

Shirley Sackett

A Dead Red Rose

A dead red rose, upon a green valley hill,
Has the wilderness of time, now standing still.
Awash are the meadows, like a clown and his mask,
Where betrayal stares back, like reflections of the past.
Alone as a nightmare stood once a wishing well,
This monument of torture, where the last petal fell.
Blackened petal stains trickle downstream,
And brings its death to a landscape's dream.
Life's spirit once flowed, as a cool Summer breeze,
Until hate's raging storm brought this rose to its knees.
These ruins of remembrance stand cold in lonely shame,
Like this rose of life, when life had a name.
In this statue of innocence, a guilty conscience lay,
Upon a darkened heart, where the haunted now prey.
A picturesque treasure, crying like the rain,
Has this soul of peace, now trespassed in pain.
This cascade of desperation, a lonely refugee,
Stands this dead red rose, for that rose is me.

Andrew Wiltshire

Decisions

Decisions, decisions; I don't know where to start!
What to wear? What to eat? What message can I impart?
Life is such a rush and the days just run away,
But there is only one decision, there is only One Way!

Decisions, decisions; where do I go from here?
As the abandoned children need more than the shedding of a tear?
Is it really enough that I set aside some time to pray?
Surely He needs to be in my thoughts every minute of every day!

Decisions, decisions; to speak or not to speak!
To witness for Jesus and perhaps be declared a freak!
God made the decision to give us freedom of choice;
So it is up to me whether I follow that still, small voice!

Decisions, decisions; I sometimes fall flat on my face!
But the answer to it all is Jesus died in my place!
He made my greatest decision and eternal life I did win;
When He chose the cross and defeated satan and sin!

Decisions, decisions; who am I to understand His ways?
And I will search for the answers all the rest of my days!
But this I do know, there is one decision I can make!
That is to follow Jesus and to live my life for His sake.

Susan M. Billington

The Search

When everybody leaves me
I wish they'd never come
They'd never pay respect on me
Respect I never want

This life such a deceitful thing
'cause I've felt many emotions
To fear with, since I was born
The joy I want was never there

I'm searching for myself
try to dig deep in my soul
Want to find my mistakes and sins
I'm sure this search will never end

There is a time when I feel so weak
No one to help no love to support
No body keeps me alive
Not even you!

This searching would be my destiny
I would face everything in this life of mine
Swear that this won't be undone
Forever...

Agatha M. Setiawan

Reflections

Now well past eighty I have time to reflect on days gone by.
I dream once more of childhood days.
Which were happy in lots of ways,
And then I give a sigh
For things past, my family and familiar things,
Our house, my mother always there
Waiting for us after school
A lovely tea to share
So many memories crowd my head
So long ago it seems,
A little tear I think I shed.
It is a lovely dream.

Laurie Watson

"Journey Of The Heart"

While you slept. I walked the stars.
The stars they walked with me.
I watched you sleep, I saw you move.
Beside you I would rather be.
To hold you close. To keep you warm.
To feel at one with you, my love, my life
I miss you
I walked the stars, a path alone
I walked a path alone.
For one wish as I walk this path
For one wish with you.
So we believe in wishes. For all our
Dreams come true.
I walk this path alone. I walk with
Thoughts of you.
I walk this path, through rocky roads
My thoughts, my dreams of you.

Douglas Burns

Untitled

Your lips are like strawberries, rounded and ripe
Your tongue is damp and soothing
Your nose is an extension of your enticing passion
Your eyes show a world beyond meaning.

Your hair is so strong, yet softly styled
To outline your face, so sexy and wild
Your cheeks warm aglow, you smile to tease
Your breath to excite, sensations to freeze.

Your hands are large and gently stroke
This human you've captured and craftily provoked
The groan as you enter into virtual excitement
The flow of your arrival and of your contentment.

These gifts you do bring me from places beyond
Are more than I'd ever wish for
You make me feel like I am alive
You make me feel like me.

Louise Sullivan

The Beauty That Is Wales

How lovely is this land
It seems that God holds in his hand
The mountains bright with snow,
Cottages nestling low, in valleys deep,
All nature seems asleep, in winter,
There, lakes, lonely, away from teeming cities.
A distant hill, the water mill,
It seems that time stand still, yet God is near
In him no fear of life in all its turmoil, and its strife
Evil seems rife, yet God prevails.
Just let me be in Wales
To gather strength from wondrous hills and vales
From eager winding rivers with water falls
And sweeping bays on golden shores,
Knee deep in heather on the moors.
This land of culture and of song,
It is for Wales so lovely that I long,
and God, who made this land,
To hold me also in his hand.

Joyce Adlington

275

A Visit To Flanders Memorial

Mists surround me. Sifting, silent
Through this moonscape earth that covers the black
Huddled ghosts of frozen forgotten armies.

Those stiff muddied ranks of innocence;
Their slow, white-faced beaten filing past the post
Where I dreamed their horror ... what of you now, ghosts?

I ache with grief that men and boys were sent
To such unimaginable deaths; lives tossed, wasted
With breathtaking ignorance onto those
Black blasted flowerless fields of France.

I grieve that I am part of that humanness.
What immortal truth have I missed that so much
Outrageous suffering was part of our necessity?

Ah necessity! How I wish that some bright biblical truth
Swayed me, eased my conscience, assuaged my reason,
But no!

Mortal man, what unthought horrors are yet ours...
I leave you ghosts with fear. I turn my eyes
To the road behind and the road ahead, and wonder:

When? Where? And in which patriot's name?

Tony Jackson

"Ziggy"

She leaps and prances up and down,
She bounces like a rubber ball.
She flings her pliant body
Here, now there,
With infinite grace - as light as air.

Luxuriant whiskers crown her brow,
Her coat is jet, her paws are white.
Each pad the palest pink - on each,
A spot of black,
How delicately fashioned in this cat.

Pale is her chin, her eyes are green,
At her tail end, a puff of snow,
Reaching for windblown leaves,
Imaginary foes,
She stands and dances on her toes.

She crunches in the grass, she springs,
She rolls upon her back with joy.
She climbs.
She stalks and hurrying out until, dear beat,
Quite suddenly, she drops and falls asleep.

Leslie Grant

Strength And Survival

On the peak of a lowly mountain,
Amongst golden-leaved trees
A beautiful creature with immaculate flight,
Swoops high over timeless seas

The rich reddy-brown of her widespread cloak,
The curve of her deadly beak
The intelligent eyes with the stone cold stare,
The intense and spine-chilling shriek

She dives to the ground as she spreads her claws,
To catch her fear-stricken prey
In the cold, snowy night she protects her young,
Then hunts their food in the harsh, windy day

Every creature fears her on those dark, mysterious heights,
But she has her fears too, for man has prized her meat
And though she has unchallenged defence,
Her species has tasted defeat

On the peak of a lowly mountain,
With golden trees that climb high
A family of strength and survival-
The eagle must never die.

Kate Evans

Untitled

I went beachcombing along the shore,
Can you guess the things I saw?
A mermaid's purse on a surf of waves,
A hermit crab that hid for days,
The shell of a cuttlefish on the shore,
A topshell, and skeletons galore!
A stargazer with electric eyes waiting patiently to paralyse,
Some ragged rocks that nearby were ending their days,
Very interesting in many ways.

As I walked nearer to the cliffs
The sand nearby started to drift, I heard a hiss!
A sidewinder swallowing a lizard! What bliss!
Further on, a Skua flew onto a rock
While angry birds soared in a flock, but the skua still did his job,
He snatched their fish one by one
Leaving the angry birds fishing in the sun.

The sun was setting and it was late, and as I walked through my gate
Watching the day come to an end, I turned the path at the bend
And said to myself, 'What a lovely day'!
And wished the world would stay this way.

Ben Scott

Personal Feelings

Now someone you love is about to die
Getting ready for that world in the sky
There's nothing you can do, nothing you can say,
If only I knew how I'd kneel down and pray
The seconds go like minutes, the minutes like hours
It's not the one whose dying
It's me that is the coward
If I could cheat God on that forthcoming day
I'd gladly give my life so this person could stay.

K. Hollings

Spring

A blackbird sings in nearly apple tree,
And daffodils dance by the window sill.
The long cold winter days ate gone.
And spring is here, our hearts with joy to fill.

The sun is high, and all is fresh and green,
The singing of the birds is loud and clear.
Lambs in the meadow, run and jump and play.
And spring is here, once more new life is dear.

Blossom on the apple tree, and may upon the thorn.
Such beauty all around us, and it's free.
Tiny chicks, and ducks, and birds in nests,
And spring is here, life's good for you and me.

Sylvia Woodrow

One For The Ode

A modern poem sounds like prose
extolling fate's eternal woes,
it rarely scans, it doesn't rhyme,
the punctuation's serving time
with phrases in recurrent strife
and sentences reduced to life,
wire-barbed like prickly porcupines,
then sprinkled with half-empty lines.
Some enigmatic choice of word
at times seems flagrantly absurd,
a pool of submarine lampoons
awash with dark mysterious runes;
no simple doggerel or sonnet
(you can bet your shirt upon it),
a theme that's often hard to find,
you have to plumb the author's mind.
So tell the writer, 'please forego it,
for goodness' sake don't be like me, I'm
one awful poet!'

Bob Charlesworth

Prue

Your loving, caring, sharing ways,
Help me forget my lonely days,
You always make us so at home,
No wonder we can never roam,
Although long miles keep us apart,
You're always near, deep in my heart,
We've had many laughs and shed some tears,
You always help us through our fears,
No wonder John became your groom,
When you alone walked in the room,
So now you've come to fifty five,
Still so much beauty on your side,
There's so much more I'd like to say,
But I'll save it for another day,
To write this verse has been real bliss,
To you, dear Prue, my birthday wish.

R. C. Ward

Son Leaving Home...

On waking I felt it
Heavy
It wasn't there yesterday
But now it's here, silence silence.
I can feel it all through the house
Can't touch it though
This invisible cloak spreads itself
Like a lion stretching in the sun
I stand and listen silence silence
He's gone
Not here anymore silence silence.
I treasured him near
His lovely presence my son my son.
now stands on his own
Learning of life's truths fears the unknown.
Presence gone removed itself
Left me with silence
Cloaked through the house
Can't touch it though silence, silence.

Marjorie Ann Warden

A Reason To Live

Throughout my life I have learn't
Of all that God has done,
That he made us the earth and
    gave us birth,
but how much is life worth?

He gave us the world so bright,
With the sun for our daylight.

The Lord with all his strength and might,
Gave us the sense to read and write.

He gave us the flowers, he gave us the trees,
He gave us the wind with its cool breeze.

But do the people of the earth
Appreciate their given birth?

Jeanette Delmore

The Quiet Coming

He comes- the gentle master- with beauty,
All healing in his wings,
Assuaging the heart's hunger.
His touch upon your brow brings Peace
All stillness is there.
So quiet, so gentle is his coming,
That even unaware it seems to you
The whole of life is vastly changed,
Transformed, and lifted up beyond all
    recognition.
His life, within your heart
So gently stirring,
Awakes a great soul-joy deep there within,
And love, great love, is born anew.

Eileen Roth

Exams

I dread it, really dread it.
I hate any exam, every single bit.
Whether it's Math, Science or English,
Just the thought of it makes me feel a little bit tinglish.
I hate sitting there in a freezing cold hall,
At those horrible desks that are either too short or too tall.
The hall fills up with nervous looking people,
Slowly, sitting at their chairs like dripping glue or treacle.
Watching their faces, some happy, some sad, some really nervous.
Some that look so silly they'd be able to join a circus.
Suddenly the examiner comes in and starts explaining about the exam,
And then someone comes in and the door goes "slam".
The tension in the hall is still building up,
The examiner says "You may now begin, and good luck"
Question after question, page after page,
All the answers running round inside your head like a mad rage.
The clock ticking by, seconds, minutes, hours.
Waiting for it to end, like watching a weeping flower.
And then just like that, it's all over and done,
Let's celebrate, let's party and bang those drums!

Kelly Etridge

Mountain Of Life

Windswept crags and rocky slopes,
Icy outcrops stretching high,
Face the climber with his ropes,
Reaching upwards for the sky.

The mountain of life holds more for me
With all its pitfalls to be faced,
Than any slippery shingled scree,
Which climbing trips are interlaced.

Some lucky ones have from birth
An easy ride and all too soon,
As they rise, we see the worth
Of supping from the silver spoon.

Not for them life's honest toil,
Working hard to pay the rent,
But what is wealth? If it should spoil
A character's development.

Pathways to the pinnacle of success,
Lie not in moments of fleeting pleasure,
Nor lavish lifestyle's sweet caress,
But deep in the foothills of endeavour.

J. A. Smith

A Slight Misdemeanour

We all collect memories, as we wander down life's way
Some sad, some happy and some funny ones - day by day
I've picked out one which I hope will make you smile
Life is so full of cares and woes - forget them for a while

I can remember seeing a strange object in my washing machine
My husband's glasses shining brightly, seemingly none the
    worse for where they had been
I took them out quickly, thinking 'gosh' I'll be in the doghouse
    for this
'cause when I examined them, they were missing one lens, so I
    knew something was amiss

I took out one sheet and pillow case, gently shaking each one,
    with care
But no luck, the missing lens I couldn't find; it just wasn't there!!!
With my brow covered in sweat, the other sheet I shook
Thought my luck had run out, so didn't dare to look

But snuggled in one corner there lay the lens whole!!!
    And without a crack
Better dry those glasses and the lens before hubby gets back!!!
He soon fixed them and still wears those glasses to-day
'Caused a lot of laughter, and here's a tip
Your glasses will last longer, with a persil
    boil/wash dip!!!!
Getting to be old and senile but must keep a stiff upper lip!!!

J. Greenacre

Seventeen

I stood there confronted by the ones I loved,
I saw feelings and emotions that I knew not of,
Nor understood.
A surge of fear and anger rose from beyond me.
I turned and ran,
But only to the sanctuary of my room.
A room that once was warm, cosy and welcoming.
Become cold, dark and treating.
The see through walls that once protected me from all
evil had shattered.
And evil came flooding in.
I broke down in continuous tears,
Lost and alone.
Lost in the maze of human life.
Yet I knew one thing
I no longer belonged here.
Not in this house nor in this town.

Samantha Madge

May Field In Autumn

Animals calling, birds squawking,
All in the Mayfield Valley,
Sun, like a ball of fire, shining on me,
Cool fresh water that glistens like a diamond.
Fresh air to breathe into my lungs,
Squirrels darting from here to there,
Like a dot to dot puzzle,
Playing hide and seek,
Long walks through the meadows,
Peaceful sounds I hear,
Feeling special like the queen of the woods,
I feel happy,
I feel as though I want to sing like a bird,
Play like the squirrels,
Wash my face in the stream,
Wake up to myself like a dream,
I feel clean, so fresh, so tired,
Time to go now, wish I could stay,
Maybe you'd like to come and join me,
.....Till then.....

Lorna Elizabeth Wood

Inside, Outside

The plain glass window, holds many memories that
  are dear to me,
The feeling of nature, and of being free,
Many hours did I spend gazing to the clouds from that
window,
Not the feeling of being trapped, from the outside,
As the feeling of being on the inside looking out
  had been quite comforting,
So now, when I see that plain glass window,
I thank it for teaching me to appreciate the nature
  and the freedom,
Now it is the opposite,
I am on the outside looking in,
I fear that this is the way of life,
As I am just a face among the crowd,
Not a voice with an opinion,
Just an outsider,
How I long to be back on the inside of that plain
  glass window.

Cara Jane Murphy

Moment

A somnolent Sunday afternoon,
Tabloid tales of busty blondes forgotten,
The old man's watery eyes close,
Gravy congeals on a chipped dinner plate,
And the sadness of eternity is caught
In the tangled leaves of a geranium.

David Buckley

A Faithful Dog

You spread your hairs all over my new suite
You walked over my clean kitchen floor with your muddy feet
You had a comfy basket to lay your head
Yet you preferred to lie on our double bed

Every time I sat down to eat a meal
You lay under the table beside my heel
You knew when I was down, you seemed to understand
You laid your head upon my lap and pushed your wet nose
  beneath my hand

You were unfamiliar with babies till the grandchildren came along
You loved and protected them as if they were your own
You let them put their arms around your neck, even pull your whiskers
You never really seemed to mind because you knew they
  shared their biscuits

You expected little in return for your loyalty and trust
Your meals and constant company were all you ever asked
Your scruffy coat held a heart of gold and a brilliant temperament
You were such a character that you made friends everywhere
  you went

Now when I walk through the garden gate, I open the door
  and stand back and wait
But you're no longer there to bound out and welcome me home
Sam, how much I miss you now that you have gone.

P. Moyes

Saying Goodbye

I never thought it would hurt so much for me to say Goodbye
I never thought the tears could flow so freely from my eyes
I never knew I'd see the day my heart would break in two
I never knew I could love someone the way that I loved you.

I never knew how I could feel so lonely and so cold
I never realized how much I'd miss your heart of gold
I didn't know how much I loved your carefree, foolish grin
I didn't know how much I loved the personality within.

I never thought I'd see the day when a song could make me cry
I never thought a picture could bring tears to my eyes
I never knew how I could feel the pain so deep inside
I never knew the hurt would be too obvious to hide.

Two hearts, two minds, one love that dies, as we both have to part
Reflections of sadness in your eyes, revealing your helpless heart.
The sun has set, the world has turned, Forever is in the past
A lifetime may pass me by, but my memories will last.

A sad goodbye, A final kiss, one last time alone
My sorrow cutting like a knife, the sea of tears has grown
The past is old, and time has left alone, two empty hearts
But the love will never leave those two souls, so far apart.

Rani Dabrai

A Rainbow Of Peace

As you meander along the glen floor
Your feet heading towards the distant shore,
Stop and let your wandering gaze,
Enjoy nature's rainbow, as it falls into place.

Looking to the hills gathered around
Cascading waterfalls replenish the ground
Where amethyst droplets, strung across heather,
Radiate riches for Bumble Bees to gather.

Pinks and whites, forget-me-not blues,
All combine for a spectacular view.
Warm, pine, scent, from the trees above
Hangs in the air with the freshness we love.

Sky and sea, sapphire blue,
The sun, a distant orb, a golden hue,
A tangy, salt breeze drifts across the hills,
Cooling the body and disturbing the still.

Sand glistening, far and away
Small wavelets lapping, keeping the heat at bay
Toes wriggling with anticipation
Of cool, damp sand and the freedom sensation!

Heather Ainley

Splinters Of The Mind

I have built a prison to house the lowest of the low.
I have bricked up all the exits,
He has nowhere to go.
I have robbed him of his memory of what had gone before,
I captured all his confidence when I laid down the law.
I drove him to destruction,
I pointed out the way.
I made him think he's useless,
With nothing good to say.
He worries for his weakness,
He waits to take a fall.
His anger can amuse me and justify it all.
He tells me he can take it and I know he lives a lie.
For all that I have done to him he never asks me why.
He tells me he's a hero and I know him as a fraud.
His doggerel disgusts me.
I read it when I'm bored.
I know one day I'll kill him and then maybe we'll be free.
He steals glances from my mirror and yes, I know. He's me.

Gareth Martin

The Wind And The Sun.. From Aesop's Fables...

One day the wind and the sun were having a chat,
'twas nothing important, about this and that
when they spotted a man coming over the hill
wearing a nice big coat, because the day was chill.
The wind said "I'll soon whip that coat off his back
I reckon I can do it in five minutes flat.."
"OK the first five minutes are yours" said the sun
Sensing that this promised to be great fun,
The wind puffed up his cheeks and he blew and blew
and really chilled this poor traveller through and through
so he hugged his big coat around him more and more
(where he had it loosely wrapped around before)
The sun stirred himself and to the wind said
"Now watch how easy it is to coax instead"
With a smile he popped out from behind a big cloud
then the chilled traveller was heard to say aloud
"How lovely it is to feel the warming sun"
and then straight away, off his big coat did come.

Valerie Ovais

Make A Friend Of Fear

When you find yourself all alone
Tired, weary, very ill and afraid
When you have faced the truth
You know the end of life is very near

When you find yourself all alone
Without a loved one or a friend
Stay calm, this is no time to lose your head
Fear not, for there will be a hand
Outstretched for you
A voice will say, come dear friend
We will travel to-gether to a new
Life at journey's end.

Sheila Lucy Wills

Talkative Echoes

My tongue is laden
Speak for me voices of the heart
Sing for me nightingales of our throats
In my sight are the talkative silences of stabbed visions
Haunting muses of fabled dreams

But in the wisdom of my tongue
  Is the muted rhythm of crackling riddles
Between my teeth are the kernels
  Of our paths in the wandering sands
And in my frail limbs
  The cramped flippers of a sutured song
  Clotting in the wisdom of my veins

Voices of my pulse, speak for me
Prancing spirits of the rheumy air
Intone my chorus in the polyglot threnody of your whispers.

Kiki Ikhisemojie

Feelings Of Pain

As he holds his empty bowl towards you,
He looks upon you with eyes of sadness.

No gleam in his eye,
Only a smile to hide his pain,
A beautiful face without a name.

Beyond his self, he feels no pain.

The dryness of his mouth,
Where no food has passed,
Still, the soil taste from birth.

He shows no joy, no happiness,
What sort of life has this child lived?
Terror, pain, all the blood shed of which he has seen.

The smell of fear,
No smell of food,
This child shall smell no food,
Ever.

What do you do to help?
You ignore his cry for help and walk away.
To your luxuries of home,
But he has none.

Ellena Marsh

Berry Tree

There is a berry tree in my father's farm
With green leaves and full of charm
Under its shade I play
Sitting in its branches bird's hail
Watching them I always say
Why don't I fly and in the air I stay
One red breast so elegant and fine
Moving her head and looking so prime
As if waving at me
Why are you here asking she
Playing her I throw a stone
Which strikes at her bone
There she comes down tumbling
And her last breath abandoning
Cursing me and remembering this I always cry
For loss of one life, why should not I die
And I always pray for this earth to thrive
For all the charm from the earth we drive
So save, save oh! Man the world from harm
With love and affection keep it warm

Sarwan Singh Deol

Seasons Analogy To Love

Winter heralds a passing,
Of summer loves blossomed warmth,
And sweet springs secure light,
Traded for dank damp dark

Winter's deep dead scene,
Bitter, lonely and void,
Can life (forget love) survive here
It does!

Carcasses of trees are all I see,
Listless stone sculpture,
Art in a mausoleum,
Is this all Loves left...?

Dead!,
And as my hope drys up,
And my weary soul thirst
Spring.

Radiant buds, hope, faith- love?
The skeleton forms have broken.

If something's to flourish, it first must rot to essence, to roots,

Patience is needed, for this tests faith, the will to live, the hope
to Love.

R. Rajkowski

Evanescent

As evanescent as a bluebell in a wood,
As dew on the petals of a meadow flower,
As a bubble from a fountain's gushing,
So I am lost in your beautiful power.

Your misty presence obscures the scene,
It dulls the senses, numbs the mind,
The filigreed clouds part in the lilac sky,
You're a fleeting statement of mankind.

A candle flame, a tower of chimney smoke,
A glittering image in a snow scene,
The holy and the mistletoe berries,
Your beauty, though outward, is supreme.

As the sun sets in a silent sky,
As the flower withers at night,
As the snow melts into declivities,
As the image sinks in my sight.

You grow old, a withered stump of time,
Your hair thins, your eyes narrow for Dante's flames,
A cheek grows red, old gnarled fingers,
But your beauty is also inner, its light remains.

Alethea Andrews

My Soldier Story

He stopped and gazed up to the stars,
Then on to his own body scars,
At the death and misery all around him
Worn out face, and an ache, in every limb.
He thought, what am I doing here
With grasses so green, so far, yet so near,
Your country, a war, go fight for it they said,
His thoughts of Mary tucked up in bed.

In trenches the stench of death all around
Yet, what was that, what was that sound
Singing voices, joyous singing all around,
A warm glow in his own body deep
The feeling of warm blood began to seep
The end of the war, oh joyous love,
As he closed his eyes to look above
Come my son, one look at Mary before you sleep
And the tunnel opened, it beckoned.

Patricia England

Foreign Travel

World travel?, oh yes it's exciting
Going to places so far away.
Spain, Italy, and the Americas,
In luxury hotels to stay.

The sphinx, the pyramids of Egypt,
And China's amazing great wall,
In India the Taj-Ma-Al?,
Oh yes, I've seen them all.

Cape town, and table mountain,
Australia's barrier reef,
And the beautiful Galapagos Islands.
Are all wondrous beyond belief

Of course, in fact, I've never been
Outside the fair British Isles
But on T.V. I have seen them all
From my chair I have travelled for miles.
But I have been to Bonnie Scotland,
To Wales, and the Isle of Wight,
Also to Devon and Cornwall,
And all were a beautiful sight.

Elsie M. Whipp

The Photo On The Mantle

The photo on the mantle is a memory cased within
A shining, gleaming, gilded, fragile picture frame
And though the memories held therein
Are yours and mine, ours aren't the same

As I glance around the room
I see that special snap
A snap that brings back memories
And as if from a water tap

They come flooding through my mind
They warm the inner side of me
As they brim me up with cheer
And help me clearly, clearly see

Just how a very special photograph
Can flick a memory switch
And radiate a warming, happy glow
That will always pleasantly enrich

A memory bank that's overflowing
With dreams that once did soar
And of all the days and times gone by
The photo on the mantle, is a dream that's held in ore

Jane Carr

Venice

Existing in a time warp, dream city wedded to the sea.
Peeling, painted facades, imaginative cardboard cut-out,
   a place of fantasy.
A theatre awaiting actors, mirage of strawberry and vanillas,
See a marshmallow confection resting on pastel filigree pillars.
Oriental style domes rise from the lagoon, interiors like eastern bazaars.
Bells ring and sing all day long in this changeless Shangri-la,
And all around water fathomless depths, a million shades of
   blues and greens.
Icing sugar palaces trailing green lace hems, yesterday's has-beens.
Deep, deep shimmering water harbouring a hundred histories
Its waterlogged heart hugging centuries of mysteries.
Everywhere gliding, gliding black-shining gondolas silver
   ferros at the fore
Symbol of the city sleek elegant shapes to last for evermore.
Seasons come and go, early in the year a carnival face, masked
   figure anonymity preserved
An enigma in sumptuous costume a place in history reserved.
Next gaudy summer trippers make a lurid postcard scene,
Tarnishing the fabric of this fading magical dream.
Then swirling eerie mists swoop, twirl and writhe from the lagoon,
Ballet of white cobweb shrouds that fade away too soon.
Maybe a figment of some God's imaginings dreamed up for
   mortals in a flush of pity.
La Serenissima, is she real? Incredible, drowning crumbling city.

Janet A. Stevenson

'Tell Me How?'

How can there be thunder without the clash,
How can there be lightning without the flash,
How can there be night without the day,
How can there be stars without the ray,
How can there be shores without the wave,
How can there be peace without the brave,
How can there be Spring without the flower,
How can there be Time without the hour,
How can there be eyes without the gaze,
How can there be mist without the haze,
How can there be feelings without the care,
How can there be breathing without the air,
How can there be centuries without the year,
How can there be sorrow without the tear,
How can there be hope without the dream,
How can there be pain without the scream,
How can there be light without the glow,
How can there be goodbye without the hello,
How can there be morning without the dew,
How can there be love without the you!

S. Hany

280

Life Is For Learning

Life is all about learning
It's not good to sit there yearning
Your negative reaction to life creates emotion
Then off to the doctor you go for a 'potion'

Look at the flower, it does not cower
Be strong and send out love by the hour
Think of a tree or even the sea
What beauty there is for you and me

Do not criticize your family and friends
Or rifts this way will never end
Anger is for those who do not understand
It's best to give a helping hand

Don't scold yourself if you get it wrong
Better just to sing a song
Remember life is about learning
Not about sitting there yearning

Joey Green

Life Ever After

A slap, a cry, where am I, light makes me squint.
Faces peering over me, buzzing in the ears, where am I.
I've come from a warm cosy place, my poor body tingles in the cold.
Someone is rubbing me, now I'm wet all over, more rubbing.
A big face peering down on me.
What are those strange noises, swish, swash.
Left all alone, come back, don't leave me! My mouth is drooping,
A loud scream, is that me?! More swish, swashing, being
lifted high.
Being wrapped in something warm, can't move my arms.
A little sob, someone patting my back, feels nice.
Being placed in empty arms. A nice warm place I'm at,
Two lips smacking into my cheeks. Peace at last,
Perfect peace, I've just been born.

I. K. Skinner

An Object In The Sky

The stars were bright, glowing in the sky, the breeze of cold
fresh atmospheric air plunged against the cold light green
mountain. A dark vehicle slammed on the brakes as a
gentle folk emerged, glazing in deep thought as he looked
up to the stars imagining thoughts of a childhood dream of
travelling among the bright glowing stars, thinking about
the possibility of life on other planets. The lights of his
vehicle reflected among the dense midnight sky reflecting an
object miles away approaching nearer and nearer, leaving
all possibilities circulating around his vivid head. He
turned with the wind grabbing his shoulders, leaving movement
difficult, from the south a blue light shone into his eyes
leaving the man blind, he cried with discomfort, he wiped
his eyes noticing a metallic circular object hovering around, the
object froze him with a force field. The object teleported
and kidnapped him, the object left at great speed heading
for a world of dreams.

Geoffrey Connor

A Gambler's Prayer

God, I have gambled, tried one last fling,
Gambled more than I thought and lost everything.
I sometimes feel that my life is cursed,
For trying for first, I came off worst,
My family is leaving, I deserve all I've got,
By trying to win, I've now lost the lot,
Despite the brave face, and this is the part,
Underneath all, I'm breaking my heart,
God, one thing I ask, please let them see,
A good husband and father I did try to be,
No excuses, nothing more can I say,
For trying that last fling, the price I must pay,
I love them, God, watch over them please,
And help me to cure this gambler's disease.

J. K. Mercer

David, A Child Of Our Times

Mine was a short life, a little stay, a happy fleeting May,
A golden visit for a while, a playful path, a sunlit smile,
A passing, transient, unsurpassing,
Joyful, toyful Peter Pan, I never grew to be a man,
At night I took my teddy-bear to bed, they called me curly-head,
I was Cath's brother, oh my mother!
Daddy made a play-pen, but how I loved the forest den!
Across the road a spell it wove for all the children of the grove,
I heard them call my name, come David play our forest game,
And there was I a little boy who longed to share their forest joy.
Oh magic to be three and play across the road and back again
for tea!

I did not know what could be fall me as I heard their voices call me,
Wistful, wishful, me and Teddy, free as a bird on limb so ready.
Swift as an eagle on the wing, I ran - and then a swerve, a
screeching ring!
It was a bitter thing, or did an angel sing?
No more to run, no more to fly, my playmates saw me die,
They said it was a Mini car, oh forest near, oh forest yet so far!
There was no mark upon my head, but on the road my blood ran red,
And me and my poor teddy-bear, we both lay dead.

Jean Mooring

Life's Song

Have you heard the leaves sing
with the rustle of the breeze?
Have you heard the loud wind
as it powers through the trees?

And have you heard the streamlet
rippling through the mossy lea
Or heard a river noisily
fall plunging to the sea?

You may have heard the small birds
making music as they fly
Or heard the sound that little
creatures make as you pass by.

Have you heard the sound of children
as their merry voices ring
In happiness and harmony
as sweet their songs they sing?

If you have heard some of these sounds
when walking on your way
My friend, you've heard the voice of life
and God's been in your day.

Jane Gilbert

K2 The Mysterious Power Of A Dream

There is a place in life or dreams,
Alison Hargreave believed.
When K2, beckoned its cong-figured shadow
At the suburbian gal, she did not flinch,
But soared like an eagle ever confident and
Upward, towards the fulfilment of a dream.

To capture a dream
Alison stands with the mighty whose tasks
Were of a herculean order.
Pursue, answered fair maidens concerned
With his safety "It is better to die like a
Hero than is live like an ox in a stall"
Upward, towards fulfilment of a dream.

The dream now captured,
Alison is the rock of inspiration.
Posthumously awarded, she lies in death
Magnificent by her enduring spirit casting
Its own shadow, beckoning those who believe
Upward, towards a dream.

Ellen Oldfield

Rain In Sarajevo

It's raining, it's raining, again today,
But nothing grows here now, any way,
The world it is watching, but soon turns away,
It's white hot metal, again falling, here today.

The constant suffering, the endless pain,
People are dying, who feel the rain,
Listen the screaming, again and again,
It's white hot metal, their only pain.

As darkness approaches, the screaming they call,
Loved one's are lonely, it's desperate, they fall,
White hot metal, lights up the night sky,
Another lost loved one, but who's left to cry.

The ground it is sodden, bright red to the sight,
Proof that hot metal, has had a good night.

Steven P. Denton

Untitled

My minds such a versatile thing,
one day it is Autumn the next day it's Spring,
one minute it's falling apart,
I just stick it together and try not to start
to let it all get too on top,
for if it gets going who knows where it'll stop;
The next day my minds out of sight,
to be with me's such a delight,
I finish each deed in remarkable speed,
but I wake up each morning not knowing
which way my mind will be going,
so I've learned to take the good with the bad,
the happy the sad, the sane with the mad,
at the same time I am glad,
for I've more of a mind than most ever had.

Michelle Anne Ridewood

Romeo's Love For Juliet

Summer's ripening breath, so sweet as true
love passion.
I bring to thee the envious moon and the
fairest stars there are.
As honourable as a bright angel's love and as
wonderful and complete as a maiden's blush.
What's in a name? So sweet and so pure
I belong to the blessèd moon.
I am proof against their enmity by my fair maid's beauty.
I am a dear saint that's been proroguèd of marriage.
Love goes towards love as birds would sing.
Dear love I refuse thy name by your brightness.
My nièsse and her wantons bird are the perfection of her beauty.
Love as deep with compliment and as wonderful
as lightning on a silken thread.
Merchandise so loving as a maiden's cry
are all put together to make her beauty.

Sara Jones

The Coming Of Spring

Out of the mist's the Unicorn came
Fairy Queen atop with fiery mane
Out of the tree's the wood nymph's appear
With fairies and elves hovering near

Gathered in a clearing below the tree
We all pay homage upon one knee
Then with a wave of her magical hand
She bring's spring back to our mystical land

Nodding her head a wood nymph sing
Whilst fairies and pixies dance in rings
Up on the hill an Elf Plays a harp
and in to the night fireflies dart

Then into the trees all start to fade
The fairy queen her departure made
Everything gone, but the coming of spring
And of course those fairy rings.........

Angela Massey

Helping Angels

My first day here, my heart was strong,
These poor kind folk had done no wrong,
They had no fight, they wanted peace,
Their families safe, they thought they'd keep.
I didn't know what to expect
As I went on and helped the next,
Children scared and crying in pain,
Cute little faces without a name.
"Hold me tight", they seem to say....
....they didn't make another day.
A mother is dying and so is her baby,
She reaches out "save me, save me".
Sometimes the stench is too much to bear,
We are locked together in a cruel nightmare.
The bodies are ploughed into a heap,
This is a time when strong men weep.
My tenth day here, my heart is weak,
I close my eyes, but I cannot sleep.
I think of home and how lucky I am,
I stand today a humble man.

Pam Davies

Ghost Writer

The greatest Dane that ever was - or wasn't - as the case may be
Was of a melancholic bent, since he could not decide if he
Was meant to be or not to be and thus form his life-style plan
And anyway, this waverer was created by an Englishman.

The keenest brain that ever set itself to solve foulest crimes
And foil the machinations of miscreants in bygone times
His deerstalker and meerschaum pipe and glass he ne'er forsook
But sadly only wrought his works in the pages of a book.

The bear a noble creature is, of legendary strength
On coats of arms and shields he features rampantly the length
And breadth of Britain, but out childhood memories retain
A fat bear fond of honey and of very little brain.

Alice and the Mad Hatter for ever will take tea
And Peter Pan and Wendy struggle to set free
The captives of the dreaded pirate, Captain Hook,
Heroines and heroes brave - but only a book.

So perhaps the smartest move, if you intend to live forever
In our imaginations, is to be indolently clever
Let some writer take the strain and scribble furiously,
And sit back and take it easy, and never really be.

Campion Carter

The Priceless Gift

Passion and promise brought life from my body,
A son for the family to carry the name.
Bathed softly and sung to, clasped into comfort,
Raised to love life, be the best, make your claim.

I prayed you'd grow slowly seeking out knowledge
And savour delights of youth's swift passing haze.
Plasticine, alphabet, numbers and bicycles.
At ten you were grown in the space of one day.

Tossed into adulthood you became carer,
Your young face so serious; mine drenched in tears.
Squaring your shoulders you promised to care for me,
Breaking my heart with the gift of your years.

We're not always masters of our good intentions,
Outside influence oft interferes.
The shield and protection I should have given you,
You took on yourself to quiet my fears.

I remember a baby, a child and that moment
When we became equals and you understood,
But, Oh, I would change it flesh of my body.
You bravely accepted it. I never could.

Jan Nicholls

Such A Love

There is a love which thunders
And roars with mighty voice.
With wondrous force into my life it flows.
Such a love as joyously o'erleaps
All obstacles between
And soars to find the one it seeks.
With such a love,
My God loves me

There is a love which whispers
And calls in gentle tones.
With wondrous sweetness on my heart it falls.
Such a love as patiently out waits
All obstacles between
And silently enfolds the one it seeks.
With such a love,
My God loves me

Elizabeth Lewis

To Dad On Your Birthday

You said you did not want a present
on your birthday, so I will give you poetry.
It is something small that can be sent
with ease, but in these words you'll see,
I hope, the love I have for you.
All my memories of you are fond:
The loving home, the laughter - you're ever new
and fresh in vision, the family bond
so strong. Mike and I as children, waiting
for you. The return of the sailor. Darkness,
the door opening. All absence fading
as you said "Hello, loves". The kiss.
You have wandered the world, come home
from the sea, to love, no more to roam

J. M. Fellows

A "Real" Man

It takes a real man to kill a child with a gun.
To watch as the tiny metallic bullet does the evil deed.
The only scar he caused is the carving on the headstone.
No conscience or guilt: A real man is proud to succeed.

It takes a real man to rape another's daughter.
No longer a virgin, she led him on, she'll never be pure.
Tormenting her dreams constantly, as a lonely old woman his
    face is her only memory.
No thought about his actions: It takes a real man to be so sure.

It takes a real man to beat up his wife
She silently accepts his punishment. No refusal, she does not dare.
Her bruised body consumes her heart as she spits out the
    bitter acid.
The loving words at the altar: It takes a real man to show he cares.

Natalie Brown

Finally Free

She screamed; her feelings took over. She
felt small, smaller than she'd ever felt
before. She felt trapped, trapped like a bird
in a cage waiting to be set free, free to
fly over the world and see how the world
had changed. Things had changed, they had
Changed for the worse, people she once knew
had died or moved on. The walls were
closing in on her; she could only go forwards
or backwards. Forwards to her home or
backwards to the dark, she didn't know what
to choose, home or the streets. Suddenly
there was a bright light; it was so pure
and beautiful, down came a cloud upon which
an angel stood. She made her choice;
she felt warm.

Stephanie Bates

See His Glory

See the spider's cobweb on a frosty morn
Drape the black hedge with lace-like lawn.
See the pale-gleaming glow of the winter sun's ray
With a mantle of gold and the stark fields array.
See the white-driven snow on the mountain bare
Like a soft bright shawl pure spotless and fair.
See the myriads of cowslips yellow and bright
Carpet the meadow with a sea of light.
See the dullness of the starling's feather
Beautified with a sheen of colours together.
See the delicate-veined tracery on the leaf of a weed
Cover its insignificance with a beauty to heed.
See the touch of God's Hand transform the least thing
So they're clothed more gloriously than Solomon the king.

Helen M. Seeley

Dark Secrets

Grey paving stones, Nostalgia,
Red brick house portray,
Of broken minds and heart,
In cold, dank dark decay.
Dim memory of something lost,
Of shredded dreams, now count the cost,
To now chastise, illusions of sane reality,
Give in to love, you can, not me.
Then beacons pose lit my way on,
Like a bonfire reflects in sad eyes,
For being away so long,
If love's, tenderness and caring exist,
Where have they gone?
Now only hatred qualifies our guilt to bear,
Your blue sky eyes,
Like a glacier in a bosom,
Chills the heart, then laughs,
As any love that's left,
Just dies.

R. Peerless

Ronan Keating Of Boyzone

All alone and wishing, now one more chance is all that I ask.
Like a new day you appeared for you're always in my heart.
Within this never ending fall my love stands tall.
For I see no lies but the truth within your eyes.
You were the one but now that you're gone
This pain lingers on but round and around I go.
Maybe I should let go but thoughts of you
Surround my every move.
No second chances but I'll fight for the love I lost.
Right or wrong I'll be missing your loving.
The sweet loving that you gave I'll surely take to the grave.

Amanda Jayne Biro

Untitled

What, fair maiden is your toil?
Your face and eyes so shrill and fixed,
Grieving as a mourner from a thousand years,
No grief shall drown your sorrowed soul,
No depths shall reach your purest pain

Once your joyous eyes were pools of love,
Now feared by a gorgon queen,
Bewitched by hands stroking your sanity in their shroud,
Backwards from your sockets, brain and grim,
Sorrow wakening by your side,
Then disappearing in the sky, I watched you flying,
Gleaming in a salty tear,
Colliding with your once friend, fear,
While sleeping on an undulation,
You drift, away from sullen recollection,
To sleep, to rest...
Not followed by your old pest, pain,
Starry, floating, crystal ripple,
Elegance, fairy, beauty be, if I were you and you were me.

Oliver Hall

The Box

It suddenly appeared.
I don't know where it came from.
A lovely box made of ... something.
When I opened up the box, a few small things fell out.
Someone's heart and someone's mind - a message in
someone's voice.
The message said:
This is your box.
Put in it what you will.
The key you'll find hidden deep inside opens the gate of fear.
Every day I put something in the box.
These are what they are.
Secrets told in confidence.
My best friend's nice warm smile.
My dreams of acting, hope and love
And the key to the gate of fear.
My box contains my bad moods,
When hatred fills my heart.
It keeps away my hate of war and
My wonder at the world.

Helen Alexander

Oh, Silver Dream Machine

Oh car, oh sleek machine,
my husband adores you!
You compete for my love.
Your bumper gleams, your headlights beam
and your engine ticks over soundlessly.

Your carburetor throbs and jitters
like my heartbeat.
You have a lovely spoiler on the rear end.
I am carcassed in a black lycra mini.

You have a smooth red bonnet, I have a black fur coat.
Your skin is gloved and polished to his touch.
My chin is patted and the lines around my eyes are noted.

You and my husband are still in the first stages of euphoria,
until the 1st of August, when he may be unfaithful,
and you will be depreciated.
And I can kick off my high heels!!!

Joan M. Emmens

In Death... In Life...

You did not get to see the golden hazy sunrise or set
Or feel the warm breeze upon your rosy cheek
Nor did the clear raindrops upon your eyelashes set
Instead the mystery of innocent death you did meet
    You did hear the voices of the ones who loved you so much
    Whisper to you the words of eternal emotion
    You did also engrave your love in just one touch
    Which will last until we will show you devotion
There are many cuddles ungiven, kisses not placed
Games not played or smiles which are lost
One day these will be given so there will be no waste
All together one day in heaven where there is no cast.
    All we ask little one is forgiveness for the past
    We would have given you all our love if we could
    When we meet next it will be to last
    In our death we lose life but gain eternal peace.

Joanne Rodgers

The Beautiful Spring

I will marry you, when birds are nesting in the trees
I will marry you, when daffodils are dancing in the breeze
I will marry you, because I love you so,
I will marry you, and never let you go,
I will marry you, and take you for my wife.
I will marry you, and love you all my life,
I will marry you, and the wedding bells will ring,
I will marry you, in the beautiful spring.

Lilian Blackledge

The Sea

The sea tumbles
With devastation.
Waves all crashing
In slow motion.
Sometimes it is silky, light to touch.
    Other times it's rough, beating against your face.
    Immovable and sincere
        So mystical with twinkle of light.
            Depths of unknowing,
                what's beneath those waves.
                You put your arms under the water
            It's so heavy to lift!
        Splashing the clear water
    With bits of sea-weed and sand.
    Salty waves approach you,
Determined to pull you under.
The sea enshrines its treasure
So it shall never be found.
    The waves extolling the heavens
        with the height of gracious elegance

Ashley Vermillio

Restless Spirit

Through profound, prismatic depths
A figure shimmers, golden veiled
Through love's strange deceits,
Each slightest flicker, glance
And gesture, evoke tingling, rainbow shivers;
The tormented delight of lovers' trance.

What yearning emptiness fills my soul
Searing through me, an intense ache?
It grips within its mad craving
To be fulfilled; yet uncertain whither to
seek, uncertain of what is to be sought.
Wandering in frantic despair,
Ever desiring a resting place, a sacred
Communion, ever withheld.

Where is your altar of peace?
Where the heady incense to sedate
the agonies of longing?
Unhappy, restless spirit,
Unnatural nomad, feverishly you seek
your oasis in a yawning; Indifferent desert.

Rosemary Merton

Untitled

Oh, a three-legged man, a three-legged man,
Lives with his wife on the Isle of Man;
Her name is Ann, his name is Dan,
And they live together on the Isle of Man;
She lives with him and he lives with her,
Both together on the Isle of Men.

They have a son, his name is Jan,
And they live together on the Isle of Man.
They have a cat, its name is Pan,
It stays with them on the Isle of Man.
They have an aunt and her name is Fan,
She too lives with them on the Isle of Man.

A three-legged man; a three legged man,
Dan, Ann, Jan, Fan, Pan,
Live happily on the Isle of Man.
One day in June with a volcanic rend,
The Isle of Man sank. . . Manx end!!
Some said it was Dan tinkering with his van.
Alas! the three-legged man now a one-legged man,
Lives all alone on the Atol of Man!

Roy W. Dalton

Whisky

Raising the glass towards my lips, your aroma strides towards me,
and my attention is instantly transfixed, on the golden beauty of thee.
A slight of colour at the base of an expansive crystal tower,
Yet the glass is drowned by your overwhelming power.
Shifting gracefully, to and fro',
yet clinging at the surface from which you go.
Oh, how delicate though, the way you glide,
seducing me to take you inside.
The tower tilts towards my lips, and gripping my tongue,
your vapour slips a hint of what is to come.
Then marching arrogantly behind, you make no subtle advances,
but claw at my tongue with fiery dances.
Now you reveal your true nature, with sinfully pleasant sensations.
I trap you there, just for a heartbeat,
absorbing you, with hesitant elation, taking time for appreciation.
Then hanging from my lips, you lower yourself down,
releasing your vapour so that my blood is drowned,
then consumes your warmth and delivers it to prickling skin.
And very slowly, your power begins to dim.
Though still to my breath you cling. Reminding me, that you are in.

David Leadbitter

A Fond Farewell

Let not my name be spoken when the children play nearby,
and when they ask where Daddy is, tell them a kindly lie,
tell them I am always with them, and will see them by and by,
please tell them that I love them, the apples of my eyes.

As you my love sleep peacefully, I'll see your lovely face,
I'll paint your dreams with rainbow colours, and silk and finest lace,
think of me for only an instant, in this timeless and endless space
you're my angel of heavenly beauty, always full of grace.

My dark haired little girl, be careful and safely play,
your beauty will blossom like Mummies, each and very day,
those big brown eyes will see wonders, on your birthday every May,
and always be, just as you are, so happy and so gay.

And you, my golden haired little boy, contentedly playing your game,
jumble the jigsaw pieces up, it will still end up the same,
each car will find a garage, each day be glad it came,
and never be like me my son, a moth to a heavenly, golden flame.

I do not leave because I want, yet I still have to go,
my thoughts of you will fill my days and endless nights aglow,
my fingers will reach out and touch you, lovingly, to let you know,
I am always with you in spirit, because I love you so.

J. S. Baracskay

Hum Of Life

Black grey clouds scudded along St. John's hill,
The breeze drummed against my ear,
I sat within the lap of the bay, watching swifts catch my eye.

Spear wort, Globe flower, Fleabane, Jenny, dance with Tom and Mary,
To Dylan, who lies above the Bay.

The tide drives the Heron skyward, the gulping wave,
Slop against the tiny boat house, in which the sodden mind
laboured.

Fat thighs labour down the tiny steps, uncaring bones draped
   with flesh,
Enter the home of spirit,
Dylan, Dylan why did you why did you, why?

Below the tide,
A voice whispers,
I'm here with Dai,
I'm here, bonny boy.

The wind touched the simple cross
Dropped to the bay,
Raced past the castle,
Into the dusty hut.

Vincent Chadwick

"Evening 'Til Dawn"

Evening's lengthening shadows deepening
o'er the land!
Pale stars disentangle from the gleaming band,
The moon astride her chariot
ventures forth anew
The darkening back-ground of the sky
Foil to her amber hue,
She gracefully surrenders to the
sleepy sun.
Who rubbing ruby eyelids
Lets his colours run,
He slips -
A vivid bruise gives to the world a picture
To gaze at but soon to lose

Anne Goldberg

The Elephant

The Elephant so grand and grey,
he wakes up early every day.
With wives and children who all follow,
trudges slowly to the water hollow.

His trunk so long, and full of strength,
is filled with water, its whole length.
He squirts it over himself, like a fool,
to keep that big, grand, body cool.

Cows, calves, and bull elephants too,
would hate being enclosed in a zoo.
They love to stroll, and wander free,
to scratch and rub, against a tree.

Elegant, graceful, free and wild,
Father, mother live with child.
The elephant is most at home,
When he is left in peace to roam.

S. A. Smith

Aftermath (The Dunblane Massacre)

Who shall account
For the senseless slaughter?
The death of a child,
Be they son or daughter.

From an act that was evil and insane,
They will struggle to make sense
Of the madness, just the same.

What took three minutes to obliterate,
Will cause a lifetimes pain.
Yet life goes on,
Even if for us - it's stopped.

Life shows no sympathy,
Hears no cry,
And offer's no answers in the aftermath,
As a grief torn mother yell's out -
   Why?...

Ingrid McGill

"Gateway To Thee"

A ghost of the grey pillar covered the courtyard.
The shadow of darkness gently caressed the leaves.
A voice from the light:
"A liar, a liar to the end".
But which way?
A silence calls,
Which way?
The silence pulls,
a patter, a gallop, a rush of despair and then free!

Day breaks the pillars,
Day breaks my heart and the wild winds around me flow free.
On north wind do blow.
Surround me, surround my soul, release me.
The angel came, took flight and the earth was free.

Heather Gorry

Silent Witness

Of blood, yet untouchable,
Separated by unspoken years
Of accumulated unknowns,
He moves along the convoluted webs of daily living,
Mature, independent, of worldly wisdom.
I know this man?

Eyes impassive until, in unguarded flash,
Torment, betrayal and pain seer their depths;
Then rapidly subside.
Like a perfectly-tuned string vibrating in sympathy
Mute anguish soars again
From the bottomless spring of my long-suppressed heartache.

In years past comfort was easy -
A hug, a smile, a plaster; but now,
Now I must witness this suffering unapproached, unneeded,
Yet bound by that cord forever unsevered
In bond of love to the last breath and beyond,
A silent sentinel of impotent maternity.

Sheila Kirkham

The Flowers Of Dunblane

Today the world is a sadder place.
For sixteen Flowers of Scotland ceased to bloom and give us grace.

They did no harm as they blossomed forth and played and
went to school.
But now they are gone and grow no more, shot by a stupid fool.

Remember them and weep for them for they were only five.
With everything to live for, they should be alive.

Our hearts go out to the parents for what will fill their void.
When the numbness goes and they weep for their little girls
and boys.

Lord receive these little children to live in heaven above.
And their teacher who taught them all with love.

And as for that man Hamilton who did this dreadful deed.
He shot himself, to good a death the likes him we do not need.

J. N. Rawlings

Timothy John

Timothy John was small and fair,
With laughing eyes and curling hair,
By the deep blue river he loved to roam,
The deep blue river, so near to his home

Timothy John went out one day
With a little toy boat, painted oh! so gay!
He wanted to give his teddy a ride
On the deep blue river - so deep and wide!

Timothy John trotted down to the bank -
With teddy on board the little boat sank!
Then a terrible splash - Help! Help! cried John,
But the deep blue river flowed on and on.

Timothy John was seen no more!
With teddy he sailed to another shore
For the 'fairies' took our Timothy John,
And the deep blue river flows on and on.

Marjorie Church

Pollution

Dirty bone in the comb
Clattering can stupid man
Wooden spoon under the moon
Bike tire barbed wire
Cardboard box plastic fox
Old shoe someone threw
Broken stick, who done it, someone thick
Dead bird lemon curd
People throw things then go
People just don't care it's not fair

Tyronne Bailey

A Wee Moment

What do you see, a question
what do you hear, no answers
but do you decide, an answer?

So out and about, not too far
In and around, all friends,
a song or a story, music all round,
a room of a difference, all one.

So will I or wonder, what can I say,
do I have answers, more questions.
So look and decide, an answer, I wonder,
like rain in the sky and a circle no end,
just like a pain, but is there an end?

From 15 and plus, another a difference
a ball and a game enjoyed by us all,
for one it was struggle, but God and its nature,
A world has decided, will I or won't I.
It's me that decides, it's me that fights all,
so yes, and a right thing,
I shall be all one, united with God!

Brendan Boylan

Untitled

Over the top of the distant hills,
a sunbeam shines on a riverside mill.
It brings to life this country treasure,
that gives to us so much pleasure.

The planks of wood on the mill are old,
Where the sun shines on them they glow like gold.
high polished by wind and rain,
rare beauty like this is hard to gain.

Under the eaves of the roof a bird nests,
a place where only it knows best.
Sheltered from the sun and summer storms,
the ideal place for young to be born.

The river turns the mill wheel round,
movement of water a pleasant sound.
A lark sings high in the clear blue sky,
While the fish in the water take the fly.

Although this mill was made by man,
a timeless beauty now it stands.
Home for one, home for all,
a home for all that care to call.

Peter Brian Ford

Self-Blues

I'm good but not that good,
I'm bad but not when I'm done,
They call me the "Jack of all Trades",
But I know I'm the master of none.

The average person,
Is the phrase that best paints me,
Because that's all I really am,
And that is all I will ever be.

I have no aims in life,
No strengths to help me along,
For everything I get right,
There's always something I will get wrong.

Now I'm stuck in a rut,
I just don't know where to go,
All the dreams that I thought I'd live,
Have disappeared right out the window.

I wish I had some hope,
But my life is such a mess,
Nothing will ever come of me,
Believe me when I say I'm worthless.

Julie Massiter

I Have Brought

I have brought mildness
For a peaceful life
I have brought goodness
To bring the child happiness
I have brought self control
To teach and preach good minds
I have brought braveness
To bring the child protection
I have brought health
For a balanced life style.
I have brought wisdom and harmony
for a good view for differences
I have brought judgement
for the child to decide on good, bad and important thing's
I brought long suffering and kindness
To put up with thing's that aren't easy.
I have brought faith
for all to have trust and to carry on.
I have brought my heart the most important one
to encourage and strengthen the wonderful child.

Sarah Adams

Love's Farewell

Rest peacefully dear love of mine your
torment now has gone.
My heart is oh so broken, my love
for you still strong.

I'm sure you knew my inner thoughts
although no words were there.
I tried so hard to help you, and show
you that I care.

I dream about you constantly, thinking
you are still near.
Then waken to reality and wipe away the tear.

Rest peacefully dear love of mine
and guide me on my way.
I know we will meet again beyond
that heavenly ray.

Valerie Deacon

Eternal Love

Our youth was short but finely lived,
Passion reigned supreme, life's reality.
The flowers of our love separated from us,
To grow and go their different ways.

Your delicate female fingers hold my face in your hands,
But you exclude me from your heart,
My love for you began beyond my memory,
Still protecting your spirit of life,
My life's value is only on your terms,
Have pity on me and love me for what I am.

Protect me from my despair and loneliness,
Expect no more the wonders of youth,
Look not to my withering flesh but the spirit of my soul
Let us now make a pact for eternity.

Keith Arbie Johnson

Dear James

Teddy bears, flowers and emotions too -
everything was present, presented to you.
So innocent and defenceless, it was not your fault -
the nation was stunned and came to a halt.

Taken by strangers away from the crowds -
you were made to conform, they being so loud.
They scared you and tortured you, just for something to do -
how could they, how dare they, especially to you.

From the bottom of my heart all my love I send -
my emotions are flowing so now I shall end.
To our James, why did it happen this way?
from myself and the nation, what can we say!

R. A. Lockley

Our Jessie

Jessie, oh Jessie, how we recall
The day you came you were very small
A pet Mum said and so did Dad
The most treasured pet we ever had
Although so small your energy so great
You ate everything we put on your plate
Then you grew and grew and before very long
No longer a puppy but quite big and strong
You stole our slippers you chewed our mats
So we bought you toys and rubber bats
Down the road and up the park
There you played and you would bark
But now you've grown old and sleep all day
And only get up for a little play
We all still love you dear old girl
As in your basket you love to curl
We think of the pleasures we had in the past
And we will do so till your last breath is cast

Mary Campbell-Bridgman

Memory

Thinking,
Numb with pain.
Just one memory,
But so vivid, emotional.
I'm always wanting to know the whole truth,
It's there but where do I look?
Somebody hurt me.
I don't know who,
The name Adam clicks, Adam, why?
Why did he do that?
Why hurt me so much?
Blocking it out is a sign of evil,
He was evil.
Maybe I'll never know when, what, how and why?
The questions that I want answered.
One memory suggests so much,
Causes hate and fear.
Is every man like that,
Like him?

Lisa Cheetham

At Sea?

Odious Captain Corpulent
On raging sea he quails
Before the common seaman brave
Ignoble, scant, he pales
What definition, precedent, elevates him thus
Above more suited, worthy men, deserved men like us.

Jack Myers

The Memory Tree

Love, do you remember
  Remember what?
Doesn't really matter - I forgot
  We both have a laugh
Well, what about when I remember
  I'll give you a shout.

To have a good memory
  must mean a lot
Sometimes a great thing - sometimes not.
Remember every minute
  Every hour of every day
Like listening to a blackbird's song
And children at their play.

Oh, how marvellous it would be
If folk like you and folk like me
Could perhaps, I say, someday
  Try to possess which, nevertheless
A little word like 'forgetfulness'
  We all should agree to invent
    word called A Memory Tree.

Ellen Littlet

Fulfilment

Considering those things that I love the most.
Whilst munching upon crisp breakfast toast,
Having nothing at all of which to complain
Content it is a beautiful day once again.
My heart is comforted and gently at ease.
Prompted by courage, feeling the spirit to please.
Priority to integrate, perform only to enhance.
Armed with an objective, now cautiously advance,
This policy causing calm solitude fly away,
Whirling in the hustle of this busy new day.
Only slowed through dull routine of detail
Eventual progress inevitably gained to good avail.
Presentation now forming and taking strong root
Combined efforts destined to bear really good fruit
There's always a job that urgently calls to be done,
No cause to ignore it, why shouldn't I be just the one.
Finding depths within and great contentment over all,
Fulfilment ensues with many memories to recall.

B. M. Hover

Hold Me

I wish I was dead, oh stop this hurt,
Buried six foot under the black slimy dirt,
Away from all the misery and painful girth,
Of living a lie on his horrible earth.

No one understands the pain felt inside,
Or the loneliness when locked in at night,
The ache in my heart is hard to bear,
Thinking of the past and wishing to go back there.

I know I can't undo all the past wrongs,
Or hold the children that I'd borne
Now dead - I wish they were at home,
I need someone to hold and call my own.

Ruth M. Young

O Summer Sun

O summer sun
    is glowing over land and sea,
How quietly the soft clouds move
    across the clear blue sky;
You can hear the summer sounds
    just around the corner:
Listen to the birds singing
    their own sweet songs so crisp and clear,
And hear the Mother bird
    feeding her noisy young ones.
As flowers grow tall the buds
    are swaying in the wind
Ready to burst into the full blossom
    of colours bright and fair.
Soon leaves are dropping
    one by one to the ground,
As the Summer sun
    is glowing over land and sea...

Sheenagh Hardie

Life

What is life?,
Big fancy jobs and cars,
A laugh and a joke with a friend,
Life to some may seem like a breeze,
The kind of breeze on a hot sunny day,
People laughing at pranks,
Pranks that mean nothing compared to life.
To others life is pointless,
Poverty and war,
No jobs and no homes,
No family to keep you safe and warm,
People who's lives have been effected by this.
Just think next time you think of life,
How lucky you are with family and friends,
Family and friends that are supportive everyday.
And then think of those with out.

Naomi Hanson

The Pilgrim's Wax

Below swirls the mist, upward, creeping softly implacable,
The wide panorama of the tangible world, dwindling to nothingness.
Only, across the valley, detached and dream like,
A hill side gleams, the trees' fine tracery
Etched in minute detail on the faint wash of the sky,
The air, a moment, full of crystal clarity,
Up sweeps the mist, gently obliterating, time dissolving,
One's journey meaningless,
Not so the pilgrims who, in bygone days, wore smooth this chalky path
Unquestioning, secure, they travelled to their goal,
Or were they, too, harassed by doubt.
Lest treacherous feet betray or clouds obscure their definite way?
Perhaps some wanderer stood as I do now,
Watching the vaporous mist enshroud reality.
Perhaps he, too, puzzled and visionless,
Found danger in his own uncertainty
And did he, as I, grope forward, hesitant,
The heart crying why and why.

Margery Bacmeister

Manchester United's Season 1993/94

Manchester United have had a wonderful season
The fans are happy with reason
Eric Cantona was awesome
Mark Hughes was fearsome
Dennis Irwin was scoring from free-kicks
Ryan Giggs was up to his usual tricks
Andrei Kanchelskis was faster than lightning
Peter Schmeichel's saves were scintillating
Lee Sharpe was occasionally injured
Then the fans became frustrated
Dion Dublin was used as a substitute centre-forward
At times Eric Cantona was a bit awkward
Gary Pallister was towering
Eric Cantona was sent-off for fighting
Roy Keane's penetrating runs were sensational
Bryan Robson was phenomenal
Paul Ince at times was a bit temperamental
In the FA Cup final Eric Cantona was instrumental
Dennis Wise gambled 100 pounds that Eric Cantona would miss
After the penalty was struck the players celebrated with a kiss

Amarjit Singh

Nightmare

I had a terrible dream
There was no beautiful sky
And the little birds found
That they could not fly

There were no twinkling stars at night
No moon at night shining so bright
In the morning we had no sun
Everyone got up looking so glum

We had no rain to wet the lawn
No Sun to ripen the fields of corn
This would be terrible if this were true
it would be a nightmare for me and for you

I got out of bed and saw the blue sky
I thought of that dream and I wanted to cry
And I saw the little birds flying so high
It was nice to see them flying in the beautiful blue sky

It was nice to see the stars twinkling at night
And the moon up there shining so bright
In the morning we see our friendly Sun
And he will shine his brightness on everyone

H. G. Booley

Cyclone

Out of control vision drifting
Unable to breathe faces shifting
The eye of the cyclone hovers overhead
Filling me with a familiar dread
Fighting endlessly to overcome my fear
Screaming silently there is no one to hear
Stygian blackness is threatening to overcome
In a tidal wave of anti-welcome
The riderless horse comes ever near
Clattering hooves the grim reaper is here
Soul and spirit are struggling still
Gaining footholds, reducing mountains to hill
The panic is subsiding, the terror beginning to ease
Slowly surfacing into less fraught seas
Completely exhausted but already seeking spaces
For hiding the horror in unremembered places
Trying desperately to forget that I thought I would die
In the frightening force of my own cyclonic eye

Susan J. Coveley-Jones

School Days

Empty chairs where friends once drank
The tables clear; the blackboard blank.
A unused coat hangs limp like rag
A broken strap, a satchel bag.

Howling wind through broken panes,
Lost voices called of school day chains.
An upturned chair; the childish scrawl,
All that's left in this learning hall.

Where once we sang, and drank, and laughed
About our girls; where phases passed.
Where fights were fought, remember them,
Until the school gates close again.

So many friends, so few are left
And we remain like men bereft.
Another group will leave this year,
The cycle leaves a laugh... a tear.

Rob Corney

Caught Between The Class

Walking along the street,
Do you blame me for looking down at my feet,
To look up seems so pointless,
What am I bound to see, people staring back at me.

Going to work is such a drag,
Riding on the train Boom Claddy Boom, Boom Claddy Boom.
I feel so sad in my own world, with no rights to be free,
But for other people this might not be so,
I keep my head down, just to avoid trouble,
One glance in the wrong way, it's too much to pay.

Do people blame me for who I am,
Having a job and money in my hand,
For the other people I'm so sorry, but I can't give you any money,
You see that's not my class to do so,
People would think, "What's wrong with her?"
"She must be a freak", "Giving the poor money"
"She's pleading for trouble."

I would like to help, one day I hope I will, in a way
I envy those people, they have the freedom to say, what ever
they will.

Amy Hooper

Late Walk

Ahead - the road, rid of the solid town,
Free as a hope on the wide future drawn;
Around - the wind, in hedge and over fields,
Talking like old tongues of untrodden worlds;
Above - the moonlit ice-floes of the sky,
Fissured with night too deep for simile.

M. J. Steadman

Fear

It paralyses, preventing forward motion.
It overwhelms, washing over us like the ocean.
Clutching relentlessly at the heart,
It pierces deeply like a dart.

Grasping, gripping, tearing,
Harsh, unloving and grossly uncaring.
Do not give in to its demands!
Fight back, you give the commands!

It will trap you like a spider,
In a web that only gets wider.
So, resist with all that you can muster,
This emotion which can cause so much fluster.

It will swallow you whole,
In an attempt to destroy your soul.
You are the captain of the ship.
Try your best to avoid fear's grip.

Rema Green

Untitled

Just as the sea recedes on sand
My love has slipped from out your hand.
You've crumpled it beyond repair,
You've killed it dead without a care.
For love is like a fragile flower
That blossoms 'neath the sun or shower,
But if it never feels the warmth
of summer's sun—just winter's wrath
It cries inside for what has been
And summer's warmth seems like a dream
It bows its head down low and sighs,
And so it shrivels up and dies.
Well, so it is with love my friend,
We cling to it until the end, and if into our hearts we delve
We find deep down within ourselves
We love the memory alone of what has been and what has gone.
And what we have is just a shell,
That's turned into a kind of Hell.
So on the grave a rose is tossed,
And I weep a tear for Love that's lost.

Norma Wilson

My Garden

In May the daffodils dip green wings
limply to rest, awaiting other springs...
while peonies, plump with promise, thrust a pace,
impatient to take over in their place.
I am filled with pleasure that I can
assist this splendid and eternal plan
with hand, and hoe and heart. And I can see
such wonder in the continuity.

As daffodil to peony gives place,
so year to year in this relentless race
of life. And with profound relief
I recognize Content will follow Grief
as Spring the Winter's pillagings reverses.
For cyclic is the blessed universe.
I would like to think some Mighty hand,
with hoe and heart assists our troubled land.

Nanette Garwood

The Enchanted Bird

Flurry of wings, flapping vigorously,
sickle flitting from branch to branch,
flaunting their wings flirtatiously,
whilst fitfully, falling from tree to tree,
high pitched twitter of tenuous song.
Sung so seriously,
Guaranteed to touch your heart,
like the over-powering colour of a rose.
Flurry of wings, flapping vigorously,
Birds flying forming into a flock,
flitting into the sunlit sky,
flying with eyes of flare.

Katie Neiman

Winter Sea

Splashing, crashing, raving, ranting,
Wind-blown spume against the sky;
Waves are rolling, rocking, reaching,
Beating up this pebbled shore.
Can you hear the thunder roll?
Successive waves come tearing in,
Boats are drawn high up the shingle
Safely berthed from vicious tide,
On the groyne a single gull
Waits for the fury to abate,
The spray leaps high; bird fades from view,
A myriad drops of trembling foam
Come lightly down to fade away,
The seventh wave has come and gone.

Mollie Joan Read

Goodbye Gran

Gran, I am in deep distress,
No longer to feel your loving caress,
Always the ready ear you would lend,
Someone on whom I could depend.

I have known for sometime it could end this way,
Always you lived from day to day,
You were old it is true but still the shock,
That the angels that day on your door should knock.

They came, Gran, to take you home,
So you wouldn't have to make the journey all alone,
And now you are at peace in Paradise,
I couldn't wish it otherwise.

Gran, I never got to say goodbye,
Or tell you I'll love you till the day I die,
But I think you know that just the same,
So thank you for memories which will always remain,
Goodbye dear Gran, Goodbye.

Sylvia Baldwin

Mum....

I wanna be like you
But I wanna be totally different.
I wanna be someone new...
A fresh alive creature that God sent.
To be strong and wise.
To give others advice.
But be someone unique,
Yet comfortable with my world.
To be polite and meek,
Though not from a mould.
I wanna touch the corners of my existence...
Tread step by step with the youth of my time.
To enjoy every breath, complete every sentence.
And explore the mysteries of life in its prime.

Sanghamitra Sen

What Shall We Have For Tea?

"What shall we have for tea?" I ask,
"Anything!" is the reply I get;
But what if I take them literally
And get the table set
With cotton wool, or shoe polish!
Would it whet their appetite?
Or perhaps a "mud pie" or "Cake of soap"
Is what they'd fancy tonight?
Somehow I don't think they'd appreciate
The things I mentioned there,
But it's just so hard to know what to have
Every day of every year!
So I ask them what they'd like for tea,
"Anything," they still all say!
And I really will be tempted
To serve them "anything" one day!

Edna Stone

The Swan

Oh majestic bird,
You glide serenely on the water with your graceful head and neck,
Your soft white feathers like silken snow,
The patch of orange burning on your beak,
You do not make a ripple as you paddle your feet.

You are a sight to behold,
When you spread your wings they are so big and strong,
Yet with gentleness they cover your young ones on your back.

You beautiful creature,
Why do they leave their fishing tackle around which harms you?
The twine which wraps around your legs and cuts deep,
Lead pellets which poison your body, hooks which pierce
    your webbed feet,
Why don't they give you a thought, oh magnificent white one.

As you glide gracefully through the water
I see you with a dainty crown upon your stately head,
For surely you are the monarch of the river.

Elsie Groves

Illusive Joy

How lovely to know people once had souls which they
    mourished and nurtured and fed,
With loving concern for all of mankind, no matter wherever bred.
How lovely to know the animals and birds, though providing
    food in due days,
Received loving respect whilst they lived on the earth, giving
    joy in countless ways.
How lovely to know that the land and the seas were treasured
    for all they could give
Of natural fibre and sentient pleasure, thus giving folk space
    to live
In peace and harmony with themselves, whilst striving with
    powers they possessed
To give of themselves in courage and hope, that tomorrow
    might be their best.

Then Mephistopheles passed this way and reared up his
    nasty head,
"Forget all that non sense and listen to me. You'll be better off",
    he said,
"If you focus your mind upon money and things it will give
    you a sense of pride,
You can have all you wish for and do all you want; you're
    bound to feel good inside".
It sounded enticing, folk listened and followed, digesting each
    word that was spoken,
But where is the happiness? Where are the souls? How sad
    they're neglected and broken.

Daphne Crack

Why?

Why? Is a question that's often times asked,
When someone so near so near to us dies.
You can't find a reason so deep in your heart,
Oh please bring them back, your heart cries.

For they've gone to a place that no-one understands,
Though I guess that we'll be there someday.
But until that time comes and we pass to this place,
We will love them more every day.

Our hearts break, we mourn, but we don't understand,
As we live but their memories hold.
Of our loved ones, God's children, we borrowed their souls,
Though their bodies were only on hold.

For our time from day one was pre-written for us,
So our Lord should reclaim us someday,
Where we'll all be united, in God's safe embrace,
And our worries will be far away.

Catherine Wilson

Untitled

There is an emptiness beyond your light
Where you may shine and yet allow the dark:
The labyrinth recesses of the human heart.
Beyond the choice to follow you or no
Lie shadows of some long forgotten wrong,
Of truths untold and secrets yet unseen.

You touch and pierce with your bright burning beam
And still the darkness blackens and resounds
While drops like tears suspended in the void
Form stalactites the residue of pain.

And though your healing hope keeps all alive,
And washes clean this dirtiest of grime,
Until you fill the chasm in the soul
There still remains an emptiness beyond your light.

Samantha Lundie

A Week In Lourdes

Last years holiday to Lourdes, was one of the very best,
A huge family of hundreds, a cut above the rest,
We visited the Grotto, where our lady appeared to Bernadette,
It's a special place for all the sick, the crowned statue is where
we met,
We went to many masses, each and every day,
With many other people, we all sat down to pray,
Again at night we gathered, with torch-light in our hand,
What a wonderful experience it was, I felt as if it was another land,
The bathes were something else, I just broke down in tears,
It cleansed me of my sins and took away my fears,
We went to see the stations, how Jesus died for all,
They were so really beautiful, lovely and gold and life size tall,
The time went by, the week soon past,
It was time to come home, it went so fast,
My heart ached not to come home, Lourdes was the place I
wanted to stay,
So I visited our Lady's statue, to pray to come back some day.

Sally Elizabeth Burton

Wings

If only I could take away your pain
And turn all your wrongs to right
If only I could climb inside your soul
And be your courage and your will to fight

If only my hands that wipe away your tears
Were the feathers of gigantic wings
If only my heart could rejoice with yours
To give you the pleasure of greater things

If only the words that I use to console you
Would do more than just dance in your mind
If only my arms were the wings of an angel
I could show you the right road to find

If only I could explain how much I care
But my words get lost in what I say
If only I could fly, then I would fly
You away to a better and brighter day

Joanne Bell

Field Of Tears

Myth! Not a stark reality of war.
The length and breathe, in the corn fields, in the hedgerow,
by the wayside, some standing proudly alone,
others huddled together in continued comradeship.

The humble red poppy chosen to be a symbol
of those countless numbers destined never to return
look, see with sweet remembrance
as from the dust
there, blossoms red
life that shall endless be.

M. Spencer

The Last Ball

The atmosphere was tense and night-time
loomed near.
The last ball was about to be bowled.
The batsman walked to his crease and
took his position.
The ground was worn down by the pounding
of feet all day long.
The bowler started his run in great big
strides.
His speed increased as he neared
the stumps.
He stopped in mid-stride and swung his arm
high into the air.
He brought it forward and let the ball
fly through the air.
It hit the ground with a soft thud.
The batsman swung and missed.
The match was over.
The last ball had gone.

Michael Mullarkey

Hold The Night

Darkness overtakes the light as day gives way to yet another night
Another night in which her thoughts will lead
To dreams where ghosts are waiting to feed her.
To feed her the blood of lovers past and others whose memories
will always last
will always last and never fade from her mind
Like the cries of those she hoped to leave behind.
To leave behind, but not forget, she'll hide in the night

And yet...

And yet once more they come again, each ghost bringing its
gift of pain
A gift of pain she cannot refuse
It's her reward, it's her's to use.
To use as once she used the others - mother, sisters, friends
and lovers
Friend and lovers who tried to reach her
Like mother and sisters - unable to teach her.
To teach her that love is cherishing, giving, holding, caring,
needing, forgiving.
Forgiving herself, forgiving the others
Mother, sisters, friends and lovers.

Denni Evans

Ode To A Chocolate Labrador

Those big brown eyes that melt my heart
Your pretty face - sets you apart
My special girl, you're so much more
My darling precious labrador.

You greet me with a bounding hug
When in the garden you have dug
You're so excited I can see
To take me outside to the tree
Where all the pansies used to sit
Now all remains is in a pit!

Into the pond you like to splash
The fish for shelter they do dash
Lilies all - out they come
You learnt to swim - Not quite so dumb.

We have some fun, my girl my girl and I
You laugh when I laugh, cry when I cry
My greatest friend - what are you worth?
You're my salvation, salt of the earth.

Eileen Nicholls

My Poem

The man looked around, knowing he was going;
No idea how he would travel to his unknown destination.
He had nothing to take, but a lot to leave behind.
Amongst all the things he loved,
There was none he could, or would take.
The truth is,... He would rather stay.

When he looks at what he loves, and has to leave,
He cries, not in secret anymore.
He thinks, or does he know,
It is not long before he goes?
He has no peace or joy to share,
Only pain and sorrow he has to bear.

Being surrounded by beauty and passion,
Is supposed to make him feel better,
But as he looks closer at those he loves,
His sorrow increases...
 ... and so does the pain.
   Ted Fleming

Hypochondriac

How are you the day?
I am fine except for
the twinge in my back,
and my rheumatism is playing upon my knee,
and do you know I can hardly see,
apart from that I am fine.

My migraine got worse,
my varicose are causing me pain,
and the doctor said my arm will never be the same again,
apart from that I am fine.

My false teeth don't fit,
and my corns are giving me jip,
and I am sure I can hear a click in my hip,
apart from that I am fine.

My hearing not so good,
my heart is a'flutter,
I am bothered with a stutter,
apart from that I am fine,
must rush 'cause there's my bus.
   Ann Armour

16 January 1991

Dawn comes softly.
  The sky in the east is peaches and cream.
  In the indigo west
  The last star lingers,
  Reluctant to leave this enchanted hour.

Dawn comes gently.
  Though the hospital never truly sleeps
  Its lights are muted,
  Its activity masked in marble and gold leaf;
  Seemingly quiescent as the desert in which it stands.

Dawn comes gaily.
  In the cool, translucent air,
  Invisibly high above my head,
  Birds are celebrating;
  Singing alleluias for the gift of morning.

Dawn comes incandescently -
  Riyadh will soon be waking,
  Unsuspecting, unbelieving,
  To a day like none that has gone before -

Bombs are already falling on Baghdad.
   Patricia Ashmore

"From This Ephemeral Plane..."

Amidst the mystic ocean of God's wrath reminiscent,
The broiling brine, my soul, doth endeavour to consume,
The beauty of that far off realm, the moon it doth illume.
To reach distant, comely land, for the stamina I hunt.

When thou art beneath my gaze, my feelings hollow as at lent,
Yet my passions rage asunder, serene and silent as a bloom,
As bewitching spells, delicate hands do weave, upon your enchanted loom,
My heart laments to capture, the sublime bouquet of your scent.

And though our paths seem oft to cross, always do you avert
Thine eyes from mine, when, like Laura, 'tis thee I do admire,
To he above, I plead, for an arrow that procures no hurt,
That together from this ephemeral plane, our souls soar ever higher.

  If, then, thou attends to afford, an admittance to your heart,
  May our affinity encircle the globe, ne'er be cleaved apart.
   Sean Chrysanthou

Spellbound By Twilight

The fiery glow of street lights
  bursts through the murky gloom
  that is our evening dusk,
  where clouds and sky merge into looming darkness.

A tranquil scene as if time has stopped;
No more is the bustle and glare of the day
  and not yet has the silent night befallen us;
Betwixt a time to contemplate, our evening.

For now is when we can survey
  the beauties that surround us,
  trees caressed by the delicate breeze,
  to a skyline of rolling hills and crumbly ruins.

This is our evening,
  when each tiny flower bows its head to sleep
  and the twinkling lights of office windows one by one go out;
So our day is put to rest.
   Helen Bates

Big Sister's Bed

I don't want to sleep in my big sister's bed,
Monsters in the cupboard she's often said,
She tells me stories that are never true,
If you were her sister she'd tell them to you,
She said alligators live down our street,
Those gators I hope I will never meet,
She said big spiders live under the floor
I don't want to sleep in her bed anymore!
   Adelle Stubbs

A Teenager

Does he belong to me?
The boy who sat on my knee.
Now he's six feet tall,
He makes me feel so small. A teenager.

He used to be up at seven,
Now it's half past eleven.
Calling out his name,
Silence all the same. A teenager.

The music, what a din,
You always know he's in.
It's not a song, it's a noise
He wants to be one of the boys. A teenager.

Now it's all girls, girls, girls
The slicked back hair, gone the curls.
Oh dear Mums are sad,
What happened to my lovely lad.? A teenager.

A few more years and he'll be grown
Fled the nest and left home.
Married then with a wife.
What to expect in his own life? A teenager.
   Avril Colville

Christmas Not X'mas

They have taken the Christ out of Christmas, it's Xmas today
in the world. With no thought for the King in the carols they
sing, Or the streamers so gaily unfurled.

They have taken the Christ out of Christmas, forgotten the
wise men of old. So with turkey and sherry, let's eat, drink, be
merry, Who cares what the future may hold.

They have taken the Christ out of Christmas, they won't let
the baby come in. Oh! There's plenty of mirth, but for Jesus
Christ's birth, There still is 'no room at the inn'

They have taken the Christ out of Christmas, instead there's a
cross cold and bare. With no meaning of love, for the Saviour
above, Who has called us, His glory to share.

Oh! Let us put Christ back in Christmas. Let him rule each
heart and each mind. With Him leading the way, then surely,
one day There'll be peace on this earth for mankind.

Yes there will be a cross after Christmas, we will all have our
burdens to bear. But that babe in the manager, will keep us
from danger if we let Him, He'll always be there.

Be it Easter, or Whitsun, or Christmas, He will solve all our
problems, and then we shall see Him in glory, and tell the old
story, With Christ back in Christmas, Amen.

Mary Dixon

North Cornwall

Come with me to a wondrous land
With wide, wide skies and sun drenched sand.
Where cliffs, slumbering in the sea
Have grandeur, power and majesty.

Where wild waves rage and pitch and toss
Just to let us know who's boss.
Where wild garlic and bluebells combine
To flood the senses; yours and mine.

Where hedges are high and narrow the lanes
And the wild foxglove proudly reigns.
Where there's not much razz ma tazz
And all that sort of jazz.

Where folk are unhurried, relaxed, at ease
Not buzzing about like frantic bees.
Where, at Port Gaverne, a bit of heaven fell
And captured many in its spell.

Where beauty, like a pain
Stabs, and goes and comes again.
Where this mystic place will always be
A bliss. A joy. A sanctity.

Simonne Dolby

All At Once There Was You

As I sit here, studying the rain
a glimmer of hope shines through
all at once I can see where the clouds will break

My thoughts are of clear things
both old and new
all at once a smile creeps up on my face

Life is ever-changing
I'm confused
which direction should I take?
Which path is there for me to follow?

The smile still remains
which means I'll make the right choice
all at once the distance of my brain is overwhelming

My life's just taken another twist
and now the sun is beaming through
it's now time to start another day
all at once there was you

Lisa Robertson

The Old Man

The old man wanders down the road, he doesn't have a care
He's used to all the people, who stop to have a stare

He hasn't any overheads, no household bills or tax
He doesn't have a telephone and never heard of fax

He doesn't have a video, a shaver or a clock
When he watches television, he does it in a shop

He doesn't have a wife, no children or a pet
He loves all the farm animals, they're looked after by a vet

He doesn't have a kettle, a teapot or a jug
The only thing in that line, is his old enamelled mug

He doesn't have designer clothes, but he has designer stubble
The last time that he had a wash, was in a rain filled puddle

He's never admired the mighty rich, with mansions and fast cars
He loves the big park benches and sleeps beneath the stars

The only assets he can call his own, is arthritis and stomach cramp
This was caused by his way of life, but he's happy being a tramp

Keith R. A. Crisp

To Imogen

If beauty was but skin deep
I would never have fallen in love with you;
But beauty stretches deep within - a smiling warming,
Like the sunlight that sparkles in your eyes of blue.
    A nod betrays innate grace of Helen
    And a face that's ten
Thousand times a greater view.

Honour forbids approach -
A useful veneer to conceal my cowardice;
Yet emotion is hard to hide
When one is inspired, moved, but lost like this.
    The spell is cast - the beguiling love potion of your eyes;
    So all I can see is you smiling and I am mesmerised.

The song of the Troubadour
- Self pity cloaked in a more respectable attire -
Provides soft comfort: Knightly tunes, some sombre, some merry,
Lyrics to match the aether of the lyre.
    It grows in and elates all I feel, all I say, all I do;
    So no part of me escapes the gentle rapture of knowing you.

Ian Macgregor Morris

In Memory Of Bounty

Somewhere in the moorland winds
Lives the spirit of my Bountikins.
Racing name Davanna Queen
The prettiest greyhound ever seen.
The jacket of red she wore with pride
It suited her to run inside.
She'd leave the traps with lightning speed
And straight away she'd take the lead.
She'd keep in front and set the pace
She knew she was there to win the race.
On the track she was rough and tough
But at home she was soft like a piece of fluff.
She stole my heart with her loving ways
But now I'm left with empty days.
I'll never forget you Bountikins
You'll live forever in the moorland winds.

Sue Davan

Winter

I open my door to see a new day
There is snow on the floor and fog in my way
My frostbitten garden, once lovely and green,
Now I must pardon for none can be seen
My bare-limbed tree covered in snow
Looks bewildered, nowhere to go
Brilliant white snowflakes glide to the ground
Mingle together, none to be found
Cries of joy ring in my ears
Children, and snowballs, and icicle tears

Jeanette Rothwell

Dunblane Carnage

Tiny children only lent
How could they know their life was spent
Beautiful flowers never to bloom
Petals crushed in a Scots schoolroom
And amongst the buds in that fateful hall
Was their Teacher standing tall
She also lost in the prime of life
A loving mother and beloved wife
Give strength to all the bereaved, bereft
Please help them Lord the families left

Tend the children who will never awake
Then help the families as their hearts break
Help them Lord as their spirits are crushed
Help them Lord as their bodies are pushed
flung over the edge with their children gone
Help them Lord to carry on

Joan Fell

I Never Thought Of Death That Way

I never thought of death that way
An eclectic feeling
An exposure to oblivion
Life's not always the right way

You know there is no existence
After that full stop, no
Continuing paragraph
that runs on in the way

And at the very point of your exposure
No one told me of the blind flash
Or the autonomous state
you reach
And at this point I had no desire
to go life's way
But to snatch back at the very existence I sought to revoke
Revealing all in one ultimate bid

I never thought of death that way
Until I threw my chance away today

C. K. Hoare

Young Criminals

It's the parents at fault, is what some people say,
If you beat them when young, then the kids will obey,
It's the teachers at fault, is what some people say,
Give a slap round the head, bring the cane back in play.

It's the law that's at fault, is what some people say,
Give coppers more weapons to use, make 'em pay,
It's the church that's at fault, is what some people say,
Let the church turn the kids who are violent, away.

So who is to blame for these kids going wrong,
Is it you, is it me, where does blame belong,
Just look at solutions that are mentioned above,
And tell me where violence stems from, not love.

S. Fryer

North Sea Thoughts

Over the seas and far away
My love for you it will not stray
It burns bright like the stars in the night
Keeping me warm on the coldest of nights
So here I am in the cold north sea
I think of you as I hope you think of me
I think of our children, I love them so much
Why does being out here have to hurt so much
The pain I endure, the work I must do
It's all for the love I feel for you
So I'm counting the days to our next embrace
When I know that our love will make our hearts race
The pain will be gone and I'll kiss you again
And tell you I love you all over again

Ronnie Paton

I Will Wait For You

My eyes want to let out tears,
and cry for this to end.
I've added days to days and come up with years,
but I'll still wait for you and for my heart to mend.

I have never missed anyone like this before,
my love for you is true.
I'll wait for the day you walk back through that door,
darling I promise I'll wait for you.

It's hard to pass days without you,
and to think of all my sorrow,
after each day I pass through,
I wait in hope for tomorrow.

My arms want to hold you tight,
never to let go.
My eyes want you in my sight,
to admire you high and low.

Every night I stare at the crescent moon,
a part of it is missing just like me.
I know it will find its other half soon,
and together we will be.

Burcu Tecirli

Untitled

Dear Lord I've sinned, how well you know
were you to show the world the real me
they'd shun me like contagious leprosy

What chance have I before I die
To make amends for all the wrong I've done
and qualify to be a worthy son

As I confess, my sorrow's real
If only your forgiveness I could feel
experience uplifting as you heal

Forgive my doubt, in guilt I find
(and who am I to question what thou wilt)
my need to merit punishment's in built

Perhaps Dear Lord you fail to see
Forgiveness doesn't qualify for me
whenever it's acquired too easily

To purge my sin, dispel this guilt
I feel it warrants punishment instead
Whilst yet I live
Too late accounting for it, when I'm dead

S. Kelly

The Death Of Day

The mauve mists lowered like a curtain, the clouds that sketched
the borders moved in wanton anger to cover the swarthy sky.
The sallow trees brushed against the ignorant world, while a
rigid wall of chill pressed close against the fabric of my soul.

Light was drawn away to be dismembered by the innocent
inevitability of the night.
As a lone bird in tides of infrequent dusk glides, I alone was
fearful of the ever increasing voyager-time. Timid was I at the
thought of my disembodied self, disunited with reality
remembered yet forgotten,

Desolate as the same cautionary mist, my journey was ended
like the night, my fate was unpreventable.
Becoming a remote figure in a plagued world.
Penetrating the skin, squeezing my breath, finally like the foul
smell of ending winter destiny collapsed upon my soul.

Birth both my life and death, a transformation of soul, day to
night was the business transacted. My beginnings fading
into an unconscious memory.
The dawn would again be a fact, but not mine. Life would be
as new as the miracle of existence. My soul's death was
complete, the fragile grip on reality which I held was severed.
My life-day was terminated.

Rebecca Harris

The Thinnest Line

Today there is the thinnest line,
between progress and decline.
As man destroys untarnished land,
all nature needs is a helping hand.

Dead fish floating on polluted seas,
rain forests stripped bare of their trees.
A drifting oil slick creates despair,
migrating birds are no longer there.

No ozone layer to shield precious life,
Ultra-Violet rays cut through like a knife.
Acid rain destroying our trees,
eroding soil and once green leaves.

Toxic waste dumped in a river,
where fish can't swim and plants just wither.
Nuclear waste and radiation,
leak from the monstrous power station.

There are solutions, so we must act now,
to stop the damage, only man knows how.
We extract Earth's resources just like a gannet,
let's stop the greed and save our planet.

Mark Nobes

Sweet Dreams

These days so long take the dust and sleep,
And shades of the night appear.
I sit and watch the sun pulled deep,
Into the glistening arms of the sea.
Clouds drift by, silhouettes in the fading light,
Then stretch out to grasp the black of the night.
Only now my thoughts can be my own.
My mind free of all but you.
Wherever you are I know you will be thinking of me too.
So till the dawn comes once more
Let's set all else aside.
We'll close our eyes and open the door
Of dreams of you and I.

Jayne MacFarlane

The Man On The Street

He looked so vulnerable, he looked so young,
Yet in his eyes loomed the signs of age.
He blamed no one, showed no hatred
Trusted everyone,
He had no sentiments of rage.
His survival was unaccompanied
No friends had he to greet,
The doorway was his solitude and the pavement made him
A Man on the Street.

His cries were ignored, his pleas went unnoticed,
And yet he sustained hope.
Maybe he understood
The reality of his life,
And knew this was the only way to cope.
His future was unknown,
Society had been such a cheat
To forget this man, accept his plight and abuse him
This Man on the Street.

Emma Denslow

High Hill, In Spring

My dog and I stand on this hill, thoughtful
The west wind blowing, but not so still
I gaze across the grey blue sea.
Where colourful yachts are racing in the breeze
I stand and stare at the wonder of nature,
The different hues, of bushes and trees,
Cowslips, blue bells, the shunned golden dandelion,
The crisp white heads of daisy's, peeping thro' the grass
One can't be too thankful, we have eyes to see
The loveliness of nature, which are given us free.

Freda Harris

My Frances Mary

I kissed you, my love, without knowing then,
That this was goodbye, you would not wake again.
I saw in your eyes, like a bright glowing fire,
A fiery red cross burning clear,
I knew you were weary, and wanted to rest,
I knew not - the end was so near.

I kissed your soft lips, you could not respond,
I kissed twice, the tip of your nose.
I gave you a hug, as I settled you down,
I watched your green eyes - slowly close.

I kissed your sweet brow - twice - as usual, my love,
Then left you to rest, by my side.
As I sat there waiting, for you to awake,
I did not realize - you had died.

I kissed you once more, your sweet lips were cold,
The truth, on me started to dawn.
Whilst I sat there waiting - to help you again,
We'd parted - my Sweetheart, you'd gone.
No longer together, death forced us apart,
But I'm not alone love, you're here - in my heart.

Francis Rennie

Mother Knows Best

She looks up at me with a twisted smile.
In a while I know she will cry.
Up come her knees, her face turns to red
She had wind, and I know, I'm a mother.

Her first day at school and she isn't sure
If she should go or stay home.
I'll do the crying, she'll be okay
How do I know? I'm a mother

Her first young man looks shifty to me.
I'm sure it will all end in tears,
She storms in the house saying never again
There'll be others, I know, I'm a mother.

The day she was married I was so proud
My beautiful daughter a bride,
She was all smiles, I was in tears
But then as you know, I'm a mother.

The daughter she had was as lovely as she
As she cradled her there in her arms.
We both cried together, and she said to me
I know it's okay, I'm a mother

Mamie K. Graham

New Year

Lord, make it more wonderful this New Year dawning;
Let the sun rising, transfigure all the dark earth;
Mist of the morn dispel with motion of white wings;
Force of the earth's founding in a New Year's birth
Let it manna with renewed wonder all living things;
Magic of Nature seen as in the first light dawning.

As in the first earth lighting be this new dawning;
Power of the one Great Star be all truth revealing;
Dwellings of mankind roofed with loving light-fall;
Testament of man's worth seen in each day's healing
Let it preach of the Wonder bedded in a dark stall;
Light of the Word seen in each new birth's dawning.

Lord, make it more wonderful this New Year dawning;
Let the sun rising, rose-red our towering darkness;
Murk of men's minds cleanse with a rainbow shining;
Spirit of the light-giving sun in renewed whiteness
Let it fire the great leaders with a fierce fining;
Prayers for peace grant in this New Year's dawning.

Ted Harben

A Kiss Is Forever

His hat hung low, over his face
I'm so desperate for his embrace.
I held his hand, once so strong
Hoping he'd stir, but I was wrong.

This man is silent, but wasn't always
Now he is distant, far far away.
I stroke his hair, and kiss his brow,
how I wish he'd kiss me now.

I felt his body, to touch is cold
his time has come now he is old
He's left my side, I'm on my own,
my world is shattered, now he is gone.

Laying awake, unable to sleep
Missing my man, it cuts so deep
I am old, belonging only to one
the one I married, in 1941.

Walking alone, I feel no fear
Everything is lovely and peaceful have,
Hearing his voice, I reach for his hands
As he kisses me now, I'm in his land.

Sindy-Lou May

The Heroine

Fire! Fire!

Everybody's afraid
Everybody's panicking
Shouting, even screaming

"Don't panic, think," I tell myself,
while watching the flames:
Leaping high, dancing everywhere, eating everything....

I forced myself to keep my mouth shut
to keep myself from screaming
to keep myself from shouting

I looked toward the phone: Red hot, melting
I looked toward the door: Flames licking at it

I looked toward our one and only window:
Thank God! It was safe, tucked away in the corner
away from the flames, away from danger

I rallied my family — though I'm only eleven
and we climbed out to safety, although nothing was left of our house
I am the heroine of the family, I saved them from a fire

Alfreda Wong

Untitled

The children are hurt,
The woman is sad,
The man she loved has gone mad in the head,
He no longer loves her,
He no longer needs her,
She remembers the happy times,
The love they once knew,
But now he can't stand her,
And wishes her dead,
Her man has gone mad in the head.

In sickness and health,
For better or worse,
The words come back to her now,
He's packing his case,
His children stand watching,
He walks out the door,
She's sad now he's gone,
And life must go on,
Her man has gone mad in the head.

A. Robertson

New World

We must not ruin our world
Every mountain, river and sea.
We must not destroy the planet
All the animals, plants and trees.
Every boy and girl, make it clear
We're polluting the atmosphere.
Everything is turning to plastic
To ruin it, would be drastic.
It's such a wonderful world,
With the flowers, the butterflies and the bees,
The elephant, bear, and tiger,
The rhinoceros, all of these.
All help to make our world
A beautiful, peaceful place.
We do not want mankind,
To call it a disgrace.

Rose Broadley

Utter Of An Insane Mind

I'm the ultimate sign of society oppression,
of women's envy and men obsession.
With my painted face, I'm often seen,
on page 3 and your TV screen,
I grace the covers of Bella, women's own
With my sultry looks in an alluring gown,
Whenever you go, you'll see me,
I'm your bondage and their fantasy.

Pretty and feminine, that's how girls should be,
Dictates this consumer society,
What if I want to be me,
Not another carbon copy,
I don't want to be painted to perfection
to become another human possession,
Don't need your approval, got my own individuality
Happy to be a woman who's broken free

V. Mohammed

To The Little Children

Don't grow up angry
Don't grow up mad
Don't grow up frightened
Don't grow up sad.

How can a world blame you
With the atrocity you have seen
In the cold light of day
Of the massacre that has been.

You are so young and innocent
Your ability to understand restricted
How could this have happened
No one could have predicted.

You must grow up strong
You must grow up happy
You must grow up striving not to blame
For you are the hopes and the future of Dunblane.

Eileen Mowat

Ode Of Life

To have and to hold, is not for me
To have and be loved must not be,
Friendships I have but do not belong
What I feel is right, has been declared wrong.

Loyalty and love was mine to give,
To the one you know I feel could be so,
But it must not be seen by those others you know.

For them their lives must glow,
But for me, this must not be so,
So, regretfully from all this I must go,
Because nobody said, I want you so.

Gwen Ladzrie

A Poem For Stewardship

We come, we are ambassadors for Christ and for His body church;
Not for ourselves we speak, but for Him,
His words are in our hearts, and on our lips -
Forgetful we may be of much He gives -
But yet we do believe that we should speak
Of all His goodness and of His great works for all mankind.

Is it too much to ask that we should offer Him
Some token of our thanks for all that he has given.
In healing arts, in wealth of harvest yield,
Our lives, the beauty of the earth, which,
    though man may do his worst,
Does yet bring forth a bounteous wealth;
In man's creations He shows forth His hand
And brings us to our knees in adoration,
Not of man, but of His works.

We are His hands to work, His feet to bring the Gospel,
His heart to beat with sorrow and compassion
At all the wickedness and misery of the world.
We are His voice to speak His word,
To sing His praise unto Eternity.

If we, the pillars and living stones, do fall then falls our Church
And Jesus Christ our Saviour came in vain.

Patricia F. Arnett

Mum

A year has passed oh so fast, since you went away.
It doesn't change my love though mum.
I miss you more each day.
And time goes by so slowly, since you left my side.
But knowing that you loved me,
it fills my heart with pride.
So I'll carry that pride with me,
until that special day.
When you'll be by my side again.
For this I hope and pray.
A mum is like a treasure, you keep close to your heart.
And even when they're for away, you never really part.
Mum's there for the good time's
Mum's there for the bad.
Mum's probably the greatest friend
a girl could ever have.
So a message to my dear mum,
and mother's all around.
You will always be the greatest
gift ever to be found.

Lynn Brown

The Beautiful Eyes Of A Child

So wonderful are the eyes of a child,
  No evil can they see.
So innocent and beautiful,
  I wish they belonged to me.

So pure they are like angels eyes,
  And the clear blue sky above,
Oh! How I wish I had those eyes,
  To see the things I love.

I once had the eyes of a child,
  I thought the world has great.
I never knew when I grew up,
  It would be full of hate.

I used to watch the flowers,
  Blooming in the spring,
And when I'd watch the little birds,
  They would begin to sing.

But, now when I think of a child's eyes,
  It makes me feel so sad,
For I wish I was a child again.
  To see what I once had.

Barbara Ann Young

Depression

Some complain their life is dull,
Some complain their life's too full,

Yet those that don't complain have passed their stage
Their hearts are full of built-up Rage.

Their eyes fill up with thoughts of fear
Hope falls down with every Tear

Depressed, lonely, in pain or sad
They long for the happiness they once had.
They feel they're locked inside a room
decorated in a shade of gloom.

Yet within this room their problems spread.
They wonder how better off is dead
Life tells of no promises nor no lies
But only makes us slightly more wise.

Our head becomes full, our hearts become hard
Waiting for life to deal its next Card.

Diane Coates

Ireland

On Celtic crosses,
Wretched wretches, retch their green bile,
'Twixt Irish eyes and smiles,
And wholehearted hearts of porter,
They plot their winsome wiles

On bloody banners, bright and borne
Torn, by hearts of thorn,
In fields where battle left its fragrant scorn,
The lonely clay, care worn

If men of mind, were men of mortal warmth
Could see the curse of kindred cant
And leave the human earth, to plant

Freed from the sinful smear
May grow a path of hopeful tears
Then yesterday may drown in cheers

Since weeping without tears
Is the saddest sadness of them all

Hugh Feeney

Always

It's all been said before,
Across a crowded room and more.
Love at first sight, a pounding heart,
Will this really be the fresh start?
Kissed and cuddled, for an age it seems,
Could she really be the one of my dreams?
Night adventured, like never before,
Truly, I couldn't ask for more.
Lover, friend, confidante,
Partner, nurse and heaven sent.
Funny how it seems like yesterday,
It's been ten years now,
Two months, forever and a day....

Colin Price

Fleetwood Skies

Amber leaves falling from fleetwood skies.
Golden feathers floating before your eyes,
Feeling twirling sensations,
Making mystic revelations,
Lift's you up with a surprise,
Beaming at the topaz sun,
The whispers of when you were young,
Reaching towards mars,
Hoping for the stars,
Suddenly falling,
Landing on the face of the earth,
Feeling the soft crumbling turf,
Gazing at the world beyond,
Named fleetwood skies.

Emma-Jane Melton

Untitled

Retirement leaves us out on Limbo
Should this happen
If we sit with arms Akimbo
Senses dampen
Rouse yourself you are not dead
So much to do
Activate your mind instead
Get off the stool

My niece is proficient and very smart
She has business acumen to a fine art
My mentor has answers already there
If not they are solved without tearing a hair

Phyllis F. Straker

Life Condensed

We've shared a life-time in only three years
We've grown close together and shared lots of tears
We've had passionate moments and gone off the planet
We've been tender and loving and sometimes quite manic.

We've argued the toss and come close to a fight
But we've always made up and it's always come right
I've waited for you for half of a life
But it's been worth every minute of struggle and strife.

We've had long dreamed of trips and excursions galore
You've brought to this life quite a lot and much more
We've laughed and we've loved and quite reached the heights
We've shared every heartache and had many frights.

At last you turned up and gave me such love
I could see in your eyes and thanked Him up above
I want only you and hope that you'll stay
I need you so much and no more can I say.

Eunice Doyle

The Music Of Life

Resounding within us, the thoughts of today
are the very music of life,
and we dance to the tunes, bad or good, they play,
composing the song of our life.

Our thought-patterns, if negative,
Cascade like chaotic cacophony,
our thought-patterns, if positive,
flow like harmonious and sweet symphony.

If the notes heard are out of tune,
our thought-patterns have composed the wrong song,
but if the notes heard are in tune,
our thought-patterns have composed the right song.

Whatever song we sing out into the vast cosmos,
the universal dome will reflect it back to us.

Rozarya Dyka-Gerard

Untitled

I have a Nana, her name is Rose
Her name matches her red rosy cheeks,
She enjoys dancing and holidays away
If she had the money she'd be gone for weeks

When I was young I stayed at her house
At week-ends and holidays too,
She was really busy looking after us all
Now she's taking the break that she's due

You see she had seven children,
Four girls and three boys as well,
Her house was always full
So she has many stories to tell

So this is about my dear Nana
Whom I really love very much,
And I'm sure the feelings mutual
As she's lovely with a caring touch.

Michelle Saini

Untitled

I feel a great weight of nothingness
Coming from inside me,
That pulls down my occasional spirits of high
Thoughts.

I feel I have everything
Yet I find I have nothing.

I exist, though not through my own choice,
I feel it o.k. to be here, but I want to go.

I'm so confused I don't know how I'm supposed to
Unleash my emotions.
It never stops or gets better - there's always
Something else.

Sometimes I wish it would just stop,
Then I could walk free alone,
Yet then I'd be lonely.

What am I to do?

Georgina Broome

Thoughts On A Winter's Journey

I love the Winter shape of trees,
And firelight shadows on the wall,
I don't mind if the puddles freeze,
I think I love the Winter best of all!

But then - I love the fresh sweet scent of Springtime flowers,
The liquid notes of blackbirds' mating call,
The freshening gentleness of April showers,
Perhaps I love the Springtime best of all?

But then - I love the warmth of Summer days,
The sound of racquet, bat and ball-
The sparkling sea through sunlit haze
So do I love the Summer best of all?

But then - I love the crunch of Autumn leaves,
The jewel bright colours of the Fall,
The dew be-spangled web the spider weaves,
So could it be, I love the Autumn best of all?

But no - For as the years go fleeting by,
Speeding me to that Final Call,
I've learnt through heart, and ear and eye,
That every season is the best of all!

Josephine Canham

Summer Palaces

They stand like an army of toy soldiers
Repelling the incoming tide
Secured by fraying old guy ropes
While supporting each other side by side.

Some look chic and lovingly cared for
With a sparkling gloss outer facade
While others hang together with a promise
Awaiting their fate on the promenade.

And who could blame them for choosing
To mount guard by the chilly North Sea
For the wind blowing straight from the Arctic
Must be faced to keep Anglia free.

These then are the Victorian Beach Huts
Of which Southwold is justly quite proud
As a haven and heaven terrestrial
Granting the front a blissful background.

So may Southwold preserve them forever
A memento of fine bygone days
To be savoured by locals and visitors
As in deck chairs they therapeutically laze.

Robert Main

Chess

The chequered board stood silent and empty,
Both sides armed and ready to attack.
A white pawn flinched; a dove of peace? Not he,
The colour of asylum walls, crazed with anger.
A Bishop of Death whispers in the black ranks,
And the black pawns slowly advance
Like night's veil sweeping the land.
White pawns become ready to defend.
Yin vs. Yang. Good vs. Bad?
Both sides clash, the raven and the dove
White knights wield swords, Swords of Truth?
Untrue, these swords are guilty of death.
An nonreligious bishop looks on like a grim reaper.
A white virgin queen turns her back in innocence.
A stake through the heart, a fall to the knees
All that is seen is death, as evil as the Black Hole of Calcutta?
A castle is left.
Covered in the blood of black and white, the castle knows not
which he is.
The blood is the same, he understands not
Why every one can't just be grey.

Rebecca Porter

The Village

What ever our legal status,
    what ever our Lordly claims;
Whether pence or pounds in the pocket
    or Smith or Jones in the names;
Right through the generations
    from earliest primitive man,
The earth has been our mother;
    the village the natural plan.

Here in the open country our forefathers toiled to live;
Delved like their grandsire Adam, span like their grandam Eve;
Built us our church with their labours,
    guided the stream to the mill,
Carted the stone from the quarry, pastured their flocks on the hill.

Now we, their children, inherit
    the buildings, the roads and the skills,
The house-hold gods of the homestead,
    the good of their lives and the ills.
When we gather in holy places, summoned by bells from the tower,
Remember the works of our grandsires and praise ye the Lord
    in His choir

Charles Brundrett

The Murder Of Duncan

Is this a dagger I see before mine eyes?
It looks genuine, yet it is an illusion
I cannot feel the dagger even though I try to snatch it
This must be trickery of the mind
Or might it be real?

Dagger, you lead me towards where I must go
Are you the instrument I must use
And on thy blade you show me blood
It is not my blood yet it could be Duncan's
Have I done the deed?

Thoughts of murder are cavorting upon my mind
The world is at sleep and rest
But I am awake and living the nightmare for Duncan
He will awake no more
And this to my gain?

I move like a ghost in the dead of the night
And take the gift of horror to Duncan
A bell rings though hear it not Duncan
For this is a knell
That summons Duncan to heaven or to hell

Neil Laman

The World Soul

O my brother, lover, sister, daughters,
In every awesome imagining,
View the world's soul in all its glory,
Mountains, lakes abattoirs, technology,
Live many madnesses for its beauty,
Love it, long for it, see it, feel it,
Awake from your long subjectivity
To its moving, glowing, radiant need,
Help it bound in chains to be ever free,
Care for this aching world constantly;
Notitia, notitia, O my daughters!
Attentively attend to its slaughters,
Breathe into the face of the world its fire,
With courage in the heart, expire, inspire!

Gillian Patterson

Caroline's Paintbox

Today, I would like to say, come in whoever you are
come on in and see my paintbox.
Red is a red, red ruby glistening like a star.
Anger I think it could be or roses sent from afar.
A red boat sailing in the sea.
Orange becomes the sun, maybe part of a rainbow,
street lights shining in the night - an orange falling into the snow.
Pink could be the colour of the cuckoo that strikes on the hour,
perhaps painting hanging on the wall - or pink flower blossoms
falling like a shower.
A memory of love in all.
Blue seems to be everywhere - the big roaring sea, a little bow
in your hair, and a blue flower seeming so small,
white is the cold winter snow,
a blank piece of paper - all the whites I do not know
but I to know of a pretty white dress that I have seen.
Gold is like a piece of the rainbow or the leaves in autumn.
Maybe someone's hair shining in the sun.
It seems like the colour of wonder.

Caroline Ashley Smith

Down And Out

A man was walking down the lane -
On his face was so much pain.
His clothes were dirty, tattered and torn.
His feet were blistered his shoes well worn.
Food would be little and not very often
Like a lot out there he would be forgotten,
That man's life must have fallen apart,
Who knows, who cares?
What he feels in his heart.
His world must have turned upside down.
So if ever you pass him on your way
Give always a smile.
And a word could you say,
Such a lot of them all living wild
Do not forget they're someone's child.

Olga Kirkup

The Seasons

Spring is with us once again as crocuses appear.
The daffodils and tulips brightly coloured, come each year.
And there is newness everywhere just look around and see
The freshness and the beauty just made for you and me.

Then follows summer once again with colours of every hue.
Flowers for the butterfly and nectar for the bee.
Hollyhocks and sunflowers, delphiniums of every blue.
The perfume and the beauty just made for me and you.

Autumn comes around once more with golden russet browns
Flowers that bloomed brightly, have given up their crowns.
But it is such a lovely time just look around and see
The loveliness of autumn just made for you and me.

Winter is here with a silence as soft snow falls around,
Many things just sleep now below the quiet ground.
But bright berries and the evergreens are still there for you to see.
The crispness of the winter, just made for you and me.

Brenda Shirley Clark

Tower Block Curtains

Blank naked faces of
concrete frozen against a
grey sky. In the wind
In the rain. In the cloud.

Don't turn your back on
the cracks in the ceiling
and the damp and the lifts
that won't work and the
stairs where dogs crap.

Don't cover your ears from
the noises of babies and
singled mothers crying and dogs
barking and young couples tiffing.

Don't hold your nose against
the curry and the bacon and
the piss in the lifts and the
blocked up loos the council can't fix.

We don't.
This is life.

Akkas Al-Ali

Freedom?

People all think they're free,
To do what they like and see what they see,
But people don't realize,
There's no democracy.

The law is always favoured to a few particular sides,
And everyone else is just taken for a ride.

You can't shout out your belief,
"Save that tree",
As people higher than you won't set it free.

If it's bringing in profit,
Then they don't give a sh**.

So now people do you see what I see?
There's no democracy to set us free.

Stand up for you rights
Be it shouting out loud or rallying at night,
Because the future is ours,
And the future is ripe.

Sarah Kent

Fit To Be Loved

From the moment you broke the threshold
I adored you,
You belonged to me
And I loved you.

We grew together yet differently
I always weak and feeble,
You the leader
And I left you.

You joined me yet were unhappy
We diverted,
You changed or was it I?
No longer my little one.

I the B****!!
What changed across the big pond?
Once again we land together
But now thousands of miles apart.

You left me
I remain
Yet was unhappy.
So sorry, what changed?

Trudy Fletcher

Fire Escape Aversion

I'm standing on a ledge, outside the window of a room
which contains my life.
Far below, I can make out the lights of the world,
going on without me.
I don't know why the f*** I came out here.
I know what's in the room though,
I know the ceiling cracks.
Every chip in every cup.
I am familiar with each and every particle of dust.
I can dimly remember an irresistible urge to flee
from there, to escape as urgently as if the
place was ablaze.
Outside now, the physical memory of this feeling
has faded from my jangled nerves, and more
than ever, the uncomfortable ordinariness of
the room seems warm and cosy to me.

I know I'd feel the same again though,
the carpet has been soaked in some cruel emetic,
the chairs electrified, and I have been conditioned...
to respond by running,
but no-one said which way.

David Bolton

As I Sit

As I sit watching the drifting, carefree clouds,
Slipping their soft, cotton wool fingers
Over the edge of the moon,

I remember the heavenly look, that used to spread across your face,
Every time my fingers slid over your shoulder,
To sensitively caress your breast.

As I sit hearing the ocean waves,
Pound and break as they hit the rocks,
With a loud hushing sound.

I remember the way you gasped with ecstasy,
Every time my pelvis thrust towards your body.

As I sit and feel the breeze that whispers in the leaves on the trees,
I remember how you used to insist on lying on the floor,
So the cool draft that blew under the doorway,
Could cool your body as our passion burned with such an ardour inside.

I remember feeling like I was burning in the fires of hell,
while lying in the cool snow of heaven.

Carl W. Pardoe

Fantasy Bachelor

My life as a Single Man,
Is not a Raunchy as one might believe,
I'm currently thirty-two years old...,
...in a few weeks thirty-three,
Out wining and dining every night,
With a different girl upon my sleeve,
Stereotyped from films and books...,
The bachelor has both Cash and Looks,
He is Cool in Every situation...,
And Never resorts to Masturbation.
Women fulfil his every Desire...,
With Every Night His Lion's A fire!.
He's the envy of Every man in town...,
Who don't have the Nerve to Fool-Around.
He Never Ages, I know Not why,
Each day of his life is a 'carefree lie,'
A work of fiction and addiction...,
This life of love, Sex and Conviction...,
In Truth We Know This Cannot Be...,
The Majority Are Dull, like you... and me.

V. Cooper

Out Of Reach

The journey is full of mixed emotions,
who will ever have a possible explanation?
'She will get no better, just worse,'
thank you, you bastard of a nurse.

Staring, wandering, sleeping, shouting,
laughing, fidgeting, moaning, singing,
coughing, slavering, choking, dying.

Just a little smile, to show that it really is all worthwhile,
but that's just too hard, there's too many people on your guard.

Your mind is deep in concentration,
it recalls everything from childhood to separation.
You just don't say a word - it's too difficult,
don't worry, everybody knows it wasn't your fault.

A touch of your hand, a kiss on the cheek,
it means so much, it's tough to speak,
I know you will always be with me,
I just pretend you have no deficiency.

You're not the person I used to know
but soon I know you'll have to go
until that day comes, I'm always with you,
even though you never recognize who this face belongs to.

Beverley Harley

Ignominy

There comes a time
When I feel like...
Can you understand that?
Can you relate to that?
I see my skin and the posters on the wall
it's the same, maybe more?
I wish I was someone famous...
So they'd idolize me when I commit suicide!
Even that is not an option in this world of...
But watch the T.V., Bill Clinton's on
and they're blaming Lebanon.
Which pissed poor old humble Israel!
I wish I was a Jew so someone would sympathize with me
And I wish I was Christian so someone would respect me
And I wish I was a Whiteman so I'd never be a minority
And I wish I was a nazi so they'd all be scared of me!
And I wish I had a thousand lovers, that I'd change overnight!
But, only Biblical prophets have such privileges...
weren't they sent by God?

Mohamed Akl Mousa

View From A Child

Why do mum and daddy fight?
I heard them falling out last night!

Why did mum call dad a bastard,
Is it 'cos' he's sometimes plastered?

Why did dad call mum Martini,
Is it 'cos' she's friends with Rene?

They call each other different names.
Is it one of adults games?

They rant and rave, curse and swear.
Yet seem to me for each to care!

They shout and call; sometimes they whisper.
Then out of the blue dad'll kiss her?

They push and shove; wrestle madly.
To bed I'm sent; be honest gladly!

Why do mum and daddy fight?
I heard them calling out tonight!

Neil C. Ormesher

Courtesan

She never loved you: now she's gone,
That b**** you called a wife.
I hope that now the deed is done
You'll realize I'm the only one
To re-inspire your life.

So welcome to my open arms
I'll love you more than any.
I'll give you full run of my charms
No other men, no false alarms,
'Till I've spent your last penny.

And when I've sucked you dry I'll go
Without recrimination.
No bitter word, no violent blow
Because I'm cute enough to know
A husk has no sensation.

David Edwards

Absent Father (Of My Children)

And so you reach out from my past
To kick me in the guts at last
Lying in your shadow cast
You Bastard

You welcome them, and show you care
With slate wiped clean, you three can share
And I can fall into despair
You Bastard

With you, no memories of rows
Of growing up, of silly cows,
So you can be their best friend now
You Bastard

Janis Brown

O Lord Art Thou Sleeping

O Lord art thou sleeping?
Pray open thine eyes
Mankind's cataclysm has blackened blue skies
Death's purpose is fickle
Resentment has guns
Pre-eminent religion is bred in our sons

Insensate the slaughter
That darkens our door
The fear of your father embowers us no more
Cast out thy staff
Dispatch brimstone and fire
Berate the masses of Lucifer's choir

Defiance be silenced
Evil be dead
Resurrect the children whose blood has been shed
O Lord art thou sleeping?
Pray open thine eyes
Annihilate the bastards that blackened blue skies

Carl Arthur Harrison

Only Close Encounters

Leaves collaged by nature's hand.

Sheep's wool webbed and fluffed
around briar thorns.

A black bird's majestic indifference
as it consumes a purple worm.

Clumsy dog as it snuffles the
ground and slashes piss indiscriminately.

Cold broken rock face softened by
purple moss.

Life given through me by purple heart.

Quinten Scallon

The Leadon

Let me stray o'er verdant bank
Rest neath serried willow rank
Cast my line on sparkling glide
Finning trout and grayling hide

Let me walk where bluebell grow
Buttercup, daisy carpets throw
Dapple shade of shadows dance
Fox-glove, orchid bee romance

Let me watch the mayflies fall
Just one night their duty call
Olives drift on spinnaker wing
To sink in void of rising ring

Let me hear tree breezes sigh
Watch yellow flags of iris fly
Zephyrs snatch at leafy bough
Whisper music reedmace sough

Let me return to valley stream
To drink enchanted magic dream
Dipping swallows surface greet
Briefly kiss clear water sweet

R. J. Charlesworth

Your Last Rights

(Gun click.)

Fear.
Love, Hate, Pain.
Tears trickle.
Hurt, Suffering.
Agonizing waiting.
Brain bursting.
The life you know, slipping away.
Black, White, Day, Night,
The Sun, the Moon, the Stars.
Galaxies drifting away.
The Universe.
God.
An age gone by, a love lost,
A wasted time, a sullen youth.
The blackest moments,
The deepest despair.
But...
You don't care.

(Gun fires.)

Claire Machin

Lucifer

Within
The vastness
That is
Space
There
Comes a point
Where
No star's ray
Can
Penetrate
The darkness
Beyond
Light

Doreen V. Saddleton

My Cat

There was a cat who was so fat
he could hardly walk
he meows when it's time to talk
he eats without a folk.
He loves the taste of pork
he always tries to eat my chalk

Bernadette Necchi

The March

Bravely they marched in file
Indian-style, each clutching each
with steel-shod claws
drawing blood, tasting good
And all around danced phantoms
with irreverent glee
Ectoplasmic ecstasy

Through acid rain they strayed
hate-sprayed from glutinous gobs
passing as clouds, dissolving marrow
from arthritic bones
Until fish-like they floundered
on the beach of each one's own despair
amid the rotting sewage there

Then swept into the sanguine sea
they spawned, mutated,
and were finally free.

Russ Andrews

"Cobweb Dreams"

If only I had the
    wings of a dove,
I'd fly to you, and
    there I'd stay,
Forever, I'd stay in
    your heart,
And from your side,
    I'd never stray;
But I've no wings,
    I cannot fly,
My life's confined,
    And so am I;
But dreams are bliss,
    So I can dream,
For cobweb dreams
    Are all they seem.
For cobweb dreams
    Are all they see

Betty Miller-Arnold

'Guildford'

High upon the rolling downs
Stands Guildford, loveliest of towns
Her cobbled streets so quaint to see,
Her castle known to history.
The river gliding gently by,
Cathedral soaring to the sky.
A school once founded by a king.
A church where pealing bells do ring.
A fine old clock set up on high,
To tell the time to passers by.
I love this town, so full of grace,
This peaceful happy dwelling place.

P. M. Baster

Does She Know?

She came towards me through the gloom,
I wonder why and where she went
With shuffling feet and back so bent.
We did not speak as we passed by
But as she looked I caught her eye.
She smiled a sad and wistful smile,
I fancied she'd remember
That day, a hundred years ago
We'd shared that warm September.
As children we had wandered free
And climbed the hill together
And rolled back down and laughed as we
Had tumbled in the heather.
    I loved her then - I love her now
Though she may never know it,
    Or has she always known I care
    And yet could never show it.

Beryl Marjorie Quinion

Billy's Broken Toy

Go to bed you naughty boy
Said mummy clutching the broken toy
So Billy climbed the wooden stair
His face all twisted with despair
As into his tiny room he stumbled
Underneath his breath he mumbled
I didn't mean to break my friend
I thought his arms and legs would bend
And we could both sit down for tea
And he could sing and dance like me
Mummy doesn't understand
I only meant to hold his hand
And take him for a little walk
And we could run and we could talk
Of all the things that we could do
But now I'm feeling very blue
My friend is lying there in pieces
And as my broken heart increases
I wish as hard as hard could be
My friend was sitting here with me

J. G. Wileman

Someone

You've nothing in this world
I'm told
Unless you have someone
To hold
The world would be a
Lonely place
If I could never see your face

You light the darkness
Of the night
You keep me safe till
morning light
you're always with me day and night
you're just a thought away

Promise me you'll always stay
And never ever
Go away
Always be my someone

M. Beynon

The Flame Of Life

The flame of life,
Flickers and eventually dies.
But it burns so vividly,
While it is alive.

So intense does it burn,
And so bright.
It almost hurts to look,
At the light.

The flame burns strong,
And its might is firm.
There is so much to give,
And so much to learn.

But soon the flame,
Grows so dim.
And it seems to have ended,
Before it can begin.

Della Nicholls

Untitled

Do watch it when the chimpanzee's
Impersonating socrates.
Since all the workings of his brain
Are geared to monetary gain,
What could this ape be out to do
But make a monkey out of you?
A dash, then, of socratic doubt
Before you dole the ducats out!

Kenneth Young

Time

Two watches lying side by side
Ticking in harmony
His and mine
Keeping the time
Like a clock work symphony.

They tick away the minutes
As we've ticked away the years
Through moments of ecstasy
Laughter, joy and tears.

As the fingers move around the face
Another day goes by.
Just like our lives,
His and mine
Gently moving through time.

Elizabeth M. Shaw

Age

Hands once firm and strong to shake
Now tremble, gnarled and twisted,
Eyes that sparkled clear and bright,
Now grey with vision misted.
No longer hearing everything
Just muffled voice and sound,
Instead of proudly striding out
Just shuffling around,
Respect him now, this man still feels,
Please try to understand.
Be patient, listen when he talks,
And give a helping hand.

Christine Radford

Peter Pig

This is the story of Peter Pig.
He had a long straight tail.
Every night he danced a jig
and drank a yard of ale.
Then one night there was a storm
Peter Pig was shaken,
he curled up his tail and ran like mad
just to save his bacon,
as he ran he had a fall,
his face went smack into a wall
that's the reason,
there's no doubts
why pigs have curly tails,
and snouts.

E. Crompton

Old Age

Days are long and uneventful,
No goal in view to spur me on,
No pressing job to warm the blood,
The dreary days stretch on and on.

Friends and family talk down to me
As to an imbecile or child,
About me, but excluding me.
As though I have no thought or mind.

Puzzles, crosswords, I'll try them all
I'll add up all accounts and bills
Yes, sure I'll keep my mind at work
The very thought just gives me thrills.

But now the children come from school
'Hi' Gran, they greet me as a mate
I've got to be in every game
I'm needed and it does feel great.

It's time for bed, the fun must end,
We've made our plans for next day's game
Happy, who cares what other's think.
I've found my place, I'm child again.

I. S. Weighill

The Beast

The beast that comes in the night.
It walks the street, it walks the road.
It stalks the very soul.
Thieves, villains, vandals and goths.
No longer at the gates of Rome.
They won't stop, at the garden gate.
Or even at the door.
The forces of evil ebb and flow.
Like the tide over sand.
Leaving no trace, only flotsam.
The wreckage of another life.
What is a victim's life worth?
Insurance remit in kind.
The worth of a victim fear.
Pain in ten pound notes.

Neville Birkett

Apart, But Still Together

We may be parted,
We may be miles apart,
But I still dream of you,
by the images in my heart.

Do you think of me?
Is it tearing you apart too?
I know it is torture,
But just think of me and you.

Together once again,
As if never parted,
Sharing time together,
talking open-hearted.

One day we will be together,
just like we were before,
But just remember this:
It's you that I adore.

Claire Smith

Who Knows

If the way
We,
As civilized beings
And intelligent animals
Treat
Other innocent life forms
The way
We do at present
We,
As well
Deserve such treatment.

We expect
To escape
Such behaviour in life.
In time,
Time will catch up
With us
And the goodness of life knows
What will happen to us.

Farld Flnzl

The Tartan

Here's to the weave of it
The cloth and plaid of it
The fighting sheen of it
The swing, the hue of it
The dark, the red of it
Every thread of it
The battle's fought in it
The honours won in it
The pride of wearing it
The men who fought
And died for it
The Scottish tartan.

George Muir

Untitled

Love is a rose
Petal on petal curled
Guarding close
Its precious centre
In early growth.

Love is a rose
Which gradually unfolds
Reveals its inner core
Petals fade, fall, decay
Adorning life's way
Perfume for friends and foes
Heedless of where scent goes.
No return it seeks, this petalled rose.

Spend itself, extends itself
Core and centre bared
Wind - blown, earth - born,
Roots itself
In life's source
And so it ever grows
love's rose.

Margaret Cunningham

Haiku

The minutes tick by
On the waiting room clock as
She waits for the pain

Lynda Winn

Obscurity

Deep is the sky
And empty the sea;
Dense is the shadow
That follows me.

Eyes that are empty
And hearts which are cold;
Time stands still
While we grow old.

Where is the warmth
That once we knew:
Made hearts beat fast,
Eyes fill with dew?

Lost in the sky
And drowned in the sea;
Engulfed in the shadows
Which hide you from me.

Jana Synek

A Near Miss

Creeping on with the traffics flow
crammed and canned in single file
beyond the bend, cars to and fro
behind a while, we stretch a mile.

Edging near, the lights in sight
wedging clear, asked left or right
seize the moment, don't hesitate
pull out now, accelerate.

The moments wrong, the times an error
a storm of wails hurls through the air,
it flashes in fury and horns in horror
as death advances in despair.

Rotates its weapon with actions swift
scrape with a screech
escape without clash
follows through with the drift
crazed and dazed and yet no smash.

Rhodri Phillips

My Nightmare!

I had a nightmare about Africa,
It took away my breath,
To see all the babies and children,
Doomed to terrible deaths!

I had a nightmare about Africa,
It was horrendous to see,
Young boys of 10 and 11,
Used as soldiers to fight and be free!

I had a nightmare about Africa,
I felt as if I would cry,
Cry for young girls and women,
That are used, abused, and then
Left to die!

I woke up after my nightmare,
I thought "Phew it was only a dream".
But then...I realised,
Somewhere out there,
It is real!

Louise Mannion

Happy Valley

The memories spanning time
Are still very strong,
Of a wondrous valley,
Not more than half a mile long.
A little dell and a brook,
With trees so straight and true,
Standing in their silent ranks,
Vertical on a sloping bank,
Their roots reaching downward,
To the water flowing through.

Where once glorious nature,
Held undisputed sway,
It has a doubtful future,
Now, close to a busy motorway.
Yet young people still go there,
To play, as those of yesterday,
Who, with happiness can recall,
The lonely valley of peace and wonder,
With its trees so straight and tall.

Ronald V. Cooper

Mother Nature

I saw the mountain's beauty
Rear up into the sky
A fairy's ice-bound palace
Among the clouds so high

Grey rock and icy waters
In sparkling shades of blue
Among the gleaming snowslopes
A quite fantastic view

Who makes this mountain splendour
Where man has never trod?
It lifts our eyes to heaven
Reminding us of God.

Lee Baker

A Silent Way

Propped upright in his hospice bed
He waved the menu card away.
Its choice of food he could not eat -
He had not long to stay.

And, ere the evening sky glowed red,
He wakened to another day
Which offered wine and offered bread -
But not upon a silver tray.

They fed him as they feed the dead
Brought back to life - a silent way;
Rejoicing in his health and peace
That timeless day.

Frederick E. Mold

A Passing Thought

I want to write a poem,
Because that's what I like,
Just a minute - no more peace
Here comes the motor-bike.

It is the son, oh what big boots,
He really looks a wreck,
And what are all those whiskers
That are growing around his neck?

His sister will come flying home,
She's trying to get thinner,
She's eaten lots of stodge you see,
"Hello mum, what's for dinner?"

My cooking's poor, with new ideas
I certainly will grapple,
They say they don't like rhubarb,
And they're fed up with stewed apple.

I think about it sometimes,
Being a mother and a wife,
And wonder what it's all about
It is a funny life.

I. J. Wickert

Mother's Driving

Don't drive so fast Fred.
And watch that car ahead
If he had put his breaks on
We could possibly be dead.

Put the wipers on Fred
Don't wait till you can't see
Remember when it rained last
You almost hit a tree

Did you check the tires Fred
Did you fix that leak
What is that bump Fred
is that another squeak.

Did you check the lights Fred
Did you check the oil
And when you filled the flasks Fred
did the kettle boil

Pull over Fred and mind that bus
and don't take the bends so fast
If we ever had a new car
I'm sure it wouldn't last.

L. P. Neville

The Gentle Executive

The gentle executive
Witnessed a twitching
That tried to hide
Within the overseer's eyes.
"I'll have to ask the men,"
The overseer said.
As expected, the men said, "No."
Later,
Shivering by a high window,
(Near edges of space),
The gentle executive
Stared
At the factory's ledge.
It invited him, (tied in a sack),
To fall outside.
But he refused.
Instead - he sighed.
It was later,
Downing a double Scotch,
He died.

John Dove

Covers

Behind a newspaper
I sit
Words
ineffectual
meaningless
sounds
irritate my ears while
I think,
An aching chasm yawns inside me
The sides gaping wide;
I drink coffee and
smoke, the haze covers
my eyes, my hair droops
to cover my thoughts
and behind my dark glasses
You fill my mind.

Sandra K. Cochrane

Precious Time

All I ever asked for
Was a little of your time
Not a bunch of flowers
Or a bottle of sparkling wine
Not hello, goodbye
I may see you later on
Or we can go out tomorrow evening
Maybe,
If you want to come

Time is of the essence
When you're mostly on your own
Having plenty of it, and
Trying not to be alone
Though you bring me presents
Which is a lovely thought
The thing I want most from you
Is time, which can't be bought

Sheila Graham

Skies

Why do they visit our earth
Was it ever the land of their birth

Are they the masters
And we the slaves

Are we afraid their superior brains
Will leave ours in chains

Rose Morgan

Our World

Today's world is becoming a wicked place
with bombings and shootings going on,
what has become of the human race,
where has all the goodness gone?

What do we see on the news
nothing but heartache and sorrow,
people starting their views.
As we wonder what happens tomorrow.

Why is our world full of hate?
with anger and tempers flowing
for this world I fear it's to late,
as violence and greed start growing.

People aren't safe in there home
children can't play in the street,
women wont walk on their own,
for fear of who they might meet.

So why can't we all stand together,
and make our lives worth living
Give us peace and love forever,
now it's time to start giving.

Janette Smith

Remembering Xmas

Xmas time comes once a year
as all of us do know

Bells ringing carol singing
children playing in the snow.

Dad puts up the Xmas tree
while mum is making pies

And there are all the children
with wonder in their eyes

The Xmas cards are all sent out
to Uncles, Aunties, and friends

And people come to visit
with the love that Xmas sends

Lets not forget it's Jesus
who made it all come true,

Because we love him very much
and he loves me and you.

Sylvia King

Untitled

Spent a restless night,
Did not sleep again
And cried, cried and cried
Wallowing in pain.

Oh, I can sing a song
Of loneliness and sacrifice,
Of longing to belong,
Of burdens, bonds and lies,

Of going without and of making do
All in the name of love -
Of disloyalty too,
Of destruction and rebuff.

I was led on a very tight rope
And now I feel the strain.
It is so difficult to cope
When all has been in vain.

Yesterday's mistakes
Haunt me today -
Life offers so few breaks
And I have thrown them away!

Ingrid Kemna

A True Story

What I have seen the other day,
I cannot think of, cannot say.
The pain and horror took my soul,
I've closed my eyes, it was so foul.

I've seen the girl, the age of five.
She has deserved a happy life,
But I've not seen her in her bed.
She lied in coffin, she was dead.

The blood has covered all her face.
A knife has left its mortal trace.
He hasn't spared a helpless kid.
Now, look, you, monster, what you did!

He has been there, I could see,
His running eyes have nagged at me,
If there is justice in this world,
Then he will mount the scaffold.

So for how long we gonna watch it,
The children being killed and tortured,
He's not a stranger, I'd rather say,
He was too close..., he was her father.

Maria A. Jeparska

Hands

What can I do for you?
With hands I have misused
But since Jesus came to me
My hands have made a recovery

My hands of love, I wish to use
To serve the Lord on high;
With hands to pray and praise the Lord,
And raise his name up high.

To give hands to care for others needs
In my daily walk of life,
In my work and in my leisure,
May my hands give full measure.

Jennifer Routledge

Magic

The romance of a summer night,
deep velvet sky and soft moonlight;
a thousand glittering stars above,
the throbbing of two hearts in love;
that's magic.

The moonlight shining on your face,
the trembling touch of your embrace;
the gentle fragrance of your hair,
just knowing that you really care;
that's magic.

Just standing there our arms entwined,
my lips seek yours and yours seek mine;
your sweet warm breath upon my cheek,
so happy I can hardly speak;
that's magic.

The enchantment of this lovely night,
two happy people, two hearts alight;
fingers trembling at each touch,
those tender words, I love you so much;
that's magic.

W. Sheldon

Space Fiction

My love,
My sweet, intergalactic love
On that unearth-like planet
Around a giant star;
Not far in my imagination,
Too far for all but love.

I am content
To love you in this way,
Content
To live two hundred years too early
For any interstellar colour bar.

Ian S. Menzies

Istanbul, The Bazaar

Tourists in the Bazaar
    shudder,
    mouths ajar;
mistaking for lovers
sister and brother
lying side by side,
    blood splattering
    their coloured umbrella.

Paying the price
    of a name
    not right
    for the leader
    of the freedom fighters.

Now, how shall I repay
    the kindness
    they showed me yesterday?

Anthony Bernard Clarke

From The Mouths Of Babes

My heart sinks in my chest
As my ears take in the words.
I have trouble believing
The sounds I've just heard.
A prejudice opinion,
From an unknowing mind.
An ignorant view
From eyes so blind.
Never given chances
To see through their eyes,
So undoubted truths
Are extracted from lies.
Too young and naive
To form their own vision,
They only know what they're taught.
They don't make the decision.
Slowly, but surely
The chance of peace fades,
As this prejudice flows
From the mouths of babes!

Lyndsey Merry

Summer Time

Summer sweet Summer
you're here at last -
cold Winter days are long past

The sun doth shine,
and all is bright
The cuckoo made
Its merry flight

Summer sweet Summer
With nights so warm,
And flowers sweet -

A clear Blue Sky
As morning dawns.
Another Day —
A summers morn.

Kathleen Simpson

English Scene

Fine blown spray high rising
From heaving, roaring waves
Dashed in furious clamour
Amid sharp rocks and caves;
Seabird's music, wildly
Swelling, fills the air;
Razor-bills and puffins,
Gulls and penguins, stare
From their rocky perches
High above the storm,
Whilst in sheltered caverns
Crouch their fledglings, warm.
Guillemots in thousands
Crowd each craggy height;
Kittiwake and offspring
Etched against the light.
Silhouettes of beauty
On a canvas vast.
Marvellous creation,
Grandeur unsurpassed!

Mary Pledge

The Long And Summer Days

I love to play in the grass so green,
In the meadow, by the stream,
The stream is gurgling oh so gay,
With flowers blooming on the way,

The birds fly over the clear blue sky,
And give a cry as they go by,
The long and summer days are here,
Let's go and give them all a cheer.

Suzanne A. Brash

The Story Of A Life

The story of a life begins
In darkness deaf and dumb,
Until such time as comes the light
And the life is seen as one.
The life is then unfolded,
Small step by tiny step
And gradually time passes
From stage to stage to stage.
As the life grows,
So does the mind:
When nonsense turns to reason
And words into rhyme.
Until the mind is wise and strong
To face what time will bring;
To help the life when things go wrong
To laugh and cry and sing.
So small a life develops on
Until the day has come
And the life once more returns
To darkness from which it has come.

Bettina Brandin

We Remember

We were there
Years and years ago,
On desert dust,
Norwegian snow,
In jungle sweat
And icy seas,
Where smoke trails met
And women serving teas...

Yes, we were there
In manhood's bloom.
Nurses to care-
Facing - facing doom.
Most came home.
Many stayed away
And no matter where we may roam
We remember those
Who had to stay.
Yes we remember
They too were there.

Les Green

Blue Bell

I saw them stretching far and wide
Among the ferns and trees
it was as if the sky had dropped
Between the silken leaves.

So blue were they, such rich perfume
Pervading the very air we breathe
How heavenly to stand and watch
Them waving in the breeze.

Brenda Joan Ostler

Merchants Of Murder

Merchants - of murder and of death
You have left no soul, no earth
That is not the victim too
Of you senile decrepit few

Bloody fingers on the trigger
Warring Mars and Midas eager
An eye for an eye and a tooth for tooth
Cannons loaded with fodder youth
Ready rockets for destruction
Burning napalm, no compunction

In senile years rotten
Old men your youth forgotten
Deprived of sense and mirth
Wither all that flourishes on earth

Hermes G. Nicholas

Just Chillin'

Capping a bucket's
Like a lifesaver.
Rescuing you
From everyday normality.
Sending you high,
Higher than a kite.
Up in the clouds,
On a fairground ride.
Just chillin'.

The fun turns to fear.
Flushed pink faces
Become pale white faces.
Running to the toilet,
To be sick again.
Collapsed in a heap,
Heart stops beating,
Body turns ice-cold.
Just chillin'.

Sarah Davison

The Golden Sand

From a far I could see
The golden sand that stretched ahead,
Where the sand glistened and wet,
That looked like golden grains.
Then one afternoon on the beach,
I held a stick in my right hand.
I then decided to write my name,
Upon the golden sand.
Then out of the blue,
Came the tide bordered with foam,
Where the little waves fret,
Leaping all over quickly,
And washed my name completely.

Marie Therese Bobe

Resting

Alone at last.
Time for reminiscence,
On what has past.
Or just to wile away the time,
Dreaming and not thinking.
Oh, how I long sometimes,
For such a time as this.
No-one wanting this or that,
No-one talking through their hat.
Just a time to sit here sat.
Elbows propped and head in hands,
Or stretched out flat, no commands.

Lin Harrison

Hope

Hope Elizabeth is born today
A sweet-faced baby girl
O, wonder, wonder, wonderment
The look of joy, on all who see
Her cherub charm, and tiny toes
The miracle of her birth.

Nana flies in from New York State
With hand woven gifts created
Grampy drives from Roman Bath
And Grandma (me) and Granddad Bone
We 'fly' by wing-ed car
Down winding roads and motorways
To hold and love this precious child.

With rosy cheeks and violet eyes
Baby Hope is here to stay
She is Hope, hope for the future
Our hope for love and peace to come
In this world of imperfection
She is our hope for all that's good
Hope is our salvation.

Barbara Ann Bridgeman

Love Fades And Dies

Side by side; so close; apart
Hear the beating of his heart
Is he asleep or feigning such
She will never know that much.

Years ago when love was young
Then they sang a different song
Harmony was then the ruler
Each one was a willing scholar

His footsteps chase her fears away
And sunshine fills a gloomy day
When arms entwine and soft lips meet
Their parting over now life's complete

How sad this situation changes
Life's harmony to discord ranges
Too busy now with household chores
No loving looks at opening doors

Indifference is the normal feeling
Nothing sets the senses reeling
Is he asleep; she does not care
All she does is lie and stare.

Elizabeth King

Our Wedding Day

Our Wedding Day is here
at last, who cares about
the weather, come rain, come
shine, come sleet or snow
my love for you has blossomed
like the seasons in the weather.

The mad rush is all
over, our plans are firm
and will set, our future
to me looks bright and rosy,
for at last we have found
true love for each other.

A day to remember for the
rest of our life together.
Time will slip by but our
memories of to-day I am sure
will never die, as long as we're
together, you see, my love, our
wedding day is here at last,
who cares about the weather.

Wendy Francis

"The Snowdrop"

Hail: Sweet little snowdrop,
thou herald of spring.
For flowers so hardy
Great praise we will sing
Your dainty white petals
Hang down in a cup, but I think
You're worthy to hold your head up!
When snow is still falling, you
spring from the earth
Which shows spring is coming and
Fill us with mirth!
What a fragile green stem, which
sways to and fro
Yet holds you quite bravely
through wind and through snow.
Hail: Sweet little snowdrop
Thou herald of spring,
For flowers so hardy
Great praise we will sing.

Beryl Probert

The Castle Of Rancorous

Soleless eyes, unblinking,
Dark and hollowed out.
Some with blinds or shutters;
Others bare and empty.
They all cry out despair.

Plaster, crippled by age,
Unwanted, uncared for.
Left to fend for itself,
Discarded by the youth,
The classes and the families.

Once bright and full of life,
Through time patched and re-patched.
Until it has no use,
Just left there, abandoned,
Ignored and feeling used.

Old houses and old men,
Die a lingering death.

Bronwen Evans

Words

The word is the thudding
    axe through the brain,
the searing acid,
    the opened vein

The world is the tiger's
    raking claws.
The words that harm
    the words are ours.

Andrea Shaw

Untitled

Butterfly, as you flutter by
Do you remember
Now, in June
How last September
You made a cocoon
And emerged in the spring
As a butterfly?

I am now in my eighty third year
And I wish that I
As the end draws near
Could metamorphose
Into a butterfly.

Winifred Adams

Mythology

Man is the myth.
God, the narrator
of a tale to amuse
the infant universe,
weaving and destroying;
is really Penelope
awaiting salvation
by her scarred voyager.
lover and killer,
aimed like an arrow at Ithaca
and Eden's narrow gate.

Michael Bell

Battered Swash

Love comes in a wave,
Crashes and envelopes me.
I am squashed by its power,
Dominated by the force.

Then it draws away, calm,
Silent battle with my heart.
I am left drowned,
Until the next one crashes.

Charlotte Dew

Valentine

The extra special feeling
As your first ever valentine
Gently glides to the floor.

Heart pounding
As you open it.
But your imagination runs wild -
They haven't signed it!

Deep in thought
You drift off to school
On cloud nine.
The day ends in a blur
Never to be seen again.

'Who would send me a valentine?'
Is all that you have thought all day.
You get home to find more.
You look at the writing -
The same.
Your mum sent them all!

Catriona Beveridge

Contrast

To, the front of the show,
seagull, give selfish cry
duck share happy story
all, take a ride on river
sliding easily by.
Shadows dance on bed of stone.
Buildings false authority
stand back afraid to bathe
as daffodil sigh in feeble breeze.
The real power,
lays in snow-capped peak
kissing clear blue sky.

Richard Wimbush

Careless Words

Eating slowly inwards.
Tearing away at my flesh,
The harsh and thoughtless taunts,
Like the touch of a burning flame,
Eating away at my confidence,
Knocking down those walls,
That I had built up.
Endlessly tearing it all down,
And there, I lie in ruins,
Destroyed by what was thought,
Just to be only harmless words.
Broken down, I cannot retaliate.
Your tongue, like the seven swords,
That pierce my dying heart.
Taking my only lasting breath,
And still your lashing tongue,
Endlessly whipping me to death.

Jacqueline Gallagher

Solace

The children of Dunblane have gone,
Gone to heaven, every one.
Evil entered their quiet town,
Evil gunned these children down.
Jesus waits for them above,
Waits to give them all His love.
He will watch them through the years,
So sad parents, dry your tears.
They are now in a safe place,
All at peace and full of grace.
The Lord above, He will provide,
For all these children by His side,
In those great words spoken by He,
"Suffer little children, come unto me".
So people of the world please pray,
For these sad parents on this day.

Jack Bexhell

Human Bodyguard

I am rippled,
Very sinuous,
Many different shapes,
Sizes, arise on my outer layer.

For the humans,
I am their life,
I keep them warm,
And shelter them,
From all the existing bitter cold.

People observe,
Day and night.
They are curious,
Very curious,
Perhaps too curious.

Most powerful one,
loved all over,
Just merely,
Life.

Neil Kashishian

Dunblane

In an assembly they sat.
16 children small, big, thin and fat.
One teacher, liked by so many.
Could any one replace them?
No, not any!

A gunman burst in
Letting off bullets here and there.
Killed all of them he did.
Families, teachers in despair.

People shaken, people sad.
People full of anger.
Anything but glad.

Everybody's still upset.
Never able to forgive the man
Who killed the children he never met.

Vanessa Sanderson

Point Of View

The world today is full of hate,
killing mankind they cannot wait.
Always cruel and unkind,
with no one in mind.
It brings lies and deceit,
promises they don't meet.
The vicious life we live today,
I wish greed would go away.
Innocent children see only war,
think to yourself what's it for.
The street's filled with poverty,
it's no good for you or me.
Illness creeps in human life,
anger only with a knife.
Arguments must stay in the past,
maybe peace will come at last.
You can see what goes on around,
therefore a solution must be found.

Sue Jordan

"Beach"

Toes caressed,
By golden sand,
Star struck lovers,
Hand in hand

Waves of emotion,
Crashing down,
Feeling of love,
Newly found,

Damian Begley

I Really Want Him!

I really like this special guy,
Who lives 6 places down my road,
He's full of heart, wit and charm,
And seems to like me through his load,
He doesn't seem to know,
Though I wish he could see,
That we'd be perfect,
Him and me,
Days go by,
Without a word,
That I'd sit and wait,
Hoping I'd be heard,
I guess I'll have to sit and pray,
And see what happens to me now,
I wish he'd come and see me soon,
Though I don't see how.

Natalie Pousson

The Tiger

The tiger, he is big and strong,
And has stripes all down his back,
His tail, now that is very long,
And always goes 'swish swack!'

The tiger, he does not purr
And he has very long sharp teeth,
He has pretty golden fur,
And soft padded feet,

The tiger, he has a great big Roar,
And eats an awful lot,
He shall always want some more,
And is not very easy to spot.

The tiger, he can see in the dark,
And run as fast as the wind,
He wouldn't like to meet a shark,
(They're very hard to find!)

Debbie Sisk

Rebecca, And "Bosorne Fox"

May his stride never falter,
May he lead you safely,
through darkness and light.
May all life's hurdles appear
small, when together you
approach the impossible wall.

May the reins of good fortune
ride with you, to hold, when
fear and doubts crowd you.
May his courage and trust
warm you. As evening shadows
cast their gloom, may his
bright eyes forever light
your memories room.

H. Bulford

Dangerous Love

Do you who seek love
Know of the pain?
How it thrusts and then stabs
Again and again.

It goes like a dagger
Straight for the heart,
It twists and it turns
Then wrenches Apart.

Pity me! I found love!
The wound's with me still,
It seeks now to slay me.
I know that it will.

If you see love coming
Keep out of its path,
Keep silent in shadow,
Maybe it will pass.

Olwen Counsell

Peace

The dream is blurred,
Hazed by morning's mists,
Hovering, ephemeral,
Fragile in bud
Bedewed with hope,
The waking self
Rejects as soft soap.
Dream wisdom's light
Fades in the sun.
Though the spirit
Sighs its needs,
In waking the
Morning soul's bereft,
Inept, burdened by days.
Monotones mute the glow:
Embers unfanned, quench.
Commonplace takes over and forgets.

Marie L. Perry

Electronic Lover

Who is this friend I've found at last,
who makes me sing his praises.
He creates no flutter in my heart
as in my eyes he gazes.

Who gives me pleasure anytime
and solves my problems many.
Who has more wisdom than a sage
and could better any.

Who is this friend to share my night
though he's not a fancy dancer
Who can tackle any quest
and come up with the answer.

Who has no passion and no wit
but absorbs my mind for hours.
Who cannot take me out on trips
and does not bring me flowers.

He's of no harm to mind or soul
no atmosphere polluter.
To whom do I refer?
My personal home computer.

John Freshney

The Consequences Of War

I'm left very hungry,
there's no food around.
With war all about me
I daren't make a sound.
My family's all ill,
my brothers and sisters dying.
I am waiting still
for your help to come flying.
Do you care?
I sometimes wonder
if there's anyone there
when it sounds like thunder.
These are my problems
and it may not show
that they are yours too,
and this I know.

Laragh Walton

I Forgive You

Binevenagh, beheaded
by a scythe of mist,
and below its stout shoulders,
harebells,
wind worn,
sheltering the minds of men
and imprinted with the hands
of heroes.
Binevenagh,
"I Forgive You!."

Hendy Foy

Mankind

I can't help thinking
It's a crying shame.
The behaviour of mankind
We're all of us to blame.
We strive to be happy.
We try to be true.
Demonstrating our beliefs.
It's killing me and you.

I can't thinking peace is overdue
Search for a solution.
Look for something new.
The way in which we do things.
Is getting out of hand
God made this earth our.
Home dear friend.
Let's respect His land.
So let's all make an effort.
We'll triumph in the end.
So precious is contentment
So precious is a friend!

Malcolm J. Trevor

Autumn

Awakened by early morning light
As dawn threw off the cloak of night
Shining rays in a sky of blue
Yet on the grass a touch of dew

Winter, spring and summer gone
It's autumn's time to come along
Branches rustle with awesome ease
Trees begin to shed their leaves
The crispy feel of an autumn day
Winter can't be far away
The nights grow dark with wind and rain
Then at last it's spring again.

Caroline Butterfield

Outcast

Stole a 'piece' from Daddy's collection
Years of torment and rejection
Kids at school as much to blame
"Never treated me the same"

All his feelings locked inside
Lay on his bed all night and cried
But today his head's held high
Ostracized "so they must die"

Resigned his life began to laugh
Before he wrote his epitaph
"Look down from heaven when I die
see if anyone will cry
I know it's heaven, I can tell
Because I've done my time in hell"

Rejoice O young man in thy youth
Seems nothing's further from the truth
When all he wanted was a friend
But now his life's come to an end
Enjoyed the dream short time it lasted
Then it was himself he blasted

Ian Timpson

Beginning Or End

Soon I will be going away
where I will end no one can say
will the heavens up above
open the gates and give out love.
Or will I end up in the
dark without any light
or even a spark
I suppose it is a mystery
and one day we all shall see
or the question is will we?

Jayne Lesley Holmes

No Memory Of Life....

In a world all alone,
In a cold empty cell,
Talk in madness to myself,
Who's life next shall be hell?
I envy the happy,
Their souls within,
I'll destroy what I can,
I'm the eighth deadly sin,
I'm made to torture,
Destroy all your lives,
Create pain and anger,
For evil's my pride,
All this was caused,
This hatred and strife,
For what happened in the past,
There's no memory of life....

Marcus Ames

Dyslexia

Emotion saturates each page:
He sees only frustration.
So many hold the key;
His pass lost,
In the corridors of his mind;

A thief,
Picking the lock
To knowledge.
Releasing only despair;

Caged once more,
A prisoner of reality
He lies dead:
A foetus
Unable to cast off mortality,
To emerge,
Purified, reborn,
From the furnace, literature.

Darren Matheson

Solitude

Solitude, sweet solitude,
  calm within my breast.
The wonder of silence,
  the world at peace, at rest
The magic of a clear blue sky
  gentle cooling breeze
Casting a confetti of blossom
  down from heavy laden tree's
Morning dew, glistening on the meadow
  crystal pearls on the spiders web
Birds footprints, in the sand
  when the rivers on the ebb
Lake with its still water.
  Reflecting the beauty of the swan
Shadows dancing, in the evening dusk
  when day is nearly gone
The quietness, the magic
  is there for all to see
I'm sure the wonders, of this world
  are not seen by only me.

Maureen Townsend

Summer Night

The sun goes down on a golden day,
Lost shadows fade away.
The bee that sipped the honeyed flower
Drones in a pollen dusted bower
And from the wracked and ruined tower
On silver spread wings,
The first-marauder of the night
Sends the timorous mouse to flight.
In the rutted lane in quiet accord
The man and dog by lantern light
Watch for the moon in the dark ford.

Tom H. Gurney

Life Is A Flower

Life is a flower,
Precious and fragile,
But yet you never quite realize,
Just how precious,
The flower is,
You grow as a flower,
Getting stronger and stronger,
And as the day goes on,
The flower becomes,
Weaker and weaker,
Until soon there is no flower,
There is only dust,
A memory,
Of you,
Of the flower you once were.

Kay French

Shouting

Shouting, we're shouting,
I'm dying, you're crying,
Soon we both will drop.

The level is rising
I'm dying but trying
So hard to stop.

You're screaming and seething
You're bawling, I'm calling
For you to stop.

You're crying but trying,
Screaming and redeeming
Your place at the top.
I wish we could stop...
I wish we could talk
And not scream till we drop,
Like we always do.

Tom Adams

The Jellyfish

I love to be a jellyfish,
Just drifting with the tide,
But when I'm pulled into the shore,
I've got nowhere to hide.

A giant crowd does gather round
They shout and rudely stare
Then poke me with a heavy stick
Life can be unfair.

I'm poked and kicked and pushed
around
Until I'm bruised and sore.
I never do a thing to them,
When lying on the floor.

Then as my last breath is dying,
The sea rushes up from behind,
Right up to where I am lying
And swiftly whisks me back in.

This endless trauma,
Is seriously bad for my health
I'd much rather be under the sea,
Baffling the sharks with my stealth!

Anna Turvey

My Life Sentence

Once I was a prisoner,
locked in misery.
Couldn't escape from the darkness,
Didn't have no place to run,
Day by day it crushed me,
Alone and empty feelings encased
within
I wondered what would become of me?

Elizabeth Roberts

Bluebell Wood

Up and over the stile
Stand and stare awhile
Look at the trees so tall
Making the flowers so small
Carpets of blue in sight
Tree colours so bright
Shaking their little bells
Make you feel like a few yells
Every year they appear
Makes you want to shed a tear
The wonder of nature is a dream
Thanks to the Lord for a lovely team

E. A. Thistlethwaite

Emotionless Curse

A world with no feeling
makes up lands with no heart,
no one is laughing
or falling apart.
There's no smiles on our faces
no grief in our eyes,
no abuse towards races
no truth and no lies.
There's no love and no loathing
there is no respect,
it's a world with no feeling
what else d'you expect?
There is no expression
in this universe,
life's just an obsession
in this emotionless curse.

Shelly Turner

"Where's Daddy"

Little girl feeling
all lost and alone
Mummy beside her
but where has dad gone

Mum says dad has left us
things didn't work out
but I'm only little
my voice it did shout

Mom said don't you worry
you have done nothing wrong
but if I'm to believe her
then where has dad gone

I've watched in the crowd
for you passing by
and every strange man
that's my dad 'should I cry'

Now I am older
I have kids of my own
but inside I'm still little
tell me "Where's my dad gone"

Yvonne Cliffe

Why?

Why do raindrops fall Mummy
One just landed on my tummy
When I cry, I lick my lip
What a lovely salty drip
What happens to the water Mommy
On my lip and on my tummy
Will the sky run out of rain
Will I be able to cry again
Where does all the water go
On the beach when it wets my toe
When water trickles down the drain
Will it ever come out again
If the rain comes from the sky
How does it get there
I must know - Why?

Pauline Clay

Daughter

Her stomach hurts.
A gnawing pain
Where the child grows
Inside.

Nobody knows her pain
As the blood pours away
And she is cleansed
And pure again.

Growing pains,
Her mother says,
As her soul slips away.
And she loses the child
And the mind
She almost never had.

Aimee Douglas

New Scoutmaster Needed

A light went out
When Peter left.
The Group must have felt bereft
Of humour, challenge, and the wish
To try a little harder, just for him.
Progress is slow in a room that's dim.

Suddenly there seemed a void,
Among the people who'd enjoyed
A leader with a forthright plan
To improve the lot of his fellow man.
Things have to change as time goes on,
But memories stay although he's gone.

Joan Novak

"Waiting For You"

Where were you last night my darling?
I waited for hours past ten
I felt so tired of waiting
I knew I'd wait again

Where were you tonight my darling?
I've waited for hours past ten
I've waited, and waited, and waited
I'll wait for hours, and then...

Tomorrow, I'll wait for hours
Just in hope of seeing you again
I know I'll wait for hours
But you won't turn up again

I have known and loved you
You know you have loved me too
If you really want to see me
You know just what to do

I'll be waiting here forever
Beside our loving tree
Waiting on through Seasons Four
Waiting, waiting on, forever more

Roy Morris

Stephen Hendry

Steady Hands,
Strong Hearts,
Sensible Habits,
Special Harmony.
Super Human,
Scottish Hero,
Supreme Hotshot,
Snooker Heaven.
Still Hungry,
Seek Honours,
Sure Hit,
Stephen Hendry!!!

Jon Perigud

Life

The child walks to the hospital bed,
Too small to climb,
And touch his mammy's head.

The mother beckons with a weary smile,
To hold her child,
Just one more time.

The father shuffles,
Bows his head.
No more tears left to shed.

The nurses, as usual,
Standing strong.
Whispers that it won't be long.

The doctor, all emotion bled,
Signs the chart,
Shakes his head.

Desmond Cain

The Swallows Of Portugal

The world is very beautiful
Our God created all
He made it all so perfect
From the smallest to the tall.

I love the flowers and animals
The apples in the fall
But nothing is so magical
As the swallows in Portugal.

Among the cliffs and rocky heights
They dart and climb on wing
I watch their flight by day and night
And listen to them sing.

I take the plane and go by train
Cross miles and miles of sea;
How can they, so small and fay
Travel as far as me?

Back home again, there's wind and rain
And I long for a spring-like day;
What do I see bringing joy and glee:
But the swallows, they've followed me!

Margaret Findlay

Words

Poems that have been written
Songs that are sung
Words that are said
To a very special and precious one

All say the words of love
Feeling what each lover feels
The greatest feeling of all
Is in each other's arms

To hold you close and secure
To kiss your lips with tenderness
To feel our passions rise
Is words into action of love

To love you then in so many ways
With horizons still to reach
Each time so precious to us both
As more depth we discover

The more we meet and love
The deeper our love becomes
A special feeling so strong
That drives our lives along.

Bobby Somerville

Untitled

Making my way across
the brook my feet froze
my hands shook,
the translucent stream
seemed to team
with bream, I cast
the line and reeled
in a fine specimen
of bream and next
time hope to
catch some brill
If it's God will

Bernadett E. Leavy

A Highland Scene

From high in these rugged mountains
with peaks covered in snow
I see a lush green valley
and the river spey below

I see the dense green forest
of spruce and scottish pine
I see wild trout in gushing streams
that glint in bright sunshine

I see the eagle soaring
so majestic in the sky
I sit so still in silence
and watch wild deer as they roam by

I look across at distant hills
beneath a sky so blue
I see the grouse upon the moor
and the heather's purple hue

I watch the winding river
gently flow through meadows green
then stand in awe and wonder
to survey this highland scene

A. V. Carlin

Gone

I didn't have you with me,
To make the cake this year,
To help me decorate the tree,
As we did, every year,
No shopping, laughs, or jumble sales,
The things we used to do,
All I have is memories,
Memories of you.
This first Christmas without you,
Will be so very sad,
Thinking of the things we did,
And all the joys we had,
But you'll still be there with me,
In every single way,
And I'm so very, very sure,
You'll be here, Christmas Day.

Laura Collingwood

Love Light

A light still shines
After all the years
Through the joy and sometimes tears
I loved you on a wet day
When together we said we'd go this way
We bought a ring
Not knowing what love might bring
Yet as the years go by
I can look you in the eye.
And know I love you more
Than when first our love did show
The sparkle and the shine
Just to know that you are mine

Mervyn D. Hill

Youth

Trapped in a shell which will neither
open nor move
Searching for something but too
scared to discover
Frustrated with
but incapable of
loyal to friends
An enemy to family
Trapped, wanting to break free
but lost
helpless without that suffocating
shelter which is offered
Experienced for youth
Inexperienced for age
Trapped.

Alexandra Frattali

Metaphorically Speaking

I was a grape
That fell on the floor
Rolled under a table
And thought of no more
I lay there alone
Rotting away
Hearing the laughs
Watching others play
Then came the time
When I was found
Dragged from my place
Across the ground
A kid thought it funny,
Put her foot on my head
After a thud,
Squash, I was dead.

Nicola Jane Tait

Always Remembered

Lift a soul a little higher,
Let it escape the funeral pyre,
Hold it there a moment or two
Enough for him to view
The loved and lovers
At their pew,
Who miss their special friend
Father, brother, husband, lover.

Lift this soul a little higher
To a plane of spiritual wonder
But in a hidden silence
Will still have presence
In a mortal's thought.
And be at her side,
His side, my side
Until it's our time
To play,
In a spiritual land
Not so far away.

Margaret Valbah

Memory Hold The Door

Memory hold for me the door
That I may remember love
And even the heartache sore
Of unrequited love

The scents and summer sounds
The sun and mist fine rain
And my love for you abounds
When I'm with you once again

Years shall pass, as pass they will
Yet still will I remember this
With a short and gentle thrill
That first soft loving kiss.

W. Brown

Winter And Summer

The winter is wet and cold,
But my love for you is warm
It lasts throughout the night
Longing for the dawn,
Hoping that today I'll see you
If only for a while.
For I long to touch your face
And see the wonder of your smile.

For you are warm and tender
Like the summer sun you shine
Your love surpasses other loves
And I'm fortunate you're mine.
There's so much we've done together
And I know our love will last.
So let's live for the future.
And try to forget the past.

Sylvia Gough

The Good Times

In the light of dawn
Deer trot across the landscape.
In the still garden
Children's voices can be heard.
This makes me happy,
I remember the good times.

Under a lime tree
Drop-outs sit on the park bench.
In the market place
A beggar asks for small coins.
I make no judgement,
I remember the hard times.

Outside the new church
Blossom drift down from the trees.
As the insects hum,
Children sing their songs of joy.
This makes me happy,
I have found the good times.

Edwards Hall

Lost Heroes

The fight has began
where have all the soldiers gone
marked off with fences
open fields, a cry
commence battle men
'I don't want to die'
bellies close to the ground
shrapnel flying by
a scream from my left hand side
Tom my boy don't die
his face torn to pieces
a wife and kids he's lost
a bloody battles continues
I must go on, I must
lost in smoke
confusion bloody confusion
my time has come
I hear a...Amen

Mark Boughen

"Friends"

Side by side we took a walk
We knew we didn't have to talk
On and on we strolled that day
We felt so much but didn't say
Our hearts, our minds
Were full of treasures
For someone who gave us
So much pleasure
Never once did our friendship fail
You always came running
Wagging your tail

A. O'Neil

Grief

When my child was born on that
cold November morn, she opened up
her eyes to see a dim silhouette
of me. How would she in later
life identify I gave that day when
better had I died that day when
they took my child away. It took
nine months to incubate this
little child I could not keep.

I cannot change the way I be,
this bond between my child and me.
Restless between two lands am I,
for in this land where I reside
the ashes of my son still lie, I
will now remain. Forget the land
from once I came, weary of this
weight I bare, but soon my son
I'll join you there.

Jane Cullen

Every Sunday

I passed a wayside church one day,
And thought I'd venture in.
My heart was sorely troubled
And my faith was wearing thin.
I didn't know which way to go,
My life was in a mess.
I'd got so many awful sins
I wanted to confess.
There, on the wall, in front of me
Some words stood out so clear
"God comes here every Sunday
Do come and meet Him here".
I knew at once, I had to stay
And open up my heart.
To ask that He would take and use
My life, in every part.
So now I've found my Saviour,
I've thrown off every care.
"God comes here every Sunday,
And I go to meet Him there.

Enid Rathbone

The Night

The night of passion came swept
my heart with excitement the heat,
run threw my body clouds gathered
lights flashes perish with me, filled
my heart with joy, I embraced all my
trust that came way, for the love
I've been waiting for.
Time just tick away after hour
after hour, it scared me has the
light started entering my room
my eyes began to fill tears that
was unexpected began to fall,
my heart began to feel numb,
I grieved but did not utter a word
of complaint I concealed my
sorrows even from myself.

Jaspal Kaur

Untitled

As each day begins with a new horizon,
Nobody knows what lies ahead,
But with life still all round us.
We must look ahead.
The values of the past are dead
Not forgotten, but there to guide us.
So meet each day with open mind.
Then it will free us from bearing
Grudges against all others.

Michael Major Atkinson

Peace?

There was hoping -
There was singing -
There was laughter -
Bells were ringing.

The sound of gun shots rent the air!

There was silence all around -
Rabin lay dead upon the ground.

There was gasping -
There was sighing -
There was screaming -
Some were crying.
Murdered by one he called his own!

Rabin who wished all war to cease -
How fragile is this dream called Peace!

Joyce Saffron

Colours

Lovely colours fill me up
Like hot sweet tea in a porcelain cup.
Duck egg blue is a brilliant hue,
Vermilion red is arresting too.
Primrose yellow makes me mellow.
Rosamundi pink I wear for a fellow.
Verdant green sets the scene
For fields of glorious flowers in bloom
Whose colours soar to a wondrous shade,
And fade the grey of life's charade.

M. S. Newlands

View With A Thought

Looking through a window
Into the nighttime sky
Pondering the universe
Trying to reason why
Searching to another place
Another time, another land
Wandering with asking thought
Unsure just where I am
Questions drifting into space
Will I ever understand

Looking through a window
Just what is it all about
What is the point of everything
Will answers give me clout
I know if you can go back
Go back through all of space
You will come to the start
The heart of all this place
Life is more than just a cycle
It is the saving grace.

Paul Quick

'The Proud Meadow Pippit'

I wish I was a little bird
Flitting from tree to tree
You'd hear my song, yes every word
I'd make you look at me.

I'd prune my feathers every day
And sand bath when I could
I hope you'd follow me on my way
As I fly to the thickest wood.

My friends I'd introduce you to
And treat you like a king
I'd be so very proud of you
I'd sing and sing and sing.

For wine you'd have the sweetest dew
And dinner would be the best
Served on a cloth of flowers blue,
I'd then take you to my nest.

Jackie Edwards

Aldeyjarfoss

The river
shoulders its way
to the final brink,
simple or rambling
in pattern or course;
drilling through lava
driving past basalt
it turns to fall,
tumbling to valley floor,
dun coloured muddy,
or dropping fine plumes
as clean as lace.

Roy Bizley

The Future

From the vortex of tomorrow
From that ever changing land
Future we can't buy or borrow
Soon engulfs us, soon to hand

Dare we face it, can we change it
Are we part of what's to be
Will it be the way we want it
Grind us down or set us free

For Kubla Khan in Samarkand
Future looked the promised land
Death was waiting round the corner
Struck him down with certain hand

A million things about the past
I've known but now forgotten
So will the future be the same
Become a past forgotten

Keith F. Lainton

Time To Sleep

Suddenly darkness - and silence,
A great hole carelessly cut
Out of the night, with a flicked switch
And a pressed button.   Nothingness.

Curl up at the edge of the hole.
Feel the rim with your hand.
It waits for you to slide in
And drown in sleep's half death.

There was light, just now, and music.
You killed them, creating this vacuum,
An empty, cavernous aftermath
Of sound, a seeping surrender.

Sink into it. Sleep. Is not silence
A basic essential of being?
The hole mends, the thread is unbroken
And life starts again, tomorrow.

Jacqui Fogwill

Ripples In The Sky

Last night you held my hand,
And loved and cared for me,
And whispered courage in my ear
As we walked beside the sea.
And as we walked, we turned around,
Looked back where I now stand,
And saw our footprints had disturbed
The ripples in the sand.

But now I know you're just a dream
And I'm awake, alone.
And so again, I dream of where
I'm never on my own.

A voice calls out, "I'm not a dream -
I'm here, no need to cry."
And where it came from, there I see
The ripples in the sky.

David Shaw

Cupid

When cupid fires his arrows
His aim is sure and true
There is no way out of it
If he has aimed at you.
His arrows have a special tip
Imbued with some strange potion
How to find a cure for it
No-one has any notion.
Once the potion gets you
You are stuck with it for life
You never can get rid of it
Not even with a knife.
It will affect you strangely
Make your heart soar on wings
You find a world of pleasure
From simple mundane things
It doesn't matter what you do
Once cupid's had his way
You'll find you'll always be in love
Yes, love is here to stay.

Valerie Lloyd

Anger

Like a wild animal,
Roaring loud and strong.
Like the thunder,
A melodious song.
Like stormy waves,
Rocking a lost boat.
Like the colour red,
Tearing your throat.
Ripping you up,
Limb, from limb,
Drowning at sea,
It's dragging you in.
No control,
None oppose,
It has no friends,
It has no foes.

Antonia Amberton

Untitled

What do you see down there,
Behind that sand,
Behind those rocks,
Behind that land.
The shimmering ocean in the
moon's bright light,
Reflecting on our earth's dark
night.
And when day breaks,
And the sun doth wake,
And the birds rise up from
their beds,
The people come from all
around,
To raise their heads to that
glorious sound,
Of the sea crashing over the
rocks.

Keziah Williams

In Sympathy (Dunblane)

Believe that on some distant hill
the sun is shining brightly still
Believe that past the darkest night
the morning waits to give its light
And you will in heavens garden meet
like children playing in the street
Happy, carefree, without pain,
everything will be fine again.

Doreen Banas

To My Parents

Through childhood days,
Carefree and fair,
I had such fun,
'Cos you were there.

Through teenage years
Turmoil and care,
I came unscathed,
'Cos you were there.

Through all the years
and every day,
Across the miles,
yes, all the way,
you were there.

And when I die,
I pray that God will
Heed my prayer.
And take me home,
'Cos you'll be there.

Patricia Abrams

Women Priests

What a great day has happened
in this century
For women priests ordained in
in the Ministry
God gave special gifts to men
and women, too,
And now this opportunity has
made a dream come true,
I know there are folk who
dislike this situation
The media has given this point
a lot of attention,
So I pray that in their work
They find little rivalry
and show they are worthy of
equality.

Doris Smith

Noel's Dilemma

It's a sin,
It's a crime
We can't tell the time,
The neighbourhood watch has been
stolen.

Noel Markham

At Home

Around the evening hearth
Flecked with blue Dutch tiles
Sit two elderly rebels by
Books, some new-made socks,
The Guardian read, and near
The quietly burning log,
Soon to be shared,
The stored grape,
The liquid sunshine
From some southern ridge,
Soft, fruity, mellow, red,
The same that cheered
A Roman soldier, tired and dry.

Quiet Sussex evenings, now and
Days gentle in the warm
October sun, while
Willing neighbours
Drive to shop and town.

Still rebels, though,
Amid the Downland peace -

John L. Robinson

The Twinkle

Have you ever stopped to ask yourself
or ever wondered why
What does it really say or mean
that twinkle in your eye.
You hardly know you have it
it's not there all the time
but when it's there I'd liken it
to that first ray of sunshine.
If you use it well it achieves a lot
like brightening a gloomy day
or bringing the lost out of the dark
and showing them the way.
It's a resource that you cannot sell
you can only give it free.
Which is why I'm always on a high
when you're giving it to me.
The beauty of the twinkle
is not obvious to most,
It has the effect of a powerful drug
but you cannot overdose.

Peter Field

Love Within Life

Leaves drop in the autumn fall,
like my tears.
Even though I may not show it,
I need to be cushioned.
From the spiral downwards,
Onto the autumn carpet.
The leaves are dead,
As I rest my weary head.
But still the tree lives,
To love another day....be it grey.
Whereas people, need people,
One day they will find.
The person, who never falls behind,
Through the rain, sleet or snow.
The comfort, they will know,
From the sun, through the rain,
Peeps the rainbow, once again.
People, need people,
like the tree, needs leaves,
but, always, one remains.

Jennifer Alexis Summerfield

Missing You!

The days are so long now,
the nights are so sad
but everything is still here mum.
Your garden of love.
My life is to you mum in everything
I do,
I live for your memory, for what
else can I do?

I feel the pain now mum,
I'm broken in two.
My life feels so empty.
Oh what shall I do?
My faith is with God now
your life is with him.
I long for the day mum,
We will be together again.

Leanne Jane Coltman

Time

Time is a path
To the end of the world
Our whole lives spent waiting,
For what is yet to come
And when a precious moment
Happens to pass,
Our life is spent dreaming
Of what we have lost.

Rebecca Grant

Silence

Through silence
We can make our voices heard
In silence
Our thoughts can strike a cord
With silence
We can reach out
And for two minutes
Our hearts will speak
A silence we respect and seek
To pay homage to all
Who sacrificed their lives
In our silence
Their memory survives

Tamar Segal

My True Love

You are my ocean,
With waves so full of passion.
You are my sun,
With warmth beyond control,
My light, my dark, my dreams.

You are my summer,
Which shines so bright.
You are my winter,
Which chills my soul.
My thoughts, my hopes, my self control.

You are the tree,
That holds down my routes.
You are the ground,
That connects my life-long path.
My direction, my balance, my world.

Mark Perry

Untitled

He has gone,
He was something that was.
This emptiness I feel,
It won't go away.
I thought we'd always be together,
I was wrong.
My life is not needed now.
Pack it into boxes,
And put it in storage.
For it won't do any good.
He's the one I need,
But I can't have him,
'Cos he's gone.
I am alone now.

Kirsty Gray

My Dream

At last, at last
The doorbell rang
I leapt to my feet
The waiting was past
Come on let's go and enjoy our treat
My friend was impatient
And could not wait
Our legs carried us fast
The excitement intense
There she stood
Graceful and beautiful
All in red
I touched her body
What wonderful curves
Temptation was great
I could not wait
She is mine at last
My wait is over
You handsome beautiful Rover

Joan Ford

The Sea Is A Wonderful Thing!!!

The sea is a wonderful thing,
Blue, green and sparkling.
Children splashing,
Speed boats racing Foam, Foam, Foam!!
The sea is a wonderful thing!!
Further on and over the horizon,
Dolphins, whales, flying fish.
Sea crashing against the cliffs,
The sea is polluted, dirty and salty,
But the sea is a wonderful thing!!!

Samantha Jayawardane

Smile!

Sitting on an old man's seat,
At the edge of Penryn Street
And Margam Road, I watched cars
Halt at a red signal light
Adjacent to the Somerset Arms.

Mind was in mysterious limbo,
Far from the warm sunny scene,
Chasing a wandering poem line
Hidden in a corner of my mind.

When a chorus sang out 'Smile!'
Escaping thought to the voices
I looked up to a school bus,
Empty save for backseat girls,
In buoyant mood for Summer
Holidays were a short day away.

'Smile' called a pretty gamine
Pressing head to the open window,
Smile I did, who could resist
Such a beguiling cry...
The bus roared into the lights

Norman G. Jones

The Weakness

I've always had a weakness,
It's caused me lots of strife
From people all around me,
It's plagued me all my life.

I've tried to overcome it
For the sake of all my kin,
It's hard to just imagine
The states that I've been in.

My children now are married
But still they can recall
This thing they had to suffer
And the blackness of it all.

Now that I live by myself,
What worries me the most
Is, I have grown quite used to it
In fact I love - burnt toast

A. V. Michalski

Loss!

That hollow feeling deep inside,
The loss of one with so much pride.
The pain and sorrow will it ebb,
Confusion, turmoil in my head.

No more discussions we once shared.
The loss of one who really cared.
Time will heal the wound they say.
I crave the dawning of that day.

The times we shared as man and boy.
The loss of one, the lack of joy.
Wishing it had been a great mistake,
And in the morn find you awake.

Alas my fear I know is right,
The loss of one, God bless, goodnight.

Andrew McDermott

No Flowers

Send me no flowers
Weep not for my death
But remember me.
For within your memory
I will live forever.

Let each memory
Bring pleasure not pain
Hope not despair.
For as each day passes
I am with you.

Keep my memory
Safe within your heart
Then, should sadness call
Search deep in your heart
And remember me.

For my memory
Will bring a smile
A new hope
That we will meet again
And I will remember you.

Lorraine Short

Trees

Earth's largest, living,
Breathing thing.
Spirit of creation,
Held in trust,
By every nation.

Host to all things,
A haven at night
Squirrels and termites,
Robins and spiders,
And weirdies on wing,

The annual round,
You choose,
Which of these brilliant hues,
Ere in one flash of autumn gold,
Fade darkly.

Bough breaks, falls, deeply,
Dead, buried,
Waits aeone's call
To earthly flame,
And dies again.

B. Walton

A Random Bus Trip

Cruising down
   a motorway
Flashing white lines
   like a stroboscope
A gnarled dead branch
Overtakes a speeding
   sports car
And a green meadow reflection
Ladders to the clouds
   in the sky.

Pilar Morales

Death Knoll

The wind howls
Screaming out its vowels.
And while the sky blackens,
My rope tightens.
And still the fire roars.
I stepped off the chair,
Remembering the whores
Who could only stand and stare.
And the wailing wind,
And the tolling of the bell,
Remind me that I have sinned,
And all that's left for me is hell.

Alison Messom

The Cruel Sea

Deep salt water rules this ode
In endless oscillating mode
Fearless friendless fierce and free
Tractless tactless truculent sea
Oft mirrored by
A changing sky
With puny vessel
Struggling by
Tolerating man's own helplessness
Or in its fury merciless
But not for me
The sluggish stream
Or river bank
To sit and dream
But foam-flecked water
Heaving high
And back I'll go
Until I die!

John Partington

Our Beauty

In our lounge we have a cage,
   With A lovely Mynah Bird.
I chat to her every day,
   But she never says a word.

When she was young,
   I could have changed her at the shop
But then I'd got to love her,
   And I thought I'd rather not.

Of all the other Mynah Birds,
   That I have ever seen.
Our Beauty beats them all,
   With her black and lovely sheen.

Now she's ten years old,
   I still would like to hear..
Just one sweet word from her,
   In a voice so loud and clear.

Eileen Hanson

Time To Fly?

How soon is it until the day
When I will have to fly away?
The days are long now,
The nights are short.
It won't be long now.
I've often thought
About the day that will decide
Upon which path of life I'll ride.

Deborah Daly

Betrayal

The promised feast of love's delight
From faith's oratory.
Pulpit preached and in life's sanctuary
Received.
Consuming Covenants,
Pious pledges made.
Assuming assonance,
Trusting promise fade.
Love's hasty need no more to drive,
Lone despair and guilt deprive
And steals away your prize.

Wendy D. Howarth

Roadside Death

Moorhen, moorhen, why, why, why,
Did you run, when you could fly?
Ten ton lorry, rumbling by,
Moorhen, moorhen, why, why, why?

G. N. Miles

So Sad

We leave the house, we're on our way
some off to work, some out to play
we're thinking of the day ahead
and often wish we'd stayed in bed

They left the house, went on their way
some off to work, some off to play
they thought about the day ahead
but never thought that they'd be dead

That awful day will always be
as long as I live forever with me
I can't imagine all the pain
but hope in my heart Please Never Again

I've wept as I have never before
I feel for them and so much more
I cannot find the words of comfort
I cannot free them of their hurt

I know the pain will ease with time
their own must be much more than mine
they've lost so much, they hurt so bad
It's all so very sad, so sad.

Christine Bankier

"Kindred"

I cannot see you,
But in my heart I know you're there.
You bring me comfort,
Enough to vanquish my despair.

I cannot hear you,
But in my heart your silent call.
You bring me strength,
Enough that I may never fall.

I cannot touch you,
But in my heart I feel you near.
You bring me courage,
Enough that I may face my fears.

I cannot know you,
But in my heart we are entwined.
You bring me solace,
Enough to grant my peace of mind.

I cannot love you,
But in my heart love knows no end.
You bring me wisdom,
Enough to cherish you, my friend.

Paul Loughrey

A Lament For A Wasted Life

A wasted life was his,
A sacrifice in vain,
An early death
Brought on by self
And other evil men.
But oh the thought,
What might have been
If he had known God,
And bent his footsteps in the road
That leadeth home to God.

What good might he
Have done down here,
How great his influence still,
Now he lieth cold in death,
An influence all for ill.
He has left behind him
Broken hearts,
And weary ones and sad,
But this need not have been
If he had come to God.

James R. Irvine

A Song Of Inspiration

Sing a sweet song from your
heart's content and lull me
to wonder. The darkest corner
of my heart will then light
from the flame of thy song.

Moments of my sadness then
will be the moments of joy.
My anguish will drift to
the unknown, leaving me to
walk into the path of happiness.

Sing a sweet song from your
heart's content and let me
sink to the ocean of peace
and tranquillity.

And the song of your
inspiration thus will be
my aspiration to live in
joy and then I can walk
along the coast of happiness.

Nirmal Chandra Deb

Restless

Days bring their own trouble
making one unsure and wobble
restless in mind want to hide
all too often thought I tried

Again one will sit all alone
no good for the body or bone
restless in mind tired brain
it's a wonder one's still sane

Scared to plunge and mingle
years fly by and still tingle
restless in mind deep inside
emotions run high as the tide

Walls protect one for quiet
are we ever ready to forget
restless in mind not to bide
now need someone to confide

Wish to be a bird and away fly
high up take clean air supply
restless in mind weep like rain
need to understand and explain

J. R. Quemard

Monsoon In Singapore

Sun beats down with heat intense,
Sears the earth and dulls the sense;
Eerie stillness in the air,
Faces grimace in the glare.

All at once, from out the blue
Looms a cloud of thund'rous hue;
Sky is slashed with vivid flame,
Rumbling crash, down comes the rain.

Mums and kiddies homeward scurry,
Clotheslines looted in a flurry:
Monsoon drains in wild cascade,
Flower borders disarrayed.

Frightened birds for shelter dash,
Tall trees cower before the lash.
Tattered kite is carried high,
Sacrifice to angry sky.

Suddenly, the storm subsides,
Sunbeams kiss the sullen skies;
Raindrops hang like crystal beads,
Sparkling on the Silverweeds.

Joe Fox

Love Forever True

My child asked in innocence
As children often do.
Tell me Mother what is meant
By 'Love Forever True?'
I gently took my child's hand
And sat her on my knee.
'How could I make her understand.
A feeling one can't see?'
Something warm and gentle
Emotional and sweet
Tender, sometimes venerable,
And often fiercely deep.
I watched my child as she sat
Contented on my knee
And knew her trust must stay intact

As I sought the truth to see.
Then I saw the love within her eyes.
That warmed me through and through.
And knew with sudden sweet surprise
A love forever true.

Sonia Santina

Shades Of Winter

Grey green is the lichened wall seen
From my kitchen window,
Stippled with sand is the bowling green
Stark and dark are the trees in
The lane
Piercing the sky with bony fingers
As the last grey remnant of daylight
Lingers - and fades.

Were these the shades of winter
When I was a girl?
Surely December sparkled with
White and blue,
The tea-time sky was a pinkish pearl
And the setting sun cast a rosy hue.
When did the colours dim and fade?
Did they change or did I?
Is it the difference the years
Have made
That make me afraid of a winter sky?

E. B. Limb

"The Machine"

I'm out of control
And in the wrong lane,
Will I ever be normal again?

I've broken down
And need to be fixed,
I feel okay-just a bit mixed.

I'm out of order
Does anyone know
What will happen if I blow?

I'm unbalanced
And going to fall,
Will my maker ever call?

Allison McKay

Computerization

In days of yore - before the war
    When needing further tonic
We simply sent - no argument
    A message telephonic.
Such simple ways, in other days,
    Gave mutual satisfaction
And also had (which can't be bad)
    Definitely quicker action.
But who am I to pontify
    On Hippocratic prosings?
When but for them I, of all men,
    Would now be decomposing?

R. E. Goddard

Without You

When I was young
I looked for love.
Looked
Among the clamour of a crowded street.
Searched
Each face,
Imagining
How I would catch your smile,
And hold it
Keepsake

Fish swim backwards
The dancer jilts his shoes
And all the snow weeps the roof dry.

I hear none of the untidy noise

The silence
Is too
Complete.

Olive Ellson

Sun Rise

Sun Rise sun shine sun set
in your lovely golden eyes.

Sun rise sun shine sun set
in your love that's also mine

Sun rise sun shine sun set
in your heart of that's in mine

Sun rise sun shine sun set
in your life of life's divine

Sun rise sun shine sun set
in your togetherness with me and mine

Carolyn Gail Lansell

I Am Your Bride

I am your bride,
happy to be by your side,
for you are always
loving me, so I return
that love and this will
ever be; from this day
until the end of time.
I am yours and you
are mine, we trust
in our loving father for
joy and laughter in all
our tomorrows, uplifting
us in all our sorrows,
we've had a perfect wedding
day, every thing went our
way. Our love shone
like a star, people came
from near and far, to
see us side by side
darling I am your bride

Lucy Green

Ode To Brenda

Your working days have come to end
Now in the garden time to spend
We'll miss your fun and caring way
Your tea and coffee every day
Suppose someone will take your place
But no one will ever fill that space
Now your well earned leisure hours
More time to spend among your flowers!
We all wish for you a well earned rest
Because for us you were the best!

P. A. Jones

On The Crossroad

Whenever you arrive
at the crossroads of your life
you hesitate and think
is this the very brink
of a line you have to cross

And you find yourself at a loss
how to decide at best
to find yourself at rest
to leave all doubts aside
be sure your stride is right

At each crossroad you waver
which turn would be safer
which turn should you take
which future is at stake

It continues throughout life
till at last you do arrive
at the final one way shore
where crossroads are no more...

Wila Yagel

Belated Valentine

Do you like the days of Autumn
When the wind is on the heath
Where the mournful trees gaze sadly
On the dead brown leaves beneath.

Or the chilly days of Winter
When Jack Frost nips every toe
Though the pain is soon forgotten
In the evening firelight glow.

Or of Spring, and resurrection
When the buds first 'chance one eye',
And the lark, God's praises singing
Tells his song, from earth to sky?

Or, the seldom days of Summer,
When the skies are brightly blue
And the flowers ever please us
With their fragrance, and their hue.

I like all the days of Autumn,
Summer, Spring and Winter too
But it's on the day of Valentine
I'll ever think of you.

Charles Charnock

Dark Secret

Looking at my reflection
At the mirror before my eyes
Overshadowed by hateful resentment
A face that is filled with lies

Trying to find an exit
Trying to find a way out
Lies, lies, lies
Is that what life is about

Worrying myself into the ground
Wondering what my next step will be
Look at me, look at the pain
Just open your eyes and see

A dark secret I bear within me
Just screaming to be known
Wallowing in self-pity
I go through this alone

Hating myself more everyday
This Feeling will remain
Until the dark secret is out
I will still feel the pain

Gulsen Ahmet

Love Exposed

As a dying rose my spirit falls;
Soul exposed and incomplete;
Where to lean you have gone my wall!
Is our love again to meet?

Without each other we are not whole;
Each is the others missing link;
Without you I'm only half a soul;
We are one in how we think.

In each others eyes what do we seek?
An anchor of hope be there?
We need not even have to speak;
In one glance our love lays bare.

Do not wilt or fall our rose;
Pray lean against your wall;
Entwine together your oneness expose;
On a pedestal seen by all.

Samantha Jones

Magical Moments

Those nights
Of sweet embrace,
The pinks and whites
Of your face.

The closeness
That we enjoyed sharing
Free of worry and stress
Full of passion and caring.

Special memories
Of two souls linked as one,
Travelling calm seas
And enjoying our own bright sun.

Dearest Lady,
You meant everything to me,
Lifting me so very high
That I swear - I almost reached the sky

Stephen Clark

Welcome Little Grandchild

Welcome little grandchild
We've waited quite a time
Now at last you've come along
Little grandchild of mine.

You've made us very happy,
Your grandfather and me
You're so beautiful and perfect,
As any child could be.

God bless you my darling
May you have good health,
A life of joy and sunshine,
Love is worth more than wealth.

Proud parents watching over you
To guide you through the years.
May the happiness you bring
Far out weigh the tears.

E. Melton

I Am Poor

My house is very cold and dark.
I have no light,
Just a candle.

I do possess a frying pan,
Though it has a broken handle.

My right foot wears a shoe, I found,
My left, it bears a sandal.

Because, I am poor.

Ian Squibbs

Loving Hours

Dining-in was a joy,
Even better was my new 'Toy Boy',
Was he loving, attentive, caring,
And strong.

Sensational all night long,
Passionate and wanting was divine,
Evening, night and morning,
He was all mine.

Elizabeth Cole

Global Warning

Pollution in the world we live,
the sea, the earth, the air,
How much more must we give?
Does anyone know?
Does anyone care?

Pumping out the dregs and waste,
Dirt and fumes, smoke and grime,
Repent at leisure, rue in haste,
Wearing away the face of time.

Will man ever learn to pay?
For his ruin of mankind
Ozone layer worn away
Is he out of his tiny mind.

Don't rock the boat
Don't demonstrate
The powers that be dictate the score,
But we must react before it's too late
Or the world will be no more.

A. Bird

Why? Who Knows

Have you ever noticed
that when things do go wrong
it never seems to just be
a little one or two
but the biggest void or mountain
that you could ever see
just one thing after another
just pile upon pile of abject misery
But then something happens
to turn this torrid tide
something so silly
that it takes you out of yourself
so that you can stand and look
to make you really see
that life is just a game
and how we play it out is
down to you and me
it's all there for a purpose
why? - we may never know
but there is a better place to be.

Roslyn Burton

Happiness

Happiness is in the mind.
An elusive state and hard to find
Though quickly born, it fades away.
Nor you, nor I can make it stay.

Comes Sadness then in bleak contrast
And Crying (- cousin to the laugh)
Replaces smiles with sombre moods
And darker passion's amplitudes.

Are these ordained and in our Fates
These Happy, Sad or Middling states?
Or conjured from Emotion's pools
Played in our minds, with us the Fools!

No! It's just that there is a norm
Where all is ordered, in due form
And Life ticks by most days the same
'Til here's that Happiness again!

Ivan Holgate

The Power Of Love

I love you, you know,
I love you so much,
I love to be near you,
I love when we touch.
I love when we lie there,
Alone in the dark,
I love you so much,
It's breaking my heart.

I love you much more,
Than you'll ever know,
I love you with all of,
My body and soul.
I love you today,
I'll love you forever,
I won't ever stop,
Stop loving you -
Never.

Natalie Ann Elliott

Tease

In the playground,
And at home,
All I hear is,
Tease, tease, tease,
The laughing,
The sniggering,
All behind my back,
Leave me alone I scream,
But they don't hear,
They just carry on,
They don't listen to me,
I repeat in my head,
My life's a joke,
In the playground,
And at home,
All I hear is,
Tease, tease, tease.

Amy Dye

Untitled

Crying is for the heart
Not the eye, not the tear.
Crying is for feeling apart
When physically near.
Profound sorrow that is deep
That does not tolerate sleep.
O heart of mine you pine
For love once so benign.

Barbara Davies

Lakeside Dawn

A golden glow through shrouds of grey,
dawn's sunlight chases mists away,
from quiet lake, peaceful, serene,
enclosed in a hundred shades of green,
gentle willow, mighty oak,
revealed as nighttime lifts her cloak,
and Brock returning to his lair,
as the sweet dawn chorus fills the air.
The earth is clothed in beads of glass,
soft footsteps through the dewy grass,
bring anglers keen to wile their time,
away from city's smoky grime.
Excitement growing, leaping wild,
just like it did when, as a child,
I fished with father, learning skills,
that long years later still fulfils,
a burning passion deep inside,
to run away from life and hide,
so silently 'twixt reed and sedge,
alone here at the water's edge.

Stephen Blake

Reality Within A Dream

Watching the first flower of spring,
Opening to let the sunlight in.
A fleeting glimpse now fades away,
As sunsets on this autumn day.

Seeing the birth of new born child,
Feeling innocence fair and mild.
It becomes corrupted with age,
As knowledge comes in each new page.

She is neither child or flower,
Her beauty won't wither with hour.
It is of everlasting dreams,
But those in reality, it seems!

Ben Brown

Harvest Thanks

Have you been out harvesting
In a garden, field or wood?
Have you enjoyed Gods abundance
Has he done you good?

Have you smelt the flowers
Long side the garden path?
Seen the effect of rain and shine
And gloried in beauty's bath?

Have you really thanked Him
The creator God above
Given yourself as humble folk
To the God of Love?

Edwin T. Kirby

True Love

O nly when it happens do we see,
N ever is one able to imagine
C larity of mind and purpose,
E nsuing such immortal happenings.

I nstantly aware in every way
N othing else could ever be so

A ligned to perfect harmony.

L ove as this is rare and true,
I nfallible in trust and understanding
F orever strong and comforting
E verlasting in its purity.
T hough few may ever find this gift
I have with grace found thee.
M y love you are my very life,
E ach day I wait for you.

Gloria Cubitt

Death Of A Young Man

Bright though the morning
No-body smiles
Hearts heavy laden
Tears dim sad eyes

Birds sing a gay song
No-body hears
Thoughts of a dear one
His hopes, his fears

White clouds are drifting
No-body sees
Angels are watching
Sighing the breeze

Young life has ended
Who understands
A grave is tended
By loving hands

Dreams are unfolding
Days long ago
Treasure him Jesus
We miss him so

B. Delves

317

2013 A.D.

Who would listen now?
They would not listen then,
If they had just taken a little care,
Those foolish foolish men.
They took resources from the earth,
Then returned them to the sky,
They sat there looking puzzled,
As around them all did die.
The Earth began to weaken,
It could not take the strain,
From all the deforestation,
From all the acid rain.
Then came the famine,
The floods from to high a tide,
The misery and pestilence,
It hit us all world wide.
And so we sit here in their future,
Waiting for the end,
And wish those people in the past,
Would have made the earth their friend.

Ronald P. Lloyd

On The Shelf

I'm well beyond the sell by date
With others I do share
Been on the shelf for some time now
So just sit here and stare

Have travelled round to country fairs
Admired and disliked too
Completely ignored by some poor folk
Not sure - by just a few

Remembered being held by one
Then dropped without a cause
Someone else just picked me up
Hushed silence then applause

I've nearly cracked up many times
With sounds of "Ugly Mug"
Shouldn't be so sensitive
I'm just a Toby Jug.

Phyllis M. Smith

The Things Of Love

The sweet, close things of love
That cling round to the heart
Wrenched off, hurt to kill.
'Tis death to live apart.

Time blissfully allows
Its balm to heal the wound,
And one will just survive
Mere flower by the tomb.

Then age will bring its frost
On bud and open flower
And reach to touch the heart
In cold and fateful hour.

But underneath the snow
Close to the old heart's core
The sweet, close things of love
Are young, young evermore.

Olga Bingham Powell

I Love You So

Why must I always wait,
Why can't you keep a date,
You know I love you so,
Why don't you let me know,
If you love me too
As I'm so in love with you
Will you love me too
As I'm so in love with you

R. Abrahams

Untitled

Whenever you're away from me
I miss you more and more
I think about you every day
Because my love for you is sure.

I know that you'll come back to me
You said you always would
That's what helps me make it through
Even though my heart is sad.

My love and trust will always be
With you my darling one
I need you more than anything
Please don't be too long gone.

Linda Howe

If You Could See

If you could see through my eyes,
what a wonder that would be.
If you could see through my eyes,
all my hopes and dreams you'd see.

If you could see through my eyes,
feel my sorrow, feel my pain.
If you could see through my eyes,
boundless knowledge you would gain.

If you could see through my eyes,
you'd begin to understand.
If you could see through my eyes,
you could lend a helping hand.

If you could see through my eyes,
if you could shed my tears.
If you could see through my eyes,
then with you I'd share my fears.

If you could see through my eyes,
If only ...

Margaret Bergin

All Too True

And like shadows we lie
The reflection of ourselves dimmed:
The man on the inside's looking in
He won't come down, he doesn't try
No need to say hello, goodbye.
The waning moon looks pale, looks thin
He hides inside; he's safe within
His own, his little said in time.
And somewhere in this darkness is me
I'm here somewhere
Nobody tell me where though
It's a game you see, it's a game
And yellow is its colour
Or brown or orange and red
But never blue, no never ever blue.
It's only a lifetime as someone said.

Alexis Croft

A Gift From God

I sit and gaze at life so still
I can't believe my eyes
For something so precious
So amazing
So real
A gift, from God, to me.

With a smell
As sweet as roses
A touch
As soft as silk
This life that I've created
My child
My love
My all.

Deborah Joy

Lily

Everyone dies in the end
but why does it have to be
Someone you love or a friend

Lily was someone I love
and now she's living up above
I'll never forget her
for as long as I live

I really did love her
just like a grandmother
and now she's passed away
I'll think of her everyday

I'm glad she had no pain
because it wouldn't be the same
I love her oh so much
I wish I could keep in touch

I'll miss her with all my might
and cry over her at night
now she's lost the light
I'm not a pretty sight.

Natalie Jane Durber

Peaceful Times

Although I'm over eighty now,
I dream of bygone days;
The happy hours we always spent,
In many different ways.
I think of all those carefree times,
And things we did for fun;
Those football and those cricket games,
Enjoyed by everyone.
Bring back all those happy days,
Of sportsmanship and fun;
No sign of crime and violence then,
Nor harm to anyone.
So let's return to common sense,
And peaceful times once more;
Let nations turn again to sport,
And not to thoughts of war.

C. W. Mardell

Retirement

Enjoy your retirement,
Everyone said,
As they handed me a card,
You will now be able to do
Everything that you have planned,
But retired friends informed me,
With wisdom in their eyes,
Don't believe life will be easier
It's all a pack of lies,
I listened with much scepticism,
To all they had to say,
And then and there vowed to myself,
My retirement I would enjoy,
Each an every day.
But somehow my plans have gone astray,
I'm on call as one would say,
Peaceful retirement without ties,
Take heed everyone,
It's a pack of lies.

P. H. Short

Harmony And Freedom

The level sword - he
takes the gate
breaking wood
The grey she takes
the hedge
side by side
they ride together.

Geoffrey M. Gardiner

Rottweiler And Master

Some people have a barking dog
That's always full of fuss,
That scatters all the garden birds
And hates the sight of puss.

But I know of a quiet dog,
You could say he is mute.
He stands and waits and makes no sound,
Until he's got you on the ground.

Then as he's chewing off your ears,
His master with a smile appears.
And when you're all inside his tum,
He takes up crumbs, with Vac-u-um.

Kenneth Broomfield

You...

Your lips on mine
Are as soft as silk,
Your kiss is divine,
Your eyes are like
The sea of blue,
Or stars that brightly shine,
Your voice is sweet
Like music,
Or sultry as the summer heat.
Your touch compares to
The greatest joy of spring,
You are my very soul,
And everything
That I ever hoped to hold,
A smile from you
Brightens, even the darkest days,
Because, I love you,
In so many different ways.

Kate West

Sunset On The Beach

Marching to the sun
Backed by music
Wavestepping from beach to light
Casting off a carapace
Of callous pain.

Listening carefully
To prayers of people
Standing on wavywet sands
Supporting my journey spiritborne

I change into a shining one
And blend
And blend
And blend
With this source of
Music power light.

Henk Van Oort

Antechamber

Tomorrow I shall conquer,
Tomorrow will be bliss.
Today may still be desperate,
But Fate won't be remiss!

And so it goes, and on and on...
I pray for things to gel;
For life to open up for real,
Although I know full well
That I am wasting time in here,
Here in this waiting room-
Behind the door to happiness
Lies nothing but dull doom.

One certitude keeps me on course,
Holds suicide at bay:
Sweet Death will surely bring relief.
And come it will, one day!

Iskander Zwaap

The Compassion Trap

Can you spare me some change?
Came a voice from the ground.
I felt in my pocket
And gave him a pound.
He'll spend it on drink
Said a man who passed by.
You shouldn't encourage them:
They're just work shy.
An old woman passing
Said that may be true
But if you were him
You might do the same too!
Who knows what his life's been.
Who cares, said the man.
I do, said the woman:
I could be his gran.
The beggar sat silently
Counting his 'winnings'
Twenty quid in an hour, he thought.
Not a bad innings!

Frances Heckler

Murder

In the blackness of the storm,
The slumped and crumpled figure,
A century from the dawn,
Murder pulled the trigger,

The mass of sodden hair,
Contemplation of this sight,
Sweeping of black mare,
That drove death's coach tonight.

The thrashing of the rain,
Sheened across the coat,
Blood that leaves the brain,
Ghost unsightly moat.

Early sirens scream,
Pierced the echoed lane,
Body warms the steam,
Trickles down the drain,

A man no face no name,
The sound of human cries,
A monster that's not tame,
The place where body lies.

Terrie Baker

"So" Donna

So little, but so dominant.
So young, but so intelligent.
So small, but so powerful.
So loving, but so independent
So time flies for us when we
are with you.

Ian Bingham

The Piano

His fingers are dancing,
For reasons be known,
Submission of senses,
He succumbs all control.
His ears caressed,
His mind awakes.
A moment in sound.
Of one he creates.
A tear has fallen,
For the unknown.
Penetrating his being,
Teasing his Soul.
His eyes reflecting,
The pain he beholds.
His ultimate release,
His thoughts unfold.

Michelle Dennis

At The Garden Pond

So still she sat there,
watching fish at play,
I thought myself a trespasser,
and walked away.

She sat unmoving,
and as quiet as stone,
so that in some strange way,
I felt bereft, alone.

Turning, I looked again,
but this time, with surprise,
I saw there only peace -
and dragonflies.

D. M. L. Wilks

A Boy And Me

Sometimes I wonder,
do we make a good combination
sometimes I think,
does it just happen to me
sometimes I say
never again
some day, that time
will come.
My heart gets broken
again and again
does it have to be this way,
I wonder.
I fall in love
he breaks my heart
sometimes I wonder
Why me?
Why me......

Gail Reynolds

For The Lost Children Of Dunblane

You had no idea
As you walked to school
How that normal day would end.
You could not know
As you skipped along
Holding hands with your best friend.
Your tragic death
has shocked the nation,
We are not ashamed to cry,
Our thoughts are with you
Little Angels
You did not deserve to die.
You'll stay among us
In our hearts
Each prince and each princess,
Sleep well
Little children,
Sweet dreams, good night, God bless.

Diane Poole

Water

What price water?
When there's not enough,
When it's crystal clear
It's really lovely stuff.
If you use it wisely
And don't waste a drop
Every one will have enough
Until the lakes fill up.

Use it once and once again
Then once more if you can,
Wash your clothes then wash the floor
Then water all your plants.
Share a bath and share a flush,
These two will save a bit.
Turn off that tap and use a bowl
Think twice before you use it.

Marian Smith

When Will Tomorrow Come?

The candle burns softly
A glow in my night
Waiting for bird song
Or the first breath of light

My heart feels so heavy
I think it might burst
Will sleep bring me peace
Or will dreams be the worst

What will the new morrow
Give unto me
Will the pain disappear
Will I ever be free

Will my love for him
Ever fade or die
Though the bruises are gone
Each night I still cry

And so it has been
For seven months now
I have to go on
I just don't know how

Emma McLeod

Questions Of Love

Will I ever see the face
that once lit up my day
will I ever touch the hand
that stroked all my troubles away

Will I ever meet the eyes
that spoke without a voice
spoke of love each and every day
without one single noise

Will we ever walk together again
quietly hand in hand
will I ever find you
in that far and distant land

All these questions remain unanswered
until the day I die
so till that welcome day arrives
I ask myself, why, Oh why, Oh why?

Christine Diamond

Freedom In A Cage

History is full of rage
Insanity on every page
Independence of the mind
Freedom given in a cage
Soil is wet with blood and sweat
Hearts are cold and feelings dead
Look at me without remorse
Sold my soul for a piece of bread
Who is judge in court of life
Who are all the advocates
Silently I heard it all
Testaments of endless hate
In this ritual caught my eye
Broken wings in cage a bird
Nothing here to testify
Silence speaks a thousand words.

Shakeel A. Khan

Untitled

Feel the minutes ticking by,
Rain is counting its drops.
Yet this misery is quiet,
Though I feel it'll never stop.

It's so long and never ending,
clouds puddles and the rain.
I can't live but by pretending
that I'll be with you again.

Alia Zapparova

My Teddy

My Teddy Stuffy is very fluffy

He can't stand up
He can't sit down
  He can't smile
  He can't frown

  Oh! I wish
  Oh! I wish
He could ride a bike
  Or drive a car
Or even eat a chocolate bar

  But wouldn't it be funny
If a Teddy came into a shop
With a hand full of money
Or he asked for a drink
  With lots of fizz
  So I guess
I like that Teddy
The way he is!

Therese Mullan

Don't Cry - Don't Sigh

Don't cry, don't sigh
I will always be there
Don't cry, don't sigh
I'm sitting on the chair.

Don't cry, don't sigh
I see you every day
Don't cry, don't sigh
I've not faded away.

Don't cry, don't sigh
I'm here always
Don't cry, don't sigh
Look at the times we've been together
With our family day by days

H. Whittaker

Losing The Rat-Race

I can't be happy
Or full of joy,
As this society has
Made me its toy.

I can't be relieved
Or breathe a small sigh,
Because all of these pressures
Are pushing life by.

I don't want to stay young
Or slowly grow old;
I want to be different,
Yet not break the mould.

I live as I can
Yet I can't help but cry -
Am I letting my life
too quickly, slip by?

Katharine Hardwick

Underground

Rattling upon the rails:
  Disinfected air;
Vast appearing Leviathan:
  People everywhere:
Grating, grinding,to a halt,
  With metallic scraping:
Humans hurry, bustling out,
  Through jaws open gaping.
Fresh intake of living bodies,
  Press tightly into space:
With hissing noise the maws are closed;
  The monster departs in haste.

Frederick Kingston

The Road To Wembley

The team warmed up
Waiting for the whistle
Knowing they would get the cup
It started with a bustle.

The others scored
Was that Roger, who
The supporters roared
You could hear the din of a boo.

When half-time
Heads hang low
The clock did I chime
When the whistle blow.

They came back on
The cup was still there
But the others had gone
They looked around with a glare.

They were the winners
They were all alone
The others the losers
And then they finally went home.

Louise Normoyle

I Desire

To awaken my sweet
in your loving arms
To press my trembling lips
against yours
So that I may feel a warm glow
permeate my entire body
I yearn for you to be free
So that we may experience
bodies entwined in ecstasy
To exhale my longing passion
so that you may quench my thirst
and relinquish my inner-most soul
Rhythmical bodies
in tune with silent music
Sweet melodies
articulated without words
Our most intimate
declarations in actions
Exquisite pleasures
I desire to be exposed.

Patricia Davis

My Friend

I do not want your pity,
I do not want your stares,
I do not want your cold, cold frown,
I only want some care.

Come and take my hand,
Come and say Hello!
Come and call on me,
Come and be my friend.

My tears they flow like rivers,
My sorrow very deep,
My broken heart will someday mend,
And then will no more weep.

The flowers will bloom in spring,
The roses red in June,
And eyes will smile and look in mine,
Because you stayed my friend.

Winifred Hartford

To Jane Who Died

My tears are shed in the night,
The lonely blackness of the night
When all is still
And only night birds cry,
When life is close to death.
'Tis then I lie
And mourn
And break my heart for you.

No tears can soothe this pain,
This cruel everlasting pain
Of bitter loss.
No matter dawn will rise
To still the night birds' cry,
I must arise
And mourn
And break my heart for you.

Edwina Chamberlin

Generations

What is the ticking of a clock?
Is it me the ticking mocks?
Time moves on when the ticking stops.

Perpetually onwards,
Ceaselessly towards eternity,
Monotonously around the face,
Speed has no meaning
Tediously ticking away
Our lives
Sands in the hourglass
Infinity beckons

Steven Siggee

True Love

I'm glad I put the white gold band
on the finger of your left hand.
Hoping love lasts till we grow old,
don't discard that band of gold.
This is the last that I shall write
in an effort to put love right.
No one knows what the future holds,
each day a new page unfolds.
My love for you cannot be surpassed,
the love I have will always last.
From the day of the white gold ring,
till the heartache of death's sting,
let my love, so great, and tall
stand by you to fight all
the troubles we will meet in life.
I love you, my wonderful wife.

Gerald Davies

Death At Dawn

A man shot the goose
one frozen dawn.
Her mate flew high
above her, all joy fled,
his sorrow one with
the ice-coloured sky.
There were garnets
of blood
on the dead bird's breast.
Folding strong
white wings the bird death dived,
lay broken, beside his mate.
Softly snow began to fall.
When the man with the gun
found the geese, he stood there
mute and sad,
watching the flakes
embalm the dead.

Anna Punshon

Horn Warning!

Honk honk beep beep faster go
Why do you have to drive so slow
If you're fearful of your life
Why put up with all this strife

Honk honk beep beep faster still
I swear I'll catch you, yes I will
Hurry up, out of my way
If you don't there's hell to pay

Honk honk beep beep faster yet
To overtake you I am set
Speeding quicker than you can
I'm a real macho man

Honk honk beep beep they regret
He'll not be home tonight just yet
He's off to have his bones and face
Put back into their proper place

Barry D. Edwards

Love Shower

Up above the mountains high
Will you hear when I cry
Faded roses faint dreams
Stop me when I fly
Listen the sweet music of life
Free from struggle hatred and strife
When you touch me or come near
Wipe off my frozen tear
Up above the mountains high
Shower on me the warmth of love
Make me dear a pretty dove
Tell me when I am out of way
Pull me out of the darken bay
My love for you is ever green
When you are the prince I will be queen
Shake my heart
And wake up my dreams

Anju Arora

Takes Time

Takes time for every little girl,
To learn to count to ten,
And time for all the little boys
To grow up into men.

Takes time for every winter
To turn into a spring
And time for every song bird
Before he starts to sing.

Takes time for every rosebud
To blossom as a rose,
And time for every seedling -
Then suddenly it grows.

So when you think that all is lost
And there's nothing left for you,
Take time to think that "Someone" cares
And "He" will see you through.

Elsie Sage

Crazy Logic

"'You can take a horse to water,
But a pencil must be lead,'
Is a quote," remarked a loony,
"Though I'm puzzled why it's said."
"So am I," replied another,
"And I'm sure it isn't right,
'cos a friend I know who's clever,
says the proper name's graphite".
"Ah! well!" exclaimed the first one,
"Now it all makes sense, of course,
Since a pencil must be graphite,
You take water when you're hoarse."

Anthony G. Pilson

The Green Spirit Of Summer

Give to me your loneliness,
And share your tears and pain
That I may give you happiness
And make you live again.

Give to me your aching heart
And I'll give you a true love
Forget the emptiness that's past,
And start again with new love.

Tell me the words you dare not say,
Give to me your sorrow,
Give to me your yesterday
And I'll give you tomorrow.

Give to me your sadness
And I will bring you laughter,
Let me have your ache-filled past,
For I am the Hereafter.

M. C. Thomas

Iris

The child must lead, 'cos pure of eye,
he cannot hear the reaper's cry.
Fear drives denial, weakness of pride,
we cannot find no place to hide.
To love the things that never die
helps if at first they are alive.
I can't be me, I have to put
my money over brotherhood.
My crust cuts out the beautiful,
fear hinders life, won't be fulfilled.
Reach out to rings from carousels
and fall and die, denial felled.

Edward Durand

Hoping Upon A Fairy Tale

A magical story
Full of mystery
Receiving glory
And making history.

A heart warming tale
To bring a tear to your eye
Nobody can fail
Or ever say "goodbye."

How wonderful it is
To escape for an hour
Sharing somebody's images
In a fairy tale tower.

As the credits role
I turn away.
Suddenly, I am cold,
Reality ruins the day.

Martina Kathryn Elizabeth Harrington

Stepping Stones

Walk, little one, don't try to run,
Take life step by step, and then
You can up the pace
And join the human race.

Tread step by careful step
Upon the nursery floor,
Then on the garden path, and out
of doors
Into the woods and down a country lane,
Further and further, exploring your
little world.

And when the time comes
For you to leave me
Walk, my son, don't run;
But do not go so far away
That there is no returning.

Cynthia M. Spey

Untitled

Today, the day seems
the same to me.
To others, death and horror
are at their side.

Whose is the finger that
points to you, and says

Today is the day that I decide,
To pull you forth for grief & woe.
Today, I decree.
That it shall be so.

Peter Manson-Herrod

Untitled

Have you ever tried to talk,
when no one seems to listen?
You get half a sentence out,
then you find they're missing.
I tried this the other day,
but my husband ran so fast,
I tried to chase right after him,
for he hadn't heard the last.
I looked for him in the Kitchen,
I looked for him up the stair,
I looked for him in the garden,
but couldn't find him there.
I searched the whole wide Universe,
I searched both far and near.
But couldn't find a trace of him,
so couldn't make him hear.
Eventually I found him,
as he walked around the bend.
I tried to finish my sentence
but forgot how it should end!

Bridget King

Eclipse

One evening in May
The Downland lay
Like a double bed
With a green coverlet
And the Moon and Sun
Became as One
The Moon she was the willing bride
And with the Sun lay close beside
Not the moon of cold, clear light
The virgin of the dead of night
But radiant in the Sun's embrace
A warmer hue bedecked her face
And both blushed red as any rose
Content together in repose
Then clouds and mist pulled covers high
And paled their faces in the sky
And Night crept in, the lovers to part
With stolen kisses in the dark

Maria Hargraves

The Baker

To sow the seeds, to plough the land,
Bread and wheat go hand in hand,

All over the world, across the sea,
A loaf is baked in time for tea,

At lunch time it's delicious too
A whole meal or cottage either will do.

Pizza's to are made with flour,
Ready to eat at any hour.

A bap with a burger,
French strick with wine,
Prawn cocktail and scampi,
A good way to dine

The world in his hands,
The Baker

June Woodhead

The Silent Visitor

When I awoke, I wondered why
My room was full of light,
On opening the curtains, saw
Snow had fallen in the night.

It fluttered down so stealthily,
One never heard a sound,
And by the time we were awake,
It covered all the ground.

The view outside was beautiful,
There were no defects now,
You couldn't see the broken wall
Or the bent and twisted bough.

The children laughed so happily,
As we did 'long ago'
And went to build their snowmen
In that lovely virgin snow.

It muffled all the heavy sound
Of traffic going through,
And looking out across the town,
The world seemed born anew.

Isobel Crumley

Shadows

Are we sure of what we see,
    Shapes, shadows running free.
Shadows reflect the light,
Change a shape, deceive
The sight.
Shadows on a distant wall,
    tell not the truth.
Make visions tall
    Day or night shadows
Appear stay awhile then
    Disappear

J. D. Smith

Untitled

I have a loving Saviour,
And a loving star,
That will guide me home to glory,
Be it near or far.
The more we see his goodness,
The more we want to be,
And be as loving as he is,
I'm sure that he means me.
So onward let us travel,
To the loving goal,
It's there that we'll find refuge,
For the unsaved soul.
Once that we have found him,
And feel him very near,
He'll be for ever with us,
And we shall know no fear.

Ruby Brawn

Sign Language

When people see a person's white stick,
They really are most kind,
They move out of the way
For they know that he is blind.
And if they find someone,
Struggling in a wheelchair,
They rush to try to help
To show they really care.
But when they shout to someone,
And he doesn't turn his head,
They wonder why he ignores them,
Is it something that they said?
Still study him most closely,
Then you might understand,
That his only communication
Is by signing with his hands.

L. R. Collins

Buzzard I

Buzzard I set off from lofty perch,
Buzzard I asleep among leaves.
Will massive wings outstretched,
Intent on a tasty search.

Then he espied a flying flock
Starlings, with rhythm ahead
Flying southward for the night,
To tall trees, out of sight.

He soared high circled and dived,
Once, twice, and thrice he tried.
All in vain were his efforts,
Closer they flew side by side.

Buzzard I dismayed went he,
To nest in sycamore tree
Away from others all alone
In retreat to try again.

Such are our life's desires.
To have and hold on high.
With inspirations fired;
Then cast down - but to ascend!

Mary Cornelius

The Thoughts Of A Country Man

Let others climb the mountains
and sail the lonely sea
but I will bide in the countryside
the only place for me

Where everything that's good in life
does spring from mother earth
how well I love this green clad land
where I received my birth

And I can roam the countryside
Where peace of soul is found
And in every field and hedgerow
Nature's bounty does abound

And in the days of summer
In each green country park
I smell the perfume of the flowers
And hear the sweet song of the lark

And when the resurrection comes
One boon dear Lord I pray
Let me be a country man once more
When next I pass this way

P. Speller

'Dear Elsie'

We'd been so happy
A true family at last,
But what you did then
Put an end to it, fast!

You were lying face down
On that carpet, upstairs,
Peeping down on dear Elsie
As she was changing, downstairs.

She was a lone invalid
Who chose us as friends,
Someone to turn to,
Our love to amend.

My eyes couldn't believe
As at you I stared,
'Cause I was at the bottom
Of those damned awful stairs!

I took my friend home
The very next day,
Never again
To ask her, to stay!

Amy Greenfield

Anything For You

My love for you grows every day
Every day that I'm away
I think about you all the time
Your love is sweet, as sweet as wine
You're on my mind as each day goes by
I'd even give my blood for you
Three pints, four pints, five pints six
I'd put myself on a crucifix
And just to show my love is true
I'd even go to hell for you
Please believe me, please do
For I really do love you
In my dreams you are each night
I wish I could hold you, oh so tight
But that day will come pretty soon
We'll sit and kiss under the moon
My love for you will never die
Please believe me, this is no lie.

David Andrew Penny

"Question Mark"

Oh, tell me does the setting sun
E'er feel a sinking pain?
Why is (inform me if you please)
A weathercock so vain?

Do stars require a gun to shoot?
What makes a bucket pail?
What tailor makes the chimney's soot?
Who writes the comet's tail?

Why is a vessel's hind part stern?
Who sings an old hen's lay?
(Please tell me for I'd like to know)
Who wears the close of day?

John Williams

Addicted

Addicted I'd become.
Addicted I would be.
They said I'd become Addicted
I said, what never me.

They say listen to your elders.
And listen to them well.
As to ignore a piece of good advice
Lands you in a place that's hell.

But I thought I knew what I was doing.
At least it made me feel good.
Even though I got told by friends.
They didn't think I should.

But ignorance is bliss.
Especially on a high
You don't see what is wrong with it.
Or even take time, to ask why.

But when you're on the road to hell.
There's only one place you can go.
So remember if you're offered it.
Believe me just say no.

A. D. Cussens

The Old Year

It goes as quickly as it came
Not noticed now, it had its fame
Abundant splendour, robed in lace
The whole world recognized its face
As it appeared, a year ago.

But now it paves the golden road
To let its offspring take the load
Its work is over, task complete
No ears will hear its mild retreat
As it slips away, forever.

Sylvia Davies

Life

Life in depth seems so full
Life itself not long at all
What time is left let's make a peace
And end this pain and misery.
Why is it that, that man must kill
to prove his power over nature's will
where once were seas and greeneries
lay motor ways and ugly sceneries
for this is not how I want it to be
surely others have sense like me
Do we want our generation to last
because time is now running out
fast for my tears alone will not save
this world but many more might heal
the pain that we have caused
　　　so open your eyes and start
　　　　to see the hurt, the pain,
　　　　　the misery.

Kelly Moriarty

Ghost

I thought that I heard you,
In the dark of the night,
Touch me and tell me,
Everything is all right.

I thought that I saw you,
Your smile shinning bright,
Could it really have been
Just a trick of the light.

Every corner I turn,
How I wish you were there,
On life's mysterious journey,
We still had much to share.

Carol Kendall

Day On A Farm - Zimbabwe

Morning dew. Sun rising
Birds awake some to song
Be quick, be quick Gregory
How doo cookie cookie
Life everywhere
Tractors on the move
The smell of tobacco curing in the air
Breakfast awaits
Expectations

Through the heat of the day
Evening creeps in
Beautiful sunset in seconds gone
Reds blue and gold
Beetles take over in music
Silhouettes of trees and hills as
The moon reaches up the sky
Time for the wild life
To roam in peace

Another day gone by.

Margaret Norman

Untitled

Autumn leaves fall,
　　filling garden bins.

Winter snowflakes,
　　biting winds,

Spring flowers and singing birds,
　　bring bliss.

Summer skies of blue,
　　sunshine's warmth,
　　　and everlasting kiss.

Leslie Gordon Knight

Senses

Every moment of every day
　　In each word I say
In the cacophony of sound around me
　　I hear you.

When I look to the sky above
　　Then to the grass below
Images pass between my eyes
　　I see you.

An overwhelming sense
　　Of a presence hovering over me
Crashes right into my being
　　I feel you.

I wonder where you disappeared
　　Without a word or sound
You touched me and then went away
　　I want you.

Kim Fisher Aaron

To Amanda

Amanda's look is fair of face
That if at me she deigned to glance
Because her form is full of grace
This poor wight would try to dance
But, knowing well that this poor frame
Could not aspire to move too long
I cannot help declare my shame
For not to do so would be wrong
I dream of her whilst still asleep
I long to hear her voice so strong
My thoughts of her go down so deep
That I with her would go along
Yet June and December cannot meet
Except as passers in the street

Tom C. F. Robinson

Alone In An Ethnic Gathering

Here with the foreign tongues
Close to my ear,
I find my own space.
A special member
Of the Human Race.
Despite the language
Isolation,
I find, I am not alone,
For I hold a
Unique
Place of my own.
Unperturbed, their laughter
Rings uninterpreted
In my ear.
I smile, my secret smile,
My humour not for their
Sharing.

Aleene Hatchard

Morning Matinee

Early morning; autumn mist
Draws a soft curtain
Across the earth,
Nothing is certain.
As tall shadows, upper stories rise
From soft, enveloping shroud,
Soaring to an unseen sky
Lost in cloud.

A grey backdrop, 'ere the play
　　commence,
Vague sounds touch the ear,
A hushed sense of expectancy
As the moment draws near.
Now! the drama of the day begins,
Curtain recedes with silent swish
As spotlight beam cuts the air,
And earth by the sun is kissed!

Lilian Davies

Reach For A Star

The sun, the moon, the stars
How distant and supreme
In their mysterious realm
Remote as a longed for dream

Though it seems that way at first
Unbelievable but true
A lucky star could change your course
A steer the way for you

Don't give up on your dreams
Though stormy clouds abound
Your troubles may be many
But they won't always be around

Always strive to reach your star
Your desires to fulfil
Keep a song within your heart
And believe some day they will

Inspiration will be your guide
Leading to that joyful day
It is just around the corner
And not a world away

Andrea Lisa Lowe

Spring Is Here

The winter is past
It is spring at last
And daffodils bloom again
The crocus head
And the tulips red
Show through on the fields of green
The sun is strong
The whole day is long
And happiness reigns once more
So we'll sing a song
As we walk along
Dreaming of days of yore.

Walter James Sermaine

"Gemini"

Existing in insulated unreality,
Heart and head unsynchronised,
Known, yet undiscovered,
Veiled, shrouded in mist,
Oblivious to all and yet aware,
Awake whilst dreaming.
Participating, yet apart,
Distantly disinterested,
Public private property,
The hidden personality unemerging,
Subdued but yet indormant,
Captive in incaptivity,
Going through the motions,
Remaining true to one's inner self.

Anita McDonnell

A Poem For You

I saw your competition
In my puzzler magazine,
I started writing straight away
I really was quite keen.

The first verse came quite easy
It rhymed on its own,
Then I had to stop and think
and have some quiet time alone.

Well that's two verses wrote
so now I'm on my third,
Thinking carefully what to write
choosing each and every word.

Now my poems at an end
I write the final line,
I'll send it to you with my love
I hope you like my rhyme.

Susan Bennett

Fear

No harsh voices,
No car so near,
No motorbike screeching!
Not a sound can I hear, hear, hear...!

The shadows envelop,
That coat on the door,
Did it not swing,
Once more, more, more...?

A sound in the room,
A footstep maybe,
Not one, not two,
But three, three, three...!

Switch on the light,
My hand reaches out,
My fingers are frozen,
With Fear, fear, fear...!

The switch goes down,
Light fills the room,
My heart stands still -
No one's here, here, here...!

Charlotte Mitchinson

"The Wild Geese"

I walk alone on Wolden Hill
when all is still
Still and silent
I think I hear your laughter
And I turn, expectantly
And run towards the sound
But you are never there at all
Only the wild geese call
Passing overhead

Eileen Blenkinsop

Somehow, Somewhere

I look in the mirror,
and what do I see.
A mass of tears
Falling before me.

A someone, a no one,
is anyone there?
Such sadness, unhappiness,
does anyone care?

A something, a nothing,
is anything there?
Such hate and tears,
does anyone care?

I look in the mirror,
and what do I see.
A handful of loneliness
Seeping into me.

Something, anything,
Nothing is there.
Loneliness is seeping
Somehow, somewhere

Rachael Veater

Why?

As I sit and contemplate
Of matters so profound
I think of metaphysics
And why the Earth is round.

What ever is our raison d'être
And why are we all here
There must be another reason
Than "we're just here for the beer"?

Alan J. Luxford

Yesteryear

On the dresser stood a wireless
With accumulators too
Today we'd think it looked a mess
But then was well to do
I miss the tanners and the bobs
And silver threepenny bits
Along with mothers home made cobs
And watching films in pits
No peggy legs and dolly tub
Or rubbing board on which to scrub
It's nice to switch the washer on
And dust around until it's done
No need for pegging rugs no more
Or sweeping muck up from the floor
No more sheltering from a raid
With bombers flying overhead
Gone the days of hopscotch
Skipping ropes and such
Yet in spite of everything
I miss them very much.

Eveline Parkin

Forces Of Nature

The forces of nature
Are stupendous to me.
The wind in the tree tops,
The waves of the sea.

A fiery volcano,
Or an electrical storm.
The rays from the sun
That keeps this earth warm.

The wonderful wild life,
The birds of the air
That nature has fashioned
For us all to share.

This world that we live in
Can bring pleasure and strife.
The forces of nature
Holds the essence of life.

Alma Dodds

Retirement

Your working life is over
It's time to slow the pace
The pen and pencil
Gets put back
Inside its leather case
The friends you've made
Will still be friends
And all will wish you health
But most of all I wish for you
All you'd wish yourself

Lavinia Evans

'That's Life'

He went down...She followed,
She drank, he swallowed.
He laughed, she smiled,
She went crazy, he went wild.

He protected, she cared,
She tempted, he dared.
He'd caress, she would touch,
They loved their baby so much.

He worked, she toiled,
Little Ben got very spoiled.
Money came, money went,
Soon every penny was nearly spent.

He'd shout at her, she'd shout at him,
She loved little Ben, he now loved Kim.
Lives so full, now so hollow,
He went off... She didn't follow.

Simon P. Ayres

The Children Of Dunblane

The world is bending with so much fear.
In prayer for children no longer here.
Oh' Lord take them and let them play.
And in your garden let them lay.

Each one you'll turn to a rose of red
And plant them in a flowering bed.
No petal ever to wither away.
Each bud, each leaf, must always stay.

Oh' comfort Lord the hands that held.
These children in their arms and felt.
Such love and purity to see.
The heartbreak Lord will always be.

Let's pray for mothers and fathers too
And ask for strength to carry through
The hills and mountains of despair.
And let them know that you are there.

Margaret Jones

"Holiday"

"H" is for holiday,
"Away from it all"
Having one's own way.
Games with a ball.
Relaxing or reading.
Whatever you choose,
Playing, competing
For fun, maybe lose!
Cooking done for you,
Just eat the meals.
Do lots of walking
wear down your heels!
Make tea or coffee.
In ones own room.
Wash these cups only.
Ne'er use a broom.
Beds very comfy,
You sleep well at night.
Out in the fresh air
You turn brown from white!

Grace Kathleen George

Life

Life is full of ups and downs,
Sorrow and strife,
Children quarrel and fight,
The man falls out with his wife,
What causes all these troubles?
I think they are just like bubbles,
Blown up, to burst and fade away,
Then comes up another day,
We are born to live,
Not knowing, what fate has to give,
The best we can do,
Is to smile, and carry on
mile for mile,
And win life's marathon.

B. Lenton

Untitled

I take what I'm not given,
And I give my life away
To a substance taking me over,
I won't be clean next day.

Bruises and scars cover me,
They envelop my arms with pain,
But every day new ones appear,
Which suck my blood 'til I'm drained

For one glorious minute
I lie semi-conscious for hours,
Thinking of ways to pay
For the next hit which devours.

Julia Babbage

My Window

I have a special window.
Where each season can be seen.
Through the leaded patterns.
I Watch natures changing scene.

I have a special window.
Where spring and summer come to life.
The country lane I've walked my son.
The fields I've walked my wife.

I have a special window.
Autumn spreads her morning mist.
I see frost upon the countryside.
Where once was summer bliss.

I have a special window.
The winter sun breaks feebly through.
Warming winters snow cape.
And glistening on the dew.

I see through my window.
What my life is all about.
For it is through my church window.
I am looking out.

Frederick Seymour

Youngblood

So young, so delicate,
Like a lambs breath,
In early spring.
So soft and pure,
Like a cloud floating in the air.
Your skin shines like the
Glittering stars in the night sky.
Smiling in happiness and harmony.
Your blood so young so smooth,
Travelling and gliding through
Your young body.
What I would give to have that
Strength and youth again,
For these hands are old,
Never to be like yours again;
But I know I will live
In your heart for all eternity
Young child.

Joanne James

Tell Me Why?

Tell me why we can't last,
why we can't be forever.
Tell me please I'm so confused,
we need to be together.

Without you life is meaningless,
my life it seems so bare.
At night I dream I'm with you,
but when I wake you are not there.

I miss your arms around me,
I miss your words so much.
I miss the way you kiss me,
and I miss your gentle touch.

Whenever I was scared or sad,
you would always calm and comfort me,
now that I have lost your love,
scared and sad is all I seem to be.

Everything reminds me,
of the times we had together.
Why did the good times have to end?
we should have been forever.

Stacy Ponder

Love

Love is a dream
You're walking on air
Life is no worry
You don't seem to care

Like a mood or a daydream
That will never fade
You've longed for this feeling
You've hoped and you've prayed

Until one fateful day
When your world falls apart
The walls begin crumbling
The walls of your heart

You feel shattered
Broken in two
It's a horrible nightmare
That Should never come true

Victoria McNulty

Forever

Stand in a shadow
Await your gaze
World goes by slowly
Yet all in a haze.
Snow falling softly
Sun shining bright
Light becomes darkness
Day falls to night.
Rains wash me over
Winds blow dry
Clouds whisper secrets
Across the sky.
Time becomes endless -
Eternity near.
Days, years, millenniums—
Forever is here.

Michelle Bennett

Untitled

So black a Rose that I have slain
Who now amongst his thorns I've lain
Whose poison seeped beneath my veins

On battlefield I now lay dead
and open wounds spew forth their red
A Rose through crimson flood

and in this field, where once I stood
Amidst this soil so stained with blood

A whiter Rose than any fleece
Shall echo now the words of peace

D. Sankey

Saturday, Too Distant

We were silent,
We were in our bubbles
For hours,
When we walked,
When we drank,
When we confusedly
Talked.
We were statues in
Front of the screen
Whilst
Wenders' angels
Were losing their
Comfortable wings
In Berlin.
We were armed
Foreigners saying
A quick goodbye in
The underground.

Mariel Lobo-Miles

The Mathematician

I am a mathematician
I can count up to one, two, or three,
But I am not very sure
If I could count up to four
But if I tried very hard, maybe

But I hope very much
You'll excuse me
For making mistakes, I regret
For if I got to
Five, Six, and Seven
It's the finest thing
I have done yet

But eight, nine, and ten
Are a problem
My brain
Has suddenly gone numb
For introducing
These very large numbers
For they are
A very large sum

A. W. Bartram

The Poppies Weep

Yesterday I left my homeland,
To fight in a Flanders field.
I thought it was my duty,
To make those Germans yield.

'Oh we'll be home by Christmas!'
The merry cry rang out,
As we left our families,
Who'd never hear the final shout.

And very soon we learnt,
Only the toughest man survives.
Though all we wanted was our Country,
And our families, and our lives

But 300 miles from England,
That is where we lie,
The sound of guns our funeral march,
As more soldiers still walk by.

It was a fight for freedom,
But so many now are dead,
With crosses and blood poppies,
To mark our final bed.

Sophie Buxton

The Storm

Thunder rumbles
Lightning flashes
Wind blows
Rain splashes
Darkening skies
Uneasy silence
Child cries
Sensing violence
Dog whimpers
Under cover
Cat curls up
Till it's over
Some are frightened
And some exclaim
At noisy thunder
And lashing rain
But all are glad
When it is finished
And celestial clamour
Has diminished

Denise Mary Twigg

Sunrise

In another day,
In another time when
I've held you for the last moment;
As I have wished to hold on,
To never let you go:
Another Sun will rise,
And I will see it without you.

If I could turn back clocks,
Go without food for your love:
Keep you close in my heart;
If I could take your hand again -
I would run to the rising Sun,
But for me it rises alone.

I cannot reach you,
Can only imagine your touch -
Feel your heart in my mind;
The love is only mine,
Against our wishes:
Remember I love and want you,
As my Sun rises alone.

Emma Wilson

Knife Amnesty Ballad

Black, silent and undetectable,
Can be tucked or taped anywhere,
Featuring a partially serrated blade,
Approach the owner if you dare.

The law is powerless,
It can't be prevented,
After someone buys them,
They can't be censored.

Nobody's safe wherever they are,
In their home or in the street,
Everyone's living in fear of,
A glint of steel, a shuffle of feet.

Deep in the heart of the city,
A bleeding body crippled in pain,
Lies unnoticed down a dark alleyway,
Only this trade is to blame.

It could be someone's
Brother, mother or wife,
Why should we live in fear,
Save a life, bin that knife.

Claire Nicholls

Bogey Rock

I looked for you again today,
Whilst gazing unto the beach.
Monument to my childhood,
Lost now far from reach.

We used to play in your shadow,
Swim around your girth.
Bathed you in our laughter,
Cling to, when waves would surge.

You stood alone,
Weathered the storms.
Like a giant tooth,
That the fairies' ignored.

Where are you now my friend?
My mind forever ponders.
Did neptune steal you from your rest?
Spirited away to the deep blue yonder.

We named you "Bogey Rock",
A title somewhat obscene.
For upon your vast head.
Sat a wig of weed so green.

Robert Swire

Yours Is As Good As Mine

There is no proof
only theories and myths
passed down through generations
Pictured so pure and innocent
more intelligent than you or I
still causing pain, torture and death
This superior 'thing' is gay
his skin colour is black
she has no religion
no personality
no real identification
It is what you make it
and has control over so many lives
always there to confide in
to listen
never giving advice
watching and waiting
learning from our mistakes.

Nahid Analoui

Island In My Mind

I caught no glimmer through
the night
like the moon shining so
bright.
As I look out at the
deep blue sea
I can see my reflection
looking at me!!

Jemma Louise Strange

Weather Wise

The gentle breeze of morning
Sighing through the trees
The lilting call of the birds
And humming of the bees

The glistening dew on the roses
The scent of flowers sweet
These are the signs of spring
Bringing contentment and joy complete

As we enter November
Some flowers linger on
But as the nights get colder
You realize that summer has gone

Soon we may have frost and snow
Winds sleet and rain
But just think in four months time
It will be spring again

R. B. Illingworth

My Love

The beauty of a sunset,
The dawn, when light breaks through;
The colours of a rainbow
Are nothing without you.

The softness of a snowflake,
The stinging of the rain;
The warmth of Summer sunshine,
I think of you again.

The roaring of the ocean,
The singing of the birds;
The laughter of my loved one
The best music I've heard.

The scent of woods in Autumn.
The laundry, freshly aired;
The tempting smells of cooking
Are better when they're shared.

The taste I have for living
Is fed by you each night;
So hurry up and find me
My dreamy phantom knight.

Valerie Finden

326

Feline And Canine Caution

Who would know
With his puffed up fur
Overhanging fences
His fat whiskered pouches
His lovely measured glances
That eighteen sharpened claws
Would spark a glisten in his eye
Following the movement
Of a dog passing by

Bent down double sniff
Not looking for trouble sniff
Tail wagging in the air
Ant up in his nose sneezing
Head up in the air freezing
Eyes meet
A little scary
Turn away
A little wary
Sensing on the fence
Malevolence.....

Anita Lazarowicz

The Blackbird

The blackbird is a happy chap,
His song is bright and gay,
He sings a joyous welcome
To all who pass his way.

He sings his happy song of love
Upon the chimney top,
And calls to all who hear him
To listen, and to stop!

He sings, that little chorister,
Upon the cherry tree,
Midst blossom now, on the bough-
His sweet Spring song to Thee.

In garden, too, or on the lawn,
That friend is ever there:
Summer days; In Autumn's praise;
On through the lovely Year!

He chirps a greeting to thy heart
And to each living thing:
Then when Spring is nigh again,
He starts once more to sing!

Jean Jane

Minnis Bay

Soaring over the broken sea
Wheeling in the gasping breeze,
Seagulls showing off their skills,
Down at Minnis Bay.

Voices raised in urgent chant,
Horns blowing, sails pulling.,
Men and women straining, shouting,
Down at Minnis Bay.

Waves dancing, foam is frothing,
As the boats tack in,
Another race has come, then gone
Down at Minnis Bay.

Ann Stewart

My Father

It wasn't his fame,
It was his name,
on his gifts I have thrived.
His every skill, well taught,
has given me success, eagerly sought.
There was joy, there was humour,
there was gentleness, there was wonder.

Linda S. Hardy

Where Lies The Soul

Where lies the heart,
But in peaceful bliss
When with thee!

Where lies the soul,
But a footstep away
From the divine!

Where lies the spirit,
But in moments like these!
Serene, as a new morn
As the warm sun lifting,
The sleepy willow,
The call of the sparrow,
The birth of a new day,
The end of sunrise
The calm cool evening air,
The dark blue sky - the sound of night!

Lisa M. Stewart

By The Water

Many times I have walked
to this distant stream
Many hours I have spent here
in thought
With my four legged companions
I've sat by its waters
So much pleasure for me
it has brought
Could there be a God
with all of the answers
For all that I've seen here
somehow
I have had my doubts
as I've sat here and wondered
But I know I am convinced
He did now.

Michael Ellis

Sister

She arrived, a screeching monster,
Writhing in my arms.
Yet she was a sleeping angel,
Beautiful, and calm.

She destroyed all my creations
With her clumsy ways,
And yet, she was my sunshine on
Those rainy winter days.

How I hate her charming grin,
Her figure, her friends;
All the things she has, that I don't,
Drive me 'round the bend'.

All that she does I hate her for,
And vice versa;
But I couldn't live without my
Sister. How I curse her.

Amy Jacobs

Fallen Nation

Taking a trip down memory lane,
Riding on this old steam train
Stepping off at a disused station
Starting to wonder about this nation
Where has all the greatness gone
It has fallen one by one
King and Queen hide in their palace
Becoming symbols of everyone's malice
No one cares for fellow man
Most people don't even give a damn
Greedy politicians with their vices
And the high street
with its prices
Where's the empire we all knew
Gone forever oh so true.

A. D. Swindlehurst

The Gull

The call of the gull means
    freedom to me.
As they fly gracefully over
    the deep green sea.

This beautiful bird poised
in flight, really is the most
    glorious sight, with
immaculate feathers and eyes
    so bright.

Don't know why I love them so
Their call is so sad and
    full of woe, but I watch
with joy as they wheel and
    glide
coming and going with
    the tide.

M. Ollerenshaw

Strutting The Lute

They found us cuddle-kissing,
Where the noisle-spring is missing.
Mums'll came all weepy-willow
Sprinkles on our sleeply-pillow
Her jowles did dingle-dangle,
As her words came spittle-spangle,
Through her wringle-wrangle teeth.

They found us cuddle-kissing,
When the puss'll started hissing.
Dads'll fumes out "Fiddle-Faddle",
Then bellows "You! Skid-Daddle!"
He's all nettle strangle-stingle
And his eye-brows crangle-cringle,
In his crinkle-pinkle cheeks.

We were tired of cuddle-kissing,
With the best bits always missing,
So we went for a bittle mingle-mangle,
Where the wild lanes tingle-tangle
And then lots'll riddle-raddle,
On old "Piddle-Puddle" Hill.

Dan Adams

Lost Love

There is nothing bubbling up from the
bottom of my heart, no love is there.
Like a pond I am frozen, ice,
a useful thing, feeling skate
across my mind, they do not
melt my ice, nothing penetrates my
frozen barrier, no one walks
upon my feelings - how I wish
they would, how I wish they
could, warm me, thaw me
make me love again.
Wrap me in a blanket of
comfort security and hope.
Fill my empty days and
lonely nights, oh how I wish
they would.

Myra Horne

Untitled

Oh Rosa, sweet Rosa
I'd love to and will
One day paint thy face
To the words he wrote
With his loving quill.
Oh, how I want to sketch his words
Of poetry and verse
With my brush I'd paint
The pictures in my mind he creates
Of the men and ladies
That lie between his pages.

R. E. Stevenson

327

Free... And Happy

I'm free as a bird
Happy as I could ever be,
Pretty as a flower
Because you always shine on me.

I cried with sorrow and pain
And you swept away my tears,
I couldn't see the truth
But you gave me your vision.

You held my hand
Because I was too weak,
You opened my heart
And made me speak.

You helped me all the way
You gave wings to the past,
You made my pain fly away.

Now I'm free as a bird
Happy as I could ever be,
Pretty as a flower
Because you always shine on me.

Marta Rodrigues

Deepest Heartbreak

My heart I gave to you to keep
You promised never to make me weep
I was so proud to be your wife
To love you for all of my life
We were so happy for many years
Then I cried so many tears
You never said you never spoke
Now my heart is truly broke
You don't know just what you did
Now my heart is truly hid
Locked away for evermore
Shut behind a tight closed door
No one can see me cry
This I do where non can pry
The good Lord up above
Sent back to me my only love
Now the sun once more does shine
Evermore his promise to be mine
For I now discover
He is my own one true lover

E. White

You

You were there when I needed you,
    You never turned me away,
You gave your time so freely,
    And helped me on life's way.

You moulded my childhood days
    With unselfish time and care,
I never needed anyone else,
    For you were always there.

I tried so hard to please you,
    Did my best to get things right.
Just one word of praise from you,
    Would make my day so bright.

My heart would swell with happiness
    When you looked at me and smiled.
I loved you with simplicity
    For I was just a child.

I wonder if you ever guessed
    Just how much I loved you then,
For you seemed quite old to me,
    And I was only ten.

Mabel Griffin

Grant

The ward was dark and silent.
Patients - all asleep.
Except for one young man alone,
Thoughts cold and hard and deep.

Operation was tomorrow.
Oh God - the site was brain!
His eyes unblinking stared ahead.
Would he ever be the same?

If only I could take your pain.
The ordeal that's ahead.
I'd give up all I own right now.
If it were me instead.

The bitter pill you've swallowed
Has been bravely borne by you.
With humour and good-naturedness
And courage strong and true.

I know at times, as parents are,
We don't say much to each other
But may I say with all my heart
I'm so proud to be your mother.

Moira Laing

Wings Of Love

Vain snow robe me in a blanket of white
Lift me up on your wings of lace
Up towards a world of infinity
Far away from the human race
To a land of everlasting peace
Here I lie where men have lived
And always fought to live
I hear a trickle of ice melting
As gunfire ceases to be an echo
A smell of smoke cascades around
Warming my face as it softly falls
I fear to rise, a worn out dog
With no strength left for the fight
Only a dream of endless rest
I wait quietly as clouds darken
I feel my body riding on clouds
With a beautiful feeling of peace
As angel wings lift up my body
My soul flies peacefully upwards
On wings of love towards the light

Barbara Hicks

Death

Like a bolt of lightning
You struck him down,
    Time ceased.
Pallid, stiff, motionless,
    At peace.
I remained alone
In my self-made night,
Adrift on the tormented waters
Of doubt and fear,
Crying in the darkness
    for answers,
Hearing only the roaring of the waves
    engulfing me,
Struggling to keep afloat,
Bereft of faith,
Clinging to hope;
Lost in the fog,
Searching for far off shores,
Where once it was day.

Gemma Beggan

Golden Thread

What is this empty shell called life,
This vacuum, void, and space,
A battle to a journey's end,
Where I, must occupy my place.

I wonder, search, and struggle,
To comprehend the meaning's end,
To reconcile, and justify,
In truth, I must pretend.

Pretend to understand,
The purpose that I seek,
Of God, of love, and the universe,
And of faith and wonder - I can keep.

And yet I'm told it's all within,
This fine, and golden thread,
That leads us to our heaven on earth,
To peace and hope - instead.

Instead of feeling life's despair,
But to search for God within,
For when we find his precious love,
Then the meaning of life, will begin.

Cheryl Iona Benger

The Sullied Sea

The sea, with ever rolling waves,
Defies man's will to harness;
Ebbing, flowing, threatening
To drown his bold assurance.

Neptune's vernal clearance
Brings flotsam to the shore;
Jettisoning, twisting,
Thrown up, of use no more.

Orgasmic swell of ocean
Foretells abortive birth;
Palpitating, thrashing,
Brings excrement from earth.

Society spreads pollution
And tides become infected
With seepage, sewage, spillage,
Harming nature's unprotected.

Perpetually pounding,
The sea upon the sand,
Lashing, lapping, splashing,
Despite the works of man.

A. Price

Thoughts On Retiring

The end of an era.
No more 1 o'clock deadlines
Or uniforms to press.
Make sure the shoes are shiny,
The hair is looking smart.

An affable expression
Permanently on the face.
Grit the teeth and swear
Beneath your breath,
Behind the Desk.

Cope with colleagues,
Nurses, patients, clerks.
People, people, people
From 1 o'clock till 5.
Keep calm amidst the turmoil

Create order out of chaos.
Solving patients' problems,
Smoothing Doctors' days.
The work of a Receptionist
Was vital to the place.

Eileen R. Elgey

I Dream, I Despair

I dream,
My soul soars light and free
It's up to me
I can be anything I want to be.

I despair,
The weight of my reality
Is very slowly killing me.
From the chains I myself made
I cannot break free.
I can change nothing
And nothing will be.

But sometimes I dream,
I could be anything I want to be
Were it not for my reality
Very slowly killing me.

Nina Ali

Ode To Anthony

Full of life and full of zest.
Anthony was the very best
of youth today.
Mum and Dad and Sister too,
Will miss him so-well wouldn't you!
What will they do without the boy,
Who was their very pride and joy.
They'll think of all those happy years,
And then they'll wipe away their tears.
For Anthony was loved by all,
But God loved him the most of all.

Madelime C. Burden

Beautiful Creation

A timely peace is granted to me
as from my window I see
"The Beauty and Splendour"
of the copper beech tree.

Joy as I listen to the birds
"in early morning song"
Delight as I see a squirrel
Jump from the trees and scurry along.

Pleasure in watching a mother duck
"hustle her ducklings with care"
To the protective covering
of the bluebells blooming there.

The scene of a true winter's night
"Stillness of fresh fallen snow".
Which glistens in the moonlight
like jewels all aglow.

Joan McKay

Untitled

Are British beef and Yorkshire Pud
A memory of the past?
They will be soon if we give way
To euro democrats.
A vote for single currency
Might benefit our race,
But will leave Great Britain floating,
Like an atom lost is space.
We will lose our independence,
Our identity and more,
'The united states of Europe'
Will then govern British law.
The conservatives and labour
Must unite to seal our fate,
And remember it's the British folk
That make Great Britain Great.

Helen Bannister

Untitled

Take thou my hand
for I can give you little more

I bring no band to bind your brow
or yet propose
a jewel strewn path to paradise

I claim no dreams
foretell no harvest in our later years
this alone my self can bring to you
an outstretched hand
with all my human frailties

I seek no queen
nor do I need a virgin proud
to bathe my feet with tender tears

I plead no cause
no garlands need bedeck my brow
nor seek I gentle words or lies
to ease bewilderment

This alone is my desire

To take your hand
with all your human frailties

Ron Hollingsworth

Amerdown Woods

Energy failed to make
the doe dance with peers;
she says.

All the pent up strivings -
past, present and future
mingle absolutely
making stag and doe feel
completely - utterly, drained.

Sap laid, peace and quiet
flow through Amerdown Woods;
leaf and twig murmur in
soft eternal breeze; life - death -

Ebb and flow of being -
nothing glib or false, no
sudden change, just the loud
falling of a leaf, the
composting of the earth, the

Seeding of the new from
the old. They are part of that.

Robert Shooter

Magic Music

Compose me a tune,
Play it only for me,
Put into your music
The sound of the sea.

Let me hear the tide surge,
The great breakers roar,
And then little wavelets
That lap on the shore

Put into your music
A soft summer breeze,
The song of the skylark,
And such sounds as these.

Sounds long forgotten,
Sweet to my ear,
Sound taken for granted
By those who can hear.

Compose me a tune,
Play it only for me,
It will live in my heart
Eternally.

Anne Kennedy

Flame

Like a child I have been bewitched,
curling, yellow gold dancing light,
mesmerised by the leaping flame,
my senses throbbing in sheer delight.
I have felt its warmth drawing me,
filling my soul with desire,
into its heart, tempting me
oblivious of the scorching fire.
I stretched my fingers into its heart,
recoiled at the searing pain.
Spellbound, I'm held by its magic
and will reach for the flame again.

Valerie Yvonne Tootal

Shattered Dreams

When I was young, I had a dream
To be an Irish Fairy Queen
But that fell through I was too big
And I couldn't do an Irish Jig.
When older I became quite keen.
To be a star of the silver screen
That failed because of just one fact
The fact was that I could not act
I changed and thought it would be slick
To be a nurse and cure the sick
Bang went my chances once again
Could not inject into a vein
A stewardess I thought I'd be
And fly the whole wide world for free,
But sad for me, I'll see no sights
Forgot I was afraid of heights.
I then thought I would be a wren
And sail the briny with the men,
No good to offer up a prayer
Yes! You've guessed it, mal de mer.

Nancy Doyle

All Must Die

Why should we mourn
and weep and sigh
and feel forlorn?
As all are born,
so all must die.

Why feel so sad
and full of woe?
Better be glad:
This life we've had,
and all must go.

So why contrive,
in vain, to avoid
death? Why strive,
since nothing live
is ever destroyed?

The wise don't sigh,
nor do they mourn
as life goes by,
for all will die as all are born.

John Walton

Mirror

One look reflects
The two. Inferior
Details distorted by
Clean cuts of the Glass.
Simple suggestions doubled
Whilst the eye attempts
To look at evident features.
Blind to corners
Or mindless separations
Ground isn't fully covered
True resemblance unknown
Simply distortion.

Tracey Rogers

The Spooky Town

All was quiet in the town
you couldn't hear a single sound.
Then suddenly, it made me jump,
I heard a crash, and then a bump.
An eerie noise, a howl, a shriek
it scared me so, I could not speak.
I looked around but couldn't see,
for it was dark, as dark could be.
Something cold brushed past my hand,
well that was it I could not stand
it any more, I took to heel
but couldn't move, my legs were steel.
A big bright light came on and then
I had to look around again
Then I saw it, what was that?
Just a dog chasing a cat.

A. Clark

On A Journey

We're all on a journey
Some know not where;
Others are so taught
They do know where.

Some will say "Not now,
We have too much to do";
Others are so taught
To seek him now.

We came into this world
For to glorify Him;
Not to seek our own glory
Or wallow in sin.

If we seek Him not
But go on in sin
He'll come with His reapers
And gather us in.

Flee to the refuge
Before it's too late;
Now is the time
To come to the gate.

Flora Campbell

A Day Of Frustration

I've had a day of frustration
I really can't understand why
It seems to go from bad to worse
No matter how hard I try

It's left me feeling frantic
Nervous and overwrought
It seems I'm easily distracted
With a feeling, I'm very distraught

Perhaps I could have prevented
In bed I should have stayed
Then I wouldn't be feeling hysterical
Bad tempered and very dismayed

I seem to get these off days
I wished that I could halt
So I hope you all kindly accept
That it's not always my fault

Though this day has been hectic
I will not admit defeat
I'll quietly sit in the office
And simply put up my feet

Dennis N. Davies

"Emozione"

In the harshness of obscurity cower,
Striped naked of all dignity and care,
And when at last I can cling no more,
I look up to find you there.

As I go through youth undaunted,
I make mistakes along the way.
But I know I have your support,
Which helps me face each day.

You were crafted from the finest,
Of all the world has to hold,
And when you were perfected,
The angels broke the mould.

You are one of a kind,
An individual to the end,
As I kiss the air and whisper,
This emozione which I send.

Sallyanne Mercer

The First Scream

Thrust forth,
Alone and naked,
I protect myself
From mirrors and maternity,
I want only to know myself
But I am forced, screaming,
Into your world of
Order, dependence and
Fear,
I will forget the
Warmth, the comfort, that
You pushed me from,
I will forget the tiny world
I alone knew,
I will speak
Your unfocused sounds,
And I will hate you
For expelling me,
Tearing me,
From your warm womb.

Christopher Long

Conversion

As I left the museum,
The dinosaur skeletons room,
By the basement door,
The sky lowered sick green
T at threatened a most dreadful doom,
Descended like a lid,
Entirely became
A monstrous squid;
Tentacles sought to draw
The breath from me,
Drain the life from me.
I called for help on every holy name.
None came.
My breath was almost gone.
With the last of it I creaked,
"Bless you," to the monster.
There was no monster,
Only three drops of blood
On the sand,
Three small red flowers at my feet.

Jean Overton Fuller

The Asylum

I am here, I am there, my mind
wanders everywhere.
I am good, I am bad, people think
I am totally mad.
I am stupid, I am bright, I get
locked up every night.
I am well, I am sick, I am just
a lunatic.

Willow Croft

The Survivor

I see him in reflective mood
Survey the statues in the park
As if departed spirits could
Assuage the sorrow in his heart.

He is a dead man on recall
Who raises the observer's doubt
Of whether he survived at all
While others perished round about.

A gentle breeze, a swaying leaf
Presages long denied relief,
But then the memory's timeless track
Plays ancient sounds and pictures back
Which fail to pacify the grief.

And so the dross of days drools on
Like poorly fashioned pearls of paste
And unexcited, unexcused
He sits bemused and unamused
Forever in reflective mood
Still waiting that oblivion would
Assuage the sorrow in his heart.

R. S. Lenk

A Friend Called Hannam

His name is Hannam
he can't half plann'em,
he's had a hard life
and now he's getting a wife,
it's gonna get worse
just like the next verse.

Hannam has a child
which has calmed him mild,
he likes to collect videos
a load of Laurel and Hardy,
he get's a lift to the pub
and drinks a load of Bicardi.

Then after the alcohol
that has severed his soul,
starts to take effect
he will neglect his mates,
bragging and slagging.
"Stop before you drop."

M. G. Smith

Ephemeral

And I saw it,
standing proud,
in the soft grey
of twilight.

A lone stag,
statue like,
its nostrils twitching
as it smelt the evening air.

Suddenly,
tossing his noble head,
as if distrusting
the very stillness.

With a flash of antlers
he was gone,
deep into the darkening shadows
where I could not follow.

Kenneth C. Mason

Verse 2

For all must die, to live again,
Leaves will fall, and it will rain.
For autumn like life sheds its tears,
That all may arise, in later years.

Alicia Anne Griffiths

Yesteryear

The artist's choice of colours
All known to them by name,
Combined with tints toward fading some
Or making others flame
To add a tint called yesteryear,
To the picture of today,
May help enhance the colouring,
Like blossom bloom in May.
As today we have some scenic views,
To behold the artist's eye,
Of concrete towers and motorways,
And jet streams in the sky,
As people speed about their ways,
In city and in town,
They resemble life's fast colours,
Yesteryear may slow them down
As when oil fuelled the cottage lamps,
And the shires hauled the plough,
Those little tints of yesteryear,
Could enhance the picture now.

David Goudie

The Ancient Drop-Out

Do you know
I can sew
But do I?

I could cook
From a book
Why should I?

I could sculpt
Such a hulk
Just don't try.

I could work
Like a Turk
Why must I?

I'm at my best
When at rest
Lazing, gazing.

I don't try
Just to vie-
So degrading.

Happy me, now to be,
Gently fading

Nansi Howells

Persecuting Society

Blessed be your soul,
Blessed be your heart,
Watch your flesh corrode,
Ripping men apart,

The fear in the street,
So murderous is their eye,
Cursed be the damned,
Hanging around to die,

Nothing to live for,
No wife or no homes,
Hippies of the suburbs,
The men sit out alone,

Riots in the streets,
No money or a life,
The pressure on the Government,
Their constituents in strife,

Politicians gamble,
And lie to save their skin,
Killing our society,
The World's biggest sin.

Ritchie Bentley

Mummy On Mummy

The funny thing about Mummy
Is that she can do almost anything
She can cook like a dream
dress like a queen
knit, crochet and sew
dig a garden and mow
she can draw and paint
can't be shocked and won't faint
can budget and juggle
can sort out a muddle
can do two things at once
be in two places at once
isn't a crossword dunce
And can stand on her head
if she has to.
The funny thing about Mummy is
she's going to have a fling!

June Wiles

Dreams

In my dreams
I am a King.
In my dreams
I'm everything.

In my dreams
I'm very rich.
I'm the best
On the football pitch.

In my dreams
Things go right;
Nothing's dark,
Everything's bright.

Oh! if life was
Like my dreams.
If only life was
Like my dreams.

Beryl Davies

Untitled

With branches well hung
You've erected your tree
But, when looking for a fairy
Please, — don't forget me!
I'll sit on the top
A bit prickly, I feel,
But the harder the prick,
The louder I squeal!!
And you won't need electrics
To light up your tree
'Cos turning it on
You can leave up to me
So, out with the mistletoe
Up with the tree
And you'd better guess quickly
This verse is from me.

Meryl Zawistowicz

Spring

I saw a little bird
sitting in a tree
it was a baby tit
and he looked so free

He tried to spread his wings
to fly across the sky
but he couldn't quite make it
oh my, oh my, oh my.

He toppled from the tree
his mummy was watching it all
she flew down like a shot
and saved her little boy.

Myrna Smokovic-Campbell

The Coming Of Age

One day I passed a mirror
And saw a man I didn't know.
I stopped to ask "Who are you?"
And saw his mouth repeat my words.
He nodded when I nodded
And smiled my kind of smile.
He pointed when I pointed
At some flecked and frosted hair.
His fingers followed mine
In a voyage around this face,
Riding waves of skin that
Broke round eyes and mouth.
Smiling through my doubt,
I wondered at his never:
Did he not know, this man,
that Youth was all, and
Age must hide its shame?
I shook my head is sorrow as I left
And was glad to see
The man had gone as well.

Christopher Churton Inge

Flames Of Loves

It was down by the
river bank my love
And I did lay,
On a bright and summer night
into the good old month of May

He told me that he
loved me, and he held
his hand in mine, he
said that we would never
part; he would always
be mine.

But the flames of love
burned brightly and they
quickly faded away
and he fled into another's
arms on a cold and dismal day

M. B. Sellen

An Old Lie

It will not be easy,
Of course I will get upset
It is true I'm suffering
But at all costs I will forget you!

Please forget that we broke up,
Forget we were together,
Forget what we passed through
And forget me like any other old lie!

After years, feeling a bit ashamed
Perhaps I'll get cross with you
Touching all your belongings,
Perhaps I'll weep like a little child.

It is true I am suffering
But at all costs I will forget you
And you forget that we were together
And forget me like any other old lie...

Yildiz Mentesh

Ants

Although ants are so small,
Together they toil,
Living in colonies,
Making nests in the soil.
Their six legs move quickly,
To keep up the pace,
Queen ants and workers,
It's as if life's a race.
They get in a line
And follow each other,
Mother, Father, Sister and Brother.

Laura Troth

Life

Being alive is all there can be.
To someone who thinks as much as me.
So I strain my ears to hear a sound.
The type you don't often hear a round.
I waste my time just sitting hear.
Until I hear the slightest stir.
People all around just look at me.
They act as though they can not see.
The pain that I'm going through.
I just don't know what to do.
Walking around on a hot afternoon.
People acting like baboons.
Shooting, killing everywhere.
Soon there will be no one there.
Death can come so suddenly,
But still people will not see.

Roger Pritchard

Sunset

I love to watch the sunset
Over the sea at night
It starts off high up in the sky
So golden and so bright
As it starts to travel
Just before it goes from view
It turns the sky around it
Into a blood red hue
And in the morning when you rise
There it is up in the skies
Starting its journey from East to West
To set once more over the sea to rest

Dorothy Howarth

Mother

When you left I blamed you
And wouldn't dare to speak
There was nothing that you could do
But my love you tried to seek

I carried so much hatred
And couldn't understand
How you could go your separate way
And leave an empty hand

That hand in which you held in yours
I never will forget
The years I turned my back on you
Is now a big regret

It was the death of granny
That made it all come clear
Without you I couldn't live
Another second, day or year

I know were not together
Though in a way will never part
For a daughters love for her mother
Comes only from the heart.

Louise McNelis

Media Age

Press the vines; read the news
Enough on this and that
Taste buds that have only ever
Tasted someone else's views

Circle around benign beginnings
Listening to toads on stalls
Never mind, the show's begun
Please be quiet - it's union rules!

Now and again a ray of hope
For what? Who knows?
"We do"
Yes
And so it goes.

Paul Emanuel

Next Summer

I'll lie for five minutes
On the yellow suede sofa
My eyelids so heavy and tired,
Gazing through smiles Constance Spry
Gloire de Dijon and Perle d'Or,
Such beauty and scent,
It's early summer again.
Ten long years my daughter lies
A short distance away
In her blue and white room,
Pretty voile curtains dance
In the breeze with dappled sunlight
Through the Catalpa leaves.
Compassion peeps through the
Shutters for the room is dark,
The sunlight hurts,
Maybe next summer.

Gillian Morrison

Alone

Here I sit, all alone,
Not a soul in sight,
Curled up in a frozen ball,
Under a dim lit light,
If only you would talk to me,
To let me know I'm here,
My life went wrong along the line,
But not through drugs or beer,
So accept me as a human,
And not for what you see,
For I once thought the same as you
'It'll never happen to me'!
But what's the use of trying
To make you change your tone,
You've all seen me here before,
And left me all alone.

Michelle Turner

Happy Anyday

Not for any special reason
nor even a happy season.
My love and deep desire,
yours alone and passion's fire
burns your name upon my breast
and longings impossible to crest,
fan my need to be with you.

Just a card, now and then,
a token of my feelings when
words seem difficult to shape,
part of me cries out agape
at many wonders we have found
and our union on hallowed ground,
a gift of happiness to share.

Leonard R. Green

Who Lives In A House Like This

Who lives in such a pretty place?
With garden flowers neatly spaced.
Thatched roof and roses around the door
Brasses polished, oh what a chore!
Curtain nets are sparkling white,
Driving passed, it's quite a sight,
Lawns are always kept in trim,
A pond with fishes swimming in.
Fruit trees further down the path,
Birds busily having their dust baths,
All vegetables she sells at the gate,
So drive out quickly before too late.
No one can resist to stop,
At such a really pretty spot,
Each day a queue, so we must dash,
Alone at night, she counts the cash.
As she makes a pot of tea,
Not long now, for her place by the sea.

Brenda Elvery

For Sale

One careful lady owner
Nice curvaceous line
Paint work looks like new
And engine running fine

Tires still have lots of tread
Passed recent M.O.T.
Very economical
With excellent m.p.g.

Perfect for a family
And really not that old
If I was a car
In no time I'd be sold!

Felicity Bradley

"In The Death Of An Old Dog"

"Sadly as autumn leaf
she let her tired head fall,
then suddenly she cocked her ears
as if she heard
her long lost mistress call"

Diana M. Oakeley

Our Car

With agile bound
And purring sound
By fire is found;
And when unwound
This furry mound
With outline round
Is fat!

Brian J. Dunn

Untitled

I seek the woods,
and flowering beds,
and nestle in amongst their heads,

Pollen here, and pollen there,
Pollen lying everywhere,
Big tall trees,
my view content,
Blossoms leaving full blown scent,
So much to do,
so much to see,
What am I?
A bumble bee.

J. L. E. Poole

The Speed Of Dance

My heart starts beating faster,
My blood goes up and down.
The energy is pumping and...
I'm whizzing round and round.

I'm moving with the rhythm,
I'm swinging to the beat.
I'm dancing with my body,
And so too are my feet.

My eyes lose their focus,
The music begins to drone.
The dance floor is now less crowded,
And I find myself alone.

My face is hot and sweaty,
My head begins to yelp.
My body is calling out,
"Drugs are not the answers",
I'm the one who needs the help!

Sarah Louise Dolphin

Loneliness

Words cannot capture
This loneliness I feel.
I cannot explain it
It's totally unreal.

It's not longing for companionship
That is making me sad,
I have the best friends I could want
Because of this I'm always glad.

But wanting someone special,
Someone just for me
That is what is getting me down.
If only one could see.
I want a face for dreaming
A face, no special one.
Beauty or ugliness,
To me these matter none.

I need answers to my questions,
So I'll ask them in this poem,
Why do some have all the luck
And why am I alone?

Claire Moore

Light

Within this house the light first came
To hand the pen was shown,
Now here I once again return
With all pens magic known.
To first revealed new born delight
In unaccustomed word,
Then slowly works flowed into lines
But truth to youth was blurred.

Time and searching found more words
yet truth was still obscure,
Some broken pens, and more mistakes
Before the pen flowed sure.

Now words no longer need be sought
The lines flow fast and free,
I flood comes from a single thought
From one love - truth legacy.

William White

This Stranger

Who is this person?
    This stranger inside of me,
I don't think I know her,
    Perhaps some old acquaintance?

She pops her head up,
    now and then,
Just to say hello,
    and scare you off,
Do you know her?
I long to talk to her,
    to ask her why?
Why does she do this?
    Why does she go?
Do I know her?

Kelly Balsdon

Breaking Up Is Hard To Do

Breaking up is hard to do
we spend years becoming whole
only to be torn in two.
A perfect heart,
now two broken sides
both damaged and looking to hide
To run away and repair the pain
maybe find another to punish and blame
So two becomes four
four then eight
are there any complete pieces
or just lots of misshapes?

Clare Eason

Presence Of A Child

Beloved child, I know you're there
Little feet upon the stair
Merry laughter fills each room
Chasing out the winter gloom

Happy face with eyes so bright
Reflecting all a child's delight
At games you play and magic weave
In your world of make-believe

When evening comes and time for bed
And pillow claims your sleepy head
All is very quiet now
The house is not the same somehow

Later in your room I'll peep
To watch you as you lay asleep
So sweet and innocent you sigh
Too quickly childhood years go by

In the morning when you wake
With early birds and chatter make
I think of all you mean to me
How lucky to be blessed with thee.

Margot Mytton

'Di'

Di is for diamond
    Brilliant and bright
Hard as the glitter
    Of stars in the night

Settings important
    Platinum and gold
Luxury hide-outs
    Brazen and bold

The world's shop window
    Centre display
Lights! Camera! Action!
    This is My day.

Warmth and sympathy?
    Yes - any amount
Sentimentality absent
    Refer expense account

We know our worth
    To the end of the line
Dug out of the earth
    with Shares in the Mine.

Bryn Bartlett

A Stained Glass Window

A window alight with coloured glass,
Commemorates sad times past.

A shipwreck picture it portrays,
Glowing in the late suns rays.

Down she sank, in ocean deep,
Too much noise to hear soul's weep.

Then the smell, as engines burned,
Pouring oil as the seas churned.

Then the silence, all around,
No sign of ship, no noise, no sound.

In the dawn's first light,
What a truly hellish sight.

On the waves, gently stirring,
Broken bodies, pleading, calling.

Rescue came, much too late,
For the man I'd called my mate.

Ashore again in hospital bed,
How to describe being warm and fed?

In the chapel, quiet and still,
None can know how I feel.

Jean M. Everest

"The Fig Tree"

Two ragged rolls,
Of rusting barbed wire,
Touching untidy posts
Of concrete stained brown,
An empty old paint tin
By a rotting wood door,
All resting gently
Amid grass and grey stones.
Then a breeze takes away
Some rising heat haze,
Moving shadows appear
Now what have we here,
One splendid Fig Tree,
Growing out of this waste,
One splendid Fig Tree,
What a pleasure to see
The waste in the shade,
The Tree, a cascade.

Yvonne I. Wawman

Current Affairs "News - 1996"

Poor Gina G. did not win
The eurovision contest
For U.K. this was a sin
Because she gave "her best"

East enders star "Arfur"
Has now come out of prison
Is there justice in hereafter,
Will he "plot" revenge in heaven?

The royals are unlikely
To remain "QUEEN of our hearts"
With stars who shine so brightly
Being just two "Tiresome Tarts."

Ma'am, because of this-n-that
"The News" has left us "reeling"
Corgies out, "'Tis year of the cat"
And that's what we are, "feline."

If this ode is just too long
It proves that I'm just 'bonkey'
And perhaps a chance to join
The brilliant "Drop the dead donkey."

Evelyn Davidson

Waking Amy

Your stillness and beauty astound me.
When your smile breaks through,
I touch you.
A miracle happens
every time you wake and start your day
I thank God for you, Amy.

Karen Bladwell

My Friend

Rushing, flowing, rippling,
The river runs down stream.
Thinking deeply, thinking
Thoughts run round my head.
Calmer, calmer still
The river trickles on,
Whilst I sit here all alone
And dream of things now gone.

The river is such a peaceful place
And I go there to think.
There couldn't be a better place,
For worries and fears to sink.
I drown them in the water
In hope they'll never come back.
The river is my dearest friend,
My ever flowing friend.

Zoe Makinson

Skyward

I gazed on high one cloudless night.
To see a passing wondrous sight
Make haste they said, for all too soon
This gleaming comet in the sky
Will be beyond our human eye.

How can they know what I may see
For when at last my soul roams free
To wander in eternity
Yet I might glimpse again sometimes
that self same comet in its flight
Below me now
Whilst I up high
Look down

Marjorie Davenport

Ending

So short and still my love does lay,
One's hands do close and pray,
Look up - look high,
The sky will dry,
No rain will pour, not ever more,
The earth does crack,
Does crumble and die,
For that is when I sigh,
The water has gone,
The lake is fake,
A picture in the sun,
The lying smile that shines so high,
With a touch that kills.
So you and I who live and learn,
By the rays of the sun shall burn.

Michael Gerald Christy

A Lonely Child

A lonely child lives
No one to talk to
To share her grief
No joy to tell
That's very brief

A lonely child lives
Blocked away from the world
Frightened and scared
If only she was happy
If only someone cared

A lonely child lives
Has no life to lead
No one hears her cries
No one will listen
A lonely child dies.

Alessia Vozza

"Hoggin The Moos"

For a lifetime I've tended cows
Through wind and snow and rain
Now through the dreaded B.S.E.
They may not see the spring again

They all have names and look so nice
As they stand there by the gate
How can a farmer tell them
What will be their fate.

My dog will be redundant
And he doesn't have a clue
There will be absolutely nothing
For the poor thing to do

My farming life is over
of the workload I'll be free
For if they will be taking all my cows
They may as well take me!

R. J. Moulton

The Meeting

I dreamt there was a meeting
Beneath the prairie skies,
Sioux cree ojibwa
And many more besides.

Magic swirled like mountain mist
And big medicine did abound,
And sitting bull with all his chiefs
Spread blankets on the ground.

As with old men everywhere
They spoke of days that are gone,
Before long knives and yellow hair
Passed on in native song.

The ghosts of all these old guys
Passed round the pipe of peace,
A heavenly peace of noble men
Not lowered by defeat.

Eventually, when they broke camp
My dream began to fade,
But I've seen the prairie heaven
Where I hope to ride someday.

Clifford Robertson

My Window Reverie

I sit and look
and watch the world go by
There once went I.
I sit and watch
The boy and girl embrace
As once we did.
No longer able now
My window is my means
To join in others dreams.
Life soon passes
As shadows on a wall
And as my shadows pass away
Life for some goes on.
Make the most of what you have
Be as cheerful as you can
God's grace is here for everyone
So watch and hope and pray.

M. A. Aldrich

Lake Huron

Maple multi-colour
edged her shore.
Reflections, now withdrawn
into my memory, lie unexposed.
Tonight I borrow nature's stillness,
toss my oars and salute
the silence of this lake.

One hour ago
red bracelets even-paced
her blue expanse.
And as I paused
between each thirsty stroke
she bled her waters from
my aching blades.

Proud lady of the night
now casts her light:
Three times ten thousands Isles
lie in her afterglow.
Until I can return I'll keep
this moment for a dream.

R. H. M. Vere

My Son

You touched my life.
So long ago: And will never leave it
whilst I live.
Many years, days, hours, minutes have
been the better for knowing you.
The ups and downs, as I look back;
have blended into joy untold.
Am I a dreamer; no this is for real.
As my hair has tuned to white,
I've watched you grow into a man.
How sad that time cannot stand still
to let us stay in such rapport.
Bless you for being you,
Thank God, for making me your mother

E. Hawes

Fantasies

I have lived a life of pleasure,
Lived a life of woe.
Loved a thousand maidens,
Slain a thousand foe.
Lived through ancient history,
Escorted Astronauts to Mars.
Unravelling the mystery,
Of a galaxy of stars.

I have experienced the emotion
Of those hailed for gallantry.
Read a thousand stories,
Written just for me.
And as I scan those pages
Life's greatest treasures there I find,
Through the presence of these fantasies
That forever dwell in mind.

Thomas Raper

The Four Seasons

Spring breezes in, turning everything
green from gold.
Summer arrives "Warm to Hot"
Makes us dream of things
We haven't got.
Autumn comes in like a new broom
Sweeping clean. Trees, ground, and air
Striped naked, branches and flower beds
Waiting to be born again.
Winter, Blustery, White gown
Spread over the earth
Come in like the roar of a lion
Now we sit and wonder why
Another year has passed us by.

N. Williams

Deep Reflection

Have you ever looked into a mirror
Beyond the staring face you see,
Reflected life of who you are
In flawless imagery.
Laughing smile hides tearful eyes,
Concealed - the disguised sorrow,
A fleeting glimpse of shattered dreams
And hopes held for tomorrow.
Life's journey through events of time
Emotions gone before.
Betrayed expressions on your face,
Etched deep forevermore.
Those we've loved, who gave us life
Not lost to memory,
Summoned forth in silvered glass
Captured, private history.
Unmasked, the face before you
With perfect symmetry,
Transparent soul depicted,
Is this what others see?

D. Conlon

Mum

Mum you were there
When I needed you.
A hand to hold
And guide me through.

Wrapped in your arms,
I was safe from all fear.
The love you gave,
I will always hold dear.

Little things that you said
Are so important to me.
They have helped me so much
And now I can see,
Exactly what it was like for you.

All the worry and heartache
I put you through.
I see it now,
I really do,
Because now I am
A mother too.

Moira Birchall

Summer Belle

Elusive is the butterfly on
shimmering translucent wings
She snatches the chance
to leave her nest;

In her fine, powdery dress
of iridescent hues
As the chrysalis transforms
her lattice papyrus shell;

Transcending her spirit of
grace to be renewed,
A humble bug reincarnated
to the belle of a summery ball;

As she whispers, the dusky petals
of the damask rose
Reveals his lonely heart;

Her brief days are mustered
from warm essence and breezes
With flight of fancy dancing
a pirouette through the exotic
gardens of summer.

P. Morriss

The Sweet Fairy

A little boy comes calling
Shouting through the letter box
Bruises on his tiny knees
Mud on his once white socks

As the door is opened
He rushes straight past me
No greeting am I given
Just loud shouts of glee

His voice calls from the kitchen
Has the sweetie fairy been
Pleading eyes look up at me
From a face so pink and clean

Together we search in pots and pans
The fairy has hidden well
Then a shout of pure delight
I have found sweets in a shell

I love to play this little game
It always goes to plan
Two small arms wrap round my neck
I love you lots - my Nan

Dorothy Spiller

I Wish!

I'd take a walk to the town,
and browse around a store.
Or have a picnic in the park,
there's nothing I'd like more!

I'd even take the dog a walk,
or stay in bed all day.
Or maybe call to see a friend,
to pass the time away.

But, as usual I will go to work,
as quietly as a lamb.
And toil away throughout the day,
cause that's the way I am.

So one fine day in later years,
when all my dreams unfold.
I'll make the best of all those things,
that's if I'm not too old!.

Christine Kirk

Crazy Crow

Crazy crow,
Cawing from that angled ash,
Ask me
What grief,
Grounded here, I groan beneath.
I, pedestrian,
Permitted publicly
One sigh,
Two tears,
You can, with noisome candour,
Tree turreted,
Full throttle,
Beat my ears with your distress.
Clarion crow,
Know below,
Silence
And so much more, not less.

Susan M. Kendall

Untitled

Life has many burdens
some are hard to bear
but we will always find some comfort
when we know there's someone there.
We do not know his purpose.
Nor can we see his face,
but in times of stress and sorrow,
we surely find his grace.

In time our burden lightens.
our sores begin to mend.
Joys and sorrows mingle,
as on our way we wend,
what brings us through our trials
and makes our troubles less
it just can be no other,
than his amazing grace.

Mary Findlay

The Dawn Chorus

The most perfect hour of day
When all around is still,
Most people sunk in sleep - yet
To those awake, or ill
The early bird-song, sweet, yet strong
Steals like sweet music
Filled with hope, upon their ear,
Giving them peace and strength
To face the coming day
As the new dawn is breaking
Outside their window sill.

Cicely M. Hart-King

Rebirth In Spring

The trees are heavy with blossom
Bumble bees out on a spree
It has been such a long long winter
Now there is so much to see

Lilac trees dressed in palest green
Hawk how the black bird sings
Search for the delicate primrose
    Ah! What frail, fragile things

There goes the very, first swallow
Spring now really is here
Back from their winter vacation
To bring us such beauty and cheer

April and may the loveliest time
When the earth awakes from its sleep
Can anyone doubt on seeing all this?
There really is life after death.

Josie Hickens

Magical Beast

Who is this, majestic elegant beast.
Who stands so proud and noble
With head held high, for all to see.
Who is this beast of royal.

A silver crown sits on his head,
His mane is soft and silky.
With deep blue eyes so wise and true,
Like sapphires burning brightly.

The magic's there, it's in the air.
Glowing all around him.
And in the moonlight you might see.
Fairies dancing round him.

Now I know, who, he can be
With his sprite wild and free.
He, who is of royal form and horn.
He is of course, the unicorn.

Elizabeth Clark

This Time

Look to the sky way up high.
See the dark clouds subside.
The rain ceases to fall
Making way for a brand new dawn.
Another day born to follow
The rainbow in search of your dream.
Life holds a special place
For each and every one.
If you believe in this.
The battle is almost won.
Look to the future.
Your sun has yet to shine.
Somewhere over the rainbow.
You'll find your dream
This time.

B. Davies

First Love

Beneath a sky of midnight blue
Grew our first night of love
With evening mists and Springtime dew
And a silver moon above.

The fire of passion as two hearts beat
On wings of love and ecstasy,
Endless kisses, deep and sweet
First love that has no parity.

A day of entrancement,
A world of enchantment,
A day of enrapture
We will never recapture.

Beryl Marvin

I Want You To Know

I want you to know that I love you,
I want you to know that I care,
I want you to know that I love you,
And for you I'll always be there.

I want you to know that I love you,
I love you with all of my might,
And if loving were seeing, my darling,
I would certainly give you my sight.

I want you to know that I love you,
That you are the rays of my sun,
I want you to know that I love you,
And through you my life's just begun.

You are my joy and my laughter,
You are my charm and my grace,
You are the one that I love dear.
You are the smile on my face.

I want you to know that I love you.
I want you to know that I care,
I want you to know that I love you,
And for you I'll always be there.

Joseph G. Mableson

Some Day

I've hardly got time to think.
Pushing my stone: to let it fall.

Men have children that grow to men,
That have children that grow to men:
They eat the grain they grow,
With the strength it gives;
They sow the grain they grow,

And I push my stone.
And so I'll do my desperate deed,
That destiny requires and fate pleads;
I'll sow my seed.

I'm a slave to:
I am bound within:
Yet I will die before,
This flesh and skin
This blood and bones.

These Sisyphus
Are your gods
Sisyphus,
These are your gods.

Anthony Harris

Night Sounds

Plump frogs croak
As sounds a metronome —
Tap, tap, tap
Then pause — silence has come.

Now it breaks
As they resume their call —
Tap, tap, tap
Again, echoes the wall.

More creatures
Stir, disturbed by the sound —
Calling birds
In trees, mice on the ground.

Ca-coph-o
Ney of woodland voices
Fills the air —
Yes night-life rejoices.

Peace now reigns,
Creatures must be sleeping —
Wise old owl
Still his vigil keeping.

Gillian M. Veale

Memories

The children were asking questions - "What's happened to Daddy" they said -
I hadn't told them when it happened - I thought they were asleep in bed,
But one of my sons, the eldest, had seen his Daddy carried downstairs then crept
Back to bed in silence not waking his brother and sister, alone in his grief he had wept.
It was midnight when the tragedy happened, when fate took a cruel hand
In changing my life and my family's - when the heart attack struck my dear husband.
My children were left with no father, and me without a lover and best friend.
How could I go on - I fought back the tears, the children asked "Why did Daddy's life end?"
I don't really know, I told them - I think God must have asked him to fly
Up to heaven to join him - for what reason I can't really understand why -
Maybe one day we will know the answer but for now we must all help each other
By learning to laugh once again and be happy - we can if we all stay together.
Since that day years ago many tears have been shed and laughter has also been present
As the children grew up new problems arose - and were solved, life is so transient.
They have now all left home - have lives of their own and children to nurture and guide
But I shall never forget the love they gave me - I was never alone, they were -
and still are - by my side.

Pamela L. Davies

Letter To A Soldier

What's the matter, why no letter, why is it that you don't write?
Maybe you've found someone better to hold within your arms tonight
Why is it that I can't please you like I always used to do?
Is there someone else to tease you? Have you found somebody new?
Can I believe that someone's taken all the love you had for me?
Or dare I hope that I'm mistaken and things are as they used to be.
Can it be that you should choose me from all the girls that you have known
Then afterwards just want to lose me, especially when I'm yours alone
Why is it that you don't miss me for I pray in every prayer
That soon you will be here to kiss me and tell me one again you care
When the stars shine bright above me, without you near, I'm always blue
Won't you say that you still love me
Because I'm so in love with you.

Joy Wingrove

Sky Watch

There's nothing strange about the sun, as is sets in the western sky,
We're familiar with our friend the moon, with its phases passing by,
But oh, the wonders of the cosmos when at last the darkness comes,
When slowly the stars peep forth with their various magnitudes,
And the thrill of a mysterious planet coming into view,
Is it Mercury, Venus, Jupiter, seen with our roving eye?
There's so many wondrous things to see, as you look into the sky.

Herschel, Newton, Messier, in the past have gazed above.
And told us of all the spectacular things that we can grow to love,
Asteroids, Meteors, Satellites all buzzing about in space,
There are so many interesting things for us to observe, and note,
A cold clear night, can reveal the constellations in their beauty,
Just take the time to persevere, if you want to improve your mind,
There's a spectacular view of the universe, seek, and you will find.

Elizabeth Udo

WK On Their Bow

Wick you were once a busy toon tho' few would ca' ye braw
They only built ye for the herring trade and in your day you were abeen them a'
Your streets were full of bustle once; with boats your harbour teemed
Where one thousand masts reached to the sky or to us boyags so it seemed,
When the gutting lassies thronged your curing yairds with their burdens brawley borne
And the cooper's hammer's ringing sound broke your sleep every summer's morn
You did not worry about tourists then with their cards and souvenirs
Nor did you cown for handouts in these fruitful verdant years
Now strangers write and sing your praise abeen names I dinna ken
But then they only know ye now not like us that kent ye then
Ye always took your rightful share of the harvest of the sea
But there is a different kind of harvest now that has no share for me
For black black oil is the master now where the herring once was queen
Where your skippers shot and hauled their nets and the drifter ruled supreme
Your skippers searched the stormy seas from shore to rocky shore
But Mother Nature let you down when the herring came no more
I would love again to tramp your braes or stand on your harbour breest
And watch the drifters run the bay when the wind was in the East
I often think of these bygone days that are gone forever now
When ten score of boats would leave your shore all with WK on their bow.

Donald Banks

Inevitable

Will the sun forget to rise or set
Will the moon not shed its light
Will the stars not gather in the skies
And twinkle through the night

Will the sea not ebb and fade away
To begin its life anew
As these things are meant to happen
So is my love for you

Let's deny our fate no longer
Let's be happy while we may
For our love will grow much stronger
Every hour of every day

As it grows we'll face together
Any heartache from the past
And look towards the future
With a love that's meant to last

Pauline Simpson

Freedom

You stole my freedom,
my right to choose.
You took my life,
and threw it away.
Now it is my turn,
I'm no longer a child.
I have a right,
to peace of mind,
And a world I know will last.

Angela Norton

Good Enough

Why should I see perfection
Since life can sometimes be tough
Considering I'm just human
I need only be good enough.

Fearful of getting it wrong
By saying it just off the cuff
I keep my opinions inside me
And wonder if I'm good enough.

To share it will help me develop
And get rid of my negative stuff
As I act as a mirror for others
I begin to feel good enough.

These skills are emerging quite slowly
Through habits that sheltered rebuff
As I let the defences down gently
I accept that I am good enough.

Dori O'Shea

Circles

Circles can be smoke rings
That fade in the air
Or a ring of sweet flowers
In a garden so fair

A walk in the woodlands
Can be a real treat,
With a circle of daisies
Down by your feet

A gold ring is a circle
On your finger so sweet
To bring love together
In a wedding so neat

But the circles I like
And it always will be
Are my circle of friends
A real treat for me

S. Fullwood

FEELING SAD

When I'm feeling sad, I feel so alone in the world.
Everybody towers over me — it frightens me so.
I want to run and run, never stopping till I am out of breath.

When I'm feeling sad, I need to be held and a shoulder to cry on.
I'm crying inside of myself and my eyes will soon be full of tears.

When I'm feeling sad, I don't want anybody to see me.
I want to stay in bed — pull the covers over my head and sleep forever.

When I'm feeling sad, I'm also feeling blue.
I see people and children all about me — they look happy.
With smiling faces and shining eyes.
But wait, — maybe they are feeling down and putting on a cheerful smile
— to hide their deep down cares and woes.

When I'm feeling sad, and I'm sitting alone at home,
I hear the ticking of the clock.
But, it makes no difference to me — for time has no respect.
The minutes tick by — just like my life.
Oh how sad I feel.

Even as I'm writing now — I've made myself feel sad.
So, now is the time to put down my pen,
— get dressed up and go out on the town.

Anna Attridge

Silas Marner

The lonely weaver wends his way through dim-lit lane and over field
And happy in his chosen craft, his love of linen is revealed
But life then deals a bitter blow and ignorance plays its own cruel part
The weaver wrongfully outcast, the Church betrayed the purest heart.

As shadows lengthen 'cross his room - the flickering firelight dancing red
The weaver's eyes rest on his loom - his body on his bed
He seeks poor solace in his gold and hoarding as a miser will
His mind grows bitter, his body ill.

Now as his figure picks its way through lane and field, his wares to sell
With body hunched and stopping low and eyes so dim they hardly see
His gold has given him no love nor kept him warm through winter night
No comfort has he thus derived from its harsh and brilliant sight.

And then one eve whilst in a trance, he wakens to the cold white gloom
To find a child so fair of face - such innocence abounds his room
He knows his gold has been returned and makes a promise there and then
He'll raise this child to be his own, his life is to begin again.

The years pass by, his faith restored - he sits and contemplates his past
How rich in love he has become, he makes his peace with God at last
As slave to the loom, his life was spent
God showed him grace, his soul content.

Stephanie Fulfit

My House Rules (By A Cat)

Before I come to live with you, there are a few things that you should know,
Actually there are quite a few, so I have listed some of them below.
If you want me to be happy, you must give me plenty to occupy my mind,
This is in addition to the usual requirements, of animals of my kind.

I do so like to play with paper, especially tissues that make quite a mess,
And wallpaper that's coming loose, now that is definitely a yes!
Please leave your pens on the table, I love to knock them onto the floor,
I also like to pull up your carpet, so that you can't get through the door.

When you're serving up your dinner, please ensure you drop a piece of meat,
And when you are in a hurry to go out, I'd like to get in the way of your feet.
If you are crawling on your hands and knees, I know you've been especially kind,
You've not put something important away, so I have hidden it for you to find.

Don't you buy me a scratching post, I'll use your furniture to sharpen my claws,
And curiosity being a trait of mine, I love to delve into cupboards and draws.
You can buy me a bed if you want to, but I like to have different places to sleep;
Don't move your ornaments from the shelves, I want to see how high I can leap.

There's one other thing that makes me happy, that's if I decide to sit on your lap,
I would want you to stroke and caress me, before I settle down for a nap.
Though I'll often ignore your chidings, I can be obedient if I really want to,
As you see I'm quite a loveable creature, I'll be no trouble if I move in with you.

Gloria Graham

"Visions"

What artist ever had the wit
To paint a moving scene,
To stipple gold among the leaves
Where once was total green
Or let his brush with bolder strokes
Draw sunbeams through the gloom
To give one last brief touch of hope
To autumn's fading bloom.

Could human mind have ever thought
Of webs with diamonds strewn
As dawn and early morning dew
The spider's work has shown
It is beyond the art of man
To so bemuse the eye
Or to design a changing world
Beneath a changing sky.

So has God's palette still got hues
That man has never seen,
And shall we, when the last call comes
See what just might have been.

Philip Creasey

The Depths Of Time

Lost memories aimlessly drift
Through infinite mind chasms
Eroding images reflect fire
Conflicting with future hopes
Driftwood on a beach forgot
Evaporates tears from the
Remorseless sea of time

Martin Latter

In The Garden

I was sitting alone in the garden,
Enjoying the lovely fresh air,
When suddenly out in the distance
The sound of a blackbird I heard.

Its voice was so sweet and so mellow,
I listened entranced for a while,
I looked, but no sign of the fellow,
Then suddenly started to smile.

There on a bush the bird rested,
It was singing its song just for me,
No other bird had protested,
It was King of the garden you see.

Somehow its song seems to haunt me
As I sit there and listen and dream,
I rest when I sit in the garden,
To the song of the blackbird, now seen.

The theme of the song never falters,
Its happiness to me seems complete.
If only he'd sing in the winter,
The doldrums of winter he'd beat.

Irene Brookes

Westward

I live in a fair city
If you come and see it
You will say it is pretty
It's where men drink tots
And I like them both a lot
Plymouth is a town of history
They say this is Drakes' county
It is said he was a hero
But all he wanted was bounty
Fame he wanted was zero.
History was made on Plymouth Hoe
Drake was a captain who
Made history on Plymouth Hoe
When you come I hope you like it too.

Gordon Richard Jennings

"Belonging"

The feeling of belonging
Came slowly over the years,
You conquered my short comings
and soothed away my tears.

Your task was not easy
But love was there to guide,
I grew up with the knowledge
You were always on my side.

To bring up someone's baby
And not know what's in store,
Brings joy and fear and worry
And should you love them more?

You probably try harder
To show how much you care,
To tell this little baby
Your love will always be there.

To be given special parents
Is something that I treasure,
I hope I've given in return
the feeling of great pleasure.

Wendy Booth

What Is Poetry?

Poetry
Highlighted prose
Chosen from language
As the need arose:
Words
To lift the heart and mind
Spoken softly
Or ranted, loud
For all to hear
The magic of sound:
Images
Portrayed by the stroke of a pen
For the eyes of all, when
Talk becomes trivial
Speech without thought
In the delight of poesy
Verse is taught:
This is poetry
A melody of words
Singing the beauty of thought.

K. M. Daugela

My Paradise

It's times like this
When I have fun,
On my own island in the sun.
It's time for thought
When I'm alone
No stress or worries
Far from home.
The clear blue sky
The palms on trees
The golden sands
The gentle breeze.
The pure white surf
On waves come in
I'm free from troubled thoughts
within.
It's paradise
No need to run
From my own island
In the sun.

James Stuart Holmes

The Future

I looked into the future,
Saw the earth aglow with lights;
The sky seemed all surrounded
With millions of satellites,
circling round the universe,
the Sun, the Moon and Mars,
Jupiter, Uranus, Venus,
and thousands of twinkling stars.
There was work for all in plenty,
Happy faces by the score,
Nobody wanting anything,
No one greedy anymore.
Meadows green and healthy,
Hill and valley gay with song,
No starving populations,
Food enough for everyone.
This is my Utopia,
True friendship be the key,
To make the Future rosy bright,
Hard work for thee and me.

E. E. Beynon

Sun Homage

What jewel rare from deepest mine
Could lustre deeper or outshine
Apollo's beam of bright blonde hair,
Aurora's golden eyesight fair.

Deepest blush on fairest cheek
Pales before dusk's crimson peaks,
Spreading radiant purples and golds,
No artist's pallet could ever hold,

See Phoebus kiss clouds rose pink,
Gathering near they watch him sink,
With vermilion fingers beds them down,
Flushing red orange in sunset's crown.

Chariots of ruby commanded by dawn,
Inflames horizon at break of morn.
Celestial pearls of lavender fire,
To fill man's eye and soul inspire.

Freely he paints his Azure sky,
Glowing embers for you and I,
The truest phoenix risen from flame,
To brighten our darkest hour again.

Anthony Ashman

Dreams

Our dreams of life are but a thread
as delicate as a spiders web
once broken, it is no more.
These dreams are precious and our own
for a future yet unknown
I lay my dreams beneath your feet
for you and all the world to keep.
Tread softly, softly
lest you break the silken threads
and forever live in dread
of what might have been
without my dreams.

Joy Orchard

Hope And Delight

Exdous my people to share the light
The clouds have broken
And in comes the light
Whirling clouds up so high
Separating as the light passes by
Only I see the flicker of hope
And delight as the clouds pass by
Hope and delight has come to stay
To wish us an our merry way
The light beams for us all to see
The path we go to see thee.

Denise Thomson

Birds Of The Air

We are of the Winds,
In the streams of soothing peace,
Peace and cool

And light of touch,
The trees echo their response
In silver backed leaves,
Limp, pale.

We are of the Winds,

Plaintive across the depths
Thin, hollow piping,
Calling, yearning.

The rushing of the winds
Buffeting the lonely sound;
Solitary in the hollow air,
Lonely in the calming streams.

We are of the Winds.
Emily Meo

In Love

If you have loved
Or loved and lost
Yet still love on
Despite the cost.

If love was like a welcome shower
A joy forever more
Crowded in one glorious hour
Then you will know the score.

If your ship passed in the night
And passing was divine
But left a saddened morning light
Just like a heady wine.

If though your love is dead and gone
You feel you're still together
Then you're a very lucky one
For you're in love forever

If you're in love then you have lived
And there is nothing greater
The outcome of the love you give
Is left to our creator
Jack Emerson

Christmas Journey

They came, trudging the dusty way.
They were expected, as always.
Every year without fail, they say,
The three, mysterious, passed.
Peter Eddleston

The Refugee

Here I stand all alone,
not knowing what to do.
The sun has gone, the moon is out,
there's snow upon the roofs.

I have no fear of the night,
for darkness serves my plight.
But in the day, the nightmares come,
and I have no strength to fight.

I have no loving home for me,
but an old wooden shed.
It's cold in there, I know it is,
but there's no one there who cares.

I have no Mum, I have no Dad,
all my family's dead.
And now the sun has gone away,
It's time I went to bed.
Justine Nicosia

"The Career"

Who cares for the Carer?
As I go from day to day,
Tending the needs of my loved one,
Who once was so happy and gay.

Who cares for the Career?
As on guard, I must always be.
Listening for the one who
every day, looks for me.

Who cares for the Carer?
Not knowing a time of rest.
Day and night keeping vigil,
Being put to the test.

Who cares for the Carer?
Could YOU take on the task
to give me a break, just one day,
that's all the time I ask.

Who cares for the Carer?
Dear God, hear my plea.
Send me a carer, of Carers
Don't leave it all up to me.
Barbara Forsyth

Empty

So dead is the night
So dead is the space I sit in
awaiting an enormous crowd
to walk in and invade my
privacy, and yet no one comes.
Nothing but stillness and silence.
As the moment passes away from me,
Death is the only awaiting friend
V. Pinkrah

Nature's Kiss

The rain pit patters
On the window pane
The spider spins her web.
Each with a rhythm
And certainty
Of what lies ahead.

Gossamer threads
Cradle the raindrops
Allowing light to bounce
From their midst.
Each tiny pearl a perfection -
Nature's kiss.
Beverley Beck

Seasons Will Pass Me By

Would you believe?
Madness looms like dark
Savages creeping.

That- who was the King Preacher
Laid down the rules.
And...Oh... I saw you fall.
And failure seeped in
Through your mouth,
And looked out through your eyes.

Freedom...
Like bird flight I
Left for better fantasies.

And here I sit for
The first time.
Praying to a God that
Has become a wall...

And here in the dark room
I wait for familiar knocking...
Rebecca Brockbank

If Only

Though I now move from Autumn's glow
to Winter's chill
And you, from glorious Spring
to Summer's warmth,
If you would only take my hand
in Lover's clasp,
The earth would move,
And sparks would fly,
And I'd relive that moment
till I die.

And you, sweet lady,
with unbounded joy,
And no wisp of regret,
will oft recall that moment,
And never never never will forget.
Beres Ford Kelly

My Elephant Friend

My name is Janice
My friend is an Elephant,
Whose name was Dennis.

They went on a trip to Venice,
Dennis was really a menace,
He kept swinging he's trunk,
While asleep on his bunk.

People think I'm nuts,
When he pinches my peanuts,
Then he trumpets so loud,
When he looks to the clouds,

But now I'm so sad,
Cause my friends been bad,
He's run back to the jungle,
to be with his lady love bungle,

Perhaps well meet soon,
One day at noon,
When I've had to much to drink,
And I see pink elephants wink.
Janice Bolton

Untitled

Weathered leaves fall on greying stone
Rustling to their final home
Their splendour gone
That adorned a tree
Just like I remember thee
I was your leaf
All fresh and new
Then my turn came
To scatter too.
Autumn leaves on greying head
Name engraved for the dead
Rustic brown, yellow gold
They have now got old
Beauty spent they rustle on
Making music on your bed
As I sit here quiet and sad
My tree is gone now
Lovely Dad
George Doolan

Untitled

My new boy friend is really swell,
I should like to think he's mine,
Got permission from my Mum
To take him home to dine,
Everything was going well,
When "shades of Aristotle"
After helping himself to sauce,
He casually licked the bottle!
E. S. Wood

My Flower

Dear, sweet scented lilac,
fresh with the morning dew,
the embodiment of life itself,
come back with your beauty,
so that I may hold
and caress you once more.
I long to touch you
and have your fragrant nectar
fill my soul again.

But for now my flower,
you are too far away,
just out of reach
and my heart must accept this.
But fear not, for we will
come together again in the near future
and then I will behold
your petals in my palm.

Martyn Tunley

My Christmas

Christmas is a good time of year
Everyone has lots to cheer
with plenty of presents
Round the tree
To see the children, all abundance
and smiling
The turkey cooking in the
oven,
chestnuts on a plate
Christmas is really a
lovely day.
To make minds and have
a drips and a laugh,
Then there's holly and ivy too.
And also the good Lord
Is looking over you -
That's my idea of Christmas.

M. Downs

The Dragon Of Cymru

Mind if you go in the valley
There's a Dragon there you see
And he's very very hungry
'Cause he hasn't had his tea.

He had his breakfast early
He missed his call for lunch
Now he's stalking round the valley
For a tasty human brunch

If you catch him on a good day
When he's had his fill
He does your toast just perfect
And he gives you such a thrill

To feel the hot flames of his mouth
The smoke from his nostrils rise
But, don't go there when he's hungry
Or you'll get an unpleasant surprise.

John William Bowen

Reflections

Reflections are in my memory
I mean well in all sincerity

Reflections of your face in the water
Reflections in the past

How I wish I had a son or daughter
Reflections of the past will never last

Reflections of the future
is a life-long task
But death has no reflection in its mask

Thomas Machin

Farewell My Love!

You'd sit by me on the sofa.
With your head against my arm,
We'd be so content together
When the fire was glowing warm.

You'd be with me in the garden,
In the heat of the summer's sun,
And you'd come to sit beside me
When my gardening was done.

We were growing old together
And your feet grew ere more slow;
I often thought, so sadly,
Of their fleetness, long ago.

It was on that same old sofa
That your life just ebbed away;
You fell asleep so peacefully
I could not make you stay.

You were just my little Tortie puss,
For twenty years my friend
And whatever life is left for me
I will love you to the end!

W. Eastwood

The Perfumed Garden

I rummaged
Countless furrows
Seeding
Weed infested lawns
Lusting to subdue
An ever-rising sap.

Now in rarer
Lucid moments
A bed-side rose
Nurtured
In clear water
Stands upright
Imbued of wondrous beauty
For the eye.

I grasp
A lurking message
Within the final threads.

Eric Donner

"Perfection"

If each of us were perfect
Life could be so sweet,
If each of us were perfect.
the world would be complete.

We'd live in perfect harmony.
No fighting and no fuss
We'd all be totally caring,
No, sin, no greed, no lust

But alas, we are not perfect,
It's a struggle to survive,
Everyone wants something,
For themselves they want to thrive.

So where then lies the answer.
that has eluded man.
There's a book that tells the story.
We should read it if we can.

Yet, do we really want it,
Such perfection, throughout the land,
If the answer's yes, to this,
Then we had better give God a hand.

Jacqueline Ann Barber

Life Is A Tragedy

Life is a tragedy;
A timeless act of sorrow,
Where death plays his part
To steal the life from tomorrow.

You'll see the world
With eyes open wide,
Then emotion numbs the soul
And your mind starts to glide.

One day you're here,
The next day you're gone.
Why does a death
Make life feel so wrong?

When the play is over,
And the tragedy has died,
Who'll comfort the loved ones
Who stood by their side?

C. P. Clarke

Untitled

Oh I feel so lonely
Now that you have gone
I touch the still warm seat
That you have sat upon
The taste of you still on my lips
Your scent still in the air
And lying twisted on my sleeve
A precious blade of hair
Carefully I pluck this gift
Most welcome to me of all
And hold it tenderly
Afraid that it may fall
For the seats gone cold
Your scent has left the air
Now I'm alone with tender thoughts
And your precious blade of hair.

Steve Edgar

Winter's Cloak

As the cold winter closes.
Spring approaches with the
Delight of the sun so bright.

Flowers appear - oh, what a sight,
With colours so wonderfully bright.

Trees with new buds that
Flourish with the warmth of
The bright, sunlight.

Oh what a magnificent
Sight, to watch the rebirth
Of the treasures once hidden,
By winters dark cloak.

Margaret Scott

That Convoluted Tree

That convoluted tree
Seems the favourite one
Of many birds; they come
And hide among the boughs.

A thrush unhurriedly
Slips into song and soon
From leaves warmed by the sun
Float coal tits piquant cries;

Sometimes a dainty wren
Appears tucked in a hole
Near to the ground; it flies
Towards deep undergrowth.

Wild birds have seldom found
In other trees nearby
The quality they feel
In these old, twisted boughs.

June M. Benians

Untitled

A little boy named Edward Bligh
Whose great ambition was to fly
Had worked out many varied ways
By which to satisfy his craze
He tried on paper wings galore
To raise his body off the floor
A little prop behind his head
Or something electrical instead
But none of these did do the trick
He merely made himself more sick
Then suddenly at last he knew
The very thing he had to do
And so to work he went his way
On this his most eventful day
So with a stirrup pump he tried
To fill himself with air inside
Then suddenly to his surprise
He saw his chest and tummy rise
Before it reached his aching head
A bang and little Ed was dead.

John D. Martin

The Tree

Old tree, old tree,
What have you seen,
As the long years passed you by,
Did lovers dream beneath your boughs,
Did you watch the soldier die,
Did you hear the children laughing,
As they sheltered from the rain,
And when the young man carved his
name on you,
Did you feel any pain,
And as they cut away the branch,
To make the Bishop's crook,
Did it leave a dreadful scar,
And could you bear to look,
And as you stand there, waiting,
Do you hear the night-owl cry,
Old tree, old tree,
What have you seen,
As the long years passed you by?

Peter Hudson

My Garden

The sky is blue with "puffy" clouds,
The sun is peeping through,
The birds are singing in the trees,
To the sound of buzzing bees
All telling me that summers come,
Warm weather's here at last,
The clematis climbing to the sky,
The roses entwining too,
The flowers blooming in their beds
In colours yellow, red and blue,
My garden, oh my garden,
I think it's at its best,
The work is done, I now sit down
And give myself a rest

Dorothy Marsh

Grandson

Adorably wet, deliciously powdered,
Gurgling and laughing,
Screaming and crying,
First smile, first tooth,
First word
Mum Mum, Dad, Dad, Nanna,

Extension of our future,
Retainer of our name,
God bless this innocent creation
Adorably wet, deliciously powdered.

Marion Olley

War

Blood on the ground,
    Planes in the sky.
People all dying,
    Why? Oh why?

"Air raid again"
    The people all sigh,
If this doesn't end
    My children will die!

Bombs keep dropping
    Like falling sky.
Food's all rationed
    I'm sure I'll die.

It's ended at last!!
    I didn't die,
The foods not rationed,
    The children don't cry.

I was lucky,
    But others were not,
Some were wounded,
    Others were shot.

Rebecca Gillies

Spring

Snowy white hands skipping along.
Primroses under hedges.
And the birds in full song.

White fluffy clouds blowing
across the sky.
Letting the sun shine through
the many bits of blue.

Daffodils yellow leaning
gently into the wind.
Hedges and trees about to burst.
Turning the world into an
image of fresh green.

Soon there'll be blue bells.
Making carpets of blue.
And golden - yellow buttercups.
Like the sun shining through.

The world is reborn.
And everything's new.
Leaving hope in our Hearts.
That summer is not far away.

Gladys Lewis

Kitchy Koo

Once there was a little mouse
Who lived beneath a rambling house
The only enemy that he knew
Was a ginger cat called Kitchy Koo

Now Kitchy knew the mouse was there
But couldn't find him anywhere
How hard he'd try to catch the thing
The artful mouse eluded him

The mouse would hide among the coal
And peep out through a little hole
If Kitchy Koo should start to wake
He'd rush off smartly with his cake

Now all went well until the day
When Kitchy Koo was sent away
Alas! A more alert cat
Was sent to sit upon the mat

He closed his eyes, though quite awake
awaiting mousey's first mistake
When mousey next crept on the floor
He pounced! And mousey was no more.

Ann Carne

Collections

Confusions and conclusions
are only in illusions
and dimensions and intentions
are asked by our own questions.

Frustration and completion
are a part of this whole nation,
yet gestation and digestion
are used in absorption.

Creation and refusion
may be made up of dilution
and stations of rhythmic syncopations
will add to your complications.

Precautions mixed with suggestions
is a segment on its own,
and all of the above translations
are thought of when I'm alone.

Josie E. Allan

Love

One of the greatest gifts is love
It truly comes from heaven above
On the darkest day the sun will
shine through
When someone whispers 'I love you'

Frances Murray

Untitled

Oh man! you're very clever -
You've accomplished many things,
You've aped the birds and given us
Mechanically driven wings;
You've linked us all by radio,
Telephone and telly screen,
So now the world's diminished
In circumference, it seems.
You speed along your motorways
In your super powered cars,
You've reached the moon
And have ambitions for the stars;
But as you're hurtling onward
Into the mysteries of space,
It's really worth considering
What drives the human race.
Try not to feel too clever
In your scientific tower,
Remember only God can give
To life, the needed power.

Jean Love

Untitled

I've talked to the floors
And I've talked to the walls
I've talked to the curtains
And the mirror in the hall

I've chatted with my pillow
Debated with my plate
Argued with the cooker
And the embers in the grate

I've asked the bloody settee
And the bookcase over there
I've even asked the windows
And the carpet on the stair

The pictures wouldn't answer
Neither would my coat
I thought I'd call and ask you
But the tears jammed my throat

So here's a little poem
It's just for you to see
The question I can't answer
Is, when did you love me?

Taff Evans

"Twenty-Five Bloody Years"

Twenty-five bloody years
Death, destruction, misery, tears
Endless killing, grief and pain
Three thousand plus cruelly slain
No more death, no more sorrow
Work together for a new tomorrow
Don't be blinded by years of hate
Stop the killing before it's too late
Put the bombs and bullets away
Let our children have peace to play
Twenty-five years, no end in sight
Innocent lives lost by day and night
The streets of Belfast filled with fear
Are the politicians really sincere
Why can't they put the past away
Sit down and talk, have their say
They must find some common ground
To which a solution can be found
If not for us but the next generation
Let's come together one united nation

Gerry Armstrong

Some Of My Favourite Things

I love the sea
I love the sun
The taste of sweets upon my tongue.
The wind and rain that blows along,
The birds and bees their summer song.
The stately trees that stand so tall,
The flowers on the garden wall.
The meandering of the rippling brook
A passage from my favourite book.
Children playing in the park,
Lovers meeting after dark.
The friends I meet along the way,
Wishing me a happy day.
The constant ticking of the clock,
The postman with his fervent knock.
The fish that swim beneath the sea,
Hot buttered toast and scones for tea.

R. C. Cotterill

Song

I love you...
such simple words
such lilting joy to bring;
I love you...
No other phrase,
No fleeting thought of spring,
No transient peace,
No passing glow
Could steal around my heart,
with all the happiness I know
and feel, since love did start.

Madeleine Weston

Bird's-eye View

O'er countryside and town I fly
Observing with my tiny eye
The wondrous sights that lie below
As on, and on and up I go.

The beauty of the great oak tree,
The ebb and flowing of the sea,
The ribboned rivers' constant flow
Into the ocean far below.

Clusters of houses, large and small,
Churches with their spires tall,
Windmills with their moving sails,
Lakes and valleys, hills and dales.

I wish that you could fly with me
And see the things that I can see,
You with your feet upon the ground
While I am soaring Heav'nward bound.

Jean Trigg

The Affair

Skin to skin
another sin
kids at play
wife is home
husband away

We are found
an awful sound
lead to flesh
bed turns red
love is a mess

Clothes black
tears held back
an end to lust
ashes to ashes
dust to dust

John Yeung

"Treasure Garden"

As my eyes explore your beauty,
 A pleasure garden I behold.
I kiss your fragrant tender blossoms,
 Sip your nectar, honey gold.
Feel your rose so gentle soft,
 Kiss its petals, feel them part.
As your softness closes round me,
 I reach down, caress your heart.
Feel my garden softly tremble,
 As a soft breeze play its part.
As more seeds I set within you,
 To new life we give a start .
Now as evening shadows softly fall,
 I relax in your sweet dew.
Had I the chance fair garden,
 All my life I'd spend in you.

Keith Harrison

Changing Coats

Pain behind the eyes
The end is a gentle bliss
Struggling against life
Daily there's less to miss

Nightmare-reality
The border seems blended
Heart petrified
A funeral poorly attended

Conciliation prize
The virile man sobbed
It promised much more
He felt that he'd been robbed

Toiled in lust
Consumed by sombre passion
Death called by name
And life ceased to be his fashion

Christopher Lance

Cherished

Your early arrival caused us a fright,
We prayed for you both day and night.
You came to us for a short while,
Baby of mine you made me smile.
A joyful bundle you came to be,
A much loved son for Dad and me.

No one could know the pain inside,
My darling cherished one you died.
No reason could be given why,
As in your sleep so peaceful lie.

The tears and pain will always be,
A broken heart when you left me.
Until that day when we'll be one,
My loves for you, my cherished son.

Wendy Byen

Thoughts From A Steam Train In 1945

Dirty and smoky, puffing along,
Red flames flaring
Flickering lights faltering;
Chug, chug, on along
In endless rhythm,
Broken by coughing,
Smoke, spluttering,
Crackle of paper
As pages turn,
Music in rhapsody,
Thoughts from the lighted coach
Out to the distant deep.
Old man in corner asleep -
What brought him here?
Over the bridge, the water,
Lights make it clear.
Movement and motion,
Just as the ocean sways
On through the countless days
Out to eternity.

P. R. D. Millns

Sweet Arrival

I yield to you, my loving babe
Be here for always, for you.
Your little life is still unmapped
The babe I love be true.
Within myself I nourished you,
Within myself you grew.
Until your time had come to travel,
For once within me,
You became part of me,
Our lives together bound.
A life we built around you,
For you to have a life.
You are my stable element
In such an unstable time.

Sally Craddock

'Follow My Leader'

Some people to a cause are wed,
While others can't that way be led
But some will only find dissent
However well their thought is meant
How strange to some the reasons given,
Why people to a cause are driven,
Do leaders strike the fiery spark.
That fires others through the dark,
A pity that so many more,
Can never stop to think before,
They blindly follow where they're led
Instead of looking where they tread.

Ronald Bradfield

The Crooked Oak Tree

In the middle of nowhere,
By a stream,
A crooked tree
Has begun to lean.
It has been on this earth
much longer than you,
First an acorn,
but then it grew.
Its branches are now
cold and bare,
Its twisted shape
is strange and rare.
It stands by the stream,
year after year,
creating a mystic
atmosphere.

Michelle Gorton

Swan Song

Solace swan of precious sight,
Soar to its glorious height,
With careful wings it glides,
And watchful eyes it rides.

Contoured lines in full suspension,
Depthless mind of new dimension,
Pastures green as it sees,
Some of many with open keys.

Under white veils of serenity,
Everlasting peace and fraternity,
An infinite bliss to harmonize,
Intangible creation - eternal paradise.

The nature of Heaven,
The garden of Eden,
Pure mystical wonderland,
Beautiful - no love abandoned.

Jay Napal

The Flood

In our house,
There's water everywhere,
It's the same depth,
Inside and out.

As I slosh around in -
My green wellies,
Picking up the things,
I knew and loved so much.

As we leave our house,
I think to myself,
Why did this happen to us?

Gemma Wright

The Words You Said

The words you said
still ring in my head.
That we would never part,
I tool to my heart.
The laughter and fun,
had just begun.
Then you went and left
me alone and bereft.
Now I am no longer free,
you have really hurt me.
What taste can there be,
In cold comfort for tea.

Joseph Allen

The Clinging Mist

It creeps so eerily o'er the ground,
Each blade of grass is kissed,
It creeps along with ne'er a sound,
That shrouded thing called Mist.

That clinging shroud of whiteness,
Sometimes sways to and fro,
It's only from a bright light,
That we may see a glow.

How it loves to paint those pictures,
When it meets its friend 'Jack Frost'
Its beauty can be treacherous,
Yet we never count the cost.

The Sun and Wind come to our aid,
That Mist has gone again,
It's left us with its patterns,
On webs and window pane.

Goodbye for now Oh' clinging Mist,
Goodbye my eerie friend,
I'll see you in the Autumn,
It's then you set your trend.

James T. Wray

Empty

I look in the mirror
What do I see?
Who is this creature
Staring at me?

With her fair skin
And her fair hair,
I look in her eyes
No soul is there.

Just a living shell
Feeling guilt and shame,
Living her life
Day to day.

Who am I?
What do I do?
If I don't know
Then how can you?

I look in the mirror
What do I see?
This creature, this shell,
This reflection is me.

Ellen Lyons

Contrary Wife And Stay At Home Husband

"It is such a lovely day
Why don't we call on May
I'm sure she wouldn't mind
And she is always kind."

"If you like."

"Or, shall we go for a hike,
Unless you would prefer by bike,
Call into a pub for lunch
And maybe have a brunch."

"I don't mind."

"I'll tell you what we'll do,
Perhaps you would like it too,
We'll go up to the moors
Rather than stay indoors."

"It's up to you."

"Now that I've thought it through
I think what we will do
Is to do some chores, have tea
And settle down and watch TV."

"What a good idea."

Joan Robertson

The Humble Bumble Bee

Relaxing on the garden chair,
This summer afternoon so fair,
Listening, watching Bumble Bee,
Collecting pollen busily,
Disappearing in the flowers,
Some of them small, some like towers,
Elegant and proud, white and blue,
Stand the tall Agapanthus new,
Fat and stripy body powers,
For Roses, in archway bowers,
Next fragrant hue and evergreen,
Garden pink, Dianthus seen,
The Humble Bumble Bee will dine,
On Aquilegia, Columbine,
And Astilbe with fine plumed spikes,
But most of all, I think he likes,
Delphinium the colours gay,
I'm sure I'll watch another day,
With fascination and with glee,
The Humble Bumble Busy Bee.

J. F. Husband

First Sight Of Spring

It was a cold day in the spring,
Bank holiday and orchard trees
Still bare without a single sign
Of plum jam in the autumn time.
We followed the slow moving line
Of pleasure seeking traffic, then
"Lets turn off somewhere soon "we said.
We turned, towards the distant hills
And there, on right and left,
In yellow beauty, glorious flowed
A host of golden daffodils.
The sky still grey, the air still cold,
But we were viewing Spring.
Then - disillusionment - these were
Just dandelions, inferior thing.
Inferior? Why dim the blaze
Of yellow by diminishing
The loveliness. "It's just a weed".
We longed for signs that winters gone,
Those dandelions met our need.

Doreen Harrison

Terry - Dactyl

The gallery was quiet
And all the lights were low.
Terry - dactyl crept from his stand
And walked toward the door.

The street was busy
And cars sped by.
Terry - dactyl spread his wings
And flew into the sky.

(To live this pitiful life
Under lock and key,
Was far too dull and boring
For Terry's life to be.)

London was live with fire
- The neon lights aglow.
Terry - dactyl flew down low
As far as he could go.

Don't fly too low little dinosaur,
'Cos humans are greedy things.
They'll want to stuff your little body
And rip apart your wings.

Tracy Ann Ferriss

Ski-ing

Cold, sparkling dawn,
Crisp, mountain air;
Anticipation.

Long slopes of snow,
Heart in the mouth;
Determination.

Out of control,
A bruising fall;
Exasperation.

Wind whistling by,
Skis parallel;
Exhilaration.

High Schwendi hut,
Hot gluhwein drink;
Recuperation.

Steam baths, massage,
Apres-ski bars;
Sophistication.

Bright memories
Of days gone by; now resignation.

Mae Jobin

Inti

If you live
in the rays
of the sun,
Rain of gold
from the skies
you have won.

If you walk
in the rays
of the sun,
All your days
will sweetly
run and run.

If you die
in the rays
of the sun,
Your life's work
and love's turn
have been done.

Lee R. Irving

The Rainbow

The rainbow is a special blend
Of many colours, from start to end,
God placed it in the sky above
A remembrance of His constant love.

We mostly see it when it rains,
Especially on dark and stormy days,
Children always look up and stare,
And wonder how it got up there.

It's not just a beautiful pattern,
Designed across the sky,
It is an everlasting covenant
God made to you and I.

The colours are the reflection,
Of the sun, shining through the rain,
And when our days are sad and grey,
He'll make them bright again.

The next time you see a rainbow,
Like a banner, proudly on display
I hope that you'll remember,
God keeps you completely in His care.

Harriet Smith

Women Only

Little girls are full of fun
and fit as fiddles all month long
but when they hit their teens
everything seems wrong.
Life is now no longer free
and aches and pains come often
but something comes to compensate
this different world to soften.
Love comes in the window
and sets her heart apace,
it makes her feel so special
and it shows upon her face.
The babies come, then babies go
she wants to cry and shout
she feels so anxious and so hot
oh what's it all about?
After the second metamorphosis
has completed its full run,
she feels just like a girl again
the world, once more, is fun.

Christina Hope

Abattoir

Lambs bleat
    Blood splashes
        Abattoir.

Sadayo Takizawa

On Reaching Eighty-Five

It's hard to write of love's young dream
Or idling by a rippling stream
The words don't come to write of joy
Of love between a girl and boy
It's hard when you manage to survive
To the great age of eighty-five
But words do come of peace and love
The joy of daughter and a son,
The words of thanks to many a friend
That's what I can so freely send.
Because I managed to survive
To the great age of eighty-five

I have food and the comfort of a home
No longer feel the need to roam.
And memories of a happy life
The joy of being a beloved wife
Living together over fifty years
We shared our pleasures and our tears.
So why complain at eighty-five
That I have managed to survive

Gladys Candy

"My Bouquet"

Shall I choose a snowdrop,
Half hidden by the snow,
So white and pure and gentle -
How brave of it to grow!

Or shall I pick a daffodil,
A ray of golden sun,
So happy in its dancing,
Delighting in the fun!

Maybe I'll choose a fragrant rose,
Pink or red or white,
Glorious in its beauty,
A rich and heavenly sight!

Or shall I pick a dahlia,
To brighten up my day,
A vivid lilac daisy one,
As summer fades away.

I choose them all -
A grand bouquet,
To cheer my heart
If skies are grey.

Marjorie Holstead

Only A Baby

Only a baby small,
    Dropped from the skies,
        One laughing face
            Two sunny eyes

Two cherry lips,
    One chubby nose,
        Two little hands
            Ten little toes

One golden head,
    Curly and soft,
        One tongue that ways
            Loudly and oft

One little brain
    Empty of thought,
        One little heart
            Troubled by nought.

Only a baby small,
    Never at rest,
        Small but how dear to us
            God knoweth best.

Robert J. Chapman

The Insurance Man

Every week he comes around,
He knocks the door and takes a pound.
He writes it in his book, and ours,
Then hurries off to Mrs Gower's.

I always think it very funny
Mum should give him so much money.
It's more than she will give to me
And I wash up and help get tea.

I asked my teacher and she said,
"He gives it all back when we're dead!"
I have to say to me it sounds
A dreadful waste of all those pounds.

Peter A. Sexton

The Angels Of Dunblane

The nation weeps with sorrow,
For the angels of Dunblane
For homes bereft of loved ones,
We share the grief and pain;
Those lives so soon were ended,
That promised all so fair,
But the buds that will not grow below,
Will blossom in God's care.

The land they leave behind them,
A safer land will be,
As other little children,
From danger will be free,
And thus the seeds of sacrifice,
A harvest yet will give,
As children of tomorrow,
Through peaceful years shall live.

T. I. Mackay

Milk

The early morning quiet is broken
By the chink-tinkle of the milk float
Carrying crates
Of white skittles.

It travels slowly
On the stop-start journey
Along its milky way
And the load grows lighter
With each pause.

The sleeping street comes alive,
White splashes appear on doorsteps
Hands reach out
From open doors.

Feathered thieves watch
With beady eyes,
Wait for the chance to pierce
With sharp beaks
The silver seals
And sip
The creaminess beneath.

Eve Kind

Too Late

It's now too late to show I love you,
Too late to say I care,
You left this world completely,
Leaving us to mourn you there,

You should have been too young to die,
But you weren't allowed to live,
Your life's bright spark has vanished,
Just like the gift you used to give,

I hope some day I'll see you,
The way you used to be,
You can see the way I wander,
Along the path you paved for me.

Bethan Jones

My Feelings

I'm upset and sad about my Uncle Les
I really miss him.
Everyone hates me
I wish I wasn't born.
I want to go away,
Live with someone else
I feel all alone
I'm scared no one likes me.
I need someone to love me,
To hold me
I love Les, I want him back.
Mum don't care,
Dad don't care,
Know one does
I wish life could go back to normal
but, no one cares anymore.

Kerry Mew

Together Again

Pure white skin, light fingertips,
Kissing gently with pouted lips.
Hands caressing silken hair,
Body and soul, totally bare.
Arms enclosing, holding tight,
Bodies straining with all their might.
Bodies shattered needing no more,
Nerves splintered, to the core.
Limbs relaxed, all energy spent.
Soul deep within, wholly content.
Now arms enfold with tenderness,
Each to hold in sleep and rest.

J. M. Cook

Life To Death

A tragedy has happened,
an innocent young girl... has died.
Her life... taken.
A night of pleasure and enjoyment
Turned out in horror...
A disaster...
Murdered by a pill...
Was it worth it?

Family and friends,
Crying in agony...
A daughter... friend... dead.. gone,
Was put in a coffin
Then buried... forgotten.
What was the point?
Swallowing a pill is
Life to death...

Carys Rowlands

The 'Corner' Shop

Up at seven,
   down by half past,
Coffee and biscuits,
   to break our fast.
Open at eight,
   school rush for nine,
Stock all the shelves
   with a best selling line.
Dust all around,
   mop up the floor,
Visit the warehouse,
   and one or two more?
Back to the shop,
   tea break and chat,
The mornings now over,
   afternoons always flat
Evenings approaching,
   no, it's gone in a flash
Lights out and lock up,
   it's time to count Cash.

R. A. D. Hudson

Who Am I?

Am I a mother?
Or the other?
A wife?...Maybe
I cook and I clean,
You know what I mean,
A housemaid?...Maybe
I can't suffer ills,
I administrate the pills,
A nurse?...Maybe
I know I've a mind
I'm one of a kind
I'm Me!

Polly Lawton

Animal Lover

As I was walking through the heather
They wordily creatures you discover.
You meet a fox and then a toad
When you walk down the road.
The fox that is so clever. The wild
Horse you could not tether.
Many a grey squirrel dashes by, but
Not a red one caught my eye.
Would it be that I discover when the
Pheasant flies for cover
That all creatures great and small
Will answer to my call

E. A. Lane

Winter

Hooves on cobbles set in ice
The icy spears hang down
Slashing through
The rose-coloured dusk
Like strange rays of light

At noon the dull sky
Is traced with tree-black,
Spidery.
Paler and remote
Swings the lamp
Of the sun.

All is quiet
Awaiting the dark
But after that
The dawn.

Anna Seifert

Thoughts

The singer's voice so rich and pure
Rang out for all to hear,
A theme of love and hope so sure
Ambitions nought to fear.

I took the road to anywhere
As freedom's choice seemed right,
And met life's tapestry full square
And changed with all my might.

Success it came as such it is;
So far across the foam
The marching years brought an abyss,
My memories of home.

The town seemed smaller so much so,
Old parents both were gone,
Our house, the school that I did know
Are thoughts that still live on.

My infant fell then rose again
His world seems heaven sent,
Persistent trials are surely sane
And fearless wonderment.

Alex Winter

Japanese Prisoner Of War (Looking Back)

I could stare forever
Pictures in my mind
Oh what of the memories
Oh what will I find

Tired eyes are sore now
Relief from a blink
Is this reality
A dream I do not think

Do you remember me
Do you know where I am
This is hell on earth for me
I am a broken man.

Sanity seems away from here
I've never felt so low
All I dream are your blue eyes
And a field full of snow.

I could stare forever
Pictures in my mind
Oh what of the memories
Oh what will I find.

Kean Turner

True Love

In 1938 I met a pilot dressed in blue,
We fell in love and got engaged
And pledged our love so true,
But then alas: there came the day
When off he had to fly
Across the sea to foreign lands,
To fight the Germans in the sky
We had a hurried wedding and a
One night honeymoon
I went back home and prayed so hard
That he would come back soon.
Then after many years had passed
he came back safe and fine,
We found our love had never changed
in that long, and troubled time.
We have had our golden wedding
with our family all around.
We thank the lord for everything
and the true love we both have found.

Suzanne Ezekiel

Living A Life

We are on this earth
To play our part from birth
We go to school eventually
To improve our mentality.

The days pass by all too fast
Soon school days are in the past
We leave and try to find a job
Now we must earn an honest bob.

As we toil we meet some friends
Who in life indulge in trends
This I find quite boring at times
I look for things along finer lines.

They think I'm being up market
When in my car I park it
How they must all envy me
For saving hard so carefully.

In this world you never get
Something for nothing not as yet
You have to work to pay your way
To eat and live another day.

M. I. Brooks

Wild Rabbits

Sniffling bunnies jumping high
running, hopping to the sky
nibbling carrots, eating veg
digging burrows to the edge
Sleeping little bunnies down below
the earthy brown ground
down down down.
Nibbling out every night
for when plants come to life.
Busy cleaning one another
bouncing playing springing
on one another.
Been to one place been to another
always alert always fast
as they scurry past.

Caroline Reed

A War Hero's Suicide

War and disorder,
Destruction and pain.
Memories you'll leave,
When you kill again.

You can't have feelings,
Not for this life.
When you guard with a gun,
And kill with a knife.

Post-traumatic stress disorder,
You won't decide.
Killing others,
May lead to your suicide.

Caroline Reeve

Sunbeams

The sun dances on the horizon,
awakes another day.
Hands they rub at bleary eyes,
wiping sleep away.
Sunbeams dance upon the water,
twinkle on the waves.
Warming up my heavy soul,
from the loneliness it craves.
To caress the world with light,
until the darkness comes
and sleep it visits me again,
when the day is done.

Gary Rudley

"Just The Two Of Us - Dol And Ball"

I'm an ancient dolmen
Standing all alone
But near a little bollard
Also in his own.

For centuries we have covered
Our master's resting place,
Constantly weathering the
Elements on our face.

No one really noticed us
Until these modern times,
When we were suddenly discovered
As "Rich and ancient" finds.

To-day we're so popular that
People come from near and far
To gaze at our strange stone shapes
And wonder what we are?

We'll keep them guessing for many
And many a day, but there's
One sure thing: We'll still be
Standing when they have passed away.

Isabel Anderson

'Does It Matter'

Conceived in mind or body,
New life, old strife, new birth.
The only certainly is its uncertainty,
What morals, what value, what worth?
Simplistic in its perplexity.

Sunbeams caress her face
Like an angel's wings.
At the altar of her unity
What then the future brings?
False hope, true love, real pity.

The leaves of time
Drift slowly o'er the grave,
A misspent life is spent,
What grace is there to save?
This life was only lent.

K. Howard

Live Like Once Before

Let this age be, my oldest sins
Let me discover, when once
All we needed was power.

I shall not forget my infant days
Where joy brought me newest ways.

My creeping fears, shall fear no more
Let me live like once before.

My heart will tame
For my fearless name
Repeating what I must
Leading life to dust.

In my sleep of death
My changes will suffer
For there I will age no more
And live like once before.

Anna Durante

Planning Awry!

Applying re-laid moral courses
and increasing psyche-volts,
social engineering
is confusing nuts with bolts.
Myopic planners have overlooked
the view from principle's steeple,
for they cant produce blueprints
to clone-organize people.
The faint, ethical divisions
between nightmares and dreams,
donate bureaucratic credence
for their impractical schemes!

W. T. Martin

Captivity

Oh God, a mind you gave me,
To ponder on my thoughts so vainly.
Day and night - this endless burden,
travels with relentless yearning.

Enticed into captivity
by softly spoken insanity,
I seek release from untold secrets
A sanctuary from regrets.

Oh youth, why did you by-pass me?
Without a thought of clarity.
Am I to dwell in timeless space?
reflected in my lonely face.

To seek this madness once again,
So far away from Bethlehem,
The liquor of my nightmare drives
away all reasons to survive.

Debbie Jane Southall

Dearest Nan, "Mrs. Teresa O'Connor"

Although no longer with us,
In our hearts you reign,
Like a royal star, never forgotten,
Forever eternally begotten,
A loving angel without wings.

Love cannot describe,
The love you gave to me,
A saint borrowed for a moment
A loving gran,
A holy angel without wings.

Your life has touched us greatly,
You shaped our destinies,
With kind words you taught justice,
With examples, good deeds,
A loving angel without wings.

Never forgotten
Though now far,
With memories, though few held dear,
You are forever near,
A loving angel without wings.

Catherine Ryan

Untitled

What is Love?
Love for a child
Love for ones family
Accepted
Expected
Part of Life's pattern

What is Love?
Love for ones friends
Ones home and possessions
Accepted
Expected
Part of Life's pattern

What is Love?
Love late in life
Love for one other
Unsought
Unexpected
Completing Life's pattern

Jeanne Jones

In Praise Of The R.N.L.I.

The sea is fascinating
beware its changing moods.
From calm to treacherous,
dark-threatening it broods.

Water sports enormous fun,
skiing, surfing, boating.
The calm sea so friendly,
a pleasurable outing.

The fishermen go fishing
all weathers - even gales.
Tell exciting stories -
some call them fishy tales!

In treacherous stormy seas,
our gallant life-boat crew
take on an unpaid task
and bravely see it through.

For outstanding courage
to them we recommend.
For unflinching service
their skills to commend.

S. Vignes

Recall

Where did I journey last night;
To wake with an aching chest,
   deep sighs, and tears
   that tracked each cheek.
Yet not with fears
   but a joyous sorrowing.
I only know there had been a parting.
   And I was moving on.
Was it leaving,
   or returning,
As I faced that crowd unknown,
With heartfelt tears, and a
   strengthening power,
I turned away to journey on,
   Spanning time,
   Alone.

   E. W. Greenslade

Untitled

Who will share my empty bed
When you are gone? When you are gone?
Who will share my lonely bed
When you are gone?

Who will hold my sleeping head
When you are gone? When you are gone?
Who will clasp my every part
When you are gone?

Who will warm my slowing heart
When you are gone? When you are gone?
Who will take me in the night?
Who will be my fierce delight?
When you are gone?

I will share your lonely bed
I will hold your sleeping head
I will grasp your every part
I will freeze your aging heart
Not with fierceness or delight
I will take you in the night
To where I'm gone. To where I'm gone.

   Ian Dunlop

Second Burial

First born,
Only born,
Still born,
Nameless son.

John brought him cortègeless
on the handlebars of his bike.
He buried him in the faith ashes
of their ancestors.

With country courtesy
he informed the priest
who, puce with rage,
commanded, "Unearth the child
for burial in unholy ground."

   Moya Hegarty

Whispering Words...

Whispering words that taunt and tease,
Ebb and flow, ebb and flow
Throughout my mind with careless ease,
Ebb and flow, fast then slow.
Whirling winds that coo and call,
Hiss and hurl, hiss and hurl
Throughout my mind with senseless gall,
Hiss and hurl, hiss then swirl.
Wailing waters that toss and turn,
Drip and drop, drip and drop
Throughout my mind with heart I spurn,
Drip and drop, drip then stop.
Whispering words, I have no more,
Breathless silence, I adore.

   Anthony Williams

Snow

Snow on the hills, brilliant
white,
Glare of the sun, shining so
bright.

Sheep in the hills, caught
in a storm,
Huddled together, to keep
themselves warm.

A red breasted robin, flits
to and fro,
On snow covered branches,
weighted with snow.

A snow storm brewing, clouds
racing by,
A wind blows so fierce, a
darkened sky.

Elements of winter, make a
picturesque scene,
Natures beauty captured,
an artists dream.

   June Cameron

Untitled

Seconds and minutes merge to
Make the busy hours fly,
Soon turning into days and months,
And so the years go by.
In retrospect, seeking to find the
Worth of our life's span,
Remembering childhood, and the day
Awareness first began.
Living again the special times
The pleasure and the pain,
The days that brought us profit,
Those deeds that brought us gain.
Close held, and unforgettable
And rare beyond all measure,
Buried full deep within the heart
The moments that we treasure.
Amid all this, what can we see
Of sterling worth to save?
Our finest, shining hour was when
We fully, truly, gave.

   Ivy Maybray-King

True Friends

I love you "Boots" more than you know
And when you leave me it will show
You've always been around - you see
When you're gone, there'll be just me.

I'm only twelve, and you're fifteen
But a livelier dog I've never seen
We walk together for miles and miles
People see us and share our smiles

I tell you all my secret dreams
And you just listen, then it seems
You nudge me with your little nose
My love for you just grows and grows

If I am sad you ease my fears
And always lick away those tears
That little sparkle in your eye
Gently tells me - do not cry.

Although you always try to please
My greatest fear you cannot ease
The time will come for us to part
I know that day I'll break my heart.

   Troy Beadle

My Shadow

I sit in a dark corner.
With just my shadow.
Looking around a lonely room.
No-where to run.
No-where to hide.
Needing some one to listen.
A shoulder to cry on
To be loved.
To have friends.
So much love.
So much friendship.
Needed to be given.
But for me it's a dark corner.
Just me and my shadow.

   Carrie Grugan

The Phantom Coach

The phantom coach that rides by night,
Not a driver there in sight.
Four grey mares with coach behind,
A relic from an ancient time.

'Tis said that on the stroke of ten
This coach will ride without its men,
Through the gloom of a dim lit street
Comes eerie sounds of trotting feet.

The phantom coach has kept its date,
On the stroke of ten not a minute late.
Four grey mares with coach behind,
This relic from an ancient time.

You stand and shiver and reason why
Should a phantom of the past go by,
With clanking chains that fill the air
And the haunting cry of four grey mares.

   S. J. Smith

Love

I sat and looked out of my room
into the dull and rainy gloom.
The sun didn't shine
The bird's didn't sing
Until you smiled at me.
And helped me see
that love was there
and that you would care.
Now I know
that the sun does shine
and the birds do sing.
   So there is love in everything
   and everywhere.

   Lauren Chandler

Sam

There is the light of healing,
Upon my face today
Casting deep within my mind
In darkness, light, a ray.
Within my heart of aching pain
So deep it holds my soul
Trapping all in angry thought
I'm dead, emotion cold.
Hold out your hands of healing
Make whole my life again
Look deep within my lifeless eyes
Search me for all my pain,
Your voice so soft upon my ears
Infuses me with hope
With you I'm feeling safe and loved
You've helped me learn to cope
Speak gently now to guide me
From broken mind see free
The person lost within this fear
Rebuild what's left of me

   Lorraine Lawson

Love And Fear

All love him,
But I hate him.
All adore him,
But I fear him.
All see the laughter,
But I see the menace.
All watch his charms,
But I cower from him.

No one - but I
Have seen,
No one - but I
Have heard
The anger and the hate;
I have felt and feared,
The anger and the hate.

All have seen,
But I am blind.
All have heard,
But I am deaf.
All hate him, but I love him.

Margaret O'Toole

Pain

Pain comes. Pain goes.
Something serious one never knows.
Pain then goes. But then comes back.
You have no time for being slack.
A new pain. An old pain.
One you have had for years
And every time it happens.
A multitude of fears.
Have you taken your tablets.
You ought to take a rest.
Why does it seem that always
All your friends know best.
Have you seen the doctor.
They are sure to say
But by the time you do
The pain has gone away.
Yes pain comes. Pain goes.
So it's grin and bear it I suppose.

D. R. Mansell

Outside The Waterzone

Outside the waterzone
I head for dry land and stone,
How long will all this last?
I have all my doubts to cast
Before they drag me back in deep
My love I will find to keep
Together forever hand in hand
Our sanctuary beyond the sand.

Fiona Jane Haines

Cats

A cat is a great friend, one
You can depend. I have just
Left a woman who has lost
Her cat; she is broken-hearted, I
Can tell you that. I have tried
My best to find her cat, tried
To find her near the railway
Track. I've also put ads in the
Hairdressers flat; my friend is
Very down today, got me a
Dinner by the way, she is a
Nice woman I must say. I
Hope and pray the cat comes
Back, and puts a smile back in
That flat, please God if it's
In your power, get that woman
Her beloved cat back to her.

David Campbell Stuart

Foal

He opens an eye sleepily,
Raising his head dozily,
Nudging the mare hungrily,
Sucking her milk contentedly,
He prances about merrily,
Chasing rabbits cheekily,
Bucking and rearing wildly,
Twirling his tail comically,
Rolling and snorting happily,
Trotting around energetically,
Nuzzling my hand sweetly,
He's the love of my life, undoubtedly.

Ffion Dewi

Darley's Darling

The sun shone in my face today
yet it was a mere reflection
of a speck I saw in your eye.

I'm lifted from the pit
of egotistical negativity
because...

To empathize with you
is to recognize and set free
the vastness of consciousness
and the fertility of creativity.

One, yet not alone.
Cradled in a fusion of love
and knowing... that its radiance
will be seen and sensed
in some time and space
by some aspiring entity
as he or she
start and end
their day.

John Bilson

The Jackpot

I've won, I've won, I've won,
I'm praying in my heart.
My world will be of paradise,
And I've know that from the start.

Mystic Meg will see my sign,
And then she'll say the words.
Then people will come running round,
And begging in their herds.

The fortune will keep me,
That money in the bank.
The holidays abroad I want,
And spending that old Franc.

The draw is to be made now,
My pounding heart does know.
The first number is a 3,
And guess what, It's Not Me!

Anna Louise Battersby

Perpetuum Mobile

He said
'Shalom' instead of 'Salaam'
So the storm arose
And disturbed the calm.

Jew and Arab,
Arab and Jew.
What on earth is
A man to do?

Surely no one
Understands
By shaking mailed fists
Instead of hands.

Wilfred Morris

Hope

Oh, at last the spring is near,
When old and such will ease their fear,
Gone is winter's icy showers,
And into view will come the flowers.

I look around and see the hope,
Of those who almost could not cope,
When keeping warm had daily tried,
The will of all to keep alive

The sun shines weakly all around,
And there is life beneath the ground,
Smiles replace the look forlorn,
It seems we all are now reborn.

It is so wonderful now to hear,
The song of birds we love most dear,
This life on earth is now so bright,
That we all forget old winter's night.

G. R. Whelbourn

Granddaughter

Not a thought, not a dream,
No hidden plans for you it seems.
Unknown to the world,
Not a hair to be curled.
No toys are a lying,
My life called enjoying.
Wild nights never ending,
Good life, it's mind bending.
The siren, the waiting,
A heartbeat, the failing.
Tolling of years,
The watering tears.
Troublesome mind, which turmoils
to slaughter
The saving of life,
Thanks to my dear Granddaughter.

Stan Wakefield

Ode To The Falkland Islands

This land so far away from home,
Is just like Scotland on a frosty morn,
Its barrenness is plain to see,
As Falkland Islanders will agree,
The lack of trees to shelter by,
Is helped by mountains way up high,
There is no problem here to see,
The islanders are now Free!

Bruce M. Long

Why Me?

Why me? Why has he chosen me?
I cannot tell, but this I know
That Jesus died his love to show.
And as I think of his great grace,
How on the cross he took my place:
This question I would now embrace -
Why me?

Why me? Why has he chosen me?
I cannot tell, but this I know
That unto death his love did go.
And as I think of all he bore,
That crown of thorns and nails so sore:
I ask the question all the more -
Why me?

Why me? Why has he chosen me?
I cannot tell, but this I know
That in his love he stooped so low.
And as I think about his pain
When on the cross my Lord was slain:
I ask the question yet again - Why me?

Stephen Hirons

Untitled

Oh lady solitude I embrace you
you are the pathway of God's few.
Tranquillity and peace lie there in
Who dedicate their lives to Him.

Oh lady solitude 'tis you I love
Listening quietly to the Lord above.
God uses you to speak to me
My soul rejoices thanking thee.

Oh lady solitude have no fear
Surround me in your mantle here
Enclosed in God's loving care
No troubles do I have to bear.

J. F. Napier

To Pat My Love

Like the ever rising sun -
    That gives the morning light
Like the brightly shining star -
    Up in the heavens at night
Like the fragrant petalled flower -
    That blossoms in the spring
Like the gently falling rain -
    That sweetens everything
Like the crystal mountain stream
    That flows on endlessly
All these things and more, dear Heart -
    Are like my love for thee

E. P. Morse

My Country

This land that I love,
Stands tall and with pride.
Fighting her battles with honour.
They tried to divide us with threats
of war,
But united we stand together!
Defending our shores like warriors
of old.
Making this land ever stronger.
The pride that I have!
The love that I have!
Is for England! England forever!

Florence M. Wells

Crust Of Earth

Crust of earth
Is dust of man,
Treasury of nature diminishes
With each life span.

Live for today,
To hell with tomorrow;
Let our grandchildren pay
With ecological sorrow.

Damian Travers

Black

Black is my son's favourite colour
Aircraft missing
Death dressing
Evil breathing
Black is my son's favourite colour.

Black is my son's favourite colour
Soft warm fur
Luck crossing your path
Dirt hiding clothes
Black is my son's favourite colour.

Black is my son's favourite colour
Dark rain clouds
Days too short
Frightening nights
Black is my son's favourite colour.

Julie Riggs

"When Smutty Mcdine Reaches Forty"

When Smutty Mcdine reaches forty
We think he will be old
He'll have a lot of wrinkles
And his tummy will now fold.

When Smutty Mcdine reaches forty
Everyone will cheer
We'll all go up the local
And perhaps buy him a beer

When Smutty Mcdine reaches forty
He will not be very pleased
If everyone laughs at him
He won't like to be teased,

When Smutty Mcdine reaches forty
He won't take part in the race
'Cause poor old Smutty can no longer
Keep up the faster pace.

When Smutty Mcdine reaches forty
We will all celebrate
'Cause one thing sure we all know
We think our Smutty's great!

Deirdre Bootes

Truth — The Reality Of Love

Winter
    Coldness
Blows around your reddened face
Endless searching, never found
By one alone a given ring.
But what I am, cannot accept
That gloveless hand upon my chest
To live
    lie
endlessly forsaken
alone
    completely
        mistaken.

Clive Campbell

Why?

Why do we want our children
to grow up just like us,
To live in little boxes
beside the river pus,
To overlook the atom-bomb,
pollution and crime,
To be ruled by machinery
and judged by time?
Do we look at them to see
a copy of our face,
To wonder if they'll muddle
through the human race,
until they have their own children
to grow up just like them,
to live in little boxes
beside the river phlegm?

Susan Margaret Palmer

It Is Time

I scanned across from left to right;
until I was blinded by the night
memories of past was all I saw
but now I think,
it's time to close the door

Now it is time to look ahead
foretell the future, before we are dead,
make believe, the world's our own,
make believe,
It's home from home.

Lisa Fox

Drinking Schnapps By The Fire

Sooty sonata,
Spattering shots like sudden
Gunfire
Across the room,
Spilling a spectroscope of heat
Over the hearth.
Sophisticated schnapps,
Sparking spirit like
Sweet, hot sunshine
In the throat.
Spilling a spectroscope of heat
Inside the body.
The wind whams waywardly
Outside,
But we are warm
Inside.

Christina Greenland

A Passing Mole

The sparrow and the hedgehog sipped
From a butter cup,
Where the dew had slipped
Into the creamy butter bowl
Where the soft earth rumbled
From the passing mole, who,
At blinding speed,
The velvet shovel, with,
Spade like hands
He digs his hovel,
Where stems and solid roots abound
In his silent underground.
No sunlight breaks to light the day,
And no worm had better
Block his way.

Alan Edward Hadley

To Fly

To burst through rain
ground fog, dense grey
into an open sunset, all oranges
magentas and pinks.
To unfold a cracked landscape
the river-beds, the lakes,
the mountains
the very sea
a mere backdrop.
To count the blue sky
as your fellow passenger,
the wisps of white your neighbour.
To hover gracefully over eternity.
To fly.

John S. Rubin

The Poetry Competition

"Write a Poem", he said,
"It's easy, you know how."
"Look, there's a competition here,"
"You could win us sixteen thou!"
"Just jot down a few lines."
"And send them in the post,"
"You've as good a chance as any",
"Probably better than most."
Thanks, for your confidence in me
But I don't know that I could
I've never entered one before
And I'm not sure that I should
"What harm can it do", says he,
"There's stacks of work you've done",
"If you can't think up one now",
"Just choose an earlier one".
So I sat and thought about it,
And decided .... Albeit elementary,
That this is the poem to be,
My first competition entry!

Kate Brownett

An Image, Never Leaving

When I wake, you are here.
When I sleep, you are here.
But only in mind.
The shadow of your presence
Still lurking in the air.

Everyday, I see you.
Everyday, I hear you.
All my thoughts are of you.
Why you left me all alone
To face life without you.

If I left, you'd still be here.
If I stayed, you'd still be here.
For my heart is yours.
Nobody else do I want.
But I can't have you.

Sarah Moore

Supposing

If every day was yesterday
And last night never was.
The moon and stars never shone
Would it come to pass?
Would the world ever know peace?
And agree to be friends at last
Think of the lovely future
Never the things of past
Today's children with that future
With jobs and careers in mind
Think of the happiness it would culture
To everyone especially mankind

P. Harrison

Sun

Sun, the power, the omnipotent one
How I miss you when you hide
In the heavens high above
When dark clouds roll
That North Wind blows
I ache and want you so

Mood swings rage when you're away
Like a lover missed
And whose return brightens up the day
To bring a smile back on my face
And warmth so fine, come burn the place
And make all things divine.

Ann Demicheli

"Return To Edinburgh"

December winds bring chilling rain
That washes through the city grey
Yet hand in hand with sweet Lorraine
To happiness I make my way

There's healing in the tender touch
As hand in hand we walk along
Or sit and quietly talk of much
And each to th'other says "Be strong"

And life is not for loneliness
In this poor world of broken dreams
When each soul does the other bless
The righteous Sun sheds healing beams

Those eyes that have looked heavenward
As windows of the spirit speak
A tender soft unspoken word
Of blessings promised to the meek

For who on earth together stand
United in our Father's favour
And walk together hand in hand
To face the world shall be the braver

Alex Valentine Jr.

Our Doctor - And Friend

A handful of people
and the wind is chill
Against the view across the hill

The vicar mumbles
not much louder than the breeze
that scatters the leaves

And all is as it was before

It is right that he should go
So quietly on his journey?
A presence, always positive
Reassuring with authority
And love.
Now does he know for sure
What made his garden grow?

Betty Norris

I Wish I Were A Spider

I wish I were a spider
that would make you
shiver. And when you're
dead the spiders will
eat all your liver.

And all the people
who are quite stout,
they will always
give a mighty shout.

And when the spider
heard the shout, the
spider climbed up
the sunny spout.
And when the
spider climbed
up the spout, they
gave another mighty
shout.

John Stephen Rimmer

Why Me?

My heart is banging
My legs go weak
They stood in a group
at the end of the street.

Some of them push me
Some of them swear
Some want my money
Some pull my hair.

They say I've to ignore them
and they'll go away
So why does it still happen
every day.

Some people are thin
and some are tall
Some are fat
and some are small.
So why does it matter
what colour or name?
As underneath - we're all the same.

Kelly Rigby

A Floating Candle Ride

I see a candle in the night
It's glowing very very bright
There it glows under my nose
So bright, so light so bright, so light
There it floats on the water side
There it floats on a lily ride
Then it becomes a beautiful bride
with another floating candle ride.

Anam Hasan

The Courageous Teacher

What unforeseen misfortune lead
To that disastrous day
Who could know what lay ahead
On that quiet ordinary day.
How could anyone just know
what trauma lay ahead
as off to school those children went
Without a thought or dread.
assembled in the gym that day
Who knew what lay ahead
as happy children content to do
What their teacher said.
The peace was suddenly shattered
As shots rang through the air
who knows the terror of that day
their little minds absorbed.
To save those little children
in vain their teacher tried
to save their lives in such a way
brought tears to every eye.

L. M. Carter

To Mozart

Music so beautiful and serene
Work more delightful has never been,
It floats - like a boat on the river
The magic will last us for ever.
To soothe and heal the mind and spirit
Nothing else will surpass its merit.
Surely it was a gift from heaven
Moving by, so calm and even,
Violin, flute, harp and piano,
Blending to wonderful concerto
Voices so sweet, in opera chorus
And we can listen to each opus.
Music comes from, and goes to the heart
Thank you Dear Mozart.

Margaret Joyce Smith

Glitterati

Painted glitterati
Limousined and glossed
Packaged by image builders
Weighed down by fortune and connections
Egged on by glamour-mongers
Pedding ego-trips
Flashbulbed by the hour
Creating news for who's who
And future memorabilia
Glamorized images for print
Work for an image hungry press
Read by adulating audiences
Vicariously delighting
In every minutiae of Hedonistic life.

M. Ridhwan Is'harc

Lady

I never heard the footsteps
of the angels getting near
To take from me to heaven
the one I love so dear
You are where I cannot see you Lady
Your bark I cannot hear
I know you walk besides me
Never absent, always near
So please stay with me dear Lady
And hear me when I call
And wipe the tears of sorrow
which on my cheeks still fall
I hold you close within my heart
and there you will remain
You'll walk with me throughout my life
until we meet again

Steve James Graves

The Spell Of The Magic Juice

The petals from a wild lily
the juice from a mountain tree.
Pour it on the eyes of a sleeping being
whatever thy person be.
When thus awakes and sees them
Instant love will be at hold,
whether it be a tiny mouse,
or a lion big and bold.

James Green

The Funeral

Today's the day for his farewell,
The voyage to a new place,
A family man they all knew well,
But I, knew not his face.

Relatives from far and wide,
All come this day to mourn,
A day when feelings do not hide,
For it is the opposite, born.

The lonesome box that carries him,
Travels oh so slow,
Pity for the next of kin,
But to me he was not known.

Such attendance was respectful,
To such a solemn place,
All eyes were very tearful,
Part lost of the human race.

M. W. Macpherson

Computer Widow

When we first met, my heart was light,
Our days were filled with fun
But then bought his first P.C.,
The nightmare had begun.

It started out with playing games
Like Lemmings and A-Train;
But then came DOS and C ++
Yet how could I complain.

The sickly smile that hit his face
When he talked of his P.C.
How could I say please make your choice
It's your P.C. or me!

Then one sad day he turned and said
'Oh Nick, my RAM's too small!
Well what a shock that was to me,
I thought he'd end it all.

So here we are with model two,
Its modem pre-installed,
With C.D. drive and scanners too;
I must say I'm appalled!!!

Nikki Read

'All In The Stars'

The night is weeping
With silver tears
Echoing of the past
And long lost years.
But like pure diamonds
Way up high above
They are cutting
Through the memories
With naught but
Gods pure love.
Till they find
A faith that is tested
Of old
And tried by fire
Till it
Comes forth as gold.

Hilary Raines

A Humble Prayer

As I kneel in prayer
Hear my humble prayer
All I've come to ask "Lord"
That man becomes prepared.

Prepared to help each other.
As he go's along his way
In the way you taught us "Lord"
In a caring loving way.

As I kneel in prayer
Hear my humble prayer
For you give us so much "Lord"
In a caring loving way

In a caring loving way
Let there be peace
Peace between all nations "Lord"
No matter the colour or creed.
Amen

Jean Gibson

My Grandfather

Our house seems so empty,
I will tell you why.
My heart is so heavy
it could make me cry.

A lovely man
whose name was Bud
A gentleman
whom everybody loved.

He had this pain
in his chest so bad
he suffered much
it was so sad.

Then God above,
held out his hand
and took our Bud
to live in his Land.

This man called Bud
who is no longer here
was my Dear Grandfather
who I loved so dear.

Loraine Sullivan

Strawberries And Cream

Little spotty sweet face
Lying in a bed of green
little blushing red heart
your beauty I have seen
each day you grow more brilliant
hiding in your lair
for weeks I have watched over you
and treated you with care
Tomorrow I will take you
and wash you nice and clean
I'll then place you on a dish
and cover you with cream
I'll then lift you to my lips,
into my mouth I'll place;
goodbye little red heart
farewell spotty face.

J. Bain

What Of The Mind?

Art is an expression of the spirit,
Music is an obsession of the soul,
Love is a possession of the heart,
Ah, but what then of the mind?
Expression of the spirit,
Obsession of the soul,
Possession of the heart;
Creations of the mind.

Mark Kenny

Sea Of Fear

Raging torrents fill my mind
sharks snapping at my heels
a silent scream, a cry for help
no-one knows how it feels

I swim around in panic
I try to escape in vain
red tears run down my face
no-one knows my pain

I swim around for hours and hours
then days and months and years
I'm reaching dry land day by day
but still I cry red tears

One day I'll face the shark
when he rears his ugly head
then when he torments me
I'll send him back to the sea bed

Then maybe I'll not be tormented
Just maybe I'll be free of the pain
I would laugh when I was happy
cry tears the colour of rain.

Brenda May Ball

Alone

I'm lonely I admit,
and I want to go home.
I can't stand this feeling,
of being all alone.

I haven't got a friend
or someone to care.
Nowhere to go
and nothing to share.

No one to reassure me
about my fears.
No one to mop up
my endless tears

I'm cold and I'm hungry,
and I want to return,
to the friends that I left,
and the family I yearn.

I thought I'd be better
left on my own,
but I'm lonely and admit
that I want to go home.

Emma Bramhill

Life

Life is a pathway broad and smooth,
A narrow rough track lane,
A pasture green where joy abounds,
A dark wood filled with pain
A long hard hill away ahead
That dragging feet must climb,
Which, yet when conquered oft reveals
A vale of peace sublime,
A wilderness of wasteland,
A garden tilled with care,
A deep ravine of hatred,
A crest of love so fair.
'Tis bones with age protesting.
'Tis healthy searching youth,
A sea of cruel deception,
A rock of much sought truth.
Life is a mighty challenge,
A gauntlet to be run,
A sport for testing prowess,
A battle to be won.

Joan B. Clay

Red Is...?

Red is the colour of love
but can be the sign
of danger.

Red is the symbol of emotion
but can be the colour
of blood
from the depth of a broken
heart.

Red is the pain of life
but can be the joy when there are
no tears.

Red is the colour of a flower,
the flower of Romance
called the
rose

Bhavnisha Mistry

Untitled

Wasted time: yet wont am I to muse
    on things that might have been.
Yet time is never wasted if a lesson
    has been learned and seen in all
    its implications.

To hold stubbornly on to something
    that has faded into past.
To be transfixed in secular space
    halfway to the stars.
    Is that any consolation?

Come down to earth and meet the
    dreadful truth of things that are.
Extract from past that part of past
    that forms and moulds one's
    senseless being.

Cynthia Barker

A Child's Letter To God

Dear God, I am but a small child,
    Whose life has just begun.
Help me to grow big and strong,
    In the rays of your great sun.
Send the rain to refresh me,
    And wash away my tears.
May the winds blow gently,
    Calming all my fears.
Then, when I've grown bigger,
    And life's turned, like the tide.
Will you walk beside me?
    Will you be my guide?
For Mommy told me you're a man,
    Whose feet have trod this way.
That is why I write this letter
    Of prayer, to you, today.

Myra Fitzell

Jamaica Inn

The wild and misty
    moorland heather
glows westwards towards
    the sea
throws salty winds and
    inclement weather
but no harm comes
    to thee.

Embers of time have embraced
    your grim coloured walls
        here history lies
            so deep within,
Mystery surrounds when
    darkness falls,
memories of Bodmin
    and Jamaica Inn.

Julie Lyons

Air Raid

Beautiful is this star filled night
With winter moon so crystal bright
Revealing street and spire and dome
And every humble little home.
Covering with a gentle grace
The bombed results of war's dark face.
Searchlights throw their beams on high
Roaming endlessly the sky
They seek an enemy who will bring
Violent death upon the wing
No cloud to hide the coming foe
Or shield from him the souls below
Who lie uneasily with fear
Of throbbing engines drawing near
And pray for snow lashed skies of grey
To help survive for one more day.

Margery O'Lone

The Summer Of '96

Death is growing inside of me
cells duplicate
unknowingly
innocently causing my pain

Contaminating my body
only doing their job
multiplying
a disgusting pregnancy of death

I would like to tear it out
to lay open the wound
and disinfect
to cure myself

A new breed of language
birthed itself with the disease
metastasis, dyskariosis
carcinoma
cancer

Susan Travis

Autumn

Gentle Autumn spins her web
Over every flower bed
Plucks each lingering tired rose
Leaving plants to sweet repose

Leaves of yellow, red and brown
Silently they flutter down
The sun is softly golden now
Waiting for Summer to take her bow

Hazy sky so softly blue
Golden days for me and you
My garden is a pleasant isle
Gentle Autumn, stay awhile.

Jean Hazelwood

Evening

Comes a peace, comes a quiet
as the long shadows creep,
And the sun slips away
as the little- ones sleep,
Here's the end of the day,
from toil we retreat,
As the blanket of night
'cross the sky gently sweeps.

Here in the evening we'll sit
you and I,
Whilst the myriads of stars
one by one meet the eye,
And we wait for the lilt of the
nightingale-gale's song,
As she trills sweet adieu
to the day now gone.

Winifred Davis

The Battlefields

Through this battle ground,
within a mist of grey,
all around lay scattered remains,
debris of yesterday.
So much pain covered by anger,
an armer to relinquish grief,
so that the struggle can go on,
to make good that past belief.
How much more shall be taken,
or how much more to give,
when all this field remains empty,
and there is no life left to live?

Janet Worthington

Untitled

Engine in line with Chassis side
Fifties found dreamer studying it.
Thought more power delivered,
If the Chassis had it athwart.

Years pass, ex trainee engineer,
Thought electric motor do trick.
Electricity made by car.
Roof solar panels help it tick.

Replaceable battery for car,
Rent one for those who can't wait.
Believed Chassis warp girders,
Up to roof and rear, strengthen it.

With weft-member joining warp side.
Finders on door bomber areas,
Restricts crushing in accidents,
Useful on buses and coaches.

Now where does this idea spring from?
The skeleton plan of tanker.
Used in warship "Kelly's" frame.
Mountbaten's ship, 2nd World War.

Gordon Ling

Militant

Capitalism, Socialism, Liberalism
'ism, 'ism, 'isms
Are the prison, prison, prisons
That entomb the Spirit.

Belief, Faith, Religion
'ion, 'ion, 'ions
Are the iron, iron, irons
That cripple the Heart.

The truth of the Brier
'ier, 'ier, 'ier
Is the ire, ire, ire
That kindles the Fire.

Peter Pugh

Why

Why oh why oh why
Do people segregate
They form in cliques and sects
In religious points relate

Why don't they realize
That whatever path they choose
They will all end up the same
It's their future they could lose

Their spirit is the future, and with
All that lust and hate
If only they could live in love
Before it is too late,

If they could live their lives in love
And personally be counted
This world would be a better place
All peoples then united.

Jessie Knox

Touch The Face Of God

Fill the void that is me
Mend the gaping soul
Seal the cavern with whispers
Make the deficient whole

Hide the cancer with plasters
The soft whisper of love
What love knows only good times
The leper who'll wear the glove?

The chasm gapes within me
Mortal is the wound
Only drowning not waving
Wave goodbye to the doomed

Hide the cancer with plasters
The soft whisper of love
What would you give for a hunter
Who cages only the dove?

Fill the void that is me
Replace the even with odd
Seal the cavern with whispers
Touch the face of God

Joanna Bryant

Awake In The Dark

In the distance roars a metal bird,
Many miles away it's heard,
Far away into the night,
Speckled by dim starry light,
Soaring over many nations,
Floating over cloud formations,
Far away into the night,
Come join me in my midnight, flight,
So far away into the night.

Ella Smith

Love Awaiting

My love is
like the Moon
in the galaxy of life...

Awaiting,
in timelessness,
the radiance
of the sun's
reflection
to burst forth
from darkness
into full nocturnal glory,

So claiming brief respite
from the shadows
and mysteries
of emotion,
which hang,
dim, suspended,
waxing and waning
in the galaxy
of life...

Margaret Mason

Park's Narsty Things

You walk through the park,
You hear a dog bark,
You slip on the grass,
People just pass,
They look at you and laugh,
You think what's wrong,
Then you smell something strong,
You look on your shoe
And you see some dog poo
You scream you shout
You have no doubt
Why can't people scoop
Their dog's poop.

Lee-Ann Kingdam

Please, Dear Friend

Please don't think of holding hands, of putting my head on your shoulder.
Please don't think of walking in mists and lying on bracken in springtime.
Please don't think of laughter-filled rainstorms as madness beyond comprehension.
Please don't think of running towards a dream we could make reality.
Please don't think of you and I shedding the sick and sad world about us.
Please don't think of midnight drives and reaching the mountain by daylight.
Please don't think of creating our space, so kind, that all is accepted.
Please don't think of the critical judge pointing their fingers towards us.
Please don't think of the jealous, the envious, who've never known true depth of feeling.
Please don't think of those who'd laugh at the poems and the romance.

Please don't think of the parting of ways, though nothing was ever started.
Please don't think of a tearful farewell, when the first real hello stays unspoken.
Please don't think of the loss of a friend, when the outlook is grey and so lonely.
Please don't think.
Please don't. Please. Please do.

Allene Norris

Balance Sheet

Debit
Ethnic minorities, housing priorities, shortages, mortgages, greed;
Lengthy recessions, paltry concessions, violence, redundancies, need.
Legal Aid rips, oil-spilling ships, child abuse freedom of Press;
Crippling taxes, bugging and faxes, corruption and arms-deal excess.
Patricide, degradation, genocide, fornication, Civil War, hatred and lust;
Homicide, drug abuse, suicide, fund misuse, morals and truth ground to dust.

Credit
Family ties, preservation, fellowship in tribulation, sincerity, sharing a crust;
Medication, education, research and inspiration, steadfastness and trust.
Love without ration, sharing, compassion, honesty, justice and care;
Charity aiding, good upright trading, strength, belief, hope and prayer.
Each of us must and can play a part to overcome all downward trends.
We hold the key to the earth's safe progress, on *us* our own safety depends.

Bessie Martin

"The Sea"

The harbour lights were a welcome sight as I hurried along the pier.
Longing to meet a loved one coming from God knows where.
I thought at first she had not come and slowly moved away,
But then I heard a gurgling sound as she lapped against the quay.
She kissed my face with her frothy lips and caressed me with a briny spray
She embraced me time and time again then slowly ebbed away.
But the breeze that took her away from me would blow her back to me some day.
I know that she will return again from that far and distance shore.
To caress and kiss me once again like a long lost love of yore.
And when I stroll along the pier in days and years to come,
I'll remember her as my first love,
My greatest love,
"My Sea."

Patrick Clendenning

Everlasting Comfort For Dunblane

Grieve deeply though you may, now that your children have gone.
No longer can they light your day, an empty void where their light shone.
The pain, the sorrow, no one can know, how deep it hurts, how hard not to show.
The other young souls looking up to see, just how to cope in such dire misery.

Go to your churches kneel and pray, pour out your feelings deep inside
The Lord will listen-whatever the day, from you the sorrow - he'll slowly divide
Death may seem final to us on earth but that is so far from right
We live in a shell, to cover our worth. Our beautiful souls safe out of sight.

Your children, never forgotten, have gone to a place beyond our Earthly belief
Released early from here - now as one. Surrounded by love, pure hearts, positive relief.
Jesus has gathered them all together; His angels will tend them while they grow
Do not grieve, it's in life's weave - our planet is small, other places we go.
   The Lord Is Here - He's with you now
   He makes a promise to this I can vow.

   "Nothing I say. Nothing will touch
   These sacred souls you all love so much."

Constance Lee

Utility, Or Ode To A Milk Bottle

Tall, cumbrous
Commonest form of man made vitreous.
Utility at its best.

Tables of the proletariat
Adorned with newsprint,
And centre piece, with faded
Flower outstanding,
Or painter's brush in dipt,
Coagulation thwarting.

Door step return,
Pristine duty waits,
Bovine juices vase.

A. M. Phillips

Soldiers Of The Lord

Soldiers of the Lord arise
to face thy mighty foe.
Lead us on to victory,
His armies we must go.

Soldiers of the Lord arise,
then on to victory.
Let us praise the Lord our God,
His glory it must be.

Soldiers of the Lord arise,
And sing thy victory.
Battle won, the day is done,
then with thy Lord to be.

Glory, glory, glory,
onwards into glory.
Merciful O mighty God,
He my Lord to be.

George R. Green

The Wild Sea Mew

The Wild Sea Mew shrieks
"Gone away, gone away.
Here by the sea
I must stay, I must stay!
Secure in my nest
I look out o'er the bay,
And twitchers they watch
Lest I stray lest I stray"

The Wild Sea Mew shrieks
"I dare say, I dare say,
They'd clip my wings too
And they may, and they may.
But one thing is certain
As night follows day,
They can't clip my soul,
Any way, any way!"

Cindy Smith

So Fragile

Tiny seeds burst prison pods
wafted on breezes soft
asking no special care
each life borne aloft

Swept away from city dust
o'er autumn fields so fair
the treasure they hold
nature shall not impair

In the quiet air
parachutes descending to earth
to rest beside a wood-land path
awaiting springs rebirth

Their beauty will live on
if blessed by sun and rain
gracing summer with golden petals
stirring joy in hearts again

Greta Craigie

Seeking Freedom

I sought freedom, freedom from the dreary routine of everyday toil.
I believed that I had found it; not intentionally, through redundancy.
But I was woven into the social fabric; not free, but not participating.
This was not freedom, merely the other side of the tossed coin;
The face that doesn't show.
I sought freedom from time; my time, usurped for another's ends.
I believed that I had found it.
Now, however, I was concerned with time.
Thoughts dwelling in the past, or formulating an uncertain future.
There is no time without thought.   Thought sabotages the meditative state.
This was not freedom, merely reformulating and justifying.
I sought freedom from ambition, the clinging to desire.
I believed that I had found it: but it was also freedom from fulfilment.
Not freedom, merely failure to distinguish ambition from destiny,
the false Gods of social construction from the inner promptings.
To flee ambition was in itself an ambition. It did not neutralize.
I gave up, stopped seeking freedom, but then I found it, really, this time.
That is, I caught a glimpse through the fog of my conditioned mind.
Attainable if this fog can be made to disperse.
It is simple. Freedom does not come through escape. It is not 'from'.
It is simply 'not seeking'.

Dennis Platten

April On The Broads

First light of morn in crisp, fresh Norfolk air, sailing deserted
waters of the Yare. Budded willows to the water weeping. Silent
spire, Hamlet's still a'sleeping.
Breakfast time - the brazen ducks on deck take greedily - ignoring
swans long neck. Crested coots, too shy to wander near, were you the
fluffy chicks I saw last year? Suddenly the water round me heaving,
with geese all making greedily sure I'm leaving plenty for all who
know this time's the best, and steal the loveliest hour from the rest.

Mood of river reflects the restless sky - clouds above fast scurrying,
while I meander past where unseen hands have hacked the reeds
now ready baled and neatly stacked.
Darkened silhouettes of leafless trees, satin river whipped up with
sudden breeze. Glorious sun lights up each tiny wave, makes colour in
an instant - oh to save. Visiting here is to another time, untouched
by greed and inner city grime.
Rough weather cannot mar the peaceful bliss. The only charge
remembering that - and this.

Last day, a perfect week has nearly passed. Can time that stands
still really go so fast? Throughout the year, whenever time affords -
I'll pause, remembering April on the broads.

Helen Jacob

Polish Village 1965

Before I came I knew this place, but I heard it had a different face.
Now unkempt roads came to converge, upon a scene, a village square
where Sundays men wore dark blue serge and Sundays girls would long to stare
at brown faced soldiers home on leave, they'd boast a little
here and there, some new promotion on the sleeve or sometimes in those
warm Septembers about their terrible manoeuvres.

I heard that all around the square were little shops, most kept by Jews
half empty now with shelves kept bare.
The sultry light through open doors, invites an ambidextrous hen or two,
and over there beside the limes, the church still slumbering in
the corner awaking only every quarter to give the time in sleepy chimes.

Out now beyond the village bounds, the graveyard still the vigils keep
by ever silent shady corner, tall summer grasses intertwined
Among the rusted crosses, they mark the places while they sleep
For those Franz Joseph's men enshrined,
Twin headed eagles, pickel helmets, all but rust away
Cry echoes of a distant day, when Kaiser's men fought
Other men, in strife both never sought
Into battles, often driven, performing black deeds, long forgiven.

Lorna Gasowska

Looking Down The Lightning

It's a force born of elements
immeasurable in their power,
building, building upwards,
growing heavier by the hour.
Colours of threatened menace,
give an eeriness to the air,
an awareness of boundless energy,
a heavy silence everywhere.

As seductive as it's awesome,
A violent explosion cracks the night,
forks shoot through the clouds,
thunder crashes through the light.
You're up there, like a God,
electric fingers taught and tight,
you're looking down the lightning,
and you rule the world tonight!

Joyce Stark

Bossy Women

I do hate bossy women
They drive me round the bend
They seem to think they know it all
Ad-lib and without end

Should you have any ideas at all
Be sure they won't last long
Bossy boots will soon stop that
She'll tell you you're all wrong!!

Oh! I hate bossy women
So there's just one thing to do
Avoid them - like the plague they are
Or it's something you will rue

Let me whisper quietly -
Just between me and you
I prefer bossy men!!!

Enid Booth

Untitled

Across the waters and far away,
I'm coming home I hear you say,
To be within your arms again,
I'll hold you close, and keep you near,
My love you've been away so long,
You'll return to me, and then it's done,
Cause now I know you're here with me,
I'll never let you go again,
And so to bring this to a close
I love you darling, now let's go!

C. L. Sutton

The Father

A drop of water
A teardrop
In your ocean blue eyes
In which
I drown myself
Such sorrow!
Such gladness!
A rose pink
Nipple

A teardrop of mick
Mother's milk
It bleeds
Such joy!
I lick it, my taste buds quiver
I shake with delight
My wife our son; myself
all one

Anne Marie Macleod

The Imbalance

All along the sleepless hours men dream within their ivory towers,
Of profit looming large as life while hunger cutting like a knife,
Precedes the reaper with his blade and fells a man who was betrayed,
Not just by 'brothers' in the West whose butter-mountains are the best,
But also famine in the East where the masses have increased,
To levels which they can't support and just to live they must import,
All food at an inflated price - an economic cash device,
Which makes one rich, another poor but all this must be changed before,
This beautiful and ancient race has disappeared without a trace,
From this our own fair Mother Earth whose nourishment about her girth,
Should be enough for all to share and feed the starving everywhere,
Here, where selfishness is rife, what then is the price of life?
For caring people seem so few yet others say: 'What can I do?'
Now is the time; become aware no longer just to stand and stare,
Act now and make a solemn vow, dying children need you now,
The sharing out has just begun, there is enough for everyone...

John Parslow

Untitled

It's nearly nine and time to go, full of fear from tip to toe.
And all around unsmiling face. No room for Love in this sad place.
My hands they tie behind my back, and over head a cotton sack.
No more for me the right to see the gentle hands that torment me.
A last, last prayer I gasp in haste, may God go with me from this place.

Gordon Hassall

You Who Are Blind.....

You who are blind to my wishes, do not ask me to see with your eyes,
For I see the beauty in nature, yet when you look the beauty all dies
You who are blind to love's power, do not ask me to give you my heart.
It is not in my power to love you, I cherish that days spent apart.

You who are blind to all suffering, do not tell me that you now feel pain.
Young people around me are dying, what right have you to complain?
You who are blind to the homeless, do not ask me to shelter you now,
I know the streets are the homes of some children, they suffer more than we should allow.

You who are blind in your judgement, do not ask me to show you the way
You flounder in your seas of illusion; even my advice will set you astray.
You who are blind through choice, do not ask me to change your mind,
For I can see clearer than you do, though I am, in the true sense; blind.

Neena Sabharwal

Dylan

I have seen the gates of hell tonight, and walked alone through tunnels dark
I have stared into the devils eyes, and had him leave his dreadful mark
I have witnessed fear, ineffable, seen terror rent on wretched heart
I have played the black minds game, seen sights absurd, stood apart

I have cried with tears of blood tonight, watched while others paid with life
I have heard the screams of fear shrill, when entrails drawn out on the knife
I have no reason for these gruesome sights, no cause to fathom can I see
I have nothing left that can ever justify, why all were slain to save but me

I have thought hard since this time tonight, what augurs now my futures part
I have wandered timeless time to find, that I know now my end must start
I have struggled this lifelong through, just to see myself loose the fight
I have tried, but Satan's won my soul, now I know I died tonight

Alan R. Speight

An Eccentric Yank

A Yank
Chewing Gum
Queued at the bank.
"This is like a prison, chum."
He said to me and my heart sank.
As everyone observed him sipping rum.
He wasn't at all concerned and looked blank,
"What's the matter with these people, are they dumb?"
"No," I replied, "but drinking here they think you're a crank."
"Me a crank!" he cried, "To such eccentricities I never succumb!
I only drink!" and from his pocket he drew out another bottle and drank!

Elizabeth K. M. Hunter

The Unknown

When night doth fall from
the sky above,
O those stars and their twinkling beams,
Rush through that sky like
spirited doves,
And help poor man to dream,
On it goes right through the night,
Its vigil none dare question,
It waits not, like the crushing wave,
Taking both weak and brave.
Er' it's gone is dawn's delight,
Farewell imagination.

John F. O'Brien

Life

Bought into the world without consultation,
A tiny baby; the next generation.
Hands of parents eagerly await,
This child now becomes a victim of fate.

Nursed and cared for in every way,
Parents watch children grow every day.
They try to do their very best,
to make that child beat the rest.

As teenage years replace childhood fun,
The next stage of battle must be won.
Parents convinced that they are right,
A strong-willed teenager ready to fight.

The understanding arrives with adulthood,
That the yelling and groundings were for your own good
Your respect now grows you forget the strife,
You realize your parents have shaped your life.

A partner arrives - a husband or wife,
Someone very special to share your life.
Then when your very first child is due,
you'll appreciate the problems your parents had with you.

Fiona Birt

Murder

Blood trickles down the lifeless hand,
And splashes to the floor,
From the centre of the blood, the heart,
That beats with life no more,
Even though the muscles tight,
The brain it lies at rest,
Set about by the blade
Stuck deep inside the chest,
The eyes lie open, as if to stare at me,
But no colours, pictures or designs,
Will those eyes ever see.
The face drained white,
The hands gone frail,
A thousand years a slave
Committed not a single crime
But sentenced to the grave.

Helen Corbett

Cottage In Devon

I fain would retire to my cot' by the sea
Where the roar of the billows comes clearly to me,
And when dusk has fallen the scent of the flowers,
Comes in through the window to brighten the hours,
The shades of the night lengthen, the cottage fire glows,
Peace - in my heart - gently steals,
Morning dawns - misty, then clear the light grows
And the glory of Devon reveals.
I'd wander along, 'twixt the hedgerows bright
Where the musk roses bloomed, afresh, o'ernight,
And the cool morning breeze fans my cheek as I go
Down to the sea, where the tide is low.
Friends of my childhood, there to meet
Seagulls! - just back- with the fishing fleet.

Amy Seagull

Final Thoughts

Seeing in believing, feeling is the
naked truth...
Did you see and believe when you
past this blue sky...
Did you feel the naked love when
truth and love unites.

Did your soul fly like a bird, free...
do you see colours flowers hear music,
can you walk...or is there silence
beyond the blue sky.

Did I really hear your voice last
night, and feel you touch my brow.
If I could see I would believe...
and feeling as I do truly is the naked truth.

You felt the naked truth of life through death,
you felt your soul rise to a height...I can't
imagine, oh! Joy to see beyond the
rainbow...I feel we will meet again!

Susan Al-Azzawi

Mountain Idyll

From rocky steeps 'neath storm-tossed sky
The mighty eagle soaring free on high
Surveys his Kingdom from on high
With mountain-matching majesty.

He sees the infant river's birth,
Then headlong down the bouldered glen
Coursing to meet the level earth
It leaps, it rests, then leaps again.

From hostile crag and slippery screes
Through heathered moorland's spreading span
With keening winds and stunted trees
By blackcock grouse and Ptarmigan.

Onward to forest's leafy glade
Through peaty pools and runs to wind,
Songbird and squirrel share the shade
With roaring stag and quiet hind.

At last the hectic race is run
To join the loch in sheltered bay,
See darting flies and otters' fun
And Lordly osprey seek his prey.

Teri Wharton

The Catalyst

Depth of thought gone unchallenged
The catalyst separates need from change
Resurrection a spoil for the chosen metaphor,
Letters of pain read like the life of Caesar
Tamed to no avail, the catalyst wanders

Closer it comes, unwinding my feelings
Never half the pain my burden unfolds
Drawn closer to earth, her smell unforgettable
Eden reckoned with by principled thoughts
The alter of you unbending and unbreakable

A Trojan heart required to break the bough of destined thoughts
How do I reckon with the catalyst
My own sweet black shadows mourn, dark as Kali's heart
As this life weaned from hurt, cowers from solitude
Pass over me like a shower of faith, cooled by love

The catalyst's inflection abiding to hope
No option given to pain
The wait immeasurable, helpless in my throes
The catalyst's season's roll into one, years to wait
As every pore spoils, my marble vault stays unchallenged.

Jamie Gordon Renton

Welcome Mat

Discarded as a doormat is, when 'Welcome's worn out weary,
    downtrodden, frayed and faded, impossible to sell.'
But the nicest piece of home I think, greeting friend and stranger,
    the first to say 'good day' to guests, the last to wave farewell.
    And when it is that wear and tear prevail
    the mat is seldom wrapped with debris other, but left to rot
    through wind and rain and gale.
It must be, though, that one day mats
    will stop and shake themselves of stone and grit
    and prove to be as fanciful as dry-cleaned hats
    that sit on cupboards or heads as uselessly as hats,
    but mats
    they learn their welcome is important,
    to shake sand free and learn to see
    the need for them on doorsteps.
First to greet the company,
    to learn of hearsay, pain and glee,
    to take the mud from soles of shoes as clues
    to puzzles of life, its people, its news
        and to be amused.
    Theresa Lamont

The Love Of A Butterfly

My Dear - you are my Butterfly:
I am the little boy trying to catch you.

You fly hither and you in a distant land,
I am the little boy trying to catch you.

You are lovely to watch in the brightness of life,
I am the little boy trying to catch you.

You light upon the flower of life and your beauty radiates,
I am the little boy trying to catch you.

You fly higher than the reach of my arms,
I am the little boy trying to catch you.

You fly into a distant yard,
I am the little boy trying to catch you.

You fly and return as my love,
I am the little boy trying to catch you.

So now, I drift slowly having captured my butterfly,
I am the little boy who tried and caught you.
    Paul G. Blacketor

Market Research

Could you help me? Where was it seen?
Did you enjoy it? How long it has been?
These are the questions to name just a few
The researchers are asking of me and you.
Was it witty? Enjoyable? Funny or clever?
Have you bought it? Often or never?
It's hard to remember and yet they implore
That you think very hard and remember yet more.
All these answers to make products more tempting to buy
To give us more service or so they imply.
So when we are dazzled by such an array
Who benefits we may ask at the end of the day?
Who's left with the bill which someone must pay?
Not the makers, retailers or the people we see
No it just boils down to us and that's you and Me!
    Alice Turner

Memories

My love, I have known you for forty years.
We read each other's thoughts like an open book.
We have shared the joy, the sadness, the sorrow.
So many things have changed in time.
The family we had have flown the nest and now we are many.
The years we have left are racing by and
still so many things to achieve.
If only life would stand still for a while
to give us chance to collect our thoughts.
    Edna Day

"The Storm"

Grief, cascading around like a never-ending storm,
A sudden sense of loss devours the conscious mind,
Clouding normality of routine existence,
Peace of mind being left behind.

Sinking deeper and deeper encased in misery,
Flailing blindly where insanity will loom,
As everyday life pales to insignificance,
Following a winding pathway of gloom.

Then a ray of hope emerges slowly,
That winter emotion yields into spring,
Through blackened clouds a shimmer of light,
From a deep, dark crevice reluctantly surfacing,

Despite the brightness, a shadow cast,
Though no longer intrusive or foreboding,
A welcome reminder, now fondly regarded,
Joyful memories warmly generating.

Now looking forward to new horizons,
A new found hope to ease the pain,
As life goes on and bereavement wanes.
That loved one, lost, did not die in vain.
    Avril Trotter

By The Window

Oh let me weep.
Do not stop the tears, flowing onto my
bare hands, drowning in my lap.
My bent head,
so full of grief for your lost life,
spent in its bloom - so young and strong.
Where you once sat, I sit,
by the window all alone.
No longer must I set a place at table
and listen to your grace.
To see your smiling face so full of love.
The very arm I need around me,
no longer here.
How could you die and leave me so alone?
Your strength was my strength.
Now I must live this life without your
love so strong.
What words shall I use to comfort little
eyes enlarged with glistening tears,
when I am so full of grief for my lost love.
    Jennifer Hedges

The Lover

A broken hearts that needs mending
A solution that not impending
I do to sleep nervously awaiting my lover to visit me
The night is long, the bell fails to ring
The haunting memories begin.

A fool I have been to no avail
Unloved, unwanted a long sad tale
I must recover the strength I once had
Separating the fool from the cad.

The journey forward must prevail
I need to walk that long hard trail
Heading forward to journeys end
I need a place to stay therein
To mend my heart been broken within.

I will move back to this place
And join once more the human race
The world out there being a joyous place
I feel a need to enter that "race".

A great contester I will be, Red Rum having nothing on me
Starting off at 10-1 what's the bet I end up odds-on!
    Lee Lowsley

357

The Tramp

Lay on a pavement in a Manchester street,
Was a poor old tramp with bleeding feet.
People just looked and went on their way,
Just hoping someone would help him away.

He must have been some mother's joy,
When he was a baby boy.
He may have grown up loving and kind,
and looking for a job was hard to find.

If the truth we only knew,
It would be a sad tale that's true.
In the winter what can they do,
Many die with cold with no one to turn to.

In the old days if a tramp you would see,
It would be a bob for the road and a cup of tea.
Many were given a little job,
They would never go out and rob.
We should have a thought for these people each day,
If we can't help, then for them we can pray.

Marie Mitchell

To A Teenager

Do not write me off because I am old
I know what life's about, I too was young
In a world full of conflict and doubt.
Your problems though different are yet the same
As the ones I encountered, striving to reach my aim,
A wish to be recognised, a voice to be heard,
To make one's own decisions, above all to be loved.
We all err at some time, both the young and old
The generation gap is not as wide as we are told
So learning one from the other, the present
And the past, the young and old together,
That should be our task.

Elizabeth Gray

The Hill That Beckons

Wherever you gather to mourn for me,
Think not only of the life I had.
Fill your hearts with love for each other;
Where I have gone, I feel not sad.

I walked life's paths for many years
And glimpsed a hill that I should climb;
To look beyond and there seek peace,
And rest with others for all time.

So gather not to feel afraid,
Let not your grief obstruct this view.
Open your eyes and with your hearts,
Seek out the hill which is there for you.

In whispered tones, tell of this hill.
Let those who mourn dwell on this sight.
For now the eyes which shed your tears,
Reveal to you the 'Hill of Light'

Constance M. Hughes

Children Of War

Innocent children killed every day,
it cannot be avoided, for they can't run away.
They do not understand and we can only ask why.
I see no reason for them to die.
They have done nothing; they are not to blame,
they should not be a part of this adult game.
A young child stands alone in a devastated street,
his parents are dead; he has no shoes on his feet.
As day turns to night, he is all alone,
in a deserted world, which to him is unknown.
His eyes search the debris, he does not ask for much,
just a comforting word and a tender touch.
As it starts to get colder, he begins to cry.
Another helpless child left to die.

Michelle Williams

Epitaph For Sadie

Your picture looks down from the TV
You lovable faithful old hound
Why did you have to leave us
We just loved having you around

There are times I forget you aren't here
And boldly cry out your name
Expecting to see you come running
And look for you always in vain

You were the odd one in the litter
As a springer you didn't make the grade
Your teeth had an uneven number
Not for you cruft's show parade

Obedience wasn't your strong point
You always just went your own way
But faithful loving simply gorgeous
Our lives stopped when you died on that day...

Jill Howard

Ebbing Tide

Glinting turquoise muted roar,
Losing a lunar tug of war.
Crashing whiteness, curling round
Stark black pinnacles
Retreat with my turmoil.

Advance again, but with each withdrawal
Calm my spirit — smooth, like the abandoned sand.
Ebb away desolation, leave the spirit free
To fly with sunbeams, an aqua reflection to the skies.

Judy Podger

Wishes For All Children - When They Are Grown

To still see in each new leaf on a tree -
    the beauty of it.
To still see in each pattern on a pebble -
    the mystery of it.
To still see in all the colours of the sunset -
    the glory of it.
To still feel in the greatness of a mountain -
    the majesty of it.
To still hear in the chirping of a grasshopper -
    the joy of it.
To still find in the simplest of flowers -
    the fragrance of it.
To still see in the flight of a bird -
    the splendour of it.
To sense in a touch, a look or a word -
    the warmth of it.
To find in the cry of a child new born -
    the wonder of it.
To find in all things freely given -
    the love of it.

Christine Sorensen

"Wastes Of Mongolia"

The ravages of time, enshrouds the land
Where stretch the empty wastes, of desert far
And sand dust strewn across the open plain
By winds of storm, beneath a lonely star.

Where once Empires stood in noble pride
And cities thrived with human toil
Wars were fought, were won and lost
Great mysteries of time unfold.

Forests that flourished, now tree-less and baron
Vast expanses of land, stand unclaimed
Whilst virgin snows on Mountain Peaks.
Hold secrets of those bygone days

As daylight approaches, and sunrise glows
Wind swept sand storms, go drifting by
Across those ghostly arid plains
To meet up, with a lurid sky.

Derek Ralph Winter

Moving On In Time

Struggle wins the fight
Pain overshadows the end
Cares, troubles are in sight
Time is solution to mend.

Bottle up regret and sorrow
Never to be feelings of peace
Without the sun will we see tomorrow
Sleep welcome, wakefulness not to cease

Walk through tunnel of Memory
Halt the dream forever more
Turn another chapter heart bearing no injury
In my mind events, happenings forever to store

Deirdre Shanagher

Northumbria

Alnwick, Bamburgh, Warkworth so small
Each with a castle so proud and so tall
Dunstanburgh Castle, ruined and shorn
Part of our history our heritage born

Priories and Churches, ancient and aged
Memories of battles and clashes once waged
Northumbria, once seat of Kings, county so Royal
St Aidan, St Bede, Christian leaders so loyal

A wall built by Romans, so brave and so bold
A gibbet on moorland maketh blood runneth cold
Carved out of history, ruled by iron hand
Born long ago, was my Northumberland.

Jacqueline McArthur

Happiness

Happiness is peace of mind, this comes from within.
If contented you will find, your life will begin
To have a brighter meaning,
You'll have more strength to cope
Try and laugh at all your troubles,
Don't give in, but hope.

Happy people always find, little things give pleasure,
Birds and bees, flowers and trees,
Can all be seen at leisure.
It's good to have ambition, but sometimes we forget,
Whilst seeking recognition, the years pass with regret.

It's good to stand and stare sometimes,
Enjoy a little peace, relaxations not a crime,
Let your worries cease, find joy and love in all you do
Then you will possess, a rich reward,
No more feeling bored, you're treasured,
    Happiness!

Dorothy Wardman

Samantha - Christina

I was part of a miracle today!
My baby was born, a beautiful girl,
I cut the cord, saw her first breath,
Heard her first cry, felt her enter my world.

I've never felt a feeling this strong,
Or a bond so true, such deep affection,
My horizons, my priorities change in a flash,
My life journeys in a new direction,

I can hardly believe it myself,
I'm a dad and it's a miracle,
I told my fourth complete stranger today,
This great "joy-love" reaching out to touch the cynical.

I'm a dad! I'm a father! I created a life!
I've found love's greatest pinnacle,
Is it all part of a master plan?
Who cares! It's a miracle...

    And I'm a dad!

Leigh Rawlins

Dawn

Water cascades from the sheltering sky,
As daybreak defeats the perilous night.
Thunder and lightning, preparing to die,
Gather together determined to fight.
A girl cries indistinguishable tears,
Masquerading themselves as falling rain.
No one realises her secret fears,
Her conscience cries in unbearable pain.
On the horizon, a glimmer of hope,
As Apollo drives his chariot on.
Perhaps after all this young girl can cope,
Supported by nature, her fears are gone.
    Out of the thrashing storm comes tranquil dawn,
    With each new day, hope and peace are born.

Joanne Carroll

Spring

Oh you spring, oh you cheat
    With your promise of heat,
You fickle made thing called the Spring.

The flowers you make grow,
    Yet you threaten with snow
And cast all around with cold winds.

One day the sun shines,
    A promise that's fine.
Next day you send rain
    And you promised in vain.

The sun it breaks through,
    Then the clouds follow too.
Oh you spring, oh you cheat
    With your promise of heat,
You fickle made thing called the Spring.

Carlton Owens

A Mother

A Mother is one who bears,
    one who cares, one who shares.

A Mother is always fair,
    always kind, always there.

A Mother is strong and tough,
    soft and gentle, never rough.

A Mother puts food on the table,
    never ill, always able.

A Mother is a special playmate,
    a true friend, never late.

A Mother is someone rare,
    when she is gone, there are no spare.

Ann Ogilvie

'Who Hears?'

Who hears the silent pleading
In those dark pools of light?
That gaze, shouting shame on our
Indifference.

In one child's eyes I hear
The elegy of Africa
Echoing across the barren space
Of the Western mind.

More immediate, more pressing sounds
Invade our eyes, our ears, our mind.
The News and Weather; a car door slamming.

'Muzak' the aural blue tranquillizer
Guaranteed to silence
The cries of the hungry
Stilling the voice of Africa
Till we hear it no more.

Madeleine Harvey

The Sun Will Shine Right Through

Although the years have passed,
Our thoughts have never died.
And all the fond memories we
share, will always be alive.

The vacant place the empty chair,
Our lives aren't right without him there.
His cheeky smile, and the love we
knew, will always be remembered too.

As Husband, Dad and Granddad
keeps within our hearts,
And there he will remain,
To walk beside us all our lives,
Until we meet again.

And on this anniversary, don't be
sad and blue.
Just think of all the happy times,
and the sun will shine right through.

Charlotte Wheatley

The Happening

Shoulders square, solid as English oak;
Yet bearing the youth of a sapling.
Would that I could have laid my eyes upon his countenance before.

His eyes, though retaining vision, possessed an irregularity of angle;
Remoulding of the cheekbones had produced a strange incongruity
Creating a mask-like appearance, not quite integral.

Communication, one felt, had somehow become impaired;
Concentration strained to its utmost limits.
His whole being pleaded, crying out to be understood and accepted.

We talked together, uneasily,
Aware that his face had become a barrier between us;
The happening had a great deal to answer for -

G. M. Beckett

Cloudsong

The strident drums of commerce beat the air,
A dirge that winds and weaves the cords that bind.
But bind no more, for I'll away to where
The Cloudsong calls, and nature's garden find.

Here crimson Eve on dappled pool reclines,
Bedecked in gold and jewelled leaves that fall,
From hanging bough the honey flow'r entwines
My love, where the sentinel trees stand tall.

With twice sung call the thrush now pipes his song
Of Eden joy, where blue-bells silent ring,
And all reflected heaven flows along
These woodland ways where winding waters sing,
    All joy rides the sky on a Cloudsong day,
    And earth's dark shadows are all swept away.

Alan Raymond Stanley

Spirit Of The Wind

The wind blows through the trees
Playing havoc with the leaves
The wind is ever changing always raging
Wind has many moods, it can be kind and gentle,
Harsh and angry or it can be playful as it plays with your hair
When the wind blows it makes a song
The rustle of the leaves, the whistle of the trees in the breeze.
I love the sound of the wind, it is so wild and free
The wind has seen many things and visited many places.
Oh how I love the wind, when the wind blows
My spirit wishes to be free to float with the wind
Wind is a powerful thing so turbulent and wise
From seeing things as it travels around, sometimes hardly
    making a sound
I wish I could ride the wind, see the things it sees
Travel to places beyond my wildest dreams
Wind, I wish to go with thee, to be free.

Tania Martin

A Box

Home for him,
A cardboard box in a doorway of a deserted shop.
With only a worn blanket to protect him from the harsh winter night,
The rain, jumping from the cracked paving slabs,
A cloud of fog worms its way between the people.
The traffic, sitting, watching, waiting,
He is his own best friend,
For only he knows the pain he's suffered,
    the loss he's lost.
Only he understands the shame he feels when a
    passerby flashes a look of pity,
His soul and body dying,
His eyes revealing nothing,
His lips a shade of death,
His heart slowing,
His world crumbling,
But he has shelter,
    A box,
        To hide him.

Rebecca Carpenter

Zilch

I sit
Papers stacked
Pen poised
I pause
Is it this or that
That or this
Thee or thou
I or is.
I ask the hazy passages of my mind.

The front door bell jangles
The milkman is paid
I sit again pen in hand
As raindrops patter on my window.

Is it that or this
Is or was
Do or don't
The moment passes as I fail
To unlock the frozen passages of my mind
My pen falls
As cheek on hand I sleep.

Evelyn Ida Henfield

The Earth

The Earth was once blue and green,
The air was once fresh and clean.
Years go by without a trace,
Until God made the human race.

Fires destroy the plants and trees,
Whilst pesticides kill the birds and the bees.
Oil floating in the water,
Fish and mammals sent to slaughter.

The Earth is now brown and grey,
As God looks down and sighs today.
The Earth is crying with stress and strain,
As it shows the face of pain.

Now the Earth is such a state,
Is this the end?
Or is it too *late?*

Phillip C. Blackstaffe

Untitled

I prayed for someone like you in '82
and you came to me in '83
but in '84, upon a foreign floor
I said the words that I will always regret,
Time will heal but I will never forget
those lessons I learnt and the teacher who taught;
For I know now that what we had could never be bought
This leaves me alone and most distraught!

Paul Crinson

The Lost Miracle

No moss encrusted stone to weep beside
For this life which grew here within,
And wearily climbing the stairs at night
Only tiny spirit footsteps trace my path.
The empty swing moves only by the wind
And no childish laughter follows in its wake,
Only ethereal lips will suckle my breasts
And phantom cries disturb my slumbers.
Frantic nursery preparation all in vain
For I never felt you move inside me,
My first picture of you dark and vacant
Confirmed you would not come home.
Now all I have are barren, aching arms
For in my sleep the angels carried you away
And now when I wake, often, through the night
I know the miracle of life is lost to me.

Caren Christophorou

Col De Soulor

Quiet and listen to a blade of grass
And a dead leaf. Quiet listen
to a symphony of silver threaded softness,
Wafer-warble thin song
And clear-brim trillness
Still and absorb rattle-dry verdant
Cricket, cluck farmland and bell-bleat fallow
Bark into order and wander again
Absorb and quivering blade point symmetry
Green-brown shading lightly to silver,
Edged gold levels mingling mellow peace
With snow capped serenity and permanence,
Splendour and majesty, meet to meadow, and wander again.

Anthea Rogers

"It's Not Fair I'm Short!"

It's not fair I'm short, "Let's chase him," shouts
the gang, "he is a baby, he sleeps with his little
Ted. Hand over your cash or I'll shoot you dead!"

It's not fair I'm short. I get pushed and shoved
out of the way at school to get to my locker.
"Get out of the way shrimp" "Here's shorty".
"Baby, baby you look like a six year old!"

It's not fair I'm short. I'm not That short! "Huh"
was their answer.

I have got to hide somewhere, now where shall I hide?
In the corridor? No way, lots of tall people there.
In my locker? No! I'll fit but a bit uncomfortable.
I guess it's just silly old shrimp for the rest of my life.
"There he is!" shouts the nasty gang.

Sharon Nourani

Future

So our time at school is at an end
To you only one piece of advice I will lend
Another part of the book of life is closed
But from the depths of the past the future has rose
The passing of time only a state of mind
Keep open your heart and the will to continue you will find
Old friends and loves you may have lost
Their absence nothing more could cost
Out of reach they all may seem
Once part of your group, the past team
Scared you may be, all alone
All that is needed is to pick up the phone
On the other end is past and future the same
Times gone by side by side with future fame
Words of wisdom heard and said
Time to remember and prepare for the challenges ahead
Life is but a game God did send
A game that can be conquered with the help of a friend.

Scott Porter

Meditation

Solitude,
Darkness pierced by golden candlelight;
A halo fading to the periphery of the mind.
Heartbeat,
Sole sound in isolation, the pumping of life.
Creator and created, meeting place.

Solemnity,
Monastic ministration, an 'Opus Dei';
Stillness, so exciting - yet so hard to find.
Alone,
In awesome passion; perfect panacea,
Listening, searching for the silent Holy Word.

Majestic,
Incessant, the power of quiet contemplation;
Placid intercession; thrice channelled grace.
Peace.
Salvation, sanctuary; redemption now made manifest;
In Paternal love, through Son and Living Flame.

Gerald S. Bell

The Storm

Small, soft voice of pregnant calm,
Prophetic phial of Nature's balm,
Foretells extravagant display
Of power unleashed.

Dull, distant ominous roar
Heavy laden storm clouds soar,
As flights of birds on the wing
Seek safer haven.

In trice the fury is released
As lightning strikes the earth beneath,
While thunder crash on ears vibrate
In deafening din.

Shrieking, mad, satanic sight,
Outwith earthly harness bight,
There is naught that man has yet devised
Beats Nature's glory.

Nessie McKinlay

"The Figure Of Peace"

How still thou art,
In peace thou depart,
No more sorrows thou shall know,
No tears, no grief, just joy where you go.
We poor beings are living through hell,
But thou, the Heavens of earth now shall tell.
What life this is? We cry and feel sad,
Because thus art gone for good from the bad.
As we stand here we plead,
"Just one word do say! Up there art thou sad?"
or say, "art thou gay?"
No answer doth come from that figure of peace,
Nothing but silence that mocks us to cease,
And so we shall wait until we do die,
To meet our dear friend in the Heavens so high.
Till then we must live through this World full of grief,
Trust in God and strong in our only belief.

Hebe Georgiades-Mitchell

Born Again

I have been consumed
By the mire of mundanity,
Have been dragged too far
Into the fire of forgetfulness.
But the proud phoenix of Inspiration
Has held me in her claws
And pulled me to a sweet moor of memories,
From whence I can stand without fear,
And contemplate the optimistic
Fields of future.

Carol O'Connor

Daddy's Coming Home

The young one's in his bed now
He cried himself to sleep
Over the daddy that he lost
Or was destined never to meet

You were coming home today
To see your little son
He'd brought his favourite down
To greet his daddy home

You'd never seen your son before
You left before I borne him
I love him dearly with all my heart
And all you could do was mourn him

Your daddy's coming home today
You should have seen his little face
Now I have to say to him
"Daddy will not be home now - he's gone to a better place"

D. Allely

Why

Why do we wonder
Why do we ponder
Is it because we have the time
To think about the past
And to work out what is lost
and to what cost

Our lives are always filled with whys
From the day we enter the world
Until the day we depart
The whys are always in our hearts
Why the sad times
And why the good times
And why the whys

Perhaps one day we will have all the answers
But what would we have left to wonder
Life might become less fun
And we would be left where we had begun

Karen Hines

Winter Slumbers

Like gnarled fingers clawing at the winter sky,
All that was left I saw as I walked by
Of an avenue of lovely limes, that had in summer been,
A shady place to walk, beneath their canopy of green.
Shimmering leaves that rustled, swaying gently in the breeze.
Alive with an excited hum of pleasure from a multitude of bees.
Lingeringly I had wandered; Oh what reverence did prevail,
This transcendent beauty quite held me in its spell.
Now stark and bare, their crowning glory wantonly destroyed,
My spirits ebbed away, I really felt annoyed,
That a beauty so sublime could so recklessly be cast away;
No insight, No planning for the pleasures of another day.
Weeks passed before I could make myself walk that way again,
Knowing it would renew my anger, intensify my pain.
I stood entranced, eyes wide with disbelief, each one
Had sprouted forth to meet the warmth of springtime sun.
No longer gnarled and old, no longer stark and bare,
But once again resplendent, proud to be growing there.

Hazel Wellman

Bush Fire

A giant, wilful, golden wave
erupts into fierce clusters of wild flames,
exuding live sparks of drifting fire.

The transfiguring wind
gathers, rolls and drops in a glowing track,
of red, raw and amber scorching embers.

Then, that thick whirlwind of black dust,
clogging the scarlet air, clouding the blue sky
and sinking the golden sun.

Consuelo Rafart

Eternal Love

You may think me sentimental
When I write to you this way
But I love you very dearly in a very special way
Because whenever I see you sad
I feel sad too
For the heart that hears within me
Will always belong to you
I never knew what love really meant.
Until I met you
That is why I keep telling you
My love is really true
So cheer up my darling and never fear
Where ever you go
I shall always be near
I shall try not to grieve
When you have gone because we both know
That life must go on.
I'll try not to be lonely or shed many tears
Because I did my best for you when you needed me most
The last few years

Jessie Tranter

Heaven

Heaven is an unknown place,
It's a place for us the human race,
It's a place that we can look forward to,
A place we have to die to do,
It's a place we think that all is good,
And no-one knows, do you think we should?
Heaven is an unknown place,
An unknown place to us the human race.

Michelle Bowers

The Passing Of Youth

The passing of youth
How quickly the pages of time have turned
A face once fair with beauty
Hair as black as ravens' wings
So light of foot and steps so gay

Alas time came calling
Like a thief in the night
He stole away my youth
Now, though suddenly it seems
A faded rose amongst new buds

Like a flightless bird that yearns to soar
How clever the snake to be free of that old skin
Emerge once again anew
Oh, how sad the passing of youth

Ann Fenton

Elusive Love

To perchance to dream of touching perfection, a golden lining
    without any seams.
Quintessential timing, a food to nurture all those tiny seeds.
Unspoken requirements of warmth, sincerity and truth.
Every quality impact, representing beauty and youth.
To be encased in all that is innocent and pure.
Resulting in a new life, a miracle I'm sure.
To reach out as heavens' golden gates open wide.
The suns' rays dart through landing by our side.
In the distance the mist caresses the contours of your face.
Yet I cannot quite reach as it gently folds into place.

There are no nets, no chains to hold it in, as I taste
That special truth, unspoken and yet interfaced.
Oh! to touch perfection, a sanctuary without a doubt.
Encased in a trust, a love that one couldn't breathe without
Yet mine is a dream, a mirage I fear.
The dawn breaks through and the stars disappear.
Love is indeed elusive, a rare butterfly.
Showering its beauty as it fans the air nearby.

Lynne Hulme

Take Heed

People rushing here and there.
They have no time to spare.
If only I could make them aware.
That they have the ability to care.
It is so unfair.
We have forgotten how to share.
True happiness today is so rare.
Married couples find it hard to stay a pair.
Our morals are in despair.
We take until the cupboard is bare.
Our selfishness is everywhere.
We even contaminated the air.
To rebel instead of conform we do not dare.
We are now so close to the devil's lair.
I have to warn you, beware.
Say a prayer.
Though he may claw and tear.
He cannot reach my heart, for dear God, you are there.

Mandy Jane Gainford

Sensual

This baby boy so close to me
grows heavier, weighty, on my knee.
Grows heavier, sweeter, in my arms.
Emulating, already, his father's charms,
Slumbering deeply against my breast.
Snuffling, trusting, his precious breath
is music to my ears.
And any sorrow he can feel
is both my sorrow and my fear.
Damp tendrils whisper against my lips
as I gently kiss his downy head.
This sweet spirit gives my heart wings
yet makes it earth bound, heavy as lead.
A surge of love deep down inside
Liquid, hot and undenied.
This baby of me
From me
Me
How can I ever cease to be
sensual. A woman.

Elaine Mellor

Memories

It isn't just the lonely nights that makes me think of you.
It isn't just the early dawn with grass wet with the dew.
It isn't just the summer rain in which we used to walk,
Or the ringing of the telephone on which we loved to talk.
It isn't just the winter winds that in the chimneys moan,
Or the single coffee cup which stands there all alone.
It isn't just the crossword with clues I find too hard,
Or looking out the window and you're not in the yard.
It isn't just walking through the Dales with no-one there to share,
Or climbing gates and stiles and not hearing "take care."
It isn't just the bad days when I need someone to hold.
For you to take me in your arms and keep me from the cold.
It's all the happiness we've shared through all the years gone by
That means that you and I my love could never say goodbye.

Beryl Williams

Inward Bound

Generally it's hard to take
Sublime, relief, never fake
Emotion holds the captive soul
Forever chastened it knows its role

We cannot escape the passage of time
Relentless motion, an everlasting crime
We pay the price these years of sorrow
Grief and stress, worry for 'morrow

Freedom from within behest
Expression outward, life of zest
Desired result, glory shines
Inside to outward from our lives

Nigel Smith

The Kiss

How can I describe you, kiss, in terms of emotion?
You govern our lives, say I, with love and devotion
   The soulful kiss,
   The tender touch,
   The merest brush,
   The passionate crush,
   The impertinent peck,
   The nuzzle of neck.
O kiss divine!
From man of mine!
How odd it is
We know such bliss!
   Yet beasts and bees,
   And birds in trees,
   And fish in the sea,
   The moth and the flea,
   Know not of the kiss
   Nor how much they miss.

Evelyn Jenkin

Age Of Innocence

Don't taint the colours of childhood with your anger,
my dreams are at the end of the rainbow.
Don't complicate my simple games with your abuse,
your witches and fairies don't belong in my world of make-believe.
Don't deny my rights with your wrongs,
'like the child,' I cry, like the child, I cry.
Don't hold me hostage with your guilt,
childhood... the age of innocence... is too high a ransom.

Irene Moore

The Chair

My finger tips are sore and shoddy
As the cheap gloves I wear,
My gauntlets against it - the chair;
War-horse of the ragged edges of pain.

My feet of clay take on ridiculous
Shapes, where they sprawl,
Instinct with nothing but a slow death.
I move the bits that move
And bruise the bits that feel,
Torn by the ragged edges of pain.

The chair sidles between me and loving,
Smugly savouring my need and my despair,
There was a woman once who flattered and fawned,
Teased and touched, but failed to stiffen
The limp flag of my desire,
Unmanned by the ragged edges of pain.

Be there when I'm tipped on the pavement,
And the chair scoots mockingly away,
When I see only rain and gargoyle-leering faces,
Then delete the ragged edges of pain.

Eunice Barnett

Disappearing Lives

Disappearing lives; half remembered memories
Fly on forgetful wings of time.
Disappearing lives; in old and faded photographs,
Faces from those happy years of youth.
Where went the childhood dreams,
The sweetness of that first love?
Where went the rosy hopes
Of happiness unnamed?
Disappearing lives; lost in the mist of passing years,
Rushed into oblivion of age.
Where went the sound of singing birds,
The clarity of colours?
Where went unbounded energy
Of happy healthy lives?
Disappearing lives; full, yet incomplete,
Cherished desires awaiting in hope.
Disappearing lives; like falling leaves of autumn,
Promises the coming spring of eternity.

Belinda Eames

Conscience

Imagine this, if you will,
A bomb so large that it could kill
A million people just like that,
Innocent lives at the drop of a hat.

Causing death everywhere,
But the warlords do not care.
A nuclear bomb I am indeed,
So world leaders please take heed.

One of my ancestors was to blame
For sending Hiroshima up in flame.
A disaster of such magnitude
Could not possibly be construed.

For one to cause such devastation,
Just defies all explanation.
It seems that mankind's lust for power
Must surely hasten earth's last hour.

If the gift of choice were mine,
I'd chance to journey back in time.
To prove to those with great insistence,
The folly of my own existence.

Carrie Williams

Morning Prayer

Thank you our Father, for the rising sun
That tells the world a new days has begun
The golden rays that sweep the bight away
And waken us to face for another day

E'er I begin to face my daily task
Keep me from sin Lord, this I humbly ask,
May something of thy character of love
Be shown through me to those amongst I move

Show me the path that Thou wouldst have me tread,
Keep me from falling, give me daily bread.
May all my thoughts and actions honour Thee
That others see something of Christ in me

I thank you for the privilege of prayer
At any hour, knowing Thou art there,
Unchanging God, for evermore the same
Our prayers are offered in our Saviour's name

When evening comes, and time has come for rest
When yonder sun sinks slowly in the West
Grant that your soul be at one with Thee
So that in peace my hours of sleep shall be

Horace Hartley

A Lifetime With Pain

My constant companion with me always
sleeping waking dreaming
never does it leave me never does it cease to be my friend
together we live we eat we work we become one
with me during the long dark nights when sleep eludes me
during the darkest days and lonely nights it is with me
we walk hand in hand together forever and ever
my friend my companion my shadow
it never treats me like a fool
never lies never deceives me
always always I know the truth it will never ever leave
our lives are as one destined to be together
together forever never to be free from one another
our lives are entwined until the end...

Christine Searle

My Place

Finding your place in this world is hard.
Most people will never find it.
Those that try may never be sure.
Those that succeed will hide it.

Barry Osborne

Reflections On Freedom

My heart bleeds for the caged bird
I panic whenever I look at him
I cannot bear his captivity
So akin to my own.
Nobody will free either of us.
It is assumed he has never known freedom
Therefore he could not survive,
I shall remain "caged" because a part of me
Is desperately afraid of failure.
How carelessly I discarded my freedom
Let it fall from my shoulders like a superfluous wrap
Nobody warned me of the impending suffocation,
The beating of frantic wings against the glass
The cry of my own insufficiency.
I take refuge in images of Dingle
Racing barefoot along endless white sands
Intoxicated by sea birds soaring above me
Clasping the blessed gift to my aching heart.

Gabrielle Maeve Whyte

The Artist

Etched with refinement upon a paletted facade,
The artistical toolpiece meticulously mars
Meandering nonchalantly across a canvas face
Illuminating the forthcoming of an ingenious piece
Gifted are the hands of this introverted man
Who dapples with oily spectre
Patience his virtuosity
Transfiguration the plan.

Wendy Osber

Your Birthday 1985

Love has come to our relationship
Often this has been apparent
Yet chances to express deep feeling
Tend to be lost in the daily round.
Thus loving thoughts remain unsaid.
Awareness of such a lapse
Encourages me to repair the oversight
And express something of my deep affection
Just some shadow measure of this attitude:
I love your patience and your care
Your cheerfulness and happy charm
Oft expressed in your gracious smile.
At our start together in a December wedding
Your bridal profile remains a lasting memory
Of your beauty and of your serenity.

J. J. MacGregor

My Chain Dream

I lay in my bed as the night drew on,
Frightening and dark was my room,
And as I lay my head on my familiar pillow,
My mind whirled into dreams of mystery.

My dream seemed to flash as I landed,
I landed somewhere dark and strange,
My vivid imagination fixed faces of fright in my mind,
And I hoped and awaited for my dreams to change.

I thought hard with all my might
To break away from my dream turned nightmare,
But the chains that held me there would never let me go,
My mind wearily slipped from dream to dream,
Just so I lay terrified in my bed.

Evil seemed against me,
What was my dream meant to mean?
I sat up suddenly with a jolt making the air quiver,
And I prayed and wished to wake up safe and secure.

As my eyes opened my mind spun back to reality,
I felt relieved and relaxed that the morning had arrived,
And my dreams were over for yet another night.

Alison Jane Flaherty

Fate, Hope, And Clarity

I'm told of tranquil torsos that tremble at my feet,
I see the Liquorice Lavender which smiles at me discreet.
Biscuit coloured beauties breath desperate bold and blue,
Troubled little Shamrocks shimmer helpless in the dew.
Golden gloves of teardrops fall gently from the sky,
Oceans of tiny crystals drop soundless from my eye.
Wrapped in Ginger Petticoats, pretty and precise,
My heart peeps through the silver clouds, I'm cold, I'm tired, I'm ice.
No more candid memories to shroud my open book,
No more bitter ingratitude from which my life was took.
Days of scented hours replace unwanted lies,
Cherries and Apple dumplings will drowned out all my sighs.
With outstretched hands of laughter that grabs my sheer delight,
We dwell on a moving pathway and travel the marbled night.
On a bed of velvet Flora, with a fragrant soft bouquet,
Our Garnet Bloods will flow as wine, our love will map the way.

S. Taylor

Father

I am angry that you didn't love me, you didn't care,
You could turn me away with just a stare.
You stole my family and my friends away from me,
You stripped away my home, my life and my security.
You sculptured my life without even knowing it,
A stubborn, hardhearted and very lonely woman.
Those feelings are deep within me now,
I've had time to think, to grow to understand.
I know now I have nothing to prove to anyone but myself,
I am good, kind and clever, to be appreciated would be so
    much better.
I'm so proud of you and what you've achieved,
And all the different awards that you've received.
I almost wish that things could have been different,
But I wouldn't be where I am now - able to understand.
I thank you for giving me life, and I know it's up to me,
To make my life everything I could possibly want it to be.
I know that things are difficult right now,
But one day we may be friends some how?

Corina Williams

Mysterious World

I sit alone with nothing to do,
That is why I write these lines for you.
I don't even know who you are,
But I write them for you whether you're near or far.
You are only alone by choice
Said the very distinctive lonely voice
You don't have to be alone this way,
Go out and find a friend today.
For there is a friend for everyone out there
It's just at this moment you don't know where
So don't get your brain all muddled and twirled
Because there's someone for everyone in this
Mysterious world.

Gary Liles

Spouse

All night the snoring it keeps me awake
Go to the cupboard some sleepers I'd take
They don't seem to work, it's getting so loud
A nudge to the ribs is the best cure I've found
A little time later, it starts up again
Who said that snoring's restricted to men
If one night in my room you were to spend
It'd be continual snoring
From beginning to end.
This constant commotion is ruining my sleep
If just for one night I could hear not a peep
I could feel energetic
Get on with my life
The problem's not me
It is my wife
She is the one who is snoring at night
So please someone 'help her'
So I can sleep tight!

Janette Harazny

Time

Beware the claws of time they said, for they have no preference
No longer will they be so kind to the face of innocents

Misuse its power on your own head and it may never be redeemed
For a moment lost is another gained, if fate should intervene

Decision it casts its cloak of shadows, letting small rays of
    light seep in
But will it guide you to the rainbow or just reveal lost souls within?

A turning left, or a turning right, which way do you propose?
Or perhaps the path to nowhere, is this the path you've chose?

Patience she waits, with love unending never questioning the aim
But time, the enemy, is unabating ready to spoil the precious gain

Fear not the question, nor trust the answer, many would debate
For the melancholy mind they say, finds reasoning too late

But what is a season compared with a year, were the words
    expressed with pleading?
Why nothing of course, you need not fear, time will never
    destroy this feeling

Janet Ling

V E Day, I Was There

I was there and I heard
As the people cheered
And laughed and cried in the sun.
It was such a great day and I'm proud to say,
I was there with everyone.
Many people laughed, but many cried
For loved ones, where had they gone?
But the war was over, it was over
"Thank God", and the world was smiling as one.

Those six dark years brought so many tears.
And filled many hearts with sorrow,
Then victory took away the fear
Of every blacked out year,
Yes, there was a tomorrow.
Let's celebrate now fifty years on,
How we won a long bitter fight.
I remember, I was there
When I heard like a prayer
'The war in Europe is over', that night.

Dorothy J. White

Shades

A pausing here, perhaps a changing face
From summer warmth to quieter autumn grace,
Glowing fires of ripened fruit and leaf
Replace the perfumed rose; a harvest sheaf
Of braided gold waits to be gathered by
While woodsmoke ascends the wider field of sky;
A cooler sun shows with softer light
Sweet days slow drifting into night
Where stars with colder flames may burn.
Fresh winds blow through feathered seas of fern
Carrying scents of blackberry and pine,
A time of shadows woven through with shine,
A memory of colours on a stream
Passing from life on the surface of a dream;
The signs of other days and other times
Of sweet and wondrous worlds, of rhymes,
Of lives cherished beyond the season's round,
The great drift of nature filled with living sound.

Brenda Hampton

Sunset At Treeton Dyke

As I stroll along by the dyke,
I hear twittering birds and a distant bike.
Each season brings its own special charm,
the red, gold and brown of the trees, on the farm.
Now a mass of grey cloud in a sky that's so blue,
as the setting sun shines on a watery hue.

The silence is eerie as the night draws in,
the birds calming down from their mighty din.
The sun's glowing warmth at the end of the day
as it sets behind hills at the side of the bay.
Then a feeling of wonder to see the sun go,
as the sky takes on a new orange glow.

But now all around is dark and dim,
and the water has lost it shimmering glint.
Still the sun will come again with the dawn,
and another new day will start in the morn
The birds will again tend their daily routine
and more wonders are there for us, to be seen.

Yvonne Gillott

Twilight Dreams

Beautiful is nice but
loved is better like
an old musty
armchair kept more
for sentimental reasons than
good taste, I'd like to wear
my worn down upholstery
like my mother's graceful middle age and
find grey hairs I
know so well tucked snug
in the corners of my dented
cushions where someone sits
always wraps arms and legs
across my body and
settles in me so I'm
sunday morning ritual or
weekday quiet time and not
loved because I'm beautiful
but beautiful because I'm
loved.

Bunmi Ogunsiji

Behind The Wall

Bright brittle scenes of summer past
As in a dream I can recall,
When the child that was me
Watched the men mow the field
Behind the hothouse wall.

My Mother and Granny searched for me.
I heard their voices call,
As distant as the chapel bell,
I didn't guess they thought me lost,
I hadn't gone at all.

The Reaper has passed and cut them down,
Those women who walked so tall
In my childhood days.
Their well-loved names are written in stone
Behind the churchyard wall.

Sometimes lost things that we yearn to see
Are quite nearby after all.
I like to think we will meet some day
In a land of light with fields of hay,
Just behind the wall.

Clare McAfee

Contrasts

Fingers dancing on the keys, moving, bending, tension, ease.
Notes chromatic to the ear are heard in colours bright
Yet to the eye perceiving them they move in black and white.

Black and white the crossword's plan
Is useless if the mind of man
Cannot with thought resolve the clue
The ambiguities pursue
Until the gaps completed stand,
Coloured by words, inscribed by hand.

Reflecting on the human state, necessity to integrate
Has touched us all to a degree
In friendships, neighbours, family.
Assimilation of all art
And cultures, fashions, views impart
A much more rational insight
Then our simplistic black and white.

I hear a purr from sofa deep where Domino has been asleep
My little cat, a charming sight,
Is really, truly black and white.

Della Nicholson

"The Glories Of War"

The cold soldier ran quickly over the barbed wire,
Then face down in the mud, avoiding the gunfire,
The lead death missing him, not by much,
Every step closer to death's cold touch,
Only eighteen, still his future to live,
But now his life he was being forced to give,
The army called him up so he was forced to leave home,
On the battlefield he had never felt so alone,
Afraid to sit still, yet too scared to run,
Confused he clutched ever tighter to his gun,
The generals sip brandy, miles from the dangers,
Playing chess, the pawns they move were lives of strangers,
The echoing gun's cry of death the only sound,
Tearing life from the battered and bruised battleground,
Not sure whether to laugh or cry,
Just determined he wouldn't die,
Remembered his mother as he left for war,
Only now knowing what it was she cried for,
Then the bullet hit him, but the pain was not the worst,
For as he died, he realized that he was not the first.

Ian Morgan

You Came To Me In Tears

You came to see me in tears and oh how I wanted to hold
you and tell you that I cared.

So I let you come in so that you could tell me that you
had fell out with him, now you find that life is so unkind
and nobody cares it has always been on my mined.

But why don't you take the time to reflect in your mined
what you have got here you have a friend in me who cares
for thee so stop feeling so lonely.

So one day maybe I could take away that pain from inside
thee and then maybe you would find that life is divine and
kind and love is all around.

For life is love and love is life so when you are feeling
lonely just call me my lonely friend.

K. Cooper

Jealousy

It makes you angry like an animal.
It makes you uptight like a flower all closed up.
It makes you lonely like a solitary leaf on the ground.
It makes you do things that you don't want to do.
Like an invisible force.
It makes you see red, like fresh blood.
It doesn't make you feel good
At all.

Simon Vowles

"Searching"

Walking around in endless circles
Looking for what I can't find.
Decisions are something out of my depth
Whirling around in my mind.

My tired, hard-worked limbs are like palm trees;
Swaying around in no breeze.
And my body feels like an oasis
You can drink from as you please.

Black cats seem to be crossing off my paths:
Leaving their bad luck to trail.
Heaven seems to be knocking at my door,
Like a chance we just can't fail

But we'll let it lie until tomorrow,
Just waiting for time to pass by.
And the angels floating over our heads
Wait until we too can fly.

Hayley Osborn

Spring 1996

The ewes, new-shorn, seek the hedge's shelter
While the blossom is wind whipped helter-skelter
From the tall old apple trees, like snow,
Pink snow - yet down below
'Cowslip and bluebell assure me it's spring.
Late but spring as the swallows swing
Down from the wires on curving wing.
The Cuckoo calls- that thug of a bird
And we go around saying "Have you heard?"
The Cockchafer - Maybug or what you will,
Died of cold on the window-sill.
Still, spring has sprung for the Flycatcher's back
Though the cold wind whistles through every crack
And I shiver in winter woollies and vest
As the weatherman talks of a frost in the West.

J. B. Dacres Dixon

Me

Voices shouting, screaming at me
A bruise on my arm, that no one can see
Is this reality, what life is about,
When all people do is argue and shout?

Eyes staring, glaring at me
Making me drown in insecurity
I need comfort, arms holding on
To this lost child in a world of her own

Ears not listening, unaware of me
Ignoring my plea for sincerity
What are you doing to this world I live in?
You're killing it - murdering everything

Feet walking away from me
They're walking to where I want to be
I want to get out, I long to be free
But you're too far away to be able to see.

Michelle Gay

Thankfulness

The sands of life sift through my hands,
And grain by grain the seconds pass,
I cannot halt the moving sands
They will become a useless mass.

The waves of peace lap over me,
And gently ease my cares away,
I drift along a tideless sea
Made ready for another day.

My thoughts fly on, soon, present, past,
No barriers to stop their flight,
No countries, nations bind them fast
They're free, thank God, to span the night.

E. Ford

I Speak God

I do not know what is inside of me,
I know I speak God.
I do not know what spurs me on,
I know I act the way of the Lord.
I do not know what my being is all about,
I know I was created by God.
I do not know what the night brings,
I know I dream of a better future.
I do not know what the inception of silence is,
I end up being religious.
I do not know what becomes of our prayers,
I know it is communication.
I do not know what death entails,
I know the body is left with no breath.
I do not know what becomes of our soul,
I do know that heaven exists.
I do not know what is inside me,
but I know I speak God.

Mary Brookman

Nightmare

Verily know I that certain place;
In dreams; where raped earth doth sigh.
Edens ravaged: O'er earth's fair face,
Wiverns, twisting, whirling, riding high.
Pandean music, wind-blown, haunting,
Over the hills and Celtic sea.
Ineluctable, overt, vaunting;
Now come the dawn, the mind's set free.
(Though wakening brings but scant relief)

J. H. Gilbert

Amy Brown

On a cold day in December
It was spring time all around,
When with gladdened hearts and thanks to God,
We welcomed Amy Brown.

The joy of growing with her,
The hours of childhood fun,
The laughter and the lullabies,
Where have these five years flown?

Our baby times concluded,
To school days now we turn,
Another great adventure
With so much more to learn.

We contemplate the future
A second time around,
As a brand new chapter opens up
For us and Amy Brown.

May the God Lord help and guide her,
May the joys of life abound,
May good fortune walk beside her
All Gods blessing Amy Brown.

M. McGowan

The Space Between

I am looking at you

We are not touching
But I am looking into your eyes

I'm stroking your face with my hand
And I'm planting kisses on your lips
I'm embracing you and feeling your warmth
I'm holding you and never wanting to let go
We are making love and it is heaven

I wonder do you know what I'm thinking?
I want to tell you so much

What was it you said just now?

I am looking into your eyes
But we are not touching

Steve Chester

Three Trees

Three seeds fell down upon the ground,
Just feet apart and striving,
Each to grow as tall and strong
As the others they were rivalling.
Each spring their leaves appeared and grew,
On branches growing stronger,
Each year that passed their limbs stretched out,
Their trunks grew even longer.
They all reached up towards the light,
And leaned to where the light was bright,
Until one day their branches met,
Their roots as well entwined and spread.
The years went by and as they grew,
Their trunks grew thick together,
And joined and turned towards the sun,
Each tree became a part of one.
Today I looked upon that tree,
Which looks like one, but is really three,
A part of the blessed trinity.

Jessica Flowers

The Black Halloween Cat

It is a dark, eerie night,
The moon is a bright circle of light,
The church bells begin a series of dongs,
Twelve dongs of Midnight.

The pumpkin Halloween lanterns,
Grin evil smiles and have wax tears,
Children shiver with excitement and fear,
And then the black cat suddenly appears.

She is sleek, sly and cunning,
She loves to kill and watch her victims running,
They will run until they are out of breath,
As they are only trying to escape death.

A swish of her tail and a lash of her paw,
The last glance of life her victim ever saw,
The reason for killing is only for fun,
This cat should be named "Oh Evil One".

Yet again like every year,
A life has been taken, full of fear,
By this black, "Oh Evil One",
Once again, it has won.

Laura Mackian

Gardeners Paradise

I call it gardeners paradise, there's plenty of things to view,
Pergolas, fish ponds, statues, a tadpole circle too,
Sounds of running water, tranquil as can be,
Making it the perfect place for everyone to see,
Now I have to mention roses, alpines and sweet peas,
Clematis, shrubs, conifers, and the two fruit trees.
When you thought you'd seen it all, the sun begins to fade,
Garden lighting then shows up, the beauty I've conveyed.

Susan White

Flowers

All the pansies have a little face,
the pinks seem interwoven with lace
roses made of velvet and silk
snowdrops painted white as milk
all are created without a flaw
with our God's love at their very core
how can we possibly ever doubt
when we see such beauty all about
what power of love it must take
just to design a small snow flake
this love of God holds me in awe
for it is His own universal law
so bless the daisy growing in the grass
for it is part of all that has come to pass
to love God is our main duty
for His existence is an eternal beauty.

J. P. Lawman

With All My Love

Once upon a time, the same way every dream's begun,
It started soon one morning till the early hours were won.
Talking till forever about nothing much at all,
While the hours passed us by and the night crept up the wall,
The fire flickered gently and its light caressed the gloom,
Our silence hung like snowdrops blooming out across the room,
Each single word was savoured like the last one to be heard,
But all through dreaming ears and so, carefully, were slurred,
The time remained to calm and the thoughts just to remind,
That things once left undone are still close enough to find,
As the sun appeared to rise again and time began its dawn,
The day fulfilled its morning with a careful soothing yawn,
As time reawoke to move again, so we did take the time,
And walking slowly, hand in hand, as priceless as a rhyme,
The time ignored this wondrous scene, and left us both until,
We could not wait for time to tell, and both took in our fill,
Our touching lips, like soothing hearts, brought comfort to the time,
Reflections held like ghostly love, by knowing that you're mine.

Elizabeth Jackson

Old Braitwaite

I read a book;
My thoughts took wing
Down leafy lanes
   — Remembering.
Of music carried on the wind;
The singing bird, the lowing herd;
Oh, happy days
   — Remembering.
The babbling brook; some days too full
Of children playing, never dull,
The men of age, their meeting place
The bridge that sees the changing face
Of village scenes
   — Septembering.
My childhood spent, my life goes on
In many other towns;
But from this book a chord was struck;
The tears fell fast
For days long past, and faces gone, as I sat there
   — Remembering.

G. Morris-Barker

Dusty

This is the name of my cat.
She is such a close friend
And sits on the mat.
She looks at me with such wistful eyes
And she is very alert when she is chasing flies
I always know the state of the weather
By the position she sits when we are together.
We all know when the rain is due
As she sits with her back to the fire
Washing her face with her paws
Wondering what else she could do.
Her colour is a mixture of grey and black
And she meows and purrs
When she is stroked on her back
When she sits up straight
She is like a wee lady
And when she is cuddled
She is like a wee baby
So now you have a picture of that
All I can say is I still love my cat.

Esther Sandford

Gardening

Where the blue lupins lift their scented spires
Weeds used to grow, a rank and tangled mass;
A rose now blooms where once the brambles trailed,
And lilies stand, where nettles choked the grass,
This being so, humanity may hope
That Man, whose hand this miracle has wrought,
Will husband the bright flower of his destiny,
And Beauty out of chaos yet be brought.

Barbara Mather

Alone

My darling I see you standing there
The gentle breeze blowing in your hair
I see your face, your eyes of blue
Oh how I wish I were with you
I walk along the lone seashore
And feel you with me, as before
I stop and look o'er the deep blue sea
Then realize you're not with me
I sit upon the soft warm sand
Where once I sat and held your hand
Then soft and warm, the teardrops start
I'll keep your memory locked deep in my heart
I look up to the sky above, and pray dear God
send back my love
Your sweet face I see, in my dreams each night
Oh how I long to hold you tight
I see you on the bridge above
I'm coming to you my silent love
Oh darling wait, please don't go away
I can't live without you another day

M. Randall

Orkney Summer

Stark next the sky stand the black hills of Hoy
In the white - water nights.
In the quiet grey town, the midsummer wind
Whistles and moans in the echoing winds
Like the mewing of gulls.
Out on the Sound, circling, and wheeling
Fulmar and petrel weave patterns in silver
On burnished grey sea.
Pale blows the thrift in the tangle of grasses
Pewter - dark seals dive in translucent light.

Smiling, you walk at my side on the shore line,
Invisible prints in the milky - white sand.
For here, in my heart, to the sea I have brought you
Showing you beauty you never will see.
This garland of islands,
Of wind and of seabirds,
The dark hills at sunset, the silent grey town,
The deathless - day wonder
Of white - water nights.

Heather Goddin

Now That I'm Eighty

When you are old and tired and full of tears,
Remember, if you will the laughter years,
When you were young and free and full of hope
And strong enough to overcome your fears.

And that remembering may lift your heart,
May give you courage, and some strength impart
To armour your worn self, and saddened soul,
That you may bravely live, and then depart.

Jane Wilson

Untitled

Autumn leaves, a winter breeze
its voice beckons me from sleep
shiny droplets sting my eyes
a heart so lonely, shivers with cries

Winter snow has yet to show
clouded skies blow winds of cold
frozen are words I longed to speak
grasp a picture that's incomplete

Springtime air, flowers everywhere
love whispers secrets that bloom
thoughts of you dwell upon my mind
longing to see you in another time

Summer heat and lovers meet
warm laughter chants in rhyme
year after year, I'll continue show
that I'm missing you Dad, and love you so.

Donna Moodey

Tree

As the wind whistles through the leaves
you get a shiver down your back,
and the shadow of the leaves look like a monster
ready to move,
and as the branches move
it is like a man waving,
and the trunk look's kind and full of life.
It's like we owe our lives to the tree that gives us
air to breath,
and home for squirrels and birds.
In the autumn the colourful leaves make the tree
look like a rainbow tree,
and the tree is reaching out to the sky so high.
And the buds, the buds ready to start life as a leaf.
And for years the tree will keep on giving us air to breath,
until the moment comes when the trees stops giving
air for us to breath,
it dies never to give life.
Again.

Ben Barnes

Home Thoughts

Grief here is deeper than the roll and sound
Of cataract waters, muffled under-ground,
And calmer yet than an infinity
Of umber plains o'ershadowed by one tree.

Here all the perched and hostile towns appear
Immeasurably far: the reapers here
Through halcyon days pile up their heavy stooks
In fields unplundered by the pestilent rooks.

Yet, at this hub, perceptibly there moves
A breeze that stirs the corn and chestnut groves;
So I, who had no memories of home,
Recall the scud, the lands from which I come.

Strange how I recollect them, barn and tree
Each poised in isolation. Summer fails
On flats where water courses twist concealed
And only the intersecting lines of field
Disturb the stubble's vast monotony.
The straits are stilled from equinoctial gales:
Untroubled now that cold, chameleon, sea.

K. P. Witney

Premonition

The telephone rings absently in the deserted room,
probing the questioning air with its shrillness.
Sharp and high the phone waits to be answered,
but the deserted room harbours only the rats,
that the tenants have left behind.
The phone that brings its news rings on,
the danger of darkness and unknown.
A premonition of danger, a phone call to warn,
goes unheeded as they are not there.
The receiver is too late with his warning,
for the crash that he saw in the morn.
The premonition of death, the people he knew,
lie dead in the crash of his dreams.
His nightmare came true, but time pays no heed,
for the time was the same, as his dream.

Beverley Zywina

Song Of Dawn

The river is high; it looks like glass.
A thin mist serenades its surface.
Along its green banks stand ancient trees,
In song they greet the ascending sun.
A duet of swans glide past in harmony,
Playing silent chords of Orphic beauty,
While riding across a red-splashed sky
A flock of geese sing their song of dawn.

A. H. Howard

Sea-Shepherds Early Morning Mist

Another grey dawn,
Another watch to keep,
Oh! How sweet it was,
To have that little sleep,
The Officer-of-the-watch,
Just as tired as me,
Glasses to his eyes,
Scans the vast expanse of sea.

The convoy to the right of us,
Slow but still on course,
Had signalled when we sailed,
That they were glad to see our force.
Three to guard a score of them to shepherd and assist,
Thank God indeed, the crews agreed, for that early morning mist.

Whilst

The U-Boat Kapitan,
Well down in the murky deep,
At least his crew were rested having had a good night's sleep.
Now they were a-hunting his hand had formed a fist,
All heard him swear, all heard him curse, that early morning mist.

Ron Green

If I Was The Leader Of The Community I Would...

Overjoyed with happiness, I take up this task;
The Gracious Lord will Guide me in this daring duty.

As you can see I take this great mission,
Hoping God will accept my perfect intention.

I will speak in soothing tones and be mild as cottage cheese;
I swear to be true and just in my words, as the stars above.

Peace will dwell here with love for thy Lord;
Love for mankind, love for one another.

Give me your views on problems faced, in the strictest confidence
they will be solved.
Don't whisper among yourselves as all thoughts will be most
welcomed.

For knowledge will stretch far as Islam encourages it.
Quizzes Debates Question/Answer sessions we will have.

Sharing the sufferings of fellow Muslims and speaking up for
your rights will be encouraged.
Islam emphasises brotherhood practising it, will be our duty.

Mother of community I will be, gentle and caring I will be,
Kind actions will be noticed it will be a happy atmosphere.

Sparkle in the building is what we need; Mosque it should look like,
With Minarets and Domes calls of prayer echoing in the air.

Oh! Saviour Oh! Saviour, watch over me, from day to day,
Keep me firm on my faith, keep me on the right path.

Akilla Ladak

Growing Old

When we grow old and our life's work is done,
Our children all married, ambitions all gone,
The days pass so quickly, no time to be bored,
The laughter of grandchildren around us is heard.

We remember the time when our children were younger,
Making plans for their future and then torn asunder.
With heartaches and tears saw them try to be brave,
When an illness o'ertook them, so courage we gave.

Many memories we hoard in that larder of ours,
Count our blessings we must, if we share in their trust.
That the good Lord is standing with arms open wide,
To give us this strength to stay close by his side.

When we start the last journey from earth into space,
The unknown won't be lonely, we have won the great race.
Life's journey was rough, it was hard but worthwhile,
No more tears, never lonely, we'll do it in style.

Lucy Hall

Thanks Dad

Thanks dad for doing so much for me
I will always remember sitting on your knee
Remember the dark nights you were always there
And switched on the light to extinguish a scare

Rubbed my hair dry after my bath
And let me stay up late - at mums wrath
Horatio Hornblower and Dick Barton on the
Radio at night
The fire aglow, cosy toes and all
Making me a happy secure little girl

Dancing lessons, swimming and riding my bike you
Taught me with care
I will always be grateful you were there

You are older now, a little frail too
But your strength shines through
Like a guiding light on a lonely lane
Saying go carefully now, you are never alone
By your side I will be to guide you home

Ann Thompson

Untitled

I am the fountain of life
Celestial water
I am the living vessel it fills
With eternity
I am cosmic consciousness
the freeing of self
I am spirit energy living vibration
I am joy and sorrow, strength and weakness
I am love and bitterness a constant battle
I am love triumphant in union with thee
I am life eternal infinite soul
I am the living temple house of God self
I am but a splinter on the cornerstone of creation

Margaret Johnson

Highland Dawn

The hills on either side of me are awakening
To the new day's morning light.
I hear only the river at the distant weir,
Some sleepy sheep,
    and away in the trees to either side of me
The wee feathered creatures at song.
Down the valley to the East I watch
    a bright theatre,
The promise of new light and warmth,
A stage of distant mountainous silhouettes
Upon which the brilliant prima donna must soon rise.

Roderick MacLean

Life, Weather, One In The Same?

Bitter winds, sunny dreams,
all come together but it's not how it seems.
My first ever memory is of rain crashing down
staring through the window in my thin dressing gown,
watching people running, not caring where they went
a shiver through my spine, is what that night sent
The next morning the sun was shining though, as though
The rain had never been, I watched for the people of
"Last night", although none of them I ever seen.
When I left the house that day my heart should have
felt free and light, but I dreaded what would happen,
when the sun went down that night, would the
rain come back in anger? Would it seek revenge on the sun?
Or would it stay behind the clouds and let us
have some fun? When you think of the weather like
this it reminds you a bit of life. You never know what
will happen, will the day bring joy or tears, it
just shows you weather, like life, has a way
of showing its fears!

Lucille Donnelly

Once Upon A Time

Once upon a time there was less smog in the sky,
Once upon a time there was no need to ask why,
Is there so much hatred and war in this land?
And why, when needed, do friends not lend a hand?
The answer to this has become clear to me,
But why, when improving things, must we pollute land, air and sea?
And why have enemies and cause war?
Because once upon a time someone wanted more.

Nicola Pomroy

The Stranger

She looked up to where the stranger stood,
His face veiled by his crimson hood.
She reached to peel back the cloth with care,
To unravel his glorious locks of hair.
She placed her hands upon his face.
With such beauty he had been graced.
She slowly traced each minor detail,
With one finger she followed the wrinkly trail,
His face so different from that of before,
Before he took his pride and went to war.
His eyes so tired, longing to close,
The dark circles hanging beyond his nose.
A faint scar ran from cheek to ear,
His whole appearance haunted by fear.
Puzzled she looked to his lips, her mind reeling,
They were motionless, starved of feeling.
Forgotten his little precious, or had he?
And then he smiled, she gasped 'Oh there you are Daddy'

Lucy Roberts

Universal Genocide

Now the atmosphere's polluted
And we have to save our land
From all the poisons that we've pumped into the ozone
What with aerosols and carbons
From our fridges, cars and cans
Not to mention all the filth dumped in the ocean

And we're felling forests daily
Then of course there's acid rain
Which kills plants - and just to add to our distinction
Some animals, the likes of which
We may never see again
Don't face survival of the fittest, just extinction

Now we didn't start these battles
They're from generations past
But we have been warned and now we have to fight them
We owe it to our children
If we want their world to last
Or there won't be any more ad infinitum

Jackie Goddard

How To Cope With Old Age, Or Elder Berry Whine

When your hot water bottle is leaking
And your deaf aid has gone on the blink
And your joint's start to creak
And you feel like a freak
And your false teeth have fell down the sink.
When your glasses steam up when you're reading
And the wheels on your wheelchair won't wheel
And your varicose veins are giving you pains
And lumbago is making you squeal.
When you've had your face lifted by Wimpy's
And your ears are on top of your head
And the wig on your nut just will not stay put
And your eyes are all runny and red
When your feet feel like two lumps of concrete
And you feel like you're going off your head
Don't kick the poor cat in the stomach
Take an aspirin and get back in bed.

Joe Kelly

Footprints

This ancient path along the ridge has
known the tread of man
Since he first left his mark upon the land,
What moments from our history, who's
famous feet have trod...?
This very piece of ground where I now stand?
Did Hadrian's cohorts pass this way
to subjugate the tribes?
With Boadicea passing by before!
Did great red bearded Vikings come, to pillage and to loot?
Their battle-axes running red with gore!
Some were barefoot, treading soft, on holy pilgrimage.
Other's clamoured o'er the ground to sate an evil rage!
Though silent now, I still can feel
their presence in the air,
they permeate the very dust of this old thoroughfare.

These well worn stones I walk upon, have echoed to them all,
A band of strolling minstrels, sad bearers of the pall.

Each had their hopes to guide them as they passed by this way,
My footprints too-will now be here when I am turned to clay!

Leonard Muscroft

The Sea Empress

T'was on the fifteenth of February,
Off the coast of South Wales,
When the sea was fierce and rough,
And the skies produced harsh gales.

A liner carrying oil ran aground,
The 'Sea Empress' was her name.
She tilted up on the jagged rocks,
Until some help finally came.

The worried sailors impatiently waited,
Until the boat would come free.
But alas! The liner was punctured,
Causing tons of oil to pollute the sea.

Tug boats tried to pull the liner straight,
But to no avail.
Booms and scrawler nets were also used,
But each method seemed to fail.

To clear up the mess,
A lot of people will have to toil,
The incident will be at great expense,
But who are we to blame?...the oil?

Emma Rickett

Wasteland

Somewhere in time
I watch myself walk through this land of shadows
Briefly touching kindred spirits
Before their lives slip out of view

Spaced out light headed
Following the river homeward to the sea
Day turning into night
Illusion close behind me

Discordant winter summer days
When warmth turns cold around the heart
And tears of ice slowly fall
From the cracked mirror of the soul

Moving pictures flicker by
Remembered days of careless laughter
A lovers kiss passionate embrace
Timeless moments captured for eternity

A valiant tree in a fallen forest
Standing tall but still alone
Watching the green shoots regenerate and cover
The wasteland that we once called home

Mignon Garrett

The Immigrant

I care not for your climate or this environment!
I find the lifestyle tedious and very much resent
The manners of your people, their pious attitude.
I find their curiosity intolerably rude.

I don't deem it an honour to be your guest at all!
Your sanctimonious compliments serve only to appal
My natural sense of dignity, my air of savoir-faire.
You're wise to be afraid of me, approach me if you dare.

My breeding is self evident, my bearing rather grand,
My pride will never let you know I pine so for my land.
But hidden by the darkness, when no one is around,
I quickly lose this noble stance and crumple to the ground.

And for a while, in sweet repose, I'm back with my own kind.
My agonizing loneliness replaced by peace of mind.
I gaze up at a different moon that shimmers through the trees
As old familiar sounds of life drift on the gentle breeze.

I fill my lungs with air so sweet, I feel my spirits soar.
At last I know contentment, for I am home once more.
But blissful fantasies of night dissolve with morning dew,
I heave a sigh and realize I'll never leave this zoo....

Eveline R. Askew

Major Gillies MacBean

Some clansmen, on seeing the bloody onslaught,
The question now lay, could they get up or not,
Several did manage, shrugging pain to one side,
Major Gillies Mac Bean, tried to get into stride,
to get off the moor, for there's nowhere to hide,
The Clan Chattan hero, would much rather die,
with claymore to hand, than a pig in a sty,
his bayonet wounds sore, but strong was the man,
his clan in retreat, to catch if he can,
Doublet all blood stained, once tartan all o'er,
tattered to rags, and covered in gore,
soon they out stripped him, nearby a wall,
he fought with such fury, with honour would fall,
six hundred yards by the fields of Balvraid,
no targe to protect him, his arm in his plaid,
Lord Ancrum's horsemen, had cornered MacBean,
"save him" he cried, but to no good did seem,
they mangled their hooves o'er the brave jacobite,
Culloden's now over, the end of the fight.

Angus Little

British Airways World Traveller

And lest you'd think it can't get worse,
Come look for my childhood on the world map.
Indian Ocean, that old traveller and his funny hood; all
   saddled up,
All alone - one last glance back as he waves good-bye.
I might've cried but you said his arm was really the red-sea.
But he might've been barring sunlight too, you know?
Did he also see orange, closing his eyes to the warm sun?
And over there, North-West: England! Blue England hanging
   above the clouds.
And that's where British Airways flies to: England in the sky.
But how do ships manage to get there?
Didn't I think beautifully when I was a kid, ma?
The cheese box enigma - I was five I think.
The round cheese box with the laughing cow, and the cow
   wore ear-rings
And the ear-rings were smaller cheese boxes, with a laughing
   cow, with ear-rings....
It took a laughing cow, hours of hypnotized trance; musing
   on infinity
But time-out folks! Cheese box is in the bin, Mom! I've grown.
All the while, steadily forgetting to ask
Why we couldn't feel "grow."
Shouldn't my limbs have tickled as they stretched? Did they?
And why have they grown so big I don't ask these questions
   anymore?

Utam Ramchurn

Eventide

At eventide when all was calm,
the air seemed filled with mystic charm.
The birds were flying home on high,
as the moon rose up and lit the sky.
From their burrows rabbits crept,
while in their beds the farmers slept.
Owls flew high in search of prey,
after sleeping through the day.
Mice excitingly squeaked in their holes,
and ran to play with sleepy moles,
The wind blew softly through the leaves;
Bats took their place among the eaves
Cats quietly walked from house to house,
hoping they'd meet a juicy mouse.
the bonfire was out in the gypsy camp,
while under the haystack slept a tramp.

Audrey E. Ridge

Shadows At Play

Deep in dimpled streams, haunting dell and dingle,
Flirting with the grass, caressing the shingle,
Where the moonlight gleams, and the waters mingle,
   Silently we pass.

Finical as chance, light as woman's glances,
Stealing one by one, through the checkered branches,
Carelessly we dance, following our fancies,
   Hiding from the sun.

Life is made for play: movement is a pleasure.
Pitied is the man, laggard in his leisure.
If you would be gay, come and trip our measure.
   Catch us if you can.

Thomas Russell

Charlotte's Day: Graduation Day

I am very proud to say
It will soon be Graduation Day
For my Granddaughter, Charlotte Marie,
Worked very hard at College you see.

For four years it was not much fun
Homework every day had to be done
Now at last she has her reward
To wear her gown and mortarboard

She will receive her Certificate up on stage
With people all around to see
But best of all her thrill will be
That Mum and Dad will smile and say
Well done Charlotte Marie!
And then she will turn to them and say
Thank you Mum and Dad for helping me.

Phyllis Chilcott

A Child

A day it lasts so very long,
A child's cry a mighty throng.
So when the clock it goes so slow,
I hope to bed at last she'll go.
A cry a sob my bath I want,
I ask myself what is the point.
So now she sits and splashes there,
To splash on me I think she'd dare.
So out the bath and down the stair,
Her golden hair so light and fair
Upon my knee she sits and smiles,
And now she's using her childish guiles.
So now in bed so fast asleep,
Alone and safe in slumber deep.
From all the world's hurt and woe,
At least she's safe from that I know.
The day will start, the clock will run,
Her little heart so full of fun.
Her smile it melts the hardest heart,
To her your love you must impart.

William Lannigan

Smile, She Smiled

Smile, she smiled that way before
Though just to ease the pain
Of circumstance, the way it was, I just remember rain
As merciless it poured on me
Into my heart it tore

Smile, she smiled it took my love
To her it was a game
Of circumstance, though taken light, my name was just a name
As coldly now she shed my soul
Like peeling off her glove

Smile, she smiled and closed the door
Though just to make quite sure
My heart was broken, cut so deep, so deep there was no cure
As finally she walked away
Smile, she smiled once more

Derek Oakes

A Promise

We're glad to have you as our guest
And promise we will do our best
To make your stay a happy time
Provided that you toe the line
So here forthwith, some odds and ends
To help us part the best of friends.

Don't slam the doors, keep down the noise
Don't bring home strangers, girls or boys
Don't leave the telly on all night
You say you won't, we think you might
And when you leave, if kind you be
Don't say good-bye and take the key.

These words are meant not to annoy
So time that's spent here please enjoy
Just one more thing about your stay
We hope you wont forget to pay!!

Bernard Greene

Ode To A Sister

Amid those fields where we walked and wandered,
Along that shore where we strolled and played,
Beside that stream that flowed swiftly seaward,
My thoughts and prayers were yours today.

I listened to the winds that stirred the waters,
And watched the waves where they met the shore.
I remembered those birds we had watched together,
And recalled how they'd climb and gracefully soar.

And there on those winds I felt your spirit -
On the winds that blew from the grey North Sea.
It was there I knew that I would find you;
Where your soul and your spirit would surely be.

God grant you peace and freedom from suffering,
And may you be as free as those birds in the air.
May I, like a wind, feel you always about me,
And may our two souls be united through prayer.

D. C. Jackson

Sleep

Sleep - that sweet visitor of the night -
Reaching forth with soft finger tips,
To soothe and calm the furrows of my brow,
Closing mine eyelids with a gentle kiss,
Leading me to dreamland, or quiet nothingness
Away from all the sorrows that beset me now.

But often she eludes me as vainly I would woo her,
Grasping forth with eager hands to draw her to my side,
Yet alas, she mocks me, as tossing to and fro,
I seek in vain within her arms to hide.

At last I cease my striving, and sadly turn away from her.
To calmly wait until the morning light.
And lo at last she tip-toes in when I am unaware,
To be my sweet companion for the night.

I. M. C. Foster

Gypsies

There are some people who just won't fit in
In a race that won't stay still.
They break the hearts of their kin
And roam the world at will.
They climb the mountains
Wade through the flood,
Must be the curse of the gypsy blood.
If they only went straight
They might go far
For they are strong, brave and true.
But they are always tired of the things that are
They only want the strange and the new.
It's the steady, quiet and peaceful ones
Who win in this lifelong race.
They are rolling stones
And it's bred in the bones
To the people who won't fit in.

Jean Russell

Autumn

I see the mist-blue woodsmoke, drifting up the air
And the old man in his garden, sweeping leaves up there;
Whilst just beyond the beech hedge, along the golden lane
Lie puddle-pools of amber, from late September rain.

I see tall chrysanthemums lean against the wall
Ready for their cutting, to adorn the lofty hall.
I hear the russet-robin sing, his clear cut crystal tune
And the daisies of St. Michaelmas are in their perfect bloom.

I can see the orchard beyond the autumn mist
Where apples glow like lanterns, and children can't resist?
While just above vague rooftops, a misty moon hangs high
And little icy starlets, float across the sky.

I can smell damp leaf mould and hay from ancient barns
Sweet clover from the cows field by the little farm.
So soon it will be harvest time, to reap what man has sown
And gather to the churches, all that man has grown.

Rosemary Diane Harving

Seasons Remembered

Remember the summer, the warm sun-filled days,
With row boats a bobbing in picturesque bays.
The soft grassy meadows with buttercups and daisy,
The warm fragrant breezes, the evenings so hazy.
Remember the autumn, so crisp and so bright,
When woodsmoke hung over each silver street light.
The frost on the pavements, that sparkled and glistened.
The crackles of bonfires, if you'd only listened.
Remember the winters, the ice and the snow,
The leaves whipped from trees by the fierce winds that blow.
The cold, lashing rain that turned into hale,
Driven ahead of the dark stormy gale.
Remember the spring, with its fresh new buds bursting,
The birds morning chorus, the songs they're rehearsing.
They take to the air, their hearts soar in flight,
To swoop and to dive from morning till night.
I well remember the difference in seasons,
But can anyone tell me the whyfores and reasons
That they should now seem to roll into one,
There's no telling when one ends, and another's begun.

Maggie Moore

Travelling

The wonder of a tiny stream,
Hesitantly flowing over untried ground,
Slowly gathering momentum and its courage
To widen into tributaries of new discoveries,
Journeying through the deep uncharted river of life,
Blown at times to turbulence, by transient winds of change,
Creating whirlpools of confusion between its sheltered banks
Navigating unexpected rapids which test the skills of compromise,
Moving purposefully on to irrigate the growth of hope
Until secure in harmony, it meets the ocean of experience,
Immense and humbling in the ebb and flow of tidal understanding.

Rosemary Austin

The Dieter's Nightmare

To all of you out there like me
Who long to be free
From the temptations out there
Which are a dieter's nightmare.

The oozing cream cakes in the bakery
Different choices for all to see
Call out to you
I am delicious try me.

The chocolate counter in the local store
Filled with mars bars and more
Makes our tummies rumble
And our minds stumble.

As our fingers fumble
And we mumble
What harm can it do
Then we realize we've just brought two.

Then as you unload to your dismay
You've brought enough for a year and a day
So you think to yourself
I'll be good to-morrow... Maybe.

Karen Anne Newman

Eruption

Like a terrible volcano, he will suddenly erupt
It could be a word, or just a look
An explosion of tremendous proportion
And I had thought I had taken such caution

Fire and sulphur spit high in the heaven
There is no way for the tumult to lessen
But I must still bide here a while
For the youngest boy is still but a child

My eyes water from the intense fog
Bile rises in my throat and threatens to clog
The sulphur burns the back of my mouth and nose
His unpredictable temper has again rose

I step this way and that to try to avoid
The inevitable lava bubbling my way with accord
I don't want to be burned again or be charred
I'm stinging with hurt and mentally scarred

Eventually I know this eruption will subside
After many a tear that I have cried
Then on tender hooks I shall have to wait
For the next time and then for it abate

Jay Baker

Life Time Continuum

1. Rain lashes my tearless dignity
   on the moorside by the windswept gash
   where we cut into Rhiannon's breast
   to lay you in coarse linen and serenity,
   robbed with the dark days of a ragged life.

2. In a pillared courtyard we fought,
   fountains of reality rippling between us
   marbled white and gold your eyes,
   veined beauty, perfect Adonis, murder caught
   as I drowned into another waking.

3. Astral high I watch my sweet triumph,
   trained dedication of a priest-king
   by whose shoulders borne, the altar stone,
   achievement of ultimate faith,
   ascends heaven's steps, apex of my sacrifice.

∞ Still, I return to infinity,
   recalled to forgetfulness and peace,
   dispassionate completion renews me.
   In the universe of my eternity
   I am feeling remembering experience.

Katherine Carington Smith

'Diaphana'

'Revelation'

White, oh! White, are the blossoms of the Cherry Tree-
Bursting from the tight-closed buds that gave away at last-
a living beauty purer than the snow,
Arising from the deep dark earth of winter long ago!

But oh! Quite soon to fade in restless breezes and
   the sun of Spring,
Yet, in so brief a time-such joy to bring.

And now, when all the petals white
have scattered on the ground below,
The budding fruit is forming the green leaves in between,
And watchful birds will eat e'er long
the cherries, where the flowers have been;

For God's creation holds a purpose far more fruitful
   than the mind of man,
That in the fading of a flower-
Lies an eternal plan!

Kathleen Edith Crosley

One Fine Morn

Stepping lightly through the corn.
Foot a tingling this fine morn
Fallen ears prick my toes with scorn.
Lightly I step to greet the dawn

Far off horizons I will seek
Where the bluebells and the daffodils meet
peer into the dark wooded dell
Where the fairies and the goblins dwell

Skipping round the old oak tree
Gnarled hands won't catch me
Filled with fear I venture on
A carpet of daises to lie upon

A friendly dormouse yawns "Good Morn"
As a shaft of light shines upon
High above the old owl sleeps
Sleepy opening one eye to peep

Chasing bees and butter flies there
Daisy chains galore to wear
Childhood wonderland I did seek
Where the blue bells and the daffodils meet

Eileen Ann Ross

The Light Has Gone Now?

A chilling rush of innocence caresses my body my entire self.
Through the darkness I reach for you, my slender arms
   envelope your magnificence.
Lust controls me, greed absorbs me, I want you more with
   each desperate breath.

Yet our room is dark now, cold and empty; I am alone in my cell.
Our love has gone now; I am stranded with haunting memories
   and squandered emotions.
I share my confusion with trinkets, objects given to me by
   your family; people fit to deserve your 'unconditional' love.
The love I have been denied. Why?
You charmed me with your passionate ideals; your beauty
   astounded me and your amazing strength urged me to give
   myself wholly and utterly to you.
You were my light but slowly you faded away.

I would have done anything for you and this you understood.

You toyed with me, making ridiculous demands, coming back
   and asking for more.
Each time I gave and gave until I had nothing left to give.
I was tired then, and depended on you more than ever before.

A 'great listener' they called you and yet you shut your ears to me.
Why have you deserted me? I loved you and believed in you!
I asked for nothing but when I asked for your help I received none.

Christ, I want you back!

Claire Anderson

Holly Holy Day: Nantwich

You should be with me here on Holly Holy Day. Nantwich's
ancient streets echoing to the tramp of gathering regiments,
The drummer's incessant beat imposing rhythmic motion on
uniformed ranks As the Sealed Knot's imitation armies muster
and move to Millfields, There, on the Weaver's grassy plain,
to simulate the town's historic siege When, for six weeks of
England's Civil War, townsfolk, true to the Parliamentary cause,
Held Lord Byron's royalist host at bay till Fairfax brought
relief and victory. So, on this anniversary day, under the
unexpected smile of the January sun, Spectators and participants
prepare for the rehearsed skirmish Which, upon the word,
starts with the stunning thunder of an artillery barrage Joined
immediately by the pyrotechnic thunder of the musketeers
Stimulating a waving miscellany of gaudy standards and
banners As taunt and challenge, cheer and counter-cheer, fill
the air with oral hostility. The two sides close and clash,
dividing into detached groups of sparring combatants,
Wheeling scrums of belligerent pikemen ploughing and
puddling the meadow's soggy turf, Opposing officers crossing
swords with disciplined pugnacity: whilst overhead, Grey
smoke, with its acrid stench of spent powder, drifts in the day's
light breeze. In time the mock battle reaches its predetermined
Roundhead triumph, The day's lusty soldiers reluctantly disengage,
reassemble and disperse; And as the cold, damp air of a
riverside dusk settles, peace returns to the memorial scene.

David Beasley

Father Time

Oh how father time makes a mockery of us all.
He builds us up allowing us to stand tall.
Then he knocks us down in front of them all.
Making us feel abashed, degraded and small.

We climb and climb to stand still.
We jump through all the hoops until
We are filled with exhaustion and still
We have not reached our destination at the top of life's hill.

Youth fills the mind with dreams and hopes,
That someday life will remove its unfunny jokes,
And the mind's shackles and chains and ropes,
And replace them with wisdom and strength like the large old
tree of oak.

Alas as Father Time keeps on working old age arrives.
It becomes clear that those aspirations to which we once did strive,
Are truly lost forever in the passage of time,
But which will live on in the tormenting crevice of the mind,
Where all our failures are stored as a constant reminder
Of our inability to always achieve that which we desire.

Rosana Henrietta Bailey

A Wonderful World!

I sigh as a warm breeze passes by me
I think this will be the happiest I'll ever be
My mind is away in a world of its own
My body has no aches and I don't groan

I pick through the branches of the trees
I see something glowing and bend on my knees
A stone so lovely and sparkling too
A rabbit runs past and stares at my shoe

Creatures watch me eyes all aglow
The stone I throw catch and again I throw
The sun through the trees shines in my eyes
I twirl around and flow into deeper sighs

Beauty and nature all by my side
The space for me is so wide
Can this be real, maybe it's not
The wonderful times that I've got

Yup! I was right, look where I am
On my bed hugging my dog Sam
Oh well, life's not so great
Until it is I can't wait

Johanne Attfield

From An Upstairs Window

I can see far from here
over sea, sand, road and people.
Sea, sand and the person I hold dear.

She comes into the view below
not stopping even to glance
from where my kitchen light glows

Brightly for the ships to see.
Why won't you climb the stairs?
Last night I nearly believed you loved me

Now I'm no longer sure
that what I feel for you
is not shared by you at all.

What can I do to save the love I gave
now as you climb back to your car.
You don't see me smile and wave.

Only the sea looks solemnly back
and returns my lonely call.

K. J. Moran

The Searcher

Never too deep
  This life that fails true purpose
Against these forces
  Flows a rare - yet simple soul
Ahead the turns and silent melodies
  Shrouded havens and cloaks of time
This mortal swirl - a pool of pulses
  Its rhythm - erratic, the player to forge
Through sighs last burden,
  Diverse pathways
Hope's last venture and chances call
  Its fragile threads - a chance to weave such beauty
A cloak for all from pulses formed
  Never defeat - mere moments weakness
Lets the life, a blaze of yours
  Venture ever with simple purpose
Never too deep nor shrouded havens
  All corners sought for melodies born
Through sighs last hurdle
  Hope's last venture, flows ever rare - ye simple soul

Leslie Downton

If...

If you can trust yourself when others doubt you
And always try to keep your head up high
If you can love and cherish those about you
You'll have treasures money cannot buy

Though hurt inside, if you can learn to face the truth
And when growing older keep an open mind
Retain your fun and with it you'll retain your youth
Be honest but remember to be kind.

Make sure your head has time to float up in the clouds
But keep your feet set firmly on the ground
Pick out that lonesome person standing in the crowd
And folk will all be pleased when you're around.

If you can balance dreams with practicality
And deal in facts but keep ideas in mind
If you can stamp your special personality
On the teeming mass we sometimes call mankind

If you can keep the special you that's deep inside you
Although you may be husband, sister, wife
You'll maybe count your friends instead of money
But you'll have a very rich rewarding life.

Cynthia Jones

The Slaughter Of The Innocents

Led one by one, they stumble on, their unknown fate to meet
These humble creatures so forlorn, an innocence complete.
Wide soft brown eyes with trustful gaze, look hauntingly about
   They smell the death that fills the air, and tremble in their
     doubt.

These trusting creatures so abused, like others of their kind
   By greed of men who without thought, have only gain in mind.
Appalling greed, infected feed, a lethal combination
   Their staggering gait, their unknown pain, has hardly touched
     the nation.

Man caused them pain, disease and death, that never should
   have been
   By wrongful ways of husbandry, unnatural and obscene.
Now to the slaughter they must go, appeasement is the game
   To those abroad, whose sole concern, is power, might and gain.

What do they know of husbandry, these city farming folk
   They care not for their animals, their ignorance a joke.
Where are the voices that should be raised, to plead for sanity
   This obscene cull of healthy stock, gross inhumanity.

They give so freely of themselves, they do not ask for more
   Than kindness, care and wholesome feed, untainted as before.
So shed your tears, and pity them, their sorry plight a scandal
   Those innocents, whose fate is writ, by men not worth one candle.

   Jane Laver

No Man's Land - Bosnia, 1992

Torn from sleep by the stutter of bullets,
They sought refuge in cellars, rat-ridden and damp,
Vainly awaiting an intermission from noise.
But dawn brought no respite.
Bleary-eyed and numbed with cold
Into the dark morning light they staggered,
Miserably wrapped in threadbare coverings,
Bare-foot children at their heels,
But one thought in mind-to flee,
Flee the horror of bomb flashes in broken rooms
And the cursed inhumanity of civil strife.
Along the road a red flag fluttered,
Marking the shell-pocked entrance to no Man's Land,
Mocking with its distant promise of silence and safety.
Painfully, they shuffled past the final road block,
Unaware of threatening rifles and soldiers' curses,
Until twenty yards onwards guns rattle again;
Bullets thud into soft, unprotected backs.
Soon they all lie limp as red rag dolls.
Our shame, their point of no return.

   John Liversedge

Miss Prism's House

Miss Prism's house is neat and tidy,
Miss Prism's house still looks like new.
Everything is bright and shining,
Done and dusted; polished too.

Our old house is like a junk yard,
Books and games left anywhere.
"It's a tip", that's what our Dad says,
"Enough to make a bishop swear"

Miss Prism's meal times never vary,
Lunch at twelve and tea at five.
Her cups are china, and the honey
Comes from a pot shaped like a hive.

Mum always tries to get our dinner
For the same time every day
But either this one's playing football,
Or that one's not come in from play.

Miss Prism's house, precisely ordered,
Gives lonely echoes when you speak.
There's noise and laughs and love in our house,
Dad says "we'll tidy up next week."

   John Chilton

You Could Never Know

You could never know how I feel inside,
What you do to me I can't describe,
I am just holding on to a dream that could never come true,
If only you knew what I feel for you.

I would love you for always if only you could see,
that when I am lost you shine a light for me,
I would give you my love because I know you're the one,
I know that it's love from this love I can't run.

Even if you're miles away I will always be by your side.
In this knot of love I am tangled and tied,
I could never forget you, you are always in my heart,
My feelings for you will never depart.

I long to touch you but you've out of my reach,
I've got feeling for you and I can't let go,
I won't let go, I could never let go.

   Hayley Redmore

Shadows

Night shadows passing
crossing the vision of the moon.
Soft night breezes
caressing sleeping flowers.
Druids of old gather in their groups.

Quickening steps,
tread lightly upon a path.
The heat of the midnight hour
cooled by light refreshing rain.
Glistening sparkles upon their robes.

A meeting of enlightened souls
encircling meet,
low chanting audible
above sky birds of the soundless night,
taking flight.

A time of exchanged humbleness
acknowledged communication between spirits.
All seeking the same thing,
to be at one with peace...

   Christine Jackson

Bullying

Bully, Bully, go away,
I'm tired of your unfair play,
You hit and kick me as hard as you can,
Why do you do it? I don't understand.

You think you're so tough with all your mates,
You wait for me every day at the school gates,
I'm tired of your hurtful names and violence,
No longer will I suffer in silence!

You'll learn one day you've made a big mistake,
People's friendship you had has now turned to hate,
Your friends got out of it while they could,
They realised you were wrong, I really wish you would.

   Nicola Lyons

Fate

I cannot understand that at the stroke
Of a hand
You will no longer hear the band,
Remembered for a while,
That certain smile,
It's as if all of us are on trial,
Life is not easy,
Life is very hard,
Life seems to be decided by the pull of a card,
Whether you're rich, whether you're poor,
It is only health that can alter the score,
But even health will not alter the fact,
That the stroke of the hand is always exact..

   Wilfred Jones

'Why Worry?'

My minds eye cannot conceive our legacy when transferred,
to the next generation,
May the gold be conveyed upon Wells, Spielberg et al,
Be they of intergalactic origin or more humble incept,
It is my fervent desire they treat it well.

Memories of a landscape, of humanity near and far,
Invading the nebula, conscience unaware,
Teachings diluted to the point of extinction,
Inanimate animation's or holograms, do they care?

Humankind, to which I belong, no saviour will permit,
that I can see,
Thoughts of nature, of families and of the Lord predominate,
Lest we hear, take heed and learn immediately,
Is it inevitable? Are we too late?

And what of our successors? If indeed we are succeeded,
Will future accountability decree we are all free from guilt?
Inexorably the fourth dimension will bear witness to our trial,
And the diminishing legacy that mankind hath built.

Tim Edwards

Brief Encounter

I've seen their tracks so many times
Along the path I walk each day.
Two sets of hooves precisely pressed
Beside the path, into the clay.

I sensed a presence in the trees,
There stood a doe and fawn so shy.
I don't know who was more surprised,
The gentle deer and fawn, or I.

I stopped, she looked and our eyes met,
So soft and full of fear.
She curved her body round the fawn.
I wouldn't dare go near.

I held my breath, afraid to move.
The dog began to whimper.
She nudged the fawn. On silent feet,
Through coppice wood they scamper.

The picture of this gentle pair
Will always stay with me.
I've stored it in a slot I call,
"My Future Memory".

Peggy Fountain

The Grim Reaper's Sales Pitch -
A Rhyme For Our Time

Sign here, Sir, please, for your place at the crem.
There're only so many to spare, at the crem.
Life's such a burden, why bother to stay?
Take my advice, and live for the day.

Heed what I say, make pleasure your passion.
Go your own way, and smoke with no ration.
Relish chips, butter, bacon, and fatty red meat,
With a gallon of ale, they'll go down a treat.

Cream cakes and pastries, what more to delight.
Chocolates and sweets, you'll guzzle all night.
Take all the mint creams, eat a packet at least.
A pint of good brandy, no less for a feast.

Suet pudding, ah yes. Nought better you'll get
For lining your tummy, and arteries I'll bet.
Never, no never, let fruit pass you lips,
Nor greens, nor beans, if you'll take all my tips.

Hark what I say, exertion is crazy.
Don't run, even walk, relax and be lazy.
Then you'll jump at the chance to get in the queue
For dispatch at the crem - with your friends in the pew.

Dennis Harrison

Seasons

Fragrant flowers bloom in spring.
The scented air smells so sweet.
The joyous wonders of hearing young birds sing
and spring lambs leaping to their feet.

Hot summer days and humid nights,
Ice-creams and lollipops; the sand and the sea.
Traffic jams and caravans are an everyday sight.
It's holiday time, and it's good to be free.

Autumn leaves fall to the ground,
gently blowing in the cooling air.
Beautiful shades of golden brown -
so stunning, no other colour can compare.

Long dark nights are closing in,
Winter's arrived once more.
Snowball fights and sleigh bells ring
and carol singers beckon at your door.

Barbara A. Lettin

A Flight Of Fancy

Oh, the birds, yes the birds, they have taken us over
Deserting the hedge-rows the trees and the clover
Preferring the chimney-pots roof-tops and bricks.
Making untidy nests to bring up their chicks.

They had multiple weddings on St Valentines Day
And made love on the roof-tops Oh, what a display,
Then watched by their mothers their fathers and aunts.
They went reeling off in fertility dance.

The young-ones are funny, treating life as a joke
They scream like a banshees and frighten old folk,
They swoop on our shopping, cooked food in their target
I've heard it's the same from Brighton to Margate.

The babies grow fat with continual feeding
And a fall from the nest is a regular thing
But go near at your peril and they soon have you bleeding
There's just one thing to do, give the bird-man a ring

So now, what's the answer, do we flee to the country
And just throw up our hands, our loss is their gain
So if we go the food goes, they haven't worked that out
now I know what the phrase means "You've got a bird brain"

Frances M. Steel

Natural

As the clouds gather high in the sky,
nobody knows how, nobody know why.
This is nature doing what it has always done,
what will come next, the rain or the sun?
Thunder and lightning a fierce storm ahead,
brilliant sunshine a scorcher instead.
The way the world works is a very strange thing,
just let it happen and see what it brings.

Mark Maulkerson

Homeless

I sit, crouched and haggard, like an old man,
Feeling the cold bite into my hands,
I've given up hope, my face is pale.
The bread beside me has long since been stale
I sit on a bag, I sleep on a box,
Long time ago was my dignity lost.
I beg if I'm desperate, I struggle and strive
Only then if I'm lucky, do I stay alive.
The street's cold and dirty; my muscles are weak.
I'm so full of anger, I don't bother to speak.
My clothes are ragged, my hair is grey,
My teeth are rotting and they're thick with decay.
My life is empty, I've nothing to keep,
Never getting more than a few hours sleep.
So as you can see, life's more than tough,
When, like me, you have to live rough.

Elisa Wright

Comment On Some Effects Of Mass Media

Before Bell, Marconi and Baird, the world condensed,
When news travelled slowly, in time with the horse,
By oral tradition was information dispensed
Giving time to consider and reason by way of discourse.

Now Through television, lives lived second-hand,
Via drama, soap and talk show host,
In political programme, hear pundits expand
On opinion and theory, with truth damaged most,

On wireless, in newsprint the experts expound,
Quoting policy documents, figures and facts.
Giving air to their views with sonorous sound,
Influencing attitudes, thinking and original acts.

Ideas are formed, and now people expect
Instant comment on issues, ill-informed to discuss,
From reality of living many people defect,
Unable to cope with life's traumas, troubles and fuss.

Mike McEwan

To Live On Mars

One day humans will venture to Mars
A stepping stone on the way to the stars
Great transparent domes will be built when they land
An interlinked network of homes, on the red desert sand
Many plants will be grown in these biospheres
For food and to replenish the local atmospheres

Mars was so different long long ago
The volcanoes were active, and the rivers did flow
But when the volcanoes finally ceased to smoke and spout,
The warm air was lost, and the rivers froze out
To terra form mars requires the greenhouse effect
The ultimate project to make Mars perfect

A day spent on Mars is very similar to ours
Turning once on its axis in just over twenty-four hours
After martian sunset, if one looks to the stars
Not one, but two moons can be seen orbiting Mars,
They are small but close, and will appear very clear
Their names are phobos, and deimos, which means flight and fear.

Stephen Norman Morris

Spring

Look around you, there's the sun
Shining down, on everyone.
Dappled light, comes through the trees
Shadows, darting in the breeze.
Birds fly high, singing sweet.
Lovely flowers, at your feet.
Wildlife scurries two and fro,
The bees, they work, the whole day through
Making honey that's so sweet
So you and me can have a treat.
Life's beginning.
Life is fun.
For the old and for the young.
Look around you, there's the sun.
Shining down or everyone.

Joan Jarvis

Jessica

Jessica hated noise.
Vile, vicious, violent, vitriol,
She looked at the rifle.
Yes, Jessica hated noise.
She found the gun primed in her arms;
cushioned as an infant.
From above she watched; distantly surprised
at her knowledge.
Jessica wanted peace.
Vaguely unaware: absolutely intent.
The rich blood flowed.
Ditto relief.
Obsidian eyes reopened.

Margaret A. Baldwin

Untitled

Soft-pillowed, sweet-scented, moon-misted dreams
Were ours in a world of some content,
For the far away voices of warning went
Unheeded until we were wakened by screams
From the dupes who had listened, year after year,
Had believed all the untruths and lies
Of those who were preaching the gospel of fear,
Lest half-happy fools should seek paradise:
And when the ill-gotten, foul womb-diseased schemes
Of the cheats have matured in the death-teeming torrent,
Now pouring blood-red through the truth-twisted vent
Of mistrust which they built on deceit-ridden seams,
Their dams of falsehood will burst to release
A hell-flaming flood; the next pseudo-peace

Robert Boswell

I Promise You

My love for you will never die
Of that I will not ever lie
For true love comes but once in lifetime
Bringing feelings for the nice times

Love letters notes presents too
Cannot show my love for you
And words alone cannot express
This feeling deep within my breast

Not a thing can match the fun we had
On outings pranks, the laughs we have
In bad times kisses cuddles too
And romantic evenings alone with you

The good times the bad times
The memories of you
Will last a whole lifetime
I promise you.

Wendy Capers

The West Coast

Ireland, my Ireland, land of toil,
On the black stove, the pan boils,
Men return from a days work with the soil,
Oh, for the sweet smell of the peat,
Oh, for the women, never to beat.

Decline to sign the pledge from the drink!
Seemingly 'tis the way to sink,
Swiftly driving a man to the brink.
Ireland my Ireland, land of toil,
To thee forever will I be loyal.

As a child, in the trim cotton frock;
And well stitched old cotton sock,
We would play and work, both hard on the land,
At times, following of with the church band.
Oh mother dear, do not fear,
I will give a hand,
For the love of you and the land.

Patricia Lawler

Moonbeams And Dreams

Reams and reams of moonbeams and dreams,
team together, forever, never ever stopping,
glowing and beaming delightful lights,
full of love from above.

Dreamy pools of light, beaming reams of delight
dreamy lights illuminating, giving gifts of life and peace
capture those lights for a moment in time.
Experiencing the magic of moonbeams and dreams

Moonbeams and dreams can soon be yours
If you open those doors to the gleams in the sky.
Melt into the gleams and glow of illuminating light,
delighting in moonbeams and dreams,
teemed up for ever with the universal dream

Jane Brewer

When We Meet Again

Near the Cotswold Hills so breezy and wide
I found a small village on the other side,
The name of the village I do not know,
But its proud little church set my heart aglow.

The name of the church I cannot recall,
But that ageless shrine was open to all,
And history spoke from those crumbling walls,
As that clarion note of victory calls.

For a family lies in that church asleep,
And each for all a tender vigil keep.
They talk of the time when they rises again
With no more sorrow and no more pain.

They radiate joy and hope and love,
Through those ancient walls to the realms above.
They know what to do and what to say,
And are fully prepared for that Judgement Day.

In this secular world we blaze our trail,
Let us never these noble sentiments fail.
Despite our many earthly ideas
Only the spirit can calm our fears.

J. M. Keilor

The Kingpin

In my embryonic days - in my crudest forms -
Before that mercurial motion sped along the highway,
Or that powered locomotion thundered along the track,
Long before the dream of that beckoning blue became reality -
I was born -
The product of parental planning,
The crafted gestation of skilful hands
And the beaded sweat of labour;
Combining strength with grace, freedom is my nurture;
When I see your endless pleasure, the depths of your love for me,
As we sail - as one - to the sunset and beyond,
Or at rest in my skeletal beauty,
I know - that I am still the kingpin;
When I feel the wind billowing in my sails,
My heart swells like that which buoyantly saves me from the
    fearful death-bed;
My eyes are moist with salty tears, for my beauty is reflected in you-
The awe and admiration of those whose unfamiliar feet trod upon my
    Well-swabbed being;
When I am gone - far from their wistful, last-glimpse gaze - they will
    Never forget me,
For I - I, the tall ship -
I am the most beautiful, the most dignified of all.

Helena Gillies

Nanny

She gave with her heart, without a second thought.
Sweets and cakes specially bought.
Presents I'll treasure for the rest of my life.
Caring and loving and listening so much.
My Nan was so special, I love her so much.

She used up her love, and now she's at rest.
Up with the Gods is where she is best,
Looking down on us, somewhere nearby,
Listening to us when ever we cry.
I know she's not with us in body and mind,
But she'll be forever by my side.

Nanny I miss you, I wish you were here.
That's one wish I know will never come true.
But nanny I will always be thinking of you.

Laughing and joking and smiling - that's what you did best,
Caring for others in bad times and best.
I love you more than words can say.
I hope you're happy with God up above.
I know he will look after you, my sweet love.

Louise Henry

Suicide

I looked around me, all was still,
I shook the bottle, out fell the last pill.
The last pill to end my life,
I could have done it easy with a knife.
I take some water and stare at the pill's colour,
Why do I want to scream for my mother?
I want to die, but I have no will,
Just in my hand a tiny pill.
Will I do it, I'm not sure,
I see Heaven and to it the door.
I walk slowly towards it,
I walk close to it.
I open the door,
I walk through.
I see a stream pour,
Of tears from you.
I have died,
You tried.
As I lie there,
I say goodbye there.

Angela Holmes

Bon Voyage (Or Sailor Beware!!!)

An unsuspecting Captain prepared for foreign clime,
A smooth unruffled passage purportedly to find,
The anchor weighed, the luggage stowed
Below deck in the hold,
He strode the bridge, chest puffed with pride,
His 'subjects' to behold.

When suddenly his eyes espied two matrons arm in arm,
With sequinned tights, and mini-skirts,
Their hamburgers still warm...
'Young free and single' slogans adorned their rakish hats,
The winks they gave the sailors, bore testament to that.
"Which way the Captain's table", they cried with Joie de Vivre,
"And afterwards I know that he will want to dance with me".

"What fate awaits me on this trip", the Captain's brain raced quicker,
"I'll do a bunk - it's not too late,
And send for Alan Whicker!!!"

M. L. Rothery

"A Roller Blind"

I am a Roller Blind,
    and you will find, that my life like yours,
is full of ups and downs,
    highs and lows.
I am yours to command,
    by the touch of your hand.
A tug on my cord, will pull me up.
    And give you light.
Another tug will pull me down,
    and make it dark as night.
Pull me half-way down,
    and like that old noble duke of York,
I'll be neither up nor down.
    If you pull me too hard
I'm liable to go over the top,
    or finish up on the floor.
Life is sometimes a bit of a bind,
    for you, as well as a Roller Blind.

Thomas Leech

Why

Why do I feel so lonely, when there are people around,
Why does it seem so quiet, when everything's making a sound,
Why do I feel like a failure, useless in every way.
Why do I have to work, there's never time to play.
Why is the world so cruel, yet so beautiful as well,
Why is the sky so blue, why do the flowers smell,
God created heaven and earth simply for man's pleasure,
So we should enjoy his gifts, in our hours of leisure,
Yet this feeling of loneliness is something I abhor,
I want to feel a part of life, a no one anymore.

R. Cocklin

Answer In Space Provided

Am I not meant to be here?
Am I just a mistake?
Was my mind made to be confused?
Was my heart made to break?
Do you know something that I don't?
Is there something you'd like to share?
Is there something I need that's missing?
Do any of you care?
Is there anybody out there?
Or am I just my imagination?
Do any of you speak my language?
Do I have a destination?
Could somebody please give me directions?
Did I miss the vital class?
Is there some sort of manual?
Did I fail or did I pass?
Did I miss the connection?
Is there a button I forgot to touch?
Would anyone like to answer me?
Or did I already ask too much?

Gemma Jackson

Loving A Girl Like You

I could always love a girl like you,
with a heart of gold that shows you're true,
Loves to listen and loves to care,
always there willing to share, when times
are good or times are bad, you may be
happy, you may be sad, you're a pretty girl
I know that for sure, with a personality
that I adore, so with this poem I'll like
to show, all my thanks that's what I want
you to know, so all I'm asking is for
you to stay in touch, because if you
don't you'll upset me very much. So
now in this poem I cannot lie, all my
feelings which could make me cry.
Everything in this poem is really true,
I could always love a girl like you...

Stephen Philip Lang

Untitled

Death and desolation, as in days of old,
Sinful man embraces, the world to enfold.
Bethlehem born, babe so fair, holy child none
Could compare; yea! He was born to die in
Pain upon a cross, so cruel was slain.

Forgive us Father for our sin, 'repentance call,'
New world begin - Lord, master, teacher,
Friend, uphold the faithful unto journey's end.
Sacrifice be not in vain; for Jesus' life our
Richest gain, dear Saviour of the world remain;
To the Son anointed king; this humble gift
Of love we bring - our life the key to
Heaven's gate. - The chosen path! Deliberate!
The Trinity! - Anticipate.

M. W. Clarke

King Confusion

Muddled thoughts control my mind,
Sanity mixed with insanity,
Misshapen thoughts block, puncture my soul
Confusion reigns, dwells upon my life
The turmoil of lives thrown into one,
pull me under into darkness
and more confusion.
My life is a disarray of mixed
emotions, mixed people and mixed loves.

The most simplistic of thoughts try
to break the barrier of my brain,
but again,
Confusion rules.

Nicola Wood

A Shadow

False hope controls my life,
insignificant as a shadow.
My mind wanders into a dark valley,
of lonely souls discarded by life.
Zombie-like faces trapped in a sea of gloom,
I cry a tremendous feeling of pain.

My life doesn't exist anymore,
all of what's left on an Almighty cloud of nothing.
I see human, but do not feel human,
more a prisoner trapped by your lies.

White, others are dressed in white,
why then am I dressed in black?
That explains my differences,
You're the followers, I'm the leader.

A. Bain

Horrious Of Peace

I see a piercing, burning light beyond which says
There must be Peace.
The discords and the factions stay but people try with everyday.
The politicians talk and delve their minds to find the way
Because they know there must be peace.
The men of violence lone stand still, still rooted firmly
in the past. Refuse to part with thoughts of hate
They dwell on unenlightened times, on all the inequalities
and want the war to last.
But even they must know they can't succeed,
That times are changing now, the spirits rise to show us how.
How to dissolve the differences and diffuse the turgid air
The doves are flying everywhere look now and listen.
For peace has such a sweeter gentler ring
And bells peel out in every corner saying,
Stop still and hear the people sing - what
from their hearts they must release
The loud tumultuous shout that rids us from this tyranny
and says again there must be Peace.

N. E. Nash

Am I The Man In The Glass

When you get what you want in your struggle for wealth
and the world makes you king for a day
Just go to your mirror and look at yourself
and see what that has to say

For it isn't your mother, or husband or wife
whom judgement upon you must pass
No, the fellow whose verdict counts most in your life
is the one looking back from the glass

Some fellows may call you a straight shooting chum
and say you're a wonderful guy
But the man in the glass says you're only a bum
if you can't look him back in the eye

You may fool the world down the pathway of years
and get pats on your back as you pass
But your final reward will be heartache and tears
if you have cheated the man in the glass

Malcolm L. B. Hunter

That Extra bit

If you care a while longer
Than is normal,
You shall caress

If you are able to be a little more human
Than most are
You shall show humanity

If you can extend compassion beyond
Merely having it
You shall be compassionate

If you give more love than
You have
You shall be loved

Craig Robinson

'Oh! Lonely Road'

Oh lonely road! my love, since you have died.
Sweet thoughts and tears for you I've cried,
Were we to know the paths, we'd take,
Would your hand meet mine,
The long long road to make!
Great riches never came our way;
Just shining truths, and trust each day,
The fires that burned inside of us,
Made sparkling words to calm the fuss
Tender moments brought the charm
That only love, means free from harm,
Sun-filled beaches, warm blue seas,
Gave us balm the hurts to ease,
Dark black clouds came, with pouring rain,
To the hearts that cared, and cared in vain,
My only love, with pain and fears
Snared in the trap of later years,
Closed his eyes in peaceful sleep,
The gentle shepherd's arms to keep
My love in sweet repose; until my lonely eyelids close.

Anne Oddie

"Far Have A Oor Birdies Gone?"

Far hiv a oor birdies gone?
The breed sits foostin on the lawn,
'Tis nae mare like when I wis young,
Fin in a frenzy they'd swoop among,
The scraps oh breed mi mither flung,

In Hospitalfield's grounds grew a handful oh trees,
It fair broke mi heart when they chappet doon these,
The cushie-doo's - descendants - bred by the monks,
Noo fearsomely compete fir their wee tickey bunks,

So far's a the birds that sang in the rain,
That splashed in the dubbies as they coursed doon the drain,
The silent sk ies are a filled with disdain,
Noo only a puckle oh their offsprings remain,
Worms noo fill the dubs far they'd entertained,

So far hiv a oor birdies gone?
And a the trees they sat upon?
They filled my gerden we sich cheery song,
His that day really come, are they a nearly gone?

They've a gone fir ever, cis we jist didnae care!
The sky now mirrors the forest, silent! empty! and bare!

W. G. Gordon

Earth Woman

I'm the woman of the ground
my soul springs through mountains and rivers.

I don't belong anywhere, then, I belong somewhere;
but my voice has the sound of all hymns in harmony.

My song is elevating to infinity
where the sea and the sky are united forever.

The wind brings me back to the origin of time;
the sun's tenderness rest in my roots, and,
I become alive again with the flowering of colours in the summer.

Hope grows up in my leaves, after, when autumn arrives
they're transformed into an ardent rainbow, flying at will
feeding our interminable hunger of the future.

The dew caress my shapes, the fountain of new life;
my blood runs like rain
in the thirsty earth of my flesh;
my bones are rocks
drawn by the breeze and the dance of the waves
as they play flirtingly in my senses.

I hear, I see, I smell, I touch
The sweet salt of the hidden secret.

Carmen Lamas Waldron

Lament

You died - unknown - upon the busy road,
Pathetic shape of fur - of black and white.
You must have crossed so many times before
While on your furtive journeys in the night.

You hated humans - fleeing from their path.
What had they done to make you full of fear?
But even more you loathed their well-fed pets
Who hugged the house when sensing you were near.

I often saw you watching from the bank -
Your refuge, p'haps, when driven off and cursed.
I hope you ate the scraps I sometimes left
Or did the friendly hedgehog find them first?

Unknown, unloved, you came. Short was your stay.
But I will miss you, cat. Poor tattered stray.

Marjorie H. Couzens

Untitled

Thy came to me with such fair face,
Thy purity shone from within;
Your smile was beauty like fine lace,
Lusty and fairly we both twain;
The sun suddenly stopped rising,
The blue sky was lost;
A shadow of darkness covered mine life,
Losing my friend, I see my cross;
Amazeth is such grief,
Confounds thy lusty soul;
Debarr'd by dateless cries,
I sigh the lack of many things I sought;
   Vouchsafe me, losses are restored,
   For thy sweet love memories are my treasure!

Sarah Brobson

Snow In March 1975

I woke this morn
At the crack of dawn.
And what did I see,
A coat of white on every tree.

The earth its self all covered too,
Was as if I had entered a world so new.
Everything there is so pure and white.
A complete change made in the night.

Daylight brings the beauty clear,
The snow is very late this year.
Oh look a beautiful bullfinch pair I see,
Happily pecking away at the buds in the tree.
Their bright red breast among the snow,
Hopping around they make a show.
It's been snowing now for hours and hours,
Has covered up all our lovely flowers.
Out of sight the world will stay,
Until the snow has melted away.

Mary Woodhams

Letter From The Heart

Turning the yellow pages,
You took my heart and began to write a new chapter
On fresh white leaves of emotion.
The printing is so clear,
As the words make their way gently across,
Red with desire and helpless like a child;
If you are looking for a reason that I should feel this way
Look no further then the pen of your smile.

You may be right in thinking that only fools
Write letters from the heart,
But I'd rather be a fool than be sensible about you,
And if you're scared of loving me the way that you want to do
Hold my hand, and I will lead you to where love knows no fear.
Loving you is not the hardest part for if it was I'd make it harder;
Open up your heart and I'll write messages for you.

Wayne Robert Ullyatt

Peace For All

I thought that war was over,
I thought the hatred done.
I remembered grieving women
Who mourned for husband and for son.

I thought, then, of the women
And girls who bravely died,
The nurses and the women's corps,
Who wore their uniform with pride.

So many years have come and gone since 1945.
Peace was declared,
But war fought on,
And each day someone has died.

For guns and bombs and bullets
Never ever care.
Be it friend or foe or tiny child,
They must destroy each one that's there.

If mankind would only pause a while,
Not heed the war drums' call.
Each mothers prayer may then be heard,
And peace could reign for all.

Ann Kelley

The Dream

In streets we played - high walls around
And brick upon brick houses there abounded
We played around the streets - oh so bare
No greenery - no trees were there.

"When we grow up" - thus we talked and dreamed
Of living in a green green land,
Where we could see the setting sun
Settle, nestling softly o'er on the horizon.

See the skyline ablaze with glory
Would this dream come true? Or just be a fairy story?
Then one day - oh joy - it happened!
Our dream house came - and there was fashioned
An area so bright - so clean -
Our very own - our village green!

Our children played and grew up bonny
Though there were times when we had little money
these were happier days. They had the green - the air - the sun
Saw the wonder in the sky when day was done

We were content our dream came true
Our home - our children and the green to view

Molly E. Martin

Still

Stranger, hello!... we meet again,
begin again. Same name, different face.
Find me still; pacing, waiting, searching crazily for a you and me,
You must be too... what else to do?!

Scrabbling around my maze - here I am! Still.
One of you, must, have that golden key
unlock my life, give me - me
freedom, safety, calmness in unity, airtight bubble of
love. A dream?...
My nightmare!

Stranger, hello!... Surname, friend?
Standing just inside the door. No!
But at the core this time; an understanding
connection, at last?
Dolly mixture of emotions offered you to
secure - me.

Still ready to run, struggling always.
You've caught me. Timid.
I'm still kicking.
Hold me still, new friend.

Samantha Dawn Clarke

Untitled

I went out to sit in my garden one day,
To brush my cares and troubles away,
I felt so low and ready to cry,
Till I saw a lovely butterfly
I watched it fly, I watched it flutter,
And thought, come on don't be a nutter.
To sit out here and watch the world go by,
When there's so much beauty like a butterfly.

M. Coogan

Untitled

When I am dead this message you'll find
To help you gain peace of mind

Lay me down in an oblong box
Without any clothes or a pair of socks

To give the ants a little treat
Cover me o'er with a clean white sheet

Take my body to its resting place
Away from this terrible human race

Cover me o'er with earth and sod
Cause I won't trouble, 'cause I'm with God.

Heather Dawn Anderton

Captive

He was born to be free
Who cares, but a few
With the cage high around him
He has little to view.

Endless footsteps of people passing
Coughing, sneezing, chatting and laughing
They have no real interest, except time to pass
Occasionally tapping upon the glass.

Stopping to peer at exhibit eight
Licking ice-cream as they lean on the gate
Liberty gone, he waits to be fed
Nothing to do, he lowers his head.

Soaring high in the sky was once his delight
He surely was a magnificent sight
Lush green pastures were his domain
Now concrete surrounds his wired frame

His captors are proud of all they have done
Large bright cages are second to none
Never the less like you and me
It isn't enough, He Was Born To Be Free.

Patricia Dare

Was It Really Us?

I go through life sometimes happy, sometimes sad!
It's funny how relationships can make us so mad!
But the fact is we need them so bad!

The smile from across the room.
Can fill you with so much bloom.
The blossoms from those red cheeks.
Compare to a ripping peach.

Then one day after he has gone away.
I look back at the way things use to be.
And you wonder whether that was really ever
you and me?

Those cheeks so red.
The things you said.
Do they really all matter to me?
Or is it just another one of those ripples in the sea?

I guess I'll never know!
So I suppose it's time for me to go?
But what I am left with is the glisten
in your eyes as you said the final goodbye.

Androulla Konnaris

"Words"

Words well arranged have beauty like flowers,,
Refreshing the hearer, as cooling as showers.
Words of kindness give us fresh heart,
Also when written to friends far apart
Conveying a message of kindness and love.
Soothing the soul like the coo of the dove.

Words that encourage and give us the strength
To travel the road whatever its length.
The pitfalls in life give most a rough ride;
Are you dismayed by the strength of the tide?
When words of encouragement are all that you hear
You will travel life's ways without any fear.

The words of a song entwining the heart
Speak of a love nothing can part.
Sheer beauty of words, the lilt of a song
Blended together sweep us along.
By using words wisely by night or by day
They'll carry the scent of a lovely nosegay.

Edgar Edwards

My Children

My children are to me
More precious than any gold could be,
Sweet happiness only a mother will know
Ah, where do those passing years go.

They laugh, they cry, they skip, they play
I see them change from day to day,
Sometimes I pause and in my mind,
I see them, childhood left behind

No riches found upon this earth
Could compensate me for their loss
The love they give me, is the treasure
God sends a mother, without measure.

Kathleen Gilmore

His - Rose Only Of 1941

He pledged to-tend was steadfast
He'd "grow-a-rose: "To-last!"
From his-patent "special" compost sprung a trusting form
Coaxed-on in warmth from that first day its seed-of-love was
  born and-meant to last
This "special" rose: To-him beyond compare!
  Though-now without his tender care
  How-can-it? Last
Ah "treasured" rose: He loved-through life yet did-not pick
For changing winds flung-us around he this-time far-too-quick
  His -last
One "cultured" rose: Alone still-lasts; in wilts-of-need
Since death has plucked "the-patient-planter" of-its-seed:
  Too-fast
An "endeared" rose: A petal-scented head of tranquil reveries
  In moss-enveloped memories
  He's-cast.

D. Gainford

Summer's Love Song...

The summer started with him, lazy, endless hours,
Thoughts of browning meadows with scatterings of flowers,
Cut grass smell and dozy bumble bees,
Scorching heat and gently scented breeze,
The salty taste of the seaside air,
The mid-noon sun bleaching his hair;
Shared ice-cream and apple tree shade
On cool ground in a hidden glade.
Confetti flowers floating down the stream,
The twilight glow brings the haze of a dream
Wrapped in his arms, the beat of his heart
Is drowned by the blackbird as he starts
His warbled serenade, telling the story
Of a couple wallowing in Summer's glory.

E. A. Parker

Silence Is Golden

I know much which remains unspoken;
Many thoughts which may never be heard;
And feelings which have been awoken,
Never expressed in action or word.

As cards are held close up to the chest;
And secrets locked safely in the heart -
Then denied is the worldly behest -
In revealing all, having no part.

To be open is the portrayal;
A virtue - being brutally frank;
Archly ignoring a betrayal;
Where does loyal humility rank?

Suspicion can grow as a cancer;
'Til tempting a direct question out -
How shattering the truthful answer;
More damaging than the gnawing doubt!

In age of assertion and chatter,
Forbearance and silence are golden,
So be not ashamed of the latter,
And to current trends, not beholden.

Roy Hammond

Il Bambino

We were no band of fighting troops in the 19th Signal Corps,
Our function was to link the groups, who fought or run the war.
The Villa on the hill looked right, a very good location.
An excellent transmitter site, for a signal station.

A shattered door, and then we saw, the woman clearly dead.
A bloody mess upon the floor, that once had been her head.
And then we heard a childish scream, a lusty joyous sound
and underneath a fallen beam, a little boy we found.

An infant of angelic mien, rounded in thigh and belly.
Like a cherub from a Bible scene, painted by Botticelli.
He laughed and smiled at everyone, his face a joy to see,
He even smiled at Corporal Dunn, the section misery.

We found some of his family, their daughter's fate to tell,
and they were overjoyed to see, their grandson safe and well.
I never made the journey back, though warm their invitation,
The simple reason was the lack of time or inclination.

The war for me was fantasy, in a different time and plane,
and all I wanted was to be in my own world again.
For when comes back the memory, of that Italian place,
'Tis not a laughing child I see, but that dead woman's face.

Lionel James Hampshire

This Mortal One

As a consequence of love and care or an interlude of passion
The foetus lies in curled up fashion in a sac, transparent;
Within the womb to be its home while development to formation
This mortal one feeds and grows in a recluse, temporary.

Formation of the human one, day by day its physical self develops:
Scanned to record the progress in centimetres and grams;
Probed and tossed by human tools, hand like spades and fingers forks
Disturbing the one content, so peaceful within the mother's shell.

So dependent on the carrier to be careful not to falter
Yet, a determination and a will to live is evident;
When time is right the play will commence, curtains back
And act by act, scene by scene, the show will then unfold.

Such drama and excitement this unborn, one, will create
When in a hurry with great zest for life, outside
This mortal one with eagerness will forcefully play its part,
Among a cast culled and trained to perform each role in turn.

Within the contemporary setting, the finale will be so grand
Of a foetus once so tiny determined to take the centre stage;
To begin a life, at first dependent on one and more for sure
Until the time is right to go and face the world alone.

Catherine O'Kane

Vision

I have a vision Lord, that every child on earth
Will one day know the meaning of laughter, joy and mirth.
No more broken bodies through famine, war and strife
Or piercing eyes and glances that beg you for their life.

Do you hear our supplications and all our endless prayers
For days of peace and happiness, a right which should be theirs.
Why should they gulp the air of fire or feel the depths of pain,
They should not play in fields of blood — their moisture
    should be rain.

I have a vision Lord, that every child will see
The colours of the rainbow that reflect eternity.
No more man made sorrows but a time to build their dreams
To play in perfumed gardens and forget their harrowing screams.

You and I must play our part and make the vision clear,
Hold the sorrowful children and tell them not to fear.
O let this world which must be theirs put right the foolish wrong,
And let the children's crying be changed to grateful song.

Judy Thomas

A Runway Of Life

Precariously balanced, a runway of life
Airports' lights are all aglow
Here I stand amidst the darkness
Red light, green light, guide my flow

Engines roaring and revving me on
Desires burning from within
The midnight sky calling from afar
My journey about to begin.

Voices past and promises calling..... too late.

Like a drawbridge, the steps have been pulled up
The door now firmly closed tight
The strain and pressures of yesterday
Are completely out of sight

Comfortably coasting across the horizon
The city stench behind me
A new beginning beckons on the sunrise
It's beauty and splendour, my destiny.

Mike Byrne

The Dickerty-Dock

Did you ever hear of the Dickerty-Dock
Who lives inside the kitchen clock?
His beard is long and his nose is red,
And he wears his hat when he goes to bed.

He places his spectacles on his nose,
And brushes the dust from off his clothes,
Then he picks up his brolly and opens the door
At the back of the clock and jumps to the floor.

He scuttles away across the hall
And nobody knows that he's there at all,
He says 'Hello' to Olga the cat
And they chatter away about this and that.

He begins to dance and does a jig,
His ears start to wobble - they really are big,
The Dickerty-Dock is a friendly fellow,
His eyes are green and his hair is yellow.

Then back he fly's into the clock
Making sure it is saying 'Tock-tickerty-tock',
He puts on his hat, says 'Night-Night' to all,
And happily snores in the clock on the wall.

V. Cregeen

Memories Of A Fleeting World

She sits in her chair, hardly saying a word,
as though life has passed her by.
She keeps her memories safely in store,
just existing in the modern world, her memories are of old.
And some times when you look at her
you can almost see a glance of the pretty young maiden
she once was in her past.
And, at times, when she tries to talk, or let's loose her silvery
laugh, you know of her sense of humour that helped her
    along life's path.
And when there's talk of romance, you see her face light up,
her eyes become all misted as she remembers a lovers touch.
Her memories are fond then, but also a little sad,
for she longs for him to touch her, kiss her, or simply hold her hand.
But he's gone to another world now, she remembers with a sigh.
And now she sits there waiting, for the time she too will die.
But don't feel sad for the lady, she's lived her life before,
These memories she treasures are hers forever more.

Katya Victoria Morgan

View From My Window

From my window an ever changing scene,
A picture new each day serene,
Of seaweed brown, of rocks and still waters,
Or waves so white and rough, spraying in all quarters.

Each day I wake and drink my cup of tea,
I gaze and gaze enraptured by the scene.
How could I ever wish to move away?
How would I endure another day?
Without the knowledge that the world does change.

Each day brings something new and some new change.
The picture never stays the same.
No painting could such pleasure gain.
No, I could never move from here,
My life would never be the same, my dear.

Elizabeth Fisher

Leaving

How well they knew these endless streets
and coal seams, where to children might give birth.
Steel cage's where men plummet to the earth;
and shapeless building's rise to meet.

As one by one the Coffin's came and went;
to leave behind the grime of distant fires,
this was all they ever knew; or desired.
And now the smell of humility; its perfume spent.

As one by one the rusting steel gates close;
as the last wagons roll on and out of sight,
the uncaring officialdom will unite.
And who will feed the sparrows.

Celia Maddison

A Way Through The Darkness

Through long years of struggle the aching heart asks, WHY?
Anger flares, followed by sorrow, then compassion;
Forgiveness abounds only to be trampled down
Under the weight of unresolved burdens.

Now comes - with that flaming anger - a sense of futility,
Hopelessness, grief. Will there never be an end
To this hurdy-gurdy of charged emotions?
Can no one help to ease the crushing load?

Yes - there is One. He sees and hears and feels
The trauma on both sides of this great conflict;
And yet He understands. He cares that hearts are grieved and breaking
And reaches out His arms to embrace.

Walk into those arms and feel the warmth
Of His all encompassing Love. Burdens remains, no outward change
But deep, deep within the soul, a spark ignites;
Courage enters the heart, growing to a flame of Hope.

M. G. Winsor

"Insomnia"

Morpheus tantalizingly stretches out his hands,
To cradle you into deepest slumber;
But elusively you escape into thoughts of wordily adventures.
Bacchus beckons you back into a land of muddled confusion.
Momentarily you wriggle into bacchus world.
Of dreams of plans and senseless confusion:
Wide awake you sense the lure of Bacchus' beckonings,
Only to realize the lesser power of Morpheus' beckonings,
Against the bitter sweet lure of Bacchus' temptations!
No sleep, no rest no respite from the grasp of
Bacchus great hands.
There's no awakening for there was no sleep.
Another day elapses and you realize that slumber
has eluded you once more!
No sweet dreams, no nauseous snorings,
Only nightmares from the muddled world of Bacchus confusion.

T. Benjamin

"Freedom"

"Free as a bird"
Is a saying so often heard,
But what does "freedom" really mean?
The air we breathe?
Or freedom of speech?
Or, go our own way for pleasures we seek!

No, it's peace of mind,
Try hard and ye shall find,
"Freedom."

"Freedom" is something money can't buy,
But with a heart of gold,
We can but try,
To earn our "freedom" as of old,
And be as free as the birds in the sky.
This is my idea of "freedom."

D. P. Franks

June Fragrance

What is this fragrance which pervades the air
scenting the evening breeze?
Now it is wafting past the door.

Ah yes! The scent is from the bush upon the wall.
Indeed, now June is here, the honeysuckle buds
Begin to pour their sweetness:
Those buds, now beautifully shaped, so delicately tinged
With hues of pink or cream,
Open out and cling upon the wall devotedly.

I feel entranced and overjoyed
To know that nature once again has grown
Those perfect blooms.
Each blossom is, in daylight hours, alive with buzzing bees.
Truly it is a hive of active industry:
Even a thrush has chosen here to hide her nest of eggs!

Sweet honeysuckle! Pure delight! O restful sight tonight!
God's handiwork indeed!

E. K. Atkinson

When One Of Us Must Go

When one of us must go, and the other must stay,
It will be as though the sunshine has been taken away,
The coldness and the heartache of being all alone,
After all the years together, since we were joined as one.

So while there is still time for us to share,
Let us show each day, how much we care,
Let us fill each moment with Love and Happiness,
Spend no time in anger, only tenderness.

So when one is left behind, with the sorrow and the pain,
There will be the treasure of every memory to live again,
To be able to remember every little act of love,
Knowing we will meet again, in Heaven up above.

Irene Bartlett

Our Silver Celebration

Today is our very special day,
Twenty five years have melted away,
We came together many years gone by,
Both of us on whom we now rely,
As time rolls on our feelings grow,
Although sometimes it may not show,
Love is always hard to measure,
And you have given me so much pleasure,
Our lives together are one and the same,
Bonded forever, not only by name,
To share our lives has been such joy
Even blessed with two girls and a boy,
May this day bring even more love,
As we work together, hand in glove,
Another twenty-five years will quickly melt away,
So we look forward to another very special day.

Trevor Reeve

Elphin Windmill

On a lonely road beside Elphin the windmill proudly stands
Its former glory now restored by the work of skilful hands
All praise to those who toiled so hard and gave their work for free
and won against the longest odds the windmill committee

It served the west in ages past before the fair or mart,
when the engine was the donkey and the lorry was the cart
Its thatched roof pointing to the sky as it overlooks Elphin
and its mighty wheels the wind will turn the corn to ground again

The teamwork spirit must be there with any task begun
to give the lie to those who say it never can be done
The tourist will be coming not to give the town a boom
a lovely windmill proudly stands where once there stood a ruin

Patrick Kenny

Eden

This fragile EDEN nestles in the shadowy corner of a tormented
soul, as it balances precariously, tossed and buffeted in a sea
of adversity, strife and pain, surrounded by the passions and
desires of materialistic frippery in this garish ugly modern
world, which would deny even the very existence of this beautiful
special place, this place whose shores are bound by the waste
and pillage of spent time.
This EDEN cries pitifully as it gasps and struggles to stave off
the encroaching darkness which chokes the pure light needed to
sustain this priceless treasure, for should it shatter, crack and
break it will certainly splinter into a myriad of broken dreams,
each lost chance sharper than a prickle thorn to tear at the soul
till it bleeds and runs to a river of red, sour wine, to then be
sold on the tread-mill of life for thirty shekels of gold.
Can we pause in this confusion? Can we stay the hand, reach
out and steady this exquisite Oasis, drawing it near, holding it
close, this butterfly of sunshine on a warm summer's day, this
intense feeling of first love, the love that promises to survive, to
last forever in the time-span of eternity, maybe it is only the
blinking of an eyelid, yet in the stillness of unending time
hope shall keep this fragile EDEN forever in our hearts.

Yvonne Ramm

Fairy Tale

The horses with ribbons and plaited manes
Are the animals being exported and killed

The dancing people drinking wine with tailored clothing
Are freezing people looking for a box to sleep in

The knights in shining armour who ride off into the night on
white horses
Are children trying to carry guns and fight for their country

Joyful children sitting around a Christmas tree happily singing carols
Are children being battered and used as slaves

Life's a fairy tale to those of us who are blind to see
And look reality deeply in the eyes.

Jade Allport

"Unforgettable Eyes"

Children in need, posters in many places,
staring big eyes, sad little faces.
So young in age but fast ageing,
such despair, so amazing.

A cry for help, with unshed tears
frightening stare full of fears.
Forlorn children that cannot cry,
the puzzled stare that asks us, why.

Why, are we children all alone,
in strange places faraway from home.
No loving family, no sisters, no brothers
and, most of all no caring mothers.

Hopeless stare, unforgettable eyes,
innocent children lost on the way.
Survivors of families torn apart,
their plight touches our hearts.

Those pleading eyes seem to say,
we need help, please don't walk away.
Join hands with others, willing hands,
maybe one day, our plight will end.

Licia C. Johnston

Peace At Last

If you look, my dear, straight up to the sky
You'll see you've a bond with that presence so high
So even though I don't visit or pick up the phone
It's because I know that you're not alone

It's a miracle how things all work out
It's a miracle, yes there is no doubt
That she's crossed the road, to a world so sweet
Where one day we all are sure to meet

Her true personality I never knew
But her good intentions I looked up to
So soft spoken with her sisterly ways
She often brought a sparkle to my days

Now she's gone, never to return
Once in a while I'll feel a heartburn
I'll miss her silent but warm company
She is dead to life, but not to me

Allah watch over and I'll whisper a prayer
I will feel no pain, shed not a tear
For she's gone onto a much better place
No breed, no colour, no human race

Clayre Bennett

In Memory of 'Richard Tillett' Our Bowls Pal

His many friends will miss that chat and cheerful face
But the spirit of our 'Dick' will live on in this place
friendly advice that he gave was appreciated by plenty,
But now without him those drives will sadly feel empty

His delight at a good bowl was so very often seen,
As he skippered us bowlers on that synthetic green
Stray bowls when delivered would gather jovial distaste,
As he'd question somewhat loudly "Your target's a waste"

From above he's now watching our progress to date,
When trying to deliver that jack shot somewhat late
But remember his laugh when our duff ones are bowled,
And do that much better like we know we've been told

The qualities of a character in this computer age time,
Makes to have known such as 'Richard' a plus human find
The green baize of this club that he so often did grace,
Will remember his big smile when delivering a dream ace

A soft spot in our memories is his big parting gift
With that old chuckle, a shout, do you get his drift
He would not want your sorrow now that he has moved on,
Just remember his laugh like an affectionate old song

A. E. J. Selfe

The Doorway

He stood in the doorway, so peaceful and still,
His back to the world, his hair to the wind,
His eye so peaceful, so peaceful until
He's begged not to go don't leave until
That daring sparkle, ingrained in deep,
A wanderer he is, far he seeks, those painful feet, longing to go,
Wherever they take him, he may never know.

He stood so still, long for movement,
His eyes alight, alight with rage, unseen until,
But not sought by all, he longs fulfilment, but not until
He wants the pearl, the pearl in deep,
Deep in his soul he's destined to go,
With some doubt in his eye, and doubt in his soul,
He must leave now, for time slips time,
The wanderer ingrained, - 'till destinies 'filled.

In the lonely doorway, of two worlds,
He has no partner, it's already left, left until
Now he must choose, which of the two,
Must destiny prove, prove right for the man, the man within,
With such charm and hope he now stands still.

Susan Byrne

Untitled

My fellah doesn't shower me with flowers and pearls,
but he doesn't look at other girls.
He is rather simple,
but he has a lovely little dimple.
I believe him when he says he loves me very much,
and shiver and shudder at every touch.
So here I stay every day,
and would be very sad if he went away.

Deborah Fairhurst

I Will Never Know

She was the sweetest girl
She never knew my name
Sitting on a high chair
Playing silly games.
She sat down beside me
Playing with her hair
She had high heels
Her skin was so fair.

Was she looking at me?
Or was she looking straight through
Was she thinking of me
While talking to you.
I felt her beside me
I felt her slightest touch
Only then I thought
I love her far too much

Was she sleeping with you while dreaming about me
Was she thinking of another was the other one me
Did I break her heart when she felt so low
As we never did speak I will never know.

Mohanish Sharma

Untitled

You can't be right, you've lost your mind
To say the things you do
Where do you get those crazy thoughts
You must have lost all sense.
You cannot change this world of ours
There is no way that you could
What actions could you take
You are so very small...
That is what you say to me.
But change first comes in consciousness
In power of mind and spirit
And in saying these words I say to you
Is the very start.

Neil P. Ashton

Untouchable

Come to me silently, I feel your need
It speaks of pain but proudly stands alone
No balm can heal your quiet hurt
No words exist your anger to atone

Come to me mindlessly, I need your hands
To feel my quickening ecstasy begin-
To hold at bay all conscious thought
And find the secret world within

Anne Robins

Someone's Mum

For years I didn't have a name of my own,
I was always someone's mum.
I fed them, and washed them,
Disliked them, and loved them,
now suddenly they're all gone.

They are grown ups now,
With babes of their own,
To feed, and wash, and love,
As well as a mum, I am now a Gran,
With more blessings sent from above.

My children will soon be grandparents too,
The cycle goes on and on,
from babies to adults in such a short time,
Where have all the years gone?

I do thank you Lord, for all that I have,
You have given so much to me.
A wonderful family, so much love,
My own little family tree.

Now, I have a name of my own, but the memories still come,
Of those precious bygone days, when, I was just, someone's mum.

Gwen Jones

Sorrow

.....But death does have dominion,
   over man and beast.
I have seen the broken, bony body of age
to the dust return.

.....But what of the spirit of man and beast?
Animal spirit consigned to the earth,
while human soul wallows in woolly clouds -

Self-indulgent arrogance.
Tears are human.
Taste their salt.
Weep.

C. A. Hill

A Forest Sleeps

A thousand feet beneath the soil
Where sunlight finds no form to enter.
Miners in hunched deformities toil
Their cyclops eyes beaming from the centre.

Here, in chambers of damp and dust
Where hell is nearer than heaven's skies.
Hewing the remnants of a forest thrust
Between the layers of rock that ties.

Ties, with unsculptured hands of stone
Unyielding as mother holding her child.
Yield's only with a tortured spirit's moan
A hundred oak that once grew wild.

In one cupped hand, ten trillion times gone yesterday
And where I stand, wild hawthorn bloomed.
When there was but God, before he formed the clay
When these were but sea and sky and earth ungroomed.

Out to the light, dusty figures grope
While through the cracks a fallen willow weeps
And high, high above a miner with the sun elopes
Hush now, before my eyes a forest sleeps

J. Haigh

'Individuality'

Mind oppressed by material thoughts,
A cloud descends and stays.
Routine in a vicious circle,
In this world, just another face.
Barriers blocking every escape,
Closing in, pushing down, no relent.
Day to day, will only spell money,
Now is the time to consent-
Consent the compressed voice inside you,
To speak on a personal view.
To display to the fake race of man what
Your unique characteristics can do.
No recognition for beauty?
Model status, genius or wealth?
Yet the hand that can tell a story,
Holds sincerity, not seen, but felt.
Confidence comes from far within,
It rides higher than vanity or lies.
Each individual is blessed with a gift,
So search and let yourself fly.

Louise A. Ryrie

The Hand That Won't Grip

The windmill turns north, south, east and west
to countries, islands, cities and towns.
We go on our way so merry and gay
quite suddenly we are struck down
For illness behind no barrier stays
Infant, beggar, maid, pop star peer
all can be hit and then know fear.
Of the arm they can lose, the leg that won't kick
The back that can break the hand that won't grip.
The gifts he gave he takes away
and makes us look another way
at everything we've ever done
with hands and feet or heart and tongue
A hidden talent perhaps we'll find
of yet a very different kind
And if we do and have the will
We'll go on turning like the mill.

Mona Wright

The Refugee

He stares not seeing
Body stiff with no feeling
Arms outstretched begging to stay alive
His world turned upside down
Mother and Father lost as the bombs fall all around
What does he know of man's greed for power
Of politics, and their finest hour;
Cold, lonely, hungry, meek, and mild
God in all your mercy
Save the child.

Flora Miller

My Broken Body

A human body is such a fragile thing
A boy racer out for a morning fling

Crashed into my car and left me entangled
For a while my life just dangled

It's 2 years now, and I'm still not mended
I feel in limbo, and deeply offended
Because my broken body will never be complete
Just when my children had left and on their own two feet

I had just begun to live life to the full
For my husband and me, life was never dull
Now my husband loves and cares for me
It is so sad, for me to see

My colleagues at work were so kind
But now, as time goes by, I seem hard to find
So take care when you do roam
Not to confine another to their home

Janet Hallam

Roses

All shades of red, pink, yellow and white
But never a blue to be seen.
Soft, curving, yielding, supple and bright
Glowing with precious sheen.

Surrounded by green of many a hue
Which sets off the beauty so well,
The deep red depicting a love that is true
As many a maiden will tell.

The thorns can take the glow away
And leave such wounded pain,
The bloom can fade at turn of day
And love can wax and wane.

But just as thorns can bring despair,
The perfume heady and strong,
Can soothe and comfort and repair
And bring more love along.

Our life is like the growing flower
Giving inspiration firm to those—
Who nurture love, with hope and power
And emulate the ROSE.

Brenda Sharp

Homeless Once Again

'Homeless once again',
The alcoholic cried,
'I have nowhere to lay my head,
My clothes are torn and tattered too,
I look around in deep despair,
A home I try to find,
At last a refuge I have found.'
'No more room tonight,' they cry.
'Why have I got this way?
One more drink,' I sigh.
At least a sleep won't be denied.
A friend I see,
But he's the same as me.
One more drink, pal.
What the heck!
Here we slump
As darkness falls,
The cold gets colder and chilly winds we have to bear.
We wake when dawn is breaking to another day of
homelessness.

Daphne Stock

A Friend

I have a special friend, he's always in my heart,
I don't understand the reasoning of why we are apart.

He's been gone a long time but I often see his face,
He's happy and he's smiling then he's gone without a trace.

I look for him and find he's back again, smiling somewhere
within my mind.

I try and take him with me, with all I feel and do and see, and I
smile as all his pain has gone and he's happy to be free.

I long to hold his little hand and lead him through tomorrow,
I reach out but cannot touch him and then I'm weak with sorrow.

I often see a little boy, forget, and think it's him,
And then the truth has cut me, I sink, my senses dim.

Although I miss him, I'm glad he's in a place where there is no bad,
No pain, no cold, no hurt, no fear yet selfishly, I want him here.

I have a special friend, who's quite unlike any other,
The little friend I talk of is my younger brother.

Even as I write to you, a tear comes to my eye,
As I still don't understand why he had to die.

Shaun O'Leary

Dreaming

I like to dream of childhood things,
Of butterflies on fairy wings.
The rumbling cart, the big grey horse.
The twittering birds, in the yellow gorse.
Paddling in a rippling stream,
Strawberry trifle, topped up with cream.
Snowdrops of the purest white,
The large barn owl, as she hoots in the night.

I like to dream of childhood things,
The sound of my mother, when she sings.
I could go on, for ages and ages,
Fill a book, with a hundred pages.
Now, I must stop my childhood dreams.
I should let them be,
For the clock on the wall chimes six o'clock,
And my husband is home for his tea!

Anna Broom

Summertime

Summertime is here at last
Thank goodness winter is now long passed
The garden's look lovely, blooms all kinds and colours
Lawns are green and trees bursting with pleasure
Birds are happy, flying hither and thither
The cat is lurking, time for his dinner
What joy to spend a lazy day
Watching children in harmony and at play
Everyone feels fitter when they see the sun shine
And dread the day when it will decline
There is lots more to be said for this time of year
But for now I'm just glad that summer is here.

Mollie Crawshaw

Star-Dust

God clapped his hands.
Nothingness erupted. Atoms flew.
Hydrogen, helium, oxygen, neon,
Carbon, potassium, sulphur, sodium,
All the elementals grew,
Collided, coalesced, clouded the void.
Nebulae giving birth
Spewed galaxies whose stars
Lived, burned bright and died.

Star-dust drifted down the solar wind -
Hydrogen, helium, oxygen, neon,
Carbon, potassium, sulphur, sodium -
All the elemental stew -
Creating Earth,
    Water,
    Green life,
    Creeping life,
    Running life,
    Flying life,
    ME.

Barbara Brice

Winter Sunset

Like silent actors in a magic play
Trees lift bare branches to the painted sky
The sun in splendour, sinks - a weary day
Prepares at last to close its ruby eye;
Across gold clouds the hungry birds flap home,
The sun's last rays alert the hunting owls
As through stark grasses small night creatures roam,
Deep in the twilight wood a strange beast growls;
While some are stirring others seek their rest
Lovers entwined, laugh in the bitter lanes,
Young faces to the bedroom windows pressed,
Watch the last glory through the diamond panes;
Soft snow sifts down to whiten distant hills
Night brings repose - and dreams of daffodils.

Rod Burnham

Daddy Dear

Beside your grave I stand with saddened tears
I listen out so carefully but I do not hear
You went to sleep without saying goodbye
I understand fully your reasons why

Trying to be strong but I'm not getting any stronger
Nothing eases the pain, I can't hold out much longer
With you daddy dear I've laughed and cried
Your true heartbeat has lived and died

Wherever I go I know you'll always be with me
Looking over my shoulder I feel you close by
So still is the darkness of this lonely night
I don't hear your voice although you're in sight.

Memories of you will always be on my mind
Why is this world so difficult why isn't it kind
Our love was so very strong, deep in our hearts
My feelings for you daddy dear will never part

Fiona Wilson

There Is Inside Us All, A Book To Be Told

"To write it you must be bold."
Are you sure anyone will find it of interest.
If you leave out the bad and write only the best?
Unless you do before it ends
You will find you have lost many friends.
Those you thought were true and kind.
Only used you till you lost your mind.
You could no longer do their bidding.
They were not friends but only kidding.
While you danced to their tune.
They made you think you could have the moon
Life is a strength affair. Then you will find those who care
When you have written the last chapter.
They will still be there.

E. Pascual

True Friendship

True friendship is a wonderful thing,
The kind that you don't let pass by,
To have a friend and to be a friend
is something that money can't buy.

To share in those good moments
When, you need a friend to tell,
Some good news, that you may have heard,
or perhaps just to ask if she's well.

A true friend is "that someone" you
know you can trust, to keep a Confidence,
Some one who is loyal and true,
without any sign of pretence.

So yes true friendship is a wonderful thing.
The kind that I wont let pass by.
Because I have a friend, and I am a friend,
You could be too, just try.

Alison Robinson

May

Her face and form they hold me captive
Entwined in bonds of charm and grace
 Unto the senses so receptive
Felt through the heartbeat's quickening pace.

How beautiful the world can be
 When heart and soul in harmony
Strike chords in mood and feelings rare
 Like some immortal symphony.

The lovely girl of whom I speak
 With laughing eyes and dimpled cheek
Her nature like the sun's warm ray
 And like the merry month they
 called her May.

J. Nicholson

"How Lucky We Are"

Although we sense that spring is near this
Place has magic through the year.
We braved the winter frost and snow with
Hail and rain and winds that blow.
Warm sunny days will slowly pass with the
Rough high bracken and soft green grass.
Then autumn too will cast its spell with all
Those colours you know so well.
We are blest with sight to see most clear,
The sky, the countryside and sea that's near.
We can touch the bluebells and tiny plants,
Hear buzzing insects, watch tiny ants.
Push through the soft leaves which adorn the
Trees, and think of honey with those busy bees.
So as we head homeward along woodland
Trails, the sky our canopy the wind our sails.
Perhaps we should just look around us near
And far then count our blessings - for how
 Lucky we are!

J. Beswick

The Unknown

Clouds of uncertainty
Filled her heart
Sheets of smoke
Enveloped her body
Unable to see
She felt the loneliness

The fugitive captured by the deficiency in self-esteem
All the things she endured
She thought she had tamed.
Ineluctable, the indestructible was created by her
The barriers strong enough to resist enquiring;
Superficial minds
Their approbious language that release unnecessary sentiments

The sentiments is inexplicable, but is one
A person of her situation can only apprehend.
Sealed from reality
Entrapped between the truth and the lies
Every ounce of strength has faded
She is unable to persevere

Ayasha Ali

Blue Bells

When'st did I see a carpet spread so blue
The bluebell glade adorned in perfect hue
The tiny bells all cramped together in sweet content
Such fragrance gives this heaven scent

Kay Spenceley

One Nine Six Six

Only as young children they were sent away
To the places they had heard no one say.
Marched in file like they had committed offence,
Out of this can you make any sense?

Live for your country and do as you are said
Shoot them five times and once in the head.
Why? These are the innocents the ones who will suffer,
While you place your order for your last supper.

When it's all over and too many are dead,
He may scream victory, "We have won our land, now we are ahead".
He served his country well but wait until hell,
You pay your price, "oh that's so nice".

So now get on with your life and go find your wife,
She can hear your nightmares of how you killed with your knife.

Every picture tells a story and so does a face,
He knows he will never forget that place.
He mumbles to himself while he cannot read,
Open wide 1, 9, 6, 6, it is time for your feed.

A. M. Jones

Take Hold Of Life

Take hold of life, don't let it slip away.
We cannot bring back, what belongs to yesterday.
Live out each moment to the full.
And you will find.
Within your heart, that peace of mind.
That peace, that makes worthwhile
The things we do not understand.
If we just reach out to our Lord
The key to life is there
Within his hand.

Martha Mynott

Wayside Beauty

The purple stately foxglove is swaying in the breeze
Below the sheltered canopy of great, sun loving trees
Who spread their proud wide branches, fingers reaching for the sky
To grasp the fading sunlight and the rain as it goes by

A heavy shower makes them dance in the summer breeze
Falling to the thirsty roots, like pollen to the bees
And at the very apex of the hill it now appears
There is a ditch now overgrown, bringing music to my ears

It gurgles and it laughs, as it winds along its way
And everything is more alive in an unexplainable kind of way
Brambles hug the area, daring people - enter in
Their thorn ever ready, like a finely honed new pin

Margarettes and daisies, one is short the other tall
Dandelions and bluebells, they all bloom at natures call
I hear you ask, where in the world is all this beauty found
Just stop your car, switch off the engine, and start to look around.

Margaret Scott

Colours

Oh what colours the eye can see.
The shapes and forms to agree.
The Yellow of the Daffodils high on the hill.
The Blue of the sky so very still.
The Green of the grass swaying to and fro,
as we pass.
Purples, Pinks and all Hues,
Green, Blues and Lilacs that come in twos.
The Old Brown Barn which you espy,
The Dusky Greys from the distance meets your eye.
Just picture these Colours in one single day,
Treasure them, before they pass on and Fade away.

G. M. Kirk

The Antidote

It is 5.15 on a summer morn,
I have watched the first blackbird swoop down on the lawn,
Pink glow to the East, the colours of dawn change as I gaze;
Apricot pink striped with azure and blue,
And sometimes a streak of grey; as higher up,
It gradually fades to the softest, violet haze.

The line of hills called Roundway Downs, are grayish-green;
The trees in the valley, pale shades of brown.
There are strips of white mist over fields of wheat,
Which is turning to yellow near home.

I think of the artist of it all - our Father in Heaven,
Who, every day paints these pictures for us.

We've a lovely view, which for days on end, I never see,
As I'm looking down on the worries and cares of mundane things.

How stupid I am! 'Cause if I looked up,
I would see the antidote!
The Artist of all our dawns,
Would blot out my worries and cares,
And lift my eyes to His beauties,
If only I trusted in Him.

Nora Ford

Hope

As long as we have hope
That we can carry one each day
With confidence we can cope
And a cherry smile to light the way.

Sometimes our Faith is shattered,
When we have to face reality,
Someone has stolen something that matters,
While we were literally having tea.

As long as you have reasonable health,
Most problems can be overcome,
You can manage without wealth,
If you can enjoy the rays of the sun.

An act of kindness is not always acknowledged,
Sometimes not even a thank you is heard,
But the look of satisfaction that is registered,
It really shows someone cared

If your action did someone a good turn
To help a person who is in need,
You never look for a thank you,
The satisfaction is in the good deed.

Harold C. Willmott

The Narrow Lane

The lane was long and narrow the trees
were green and still we were just
out walking, talking as couples will.

We strolled along together
the air was fresh and good
such a perfect - evening for a couple so in love

I felt your hand in mine
you looked at me and smiled

Oh Peace so quiet, so contented, to let the world rush by.

If only it could be like this, the world to
slow down to walking pace, we would
have the time to look around us to see the
things we miss.

But alas the time is now in the
Lane so long and narrow

If we could walk along life's way and
try to help each other, I'm sure somewhere
we would find the Peace we felt in
that lane So Long and Narrow.

Isabel Platt

On Loss And Hope

Who can gauge the ache of loss
When loved ones have to part
Who can truly know the pain
That lives within another's heart

Who can measure the empty space
With its traumatizing sorrow
The longing that dwells within the soul
For just one more to-morrow

Only those who've lived the void
And experienced the grief
Will know this deepest anguish
When tears bring scant relief

How can we endure this emptiness
And anaesthetize the pain
When someone dear leaves our life
Never to return again

We can only accept our suffering
But reverently we can pray
That empowered by love and faith and hope
We'll meet again, dear God, some day

Tricia Sinclair

The Hardest Task

Hold me when I am afraid
Wipe my tears away should I cry
When darkness is all I see
Shine some light on me
If I am wrong please put me right
Make me smile when I am sad
Give a little love
With no words asked
A kiss to say a thousand words
On you falls one of life's hardest tasks
Until our end to be a friend.

D. Ward

Tree In The Wind

Listing in the wind.
Movements of solid grace.
Reaching out into thin air.
For someone to hold its hand.
Playful encouragement calls me,
But out there I could not stand.
The wind might lift me like a paper bag
And God knows where I'd land.
The casual sway of its branches,
Does not reflect the powerful force
With which it dances.

Someday, when we are both old and frail.
And its dancing partner is much too strong.
The poor old thing will sway its last.
Never again to grace the skies
Like an opera star on a permanent ovation,
But to lie down gracefully,
And move, only when told to,
By the wind.

David Graham

Ronnie

Where was your bitterness when you were told
That your medical treatment had failed?
I watched, an outsider, for the truth to unfold
And saw only your shadow was jailed.

Your humour stayed healthy and strong to see
Your body and spirit grew weak
And I, an outsider, wanted you to be free
From your pain but did not speak.

Your wife was by your side that day
When Humour had earned its rest
And, the Outsider, could only watch and pray
But where was your bitterness?

Joan Peck

I'll Go If I Must

The house is empty - furniture gone
Just the case I sit upon
Cardboard box, next to the door,
Carpets lifted from the floor,

I can take my photos - well three or four
Of course my clothes - but not much more
A painting? Well maybe, just,
If I feel I really must

I'll be alright, I know I will
Of course it won't be all downhill
Dad wouldn't like this doom and gloom
You said love,- you haven't got the room.

You'll come and see me like before
Once you're back from Singapore.
I'll make new friends and eat my greens
And promise - no unpleasant scenes.

Here's my transport - they've sent their bus
No love I won't make a fuss
I'll wipe my eyes, I wont be tearful
They like their residents to be cheerful!

Michael M. Swaddle

Anniversary

You have been dead a year and I am numb.
Thoughts of you unbidden come
Of how you were long years ago.
Love and laughter - your hand in mine, just so.
That loving smile,
All mine for just a while.

Oh, I would blot out the failing years,
The sadness and the bitter tears;
The knowledge of the end
When you, my love, my dearest friend,
Would have to journey on alone
And leave me sadly on my own.

But I must carry on from day to day.
Press on regardless, as we used to say.
And maybe in a dream sometime when
I least expect it, you might come home again,
To hold my hand and smile at me
In the way that once we used to be.

Eileen M. Lodge

Untitled

Banners, bunting and flags by the score,
All this to celebrate the end of a war,
The bombs have stopped falling, peace here in sight,
No more young men will march off to fight.

So many here in fancy dress,
Each one trying to look their best,
Street party tables are laden with buns,
Adults and children all having fun.

Old men with medals across their chests,
Old lady's wearing their Sunday best,
It's fifty years since the day of V.E.
I was a child so have no memory.

They say we've had peace for fifty years,
Hard to believe when I shed my tears,
As the mother of son's who marched off to war,
The Falklands: The Gulf, Ulster as well.

As I see the flags waving and hearing the cheers,
Lets put an end to every ones fears,
So no mothers son or small child's dad,
Will go away and never come back.

Maureen Newton

Untitled

The sound of silence, lost in the night, of soldiers
putting up a fight, of children not knowing wrong from right
All for the need of Love.

Of children looking up, to us in trust, of things that parents
would rather not do, but must, all for the need of Love

Of happiness and wealth untold, of a lifetime
worth its weight in gold, of memories from young to old
All for the need of Love.

These things can surely all be ours when
the fighting of soldiers, be replaced with flowers
All in the name of Love

When by firmness, or by gentle guidance brings normality within the
laws of obedience when all the wars, come to subsidence
Then surely we'll have Love

The love of fellow man, bereft of greed,
The love of each other, plus race, and colour,
and creed, once we learn of our simple need, merely
the need for Love.

This thing called love, we cannot buy,
it comes from way beyond the sky where a thousand years,
may just be a sigh, whilst we learn the true meaning of Love

M. Brownlow

Passing Thoughts

I want to tell you how I feel, but fear prevents me saying how,
I look at you and all my senses seem to let me down somehow.
I yearn to be of one sound mind, to go and travel all my ways,
But loving you makes me stay behind and doom myself to solitude.
I long to hold your warm soft form, to feel your hands caress
    my breasts,
To be so young, to hold your child, to hear you say "I do love you".
I want to share your deepest thoughts, to be a part of you me,
To hold you tight forevermore, never more to be lonely.
I do love you with all my heart and wish these things would
    come to pass,
But pass they must, as so must time.
Yet for the moment wait awhile, leave me not for lest I perish,
At the hands of my own thoughts.
Love me now as you know how too,
I shall be content with that, loving you forevermore.

Christine Seymour

Untitled

He's got a crazy walk and a lovely big mouth
Oh I do like him so much
With those looks he's got.

The sorry face he had
Before he did decide to leave
He made me feel oh so sad

The last words I hear him say
No, no, no
I think oh please don't go as I do cry

Too late he's gone
Before I had chance to speak
I feel the tears rolling down my cheeks
Will he be back
Oh I hope he is
Just to see him one more time
Oh would be so nice

Did he leave cause of me or of the police
Please I hope it was not me
I wish I had a chance to say good bye, but no
Now every time I think of him I just cry.

Nicola Thompson

Spring

Spring comes once a year.
Golden daffodils and leaping deer.
Croaking frogs, all day long.
Fish splashing, water songs.
New leaves growing on the trees.
Lots of new grass sparkling in the breeze.
Every day a new bud grows.
The plants are glad.
There's no more snow.

Gregg Lawtey

Hand Prints

Here are my hand prints for you to keep,
They'll make you smile or even weep
Because you won't find them just anywhere
I can't put them here or there.
You've never found them on a window pane,
Or planted neatly on a white door frame.
My sticky fingers, my grubby paw.
Gradually rising on a nice clean door.
I can't walk and I can't climb.
To put my marks where only you can find.
I've put them on the mirror a time or two,
When I've looked at baby with you.
And popped them on my feeding tray,
But they are soon washed away.
So, I thought I'd put them on paper for you.
To keep and to cherish because
'I love you.'

Joan E. Jones

Devastation

The rain poured down that day
As we embraced outside the station
When you broke my heart
Saying that it had to stop and
That we could go no further
(But you hoped we could be friends).

I swallowed, screaming silently
Through the lump in my throat
As I rushed to my car
(Parked with discretion)
And screeched away
With noises in my ears and my radio strangely mute.

The rain poured down that day
As I drove home without seeing
Never before having known such pain
As the day when my world collapsed;
But I decided I would fight on
And would one day win you, for my own.

Suzanne Heathman

"Crazed Tigers"

Jealousy came to visit one day,
but I was not pleased to see her.
Nonetheless, I fed her fried pride
and sauted shame.

She ate, and enjoyed,
but felt that there ought to have
been a bit more herbed humiliation.
Tigers, crazed, ripped through my body
as she spoke.

She smiled, perceptive of my demeanour.
I tried to speak with careful calm,
yet heard staccatoed senselessness.
Marriages beware!
Jealousy entwined with Domesticity,
breeds Chaos and Folly.

Kenia M. Nottage

Treasures From The Sea

Abraded and smoothed by high and low tides
Stony beaches with beauty, it sometimes hides,
A black, and white pebble found on the shore
Cherished and polished to add to my store.

Trails like icing on pale grey stones
A small creature's creation while the sea moans
Sometimes a fossil is eased from the cliff
Eons have passed and this still exists.

Drift wood floats in on a turbulent wave
Fashioned by the sea from a watery grave
Animals, birds, sometimes human in form
Cleansed and treasured, now reborn.

Shells of all kinds are found near the sea
All over the world strange shapes to see
Nature an artist beyond compare
Exquisite, lovely and some very rare.

Held by the sea many secrets abound
Submerged under water wait to be found.

Evelyn Sharman

Why?

The world is one, but the people are not.
It's like an over ripe apple beginning to rot.
The heart is in shadows and decay has set in.
We're fighting for nothing, what is there to win.
Conflict between countries, land and race.
Competition for power, but who sets the pace.
Weapons are made, and restrictions applied.
Divisions are settled, but who can decide.
Why fight our own people, we should unite as one.
For we all share the same earth, moon and sun.

Clare Tillyer

Envoy's Report To The Count

My Lord, the Duke shewed all the niceties
And spoke - as to yourself - no condescension
To an envoy - but direct to you.
His palace, like many in Ferrara now,
Was short of that good care and finish
Conferred by Mistress' hand on reins -
Now slack and careless held - and lacking
Dowry to renew its state and quality.
Your daughter would be welcome as a thaw in Spring
After the ice has held the land in thrall.
But melting should be held in check for those around,
And only to the principal attention paid
Lest ice break bounds and settle in her heart.
No guidance will he give as to his wishes,
To stoop thus far would offend his pride.
But, like the hawk, if prey offend
He'd take the living heart from untaught lure
And hold it in a crystal cup; where lacking
Warmth and love, 'twould languish to a lonely
Death, enshrined in unrelenting icy pride.

E. G. Macquire

Hue-Manity I Love Your Tu-lips And Chimneys

Hue-manity I love your tu-lips and chimneys,
Your odd, unlovely bard (arresting broads).
Post-impression actualities (half-stooping)
Would you stone a passing woman with a child?

Hold on tight here for one moment-leaf you only
I guess so far your whistle-time is over.

Hue-manity I love your upland drumming
Your pretty-baby-blue-eyed boys, no thanks!
Lets take the train dear for because I fancy
A day of long canalways running now;

Hold on tight-lean every different body to me,
That's how I know your one rhyme dies alive.

Neil Gooding

Sagacity

Winter abed with Autumn gold
Plucks the late fruit touched by first frost
And drinks a wine more subtle and divine
Than any tried in youth.

Revived, old winter drinks again
All season's kaleidoscope into one
And sage tranquillity attends his final hours.

Thelma Easterby

Mermaid's Purse

When you think of so many different lives
All living in harmony side by side
With all the fights and wars down through the years
All the hatred the bloodshed and all the tears
It's strange how life battled through the rough and smooth
We reproduce so we can't lose
But how many times can we come close
Before we destroy the things we should love the most?

Life, it seems to be so strange
Our fate seems hard to rearrange
Life, it seems to be so short
It seems our futures have all been bought
Life seems amazing to so few these days
Taken for granted in so many ways

Yet in spite of it all life keeps on burning
And through our ignorance we shall keep on learning
And when everything has been said and done
We're still only a rock spinning round a sun
In the ocean of the universe
We're just a tiny treasure in a Mermaid's purse

Simon Ellis

Night After Night

Night after night I sit and wait for you,
Expecting doors to open and you coming in.
Night after night I feel so sad and blue
Because I know - you never come again.

Night after night the shadows of the past
Will make their way across the stage - my mind!
How long must our separation last?
Oh God of love, I beg you to be kind.

The lonesome nights, when only tears
And loving memories will keep me company;
These are the times, when doubts and fears
Build shadow monsters right in front of me.

My eyes are searching for your image here.
My empty arms, outstretched, aching for you.
And down my cheeks comes tear now after tear.
My heart is heavy, it is crying too.

Come, hold me close, and love me once again.
Please, never leave me. You - to me - are life.
Come to me now, and kiss away the pain.
Forever I am yours - I am your wife.

Helga I. Dharmpaul

Summer Dream Or Reality

Summer in fresh prime infancy.
Sun drenched bodies,
And the shadow of heat.
Squinting eyes floating through haze,
My eyes meeting another.

Fleeing from confusion, finally alone.
Awesome golden rape seed.
Open vast fields of mystery.
Summer love bewilderment,
I seek to know you.

We lay underneath the boundless blue sky.
Time likened to the air,
Drifting endlessly through eternity.
My love was quixotic, but real?
The beginning of our lustful story.

The love of summer is an apex.
The endless days are ending.
Ebbing away, we swam the laughing sea.
Lonely days have just begun
Dreamlike days are winters to be.

L. R. Nicholas

Colours

A garden filled with summer flowers.
A rainbow in the sky
Plumage of exotic birds
A pretty butterfly

All around us we can view
Colours bright of every hue
In the clothes that children wear
In the market, at the fair

Grown-ups, too, have caught the craze
Umbrellas bright for rainy days
And in the sun, dull dress has gone
It's colours now, for every-one.

At football matches, watch the play
Of teams in strips so bright and gay
Fans, and rivals, girls and chaps
Wear coloured scarves and woolly hats

But, on the modern cricket green
The strangest sight is to be seen
It's blues and reds - all colours bright
There's not a single white in sight!

V. Tank

Untitled

I told myself I didn't want it,
Rubbished all the Shakespeare sonnets.
Told myself I didn't care,
As I ran my fingers through your hair.
Took on board this reluctant glow,
I silently watched this feeling grow.
It meandered through my sullen thoughts,
Walked across all I'd taught,
Myself to be,
I wondered quietly,
Is this me?
I want to know you inside out,
What took away my mellow doubt?
I played with words endlessly,
Wondered what you took them to be.
I felt the pain of letting go,
Of what I thought I'd never know.
Please don't take away this flame,
I know my life will never be the same.

Christina Urso-Cale

The Lull Before The Storm

The burning sun;
The streets no longer crowded,
People smiling, content with life;
Satisfied... life is Ok.

Wind, so soft blowing,
Running through hairs,
Warm.

Smoke...
No longer vile, no longer putrid,
No longer existent.

Bus rides,
So joyously joyful;
Smooth sailing, smooth riding,
With seats abundant.

The abyss of metropolis,
If only life can stand still, all peacefully quiet,
Yet, at 4.30 p.m.
I, as everybody else knew,
The familiar, pleasant serenity,
Is nothing but the lull before the storm.

Amir Al Fatakh Yusof

Kit

Mute words of Love
Calm comforters to steady a bolting heart,
Soundless words of Love
Dry the sudden breaks of sweat,
Silent words of Love
More treasured now unspoken,
When memories of your creeping cancerous Death - Resurrect.

Ann Kitson

Just Walk With Me

Come give me your hand and walk with me
I will show you peace and tranquillity
The green of the grass, the blue of the sky
The sight of the Eagle, as it soars on high
The silver stream, as it meanders along
The sweet soft sound of the birds in song
The fleeting touch of the breeze as it passes by
The eerie sound of the owls haunting cry
The kiss of a snowflake upon your cheek
The crackle of twigs beneath your feet
Snowcapped peaks of the mountains, in sunshine glowing white
Frost glistening in the trees, In the bright moonlight
The gossamer cobwebs, heavy with dew
These are the treasures, I will show to you.

Rosemary H. Henderson

Comfort

Think of me as a Spring day, with Daffodils gently swaying in the wind
And do not tell yourself, you cannot enjoy because I've gone away.

Then Summer skies will surely follow, and long warm lazy nights
And do not feel ill at ease, because they make you feel so bright.

As sure as Summer comes and goes, then Autumn breezes in
With falling leaves and rainy days, it really can be dim.

Then Winter strikes, its firm hard hand
The dark nights, soon appear
Though snow may fall, and trees are bare
But yes - I still am here.

Though all the Seasons come and go, with changes in our lives
As each day passes, ease shall flow
Remember me with a smile.

I'll be your flowering Daffodil and your Brightest sky
I'll also be the wind that gently lifts your spirits high.

This one thing you can be sure
As winter follows Spring
I'll stay close to you in your heart
I'll be your everything.

Carol Kennedy

'Sad Little Dreamer'

Ways of escaping, contemplating a better life,
free of poverty, of loneliness
free of a troubled mind a little sunshine to find.
So the sad little dreamer, the schemer,
Who reads the paper and watches TV
longs to break free from dreamland and break into reality.
She's found her fairy tale, her dream man, the one and only
Prince Charming.
yet the bells of reality ring loud and alarming.
Because all she does is dream,
too shy, too insecure to break free.
So the sad little dreamer will never see
that glorious holiday party in the sun,
none of those beautiful people,
film stars and musicians having fun.
She'll never have that glorious wealth that brings security,
in this Cinderella story, Cinders can never break free;
after all, this is the painful world called reality.

Caroline Macrae

Peace At Last 1918?

It was the eleventh hour,
The eleventh month,
Guns fell silent in France,
The Western front.

No more war,
So we were told,
Farewell to the rifle, the bullet
The politicians spoke so bold.

Homes fit for heroes,
Work in plenty too,
Disillusion, disappointment came soon.
Who was fooling who?

The fields of Flanders are not for food,
The seed grow corn, and poppies too.
Battles of guns, cries of pain
Home to hunger, poverty, whom do we blame?

A fight for a home.
A citadel of our own;
Social war now rages
We seek only regular wages.

Steve Webb

Untitled

You've touched me deep inside,
my emotions I just cannot hide.
Everything you do and everything you say,
keep unhappy feelings at bay.
Even when you're angry you warm my heart,
that's pierced by your words like a falling dart.

I'd love to be with you night and day
but as my feelings grow deeper, you drift further away
I need your love it fills me with life
However your actions are like a blunt knife
Twisting and turning tearing apart
Unlike arrows that fly sharply through my heart.

When thoughts of you fill my mind,
I see nothing else for love is blind.
You can guide me through the maze of life,
Keep me away from trouble and strife.
You are the grape and I am the vine,
We depend on each other to make the wine.

Amelia Streeter

Whims

"Words were heard on a high mountain-
And the same became snatches of conversation-
That where picked up by a "Babbling Brook",
Who told the "tale" to the stream-
For whom it became a philosophy,-
The stream spread the message to the river-
Who told it from bank to bank.
Then the riddle was carried to the sea-
Where it was dispersed far and wide,
And the seas confided it to the oceans-
Who debated it amongst themselves-
As they were thought of as deep and wise;
While the whole concept was turned over and over-
Being looked at from many angles-
When finally the wind caught its drift;
And carried it aloft the better to see its insubstantiality-
But the wind soon tired of the mystery too-
So it dropped a few words to the breeze,
Who hid them in a cache on a mountain-
And so they became overheard by a brook...

H. H. Lewis

Naw Really It's Great Being Unattached

Naw really it's great being unattached
Nae pressure, nae hastles, lovers' tiffs 'n that.
Nea hiding, lying, pretending, offending,
Aye 'n nae big brother tae kick yer head in.
Nae wan there, unpainted, unmasked
'N nae probing minds bringing up the past
Nae old flames, growling 'n making eyes.
Aye 'n nae need fur telling blunt faced lies
Nae guilty thoughts, nae presents bought
Nae wan tae know if ye did or not.
Nae wan 'a taw. That comes up tae scratch
Naw really it's great being unattached.

Naw really it's great being unattached
Ye know waking up on yer tod 'n that.
Nae wan tae occupy yer mind
Ye know some wan who's always on yer side
Nae hands tae hold, nae stories told
Nae wan there tae keep oot the cold
Nae mate, pal, nae best friend
Aye 'n nae understanding ear tae bend
Naw really it's great being unattached

John Houston

That Woman

I look in the mirror
But what do I see
A face that's familiar
But it's really not me
The hair on her head
Is lank and so dry
There's a puffy dark look
Under each eye
The skin looks weathered, quite taut and tight
The droop at the mouth, just isn't quite right
I stare at the face, it stares back at me
Between us runs a bond, of great sympathy
A gradual awareness pervades the air
I do know this woman, who can still only stare
She once was attractive, or so people said
But she never ever let it go to her head
Now here she is, for all the world to see
And I've got to admit it, that woman is me.

Jean Kennedy

Untitled

The years have passed yet all but seems
like yesterday
When first we met
Another time, another place.
And thro' those years my heart has found
Such peace of mind for me to say
that in my days, alone,
I found that peace when thinking of your face,
For it's the one I love,
And all the joy it gave to me
along the years when worlds apart were we -
Till now - to-gether here - residing in
Our Home of dreams,
I think once more how only yesterday
It seems.

J. Hinde

Friendship Rare

I have a friend with hair of flame,
And one of raven's black.
Who fill me up with smiles inside,
In sadder times, my tears they've dried.
We've shared our hopes,
Our secrets, our dreams.
In midday shine, in moonlight beams.
So this short verse I wish to devote,
To two dear friends on whom I dote.
To tell them both how much they mean.
To tell them each how precious they've been.
Here's to future encounters,
To moments of pleasure.
To past endeavours,
I cherish and treasure.
Here's to my friends one dark, one fair.
Of friendship true and often rare.

Karin More

A Tribute To My Gran

Gran, I'm going to miss you lots; we all think you were a dear,
So on this day of memories I'm sorry as I shed a tear,
Thank you, Gran, for all you did; you helped me in a big way,
I'm sorry I didn't manage to tell you all I wanted to say.

A Heart of Gold was what you had; you'd help each and every one,
Kindness, help, advice and love you'd give out by the ton,
While we're apart I'll think of you and all you used to say,
Don't lie down and let the dogs eat e' face life day by day.

Thank you, Gran, for being there; seeing you was a real treat,
I'll never forget your cheery ways and until again we meet,
Rest peacefully, Gran, we all agree you certainly were the best,
Gran, we'll always love you even now that at peace you rest.

Michelle J. Dymond

Shout

May I shout it from the roof tops
may I go to the bloody hell.

Maybe if I go ahead,
maybe of hurting you is what I'm afraid.

Should have been an ugly swan,
Instead of this bloody one.

Frog escaped from a fairy tale
or soul confined in a jail.

What if a kiss would come?
Wonder what this frog would become.

What if anyone would open the gate?
Wonder if freedom would be my fate.

Why should I become a bunch of nerves.
Why, why? When only nature explains.

I just wish I could try
but not by making a star fall from the sky.

Elsa Casanova

Night

Darkness falls,
The sky draws close its eyelids, ebony wash.
Nothingness but not emptiness
Endless but with depth
A black shroud, an enraptured world
A cocoon spun of treacle black.
The lid has fallen once more
Light has lost.
The impenetrable shield of the night
Only the moon offers to do small battle with this almighty foe
Jet black, soot black
With the closure of the day comes silence, rest, dawn.
The night peels back
Retreats, withdraws his presence
Overthrown once more
The dark kingdom vanishes
Sunlight dissolves his enemy
Encroaching his territory
But the vanquished shall return.

Diane Wood

Telegraph Pole

Standing by the side of the road, lonesome, bare.
Surrounded by memories of my former glory.
Steel footholds mock my once resplendent branches.
I used to have children playing in my branches;
Now all I feel are the thunk of heavy workmens boots.
Impotent, my unliving existence a permanent winter
Erect, feigning life but really dead.
A Zombie.
Stripped by man, deprived of life,
Serving without choice,
A Zombie.

Leo McHugh

Cat

Bright eyes that shine with fervent glare,
What mysteries hide behind your stare,
The world around you does not see the beauty that you shine on me,
For you are quite beyond compare with your appealing distant air.

You wander off into the night to disappear in fading light,
Who knows the trail that you are on - we only know that you are gone.
Maybe at dawn you will return, but still forever I will yearn
To learn the secrets that you keep, beneath your mask of self conceit.

You sit aloof and so serene, more gracious than a king or queen.
Your hunger I can satisfy, and comfort you will always find
When you curl up by my fireside.
But there is more to you than that, although you are only a cat.

B. Carrott

Strength To Survive

They say life is what you make it,
But it can be so, so cruel,
Some people have it all,
While others struggle until they fall,
When financial ruin is upon you,
And you don't know where to turn,
You wish for someone else's help,
To give you some advice and learn,
How can life be what you make it,
When you feel you've done all you can do,
You want to make it easier,
But feel like falling through,
When children also depend on you,
They look to you for hope,
This signifies the strength you have,
To make you want to cope,
Then you realize you have to strive,
To fight for a better life,
Not just for you - your children too,
You know you have to survive.

Angela Powell

What Happened To The Promise?

The dreaded news was conveyed to the nation,
Glazed eyes stared back at the cold, hard screen.
People stood motionless, and their elation
Was lost from the months when peace had been.

The murders and hatred had started again,
And bombs became weapons destroying all life.
For one man, his fight now seemed almost in vain:
Once more, Ireland's feud had returned all the strife.

The echo of fighting brought back all the hurt
To the young man whose life had almost been grasped.
When he'd flown over Ireland, a danger alert
Had come just too late for his freedom to last.

Now a wheelchair imprisoned his sad, forlorn soul,
Down the length of his limbs, great scars did remain.
Yet he knew that if he could regain control,
For people and country he'd suffer again.

Faye W. Tattersall, aged 15 years

The River's Life

When I was free, when I was young
My body weighed over a hundred tonnes.
I sped past roads, bridges, and cars
I slept under the moon, sun and stars
I ran into springs and out again
Life was good, I wish it was then.
But then things started to go wrong
People walked past and said "Oh, what a pong!"
They poured their pollution into me
Now you can hardly see me.

But people thought that nobody knew
That behind the houses and bushes too.
That I was being used as the city dump
And that my life was ending as a garbage lump.

Debbie McIntyre

Memories

Sitting by the fireside all snug and warm,
A flicker in a flame stirs a distant memory
A field full of daffodils, Two people walking by,
Their love so bright and full of hope glows from up high.

Time passed by so fast, where did it go?
So many happy times and sad ones too,
Glancing back into the fire a flame dances and glows.
It's trying to tell us what already know.

Black ashes are the past laying in the grate,
The flames are the future love that grows with time,
These will be more memories or yours and mine.

Hazel Collins

Mummy Come Home

I'm a little girl in a children's home,
all that I want is a Mum of my own,
Some Kids are adopted, they leave, I'm left alone
and all that I want is a Mum of my own,
I want someone to love me,
I want someone to care,
To hold me tight and hug me, when
teardrops are there,
To tuck me up at night and cuddle me tight,
This would make me happy,
My life would be alright.
Please, come back to see me Mother,
you've been gone away six years,
In that time I've cried so many tears.

P. D. Cropley

Untitled

Autumnal wiles, described with glee
By Weather-Persons on TV
As "this could be" and "that may follow"
(Surprise! Surprise! - A fey tomorrow.)

With phases of "High Pressure here"
And "Movements of Low Pressure" there,
I crave the need for poesy,
When brown leaves on the ground I see.

On Brook Green, near the tennis courts,
By a grand oak tree? Of sorts,
So old that King Charles may have been
Privy to her silent paean.

When Autumn lends to the relief
The lovely smells of burning leaf
For those who happen by that way
A perfume for the gods, I say.

But there to end, and here to lease
The end-line from a song called "Trees"
Dendrology - my hat to thee
"But only God can make a tree."

T. L. Cahill

An Old Lady's Thought

Looking back through the years
Remembering times, I knew no fears
Strong and blithe, patient and kind
Now I nurse an ailing mind
My looks once striking now wither and fade
The mirrored image of a wizened old maid
Oh it's true I hear them say
"She'll have to accept she's had her day"
Am I not the same person then?
Does spirit leave at four score and ten?
Do my eyes not dance and shine
When I recall memories that are only mine?
If only the young could comprehend
The ways of my youth, these times would mend
I ask not for your pity or tears
For you will be me, in a few years

Julia Watkinson

Untitled

Words guiding hands to deeds of violence and shame,
Is that the message to children in Ireland's name.
History will acclaim, to history we are bound,
Bitterness is strength we read, but no compassion is found.
Oh many splendored country of beauty and love of words,
Peopled with dreamers and the humour of Gods.
Stop this misery of bitterness and strife,
Bring your children out of darkness into light.
Wave your flags for the future without the clouds of the past,
Light the glory of your martyrs with the light from above,
Let peace have your children and hold them fast.

Doreen Richards

"With God's Help"

Whilst working in my greenhouse.
I had some time for thought.
To put my hand to growing plants
Which other years Id. bought

I took these little seedling
And broke open little pods!
My grandson said where do they come from granddad
They were sent to us from. "God"!

I'm just one of his little helpers
To rearrange what he has sent
Some plants they all stand upright!
And other plants are bent.

Just look at all the colours.
From the seeds that I did sow
And thank you God for all your help
For helping them to grow

The plants are all shapes and sizes
With God's help they are doing well
He just did not give them colours
He gave them a welcome smell.

Brian Johnson

Teachers' Lament

I am anchored to my desk,
manacled by a leaden will.
I strain to see and breathe through murky depths,
to surface above scrambled lines of black and blue,
of sheaves stacked, desperate for recognition
dug up from some distant conscience
to be dragged to present need.
I am prisoner to paper and scrawl
and question the relevance of it all.
Misquoted lines and pseudo paragram,
desperate to master some forgotten bard,
half rhymed lines from centuries past.
This like some dead King's ghost
returns as in some vague memory
to haunt prisoners on both sides of the wall.
I weaken and slump into the spidery morass
as mechanically I tick and cross
and make my mark on all.

Richard Brebner

Choices

A breeze of icy crystals,
A night as black as pitch.
A million glittering stars,
Poised in an infinite void.

A snow enveloped night.
A night laced with wonder.
A night so intense
you can feel it on your skin.

A train track born from shadows.
A shadow as thick as night.
A challenge to the brave
to seize the chance while it exists.

A track pointing to light
A light that glimmers far away.
A light within reach
of those who will run to grasp it.

Picture yourself waiting there, in the snow.
Answer me this, now you know the choice.
When the train comes for you,
Which way will it go?

Kristi Beak

Wer Beim Juden Kauf...

Listen to the screams and shouts you hear,
Try to ignore them and muffle your ear.
You'll get use to anything given time,
Their lives are no longer at their prime.

Puff puff an incoming train,
They come in all weathers be it wind or rain.
Those unfit to work were sent to be gassed,
Quickly quickly this must be done fast.

All pushed into a space,
"Please sir what is this place?"
"Never you mind boy do as I say,
Or you'll never see the light of day."

Is there any justice?
What did we do?
"No one cares because you're a Jew."

Becky Jones

The Dark End Of Life

A turmoil of tear gallops through my head
As the words are frighteningly and coldly said.
The church bell chimes the song of soul,
Whilst the pendulum dances to and throw.
The nighttime cries as daytime breaks,
The lonely sigh as their shattered hearts ache.
The tunnel of light is now dark with fear,
The end of love and emotion is near.
The sweet song sang is now moaned with shame,
As the teary and dismal survive through pain.
The old and aged walk in a zombied state,
As death now seems to arrive too late.
Nothing is left in this world to gain,
And all that's living slowly go - insane.

Michan Jean Clancy

Untitled

The field mouse brought the town mouse
Up to the country to see
What wonderful things in the country
There are for you and me
They climbed the hedges and over the stile
They ran and ran for almost a mile
They saw the poppies and corn a-glowing
They saw the carrots and onions growing
They climbed into an old straw hat
Then they saw the farmyard cat
As big as a tiger to them he seemed
With eyes like slits he sat and dreamed
But the mice were off
They wouldn't stay
For pussy to wake and ask them to play.

E. Stocks

Love And A Father

Love in a book is a torment, a tempest,
A torrent of feeling, too strong to ignore.
Love of a father is quiet and gentle,
Knowing him, seeing him. Can you want more?
There to be talked to, ranted at, raved at,
There to be joked with, share laughter and praise;
There just to look at, to smile at, to lean on,
There for your comfort to the end of his days.

Love of a father is quiet and gentle,
There, without knowing it, till he has gone.
That love of a father tears heart from its moorings,
Leaves you weeping, and lonely, and oh! So alone.
Not there to be talked to - the chair is now empty,
No one to joke with, joke's aren't funny at all.
Where now the smile - the love that you leant on?
Gone - to your sorrow - to the end of your days.

Margaret Cable

Crying Time

Crying time is when the hurt shows through
All the things I could not do
I could not stop a baby crying
I could not stop a man from dying

So many things I would like to do
Just to let the sun shine through
To put a smile on a little face
To make the world a better place

To try to protect the weak
To help a little baby speak
These are the things that I can do
To show I care for you and you

Jeffrey Price

Focus On This

Focus on this and dream me a dream
Let me burst from the ground
Like a flesh mountain stream
Let me dive the deep oceans
With speed on my side
And await my return on the turn of the tide.

Focus on this and inspire my mind
Let me warm like the sun
Let me shine on mankind
Let me paint you a rainbow
To colour the skies
And await my return when you open your eyes.

Focus on this and teach me to learn
Mould me and shape me
For knowledge I yearn,
Let me be wise
In this world of despair
And await my return on the breeze of repair.

Dawn Reed

That's Life!

As life unfolds it opens out the pattern that you'll follow,
The jumps you'll take, the choices you'll make, the happiness
and sorrow.

You'll think it isn't easy as you travel through the years,
The high times, the low times, the smiles and the tears.

The sadness you may see as you go along,
You may make mistakes and could be in the wrong.

Whatever the outcome, you will reach your goals,
You'll meet some interesting, sad and happy soles.

Never count on any luck, or at least not that alone,
You have to help yourself along at work and at home.

Believe that you're successful, know your good points too,
Never wander aimlessly in anything you do.
Teach yourself to handle life like a peace of fragile china,
Because in the general scheme of things there's nothing any finer!!

And that's life!

Michelle Kirsty Beddoes

Snowscape

For weeks the snow has lain,
    as far as the eye can see,
Greedily draining every drop of colour,
    trapping it in a crystal prison.
Even the trees seemed black
    against the grey clouds.

Today the sun is shining,
    the sky is a brilliant blue,
And look!
    the snow is dancing -
Every flake with a delicate edging of green.

Pauline C. Roe

Breathing The Changes

When times of Change are Winter sorrow,
Hurt drifts, hollow and deep,
Pain inside, gnarled and ragged,
The light fading; dark and barren.

The road long, grey and endless,
Vision blurred; wet raining Tempest,
Anger driving on relentless,
Confusion smouldering in the half-light.

When times of Change are Winter fading,
And Dawns early light is breaking,
Hope glistens meekly through the dimness,
And tomorrow gently eases forward.

Fresh buds shoot up from out of nothingness,
The sky becomes awake with brightness,
The land lies fresh with new beginnings,
New life roots deep in Natures soil.

Andrea Oakman

Adieu

I had a duty- it was my task to do
To tell this elfin child
Of a certain sort of sadness, altogether new.
And how was I to say to her,
"Your Nanna's dead, she died today,"
(Released from a pain you cannot understand)

I told her: and she looked at me,
The large grey eyes, as yet no tears,
"And why is it?" she questioned, restlessly,
"The sun's still shining, the day still warm
But inside me it's all so cold
For Nanna's dead and she is gone."

Audrey Roberts

Our World

Trees down and paper plenty
What shall we do when our world's empty.

Forest all gone and animals too.
That's when we'll have to visit the zoo.
Joining life's big long queue.

No plants, no trees no evergreen
The thoughts to ugly to be seen

Water's polluted and fish all dead.
Man's got - a lot of worry upon his head.

Greed and lust is out of hand
What a mess we're making of God's land.

O, how I wish I had a golden spell
I think I'd send them all to hell

Crocodiles and elephants too
They shouldn't be kept in a zoo.

Freedom is the name of the game
So let them live a life that's free
And maybe man can live in - harmony

Dorrie Dee

A Brave Little Girl

"There's a tear in your hair mummy"
She softly said, as she touched it gently
From her hospital bed.
It was her tear you see, she wasn't well today
"It's the chemotherapy" that's what they say
Her own hair gone, her colour too,
A brave little girl with eyes of blue.
As mummy slowly turned her head
The tear was like dew on a spider's web.
Please God give her the strength to fight
The pain, and one day soon be well again
So she too can have tears of joy in her hair
Not just in her eyes so big and blue

Jill Gilbert

The Reunion

The room was full of heroes
and they'd laugh if heard it said,
there were others should have been there
but I'm afraid that they're all dead.

I looked at all their faces
and their sparkling shining eyes
I could still see - through the ages,
they were once some daring guys.

They asked me - would I tell them
Why I joined - and what I did?
How I helped to keep our freedom -
when not more than just a kid.

Well, I told them - there were others
who could tell of deeds well done -
and even they would argue...
"Oh I'm not the only one!"

Yes, the room was full of heroes
and I know them all by name
I'm so privileged and I'm honoured -
and they're in my "Hall of Fame."

Charles E. Sleigh

Someone By My Side

Someday's I feel so lonely inside,
like a baby left on its own to cry,
and a bird on its own in the sky,
I wish someone was by my side,
to hold me when I don't feel alive.

I want someone to love, which will love me too,
I'd be there for them when they want me too,
I'd care for them every minute of the day
and hope to God they won't go away,

Some days I don't want anyone there,
but I think that's because I'm too scared,
that they'll go away and I'll be on my own again,
like a child stranded on its own to play,

One day I'll find someone that will stand by me,
and we'd be together for eternity,
I'll love him and he'd love me,
We'd be happy as can be.

Kerry Shuter

Ode To Endogenous Depression

Go away depression, go away today
Go away depression and go away to stay.
I can do without your doubts and its attendant fears
I can do without your misery and its ensuing tears
I can do without your hovering to disturb my morning calm
I can do without your repeating of the same familiar psalm.

You're a pain and you're a horror, and the ultimate con-man too,
Giving not much joy, nor peace of mind, just a mood
that's blue, dark-blue.

Go away depression, go away today,
Go away depression and go away to stay.
I can do without your fear colouring my thoughts and deeds
I can do without your intransigence making a mockery of my needs
I can do without your anxiety, playing on my nerves,
I can do without your uncertainty and the cause it serves.

You're a spoiler and you're a tyrant and a great seducer to sloth
Giving not much joy, nor peace of mind, and I'm so in need of both,

Go away depression, go away today,
Go away depression and- please, please, stay away.

Mary Bane

Do You Ever?

Do you ever get the feeling there's a ghost in your hall,
A demon in your cupboard next to your ball

Do you ever get the feeling there's a snake in your sink,
Waiting for you to get thirsty and go for a drink

Do you ever get the feeling there's a witch on your path,
Casting spells over her cauldron which sits on the grass

Do you ever get the feeling there's a wizard in your loft,
He's smoking a pipe, you can hear him cough

Do you ever get the feeling there's a dragon in your cellar,
Who breathes out fire in the cold...cold weather

Do you ever get the feeling they come out at night,
Are you ever scared? Do you think they might?

Do you ever get the feeling there's a ghost in your hall,
Then you wake in the morning and there is nothing there at all!

Hazel E. McDonagh

The Lonely Wheelie Bin

They've given us a Wheelie bin, it really is a scream!
I've decorated mine with flowers in Blue and Pink and Cream.
I've christened her "Griselda" - a name which seemed to suit...
The neighbours all poke fun at me but I don't care a Hoot!'

One sunny Sunday morning I was cleaning out my bin when
all at once a tiny voice came bursting from within...
"I'm lonely!" cried Griselda." I really need a friend to laugh
and talk and joke with, or else my life will end!"

"I like that bin right over there. He's handsome and he's clean.
I really dig his shiny lid. I'd love to be his Queen!"

The Wheelie bins were married and now stand side by side!
"Big Al" gave his permission. True Love can't be denied!

Sheila Tomkins

Home

Where ever you run, where ever you roam,
Just remember, you're never far from home.
When you move out into a home of your own,
Just remember, our house is always your home.

And in time when you take a wife,
We will invite her into our life.
No matter what you need to loan,
Our house is your home.

If you can't get home so much,
Just remember to keep in touch.
Write a letter or use the phone,
Because our house is your home.

Donna Taylor

Life Without A Loved One

Why can't life be simple?
And why is it so plain?
And because of this it drives us all insane;
Why is life a struggle?
And why do we always die?
We lose our most dear loved ones,
And then we always cry.

The children sing, the children play,
The children dance, the children pray,
The children sing, and children shout,
And soon our children will all die out.

We wish we could die
When our dear loved ones disappear
Our hearts sink, our eyes blink,
So why do we always die?
Because life without a loved one is so unfair.

Katie Burleigh

A Wistful Dream

I dream of a world of perfection.
Its people good and kind.
All keeping the ten commandments.
Moses brought down the mountain side.
Just imagine, no murderers, rapists, rogues or thieves.
With wide open doors, we could tackle our chores
Do as we please, with comfort and ease.
With pleasure and relaxation,
we could stroll down country lanes,
no need to look over our shoulders,
for fear of being caused pain.
It's unbearable the stress that fear causes,
it makes our health below par.
The soft touch of the powers that be,
are certainly no good for you and me.
Real punishment to fit the crime, I say,
like strokes of the birch, where it most hurts,
that would soon keep crime at bay.
But it's only a dream of perfection,
a dream, I dream every day.

Peggy Johnson

Untitled

Escape the confines is your wish
Imprisoned by these walls of life
Love's beat heart desire will roam
To soar bird-like with free soul
Elegant, graceful and purpose know
Hunting for the one true goal.

Break the chains that hold you down
Restrained by frantic thoughts abound
Love's labour price for you will race
To power swift your warm embrace
As caring as a summer breeze
To think of it is but a tease.

Imagine not too much of what may be
And do not idle sit to wait and see
For nature fashioned the birds and breeze
As sure as nature made you and me
So lift your head and with stalwart heart
Go forth and follow Cupid's dart.

David Porter

Camaraderie

Two friends sat in silence before the fire
Only voices of boatmen faraway in the lagoon
Singing fitful and gentle on the calm water
The lamps on the boats were burnished red glows
Nebulous first, then flickering out and voices ceased
Land and water slept unstirring, invisible and taciturn
Glitter of stars remained streaming, ceaseless and vain

A plaintive murmur arose saddening and startling
The great solitude of surrounding woods
Whispering their wisdom of immense, lofty indifference
Sounds floated hesitant and vague shaping into words
Flowing gently, a murmuring stream of soft, short sentences

They sat motionless under the sheen of stars
Each speaking in low lengthy dreamy tones
For where can we place
The ponderous burden of our troubles
But in a friend's heart

Priyanka Senadhira

Childhood Days

How well I remember that part of my life,
Everything seemed so wonderful no trouble or strife.
We would run through the cornfields and play in the wood,
The world seemed so happy blissful and good.
Our mums and dads knew we would be o.k,
I wish I could say that of our children today.

J. Derbyshire

Stranger

I was a stranger in a strange land,
to be cold and formidable was my right hand.
Oh, how generous was I who felt so grand,
when all around, heads bowed in solitary stand.
My power was all prevailing,
my conscience knew of no failing.
Yet, there were times, that my heart knew true,
many the man loved, but seldom by few.
Could cast-away his failing,
by pretending, not staying.

I am a stranger in a strange land,
kind and reverent to my fellow man.
Never to deny these people my hand.
No longer to see their heads bow low,
in love and humility, I do try to grow.
The stranger is no longer the stranger within
he is at peace, he is at one with his fellow-man.

Julie Bright

War!

Night has fallen in the streets of Sarajevo
As child sleeps bombs hit the ground.
A family's pain and suffering is the only sound
Mother runs in with tears in her eyes.
Child beneath rubble there's no reply.
Why have war? You should all get along.
Stop the fighting and the pain, you've got it all wrong.

Starving children begging in the street,
If we don't stop the war the ending is bleak.
People in the street walking in fear.
They look back and know death is near.
Why have war? You should all get along.
Stop the fighting and the pain, you've got it all wrong.

Land mines taking people's lives
Death by bombs, guns and knives.
War isn't a film performed or narrated
By the majority it is hated.
Why have war? You should all get along.
Stop the fighting and the pain, you've got it all wrong.

Oksana Mykolyszyn

Ringing Of The Bells

The ringer walks down to St. Werburghs
church and looks at the raven sat on its
perch, and hears the bells and their very
loud toll as they echo around the belfry
walls, up and down around and around
the bells are speaking throughout the land
saying "listen, listen, hear our song we
are the bells big and strong the ringers
our guides the belfry our home come
listen, listen and hear us all" the bells
need ringers to help sing; the ringers need
bells to do the same things so beautiful
music comes out of the towers for
hours and hours and hours and hours.

Katie Dore

"Yesterday"

I look out my window, what do I see,
A reflection in a puddle, the reflection is me.
I stand back, I look hard in disgust,
I look like a used car suffering from neglect and rust.
My eyes are tired, my skin is weary,
I look at my face, a face that's quite scary.
My body is used, run out of miles,
All I have to look forward to is arthritis and piles.
I used to be pretty, slim and fair,
But now I've wrinkles and grey hair.
People look at me in quite a different way,
It feels just like I was young yesterday.

Theodora Lourida

Death...

Who am I?
Why am I here?
For I know too much of sadness,
Too much of pain.
I am not like you,
But I will haunt you, for I am lonely,
Tired, and weary of wrong.
But so too are the seas, the skies, or not?
I will torment and anger you,
Cherish and love you.
But who am I, I ask you? Yes,
I am lost in this world.
But I will meet you, you will face me.
Then who will you run to?
Only to your shadow who will laugh,
For when you meet me you will cry,
Until the bright light - shines,
And you smile again.
Forever!

Clare Mooney

The Magic Of Faith

Count your blessings while you may,
Make it a habit every day.
Believe it's a necklace of expensive beads.
Each one designed to meet your needs.
Wear it with pride, and at its centre
Have one called faith, a golden mentor.
For this is special, it gives you strength.
When weakness invades you, and troubles arise
It makes you climb mountains, and reach for the skies.
It casts away doubt, and makes you see
There's an answer to everything, and it's free.
God helps them that helps themselves,
For He will guide us all the way
And help us in our faith to pray.
Faith is like a shining light
It helps to keep things fair and bright.
It spreads its rays through-out each day
And helps us all along life's way.
When all the world seems sad, and tragic,
Spread your faith to all, it's simply magic.

K. Rhodes

Paper, Chain

School began, you found me
life was cool, we were free
You took me in your arms
I was baffled by your charms
A paper chain you hung around my neck
And a worthless ring you placed on my finger,
And asked me to wait for our wedding day.
Still this paper chain hangs around my neck.
And this worthless ring on my finger
And the waiting is the dying
When you just feel like crying.

Sarah Louise Spencer

A Moment In Time!

The warning siren would wail
The child stands staring, watching her mother, and sharing
The fear   waiting to hear _____ the hum _____ then silence
Her mother is crouching hands over her ears
The puzzled child watches her fears
She fears silence
Then comes the explosion ——— the whole house shakes
What a loud noise it makes

The child still staring, runs under the table, crouching unable
To share her fears with her mother, or any other.

At last the all clear siren wails, her mother is now able
To stand and say "we live to see another day."

Gwendoline Green

401

Spring Is Here

As we are shrugging off winters last
bitter blast
A faint reminder of spring appears in
lush green meadows
As all around us there occurs a series
of mini explosions
In wild and dynamic colour as the softly
Defined shapes of newly developing
flowers
Quiver ever so gently in a mild
freshening breeze

Birds sing aloud their chirpy tunes to
Announce the season that every living
thing yearns
Once again natures rejuvenating light
Falls to earth in warming beams of
sunlight
Reawakening all of Gods sleepy
Creations whilst lovingly
Giving life to others

Garry Veal

A Sense Of Freedom

'Twas as I wandered on the Downs,
And looked o'er valleys, hills and towns,
Saw busy streets and peaceful lanes,
And flashing cars and streaming manes,
Saw winding streams and great wide sea,
I felt this sense of being free.

The loss of love of liberty,
No man could compensate for me,
The right to wander where I please,
To seek the sun or shade of trees,
To wander on, the world to see,
And know the joy of being free.

Free as the birds, aloft on high,
That gently sail the cloudless sky,
But freedom doesn't mean "just one,"
It's sharing life and all it's fun,
So hand in hand just let us be,
Always together - always free.

Peter J. Adams

Jim From Milwaukee

The canvas tent was olive green
His camp bed inches high
This yankee captain so supreme
His sea an open sky.

He sneaked me to his D.C.3
And threw me though the door
So I could feel and smell and see
And hear the Cyclones roar

"I can't take you for a flight," he said
"Just a spin across the field
If we're caught I'm as good as dead"
As the rudder bar he heeled

The Reich didn't last a thousand years
Thanks to men like Jim
Who laughed and fought and shed their tears
And put their faith in Him

Half a century since I met this man
Over ten foot tall to me
Forever I'll be a loyal fan
Of my "Captain Milwaukee"

J. G. Matthews

The Suppression Of Emotion

Silent, lonely, tears fall gently down my cheek,
My black mascara runs, my lipstick soon will slowly fade.
My well practised flattering smile now wrinkles up with pain
For life and people I work as a bitter slave

For a second time, I work a ball of mousse into damp hair
and rough dry with a diffuser.
My mascara and lip balm are freshly applied,
I feign a dazzling smile, my eyes seem wide with wonder,
With people I appear pleasant and joyful,
They don't realise it,
I lie.

I take one final glance in my narrow mirror,
I look myself up and down
Once again I'm ready to act in front of the world, pretending
to be happy
Outside people are expecting me, waiting on me, relying on me,
But nobody out there is familiar with my inner self,
If I were alone in the world just now -
I would curl up and die

If only I could lock myself away for twenty minutes,
To me that would be twenty minutes of heaven.

Michelle Martin

Myself

I am a daughter
and a grand-daughter,
a niece and a great niece,
I am a sister and a cousin,
the list goes on and on,
but all these names cannot describe
the real me, the me inside.

I have feelings, emotions too,
things to say,
and things to do,
I have memories locked up in there,
and dreams of hope and dreams of despair,
the things I hate,
the things I like,
my worst fears,
my greatest delights.

I have a picture inside,
of how people see me,
but do they really see the me
that I think they see?

Sarah Gaustad

Matthew A Gift Of God

He is the sunshine of my life,
This special son of mine, I know the love I have for him,
Will stand the test of time.
All the hard work and the worry go into obscurity.
When he puts his little hand in mine, and looks up so innocently.
Many times we've sat by his bedside and willed him so hard to live
And then prayed to God for the help, that only he can give.
But it hasn't been all sorrow and
Sadness, as one might be led
To believe
But happiness, joy and much
Loving, in abundance from him we receive.
Everything we have to do for him,
It's not hard when you love him so.
Just to hear the sound of his laughter,
Makes you want to keep on the go.
The Doctors say he's a fighter, with
This I must agree,
So however can I give upon him
My son, my little Matty.

Shirley Carter

Hope

The flowers of summer lie dead upon their stems
Their sap is spent, their glory lost,
The song of birds is muted, sad and joyless.
The veil of the summer sun is drawn as
The daylight ebbs, sped by the menacing clouds.
Grim, implacable, irrevocable reaper, scythe in hand
Stealthily, surely advances, his blade bloody
With the precious life force of dear, loved souls,
Silent their voices, lifeless their corpses
Like lilies in their vases under heavy headstones
Whose trumpets upon brittle stems cry faintly
For former warmth and soft caress of bees.
Whilst leaves like bitter tears fall sadly to the sod
Trampled, crushed beneath heedless feet peering at epitaphs.
Long, aching, empty months of winter stretch unending
Until, as promised, the world is new again
And the icy grip of death released at last!
The sap rises, nature and life rejoices
Our grief is forgotten. God smiles down in love
Upon his chosen blooms risen from their darkest tombs.

> *Dorothy Fenwick*

Epitaph To The Elm

The sallows in the spring flaunt their golden palms
Diamond-pitted boles and silver-budded charms
But choose me the sovereign to steer the helm
Now that Nature's mint has withdrawn the elm

While lovers still carve their initials on the beach
And more and more conifers skywards reach
The spirit of Browning is laying the wreath
To the last of the elms in tiny leaf

The willows of tomorrow will cut and glance fours
The noble pine's paper will record the scores
But what will become of the lepers in the lane
Stripped of all life in a leafless reign

Whitebeams and cherries and Trees of Heaven
Will beautify the streets of Durham and Devon
But name me the tree in this fair realm
To stand in the hedgerow after the elm

No more to flower when February's done
Or giving shade to cattle in the July sun
Farewell dearest elm, arborescent saint
Deified forever in Constable's paint

> *Roy A. Skelton*

Nasturtium

The withered pale and limped stalks
Once sun-kissed nasturtiums,
Cut down by a cruel October frost,
I gently carried them away to a corner by the river.
I felt as though a friend had
-Died-
And I wasn't there to see him
-Go-
For on a cold foreboding morning I mourned the sight.
Sweet Nasturtiums, orange, red and yellow
Turned to brown.
The leaves still green were dead
The knife-edged frost had ended
-Life-
Drained the colour from every flower
Left a dark and lonely bower where I alone did grieve.
For who else cared but I -?
Who tended for so long, from seed to bloom
Once a blaze of colour, then cascades of death,
Leaving shades of gloom.

> *Mary Josephine Devlin*

Twelve Forty One

What a dreary day! It's twelve forty-one on Salford precinct
They rebuilt it inside out, clean, neat, shining, complete,
It's twelve forty-one on Salford precinct
A young woman with three bags, three kids and a
million troubles, trundles to the shops
Still at least they're clean and neat,
Nike trainers plushly winking from dust-stained feet.

It's twelve forty-one on Salford precinct,
Albert is about and heading for the Pub
It's a major item in his pension book
His clothes pressed clean, neat.
He's with his people, among the hub.

It's twelve forty-one on Salford precinct
A bilious orange and white bus presents itself
Clean and neat, shimmering in cold damp heat, Oh no!
It's scruffy and stuffy and reeks
The poor lose; and the rich
And the rich around here are bloody extinct
But who's counting, who's crying
It's now twelve forty-two on Salford precinct.

> *Andrew Thompson*

A Night At The Club

We went to the club some years ago,
Where the "turns" were voluntary,
I did not expect Frank Sinatra, and so,
I relaxed and sat back with a sherry.

The first turn, a lady, had quite a nice voice,
And gave us "The miller's daughter",
I would have preferred a different choice.
Something like "Afton water."

I finished my sherry and went to the bar
For a refill, and one for the wife,
The evening had been very quiet so far,
But then came the laugh of my life!

The next turn, a man, appeared in her place,
They said that he came from Guiana,
Bow-legged, long arms, a Simian face,
They announced he would sing "Nirvana."

Now "Nirvana" is a lovely old song,
But the choice of it not of the best,
For the opening line, that we've known for so long
Is "I have come from the silent forest!

> *Stanley Gott*

A View From A Gate

The swinging gate. With hinges old.
Stands firm and strong against the cold.
Where lovers stand to coo goodnight
Or others face and curse the flight.

And from its bars, a mountain high,
The seas below, a curlew's cry,
'Twas on those rocks that great men
Stood, most for evil, some for good.
With plots or schemes, all underhand.
Or how to rape the thriving land.

So now the autumn of the scene
Vanishes rapidly, ancient green.
To know that soon no dog will
Bark and no more children in the park
Now fish that swam in crystal pool,
Are just as absent as the schools.
For feeling are no longer fine
As fat contractors rub their hands
And scar the face of our own land.

> *Michelle Holtom*

A Memory In The Dark

Where have you gone to, light of my life?
Who heard my troubles, shared my strife,
Who wiped away each dreary tear,
Who held me close when danger was near,
Whose beaming smile I took for granted,
Whose radiance kept me enchanted.
When I see a star shining on high,
I close my eyes and wish that you were nigh.
But I know you have been laid to rest.
My beloved mother, you were the best.

R. Tucker

Faded Dreams

Where is she now - that girl of my youth
Whose face beamed with joy, who spoke only truth
Whose dreams and ambitions, hopes and fears
Were to shine like a beacon down through the years
Life was good to her, life was kind
So much to think about, lots on her mind
Tomorrow was still a day untouched
Tomorrow was when she'd achieve so much
Alas - tomorrow came and went away
Tomorrow, too soon, was yesterday
The dreams long faded - ambition spent
Seems the girl of my youth just got up and went
And left in her place for all to see
This arthritic, bespectacled, O.A.P.

Pauline Beer

Remembering

Now that my sight grows dim,
Stronger is the light within,
That shines for times of long ago,
Of joy and sadness that I used to know.
Shuffling my feet through fallen autumn leaves,
And raindrops falling on the outer window sill,
And splashing upwards like so many little crowns,
Things like that I remember so clearly still.
The big thick skipping rope across the road,
While young and old jumped in to skip and run
Some mums with children in their arms took turns in all the fun.
Much fun and laughter as the game went on,
Strong arms at either end the rope to turn.
And passes by would stop awhile to watch and cheer,
Milk men, dust men, coal men, post men, from their duties too
   would pause a while,
To enjoy reflected joy, they too would smile,
As I smile now remembering.

Azile Enid Carr

Forever In My Heart

Why is it there are so many things,
Destined to tear us apart,
Even though I know you'll be
Forever in my heart,
Aren't we good enough for each other?
Or is it because they can't see?
All the love I have for you,
Welling up inside of me,
You look away abruptly,
Whenever you catch my gaze,
Although not in a nasty way,
You just try mastering my emotional maze,
My heart warms up as you walk by,
And nod to say hello,
And as I look into your eyes,
They fill me up with woe,
'Cause we'll never be together,
Only ever torn apart,
But you should know you'll always be
Forever in my heart.

Claire Piwowarski

Many Faces

I am the pillar that stands so strong
A maypole that all revolves around
My hands perform many tasks
I have many faces each with a different sound

I'm somewhere between a teacher and carer
Maybe even a cook, nurse or dressmaker
I project so much strength and inspiration
I'm surely a preacher or a possible peacemaker

My job description requires numerous skills
From listening to loving among lots of others
My vocation is one that is not given full dues
It's a God given gift to be chosen as a Mother.

Veronica Harley

The Last Day

To go to bed
Never to wake to another morning, never to see another day
Never to experience or express another emotion
time stood still, motionless, silence falls
soon it will be the end of the day, the end of life
Seeing the ones you love and bringing together
friendships old and new for the last time
Let there be Harmony, for after tonight, life will cease
those who suffer in pain will suffer their burdens no more
those who hurt will hurt no more
those whose hearts are broken will shed no more tears
those who cherish loved ones will cherish them dear
in that precious moment, night falls
We sit together, waiting
crawling into bed I curl up like a child
I find security, comfort and the warmth surrounds me
staying calm, a sudden thought for loved ones
I hold that memory like hypnosis
my eyes close, I cannot fight
its power overwhelms me, there I sleep, till I am no more.

Diane Cooper

The Little Fisherman

Down to the stream at the foot of the hill,
It's the best place on Earth for a boy,
A net and a jar, it's not very far,
Come on and I'll show you pure joy.

'Course, big boys use fishing rods,
one day I'll have one, just like my
big brother and Dad,
But for now I'll just treasure,
these moments of pleasure,
That's enough for a little lad.

One day I'll grow up, an' I'll buy a big
boat, an' I'll catch all the fish in the sea.
Till then, what the heck, I'll catch
tadpoles int' beck,
That's enough, at the moment for me.

V. Conley

Untitled

As I walked on through the stormy waters,
I heard the angel's cry.
It floated down to greet me
and echoed through the sky.
Its cry was sweet and tender.
I knew I had no choice,
I had to follow the voice.
The path was hard and lonely
and often filled with war.
But all the while it was worth it,
for I knew I had the best,
The best this world could offer
The path of life may be hard and long,
but that will surely pass.
When it does you're sure to find,
the key to happiness.

Elizabeth Hall

With All My Heart

Listening to the sensual music that plays
Lifts my spirit and makes me sway
The love we share together
Will keep us happy forever
When your hand touches mine
We are suspended in time
Here and now is all that we share
The love and tenderness is just to show how much I care
When your lips touch mine
I can feel the tingling down my spine
When we lay next to each other underneath the cover
The fire burning deep inside will never subside
As the tenderness of your touch
Makes me tremble so much
I will always love you my heart stays true
Please believe me when I say
I want you here with me to stay.

Amanda Bland

My Diamond Daughter

A Priceless jewel that shines so bright,
She'll break a few hearts, you'll see I'm right.
A world of happiness from her tiny smile
Spoil her rotten, once in a while

Dry her eyes of tiny tears,
Protect and guard her through the coming years.
She has herself so much charm,
Always keep her safe from harm.
Always be there, always share
Her ups and downs
Her laughs, her frowns

She's only three,
She means the world to me,
My beautiful daughter Natalie.

Steve Kenny

In Memory

You and I were children long ago,
brother and sister from a time gone by.
Not for us a well filled silver spoon,
though young,
to wise to cry out for the moon.
We never thought to question men of power,
who would pander to the rich and scorn the poor,
did we know somehow our day would come!
When war and danger knocked on every door.
An underprivileged childhood
some might say.
But we had much the young have not today,
the fields, the trees, the flowers, the open sky,
the streets to play in, not a place to die.
Though you no longer walk this earth
my brother,
perhaps your spirit wanders where we used to play,
perhaps you see us as we were
as children,
perhaps, who knows, we'll meet again someday.

Linda Gubbins

Winter Now?

If all the poets that have gone before
Have drawn on images of summer,
What is left but the autumn of ideas?

And if I should plant seeds in this ground,
Over-cultivated and untilled,
What could grow there now but poor frail blooms,
Shaken by the cold winds of winter?

But still my Muse drives me to write,
To till, to plant and to water;
Still she tells me spring must follow.

Philip Cooke

Alien

Why do we laugh?
Why do we cry?
These special feelings of love,
Perhaps we'll never know why.

Each day passes through,
Each month lingers on,
I close my eyes and try
To remember the good times and write this song.

The feeling of emptiness, of being alone
Surround me from head to toe,
I plan what to say and pick up the phone,
The words just stick and don't seem to flow.

I practice, I pray, I plead, I preach,
Maybe, if, why not, in fact, I don't have a clue.
My thoughts are right, my words are wrong
And all because I'm trying to say, "I love you".

Helen Slade

Eleventh Commandment

The girl who is transparent
hides away in her room.

The girl with no voice
has forgotten how to speak.

The girl not blessed with intelligence
never goes to school.

The girl who will never be beautiful
starves, purges, punches, screams and bleeds.

The girl who cannot pull herself together
Is threatened with the sanitarium.

The woman who can cry
is repeatedly asked not to.

The woman who is not ignorant
does not really know anything.

The woman accepted as herself
is unable to do right.

The woman liked for her sensitivity
is far too quiet.

The woman who is host
is an intruder in her own home.

Joanne Pearson

Paris

Beautiful Paris, salutations
This wonderful morning in spring
They come people of all nations
To you homage they bring.

Your magnificent buildings delight me
With their grandeur and beautiful shape
What time I shall need all their number to see
And at their immensity gape.

Paris I worship your scent and flowers
With aromas the air is laden
From your perfumeries and your bowers
And from many a passing maiden.

Treading daintily your wide sentiers
Ladies with their haute couture
Every eye looks, heads turn their way
Mesdemoiselles with steps so sure.

I enjoyed my visit to Paris
When I fell under her spell
A flag for her I will now carry
And of her enchantment tell.

Lucy Mary Ronchetti

The Milk Maid

Spurts of white into the pail do sing
Her hands so nimble, her voice gently sings
Nestling her head in velvet brown
Tenderly murmuring, she steadies her down
As she milks the old brown cow
She dreams of love under the apple bough
With the man she is soon to wed
On she dreams in the old cow shed

Bucket full of creamy milk
Smooth and white, like fairy silk
Straightening up her aching back
She gives the cow an affectionate slap
Pouring white into silver churn
Come on, Nellie, now it's your turn
Just one more, then she's done
Sky is golden, with the morning sun.

Jean M. Aldridge

Unknown

I do not know you, you do not know me,
You are but a name I see before me.
Gone from your life - I know not why,
To live another life, so young to die.
You were seventeen years old when you died,
    What for?
Snuffed out like a candle when someone slams a door.
A stone is carved which you cannot see,
There is no name standing here before me.
"Missing in action" is all that is said,
You went full of fear, but came back dead.
Here is this young man - before me he lies,
I would love to have seen you with my own eyes.
I do not know you, you do not know me,
You are but a name I see before me.

Kevin Somerfield

Picture Simple Love

The picture would be simple
Painter perhaps could carelessly caress
The welcoming canvas
Beauty, grace, elegance would adorn.
Everlasting splendour
Happy ever after imagination yells
The queen will have her king
Their palace engulfed with glee
Passion would abound, infatuation.
Everlasting joy
Life reveals a different picture
Untouchable beauty, a fortress
Never to be breached, this king
Will never be accepted, hurt, sorrow, grief.
Everlasting pain

Andrew Gavigan

Our Treasure

Sapphire in the sky at night
Ruby of glorious dawn
Topa'z on the aqua' seas
Garnet hills and emerald lawn
Diamonds in the space of time
The golden circled sun
Tall and rustic shaded trees
Where the songs of the breeze were sung
Opal horizons silver moon
Turquoise and coral beds
Golden sands and clouds of pearly white
Agate bloodstone rocks more still, than dead
What more is there to look upon
And all for nought, thy pleasure
With these riches all around
Our world is full of treasure.

Agnes

Time On Time

Once upon a time
Man's time
Time went Tick Tock
Sometimes a relaxing sound
Other times
Migraine times
A thunderous sound

Modern Man's time is silent
Pulsating time
Quarts time

Man controls this time
Putting time forwards
Or backwards
Stopping time altogether
To bring his time in line with atom time

There is a time however
Man cannot control
It goes on and on and on.....

Rodney George Priest

Time On Time 2

Time goes by so slowly
Yet passes in a flash
One minute we have all the time in the world
The next we have to dash

Sometimes, there are not enough hours in the day
Especially, when harvesting hay
Other times, too many days in the week we say
Especially, when waiting for our pay

Work time, Monday to Friday
Play time, Saturday and Sunday

This is Man's time

There is a time however
That has no beginning and no end
Not governed by five days in the week
Or two days of the weekend

This is God's time

Find the time to know this time
And you are finding the time
To know God
And God's time

Rodney George Priest

Colours Of The Seasons

Gold is the colour of spring.
Primrose, daffodil, crocus ring.
Forsythia, kerria, golden sun,
Pink blossomed trees, now winter's done.

Blue is summer, high, cloudless sky,
Forget me not, corn flower, frail butterfly.
Tall delphinium, fragrant rose,
A rainbow of colours. By summer's close.

Riotous autumn in russet and reds.
Crinkly leaves, dried flower heads,
Fruits, nuts, berries, bales of hay,
Glorious sunsets, to end the day.

Winter, Grey, brings snow overnight,
Clothing our world in dazzling white.
Silvery frost, rivers of ice,
Transforming everything, in a trice.

Each season shows a different face,
Ever changing, to keep pace,
Blending one, into another,
Yet, staying unique, with its own special colour.

E. M. Eagle

Temptation; The Way Of The World

...Below the rocks, where the fair verdures stretch'd,
and in a wild profusion, fields of bloom -
The ambient air ambrosial, and full of sleep -
Without regard of man, a mystic Torrent ran
Past citadels, - scant pastures of the world -
and by a hundred crowds; - oh, happy throng
that look'd so well unto their happiness!
And to these citizens, one Tree beside the Torrent
yielded a fruit so hard - like gall - and full of stones.
And yet, some thirsting soul would on occasion come,
and pluck with palsied hands the Tree,
to taste this fruit; and straight would come
a thousand fairer fruits before his roving eye.
To quench his thirst, he then forsook his first desire,
and reached, and ate, with eyes afire.
The silent Torrent, flowing by, would fain have quenched
His sore dissatisfaction; still he ate; and burned within
And then, a Darkness came: his Helping gone,
he sigh'd, lay down beneath the Tree, and slept.
The ambient air ambrosial, and full of sleep.

Verity E. S. Dibben

Bear

Propped up on pillows
Bear sits.
Still and silent.
Staring brown eyes, simply plastic yet
Witness to so many years,
Always there, yet sometimes forgotten,
Bear fulfils his roles,
Eternal ear, forever friend,
Bringer of warmth and security,
His fur matted through fever and grief,
Still soft though old.
Discarded when a lover takes the bed,
Bear is quick to forgive,
Assuming his place when the rival has left,
Ready once more to catch the tears...
Strange to think he affects me so much,
When a bear is just some
Fur, filled with fluff.

Ruth Walley

Children Of War

Deaf, dumb and blind,
Could anything in life match the horror of knowing,
The cruel ocean accepts the sacrifice of young sailors,
We sow terrifying crops in the fields of war,
A cold and dark embrace,
From a strange and unwelcome guest,
No one wants what's bound to come,
As fat generals dine on young men's souls.

Jason Sutcliffe

The Storm

The rain came crashing down upon the window,
As she snuggled up in bed,
It began to sing in little solo,
She raised from the pillow her tiny little head.

The wind began to race the streets
So she turned to Ted and Golly,
Another roar, she jumped the sheets,
She didn't find this very jolly.

The wind and rain got really fierce,
but alas, she couldn't reach the handle,
Then mummy heard her daughters tears,
got up and lit a candle.

The door swung open,
And there she stood weeping
Mummy rocked her in her arms
And before she knew it she was sleeping.

H. Conti

For My Son

A million tears to cry, a million more in the why
before you'll know so many more,
Can you give them all to me?
In its hour the answer pure and simple
is burning as a flame, burning in desire
For you to see.

I feel your love and understand in what it is,
Disrobe the blame, disrobe the game,
For I am with you always, as you are of me.

Though I am not what you see,
In love or hate I am the void of what it is
The existence of the heart and soul.

A million tears we cry from a million questions
asking why,
Of father, of son, a circle begun

But in truth, the answer always there,
Beckons,
'til our last embrace.

Kenneth Herbert

Solace

A single cross
Two candles lit
In front of me where I sit.
You take my hands
And bow your head;
Not a word spoken, nothing said.

My eyes are closed
I know you pray
Your gentle warmth has much to say.
I hear you sigh
My pain has fled;
Not a word spoken, nothing said.

I see green fields
And blue skies
But tightly closed are my eyes.
Your warmth is deep
You cross my brow;
Words "God bless you" are whispered now.

Jenny L. Treacher

For Norton And Mia

My life is more fulfilling
Since you two were born,
You're my reasons for living, laughing and crying
And getting up at the crack of dawn.
Each day is so special,
I'm glad I spend them all with you
It means I get to treasure
The little things you say and do
When you first learnt to crawl and walk,
How you tried and tried,
And when you first said 'Love you, Mummy'
I remember that I cried.
You both have lovely personalities,
You live, learn and enjoy.
You're happy, contented and smile a lot
You are my pride and joy.
I really love you both so much
I don't know what I would do,
If I hadn't been so blessed to have
Two children as wonderful as you.

Marie Whyte

The Runner

On a lonely beach of soft, damp, sand
Which the curling waves had swept
Was a figure running - and he was alone
While the land by the seashore slept.
Running from what? And running where
Was a secret he alone kept.

And the footprints that the runner made
In the damp and yielding sand
Were washed away as the sea came in
How could the waves understand
Why that figure ran, in the early dawn
At the very edge of the land.

Was the runner hastening on to meet
Someone at the days first light?
Or running from something, causing his feet
To keep on in a headlong flight.
As the waves came gently, creaming in
The figure ran on, out of sight.

Molly Rodgers

Peaceful Place

This hill on which I sit,
Consists of stone from down the pit.
It has been here many years, now grass has covered over,
I lay down my head and rest, upon a bed of clover.
As I look up I see some clouds,
They're quickly passing by.
Just for a moment I think,
Of all the wonders in the sky.
Bright clouds, bright stars, bright moon, bright sun,
Wonderful, beautiful, every one.
I hear a bird sing in the trees,
It brings my thoughts to ground.
I see the shallow pond in front of me,
And hear a quiet rippling sound.
The wind is blowing, the air is cool,
Cool upon my face.
I feel so contented here,
This lovely, peaceful place.

John Millar Kent

Sanctuary For Two Stray Cats

Where would we be if it weren't for you?
Under the earthy ground
You fed us, you loved us, and for us a home you found.

We have our own little garden which is a great delight
We scamper around, or lie quite still and sometimes
We have a fight.

We have a blanket to lie on, and a pillow for each head
It's snug and warm and cosy when it's time to go to bed.

So thank you all sincerely, it's better than a toy
Thank you from little Lily and from me a grateful boy.

Doris M. Herring

The Christmas Card

Your Christmas card brought
   endless cheer.
To walks of life both far and near
Though flowers appear and cheer.
Your card's a flower all the year.

And as I journey on in life.
And see around a change.
When flowers have failed to be
still goes on the "Hand" of man.

Of everything by man installed.
Be flowers - and what's on the bench.
There still goes on the hand of love
"A Christmas" card's a flower all the year.

Elsie Margery Robinson

The Girl In Green

There's a girl in green at the end of the bar,
she appears to be upset,
too pretty to be out alone, her boyfriend's late I bet

There's a girl in green at the end of the bar,
she's been there quite a while,
should I try to catch her eye,
raise my glass and smile?

There's a girl in green at the end of the bar,
still no one by her side.
I'd like to go and talk to her,
but rejection hurts my pride.

An hour has passed,
the girl has gone,
I never said hello,
although I think I caught her eye as she turned to go.

There's an empty glass upon the bar,
standing on its own.
I romanced awhile to no avail,
and like the glass I'm here alone.

Gavin Bradley

"Your Eyes"

Your eyes I love when they sparkle in their love for me.
Ablaze in azure splendour, neath the curtain of dark lashes.
Their constant changing shades contain more hues than any sea.
Your eyes I love; when from their depths love flashes.

Longed for glimpses, when lost beneath the flutters of your lids;
To Morpheus' arms you silently succumb with yawns and sighs.
Blind sleep a thief! Curse him and every mortal whom he bids:
Yet - grateful for the mortal vision, which lets me love your eyes.

Pitied them, when streaked with tell tale red, I know your tiredness.
Hair veins fan out from each small centre,
Moist with beauty lie like tiny blood strokes on cornea snow.
Arouse my cries that Nature with her treasure should be gentler.

Surely Argus would have traded all for two like thine.
Heaven will be your gaze forever into mine.

Charles Robert Toman

Stress

If you have a friend, upon whom you can rely,
Then stranger, you are far better off than I,
For all around me are circus clown's,
Grey cells of them are quite unknown,
Not one charitable thought in their head's,
It surprises me, that they can even, get out of their bed's,
And for sixteen hours while they're awake,
All around in their wake,
They make life, very hard to take,
Always leaning on others for support,
By themselves, capable of naught,
For a willing horse can be flogged to death,
And my breath is stifled by these living dead,
Now I'm not talking, sick and afflicted,
Just people, that are downright stupid,
Idiot's of the first degree,
Who I don't need to meet, or have meet me,
So all cretin's, keep away,
And I'll stay sane, for another day.

A. P. Rempel

Prison

Intimate thoughts of lifestyles before
Pondering memories that fade into past
Distress and despair reigns with the boredom
As hope's golden flame fades into the darkness under the bed

Coldness echoes round this hardened hole
Breathing fumes that choke with remorse
Tears of frustration rimming your eyes
As you fight for your sanity under emptiness pressure

Louise Kitchen

Playing The Game Of Life

High above in the clouds,
light so bright I cannot get out.
Help is near as angels call,
my life begins, now I will not fall.

Then I wake up and I wonder,
Is this what will happen, or will I really fall?

Hole dug deep to me they call,
"It's time to go Cinderella, It's time for the ball".
Forceful pull I cannot escape,
unwanted help just throws me in.

Darkness falls down here as dawn breaks up there,
shivers down my spine, It's time to fear.

For those of you who live in grace,
another good life for eternity awaits.
I've sinned on sins and now I pay,
death after life is the game I play.

Shabnam Iqbal

A Poem

Never have I loved a man,
The way I loved that boy.
My mind would never let me rest a day.
The things he planted in my soul
That grew to shine so bright
Will never shine again to make me stay.

One day I hope to meet someone
Who'll light that quiet flame,
Who'll make my heart burn bright again inside,
So I can put my feelings by
For that boy long ago
And fill another's heart with loving pride.

Naomi Turner Rankin

Going Back

I came back today to the home of my youth
where from a child I inherited the value of
truth, from a father since passed and a mother
alone our search goes back to days that are gone.
We look up to the mountains and down to the
lough remembering mother on our runaway horse.
For all of a sudden she's young once again
and I am a child bordering on ten.
The twittering swallows in the barn overhead
parts of a comic that once had been read
by a child now grown up with boys of her
own who might one day return to their
youthful home.

Muriel R. Graham

Poli Poli The Elephant

Great Colossus
Your life evolving
From Nature's slow gestation
To a grand matriarchy
Indomitable and tender.
Lumbering your way across
The African plains
Into the age-old imagination of mankind.
So full of fear and envy,
For you carry your wealth
For all to see.
Proud tusks thrusting forward
Not hidden like ore
beneath the earth
Your trunk bellowing
The trumpet of a thousand warriors
Yet felled to the ground
By puny man's desire
For a back street dagger.

Bell Diamond

Tutankhamen's Love

When we were alive,
I knew how much you loved me.
And now, from your adorned sepulchre, you compassionately enter,
With protestations of love greater than ever before.

But why Tutankhamen, in my state of deadened eternity
Do you wish to declare your deepened love,
For though my body has been saved from violation,
My heart has been gnawed with guilt?

Keep me covered, for though you have no eyes,
I dread your glare,
And though my heart has long since stopped,
My fear is such to trigger its beat once again.

Stop! I cannot conceive your forgiving presence.
Come no closer to my ungendered body,
For my guilt must surely be as translucent
As your alabaster wishing cup.

Yet you still draw closer.
And while I die further,
You serve not to judge
But to love, even more...

Sarah Borg

The Search

I long for peace of the aesthetic kind
A spiritual need, to ease my mind.
Make sense of being, to see the light,
To not be lost, in this endless plight - of empty unknowing.

Many before me have longed for the same,
They too were lost, stumbling and lame.
Treading the path, short of what will be,
Deep in sadness, such a need to see - where it's all going.

I hope some day that I will find, what eluded them, my soul to bind,
To a sense of purpose, a glimpse of truth,
Where for and what for, so troubled since youth - but I need showing.

I've looked for myself but with no success,
The more I see, the more I know less.
Why should it be that I remain so blind,
Seek ye and seek ye but I never can find - the seeds for sowing.

In this infertile ground of my sanity,
To take and to bloom, to set my soul free
To flower and show me, appoint the right day
To flourish and shine and enlighten my way - for the need is growing.
and - my life is slowing.

Anthony M. Morgan

Let Me Be The One

Let me be the one to hold you, and keep you warm at night.
To kiss your lips forever, and cuddle you so tight.
Let me be the one to love you, and cherish you all my days,
To keep you and look after you, in every single way.

Let me be the one you're wanting, give me all your love,
You take my breath, you took my soul, you gave my heart a shove.
Let me be the one you lay with, so loving all the time,
I'd love you like no other could, just say that you'll be mine

Let me be the one you walk with, on and on we'd go.
And always be the one you talk with, I will listen so.
Let me be the one you care for, always on your mind,
Your hearts so pure, you're so sincere, and always very kind.

Let me be the one to listen, and sooth you when you're blue,
I want to live a life of love, and that means loving you.
Let me be the one to share with, all the love you give,
And that means sharing life together, as long as we both shall live.

Barry Clark

My Poem

Body: My fear is one of the unknown
    Death is a vast sea with many secrets.

Soul: For every sea there is a shore
    For every journey there is an arrival.

Body: But how will I know when I have arrived?
    Who will welcome me?

Soul: There will be sleep beyond the sleep of men
    And peace beyond aspiring.

Body: If my eyes are closed you will leave me
    And death will inhabit in your place.

Soul: This is the contract. I have lived within you
    But you have been a temporary dwelling.

Body: Is there no union more lasting?
    Must it crumble away into nothingness?

Soul: It is inevitable, but do not despair.
    You have loved me well - I shall not forget.

Body: Embrace me. Do not abandon me
    The flesh is weak in the face of destiny.

Soul: Come, look on me - I am your face of love
    I will stay with you until you sleep.
    Ann P. Whitmore

Treasures In My Garden

How lucky to have in my garden
Squirrels so cheeky and bright
Giving the pigeons and blue-tits such a fright.
When the birds fly down for the nuts
A squirrel will suddenly appear.
So up fly the birds to a higher branch
While it leads them a merry dance.
Swinging down it shakes the nuts
With a crash they fall to the ground.
It takes them one by one
Digs a hole and hides them until the winter comes.
Along behind it creeps a magpie
Digging up the hidden treasures.
There in a branch above
Watch the two collared doves
Waiting their turn to fly down to the ground along with the jay
Who has his way of dashing down
When there are nuts to be found.
With my camera I crouch and try to remain still
To capture these moments gives me such a thrill.
    Patricia M. Farbrother

Depression

It's been with me now so many weeks
The tortured mind within
Its presence claims me for keeps
Oh, how I must have sinned.

Each moment of each and every day
The nagging thoughts abound
What life is left? I cry, and pray
A solution can be found.

At night not much respite is there
For dreams are hideous and scary
I wake sobbing and shaking at another nightmare
Of sleep I become wary

I am out of touch with reality
Deeper and blacker it gets
No-one understands the frailty
The lost soul frets and frets

Slowly through medication the day returns
Eight months was quite a while
The pleasure of life once more is earned
My face learns again to smile.
    D. W. J. Golds

Poetry In Motion

Write me a poem you say
A poem about what?
About anything you say
But I don't know anything
Except - that you are asking the impossible
Asking me to write a poem is like asking me to fly
I might dream of it
I might wish it with all my heart
But that doesn't make the landing any less painful or embar-
rassing.

The branch begins to sway
Jump you say
It's too high
Jump
I'm scared
Try
Will you hold my hand? Will you catch me?
Maybe
Write me a poem, you say
I close my eyes and jump...
    Lynn Donovan

'Childhood In Venezuela'

I remember the voices in the old Homestead,
Hours of joyful intimacy
Trees that would sway in rhythmic slumber,
While the to and fro of the waves outside
would fill our souls with a restful aroma.

Caribbean sea,
Intimate friend of my early years
Your secret depths seemed to share
a communication of restful odour.

There are memories which bring
Sighs of time gone by.
Tears like pearls
that wash the face.

Memories that time has taken
with the blue sky of transformed clouds
in the pure illusion of a lost era.
Which enveloped was in a sweet perfume.

The wind seems to whisper the names of those behind
linked intricately and forever
with those bygone times.-
    Millicent Burman

Thankless Monsters And Charming Cherubs

The battle cry of "I don't wanna" rings around our home,
With two of you and one of me - I sometimes feel quite alone.
"Can that be me?" I ask myself when I hear shouts and bellows,
Perhaps it's not - perhaps it's the two little fellows.

All year 'round the war goes on without stopping to reload.
It's hardly surprising really - we're out of the same mould.
Yet something stirs inside of me as Christmas time draws near,
My mind is filled with images so vibrant and clear.

There are Christmases past when you were babes, when your
    innocence shone through,
But the boys that stand before me now - guess what? They're
    still you,

For a few short days there's a cease fire, you've other things
    on your mind,
Like stocking and parties and paper hats and adventures of a
    most pleasant kind.
You're ready for action - you want 'to do' - not planning an assault,
But trimming the tree and wrapping the gifts - and you're
    pleased with the result.
I watch you giggle and dance with glee, at the most innocent
    little things,
And I wonder - deep in my heart - what future Christmases
    may bring.
    Yvonne Hughes

Adas

I am here, you are there
You are here, there I am
There you are, here I am
Lies the crisis of the modern man

We share the same air
We share the same sky
We awake by the same light
The same moon that guides us at night

How can I continue to live
How can my heart continue to beat
When you have the other half
Give it me back
As you only live across the street

I don't understand
I'll never know why
We don't share the same feelings
But yet we've shared the same piece of sky

Andrea E. Cope

Images Of London 1st January 1995

Tramps huddle in their cardboard carton lairs,
While Big Ben's chimes ring out the brave New Year,
And ladies of the night wait 'neath the stairs,
While drunken louts pass, shouting, full of beer.

The empty streets resound with wind-blown cans,
And stars reflect in oily puddles near,
Obscured in turn by flashing neon signs,
Whose advertising brightness fails to cheer.

The morning creeps on lead-polluted feet,
Weighed down by fumes of traffic passing by;
The faceless crowds who jostle and who beat
A steady progress, while they turn a blinded eye.

And high above St. Paul's Cathedral seat,
The dome proclaims 'Behold, the Lord is nigh!'

James Bailey

Love

Words have been written in songs and rhyme
of this thing called love and endless time
and yes, it will last a whole life through
for true love is a bond between just two

It's strong and demanding and causes pain
it's tender and gentle like summer rain
without it, what would life be worth
there is nothing quite like it on this earth.

It's the meal that we cook, and the present we buy
it's the touch of a hand or the wink of an eye
it's the ache in our heart when a loved one's away
the contentment we feel at the end of the day.

Some have been known to die in its name
and others have treated it just like a game
it's a powerful emotion, not quite understood
it is a feeling divine, so hats off to love.

E. R. Ross

Winter Remembered

I look across fields that
are like a white tranquil sea.
Eyes strained.
Searching for a light house amidst
the islands of trees.
I walk the bleak road, treacherous
as any rocky coast line.

Exhilaration and fear mix as the
wind whips the snow into a frenzy.
Appreciation of a beauty that is only momentary.
A longing to be home to the warm
harbour of a cosy kitchen, where
appreciation of the winter storm can be retained.

Sheila Regan

Fittleton

With jackstay rigged and heaving party strung along the deck,
The ship came close the MERMAID's stern: the captain made a check.
On parallel course, but too far out, the fated move he made
To bring the 'sweeper closer, yet failed to heed the warning.
As water swirled and surface boiled, the ships were drawn together
And FITTLETON, caught beneath the stern, was brought to overturning.

Proud ship lay prone in dreadful pose as crewmen met their doom:
Near half a score were quick to die but those in Engine Room
Were trapped alive and frantic taps were heard upon the shell.
But FITTLETON could not be held and soon all rescue bids
Were scuppered as the ship went down and hopes were sunk as well.

Thus ended FITTLETON's days in misery and shame,
Her damage found beyond the price of reasonable reclaim.
Now from this tragedy must surely come the good that follows ill:
Authority must see that never more can such a loss befall,
That extra care be taken as ship as these come near,
That better training and design be targets for us all.

Malcolm Oliver

My Man I Love

My man to my imagination, once I knew,
He shone like a star, was born new,

The sparkle of his eyes, was the early morning's dew,
Like the rainbow, he came, and I lost him in the gathering of few,

Search was on for the man I lost,
Gathering fled, so did the rainbow's host,

Storm in my eyes, made the rumbling noise in the ears, did its duty,
All alone I stood, even shimmer was gone, and taken all beauty,

Essence of my love, lost its flare,
Erratic beats of my heart, gave the sign to beware,

Bewildered I was, left with no pride,
I temper my self, for the astonishing tide,

Timid was my body, soul left to lurch, The green grass, I'll
never walk again, for I was a made a rod of birch,

Vibration of the storm, erupted the volcano of my brain
Evidence of erosion became, positive as long as train,

What device can I use to erase the memory of enmity,
Can the faith be found, in love the only cure, in the pity,

Determination is to mend the broken destiny, of one's fate,
Very easy to say, love and devote, one another, not to hate.

K. Bahra

Have You Ever Sat And Wondered

Have you ever sat and wondered about the way a woman lives
Why she has to be broad-shouldered, rarely takes but always gives
When she's little she is acting out the role of being a mum
When older she has found her man, the best is yet to come.

She leaves her home to live in bliss and does for quite a while
She's cooking, cleaning, washing, ironing, all done with a smile
She is happy to participate in this new game she's found
To care for and to dote upon the man to whom she's bound.

But what happens to us women who have done this all along
Who have sorted out the bills to wonder where the money's gone
Who have sorted out the meals to be eaten in the week
Who feel completely shattered but still standing on their feet.

Just think about the housework done when you walk through the door
The grass is cut, the car is clean, you couldn't ask for more
A meal prepared awaiting to be eaten up with glee
You haven't had to cook it — that's pure ecstasy.

When finally all is said and done, what else is there to do
This has been a woman's life from all the ages through
But just a little encouragement or praise for what you've done
Would make you feel of value — not just a wife and mum.

Ann Cashman

Talk And Try

To-day our world is totally confused
Mother earth is polluted and most abused.
Many children cry from famine and plight
We look on and say how can this be right?

Each one blames the other
For all that has gone wrong so lets all get together
And work from here on in to stamp out the flames
Of hatred and greed before these wrongs
Destroy mankind

Our Young generation has got to prove
That sorrow and evil the power of love can move
We shall do all we can our very best
To make this century better than the rest.

We must talk, we must try we must strive with
all our might we must fight to
make them see the light yes! We must get it right.

Angela Moore

Violent Flowers

Violent flowers were your parting gift
In that jealous garden
Suffocating aroma of unforgivingness
And bruised petals of hopelessness
Were your accusation.
"Their leaves never shed"
You said,
"They never die
Just lie
And they need no care, no love
No tenderness
No happiness
Unlike me".

And you turned away forever
Clutching your severed heart
Betrayed and torn apart
And left me with that bouquet of bitterness
Crying and bleeding on my condemning weakness.

J. E. Read

Thoughts - On Life

Is life just a dream, for that's what
It sometime seems.
Do we live and breathe, or are our
eyes there only to deceive.

Is life just a dream, and we are but a
cloud, way up in the sky, just going
round and round.

Is life just a dream, and when each dream
is past, do we just evaporate, then make a
brand new start.

A. G. Taylor

To Love Again

To meet you now, with in my life
Is all I ask.
To care for you now, through out our life's
Is that my task?

I dreamed I was with you,
All day and night.
I dreamed I could love again,
But I awoke in fright.

To get to know you, your hopes and dream's
To talk all night, of deep and spiritual things.
With in your hopes, with in your dreams.
Could there be a place for me?
Just look my way,
Then maybe some day,
You'll hear me say,
I'm in love again!
Yes! to love again.

P. S. Barlow

Steve's Mind

Questions - no answers
Crying - no tears
Understanding an addict
Don't rebuke me, don't sneer

Words spoken from an addict
How can you understand you are merely my mum
Don't know how I am hurting, life ebbing away like sand

Falling like a star in the dark of night
How can you possibly have the slightest insight
You have no conception of the craving deep in my soul
Leaving the powder alone I cannot feel whole

Do you sincerely believe I enjoy living this way
Sometimes I do not want to wake to another day
Wake up in the morning and try not to score
Like fighting with yourself, your own private war

I feel so alone, no support, no-one to care
This is how you think Steven, I am totally aware
I know more than you think, know what you are going through
I once was an addict - different drug - but
I have been there once too!

Eve Thirlaway

A Spring Morning By The Stream

Cool Clear water billowing down the side,
Bulrushes and pebbles dragged by the ebbing tide,

A fresh new morning the sun, a blaze of fire,
The cloudless sky, the dew dropped grass, bows to its desire,

The touch of pressed satin, the spiders silken weave,
The glimpse of a golden sunbeam through the delicate thread
they leave,

A silent moment of stillness, everything stops its thrive,
A sun-sweetened Butterfly pauses to whisper......

He Is Alive!

Esther J. E. Lockwood

A Tiny Spark In A Fire

We exchanged chemicals in the warm
    Summer's dusk,
The night still young like our love;
An eternal flame; forever burning,
Warming me every moment separation occurred.

Ears burning, the tree
Listening, the grass beneath our
Footsteps....
    Whispered.

Love was among us that August night.
Your words of wisdom woven in
Feather and grass.
Your love died; mine did not.

Zoe L. Gray

The Rich Man And The Tramp

There was a pauper by the road,
whom a rich man, upon a horse which strode
past, always gazed upon and watched eat
the food people cast at his feet.
One day, providence ordained
he should receive a feast fit for a king,
and on gold platters it was served,
with wine, sauces and every finer thing.
Instead of sneering, as he had oft' done before,
the rich man was enraged at what he saw,
and, dismounting, kicked him in the teeth;
and the dishes, with all the food, he scattered around.
The poor man, who lay bleeding on the ground,
cried, "That is the only thing I have had in my life!
You have everything: Wealth, a mansion and freedom from strife!
Am I forbidden but one consolation,
when all I've ever known is desolation?"

S. P. Lloyd-Price

Beyond Archaeology

With humble tools we scrape the crust, and beneath
Lies promise of pure language, oracles
Concealed in ancient cities and caskets,
Skulls entombed in a fusion of tenses.

Smoky columns rise from burning pyres,
Statues rust and crumble, monuments ruin,
Stepping stones, once so firm, dissolve and fade
Into desert sands and silt of oceans.

In this wide vault the leaves of Shakespeare lie
Among the ghosts of Plato and Darwin.
Adam grips a crucifix and weeps as
Urns spill over with the blood of armies.

From fragments we compose our history,
But never perceive the glowing core itself,
For truth is masked, and like some distant star,
Appears as a vision, indefinite.

Giles Fletcher

Long Time - No See

Sid! Hey Sid - I was sure it was you,
what brings you back here?
Looking so blue.
It's got to be years, since I saw you last,
Remember the antic's that surrounded our past.
We got so legless, we could hardly speak
and the girls we walked out with
we never could keep.
You did alright though with Maisy Norris,
After you left, I hitched up with Doris.
We had some good years, she was always a laugh,
She's not long departed,
ne're broke me in half.
But you did alright Sid, so I've been told,
All them houses you bought, did up
and sold,
I've got my allotment, it's what I do best,
growing me veg, then have me a rest.
Off now Sid, mind how you go,
it's sure nice to see you - cheerio.

Deborah Harbach

With Thanks To The Brave Firemen

This is a tale which took place in World War two,
When firebombs rained down on us and Granddad, seventy flew
Around with sandbags, a solo fire squad played,
Whilst all our younger neighbours, quaking in their shelters stayed.
The Home Guard headquarters was in the local pub,
Well, that's where Dad reported, nightly after grub.
But not before he proudly, standing at the gate,
Watched me running to the Depot, as usual somewhat late,
To travel with mobile canteens of W.V.S. fame,
Dispensing cups of tea outside buildings well aflame,
Into the numbed hands of firemen, wearing jackets still
Soaking wet from last night's fires, uniforms which will
Be just as cold and wet tomorrow night, when
The sirens will sound and bombs rain down again.

Margaret Doran

Untitled

One morning you wake up and there it is -
A baby - well, you had it yesterday
(A rather medical experience
Like going to the dentist, not much more).
And so it grows, through nappies, sleepless nights,
Tempers, schools, vaccinations and the rest -
The pangs of adolescence - to a man
Who may perhaps write novels, and in them
You figure, as a mother! Who'd have thought
That such a casual event as birth
Would make you one of those? For still you feel
A girl, with life to come, and these grey hairs
Most unconvincing substitute for age.

Diana Richardson

Solution To Pollution

Come on everyone, and act on pollution.
You know there really is a solution.
So come on now, let's get together
To find the solution, face the weather

Let's face facts,
Come down to earth,
Follow the tracks.
Let's take a walk.
Take a leaf from the good book,
Don't be afraid to take a look
Into the greatest book on earth.

It's action that's needed and not
too much talk,
Into the park we can't really walk
To enjoy the flowers, bees and birds.
So let's act now on these reliable true words

Michael Charles Philp

Happy Day

Let me tell you how I feel about you on this day
I love those tight blue jeans of yours
In such a special way
Every time you take a step
Those "Cheeks" just roll together
And as for that lunchbox of yours
I could have your "Dish of the Day" forever

I love the way you look at me
Through your oriental looking eyes
And the way you run your hand upon/between/up
My "Smooth and silky" thighs
You press upon my buttons and I'll show you the real me
The real me that no other man has been privileged to see

Boy I'm daring you today/tonight to knock on my trap door
And if you're lucky to get inside
You'll be shouting "I want more"
"I want more of what you're giving me now that I am inside"
And I'll be saying, yee ha babe, I'm gonna take you for a ride!

Sharon Clennon

To My Grandchildren

You lie in your cradles so small and so sweet,
And gurgle and smile as you play with your feet.
You creep and you crawl; then you're standing up tall,
Watch out! Watch out! There's a toddler about.

Life is such fun as you walk and then run,
You chatter and play through each bright, happy day.
Then, almost before my head can turn,
You're off to school with so much to learn.

School days will pass and you'll grow strong and tall,
And you'll learn about things that I don't know at all...
You'll dream youthful dreams and try out new schemes,
But as you're maturing, I'm starting to fail.

While your strengths wax, so mine must wane,
Since the world began it's been the same,
But you, dear grandchildren, the future must frame,
To make the world a better place. Do it well!

Valerie J. Owen

"A Love In A Leave Of Its Own"

Loves came loves go; for years of love I want you to know
Our love is special, for me just right it's you and you
only I want and need in my sight.

Just like a circle no beginning, no end you are my
very best friend and sunset, no room at night.
What goes wrong I thought of you make it alright
for our love.

I am full of pride, I am accomplish for anything
when you are by my side.

Nadine George

Quiet Query

They have been dormant during the winter,
Keeping their heads low and warm.
Accumulating strength, for their stalky length,
When they finally 'peep' in the morn.

Often the welcome that awaits them,
Is the blasts of frost, and snow.
Not to be daunted, they continue to grow
In clusters, thus providing a colourful show.

Cold winds shake them violently,
In appearance, they look droopy, and sad.
A kindly hand has reached down, and cut them.
Now revived, they're displayed in a friendly warm grange.

Part of their form is a trumpet
Ample length, but silent in song.
They're endowed with a scalloped border.
Brilliant yellow, diffusing cheer all around.

One of God's wonders of nature
Quietly determined, opposing the storm.
Sharing its natural beauty with humans.
Daffodils. Herein is an example without a sound?

A. R. Harcus

Only In My Dream

Once I had a dream, with omniscience,
leaving the real world,
seeking to leave the crossroads I am at.
There I saw the sun, the moon, the stars, from where I sat,
assuredly promising their eternity of time,
I, that length making you mine.
All knowing of my heart's desire, moulded you;
quenched my burning fire!
Blissfully alone we watched the sun finally set,
the moon rose higher, the stars glowing with consent.
Blooming love in the tranquillity and joy,
us, and you so sweetly coy, (ha?)
Harshly to reality I came back.
On reflection, interpretation;
Once again, you, no nearer than the sun, moon or stars!
All I hold is that short moment of wonder and all knowing,
no matter how much I try to recall,
this reality is where I stay, my
wishes only in a dream...

M. L. Gallacher

A Cry From The Mount

I, Mother Mountain, with head held high
Looking down, protecting lochs, and birds that fly so high.
Who are these people who invade my space,
Who have no respect for my hilly braes?
They climb up my crevices, my seems are crying out.
Why don't you go away, leave me in peace, let me heal the scars
you've created. I am tired of your egotistic bravado.
You pillage my sides, my back is getting sore.
I, the Omega, the beginning, the end.
You really don't know it - I am your friend.
I've kept you safe, protected your lands.
If I fall down, you'll be a sorry man.
Who will protect you from the wind and rain,
Hold you together when evaluation comes?
Again, the ozone layer is getting thin, my green lands
are polluted by waste.
How I feel sorry for the human race.
The greed you have, has blinded you to a false way of life.
Be content with Mother Earth, give back what you have taken out,
And be advised from the Mount.

Anne Sharp

Sonnet

You loved the things I loved—the golden light
Of sunshine on ripe cornfields and the still
Quiet beauty of a fragrant summer night,
The deer, the silver birch trees on the hill,

Sunlight on snow, its soft blue-shadowed lines,
Snowflakes, star-shaped, that nestled on our hair,
Bright moonlight and the wind among black pines,
I loved these things the more for you were there.

I cannot let you go. You are a part
Of me. Dark whispering trees 'neath star-sown skies
Know how your kiss first woke my sleeping heart,
And I looked with love and trust in your dear eyes.

Let me not feel now bitterness or hate.
I cannot let you go—and time grows late.

H. Stevenson

Foregone

Of all the many words we use each day
There is one we sometimes find difficult to say
It is a word which is unique in a power which
    it holds
That is found in only this world alone

Forgive is the word which holds such power.
That when used could bring relief and happiness
    in the darkest hour.
And if given sincerely with a heart that is true
How wonderful what this word could do

It could perhaps bring families and friends
    together again.
After many years of loneliness misery and pain
Why don't we try and use it more often, then we
    may see.
What a lot more happiness, instead of sadness
In our lives there may be.

V. Thompson

Invoking River

Sentinel, you are on heights,
Catch our city in your sights.
Through time's true-eye cast your gaze,
Find for us our Golden days.

Flowing outward ever still
I see the embers in your sil':
Lowing cattle markets sift
Watt's child's screaming-puffing fit.

Tiered-past's plateaus your waters lap,
Echoing aeons bridge the gap,
Hindsight's heroes wars divide,
Cultures' multi-spirits bind.

Town Hall, Library, Art show
As stars in fountain's deep glow.
Basked in waves of saffron light,
Vision flows from city mights.

Sentinel, you are on heights,
Catch our city in your sights.
Through time's true-eye cast your gaze,
Find in us our Golden ways.

Pat Healy

Untitled

The boy knelt down on the cold, damp earth,
On the spot once stood his place of birth.
He thought of his family who had once been there
As he bowed down his head in silent prayer.
The tears had flowed and the grief all gone
As he prayed for the strength to carry on.
The Lord looked down from heaven and smiled
Because there stood a man instead of a child.

Kenneth B. Hetherington

Value Of Life

Have you ever wondered,
exactly what you're worth?
I do it all the time
Though I never amount to much.

I'm just another human being,
give me a number instead of a name
whichever one I go to try,
I'm really just the same.

Would it make much difference, I wonder,
if I were to disappear?
Would anybody notice,
if suddenly I'm not here?

Do people really like me?
Or pretend, to shut me up?
People think I'm weird,
just another crazy nut.

Jaclyn Mayne

"Thoughts In Flight"

Today's the day, up, up and away
From my seat on the plane I can dream and survey
The cotton wool clouds as they slowly drift by
In the tranquil peace of the wondrous sky
There's the gold of the sun midst the blue of the scene
I muse - three score and ten, what has life come to mean?
I guess just to be there, to care and to share
In the lives of those dear ones with problems to bear
Still, first there's the landing, oh dear - all that weight!
No, don't be so silly, the take-off was great;
To think their sweet faces so soon I shall see
No more writing and waiting, they'll be there for me
The children will laugh at the funny old lady
Who melts into tears at the sight of the baby
No matter, the happiness surely will shine
As their hands are lovingly placed into mine
A final thought now, come what may
Thank you, Dear Lord, for this day.

R. M. Green

Entangled

The essence of love comes from deep within,
An entangled web of hearts,
Bound together through desire and joy,
So frequently endured by both girl and boy,
Their destiny unknown each embarks.

No true explanation can ever be found,
Of an emotion held so dear,
But a burning passion can so easily create,
A lust that turns to jealous hate,
And a love so easy to fear.

Angela Browne

The Seasons

In the green underwood on soft mossy beds,
Violets and primroses lift their sweet heads.
A soft perfumed breeze rustles the trees,
Birds sing - 'tis spring!

Light warm breezes and flowers arrayed,
Bright golden sunshine, hours to play.
Nightingales sing 'neath starry skies,
Love-filled eyes - 'tis summer!

Leaves on the trees, russet, red and gold,
Stirred by a wind that is brisk and bold;
Over the meadows they dance and fly,
Swirling high - 'tis autumn!

Frost is sparkling o'er hills and plains,
Streamlets bound in icy chains.
Banks of snow; North wind blows,
Fires glow - 'tis winter!

Muriel Mary Green-Davis

Emanon

Is there a place where nothing lies?
If so what would it look like?
As comer of an empty room; as it seems,
In fact not so empty or desolate; filled with life,
To which one meaning is unknown.

Would you be blind to this nothingness?
Would it render you powerless;
Choking for one last breath of air
Would you fall or fly, live or die.

Nobody knows the meaning of life,
The answer put at 42 or 90,
Seems like another puzzle to solve.

Maybe that's the meaning,
Everything is never ending,
A cycle going on forever,
How long is forever?

Infinite........

Does time end, did it ever begin?
What is time?
What is our purpose?

Lindsey Barker

Naked

He was overcome
and although I never met
the question is
what are you waiting for
a massive black hole at the galaxy's heart.
I keep forgetting how
as always
your sad tragedy
in midsummer,
on the roadside
closer to the sea.
It looked briefly as though
also in the evening sky
cultures lose their souls.
He was just amazing
determined
when I wept
there is no need for
the end of our journey.

Pauline Anderson

Waiting

Hidden by the poker-faced surfaced, the restless power
twitched again.
Like tensed muscles beneath skin
The water was still. Waiting.
Another twitch. A cat about to pounce.
The flicker of an evil grin. Waiting.

The boat's gaudy hull broke the whispers of waves.
A foreign object, lost in the everlasting expanse
Arrogantly oblivious as the tourist
Our vast pink flesh drowned the deck
A sacrifice to the sun. Unwittingly we basked.
A breeze rippled the deceptive calm lulling the naive.
The hidden turmoil waiting

No longer
The spirit loosed came smashing, crashing, roaring.
Untamed she clawed at us. Icy fingers grabbing from above
Primitively hungry, the magic force drew us down
Deeper, deeper, enveloping us. Our feeble bodies bursting with
Awe, admiration
And, too late, respect
We surrendered.

Eleanor Horsman

Legacy

You've gone from me and now
I cannot tell you how in awe delight of you
Has swiftly sped the day
Of the hours I embrace again
With complete approve your face again
And dwell in eyes that mesmerize me
With the secrets kept therein
    Dying with summer was never in the plans we made
Intimate on idle days of August's warm profusion
When — as if impatient to accompany departure
Suddenly and with it you were gone
But I have witnessed in a quiet place
Upon your lips — your still exquisite face
That seemed to me to linger there — a smile
That with me lingers still the while
You went sweet love with summer
And truth bears it no thought of bliss
But bleak and strangely cold it feels
Like those closed lips in death I kissed.

Victor Maynard

"Creation"

Through life we hear of courage, humility and strength,
Yet not in all the world is there a feeling of such wealth,
As when we stand in green fields, a glory to behold,
Each blade of grass so perfect, in itself a prize of gold.

The sun, the moon, the stars and sky
Are there for all to see,
The flowers in their splendour, the honey and the bee,
For the hand of God has made its mark
In this world which we all know
And when we look upon it, 'tis with wonder, and with awe,

When we see a distant ocean, or spy a distant shore
We wonder how they came there, yet everybody knows,
'Twas the hand of God that made them, and he has many ways,
To show what he created, in only seven days.

L. Sheard

The Silver Rain

Shining like a mirror on the roof behind the tree,
Almost reflecting the sun and the sky.
Soaking the grass, the blossom and the lea,
Running down the windows and pausing on the glass.

Dripping from the roof the branches and the hedges,
Droplets on the flowers, sparkling as bright gems
Circles in the pond, spreading to the edges,
Spitting on the windows and splashing on the trellis.

Puddles on the concrete and water on the flowers,
Sunshine coming out and shadows on the path.
Clouds in the sky and long quiet hours,
Birds singing songs when they know the rain has passed.

Ruth M. Joyce

Book Of Kells

Anonymous fingers held the quill,
Formed the letters with great skill,
Flowing shapes and wondrous creatures;
The modern world's never seen their features.
Complicated Celtic knots adorn the pages
A lasting link with dark medieval ages.
A tenuous thread that survives
To bring colour and hope for our lives.
Bright gems that embellish thoughts,
Finely printed, carefully wrought
To bring praises to that monk's Lord.

Amidst the chill dull walls
Vibrant pigments glowed like jewels
Adorning intricate initial letters.
But did that scribe feel the fetters?
That today men would find bind tight
Valuing freedom more than God's light.

E. A. Morris

Wounded Womb

Like those munich mannequins she wrote of
But not so perfect
Starving for the essential,
the necessity for perfection:
A child crying in warm arms
Struggling to succeed in the fantasy which rules the life.

That hand!... oh God that hand!

Mutated by passion, wounded and bleeding.
Crying,
Desperately trying to catch air like a babe's first gasps.
Suffocated by the gentle hand that reaches out
and screams silently from the manacles of love.

Terrorizing to mind,
And heart pounds, a head throbs and the music plays on and on and...
... the blood-smothered hand clasps my heart and rips it to strips.

It flashes before me, again....
and again. Like lightning - sharp to the senses.
The familiarity of the mumbling thunder that consoles me and
softens my emotions, that echoes: I love you, I love you;
and closes my eyes to the hand.

Donna Lee

Middle age or menopause.

There is a big decision to make,
Which path at the crossroads do I take?
Redundant mother, past sell by date wife,
What do I do with the rest of my life?
Remembered ambitions, put aside schemes,
How far can I get before realizing those dreams?
The path that's familiar, life in distress,
Streets of depression, boredom and stress.
I know the path I want to take,
So why do I hold back and hesitate?

Georgina Abbott

Devon

Wild ponies and young fools on the Moor's Running wild and free
In the woodlands squirrels scampers in the trees
Sun warm and all a glow
Birds sitting in the hedgerow
Singing sweetly their songs does sound
Bluebells white daisies in the green grass hard ground,
People having their Devon Cream Tea, of scones and strawberries
Or drinking scrumpy that makes you feel quite merry
So much to see in this beautiful Devon
Makes you feel with its peace that you are in Heaven

D. J. Newman

Snowtime

The world slept deep throughout the night
As natures coverlet fell silent to the ground
The virgin whiteness shone in morning's light
A new beginning had been spread around

Radio voices crackle through the box
Warning the world to stay at home today
I roam the fields and see the track of fox
And rabbit in their search for food or play

The veg. plot sleeps turned ground is covered level
Awaiting nature's call of spring
When seeds may sprout and plants and flowers revel
And nearby Canterbury bells may ring

Meanwhile I look at nature's beauty all around
Tall firs stand dusty white along the river bank
Mother Cary's chickens come to ground
The ice is thick upon the water tank

My footprints in deep snow around the pond
Reflect man's journey 'cross the world each day
Later in sun's warmth they will be gone
As man himself must leave to tread the Heavenly Way

J. Rowat

416

Woods

Hearing the cracking of twigs as we walk,
a time to listen, a time to talk,
the sunlight drifting on the ripples of the water,
the smell of flowers and the sound of laughter,
happiness here is all around,
from the green tree tops to the ground.

How fast these days go by,
like a cloud in the clear blue sky,
things would be perfect if you were here,
never seeing you again is my greatest fear.

A bird flies through the trees,
you can't imagine the beauty I see,
a swan swimming with her signets,
a little girl with her hair in ringlets,
judging by these sights around me,
the best things in life are definitely free.

The only thing I need is you,
don't stop loving me whatever you do.

Rachel Curd

Search Dog

Who would know? To see her stand, perhaps to stare...
Gingerly sniffing winter Lakeland night air,
She alone can sense where fragile life has lain,
Under flimsy floating fog, or mystic rain...

Who would know? If 'neath any icy bed of snow,
Hard-packed, where human rescuers feet trudge slow,
A climber's heart may beat... or is it still?
Will Mother Nature's mountain claim another "kill"?

Who would know? Above all whispered prayers...
Frenzied digging...layer to deeper layers...
Striving...to set free the soul which makes no sound..
Canine instinct drives her deeper underground...

Who would know? Set deep in Winter's final cast...
Where to dig, now death white avalanche has past
She tugs an arm...'shows' the climber...safe..below...
Barking to the Rescue Team...'I told you so'...

Alexander Crawford

Untitled

A girl named Jill read J. S. Mill upon a hill near Brill
for her M. Phil at Somerville, she sat quite still until
a storker with an evil knife
in cold blood took her happy life:
Oh! Who could spill, with such ill-will,
the blood of tranquil Jill?

Paul Rand

Untitled

Oh have you heard the scandal,
It's all round our estate,
That Mike who's married to our Jill,
Pure havoc did create.
It was at Emerald Club house.
His Daughters Eighteenth party
A little bit too much to drink,
He thought he'd be a smarty.
The Stripper song it started swell,
But things progress and they could tell
The shirt was off he looked quite keen,
He thought he was a sex machine.
Poor Jill not waiting till much later,
As Mike fell back on radiator.
Broke it too as we've heard say,
His back was black the very next day.
Poor Mike he really felt quite queasy,
Perhaps next time you'll take things easy.

Janet Tovell

Heat

The crows were heralding another tumid day,
The wind was hot and dry -
Scorching every thing in its path.

The caves on the trees curled up and turned beige,
or the fiery blast.
The perspiration poured -
as they node across the desolate land.

No other living creature was to seen
in the burning sand.

The dams were almost dry,
when will it rain? They try!

A prayer goes up -
oh please, please, let it rain -
but in vain.

Jess C. Cane

Luke

Sunshine bursts into the room
Eyes a twinkle, smile full bloom,
Hiya Nana, how are you?
Have you thought what we can do?
Shall we play this
Shall we do that?
Will you read for me
Can I wear your hat?
His laughter rings like a tinkling bell,
Suddenly I feel so well.
Then, "Come on mum it's time to go,"
Darling child, I love you so.
Now the sky seems dark and grey,
My aches and pains are back to stay,
But he'll be here another day
I'll just sit and think what we can play.

Patricia C. Bowers

A Struggle

I am no beggar, but I feel like one
No one to turn to, now I'm on my own
Trying to live in a reasonable way
But it's only a struggle day after day
Watching the pennies, as best I can
Live is real hard, since I lost my man
But I'll carry on, what else can I do
'Cause I will not beg, from only of you
I cannot believe what's happening to me
Too old to work, and not yet sixty
I'd love to be up at the crack of dawn
That's early says you, stifling a yawn
But to be at work, for a few days at least
Would you give me great pleasure, and also peace
For then I'd be sure, I'd be poor no more
I could live much better and that is for sure.

Sheila Wall

Just Us

You came to me to share my life
With no thoughts of wanting another wife
Sunk deep in sadness, so forlorn
You never guessed that I too was alone.

Strangers thrown together, how were we to know
That respect for each other to such heights would grow
With trust and companionship we share our days
Pleasing ourselves in so many ways.

The sadness is passed, each other's memories confide
Constantly caring with no secrets to hide
Our families, our friends all agree
They put us together, you and me.

So whatever the future, we know we belong
Be our days numbered short or long
Continually blessed by the one up above
Who must have known we both needed love.

Vi B. Beck

Memories

Oh, how I remember; how it used to be
memories, the good, the bad.
yesterdays forgotten, but remembered.

I still remember
The pain, the anguish, the anguish inside.

Some laughter, some cries, I still remember
Some time and some times;
the reaching out, the pressing in; that time.

Different now, it is
yet, still I remember.

Memories, the bad, the good, the better.

Oh, how I remember,

The times, this time and times to come
I still remember

Ifeoma C. Uche

Solitary Man

Behind those saddened emerald eyes,
Behind the bedraggled lonely disguise,
Is a man whose life remains a mystery
To all whose eyes just cannot see
Beyond the image they are made to face,
The ignorance surely, is their disgrace.

The old man, he shrugs, he heaves a sigh,
As his life, with its time, passes him by.
Loneliness and solitude become his only friends,
All he relies upon, faithfully depends
Unlike those who trod him down,
Left him to the streets, the roughness of town.

Alone he travels, no family to care,
No welcome awaits him, it seems so unfair.
Yet he turns to no man, rejections cause sorrow,
If carried along, he will face no tomorrow.
When once again he'll raise his burdened head,
From the rolled up rags on a bench for a bed.

So spare a thought, if a tramp passes by,
It was us who put him there, and only he knows why!

S. E. Foreman

One Player To Another

The long-rehearsed production has been played;
Performances given, we have at last
Acknowledged the perfunctory applause
And shed the paint and powder of our parts.
But something yet remains that will not fade:
A sad and lasting indent which lies cast
Firm in my heart, Lady, without a cause
But that which should have ended with our arts.
The trappings of a sentimental play -
A Summer night, a song we once had known -
Still prompt unjustifiable dismay,
A fear that I remember them alone.
And though we do but mirror life's design,
Some touch of this will always now be mine.

John Boud

WAR

There is a question of which I always wonder,
Were War and hate just God's blunder?
All kinds of people offer their lives,
Only to fall to the enemies' lives.
Even when a weed strangles a flower,
War again displays its power.
The evil of war is everywhere,
Children learn to fight before they learn to share.
As long as there is hate there will always be war,
Until the day that we exist no more.
It is the war within us that will be our downfall,
It is the war within us that will kill us all.

Nick Poturicich, late 1993

Hope

Hope is the light at the end of the tunnel,
   That keeps us journeying on our way.
Through the dark and gloom we strive to reach the light,
   In search of a brighter to-day.

Hope is the life-buoy that keeps us afloat,
   'Mid the perilous waves of life's sorrow.
Riding high above the ups and downs,
   To land on the threshold of a brighter to-morrow.

Hope is the star that shines through the dark.
   When life is dull, empty and cold,
It gathers us up in comforting arms,
   And awakens in us dreams untold.

When the fire of life is dying out,
   And zest for living is running low,
Hope is the fan that livens the embers,
   And restores the flame to full glow.

Hope is the jewel afforded to all.
   It carries us through all trouble and care.
Without that little sparkle to light up our lives,
   We might all lie down, and die of despair.

Roisin Christie

Snapshot

See the photograph which is faded and worn
That treasured second that was dead when born;
Lost image and time of another land
Focused and snapped by whose dear hand?
Remembered.

The street that is busy without many cars
But still nestling under the self-same stars;
A dangerous corner seems so serene
Black and white its colours unseen
Remembered.

Covet the portrait hanging with loving care,
And was it the wind that ruffled the hair?
A jumble of long forgotten places
Hope and fear in those dear faces
Remembered.

Those evocative prints from which we must part
Are still stirring, and stay lodged in the heart.
The vision is fixed but the feelings fade
Into the past, a past decade
We can remember.

Alan Dickson

'The Circus King'

The crying heart, of the laughing clown
The world thinks he's up, but he knows he's down.
For a short while in the sawdust ring,
He plays his part of the circus king.

Children laugh and shout - everyone is gay
A fitting end to a fun-filled day
But when the lights are all turned down
Does anyone think of the laughing clown

Where does he go to, where does he stay
Until he returns to the circus next day?
Once, he sped home to his perfect life,
His cottage - his children - his loving wife

His heart aches now, as he thinks of the past
Bereft of the joys, that he thought would last
But, he'll carry on - all troupers do
Behind a mask that you cannot see through

To the crying heart of the laughing clown
The world think he's up, but he knows he's down.
He travels the world with the sawdust ring,
Known and loved by all as the circus king.

D. E. Brooker

Untitled

Each person that's born is given a gift,
Given by God above.
Some are given a silver spoon.
The lucky ones are given love.

Sometimes we find it early in life
Sometimes it has to be won.
The greatest gift God gave to me
Was my beloved son.

Susan Irene Brown

Lest I Forget

I won't forget you Timmy, I won't forget your pain
I know my mind will see your face time and time again.
I'll not forget you pleading, as the anger in you grew
And your eyes revealed a hurting child, seen only by a few

I won't forget you Timmy, nor the tears you let me see
I won't forget the drugs that torture you once tortured me.
I'll not forget you saying that no one really cared
As I saw your wounded spirit in the poem that you shared.

I won't forget you Timmy, you've no love, no home, no bed.
I won't forget you fighting with the demons in your head.
I'll not forget you screaming as the fire inside you burned
As compassion in me took control of everything I'd learned.

I won't forget you Timmy, and I'll pray you'll live to know
The reason that I'm weeping is because I love you so
And although the world rejects you and calls you rough and wild
I know the homeless addict is a frightened desperate child.

Lyn Bacon

"The Storm"

The glowering sky broods darkly o'er the hills
And a deathly silence dulls the air it fills
Beast and bird doth homeward slowly flee
Whilst gently the wind shakes the aged tree.

Suddenly, the sky is torn apart
As lightening rips across an angry cloud
The hare, in his form, shakes with a trembling heart
And the stag, with fury, summons his herd out loud.

At last, it comes! The unrelenting rain
Beating the ground, as if to cause it pain.
The aged tree - no longer in its prime
Groans as it succumbs for the last time.

Slowly the needles of rain ease as they fall
A soft grey veil descends upon the hills
And like a message sent to one and all
The golden sun with warmth the land soon fills.

Sally-Anne Hardie

Himself And Church

He seldom prayed in churches
But he believed in "God."
The father son and "holy ghost"
His life was based upon.
He said one could pray anywhere
Or say a rosary.
While strolling quietly through the woods.
Amid the greenery.
He marvelled at creation.
Believing as one should
That "God" created everything
That's beautiful and good.
When things went wrong he did not flinch
or moan about, bad luck
He said these things were sent to us,
to try us and our trust.
Though he did not pray in churches.
It was very plain to see
The deep faith that he had in "God" and christianity.

B. Walker

The Rock Face

I started life so grand and so tall.
Then the wind started blowing the sea to a squall.
Up come the waves and sand at a pace
It found a weakness one side of my face.
Out come the sun and near made me smile
This was only short lived for a while.
With a vengeance the wind and the rain come back and turned the weakness
into a large crack.
Sea crashes forward wave after wave
Turning the crack into a large cave
Years of pummelling made the cave a huge arch
My once grand tall face becoming a farce
The arch began crumbling from the wind and the sea
I was becoming something that was not me
There was nothing about it that I could do
I felt so bad and it made me blue
My arch now worn to a very large stack
Out there in the sea all alone in the dark
Then surely and slowly without warning or sound
The stack is gradually worn to the ground
It just disappear right into the sea
Away goes the part that once was me

B. Wood

The Cry Of The Earth

You cut down my trees without a care
You belch your smoke into the air
You pollute my rivers, you poison my sea
Don't you hear me when I cry, "You're hurting me!"?

With aerosols and pesticides you gaily spray around
In house and garden, where ever life is found
When you kill the fly you kill the bee
Can't you here me when I cry, "You're hurting me!"?

My fauna you kill for your sport
My rarest species count for naught
With the damage you do, can't you see?
You're hurting yourselves when you hurt me.

You could have a paradise here on earth
If you treated me right and valued my worth
Stop acid rain falling on plant and tree
Please here me when I cry, "You're hurting me!"

Eileen Root

Fast Lane

Why go so fast, what will you gain
You cause so much suffering, you cause so much pain
And what did you do, what did you care
You just stood and looked when you saw the despair.

Why did you do it, you could have slowed down
You saw the red lights, when you spend out of town
And what did you do, what did you care
You just stood and looked as my loved ones lay there.

You've caused so much sorrow and hardship and stress
Our lives have all changed, just by your selfishness
And what would you do, what would you care
If yours were the loved ones you saw lying there.

Pat Whitmarsh

Untitled

The lift of a promise, like the teasing of a breeze.
Soft and caressing, always aiming to please.
The words spoken so true, full of calm and of love,
Like the angels have sent you from heaven above.
A lingering kiss, that's saying so much
Trembling and melting at the thought of your touch.
Like a feather you trace the heart of my being
Softly, softly, the passion I'm feeling.
As we become one, entangled together
I know in my heart, we will last forever...

Zoe Ferguson

"It's No Chore"!

A bag of nappies, a tin of milk
   some baby oil to make skin like silk
A dusting of talc, a blob of cream
   so Lauren Mae is ready to dream
One last coo, a smile, then goodnight
   God bless my darling, teddy held tight
A new day dawns, a noise from the cot
   my lovely sleep, I've had my lot
All systems go, bottle in hand
   my little Lauren looking ever so grand
Clean clothes a'wash, a brush of hair
   wide gaping eyes having a stare
So much to see, do and learn
   noises and bangs to make my head turn
Then those words are spoken at last
   my goodness, they grow ever so fast
A trip to the shop for more supplies
   a dirty nappy, there's tears in her eyes
A dash to the mothers room, change of bum
   then into arms for a cuddle with mum.

Deborah Bearman

Heartache

Here with you I have known all of living,
The heights and depths,
Laughter and tears,
Moods light and deep depressions,
Shared hopes and fears,
The untold nameless trifles of our years;
And here with you have found
A love which could not change or falter.

And now the dear companionship is ended
And life must know a sadder, greyer hue,
For all the quiet happiness of living
Is faded now - has fled, alas, with you.
No eager welcome greets my home returning,
In mem'ry only do I see your smile:
Lonely I wander through the house
And emptiness of room and chair
Finds echo in my empty heart.

Eileen Mason

Heaven On Earth

A life of love and caring, These are the things we all need most,
No War, No Hate, No Hunger, Would be something we could boast.
But life is not so simple, And we all are not so free,
To take these things for granted, To see a flower or tree,
For there is war and hunger Poverty and Tears.
It makes your heart just ache and ache to see the flow of tears,
But there is hope and sunshine if only we could try,
Beyond our dreams, Our destinies, Like a bird about to fly,
For we could love each other, Then war would be no more,
In a peaceful world together, will the last one close the door.

Jennifer Jones

My Life Is ... A Wall Of Confinement

My life is a wall of confinement,
Following me, chasing me,
I cannot escape my solitude,
All thoughts trapped,
Bubbling to be free.

The loneliness surrounds me like darkness,
But the light to my dreams cannot be switched on,
The blinds to my thoughts are pulled tightly shut,
Secured by hands of disability.

I shall never sing the sweet songs I hear,
Or laugh the deep laughter of happiness.
I will never express my true feelings,
Of love, fear or sorrow.
I'm alone with my thoughts,
Imprisoned by people, when I cannot tell my name,
Because the key of my voice was lost at birth.

Sherron Houghton

'The World Tonight'

'The World Tonight' How can it be?
For our dear John gave his life that we might see
And hear of all the atrocities.

The innocent always prove
That "God is Love" this cannot be denied.
It is the wickedness of the land
That raised our John so high.

Why cannot they see how cruel they can be?
To shoot, throw stones and jeer,
For the peoples of the land cry, Oh God! Come here.

In all his tender years John lived his life to full
And accomplished more than many
On the way to that Green Hill.

'The World Tonight',
How can it be the same without our John?
One bullet did it take for such grievously bodily harm.

But, oh! The World
It must go on until all hostilities cease.
It is only then 'The World Tonight'
Can report - "Everlasting Peace."

Ruth Evelyn

In Memories Dreams

Long have I loved you in memories dreams,
In my heart all my life have I loved you it seems;
When shadows have fallen each night as I slept,
My memories wakened and silently wept.
They remembered our love, long ago, back in time,
When we said "Please remember, you'll always be mine;
I shall love you forever, each life we shall meet,
We will know and remember, this promise we'll keep."
When we walked in the Heavens we saw and we knew,
That, this time, when we met, all our dreams would come true;
We knew that the love that we kept in our hearts
Could not rest on this Earth, while we two were apart.
Then we parted in Heaven, returned here to Earth,
To repay all our debts from the time of our birth;
Then the sun and the moon wept no more, it was done,
The debts were all paid and the angels said "Come,
You have known and remembered, you both have believed,
It is time, it is written, the stars have decreed,
On this day, at this hour, 'tis the time you will meet
And your love shall be blessed and no more will you weep."

Jennifer Anne Butler

Granddad

I wish I could've seen you just one last time,
I wish I could've said goodbye,
Not a day goes by when I don't think of you,
Nor at tear drop is shed from my eye.

Why were you ill? Why did you die?
It's just not fair, why did you have to go?
You had to go away,
And now I am so low.

You haven't been gone a year yet,
But I miss you so much right now.
And one thing that I can promise you,
Is, I love you forever - I vow.

I know I didn't get that chance,
That chance to say goodbye,
I never will forget you granddad,
So just you let me try!

I miss you so much granddad, and love you I do forever,
And one day I might join you up there,
Up with you in heaven.
I love you forever granddad.

Karen Baumber

420

Love Hurts

There it is lying there
  So pure, so fair.
The mother picks it up to share
The beauty of its special stare

Its hands are so petit
  So are its little feet
Its fingers are so shiny
Its toe's are so tiny.

Your smell is full of joy
That's because you're my little boy
Your heart is full of grace
I'll never forget your innocent face

She clenches her fist's and starts to pray
That you'll remember me again some day
After that she gives a sigh,
and then begins to cry.

The paper's are signed
She looks behind
There's nothing there
but all she can see is her babies stare.

Shona Macintosh

Jesus S.O.S. Christ

The "Saviour of souls" is what You are,
With "Men" on earth and God afar;
Though far away You are so near
To all mankind dispelling fear:

You're in my heart where'er I be,
Guiding, helping, instructing me;
When I need help I turn to You,
I talk with friends (their Saviour too)"

I'll trust in You when I'm unsure,
For You're my Lord and know my cure;
Lord You are near, when I show fear,
You always care my Saviour dear:

I know I'm safe when trusting You,
I've faith then Christ in all I do;
For when I'm weak, You are so strong,
My trust and faith in God belong.

God loves all "men", for them He died,
Dear Jesus Christ was crucified;
His life he Gave all "men" to free
For God incarnate was Him you see.

John W. Hopkins

1940's

A time to laugh, a time to cry
A time to say one last goodbye
A time for prayer, a time to act
A time to heal, or seal the pact
A time to dance a time to sing
Thankful of the joys that others bring
A time to hold, a time to fret
Of lost tomorrow's without regret
A time to wish, a time to feel
A time to grasp life's steering wheel
And hold it still, against the tide
Of in-humanity - a roller-coaster ride
A time to age, a time to wilt
A time to strengthen that already built
From times spent in different ways
Through peace-time, war-time, and halcyon days
That time to dream, to be with friends
To shake the hand that friendship sends
A time for truth. Alas, a time to lie
The world, left in darkness, alone to die.

Andrew M. Webster

One Moment

Last night I saw you in loneliness
Through a picture of perpetual charm
A picture of divinity
Filled with natures natural beauty
And as fickle as a distant star
Gaze into these radiant eyes
See them shimmer and flit like fireflies
Light up the night in my sunken path
Give me your presence
Full bodied in unheard stillness
Paralleled in radiance as a jewel suspended
Through the curtain of the night
Fragmentation of my memory,
Resurrected, captured eternally
For one moment in time.

Peter Murray

When I Die

When I die, let it not be in spring
when snowdrops make way for tulips and daffodils
and green haze shrouds the trees as new buds come,
when blossom pink red and white spreads like good news

When I die, let it not be in summer
when roses and delphiniums make perfect the backdrop for
pansies, salvias and tiny yellow marigolds
when beauty unfolds before us, while children play in the sun

When I die, let it not be in autumn
when green turns to gold, and red, and bronze
when children run merrily through crackly leaves,
when country lanes wear mantles of fire - unreal, as in a dream

When I die, let it be in winter
when trees are bare and winds and snow depress,
when icy roads make old folk tremble lest they fall,
when all is still, and everything waits — let it be then.

Mildred Hemmings

Bluebell Wood

Bluebells unfolding in a wood of old,
  No sight or sound of man's mould,
Treasures forgotten beneath your ground,
  Step by step enter perfumed surround.

The woodland trees are part of you.
  Soft breezes sway a branch or two,
Shading your light of violet and blue,
  Continue amidst the perfumed hue.

Ellie Gibson Reid

Willow In The Whispering Wind

Willow in the whispering wind
Can you remind me of this day
Long gone but never forgotten
I still recall those things you used to say

All those mirages everywhere I run my head
Some keeping their faces in disguise
Whenever once of them catches me
It's time to face up and pay the price

You were an illusion all along
Fading away as quickly as you came
It was love at first sight and now you've gone
There's only me left to blame.

All those "so called" friends I met on my way
Not even a handful of them were here to stay
Didn't you tell me you'd stand by my side?
Then trouble runs along and you sneak away to hide.

Willow in the whispering wind
I'll face it all with a smile and I wont be afraid
My life is only about to start
It's never too late.

Vanessa Mehrabian

Thoughts

Your feelings smash off the wall,
You've never heard any thing so loud,
Emotions run through your head,
You've never felt anything so powerful
Yet painful.

Thoughts of the past,
Thoughts of the present,
Thinking of everything you have done,
Whether it is joyful, hurtful, painful.

You never knew you could feel this way about -
Things of the past, present or future,
Whatever it is, it cannot be explained,
It's a feeling out of this world,
But you might never experience it again.

Therese Ryan

Silence

As you form
Your soup like apparel emulates peace and tranquillity.
A blanket forming to silence the world.

As vision is obscured, the senses sharpen,
You hear everything yet hear nothing.
You see nothing and yet see everything.
We touch you, we taste you,
Your smell is distinct, inviting, tempting.
Your mass allows obscurity, anonymity,
Yet ensures identity through discovery.
Within you I vanish,
Those surrounding disappear.
We are alone yet they are near us,
Together we stand divided.
At your border we are excluded,
Longing but fearing to be at one with you.
Our need to feel you overwhelms,
We dive into you,
Hidden from each other and ourselves.

Zena Vater

Crufts And Scruffs

The Dogs are in the field ready to start
You can tell the pedigree from mongrels apart.
There's a fifty seven with legs long at the back
His nose is muzzled with a piece of old sack.
The next one along a pedigree for sure
Sitting politely raising a paw.
The judge calls him out to show him a trick
But he won't even run after a stick.
The mongrel is wagging his tail to and fro
He breaks his leash and off he does go,
To fetch back the stick the pedigree won't get
Dives into a pond - now everyone's wet.
He drags out a stick not the same one we see
It's an enormous log, half a tree!
He drags it to his owner from behind
The judges are laughing but they don't mind.
They have made their decision it's plain to see
That not all top dogs are pedigree!

P. S. G. Kusionowicz

A Poem For Derick

God saw you were tired and took you away
To sit with him each blessed day,
But if we had known you were going to die
We could at least have said 'goodbye'.
Those words, unsaid, I will always mourn
As surely as the coming dawn.
I'll love you always. But I pray
That time will ease the pain away.
Now, as the wind sighs through the trees
All I have left are memories,

(of you).

Valerie Edwards

Untitled

With the wind in my face and the sun on my back,
I cycle along the road.
The lorries fly past at a terrible speed
As though they were empty of load.
I am happy today; my heart feels free
From worries and gloom and care.
I sing a light song, which expresses my mood,
Free as feathers blown in the air.
Don't think of tomorrow, I say to myself,
Let that be a future surprise.
Today, this moment is all that I need.
Forget the past say the wise.

Up the hill I puff and blow,
I cannot think of more
Because my breath is harsh and loud,
My knees are feeling sore.

At last the top of the hill is reached,
I see the road descend.
What bliss to feel the wind in my hair
And the journey is nearing its end.

Katharine Jewitt

My Fear...

If only it was that simple
The life would show us the way,
Why such strong hatred?
I am scared of the dark, I am scared of being alone.
I posses my worst enemy-
Maybe it will scar, or is it old?
I fear what I do not know,
And I fear what I cannot own.
Surely this is all I want?
Surely this will be the world?
For I know it regards me as here.
I know I have shown I am the salt of the earth,
As we all surely were. I know I have a hope,
For I know hope is borne by loss,
But I have challenges, one of which is me.
I know that terrifying stranger,
The one you never want to meet
Is always close to your heart,
I know, I am truly scared of me.

Tiffany Bryan

Discovering Yourself - The Point Of Life

Life is like a sword
Kept always hidden in its sheath
The outside's clearly visible
But what is hidden underneath?

Is it dull and rusty
From never being cleaned?
Or is it bright and shiny
With a glistening sheen?

Is it a treasure to be proud of
Or a thing to hide away?
Do you see yourself as 'rusty'
Or good enough to display?

Do you 'plod' along uncaring
Or are you always reaching for the moon?
Do you have energy and ambition
Or are you full of doom and gloom?

When thinking of your own life
Compare it to the sword
You should be proud of who you are
And reap all life's rewards!

Joanne G. Wilding

In Loving Memory

I look into your eyes.
I know I've got to say goodbye.
Your time in this realm is
coming to an end.
So goodbye my dear friend.
To a place you will go,
where pain you will no more know
But still it's not easy letting go.
I remember all the good times
You'd cheer me up if I was feeling down.
You used to give me the run around.
You were and still so precious to me
In life a precious jewel,
and now in death an ever so
precious memory.
So goodbye my friend
I'll never forget you
love and Empathy always

Clare Porter

Winter

Now cold winter knocks on the door of the year.
His beard hoary with frost, on his head a cap of snow,
    Clothed in rain clouds dark and drear
He wanders where the north wind bids him go.
Upon your window paints with icy finger
Delicate patterns of scrolls and leaves.
Hangs icicles like glistening swords from ledge and eaves.
Glides with frozen feet o'er dyke and pond-
bemused Ducks slip and slide, feet a-skew.
Breath of Horse and Cattle rises like smoke
Warming stable and byre, while cold winter waits.
He calls upon the Snow Queen, bids her lay a carpet of snow,
Silently she drifts through the night.
Morning finds a pale Sun,
Tall trees cast long purple shadows, Nature sleeps.
    Winter has wrought—Beauty.

E. Cartwright

Untitled

You back yourself into a corner,
You push the world away,
You've created your own private hell,
And lonely you shall stay.

Through the mysteries of life you wander,
Upon your mistakes you ponder,
Plenty of time to sit and think,
And deeper inside yourself you sink.

Now you realize,
No need to run away,
For it's you you're running from,
And you are here to stay.

Bethan Wilcox

"You're"

Like a ship in the roughest of seas.
Isolated, alone, yet strong.
Alive in an ocean of nightmares.
Shipwrecked in life's esteems,
Silenced by a time gone too soon,
Reminiscent echoes, future thoughts.

The never halting clock ticking on,
Continuing a ready planned course,
With no stops, delays or returns,
Ploughing straight ahead,
Catching short glimpses, or a moment or two
Of scenery passing by,
But feeling anticipation,
In awaiting a new lease of life.

Nadia Hafiz

To My Garden Friend The Robin

When you visit my garden, with your sleek red breast
I hear you sing with such cheerful zest.
Of all the creatures which God has made,
You are the one that sits on my spade.
While I tend the flowers and dig the ground
You keep me company as you hop around.
When on my garden seat I choose to laze,
You watch me closely with your beady gaze.
It will always be a mystery
Why you should seek my company.

Joyce Boast

Facing The Sea At Midnight

Facing the sea at midnight
A pair of lovers part
Following a tragic fight

Harsh words, she leaves in a rush
He says nothing, no words, just hush

He retraces her parting footsteps
Those he so desperately tries to mark
Feelings of guilt and regret
He weeps alone in the dark

As the days go by, moments in sadness go past
Living without her
How long can he last?

Tragedy strikes
He learns of her death
He cannot bear the thought -
Not his Beth

A year since has passed.
He recalls her leaving, gone, out of his sight
He does this, whilst
Facing the sea at midnight

Nathalie El-Korashy

A Tribute To A Wonderful Mum

Oh Mum I miss you so. You had so much get up and go.
Before you were ill, and had to lie so still.
Often I shed a tear, when I remember from year to year.
When we had problems and things were bad,
Also the laughs and jokes we had.
You were a kind and gentle lady, wife and Mum
And made a happy, secure home for your husband, daughter and son.
The pain of loss gets more intense
And sometimes life just makes no sense.
Mum, I know you are still with me.
Your spirit helps and guides me.
The warmth of your presence surrounds and protects me.
If I am sad and lonely you comfort me.
If I am happy you share it with me.
Mum, we thank you for all your sacrifices and love,
And know you are safe with our Lord up above.
I know we shall all meet again,
When our span of life on earth is through.
In the meantime I will be honest and true,
And try to follow God's word in all I do.

Jenny Scales

On Reaching Seventy

Now all the seasons pass too rapidly,
And do not linger, as they used to do
When I was young and time stretched far ahead
Beyond my careless and untroubled sight

But now, when I see Autumn's lovely hues,
Or beauty of a perfect day in Spring,
I feel a sharper poignancy and pain,
Sensing the moments slip away from me.

Marjorie Boardman

The Open Countryside

The flowers bloom in all their glory,
  The glittering green grass glows.
The leaves on the trees slightly shiver
  As a cooling breeze gently blows.

The sun beats down mightily on the calm fields,
  How still is the water in the stream,
This relaxing place feels tranquil, warm,
  A long, forgotten dream.

Wild rabbits roam the grassy hillocks,
  Playing amongst the snowdrops,
Whilst the sun slowly moves from a field
  To shine again in a tiny copse.

The sky is blue and there are no clouds
  And the breeze has almost died.
Tell me, is there a place more tranquil and pretty
  Than the open countryside?

  Richard Martin Taylor

These I Have Loved

The crunchy taste of crisp ice-cream cornets,
The vibrant colours of flowers in a summer meadow,
The smell of a freshly mown lawn,
The touch of silk,
The sound of the sea as it ebbs and flows,
The fresh, cleansing breeze on my face when walking in the
country-side,
The blaze of the setting sun;
These I have loved.

  Helen J. Shaw

Untitled

Like a bird searching, I fly
For what and where I do not know

The ultimate mountain, steadfast and secure
An enchanting forest, warm and alive
Or the windswept peace of the plains

But I am lost and weary,
How long will I be left
Encircling the sun?

  Ellen Porter

Home From Abroad

'Home is where the heart is'
or so the saying goes.
But if you leave your heart
where your roots lie deep,
then a yearning grows and grows.

For a country lane to walk down,
golden sand on a Cornish beach;
cobwebs on a frosty morn,
tea with friends, too long out of reach.

But now your roots have drawn you back,
we hope no more you'll roam.
You'll stay with us, grow old with us,
this place your heart calls home.

  Linda Cragg

Friends Forever

Friends forever, you and me.
I never knew how strong a friendship could be.
We've been friends for such a long time.
We've had many mountains of trouble to climb.
Together we've been through thick and thin.
But in the end, together, we always win.
A friendship that grows stronger every second of the day.
A friendship where fear is kept at bay.
A friendship that keeps us together.
A friendship that will last forever.

  J. Battles

Ode Is A Robe

Thin as I am and don't I know it,
My brain is still sharp and so is my wit.
When not too full of food but still feeling good
Come my best inspiration and greatest creations.
I think very clearly of things that so dearly mean ever so much me,
Like writing and reading and singing and
  playing and sometimes cooking too.
It's wrong I know to be as thin as I am and
  to feel the cold as I do,
But I've been through it all - the stuffing and drinking
And eat up dear, please do,
But believe me I'd rather get by on my
  diet of eating whatever I can,
than filling myself up with food I don't want,
And giving my poor tum a pain!

  Delphine Elizabeth Williams

Time Spirals

From beginning to beginning, currents ebb and flow,
Breathing softly, sketching lightly, patterns here below.
Liquid moments gently smoothing shadows into light,
Gleaming seconds, glowing briefly; day embracing night.
Sweet, eternal promise brought by each returning Spring,
Softly-perfumed Summers fleeing; swiftly taking wing.
Golden, graceful Autumns, shedding dignity, depart,
Winter's ermine mantle shielding earth's stiff, frozen heart.
Coming, going, turning, flowing in hypnotic dance,
The rhythm of the seasons, nothing left to chance.
Kaleidoscopic patterns, in ever-varied hue,
The cosmic dancers swaying to tempos soft and true.
One moment horizontal, they move with measured tread,
Then vertically, beckon, passing overhead,
In endless, twisting movements, twirling one by one.
Beginning and beginning, the dance is never done.
They catch us in their rhythmic net; move us to and fro,
Descending and ascending, round and round we go.
Turning and returning, still they make us bend,
Prisoners of the spiral dance; captives to the end.

  A. M. Atkins

"Whales Versus Plants"

No need for the killing of whales,
for a certain plant that grows,
it is called the jo jo ba,
and it grows in Arizona,
and the deserts of
Mexico and California.
They kill for the whales oil,
but this really is no spoil,
for the jo jo ba plant gives you better oil,
so the attempt I would try to foil.

  M. Pringle

The Cosmic Question

As I sit here and watch the sky,
Things go through my mind, I wonder why.
Do I really exist or is it a game?
Could I be a part of a much bigger plane?
I drift from my body and look down on this place.
It's really quite small from out here in space.
I do not feel cold, alone or afraid,
I just want the answer, how was it all made?
The stars, the planets, asteroids in a gang,
Did it all come from one great big bang,
Or is it much easier to understand?
Is there a God, did he lend a hand?
Some would say yes and some would say no.
Some would say simply, "I really don't know."
But there's nobody out here to ask or debate.
Nobody out here, the truth to relate.
So I'll fall back to earth and I'll watch the sky.
Things will go through my mind and I'll wonder why.

  Alex Cliff

Brown Eyes

My breasts, they are the rolling hills,
The thunder is my heart.
I will hold you through the long, dark night,
And we will never part.

Your eyes they are so deep and dark,
They are blacker than the mire.
My heart is so in love with you,
It is burning like a fire.

You speak a tongue that is so sweet,
That I can hardly understand.
My bitter ears have never heard,
Such sweet music in my land.

After the heavy shower of rain,
The hard bud became a rose.
It still lies with dew upon it,
Beside me as I doze.

Just like a field, that is newly ploughed,
I opened myself to thee.
If you could love me outside my dreams,
Then our love could be.

Donna Melinda Sloan

Butterfly

Touch the warm, beautiful silk,
That is your love
And silently, whilst you sleep,
I caress you and say that I love you.
At night bare my soul to you and cry,
As I sing softly the sweet sound of what I feel inside.

Blowing gently on your hair,
I feel the comfort of your body next to mine.
Darkness and the cold night destroyed, By the touch of you.
Thinking of a thousand kisses, shared days and happy,
laughing memories,
Then another thousand kisses
And the deep, drowning passion of my love for you.

All my senses guided towards your silent, sleeping shape,
A light within a dark tunnel.
Sheltering inside and searching further
For the extra bond that holds me so close to you.
Forever I look at you as you sleep peacefully,
Forever I love you.
My choi-choi, my butterfly.

Bobby McPherson

Mice

I know of a story that's certain to please
Of a Grand Mouse's College at Cheddar-on-Cheese
Where all the best rodents parade every Term
To compete for the coveted prize "A Tail Perm"

Old Mr. Chewchops the Master of Maths
Taught in his Class all the best Larder paths
Whilst Young Mistress Whiskers - the best teacher there
Told all her young pupils how and when to take care

She related the horrors of cats big and small
And was greatly adhered to by mice one and all
She said to be careful of traps set to spring
And showed removal of cheese with a stick and some string

The Great Mouse Headmaster taught the top class of all
And kept mice enthralled when he would recall
The time he escaped by only a fraction
After the Cat's owner demanded "More Action"

He said to stay hidden, to keep out of sight
And only to feed in the Kitchen at night
Their greatest reward if they did all these things
Would always prevent them from wearing "Mouse Wings".

D. Randall

The Fiesta Is Over

The horse's tinkling bells are silenced,
Not an echo left of crazed ole,
There is but a shadow left Senor,
Of your sombrero at dance and play.
Stop the flowing vino, not a single drop more,

Paloma milk, with head beneath her wing of silk,
Sighs at the moon, drinks in the peace.
No more clapping, no stamping, no flamenco castanets.
Dry your pearled tear Senorita, the fiesta had to cease,
Bid adios to him, that laughingly has your passion whet.

The arena, sand and blood mingle to form one.
Silently on the dying breeze, I hear on her breath, the bull's cries.
It is over for him, the pain, the sorrow of not knowing why.
For the joy of the fiesta, for the joy of you Senora,
he kneels and dies.
At this time, even the beast has brine within his eye.

The feria is over for another year, gone with the mist.
The blood carnation flung into the corner of the sun,
dejected, in pain.
Silence rules the sleepy village, the sky nods, the sea sleeps.
Slumbering now, until the fiesta lifts her skirt of frills again,
When the bull shall cry and the fatted lamb sadly bleats.

Susan Greta Read-Lobo

Rules

To demand an explanation
from them up there so high
would challenge their authority
and they may well ask you why

There are rules for us and rules for them
with few rules in between.
There are rules that they might try to hide
and those that can't be seen

See those of them that make the rules
they know not what they do
to enforce their laws upon the many
Just to please the few

They make the rules then break them
well with this we disagree
because if they can do it so can I
and that's alright by me

A. J. Arthur

Glutted With Reproaches -
(Dialogue Between Jesus And The Soul)

My Heart is glutted with reproaches, the pain cannot be eased:
For sinners it was pierced and bled - of Me, they take no heed.
For mundane power and glory, riches that cannot last,
They barter their souls' own treasure and break My sacred Heart.

In selfless love's endeavour My life on earth was spent.
In toil and tribulation, hardship and contempt,
To ransom poor sinners who would on Me but hope.
To save them from eternal death, I died upon the Cross.

Misunderstood, maligned, rejected and despised,
Pure love so cruelly thwarted, betrayed and then denied.
My Heart is glutted with reproaches, in loneliness and pain,
For souls that once did love Me have turned for other gain.

In longing expectation - I beg, entreat of thee
Stay and keep My company, come and comfort Me.

O Lord our God, our love, our life, we heed Thy plea of pain,
We ask for Grace to love Thee and follow in Thy trail.
For glutted with reproaches, we too are sore beset
Bearing Thy sacred imprint wherever we are sent.

No closer bond can thus unite, no force nor power can sever
A love so strong and true as Thine, though few there be that follow.

Jeannie Hay

Mother Love

A little mound in a quiet field
A little angel above
A little bunch of forget-me-nots
Token of mother love
A little child whose feeble strength
God knew could never weather
The storms and battles that on this earth
Walk hand in hand together
Back to his heavenly home he called it
The mother grieved full sore
But she knew that when her time did come
She would see her babe once more
And so upon that tiny grave
Pretty flowers lay
Put there by a mother
Who loved so well
Fresh gathered day by day

W. Luff

Bereavement

Our work well done
Years of blissful leisure lay ahead.
Hand in hand in happiness
The time so swiftly sped.
Little thought we gave to those who were
The lonely ones.

But now you've gone
And I alas must face the lonely years
Engulfed in sadness
And with ever falling tears,
Knowing anguish and the pain to be among
The lonely ones.

D. Butcher

Love Eternal

Life is living,
Love is giving;
To care is sharing;
Daring to bare one's soul.

To share a life with you,
Is all I want to do
My life, my love, my all.

How can I share my life with you,
When you no longer live?
To be with you again, my love,
My own life I would give.

But life is living,
And I am giving my love to you to share.
Beyond this life, where man and wife
Can share one's very soul.

Jean M. Senior

Thoughts

Forgive me friends if I seem down
And instead of a smile I wear a frown.
You come to visit me every day
But after an hour you go away.
Strange thoughts go on inside my head
As I lie here in my hospital bed.
I know it's hard to comprehend
The tedious hours that I spend
Gazing at the same four walls
And watching as a petal falls.
The flowers you bring are gay and bright
They really are a lovely sight
What I would give to pick a bunch
And then to take you out to lunch.
God, give me courage to go on,
The chance to greet another dawn,
My health and strength renewed at last
And all my trials in the past.

Nan Watson

On Awakening

I awoke this morning to a new day of life
    in which the intake of sweet air, peace without strife
    invaded my mind with the force of a wife
    whose determination, in simpler times, was focused on work.

The labours ahead, the day unlike others, was more
    a delight than a burden or chore,
    but a life-style itself when devoted to others, or a door
    of opportunity, unlocked, inviting, as a Kirk.

So I examine my potential to utilize
    each sense I possess to smell, hear, touch, then my eyes-
    which have not yet opened to assess the great prize
    of sight - and its attendants which taste and test, as a perk.

To promote, provoke, petulantly persuade my whole being
    into motion, as it follows - sensual and preoccupied - to sing
    the praises of one who sees, in the great and astonishing
    world, simple existence as a foundation on which to build.

Yes, a greater, more useful utility of that essence of time
    combined with these senses that direct my body to mime
    other organic creatures. Fingers, flex! Mind, leave off rhyme!
    Commence your day by reading Braille, friend, for you are blind.

Walter P. Stewart

No Man's Fool

Sitting in the trench,
Engulfed with loneliness and fear.
Mud sloshing round your knee-caps,
Wondering why on earth you're here.

They say we'll return as heroes,
If we return at all.
Probably meet our death in no man's land,
When the most terrifying is called.

Go over the top! the general will shout.
Forward! Advance! Attack!
We all clamber out the trenches with heavy hearts,
knowing we might not come back.

There are cries of 'Help!' and 'Save me!',
As we are running through the sludge,
Soldiers dropping down as shots ring out,
While others are drowning in the mud.

'Retreat! Retreat!' shouts the general,
and back to the trench we go.
Back through the dead and the injured,
To the hole in the ground we call home.

Sharon Paskins

War!!! Why???

Do all the people in the world think the same as I,
That all the men who go to war, go simply to fight and die,
They go, they die, one by one not knowing the reason why
obeying orders without question for theirs is to do or die.
People who were left behind to grieve for husbands and sons
were asking why should their men be the ones behind the guns,
To be killed by total strangers in a land so far from home.
While the men who should be fighting meet, and talk behind closed doors.
Still men go to war, men kill, some maybe lucky and survive
yet thousands on both sides have given up their lives.
Do the scars of killing others ever go or do they stay
memories of families and friends, who died, will never fade away.
Our rulers have a lot to answer for in the count of lives lost
is war always the only answer has death to be the cost.
Why do the heads of nations, the ones who can not agree
always send the innocent to do their dirty deeds.
If this must always be the cost, then the cost is much too high
But this is the price of war my friends, good men having to die
Is this what you want in the future for your husband and your sons
Start asking for the reasons now before their time must come.

Sylvia Roberts

Memoirs Of A Golf Ball

I was all teed up in the morning mist
Awaiting the off, through a flick of the wrist
Ouch! what the hell was that?
I think an elephant kicked me in the back
It was only the club, didn't hurt at all
That's why I'm here, I'm only a golf ball.
I fly through the air for all to see
Jet propelled, fore! Look at me!
Now I've got as high as I can go
I've got to come back down again though
I know I've been hit with plenty of loft
Where I come down, hope the landing is soft
Now I'm down and rolling through the grass
In places it is a wee bit sparse
Now it seems to be shorter still
I think I'm falling down a hill!
Where am I? It seems awful dark
This time I think I've made my mark
Yes! That was my good deed done
I got the boss "A hole in one".

Maurice Mann

Untitled

Throughout life there is heartache and pain
but throughout the heartache and pain
a new beginning will unfold
As it unfolds it will take away all
the creases of pain and heartache with it
and a new brighter future will begin.

Ruth Kiltie

Untitled

Crying low on bed of pain,
Will I ever walk again?
Doctors, nurses, physios too,
"Sure you will. It's up to you"

Wheelchair first - you'll have to learn
How to drive and back again.
Gadgets next and yes, a zimmer.
I begin to get a glimmer
Of how things are going to be,
Although it's pretty hard to see.

The main thing is, you musn't fall.
That would never do at all.
Now, on sticks, I'm on my way.
Yes, I live to walk another day.

Jean Morris

To The People Of London

London, greatest city of all time,
  Now facing war in all its grim reality,
Against the darkness doth your spirit shine
  And lightens up the Huns brutality.

Paris, yes, and many more who fell
  The prey to evil vultures of the night,
In kind of warfare that we know so well,
  By men who cringe when met in open fight.

Historic buildings that you loved so much
  Have all been smitten by that tainted hand.
Foundation and morale they cannot touch,
  So stand together, one united band.

In every corner your great empire knows
  You wanted peace, but you were sorely tried.
That peace will soon be welcomed by your foes,
  Whose blood doth trickle from a wounded side.

Fight on great people, 'til victory is won,
  For freedom and for peace, we all desire.
To foes, the day of reckoning will come,
  The victims of their own unholy fire.

Joseph Neville James

The Fertility Of Nihilism

Were we called into this labyrinth to forgive the past?
Were we called to breathe fresh the wind of silent love?
To bury the vile shadows, coiled thick and murderous
Around our dying hearts?

We are invited to declare our freedom from the tyranny of words
The prisons of system and rigid ordered lust.
Come sweet richness we welcome you
We search your luscious waters
We seek your smooth love.

Can we imbibe this rich light?
Can we embrace the rolling dawn?
This woken new flowing stillness.
Here in this cool blue river the nymphs have woken
And in our mad eyes vast kingdoms reveal themselves in splendour.
Could I believe these trees and rivers, this wind and the high
mountain, would rejoice and sing as now I see they do?

Jonathon Tillotson

The Henrietta

She was built to last by men of old,
A ship that stood so tall and bold.
She spent her life upon the sea,
The only place where men are free.

She served her masters faithfully,
And led them where they sought to be.
Her sails were spread to fight the gale,
As off to foreign climes she'd sail.

Through wind and storm she rode the tide,
Her masts held high, her hull so wide,
From north to south, her sails unfurled,
Proudly she sailed around the world.

But men fought wars, for fame and greed,
Her guns burst forth to serve their need,
In battle sore she met her end -
And no man left to call her friend.

So now, forever she will lie,
Her masts still pointing to the sky,
Her soul, where it should never be -
A thousand leagues beneath the sea.

Mary Baird Hammond

Striking Glaze Ripple

Striking glaze ripple all colours casted blue,
so peacefully from the midst a swan swims through,
Like a stick its neck stands firm,
But to touch thy hand would burn,
as striking glaze ripple and part each way in turn.

Maurice Lucas

Changing Seasons

After Winter's sleep
The Earth awakes to Spring,
Flowers and hedgerows start to grow
And birds begin to sing.

When Summer's heat wafts o'er the land
The earth is full of flowers,
The days are long, the nights are short
You barely can tell them apart,
This season is so grand.

Days are closing in again,
The air feels cool at night,
Morning mist leaves her dew behind,
Autumn Sun shines with all her might,
Trees are blowing in the wind.

Snow and frost now paint the land
White and glistening in Winter's pale sun,
The robin appears with his head cocked high,
The cold weather really has begun
In this Winter Wonderland.

M. Vivien Holden

The First Time

She is nothing much but fur
with two eyes of green
and there are many things
she has never seen.
She looked up at the ceiling
and saw two busy flies
She looked inside the mirror
and saw tow gleaming eyes.

She looked at the floor
it was very very cold
and there are many things
the kitten does not know.
She looked up and saw
she was not all alone
it was a funny ringing phone.

She lapped up a bit of milk
and slept on cosy silk
she saw the silk was green
as green as a lime.
These were the things that happened at the first time.

Sharon Widdowfield

A Countryman's Sorrow

The trees weep for him
Teardrops glistening as they fall
fog shrouds the land
A fitting pall
for the passing of a great man.
The sun breaks through
And we see again the glory
Of past deeds of pageantry
And pomp - of battles won
Echoes into the future
Of a man who in our darkest hour
Gave us the courage to fight and live on.

S. Venable

Within The Valley

In a far off valley, in a green display,
No bitterness, no sadness and no decay.
With the whispering breeze and the solitary trees,
A beautiful surrounding is all he sees.
Drenched from dewdrops in the morning sun,
A wise man seeks purity, with no wish to run.

He swallows the goodness in each new day,
Embracing nature in every way.
Alone, as he rises, the birds sing with glee,
He's at home in the valley, it's his place to be.
At one with all nature, at one with his life,
His thoughts are his children, the earth is his wife.

Paula Greaves

Elvis Presley

With a voice so magnetic
and him so energetic
Who am I talking about?
Why Elvis of course.

He could 'Love You Tender'
get you 'All Shook Up'
call you a "Hound Dog'
and be 'Stuck on You'.

So 'Don't Be Cruel'
those who don't understand,
For this man is in all the fan's hearts,
there's nothing can tear us apart.

The 'Burning Love' we have for him
will surely never dim,
His face form and figure is
an 'American Trilogy'.

Helen Barrie

"In Loving Memory"

All she remembers now are her childhood days.
She is in a time capsule, no one can erase.
Familiar Faces mean nothing to her now
Her memory fails her here and now.

Family come to visit her so fragile, so thin.
Sitting, staring without a care in the world.
Far removed from the world outside
Her memory fails her here and now.

Gone are the happy times we used to share.
Gone are the loved ones we knew before.
Gone from the house, that homely feeling
Her room, tea pot, chair have no meaning
Her memory fails her here and now.

I stroke her hand and feel her pain,
I want her to know I love her still
And feel, unable to help her now she is ill.
She has no time left on her side.
Her brain is dead, her body barely alive.
God above in your heavenly home
Grant my mum peace and take her safely home.

Alison F. Branch

Mother Of Dunblane

She's still sleeping as dawn is creeping underneath the door,
She had a dream that mattered but it doesn't anymore.
And one day she will notice that there's still a world out there,
For now her only link with life this tear-stained teddy bear.
And in her sleep she's gluing dead leaves back onto the trees,
And in her slumber holding back the waves of giant seas.
And in her dreams she's dragging back the stiff hands of the clock,
And in her nightmares fumbling with keys too small for locks.

She's still crying though her tears are lying frozen on her face.
"Leave a little light on in the window, just in case".
And one day she'll remember deep inside her is a smile,
For now each weary footstep, every movement is a mile.
And in her sleep the soft skin and the scent of baby's breath,
And in her slumber signposts pointing every way but death.
Courting the impossible, praying it's not real,
Trying to make safe something that she thought no-one could steal.
Reaching out for reasons, breathing out the pain,
Reality has changed her shape, she'll never be the same.
Infamy her burden as the world whispers her name,
No more just a mother but a Mother of Dunblane.

Annabel Lamb

What Is Life?

I've heard it said, "There is no GOD, it's all a matter of science,
All things can be explained by using some form of appliance"
Plants grow from seeds, bulbs or little corms,
To show their beauty in many lovely forms,
  But then I ask - just HOW?

Birds that sing sweetly with feathers colourful and bright,
Are regularly hatched from eggs by sitting long and tight,
In cosy nests each lovingly made to a neat and tidy plan,
A very intricate task, unaided by hands of man.
  But still I ask- just HOW?

That pretty fluffy kitten, appealing puppies' charms,
The wonder of a newborn babe, snuggling in your arms,
So soon to grow to each respected shape and form.
We take all this for granted, as if it's just the norm.
  Again I ask - just HOW?

No man, however bright and intelligent can find
The wondrous secret sought by many of mankind.
The spark of life with which animals and plants will grow
And reproduce their special gifts for each and all to show.
  I truly say - IT IS GOD!!

Doris Peck

Pen-Friend

Julie is my pen-friend's name,
She used to live here in England,
but now she's in a far off land
many, many miles away.

Australia is her home now,
With the blazing hot sun,
and scorching yellow sand,
Oh, what it's like to be in paradise
Well, I'd like to be there right now, but how!

We've written to each other,
for a very long time now,
and oh how the years have flown,
and with it our friendship
has grown and grown

Sara Crump

The Four Seasons Of Love

Love is like the four seasons
In spring all bright and new
Having said so shyly those magic words
Darling I love you.

Next the summer of your love
Still all glowing and still so new
But now so much stronger are those little words
Oh I do love you!

Here comes autumn
All browns - yellows and bronze
That starts to make you both feel
This is where we both belong

Now it's winter
All white and pure
We now know that we are so much in love
And that we want to share our married life
Together forever, that is a fact for sure.

Margaret Priest

Somewhere Not Anywhere

I met a man the other day
Who he was he wouldn't say
He asked me if I knew the way
To 'Anywhere' - He wants to go
I'm afraid dear sir I do not know
The cost is high and the journey long
By the looks of you, you're not strong
Now 'somewhere' that's not far
For someone like you it's on a par
When you reach 'somewhere' - the people there
Give every care, the food is good
There's lots of love
Miles of smiles
It's all there at 'somewhere'

Sidney Wilson

The Web

The butterfly flew from flower to flower.
Enjoying every sunlit hour.
But oh across the stems of brown,
A spiders web as light as down,
Was woven there, transparent, light
To trap small creatures in their flight.
The butterfly just failed to see.
This trap might seal her destiny
Swiftly, brightly, heed forgetting.
Flew into the spider's netting
In a trice, and full of fear.
She tossed and turned the net to clear.
The spider watched, his wicked eyes shone,
He'd have her for tea, she'd soon be gone,
But I thought it too bad, and terribly sad
For that butterfly frail to die.
So I broke up the web, and the old spider fled,
And the butterfly waved me goodbye.

Katie Coolen

Welsh Borderland

In this tough world of hard work and toil,
There are still simple pleasures for all to enjoy.
I have no wish for the fast lane of life,
So explore the Welsh border, where none can destroy.

I journey along the quiet country road,
The pastoral scene is always complete
With high hedgerows and teeming wild life in profusion.
What a joyous sound, bird song, bleating of sheep, oh such a treat.

One minute a wonderful expanse to the horizon
Of hills far away all misty and blue.
Then suddenly a narrow lane bordered with trees,
With the sun glinting through, so perfect and true.

At ones side a gentle sparkling rill,
Maybe a pheasant or rabbit runs by,
Or perhaps a squirrel jumps from tree to tree.
No man makes such beauty however hard they try.

It is up to us to keep it that way.
Our transient life an inheritance must leave,
As little has changed since King Offa's day.
On the border of Wales, natures patterns to weave to eternity.

Barbara A. Freeman

The Last Chance

I was hoping for a sunny day but afraid it was not to be
But thought it best to make the most of it as we don't get
much chance you see
So after dinner we all set off for our walk along the lane
Afraid it was Damien's turn today it was his turn to be a pain
But once we got started he was ok
So really must make the most of this day.
All along the hedgerows are spring flowers bright
To me they really are a wonderful sight
At first as we went up through the woods we thought there
were no blue-bells out
But took another turning and found plenty about
The path we took we'd never been before
But a little further on was a real treat in store
For growing there in all their beauty were lovely marsh marigolds.
A sight I hadn't seen since I was a child a glorious sight to behold
It took me right back to my childhood day's to the country
side of Devon
The days of my youth I shall never forget looking back it was
just like heaven
Those far off days are precious to me
With my parents, my brother my sisters and me
So just a little thank you for the chance to see
The beauty of the Spring time in all its majesty

Olga Giblin

These Colourful Wonders

I have so often had the yearn to write
About those things of sheer bliss; and pure delight
Like the sun that rises, and the morning dew
And about the lovely gardens, that are at kew.

The beautiful flowers and the Chelsea show
With such gorgeous colours, and all aglow
The rivers that run through pastures green,
And the countryside that is so serene.

The blossom on the trees, is such a lovely sight
The air is perfumed and fresh, and truly a delight,
And the magical appearance of the rainbow in the sky
With its brilliant blend of colours that really make one sigh.

The moon and stars on a crisp clear night
Just to see them shine, and ever so bright,
For their brilliance is there, for all of us to view
The wonderful things to see, are not just for the few.

The glorious setting sunset with its vivid crimson glow
Is surely nature's way, to simply let us know,
That a most delightful day, it has really been
And for these wonders, that we all have seen.

G. J. Stubbs

Star Of Bethlehem

Gang raped by society, where freedom is a threat
Experience job insecurity,
They'll plug all loop holes yet,
Your lot's the middle England - plugged into internet.

A shallow,
Twisted mass of
Hurt, rejected souls
A deep freeze full of feelings,
Eyes of burning coals

Angry, desperate, hopeless
Am I now like you?
I thought I wasn't, sometimes better, mixed with déjà vu.
Now I start to question, "Am I spiritually poor?"
"But others have suppressions which are rigid to the core!"
My little cat he comes to me whom I feel my heart will break,
I think it is affection but he really wants some cake.
Mind games I've been playing when my feelings were ignored,
My ego craved distraction when my intellect was bored.
Now what will fill the big black hole where my
Feelings all were stored?
    Stevan Jalabhai

Untitled

I like walking, now it's spring,
It's nice to hear the little birds sing,
Smell the blossoms in the air,
As I walk on without a care

Ever since I was a boy,
Springtime brought me so much joy,
Gentle breeze upon my face,
As I walk on at a steady pace,

Lovely flowers all around,
The birds they make a lovely sound
Pleasant sunshine everywhere
As I walk on breathing in fresh air
Everything is wonderful
Everywhere bright, nowhere dull,
The countryside is great for me,
All the best things in life are free
Though the dark clouds bring forth showers
I could walk for hours and hours.
    Cedric Lamb

Untitled

  O me O my
I am tired, and weary.
I live all alone.
I've got no money. I've got no home.
I shed my nights. In the bright city lights
I roam the streets by day
It's there where I most
A beautiful girl bright and gay
So I asked to marry her straight away.
And she said that made her day.
I said that I would do everything I can
and act like a gentle man
She said that her name, was called brown
And that she came from the town
She looked at me and smiled
And I said would you be my Darling Bride.
  O me, O my
I am not such a lucky guy as she said
it wasn't me she admired
It was my beautiful tie O me, O my.
I just bowed my head and cried O me, O my
    Kevin Dinsdale

Dunblane

I think hard and wonder,

What if that was me with a gun
pointing to my head!

But why must it have been 16
Innocent children without a worry in the world?

A sick man with 4 guns
Shooting 16 children dead!

It was just a normal day until the
Murderer came and shot them dead!

Children in search for shelter not
to get hurt, screaming, crying for help!

But now shot Dead!

Why the children of Dunblane why!
16 children around 5 yrs old!
They had their whole life ahead of them,
But it's wasted forever!
No longer cheerful children playing but silence
May you rest in peace
Children of Dunblane!
    Rebecca Pugh

Seeking

When jet and probe tear the skies,
and satellites the heavens rip apart,
piercing the distant planets and their stars;
when man takes knife to coloured man
fist to face and boot to groin;
when women nag and children scream,
and cities spread their septic scabs
o'er valleys where the corn once stood;
and seeds lie unfulfilled beneath the concrete strips
that hide them from the rising sun;
I envy then that man of simple faith,
and long to rest my head upon the knee
of Him to whom the answers are all known.
    J. M. White

Tribute To Spring

How nice to feel the warm spring breeze,
Trying to awaken the sleeping trees,
Gone is the icy winter's blast,
Spring has arrived it's here at last.

The primroses awaken and lift their heads,
Green leaves appear on their mossy beds.
Even the birds are gay on the wing,
And everywhere heralds the coming of spring,

Oh warm gentle season awakening the earth,
With your beautiful flowers and sweet songs of mirth,
I think you are the season, beloved by all,
with the promise of summer before the fall
    Hazel Lawrence

Farewell Sweet Rummy

We all awaited your last performance
Now it's like a stage without a star,
We loved you and we backed you right
    till the Eleventh hours,
We'll miss you, how we'll miss you
  But the show must go on,
In all our hearts we'll be feeling, where's
  our Rummy gone?
You're the greatest, the very greatest
And you'll always wear the Aintree crown
For had you been able to be there, you would
  not have let us down.
Farewell and happy retirement on Southport shore
For there can never be another Rummy Evermore,
Finally you have been taken to rest
Now you will go into history books
    Enid Wyles

Werecat

So many ages past; long now the last of nine lives gone
Yet still there lingers on in me an empathy...

I gaze beyond unblinking yellow eyes and, in that steady stare,
Am well aware, aloof in amber depths, a kindred spirit lies.
I too have sung a throaty purr
And known the sensuous pleasure that she feels -
My fur caressed by human hands.
On nightly prowls I long to stalk upon her heels -
Go stealthily on secret cat-concerns,
Mysterious once more in lurking lands.

Awakened instincts urge anew and call me,
Through dark spinney and green glade,
To pad along on silent, moonlit tracks.
My daytime frame is much too vast -
It lacks the lighter tread that finds old haunts so often forfeited;
But... come this eve's full-lunar light,
My velvet paws, my curving claws
Permit me share her furtive schemes
And live again, immutable alongside hers,
Primeval, longed-for, feline-daytime dreams.

W. Roy Harvey

State Of The World

As I look around in this dull, bleak, black world what do I see,
I see guns, knives and fingers all pointing at me,
Children crying in the street
Without the food they need to eat,
Crime like cancer a runs through the town.
Looking upon this world it makes me frown.

As I look around in this dull, bleak, black world what do I see,
I see guns knives and fingers all pointing at me,
Death and destruction at every door,
rape, murder and war,
Man chastised for the colour of his skin,
What should count is the soul within.

As I look around in this dull, bleak, black world what do I see,
I see guns, knives and fingers all pointing at me,
Disease being spread without concern,
Oh, how I wish society would learn,
Rainforests falling all over our planet sphere,
Won't someone help me get out of here,
What has happened to make this world sour,
The answer is man's great weakness, power.

Alison Tilley

Halcyon Days

Today I sat by the waterside
As I did when I was a child
I felt the rough grass neath by feet
From the moor so rugged and wild

Again I was back in my girlhood
Swimming the "Tibbies Brig" pool
Changing my clothes 'mong the rushes
Spotted white with cast off sheep's wool

Oh the joy of hearing the water
Flow over the rocks smoothed with age
The smell of the gorse and the heather
And flies buzzing round in their rage

I could hear the lambs' cry for their mother
Those sounds I could never forget
The sweet calling song of the skylark
When the evening sun started to set

Oh I'm loathe to leave this Valhalla
And my thoughts of Halcyon Days
But inside me this girl lives forever
In my heart the memory stays.

Elizabeth Wyllie

If The Darkness

If the darkness tries to grab you,
and you can't close your eyes to sleep;
if your dreams turn into nightmares,
and you see demons 'stead of sheep.
When the night-time does not comfort you,
in peaceful slumber you can't go;
if the moon and stars give little light,
and it's not your friend but foe.

If the dark nights ever haunt you,
and into terror you are thrown;
if there's no one there beside you,
and you're lying on your own.
When the night-time seems to frighten you,
as the devil's time covers the land;
just call on me and I'll be there,
to hold on to your hand.

Stephen C. Cuttell

Sunset

I saw an autumn sunset die tonight,
A blood bespattered canvas painted gold,
I tried to cling onto that magic sight,
Before it vanished far behind the world,
But all too soon my vision of Midas sacked,
A hand has come and plucked it from the sky,
Please for me bring Arcadia back,
And put it where at night it cannot die.
I wanted to hold the sun within my hands,
To drink the sunset like a glass of wine,
To feel the stars beneath my feet like sand,
To stop the very hands and cogs of time,
And I wanted to run barefooted like the free,
But I could not and how this saddened me.

Christopher Bishop

Trail Of Thought

From a bird in the sky
To the sky's infinite blue
For blue is the hue
Of a mood and a sigh.

From a bee buzzing again
To a flower's colourful beauty
To the heart's inner beauty
To the evil lurking in the hearts of men.

From a kettle boiling
To the water itself breaking bonds
To what's right and what's wrong
To judgment day's final dawning.

From a foretold lie
To lying to yourself
To the dissipation of health
To when we all die.

Nikesh Shukla

Untitled

Awkwardly
I hint at why,
All of a sudden
There seems to be
An intense interest on my part,
And I apologize for the words I chose.
You must excuse my easy heart.
Because in the sober light of day
I should never have said I felt that way,
So now I'm taking back what is mine
As if you never read a line.
I didn't live or breathe you
I only momentarily had you,
I didn't love or leave you
I didn't even have to.

Jacqueline Harrison

431

"O' For A Breath Of Air"

I sit at night upon my chair
Gasping for a breath of air.
To look out the window
And see the washing blowing in the wind
I know there is plenty of air outside
but at last where I sit in my chair
As I grasp for a breath of fresh air
You here the people say
From Land's end to John O'Groats
The air we breath is free
But how I wish my lungs could
Fill with a breath of fresh air
I would love to get out amongst
The people from lands end to John O'Groats
In stead of being confine
To my old chair.
Gasping for a breath of fresh air.

Sam McLaughlan

Words Of Command

Heel, sit, down, come, stay, leave
Those are the words of command I believe
The dog will respond to each one in turn
As long as they're said not softly but firm
To make sure the dog his work he won't shirk
It's out on patrol and a spot of man work
We patrol in a manner that's quiet and alert
He picks up and indicates it's time to divert
Out of the banking an intruder he climbs
My job at this point is to shout halt three times
My shouts fall on deaf ears, he's running away
It's time to release and chase I will say
The chase is fast and direct for the arm
Stand still right now and you'll come to no harm
The command to leave I will give right away
Then I'll say come, heel, sit and then stay
Now to escort the intruder away
He's been warned not to run, he's unleashed I will say
It might only be training you must understand
To work as a team you need words of command

Colin Henderson

The Clock Ticks On

I watch the hands sweep round the clock
and I wonder, when for me those hands will stop,
"there's plenty of time" so I'm told,
"to worry yourself about growing old."

I hear the pendulum swing to and fro
and I wonder, when for me that swing will slow.
Tomorrow is here and then it's gone.
As I sit by, the clock ticks on.

Lorraine Gouland

Why Do I Love You?

Why do I love you? Now, let me see,
It's all the things that you do for me,
You're so considerate and understanding,
It must be hard, I can be so demanding.

The way your eyes sparkle, and that cheeky grin,
That cheers me up whatever mood I'm in,
And you've got that laugh, when your face seems to shine,
I just can't believe that you are all mine.

I love to be near you, and then when we kiss,

It leaves me in a state of such total bliss,
Those strong arms that take me and hold me so tight,
Make me want you to stay with me all through the night.

I just wanted to tell you how much I care,
If you want me, or need me, you know I'll be there,
In every little thing that you say or do,
I can tell you're very special, and that's why I love you.

Zoe Bellass

Why The Angel?

Today like any other, a smile proceeds the face of the angel,
Hiding away any anguish from the outside world.
A soul so sweet, so pure,
Untarnished by life's evil vices.
An idealistic portrayal of nature's ability to produce beauty
like the moment the sun's rays catch the clear water,
Illuminating the earth's bloodstream.
She generates her warmth deep from within her heart,
Looking to share, rather than keep for herself.
She is the earth's eighth wonder.

Lost and confused, she is encaged in a pit of despondence,
her frame of mind being unmercifully disintegrated,
By the unwanted bad fortune that surrounds her,
Hope and the will to overcome she seeks,
As she longs for a return to normality,
Her optimism portrayed in a manner of realism,
Nature forbidding surrender
No being on earth is deserved of any such plight,
why the angel?

Steven Archibald

Musing In An Empty Classroom

Tired and weary of being pushed and pushing, Jaded with
the March of time, Weighed down by world pressures,
　is mankind a lie?
Deafened by car homes blowing
Harassed by education musts which enter,
From every side-road I must cross.
This world is a crowded city centre
And if a wish I could be granted
With the speed of an arrow from a bow would I fly!
Into the arms of a sight that I shaded, from the human mind is closed.
Where there is no premeditated rendezvous but liberty and
　felicity shining through
Oh! For that world of quiet peaceful time, where sounds are leaves
that rustle: and fantasies come, impossible to choose the
　nature of them,
never wanting to refuse to view the images that are imposed
Suddenly with momentary shock; I feel regret, unease
As once more to my day of toil, shattered
Silence once more reigns
My classroom door slams open, my children burst inside.
Interpretations ventured but soon forgotten
As my dream world retreats. Visions disbanded I do not understand.

Marisa Dale

One Life

So, what's it all about, this life, whether short or long,
Who deals the hand that gives some all
And others to forever strive
　It's wrong.

If only we could change the roles
Even for the shortest time,
To experience the pain of want
Feel humbled for a while
　That's right!

The greatest pleasure is to share
To see a smile the prize
To know you're needed is reward
Your living justified
　You know

Don't preach but practice; love, don't hate
Don't wait, don't count the cost
The hours, the days, the years are short
The last sleep ever long
　One life one chance

J. H. Drury

I Wish I Was Young Again

Now I am old, I seem to depend,
On people I know I send round the bend.
Poor old Fred, he was my husband you know,
Died a few months, or was it years ago?
I can't seem to remember,
My memory's not like it used to be,
People keep on staring, they keep looking at me.

I only have one grandchild, he's called Ben,
Ben is young he is only ten.
I remember when I was his age,
Playing with friends, the sun on my face,
Those days are gone now, gone without a trace.

Now dark days are upon me,
My husband is dead
I look to the future and I shudder with dread.

Jenni Allen

Blood, sweat and tears

Think just think, of all the blood, sweat and tears
London has shed with the passing of years,
The dirt, dust and smog, the noise and the grime,
Poverty, slavery, squalor and crime.

Ambitions and hopes, mad schemings and fears,
Disease, depravity, vice, wines and beers,
Arts and culture can pass the test of time,
City of contrast from base to sublime.

Historical monuments, long endears,
Symbolize prestige of people and peers,
Noise of the traffic and church bells still chime,
Rags next to riches, cultures rise from slime.

Millions of people have lived, worked and died -
London remembers few only with pride.

Susan Mary Robertson

So Beautiful, So Sad

Look out across the lush green meadow
Where butterflies flick the air
To the straggly, multicolored hedgerow
Bees, buzzing around the flowers so fair.
Above the lurching poplars
The grey stone church tower stands
Its bell chimes so melodious
Across these peaceful lands
The skylark sings so sweetly
In a heaven of azure blue
And lovers, hand in hand
Walk with hearts that are so true.
Why then so melancholy
What is this sadness for
It is, that I feel the last sight
Of so many
Who left to die
In the Great War.

Bill Muirhead

The Secret

As the haze fell over the water's edge,
And the stars shone bright in the cold dark night;

She came again and here she did weep,
Her tears falling into the bulrushes at her feet;
And there for a while she did sit,
singing in the rain.
Then on the surface of the forest pond.
she laid a lilac chain.

As the dawn began to break,
And the mist was gone,
She ended her magical fairies song;
She dispersed just as the haze had done,
Before the first rays of the morning sun.

Lucy Rainford

A Father's Son

I remember the days were long,
The nights too soon came on song,
Dancing, singing, playing games,
All the faces, names remain.

And yet as life, time went on,
And still the fun carried on and on,
Too soon age and living make their mark,
And still the memories are sharp.

Growing, learning day by day,
No knowledge of the role to play,
Childhood life too soon is past,
Hold on tight and make it last.

And all at once a new life is born,
And all the memories to dawn,
To stand, to watch, to see him grow,
And feel you felt what he will know.

What joy, what hope, you can't describe,
But life goes on and builds with pride,
And will a father's son know too,
In time the life that was blessed on you.

K. Rowan

Fears In The Night

A storm comes hurtling through the night
With such a greedy appetite.
Wakes the child lying in his bed,
He cries, pulls the covers above his head.

Rain pounds on the roof
Lashes at the windows.
Wind, howling, frustrated,
It lifts and pulls, twists and turns.

Thunder echoes from a distance
Rolling nearer and nearer.
Lightening flicks its eager tongue
To strike, scar and burn.

Anger explodes and breaks
Unleashed, untamed, unashamed
On its furious, frantic journey it goes
Until, one last disdainful lash of its tail.

Then all is calm,
A soothing hand sweeps across the countryside.
The child sleeps.
Dawn is breaking.

Angela Wooldridge

Ups And Downs

Another morning another day,
What will this one bring,
I sit and say,
Will it bring sunshine,
Will it bring rain,
Will it bring happiness,
Or will it bring pain.
Life is a pattern of ups and downs,
So if you have an up,
Help those who are down.
I guess our creator could not give us all ups.
Think about it,
One pattern could drive us all nuts.
Now if it is your turn for a really rotten down,
Read this again,
And a smile will take that frown.
Then remember,
It is your turn for a really good up.
Life is a puzzle,
And not all good luck.

Joan Wallis

Snowflakes

Curtains draw up, the stage is set
Eyes to view, smiles that met
A million crystal dancers
Ready to perform like romancers

With the crystal dancers opening in flight
Views now comparing the differences through sight
Mathematically, chemically you see true
Geometrically symmetrically falling from view

I view through different eyes
A delicate crystal ballet dances through the skies
Fluttering and caressing willing to stay
Alas descending now to earth in a graceful way

Then the precious moment when our eyes unite
Beholding the wonder in this miraculous flight
As the snowflakes will fall and eventually disperse
As will our souls together dance with this earth

Margaret Bell

The Hand

The greatest of man's limbs is his hand,
It conveys so much we can understand,
The hand can beckon - or wave "goodbye".
It can mop our tears when we tend to cry.
A hand on the shoulder comforts another
Offering welcome to man as a brother.
It can bid at auction - restrain a child,
Clasp another hand when reconciled.
It can feed the owner - or blend in prayer.
Comforting the sick conveying our care.

Kathleen Croall

"The Anticipation Of Transformation"

O' lonely Caterpillar, how you crawl through life.
So vulnerable, so easily torn apart by the greedy.
With no defence, just humility to see you through.
But you yearn for nothing more than a leaf from the Tree of Life.

But when times get tough enough, your tactics are seen as weak.
But in the face of adversity, strength is what you behold.
A barrier so delicate yet so strong to hide your feelings.
Your chrysalis protects your emotions from those that wish to hurt.

While others see you as lazy, you work hard within your home.
To enter a state of transformation, so that you may.
Take on the world in a different new life.
For you know you can fly to higher heights.

You do not hurry to change your being.
But when the time is aligned to forces of change.
You break forth gently from your self made enclave.
To take flight as a refreshed, experienced being of freedom.

Jason Hood

The Dance

In this internet of confusion,
We could easily lose our minds,
But one thing keeps us sane;
that is the dance,
the dance is our path to the future,
the future is our path to the stars,
we become the future, we become the stars, we become the dance.

The dance lives on past infinity,
the beat stronger, stronger than before,
the universe and the dance combines,
And just for a second, we feel united,
united as a generation,
We become the dancer and we become the dance,
We become the writer and we become the written,
We become the creator and the creation,
We become the uniter and the united,
But generations come and go,
And the dance lives on.

Jaime Winfield

Sensuality

Ever tender touch sends echoing shivers of pleasure throughout the whole of my body,

Like ripples through a pond.

Spasms of pulsating pure energy released in sweet anticipation down my spine,

His touch sets free my senses, gradually unleashing the secret of ecstasy and the power of sensuality with every pounding beat of my heart

The essence of intense sexual desire flows rhythmically through every inch of my body - so much so I can almost feel the pumping rush of blood spreading through my veins

Visions of pure emotion cloud my judgement and the overwhelming sensation of surrender overcomes me,

As I draw him closer I can feel his heart beat next to mine

His touch, his smell,

His light, loving kisses touch my face, my lips,

Like cold, soft snowflakes fall upon the ground,

Our hands caress every part of each other, exploringly, slowly and intimately- his touch is electrifying.

Our naked bodies lock together in a slow, rotating movement, and I lose all control as we make love.

Gemma Stockton

The Morris Dance 1996

Fair Shelley sold sea-shells along Southend Pier,
The way she had sold them for many a year.
She just sold her sea-shells and paid up her VAT,
A law-keeping, hard-working, tortoise shell cat. Ah.

The EEC heard about Shelley's success.
They cried: "Now what shells do the British possess?
Brit cats have no right to trawl off British shores!
So one thing is certain - those shells are not yours! No!

"We warn you to leave all those sea-shells alone.
Southend will be listed a 'sea-shell-free' zone.
Your cattle we zapped and your fish we did steal.
Now we have your sea-shells...but you can appeal! Ho!"

"It will do you no good, 'cos out-voted you'll fall!
Let kind EEC just look after us all!"
Said Shelley: "Your motives, self-seeking, not daft,
Breed rules so quaint-sounding they make a cat laugh! Ha!"

"European Commission! You know quite well
You should be renamed the Commission from Hell.
You say that for all EEC will provide?
But the price will be Freedom! and that's suicide! Ooh!"

Rachael Esterson

A Springtime Poem

The winter is over
Springtime is near,
I look through my window
And see that it's here.

A peaceful, sound morning
Birds resting in trees,
Entwining their homes on an ever-fresh breeze.

The colour of the grass darkens,
Flowers start to bloom,
An amazing bright light
Gracefully fills the whole room.

I wash and get dressed
And go straight outside,
A long walk ahead of me fills my mind

The night-time comes,
And I go in for tea,
I think of the day I'll be leaving behind,
And the one that's ahead of me.

Nicola Tipping

A Once-Was Life

Humdrum days have extinguished the spirit
Of a once bustling mind.
Quiescent eyes now see a life become flavourless,
While the rigose lines on tired face
Chronicle this life's wearisomeness.

Now that the horizon encircles swamp like
With predictable monotony,
And expectations drop into empty nothingness
Life's rich nectar turns to watery tears
Masked behind an etched smile.

And so sepia shadows devour the colour,
Clothing the times in dullness
To match the languid mind, recently tamed
By bankruptcy of simple notions;
Mapped out in some headier time.

Christine McNamara, pseudonym - Elizabeth Smith

A Place Called Heaven

I lay awake at night and ask where is this place?
Where all our loved ones are gone without a trace
Please listen to me and take me there
So I can tell them that I care.
When I fall asleep at night
Please take me on that special flight
Into the unknown.
My son's new home
Through a large tunnel, at the end a light
Where everything is peaceful, pure and white,
All around is filled with love and harmony,
But alas this wouldn't be for me,
For I still have many lessons to learn,
And more bridges to burn,
So in the meantime all I can do,
Is love and think of you.

S. C. Budd

Time For Renewal

Spring, the first season of the year.
Comes with it hope and brings us joy.
A time to think and our thoughts employ.
A time to trust and dispel fear.

A time for love to flow and rebound.
Like a flow of water from the ground.
To those who suffer lend a listening ear.
Courage to recover their loss without fear.

With fresh hope and a spring from our heart.
Replenishing our body with material need.
Refreshing our souls with spiritual feed.
Working for a land where all feel a part.

We'll endeavour to treat others with mutual trust.
Cross community efforts, helping others is a must.
Living to-gether in harmony and not harbouring hate.
Putting others first in a considerate way.

God's plan for us we must surely perform.
Life's too important to destroy or maim.
Jealousy and arrogance expel, let love be the norm.
Courtesy and consideration to spurt and be the aim.

Elizabeth Swaile

Rebirthday

In Europe's deepest valley, impossible to forget,
Snow fell over spring flowers when we first met.
On the heights, too, later, that lovely white lay strewn
Where three of us watched pinnacles,
Black birds, and a daylight moon.

A hemisphere and year away, just now I do not mind
Whether snow is falling again where you to two were kind;
For certain in those mountains, in some deep glacier's cleft,
Snow shields one fallen ice man,
And one live man is left.

W. D. Hamilton

Reversal

It seems but yesterday when dreams were the future
Waiting to unfold.
Childhood seems so near to age
Despite the years between that rolled.

It seems but yesterday when fully grown in stature
And so sure of right and wrong,
That we could put the world to rights-
We were so sure and strong.

It is but yesterday and we are now mature
In mind, and less inclined
To feel we have all answers that will cure
And save mankind.

It is today. So many yesterdays, and yet
So few tomorrows.
The farthest yesterdays away are those we least forget,
The nearest are for sorrows.

Tomorrow never comes, 'tis said, for each and every day
Becomes today. Oh would that our tomorrows
Could become our yesterdays. That way
Old age could give to youth, the wisdom life begat.

Doris A. Mahon

Hands In Prayer

The hands are a part of the body
That God created with care
There's nothing that looks more beautiful
As when they're together in prayer.

For the use of the hands there are many
Carpentry, tailoring or repair
They will never be more useful
As when they're together in prayer

In everyone's life comes a moment
When you sink to the depths of despair
Just put your hands together
Spend just a moment in prayer

God listens to those who are anguished
His love you can never compare
So put your hands together
And speak to God in prayer.

Florence Phillips

Parental Wonders

My little girl asked me if God was crying
She asked me if all the trees were dying...
She brought a lump to my throat
While tugging at the bottom of my coat...
Waiting for the answers by impatiently sighing...

Now the rain has turned into a dry spell
The golden autumn leaves have all fallen...
Now my little girl has grown
She has a little girl of her own...
The secrets of the universe are hers to kiss and tell...

One day my little boy lost a tooth
He said to me his friend had found proof...
The tooth fairy does exist
I said how do you know this...
His dad saw her one night and told him the truth...

Now my little boy plays the fairy for himself
As his children slowly take away his wealth...
Gold coins glint in the light
That appeared mysteriously in the night...
Now they rattle in the piggy bank on the shelf...

Keith Tissington

A Series Of Links United

As I read 'concatenation' caprioled off the page and hit me in
  the head.
And it read as new, as never seen before,
Which sets in train analysis.

Con is with and cat is, well, cat. With cat?
Tenere to hold. Withholding cat? Poor cat.
Nation. Nation? Country, my soul there is a country.
Land - land of hope and glory, realm, coin of the realm.
State - state of the nation.

Nothing like the dictionary definition.
That's not half so much fun though accurate.

Can't, cant, cent, cone, cine, cite, cotton, Cato - republican.
Cato Street conspiracy,
Catesby, Robert Catesby conspirator, gunpowder plot,
And we're still only at 'c'.

I want to have that word 'concatenation' for my very own not
  share it.
There are other words like that - they're mine.
I don't talk about them in case anybody else gets in.

Jennifer Herd

Planet Earth

There are wondrous things to behold,
On this land we call earth.
Like a baby's first cry soaring skyward,
As its mother has just given birth.
Pretty flowers, trees and bushes,
Far too numerous to tell.
Lots of creatures roam around,
Some we know, others not too well.
Many lakes, hills and mountains,
Surround a vastness of seas.
Countries of all nationalities,
Speak many tongues with ease.
The beautiful rainbow that follows the rain,
Curves across heavens so high.
We gaze at the lovely colours,
And marvel as we pass by.
So many things on this planet abound,
With its majesty and all it implies.
We mortals can only guess by half,
For it's here that our destiny lies!

Betty Munro

Nature's Balance

I look up my garden and what do I see,
  so many colours up there in the tree.

The birds are all roosting, the doves near the top,
  not one of them eating, oh! why did they stop?

They suddenly leap up, and all fly way,
  I see a bird coming; it's only a jay.

But there looking down, flying high in the sky,
  it looks like a hawk, now a creature will die.

You can see her swoop down, she's after her prey,
  Oh! Why does she kill it; I must look away.

Her chicks are all hungry, so that's why she came,
  they only eat meat, so she has to catch game.

But nature's well balanced if you stop to think,
  for all living creatures must have food and drink.

The hawk took the slow one, the weakest must go,
  the same thing is practiced on the earth here below.

No unsightly corpses are lying around,
  the carnivores take them, so nothing is found.

The balance of nature no one can dispute,
  who would clean our earth if they only ate fruit.

Muriel Richards

Lost For Words

A friend of mine called by today,
to say a loved one had passed away.
I said, "I know just how you feel,"
that given time, the pain would heal.

My words seemed to have an hollow ring,
how much comfort could I bring,
to a badly broken heart,
to one whose life had just been torn apart.

How could I her sorrow share?
I can't see that empty chair,
Or feel the hopelessness within.
It would be so easy to give in.

And so I just sat quietly, as out her heart she poured,
the sadness of the final days, and how hard she'd fought
to be brave, and not let show
the tears that at any time might flow.

Yes, I know the feeling, that losing someone brings,
the sorrow that wells up, over silly little things.
And yet it isn't easy, to find the words to say,
to give someone the courage, to face another day.

M. Boden

Kaleidoscope Upon Tring Park Bridge

Spinning cars shoot straight lines
Under a man made bridge
That broods upon Autumn;
Cold steel cuts the motor-way
in two,
Trees, either side, fan September skirts
Against quiet grey.....
Rooted formation dancers await their cue
To rustle the fabric of dreams.
October passes, leaves in a misty swirl
Loosen lace shifts,
And unveil November.

December hills catch fire burning timber,
Clouds shape Winter charcoal
That sinks, while embers drift
Cradled in sightless branches;
Wind blows boughs, four ways.....
Criss-crossed
Benediction.

Dhoon Casstles

Caring

First as a stranger then as a friend.
We would sit and talk for hours.
He full of tales of long ago days.
Me so full of awe.

He told me tales when as a child
Then later as a man.
Encounters with the mau mau.
Deeds in far off lands.

First on a crutch then in his chair.
His tales still outward poured.
When he had a good day.
My heart would gladly soar.

I nursed him through his illness.
Watching his sad decline.
Then at the end I held him.
Close within my arms.

His eyes told me he was not afraid.
Of the journey still to come.
But as life ebbed away I wondered.
What adventures still had to be overcome.

Ann Phipps

Separation

They told her he'd been very brave
And stuck a medal on his chest
And fired their rifles in the air
And said a very solemn prayer

But that was very long ago
A frozen moment in the past
Distorted through a memory glass
And yet the moment failed to pass

An ageless smile that never fades
Unblinking eyes that ever stare
His sepia face she wets with tears
As twilight thoughts draw back the years

Her ritual done she climbs the stair
Her aching limbs and bones to rest
To find in dreams her hopes fulfilled
A meeting of two souls distressed

Matthew T. Calderwood

Seasons Of Sanctuary

Spring is the first season of the year
It is when the yellow daffodils appear
The first new lambs are also born
And bound and leap amidst the dawn

Summer is when the sun shines high
With the white fluffy clouds up in the sky
The ocean is so blue and white
And the children playing with their kite

Autumn is the season next
When the leaves fall from their leafy nest
The smell of bonfires burning bright
With fireworks lighting the Autumn night

Winter is when the cold winds blow
With snowmen standing in the snow
The robin shelters in the barn
so the cold winds and snow can do no harm

Hazel Paginton

VE Day 50th Anniversary (A Veteran's Thoughts)

I looked and I wondered, I laughed and I cried
why was I here when so many had died?
So many more worthy far braver than I.
I don't know the answer I just wonder why.
If life's just a gamble, a throw of the dice
who are the winners and who pays the price?
If there's a purpose it's hard to relate
to the way that things happen if it's just fate.
In the midst of battle does God pick and choose
who shall be winners, who's going to lose?
With so many praying for self to survive
which of those praying will come out alive?
Maybe God leaves us in total despair
to sort out our troubles, for why should he care?
He gave us freewill so we've always a choice
if we'd only listen to that still small voice.

Jack C. P. Rowe

The Lost Leader

But for a couple more voters she left us,
   Faced with defeat in the very first round,
Forced to resign, thus misfortune bereft us,
   Upset the market, devalued the pound.
Government's confidence challenge by Labour
   Offered the gift of a golden retort,
Slew her opponents with sharp witted sabre,
   Relished command of her literal sport.
What had they done to desert such a leader?
   Full of self-interest, loss of their seat?
All now deserve de-selection procedure:
   Blot out their names, let them fear for defeat.

Geoffrey Daish

Autumn

Leaves of russets, green and browns
Descend with speed before winter frowns
Its sheen of white upon the ground.
Beneath, hibernating animals sleeping sound.
Shimmering, sparkling, the gossamer thread
Cradles the unsuspecting prey - now dead.
A gentle breeze whistling through the tree.
The beauty of the Autumn for all to see.

Patricia M. Kennett

To My Husband...Gilbert

Fifty years have flown and I am left alone.
My love, my life has changed overnight.
What love, what companionship could compare?
A casket full of jewels would not replace the void in my heart.
Alas it aches!
Two lives as one entwined, then estranged.
What cruel games life plays.
The tenderness and bravery of an illness not to be
defeated, which claims its victim in its own time, to a
sleep from which one never wakes.
Eternal and final.
Their richness of a marriage strengthened through the
years, the fears and tribulations endured.
A family of joy, so good to behold, maturing as the years
began to unfold;
Gave support when needed.
Oh my love you have journeyed so far away;
God rest you and keep you until my final day.
Do not cry when the sun sets, for your tears won't let
you see the stars.

Jeanne Byers

An Elegy For Alex

Just for you my darling, these few words come to say,
That you are always in our heart's, forever and a day.
You came to us a precious gift, to join our family,
But for reasons, quite unknown, this was not to be.

For those of us that saw you, and held your tiny form,
And for those of us that didn't, were left feeling so forlorn.
To never hear your laughter, or see you smile and play,
We had so much to share with you, as you went on life's way.

We've all been robbed of knowing you, and this is hard to bear,
So we're left to find the answers, in these sentiments we share.
Only time will heal our sadness, our sorrow, grief and pain,
So we ask that Jesus,...
Guard your soul with love,
Till we meet one day, again

Lynda Jaunzems

Tranquillity

Lying in the meadow, watching clouds go scudding by,
Songbirds flying over head, making music in the sky.
Tranquillity

Sailing down the river, trailing fingers from the boat,
Sunbeams on rippling water bring a lump into my throat,
Tranquillity

Walking barefoot on the grass, the dew upon my toes.
The smell of new mown hay comes drifting to my nose.
Tranquillity.

Early in the morning, watch the sun rise in the sky,
The flaming orange ball brings a tear to my eye.
Tranquillity.

Lying in the bath tub when there's no one else about.
To knock upon the door and shout "hurry up, get out"
Tranquillity.

Knowing that it's Sunday, no need to rise at dawn,
Jack Frost at the window, but in bed you're nice and warm.
Tranquillity.

June Davies

To Have And To Hold

With his touch her heart he took
without a thought to how she felt.

With his eyes her body he undressed
without a care for her shyness.

With his words he persuaded her
without a feeling for her guilt.

With his passion he seduced her
without wanting her to care.

With her response she gave him all
not waiting to hold back.

With her kisses his body she explored
not liking him to move away.

With her words she begged him stay
not wanting him to go.

Having given of herself surely his
time was hers if not his heart.

But having taken and enjoyed his time was up,
passion spent, desire satisfied.

Whilst for her sweet memories remained of what might have been
if only time was theirs to keep and his heart was free to give.

Alex Murray

An Affair Of Conscience

Night falls, the curtains draped, blackness fills the room.
I lay awake listening to the wind, calling, telling all untruths.
Tightening my eyes, squeezing my face, I lay not moving,
   too scared to make a sound.
Counting sheep, can't concentrate, frightened and guilty of deceit.

I lay wanting, willing myself to sleep, no words or actions
   can be heard or seen.
Thoughts rush through my head, questions, answers,
   not wanting to be told or said.
The ticking of the clock, the creaking of the floor,
   something blowing in the wind.
Silence is so dense, yet so fragile.

My body tired, weak and frail, my conscience alive and burning.
My head aching ready to explode, willing a thought to light
   the fuse to enable me to sleep.
Why only I can tell, but no one is to be answered.
The secret shall remain!

Patrick Anthony Williamson

Life

It's all out there in colour and sound
fabrics made up of many mediums
an ever-lasting piece of perpetual motion,
that never adjusts its speed or direction
only through age does it quicken.

Grass, concrete, tar and wood
the yield that keeps us all living
anxiety, depression, laughter and grief,
the other side of the coin
but to give in, involves no future.

A rainbow of shades and shapes
rough, smooth, grainy to touch
that brings all our senses into action,
and programmes our every thought
before that final date.

Today as it goes faster and faster
our body clocks now go out of time
the process of evolution; can't cope,
and all these words about life
have the human-race punch-drunk on the ropes.

John Downie

Ruby Wedding 18th February 1995 George And Joan

It was a little iron gate I opened and walked
   through.
Behold the sight before my eyes - too perfect
   to be true.
Rows and rows of crocuses mixed orange,
   purple blue.
Beside the path I walked upon - edging green
   lawns two.
The colour and conformity so evenly
   displayed!
To lift your heart, welcoming, perfection for
   this day:
As if they knew it had to be, for 40th
   anniversary.
   L. G. Goss

Emotions

The pain, the anger deep inside me,
The hurt of my losses bellows and cries,
My feelings tormented by hope and fear,
The way which I feel I really despise.

I feel cold, empty and always unwanted,
In this life all on my own,
Threatened by all the turning confusion,
How could they leave me all alone.

I'm trapped by betrayal and humiliation,
I can hear their teasing and whispering taunts,
I want so badly to forget these frightful days,
Why me, must this terror always haunt.

I searched through hours of light and dark,
For something I knew could never be found,
My hope for loving from someone so dear,
Lay far beyond this tearful ground.

Sarah Moore

Illusions

Love is one of our greatest illusions
it sets out to conquer like a 'Quest for Truth'
knights on horseback - the wings of a dove?
We are all unconquered for in our Quest we
lose ourselves a part of our soul is taken away
on a whim - a never-ending dream of true romance
Perhaps if we stood still and looked within
we would find that love is no more than a
search for recognition associating our emotions
with those of another person
What vast amounts of energy we expend in always
trying to reach the unobtainable
moving our goals to extend our horizons
Very seldom do we feel the complete
satisfaction or pleasures of pure love
because like every other emotion
it very rarely stays still long enough
for us to evaluate or feel its true connection
We have entered a world where shadows lie
on the brink of our happiness, it always remains unjustified.
   Jenny Bickers

Why "Greenpeace"?

A polluted world!
How long will it take?
No clean water,
Or fish in the lake.
No pure rain,
But a world filled with acid,
How can we remain so placid?

Why support "Greenpeace"?
Some of us know,
They want the clean water
To continue to flow.
They want the fish
To continue to swim,
Support "Greenpeace" and help them to win.
   Linda Sylvester

The Freedom Of Choice

Floating, serene, cocooned in my cloud,
Peacefully drifting, no noise that is loud.
Wrenched back from my haven, on to a hard bed,
Confusion and throbbing sounds circling my head.
Jumbled up voices rebound off the wall,
Some I have loved; others I know not at all.
I yearn to go back to my cloud in the sky,
But I am unable to utter even a sigh.
Rushing feet, muffled words, I am too bewildered to think.
Despair and frustration fill me - if only I could just blink.
My soft white chariot draws me, clear of all pain,
Safe and calm, slowly drifting, at peace once again.
Back in my prison, my jailor': machines and drugs.
My frail hold on life, just a set of old plugs.
Trusting only in God. Would it all be in vain?
I am surrounded by sorrow and continuing pain.
Man will play God here on the earth,
Test tube babies, donor eggs - to create birth!
Silently pleading 'Just let me go'; the answer I know will be never.
My only prayer, to float on my cloud, for ever and ever and ever...

Joan Townsend

Emily's Sheep

The wintry morning was bright but cold,
The view from the hill a joy to behold.
Old Emily Jones watched her dog lolloping ahead
And pulled her hat more firmly over her head.
As always, they'd enjoyed their walk,
But now Emily Jones was turning her thoughts
To her cosy kitchen with glowing fire,
Where she'd warm her toes as flames leapt higher.
Sheep grazed on the slopes as Emily made her descent,
At the bottom against a hedge, trembling, head bent,
A sheep stood alone, fleece and thorns entwined.
Emily put thoughts of her kitchen out of her mind
And painstakingly tugged at each fleecy knot,
Then, suddenly free, the sheep to the ground dropped!
With legs too weak to support him and a hopeless look in his eye,
Emily helped him to his feet pleading "Please don't die".
He stood unaided, then with faltering steps, joined the sheep
Grazing on the hill, as Emily breathed a sigh of relief.
She then headed for home, dog at her side,
Thanking God in his Heaven that the sheep hadn't died.

Christine Jarvis

Limited

A solitary flower rising up,
Struggling to pull away,
Caught up in a web of thorns,
Keeping her at bay.

A tiny bird takes a leap,
Trying in vain to soar high,
She is beaten down by brighter wings,
And falls helplessly through the sky.

A humming river winding through the hills,
Wanting to run her own course; to be free,
The peaceful humming is soon drowned,
By the mighty roar of the sea.

A frightened lonely girl,
Opens her eyes to see,
But is blinded by a vibrant light,
A light in which she longs to be.

The light is dimmed by a cold mist,
The saviour is fading fast,
The girl tried to sever her chains,
But, again, her chance has passed.

Meg Nash

An Appreciation Of Janet

Mother Theresa of the South that's Janet
No one I knows cares more on this Planet
All her concerns are for others
Mums, Dads, Sisters and Brothers

Mother Theresa of the South that's Janet
Church work, Samaritans, she'll plan it
Such devotion has me worried 'bout her health
She seeks neither promotion nor wealth

Mother Theresa of the South that's Janet
She even cares for me, a gannet
How does she manage to appear so serene
When many around her are so mean

Mother Theresa of the South that's Janet
If I could harvest her love I'd can it
Lord in your mercy her do bless
As for me may I her oft caress.

Alan Ferguson

Persuasion

Come with me
And I'll show you peace.
Stand with me
And you'll feel tranquil.
Sit with me
And you'll hear only silence.
Lie with me
And you'll know great love.
Look with me
And you'll see pure beauty.
Walk with me
And you'll be my life.

   All my thoughts I will share with you.
   All my feelings will be yours too.

Paddy Jupp

Head Piece

Small fishes swim from sockets, where once eyes
Looked out eagerly to scan the war torn skies
The skies that hid the cannon from a plane
That ruptured flesh, broke bones, and pulped the brain
The brain that thought as many had before
That only other people died in war
The war that seemed so very far away
From cosy cockpit on that sunny day
That sunny day that could have been enjoyed
Had not the bombs and bullets been deployed
Deployed by men of unrelenting greed
Used by puppets who could never share that need
That need to own what other people had
A feeling so intense, it drove them mad
Mad enough to organize a war
And push the common people to the fore
Fore, came the cry from Berlin, London, Rome
And caused this skull to be a fish's home

Lew A. Gray

JCB

Relentless dragon
Slithers from cocoon of clinging clay,
Snorting lethal fire.
Devours with avid jaws calm unsuspecting
Meadows, flaunting summer opulence
Of buttercup gold.
Sheds in its wake a raw and gaping wound
Which fresh green filaments of time alone can heal.
A tree sprawls, shamed in alien stance,
Limbs bunched, grotesque;
Its severed roots, up-tilted, bleed to death.
A trembling hare, fear-frozen,
Surveys with hopeless eyes its shattered world
Where soon will rise a concrete Legoland
As nature's shrinking soul hands out
The price of progress.

Anne Leask

Just Before I Was Born

My father fell one winter's morn
And through the dark a rent was torn
And sunlight fell upon my cone.
I pushed my feet into the earth.
And craned my head for all its worth.
I spread my palms to face the sun,
Any new my life had just begun.
My nursery days came and went.
As I raced my twin, to fill, the rent.
Our bodies strong arms drawing power.
We grew into majestic towers
Side by side three hundred years
Then my brother shed his tears
Up and down I looked about.
And there, through his trunk a road cut out.
He leant on me, I took the strain
and than I felt the searing pain
Again, I felt the puny thunk
two ants were chopping through my trunk
I'm lying now on the forest floor, majestic tower to be no more
One ant is sad, why should this be? I'm just another redwood tree.

Henry Fell

The Children In Tiananmen Square

They were foolish, brave, courageous,
    "the children" in Tiananmen Square.
For the dreamed of things, shh; "almost forgotten"
    truth, freedom, "they dared!"
Fasting, singing songs, as though at a banquet,
    hearts overjoyed, at one!
Oh! The memory of those children, can't be a bitter one.
What joy to have known them! Were they kin?
    Brother, Sister, Daughter, Son.

The world is richer, that those spirits, sung their song,
    so clear, for a while, in Tiananmen Square.
For they possessed spirits, so rare, so rare!
    "the children who dared" to sing, in Tiananmen Square.
For none can destroy the memory: innocence, love, "Oneness"
    reigned.
They'll sing again one day, those spirited brave little children,
    "who dared" to sing in Tiananmen Square.
Fathers, mothers, dry your tears,
    "your children" have found the way,
Their spirits will live on,
    long after, Tiananmen Square has decayed.

June 1989
Hong Kong
Alice Recton

In Flight

Emotionless
Flat and bittersweet.
Roslynn like a dream of eternity
Between a cognac and Nairobi.
Does she think of me still
Or is the reality too harsh
As she dusts the china dog?
Like Prufrock
"Dare I eat a peach
Dare I disturb the universe"
Dare I tap the traveller in front
As he sips his port
Served from left to right
To tell him a Roslynn and the secret of life
All in one breath?
Have I the right and have I the reason?
Blue blue eyes and old, cold heart
(My heart is elsewhere)
High in the sky
Zonked at altitude.

A. J. Gordon

Flaunting An Old Planet

The rapidly melting countryside,
Of deep Green pastures, lily filled ponds,
slow lazy rivers, sharp cut lawns;
Heavy smelling machines, cut wedges,
Dump foul rubbish and sweaty bitumen;
Pale Blue skies, wave smashed beaches,
Dark round mountains, a long road breaches;
Luminous toxic waste, concrete slabs.
Selfish men in many stale state labs;
Eroding green belts, wearing fur lined pelts;
Six legged lambs, two headed deer,
Drooping Red trees, the plough turns up a gear;
Acid covered lands, ghost haunted cities,
Hard fought plans, self inflicted pities;
Deserts of black ice and Yellow-Green sand,
At an enormous price:
A fancy sounding band plays a haunting lament,
To the flaunting of an old planet:

Paul Gallagher

Cassino-1943

Once where honour bled in green fields there lies still,
One at least I knew,
Whose every drop of blood was shed, that we might climb the hill-
A grim memorial there remains, a careless cross, a helmet,
flowers to recall lest we forget, the toll of those last hours.
No tears, no sorrowing no funeral bell, can remove death's shroud,
nor the Very lights at dawn produce another fear;
the shadowy clouds cast not a tear,
to animate him who fell.

Let Honour invoke a Silent Prayer and Peace to his Martyred
End of Strife.

Ronald Salter

Morning Call

This morning feathers tell the story:
The ground a triptych of distress.
The urgent summons was a call
To carnage, broken bodies, last fading breaths;
Memento mori in the watery dawn.
This was siege slaughter; rampage; medieval.

Myth figures statuesque in the moonlight,
Grey sentinels who turned their backs,
Were dreamers betrayed into rear guard action.
Later we searched the silent garden
Without hope; haunting the refuges, guilty among the dead.
All day, the leaves stirring in uncertain dread.
Too late. The cockerel's anguish and tumult cries
Wake us at morning to a bloody assize.

Mike Evans

The Candidates

Heavily falls the rain
Like bullets resounding on a tin can roof.
Persistently pattering, pervading the air.
Leaving it chill and damp adding to the despair.
While in the room the candidates wait
Troubled and pensive not knowing their fate.
Time travels slowly as the tension swells.
Last minute cramming, nails chewed to the bone.
Heads bowed, absorbing knowledge
Individuals alone.
Isolated and silent, coping with stress
As intermittent twitches withhold the calm.
No point in bolting, causing alarm.
While one by one to the slaughter they're lead,
Foreign conservations infused in their head.
Heels tip-tap on a vinyl floor
Followed by a soft-shoe shuffle as they reach the door.
Slowly it closes as the butterflies churn
Recognition, realisation.
The point of no return.

Glenys Fishburn

Embers

You left me, sitting by the fire,
Shadows drawing, with winter coming.
You left me by an ash grey pyre,
To face the chill, so surely growing.
And yet, I lived.

You took all I wanted with you,
Hope and light and the need to live.
You took all these as your final due,
The very things that I dared not give.
And yet, I gave.

You tried hard, with your final look,
To mark my mind, for the lonely years.
You tried hard, by the things you took,
To leave no trace, or relief in tears.
And yet, I wept.

You went away, through the mists of time,
Winding perhaps, to your final shroud?
You went away, with no other sign,
But in my mind dear, clear and proud,
And yet, we live.

C. R. Jury

Fog

The damp swirling mist was all around
Blotting out the familiar landmarks of the town
The muted sounds of the traffic on the street
Like ethereal beings drifting in and out of focus as they creep
Was echoed by the hollow footsteps of passers by
Like Zombies with hidden faces - distant yet nigh
The icy fingers of penetrating cold
Were identified by both young and old
With hunched shoulders and coat collars turned high
Hands thrust in pockets as if nature itself to defy
As evening drew on the sombre darkness deepened
Producing eerie glimpses of lights as if imprisoned
Within a veil of encircling gloom
A foretaste of impending doom
Quiet sounds were faintly heard
of ghostly footsteps and the stilted word
Night came with a new dimension of strife
Like an Alien planet devoid of life
It was silent - all at home safe and sound
Similar to a fox evading the hunt and gone to ground

Alan G. D. Matthews

Untitled

Locked in my head are thoughts
Clamped tightly as if with a key.
To express some emotion, some feelings
Seems now far too taxing for me,
Sometimes I feel happy, sometimes I feel bleak
But never before was unable to speak
Of the joy, of the pain, of the loss, of the gain
And put it in words on fine paper to keep.

Mid life crisis what a thought
It could be "writer's block" but not.
Lack of practice seems the reason
Or stale of spirit, heart just freezing.

Let me loose to soar once more,
Heat me up with passion raw,
Let me find my heart just bursting
My spirit and my soul just thirsting.
Words and memories let them flood
Until they fall like rushing blood
From cuts so deep within my soul
My thoughts and dreams in torrents flow.

Susan Parkinson

Inside The Asylum

Terrorized, brutalized, victimized,
The eyes,
The tears, the fears.
The abused and confused.
The addicted, restricted, from the fix
They are craving.
The guilty in silence;
While the unrepenting are unrelenting
And raving.
Hell bent on destruction.
The unkempt and demented,
Unloved and tormented.
The tortured, the haunted, the fraught,
Frightened, still fighting, they fought,
The captors of their minds.
The depressed, the oppressed, obsessed
And despairing,
And most still uncaring,
Outside those high walls.

Susan Belinda Butcher

The Rose

O Beauteous Rose, O mystical Rose,
So precious, so tender, so full of repose,
Displaying your colour of many a hue,
Spreading your charm to all those who view.

Your raiment of petals, like velvet, unfold
More precious than silver, more splendid than gold,
Opening your centre — a heart so serene
Adding peace and contentment to many a scene.

You spread an aroma so sweet to the sense
Evoking fond memories of just such a scent.
It touches the heart and gladdens the eye
I treasure my Rose — now sweet rose good-bye.

Angela Murphy

The Sidings

Years ago, it was a very useful piece of land
Kept as a Railway Siding
Storing coal for trains, that come and go

Then much later Ownership was re-assigned by hand
A Builder took a liking
With a vision of houses in a row

Very soon it became work-place for a toiling band
So many skills providing
Shape, midst dust, noise and dumpers to and fro

And now the transformed area really is quite grand
Red hand fashioned bricks rising
Into homes, where commuters rush and flow

But one is extra special, has pets and pit of sand
There, children are residing—
Have lovely eyes and faces all aglow

How different now that very useful piece of land
Kept as a Railway Siding
Storing coal for trains, that still come and go

Ellen Wayland

Untitled

In Manchester where I was born
None had time to be forlorn
Where there's muck! There's Brass Old Ted
Would say - but I want grass on which
to play - not scrub and clean pavements
every day! I shouted at him.
Then be off and find it the Old Sod!!!
Said; Out came my tongue - was his face red!
Soon I will be 4 score and seven
live in the South. It's really heaven
except for the pavement's looking rum
a gift from U.S.A.? Say some Mancunian's "Eh" by "Gum!"

Ida I. Radford

My Life

I could not live without you, my love of many years.
Beside me as my husband, allaying all my fears.
I wouldn't want to leave you - not voluntarily,
Sometimes it just happens, if it is meant to be.
I want to tell you darling, you mean the world to me,
Each year, each day, each hour, a lifetime of harmony.
Our loving warm companionship, just the two of us alone.
Together when our family left to build their loving homes.
You listen when I talk to you, hold me when I'm sad.
I value all the special times, the joys that we have had.
We've trodden down life's path we two, love's foundations
  built on rock.
We've let the sunshine come right through, have weathered
  stumbling-blocks.
And so my dear, if it should be that you can't see me any more.
Remember darling I am there, in your heart for sure.
I'm only just a thought away, behind Gods heavenly door.
Close by and always waiting, until we meet once more.

Anne Baker

Bullies

Day by day,
Always walking away.
How much to take,
When to break.
Can't take no more,
Life or moored.
She stares again closer she comes,
Shouting and screaming.
Standing and leering.
How much to take,
When to break.
Tell a teacher they say,
Laughing and sneering, dying for a fight.
Walk away I say,
Leave the bullies alone.
No more, I can take,
No more, I shall take.

Maria Jones

The Outsider

The cold, westerly, wind whips my cheeks,
How long has it been? Years, days, months or weeks?
As I stand alone in this desolate land
The things I feel, are with my heart, not with my hand.

I am abandoned, deserted, in this hellish place,
Myself and my visage, my drawn, gaunt face.
I run and run, and pound my fists on the ground,
And now I see a window as I turn around.

Inside, there is a family, with warmth, love, and who care
I stare, and I sigh, and I wish I could be there.
I tap on the window, hoping they will hear,
But why would they want me, need me or care?

My solitary confinement is to a life of confusion,
In my head I create a world of love; the window, an illusion
I am all alone, scared, as my eyes grow wider
With no family or friends, I am an emotional outcast, the
outsider.

Melissa Teale

Untitled

I have a friend with lovely red hair,
A very dear friend who shows that she cares.
She is good and she is kind which is terribly rare.
We go out for walks and we look everywhere.
We look at the flowers and the scenery around.
We talk of our childhood and the things
that we've done. The good things the bad things
for we are not nuns. We laugh and we chatter
of our childhood days and at night we thank God
for a lovely day, and the last thing we do is
we gently pray to that God up above for a Beautiful Day.

C. T. Krapp

Written On The Beach

He made the earth, the sea and the sky;
He made the sand and the seagulls cry.
He made the boats, that rock on the gentle foam,
For we are His hands, our hearts His home.
Rebel we might, but when all is said and done,
Without Him we're nothing, we rely on Him alone.
He made us all and to Him we must return
And render our account of life's sojourn.
Then we must face the sinless Ones -
Father, Son and Holy Spirit -
When their continued love we hope we'll merit.
Then we'll leave the earth, the sea and the sand
And enter, we hope, into God's happy land.

Pamela Flavin

The Untold Story

The start begins to fade
As my memories eye closes
Upon the pages earlier made.
No longer do I remember
When the chapter of childhood was closed,
And my life now, crept out from under
The cover of innocence, out into the cold.

My life, my future like chapters of a book
One page read as each sun sets,
Yet to finish but I cannot look
To see what fate has in store,
As it's only the last page of my book that can tell
Of how life closes its final door.

Each day a new page unfolds
To let me read a little bit more
Of what my future holds.
How many pages have I left to read
Of this book - thick of thin?
Will I at last in my life succeed?
Why can't I now be told?

Lisa Robinson

Dogs Island

I wade into the water with some trepidation.
He keeps telling me to go out
Farther or the gun will kick too much.

So I have to be on flat ground.
My slight and blurry vision doesn't help,
But you see, the bright light hurts my eyes
He never remembers that.
'Call when you're ready,' he says.
He sits like a king
He seems excited I can handle this gun so easily.
I aim towards the sky, brandishing
The hot metal to my cold cheek.
Just to burn me a bit.
It makes me more accurate
Then I pull,
And fire.

Jessica Freels

Evening Sky

You, beautiful sky this evening,
You are not true, you are deceiving.
Adorned in pink edged indigo dresses,
You lure me, I long for your caresses.
I know you are trying to make me believe,
You are the arms, to embrace and receive
Me, into heaven when I die,
But I know differently, in final goodbye,
There'll be no heaven, there'll be no hell,
With all other dead I will dwell,
Nowhere, just dissolved into eternal peace,
As happens, when all lives cease.
You do not fool me, ethereal sky,
Although so beautiful, you are false and a lie.

P. J. T. Porter

Untitled

The faded bricks of the old court yard
Warmed by the sun over countless years
There sleeps the cat like a ball of fur
But not unaware of the black birds call
Too old to bother his aging limbs
For he knows he can no longer win

The lilac tree with its shading leaves
A shelter high above earthly things
The lovely blossoms their scent imparts
Memories so dear to the heart

And then as evening shadows fall
Still enclosed by those old brick walls
Are all the joys of by gone days

We feel more safe when night must fall
as we lock up the gate in the old yard wall
We hear the rustle of the tree as the
wind stirs the branches to let us see
That through sun storm and moonlight there still remains

The sun warmed bricks though faded and old
To guard what was planted so long ago

Mildred Reid

The Romance And The Reality

For Christina

We sat that morning,
Do you remember?
Our cold hands clasping,
the cafe coffee cups.
We watched the dawn come up,
above the grey horizon of November.
With colours brighter than we'd ever known.
As if God was painting us a brand new world.
And in the corner of your eye,
I saw a trembling tear, like a diamond in the moonlight.
I thought for one moment, that it was our love, or maybe me.
But I knew that it was only the coldness of the wind.
Then softly I heard
your far away voice say, "Come".
And gently you took my hand in yours, and said...
"I've got to go to the dry cleaners".

A. Oram

A Zoo-Illogical Tale

When the boss of the circus said "Hop it!"
  As he fired the old grey kangaroo,
His soft-hearted wife pleaded "Stop it,
  Let's donate the poor thing to a zoo."

So the musical 'roo found a niche at the zoo,
  Where he sat on his tail every day,
Playing outside the loo on a didgeridoo
  In its own very primitive way.

With a tempo so wild that the crocodile smiled,
  Every chimp feel about like a chump,
The hyenas laughed till they nearly went daft,
  Though it gave both the camels the hump.

Big elephant feet stamped in time to the beat,
  Six cobras swayed high in a trance,
All the polar bears clapped as they listened enrapt,
  And the penguins joined hands for a dance.

But the didgeridoo was upsetting a gnu,
  And the keepers' nerves started to fray,
So they paid the 'roo's fare to Australia, by air,
  With a pouch full of lager and hay.

Alex McLeish

Untitled

I wish I loved the Human Race,
I wish I loved its silly face,
I wish it would find another place,
And jog along at a steadier pace.
I wish I knew where it was going,
I wish I knew what it was doing,
I wish I knew what it was brewing.
As it takes us along the road to ruin,
Its latest plan must not prevail,
There must be no human eggs for sale,
There are many flaws that might entail.
It is a very wicked innovation,
To take the soul out of the Nation,
And leave alone with mass creation,
And lives to be spent in desolation.
Oh! May there be a little cheer,
With a change of fortune in the following year,
A chastened mien, a little grace,
Return at last to that human face.

G. I. Webb

Lost Ages

I found them on an island
in a lake poisoned by acid rain
It had been a long hot winter
and I could wade to the ruin there

It was a place long forsaken
overgrown with bracken and thorn
But if my mind hadn't been broken
I couldn't have opened the door

They blinked as I came near to them
eyes grown accustomed to night.
Said, "Who wakes this sleeping king and queen-
What need to have of Light?"

I did not know what to make of them.
Were they real, or mad-what was I?
From all around and about I heard laughter
Noticed a promise clenched tight on their lips

Then I watched them become dragons
rise like angels upon the dark wind
yet where their breath touched the scorched earth
sprang a garden of flowers

P. J. Thompson

The Last Flower

Ah woodbine, wild honey suckle the sweet scent of your
bloom drifts upwards on the warm evening air to enter my
room and lay my heart bare. How often I waited by cottage
gate and smelled your perfume growing stronger as the hour
grew late, then fading in the cold and silence of early dawn,
leaving my poor heart wretched and forlorn. Three times the
honey suckle bloomed, three times I felt my love was doomed
there was no word, how can this be-how can this be? My heart
trembled with lonely dread, dear Lord let him not be dead! Three
times the honey suckle bloomed, three times I thought my
lover doomed yet in my heart he came to me, how can he not
live, how can he not be? his eyes aglow with love for me, and
sword affixed with silver buckle glinting neath the honey
suckle. As the flowers faded once more I waited-yet with little
hope. A messenger came-the last flower fell, my anguished
heart broke. Ah woodbine, wild honey suckle hold my lover
fast that I may go to him at last, there is nought in life to bind
me here but remembered love and lonely tears I wish only to
die that I may be with my love through all eternity. I shall go
to where he waits for me, proud in uniform with silver buckle
'Neath the woodbine, the wild, sweet, honeysuckle.

Christine Yeoman

443

"The Birth"

The night was cold, the sky was bright
Up above a shining light
Jesus was born it seemed to say
It turned the night into day

Church bells were ringing far and wide
Showing the way to Jesus Christ
Christmas Eve has come once more
A time for rejoicing, all grief must go

The candles in church, show of new life
God's gift of his son, after all that we've done
All that he asks is for peace in the world
For all enemies and foe to talk once more

The peace in his message brings warmth to our souls
Helping us achieve our goals.
The greatest gift of all he gave
Was love and forgiveness for all our sins

Helen Lennox

The Seasonal Year

The first season of the year
Beautiful spring is in the air.
The coloured flowers come to light.
Some are pastel, some are bright.

The second season of the year,
When the sun is warm and clear.
Holiday time for fun and pleasure,
Lots of memories to treasure.

Third season of the year,
When green turns to gold,
Because autumn is here.
The leaves curl and tumble down.
To come to rest upon the ground.

The fourth season of the year
The weather is cold with chill in the air.
But then comes joy and happiness
For it's Christmas Time, and all is Blessed.

Shirley Grant

Vast Is The Universe

Heavenly bodies inhabit the sky,
Astronomically way, way up high,
Patrolling the heavens, making no sounds,
Each keeps within its own limited bounds

So many millions and so far away,
How we marvel at their splendid array!
Who was it made them? Who planted them there?
What is their purpose? Do we have a share?

Many we know and to them names have giv'n,
Millions of others are dotting the heav'n;
The span of the sky is beyond our ken,
Its countless secrets not all giv'n to men.

A tiny, wee body is Earth up there -
Just a speck in the Universal air!
Look up and ponder - you'll surely agree
Vast is the universe, so small are we!

B. F. Smyth

Me

I'm a pretty blue-eyed girl
With a natural curl
I'm a size eight figure
But I don't hate what I see in the mirror
All my friends take me for what I am
If I get a spot they don't give a damn
I haven't got a boy friend but I don't care
My time will come when I'll have my share

T. Mason

Spring Song

A windy day and the rooks fly high
Catch if you can, they seem to cry
Twisting and turning, I love to watch
As those blue black birds play their game of touch

What are they dreaming of up above
Nests to build? A mate to love?
For once a bird has his chosen mate
It's till death us do part, no quarrels or hate
To dull the sparkle of two bright eyes
As they follow their partner through wind-tossed skies.

So many elms, dying and dead
Where will they roost, can their young lay their head
Among pines straight and tall
Please rooks decide, there's room still for you all.

Edna Buckner

The Junction Road At Dusk

The light still lingers on,
    While bamboo and sugar cane
    Stand etched against the sky.
The night grows darker, and I dimly see
    Sheer cliffs, and rivers either side.
A country bus belches black smoke
    And homebound cars
Move slowly along the tortuous mountain road.
    A crescent moon shines brightly overhead...

Tonight I'll dream of sunlit surf
    Pounding on sandy shores,
And shining palm trees waving in the wind,
And feel a deep and heartfelt thankfulness
    For these remembered joys.

E. Prince

Midden Hills

Hysteria grabs us in media alarm,
The animal feed poisoned at the farm,
This revealed, what about the rest,
Vegetables with pesticides, to make them the best,

Chemicals are added to everything we eat,
Gives us diseases, demolishes our teeth,
Chemicals in tap water can dull the brain,
Liquid brain disorder, from the water main,

Go out of the factory away from the fumes,
Inhale the air, in polluted plumes,
The factory smoke forms acid rain,
Which kills the trees and green terrain,

Illnesses caused from electricity power stations?
Atomic plants, hospital creations?
Is it economical schemes,
Which tantalize our ecological dreams?

Paul D'Gama

The Cashier's Retirement

Thanks for the funding we have had,
Emotions at present are sad,
The future can only be bad,
but for you 'retirement' can only be glad,
Enjoy the Sun, Relax in the garden,
drink champagne, whoops beg your pardon!
Stretch out and reach for your Sunday magazine
Take time and read all the latest scenes.
For your honour, a cake or two,
nothing too fancy, a buffet will do!
A drink or two with friends that you have met,
over the years, there's bound to be tears,
So dry your eyes and eat your pie,
dab with a hanky and enjoy your retirement party.

Andrea Jackson

A Love Burning Without Desire

Then when the morning light hits your face
and your heart is full of praise.
I Thank the Lord that you are mine
and hope you feel the same as I,
and when the leaves fall off the tree
I know that winter is on its way.
Let's talk about the birds and bees
because only your breath can set me free.
My love for you is like a fire, burning without desire.
Oh let us make sweet love all night long
and make the world go round and round.
So let it be just me and you and
let the world go round and round.

Chris Michanicou

The Highway Man

Down on the road, by the old turnpike, in the dead of
night, the clatter of horses hooves, but only long shadows to
be seen, cast by pale moonlight.

Then they appear, to those who can see, the foraging
fox, and the tawny in the oaks rambling ivy.

Mounted on a phantom steed, a black cloak and a mask
so thin, he makes his way to the village and his favourite
coaching inn.

Passing by, the sound of laughter wakes the night from its
slumbering lull, the smell of well stoked clay pipes, and pewter
tankards brimming full.

Ever onward past the church, for him no chats by the
fireside or well woven tale, no mortal pleasures, no feather
bed or pints of warm flat ale.

As if beckoned ever further, up the winding road
where the coaches once ran, no more ill-gotten gains or
flashes in the pan.

Then climbing the hill, where the gibbet, long gone
once stood, he heaves a sigh, then melts away into the
shadows, of the ancient tangled wood

Steven Travar

My Sorrow

I gaze from my window - and what do I see?
Never the moonbeams that dance on the tree,
Nor the swift owl as it swoops in to land
But the ghosts of our soldiers on some foreign land.

The crashing surf took them that terrible day.
It was: "Over the side, lads." and "Away, boys, away."
With white anxious faces they struggled ashore
Against mighty odds to enter the war.

Several survived, but thousands were lost,
Battles are won - but what of the cost?
What of the mother, and what of the son -
There is no future now for her beloved one.

Whatever the reason, whatever the rhyme,
The pattern of war takes men in their prime.
Life is so precious, oh why can't there be
A better way for mankind to live free?

Patricia Farr

Come Take My Hand

Come take my hand and walk a while along a beaten track,
It may be to the promenade to the sea and back,
Or we could walk through country lanes that wind to views unseen,
Come take my hand I'll lead you to where you've never been.

Walk along a river bank on a sunny day,
Ripples with sunlit riders meander on their way,
A gentle breeze to caress your face and whisper through your hair,
Come take my hand and walk a while and I will take you there.

Brian Ashton

Father

Son (question)
Father, dear Father where have you gone?
For here I sit I am your son!
No care for one second, one moment's embrace
You have given me life, and this human face
I do not know of you, I would like to I'm sure
Not to dislike you, but to know you more
My mum's tried to show me through threads of tapestry.
Why doesn't she face up to it, and come and tell me?
I've known for a long time, but held it inside
This thing you will not, and cannot hide!
Father, dear Father, where oh where how tall are you?
What colour your hair? We can't say we're sorry.
What's done is done but at least I can say, I'm my mother's son.

Mother (answer)
To answer the question that torments your mind
I could say so much, but leave so much behind
How can I tell you? Would you understand
How wonder love become sifted sand.
How tall was he? What colour his hair?
Like you my son, tall and very fair.

Paul Atherton

Fly Free

14th. January, 1944.

Perfect love was there in that soul - uplifting air
On you soared - to only God knows where
All that was precious banished from the dedicated mind
Gloriously set on course to save mankind as
Knowingly, laughingly cavorting in
the dance of death - and caught -
In that single, terrible, sunlit moment
by the hunters gun
Oh, the price was high to partake in such a sky.

And afterwards all hidden memory
denied its rightful place
And frame succumbing early to the years
Reverberations reaching out to touch the furthest star
Of what you were and are
How dare they judge, they who would have you conform
To what was regarded as the norm,
No pain now, no tortured nightmares heard
Fly my love, my dearest love,
Fly free, free as a bird.

E. M. Clayson

Memories Of Long Ago

As I stare out across the moor, there is inner peace throughout
  my soul.
I lay down upon the dampened grass, and watch the day
  slowly pass.
The clouds are floating way up high, my eyes begin to fill,
  I start to cry. I remember the days I was young,
With Mum and Dad, and the family, I remember when we all sung,
At Christmas time around the tree,
I remember the smell of fresh baked bread, the washing on the
  clothes horse or the back of the chair
The crisp cotton sheets that lay on my bed, my little brown teddy bear
My first day at school when I cried so much, my little red
  dress that I loved to wear
That gentle kiss, that special touch.
My family showed me how much they care.
Life is so simple when you are small,
You are given the world and you take it all.
If only I'd given a little bit more,
My innermost self, right to the core.
The sky has gone dark, and begins to rain,
My memories will have to wait again.
But in my mind, they will always stay, for recognition another day.

Ellen Jane Duvall Thompson

Untitled

Hours and minutes tick away
The last mill will close today
Winders - spinners - machines stand still.
The eerie silence of the mill.

Jute and stour got everywhere
in your clothes in your hair.
Women in aprons standing still
The eerie silence of the mill

No laughter, no smiles, only tears
memories of the past forty years.
Here I stand with my brother Bill
The eerie silence of the mill

Hugging and saying farewell to each other
Glancing around I see my mother
  Come Bob, come Bill
The eerie silence of the mill.

Pamela Glen

Requiescat In Space

There was a smile on every face
As the shuttle left the Earth for Space.
But, on that fine day in September,
Which millions have cause to always remember,
Seven brave astronauts flew so high,
Little knowing - so soon to die!

Were their lost lives but tragic waste,
The sad result of too much haste
As mankind strives to reach the stars,
First the Moon, then Venus and Mars?

But futile thoughts just bring despair,
We have better ways to show we care.
So let us hope and let us pray
That success will bless "Discovery"!

Joyce Lindsay

To Ann

Thoughts from the heart are good to read,
each shrinks miles between plain and hill.
Grey matter leaps as words cry out,
flinging stories of years before
to heights unseen encapsulating sine waves
of a voice unheard but ever felt.

Skies a'fire, a drowsy breeze,
cumulus floss, on a winter's eve.
Sleek, black crows make silhouettes,
a palette so grand in December's brief.
Shadowy ghosts stalk fleeting tints
but peering eyes stare transfixed.

As day retreats life's orb sinks
to peace, darkness and gentle sleep.

Evelyn Wilkins

What Would'st Thou?

I am weary treading city streets
Worn with the tramping of countless feet,
The deafening roar of traffic sound
The jolting and pushing all around.
I'm sure, like me, you too would frown,
Sigh for rivers running down
To meet the sea, and there unite
In spraying seagulls on their flight;
Or linger in some woodland bower
Where quiet reigns for hour on hour
Where rippling brook summer breeze
Join in melody with the trees,
Singing "God hath made this glad retreat
'Tis man who made the busy street.
Here one can write, or muse or play.
Chase all worldly stress away.

Therese McVey

Henpecked

This is about a battery hen,
who sits all day and wonders when,
someone will come to set her free.
How nice a breath of fresh air would be.

Her life is so different from hens on the farm,
she is cooped up all day where it is warm,
sat in a row with her unfortunate friends,
in a perfect line that never bends,
of small compartments like tiny cells.
They're very hot and each one smells.

This restricted life is no good on the legs,
but no one cares so long as she lays eggs.
Certainly a real jailbird,
she's that in every sense of the word.

A glimpse of daylight would be just fine,
the pure clear air would smell like wine,
though there is no hope of any change,
her favourite dream is to be free range.

F. Patricia Firth

Untitled

I try so hard, I try in vain,
But, nothing seems to ease the pain.
It grinds away deep inside,
As tear drops flow from my eyes.
Nobody seems to understand
As pain is something no-one can,
It is not something we can see,
But from within, that we must deal,
I'm tired now and so worn out,
I do not have the strength to shout.
To tell, to plea, to disagree,
I just want, to make these people see.
Maybe one day they'll show concern,
To do that they will have to learn.
Must I teach them one by one,
A lesson with each rising sun.
As each dawn breaks, a new day is born,
And with it should melt a little forlorn.
We must hope one day, laughter it will bring
Happy faces, smiling eyes and voices that sing.

Gretta Geoghegan

Loss Of A Friend

The house is so empty without you,
I don't have to run for a chair,
But it's hard to come to terms with
The fact that you're no longer there.

My tears still fall, for I miss you
When I look at your photo, I cry.
My sad eyed gentle giant,
How my years with you flew by.

That terrible day was a nightmare,
I had prayed for your life, all night
I hoped against hope, as we carried you in,
A miracle would make you alright

I knew what the vet would tell us,
I listened, not wanting to hear,
You cried out in pain as he checked you
It was all just too much to bear

He shook his head, as I knew he would
I had to say Good-bye,
I wept, and held you, and told you I loved you
Then I had to watch you die.

Jane Ricketts

This Curse

Unwritten dreams play across his mind as a way of
escaping the real world. Ray-ban shades cover his eyes
in the hope that he can fool the man in the mirror.
A permanent frown is tattooed on his heart as a
distant memory rolls around again. It may be only one
word but at one time or another it's broken everybody's
heart. He remembers everything about her like it's
branded on the underside of his brain. Her name those
three letters still haunt his nightmares as he's tried
everything from trying to out-drink it to meaningless
sex to erase her memory. If she were here she may
think it funny that the only lesson he's learnt is
that making love is so much easier when you love the
one you hold. But then she never loved him for as till
now he always doubted love was real.   Then if that were
true what's tearing his heart in two. Her smile calls
him from the far reaches of his mind and as he tries
to run away he falls to his knees and prays in the
name of mercy to be released from this curse called
love.

G. Turner

Our Passing Out Parade

How long we've waited for this day
    and now it's here at last,
The doubt's and fear's, blood, sweat and tears
    are behind us in the past,
This is our day and we are proud
    for we have given our best,
We've worked ourselves into the ground
    now we deserve a rest,
Looking back on thing's we've done
    since first we came down here,
Sometimes they really got us down, each day seemed like a year;
But we've won through and passed the tests we've really
    made the grade,
So here we stand with head's held high on our passing out parade,
Our parents, friends and loved ones are here to share our day,
We see their smiling faces and sometime's hear them say,
"Just look how smart our son is, oh! don't they all look great,
I think I'm going to cry love, they really are first rate,"
But now at last we can relax, our day is at a close,
We've worked, we've sweat, and we've passed out
    But How! God only knows.

Carole J. Matthews

A Female's View

The morn has broken life awakes
Gone the night, you've got what it takes
Arising for work to face another day
To toil and graft it won't go away.

Some routine the monotony of life
Thirty years of being a wife
Gone the kids they flew the nest
Only the husband the biggest pest.

Lounging around watching the box
As I wash his sweaty socks
The house again is spic and span
Why do I have such an idle man

A helping hand once now and then
Fat chance, he's asleep on the couch again
One day, I say I'll pack up and leave
Who am I trying to deceive.

Sixteen hours feeling rather dead.
Another day over, time for bed
Crawling into sheets satin and blue a kiss goodnight
I do it all for the love of you.

R. J. Baird

Reminiscent Forever

I walked into the stone cold house
While the sun was blazing out;
The noise of the ice-cream van fading
As the door closed behind me.

Adults wailing left and right,
Up and down and all around;
Women revealing their deepest grief
With straight-faced men by their sides.

Children's laughter echoing in the house,
Oblivious to life's ultimate chapter;
Looking through their sorrowful parents
Without a care in the world.

I walked passed the crowds of people
Towards the once live body;
A sight both horrific and peaceful;
A sight reminiscent forever.

Vathani Nathan

Hunger For Peace

The other day I saw a sight
    a frightened rabbit poor wee mite
Taking scraps from human hand
    in a snow-covered winter land
It shows that hunger can cure fear
    when thoughts to run all disappear
It made me think now our world depends
    on each of us all being friends
The act of this rabbit now has brought
    the answer to those wars being fought
The fact that friendship is a must
    so we should keep it oiled it doesn't rust
Let us all join hands and pull together
    through troubled times and stormy weather
If we all put our shoulders to the wheel
    this world will keep an even keel.

Lachlan Taylor

The Children Of Dunblane

They were the future
They were the hope
For a world expunged of misery.
Yet, in a flick of an eyelid in time
Those dreams of temporal utopia are gone.

But can we accept that the end of such sweet innocence,
Limited only by its earthly influence of five short years,
Has left no legacy, no justification of their being?

Or could it be, encompassed within that chaotic order
So incomprehensible to our understanding
Lies their raison d'etre; limited in tenure and of unthinkable
    finality
Yet, in the very enormity of its abhorrence
We who are left re-awaken our will to conquer evil with good
And with such awakening comes inching progress in our civilisation.

They are our future
In death, they are our hope.

E. R. C. Lunn

Today

When darkness falls, or clouds obscure the sun,
When nights seem endless, and the day is done,
And every hour you fill with things to do,
You know that sadly there is only you,
You think of all the happy times when there were two,

No one can understand how much you miss
The ordinary things, the hug the kiss,
The memories are painful, always there,
Thank God you had so many years to share,
And as with spring the days move on and grow,
Morning will brighten and the clouds will go,
Each day will be a mountain you will climb,
But healing won't be hurried, it takes time.

Nadine Cope

I Did It My Way

A body that used to be taut and lithe
has now gone all rusty decrepit and stiff
Lustrous hair and skin simply glowing
instead I see wrinkles - and grey hairs are showing
I gaze in the mirror, it's now plain to see
That "Old Father Time" has finally caught me
I turn round the mirror, calender too
My fortieth birthday! The postman now due
I race to the front door, cards flooding in
I gather them up and head straight for the bin
all traces of evidence must be disposed
the bin men arrive alas I'm composed
Exercise, face creams, the experts all say
will help keep us younger and wrinkles at bay
but my way's more simple - I reach for the wine
and suddenly dismal days brilliantly shine
Wrinkles now vanished with this magic potion
music now blaring stiff joints in motion
I'll slip on my mini and hold in my tum
and grow old disgraceful, to me it's more fun!

Patricia Wilson

Memories Nine Elms Depot 1956

In the yard at nine elms depot they lay a dozen strong
Shrouded in steam and drifting smoke, a noisy, hissing, throng.
The Red Knight and Sir Kay were there and along with proud
   Queen Guinevere
Okehampton, Whimple, Joyous Gard and Appledore were seen.
Lord Anson, Charterhouse and Stowe with safety valves
   about to blow
Mixed with Bulleid "Channel Packets" smartly painted
   Brunswick green.
Those Arthurs, Schools and Nelson are now but just a dream
At rest in Nine Elms Depot in the days of Southern Steam.

Down in Nine Elms Depot, it's many a year ago
Since wisps of steam from sleeping giants wafted to and fro.
With the smell of smoke and oil and men grimy from the toil
Of preparing Elder Dempster Lines for the run to waterloo,
And the glow from the firebox and a roar from the cylinder cocks
As the engine backed down slowly with a wave from the
   cheerful crew-
A grizzled veteran and his mate, a skilful top-link team
Now gone from Nine Elms Depot along with Southern steam.

Mike J. Thurbon

Vincent Is Sitting In His Room And Weeping

Music that burns with righteous passion
From behind locked doors with broken hinges
I watch her like television
She opened her eyes and smiled
Eyes wet with sentimental tears
Most beautiful of women
I paint you better and better
"I am a door" I heard her say
"You may walk next to my wall".

Michael Leonardward

Time

Time is passing by too quickly
I have not done the things I wanted to do
And not wanted enough to do the things
I should have done
Is there time
The days are crowded
Hours are wasted
Hours are enjoyed
Should people be chosen to share your
Precious time
Or should they be tolerated and made the
Best of
Who decides what path of life we chose
Yourself you are your own master

Lillian Halliwell

Amaryllis

Not having green fingers
(Killer even of cacti!)
I was chary of the Woolworth's bulb
Presented by my sister at Christmas.

I followed instructions.
And was reminded of her daily,
Now in Denmark,
As the thing began to burgeon
At an alarmingly pleasurable rate.

I sent her a postcard
To inform her of its progress.

It became a joke
Among my friends
Who giggled at its gorgeous trumpeting
  priapic obscenity
Erect on its firm green stalk.

The flowers have faded
Though shoots continue to sprout.

It is a shame that I have to lay it flat
In some dark place.

Agnes L. Conway

1066 Or Something Like That

Cromwell's crumbling castles,
neatly nestling on well-kept lawns,
all misty murk on a cobwebbed morn.

Abbots abbeys and archbishops arches,
holding flat topped towers, like table mountains.
And spurting spires like static fountains.

Foundering foundations and foundering beliefs,
while a nearby church is preyed on by thieves.
Rolling lead like a carpet of grey.

Carved capitals on corinthian columns,
supporting leaded windows of saints and kings.
Like lattice veined damsel fly wings.
A gleaming lustre in a kaleidoscope cluster.

Tombs and catacombs, manuscripts and dusty crypts.
The crowd pay there entrance and rush in quick,
if it's sunny today we will have a picnic.

His holiness woken from centuries unknown,
as a car alarm screeches in a monotonous tone.
The last time I was awoken was when the church bells rang late.
but that was just the black death in 1348.

Peter Anthony Kelland

Mother

We shared good times, my mother and I,
Sad times too came into it.
Hers was a shoulder on which to cry,
She made me laugh with her undulled wit.

Eighty-six, but young at heart,
A dancer in her younger days.
Nimble, upright, oh so smart,
A little vain in some of her ways.

Back from one of her flying jaunts,
She took ill, then took to her bed.
For me the change in her still haunts,
No more her dainty tread.

She refused my goodnight kiss one night
And turned her head away,
I joked, with my fingers on lips in flight.
I'll blow you one anyway.

Was there something she kept from me?
But bravely would not say?
To me, a hurtful mystery
She died the very next day.

S. Coughlan

The Magpie And The Crow

The Magpie and the Crow watching over me like doom and woe
They are there one minute then off they go

One returns but you know the other one's not far away
Doom and woe sent to darken your day

Magpies are birds you rarely see in two's
Just one for sorrow aimed at you

I could say 'I don't believe in superstition
But what if the superstition is true?

My luck is bad as it is
I don't want to tempt more would you?

The Crow sits watching over you with its beady eyes
Like a vulture waiting for his prey to die

The Magpie and the Crow watching over me like doom and woe
They are there one minute then off they go

Sarah Beverley Brown

Only A Heart Beat Away

I won't shed any more tears, love,
Because you're only a heartbeat away,
I'll smile when you're near me in the evening,
Because you're just out of sight through the day.

You're watching when I am sleeping,
Hearing me when I pray,
Sending your love to be near me,
Because you're only a heart beat away.

I'll dry my tears and smile again, love,
Remembering the happy times we've known,
Guarding the joy we discovered,
Like the love that was planted and grown.

The road will be lonely without you, love,
The future before me looks grey,
But I won't travel the road alone, dear.
Because you're only a heartbeat away.

Florence Turner

The Fish And The Elephant

He had no fear as he swam by
For he saw the gentleness in his eye
His huge frame a silhouette against the evening sky
He slowly lowered his head to drink his fill.
He let his fin tickle his trunk
So he knew that he was there
But he drank and drank till the pound was dry
And left him, gasping for air, floundering
High and dry.
As he turned around and ambled off to his rich.
Domain, the giant of the jungle. He felt no shame
But as sure as the mountains kiss the sky
And the sea's caresses the shores
For as long as I live
I'll never know why this poor fish had to die.
For in this world, were the tory lies.
And democracy rots like a dead fish.
Before your eyes.
Surely, the law of the jungle.
Still applies.

Michael Housley

The Swallow

Little swallows flying by
Cheer you up when you want to cry
Wings in the air which set them free
No problems like you and me
Crumbs of the earth is all they need
No fighting of wealth and greed
I wish I were a swallow flying from roof and tree
Looking down from above
On you and thee!

Mae Winterburn

Remembering The Land So Faraway

I remember the land so far away
that stays in my heart even today

It's filthy and dirty smells oh so bad
and yet I will say what a nice day I've had

The heat, the dust, the flies on the way
why do I love this madness I say

The marketplace noise, the rickshaw bells ring
the music so loud, and the beggars who sing

"Madam do come", the vendors would shout
"I've got the best food, should you want to eat out"

Poverty, greed and corruption you'll see
Yet the people are still happy and free

And late at night you will hear the loud cry
Of the man praying to the God in the sky

The mystical sounds and the heat of the day
makes me remember the land faraway.

J. H. Howell

Back Home

The children sat in fear and gloom
As the broken man came in the room
And as he paused to get his breath
They saw the medals on his chest.
One arm had gone and he was lame
His head was bowed with fear and shame
They did not know this broken man
And then he spoke to each of them
How did he know all of their names
His voice familiar, very strange
But then he smiled and then they knew
What this great man had just been through
They rushed to him will abated breathe
and threw their arms around his neck
Their eyes ablaze, like a shining star
This man their Dad, had won the war.

I. C. Cole

Untitled

He stumbles aimlessly along the road.
A lonesome figure to behold
A mind that's wrecked, by alcohol
Remembering little, if not at all.
But there he walks, his head held high
This poor pathetic, little guy
Looking close, you'd never guess, how he came, to such distress
Nor does it matter, you may say
Just how he came, to be this way
His only release, from a distant past
Is every time, he downs a glass
A smile, a wink, a nod, a cheer
Just watch him beg, for the price of a beer
A tragic sight, and no mistake
His mothers heart, would surely break
To see her son fall so low but then she's gone, so who will know
One more casualty, in our streets, dirty clothes drunken dead beat
No help given, as on he trudges
From simple minds, of you -
The Judges

Samuel Wright

Us

Husband, Lover, Companion, Friend -
none of these will ever end,
Here on Earth or beyond the Grave,
Unending love will always save
the Bonds, the Chains, that hold us tight,
from early morn 'til dead of night.
When darkness closes in on us,
Love holds us close, just you, me, Us.

Marilyn Leatherland

Music

Music is enjoyed around the world, in many different ways.
It's played and sung by young and old, every minute of the day.
Joy and laughter, sadness and tears.
Music brings feelings to everyone's ears,
Lullabies for babies, romance by the fire,
Pop for the children, hymn's for the choir.
There is rap and jazz, we can swing or sway.
Some that we sing, some others we play,
Orchestras, bands, quartets and trios,
Choirs, barbershop, duets and solos.
Sopranos, altos, tenor and bass voices,
Composers write ballads, marches and waltzes.
Quickstep, polka, the twist and the jive,
Feelings of happiness, glad we're alive.
Clapping our hands, stamping our feet,
Listening to Buskers who play on the street.
Film music often brings fear to our hearts,
All over the world music plays a big part.
When we are alone, music's often a friend,
It's there in our lives, from beginning to end.

Lenore E. Tomsett

The Cheetah And The Gazelles

Across from the early morning light
a herd of Thompson's gazelles leap out in sight and spread
across the plain,
and in a distant shade,
a cheetah's tail can be seen
moving across the grass,
then alerted by the presence of prey the cheetah leaves cover
and begins to stalk their way
the herd spot danger and flee
sounding the alarm for all prey that may see
The cheetah jumps out and chases the young
until one strays away,
and after a struggling fight the cheetah grabs hold with a
strangling bite to the throat of its innocent prey,
the gazelle falls down with a sharp piercing pain, and dies.
The herd watches on and grieves for the prey
as the cheetah drags off its food for the day.

I. P. Smyth

The Fight

I find myself within a fight.
  Is it wrong, or is it right?
Who will loose? Who will win?
  When this bout is held within.

I could say 'just wait to see'
  But this fight is within me,
With myself, and, against myself,
  Not to be put upon the shelf.

This, I know, is the fight of love.
  Should I stop? Am I strong enough?
These are the questions which I ask,
  As I face each coming task.

One thing I know, and can easily see,
  There is a faithful, honest, referee,
Reigning within the most treasured part,
  Which, my friend, we call the heart.

James K. D. Adams

Space

Infinite emptiness,
Limitless loneliness,
Lifetimes of nothing on every hand.
A silence unbearable, incomprehensible.
Silence profounder than absence of sound.
And yet all about one a light unbelievable,
Light from a myriad swirl of suns;
Forever the same yet forever receding,
Some forming, some fading, since time began.

Richard Todd

The Empty Cradle

Fallen leaves
Empty trees
Standing lifeless in the breeze
Cold and lonely mourns the empty cradle

Forest sleeping
Winter stays
Desolate grieving fears remain
Tears roll down upon the empty cradle

Barren land
Bleak and grey
Hoping yearning day by day
Frozen wind blowing free rocks the empty cradle

Spring-time blooms
Darkness fades
Heaven smiles it summer rays
Warm and loving giving free God fills the empty cradle

Sandra Donaldson

Untitled

All alone, nothing to see,
No one here, only me.

Been deserted, lost without trace,
Friends all gone, a lonely face

Want to get out, want to be free,
Want to be popular, want to be me.

Can't stand the heartache, can't stand the pain,
Please let me out I'm going insane.

No-one to talk to, no-one around,
Please break the silence, I need a sound

Just one more person, we'll be a team,
I need a friend or I'm going to scream.

So please don't hesitate, please don't delay
I need someone soon, I need them today.

Someone who's pleasant, someone who's fair,
A boy or a girl I just don't care

And when that day comes and I meet the one,
I'll remember this day and what you have done.

Rebecca Smith

The Boy Seaman

To be a sailor was my intent,
To "HMS Bruce" I was therefore sent.
My first meal there was green pea soup,
That nearly made me "fly the coop."

In bellbottom trousers of navy suit.
I had to march and then salute.
I learnt to say Sir and Marm,
When taking my pay in the palm.

First leave came and home I went,
To be a "Jack Tar" was now my bent.
In uniform all blue and white,
To bring tears of joy to mother's sight.

Into a "pub" was now my desire,
Of my age, they would not enquire!
In naval uniform I look'd the part,
To refuse to serve they hadn't the heart.

"HMS Ulster" was my first sea ship lent,
To Pentland Firth "she" was duly sent.
Regulars said I would learn quick,
But the sea was rough and made me sick.

Graham Smith

My World Of Heaven

Call me an angel and listen to the flutter of my wings,
For the heavens shall be my entire world someday.
Your inquisitive smile will ask me a thousand times,
But only an answer that brings you a dream shall
Collect the love you send.
Entranced by emotions that deflect your true feelings
May open eternal beliefs.
A frail road to another world is the path we walk along.
Let tides turn and file away, as the shore may cast
Its coast.
A dreaming love I lie for you upon my golden pillow.
If in flight my wings do fail,
I'll hide behind my clouds of steel.
For my sword may draw its blood,
My hands I reach to touch your love.
Beside your smile and golden charm,
I spread my dreams before your arms.
You look upon my heart's desire,
For flames of hope that burn like fire.

Duncan Burrows

How Great Is The God We Love And Serve

How can we measure a love so great
Beside a life so small
Your everlasting love for us
When unworthy are we all
But when you touch us with your love
And lead us by the hand
Our lives become a temple
Where the holy spirit stands
The power of your love
And your everlasting strength
Becomes so strong within us
We are filled with deep content
We can cope with all our problems
We are happy, we are free
Through you we are all things
You just want us to be
Jesus, we thank you, for paying the price
With your life, you so willingly gave
At Calvary's cross, you paid in full
For a debt we could never have paid.

Gladys Duriez

I Heard A Robin Sing

The spandau snarled and death searched
everywhere,
The valley froze, expectant, waiting there.
Grey clouds of smoke enshrouded everything.
And yet above it all, I heard a robin sing.

Metalled lead questing deep for blood,
Carnage now where once my friends had stood,
The spandau snarled a last defiant fling.
And yet above it all I heard a robin sing.

A Shropshire lad, among the trees I lay,
And dreamed of home. It seemed so far away.
The spandau now had spent its lethal sting.
But I had lived, because I heard a robin sing.

Brian Furber

Tormented Child

Behind the doors of unnoticed fear,
A child's cries I forget to hear.
Daring my life to close the door yet
Dreaming of what I forgot I saw.

Reliving the horror of a simple mind,
That even lost souls stay slumbered behind.
Ripping up the efforts of all my tries,
My childhood nightmares unfolded - still lies...

...So open your mind and hear my cries.

Catherine Bak

Dawn

I sit here in the morning light,
A new day begins, gone is the night.
The birds fly down to feed and drink,
I love to just sit here and think,
Of the happy times that we have seen
And different places that we've been.
I love this morning solitude
It fills me with a joyous mood.
It's so quiet and still and all you can hear,
Are the birds singing sweetly, their songs so clear.
It's a wonderful time, the start of the day,
No traffic about, no children at play.
The world will wake up soon,
The new day will start,
But the splendour of dawn
Lives on in my heart.

Sheila Herbert

The Video Game

I am a giant wizard and I can cast a spell,
To banish all these demons
Back to the gates of Hell.
I am the greatest warrior who ever strode the land,
And with my mighty sword I've hacked
Off heads and crushed them into sand.
I drive the fastest racing car there ever was and then,
I climb aboard my space-ship
And fight with small green men.
I am an elf, I am a dwarf, I am both great and small,
Just plug me in and off I go -
Not human, after all.

Kate Stuart

He Is My Man

I know he hears me...
Sees me in his dreams;
A harmless obsession.
But now I begin to see,
I care for him too.
Whether I like it or not....
He is my man; we need one another.

I shiver when he is near,
And yet I am not cold.
The butterflies brew up a storm within me,
Yet I am safe....
He trusts in me and I in him.

We have a common interest
But that doesn't matter,
We'd still feel for one another
Even without common ground.
We see eye to eye...
And even when we don't;
There is no friction
No stressed, uncomfortable air.

R. Bridge

A Star Is A Star Albeit A Twinkle

Stars were stars, a twinkle when I was little
Then enigmatic when questions I did ask.
The pictures told me they were not just twinkles
But bigger still, and perhaps dead many aeons.
They were far too far for me to imagine
Or for man to travel
Or count for that matter.
Why learn to count, I asked,
If I couldn't count my favourite stars?
The mysteries intriguing ever muddled...
And then along comes the Hubble!
And Lo! it captures a star being born.
Did I rejoice, did I care?
Only to discover the star may no longer be there?!
Born and dead a million years.. and I despair.
To console my heart I go back to Basics...
A star is a star, albeit a Twinkle.

Mandeep Bhogal

Little Pink Dress

Why do I have to be a girl, an adolescent, a woman?
Why do I have to be this gender, I wanted to be born a boy.
I don't want to be like this, I want to be like my brothers,
   not my sisters.
I want to be free.
I don't want to have to wear this little pink dress any more.

I don't want to be sexually abused,
I don't want to be beaten by my brother, my father, my lover,
   my husband,
I don't want to have to bleed every month,
I don't want to be sexually harassed,
I don't want to be raped,
I don't want to have to carry babies in my womb,
I don't want to have an abortion,
I don't want to get breast cancer,
I want to be free,
I don't want to have to wear this little pink dress any more.

I want to be like you.
I want to have your freedom.
I want your life.
I want to be free.
I don't want to have to wear this little pink dress any more.

Dawn Elizabeth Rowley

Pippa

I've said goodbye to a special friend,
Who was loyal and faithful to the end.
The time had come for us to part -
A lump in my throat, a knife in my heart.
I said a silent, secret prayer,
That I'd be strong to comfort her.
I held her tiny panting frame
And softly, softly spoke her name.
The lethal needle took its toll
While down my cheek a tear did roll.
We said goodbye on a winter's day
But always in my heart she'll stay.

A. Astles

Times Retraced

In the autumn gloom
of my small room
a soaring voice takes over:
from musty cover I discover,
suddenly, joy I can't define,
that wondrous early zest of mine.
Forgotten long these records old
and half my youth the tales they've told,
for what I chose long years gone by
was me, then; and now I sigh
for the me that was then:
the record plays over again and again
and the dreams return - and the love -
and the pain
but the love will remain.

Pamela Broster

"Eloi, Eloi, Lema Sabagthani"

Not an agonizing death on a frame of shame
But the selfless supreme sacrifice with unsought fame
"My God oh my God thou has not forsaken me."

I'll prostrate myself before thy divinity to be judged
My sins and goodness in thy scales thou shalt weigh
When eternal night blacks out the day of my short stay
After through life's lows I've wearily trudged.

'Tis the straight and narrow path of Calvary I seek
To Golgatha the cross of my shortcomings I must have
Sharp stones they redden each barefoot's sole
Humble is my proud arrogance and I'm meek and weak
Enough to need thy staff lest I fall and I'll call
"My God oh my God suffer me thy redemption to make my
broken spirit whole."

Christopher P. S. Richards

The Sea

Cold and dark.
The water calls the ghastly figure.
Drawing him closer.
Enticing him towards his doom.
He cannot escape its briny depths.
Shimmering in the moonlight.
The waves lap against the shore.
He is pulled deeper and deeper into the murky sea bed.
Despair.
He lurches violently in a valiant survival attempt.
Unsuccessful.
His attempts have been in vain.
He is suffocated by the weeds of despair.
Any residual life is squeezed from his body.
Death is the only option.

Jonathon Nobes

War

The former Yugoslavia,
The birth of World War Three,
The death of innocent civilians,
Of people like You and Me.

The Earth, its cells, they suffer,
This War is but a Cancer
Upon the surface of Gaia,
The result of Modern Warfare.

A Cancer raging beyond control,
It's 'cause an uncertain certainty,
The Ego with its dreams untold,
As plans for Genocide begin to unfold.

The renegade Ego marches on,
Gathering followers along the way,
With death and destruction its desperate toll,
The Ego surges beyond control.

The stupidity of Ego, the tragedy of War,
To illuminate the Dumb, and enrich the Poor,
While the surplus lie dead and buried,
LET'S NOT DO THIS ANYMORE!

Shaun Savage

My Old Hat

I retrieved my hat from the bottom drawer
And decided I would not need it anymore
But to throw it in the bin
Would surely be a terrible sin

Why not give it another chance
A piece of ribbon to enhance
I could add a fancy feather
Which may induce some fine weather

How about a pretty pink bow
To add to the feather just for show
I could of course visit the shore
And probably buy a summer straw

It has served me well over the years
Attending weddings, and shedding tears
I really will have to make a stance
And give the dear old thing another chance.

Sylvia Spicer

Early Days

Five thirty is illuminated on the digital alarm,
It's hello to the turbulence, goodbye to the calm
As tiny pattering precedes a tug on the quilt,
He executes his entry with no feeling of guilt.
You cling to your life-line as he claims more of the bed
- The two year old intruder with 'quack quack' and 'ted'.
He employs lunging tactics to conquer more space
And lies perpendicular with his feet in your face.
But the unsociable pamper starts to waft your way.
His chemical warfare has started the day!

Angela Tooby-Smith

452

Reflections

Your eyes reflect the depth of your soul
So deep
So cool
Yet
Passionate.
When I linger there
Glorying in your self control
You loose it...
The heat of your passion wells up
Overtakes any calculating thoughts.
There and then you see only me,
And for all that time,
I am the centre of your universe, your only thought.
Expression purely physical
All powerful
All consuming
Is the epitome of love.
Our love
Is never greater than when we possess each other.

Carolyn Carter

From Mother To Daughter

Everyone said it, wouldn't last
But 30 years we've been married,
When 7 years flew past
Then a baby I carried.
Our hearts was in a whirl
When we had a baby girl.

It doesn't seem so long ago you were small
Then one day a boy came to call,
He fell in love with our little girl
Setting her heart and life in a whirl.
We knew he was the boy for you
And one day you'd say I do.

In a carriage you rode through town
Wearing your beautiful wedding gown,
We were so proud as Shaun took you for his wife
Now you start your own married life.

Then 3 years after you marry
Our first grandchild you carry,
Happy and proud we wait for the patter of tiny feet
Thank you Sarah and Shaun for making our family complete.

Joan Wheatley

The Results Of Fire

The inner fire; the inner danger,
The havoc it wreaks, the destruction it brings,
It summons energy and power from its fuel,
The driving force of its ferocity.

It laps up family treasures,
Invaluable belongings destroyed,
Years it's taken to build up this collection,
But fire only takes seconds to manipulate them.

Fire is an element, a natural element,
It gives off choking billowing smoke,
A mother's sincere distress, her baby engulfed,
In thick black, life-threatening smoke and pure fire.

She screams with distress,
Tears pour down her cheek,
Nothing can replace her baby,
Abused by the vicious fire.

The foolish action; one gas lighter,
Is all it takes to rip through... anything,
The fire's extinguished the suspense,
As she searches the smouldering remains... nothing.

Shaun Worth

The Junk Shop

There's a Junk Shop on the corner of St. Mary's Street,
And inside a lady so gentle and sweet,
Who waits there to serve you and answer if any,
The numerous questions that come from so many.

Inside the door, stands a Grandfather clock,
An old fashioned chair that used once to rock,
There's a neat little tray full of trinkets and rings
Inside the window, among other old things.

There are lots of old pictures and modern ones too,
Also old clothing including some shoes.
There's an old fashioned shawl such as Grandma would wear,
Without a hole or even a tear.

If you should be walking down this little street,
Do not pass by the window so neat,
Spare it a glance, you'll find if you do,
You'll go right inside for a minute or two.

Inside you'll imagine the bye-gone days,
And compare all the trinkets with jewelry of today,
Which, one day who knows, may take their place,
In this neat little window of this quaint little place.

Amy Wills

Untitled

As I sit I see the land
Which was once green, now turned to brown sand,
The playful laughter of children once heard,
Replaced by the screams of a dying bird.

The flowers once bright, the trees once green,
But now not a petal or leaf to be seen.

Instead of white clouds or blue sky
Grey smoke from slums drifting by.

Factories trying to save money instead of mirth.
It's costing us a lot, in fact, the earth.

Angela Taylor

The Sacrifice

He knelt there raising fear filled eyes, Father, can this be?
Must I, Thy Only Son, be nailed upon a tree?
Oh God 'My God' the tears of blood slip slowly down my cheek.
Father, give me strength, sustain me, let not my will be weak.
You sent me, mortal man, to taste the cruelties of sin
Oh 'God' do not forsake me now, let not Satan win

I asked them to watch with me to ease my bitter fear,
But Father they are sleeping when I longed they would be near.
He looked upon the men asleep as the night wind sighed.
"Where were you, my friends in my darkest hour
when my soul near died."

The light crept slow, He stood erect, the tears were gone.
About His pale and Holy Face Heaven's aura shone.

Fran Vincent

Come Close

Come close and taste the sweetness that is me
Inside me there's a yearning to be free
Come close, unlock the door to where I hide
See the love that's waiting there and come inside

Come close and very gently take my hand
And lead me from the darkness where I am
Come close, so I can see a brighter day
That's waiting if you'd only lead the way

Come close and mend my battered, broken wings
And hold me till again my heart it sings
Come close until you're very, very near
Until at last my heart learns not to fear

Come close and hold me till I run no more
And whisper that you'll love me evermore
Come close and make me know that love is true
Till finally I trust and love you too

Linda Patterson

453

"My Son"

I had a baby, a darling boy, he was my world, my hope, my joy.
He gave a new meaning to my life, a love so different
  to that of a wife.
I missed him when he went to school, stayed at home and
  wept like a fool.
Christmas and birthdays he'd make my day,
Bringing me gifts, "I love you", he'd say.
How the years pass and boys become men,
Where's the time gone and the love we shared then?
Who took my place, a pretty young miss?
No, I think not, I could have borne this.
Mates and motorbikes, cigarettes and drink,
  all led to his downfall I think.
From being kind and happy he became cruel and mean,
  he seemed to live in a permanent dream.
Dreams travel fast like a run-away train,
  turning to night-mares and I take part blame.
Why did he turn to his love of drugs,
Making friends of thieves and thugs?
I want the return of the boy I once knew, smiling face,
  eyes of blue.
Set him free Lord, free of strife, free to learn to love real life.

Marna Harrison

Portrait Of A Debtor

It seems to me there once existed,
two small angels who persisted
in giving me all the love and joy I needed,
and succeeded,
and still do,
it seems to me.

It seems to me in this same weave,
another angel I perceive
whose open arms were ever ready to receive me,
and relieve me
through and through,
it seems to me.

It seems to me that I had better
clear myself from being a debtor,
by returning all that love and joy and pleasure;
in full measure.
Two-fold too.
It seems to me.

James Caldwell

The Old House

The leaves lay scattered on the floor
A little mouse sat by the door
The old folk watched the wind blow
This was their home of long ago
And as they looked amid their tears
Their thoughts winged back to yesteryears
Some were good, some were bad
And the little house seemed so sad.

Rose Mary Reddish

Memories

Our first meeting,
filled with anticipation and hope.
A quiet drink, shared laughter,
memories, a mixture of good and bad.

The natural way you caught hold of my hand
as we left to walk to the car.
Feelings of well-being, belonging,
things being right at last.

Our first kiss
still talking, so fleeting it barely happened.
Tender, soft as velvet,
a foretaste and promise of things to come.

Angie Smith

To Kerris

A granddad, who me! In the true sense of the word,
I cannot believe the words that I've heard.
In these times of doubt, uncertainty and grief,
You've made me happy with joy and relief.

You say in proxy I am already one,
But that doesn't compare with the joy you have done.
You are very special and no words can say
How much you have made me happy this day.

Whatever it be, either girl or boy,
No words could express my happiness or joy,
As long as all things turn out well
My latter years will be heaven, not hell!

I'm as soft as they come, but you know that by now,
And the news today has me flying and how!
I meant what I said at your reception that day,
Your happiness means more than mere words can say.

If you are happy, as I am today,
I cannot express or attempt to say,
How you have brought so much hope and joy
You are number one, who could ask for more.

Alan E. Ashwood

The Litter Lout

I dreamt I was back at school again in days
of yore, when people were poor and there was
no litter about. I woke with a start and to
play a part decided to write a poem
Look out! Look out! The litter bug's about because
he lives in the land of plenty his Tummy is full
but his head is empty he's dumping here he's dumping
there he's dumping almost everywhere
he does not care for you and me
he does not care for land or sea
"I say" he says it is not me, it comes from
outer space you see'
but one of these day he is going to be canned
I don't mean like a spaghetti or baked beans man
his days are numbered and that's for sure
because of what he has made us endure
recycling is coming in he is going out
good riddance to the litter lout.

James McFadden

The Urban Zoo

Look at a city that's beaten and broke,
See in the future no reason to hope,
Delinquency, truancy, violence, despair,
Knives on the street and drugs to spare.
Exam passes unheard of, an 'E' a surprise,
Teachers just sit tight and pray to survive.
Homes that are filthy, unhealthy and foul,
Where anger is drunken and love wears a scowl,
Streets full of weirdos, beggars and sluts
Pleading for mercy as caged monkeys for nuts,
But all the crowd does is glance in dismay
And ask why the captives bother to stay.
While those who've trapped them don't feel the pain
As their policy meetings commence once again,
They don't know the anguish, the futile endeavour,
But they have no money; the zoo will open - forever.

Sarah A. R. Adam

The Christmas Tree

The prickly pines the straight lines of branches from the stem
and at the top a star that stopped to guide the three wise men.
The tiny lights that shine so bright the presents on the ground.
The glittering glow of sprinkled snow sends a brightness all around.
The tinkering bells a story tells of a christmas tree.
And it stands so bright in the window light for all the world to see.
And one thing I know it will never go it will stay till eternity
for the tinkering bells a story tells of the wonderful Christmas tree.

P. Tanner

Life Goes On

Life is a misery, which avoid we cannot
    Journey begins with baby born into Mother Earth,
Pure as the rustling wind, shrieks with a cry,
    breaking the anxiety.
Cry of joy and happiness follows.
    'Is it a boy or a girl?' The question is asked.
I tell myself, "Who needs this?"
But down inside me, it hurts to think of what misery
    lies ahead.
Poor little creature.
Pollution, disease, corruption, lies, damn lies, injustices,
    inhumanity to humanity, war, famine, poverty and persecution.
The end is near, age catches on, death calls,
    Sadness and misery again follow,
The journey began is ended,
    Life goes on.
    Solomon F. Ezobi

First Love

I remember you dear Brenda
    So sweet and tender
I remember the joy of school
    Of helping wind your wool
I remember the laughter and tears
    Of Sunday teas of yesteryears
I remember your favourite songs
    And of course my wrongs
I remember when I saw you last
    For three minutes - it went so fast
I remember my heart was aglow
    Those brief minutes years ago
I remember it changed not your heart
    For we just drifted apart
I remember it all so well
    And through the years I always shall
I remember you dear Brenda
    My very first love — sweet and tender
    K. H. Peacock

Untitled

Heart said to Head,
"I ask not for bread,
"But the gift of grace, our life to sweeten."

Head said to Heart,
"I have no deep art
"To recall the years that the worm has eaten."

Soul said, "Leave tears.
"God's hammers, those years,
"And by them are we to His pattern beaten."
    J. W. Dickson

Sea Gulls On The Shore

At low tide
They take possession of the unfurled sands,
Scrabbling greedily for fish-heads
Cut and thrown by boatmen when they come ashore.

Their screams are raucous, air-pervading;
Unblinking eyes
Straddle jutty yellow beaks that
Probe and wrest the flesh from pebbly morsels.

A perky, motley little terrier of a dog
Runs towards their watery patch of beach,
Eager for sport and conflict.

The birds ignore him,
Tearing and gulping the last fish remnants till
No more are there. Then with contempt
They note the nearing dog and slowly spread their wings,
Lifting easily and heading seawards,
Effortless above the lapping waves.

The dog stops short and yelps
Impotently.
    Bryan Samain

Colours

If black is black, and white is white,
Then who can tell me why
Envy is always depicted as green,
And yellow the streak down my spine?
Why patches are purple and studies brown,
And clouds are grey when my luck is down.
Why herrings are red, and letter days too,
The colour I see when my tempers high.
Or who would think that elephants are pink
To a very tipsied eye?
I'll put on my spectacles (tinted pink too)
And look at the world 'til I'll think it's true,
That letters are red, and envy green,
And even - Well! Yes!
That the moon is blue.
    M. Wharton

Upon Your Face

Though you're not here I see your face
Smiling with your gentle grace
If you were mine then I would be,
In love with you for all to see
When we're apart then I am lost
And morning brings a lonely frost
For sorrow dwells upon my face
As I sit inside my lonely place
You cast your web and I was caught
Never breaking free and wanting not,
This endless pain, no hope in sight
As here alone I sit at night
And count the stars which have been placed
beneath your eyes upon your face
    Graeme George

Freedom

The freedom you offer is a pleasure to take,
    and with it comes hope,
        which is our time to come;

The love that you give is held in my heart,
    where it is nurtured,
        and tendered with care;

This feeling of calm is borne of your smile,
    which radiates peace,
        and smooths out our cares;

The joy of the morning is to see you there,
    fresh and alive,
        awaiting the day.

For all that you are, my spirit of joy,
    I smile with my eyes,
        so you can feel free.
    Louis Parker

"Our Wedding"

We are two people in our reclining years,
    both over sixty, may I add,
We met each other, in the five ways club,
    of this, I am extremely glad;
        so, once again a life to share
The simple things, to love and care;
    we're getting married 27th September,
This will be "Our" day to remember;
    with many friends, from near and far,
Some travelling by train, but most by car;
    Me! The bride, dressed up in pink,
I must admit it makes me think;
    just how "Wonderful," it is to care,
    to see, my intended, standing there;
Dressed up, in his kilt attire,
    it really sets my heart on fire;
I hope, we, shall have a "long" and "happy" life,
    I'll be, so proud, to be his wife.
    Harriet Rose

455

Growing Old

When I am old I could look back
On life so brief but sweet.
Great changes I may have witnessed
friends would have come and gone.
I may have had a family with children of their own,
living at some distance; leaving me alone.

I hope I won't be lonely,
which isn't the same thing.
With good memories for company,
My days could be rich and warm;
The passing years leaving, their legacy of charm,
My twilight time spent, in tranquillity and calm.

I would wish each person life
Could be passed like this,
but the future we cannot force,
Life could be much less kind,
And left alone in a lonely world
I might well only find
that memories of a bitter sort
remain to haunt my mind.

Emma Wallwork

Pandora's Box

Sappho her divine form unadorned slumbers
In rapturous embrace, her
Glorious arms perform
Who dares disrupt, with honeyed tongue
Her bower to invade with
Unhurried bliss and
Makes lover thrice fold
Lesbos donates this adam's rib
But what of adam, he must flee
And leave the lovers in
Harmony of chaste delight
With all impurities banished
Their joyous symphony
For all to hear
And the world shall fall
Into peace.

J. Hutchinson

Voyeur To Observe

Leaf to the ground erotic twist
Friends on the bough surely missed
Falling free, control, engage
Animal wild escapes life's cage
Spiral dive shape obscure
Natural gift there is no purer
Confused amused ruthless edge
Trying to fulfil an unknown pledge
Frightened frustrated emotions sedated
Unconscious heart chromium plated
A need to belong reject and replace
Gravity pull grand central space
Labyrinthine challenge burning core of desire
Lust, like fuel enrages the fire.

Paul Murray Watson

A Thought From Nature

Rust and yellow, red and brown
All gleaming in the autumn sun
Floating gently to the ground
Falling leaves, their life span done.

Mist swaying peacefully o'er a stream
Hangs like a veil 'twixt life and death.
The living and the dead it seems
Are linked by loves eternal breath.

For the tree of life can never die
Its roots are deep, its sap secure
Its leaves may fall as it gives a sign
Yet spring arrives and it blooms once more.

Jack Kirby

The Rose

There is nothing quite like a rose
Its beauty perfect in full bloom,
Swaying gently, silently in a pose
Oblivious of its future doom.

The deepest red and velvety bright
Covered in a refreshing dew,
After the dark restful night
To awaken as good as new.

In the heat of a glorious day
Happily sun-kissed and tinged with gold,
Buzzing bees calling on their way
Working so tirelessly, busy and bold.

Everywhere the air is sweet
A butterfly calls by to rest,
Relaxing in the gentle heat
A still and trusting graceful guest.

Unknown to the rose, tomorrow brings pain
Its beauty suddenly starts to fade,
Washed away by the torrential rain
Dearest Rose, I'm glad you were made.

Anne Carter

Innocent Victims Of Sarajevo

With haunted look on saddened face
Our hearts do ache for this proud race
Where families strolled, and children safely played,
Midst ancient buildings, with majestic domes.
Reduced to ruins now, on blood-stained paving stones.
Where man killed man, whom once as brothers lived
Humans herded into battle, ends in march to death.
No goodbye's allowed, before they massed beneath the earth
Women wait and weep for loved ones' safe return -
Not knowing of torture brutally and unrelentingly, enforced
By unfeeling war lords, obsessed with territory gains.
Unconcerned, that children also suffered injury and pains.
Some watched in horror as bodies ripped apart
Lost their innocence, with disillusioned heart.
Is life mapped out for all, with one pre-destined plan.
Or, are we led a merry dance, with man's inhumanity to man.
Do we have our own steps to hell, or climb an altruistic path,
To find eternity with loved ones, none existent wrath
When innocents starve, and tortured souls must die,
Whilst idle rich in silken sheets do lie.

Sheila Barton

The Knowledge Tree

The tree was planted years ago
In a pit they called The Grey.
Where miners and their children worked
For a pittance of a pay.

The men they worked the two feet seams
In dust, and damp, and grime.
Twelve hour shifts they were forced to work
For the owners of the mine.

The tree it grew so slowly.
In the darkness down below.
Its roots were fed with sweat and tears,
Blood and broken bones.

The tree was the Tree of Knowledge
That the miners all agreed
Was the right of education for each man's family.
The right to join a union one vote for every man.
A charter for the workers in this oppressive land.

The Grey is gone now long forgotten in the realms of history.
But the ghost of those old miners still look down on the
    knowledge tree.

John Lewis

The Magician

He holds his hands out to the air
And cards appear from anywhere,
A silken scarf, beneath his chest
Upon its edge a ball will rest.

A parasol in colours bright
He holds up to the beaming light,
And as he swings it sky to floor
You'll see it's not there anymore.

A snow-white dove flies through the air
And perches on an old cane chair,
He says a magic word or two
And changes dove from white to blue.

The audience is breathless now
And then the young man takes a bow,
And though his act is nearly done
His fingers light up one by one.

The people clap and whistle out
They don't know what it's all about,
They'll wonder how it all was done
But hasn't it been magic fun?

D. Thomas

Thoughts Of First Love

The wind whistles down the chimney
The bushes sway and dance
Leafless branches cavort on the trees
Not a morning to think of romance

Yet I sit here and think of my first love
Walking hand in hand by a stream
Thoughts only of each other
A kiss stolen, as if in a dream

No thoughts too far into the future
Wrapped up in a world of our own
There is nothing to compare with a first romance
It has a magic for us alone

After a while we drifted apart
Even good things do not last
What brought back these thoughts today
Memories from the past

Perhaps it's a sign of growing old
That was fifty years ago
The winds of time have stirred my memory
And the gale continues to blow.

Peggy Hunter

Choosing Sides

I cannot go into battle,
although I'm fighting for my life,
I have no back-up forces, she's protected,
she's already won the fight.

I thought you were my shining knight.
Sadly, I was mistaken.
You turned from me so suddenly.
My life force you have taken.

Time will heal these gaping wounds of mine,
they are hidden out of sight.
Love, you are a warlord,
you plague my soul throughout the night.

You'll see no blood-red poppies growing
in our wild green field,
you have thrown away our precious sword,
while I still hold the shield.

Now that it's all over
to the victor go the spoils.
It hurt, you chose security
when it came to choosing sides.

Margaret Casey

Loneliness And Love

The remains of my life and past are gone
Very cruel, bitter but at times it shone
The children I bore and loved abandoned me
All streets of loneliness and filth I came to see
A homeless desperate drunk for quiet sometime
I started to see, and fought back for what was mine
Trying too hard already in my lonely fight
My heart gave in with yet another fright.
Very ill and ashamed of all that was lost
I found a friend that did not count the cost
So in my twilight years I have really found
At long last a love so very sound.
Music to my heart and soul
Loneliness gone finally found my goal
Now I hear the birds sing
And fear no more of what the future brings
Happiness is what I have now at last
No more fear of the lonely past
Thanks Tony to my dying days
For you healed my lonely ways.

Marianne G. E. Van Rhee

Euphoria Remembered

Peace is a garden of sweet-scented flowers and trees.
Peace is a garden with the sound of birds chirping,
accompanied by a chorus of bees.

I sit relaxed, with serene tranquillity in the warmth
of the sun, whilst a gentle breeze caresses my skin.

I wish I could contain this feeling forever in a golden box,
and retrieve whenever needed.

My gaze beholds the whole colourful scenery.
I observe the lustrous grass so green, where there
is much activity from little black ants.
Their purpose in life, to feed their queen.

A red petal gracefully falls
from a geranium gliding gently down onto the soil, oh dear!
A fly has flown into a web under the window sill.
The spider scurries down to the victim and claims its prey,
which struggles to be free.

Suddenly the sun is engulfed by a dark cloud.
The breeze has chilled. The silence of the birds is
followed by an echo of thunder in the distance.
My euphoria whisked away by the change in the weather.
If only good feelings could last forever.

E. Dobie

Llangollen Esteddford

Mountains rising high in the skies.
Overlooking the river below
A picturesque village, full of surprise
O'er the bridge where the traffic still flow.
yet it's a field full of wonder,
A land full of song.
All the world takes part in its joy,
Beautiful voices echo around,
Each year for all to enjoy,
In national costume, they sing and they dance
Bringing love, to those who attend.
Some people have met, in a ring of romance,
And locals have found, many a friend,
So may it continue, down through the age
And may every year write one more page,
In a book of romance, as years come and go,
For this is Llangollen, so proud and so strong,
Bringing us together,
In their land full of song.

Win Davies

From Beginning To End

The daylight dawns; the morn is here;
  My heart beats out, you to cheer.
O Love from morn to night
  I await your charm's delight.

Years roll by, but there's no fear -
  Always in my heart you are near.
I keep in mind a picture for my sight
  Forever there from dark to light.

Wrinkles come, grey hairs too, my dear,
  Young ones think it funny and jeer;
But that's no need for cause of fright -
  To me you will always be young and bright.

One thing to me is very clear -
  Our Love has blossomed from year to year.
So when, my dear, a new dawn may alight,
  We together will greet it with that same delight.

  Joan Hill-Lewis

It......

Print it, sign it, date it, time it,
rules of life for earthly primate,
want it, need it, buy it, feed it,
material wealth for the climate.

Use it, lose it, forget it, misuse it,
the way till now excluding fate,
make it, break it, give it, take it,
how easily lured to the bait.

Accept it, do it, ask it, review it,
let the heart feel the vibration rate,
think it, say it, express it, pray it,
for it is never too late.

Find it, send it, mind it, lend it,
you are given time to cultivate,
sow it, reap it, store it, keep it,
forge ahead, no time to waste.

Seek it, share it, spirit spares it,
it has been there since your birth,
absorb it, digest it, explore it, test it,
use it wisely on planet Earth.

  Graham Stuart Broughton

Today

Today, perhaps today will be my last.
As I get old each dawn is a surprise.
"Appreciate the day," I tell myself,
The sun may never yet again arise.

And yet to get new memories to work
Is harder, yes, is harder every day.
The aches, the pains, they never will give up.
You try and try, and yet there is no way.

So how to keep what's left endurable?
Old memories are long, and Oh! so sweet.
The best of life has gone, but it's still there,
Just lying there, your old, old eyes to meet.

If you can see the funny side of things,
Then every minute's worth what your life brings.

  Peggie Hannen

Dad

I loved Him dearly with all my heart,
they said it wouldn't be easy when we had to part,
he helped me and encouraged me in everything I did,
whatever my problem it was never to big,
we had lots of hugs and many a good laugh,
sometimes I think people thought we were daft,
there were bad times I couldn't have got through without him,
I know we both shared this special thing,
they were right and it really was bad,
when I had, to say goodbye to my dear old dad.

  R. M. Wilcox

Grace

What matter where these toiling footsteps tread
how far along each lonely, thirsty mile.
Who cares for what may lie ahead
when eyes have seen the wonder of your smile.

Though memory only spans the gulf of years,
and dim uncertainty of time and space
leave yet unshed the unavailing tears.
Have not these fingers softly touched your face?

If in slow trial of strength this arm is bent,
while patient vultures wait and wheel above,
it will not be in vain this life was spent.
This heart has known the beauty of your love.

  R. G. Davison

Untitled

Lying here on my own,
alone in the darkness.
Thinking of the good times
that I used to have.
Why can't they see
that I'm alone in the darkness,
they don't realize what it means to be free.

Why can't they set me free?
They could just let me die.
They can't see that I'm suffering,
they don't hear me cry.
They keep me hanging on
letting all hope fly.

Why can't they see?
Think of my point of view?
Try to remember just what I could do?
They think I can't hear them
and they think I am dead.
They'll never hear my screams
because they're inside my head.

  Michele Eisenhauer

Autumnal Fancy

I let my heart go wandering away.
The bouncing winds a mischief caught it up
And danced it sore for many a sun-kissed day
Then tied it to a high-hipped buttercup.

Oh! Fools may catch the fancy for a space
Like random winds no more sincere
And summer's breath leaves no sad trace
Lonely the heart is waiting here.

  Ena Brason

Thoughts

Wind and sea gulls, sand and salty spray;
lonely shores that curve away
into a lonelier sea.
And what for me? Misery and gloom?
No! Memories give peace and quiet joy.
Memories sweet - of dancing; dinner; pies in pubs
and chiding when my shoulder rubs
against a gown. Chiding spoke in lovelier tones
than when the gentle spring condones
rude March for breathing hard upon her Mabian dress.
And bluey eyes, kindly none-the-less
when clumsy feet
destroy a beat
when dancing to a new refrain.
A drink. "Let's dance again."
A kiss, the first - the last?
Then running fast
to ride in cattle style
to where, for a while,
we had a place to be.

  Maurice Gubbins

The World's End

The Earth floats in space
Fresh, green and new
Then the lava clashed with the sea.
After came people like you and me.
We built our houses and built our mines
And computers and work infested our minds.
Our life grew easy but wars began
And deforestation covered the land.
We grew weak to this very day
But very soon we will have to pay.
The Earth will end in fire and water
With flood, flame and mass slaughter.

Peter Norman

Cry From The Heart

It's me, it's me, I'm all alone,
it's me alone and far from home,
I'm sitting here, and moving there,
There's only floor, just floor, no chair.
No windows in this room so small,
no windows, just a quilted wall.
It's me, it's me, am I not well?
My God I'm in a padded cell.
A padded cell, why me? Why me?
I just tried hanging from a tree,
I only cut my wrists, so small,
Blood making patterns up the wall.
The tablets, well, they looked so good.
A bottle or two, taken after food.
And then, before I went to bed,
I heard these voices in my head.
Hello, hello, it's me, it's me,
I'm sure you've thrown away the key.
If someone's there, please listen do.
I really need some help from you.
Just have a look to find the key,
Please help me find my sanity.

Jill McClean

Sunset From The Churchyard

I stand among the headstones and turn towards the west
The sunlight dies around me, the day is near undressed.
I feel the evening breezes a-whisper in my hair,
And see a kneeling body of all the souls at prayer.

I sit upon the seat and watch the daylight fade
From the velvet-curtained sky of turquoise-blue and jade.
Then slowly sinks the sun full down on to the wave,
And tips with purest gold each tomb and grey-stoned grave.

I see a crimson cloud trimmed with gilded lace,
Embroidered wisps of cirrus leave a fiery trace.
The burnished orb has vanished far beyond my sight,
I stay and watch the shadows as they form the silken night.

For here is peace and stillness and glory all around,
On this earth blessed with beauty - a sanctuary profound.
Here I'll rest for ever when the sands of time have run,
And know my bones will feel each setting of the sun.

Jeanne Webb

The Willow Tree

Why do you weep when all around your feet
Tulips and daffodils dance and sing
To greet the newly - wakened Spring?

Throw back your hair and lift your streaming eyes
To see unfolding pageants of surprise
More colourful than anything portrayed by man -
Living; enduring; formed in the immortal span
Of God's creation through the ancient years.

You should rejoice...
This is no time for tears.

Anne Wheatley

Elusive Beauty

The greatest gift afforded mankind,
Gives ease to the heart, and peace to the mind.
It's elusive, charismatic and sought by us all
We're fulfilled in its presence, we respond to its call.
Our senses develop, seeds of awareness are sown,
In a fertile mind, to be nurtured and grown,
Till at last comes reward, the search has bourn fruit,
Beauty strikes to the core and from there will take root.

It surrounds and beguiles us all of our days,
Touching our lives in so many different ways.
We experience the magic, in shades of shadow and light,
By touch or by sound, by taste or by sight.
A moment of truth? A reflection of glory?
A hidden depth? A wondrous story?
Whatever it is must be held and savoured,
For, whilst we grasp it, we're greatly favoured.

Should we loosen our hold, it slips through our fingers
and all we are left with, is a memory that lingers.

So unlock the mind, seek this treasure each day,
Find this sought after wealth in your own special way.

M. Rodgers

Westminster Bridge

He stands alone there great and bold
Very, oh so very often left in the cold,
If he could speak what tales he'd tell
Of the folk that all around him dwell.

Many kings and queens have passed his way
To brighten up a dreary day,
But alas sometimes sad, I must relate
Is when they pass his way to lie in state.

The houses of parliament are in his wake
Along his road some ministers take,
The wise old bridge with his grey grey look
May sometimes wish it was another road they took.

He bears a real tremendous load
Along his long and dusty road,
The cars the wagons and horses too
And ordinary folk like me and you.

The day is over and night has come
And work has started again for some,
But the bridge carries on through night and day
Let us to this great friend our respect pay.

Margery Brett

Sea Music

There's a swishing and a shushing and a hushing from the sea,
And the waves are foaming palely while the gulls are flying free.
I hear trebles on the pebbles, I hear singing from the sand,
With the shingle drumming softly like a military band.

There's a splashing and a lapping and a tapping on the shore,
As the shells are humming mutely with the muffled ocean's roar.
I hear breakers, music makers, I hear shifting rolling stones,
As a spirit winging leeward stirs my antiquated bones.

There's a surging and a sifting and a drifting 'neath the swell,
While the skies are dark'ning swiftly to the danger warning bell.
I hear thunder up and under, I hear rumblings t'ward the strand,
And thick purple pulsing channels blight my tightly knuckled hand.

There's a lashing and a crashing and a flashing in the sky,
Now the clouds are gath'ring closely while the sea-birds
    shoreward fly.
I see lightning stark and fright'ning, I see raindrops on the beach.
And the dimpled patterned grains slip slowly out of reach.

Soon the pounding and the pelting and the belting storm
    throes cease,
And the dark is greying slowly and the mist is bringing peace.
I hear noises, I hear voices, I hear choirs o'er the waves,
And old shanties drifting sadly from a million watery graves.

Bryan Borgeat

Shadows Of Pain

Pain is felt in many ways, in love, in memories
It hides itself in shadows, like sunlight lost through trees

It strikes the old and young alike, no pity or remorse
No warnings, no exemptions, it's always right on course

There's pain in loving someone, who can't show that they care
There's pain in living all alone, when your heart just longs to share

There's pain in having words to say, when silence must prevail
To have to wait, till the time is right, yet to do so is to fail

There's pain in being blamed, for something that you didn't do
There's pain in trying to be heard, when no one want's to know

There's pain in separation, from the ones you love so dear
Not being able to explain, to ears that long to hear

There's pain in when you can't hold on, to all that you've achieved
To face injustice of a kind, that's brought you to your knees

But God in all his wisdom, will ease that pain one day
And bring the hope you've longed for, in a monumental way

He'll wipe away the shadows, and the pain will disappear
And your life will be returned to you, to live and love and share

Beryl Sumpter

The Question Of Living

Scavenging Vultures that circle above,
They're waiting to get you, waiting in line.
No questions are asked, they're after your blood.
A sign of a struggle and they're at your demise.

It's a jungle out there, only the strong will survive,
If you struggle and fall no matter the cause.
The Vultures that circled are now by your side,
As the bounty is fought for, then nothing remains.

The scavengers survive they've swallowed their pride,
They live off the land protected for life.
While the pickings are rich they're happy to scrounge,
But tighten the belt and they're the first to complain.

If you do have some pride and you want to survive,
No mercy is shown if you struggle and fall.
Help is not given to those who have tried,
To live out this life without help from the land.

The answer to life seems therefore to be:
A scavenging Vulture that scrounges a life
And relies on the land to feed and to house them.
Or be King of the Jungle and take what you please.

Michael Staples

To A Nature Lover "Remembering"

At times you think life's not worth while
You're feeling sad and blue
Just stop and think what nature's done
That makes life bright for you.

Just walk along a country lane when summer time is here
And see the sun, on flowers, blooming, the whistling of birds
so clear.

The streamlets and rivers, all rippling and singing, the children,
they laugh and play, look at the green fields, the flowers, the
blue sky, for this is nature out on display.

In winter you'll see, the very same scene in a different kind of way,
You'll see the green fields in a blanket of snow
And the skies won't be blue, they've turned grey.

The bushes and trees, with icicles on all look like glass Chandeliers.
The rivers you'll see with the skaters on, and then when the moon
appears every where glistens, in a different light the people they
drift away, the moon shines on in the still of the light, but is
gone by the break of day.

Nature does not stop, it goes on never ending,
As you can go on, just keep on remembering.

A. Harrington

Kismet

Words cannot convey these feelings so rare
Or explain the inexplicable intensity we share
Its passion reflected in the eyes dark jewel
Destiny the force, Intoxication the fuel

Absorbed in its aura and consuming powers
All cares abandoned as desire devours
Its touch exotic caressing our frame
Chemistry the fusion, Vitality the flame

Satiated we lie whilst serenity descends
As love encircles, entwines, intends
Its mantel warming as our hearts pace
Ardour the fire, Utopia the face

Fulfilment depicts the devotion we hold
And eternity the embrace, as we grow old
Its image etched forever in our mind
Division the fear, Euphoria the find

Deborah Webber

Joy (Or The Optimist's Prayer)

Sail into the wake of life,
Never fear death will drown you,
Blessings are in abundance,
Misfortunes merely but few,
Enjoy the gifts that nature brings,
Cast out hatred that surrounds you,
Give time to loved ones,
Take a problem away to solve.

Heal pain with mind's hope,
Strengthen the spirit of survival,
Weep not forever, good is for remembrance,
Sadness be given little meaning,
Warm to feelings of others,
Share pleasures in success,
Work hard at a smile and gain happiness,
Change wrongs to right for all sake.

Treasure possessions for a short time,
Linger not on what might have been,
Go forward with a positive force,
Then know the joy of living.

Christine Semark

Career Confusion

Walking away that day with my severance pay.
Wondering to myself what do I do now.
Happy and sad both at the same time,
but with a fear of not knowing what will happen next.

I threw away on purpose my livelihood,
to persuade myself to stay where I could not endure.

"Oh come now" I say "You will try harder
next time." Next time would it not be
more reasonable to do what I know best.

To have a home a career a family
a life, others can do it why can't I.
I just suppose I am a woman for
whom this is too much.
The only acceptance of myself lies within me.

Saira Khan

Time

A I look around me
On this planet we call earth,
I think of the destruction
That I've seen since my birth,
There is so much we have destroyed
In the name of man.
But at the end of the day somebody must pay
Someone must take the can
Bigwigs no never
Because they so clever
It's always the working man

Betty R. Sewell

Union

The child-father savagely beats the walls
to punish them for the world's indifference.
The whitewash dust drifts in the sunlight
and settles slowly on the uncaring floor.

The wall's blood must gush forth in streams,
the agonizing screams must fill the space.
The world must beg relief and ask forgiveness
for all those long suffering days it caused.

Then tiredness comes: it always does - at last.
The aching arm drops, the rope falls away,
the pain relieved for a while: then guilt flows.
The amused sun stares in to bless the scene.

The father - child sees it still: the drifting dust,
the swaying trees, the indifferent staring world,
the sweating walls, their white blood drifting;
that mocking sun, the uneased pain, the unknown loss.

He reaches back across the years to stand beside
and touch the shaking child: to smell his pain,
to touch his brow, to hold him close.
He knows the loss and can calm him now.

Terry M. Thorn

Easter Blessings

Holy Father, you gave us your Son to love
And He gave His life for our sins,
To teach us to share our love with others
To make a better world to live in.

He died that our sins be forgiven
To spread His word throughout the land,
To help draw us closer together
As a loving and caring band.

To share our love with others
Is all that He asks of us,
And to teach the little children
To live and grow in His righteousness.

Easter is a blessed and joyous time
For Jesus he did arise,
So we must count our blessings
For with Him are our Spiritual ties.

Marian Bates

A View To A Kill

As she creeps up slowly, they look around,
Looking and waiting for a sign of her.
Listening attentively for a sound,
Grazing quietly, trying not to care.
She lies down low, watching their every move,
Keeping still, until she knows it is time.
She knows which one she is going to choose,
The slowest and youngest are in their prime.

They see her now as she comes into view,
They all move at once causing a stampede,
And the cheetah knows she will have her feed.
They are all gone now, except for a few,
There on the ground, as silent as can be,
A young wildebeest, she has victory.

Claire Barnes

Life

Series, dramas, films and soaps,
Related to life and all its hopes.
Cartoons, comedies and sci-fi themes,
Built up in our heads and displayed in our dreams.
Swearing, violence and psychological thrillers,
Cause the breakdown of life and societies pillars.
Musicals, mayhem and media,
Are the writings of life's encyclopedia,
So others can learn from our mistakes,
And put back in life what it takes.

Chris Thomas

Take Time

Take time to greet each day, with thanks for being alive,
Through its strengths and its weakness, you'll find a will to survive,
Take time to hear all others and what they have to say,
As it takes all kinds of words to make or break a day.

Take time to see each man that passes by your side,
Don't judge him by cover - real beauty lies inside.
Take time to spare a thought, for the other way of life
The starving, the homeless, and those in pain and strife.

Take time to show you care for those that you hold dear
Don't leave it 'till tomorrow even though it seems so near
Take time to say "I'm sorry," for things you've said or done
For each man from his conscience can never ever run.

Take time to smile or laugh - it brightens the darkest day,
And just for that one moment your troubles fade away
Yes - taking time to do these things will be easier said than done but,
You'll have fought the hardest battle and indeed you will have won!

Jacqueline Deveney

The Cooker And The Cuckoo

As I was riding out one day,
I saw a Cooker in a field;
There it stood so lonely, and very much in need.
Along came a Cuckoo,
And perched upon the Cooker said;
"Hello little Cooker, what are doing here?"
"I'm waiting to be cooked upon"
The Cooker replied,
"Should you have a little need."
Said the Cuckoo,
"My need is for the air I breath,
The grass and tall thick trees,"
Then flying off, left the Cooker standing there;
Still very much in need.

Arnold Monk

For Kathy

So sad a countenance, my friend, so hard the sobs, so hot the tears,
Oh how you crave to quit this world that's held you captive
    through the years
In bonds of worthlessness and strife.
You feel that's been your lot in life.

So temptingly oblivion calls, its icy finger beckoning.
To sleep and never stir again until the day of reckoning.
Oh heavy heart, you do berate,
Release you from this anguished state.

But don't despair, the cloud will lift, the heart will melt, the
    tears will dry
And you will see your real worth, your value through
    another's eye.
You do so much for those in need
And comfort both in word and deed.

You hold a place in many hearts, don't ever underestimate,
And just how much those kindnesses we all of us appreciate.
Oh Kath, my friend, what would we do
If we should lose a friend like you?

Patricia Atkin

February Fill-Dyke

February Fill-dyke, either black or white,
The days are cold and dark, season of half light.
My eyes are weary as the scene I scan,
And yet this desolation is part of Nature's plan.

As in our lives we find a quieter pace,
And slow our feet to halt their hectic race,
The flowers fade as Nature holds its breath,
And summer's joys lie withered by Winter's misty breath.

But soon, the newly rising sap will resurrect the trees,
The lilac blossom's perfume distils in fragrant breeze,
The shoots of pure white snowdrops push bravely through the earth,
Their tiny buds proclaiming the season of re-birth.

Kathleen Wood

Nature's Mosaic

Through country lanes, in the rain, the wet leaves shining,
globules of water, bead-like hanging on grasses
and cars making passes to each other...
All in a hurry, we to Wateringbury,
where moored is a miniature home...
Kettle and cups, coffee or tea, for you for me and family..
Green flotsam of mini-plants floating in waves,
from hidden depths and fishy caves...
The spit-spotting rain causing water-grain circles,
that expand and bump into each other,
forming another ring...
On either side, in meadows wide, sheep graze and gaze into
the dampness...
Birds sing and wing skywards, as we glide in peaceful motion,
on the water's surface,
nature's mosaic, perfect...
Such is earth in beauteous drape,
In oasis moments, when we escape...

Ruby Buckle

Tomorrow's Child

Those infant Babes in cribs or shawl
guarded with such loving care
shrill voices heard on teachings call
those schooling days they have to share.

Learn from the learned and confide
to instil the power in the mind
the trust and virtues they provide
to children of all class and kind.

The will to win and how to lose
teenage years are hard to bear
those rights and wrongs, which to choose
till time to leave parental care.

They tread the arduous paths of fate
exposed to the dangers that unfold
the joys and sorrows that relate
to reach their adult goal.

The loves and passions of marital care
where family tremors are unfurled
the wealth and poverty they will share
in this unstable modern world.

K. C. Burditt

Kent - Sea And Sky

Amongst the Wolds and blossoms of Kent,
the peoples enjoy the views and scent.

Gone are the days when our Navy was seen the be strong,
now we are left with memories long.

The sound of the battles were clearly heard, the roar of the engines
and rattle of guns where the young boys fought high in the sky.

They stood on the streets and fields of work,
and cheered when they won and cried when they died, for our
boys in blue who fought in the sky.

The sound of the battles have long gone away,
and the boys in blue have all gone away.

Now we are left with the sound in the sky from the Jets
who speed on their way never a thought for the boys in blue,
who fought alone high in the sky.

Long ago their foreparents would stand by the shore
to watch their men go to war.
Against the French, the Spanish, and all, in their ships
of wood, of yesteryear.

Now there is no Nelson, no Collingwood or the Jones'
we have no Navy to watch by the shore.

Peter Charles Knight

Moving On

In each book of life there are chapters
Pages we wish we could change
Others we yearn to recapture
Yet that we can never arrange
A new testament can only begin
By leaving the past behind
Believe in yourself and you will win
With faith in heart and hope in mind.
When our world's turned upside down
All our efforts seem fallen in vain
We should never stand still but keep walking
Then in time we will run again.
We can't retrieve the life that has gone
So as months turn into seasons
We learn again to laugh and sing,
To love life for different reasons.
So turn the page over - begin again.
The world has the paper but we hold the pen.

Valerie Reid

Dream

I lay within some bracken moist with dew
Upon a lonely hill, close to the sky.
I could have touched the clouds that passed me by
But I was fearful, of the things they knew.
Afraid that they would carry tales to you
Of all my plans, to make the earth now cry
For beauty, where no beauty seems to lie
But creeping shadows whisper, and accrue.

The earth has grown so weary at her plight
I thought I'd rouse her from her apathy
But dreams must now remain as dreams for me,
And I will put my foolish thoughts to flight.
For how can I provide the earth with light
To see through all her great complexity?
And how can earth, and you, belong to me
Enfolded in the darkness of the night?

John Fernley Sing

England's Pride

If I should tell thee of my greatest fears,
Please do not scorn, or criticise my words.
The pride I feel in England is so great.
This feeling; swells my heart to such extent,
That I cannot smother this growing bubble.
This war that I shall now go out and join,
This bloody war. It brings nothing but grief
The lives it takes; oh those innocent lives.

For this is all it does. It takes, and takes,
And takes again. It only causes grief.
I shall fight for the freedom of this land.
Though if I loose my life in vain. Please do
Not grieve. I think this is my only fear.
Grief is just a feeling, pride makes this land.

Andrea Michelle Parks

Easter Passion

Behold, that grim and holy hill 'neath the low'ring sky,
Without the city walls of Jerusalem, it lies.
Golgotha...Oh, Golgotha...Place of Christ's Calvary,
Where passion ran its course to His Final Destiny.
...Eli, Eli lama sabachthani?.....Impassioned
Cry, echoing down two thousand years and, like fashioned,
Again I hear...My God, why hast thou forsaken me?
And the despair, in many tongues, repeats endlessly.

Oh, Crucifer, Crucifer....You who carried the Cross,
Toiling, stumbling thro' streets of faces leering so close,
To that Place of Skulls, you went, to reach His Final Tryst;
Such a noble heart did beat strongly within your breast.
And what thoughts did pass thro' your mind that long, long sad day,
When you were chosen to bear the Cross and make your way
To that stark crowded hillside, where jackals bayed for blood;
What perceptions did you embrace in that dark'ning mood?

Gwen Douglas

462

Trees

Hidden deep inside the trees are souls I think
Souls that grow and change like the trees
Each leaf is so quiet inside it's seen things no-one else has
A memory of moments, nobody ever listens
Or ever takes the time to think that the way they sway
And rustle is a hint they want to speak.

Once they might have tried to whisper softly in someone's palm
The memory of a girl who carries a hole inside her
But nobody's there to listen or care that maybe, just maybe
That tree knows that something's horribly wrong
Maybe it wants to talk about the sadness that it's seen

Perhaps the world should take a long walk
Deep into the woods and look carefully, closely
At the patterns, the tiny maps printed in the leaves
The dirty footmarks and stains
Flattened to the ground, can they not see
The leaves shaped like tears, the design of the fallen needles
Maybe they will lead the world to the one who made the hole.

Rachel Lloyd

Mischief!

Eight paws scamper across the floor.
They have heard the sound of my key in the door,
Two little tongues lick my hand,
They give me a greeting that is really grand.

Basil and Polly are their names,
They delight in playing games,
Rolling on the muddy path,
They really hate to have a bath!

Lucy watches them at play,
And guides them if they go astray,
God is very good to send,
These three dogs me to befriend.

Edna L. Shotter

Insomnia

You're scared, and you'll not sleep
You don't know, and so you're down
You're walking, but now you're falling
You're thirsty... but soon you'll drown

Voices in the air around you
Speaking words without a meaning
Sentences of good intention
And understanding could be believing

You're tall, but now you're cut down
You're aware, of the pain in the fight
You can't help but stare at the sky each time
That the daylight fades to night

You're still scared, and you'll not sleep again
'Til you can find a way to really learn...
You're dreaming, but again you're waking
You're so cold... but soon you'll burn

Paul Bowler

Bring In The Spring

Hail in the Spring a start of new beginnings,
Creativity awe-inspiring, gives a reason to be living.
Plant life showing life anew, a wonder to be found,
New born lambs playing in the fields, birds nesting all around.
People enjoying the Sun and warmth, feeling good to be alive,
Spring gives a purpose to our lives, a touch of Paradise.

Fulfilment and contentment as the days pass idly by,
The strong aroma fills the air, as Spring flowers catch the eye.
The ducks on the water with their families new,
The whole of nature seems to be bringing to you,
A joy of things that will unfold as time goes by,
That Spring gives each and every one of us a piece of Paradise.

K. M. Sutton

A Dog's Tale

My very best friend, so true to her end, through parks and
down lanes we would wander. 'Long riverside walks, knew
where the path forks, always led to an inn way out yonder.
On one of those rambles, fed up with the brambles, took my
through to the back of a pub. There a lawn full of creatures,
as one of the features, was to judge the best entrant out there.
Nineteen dogs, even rabbits, pets with all habits, just fancy, a
tortoise was there. She was mixed up, cross bred, but let it be
said, end result was a jewel, most rare. Though uninvited, she
stayed, and sat at my feet, composed and enjoying the rest.
She wasn't to know, that the judge, local vet, had watched her
with much interest. To shorten the tale, after doing her tricks,
he checked her from nose to her tail. Then to my amazement,
he gave the awards, 1st 2nd and third to my Queen. But that
wasn't all, disbelief, after all, I got the best handler's Rosette.
Not even my dog, my neighbours she was, but we shared her
love through the years. But it wasn't to last, for age catches
up, and she left, just seven months later, to go to the canines
creator Now, we're left with our tears, and the thoughts of
those years, of the pleasure and joy that she gave us.
Though time's a great healer, and while we still feel her, still
close we remember the best.

Epitaph. 'Young or old, always beware, of giving
your heart to a dog to tear.

Harry S. Stewart

They Came To Say Goodbye

The Church was full, the memories hurt,
The loss so great, so hard to bear,
We loved her so, our dearest one
Her way, her touch, no longer there.

She left too soon, they felt the loss.
No words could mend their breaking hearts,
"Be brave" she said, "I love you so.
Such joy we had, I didn't go."

Remember times of happiness of roads we walked together,
Those days were ours they'll never end,
Well have them now forever.
Don't cry my loves, remember me.

The wind was soft, her smile so bright,
Her scarf waved a last farewell,
"Be brave" she said, "You musn't cry,
I'm here with you, I'll never die".

Patricia Kaariainen

Nightdrive

Red, through amber, now greenlight,
Accelerate into the night,
Increase the tempo of the stripes
As speed turns strobe the bright streetlights.

Met with rhythm of the wheels,
Pulses as the tyres feel
Silent road marks that conceal
Chants that speeding cars reveal.

Deeper now into the night,
Further still into my flight,
Driven far from city's sight
Amber turns to pale moonlight.

Dazzled now by unchecked beams,
Dark and light at great extremes.
Cat's eyes staring from the seams
Of the roadway that redeems.

Till lastly I decelerate
Into the village and the gate
Where you so lovingly await
To shelter and encapsulate.

Timothy C. Jefferies

The Outcast

Do you believe in bad luck or fate?
I do, it is not my fault I am in this state,
I remember life how it used to be,
Never did I think this could happen to me.
Years ago I had a very good life,
It may have been different if I had a wife,
I had a house and a good job too,
But all my plans went wrong and feel through,
Sleeping rough along by the river bank,
I cannot believe how low I have sank,
Freezing cold in the wind and rain,
I have had my share of heartache and pain.
I collect old newspapers for some cover,
Often I think of my dear old mother,
She would have told me where I went wrong,
Oh, for the good times I really long.
How on earth did I end up like this?
A bottle of drink my only bliss.
People look at me with utter disgust,
For me they have no time or trust.

    L. Turner

Angel Hands

God sent me an angel, a lovely baby boy,
  I looked at him, and loved him,
  he filled my heart with joy,
when I awoke at night to lonely baby cries,
  I held his hand and rocked him, and sang
  him lullabies

When he was trying hard to walk, I held his hand in mine
And then it was not very long before he learnt to climb
Before he started school, we had a lot of fun, of
days filled with happiness, of beaches, sea and sun

The day he started school he was aglow with pride,
  and I released his hand, went home, sat down, and cried

The day that I entrusted him to someone to walk
  him home, she did not think to hold his hand,
  so he was left to walk alone,
A madly driven car came speeding round the bend,
  it took my blonde haired boy away,
It caused my dreams to end;

When I go to heaven to the Lord I pray, that my
  angel takes me by the hand, and he will show the way.

    Renie Moran

My Song

The music in my soul has descended to a minor key
  And has softened to a muted and slow tune.
For now the early promise of youth has gone from me,
  The present times are flat and echo gloom;
    But the music murmurs on.

It seems only yesterday that each hour played a symphony
  Of such joy to uplift and make my heart sing.
My solo kept company with the merry melody
  That the daily events in my life would bring,
    When the tempo swept me along.

But now fateful drums boom out time's awful timpani,
  While the clashing discord of life deafens my ears.
I dread the shortening interval before my Judge's decree,
  Could I be condemned to silence, while bitter tears
    Mourn the loss of my song.

I do not know who conducts this constant harmony in me,
  For it remains faithful despite all my fears;
But I trust its variations will sing through eternity
  To swell the chorus of praise the Great Composer hears
    From all of creation.

    D. M. Smith

Rough Justice

If extraterrestrials, superior to man,
land on Earth and decide to stay,
what part shall we play to serve them?
Perhaps if we're pretty they'll let us be pets
(though to be a best friend there must be trust,
a problem for man through the ages)
or our weirder ones could go on display
in various compounds and cages.

It might be thought best to use us to test
their cosmetic lotions and health-giving potions
or take us apart to see how we tick
then, when they fall sick, they can use spare bits
in hospitals for transplantation.
Some of their kind might find this unfair
but all they will gain for their pains if they shout
is a 'crackbrain' reputation.

My earnest hope, and no doubt yours,
is that if they do come they'll be herbivores.

    Margaret Stead

Georgie And Me

We strolled across the hilltop, Georgie and me,
He wore a blue suit - Air force blue
And under one arm he'd tucked his cap, flat topped with a peak,
The other he'd placed about my waist,
Uh-huh, Georgie and me.

We stopped at a stile, and oh the air was pure, so pure.
We surveyed the scene: beauty unbound!
Then he stooped and picked a blade of grass
  dark green and pointed, and
Just then he turned and looked into my eyes:
Uh-huh, Georgie and me.

We were only good friends when me parted, Georgie and me.
He was so shy. An Airman? Gosh!
Only a blade of grass in his hand - but to us the world...
He couldn't find words, but I knew...
Uh-huh, Georgie and me.
He went off to war and we never met again.
Sometimes I stand, here at the stile
And think of that time when the grass was green and love but a dream;
Now all that is left is the blue of the sky.. Per ardua ad Astra....

    Connie Francis

Fear

I live in fear from day to day,
Why I never know.
Each day I live the more I fear;
I cannot let it go.

The more I hide, the worse I feel.
It's building up inside;
The thought of never being free; the fear of being alive.

Afraid of being in darkness, afraid of seeking help;
Afraid of every living thing,
Especially fear itself.

If only I could face them, to be brave and kill them dead;
After all, 'twas I invented them
And they're living in my head.

I'm deteriorating slowly,
I have so much to give.
The fighting of this battle
Makes me yearn for strength to live.

Oh God, I'm going to fight this fear
A little at a time
Until it's conquered to the end and prove my life is mine.

    Eleanor O'Neil

Waterloo

You're valiant, courageous, a lover, a friend,
We lived, loved and fought, so why did it end?
When you left my side it near broke my heart,
You hero, you war Lord, you true Bonaparte.
Tell me Napoleon, what was it all for?
I lost the battle but you won the war.
You won the battle of sexes, not I.
Now you're fighting with men, you live or you die.
You'll not find compassion in Wellington's eyes.
You cope well with deceit, mistrust and lies,
The proud iron duke chose his spot well,
Your men came in thousands, they fought and they fell.
They charged in the rain, and ploughed through the mud,
The air was all smoke from the cannon,
The earth a red blanket of blood,
You marched on and on through torrential rain.
Your body a furnace of anguish and pain,
You and your army fought hard it is true
But fate wore a red tunic at Waterloo.

Kathy Karlikowski

Somersal (1964)

Somersal's like a posy the children jock in may.
It's small and neat and fragrant,
And hidden quite away within fringe of
green leaves, far from prying eyes,
But like a children's posy, it's full of sweet surprise.
　The hawthorn froths its hedges,
　The wild flowers deck its feet,
　No discord mars its beauty,
　Only the merry feet of children and their
　Laughter disturbs this quiet retreat.

When I am back in the tumult and turmoil
of the town.
I shall see again sweet Somersal
In her shimmering. May day gown,
And hear the sounds of husbandry
And the children at their play,
And the quiet patient cattle
As they pass along the way.

R. Dawtry

Life's Lesson

We still can remember friends we have lost,
And memories that we have loved the most.
But it's no good grieving for things that are gone,
It's no good longing for days that are done.
The road of life still stretches ahead,
And this is where our feet must tread.
Greet each day as it comes in view,
Old friends are gone, make friends anew.
Make the most of each day of your life.
We only live once don't live it in strife.
Live it in loving your friends and kin.
Open the door-let happiness in
if you give folk a greeting and a smile,
You'll help to make their life worthwhile.
You'll give them joy, and yourself too,
Love will guide you, your whole life through.

Eileen Meadows

The Skater

Her cheek was quite cold, her lips were blue,
Her whole face flushed with strawberry hue;
Skitting and skating, a dancing sprite,
Muslin and lace drift into the night;
Flimsy snowdrop with dreamy dark eyes,

Breathes sullen and silent mournful sighs,
The song of the swans in singing death;
Fairy-like tremors of dying breath,
Bending and bowing, beauteous bell;
A crumpling and crying Little Nell.

Gehanne Erian

Untitled

I sit here each night and wait for the sun,
I pray the Lord every new day will come,
Some come fast and some come slow,
Some won't leave and some just go,
I'm not saying there's much I can do,
But sit around here and think of you,
I'm not saying there's much I can write,
But give me a chance and I'll try all night.
I would sail the highest mountain,
I would climb the seven seas,
If you would be my lady,
I would get down on my knees.
I would die for you,
I would cry for you,
I would do anything you want me to.
I would live for your smile,
I would die for your kiss,
All I ask for is the girl I now miss.

Stuart Hurst

Man Dog God

The 'sands of time' are running low.
Deserts freeze and icebergs glow.
Greenlands parched, we sow in vain;
reap our harvest, 'acid rain'.
Uranic waste unto the sea,
eyeless fish on poison feed.
Diseased sheeps brain for bovine beast.
Children perish; Christmas feast!
Wipe the forests from the earth,
pulp to paper, what's its worth?
To feel the snow in summertime;
see the ebb of winters tide?
We drilled a hole right through the sky.
Carbon poison. Watch us die.
In lands to scorch by midnight sun.
To hide in taverns on the run;
in hope of mortals death delay,
which God, made light, a cancerous stray?

James L. Pomeroy

Big Sur

The road winds on - beckoning - eager to reveal its treasures.
The sky, wide-angled, with curved blue arms,
Cradles me to the edges of the earth.
I draw a breath as I kneel to the dancing silhouette of golden grasses
Graceful, glorious, slender stems
That hide a darkness of slow falling rocks-
And suddenly terror, there is terror, here.
A pristine beauty, generous, an unmeasured magnificence
Which time has nurtured.
Then cruelty beyond belief grasps my heart in a moment of
tortured memory.
A telescopic vision, tunnelled, black, spins my dreams, my hopes
And spirals them beyond the boundaries of touch or sight or colour.
The mountains, misty grey, swirl and grow
As pink/orange/blue/green/purple
Light suffuses sky and sweeps away the remnants of early morning.
I stand, heart stopped with joy as I become a part of nature's landscape.
Peace...beauty ...the silence of space.

Oh! But the joy is broken, shattered into black-daggered grief...
As time becomes the enemy and beauty cracks
To show the rotting corpse pinioned beneath the wide-spread arms.

Elizabeth McOwat

You Will Never Notice

Every touch that could never reach.
Every tear that was never to be seen,
Every smile that died and rotted to a
Scowl before it could reach the surface.

Every confidence that was beaten to the ground
Will dissolve into the air,
You will breathe them for the rest of your life
And you will never notice.

Alex Butler

Winter's Night

I stood by the window, looking into the night
The garden was covered with snow
The trees were all glistening, from the rays of the light
And - the moon seemed - to be saying "Hello"

The stars were so bright in the cold of the night
No clouds to interrupt my view
The tall trees were swaying, as if they were saying
Please play us a nice soothing tune.

The children in bed, and the animals fed
The birds were asleep for the night
No animals frisking in the new fallen snow
Perhaps none of them were in sight

As I closed the curtains on that starry night,
I'm sure the moon seemed to say
Go rest for the night, I'll see everything right,
Tomorrow's another new day.

Alcock

Bobby's Dad Who Has Gone To Heaven

Poor Mr. Timms, what a din
you will have to fetch the dustbin in
those groaning noises you do make
They really make my stomach ache.
You are a neighbour brave and bold
God Bless 'em all when you get old
your famous stick as I pass by
makes me shudder, I wonder why?
I do not dislike your tramp-like face
but I hope one day you can find a place
where you can smile without a scowl
you silly wee-man that makes a noise like an owl!

Freda Cox

Similarly To Animals

I know how dogs do it.
Cats do it
I'm pretty sure how rats do it,
Elephants, tigers and bats do it,
But
Birds of a feather? Never!

I'm even sure that dogs adore
The method they've adopted
It would be no surprise to realize
That cats could be co-opted
But birds? Birds? Pigeons and things?
Do they live like us. Have final flings?
And does she really - the lady hen
Entertain in her little den?

And if it's a fact, they get into the act
How does he get under the feathers?

A. Sampson

The Ghost

She came when the world was all asleep
A shimmering spectre, pale, discreet;
    She floated across the airy room
    And sat beside her musty loom.

Her finger touched the spindle shorn,
Her finger touched the cotton torn;
    The ghostly hand which once was gay,
    Silently lifted the cobwebs grey.

A sound came through the cold night air,
A breeze uplifted her silken hair;
    She ceased to ponder over her loom
    And gazed across the gloomy room.

A shout rang through the empty house,
She cowered like a frightened mouse;
    She rose she listened, made a dash
    And now was off in a momentary flash.

John F. McCartney

A Sonnet To Kieselguhr

When rising throats forgo the unforseen,
Take all their cares to call the rusting claw,
For journeys may be cautious or obscene,
And fancy fires create the blemished law.
If mine calls twice it must not sink again,
Or paler smiles than Orpheus can ignite,
While hope can be outraged by powdered rain,
Shading against the autumn circles light.
Grey-purples tinge - and crawling on a thread,
What shall deny the symbol's comely rest?
Though fitter lays bemuse and never dread,
Their wily ones recant the royal jest.

Give heed to he who draws the ample guise!
It merits not the waking feast of lies.

John Spooner

The Antique Restorer

Surrounded by the bustle of a modern time,
He rests on seat of ancient yew,
Within his kingdom of a bygone age,
And reminders of a world more true.
His hair, now grey, becoming sparse,
His face, moustached and gently lined,
His hands, still deft to ply his craft,
Restore past beauty left behind.
He ponders on the history of each piece,
Caress each smooth and polished face,
Of well loved chest or table bare,
Fashioned with no lack of grace.
His fingers run o'er crystal glass,
Lovingly trace some silvered art,
Note work of adzes and chisel point,
For of his life are these all part.
A long life he's spent, in helping save,
The works of masters, long since past,
With knowledge that his talents, used,
Will surely make them, his outlast.

E. B. M. Ushaw

"Change At Bank For Waterloo"

No paper to read or book to devour, anxious to avoid contact
with my fellow travellers,
my eyes begin to wander the classified in the carriage.
"Change at Bank for Waterloo"
An interesting thought.
I wonder what change my listening bank would give for
Waterloo, and at what exchange rate?
I wonder what Wellington might have thought...
Interesting; going to work on the tube.

Janice Hand

Paint Me A Picture

Paint me a picture of mountains and heather.
Paint me a picture of ever changing weather.
Paint me a picture of bag pipes and skirls.
Paint me a picture of bonnie dancing girls.

Now wash out the brush, the colours of deception.
And put brush to canvas, the bonafide conception,
By using the paints within this black box,
Their malignant hues the true image unlocks.

Now paint me a picture of steelyards closed down.
The wandering homeless in the centre of town.
Boarded up windows of a once busy shop
Five hundred workers in line for the chop.
The once mighty shipyards that did us all proud,
lying dead and decaying, in a death coloured shroud.

All this is just part of a far bigger puzzle,
this attack on Scotland, like a pit bull unmuzzled.
To be helped only when the government see fit.
Then discarded like the needle, of a junkie's last hit.
Now take this painting and toss it in the bin.
It just wouldn't look right on a shortbread tin.

Duncan Greer

Friendship

I found a life unknown, a love to share,
Each moment but a pleasure deep to bear
And all the ecstasy of each day's swiftest passing
Born in friendship's name.

A jewel rare, a joyous wond'ring care,
A thing so great that ev'ry star must stare
And each green blade of grass must needs go graceful
dancing
Because of friendship.

I humbly ask this priceless gift so fair
To stay with me, to have, to hold, to wear;
I trust it for my heart goes always onwards prancing
So to possess it.

Throughout the years my ev'ry load of care
Will lighten for kind friendship's hand is there;
Together bound, with sorrows shared, with joys enhancing
For dear friendship's sake.

Alison Spence

Bedtime On Holiday

There's a hush along the east coast where the shingle meets the sea,
Like a lull before the storm begins to break,
And shadows out of history books pass by inquiringly,
Lord Nelson, Kitchener, Raleigh and Drake.

There's a murmur in the harbours all along the east coast towns,
There's a humming in the shipyards and the docks,
There's a wind sweeping seawards knowingly across the fens
    and downs,
And whispers to the valley and the rocks.

There's a hush of evening fallen on this turbulent old day,
But in the sky there shines a crescent moon,
And the waves beat out a lullaby in every creek and bay,
To remind me that it's bedtime very soon.

So my darling close your eyes and of me gently dream,
For my thoughts fly out to you on wings of gold,
And we will meet again my dear, when the suns light is a gleam,
With the exchanging of a new day for the old.

Louis Shellard

Do Not Speak Again

Do not speak again, do not speak,
Let the soft veil of silence fall,
Hush sharp-edged words that drop as stones.
Desperate words beyond recall.

Later, with wounds perhaps time-healed
Anguish paces down the years,
The underlying scars remain,
Memory throbs, bitterness sears.

Unknown black thoughts had broken through,
Stirred by blind emotion from the deep
And hidden crannies of the mind.
Alas, we should have let them sleep,

Lala Lloyd

The Beggar

I saw a man beneath a railway bridge
Sitting arched below the wall
The rain ran in a gutter above on a ridge
And splashed the stone at his feet,
He had a sack which served him as a seat.

"I must hurry fast to get my train
No time for a man just sitting in the rain."

His glance met mine just once - no more
His eye was twisted as if to see
Death coming closer by one door
Or at another - he had chalk pictures of a cat,
A yellow one, a sunset and an empty hat.

J. S. Malpas

Winter Wonders

A winters morning crisp with snow
People walking oh! So slow
Picture book houses up and down the street
The snow plough races its work to complete.

Remember the poor animals though
Where can they get out of the snow
Ducks and birds peck the ice
Frantically looking for something nice.

Children's shrieks of joy resound
For them rare snow is all around
Snowmen all shapes and sizes
Constructed well in many guises.

Lovely though the snow may be
We are not used to such a low degree
Old folk shiver in their beds
Wondering if they will get fed.

Soon the snow will melt and go
Leaving only memories and slush to show
Then we look for brighter days
So all can enjoy the suns warm rays.

Trixie Jennings

Trees

There's nothing so majestic as the tree
Just look around and you will see
Notice the great oak that grows from little acorns
And next, admire the lofty forty years Hawthorns
Cast your eyes to the maple and sycamore
All these trees, you will come to adore
See the conifers, such lovely evergreens
Make some of the prettiest of ever scenes
They bring parks and gardens back to life
After a bare cold winter, full of strife
In spring the horse chestnut comes into flower
Lovely small petals and crimson dots, they endower
There are so many, we cannot count them all
They come in all sizes, big and small
And not to forget our blossom trees
Which in the autumn, bear fruit to please
Apples, plums, pears as such
Bring to our trees a final touch

Jean Linney

Forever Love

As the golden sun appears, at the start of another day
I find myself still wondering, why you had to go away?
In one agonizing moment - you had to go
Taking with you, more than you'll ever know!
Was Paradise so needy, for a bright and gracious soul?

So tender was your touch, your smile to warm my heart
And as a Butterfly emerging, you were as beautiful,
why are we apart??
Always words encouraging, forever true
Nothing will quite compare, to the trust I had in you.

Each line on your face, showed the stages of your life
I have so much to thank you for, but cannot in this life...
So special was your presence, captivating many along your way
Whenever I would meet with you, endearing things you'd say
I go on without you, I cannot change, I must accept
Time will never take away memories, locked deep in my heart
    and kept

To stop loving you, I must ask the sun not to rise...
The birds not to fly, never a tear to pass my eyes...
I'll see you someday my beloved me
When all earthly ties for me are done.
You can't hurry time and there's things still to do
So I send you a kiss and all my love for you, too.

Christine Peers

Sea Spirit

Down where the black flecked wavelets lap the sand
Where stick legged seabirds forage for their fare
Where age and youth go walking hand in hand
Wrapped in a timeless moment free from care
Where sun on water cuts a glaring cleave
Almost unbearable to naked eye
Which in soft shoal and shadow seeks reprieve
And climbs on endless wave crest to the sky
There would I sit and wile away the hour
Content with nature in its basic form
Free from the grim facade of concrete tower
From endless social rites in uniform
When daily pressures force my spirit low
When living tends toward despondency
There is a special place where I can go
Where land and cares are swallowed by the sea
So give me sea and sky and solitude
And I will be content I need no more
Than sinking softly into nature's mood
To free my soul and let my spirit soar

A. Begg

Of Passage

Gliding... then, of a sudden, gone... fading
from view... a Massachusetts sunset played
bright under belly and throat. These birds float
by on a summer evening's sky, softly
serene on Beacon Hill, silent, remote.

Many years passed... looked up... a gull flashed
just over the roofs in the brilliant blue
of a Norfolk winter. My thudding heart knew...
it knew not what. But something immediately true.
Was it only hope leapt up? That shining day
what could a gladdened mind know of dismay?

Is time ever brought to heal? Can we come to truth
in a moment? And do we feel its presence,
or capture its flight? We pause... like John Keats,
one with the birds, caught in a brief illumination
of life, sharing in innocence, sensing we are
unaware, but passing down columns of air.

Those Boston days were a rediscovery
of poetry's heights of happiness, no augury
of death and the slow knowing of how unaware we are.

J. K. Coleridge

All At Sea

O' to escape the concrete and dirt of dry land
for dreams of drifting upon waters divine,
to rid oneself of all things shallow and bland,
to tread barefoot across warm silken sand,
and plummet the depths of the beckoning blue brine.

O' to wade the swirling white foamy sea,
to float endlessly atop the ocean so clear,
to heed the call of the turquoise tranquillity,
exchange grounded madness for watery serenity
and witness the shoreline slowly fade and disappear.

O' to make blue infinity the desired destination,
trail the sun's shimmering stripe its rays have set gleaming,
toast oneself in the drink with spellbinding elation,
plain-sailing the surf unto the unreachable horizon,
ridding the crest of life's waves to where time has no meaning.

O' to ceaselessly coast from all things polluted and manic,
get lost at sea, cure the craving for fresh sea air,
hearing only the swoosh, splash and ripple of all sounds oceanic,
beholding beatific aquamarine shades of aquatic panoramic,
leave with the tide, into deep blue oblivion, on a slow boat to
Nowhere.

Roger Phillips

"The Man"

He is a man of thirty three
Yet like a child he laughs with glee
In a special place does he live
Ever willing is he to forget and forgive.

Readily we'll conjure up a smile
Without a complaint he'll walk a mile
His life is filled with constant laughter
He lives for the moment, not for what comes after.

But so much of life has passed him by
It makes you want to sit and cry
Does he know how to appreciate life?
Though he has lived it without much strife?

Yet one can't help but envy him
He has happiness filled to the brim
He's been spared from feeling sad
On the whole, his life ain't so bad...

Shireen Batcha

'London Pride'

An old tramp plays by the embankment stand
Nobody listen's or ever gives a dam.
His greasy cap placed upon the dead concrete ground
While stained nicotine fingers play the harmonica sound
The soles of his shoes are tattered and worn
Purging with news paper 'Yesterday's News'
Like his youth come and gone
Two fold the music, none stop he plays.
While the blackbird joins him in full array
One satisfy's his restless soul while the other his drinking.
Like the fish in a glass bowl.
From the thames cool breeze, the almond trees in full bloom.
Sway gentle to the rhythm of his begging mood
While petals fall dancing around lovers feet,
For him heavens his only retreat
Not even Beethoven at the festival hall
Can compare to the loneliness of his harmonica call
On and on the nostalgic sound
'London Pride' on the embankment is found

Celia Ashton

Mummy Watched You Die

A delicate tear falls upon her soft pale face,
Her hand reaches out,
but all she can hold is a hanky full of grief.
Baby in a cradle,
The innocent games you played.
Toy soldiers, your death.

Mummy watched you in the garden.
She watched you pull the trigger on your plastic gun,
and the stone you through, which was your bomb.
Mummy laughed as you rolled in the mud.
Then the garden turned into his grave.
Her boy was marched to war.

The gun you fired killed innocent young men.
The bomb you through, blew up the trench.
The mud, his blood, choking drowning.
Her baby now a stone cross,
As mummy watched you die.

Sarah Watson

Floral Tribute

Fresh bloom the daffodils upon your grave
Springing from fertile soil enriched by you,
Mirrored by sunlight in the polished stone,
Framing the golden letters of your name.
I stand here, remembering.

"Give me flowers while I live", you said,
"Not when I am dead".
My dear, I do, I do;
Though mortal residue lies here
Your spirit lives and ranging free
Loves and remembers too.

Thomas S. Hicks

A Mother's Prayer

As I kneel and pray on Christmas Day
For my loved ones, so far away
In this house, now so dark and void
I might hear again the laughter in a boyish voice

The firm tread upon the stair
A husband's greeting "Hello dear are you there?"
A tiny whimper from the cot across the way
A young mother's voice raised in sweet refrain
A proud father looking down upon his tiny son

Oh why did you have to die so young
As I walk my weary way
My heart goes out to you all in vain
God bless you all until we meet again.

Joyce McGrath

Drugs

So many tears are falling slowly
Most everyone is sad and lonely
The people of the night
Are looking for the light
And clutching stars that glitter brightly
We bend our knee to fantasy
And linger in our golden dream,
Forsaking thoughts that this might be
The nightmare of our yesterday

And when the stars of night are sleeping
The morning wakes and brings the pain
Of facing one more day of - nothing
And waiting for the night again!

M. Fromhold

Like The Waves

Splashing on the sand,
Towards me.
An offering, I thought,
So I took it.
Maybe it is what I've been looking for.
Soaking into me,
I touched its silver, smiling ripples,
Slowly and gently.
And inhaled its salty scent.
But before I could hold it and keep it,
It of its own mind, fell purposely,
Shattering into a million pieces of worthless crystal.
It backed away from me,
Not wanting my company,
For I misunderstood its meaningful gesture and shine.
In silence, I try to forget,
Push it away, out of my thoughts,
But I can't,
Because I'm trying to mend a broken heart.

Sharon Cheng

Friendship

There is nothing quite so precious as a friendship,
another spirit who helps in times of strife,
Who laughs and cries and comforts you through
the ups and downs of life.

They'll walk beside you in the sunshine,
down a winding country lane,
Or they'll write letters to a far off place,
till you come home again.

A friend can say whatever's needed,
even though the truth might hurt your pride,
They'll keep their place while you recover,
then fall in step right at your side.

When you feel the world's against you,
that there's only trouble left in store,
A friend will take your hand, and firmly place you
back in the stream of life once more.

Sheila Hawkins

Riddles Of The Universe - One

I pity not the man who fails
and overcomes to leave his mark.
Whose destiny as it unveils,
sheds light where all before was dark.
To rend the Oak receives the power
and understanding man's conceit
learns nothing when his vision pales.

Laments are pointless for the earthly dead
that choose to leave consumed by their own passion.
as corn that rots renews the daily bread
so who will rise again in heavenly fashion.
There is some merit in this self deceit
for rotting bread can make all man replete,
renewing birth his journey lies ahead.

If knowledge is within then what's without?
All sight and seeing? Is there room for doubt?
And does all time reverse itself at midnight?
reliving all this sorry human plight.

Thomas Moore

Rebbeca

A babe was born to my wife and I
Healthy and whole, well able to cry.
We shared in our love, complete and repaired
I felt forgiven, wanted, our marriage saved and spared.

A boy and a girl, a home and a wife
A job and a future, perfection - rare in life.
One day I came home, relaxed with a coffee
"Won't be a minute" she said, "Just go check the baby"

I stood up to join her, share joy in the sight
"Tooommmmmm!" came her shriek of fright.
Ran to the bedside, "Rebbeca's gone blue"
Sheer shock and horror, great chills going through.

Snatched her up in my arms, "Ring an ambulance!"
Cold floppy rag doll, but not dead in my glance.
Sheril shrieked into the street, screaming "Rebbeca, Rebbeca's dead!"
Broken completely by that sight, and I almost out of my head.

Tear drenched babe, I blew in your mouth
'Til the ambulance came, then there was no doubt.
Now all is lost, and now all is gone
Love left with Sheril, so I'm all alone.

Thomas Henry Ledger

Little Angels

Parents, relatives and people of Dunblane
Why have you been given such a grief and pain?
Your question to God will be why my child?
And how was this monster allowed to run wild?
They were sweet and innocent, just wanted to play.
Now these dear children have been taken away
Your heart will ache and your eyes will never be dry.
These feelings will be with you
until the day you die.
You'll feel like yelling and screaming out loud.
For now you're locked under this dark black cloud.
You'll tell yourself wake up, it must be a nightmare.
Deep inside, you'll be saying,
Life's just not fair.
They brought you joy, think of
all the good times you had
My heart goes out to all the
parents, relatives for I to am a dad
They're not alone, when they left, they all left together
Now they will play in heaven, little angels forever.

James O'Brien

469

Untitled

'Twas one cold day, in the month of May,
I stayed at me grandpas house.
As I came down the stairs he called apples and pears
I say a big fluffy grey mouse.
So I got very bold, and when it felt cold,
By the fireside is were I laid it.
But it didn't reveal the most tiniest squeal,
It never moved one little bit.

So I put on me coat, and I wrote out a note,
Poor mousey's life's come to an end.
And took me old spade to dig it a grave
At least it had one little friend.
I went back in the house crying tears for me mouse,
And saw grandpa sitting down to is kipper,
Oh there you are Sue I've been looking for you.
Have you seen me fur ball off me slipper!

Linda Otton

Reflections

Years past come rushing, like the tides from far off shares.
  Happiness, pain, sorrow like the waves that roar,
Children's laughter, distant, hollow like sea-shell to ear.
  Times gone by, so far and yet so near.

Sunny afternoons in gardens, perfume filled
  Where to each other our hearts over spilled,
Moonlight illuminating waterfall
  Love in abundance for all.

Christenings, weddings, funerals, and all happenings between,
  Life is but a circle, yet a dream,
Wishing, wanting, waiting, and what for?
  The hand of God is all that one will need when life is o'er.

Mary Connaire

Take That 1991-1996

You think they'll always be there forever
but suddenly they're not there at all
and the pain you feel when they're finally gone
it's like your heart's been wrenched from your soul

They've been with me five long years
made me smile when I'm feeling down
The joy they gave me - I'll never forget
and it will never be far from my heart

Nothing will replace that feeling of joy
when their faces appeared on the screen
nothing will take the despair I felt
as they walked away so far from me

I'll never get to see them again
but the memories they will live on
I'll close my eyes, remembering good times
dreaming of all their songs

Allie Davey

Patience

She had no patience, couldn't wait
Just leave her future up to fate
Spending five pound notes and tenners
On tarot cards and fortune tellers
They all had different things to tell
She even bought a wishing well
She's wish for cars and handsome men
Lots of kids, nine or ten
While shopping, something caught her eye
This was one she had to try
While climbing for the crystal ball
She fell head first into a wall
No amount of money spent
Prepared her for the way she went
For years her coming fate she sought
She found out sooner than she thought.

Mary McShane

The Telegram

Alone she sits each day,
Her eyes alive in anticipation.
Searching the lost souls beyond
For her love to return in jubilation.

Countless springs and summers
Have walked gaily outside her door
New houses, new faces, new lives;
But she is not aware anymore.

Her frail body guides the rocking chair,
Probably insensible to her motion;
Only those eyes search the pavement
For he who went missing in action.

The telegram sits shyly at her feet.
Never intruding, still waiting for the moment.
So many years gone, so many years
Yet still she sits and waits for her gent.

My eyes glance down as hers rise up
No words for her hope can I give,
But I will pray, as she, for his return,
For as long as she shall live.

Sayeda N. Abu-Amero

Sun Of 85

Our lives like straws we draw, seem to parallel each others
very different yet we mirror one another.

Each turn we take has been mapped,
yet something tells me you have been down this path before me,
like a lighted pathway you guide me, helping me unravel life's
mysteries, "come my friend," you tell me, "I will help you
discover this strange land."

I come from a different world, you came here taking a different
route yet we meet at this crossroad,
and the blood which runs through our veins tell us we are one,
you tell me about your life, and that life is my story too.

My culture has served as a force to rush me in
and keep me serene amidst the currents of this new age,
yet I seek your ways, your lifestyle, only to find that we aren't
too far apart.

We sometimes speak in different tongues, still yet a common
thread binds us, we have the same dreams, we share the same
fears, we aren't too far apart.

Something whispered in my ears by my ancestors long gone,
tells me that you and I can find mutual ground
perhaps because we rose on the same dawn.

Sokunbi Sowunmi

"The Journey Of Life"

We are born to our Mothers and reside on this earth,
Our lives can be sad or filled with mirth,
We travel our paths full of hope and life,
We can also encounter some days of strife.

We all tend to go our own private way,
Some straightforward, but some do stray,
Some of us find the journey serene,
Others are wondering what might have been?

It may be best just to look ahead,
Completing the tasks and thoughts unsaid,
This way our lives will be fulfilled,
Never dull or empty, but like a field just tilled,
Ready to cultivate new ideas,
Looking to the future without any fears.

If we can live our lives on an even keel,
As we journey on, see someone to heal,
Our time on earth will have been well spent,
As the scriptures say, we are only lent,
When at last the day comes for eternal rest,
We can look down on our offspring who are put to the test.

Kathleen Hale

Loneliness

As the mist thickens to a heavy fog
The old woman peered through the curtains she shivered.
Another long long night alone
Her only company, a green eyed black cat
Purring by the empty fireside.
A creak in the roof space - the cat stretches
And the woman looks around.
Pale faced sweating she reaches for her chair.
Into its comfort she sinks hoping to fall asleep
Wishing the morning to come.
If only a neighbour would come to pass an hour
To talk, and have a laugh but no one came.
The cold air crept down the chimney and under the door
It filled the sparsely furnished room
And settled on the old woman she shivered
The cat moved onto her lap and snuggled close
She reached for a rug and covered them both
Settling for the night she slept a long sleep never to waken.

Sarah A. P. Gallagher

Me, Myself And I

Who am I? Who should I be?
The whole of my life yet to live
Why is so much expected of me?
I've only got so much to give.

You must be perfect, you must be strong,
Society says that's how you should be.
And how I've tried to for so long,
But I can't do it, that's not me.

Confident, happy, is how I appear,
Clever, talented, young and carefree,
Yet deep inside I'm full of fear
That's just the surface that they see

Negative, selfish - a misconception
Unhappiness and deep despair
This child inside me craves protection
Does anybody really care?

They can judge me, have their view,
But I'll survive, I know I can,
If I remember my own value,
I am what I am, I'm only human.

Amanda Cole

Snow Garden

The paper lies before me - stark purity of first fall.
    White emptiness. Am I snow blind?
Words slide and tantalize beyond recall,
    Blue cats caress the shadows of my mind.

Fat tabby nuzzles, then evades the hand
    Seeking to hold, manipulate, possess.
Snow garden is a secret land
    Of magic or of emptiness.

Warm pads pass hesitant across the snow,
    Pale sunlight slides over the icy day.
Words, indentations, follow where they go,
    Cats in the garden showing me the way.

Svelte siameses stalking metaphors.
    Grey smudges formed by phrases half forgot.
Clawed assonances sheathed in velvet paws.
    Cats fighting. Words all in a knot.

Tails form a question mark in time and place,
    The cats are playing now in open sight.
Snow garden, white page, both defaced
    By footprints and by words I write.

D. A. Hipwell

Perverse

I didn't want to walk so near the sun,
I like the ocean.
I didn't want to really learn to run,
I'm used to crawling.

I didn't want a numb and airy bliss,
The hurt's inspiring,
I didn't want to shelter in a kiss,
The bruise becomes me.

I didn't want the bed of petals softness,
Nails are sharper.
I didn't want your flowing printed dress,
It didn't know me.

I didn't want envy in their eyes,
Pity is kinder.
I didn't want the tear that quickly dries,
Sobbing's a blanket.

I didn't want to cultivate rare lilies,
Daisies are brighter,
I don't want life to be easy,
I want to fight her.

Nikki Lightly

Beauty

A picture one does not very often see,
a combination really quite so rare.
Eyes that seem just pools of mystery,
head crowned with black and silky hair.
Oval face, carved as if out of marble,
lips like a bow, full and soft and warm.
Figure of a heavenly dream-like marvel,
perfection of a child just newly born.
A voice that's soft, low and full of meaning.
A smile, offering confidence and trust.
A mind so full of love and willing dreaming,
a heart wherein love lives and simply must.
And so, she moulds and plans her life
with one she loves and knows could not be better.
He will rejoice to call her just 'his wife,'
and Isaac finds again his own Rebecca!

H. Herring

March 1996

The crocuses are out!
Bright yellow egg-yolks in the grass.
Catkins wriggle in a playful breeze
Primrose sun in a pale blue sky.

Kittens roll in ecstasy
On the warmed garden path
Old dog snuffles and snorts in the rich earth
Prances on the damp grass.
Old cat blinks and licks his lips
As birds flirt and fly
In joyous living.

Spring is here,
The crocuses are out
I am alive again!

E. A. Caton

Word Processing

Flirting with fancy and flippant frivolity,
Boisterous banter with jokes, japes and jollity,
Cheerful chuckles and chortles, of charity,
Cut out this hysteria, this hearty hilarity,
These giggles and guffaws, yes, even garrulity,
Quirks, quibbles and quips beyond all credulity;
Such trivial toying with words tries my temper,
Like the witless whining from a dog with distemper.
Must one swallow such stuff like grouse out of season?
It has alliteration and rhyme but no reason!

M. Ebbage

A Greek Sunrise

I watched the sun come up this morning,
golden, golden, unfolding.
Catching the Aegean half asleep.
Pushing, stretching the Aegean deep.
Chugs of elf-like boats go by,
holding ageing faces with silent sighs.
Mountains now visible dusted lightly in cloud.
Motionless Islands in the distance now found.
The sea splashed yellow with the awakening sun,
now gurgling pleasantly like new life begun.

Jose M. Bradley-Giakoumakis

Optimist's Eyes

What do you see when you look at the sky at night?
I see a silver sickle moon shedding her light.
I see shimmering stars floating on high.
That's what I see when I look at the night sky.
Ethereal clouds, shooting stars on a midnight-blue background.
A timeless perpetual pattern totally devoid of sound.

What do you see when you look at the winter weather?
I see filigree snow-flakes as soft as a feather.
I see diamond icicles that shatter and splinter.
That's what I see when I look at the weather in winter.
Crunchy-crusted snow like sugary meringue that decorates all.
Tinsel topped twig complimenting fruit and berry bauble.

What do you see when you look at a rainy day?
I see a soft blanket of cloud in shades of grey.
I see splashy puddles, rivulets and gurgling drains.
That's what I see when I look at a day of rain.
Natures life-giving liquid, washing, cleansing and quenching.
Zillions of droplets damping, dowsing and drenching.

D. McLoughlin

Sweet Soft Was She

Sweet soft was she like cotton clouds above,
When touched by special moments of her bloom;
As I was touched a student of her love,
To find a heart which thought itself immune.
Where she's imposed a difference that is strange,
To change a former self I knew before;
And I am left a stranger to that change,
My heart aware but now my head unsure.
What price that lady's love, then is today,
Who takes her passion from the stars it seems;
Cold as the light they shine she is to me,
The substance of and total to my dreams.

R. S. Blackshaw

The Summer's Wedding

The bride is be-decked in the snow-white flowers
Of dainty filigree Queen Anne's lace,
Hawthorn and meadowsweet scent the air,
Chestnut candles, pink and white
Sway above in the summer breeze,
Buttercups strewn on the bridal path,
And the daisy opens wide her eye
To see the glorious panoply.

Choirs of chaffinch, blackbird and thrush
Fill the air with joyful sound,
Flights of swallows dip in salute,
And blossom petals softly fall
Upon the happy wedding scene.

And waiting for his summer bride,
Stands Autumn, mellow, russet-crowned
His gift of harvest gathered in;
With glowing face, in gentle voice
He promises fruitful days to come,
And fulfilment of the Summer's dream.

Doris A. Dowling

"Peaceful Departure"

Life was slowly ebbing
From my kindred mother.
Fully alert and wide awake
She gave so little bother.
Content with all the little things,
My hand upon her brow:
"How good it feels", she kindly said.
Could we only do it now.
If she would only stay alive!
Oh! How selfish human nature,
To do our best to keep her
From a much more peaceful future.
Her kindness flashed before our eyes,
We knew, but feared to think,
Those welcoming arms would soon be cold
'T would only take a blink.
So precious is life and yet it goes so quickly.
We held her living person there,
But the hand that held her hand
Was slowly made aware.

Bernice McCallion

In Hospital

The Wards are quiet as patients drift to sleep
The lights are dimmed as Nurses watch do keep
The noisy sounds that permeate the day
Have vanished now and only sleep holds sway.
But suddenly a patient calls the Nurse -
Reporting that her pain is feeling worse.
Then others in the room awake to hear -
And they themselves experience her fear.
But soothing words from one who must know best, -
Affects them all, as they return to rest.

Those Angels in our lives when we are ill, -
Can never really know, the gap they fill -
When reassuring us with gentle word
Not showing us, how their hearts are stirred.
The Doctors too - and all the others teams,
Their reassuring skills, like golden beams-
Uplift our hearts and calm our inward fears,
Cheering us up - when we are close to tears!
Devotion of this calibre is rare
And merits acclamation far more fair!

Marguerite Brassington-Griffiths

My Mysterious, Secret Love

Pale azure with a cobalt cast, your eyes found and captured me, from behind soft lashed you held my gaze. But my darling what 'did' you see? A lonely soul with a place for you? A heart that yearned for passion? A woman charged with a burning need for a change of routine and fashion? Or a discontented housewife? Suppressing dreams of breaking free? Oh to climb beyond those eyes to know what you see in me. Your gentle voice...it calms me, and slows tumult life I escape my role as mother, gone is my duty as wife. Your whispers of love...they melt me, and I'm a woman once again, I rely on you now to release me, from a world that's routine and mundane. In your arms I'm 'allowed' to be me, I can vent the want inside, then I lock it away on my return home, but it's often hard to hide. You're the reason I'm sometimes anxious, you're the smile I can't explain, like a ghost you'll drift around me, slipping in and out my brain. My company at the kitchen sink, my inspiration when I'm down, you're the memories in my laughter, the pain etched in my frown. In my thoughts whatever I do, every hour every second you're there, you're the reason I put on my make-up, the reason I style my hair. Without you now there would be no magic, in the moon or the stars up above, you're my other life, my anonymous friend. My mysterious secret love.

Jacqui S. Starkey

The Caring Mind

Through timeless aeons, the age old tale-
Menage-a-trois best sums it up -
Yearning, excitement, resentment too,
A tangled web of love and lies,
Prevarications
Interspersed with declarations,
Avowals new.

The single thread of love is all
That gives the man (The woman too?
Who knows? - She will nor say, or can't)
The where withal to open up his life afresh,
Commit himself with no regret,
Accept what Kismet has in store,
To leave an ever open door
To gardens of delight, not rich,
Yet, if only she can see it, which
Lead on to riches unforeseen,
Fulfilment of a different kind
Existing in the caring mind
Of love.

David Selway

The Feathered Friend

The canary was a good friend to me
As she flew from perch to perch
With no idea of how I felt
Of my thoughts and relentless search
To find the person that I once was
Mixed up and so confused
But to hear her chirp and whistle, was
Something that made me amused
She was something special, this feathered friend
who could offer no advice as such
Just watching all her actions
Taught me so very much
It seemed as though I was being told
To carry on with the fight
Don't give in to all the stress
Everything will turn out right

Clive Bloyce

Piano Magic

Sensitive fingers touching Ivory Keys,
Opening doors of Magic-creating fantasies,
Pounding the beat into someone's brain,
Injecting the tune into every vein.
Reaching a point where thoughts collide,
Telling without words what's felt inside,
Changing thoughts into notes and notes into hearts,
Spilling over the joy the music imparts.
This mastery, this art, this compulsive obsession,
To create gentleness, love or even aggression,
This way to express what life's all about,
To keep your lips sealed - and be able to shout,
This wonderful drug that knits hearts together,
Is yours in your hands, clasp it forever.

Pauline Fenn

One Day For Me

Two long years I looked out from the shore,
am I to spend my life here evermore?
My daily quest for food and drink,
gets harder ever as I sink,
into this mood of pessimism,
as I scan the horizon through this prism.
Behind me lies the Mountain high,
wooded steps up to the sky,
would I climb them every day,
but my search for food stands in the way.
One day perhaps a ship I'll see,
will I faint or jump for glee?
God give me the chance, that I can see,
it coming ashore one day for me.

J. R. Cubitt

Deep Within

The day begins with startling light
Through sturdy boughs of frosty sheen,
Encapsulating a world of peaceful sight
Whilst deep within the snow, life sleeps.

Well defined it smoothly flows
Over ditches, hills and moorlands,
Supplanting white in cascading rows
Right to the heart of our inner souls.

This beauty we are indeed aware
But still our breath escapes us
A delicate frond, tall grasses to share
Encrusted with a mantle.

The sun fades quickly in the sky,
Dark frowning clouds replace it
The blackbird swings on branches high
Undaunted by the prospect.

As the last vestiges of light
Draws all into its embrace,
Alone the wind with a driving bight
Ensnares us with a chilling fear.

Agnes McRae

Bluebell Magic

Life is like the bluebell wood
One can never really claim it.

Somehow it springs from bushing shrub
And scents the air with heavy hyacinths
Guide electric deep and damp from harms
Springs the heavy smell;
Pleasing themselves from where they sprung
And can be dormant then appear and startle
A law unto themselves and giddy from a lesser smell
Mid coppiced wood and ditches lived with oxlips
Rare birds nest above ditches keep and dank
Strange stunted hazel groves, miles of paths and tracks
The changing moods, mid bramble and bracken
Hiding, the badger sits,
Glimpses of this strange and secret place,
Seldom ventured, we're invited on a sheltered path,
In this rarest place we halt and listen to our bodies.
Then known a peace as on some dark night
Commencing with the dormant forest now spring.

Doris Prescott

Yesterday's Children

Up with the lark
Not afraid of the dark
No demons round every corner
Run and jump like a hare
Hide under the stair
No fear to go for a wander

Laughter all around
No frightening sound
To make you stop and ponder

A warming fire to welcome you in
Hot soup in a great big mug
But better than that
When you took off your hat
Was the lovely welcoming hug

No pushers or pimps
Nor dirty fly winks
From the sleaze that stands on the corner
Your neighbours were friends
Right to the end
And everyone's smile was warmer.

Roberta Preston

This You Must Know

It doesn't matter what you do
I'll never be the judge of you
There is a place where you can go
I'll never fail, this you must know

I'm sure there's times, I'll disagree
And times you'll not see eye to eye with me
But as you live and learn and grow
I'll never fail, this you must know

I'm very proud of my sweet bud
For as you blossom into womanhood
Who knows which way your life will go
I'll never fail, this you must know

I'm there beside you every day
And hope one day that you can say
That when it's time for me to go
She never failed and this I know

Eileen Furbank

'Legend'

Common men dream of humble means,
Politic schemes by priestly means:
Feeding legend to thee and me.

The horsemen... rise... unabated:
Balkan men thus berated... destroys his brothers:
Breaking hearts of their mothers.

Widows, orphans thus created:
Steeped in legend be.

On homespun fields and cities red:
Mars lay down his youthful dead.
Willows weep and birds lament;
Statesmen cry 'twas heaven meant:
Believing God... to them had sent,
His might squander thee.

K. J. Rual

The Uprising

Greed, power, abuse of man,
    weakness, exposure, a total sham.
Whatever the cause, the tale's the same,
    as timeless as the earth.
Oppression, revolt, bloodshed and horror,
    a twisted sickening dearth.
The quest for freedom to overcome
    a human despot's rave.
A driving force and justice won
    and carried to the grave.
Courage, fear and life itself,
    emotions all supreme.
Can these be snuffed from man by man,
    so easily it seems?
Or am I just deluded thus
    with dreams of self deception.
To rid the world of cruelty
    in search of true perfection.

Eileen Ramsey

Untitled

Our whole lives have now changed
Nothing in this world will ever be the same
Seeing you, lying there
So pale, so cold
It's just so hard to see you go.

Death is such a sad thing
Why does it have to happen?
Loosing you, loosing others,
I just don't think I'll recover,
Then of course, my time will come
And I shall be the next one.

Carly Obee

Henry's Christening

Lent

In his ceremonial christening gown
The miracle of life so good, no frown
The innocence of a newborn babe
Big blue eyes opened wide.

No one can tell of the depths inside.

The organ music softly played
By his loving Dad so proud so staid
Cradled in Mother's arms, so cosy, so good
While proud Grandparent's by her side they stood.

Loving relations and friends joined in to sing
Prayed sincerely with prayers and hymns
To Lent and the coming of Easter and Spring
When sadness and glory of our Lord this day

For new life blends softly with the old
Whether the seasons blow hot or cold
True love is always here to play
It's part of Heaven and Earth today.

Mabel Smallpeice

'Time'

Birds of freedom how do you know
When it is time for you to go
Far away flying night and day
To beat the winters snow.

Through the bars of my cell
Without freedom I gaze
And watch as you fly free,
I'm hoping one day you will pause from your flight
And share your adventures with me.

Each long lonely day the hours tick away
And I dream of the time I'll be free
To go where I may any hour any day,
Oh what a joy that will be.

Goodbye all my friends now
The summer time ends distant
Lands are calling you I see,
Take care as you go though
Stormy winds blow, and think just
A little of me.

Olga Johnson

Letter To Our Children Overseas

To offspring four whom we address, we do not aim to lecture
But to give to you our closest thoughts, on which you can conjecture;
Now you are all so different, nature made it so this way,
Though to us each one is special, that is our thought each day.

With every move that you may make, success comes to us too,
Reflected glory reaches us in all the things you do,
For though you are so far away in other climes and lands,
We know that you have kept the rules in ways you understand.

The first and foremost of these rules, yourself do not delude,
The next have faith within yourself, let others not intrude,
But most of all, fate's changing moods, but not afraid to face,
Just grasp the nettle by the sting, and put it in its place.

Now through these rules you've reached success, whatever expectations,
Without our help, fulfilment reached, we praise the culminations,
How could we not be proud of you, for courage you have plenty,
Your love transcends all distances, without it life is empty.

We all know life's no rosy hue, which shines on us forever,
If without hurt you'd reach today, you'd have to be quite clever,
So when life seem to drag you down, don't hold your head in sorrow,
Just lift it up, throw shoulders back, look forward to tomorrow.

R. J. Smith

Sewage System

I've got nothing to lose,
But I've said that before.
No opportunity to choose,
I shouldn't expect more.
No talent to use, nothing to fight for;
All I want is gone, taken without question.
Left with none, merit no mention.
Last move done,
No hope of salvation.
I don't matter,
It seems so bad.
Down in the gutter,
Life seems sad.
Starve to get fatter,
Lost all that I had.
Conquered in spirit,
No longer free.
Must put an end to it
My vocabulary escapes me.

Tim Challis

Moving On

The early winter dusk cast a shadow on the garden
He saw the swing silhouetted on the skyline
And the sharp bare branches of the apple tree
With the rope frayed, swaying and forlorn

He drew in his breath sharply, and held it
As busy hands dissembled his bed,
Tore the stickers off his door,
And jumbled up his precious soldiers

Dear old Neddy, and Woolly Rabbit,
Soft, warm and comforting,
Relics of childhood, too swiftly passing,
Resentfully he placed them in the box

Teddy Bear, ear all chewed,
Dear Edward, beloved friend,
You shall not go in with the rest,
I need an old pal to-night.
Goodbye old house, and childhood joys
Memories I will keep forever,
On now to adventure
Tomorrow I'll be eleven - and adult.

Jackie Westing

Quiet Walks

I am the bluebell,
   my fresh-blown blossoms are thine,
   For you to behold,
      When awakened spring is mine,

Set fair by the wayside,
   Or to the walks of a wild wood green,
   My trailing magazine carpet,
      Gathers sunbeams to gleam.

Let me abide here awhile,
   Let hand not idly deface,
   All that which by right,
      Is mine own state of grace,

Lightly tread where your footsteps
   Would lead you to stray,
   That others may pause,
      To share my smile the day,

For my ephemeral mantle,
   Is fleeting sent to ever cast,
   Sweet recollections,
      To memorably last!

J. A. Andrews

When You Are Dead

When you are dead how do you feel?
Cold and lonely
afraid, unreal.

When you are dead how do the people that loved you feel?
They've lost you forever,
they can't get you back,
their sadness remains
their happiness lacks.

When you are dead what do you do?
Do you think of the loved ones
that you've left behind
who's lives at the moment seem cruelly unkind.

When you are dead how do you and the people that loved
you feel? What do you do?
These questions still elude me,
but they don't elude you.

Gemma Skinner

Romance With Nature

Together, we walk hand in hand,
Down winding lanes, so full of colour,
Across fields, with sweet scents of summer,
Oh so beautiful, is our native land.

Meandering rivers, slow tumbling streams,
Breath taking scenery, all around,
So much to see, wildlife abound,
All evoking, such wonderful dreams.

Trees and bushes, their leaves so green,
Dawn till dusk, birds are singing,
Oh what joys, nature is bringing,
Such wonders, are there to be seen.

Then I awoke, reality I must face,
Dreaming it was there for us to see,
But romance with nature will never be,
Because together, we live in this rat race.

D. A. Rye

Just Another Sad Love Song

Like a whisper in time, but then so swiftly gone,
A moment in my life that can never return,
For once you were mine, but now things have moved on,
And now I'm alone, but for you I still burn.

A quick burst of summer that captured my heart,
Why it had to fade away, I guess I'll never know,
For then a long cold winter that tore me apart,
And left me so empty, but still I cannot let go.

I long to forget, to put it all behind,
To let go of this pain I've been sent,
I've nowhere to run and I've nowhere to hide
And I wish I could forget whatever love meant.

Let the pain go, let me forget,
What life ever sent,
Or love ever meant.

K. Stringfellow

The Bell Of My Lover

The eyes of my lover are sweet as melting chocolate,
the hair of my lover is like the sand on the beach,
the lips of my lover are warm and full of promises,
the words of my lover are like the wind amongst the trees,
the smile of my lover is mischievous and arresting,
the skin of my lover is like honey in the sun,
the hands of my lover are strong and demanding,
the fingers of my lover are like the flakes of the snow,
the laugh of my lover is mocking and engaging,
the belly of my lover is soft and yielding to the touch.
The thoughts for my lover are like the pebbles in the river,
the love for my lover is like the thunder in the sky.

Paola Lamborghini

Orchestra

The wind through the reeds doth blow, while
in the fields the spring lambs dance.
The lilt of the flute, the growl of the oboe,
ponies by the mother mare prance.
Trumpets beckon and herald the storm,
the changing scene as dark clouds are born.
The baton rises, the mood is stressed, enter
trombone, brass, tuba, French horn.
Drums roll like thunder, rain sweeps the fields,
the brook no longer meanders along, as
droplets in widening circles embrace, bow and string,
violin and song.
with emotion, feeling, rapture and sorrow,
the composition cascades in shimmering pieces,
with tempestuous accord the movement rages.
the baton moves and the tempo increases.
The strings of the harp and bow now wait,
as the cymbals clash and the brass vibrate,
to the zenith, to the peak, and then abate.
The sun shows through, the brook is calm,
the music flows on, the appetite to sate.

K. Ainsley

City Chaos

Glass, steel and concrete standing tall,
Graffiti intruding on each subway wall.
Arcades and alleys like darkness and light.
One thrives in the daytime, the other at night.
Taxis and buses bulging with fares,
Trains that defy daily road traffic snares.
Pizzas, burgers, donuts, chinese,
Indian, traditional, cantonese.
Smells that appeal to each personal taste,
Bins overflowing with take-away waste.
Keen shoppers charge to the front of the queue,
Forming ranks that deny passers-by access through.
Brollies and bags become weapons of war,
As rash bargain hunters take over a store.
Buskers betraying the roar of the crowd.
Street sellers trading where they're not allowed.
Dusk brings relief to shop weary souls,
Seeking bus, train and taxi in burdened shoals,
Now lacking the will to put up a fight,
As they clash with the hordes who arrive for the night.

T. J. Hill

My Gift To You

My poetry is a gift to you,
I share my thoughts and feelings,
It's often I ponder about my life,
And jot down lines so you can read them.

My secrets begin to slowly unlock,
You sit and feel it's you,
I like you have had days of luck,
But unveil my hidden truths.

I'm caught up in a time warp,
My life's slipping away,
I've no one to turn to,
So I write through my day.

Like great world poets I've confessed,
Things I'd never tell my dearest,
I write to please and do my best,
It seems to bring friends nearest.

Now if you've never done it yourself,
Put pen to paper and try it,
You'll probably create a masterpiece,
And touch people's hearts like I did.

Diana Dooner

Let's Sing Praises To The Baby Born In Bethlehem

Let's sing praises to the baby born in Bethlehem
Let peace reign
And war end
And love be for men
Let's pay homage to the only true
King among men
Let the world join together
And sing out A-men
Let Jesus the Lord
Be loved and adored
The Baby of Bethlehem
Be thy sword
To conquer the world
With love and not war
So let us love him more

David Brinley Childs

Prisoner In The Home

I watch the people, go by the window,
I sit in despair and wish it was me.
Oh why! Oh why! Can't I go out,
The answer is this, I'm agoraphobic.

With in these four walls, I sit each day,
Bored and frustrated, relying upon people, to do my shopping.
I know I can not live, like this forever.

Everyday I try to combat the problem
How hard I try, it seems impossible,
Only reaching, far as the front door,
Just standing there, dreading, going outside.

I open the door,
I wish I could close it,
I know if I do, I'll only be failing.

I'm no loser, I'm going to beat it,
for I'm going to try, to get my life back.

Lucy Shaw

My Autumn Years

Have you ever seen the colours of a late September morn,
The greys and pinks and beauty, we get with each new dawn,
I walk slowly through the sunset and marvel with each step,
At natures autumn beauty, so much I won't forget.
The shaded hues of golden leaves scattered on the ground,
And I look back upon my life, where is that girl?
I've lost the natural speed of youth, but my mind's back there,
Oh yes my mind's still there.
And in my heart a young girl sings like echoes from the past,
I may not recall that voice I had, but memories always last.
Time hurtles by with frightening speed, I know not where it's gone.
Though in my mind I'm still that girl, the timeless breath of rain,
I would not change my autumn years to be that girl again.

Pauline A. Burbidge

Dad

Whether in the Garden
Or puttering in your shed
Watching all your war films
Or "resting your eyes" up in your bed
Tinkering with your models
Painting all things red
Talking to each one of us
Those words of wisdom to be said

Most times you'd make us happy
Or "debate" until we're sad
But your thoughts or "bloody-minded-ness"
With best intentions to make us glad
Now empty autumn, winter, summer
And spring will be so bad
We'll miss you not here beside us
Because you are forever, forever are our Dad

Paul Hanley

476

Food For Thought

She twist his brain and turns his head.
Plays games with his mind.
She leads the dance.
He's in a trance and stands no chance.
In the game of love, he's lost.
She takes it all and gives none back.
He contributes so little.
She bobs and weaves a web of silk.
Sucks him in for food for thought.
Then eats his head, after they've made love.
With eight long arms she extends her charms.
Then crushes him to death.
And the game of love goes on and on
and on and on and on.

Robert J. Miles

Life

Today the clouds of sadness dull our lives
And not a chink is visible in the haze,
But through all the trouble and the strife
We keep on hoping that we'll see the sun's
  bright rays.

Too many times life's happiness is marred
By worry and so many little things,
But I'm sure that if we try to make a path
We will be rewarded by the joy that life
  can bring.

And now it seems the clouds are passing by,
A little shaft of sun is peeping through.
It's just as though we've had our little cry,
And now our sky is coming clear and blue.

Helen B. Lyon

Summer's Day

The sun is golden and aglow,
It always lifts my spirit so,
The gentle warmth of summer sun,
Oh! So relaxed have I become,
Birds are sleepy in the trees,
Listen to the hum of bees,
Shadows falling all around,
Making patterns on the ground,
Flowers turned full faced towards the sun,
Butterflies with wings spread wide,
Dart about the countryside,
Sadly now, all too soon,
Summer fades,
As comes the autumn moon.

M. A. Hadlow

Vision Of Peace

Slowly, gently, incoming streams
Of fragments of Peace are trickling in
All over the earth. There is positive thought,
Compassion, care and love in the heart.
There are those who know that all are ONE.

These are the ones who work with the Plan
To bring in a golden age for man,
With food and home for health for all,
When rulers will care for all living things,
And will govern with their spiritual selves.

Then every soul in every land
Will have learned to love his brother-man;
And truth and justice, hand in hand
Shall walk upon an earth at peace;
And all will realize, more and more
Heaven is no place or need for war.

For all will be strung on the silver cord
Of Love-and the earth will be transformed.

But peace on earth can never be
Until it starts with you and me.

Nancie Grant

Spring Forward - Never Fall Back

Can you feel the vibrance that's tangible in the air
What a beautiful, Inspirational time of year,
Everything is waking up all part of a great plan
Perfectly designed to live - no help at all from man,
Slowly tiny buds appear, pushing through the ground
Evolving, bursting forth, Silently with no sound,
To explode into beautiful colours, yellow, blue and red
Clustered together, nodding their heads to make a flower bed.
Lambs frolicking about and joyfully having fun-
Playing in the fields so green, under a smiling sun.
April showers, cooling all, silver droplets rain from above,
Men and women all over the world meet and fall so in love
The hour changes, days grow longer Evenings are much brighter
Smiling faces, such happy people with hearts definitely lighter
Trust that everything in life happens for a reason
Just as surely as the changing of a season
When stark winter arrives it brings about a sadness
Then along comes springtime filling us with such gladness
At this Incredible time of year all your wildest dreams come true
Think positively-follow your heart-that's all you have to do.

Sarah Louise Hall

"Cutchy-Cutchy-Coo"

One morning very early, out of my cradle I
  did see
A man a-bending over, a-looking down
  at me;
He said that he would wait for me if I would
  grow up fast!

He said, 'Oh! Grow up quickly, the spring is
  almost here;
The days of wine and roses are drawing
  very near.'
So I leapt up from my cradle and grew and grew
  and grew
Till at last I was awakened by his words
  so soft 'tis true;

He said that he would teach me the art of love he knew
And now I'm learning more and more, and more
  and more and more,
But not of what they teach you at the seats of
  learning true
But oh! So much, much better than "Cutchy-Cutchy-Coo."

'Jillie'

Rules Of Love

Reassure me when I'm afraid
Miss me when I'm away, keep good
The vows you made, believe in what I say.
Laugh with me when I'm happy, cry with
Me when I'm blue, and when you love me....
Really love me prove your love is true.
Correct me when I'm wrong, stand by me
When I'm right, think of me in the morning,
Dream of me at night.
Comfort me when I'm lonely, have faith in what I do,
Follow me to the end of the earth as I would follow you.
Kiss me softly and tenderly, hold me gently but tight.
If I should lose my temper, please— don't let us fight;
When you say you love me - mean it with all your heart.
and - if you really mean it, even death can't make us part.
Forgive me when I'm not myself, try to understand,
Just put your arms around me, or tightly hold my hand.
God bless you when you say your prayers,
The way I pray for you, and tell him
With all your heart to keep our love - true.

Sonya Bartlett

Wash Day

Clouds of scented steam,
Rise slowly out of the open window,
The copper bubbles and burps like a boiling volcano,
Mother stands at the wash tub-flowing with soap suds,
Scrubs at the clothes with her red and swollen hands,
Different bowls of coloured liquids, wait enticingly,
Ready to rinse, starch, and bleach.
The whole atmosphere is cocooned in a liquid of mystic mist,
Linen gasps as it meets the great rumbling wheels of the mangle,
Only to plop out paper thin the other side,
Sheets tug, stain and bellow, like great
Sails on the clothes line,
Fathers long-johns dance a little jig,
Then twist one leg round the clothes prop,
    Monday is wash day,
    Cold meat for dinner.
        Jenny Taylor

In Memory

Where do I start to explain how I feel
I can't believe it, it still isn't real
You changed the lives of all those you met
And those who you met will never forget

Words can't bring you back again
I know because I've tried
And tears won't help to ease the pain
I know because I've cried.

No one knows the heartache of what your leaving costs
But angels up in heaven have gained what I have lost
My love will last until the end of time
For a Dad that I'm so proud was mine.

Words can't tell the heartache
Or stop a silent tear
Or take away the memory
Of a Dad I love so dear
        Tammy Chester

Dunblane

Like a thief he came and stole their youth.
Their days and all their tomorrows.
They touched our lives but briefly.
Their beauty short lived.
Like beautiful fragile butterflies,
They filled our world with their wonder.
And were gone in a flash.
Corridors that once rang with their happy childish chatter
Are now empty and still,
A silent tribute to their passing.
Time will not fade their beauty,
Or dim their memory.
They will live in our hearts forever.
And still the flowers come,
For God's little angels.
        June De-Bont

Sudden Glance

I suddenly looked at the sky
    And a million things I had
        quickly espied:
Young twilight was laying the table;
He messed light crumbs of cereal
And turned purple cloth sidereal!
Like misted with dew it merely twinkled
These glittering diamonds on veil were
winking;
Nice spoonful of cream was splashed by the
wind
And merged into white cool spring
But sage father moon was snoring while
thinking
Of myriads of things known only by him.
        Vera Kurashova

Me

A busy working life was all that I knew,
Until overcome by an illness akin to 'flu.
Bed for a few days I thought was the cure,
And back to school in a week to be sure.
To teach the children I loved dearly,
Was in my mind ever so clearly.
Not so, alas, as the 'flu did persist,
And muscle and joint paint pain were added to the list.
A year off work and every C.T. scan,
Told me that work was now on ban.
My doctor's prescription was retirement and rest,
If I wanted for Me to do my best.
Myalgic Encephalomyelitis is the illness to blame,
Chronic Fatigue Syndrome a truer name.
Whatever it's called it is most certainly real,
Although many sufferers receive a raw deal.
From doctors and consultants who simply don't believe,
The daily pain and suffering their patients receive.
A eminent Professor proclaims help is around,
A cure is near at hand and medicine will be found.
        Kirsty McArthur

My Little Piece Of Heaven

I'm married to an angel,
A piece of heaven came my way,
How much I love my angel,
There are no words to say.

Why he stays with me I cannot tell,
For I'm no picture to be true,
But he holds me close and speaks my name,
And I'm content....I can't be blue.

I cannot walk — it makes no difference
He loves me just the same,
He says my disabilities
Are just part of life's game

I'm lucky — and I know it
An angel came my way,
And I thank my stars each dawning day
That my heaven's here to stay.
        Margaret Fowler

Deja Vu

The fourth time this week,
My love comes (drunk) to me.
It must be Thursday.
He brings more drink, always takes too much,
Slaking nothing but imagined thirst.

And so he drinks; my mouth runs dry, with
Deja vu of slurred insults and calumny.
He will not eat, prefers to sleep
While I, exhausted, find
But the kitchen for my comfort.
I feed but still stay empty;
I am sadness deep inside.

He says he wants me,
But for what? Unwilling witness
To his destructive display?
He says he needs me,
But for what? Must I always
Be there for him each "next day"?

He says he loves me ...
        Philip Docherty

It Was Just One Of Those Days

It was just one of those days,
the air was sweet and it was May.

The apple blossom swayed in the breeze,
the orchard was full of these lovely trees.

Wandering through the orchard pass,
treading on the new mown grass.

Leading to the field beyond,
where there's a delightful pond

Ducks and moorhen swimming there,
as if not a single care.

Lambs a-bleating for their mums,
who would gently call them - come.

Onward then to see the growing corn,
green and sharp and not forlorn.

The sunshine now with warmth and so bright,
the whole farm looks a wondrous sight.

Elizabeth Russell

A Token Of Love

The planting of a willow tree
Is a symbol of your love for me
And in every growth and branch anew
It also bears my love for you
A token of our years together
Digs deep the roots of love forever
It treasures these secrets amongst its leaves
Whispering softly in the gentle breeze
And as our love doth flourish and grow
So too does the meaning of the Weeping Willow
For in the earth below the ground
Reflects a love that's true and profound.

Paula Marozzi

The Queen Of Spades

The orange light bathes her
as she searches for something which isn't her own,

And the pavement glints in the moonlight
obscuring her dreams.

As the Queen of spades stares back at the moon's face
a white rose drowns in blood.

The lovers follow a path in the darkness
made by the embers of a dying fire.

Which glow
like her heart,

And the sea gives her advice
but her lips turn black
from shame.

Catherine Stephens

On Entering The Third Age

Slowly, imperceptibly the years were creeping on;
I'd reached the middle sixties, the family had gone.
"Get on your bike" said one M.P., it sounded fundamental
E'en so, I bought a cycle - it was just experimental!
Down at the Leisure Centre I took up a P.E. Session:
At sixty-six I learned to swim, now back-stroke's my obsession.
A trip at seventy-four to California, U.S.A.
Made my wildest dreams come true, for there in 'Frisco Bay
The Golden Gate Bridge beckoned me, a magic, misty moment.
And now I'm in the Third Age, my life is well content.
Take note, I joined the U3A, my latest seat of learning.
At seventy-six my life is full - this lady's not for turning.
My 1930's typewriter's been replaced by Word Processor.
The O.U. calls, perchance I'll be an Octogenarian Professor?
Slowly, imperceptibly time goes, there's no disputing:
My Centenarian aim is How To Beat That Damned Computing.

G. E. Foxon

Untitled

Kiss me and tell me you hate my touch
Touch me and tell me you loathe my caress
Caress me and tell me you have no want
Want me and tell me it's not enough.

Embrace me and tell you cannot feel
Feel me and tell me I do not entice
Entice me and tell me you have no desire
Desire me and tell me it's not enough.

Entwine me and tell me there is no thrill
Thrill me and tell me you have nothing to miss
Miss me and tell me your heart cannot trust
Trust me and tell me you care enough.

Paul Hinds

Winding Down

Sitting by the window, waiting to get tired
All alone as recently all local life's expired
Counting stars winking down and watching as we sleep
A nervous cough, a look around, who else will have a peep?

Silence in abundance except the insects wing beats
And the leaves that rustle always, natural wind cheats
A light flicks on, I try to see who is there behind it
Then it's off again as if to say, not my business, don't mind it.

Rapturous in loneliness, content in silent wonder
Activity and interest of the day now all tucked under
Mattresses yield to urgent press as sleep gets ever closer
The next event is breakfast when we activate the toaster.

As I sit quietly overlooking my new found realm
Considering my life's direction, and who is at the helm
I keep looking and listening for the merest sign of life
The quiet and stillness are so thick you could cut them with a knife.

The coffee sitting beside my arm has long since lost its steam
The night surrounds so totally I may be in a dream
But I'll still sit by the window waiting to get tired
And son enough, all signs of life, in me, will have expired.

Robert J. Scholes

Retirement

Having, as one does, the time to ruminate on life and how
the Gods do choose to show the rhyme and reason for
our misdemeanours, now!
"I told you so" trips fast across the lips of friends and
colleagues caught within the self same round. The chips
are down and only God's good grace will spare them
my unnerving glimpse of that swinging scythe.
But yet they try to bolster shattered nerve brought
on by my experience, with "I told you so," as if the curve
of their indulgence does not mirror mine. And as if
their hearts are proof against tobacco and the products of the vine.
I grin within to see them posture so and feel they
should recall as I so clearly do the pulsing blue;
the sirens wail. Others dedication saved me from
my self-inflicted wound; lets hope for them.

David Scarfe

The Swimmer

I walk into this place I feel cosy and warm.
I climb on the block ready to perform.
I go down gaining some power.
Then, Bang!
I go up and out to start my hour.
This is my time to show what I am.
So I swim through the water as fast as I can.
My arms fly high for my butterfly.
My legs go low, then I turn with the flow.
As I push off I feel like a fish, this is what my
Swimming does consist.
At the end when I touch the side I look around
Hoping for a prize.

James Parker

Rain

I wandered down the country lane
To see the beauty of the land
And heard the rustle of the leaves
And knew the sign for rain.

These signs make glad the heart of man
When winter has been hard and dry
The gardener and the farmer too,
Give thanks for the blessed rain.

'I do not mind the aches and pains'
Old Ben the gardener smiled
'For what is a touch of backache
If we get a shower of rain.'

Where shall we find our flowers and grain?
Even the trees cannot survive
To give us homes - we cannot thrive
Unless we have the rain.

At least the rain floods through the land
And rivers wash away the silt
And nature drinks regenerate
By God's Almighty hand.

Rose Finch

Nostalgia

Empty space where it used to be
The air is still, there's only me,
Only me how can that be?
When voices speak and there I see

The dear sweet friends I tried and tried
To conjure up in my third eye,
The laughter tears and sometimes sighs
As mothers call when night is nigh.

They are my childhood chums
No more school 'til Autumn comes,
Swift of foot we run and run
Round the building and up the burn.

Jump the burn there Tommy goes
Missing edge just by a nose
Stifled laughter dripping clothes
Home to face our mothers' woes

Aching longing bitter sweet
Slow of foot and down the street,
Empty space where it used to be
The air is still, there's only me.

Elizabeth Wilkinson

Broken Mood

A plate of cold roast mutton
A half-dozen pages of Lamb,
A half-gallon of strong cold cider,
A supper fit-for a man.

No thrushes song now disturbs me
No children's game cries out
No blackbirds trill now grates me
The moon is now long out.

My tankard stands half empty,
I now muse on Omar Kyam,
A cold nose in my hand disturbs me
The dog views the house with alarm.

The door is violently flung open
My table is viewed with disgust
The evening spell is sore broken
I lay condemned by the just

Do not begrudge me my tankard of cider,
Nor resent me my odd volume of verse
And when I want to be in my garden
Please don't let your manner be tense.

A. N. Gilkes

My Favourite Place

There are patches of orange, white and red;
With blue and pink in my flower bed.
In the lavender there's the buzz of a bee,
And birds are singing high in a tree.

A pigeon comes down for a bath,
Ants are scurrying along the path.
The grass is cut, with edges neat,
As I sit here on my garden seat.

The sky is blue with clouds so white,
They drift across, way out of sight.
The sun is warm upon my face,
As I sit here in my favourite place.

The Buddleia attracts the Butterflies,
I sit and watch them with shaded eyes.
The smell of Roses I breathe in deep,
As I drift off into a peaceful sleep.

I awaken again and stretch myself,
And say thank you, God, for all this wealth.
Not of money, but for the beauty we see,
For the birds and creatures given free.

Barbara Dalton

Gala Day

It's mother's turn to 'phone.
Breathless she asks, "How is it now?
How was the Gala Day?"
"He disappeared the usual two hours."
"My God!"
"I saw her pass quickly in her car.
Made-up, sunbed tan,
Hair dyed, she looks a million dollars.
'Never better' people say.
She's so happy to have my husband.
He's tortured, cold as ice.
The kids have cottoned on.
I'm going to be a one-parent.
They ran to him when he appeared
After the races. To me he said, 'So what?'
What can I do now, mother?
All the time there's a pain at my heart,
She was my best friend, my confidante,
And he and I were the toast of Kintail."

Margaret Wiener

Life From The Bubble

In the beginning there evolved "The Word,"
that was also of God;
Living came, in his name.
The seed was from a pod.
The Holy Bible's word makes one's blood stirred.
Albumin in the sperm,
it has the proteins like a worm.
Blood is the life,
penetrated into your wife.
She incubates,
nine months wait they anticipate.

A bubble we are in and we are not free.
O' life is in and from a cell,
we grow, dependant on the living waters from the well.
The word, and water sustains life,
Want of it leads to strife.
Life's sentence everlasting,
we will all be gasping.
In our need for a belief,
O' our creator, is there no relief?

Elizabeth Hookey

The Versifier

The country poet sits in his hall of fame
through his window
the sunset dusk begins to turn to flame
and mirror all his thoughts

He has no need to search for fortune
Nor make himself a name,
At any time
Free is he to apportion praise or blame
As he thinks fit
As it appears to him.
For so it is that his own story
Is enshrined in his home;
And what he pens is no great glory
But is just written in his open face -
A face which now is lined with age,
Mellow, and full of character.

Vyrnach Morgan Griffiths

Pitch Black

I'm hungry, lonely, scared,
The wind is blowing hard,
I'm cold and wet with frost bites.

I'm in a room of my own it's pitch black,
I feel someone is watching me,
It's late I hear people praying.

I'm relaxed but worried,
I hear tiny footsteps coming towards me,
But I can not see them.

I'm in a very deep sleep,
I'm in a world of my own,
It's like I'm in a hole a tight hole.

I can't get out,
I kick and scream,
But no one hears me

Holly Findell

Untitled

So calm and cool the garden stands
In early morning light
As from my bed I look around
At this most pleasing sight.
When first I came the garden stood
So lonely and forlorn
Beds down each side and in the middle
A much neglected lawn.
'I can't live here', my heart cried out,
'You must', was the reply.
'Just do your best and leave the rest
To One who dwells on high.
The lawn has gone, pink paving lies,
The beds are full of bloom.
A little ponds reflects the skies
Arched by a golden broom.
A garden seat is painted white
To hide the dark brown wood.
I love my garden's peace and quiet.
I never thought I could!

B. C. Neave

Untitled

Crying, they are crying....they are dying
With no hope, how can they cope?
Each tear which flows from the flooded eye...
Is full of a new fear no matter how hard I try.
Bosnia, Northern Ireland, Sarajevo and Kashmir
    everywhere I see...
People are crying and dying
"It will stop, it will stop" When will the politicians
stop lying?
If only...I could stretch my arm
    and help them escape from all this harm?

Umbreen Zulfequer

"The Need To Love"

Love is a joy that makes life worth living,
Especially if you are one that likes giving
Kind thoughts that cost nothing, but play a big part,
Just show your true feelings are straight from the heart.
There are so many sad things in this world today,
We should try and help people in some small way,
For doing just that will give you much pleasure.
Seeing smiling faces would be a sight to treasure.

G. Watson

A Flight Of Fancy

Tired in mind, weary in limb, yet came not sleep.
Restlessness tossed my brain from thought to thought;
yet heeded not the deeper call within, the quiet release it sought.
Noisy the clock upon the shelf, seemed as a drum to my
    unwilling ears;
pulsing my brain into extremities of thought.
Yet in that visioned, wakeful dream, came trivial thoughts,
and thoughts with greater themes; came questions, who's
answers I could never know; came quaint ingenious schemes.
Truth, the reality, abandoned I; to climb the starry carpet of the sky.
On wings, imagination took me up, to soar into the airy night's expanse.
From Moon to Mars in one sharp leap I'd fly.
Prodigious mountains, barren seas between, and weightlessness
    defying gravity.
There creatures hitherto unknown to man, hideous in extreme,
of vast expanse, roamed o'er the trackless wastes, that cratered calm.
Then suddenly, as if by magic, Earthward bound, reality engrossed
my inward calm, and drove the vision surging from my mind.

A. P. Huggins

Gypsy Girl

The gypsy girl travels the road
In worn out shoes
And tattered clothes
Selling gypsy wares from place to place
She's young at heart
But old in face.

She travels around in her horse-drawn van
With her gypsy kids
And gypsy man
Telling fortunes of what's to come
Will you dwell in a palace
Or live in a slum?

She's happy with the life she leads
Selling ribbons pegs and seeds
Seeds of fortune
Seeds of woe
Seeds of the gypsy girl
Far to go.

Katherine Erswell

Aging

Let me lie within your arms
And whisper that you love me
Tenderly and sweetly,
As you did in days long past
When first we met.
Days of promise for the future
Stretching year on year before us
Filled with excitement of the unknown.
With the vigour and naivete of youth
We lay then.
Strong heartbeat upon strong heartbeat,
Our young bodies eager for the adventure
Of fulfilling our desire.
The years have fled, we now are old and grey.
Your back is aching, stiff and sore,
My arthritis is killing me once more!
The convolutions of supple bodies on a bed
No longer possible.
So, let me lie within your arms
And just whisper that you love me, as I do you.

Robin Illman

The Box

This box could be a
racing car
speeding along
going quite far
(but to me it's just a box)

This box could be a
spaceship
going through space
down a deep dip
(but can't you see it's just a box)

I think I stare
I pull out my hair
There's lots as things this box could be
but it's just a box to me

Karen Lees

Flower Power

You handed me a single red rose
And said nothing.
No questions.
No accusations.
No judgments.
Words.
I thoughts words were the answer.
I thought I had to hear you say
"It's all right. Everything's okay."
I would know by your voice if you meant it.
I know you so well,
The slightest hesitation or insincerity and I would know
I had let you down.
But you said nothing,
And in that silence said so much.
You told me that you loved me;
You handed me a single red rose,
You gave us a future.

Rebecca Dunn

The Waves

Then the sea lapped softly against his legs
As he moved away and lay in the wet sand
Enjoying the eternal ebb and flow of the tide.

It seemed strange to him that life lost its meaning
When the pebble of joy burst in his hands
The deep passion of life destroyed by its terror.

There was nothing left but to count the waves
As they came towards him, one by one.
He could only meet them sadly, with an aimless walk.

Suddenly a large expanse of water hit him
Seeming relentlessly to tear him limb from limb
Dragging him down as it closed over his head.

He could not move in a useless struggle against the sea,
His deepest feelings in the power of something else.
Clutched by an alien force, he surrendered himself to the waves.

Like a moonbeam trying to penetrate a cloud
His mind struggled hopelessly for consciousness.
Like a cloud passing over the moon, fate darkened him forever.

Anthony Rodway

The 07.31

A smile is stretched over a mask of pain
And fixed into place with a pink ribbon bow
Heads nod in sync with the jolt of the train
As broadsheets and tabloids form row upon row
Of smiles tied onto expressionless faces
When one stands out and murmurs "Good Morning"
Faces and braces and blank briefcases
Turn as one and the one they are warning
Sighs and turns back to his mind full of files
And the sea of smiles stretches out for miles

Alison Miller

Untitled

Who can I turn to when I'm feeling down
No one beside me when I act like a clown
People tell me their problems, they say I have a good ear
But when I have some troubles there's no one to hear
Pals I have plenty, but friends, I have none
No one to talk to when I finally go home
I once had a lover he loved me so true
Now he's gone and left me for somebody new
Sometimes I question the meaning to life
No thanks or gratitude only troubles and strife
My family, they don't need me I know that is true
They seem to ignore me, that's why I feel blue
Sometimes when I'm sleeping I see in my dreams
A place filled with love and all special things
A cottage in the country with flowers round the door
And people who love me I'm happy once more, I wish I could
Stay here, I don't want it to end but then I wake up and
I'm friendless again my world feels so empty there's no one
Who cares about me or my life and the love I could share
I need someone who's special, to be by my side
Just someone to love me for the rest of my life

Liz Douglas

Observations

Comes the morn and bright is the light
chasing the dark shadows of the night
and we awaken, our dreams now out of sight to greet the dawn

Way up on high a lark is singing
Heralding the day with notes a'ringing
'Twould seem to us a message bringing a new day is born.

The distant hills viewed from afar
Seem like dreaded sentinels of war
which saddens our thoughts and evokes despair leaving us forlorn.

Beside the lake so calm and deep
Where 'mongst the reeds small creatures creep
And hide to escape the heron's vicious beak to survive the morn.

From such scenes we pause in time of ponder
and inevitably we allow our thoughts to wander
from nature's laws: But always we wonder with patience worn.

With sorrow we accept but don't disclaim
for we also destroy in our quest for fame
to reach the pinnacle: It's all a game but hearts are torn.

Matthew Brown

Metamorphosis

My son, just how I feel for you, I thought you'd never know.
From the moment that I held you, oh how I loved you so.
The panic I experienced when you were sick, or ill,
I can't forget the anguish, I think I never will.
The joy when you depended on that comforting from me,
You'd want a kiss and cuddle and climb up on my knee.
Too soon that sweet dependence you chose to cast aside,
You'd be a man, not want your Mum - oh damn your boyish pride!
So many disappointments throughout your teenage years,
A gangling youth so scruffy, for your future now I feared.
But all things come to those who wait, 'though it may be hard to cope,
How glad I am I waited, that I never gave up hope
Of that chrysalis creating, not a thoughtless selfish form
But a kind and gentle, loving son for which I'd yearned so long.
And now when you confide in me, or show me that you care
I see that in those middle years you simply weren't aware.
You're half way there, almost a man and warm and caring too,
You accept at last the love I have, have always had for you.
Throughout the years, whate'er betide, that love will never sway
And son, I know you'll feel the same when you hold your child
someday.

Judi Lawton

A Dream

Last night I had a dream, that dream it was of you,
And I was there, we both sat by a tree,
It was a Summer's day and the sky was blue.

We had all day to be together, and we talked and talked of
    times gone by,
I've never seen you laugh so much at
The things we did, just you and I.

We talked of the future and what we'd do, in years to come,
    just you and I.
At least we'd always have each other
To talk to, laugh with and cry.

Whilst there I picked some flowers, those flowers they were for you
I closed my eyes and made a wish
A rainbow of colours - orange, purple and blue.

I wished that for every flower I'd picked, you'd find love,
    such love you'd find,
And those flowers there were hundreds
For you my sister, my lifelong friend.

Today I have a dream, and that dream it is ours
And in that dream what belongs to us,
Is a rainbow of colours and those beautiful flowers.

Ciara Bond

My Everything

Like a star in the sky, you shine so bright;
To darkness you bring a splendour of light.

Like flowers, you are full of colours that gleam;
As the sun's rays upon the ground, you beam.

I will love you for life, that I want you to know;
The feelings I have for you will always grow.

Life will end one day although my love will never die;
For you it will last until my blood runs dry.

I wish you could see how much you mean to me;
And how much I hope and pray that it could be.

I'd give you the world if it were mine,
For you I would wait until the end of time.

Flowers will always grow, birds will always sing;
I will always see you as my everything.

C. Panayiotou

Ted's My Name

I was loved and I was cherished,
I was hugged and I was chewed.
I even lost an ear one time
And it had to be renewed.

I was dragged and I was carried,
I was bumped down every stair.
I even lost an eye one time
And received another pair.

I was kissed and I was cried on,
I was fed all sorts of things.
I had to have a stitch-in-time,
After bursting out my seams.

I was grubby, I was scruffy,
And I had to have a wash.
I was dried and brushed and cared for,
Until I looked real posh.

I've been talked to, I've been cuddled,
Even though I'm now quite old.
I've never lost my use in life
There's much - I could have told!

Diane Knapp

Sowing The Seeds

My brother sleeps sound in Combe Down
His loving wife rests softly beside
The warm fire turns into nighttime hands
Gently caressing their distant dreams
The smoke rises through old tudor pot
Hiding the frost hung moon from shadowy roof
Curling over thatch-covered barn and the pigs pen
Saying goodbye to Jersey Lil and Saddleback Pete
Both resting in the land of Combe Down

I lean forward in my father's chair
My hands gripping dark stained limbs
Scorched black by my father's brooding sins
Unable to raise his eyes to mother's tears
Her death became hope, but not for me
I look into a mirror's celibate image
No joy or passion returns the gaze.

Leonard Crofts

In The Church

In the old wooden door,
Is the entrance to God's home.

On the carpeted floor,
Are the gravestones lying.

On the decorated cross,
Is Jesus dying.

In the pulpit,
Is the priest, saying a prayer.

In the stained glass windows,
Is Jesus showing love and care.

At the beginning of the service,
Are the church bells ringing.

In the organ, that plays so loud and clear,
Is the voice, that shows there's nothing to fear.

In the long wooden pew,
Is the praying nun,

In the candles,
Is the shimmering sun, sun, sun.

Claire Betts

Was I There?

Was I a follower, a disciple one of twelve?
    Who gave up trades and fishing, to teach and pray themselves
Was I among the angry crowds that shouted 'crucify'
    Release to us Barabas, but He the King must die?

Did I have the Pilate's hands, I washed to pass the blame?
    For I found there was no blemish upon His Holy name
Perhaps I was the Judas man, who sold Him for a fee
    As He walked with His disciples in cold gethsemane

Was it I denied Him thrice, before the cock did crow?
    To turn my head, perhaps in shame, I do not really, know
Was I at the table as they sipped the royal wine?
    When He broke the bread and gently said, "This is my body
    on which you dine"

Maybe I was the soldier who made the thorny crown
    And placed it firmly on His head, and watched the blood run down
Did I wield the hammer that nailed Him to the cross,
    Then ripped up all his garments, and for his robe did toss

Did I meet Him in the garden, after the stone was rolled away?
    For they said that He had risen, and would return another day
As I begin to wonder, was it all but just a dream
    Then I see it - much more vividly - Was I there - I must have been.

N. S. Howells

A Dream

Prepare the ingredients for this surreal potion,
Take the complexion of a full moon at night,
Take the deepness of the oceans,
Take the colours from a peacock that shimmer bright,
Take the slender curves of a snake,
Take the juice from passion fruit,
Take the energetic life of a lion-cub,
Take a desire that could never be stubbed,
Take the beauty of a rose,
Take the beauty that does not show,
Take an inspiration,
Take a heart, soul and life, ready for devotion,
Take the powerful, yet controlled, youth of a fresh-flowing stream,
Take a vision of a dream,
And behold, a perfect description,
Take the description to be you,
It is surreal no more..

Wajid Hussain

Dawn

I awoke at dawn and looked to the east
There, on rare beauty my eyes to feast
From beyond the horizon the sun slowly came
And painted the sky with brilliant flame.
So I walked in the garden this bewitching hour
And saw sun reflected behind every flower.
The sun rose higher, the colours all changed
From red and orange and yellow they ranged.
I stood enchanted such a vision to see
While a blackbird trilled in the old apple tree.
A gentle breeze caressed my face
I felt far away from the human race.
I saw the dewdrops there on the lawn
All turn to diamonds this mystical morn
And an inward voice to me seemed to say
Be happy and enjoy the newborn day.

D. Blanthorn

A World Of Its Own

The gallant and bold pig gives a welcoming grunt,
He searches for food in such a useless hunt.
The lonely sheep wanders in search of new grass and juicy hay,
On her own she'll wander - day after day.
The cow stands patiently, occasionally porting the ground,
Waiting to be milked, without uttering a sound.
The cockerels crow is sharp and brave,
He's unaware that he's perched on his unmade grave.
When the sun shines brightly in the morning sky
The ducklings feel no need to walk as they've discovered how to fly.
When the sun has cast its shadow - no life is left on the farm,
All the animals have gone to sleep, treasuring such a unique charm.
They'll wake again tomorrow and start all over again,
Even if it's in the sun, the snow or the rain.

Sarah Kind

A Grain Of Sand

A grain of sand on the ocean floor
or maybe on a silver strand
waiting lonely out there, for a foot print or
a hand.
Maybe for a child to play with a God-like
innocent hand.
To gather more along with and make castles
in the sand
But others come to despoil it
with their litter of broken glass
but leave it not a grain of sand
but a heap of ugly morass
oh lonely grain of sand
where God himself put you
should we not lowly mortals
just leave what you are, a grain of sand.

Joseph O. Sullivan

Opposites

Elation, joy, emotions rife,
You take me as your wedded wife.
Our joy complete, we have a child,
Is it that which drives you wild
Enough to leave, to find another,
A more complete fulfilling lover?

You leave and go to pastures new,
Is it such a better view?
My love for you knew no bounds,
But you never came around.
Now, when I need you, you're never there.
So, in the end, Despair.

A. M. Baldwin

Nature's Footsteps

Just for now
   Just for today
Let us throw our cares away.
Let us walk in nature's footsteps,
   Let us see things nature's way.

Simple beauty, God's creations
   Trees in blossom, flowers on display.
Birds are singing, skies are blue.
   The sun is shining out for you.

Gentle rain falls from above
   giving life to things we love.
If your pleasures are but few,
   look around, see things anew.

Even on a windy day
   let it blow your fears away.
Watch the clouds across the sky,
   magic mountains floating by...

Cherry Eccles

Missing You

Do not stand looking for me on your way,
Sadly I am not here...
I am a thousand miles away from you.

Do not try to find my face,
In those of hurried people on the busy pavements.
Do not try to find me sitting on a deck chair in a park.

For a short while, I cannot be with you,
To share laughs as we usually do,
To share secrets on our why back home.

But...
I will be in the wind that blows,
In the rain that gently touches your window,
In the leaves falling with the coming of Autumn.
I will be with you in my thoughts,
In places we used to be together.

Sadly I am not here...
I am a thousand miles away from you,
Thinking about you...missing you.

Maria Lucia Da Costa

Life

A wave of insecurity washes over me
I'm drowning in a sea of inexperience
Stood alone in a maze of wrong choices
Cutting my feet on shattered dreams

No-one warned me it would be like this
I worshipped too many false idols
believed too many lies.

Now I believe in nothing
I'm looking for a light to guide me
How can I know if the path I choose is the right one
before it's too late to turn back?

Louise Morgan

Seasonal Heartbeats

The Summer sun's rays have reached my heart...'twas love,
my breath engulfed by havoc play of heat
cooled by the first Autumn showers from above,
teardrops proving the existence of cheat.

Against Winter chill there's a coat and a glove,
but my now cold heart no warmth could it meet
'til peace filled the air with the grace of a dove
and Springtime blossom forgetting defeat.

Ass time passes by, the cycle repeating,
my heart remains blind under love's domain
though many a pain it keeps on receiving.

And yet it keeps on beating without an aim
for a man whose love's worth going insane
when giving or taking is only a game.

Mariella Ellul

1995 VE Day + 50

What did you do in the war, Granddad?
Did you fire a gun?
Did you shoot them dead, Granddad?
Why were they called the hun?
Did you drive a tank, Granddad,
Or fly in an aeroplane?
Did you sail in a warship
Or dive in a submarine?
Why did you go to the war, Granddad,
All those years ago?
Grannie said she cried, Granddad,
Because she loved you so.
Have you some medals to show me, Granddad?
Why do you hide them away?
I'm very proud of you, Granddad
And glad you came home safe to stay -
Will there be war again, Granddad?
Will I have to fight?
I hope I'm as brave as you, Granddad,
I'm sleepy now - God Bless - Good night.

Joan Townsend

"The War We Knew"

Oh! How we enjoyed "40's" although there was a war.
We even new our neighbours, or the folk next door.
There was very little food, and a scarcity of coal;
And sometimes we'd come from the shelter, to find another hole.

Yet, we were all quite happy, in a funny kind of way,
Getting on with the job, of living for each day.
Waiting for a letter, that sometimes didn't arrive,
And thanking God that we, at least were still alive.

Somehow we grew accustomed, to what went on each day.
The one thing we longed for, was for peace to be on the way.
Longing for our loved ones, to come home again once more,
Praying with all our hearts, for the ending of the war.

No good would ever come, from getting so involved,
There is never a winner, and nothing's ever solved.
By killing one and other, that's always been in vain,
So please dear God we pray, it never happens again.

Rosina D. Warren

Touch The Earth

People donate their mark bestow
their imprint on the planets sod.
Hushed benefit for history's account.

For nations are born as nations die
false standards rife are fitted to theory
will we know final victory?

Or, love shall wilt and towers crumble
years move by we sleep. How can we know
the quest of Genesis awake awhile?

Herbert Wilson

"A Promise Kept"

Two roses bloom in the bright sunlight,
One is yellow, the other is white
Planted by a husband and his wife.
At the beginning of their married life.
year by year the roses are cherished
Watered and loved they never perished,
The husband has died,
His wife is alone
She tends the roses,
Where love has grown,
A promise was made, long, long ago,
That they would grow
Until the end of their life,
Two roses side by side,
One must be yellow, the other white.
To change the colours would not be right,
The memory lives on, the roses a delight,
something precious, a beautiful sight.

Florence Walton

"The Dream Of Life"

The ocean waves smash and roar,
'Til trickling waters reach the shore,
and boats that glide upon the deep,
where fishes swim and dragons sleep.

So, tell me friend - where does it start?
But then again - where does it end?
Like life itself, we do not know,
We just go forth along the flow.

Madelaine Ratcliffe

Birds World

Hear the tumultuous song of birds at the morn
The hurrying, flittering, scurrying,
of beings as bright as mortal might,
Of a world as real as ours.

Look to them as they fly in the sky,
Borne with the breeze that sings through the trees,
They fly with the wind, and sigh with the wind,
And laugh in the noonday sun.

Arising from rest, they leave their nests
Then poise with twittering noise
And so do head for the blue.

Hours filled with roving, loving, and shoving,
Tom tits gathering, starlings chattering,
Magpies thieving, cuckoos leaving,
Their day so busy; at night housed so cosy;
In their world as real as ours.

Grace Whitehurst

Conformity

A poisonous spider spins her web,
The signs and symbols upon it of a different era,
She spins, the web grows bigger-to strangle, capture, and take hold.
A master plan she has devised.
Do what she says.
Her web unfolds.

Grey crowds march through the streets,
The web is thick; a herd of sheep.
Don't look at each other and don't ever catch anyone's eye,
The web is thick, they must conform. Ignore the man in the
yellow shirt and red jeans.
"We are individuals too", they say "but we'd never dress like that."
"It just isn't right!"

The old spider laughs to herself,
Robots do what everyone else does.
Doesn't matter if the meaning is lost,
It's the thought that isn't there that counts.

Louise D'Cruz

Decision

As the train rolls on by, I take in the scene,
Watching, yet dreaming of who I had been.
My life has no meaning, no niche yet been formed
But it begins to take shape now as night rolls into dawn.

A hand reaches out, beckons me through
Lights burning brightly, a dream coming true,
But as bells start to ring and I open my eyes
The clock says it's morning, my life says goodbye.

All that it takes is the will to go on,
But people give up, do no more, and are gone.
If you know it's important, the dream will unfold
Draw you in and, at once, there'll be love in your soul.

A part of your soul, of your heart and your mind
A deep sunken feeling you can't leave behind,
Then I'd realized my dream, what I had to do
And the shadows grew lighter, black became blue.

I know that I have to, I know that I must
To keep me alive, not crumbled to dust
for somewhere out there is the chance I must take
Make the choice, take the plunge, before it's too late.

Josie Bell

Friends

Right from the tender age of eleven,
Our friendship formed, a gift from heaven,
Through hardships, fun and adolescence,
Our bond just grew and grew,
We kept in touch throughout the years,
And shared our joys, and shared our tears,
Together, conquering all our fears,
And braving days to come,
And when were old, I know we'll be,
As close as ever, you and me,
And over cups of sweetened tea,
We'll chat of days gone past,
And even now, I'd like to say
Your visits brighten up my day,
I'd like to thank you for being my friend,
And in return I can lend,
A shoulder to cry on, an ear to bend, if ever you may need,
And whenever you are far from me
In my thoughts you'll always be
Just close your eyes and think of me, and I'll be there my friend.

Rhonay Terri Barter

Travelling By Bus

I travel by bus five days a week
Peace and quiet is all that I seek
But can you get it, no siree
It's the other passengers along with me

There are the ones who carry a pack on their back
They turn without thinking and you get a whack
Others with packages taking up a whole seat
When all you want is to rest your feet

Then there are some with feet stuck in the aisle
When you fall over they look up and smile
I've seen people caught in the automatic door
When the bus gives a jerk some end up on the floor

There are cans and rubbish all round your feet
The odd piece of gum stuck to the seat
The personal hi-fi - well that is a laugh
Some you can hear for a mile and a half

Yes, travelling by bus is fraught with danger
Your life's in the hands of a total stranger
I can see if I want to stay alive
I'll just have to try and learn to drive

M. Scott

The Candle

Tear-shaped flame, dancing as if suspended above a white wax pillar,
Alive, glowing brighter, bringing warmth into the cold darkness.

Comforting the woman in pain, as a new soul struggles for life,
Then the flame burning in thankfulness for the safe journey of
that soul.

Soon a light burning a bright and warm welcome,
As the soul is accepted into God's family in baptism.

The same flame though small and delicate, burns gaily on
The birthday cake. Burns again above the young bride and groom,
And again burning strongly to bring comfort to the sick and dying
In the winter of their lives,
And finally around our mortal remains,
When we leave this life.

It has accompanied us from the beginning and is still with us
At the end.
It may have flickered and dimmed as we journeyed through life
But now it shines brighter than before,
Bright as the new light that is almighty God.

Neil Doherty

Whispers

A whispered perception
A reconstructed apparent that renders me free
The whispers of a joyous conjurer
Guiding me, igniting my destiny
I gasp aloft a solemn being
Cast and moulded within the rhapsodies of time
Extradited from such I remain in touch
With the vision that is mine, pure, sublime
Distraction, abstraction, distraught in thought
I breathe incessantly to ignite the embers of my whispering world
Consider my mind as the womb of inspiration
So within a confinement I can nurture and protect
The prevalence of majesty and wonder, as is mine
The shining of this immortal coil will only be shuddered at
Through the eyes of those whose faith is compatible
With the merest glimmer of hope
Whispers become unified within the symmetrical images of faith
The conclusion is mine to draw, true whispers of belief that elate
Eradicate the whispers deep within my soul, a temperance
shall predominate.

Jane Boyce

Goodbye, Cambridge, My Lovely!

I pick up my bags with tears in my eyes,
Gently enough not to break her sweet night,
And throw a kiss instead of saying goodbye.
The lovely past first comes back to my mind:
Her grace stopped my pole on my first punting time.

In the summer flowers is her streaming hair,
With her green gown loose down to the fresh air,
And through many bridges rustle her white feet bare.
Proud swans deep lower their heads around her nearby,
While ducks keep silent and stop the wild cries.

In the strange land, some dogs barked at me here,
And even young drunks shouted at me there,
But calmed them down her pats light with much care.
Mad drivers slow down a lot in front of her gate,
And porters shut the doors much light and late.

Her beauty moves my heart and changes my mind,
But she was born to the Cam under the English sky,
Though I decide to win her hand through all my life.
I can't control myself, with tears in my eyes,
And cry out from my heart, my lovely, goodbye!

Wang Zhi-Jun

486

Nature

When the sun arises at the dawn
   I turn to awake to the morn;
When all at once I turn to see -
   The birds a'flying to the trees.

I stand and stare and watch with glee:-
   All the birds sing unto thee,
And still I stare and watch to see
   What nature will next bring to me.

Suddenly, I glance to see a squirrel,
   He races up a tree, shaped like a spiral:
Again I turn and see a fox,
   Scattering down the rill and rocks.

The rill on which rushes through rocks
   Conveys its fish like its flock.

Then I would say unto thee,
   "Give nature first prize, for all its glee:-
Nature is beauty, sound and sight,
   For what it gives us, morn till night..."

   Denise King

Remembering 1979

1979 is the year of the child
The baby, the toddler, the girl and the boy
The dark and the fair, the weak and the strong
The blind and the deaf, the lame and the slow.
Children the world over are needing our love.

Some of them have all a human can need
Some of them very little they need
Some are so strong they can manage alone
Some are so frightened they daren't stay alone.
Children the world over are needing our love.

We can if we care give some of our time
To think and remember the needs of the child
They need to feel wanted, they need to be loved
They need the security of knowing we care.
Children the world over are needing our love.

So let us together go forward in strength
To build a new world of beauty and love
A world where the child can take his rightful place
Then he in his turn will care for his child.
Children the world over are needing our love.

   Jessie Lowden

Solitude

The busy street, the hurrying throng,
chatting, smiling, as they go along
Their several ways, each hurrying homeward
Knowing someone will be waiting there
Wife, husband, parent, children dear,
with love surrounding all.

   But I am not of these...
Bereft of you, I wend my way
Not caring for the folk I see,
Blind to the boys and girls at play,
Blind to all things, save you and me,
The memories I hold most dear —
your loving heart, your kindly touch,
your presence always hovering near,
your gentle eyes that told so much.
But I am left alone to dwell
on "Might have been", I must confess
I thought I saw you standing there...
But no, with heavy heart, I turn again
   To solitude and loneliness.

   Annie Whitehead

L Of An Experience

I'm only a little swallow, the youngest of the brood
Mum is calling me to follow in the search for our food
She said she had to fatten me to fly a long long way
I like it here beside this tree, don't want to fly today
I'm only a little swallow, the last to try to fly
My stomach is very hollow, my mouth is very dry
With open wings and eyes tight shut I take a great big breath
Start to launch myself in space but, Can't do it, not just yet
The others call come fly come fly, it is a wondrous thing
To wheel and dive, go flashing by, while you sit there sulking
I am so intent on watching I didn't notice Dad
He really caught me napping and now he's made me mad
He pushed me off my blooming perch, now I'll have to fly
I fell and twisted with a lurch, my short life flashing by
And then I opened up my wings, found the power of flight
Oh what joy how my heart sings as I fly fast out of sight.

   Sylvia Cornforth

To My Grandfather

I must walk now, into the dark alone.
Although I fear, I will accept the knife;
It twists, it tortures, but I must not moan
As life pulls me deeper into its strife.

In looking back to see the little light
Poor soul, it fades as death stabs the darkness
And there is no escape from what is right
So, go on and on; there is an abyss.

And you will fall into the endless black hole
Of memories: after the frantic pace,
Bustle of the funeral rites, closing doors
Seeking a reason, a release, an escape.

There is a release, an escape, a breath.
Note: each day we all come closer to death.

   Alison Phillips

Untitled

A joy to behold, our existing life,
Fifty-two years married, luckily, with little strife,
Ups and down we've had, like many other couples,
Although discussion sometimes gets rid of the ruffles,
We're always together and happy to say,
Best of friends we'll be forever and a day
We can't imagine life without each other,
Hoping to be together forever and ever,
Time will arrive, when we must part
Unfortunately, one of us will have a broken heart
Morbid perhaps - when read, by others,
Re our wonderful life, enjoyed by two lovers
We've been lucky, finding our perfect match,
Simply made for each other and that's a fact,
Two daughters we have who are proud to see
Their Mum and Dad, still as happy as can be!!

   E. Pickard

The End Of Love

The end of love is something to resent.
A trying time of discontent.
A time of solace, silence and repent.
A time to wonder where the wonder went.

A love that's lost no longer can enthral.
The dreams of past delights begin to pall.
And we find it hurts when we now recall
With wonder, the wonder of it all.

The end of love is an awesome rent
That forced two lives asunder.
Something said that was never meant,

Or some other kind of blunder,
Which the lover who meant no ill intent
Is sadly left to ponder.

   Terence Jacob

My Winner

As she circled the paddock I studied the mare,
So much smaller and lighter, but who can compare
The refinement of beauty with muscle and power?
She was fresh as a daisy, a delicate flower.

Her gaily pricked ears, as she jogged to the start,
Showed everyone watching she loved playing her part;
But the bookies were anxious, the ground was like mire,
Would the mare take the trip now she'd lost to Karl's Fire?

At the drop of the flag, the field was ago,
They all cleared the first fence, taking it slow;
The second went faster, but three horses fell,
Would Ciao Baby make it? No one could tell.

They rounded the bend doing twenty or more,
The jockeys were urging, the crowd was a'roar;
I watched in amazement as Ciao Baby fought
To take up the running, Delanto was caught.

As I led my mare back to unsaddle, a cheer
Went up from the crowd, but my eyes filled with tears,
To think how she'd suffered to give me her all,
Then I looked in her eyes, and I felt ten feet tall.

Jenny Chryss

A Whirling Dance

When dawn is breaking golden rays awaken me
by bombarding my face with all their might.
I hope they bode a wonderful day, and promise much more
some happiness in store. So I accept this as an invitation
to a dance for a day - a whirling dance to get me up at once.

Indeed, as the day progresses I am here and there,
meeting many people who greet me with a smile.
As I smile back I feel I open their hearts to pour all their love
and to give me a wonderful time - and much much more,
to make me realize life is really a whirling dance to be enjoyed.

In the evening when I recall the events with pleasure
The sweetness of the flowers wafts in the air. While admiring
their beauty I cannot help but see an embodiment of numerous
hearts of those who care. So I am ready to sing as loud as I can:

"That's been a wonderful day to instil a belief that tomorrow will
bring much more happiness than I thought would ever be
in store for me". Thus I invite it with all the optimism
I can muster and say: "Oh come another wonderful day
to take me to a dance again - a whirling dance-
To be enjoyed no matter what comes".

Lucy Carrington

Night Wind

The night wind slips by,
My bedroom window,
Down the alley, past the trees,
Bearing on its ghostly rush,
Whispering tales, endless hush.

Like a king the harvest moon,
Mounts the still and silent pines,
As through the night,
They listen
Shadows falling, filtering light.

But restless sleeps the valley streams,
O'er their gravel beds are weaving,
Swishing lowly,
Weeping willows,
Speaking to the wind of night.

What they say, must we know,
Do they sing, or do they moan,
Do they sigh, or do they groan,
Knocking on my bedroom window,
In the dark of early night.

Noel Teague

To Share Perfectly

In a world of perfect peace,
    All beauty lives; and endless to cease:
And here am I, to view behind the ever ending road,
    To enjoy this life on earth I've trod.

Before me is the - Heavenly gate,
    Behind, is all the faith that carried me,
I've seen, (not only within) changes of love and hate,
    Yet, I've still tried to see...

    The reasons for so many wrongs,
    The weakness to make me strong,
    The patience to endure a trial,
    The long-suffering yet a smile.

A love that surpasses all understanding and knowing,
    I've found and been shown, deep within my heart,
And I'm filled with that joy, ever growing...
    Every day, every season, every part.

Prayer: Bless a World which starves - whilst another just wastes,
    Teach them how to break halves - then all can share the taste.
    Bless all the poor - that they might enjoy more,
    And we'll have learned to share perfectly, for sure!

Paul S. Gordon

Those Who Shall Never Really Belong

The sun rises o'er Somalia
Children seen hugging around a bowl of rice,
this is their only meal of the day,
and it must last.

In the distance a mother is seen cradling her child
who died during the night.
She is too shocked to cry, or is she?
She knew - she had to know that her child would
probably die.
A desolate women, who cares.

A father buries his one and only son.
He holds his body aghast - hands beckoning to the sky -
why? Why?
He falls to his knees, a defeated proud man,
what has he got to live for?

There is no peace wherever they go.

We sit here on comfortable chairs, yet horrified at what we see,
but at the end of the day,
we are here - they are there

They Who Shall Never Really Belong
Donna Hope

On The Beach

Grandma is sitting, busy,
    with her knitting,
Granddad is snoozing
    with his sun cap on.
"How about a swim?"
    calls Daddy to us,
"Yes" comes the answer
    we're off like magic.
Down to the water,
    warm and inviting.
The children jumping, gaily laughing,
    our toes sinking,
    deeper and deeper,
    with the tide trickling
    over and over.
The sun is shining,
    oh for a swim, so relaxing,
    now it is time to return.
Grandma is waving, Granddad has woken,
Now for the ice cream, lollies and pop-corn.
Morag Dyer

Valldemosa

The dusty road winds steeply
Up the terraced hillside between
Olive groves with ancient trees,
Their thick trunks split and twisted,
Their grey foliage swaying in the breeze.
A ruminating donkey idly munches the dry grass
The only sound is the tinkling of his bell.
And there, at the top of the hill
A town, its houses of golden stone
Glow warmly in the noon-day sun
Its blossoms perfume the evening air.
And standing proudly on the summit
The Monastery, like a benevolent parent
Watching over a much loved child.
This place, untouched by worldly sophistication
Is Valldemosa.

Anne Crofton Dearle

Gassed

All the noise around me is weeping
Whilst the rest of the world is sleeping
You hurt me, but you don't care
You laugh and laugh, in my face

Why oh why won't the world help?
You shave me, and strip me
I beg for mercy, but you just keep on
What did I do wrong? Being a Jew?

You try chemicals on me, that you know will do wrong
You put my friend in a room full of gas
A few seconds later she dies, you'll do it to me next

They put us in a carriage, full of dirt, with pigs and cows and sheep
They treat us like a bit of rubbish, we try to hide from you

You put us in camps, with hardly any food
You're killing us because, we believe something different than you

"Next" they call and someone dragged me by my ear
They put an injection in me and put me in a room
You tied up my hands you tied up my feet
You gassed me. I can't remember anything else. I coughed.

They Killed Me!

Amy Bernard

Dartmoor

The feet tread softly o'er the verdant sponge...
Cool music quenches mind of thought and care.
The pillar'd line is sharp!
A ribbon gleams.
A sanctuary of spring; of peace.

Yet all is bare

Denis J. Butt

Longing For The Past

There were times at night, when all I'd do was weep,
But you were there to lull me to sleep,
And guide me, and comfort me, and hold my hand,
You would pick me up when I couldn't walk or stand,
But now, into who's open arms do I fall?
When I'm so much older and I "have it all,"
Please look harder when you step into my golden world,
For beyond this mask, still sits a little girl,
This child can not take the grown up pain,
And needs a thousand kisses to make it go away,
A glimmer of perfection and nothing less,
She became a whole new meaning for happiness.
Never again could I bring so much pleasure and delight,
As an infant could create a technicolour glow over night,
Now chaotic mountains and fading stars loom,
Replacing the love and laughter, the sheer magic that bloomed,
Inside of this adult shell will always haunt the little girl,
Enchanting as any diamond, as precious as any pearl.

Emma Davidson

Beware The Time Is Near

The poor are going to be hit again
the Labour Party will inflict the pain
its plan is simple or so it seems
make unfortunates our streets to clean

The next set of people that they attack
the council workers who get the sack
Then forced to earn their misery dole
are given their old jobs as their roll

It's good it's great it works a treat
the proof is in our cleaner streets
and our wage bill has; gone right down
now that is settled lets look around

Who is going to be next for the chop
The Banker or Artist the man in the shop
The list is endless where will we stop
When all awake too late; (it's comi-rot.)

It would be reasonable for us to say
a jobs a job we should have fair pay;
It may be the best thing to sack the lot
We certainly do not want this comi-rot!

E. F. Heyward

Outside The Door

There are a thousand people outside the door
A thousand people or maybe more.
A hundred schools for them to learn,
A handful of counsellors full of concern
There's a hundred labels for every child,
From 'hyperactive' to 'sensitive' and 'mild'.
A hundred doctors to care for their health,
A hundred bankers to spend their wealth
A hundred teachers to say who's wrong.
A thousand white lies three meters long
A handful of no hopers that will end up nowhere,
A handful of no hopers who don't really care
Several who will lead and each they aim high,
Striving for success and for the sky
A thousand people outside the door.
Frightened and scared by nuclear war
A thousand people of every creed,
Tempted by promise fed by greed
Just one decision from one single mind
Open the door, there's no one behind.

Claire Valkhoff

Empty House

Dark figures drift in and out
Atmospheres oppress me all about
Like ghosts furtive in the wind
Which blows through each room like a restless spirit
The cold is cruel and the silence mocks

Shadows around me whisper quietly
And break the uneasy fitful peace
Their words unassuring and full of dread
An owl shrieks a warning shrill and clear
Leave this house - this place of fear.

Alasdair Cowie

Peace

The sea with all its vastness spread out before me
rolling in on unresistant sand;
it beckons...
TO GIVE ME PEACE

The cool water embraces my body
gentle and caressing waves hold me with tenderness;
it beckons...
TO GIVE ME PEACE

The waves roll and ebb in harmony washing away my pain
I am unresistant;
it beckoned...
AND GAVE ME PEACE.

Jean Aspin

The Old Inn

A building burnt with age
  Where winds blew with rage -
This old inn once with joy and mirth
  Now tumbles down to earth -
Its stone and timbered walls
Knew some day they had to fall -
  A roof clad in tiles bright
Now slip and slide down. This wasn't right -
  To watch them tumble and fall
Before the crumble grey stone wall -
  The door of strong old oak.
With latch and hinges rust and broke -
  Tables and benches made of beech
Once held people with songs and speech -
  Now they're old and broken
  Where not a word be spoken -
Though Winter - Spring - Summer - Autumn
  With all the years of joy to some
    For now to farewell goodbye
To be replaced by a motor way

L. M. Gale

The Grey Geese

Flying the Northern night
They set uneasy cattle
Starting in the stall.
Troubled chains rattle in the dark,
And sudden, a yard dog barks.
Against the winter sky.
The long byre roof is black,
Yet darker shadows now
Erase the frosted stars.
High the Host is flying.
Their calling, a stirring in the blood.
They trace an ancient course,
Untroubled by the times and tides of men.
They are Eponas' company,
The Grey Geese.

T. C. Blenkharn

Mother Nature

Everyone's wearing a smile once more,
Our gardens and plants have survived.
The summer has turned up at last,
We thought it would never arrive.

The winter seemed endless with cold winds and snow,
Our plants and bulbs took forever to show,
But Mother Nature has surprised us again,
with her wonders and magic galore,
It's just the rain measure she seems to have wrong,
So please could we have a little more.

Maureen Finn

Untitled

The sandman laughed surprisingly loud.
when he read the contents of my sleepy head.
he said Dreams prepare you for the day to come,
but with dreams like yours you should stay in bed
for you dream of a world full of love and caring,
when the world out there's full of contempt and hate,
and in your world there is food abundant and plenty
whilst thousands here stare at an empty plate.
This dream world is lacking in greed and war,
whilst countries here are divided by the wealthy and the poor,
This world you dream of...there is no such place!
I looked at him knowingly and smiled at his face,
saying Look deep into the dreams of all who sleep.
And this land that I dream of you will find.
For many dream of this world of hope,
so I know I'm not crazy or losing my mind.
He smiled sweetly back saying "Have it your way.
And may this hope that you dream of get you through each day."

Josephine Jackson

Your Heart Of Gold

You may never be a brilliant star
Or into the heights of fame travel far
But I can assure you your heart is of gold
Which does bring comfort to the old

A very old o.a.p. such as me
It has brought love you will see
Now I find life is worth living
Since you came along so full of giving.

What could have happened before you came
As I drifted along with heartfelt pain
Then you came by with your heart of gold
Determined to take me in from the cold

For this, "Allison", I will bless you forever
I cannot try to be too clever
But you deserve a tribute from me to you
For without your help I haven't a clue

I do hold great love in my heart
So would dearly miss being apart
However such devotion could I repay?
One, I shall remember till my dying day

William Anderson

Our Holiday

On the day we arrived excited and keen
To enjoy our short stay with family we had not seen,
For several years.

Our trip was by plane so quiet and serene,
As we drifted into land.
We were met and greeted with joy and happiness,
And so our short adventure began.

We travelled by car for several hours,
Through small towns all lit up for christmas.
It was like fairyland. Nothing like our home.

The shops and towns were all lit up,
And you felt like a child again.
We stopped at Las Vegas for two wonderful days,
Had a gamble, lost and won.
Oh was fun it was.

Now our stay is coming to an end,
Cases to pack and good byes to say.
A few tears will be shed.
And all that we will be left with are our
Memories of a wonderful trip.

Margaret Wood

Thank You

There are many things to thank you for
In the short time we have known.
That first sweet kiss and soft caress.
When the seeds of love were sown

Now everyday that love grows stronger
Along with laughter and some tears,
And as the months grow ever longer
So will the coming years.

There are many things to thank you for,
All that love which you have shown.
The hope that you have given me,
And all the worries that have flown.

There are times I may have hurt you
By things I've said or done.
But the love there in your eyes,
Can forgive me everyone

There are many things to thank you for
So as the years go through.
I'll walk beside you hand in hand,
Just thankful I found you

David Whitmarsh

Suppressed Love

I remember the love of my youth,
The happiness, the shared moments, the love.

But it was all stopped.
Suppressed by our parents.
Old people who believed only bad about the young.

We tried to fight, hoping to keep happiness,
To hang on to our island of love,
To stop it getting washed down-stream,
Along with our dreams.

We lost the battle.   And flowed away with shattered dreams.
My parents hid the matter.
Locked it away in a box, never to be opened,
They tried to suppress my memories,
Stop my thoughts.

They can't kill my memories like they killed my love.
I can still feel the pain now,
In my broken heart.

I'll never understand my parents,
Why they killed my love to prove theirs.
Or why we had to lose our dreams and be left only with pain.

Vikki Kitson

Road Rage

Tarmac, concrete, chippings and stone,
Great crawling cat and fierce gleaming ram,
Meadows stripped, no cattle roam,
On birds and butterflies, a complete ban

Roaring spoilers chalices mix and go,
More sober liquid roads to hide,
Our drunken lanes we love and know,
Ancient home and hedge on their mad tide
Traffic in poison pollution and smog,
Careless of season,
Migrating millions of wild eyed road hogs,
Bereft of all reason.
Where will it lead this quest or destruction,
As it began, there it will end,
When we learn to heed on instruction,
Will this ever be, that will depend.

Michael Thomas Duckett

Sonnet LXXXIV

The week that's passed since last we kissed goodbye
Seems like a year by idleness made long.
Each minute slow expiring with a sigh,
Resigned to suffer time's remorseless wrong.
And will these smiles I see be here to-morrow,
When all the world is chastened by my tears?
Can people then ignore another's sorrow?
Can laughter still the trembling of my fears?
For though with each departure we pretend
That absence being finite will conclude;
How sure are we that this time it will end
Ere death snuffs our brief living interlude?
   And yet I swear the calendar is wrong
   That calls this lonely hell but one week long.

Peter Cressall

Good Neighbours

We've lived next door for many years,
We've shared your laughter,
And shed few tears.
You're eighty now - that's no surprise,
Your smiling face - those shiny eyes.
You owe all this to your good life,
Not forgetting your dear wife
Who's helped you through the thick and thin,
You knew because of her - you'd win!
Enjoy your day - and many more
At least until you're ninety-four

Dorothy Eileen Kershaw

One Day, One Night

Today,
Tonight
Is all I want to leave it at.
Memories.
One day or one night
I will look back seeing all I had
one day, one night
Every thing I dreamed, everything I wanted,
left behind.
Only in my mind...
Everything we have to leave
One day, one night
But we don't, do we?

Narielle Robinson

The Humming Bird

Did you come, did you hear me sigh?
Did you know of my deep pain
That required some form of farewell?
A brief visit but enough for me to understand
You would not go without a kiss goodbye.

Eye to eye, in wondrous silent song
Within my grasp but out of reach
Gossamer wings humming gently just for me
You said "adieu" my heart was free
I spoke your name and you were gone.

Pamela Soley

Who Am I?

Who am I?
Am I the bird that flies
or the fish that swims?

Oh God tell me who I am.
Am I alive or am I dead?
Can I breathe or can I hear?

Who am I?
Am I the flowers that grow?
Or the mist that beckons the fields?
Am I the blue sky or the green grass?
Am I the worm that wheedles its way through the clay?

Oh God tell me who I am!
I am all these things.

I am the sun, the sea, the sky and the earth.
Oh God tell me who I am?
Shall I live or shall I die?

Natasha Marie Asker

This Child

Tears in the eyes, of a child that's blind.
Love that's given, by people so kind.
Sun and blue skies, this child cannot see.
Inside this child, his heart flies free.

The tender touch, of a child that's blind.
Visions of the world, put into his mind.
Dreaming of colours, red, blue, and green.
Things of this world, this child hasn't seen.

The imagination of a child, that cannot see.
Things we take for granted, the likes of you and me.
Trying to describe, the colours of a rainbow.
Or the gentle touch, of falling flakes of snow.

Love is given, by this child who is blind.
Questions, information, to fill up his mind.
What's time, what's that, things he wants to know.
Information given, makes his dark world grow.

A darkened world, for a child who cannot see.
Questions that are asked, answered by you and me.
This child so tender, radiates so much love.
This child will see these things, in Gods heaven above.

Kevin P. Collins

Life

We start the journey of life with hope
Thinking there's a lot of scope
But when the struggles get hard to bear
And no one ever seems to care
A light shines through the gloom and doom
Our spirits rise as high as the moon

So now a new horizon's here
Forget the past and all your fear
Think of the future
Let tomorrow come
Then all the things you love
You'll find you've done
Joy Christopher

Before

He invaded my body,
I could feel him rip through everything I am,
   everything I was, everything I will ever be, gone.

His hands haunted my mind,
   the feeling of them searching my body,
His eyes pierced into my chest,
   like a knife into an orange.
The pain he inflicted into me,
   was a memory I could never forget.

The recollection of him,
   breathing heavily into my face and neck,
Was sometimes to much to with stand within myself,
And I would wake up screaming out.

The scream was nothing compared to the pain of the nightmare.
Every time I went to sleep I would relive that fearful night.
Zahra Dhamani

Curtains

Oblivious to time of day,
heart has gone fishing with my mind.
Turning a blind eye to conscience,
it was fatal to look behind.
Love's a river I cannot cross.

Dust-clothed corridors of my mind,
ghosts of regret have nestled in.
Round every corner of my heart
I'm lured into cobwebs of sin.
Love is a dream through which I'm tossed.

My ultimate destination
necessitates a path of pain.
I doubt my soul has what it takes
to survive redemption's terrain.
Love's a gamble I've always lost.

I am guilty of the passion
but did I commit any crime?
The veil of darkness draws closer,
ridiculous becomes sublime.
Love demands far too great a cost
Pauline Ilsley

Build On Your Dreams

Build on your dreams.
Let them take you to the places
You've always wanted to reach.
Fulfil your definition of success.
And let your hopes guide and inspire you.

Build on those dreams of yours.
Don't lose sight of all that could be.
Meet every challenge in the best way you can.
And make your plans turn out beautifully.

Build on your dreams.
The future is there, just waiting for you.
And keep happiness in your heart
   All the days of your life.
Roochi Khullar

Untitled

Dear Vera, I'm sorry I can't come today
The pains all o'er me won't go away
I lay weeping through the night
Now I look a dreadful sight
So I sat me down and wrote this letter
Me - thinks os-te-o-por-o-sis won't get better
I like you much, so before it gets worse
I'd tell you that: Unless you'd like to Nurse
Instead of smiling chap living by the sea
A grumpy old Bod in wheelchair I'll be
and though I may go on for years,
This Friendship might just end in tears
for one day you could come to door
Find me near life-less on the floor
So my dear please don't you cry
Let's kiss (if you want) and say goodbye
God Bless you, for all you've been to me
and this little old lad beside the sea
Will smile (as always) and leave the D.H.S.
To come in here: Clear up the mess.
Eric G. Watts

Silence Sounds

I rode a spiral last night,
And
Dropping inward, became a sound beneath the surface.
From whence did one become?
Beyond the blanket, traversing
A long known outcome,
When,
Out of blackness
A shout, and
Into blackness fell.
Silence reigned.
Even behind the silence, I could hear the drip,
Dripping of thought exploding onto surfaces
I couldn't even begin to explain.
The rusted bars of reason couldn't
Hold sway much longer, and,
Creaking.
Reason gave way.
All there was sound.
Philip Noise

Seasons

Spring is such a lovely time, I'm sure you will agree,
The days filled with such beauty for everyone to see.
A time of great awakenings for all nature's treasure,
A time for blossoms on the trees that bring about such pleasure.

With Summer comes long, lazy days relaxing in the heat,
With flowers blooming everywhere this land looks such a treat.
The beauty of a summer's day takes second place to none,
The flora and the fauna are so loved by everyone.

With Autumn there's a golden glow, deep russets everywhere,
I love to walk through crunchy leaves and kick them in the air!
The farmers harvest in their crops to beat the wind and rain,
You'll see many a bonfire to prepare the fields again.

Last of all comes Winter, let's wrap up against the cold.
Jack Frost leaves wondrous patterns for us all to behold.
We've Halloween, November 5th and Christmas celebrations,
No wonder that, despite the cold, we all feel such elation.

Which season now do you prefer? I know I cannot choose,
I feel that there's not one of them I'd be prepared to lose.
For any of our seasons would be greatly missed, I fear,
And I, for one, find pleasure in each season of the year.
Janet Samwell

Words

Words, words, words, words.
What a wonderful thing is a little word.
It may be funny, it may be absurd,
Or the loveliest thing you've ever heard.
What a wonderful thing is a word.

When your dear one is loving and whispers sweet nothings,
Then life goes along all serene,
But when feelings start rising, it's not so surprising
If words paint a different scene.

So, each one that you use most carefully choose,
Unless one day you regret it.
An ill-spoken phrase you may rue all your days,
And it's likely you'll never forget it.

So, take all the nice words, the sugar and spice words,
And leave all the others behind.
Reject all the bad ones, the ugly and sad ones,
And try to use words that are kind.

Anthony Redbridge

The Mirror

We think nobody knows we gamble when we talk,
    anticipate or dread,
We strive to hide our weaknesses, then hope that they are dead.

The mirror speaks. Repeats familiar shapes, unnoticed blur of time.
We organise and front a smile.
But others see the frown, the relic of the snap reply, the sneer.

Our profile is the enigma. Unknown, it does not live.
There are no eyes, no windows to exchange their light.
Turn aside to hide the spirit, wisdom, heart. To cover secrets.
But the side face is not bare. Life is there. And others see.

We interact. A happy man believes that I am too.
He makes me laugh.
I sympathise with sorrows, and troubles that seem to be mine.
I become a comfort. An echo from a sounding board.

Our outward show is made by others. 'I' am interred.
Have I another life that differs from the one I know?
Is the outside part of the inside, integrated, whole?
Or is the inside constant? And the shell all things to all men,
Reflecting them?
The mirror lies.

Valeria Chapman

Thoughts For Mary

She's like a star she shines so bright
And help my dreams into the night
Where ere I go I want her more
Of this I know of this I'm sure.

As weeks go by we've grown together
Just like the downs that grow the heather
No never must we be apart
Me and my own true love, dear heart

When at times we must share sorrow
We say there'll always be tomorrow
And hold together each other close
Then pray as silent as a mouse.

We ask that this great love be spared
Many more years to be shared
Then in the twilight of our years
We will not shed any tears.

For we know we'll meet again someday
When once again we'll laugh and play
For we know that this we've done before
Of this we know, of this we're sure.

D. Stubbington

Contemplation Of Desire

What is he thinking, what does he feel
How can I tell which emotions are real,
Does he not know how good my love could be
When he is sleeping, does he dream of me.

Is he the same as the rest of his peers
Is he contented, or drowning in tears,
Is time what he needs, solitude, empty space
In his heavy heart, could he find me a place.

Should I forget, push him far from my mind
Think of the future, a new love to find,
Waves of emotion are building inside
What must I do, should I run, should I hide.

This man needs this woman to help him forget
To make him feel wanted, to comfort him yet,
The past hurt inflicted is with him to stay
His desperate sorrow won't wither away.

And so, for the moment, the woman must wait
For his pain to subside with his anger and hate,
She dreams of the passion, the pleasure he sent
and clings to the memories of times they had spent

Debbie Thomas

Love

Betwixt life's sway, blows love and passion,
Each so tender, wondrous; And fragile be
This fair sense, bear with it compassion
For those less fortunate creatures; See
What life begrudged the servant chain
Let dignity and worth remain
To us passionate lovers, a Mystery
Come, let us re-live Love's history.

Patricia Naughton

How Deep Is My Love

Like cornfields that reach for the sun above
Like the oak tree searching for waters life
Like the homing sense of a returning dove
    So strong my love for you

Do morning birds sing when the sun cuts the dark
Do kittens purr when warmed by the sun
Do squirrels climb trees by use of the bark
    So definite my love for you

How many fish do the wide oceans hold
How many birds fly south for the winter
How many penguins love to swim in the cold
    So expansive my love for you

How deep is my love
It knows no bounds
How deep is my love
It knows no grounds.

John Weafer

Tune In Your Mind

Treat your mind like a video
Record only what will enhance your life
Like wave bands tuned into radio
They can bring either happiness or strife

Tune in your mind like a video
To what is pleasant to both see and hear
You'll find that in life's heights and lows
It will bring happiness throughout the years

The mind, like an activated video
Dictates only what is recorded within
Violence and wars may erupt like volcanoes
But only with peace and love can your life begin

Be wise and true thoughts as you would a video
To what is pleasant and on how noble to be
As years roll by you won't feel so slow
If your mind is untrammelled and carefree.

Liam G. Lynch

493

The Journey

Copper heart
Poison dart
Straight to the point
With love to the joint
A blanket of broken kisses
An eternity of near misses
Entering the corpuscle red
All the white have been shed
I feel faint and sick
My will for now has been licked
The room now appears cloudy and blurred
But somehow I feel unperturbed
Close my eyes and count to ten
The sheep are unicorns searching for zen
Drifting further into the deepest sleep
I hear sounds of people starting to weep
Do not despair my dearest friends
I travel light and make amends
With heavenly creatures from pastures new
Don't forget me my darlings, I will always love you.

Carole Patricia Smart

Reality?

How deep the night
That changes all reality to dreams.
And sleep-abandoned pain
Sinks into restless peace.
In those lost hours
We cease to live.
Yet into a world unknown
Do we invade
And seek the paths
So hidden from our minds.
We cannot know
In taking part they are but dreams.
Yet with wild fears
On leaden feet we flee.
Or falling, never reach the chasm's end.
Fantasies so wished
We could not spell them out;
For as morning breaks
'Tis then we do become
But shadows of our true identities.

C. Doig

To Dad

Your sigh signals you want me to speak,
but silence had become my language,
when all you can do is hear time passing.

Katie Phillips

Guilt

He came in my life like a breathe of fresh air,
The understanding and affection he shared,
Comforting and loving was he,
But oh no, I didn't let it be,
But who am I to complain,
For it was I who made the pain,
I wish I had made him stay,
I handled it the wrong way.

Now I'm on my own,
I shouldn't really moan,
My feelings are still here for him,
Without him life is dim,
My heart is broken,
His love was like a golden token,
But now it's too late!
All he feels for me is hate.
Now he's gone away,
And there's nothing I can do or say.

Labinder Kang

Separated Love

We are separated by seas, sky and land, but I can imagine us still hand-in-hand.

Through these lonely nights I can dream and change myself into whatever I deem.

Tonight I come to You as a Great White Dove and soar down to You my true Love.

As the spirit bird I can only look at You, but to touch Your tender skin is what I love to do.

These dreams I have every night keep my heart alive with love and together we will always be, in body or as the spirit of the Great White Dove.

Terry Bruce

Lest We Forget

Empty chapels, fractured lives
a new generation strives, with
Shouts despairing, "Where's our jobs?"
The older generation calling them yobs,
Not always true, we have to confess
It doesn't really matter if we think they're a mess.

With designer gear all around
Where is the money to be found?
To dress the young as they like to dress
They are just as we were more or less.

Let's remember when we were young,
to Nat King Cole, or Beatles sung,
with the latest hit or fashion agenda.
Lest we forget, and not wish to remember.

Pat Morgan

"The Beginning"

Cold clear sunlight, black lace boughs against the sky
Long yellow fingers from the sun, creep over the barren hills.
A blanket of warmth spreads and recedes silence.

Small ruined houses squat in the green fields
The dark earth spews its grassy cloak across narrow roads,
Pavements crumble - split open silence.

Rivers run unchecked across flattened banks-
Stones polished by a million years of watery caresses
Shine like glass on the dry beds silence.

City life - No life - dark shadows play in the bright light
Stark twisted shapes stretch towards the smiling heavens
Colours play on colours - red - brown - black silence.

Nothing moves, no sound, a vacuum this bright and chilling place-
No leaf to fall, no flash of wings disturb the empty air,
  Just silence-

In some place amid the brooding hills, a silver dish stares blindly at the sky. Within its heart of black and twisted steel a small pulse beats within a feathered breast, and, all around is music as it coos, in the silence.

J. Ferrill

"My Land"

I wander o'er the heather with a heart that's full of joy
for soon I hope to meet the one who has filled my dreams,
my own darling boy.

We parted some time ago with vows that we would meet
each to fulfil our destiny whatever that might be.

His has taken him across the lonely sea,
mine has been to wait and wonder endlessly.

Somewhere in the distance I see someone,
I wonder is it he will he recognize me.

As he gets nearer I whisper God please let it be,
the same sweet lad who left two years ago today.

Mary Shaw

Untitled

Don't make a sound, don't wear a frown.
For times are changing.
Smile for a while.
Don't cry my darlings.
When nature calls you will hear it all.
The sound of something new for you.
The kestrel will call. The shrieking sound.
It will be all around. Oh! That beautiful sound.
Then beauty will reign again. Upon this planet abound.
No more noise in the air. From cars or planes,
No more hustling and bustling, only the sound on the ground,
Telling us all that we are safe and sound.

Friends we know come and go.
They keep you sane and tell you what you do is not in vain.
We treasure the moments of peace we have.
We walk and talk. And know what should be said.
With love in our hearts. We can make a new start.
To be happy, instead of mad, or bad,
We will shine like the sun.
And be at one, and listen for tomorrow's song.

Julia Jacques

Terrorism

A bright, beautiful day - nature made no error,
Then the peace is shattered by an explosion...TERROR!
A bomb in a car - the blast rents the air,
Bits of steel, pieces of flesh - people scream and stare.

Running the gauntlet of flying glass and metal,
Counting the cost as the dust starts to settle.
Here a broken body, there a bundle of clothes,
Death of innocents, why? - nobody knows.

What a cowardly deed - to kill and to maim,
People that never caused anyone pain.
Ordinary folk - not politicians - not soldiers,
They carried only life's burdens upon their shoulders.

They made no decisions - did not govern or rule,
Yet lost their lives - to a fanatic, a fool.
Would an "eye for an eye" even the score,
Or would that forge a circle that rolls on, ever more?

What hope is there for the human race?
Who then will plead the plain people's case?
Must they walk with fear, 'til one by one they're killed?
That cannot be the way, the creator willed.

Kate Cliff

A Kind Of Consolation

How unlike the solitary bee
feasting on copious cornucopias
and the heavy scent of honeysuckle,
We try to pick out one specimen
from a dense cloud of insects,
To identify one pair of wings —
To stay the slip of quicksilver —
To sift one solo song amid
the senseless sea gulls clamour —
To breathe one clean draught of air
from the cigarette smoke and the smell of ale.

But somewhere in the crude ingredients
there lingers yet some love and loveliness,
a curtain of remembered kindness,
a quiet companionship of flowers
opening over the brambles of lost time —
and somehow, somewhere, sometimes
our little anger is humbled by the thunder
and a quietness, a kind of consolation
eases into the secret space behind the pain.

Douglas Dunker

Facts Are More Potent Than Assumptions

Drugs dealers do not care how often the death knell tolls.
Nor yet the misery caused, to so many kindred souls.
Dangerous drugs, like deadly bugs everywhere cast their blight.
Children being initiated, into an evil rite.
Come along now, do not tarry, you are going off to jail.
And for the crime that you have done, I trust there is no bail.
Once inside prison walls, you will know you are doing time,
For anti-social behaviour and head strong drift to crime.
For those who step out of line - primarily beginners.
The chance to get back into step, is greater than for sinners.
In future do not be tempted nor take up on a dare,
Less the folly of that action leads, to anguish and despair.
And for those who's life is geared to another quick fix,
You should realize that, the dangers you cannot trick,
And when the usual dose, brings the final curtain down,
Remember then, there are those, who mourn not, for a clown.
Taking time for reflection and to regain lost pride.
May well bring hope and wisdom. Enough to turn the tide.

John J. F. Cooney

Fate

I've watched the blossoms forming on the trees,
And fluttering downwards with the breeze;
Have seen the bluebells bloom,
And fade away so soon;
Nature gives, then takes away,
Regardless what we do or say.

Have noticed people praying on their knees,
Yet suffer awful tyrannies,
Seen children laugh and cry,
Suffer, shrivel and die;
Nature gives and takes away,
No matter what we think or say.

Most people search and strive for precious peace,
Others are restless with unease,
Wild wars proliferate,
Sending souls through Hell's gate;
Man can give or take away,
Regardless, oft, of what we say.

Elwyn Williams

Lonely

Lowered, rejected from life's few selected,
Orchestrating suggestions to Political conceptions,
Narcotics and drinking infesting the thinking,
Encouraging failure to look to a Saviour,
Limiting hope to a four letter word,
Yell Life! with a purpose, reach out and be heard.

Chris E. Long

Fjord

Low skies and hung waters
Harmonise - Nordic
In a rhapsody of blue.
Shaded mirror images catch the light
Reflecting Spring peaks.
Fast disappearing snows are captured
In luminous ripples drizzled-silver.
Harsh lines of silent inland seas soften.
Hard ice meets the melt, merging subtlety
And splendour with the shock
Of shelving shores.
Broad horizons hyphenated shrimp-pink
Hold fast in a state of inverted suspension
Soft-focused, this world stands still.
Timelessness laps a heartfelt calm.
Quiet understanding and peace
Reflect a rare tranquillity;
A profound power-
A mystery untold.

Eileen Allsopp

Shocked Into Reality

I felt so well and fit - I still could run
And sometimes touch my toes, when day begun
I tried each day to help a friend in need
Remembering to do my day's good deed.

And I was in my prime, or so I thought
I loved to cook - no cakes were ever bought
I could enjoy a laugh with anyone
And e'en when working hard life could be fun.

But then I heard the news, and felt so sad
A dear old lady hurt, that must be bad
A dear old lady - wait! - aged sixty-eight
But I am seventy-odd - could this be fate?

Informing me that I am really old?
And shouldn't run about or catch a cold?
Oh! Horrid thought and grim, I cannot bear
To ponder on my age or my grey hair.

Yet I'm still well and yes, I still can run
I still enjoy a laugh and life's still fun
So I'll forget my age and my grey hair
And do the things I like - and those I dare!!

O. G. Beck

Bird Flight

It came from the sunshine by the smaller door,
fluttered in the darker shadow, stalling,
flying to the windows high above the floor;
someone looked and saw a feather falling.

A creature of clear air and open space,
now climbing, gliding, with swoop and wheel,
panic-fraught in the enclosing work place;
colliding through trusses' forest steel.

Slowly attention changed from tasks in hand;
machinery fell silent, tools were still,
and workers stood together in a band
as if to help the bird by force of will.

It circled lower now, into a breeze
that blew in from another open way
and, sensing freedom, flew with better ease
to rest upon an angle-iron stay.

Rested, it preened; then, wings unfurled,
with sudden dive it plunged towards the light
that streamed from outside open world
and climbing in the glare, was lost to sight.

Roy Thompson-Holland

It All Happens In Bed

Within a warm bed we start out in life;
When first we're fed, it's by our Dad's wife;
And, thinking to wed, thoughts take us to bed
Where many a trouble has been shed.

Where do we go when we have our woe?
Where many a poor soul has been bled.
To have a quiet think, or have forty winks,
There is no better place than in bed.

When we are ill and we've swallowed that pill
It's a comfort to flop on our bed;
It's a port in a storm, a place to keep warm
With a pillow to rest that sore head.

Whatever your age, in the words of the sage,
This world's not so bad as it seems -
Lying warm and cosy - awake or dozy -
It is heaven alone with our dreams.

It all happens in bed-
Lying, sighing, crying.
It all happens in bed-
Being born or dying.

C. J. Geater

Those Who Came Back

Their nights are not like our nights
Soothed by the serene sky into gentle sleep
Their nights are still filled by fearful sights
And into their dreams old terrors creep.

Their dawns are not like our dawns
A joyful prelude to a happy day
But grey rememberings of other morns
Beseeching eyes, swept ruthlessly away.

Their ways are not like our ways
Paltry and meaningless
Forgotten Elite of a phantom world
Their eyes are pitiless.

Confronted by sombre twilight
They chose the torch of liberty
Knowing full well this decision might
Drag them through Hell to Eternity.
Eternity refused, they trod their way
With measured steps to the Break of Day.

Doreen Objois-Peel

"A Prayer For Peace"

Guns are blazing, Lord, all around -
Children hiding, Lord, underground.
Not enough food is there to go around -
Oh Lord, give them peace.

A frightened mother, she sheds a tear -
Santa Claus won't call this year.
In a war, no Christmas cheer -
Oh Lord, give them peace.

No more gardens, Lord - Nowhere to play -
A sea of mud to greet each day.
And who will take the guns away? -
Oh Lord, give them peace.

Night is falling, Lord - deep and dark -
Far to near, the cannons bark.
You can see the fuses spark -
Oh Lord, give them peace.

Children huddled on a mat -
Outside the guns go "boom" and "splat."
What kind of lullaby is that? -
Oh Lord give them peace.

Kate Brookes

Just Visiting

You, with your southern charm and easy ways,
Asking nothing, taking nothing - giving everything;
Your love unconditional, solid and true.
And time, always there was time.

That day when you made safe the old black bicycle,
Shiny, shaking, wheels wobbling down the lane,
While I stood laughing and so
Secure in your existence.

Long deep winters when nothing moved;
You splitting and stacking great logs,
Plodding, crunching, silent white.
Your hand, strong, guiding and protecting me.

And now in this peaceful place you lay;
Under cool green shadows of church yard pine.
I gaze towards patchwork hills beyond,
And memories surging, catch my breath.

Childhood tongues speak not
Of love and thankfulness;
But today, just visiting,
Will you hear and - know?

Mary Maguire

Nemesis

Alas, alack, who would believe me
I never thought she could deceive me
Though it was obvious from the start
That he'd won her fickle heart.
Choicest tid-bits, the best of fare
To tempt his palate - steak tartare.
But for me, any old trash
I'm sick and tired of sausage and mash
He's seized my slippers, she doesn't care,
Now he's dozing in my favourite chair.
Spurned, rejected, the final slight
She took him to her bed last night.
With jealousy, my heart a flame
I'll put a stop to his game.
Destroy my marriage, enslave my spouse
We'll see who is master in this house.
Now at last - my mind made up
I'll build a kennel for that dammed pup.

Brenda Broughton

Ode To Something Important In My Life

Oh! Curer of chaos,
Anathema to anarchy,
Opponent of outrage,
And soother of troubled minds.

You consist of
The leaves of an unimportant shrub,
Tanin,
And water (boiled, of course)
And, upon request,
Saccharin and lactic additives.

When I returned home from my last exam,
I drank to my success in a cup.
When I heard my grandfather, my mother's father, had died,
We sat her down with a cup to comfort her.

Whether your tea bag is round or perforated,
Or you use loose leaf tea from the box,
There's something so wonderfully British
About a good old cup of tea.

Andrew Fisher

Spaghetti Kids

Spaghetti spaghetti, all over the place,
up to my elbows up to my face.
Over the carpet and wound around the chairs.
Into the Bedclothes and all down the stairs.
Filling the bath tub right up to the taps.
Making the sofa a mad mushy mess.
That flat is all ruined, I'm terribly worried.
My guests have all left.
    (Unless they're all buried).

Julia Tedde

Here Today...

As our journey through this life we take,
We're ageing-and make no mistake!
When, to birthdays galore,
We add more and more,
'Til the candles cost more than the cake!

But let us not foster dismay
As 'Homeward' we make our sure way,
Just keep memory the store
Of kind deeds galore,
To enjoy at the end of the day.

Like, whenever you feel you have cause
For taking a stroll out of doors,
And someone comes nigh
With no smile, why not try
To give that poor soul one of yours?

David Hester

Dunvegan Dungeon

If you ever go to Skye and get bad weather,
And wonder what on earth you're going to do.
  To change your holiday venue's too much hassle;
So to pass a day you see Dunvegan Castle.

The longest ever lived in by one family,
  The Clan McLeod for seven hundred years.
After driving through the clag you will see the Fairy Flag,
  But of all the sights the Dungeon is the worst.

For if a local peasant goes a-poaching
  And has the great misfortune to get caught;
He doesn't go to jail and he gets no chance of bail,
  There's just one way his freedom can be bought.

"Get you to the dungeon with the rats and all the slime;
  The visitors will think you're just a dummy.
When you know you're not alone fetch a realistic groan,
  A sound that's not expected from a mummy."

The tourists go their way having passed a pleasant day:
  They marvel at the castle's electronics.
But it isn't an adaptor, just the poacher and his captor
  Should be thanked for such sophisticated phonics.

Bill Todd

Untitled

A wonderful dream "Khayelitsha" my home,
My roots I will plant here, no more will I roam,
I have made my choice where I want to be,
My sons will be born here, free ever free.

Though part of me will always remain
In the depths of the jungle, from whence I came,
For my children my hopes for a bright new morn,
With courage I'll make it, fresh hope newly born.

Then I found all my dreams were made of clay,
"Khayelitsha", "Khayelitsha", I never can stay,
Suppression and poverty here rules the way,
Violence and hatred, I see every day.

My thoughts take me back, to where wild birds fly,
South African sunsets, mystic glows in the sky,
Sounds of the wild in the dark velvet of night,
Oh God lift the shadows, show me the light.

My struggle for freedom goes on and on,
"Khayelitsha", "Khayelitsha" never my home,
Blood of my forbears runs strong in my veins,
I live for the day when equality reigns.

Mary Adamson

Christmas With A Broken Man

They've gone, the children of my life,
Gone to share their Christmas, with their mother, my ex-wife,
She will share their laughter, she will see them smile,
Will they think of Daddy, for just a little while.

My hours stretch before me, theirs will fly so fast,
Christmas now, is nothing like, our Christmas in the past,
This year no early waking Christmas Day, for me, an empty time.
My table bears a single plate, and a single glass of wine.

No playing games, no sharing meals, no sitting by the fire,
No loving glances round my kin, as the day begins to tire,
For them the day begins to close, and their celebrations cease,
I turn to Him, and ask Him, why can not I share their peace.

They seem to be a far off dream, those Christmases long gone,
When as a family we would spend, our Christmas Day, as one,
Now we are 'split asunder', a broken home, with broken dreams,
No more the loving comfort, no more, no more, it seems.

I pray, I pray, I pray, for what I'm not quite sure,
They say some day "all will be well", if only I endure,
People try to comfort me, and offer drinks of tea,
When all I want for Christmas, is my children next to me.

Alec C. Carrotte

Night

'Tis magical to stand alone on a clear and cloudless night,
In a cornfield, who's golden grains are swathed in silvery light!
The sun has set with garish light - red flames that scorched
   the sky too bright;
Then gently crept a silent mesh - the curtains of twilight!

   The moon has cast her mystic beams
   To steal the colours from day's dreams;
   And thus the canvas of the dark
   Is hidden even from the lark!

So stand quite still and hark the sounds that come with night alone:
A fox will bark; a night-owl call; a badger moves a stone!
A breeze may drift within a swirl to waft across the corn,
That sways with gentle rolling waves, to startle a young fawn!

   No storm to rent this summer's sky!
   The night-jar's safe to home-ward fly
   Across a starlit theatre's stage...
   The World has turned another page!

   These wonders of the night may tear
   The heart-strings of your soul with fear -
   For suddenly there comes the thought:
   Supposing daylight comes to nought?
     D. R. Payn Le Sueur

"Wittering" (West Sussex)

Where the tamarisk bends before the wind
And the sea pinks nod though winter thinned,
Where over timber groyne breaks the sea
That's where we long to be .....to be.

Here we can watch on starlit night
Brave Nab's bright and warning light,
Long sands stretch to Selsey bill
North eastwards stands the Southdown Hill.

To starboard lies the Isle of Wight,
Sandown Cliffs when seen so white,
Between luff dinghies from Bosham Haven,
There dives the gull, flaps solitary raven.

Form the west sand dunes run the conies
In the briny grass, as free as ponies,
That canter and gallop to Bracklesham Bay.
You'll understand now why we long to stay
    Wilfred Purton

My City Of Dreams

The whisper of my name is heard
as my eyes closed in slumber,
Reaching out my hand, I glide along,
The sand in this glory's dreamy wonderland.

As this magnet draws me closer,
To this misty city that I'm over,
Along the sea of glass, where everything
has passed into my city of dreams.

There is no sorrow or pain,
No darkness or rain,
Streets have no names
everyone remains the same,
as I float in this transparent frame,
In my city of dreams

Peace and security I have found,
on this magic merry-go-round,
where life drains, and love remains
(Until) that inner force calls me back,
from the city that's in my heart,
my city of dreams.....
    Rosaleen Dunn

Time

Time is a thing we all seem to watch,
Not just a clock or a pocket watch,
Time in a day, or all the year round,
When we are born, or plants front the ground.

We start by knowing when it's time to be fed,
When it's time to play or go to bed,
Then for our lessons and our play,
Oh! The things we can do in a day,

As we get older and work all day,
We don't have as much time to go and play
Time goes more quickly, months turn into years,
We are living in time, sometimes laughing sometimes tears.

So as each day passes and you think you have time,
To do this and that, then you hear a clock chime,
Don't put off hill tomorrow what can be done to day
Even if it means losing a lot of your play
    Enid Vickers

Life

Life?
Life looks like an exciting, hopeful journey when you're a bairn
"Daddy, foo...ottee" cries Jonny excitedly
"When you're older, Jonny, when you're older", answers Daddy
"Not fair! You just wait until I am older", thinks Jonny
Jonny continues to pester, but he's now at primary school
"Dad, guess what? Sammy is having a birthday party. Please
can I go?" pleads Jon. "Yes, alright Jonny." Replies his Dad.
"It's Jon. Thanks, Dad." "That's ok son".
Jon is now beginning to grow up, and life is turning into a
complicated, magical, mystery tour
"Life's a bitch, isn't it Cath?" he says questioningly to his
girlfriend, Catherine. "Yes, it certainly is,"she replies
He is going through the wonderfully confusing aspect of life
being a teenager and beyond
"I am now seventy-four and am looking back on my life."
"I now laugh fondly when I look at how complicated life
seemed when I were young
"It's now that you realize that life gets easier when you are
independent and in your twenties,"
"I can still see those happy faces in the dance halls. Mm, "In
The Mood" (laughs softly) "Pennsylvania 6-5000."
"Aye those were days - yes I were fighting for my country,
but I were proud, we were a strong and happy bunch."
"Well, I'm coming to the end of my life now, and it's b'en a
happy one, lad!"
    Jenny Dixon, Elvington, near York

Man Sees With New Eyes In Flight

Deep within a forest burning, pounding heart and stomach churning
Driven farther in a lather upon this night within this year
Through tangled trees and underbrush, onward, inward I must push
I lurch in search through brush and birch, fighting back my fear
Ahead I see a hole aglow, from unknown places they bestow
Wild delights this dismal night, hide within this hole I peer
Radiating spectral light, from deep within this hole I peer

Vibrations rise through burning eyes, as lights dance in the skies
I sense the air in oscillation, electrostatic radiation
Red energy in flight turns white, tuning into violet light
Great auras of electrons roaring, brighter faster swirling on
Waves of heat force my retreat and gently lift me off my feet
Dimensions bending, blending in, as gravity is overcome
Suspension of our linear time as gravity is overcome

My mind is stretching, melding, morphing, activating new endorphines
Upon my senses, no defenses, molecules are quasi-fluxing
Energy is now releasing, metamorphosis near completion
Feeling weightless, fateless, feel electrovalence in eruption
Down some cosmic road I'm racing swirling strands of light encasing
Quantum dreams in constant stream, zero's and one's seduction
    Grae Laws

Courage

For Jaymee B—An Epitomy of Courage

Courage is one of the virtues which cannot be bought or sold,
History is full of courage and as children we are told,
Of tales like our Patron, St George, and the dragon he did slay,
Such courage allowed his people to live on another day.

As David stood and faced Goliath courage came to the fore,
Calmly he guided his sling and the giant fell to the floor.
But courage is not unique, though, to any beast, race or creed,
Animals need courage when they have young to protect and feed.

The world is full of courage and has been since the days of old,
So many past and present heros have been so very bold.
Those that are born with courage must be among the chosen few,
Who provide the inspiration which will help pull others through.

Courage I admire most is shown by children everywhere,
Disease is so rife in this world, despite lots of love and care.
If fighting any illness take heart from little Jaymee B,
She fought just like a lion and stands aloof in history.

Paul Andrew Younger

The Gambler

The cold winds blew with loneliness hate,
He struggled on against an unknown fate,
His courage grew with each cold blast.
He knew he would make it at last!
A gambler born to fight the wrong.
That rang around him like a song.
The traitor stepped up into view.
Up went his gun and he shot true!
The traitor fell in mortal pain.
Shouting out the devil's name.
But true the gamblers luck ran out.
And in his ears he heard a far of shout!
"You've played a great game and won my son".
So come and join us in the sun,
His fading eyes they saw a sail,
Approaching fast like in a fairy-tale.
He saw his comrades from the past.
He smiled a smile of peace, on deck at last!

Gordon Paul Epitaph

Lady Luck

If lady luck were to shine on me
My friend for life you would be,
I'd hope for more, but hold friendship dear
And be content to have you near.

So, my inner thoughts, you'll not know
As I watch you come and go,
But if lady luck were to shine on me
My love for life you would be.

Alan Harrison

You

Your tail lined with gold as the soft water rolls from it
Your soft silky skin as you rise to the cool clean air
In the distance the faint call of a songful sister nursing her calf
I wonder what it's like to be you.

The horizon lifts and falls around your humble abode
The sun dancing with you, displaying your striking motion
Rippling tides lapping around your body
I want to be you.

And yet I know there are those who will kill you
And travellers with their many men after you
But you're special, and a creation by God
I wish I was you.

I won't forget the time we spent together
I'll always remember your affectionate expression
So fine and so sure, along with so free
I wonder what it's like to be you.

Karoline Fisher

London

City of scars, cars whizzing in and out of polluted sinewed streets.
Where sleazy cafes compete with the British Museum.
Buckingham Palace now a Mausoleum,
Royal residents turned into Wax,
Hiding in Tussauds, avoiding the Tax.
Houses of Parliament awaiting the Axe.
Fat cats relax in the Cocktail bar, viewing their spoils from afar.
"Eros smiles at the trekking homeless,
Addicts gaze at skin and bone arm, Eros' arrow could never pierce.
Gays march down the Mile End Road,
fierce shrieks strangled by red ribbons, Some already on crutches.
Underground train plays host to a suicide,
Far better in prison, supping the Bromide.
Walk on the 'sunny side' to the D.S.S.
Buy a Porno video, Relieve the stress.
Guitar player slumps on the pavement,
Drunk on stolen wine while in slavement to 'Cash and Carry'.
Will someone marry me? Gotta have two children first,
to quench the thirst of never, never land.
Even Jack the Ripper, with knife in hand, would walk in fear
In this fair City, called London.

Betty Fenton

Indian Epic

There was Hiawatha and Lowawatha and Wathas in between,
Minihaha and Maxiehaha and Hahas fat and lean.
Wig-wams where they whammed wigs on bald and shining pates,
each Cherokee that one could see was paid on daily rates.
The cost ran into millions with five thousand extras found,
the time they made a film called "The Happy Hunting Ground".

The set was full of Indians from many Redskin tribes;
Sioux, Algonquin, Mohawk, Crow, Mohican, Cheyenne; all on
show with Navajo and fierce Apache.
In that world of paper mache sets and totem poles,
many were the famous stars who played the leading roles;
Pontiac and Crazy Horse, Cochise, Geronimo;
Pocahontas... she who dearly loved a white man so.

Laughing Water, Running Water, Fleetfoot, Sitting Bull;
squaws of every shape and size, papooses plump and full.
Whirring cameras, microphones and all the paraphernalia
of props and costumes that ensured each tribe its right regalia
Brave were the braves;
no white men's slaves did they have wish to be.
Yet at the last, all the cast were slaves to filmed T.V.!

Edward George Freestone

Dog Show At The Village Fayre

Tightly enclosed in a circle of humans
Were dogs of all kinds and colour and size,
Thoroughbreds boasting superior breeding,
Little ones eager to win every prize.

Some tails were a-wagging with feelings of joy
Greeting old friends on this fine summer day,
While some tails were sluggish until set in motion -
Manual rotation got them under way!

As the dogs in their turn were called to their class,
They lined themselves up - reluctant to go,
Manhandled by owners to face the right way,
Or nipped into place by tweak from a foe.

Instructions were given, some quietly, some loud,
Man kneeling to dog to whisper in ear,
Or dog rising up, front paws on child's shoulder,
Lingering licks saying 'I'd rather stay here'.

A few left for home displaying their prizes
But most were content with words of praise said.
Then raffle wins claimed, to the strains of the band,
Dogs led owners home - for hugs, bones and bed.

G. M. Harvey

The Shooting Of A Coward

Oh my brother,
Where does your broken body lie?
I've search from the fields of Flanders
To the slaughter of Cambrai.
Now blowing poppies and sorrowing sky
Treasure the place where you were thrown down to die.
Did you not cry out in despair
At the sound of death filling the air?
Cry out against the reaping of so many sons
To be crushed beneath the wheels of the charging guns;
Tormented by marching voices in deaths attire
Singing back dead from the putrid mire.
Oh in that awful dawn,
The order was given and the pistol drawn.
Oh why could I have not been there
To cradle your head and calm your fears,
All those things you did for me in my childhood years.
Oh tender brother you did your best.
So sleep my brother, sleep in the eternal rest.

Jim Jefferies

Motorway Morning

The pigeon calls softly
And small deer do roam
This is the place that the badger calls home
Centuries old the beech woods still stand
While the roads for the travellers
Take over this land
And you, as you hurry
Cocooned in your car
Catch a glimpse of my woodland
Though you look from afar
But we are all travellers
Yet we wish not to be
And all search for a place where we can be free
Often I've travelled the same road as you
And glanced at your forest
As I passed by, too.

Jill Evans

Callanish-An Claich Mor

Pink veins glow in the grey gneiss
Clear again of lichen,
Stark and alive.

The turf neatly edged to outline
The concise stonework.
Coffins sink in the peat.

Almost it stirs again in sleep,
the power of the stones in place.

(Just to be there, stone, just to be there.)

Alasdair Macinues

Sam

He was my life, his name was Sam,
He was simply a very caring man,
He gave me love he gave me life,
Until his body was racked with pain,
And even then he thought of me,
He said he had to go he could fight no more,
Holding my hand he asked me to let him go,
In saying yes it broke my heart,
Because I knew it meant we had to part,
And in the end God took him home,
My life my love now I'm alone,
A year and more has now gone by,
So much hurt and pain to understand,
Yet knowing Sam was a wonderful thing,
He gave to all - his love his time,
He gave so much and asked for little,
This man I loved,
This man called Sam
He was simply a quiet and wonderful man.

Agnes D. Craig

How Nice It Is

Oh how nice it is, to be healthy and free.
Oh how nice it is to have someone who cares.
How nice it is, to see a smiling face
and hear the birds singing in the trees.
How nice it is, when you are young and strong,
and can walk upon this beautiful land.
Oh how nice it is, when you can greet each morn
and watch the roses greet another dawn.
How nice it is when one can step outside
and look at the rainbow across the sky.
How nice it is when you can reap the good things
that you have planted with your own two hands.
How nice it is, when man is free,
to see, to hear, to sing.
How nice it is to dream;
and wake to see the things that real.
How nice it is to hear men sing and pray,
giving thanks to the one who gives to us,
this wonderful land.
    How nice it is.

Winston Samuda

The Cleansing Tide

Wild, sweeping, gracefully, upon the tide,
Rebellious horses on your milky way;
Leaping joyfully, with fearsome surge,
Then sighing in the settling spray,
King Neptune's chariot can hence be seen,
If one should close the eye.
Dancing, and laughing mermaid's cavorting
Throwing seaweed garlands to the sky
Only obvious to discerning humans such as the seeking "I",
Laughing surf, sweeping sand and pebbly rocky shore
Washing clear the debris before receding once more
Egged on by the cumulous of clouds across the sky
Sweeping across the ocean's roaring down the bore
The whole majesty of movement, enhance the life of such as I.
Oh rushing tides of life, roll on,
Erase the scars we bear.
For blood so pointless shed for war,
Upon some alien shore.
Refreshing spray, wash clean the world,
Lest all, but you, should die.

Olivine Thompson

Working For Imports And Exports

I work in a Section called Imports,
And exports are covered as well.
I thought it might be interesting
But conclude it's like being in hell!

With ships coming in at all hours
And ships going out on the swell,
The documents pile into towers,
Passed to me by Manager, Mel.

I groan from the weight of the paper
Which has to be sent through the fax,
And my 'phone will start ringing, I wager.
Oh! When can I sit and relax?

We've arranged for a loaded container
To go to Japan on the sea.
It got lost and was found in Malaya,
Now Mel and I have had to flee.

So if anyone wants to do imports,
Exports must be covered as well.
There are now two suitable places
Awaiting you right here in hell.

Jeanette Arnett

The Reason Why...

I thought that we were friends, content to chat,
And sip our wine on Sunday evenings; to me they meant so much.
But when you went to France, all's changed, and that
You broke your promise, to 'keep in touch'.

Your silence mystified and hurt; was it the knell
Of a friendship by which I'd set such store?
But now you're back, all's change, and maybe now you'll tell
What went wrong: was I such a very tedious bore?

Yet I shall not forget that ten long months ago
When black despair engulfed me, and suicide was near,
You it was who saved me then, to show
Me life goes on, and hope may conquer fear.

This evening we have met, and talked the problem through.
Your explanation was so very clear and neat.
A lover, younger than me or even you!
So now we're just two neighbours, who share the same quiet street.

G. C. Oxley-Sidey

Remind Me

Remind me that this was the month
  I promised to remember,
The misted hills and purple shadows,
  the scent of woodsmoke in that far September.
There was sunlight and children's laughter,
  then suddenly the beaches were empty,
  the children gone and only silence after.
I remember the sea rippling in over the white sands,
  and the air filled with gulls cries.
How strange that I should remember all these things
  when I have forgotten the colour of your eyes.
Remind me that there was love and tenderness
  in the warm night,
and how we owned the earth until the morning light.

Lilian Unsworth

'Cried And Tested'

In my cage you leave me here,
From my eyes another unnoticed tear.
To test on me is so unfair,
Do you have any feelings, do you really care.
The hatred, the evilness built inside of you,
All of us, once animals running free,
But the ones that escape you are few,
Do you enjoy it, maybe find it funny,
My question I ask is how can you do this to me,
Such a defenceless bunny.
You poke me about, blind me and hurt me,
Why do I have to pay this painful fee,
What did I do wrong most would agree that it is unkind,
To make a bright life full of pain, and beautiful eyes blind,
One thing that I know is that God missed me when he was
  giving out love,
Because I shouldn't be here waiting to die,
I should be out flying as free as a dove.

Gemma Priestley

My Love

You're in my thoughts day and night,
I feel your presence though out of sight.
I see your shadow beside of me,
My love and kisses I gave to thee.
The love you give is the love I take,
The love you take is the love I make.
Although we may be miles apart,
You're in my mind and in my heart.
Many years will slowly drift by,
Tears for laughter and sadness we'll cry.
But I know these tears will only be,
Shared by you and shared by me.

Claudia Dolente

The Village Fete

The fete was o'er, 'twas time to go,
His love for her still undeclared,
They would be home in a short while,
His secret feelings must be shared.

They stood beside the water's edge,
While twilight shadows lengthened fast,
He took her hand, the time was right,
Alas; his courage failed, the moment passed.

He left at dawn a train to take,
To a fighter squadron far away,
He left a note for her to find,
And vowed return another day.

He'll not come back, his plane was lost,
But Jane still meets him at the fete,
For she to was killed when bombs were dropped,
Their love they now pledge by the lake.

If you should be in the park alone,
And you tarry awhile till the moon is bright,
You perhaps may see them holding hands,
It maybe however a ripple of light.

Adrian Long-Price

Epitaph To A Dead Snail

Here lies a poor snail
Whose sad fate, I bewail.
A garden roller, stood in his way
Someone pushed it, lackaday.
No more sweet strawberries will he taste,
The gardener now has time to waste.
Thrushes now, seek him in vain,
They always sought him after rain.

R. D. Dick

"Grieving"

I feel so sad and so bereft
Now my beloved is laid to rest
The pain the anguish he endured
From an evil cancer they could not cure
The prognosis given was hard to take
At times I felt my heart would break.

The strength and courage he displayed
One could not help but be amazed
His only thought was to save me worry
So his affairs he dealt with in a hurry
In the face of death he was an inspiration
But to those remaining it is little consolation.

The utter loneliness and despair
Is really becoming tough to bear
Friends are kind and wish to help
But the answer must lie within one's self
How can you explain that all you really yearn
Is for your loved one to be returned.

L. J. Williams

Number Please

The phone brings you together when you're really on
  your own
Your lover seems so close to you, you don't seem
  all alone
The time goes by so quickly as you whisper words
  of love
I do feel very downcast when I have to give
  a shove
To end the conversation when I have so much to say
To tell how much I love you, that the ache won't go away
But when the call is over, and the room is very still
And once again you're on your own with lots or time to fill
I pick up pen and paper, and maybe give a curse
Then I got to thinking and I wrote this
  little verse.

Ron Bate

An Ode To Marie

The time has come, dear Marie, to take a well earned rest
For twenty eight years or more, you have always done your best
A scotch, a pint, a brandy too, you have served them all
With expertise and vigour, answering everybody's call
We hope the future holds for you, happiness and more
Good Health and Wealth in all you do, there's plenty there in store
Best wishes come from one and all to greet you on this day
And may there be good memories for you to take away
We hope that you will accept this gift, for giving is a pleasure
And hope that as the years go by, it's something you will treasure

Lynne E. V. Moss

Springtime

Dear Lady Spring, most welcome are you,
Dancing and prancing the live-long day through.
You bring sunshine and showers, such myriads of flowers
Delighting our senses with bright scented bowers;
So go now, dull winter, take sadness and gloom
To the realms of forgetfulness ——
For you there's no room!

Dear Lady Spring, you are welcome indeed;
The birds sound so joyful as babies they feed,
While animal parents take care of their young -
So sweet and defenceless, with so much to learn!
The trees provide shelter, much beauty as well,
And green grass clothes the earth on which all dwell.

Dear season of happiness, we all are so glad
To know you are with us, bringing colour to clad.
Only God in His heaven could bring us such joy
To lighten our hearts - such variety employ.
So to Him we give praise, our thanks we will sing
For you, O most welcome, most welcome Lady Spring!

Betty Bussell

Toast To A Tourist

Take a glass and make a toast
That's what a whiskey's for,
Hold it high and wish them well
Our boys are off to war.

Yet we are only spectators
Standing on the outside looking in,
It's not a game of soldiers
For you fight a war to win.

No, we don't know the fear you fear
Nor do we know your pain,
But we're proud of you and as they say
"When will we see your likes again?"

So will you return a different man
Because of where you've been?
You can drink a thousand drams my dear
You can't forget the things you've seen.

So when the streets call out to you
And they put a gun in your hand,
Remember you're just a tourist
In someone else's land.

S. Arnachellum

Coast Town In Winter

Coast town in winter, deserted beaches,
Ghostly sea mist; pounding wave reaches
Over the sea wall on to the walkway
Drenching lone watcher with salty sea spray.
Grey gulls are wheeling, gliding and turning,
Plaintive cries sounding like lost children yearning
For warm summer sun on soft golden sand;
But hard pebbles crash in tympanic band.
Then from dark clouds the sun pushes through,
Angry red, tinting with sullen hue
Sky over sea, then softly sweeps
Through purple to black, and fitfully sleeps.

Jessie Kempster

Double Egg And Bacon

A murky bottle of vinegar
Flirts with the salt and pepper
as the smell and sound of toast
pop up to support
a Cumberland pork sausage.

A multi stained apron hangs from a neck
which runs to a hand
which artfully spatulas an egg.
Over it goes to create that noise
which blends in nicely
amongst the coughs and rustling of national tabloids.

Tables with metal legs
housing chairs and builders legs.
"Tea please love,"
cries a solitary soul who's deep in debt.
30 cost a cup of tea,
"Sod it, double egg, bacon and beans,
I've a ceiling to plaster next week."

The cafe door opens and lets out a cloud of heat,
and the stones jamming on the radio.

A. J. Smith

A Bather's Lament

To the Management of this hotel, I simply wish to say
Your accommodation's quite superb in almost every way.
But there's one specific feature that has got me in a lather,
For your bathroom's shower accessories are of no use to a bather.

You see, there I was at six a.m., the middle of the night,
Stumbling around an unknown loo and searching for the light,
Stripped to the buff and quivering, like your average flabby male,
Or a wrinkly porker posing as a beached and stranded whale.

Now, I'm one of those who love to steep in water to the nose
While we contemplate our manly chests, our navels or our toes.
So imagine my frustration when I groped for soap and found
That the stupid damned dispenser was screwed five feet off
the ground.

Can you picture the gyrations as I gamely tried to cope,
Splashing and bobbing up and down to get a dab of soap?
All of it doomed to failure, though, for if the truth be told,
I'd barely cleaned my armpits when the water had turned cold.

So in future please consider all the reps who like to soak,
For these frantic dawn aerobics are, quite frankly, past a joke.
There's an obvious solution to this highly vexing matter;
Leave a bar of soap beside the bath, much closer to the water.

Iain Hirschfeld

Another Folly!

He said "She'll not leave you" but I shook my head,
He said "She will love you and never stray",
But I knew the heartache such words could convey,
I knew she would leave me, 'Twould not be my doing,
There'd come a time when she'd leave without knowing.

One friend just gone, years too quickly passed,
A lifetime of deep love finished at last,
How could I stand to lose another, and surely she
    was too young to leave her mother?

He said "She'll not leave you" (How deep brown her eyes),
He said "She needs you, you need each other",
So I put out my arms, I always was weak,
They've only to look and don't have to speak,
They ask for nothing and take what we give,
Perhaps fifteen years together, if lucky, to live.

(How Deep brown her eyes)

Oh dear, what folly,
I've fallen again for another Welsh collie.

Jeanne E. Dibley

Life

Life is now
So live each minute to the full, for life is now.
It's not the past, for that is just a memory
to cherish on your way, but life is now.
So if you see a friend in need,
And you can lend a helping hand,
Do your deed, the time is now.
You will not pass this way again
This instant is still fleeting
do not miss your chance in life, for life is now.
Find joy in all the lovely things
which god has made our heritage.
Blue skies, the sea, the dewdrops on a flower.
A field of corn, the first new buds of springtime
A baby's smile, the early dawning hour.
Be kind to one another, as you would they to you.
And live and love and laugh, for life is now.

Betty Williams Baldery

Love Means...

Love means just one single thing
to me: it's giving everything.
Expecting nothing in return.
Waiting and hoping, while my eyes burn
with unshed tears. Hiding my fears
and pain behind a smiling face.
Caring and loving - and with grace
accepting the one who took my place.

Love means: To suffer. How it's true.
Sorrow and pain, caused by one who
does not care any longer for me.
Still love remains within my heart.
My eyes are dry. My lips won't part
to speak words that are bitter and hard.
'Cause love means just one single thing
to me: it's giving everything.

M. Smit

The Fox

The horn blows foretelling that the chase has begun,
Myself the victim, hunted, sought out
Mounted horseman, clad in blood red,
The colour the liquid of my life will flow, if caught.

Through green fields as carpets beneath my feet I flee
Under hedges, boundaries, separating grass from crops
The blowing wind intensifying my scent
with my hunters advancing at my heels with zest.

Too late to redeem myself
For I too am the hunter, foraging and stealing
But I, to sustain the hunger that ravages my body
Not just for the thrill of the kill, as man.

Tiring my body grows heavy, weary
I can feel the hot breath of death on my face
and I know the end is near.

Susanne Newton

Untitled

They have never seen the sun
They have never felt the rain
They don't know how to run
or play with dolls or trains
They have never tasted choc-bar's
or had a stick of rock.
They don't know what a cuddle is
or someone to touch.
So don't forget the babes with AIDS
as princess Diana has said,
They all need a cuddle and a love
to make them smile again
who are these babes you have not guessed
The Romanian orphans- how soon we forget.

O. M. Eaves

Love

Love is such a beautiful thing,
You feel like an angel with white sparkling wings.
With one flap and you're up and away
Gliding over the sunset bay.

Or maybe sitting on a cloud so high,
Watching the sun and sky go by.
Or admiring the twinkling star's and moon.
Maybe in sunburst June.

When you're in love you feel great.
You do go out with him but not as a good mate.
The sun send's down its bright gleam on you.
And your heart is no longer broken
but a soft melty goo.

Suddenly every time you go out
a bit of eyeshadow on the eyes
and a bit of lippy on the mouth
you really love this lad with all your heart.
After all you've been hit with cupids dart.

Gillian Curran

Untitled

I'm here, for years I've been
dreaming of being here,
Finally boarding the plane,
Although memories,
memories of the time before.

Will this be my doom?
Will this be my end?
Maybe, maybe not,
fear was walking straight towards me.
My family, I would miss my family,
my friends, my life.

If I came to my doom,
I can't complain,
I had an enjoyable life,
He'll find a way, if not today if not in
this way then soon,
and in another way.

I'll go, I'll try it, if I'm meant to go,
I'll go, there's nothing I can do to change it.
But like a child it still scares me.

Kelly Harding

Dreams

Life is wonderful, loving and giving
Life is hard, cruel and sometimes misleading

The truth is buried beneath anger and jealousy
Sometimes lost in a torrid world of
Confusion and insecurity

Emotions run high and feelings run free
There is no secret place for us to be

Among all this hate, fear and pain
We need to escape and start again

One more chance is all we need
Let me prove to you there is a seed

Let us grow and learn from each other
The best thing in life would be to love one another

I was in turmoil and you set me free
For those few hours I knew me

I looked up to the stars and the moonlit sky
At last I was at peace and I knew why

If your heart can find forgiveness
Who knows maybe in time, our seed will have grown
And you will be mine

Carol Quinn

Dream Of Horses

Like the beginning of time in a crack of the earth
creation gave the horse its birth.
Down and down in the drifting sleep
through long shadows dark and deep.
Misty clouds come leaping past
travelling far, and free and fast.
Forming froth that fury spat
from the cauldron to the vat
racing gracefully, slick and smooth
minds he'll settle, nerves he'll soothe
through muddy waters of silt and clay
they slip and slither, roll and play
all together they follow and run
just like children having fun.
With pointed toes and high held heads,
they mock and jeer with carefree treads
through the furnace of fire and flame
the cowards retire and the young brave claim.

Susan Young

My Mum

She had me in pain,
But loved me just the same.
She fed me when I couldn't,
And dressed me when I wouldn't.
She hugged me when I was sad,
But still loved me when I was bad.
she protected me when I was wrong,
And still protected me when I was strong.
She smiled when I left her life,
But only for my wife.
She taught my wife to cook,
But not from any book.
She left me one sad day,
Now I can never repay.
She came to visit me one night.
That's when I saw the light.
She looked so young and fair,
And told me not to despair.
She comes to me as a butterfly,
I know I shall see her when I die.

T. W. E. Butler

The Chick

Unsure, unknowing
A headless chicken amongst the one-way traffic
A pang of hurt volts through my head
The head of a headless chicken.

A ball of knowledge
of which I know none.
A herd of elephants
of which I am not a part.

The headless chicken sits all alone.

Laura Bishop

M.P.F.

You may think I'm mad but in my head I know I'm not,
You ask me things from the past
That I almost forgot not!
Bad things happened that you may think are gone.
Then someone drags them up once-more,
And the nightmare begins again
Physical abuse turns to mental abuse,
And together that is mad,
But I am not and won't ever be 'cause I've had the lot,
I hate the past, but know it will never go away,
I am who I am, take me as I come,
To you mad,
To me, I am a totally screwed up child
Mind aged 12 years in a body of 21 years.

Jodi McMillan

Don't Change

Run free, run wild,
Walk tame, walk mild,
However you live, who ever you are,
Your mind will be free, your mind will be far.
There will be a day, a day in your life,
A game of wild play, takes place to entice,
Entice you to live, entice you to die,
What ever it tells you, it tells you a lie.
This message I bring, this message I've brought,
Be what you are, not what you're not.

Mary C. McGregor

A Natural Law

When destiny extends its hand,
 From the heavens as a dove it flies;
Its vibratory nature can only reveal
 Its cosmic identity and definite role.

When destiny extends its hand,
 Electrons unite to form atoms;
And atoms give forth molecules
 All is matter, the indestructible.

When destiny extends its hand,
 Two hitherto unknown worlds collide;
They seem to reel toward same purpose,
 While each guards their natural form.

When destiny extends its hand,
 Harmony and peace is all it wants;
That each infinitesimal play its role
 In the cosmic scheme of God's creation.

Claire

She's Leaving Home

I walk into her bedroom
And clutch my heart with fear,
My thoughts are naught but doom and gloom
I feel the trickling tear.

The trunk is packed, her treasures all
Are wrapped with tender care.
The photos, racquet, shoes and doll
And grandma's special fare.

It seems a short, but precious time
Since my little girl arrived
A tiny baby loved, and mine
She must never be deprived.

Her favourite meal on table laid,
We try so hard to eat.
Few words in conversation said,
So soon her vacant seat.

The day of parting comes too soon
We bid our fond adieu,
Our home is badly out of tune
The sight is sad to view

Doreen Cruickshanks

A Dedication To My Wife

She's one in a million, she's quite debonair,
She's kind, she's gentle, and I wouldn't care
To travel life's road if she wasn't there.
She has beauty and virtue the like I've ne'er seen,
No fair summer's rose compares with my queen.
When I'm down on my luck and haven't a dime,
I've little to offer this angel sublime.
Yet, when I gaze into sparkling eyes,
I know that she loves me as the birds love the skies.
She brought me a heaven, she gave me its key,
Life's greatest pleasures, she brings them to me.
At the end of my life, when I've reminisced,
I know there are times, I ne'er would have missed,
In those wonderful years, the best of my life,
Which I shared with an angel - my beloved wife!

Henry Ward

Soul Searching

The real flower blossoms, Autumn and May
Never never dies, all season stay

Every noble one wakes up, somehow, someway
If you like to reach a love searching day
Hold my hand I will show you the way
With romance in your heart, a most exciting day
Whatever your wish, why not say?

We are in Spring, the golden cup is the heart
Once you are in it, dare you depart
That is all yours, you are my heart
A poem is for me the most romantic art
Which pulls me forward to your heart.

If I cannot create the life given art
I shall lose forever, I shall be a coward
A dreamless person who never holds the card.

Before the sun, moon and far away lifeless star
Why don't you search your mysterious heart?

T. Kaplan

I, The Wandering Cloud

I the wandering and mysterious cloud
Whom does roam this terrestrial earth
From time to time I unveil my airy shroud.

I was born the daughter of streamed water
Destined to nurse blue filled skies,
Although I do change but cannot die.

I bathe dried earth from unleashed wings
Whilst waving a breeze over stretchy oceans,
Along with my guiding, and sweeping motion.

I bring a shower of fallen endless rain
That heal the limbs of thirsting flowers,
Under my spell of streaming power.

I bear a cooling shade for crinkly leaves
As they seek under my roof like shelter,
For an avalanche of dewdrops that pelter.

I observe and whisper faraway high above
From my foamy world of clouded loneliness
Throwing down a smile of speeding lightness.

When I sleep in the arms of heaven above
I float restfully like a peaceful dove...

Amanda Jane Martin

Take Heed Lest Ye Fall

When all seems well and everything's honey,
Nothing to do and plenty of money.
Be careful, be steady and also be wise,
For something will bring you down to size.

When you're a champion - top of the league,
And do not suffer from any fatigue
Beware of the underdog, he is no clown
'Cos he will surely bring you down.

So when you're right at the top of the tree,
An example to others you have to be.
Act sensibly and don't be a chump
'Cos if you don't you'll land with a bump.

When you reach the top of the class,
And all exams have duly been passed.
That's when you think you know it all,
So take heed my friend, lest you should fall.

So when you're on the highest plane,
And everyone else has much to gain,
Be careful when you're standing tall
Remember: "The higher you are, the harder the fall."

Alan Cox

Country Play Days

Hopscotch, skipping, games with a ball
Bowling hoops, marbles hand stands up the wall.
Cricket, football, team games on the green.
'Come on' John, Sue, Tom be on my team.
The swing the boys made with old tyre and rope
Hang down the side of the old great oak.
Daring boys climb high in the branches
Showing off to the girls that they fancy
Gathering flowers to take home to grandma.
Filling the cottage, bluebells in a jam jar.
Fishing, paddling splashing in the streams.
Lazing in sunshine, having day dreams.
Finding a bird's nest in a high hedge
Waiting and watching to see the young fledge
Feedings the ducks down on the pond
Cooling our faces with a fern frond.
Helping the farmer take cows home to milk
Touching the calves, their coats like velvet and silk
Shadows lengthen on the old orchard wall
Time to go home now, as we hear grandma call.

Jean Parker

The Highlander

Alone and dying in the desert
There lies the figure of young McPhee.
Clothes soaked in blood, wracked with pain now,
No longer part of the battle scene,
How he longs for the highlands of Scotland.
Running over the heather clad hills,
He's Rob Roy that dashing hero, clad in tartan, set to kill.
Waving his sword "Look out my laddies", he hoots and
    hollows down the brae.
One day he will be a hero, never thought it would end this way.
Now the pain tears through his body hears the piper's slow lament.
"Fight no more, my bonnie laddie."
"Come rest awhile, find sweet content."
Calm and quiet all around him, no more noise of battle calls.
Hear the song of thrush and lark now.
Drifting downwards, the piper calls.
There's the highlands locks and heather.
Smells of pine woods, sweet perfume,
Rest bold laddie, find your peace now.
Welcome laddie, now you're home.

Lucille Woods

Hampshire

Your leafy lanes and golden beaches call me;
Your ardent rivers, flowing to the Sea.
The speckled trout, in crystal waters gliding -
The mayflies waltzing one brief, hurried spree.
The leafy Downs, where Chalkhill-Blues are dancing,
The golden haze, the poppies' scarlet blaze;
The skylark's joyful singing, high above me,
The smell of grass on glorious Summer days...

Joan Lambert

'Walk With Me'

Take me by your side, Lord, guide me on my way,
Keep me on the right path, never let me stray,
Show me all the good things, spare me from the bad,
Help me to be thankful for all the joys I've had.

Teach me to be honest, teach me to be true,
Save me from the pitfalls, for I trust in you,
Let me be your servant, let me be your friend,
Trust me to be faithful and all my sins amend.

Hold me to your bosom, clasp me to your breast,
Let me prove I'm worthy, put me to the test,
Grasp my hand and show me that you understand,
Listen to my plea, Lord, show me where I stand.

Judge me by my faith, Lord, as we journey on,
See that I am willing to reach the goal beyond,
Light the path I wander, keep all harm at bay,
Guide me by your wisdom, till the judgement day.

Richard Thomson

505

Life

Another day different to the last.
Our present already in the past.
As we walk through our charted waters.
Be fathers, mothers, sons or daughters.
We give life and love to those we care for.
But sometimes we want more.
We want eternal life to be together forever
As we walk from one life to another.
Our memories however long or short
Remind of the things we've been taught.
Through this great journey we can learn
From those whose destinies take a turn.
To those whose lives have ended sadly
We learn how life can treat us badly
To those who live with devastation
We learn that this is realization
However long or short your stay
Life goes on day by day.

Katy Foster

On A Sunny Doorstep

Relaxing, sharp-angled, I pined, hauntingly gilt-wrapped,
On sun-hued chair in yellow haze,
Remorse-bent, while pine-toned Burmese cat encircled
Golden dreams.

Sitting, stiff-jointed, I reposed, craving summer-seepage,
Seeking purgation of hoary winter mind.
Minding the unviolated peace of Aurora's somnolent curves,
Repressing emulation.

Perching, taut-limbed, I reclined, imitating natural ease,
Hope-rays warmed fleetingly between exclusive clouds,
Pierced-glitter eluding glorious absolution,
Prickly comfort.

Lounging, straight-backed, I mused, envyingly sun-trapped,
Resisting urges to kick the coiled complacency,
In thoughtless voids the cat luxuriated with feline facility,
Purring contentment.

Julia Clyde

Divine Wind

The day she slit her wrist,
was the day I cleared my throat,
and felt the relief of withdrawn weight
from my shoulders.
Feelings of sincere relief easily overcame sadness and regret.
No element of guilt or suspicion entered my mind.
In fact only redness of roses,
and licks of laughter infused my brain.
Brainless relief, relieving laughter, laughing at itself.
Smiling high, and rubbing hands with delight,
I sat and enjoyed coffee,
noticing granules, grown then grained.
I thought of this and then,
and here and now nut shelled.
The relativity of now was nicely bizarre,
and comforted by the safeness of then
already lived, lived through,
and experienced, still here, unlike her.
She now lies motionless, stiff and grey, or
are her ashes blowing in the wind.

Steven Hogarth

Parting

At the moment of parting we stand,
When gifts are pressed into loved hands.

These are my gifts — tears;
A poor man's pearls,
Strung endlessly to show
How my heart weeps when you go.

J. L. Hancock

The Essay Writer

I sit, nearly rigid, eyes blurring, characters monotonous,
Gazing momentarily on a clock face set on my wall,
It is the hour of midnight, just two more hours needed.

My mind is blocked, illogicality follows,
My hopes and dreams are dammed, like a mighty river.

A world in my head, dry as a desert,
Tired as a marathon field at the last mile,
Exhaustion seeps, like plasma from a wound,
I am done, communication and idealism flow through my pen.

Joseph Reilly

Life With Meaning, And Without

You're a jumping jack in an enclosed box,
Blood thirsty hounds hunting a fox,
A deserted girl in a crowded world,
A hissing serpent writhing on the ground,
Too hateful to move, too spiteful to need,
To crave would be to open,
To love would mean your grave,
You dug your own plot and now in it you must rot,
Rest in peace and sincere and don't get caught,
And don't come back to confuse and instill-
Stay away and hinder the broken, on the window sill,
You're a doomed truck falling over a cliff,
You're a dumb chick with too much brains to live,
A rocket scientist in his own biosphere,
A school ma'am full of self-inflicted fear.

You're sunshine, rain, a dirty frog lying in pain,
Since you're so full, come share and exclaim -

Julie Anne Cullen

Because Of Love

It's the reason that makes,
My legs get the shakes,
And also why my whole body quakes.

My arms get weak,
I feel oh so meek,
But nowadays, my thoughts aren't so bleak.

My heart beats so fast,
I think that at last,
I'll leave my single life in the past.

My eyes are so starry,
I don't want to tarry,
So now I think that we should both marry.

I don't want to wait,
So just name the date,
When you will become my lifelong mate.

It's not because of a turtle dove,
It's not because of God up above,
It is my darling because of love.

M. Younger

The Windmills

I walked on alone through the milling crowd.
Past all the houses and pubs, shops and grills.
Then spied with shock, high on the hills, a proud
Far away group of war-like white windmills.
Running along the pale blue-grey sky-line
Manifesting the tawdry way they stray.
Uniform they're tall, smooth, unapt outline
Reaching out to a far distant highway.
The grass soft beside their solid pathway
Its timeless green-peace colour contradicts
These new wind-fed humming towers so fey.
But, I realized, how my needs conflict

And stared, knowing I should give some support
For all the cheap electricity they brought.

Susan Holmes

Untitled

It is good to greet
  A brand new morn,
Each new dawn that appears.
  To see it shed its dew,
Like I often shed my tears.
  for every time I see a thing of beauty
That is when your face it nears.
  I cry out loud, but no one answers,
For only nature hears.

Len Worrall

Correspondence

I'd like to send a message to you,
One I know you'd read.
Of my pain and of my suffering.
Of my hunger and my need.

And, when you've read the final word,
You'll say, "you meant that, didn't you?"
And I'll repeat the thousand times
I spoke those words to you.

A letter about the way I feel.
Of concern and trouble and fear.
Or a phone call from the darkest vaults
Of things you'd hate to hear.

Yes. I'd like to send a message to you.
One I'm sure you'd read
Of my pain and of my suffering.
Of my hunger and my need.

Kathryn Moores

"Mine"

The gloom of temper tantrums is dispersed by winning smiles,
As they squeeze into your chair to huddle snug,
And the radiance transmitted excuses many wiles,
When they end a scolded silence with a hug.

They aggravate a weary you, then shed a soulful tear,
When your temper barks chastisement at the mites.
All at once you are an ogre, attacking frightened deer,
Ravening their tender psyche with cruel bites.

Then some days are simply magic - they heed your every word
As you analyze the wonders they can see.
Soon you come to realize the untruth of what you heard;
Of how parenting held only misery.

For the glow you see deep in their eyes, when you get it right,
Is the closest you can get to the divine,
And if they're loved enough, they'll always bear that certain light,
So that proudly you'll exclaim - "Those kids are mine!"

Perry McDaid

Mountain Mover

Altho' there be nothing in the kitty
One can still sing a ditty
For God has said he will provide.
Now mohammed couldn't do it
As he worshipped the wrong God he blew it
And the apostrophized mountain continued there to abide.
But God has said that every little sparrow nestles in his care
And the lilies in the fields of worries are unaware
And are men not worth a great deal more?
The mustard seed will sprout
Invested with divine clout
If we but have faith his blessings lie in store
Like those lilies we too can be arrayed in glory
If our life script is a credible story
If we focus on God's love and grace divine.
Albeit burdened by life's sorrow
Let us salute each shining new tomorrow
And one day God will say "My child thou art mine."

Michael John Fee

The Dewdrop

Lulled by the breeze
Excited by the wind,
This tiny fellow
Has no fears, is not ill at ease.

Behind the eaves and on the gutter,
Frozen in Winter, almost sizzled in Summer,
Boldly, he will not utter.

From the leaves on high
When a storm is due,
He will not be angry - or frightened
To realise, God's work must ensue.

F. Dee

Depression

I wish all people understood just what depression is,
Instead of thinking we are mad, and giving us a miss.
Our thoughts turn in, our world is black we cannot see the light
We pray the mist will go away so we can see the light.
Everything's distorted, we believe ourselves so low
We need to talk, and listen to let the darkness go
Some of us are fortunate with friends who lend an ear
Others aren't so lucky, alas no longer here!
Tablets, pills and medicines to help us on our way
No! They don't work miracles but see us through the day
Imagine how were feeling, we hate to be like this
Sometimes all we really need is a smile, a hug, a kiss.
So when we have our bad days thank God they're very few,
Don't turn away, just talk to us, next week it could be You.

Jennifer Bollington

Alphega

Have we lived before? Is a question often asked
Somewhere down the centuries, in the deep and distant past
Is death a transformation? From one level to the other
From being a human in one, to an animal in another

Living before! Would explain things already knew
The 'I've been here before', the power of Deja-Vu
Does existence really end? With innervation in the grave
Are ghosts left to remind us? Of heaven's place we are still to save

Is sleep a look into death, a glimpse of what's ahead?
The next step in our progression after we are dead
If you've been to a place before instinct let's you know
A flash of another time, another life in a growing row

When the eyes close and breathing stops - our next journey begins
Where we do end depends on goodness or sins
Down the dark tunnel the spirit does go
To enter the light and be met by people we know

The years are a circle, turning like the wheel
To come back again is maybe our spiritual deal
Our existence being short, ending like a season
Making way one for the other - is a logical reason.

Paul Muir

The Dream

Oh tell me did you ever dream of a world.
Where nobody starved to death.
Where no children were beaten, and cruelly used.
So that greedy folk. Could amass wealth.
Or if the day ever came when the races combined.
To treat each other as friends.
But as human nature has that free will
To be good or bad as they choose,
Things will not change in east or west.
There will always be abuse.
If wishes were horses the old saying goes.
But they're not so what can we do?
All we can do is our best in this world.
So one day these dreams may come true.
If that ever happened one wonderful day.
I'd like to be there wouldn't you?

A. L. Price

Untitled

Then when, my love, can it come true,
our not-yet-written fairy-tale
that sustains the hope
of what we want to be?

The loaded books try to tell us
in syllables that run, burning
endlessly through the lost pages
of our consciousness.

Yet, like elusive harpsichord notes
on the sprung breeze across an island,
the meanings are breathed and dropped
across the hazed horizon.

And we cannot run to catch them,
for the past anchors, that hold us
always from the truth of the fairy-tale,
are locked too deeply in the sea-bed depths
of what we wish did not exist.

John Tildesley

Naked Mind

Your watery blue eyes idly wander in my mind,
Searching, probing, leaving no stone unturned,
Then, you find my innermost thought,
Cowering away from you,
It is my love, my love for you.
You tear it apart, throw it away like waste paper,
Snatching it like a greedy child, a child that aims to hurt.
I have no control over you, you have taken my
Thoughts of love for you away from me,
And left me with a naked mind.

Elspeth Oram

Dreams

I'm torn inside by the two worlds in
which I live in,
In one I can breath freely, in the other
the air grow's thin
Why risk living, this life, suffering rejection
and fears.
When we can escape to the next avoiding
heartache and tears,
Why can't I escape to the land of peace,
Where I could remain till the end of time,
Instead of wasting precious year's in a world
of death and crime,
When I leave this bitter world, which is
enveloped in resentment,
My body floats away with a feeling of contentment,
How I hate to awaken from a land of
peace and immortality,
To return to a world which breeds
hate and violence,
This place I call reality...

Lisa Palmer

Timothy

Many a magic morning has he walked
But not at heel and docile at my side,
And when we're resting often we have talked
Of rabbits and the deer the heathers hide.
He roams sharp-eyed on moor and through the wood
On paths he knows by heart from infant days,
Alert for any sign of life that could
Attract his interest enough to stay.
Perhaps along the valley by the brook
A plunge, a splash, but never any prize,
A fish is always worth more than a look
But never does he register surprise,
For him the chance is there just for a swim,
The golden retriever we all call Tim.

Bernard Jones

Memories Of My Younger Days

It was on Greenhow Hill Yorkshire, where I was born,
With only fields of grass, and no fields of corn.
The houses were built of stone, and not brick,
Some quite solid, and some quite thick.
I was living on a farm, in a village near by,
Where other country folk lived, some rather shy.
There was a church, and an Inn, a shop, and a school,
Where children attended for lessons, and did not play the fool.
It was quite safe to cross the road, in many ways,
There was not much traffic on the roads, in those days.
Only the odd Lorry, and Horse and Cart,
And only a small, playing park.
Which had a pavilion, a swing, and two wooden see-saws,
For children to play on, outdoors.
I had seven brothers, two sisters, a dad and a mum,
Me being the youngest, had lots of fun.
But we did get punished, when we did wrong,
Which made us grow up, to be respectful, and strong.

Dennis Calvert

Reflections

When a child laughs through the misery of war.
that is hope.
When a woman prays by a hospital bed,
that is faith.
When a man can smile amidst utter chaos,
that is peace.
When a family can grow old together,
that is happiness.
When a baby cries for the very first time,
that is joy.
When I look at your face and deep in your eyes,
I see all these things and more
that is love.

Wendy Westall

Time

I remember the joy of our days by the sea
And painting our dreams by the setting sun
But life turned around as you walked away
How could you leave and give her our world
My heart is exhausted-
Why does love have to hurt and time slowly unfurl

I hear the waves crashing near me
On the warm rocky shore
The white foaming water calling me, calling me-
With the sea all around no more struggle or pain
My mind is exhausted-
Shall I stay with my soul and let time play on its own

I close my eyes and let the water caress me
I dance with the sea and there's music around
My limbs won't obey me but I no longer care-
Then strong arms surround me lifting me high, higher
My body is exhausted-
As fate shows her hand there's another term to go
Time is in control again

Mary Hammond

Dusk

I am going out alone into the scented twilight
To where the apple-blossom lightly stirs
And the wind that has kissed the violet and aconite
Plays now among the firs.

I am going out alone to where the poplars
Stand on parade against the evening sky,
To smell the rain-washed air near the magnolias
And hear the night-bird's cry.

Then as the blue-dim night slowly effaces
The fading memories of a day that's dead
I mingle with the half-remembered faces
And softly sigh the words I'd left unsaid.

Constance Kenny

508

Nature's Gift

We live in a world where seasons change
The summer sun, the winter rain
The snow on the hills, the valleys green
Precious sight's that we have seen

Nature waves her wand across the land where we live
She gives to us these precious gift's
She ask's no favour in return
Other than to live, love and learn

She is the one who gave us life
We are the one's who cause the strife
But now and then we get it right
When a little child come's into sight

A little child with love in her eye's
Who always smile's and seldom cries
She ask's nothing in return
Other than to live, love and learn

With the help of her father and mother too
She will grow strong, loving and true
Nature perfected only a few
Sarah Jayne, she chose you.

P. Parsons

Oh Deer

No light for leaves,
No wind, no breeze,
Restricted and confined,
Time bomb ticking in my mind,
Got to get out, got to escape,
Dense foliage canopy, velvet drape,
Wide open iris, no light inflicted,
Searching intently, but nothing depicted,
Straining drums listen with vim and vigour,
For the crack of a twig, the twitch of a trigger,
In it comes rushing, the thump of explosion,
The snap of taut skin, the rib cage implosion,
The huntsman's hound thrashing through heather,
This cannot be happening no, nay, never,
Beaten and bleeding, with antlers sawn,
To heaven I rise, my new day is dawn.

David Beesley

My Philosophy

Violence, violence we cannot accept
Not for us our children or even our pet
The world is unhealthy, where did we go wrong.
Don't get depressed try singing a song!
It's the good deeds that count
Of that there's no doubt.
Spread a little happiness when you're out and about
Elated, cheerful, no thoughts of trouble
Don't let anyone burst your bubble!
We live - we die but in the meantime
Say hi! Say hi!

M. J. Stapleton

On Choosing A Book To Read

Volumes of words composed of creation,
Oceans of ideas; streams without banks.
Torrents of titles awash with allure,
Literary giants in snug serried ranks.
Girded in leather, in linen and pulp,
Some gilded, some tattered, some dust-jacket clad.
Favoured ones frequently fondled and read
Others stand silent, disconsolate, sad.

Which were the stories succoured with sweat?
And whose are the tales untortured with toil?
How lately did musings emerge from some mind?
Does dusty tome signify musty tomb's soil?

Consider the reader; which instinct is strong?
To fancy the Singer or go for the Song.

Katie Preston

'Quiet Interlude'

I felt the sun warm on my face, heard the sough of the
    wind in the trees,
I relived my memories of years gone by and, I dreamed my dreams.

I took time off to think, not of problems looming near
I thought about the future, of those I held most dear
I allowed the soft and gentle air to caress me as it passed
Feeling touch of another Presence offering strength, unasked.
I was aware of a Peace then, unrivalled in its power
I was surely not alone as I worked among my flowers!
I felt in tune with Nature as a bird went winging by
I heard the hum of insect, saw the flight of butterfly,
I wanted then to feel the joy of a light and grateful heart
As I took the time to meditate, to quietly play my part.
I offered up my deepest thanks for what I had received and,
I prayed I'd not be wanting when others were in need.

I felt the sun warm on my face, heard the sough of the
    wind in the trees,
I relived my memories, remembered my past,
    and I dreamed my dreams.

Ruth M. Gilbert

The Showdog

With swishing tail and pride in stride
By stylish glamour, he commands the scene
Away to the front, out and around the side
A racing glide, lines swift and clean

Aloof, he scorns the watchful throng
Cock confident of the treasured goal
Sports gleaming coat and head held strong
To catch the eye and snatch the soul

Harmonic vision, a pure spirit forth
Blithe spectacle of divine creation
Epitome of the true breed worth
Bold symbol for his generation

The prospect firmed, the prize in hand
The victor bounds his exultant lap
The judge pens notes as the finalists stand
The ringsiders sound their ultimate clap

No humans attain their own perfection
They learn their failings, accept the strife
But honour to those who, by a different election
Seek to nurture ideals through another life

John Ellis

War

I hear the distant sound of a gun, and realise that a war has begun.
Standing to attention I pick up a gun,
A mother cries for her only son.

Everybody slain, so plain to see it's like a death train.
Guns in every hand, fingers pulling triggers.
Boom bam boom bam, bombs exploding.
Dust kicking, bodies flying, everywhere nobody picking.
Boots crunching, doggedly marching, grenades launching.
Faces, deadpan expression, battle zone total collision.
I sit in the dark, waiting for a foe so I can let go.
I hear the bullet zip through the still dark night.
I hit a target, I see him fall, what a bloody sight.
The young lay dying, everybody crying, the whole world sighing.

I choke at the horror, and the holocaust I have come to represent.
But in the name of war I go down as a hero.
Sure they can say all that and more, just to boost up my ego.
If fighting a war means right, then I would rather be wrong.
Innocent lives have been killed, whilst a handful are playing warlords.
In my book men are dead, and many more may die.
I feel so depressed, as humanity becomes suppressed.

Mohammed Turay

Ode To A Dead Hawthorn

Peace o' fallen relic of this lonely heath
Whom bleak and windy seasons have unrelenting tossed
Since your infant mouth first suckled here beneath

I wonder not your twisted limbs portray the pain
As of striving to raise your thorny brow aloft
And God beseech your supple youth again

What force benign would preordain your lot
Unseen to rise and wither in distress
Unsung to die in this forsaken spot

Did summer never chance to come this way
One errant beam illume this wilderness
Your blossoms once be never blown away

Did once a bird defy these lowering skies
And soothe with song the rigours of your plight
Or did the dawn, too late, repentant on you rise

If you were not intended to persevere in vain
And be as man refashioned of beauty and delight
We may yet communicate upon some kinder plain

A. E. Dyson

Dreams

When you close your eyes
You live another disguise
Travelling on many trips
With no sound from your lips.

In a dream, it's funny, your feet
They never seem to touch the peat
You walk without a cut at all
Through a stained glass wall.

The vision, isn't clear enough to see
The images, obviously are not me
It's not about love or money
Nor about anything funny.

Would you call it a nightmare
When you can't see, touch, or hear
And teardrops dampen your pillow
From dreams of pain and sorrow.

Sometimes dreams are hard to explain
When you wake up refreshed again
But you know your dreams aren't worth keeping
Because they're all in the art of sleeping.

Jacquie Smith

To A Daughter On Her Christening Day

O tiny child content and warm,
A precious gift from God.
How perfect is your tiny form,
You're beautiful to behold.

With love you came into our lives,
Entrusted to our care,
We'll nurture you with joy and love,
Such happiness we'll share.

Good parents we will try and be,
We'll guide your steps each day,
Just put our trust in God above,
He'll surely show the way.

'Sarah Louise' is your chosen name,
And in God's holy place,
We dedicate your life to him,
Who's holy name we praise.

We thank you Lord, for this precious gift,
Watch over her we pray,
And as she travels on life's road,
Please guide her, show the way.

Joyce Willis

Thank You For Being There

I didn't really get a chance to tell you how grateful
I was for your love and support, throughout my unhappiness.
I didn't really tell you how your calmness and faith in me
strengthened me, and helped me to believe in me again.
You were there for me strong and true ready to protect me
and all that I am. Never doubting, never asking why, just
believing in me; and gentle hushing away my tears.
You were for me the strength during my weary midnight,
my encouragement through my deep pain. The friend that I
could not have come through without.
So now I would just like to take the chance to thank you
for.. reaching out to me, for reaching down with me and
for sharing my pain.
Thank you for being with me in thought, even when you
could not be in person. Thank you for holding on and
thank you for loving me.

Angel Mullings

Finding God

No thing of beauty ever made by man
Is greater than the man who formed it so.
No wondrous art or skill, however fine
Can be so strongly wrought with mystery
As He who's power of thought can give it birth.
Such kindness as can fill the heart of man
Brings forth in him the height and depth of love,
Self-giving love to other men out-poured.
Yet this is mere reflection of a love
That far exceeds the limits of our sight.
For He is love's creator, He the source
Of all that's best and finest in man's soul.

Mary Culverwell Smith

These I Have Loved

At Sunday tea we always had fruit and jelly,
Must have bread and butter, but there was no telly.
Fruit cake was a must and jam tarts too.
Those were the memories not but a few.
The coal fire was burning flames red as hell.
We all huddled round there, stories to tell.
I still hear the radio singing songs of praise.
We all had lovely voices and these we would raise
I think of the holidays, just Mam, Dad and me.
Every year June or July the sand and the sea
Bucket and spade, oh I kept them for years.
I grow plants in the bucket, though no one cares.
The seasons all came, the seasons all went.
We knew them all well, all heaven sent.
To remember these things that were all in the past
Brings peace to my mind, the memories to last.
These are some of the things I have loved.

Sylvia Baddon

East

Mystery people in a mystery world
Sitting in windows - standing lonesome in doors.
Surrounded by power they have no shame,
Standing and staring they're not to blame.
Mystical magic in a mystical age,
Shining example of a life in a cage;
Shutting my eyes dreams flood so near,
I reach out and touch them releasing emotions of fear.
Like clones they walk through the street,
Downtrodden souls with downtrodden feet.
Like puppets they hang in mid air -
No-one to turn to and no-one to care!
Flying over hills smiling up to the sun,
Rising higher reaching up to the stars;
Looking down to the world - patchwork landscape below
Like fireworks light up the sky bombs silently explode -
Sending flashes and sparks way up so high!
If not for death it's a wonderful sight -
But I wonder how many Heaven's claiming tonight?
Gates left permanently open - it's a never ending fight!

Deborah Mary Booth

I Remember

I remember when you held me in your arms all night long.
I remember the look in your eyes, when you told me you loved me.
I remember the touch of your hands gliding over my body.
I remember, I remember...........
I remember the feel of you deep inside me.
I remember my body wrapped around you.
I remember our desperation, our need to be one.
I remember, I remember...........
I remember the fun, the laughter, the secrets we shared.
I remember wanting your happiness, more than anything else.
I remember the contentment, the joy, of just knowing you cared.
I remember, I remember...........
But now you are gone, torn away from me,
leaving a gaping wound that will not heal.
My body cries out for you in the night,
my heart sinks deeper in despair with each passing day.
The pain grows stronger, time is no healer.
You are so near, I can feel your presence,
it surrounds me wherever I am.
There will be no peace for you or me,
time and space cannot separate us.
I will live in your soul and you will live in mine, forever.

Elizabeth Laffeaty

Time

Time runs away with life, it hastens along its path,
We cannot believe or, quite conceive, where yesterday has gone.
The daily hours they shrink so as through the week we go;
So many things we mean to do, but time gets in the way.
There is always tomorrow, or so we often think,
Another beginning, another day, and yet another link.
The next will not be longer, or though we wish it were.
So use each precious moment as if the last should be,
Treasuring the days as given; freely to use and only ours to see.

June A. Fuller

How Much Will It Cost?

Let's take a journey down memory lane,
When the air was clean and no acid rain,
The forests and jungles were dense with leaves,
Giving off oxygen for us to breathe.
Sheltering animals, who all had their place
Before poaching became a human disgrace.
The rivers ran clean and the water was sweet,
No poisonous chemicals on food that we eat.
When we took from the land just enough for our needs,
Before man became selfish and bloated with greed.
The forests are dwindling and now in their place
Are acres of land which are all laid to waste.
We needed the oxygen from all those dead leaves,
The animals needed their homes in the trees,
Rivers and streams are no longer safe
Being filled with rubbish and foul smelling waste.
Some species of animals could soon be extinct,
And fish will soon follow if we don't stop and think.
We're killing our world slowly each day by day,
And sooner or later we'll all have to pay.

Thelma Dinham

The Cook

I listen to her raucous laugh,
Sometimes I think she's a little draft.
But nevertheless no kinder soul you'll meet
So busy, she's never off her feet.

No fairer cook is in this land,
No machines, it's all done by hand.
Her face glowing from the oven's heat,
The once tidy kitchen now not so neat.

Her greatest delight is a knock at the door,
It gives her a chance to bake some more.
To replenish the stock she keeps in the tin,
For waste to her is the greatest sin.

William Frazer

The Last Supper

Wisdom, is for those who see the sun, he said.
I feel the weight of his body, bearing down upon me,
as weighty as a sandbag.
Religion is for those who fill the need,
to worship, I said,
Glory unto you, he said.
I hear the sweet purity within his voice,
a penetrating lightness of being,
within the cup, of darkness,
How can you drink bacchus, would you not give me back my son,
He lies in his grave poor wretched soul,
A child he may be, clad in purple,
buttered gold and vermilion, but he is mine.
His bones are yours, to keep,
deep in the bowels of the earth buried,
the cage of ribs creak and whine,
As you my saviour dine upon the little ashen birds,
Mother, mother, I cannot find him,
He blossoms around us all,
He is my son, the son of God, the sun of all.

Melinda Dunseith

Sad Memory

Which way to light, our love was cursed
my body is a tomb, enclosed in memories
of smiles that laced around her womb.

The blood that poured it was once life,
But dried upon the earth
it sunk to feed the roots of time
that grew into my world.

Alone I stood all dressed in black
the blue-print of a man.
My weakness was I never took
the time to tend my land.

And now I take the ocean air
and walk upon the sand,
no more to think of harvest
time or animals to brand.

Suzanne Jones

From A Hopeful Lover

I see a spark of love for me
showing in your eyes
Reflecting thoughts that lie within
and dreams that may arise

Please, please, kindle that little spark
till a glorious flame appears and
Do not keep me in the dark
but chase away my fears.

Sarah Pridgeon

Untitled

You came, a tiny pretty girl, on my doorstep, my first sight of you,
You were so frightened, yet did not need to be.
You knew your name and 'out' and that was all.
I loved you then, I love you still,
You brought me happiness and joy and love.
Gradually you changed and learned to trust and also understand
the words I spoke,
We went for walks, I did not dare to let you off the lead
For fear you'd run if another dog or traffic startled you.
This was your home and garden too,
You learned to play, though not with ball,
You came upstairs and followed me, my silent shadow,
Rushing by to get there first.
You suffered pain, we tried so hard to make you well, but could not,
So farewell my own sweet Cleo.
One last quick kiss from you I shall remember always.
You came, you stayed so short a time,
Just three short years, my darling,
One day I hope we'll meet again.

Joan M. Wood

Deep Within The Twilight Wood
(A Childhood Dream)

Deep within the twilight wood
A little silver winged fairy stood,
By the roots of an old oak tree,
Surrounded by a bluebell sea.

On her head she wore a crown
Which sparkled when she fluttered down,
From the sky at the break of day.
Before the stars had run away.

At the touch of her wand, the trees would sing,
And the bluebells would start to ring,
Even the wind would joyfully cry,
As he pushed the white clouds by.

In the afternoon, her friends would come
Then the fairy folk would have such fun,
Drinking early morning dew.
From acorn cups, till the day was through
And when it was time to go to bed
Our fairy Queen would raise her head.
Then the Sun would wink his eye
And turn his light out in the sky.

Jeremy Westley

Homage To Nature

I meditate along the winding path
Grassy, glassy, mulchy
Of recent rains the aftermath.

Silence breaks way down a little
With hidden view it's vague yet brittle.

I pause to peer through forest thicket:
I listen to the eerie sound
Of water somewhere near my ground.

The mist is rising faster now:
A shaft of light creeps through the bough ahead of me;
the sky I see
Glimmering, shimmering sunlight pale:
I pause on pebble, rock and shale.
A crazy waterfall of hail like snow
Dashes, crashes to slower flow
And quietude of pool below.

A rainbow then appears across that fall:
An iridescent offering; a barrier
To nature's impenetrable wall.

I gaze and gaze, enchanted and awe-shrouded
the mystery beyond remaining clouded.

Helen Anna Zurlinden

The Alphabet

Alpha Bet sounds quite grand,
of Poet's corner, writer's cramp
The twenty-four complete the course
Melanch'tlon a golden source

Of Homer's works, a class apart
Shakespeare the only rival bard
Him speedy Argonauts employ
For them the Sirens would destroy.

Josephus words in Grecian tongue
of wars and death and Herod's sons
And from the safety of the lair
He bore a consequential air.

The Hebrew tongue of twenty-two
The Aleph-Vau of sacred hue
All other language would eschew
Any dialect from Goy - only sent us to annoy.

Enigmatic, strange but true
Pythagoras and Horace too
Expressed their calculations drew
In the limits of words knew.

Richard Cummings

Good Friend

Through trouble and strife, down all the years
You were there, you soothed my fears,
Arms outstretched you wiped away all tears,
you were there for me, my friend.
For you it's been no bed of roses,
You too have your share of life's pain,
I'll be strong, I will help carry your crosses,
I will be here for you, good friend.

Elizabeth Furlong

The Farmhand's Daughter 1952

My childhood meant to me,
Sitting on my daddies knee
When he could spoke the time.

A farmhand dad who played piano on a sabbath night
whilst neighbours came and sang by warm fire and
flickering glow of pale gas-light.
Aunt May got out the rubbing board and fill
could play the spoons,
mums saucepan lids and comb "kazoos" accompanied the tunes.
Stone-flagged scrubbed farmhouse kitchen floor
Dads ex-army great coat on the back of the old stairs door,
Scrubbed white farmhouse table on oak legs carved and black
Standing boldly astride our worn out coconut mat.
Billy Paver and Alan Quinn sang, mostly as duet,
Oh those happy Sunday nights I ever will forget.
Then dad would play that same sad melody
in the evening glow.
I'd cry, with a mouthful of home baked scone,
and off to bed I'd go.

C. D. House

Untitled

Never book your holidays the week that I am going,
For even if you go to Rome, it's certain to be snowing.
The temperature will surely drop on beaches I have chosen,
And if I don't wear woolly clothes, I'll probably be frozen.

I buy some tanning lotion, in case my skin should peel,
But even as I spread it on, I know it will congeal.
I take my winter anorak and wear it every day,
It protects me from the tidal waves that roll in from the bay.

"You should have been last week, every day was great"
I know, I've heard it all before, it doesn't help me mate!
But worst of all, when I get back, my neighbour says. "My Dear,
You should have stayed at home, because we've had a heat wave here."

Summer suns are glowing,
But not where I'll be going,
Storm-force winds and hurricanes and north winds will be blowing.

The weeks I spend away each year, it always pours with rain.
The weather always lets me down, specially in Spain.
It's up to me to warn you, and so again I say,
Never book your holidays the week I go away.

E. Beaman

The Wolfman

The Wolfman comes to me at a full moon.
His whistle is as soft as any tune.
In the dark, you cannot see his face.
When he is gone there is hardly any trace.
His breath is so hot and steaming.
Am I awake or have I been dreaming?
He is gentle yet strong.
In whose world do I belong?

Does he want my blood?
My tears flow like a flood.
The birds are singing up in the trees,
And I'm sure I can hear the humming of bees.
It's time for the Wolfman to go.
He shakes his head, I scream no!
It's the coming of dawn,
And my heart is forlorn.

Carol Brown

512

The Cup

Living hands created these old dead vestments:
long-gone, they embroidered symbols of life;
perfection of circles, vibrant whirls and spirals,
expressing spinning Sun or powers of elements.

Then that rose, the only one of that strange salmon-pink
of petals, prettily outlining the cup-shape,
broad but deep, turning gold, then old-gold in its deeps.
A humble-bee alighted, so agile, stopped to drink.

Tracing its footsteps, I began to follow
its journey around those petals, delicately;
they moved as I moved, a slow-spin I paced,
faster and faster into that sweet hollow.

Deeper and deeper, deep-down, not up,
I danced against upspringing rhythms, spiralling:
spinning with the whirls, intoxicated with nectar
of praise. Then heard, "I am the cup".

Edward A. Marshall

The Game Of Life

Face life with a smile and a happy song,
Seek ever the best, to the good belong,
We are here to learn, to evolve and grow,
But there's a deeper knowledge we should know.

Know your real self is not the thing you see,
Just realize your own divinity,
All life is on the path, the upward way,
That to perfection leads some distant day.

This single life is but a day in school,
So do your best, don't be a selfish fool,
Choose the good law, the right, the good, the true,
If you want inner peace to come to you.

Do not live just for money and success,
If you want happiness give happiness,
You have free-will, the good or bad to choose,
So blame not God if you choose ill and lose.

Love all, and play life's game with heart and soul,
Think less of self, win the Great Golden Goal,
Then only can you say goodbye to this.
And enter love and joy and perfect bliss.

George F. Walters

A Plea For Humanity -
And The Creatures Of The World

Was not the life that people led
In those days, many years ago
The way that we would live today
If only we could make it so?

The pleasant life, the peaceful life,
The love and wonder of the land
Which gives us all we need to live
And answers to our skilful hand

The lovely skies, the stars by night
The beauty of all creatures, too
Dear God, we need but little else
Please make it so - please make it true.

We do not need the modern ways,
No electronics - none of these
None of the gadgetry which comes
With modern living - aimed to please.

For we are heirs to all things past
Inheritors of time are we
And in our turn do we bequeath
Eternity.

C. M. Chaplin

The Old Fashioned Farm

While children played aloft
Cows, Daisy, Peggy and Sally munched sweet hay
The Farmer milked, slurp slurp into a bucket.
Children laughed,
A bull comes to call, making
a clatter,
Daisy has a calf Heifer or Bullock
doesn't matter,
Everyone smiles,
No Artificial Insemination
No Chemical Feed
No Cattle truck across the sea
No B. S. E.

Lucy Hood

Days Outing With George

We sat by the road at Dunguness
looking across to the sea.
The sky line is scattered with funny old huts,
fishing boats, an odd car, but no tree.
On the sea many sailing ships swiftly passed,
and farther out tanker's went by.
The sea it was blue, white horses showed up
in contrast to a pale streaky sky.
Some fishermen came, loaded up to the hilt,
back to their cars to go home.
They talked in groups of the fisher's they'd caught;
and other's that were lost in the foam.
There weren't many birds, around where we were,
just a skylark, and one or two gulls.
But I'm sure when the fishing boats
landed their catch,
there were plenty to fly round their hulls.

Mollie Daw

Sea-Moods

Calm and serene no mortals to command
Blue-sky reflected, o'er the golden sand
Crystal clear in beauty priceless yet so free
Sun-dappled waters just one mood of the sea
Then as dark clouds gather and change the blue to grey.
The wind lifts up the waves and tosses high the spray.
Till rolling and dashing against the old sea - wall
Gives vent to all its anger, as the tide must rise and fall
This then - another mood - evil as may be
Yet once again so wonderful and worthy of the sea
Then just as if by magic calm returns anew.
The evening sun's declining rays set up a purple hue
And in the darkening waters, deep with mystery of the night
Tho' quietly in slumber, now radiates with light
Moon beams dance and shimmer stars sparkle down with glee
Together make perfection in the glory of the sea.

Marjory Rosetta Blake

Royal Reality

"God save the Queen", the anthem peals:
But saved for what? It sometimes feels
We ask too much, accept no flaws:
Those constant probes behind closed doors!

We criticize her way of life:
Is she a good Mother? Is she a good wife?
Has she spoilt her son and heir,
Our future monarch? Do we care?

Is the Palace out of touch?
The younger Royals indulged too much?
Must the Queen take all the blame
For let downs to the family name?

She dedicates her life to us,
She never falters, makes no fuss;
So, when we sing "God save the Queen",
Remember just how tough life's been.

Corinne Lovell

For A Kind Lady

Because you're special and kind to me, I gave you
something round and sacred.

My tears of frustration you have seen,
and wiped away.

My inner self, I have revealed to you,
you and I carry the card and key to an unknown future,

But I'm not scared, if you'll walk with me,
when you're sleeping I gaze deeply.

When we curl up together, nothing can
touch us, and the spirits are silent for a while.

I hope we can play it together, if not,
when you're dancing,
close your eyes, feel it pulsate in every
nerve, then take it and throw it high,
and it will fly and never come down.

For I have given you the card that
is round, it is my heart, my dreams,
my thoughts, my future, my perception, and my loving
please be careful and don't be scared.

Simon Dinçalp

Perspective

Dream of all you wish and adore
Through each misty cloud that implores
Rise through each doldrum you endure
And find yourself on some far off distant shore

Ride along each silvery trail
High beyond the plane that impales
Warm within wants thoughts assail
And find yourself in some timeless nurs'ry tale!

As life goes through perspectives anew
Help you ease a moment of strain!
And as you soar, new energies pour
Forming meanings on a higher plane!

Then, as you reach conclusions that teach
Tones tend a more settled score!
And new resolve, that such process evolves
Feelings form a further encore!

So, fly within your halcyon hues
Far beyond each boundary's blues
Freed from all atmospheric views
And find yourself through perspective anew

John Byron-Evans

In A Child's Face

The nameless child, her birth he never knew,
Oh! Parent of joy, his angered hope, dutiful task due.
Mother's ill-dissembled hate, upon her lips of fear,
bring forth angels, love of heaven, tomorrow appear.

She fled from him, alone but for a child,
a lonely man's revenge ascends a fiendish smile.
Mother bade her infant suck, while dying in her silent pain.
This miser brought forth another woman, to bear her scorn again.

In eager hunger further loathe, burden maternal earth,
the madness of a hypocrite, the insult of a second birth.
This mother who weeps, oppressed of woe,
an outcast of falsehoods, fear we know.

Child of scorn, woman betrayed,
in a child's face the future made.
Child - successor to freedom and truth,
God's love is in the face of youth.

Suffer the children, for your parent's scorn,
heaven and hell on earth, a child of glory born.
In a child's face there is hope and love,
seek faith in God, or a child's epitaph.

Beverley J. Wright

A House Wife's Dream

I've always wanted to go to YORK,
But all I do is talk, talk, talk,
About going to York
I dream of lofty spires and cobbled streets,
Old world inns where the locals meet,
With weathered eyes they sit and stare,
At hordes of tourists everywhere,
Ghosts stalk. Ulph's Horn may be heard on a breathless night,
While Guy Fawkes passes flying his kite.
Dick Turpin thunders by for kicks,
Could it be him or was it swift Nicks?
I search in the library to find out more,
Much better this than household chores.
A flick through the brochures for the quickest way,
And my dreams are released as I book for my stay.

Mary Allen

One Aspect Of The Lake District

Blue mist shrouded are those mountains so high,
Humped back whales, buck furiously at the leaden sky.
Slow moves the weather-vane in the still of the day,
As plumes of spumy water, five miles high,
Fall as spray, or even more dramatic measures,
Over the land at Highfell; moss-green; or through the leafy trees,
Drenching any occupant of such land they travel on.
Sheep don't even notice, for they're used to it - you see.
Soggy, boggy places they'll give a miss that day,
And shelter by a boulder of slate hard grey,
While they inspect the grass,
And dream of more pleasant ways,
They can chew and watch you pass.
A canny animal which sometimes makes you laugh.
They will eat the wild herbs, even the endangered flower,
While we look on dejectedly from under a fern-strewn bower.

Susan Johnston

Prelude

I hear the prelude, simple and easy
Like our life together
When you were young.
The dialogue flowed and soared
Played as notes on the organ,
All was harmonious, I was omnipotent!
You, my darling girl-child; I, your mother.

Listen! that tune is finished, for now the fugue is being scored,
Your life weaving and ducking around mine
In imitation when we blend;
Suddenly, utter discord, the notes harsh and strident
Like our ideas and passions, structured on different levels
Dissonant and in conflict, seeking a new motif
You pulling your way, my part lessening -
Not major, but minor, our strain not in unison.

When we play our new theme, will it be in harmonious rhythm
Together?

Anita Ling

People

It doesn't matter what your colour is,
It doesn't matter where you're from,
We all have legs and arms and eyes,
We all have secrets and we all tell lies,
So what's the difference in the colour of skin,
What does it matter?
We're none of us tin,
Black or white, yellow or pink,
It's only a colour,
So where is the link,
Between colour of skin and colour of soul,
Being black on the outside and having a heart of coal,
Just because you're white it doesn't mean you,
Have a halo on your head and are an angel all year through,
Every body's different but we're really all the same,
So when will people realize,
Racism's not a game.

Emily Plumtree

Looking Forward

Growing old, a natural progression which no-one likes,
But don't despair - it need not be too bad,
With reasonable health and a lively mind
Life can be enjoyed and new pleasures had.

Try different foods, pasta can be fun,
If you really don't like it you don't have to eat it!
A glass of wine, careful, no more, enjoyed daily
We're told is good for one.

Learn a new skill, try typing or pottery,
Be aware of others needs and try to support.
A listening ear, sympathetic words
And a cup of tea can mean a lot.

Wear bright colours to lift your spirits,
Present the world a cheerful face,
Be glad to have lived in this momentous century
From Victorian cobbled streets to Information Highway Interface.

In 4 years time will be the Millennium
To celebrate which great things are planned,
And in 2002 we'll rejoice with thanksgiving
Queen Elizabeth's Golden Jubilee.

Joyce Page

Bright Future

Small green buds emerging
From Winter's inertia.
Decorating bare branches with verdant gems.

Some Spring days grey, cold, foreboding,
Others, blue skies and white fluffy clouds.
Ever changing, ever hoping.

Bulbs slumbering under an earthen duvet
Preparing to burst forth like a giggle.
Cajoled by the sun's warm caress.

The earth, a dark casket from where
Yellow flowers tumble out in profusion,
Like golden nuggets from a treasure chest.

Birds busy in the gardens
Searching for food and socialising,
Looking for nesting places to procreate.

My hopes for the future rekindled,
Gazing out on this annual rebirth
I glance at my new baby and feel joy in abundance.
Jonquil, my personal Spring issue.

Brenda Faruque

The Butterfly

A caterpillar bit into a juicy leaf,
And lay in the lovely hot sun.
She spotted a bee flying past her
And thought, I wish I had that much fun.

The bee has wings so she can fly,
A lot of luck she has caught.
And I can only crawl around
The little caterpillar thought.

Months went by and the bee was still
Collecting pollen from flowers.
And still the caterpillar prayed and prayed,
And hoped and hoped for hours.

At last it was time to build a cocoon,
The caterpillar didn't know why.
But anyway she built it up,
Very, very high.

She spent a long time curled up in the cocoon,
And then at last she burst out.
All those colours definitely meant
She was a butterfly, no doubt!

Tracey Diamond

Waiting For The Sunshine

The birds and I were waiting,
For the coming of the sun,
(softly,) from the clouds, heavy, and grey,
I watched with a wonderful, feeling
The darkness, slowly passed away-
Soft blue sky, like a vision, as in a dream
slowly, but surely, the dream became truth,
Form the heavens, once dark and grey,
The golden light with its warning ray
covered the land, and the sea
God was here in his golden light
The birds began to sing a morning hymn-
Thank you heavenly father,
For your radiant light
All will be well, when your are here
Changing grey skies to beautiful blue.

B. V. Robinson

Thankfulness

Once more dear, Jesus, I send my thanks to thee,
For sweet sleep, that took away my fears,
The worries of the day.
Composed, in the arms of sleep,
When all is calm, and peace,
'In prayer,' I brought all my troubled thoughts,
and troubled heart
And lay them at your feet,
You gave gentle rest,
The night passed away,
Once again I give you thanks,
For the coming of the morning light
Teach me gentle Jesus your pathways to keep

When the clouds cover the light,
And stars are gone,
You will be ever near,
To guide me softly through
Both day, and night,
My heart and I say thank you,

B. V. Robinson

Into The Countdown

Research - into every aspect of life
Has progressed at a breath-taking pace:
To protect and conserve organisms and cells
Thus embracing our own human race.

Sex changes, at transplant, an artery by-pass,
Hip replacements - confirmed by a Scan,
In Wards of a Unisex structure
Regardless of woman or man...

...leaving much to be done in a far reaching Science,
Of concern to the males - heaven sent,
When the Newscaster, Peter Sissons, announced
That the sperm-count is on the descent.

Margaret R. Lawrence

The Diviner

Here I sow them, seeds of a deprivation limitless, private,
In the rejection of this landscape where the rock burns
And no tree shelters the lonely, the abandoned,
Where the bushes, a dry menace, crouch close on the bone-
    hard ground.
From the spindle-shaft of the burning scrub cut then the twig
    of the dowser,
Hold it as an offering of passivity, and power,
In your perambulation of this landscape more than a companion,
A prophet whose cry is silent.

Who dares to prophesy against the lightning's
Ceaseless flaunting of an unattainable horizon?
Yet I follow; await the arch of the descending rod.
For one day I shall dig deeply
And on that day I shall carry water
To the hidden, the indestructible seed whose fruit is joy.

Lorna M. Armistead

515

An Ode To Spring

The daffodils show their trumpet like heads
And the gaily coloured crocus, from their wintry beds
Nature bursting to life on the bushes and trees
And the birds singing gaily on the still cool breeze
The magpies build their nests in the trees so tall
Whilst the bluetits examine the box on the wall
Soon a pecking sound is heard, as they prepare
The box - to nest, for their children to bear
When all this is over, they fly away
Perhaps to return, on another day
Garden seat emerges from its wintry cover
And made ready for use, in the oncoming summer
At last winter's over, let's rejoice and cheer
For at least until it returns again, later this year.

H. Street

The Town

Leaves are falling in the empty square;
Nothing else left now
But these rustling witnesses, joining
Scraps of discarded paper in the breeze.
Gone are the happy voices of buyers and sellers,
Gone the shouting, quarrelling, eager crowds.
Gone with their busy, restless lives
To hide another night away
In their stone castles.
The sun is sinking over the small town.

But to-morrow they will be back;
Re-awakened by the dawning day
To possess again the empty square,
Swept clean now of leaves and litter,
To make room for another day's living and laughing,
Noisy and vibrant in the autumn sun;
Uncaring of newly falling golden leaves;
Unheeding of the brevity of day,
Unmindful of the dark forgetfulness
In the embrace of an enduring night.

Irmgard Cameron

Daffodil, Daffodil

Daffodil, daffodil you are new,
popped up with the dew.
Daffodil, daffodil you are sweet,
shooting up for me to greet.
Daffodil, daffodil you are yellow,
swaying down low and
waving to me, saying hello,
Daffodil, daffodil you are dying,
look at me now I'm crying.
Daffodil, daffodil you are dead,
no more to be, curled up for the world to see.

Maybe next year you will come back for me!

Jordan McMillen

My Special Friend

You gave of yourself, when love was needed.
You cared and brought some happiness, when no one else heeded.

You wrapped your arms around me, and understood the pain.
I knew that when I needed you, that you'd be there again.

You were the one, who made me feel a special person, once more.
All my tears and troubles, onto you, then I did pour.

We laughed, we sang, and all that silly talk.
The country walks, the lovely meals, the tender words we spoke.

It seems so long ago now, when you came into my life.
Lifting up my spirits and easing all my strife.

Perhaps within another life, we'll meet again someday.
And love each other then, but in a very different way.

I always will be thankful, to you my special friend.

And in my prayers, and thoughts of you, my love I'll always send.

Valerie Lees

To Doris On Her 70th Birthday
(A Long Way After Louise MacNeice)

February has come and I wake
And I think with joy how, whatever now or in future the system,
Nothing whatever can take away our relationship,
Not even death - for that effects the flesh only.
The mental and spiritual links remain: We shall always be sisters.
The conditions of love will be changed and its vices diminished.
Affection will not lapse to irritation nor its flow be hindered.

February has come: It is hers
Whose vitality leaps in the spring.
Whose nature prefers woods with anemones and climbs over stiles
So I give her this month and the next, though the whole of my
years should be hers
Whose rendered already so many of its days crammed with blessings,
Who has left a scent on my life in my ears, and all of London
Is littered with remembered outings,

So I am glad that life contains her with her courage and humour
Whose mind is lucid like a Mediterranean pool,
Whose eyes are candour and whose mouth reveals tenderness.
To whom I send my thanks
That she was born in Aquarius.

Mollie Helen Pitts

Another World

As you gaze into the blue horizon
I wonder what each of you see
Do you see only blue skies and clouds
Or can you see much further - like me

Can you imagine another life in the distance
With people perhaps like our own
Carrying on with their own existence
And calling their planet their home

Do they also gaze out on their own sky
And see life in a different light
Does a sun perhaps shine in the morning
And do they ever have night

Earth as we know is smaller than some
Are we sure we alone do exist
Why not Saturn or Jupiter or many more
We can never be sure of this

So if you happen a glace some starry night
Look closer - think longer - why is that star so bright
Could there be someone - just a bit like you
Thinking - Is there life out there - Could it be true

Irene Sutherland

Farewell To A Loved One

Why did leave me? Why did you go?
Your death came to soon and I loved you so.
I miss you so desperately with each passing day,
I try to be busy but the pains here to stay.

The good die young so the old adage goes,
You were one of the best love, as everyone knows.
A loving husband and father, great son and brother too,
loved and respected by all who knew you.

You loved all the sports, though rugby was your game,
Your name will live on in that hall of fame.
Our families are wonderful yet I still feel annoyed
My life is half empty my heart is a void.

No one to talk to, no one to scold,
No shoulder to lean on, no arms to enfold
No one to laugh with to hug and to kiss,
No one to fight with, no moments of bliss..

I need you to love me to show that you care,
To hold and caress me, life's so unfair,
When I open our door love, I still hear you hum,
I miss you my darling, my very best chum.

Maureen Rosemary Lane

If Only

If only the world could stand still for a day,
If only the moon and stars could come down this way.
If only the seas could dry up for a day,
To bare what lays beneath the spray.
If only one day there was coloured rain,
To trickle down the window pane.
If only all wars could cease for good -
And man turned hate to love as he should.
If only each one had an equal share,
Food, clothes, a warm bed and someone to care.
If only we could live a simple life,
No governments to argue and cause such strife.
If only a cure was known for all ills,
No more need to swallow pills.
If only we could live our lives as free -
As our feathered friends that live in the trees.
If only we could be content with all that is free -
Then God would bless you and bless me.

Margaret Bowles

Noble Art?

The noble art of self defence,
Is often just a sly pretence,
To use our strength, impose our will,
To show off pugilistic skill
When to the ring a boxer goes,
To enter combat with a foe,
With whom before he's had no quarrel,
Where then is the noble moral?
Intent on breaking jaw or nose,
Bruising eyes to make blood flow,
To damage brain beyond repair,
Does the public really care?
God gave us gifts of strength and health,
And liberty to use this wealth
In any way we felt inclined,
Through the impulse of the mind,
But 'twas his will it's plain to see
Through the evidence of Calvary,
That we should love each other so
That sin should be our only foe.

Peter Spear

Untitled

Wavelets lazily lap the concreted walkway
Shared with cyclists and dogs and anglers on lieu days.
Ducks busily grooming each feather into place.
Almost unnoticed, two lovers share an embrace.
Scaring above a plane drones on the air waves
Mercifully free of disc jockey tirades.
Banks of buddlia, briar and tasty blackberry
Effectively screen warehouse and factory.
Gone are the king fisher, warbler and dragon flies
We're left with the midge of pester and terrorize.
A pleasant enough walk to test your leg power
From Churchill to Newbridge you'll need a good hour.

G. Davis

The Guitar

Twang! Twang! - A broken string,
Oh will I ever learn this thing,
They say the key is perseverance,
I'm probably musically illiterate by chance.

Strum! Strum! It's better now,
I've kept the practice, I don't know how,
But patience is pushing me through,
without determination what would I do.

Trinkle, Trunkle, I know the flow,
So this is what I have to show,
For now I am a super star,
And all thanks goes to my guitar.

Vera Power

The Old Armchair

I'm always sitting in my chair,
Wishing I'd been here and there.
My legs are weak but my brain is still strong
As I keep wondering where I went wrong.
I would love to have seen the sky in Rome
And France, not so far from home,
Gay Paris with its dancing girls
Who throw up their skirts with their twists and twirls.
Beautiful chateaux standing so grand,
Looking out over the land.
Vine yards bursting with promise of wine
Which I used to love when out to dine
I wonder what it's like to see Hong Kong
With its many shops and busy throng,
India and the mystic east,
The colour of their clothes giving the eyes a feast.
Africa with its animals, rivers and falls
And at night a host of strange weird calls.
I dream of it all but never get there
And still keep sitting in my old armchair.

Dorothy Mabell

A Mummified Hand At Chiddingstone Castle

This little hand so still and hard and brown,
The palm obscured by fingers stiffly pointing down,
Plucks at my sleeve across the centuries.
It housed a pulse once, and its flesh
Was supple, fresh and smooth.
Brushed away tears, clapped over lips in laughter,
Listened to Dramas, clasped in its sister hand,
Followed the rhythms of drum, flute and cymbal.
Cooked, wrote, picked flowers, maybe toiled in fields.
Struck out in quarrel, stroked a cheek in love.
Stretched out in worship, marvelled at the sun.
Made shadows on the wall under the moon,
Had lines upon its palm, marking its future.
But did those lines predict it would lie here?
My hand lies over it and mirrors it.
The glass case part us. All the same, we're one,
Perhaps I knew you in another lifetime,
Centuries ago and another land.
And then the thought occurs - perhaps I *was* you -
Good grief! Perhaps I'm looking at my hand.

Anita Silverbirch

"The Unborn Child"

Life began as life begins
Unknown yet wanted
Their eyes hidden as the love awaits
    the cry of life
Yet that cry would be a peaceful smile
If only reality could be where life begins

Heart beats for ever reaching for the
    unknown world
A life lying still, hidden to what only
    could be
Yet beauty so radiant as with loving
    kindness
Reflected the love - the fears and unknown care

Moments of pain, moments of splendour
Gave joy only to be remembered
That cry, that smile as real life reveals
The radiance of the unknown child

The longing shared by all who know's
and may all dreams he rewarded by
the kindness everyone should show.

J. S. Mitchell

Lost

Mounting confusion overwhelms the mind,
Searching for something impossible to find.
The tide goes out, leaving a wilderness of sand,
A never ending path, obtrusive land.
Surrounded by people, and yet all alone,
Suddenly afraid of the love she's been shown.
Once so protected from hurt and from shame,
Now she is drowning in an ocean of pain.

When sunlight has gone, darkness brings fear,
Alone, with nothing to cling to, no-one near.
The world is so distant, a far away shore,
Her desperate cries unheard, ignored.
Free as a bird, but somehow trapped,
Raised up on high, then downwards slapped.
Engulfed in the waves, the sea of strife,
She asks herself why? What's the meaning of life?

Mandy Montague

"Please Santa"

Father Christmas reined in gently as he approached the
   rooftops low,
The sound came quiet distinctly across the ice and snow,
He heard her softly crying as she lay tucked up in bed,
'twas Christmas Eve and not the time when a baby's tears are shed,
She should be waiting there for Santa to bring toys and all
   good cheer,
But her poor little heart was breaking as she whispered in his ear.
"Father Christmas won't be calling Mummy told me tonight,
She was crying when she told me and tucked me up so tight,
The policeman had told her gently, the driver was a drunken lad,
and only God in all his Mercy can bring me back my dad.
So Father Christmas if it please you, you can make me and
   Mummy glad.
With your sleigh and all your reindeer, please bring
   back my Dad.

W. H. Allen

The Daisy

Out walking very early on a calm and peaceful morn
I spied a child, lying flat, face down, so quiet,
   so still.
In trepidation, hesitation, call it what you will -
I slowly, quietly, moved towards the little form -
Now quiet enough, she moved little finger to her lips -
I am waiting for the flower to open, as indeed it did
A simple daisy, so white, so fresh - as pure as the
   child herself.

We walked together to our home -
She is my child you see -
Her Mother is awaiting us and greets us happily.

The Universe is ours today - a day of calm and peace
A daisy small, a child's delight - a Happy Family.

E. B. Woodman

Distance

They say they do...
They spoil, pollute, assume
No Responsibility.
They lie
And slyly, quietly condone
politics of violence and greed,
Mutter phrases of 'Economic Need and Stability'.
They take, they waste, make endless trails........
of destruction
wherever they may go........
But don't you know
We sigh,
And try Ideals
lead-free, save whales, the trees;
Ask why, donate, lay blame...
Forget to see that 'They' is you and me.
They steal.

Denise Fox

The Match Stick Girl

A life of sadness is all she has,
Down in the darkest nights,
A life of sadness is all she has,
Low spirits shading the lights.

The way she walks is slow and sad,
Down the running track to hell.
The way she walks is slow and sad,
Armed with her match sticks longing to sell.

The way she cries drives daggers through hearts,
She falls, she falls.
The way she cries drives daggers through hearts,
Finally the vale of sadness envelops her.

Shelley Francis

No Music

We go to lots of places to sing and play for folk,
We love to join them for their tea and chat and have a joke.
But everywhere I go I have to carry such a load.
I'm very glad to go by car and not walk down each road.

Oh how I envy clever folk who can play just anything.
You call out a song - they're never wrong - and everyone can sing.
But me, I bring just lots of songs and when folk start to sing,
They ask for a song that I haven't got or else forgot to bring.

We went to a Music Museum once when in Germany one day,
The girl touched a switch - organs, flutes and pianos like
magic, all started to play. She danced with my husband to
music so gay, He enjoyed every moment it quite made his day.
A beautiful grand was standing there and I wished I could
play it without a care. Oh how I longed to remember a tune by
Schubert, Novello or Strauss - But Happy Birthday to You
was all I could do - I wished I could hide like a mouse.

So unless I tuck music inside all my clothes -
Blue Danube, Mikado, and To a Wild Rose,
And say with a smile - "Oh look what I've found" -
And hope I can reach it before they turn round!

Ena Matthews

Cambodian Legacy

Shatter the ice from crystal black windows,
twisting and turning like Moths round the moon.
Bow down to ashes of yesterday's childhood
and tear out the pages of days passed too soon.
Lap the dark earth from the roof of the abyss
and drown with the Whale on its flight to the sun.
Hide in the shadow of searing black Arc-light
and laugh with the knowing that hell hath begun.
For the once stolen seconds midst ivory pagodas
now scream with the teardrops on red sharded grass,
and the child that once danced to the windsong of silence
is frozen forever as the horsemen they pass.

William Marshall

"Worlds In Time And Space"

As evening draws its darkened veil
Another day goes by
And stars appear through ragged clouds
Skimming the endless sky
I often gaze in pensive thought
At those jewels of the night
Which light out world so sad and grey
With their constant, steady light.

Are they worlds like ours as such we know
On which young beings thrive and play
Or just gaseous specks of distant light

As our learned Boffins' say

Surely we can't be the only form of life
Amongst those distant galaxies in space
And someday we might prove for sure
We're not the only living race.

Susan Elizabeth Ault

My Moulana Baba!

You're the symbol in our lives.,
You've filled our heart full of joy.
There is no doubt,
As long as love and memory last
You're the nicest "Baba" to love.
You're the love, support and guidance
Gave us a tower of strength to do well.
Without your help our lives would be miserable.
You're always deep in our heart.
You'll live now and forever.
I admire you more than ever.
Your fame will never leave us.
We saw your image,
You smiled and said:
Don't worry folks, I'm always with you.
One day I'll meet you in heaven
Where you take rest.
God — bless, I remember you always
We love you now and forever.

Shafi Ullah

"Sara"

I sat and watched you sleeping tonight,
I think of your funny little ways,
Your cheeky little face, almost hidden by strands of your hair,
As I brush it aside
You screw up your nose in the indignant little way you
did today when you couldn't get what you wanted.
I can still see the look on your face when you took
your first step-
You were so proud - I was too.
You were always what I wanted you to be - so full of life
and expectancy of what it all could be.
Oh, you've had your moments,
but you remind me so much of me
Headstrong? stubborn? sensitive? maybe even a little insecure
Sometimes you send me into total despair,
but I wouldn't change you for the world
You're part of me, part of my life
and I love you -
Unconditionally!

Amanda Jayne Taylor

Flight Of Fancy

Against the cool, clear blue of the sky
The small white clouds are peaceful and still.
The leaves of the trees swirl, round and round
Along the paths and down the ground.
A flock of birds, gathered high in a tree
Huddle together with chatter so loud,
Then suddenly soar up into the air
To return once again, and settle back there.
Up above, in the cool of the sky
Wild geese fly by in strict formation.
Small birds follow, moving together - wings lit by the sun
Flash gleams of silver, as they fly, steadily, silently on.
High up, and above, there are glistening aircraft,
So high, so silent, with jet trails behind,
Yet large and so complex, with engines that roar
As they carry the travellers to far distant shores.
To tilt the head and study the sky, to ponder the wonder of flying,
Is to sense the great height of the air up above.
To soar free as the birds, from earth's trappings below
Or in flight of fancy travel to where the travellers go.

S. M. Green

The Smile

It leapt on my face like deadly disease
It stretched its way out like an oncoming tide
It opened up like an oyster to show its white pearls
It pushed out the cheeks like a bird does his breast
It reddened the surface like a rose bush blooming
As it sang out its song of joyful laughter.

Rachel Clements

Green Glory

"Trees tell me nothing, men are my teachers"
Was Plato's laconic statement

But legend says trees are almost human
Appreciating what goes on beneath their branches
The loves, dreams and misdemeanours of men and women
Perhaps they can forgive while men and women lacking
In imagination are unable to do so
Maybe the trees are near deity as much as we are

How they must laugh, sometimes in derision too
Trees with affection watch those who understand them
Listen, when winds caress branches and whisper in your ear
Interwoven tessellation of foliage hide rocks
That smile upon the gurgling, glistening waters below
These are places where one can dream
Of beautiful entities mostly unattainable in reality

The statement of Plato is one I cannot agree with
I hope you can see what I see
The glory of a tree

Shireen Senadhira

The Re-Awaking

A few, soft, spoken words, the breath of a kiss to his head
The tremor and pressure he felt as someone sank gently,
    onto the bed.
His eyes flashed open, the hope plain in them to see,
    looking, searching
For the one that he dreamed of... but, again, it wasn't to be.
As his eyes scanned the faces of his family gathered there
Their luster and gleam faded and returned, to their oblique stare.
"It's been so long now", he thought, "my missing you
    'causes me pain.
How long must I wait for you to hold me? And tell me, you
    love me... Again."
Our children are here, they won't let me be, our grandchildren too!
As I'm sure you can see.
I've told them all about you and about a mother's love and they
Remember you so clearly... as do I... Mary, my love.
The years have been hard since you passed away and I think
    of you often with each passing day.
I'm tired now... I find it hard to carry on, I want to be with you...
It's where I belong.
The children who watched that tired old man were amazed
    when he spoke and reached forth a hand.
The words that he spoke were to Mary, his wife.
Then he lay back and smiled... and thus, ended his life.

Gerry Brady

A Horse

A horse was standing in the field across the road
Her foal was only a few weeks old.
A stranger arrived upon the scene the mare she began to scream.
She knew it wasn't time for her feed.
This man was out to do a dirty deed.
She threw back her heels and tossed her head.
The man became so hot and red.
The mare she kicked and jumped around.
This sent the man falling to the ground.
She showed the man that she was boss.
And standing there would be his loss.
She stood her ground but cut her side.
It wasn't deep or very wide.
The stranger began to feel ill at ease.
And he was aching at the knees.
He had torn his coat and cut his hand.
So he got up and left the land.
The mare she stood there full of pride.
Her foal standing by her side.
She groomed his neck and nudged his head.
Now my dear it's time for bed.

Esme Trickett

Untitled

There she stands in skin tight jeans,
A replica of what I had been.
Slim and beautiful with hair of gold,
What a shame I'm getting old.

Youth flashes by like a flash of light,
All we have left are lonely nights.
The Photo Album is a source of joy,
All my memories of my girl and boy.

From babe in arms to wedding day.
There's nothing more for me to say.
Just close my eyes and dream again.
That the boy is eight and the girl is ten.

L. B. Yates

Black Dawn

I can hear nothing, but the stillness.
The deep stillness which drowns every mortal breath.
I can see nothing, but the darkness.
The thickening darkness which suffocates the gasping pupil.
I can feel nothing, but the cold.
The clawing cold which numbs the throbbing body.
I can smell nothing, but the fear.
The possessing fear which clutches the weeping soul.
I lay here, trapped in the rebirth of a new dawn.
Time is non existent, as is mankind.
The debris of this fallen race encircles me,
Their pungent smell of want, envelopes the dense air
My soul lays heavy, contained within this motionless shell.
I wait, a sickening pain pulsates through the
untouched depths of my mind.
Sorrow.
All that once was can never be again.

Sarah Rushforth

Echoing Promises

Someone was close from the very first breath
Waiting and feeling you there
Somebody special was longing to give
Fulfil your every prayer
Anticipating the warmth of your touch
Feeling the silk of your skin
Strong for your happiness, weak for your tears
Willing that life to begin

She was so close when you opened your eyes
Reflecting a world, oh so new
This day that you celebrate is not your own
It was special for someone else too

Warm were the memories, of holding you close
As seconds and hours stole each day
Filling the void, that left scars on her heart
As childhood slipped gently away
Echoing promises still in our ears
Embrace the dreams we renew
You'll never forsake her, that sweetest of loves
Whose life was worth living... for you.

Maria Ford

All The Wars

We remember our dead with great respect
If they were to come back what would they expect,
A peaceful life for which they fought
And freedom of life with death and pain they bought,
but we still have wars that cause pain and strife,
for which all these young people gave their lives.

So what was it all for at the end of the day
No one is sure but with their lives still pay,
For the freedom of life they still fight every day
If we could all speak calmly together,
perhaps we could have peace forever
What a dream this is,
for the dead and maimed a kiss.

June Centauries

Faith, Hope And Charity

Feel the gentle breath of God, in every breeze that blows,
See the wonders of his works, in every single rose,
Hear the singing of the birds, as each new day is born,
Marvel at the glories of the sunset and the dawn.
Treasure every memory of happy day gone by
Raise your eyes and wonder at the mystery of the sky,
Stoop to pick a daisy, and scan its perfect face,
No imperfection you will find - it too, is blessed with grace.
Stand in a Cathedral, take in its artistry.
Who, but God, could fashion that monument for all to see?
Thrill to sounds and silence, for each one has its place,
Look for good, not evil, in every human face.
Touch a leper, you will find the answering touch worth while.
Wonder at the miracle of a baby and its smile.
Read again the story of the cross, and all it meant,
Question not his actions, and your heart will be content.
Know that he is always there, to tell your troubles to.
Have faith that he will listen, and give you hope anew.
Thank him for his love for us, sinners though we be.
Bless him for his promise that we shall have eternity.

M. D. Schofield

Back To Sea

Take me back to sea once more,
On the wild coast and rocky shore,
Where the roaring waves and salty spray,
Are flung ashore on a stormy day,
Where sea gulls circle around on high,
I hear the sound of their mournful cry,
The lighthouse with its flickering light,
Warning the ships that pass in the night,
To see the ominous leaden sky.
Picture the storm clouds rolling by,
Jagged rocks both stark and bare,
Shipwrecked crews have perished there,
When all is still, and mist comes down,
The fog horns blast their raucous sound,
For these are the sights and sounds of the sea,
That bring back pleasant memories for me.

R. L. Todd

Mother

To you I owe everything;
My life, my love, my heart,
My will, my determination and my knowledge,
For you are my strength.

From you I've gained everything;
My faith, my dreams, my hopes,
My spirit, my morals and my values,
For you are my inspiration.

To you, I give everything;
My thanks, my love, my heart,
My devotion, my support and my encouragement,
For I am part of you,
For you are my mother.

Christopher James Francis

'Dance Of The Butterflies'

Meeting in union, fluttering on the summer breeze.
Delighted to be as one.
Liberated together in utmost splendour.
The silk of the wing untorn by the rampant activity of their exertion.

Their brief encounters disturbed by long durations apart.
Durations of solitude, distress and torment.
...Of desire, passion and restlessness.

When once again they reunite,
Joy, devotion and love, though invisible, blind all with their light.

Leaving no doubt
That together they belong,
That together they should be.
The dance of the butterflies radiate love for all to see.

Kirsty Pritchard

The Junk Shop

Rows and rows of dusty shelves,
Beckoning, encouraging me to delve,
Odds and ends, what will I discover?
This vase was once a pair. Now where is the other?

What about this broken chair,
Just waiting for someone to care,
Examine more closely it's not too late,
It can be rescued from a sad fate.

Large black kettle, take over to the light,
By jove! It's copper, soon have it bright,
All these things from someone's treasured past,
I spy a cup and saucer, my Mother had one like that.

To my home I happily wander back,
With the kettle that is all black,
Next week I think I'll buy that broken chair,
That is of course if it's still there.

Marion Fearn

Dunblane

Today sixteen children were shot and died,
Is there someone up there to be their guide.
What did these innocents do to deserve this,
and how their parents will miss,
that smile, those eyes, that sweet face,
this is a human disgrace.

How mothers and fathers will suffer for years to come
Who can understand this man with a gun.
Questions will never be answered as he shot himself.
What a waste the little ones had such wealth
of happiness and laughter to give to the world.
But into the unknown they were hurled.

We think of those parents this night
and wish we could help them in their plight.
The pain will be deep within
who will pay for this most terrible sin.
Is it society that is to blame?
We must stop this from ever happening again.

Paula Britt-Compton

Untitled

Like two rivers we flow through life,
separate, but towards the same destiny.
You, a raging torrent,
carving your way through rock and stone,
forceful, fast and furious,
I, a meandering stream,
flowing this way and that,
I am still water, but I am deep.
Then we meet and our paths become one
you add pace to my flow
I add calm to yours
and so we flow towards the sea
twisting turning together.
Forever.

Kell Lunam-Cowan

Untitled

I wish I was a poet
who could win 110,000 pound
but, if it was meant
for me, I would be dumb founded.

I am sure the winner will be brainy
not like me an 'o' level type
If only I could be handy
with pen pencil and type.

Oh! to be the winner,
but, I'm afraid I will be a sinner,
and with for what in not going to be mine
but, will in time be thine.

Gwendoline Standen

November Thoughts

The fog came down like a blanket and shrouded the earth below,
All sound was muffled and far away - the lights were a dim,
dim glow. A feeling of solitude crept o'er my mind and
eventually covered my soul, I felt cut off from the rest of the
world and afraid that I'd lost my goal. The world had a
shadowy feeling, aloof and so far away, I looked at my fellow
humans, but what, Oh what could I say? I couldn't communi-
cate with them, I couldn't reach out my hand, I felt I had been
deserted and left in a far away land. A feeling of horror
engulfed me, and pricked the top of my head, When suddenly
deep from within me a voice came and simply said - "I'm here -
I will never desert you - alone? no that never can be, I yielded
my life for my brothers and died that you all may be free. And
my Spirit now lives deep within you to comfort you now and
always, Away with the gloom and the terror, take hold of my
Name now and pray" A warmth flooded quick through my
body - a feeling of joy filled my soul, I am loved by a dear
loving Saviour whose sacrifice has made me whole. The fog
in the world was still thicker, but no longer could I feel afraid,
With the hand of the Lord there to guide me, the ghost of my
fear was now laid.

Eira Smith

Image Of Man

To-days Man is clever, very clever indeed,
To busy working, thinking for his financial need.

Goals to reach! he is very specific,
To Kill, Rape, and Thieve, he is very terrific.

Live as Gay Lesbian, or without a Ring,
Committing a sin! there is no such thing,

Morals, Immorals, right or wrong, a thing of the past,
To abuse, Mother, Father, Brother, Sister or Child, has
come into fashion, very fast.

Has high hopes to live on Moon or Stars,
But Brotherhood on earth has gone, as far as Mars,

Pride, Shame, Loyalty or Respect are nowhere to be found,
With Laws of Selfishness, Degrading, Disloyal we are bound,

Rachet HUMAN has taken the earth in control,
For his Satisfaction, Animals, Birds, Beasts of the
jungle, he takes his toll.

Civilized he calls himself, without sense,
he might as well be dead, to Love, Care, and Protect
he leaves to the Almighty Head.

Kulwant Bahra

The Mother Country

The times I look back over,
To me they were the best.
The two wars that have passed us by,
Have now been put to rest.
The future could be brighter,
We all would like to see
Away from brussels silly rules,
Great Britain, for you and me.
We managed before Europe
The common wealth was great
Our goods were sold all over,
Our respect was also great.
Our friends were always grateful,
For where we use to help,
Europe didn't need us then,
All they did was yelp.
God surrounded us with water so that we could stay quite free,
Please look back my daughters I'm sure that you will see.
No more invasions from the Europe, as went on in the past.
Bring us joy and happiness, and God please make it last...

T. Lawrence

521

Misty Clouds

Through each day of toil and stress
We look through clouds of mist
To find the glimmer of better things to come
But clouds of closer density remain

Frustrations, bad tempered thoughts take over
But still we strive for new beginnings
Whatever we do, whatever we say, still bring
Just shrouds of darkness.

Until one day we realize we shall grow
Too old to enjoy what the world has to offer
It is through the strong bonding of love
That keeps us sane and clear-headed
To fight that road of sheer hopelessness.

But just one day there might well be
that chink of glorious light.
The garden of Eden to which we can all rejoice
Alleluia!

John Jordan

The Web

I am caught in your web -
all this time I have managed to refrain
from your hypnotic encounters.
I have remained in control of my feelings about you
have kept myself safe -
from this fatal attraction.

I have often wondered what it would be like
to be embraced in your magnetic power.

Now - here I am
shrouded in your veil of charm.
I am being drawn closer.
I should keep distance between us
but I can't -
I cannot escape you.

I move nearer
my head is spinning
my heart is pounding
our eyes meet and lock
I am entranced
take me - I am yours.

Shirley Jones

Storm

The lonely mist descends
Isolating the weathered tree,
Its leaves shedding green silvery tears
As they are lashed by the rising storm.
The wind's angry murmuring
Shrieks to a crescendo
As the tree bends to its master
And twisting, twirling leaves dance
To the howling tune.
Slowly, the storm begins to fade
Till, with one last bitter whine
It tears its way aloft
Leaving the icy, swirling mist.
And the tree
And the gentled, howling God
Live again in harmony.
I am that tree.
He is the wind.
And so we lived, till that next storm
When the tree bends before the wind or uproots and dies.

Pamela Smith

Oblivion

Swirling depths,
Wherein no eye can see the tragedy that lingers,
And awakens all who sleep.
Within the mighty roar
The soul bursts forth the wrath of evil,
And descending strikes.
A judgement on all men
Who fail to recognize, when life they see,
That forces far beyond the source of man
Are reasons for our destiny.

But what of those who do perceive,
and seek to change the unrelenting need of fear.
To still the mind, releasing from within
The tortuous bonds.
And yet what choice remains.
Is not to end, the same as to begin?
And who will seek the glory
After the masquerade,
When hell in all its fury
Becomes the communal grave.

A. M. Gattenby

Last Chat Before Going Into The Community

Betts come along-a-me, 'cos I got to go to the 'munity,
They say it's better out there, but guess what?
My bedroom's up the stairs!
They have not thought of my poor legs, but say,
They'll put a lift in any day.

Betts, what am I going to do?, 'cos me and Joaney
Bin' a long time with you.
Do you think them others will know, about my moods,
And how I like to fold my clothes, which takes me time,
Not be in bed 'fore half past nine?

Betts, don't go, don't 'tire, 'cos you're too young,
Me and Joaney won't have much fun, if you're not there.
Where did you say you're going to? It's not fair
We want to come too. Australia's a long, long way,
Why you want to go, I don't know.

Betts please! come along with me, for how will
Them new ones know, that I like sausages with beans,
Not pies, and them sort of fings'.
Can I take my old bike too? Oh! I wish that you would come.
Betts, what are Joaney and I to do, without you?

June R. Macbeth

"Love Forever"

I feel your breath as fresh as dew,
a warm feeling kissing my neck.
As you sleep, my thoughts of you
run so deep within.

You hold me so tight, to never let go.
Your legs wrapped around mine,
a sensation so fine.
Deep within my heart, you'll always be mine.

You opened your eyes and then you smiled,
Our love will never die.
You sealed it there,
with one lingering kiss.
So full of bliss.

T. A. Bonner

Wandering Star

Driving down the highway miles away from home
Cars are bustling by me, as once again I roam.
Far from home and family, friends and places known.
On my way to nowhere, friendless and alone.
What can it be that drives me down that endless track
No tears or pleas or sorrows can hope to hold me back.
On and always onwards with the wind upon my face,
Lost forever lost, like an astronaut free in space.

Rita Dianin-Mair

Spring

Although it happens every year,
It never fails to amaze,
Starting with snowdrops shedding a tear,
Right through to the end of May.

With crocuses of various hue,
And primroses of delicate shade,
Daffodils and tulips too,
Add to the wonderful cascade.

And as if this is just not the best,
For our eyes to really see,
The trees get on their summer dress,
And we have blossoms on the trees.

Oh wondrous seasons that we bear,
Each one with its wondrous ways,
But Springtime really is the best,
And gives us beautiful, beautiful days.

D. K. Terry

Shepherds Beware!

Like wine dripped drop by drop in water
suffusing it with a faint rosy hue,
infiltrates dawn, which rises from the night
Until it colours every bit of day.
At first it drips upon the edge of dark;
it steals the light from Venus and the stars.
Then changing, sets the mountain tops on fire,
turns snow to red, to rose and then to gold.
This must be the work of an enchantress!
Ah! Here she comes! Still sleepy eyed and pale,
to dip her finger in the make up box 'Morning',
gilding the clouds and braiding them with silver.
Faintest wisps of smoke that rise from chimneys,
she charms to coral for her lovely hair
and then she takes an aircraft's vapour trail
and it becomes a diadem of jewels
to lie, resplendent, in her golden locks.
  She rises like a flame, in her best clothes,
  fit to meet the world in all her glory.

J. A. Burton

A Wakened Love

She settled on us gently, like a warm summer breeze,
Venus, goddess of all hearts, was seeking whom to please.
In her hand she held a torch, of incandescent fire,
Offering, her Flame of Love, to kindle our desire.
Its radiance, piercing, through the black despair of night,
Arousing all our senses, with an iridescent light.
She played her flame upon our minds, and bade them be as one,
Burning through the loneliness our lives had once become.
She passed her flame before us, and willed our eyes to meet,
Thus held, a tender passion born, still burning as we sleep.
She played her fire upon our hearts, behest our fingers touch.
To share the joys and pleasures, which we had sought so much.
Her fire consumed our empty souls, minds and bodies wed,
Sealed in a mutual harmony, high on a spiritual bed.
Her torch held high in triumph, soft whispered, have no fear,
Don't let this love I've offered you, just vanish in a tear.

Richard Lewendon

Life From The Heart

The world is amongst the thoughts from our mind
of why such things are so unkind
As we travel along the paths in life
to which have gained the cracks of strife
We come to realize there is something to find
that can only be seen if faintly outlined

I often think of the things upon earth
that came to us on the day of our birth
Of which represents a feeling and thought
that can not be shown or let alone fought
Of who gave us life and what it is worth!

Victoria Bancroft

Untitled

So much to see
So much to do
Why should there be so little time?
The years go by and the days that seemed so endless
Now pass so swiftly

Which way to turn
Can we ever know?
When the despair of all our follies ceases to be
Can we find the peace we so desire?

Seeking the happiness that once was so rare
We watch as day by day the morning light ascends from the
  darkest night

There is no time to wile away the hours in reveries
So much to see
So much to do

Sarah Marriott

The Old Railway Line

After the rain and the gales
I walked along the old railway line.
Underfoot the grass was wet, and sludgy clay
imprinted with ponies hooves
paw prints of many dogs and others who
had passed the same way.

Dead leaves, battered by storms-
branches flattened - blackberries all awry...
streams and pools left torpid in the growth..
Yet butterflies of many hues still flew
from one wild flower to the next -
and the hum of insects was there.

In nearby soggy fields
the sheared lambs were strangely nude.
A fox's hole - exposed by wind
the night before - I never knew was there!
The smell of Autumn in the air
recalled a fleeting summer gone...

Constance E. Findlay

The Sweet Season Of Spring

My favourite season has to be Spring
When the daffodils bloom and the bluebirds sing.
When the sky stays blue day after day,
and children laugh and come out to play.
A time when lambs are newly born,
fresh green grass beneath their feet, they
follow their sheep with their fluffy
coats; a sight to behold so innocently sweet.
There are babbling brooks, streams
and trees, pretty flowers and pea
green leaves. Singing birds, long sunny
days, everything seems a blissful haze.
Oh Spring is such a joyous season and
to be happy needs no reason; for new
life is here and the world is bright,
Yes Spring is wonderful, a true delight!

Linda Kerfoot

Noises

Have you stopped just for a moment to listen all around,
Stood a while in silence without uttering a sound,
Can you hear the gentle breezes as they whisper through the trees,
Heard the swish of eagles wings as they soar above with ease,
Listened to the cockerel, crowing at the dawn,
Little chicks a chirping from their eggs as they are born,
Gentle pitta patta of falling summer rain,
Maybe heard the trot of horses down a quiet country lane,
Perhaps in the city as it wakes up from its sleep,
The rumble of the traffic as it moves along the street,
There's quite a lot of wonder in the noises all around,
And the magic maybe something in the new sounds you have found.

B. P. Willetts

The Old

Mind crisp as wine
Demented or just cold
Wise and serene
Accepting, depressed
How will we look and feel when we are old.

Keep me company
Make me a drink
You will tell me if my clothes stink

Speak to me kindly
Hold my hand
I'm nearly at the end of my time
And when the evening shadows fall
I hope you'll be there when I
Give you a call.

Philomena McAllister

"My Lonely Toys"

My dolly is lonely for someone to play with
the puzzles have fallen asleep
Dolly has gone and fallen over and forgotten
to go 'bo peep'
The pram in the corner, is going rusty because it
has not played.
I wonder if my teddy in the cupboard would
like to come out and play.
My skates have gone all squeaky since they
have been away.
Perhaps someone else could take them out.
And clean them and dust them, then take
them out to play,
The toys would shout with joy
'Hip hip' "hooray hooray hooray"

John Etridge

A Fleeting Moment

Life is but a fleeting moment,
Each precious moment a gift from God,
Enjoy the beauty of living full and free,
Take today and change it to all your
    tomorrows
Today is special, take the life you have
    give it freely,
Today is a meaning, tomorrow there is more
    to come,
Enrich the life you have, take beauty as its
    course,
Life and all its glory, life its splendour and
    majesty,
Yesterday, to-day and tomorrow
    a precious moment to enjoy.

E. R. Jones

Think Before You Say

'I always say just what I think.'
A lady said to me one day.
'I'm sure you always, always don't',
I interposed, 'for what I think
Is not always what I say.'
'Green? But you look so nice in blue'
'I wouldn't wear that if I were you'
'You've got to be really slim for those
 High-legged boots as everyone knows'
'What a naughty child you've got'
'I say, my dear, is that a spot?'
'This Yorkshire's sad, the roast beef tough,
Gravy's lumpy - I've had enough'
'I don't like that' 'You look quite fat'
'What a mess you made of that.'
Thoughts like these are best not said,
So keep them to yourself instead.
Voicing them could spoil one's day.
If you must say just what you think
Make sure you think before you say!

Adina Jane Dring

For Benevolent Societies

A man of feeling you cannot be
Whilst war abounds around thee
You have to kill with obedience
Whilst your heart cries out for lenience
The saddest thing that can aspire
Is for a man of conscience to open fire
He may not know what his actions achieve
But in times of quiet his mind will grieve
Just the thought the dreadful obscenity
He may have killed without humanity
To God bless-ed men, who feel this way
There is but one kind thing to say
Fear not, dear soul, your God can see
The awful anguish, that haunteth thee.
These kindly words, although well meant
May only serve, to further augment
The tortured sensitivity
That follows a kindly heart, to infinity
So brave heart do not despair
We know your problem, and we care.

William G. Thomas

So Long, So Far, Not Good

For years I've known your presence, been dependant on your
charm, yet my dreams of pipe and cloud cuckoo's dwelt, have
never done me harm yet that was when you were near me, just
the whitest lie away, but they've dropped the final curtain, for
my role within this play.

You were sought a life of honour; her joy and understanding
for the sands of time in her pledge of fate, were all too damned
demanding. So it appears this worm has turned again, upon
his selfless gesture for now is the time, for him to enroll as
life's appointed jester.

So now I lie defeated, where once in awe I stood, for it
seems those years of practice, have done me no such good,
So I bid you all the best my dear, in this farcical fated scheme.
It appears that maybe not all cats are entitled to their cream.

But rest assure, irrespective of location, my memory's there to
linger for you'll need more strength than her band of hope,
around your wedding finger for your restless gaze and
treacherous embrace will never satisfy you. For there's no
such place in your furtive mind for a table made for two.

Lucy Jayne Parish

Within His Hands

Oft as I sleep - I dream away
I wander off to the Bible's day
In sun-drenched sea and sand
Sublime - in that exotic land

Within my dream - so bright and clear
Without fear - I walk with God
His arms outstretch and take my hand
To heaven's fields - this chosen land

He confides in me and soothes my soul
And knows my secrets one and all
From those cradle days of well begone
Unto the depths - unto the pall

A mass of shining light - revolves about
Travels my mind - solves my doubt
This new today - has dawned at last
All yesterday's sins - ebbed and passed

Then comes the morn - I stir and wake
Adorned to cope with life's intake
I greet the day with its demands
I leave my life - within his hands

Robert Jennings-McCormick

To Dad Retiring After A Life's Time Of Service On The Railway 1963

Ribbon rails as time behind me, youth that sped
Along with time,
Aching back and shifting
Footplate, sweating, shovelling, cased in grime.
Station through a pitted window, gently now the brakes applied,
Whistle sounding, throttle open, passengers are safe inside.
Hall and king and castle numbers these are
Little boy's delight, waving hands, and shining
faces, speeding by and lost to sight.
Steam and I are now retiring, products of a bygone age,
Time and pride and memories motion, turning over history's page
The cup of life is full and so can hold no
more, review of life as through an open door.
The rails are straight the points are set, the
signals pointing down, open throttles rails of
life, traverse your varied way, more time, more
leisure, and then a longer day.

Geoffrey Hale

L'Escargot

Are
you aware
that despite being
thought of as a slimeball
by many people, I am
in fact, considered
a rather tasty morsel in some
french quarters!!

Charmian Bayly

Memories - New Zealand, 1995

My thoughts and memories took me back,
as I wandered down that lonely track,
To homestead graves, one can be seen,
"Did not return from France - 1914".
Again one's memories unfold, to diaries
Written, ages old, in that same war.
The loyalty of those so bold was there
and did explain, that it was right - no personal gain.
What matter - thousands of miles apart -
the call was there right from the heart.
The years passed by and, as before, the
call came again and "off to war",
And so they're spread in distant lands,
many in the 'fighting sands',
And still the faceless ones appear, to pay
homage, so they say, each year
And bend the knee to those who cause the
lonely crosses on far distant shores.

B. A. Howlett

Misty (A Sealyham Dog)

Very brave and bold you were as you strolled across the room
You were the pup for us, the pup without a care
Unique and beautiful beyond compare.

We love you oh so dearly,
People can see so clearly how friendly you are.
You wag your tail which encourages friendship without fail
Your eyes so beautiful and dark, show
mischief, even spark.
Though now they are glazed, you do not see so well
The cat upon the lawn, to chase or not?
It could be ours as well
You peer deeply into the darkening day
Youth has had its fling, but there remains the little rays
Of life, and spark, and ferocious bark,
To prove to all this dog has not yet had its day.

Ann Cundall

Awaken

I awoke in tear's and pain,
Listening to the wind and rain,
I turned the radio on,
The DJ played an old favourite song,
memories of youth and day's long gone.

My husband came in with tea and a smile,
with flower's card's in a pile,
I was sixty today, no big deal,
But then they say, one is as old as one feel's

The phone rang, six little voices sang,
Happy birthday, we love you Nan.
I no longer cared about rain if pain
I felt loved, cherished no need to complain
The wind would ease, gone with the showers
I would sit in the garden, admire the flowers
Walk on the beach, feel the sun,
Count my blessings one by one,
Thank God in heaven above,
For my life, my family and his love.

Philomena Eastlake

"Deirdre"

In different ages many roles you played,
High priestess, witch, and old maid;
In present time a mother with daughters three,
Who could watch a leaf fall to eternity.
You were gentle with a loving heart
And happiness was mine till we did part;
I believe we loved in ages past,
And in some future time maybe; it will last.
Just flotsam on the river of time
Together we loved, apart I pined;
But striving too much for earthly gold
You wandered from the spiritual fold.
Go back before life's course is run
And bathe again, in the spiritual sun;
Then you and I down the river of time
Once more will love; no more I'll pine.

William Donovan

Escape

Gliding through the murky deep the dolphin guards his ground,
Swimming through the glistening shores aware of not a sound.
As shadows pass above the shore danger lurks nearby.
Then all is quiet for a while, then it comes, the thing they call
    the net, crashing through the water.
The dolphin starts to move, he moves faster and faster still not
    aware of what's behind, coming in faster still.
It scoops him up near to the surface, he tries to struggle,
    but it's no use.
He sees an opening, darts for it and, yes, he escapes. For the
    time he's safe from the dangers of the deep.

Karina Robins

Untitled

Waiting for tomorrow that never arrives,
idly dreaming every day of our lives.
What are we searching for, does anyone know
which way to turn, which way to go.

We sit, gaze, think and ponder
is there any doubt why we wonder
what life has in store for us all,
while we are waiting for the heavenly call.

Who is free to be himself,
we're just like ornaments on a shelf.
Pack us up, turn us loose
we're so confused, it's like being in a noose.

Our bodies ache, our bones are sore,
life at times seems a meaningless chore.
charged up in the morning, run down at night
our tormentors say everything is alright.

Raymond George Smith

The Olden Days

It was Xmas time in liverpool, in the God forsaking poverty years,
there was no room for laughter, nor room for any tears,
On searching ones own stocking, there was ashes to be found,
that's the way Santa Claws treated children,
that have been naughty all year round.

Still there was an apple and a orange, also a brand new penny there,
so we carried on regardless, it's as if we did not really care,
Christmas dinner was a change, from a rabbit or a hare,
Given by the goodwill brothers, otherwise the table would be bare.

My share of Christmas dinner, which had to go around the
family plate,
Being eight of us for dinner, the head was mine at any rate,
we still said our prayers, to thank the good Lord up above,
it's not so easy without a mother, to spread her loving love.

So we all sat and smiled with each other,
We tucked into our lovely grub,
and hope the good Lord is looking,
as he takes care of our Dear old mum.

H. Howard

Life's Companion

My dear companion such time has passed
Since last we've been together,
And our parting, so sad and 'er so final
seems almost too much, it's so unfair.

When in the still of the night,
My hand reaches out to touch you
And you're not there.
When day breaks, and the morning sun
Kisses away the dark night shadows
I turn towards you,
And you're not there.

The secrets that we once shared together
The laughter and the tears
Words unspoken, glances stolen,
Our hopes and our fears
It's these small memories that bring me comfort
Makes life easier to bear,
So, until we meet again my love
Goodnight, God Bless, take care.

M. K. MacMillan

The Horse...

Trotting, slow movements that are so graceful.
See the legs pounding the brown earth.
Suddenly, a noise makes him stop..and listen.
The fear moves through his body,
See him tremble.
His body rears up and his legs kick out at an imaginary being.

Now he's galloping away.

Leg's move faster..faster.
Sweat runs down his neck and settles in white lines,
Eye's are wide and staring, there's nothing to see but his fear.

He runs into the undergrowth, and once more feels safe.
Panic is fading from his eyes,
And once more his wet, heaving body calms down.

All that is heard, is the pounding of his heart...

Lorna Harrison

Cold Paradise

Sparkling,
  Glinting as it falls from the skies,
An icy cold sheet of continuous white,
Snowflakes dazzling like a world of crystal
  clear ice.
A shiver as frost shatters to the ground.
Snow drifting slowly, falling in foot prints
To make the ice sheet complete again.

Rochelle Allison

The Fisherman

Silent and intensely still, oblivious to all,
His elegant artful rival dives,
Accomplishing his goal sits and preens.

Through the quiet rustle of reeds,
A whir of reel and splosh of cast,
The twitch, the anticipation of his strategy.

He strikes whistling line in wind,
Taught with the weight of his prize,
The battle commences.

The sudden glisten of a silver flash,
Disappearing again beneath the surface,
Momentarily he faced his foe.

Artfully his captive is netted,
Caressed respectfully while unhooked,
All thoughts of battle gone from mind.

Gently now his prey replaced,
With a swish of tail tastes freedom again,
Again he is still, awaiting his next opponent.

Pauline Allan

The Lord Is My Shepherd I Shall Not Want Anymore

He was there with me when the doctor refused me attention
He gave me his greatest of medical attention
He looked deep into my eyes that were like mince pies
At the sight of the Lord himself with his eyes

He deterred me from going into that great place heaven
By giving me my life back before going to heaven
He took me by my left hand to bold on pit fire
Which was my desire to help my fellow man in fire

He then led me to William pit white haven fire
Then to easington pit disastrous pit fire
Where his unseen hand came to my desire
He stopped me from going into the fire

As all the lives were lost in one great fire
He gave me great help in my great desire
To help my fellow man with the great fire
Although he sits upon his throne with desire

He gives out great help in his worthy attire
His helping hand is a very great umpire
When one is caught in such great fires
His help is there for all who may apply fire

Fred Scott

Our Heritage

God's many generous gifts are sure to please -
Not least among them, always, are our trees;
So richly clothed, resplendent in their green,
Some bare, when winter winds have been.

Bright autumn tints, breathtaking in their hue,
Much beauty, to enrich our lives anew.
And later still, for most of us to see
Delights of sparkling winter tracery.

Just imagine, should they not be there,
A vast expanse, so cold and bare;
No vista of beauty, no dappling shade,
No blossom or berries or favourite glade.

No rambles in forests, or tranquil Pinetum,
No food for our Wildlife -
Or cool Arboretum!

The message for me is simple and plain -
We nurture our trees, again and again;
We nourish and care for them, keep them free -
And treasure God's gift, a beautiful tree!

Joan Adams

Hidden Love

How can you love someone who doesn't know,
Think about her wherever you go,
Look at other women you still see her,
Never out of your thoughts,
Never out of your dreams,
Always and forever,
That's what they say
But how can that be when they don't even know.
You want to tell her your thoughts,
Whatever they are,
Let her respond by looking into your eyes.
Seeing her smile and her sparkling eyes,
Looking at love and making you cry.
Crying for what you know should be.
Love forever our destiny.

Shaun Tester

Lost Youth

We were young, those of our generation,
too young to fight during the years of devastation,
but we had survived the time of bomb and black out
of rationing and going without.
Now the war was over and for us, and end to strife
and into our hearts came new life,
life that was joyous and without cares
and ahead, those few short glorious years
which then were ours to enfold.
So we laughed and danced and loved
and sought the passing years to hold.
It seemed that they would never end,
that time would always be our friend.
Alas, such foolish thoughts and youthful dreams,
for nothing is what at first it seems.
Too late we find,
those dreams were left behind,
whilst life itself has passed us by
and we ourselves can only wait to die.

Marion Bradfield

The Beginning

Water and lightning
Folded and wrapped together
The mountain rocks parted
The water trickled down and through
And then she grew.

Her hair trickled over her head and down her back.
Thickening everyday, every hour, every minute, every second.
Her features and her emotions grew
The pace of the water sculptured her features
The power of the water feed her emotions
Animals and plants grew to love her
And then one stormy day in May I arrived
She frowned at me, then looked out to sea.

Hayley Hughes

Poetry!

Poetry is like a Jewel.
It glistens as you read it.
Such magical words that are put on paper,
No-man should ever forget.

The things that one may read in a poem,
are always something special
The things that poets write
about always seem so real.

A poet should always be,
proud of their work.
Even if it is no good.
As long as they have put their heart in it.
It will always be classed as art.

A poet should always be as proud as can be.
Then they will be classed,
as a true supreme artist

Demelza Willey

Frustration

Every twist, every turn, reasons why not.
An overwhelming urge to scream, to make the mirror crack.
Shards of thought all around,
That cut and pierce every bit as much as glass.

Thumping heart, breathless eternity lasting mere seconds.
Fearful emotions breeding fear of resulting consequences.
Controlled uncontrolled, fooling everyone,
Except the keeper of the key.

Smile or curse, flail out with shaking fist,
The Demon remains untouched.
No impression, nothing alters.
Defeat brings hurt lasting far longer than the fight.

Frustration's echoes haunt,
    Reverberate,
       Return once more,
          To mock, to laugh, to taunt.

M. K. Green

Doctor Henry

Doctor Henry, who is she?
A lady of integrity?
Has she got a clever brain?
Is compassion part of her fame?

Humour, understanding and wisdom are needed.
I need patience for the patient
And courage, oh Lord, to accept
Thy will be done.

When the road gets tough and I don't feel strong
Give me serenity and courage
And the grace to accept my fate
And to accept that I can be wrong

Give me dignity and hope
To be myself and not be a dope.
May I learn to praise and to liaise
To find a common ground where love is found.

Gladys F. Herberts

My Love

The time had come, my love had to go
Never again would I say, 'I love you' to him
I lost him in seconds yet it seemed like hours
Don't go I whispered, don't leave me please

His hand seemed so protective, he took his last breath
That breath seemed so useless now
His eyes seemed sad yet so warm and loving
He looked up and said, 'love you' and closed his eyes

I shook him, but he would not stir,
He would awaken from this endless sleep
I had lost him forever, tears stung my eyes
He seemed so peaceful lying there, his hand was still warm

I whispered, 'I love you', but had he heard it?
That thought shall haunt me forever
I lay a kiss upon his forehead, I'll never love again
I thought, and slowly I walked away.

Samarah Haq

Village War Memorial

His name's not there but I am led to dream
Of all the happier things that might have been
Had he not rushed - but waited for his call.
So young, just twenty one when he was killed;
So much of life's potential unfulfilled,
His oyster's pearl unclaimed.
Yet 'better dead' he'd say than sadly maimed.
All thousand of his shipmates joined in sleep
Their resting place is 'neath the ocean's deep.
His name's not here but I am led to dream
Of all the greater things, that could have been
Had all the brave survived!

Bee Kenchington

The Reason For Your Love

To My Wife

Hills abound where I would be...
The golden sand would kiss the sea...
Then I would ponder silently... the reason for your love.

A rippling stream to help unwind...
A gentle breeze for peace of mind...
A quiet place where I may find... the reason for your love.

A sunlit land where hills will flow...
A field of corn with summer's glow...
A peaceful heart where I may know... the reason for your love.

The sound of bird-song in the air...
The still of twilight everywhere...
A burning wish that I might share... the reason for your love.

The green of trees that whisper soft...
The passing thought that's borne aloft
And weaves a dream much more than oft... the reason for your love.

The slowly moving hands of time...
The sharing moment, warm, sublime...
Then oh, at last to know that I'm... the reason for your love.

Ken Allen

Shadow Of Doubt

For days of wonder, I now grieve;
Shadows around the relic self arise;
From here I see so little to believe.

I have waited, eager to receive
times lessons, hoping they might wake me wise.
For days of wonder, I now grieve.

But no; that cruel teacher will deceive
innocents seeking an uncertain prize.
From here, I see a little to believe.

I'm alive now, this instant that I breathe;
The past's a tomb, filled as the present dies.
For days of wonder, I now grieve.

The unborn future no power may perceive;
The futile prophet seldom thwarts surprise.
From here, I see so little to believe.

Myth and truth a fragile fabric weave;
Life's cloth a random mix of facts and lies!
For days of wonder, I now grieve;
From here, I see so little to believe.

Jonathan Preece

The Handicap

The smile expands
grinning, laughing, joking
such a complex brain
but yet so simple.
Watching her you see
a face of concentration,
yet the hand not writing.
For us - we think, we write.

For them - they think, but it is kept inside.
Some think they have no sense
but they are more intelligent
than the most educated man.
They would not start a war -
their simple world is a world of peace.
They are content with what they have,
no greed, no anger.
Happiness is all they have
and they know no different.
Maybe such a world as this
would make us as intelligent as them.

Phillipa Meade

Postcards

The poetry of postcards fills the missing link
Of space that is between us and tells the way we think.
Enjoying ourselves on holiday the picture postcards show
All the interesting places where we want to go.

Telling how we like it - "Visit here you should,
Perhaps come and join us the food is very good."
Writing letters can be tedious and difficult for some
So "Drop me a postcard to say when you can come."

Collectors too like postcards, the very old, the very new,
The quaint, the unusual, and sometimes naughty too!
It gives them great pleasure to browse and reminisce
And to remember all the past times that they miss.

Tucked away in boxes how precious that they are
Giving us a history which goes back very far.
There are special times when postcards mean so much
Christmas, Birthdays, Weddings when we need to keep in touch.

Valentines and Get Well have a message of joy and hope;
All these are very special and come in an envelope.
Postcards are a part of us so let us celebrate
The postcard's 100 years or more before it is too late.

Barbara Fosh

The Albatross

It was in Southern seas that I first saw him glide,
he followed our ship never trying to hide.

So graceful he looked as he flew to and fro,
always knowing which way he would go.

He never seemed tired or in need of a rest,
just as well, it was far from his nest

Hardly a flap came from those long slender wings,
he had great ease of doing things.

As the sun went down on his back at night,
what a picture it made, what a beautiful sight.

His wings were black and his plumage white,
so those colours can live together and be alright.

Soaring so high he would fly for the sky,
then dive for the sea as straight as a die.

Two thousand miles we could be from land,
but that flying wonder never needed a hand.

How could God make such a creature as this,
then give man a gun just to kill for his bliss.

In those southern seas he was always there,
I would love to think he had not a care.

Thomas Wheeler

Fire

A tiny spark falls
Red and yellow flames leap into the air
It is so fierce
Like an angry lion.

It has a never-ending thirst
Ever growing, ever drinking
The hunger escalates
It roars through the land.

An animal just ready to pounce
Weighing out its chances
Every ounce.

The pain and anguish
It contains
As it eats away
Yet still remains.

It licks its flames preparing for its prey
Sending out smoke signals
Before shaking its mane
And leading the way.

Nicola Armstrong

Isle Of Skye

Breathtaking - like a dive into the cool blue waters
Wildly windswept - by gales that cease, to amazing calm
Mountains that roam beneath the clouds, snowcapped unruly
This wild surround

Where rivers rush by us and meet the sea
Otter, deer, birds of prey, live their lives as it should be
Completely natural - totally free

With the spring come flowers galore, they cover the land
From croft to shore
No sun drenched island that's been kissed
But still a paradise of covered mist

Linda Garland

The Place Of A Thousand Beds

The visitors have all left
The lights are dimmed,
I have drunk my cocoa and I feel bereft,
Strangely alone in this place of a thousand beds.

I gaze idly at the ceiling,
Follow the patterns thrown there by the light,
It's good that the walls have no feeling
The scenes they have witnessed would bring them tumbling down.

I hear the wheels of a trolley,
Night sister's voice so reassuring,
She stops by my bed, dispels my folly,
Dispenses night medicines, the boon of sleep.

All is quiet again
And I seem to hear a thousand sighs
The moans of those in pain,
But not for long; sweet sleep creeps up on me.

Margaret L. Clabbon

Tell Me A Tale

Tell me a tale that I love to know
Where places are far off and places I know.

Where life is a tale in its own way
And is magic and gay.
That never begins and never ends.

A tale of good luck
And of Good Fortune.
Where there's music and dancing
And romance.

So tell me a tale of the past and the present.
Things that have gone and things that have happened.
To You and Me.

Tell me a tale of the Light and the Glory.
Where worlds are a fantasy in your mind.
Where dreams are a land of their own.

So tell me a tale of no one at all.
Just tell me a tale.
That's all.

J. Hearl

The Ways Of The Ocean

The calm and the wild that is what the sea is.
A wild spirit of mother nature
so deep are her waters with its own kind of life.
She can be ruthless, she can be kind,
whoever wants to take her on.
Many a life have been taken from her shores
by this spirit of life.
Her elegance that lies beneath the waters
only certain eyes will see.
Mother nature's own treasure lies here beneath the
ocean of life.
And if man wants to take her on let their
lessons be learnt.
From the greater power that has been here longer
than man themselves.

Dee Lean

Together In Thought

So close and yet so far apart;
In thought together, living with one heart.
We grow - one unit formed of single souls;
All sharing, proudly, in each other's goals.

Nurtured from infants - now are men;
Our childhood dreams we shared, and then
Survival called; we went our separate ways;
Thoughts stayed, nostalgic for our childhood days.

Our hopes, our dreams, now distant in the past;
But closeness such as ours will always last.
We learnt together how to live and love;
To cherish joy; each pain to rise above.

This bonding, formed so long ago,
Impermeable, lingers, thwarting every foe;
For love of family is the utmost aim -
Without this, life would never be the same.

Mary Farrell

Nations

Eternal is the flame that always burns
Forever is the love that never learns
Distant realms of light from echoes past
Vacillations are dreams for a tempest outcast.

Mirrors of shadows reflect the stories untold
Dissected but together are the souls three-fold
Transparent visions breed the negative walls
Savage is the human till society falls.

Nature's cosmic clouds they cry in pain
Ignorance called misanthropes create the acid rain
Automatic earth is in danger of dying
Deformed images show the world is crying

Chaos is an entity that breathes hate
Diverting the truth and blinding our fate
Apathy is rife, it thrives on the young
Depriving the taste of the pilgrims tongue

Obscure forms of life are always found
Panchromatic are their eyes, they absorb sound
Inner worlds of wisdom inhale the faith
Unity is the angel God's given wraith.

Daniel Dulewski

Conquerors?

"I will not, never, ever will I!" She promised and the words
were not a lie. The flag was replaced and a shadow was cast
deep and grey, large and ominous from the mast.

"This Isle is unto itself sovereign!" He shouted, rousing
courage amongst his kin. "Remember your parents, they are
dead." The anguish and anger escaping his head.

"Banished to Australia, beneath the clay, on ships to 'Merica;
home again they'll ne'er lay. Starved us they did, greedily,
cowardly for their gain" she cried, her tears lost in the rain.

Some time later when more were dead, they met by chance,
and in sorrow Revised their lament, like lead they moulded;
ideas also, to face the morrow

We'll stand together, love, shed not tears for the Almighty
witnesses and hears and will help. Stand up, love, "The truth
be known that peace is a dove"

"The bird so white will carry our plight? "Yes, woman, victory
without a fight!" "They are the devil, seeking retaliation?"
"Yes, love, but resist hate and come salvation!"

The wind blew, the sea chopped, lightning seared, guns fired,
bombs blew, many feared, but they hold each other close
forgiving and pitying. Who? Those.

Gerald Peter Wickham

Disorder

I am tired and the tiredness
Has numbed the fingers of my brain,
With which I grope, in fog,
Through subterranean halls of pain.
No sense of what is perfect can impede
My stumbling forward progress,
Which will only heed
A wild unbridled foraging of fantasy.
My vision is a lattice-work of fire
Through which I perceive the grey-green goblins of insane desire
Cavorting on obscenely swollen limbs,
Fat from a too rich diet of fevered dreams.
With wobbling bellies they delimitate the farthest point of my
Ambition, piped to a thin and meagre dream
By the unfailing flutes of an infallible attrition.
Time is a taut and supine silence,
Livid with the scars of suppressed screams.
And lesions dripping out the bright red blood of hope
Drown the fading glory of my former days
In a corrupting sea of lurid crimson haze.

Derek Creighton

Special People

Friends are very special people
They help you out in times of need,
They're there to help you when you fall
They never fail to hear your call

I have friends old and wise,
Stretched across the world so far
They've been truly tried, a long long time,
If I should need them,
They'll be there.

Friends and time go hand in hand,
Truly tried, friends are rare,
Special people.

Moira Kirkland

Final Thoughts

As I lie in my bed just before sleep,
I think of my childhood and silently weep,
for then, I had my family and friends,
we played, and laughed, and sang together,
Now I am old and live alone, my family gone forever,
they are in heaven with the Lord above,
and soon I will join the ones I love.
There's a young lady who visits me,
I don't know who she is, but she makes me some tea,
she helps me to dress and puts me to bed,
she dresses like a nurse, and makes sure I'm fed.
Sometimes I ask if she will stay, but she is always
to busy and must be on her way,
where she goes I do not know,
but soon, it will be my turn to go.

Myra Zoboki

Tightrope

From the increased distance and altitude rising
Sooner or later,
I am surmising,
A fall will be made
By you or I.
A push or a shove.
The breath of a dove.
To send us tumbling
Head over heels out of love.

A tightrope
With a slight slope
To send us tumbling
Head over heels out of love.

Iain C. Davidson

Time

Time the eternal, the ever present
Time, the here and now, the yesterday
Time, that can pass as a snail
Time, that can speed as light
Time, you cannot stop or capture
This very moment will pass and in a
flash will have gone forever with these and
other countless moments

Time, the master of all events past and present
Time, the governor of life and death
Time, the ever present threat to man's immortality
Time, has no beginning and no end
Not like man who lives but a trice and who is gone
in a second of eternal time

Time, the ever present ever moving enemy of man
When all things on this our earth cease to be
One thing will remain inevitably moving onward, onward
Indestructible, unstoppable, unforgiving, Time

Keith Nixon

Untitled

I open my eyes quickly, sit slowly up in bed.
The sun pours through the curtains.
What thoughts run through my head.
Feet feel through lush, blue carpet, family, friends must be met.
Cold water refreshing on my face.
Coffee will be waiting, sweet, strong to taste.
Strolling happily, car left at home.
No one to bother me, no mobile phone.
Peace from all technology.
I am myself, there's only me.
A friend's caring smile brings happiness to heart.
Closeness, love, compassion complete in life, all part.
Days carry on, from beginning to end.
We cannot get on without family or friends
I close my eyes slowly, sink quickly to bed
No more thoughts running through my head.

Julie Airey

Epilogue

Just here, and there, with dogged air,
The stem retains a leaf,
Most glory gone, though how it shone,
In splendour bare belief.

So, dull and drear, and brown and blear,
The span comes to its close.
The journey spent, now old and bent,
It settles in repose.

A fleeting phase, those summer days,
The snows came all too soon,
That great desire, aflame with fire,
Waned wanly as the moon.

One should not miss, those days of bliss,
So plough the furrow deep,
And plant the seed, enjoy the deed,
One is too long asleep.

L. Dennis Foote

A Touch Of Vim And Vigour

Looking from my window
I see children playing in the street
And hear the pitter patter
Of happy little feet.

The bright and shiny faces
Smiling sweetly there
Hide a simple weariness
That flops down in a chair

"Hi, mum, I am hungry", a little voice declares
Then, out again to see his pals with whom a drink he shares.

David J. Rigg

Untitled

Weep for me my darling - but only for a
while - then chase the road in front of
you - enjoy each happy mile -
Tread the ground we walked together
feed the birds that sing -
keep warm thoughts in Winter - and
turn them into Spring.
Touch a tender rosebud; watch its petals
grow - feed the birds for me, my love, when
the ground is thick with snow -
I'll take care of heaven - till you join me
there - I'll buff the stars up nightly -
shine the moon we'll always share.
You take care of things below, for they will
need your love - I will shine to guide you -
from the moon-filled skies above -
So weep a gentle teardrop to make
our roses bloom - while I sit and
wait for you - I'll polish up
our moon.

  Eileen Cree

A Soldier's Prayer

Come the dawn with all its hues,
And God's light bathes the sky;
Then I shall know in this heart of mine
That the time has come to die.

This heart that's but a pulsing mass,
Of tissue, blood and flesh;
Yet served to show such tenderness
To those that I would bless.

Yet served again with throbbing hate,
When enemy I'd face; to give me strength,
To give me cause,
To save me from disgrace.

Serve me to the last brave heart,
Fail me not my end;
When faced with those my life to take,
Let my dying not offend.

  S. J. Keen

The Cherry Tree

Cherry tree, you luscious pink
Blossom of May;
Brimming rich with ripe treasures,
Opulent fruit on the ethereal wing of Springtime,
Lark to herald the dawn of
Warmer months and sunlit hours
Beneath the golden towers of boughs and foliage
Interlaced with pollen-threaded honey charms,
Woven by an unseen hand
Which plants enchantment through our land.

Sweet cherries, you, glimpsing
Paradise through Nature's bosky eye.

  Lynn-Marie Cody

A Flee Tae Catch Yis A'a

Tak stock o' new sassanach flee like the prey.
Dressing up and doon gie reluctantly.
Ca'd a wine gobbler has red boggley beady een.
Busked on double size twenty hook barbs honed keen.
Built winged rainbowed marabou tae lang flutter away.
Tails are a fu shaving brush weel worn tae splay
Body o wine cork is motley bottle green.
Legless yet troot fill yir waders whenever seen.
Hid soberly as true sportsman jist no fair play
So joins ither specials in hat festooned tae stay
Daft multi coloured type busby best front been.
Dra's fae attention sodger palmer roosted
Auld peen.

  Tom McConnachie

A Poem For Pennies Or Lakeland Moods

These Lakeland Hills
So varied in their moods,
Can match my thoughts
And ease all ills.

Often alone amongst them I would roam,
Lost in sorrow and grief,
But their all powerful majesty
Gave peace and solace to take home.

The dull days when I was conscious of my single state
With parents and brother passed away.
The happy days with sisters, nephews, cousins,
When the sunshine and scenery made me feel great.

Now as I wander, not alone, nor in a crowd
But with my husband, content and happy
Enjoying the friendship and support,
I want to thank the hills and shout aloud.

  Angela Robinson

Church Of Dreams

There's a church built on a hill, and its doors are open wide.
Above the door a message, "All are welcome, come inside."
It shows no denomination, and its style gives not a clue,
There is nothing that could tell one if its Muslim, Catholic, Jew
It could be Protestant or Hindu, or maybe none of these,
Yet its beauty when one sees it, brings them slowly to their knees.
If one climbs the hill and enters, they know it's a place so rare,
A house of God, Muhammed, Allah, and Jehovah, all are there.
It has no denomination, it's a place where all can pray,
A refuge from a violent world where none are turned away.
Should you need a place of worship, then just gently climb the slope,
For this Church is near to heaven, It is Peace and Love and Hope.

  Susan Gibbs

Untitled

I couldn't find a card for you
That said the things I wanted to:
So, deciding to take up the pen
And write myself, I found that then
The things I feel and rarely show
Can't be told in those few words I know;
So it's not surprising it's so hard
To find them printed in a card.

I'd like to give the hope of dawn,
Brought by the sun each day is born;
The peace you find in quiet night
With distant stars the only light.
A love of life that makes each day
A great adventure, in its way;
And faith to know, whate'er you do
I'm always here to comfort you.

  Sue Baker

Prelude

First thing you notice is the silence,
Silence beating back from the walls,
The shuttered shops, the suddenly alien houses
Turning away, unwilling to get involved;
And your footsteps echo, guilty, fearful,
In the deserted street, for somewhere,
Somewhere, perhaps, there are eyes watching,
And slippery fingers clutching weapons,
Sweaty, shaking with fear and bravado;
All hell awaits...
            but you think rather:
How'm I going to get back home,
Now the trains have all stopped running?
Is my family safe? Have we enough food?
Who, of the people we know, are in danger?

But the indifferent, hostile buildings give no answer;
The tense and frightened city holds its breath,
Silent as death.

  John H. M. Butler

531

The Fledgling (A Bird's Tale?)

Gaping, oversized beak, mesmerized, still.
Shiny, brown, frightened eyes - listen mother's shrill!
Away from the nest on a wing-testing flight
Suddenly alighting, landing in fright.
Mad scrambling, crashing - feathers amiss.

Back in the nest everything's calm.
Emptiness, quiet - no little bird's song.
What good a nest when everyone's gone?
Mother is worried father as well.
Is young frightened fledgling feeling the stress?

With beak full of food mum follows along
Her wanting to help, the strength to fly on.
His new found freedom finds intrusion a pest
His only intention, to build his own nest.

With babes of his own our fledgling returns
The scrambling, the crashing it seems so much worse.
To think in the past we had energy like his
We now just look on our mouths all aghast.

Gerald Christopher Lavers

My Spouse

She keeps my seven children as well as I
could e'er desire, although no labour I do try
no dirty work or hire, as I laboured once in farming
no riches I am amazed.

A menial I disdained to be and keep my vow unto the
last. As I ceased to labour in the land,
since e'er I noticed to my spouse I will remain an
idle and contented man.
And will endureth to the longest life.

My musket-loving wife, indeed,
in whom I faith fully do believe,
she's able to still to earn my bread
and oor will, she will not e'er deceive.
I have no lack of linens fair
and plenty clothes to serve my turn
and trust me that all worldly care
now gives me not the least concern.

William Napier

Poverty

You look so smug, what does your man say?
No prospects, in a crowded room, with lives so grey.
He'll have no opinion. He cares not either way.

Spare a muse for that poor little mite.
Coiled, warm and drifting, safe and tight.
Till bloody, it bursts upon its destiny's blight.
Its mystery gone after the first sight.

Let it feed and be nurtured while I can provide that for free.
I will wait for the season it will love and tend me.
You say the child will be a proud branch on the Family tree,
I think it just joins you, another victim of poverty.

How you must have been neglected of love
To seek it from each kin.
Why can't you realize
You only get out what you put in.

Carol Zlotowitz

Starfire

Standing on the edge of the world watching stars shoot by,
Seeing the milky way, splay through the universe,
Riding the tails of comets,
Stars twinkle in the firmament.
I am a sailor on the edge of time,
An archer to the stars.
The oldest firefly in existence, older than Methuselah,
A pendant on the star of forever,
Riding the highways and byways of the stars.
My life story is written in the galaxy and constellations of
outer space.

Jonathan Schiff

Help!

Unemployed, no hope,
Paranoid, and broke.
Interviews, futile,
Dole queues, meanwhile

No trade, just brawn,
Hopes fade each dawn.
Distraught, debts mount,
Food bought, "on account".

No smokes, no beer,
Evokes, no cheer.
Must try yet again,
Sanity, retain.

Ostracize resignation,
Exercise motivation.
Attributes evaluate,
Worthiness accentuate.

I'm strong and healthy, work hard too,
I'm trustworthy, in all I do.
Someone out there, can't you hear?,
If you've got jobs to spare — I'm here.

Eileen Moores

"Body Music"

As we face a new millennium,
Like winter gives up to the spring,
I can hear her softly singing,
The new queen flies on the dragonfly's wing...

Through bluebell forest and butterfly laughter,
You can spy the trembling spring,
As rivulet it gives way to summer,
See him come, the helmeted king...

Chain by chain, the daisies restrain him,
Irises spear through water bed,
The new queen dances slowly toward him,
Body music is in her head...

See them moving like a mountain,
Hear them breathing like a tree,
Dancing barefoot round the fountain,
Spraying jewels on you and me...

Spreading out from the centre,
Making loving hearts pound,
Is a rhythm born of timing,
Known as body music sound....

Peter Vaughan Williams

Poetry

Yes, I know it, I have no artistic talent or sense of rhyme
Methodical worker, never, never a poet,
Terrified school days, spellings, comprehension, dictation,
Stones, reading aloud; frozen, stuttering in fear,
Inside I longed to dance off my silent tangled fear
Outside the passive smile, my well accomplished masking tool,
Skilfully showing a convincingly happy roly poly child,
Unimaginative, with limited literacy skills,
Moulded by an intrinsically manufactured mathematical will,
Imprinted with "I can't do English"
That timid, desperate victim, produced to thrill,
The forward scientific age, mateless, soulless
Alienated from the elaborately, expressive wahay gangs
Stop Press, news for you, I have my own wish,
Yep, that once terrified tongue - tied child, who was locked inside,
has exploded, explored, designed and created art,
An inner talent, irrepressible, no one can ever steal,
For it's treasured forever, deep within my heart... for real,
It's time, for my child and I to flare to our heir, I can do poems!
I will! I will!

Nicky Linfield

Mother Of Pearl

When you are young, the world is your oyster;
to be opened at will and its pearl taken and grasped between
the fingers and held up to the light, its colours dazzling the
eyes of the beholder.
But the ocean is deeper now
and the ocean bed lies littered with empty discarded shells.
To find your oyster now the search is hard;
Deeper breaths, holding on, swimming to new depths,
searching for the oyster of your youth once more.
Some find it - in new love, in new hope, in new faith, but many fail:
They float back up towards the sunlight with no pearl grasped
between their fingers,
No colours to admire.
Mother of Pearl you've tricked us into thinking that we had
you forever within our grasp.

Mike Preston

Back To Front

Because I loved I was able to grieve
The darkness left will become friendly,
So do not fill the hole with emptiness.
Though I cannot now touch or see you
The empty space will not divide us,
For love's strength reaches out in its simplicity.
Still the dreams take shape
Of the things we did and did not do,
So quieten your soul then harmony is found,
Which links us to life once more.
Two hearts still beating in rhythm
Across and through nature's time.
Listen to me and you shall hear the symphony,
Of a blessed melody released,
Holding just a beautiful memory.
Silently cushioned forever in your heart.

Anna R. Mulroy

I'm Late, Sir, Because, Sir .....

I'm late sir, because, sir
Last night an alien came to my house.
It was tall, thin and green and squeaked like a mouse.
Starving and lonely, its spaceship had crashed
Into our duck pond it tumbled and splashed.
My Dad, a mechanic, with a heave and a shout
And lots of blue language, pulled the craft out.
He stripped the ship down, right to the motor;
He spotted the fault - it required a new rotor.
All the shops were shut, though we searched near and far,
Then we thought of the garage and out motor car.
After raiding the engine, we got the right bit,
Transferred to the spacecraft and made it air-fit.
The alien thanked us and went off to his star,
Leaving us, here on Earth, with a broken-down car.
And so it transpires, by the strange hand of fate,
That this is the reason why, this morning I'm late.

Lynne M. Robertson

"Just Scream"

The last rose of summer floats blind,
Through the stream of life memories left behind,
Emerald spirals eager to form,
Through your eyes my spirit is born,
I'm restless and dark but always sure,
When you crumble to dust, that I can't endure,
Trapped souls steal my ebbing breath,
Slow and painful steel chains quicken my death
My wound cries out for fresh air,
Rapped in silk my fingers fall from your hair,
Spikes run through my veins, too much to bear,
Enchanted gardens, am I really there,
Tell me what am I meant to see,
My body lifeless, what am I meant to be,
Your eyes dark holes, cold and still
Your dreams shattered by that easy-way-out pill,
  Just scream.

J. G. Doherty

'Friendship'

I see them stand above my grave
And feel the weight of all the pain.
It's not your pain; you do not cry,
The sorrow emanates from I.

I slowly come to realise
How you all fake your love for the one who dies.
My life didn't hold any weight in your heart
Yet you act like you loved me now that I have parted.

Ashes to ashes and dust to dust.
You don't give a damn, 'cause you had no lust for my life.
Well, be happy for now I am dead.
So now you can let your hate out of your head.

I tried to care but you just spat it right out.
I tried to share but you just kicked me about.
At least now I know that nobody liked me,
You just acted that way. Now that I can see.

Goodbye, my old 'friends', thanks so very much.
It's so nice to know that there's no-one I touched.
Still, at least I can smile for I know you will pay,
For the same thing will happen to you, one fine day.

Daniel Pearce

Progress

A town nurtured on shipyards. Iron and steel,
Its founders men of vision with ideas so real.
Once proud shipyards erected skeletons of steel
Hundreds of sweat stained men laboured to lay down a keel
Iron foundries, rolling mills, and coke ovens of might,
Illuminated skies with their glow on the darkest of night.
The hill's were a honeycomb, as miners in the earth did bore,
With bent back, pick and shovel. They sweated for ore.
But now the mines are silent, the air quiet and still,
Maybe ghosts of past miners still trudge up the hill,
The shipyards are empty slipways and dry docks all laid to rest,
But this was progress, promised as all for the best.
With foundries all quiet, and furnaces cold and still,
The bulldozers of destruction moved in for the kill.
There was history in the rubble, sweat among the dust.
And this was the era of progress, no matter what the cost.
They wounded the heart of Teesside, as they took away Its steel.
And like some badly injured beast, on its knees was forced to kneel
Its once proud head will be raised again. Its roar echoing
  across the seas.
For this beast is a lion, mighty king ruling the tees.

L. D. Catterick

A Gate From Morocco

In my hand
Cool smooth, comforting.
Weight, solid.
Timeless, old as the earth.
One of creation's rocks.
Fashioned by man for his pleasure,
Formed deep within the earth.
Opaque mysterious,
Layers of years upon years
Beyond my understanding.
Earth colours of burnished browns and greens.

Here in my hand
Eternity, safe solid
Hope? Buried, hard pressed,
And at the end,
Timeless beauty, splendour,
Decorating man's temples
  to his creator.
Courts of kings
Here in my hand.

Pauline M. Leyland

Dunblane

Smiling faces, lives of sunshine -
living in peace, harmony.
Every day was a kind of game.
...today, a game of war.
Pounding footsteps; Stranger.
Clutching life takers, blast machines -
he entered the room of sunshine.
The smiles turned to confusion...
Fiend? Friend? Foe?
They jumped, played and skipped into
the ray of the stranger.
Laughing, sunshine, blasts, silence
Sunshine to sorrow - Peace to pain.
Tears began as lives ended.
The stranger? Gone.
Later, more destruction, confusion - the
room of laughter... gone.
In its place a garden, garden of hope
flowers, memory, sorrow.
Nettles to daffodils - Darkness to light.

Sarah-Ellen Almgill

New Age Symbols

Ever wondered of the new age we'll meet
Where shifting shadows are forced to retreat
Re-born souls heal and cleanse
Holy authority shatters pretence
Aerial powers arrange for truth
From shades of surrealism to simply sublime
Our breadth of vision stirred to breeze
Release and liberation search the soul
Destinies glow and reveal their paths
Imagine the strength but measure the cost
Quakes can quiver yet evil will shiver
Nature responds for justice to deliver
Intuition learn to trust
Magnetic music make we must
To coincide with new age symbols.

Tony Roberts

The Capricious Oddity

Hither thither zooms a figure, very swift full of vigour.
Saucy, nosey, full of tricks, light as a feather; what
   makes him tick?
Who helps the knitting wander astray, at any hour of any day?
Who stalks butterflies on the breeze, has to be checked
   chasing bees?
Who gets tangled in long lace curtains? Has to be him,
   that is certain.
Who hides to jump out on folk unaware? That's him, he's
   always there.
Who chases shadows like a fool, tires himself, starts to drool?
Who looks so innocent, with a temperament loving and mild?
Indeed, it's that puss, playful not snappy. He has
   a name...
It is
Meddlesome happy

Penny Beddard

Untitled

I heard a scream and it was me
I screamed o'er land and across the sea
I screamed at the wind and driving rain
I screamed at the whole world again and again
I shouted the house down, I banged on the doors
Went into the wild land and screamed 'cross the moors
I screamed and I shouted, I shouted and screamed
Then I lay down and I slept and I dreamed
I dreamt of lost treasures locked under the sea
I dreamt I was flying away to be free.
As I slept I heard screaming, but what could it be?
I dreamt I heard screams and the screams came from me.

Ken Gray

Henry My Bassett

I often think of my beautiful bassett hound
He was large warm cuddly and a rascal I'll be bound
When left on his own he slept in fact a little Angel
On my return home what mischief he would cause I could not tell
His loved the phone to ring and thought that's my cue
Mums engaged so I'll grab anything does not matter whether
   it's old or new
Once he stole a large piece of raw beef which was ready for
   the oven
He bolted outside as the door was left open
On one occasion he stole a string of pork sausages
Dragged them upstairs to devour with me to clear up the mess
Everyone knew Henry and he loved to be admired
After going for his walk he would come home tired
At last some peace but not until he was sprawled on my lap
He loved to cuddle up close and tight for his evening nap
Sometimes during the day I could hypnotize him to sleep
I would say, Henry, you are tired, stroke
him, and suddenly not a peep
We all miss that lovable bounder and
have many funny fond memories
of him I can tell my grandchildren
endless, laughable stories

Dorothy Stevens

I Wanted To See Africa

The fickle shifting of the surf
as bending palm fronds lean to kiss
the white sands of Africa.

Abundant flowers fill the sky
cascades of green burst through the dust
the red earth of Africa.

Looming early from the mist
panting on the white hot plain
the wildlife of Africa.

The endless calling of the night
echoing softly through your dreams
the sounds of Africa.

Kind and smiling in the sun
reaching out to make a friend
the black faces of Africa.

Just a memory in the span of time
one day I will return
to Africa.

Jennifer H. Fox

My Life As An Individual

My world revolves around hopes, wishes and dreams,
What I want the most never lasts it seems.
I'm cocooned by society with tied restless wings,
Always having to abide by whatever authority sings.
So the only way I'm alive is the thoughts in my head,
My escape from the truth or life,
Or being dead.
I know it's unnecessary to feel or want to be someone else
instead,
But being me is what I most dread.
They may not approve of the life I'd rather lead,
So I must blossom from someone else's seed.
So who can I act like?
Who can I be?
Someone with no troubles and insecurity.
Only tomorrow can ever release my true soul,
Let me be myself without paying the toll.
And when that dream,
My seed of life does grow,
Then I will eventually be the me that I know.

Julia Dalby

Irish Box

Galley's steaming brew sheds chill
from fingers I forget
whilst hauling at the nets.
Oilskins leaking rivers down my neck,
wishing I was home boy
Scriddlin' with the cats,
stockinged feet, blazing fire,
Missus knitting, click, click, click...
Stead of which, I'm out here boy
in the bloody Irish Box.
Over the quota, over the side,
white bellies float, dead
just to conserve the stock.
Fishery Protection vessel, nosy bugger,
grey, gossiper peering
behind curtains, of a foreign, weave,
Today, they let the Spanish in.
The bloody Irish Box... Olay!
Knacker'd and castinettas, clack, clack, clack,
Oh, I wish I was home boy a'scriddlin' with the cats.

Dudley Ward

Is It Really Heaven

Is it true what they say
Is there really a land far away
Where love and only love reigns supreme
Does anyone know or is it just a dream.

They say we know no pain
It's a place where we meet our loved ones again
When we are small, full of play and tended with care
We believe, oh yes we really believe it's heaven up there.

As children grow older, with more responsibility to shoulder
Seeds of doubt begin to grow
Perhaps until we leave this earth below
We are not meant to really know
The secrets of that land above
So let us learn to live and love.

As childhood dreams are left behind
We find the world around us isn't always kind
The world can become a frightening place
Such violence and hate among the human race
So if we are to keep those childhood dreams of love
Surely we must believe in that heaven above.

Mary Wells

My Winter Walk

We took a walk this afternoon
My little dog Shep and me
Across the snow covered country side
Just before we had our tea

What beauty we found on our snowy walk
No picture quite so fine
Than these mother nature had painted
And today they were mine, all mine

Hedgerows and fields wore blankets of white
Here and there blades of grass peeped through
And the old thatched barn at the end of the lane
Was housing a robin or two

Our little village nestled in the downs
Thatched cottages and church so fine
Held beauty in its winter cloak
And today that beauty was mine

Oh, thank you Lord for my snowy walk
And the beauty all around to see
Thank you too for the warmth of my home
Though humble it may be

P. J. Puttick

A Great Wind

A great wind rips and roars,
Uprooting tall trees in its path.
Leaves are plucked, and skyward soar,
As the air blasts on in wrath.

How each branch, creaks and groans,
As the violent gusting tears,
And leaves rattle, in a dying moan,
When shorn from limbs laid bare.

The wind howls its clarion cry,
As it pummels, plucks, and beats.
It hurls and shakes, all who lie,
Within its roaring reach.

It sometimes convolutes into gigantic rings,
In a vortex of violent motion,
Or with great turbulence it also brings,
A hurricane of destructive proportion.

Like a mighty bellows blowing,
It howls its wrath at all.
That pounding wind is showing,
How devastating is its call.

L. Owen

My Retirement

I thought when I retired
There would be nothing left to do
But strange enough, I do not have time
To do the things, I intended to

Now I have time to wander around
To look for bargains and such
Time to read and time to write
To look up friends, and keep in touch

I find myself more cheerful
And do not feel so sad
At having had to give up work
Things have not been so bad

So all of you whose time has come
To lay down all your tools
Do not weep or moan, friends
Just make a few more rules

Just get around and fill your days
With happiness and laughter
Then you will find that life's worthwhile
And that is what you're after

Mavis Mary Hall

Return From Jeddah

Belatedly I climb the stairs to the howling eagle's belly,
The icy air-con blasts me to my seat,
The doors thump shut, the straps go on, my muscles turn to jelly,
As the desert disappears below my feet.

O'er Red Sea, Nile and Pyramids, to Cairo's gathering gloom,
In the western sky the sun will soon retire,
On over the Med' the sky turns red, the sea is clothed in blackness,
'Though our whole world above is bathed in fire.

Cross Sicily to the coast of France confirming our position
Great Mont Blanc burns on our starboard 'tips
Full speed ahead in darkest night the lights below a-twinkle
But we spurn Paree's seductive blips.

From on high the roar subsides as we join our Heathrow glidepath
Beachy Head reflecting the harvest moon
Turning left at Tunbridge Wells and a glide down Oxford Street
And thud! ... We're back to a "Muzak" tune

Chris Hudson

535

All The Day Long

You are in all spaces, and without even
Thinking, I move within my God
　All the day long.

Nature, like other people, is seen as
separate and apart from me;
　but we are One.

The ever-present, invisible You waits for a sign
That we understand; we have a song
　of oneness to sing.

In a great deep, a silence, like a mighty door
That we alone can open;
　Even a chink will let You in.

And we are stunned by the simplicity,
　of the one 'I AM' in All.

In the rush, tear, and confusion of living,
It is hard to hold on to that
　one 'I AM'.

But without even thinking, I move
Within, and gaze upon my God,
　All the day long.
　　Barbara E. Hawkins

Untitled

Memory brings back thoughts of you,
On days when I was feeling blue!
Then you would smile and always say:
Here I am, in my same old way,
Ever here to bring you cheer.
Rely on me, I'm always near;
Send misery off and show a smile!

Don't ever forget for a tiny while;
Always, together we've come right through
You know that when the rent falls due

Never have I spent the lot
In buying things I haven't got!
Now let us try to think about
Everything without a doubt
That in all those lovely sixty years
You know that all those silly fears

Stay buried deep with many a thought
In love we both have really caught
Exactly what life's all about!
　　John G. Brooks

Reflection Within

As I feel you grow sweet sour child
It makes me calm with waves of wild
The moods of Wind' will change our ocean
And storms pass by when your eyes become open.
The Fear of change' my waters cover
My fullest of genda exposed to my lover
I start to disfigure as you Build your shell.
For your health in return I wish in your well
I look deep within to Imagine your feature
And shadows appear with silhouettes of my creature
The weight of worry lifted from my mind
As you float to surface and your figure I find
When I hurt do you cry? like a sea with Emotion
Or a devil disguised? and you give all such potion
You reveal all you are - when your Sea heads shore
Then my rain drops will wash my love to pour
The depth of My body you need to survive...
My breath and my blood will keep you alive
You have your own instincts so I wait as your tutor
The one who gives life will decide on your future.
　　Rebecca Baker

Our Faded Love

　It seems that I'm not good enough
to be a part of you.
　I love you more each day, now all
I need is for you to love me too.
　You used to love me once, though that's
all in the past.
　I hope each day you will care again,
but alas,
　It's not meant to be, it never will,
you've moved on from me now.
　I try to fit in with those you like,
but just cannot see how.
　I'd give everything I own to have
your tender love and kiss.
　I remember all the old times we
shared, they used to be such bliss.
　I know that I should face up to
the fact that it's all gone,
　However I keep thinking that you're
the only one.
　　Joanne Eve Lusty

Cueva De La Pileta

We shuffle unsteadily along stony passages,
Herded together.
A primeval instinct in a primeval place.
Flickering lamps hold back the dark,
Symbolic of man's history.

Ochre, black and yellow on the surface of the limestone.
Scratches proclaiming our presence
Tiny in this cathedral created for no God.
Placatory symbols soothing the elements.

Who were these people, living in the dark,
Proclaiming life in ochre, black and yellow,
Outlining living creatures, keeping a tally of their days?
Man the hunter, man the supplicant
Captured for his children a synopsis of his life.

And we, shuffling along, what mark do we leave in these caves?
A handrail, stone steps, coins in the pools
For future visitors to say:

Who were these people who travelled these paths with care?
What was the measure of their progress?
And were their gods placated with these coins?
　　Linda M. Terry

A Celebration

The countdown to the year 2000 has begun
And 'though I may not make it to the fun,
I live in highest expectation,
That I may join the coming celebration.

I now review, but not with sadness nor regret,
A life that (clearly) has not ended yet
And find throughout those bygone ages,
I have enjoyed my role through all its stages.

My childhood first, with all that Devon had to give,
In farmhouse old and cottage primitive.
Exploring daily all there was to see,
And, sampling all, foundations laid for me.

School first, the Royal Navy follows,
Self confidence provides, to pull me through life's hollows.
Marconi's Research next and I walk tall.
A wife, two boys, good friends, I have it all.

And me, what do I wish for now? That I will not a burden be.
That you, my family, will look up to me.
That you may oft remember me and in the century now due,
Will celebrate with pride those gone before and those who
follow you.
　　A. B. E. Ellis

Thin Ice

'Come here', shouted the children by the lake
'This notice says "Beware, ice is thin"'.
And so it was, pearl-grey and water-slithery.
'You said it might be thick and we have brought our skates;
You told a lie', they challenged bleak and narrow-eyed.
Their guardian pointed to the notice,
'Is that always true?' she asked.
The energy of childish anger clamoured to be heard.
'No', the first child stamped, 'Or we could never skate'.
'But that's not what it means', the second cried and
'If we disobey we might fall in'.
'Who says we must believe it?' shrieked the excited third,
'It may be thin for grown-up men but we are very light, let's try'.
Their guardian tossed a stone onto the ice.
The ice splintered and a bubbling puddle formed.
'That notice is just wrong', the first child growled,
'They really mean this ice is thin'.
'But what does it matter?', scoffed the second child,
'It's obvious what they mean'.   The third looked thoughtful,
'Can you always test things out and, if you can't,
How do you know when you must just believe?'.

C. Marjorie Carpenter

On A Cornish Beach

Passing midnight blue sand, cold as snow to bare feet
Cross naked, silver in the half light
of a bigger moon.
Set central observing the distance
Shameless face, smiling, laughing even.
The water is cooler, cooler on the spirit
Than the stars glittering, reflected
on my stomach.
Not a crack in the mirror pool, lapping
Edged in a ring of darkness
Across the body so still in the silence,
which is not really silent
But enveloped in a calmness of ancient tides.
The moment, a pointer of time signifies completion.
A fulfilment of promises, of a wholeness which shines
Like a pearl surrounded obscurely by inky clouds.
A moment of dreams, whose utterances
touch a simpler reach
becoming by body afloat,
Passing through midnight blue.

Jo Connell

Lush

Laying sprawled out on the bed
three sheets blowing wildly in the wind.
Libation intemperance addling brain cells
leaving behind only crapulence.
A picture painted by ignorance and naïvety
by an onlooker leading with a blind eye.

Honesty begs me to twist my sobriety.
Far from being detrimental
my bibulousness lends a hand to my insecurities,
banishing paranoia and anxiety for a little while.
Step into my convivial world
and let me take care of you here.

An inebriate to a rechabite
life oscillates without meaning, beginning or end.
Living in love's sweet exile
waiting for the injection of motivation
to take me away from my downward mobility.
A futile existence based around a weekly routine.
There must be more to life than this.

Mark Cope

If Only

Instead of turning to violence and lust,
If only more people would just
Look around and see the love of the Lord,
I'm sure they would never, ever be bored.
So much to do, when you walk in the light,
Be happy and friendly instead of wanting to fight.
Peace and contentment, and the love of good friends,
And knowing more about Jesus, whose love never ends.
If only more people would worship his name
I'm sure they'd find happiness and love, never pain.
He helps us to see things clearer by far,
That wonderful saviour bright morning star.
So Look to the Lord friends don't take flight
Only he can make everything turn out right
Believe me good people, the Lord does listen
And he knows in a second when a lamb is missing.
If only more people would enter the fold
I'm sure life on earth would be a joy to behold.
Let us pray to the Lord then, In Jesus name.
And say Lord if only more people would do the same.

Joan Hillan

Untitled

You didn't take my lungs out
With a carving knife
So how come I can't breathe without you?

You didn't take my Heart out
Although it feels that way
So how come I can't live without you?

You didn't take my Nightmare
Or put matchsticks in my eyes
So how come I can't sleep without you?

You didn't take my Brain out
Or stab me in the Head
So how come I can't love without you?

You took the only thing I had
You made me happy, made me sad
You crippled my emotions
Took all I had to give
The only thing you left me
Was me with me to live.

Nadia Robinson

Why Take My Life?

Why is my life not my own?
Why am I governed, never alone?
Constantly glared at,
Tediously stared at,
What must I do?
Why is this me, and not you?

So discreetly they spy,
Deviously they lie,
So full are they of deceit,
I'm falling apart, so incomplete.

If only I could see,
a way to pull free,
For I know the lock, but am lost without the key.

All my decisions are carefully compared,
All my possessions are equally shared,
Why am I cheated?
Does nobody care,
Why is my life, so wrong and unfair?

Karen Rehill-Pott

Home

A place to rest after a busy day,
lovingly thought of when you're away.
Our children echo in every room.
They're growing and leaving came all too soon.

This house that we've lived in.
Those years left behind,
will always be special in our hearts and our minds.
We remember it now, so crystal clear,
the' times of our life', memories so dear.

And now once again, our homes filled with pleasure.
The family returns, Sundays: hold more memories to treasure.

So it goes on with each passing day,
the cycle of life: Generations,
in a home where love is hear to stay.

Tricia Rowley

The Winter's Dust

The winter's dust
lays its bed
Flakes of soft white
Harsh, but with a look of gentility
As it harbours its base
with its cold white face.
It falls like diamonds from a sky that sings
As it spreads its wings
When it melts it knows it must
Until the next sprinkle
of winter's dust.

Saranne Morrissey

Parents

Why do parents go out of their way
To mess your life up every day?

They never let you use the phone
And ground you if you so much as moan.

Tell you what to eat and drink
As if you haven't a brain to think.

Never let you stay out late
Timing you as you walk through the gate.

Boyfriends are a definite no
At the slightest hint their tempers blow.

Complain about the clothes you wear
And show your friends your first teddy bear.

They smother you like a hand in a glove
And say that this is done out of love.

Shelley Wright

Profound Thoughts

Life I'm sure is a frame of mind
Completely encased in a molecule of time
Our bodies are substance that were born and will die
These are my thoughts as time passes me by
Our spirits could be of a deeper mind
To express into life time after time
The Egyptians believed in a cosmic plain
Pyramids were used to be reborn again
My memory's failing but my thoughts run wild
Where did I come from before I was a child?
Are there more worlds than just ours?
Beings somewhere with super powers
Vain we would be to think we're supreme
Not all in the sky is as it would seem
Only now are we beginning to know
Civilizations lived on earth long ago
Strange myths passed down by word of mouth
Enigmas found from North to South
Science suggesting with every trace
We've had visitors from outer space.

Val Harvey

Disappearing Beauty

The winds blow softly through the trees
They seem to whisper on the breeze
Whispering thoughts of long ago
Centuries of change they have seen come and go.

Moonlight glistens along the milky way
How different planet Earth looks today
Evolution and time have set the pace
But what of us, the human race?

What points in our favour?
What points have we gained?
How much of our planet
Have we not destroyed or maimed?

Our animals, fauna, birds and wildlife
Rainforests and man all bear the strife
Of our so-called achievements in the name of progress
Is this why our world is such a mess?

Progress means pollution, dust and decay
Is this man's intended way forward today?
This beautiful planet, the air and the sky
Most surely from under us one day will die.

Lin Nicol

The Creative Urge

You're there like the devil inside
Festering away.
You gnaw at my insides 24 hrs a day,
And you won't free my mind to
Think remotely normal thoughts
Like what to have for dinner.
You constipate me and it takes days of effort to
Crap you out.
My life becomes a state of temporary insanity,
Every woman a Lady Macbeth
And pretty young boy a Rosalind.
At the time of outlet my brain hides in some
Dark recess of my head,
Whimpering.
And when you do want to come out
You are like a laxative taken
At the wrong time
And I have to run to write you down
Before you disappear again.
God it's good to dump you out.

Sarah James

Me Mum And Dad

They have long since passed on, me Mum and Dad
and I didn't always do as I should, when I was a lad,
Times for them were hard, with a large family to keep,
And for us, two or three to a bed, when time came to sleep,
No work for Dad, and his dole had run out,
For thousands like him, there was no work about,
The twenties and thirties were really hard years,
For the parents of many there was nothing but fears.
Christmas and birthdays were like any day,
There were very few extras because Dad had no pay,
Though it must have been hard, Mum did her best,
    And after a lifetime of struggle, with Dad she's at rest.
Please bear with this old man as I turn back the years,
There were times of laughter, and quite a few tears,
That large family of ours has got quite small,
For like mum and dad, others have answered His call.
I remember them all with fondness and love,
Who are now part of that great family above,
And if it's still not too late for this old lad,
I'd like to say thanks, to me Mum and Dad.

Tom Turner

538

In The Still Of The Night

From a yawning chasm of black shadows
a phantom's finger plucked at my shades of sleep
persistent, insistent that I should wake,
and in the wink of an eye It succeeded
in giving me such a shake

A sixth sense warns me to be still - quiet -
so I lie inert, alert, receptive to
whatever felt It had the naked right
to trespass, and terrorize in Its passing
the stark stillness of my night

My attentive ears strain only silence,
but the solid beat of my heart's pump resounds
in disquiet thump, a bump in the night
betraying my secret quietude, wherein
It could furtively intrude

Before the mists of Time It had emerged
from eternal pits of slime; somehow I know,
now with superstition reawakened
I pray that this Dark Angel would beat Its wings
and just as suddenly - go

Des O'Donnell

Wise Old Tree

Oh God my heavenly father, I come before you now,
With all my heart and soul, in humbleness I bow.
Make me like the tree, planted by streams of water,
Show me the paths of righteousness, stop me if I falter.
For my seed was planted, not even a year ago,
Though I've grown and rooted, I'm not that strong you know.
I pray for the first ring in my tree, to become solid and complete,
Oh to be that wise old tree, stood firmly on his feet.
From the warmth of the sun, and the moisture of rain,
let the likeness of you, flow through every vein.
Please make me strong, by day and night,
let me nurture, from your loving light.
Is it a lot to ask for, tell me am I fair,
I long to hold my branches out, and touch you in mid air.
"Have faith" I hear you Lord, Trust in me and I will act,
I feel your presence Lord, that's a conscious fact.
You've touched my heart that's special, I will never forget,
On your law I will meditate, for the best hasn't happened yet!
Amen.

Donna Woolley

Scarlet

She tossles her head to jumpstart her brain.
Takes a happy pill to erase today's shaking.
Smears rampant red on her lips, for her self,
Fingers her last Cigarette that lies on the shelf.

Lighting it, she looks around in bleak despair.
Inhaling the nicotine fumes deeply.
She pauses, pouts, and again she ponders.
Grabs a scissors, and into the bathroom she wanders.

Clutching a tuft of her ebony hair.
She shears in orgasmic movements.
Glancing down at her dress, now slightly spotted with blood.
Sanity returns and she begins to scream as loud as she could.

Scuttling into the bedroom.
Holding her scalp all bloody now,
Curling up like new born kitten on the bed
Swearing angrily to the ghosts of the dead

Wake up, sweet scarlet!
Does anyone take care of you.
I cradle your wretched body.
O Scarlet, that's all you'll let me do.

Marie Keegan

Infertile Imagination

My tears are falling, like the rain - almost constantly!
Why didn't we try again? Although
Deep down I knew it wasn't to be.

Oh little one I wanted you so much,
To hold you and to touch.
Your smiling face, while you sleep
Eyes shut tight against the sun.

It's better to have had and lost.
Than never had at all.
Some might not agree with me,
But some just have it all!

The grief and sorrow I've to hide,
I can't let it show.
It's such a barren empty word,
It's infertility you know.

What a vivid picture I can conjure up
As I sit and pray,
They'll find a child for me in heaven
Maybe some day.

M. MacKenzie

Whilst It Happens

No motion, no sound,
A silent atmosphere,
Black, nothing,
Spherical atomized masses,
Circling round a sun,
A blue sphere of life,
Through the clouds,
Down to land,
A girl and boy play in the sand,
On the streets behind them a marching band,
A carnival, jamboree,
Life's living laughter joyful and happy,
A noise a chaos, a happening,
Back on the beach the children stop their play,
The sea washes their footsteps away,
They go home it's the end of their day,
A dark night sky full of stars,
Beyond them black nothing,
A silent atmosphere,
No motion, no sound.

Paul Waldock

The Refugee

Driven from home in haste and fear,
    Journeying on, I know not where,
Surrounded with noise of gunfire I flee;
    This is the life of a Refugee.

What lies ahead one cannot think
    As ones heart and spirit continues to sink;
Will there be food or rest ahead?
    Somewhere to sleep? Some sort of bed?

First in ones thoughts is for safety sake,
    Which way to go, which turn to take;
Shell fire surrounds, and bombs explode,
    Closing the bridge and the safest road.

So far there has been no time to look back
    Or think of the many comforts I lack;
It's just a struggle to save my life
    And escape from all this war and strife.

Shall I ever see friends and home again?
    The parting that gave me so much pain.
My favourite pets that I love to please,
    Oh God have mercy on all Refugees.

Bridget Monahan

Evening Concert

A summer evening spent with friends,
We spread a picnic on the grass;
Red wine we shared, and bread and cheese,
And listened to some mellow jazz.

The evening sun lit up the scene,
A sea of faces round us glowed;
Each one relaxed and at their ease
Enjoying the music as it flowed.

Then with the slowly setting sun
A hush descended on the crowd,
As in the dusk, like fireflies,
A myriad cigarette ends glowed.

I watched the harvest moon rise high
And felt a chill creep round my bones,
And death caressed me, like a sigh,
And in the crowd I felt alone.

Wrapped in my rug and reverie,
The band played melancholy airs;
I missed you then, and wondered if, like me,
You too were lonesome, looking at the stars.

Vera Meister

You're To Blame

Confronting you came out of the blue,
A surprise to both of us,
Yet there I was face-to-face with you.

Look left, look right, what else could I do?
Every day I crossed that road,
But never before encountered you.

Your face is now implicit on my mind,
No image could be clearer,
My brain could not be more confined.

Only now has it become real,
You got to test your engine,
But I ended up with the worst deal.

Day in, day out, here I lie,
Dumbfounded, no emotion,
No more happiness, I can't even cry.

For me I might as well be dead,
I am motionless you see,
And to my family 'sorry' is all you said.

Neither of us had planned it when you came,
I was innocent, your speed was guilty, you're to blame.

Rosie Asher

Please! - No Storms

There is a storm in the trees,
I'm disturbed and terrified
By the awful havoc and ruin it brings
To things outside.
Borne on the wind is a terrible sound,
   frantic, desolate cries,
As destruction comes crashing in
And something dies.

The oak tree's guarding the garden, beseeching the sky
Too far away to care when danger threatens us down here.

The storm dies down and lighter is the sky,
And somewhere out there a bird
Is setting out to fly to a safer place,
Where the air is warm, with shoots and buds,
   where insects fly
Round in a golden swarm.
Borne away on the wind goes the scent of hear,
And in the sudden silence there
The murmur of a million things, I fear,
Freed from their despair.

Rosemary Walsh

Pumping

Just in a day the buds spat green saliva;
Saturday's sun made sure of that. The trees
in Lennox Road yodelled a thousand leaves,
dynamited by the sudden sap. Now

we can exhale, knowing we have their low
or vivid tones to hear; or feel the bucket
of hot blood rising when we see those two
early swifts cutting the sky's throat. All this,

as we hit against the crossroads and (holding
tight our tongues), clock the zebra where yesterday
you, a stranger, lay wombed in blue light. Police
snarled, and hyenas of the urban kind
closed for the kill. Kneeling, a nearly-neon
paramedic pumped you full of Winter.

Fabian Peake

Untitled

You grow on me like ivy on a tree
Your roots go deeper and deeper into my heart
I hide behind your beauty and can stand tall
and proud knowing you are with me.
Your whole being surrounds me, almost
suffocating me,
Yet I cannot pull myself away.
But, perhaps I am the ivy and you the tree.
I cling to you because you are strong.
I lean on you and gain the support I need.
You stand almost unaware of my presence,
Exciting in the promise of Spring;
magnificent in your summer splendour;
Regal in the reds and golds of autumn.
But in winter when you are alone,
Your leaves have fallen, your branches are bare,
The birds have flown,
I will be there, I will always be there.

Maura Coleman

Life And Me

It's life and me
A prolonged moment of agony
No words to sing
Stand cursing the Sun Rising
I can't believe
That I'm this confused or naive

Come back king kong
Tear down the building, they're all built wrong
Twist to my fate
I'd catch the rope but it swings to late
It will go dark
I know a species that should have missed the Ark

Drink to the end
Then flush the artists around the bend
Sink into sleep
And bury progress six feat deep
What will there be
At the end just life no me

Simon James Hayes Jr.

Anger

Your sudden anger traps me into silence.
The words pile up in my mouth.
My eyes remain calm, and look at you with love.
I move closer but scalding sentences
Pour from your lips and tangle in my hair.

I am full of compassion. My fingers ache
To touch your cheek frozen now
With self-induced, hurt pride.
It is too soon for my warmth to melt you.
I must wait until your stone eyes see me again.

Joy Matthews

The Torture Chamber

Cold stone steps leading down below.
Dim lighting as we descend into history.
A time gone by where horrors were known
to have happened, a time where feelings were lost.

"Here lies a place where there is no God"
was the sign that was hung above the door,
leading to a chamber where emotion was rife
yet compassion was none.

Atrocities occurred we can only imagine
the horror and torture of human life.
Abused and scorned, destroyed then mourned
by loved ones that were left behind.

The scorching coals against the skin.
The perpetrator submitting to evil sins.
One more soul - they do not count.
This has become a way of life.

Afi Beheshti

The Turning Away

Obscurity reasons with fate,
in a world of intense hatred and subtle desires.
On the turning away from stoicism and solidity
    there is a suicidal leap into the transitional.
Light changes to shadow,
Love is extinguished into loss.
Raw nerves burn away human feeling,
    leaving only an empty space,
A void race.
Non-committal, non-feeling.
No more turning away is but a dream
    in the eyes of neo-hedonists.
Life is a sacrifice.
in which we become the altar.
With no God religious devotion,
    becomes pure fantasy.
The grass is green, the sky is blue.
The world revolves, as we fade into the pale
    structure of the past.

Jessica Milne

Life Givers

As the wind of the world goes passing by,
It creates new life but some must die.
It brings rain to the land to help crops grow,
It brings rain to the land to help rivers flow.

Many people have an aversion to rain,
Although without it all life would be in vain.
Without the rain we could not exist,
For no food could be made to be held in our fist.

Last comes the sun to heat up the land,
A giver of life since the first grain of sand.
A phenomenon of God we shall always need,
To help keep alive every culture, every creed.

As the tides of change are coming around,
By the laws of nature we shall always be bound,
Therefore we must realize how lucky we are,
That life is so precious, as beautiful as a star.

Jon J. Rogers

Farewell To Poppy

You have gone so far away from this place of damp and cold
To a land across the sea where the sun shines ever bright and bold.
In your going you left behind a void, an emptiness
For you tiny hands held my heart, all my life's existence

My love will always walk beside you though I'm out of sight,
I gaze upon your picture and yearn to hold you tight,
Be happy little Poppy, I pray your star sines ever bright.
May your future days bring laughter, joy and love's delight.

Jan Ziemba

Happy Birthday

Sixty years ago today our Lily had a daughter
She grew and blossomed through the war, her curly-headed Irene R
"I want to be a nurse" she cried and so she did and qualified
and women in their labour cried, "I want Doreen by my side"!
So these same words were said by Ted, THAT day
when he and Doreen wed
So happily, the years rolled on.....
And then she thought "I'll try for fame and Badminton shall
be my game" but this alas was not to be........
"Oh Barbara!" she would exclaim (when really B was not to blame)
But then her talents turned to song- her lovely voice -
it thrilled the throng
With all her love and fun and laughter
she's our Doreen and Lily's daughter.

Angela M. Laws

Pete Townshend

I remember the night The Who played Paradise
my eyes homing in on a laser beam
to the spotlight splash where he stood swimming
beating the wave with his one good arm
riding the music like a jockey

Frustration flung across the sky
like a small bird by his windmill blast
swinging the boot in a boiler suit
stoking his furnace of feedback
that burned me with the iron of truth

His music was always in my head
and now I am stunned
by the stark amplification
of what I knew but never said
his words were always in my head
On the stage it is me for a moment

George Damian McNutt

"Coming Down The Mountain"

My name is young Jud Nickson,
I live on Stainings Hill,
Just down from Waltons' Mountain,
To a smaller shack, but still.
It's with this darn depression,
The lumber yard ran dry,
So we were forced to sell our goods,
And our moonshine made with rye.
The young-uns kinda like it here,
They School in Walnut Grove,
But not before my Sammi-Lee
Makes victuals on the stove.
I've found more work with timber,
Puts food on our tin plates,
And keeps us warm on chilly nights,
With logs thrown on the grate.
I'm settled now, I've found my way,
And a man could want no more,
Than a handsome wife and five Young Kin,
Come to greet me at the door!!!

Sonia M. McBride

It's A Wonderful Life

Modern day life brings its modern day strife;
We go from our nine to five jobs to our five to nine wife,
We watch artificially tanned bodies and collagen lips,
And away from the T.V. we take nostalgic trips,
To the homes of our Ancestors, living and dead.
And we weep crocodile tears for the children unfed.
We have gadgets for everything under the sun,
And we pretend that computers are simple and fun.
We live under the threat of a nuclear age,
Where one press of a button by some self-righteous sage...;
Whom we elect for their morals and Utopian guarantee,
Or through a process not dissimilar to 'pin the tale on the donkey.'
Why suffer the hypocrisy for what is life but a lie,
The only reason we are born is so that one day we will die.

Paul Piercy

Meditation In A Garden

A secret door into a garden - a spell is cast,
Glimpses of an enchanted past - if only it could last,
I can sit enraptured and enjoy the silence found.
Where rippling brook and bird's song are the only sound.

Contemplate and view the world, as from another sphere,
The sound of human voices no longer in my ear,
Wood pigeons cooing in trees that touch the sky,
Ornate bridges, rockeries, woodland pools where fish abide.

The singing waterfalls where live the nature sprites,
Rustic seats that bid you linger, despite late summer's fading light,
When the outside world intrudes upon the peace found here,
I silently leave this bower of green velvet glades,
and tall trees that tower,
Refreshed within by the solace found where time
stands still when the heart so desires.

H. J. Hoope

The Flight

It was a dark and silent night
As crews prepared to make their flight.
Engines roared on that fateful night,
As steadily the 'planes took height.
Then Germans announce 'Enemies in sight'.
The bombs rained down with fearful might
Over that city raged the fight
One pilot thinks - this can't be right
As he prepared to regain height.
His friends he knows not of their plight
Whilst limping home in his damaged kite
He struggles on with all his might,
Then he touches down in the still poor light
And once again it's a silent night.

Patricia Jane Hayes

Who Am I?

Who are you?
When you haunt my dreams, and seek
to wake me, with your icy touch upon my cheek.
Who are you?

What are you?
With the sounds you whisper in my ear,
with spectral words I've grown to fear.
What are you?

Why do you?
Entomb me in your ghostly hold,
embraced within your chilling cold. Why do you?

Why should I?
Accompany you into the night,
go with you on your phantom flight. Why should I?

Why do I?
Merge with you, and come to worlds unseen,
to where no man has ever been. Why do I?

Who am I?
Now you're part of me, within my soul,
our spirits one, we are a whole. Who am I?

Irene Carss

The Children Of The Third World

The Piteous Cry of such tiny children.
Their faces solemn and overflowing with hunger,
Hunger that only they have experienced.
Unimaginable pain known to them only too often.
Nothing to live for and nothing to hope for,
Their world is silent as if on pause.
Each new day death shadows them,
Each night is filled with sleepless worry.
Their clothes tattered torn and dirty.
Everyone of their bodies, plagued with disease.
All they hope for is a chance to live,
Opportunities that others knock back.
The Children of the third world.

Rebecca Karn

The Pride Of Liverpool

The dawn had just broke over Hillsborough.
The sun was high in the sky.
The Liverpool fans were just awakening
For the day they all planned.

With hats and scarves and banners
To follow their heros again
They were all on the road to Hillsborough
To shout for Daglish and his men

For Wembly was just round the corner
Just 90 minutes for a final again
But God help the anfield supporters
God comfort each mum and each dad
God give them the strength to stand up and face
Say my son was a Liverpool fan.
He died for the name.
May long be his fame
For my son was a Liverpool fan.

Katherine Edmondson

War Trauma

Parents receive words, 'Your son is dead'
Emptiness is all that is left
Nobody is winning, all suffer loss
Hospitals full of wounded men
Trenches full of death
Tortured minds and bodies, interrogated
What good is it doing... this war?

Bombs falling on the innocents
To the shelters, must take cover
How will it all end, when will it all end?
Look out! Oh, it's O.K, it's one of ours
Shell shocked, Traumatic war
Why do you cry Mummy... When is Daddy coming home?

A man sits in a corner laughing madly
His mind unable to accept anymore
A woman holds her dead child
The child soaked, with blood and tears
What is it all for... this war?

Anthony Steven Green

Evening Song

Birds in the trees sing their evening song
One sits and wonders how could anything be wrong
A young couple look into each others eyes
And a flock of sheep graze under the evening stars
In this country scene there is no strife
It's all at peace and in love with life
So spare a thought for those faraway
Who only live from day to day
They suffer in pain and stand and cry
As they watch and see their country die
They are not strong they are not weak
Just wish we would listen when they speak
So pray for peace in that land faraway
And let us listen when they say
When from our homes and towns were leaving
Give us peace and love in the evening

Ken Causebrook

Late Night Ramblings

The art of Philosophy can, I'm sure,
Justify the need for war.
The study of Science can, I bet,
Equate and explain the pain I get.
And nature's heart, so stark and straight,
Has cast the parts and set the bait,
To determine who I love and hate.
But no-one on this earth has shown,
Why my love has left me all alone.

Dean Smith

542

Dovedale

Down from Thorpe cloud and into the vale
    Bathed in the summer sunshine gay,
I'll take the track to the stepping-stones
    Where the Dove doth wend its way.

Rivulet chattering to limestone bed;
    Twisting, bending between each bank
Till the dale begins to hem one in
    A verdant glen; moist and dank.

Oft-times have I followed this stream and walked
    Pensive or care-free for nigh an hour,
Yet rarely traversed to the Ilam Rock
    For the "Straight" grips me in its power.

Grandeur in miniature! All around
    Towering rocks guard silent pools
Where trout and grayling rest in shade:
    Each leafy spray the causeway cools.

Lush foliage in this gorge abounds-
    From high, cracked crags yews scent the air;
There can be nowhere else on earth
    Such sylvan beauty to compare!
        Thomas Granville Pickett

Changes

We're not the same as we used to be,
There's a different you and a different me,
There've been a lot of changes in the past few years,
We've changed our hopes and changed our fears,
There'll be a lot of changes in the future, too,
Changes to me and changes to you
The past has passed, the futures to come,
How will it be when we are done,
What will have changed, what will be the same,
What will we lose and what will we gain,
Sometimes we'll laugh, sometimes we'll cry,
Sometimes say 'Hello', sometimes 'Goodbye',
But whatever happens there'll always be a place,
In our hearts, for memories we can not erase.
        Hazel Woodruff

The Beauty Of Darkness

There is a beauty in this darkness
That we seem to share
An everlasting desire
To show how much we care
Through touching and holding
And the visions in our hearts
This beautiful feeling can never come apart
Because each darkened night
Follows a bright day
And all the shadows awake in us
Tell us don't be afraid
There is never sadness without the tears
Or smiles without laughter
But as you and I grow closer together
We will form an ever after
        Eva McDonald

Untitled

Surface of blue; sparkle of sun
Ripples on sand; holiday fun
Soft summer haze; salt scented brine
I saw the sea with these eyes of mine

Moon shining down on a silver sea;
Breeze that ruffles that filigree;
Lights that wink and flicker and shine.
I saw the sea with these eyes of mine.

Cracking of timber! A cry of doom!
White mountains tower o'er a cavernous tomb
Rocks reach out. The ghost winds whine.
Oh, how can I look with these eyes of mine!
        M. M. Morey

The Earth

Lying down on the grass, I spoke my soul to the sea,
    I felt its coldness and wetness,
The saltiness of the sea. The seals that swim down,
deep under, to tickle the earth's belly, I also feel the loneliness.
The volcanoes that warm up the cold waters,
    the rocks that are smashed
As the sea crushes them from above. But Then -
    I suddenly feel the pain and anger
of the sea, as oil and waste is dumped into the sea
Which contaminates and kills all life, the creatures that cry out
"Save us! Save us from death!" as they are engulfed in darkness,
Then as the cloud leaves, the sea bed is littered
    with dead and dying animals,
The few that survive don't dare to scavenge, as they know that
They would die of infection. They swim about desperate for
    food, but
Eventually they die. The cloud spreads.
The remaining animals group together and beg for mercy to live.
Some humans help, while others dump more and more rubbish, until
Every sea is black.
The humans fear it's too late, because
Man has made life in the sea extinct.
        Robert Yates

Knockbrack, Knockbrack

Erin, you are mine
you are fresh and you are green,
the ebb and flow of the tide of peace and love
and song and pain, does nourish your people so.

The little walls of stone, in the Athenry fields,
like ancient corridors lined my walking way
as I trod upon your earth.
Knockbrack, Knockbrack, my house, my home,
How I love you so.

You waited for my return, old and cold and worn,
you waited for my return.
Another winter, and you will be gone forever,
for the birds have come to nestle in your rafters.

The thatch is growing old, your white-washed face
is cold and grey, and the fire no longer lives in you,
But you waited for me,
and I love you so.
        Denise Coen

My Friend

Do you have a really good friend
Who understands your pain,
She's always there to listen and help
And doesn't look for any gain.

She will volunteer her husband
To taxi you here and there,
But she can be very stubborn
When you offer to pay your fare.

She is one of the best who was ever born
With her happy outlook on life,
And after a few minutes with her
You forget your trouble and strife.

She is also a jigsaw fanatic
And her hubby thinks it's a joke,
To see her try to fit pieces in
After a few voddies and coke.

So I raise my glass to Elsie
May she reign for many a year,
To my good friend and confidant H.M.
See you later to whisper in your ear.
        Agnes Carlon

Fading Shadows

Dreams fade in the light
never so real are the things of the night.
Things that might have been
may never be seen
as shadows fade from the night.

Whistling wind blows through the trees
haunting sounds have you down on your knees.
Empty promises made in the night
disappear as shadows fade from the light.

Fool's paradise is made in the dark
letting cold spirits leave their mark.
Wake up in the morning from the fright
as shadows fade from the night.

Yielding wounds that no-one sees
asking questions like a searching breeze.
Never seeing what was in sight
as shadows fade from the night.

Liz Grant

Through The Window

Like a cannon your vision is hurled,
Through the dividing window,
And into another world,
The world of abuse, violence and theft,
A place where disease,
Might as well just mean death,
To a place with no sun, where all dreams are broken,
Where insults and "You're Nicked",
Are the only words spoken,
Where kids sell their souls for the price of a pill,
So they can risk their own lives,
For a quick magic feel,
A land with no tears because they're just not worth while,
But it's easier to cry,
Than to manage a smile,
But now you've seen too much so you just close the curtain,
But the other side is still,
Dark, frightening and uncertain.

Clare Fletcher

The Little Things

It's not the thought of dying
Or even being dead
That fills my heart with sorrow
And puts pain inside my head.
It's not the ageing process
That brings me to my knees
And as for all the little things that gall
It's none of these
That cause me so much heartache
And fill me with despair,
It's the lack of understanding
From the ones who say they care.
A kindly word, a tender smile
Would lighten up the way
And give me all the strength I need
To face each passing day.

V. Flintoff

Wanton Are We

Have you ever watched the glimmer of an eye?
Have you ever watched an eye that is to die?
Did you see the darkness cloud the light therein?
And a question, where are you, where have you been?
It's so dark and I cannot see, please stay by me,
Hold my hand don't let me go, please hear my plea,
I must rest now, eyes are heavy, I can sleep,
Before I leave please wipe away, the tears that keep,
Will you kiss me, hold me tight, once and for all?
And enclose me really tight, so I don't fall.

V. V. Oliver

Bloody War

Oh, the mindlessness of war,
Just say what you feel, because you feel what you saw.
Those smoking guns on a dark damp morn,
The stench of bodies - limbs broken and torn.
Dull haunted eyes staring into space,
Thank God you at least are in a better place
But what of us who are left to fight?
Who cares if we think it's wrong or right?
Hour upon hour, and day after day
No matter how hard we fight or what we say,
The results are the same for the whole human race.
Can you understand or look me in the face?
This is not the way to bring about peace.
How I wish this bloody war would cease.

Anne Naylor

Remembering Tim

The shopping bag that lies in tatters
The semtex bomb that maims and shatters
The blood and ruin all around us
No longer shocks us or astounds us.
We take it all for - granted.

There's grief and pain and shock and terror
But who feels shame or guilt or error
It's all for freedoms sake some cry
It's just too bad some kids should die

If peace should come and bring redemption
Will damaged lives receive attention
We better get it right this time
And not sink back in hatreds slime

If hope can spark and start a flame
Of peace and understanding
We have to keep that flame alive
No matter how demanding.

Eric P. Burns

My Mirage Of A Fable

I walked in the country just after dawn
At peace with the world and glad I was born
Entranced by the scenes nature displayed
As I walked by a brook leading on to a glade,
It flowed into a pool where I got quite a fright
For drinking its fill was a horse of pure white
It shied up in the air then I suddenly knew
For I looked in its eyes which were flashing and blue
While from its head was a glittering horn
That it was not just a horse but a white unicorn.
I stood there amazed as a fable came true
Transfixed and wondering just what I should do
But the wonderful beast sensed I meant it no harm
Came up close to me and nuzzled my arm
Then quietly it turned and with a soft neigh
Trotted into the wood and just faded away,
As it vanished from sight I heard a faint sigh
And a whispering sound like a wish of goodbye
I shall always be grateful I went out that morn
And was lucky to see the white unicorn.

A. W. Jones

Unemployed 1993

In this doorway I have slept
Through snow, frost, heat and biting rain
Until the policeman ordered,
"Move and do not come again".

In palaces I was employed,
In University qualified,
Now poor, lonely, worried thin;
Very, very, very tired.

No one cares: no one will.
How can they understand the pain?
All is lost beyond repair:
No wife, no job, no hope-just rain.

Sydney

Getting Better

I'm getting better, yes I really am
and when I'm with another,
my mind is far away from you
and we that had so much.

What happened to us, that time ago?
who dealt the blow, to part us from each other?
Fate is unkind, it shattered all our dreams,
it took away our hopes and all it means
to be in love, to find someone to care.
I'm with another, but you're not there.

Perhaps in time I may forget, a little
Of the love I've lost.
I hope you're happy
found love again,
For me I'll never be the same,
I didn't know of love so brittle.
I'm getting better. Yes, I really am
and now I'm with another,
who says he'll always love and care for me.

I have to trust implicitly.

Sylvia Peile

Never To Forget - 10th February 1996

At Canary Wharf in London's Dockland at one minute past seven,
The 'Peace process' was shattered, two people died and went
  to heaven.
Over a hundred people were hurt and windows in buildings
  were blasted out,
As the IRA's bomb went off; thankfully when many more
  people were not about.
If it had been earlier, many more people would have died,
But it still left the young and old hurt, bruised and all had cried,
About the fanatics that had felt the democratic process slowly
  overhauling them.
So Sinn Fein broke the peace deal to forestall the election
  curriculum.
Northern Ireland's countrymen must make their hatred of the
  bomb and bullet clear,
Shout it from the rooftops to demand peace back again to adhere.
British and Irish Prime Ministers have to learn to work together,
So our peoples will live and work in peace, today, tomorrow
  and forever.

V. A. Marshall

Generations

Will men destroy the things they love,
With iron fist in velvet glove?

The young believe. The old know best.
The young want change. The old want rest.
The young feel sure they should hold forth,
With all their most compelling wrath,
Against the laws the old ones made,
And try until their numbers fade,
To change by ballot box and vote,
The very things their fathers wrote.

Yet hist'ry shows, down ages past,
Unless they turn and kill at last;
Their values and their ethics spurned,
They'll find at last they have been turned,
From activists, to passive fools,
By elder's democratic rules.
So, each oppression then oppressed,
Without a fight, can't reach its crest.

Men will destroy the things they love,
With any fist, in any glove.

Graham Dyer

Wars

Why oh why must there be wars?
Why can't we all live in peace together?
Why must one Nation strive to be stronger than the other?
Innocent lives so needlessly lost,
In the pursuit of territorial gain.
Old and young alike,
No-one is spared this dreadful pain.

In the end all that is left is total devastation.
The survivors have lost their habitation.
Loved ones and friends gone forever.
Whilst they must now try and live together,
With people once their enemies
In peace, love and harmony.

Forgiveness is such a hard word to extend,
To the people responsible for your pain,
Who now want to be your friend.
But the only way forward
Is to let discussions replace bullets
So instead of tears there are smiles.

Pat Jones

A Child Of The Millennium Fold!

Bells! Bells! Bells! Bells! Bells!
Rachel, dear grandchild, awake! arise!
Though Midnight's our hour has just arrived, come, hear yourself
Two-thousand Millennium bells being rung out mighty strong -
Ding-dong; ding-dong; ding-dong; ding-dong; ding-dong-
  ong-ong-ong!
And Hark, the Peoples sing in many Tongues, but in joyous unison
To greet in the New Year two-thousands and one!
A new world for you, not yet five!
Come, see the first dawn break in the sky,
And know another thousand years from Jesus' Birth has just
  come alive!

What new wonders would you behold? Wonders never
  cease, we're told!
What new joys; new hopes for you and yours, alas!
After the upside-down two-thousand years just past!?
But hopes never die, just fade away, so they say!
For discoveries new, what fun, just to clip on your very own wings
And fly to freedom, when and where you will...indeed a thrill!
Space age revealing new wonders, e'en new black holes as well!
Come what may, be not afraid, with Jesus hand-in-hand
Make your own new world a new better place, if you can,
'Cause Jesus sacrificed His all, to give the best to woman and man!

P. M. Gwynn

The Despoilers

There's all kinds of waste
In the world of today.
There's a life taken
In a flash, on the motorway,
Leaving behind, Mother, Father or wife,
Husband or sister or brother,
What a waste of a life.
There's the rubbish that's thrown
Without thought or care
And denudes our countryside
Of the charm that was there.
There's the wastage of values
Now sadly all gone,
Morality, honesty, compassion too
And so many more I could recite to you.
There's the countryside in front of our eyes
Concrete, replacing once an earthly paradise.
The wild life are finding it hard to live
And I who am a conservationist -
Find it hard to forgive.

Anne Haldane

Reverie On A Smile

She shows to the world a warm tolerant smile
The cares of her life she plays down.
The sorrow, the heartache, the hurt and the strife
She hides under a mask - like a clown.
It's not for the want of a dream coming true
For that's hardly likely to be
As time and again the dreams all turn out wrong,
So counting on them isn't real.
Perhaps a far-distant star, proclaiming her fate
As part of its own dynasty,
Is really the culprit and largely to blame
For the way things just have to be.
Or, was there a turning she just didn't take
Some sign she just failed to see,
A guiding hand that she overlooked
In her fight with adversity.
Today as I sat by my mirror
A face so pale and sad gazed back at me,
I gave her my warmest reassuring smile
And she smiled back at me.

Vida Chatham

Faraway Eyes

I have a feeling, one that shows in my own
faraway eyes,
   One that's trying to forget, all those
heartbreaking goodbyes.
   The goodbyes that took away everything, all that
I felt should rightfully have been mine,
   And all because they seemed to have been said, to
the wrong person, and at the wrong time.
   Who was to be my valentine, when February
comes around?
   All these feelings left to discover, now how will
they ever be found?
   I thought things could never be the same, my life
instead filled with, heartbreak, tears and pain.
   Well the pain has barely eased and I'm still
waiting, praying for someone to take me by the hand,
   And take me away to the faraway land,
   The land that I can see, see through those faraway eyes,
   Those eyes that belong to me

Maria DeCosimo

Unborn Child

Voices echo, sounds changing all the time
My vision isn't clear, but I see more every day
Sometimes it's so quiet, now and then I jump with fright
Where am I? What am I doing here?

Please don't have that again, it tastes awful
This is great, somersaults, karate, I'm getting my own back
I'm growing quickly, discovering extra bits each time I wake
That's better, something sweet, some more please

Not as many new things now, it's a tight squeeze in here
Not as much room to move, I can't stay here much longer
Someone's poking about, oh can't they leave me alone
I need to sleep a while, will they ever go away?

Today feels different, tastes different, sounds different
A tunnel has appeared, it looks narrow and small
Do I go in there? It seems I have no choice
Ouch! It's a bumpy ride, but I can see a bright light

I feel closer to it now, nearly there, here I come
Wow! It's cold out there, things look weird
You sound better than before - I know you!
That's nice, it's warmer now, cuddle me closer I Love You Mummy!

Arlene O'Donnell

Destruction

As he pulverises the immortal carcass of the zamyboar, he has
death and evil, in his onyx black eyes, as his head delves into
the carcass a crown of blood appears.
His black cloak of dry blood gets longer and longer, the more
innocent creatures he tears apart with his razor sharp beak,
like a knight's trusty sword.
His collar which once was snow white is covered with the
sinus of his last meal,
Chewing chopping like a sharp, steel, strong, sturdy weapon
of death, as he glides across the moors with his wings of
anthracite black silk, on a cold winter's day wondering and
waiting who and what defenceless creature will be his next
feast of joy.
His claws are as sharp as knives and like red rubies his legs
like an old man's wrinkly face.
His nest is perched up high in the sky where no good can
reach, his pray all pay him homage as he wishes, when they
have paid their respect he grins and laughs. Nothing would or
has dared to outwit this mass amount of intelligence, as if they
dare they may not live to say.
But all good things have to come to an end, his rival MAN
kills his pray, pollutes his air, destroys his home, and kills his
mate, he has a long lonesome death where he learns what evil,
death, destruction, and consumption means and feels like.

Marie Lewiecki

Paternal Instincts

I've just been the doctors and found that I am with child
When I tell my husband he'll go really wild
It's not that he gets morning sickness or any kind of pains
And neither will his figure change with all the pounds he gains
No-ones going to stare at him or laugh about his bump.
So why do I ask myself is he going to take the hump.
He doesn't have to go off food or get any kind of craves
no-ones going to stop him drinking or going to his raves
So why should I worry when I tell him again
one more won't make a difference we've already got ten.

Julie Jenkins

Reflections Of My Mind

It stands alone, impressive and white.
The sun reflects through the window,
As I wander in thought, through the trees,
Listening to the birds mocking,
As the river's gentle flow
Ebbs through my mind.

It doesn't seem far across the way
To yonder green hills, lazing,
Beneath the gentle wind's blow,
As it dances the grass, back, forth, to and fro
While the sun makes it glisten
Like silvery snow.

The trees are changing their colours today,
From green through to red and blowing away.
Swirling high like birds on a wing,
Then floating to ground as cover till spring.
Trees bare of leaves standing proud and stark,
Seen through the mist are like ghosts from the past.

Margaret Metcalfe

The Mountain

Lonely she stands, her skirts of mist swirling around.
Ethereal splendour, her constant companion.
The eagle, her only visitor, on dark, undefined nights.
Shades of light pattern and flicker across her face.
Her sun seeking summit, pierces the blue orb above.
Warmth on the breeze, brings human visitors,
Tolerated, only barely, they stay but a short while;
Her friend the rain, ensures her solitude again.
The peace returns, and lonely she stands
Island mountains, on windswept barren land.

Isobel Francis

My Dog - Shan

Still now in grave, in beauty lies,
Adored within my watered eyes.
I mark the grave which marks my heart,
And curse the time we have to part.

Gone is the light along the way,
Gone is the form I saw each day.
Now in my thoughts I search for you,
Gone, not from my heart but from my view.

Wishing you peace and tranquil rest,
In knowing you I was greatly blessed.
Wanting your presence ever more,
Tears in my eyes to show the sore.

The days, the weeks, the months go by,
Nothing on earth can dry my eye.
Wouldst I could be once more with you,
To know again a love so true.

Without you life has lost its spark,
I wander on as though in dark.
My hope is, after my life span,
Again I'll see you, my dog Shan.

A. Bourne

As Man And Boy

Silently, he came in the middle of the night,
An image of innocence long since demised.
Softly, he spoke to me as he lay by my side,
Words of a language I had left far behind.
Recollections of splendid adventures enjoyed
Flowed from the lips of this willowy boy,
He seemed so familiar that I did not feel fear,
As my inner reflections became very clear,
This was the boy who had become the man.

Suddenly, emotion clouded the sky,
Forcing confessions of childhood lies.
Words flowed freely like salt tears in the night.
As the clock kept time he slipped from my sight.
Where is the spirit that stood by the door,
Reaching within me the man who was boy?
Just for a moment, I saw him once more.
He smiled as he faded and my heart filled with joy,
For I had lived life with passion both as man and as boy.

Susan J. McIndoe

The Temple Of Poseidon At Sounion

Sounion I always will remember
Silent beside the silver sea
Its snow-white marble gleaming in the moonlight
Superb and stark in its simplicity.

The beauty of its columns rising sharply
Pointing their fluted fingers to the sky
One of them scarred - that earliest of vandals
Who carved his name and idly passed it by

This Grecian tribute to the great Poseidon
Whose temple this was - Lord of all the seas
Who ruled in splendour garlanded by mermaids
Enthroned - and holding court with such as these

A ruin now - shadow of former glory
Whose elegance has stood the test of time
A landmark in a land of living legend
Whose legendary grace remains sublime

So stand and gaze upon its noble marble
Picture again this time-forgotten place
Which sears its way into your living memory
Like someone's lovely half-remembered face.

Leon Coleman

Marriage Of Love

as you are joined
as man and wife
to live in *love* together
for the rest of your life
remember *love* is a gift from God
the most precious gift the world can afford
may *love* fill your heart,
your home and your life
in moments of joy and in moments of strife
when strife comes along as it surely must
may your *love* for each other
show patience and trust
may your *love* endure as the years go by
on the wings of *love* may you ever fly

Margaret S. McAlpine

Time

We do not shape our destiny
the time on earth is only lent
but during that life span
we decide how it is spent.

Some have ambition, and reach for the moon
some get sick or face death too soon
some invent, write, paint, some build and fix things
some like to travel as if they had wings.

The world is a stage they say this is true
the way that you act it is up to you
the pace that you dictate that your life should be run
is sometimes guided by the stars or the sun.

When life reaches its last final page
when hopefully you've reached a ripe old age
just think back to this time only lent
I hope I can say I am very content.

Patricia Steers

In Gloucester Cathedral

The stones beneath us many a saint has trod:
But in this Cotswold shrine, where tinted light
Ripples and quiet echoes tell of God,
Has truth been sensed beyond the pale of sight?

The brooding hills and languid Severn River,
Outflux and link of homelands to the sea,
Revealed in human hearts a bow and quiver -
Uniting thoughts of how the world could be.

A social club and concert hall remain:
It's gone - the heady wind that stretched the sail.
When shadows spur the bold to seek again
Shall inborn conflicts lead where angels hail?

David Bowers

Song Thrush

How pleasurable that forceful song,
So indefatigable, livelong,
That's the Throstle, on top branches sat,
Its favourite singing habitat,
Thriving its voice on iteration,
Vocalist without relaxation,
Such vigorous communicator,
And, of the Spring, prognosticator,
Experienced snail depredator,
The latter mercilessly battered,
Shell, scant protection, so soon shattered,
And fragments willy-nilly scattered,
Gastropod molluscs a delight,
And so surely the most relished bite,
They tickle the turdine appetite;
Most handsomely spotted on the breast,
In our gardens a most welcome guest.
Strange that its namesake is an inflamed throat
When from that bird such tones melodic float.

Frank Dobinson

History

One, two, three, it was Victory,
Four, five, six, the two Davids didn't mix.
Seven, eight, nine, only Labours new colours are fine.
And, No. 10, it was not for the men.

It had to be a Major to proceed Margaret Thatcher.
For Neil and Paddy, not one could match her!
Neil-Kin-Nock at No. 10.
For Johns in residence with his men.

Conservative victory once more to make four.
Why once more? Well let me say,
Neil and Paddy would give all Britain's power away!
So Neil can Kneel for No. 10, and Paddy can think again.

Kinnock went, alas, John Smith, such a nice man,
It was not to be for Labours plan.
Enter Tony Blair, who seems quite fair,
But his party already divided and in despair.

Keep the red flag flying they say, it will be their defeat on
voting day.

Vote for Neil, go more red,
Sign a treaty before anyone said!
Vote for Paddy, red and yellow,
Copy Neil but a little more mellow.
Vote for John, keep in the blue,
Backing Britain, it is true.

Margaret Oakley

The Silent Communicator

He waits impassively for me to begin
Mouth shuttered in silent refusal.

Words unformed
as thoughts stay caged
behind the childhood cruelty
of being seen, but never heard.

Adulthood beckoned,
bestowing on him the highest accolade of Irish acclaim;
a quiet modest man.

My quiet modest man.

These chiding words
haunt the ever-changing consciousness
of my plight,

I want his quiet presence
Not his screaming silence.

Maria Thompson

Last Quarter

I could not sleep, so left my bed
At 3 a.m. to pace the room,
When, through the window, I beheld
My former cheerful friend, the Moon;
But now, alas, how thin and old
He had become, his light so faint
He hardly had the strength to shine,
The smallest cloud could smother him.
"Dear Moon", I said, "I feel for you,
I too am old and dull, and tired,
And have no strength to fight the clouds
That seem about to smother me."
And then I thought he gave a wink,
As he had often done before,
And said in my attentive ear:
"Look West in seven days' time, my dear,
And you will see me young and bright
And growing stronger every night.
Go back to bed and close your eyes,
And sleep will come before sunrise."
And so it did!

Joyce Miller

Stages

When people are young depending on age,
The degree of intoxication will change at each stage.

A tiny baby is so overcome,
It's unable to cope and depends on its mum.

When they grow older about two or three,
They fall and they stumble like men on a spree.

At five or six they are walking okay,
But like men who take drink they are full of horseplay.

Then growing up they reach their teens,
Getting more sense making less scenes.

More sober thinking mind more alive,
Head should be clearing when they reach twenty five.

But some go through life when these stages are over,
Just that little bit drunk, they never get sober.

T. Black

A Dream

I dream that drummer is up in the stars above me,
But he still in my heart,
And I still love him in the same way.

He still might recognize me,
But I do not know.
I believe he is in my heart, And in my soul.
The only way I know is because I can feel him,
All day and night through.

If he can still hear me, and listen to me,
I love you very much.
When I look up to the stars,
And see a bright glow,
I know that drummer is saying something to me.
Drummer
That bright star

Kayleigh Katherine Ellis

Living

Striving to live, striving to learn,
To cope with feelings, pain and emotions.
Taking each day to see what it sends.
To get through, and emerge with a smile.

Getting older losing family and friends
The kids have left home,
Finding relationships of their own,
Life changes, but still we go on.
No good looking on what might have been,
If I had done this,
Or I had done that,
The years have rolled by oh so fast,
But so what, we survived
Don't give up, enjoy your life,
It's all we've got left,
Let's forget all the strife.

Mike Govier

Two Bands Of Angels

Like a band of guiding angels they swooped upon his bed
Quickly quietly, as a team, not a word was said
Hidden behind the curtains pulled shadows on the wall
Surgical equipments, a softly spoken call
Curtains bulging in and out-more angels flitting in
They worked and worked oh! How they worked
For they had got to win.
But another band of angels were waiting by the side
Watching this mortal battle, they did not need to hide
Behind the curtains now all limp with quietness creeping in
They knew from the beginning this battle they would win
   No one won this battle
   No one lost it, too
   But there must have been a victor
   I don't know - do you?

R. P. Pye

Child

European Child of four,
Weight two stones each day gradually more.
Toys strewn across the floor —
Abdomen excess flesh protrudes,
    Chocolates Lollies —
But only after all vegetables have been consumed,
Food which falls upon the floor, disgraceful Offensive!
To be eaten no more.

Father Mother, Brother Sister,
All eyes to show they care.
If anything Child wants not needs,
Attentively they'll be there.

Oh God how they care!
Take for granted what is there.

Outlying in another Land, was born a Beast,
As I went nearer, I saw it was Man,
When I came nearer still, I saw it was my Brother ——
An Ethnic Child of 5, sorrowful disturbing, wandering eyes,
Carcass weighing 12 lbs or more,
This body lies upon a sandy floor.

R. Sira

Matter Over Mind

I hope that I shall never be
as horrible as a wizened tree,
Lying around in my nakedness,
Frightened as a bird that is free.

The face I saw in my mirror
was not quite mine but, thicker,
It was like the face of the devil
I looked upon it with horror!

It was sometime later, in spring,
My mind wandered back to that awesome thing
The wizened tree, this filled me with terror,
Seeing a raven wing its way to the firing.

What shall I do when friends find out
that I am the demon round about.
I in my nakedness will show them
The way, though I be a dolt.

My nakedness was of the mind,
The face in the mirror was devilishly unkind,
Wizened though the horrid tree,
Please, dear life, forgive me!

Alma Montgomery Frank

Reflections

I've lived half my life and I've lived it hard,
Struggled on for every yard.
Known the times when I could cry,
Faced with nights when I hoped I'd die.

Seen the days when I've been too weary,
to end this life that I thought so dreary.
Passing through those dirty Towns,
Shrugging off the ups and downs
Of a life not worth having, God knows why,
I wish sometimes He would let me die.

But I can't let go, not just like that.
For life can be sweet no matter what.
A fond hello, a simple smile, seems to make it all worthwhile.
The funny jest, the spoken word,
The bleet of a lamb, the song of the bird.

The feeling of warmth as you hold someone near,
Of knowing you're wanted when you're called My Dear.
If you happen to read this, my friend, take heed,
For the likes of us there's always a need!

Ray McLeod

Hurricane

Far out in the calm sea
the hurricane twirls with great glee,
it throws itself forwards, towards the
island with awesome power.

Rushing like a spinning top,
knocking down the trees,
bananas flying with this destructive breeze.
The hurricane zooms from the island,
leaving not one tree.

But if it comes again it will
never lose this horrible destructive power that
all hurricanes have. It's like a big black cape
tearing across the land, nobody can escape
the deadly hurricane that twirls in Gods hand.

Carl Roberts

Happiness

When in love you think of spring,
the flowers grow and love starts blossoming,
you wonder what is happening.
Your heart beats at a pulsing rate,
as you rush right through the gate.
Your only thought, in those days,
is happiness in lots of ways.

The bubble bursts and you fall,
shedding tears like a waterfall.
Not wanting to find someone new,
but all to soon, your heart heels fast,
you knew it would not last.

Ready not to face the world out there,
feeling you should be aware.
You go around head held down,
feeling sadness and wear a frown.
Then you meet a new soul mate,
fall in love, that is your fate.

Jean Talor-Watson

A Spring Flower

Would nature a crocus had wished me to be,
To awake the dawn when I could see,
the sun in the heavens waiting to pass,
enhancing my colours that puts to the grass,
So envious since that last restful day, when did nature,
with a smile on her face cascade colour all over the place,
On her favourite the rainbow, did most of it fall,
while the crocus, so patiently waiting her turn, was pleased
when nature did at last discern, such a promising beauty so
early in spring,
Then God, his work finished at last, suggested that with a
canvas so vast, she should use just one colour to paint the grass,
And ever since the eve of that day, after all his creations
had been, she looked, and searched all over his world,
But all she could find was green.

James Cuthbert

Death

It hangs over him like a dark cloud,
He sighs and weeps and cries aloud,
The cloak he wears is long and black,
He stoops and walks with a crooked back,
His skeleton look scares people away,
Though he does not mean it in any way.
His ghostly body floats above the ground,
Making sure he does not make a sound.
This man you see is full of death,
But is hanging on with each and every breath.
His grey hair is long and straight,
No-one can determine what will be his fate,
The wind is strong, the air is cold,
His fingers and toes are covered in mould.

Laura Carroll

The Human Brain

The human mind, the brain, the soul,
Encapsuled in a secure home.
From birth to death, this miracle endowed,
To serve its human owner proud.

All feelings; touch and smell and sight,
Come easy to the human mite.
He knows not where he is, or how,
Or why his mother's furrowed brow.

The journey through his life depends
Completely on the brain, that sends
The signals through his entire frame,
For every action in life's long game.

From the very beginning, it seems,
Man's search for love, fulfilment, dreams,
Has been a lottery- light and dark.
The good was great, the bad was stark.

In nineteen ninety six A.AD.
He's climbed near the top of the massive tree.
The danger of falling is always there.
His brain responds; It warns - Take care!

T. S. Totten

Tranquil

The serenity of my garden,
My own pleasure in paradise,
And through eyes of other people
It's looking rather nice.
This land ablaze of rainbows,
Now spring is on its way,
Everything so active every minute of the day.

In between the trees, foxgloves gently peeping through,
Orange blossom, lavender, roses,
Their fragrance drenched in dew.
A friendly Robin chirps by your side
As you gently fork the soil,
He's waiting for his next meal.
Regardless of your toil...

So many exciting changes.
Challenges often new,
Left alone, content in my garden,
Is the choice of quite a few.

Joan Purcell

Stay

It's not that after you're gone I can't carry on
and pick all the pieces up
it's not that I can't start again or find a new friend
or that I can't be strong

I'll still be all I can be, but just I - not we
will be making the plans that we made
It's not that these tears I cry won't eventually dry
without leaving a trace

It's just seeing you as you are, your bags in the car
your hand on the door set to go
and as your lashes you raise, for one final gaze
I want you to know:-

It's you, it always was you, will forever be you
in everything that I do
and if this day we should part, I'll no longer have
a need for a heart

don't go! Pleads an inner voice though not a sound
is heard from my lips there is nothing more I can say
but before you I'll stand, and hold out my hand
and pray you'll take it, you'll hold me, you'll stay

Dawn-Marie

Sea Of Love

A calm ascends across the waves,
gentle ripples form across the surface
like a love that's new and unfounded,
as clouds gather across the sky,
the waves begin to quicken
trying to reach something far beyond.
The more the waves try the angrier it becomes.
Lightning strikes the skies, the storm has arrived.
wild crashing waves go on and on,
reaching for that something.
At last the waves slow down,
content with its capture,
and once again descends into a calm
gentle ripple,
happy until the never ending sea
Seeks for revenge once more.
Like a heart searching for love,
never fulfilled or contended,
the waves of the sea
will never end.

Elizabeth Mitchell

The Blue Bell Walk

I love to tread the leafy mould of woodland glade,
That lies betwixt the patchy seas of bluebells.
And, there to kneel among the soft green moss,
And, pluck the sweet windblown anemone.

'Twixt primrose banks a river running by,
Above its cool reflection, flits a dragon fly.
While in the depths, the stirring reeds reveal,
The speckled trout, they dart in all directions as I draw near.

Whilst in the trees, a 1,000 beaks in song
Blend with the breeze, the rustling leaves and the cuckoo's call.
Yet there's a stillness reigning there, a tranquil peace sighing
in the air,
Held in the beauty of this lovely glade far away from the city
man has made.

Rosalind Ozga

Praise To The Lord

The world is full of beauty if only we would look-
The mountains and the rivers, the gentle babbling brook
The arctic snows of winter, the gentle summer rain,
The glory of the sunset across the desert plain.

But man is far too busy in his search for fame and gold
To thank the Lord above, these wonders to behold.
If only he would pause awhile and take a look around
He'd see the lovely things of nature that abound.

If only he would spare a moment to thank the Lord above
For all this lovely beauty which shows the Father's love.
When one looks at the stars at night and planets out in space
With just a little bit of faith we can also see His face
The Maker of this Universe, of birds and beasts and man
The blessed God and father with His Master Plan.

Inez M. Henson

An Old Man

Just an old man sat on a seat watching the world go by
Deep in thought of memories that linger with every sigh
Wonderful days to treasure, childhood dreams in his sleep
School days of long ago when rules were made to keep
Defending king and country he proudly marched off to war
Parted from his family and sent to some far distant shore
Returned safely from battle and married his girl back home
Behind him the bloodshed and tears, no more the world to roam
Having children and raising a family, working hard all his life
Holidays, laughter, lots of fun, the love of his darling wife
Into old age, then retirement, oh! how the years have rolled by
So many good times to remember, where have they gone and why?
Youth brought him love and happiness, he held the world at his feet
But as we pass him by, he simply remains just an old man sat on a seat

Patricia Hartas

In Search Of You

Never before has a love so great in its power been born
nor as pure, as the love I give to you!
Oh! the years that have passed, though we maybe weather worn
yet my love, remains as fresh and new.
As though, it had just begun, untarnished by time,
my love comes shining through.

I am a burning fire of love for you, you're the blood within my veins.
A pure white hot flame of emotion, burning brightly and eternal,
Unquenched by the water of an ocean, nor by a cascading waterfall.
Still burning through a global downpour, of thunderous rains.
So hot! Such power, my love for you proclaims.

No power upon this Old Earth, could break the bond of my soul,
as my love floats in ethereal tendrils to you, on a current of air.
Bringing with it the happiest mirth, and the knowledge of my goal,
to love and care for you, for as long as time is still there.
With such a great fire burning within me,
It's a wonder I am not engulfed by the flame.
As my love bursts forth in search of you,
my heart whispers in the wind, calling out your name.

D. R. Breach

Insane

I knelt down beside her, holding her bony hand: limp and weak
Sound of her heavy slow breathing: long gasps deep gasps,
    unearthly gasps,
Her floral dress smudged with what looked like blood
Oh! how my imagination is running away: cowardly,
What do I feel? All of my deep emotions are pouring out
escaping into the dark room; like the blood is escaping from
    Her body!
Scared? Tearful? Powerful? Weak?
What do all of those emotions say? Mean?
What are they telling me?
I am confused, muddled, my emotions are mixing, intermingling!
I do not understand!
"Help me please!" Am I going insane?
Whom is this old lady holding my hand?
I am hungry. I dare not eat,
I feel sick, ill, depressed, lonely,
No one loves me!
I am cold, I feel a change,
My heart is going black!
My eyes misty with tears: perhaps of blood: perhaps salt:
    frustration!
I have changed! Insane has spoilt my life!

Caroline Simpson

The Mortal Coil

Why do people kill one another?
What makes them shoot that gun?
Someone went and murdered their brother;
close the eyes of the sun.
And please shield us from reality,
I really do not want to see,
That it's become a necessity,
to kill people like you and me.

My life is a staircase without a wall,
The further I go, the further to fall,
For the steps they crumble,
as onwards I stumble.
Through my life.

What's this life we lead?
For how long can we bleed?
No-one ever explained to me just how hard it would be,
To grow up and to see that this person inside is me.

The only place where I'm at peace.
I'm dressed in lace, reality ceased.
I'm dreaming.

Rachel Battersby

The Church Coffee Shop

There is a little coffee shop down my way
Run on a volunteer basis day by day
After retiring I had some hours to spare
So decided to use them by working in there
It's something I'd always wanted to do
And it was a chance to make my dream come true
Of helpers they are always short of their quota
So were only too pleased to add me to the rota
My colleagues are friendly we all get on well
And share in the serving of things that we sell.
Some folk like some coffee or maybe some tea
Which we serve with a smile and a hope that we please
There are biscuits on coffee and homemade cakes too
Or if you prefer perhaps a tea cake would do
If you are hungry and would like more to eat
We have soup, flans and pies and lots of nice sweets
I have made lots of friends with the people I meet
And some of them come to see us each week
I really enjoy my hours spent there
And it's great helping others by doing my share

S. C. Talmadge

The Regression

I said to myself,
I've been here before,
As I opened the door
Of this old house.
I had a strong feeling I knew the layout.
My head started reeling, I almost passed out.
Something vehement happened.
And I seemed to know,
I could see a pool of blood on the floor,
In every room there was more and more.
I could feel myself being attacked
By a man with a knife,
I begged for mercy to save my life.
But this madman was intent on killing us all,
I could hear screams through every wall,
Until at last no screams at all.
I started to feel a very sharp pain,
So I got out of that house,
Before he comes again.

D. G. Field

Ode To A Chimney

I am one of Millions even Trillions
No longer in use I am out of date
Across my top does lie a slate
Sadly this now is my fate

In days of old when burned black gold
I sent smoke spiralling across the sky
The wind would catch it and toss it around
Did it ever return to ground

Cats prowled all around me
Miaowing and sheltering falling asleep
A lovely aroma of burning peat
Birds of all sizes used to meet

Sadly 'twas said I caused pollution
The powers that be found a solution
Redundancy loomed we were all doomed
Smoking was banned all over the land

One thing for sure they cannot remove me
I am part of tradition for all to see
High on the rooftops plenty like me
Conserved for posterity happy to be

Mary D. McClellan

551

Spring Island

Tranquillity encases the secluded world,
A cool breeze caressing the lofty blades of thin grass,
Teasing, dancing around the bony arms of a tree,
Its green leaves, visibly shaken, tilt towards the sun.

Seclusion sends sensations of nature buzzing into space,
Tireless rays of melting sun touch beautiful petals,
Ripe buds, bursting to open, combat for the sun's affection,
A gigantic cloud of orange stretches across the clear blue sky.

Contrast of colours content the sunset,
Precious jewels gleam at the water's surface,
Flowing out towards the mouth and the eternal light,
Shining, shimmering, creating a perfect harmony.

The sky slowly dies, surrounding the world with bright stars,
Flowers and trees mourn in silence with bowed heads,
Stillness whips around the sleeping island,
Tranquillity encases the secluded world, the world of Spring Island.

Louise J. Crowley

Untitled

She stands before me
Such an exquisite sight to behold
That my limbs fail me
and I gasp for breath.
"Avert! Avert your gaze", I tell myself
Lest I become powerless with intoxication.

Can this perfect embodiment of physical beauty.
Be the result of the accidental union of two mere mortals?
She can only be the creation of the Gods
of Lord Shiva and Parvati
when in passionate embrace
Therefore timeless and immortal
and in that knowledge I rejoice.

C. P. Viswanathan

Heart In Peace

Several faces, sound and noise
But all I'm hearing is an inner voice,
Detaching me from those around me
Giving a feeling of warmth and serenity.

Thoughts are more but feelings many,
Love and pain and joy if any,
Something within needs to come out
In my usual silent shout.

Mingling passion, endless love,
The inner strength from the One above,
Sunny rays to warm my heart
Of an intense phase this is the start.

Wandering thoughts, carefree mind,
This day might be a little kind,
Lightened soul and me at ease
And for some hours my heart in peace.

Fleur Balzan

Dreams

Somewhere down in the twilight world
Between consciousness and sleep
Where forgotten voices whisper your name
And half formed creatures creep
There exists a world beyond your ken
Full of faces you cannot recall
So clear and vivid at the time
But on waking you can't remember at all
A twirling, whirling kaleidoscope
Like characters in a play
Dramas that unfold one by one
That are forever unable to stay
Anything can happen in wondrous dreams
Where vision and imagination defies
So many things in the actual world
Disappear with the opening of your eyes.

E. Timony

Never Give Up Hope

It's the time of the month again, when you should be glad
But instead deep down you're crying because you're sad
A life within was meant to begin, life month by month would
grow but once again you must put on a smile, you hurt so
much nobody knows

At least two years have passed and still no signs
That appointment with the Doctor, now is the time
But from there it's the specialists who would check you out
If all is not well! They'll explain what all the options are about

At the end of the day, you want to carry a child
You want to try whatever it takes, from now on it could be
make or break
The blood tests will begin, then the wait for results to come in
Then it'll be time to decide, should you go ahead
Should you apply for IVF.
It could take months or even years
it could even all end in tears
but one must never give up, never give up hope!
Whether it happens naturally or with medical help
Somehow you'll find the will to cope.

Alexandra Campbell

Home

When we die, where do we go
I used to wonder, I didn't really know
Is there a heaven, is there a hell
Religion says yes but how can we tell.
Then it happened and I had to face
It comes to all of the human race
That searing pain, seemed there to stay
But it went, as the spirit skipped away
Now I was floating, through the air
All my troubles gone, I didn't have a care
I was free like a bird, on the wing
I was happy, like a child on a swing
I had a beautiful feeling of content
As my soul reached out, for heaven's scent
A feeling of peace, I never knew
There is a God, I know it's true
So this is what it's like to die
The voice my own, I heard the cry
There was no fear, of the unknown
It seemed at last - I was going home

B. J. Hendry

Cheviot View

Oh! bleak mysterious stone standing afar, like a long
forgotten home.
Who would live there long ago?
Defending it.

Gentle shepherd or warrior race, magician, poet or
lady of grace.
Imagine them on that stark hill,
defending it.

Surviving winters cold,
straw for warmth, beasts in the fold.
Children crying, dying, but still
defending it.

Home now to grouse and sheep, no wild wolves to
disturb the sleep.
Only the jets and keepers around,
defending it.

Believe that the spirits who once live there, will
know that we care.
Time and distance as nothing,
in your defence.

Jean Mather

Watch Your Bounty Grow

When I look back on yesterday, on my past attempts at life.
I recall a lot of happy times, with interludes of strife.
The efforts made to give my best,
Those souls who put me to the test,
I laugh, I cry, I smile.

Rough patches were the building blocks, that made a stronger me.
Good times were had more often than not,
but somehow I could not see.
The loves I've know,
The way I've grown,
Oh soft soliloquy.

Thank God for where I am today, for a light so brightly shone.
The wounds and scars that hurt me so, I look within a find all gone.
A gentle wave washes me clean,
A soft caress remains unseen,
Along this highway long.

Mother, Father look at me now, be as proud as I am so.
Realize the hardest thing about giving life, is sometimes letting go.
Weep tears of joy not sorrow,
And praise a new tomorrow,
And watch your bounty grow.

Joanne Managh

A Reflection On Life

An image in the mirror
  A shadow on the wall
The light at the end of a tunnel
  You must have seen them all,
The tick of a clock, telling us the time,
  A river running by
An ocean full of beautiful life
  That stretches as far as the sky
The sun that gives us light
  and heat through out the day.
A lonely green meadow
  The smell of fresh cut hay,
The flowers by the wayside
  The leaves upon the trees.
Hold out your hand and feel,
  The soft gentle breeze
Then by yourself spend a moment
  And reflect on all of these.

Christina Leasly Parish

To My Mother

This lady that I loved
Enters the twilight, where my veiled eyes see
A person worn and proved
With greying hair and age-bent poverty,
I'd weep to see her but that this I know
All thither go.

She turns once more to me
Against the woods alight with dying gold,
Spindle and dogwood tree,
Cadence of scarlet, crimsons manifold
That fade to weariness and whispering lie
Bidding goodbye.

Leafless the trees and grey,
Elfish with moss, bereft of life and cold
Where she goes eagerly
Under a frail moon poised, star-struck and bold
And in her hand outheld at this dark hour
A crescent flower.

Katharine Lethbridge

The Enfolding Silence

Mist falls, and the peaks, tooth-pointed, waver and fail,
Vanish in their wisps of grey, then loom, wrapped
In thistledown balls of cloud. Magic they are, and strange.

So comes the enfolding silence, curling
Tightly around me, lapping in thick
Stealthy layers, me, poor chrysalid.

Thin spires of sound. A creak.
The chair where he used to sit.
A door swings softly
No presence, a wind, a breath.
Suddenly a bird cries.
Piercing sweet it soars,
And one gold ray
Dips at my feet.

G. R. Sandberg

My Son

I suffer, as I feel your pain.
Rejoice with you when you gain acclaim.
Inside, unseen, I cry for you,
When the world turns its cruel face.
I laugh with unleashed joy, when fate smiles kindly.
My heart, my soul, my nervous breath, follow your
Every move.
Even when I know nothing of your position
I fear for you, and in my troubled mind clothe
you in a warm, unseen, protective shield.
These apron strings, you held so tightly, when
young hang loose about me now.
Take care my soldier son.
I do not care to let you go, to stand for
Queen and country in a foreign land.
But go you must and with saddened heart
I follow you with pride.

Joan Jarvis

The Verge Of Defeat

Continuous conflict and no compromise,
Attitudes, different views,
And here am I on the verge of defeat
And I see all that I have to lose.
The pressure and strain is weighing me down
And eating away at my will,
I'm losing this battle, morale is so low,
And yet to survive I would kill.
I try not to waiver because I have sworn
Allegiance to you as my queen,
So I soldier on as I search through my heart,
For defiance that's as yet unseen.
A silence that deafens, a cold so severe,
Are constant on this battlefield,
But then I recall why I'm fighting at all,
And I know then, that I'll never yield.

Allan Wilson

Starsigns Of Love

To My Inspiration

You are a Sagittarius, I am a Gemini,
You struck me with your arrow
And left me there to die.
Dying not a death, but for love towards you,
I'm so glad you chose me and not the other few.
I can't help but to think of you
All day and also all night,
You twinkle in my mind so much
Like the stars that shine so bright.
When you're not around me, I think of you in my arms
Deserted on an Island underneath the many palms
I see us both so happy
In the life that we have together
And I hope this happiness will last
In the life to come hereafter.

Shajan Miah

A Certain Sadness

I'm off to where my loved one lies
  before the bells of morning
I'll speak her name and hope again
  to hear her soft voice calling
Flowers where my sweetheart sleeps
  invite a questing bee.
and in the silent search it keeps
  it seems that bee is me
The hawthorn gently sighs for her
  the lilac heave's a sigh
The fir tree touched by sorrows breeze
  provides a moistened eye
I tell the nearby willow tree
  that shares my silent sorrows
of today a tiny island
  in a sea of no tomorrows

    L. Chatwin

Josephine

There's times you can annoy me,
There's times you make me cry.
There's times when I'm in heaven,
When I'm walking by your side.

We know we've something special,
Of that there's little doubt.
Our eyes can sometimes sparkle,
At home or when we're out.

I know I'm sometimes distant, Jo,
It seems I do not care.
But really Jo I want so much,
For us a home to share.

All of your love I'll never get,
And this I understand.
Your heart is up in heaven,
Where I'll take you by the hand.

    John Cosgrove

Penny

She was as cuddly as a teddy bear.
She ran walked and played.
She was tired after running
and in her bed she laid.

To me she was a cushion
so cuddly and fine.
The tears trickled down my
face, as I said goodbye.

Penny was a happy dog.
So lovely sweet and warm.
That special day had come to me,
when Penny had been born.

There is something I would
like to say, now that Penny
has gone away, I would love
to see her one more time,
I just wish there
was a way.

    Leanne Lesley Wylde

Caring

Who cares for the carers.
  Lonely, desperate.
Who cares for the carers.
  Tired, weary.
Who cares for the carers,
  Only themselves.
They care for others
  And have no life,
Who cares for the carers
Death cares for the carers
  The only respite.

    Robert Edgar Evans

Just Dreaming

Don't wake me yet,
I'm fond of this dream.
I'm seeing you smiling
Or so you seem.
Don't wake me yet,
It's so quiet here.
I'm seeing you laughing
And I want you near.
Don't wake me yet
Because I don't want to miss
Your gentle loving lips
And an enchanting kiss.
Don't wake me yet,
Because your arms are around me
Softly caressing my face
As we used to be.
Don't wake me yet,
But you whisper you love me,
You are fading away
And setting my heart free.

    Teresa Carlow

You

You are the sunlight in the dawn
Awakening minds that weep and mourn
You are the Fountain, soaring high
Sprinkling Truth and Love; and why?
Because every faller needs a helper
Every soiled path needs a broom
Every lost child needs a guide
And every strangling rose a prune
You are the helper
You are the broom
You are the guide
And, I am the prune!

    J. Parry

The Dream

The sun is shining in the sky.
The birds are flying way up high.
Wind rustles gently, through the trees.
As I dream of you, my sweet Louise.

Fair of face, and sweet of tongue
But oh, you are so young,
Your long brown hair, lies in a plat,
Coming halfway down your back.

As I sit beside the gentle stream,
Still of you Louise, I dream,
Childhood days full of fun,
How I loved, to see you run!

Sadly dream's don't lost for ever,
Not in our stars, we'd be together,
When I close my eyes, I see your face,
And no-one else will take your place.

    Mary Winifrid Taylor

"A Wife"

What is life without a wife?
It is just like a kitchen
without a knife
all struggle and strife
no one to rule.
You just feel blue.
Because you have not
got a clue.
To do the things you
would like to do.
A kitchen without a wife
is not much life
just like a kitchen
without a knife.

    E. J. Wheatley

Butterfly Wings

She was a shimmering butterfly,
To kiss her, he did try,
She danced away on Gossamer wings.
He followed clutching golden rings,
And watched her as she flew.

She wandered down summer lanes,
Her colours washed by gentle rains,
Aimlessly following, no direction.
Overawed by endless selection,
She didn't stop for long.

His eyes admired from afar,
like a planet does a star,
He stayed in orbit did not crowd,
Sometimes he heard her laugh too loud,
And knew it was him.

He had the occasional fling,
A relationship without a ring
Waiting for his butterfly to settle.
On a cactus, or a nettle,
But she never did.

    Ruth Gerring

Untitled

Mothering sunday is a lovely day
As we sing hymns, and all feel gay
God makes it such a happy time
It is so beautiful and sublime
We forget all our worries and strife
To give our children a happy life
And as we pray to God above
He surrounds everyone with his love

    Mary E. Hague

For My Daughter

Life is to live and not avoid
The passive stream of life
There is so much one can repair
But never lose the thread!

Put thoughts into the future now
And realize it is for you
Be yourself and find the plough
Just think and start the day anew

Tomorrow is another day
Do not despair there is a way
Which one will find when one
  descends upon the ray
Of sunlight on your mind

    Shirley Swinn

The Rooks

For all the things I wish I was
I'm glad I'm not a rook.
Because the man with gun he came,
Now I lay dead in the brook.

He shot and shot up into the air
My body he did hit,
And as I plundered to the ground
I prayed my babies in the nest did sit.

Who will feed them now I've gone
How will they survive,
Who will tell them I am dead,
Who will keep them alive.

I used to fly up in the clouds,
My shining feathers alight.
Now it's dark and cold, no sun,
Today is forever night.

    Christine Rowlands

Too Late

Trapped, by fire!
Wrapped in fear,
Danger here!
Sirens sounding near.

Painful breathing.
Chest, lungs, heaving
Consciousness leaving...

"Dead, I fear!"

C. A. Lee

Sunset Of Angels

Apricot clouds with a rosy hue,
Pale green patches turning blue,
Horizontal bands of red
Like ribbons gay stretch overhead;
Patches of rich deep purple too
Turning quickly to greyish blue,
Pink sugary clouds come sailing by
Like icing cakes across the sky.
And now, rich rainbow coloured bands
Wiped across with angel hands.
White gossamer angel wings unfold
All richly edged with shining gold.
Small dusty feet come dancing now
Ribboned to a multi-coloured plough;
Dark puffs of cloud from angel men
Smoking inside some angel's den,
Then burning fires hot mixed with gold
The heart of heaven itself; unfolds.
And as the sun's last rays depart,
I'm left with dull and faded art.

Nancy Worrall

In The Blink Of An Eye

In the prime of his life,
Dead, gone;
Taken away.
In the blink of an eye
Is what they say.

But what is the meaning
In a blinking eye?
It's a life;
A heartbeat.
It's from where I can't cry.

And what now would a heartbeat mean,
When the lid is shut
And the eye unseen?
Nothing now.
The lids are dry.
His eyes don't blink,
Don't move;
don't sigh.

Rachel Mann

The Flirt

How snug was I
Impeccable and safe
Blandly avoiding the trap
Measuring love for comfort's sake
Ignoring old lesions.

Inside a hundred seconds
The icing cracked.
A small caprice
A missed encounter
And pain came gnawing
Once again
Through pain delivered thoughtlessly.

How sly the sand
Heart's ease would build upon.

Ursula Warwick

The Dancing Champ

Easter Monday was the day
The holidays were under way,
A pint or two I had that night
Just to get the feeling right.

The irish league was my last call
I held the bar so not to fall,
Looking at the stage I saw
Some people dancing, watch them go.

It was an irish jig I found
Asking those who stood around,
One chap he stood out a mile
You could tell that he had style.

I asked the barman who's that there?
Dancing round he's light as air,
That's Jimmy Fegan didn't you know
The dancing champ of County Mayo.

Ronnie Howarth

A New Identity

I have pack my bags and I am
leaving, leaving this place I
used to call home, with all its
bitter memories, and what might
have been, I know I could never
live this down.

I am heading off into the
unknown and I am never going
back, I am going to assume a
new identity and take it
one step at a time.

Eve Paige

Eyesight

How green, how green is the grass.
God preserve to me my sight:
Gone would be sweet spring's delight
If the time should come to pass
When I could not see this grass,
Nor the insects crawling through,
Nor the airy sky's bright hue.
Not see wild violets grow
In the shade of thorn hedgerow,
Nor the lovely moving frieze
Of the skyline's bare-armed trees,
Tossed in young wood-scented breeze,
Nor the golden new-turned earth,
Ripe to give the grain re-birth.
If I could not see these things,
I should taste some bitter springs.
Therefore let my prayer be:
While I live, I also see.

C. A. Hutchinson

You're Mine

I miss you,
you're sleeping.
It hurts so,
I can't bear it.
You're so close,
yet so far apart.
Can I kiss you,
you're next to me.

Just a word,
in your ear.
Do you feel it,
are you scared of me.
I can see inside,
don't be frightened.
The reason that keeps me,
that your heart is mine...

Ruth Horner

This Time

Too much, too soon.
Anticipation of love and hot romance.
Desensitized by butterflies
And lot in hope and winning smiles
Of physical attraction.

Bemused by odd behaviour
Of one whose inane grins
Betray the truth.
The liberating warm content
That numbs the fear
Of pain
That could result.

But no, not time
To fear 'what if'
Instead a time to live and laugh
So just for now
Relax a while
Be happy
And enjoy
This time.

Avril Patterson

The Photo

Still, no movement,
Colours join together.
Smiling, joy, love
and happiness,
The date, time and place
Means so much.

Still, no movement,
Memories, kept forever
In the heart.
This still picture
Is the past, present
And the future.

Claire Wright

Blue Eyes Burning

You came to me one morning,
In the still and hazy light,
Your tiny form so perfect,
Your blue eyes burning bright.

You broke the peaceful silence,
Unsure and unaware,
Drifting into consciousness,
Your soul laid open and bare,

You can hear the voices,
You can feel the love,
Put your trust in me now,
And have faith in the world above,

The beauty that you radiate,
The joy and peace inside,
Your tiny fingers touch my heart,
Your life envelops mine.

You came to me one morning,
In the still and hazy light,
Your tiny form so beautiful,
Your blue eyes burning bright.

Elizabeth Kerry

Thoughts From A Window

When I look from my window,
Across the rising hills,
The rays of sunlight glisten,
On each and every peak,
I hear the lark that soars on high,
The rolling stream goes running by,
And time stands still, as if to say,
It's great to be alive today.

M. Dickin

555

Through The Eyes Of My Mind

I asked if he remembered
The time we went away,
He looked at me with tenderness
Not knowing what to say.

His eyes were bright and questioning,
He was waiting for a clue,
So gentle hints I offered him,
Well what else could I do?

I knew it would be difficult
Recalling where we stayed -
The country farm - the seaside town
The beach where children played.

And when the light began to dawn
Through my cajolery and tricks,
His face lit up - remembering -
Not easy when you're six.

Oh Nana, I do remember now,
But it was very hard to find
'Till I looked and saw our holiday
Through the eyes of my own mind

D. M. Rothery

Winter

Winter smiling palely bright
Trembles at Autumn's dying
Then clad in sables white
She rides the north wind sighing
Till hard beneath her breath
The earth grows cold.
Peaceful as in death
Wrapped in a snow white fold
A shroud bestrewn with Jewels
Cast from the virgin's breast.
Sad lady made more cruel
Autumn is dead and she is left.

Tom Gurney

My Child

I remember the day that you were born
And I held you in my arms
Nine pounds of lovely baby girl
Now, for you, I mourn
I thought that I would watch you grow
For many years to come
But fate said that was not be
And God knows I miss you so
You were so lovely and so bright
It really was a waste
That you should have to die so young
But not without a fight
You clung to life, so brave and true
For many painful hours
But then my love, you had to go
For Heaven wanted you

Mary Evans

Jasmine And Flowers

Perfumed jasmine - kissed with dew,
A token of my love for you.
Marble white like woodland dove,
To greet you with the dawn my love.

Pale bluebell - from leafy dell,
In golden hair to weave a spell,
around my heart forever, aye
arise - oh! sun - this is my day.

Blood red roses - sunset high,
Day is ended - moon hangs high
In your dear eyes I gaze and say,
Thank you for a lovely day.

M. M. Taylor

You May Say Equal

God says all men are created equal
That may be true
But women are ahead of you
From the wedding day on
They will sing their song
as long as you string along
But when the rivers run dry
She will run away
And leave you to cry
With the echo of that song
You thought you shared
Divorce day so near
And still shedding a tear
She will strip you bare
And not even the children to share
Children filled with poison and hate
Minds bent beyond repair
But they are too young to know
It was not I that had to go.

Paul Volante

Mother Tree

Rake the sky so wild and free,
Strip the bark upon the tree,
Burn the leaves that crown the top,
Hack its trunk they never stop,
Tree to stump a sight so grim,
Like a human's severed limb,
Plain is empty once was green,
People look they hadn't seen,
Metal came and bricks have won,
Mother Nature lost her son.

T. V. Lattimore

This Is...

This is my work
These are my words
This is a moment's thought.
This is my pen and paper
I write with and upon,
This is my hour
This is my day,
These are the words
I want to say.
This line is mine
The next one. Two
This line I think
I'll share with you.

This is a space
I've left above
In case I think
of Something good.
This is, the end
Or, is this, the start
Is this? Is This? This is!

Len Goodwin

No Need To Say Goodbye

A friendship like ours is hard to find,
It's a friendship made in heaven,
It's a world that's mine and yours,
That no-one can ever enter.
Even though we are worlds apart,
We are still together in our hearts,
You were there for me when I needed you
You wiped away my tears,
I don't need your memories to last,
As you live forever in my heart.

Majella Meade

Help Me

There is this vision.
This vision in my brain.
It's driving me, totally insane.
Because now.
I can see, the evil of men.
But I don't want to fight,
These criminals again.
Nobody don't know,
What I have to do.
It's to kill the criminals.
Or watch him?
kill you.

Melvin Williamss

Come With Me

Come come come with me
See all that I can see
Trees flower's birds and bees,

Young or old
Come with me,

You'll see his wonders here
That God has created

Have no fear,

Come come come with me
Wind rain gentle breeze
See them all touch the trees,
Trees bring life to us all

Don't chop them down
Don't be a fool

Or there be no life at all

B. M. Fuller

Upon Awaking From Sleep

The earth went to sleep;
Then it awoke bursting into glorious
Springtime, and nature became
Magnificent in all its beauty.

Jesus went to sleep;
Then he awoke in life eternal
Bursting into glorious resurrection
And radiating perfect love.

One day I will go to sleep
And when I awake Jesus will
Be there in all His glory
To welcome me home.

Joyce Marrable

Come Play

Come play - play with me
Tonight, tomorrow, all day long.
Your touch - a secret,
Never to be shared.
Your kiss - a taste.
Of a passion so great.

Come play - play with me
Tonight, tomorrow, all day long.
Your body - a toy,
I've always longed for.
Your heart - a place,
I can rest in.

Come play - play with me
Tonight, tomorrow, all day long.
Kiss me, tease me
Tempt me with your sin.
Come play - play with me
Tonight, tomorrow, all day long.

Tanya Richardson

Love

Meeting you
I feel there's so few
A rushy shiver
I welcome inside
All around
My frozen up mind
I feel so free
Like I could fly
I become so close
To your sparkly eye
I see life, fantasy and courage
In you
I hope you feel
The same way to
I know in the darkest doomy days
When life just seems
A changing face
I know that you are there for me
And forever eternity...

Samantha Blasdale

Mediocre Me

I'm not good looking
And I'm not tall,
But I'm not ugly
Nor am I small.

I'm not very clever
And my wits aren't quick,
But I'm not stupid
Nor am I thick.

I'm not well dressed
But I'm not scruffy,
I'm always tired
And my eyes are puffy.

I'm not very happy
But why should I be,
I'm just really rather boring
Mediocre me.

Fred Neville

Be My Lover

Let me be your lover
Let me be your dream
I want you to love me
In peace and harmony
I want to feel your heartbeat
So close to mine
That it'll be like one
We will both shine
Forever we shall last
Forever it shall be
The way you make me feel
The way you talk to me
The sparkle in your eyes
The cuteness of your smile
Give me one chance
And you will see
That we were meant to be together
For eternity

Sarah Green

Untitled

There is a start,
There is an end,
Unless the two combine
Which is fine,
That way, both parts remain
A chain - which links
Nothing sinks - but a
Circle joining
Has us rejoicing

Marjorie M. Wheeler

The Coldness Of Lung Cancer

In I creep, in I crawl
there my roots will spread
to cause such pain and illness
then weigh you down like lead.

I feel I'm grey and ugly
so in here I will hide
I'll break your strength to weakness
till nothing's left inside.

I'll grow as you will wither
in you I've always been
I thrive on nerves and worry
and deadly nicotine.

You may think you can stall me
or cut me with a knife
but I'll return to get you
and finally take your life.

J. Davidson

Seasons

Autumn is here,
There's a chill in the air,
Leaves on the ground
Branches all bare.
Soon the hard frost
Will cover the earth.
Birds find shelter
As they twitter and chirp.
Then it is Christmas,
Windows aglow
With trees and baubles
And cotton wool snow.
But let us remember,
Amidst all the joy,
The birth, long ago
Of a dear baby boy.
Born to be our saviour,
He gave up his life.
Think of him now,
And let peace take over from strife.

Jean Petty

Last Thoughts

Once I had a future
I was brave and I was strong
years took that away
and they just keep moving on.

I see people from my window
for me they care a lot
a young bay and his mother
will stay forever in my thoughts.

You see I am now old
my body feels the pain
I would like to leave this world
so I may live again.

Please understand my friends
pray God my soul to take
but another year has started
so this decision I must make.

I sit down by the river
I have known for many years
I think of those who love me
as I cry my last few tears.

Madeline Mullan

Untitled

The city awakes,
Traffic stirs
amidst the hustle bustle of the day
expectations, hopes and fears
award the weary traveller.

May Walker

The Echo

I lie awake at night and
Listen to the echo of the day
The sound of birds still
Touch upon my ears
Earth's heady perfume swirls
And curls at will
Face still flushed
With summer's sun
The glory of the day
Lives on behind my eyes

Patricia Kelly

Waiting

The clock ticks,
Echoes through a lonely house,
Lying here I wait,
Wait for sleep to come,
To take over.

I wait to be led,
Led by the hand,
Deep into a world of mystery.
A time of enchantment,
Flying over rooftops,
Staring in the face of death.

So I wait.
Wait for sleep to come.

Emma Boolaky

So It Ends

All but a few lines
in time go by.

And Arthur king and arch.
Warlord Duke of Britain
Passes by and passes
On.
Merlin and Lancelot and
Palermeads and also Bedwean
Guinevere and as time and
The mists of Avalon come
and go.

This part of our heritage
and History goes but leaves
its mark for all
to see.

England oh England if
only
You could be again the
place that you once
were.

Malcolm Form

A Smile

A smile it is a funny thing!
It wrinkles up your face!
And when it's gone, you never find its
Secret hiding place?
Far but better and wonderful it is!
To see what a smile can do.
You smile at one - he smiles at you.
And so "one" smile makes two.
If we noticed little pleasures
As we notice little pains.
If we quite forgot our losses!
And remembered all our gains;
If we'd look for people's virtues,
And their faults refused to see!
What a Happy, friendlier place
This world of ours would be?

B. Gilman

Life Passes By

It all seems like a dream
Those years that came between,
Days full of love and glee,
That's how life was for me!

A baby from the war,
(But glad it was no more)
Living in peace again
Together did remain.

Days at school came and went,
Then on to training sent,
Work came, and money too,
Life was rushing me through!

Time came for married bliss,
Then boy and girl - our wish,
Now grown up - moved away
Yet still around today!

Now I am all alone
My husband, too, has gone,
Yet, I have thoughts and dreams
Life's not quite what it seems.

H. R. Stuart

Untitled

I met him once
He came to collect
I think
One cold dark tragic night
Dimly collected sound
The smoke, the heat, the fright
I lay and prayed
For strength, for air
Faint images of light
He was there
Beneath the thatch with me
I felt his breath
Cold and black
I struggled, the weight upon my back
And then a hand, a voice
Whose I cannot say
I did not need to see him go
I felt him shrug
Then turn and slowly walk away

J. P. Platt

Pica In A Western Jamaican Woman

I am gnawing my way very slowly
through my daughter's miniature
Nigerian soapstone rabbit
I have already eaten the rhino
the elephant is next in line

Why the urge? How long possessed?
What prehistoric desires
link with ancestors, dust to dust?

The musk of newly rained earth
made my mouth water
as a child, and still does

Going towards Eastbourne in the train
the sight of a chalk cliff face
stirred up longing
like for chocolate or sex
for living or for dying

Like all these things
I could do without
my piece of soil
but I will always want

Audrey West

"Stolen Dreams"

Each night I have a visitor who steals from me my dreams.
He will not let them see the daylight, or to me that's how it seems.
But one night he was disturbed, as he was sweeping through my mind,
As he fled into the darkness, a split second of a dream was left behind.
It was only a very small fragment, perhaps a fleeting glance,
Of a brilliant flighted halcyon, sitting on a branch.
And gentle ripples on a secret pond, where the sunbeams danced upon.
The majestic flowers swayed with the rhythm their cares all now long gone.
Then a strange exotic sunlight through overhead leaves filtered down,
Enhancing every shade of their yellows, green and brown,
As a million glittering rainbows the light was shining through
Every single crystal drop of the early morning dew.
But the stealer of my dreams, he has hidden them well out of sight,
As I search the cobwebs of my mind, one day they may come to light,
From my pen the stolen dreams would then begin to flow,
And the poignant tenure of my dreams would set the page aglow.
This stealer of my dreams he knows of my despair,
The other aspects of my life he neither feels or cares,
For never on his visits steals, my grim grotesque nightmares.

R. V. Denton

The Unknown Awaits

Empty faces staring ominously out of windows gently glazed with frost,
Inquiring minds exploring the world which lies outside their door.
What goings-on are there looming in the lives of passersby?
Only the snug harshness of life indoors reveals itself to those
sheltered inside;-
Inside those leering walls of cement. But do these walls protect?
Or do they really block out that vital knowledge which lies outside;
Preventing closeness between families, and contact between
neighbours.
Only the unknown lies outside those frosted panes of glass...

People wander aimlessly among unfamiliar streets,
Curiously obscured to those indoors.
Each is trapped in a world of desolate desperation.
No voices of comfort cry out, only the isolated footsteps of nearby strangers.
And to these the indoor world is hidden,
A parallel universe where others sleep and eat alone.
Yet somewhere in the vast unknown two people lie together,
Their lives intertwined, unseen by those outside.
Innocence protected from the alienated race outside.
Enclosed by warmth and love
and still outside
the unknown awaits.

Emma O'Hare

It's....

What is the essence up-holding existence, is it of time, yet timeless?
It's the spirit within On - beyond the physical - yet of it.
It's the sound found within silence - the unseen, within the seen.
It existed before the first seed, yet is the first seed.
It's within the microcosm that germinates the microcosms.

It formed the foundation from which its envoys, between water, fire, earth, and sky, flow.
It's in the light that illuminate the darkness; seasons, days, bows down before it.
It's the shadow passing the sun; cry of the new born, hues clothing the rainbows.
It's the early morning bird song; the dew that gently crowns the earth.
The lake that walks, yet, goes nowhere.

Its desires are fulfilled, allowing minds to flower, to seek freedom.
It instils knowledge - causes the mind, hand, to work at its command.
It's the drumbeat, kernel, that gives birth to language, civilization, and kingdoms.
It's in the breeze that moves the prayer flags - 'will' is under its control.
Forms, boundless, the instruments upon which it plays its music.

It resides within contemplation - is the many within the whole.
It's tangible, yet transient - the limitless within the ever lasting now.
It's within the order that controls chaos.
Is in the 'I' of 'me,' exulting the power of the omnipotent mind.
It is the ultimate - supreme - 'I am,' of all existence - spirit life.

P. Tebay

Bedtime

A limp lettuce,
I sprawl between the sheets
Of my bed-sandwich.
A tired filling,
I lay my head on the
Soft crust of my pillow.
Only too happy to
Let the night sink its teeth in,
Munch, and regurgitate me
Unceremoniously
In the morning.
Charlotte Coleman

Animal Lover

As I was walking through the heather
They wordily creatures you discover.
You meet a fox and then a toad
When you walk down the road.
The fox that is so clever. The wild
Horse you could not tether.
Many a grey squirrel dashes by, but
Not a red one caught my eye.
Would it be that I discover when the
Pheasant flies for cover
That all creatures great and small
Will answer to my call
E. A. Lane

Winter

Hooves on cobbles set in ice
The icy spears hang down
Slashing through
The rose-coloured dusk
Like strange rays of light

At noon the dull sky
Is traced with tree-black,
Spidery.
Paler and remote
Swings the lamp
Of the sun.

All is quiet
Awaiting the dark
But after that
The dawn.
Anna Seifert

Thoughts

The singer's voice so rich and pure
Rang out for all to hear,
A theme of love and hope so sure
Ambitions nought to fear.

I took the road to anywhere
As freedom's choice seemed right,
And met life's tapestry full square
And changed with all my might.

Success it came as such it is;
So far across the foam
The marching years brought an abyss,
My memories of home.

The town seemed smaller so much so,
Old parents both were gone,
Our house, the school that I did know
Are thoughts that still live on.

My infant fell then rose again
His world seems heaven sent,
Persistent trials are surely sane
And fearless wonderment.
Alex Winter

Adrift

The world is such a lonely place, without you being here,
Oh, how I long to feel your touch, to hear your voice so dear.
You were always such a comfort through the "ups and downs" of life.
And singing "My Old Dutch" to me, made me proud to be your wife.
You always said that "life is sweet and every day a gift"
I try so hard to think like this - but - my moorings are adrift.
We found such sweet contentment, in everything we shared,
We didn't have to speak at all, to know each other cared.
Now you are in Heaven-and God is by your side,
I hope there's golf and horses and much, much, more besides.
You are softly, safely, sleeping and there is no such thing as time,
But God will say "Come to me" one day, then we'll close the Great Divide.
Margaret Standen

An Alternative - Heads Or Tails

For Colin

As spontaneous our first meeting went, with fervour strong and intentions meant,
We found our conversation flowed, and wanton needs physically showed,
But still our minds could not say yes, for reasons, ourselves, separate but lest
We are so different, but in effect the same for desiring each other; then what's to blame
For pulling apart something so new, no time to find it could all be true,
But just as mentioned in words afore, relating to history, what's happened before,
Take away the prejudice actively shown, else we might find days spent alone,
And that my darling is too much to bear, to never discover how much we care,
Perhaps this really was never to be, and into the future I cannot see,
Life already is a struggle to breathe, our senses need to abandon and leave,
About impulsion when we were young, and the consequences? Got to be done,
An age we are at, should we play around, or settle our lives on more even ground?
Whatever the answer, no matter what, don't let this position be only our lot,
For deservedly more both should expect, rewards of ourselves, no more to collect.
Michelle Dance

A Tribute To Jane Austen And Pride And Prejudice

Dear Jane, we owe you such a debt and one that we will not forget.
You took us back to gentler days with all their simple country ways,
And parents children young and old, they flocked to watch your tale unfold.
Sweet 'Lizzie' with her surly swain, yet what a Hero he became!
And though' he was an utter snob he made all Maidens hearts to throb!
And wasn't Lizzie quite superb the way she dealt with Lady de Bourgh.
And what about that 'oily' Parson who Lizzie found so very tiresome.
And here I have no qualms in stating He really was quite nauseating.
That silly Mother with senseless chatter about things that really did not matter.
Poor Father he had much to bear, though' he was really quite a dear!
Then there was nice sister Jane, they called her good looking, I called her plain!
The younger sister, she went astray and caused the family great dismay.
But 'Darcy' to the rescue came, and all was very well again.
In the end we were made to see how he won over his Bride-to-be.
Oh, T.V. Producers cannot you learn that for more of these plays most of us yearn,
Instead of the Violence, Sex and Crime which come on the Screen time after time.
Mary Hayward Browne

Found

Nervously at first and yet, willing to try a new start.
The only way forward is to take the step, to be free from the pain in your heart.
Through the shadows comes the light, and at first it hurts your eyes.
So used to darkness of living in grey, to be hurt by the light's no surprise.

Then as the rays begin to flow,
Slowly at first till you're used to the glow.
You see things in a different light,
The world around you begins to look bright.
Now instead of living in constant dread,
You start to look forward to the future ahead.
You see how much of life you've missed, you see how much you're worth,
Your heart is filled with a sense of love, at the miracle of your rebirth.

No one can take that away from you, you've got it till the end,
And with it comes the heartfelt warmth, of finding your own best friend.

Someone who you can depend on, to stand by with a love that's true.
Who'll stay at your side no-matter what, the best friend you've found is in you.
And now no-matter what life brings, you'll not face it on your own.
You'll see it through and you'll survive, and you'll never be alone.
Christina Taylor

The Lily

My favourite flower if I were asked
Would be a Lily fair,
She is so regal and sedate
With head high in the air.
And on a gentle summer breeze
She nods her pure white crown,
Then wafts her fragrance round about
To cast away your frowns.
All who see her hesitate
Their praises have no end,
Again she nods as if to say
"But you are all my friends!"
She cheers the saddest faces
And should I be so bold,
To say - you can't be miserable
When her beauty you behold.

Joyce T. Newman

Untitled

I love the English countryside
Hedgerows flourish, rabbits hide

Fields and fields of corn around
Tiny hamlets to be found

The pace is leisurely it seems
Time to hold on to your dreams

The local pub, the village pond
Things of which I'm very fond

People are so friendly here
Time to talk; no stress or fear

This air so fresh will do for me
There's no place I would rather be.

Brinley Jones

Faith

The world was peaceful long ago,
no need to fear,

Then came wars and people dying,
people killing far and near,

Racism between blacks and whites,
Jews and other faiths,

People starving,
getting cold.

All losing their faith.

Katie Lamb

The Four Seasons

Spring flowers shake their sleepy heads
Buds yawn and stretch along the branch
Blossom a shower of confetti
Birds two by two with love in mind

Sizzling sun with happy memories
Cornfields a golden glow
Earth baked hard and crisp
Laden fruit trees with aching arms

Autumn trees raging in the winds
Rain thunders to the ground
Snow scratch past the window panes
Streams flow like small veins

The earth a blanket of snow
Birds flying snowballs
Lakes frozen mirrors
Icicles a fringe of crystal
A frozen silence

Phyllis Baldwin

Untitled

The life span of an average Gnome is about 400 years!
We've been around forever and we see things very clear.
We're often asked why do we smile? And now's the time to tell.
You humans just confuse us, and we don't know you very well!
We've lived through your wars a disputes but we've never understood,
why the young are forced to fight them, when those who start them never would.
Why make your artists and poets famous, but mainly when they're dead?
Yet ignore their talents when they were living and ignore what they had said.
You say you love all creatures, and that you really care.
Why then do we tend so many, caught up in your snares?
We nurse all wounded creatures - some wounded by your gun!
And why chase the fox, until it drops - in the name of sport and fun?
Why waste your time with quarrels - all that pressure - all that
strife? Learn the great importance of a happy, contented life.
So, next time you see a Garden Gnome, please, don't ignore his smile.
And although many of you may not like us - at least admire our style.
We're happy and contented, because really, there's a need
To learn to live together in a world that has no greed!

Les Clark Jr.

May 1996

When I was young the world was good, we used to play Robin Hood
Cowboys and Indians, and pirates too, I saw the world as children do.
The snows of winter held no chill, frosted windows made me thrill
For out there in that world of white I could have a snowball fight
And snowmen with their coal black eyes, watched over us; there were no sighs
Just squeals and shouts from having fun, as we hurtled down the sledging run
The fastening sleds on ponies backs, we led them up the powdery tracks
Until we reached the top and then! Careered back downhill again
At night beside a crackling fore, we watched the snow grow higher and higher
And knew that when the morning came, all of today would be the same
The world again a crisp white sheet, only touched by fairy feet.

I'm older now, though not yet old, the world it seems so very cold
No care or kindness from anyone, too many clouds! Can't see the sun
The place seems evil, it feels so bad, can you wonder why I'm so sad
But: is it me, or is it you, do I still see the world as children do.

Maggie Craig

Life?

Shouldn't life begin at forty? If that's the case it's late,
Perhaps I should have thrown a party? But then who would I invite?
My mother, father, nanna, my brother and his wife,
I really don't have many friends, my children are my life.
They, the business and our home, keep me busy through the day,
But my evenings I spend all alone, and I'm just not made that way.
I know life won't knock at my front door, I don't expect it to,
Still I've looked and tried till my heart is sore,
I don't know what else to do.
If life is truly what we make of it, I must have the wrong recipe.
I've put everything I have into it, where is that someone who'll love me.
Someone to share those quiet hours, when the children are asleep,
The companionship which blooms and flowers, when love is true and deep.
Someone with whom to laugh and smile, support each other should we cry.
Sometimes together, sometimes apart,
Yet never lonely, for in our hearts, we would share our thoughts and dreams.

Ann Whittington

Across The Miles

I sit and gaze thro' checked windows, into a dark and starless night,
Across the miles, across the oceans, my mind floats out - I think of you,

In this room, which is my ship, I steer my course to battle through
All my worries, all my heartaches, my mind is drained - I journey to you.

You are with people you should be with, your friends, your family, a life to you,
In your voice, I hear a happiness, my mind is worried, but - I'm glad for you.

When you speak, you sound so happy, but out comes sounds - strange from you
Or is it really how it should be, my mind is questioned - I'm sad for you.

When you're so far from me, I'm lonely, lost and so afraid,
yes dear friend, you do effect me, my mind is quite - I'm missing you.

So I sit, gazing thro' these windows, it's still a dark and starless night,
Across those miles, across those oceans, my mind still floats - I dream of you.

David Turner

Storm's Wife

Storm brewing in a tea pot
all day long,
stains all over the tablecloth
from hurled and full things,
all down the nets.
The table could be in high seas,
pitching, tossing, wobbling under adamant
fists.
She, braving the thunder cracks,
rides the storm with her nose up
like a periscope to save herself from
drowning.
Even baby Storm wails and rages
all day long.
She hears nothing
but as if a sea shell had been placed
at her ear, comes the sound of her life
slowly heading for the rocks.

Susan J. E. Fowler

Harry Pointing The Way

Turning handle to baying alarm
Escort sighted brings tranquil calm;
With trembling excitement passion shows.
Venturing outdoors fondness grows.

With fatherly nature and stoutly figure,
Crosses sands with surprising vigour;
Amidst heathery shades and prickly gorse,
Continues onwards with daily course.

With discerning head and raised tale
Riveted stance depicts sculptured hale;
With fur flecked and black patches,
Nose twitching, rabbit matches.

Returns fatigued, impatiently hums,
Raises paws like beating drums;
Ascending stairs with hungered pace,
Dined and contented, has smiling face.

Dennis Peter Nicolle

To Wonder Why

I often think and wonder why.
Things couldn't be better if we try,
A helping hand, a listening ear,
To give some hope to those who fear.

I've seen the pictures on T.V.,
Of children starving and misery.
When battles rage and cause such plight,
God only knows that can't be right.

It's hard to see what we can do,
Knowing all they are going through.
If only to take away the sorrow,
And give them all a new tomorrow.

Our thoughts go with them everyday,
And least of all we can but pray
That they'll get courage and strength to find,
A happier life and peace of mind.

Robert Connor

The Blessing

Days loveliest gown - the cloak
of velvet night adorned with stars
of brilliant profusion,
like new souls from earth shine
forth last benedictions
and come the dawn pass on
into the eternal light
of heaven.

Jeannine Anderson Hall

A Widow's Prayer

Lord, give me light to guide me through the darkness of my sorrow,
Give me hope that I may cope till there dawns a brighter 'morrow.
Help me through the lonely days and more so, lonely nights,
Take me from these saddened 'lows', help me reach the heights,
Give me strength that I may face the life that lies ahead,
Without my 'love', how shall I be, the thought holds nought but dread.

I loved him then, I love him now, I'll love him evermore,
I'll love my darling always as much as ever before
So Lord, give me a dream that it will seem that he is beside me still,
Until I meet my love again on some other brighter hill.

Nancy Castle

An English Rose

This beautiful flower, the English rose, renowned throughout the world,
In spring it buds and under warm May sun, its splendour is unfurled,
Its summer bloom comes in many hues, each as wondrous to behold,
But the autumn mist gives it jaded look, and it dies in winter's cold.

This heavenly creature, the English rose, so pure and undefiled,
In the spring of early life she blooms, from babe to innocent child,
Too soon to tell though at this time, no sign one way or the other
Some will say she's like her father, and others like her mother.

In the season of her youth she grows, with elegance and poise.
Although she is but one of the girls, she has centre stage with the boys,
During her summer years she blossoms, more lovely with each day,
Catching eyes wherever she goes, and desired in every way.

The autumn of her life arrives, much too quickly, alas, it seems,
And though she has lived it to the full, she has not fulfilled her dreams,
The lines of age are showing now, but her beauty still remains,
Mature and confident she's seen it all, the losses and the gains.

Time's harsh winter takes its toll, the lines much deeper now,
Age is showing around her mouth, and on her furrowed brow,
But our flower still has no equal, for true beauty never lies,
And the memory of this rose will linger, beyond the day she dies.

Maurice Bingham

In A Darkened Room

My feelings that morning, as I staggered round yawning; just nerves
crashing through me in torrents, like never before, I thought more and
more, had men openly signed their death warrants, the mirror on the
shelf, where I glanced at myself, offered a reflection with black,
tired eyes, I turned away quickly feeling haggard and sick, but the
state I was in... no surprise, as much as I tried, my head thumping
inside, to remember the course of that night's events, with my mind
in a daze, memories clouded in haze, odd recollections just didn't
make sense, I had no excuse, to lie was no use; the drink was not
solely to blame, I'm sure she first approached me, or so says memory,
but that was incredibly tame, so I sat down and waited, directing
anger and hatred at myself for the way I had acted, the only sound in
our home was my heart's thudding tones; a key turned in a look.... I
retracted, so quietly she entered, her mind tensely centred, on what
she had, no doubt, been told, I saw the
tears that she'd shed glisten under eyes in an expression so cold,
her near inaudible voice whispered I didn't have any choice but to
let her go her own separate way. Throwing down her gold ring, she
packed up her things, walking out with no more left to say, as I
retrieved that small ring, it didn't really sink in, and I expected
her to walk back through the door, then reality loomed and in that
darkened room, I realized I would see her no more, is that all it
takes, just one drunken mistake, for a relationship to come to a
close? Slowly closing my eyes, the picture come in my mind of the
night I finally proposed, her face lit up with pure pleasure, a
memory I'll treasure; she said yes, I was stunned and wide-eyed, that
joy and elation is now a past celebration and alone in that
room....how I cried.... I'm not ashamed
to admit... how I cried....

Philip O'Day

Dreams

Dreams can be really good,
Dreams can be really bad.
Dreams go round,
Extremely fast in a bag.
They jump in and out,
Of your empty brain.
This is why they are big pains.
Dreams can be happy,
Dreams could be sad.
Either one of the two,
I mostly dream of good news.
I hate dreaming about family,
As it always panics me.
I hate to wake up,
To find I am alone.
Parents all the time,
Are in a world of their own.
I try to make them notice me
This can not always be!

Katy Tye

Untitled

I never knew what was in store
Until you came a knocking on my door
I looked down and saw your case
You'd come to move into my place

Come hold me tight in your embrace
Until there's not a single trace
Of sadness, pain or any tears
Lets make the most of all the years

We'll hold our heads up with pride
Now at last, we're side by side
We've loved each other for so long
This must be our own love song

I give to you, all my heart
Never, never more to be apart

Penelope June Schoobridge

Deep Sea

A deep sea diver that is me
magnetic pull to waters deep
yearning to go beneath the sea,

Where Neptune waits in raptures sweet
ethereal addiction flow
and Davy Jones his locker keep.

Pandora's box is there I know
Intoxicating, lures me in
my piscean friends told me so.

To revel in such sumptuous sin
into the womb of mother earth
where many forms of life begin.

Evolution to name gave birth
this deep sea diver found its worth.

Margareth Richards

On Ice

The wine, in its bucket, was waiting,
Two glasses were there, side by side,
I was dressed up in my Sunday best,
Bristling almost with pride.

None of us knew you'd deserted,
Wouldn't come as you'd promised to do,
That the words I'd rehearsed
Would stay locked in my head,
On ice, like the wine, without you.

Joyce Walker

'Two Small Tears'

 With outsize shoes and baggy pants - he'd stride the circus ring,
With a cheeky smile and a big, red nose - he'd stride the ring - a king.
 For the solid sound of laughter was music to his ears,
He did not speak and on his cheek were painted two small tears.

 His life and love was his love for life, with a grandly painted smile....
His clowning and his antics seem to lift him for a while,
 He was quite the funniest of all the clowns - he'd played the part for years.....
Always on his face a smile - on his cheek the two small tears.

Then one show, quite some years ago - as he made the audience roar,
 The show was filled with laughter, but his heart could give no more
For he'd lost Marie that fateful night and his one and only son,
 And to the sound of cheers and laughter, he bid the show go on.

He gave his greatest performance, he sent the big top wild,
The tent was packed, but through his act saw only on his wife and child,
 He did not hear the finale, the acclaim or the shouts and cheers,
On his ashen face, a knowing smile.... on his cheeks were two small tears.

Tony Armitage

Christ's Incarnation, The Miracle Of Love, Emmanuel

Are we not made by God - His Noble Image - Our Holy Predestination
To freely accept His gift of life and limb with mutual appreciation!
But in return, alas! We disobey and yield to passions and desecration.
Who will rescue us? Jesus Christ, Son of God, Son of Mary, Our Expiation.

You took upon Yourself, O Lamb of God, our sin, our blame, our shame;
Such Love all compelling, such Love all excelling, to restore our name.
Jesus Christ, Son of God, Son of Mary, God Incarnate, in grief and pain,
You paid the price, you restored our life, may your Kingdom reign.

Who can grasp the height, the depth, the breadth of love and life so sublime?
Not enough He should descend as one of us so amazing, holy and divine.
Jesus Christ, Son of God, Son of Mary, His Spirit within us for all time,
And His very Own Self in food and drink, in consecrated Bread and Wine.

Let's raise our hands in praise and worship and humble adoration!
Let's raise our voices with hymns in awe and wonder and proclamation!
To Jesus Christ, Son of God, Son of Mary, our thanks and jubilation,
Behold a Holy People, the Spirit's Power, Destined for His Glory,
 A New Creation!

J. Henkel

Untitled

This is the story of Lancaster Court, where flats are sold and can be
bought idyllic surroundings or so it would seem, you've got to go
back once you have been

Our tale begins with the passing of years, and a colony of lepers
brought here with their tears a hospital near there had to be which
now the White Lion with its long history

Lancaster Court then came into being with the original gate and
wall still there for the seeing the old with the modern is now what we
have but who can fault this building we brag

But......

The corridor stalker rings bells in the night and with fleet of
foot as the shroud is of white the shadows are whispery as they make
there, where howlers they howl and spirits they wail

It is a ghost of years gone by, of a lonely leper who lived nearby
or is it a mortuary figure unveiled, escaped from the coffin in which
he was nailed or could it be Mistress Nutter of Witch Trial fame of is
it a poltergeist playing a game it could be a leper whom they once
called 'Old John', letting us know that he has not yet gone

The lights they do flicker and make shadows on floors, the spirits
of night glide past rattling doors the ringing of bells goes on 'til
the dawn, whom ever it is, we will meet in the morn

Take heed then if ever you hear this defective, call at once for
the 'In House Detective' It's time that this nuisance was told to abort
and happiness shall reign once more at the Court.

Dorothy Nicholas

Sun Homage

What jewel rare from deepest mine
Could lustre deeper or outshine
Apollo's beam of bright blonde hair,
Aurora's golden eyesight fair.

Deepest blush on fairest cheek
Pales before dusk's crimson peaks,
Spreading radiant purples and golds,
No artist's pallet could ever hold,

See Phoebus kiss clouds rose pink,
Gathering near they watch him sink,
With vermilion fingers beds them down,
Flushing red orange in sunset's crown.

Chariots of ruby commanded by dawn,
Inflames horizon at break of morn.
Celestial pearls of lavender fire,
To fill man's eye and soul inspire.

Freely he paints his Azure sky,
Glowing embers for you and I,
The truest phoenix risen from flame,
To brighten our darkest hour again.

Anthony Ashman

Dreams

Our dreams of life are but a thread
as delicate as a spiders web
once broken, it is no more.
These dreams are precious and our own
for a future yet unknown
I lay my dreams beneath your feet
for you and all the world to keep.
Tread softly, softly
lest you break the silken threads
and forever live in dread
of what might have been
without my dreams.

Joy Orchard

Hope And Delight

Exdous my people to share the light
The clouds have broken
And in comes the light
Whirling clouds up so high
Separating as the light passes by
Only I see the flicker of hope
And delight as the clouds pass by
Hope and delight has come to stay
To wish us an our merry way
The light beams for us all to see
The path we go to see thee.

Denise Thomson

Hear This Despot

It thinks itself a bird
The butterfly of varied colours
For that it challenges the kite
Flight is the game,
So they did fly
But the thorns made
A rag of the butterfly

It wriggles like the snake
And swims like the cobra
The snake fish of smooth skin
And so decides to hunt with snakes
But when the snakes find not a game
They feast on the snake fish

He parades himself like a God
The tyrant of battered conscience
And makes his subjects groan with pains
But let him not beat his chest
Lest he crumbles from his height
Crest-fallen like the rain-drenched rat

Solomon O. Iguanre

Bus Stop Waiting

Diamond shiny sparkles glint and glitter, spearing nose and throat.
Ice sheen, icing sugar frosting, on pavement, road and window ledge.
Peering through cold-watered eyes for the oblong warm bubble rising up the road.
Eager to rest numb feet on a heating tube,
Relax tired, shivering muscles within the soft, body-dampened air.

The moderate sun, dipping behind the facades, decides on one last fling,
Leaping from windows and dancing across stonework.
Long shadows cross the road, clamber up bright walls;
lambent clouds traverse a tricolour sky.
A fresh breeze chases the waning sunlight, pirouetting with a paper bag.

The gutter lies dredged with dust; insect tracks criss-cross the sandy veneer.
Baked air, thick with fumes sweat and flies, torches mouths. Later
The clink and chatter of the cafe drifts over Friday night crowds,
Melds with the murmur of people meeting, revellers hailing companions;
A delighted squeal fades into memory, and somewhere, the diminuendo of
a motorbike burr adds its cadence to the evening's rhapsody.

Clouds look overhead, muddy black, like slushy, dirty, trampled, half-melted snow.
Aircraft shuttle between them, dragging transitory vapour trail threads
That expand and merge into the atmospheric tapestry like watercolour on wet paper.
Sluggish drizzle dampens the concrete; a lamp flickers into pink-red life.

Richard Winpenny

Mortality?

When a dying man lies dormant, there is much we do not know;
Does the brain live on in torment when the blood has ceased to flow?
  Is the character reposing as they sound the funeral knell?
If the mind was one of vigour, must its knowledge then be lost?
When the flesh is cold with rigor is the soul benumbed with frost?
  While the corpse is decomposing, is the intellect as well?
When a thinking man lies dying, it would seem a little odd
Were it just the body trying to appear in front of God;
  Is it but a chapter closing with the toll of heaven's bell?
  Only dead folk know the answer, only dead folk never tell!

Is there nought but dark oblivion for all that he has been?
Is there nothing to revivify what he has done and seen?
  Does the virus or the cancer finish aught within the shell?
Though he lived as a believer, there is still a vexing doubt:
  Life may not go on forever after death has laid him out,
  Is there none but the romancer who can rise from where he fell?
Though the voice be quiet and wordless with the final gasp for breath
Do the thoughts flow on regardless through the currency of death?
  Will there be another stanza out of paradise - or hell?
  Only dead folk know the answer. Only dead folk never tell.

Rodney Barnett

The Tapestry Of Touch

On our journey to the grave from the cradle,
We experience innately, as soon as we are able
A whole plethora of contact... a tapestry of touch.
When other senses fail, it still conveys so much.

The caring, protective arm placed around elderly kin.
The kiss of the surgeons knife, enabling new life to begin.
The street urchin absorbing the bustling comfort of the exhausted nun.
The pulsating pain of reviving feet that were cold, blue and numb.

The cleansing of the virgins bath and the prostitutes evening douche.
The child smearing on mummy's make-up, while the clown rubs on rouge.
The trembling flutter of a puppy, whose excitement begins to grow.
The prick of tears when a lover turns to go.

The skilled craftsman's dextrous hands needing no luck - Touch wood!
The inspiration stimulated by the gifted, the great and the good.
The easy horse-play of brothers bound by cord from the same womb.
The humane hand that eases us at last into the welcome tomb...

Linda Miller

Untitled

The bright summer sea embraces the shore
They dance together a stately quadrille
He gently moves toward her then he retreats
A little closer each time until she's won over
The bright summer sea is a tender lover

The cold winter sea is a violent lover
He batters the shore and shouts his anger
The stones on the sea shore tumble and fall
In their haste to run away from it all
He rapes the shore then throws her aside
The sea doesn't want a passive bride

Summer and winter sea and shore
Life is exciting or a terrible bore
Tender and loving violent and cruel
Love in its guises is always surprising
So beloved when you come to me
Love me gently, gently as the summer sea

Sheila P. Shaw

Waiting For The Bus

I stand here waiting, on a cold, wet morning,
Outside the shelter, the rain is pouring,
Cars go by, out on the road,
Birds above fly, the traffic has slowed.
The rain is slowly turning to sleet,
Gathering round my frozen feet.

Up the road the bus is coming,
I can now see, that it's service number 3.
A shabby little bus, an old single decker,
But you can't complain, at least it came.
It pulls up beside the small little shelter,
The bus is coloured blue, none of them have a clue.

Thinking what's ahead, what lies in front,
Another whole day's work, what is the point?
Who made school? Why was it made?
Who was that fool? My ideas fade.
The bus drives off moving from home,
I'll have to get off soon, but I'd like to stay on.

Chris Jansen

First Day Of Lent

'Where are you from?' The Parish Priest
asked with friendly interest as
I, not finding a match,
hesitated near the alter on
the afternoon of Ash Wednesday.

Where am I from? That's not a big
problem, I am clear on that point.
Where I am going, or
if I've arrived yet is
something quite different.

But just for this moment,
To light up a candle is
what I am here for,
To leave a small radiance.

Daphne Kirkpatrick

The Missing Link

I could never find that missing piece,
for years — what country was it again?
So the jigsaw hung there with its gap gaping.
It spoke of a loss much deeper —
then the game of a puzzle.
    Unsolved indeed it stayed
until you came.
"What's this wedged into your sanded floorboards?"
Blond tuft of hair falling in your ocean blue eyes,
I reframed it and rehung it in my bedroom where,
Your eyes reflected in the glass and smiled.

Lisa Ellis

Demon's O' Hindmaist Day

Nae food nae water, only starvation,
Nae Angel's nor Sanct's, for oor salvation.
Devotin' his time tae life's damnation,
Unhailie nemesis tae God's creation,
Famine, killer o' land's his only station.

Surrounded by rottan's, guided by flies,
Poustit an' pain wi' pitiful cries.
Disease I spread by touch an' air,
Smilin' wi' glee for I dinna' care.
Pestilence, fore'er waitin' within his lair.

Encased in armour fae head tae foot,
Nae sign's o' life thro his metal suit.
Wi' airmy's at battailze, wi' glaive in hand,
Taken' men's souls at Sathen's demand.
War, on constant watch thro, out the land.

Cloak as umbrakle, dark as night,
Since birth wi' us a constant fight.
Followin' alway's wi' hand on scythe,
Fore'er waitin' tae take yer life.
Death, gaither'er o' the dead on Hindmaist Day.

Stuart McAllister

Yesterday's Hero

His shoulders now more rounded
    than the tunic he once wore,
No more military two-steps,
    no more sweeping 'cross the floor.
Yesterday he stalked the battlefields,
    he courted ladies fair
Now robbed of youthful vigour,
    and imprisoned in his chair.
Is that why the young so mock him?
    and why they paint in scorn,
Can't they see his body's broken?
    Can't they see his banner's torn?
Once he was a hero, ranked amongst the best
Now alone, and on ribbons hung, his life across his chest.
Desperately he clings to life, his memories to save,
Without a wife or family he fears the lonely grave.
There he is, no more the hero, no longer of the best.
Who will see his medal ribbons? Who will know his place of rest?
But someone will remember, this lonely, unknown man,
A hero will always fill our hearts, loneliness never can.

M. Hood

My Poem

I thought I'd write this poem.
    Different from my 'others'
Not too 'deep' or 'meaningful',
    of families, friends, or mothers

Nor of British weather,
    which really gets me 'down'
or even, the ideal, 'getaway place'
    Miles from any town!

I've done 'all' the seasons,
    'springtime', 'Christmas',
Even, about the 'sea', the wonders of nature,
Day and nighttime, are written subjects for me

About this crazy world,
    Where sometimes, wrong rules over right
often, are hidden meanings, a message,
    behind the words I write

But, this poem, will be different.
    A cheery, happy one,
Light-hearted, to the end.
    After all, it's just for fun!

Colleen La Roche

A Day In Springtime

Flying high, like a bird on the wing.
  On a warm bright spring,
Hear them sing, a song in the air,
  We're to happy to care.
Sitting around with the wind
  In our hair.

The sky above, a blanket of blue.
Lying here, dreaming of you.
On a winding path, lies a butterfly.
Moving along, like a bird in the sky.

So when in spring, I hear the birds sing.
I remember all the joys of spring.

    Eric Donaldson

What Shall I Wear Today?

Should I try on the tartan smile?
After all, it is the latest...
The P.V.C. grin
Is in for the season, too...

I could try on
The ecology friendly face...
No! Too worn out to be repeated,
Slightly out of place.

Maybe the sexy, strapless evening wink...
Or the luring lycra leer?
There's always the little back pout
To fall back on...
That's never out!

How about the dependable denim daydream,
Or the natural fibre demanding stare?
The polyester prim look would be fine
I suppose....or the chic, glittering glare?

Heavens! Isn't life difficult!
Especially after discovering
You've got Nothing Decent To Wear!

    Margaret B. W. De Araujo

Sapper Charles Johns Killed In Action 10 July 1916

I have never met you
Yet I know you so well.
I know how you think
And what stories you'd tell:
What games you would play
And just what you would drink.

Why did you so die
Unknown where you lie?
It's cruel, senseless - so hard to believe
With bugles, prayers and a simple wreath.

    Charles Johns

The Bride

She stands at the church door attired in white
Her dress is made of lace and silk
Her veil like pearly ice,
The smile begins upon her lips
But does not reach her eyes,
The guests are full of happiness
The bride is full of lies.

She looks into the distance and wonders what the future holds
Her mind recalls dim memories
But the love for him is cold.
People push her forward
She feels the sudden fear,
Her grip on reality slipping
From within her slides a silent tear.

In her mind she turns away
And runs to reach the outstretched hand,
In the cold hard light of day
She admires the false gold wedding band.

    Julia Kendrick

The Chain Of Life

When God made the Earth, He planted the seeds
of all Earthly Life and of all its needs.
The first blade of grass, the first ant and man
and all that now lives were part of His Plan.

The first Seeds of Life at the Beginning of Time,
to the last living person and the last drop of wine;
He programmed it all, in making the Earth
and the Chain of Life He brought to birth.

Life is passed on in all life you name-
in Man, Beasts and Plants, the Chain is the same;
the grass spreads its seeds and so do the trees-
we get food and flowers helped by Earth's Bees!

All that we use in our Earthly Home,
comes from the Earth below Ozone's Dome;
but Earth's Great Resources are too precious to waste-
what God made in patience we devour in haste!

Let's value Mother Earth and all God's Creation,
treasuring His Handiwork without desecration;
Extinct Creatures, Lost Ozone, the scars of our crimes-
shout WARNING and DANGER for Earth in Our Times!

    Michael Simmonds

Vampirehood

Suffered a fear
imagined the world in white
soon put that right
Envisioned Denzel Washington as a vampire

Hunting in broad daylight
invisible in the heat of the sun
save teeth
and white of eyes

Sucking the hate out of bodies
without blood
draining the fear
of true parity
swallowing the greed of power

A kinship
beyond colour
or sex
a life
beyond the pale

    Delroy Williams

Sisters

We were born at different times,
So these years form a divide,
When I was born the youngest child
One of you cheered,
The other one cried.
Both loving and jealous thoughts crossed your minds.

We seem to be so different
Yet we manage to stay friends
And when arguments set in we always make amends

How can we all be sisters
When our lives take different paths
But despite all of our quarrels we still, can share some laughs!

Being the youngest sister
I appear the lucky one,
As I'm never the victim of two against just one.

All sisters have their quarrels, fights and stupid rows,
And I think we always will
But despite all of our problems
We remain good sisters still.

    Anne-Marie Mainwaring

565

Without My Lord

Without my Lord
I could not foresee
The things of this world that I would face
Its pains, its woes the tears and fears
The darkest days replaced with light
The peace he gives me
Every day, the hope the joy
When I know he's near
He'll never say, I have no time
To listen to this child of mine
Without my Lord, my prayers to hear
Rewards are great when he is near
He'll never leave me night or day
He's in my heart, he's there to stay
No one can ever take this place
He knows your name
As he knows mine, this Lord of mine
Can be yours today just ask him in
To your heart today.

Freda Trimble

A Typical Granddad!

A small wrinkled face hides behind a newspaper,
Puffs of smoke appear, then drift further and further away.
Slipper covered feet rest lazily on an old battered stool,
The gramophone crackling, not able to operate smoothly.
The newspaper crinkles,
His grip tightens.
The newspaper lowers to reveal an old, worn face.
Small blue eyes gleam like stars,
A maze of wrinkles cover his forehead.
With bushy eyebrows spread over and on his eyelids,
His nose is curled up and creased.
The strands of white wispy hair lie flattened over his bare head,
With tiny little ears poking out from under tufts of hair.
A wooden pipe is positioned in his mouth with precision.
Stumpy grey hairs are growing out of his chin.
The old man looks up and sees me,
He gives a slight smile, uncovering two gums.
Only one old, grimy, yellow tooth remains!

Kate Harvey

Feelings

I'm a domestic pet,
Too tame to follow my heart.

With each brick of time I built a tyranny,
I gave the oppressor a throne in my head.
But this power made him drunk
And with his sceptre he ripped my heart.

Now,
In the hollow chambers of the wound,
Grief is echoing, echoing, echoing.
- his conscience is stained with blood.

Aldo Zammit

The Depth Of Beauty

Ships at night in harbour
At rest from tossing waves,
Recline in glowing ardour
From sunset on the caves.

With funnels gently oozing,
The drifting smoke doth float
Into colours soothing,
Each cloud, a painted moat.

How tranquil as the gulls fly,
The trippers stand and stare,
Then twilight warns that night's nigh,
So record these sight's so rare.

Only artistic contrasts,
On canvas tells the scene,
No change from days gone past,
Perchance, an enlarged screen.

John Webb

The Prey

As I sat in the African plain,
I sensed a fear.
A fear of death,
for I could smell the scent of a tiger.
Was I to be its feast?
To be torn apart and eaten alive,
No!
The scent became nearer,
my heart pounding, for the fear of my life,
I ran.
I ran as fast as my little dear legs could run.
I fled in time,
for I am still alive and the tiger still hungry,
let far behind.

Silpa Chauhan

I'm Sorry

Your eyes are a clear night's sky and your tears are
Silent comets that race bearing the fruit of emotion.

My foolish words, sparks from a selfish fire, do not
deserve such gifts. Alas my heart befuddled my tongue
And spawned barren words, void of truth and
direction. They run snapping around my love for you
seeking importance where none is deserved.

Let my regret sweep them aside like dead leaves so
That we might walk together unhindered.

Martin Hugh Myall

When I Win The Lottery

When I win the lottery a miracle that would be
Imagine the finger pointing to say it isn't you it's "me"

A holiday's first priority with sun and booze and sea,
Will all my friends and family the honours are on me.

Of course a bit to charity a donation I would give,
New houses for the homeless a decent place to live.

Shop till I drop, takes on new dimensions,
New outfits there would be,
Of course there would be a bigger house
There would have to be, to accommodate
My wardrobes that numbers one, two three.

Alas my dream disperses, the bubbles burst for me
Interrupted by the screaming of mum, where is my tea?
And where's my jeans that's faded, can you iron them for me?
"Don't worry I'll buy you a new pair.
When I win the lottery".

Diane Edwards

It's All In The Mind

All week I've wondered if I dare
Go and sit in the dental chair,
I enter the waiting room to await my call,
There are posters of "Teeth" placed along the wall,
Then the dentist appears and says "Please come through
Sit down, now what can I do for you?"
Try to relax and open wide
So that I can see just what's inside,
There's a very large cavity, so I hope you'll be willing
To have an extraction instead of a filling."

The dreaded needle - here it comes
Penetrating deeply into my gums,
I'm given five minutes of relaxation
He then brings the forceps into operation,
All I can feel is a gentle pressing
And on the whole - it's not too distressing.
"There - says the dentist - your tooth is out".
"Oh three cheers kind sir" - I would like to shout.
I'm so relieved that I could start to sing,
Simply because I didn't feel a thing.

Phyllis White

566

Deliverance

Where hides the wind?
The icy sheet that can cut steel.
Lost in the raging torrent of life
And now shattered as a frail egg shell.

Shadows cast over a land,
Once so fresh and vibrant.
Paths now strewn with diversions.
Never ending waves lapping at the shore.

Embittered by life.
Chipping away at the bold rocks.
Craters registering an existence long past,
But not forgotten.

Speak softly to me,
O gentle breeze.
Carry me on your whim
And make me invincible, immortal and wise.

Pat Stone

Untitled

When we are young we all have dreams,
To wed and raise a brood,

The most of us are taught this way,
And told, it's what we should,

But real life has a funny way,
Of putting you in a spot,

It changes all our best laid plans,
And dreams are all forgot,

At first this seems disaster,
But very soon we learn,

That even tho we make our plans,
Our dreams, from life, we earn,

And then upon reflection,
This life is not so bad,

But the loss of dreams, I never earned,
Sometimes makes me sad..

Irene Whitehall

The Thoroughbred

Pulsating veins, nostrils wide,
you look majestic in your stride,
eyes a glare and oh so sharp,
your ears pricked you hear the lark,
when at the gallop you're so smooth,
your hooves they pound the soils groove,
at one with the lad high on your back,
you look so smart in all your tack,
your sweat it lathers on your chest,
you pass that post and you're the best,
it's then I cheer, I'm oh so high,
and you my lad, you know just why,
for as a little foal we ran,
together, you, me and your mam,
and now just as I watch you race,
I see the look on my dads face,
he's oh so proud of you he bred,
a most majestic thoroughbred.

Catherine Anne Martland

Wings Of Eternity

Wings of eternity — high in the sky.
Spreading their feathers far and wide.
Chariots that race on silver cloud
Spreading their shadow across the sky.
Wings of tomorrow — eternity high
Coming to enfold you, and keep you from harm.
Tired arms that reach out — and grasp.
Evermore at rest, beneath the bosom of death.
Wings of eternity — high in the sky.
Gathering their feathers, from far and wide.

Doreen Ann Mear

The Hidden Treasure

Who does compare? so we can feel and touch,
do not hide "oh treasure mine! which brings
sweet music to my ear, open my eyes
lover mine, please out my aim, to see
your design, oh calm the storms
of life - to bear what will be
my portion here, so oh merciful one
please take away the things which
don't fit in to your beautiful design,
so it will "well" up in us, praise to you
oh my Lord God - your spirit "Groans" within my
heart - which will put me right for you to plan,
so "Groan" the more my beloved - to warn me of
your disapproval, so you can warn my heart
to do what's right "which is country" of your trust
"in me", - oh steady love who merely spoke and
the heavens where formed, and all the glorious
of stars, he made the "oceans" pouring them into the
just reservoir - so as you project your love
to me help and shield me in such awesome wonder

Norman Crawford

Brave Heart

Brave Heart beat fiercely in a pre-destined breast,
Fate led him into battle
fighting for the right for freedom of rule,
No usurpers to beat Brave Heart

Brave Heart fought and killed with his bloody sword
the usurpers slain by his hand,
But still the regal knave fought on
to capture the Heart of the Brave

Brave Heart died as he lived
fighting for men to be free,
His blooded core rent from within;
His warrior cries echoing down
the long corridor of history and time

Brave Heart lives on in a million free hearts,
The blood has since run dry;
The spirit uplifted by freedom's song
"Scotland the Brave".

None braver than Brave Heart....

Irene Anderson

Villanelle Of Autumn

As cascading leaves carpet the earthy stair
The autumn colours burn like a fire ablaze
Leaving branches cold and bare.

The crisp morning dew layers the ground with care
Sleepy grass awakens, green and fresh
As cascading leaves carpet the earthy stair.

The hazy dawn sun shelters while rain clouds tear,
As Autumn's golden snow coats the land
Leaving branches cold and bare.

Engraved in the sodden ground are paw prints, small and rare
From squirrels, scurrying, starting stores for winter
As cascading leaves carpet the earthly stair.

A solitary figure strolls; the soft breeze through her hair
The wind blows leaves around her small and huddled frame
Leaving branches cold and bare.

The sun on the resplendent leaves, making them flare,
The drowsy world, reluctant to arise
As cascading leaves carpet the earthy stair
Leaving branches cold and bare.

Rebecca Mary Heayn

567

Dad

I see him stumbling down the road,
In his delirious state of drunken glory.
My body slumps with surrendering acceptance;
I sigh and my breath steams up the glass.

His clothes are not coordinated, as if
Blindly pulled on under poisons influence.
I recognize the vacant mist over his eyes
And recall days I wish were dead; memory is so cruel.

I open the door and he grins like a
Sheepish child and can't even see the tears
Forming or the stains on my cheek or
My castles in the air forming bigger cracks every second.

He used to be my hero, the man I respected so much.
I felt secure and safe and warm in his loving touch.
Now I walk down the road with a stranger by my side,
It seems I've resigned myself to accept that I can no longer hide,
from the fact that this man's chances of escaping are very slim,
The liquor of darkness has found another victim.

Helen Lynch

Forever

I see in your eyes how life is deserting you,
each second, each hour, each day and still
you look at me and smile.

The Hospital has became your school, your
playground, your second home and still
you take it as it came, with no complaint.

I wish I had the strength to let you go,
to live with out your warming presence,
to look at you and say good bye.

But I can't, my anger grows with
your suffering. I close my eyes
and scream aloud; why? Why?

I wait long time under the pouring rain.
Looking at the flowers that adorn your
new bed, wondering how would they feel.

I wish they knew that with them, an angel
sleeps with no more pain, waiting for
the day I will join him...forever.

Ruth Esther Arrola

My Love My Life

My husband was dying, what could I do, just keep repeating,
I love you, deep inside I was screaming, don't leave me alone,
I will look after you, please come home

Those three little words, don't seem much to say, I love you, I
love you, please don't go away we had forty four years living
as one, what will I do now you are gone

I wake up each morning, and you're not there, only the memories
we used to share how long will this ache in my heart go on,
the pain the longing for my dearest one
I thank God for my family and friends who care, their love and
understanding are all too rare

I feel I could have done more, if I had really tried
Forgive me my darling, now you're not by my side

I did my best, the only way I knew how
Dear God if only you were with me now

What would I change, what would I do,
I really don't know, except I truly loved you

Your patience, your trust, your belief in me
Never questioning, never doubting, your love was plain to see

A faithful husband, a loving dad, I realize what I really had
If I didn't before, I truly know now

Wait for me darling we will enjoy once more
Our togetherness, our love, just like before.

A. P. Gallifant

The Land Of Wales

The land of wales is special to me, travelling around was able to see
Mountains, high valleys - so green and deep,
People: Warm, friendly, always pleased to speak.

Strolling along a path on a mountainside,
Passed lots of trees and flowers - with exciting colours, growing wild
Walking at a very slow pace, enjoying
the silent 'hush' that surrounds this beautiful place.

Softly the wind moves high among the trees,
Making music with all the dancing leaves.
Time had no meaning - it just went by
as I gazed into a rich, blue sky.

A running stream seemed to be quite near.
It's rippling voice became very clear.
My eyes closed and I stood, so still - soon my thoughts
were lost to the magic sounds of the rill.

With the sun upon my face and a breeze gently going
Through my hair: It felt good - as though I hadn't a care.
Having my mind in such relaxing and peaceful way,
Wales had made me The Perfect Day.

A. C. Blakeman

Ode To Psalm On Red Nose Day

His name is Pete and on his feet is thinking all the time...
And now for my part I must start to make the next lines rhyme.

His work in Psalm brings such sweet pay-
but Peter won't a lolly lick...
Though he could have a field day with (pause) a chocolately picnic.

If at times he's in a hurry, and here's a gentle hint,
Pete may just find he has the time to consHULME a murray mint

Football's the name of Peter's game, he plays a bit like Gazza
Now here's my chance to drop more names
Johns 1 & 2 big Al and Muzzer

Some days when the hour is past eleven with manual on his knee
He'll sit and dream of heaven and... perhaps a Galaxy.

So when the system's up and running, he sits and hums and hars
And then with delectation stuffs his face right full of Mars.

No one else has seen the like he does it with aplomb
A really sticky joyful treat-a Mars bar 'Hole in one'

He doesn't like loose women or very fast motors cars
but as many here can testify he can really stuff a Mars.

So here's the final question for Pete so hale and hearty
What would he find to do right now with one small chocolate smarty!!??

Allan Eves

Spiritual Momma

Momma is love
  I feel her around me, she's cool about me
Momma is love
  But I don't mind, I love her near
Momma is love
  As she was a dear
Momma is love
  She cares for me even when she's above
Momma is love
  She flies around like a dove

Momma is love
  In the spiritual world is she
Momma is love
  In the world above with flowers all around her
Momma is love
  A sweet smell of perfume around her

Momma is love
  She flies like a dove
Momma is love

Barbara Ann Linney

When I Was Young

When I was young I could run I could skip.
I jumped and I hoped but now all
I can do is sit!
Sit in the cell which I call home
And wait and hope till the day
That I die.
When I can be free
Free of this cell and
All of this pain
When I can just remain
In peace!

Nicola Croft

Our Future

Another storm with wind and rain
Dark and gloomy with the weather vane
Spinning in circles at fantastic speed
It's dangerous out so better take heed
As the weatherman says don't venture far
Especially if you are driving a car.
The trees are all bending and starting to sway
Many will fall by the end of the day
It's scary having these winds so strong
And at this rate it won't be very long
Till we move underground to avoid such a storm
That we humans have caused by upsetting the norm
The ozone layer is wearing away
Destroyed by emissions and aerosol spray
We've not heeded warnings to cease our behaviour
So now we're seeking some kind of a saviour
To help us to save our planet earth
I hope that we can as it's surely worth
Changing our ways to preserve habitation
So we've something to leave the next generation

H. P. Bunker

Selling Yourself To The End, My Dear Friend...

I walk down this street, almost once every day,
The pavements are littered, but some people are gay.
There are lights all around, from the sex shops come sound,
Of music in beat, on that dirty street.

Some looking for love, some looking for dope,
Some, looking for someone to give them some hope.
Some, they are rich, just having a fling,
Not knowing the hitch those young people are in.

Behind that stoned look, behind that deep well,
Those people I see, in their private hell.
I feel them you see, and I'm glad it's not me,
But I've sorrow inside, for their loss of pride.

I go through this street, and my heart, like it, beats
Out a prayer every day, "Not to see you again,
Selling yourself, to the end, my dear friend".

1983-Denmark

Barbara Byron-Rasmussen

Tell And See

It's amazing what I thought, it's amazing what I did,
don't know why but I just hid.

Did you feel the room go warm, did you see the calm.
Everyone's in a spin to the music within.

Tucked away inside, in a corner,
tucked away inside, our love's forever.

The other night you were away but you're here with me today.
Could you smell me - I could smell you.
Could you see my thought - you're such on inspiration.
Like a flower opening and a dawn rising, let's tell and see.

Mark Haffner

Exodus

You came, soul-naked and with weary heart
  To my oasis.
And there, drank deeply of the age-old waters.
I held you - in my shade, and, whilst you sang
  Your song of sadness.

You did not come to stay, only to part
  With phantom faces.
To tend your wounds, and arm against new slaughters.
You laid your burden down, my desert rang
  With your sweet madness.

You rested here, awhile, and then were gone.

The desert sands drift on.

Stephanie Ann Noble

What's The Rush?

Hey! What's the rush? No need to run and run,
Take your time, relax, feel the sun.
I know you need to earn your pay,
But no need to do it all today.
Why do you go so fast?
Enjoy the good things, make them last.
Do you need the stress and strain?
It's in your chest you'll feel the pain.
Take time to see the flowers and trees,
Don't let your work bring you to your knees.
What about the things you haven't seen?
All the places you've never been.
What about the books you've never read?
Much too late when you are dead.
Hey there! What's the rush? No need to run,
Life's for living, slow down, have some fun.

James Stuart Denby

Malindi Child Of Africa Ode To A Zoo Lion

The sandy richness of her coat
Like the African soil she has never seen
The gleam in her eye like a desert star
Her teeth as white as the moon's place beam.

The beat of her heart... like an African drum
The pad of her paws so soft in the night
The cry of her cubs cuddling close
The mist of their breath in the dawn's pale light.

The soft sweet touch of the African wind
That streams across the Mara plains
Pricks her ears, stirs her tail
And runs like a fever in her veins.

Queen of beasts, and of my heart
Embodiment of all that's wild
The sweet kiss of Kenya touches my soul
As I stand before you... Africa's child.

Clare Snead

Soldiers Brave

Upon a field a soldier lies,
His fight for freedom done.
His face lies buried in blood soaked land
Beside him lay his gun.

He fought with valour and with strength
He fought with heart so bold,
But where he lies, 'tis scared ground
Though body lies so cold.

The snow and rain and hail beat down
And wind blows through black hair,
What purpose for did hero die?
Leaves friends in deep despair.

His body will be lifted
To be placed in heroes grave,
To where all comrades rest in peace.
Where God doth guard the brave.

J. D. Tarling

Life To Death

Did you have a good life when you died?
With the living there will always be the dead.
Getting closer to God, what a view can be seen,
Halfway to hell, almost in heaven.

The dancing fools has no fear of death and the face of God.
He kisses the shrine of all that is out of focus,
Broken and sinful but loved by humanity.

People you meet in the walking hour of life,
Become just echoes in the stars when you are no longer.

Is death fear of God?
Life is fear of death.
An inseparable trap that we have weaved for ourselves.
Beware the weaver.

Freedom is the ability to say I alone am not afraid of death,
Therefore, not afraid of the infinite.

Freedom Follows.
The soul is but energy wanting to travel the infinite, like a
lonely atom, gone.

Andrew Rich

Me My Dog And My Cat

We have such fun we three
The dog and the cat look at me
As if to say what is it to be.
Shall we all try to climb that tree,
Yes for we are little devils, yes indeed we are three
The dog looks at the tree, then he looks at the cat
As if to say, what are you laughing at.
Then the cat climbs the tree
Yes it's easy for him for he has claws you see
Then I say I can climb that tree
Although I am only three, then the dog chases the cat
Then he sees daddies old hat
Golly he makes a right mess of that
Then the dog lies down flat
As if to say I have had enough of that
Then I am saved from climbing that tree
For mother calls it time for tea,
Well who wants to climb a silly old tree
I must go on now or I shall have a right row
Yes we shall? We three.

George Delancey Attwood

Battlefield And Heartlands

Shall we just be,
only young dreamers,
remembering the rhymes of forgotten times?

Farewell to battlefields and heartlands,
twelve thousand miles and burning smiles.
Yesterday's sanctuaries, sainted portraits tainted,
long past reflections now cursed down in torment.

Distant angels sense their virtue,
while life hangs in dumb silence,
they murmur in grey corridors,
shallow tears drip the red stained floor.

Lost in dungeons of June,
morning light never comes too soon,
cats clawed at wailing moons,
between a nightmare and a dream
to fusions of tranquillity,
we dance in a masquerade.

Remembering the rhymes of forgotten times,
shall we just be,
only young dreamers?

Neil Jones

Address Tae Stovie Tatties

Great Patron Saint o' Ingin Johnny,
May ev'ry blessin' fa' upon 'ee
'Ee mak a meal, as guid as ony,
　　Tae pass the lips,
And whit a drouth 'ee pit upon me,
　　For pints and nips.

Weel pairtner'd wi' yer cronie, Neeps,
'Ee lie in glorious, steamin' heaps,
Yer odour, tantalisin' seeps,
　　'A through the place,
Each tastebud, helpless, softly, weeps,
　　Quick - say the Grace.

Within that pot, 'ee've jist been born,
O'or ready wi' John Barleycorn.
Let's live the night, forget the morn,
　　Ah, - Deo Gratis!!!
Mae man nor mither's son could scorn,
　　Thae Stovie Tatties.

Robert Donaldson

The Trawlerman

The sea is blue
The sea is green,
The sea can be angry and grey,
Fishermen have to be brave and strong
to fish in deep dark water for their
Work to be done.

The silver fish has lined pockets with gold
But the loss of life is a price untold.
There is no chance with angry seas
When they keel over strips with those
Who are brave,
Remember always to respect the sea for
there is no way out in this cruel grave.
Lost, but forgotten they will never be,
These knights of the deep blue sea

Mavis P. Wegg

Winter

Days of darkness,
Months of mournful lament,
season of solitary discontent
of fading heartfelt anticipation of
lasting light that will now never shine,
hoping to have been bathed
in the light redeeming glow
a broken promise of deliverance
from the misty depths of despair,
to have been wrapped in warmth
and to sleep in sweet silence,
whilst the ebony embrace of
early evening enfolds.

Brian J. Henry

Progress?

The singing of larks rising, on hazy summer days.
　　The distant voice of the cuckoo in leafy forest ways,
The squeaking of bats at dusk, in the soft quiet air,
　　The slow country ways and time to talk and stare.
The lowing of brown cows, single file across the lea,
　　Too intent to notice my old dog and me.
These are the things I enjoyed, when first I moved from town.
　　Away from the noise and the crime.
And facing each day with a frown,
　　But the town has spread up around me.
The buses pass by my door.
　　No longer the sound of the cuckoo.
The larks are heard no more.
　　Just the screams of children playing.
And traffic non-stop gets me irate.
　　Because you see, I live now in the middle
Of a great sprawling 'housing estate',

B. S. Martin

The Way I Feel

God made the sun to shine so bright
That brings trees and flowers to our delight,
The rain that makes the gardens grow,
How lucky are we to get all these things,
To see God's creatures and birds on wing.
To have him about us all to love
And keep us in his tender care,
He gave us all these things to share
Amongst us all if we only care
So we thank you God for just being there

E. M. Cowley

Untitled

Shiny wet roofs framed by a rainbow.
Squat white houses fixed in time.
Derelict cottages with dead eyes.
Swift clouds changing the mood of mountains.
Sheltered bays with necklaces of lobster pots,
White capped waves caressing wet sand
Almost hiding lonely footprints.
Grey and white pebbles
Inviting you to pick them up.
Amber coloured seaweed scrunching underfoot.
Lush green shrubs interlaced with fuchsias.
Occasional sighting of deer.
The soft silence broken only
By the clip clip clopping
Of the horses pulling the jaunting carts

Patricia Edmead

Global Suicide

Oil upon the beaches, poisoned sewage in the seas,
Exhaust fumes in the air and all around.
Nuclear waste and radiation, toxic slime and CFC's.
Pollutants in the streams and on the ground.

Waste paper on the pavement, broken bottles in the street,
Polystyrene packing strewn in every place.
Rain forests disappearing, burning wood and coal and peat.
As we strip the Earth, we kill the Human Race.

Ozone layer depletion means that global warming nears
As we fill our skies with smoke and toxic fumes.
We feed our lust for power, but does anybody hear
Our children cry as they watch us seal their doom?

The ice-caps gradually recede,
The seas begin to rise.
The Earth is slowly dying,
But we're heedless of its cries.

Mark Williams

The Book Of Me

The book of my loves and lives long gone is now dust on my shelf.
Old days of tomorrow that would see my heart come and go,
How they spoke of me, yet none were mine, nor was my self,
Nor the days I spent, the love I thought would surely grow.
But how much should it grow? And to what end?
Life, behold, the book I am writing I have only borrowed.
All the time more chapters to follow, tears to be swallowed
Tears full of awe and such awful pain.
Yet out of it all, a taste of strength there is growing again.
Where the passing clouds like to reveal
the dark, dark sky and the stars do not mind;
Their moon has nothing to say to me either.
No but's, no why's, and never an answer.
Not even a question for me to find
To the span of my life, turning into a widening circle
forever transforming, hardly perceptible,
An endless end of moment upon moment
Like page upon page, resting on that shelf -
firmly unturnable,
turning, turning, and turning itself.

Iris Teichmann

Why?

Why do people have to stare,
and walk past me as if I wasn't there?
Why do they sit and snigger?
Could it be my figure?

Why does everyone point at me?
They're starting to bring me to my knees.
Why do they have to frown.
Just because I'm brown?

Why are they always avoiding me?
as if I have HIV
Why do they make me feel so weak?
They look at me like I'm a freak.

Why is the world so poor?
Maybe it's why I sleep on its floor?
Why don't I have a roof over my head?
Most of the time I wish I was dead.

Why do they kick dirt in my face,
is it because I'm not their race?
Why oh why are things this way?
It's always us homeless who have to pay.

Hannah Sheen

Untitled

Oh Man of Past and Future Generations
With helping hands for soft and brutal Creation
You hold your pain as if it were a lesson
To show this world that life is but a sphere
We travel and we stumble for a reason
We question and we kill and yet remain
We live, we love, we learn how to be tender
And every time we do a mask we gain
While trees grow and seasons change
Our silence shouts
Our words melt
Our eyes cry
Our bodies die
Only our souls remain.

Look upwards
Eyes are dying
Be outwards
Hearts are sighing
Be gentle
Someone's crying- somewhere

Lynn Allen

4 O'clock Shadow

Twenty-eight years was what she had,
Her fight now through, tired and weary,
After all what was life?
A joke?
A ridicule?
A farce?
Where was the point of life?
There was no point.
Full of hopelessness and hate,
Why did they hate her?
Why did they not love her like they had said they did?
Why was she born to be so evil and bad, was she?
No-one knows; a volt runs from her head to toes
Relief or excitement or both.
The clock strikes 4 am not long now; a smile, a tear,
A kiss for the child she's loved for only one year.
Take your life and be at peace,
As peaceful as the baby that sleeps in your arms.
God bless you child, may the world be good to you
And remember mummy will always love you, goodnight.

Sally-Anne Cousins

The Show House

If ever a girl deserved first prize
It must be a girl called Fran
Her house is so tidy and everything gleams
I suppose one could say "Clinically Clean"

Everything in order and not out of place
"Excuse me" guests say I'm a little confused
The kitchen so neat "Is it really used!"
Pots and pans, usual clutter no where at all to be seen,
Yes this house is 'Clinically Clean'

Every room so neat a joy to behold
People must walk carefully with unshoe'd feet

And if you sit you're on the edge of the seat
No indication that anyone's been
Yes there's no doubt about it she's "clinically clean!"

Clive Howard Litten

In My Garden

In my garden I can see,
Flowers and a chestnut tree,
Lawn, rugged and forlorn,
Shining, with dew in the dawn.

Weeds are protruding amongst the flowers,
Growing bigger with the April showers,
Waiting to be up rooted by the hoe,
Then they will be laid very low.

Great hyacinths are coming through,
Crocus too, tulips don't know what to do,
Too cold for them at present,
Waiting for weather to be more pleasant.

Sylvia J. Codd

Alien Thoughts

Earthlings enjoy multifarious guises,
Contrasting colours and differing sizes.
Speak in strange and varied tongues,
Utter slights, avenge, imagined wrongs.

Collectively known as human-kind,
Mean of spirit; blinkered narrow-mind
Body-suit of thick and selfish skin
Hides a functional likeness there within.

Embracing Christ who died but lives again,
Buddhas' outstretched arms-amen, amen!
Virgin mother most pure and chaste;
To Islam all are subjugate.

Bigots, zealots all fanatical creeds;
An excuse for war hate and greed.
Agnostic, pagan, heathen vilified;
Hearts are brave, mind open-wide.
I am spangled star, the shining sun and moon,
An ebbing tide, the wind and rain, a flower in bloom

Eternal, ceaseless, endless time and space.
Black hole of a dark, expanding universe.

M. Goodwin

Devotion

The way your eyes smile
I want you to stay awhile
The way you kiss me.
Makes me feel I'm drowning at sea
A sea of love and hope. Excitement and desire.
When you hold me my body's on fire.
You know me so well, you can read my mind
A love like ours is hard to find.
So hold me close, and whisper in my ear
Whenever I'm with you, I feel no fear.
You're always a friend, but so much more
You're everything that I adore.
Your lips are sweet, your touch divine.
So I'll be yours and you be mine.

H. Speight

Jobless Blues

Times of heartache time of pain
times of living your life in vain,
times of struggling to make ends meet
Just to keep yourself on your own
two feet, heartache hiding behind
big smiles as together we try to
make it through life's trials, But
together we'll make it through this hell
on earth and find the peace we all
Deserve.

Anthony Charles Whitehead

Our World

What a wonderful world we inhabit!
Its beauty in light and in life,
All things from the smallest and greatest
Perfection for each in its place.

In nature all things chase fulfilment
The answer is there for their needs,
For some it is harder to find it
But sooner or later it comes.

One poet gave voice in his writings
Where all that is good gives delight
"'Tis only mankind that is evil"
A judgement too sweeping to make.

Yet, think you, there's so much of truth in't
Its sadness infiltrates the heart -
With all that there is to delight us
Why must greed cause hatred and war?

G. Drysdale

God's Blessing

Open your eyes once again my Darling
See the sun on the window pane
The Angels of God are coming
To relieve you of all your pain

Go with a smile on your lips my dearest
For those who would keep you in vain
We'll never forget you
In sunshine or in rain

We'll walk with you on the mountains
And by the riverside
In sunshine or in shadow
You'll be ever there at our side

Mary Joan Sheard

Charney Bassett

Elegiac, a dying fall...
Does the fact they leave you out
mean you are not there at all?
Will I find you if I search
beyond the lawns, the manor wall
to where the local ladies play
their dazzling tennis, four by four?

The people here are kindly, sure,
believing in the good of all
but in the house there beats no heart,
no loving, living, dying Lord
to grace the solar, pace the sward;
no wine for blood, the gift of love,
transcends our state.

Mere history cannot replace
the light upon that hallowed face,
no miracle of air or space,
earth or water, or the touch
of human love can compensate
if there is no redeeming act...or ever was.

Penelope Flint

I Hear You

I hear you calling, I hear you call my name
Each whisper though silence, calls softly to me again
I hear your echoed laughter, and ache to see you smile
This distant between us, feels like a thousand miles
I feel you inside me, like it was yesterday.
Completely, so deeply, you are my, night and day
When you feel movement, all around you
Don't let go, of the love, you've found
Make a stand, for who you are
Don't give it away now, you've got this far
I can taste, more than fear
The burning, inside me, is so real
I can almost lay my hands upon
This warm glow, that lingers on
My soul on fire, lead me, by the hand, to infinity.
There's so much that you, can rise above
Shot in the darkness, my wound allowed, to cry, tears of pain
Helps my body die, stumbling, forward, to the ground
The sound rings through my ears I feel so cold, so far from you
And all I see, are fears, my joy, one caress, a higher love

Michael Crawley

Chloe Joy

She has lovely blonde curls and a cute little nose,
Her cheeks hold the blush of a sweet summer rose,
Her eyes are like jewels all sparkling and bright,
The lovely dark lashes are curled round just right,
Her smile as she greets me is something to see,
Gran-Gran may I please stay for my tea?

We walked round the garden her hand clutched in mine,
The Clematis nodded, the bees hummed in rhyme,
She sang me a tune and danced round the trees,
Her pretty pink dress caught up in the breeze.

We played with her dollies and then hide and seek,
She just could not resist move her fingers to peek,
We went in for tea around half past four,
Soon after that Mummy came through the door.

With her warm little arms she hugged me goodbye,
The sparkle was still in her eyes,
She skipped down the drive, blew a kiss - and was gone,
And so had my sheer paradise.

Cynthia Fenwick

If

So many words going round in my head
So many things that I should have said
So many feelings that I should have shown
So many good deeds that I could have done
If only there had been time.

So many friend with whom I lost touch
So many people who I loved so much
So many Seasons and years travelled by
So many times I had reason to cry
If only I'd found the time.

So many summers that I have missed
So many lovers that I could have kissed
So many memories around in my mind
So many ways I could have been kind
If I'd had the time.

So many places that I could have seen
So many pathways where I haven't been
So many dreams I had now are gone
So many sorrows - I left it too long
If.. I should have made time.

Mary Brooke

Mollie Mine

The puddle I found garnered in a ridgy rock
Became for me (in boyhood fantasy)
My Loch na Peiste,
Except that she (a Hairy Mollie)
Lay stranded on an island,
Waiting for the sun
To dry her way to heathered home.

Stepping stones (placed close) failed to wake the slothful ball,
And when, eventually, I prodded with a twig,
She rolled right in, and drowned.
So now, the beast was in the boy,
Urging him, "Destroy, destroy."

Maggots which he loved to pull and break and mutilate,
And conies snared,
And plump-voiced pigeons
Blasted from the trees

All led (decades on) to loves betrayed by restless eye;
Pace, Emer, Carmel, Kate, Sinead...

Beastly Moll, did you really have to die?

Joe Neal

Dear Sahara

In summer, 1994,
You burning Desert Sahara, Your endless expanses of nothingness,
witnessed the beginnings of life.

I was a desert myself,
forlorn in your embrace, alone in the human race,
not realizing the life growing in my uterus.
You were inhospitable as Nature ever could be.
You let me down; I felt like dying.
But You let me survive, and my fetus be born, "perfect".

Now we are in prison alias London,
deprived of all the natural rights, crushed by all the human systems.

Oh Sahara, save us, me and my son,
whom You didn't let rest in peace with you,
whom You won't let perish in damned civilization.

Let us return to You, soon. In chah Allah!
You shall see Dahmene,
whose invisible life You blessed for seven months before birth,
whose inviolable little life You haven't known yet since birth.
Dahmene, my beautiful son, another of Your child,
Child of Nature.

Naomi Kawaguchi

Loneliness

I am designed to function
Like a chess piece, there are many of me
I am
Moulded
In many forms
I can't move
But - can be moved
In many ways
Sometimes
I remain
Sometimes
I am taken
But always
I am replaced
Always
I am the same
Functional

Why do people want to mend you
When you're not broken?
Why can the species only reproduce now?

Martin Stubberfield

Band Of Gold Ageing Thin

Unknown female, unknown place of abode
From the tag on her big toe, this story is told
Post mortem established, she's not eaten in days
Abuse of the body showed in many different ways
Looked like she'd been in a fight with King Kong
Black Eye, split lip and tongue, she couldn't have talked
Feet covered in blisters from the miles she'd walked
Yet on her finger a band of gold, ageing thin.
As if trying to hold to the past, but unable to win
A lot of the marks were far from new
Did that band of gold justify what she'd been through
Stretch marks show, at some stage, she bore a child
Was that what unleashed the beast insanely wild.
Or a circumstance out of her control, like drink.
His being redundant and needing cash, the missing link.
My eyes go back to the mark of the ring she wore with pride
No set of circumstances this end could be justified.

Desmond Howe

Twenty Three Hour Cell

My mind cries with hunger
but not a morsel of literature can I find
and my imagination leaps and bounds like a
gyrating giraffe.
I feel like an actor
pregnant with clichés
starring in a silent movie.
The silence deafens me
like the roar of a machine
that sows the seeds of philosophy
that germinate in my brain and come bubbling from
my lips like wine
but who is there to sip of it?
Only myself
and I have already drunk myself sober.

Alexander John Sansome

Eyes Of Truth

Look into my eyes and tell me what you see,
Happy, sad memories deep inside of me.
Hurt and pain are scarred inside,
Which pleasures try to mask and hide.

Looking in your eyes I'll tell you what I see,
Mysteries and secrets of what you want your life to be.
Hurt caused by heartache and shattered dreams,
All roughly placed together and sewn at the seams.

Eyes which are full of hurt, lies and pain,
Hide feelings deep inside which are driving me insane.
Good memories were made by you and me,
Being lost in those memories is where I want to be.

Look into my eyes and tell me what you see.

Sofie Paton

Spring

Dark winter's days are gone,
His dark cloak, no more draping the sleeping land.
Behold bright Spring, pale nymph of life,
her robe a myriad of spring flowers.
Caressing now the still earth,
her quiet whispers calling back the distant birds,
to witness nature's rebirth.
Awakening plants, push forth,
basking in the pale sun's glow.
Skeleton trees, once bare, bring life,
and blossoms erupt in joyous triumph.
Yet Spring, pale and fragile, lasts an instant.
Summer strong, seeming never-ending, slaying mild Spring.
But still the Seasons run, and Spring forgotten through
Summer's heat and Autumn's fruitful bounty waits.
And as Winter's icy bones again drape the resting land,
Spring lies sleeping, snow-drops in her hand.

Margaret Ann Peake

In Sight Of A Robin

The song of a mocking bird makes you look around, then when in sight of a robin you hear a difference in sound as the leaves high up in the trees flicker all around, you stand still on the ground feeling the cool breeze brushing over all that is around then you open your eyes, and realize that in the world of today, there's not enough self sacrifice when the cool breeze brushes across your face you can't help but feel for the human race. At times like this you see the looks and expressions on every-one's face this makes you see that life is nothing more than a matter of taste unfortunately for some it is nothing more than a matter of waste, of these people what may I say besides there is no one left to show them the way their life is extreme in every sense, and their way of life is considered to cause offence, signing their names to the forms required in this life enables the people in power to give them nothing but humility and strife but some-how they can still hear that mocking bird singing its song and observe the small robin as it hop hops along and like the leaves being caressed by that cool gentle breeze quite often all they want is to be free. Instead of leading their life through rules and regulations of societies what is it that these people see a government full of hypocrisy people in power who lack in the practice of integrity.

George Clarke Lyons

A Scorpion's Tale

His voice weapons were words of cold blunt granite
chilled in the freezer compartment of his brain
which he fired off to browbeat others into submission.

His first volley caught me unarmed and unaware
peppering my acute sense of injustice.
His second bounced off the rubber shield that was my spirit
which deflected and parried with a silent ease.
His third salvo meekly melted, forming a puddle at my feet
which I stepped out of so as to steady my aim.

Voice weapons! my technology was far superior.
Loaded and ready I turned to face my selfish adversary.
I was armed with words of steel, arrowheads with acute
    cutting edges.

My first volley sliced through his arrogance, piercing his pride.
My second hit him in the ignorant region rendering him deaf,
My third salvo brought him down with a direct hit on his
    inconsiderate nature,
rolling over, a muffled sound emitted from his motionless frame.
I walked towards him, and bending down dragged the white
    flag of surrender from his mouth.

Glynn Taylor

Meditations

Vast are the regions of my soul
From which the vine of wisdom climbs
Bearing the fragrant flowers and fruit
Of distant worlds and different times.

Fountains of happiness cool and refreshing
Spring from the mountains in joyful elation
Flowing through forests of fir tree and Pine
Bringing their message of sweet liberation.

Magical moments of musical splendour
Cascading in waterfalls down to the sea
Golden notes soaring high in the cosmos
Ecstatically tuneful delightfully free.

Spectrums of colour scintillate brightly
Flashing and spiralling out into space
Healing rays glide over rainbows of satin
Weaving a mantle of gossamer lace.

Blue Crystal Pools lying tranquil and deep
To which I am swept in a torrent of tears.
Inspired by beauty enveloped in love
My being dissolves and my Self disappears.

Margaret Stubbs

Nursery Rhymes

On slender stems they grow upright,
and fill the parks so green,
their golden heads nod day and night,
stark contrasts glow serene.

Men grow these plants, we hear of words
said in their sheds or shack,
but I have never, never heard
one nodding head talk back.

They are supposed to grow supreme
for entries into shows,
I've even seen these fingers green
that dig, then plant in rows.

Each day I try to say a lot
to individual flowers,
and even given them a tot
above their copious showers.

My entries never win a prize,
I was informed as such,
bulbs only rise, then rise and rise
If you speak to them in Dutch.

J. S. C. Webb

Poetry Comp

Sandy McTavish was a Scotsman bold
He had a shilling he couldn't hold
So with that shilling he has to part
And that broke poor Old Sandy's heart

When Sandy died he went to heaven
Where all his sins would be forgiven
But on his way he met a jew
Who said he was bound for heaven too.

When Sandy arrived at the golden gates
St Peter said you will hate to wait
For the golden gates have gone and bust
It must have been caused by the action or rust

So Sandy went down the ill trodden path
And there he met the devil's wrath
It was a fire so terribly hot
And over the fire was the devil's pot

So all you children do beware
Please be good and also fair
Just remember Sandy's lot
And do give it another thought.

Robert Wilson

Autumn

Autumn leaves fall all around,
Lying scattered on the ground.
Boughs and branches stripped naked, bare,
Dancing midst the moist, cool air.

Robin redbreast does appear,
With melodious song for us to hear.
Acorns dropping one by one,
Provide old squirrel with much fun.

Contrasting tones do abound,
Red, brown and yellow to be found.
Ripe berries and nuts hang plentiful,
For bird or beast to take his fill.

Dew and mist now re-appear,
To mask the antics of the deer.
Old badger and bunny hide away,
During the brightness of the day.

Red sky at night shouts out its glory,
But nature tells her own sweet story.
For winter's wrath is drawing near,
And we must make for winter cheer!

Patricia Drew

Dreaming

The constant tick of the clock at my side,
sends me sleepily towards my dream ride.
A roller coaster of sounds and sights,
fill me with both dread and delight.

Floating through mysterious scenes,
weightless, I drift like a bodiless being.
Laughter, singing, cries and screams,
I know not what these images mean.

Abstracts from the days events,
are just a few of the elements,
which make up weird and wonderful dreams,
a mixture of different plots and themes.

Dangerous adventures, wild romance,
luxurious living, song and dance.
To nightmarish visions, demons and ghouls,
haunted buildings, heroic fools.

I awaken, my room's a misty haze,
when it returns to normal, I'm quite amazed.
My dream had seemed to last so long,
but yet only an hour has been and gone.

Emma Louise Barker

Imaginary Universal Travel

Floating from Earth exploring beyond darkest depths to
    heavens on high
Touching the moon or stars by hand within one's mind and
    not one's eye
Calmly slowly toward bright light
Wishing to touch a dream, he concentrated, then waited.
Resisting an urge to glance to Earth, he looked upward
He was inclined to charge his mind, yet refrained from temptation
This he knew was to be his dream
The journey of his Imaginary Universal Travel.
Quietly watching him the Great Bear moved aside
While the North Star lit the Milky Way to keep the cosmic dust away
Leading him ever deeper into the Cosmos
Never had a sight caused such delight until this night.
Enveloped in wonder his every sense, eyes intent on seeing more
Everything within his grasp passed by so slowly
Astrological signs of old, so bold, beyond compare were there
The Fish, the Archer, each in turn passed in starlight and smiled.
Longing so much to touch the moon, too soon, too soon to yearn
He woke thinking of beautiful Diana, would he ever return
The Universal dream had gone in sleep
Imaginations wish a kiss from the moon forever lost to memory

V. Griffiths

A Tribute To An Island

I rode across the water,
To an island in the sun.
To see some racing, and have some fun.
To stand on the spot,
Where Mike Hailwood had done the ton,
As I stood at Ballacraine.
The Ducati coming like a bat out of hell,
The sound was music to my ears.
Just like a blur of red,
He's out of sight, but definitely not out of mind,
He left a legend behind.
As the tears roll down my cheek,
The words I can not speak.
For all those who follow and try,
Some will fall and surely die.
This is meant for one and all,
The islands final role call.
Lift up your eyes and say with pride,
It was an honour to see these great men ride.

Leslie Winterbone

Mr. T.V. And Video

Mr. T.V. and Video - You know who you are
The most laziest person by far
Won't get up to close the door
Ignores the draught - it stays afar

Mr. T.V and Video - has no big ideas
Never reaches for the sky
Just as well - they'd be written in that jotter
He forgot to go and buy

Mr. T.V and Video - I'd like to blow your mind
A mercy killing, to be kind
It won't take speed, or sticks of dynamite
Just a spanner in your rewind

Mr. T.V. and Video - You're the sloth of inspiration
Dreaming about dreaming, whilst sleeping
Thinking about nothing at all
Except T.V and Video

Mr. T.V and Video - Mr. Boring
You know who you are
Whirr whirr, dick dick,
The most laziest person by far.

Steve Bagshaw

Mystery

Voices muttering in the breeze,
Falling grains of sand,
Oh! how the fates do love to tease,
and keep the upper hand.

The current flows, but the tide can turn,
Who knows where it leads?
Will the harvest we reap, be bitter or sweet?
It depends on who sows the seed.

Design, and chance, stand side by side,
In answer to the eternal quest,
At our darkest hour, do we leave our shell?
or stay inside, and rest?

As our journey began, we had much to learn
Yet much we already knew,
Is this our maiden voyage?
or are we a seasoned crew?

To probe the enduring mystery,
has always been part of our history,
So we ask ourselves, every now and then,
What? where? why? and when?

Richard Stalker

I Have A Faith

I have a faith, oh such a faith,
I wish to others I could tell.
I can't explain, but it is by faith
I am guided through life so well.

Each morn I find another day
Is blessed again you see.
For in this beautiful new day
I can do what the Lord wants of me.

To be there at hand when others talk,
To help a friend in need, or foe.
To just be there, and give a prayer
When someone's full of woe.

Prayers reach up, joins God to those
Who cry out in their need.
Prayers are a link with God's will,
Helps His hand to intercede.

I have a faith, oh such a faith,
I wish to others I could tell it.
help them to know of the Saviour I know,
The joy - and the benefits from it.

Eirlys Green

Have A Heart

How sad is Mother Earth? How she must cry
For all her lost children living under her skies.
She hears the screams of her beloved. The whales in her seas
Can know no sanctuary from the harpoon boat.
And newborn seals on her shores,
What agonies must they endure? For a coat? She hears them all.
She hears the helpless crying and howling and screaming of her
innocents, of mice and rats and monkeys and cats, imploring piteously,
in laboratories all around her, for mercy. Her finely tuned ears
perceive new agonies, as the trees in her rain-forests succumb
To technology and machinery that poison and pollute
the very atmosphere the trees exist to clear
of poisons and pollutants so that all life may breathe.
How long can she sustain a life-form that causes so much pain?
Her very heart needs to nurture and to care for all life. Her
abundance is to share. We do not have the monopoly, just a tenancy.
She hears all, she feels all, she weeps for all.
For 'Earth' and 'Heart' are the same word, don't you see? And 'Ear'
and 'Hear' and 'Tear' sparkle from within like a pearl. Of wisdom?
Maybe a pearl we would do well to contemplate, before it's too late.

Helen J. Wright

A Tribute To Freddie Mercury

His name was Freddie Mercury, the best by far this century,
Joined Brian, John and Roger, to form a band called Queen,
No finer artiste anywhere, a voice so powerful and rare,
Unique, he was to say the least, the best there's ever been,

Living life in harmony, those boys and Freddie Mercury,
Turning out those records, like the world has never seen,
From Wembley to Budapest, they proved to all they were the best,
Four lads a cut above the rest, had joined the music scene,

There is no one who could replace, forever more there'll be a space,
For no one has the talent, that was the King of Queen,
He left his fans a legacy, that brilliant Freddie Mercury,
A collection of his music, and videos for our screen,

Yes he'll go down in history, be there for all the world to see,
With the rest of his family, those boys, the mighty Queen,
A legend forever more, remembered, that is for sure,
Roger, John and Brian, have showed us that they mean,

They've shown their fans their loyalty and respect for Freddie Mercury
The greatest showman ever, to perform upon our screen,
The promises they made that day, when Freddie sadly slipped away,
The greatest tribute ever, not to replace the King and Queen.

Margaret Plant

Missouri River

Gaze up to the tall Pines seemingly touching the blue skies,
Here, God's creation, mother nature and tranquillity lies.
The calm waters of its winding river, stretch through utter wilderness,
Canoeing along Sioux country, my heart is lost in its loveliness.

Moving on, now miles from civilization, I pitch my tent,
Relieve myself behind a bush, my personal need to remain decent!
A fluffy skunk decides to join my bathroom floor,
Thank goodness it did not leave its appalling scent at my door.

The stunning black silhouettes of the scenery against the red sky,
Reflects on its River as the evening draws nigh.
The shrill of the musical crickets and the mist from the water's edge,
Accompanies the howling Coyote under the moonlights pledge.

I lay my head down on the heather picked pillow, spiders and all,
Morning brings strong winds, storms and heavy rainfall.
Petrified, I paddle though treacled waters, my plan now alters,
Blabbering something resembling a prayer, as God never falters.

Bewilderment engulfs me, with sheer exhaustion I await for help,
Golden Eagle Scout with infinite wisdom saves me from the cards dealt,
My dice with death, experience and true grit,
Now that I live to tell the tale, I wouldn't change one minute of it

Deborah Lockwood

A Probing Curiosity!

A probing curiosity!
'Black' mother, 'white' father!
Torn between such extremity!
Who's better, who's right who's culture?
It's an endless fight...
But what of me, a silent observer, a fence - sitter,
A mere spectator?
No! I was cajoled into life...
But I was innocent
Where's the justice, where's the law?
Half - breed, hybrid, mongrel, mule, comma five,
A gloomy experiment!
Yet behold! I breath, am alive!
A parent is a parent.....
But I, a sacrificed individual, confecting views,
Oh cruel struggle, such sweet abuse....
I'll not tolerate it! Who am I?!
I'll seek, search, find myself through my own eye!
My conscience clear, my morals firm,
And low, I'll rise victorious!

Bridget Tania Rose

"A 'Buck' Or Two Passing Hands!"

Last week .. I gave you .. a "Buck" from me -
which you've kindly handed... back this week!
It could easily go towards cake for our tea -
But, I simply do not have the cheek!
I really appreciate your very kind offer -
But lolly I have, tons, of mine... and Dad's!
Thus.. I'm not short of.. a single coffer -
of which, I'm rather, frightfully - glad!
May the "Buck".. go back to you?
To feather your nest - I'm sure you'll agree -
For you to be money-bags, one day, too!
with lots of love... for you... from me.

Meg Gaspar

Lilliputian Fairyland

Summer's evening a warm whispering kiss
Of breeze upon my cheek
I walk through damp grass
And smell honeysuckle's heady scent
The whirring wings of hawk moths.
Attending each flower like airborne waiters
In flights and then before me I behold
A village in miniature of tiny lights
Like Gulliver I feel as I look down upon them
Gleaming jewels of mint green
The glow worm's beacon of love
To its suitor up above
They meet and pair
With saddened air. And then dimming theatre lamps
They part and die. But not in vain
The eternal return of terrestrial stars.
To catch the eye

Michael Joseph Lafferty

Forgive And Forget

Your life's a glorious cycle of songs,
for my love thought I was a dunce youth.
And love is a thing that couldn't go wrong,
for if my darling only knew the truth.

For I laid my only heart in your hands,
as I laid beside the crystal brooks,
I watched it fade away like golden sands,
and held the silken lines and silver hooks.

My everlasting love will never end,
for my darling looked very elegant.
Her love is my gold that shall never vend,
I knew your love could never be supplant.

So let our love blossom like a rose,
for what we have is too precious to lose.

David O. K. Fashakin

Final Love

I yearn for the day
When a velvet-black horse appears on the horizons,
Its tail floating in the wind of racing darkness,
Its rider a silken fantasy to my dreams.

A rose between his teeth, the man would watch
With smouldering eyes,
His dark hair shadowing the path of the horses tail,
His eyes the colour of waves crashing to the shore.

His gloved hand would reach out to mine,
And I would take it, my dress rippling in the frosty air,
As I straddled the horse behind him,
Freedom calling through the dawn
As the moon gave way to the sun.

Together, a huddled twosome on a whinnying horse,
We would gallop through the heather-clad moor,
A universe in front of us,
The dreary dark past banished forever.

Cheryl Banks

The Hardest Thing To Do In The World Is...
Write A Poem

You can't think of a word to write
Or think of a title that'll sound alright
Looking around the room and it's making you sad
It's the poem's fault - it's driving you mad!
Finally you've got your very first line
Then someone shouts "Hey, you've copied mine!"
Tearing up your paper, you take another shot
The teacher approaches, "What have you got?"
You answer "Sir, I haven't a clue"
Then all of a sudden you know what to do
Picking up your ball-point pen
You start to write your ballad, when....
Your mind has gone blank
Your ideas have just sank
Those great suggestions you've now forgotten
You begin to feel depressed and rotten
You decide to take a final try
Before you break down and cry
Sighing, you wish you were a poem whiz
Because, the hardest thing to do in the world is... write a poem.

Laura L. Nisbet

The Rogue

Found him Thursday night.
Black and White. Full of fright.
Took him home and gave him tea.
Thought he'd stay a while with me.

After meat and milk,
He stretched upon my bed of silk.
Then I showed him round our home.
Thought he'd like it. Might not roam.

Well, he stayed for days. We fought in ways.
Had to have the flea sprays.
A collar too, of purple royal.
And he tried hard to me be loyal.

But then the sadness to him came.
Here with me not quiet the same.
His inner thoughts, I did not know.
Even 'though I loved him so.

For love there is no cure. After this, I'm sure.
With early start the following morn.
From me sadly Roamer had gorn.
Back to his home. The next road alorn.

Caroline O'Neill

A Stranger, Not Unknown

Have you ever been touch'd by someone
you don't know,
A stranger, quite of whom you still know all
That matters,
Who carries a tragic air?

It may be beauty but a little flaw'd,
Marr'd by some tiny imperfection
That stands out all the more from all the rest;
Perhaps a smile that hides a pendant tear,
Perhaps eternity shows through,
A mortal immortality that cannot last a year,
A glimpse of fear.

I saw a girl as such the other day,
So beautiful, but not in earthly way:
Fair, yet so fragile melted by heart away
But not with love, only with sorrow
For all her kind; for ev'ry down that comes
Before the morrow.

Thom Aitken

Spring Awakening

Awake, awake it is the Spring,
Cold damp winter days have flown,
The heavens are filled with birds who sing
And nature wakes to claim her own.

The trees spread up to greet the sun
Whose gentle rays warm field and dell,
The gambolling lambs are full of fun
As they scatter wide o'er field and fell.

The ice and snow are melting fast,
And fill the brook which sparkles by,
Beneath the bridge it hurries past
To join the brimming river nigh.

The Shepherd with his dog Carew
Gathers all his wandering flock.
His whistle tells him what to do
As they work together round the clock.

The birds return and mate in pairs
The buds break forth in grand array,
The scent of blossom fills the air
And all around is bright and gay.

Norma Verney

Untitled

Trees stretch before me far ahead,
The ruined gazebo stands alone,
Pond left to stagnate.
I walk through parched grass,
Past overgrown hedges,
Clinging vines climb grey crumbling walls.

A child's face (a sharp contrast),
Shatters this sorrowful scene,
Bright eyes (full of life) twinkle
mischievously.
This place is a stage,
And she an actress,
To her there is no death,
life is for living,
No time to stay still.

She finds a red bloom amongst the nettles,
And puts it in her hair,
She dances and twirls through the fallen walls,
The wind in the trees join in.

Julie Russell

Bluebells On The Tube

This new life, this new world,
all would be rosy, we were told.
Shinning apartments, snazzy cars,
no chance of unveiling societies scars.
Dinner parties and birthday treats,
expensive holidays and ruffled sheets.
Happy children, smiling pets,
forget the mortgage and the debts.
Slowly the dream faded away,
rainy days, although it was may.
Committing suicide was in my thoughts,
from a bridge, just in shorts.
I took the tube to Waterloo,
for anything but that same old view.
Things changed near Parsons Green,
with bluebells, the loveliest I'd ever seen.
In their hundreds, in full bloom,
looking serene, in a rail siding tomb.
Their blueness affected me in a way,
perhaps now I'll die another day.

James Loxton

What's Happening?

Is everyone blind, can't anyone
see, what is now, and what is to be,
The world is growing smaller and
smaller, our population is mounting taller.
The world is ashes turning to dust,
just like car engines turn to rust,
it's not only us living on this world,
we have other things to consider as well,
children are dying, can't you hear
the earth crying, as the sun drowns into the horizon.
I can do nothing, but it will soon be rising-soon the
world is going to end,
but the problem is,
no one knows when?

Gemma McGonigle

Genises

The planet of genises the bringer of life
Casting doubt on the solitude planet
Life is there but in horrific storms
Fleeing people underground to where it is warm
Children asking where abouts is dad
Mothers giving no answer but the face expressions sad
The rest of the men all out trying to find food and water
No time for greed in these to parties the only system is to barter
The strongest men that are loners don't seem to survive
But the ones that join in groups are the ones that seem more alive
All joining together to help with any need
Like a big family with no hate and no greed
The love of this place is based on the people
It's just the planet that's gone wrong
Are planets like us where without love grow feeble
But with care and health will grow strong.

Stuart Haworth

Hold That Dream

There is this Dream I have each night,
It is a Dream of a Better world;
Where Peace will Reign, throughout the Earth,
When I wake up, I see tears and Pain;
Wailing Mothers, and Starving Babes,
Sons and Daughters, takes years to Rear;
They are Burying them in a Skeleton's grave.

Still the Dream returns, most every night,
It is that Dream of a Peaceful World;
A world where Peace will Reign Supreme,
So hold that Dream, never let it go;
And so walk on, to that Better World,
Maybe someday, when I wake up,
I'll find that World is Here at last.

Adlin Watkis

Distantly Lost In Your Fears

If I could express as much as I love you
all the roses and poppies in the country
will flower with painless thorns,
all the love that I have given...

Golden are the dreams of his belly
when she caresses his face, I want to show
as much as master as the birds to liberty.

You come to me as my shy boy
you come to me without rancour
you come to me happily and then
you won't cry, never ever again, my child.

As to find you have murdered
the sad pain of golden carnations

He feels the fear as it catching
he pretends feeling the beautiful sensation of to sleep close,
to another human being

So... Who is going to advise you, boy?
  when you remain alone ... Even to die
  don't you understand that you grew up?
  Then never ever sleep in my bed again.

Elizabeth L. Faitarone

Autumn's Promise

The leaves of gold, yellow and red
Fall from the trees and foretell ahead
Of winter, with its long cold nights,
Stretching continuously with days of sparse light.

My heart sinks at the sobering thought
Of trees dressed daringly in nought
But branches, reaching to the sky
Desperately, but unaware of exactly why.

Winter is usually quite barren and bare
Bereft of colour and the suns bright happy glare
This year the tenth month is still very warm
Which, hopefully, will delay the oncoming storm.

I believe I was born a child of the sun
Which is why I detest winters glum
Unforgiving ways, with conkers, underfoot crisp rustling leaves
And a bitter wind whistling under the eaves.

How I yearn for days of winter to pass
Rapidly by, and allow me to once again bask
Under a vivid blue sky in the warm summer sun
Warming my body right through to the bone.

Marie Jacqueline Walker

Despair

Sky overcast
Face downcast
A man walks alone
He thinks of his past

Not much money
But jobs to be had
Collieries working
It wasn't so bad

The man looks up
Despair in his eyes
No chance of a job
No clear skies

A ray of sunshine from the sky
A sign of hope, no time to cry
A glint in his eye as he hurries his pace
A hint of a smile on his careworn face
The sky is blue, there's a new life ahead
He'd show them all
He's not yet dead.

I. B. Evans

Mother Miracles

Thy gift of life received from God
For nine months I was blest,
My child, was one with me
Joined by a cord of flesh
Two hearts did beat two souls did shine
One was my child's, the other was mine
Within my womb a spirit of five
Clothed in flesh and filled with desire
Entered this world naked and divine
The cord was severed the miracle was mine
You came into this world with a cry of distress
To face the material and do your best
Challenge this life with a humble heart
Never lose faith God takes your part
These words, with love, I give to you
Forgive, share, be kind
And all that's good returns anew
And will give you peace of mind

Mary Ann Paterson

Revolt

One man standing alone,
Facing a barrel of cold steel on his own,
A row of mighty tanks stopped in their tracks hold fire,
The small individual waits, refusing to retire,
The man demands, urges the soldiers to retreat,
Knowing the movement for freedom will not be beat,
He wants reassurance, calm and peace,
For attacks on defenceless men and women to cease,
More tanks, trucks and troops roll in ignoring his pleas,
They threaten, cajole, shoot, bludgeon, killing with ease,
Mayhem and carnage are the scenes,
The world watches shocked and horrified on TV screens,
The slaughter in Tiananmen Square continues,
As the West sees the savagery on innocent, unarmed civilians,
Old men in a closed temple room,
Deciding democracy is doom,
Communism is the way ahead,
Those against should be jailed, brainwashed or dead,
China's student revolt is crushed in a bloody attack,
The way forward in June 1989 became the way back.

Steven McElroy

The Poet?

The poet? Bends to his thankless task,
Scribbling his muse, across acres of paper.
Words tumbling forth, hastening as years speed by,
To leave a desperate mark, before his span is done.
Not, for monetary gain or fame, although some do,
But rather for art or hobbies sake, one day, perhaps?
To see a line or two of his thoughts,
Hopes, desires, dark imaginings, appear in fine print.
To show his friends and leave to children's, children.
And by so-doing prove - he also lived, and life was not a dream

A. G. McRobb

Lost Mail Or Black Hole

Auden wrote of Night trains, and Bejethmen too
but my questions different, although not new..
what do you think happens to the mail that disappears?
Where does it go to, it must go some where,
rather like the 'dd socks' which in my wash appear,
each year I have a basket, I don't know from where...
I don't understand physics, quantum theory's or black holes,
I listen read and hear a lot, but it doesn't really mean a lot..
you see I have a problem of my very own
What happens to that letter they said was in the post.
What happened to those tickets, now those really were no joke,
then there was that cheque they sent...that too never came
What that happened to that parcel they said just the same
What happened to that second sock....that too has disappeared
then there are those little spoons- I know that they were there
now like all the other things, they're nowhere to be found.
Could there be a black hole somewhere around?

Lilia Baillie-Hamilton

Love And Learn

Is it just a vision, or could it be a dream
is it just illusion, or is it very real
Can you touch it with your wisdom
how does it make you feel
If you're happy in this confusion
C'mon help us turn the wheel.

Go greet yourself tomorrow go meet yourself today
ask yourself the question what makes your life this way
you can touch it with your wisdom
but you've got to keep your faith
an open heart is vital
and so is give and take

Get down to new age thinking because
it's destiny it's fate
new doors they are now opening
don't hesitate don't wait
the reason for you being here
is deep inside your mind
consider nature's calling
before the end of time

Vincent Rees

Untitled

I sit here all alone and wonder why
It was you my darling that had to die;
Your loving smile and caring way
I'll remember, to my dying day;
Unemployment came to you;
And work with them I had to do;
Now I've retired, and what we planned to do,
Alas now I'll have to do without you;
I feel your presence all around,
Having seen your body placed in the ground;
The times we had together were good;
The tears must stop, I know I really should;
I'm trying, yes trying very hard,
Even though my heart is scarred;
I have memories which I will always keep;
Thinking on them, I sometimes weep,
I will try my best to carry on;
It's now so hard, now you are gone.
Until we are united once again;
I must remember, your life was not in vain.

Janice Jackson

Who Would Be A Mother

After the pain of child birth
Having to wake at 3 a.m. in the morning
With a screaming baby pacing the floor making formulas
Who would be a mother?

As they have grown she lies in bed waiting
For her children to return home
Sting up lightening to the cars in the distance
Is that a taxi? The relief of the key in the door
Who would be a mother?

She settles down in bed
And as she drifts off to sleep
She realizes she would spend many more like this
She whispers; who would be a mother?

Mum, I am sorry, I am having a baby
Angrily she shouts at her daughter, but what good is anger
For she hears a little voice nan! nan!
Her grandson comes running up to her with a broken toy
With pride she kisses him softly on his cheeks
Life is the most precious gift a mother can ever give
Who would be a mother? I would

Irma Lewis

Untitled

Lonely and loveless I stand,
So much to say, but no-one to hear,
So much to give, but no-one to receive,
Down trickles one solitary tear.

Amongst all the confusion and dreams,
I try to hold on to reality.
Amongst all the pressure,
I try to retain my individuality.

I try to find love and friendship,
I search for warmth and trust;
But I am met with indifference -
I am desolate, forlorn - lost.

So I travel through this bleak and hostile life,
And pray the Lord my soul to keep;
For the road of life is long and lonely
And I have no tears left with which to weep.

Tagreed Mohammed Ismail

Who Are The Animals?

As I look upon the fish,
Their faces fill with despair
Covered in all that oil,
Is it really fair?

As I look up at the birds,
I notice that look of fear.
The fear of people shooting,
But we just stand and leer.

Gentle creatures with long white tusks,
Glistening in the sun.
But now they are just a target,
For poachers with a gun.

Cute little puppy dogs,
Bred to fight and win.
I do not find this sporting,
In fact it is a sin.

Animal killing is not a sport,
What do the animals do?
I do not think it's fair,
But then it's up to you.

Lisa Devere

In My "Country"

I was a lonesome little waif
When I found my wood of Oak and Beech
How their spreading branches lowered to my reach
As if in their majesty they bent so strong
To the simplicity of a waif
And swayed to the lilt of her happy song.

I gathered sticks 'neath those silent friends
To take to my foster-mum living alone
To look after her was my childish boast
"I'll bring sticks for a cosy fire
And brown bread toast!"

One day a stranger came to my wood
My instinct sensed he meant no good.
I sought the refuge of my majestic Beech
Moving away from his cajoling reach.
Suddenly, a shot rang out beyond the fence
The gamekeeper, who from all his duties thereabouts
Came in time to my defence.

From that day, my faith has held a firm belief
That God too was there, in my "country", so brief.

Rachel Y. Booth

Spring Time Lamb

Skipping, running, leaping into the air,
Straying from their Mothers as far as they dare.
Exploring, playing, finding their way.
Four more playmates were born today.
This is the season for everything new,
Spring is here. The cold spells are few.

A new life beginning with each Sunrise,
Most are the same, in looks, shape and size.
Which one is which? No one can tell,
Apart from their Mothers, and they go by smell.
Some may be black, but most will be white,
Crying out loudly, when they take a fright.

Of what am I talking? I'm sure you all know,
They're born just after the last falls of snow.
Look in the fields at Spring Time and see,
These cute little creatures jumping with glee.
Their Mother the Ewe. Their Father the Ram.
The season of Spring. Of course, it's the Lamb!

Tracey Beacall

Is That Mr. White?

'Hello, is that 3, 2, 1, 7, and are you Mr. White?'
"Well, yes, you have my number but That Name isn't right
You rang me twice on Saturday and again last night
So Please don't telephone again, it gets me so uptight

Would it help you if my name were Green or Pink or Red?
(But don't ring up at midnight and drag me out of bed)
You have a charming female voice - are you an old flame?
Because you're asking who I am, but didn't give your name

You didn't ask if I were married, and by the way, are you?
Tell me what I'm missing, maybe I'll turn Blue
If you're after money, if you're treasure trove
Darling, I have news for you, my name could be Mauve!

So now we've sorted that one out, whatever made you ring?
Have we been quite close, we two, you want a final fling?
No, dear sir, I'm going to tell you something quite amazing
I'm not what you think I am - I'm selling Double Glazing!

Stan Blake

The Factory

Monday morning five past eight
Weary and tired, I crawl through the gate
Production line? Where am I going.
Still young party throwing
Why am I here?
This is not for me.
The dreams I once had
Weren't of factories
Working my soul in the ground
Put through hell for an honest pound.
Long live Friday
It waits for me
To be with my friends
To laugh and be free.
I count the minutes, I count the seconds
Five more days Friday beckons
One of the days I'll be free
I'll be free from the factory.

Jason Ryan

Perfect Deception

The perfect look of perfect eyes
that kiss you as they tell you lies.
A face of Angelic innocence
Sprinkled with a look of in offence.
A devil lurks behind that face
Whose only want is a disgrace.
The web of lies which has been spun
was told by lips as beautiful as the sun.
Not all is ever what it seems
Perfect deception deems.

Anna Maher

Loss And Gain

I finally decided to sell the statue.
And I convinced myself I wouldn't care
If the buyer threw up her hands, rejected,
and said, "No way!"

So I wrapped it carefully, saying goodbye,
Sparing a few, quiet moments to remember
When we had bought it in that open air market.
Then, 'it' was 'they'. A man and woman casting their nets.
Frozen forever in a graceful swing of arm and body.
Now, I was parting with him. She had gone long ago.
Both, memories of a past I'd been glad to leave.

And so, because of that, I'd no regret
In seeing him placed on the shop's high shelf,
Who knows? Perhaps one day he'll meet his fisher girl again,
Then they'll stand together, proud before the waves

Evelyn Ross

Untitled

When you've glanced at me I've already stared at you,
When you've drunk from me I've already eaten you,
And when you've hit me I've already killed you.

Just because you can't see me it doesn't mean I'm not there,
a blind man can't see but a deaf man can stare.

You see a thorn I see a rose, do you see the corn
or do you the crows?
You think it's cheap I know it's free,
Do you see a face or do you see me?

I think I'm silver but I may be black,
I think I'm a highway but I may be a track,
I think I'm drunk but I may be straight,
I think I'm too early I know I'm too late.

You think you've seen me but you've only looked at me.
You think you've felt but you've only touched me.
You think you've killed me but you've only shot me.
You think you see daylight but it's only the sun.
You think this has ended but it's only just begun.

Lauren Joy Dunwoody

Dartmoor

Oh, Heather moor, "Where do thy secrets lie?"
In Spring and Summer, Autumn, Winter,
Time cannot fade thy awesome shade.

Oh, Heather moor, your tors, your fields,
Your beauty enhanced,
While we walk in a trance.

Oh, Heather moor, time will not fade in tomorrow's days,
From Hay Tor to Hound Tor,
From Easton Tor to Kings Tor,
The wildlife roams in a place made its own.

Oh, Heather moor, your beauty belies the secrets you hide,
From 'Janes' Grave' to the prayer rock of a bygone age.

Oh, Heather moor, history does not record,
The harmonious accord of many who say,
"It has always been done that way".

Oh, Heather moor, fane would I fathom,
Thy nature's chasms,
Always would I rather thy nature treasure.

D. J. Squire

Spring

Spring is very nice and clear,
People don't have any fear.
Rivers are very blue and cool
I can swim in a swimming pool.
Naughty children play pong ping
Gay is the word to pronounce it's spring.

Danielle Livesey

581

The Cat

He lay in wait like a black shadow cast,
Waiting for the wing that wasn't so fast,
Will it be blackbird or tiny sparrow,
To find its doom in the garden farrow,
Is it for pleasure or instinct long past,
That I'll not know of the black shadow cast,
Mother of the doomed cry with fright,
Search all day and into the night,
Hoping its offspring might still be with life,
Cry no more but start with new strife,
As it lay in wait like a black shadow cast,
It maybe the first but it won't be the last,
As he lay in wait like a black shadow cast.

A. E. Carr

If All

If all the world's butterflies came together
wouldn't it be a wonderful sight
what a show of splendid colours
with their wings all outright

If all the world's songbirds sang
altogether in one song
what a sound it would be
maybe we could sing along

If all the world's people joined hands
and lived in harmony
and learned to care about each other
what a peaceful world it would be

Andrew W. Green

"Green"?

How green was my valley?
Well it was never "green"
It has always been "Black"
My father's face was always "Black"
He worked in the local coal mine
When I was a small child he would
Go to work in the mornings when it was
"Black" and return in the night when
It was "Black", at his funeral we were
All dressed in "Black" the hearse was also
"Black". When I was old enough to work
I also entered this "Black" work place
"Black, black bloody black!"
"Black" and "Blood"
"Black" it was not "Green"
How green was my valley?
How green were my people?
My blackened green valley.

Mario Francesco Flynn

Our Frailty

Next time you meet
A person frail and bent,
Remember this is not
The way they were heaven sent,
They arrive here just like you.
A little boy or girl dressed in pink or blue
They grew up tall
Thought they knew it all
They danced they drank
They met their mates
To grow up they could not wait.
So next time you see
Them shuffle down the street,
Remember our maker we all must meet
Extend to them a helping hand
to beat them up was not the plan
the die you cast will follow on
before very long it's you
who will not feel so strong
as you struggle hard just to belong.

Gabrielle Carroll

The Cryer

Holding court, amongst the crowd the cryer takes a bow
The act we watched can't be denied for attention pity and how
She held us all in trance-like state until she stopped the show
A dozen hankies raining down, she wipes away the flow.

And whilst this spectacle goes on the crowd doesn't see as well
The mask of pain which lines the face of the dry-eyed girl whose shell
Has wrapped its grief around her life, a hard and bitter coat
She wants to cry, no tears will come, so long has her grief been stowed
Away in a dark and secret place where no one dares to go
A place where only she can hide, where only she can know

So silently she walks away and leaves the show behind
If only she could hold 'that' court, but people are so blind
They only see the outward pain with no real wish to delve deeper.
So time and time again they console
The self-indulgent weeper.

Mandy Flower

The Everlasting Flower

At the base of our plant is the stem,
There is only one path which is bold and clear,
Higher up the stem breaks into many branches,
Each springing forth in a different direction,
You choose your own branch leading onto others,
At the end of everyone's journey,
There, at the highest tip,
Is their flourishing flower,
Yours is the Orchid,
So delicately light,
Its soft white petals show through the rosy tints of your inner charm
I have dipped this flower in gold,
Though the gold is not as precious as you, it captures all your beauty,
Even if your petals perish with time,
All I see is your golden smile,
It is,
The everlasting flower.

Puja Loree Chadha

A Last Farewell

I stood in the room with the curtains half drawn,
Sunbeams tried to give solace to my heart,
The silence, an awesome weight on my shoulders, at dusk and at dawn.
A silent tear, so shameful and yet so right, tearing my soul apart.
No sound exists, no breeze, not even the cry of a bird -
Only silence and emptiness filled up the room, and my aching heart
Filled up with hurt.
Your smile has gone, no hand to grasp.
I look at you with tearful eyes, I kiss your face, A last farewell
And my last task:
Good-bye my love, I won't despair,
'Though you've gone - we'll meet somewhere

Helmut Koehler

That Dreams Are Made Of

That I could fly, and glide, and float at will, the envy of the birds on high.
That I may drift with timeless speed between the stars in silent sky,
and view at will in close delight, the magic of their gleaming light,
to reach where man's endeavours fail as yet, without the need to
breathe or fret, at searing suns, nor icy moons and yet be clear of
eye with senses keen, no need for eyes to close at intense gleam.

Ah! But mortal creatures we, who know no boundaries in a dream.
But I have travelled dare I say? To distant planets far away.
For now I know our lives are dreams, 'tis but a lesson learned it seems.
To swell the store, in future lives to use, each life but the smallest spark—
and more, to contemplate the Cosmic path, and muse—how
small we are, how great the task, to worry and confuse.
Whither are we going—many of us ask.

Terry Ward

November

The drenched foul earth below commands the leaves to fall,
The frost bites at their stems, and the cruel wind beats them,
Screaming with its shrill voice "leave the trees and fall."

The weak give way, their lives at a close,
   they lose their hold and tumble,
Battered by the blustery storm, down to the earth below,
For some the fight is not over yet, the frost may bite,
   the wind may scream - but they won't let go

For those below who have left the branch,
They still have time for their drunken dance,
Round and round they spin and swirl on the cold sodden
   earth below
Red, brown, yellow, orange, green, their lives end
   dancing dresses spin in dizzy delight,
As the orchestral wind cries its musical call.

Floating gently downward on their lives' last journey
   like coloured snowflakes to the earth.
Even when, the dead, the dying - dancing leaves are bundled into
sodden heaps. Still they fly with grace and ease, aided by the
smallest breeze, their whispering voices laugh,, as if to say
"we'll dance yet for another day"

   M. Kemp

"Sweet Life"

As life goes on, and you're getting older,
The sun loses heat, you feel so much colder,
So many things have happened,
Having witnessed both good times and bad,
Experienced times of sheer delight,
And times of grief and being sad.

Each person is a very special person,
Conceived between woman and man,
Look around and see what God gave you,
Try and better it if you can.

Life on earth lasts as long as fate decides,
It's up to the individual to make the most of low tides,
Each and every day should be treasured,
That day will surely not come again,
Appreciate the sunshine, birds, and flowers,
And welcome the refreshing rain.

Life is sweet, you will never pass this way again,
Enjoy the things you love, do forget the pain,
Each person has their share of sorrow and grief,
But life on earth is so very brief.

   Gwen Dalley

Gettyburg's Legacy

As the general's gaze searched for wisdom
And the hard ground ate up the blue and grey
On marched the flags of poor and rich
On this their dying day.
"Straight through the center" cried Johnny Reb
"Into their midrift, that's where we will go.
Push them back, cut them down", cried yank
I'm afraid it must be so.
"Lead us to victory canon",
"Let Washington hear the sound of our muskets".
"Hold for our beloved capital. Fix those bayonets private
And do what you have been entrusted".
Open fields was defences sheer delight.
Where onward they came, to stand and fight.
Mercy forgotten and rage fulfilled.
Where men became ghosts, when justice was killed.
Wielding swords of fury, with hand fist and boot
did they take away their brothers' limbs to gather lusty loot.
When silence broke, and settled was the dust for all.
Not both of us, not all of us, was written in the stony wall.

   Robert Connolly

Gaze

The rays of the sun-set lit up your eyes
Your gaze was sharp as I felt your heart throb
Then a wave of the autumn breeze stroked my hair
And the gentleness of its touch brought reality to my heart.

Beautiful, you are, and sweeter than the wine you served me
Spontaneous and innocent, but a gap of differences separated us.
Was it fear or reluctance that pulled me away?
Or was it arrogance and pride that filled my mind!

I glanced at you and denied my whim
I dare to join you, but behove to behold.
Old as the sand and deep as the sea,
Yet you're clear as mid-summer sky and young as every spring.

You share my tongue and could share my sheet
Was it fate or a chance that we should meet?
For flesh, I know, is a perishing phase,
Still bewildered I fell looking up your face.

When a vow to depart cannot be denied,
Behind me all leave an empty space.
Look at it... remember me, there might be a trace,
For, I will as time goes by, remember your gaze.

   Sherry Noman

Here We Go Again

Beads of perspiration prickle on the brow,
Tickling, trickling, creep down twitchy nose;
Globules of sweat blob down upon the paper,
Like raindrops falling on a budding rose.

A scrap of paper clenched in trembling hands,
Cold-clammy, fumbly-fingered hands that hold
The passport to a paradise of wonders,
The key to Eldorado, lands of gold.

Narrowed eyes, transfixed, glued to a T.V. screen,
Watch coloured balls and numbers tumbling round;
Mesmeric, rising, falling, colours, numbers,
Entrance, excite emotions, sight and sound

Anticipate the button pushed, the drum-roll -
Expectations swollen now to fever-pitch;
Then, one by one, the round bits of plastic
Shatter the dreams of one who would be rich...

A scrap of paper ripped up, torn to tatters,
Tossed, petulantly, into the nearest bin,
But I suppose I'll do the Lottery again next week,
And, who knows, perhaps, maybe next week I'll win!

   Angie Creed

The Poor Woman

Tischer is my name. The poor woman.
I live in the olden days.
Most people think I'm odd. I seem to be, but I'm not.

Day by day I look in the mirror
and I see scraps and pieces falling from my face.
I smell the smell of stale beer on my body.

Sometimes I would beat myself because I was ashamed of myself.
Before when I wasn't poor
I had a family, I had kids but now they're gone.

Now I know it's true what they say that to be poor is a crime.

Everyday I hear the sounds and the vibrations of people
Looking and talking about me.
Everywhere and talking about me.
Everywhere I go people treat me like dirt.
I sometimes ask myself this question:
Do I really belong here?

Sometimes I feel like killing myself
So it could take the pain away that I'm suffering.
I feel like I don't know myself any more.
I feel like I'm locked up in a cupboard somewhere and I can't get out.

   (Wanya) Benjamin Kusi

Jersey

The largest of the Channel Isles,
From France it is fourteen miles.
For holidays Jersey's the ideal place.
Les Landes is where the horses race.

Trinity, where the Zoo is found;
Surrounded by landscaped ground.
The Orchid Foundation is near;
It is worth a visit, whilst here.

There are many choices of where to eat.
Vegetarian dishes, seafood varieties or meat.
Opera House, Museum, Art Centre too.
The Living Legend, amazing to view.

In August is The Battle Of Flowers
It almost guarantees 'no showers'
Most people who visit this lovely isle
Want to return and stay a while.

Valerie C. Park

Made For Her

Could she be the brightest, the most beautiful and loved?
For she turns my pain into glee.
Yet joy cannot even express such enhancement.
Such excitement,
Such wonderfulness.

As laughs are plenty but tears are few.
Even they dance a delight.
Warmth shining and charming itself.
And again a laugh,
And again a laugh.

Yet here lies mystery and here lies doubt.
And pools of darkness swimming in secrecy.
Paleness so pure.
Such excitement,
Such wonderfulness.

And I am contented here and I am at rest.
Peace sleeps around my ankles.
And touches my mouth with a kiss.
And again a laugh,
And again a laugh.

Luka Isherwood

Love Is Blind

Oh! Perfect love is being played
The bride gloom waits quite unafraid
The best man stands there face all white
Thinking of the previous night
They lived it up gag after gag
They'll never forget that last stag
Because from now on the bride is here
No more snooker no more beer
When the words are said I do and I will
That's the beginning you are climbing the hill
And there at the top will be your wife
Get out you fool and run for your life

F. Wright

Dignity

Society says I'm old now, and yes I feel that way.
I've worked hard all my life, and now I've had my day
The state gives me a pension, but I find it hard to cope.
Don't get me wrong, I'm grateful, and never give up hope.
But winters do seem colder, and food is awfully dear.
So I'm careful with my money and wish the spring was here.
I get a bit confused now with all these forms to fill,
The council tax, and D.S.S. Sometimes it makes me ill.
I don't want to die yet, but maybe when I do,
I won't be such a burden on both the State and you.
I've spent a lot of time on earth, and 'though I'm old and grey,
I wish the world would realize, I've got a lot to say.
Muddled I might be at times, but I've got a lot to give.
Give me back my dignity, And I'll teach you how to live.

Penniluck Nicolson

The Deep Lagoon

The Vanishian carousel, the ancient atoll,
Chequered, fluorescent and coloured with glee,
Colours through glass distilled and perplexed,
Ice in the summertime melting to dust,
Sea in winter cold and robust,
Its scintillating fury and lavish finesse, ravishing
anger then cool arrest.
Swishing and swaying and dancing in the light
then zealously salacious and smoothly ignite,
The sun in the distance beating down heavy,
The moon in its corner humble and steady,
Cupid's last arrow fired into the night,
Readily stumbles and falls out of sight,
His hands are but withered, his wings are worn through,
for most Cupid's arrows sink in the deep blue.

Tony Michael

What Is Old Age?

Old age is remembering the things that you did
when a teenager or only a kid.
When people respected the law and the police,
and Woodbines were only a ha'penny a piece.
When four pence on a haircut was all that you spent;
but now your "get up and go" has got up and went.
You know it's old age when your knees start to buckle
not the belt round you waist,
and food seems to have lost that old-fashioned taste.
Mint balls and slippers, seems always the gauge
of what you would want as some think of "old age."
You know it's old age when
pretty young ladies pass you in style,
and all you can raise is your hat and a smile.
No curries or lasagna or Italian paella's
Just attics and chimney-sweeps, pac-a-macs and cellars.
But in this Third age of Life with experience of the past,
it's the brightest of times with memories that last;
some linger on of what you did aged ten or eleven,
are as fresh as tomorrow when you're eighty-seven.

Ray Oldham

Untitled

I remember the playing cards and the crafty grin,
The whisky, light and bitters, and tobacco tin,
The rolled up cigarettes he made with care,
The hat, and bike and of course "His chair,"
The mysterious pictures that hung on the wall,
He seemed to have a story for them all,
I still remember being sat on his knee,
I must only have been about two or three,
But the love he showed then; he showed till he died,
And all the above memories made sure that I cried,
The tears will soon go, but the memories will still be there
Of the Granddad I loved sitting in his chair.

Gary Grange

Guess Who Is This?

This poem is dedicated to Miss Edda Endrigkeit

Ever seen such proud, charming beauty?
Do have a look at this young woman,
Do give her your praise and admiration,
And she's upright, smart and pretty!

Ever seen an example of untold courage?
Never giving in to any kind of temptation,
Do give her a gesture of sheer adoration,
Raving belle, no one succeeds to manage!

I never met a woman of such fiery temper,
Going about her business with such fervour,
Kind and friendly, and no mean demeanour!

Ever seen such a virtuous determination?
In Lord's Prayer she'll find salvation,
To grant her heart's burning wish realization!

Anton Ales

Pictures

Life holds many wonderful things,
Gurgling brooks and fairy rings;
Rounded pebbles and rosy dawn
Verdant grass and golden corn.

Glistening raindrops zephyrs cries
Billowing clouds and starry skies;
Sun drenched flowers and singing birds
Pictures which cannot be framed in words.

Life holds many wonderful things
Joy which children's laughter brings;
Friendship bound with a golden cord
A beautiful song; a kindly word.

Children's trust, a hard earned rest
Comrades playing a game with zest
These are works of art indeed
To help us in our times of need

Eleanor Hossack

Night Fall...

Darkness falls and the angels cry
evil awakes for the city to die
shadows smile, and a prolonged scream
makes nightmares spiral down over your dreams....

Darkness calls the voices in your head
permission granted, revenge for the dead
turn to your lover to grasp the light
candlelit visions brighten the night....

Darkness beckons the earth's satellite
the devil's laughter fills the night
the daylight is dead and the curtains are drawn
victims lie in wait to become the unborn....

Darkness shows the narcotic smoke filled air
and the smell of sex without the care
a wind of thought blows through....
and dream filled rain falls deep....
Night Fall is now upon us, go to sleep....

Lee Cooper

World Affairs

Sitting down watching the television
Falling asleep, having night visions.
Parents work, while children play
Oh, what a tiring day they say

Children murdered, children abused,
Men and woman all being used.
Earthquakes and wars are on the land
These are signs that God is at hand.

Marriages are made, marriages are broken
Leaving children behind as token.
Films about sex, films about violence
It's no wonder our children are easily influenced.

The elderly are poor, and are lonely
Yet they're told lies and robbed of their money
Oh the pain, the pain of it all
Still some say they're having a ball.

Take a good look at the world around you
There is something we all can do
We can show love to each and everyone
Letting them know they are not alone.

B. Chattoo

Happy Mother's Day

Happy mother's day
And many many returns
People love you
People care for
You
Mum there is No
Other greater
Than you
Here is an
Everlasting
Righteous
Song
Don't go changing to try to please me I love you just
    the way you
Are
Yeah!

Angelena O'Selle

Untitled

When I am alone and feeling blue,
My thoughts tend to wander, I think of you
So very much happiness you've given to me
I still sit and ponder and fail to see
How long it will last, I'm frightened to say
For ever and ever I just hope and pray.

For so many years, I accepted my fate,
And then I met you and now it's too late

There must be thousands just like me
Who love but once and hopelessly
I wonder if they've tried like I.
To leave you and say goodbye
Each time I attempt it you suddenly do
Some crazy gesture which draws me to you

Bessie Huddy

Avebury Stone Circles

Silent solitary stones, each one a time-warped memory of the past,
For in your structure, events, storms and sunshine's light is cast.
What stories can you tell of futile battles fought by men,
Of nature's children borne from her womb of love,
All earthly creatures
And the graceful flight of birds above?
In atoms store all is remembered.
In truth can each story soon unfold
Recalling deeds of honour contained in minds of ancient
knights so bold?
Or perchance in your memory still contained
Religious vows to some deity unknown
Worshipping of morning's light, in heaven then ordained?
Perhaps in ages yet to come your scrolls of stone will tell their
stories yet to be unmasked.
Will you then in truth impart
In light's golden glory......as magic key unlocks
each secret chamber of your stony heart?

Jack Joseph

Beauty?

The new town is spreading, its face to wind,
With great, green parklands and open spaces behind
The single-deck shops and tall office blocks,
The angular pavements and mounds of bricks.
The town is fast a'growing
And the land is not germinating
The grain we are all needing.
Litter spatters the green
On which are necking
The young of today:
They will inherit this town
And then they will care;
Only time will make them cry
'Halt' to the ruin of the land they now
CURSE.

Lavinia M. Harris

Village Life

The dreariness of winter gone
The grass is nice and green
Children playing in the park
A sight worth seeing
All the gardens were quite full
With spring flowers, I declare
Primrose, bluebells everywhere
Pollen fills the air
Water in the village pond
Was seemingly quite shallow
Mallards did not seem to care
Flashing their lovely colours
Village shops are now quite rare
Big stores taking over
It is really such a shame
They may be gone forever
Who cares about the bustling towns
Village life is great
There are always those who care
A thatched cottage is my mate

Colin J. West

Realism

Triggered by an endless spiral
Slow spinning to get some pace
Spiritual guided through time
And eventually lost in space

Turning in all directions
Never knowing when it will end
Like life it's so eternal
Go straight for a while then bend

Reaching out to every sphere
Touching at one single point
Question is? Where from here
Another chapter for us to anoint

Words that have no real meaning
Created in images of man
The thoughts cannot be out-dated
Just held fast by God's right hand.

P. A. Robinson

The Sparkling Lake

The sparkling lake by dawn
And by dusk the lights
Shimmer is gathered.
It's beauty by moonlight
Is truly unique.
The ripples and waves are fantastic.
The swans swim so gracefully.
The ducklings wait for
their mum patiently.
It is undoubtedly poetry in motion.

Shumon Momen

Contents Of My Mind

My hair is awful,
I have no clothes.
Don't shave fully - am I a man?
Immature in appearance,
Oh, and in thought.
Yet worse than me prevail.
Settle down - a car - a house
These people are happy,
life is simple - easy.
They never question or disagree
Enjoy life, so mother says
But how can I enjoy
Something with understanding,
why or what it is?
Give me the solution - the code
to this maze,
    People call it life

Daniel Martin

Monkey Business

Can they imagine...
as the wire trap tears at their limbs
and their terrified screeches haunt the forest?
Do they cry for their stolen freedom,
or do they fear the future?

Can they imagine...
incarcerated, separated and cramped?
Their terror is vocal until resignation silences them,
and, with the realization that the bars are not tactile,
they groom alone.

Can they imagine...
the tastelessness of being a living delicacy
to line the stomachs of the rich?
The inhumanity of being exploited to further our knowledge,
at a price to line the purses of the desperate.

Can they imagine...
Can you?

Penelope Tilzey

The Old Year Passes

Over the snow-laden fields
Measured time sweeps
Its dark skirt of sequined half-remembered days
Towards the threshold;
Music fades, murmurings are stilled.
As cattle on summer-drenched afternoon
All face the Sun-God
All eyes seek the gold-lit tower
Ensnared by the silent progression
Of fingers across the dial.
Anticipation grows, is tangible.
Heads lift to the keen scent of future;
Some hang, reluctant to discard
The old, familiar and well-packaged past.
    The sharp air trembles
Rippled by acid chimes, climbing
To the inevitable climax.
The great hand holds the smaller in embrace
While twelve apostle notes rend the dark
Moving the stone to reveal the unmarked path.

Edward Denyer Cox

Confusion!

The mix of emotion is burning inside,
My state of confusion becoming hard to hide,

Should I laugh or should I cry,
If I told you "I love you" would it be a lie,

How I feel right now I'm just not sure,
My feelings for you aren't the same any more,

Jumbled thoughts my mind is a mess,
If I told you my feelings would you think of me less,

These feelings and emotions are driving me insane,
Although each time when I search my heart I come up with the same,

If I let our love pass would I be mad,
I wouldn't get you back after treating you so bad,

I wish to end my state of confusion,
But if I think anymore would I find a conclusion.

Jody Partridge

Her Love Can Never Be Replaced

Her endless love knows no bounds
 e'en though she's gone away,
I feel her all around me,
 every minute of the day,
I hear her voice so dearly,
 in gushing water streams,
I see her in the stars at night,
 and always in my dreams,
I smell her in the flowers,
 and on the summer breeze,
and in the heady perfume
 of the fragrant blossom trees,
I feel her gently stroke my face,
 lips whispering her love,
I know she's in a better place,
 with angels up above,
Her love can never be replaced,
 nor compared with anyone,
I loved her oh, so very much,
 my beautiful one, my mum.

  D. M. Morris

The Last Baggage

Dedicated to his 6 grandchildren

A baby is born
All soft and pink
Nappies and bibs
To body adorn

Soon turns a youth
Handsome and bright
Denims for jeans
Tight yet not uncouth

Day and night only goals
Money mansion never content
Ups and downs steered by luck
Counting dough in metal and rolls

Desires getting lower
Hair thinning faster
Oh! The mid-life cage
Sad the inadequate lover

The last journey yet to be
Time and date never clear
Memories flash good and bad
Only baggage to accompany

  Nagy N. Rao

Life Time Future Thoughts....

Who knows what
The future holds?
Nothing's written
Your dreams are bold.

Slowly stepping
Across new ground.
Reaching forward,
Never frown.

Choices chosen,
Decisions made.
Forming visions,
Nothing fades.

Make your future,
Have your say.
As time goes by,
You'll find your way.

The things you say
The things you do,
In the end,
They all make you...

  G. Trowbridge

August

Plump tassels of the Buddleia, rich purple,
Star-flower-packed, each floret tipped with crimson,
Vibrate and boom and clash their deep percussion.
On sour-milk powdered wings the Cabbage Whites lurch,
Zig-zagging, frail and feckless little Pierrots,
In and out they weave their tinkling grace-notes.

A ginger cat comes mincing up the garden
Cadenza in this summer-mad concerto —
He crouches flat, the hind legs giving purchase,
Then up he springs and twists as he soars skyward.
What pirouettes! Nijinsky in fur trousers,
He grasps at butterflies with up-stretched claws.

Sun splinters on his pelt as, leaping, turning,
Against the backdrop of the Buddleia,
While hollyhocks and roses watch in wonder,
He drolly dances in the heat of noon.

  Ann Wharrier

Beyond Sleep: Sacred Icon Or Oblivion?

Theme:
"Women and men do not survive on bread any more;
but blossom on the power within their dreams".

Wave upon waves of peaceful slumber,
Ghosts of darkness, that never leave us;
Geysers of memories - past or future,
Emerge into our present to inspire us.

 Sleeper, Listen intently!

Leaves upon trees of amorphous shapes,
Grow from muscles of psychic energy;
Silently, the mythical fantasy explodes
Yet before I begin dreaming, am I born free!

Dreamer, recall the instant
Whispers of survival from nightmares - surface,
To recall the hellish trauma of fears, that hiss;
Snoring cobras that sleep in coziest of places;
Can kill with deadly sting, the careless.

  Bento J. D'Souza

Untitled

There's many things we face in life, the stresses and the strains, the joys, the fun, the laughs, the ups, the downs and many pains To speak of one on its own, how bad upon your scale, of pains that reach your deepest soul when love does not prevail? I cannot answer that for you, that is for you yourself, how bad your scale of hurt when love's left on the shelf? There are two ways to look at this, but, which one hurts the most? The pains can be as bad both ways when love's a fading ghost. There's hurt when love is not returned, when two were not united and then the hurt when love has gone from one, love unrequited. I've known both ways along my road of life I'm sad to say, I hope for you it never strikes, my heart is easy prey. I'm not alone, maybe you too can see a bird, a dove, who sometimes lands upon your heart and builds its nest of love. So joyous for the time it's there, sometimes it stays so short, lies break the nest of truth and love, the dove becomes a hawk. With talons sharp it rips and tears into your deepest soul, what is there left when hawk has flown, an emptiness, a hole? A time of shades from grey to black? No sunshine does get in, a mask of sadness from grey to black? No sunshine does get in, a mask of sadness worn outside, a mask that does not grin. Although you wear the mask all day, some people never see the gaping hole where once your heart was full of love so free. Once in this state people fill the space with other things, some put up bars and wire mesh with padlocks, chains and rings, Let no-one in for evermore, the space becomes a vault, they will not let a new dove in, it might become a hawk. That's true enough, you never know when first a dove does land, some doves are hawks but none in disguise when you extend your hand. You will no know in love's first bloom, a hawk may not appear and if you let one in, or not, you always live in fear.
There is no answer, none at least that I have ever known, all I can do is let doves in and pray they stay at home.

  Richard I. Baum

587

A Vision Of Heaven

We are born with vestigial memories
Of horrors of time immemorial
The shabby detritus of human life.
And, as the years accrue,
Fresh layers are added.
The holocaust, refugees, faces
Of starving children.
Drowned cattle, tortured bodies.
Will heaven be the total expunging
Of the great undertow of human suffering
Submerged within us
And the soul be at peace at last?

Joan Sealey Wayman

Witness For The Defence

Mischievous, you patter on the roof,
play hide and seek about the trunk of cherries, tall and bare.
In frantic haste to raid the winter store,
bulbs are scattered,
uprooted plants the victim of a memory blip.
Scrabbling and nibbling, the energy gleaned
from one nut is dissipated in the effort...
mere peanuts set against the scamper of your life.
Yet now and then, glimpsed motionless upon a stump,
ears a-prick, thick tail furled,
the whiteness of your waistcoat bearing out
the cosy stuff of children's stories,
I cannot brand you rat or persecutor of The Red.
A creature will survive as best it can,
oppressed by elements, spurred on by need for food.
The fault lies elsewhere for your arrival here
and, though no one denies Red's scarcity and charm,
a gag on the grey's flag-waving chatter
(directed at cats from its ivy-clad drey)
would leave a gap in our garden life.

Sheila E. Smith

Supernova

The thing to do, the crowd to follow,
pier pressure kicks in and the mind is hollow.

Cadaverous body, eaten from within.
skeletal structure, devitalized skin,
The distorted mirror image is shouting back lies,
concealing the truth from her deep inset eyes.
Lack of excuses and suspicions conveyed,
Family in turmoil, illusion mislayed.

Push it aside?
And chide the world where ignorance is cloaked by image,
retuff the trend
and attempt to mend your emotional control

So was in inconceivable? Does that saying still remain,
'It'll never happen to me,' repeated once again
Discussion about the persons, deciding on your fate,
Should it really be up to them,
   can you contemplate?

Anna Murrells

Waiting For The Sunshine

The birds and I were waiting,
For the coming of the sun,
(softly,) from the clouds, heavy, and grey,
I watched. with a wonderful, feeling
The darkness, slowly passed away-
Soft blue sky, like a vision, as in a dream
slowly, but surely, the dream became truth,
Form the heavens, once dark and grey,
The golden light with its warning ray
covered the land, and the sea
God was here in his golden light
The birds began to sing a morning hymn-
Thank you heavenly father,
For your radiant light
All will be well, when your are here
Changing grey skies to beautiful blue.

B. V. Robinson

Thankfulness

Once more dear, Jesus, I send my thanks to thee,
For sweet sleep, that took away my fears,
The worries of the day.
Composed, in the arms of sleep,
When all is calm, and peace,
'In prayer,' I brought all my troubled thoughts, and troubled heart
And lay them at your feet,
You gave gentle rest,
The night passed away,
Once again I give you thanks,
For the coming of the morning light
Teach me gentle Jesus your pathways to keep

When the clouds cover the light,
And stars are gone,
You will be ever near,
To guide me softly through
Both day, and night,
My heart and I say thank you,

B. V. Robinson

Society

Live in harmony, strive to love,
In this desperate world of hate and greed,
No morals, no peace, kill or be killed,
What about the children, the mouths to feed?

To what end, and when will our conscience see,
That such pleasurable darkness and mental pain,
Is so wrong in this oppressed time,
Where is our hope? The world is insane.

When all is lost and death knocks your door,
When you conform to your God of this land,
Mankind inventions and road you will strive,
Surely you will be die and add to earths sand.

No-one seems to laugh anymore,
As hurting is much more fun,
Evil is our very best friend,
From this we have nowhere to run.

There is a hope from a very special friend,
Who can give joy in the spirit to all men,
He gives life beyond the life of mankind,
From our birth until the very end.

Darren Riches

Biographies
of
Poets

AARON, KIM
[pen.] Kim; [b.] 10 September 1956, Bombay, India; [p.] Horace and Ruby Fisher; [m.] Belisha Lasky Aaron, 24 November 1979; [ch.] Horace Stewart and Tranel Chambers; [ed.] Baccalaureate, France Secretarial Diploma, Studied French and German; [occ.] Decorator, Handmake Artificial Flowers and Decorations; [hon.] Several athletic, elocution and drama awards; [oth. writ.] Short fiction stories and children's stories; [pers.] Life is a learning game. We never stop learning. One must be able to rise above a situation. Do unto others as you would have them do by you.; [a.] Mombasa, Kenya

ABBOTT, ANNE ELIZABETH
[pen.] Tessa Merlin; [b.] 17 February 1952, Smethwick; [p.] Fred Abbott, Vera Abbott; [ed.] Secondary Modern, Oldbury; [occ.] Office Clerk in Local Youth Charity; [memb.] West Midland Bird Club, Local Dog Training Club; [hon.] City and Guilds in Photography; [oth. writ.] Poem published in anthology and poem and limerick in general collections; [pers.] I have many interests in addition to writing which include painting/drawing and craftwork, photography and animals and natural history. I try to capture the beauty of nature in all my work.; [a.] Warley, West Midlands, UK

ABRAHAMS, MRS. ROSE
[b.] 11 November 1918, London; [p.] Dead; [m.] Jack Abrahams, 1956; [ed.] Retired; [oth. writ.] Lighte Opereta two verses, verse has been accepted by you as a poem. Where are you now my love. Second verse. Called why must I always wait. I have music.; [pers.] I have twisted fingers I play with one hand on piano. I cannot read or write music. Please excuse writing.; [a.] Westcliff on Sea, Essex, UK

ABRAMS, PATRICIA ANN
[b.] 3 December 1938, Devonport; [p.] Henry Abrams and Edna Abrams; [m.] Kenneth Caulkett (Divorced 1990), 15 July 1957; [ch.] Stephen, Karen Debbie, Timothy, Kenneth, Andrew and Charles; [ed.] Hilsea Modern Girls School Portsmouth; [occ.] Assistant Cook; [hon.] Dog Breeders Certificate, Institute of Canine Studies; [oth. writ.] Short Story, Dog Training Weekly 1987; [pers.] Good example is a language and an argument which understands Bishop Thomas Wilson, this is how I was taught by my parents to whom my poem is dedicated.; [a.] Didcot, Oxfordshire, UK

ADAMS, DAN
[b.] 22 July 1929, Yorkshire; [m.] Pamela Joan, 1955; [ch.] Five; [ed.] Veterinary Science - Liverpool University; [occ.] Retired Vet.; [memb.] Opera, R.S.C. and Literary Clubs, Walking Groups, Rotary, Member Royal College of Veterinary Surgeons; [hon.] Bachelor Veterinary Science; [oth. writ.] Poems and short stories; [pers.] I like poems that have "energy" and an inner music.; [a.] Burghill, Herefordshire, UK

ADAMS, PETER
[b.] 29 April 1931, Hastings, Sussex; [p.] Robert Adams and Elsie Adams (by Adoption); [m.] Virginia Mae Adams, 5 March 1955; [ch.] Dennis Robert, Stephen Richard; [ed.] Bedford And Hastings Modern Schools, continued Education under Service Education Systems, Cranfield Institute Courses, Henley Staff College Courses; [occ.] Retired Aviation and Airworthiness Consultant; [memb.] Engineering Council, Royal Aeronautical Society, Institute of Quality Assurance, British Association of Aviation Consultant; [hon.] Chartered Engineer, Fellow of R.Ae.S., Member of B.A.A.C.; [oth. writ.] Numerous technical publications and papers concerning aviation engineering, operation and management, maintenance systems and philosophies, aviation law and legislation.; [a.] Biggin Hill, Kent, UK

ADAMS, ROSY
[b.] 15 July 1977, Builth Wells; [p.] Caroline Body, Steve Adams; [ed.] Brecon High School, City of Bath College; [occ.] Student - French and English Lang. 'A' levels; [memb.] British Hangliding and Paragliding Association; [a.] Bath, Avon, UK

ADAMS, TOM
[b.] 14 December 1966, Glasgow; [m.] Pamela Adams, 13 June 1991; [ed.] Woodfarm High School, Langside College, Central College; [occ.] Operations Supervisor, Motoring Organization; [oth. writ.] Many poems on all subjects of life, shouting is the first one attempted to be published, many more to follow; [pers.] I have written many songs and poems, I am inspired by people, places, politics and life. The world is waiting for new talent to appear, now is the time for us all to make ourselves known.; [a.] Giffnock, Glasgow, UK

ADAMS, WINIFRED
[b.] 16 September 1913, Northampton; [p.] Charles, Jessie Law; [m.] Donald A. Adams, 2 November 1939; [ch.] John and David; [ed.] Northampton High School, St. Katharine's Training College; [occ.] Retired; [pers.] English Literature has always been my favourite subject, especially poetry.; [a.] Carlton, Nottingham, UK

AHMAD, OMER SHUJA
[pen.] Omer Ahmad; [b.] 5 March 1980, Edgware; [p.] Shuja and Tehmina Ahmad; [oth. writ.] Many poems and short stories but have not been officially published.; [pers.] If you want to write a poem for a hobby or for any other reason then this is what you need to do: Write about a true life event which you have experienced in an appropriate but simple style and give it a good title.; [a.] Kingsbury, UK

AHMET, GULSEN
[pen.] Gulsen Ahmet; [b.] 23 April 1973, London; [p.] Ahmet Osman and Emine Osman; [ed.] B Tec National Diploma in Business studies; [occ.] Saves support/Admin.; [pers.] Thanks to everyone who supported me, especially my mother 'Emine' who kept on pushing me and never lost faith in me, I love you dearly.; [a.] Enfield, Middlesex, UK

AIRD, DAVID
[b.] 8 May 1972, Livingston; [p.] Agnes Aird, David Aird; [ed.] St. Augustines High School; [occ.] Unemployed; [oth. writ.] A few unpublished poems which have only been seen by friends.; [pers.] I have found it easier to explain something through poetry which would otherwise be difficult to explain in conversation. The little poetry I have read, Crowley and Baudelaire are favourites.; [a.] Edinburgh, UK

AITKEN, THOM
[b.] 14 April 1923, Aberdeen; [p.] Tom Aitken, Margaret Aitken; [m.] Mary Jane Aitken, 30 December 1949; [ch.] Thomas, Mark, Grigor; [ed.] Robert Gordons College, Aberdeen University, Edinburgh University; [occ.] Retired - H. M. Colonial Service, The British Council; [memb.] Blairgowrie Golf Club, The Royal Lisbon Club, Johannesburg Country Club, The Four Seasons Country Club, Marbella, The Probus Club, Blairgowrie; [hon.] M.A. (Lang and Lit - Aberdeen), M.Sc. (Appl. Lings - Edinburgh); [oth. writ.] Several poems - poetry now ('92, '93, '94) - "Sonnets from Soweto" Univ. of the Witwatersrand 1990-'91, Radio Plays and book reviews - N.R'Zambia Broadcasting Corpn. (1960-'68); [pers.] I write poetry to counteract my increasing cynicism and to support and amuse my friends.; [a.] Blairgowrie, Perthshire, UK

AL-AZZAWI, SUSAN
[pen.] Arden Lee; [b.] 23 May 1956, Falmouth; [p.] John Kennedy and Lorna Kennedy; [m.] Fouad Al-Azzawi, 3 February 1989; [ch.] Zainab and Philip; [occ.] Housewife and Mother; [oth. writ.] Many poems never seen are in my personal diary; [pers.] "Final thoughts" was written for my Dad who died on 7 September 1995. Through his illness he showed how to be brave when dying. He inspired me to look beyond what we see.; [a.] Carlisle, Cumbria, UK

ALBAGHDADI, TAJIA
[pen.] Tajia Albaghdadi; [b.] 22 November 1944, Baghdad; [p.] Jawad Ali; [m.] Ahmed Kaldi, 12 September 1970; [ch.] Ali, Dina and Zaid; [ed.] College of Arts, Baghdad University; [occ.] Teacher, King Fahad Academy - London; [hon.] BA in Arabic Literature; [oth. writ.] Poems published in Alsharo Alawsat, Aligtirab Aladabi, Alowafil, Durer Sharqia. Articles and books review in few Arab Magazine.; [pers.] I believe in humane literature that stand against big lies. I love poetry which disclose the simple truth. I have been influenced by T. S. Eliote and Almutanabi; [a.] Greenford, Middlesex, UK

ALDRIDGE, JEAN M.
[b.] 7 July 1931, London; [p.] Deceased; [ed.] Grammar School; [occ.] Retired; [memb.] Winsley Social Club, Travel Club; [oth. writ.] Poems published in local paper and magazines. I try to paint a vivid picture with my poems. I've also started to write a novel I love the older style of poetry such as Wordsworth; [pers.] Everyday events help me when writing my poetry; [a.] Winsley, Wiltshire, UK

ALLEN, LYNN
[b.] 29 October 1948, Oxford; [ch.] Four children; [ed.] Comprehensive; [occ.] H/W; [oth. writ.] Poetry, Song; [a.] Oxford, Oxfordshire, UK

ALLEN, MRS. PEG
[b.] 8 November 1926, Guiseley, Nr Leeds, Yorks; [p.] Mr. and Mrs. William C. Rogers; [m.] Benjamin Allen, 9 June 1948; [ch.] Lynda, Lizanne, Peggie, Micheal, David and Ben; [ed.] Rutland High School Dublin and The Dublin Art College (1942-45); [occ.] Housewife; [memb.] Irish Country Woman's Assoc. Oasis Literary Club, Dog Showing and Judging at Championship Level, Drawing and Painting Clubs.; [hon.] Have had several articles and poems printed in Oasis Magazines and also in Dog Breed Magazines. Had a poem "The Dachshund" in an English "Dog Anthology" a few years ago.; [oth. writ.] I am in the middle of writing my autobiography which I am informed should be of "Historical Interest" because of my advanced age!; [pers.] I have a great belief in God and am told that this comes through in a lot of my poetry, which pleases me greatly!; [a.] Blackrock, Dublin, Eire

ALLOTT, REBECCA
[b.] 4 December 1980, Barnsley; [p.] Dorothy and Trevor Allott; [ed.] 5th Year at secondary school (Kirk Balk); [occ.] Still at school; [memb.] Press Pack, International Pen Friends Association; [hon.] Won two ten pound vouches on teletext.; [oth. writ.] 2 Short stories published on Teletext as part of a competition piece; [pers.] I wish to show that through the horrors of war we can only amend our mistakes. I have been greatly influenced by the great war poet Wilfred Owen; [a.] Barnsley, South Yorkshire, UK

ALLSOPP, EILEEN
[b.] 11 August 1951, Doncaster; [ed.] Maltby Grammar, Sunderland College of Education; [memb.] Le Cercle Francais De Doncaster; [oth. writ.] Introspective verse and work emerging from photographic images of the natural world, particularly on the theme of trees and timber.; [pers.] Poetry became a spontaneous vehicle for the expression of my moods and those of the elements after a number of years spent learning to manage M. D. Words, wood sculpture and paintings are complementary; [a.] Doncaster, South Yorkshire, UK

ALLWYNN, DOREEN
[b.] 4 April 1926, Bedfordshire; [occ.] Retired; [pers.] These verses were written to insert into a humorous birthday card. Sadly he passed away on the 1st December 1995. They are now a commemoration to him.; [a.] Havant, Hampshire, UK

ALMGILL, SARAH-ELLEN
[pen.] Sarah Almgill; [b.] 15 September 1984, York Districts; [p.] Lynne and Bruce; [ed.] Langfoss Primary School, Pocklington Grammar School; [occ.] Schoolgirl (pupil); [a.] Fangfoss, Yorkshire, UK

AMODIO, JACQUELINE ANN
[pen.] Nee Phelps; [b.] 27 May 1965, London; [m.] Anthony Amodio, 11 May 1985; [ch.] Paul Amodio, Danielle Amodio; [ed.] Parliament Hill School for girls; [occ.] Care Worker Buchanan Court Nursing Home Harrow; [pers.] To friends Pamela Weight and Tess Mariapa for their faith and encouragement, I give my thanks.; [a.] Northolt, Middx, UK

ANDERSON, IRENE
[b.] 1 January 1951, Lampeter; [occ.] Medical Secretary; [oth. writ.] Two poets published in anthologies in 1993-1995.; [pers.] Courage in the face of adversity.; [a.] Glasgow, Strathclyde, UK

ANDERTON, HEATHER
[pen.] Dawn Fontaine; [b.] Slough; [p.] Albert Crabtree and Rosina Crabtree; [m.] Gerard Anderton, 22 April 1970; [ch.] Martin Gerard, Steven Gerard; [ed.] Orchard County Slough; [occ.] European Finance Manager; [oth. writ.] Short stories and several poems.; [pers.] Treasure the gifts given as they are so easily taken away.; [a.] Taplow, Berks, UK

ANDREW, CELIA
[b.] 25 January 1921, Sheffield; [p.] William Heppell and Emly Ann Heppell; [m.] Frederick Andrew, 9 November 1943; [ed.] Abbeydale Girls' Secondary School, Sheffield - Brentwood Teacher Training College - London University, Goldsmiths College (Part Time); [occ.] Retired; [hon.] B. Mus. (Hons) London University. Associate in Music, Trinity College London. Licentiate, Trin-

ity College London. Diploma, Education of Handicapped Children. Teacher's Certificate, Cambridge University; [oth. writ.] None; [pers.] Cast thy bread upon the waters: For thou shall find it after many days; [a.] Bridport, Dorset, UK

ANGLIN, VIVIAN
[b.] May 28, 1952, Kingston, Jamaica; [ed.] St. Michaels, Ray Town, Kennington Secondary for Boys, South London; [occ.] Reclusive Poet; [oth. writ.] Poems published in two anthologies ("A Kaleidoscope of Verse" and "Love Lines") and prison magazines. Also four volumes of poetry independently published. Titles: "Caught In The Rhyme", "The Outpourings", "Scenes from a Prison Cell", "Sonnets".; [pers.] I see poetry as the highest art form simply because it can say so much with so little.; [a.] South London, UK

ANUMIHE, CHRISTIEBELLE
[pen.] Christiebelle; [b.] 5 September 1970, Nigeria; [p.] Mr. and Mrs G. Ahamefula; [m.] Divorced; [ch.] Jasmine Anumihe; [ed.] Brunel University Cleveland Road Uxbridge Middlesex UB8 3PH, College of North West London NWD; [occ.] Full Time Student; [memb.] Union of Brunel Student; [hon.] Studying for LLB Law; [oth. writ.] Unpublished.; [pers.] An avid reader. Greatly influenced by the African poet wore Soyinka. The poem is written for my child Jasmine. Tying to come to terms with her speech and certain development difficulties.; [a.] London, Acton, UK

ARBUCKLE, JOHN
[pen.] John Arbuckle; [b.] 3 March 1930, Bellshill; [p.] John, Mary Arbuckle; [m.] May Arbuckle, 3 March 1956; [ch.] Yvonne and Stewart; [ed.] Hallside Primary Gateside, Secondary; [occ.] Pensioner; [hon.] Glasgow, and Strathclyde, Poetry, Anthology, Unabridged, V.A.P. Publications; [oth. writ.] "A Mother's Son", "A Pounds, Worth of Pleasure", "The Three Whales", "A Lad from Ayrshire", "Happy Birthday Rabbie", "A Day at Yarmouth"; [pers.] As I go out-walking every day, I record simple things along the way. Like the birds and bees the flowers, and trees. Inspiration I get from all of these.; [a.] Glasgow, South Lanarkshire, UK

ARNOLD, MAUREEN B.
[b.] 19 July 1939, Edmonton, N. London; [p.] Beatrice Goodrich, Alfred Goodrich; [m.] Brian Samuel Arnold, 5 March 1960; [ch.] Tracy and Ryan, grandchildren: Daniel, Joqui, Shane; [ed.] Hazelbury Secondary School; [occ.] Ancillery Worker at Local Doctors Surgery; [memb.] Royal British Legion, affiliated member local branch.; [hon.] Certificates for the piano, as a child.; [oth. writ.] Poem published in the anthology The Other Side Of The Mirror, several poems also in our local British legion magazine.; [pers.] I feel I am a very emotional writer. I am a great admirer of Pam Ayres. My ambition is that one day somebody will ask to see my Portfolio, and who knows perhaps I might become "recognized."; [a.] Enfield, Middx, UK

ARSCOTT, BRIDGET
[b.] 7 March 1935, London; [p.] Harold W. G. Arscott and M. A. McNeal (Deceased); [ed.] 1942-1948 Mary Datchelor La Retrate High School Balham, St. Joseph School Launceston SW 12; [occ.] Teaching Religious Involved in Voluntary Work (Prison Hospital); [memb.] I am a member of a religious order (La Retrate) for 40 years. Have taught in Africa - followed a writing course in

Berkeley with Pat U.S.A. Sckneider; [hon.] Teaching Certificate (1968), Certificate for Spirituality and Worship Programme (Berkeley California.); [oth. writ.] A story for children in Quatemala "The Gift" not yet published.; [pers.] Writing unlocks the door and is the key to inner freedom, growth and happiness. I have been greatly influenced by "Living by the word" Alice Walker.; [a.] Bristol, Avon, UK

ASHMAN, ANTHONY
[b.] 8 June 1960, Birmingham; [p.] Kate Ashman, Charles Ashman; [m.] Sonia Ashman, 28 June 1985; [ch.] Jessica, Cassy, Shane; [ed.] Comprehensive - School Heathfields; [occ.] Assembler; [pers.] Poetry as positivity, spirit building, is my writing's objective. Influences Coleridge, Shelley, Homer, music, cinema.; [a.] Selly Oak, Birmingham, UK

ASHTON, NEIL
[b.] 10 July 1965, Whiston; [p.] James Ashton and Joan Ashton; [ed.] Knowsley Higher Side Comprehensive; [pers.] Be open and true, and with understanding will come universal love.; [a.] Prescot, Merseyside, UK

ASKER, NATASHA MARIE
[pen.] Just Natasha Asker; [b.] 11 November 1975, Te Aroha, New Zealand; [p.] Richard and Erna Asker; [ed.] Uplands C.C. Wadhurst College, Hastings C.A.T. and Cyprus School of Art; [occ.] Artist/painter, taking Visual arts Degree at the University Nil College Scarborough; [oth. writ.] I have written a number of poems which I hope will be published. I a m much influenced by William Blake, Keats, and Lord Byron.; [pers.] I would like my work to create a feeling in the readers mind. When I write I escape from my own life into a poetic dreamer's world. Whether my poems express sadness or happiness, they are more a reflection of my own life and the world in general.; [a.] Rye, East Sussex, UK

ASTWOOD, VERONIQUE
[pen.] Veronique Astwood; [b.] 13 September 1973, Gravesend, Kent; [p.] James Astwood, Annie Astwood; [ed.] St. Theresa's R.C. Convent School, University of Westminster; [occ.] Student, Artist; [hon.] English Literature; [oth. writ.] Short stories, I am presently compiling an anthology of my poems.; [pers.] I dedicate this poem to Darren.

ATKIN, PATRICIA
[b.] 11 November 1946, Klagenfurt, Austria; [p.] Albert and Ivy Golder; [m.] Michael Atkin, 17 October 1970; [ch.] Justine Marianne; [ed.] Carlton Le Willows Grammar School, Nottm.; [occ.] Housewife; [hon.] Cert. for winner of 1995 PIBI Open Poetry Competition.; [oth. writ.] Poems published in 'Poetry Now', 'Poetry Council of GB', 'Poetry Institute of British Isles' anthologies.; [pers.] A lover of traditional rhyme and rhythm, I feel that a poem should still the reader's emotions - joy, sadness, sympathy, humour, and that it should linger in the mind long after it has been read. If my poems achieve this then I have realized my ambition.; [a.] Lambley, Nottinghamshire, UK

ATKINS, MARY
[b.] 9 April 1932, Merthyr, Tydfil; [p.] John and Nancy Lloyd-Atkins; [ed.] Cyfarthfa Castle Grammar School, Exeter University, The Council of Legal Education, London; [occ.] Barrister - Re-

tired; [memb.] The Honourable Society of the Middle Temple, The Poetry Society; [oth. writ.] Several poems in other anthologies.; [pers.] I love words, rhythm, and rhyme. I am drawn to the natural world, abstract ideas, metaphysics and mysticism.; [a.] Merthyr Tydfil, Mid-Glamorgan, UK

ATKINSON, MICHAEL MAJOR
[b.] 31 March 1944, Lancaster; [p.] Ruth and Maurice Atkinson; [ch.] Graene Atkinson, Stephen Atkinson, Gillian Atkinson; [ed.] St. Mary's Kirkby Lonsdale, Kandal Col of further Educ. Lancaster and Morrcambe Col of F.E.; [occ.] Technical and Innovation Manager, Shoe Manufacture; [oth. writ.] First work.; [pers.] A time in my life when I needed to lift myself from the past into the future and poetry served to be a positive way of expressing feelings with meaning.; [a.] Boeton-le-Sawy, Lancashire, UK

ATTRIDGE, ANNA
[b.] September 3, 1957, Windelsham, Surrey; [p.] David Haslam, Freda Haslam; [m.] Joseph Attridge, August 3, 1985; [ed.] Bishop Douglas Comprehensive School; [occ.] Word Processor Operator/Audio Typist; [oth. writ.] I had a previous poem published in a book of anthologies.; [pers.] I thoroughly enjoy writing poems. I also write short stories and poems for those in my office when they leave. I hope one day to own a computer and printer; [a.] Enfield, Middlesex

ATTWOOD, GEORGE DELANCEY
[pen.] Delancey; [b.] 9 March 1913, Delancey Hospital, Cheltenham, Glos; [p.] Albert Attwood; [m.] Frances Attwood, 17 June 1935; [ch.] 1 daughter and 1 son, 5 granddaughter, 1 grandson, 2 great grandson, 1 great granddaughter; [ed.] British School, Abertillery; [occ.] Retired Miner; [memb.] Local Writing Circle, Tilley Writer Circle, Ebenezer Baptist Church, Over-Sixties Abertillery, Old Age Pensions Cumtillery; [hon.] Medals of Battle of Burton 1945, Italy Star, Battle of the Atlantic, Star, Bar for France and Germany, Italy North America Battle of Atlantic Veteran.; [oth. writ.] Poems in local paper, Church magazine, I am a Pratishen Baptist, Poem, "I Came This Way To Kneel And To Pray."; [pers.] I think writing consists of patience, observation and imagination. Poets I like Watsworth, Kipling Shakespear, "I Believe In God"; [a.] Abertillery, Gwent, UK

AUSTIN, MISS JENIFER ELLEN
[b.] 29 March 1965, Sproxton; [p.] Mother is alive, father died on 23 December 1970; [ed.] Primary from 5 years - 11 years old. Then to Secondary Comprehensive school from 11 years - 16 years old. Both local; [occ.] General Domestic; [oth. writ.] None (except some more of my own unpublished poems!); [pers.] From one victim to another. In silence, in solitude, with union we all stand together. I believe in every one of us has a personal unique gift. Some will find it, some will find it, some will not. Some will use it some will not.!; [a.] North Yorkshire, UK

AYRES, SIMON PETER
[b.] 29 May 1957, Ilford, Essex; [p.] George and Kathleen; [m.] Janet Ann, 28 May 1988; [ch.] Sean (11-5-89), Michael (12-5-92); [ed.] Ilford County High Grammar; [occ.] Eurobond Operations Manager; [oth. writ.] Won radio poem competition, write for company annual report.; [pers.] Think it, believe it, write it, let it be read and enjoyed.; [a.] London, Essex, UK

BAGSHAW, STEVE
[pen.] Baggy; [b.] 26 October 1962, Glossop, Derbyshire; [p.] Harry and Hilda; [ed.] Hyde County Grammar School, Leicester Polytechnic, Newcastle University; [occ.] Warehousesman; [memb.] Socialist Workers Party, Anti-Nazi League; [hon.] H.N.D. Public Administration, B.A. (hons.) Politics degree; [oth. writ.] Alienation (The Poetry Guild); [pers.] Oh the irony - he who inspires nothing and no one, compels one to write! Mr. and Mrs. T.V. - switch off your set, switch on your life. Live it today or view it away.; [a.] Hadfield, Derbyshire, UK

BAHRA, KULWANT
[b.] 14 July 1947, India; [p.] Ajit Kaur and Chanan Singh Sagu; [m.] Satman Singh Bahra, May 1972; [ch.] 2, Manminder and Amandeep; [ed.] Brudnell County Secondary, Leeds Yorkshire, College of Technology, Leeds; [occ.] Company Director (MD); [memb.] Inst. of Directors, Nobility Staus in the Hutt River, Principality of Queensland, Australia; [oth. writ.] None published; [pers.] It is my aim to try to reflect the reality of life in all its aspects.; [a.] Sutton Coldfield, West Midlands, UK

BAHRA, KULWANT
[b.] 14 July 1947, India; [p.] Ajit Kaur and Chanan Singh Sagu; [m.] Satman Singh Bahra, May 1972; [ch.] Manminder and Amandeep Bahra; [ed.] Brundell County Secondary Leeds Yorkshire. College of Technology Leeds; [occ.] Company director (MD); [memb.] Institute of Directors, Nobility Status in the Hutt River Principality of Australia. (Queensland); [oth. writ.] None published, several written for family and friends; [pers.] It is my aim to try to reflect the reality of life, in all its aspects.; [a.] Sutton, Coldfield, West Midlands, UK

BAILLIE-HAMILTON, LILIA JULIA
[b.] 16 November 1933, Saint Lucia, West Indies; [p.] May and Alan Peter; [m.] Alexander; [ch.] Six - 3 girls, 3 boys; [ed.] Ursuline Convent Barbados, West Indies, Loretta Coledge, Toronto Canada; [occ.] Artist, Water Colours - China Painting; [memb.] Poetry Club, Maidenhead Berks; [oth. writ.] "China Painting" article for the Artist and Illustrator and also for the British Chiner Painter Mag.; [pers.] While painting I have for 20 years scribbled my thoughts and little poems on to the margins of my work. These reflect the different countries I've been to recently. (I travel constantly) now I've started to put these together starting with my West Indian childhood.; [a.] Maidenhead, Berks, UK

BAIN, ANGIE EMMA
[pen.] Angie Bain; [b.] 12 October 1980, Pembury; [p.] Vivien Bain, Stephen Bain; [ed.] Wrotham School; [occ.] Student; [hon.] None of Great Importance, but I have many Certificates of Various Achievements; [oth. writ.] None so far I'm still at school, there is plenty of time to do that.; [pers.] If I cannot find an answer in my heart, that is when I write poetry. Although, I find Shakespeare's poems very moving.; [a.] West Malling, Kent, UK

BAKER, ANNE
[b.] 3 June 1936, London; [p.] Arthur Insall, Gertrude Insall; [m.] Brian Baker, 6 June 1959; [ch.] Gillian, Claire; [ed.] Princess Rd Sch. Regents Pk London, Later Long Crendon Sec. Mod. Bucks; [occ.] Account's Assistant Part-Time; [oth. writ.] Poems published in several anthologies. Childrens stories - for my grandsons; [pers.] I try

to write from the heart, to convey through my poems, my thoughts and feelings, mainly for my own pleasure, but also I hope for the enjoyment of others. Influenced by poetry readings in school.; [a.] Abingdon, Oxon, UK

BAKER, JOAN HELEN
[b.] 3 August 1922, Northampton, UK; [p.] Jessie and Cecil Whittle; [m.] Dennis Rogers (Deceased 1977), 30 October 1945, Gilbert Baker (Bishop of Hong Kong 1966-1980, Deceased 1986), 3 September 1980; [ch.] Mark Anne Clare; [ed.] St. George's Intermediate School, Northampton, Edinburgh University former occ. Law Writer - Tracer - Youth Worker; [occ.] Active Retired; [memb.] Friends of the Church in China, Hong Kong Anglican Church Association, St. Martin's shared with Methodist Church Dorking, University of the Third Age, Dorking Branch; [oth. writ.] Poems published in various magazines and used for broadcasting in Hong Kong. Published in Arrival Press U.K.; [pers.] I have been writing poetry seriously since 1966. I took part in fringe poetry events during the Hong Kong Arts Festivals of 1976 and 1977. Reflections Poetry can distil thoughts and feelings. It can often communicate beyond the word. It can inspire individual interpretation.; [a.] Dorking, Surrey, UK

BAKER, LESLEY
[pen.] Maddy Thomas; [b.] 24 June 1945, Hillingdon, Middx; [p.] Victor and Jean Cooper; [m.] Raymond, 31 July 1965; [ch.] Simon Andrew and Lisa; [ed.] Harlington Secondary Modern; [occ.] Administrative Assistant; [memb.] Wells Gardening Club St. Mary's Flower Guild; [oth. writ.] Several poems published in Anthologies and Local Magazines.; [pers.] I try to reflect on the deep and innermost feelings of mankind in my writings, which cover a range of subjects from the part to the present day.; [a.] Street, Somerset, UK

BAKER, MRS. JANICE MAUREEN
[pen.] Jan Clark; [b.] 5 May 1950, Brighton; [p.] James Clark, Marjory Clark; [m.] Keith John Baker, 1977; [ch.] Peter, Melanie, Melissa, Mark; [ed.] Secondary Education; [occ.] Housewife; [memb.] Hobbies include gardening, reading, writing poems and short stories; [hon.] GSES in Maths Art English Religious Education English Literature; [oth. writ.] Poem published "Neglect" in between a laugh and a tear; [pers.] I strive to reflect the beauty and sadness of our lives in my writing.; [a.] Little Hampton, West Sussex, UK

BAKER, RONALD JAMES
[b.] 16 May 1963, Liverpool; [m.] Linda Ledsham Baker, 16 September 1994; [occ.] Unemployed; [memb.] Completing Course with the Writer Bureau Ltd. Manchester; [pers.] 'To breathe is to be alive to be alive is to experience greatness.'; [a.] Church Stretton, Shropshire, UK

BAKER, TERRIE
[pen.] Alice Hart; [b.] 10 August 1970, Middlesex; [p.] Anthony J. Fox, Gillian F. Fox; [m.] Mark Phillip Baker, 27 January 1988; [ch.] Frances Ann/Phillip Ronald; [ed.] Treviglas Comprehensive Newquay Cornwall; [occ.] Full time carer for my son who is autistic; [memb.] Readers Digest, National Autistic Society; [oth. writ.] Report concerning local roads in news, letters, poetry for fund raising. Looking to get unpublished poetry by the hundred out into the public eye.; [pers.] To want to know why we are or cease to be, to value faith and understand even things we cannot prove or justify.; [a.] Saint Austell, Cornwall, UK

BALDWIN, SYLVIA
[b.] 5 July 1944, Watford, Herts; [p.] Grace and Arthur Bugbee; [m.] John Baldwin, 3 October 1964; [ch.] Avril, Simon and David; [ed.] Victoria Sec. Mod. School for Girls, Watford, South West Herts College of Further Education, Watford; [occ.] Housewife; [memb.] British Balloon and Airship Club; [oth. writ.] Several poems as yet unpublished.; [pers.] In writing poetry I am expressing emotions that surface when I look at a situation, and hope others can relate to and draw comfort and pleasure.; [a.] Watford, Hertfordshire, UK

BAMBROOK, JOHN
[b.] 4 September 1944, Portsmouth; [p.] John and Gwendoline Bambrook; [occ.] Local Government Officer; [pers.] I try to record my wonder at the beauty of creation.; [a.] Theydon Bois, Essex, UK

BANKS, CHERYL
[pen.] Sheryl Balcleef; [b.] 3 February 1981, Chichester; [p.] Sylvia Banks, John Banks; [ed.] Wykeham House School; [occ.] Student; [memb.] Young Nadfas; [hon.] Art; [pers.] This is my first publication and hopefully a promising start to a fertile career in writing and art the influence for my work is imagination, not experience; [a.] Emsworth, Hampshire, UK

BANKS, DONALD
[pen.] Banker; [b.] 29 October 1925, Wick; [p.] James Banks, Margaret Banks; [m.] Elizabeth Banks, 11 January 1949; [ch.] James, Catherine, Donald; [ed.] Wick North School, Wick High School; [occ.] Retired Atomic Worker; [a.] Wick, Caithness, UK

BANKS, MRS. JACQUELINE
[b.] 26 May 1943, London; [p.] Frederick W. G. Wise (Deceased), Lilian B. Wise; [m.] Divorced, 4 July 1964; [ch.] Christopher Neil (28); [ed.] Grammar School; [occ.] Career of my son who is disabled with Cerebral Palsy; [memb.] British Diabetic Association (I am diabetic); [hon.] Prizes for English and French G.C.E. Results (Top Marks in Year) and one Competition Prize Based upon a Poem; [oth. writ.] Two other poems published, several letters published in local newspapers and diabetic publications.; [pers.] I have found my garden to be a constant source of pleasure, and of immense therapeutic value in times of stress, it was also the inspiration behind my poems - "A Day In The Garden."; [a.] Rayleigh, Essex, UK

BARBER, CHARLES JOSEPH
[b.] 25 December 1921, Brockley; [p.] Florence and Joseph Barber; [m.] Alice Barber, 22 December 1951; [ch.] Sandra Linda; [ed.] Mantle Road, Elementary; [occ.] (Retired) Ex. Postman; [oth. writ.] I have written poems of some of my family. But only for the pleasure I derive from them. I have never had any published, some are lengthy.; [pers.] I enjoy reading poetry, good books also like writing long letters. If my family enjoy my entry, it's going to give me great joy and encouragement.; [a.] Woolwich, London, UK

BARGE, ROBERT HAMILTON
[b.] 6 November 1936, Stone, Glos; [m.] Ann, 24 March 1962; [ch.] Jackie and Steve; [ed.] Thornbury Grammar School; [occ.] Management Accountant at WWT; [memb.] Gloucester R.F.C.; [hon.] FMAAT; [oth. writ.] 1 poem published in works magazine in 1978. I have written scripts for boys brigade displays. I have mostly written

poems for special occasions involving family and friends generally of a humorous nature.; [pers.] I am influenced by my country upbringing writing about nature. I also like to use humour based on actual everyday happening.; [a.] Stroud, Gloucestershire, UK

BARKER, EMMA LOUISE
[b.] 17 October 1978, Sheffield; [p.] Kenneth Barker, Patricia Barker; [ed.] Herries Secondary School, currently at the Loxley Centre of the Sheffield College; [oth. writ.] A poem called 'War Isn't Fun' published in 'Young Writers Write and Shine' regional anthology for South Yorkshire; [a.] Sheffield, South Yorkshire, UK

BARLOW, BRIGIT
[b.] Wendover; [m.] Erasmus Darwin Barlow; [ch.] One son, two daughter; [ed.] University career ended when I gave birth at the end of my firs year! Evening classes, music and Russian, were my education; [occ.] Writing/Housewife, Grandmother; [memb.] Kettles yard, Granta Opera Goers., Horticultural Club, Lib/Democrats; [hon.] Prize for radio play 'The Great Thaw'. (This play combined my love of music and Russia); [oth. writ.] A novel. An autobiography, short stories - 3 for Morning story B.B.C. poems published in magazines. Articles on the business world, governing, bird watching. Music criticisms.; [pers.] I like things to be simple. I don't like adjectives and adverbs. They should be used sparingly. My poems are mostly light hearted short stories that happen to rhyme.; [a.] Ashwell, Herts, UK

BARLOW, PAUL
[b.] 27 November 1958, Bolton; [p.] Alan Barlow, Sylvia Barlow; [m.] Divorced; [ch.] Matthew Barlow, Elizabeth Barlow; [ed.] Radcliffe High School; [occ.] Residential Social Worker. Bury Social Services; [memb.] Radcliffe Chess Club; [hon.] Dip in Industrial Studies; [pers.] I want people to know, that in this world full of sadness and despair, their is people, who care for humanity, and if sharing my thoughts. And poems can raise our awareness, that to share is to care, then maybe their is hope for mankind yet.; [a.] Radcliffe, Gt. Manchester, UK

BARNES, DAVID EDWARD
[b.] 19 February 1936, South Wales; [p.] Alfred and Elizabeth Barnes; [m.] Dorothy Barnes, 26 March 1960; [ch.] Amanda E. L. Barnes; [ed.] Royal Merchant Navy School, (Bearwood College GE); [occ.] Maintenance Dept. at Psion Ltd.; [pers.] Like my father before me I served in this Merchant Navy, that is why I wrote "The Hogarth Company" in memory of all those brave men who have no known Graves but the sea.; [a.] Northfields, London, UK

BARNES, MRS. C.
[pen.] Nannette; [b.] 23 April 1946, Riber, Matlock; [p.] Mr. and Mrs. G. Marchant; [m.] John Barnes, October 1974; [ch.] Three, youngest 20 years old; [ed.] Ernest Bailey Grammar School, Matlock; [occ.] Domiciliary Services Organizer; [oth. writ.] None published yet. This is the first poem I wrote.; [pers.] My husband plays golf my family are grown up and I wanted to have something that was mine so I started to write.; [a.] Matlock, Derbyshire, UK

BARNES, MRS. CHRIS
[pen.] Annette; [b.] 23 April 1946, Matlock; [p.] Mr. and Mrs. Marchant; [m.] John Barnes, 19

October 1974; [ch.] Kay Andrew and Christopher; [ed.] Ernest Bailey Grammar School; [occ.] Domiciliary Services Organizer; [memb.] Matloch Writers Club; [oth. writ.] None published; [pers.] I recently reached a special age, my husband plays golf, my children have grown up so I started to write. You are never too old to try something new.; [a.] Matlock, Derbyshire, UK

BARNETT, HENRY ARTHUR RODNEY
[pen.] Rodney Barnett; [b.] 9 December 1914, Chesham; [p.] Arthur Henry Barnett and Amy (nee Heilbron); [m.] Joan Platts (Nee Richards), 31 August 1946; [ch.] Two daughters: Fiona and Hilary; [ed.] Mill Hill School; [occ.] Retired Actuary; [memb.] British Chess Problem Society, Fellow of Institute of Actuaries, Fellow of Royal Statistical Society; [hon.] Institute of Actuaries Finliason (Silver) Medal, Testimonial by Royal Humane Society; [oth. writ.] Several professional papers published in Journal of the Institute of Actuaries. Paper on "Errors in the Gregories Calendar" published in Volume 2 of Transactions of the 15th Conference of the International Association of Consulting Actuaries.; [pers.] I believe, like Voltaire, that if there is no supreme being it is most important to invent one.; [a.] Bath, UK

BARRINGTON, MR. PETER DAVID
[b.] 25 May 1951, Bridgend; [p.] Haydn Gwyn Barrington, Audrey; [m.] Helen Elizabeth Barrington, 20 July 1974; [ch.] Laura Elizabeth Barrington; [ed.] Bridgend Grammar, Cardiff College of Education, Cardiff University; [occ.] Deputy Head teacher, Trelales Primary School Bridgend; [hon.] B. Ed. (Hons.); [oth. writ.] Poem published in "Up And Running" poetry. Communication across the barriers.; [a.] Bridgend, Mid-Glamorgan, UK

BARTER, RHONAY TERRI
[b.] 8 May 1969, Peterborough; [p.] Terry and Susan Barter; [m.] Deceased; [ch.] Shaun; [ed.] Orton Longueville Comprehensive School; [pers.] I wrote this poem for my dear friend Kim Moller, who gave up everything to travel around Europe alone. No richer could one be, than to have a true friend.; [a.] Peterborough, Cambridgeshire, UK

BARTLETT, IRENE
[b.] 5 May 1933, London; [p.] Jane and Frederick McCarthy; [m.] Christopher Bartlett, 31 May 1952; [ch.] 2 son and daughter, Jane and Christopher; [ed.] Stroud Techinical College, Glos; [occ.] Retired Nurse and Typist (I am now a widow); [memb.] Captain of South Cerney Bowls Club, Committee Member of National Assoc of retired Police Officers, Member of Glos Police Bowling Club; [oth. writ.] Poems, Childrens Stories; [pers.] I write as an expression of my thoughts and feelings. The children's stories I have written for my children and grandchildren and hopefully they will go on for generations; [a.] Cirencester, Glos, UK

BARTON, MRS. IDA
[b.] 12 October 1931, Snienton Dale, Nottm.; [p.] Both Deceased; [m.] Mr. Colin T. Barton, 17 March 1951; [ch.] Elaine and David Barton; [ed.] Peveril Bi Lateral (now the Manning School as play), then Trent Poly (now Nottm. Trent University) for Degree; [occ.] Now retired (both); [oth. writ.] "The Architect" and other poems (1960's) not published. Poem on War - to British Legion Magazine, "A Life Cut Short by War"; [pers.] I wrote this poem to the Nottm Evening Post, then

heard from your publishing, or it may be the war poem. I sent to the Legion Magazine, thank you very much indeed.

BARTON, SHEILA
[b.] 10 February 1930, Birkenhead; [p.] Alfred Dorrity - Dilys Dorrity; [m.] John Barton, 1951; [ch.] Susan, Amanda, Nicholas; [ed.] Birkenhead Secondary School, Art College Nursing St. Catherines Hospital; [occ.] Part-Time Antiques Full Time grandmother of four; [memb.] Gilbert and Sullivan Opera Society, W. Hove Golf Club, Support - Amnesty International IFAW; [oth. writ.] Have seven poems published with arrival pression different anthology's in last four years when started writing poetry; [pers.] Care deeply for people's lack of freedom of speech and movement - ABBOR. Injustice cruelty - Bigotry always optimistic of future believe good will come, when love is shown; [a.] Brighton, East Sussex, UK

BARTRAM, MR. A. W.
[b.] 21 March 1924, London; [p.] William and Ethel Bartram; [m.] Elizabeth Bartram (Nee Duffy), 4 October 1958; [ch.] One - David John; [ed.] Tollington Park, Secondary School, Islington - North London; [occ.] Retired; [memb.] Royal Society for the Protection of Birds, Butterfly Conservation Society; [oth. writ.] None published; [pers.] I firmly believe that if man is to survive on this planet, and as a 72 year old Cockney, I hope I am wrong the environment is so vitally important city.; [a.] Norwich, Norfolk, UK

BATEMAN, MILDRED
[b.] 8 October 1921, Tipton; [p.] Richard Harper, Mildred Harper; [m.] John Dudley Bateman, 10 April 1943; [ch.] Lesley Jane, Mark Dudley, Andrew John; [ed.] Kings Norton Grammar, Wednesbury Commercial College; [occ.] Free Lance Journalist, Poet and Playwright.; [memb.] Former Brierley Hill Choral Society, L. Chair. West Midlands Writer's Circle, Officer of Christian Church. Present: Royal Agricultural Soc. Eng., N.T., R.S.P.B.; [oth. writ.] Poetry collections Play, T.V. and Radio. Chiefly, Non-Fiction on the British Constitution.; [pers.] As Pacifist, republican, humanist, I am scientific ally opposed to the existing British Constitution; [a.] Kingswinford, West Midlands, UK

BAUM, RICHARD I.
[pen.] Rainbow; [b.] 20 December 1950, London; [p.] Yes!; [m.] Not any more! Don't wish to be reminded!; [ch.] Two; [ed.] Mostly the university of life and hard knocks!; [occ.] About to be discovered literary genius!; [memb.] As per Groucho Marx "I wouldn't want to be a member of any club that would have me as a member!; [hon.] Only those I award myself - currently awaiting other poeples awards for my works!; [oth. writ.] Currently unpublished autobiographical "expressions and observations" of the life of an alien who sometimes think he might be human! publishers wanted!; [pers.] My expression and observations" (poems) are simply the result of my thoughts transferred to pen and ink resulting in instantaneous verse on any subject of or suggested!; [a.] Towlester, Northants, UK

BEACALL, TRACEY
[b.] 11 April 1967, Bedford; [p.] Anthony and Marilyn Wildman; [m.] Reginald (Reg) Beacall, 23 September 1989; [ch.] Harry (born October 1990) Luke (born 19 August 1992); [occ.] Housewife and mother; [oth. writ.] Have had work published in my husband works magazine; [pers.]

I have written poetry and stories for pleasure. And for my family and children and would now like to start taking my writing further.; [a.] Bletchey, Milton Keynes, Bucks, UK

BEADLE, TROY
[b.] 19 July 1981, Farnborough, Kent; [p.] John R. Beadle and Lindsay Beadle; [ed.] Ravens Wood School for Boys; [occ.] Still School Student, studying for GCSE's; [oth. writ.] Published poems include "Lying In The Hay" - Squat Diddley Kent and East Sussex young writers anthology and "Memories Of Hell", poet soup.; [pers.] I strive to reflect personal experience in my writing and thank my parents for their continued support. "True Friends" is my favorite piece of work and "Boots" will not be forgotten.; [a.] Orpington, Kent, UK

BELL, GERALD S.
[b.] 16 October 1938, Sheffield; [p.] George Bell and Doreen Bell; [m.] Helen, 8 August 1964; [ch.] Two sons, Matthew (25) and James (20); [ed.] High Storrs Grammar School, Sheffield; [occ.] Bursar at St. Clement's High School, King's Lynn; [memb.] Associate of the Chartered Institute of Bankers, Oblate of the Abbey of Our Lady & St. John, Alton, Hants; [oth. writ.] Several 'Local Interest' and 'Personal Odes', including one, 'The Sharpened Sabre', on the them of redundancy, published in local weekly newspaper.; [pers.] Over a number of years, I have been motivated to write poems and odes about humorous or tragic events encountered in daily life. In recent times, however, I have found inspiration to write in a more serious or 'pensive' style.; [a.] King's Lynn, Norfolk, UK

BELL, MRS. NORMA
[pen.] Norma; [b.] 22 November 1943, Newcastle; [p.] Georgeina and William Graham; [m.] 29 May 1965; [ch.] Leo Marco; [ed.] Comprehensive; [occ.] House wife; [memb.] Free Church, Arts Crafts Gateshead Collage also computers.; [hon.] Bible Study Teacher; [oth. writ.] Author, writer of several poems published in our local magazine Christian songs which I have had recorded for friends and local church.; [pers.] I strive to reflect Jesus in my life through the poetry and songs I write also the magazine I compose, bearing witness to what my savior has done for me and so passing on to others the great message of salvation to whom I can.; [a.] Whickham, Tyne and Wear, UK

BENGER, CHERYL IONA
[oth. writ.] I have composed several gospel, spiritual songs, which are essentially, about how we can try to be kinder to one another, and how I see our live's - As a journey which depending on how we travel that journey, will determine the strength of will-we gain. Also, about the good and simple thing we have around us which we don't always acknowledge or appreciate.; [pers.] In my poem, I have tried to express and reflect the emptiness, despair, and uncertainty that we all experience at some time in our lives, but I "Do" believe that there is a `Love' there that will hold us together, if only we can reach inside for that inner strength and purpose, that is within our very souls.; [a.] Cardiff, Wales, UK

BENNETT, CLAYRE
[b.] July 1, 1969; [p.] Jean and Rudolph Bennett; [ed.] London Corporate Relations P.A. for BT; [occ.] Poetry Society, BSHA (British Street Hockey Association); [oth. writ.] Several RAPs, poems

published in "Voice" newspaper.; [pers.] Good things come to those who wait and yes I've waited with wholesome faith, now my work is to be published, the world will see, my face through my lyrics and all I wish to be.; [a.] Edmondon, London,

BENNETT, FRANK
[pen.] Francis Bennett-Diss; [b.] 27 April 1930, Acton, London; [p.] Ethel Mary, Christopher John; [m.] Sylvia Rose Bennett, 8 October 1955; [ch.] Jacqueline, Jillian, Denise; [ed.] Finchley Grammar, St Alban's College, Hertfordshire University, London University Goldsmiths; [occ.] Freelance Journalist Professional Artist; [memb.] Freelance Press Services, Brent Artist's Register, Brent Visual Arts Committee, Vice Chairman Dollis Hill Arts Group, B.A.S.C., C.P.A., M.Z.A.G.B.; [hon.] Cert. Art and Design (Access) Cert. Art and Design, Cert. Art and Communications; [oth. writ.] Poems 'The Old Man's Nurse' - 'Old Jock' Short Story, 'Nearly Mine', Novels 'All Fall Down' and 'Freak Out', short stories 'The Rewards Of Labour' and 'The Born Again Biker' (etc.) and articles press. (etc.); [pers.] I believe that poetry today, like art, should be about situations we find ourselves in and places we have visited. But more importantly about the emotions we have experienced.; [a.] London, Middlesex, UK

BENNETT, GEOFFREY
[pen.] 23 July 1962, Coventry; [p.] Alan Bennett, Barbara Bennett; [m.] Miss Helen Jones (Fiancee); [ed.] Coventry Polytechnic, Coundon Court Comprehensive School; [occ.] Analyst/Programmer; [hon.] BSc Mathematics; [oth. writ.] Published in four other anthologies.; [pers.] I relish, sound and mood in language. My fervent wish is that others love poetry as I do. I want to help them.; [a.] Huddersfield, W. Yorks, UK

BENSON, KATHLEEN HOSEY
[pen.] Kathleen Hosey; [b.] 13 July 1932, Achonry; [p.] Michael and Lily Hosey; [m.] John Joe Benson, 18 July 1953; [ch.] Six; [ed.] Leaving Cert.; [occ.] Housewife and working on the farm; [oth. writ.] I am currently writing a book, (all about growing up in the war years); [a.] Tubbercurry, Sligo

BERRYMAN, DAVID
[b.] 9 November 1950, Hessle; [m.] Janet Elizabeth; [ed.] Hull Grammar School, Loughborough College; [occ.] Retired Deputy Head Teacher; [hon.] Cert. Ed. D.P.S.E. (Management); [oth. writ.] None published.; [pers.] How is it possible for a species to evolve so far, know so much and yet learn so little? Nature knows best!; [a.] Hessle, East Yorkshire, UK

BEVAN, JOAN
[pen.] Joan; [b.] 12 July 1918, Rhondda; [p.] Daniel Aneurin Powell, Jane Powell; [m.] John Bevan, 24 March 1947; [ch.] David Andrew, Ann (Dr.); [ed.] Hendrefadog Girls School; [occ.] Retired Nursing Officer; [memb.] Samaritans since 1974 Founder Member St. David's Foundation (Hospice at home) since 1979 W.I. over 50's Club Community College; [hon.] S. R. N. Midwifery Certificate "Sociology and Psychology" in Diploma of Nursing.; [oth. writ.] Some poems - unpublished short articles - unpublished monthly report for "Link" local methodist magazine.; [pers.] Influenced by my early life. My involvement with people and my love of people and nature.; [a.] Caerleon, Gwent, UK

BEVERIDGE, CATRIONA
[b.] 29 March 1983, Hastings, E. Sussex; [p.] Joy and Robert Beveridge; [ed.] Robertsbridge Community College; [occ.] Student; [pers.] Older sister, Donna, older brother, Neil; [a.] Hurst Green, East Sussex, UK

BEXHELL, JACK
[b.] 3 October 1930, Hastings; [p.] Jack Bexhell, Anne Bexhell; [m.] May Helen Bexhell, 2 August 1948; [ch.] Jacqueline Lilian, Linda May; [ed.] All Saints Hastings, Central School Hastings; [occ.] Retired; [memb.] Royal British Legion; [oth. writ.] Local Parish Magazines; [pers.] I try to put into words. How I feel about what I hear and see. I like to write for people, poems. About themselves how I see them and the place I live.; [a.] Hastings, East Sussex, UK

BHAKER, GURHAM KAUR
[pen.] Harry; [b.] 9 October 1973, Nottingham; [p.] Surat Suwali, Biant Suwali; [m.] Kultar Singh Bhaker, 10 September 1994; [ch.] Sanjay Singh Bhaker; [ed.] Manning Comprehensive School (Nottingham); [occ.] Product Assistant in Aromatherpy Oil; [oth. writ.] A poem written for my weekly magazine.; [pers.] I thank God for his humble gift of writing. And for such talent he has bestowed on me. I dedicate my poem to my loving husband and my beautiful little son Sanjay.

BICKERS, JENNIFER ANNE
[pen.] Jenny Bickers; [b.] 1 July 1962, Grayshott; [p.] Jill and Norman Kelbrick; [ch.] Jason Alexander and James Cameron; [ed.] Copleston High School Ipswich, Suffolk; [occ.] Mother/Trainee, Aromatherapist; [memb.] Stowmarket Junior Chess Club, Suffolk Poetry Society; [oth. writ.] Several poems published in eastern light magazine sold in East Anglia, poems in two poetry now anthologies.; [pers.] My poetry aims to form a bridge between the physical and the spiritual sides of human nature in clear indentifiable terms.; [a.] Stowmarket, Suffolk, UK

BILLINGTON, SUSAN M.
[pen.] Susan M. Billington; [b.] 9 August 1947, Oldham, Lancs; [p.] Ellen Billington (Deceased), James Billington; [ed.] Elizabeth Girls Technical High, South Australia; [occ.] Secretary - Personnel YMCA Training; [memb.] Assoc. IPD; [oth. writ.] Book: "A Letter To Cliff!", shortly to be published. My testimony incorporating musings and poems.; [pers.] In all my writing I try to express my joy of loving God but more importantly God's love for all mankind. My aim is to show that His love is just as relevant in today's modern world as it was 2000 years ago.; [a.] Manchester, UK

BISHOP, MARGARET
[pen.] Etheldra Bishop; [b.] 13 January 1939, Birkenhead; [p.] Etheldra and William Johnson; [m.] John Stuart Maxwell Bishop, 31 August 1963; [ch.] One son born 14 December 1964; [ed.] Birkenhead Girls Grammar School; [occ.] Disabled/Cartomancer/ Lupus Contact - Counsellor.; [memb.] Lupus - UK, Lupus Inc. of America, Left Handed Club.; [hon.] Police Force Awards, (Very Negligible II); [oth. writ.] Small features, items letters to 12 leading woman's magazines and letters in reply in the daily express (roll published); [pers.] During my days of adversity, I find relief with a kind word, a happy thought and a positive action. Writing is my relief from daily stress and pain.; [a.] Reigate, Surrey, UK

BIST, VIPULA
[b.] 15 August 1964, Delhi; [m.] June 1989; [ch.] Two sons, aged 2 and 5; [ed.] LLB Law (Hons); [pers.] To me, poetry is like beautiful music filled with a rare degree of unforgettable imagery. It strikes to the deep places of the human heart and awakens the perpetual spirit of delight.; [a.] Greenford, Middlesex, UK

BLACKBURN-EVANS, MISS RUTH
[b.] 3 August 8, 1931, Liverpool; [p.] Jenny Evans; [oth. writ.] Book Poems from the Heart, two, manus. just completed; [a.] Poulton-le-Fyld, Lancs, UK

BLACKETOR, PAUL G.
[b.] 10 February 1927, Birmingham, AL; [m.] Irene Blacketor; [ch.] Three - one daughter and two sons; [ed.] B.S. - Samford University - USA, M.S. - Auburn University - USA, M.A. - Auburn University - USA, Doctorate - Auburn University - USA; [occ.] Professor - Keene State College - University System of New Hampshire - USA; [memb.] Kiwanis, Veterans of Foreign Wars, American Legion, American Association of University Professors, National Education Association, Association for Supervision and Curriculum Development, New England Confidence of the Philosophy of Education, National Council for the Social Studies, National Council of States; [hon.] Kappa Delta Phi, Kappa Phi Kappa, Phi Delta Kappa and Phi Alpha Theta, Kentucky Colonel, Citation from the New Hampshire House of Representatives, Citation from the Kentucky State Police, and others.; [oth. writ.] Blacketor, Paul G., and others, Senior Researcher, International Study of School Leavers - 1960-61 to 1992-93 (UK) - in progress, National Study of Public School Drop Outs - 1960-61 to 1992-93 - in progress, Sketches of Unusual Events and Significant Contributors in the History of the United States, (Currently in progress.), History of Vermont Baptist Churches, Vermont Baptist State Convention, 1988, The American Baptist Bi-Vocational Ministry in New England, Massachusetts Baptist State Convention, Boston, 1987, Basic Statistics For Teachers, Edwards Brothers, Ann Arbor, 1974. (Revision in progress), Career Opportunities In the Greater Kenne Area. Stone Press, Chamber of Commerce, Kenne, 1970., The Extent of Certain Supervisory Activities of Selected Public Schools in alabama, Auburn University, 1966., The Policy of the Greenville Advocate, 1872 - 1892, Auburn University, 1965., The Off-Campus Student Course Offerings and Scheduling by Auburn University in Alabama, Georgia, and Northern Florida, Auburn University, 1954. Various other articles.; [pers.] My wife, Irene, was the inspiration for "The Love Of A Butterfly".; [a.] Enfield, Middlesex, UK

BLACKMORE, SYBIL JOYCE
[b.] 21 February 1929, Brompton Regis; [p.] George Bale, Maud Mary Bale; [m.] George Henry Blackmore, 19 March 1966; [ed.] West Central School, Bath., Bath. Technical College; [oth. writ.] A selection of poems and stories written throughout her life, never sent for publication.; [pers.] Sybil had the magical quality of being able to see life through the eyes of child and the ability to interpret their enchanting humour.; [a.] Culmstock, Devon, UK

BLACKSHAW, RONALD
[b.] 30 March 1935, Fulham, London; [p.] Samuel and Hannah Blackshaw; [m.] Jean Rachel, 7 March 1970; [ch.] Garry, Laura, Jean; [ed.] Henry Compton Secondary Modern; [occ.] Retired Printer; [memb.] Royal Horicultural Society, Water Colour and Acrylic Art Group; [hon.] United Nations Medal Korea General Service Medal Kenya; [oth. writ.] Various poems in community association newsletters and fanzines.; [pers.] This is my first serious attempt to publish a poem at the age of 61, I thought it was better late than never.; [a.] Woking, Surrey, UK

BLACKSTAFFE, PHILLIP CHARLES
[b.] 6 December 1973, Birmingham; [p.] Rod and Dawn Blackstaffe; [ed.] Dartmouth High School B'ham Sandwell College - Change Campus Smethwick; [occ.] Security Officer; [memb.] Scout Association Junior Astronomical Society National Mini Owners Club; [hon.] NVQ Bricklaying; [pers.] A poem has a rhyme and a rhythm. If it hasn't got either then it is not a poem.; [a.] Birmingham, West Midlands, UK

BLAKE, STAN
[b.] 10 January 1912, Gillingham, Kent; [p.] William and Edith Marsh; [m.] Eileen, 6 May 1995; [ed.] Richmond RD Primary and Secondary Schools, Gillingham further Education Royal Navy; [occ.] Semi-retired; [memb.] RAOB, Royal Br. Legion; [hon.] Royal Society of Arts Diploma in Italian, Hon. Member Royal Life Saving Society Italian Equivalent; [oth. writ.] Autobiography published November 1994 by bound biographies, London, various poems to residents association magazines and local press.; [pers.] Peacetime 1927 - 36 Royal Navy, Wartime 1940 - 46 Army Intelligence then into salesmanship. Currently pensioners club committee.; [a.] Tilbury, Essex, UK

BLAKEMAN, ANTHONY CHARLES
[b.] 19 July 1933, Cardiff; [p.] William and Gladys Blakeman; [m.] Ada Megan Blakeman, 25 September 1953; [ch.] Peter Ruby Richard; [occ.] Heating and Pluming; [memb.] Cardiff Athletic Male Voice Choir. Cantonian Singers; [oth. writ.] Member of the Royal Signals 1950. Taken part in concerts in America Canada Belgium France Holland with Cor Mibion De Cymru; [pers.] I was influenced by Dylan Thomas poem Rev Eli Jenkin's from the book under wilkwook.; [a.] Cardiff, Glamorgan, UK

BLANEY, THOMAS PATRICK
[pen.] Scotchtommy; [b.] 15 September 1929, Coatbridge; [p.] Deceased; [m.] Beryl O. A. P., 1954; [ch.] Two sons; [occ.] O. A. P. was Komet Sock Mc Operator Knitter; [oth. writ.] Poets, anchor, untitled, one of the many unknown soldiers, by Scotchtommy editor - Andrew Head Poets 1995 1-2 Wainman Rd, Woodston Peterborough PE2 7BU; [pers.] Scotchtommy

BLASDALE, SAMANTHA RACHEAL
[pen.] Rupert; [b.] 3 March 1979, Rush Green; [p.] Anne Blasdale and Robert Blasdale; [occ.] Shipping Clerk; [oth. writ.] This will be my first published poem.; [pers.] My work is inspired by a natural outlook on life. I like to study all different categories whilst writing my poetry it is also based around different views on everyday living life.; [a.] Essex, UK

BLOORE, MRS. HELEN
[pen.] Helen J. Wright; [b.] 6 July 1964, Leicester; [p.] Colin J. Wright, Anne Wright; [m.] Mr. Peter Bloore, 19 June 1991; [ch.] Cathy Anne Jane, Christie Hannah and Jack Stanley; [ed.] Newark Girls, Leicester Bosworth College, Desford; [occ.] Market Trader; [memb.] B.U.A.V.;

[pers.] In this new age, man now has the capacity for total destruction. I know however, that if enough of us can open our eyes to the universal truth that love and self-knowledge are the only things that truly matter, then we also have the capacity to achieve "heaven on earth" we owe it to ourselves and our planet to seek that truth.; [a.] Elmesthorpe, Leics, UK

BLOYCE, CLIVE
[b.] 29 October 1946, Little Heath; [p.] Robert Bloyce, Margery Bloyce; [ed.] Little Heath Primary, St. Audrey's Secondary Modern; [occ.] Carpenter and Juiner; [hon.] City and Guilds of London Institute; [oth. writ.] Three other poems published in 'A Treasury of Modern Poets'; [pers.] No-one should be denied the right of humour; [a.] Potters Bar, Hertfordshire, UK

BOBE, MARIE THERESE
[pen.] Marie Helene Permal; [b.] 11 August 1949, Mauritius; [p.] Orelius and Daisy Pierre-Louis; [m.] Divorced, 2 February 1977; [ch.] Sarah L. Bobe; [ed.] Riviere des Anguilles Primary Schl., St. Helena's College in Mauritius; [occ.] Registered Nurse in Tower Hamlets, London; [oth. writ.] Several short poems I have written for my friends and family; [pers.] I want to reflect the goodness, compassion and joy which each one of us seek to accomplish.; [a.] London, UK

BODYCOTE, SALLY
[pen.] Sally Marriott; [b.] 16 March 1940, Melton Mowbray; [p.] Thomas and Norah Bodycote; [ed.] King Edward VII Grammar School Melton Mobrary Leics; [occ.] Accounts Manager; [memb.] Associated Retired Persons Over 50; [oth. writ.] 6 poems published in "Spring Poets '74"; [pers.] I find it so much easier to express myself in the written word.; [a.] Nottingham, Notts, UK

BOLLINGTON, JENNY
[b.] 12 February 1937, Ninfield; [p.] Harry and Mabel Seymour; [m.] Now Divorced August 1956; [ch.] Victoria; [ed.] Ninfield Church of England Primary School; [occ.] Hospital Domestic; [oth. writ.] Have had poetry published in local health authority magazine. Selection of other poems and writings as yet unpublished; [pers.] All my work is an expression of my own personal moods, and circumstances, influenced by feelings ranging from joy and pleasure through to suffering and depression; [a.] Eastbourne, East Sussex, UK

BOLTON, PENNY-LOUISE
[b.] November 19, 1986, Portsmouth; [p.] Sarah Anderson, Terry Gaunlett; [ed.] Cottage Grove Nursery, Cottage Grove Primary, Goldsmith Primary, Fernhurst Junior.; [occ.] At School; [memb.] Dancing school; [oth. writ.] I have written many other poems.; [pers.] I enjoy reading and writing poetry and I try to include a message in my poetry. I also try to include interest and fantasy. I hope to continue writing poetry.; [a.] Portsmouth, Hampshire, UK

BOLTON, YVONNE ANNE
[b.] 9 June 1947, Manchester; [p.] Dorothy and Hugh Byrne; [m.] Geoffrey Bolton, 2 March 1968; [ch.] Paul, Warren and Craig; [oth. writ.] 4 Novels, several poems 25 short stories: Sadly yet unpublished. Many articles published in newspapers, magazines etc.; [pers.] Old fashioned as it might sound. I wish only to be recognized as a good wife, mother, writer in that order. Achieving greatness would be a bonus!!!; [a.] Penysarn, Gwynedd, UK

BOND, CIARA
[b.] 3 May 1970, Derry; [p.] Michael and Patricia Bond; [m.] Mr. Eamon Doherty, 18 March 1995; [ed.] St. Brigid's Secondary School, North West Institute of Further and Higher Education; [occ.] Personal Secretary, Western Health and Social Services Board; [memb.] Institute of Qualified Private Secretaries, Pat Henderson Academy of Irish Dancing (Teacher's Certificate Rinci Gaelacha); [hon.] Private and Executive Secretaries Diploma, Grades I-VI - honours Irish Dancing; [oth. writ.] Several writings but none published as yet.; [pers.] I have a great love and respect for life and can express my emotions best on paper. I will keep on writing - after all, writings is part of who I am.; [a.] Derry, Derry, UK

BOND, DORIS R.
[b.] 21 January 1935, Frimle Green, Surrey; [p.] John and Noara Wonham (both Deceased); [m.] Keith Bond, 21 July 1956; [ch.] 1 Son 2 daughters; [ed.] Old Woking Primary School, Kingfield Sec. School; [occ.] Retired; [oth. writ.] Several poems published in ex-firms magazine (J. Player and Son); [pers.] I write purely for pleasure hoping it will bring someone a little pleasure too.; [a.] Nottingham, Nottinghamshire, UK

BOOLAKY, EMMA
[b.] 22 May 1981, Croydon; [p.] Rajindraparsad and Kathleen Boolaky; [ed.] Woodcote High School; [oth. writ.] Poetry and stories for the school magazine.; [pers.] I want my poems to enable people to see things they have seen many times before in a different light.; [a.] Coulsdon, Surrey, UK

BOOTH, RACHEL YOLANDE
[pen.] Rachel Booth; [b.] 6 August 1922, N. Derbyshire; [p.] Wilde Fostered by Minna Fearn 1929; [m.] John Henry George Booth, (Deceased), 18 September 1948; [ch.] John Spencer, Yolande Robertson Booth, George Booth, Roger Booth; [ed.] Church of England Girls' School, School of Art Derby, Wartime Training: Hvy. Ack-Ack. Btn. Command Post; [occ.] Retired but have family responsibilities; [memb.] Life-Long Womens Inst., "Royal Ntl Rose Society"; [oth. writ.] Varied contributions to local paper, a poem of so for press.; [pers.] My letter-writing is my hobby - a challenge for my life-long self-discipline. Always alert to humorous incidents!; [a.] New Tonmore, Invernesshire, UK

BOOTH, WENDY J.
[b.] 27 May 1954, London; [p.] Frank and Vera Smith; [m.] Mike Booth, 16 October 1971; [ch.] Jason Philip and Sarah; [occ.] Order Office Clerk, Allied Mills Ltd, Tewkesbury; [a.] Tewkesbury, Gloucestershire, UK

BOWEN, JOHN W.
[pen.] David Liam Shane; [b.] 19 December 1948, Bugbrooke; [p.] David Bowen and Hilda Bowen; [m.] Stephanie Bowen, 4 November 1972; [ch.] Kerry, Steven, Ben, Simon and Victoria Liam; [ed.] Bugbrooke C.P., Duston, S.M.S. Northampton College, Ruskin, College Oxford; [occ.] Student; [memb.] Bugbrooke, R.F.C. Hon: Member Mature, Students Union Rep. Committee, Member Bugbrooke Playing Fields Association, Oxford Union; [hon.] C&G I, It word processing studying at present, to go on to University, to read philosophy and politics; [oth. writ.] Publications in various poetry anthologies throughout Great Britain and Europe. Written for David Shepard, Elephant Trust. And for relief for

Rawanda, refugees and the late R.H. John Smith MP.; [pers.] To write for the benefit of a better world, and for the future of our children, and the environment, most influential author, to date Robert Tressell.; [a.] Northampton, Northamptonshire, UK

BOWEN, VIVIEN PFEIFFER
[b.] 1 January 1953, Liverpool; [p.] Eric and Beryl Jarve; [m.] Norman Pfeiffer Bowen, 27 July 1991; [ch.] Sarah, Sean, Lydia; [ed.] High School Wigan Road Ormskirk Lancashire, Deyes Lane High School Maghull Nr. Liverpool; [occ.] Medical Receptionist 2 inventor; [oth. writ.] Many more poems throughout my life. I also write song lyrics and compose music. After this my first try of publication I shall endeavour to strive on.; [pers.] At 43 yrs. of age I have been through the university of life. I have my own philosophical Viewpoint that age is but a time of understanding and understanding only comes with age. I have not been influenced by any one other than my feelings.; [a.] Skelmersdale, Lancashire, UK

BOWERS, PATRICIA CONSTANCE
[pen.] Patricia Bowers, PCB; [b.] 4 June 1940, Stockport; [p.] Thomas Froggatt, Constance Froggatt; [m.] William Bowers, 3 October 1964; [ch.] Gail, Michelle, Billie-Jean, William; [ed.] New Mills, Comprehensive; [occ.] Retired Nurse; [memb.] Served in "The Women Royal Navel Service" for four years; [pers.] I write mainly for my own pleasure and satisfaction. I am influenced by my very close and loving family. I am disabled after suffering a stroke, and am forever grateful to my wonderful husband and children, for all their help and caring.; [a.] New Mills, Derbyshire, UK

BOWLES, MISS JUDITH ANNE
[pen.] Judi Bowles; [b.] Helensburgh, Scotland; [ed.] Grammar School, and College of further Ed.; [occ.] Amateur Writer and Secretary; [hon.] RDS Artwork; [oth. writ.] Only roughwork, 12 short story child's.; [pers.] The magnificent creativity of nature has been marred by the materialism of industrialists.; [a.] Bedington, Wirral, M'side, UK

BRADFORD, AUDREY EILEEN
[b.] 2 November 1922, Otley, Yorkshire; [p.] William Stringer, H. Ida Stringer; [m.] Robert Earle Bradford, 28 August 1965; [ch.] (Step-children) Jon Baker, Gregory Earle; [ed.] Roundhay, Leeds University (BA Hons German), Erlangen University, Bavaria (Teaching and Medineval German Research), Queen's University, Belfast (German Staff), PGCE (Leeds), Associateship London Institute of Education (TEFL 1987), MA Icelands studies (Leeds 1973, Emphasis on Nurse Vikings and Sagas); [occ.] Retired Senior Consultant of British Council's Overseas Career Service, now freelance; [memb.] First Division Association, Victoria Service Club, Friends of West Yorkshire Playhouse, National Trust, Red Cross, Oxfam, Amnesty International, Green peace, RNLI, IFAW, SCF, Children's Society, etc; [hon.] OBE 1973 (Buckingham Palace); [oth. writ.] Reviews "German Life and Letters", Education articles in English, Indian, Thai, and Nigeria English-language, publications, a group of poems for the Government of Kerala, South India, to use in primary schools, "A Survey of the Funding of the Arts in Australia" for the then Arts Council of Great Britain (C 1977/8), an ongoing series of poems (unpublished) from 1977 to date, mostly longer, few short; [pers.] Very varied career from W.R.N.S. in war time WRNS to educational work at University and Institutes in

Germany, Belfast Switzerland, SE Asia and Nigeria, Indian led to a deep concern for young people and their teachers in "developing" tropical countries. Their warm affection has inspired me to an every growing and deeping conviction that only love and compassion to all are what matter in life. This under lies my love of travel, people, drama, classical music, and poetry.; [a.] Leeds, West Yorkshire, UK

BRADSHAW, RICHARD JOHN
[pen.] I simply include John as J.; [b.] 31 July 1935, Wood Green, North London; [p.] Edna and Harold Bradshaw; [m.] Ann Bradshaw (Nee Haynes, Deceased), 19 October 1968; [ed.] Hazelwood Lane Infant and Junior School: Winchmore Hill Secondary Modern School: Southgate County Grammar School: Trent Park College (University of London); [occ.] Retired Primary School Teacher; [memb.] Felixstowe Branch 'Cancer Research Campaign' Committee: ARP/050: Eagle Society: Suffolk Wildlife Trust: Friends of the Pavilion Orchestra; [hon.] Voted best poet of 'Isthmus' poetry of Magazine (Issue 2) two certificates of further professional study (Cambridge Institute of Education) in (A.) Ecology (B.) Sociology; [oth. writ.] 'Quartet in B' (PFC publications) poet's England - 15 Suffolk (Brentham Press) various imprints of forward press: 'Best of British' Magazine: 'Isthmus' Magazine: Various house journals and parish magazines; [pers.] No underlying hidden messages sad or humorous, I simply try to paint with words. Subject matter quite often Nostalgic. A lover of Betjeman's work. Most work in rhyme.; [a.] Felixstowe, Suffolk, UK

BRAMMER, LINDA-MARIE
[b.] 27 September 1945, Manchester; [ch.] Darren Anthony Brammer; [ed.] Poundswick G.S. St. John's College Manchester; [occ.] Personal Assistant; [memb.] Former member Acton Bridge Cruising Club, Weaverham, Cheshire; [hon.] RSA Shorthand/Typing Distinction; [pers.] Dedicated to my late son Darren Anthony, without whose guidance and inspiration from beyond our world as we know it, my pen would not move.; [a.] Ashton, Lancashire, UK

BRANCH, MRS. ALISON F.
[pen.] Mrs. Alison F. Branch; [b.] 23 February 1950, South Queens Ferry, West Lothian; [p.] William and Janet Temple; [m.] Raymond H. Branch, 24 June 1972; [ch.] Annabel J. F. and Jennie M.; [ed.] Lasswade High School; [occ.] Registered child minder; [memb.] Bonnyrigg C/M group Scottish C/M Association. Dalkieth Hortcultural Society; [hon.] Scottish Certificate of Education, English, Award 2, S.C.O.E. Higher (Revised), D. Scotvec Introduction to Literature the Cameron cup of the D.H.S. 93, 94, (Baking); [pers.] I wish to dedicate this poem to my beloved parents.; [a.] Bonnyrigg, Midlothian, UK

BREBNER, RICHARD
[b.] 27 April 1955, Bulawayo; [p.] Gerald and Nan Brebner; [m.] Debra, 6 August 1983; [ed.] "A" levels in English, History and Geography. B.A. Eng & Geog (University of Rhodesia) grad. C.E. (hons.); [occ.] Professional Safari Guide; [oth. writ.] Have never submitted any of my other poems.; [pers.] I am inspired by nature and wild life. The poem "Teachers' Lament" came at the end of 15 years of English teaching in Zimbabwe.; [a.] Bulawayo, Zimbabwe

BREEN, BRIDGET
[b.] October 9, 1925, Donegal; [p.] Thomas Gallinagh, Margaret; [m.] James Breen, March 1, 1949; [ch.] Six children; [ed.] Primary School until age fourteen, thereafter the School of Mankind and University of Life, no academic qualifications.; [occ.] Housewife, [oth. writ.] Few articles to magazines, papers, etc.; [pers.] I looked after my mother in her own home. She died last year, aged one hundred and two. Her death gave birth to my poem "The Passing Of A Centenarian"; [a.] Donegal

BRIGHAM, JOHN EDWARD
[b.] 1 June 1912, Darlington, Durham; [p.] John C. and Eleanor Brigham; [m.] Lily (Pat) Askwith, 27 March 1937; [ch.] David, Mary, Eleanor; [ed.] Polam Hall School, Darlington, Darlington Grammar School, Ackworth Sch. Bootham, York, Durham University/Sorbonne/Cambridge; [occ.] Retired Headmaster; [memb.] Religious Society of Friends National Trust; [oth. writ.] Translated (from Dutch): Books on M.C. Escher The Elite and the Welfare State (Prof. Thoenes); [a.] Cambridgeshire, UK

BRITAIN, MARY GWENDOLINE ANNIE
[b.] 31 March 1910, Pickhill; [p.] John and Gertrude Britain; [ed.] Pickhill, Nr Thirsk, Church of England School; [a.] Thirsk, North Yorkshire, UK

BROADLEY, ROSE
[pen.] Rose Broadley; [b.] 1 August 1938, Hull, Yorkshire; [p.] Charles Barnes, Irene Barnes; [m.] Brian P. Broadley, 26 December 1959; [ch.] Philip, Marguerite, and Jane; [ed.] The Convent of Saint Agustine Hull. Hull Regional College of Art and Crafts; [occ.] Housewife; [hon.] National Diploma in design; [oth. writ.] Twelve poems published in Nottingham evening post; [pers.] I like to write about nature, in particular, the seasons, plants and flowers.; [a.] Nottm, Nottinghamshire, UK

BROBBEY, JACOB ASARE
[b.] 2 November 1955, Kumasi; [p.] Dinah Arkaifie, Jacob Brobbey; [m.] Otilia Mariana Brobbey, 29 October 1988; [ch.] Nerissa Adela Isabella; [ed.] Mfantsipim Secondary School, Presec Legon, in Ghana Faculty of General Medicine, Bucharest, Romania; [occ.] Medical Practitioner; [oth. writ.] Several poems published in Ghanaian National Papers. Drama for Theatre.; [pers.] There is beauty in poetry and drama.; [a.] Accra, Ghana

BROCKBANK, BARBARA J.
[b.] 29 July 1918, Stockton Heath; [p.] Grenville Hodgson, Dorothea Dee Bracecamp; [m.] Robert Alston Brockbank, 7 January 1950; [ch.] Robert, Grenville, Jill Henton (now Schofield); [ed.] Winifred's (Woodard School), Llanfairfechan, Bedford Physical Training College; [occ.] Retired, Widow Family Archivist; [oth. writ.] Rhymes for family birthdays etc!; [a.] Lowestoft, Suffolk, UK

BROCKIE, LINDSAY THOMAS
[b.] November 18, 1953, Dumfries; [p.] Alexander and Sheila; [m.] Lesley Irene, September 6, 1975; [ch.] Claire Louise; [ed.] Annan Academy Dumfries Technical College; [occ.] Carpenter and Joiner Self-employed; [memb.] Powfoot Golf Club; [hon.] Being accepted by yourselves; [oth. writ.] 'Snowflakes' (unpublished) several testimonies in verse; [pers.] To live to the full, and to try anything at least once, more importantly, when meeting new

people through life to always leave them with a smile on their face; [a.] Annan, Dumfriesshire, UK

BROOKE, MARY
[b.] 1 October 1943, Rushden, Northants; [p.] Ted and Kathleen Smith; [ch.] Neil Robert, Brynley John; [ed.] Wellingborough High School, Northants; [occ.] Foster Career, Social Services, Lincolnshire; [oth. writ.] Several poems published in anthologies and poetry magazine.; [pers.] I see my poetry as a reflection of life in our current society; [a.] Horncastle, Lincs, UK

BROOKES, KATE
[b.] 7 March 1964, Cambridge; [p.] Mary and Tony Fowler; [m.] Paul Brookes, 6 April 1996; [ed.] Willingham Primary School Cottenham Village College, Cambridge College of Further Education.; [occ.] Unemployer, but I am a Navy - between contracts; [memb.] Redditch Folk Club, Trinity Church Choir, Bel Canto Singers (Choir) (With my husband, in all of Redditch Otters swimming Club for the Disabled); [hon.] Caring skills in the community, 6 Differents Training certificates, in the Scout Movement, as a Club a Leader and Beaver Leader; [oth. writ.] Had a poem in "New Poetry 1981" had letters in "Cambridge evening News" constantly for years. Had true story published in "Take a Break" magazine August 1996. Short true Story in an anthology of Pet Stories - called "Tips and Taps, 1988; [pers.] I have wanted to be a writer since I was a child. The idea of other people reading, and enjoying something I have written fills me with pride. I want to be a poet and author.; [a.] Redditch, Worcestershire, UK

BROOKS, MARCIA I.
[b.] 13 March 1923, Sleaford; [p.] Harold and Anne Taylor; [m.] Ellis E. Brooks, 25 July 1942; [ch.] Vincent Peter; [ed.] County Secondary School, Sleaford; [occ.] Housewife; [hon.] Honary Awards for Poetry; [oth. writ.] Several poems published in other anthologies.; [pers.] I enjoy writing poetry to try to express my feelings, and to reflect on some of the good things in life.; [a.] Bourne, Lincolnshire, UK

BROTHWELL, DAVE
[pen.] Al Davonne; [b.] March 1, 1945, Nr. Sleaford, Lincs; [p.] John and Rose Brothwell; [m.] Yvonne, March 1, 1979; [ch.] Helen Marie; [ed.] Carre's Grammar Sch., Sleaford, Lincs; [occ.] Mini-Bus/Ambulance Driver (Mainly Elderly and Disabled) working for local authority L. C. C.; [oth. writ.] None - this was my first serious attempt; [pers.] Lover of wildlife and all animals both wild and domestic.; [a.] Grantham, Lincs

BROUGH, CHRISTOPHER
[b.] 10 July 1957, Uttoxeter; [p.] Dennis and Barbara Brough; [m.] Divorced; [ch.] Emma, Rebecca and Charlotte; [ed.] Alleynes Grammar School, Uttoxeter; [occ.] Line Technician; [oth. writ.] Poems and several short story; [a.] Fenton, Stoke-on-Trent, UK

BROWN, JANIS
[pen.] Janis Brown; [b.] 4 September 1950, Rochford, Essex; [p.] Charles Sapsford, Rosina Grant; [m.] Divorced; [ch.] Lesley, Janey and Daniel; [ed.] Wentworth High School Southend-on-Sea, Heriot-Watt University, Edinburgh; [occ.] Final (4th) year student studying MPHYS physics

degree; [memb.] Institute of Physics; [oth. writ.] Written many poems but this is the first that I have submitted one for outside appraisal.; [pers.] I have been influenced by my personal observations of life around me and not by any one particular poet. I am also Vegan which often influences me.; [a.] Edinburgh, UK

BROWN, MARY B.
[b.] 29 February 1932, Ireland; [p.] Bill and Bridie Downey; [m.] John William Brown (Deceased), 10 September 1960; [ch.] Malcolm, Yvonne and Anne; [occ.] Retired; [memb.] Sometimes I write, sometimes I garden and sometimes I have a go at house maintenance; [oth. writ.] A publication in local newspaper, London poets What's The Score? Broadcast on Robbie Vincent - L.B.C. Publicity - Royal Festival Hall.; [pers.] Words cost us nothing. They mean a lot and can cast pleasure in ever-abundant streams.; [a.] Manor Park, London, UK

BROWN, MHAIRI JARVIS
[pen.] Mhairi Jarvis; [b.] 6 July 1943, Dundee; [p.] Bridget McConville, George J. Arvis; [hon.] Editor's Choice Award from International Library of Poetry for 'Aftermath' in Voices On The Wind; [oth. writ.] Eleven published poems, 2 short stories, published.; [pers.] 'My Friend' - is for Nan who came into my life for 4 years. She touched my life and helped to make me who I am.; [a.] Dundee, Angus, UK

BROWN, SARAH BEVERLEY
[pen.] Sarah Brown; [b.] 18 December 1966, Slough; [p.] Francis Leonard and Maureen Anne Brown; [ed.] Heathend Secondary School; [occ.] Service Switchboard Operator; [oth. writ.] My personal collection of poems I've written over the years. I have submitted one other poem to a competition and that was published in the 'Best Book of Life and Love!; [pers.] I seem to have acquired my own style of writing and can't say that I have been influenced by any other writers. I get an idea in my head and just have to put pen to paper. I am pleasantly surprised that my poem has been chosen for publication.; [a.] Aldershot, Hants, UK

BROWN, WILLIAM
[pen.] Guillaume; [b.] 6 December 1943, Ayr, Strathclyde; [ed.] Whittinghame Boys School, East Linton; [oth. writ.] "Love Positive" International Society of Poets", A Passage In Time", "Teach Me" "Poetry Now", "Up And Running", "Loneliness" and "Memories Of Love" A treasury of modern poets 1975. "Regency Press London.; [pers.] I have been influenced in my writing by the Scottish Bard Robert Burns and R. W. Service. Still with us in verse.; [a.] Ayr, Strathclyde, UK

BROWN, YVONNE
[b.] 25 July 1977, London; [p.] Pansie Brown; [ed.] Convent of Jesus and Mary High School, currently at Hertfordshire University; [occ.] Student at Hertfordshire University studying Art and Design; [memb.] Harlesden Keinya Self Defense Club; [hon.] English Literature, Art and Design; [oth. writ.] Currently writing a personal anthology; [pers.] I endeavour to reflect the reality of experience in my writing and regard poetry as an instrument of expression. My influences have been the modern poets whose veins on emotion, culture and belief I share; [a.] Harlesden, London, UK

BROWNE, REV. JOHNNY ADAMSON
[b.] 24 June 1923, Banana Island, Sierra Leone; [p.] Maria Browne; [m.] 1st Fanny Macarthy, 2 January 1952, 2nd Adel Iyamode Macauley, 6 September 1990; [ch.] Ten; [ed.] 1. General English type Middle Grade, 2. Government Trade Center Sierra Leone I.L.O. Technical Institute Turin, Italy-Slough, England, 3. Sierra Leone Theological Institute; [occ.] Minister of Religion and Superintendent of West African Methodist Demonstration Churches in Sierra Leone; [memb.] Sierra Leone Rural Area District, Council West African Methodist Church, Minister's Fellowship; [oth. writ.] The Spark and other poems. Published by Arthur Stockwell, at Illfracombe Devon 1952. 1. Influenced by Elizabethan Poetic and Prose writers, 2. Wallace Johnson of Sierra Leone; [pers.] Whatsoever a man sows, this he will reap. I believe that there is a God who made all that constitutes this world in which we live, whose power is unlimited whose purposes for mankind is always for his good.; [a.] Freetown, Sierra Leone, UK

BROWNE, REV. JOHNNY ADAMSON
[b.] 24 June 1923, Banana Island, Sierra Leone; [p.] Maria Browne; [m.] 1st married Fanny Macarthy, 2 January 1952, 2nd Adel Iyamode Macauley, 6 September 1990; [ch.] Ten; [ed.] 1. General English Type Middle Grade, 2. Government Trade Center, Sierra Leone, I.L.O. Technical Institute Turin, Italy, Slough, England, 3. Sierra Leone Theological Institute; [occ.] Minister of Religion and Superintendent of West African Methodist, Demonition Churches in Sierra Leona; [memb.] Sierra Leone Rural Area District, Council West African Methodist Church, Ministers Fellowship; [oth. writ.] The Spark and other poems, published by Arthur Stockwell, at Illfracombe Devon 1952. Influenced by Elizabethan Poetic and Prose writers, Wallace Johnson of Sierra Leone; [pers.] Whatsoever, a man sows this he will reap. I believe that there is a God who made all that constitutes this world in which we live. Whose power is unlimited, whose purposes for mankind is always for his good.; [a.] Freetown, Sierra Leone

BRYAN, TIFFANY-LEANNE
[pen.] Tiffany Leanne Pexton; [b.] 18 July 1980, Tittensaw; [p.] Lyn and Mike Bryan; [ed.] St. Annes Primary 1984-1987, St Patricks Primary 1987-1991, Weston Road High 1991-1996; [occ.] Student; [hon.] Poetry now Young Writer Awards "Write and Shine", 1995 and 1996; [oth. writ.] A few short poems published in regional anthology; [pers.] All my life I have felt a natural yearning to reach success and reflect my deepest thoughts through the best way I personally can - through writing.; [a.] Stafford, Staffordshire, UK

BRYANT, JO
[b.] 6 May 1963, Liverpool; [p.] Jacqueline Bryant and Alan Bryant; [ed.] Goldsmiths' College, University of London and Cardiff University; [occ.] English/Drama Teacher, Willows High School, Cardiff; [memb.] Director/Producer "Scream Theatre Company" Willows High School. Willows Word Wizards Publishing Company. (Local History Books written by Pupils, Supervised, Edited by Myself; [hon.] B.A. Hons English/Drama, P.G.C.E.; [oth. writ.] Many but this is my first attempt at publication. Barclays bank `A' level essay prize winner.; [pers.] Limits limit! If you don't reach for the stars you can never hope to touch them. Live your dreams!; [a.] Cardiff, UK

BURDITT, KENNETH C.
[b.] 30 May 1931, Market Harborough; [p.] Harold and Winifred Burditt; [ed.] Market Harborough Grammar School; [occ.] Retired; [hon.] Award of Excellence (Poetry).; [oth. writ.] Several poems published in local newspapers and anthologies.; [pers.] I enjoy reflecting the present day happenings and events in my writings.; [a.] Rugby, Warwickshire, UK

BURNETT, MRS. E.
[b.] 8 June 1937; [p.] Deceased; [m.] Mr. T. Burnett; [ch.] Four daughters and two grandchildren; [pers.] I am a middle aged woman. I work with young children. One of my strongest beliefs is that whatever I do, I do to the best of my ability. I try not to dwell on the negative aspects of situations that arise, but to find some good out of everything. My inspiration arise from everyday events around me, and also from my own personal life experience.

BURNS, DOUGLAS
[b.] 22 June 1955, Patriotic Scotsman, Stafford; [p.] William Burns and Elizabeth Burns; [m.] Jacqueline Burns, 22 December 1995; [ch.] James Buns, Lisa Burns Claire McCarron, Theresa McCarron; [occ.] Auxiliary Nurse; [memb.] School of Life; [oth. writ.] None - other than for personal reading/pleasure my poetry is for pleasure. If other people take pleasure from the writing, then fine.; [pers.] Be at peace. Be free. Be alive. Be happy. For you.; [a.] Cromer, Norfolk, UK

BURNS, JAMES PAUL
[b.] 23 June 1967, Liverpool; [p.] James Burns, Monica Burns; [ed.] Secondary Modern School, Liverpool; [occ.] Royal Mail, Liverpool Copperas Hill Sorting Office; [hon.] Dream of a snowflake published in 'Awaken to a Dream' anthology; [oth. writ.] Songwriter and musician various poetry (unpublished).; [pers.] I like to touch all aspects of life and observe and use imagery to escape for a while, if the day doesn't offer a happy alternative.; [a.] Liverpool, Merseyside, UK

BUTLER, ALEX
[b.] 29 June 1976, Manchester; [p.] Paul and Sheila Butler; [ed.] St. Benedicts Upper; [occ.] Student, University College London; [pers.] For E.J.C. thank you to D.L.H. "We are all in the gutter, but some of us are looking at the stars." Thanks Oscar, Leonard and Richey.; [a.] London, UK

BUTLER, ANGELA
[b.] 25 March 1936, Halifax; [ed.] Elland Grammar School Leicester University; [memb.] Grange-over-Sands Music Society, Leisure Centre; [oth. writ.] Many poems published in regional and National poetry anthologies. I have given considerable help towards the writing of 2 christian books by Evelyn Booth-Clibborn.; [pers.] My concern is to reflect the christian message and hope through my poetry - not in a didactic way, but less obtrusively through pattern and image and positive outlook.; [a.] Grange-over-Sands, Cumbria, UK

BYRNE, MIKE
[b.] 13 May 1962, Birkenhead; [p.] Thomas and Vera Byrne; [ch.] Laura Jane; [ed.] St. Hugh's High School Birkenhead; [occ.] Math-Teacher Training, John Moores University; [memb.] Guitarist of R plus B Band 'Waterfront'; [pers.] My inspiration for life. 'Laura' our beautiful little girl.; [a.] Wirral, Merseyside, UK

BYRNE, SUSAN
[pen.] Serendipity; [b.] 14 October 1978, Cork; [p.] Mary O'Connor Byrne; [ed.] Children Hse. Montessori Sch. Waterford, Our Lady of Mercy Convent Secondary School, Waterford; [occ.] Student; [memb.] Royal Dublin Society Irish Pony Club; [hon.] Honour up to bronze medal in Speech and Drama and Speaking of Verse and Prose; [oth. writ.] Several poems published in school magazine.; [pers.] An open mind is a mind for eternity.; [a.] Waterford, Waterford, UK

BYRON-EVANS, JOHN
[b.] August 28, 1946, Southport; [p.] Mary Klass Evans; [m.] Dot Byron-Evans (Divorced August 31, 1983), August 8, 1970; [ch.] Aldene, Scholka, Kwei (girls); [ed.] St. Philips Primary, S/Port Holy Trinity Primary, S/Port Meols Cop Secondary S/Port, Mr. Richard Smith, (Music Teacher); [occ.] Patient, and Pupil at Ashworth Hospital, L/Pool; [oth. writ.] Several poems and songs, unpublished.; [pers.] Life is all to everybody! The only thing is to be confident, comfortable, and at peace with the world, and yourself, using consideration! Poetry, through it's perspective, helps me to achieve this goal.; [a.] Liverpool, Merseyside, UK

BYRON-RASMUSSEN, BARBARA
[pen.] "Barbara-Anna" (Music name); [b.] 1 March 1944, Lewes; [ch.] Diana, Denise, Debbie, Karl; [ed.] Mountfield Road Secondary School, Lewis, Sussex; [occ.] Early retired voluntary worker; [memb.] W.R.V.S., Red Cross, Age Concern; [oth. writ.] 400 of more poems - odes 50 songs, 3 prayer books, life story in poetic form, available for publication.; [pers.] Inspired to write by a big life, home and abroad - and the people have met from many nationalities. I did not choose to be a writer. I just am, influenced by other poets. Coming from the heart!; [a.] Brighton, Sussex, UK

CABLE, EMMA
[b.] 20 April 1976, Pembury, Kent; [p.] Peter Cable, Pamela Cable; [ed.] The Cavendish School, Eastbourne Chichester College; [occ.] Drama Student at the Academy of Live and Recorded Arts, London; [hon.] L.A.M.D.A. Gold Medal for Acting and Associate Acting Diploma, A.L.A.M. (Hons).; [oth. writ.] Several poems published in anthologies by poetry now; [pers.] My writing comes primarily from a burning desire to feel expressed. I am influenced more by song lyrics than classical poetry, and ordinary people inspire me most of all.; [a.] Eastbourne, East Sussex, UK

CABRAL, ANANIOS
[pen.] Nani; [b.] 23 November 1975, Luanda; [p.] Jaime Cabral, Carolina Miranda; [ed.] GNVQ - BTEC Foundation in Business - Southgate College, Esol - Intermidiate - Barnet College; [occ.] Student; [memb.] World Books Club, Children Aid Club; [oth. writ.] First published; [pers.] My writing comes from innocent and lovely nature, children, their creator, and my heart and soul love to them and the wonderful things they give to us.; [a.] London, Enfield, UK

CAIN, DESMOND
[b.] 27 June 1951, Port Clarence; [p.] Joseph, Geraldine Patricia; [m.] Janice; [ch.] Lucy Patricia, Sara Fiona; [ed.] St. Mary's College, Middlesbrough, Teessire Polytechnic; [hon.] B. Sc.; [oth. writ.] Collections: Vietnam: A Million Tears (words and music), Bayonets High (words/music), Songs for Children between the ages of 3 and 9 1/2 years.

CAMERON, JAMES STEVEN
[pen.] James Randolph Scott; [b.] 17 April 1954, Lutterworth; [p.] Kaye Brierley; [m.] Divorced and Separated; [ch.] Four children; [ed.] Lutterworth High School and Lutterworth Grammar School; [occ.] Self employed, writer, artist and poet; [hon.] City and Guilds in Plumbing and Heating, Passed with Dist, Registered Healer; [oth. writ.] One poem published in national verse "A Beautiful Dream" one romantic novel titled "Venus And The Pearls" three children's books "Togglebolts" one book of poems and songs, "Reflections Of My Mind" 100's of songs and poems illustrations and design etc.; [pers.] "Love is the greatest liberator known" "Love shall conquer all dark places known" "When mankind appreciates nature, then he has found wisdom at last"; [a.] Ramsey, Isle of Man, UK

CANDY, MRS. GLADYS AMY
[b.] 17 June 1911, Kennington, London; [p.] Francis Joseph and Amy Eliza East; [m.] Regnald Arthur Candy (Deceased), 4 May 1935; [ch.] Brian R. Candy and Angela Mary Burton; [ed.] 1. John Ruskin Elementary 2. St Saviours and St Olaves, Grammar School, New Kendro London; [occ.] Retired; [oth. writ.] School Mag. (1922-29); [pers.] Living in a residential home for the retired I am called on to write for special occasions. Several 90 years birthdays; [a.] Maidemtean, Berks, UK

CANE, JESSIE C.
[b.] 11/4/1927, Carlisle, W.A., [p.] Archibald H. and Jessie M. Paton; [m.] divorced; [ch.] 2 adult sons Garry and John; [ed.] To Eighth Standard. and then on to a business college for a year; [occ.] Home duties; [oth. writ.] "My Garden", "The Spider", "Tears", "Sleep", "Noise"; [pers.] Am a very new verse writer. Do like humerous odes.; [a.] Geraldton, Greenough, W.A.

CAPERS, WENDY
[b.] 13 November 1960, Coventry; [p.] Les and Sylvia Insley; [m.] Richard George (Deceased), 11 August 1978; [ch.] Deceased; [oth. writ.] Several unpublished writings.; [pers.] Inspiration came as a way of expression from several personal tragedies.; [a.] Leamington Spa, Warks, UK

CARLOW, TERESA
[b.] 27 May 1966, Gravesend; [ed.] Northfleet School for Girls, Hall Road, Northfleet, Kent; [occ.] Careworker to adults with learning disabilities.; [oth. writ.] I have many unpublished poems but together by myself over many years.; [pers.] I have been writing poems since a teenager and my work has been inspired by my own personal experiences in life, whether they be of joy or sadness.; [a.] Dartford, Kent, UK

CARNE, ANN
[pen.] Annie; [b.] 3 August 1964, Kent, England; [p.] George Carne and Sheila Carne; [ed.] Clark's College - Bromley, Bromley College of Technology; [occ.] Financial Services Asst.; [oth. writ.] Only as A hobby and my diary. Never tried to have anything published before this.; [a.] London, UK

CARPENTER, C. MARJORIE
[b.] 19 February 1925, Manton, Notts; [p.] John Rutter, Florence Rutter; [m.] David A. Carpenter, 14 May 1948; [ch.] Anne Hazel (1953) Stuart David (1956); [pers.] My poem 'Thin Ice' is part of ongoing, private research concerning images and the brain. It was written as an attempt to 'lay

out the fundamental questions of philosophy in a simple, uncluttered way,' cf. Editorial: Philosophy and children. The journal of the Royal Institute of Philosophy. Hon. Ed. Professor O'Hear (April 1996 Vol. 71 no 276); [a.] Llonerfyl, Powys, UK

CARR, ANNE ELIZABETH
[pen.] A. E. Carr; [b.] 26 August 1945, Britain; [p.] T. F. Binley and V. L. Binley; [m.] Donald Raymond Carr, 7 September 1963; [ch.] Rebecca Claire and Dorian Lee; [ed.] Kettering Girls School; [occ.] Director of Camping Business; [memb.] Guild of Master Craftsman; [oth. writ.] "May Flower" 1996 anthology. Process of being published "It" same publisher.; [pers.] The environment and treatment of animals.; [a.] Kettering, Northants, UK

CARR, AZILE ENID
[pen.] Azile Arnett; [b.] 22 July 1909, Bridlington; [p.] John-William and Gertrude Lily Creaser; [m.] James Edward Arnett later Carr, 17 March 1932, 5 June 1978; [ch.] Ian, Wendy, Clive, Robin; [ed.] Elementary School; [occ.] Housewife and Painting; [oth. writ.] Other poems not published; [pers.] I have been writing poetry for many years, during quiet moments of reflection and peace.; [a.] Hull, East Yorkshire, UK

CARR, PETER LESLIE
[b.] 8 September 1958, Grimsby; [p.] Myra Carr, Leslie Carr; [ed.] Western Secondary School; [occ.] Unemployed; [oth. writ.] Several poems not yet published also several songs.; [pers.] It is my hope that people enjoy my poems and my songs but more important than that I hope they understand.; [a.] Grimsby, Lincs, UK

CARROLL, JOANNE
[b.] 3 January 1974, Droylsden, Manchester; [p.] Dennis and Janet Carroll; [ed.] Fairfield High School, University of Keele; [occ.] Clerical Supervisor; [hon.] Joint Honors Degree in English Classics; [oth. writ.] Poetry published in anthology "Quill and Ink." Short listed for award in "Writing Magazine."; [a.] Manchester, UK

CARROTTE, ALEC C.
[b.] 22 February 1943, Sheffield; [p.] Alec and Eileen Carrotte; [m.] Barbara May Carrotte, 25 August 1990; [ch.] Greg, Laura, step-children: Simon and Chris; [ed.] Firth Park Grammar, Sheffield, and Sheffield Polytechnic; [occ.] Lecturer Bournemouth and Poole College of Further Education; [pers.] Learning and understanding through reflective writing.; [a.] Ferndown, Dorset, UK

CARTER, LORNA MAY
[pen.] Lorna Maye; [b.] 9 October 1920, Long Eaton; [p.] Thirza and Robert Marshall Cooling; [m.] John Carter (Deceased), 4 May 1945; [ch.] Educated at the Wellington St, school for girls, Long Eaton, Notts; [ed.] Housewife; [oth. writ.] Dedicated to Sean Wilson and the Saffron Crocus.; [pers.] I love writing poetry about anything and everything particularly about animals I read a lot do embroidery I also paint, I love walking particularly in the country and also love good music.; [a.] Long Eaton, Nottingham, UK

CARTER, SHIRLEY I.
[b.] 19 December 1935, Belper; [p.] William and Dorothey Bowler; [m.] George Carter, 6 February 1954; [ch.] Julie, David, Tricia, Mark and Mat-

thew; [ed.] Grammar School; [occ.] Housewife and Mother; [pers.] I hope this little poem, for what its worth, shows hope can come from fear and love from what seems a tragedy.; [a.] Belper, Derbyshire, UK

CARTER, WENDY ANN
[pen.] Wendy Ann Carter; [b.] 9 March 1942, Cornwall, England; [p.] Doris and Raymond Paradise; [m.] Orville John Carter; [occ.] Retired; [oth. writ.] Several poems and a short story; [pers.] I started writing poetry at age 14. Inspired by the Mystic Beauty that is Cornwall and the Majestic Beauty of Canada where I lived for many years.; [a.] Camborne, Cornwall, UK

CASSIDY, RICHARD
[b.] 9 October 1976, Bellshill; [p.] Edith Cassidy; [ed.] Abronhill High School; [occ.] Administrator; [hon.] Group Awards: Business Administration Level I, Business Administration: Administrative Level II; [oth. writ.] Short stories/Poems runner-up in 1986 with "Captain Peter and the Gingerbread Men" Competition with Kirriemuir Gingerbread.; [pers.] I write almost with my eyes closed as I try to be influenced only by my heart. I hope my poems move you as much as I was moved to write them.; [a.] Cumbernauld, Dumbartonshire, UK

CATALANO, M.
[pen.] The Poetic Cat; [b.] 9 October 1947, Italy; [p.] Giuseppe and Stella Catalano; [ch.] Pino and Gianna; [ed.] Technical Industrial Institute - Bari, italy; [occ.] Mechanical and Structural Designer; [oth. writ.] I'm having my complete collection of poems published by Minerva Press Publishers hoping to share my feelings with the publics.; [pers.] I believe that live is a very powerful force in the universe and a source of inspiration, and love inspired my writing, dedicating it to those who have loved.; [a.] London, UK

CATON, ELIZABETH ANNE
[b.] 17 September 1941, Solihull; [ch.] Philip, Deborah, Richard; [ed.] Royal Grammar School Brockenhurst, Slough High School, Eastbourne Training College, Open University; [occ.] Tutor; [memb.] A.T.L.; [hon.] B.A., D.A.S.E., A.L.A.M.D.A., Dip Ed.; [oth. writ.] "A Year In The Garden From Darkness To Light," "Plan Accordingly."; [pers.] I have been writing poetry for purely therapeutic reasons to help me through a recent "bad patch" in my life. If my experiences, progress can be of help to anyone else in similar circumstances. I would be only too happy to share them. I find my greatest comfort in the natural world.; [a.] Blackburn, Lancashire, UK

CHADWICK, VINCENT
[pen.] Vin Chadwick; [b.] 6 October 1934, Salford; [p.] Thomas Chadwick, Esther Chadwick; [m.] Alison Chadwick, December 1983; [ed.] St. Gregory's Grammar, Mancester Univ. (De La Salle College); [occ.] Teacher; [memb.] R.S.P.B., N.T., R.A., Care; [oth. writ.] Many poems not published.; [pers.] I wish to reflect my spiritual anger for the death of man's soul and the uncaring modern society.; [a.] Gravesend, Kent, UK

CHAFFEY, JANET
[b.] 31 July 1930, Wheeler End, Bucks; [p.] Florence and Charles Simmons; [m.] George William Chaffey, 5 April 1952; [ch.] Christopher, Jacqueline, Peter and Caroline; [ed.] Lane and Primary Amersham College of Further Education;

[occ.] Retired; [memb.] Buckinghamshire Archaeological Society - Chess, Valley Arch. and His. Soc. - Association For environmental Arch.- Medieval Pottery Research Group - Council For Independent Archaeology; [oth. writ.] Articles for chess. Valley Arch and Hist. Journal.; [pers.] I write about the things I see and how they make me feel.; [a.] High Wycombe, Buckinghamshire, UK

CHALLIS, TIM
[b.] 22 March 1970, Maidstone; [ed.] Maidstone Grammar School for boys, The University of Kent at Canterbury, The University of Greenwich, the University of Brighton, the Open University.; [occ.] Occupational Therapist, London Borough of Redbridge Personal Social Services.; [memb.] Occupational Therapy for Elderly, People National Specialist Section; [oth. writ.] Work included with numerous anthologies of poetry and the British Journal of occupational therapy. Collection of Poetry due for publication late 1996; [pers.] My ambition is to set up a publishing company catering for small, specialized groups. My written work is influenced by the experiences of those with whom I work, and the trends from within wider society. My particular area of interest is the position of the elderly and the role they play in the community.; [a.] South Ockendon, Essex, UK

CHAPMAN, JOHN STUART
[pen.] Biro; [b.] 23 December 1946, London; [p.] George, Edith Chapman; [m.] Susan; [ch.] Steven, Mark, Lisa, Martin; [ed.] Spencer Park London, Arthur Mellons, College Peterborough, Isle of Ely Horticultural College, Eynsham Police College; [occ.] Retired Police Officer, Housing Association Administrator; [memb.] Co-Ordinator of the Skorpios Project (Breach Marine Protection), Mayhem Street Theatre, The Rusty Relics Scythe Dancers, The Fun Jug Band, The Fenland Eelbilly Band. I am the Simon May Fan Club; [hon.] Cert., for winning the 4th Battersea Cubs Egg and Spoon Race; [oth. writ.] Twice upon a time (a collection of short verse) yet to be published.; [pers.] When I die, on my headstone wright, "We will never forget you," but write it in chalk.; [a.] Wisbech, Cambs, UK

CHARLESWORTH, BOB
[pen.] David Charles; [b.] 16 June 1922, Crewe; [p.] Wilf Charlesworth, Gwyneth Charlesworth; [m.] Amy Charlesworth, 27 December 1944; [ch.] Ian Charlesworth; [ed.] Crewe County Secondary School, spare time education post 1946; [occ.] Retired; [memb.] Secy. Hull Jazz Record Society Institute of Trading Standards (Retired member); [hon.] Institute of Trading Standards Certificate Diploma in Municipal Administration; [oth. writ.] Several articles in Jazz Magazine, Jazz Newsletters.; [pers.] Amateur painter, write occasional poetry for amusement; [a.] North Cave, Brough, East Yorks, UK

CHARLESWORTH, RICHARD
[pen.] Charlie James; [b.] 15 March 1952, Cheltenham; [p.] Malcom, Gwendolyn Charlesworth; [m.] Sally Charlesworth, 21 September 1974; [ch.] Bethany Jane, Oliver James; [ed.] Arle Secondary Modern, Gloucester College of Art and Technology (Gloscat) O.U. Technology Undergraduate; [occ.] Project Engineer; [memb.] British Association for Shooting and Conservation (BASC) Cheltenham and District Clay Club (CDCC), University of Life; [oth. writ.] Several poems published in other anthologies; [pers.] In-

fluential poets include: W. H. Davies, Lord Tennyson, John Masefield, C. Patmore, C. Kingsley, some Shakespearian sonnet. "Treat the earth well, it was not given to us by our parents, it was lent to us by our children.; [a.] Tewkesbury, Gloucestershire, UK

CHARLTON, BRIAN JOHN
[b.] 14 February 1944, Hull; [p.] Ronald and Edna; [m.] Janice, 19 December 1970; [ch.] Gemma and Paul; [ed.] Consett Grammar; [occ.] Local Gout Officer and E/T Marker Researcher; [memb.] Amateur football clubs; [hon.] Various football honors and Insurance Sales Award, 7 ECE '0' levels, Civil Service Executive Examination; [oth. writ.] Various school and company magazines. Several unpublished childrens stories, previous poem "At The Crossroads" published in "Voices in the Wind".; [pers.] I rate myself as a beginner but fell that personal experience and empathy help a great deal in poetry writing particularly.; [a.] Reading, Berkshire, UK

CHARMAN, MARILYN
[b.] 9 September 1947, Ombersley; [p.] Mrs. A. Spragg and Mr. H. Spragg (Deceased); [m.] Anthony Charman, 5 October 1968; [ch.] Timothy David, Grant Anthony, Lisa Victoria; [ed.] Samuel Southall Secondary Modern School for Girls; [occ.] Various; [pers.] As stated I am just a wife and mother I have no special qualifications or degrees. Writing poetry helps me to relax and keeps my mind alert. My work and family take up most of my time. But I will think in the future try to get more poems published.; [a.] Nr Droitwich, Worcestershire, UK

CHARNOCK, MR. CHARLES
[pen.] Mr. Charles Charnock; [b.] 24 April 1907, Bolton, Lancs; [p.] Mr. Charles Charnock; [m.] Mary Elizabeth Barnes, 16 January 1932; [ed.] Elementary St. Edmund RC Bolton and evening classes, Military to General Staff Clerical Distinction in Hygiene 0 98 and 98 clerical; [occ.] Retired; [memb.] Royal British Legion; [oth. writ.] Soldier on the move ISBN O 952 4324 O 4 Publisher Sandra Hoad; [a.] Darwen, Lancashire, UK

CHATTOO, BEVERLY
[b.] 5 May 1953, Jamaica; [p.] Joseph Brown, Elesia Stanley; [ch.] Sonya Lorraine, Louise, Hannah; [ed.] Firs Hill Primary, Hinde House Comprehensive, Grandville College; [occ.] Unemployed, Mother; [oth. writ.] Poems, articles printed in church magazines.; [pers.] I have always loved writing. I have been inspired to write poems through events happening around the world and reading the bible of which I have received great insight.; [a.] Sheffield, Yorkshire, UK

CHATWIN, LEONARD
[b.] 16 September 1919, B'ham; [p.] Mr. and Mrs. H. I. Chatwin; [m.] Mrs. Annie Chatwin, May 1949; [ed.] Elementary; [occ.] Retired; [memb.] Ward End Ex. Servicemen Club, Ex. Service R.Af., "Y" Service, can't say more because I have signed the secrets act; [hon.] Only the one you bestow on me and just wartime medals; [oth. writ.] Several other poems unpublished.; [pers.] I like to hear words in their best order I strive to accomplish this.; [a.] B'ham, Warwickshire, UK

CHAUHAN, SILPA
[b.] 2 May 1978, Leicester

CHEETHAM, LISA
[b.] 14 April 1981, Bridgewater; [p.] Peter Cheetham, Linda Cheetham; [ed.] Taking GCSEs in summer of 1997; [pers.] My work reflects the lives of myself and others. I hope that my writings will help people understand the emotional feelings that many experience.; [a.] Potters Bar, Hertfordshire, UK

CHELL, ALAN
[pen.] Alan Chell; [b.] 18 October 1933, Hanley, Stoke-on-Trent; [p.] Harry Chell and Louisa Amelia Chell; [m.] 1st Patricia Davenport (Deceased), 2nd Diana Hemmings, 1st 31 March 1957 (W), 1985, 2nd (M) 29 May 1987; [ch.] 1st Paul, Adrian, Chell; [ed.] Cobridge C.E., Stoke-on-Trent, St. John's C.E. Burslem, Stoke-on-Trent; [occ.] Retired Medically 1980; [memb.] Radio Society of Great Britain; [hon.] City and Guilds (Amateur Radio) Call Sign 96 AYG; [oth. writ.] Poems published in medical magazine.; [pers.] Try to reflect the plight of the less fortunate in some of my writing. I owe a great deal to my GP doctor David French and all the staff at Kidsgrove Health Centre, Stoke-on-Trent for their encouragement.; [a.] New Chapel, Staffordshire, UK 4PU

CHENG, SHARON S. F.
[b.] 5 January 1983, Inverness; [p.] Yung Sang Cheng, Yuk Chun Cheng; [ed.] Muirtown Primary and currently in Charleston Academy S3; [occ.] A paper round; [memb.] Highland Budokan Judo Club; [pers.] I believe that the heart should be deeply explored, feelings should not be hidden. I admire the way that sometimes it only takes a word or a few that says it all.; [a.] Inverness, Scotland

CHILDS, DAVID BRINLEY
[b.] 23 October 1933, New Tredegar; [p.] Charles Childs and Edith Kate Childs; [m.] Ceri Orinda Childs, 18 July 1981; [ch.] Russell Owen and Charles Childs; [ed.] Cardiff University, Columbia Pacific University, Mus. Dip., M.A., Ph.D.; [occ.] Retired School Master; [memb.] Caerphilly Male Voice Choir, Member of the College of Preceptors M. Coll. P., Member of the "Associated Board of the Royal Schools of Music"; [hon.] Fellow Royal Society of Arts - F.R.S.A., Fellow of the London College of Music F.L.C.M., Fellow of the Curwen Memorial College F.T.S.C.; [oth. writ.] Christmas Carol book 1991, "They Rejoiced With Exceeding Great Joy", Christmas Carol book 1992, "Hallelujah The Lord is Here", Catchy Christian Songs 1992 "Sing! Children In The Name Of The Lord".; [pers.] To praise our Lord Jesus in music links us with the heavenly choirs above. This in my opinion is a great privilege. I have been greatly influenced by the Bible.; [a.] Penpedairheol, Mid-Glamorgan, UK

CHRISTOPHOROU, CAREN
[b.] 11 November 1959, Altrinc Ham.; [p.] Bill and Eileen Grindrod; [m.] George, 14 February 1995; [ed.] Brookway High School, m/c, Fielden Park College of F.E., m/c; [occ.] Education Co-ordinator; [hon.] Ams certificate in Medical Secretarial Studies, m/c T.E.C. Business Enterprise Programme Certificate; [oth. writ.] Poetry published in "Lift The Veil" (Writers Bureau Anthology, 1994) and "Island Moods and Reflections" (Poetry Institute of the British Isles, 1995); [pers.] This poem is dedicated to Sophia and Gabriel in the hope of immortality through these words.; [a.] Manchester, Lancashire, UK

CHRISTY, MICHAEL GERALD
[b.] 25 February 1973, Saint Asaph; [p.] Violet Christy, T. P. Christy; [m.] Marian Lloyd Christy, 17 November 1994; [ch.] Aidan Wyn Christy; [ed.] Ysgol Syr Hugh Owen; [oth. writ.] Poems published by Anchor and Triumph House books; [a.] Caernarfon, Gwynedd, UK

CHRYSS, JENNY
[b.] 19 October 1955, London; [p.] Basil and Mary Chryss; [m.] Barry Barnes, 17 May 1986; [ch.] 2 step children, 3 step grandchildren; [ed.] Haberdashers 'Ashes' Girls School, Huddersfield Polytechnic; [occ.] Journalist, BBC Radio Slive, Social Affairs Specialist; [hon.] 1988 Local Government Journalist of the Year (shared) run by Local Government Information Service.; [oth. writ.] Numerous Articles New and features in Local papers.; [a.] Thame, Oxfordshire, UK

CLAIDEN, A. K.
[pen.] Alfred K. (Daniel) Claiden; [b.] 2 July 1919, Richmond, Surrey; [p.] Alfred George Claiden, Rose Elinor Claiden; [m.] Liselott Claiden, 24 February 1945; [ch.] Nichola, Susannah; [ed.] St John's School Richmond, Richmond Central School, LLA Tamburrini: Monumental Masons; [occ.] Arts Lab Explorations of Empathy Stresses from Media Presentations of Civilians in War: Convalescence from Stress-Induced Physical Consequence; [memb.] British Psycho-Drama Association, Friends of Imperial War Museum; [oth. writ.] Poetry as a normal part of language is in constant use as a tool of concentration. Self-published 'The poets were not there' is held in the achieve of the 'Imperial War Museum', and the Normandy Memorial Caen.; [pers.] Heavy Emphasis on voice for the person beneath the organization.; [a.] Woodland, Devon, UK

CLANCY, MICHAN JEAN
[pen.] Channy; [b.] 24 October 1978, Guy's Hospital, London; [p.] Mr. Stephen Clancy, Mrs. Jackie Clancy; [ed.] I am at the moment studying for my English literature and language A - levels, 1 achieved 5 G.C.S.E's above C; [occ.] Student, Part-time cashier/sales assistant in Tesco's; [hon.] I achieved awards during my time at secondary school, I also completed and was awarded for a mountaineering and survival course during a stay at Wales; [oth. writ.] I have written many poems but I've never sent any off to be published before.; [pers.] Something like this achievement has never happened to me before. I am very honoured and proud that my poem is to be published, it is quite hard to believe, but it's great; [a.] London, UK

CLARING-BOULD, MRS. BARBARA HELEN
[b.] October 30, 1930, Hounslow, Middlesex; [p.] Both Deceased; [m.] Mr. Earnest Walter Claring-Bould, August 30, 1952; [ch.] Stephen and Stephanie; [ed.] Hillingdon High School Middlesex; [occ.] Matron Proprietor of Residential, Home for the Elderly (86 Maison-Dieu Lodge); [memb.] "Young Wives" and "The Women's Institute", during the 1950's when I was first married; [hon.] Several certificates in Music Associated Board of the Royal School of Music, also Red Cross Nursing Certificate, also Secretarial Diploma, "Guildhall School of Music and Drama", also A Rivera School of Floristry and Flower Arranging; [oth. writ.] Several "Readings" for friends in the church, about their life, etc., also poems read out by The Vicar, including one for my mother when she died, to explain a little about her life during the war yrs.,

also a few poems written at Lib., in my possession.; [pers.] As a child of five years old, I was chosen to stand up in the classroom and recite: "Big Steamers" by Rudyard Kipling, also "Someone" and many more poems which I have taught to my children and grandchildren, also several other poems, to help them at school.; [a.] Dover, Kent, UK

CLARK, BARRY
[pen.] Barry Clark; [b.] 6 February 1951, Wyke, Bradford; [p.] Minnie and Stanley; [m.] Maureen (Estranged), 10 October 1970; [ch.] Brian, Tracey, Tina; [ed.] Wyke Manor Comprehensive; [occ.] Fitter, Welder; [memb.] Mirfield Pool League, Westfield, Pool Team; [oth. writ.] Numerous poems which I have not yet submitted for any kind of publication. But hope to do so in the near future.; [pers.] I love to write as the mood takes me. The works of Robert Browning is my greatest influence.; [a.] Bradford, Yorkshire, UK

CLARK, LESLIE M.
[pen.] Les Clark Jr.; [b.] 12 September 1941, Farnham, Surrey; [p.] L. M. Clark Sr., Joyce Clark; [ed.] Gordon Boys School West End - Working Surrey Army Training School; [occ.] Unemployed Poet; [memb.] Isle of Wight Snooker Club; [oth. writ.] Seven poems in a limited edition of five hundred books called "Reflections" (1 produced the book myself.); [pers.] I try never to use a word that may send my readers to a dictionary! If they can find their own identity somewhere in my work, if they can say "Yes I've Feel Like That" then my poetry is worthwhile. I have been influenced by no-one, but encouraged by many.; [a.] East Cowes, Isle of Wight, UK

CLARKE, M. W.
[b.] 22 January 1922, Croydon; [occ.] Retired; [memb.] Pawsons Road Baptist Church, Hard of Hearing Christian Fellowship; [oth. writ.] Several poems published in Church News Letter; [a.] Croydon, Surrey, UK

CLENDENNING, PATRICK
[pen.] Rick Denning; [b.] 26 October 1926, Ballykinlar, Co. Down; [p.] Henry and Mary Josephine, both deceased; [m.] Bridget May Rafferty, 16 July 1959; [ed.] Ballykinlar Public Elementary School October 1932 - December 1940.; [occ.] Part time Commissionaire Slieve Donard Hotel Newcastle; [oth. writ.] Romantic/ Thriller. The Silver Crutch 114,000 words publisher has promised to read it. I have written several other books including Western, Thrillers/ Boys and Childrens require to be re-typed.; [pers.] Clendenning, Patrick pen Rick Denning, 26 October 1926, Primary School Education. Ex. rep. "Trebor Confectioner", Retired 1991. Intend to spend more time writing.; [a.] Newcastle, Down, UK

CLENNON, SHARON
[pen.] S-Teem; [b.] 11 July 1975, London, England; [occ.] Production Assistant for a Large Marketing Research Agency.; [oth. writ.] First poem published in school magazine (secondary) went on to win 'Voice Newspaper' Rap Poetry Competition '94. This poem was also published in Artrage Magazine and recorded for BBC World Service.; [pers.] Through my writing I hope to bring happiness, hope and humour into the lives of "Everyday People".; [a.] Middlesex, Ealing, UK

CLIFFORD, JAN P.
[b.] 21 June 1960, Bristol; [occ.] I am medically retired from my career due to ill-health.; [oth. writ.] I am currently writing a book about the trauma of having M.E. the illness from which I suffer. I adore writing poetry and have done so for many years, although this is my first entry for a competition or publication.; [pers.] I love to write poetry that touches people's hearts and feel great contentment when emotions are evoke. This inspires me to continue my love of writing.; [a.] Bristol, South Glos, UK

CLINTON, JEANETTE
[pen.] "The Sea"; [b.] 15 November 1955, London, England; [p.] John Stocker, Dorothy Stocker; [m.] Michael Clinton, 26 July 1986; [ch.] Sara Louise, Wendy Jane; [ed.] Walthamston High School for girls; [occ.] Housewife; [oth. writ.] Poem published in anthology. Have written first novel-still awaiting response from publisher.; [pers.] Words are a reflection of mood or thinking, poetry expressions of heart.; [a.] Preetz, Germany

CLOKE, MRS. PEARL
[pen.] Fern Brooks; [b.] 19 March 1942, Penberth; [p.] Ted and Eva Matthews; [m.] Arthur Wolsely Cloke, 25 June 1960; [ch.] Dawn, Mark, Heather, Shem, Lee; [ed.] Left school at 15 went to a Secondary Modern School.; [occ.] Work in the Laundry of Penzances Biggest Hotel "Queens"; [oth. writ.] A few poems printed in Women's Magazine and two short stories; [a.] Penzance, Cornwall, UK

CLYDE, JULIA MARGARET
[b.] 4 April 1937, Holsworthy, Devon; [p.] A. E. and S. M. Axtell; [m.] Robert McCallum Clyde, 9 July 1960; [ch.] Deborah, Hamish, Cassandra, Angus, Elizabeth (Adopted); [ed.] Stella Maris Convent Bideford, Devon. No Formal Education After 'O' Levels; [occ.] Editing newsletter for (mainly) British Ex. pats in Brittany; [oth. writ.] Novels, plays, poetry, short stories all unpublished.; [pers.] I like there to be a creative element in everything I do. Personal relationships on a meaningful level are of utmost importance to me.; [a.] Pontiuy, Brittany, France

COCHRAN, ELIZA
[pen.] Betty; [b.] 24 February 1921, Jarrow-on-Tyne; [p.] William and Elizabeth Beattie; [m.] Married twice, (Both Deceased Unfortunately); [ch.] Two and one stepson; [ed.] Church of England School; [occ.] Housewife; [a.] Dunfermline, Fife, Scotland

COCHRANE, SANDRA K.
[b.] 9 January 1944, Heanor, Derbyshire; [m.] Thomas A. Cochrane, 27 July 1968; [ed.] Swanwick Hall Grammar School, Swanwick, Derbys, Furzedown Teacher's Training College, London, SW17; [occ.] Retired teacher; [memb.] Brooke Hospital for Animals E.I.A. (Environmental Investigation Agency), World Society for the Protection of Animals, Born Free Foundation; [oth. writ.] I am a new writer, 'Footsteps' - 'Inspirations from Eastern England.'; [pers.] I write about aspects of creation to which I am drawn, about thoughts, often unspoken, and experiences both emotional and spiritual.; [a.] Peterborough, Cambridgeshire, UK

CODD, SYLVIA J.
[b.] 2 August 1935, Spalding; [p.] Mr. and Mrs. Stephen Featherstone; [m.] Arthur Henry (Sam) Codd, 23 August 1986; [ch.] I have 5, 3 boys, 2 girls, by first marriage; [ed.] Primary, Pinchbeck, Secondary School, Spalding; [occ.] Retired, was out service; [memb.] Forward Press Ltd., Poetry Company, Peterborough; [hon.] I had a certificate award for passing an exam on "Pride And Prejudice" in my teens; [oth. writ.] I have had a two poems published in two local papers An Day Care Magazine; [pers.] I write poems as I see life and every day happenings.; [a.] Bourne, Lincolnshire, UK

COFFEY, DORIS
[b.] 24 August 1944, Belfast; [p.] James S. Woods, Margaret Woods (Both Deceased); [m.] Hugh Coffey, 17 August 1968; [ed.] Rosetta Primary School Belfast, Shaftesbury House, Tutorial College Belfast; [occ.] Clerical Officer Radiology Directorate, Aros Hospital; [memb.] Kircubbin Accordion Band (Enter championship competition in Ulster Hall Belfast); [hon.] Pitman's Shorthand certificates (90, 110 and 120 wpm), Royal Society of Arts, Typewriting certificate Stage 3 (advanced); [oth. writ.] Small poem published once in Belfast Telegraph competition (1st prize winner); [pers.] Reading poetry gives me untold pleasure whilst writing it enables me to portray my innermost thoughts and feelings.; [a.] Newtownards Down, N. Ireland, UK

COLE, JOHN
[b.] 29 May 1921, Chelsea, London; [p.] Ernest E. Cole, Grace A. Cole; [m.] Grace M. Cole, 9 August 1941; [ch.] Martin John, Peter Bryan, Andrew Ernest; [ed.] Merton Park Council School, Beverley Central School; [occ.] Retired, Ex-Toolmaker: Aircraft/Automobiles; [memb.] Founder Member of the Swindon "Folksinger's Club" Wiltshire; [hon.] Self taught glass engraver (Non Mechanical), Harmonica Player (Blues and Jazz), featured on Granada TV, Records: England, Australia, USA; [oth. writ.] A published poem "My Valentine" to my dear wife Grace.; [pers.] My writings reflect my family feelings, concerning my spiritual values during our marriage vows, "for better for worse", as my wife was severely paralyzed 42 yrs ago, (18 months after our youngest son was born.) She was my only girlfriend, mother and wife for 55 years.; [a.] Swindon, Wiltshire, UK

COLE, SHIRLEY
[b.] 27 December 1973, South Wales; [p.] Brenda and David Cole; [ed.] I am currently reading for a degree in special Chemistry with drug design and toxicology. I will graduate in June 1997.; [memb.] I am looking to be a member with the Royal Society of Chemistry.; [hon.] Gained an award in a B/TEC Higher National diploma in Chemistry.; [oth. writ.] I have written numerous poems for my friends and family in the past but never gave a thought of publishing any as they were on a personal level and for those people only.; [pers.] My poem is about emotions and how cruel they can be. A lesson we should all learn is to say exactly how we feel and not worry about the consequences if only. We should be honest with others, but most importantly with ourselves.; [a.] Blackwood, Gwent, UK

COLEMAN, CHARLOTTE
[b.] 25 April 1970, Merton; [p.] David C. Coleman, M. Gillian Coleman; [ed.] Urdang Academy Middlesex University; [occ.] Dancer; [hon.] BA Honours in Dance and Spanish; [oth. writ.] I have written several poems but have not yet submitted any for publication; [pers.] I hope to be able to entertain and amise through poetry: Also to deal with issues/incidents which people can relate to universally; [a.] Wollwich, London, UK

COLEMAN, LEONARD T.
[pen.] Leonard T. Coleman; [b.] 10 July 1916, Frant Tunbridge, Wells; [p.] Thomas Coleman, Margaret Jane Coleman; [m.] Pamela - nee Roberts, 23 September 1972; [ch.] David (aged 51), by previous wife; [ed.] Skinners Company's School, Tunbridge Wells; [occ.] Retired L. Gov't Officer War Service - Raf.; [memb.] Bomber Command Assoc., 75 (N2) Squadron Assoc., Eng. Assoc., Member Welsh Academy; [hon.] Queens Silver Jubilee Medal 1977; [oth. writ.] Poems, Reviews - Local Press, Anchor Books - Forward Press, own collection 'A Procession Of Words' (Minerva Press 5.99 pounds).; [pers.] Like early romantic poems, V12 Wordsworth, Pupert Brook, Christina Georgina Russetti, etc.; [a.] Crawley Down, W. Sussex, UK

COLEMAN, LEON
[pen.] Leon Coleman; [b.] 10 July 1916, Frant, Sussex; [p.] Tom and Margaret Jane Coleman; [m.] Pamela Edna Coleman, 23 September 1972; [ch.] One - David; [ed.] Frant School then Skinner Company's School Tunbridge Wells; [occ.] Retired local Gov't Offr; [memb.] AA, Bomber Command Assoc, 75(NI) Squadron Assoc, Assoc M Welsh Academy; [hon.] Defence medal, Gew war, 1977 Queens Silver Jubilee medal, for L.G. service; [oth. writ.] "Night Guard", "Mitterand", numerous poems in anthologies Poetry Now, Int. Lib. Poets, Anchor Books, own book "A Procession of Words" publ by Minerva Publ 5.99 pounds.; [pers.] I first write poetry encouraged by my English master "Jock" Grierson at the Skinners School. Many years S/Pro Musician in dance bands - piano, trumpet, then saxophones, clarinet, few lyrics.; [a.] Crawley Down, W. Sussex, UK

COLERIDGE, JOHN
[pen.] Sam Taylor; [b.] 26 July 1926, Leigh-on-Sea, Essex; [p.] Alfred and Violet Coleridge; [m.] Myrna Coleridge, 22 September 1979; [ch.] Two sons, one dead, one stepson; [ed.] King's School - Bruton, Somerset, King's College, Cambridge; [occ.] Retired writing novels, biographies and poetry lecturing; [memb.] Various Wells Societies, University of Third Age, Graduate Members of Cambridge University, Golf, Royal West Norfolks The Pedagogues; [hon.] None apart from (Naval RNVR), Inevitable Wartime Ribbons; [oth. writ.] 1 1/2 novels. By end of this summer I hope 2 hardback volumes of History of Sheringham and R.W.N. Golf Club's Centenaries. Articles on Williamson, Henry Davidson, Stiffkey (church and marches). Edition of Emily Dickinson with U.S. Published; [pers.] Poetry has always been important to me since I began writing aged 15. Now I'm past to silence and space and its eternal become more important. (See Dickinson interest); [a.] Wells-n-t-Sea, Norfolk, UK

COLES, ANGELA
[pen.] Alicia Devereaux; [b.] 31 October, Liverpool; [ch.] Liegh and Victoria; [ed.] Comp; [occ.] Artist/Writer; [hon.] O and A Level Art; [oth. writ.] Short stories 100 poems.; [pers.] To have my own 100 poems in my own book. And dedicate Shady Days to Aussie X.; [a.] Liverpool, Merseyside, UK

COLES, MRS. B. M.
[pen.] Betty M. Coles; [b.] 29 June 1927, Farnborough, Hants; [p.] George Edwards, Ethel M. Edwards; [m.] Peter Coles, 16 August 1947; [ch.] Susan Joy, Janet Clare; [ed.] Guildford County School For Girls; [occ.] Retired; [memb.] Peterborough Pensioners Assn., "Prime-Timers" Singing Group, St. Barnabas Community Church; [oth. writ.] Poems for charity anthologies; [pers.] I seek, through my own experience to communicate to others.; [a.] Peterborough, Cambridgeshire, UK

COLLIER, DEBBIE
[b.] 1 May 1973, London; [p.] Audrey Collier; [ed.] Bexley Grammar School; [occ.] IT Technical Support Advisor; [pers.] Grandpa said "Many days it may rain, but eventually the sun has to shine" - and behold, it did! I dedicate this, my first published poem to my Mum for all her love and support and to Granddad for his wisdom and kindness.; [a.] New Eltham, London, UK

COLLINS, FRANK
[pen.] Frank Collins; [b.] 5 November 1927, Welling, Kent; [p.] Albert Collins, Florence Collins; [m.] Eileen Collins, 25 March 1950; [ch.] Maureen Catherine, David Eric, Brenda May; [ed.] St. Paulinus (Crayford), Crayford Secondary Modern, Army Apprentices College (Beachley); [occ.] Retired 1994 (was Senior Technical Clerk with Babcock Energy Ltd.); [memb.] Beachley Old Boys Association; [oth. writ.] Several poems published in army regimental magazines as far back as 1942.; [pers.] In all of my poetical efforts, I try to write with sincerity, and honesty.; [a.] Erith, Kent, UK

COLLINS, KEVIN P.
[b.] 4 November 1945, High-a-Walton, Nr. Preston, Lancs; [p.] Peter and Catherine; [m.] Eileen, 12 November 1995; [ed.] St. Mary's Secondary Modern School, Bamber Bridge, Nr Preston, Lancs; [occ.] Security Officer; [oth. writ.] Poems published by "Anchor Books", "Triumph House Books", both at Peterborough, also poems published by "The International Society of Poets", and "The International Library of Poetry"; [pers.] My main hobby is writing - my ambition is to have a book published - I also write songs - country/ western and ballads.; [a.] Melbourne, Nr Royston, Hertfordshire, UK

COMMON, LEANNE
[b.] 7 January 1982, Brighton; [p.] Sandra Common, David Common; [ed.] Currently Studying for GCSE's at Tideway Secondary School; [occ.] Student; [memb.] Invited to become a member of Mensa; [pers.] Reports of Racism and prejudice in the media influenced me to write my poem. I hope that someday people will not be discriminated against and the world can live in peace; [a.] Newhaven, East Sussex, UK

CONLEY, MRS. VALERIE
[pen.] Valerie Conley; [b.] 28 October 1947, Leeds; [p.] Mr. Dennis and Mrs. Lilian Greenwood; [m.] Mr. B. Conley, 21 December 1985; [ch.] One son - Shaun Reynolds; [ed.] Secondary Education Burton Stone York; [occ.] Sheltered Housing Warden; [memb.] Hollybush Christian Fellowship, Thirsk N. Yorks; [hon.] First Aid Basic Food Hygiene G.E.M.S. Course (Further Education) 0 Level English; [oth. writ.] Several poems printed in community magazine which I used to write for clients.; [pers.] If I can but give others a glimpse of hope, a touch from the masters

hand then all of my unshed tears, written in poetry will have accomplished that whic they were meant to do.; [a.] Keighley, West Yorks, UK

CONNAIRE, MARY
[m.] Vincent, 1 February 1969; [ch.] One teenager son - Kevin; [ed.] Our Lady's Bower, National and Secondary Schools, Athlone; [pers.] My mother-in-law and father-in-law died within a short time of each other, then my own mother took ill while on holiday in a seaside resort. After these events I wrote this. My first poem.; [a.] Athlone, Westmeath-Eire, UK

CONNOLLY, ROBERT DANIEL
[pen.] Robert D. Connolly; [b.] 24 July 1969, England; [p.] Charles Connolly, Eileen Daly; [m.] Partner: Phillippa Elie; [ch.] Zhane Connolly; [ed.] St. Thomas More Secondary School 1980-1985. No qualifications. None taken.; [occ.] Nat West Bank. Bank Clerk; [oth. writ.] I have nothing published. But nearly 200 short and long poems. With various these, and a considerable number of quotations, and other writings.; [pers.] I believe in darkness and light entwined inside the magical mirrored dream.; [a.] London, UK

CONNOR, ROBERT JOSEPH
[b.] July 2, 1962, Bellshill; [p.] Francis Connor and Margaret Connor; [m.] Angela Connor, July 7, 1995; [ed.] Cardinal Newman; [occ.] Corporal, British Army.; [memb.] Royal Yachting Association. Mohnese Sailing Club. Royal Logistic Corp association.; [hon.] UN Medal and Clasp. General service medal (N.I.) Foreign, Liberation of Kuwait medal, Saudi Defense Medal, Gulf Medal; [oth. writ.] Poem put on display imperial museum, gulf war. Published, edited, own magazine for previous regiment; [pers.] Sadly, my best work is written whilst serving in conflict war zones around the world. The inspiration despair and the glimmers of hope that sustain.; [a.] Crumlin, Antrim

COOGAN, MISS M.
[pen.] Margaret Ann Coogan; [b.] 1 October 1951, Newcastle; [p.] Pauline Stafford, John Coogan (Deceased); [m.] Partner: Terence Horspole; [ch.] Foster/Kenneth Smith, Claire Turnbull; [ed.] Welbeck Road Secondary Modern; [occ.] Self Employed Foster Parent; [hon.] GCSE Maths open University Certificate/Caring for children; [pers.] Fostering children can be heartbreaking at times, but the rewards far outweigh the bad times.; [a.] Newcastle, Tyne and Wear, UK

COOKE, JUNE E. R.
[b.] 14 June 1921, Egypt; [p.] Medical Missionaries In Egypt; [m.] Deceased, 2 June 1948; [ch.] Five, twelve grandchildren; [ed.] Laurel Bank School Glasgow, Scotland; [occ.] Water Colour Artist, Amateur and Writer, Amateur; [memb.] 1. Oban Art Society 2. Appin Art Group 3. Glasgow Society of Lady Artists 4. Paintings Shown In The Fitzroy Gallery; [oth. writ.] 1. 'The Scots Magazine', 2. Poetry Anthology, 'Simple pleasures' 3. 'Scottish Poets 1995' 4. Local Magazine; [pers.] Written poetry since age 5 years. Started painting (Water Colours) After gap of 43 years. I wish to show the beauty of Scotland in Art and writing.; [a.] Port Appin, Argyll, Scotland

COOKE, PHILIP
[b.] 5 November 1968, Doncaster; [p.] Philip and Shirley Cooke; [ed.] Danum School, Doncaster, University of Bradford; [occ.] Revenue Assistant, Inland, Revenue; [hon.] Modern Languages

(French and Spanish); [oth. writ.] Poetry, short stories and essays, none published to date.; [a.] Bradford, West Yorkshire, UK

COONEY, JOHN JOSEPH FLYNN
[pen.] Wee John; [b.] 10 October 1926, Bothwell, Lanarkshire; [p.] Alice Cleary formerly Mrs. Cooney and Bernard Flynn; [ed.] Orphanage (Sisters of Mercy) sent to working boys home in Edinburgh, aged 14 years.; [occ.] Retired; [oth. writ.] Many poems (none published) this is my first attempt. Any subject, topical or otherwise.; [pers.] Personally, I would feel like a Gaudy Child in the realms of the artistic world. But I hope I can show the disadvantaged - like myself, - that we all have something to contribute; [a.] Glasgow, Lanarkshire, UK

COOPER, EVELYN MARY
[pen.] Eve Cooper; [b.] 13 June 1930, Marylebone, London; [p.] Susan Caroline, Albert Edward Denham; [m.] Edward James Cooper, 10 December 1949; [ch.] Four boys and two girls; [ed.] Secondary Modern, Whinchcombe Road Carshalton, Surrey; [occ.] Retired; [memb.] V.3.A. Croydon; [oth. writ.] Twenty poems none ever sent for publication; [pers.] I write mainly about lives of people I know; [a.] Purley, Surrey, UK

COOPER, PETER S. A.
[b.] 16 March 1915; [p.] H. Charles Cooper (of Manchester) and Louise Florence Cooper (nee Smith) (of Plymouth); [m.] Angela Cooper (Nee Stranzi of Austria, Deceased); [ed.] St. Christopher's School, Letchworth; [occ.] Free Lance Translator, Chief Translator at General Electric Co. (1948-1963); [memb.] English-Speaking Union, Institute of Linguists, Publicity Club of London, Anglo-Austrian Society, Trollope Society, Georgian Group, Irish Georgian Society; [oth. writ.] "Irmgard und Ian" (Munich, 1961) German translation of "Lake Isle of Innisfree" (W.B. Yeats) in "The Linguist" (1990). Since 1994: 8 poems published in anthologies by Poetry Now (and Anchor Books) Peterborough and 1 by Beyond the Cloister Publications, of Brighton.; [pers.] Flo, the subject of all my poems, hails from the emerald isle, lives on the Sussex coast and has most wonderfully transformed my life.

COOPER, VINCENT
[pen.] Vince Cooper; [b.] 16 January 1963, England; [p.] Ken Cooper, Ann Cooper; [ed.] Rongotai College (N.Z.), St. Helier Boys School (Jsy.), Hautlieu College (Jsy.); [occ.] Trust and Company Administration; [memb.] Camra, RBL, Modern and Military Arms Association; [hon.] None to date - however, I am in the process of enrolling on an 'Open University' course that will result in my obtaining a 'BA' relevant to my Occupation; [oth. writ.] None published.; [pers.] I have read and experienced a great deal and compose my writings from a combination of my knowledge and experience.; [a.] Saint Lawrence, Jersey, CI, UK

COPP, FRANK
[pen.] Armie; [b.] 11 November 1918, Appledore; [p.] Frank Henry Copp, Lillian Blackmore; [m.] Erika Copp, 23 November 1948; [ch.] Lillian, Susan; [ed.] Formal; [occ.] Retired; [a.] Barnstaple, North Devon, UK

CORBETT, HELEN PAULINE
[b.] 10 September 1980, Colchester; [p.] Capt. Peter Corbett and Heather Mary Corbett; [ed.] Hockerill Boarding School, Thomas Lord Audaley School; [occ.] Student; [memb.] Modern and Ball-

room and latin dance groups; [oth. writ.] Poems published in local magazines; [pers.] I try to write simple poetry which should chill the mind, but at the same time touch the heart.; [a.] Colchester, Essex, UK

CORBETT, PETER
[b.] April 13, 1952, Rossett, North Wales; [p.] Dr. and Mrs. J. H. Corbett; [ed.] Liverpool College, Mossley Hill, Lpl 1970/71 Liverpool College of Art of Design (Foundation), 1971-74 Manchester College of Art and Design (BA Hons), 1995-Studying for Ph.D Liverpool University; [occ.] Artist, poet, student; [memb.] Maison Internationale Des Intellectuels (Academy M.I.D.I.) Paris, Hon. Professor of the Academie dess Sciences Universelles Paris, Life Member of Design and Artists Copyright Society (D.A.C.S.); [hon.] Purchase Prize - Merseyside Contemporary Artists Albert Dock Liverpool, Certificate of Merit for Distinguished Service to the Community (IBC Cambridge Sept. 1988); [oth. writ.] Articles for 'New Humanity Journal' London, "Art of the Post Modern", "The Turning Point", "1993 Poets" - in poetry now, "Undercurrents" - poetry anthology, strange publications Liverpool 1990.; [pers.] In my painting and poetry I have endeavored to express and reflect a higher dimension of reality which I experience in meditation, and from the springboard of external events which I feel are connected to it in some way.; [a.] Liverpool, Lancs

CORNFORTH, SYLVIA
[b.] 20 September 1940, Roundhay, Leeds; [p.] Ada Ruby and Joseph Hall; [m.] Brian Robert; [ed.] Richard Hind High School, Stockton-on-Tees; [occ.] Housewife, Calf Rearer; [oth. writ.] Nothing published, but poems and short story of a mastectomy operation am writing a book on the funny side of farming.; [pers.] I like to walk in the countryside and take delight in the flora and fauna. Much prefer the funny side of life.; [a.] York, North Yorkshire, UK

COTTERILL, ROSEMARY CLEATUS
[b.] 19 September 1927, Appleshaw; [p.] Charles and Winifred Barlow; [m.] Robert Percy Cotterill, 24 October 1992; [ch.] Helen; [ed.] Secondary Modern School for girls Andover Hampshire; [occ.] Retired; [memb.] Outdoor and Indoor Bowls Clubs over sixties Club Treasurer; [hon.] School honors; [oth. writ.] Children's book not published used for reading in Clarendon School. Also other poems as a hobby.; [pers.] I write to express my love of nature, for the simple pleasures of life, incorporating all I see and feel.; [a.] Tidworth, Hampshire, UK

COUNSELL, OLWEN HOWELL
[b.] 11 November 1925, Todmorden, Yorks; [p.] Albert Bush Margaret Bush; [m.] Kenneth Counsell, 19 November 1941; [ch.] Andrew, Beryl, Olive, Gillian; [ed.] 'Holy Saviours' Catholic School Nelson Lancs; [occ.] Retired; [oth. writ.] Several poems published in 'Triumph House' Magazine Peterborough also 'A passage of time' anthology.; [pers.] Persue what is good, reject what is bad, always have music in your heart.; [a.] Cleveland, Lancashire, UK

COUSINS, MRS. SALLY-ANNE
[b.] 21 February 1967, Middlesbrough; [p.] Mr. and Mrs. R. Paxton; [m.] Mr. Mark Cousins, 26 August 1989; [ch.] Samuel - 5 years, Ben - 2 years; [ed.] Nunthorpe Comprehensive School; [occ.] Housewife/Childminder; [pers.] My poetry speaks

from within, and opens windows into places people dare not lock.; [a.] Richmond, North Yorkshire, UK

COWLEY, MISS EVELYN MAUD
[pen.] Poet Cowley; [b.] 24 November 1926, W. Midlands; [p.] Maud and Frank (Deceased); [ed.] Secondary Modern School; [occ.] O.A.P. (Retired); [hon.] Cup and Medals for Dancing (Ballroom); [pers.] Feeling at a low ebb, I composed this poem of how I felt after losing my mum of 95 years, whom I cared for. I am still caring for my handicapped sister of 67 years. Afterwards it made it a little easier to cope.; [a.] Oldbury, West Midlands, UK

COX, MISS FREDA
[b.] 6 December 1925, Birmingham; [m.] Siliculter McJohn Moore; [ed.] Ordinary; [occ.] Old age pensioned 40 years; [hon.] Have won small awards; [oth. writ.] In book several times; [pers.] I have wrote poems since the age of 14 I know Royalty people on the TV but I would rather this was not printed.; [a.] Halford, Nr Shipsto, Wancks, UK

CRADDOCK, STEPHEN
[b.] 26 April 1976, Northampton; [p.] John and Denise Craddock (Nee Brown); [ed.] Weston Favell Upper School Northampton College; [occ.] Part Time Shop Assistant but I am a qualified baker; [oth. writ.] Many poems but nothing published before. A short story was published in a school competition - I won third prize.; [pers.] I have been writing poetry for 10 years or more, it is a natural outlet for my emotions. I find peace a comfort in my writing which I hope to share with others.; [a.] Northampton, Northants, UK

CRAIG, AGNES D.
[b.] 28 September 1936, Coatbridge; [p.] John Reid, Agnes Reid; [m.] Samuel B. Craig (Deceased), 14 December 1957; [ch.] Samuel J. R. Craig; [ed.] Coatbridge High School, Langside College; [occ.] Social Worker; [memb.] Institute of Management, Arthritis Care (Welfare Officer), Friend of Scottish Opera, The Folio Society, Ltd.; [oth. writ.] Several poems and items in church magazine.; [pers.] I love to read poetry and write only for pleasure and occasionally for special events in birthdays, weddings etc., I have never had anything published before I have never entered before.; [a.] Carluke, South Larnarkshire, UK

CRANE, NINA
[b.] 25 September 1975, Sidcup, Kent; [p.] Margaret and Dennis Crane; [ed.] The best Education is life and living it; [occ.] Administrative Assistant for Met. Police; [memb.] About 20 Animal and Conservation Groups plus the Myth and Magic Society; [oth. writ.] I am writing a book, have been since, my early teens and I hope to get it published one day. It's a satirical look at life.; [pers.] I write poetry because it's the best way to get things out of your system. This one I wrote on a hot night when I couldn't sleep. Edgar Allen Poe is my poetry hero.; [a.] East Ham, London, UK

CRAWFORD, ALEXANDER
[b.] 30 May 1943, Carlisle; [p.] Scottish; [m.] Brenda Ann Crawford, 5 July 1980; [ed.] Carlisle Grammar School, Cumbria College of Art and Design. Rat Medical Colleges of Nursing; [occ.] Writer; [memb.] Rafmra Royal Air force Mountain team Association. British Gordon Setter Club;

[hon.] Meritorious Service Award for resulting injured climbers in Snowdonia whilst in service with Raf Search and Rescue Helicopters (22 Sqn. Raf Valley); [oth. writ.] Autobiography 'Audible Glue' Novels: 'Mush Mumkin' - 'Hill Troop' - and currently 'Sand in my Shreddies' regular writings for the British Gordon Setter Club... 'For the good of the breed... and all it stands for....'; [pers.] Proud of my 'Border Heritage' I strive to save as much as I can for my God-children so they may enjoy it as I have.; [a.] Carlisle, Cumbria, UK

CRAWFORD, MR. EDWARD
[b.] 23 March 1941, Glasgow; [p.] Lillian Hill, Edward Crawford; [m.] Helen McCance, 28 April 1965; [ch.] Edward, Lorraine, Brian, Ian, Coles; [ed.] Passion Park Grammar, Erlean College; [occ.] Decoration; [memb.] International Steel Stand Association: I.S.S.A.; [hon.] Sociology Psychology (Hon) Some of my poetry has been on imagination at seal island, and Scotland; [oth. writ.] Last Trass to Sainty; [pers.] All talent inspires me. Although I have a penchant for Voltaine. Plato: Writings; [a.] Bronx, London, UK

CRAWFORD, MR. NORMAN
[b.] 27 July 1920, Stewton, Near Louth, Lincs; [p.] Mr. and Mrs. Crawford; [m.] Doreen Mary Crawford, 25 November 1978; [ed.] Primary and Secondary Basic Education; [occ.] Retired 1983 Ex Motor Mechanic; [memb.] Methodist Church, Ex Salvation Army and Pentecostel (Gathering); [hon.] 2nd World War, 8th Army Medal, El Alemain 1942 to Tunis with 12 AA Brigade Royal Signals, medal now lost; [pers.] Happily married for 17 years at a ceremony in the salvation army in uniform. (A Louth Corp I was previously married to Annie who passed on after suffering a severe stroke for a few years Doreen and I, still follow are believe in God; [a.] Marblethorpe, Lincolnshire, UK

CRAWLEY, MICHAEL
[pen.] Mickey; [b.] 1 September 1936, Belfast; [p.] Thomas, Helen; [m.] Betty, 31 March 1962; [ch.] Pauline, Philip, Jason; [ed.] Christian Brothers School Abbey Newry Co Down Northern Ireland; [occ.] Engineer, Self Employed; [hon.] Army Boxing Champion Army TA, Cross Country Champion, Athletics 1/2 Mile and one Mile Champion 1960 Boxing Champion 1964, Now ABA Coach England International University, Team Manager and Coach train many champions at school-boy and senior Level; [oth. writ.] Sports reports for Local newspaper on boxing and radio shorts stories; [pers.] To write something beautiful, for the pleasure of other people to enjoy reading and for peace, in this trouble world; [a.] Kidsgrove, Staffordshire, UK

CRAY, ALISON
[b.] 3 October 1967, Lancing, West Sussex; [p.] Albert Cray, Joan Cray; [ed.] Salford University, Electrical Graduate; [occ.] Tendering Engineer, South Wales Transformers; [memb.] Petty Officer in the Sea Cadet Corps, Rhondda; [hon.] Electrical and Electronic Honours Degree; [oth. writ.] My other poems are specific to events or people and are therefore only relevant to a few.; [pers.] Brian, Jan and Michelle, my inspiration comes from relatives and friends, their guidance, enthusiasm, hopes and dreams.; [a.] Abercynon, Mid-Glamorgan, UK

CREED, ANGIE
[b.] 22 April 1953, Eastbourne; [p.] Mervyn and Doreen Simmons; [m.] John Creed, November 1980; [ch.] Joanna Clare; [ed.] Eastbourne High School, Eastbourne College of Arts and Technology, Sussex University; [occ.] Student/Housewife/Home Help; [oth. writ.] Several poems published in anthologies and local paper a play on T.V. - aged 16; [pers.] I write because I can, and get so much pleasure from it. Nothing more complicated than that!; [a.] Eastbourne, E. Sussex, UK

CREEDON, DAVID JOSEPH VALENTINE
[b.] 14 February 1926, Waterloo, Nr. Liverpool; [p.] Septimus and Elizabeth Creedon; [m.] Alice Nora Fitzpatrick (Nee), 1 October 1966; [ch.] Sean Anthony; [ed.] St. Mary's College Crosby, Merseyside, Lanc's; [occ.] Male Nurse SRN - SRMN - SRMH; [pers.] Son Sean writing of his deceased Dad "As a lover of nature David may have witnessed the passing of the seasons with a touch of sadness-however a ray of hope would have always shone through".; [a.] Alvaston, Derby, Derbyshire, UK

CRESSALL, PETER
[b.] 28 December 1930, British Guiana; [p.] Frank and Olga Cressall; [m.] Daisy Cressall, 15 March 1958; [ch.] Francis, Victoria, Diana and Stephen; [ed.] St. Andrews School, Pangbourne Queen's College, B. Guiana, Lodge School, Barbados Cranleigh School, Surrey Aston University, Birmingham; [occ.] Farmer; [memb.] Canning Club Historic Houses Association National Trust, Royal Academy British Museum Hurlingham Club, Buenos Aires; [hon.] B.Sc.; [oth. writ.] Four volumes of poetry and an anthology of verse, all privately published; [pers.] I believe, as Robert Frost said, that writing free verse is like playing tennis with the next down. I am afraid that it has also become fashionable to dispense with the ball; [a.] Aston Munslow, Shropshire, UK

CRIGHTON, LORRAINE
[b.] 15 January 1958, Dundee; [p.] Tom and Alexina Donegan; [m.] Stuart Crighton, 10 March 1979; [ch.] Mark Paul and Brian Neale; [ed.] Harris Academy, Dundee University; [occ.] Senior Analyst Programmer, Scottish Hydro-Electric Plc; [memb.] Unison Branch Executive; [pers.] Someone once said "Each moment is the right one to be kind" I would change the each to every and hope mankind could learn to live that way, for then the world would be a better place.; [a.] Aberdeen, Scotland

CRISP, KEITH
[b.] 30 September 1950, Petworth, Sussex; [p.] Mr. Tom Crisp, Mrs. Ellen Gibbs; [m.] Brenda Crisp, 11 April 1970; [ch.] Mark and Darren Crisp; [ed.] Lancastrian School for Boys, Chichester, Sussex, HMS Ganges, Shotley Gate, Nr Ipswich, Suffolk; [occ.] Supply Technician II, British Aerospace; [memb.] British Legion, R.A.O.B.; [hon.] Royal Navy Long Service and Good Conduct Medal, Herbert Lott Award for Achievement (HM Submarines); [oth. writ.] Own collection of poetry, written over the past 6 years, this being the first poem entered in any competition or publication.; [pers.] I enjoy writing poems of everyday life and things that are taken for granted all around us. Living and material things.; [a.] Chichester, Sussex, UK

CROFT, ALEXIS JOHN
[b.] 25 February 1966, Winchester; [ed.] Bishop Wordsworth's Grammar, Salisbury, Florida Insti-

tute of Technology, Florida; [occ.] Managing Director of a Production Company; [memb.] R.N.L.I. Governor; [oth. writ.] Huge Amounts of Brilliantly, un-published poems and songs; [pers.] Spinning like a spider's web drifting as the ocean ebbs its way through tangled times, that's me.; [a.] Bream, Gloucestershire

CROFT, MRS. DAWN
[b.] 14 October 1962, Walsall, West Mids; [p.] Ken Gough, Olive Gough; [m.] Mark Croft, 1 March 1983; [ch.] Nick Croft, Martin Croft, Dale Croft; [ed.] Queen Mary's High School Walsall; [occ.] Special Needs Assistant, New Milton Junior School; [pers.] I enjoy writing poems about things that happen in everyday life. having three children of my own and working with children I have an insight as to their feelings.; [a.] New Milton, Hants, UK

CROFT, NICOLA
[pen.] N. M. C.; [b.] 26 March 1995, North Tees; [p.] Alan Croft, Valerie Croft; [ed.] Primary School Sats/tests; [occ.] Student; [hon.] That people have recognize my talent and that it has been liked.; [oth. writ.] Poetry. The Sea Is At Treasure, Getting Older and a number of other poems. Big Move When The Raven Lost His Beak, The Victory and more!; [pers.] I get a lot of satisfaction from writing my poems and stories. I also get satisfaction from people reading my work and enjoying it.; [a.] Billingham, UK

CROPLEY, MS. P. D.
[b.] 30 September 1935, Bognor Regis; [p.] William Cropley, Doris Cropley; [m.] Divorce; [ch.] Terry, Angela, Jayne; [ed.] Secondary School, Adult Education; [occ.] Writer painter; [oth. writ.] Book of poetry (unpublished) Autobiography (un-published); [pers.] I write about life as I see it, and through my own experiences of life and love etc.; [a.] Twickenham, Middlesex, UK

CROPLEY, PEARL D.
[b.] 30 September 1935, Bognor Regis; [p.] William and Doris Cropley; [m.] Daniel Benjamin, December 1954; [ch.] Terry, Angela, Jayne; [ed.] Secondary School, Adult Education; [occ.] Housewife; [hon.] Art; [oth. writ.] Book of poems (unpublished); [pers.] I write from my own experiences of life and the world I see around me.; [a.] Whitton, Twickenham, Middlesex, UK

CRUMP, MRS. SARA
[pen.] Sara Crump; [b.] 2 February 1967, Oxford; [p.] Charles Tucker, Pat Tucker; [m.] John Crump, 1 November 1988; [ch.] John (10), Helen (8,) Laura (6); [ed.] Henry Box School Witney; [occ.] Housewife and Mother; [memb.] The Tiger Trust British Country Music Association; [pers.] I love writing and only write from the life experiences.; [a.] Eynsham, Oxfordshire, UK

CRUTCHLOW, KAREN-SUE
[b.] 19 November 1963, Dundee, South Africa; [p.] William and Pat Will; [m.] Jeffrey Crutchlow, 2 June 1984; [ch.] Rachael, Annabel; [ed.] Medina High School, Isle of Wight College Arts and Technology; [occ.] Special Needs Assistant Primary School; [memb.] West Wilts Parachute Club, Bembridge Windsurfing Club; [pers.] I am influenced in my observations of all I see and how I feel within.; [a.] Bembridge, Isle of Wight, UK

CUNDALL, MRS. DOROTHY ANN
[pen.] Emma Whitehead; [b.] 4 October 1940; [p.] Florence and Herbert Turner; [m.] John Cundall,

24 July 1971; [ed.] Easingwold Grammar/Modern School Sheffield Polytechnic College; [occ.] Retired; [memb.] Nation Union of Teachers (Retired section), Easingwold Catholic Women's League; [hon.] Teacher of special need's child ren, studied a part time course entitled "Children with learning difficulties in the ordinary school" Picus other related part time courses; [oth. writ.] None published before.; [pers.] I love the beauty of the country side, and coat, birds and animals, and therefore try to express my feelings through poetry, and attempted stories, I also like to write about life, emotions and people (Characters).; [a.] Easingwold, York, N. Yorkshire, UK

CUNNINGHAM, MARGARET
[pen.] Kiltoon, Carrownderry; [b.] 19 January 1936, Athlone, Ireland; [p.] Patrick Cunningham and Winifred Mannion; [m.] 17 August 1960; [ed.] B.A. Degree Hons., H. Dip. Honours, M.A. Honours, Glanduff N.S. Mercy Convent Roscommon University College Galway Milltown Institute Dublin; [occ.] Retired Teacher early retirement due to asthma.; [memb.] I am a Sister of Mercy. A member of The Remedial Teachers Associations of Ireland. A member of the Provincial Archivist Team of Mercy Sisters Western Province Ireland; [hon.] Intermediate certificate: 5th place in Ireland, University Scholarships each year in University College Galway, M.A. (Hons) Milltown Institute of Higher Education; [oth. writ.] Catherine McAuley: Now Insights into her Spirituality. Several other unpublished poems.; [pers.] Appreciate life. I have found happiness in making every effort to ensure its happiness of those I meet and work with, my religious sisters and my families.; [a.] Athlone, West Moath, Ireland

CUNNINGHAM, THOMAS
[b.] 13 December 1919, Strathaven; [p.] Thomas Cunningham and Mary J. Cunningham; [m.] Ida (Deceased), 23 June 1945; [ch.] June; [ed.] Strathaven Academy, Hamilton Academy; [occ.] Retired Local Govt. Officer; [memb.] Parachute Regt. Association, Wakefield, Parachute Kegt. Assoc., The Royal British Legion; [hon.] Military medals and campaign stars for service in H.M. Forces in U.K., North Africa, Italy, France, Greece and South East Asia with the Parachute Regiment; [oth. writ.] Poems published in "Pegasus Journal", Magazine of Airborne Forces. Articles published in Saga's "Letters" magazine; [Pers.] I dedicate the poem "reflections" to colleagues who lost their lives serving with the 6th (Royal Welch) Parachute Battalion in the second World War.; [a.] Hemsworth, West Yorkshire, UK

CURRAN, ANDREA SHANELLE
[b.] 5 January 1982, Baguio City, Philippines; [p.] Mrs. Judith and Mr. James Curran; [ed.] Brent International School (Grade 9); [occ.] Student; [pers.] I write from my heart and I try to bring my feelings out onto the paper.

CUSSENS, MR. ADRIAN
[b.] 30 April 1968, Erith, Kent; [p.] Mrs. A. M. M. Cussens and Mr. R. S. E. Cussens; [ed.] Comprehensive and College; [occ.] Chef Royal Navy; [oth. writ.] To date, had a different poem printed in another anthology. Plus one printed in a local paper. And another read out on T.V.; [pers.] Poetry a hobby I do for fun either reading or writing it. So others may share the enjoyment and experience. I enjoy so much myself; [a.] Ashford, Kent, UK

CUTTELL, STEPHEN CHARLES
[pen.] Stephen C. Cuttell; [b.] 8 February 1971, Ilford, Essex; [p.] Ronald Cuttell and Janet Duncan; [ed.] Priory Meadow Boarding School, for children 11-16 Y.O.A. with learning difficulties; [occ.] Former Painter and Decorator - Presently Receiving Invalidity Ben.; [memb.] The Loxford Social and Snooker Club. Play Pool for two pubs; [hon.] None as yet because I have only just taken my writing seriously; [oth. writ.] Have written approximately 250 poems on various subjects and am at present near completion of my first novel. This is my first attempt for publication.; [pers.] I always write from the heart, and believe that if your heart is truly in what you create, then you can accomplish most things in life through your work. Believe in yourself as well as others, there is a market out there for everybody.; [a.] Plaistow, London, UK

CUZEN, MISS ELIZABETH
[b.] 3 June 1985, Stanford-le-Hope; [p.] Alan Cuzen, Susan Cuzen; [memb.] I belong to a Children's Video Production Club; [oth. writ.] I have been published in "Hear My Voice" 1994 a poetry anthology by Essex School Children.; [pers.] I gain pleasure and fulfilment by putting my thoughts and dreams into verse.; [a.] Stanford-le-Hope, Essex, UK

D'GAMA, PAUL
[b.] 31 August 55, Birmingham; [p.] Tony and Theresa D'Gama; [m.] Carmel D'Gama, 2 August 1986; [ed.] St. John Wall, Secondary Modern, Warley Technical College; [occ.] Chemist; [oth. writ.] Numerous poems.; [pers.] Carmel is my Inspiration.; [a.] Birmingham, West Mids, UK

DA COSTA, MARIA
[b.] 12 August 1936, Cabo Frio; [p.] Aracy, Nazareth Machado; [m.] Carlos Eduardo, 26 September 1960; [ch.] Carlos Eduardo, Teresa, Claudia, Paula, three granddaughters: Stephanie, Rebecca and Caroline; [memb.] Friend of the Royal Academy and National Art Collections Fund; [oth. writ.] "A Bouquet of Memories" (book), "Breath of Life" (35 poems in English and Portuguese), editorial team of "Leonora Age Concern Special", supporting poetry and short stories. (Magazine); [pers.] Do not let precious moments of your life be grabbed by life like strong winds in a stormy day...live them to the fullest, time never returns.; [a.] London, UK

DAISH, GEOFFREY
[b.] 28 February 1920, Ealing; [p.] Thomas Daish, Joan Daish; [m.] Elizabeth McCall, 25 April 1942; [ch.] Judy, Lesley; [ed.] Tonbridge School Cambridge University; [occ.] Retired Engineer; [memb.] Guild of Aviation Artists Priory Theatre Company, Kenilworth. British Limbless Exservice Men's Association; [hon.] M.A.; [oth. writ.] I have published privately 3 booklets of poems covering 50 years of endeavour, namely for rhyme or reason more rhyme or reason yet more rhyme or reason; [pers.] It all started in May 1943 at the 31st. Station hospital run by the U.S. Army Group of 2nd Corps attached to the British 1st Army in North Africa having been recovered by Americans the previous month, wounded.; [a.] Kenilworth, Warwickshire, UK

DALLEY, GWEN
[b.] 2 August 1938, Gloucester; [p.] Harry Dawe, Phyllis Dawe; [m.] Geoffrey Dalley, 30 August 1958; [ch.] Shirley, Pamena, Leslie; [ed.] Castlemorton C/E School Nrmalvern Worcs; [occ.]

Housewife; [memb.] Morris Minor Owners Club; [pers.] I have written poem entered and others since my mother died recently and whilst visiting my father in hospital where he nearly lost his life. Something inspired me.; [a.] Ledbury, Herefordshire, UK

DALLIMORE, MR. DAVID R. J.
[pen.] Dave Dallimore; [b.] 20 May 1973, Kingston; [p.] Mrs. Sheppy and Mr. Dallimore; [m.] Mrs. Claire Dallimore, 3 June 1995; [ch.] Daughter: Shannon Jade Dallimore; [ed.] Southborough Comprehensive School; [occ.] Royal Navy, Seaking, Helicopter Mechanic; [hon.] Earned United Nations Medal, serving in the Former Yugoslavia; [pers.] I am influenced by the experiences of life, and wish to capture the moments in my poetry.; [a.] Yeouil, Somerset, UK

DARLINGTON, ELAINE
[pen.] Elaine Darling; [b.] 4 November 1955, Plymouth; [p.] Ronald and Pamela Edmonds; [m.] Ian Darlington, 13 February 1993; [ch.] Darren, Hayley and Dale Willis; [ed.] Public Secondary School for Girls; [occ.] Amateur Artist; [hon.] Art included in CMHSD 1996 Calendar, Certificate Awarded by MP David Mellor, current owner of artwork titled 'The Heat of Grenada"; [oth. writ.] Poems including titles `Is This Reality Or Dream', `Life's Journey', `Moving On', `Fulfill Your Destiny', `Seeds of Chaos', `Universal Government' and others all as yet unpublished.; [pers.] A painter does not paint one masterpiece, a poet does not write one poem, a composer does not compose one song. A creator does not create one being, one planet, one star, one universe.; [a.] Newquay, Cornwall, UK

DAVENPORT, MARJORIE
[b.] 6 April 1928, Oakworth, West Yorkshire; [p.] Harry Pakes and Elizabeth Pakes; [m.] Frank Davenport; [ch.] Daughter Bronwen and Granddaughter Emma and Joanne; [ed.] Secondary-Modern; [occ.] Retired; [oth. writ.] None, but worked as a voluntary braille transcriber for several years for Library for the blind.; [pers.] My first poem inspired by the appearance of the comet in spring 1996 and my answering belief in a spiritual after life.; [a.] Rustington, West Sussex, UK

DAVIDSON, LORRAINE
[b.] 16 February 1960, Douglas; [p.] James and Susan Davidson; [ch.] Lindsay Davidson; [pers.] To dedicate my poem to my father James Davidson who died of lung cancer on the 24 January 1996.; [a.] Glasgow, UK

DAVIDSON, ROLAND CHARLES
[pen.] David Davidson; [b.] 21 May 1924, London, SE; [p.] Minnie and Joseph Davidson; [m.] Jean Freda Davidson, 10 April 1950; [ch.] Paul Joseph; [ed.] St Pauls Church School Cofe. London S.E. Left school 14 years age. To begin employment hotel page; [occ.] Retired Founder Boy, Company Chairman; [oth. writ.] Children's Verse Children's Stories in Verse Form. Short Stories. "Conversation Pieces."; [pers.] To write as a pastime is a joy - to write for a living is only a job.; [a.] Cambridge, UK

DAVIES, BERYL
[b.] 4 July 1946, Carmarthen; [p.] Thomas and Rachel Davies; [m.] 4 April 1970; [ch.] Heddwyn, Heulyn and Eurfyl; [ed.] Lampeter Sec., Cardiff College of Music/Drama; [occ.] Housewife/

Mother; [memb.] Organist since '73-Soar Y Myndd, Nr. Tregaron, Dyfed; [hon.] SVRL Prizes 'Eisteddfodau' - Hymn writing incl. $100 prizes; [oth. writ.] Many Hymns in song books.; [a.] Tregaron, Dyfed, UK

DAVIES, BRIGIT
[pen.] Britt; [b.] 16 September 1943, Ireland; [p.] Patrick and Katie Morrissey; [m.] M. E. Davies, Valentines Day; [ch.] Two; [ed.] Convent School and College also colleges of further education to study various subjects and languages; [occ.] Receptionist; [memb.] R.B.L., R.S.P.C.A., B.C.M.A., Chorley Sport and Leisure Club; [hon.] Lancashire Aikikai, Las Vegas Airlines, Award, National Travelworld British Airways Award, both explorer rewards; [oth. writ.] Arrival Press (Book), Gabriel Communications Ltd. (Mag.), these are books and magazines in which I have had some of my poems published.; [pers.] I write on many topics but, my favorite is inspirations. I believe we are all inspired by something.; [a.] Preston, Lancashire, UK

DAVIES, DENNIS N.
[b.] 20 February 1937; [p.] Mr. B. Davies and Mrs. E. Davies; [m.] Mrs. M. Davies, 16 June 1962; [ch.] Jason D. Davies; [ed.] Secondary Modern; [occ.] Production Worker; [oth. writ.] Goodbye Friend, book title anchor lines by anchor books (publisher); [pers.] Born in West Bromwich-Serverd in the British army in Egypt. Trpoli moved to Telford in 1965. Worked at G.N.N. Sankeys for 30 yrs. as a production worker. Took to writing poetry when my dog died; [a.] Telford, Shropshire, UK

DAVIES, GARY PEER
[pen.] Gary P. Davies; [b.] 28 July 1970, Liverpool, England; [p.] Ann Davies, Peter Alan Davies; [m.] (Fiance) Engaged to Ms. Elizabeth Stevens; [ed.] Lawrence Rd Lower, Sefton Park Boys, The Holt Comp. School, Millbrook College High 1986-1988; [occ.] Senior Local Govt. Officer - Liverpool City Council; [memb.] Liverpool District 147 Snooker Club (ex under 21 Club Champion), Unison-Local (Liverpool Branch) Trade Union, Chairman of Local and Office Fantasy Football Leagues; [hon.] 5 "O" Levels, 4 CSE Grade Passes, School Poetry Awards, Seniors Champion. English Language, English Literature and Poetic Studies achievements. BTEC National Award full credit pass in business, finance and economic studies.; [oth. writ.] Personal poems printed in local press, magazines and competitions. And also write free-lance for individuals for special occasions eg. weddings, birthdays, achievements, romance, general topics too.; [pers.] I like my writing to leave the reader with emotions and after thoughts. Also life is like the weather - `Unpredictable' often stormy with never enough sunshine!; [a.] Liverpool, Merseyside, UK

DAVIES, LILIAN
[b.] 7 May 1924, Birmingham; [p.] Thomas and Gertrude Maynard; [m.] Kenneth John Royston Davies, 13 October 1943; [ch.] Christine Carole and Gail Louise; [ed.] Tinkers Farm Secondary Modern, Northfield, Birmingham; [occ.] Retired; [oth. writ.] Several poems published in a quarterly book called 'Poetry For Everyone' and several in the local paper the Redditch Advertiser.; [pers.] I like to write of nature as I see it and also things which are spiritual. I also write poems for my lovely family from whom I have always received much support.; [a.] Redditch, Worcestershire, UK

DAVIES, PAM P.
[pen.] Kerren Claire; [b.] 14 June 1950, Birkenhead; [p.] Peter Bickley and Winifred Bickley; [m.] Roy Davies, 1 November 1970; [ch.] Kerrie, Warren Claire, Graham, Granddaughter Lois; [ed.] Prenton High School Carlett Park College; [occ.] Practice Manager - General Practitioners; [memb.] British Association for Counselling; [hon.] Studying presently for diploma in counselling final year; [oth. writ.] I have been writing poetry for as long as I can remember. Occasionally I share them with my family.; [pers.] I am influenced by my emotions and deeper feelings towards happenings in my life, my loved ones or for strangers I may never meet.; [a.] Birkenhead, Merseyside, UK

DAVIES, PAMELA LILIAN
[pen.] Lilian Holme; [b.] 21 January 1929, Crosby, Lancs; [p.] May and Louis Routledge; [m.] Stanley Davies (Deceased), 29 March 1952; [ch.] Robin and Timothy, Carol; [ed.] Waterloo Grammar, Southport College; [occ.] Retired P/A; [memb.] W.R.V.S. New Era Club (Early, Retirers), Voluntary Worker for Disabled, Ramblers, Gardening Club; [hon.] Dipl. Personnel Management; [oth. writ.] Short plays for Local Club - usually comedies quarterly news magazine for resources centre for disabled. Poems. News items for local paper of New Era Club.; [pers.] Since retiring from a busy P/A (to M. Dir's) position - I need to express myself and find that writing helps to release my emotions - both humorous thoughts and serious feelings.; [a.] Prestatyn, Denbighshire, UK

DAVIES, THOMAS NOEL
[pen.] T. Noel Davies; [b.] 21 September 1959, Bromborough; [p.] William Peter Davies, Hilda Davies; [m.] Samantha D. T. Davies, 4 August 1984; [ch.] Glenn Roen Davies and Adam Jonson Davies; [ed.] Anthony Gell School, Wirksworth Ecclesbourne School, Duffield Yale College, Wrexham Dundee University; [occ.] Dental Surgeon (BDS); [memb.] Thornhill Baptist Church; [oth. writ.] Several poems published in local magazine. Several poetry orations. International Library of Poetry Quiet Moments and Sound of Poetry.; [pers.] I wish to write poems in various styles. Invariably my deep Christian faith is expressed. I hope to published my own anthology entitled 'Insite at Midnight.' I enjoy music especially from singer/song writers.; [a.] Southampton, Hants

DAVIES, WILL
[pen.] Will Davies; [b.] 25 April 1950, Bradford upon Avon; [p.] Mr. and Mrs. Dal and Gwen Davies; [occ.] Laboratory Tech; [hon.] Books: 'When The Countryside Is In Your Blood' used for 'Book For The Blind' major personal goal.; [oth. writ.] Classical country collection entailing four traditional country pursuit pictures enhanced with own poems (LTD Edition 250) published book 'When The Countryside Is In Your Blood ISBN No 095219600X; [pers.] 'Today is the first day of the rest of your life'; [a.] Westbury, Wiltshire, UK

DAVIES, WINSTON
[b.] 10 May 1940, Bristol; [p.] Both Deceased, April 1990; [occ.] Factory worker; [oth. writ.] "A Glow in Autumn" March 1994, a short story "The Dropout" June 1995 "The Dropout" a play "Love Has Many Turnings" December 1995, a play "Spring is Coming" February 1996, a poem "Under Medical Advice" May 1996, a play; [a.] Portishead, North Somerset, UK

DAVIS, MURIEL MARY
[pen.] Muriel Green Davis; [b.] 6 September 1914, Woodlands, Nr Frome, Somt; [p.] Mabel Green, George Green; [m.] Francis T. Davis, September 1939; [ch.] One daughter; [ed.] Christ Church Girls School and School of Art and Science; [occ.] Retired; [oth. writ.] Two poems in magazines; [pers.] A true daughter of Nature - I love my England and its beautiful countryside, may she always remain the same.; [a.] Frome, Somerset, UK

DAVIS, WINIFRED
[pen.] Isabella Fagentees; [b.] 29 September 1921, Bishops Stortford; [p.] Lilian and Thomas Francis; [m.] Philip Seymour Davis, 11 October 1947; [ch.] Son and daughter; [ed.] Essex and London - also trained as a Nurse and Radar operator during war 1939-1945; [occ.] Retired; [memb.] Hon. Member A.E. Housman Guild, Ludlow, Shropshire; [hon.] 3rd place in an International Amateur poetry Competition in the 70's; [oth. writ.] Many poems published in magazines and newspapers, and also many works published in eleven other anthologies. Internationally; [pers.] I have always enjoyed writing, and during the war years - on active service - I found the beauty of words, and the rhythm of poetry a release from the stress of those times.; [a.] Selsey, West Sussex, UK

DAWKINS, TRACEY
[b.] 3 November 1977, Hackney; [p.] Evadney Dawkins; [ed.] Hackney Community College; [occ.] Student; [oth. writ.] Write Articles for the Local Newspaper and Magazine.; [pers.] Your brightest star, can sometimes be so far, have faith within yourself, if you feel the star is near.; [a.] Stoke Newington, Hackney, UK

DAWN-MARIE
[pen.] Dawn-Marie; [b.] June 1969, Dulwich, London; [ed.] St. Saviours and St. Olaves Grammar School for Girls, also an RSA qualified Fitness instructor; [occ.] Mergers and acquisitions database operator and researcher in Investment banking, also a fitness instructor in spare time; [oth. writ.] Other writings include 'Leave The Words at the Door', 'Don't Judge Me', 'Awakening' and 'True Colours' amongst many others; [pers.] For me poetry is very spiritual, I just close my eyes, look within and write from the inside out.; [a.] Camberwell, London, UK

DAWSON, MARGARET
[b.] 7 October 1962, Cardiff; [p.] Christopher Brockway and Elizabeth Brockway; [m.] Paul Dawson, 29 August 1992; [ch.] Matthew Dawson; [ed.] Bishop Hannon R.C. High School, Rumney Technical College; [occ.] Housewife; [pers.] This was my first attempt at writing poetry. My inspiration I must say was my son Matthew aged five. I have to admit I am totally surprised at it's success but very pleased indeed.; [a.] Cardiff, South Glamorgan, UK

DAWTRY, RHODA
[b.] 17 June 1911, Wolverhampton; [p.] Mr. and Mrs. Dawtry; [ed.] St. Annes Convent High School, Birmingham, Sisters of Mercy; [occ.] Retired (music); [memb.] National Trust, R.Digest, Book Club, History Club; [oth. writ.] A private book for family and friends of poems, privately published.; [pers.] Loving all my life - Music, Art and the simple pleasures of the Countryside.; [a.] Welington, West Midlands, UK

DAY, DEREK JOHN
[b.] 3 November 1944, Ilford, Essex; [p.] Henry Hawksworth Day, Grace Victoria Day; [ed.] Richard Male, Hertford Herts; [occ.] Claims adjuster at Lloyd's, London; [memb.] Member of Lloyd's, Domma Groups, Church Warden, World Wildlife Fund, Environmental Groups, etc.; [hon.] 'O' levels /A levels and "University of life"; [pers.] Inspiration drawn from people situations and life in grandral I have travelled widely this also inspires.; [a.] Ware, Herts, UK

DAY, LESLIE
[pen.] Leslie Aisne; [b.] 16 May 1933, Dover; [p.] Thomas and Emily Day; [m.] Joan Margaret Emily Child, 27 August 1955; [ch.] Five - Graham, Christine, Beverley, Karen, Angela; [ed.] Primary and secondary school, St Mary's Boys School, Dover 1938-1948; [occ.] New Romney Junior School Caretaker; [memb.] New Romney and Littlestone Cricket Club, Royal Air Force Association; [hon.] Royal Victorian Medal (silver) for 26 years service as Police Constable at Kensington Palace, New Year's Honour List 1980; [oth. writ.] Several poems published in local magazines; [pers.] If just one person enjoys my writings then I will feel that I'm successful. I consider poetry as the true language from one's heart.; [a.] Lydd-on-Sea, Kent, UK

DE ARAUJO, MARGARET
[pen.] Peggy; [b.] 9 April 1952, Bangor, Wales; [p.] Margaret N. and David T. Williams; [m.] Mario De Araujo, 28 April 1973; [ch.] John Michael and Daniel James; [ed.] Llangefni County Secondary School, Hollings College, Manchester; [occ.] Partner in a Consultancy Firm, Teaching English as a foreign language; [memb.] Oporto Cricket and Lawn Tennis Club, Oil and Water Painting Classes; [oth. writ.] Various poems (unpublished); [pers.] I attempt to analyze my personal opinions on personal experiences and current trends and topics. Influenced by my ex-headmaster who introduced me to the Metaphysical poets and Margaret Drabble novels, also love Portuguese writers and Visual Poetry.; [a.] Braga, Minho Region, Portugal

DEE, MISS DORRIE
[pen.] Miss Dorrie Dee; [b.] 3 February, Nottinghamshire; [occ.] Unemployed; [oth. writ.] Written several other poems throughout my past years which has enabled me to express my inner feelings and thoughts to the people of "Our World."; [pers.] My creative ideas have been influenced by my work including my spiritual believes and awareness.; [a.] Arnold, Nottingham, UK

DELE, MR. NIRMAL CHANDRA
[b.] 31 August 1942, Sylhet, India; [m.] 11 March 1973; [ch.] 3 children; [ed.] Diploma in Journalism and Writings; [occ.] Warehouse Assistant; [oth. writ.] I write in both Bengali and English languages. My work has been published in various news papers and magazines. My books are 1. Chander Alo (Book of Poems in Bengali Language), 2. Moonlight, 3. Summer Wind, 4. Gentle Breeze, (Book of poems in English), 5. Nitur Biye (A novel in Bengali Language) and others.; [pers.] I would like to struggle for the cause of humanity.; [a.] Hendon, London, UK

DELMORE, JEANETT ANN
[b.] 2 July 1958, Croydon, Surrey; [p.] Eric Gibbs, Sheila Gibbs; [m.] Gary Mayo, 24 May 1994; [ed.] John Ruskin High; [occ.] Administra-

tion (Solicitors); [hon.] Studying Egyptology; [oth. writ.] Path Of Time, and Second Change.; [pers.] The inspiration for writing, and indeed writing poems, is life itself.; [a.] Wickford, Essex, UK

DENBY, J. S.
[b.] 15 March 1948, Hornby; [p.] Colin Denby, Dorothy Denby; [m.] Jean Denby, 1 September 1967; [ch.] Kathleen, Jacquline, Annette; [ed.] Grassington Secondary Modern; [occ.] Carpenter; [pers.] I try to see the humour in everything.; [a.] Sunderland, Tyne and Wear, UK

DESILVA, DENNIS RAPLH
[b.] 12 December 1919, Calcutta, India; [p.] Herbert C. J. deSilva, Hattie Jane deSilva; [m.] Joan N. S. Brodie, 29 June 1957; [ch.] Brian Charles, Michael, Ralph; [ed.] Senior School Certificate, Cambridge University; [occ.] Retired; [hon.] Burma Star, 1939-1945 Star, War Medal, Defence Medal; [pers.] Every individual is capable of producing a memorable print out either as an autobiography or a poem of their experiences when motivated. The 'Poetry Competition' advertisement caught my eye and the result was 'Reality'.; [a.] Walton on the Naze, Essex, UK

DEVENEY, JACQUELINE
[b.] 27 November 1972, Craigavon Area Hospital; [p.] Kieran and Maureen Deveney; [ed.] St. Patrick's High School Keady; [occ.] Manageress, Birthdays Armagh; [a.] Keady, Armagh, UK

DEVERE, LISA
[b.] 7 February 1981, Enfield, Middlesex; [p.] Charles and Susan Devere; [ed.] Southgate Secondary School; [occ.] Student; [pers.] As I am against all ill treatment of animals, I have tried to express this through my poem.; [a.] Southgate, London, UK

DHILLON, JASVINDER SINGH
[b.] 22 July 1969, Birmingham; [p.] Joginder Singh, Harbhajan Kaur; [m.] Sarbjit Kaur, 26 August 1989; [ch.] Ravi Dhillon, Aaron Dhillon; [ed.] Handsworth New Road School, Handsworth College, University of Central England; [occ.] Driving Instructor (Jazz School of Motoring); [memb.] Association of Freelance Writers; [oth. writ.] Several pieces published in various papers, poem published in another book.; [a.] Birmingham, West Midlands, UK

DICKIN, MRS. M.
[pen.] "Meg Francis"; [b.] 21 September 1920, Herne Hill; [p.] Mr. and Mrs. Lindsay; [m.] Mr. G. Dickin, 2 February 1946; [ch.] 3 daughters and 1 son; [ed.] Clark's College, Ilford, Essex, St. Winifreds, Goodmayes; [occ.] Housewife; [hon.] Medals and Shields for Ballroom and Latin American Dancing; [pers.] I have a great interest in the arts (e.g.) literature and dance. Served in the "Wraf" during 2nd World War.; [a.] Bagshot, Surrey, UK

DICKSON, ALAN CORNELIUS
[pen.] Alan Dickson; [b.] 21 October 1927, London; [p.] Maxwell Dickson, Phoebe Dickson (Nee Scudamore); [m.] Maureen Dickson (Nee Hartley), 21 June 1976; [ch.] Timothy, Penelope, Sara; [ed.] Addey and Stanhope, Grammar; [occ.] Retired Bank Officer; [memb.] Royal Air Forces Association Union Jack Club; [hon.] F. Inst. BA, FAI Gliding; [oth. writ.] Poems published in poetry, Now, Oceans Apart, A World At War, and poets in Wales anthologies.; [pers.] A project

correspondent for "Poetry and the art of Medicine" University of Bristol; [a.] Rochester, Kent, UK

DICKSON, JOHN WANLESS
[b.] 31 July 1920, Westgate on Sea, Kent; [p.] Ivan Wanless Dickson and Helen London; [m.] Evangeline M. L. Sladen, 18 August 1949; [ch.] 3 children; [ed.] University of Toronto Schools, University of London.; [occ.] Consultant Orthopaedic Surgeon (Retired); [memb.] Fellow, British Orthopaedic Ass'n.; [hon.] Hunterian Lecture, Royal College of Surgeons of England; [oth. writ.] Various pieces from 1947 onward, none published.; [pers.] Early works influenced by Christianity Later Secular.; [a.] Westerfield, Ipswick, Suffolk, UK

DICKSON, KIRSTY
[b.] 13 April 1982, Newcastle-under-Lyme; [p.] Pat Dickson and Jack Dickson; [ed.] At present at Newcastle-under-Lyme School; [memb.] The Jill Clewes Dance Studios; [hon.] Distinction Senior grade two English Speaking Board Exam; [oth. writ.] Poem: 'Mercurius - Messenger of The God's' printed in the aiming high multi - arts project booklet based on the solar system for year 9 students across North Staffordshire; [a.] Newcastle, Staffs, UK

DIDCOTE, LOUISE HANNAH MORRIS
[pen.] Louise Didcote; [b.] 9 October 1980, Gloucester; [p.] Jayne and Brian Didcote; [ed.] Bilson Infant School, Latimer County Junior School, currently doing my GCSE's at Heywood Community School; [occ.] Student; [hon.] Head pupil of year 9 and School Newspaper Award.; [oth. writ.] Writings for Heywood Hearld School newspaper. Writing for the forest of Dean Newspaper. Wrote and edited a report on Shakespeares 'A Mid Summer's Night' dream production for local radio.; [pers.] Take every opportunity as it comes and live life to the full.; [a.] Cinderford, Gloucestershire, UK

DINÇALP, SIMON
[b.] November 11, 1968, Gloucester; [p.] Andrew and Jennifer Light; [occ.] Student; [pers.] "To fly the free trail", is a state of subconscious beauty, an experience of sublime freedom.; [a.] Grimsby, North-East Lincolnshire

DINHAM, THELMA
[pen.] Leslie Coleman; [b.] 27 December 1937, Plymouth; [p.] James Reynolds, Myrtle Reynolds; [m.] Peter Dinham, 1 July 1978 (2nd marriage after being widowed); [ch.] Martin Graham, Alan Jeffrey, Helen Elizabeth; [ed.] Davonfort High School For Girls; [occ.] Retired Local Government Officer; [hon.] Left school to start work before taking examinations but a graduate from the University of Life.; [oth. writ.] A variety of poetry written for my own pleasure, not submitted for publication as yet.; [pers.] I am very concerned about the destruction of the environment-forests (The Lungs Of The World) and The Wild Life. Some of my poetry reflect my concerns.; [a.] Plymouth, Devon, UK

DIXON, IRENE
[b.] 15 April 1917, Finedon; [p.] Harry and Helena Walker; [occ.] Retired; [hon.] 2 Mensa Certificates one aged 75 (1992) and one aged 76 (1993), Awarded the Good food Award, "The Mallard" Scunthorpe 1979; [oth. writ.] Poem published in local charity book.

DIXON, MURIEL THWAITES
[pen.] Muriel Thwaites Dixon; [occ.] Early retirement due to health; [memb.] Royal Forestry Society of England, Wales, N. Ireland; [hon.] Nil; [oth. writ.] Several poems and articles in my local newspaper in England.; [pers.] My deep love of the countryside and all aspects of Nature. Every spare moment of my life has been spent in this way.; [a.] Oban, Argyll, UK

DOBINSON, FRANK
[b.] 5 July 1916, Birkenhead; [ed.] Elementary School, Secondary School, Technical College, Newport, Mon., now "Gwent"; [occ.] Retired Civil Servant (H.M. Customs and Excise); [memb.] C.S.M.A., R.S.P.B., Devon Birdwatching and Preservation Society, Cornwall Birdwatching and Preservation Society, Somerset Ornithological Society; [oth. writ.] Book - "Strictly For The Birds", published 1995, Contents - verses about birds, and birdwatching. For some years I wrote Holiday Verses which were (recited or) sung at weekly concerts.; [a.] Barnstaple, Devon, UK

DOBSON, GEORGE WALTER
[pen.] George Montgomery; [b.] 20 September 1927, Darlington; [p.] Mr. George Walter, Dobson Sr. and Mrs. Lavinia Dobson; [m.] Mrs. Jean Mary Dobson, 29 December 1994; [ch.] Two stepson; [ed.] University of Life; [occ.] Retired Accountant; [oth. writ.] Several poems published in local newspapers. English Heritage: Circulars prince of wales and Lord and Lady feversham of duncombe Park Helmsley N. Yorks; [pers.] When inspiration comes to me tis then I write my poetry. Thoughts aroused then fill my mind with al the memories it can find expressed through words. I feel inside and inspiration as my guide; [a.] Stockton-on-the-Forest, York, UK

DODDS, MRS. ALMA
[pen.] Alma Dodds; [b.] 8 October 1925, Taunton; [p.] William Vincent, Mabel Vincent; [m.] James Dodds, 19 April 1950; [ch.] Ian Kennedy; [ed.] Holy Trinity School, Taunton and Askwith School, Taunton Somerset; [occ.] Housewife; [oth. writ.] Three poems published in anthologies. Poetry now 1995, British Poetry Review 1995, A Trouble Shared 1995, small booklet of fifty poems. Feelings and reflections 1980; [pers.] Born and brought up on a farm close to nature I have a deep love and understanding of the countryside. This gives me inspiration to express some of my feelings in poetry. It also has therapeutic values.; [a.] Langport, Somerset, UK

DOERING, PETER
[pen.] Thalassus; [b.] 22 October 1954, Willington, Cheshire; [m.] Kate, 21 September 1979; [ch.] Karl and Stuart; [ed.] HMS Conway MN School, Open University; [occ.] Navigation Officer, Merchant Navy; [memb.] Institute of Physics the Planetary Society; [oth. writ.] A huge Collection of works, yet to be submitted for publication.; [pers.] Poetry should flow freely from the heart and the pen, and not be constrained by the ideals of critics. It is an expression of life.; [a.] Upton, Merseyside, UK

DOHERTY, DENISE CHRISTINE
[b.] 2 March 1949, Oldham; [p.] Mr. William Buckley, Late Mrs. Veronica Buckley; [m.] Mr. James Francis Doherty (Divorced), 1 October 1966; [ch.] Vincent, James, Bernadette, Shaun, Marie, Lee, Antony; [ed.] Comprehensive Education, always first in cooking and needle work;

[occ.] Unemployed; [memb.] Daniel O'Donnel famous Irish Singer Fan Club; [hon.] Basic - Hygiene Course; [oth. writ.] I never send any poem before. But I have wrote lost and keep them myself. I just like to try my hard its to succeed in life.; [pers.] I have often, enter magazine quiz competition, just for more knowledge. As my English was very poor at school. Even though I try hard. I found hard subject.; [a.] Manchester, Lancashire, UK

DOHERTY, JEREMY GORDON
[b.] 12 December 1971, Rochdale; [p.] Rod and Jean Doherty; [ed.] Primary and comprehensive schools; [occ.] Rotary Screen printer; [pers.] I cannot be denied, that the draw-bridge of a persons mind can pass from one world to another, and the partition between the two worlds is the light, or rather the mist, in which hoped-for things obtain substance, the unseen things become evidence.; [a.] Rochdale, Lancashire, UK

DOHERTY, NEIL
[b.] 26 September 1936, Ireland; [p.] Neil and Lila Doherty; [m.] Helen Gately, 5 August 1961; [ch.] Jacqueline, Caroline and Janice; [ed.] St. Columba's National School and Buncrana Vocational School; [occ.] Retired (Shirt Manufacturer); [memb.] Buncrana Pantomime Society Producer for 20 years. First Pantomime was 1976. Have scripted two original Pantomimes; [oth. writ.] Several poems published in Local newspaper also lyric's for several songs.; [pers.] I encourage young and old to develop what talent they have and to use it!; [a.] Buncrana, Donegal, Ireland

DONALDSON, ERIC ALEXANDER
[pen.] Eric Donaldson; [b.] 16 February 1955, England; [p.] Danny MacLellan, Mary A. White; [ed.] Secondary Education in South Vist, Scotland. My education was very poor.; [occ.] Unemployed due to spinal operation.; [hon.] None, I have only just started in poetry, so this is my first article. I have written others, but have not yet submitted any.; [oth. writ.] A Lasting Peace, A Day for Peace, Springtime, A Rose, Whatever Life.; [pers.] I'm not that good at poetry, and it does not always work for me but I do try to write, about the world in general. I also write short stories, etc. Thrillers, horror, and comedy. So poetry comes new to me.; [a.] Worthing, W. Sussex, UK

DONALDSON, ROBERT
[b.] 31 December 1923, Galashiels; [p.] Charles and Mary Jane Donaldson; [m.] Olive, 20 August 1949; [ch.] Irene Wright Rigg; [ed.] Galashiels Academy, Kelso High School; [occ.] Retired Chartered Accountant; [memb.] Royal British Legion Scotland, Kelso Golf Club, Kelso Curling Club, Kelso Burns Club; [hon.] Life Member of Royal British Legion Scotland (Awarded 1967); [oth. writ.] Various poems on Golf, British Legion, Farming, etc., none published.; [pers.] My life-long interest in the life and works of Robert Burns has spurred me on to write poetry along the same lines (but not nearly so good); [a.] Kelso, Scottish Borders, UK

DONNELLY, GWENNETH EMILY
[b.] 18 April 1948, Loveday Street, Birmingham; [p.] Emily Wilcock and Albert Edward Sidebotham; [m.] Leslie John Donnelly (Divorced), 31 December 1971, (I am 3 years apart); [ch.] Gary Edward Donnelly, born 7 September 1972; [ed.] Leigh Road Junior and Infant School, Ward End Hall

Secondary Modern School; [occ.] None, was dragged off to Highcroft Mental Hospital for shouting at Stone Throwers, went before a tribunal and was discharged. Although being hit by the stones I have never thrown any back. I wrote two poems instead one called "Injustice", one called "The Stone Throwing Continues". These have not been published, I did throw some rotten eggs at the Stone Throwers House, I saw my mothers house smashed up as she sat in a wheelchair. I lost my temper with them.; [oth. writ.] Translucent Memories, No Confinement Please, Mock Orange, The Fallen Tree, A Mothers Love, Reverberating Halos, E.T.; [pers.] We are all our Lord's children, No Stone Throwers Please, Erythroblastosis Foetaus Babies Have Feelings, my work comes from my heart.; [a.] Birmingham, Warwickshire, UK

DONOCKLEY, ANNE
[b.] 20 February 1948, Urmston, Manchester; [p.] Annie and Isaac Braithwaite Donockley; [ed.] St. Paul R.C. Comprehensive - Stretford, Liturgical Institute Carlow - Eire; [occ.] Religious Sister of the Augustinian Order - Grange Over Sands, Cumbria; [hon.] Diploma in Sacred Liturgy, (Cum laude) (Maynouth) from Carlow Lit Inst., Am currently studying for a B.A. (Hons) in Theology and Ministry at Ushaw College-Durham; [oth. writ.] Music composition - music for our monastic, offices psalms and antiphons. A set of 11 hymns based on the writings of St. Augustine (words and music) book entitled "songs inspired by the writings of St. Augustine.; [pers.] I believe in the presence of God in everything and in each person and pray that my writing and music may help individuals to recognize the God within and to live life accordingly.; [a.] Esh, Durham, UK

DONOHUE, KATHLEEN
[b.] 29 November 1940, Essex; [m.] John Donohue, 10 June 1961; [ch.] Maria, Tony, Tracey, Darren and Glare; [ed.] St Mary's R.C. School, Tilbury, Essex; [occ.] Housewife; [oth. writ.] This is my first poem to be entered into a competition. Or published. I do have other writings.; [pers.] As a spiritual healer I know that living is all about, caring, and loving our fellowman. This way of thinking has influenced my writings.; [a.] Grays, Essex, UK

DONOVAN, WILLIAM
[b.] 15 May 1930, Cobh, Co. Cork; [p.] William and Elizabeth Donovan; [ed.] Early Education Cobh National School, finished education, Rosminian Order; [occ.] Retired; [oth. writ.] Twenty other poems.; [pers.] Its time, that the winged Eunuchs, who flutter around the throne, were sent down, to put some meat upon the bone.; [a.] Cobh, Cork, UK

DOOLAN, GEORGE
[b.] 25 July 1937, Hammersmith; [p.] James and Norah Doolan; [m.] Maureen Doolan, 10 October 1960; [ch.] Six; [ed.] Secondary Modern St. Jame's Marylebone Lane; [occ.] Porter Town Hall Luton; [pers.] To try and say the things you would have like to have said at the time, about people that are no longer here. Who you loved; [a.] Houghton, Regis, Beds, UK

DOUGLAS, GWEN
[b.] 5 October 1948, Hull; [p.] Kenneth and Jean Hayzen; [m.] Edward Douglas, 15 July 1995; [ed.] Estcourt High School, Hull College of Technology, College of Humberside; [occ.] Chemical

Analyst, Hull; [memb.] Leven Walking Club; [oth. writ.] Another poems to be published by yourselves in "Between A Laugh And A Tear" two other of my poems are being published by another publisher in September.; [pers.] I write about what I know, feel and reflect. Then I know I am being true to myself and to the people who may read my poems.; [a.] Hull, East Yorkshire, UK

DOWNIE, JOHN
[pen.] John Downie; [b.] 16 March 1960, Dundee; [p.] James and Janette; [ed.] Blairgowrie Hill Primary, Alyth Secondary; [occ.] Unemployed; [memb.] Scottish Wildlife Trust Greenpeace; [hon.] H.N.D. Conservation Management; [oth. writ.] One other poem published in 1994/95 Scottish Anthology for new poets.; [pers.] To highlight the social pressures which affect the human race, and the environment in which we all live. I have been influenced by the writing and poems of Spike Milligan.; [a.] Blairgowrie, Perthshire, UK

DOWNTON, LESLIE
[b.] 9 August 1952, Stourbridge; [p.] Deceased; [m.] Silvia Downton, 2 July 1983; [ch.] Two; [ed.] Audnam Secondary Modern School Near Stourbridge; [occ.] Warrant Officer British Army; [memb.] NIL; [hon.] Gulf War Medal, Un (Bosnia) Medal, Northern Ireland Medal, Long Service Good Conduct Medal Kuwaiti Liberation Medal, Saudi Arabia Medal; [oth. writ.] Minerva Press Small Book called "Unclassified" 17 poems written whilst in Bosnia, Poem called "A Corner Rose" published in "Voices On The Wild" by "Your Goodselves".; [pers.] Old soldier - who decided to write poetry at 42 years of age - but only gets time to write when on "Operational Tours" such as Bosnia and Currently Northern Ireland.; [a.] Dungannon, BFPO 803, Tyrone, Northern Ireland

DOWSETT, LINDA
[pen.] Christine Linden; [b.] 7 August 1946, Bath; [p.] Evelyn and Jack Christian; [m.] Gordon Dowsett, 7 June 1975; [ch.] Christopher and Denise, Martyn and Beverley; [ed.] Grammar School, "City Of Bath Girls School"; [occ.] Self employed, Fancy Dress Costume Hirer; [oth. writ.] My friends and relatives have asked me to write for special occasions. All complaints I have made have been in poetry. I have never had anything published before; [pers.] "I am a `People's Poet'" (I write poetry when I want to make a statement about, or to, a person).; [a.] Trowbridge, Wiltshire, UK

DRAIN, LAURA
[pen.] Laura Drain; [b.] 1 March 1989, Margate; [p.] Hugh and Denise Drain; [ed.] Central Primary School, Limavady; [occ.] At School; [a.] Limavady, Londonderry, UK

DREW, PATRICIA
[b.] 24 March 1949, Watford; [p.] Thomas Scanlon, Hilda Scanlon; [m.] Brian Drew, 12 July 1974; [ch.] Joanna Louise; [ed.] Rickmansworth Grammar; [occ.] Writer, Parrot Breeder; [memb.] Parrot Society, National Council Aviculture; [oth. writ.] Several poems published in books and magazines, articles for bird keeper monthly magazine, articles for Parrot Society Magazine, article for the Australian Bird Keeper Magazine.; [pers.] My writing is drawn from personal experience, a deep from personal beauty and wonders of nature and our need preserve and protect our planet.; [a.] Rushden, Northamptonshire, UK

DRING, ADINA JANE
[pen.] Denia Dring; [m.] Reg Dring; [ch.] Dennis, Dawn, Diana; [occ.] Housewife; [memb.] Member of the Salvation Army; [oth. writ.] A series of humorous articles on family life and several poems published in local and national salvation army magazines.; [pers.] I believe a sense of humour is a very necessary ingredient in every day christian living.; [a.] Sandiacre, Notts, UK

DRYSDALE, GWEN C.
[b.] 12 September 1902, Hull, Yorks; [p.] A. and F. Clifford Smith; [m.] A. Drysdale, 17 June 1935; [ch.] Two sons and one daughter; [ed.] Three boarding schools (one bombed out in 1914) Royal Academy of Music, London; [occ.] Retired classical pianist; [memb.] R.U.S.P.A., French Twinning Assoc. Speaker's Club, Institute Advanced Motorists - Safe Drivers Association; [hon.] Royal Academy of Music - Bronze Medal, LRAM; [oth. writ.] Nothing published - just ordinary correspondence; [pers.] I believe in a Creator God - I believe good and evil are at war in the world, and in God's good time good will triumph - The answer is governing love.; [a.] Ayr, Ayrshire, Scotland

DUCKER, BRIAN
[b.] 20 March 1939, Dudley, Northumberland; [p.] Gladys and Mason Ducker; [m.] Helen Ducker, 8 April 1962; [ch.] Helendane, Owlen Elizabeth, Brian Owen; [occ.] Early retired; [memb.] British Red Cross, Ramblers Ass. Wooler Epilepsy Support Group.; [oth. writ.] 26 poems published by five others publishes plus several published in magazines and newspapers.; [pers.] My poetry is influenced by my wife as a country man. I feel that poetry is an extension of the person.; [a.] Wooler, Northumberland, UK

DUCKETT, MICHAEL THOMAS
[b.] 8 May 1932, Stalybridge; [p.] Frederick and Rosanna Duckett; [m.] Winefride, 27 October 1960; [ch.] Richard, Dominic, Rapheal, Hilary; [ed.] Man. Univ. Nottingham Univ.; [occ.] Artist Painter; [memb.] GED Society; [hon.] D.P.E.D.; [oth. writ.] Various; [pers.] I am my brothers keeper; [a.] Luton, Beds, UK

DUFFY, MICHELLE
[b.] 17 November 1983, Solihull; [p.] Anthony and Sheila; [ed.] Yardley Junior School, Cockshut Hill Secondary School; [occ.] Student; [memb.] Tennis Club, RSPCA Animal Action Club; [oth. writ.] Poem published in 1996 British Poetry Review book and poem published in "Family Pets" book; [pers.] As a poet, I try to express my feelings and my visions; [a.] Birmingham, West Midlands, UK

DUNKER, DOUGLAS SIEGFRID
[b.] 15 March 1913, Rugby; [p.] Louis Dunker - CBBA Nordensson; [m.] Christine Dunker, 2 September 1939; [ed.] Hanley Castle Grammar School, Clarks College, London Central School of Art, Cranage (Raf) College Burderop Park College (Min. Ed); [occ.] Retired Schoolmaster, Ex Staff Navigator RAP; [memb.] Navigation Examiner RAF, P.R.M.E.R.S., F.C.I., R.B.S.C., F.S.C.T., Chairman Midbucks Exams Committee, Member Amateur Artists Society; [oth. writ.] 1 Small books of poetry published some poems published in magazines prize in local poetry competition some poems written for and read in church services; [pers.] A life-long interest in study of language the wonder of words. Literature of poetry the belief that poetry should have a spiritual in it's widest sense.; [a.] Aylesbury, Bucks, UK

DUNKLEY, HAZEL V.
[pen.] Knight Hazel; [b.] 12 April 1944, Surrey; [p.] Violet Knight and George Knight; [m.] Divorced; [ch.] 3, 8 grandchildren; [ed.] Ruxley Comprehensive School; [occ.] Writer, Artist, Poet; [hon.] Art Scholarship; [oth. writ.] Poem "Love Hurts" recently published.; [pers.] My poetry reflects my emotions and feelings. It is a wonderful way of expressing them. Favourite poet. Alfred Lurd Tennyson.; [a.] Pagham, Sussex, UK

DUNN, BRIAN
[b.] 22 March 1937, Plymstock; [m.] Julia Christabel, 25 October 1965; [ch.] Tracey John, Joantha Carowne, Alexander James; [ed.] Birrenhead School; [occ.] Recently Retired; [memb.] Port Sunlight Players, Church Lad's and Church Girls's Brigade; [hon.] Noda 35 yrs. Medal and Bars; [oth. writ.] Letters and articles in House Journals and Parish magazines; [pers.] Poetry for pleasure, not pretention.; [a.] Birkenhead, Merseyside, UK

DUNN, MISS LYNETTE
[pen.] Lynette John; [b.] 11 April 1972, Bristol; [p.] Gloria Dunn and Leonard Dunn; [ch.] Amy Louise Elizabeth Dunn; [ed.] The Grange Comprehensive School, South Bristol College, Alfred Marks Technical College; [occ.] Single Mum; [oth. writ.] Several Poems published for poets corner in local paper. Poems published in other anthologies other work produced for specific occasions.; [pers.] Great satisfaction is obtained in reflecting personal experiences, and poetry is my way of self expression my work is dedicated to my daughter Amy.; [a.] Weston-super-Mare, North Somerset, UK

DUNWOODY, LAUREN
[b.] 11 August 1980, Lymington, Hampshire; [p.] Linda Dunwoody, Joseph Dunwoody; [ed.] Hordle C. E. Primary and Arnewood Comp. New Milton - Brockenhurst College, Hampshire; [occ.] Student; [hon.] GCSES - A Art, A English Literature, B English Language; [oth. writ.] Other poetry (not published); [pers.] If you've got a feeling inside your head then release it before it goes again otherwise you'll never have an argument to prove!!; [a.] Lymington, Hampshire, UK

DURAND, EDWARD
[b.] 21 February 1974, London; [p.] Rev. Sir Dickon Durand, Lady Stella Durand; [ed.] St. Columba's College, Dublin The Milltown Institute, Dublin University of Ulster, Co. Derry; [occ.] Philosophy Student; [oth. writ.] Poetry, music reviews, and articles in "Muse" fanzine. Poem in College Magazine.; [pers.] In my writing I strive against inequality, conformity and capitalism, I see most of mankind's problems as coming from the concept of possessions.; [a.] Sugo, Sugo, UK

DURIEZ, GLADYS
[b.] 6 January 1931, Birmingham; [p.] Richard and Violet Collins; [m.] Charles, 15 March 1969; [ch.] Julian Martin, David, Graham and Ian, also six step-children; [ed.] Birmingham Sec. Modern; [occ.] Retired Nurse; [memb.] Deaconess - Presteigne Baptist Church - Leader and Treasurer of Day Centre for Physically and Mentally Disabled, Voluntary, Sec. and Treasurer of Local Branch for ARC Research; [hon.] Long Service Award for work with ARC Research; [oth. writ.] Several poems published in local church magazines also broadcast in California on radio. Inspirational hour by a pastor friend.; [pers.] My

inspiration to write comes from knowing Jesus Christ as my Lord and saviour, I pray others may be influenced and encouraged by my writings.; [a.] Presteigne, Powys, UK

DURRANT, ALFRED AUGUSTUS
[pen.] Phega Bakka; [b.] 31 July 1950, Kingston, Jamaica; [p.] Mrs. Caroline Smith, (Late) Uriah Durrant; [m.] Maureen Durrant, 31 July 1982; [ch.] Elfleonardo Jason, Caroline, Tracy; [ed.] St. George Boys (Bristol) Rolls Royce Tec. Filton Tec. Bristol; [occ.] Aero Engineer; [memb.] Former Empire Sports Bristol; [hon.] Seven CSSE Passes, Apprentice of the Year, award city and guilds Engineering Craft and Tec.; [oth. writ.] Several unpublished poems E.G. "Living," "Guilty", "Pandora", "Sings", "Sleep", "Empty", "Tree", etc.; [pers.] Poetry reflects inner-thoughts fed by observation and personal experience. My aim is to induce positiveness in mankind. Influenced by the poet Rud Kiplin.; [a.] Bristol, Avon, UK

EASSON, HELEN ANTONIA OAKLEY
[pen.] Kara Lee; [b.] 25 March 1982, Stockport; [ed.] Cheadle Hulme School, Cheadle Hulme; [occ.] School girl; [oth. writ.] Occasional input to school magazine; [pers.] I try to write what the human eye cannot see.; [a.] Prestbury, UK

EASTWOOD, WINNIE
[b.] 7 August 1914, Greetland, Halifax; [p.] Clement Eastwood, Edith Eastwood; [ed.] Greetland Council School, Greetland, Halifax, West Yorkshire; [occ.] Retired; [hon.] 1st prize for an essay, at age 11, at a local event; [oth. writ.] Oddments of poetry, just for my own entertainment; [pers.] It has taken me 82 years to get any of my work published, in spite of being told of early great promise!! I enjoy composing short verses, especially to comfort those bereaved.; [a.] Elland, West Yorkshire, UK

ECCLES, CHERRY L.
[pen.] Cherry Stone; [b.] 27 December 1944, West Bromwich; [p.] Joan and John Judd; [m.] Ron, 1964; [ch.] Matthew, Emma, Francesca, Gareth; [ed.] Great Barr High; [occ.] Houswife/Mother, Poetry writing for pleasure; [memb.] 'Friend' of the Poetry Society, Jose Carreras Society, RSPB Fellow; [oth. writ.] Small poems in Pen friend magazine; [pers.] My lighter poems have been influenced by the writings of patience strong. My other poems are deeper, straight from the heart.; [a.] Nr Llanfechain, Powys, UK

EDGINGTON, STEPHEN
[b.] September 20, 1958, Reading; [p.] Maurice and Judith Edgington; [m.] Linda Ruth, March 18, 1978; [ch.] Jeremy John, Rowena, Michelle and Gemma; [ed.] Oxford Boys Grammar, Ox College of F.E.; [occ.] Computer Systems Engineer and Trainer; [oth. writ.] None published; [a.] Oxford, Oxon, UK

EDMEAD, PATRICIA
[b.] 1 March 1925, Bristol; [occ.] Retired; [oth. writ.] Wartime love story newspaper articles memories of cinema (published); [pers.] Poem inspired by an autumn holiday in Ireland; [a.] Bristol, UK

EDWARDS, DIANE
[b.] 7 November 1954, Tredegar; [p.] Eve Jones, Stanley Jones; [m.] Alan Edwards, 27 August 1979; [ch.] Leanne Edwards; [ed.] Crosskeys College of further Education, Ystrad Mynach

College of Further Education; [occ.] Owner, Manageress of Keltic Fine Art; [pers.] A humorous, and personal reflection of everyday aspirations of a working wife and mother.; [a.] Blackwood, Gwent, UK

EDWARDS, STEPHANIE
[b.] 14 October 1967, Derby, England; [p.] Mr. and Mrs. N. A. Edwards; [ed.] Educated to basic secondary school level. Taken and passed several counselling courses. Presently taking the 2nd yr. of my diploma in Counselling.; [occ.] Project Worker. Working with children from social services; [oth. writ.] 1. "The Tears Beyond the Door", 2. "She's Grown Up Now, but She hasn't Forgotten", 3. "The Hypocritical Mentality", 4. "Pain", 5. "Relationships"; [pers.] Life is lots of roads, with lots of signs. Those signs are choices. One incorrect choice is merely a lesson, stop look and learn then move on. Never look back look up!; [a.] London, UK

EILEEN, ATKINSON
[b.] 6 January 1913, Stratford-on-Avon; [p.] Kate and Harry Playdon; [m.] George Steele Atkinson, 30 September 1946; [ch.] Andrew Harry George; [ed.] Kings High School Warwick Furzedown College, London; [occ.] Retired Teacher Taught for 37 /12 yrs in Primary Schools; [memb.] Conservative Association; [hon.] Distinction in Latin and French, Good Credit in Creek at Furzedown College 1934; [oth. writ.] Several poems published in "Garland of Poetry" (Poetry Press Ltd); [pers.] The wonders of nature have always fassionated me and the effect this has on life in general. I am particularly interested in human nature and the effect that environment has on thought and action. This psychological thought forms the basis of most of my poems.; [a.] Leicester, Leicestershire, UK

EISENHAUER, MICHELE
[b.] 10 April 1974, Rush Green; [p.] Michael Eisenhauer, Carol Eisenhauer; [ed.] St. Edwards C of E Comprehensive Anglia Polytechnic University; [occ.] Primary School Teacher, Furze Infants School; [pers.] I strive to prompt a personal emotional response from the reader in my writing.; [a.] Romford, Essex, UK

EL-KORASHY, NATHALIE
[b.] 14 January 1977, London; [p.] Ahmed and Bienvenida El-Korashy; [ed.] St. Angela's Ursuline Convent School, Thames Valley University; [occ.] LLB Law Student, Thames Valley University; [memb.] Law Society; [hon.] English Literature; [oth. writ.] Poem published in church newsletter.; [pers.] I believe poetry is the placing of short stories or personal feelings into words. I have been greatly influenced by the work of William Wordsworth and John Keats.; [a.] Manor Park, London, UK

ELLIOTT, MARY AGNES
[b.] 17 March 1924, Irvinestown, Co. Fermanagh, N. Ireland; [p.] John and Alice Magee (Magilly); [m.] John J. Elliott, 13 August 1945; [ch.] Josephine, Maureen, Leo and Tony and 8 grandchildren; [ed.] Fermanagh Technical College; [occ.] Housewife (Now a Widow); [memb.] Co. Donegal Historical Society, Irish Country Women's Association, Letterkenny Writer's Group; [oth. writ.] Have had many short stories and articles (mostly historical) published through the years. Began writing poetry, 4 years ago on joining Letterkenny writer's group.; [pers.] Reading has been one of my greatest pleasures in life - including reading poetry, old and new. This led to my writing.; [a.] Castlefin, Donegal, Republic of Ireland

ELLIOTT, NATALIE ANN
[b.] 21 April 1969, Glasgow; [p.] Carol McSorley, William McSorley; [ed.] Kilwinning Academy, Kilmarnock College, I.C.S. College Glasgow; [occ.] Nursery Nurse; [oth. writ.] Currently compiling a book of my own, as yet, unpublished poems.; [pers.] Emotions and thoughts often go verbally unheard. Writing them down allows others to listen and understand.; [a.] London, UK

ELLIS, KAYLEIGH KATHERINE
[pen.] K. K. Ellis; [b.] 4 June 1986, Notts; [p.] Tracey and Shane Ellis; [ed.] Heathlands first school, Rainworth, Notts. Berry Hill Middle School, Mansfield, Notts; [occ.] Full time student; [memb.] Oakmere Park Golf Gourse, Oxton, Notts British Show Pony Society. Oaktree Lane Torgwondo Club. Warren Ridding Club.; [hon.] British Show Pony Society Awards. Overall Supreme Pony Championship Ridding Club. Taekwondo Trophy Awarded Honorary membership of Oakmere Golf Gource; [oth. writ.] Poem about chocolate. About haven about Granmas, some about trucks. The Iron Man Poem. About dads and my dad.; [pers.] After tragically losing my pony "Drummer" I felt so many emotions that I felt the need to write.; [a.] Mansfield, Nottinghamshire, UK

ELLIS, LISA R. P.
[pen.] Penelope; [b.] 12 October 1967, Singapore; [p.] Ilse and Brian; [ed.] BA Hons Degree in Theatre Studio at London University, P.G.C.E.: Media and Drama Reading University; [occ.] Teacher (English) in Stafford East, also actress (stage); [memb.] Theatre and Writing based Youth Groups around London where I contribute and all involved in community plays for example Stratsford Theatre; [oth. writ.] Unpublished short stories, teenage novel, film synopsis.; [pers.] My poetry truly strives to express my perceptions of life around me often bitter and ironic, yet sometimes surprising and hopeful lifting my spirits. I believe these is always an answer to experience.; [a.] London, Islington, UK

ELLIS, SIMON
[pen.] Elliot Simons, Simon Antony; [b.] 22 November 1973, Southampton; [p.] Anthony Ellis, Margaret Ellis; [ed.] Weston Park Boys' School, Southampton, Itchen College, Southampton; [memb.] Federation of Goju-Ryu Karate, "Swatch-the Club"; [oth. writ.] Over 60 song lyrics, various other writings, including short stories and factual articles; [pers.] I am now actively, looking to break in to "The big time" and to find parties who are interested in my song lyrics. I believe we all have the potential to realise our dreams, it's just a shame that most are quite happy to let life pass them by; [a.] Southampton, Hampshire, UK

ELLSON, OLIVE
[b.] 13 August 1923, York; [p.] R. J. Young, E. M. Bell; [m.] J. A. Ellson, 14 August 1948; [ch.] Kathryn, Shirley, Colin; [ed.] Mill Mount - York, Dartford College of Physical Education; [occ.] Enjoying Retirement; [memb.] Worthing Bridge Club and Friends of Worthing Museum and Art Gallery; [hon.] Phase 1 County Hockey Netball and Welsh Golf Trials, Phase 2. Poetry Readings Jabberwocky, Radio Merseyside and Local Societies, Phase 3. Competitive Bridge; [oth. writ.] In the Early 80's brought out "Take Me With You" to be followed by "Come With Me" - if I ever get there! And of course the inevitable unpublished first novel. Also poems in magazines and poetry now.; [pers.] To rely on others is a mutual disaster which explodes the myth of self sufficiency into a paradox.; [a.] Worthing, West Sussex, UK

ELLUL, MARIELLA
[b.] 20 March 1975, Pieta, Malta; [p.] Anthony Ellul and Emanuela Ellul; [ed.] St. Joseph School, Paola Primary 'B' Sandhurts Junior Lyceum, Paolino Vassallo Upper lyceum; [occ.] Clerk 'B' - Central Bank of Malta; [hon.] Runner- up 13th Edition of the "Giorgio La Pira" International Italian Literature Competition - Pistoia - Italy; [oth. writ.] Several novels and short poems for competitions or a hobby in both english and italian languages.; [pers.] In my writing I try to express my feelings and my deepest thoughts which I find quite hard to release only by direct speech.; [a.] Paola, Malta

ELPHICK, MISS AMANDA SARAH
[b.] 10 December 1976, Gloucester; [p.] David George Elphick, Brenda Joan Elphick; [ed.] Brockworth Comprehensive School, Brockworth; [occ.] System Operator, UCAS, Cheltenham; [memb.] Heroes and Villains Line Dance Society; [oth. writ.] Had three poems to date published through arrival press, Peterborough; [pers.] Through my writing I have found my inner self which has taught me understanding and much pleasure; [a.] Hucclecote, Gloucestershire, UK

ELWELL, BERNARD DENNIS
[b.] 26 August 1944, Birmingham; [p.] James and Winifred Elwell; [m.] Avril Elwell, 19 July 1969; [ch.] Craig Elwell, Dean Elwell; [ed.] Secondary Modern; [occ.] Distribution Manager; [hon.] Excellence in Distribution; [oth. writ.] A selection of poems relating to family and life. Memorable times etc.; [pers.] My poems are my way of expressing my personal feelings and thoughts.; [a.] Redditch, Worcestershire, UK

EMERSON, TAMMY-SHEREL
[b.] 19 October 1974, Belfast; [m.] Andrew John Rankin; [ch.] Karol Elizabeth Rankin; [occ.] Housewife and Mothers; [a.] Whitehead, Antrim, UK

EMMENS, JOAN M.
[b.] 12 May 1952, Woodbridge; [p.] John and Margaret King; [m.] Chris Emmens, 22 May 1993; [ed.] Farlingaye High, Suffolk College, Trent Polytechnic; [occ.] V.D.U. Operator; [memb.] Breast Cancer Care, Melton W.I and V.P.A. Deben Camera Club, Belstead House Camera Club; [hon.] Various, C.S.E., R.S.A., G.C.S.E., 'O' Level and 'A' Level Art Passes; [oth. writ.] Poem "Thoughts" Island moods and reflections (anthology) "I feel I can almost remember", in sunlight and shadows. 'The kite' into the spotlight; [pers.] I enjoy putting 'pen to paper', and trying to fulfill my dreams, and inspirations, in my poetry, and short stories.; [a.] Woodbridge, Suffolk, UK

ERIAN, MISS GEHANNE
[b.] 3 March 1976, Whitehaven, Cumbria; [p.] John Erian, Jennifer Erian; [ed.] Farringtons Girl School, Chislehurst, University of Kent at Canterbury; [occ.] Student: B.A. in English and American Literature; [memb.] Agatha Christie Society; [oth. writ.] Several poems published in anthologies; [pers.] I agree with whoever said "a poem should not mean, But be." I do not expect one single meaning to be derived from my poems, but if they have roused any emotion whatsoever, then I am content.; [a.] Keston, Kent, UK

ERIAN, MICHAEL
[b.] 14 October 1974, Redhill, Surrey; [p.] John Erian and Jennifer Erian; [ed.] Eltham College, London Warwick University, Christ Church College Canterbury; [occ.] Student; [hon.] BA (Hons.) English, Literature (First Class) from University of Warwick; [pers.] I would like to make people nice again. J.L. Carr and A.E. Housman are two particularly important heroes of mine.; [a.] Bromley, Kent, UK

ETRIDGE, JOHN
[b.] 11 September 1933, West Ham, London; [m.] Edna Dorothy, 6 July 1957; [ch.] Lesley and Kina; [ed.] Secondary; [occ.] Self Employed; [pers.] A lovely means of releasing ones imagination and inventiveness; [a.] Croydon, Surrey, UK

ETRIDGE, KELLY
[ed.] Student at Kingsdale School, Alleyn Park, Dulwich; [memb.] Dulwich Youth Orchestra; [pers.] My ambition is to be a writer and a teacher of music.; [a.] East Dulwich, London, UK

EVANS, CYRIL C.
[b.] 4 August 1904, Ebbw Vale; [occ.] Long retired Local Government Servant; [oth. writ.] Local poems; [pers.] Sony Rather hurried to catch post.; [a.] Ebbw Vale, Blaenau Carne, UK

EVANS, MARY BERNADETTE
[b.] 19 June 1950, Birmingham; [p.] Bert and Eileen Stevens (Deceased); [m.] Kenneth, 6 June 1970; [ch.] Julie, Connie, Justin and Natalie (Deceased, 1995); [occ.] Studying Hypnotherapy and also the After-Life; [memb.] Sunrise Child Bereavement Centre; [oth. writ.] Two other poems published.; [pers.] I write my poems to release my feelings about the death of my youngest daughter from Leukemia in March 1995. Natalie was 13 years old when she died and her death devasted my life.; [a.] Birmingham, West Midlands, UK

EVANS, ROBERT EDGAR
[b.] 22 December 1953, Bridgend; [p.] Edgar and Elizabeth Anne; [ed.] Ynysandre Comprehensive School, Bridgend Technical College, Polytechnic of Males Thefonew; [occ.] Council Employee; [hon.] City and Guilds Cert Class I, Mechanical Technical Certificate, Certificate of Mechanical Engineering (HVC); [oth. writ.] I have written a number of poems, but have never strived to have them published.; [pers.] I am greatly influenced by personal occurrence, and feelings, that I have encountered in my life, and by the problems and daily hardships of living.; [a.] Bridgend, Mid-Glamorgan, UK

EVANS, VIRGINIA
[b.] December 7, 1941, Wirral, Cheshire; [p.] John Hopkins, Winifred Hopkins; [m.] George Evans, June 7, 1969; [ch.] Martin Richard, Deborah Louise; [ed.] Park High School for Girls, Birkenhead; [occ.] Clerical Officer, South Cleveland Hospital, Middlesbrough; [hon.] Diploma in Public Administration; [oth. writ.] Early poems published in local newspaper. This is my first "National" publication.; [pers.] I abhor cruelty to any living creature. I hope for tolerance and understanding on personal and international levels.; [a.] Yarm, Cleveland, UK

EVANS, WILLIAM
[pen.] Curley Evo; [b.] 10 August 1955, Liverpool; [p.] John Evans, Margart Evans; [m.] Jennifer Evans, 24 December 1976; [ch.] Tracy Gemma, Paula, Philip; [ed.] St. Kevin's Comprehensive,

Halton College of Further Education, Runcorn open study centre; [occ.] Store keeper, Gidding and Lewis, Kirkby; [hon.] City and Guilds, for Community Care Practice, R.S.A. Certificate in Continuing Education; [pers.] By caring and sharing my feelings they flow by this publication my feeling's you know.; [a.] Widnes, Cheshire, UK

EVES, ALLAN
[b.] 21 November 1934, Macclesfield; [p.] William Eves, Doris May Eves; [m.] Gwynneth Mary Eves, 1 February 1958; [ch.] Pauline Mary Eves; [ed.] Macclesfield Central School; [hon.] Youth Trainer's Award, Awarded September 1990 - by the City and Guilds of London Institute; [oth. writ.] "My Money Making Secrets" published by Chartserch Ltd in 1986.; [pers.] The poem in this anthology was written to raise money on red nose day. Pete's party piece was to eat a whole Mars bar in one go! I wanted him to get colleagues to sponsor him to do this and then I would write a poem to commemorate the event and possibly raise more cash by selling copies of the poem to those who watched him do it. Pete worked in the dept called "Psalm" which means "Professional Selection And List Management" and is a large computer agency database. Pete was part of the computer technical support team which included Johns 1 & 2, big Al, and Pete's boss Murray Hulme (Muzzer). I think that the party piece helped to relieve some of the boredom for him. [a.] Macclesfield, Cheshire, UK

EYRE, GILLIAN
[b.] 22 November 1957, Chesterfield; [p.] Darrell Athey, Evelyn Athey; [m.] Stephen Alan Eyre, 9 April 1994; [ch.] Christopher Wayne; [ed.] Eyre Tech. High School, Whyalla, South Australia; [occ.] Unemployed; [oth. writ.] I have written many poems not yet published; [pers.] My poems reflect the body and soul coming together in beautiful words of meaning. "A Tribute To My Father" was a poem I wrote for my father who I deeply miss and love.; [a.] Chesterfield, Derbyshire, UK

FAHEY, CONSTANCE
[b.] 14 July 1921, Manchester, NE Stanton; [p.] Jack and May Jones; [m.] John Michael Fahey, 30 January 1967; [ch.] John Michael Stanton Fahey; [ed.] Elementary at 14 years Left School; [occ.] Housewife, Pen; [memb.] Member of the human race with friends in U.S.R - S.A. Can., Ireland, Israel and the Cametoons. So the ILP, will be at home, on my book shelf and I look towards to reading and perhaps finding new friends in its pages.; [oth. writ.] Nill - published, never sough. I have just written on events that appeal to me and my poetry has become my diary down the years.; [pers.] I often communicate with my friends in poetry. Particularly when I with he make a point, many tell me they injury it. Poetry for me is a great way at talking to the people I meet.; [a.] Stockport, Cheshire, UK

FAIRCLOUGH-KAY, MATTHEW
[b.] 30 October 1977, Manchester, UK; [p.] Catherine and Johnathon Fairclough-Kay; [ed.] Cheadle Hulme School, Currently attending Lancaster University; [occ.] English Literature and Theatre Studies Student; [oth. writ.] Various poems published in school magazine, a small number of articles for a local newspaper.; [pers.] I am an idealist in an unideal world. Therefore, I try to strike a balance between practicality and sensitivity, philosophy and survival. I have been greatly influenced by James Fenton.; [a.] Chapel-en-le-Frith, Derbyshire, UK

FASHAKIM, DAVID O. K.
[b.] 20 June 1982, England; [p.] Florence B. Fashakim; [ed.] Still at School, "Preston Manor High School"; [oth. Writ.] "Quotation From The Heart", "My Darling, My Love", "The Runaway Slave"; [pers.] It is my hearts desire to be a successful poet I pray for God's grace and mercy to help me realize this ambition.; [a.] London, Harrow, UK

FENWICK, CYNTHIA
[b.] 29 Sept. 1929, Scunthorpe; [p.] George and Maud Camplin (Deceased); [m.] Dennis (Deceased), 19 Sept. 1951; [ch.] Peter John and Joy Elaine, granddaughter Chloe Joy; [occ.] Retired Legal Cashier/Accountant; [oth. writ.] The Gardener?, Ward 22, Villains, Sixty Something, Frosted Lace, My Bundle of Joy, Grammy's Face, Why?, Childhood Memories, First Class Reunion, Freedom, Chloe Joy; [pers.] I see a rose in morning dew, A honey bee comes into view, I get an inspiration then, once more I reach out for my pen.; [a.] Scunthorpe, North Lincolnshire, UK

FERGUSON, MISS CLAIRE
[pen.] Lisa Scott; [b.] 19 Feb. 1981, Ipswich; [p.] Ian Ferguson, Liz Ferguson; [ed.] Queen Elizabeth's Grammar School Horncastle, Lincolnshire; [occ.] Pupil Year II; [hon.] Musician, piano - gr. 7, flute - gr. 6, recorder - gr. 7; [pers.] This is my first serious attempt at poetry, in which, 'Wake Up Shake Up' reflects the sequence of events for most teenagers in their hectic lifestyle at school.; [a.] Coningsby, Lincolnshire, UK

FERRISS, TRACY ANN
[b.] 9 May 1967, Hampton Court; [p.] Ann Ferriss, David Ferriss; [ed.] Waldegrave Girls, Richmomd upon Thames College; [occ.] Local Government Officer; [memb.] Associate Member of the Association of Reflexologists, Member of the Pagan Federation and Musicians Union; [oth. writ.] Currently playing bass guitar and co-writing songs in a band; [pers.] "Tread Lightly on the Earth"; [a.] Twickenham, Middlesex, UK

FIELD, PETER THOMAS
[b.] 26 October 1954, East London; [p.] Fredrick Arthur Jack Field, Leone Elizabeth Field; [m.] Christine Teresa, 5 June 1976; [ch.] Mark, Luke, Grace, Amy; [ed.] Pretoria Secondary Modern; [occ.] Civil Servant; [oth. writ.] Many, mainly personal and unpublished; [pers.] Influenced mainly by honesty and innocence; [a.] March, Cambs, UK

FINCH, ROSE
[b.] 29 September 1907, Dorsington; [p.] Christopher and Rowena Finch; [occ.] Retired (Trained Nurse)

FINDLAY, NEIL S.
[pen.] Neil Findlay; [b.] 24 July 1974, Malta; [p.] Larry Findlay and Gwynne Findlay; [ed.] King's Park Secondary School; [occ.] Sales Representative for a stationery company; [hon.] Only Scottish winner of 1988 BBC-Sport Aid-John Craven's "Newsround Newshound" competition. Resulting in making a documentary film in the Philippines for BBC Television.; [oth. writ.] Experimenting in various styles of poetry writing, compiling a portfolio but having no poems published yet.; [pers.] All too often we take for granted the things in life which really mean so much to us, i.e. family, friends and even our surrounding scenery. Reading Wordsworth and Burns, ignites the need to recognise what we have, as well as inspire us to pen our own feelings.; [a.] Cathcart, Glasgow, UK

FISH, GEORGE HENRY
[pen.] Kipper; [b.] 8 August 1941, Newport, Gwent; [p.] Dorothy Victoriouse - George Henry; [ch.] Andrew John and Darren; [ed.] Corporation Road School, now, St. Andrew Secondary School; [occ.] R.S. Man Llanwern - BSC Newport Gwent; [memb.] RTB Labour club; [hon.] Gold award, for giving blood 32 year service in Llanwern Steel Works BSC 10-2-64; [oth. writ.] I care a lot for my family. My self I want nothing but good health, I hope; [pers.] I make sure my mother want for nothing, my father is dead God bless him, also make sure, my two son, Andrew Darren, daughter in law, Tania, grandson (Oliver) want for nothing at all; [a.] Newport, Gwent, UK

FISHER, ANDREW ROBERT
[b.] 9 November 1974, Worlingham, Suffolk; [p.] David and Miriam Fisher; [ed.] 10 GCSES including English Literature, Information Technology course, Writing Correspondence course; [occ.] Freelance Fiction and Poetry Writer; [memb.] National and International Computer Clubs; [hon.] Poems published in recent anthologies - Island Moods and Reflections by the P.I.B.I. and Poetry Now 1996 Eastern Anthology; [oth. writ.] Articles on Home Computer for National Computer Magazines and Fanzines. Recently completed is my first novel, a comic fantasy adventure called "Brian the Barbarian"; [pers.] I have recently started writing lyrics for a band, and hope to find a publisher for an anthology of my poetry and a short story collection.; [a.] Cambridge, Cambs, UK

FISHER, CATHRINE
[pen.] Kate Austin; [b.] 7 September 1934, Barnsley; [p.] Jack and Edith Sheehan; [m.] Rowland Austin Fisher, 8 April 1982; [ch.] Jane Marie and Michale John; [ed.] Catholic Sec. Mod., Holy Rood, Barnsley; [occ.] Housewife; [oth. writ.] I have written many things, but this is the first piece to have been submitted, I am at present writing my own biography.; [pers.] The love I have for my family prompted me to write my poem. I rely would not like them to be sad when I am no longer with them.; [a.] Barnsley, South Yorkshire, UK

FITZELL, MYRA
[b.] 3 October 1944, Birmingham; [p.] Albert Yeomans, Hilda Yeomans; [m.] Robert Barry Fitzell, 7 July 1990; [ch.] Rebecca, Matthew, Lisa; [oth. writ.] Several poems published in local magazines; [pers.] I am inspired by the wisdom and spiritual knowledge of the native American Indian, I strive to reflect their philosophy into my writing trying to touch upon the spiritual side of mankind.; [a.] Birmingham, West Midlands, UK

FLAVIN, PAMELA ANNE
[b.] 20 December 1932, Derbyshire; [p.] Miner's Daughter; [ch.] Kevin Francis, Trevor John, Jeannine Mary, Rita Bernadette, Michael Dominic (5); [ed.] Grammar School, College of Further Education; [occ.] Compiler of Crosswords; [memb.] Secretary, Catholic Women's League, Secretary, Christian Aid Group, Member, Yate Writers' Group; [oth. writ.] Poems in various anthologies. To be published: (books) "Comedy in the Cloisters", "Trilogy of One-act Plays", "Tori the Lion Cub's Adventure", "What He has Done for Me...", "An Alphabet of Saints", "The Two Little Princes", "Book of Essays and Short Stories", "Anthology of Poetry".; [pers.] On the departure of the last of my five children, I decided to devote myself to voluntary work and continue

with something I had only dabbled in previously - writing. I was encourage in this by a Nun, the Head of a religious Order, and was lucky in obtaining the post of complier of a crossword for a weekly religious newspaper, which helps keep the wolves from the door!; [a.] Yate, Bristol, UK

FLEET, PAULA
[b.] 5 May 1969, Chesterfield; [p.] Rodger Wheatcroft and Lesley Wheatcroft; [m.] Martin Fleet, 27 March 1993; [ed.] Newbold Green School Chesterfield, Chesterfield College of Art Bretton Hall Wakefield; [occ.] Painter; [hon.] BA (Hons) Fine Art; [a.] Ely, Cambridgeshire, UK

FLETCHER, JOANNA
[b.] 31 July 1968, Kidderminster; [p.] Roy Fletcher, Jeanette Preece; [ed.] Stourport-on-Severn, High School; [occ.] Trainee Councilor; [memb.] The Ring of Truth, the Nurse Circle; [pers.] As a chosen priestess of Odin, my aim is to awaken the old tradition of Asatru through my poetry - through Asatru anyone can become one with themselves and one with nature as I have.; [a.] Kidderminster, Worc's, UK

FLINT, PENELOPE
[pen.] Penelope Flint; [b.] 26 December 1951, Prestatyn, N. Wales; [p.] Valerie and Geoffrey Green; [m.] John Harvey Flint, 12 August 1978; [ch.] Timothy (14), Sarah (12), Charlotte (9); [ed.] Howell's School, Denbigh, Clwyd, St. Hugh's College, Oxford University (1970-1973) English Honours; [occ.] School Administration, Freelance Writing; [memb.] Oblate of St. Mary's Convent, Wantage, Oxon since 1989, member of Pangbourne College Chamber Choir; [hon.] Poetry Society Gold Medal (for performing poetry), LGSM (Guildhall Performer's Diploma in Drama) 1969, M.A. in English 1974 - Oxford University; [oth. writ.] My spiritual autobiography - "All The Days of My Life" published under Spire Imprint, Hodder and Stoughton 1989, (this includes a number of poems), my poems `The Bridge' reprinted from above in Michelle Guinness' recent poetry compilation - `Tapestry of Voices'; [pers.] Artistic and spiritual interests provide the keynote to my work. I try to express spiritual values which I believe uphold and permeate our lives. Literature, music, philosophy, psychology and current scientific thinking all contribute.; [a.] Pangbourne, Berkshire, UK

FLYNN, KAY
[b.] 12 February 1928, Liverpool; [p.] John Doherty, Susan Doherty; [m.] Tom Flynn, 22 July 1953; [ch.] Clare, Thomas, Joseph, Eileen, Anne-Marie; [ed.] Notre Dame Convent Liverpool, Endsleigh Training Teacher Coll Hull; [occ.] Retired; [memb.] Norwich Poetry Society Hoveton Bridge Club; [hon.] Distinction in Eng. Lit. Music and Teaching at above College.; [oth. writ.] Poems published in Norfolk Life magazines and two broadcast on BBC; [pers.] From childhood I have loved drama literature and even aged 8 was writing childish "magazines" and plays. Alas I am a lazy writer! Too much socializing and bridge. I love people.; [a.] Norwich, Norfolk, UK

FLYNN, MARIO FRANCESCO
[b.] 28 September 1958, Mountain Ash; [p.] Raymond Birch Flynn, Rosina Maria Zeraschi; [m.] Catia Motta, 27 December 1981; [ch.] Luciana Francesca, Fabrizia Alessandra; [a.] Mountain Ash, Mid-Glamorgan, UK

FORD, GEORGE J.
[b.] 3 July 1931, Edinburgh; [p.] Patsy Ford, Christina Ford; [m.] Celia Ford, 1972; [ch.] Kathryn and Alan Ford; [ed.] Belevue Secondary School; [occ.] Micro-Film Operator, National Utility Services Ltd.; [memb.] Duddingston Golf Club, Forth 66 Golf Club; [oth. writ.] 2 Ski Magazine, Edinburgh Ski Club 1960 Approx.; [pers.] A poem is a poem a rhyme is a rhyme, Would like it in book form, if you publish mine.; [a.] Edinburgh, Midlothian, UK

FORD, KATHERINE NORA
[pen.] Kitty Binns; [b.] 13 December 1917, Kenya; [p.] Rev. Alfred and Mrs. Grace Clarke; [m.] William Mason - 1947, William Ford - 1962; [ch.] Katherine and James; [ed.] St. Michael's School, Limpsfield, Surrey; [occ.] Retired Nurse/Midwife 5RN/5CM; [pers.] I feel, I write, and I like to share.; [a.] Devizes, Wilts, UK

FORD, RICHARD CHARLES
[pen.] "Ricardo"; [b.] 24 April 1921, Sunderland; [p.] Richard Ford and Louisa Ford; [m.] Barbara Smailes, 9 September 1942; [ch.] Ronald, John, Raymond, William.; [ed.] Educated at Commercial Rd Senior Boys, studied Science, Maths, English, and Psychology. My favorite subject was English.; [occ.] Retired, previous occupation, Jewellery repairer.; [memb.] Sunderland Magic Circle, Fellowship of the Services; [hon.] War Medals (4) ie. 1939-45 star, Italian Star, 1939-45 Defense Medal, 1939-1945 Service Medal. 2 Engraved Plaques from Fellowship, 1st prize 1972, 2nd Prize 1994. For newsletters in competition; [oth. writ.] Poems published in local press letters of topical interest also published. Items of effects published in magic magazines.; [pers.] I am an Almoner in the fellowship and visit the sick at home and in hospital, also give help and comfort to the bereaved members. My simple philosophy is, "Do unto others as you wish to be done by"; [a.] Sunderland, Tyne and Wear, UK

FORMAN, ALAN
[b.] 9 November 1948, Leicester; [p.] George William, Elsie Mary Forman; [m.] Valerie, 18 December 1992; [ch.] Two Daughters, 1 Step Daughter; [occ.] Electronics inspection/quality control; [memb.] New Parks Methodist Church, Institute of Super vision and management; [pers.] In life is a book I'm in no hurry to read the last chapter.; [a.] Leicester, Leics, UK

FOTTRELL, MICHAEL
[pen.] 12 February 1948, New Ross; [b.] Matthew Fottrell (Deceased), Julia Cody; [ed.] New Ross C.B.S., self taught Musician and Music Teacher; [occ.] Self employed as a H.G.V. Hauliers Agent; [memb.] Silver Sounds (The New Ross Band), A Volunteer Wind and Percussion Band, Irish Association of Brass and Military Bands (An Umbrella Group); [hon.] Nat. Award HFC BB New Ross 1966, Nat. Award Arklow Silver Band 1972, Nat. Award Arklow Silver Band 1973, Nat. Award HFC BB New Ross 1973, Nat. Award New Ross Silver Band 1989, Nat. Award New Ross Silver Band 1990, Nat. Award New Ross Silver Band 1991, Nat. Award Silver Sounds 1996; [pers.] Each one of us is as important as anyone (Bar none) who has lived or will live: Not more, not less, just as important.; [a.] New Ross, Wexford, UK

FOULDS, BEVERLEY
[b.] 2 June 1958, Guernsey; [p.] Thomas Le Huray, Nancy Le Huray; [m.] Gordon Foulds, 23

July 1993; [ch.] Rebecca, Jamie; [ed.] Grammar School for girls Guernsey; [occ.] Housewife; [pers.] My poetry portrays personal experiences in life. Since writing "Reflections" I can as certain that dreams can come true.; [a.] Guernsey, Channel Islands, UK

FOULKES, JASON PAUL
[b.] 8 August 1974, Brighton; [p.] Barry and Shirley Foulkes; [ed.] Lewes Priory School Lewes Tertiary College Brighton Itec.; [occ.] Multimedia Producer; [memb.] Lewes Chess Club; [oth. Writ.] "The Joy To My Heart You Bring" and "Valentine Card" published by Anchor Books.; [a.] Lewes, East Sussex, UK

FOWLER, SUSAN J. E.
[pen.] Susan J. E. Fowler; [b.] 22 May 1962, Sheffield; [p.] Mrs. Margaret Fowler, Dr. Peter Hollis Fowler; [m.] Nabil Iddir, PhD, 25 September 1991; [ed.] Notre Dame High School Sheffield, Richmond College, Sheffield, Castle College, Sheffield, The open University; [occ.] Receptionist; [pers.] I draw calm and inspiration from the English countryside, from seascapes and unspoilt Landscapes.; [a.] Sheffield, South Yorkshire, UK

FOX, DENISE
[b.] 1 May 1950, Yorkshire, England; [ch.] Four boys; [ed.] B.A. Community Ladies Iltley College; [occ.] Writer (Struggling) last/found in Brittany; [oth. writ.] Poetry, short stories and songs; [pers.] Am still alive and learning.; [a.] Persquen, Morbihan, France

FRANCIS, CONSTANCE LAURA
[b.] 15 November 1916, Plaistow, London; [p.] Annie and Louis Romano; [m.] Edward Frank Francis (Deceased), 30 March 1962; [ed.] Primary School, West Ham Night School, West Ham obtained top marks for English at school, but did not go to secondary school; [occ.] Retired, but still studying: Psychology; [oth. writ.] Have written over 100 other poems, but am too self-critical to try and have any published; [pers.] When something (or someone) inspires me I get the urge to express my feelings in pen and ink. I passionately love children and animals, and acts of Heroism. At school I was called: "Romantic Romano"; [a.] Great Yarmouth, Norfolk, UK

FRANKLIN, AMANDA
[pen.] Delores O'Neal; [b.] 22 November 1981, Bath; [p.] Michael Franklin and Janet Franklin; [ed.] Currently a student at The John of Gaunt School, Trowbridge. Studying GCSE's; [occ.] Student; [pers.] I base my poetry on everyday life situations and each poem I write has a hidden message. I believe poetry is a beautiful way to express any message, whether it is to the world, or simply to a loved one, as is the case in 'I want to be with you'.; [a.] Trowbridge, Wiltshire, UK

FRANKS, DOROTHY PEACE
[b.] 22 November 1918, Kent; [p.] Clara Higglesden, Frank Higglesden; [m.] Merlyn Franks, 4 April 1953; [ed.] Retired; [pers.] I endeavor to introduce my own personality in my writing showing love of nature and everything it stands for.; [a.] Bristol, South Gloucester, UK

FRASER, CAMILLA
[b.] 21 July 1977, Oxford; [p.] William Fraser and Inger Fraser; [ed.] Ladymede School Pipers Corner School; [occ.] Student at Edinburgh University; [memb.] Edinburgh Uni. Poetry Society;

[hon.] Prize in National Junior Poetry comp. various School Creative, Writing Awards; [oth. writ.] Various poems published in school magazines; [pers.] I have always been entranced bagpipes and the story of a distant cousins being "lifted" from first world war trenches by their music provided the inspiration the lines seemed to write themselves.; [a.] Nraylesbury, Buckinghamshire, UK

FRASER, YVONNE
[b.] 17 October 1960, Dundee, Scotland; [m.] Ian James McKenzie, 8 February 1996; [ed.] Madras College (Kilrymont), St. Andrews Fife, and Dundee College of Commerce; [occ.] Health Care Assistant, Perth Royal Infirmary; [memb.] Girl Guild Association; [oth. writ.] My Thoughts Of A River - Anchor Books, Shipwreck - Triumph House, Beachcombers Paradise - Anchor Books, The River - Arrival Press, Restore In Me A Faith - Triumph House, The Fisherboat - Arrival Press, Sad Story Of Woe - Anchor Books, My Wedding And In Laws - Anchor Books. In process of being published. Voices of the Wind - International Society of Poets.; [pers.] I have been greatly influenced by my love of Scotland. Supported, strongly by my husbands encouragement. I've written my thoughts on to paper.; [a.] Perth, Tayside, UK

FREEMAN, MRS. BARBARA A.
[b.] 4 December 1936, Ross-on-Wye; [p.] Sid and Doris Woodroffe; [m.] John M. Freeman (Deceased), 26 March 1960; [ch.] Son and 2 daughter and 3 grandson; [ed.] Haberdasher's Monmouth School for girls - Kidderminster High School - Halesowen College; [occ.] School Administrator at Sladen, Kidderminster; [memb.] Several Genealogical and Family History Societies, Church (Organist); [oth. writ.] Articles for several genealogical, Societies, Articles for country quest; [pers.] Strong desire to keep my native Herefordshire and into Wales unspoilt. Much as it was when my Caldicott ancestors milled there.; [a.] Stourbridge, W. Mids, UK

FREEMAN, S. N.
[pen.] Sidimus The Scribe; [b.] 25 June 1919, Lewisham SE, London; [m.] Ellen M., 4 October 1952; [ed.] Comprehensive Schools; [occ.] Retired; [memb.] The Royal British Legion Colchester Branch; [hon.] Army Medals Served 22 Years. 1938-1960; [oth. writ.] "Shuaba" (ARR Wal In Iraq 1941); [pers.] I write to please someone, any one.; [a.] Colchester, Essex, UK

FREESTONE, EDWARD GEORGE
[pen.] George Freestone; [b.] 17 November 1919, Cambridge; [p.] Arthur and Florence Emily Freestone; [m.] Olive Doreen Digby (Deceased), 24 April 1941; [ch.] Paul, Jill Linda, Deborah Jane and David Madeline; [ed.] Cambridge Central Higher Grade; [occ.] Mainly retired. Keep up music interests; [memb.] Performing Right Society, British Academy Songwriters Composers and Authors International Songwriters Association; [oth. writ.] Works for the Theatre, Children's songs, Satire and Comedy; [pers.] Humour and social comment with an optimistic slant pervades most of my poetic and songwriting work.; [a.] Newmarket, Suffolk, UK

FRENCH, KATHY
[b.] 11 June 1926, Sheffield; [p.] George Albert and Elsie Ibbotson; [m.] John Peter French, 12 April 1947; [ch.] Three; [ed.] P.G.S.; [occ.]

Housewife; [memb.] Women's Guide B. Legion; [oth. writ.] Children's Book. Baby the Little Water Hen. (Ex Land Girl); [pers.] I enclose a book with a proof on the back which you may use. The book is complement to you sir.; [a.] Nr. Huddr, West Yorkshire, UK

FRENCH, LOUISE SARAH
[b.] 3 January 1989, Keighley; [p.] Andrew Robert French and Wendy Ann French; [ed.] Attends Carleton Endowed Primary School; [occ.] School girl; [pers.] I like reading books and writing stories, and was really pleased to have my poem chosen.; [a.] Skipton, North Yorkshire, UK

FRESHNEY, JOHN
[b.] 25 May 1955; [p.] John and Mary Freshney; [m.] Hilly, 28 December 1995; [ch.] Leo, Ian and Brett; [occ.] Management, Development Officer; [pers.] My poems are dedicated to my family, past, present and future.; [a.] Redditch, Worcestershire, UK

FREY-MICHAELS, MILDRED
[b.] March 18, 1917, London; [p.] Louis and Fanny Michaels; [m.] Maurice Frey, September 13, 1938; [ed.] North London Central School; [occ.] Retired; [hon.] Dame of Justice for Service to Humanity. Bronze export plaque city of Valencia [Spain Gold Medal 1963 (Valencia) for export], Bronze medal IGEDO Dusseldorf Germany 1965; [oth.writ.] Gold medal "Salon D'Enfance" Paris for design; [pers.] Always maintain optimistic outlook.; [a.] Hemel Hempstead, Herts, UK

FRYER, SANDRA
[pen.] Sandy Fryer; [b.] 21 January 1954, Luton; [p.] Bob and Jean Fryer; [m.] Divorced; [ch.] Claire Louise; [ed.] Ashcroft High School; [occ.] Manageress of all regions glazing, emergency glazing service; [memb.] Social Clubs; [hon.] Several Awards, for Ballets and Athletics; [oth. writ.] Nine poems published in books.; [pers.] Most of my poetry has a twist at the end or is humorous or hopefully makes a statement in an interesting way.; [a.] Luton, Bedfordshire, UK

FULFIT, STEPHANIE
[b.] 20 April 1947, Plymouth; [p.] Doris and Fernley Sargent; [m.] Gordon Fulfit, 12 November 1966; [ch.] Glynn Stewart and Timothy Alexander; [ed.] Penlee Secondary School; [occ.] Ex-Civil Servant, Inland Revenue; [oth. writ.] Children's poems and short stories - nothing published.; [pers.] Inspired by one of George Eliot's finest works and coupled by my fascination of the past, I felt compelled to express this very human story in verse. Dedicated to my late mother who shared my joy of literature.; [a.] Plymouth, Devonshire, UK

FULLER, MRS. B. M.
[pen.] B. M. Fuller; [b.] 29 December 1933, London; [p.] Lily Dean and John Shea; [m.] Leslie James Fuller, 14 July 1977; [ch.] My son died 1986 age 23; [ed.] Church School London back at School age 50 O'Level Art and Craft; [occ.] Retired; [memb.] The Society of Amateur Artists; [hon.] O'Level Art and Craft Painting Hang in Westminster Gallery, and in Walsall Gallery. Poems Publish; [oth. writ.] Poems; [pers.] I married in 1950 age 16 married for 26 year's husband died 2-12-76 age 47 one son died age 23, in 1986 remarried in 1977, hobbies, art, wood carving, sculpture, painting, cross stitch, many other hobbies.; [a.] Walsall, West Midlands, UK

FULLER, GLENN
[b.] 19 February 1968, Guildford; [p.] Len Fuller, June Fuller; [ed.] Fernhill Comprehensive School, Farnborough; [occ.] Credit Analyst; [oth. writ.] Editor and Main Contributor of Silverton Football Club's Periodical Publication "The Mini Mag".; [pers.] Don't compromise your principles to conform with the majority of authority. Have faith and self belief to be loyal to your feelings.; [a.] Farnborough, Hants, UK

FURBER, BRIAN
[b.] 16 August 1923, Much Wenlock; [p.] Mr. and Mrs. Frank Furber; [m.] Mary Elizabeth Furber, 30 July 1949; [ch.] 3 girls and 1 boy; [ed.] Church of England School; [occ.] Retired; [oth. writ.] A few poems; [pers.] I am an exfrontline soldier of WWII and I have seen many awful things including the liberation of Belsen about which I have written a poem. I have also been a game keeper and I care for all wildlife.; [a.] Shrewsbury, Shropshire, UK

GALE, DAVID
[b.] 18 December 1946, London; [p.] Evelyn Gale; [m.] Katherine Gale, 2 September 1972; [ch.] Timothy David, Peter Thomas; [ed.] Walpole Grammar, Ealing, Keswick Hall College, Worwich; [occ.] Primary School Headteacher, Spalding, Lincolnshire; [hon.] Certificate of Education (Teacher); [pers.] My writing is a reflection on life as I see it around me.; [a.] Spalding, Lincolnshire, UK

GALLAGHER, PAUL
[b.] 9 March 1964, London; [p.] Patrick and Susan Gallagher; [m.] Deirdre Cahill, 1 July 1994; [ed.] St. Bernadettes NS Perth, WA, St. Fergal's BNS, Finglas, Coolmine Community School, Clonsilla; [occ.] Maintenance Fitter, AER Rianta, Dublin Airport; [a.] Swords, Dublin, UK

GALLAGHER, SARAH
[b.] 28 March 1962, Garrison; [p.] Eugene and Sarah Cullen; [m.] Jim, 5 September 1987; [ch.] James Sarah Rachel; [ed.] Mount Lourdes G. S. Enniskillen; [occ.] Registered General Nurse; [oth. writ.] Poems; [a.] Bellanaleck, Fermanagh, UK

GALLIFANT, MRS. PRIMROSE
[b.] 19 April 1927, Sunderland; [p.] John Nicholles, Maud Nicholles; [m.] Reginald John Gallifant, 26 March 1949; [ch.] Robert John, Dean Fracios; [ed.] Comprehensive School Lavender Hill Battersea; [occ.] Retired Opers.] I have been greatly influenced by my own personal experiences.; [a.] Battersea, London, UK

GARDINER, GEOFFREY M.
[b.] 6 September 1947, Birmingham; [p.] Allan F., F.N. Margaret Gardiner; [m.] Divorced; [ed.] King's Edward's School, Birmingham; [occ.] Inventor; [memb.] Old Edwardians Association, Institute of Patentees and Inventors, CPRE, CMA; [hon.] Royal Lifesaving Society Medallion; [oth. writ.] Several poems - 1 published; [pers.] When your shadow meets tomorrow coming, You are one.; [a.] Birmingham, W. Mids, UK

GARRETT, MIGNON
[b.] 1 March 1931, London; [p.] Frances Morgan, Henry Morgan; [m.] Roy Sidney Garrett, 24 December 1952; [ch.] Jane Victoria; [ed.] Benhilton College Surrey, Sutton High School G.P.D.S.T. Surrey; [occ.] Retired/Author; [memb.] Pendragon Writers Workshop; [hon.] Matriculation in English Literature and The Arts.; [oth. writ.] Poetry (various publishers) short stories, two novels.;

[pers.] I find the fascination with the purpose of life quite compelling and try to express my feelings and emotions trying to deal with these complexities in my poetry.; [a.] New Quay, Cornwall, UK

GASOWSKA, LORNA M.
[b.] 2 February 1920, London; [p.] Charles Stuart, Edith Stuart; [m.] Marian Emil Gasowski, 11 April 1942; [ch.] Peter Gasowski; [ed.] Village Elementary Plus Technical Schools; [occ.] Architectural Technician now retired; [oth. writ.] Two articles for journal - 'Bygone Kent.' One Novella Under Pseudonym of Leon Grosz - not yet published.; [pers.] I have always had a deep feeling of understanding and sympathy for the groups of people caught up by fate in the misfortunes and injustices of wars and politics. I have a great liking for the works of Laurie Lee.; [a.] Ruislip, Middlesex, UK

GASPAR, MEG
[pen.] Tosca, Lulu, Hot-Hot Lady, Shortie, Meggie; [b.] 24 August 1947, Salisbury, Rhodesia now Harare, Zimbabwe; [p.] Jack Donald Baker, Sophia Elizabeth Earle; [m.] Manuel Domingues Gaspar (Deceased, 11 April 1993), 8 June 1968; [ch.] Mandy Elizabeth (adopted 15 years), Anthony Manuel (natural 28 years); [ed.] Six years junior School and only one year and two months high school - due to parents divorcing!; [occ.] Live-in Home care... with two counties community care; [hon.] First prize for first poetry comp. I entered in Africa, 1993; [oth. writ.] I adore gliding a pen over paper! Have had no poetry lessons am an amateur!; [pers.] I am a totally philosophical person - my faith comes from God - he is my sustainer: I am grateful to be a poet - to be able to see, what other's cannot!; [a.] Coggeshall, Essex, UK

GAULGAN, ANDREW
[b.] 26 February 1978, Dublin; [p.] Patrick Gaulgan and Anne Gaulgan; [ed.] Milltown NS Mercy Sec. School Ballymahon; [occ.] Student; [pers.] Influences include W.B. yeats, Dolores O. Riordan and Noel Gallagher; [a.] Mullingar, Westmeath, UK

GAUSTAD, SARAH
[b.] 30 January 1984, Cambridge; [p.] Mr. John Gaustad and Mrs. Clare Gaustad; [ed.] Crown Woods Comprehensive School, (year 8 - aged 12); [memb.] Greenwich Youth Dance and Greenwich Community Performing Arts Project; [pers.] I enjoy all performing arts especially drama and English is one of my favorite subjects at school and I enjoy writing poetry and stories at home in my spare time.; [a.] London, UK

GAY, MICHELLE
[b.] 17 March 1981, Solihull; [p.] Patricia Gay, Nick Gay; [ed.] The Woodrush High School; [occ.] Still at school; [pers.] All my family and friends have been totally behind me all the way and I would like to thank them for being there for me.; [a.] Birmingham, Hereford, Worcester, UK

GEORGE, GRACE
[b.] 5 December 1934, Newbury; [p.] William and Grace Lewendon; [m.] Brian George, 27 July 1966; [ch.] Alison and Maureen; [ed.] Speenhamland Primary School Newbury, Newbury County Girls Grammar School Newbury; [occ.] Housewife; [oth. writ.] Several other poems (unpublished); [pers.] I appreciated poetry at primary school, much of which I still remember, countryside themes mainly. I thank the Lord for his inspiration ...I couldn't do it on my own!; [a.] Reading, Berkshire, UK

GEORGE, GRAEME
[b.] 16 February 1976, Glasgow; [p.] Maurice George, Helen George; [ed.] Dumbarton Academy, University of Paisley; [occ.] Student Attending Paisley University; [hon.] BSC in Chemistry; [pers.] This poem is dedicated to the first, and only, girl who I will ever love.; [a.] Dumbarton, Strathclyde, UK

GEORGE, NADINE BELL
[b.] 21 January 1980, France; [p.] Mars Borbillo and Hortense; [ed.] The Langham School I just finish giving my GCSE exam; [memb.] New (Model Agencies) I have been modelling since the summer of 1995.; [pers.] I am 16 year old a model who lived with her parents, my dad Mabs my steps mom Horense and my step two year old brother Archange, I just finish giving my GCSEs exam. I have been modeling since the summer of 1995 and I have received certificated for modelling, next year I will be in college studying media after year of college I would like to be a successful journalist, my ambition is to be happy healthy and to make enough money to look after my families. My best friend Reyhan always tells to believe in myself hopefully my dream would come true one day. I think everyone in this world got talent for something, something they really want always keep they finger cross to make come true.; [a.] London, UK

GERRING, RUTH
[b.] 24 March 1947, Wantage; [m.] Married; [ch.] Two sons; [ed.] Greycotes School, Oxford; [occ.] Therapy Assistant, at Local Hospital; [memb.] Morris Dance, Display Team, Amateur Dramatic Society caller for a Barn Dance Band; [oth. writ.] Poems published, in, farmers weekly, and several local magazines; [pers.] A farmers daughter born and brought up in the English countryside, I am interested in all aspects of countrylife, my poems reflect this.; [a.] Faringdon, Oxon, UK

GIBSON, ANDREE
[b.] 21 April 1916, Amsterdam; [p.] Robert Welch and Olga Welch; [m.] George Gibson, February 1953; [ch.] Robert Gibson, Antolin Gibson; [ed.] Streatham College Dulwich High School, Somerville College Oxford; [occ.] Housewife; [oth. writ.] I have a small bookcase full of folders with work at various stages - poems long and short; [pers.] And the manuscript of a book for children of all ages. Belatedly, I am now able to correct and complete what is virtually the output of a life time that has required too many practicalities.; [a.] Windermere, Cumbria, UK

GILLIES, HELENA
[b.] 13 January 1948, Edinburgh; [p.] Ernest McCabe, Lena McCabe; [ch.] Helena Teresa, Angela Dawn; [ed.] Holy Cross Academy, Torphichen Commercial College, Edinburgh; [oth. writ.] Newly-published book 'God, Atheism And Injustice the Dove Collection', several poems in 'Poetry Digest' and 'Host' magazine.; [pers.] My writing reflects the kindness and beauty in our world, highlights the injustices to human and animal kind, and argues the existence of God.; [a.] Edinburgh, UK

GILLON, MAGGIE
[b.] 7 November 1958, Saint Helens; [ed.] 8 O Levels 2 A Levels, B.Fd Music and Math, Grade 1-VIII Piano, Notre Dame High School, St. Helens De LaSalle College; [occ.] Computer Lecturer; [oth. writ.] 2 articles in IDPM Journal (Institute of Data Processing); [pers.] I like to provide a differ-

ent perspective on life and events, I play indit, classical and N&B in many different choir, play guitar.; [a.] Manchester, UK

GIRT, MR. G. W.
[b.] 2 September 1923, Aldershot; [m.] Widower, 23 June 1943; [ch.] Two daughters; [ed.] Edgworth High School; [occ.] Retired since 1988; [memb.] Blackpool Writer's Circle, Chairman Blackpool Writer's Circle 1995-1996; [hon.] Winner - Blackpool Writer's Circle, 1996 - Short Story Section, 2nd and 3rd - Blackpool Writer's Circle, 1995 - Article Competition; [oth. writ.] Various articles in following magazines: - "Lancashire Magazine", "Yours Magazine", "Good Stories Magazine" and regular contributor to "Fylde" and The "Fleetwood" Magazines.; [pers.] I took up writing as a retirement hobby. I was a Royal Naval Wireless Operator from 1939-1954. Worked for AEI and GEC in Telecommunications. Had my own business from 1969 until retirement 1988.; [a.] Bispham, Lancashire, UK

GOLDMAN, ANTONY J.
[b.] 28 February 1940; [m.] Anne R. Goldman, 1964; [ch.] Three sons; [ed.] Marlborough College and Peterhouse, Cambridge; [occ.] Civil Servant; [memb.] Haslemere Musical Society; [hon.] Companion of the Bath (CB); [oth. writ.] Collections of verse, privately printed.; [pers.] I try in my verse to combine conciseness of expression with simplicity of style, and usually an element of honour. (This poem is a rather solemn exception).; [a.] Godalming, Surrey, UK

GOODING, NEIL PETER
[pen.] Lance Stephenwolf Kimberly or L. S. Kimberley; [b.] 19 October 1957, Port-of-Spain, Trinidad; [p.] Mr. Angelo Gooding and Mrs. Janette Gooding; [ed.] Comprehensive School Education, St. Thomasmore; [occ.] In a Psychiatric Hospital at the moment. St. Andrews Hospital, Northampton; [memb.] The John Clare Society; [oth. writ.] A few poem, The Minnie - Master Singer, The Song Of The Side, Stealthy Beggar, All Gold Olympians Of Metrical Verse, Before Tabernacles Ponderous Moon Belongs, Below A Time...; [pers.] It is nice to know that people are still writing poetry, the mainstream of which is current.; [a.] Northampton, Northamptonshire, UK

GOODWIN, LEN
[b.] 24 August 1940, Sheffield; [p.] Leonard Goodwin and Amy Goodwin; [m.] Lynne Goodwin, 18 September 1982; [ch.] Mark Goodwin; [ed.] Hucklow Grammar School, Sheffield; [occ.] Proprietor Promotion and Record Company, Tram Promotions/Gable Records; [memb.] M.C.P.S (Mechanical Copyright Protection Soc.), P.R.S. (Performing Right Society), P.P.L. (Phonographic Performance Ltd.); [oth. writ.] Many songs published and recorded also produced and recorded a 4 track. cassette and co-wrote title song "Good Old Coronation Street", performed by The Houghton Weavers, recently finished a text book about songwriting and the music business.; [pers.] I enjoy writing songs and poems and take pride in seeing these works made available through retail outlets in hopes that they give pleasure to the general public.; [a.] Bolton, Lancashire, UK

GOODWIN, MAUREEN
[pen.] M. J. Matthews; [b.] 1 January 1958, Chesterfield; [p.] C. Goodwin and J. Goodwin; [m.] John Goodwin, 27 September 1989; [ch.] Matthew James Goodwin; [ed.] Whaley Thorns

Secondary, Mansfield, Notts. Mansfield and Workshop, School of Nursing, Notts.; [occ.] Nurse, White Rose Centre, Hucknall; [memb.] Sutton Saxon's, Motor Cycle Club, Sutton-in-Ashfield, Notts.; [hon.] Three certificates of merit from bassetlaw association of arts; [oth. writ.] Several poems published in Midland anthologies also short story; [pers.] Try to reflect life as I perceive it.; [a.] Sutton-in-Ashfield, Notts, UK

GOREN, INA MARGARET
[pen.] Maggie Goren; [b.] 24 October 1937, London; [p.] Herbert Evans, Molly Evans; [m.] Arnon Goren (Israeli born), 24 October 1970; [ch.] Adam, Matthew, Daniel, Benjamin; [ed.] City of London School for Girls, Hendon Technical College 10 years studying Philosophy with Paul Beecham (adult education); [occ.] Housewife, Voluntary Community Work, Editor Parish Magazine; [memb.] Midlands Festivals Chorus the Stour Singers; [oth. writ.] Booklet of poems, comic sketches, monthly editorial for Parish magazine (editor for 18 years) currently writing children's book; [pers.] Many people have creativity in their hands and heads that never reaches expression. Education to develop the whole person is essential. Opportunities exist - time and self-confidence are often lacking. People who help open doors for others for creative development are helping, towards a healthier society. I believe there is a spiritual renaissance in our aspiration towards beauty and human fulfillment.; [a.] Brailes, Warwickshire, UK

GOUDIE, DAVID
[b.] 28 July 1925, Paisley; [p.] James Goudie, Catherine Goudie (Deceased); [m.] Jessie (Picken) Goudie, 6 June 1947; [ch.] Two Boys; [ed.] John Neilson Institution, Paisley Technical College, Stow College Glasgow, Elect. Engineering, 5 year Electrical Apprenticeship; [occ.] Electrical Contractor; [memb.] Royal Society for the Protection of Birds (RSPB) (Specialize in Study of Sea Birds); [oth. writ.] Asked by parties to compose short verse on events. (Weddings, silver-golden) and other occasions.; [pers.] Tenor singer. Lover of Robert burns songs and verse I always believe that it is better to strive for quality not quantity.; [a.] Pailsey, Renfrewshire, UK

GOUGE, DENISE
[b.] 27 July 1958, Battersea; [p.] Patricia Madden, Charles Madden; [m.] Nicholas James Gouge, 31 May 1980; [ch.] Hayley Louise, Lisa Jay, Amy Charlotte; [ed.] Dagenham Priory Comprehensive School; [occ.] Greetings Cards Retailers (Partnership); [pers.] I write my poems to suit an occasion. For my children and husband, for fun. For very special times. This very first publication is for a very special grandmother.; [a.] Harleston, Norfolk, UK

GOVIER, MICHAEL
[pen.] Mike Govier; [b.] 25 October 1949, Street; [p.] Marcus Govier and Joan Govier; [m.] Noreen Govier, 17 February 1996; [ch.] From first marriage, Darren, Louise, Kelly, stepson Dion; [ed.] St. Johns School, St. Dunstans both Glastonbury Schools; [occ.] Theatre Caretaker; [hon.] Courses in Agriculture; [oth. writ.] Have only just started writing. Completed a number of short stories this is the first publication also have a selection of more light hearted poems.; [pers.] Find enjoyment in writing. Maybe more humorous material. Have always liked Pam Ayres Poetry.; [a.] Glastonbury, Somerset, UK

GRAHAM, GLORIA
[b.] February 11, 1947, Ashford, Kent; [p.] Peter Muckle, Gwen Muckle; [m.] George Graham, August 5, 1972; [occ.] Rye Secondary; [oth. writ.] Poems recording personal events (Weddings, anniversaries etc.) Mainly for relatives and friends. Other miscellaneous poems. None published to date; [pers.] My 'Personal Event' poems are usually presented framed. I also find that some of my poetry is instigated by a particular subject. Other miscellaneous poetry is done in a lighter vein; [a.] Bognor Regis, West Sussex, UK

GRAHAM, MURIEL
[pers.] Influenced greatly by the "Bronte's" whose homeland was near Bandbridge in Northern Ireland.; [a.] Lisburn, Antrim, UK

GRANGE, GARY LEE
[b.] 5 April 1963, Muswell Hill; [p.] Jean Ruth, Terence Frederick; [m.] Gillian, 15 April 1989; [ed.] McEntree Secondary School; [occ.] Customer Liaison Manager, Royal Mail; [memb.] Docklands Business Club; [hon.] NVQ Management Level 4; [oth. writ.] None - only personal poetry never published.; [pers.] This poem was written with mixed emotions shortly after the death of my granddad, Fred Bambridge. Happiness of my memory of him and sadness of his death combined to give me the inspiration.; [a.] London, UK

GRANT, KEVIN
[b.] 20 Sept. 1972, Aberdeen; [p.] Yvonne and Norman Grant; [ed.] Harlaw Academy, Aberdeen College; [occ.] Replenishment Assistant (Nightshift); [hon.] HNC Business Studies; [pers.] Dreams are made to be broken or brought to life. Always remember what might have been but at the same time look forward to what could be. One of my own dreams has now come true - to see one of my works in print.; [a.] Aberdeen, UK

GRAY, KIRSTY
[b.] 14 January 1981, Market Deeping; [p.] Richard Gray, Carole Gray; [ed.] Presently at Queen Eleanor Secondary School; [memb.] Once a girl guide also applied to be a perfect at my school.; [hon.] Certificates in Spreadsheets, Word Processing and Databases; [oth. writ.] This is my first piece to be published.; [pers.] I am particularly proud of this honour and privilege.; [a.] Stamford, Lincolnshire, UK

GREEN, ANDREW WILLIAM
[pen.] William Andrews; [b.] 13 August 1957, Pembury; [p.] Earnest Green, Gillian Green; [m.] Gina Denise Green, 21 July 1990; [ch.] Jordan James, Rebecca Charlotte; [ed.] Hayesbrook Secondary; [pers.] I like to write about everyday life, and about past events of history as I am a great lover of old fashioned things; [a.] Paddock Wood, Kent, UK

GREEN, ANTHONY STEVEN
[pen.] Steve Green, B. Sc.; [b.] 21 Nov. 1962, Leicester; [p.] Terence Green and Sheila Green; [ed.] New Parks Boys School, CSE's, Charles Keene College, 3 'A' Levels, Bolton Institute of M.E.; [occ.] Psychologist, writer and artist; [memb.] The British Psychological Society (based in Leicester); [hon.] A bachelor of science honors degree in Psychology from the Bolton Institute of higher education; [oth. writ.] 5 songs not yet published and 35 poems not yet published. A lot of various length, form, subject matter writings yet unpublished.; [pers.] My life experience and psychology background, steer my poetry, which is empathic and anxiously abstract.; [a.] Leicester, Leicestershire, UK

GREEN, EIRLYS

[pen.] Eirlys Green; [b.] 22 February 1935, Treorchy, Rhondda; [p.] Edward and Mary Ann Howels; [m.] Douglas Green, 27 July 1951; [ch.] Allan and Deborah; [ed.] Qualified Teacher (primary age), Attended the Local Grammar School in Rhondda Pentre Sec., went to Fishponds Bristol College; [occ.] Retired teacher, grandmother (manage) to three little granddaughter; [memb.] Joanna, Samantha and Jessica - Deaconess at local Baptist Chapel (Salem) in Tonteg; [oth. writ.] Religious poems (2), 1) Calvary Walk, 2) Time, Ballads and a hymn, have also, almost finished my first romantic novel on my life in the Rhondda, where my dad was killed in he mines.; [pers.] My writing and songs to date, have been on my religious beliefs and feelings, and through them, reach out to others along the way. My novel has given me great joy in that it has helped me to accept the past and lock forward to the future.; [a.] Tonteg, Mid-Glam, UK

GREEN, JOAN

[pen.] Joan Miller; [b.] 1 October 1942, Glasgow; [p.] Noel Miller, Margaret Miller; [m.] William Green, 12 March 1966; [ch.] Derek William; [ed.] Bearsden Academy Cumberland College; [occ.] Admin. Assistant; [memb.] Jubilate Choral Ensemble, Apex Players Dramatic Society; [oth. writ.] Several poems and short stories, as yet unpublished; [pers.] My inspiration has come from spirit, through my spiritual healing, and my influenced to write has been passed on by a relative from my family history. i.e., (Hugh Miller, Cromarty Stonemason, writer, Theologian and Geologist 1802-1856); [a.] Cumbernauld, Lanarkshire, UK

GREEN, MRS. LUCY D.

[b.] 19 December 1922, Belper, Derbyshire; [p.] Stanley and Alice Whawell; [m.] Alan Albert Green, 9 September 1995; [ch.] Mrs. Angela Horsman, Robert Richardson; [oth. writ.] Sacred poems published in church magazines also many articles; [pers.] I base all my poems on thought which many times is more dramatic and beautiful than romantic fiction.; [a.] High Wycombe, Bucks, UK

GREEN, REMA

[b.] 5 July 1962, Mandeville; [p.] Isaac and Zetta Green; [ed.] Manchester High, Knox Community College; [occ.] Secretary - Jamaica Public Service Co., Mandeville; [hon.] Secretarial Science; [oth. writ.] Several poems, not yet published; [pers.] The mind is a very powerful tool, use it with care and caution. Use it wisely and you will become wiser still.

GREEN, SARAH ELIZABETH

[b.] 1984, London; [p.] Gerald Green, Stephen Green; [ed.] Corthall School for Girls; [oth. writ.] Other poetry not published yet.; [a.] London, UK

GREEN, TERRY

[b.] 25 May 1949, Sidmouth; [p.] Charles and Nellie Green; [ed.] The King's School, Ottery St. Mary; [occ.] Local Government Officer; [oth. writ.] Other poems include: "Dream On...", "Picture Of An Elegant Lady", "This Thing About Believing..." and "Draw The Dark Curtain".; [pers.] I like to think of myself as a man of words and of emotions never a prolific reader but influenced over time by Shakespeare, Betjeman, and more especially by the first World Ward poets who wrote in an arena of emotions almost beyond imagination!; [a.] Sidmouth, Devon, UK

GREENACRE, JOAN

[b.] 13 May 1920, Norwich, Norfolk; [p.] Mr. and Mrs. C. F. Prake; [m.] E. R. Greenacre, 13 April 1946; [ch.] One son and one daughter, three grandchildren; [ed.] Notre Dame High School, Norwich, Norfolk; [occ.] Retired; [memb.] 1) Gt. Yarmouth Organ Society, 2) Founder President Gt. Yarmouth Ladies Probus Club (for retired business people), 3) Secretary of our Local "Meals on Wheels.; [oth. writ.] "Past Recollection" published last year 2 more in the pipe - lime one of which is a xmas carol for which I've written the music - in the final!; [pers.] Get great satisfaction from writing poems mostly funny incidents which have happened to me, and caused great laughter. keeps the mind active and me - young in heart! Also swim 3 times a week.; [a.] Gt. Yarmouth, Norfolk, UK

GREENFIELD, LEO QUENTIN

[pen.] Quentin Greenfield; [b.] July 1942, Swansea; [p.] Mother - a teacher, Father a farmer; [ch.] One daughter; [ed.] Attended Local Grammar School, University of Wales Cardiff, Teachers T. College, Sunday School Teacher, Children's Remedial tutor, Trained Teacher of Hearing, Impaired Qualified tutor of Adults with learning disabilities. (Vulnerable to Sexual Abuse); [occ.] Retired Teacher, 1995, (In colleges - specialized in English/Art/Theology and the Welsh Language.); [memb.] MENSA; [hon.] 1. University of Wales Cardiff Teachers Certificate, 2. 9 Certificates for piano playing and theory from Royal School of Music and Trinity College of Music, London, 3. Certificates in Education and Training in Developmental Social Work. 4. Woman's own' diploma for best entry in handicrafts competition, 5. St. John's Ambulance Diploma (Community), 6. Certificate of Merit Mensa; [oth. writ.] Former Press Correspondent for Local Associations, Poems: They Didn't come?, Another Sad Day, 'Time To Get Out', 'Lazer-Light Music and Seagulls', 'Life Without Caring', 'Oh! Copper Beech', 'Missing You Already', History of the Amman Valley and it's religions. (in Welsh); [pers.] Kindly thought so often helps a sad heart on its way, although we cannot always see the good it does that day.' God never or sleeps and is therefore always aware of any deliberate in justice.; [a.] Swansea, West Glamorgan, UK

GREENHOUS, PATRICK

[b.] 18 February 1919, Bishop Castle; [occ.] Retired; [oth. writ.] Started writing poetry in Stalag Luft III when I was a P.O.W. having been shot down over Holland. Have recently recommended writing verse.

GREER, RON

[b.] 8 October 1950, Glasgow; [occ.] Consultant Biologist, part time Museum Curator, Bar Steward; [oth. writ.] A book on angling 'Ferox Trout and Arctic Charr', several articles on angling and environmental topics in specialist magazines and national press. Various poems and songs on Scottish history/nature; [pers.] My writing is stimulated and tries to reflect the diverse nature of Scotland's history, culture and natural environment.; [a.] Blair Atholl, Perthshire, UK

GRELLIER, EMMA

[pen.] Emma Grellier or EJ; [b.] 7 October 1982, Chirk; [p.] Mrs. Juile Grellier; [ed.] Rhyh Park School - (St. Martins); [occ.] Help teach the 1st St. Martins Brownies; [memb.] Swimming Club; [hon.] Swimming and life saving awards, dancing awards and fitness medals; [oth. writ.] I have many other poems which I have written such as: Inner Mind I and II, Dreams and Don't Forget.; [pers.] Because I'm a kid I'm not trying to say anything in my poems. I write poetry because I like it. Thanks to my friend and teacher Miss Sharon Davies for helping with my problems and to my mum for her support.; [a.] Oswestry, Saint Martins, Shropshire, UK

GRIFFITHS, LISA

[b.] 8 December 1953, Taunton; [p.] Evelyn Kimmins (mother); [m.] Paul Griffiths (Builder), 1 April 1971; [ch.] Mark (25), Paula (23), Shane (13), Aaron (9) and 2 Grandchildren Tammy and Kyle; [ed.] Comprehensive School (Castle); [occ.] Housewife; [memb.] Belong to Local Library, I love books and find reading very relaxing; [oth. writ.] Have written other poem's and write my own verse's in Family Birthday and Christmas Cards.; [pers.] I only felt compelled to write poems after the death of my much loved Dad "Ernest Kimmins" and would like to dedicate this poem to him.; [a.] Taunton, Somerset, UK

GRIFFITHS, SONIA

[b.] 4 January 1940, Cwmgwrach; [p.] Rachel and William Hart; [m.] Malcolm Griffiths, 18 August 1962; [ch.] Karl, Wyn, Leah; [ed.] Neath Grammar for girls, Trinity College, Carmarthen (Teacher Training College); [occ.] Retired School Teacher; [memb.] Amnesty International, Action Aid Sponsor of Child, Cancer Relief McMillan Nurses, IFAW, R.S.P.C.A., B.U.A.V., Compassion in World Farming; [oth. writ.] Poems published in Rhyme Arrival. Pursuing A Children's writing course.; [pers.] Lincoln said: "I am in favour of animal rights as well as human rights. That is the way of a whole human being" I would like to promote this in my writing.; [a.] Glynneath, West Glamorgan, UK

GRIFFITHS, VALERIE DIANE

[pen.] Valerie Griffiths; [b.] 30 March 1954, Manchester; [p.] Harold and Winnifred Griffiths; [m.] Divorced; [ch.] Nicola and George Eastham; [ed.] Ladybarn Secondary Parrswood High Fielden Park College; [occ.] Hotel, Travel and Administration Assistant; [memb.] Library, Book Club, Sports and Social Club; [hon.] Business English diploma English - word processing Business studies - shorthand - typing - each obtained for the necessity to work not for pleasure; [oth. writ.] Nothing published as I usually write for myself the same as I water colour for my enjoyment.; [pers.] I believe imagination and sight are arts. One draws a picture from their mind then seeks a way to describe it.; [a.] Manchester, Lancashire, UK

GRIMWOOD, IAN

[b.] 27 April 1939, Hampton; [p.] Emily and Alfred West; [m.] Fred Grimwood, 30 March 1963; [ed.] Thames Valley Grammar; [oth. writ.] Monthly column in dog magazine; [pers.] Started writing poetry about 18 months after my husband's death. With my faith at rock bottom, expressing myself on paper helped give some answers to the question - why?; [a.] Tackley, Oxon, UK

GROVES, FRANK BRIAN

[pen.] Brian Groves; [b.] 6 October 1931, Southport, Lancashire; [p.] Miriam and Frank Groves; [ed.] Edensor School, Longton Stoke-on-Trent Staffs University O.U.; [occ.] Civil Servant;

[memb.] Lancashire County Rugby Union-Life Member Lancashire C.C.C., Longton RUFC, Civil Service Club; [oth. writ.] Several poems published in the Middle Way and other magazines; [pers.] My poetry is the result of a half a life times interest in Buddhism (particular zen) and the belief that all creation is an integrated whole. We are all members one of another.; [a.] London, London, UK

GUBBINS, MAURICE REGINALD
[b.] 24 November 1919, Boscombe; [p.] Ethel and Reginald Gubbins; [m.] Dorothy, 10 August 1951; [ch.] Juliet and Nicholas; [ed.] Bournemouth Grammar, Bournemouth Municipal College, College of the Rhine Army, Folkestone Training College; [occ.] Retired Head Teacher; [memb.] National Union of Teachers Andover Wine Maker Circle, National Assoc. of Head Teachers Wiltshire Trust for Nature Conservation University of the Third Age; [hon.] 1939-45 Star, Frame Germany Star, Defence Medal, War Medal 1939-45. Territorial Medal, Market Garden Veterans Assoc. Medal; [oth. writ.] Articles for local magazine. Various poems and short stories (unpublished).; [pers.] Since my school days, I have been interested in reading a wide variety of poems. My own poems have been composed after strong emotional experiences.; [a.] Wroughton, Wiltshire, UK

GUILBERT, LUCIE
[pen.] Theodora Goatbox!; [b.] 21 November 1975, Guernsey; [p.] Peter and Valerie Guilbert; [ed.] Ladies College, Guernsey, York University; [occ.] Student (Archaeology); [memb.] Queen Fan Club, Archaeology Society, English, Heritage; [hon.] Mallett Trophy for Poetry (under II) x 2, Prix D'Honneur for Poetry x 3 (2 - poetry, 1 prose), School English Prize x 2, music prize x 1, 1st prize Local Library Comp.; [oth. writ.] One poem published in 'Diapers and Dimples' by Arrival Press. Many poems printed in school magazines!; [pers.] My poetry is inspired by extreme emotions, deep thoughts, and by great love, for nature, children (especially special needs), the down trodden, animals, and above all, God.; [a.] Guernsey, Channel Isles, UK

GWILLIAM, JEAN K.
[b.] 13 April 1916, Calcutta; [p.] Mr. and Mrs. Alexander Shanks; [m.] Frank Gwilliam, 15 August 1938; [ch.] One boy and One girl; [ed.] Educated in Scotland Dumbartow Academy Scotland; [occ.] Retired; [hon.] For Art and Music; [pers.] I have had great satisfaction in self expression through the helpful consequences of "outside influence"; [a.] Neston, South Wirral, UK

GWYNN, MRS. P. M.
[pen.] Peggy Gwynn; [b.] 27 February 1923, Madras, India; [p.] Andrew Satur, Hilda Satur; [m.] J. P. L. Gwynn, 27 June 1959; [ch.] John J. L. Gwynn, Robert C. P. Gwynn; [ed.] In Madras - India; [occ.] Housewife from the day I married; [memb.] (a) The National Trust, (b) Member of St. Edmund's Roman Catholic Church Chorale of Liturgical Sacred Music down the ages, (c) Member of the Churchill Library - Bromley, South, Kent; [oth. writ.] Other poems not published yet. 3 articles published in the Roman Catholic Booklets ("Jesus Caritas"), entitled (a) "Living In England," after 21 yrs. permanent stay in the U.K. comparing it with the totally different lifestyle I had in India!, (b) "An Indian Grandmother" vis-a-vis community living in India, (c) "What We Sow We Reap" vis-a-vis with a query of should children

be brought into this world?!; [pers.] To me, poetry becomes the easiest and best medium for expressing what I feel deeply. I keep my poems concise, still feeling capable that my messages to the world can be grasped clearly. My best poems are centred around the redeemer of the world!; [a.] Bromley, Kent, UK

HAFFNER, MR. MARK
[pen.] Mark; [b.] 8 January 1973, Haddington, Scotland; [p.] Lynn Haffner, Jon Haffner; [ed.] Earl Shilton Community College; [occ.] Research and Development; [oth. writ.] 60 other poems yet to be recognized.; [pers.] Over the last year and a half, I have been writing poems which reflect different events in my life being from the heart and from the mind.; [a.] Hinckley, Leicestershire, UK

HAFIZ, NADIA
[b.] 10 October 1976, Hackney; [ed.] Middlesex University; [occ.] Student; [pers.] People often find that poems reflect their inner feelings and experiences. Therefore I see poetry as a window to peoples thoughts and a comfort to those who read them.; [a.] Walthamstow, London, UK

HAGUE, MARY ELIZABETH
[b.] 31 December 1914, Barrowford; [p.] Deceased; [m.] Deceased, 23 December 1939; [ch.] One; [ed.] C of England; [occ.] Housewife; [oth. writ.] For family and friends and other subjects; [a.] Elsecar, Yorkshire, UK

HALDANE, ANNE
[b.] 29 March 1923, Bonnyrigg; [p.] Robert and Annie Haldane; [ed.] Temple School Scotland; [occ.] Retired; [memb.] Member of Writers Club Musselburgh; [oth. writ.] Parting The Seas, published by Triumph House, Childhood Memories published by Arrival Press. A Passage in Time published by the International Society of Poets. Poets of 1996. Triumph House. Library Anthology of East Lothian Poets 1996.; [pers.] Yet to be published. I am very grateful to still be able to compose poetry. Having had a stroke in January 1991. I have written poetry since I was four years old. But did not publish until 1991 submitted several to church magazine Aberlady.; [a.] Musselburgh, East Lothian, UK

HALE, KATHLEEN
[b.] 12 March 1923, Wallasey; [p.] William Pell, Eveline Alice Pell; [m.] Benjamin Hale, 20 March 1965; [ch.] Anthony Hesketh Barber; [occ.] Housewife; [memb.] University of the Third Age; [oth. writ.] Poetry allows me to think deeply, and I hope my contribution will give your readers the same satisfaction and enjoyment which I receive.; [a.] Halifax, West Yorkshire, UK

HALL, EDWARD
[pen.] Edann; [b.] 13 May 1937, Rossendale; [p.] Joseph Hall, Jennie Hall; [m.] Kathleen Ann Clews, 7 September 1957; [ch.] Kevin Beuce Stuart, Sandra Denise, Karen Jacqueline; [ed.] Bacup and Rawtenstall Grammar; [occ.] Retired (Ex RAF); [memb.] Pendle forest Association Royal Air Forces Association; [oth. writ.] Various items on Scottish history and anglo-saxon history, none published as yet.; [pers.] I write for pleasure and like to extol the virtues of my native Lancashire.; [a.] Rossendale, Lancashire, UK

HALL, JEANNINE
[b.] Lancaster; [p.] Margaret and Percival Anderson; [m.] George Hall; [pers.] Poem taken from a selection entitled "The Flowers of Heaven" in cherished memory of my beloved daughter Sheralyn and for all who suffer the "Seeming Loss" of a loved one particularly a child.; [a.] Blackpool, Lancashire, UK

HALL, OLIVER
[pen.] Oliver Hall; [b.] 26 December 1980, Nottingham; [p.] Elizabeth Williams, Nicolas Hall; [ed.] Berry Hill Primary School, Mansfield Bracken Lane Primary School, Retford King Edward VI Secondary School, Retford; [occ.] Student; [memb.] Newstead Abbey Cricket Club; [oth. writ.] Two pieces sent to Whsmith competition, no confirmation of any results yet.; [a.] Retford, Notts, UK

HALL, SARAH LOUISE
[pen.] Sarah Louise Hall; [b.] 15 February 1962, Norwich; [p.] Shelagh and Eric Hall; [ed.] Eaton City of Norwich School; [occ.] Video Shop Proprietor; [memb.] Salhouse Equestrian Centre; [hon.] Dancing - Bronze, Silver - Gold - Gold Star Medals; [oth. writ.] I have written several poems but have not sent any off before.; [pers.] I write from my heart.; [a.] Norwich, Norfolk, UK

HALLAM, JANET
[b.] 9 November 1945, Derby; [p.] Leonard and Marion West; [m.] David Hallam, 5 June 1965; [ch.] Anita 29, Adrian 26; [ed.] Secondary Modern and further Secretarial, Public Administration (ONC) at Bristol and Derby F.E. Colleges; [occ.] Secretary; [pers.] My poem reflects my true feelings after experiencing a very serious road accident. I would be very happy to think that it might just make people stop and think, in this very fast and competitive world, before speeding off by car to their next urgent destination!; [a.] Belper, Derbyshire, UK

HALLETT, MARY
[pen.] Mary Woodhams; [b.] 6 January 1911, Cotchford Farm House; [p.] Sophia Woodhams, Henry Woodhams; [m.] Onessemus Knight - 12 December 1935, Leslie Hallett - 1 June 1948; [ch.] Elizabeth and Derrick, Pauline; [ed.] Small Village School C of E. Hartfield; [memb.] Member of Brian Jones fan club He was of Rolling Stones and He drowned at Cotchford farm, He was a very kind young man I knew him very well a very good friend; [oth. writ.] "Our World" entered into outposts poetry competition 1981 printed in A Garland of Poetry.; [pers.] One of my favorite poets is Patience Strong.; [a.] Hartfield, East Sussex, UK

HALLIDAY, SHEILA
[b.] 5 March 1925, Maltby; [p.] Annie and Bernard Heafield; [m.] Alexander Charles Halliday, 26 December 1946; [ch.] Jennifer and Paul Halliday; [ed.] Comprehensive School; [occ.] House wife; [a.] Maltby, South Yorkshire, UK

HAMMERSLEY, BRENDA
[b.] 16 December 1940, Bedford; [p.] Alfred Rollo, Ivy Rollo; [m.] Brian Hammersley, 21 April 1962; [ch.] Tracy; [ed.] Cuckoo Hall County Secondary School. Hertford Regional College; [occ.] Optician's Receptionist.; [pers.] I find writing poetry therapeutic, and it is an enjoyable way to express my feelings.; [a.] Cheshut, Hertfordshire, UK

HANY, DR. S.
[pen.] Hany; [b.] 4 May 1946, Ghana; [p.] Both Lebanese; [m.] Jean Ritson, 26 November 1981; [ed.] Brummana (Society of Friends) High School, Lebanon, Medical School, Cairo University, Egypt; [occ.] Pediatrician at Fairfield Hospital, Bury. My father won the BBC's first prize in 1948 for the Arabic Speaking Poets residing outside the Arab world. Naysam (Soul of the Breeze), Nima (Nature's Prosperity), Ramaya (Sound of Falling Rain). Worked as a 'Desert Doctor' for 2 years in Saudi Arabia in the early 70's. Came to U.K. in '76 for 4 years then back to Mount Lebanon for 7 years during the Civil War. Now in the U.K. since 1987.; [pers.] "Influenced by Gibran and Keats."; [a.] Milnrow, Rochdale, Lancashire, UK

HAQ, SAMARAH
[b.] 30 March 1980, Bristol, England; [p.] Ibrar Ul Haq, Salma Haq; [ed.] Boroughnuir High School currently in 5th year doing 4 highers; [oth. writ.] Wrote a poem for the parents of the children who died in Dunblane. Poem was read out at radio 4.; [pers.] I have only just recently started writing my poems. Poetry is how I express my feelings. I was encouraged by my family and friends to keep on writing poems, I would like to thank them all.; [a.] Edinburgh, Scotland

HARCOURT, GEORGE
[pen.] George Harcourt; [b.] 15 August 1909, Evesham; [p.] George Harcourt and Elisabeth Andrews; [m.] Muriel Ottoway, 12 August 1959; [ed.] None since leaving a council school in 1924/25; [occ.] Retired; [oth. writ.] Various poems published by forward press of Peterborough. Also poems published in Parish Magazine of all Saints Church - Evesham.; [pers.] I have to adult that I write poetry because I enjoy doing so may I say that I just write as I think and feel. To give pleasure (I hope) but never in an attempt to please any particular person or group.; [a.] Evesham, Worcs, UK

HARDWICK, KATHERINE
[b.] 10 July 1978, Bedford; [p.] Ellen Hardwick, Richard Hardwick; [ed.] Wootton Upper School, (Due to start in Sept.) University of Warwick - BA in English and American Literature; [occ.] Student; [memb.] Duke of Edinburgh, Award Scheme; [a.] Bedford, Bedfordshire, UK

HARFORTH, OSWALD STUART
[pen.] Oswald S. Harforth; [b.] 28 April 1941, Middlesborough; [p.] John Ausbert Harforth, Dorothy Margaret; [ed.] Ampleforth College a large public school and Benedictine Abbey, I was a day student; [occ.] A variety of occupations but unemployed at present; [hon.] 5 GCE 'O' level subjects plus prize for top of the upper fifth in General Science; [oth. writ.] I read and write quite a lot of stories and poetry etc and I read books and many subjects but this is the first poem I have sent for review and I am pleased it has been received for publication it is the first poem or story of mine published thank you; [pers.] Do ones best for others and oneself and have love, comforts and pleasures and give thanks. I also was influenced by the poets of the past and the peaceful romantic poetry of Wordsworth my real first name is Stuart which I am known by so I would like Stuart or S. included in my pen name; [a.] Helmsley, Yorkshire North, UK

HARMONY, ANASTASIA-LEE
[b.] 12 May 1974, Chertsey, Surrey; [oth. writ.] My poem Alone in Pain!; [pers.] I want to dedicate this poem to survivors of rape and abuse. Al my

inspiration comes from my own life, my poetry is about things I've had to deal with myself, expressed in a very direct way that other people can share.; [a.] Milton Keynes, Buckinghamshire, UK

HAROLD, JOHN-PAUL PHILIP
[b.] 2 December 1976, North Shields; [p.] Kim and Paul Harold; [ed.] Beckfoot Grammar Bingley; [occ.] Student (eventually going to Aberystwyth); [oth. writ.] Some failed scripts and school mag. contributions aside, I wrote another 'poem' called "The Original Design". I mainly composed songs.; [pers.] Aleister Crowley said it all "Every man and woman is a star". I aim to be honest about myself and so what I write is often sombre, but I don't think its depressing, I simply expect failure as much as I do joy.; [a.] Shipley, West Yorkshire, UK

HARRIS, JANET
[b.] 10 September 1978, Nottingham; [p.] Geoff Harris, Diane Harris; [ed.] The Gedling School High Pavement Sixth Form College; [occ.] Student, Healthcare Sales Assistant; [hon.] Grade 3, 4 and 5 in flute; [pers.] Just do it. You only regret it if you don't.; [a.] Mapperley, Nottingham, UK

HARRIS, PATRICIA F.
[pen.] Patricia F. Arnett; [b.] 1 October 1923, West Bromwich; [p.] George and Florence Arnett; [m.] Harold Harris (Deceased 1982), 16 May 1955; [ed.] Board of Educ. Drawing and Painting - N.D.D., Diploma of Fine Art, Univ. of Lond Slade School D.F.A.; [occ.] Artist, Retired Art Tutor period Scenic Artist Stratford; [hon.] NIDD, DFA 1st prized design and for drawing slade school, 1st prize dudley spring exhibitions Richardson Scholarship Univ. murals for public buildings exhibitions in several galleries wolvenhampton 1992 who bought a painting for then collection; [oth. writ.] Self published a collection, of early poems 'Vision and Reality' have considerable number of other poems in process of illust collecting into booklets some poems in church magazine.; [pers.] In my poems I express thoughts not possible to express in my paintings concerns are with mature, ecology, philosophical and religious.; [a.] Tipton, Staffs, W. Mids, UK

HARRIS, RALPH LESLIE
[pen.] Ralph L. Harris; [b.] 26 January 1936, London; [p.] Mark Harris, Annie Harris; [ed.] Central Foundation Sch. of London Matriculation, open University; [occ.] Company Director; [memb.] Member of Institute of Patentees and Inventors; [hon.] 3 U.K. Patents and 2 U.S. Patents, several achievement awards as financial consultant.; [oth. writ.] Other poetry published in local press. Instruction manual for playing snooker.; [pers.] I prefer light-hearted poetry, but do also write about more serious world events. I am an avid participant in crosswords and Mensa puzzles and bridge problems.; [a.] Luton, Bedfordshire, UK

HARRISON, LINDY
[pen.] Lin Harrison; [b.] 1 October 1944, Evesham; [ed.] Hereford Teacher Training College; [occ.] Postal Officer; [hon.] Teacher Training Certificate; [oth. writ.] Poem - Waiting Golden Eagle Press; [pers.] Nowness is the only now for in this I am.; [a.] Birmingham, West Midlands, UK

HARRISON, LORRAINE
[pen.] Clara George; [b.] 20 February 1958, Warrington; [p.] Doreen and Terry Albinson; [m.] Charles Samuel Harrison, 14 January 1978; [ch.] Nicola, Charles and Daniel; [ed.] English Martyrs

Roman Catholic Secondary School, Warrington Technical College, Myerscough College; [occ.] Farmers Wife, Mother, Secretary; [oth. writ.] A number of poems, approximately 35, my aim being to have enough to compile a book. Some written for other people, some written for reading in church.; [pers.] Influenced by my own personal feelings and sentiments, I get great relief in writing my feelings down in poetry, some silly, some from my heart, but always with sincerity.; [a.] West Houghton, Bolton, UK

HARTLAND, JOAN
[b.] 9 September 1931, Sunderland; [p.] Margaret and Robert Mackel; [m.] John William Hartland, 24 September 1977; [ed.] Secondary School; [occ.] Retired; [memb.] HF-CHA Hiking Club RSPB, International Fund for Animal Welfare, Ramblers Association; [oth. writ.] Poem - Who knows My Shangri-La, So Lonely, The Me The World See, Abarmaids Reverie, Anguish Seasons Of My Life, Divorce, The World Today.; [pers.] I found writing my poems helped me find some peace through my darkest days and I have I hope become a help to others going through their dark days.; [a.] Doncaster, S. Yorkshire, UK

HARTSHORN, BARBARA
[b.] 18 January 1938, Holsworthy; [p.] Susan and Walter Symons; [m.] Geoffrey Hartshorn, 24 June 1956; [ch.] Three; [ed.] Holsworthy; [occ.] Secondary Modern School, Holsworthy North Devon 1949-1953; [memb.] Housewife

HARVEY, JACKIE
[b.] 6 June 1945, Northing; [m.] Terence Harvey, 23 October 1965; [ch.] Steven Mark Harvey; [occ.] Personal Assistant to Admiralty Lawyer in Brighton; [oth. writ.] Several short humorous articles for Joanna Hollis' "Fact and Fiction" series on BBC Radio Brighton (a few years ago); [pers.] My inspiration comes from feelings, observations and emotions which touch my heart.; [a.] Sompting, West Sussex, UK

HARVEY, KATE
[b.] 16 June 1984, Bristol; [p.] Lesley Harvey, David Harvey; [ed.] St. Johns Primary School, Clevedon. Clifton High School; [occ.] Year 7 pupil at Clifton High School; [memb.] W.E.S.T. Elite Swimming Team, Weston-super-Mare Swimming Club; [hon.] Examination Scholarship (CHS) 10 Trophies, 2 Plaques, 40 + Medals (24 Gold) for swimming; [oth. writ.] Many poems and a few short stories; [pers.] I hope to produce poems which many people will enjoy reading and that will encourage them to do the same!; [a.] Clevedon, North Somerset, UK

HARVEY, VAL
[pen.] Val Harvey; [b.] 18 March 1945, Amersham; [p.] William and Florence Podbury; [m.] Brian Harvey, 1 July 1967; [ch.] Belinda Louise; [ed.] Dr. Challoners, Grammar School, Amersham, Bucks; [occ.] Residential Social Worker; [oth. writ.] "The Mists Of Time", poem published in "Between A Laugh And A Tear", "Pennies From Heaven", a short story published in a local paper.; [pers.] I am a deep thinker and I am fascinated by stories of the unexplained; [a.] Chesham, Bucks, UK

HASAN, JILL
[b.] 25 August 1946, Quinton, Birmingham; [p.] Amelia and Eric Parry; [m.] Ahmet Hasan, 17 August 1968; [ch.] 3 grown up sons; [ed.] Oldbury Grammar School, Oastler College, Huddersfield;

[occ.] Primary School Teacher; [oth. writ.] Poems, short stories, book reviews for "Scottish Field"; [pers.] My poems are written for family and friends anniversaries, birthdays, etc. The short stories are of a supernatural nature, with a twist in the tail.; [a.] Oldbury, West Midlands, UK

HASSALL, GORDON
[pen.] Miles Platting; [b.] 5 May 1938, Manchester; [p.] John Hassall, Edith Hassall; [m.] Glynis Hassall, 29 June 1996; [ed.] Sec. Mod.; [occ.] Ret'd. (Early); [memb.] Radio Society of Great Britain; [pers.] A semi literate working class plonker with delusions of gran-deur.; [a.] Manchester, Lancs, UK

HAWKINS, SHEILA
[b.] 13 Sept. 1934, Newcastle-on-Tyne; [p.] Frances and George Gray; [m.] Douglas Hawkins, 25 June 1955; [ch.] Stephen and Nicola; [ed.] Chisnick Polytechnic; [occ.] Ceramic Artist; [oth. writ.] Several poems published in anthologies. Full length novel awaiting publication.; [pers.] Christmas poems, written exclusively for family and friends, have become an annual tradition.; [a.] Bledlon Ridge, High Nycombe, Buckinghamshire, UK

HAWORTH, STUART
[pen.] Stuart Haworth; [b.] 28 August 1973, Blackburn; [p.] Eric and Bessie Haworth; [pers.] Its a nice thought to think that someone out there appreciate my work its just a shame I could not send more work in?; [a.] Blackburn, Lancashire, UK

HAYES, SIMON JAMES
[pen.] Simon James Hayes; [b.] 5 March 1970, Coventry; [p.] Simon and Kathleen; [ed.] Cardinal Wiseman Boys School, The Butts College of Further, ED; [hon.] English Literature; [pers.] Communication makes people special and different from other creatures, poetry in my opinion is the highest and most beautiful form of communication.; [a.] Coventry, Warwickshire, UK

HAYWARD-BROWNE, MRS. MARY
[b.] 29 April 1903, Hertfordshire; [p.] Walter Errington, Grace Errington; [m.] Benjamin Hayward-Browne, 30 April 1935; [ed.] Governess! Finishing School-Switzerland; [memb.] NADFAS (Lecture Soc), First Aid Nursing Yeomanry F.A.N.Y. drove all thro' 2nd world war, drove General Commanding S. Area famous polish general also General Sykorskie! Also ambulances etc.; [hon.] Medals for War Service; [oth. writ.] Poems and articles for local magazines; [pers.] I write poems mostly about the beauty of nature - also some comic ones to amuse my friends. I am greatly influenced by beauty in all arts. Particularly pictures, music etc.; [a.] Nr Exeter, Devon

HAZEL, YVONNE PATRICIA
[b.] 16 October 1949, Barbados; [m.] 31 July 1971; [ch.] Sonia Lynette and Joella; [ed.] Modern High School Barbados; [occ.] Ex. College Lect. Ret. Midwife; [memb.] WR vs Stroke Ass. Ousevalley Headway Progress Ass.; [oth. writ.] Local Events, Local Magazines; [pers.] Influenced by reflection: Inner Therapy Spiritual and Philosophical: The beauty of life in the midst of ill health.; [a.] Bedford, Beds, UK

HEARN, ANDREW
[b.] August 28, 1969, Manchester; [p.] Al Hearn, Sandra Hearn; [m.] Elaine Savides; [ch.] Georgina Alice; [ed.] Warbreck High School Blackpool and

Fylde College Of Higher Education; [occ.] Retail Sales; [memb.] Poulton Chess Club; [oth. writ.] Several poems published in Poetry Magazines and Anthologies; [pers.] My poems tend to drift towards the darker side of life; [a.] Blackpool, Lancashire, UK

HEAYN, REBECCA
[pen.] Rebecca Heayn; [b.] 3 July 1981, Truro; [p.] Roger Heayn, RoseAlynde Heayn; [ed.] Archbishop Benson Primary, Penair School; [occ.] Still attending school; [memb.] Truro Cricket Club; [hon.] School prizes for English, religious education, humanities, languages, religious education, geography; [oth. writ.] A poem published in a regional anthology, articles for local newspaper; [pers.] I would like to thank the English teachers at Penair School for all their help and encouragement with my poetry writing.; [a.] Truro, Cornwall, UK

HEEL, MAVIS
[b.] 10 May 1925, Leeds; [p.] William and Nellie Beanland; [m.] Arthur Joseph Heel, 24 March 1945; [ch.] Lyndon, Judith, David Heel; [ed.] Leeds Commercial College Shorthand, Typing, English, book keeping; [occ.] Retired; [oth. writ.] I have written a romantic novel published by the pentland press in 1993 titled "The Pendant"; [pers.] I was born in leeds Yorkshire and lived with my husband for a while in India. I now live in solihull with my two docs. The beautiful flowing words of poetry has always meant so much to me.; [a.] Solihull, West Midlands, UK

HEMMINGS, MARGARET
[b.] 10 August 1944, London; [p.] Fred and Mabel Dymond; [m.] John Hemmings, 2 July 1966; [ch.] 2 Adult; [ed.] Modern Arts Degree (Honours) English Kingston University; [occ.] Teacher of Adults; [hon.] Honours English Degree City and Guilds 730 Teaching Adults; [oth. writ.] Short Story published in 'Best' Magazine.; [pers.] My poems help expel my emotions and are therefore beneficial to me and, I hope, readers of them.; [a.] Leatherhead, Surrey, UK

HENDERSON, COLIN
[b.] 26 October 1962, Edinburgh; [p.] Sheila and Jack Henderson; [m.] Irene Henderson, 27 June 1987; [ch.] Daniel, Kayleigh and Ross; [ed.] Forrester High School Edinburgh; [occ.] Ministry of Defence Dog Handler; [oth. writ.] Awaiting publication of my brother and a gift of life.; [pers.] Live and let live, forget and forgive but always keep a record its nice to look back on your thoughts in verse a life so chequered.; [a.] South Queensferry, West Lothian, UK

HENKEL, JACK
[b.] 22 May 1919, Smethwick, Birmingham; [p.] Robert and Winifred Henkel; [m.] Shirley, 26 February 1954; [ch.] Michael, Ann, Christine, Stephen; [ed.] Retired; [a.] Huddersfield, Yorkshire, UK

HENRY, BRIAN JAMES
[b.] 17 May 1966, Farnworth, Bolton; [ed.] Hayward Grammar School 12-09-77 to July 1982. IQ of 126, Officially tested autumn 1992 by Mensa in Manchester.; [occ.] Security Officer. N. Gatwatch of Swinton, Manchester; [hon.] Guard of the month May '91 with a previous security company two "good work" commendations in 1992 from the same company; [oth. writ.] None previously completely new to poetry and literature; [pers.] I'd like

others to share my feelings and thoughts through studying and reading my work, poetry is inspired by one's deepest emotional response, to a person place, or whatever inspires.; [a.] Bolton, Lancashire, UK

HEYWARD, ERIC
[b.] 18 October 1946, Exeter; [p.] Colin Heyward, Brenda Heyward; [m.] Lynne Heyward; [ch.] Rhett William, Kelly Ann; [ed.] Toddington Comp. Luton College; [occ.] Salesman; [pers.] I like poems and songs that tell a story or give a message, a wide range of topics. Which evoke strong thoughts or feelings, preferably both.; [a.] Plymouth, Devon, UK

HICKS, THOMAS S.
[pen.] Thomas S. Hicks, Tom Hicks; [b.] 7 January 1923, Mevagissey, Cornwall; [p.] Samuel Hicks, Mary Hicks (Nee Hunkind); [m.] Mona Hicks (Nee Phillips died 30 August 1993), 26 June 1944; [ch.] Barbara S. Hicks, Margaret A. Gary, Rosemary Hunsperger, Philip John Hicks; [ed.] Mevagissey Elementary School, St. Austell County Secondary School; [occ.] Retired Civil Servant, Wartime Submarine Officer; [oth. writ.] Poems included in a number of Anthologies, in church magazine and book of 80 poems published for Church Centenary; [pers.] I write for enjoyment and to express my feelings and views hoping they may strike a helpful chord with readers.; [a.] Preston, Lancashire, UK

HILL, C. A.
[b.] 10 August 1947, S Wales; [p.] Raymond Day, Olwen Day; [m.] Gregory Hill, 16 March 1968; [ch.] Three; [ed.] B.A. (Open) Sociology; [occ.] School Librarian; [memb.] Amnesty International; [pers.] I enjoy fitness training and am an animals lover.; [a.] Garway, Herefordshire, UK

HILL, RICHARD
[pen.] John Neville Walsh; [b.] November 2, 1955, Bangor, North Wales; [p.] Frederick Hill, Dorothy Hill; [partner] Simon Hawthorn; [ed.] Llanidloes High School; [hon.] Lord Brock Memorial Trust Historical Essay Prize (Special trustees of Guy's hospital); [oth. writ.] Articles of local history; [pers.] "But oh, beamish nephew, beware of the day, If your Snark be a Boojum! For then, you will softly and suddenly vanish away, and never be met with again!" (Lewis Carroll - The Hunting of the Snark).; [a.] Slough, Berks

HILL-LEWIS, JOAN
[b.] 2 October 1918, Rochdale; [p.] John and Elizabeth Hill; [m.] James Hill-Lewis, 24 August 1972; [occ.] Housewife; [memb.] Civil Service Club, London. Civil Service Retirement. Fellowship Club. Manchester Branch. Rochdale Cricket and Squash Club; [pers.] Born in Rochdale, Lancs. Where I lived until recently moving to the out skirts, Whitworth. I would like to dedicate my poem to my husband and niece, Nadia Elizabeth Hill, Solihull.; [a.] Whitworth, Lancashire, UK

HILLAN, MRS. JOAN
[b.] 4 July 1939, Carlisle; [p.] James and Annie Jackson; [m.] Jack Hillan, 9 January 1963; [ch.] Brian, Gordon, Lynn and Martin; [ed.] Robert Ferguson Secondary School; [occ.] Housewife, Mother, Gran; [memb.] Bonkle Women Guild Secretary; [oth. writ.] One prayer, printed in Bonkle Church of Scotland Magazine; [a.] Wishaw, Lanarkshire, UK

HIRJI, NAZNIN
[b.] Tanzania; [m.] Nazir; [ch.] Farhan, Amar; [occ.] Researcher Editing; [memb.] CG Jung Analytical Psychology Club London, Calamus Foundation; [oth. writ.] Articles, Research Papers, Poems; [pers.] The most important thing in life is to be aware of each moment, for each moment is dynamic, alive with movement, shifting all the time and yet, within the movement, there is utter stillness, utter calm. Every moment, every day.; [a.] Millhill, London, UK

HITCHMAN, DOROTHY FREDERICK
[pen.] Dorothy Frederick Hitchman; [b.] 17 April 1925, South Shields; [p.] Margaret and Frederick Swann; [m.] Granville Hitchman (Deceased), 20 December 1951; [ch.] Paul, Mark, Timothy, Andrew; [ed.] South Shields High School for Girls 1936-1943 Sunderland Teacher Training College 1943-1945; [occ.] Retired Teacher in England and in Bermuda; [memb.] Former member and President Tancersley W.I. member N.F.U. Countryside; [hon.] Qualifications School Cert. higher School Cert. Board Education Teaching Cert.; [oth. writ.] Numerous poems published in anthologies of contemporary verse, local newspapers and church magazines.; [pers.] I am a nature lover and conservationist.; [a.] Hoyland, South Yorkshire, UK

HOARE, ROD
[b.] 11 June 1945, Luton; [p.] Donald Hoare and Georgetta Hoare; [m.] Judith Hoare, 5 March 1966; [ch.] Tanya Kim and Darran Mark; [ed.] Dunstable Grammar School, Luton College of Further Education; [occ.] Head Gardener Nettleden Lodge; [memb.] Professional Gardeners Guild Leighton-Linslade Royal Naval Association. Beds and Herts Submarine Old Comrades Association British Country Music Association; [hon.] City Guilds Electronics, City Guilds Gardening, Long Service and Good Conduct Medal Royal Navy.; [oth. writ.] Articles and poems published in local royal naval association news letters; [pers.] Ideas for my poems tend to come from reflective moods when working in the garden, or from incidents that happen to friends, the later tends to be my main influence; [a.] Leighton Buzzard, Bedfordshire, UK

HOBLEY, LAURIE
[b.] Leamington Spa; [p.] John and Mildred Parkes; [ch.] Tomi Gardner and Nicholas Hobley; [ed.] Priory High School for Girls, Teacher Training Unit; [memb.] National Trust R.S.P.B.; [hon.] RSA's in English and English Literature; [pers.] 'Can you exist?' is a poem straight from the heart. I have written at various periods throughout my life from quite a young age, stories and poems, but never tried to publish.; [a.] Coventry, Warwickshire, UK

HODDER, RUTH
[pen.] Ruth Hodder; [b.] 1 April 1949; [m.] Malcolm Hodder, 21 December 1968; [ch.] David, Paula; [a.] Berkshire, UK

HODGE, ROSEMARIE EVANS
[b.] 11 November 1935, Leeds, Yorks; [p.] Iris and Leo Evans; [m.] Derrick Hodge (Married 23 yrs.), Divorced 1977; [ch.] Timothy Ed, Shaftebury; [ed.] 1st Crunpsall Lane County Primary School Manchester, 2nd Norcliffe Private School Hr Broughton Salford; [occ.] Housewife; [memb.] Serve on four management committees. Multiple Sclerosis Society, Leonard Cheshire Foun-

dations; [hon.] Bronze Medal, Elocution Speech and Drama, was accepted at Birmingham Theatre School 1952 unable to go recommended for R.A.D.A.; [oth. writ.] Several poems published in magazine, articles in various monthly magazines and weekly papers edited magazine for 8 yrs.!; [pers.] US since 1966 - was service wife for 20 years. Travelled extensively 'I try to love the unlovable and forgive the transgressor'.; [a.] Loughborough, Leicestershire, UK

HODGKINS, ERNEST GEOFFREY
[b.] 25 November 1916, Woolwhich; [m.] Edith Hodgkins; [occ.] Retired; [memb.] Rating member of Labour Party; [hon.] France, Germany, War Medals; [oth. writ.] Strictly verse; [pers.] To be patient and thoughtful, brings peace of mind.; [a.] Nuneaton, Warks, UK

HOFFIN, KEVIN PETER
[b.] 28 September 1987, Stoke-on-Trent; [p.] Linda and George Hoffin; [ed.] Howitt House School Hanbury, Nr. Burton-on-Trent, Staffs; [memb.] Joanna Bivens School of Speech and Drama; [hon.] Elizabeth Haynes Trophy for original poem under 12 years at Burton Music and Drama Festival, 1996; [a.] Burton-on-Trent, Staffs, UK

HOFFMAN, PAUL
[b.] 14 September 1960, Leigh, Lancs; [p.] Herbert Hoffman and Bessie Hoffman; [m.] Carole Lesley Hoffman, 27 September 1986; [ch.] Lauren Hoffman; [ed.] Fred Longworth County Secondary Tyldesley MC/R; [occ.] Long Distance Lorry Driver; [oth. writ.] Several poems published relating to trucking and life in the North.; [pers.] I try to write poetry with a trucking them and it's effect on my family life, often with a humorous or poignant message.; [a.] Wigan, Lancashire, UK

HOGARTH, STEVEN
[b.] 26 July 1975, North Sheilds; [p.] William and Ann Hogarth; [ed.] Astley High School, Newcastle School of Performing Arts; [occ.] Actor, Writer; [memb.] Actors Center NE, Newcastle United Football Club.; [oth. writ.] Ether, Seashell, Fifty/ Fifty; [pers.] I'm kicking like a Kung-Fu Shakespeare.; [a.] Newcastle upon Tyne, UK

HOLMES, MRS. MYRTLE E.
[pen.] Myrtle Holmes; [b.] 30 January 1927, Peatling Magna; [p.] Francis Henry and Cicely Mary Spokes; [m.] Charles Raymond Holmes, 2 June 1955; [ed.] Lutterworth Grammar School; [occ.] Housewife; [oth. writ.] A poem in "A Passage In Time", 2 poems in Anthologies for poetry now; [pers.] I just write about birds and animals, in fact what I see when I look out of the window.; [a.] Oadby, Leicester, UK

HOOD, MICHAEL
[b.] 23 June 1943, Stoke-on-Trent; [p.] Enoch Hood, Violet Hood; [ch.] Andrew Michael Hood, Robert Hood; [ed.] Stanfields Technical College; [occ.] Retired; [oth. writ.] Private Commissions for Birthdays, Anniversaries or Expressions of Love and Remembrance; [pers.] Introduced to poetry by my late grandfather, I retreat to poetry as a personal expression of beliefs, emotions and the impact that life sometimes has on us all.; [a.] Stoke-on-Trent, Staffs, UK

HOOPER, MRS. HAZEL JUNE
[pen.] Avalene Lyle; [b.] 8 June 1928, Newton, Abbot; [m.] 26 July 1958; [ch.] One daughter;

[occ.] Retired; [oth. writ.] Poetry Reflections Of Life Book 1, Reflections Of Life Book 2, Poppies Of The Field, A Time For Dreams; [pers.] To take what life has to give and make the most of it.; [a.] Bournemouth, Dorset, UK

HOPE, CHRISTINA
[b.] 18 December 1946, Cheshire; [p.] Edna and Reginald Poole; [m.] Stephen, 22 July 1967; [ch.] Matthew and Michael; [ed.] Secondary Modern left at 16; [occ.] Mother and wife; [oth. writ.] None published but many kept personally; [pers.] Drawing on experience of life and its many trials, I find relief in expressing my thoughts as a poem.; [a.] Nantwich, Cheshire, UK

HOPKINS, GARETH
[b.] 16 April 1967, Neath; [p.] Roy Hopkins, Maureen Hopkins; [ed.] Cefn Saesan Comprehensive School, Neath College, Aberystwyth University, Cardiff University; [occ.] Probation Officer; [memb.] Cameo Club; [oth. writ.] The Estuary, Christmas With Grandmother, Baggage, Wild Swans At Home, Tough Guys Don't Dance. - Poems.; [pers.] Look in the mirror every now and then. See things as they really are.; [a.] Cardiff, S Galmorgan Wales, UK

HOPKINS, IAN RUSSELL
[pen.] Ian Russell; [b.] 1 November 1965, Lancashire; [p.] John Hopkins and Jill Hopkins; [ed.] Deyes High School, Maghull, Liverpool; [occ.] Foreman Bricklayer; [oth. writ.] Published in 17 difference Anthologies, published are Poetry Now, Anchor Books, Arrival Press; [pers.] Most people don't read poetry, so let's persuade their ears to bring them to the book shop.; [a.] Maghull, Merseyside, UK

HOPKINS, JOHN W.
[b.] 29 October 1918, West Stanley Co., Durham; [p.] Deceased; [m.] Mrs. Marjorie E. Hopkins, 17 August 1946; [ch.] 1 daughter and 1 grand son and 1 daughter; [occ.] Retired; [memb.] Fellow of the Institute of Business Administration; [hon.] (6 medals for service in H.M. Forces). (Including the T.A. 5th Survey Regiment R.A.), (1939/45); [oth. writ.] Had a book published in 1995. Entitled "The Man Who Gave His Life" (religious verses, prayers and lyrics, 72 pages), (You may have a copy if required two other songs published by the Salvation Army. Others pending.; [pers.] Kindly note that all my work, be it Poetry or music, is done to the glory of God through His Son Jesus Christ, for he is my Savior and guide, throughout life; [a.] Christchurch, Dorset, UK

HORNER, RUTH
[b.] 17 June 1973, Letchworth; [p.] Mr. Peter Nunn and Mrs. Ruth Nunn; [ed.] Comprehensive; [occ.] Student; [memb.] Libraries and Night Clubs; [oth. writ.] Feeling Deep Down, poem is being published with Anchor Publishing Company in their book called My First Love.; [pers.] I write poetry because I do have feelings very deep feelings and I have expressed in poetry that other people can't express my poetry's from the heart not just my mind.; [a.] Letchworth, Hertfordshire, UK

HORNEY, RICHARD
[pen.] Richard Lockley; [b.] 3 January 1965, Home; [p.] John and Auril Horney; [ed.] Manor Farm Comprehensive, Midland Rd Centre, Walsall College of Tech; [occ.] Caretaker, (Midlands Rd

Centre); [memb.] Calderfields Gold Club; [oth. writ.] Self-published a poetry book.; [pers.] My writing has been influenced by public and media, which has allowed myself to meet such high standards while aiming for one's ultimate goal.; [a.] Walsall, West Midlands, UK

HORROCKS, JUDY
[b.] 17 April 1932, Otley, W. Yorks; [p.] Francis Raymond Glover, Janet Hawkins; [ch.] Three daughters, one son; [ed.] Otley Infants, JNRS, Secondary then Commercial Training Bradford and Ikley; [occ.] Retired Civil Servant; [memb.] Health Problems and Rural Isolation, prevent any membership! But do I need them? Very creative, unusual Handsewn Cushions decorate my walls.; [hon.] Civil Service Typing Skills, Audio, etc.; [oth. writ.] Small, booklet of twelve poems published '91. Writing talent sprang to life suddenly.; [pers.] Very much aware of the earth's beauty, sun sea and moon, weather patterns, creature's 'Great and Small'. If my inner soul is pierced then I will write.; [a.] Norwood, North Yorks, UK

HOSANOO, SHAROON
[pen.] Sara Malleka; [b.] 13 July 1973, Scotland; [p.] Adam Hosanoo, Rashida Hosanoo; [ed.] Greenfaulds High School, Loreto Convent Curepipe College; [occ.] Consular/Immigration Assistant for the British High Commission; [memb.] British Council Library (Mauritius), Body Tic Fitness Club; [hon.] Brains Trust Debating Award; [oth. writ.] Some poems published in school magazines, articles on various topics.; [pers.] I feel that poetry is a splendid way to portray one's innermost thoughts. My inspiration comes from the realistic chain of events surrounding us.; [a.] Curepipe, Mauritius

HOSSACK, ELEANOR
[pen.] Eleanor Hossack; [b.] 30 August 1916, South Shields; [p.] George and Margaret Ternent; [m.] Harry Hossack, 29 August 1942; [ch.] Two sons John and Richard; [ed.] Westoe Secondary School So Shields St Margarets Buxted Sussex; [occ.] Housewife; [oth. writ.] Several poems published in poetry now; [pers.] I attempt to encapsulate beauty in words; [a.] Harrogate, N. Yorkshire, UK

HOUSLEY, ANDREA
[b.] 11 July 1941, Huddersfield; [p.] Arthur and Evelyn Hamer; [m.] Harry Housley, 18 March 1967; [ch.] Richard, Joanne, Deborah; [ed.] Deighton Secondary, Huddersfield, Yorkshire; [occ.] Housewife; [pers.] I have always marked any significant events in my and my family's life by writing poetry verse seems the most natural way of expressing myself.; [a.] West Kirby, Merseyside, UK

HOUSLEY, MICHAEL
[pen.] Michael Housley; [b.] 15 June 1937, Sheffield; [p.] Mother; [m.] Laurel, 31 August 1994; [ch.] Four; [ed.] State education; [occ.] Art Restorer and Antique Dealer; [memb.] Royal Beauchief Gold Club, L and PAD Association; [hon.] GSM Cyprus medal; [oth. writ.] Morning Haze, You are My Friend, Nightingale, Let's Go to War, Who am I (Is this Me?), Yew Tree Windsor; [pers.] My poems allow me to express freely and uninhibitedly my many frustrations which I find in today's modern day society.; [a.] Sheffield, South Yorkshire, UK

HOUSTON, TURID
[b.] Bergen, Norway; [m.] 1962; [ch.] One daughter, one son; [ed.] University of Bergen, Sorbonne, Paris, University of Edinburgh; [memb.] Anglo-Norse Society, Grieg Society of Great Britain; [hon.] French Language and Literature, Provencal Language and Literature; [oth. writ.] Poems published in Norway and France; [a.] Ashtead, Surrey, UK

HOWARD, ALAN
[pen.] Alan Howard; [b.] 22 November 1936, London; [p.] Harry Cox and Lena Cox; [m.] Mavis Howard, 19 February 1983; [ch.] Mavis, Natasha and Naomi; [ed.] Sloave Grammar, Acton Technical College and Regent Street Polytechnic; [occ.] Security Warder, British Museum.; [memb.] Ranelagh Runnine Club; [hon.] 'Reporter of the Year' for 'Norcros News' (Magazine for group of companies) in 1979; [oth. writ.] A couple of short stories were published in Australia and another two in the 'Norcros News'. At the moment I am just finishing a set of six stories on Australia, narrated by a peripatetic English man. The book totals about 90,000 work; [pers.] Writing for me is what prayer is to a Benedictine monk: an essential part of everyday life. I believe mental creativity. My major literary influences have been: prose, Norman Mailer, and verse, William Wordsworth.; [a.] Richmond, Surrey, UK

HOWARD, DECKLAN
[b.] 4 May 1972, Tralee; [p.] John Pascal Howard, Teresa Howard; [m.] Andrea McAllister; [occ.] Registered General Nurse; [pers.] If I have seen more, it is because I have stood on the shoulders of giants; [a.] Watford, Hertfordshire, UK

HOWARD, HAROLD
[pen.] "Bill", "M.O.S." (Misenlet Old Sod); [b.] July 18, 1910, Liverpool; [p.] Deceased; [m.] Deceased, February 8, 1936; [ch.] Five; [ed.] St. Philips C. Off. Church School, Litherland Liverpool; [occ.] Retired; [memb.] Life Member, Dunkirk Veterans Ass., Bro., R.A.O.B. initiated 1933 Abbassia.; [hon.] Medal Col. from World War II and Palastine 1936.; [oth. writ.] Poems and short stories but none published yet.; [pers.] Poetry is: "Sounds from the soul", not "Cymbals of Interlectualism".; [a.] Bramber, West Sussex, UK

HOWARTH, RONNIE
[pen.] Pipe; [b.] 28 September 1941, Nelson; [m.] Divorced; [ed.] Primet Secondary Modern School Colne; [occ.] Made redundant 1993; [oth. writ.] The Choir Boy, What's In A Name, The Blocked Toilet, Fifty, Just A Snip, Black Gold; [pers.] My poems are about things that happen in life.; [a.] Nelson, Lancs, UK

HOWARTH, WENDY DAWN
[b.] 25 May 1953, Moreton-in-Marsh, Glos; [p.] W. Albert Howarth, Betty Howarth; [ch.] Thomas, Duncan and Charlotte; [ed.] Chipping Campden, Grammar School, Worcester College of Higher Education, Open University; [occ.] English Teacher, Manningtree High School; [hon.] B.A. Hons (English), P.G.C.E. (English, Secondary); [pers.] Inspired by the mystic melancholy of years and the sensuous spirituality of Hopkins. Creativity comes from the soul.; [a.] East Bergholt, Suffolk, UK

HOWE, DESMOND
[b.] 9 February 1933, Canada; [p.] Ana and Leo Howe; [m.] Wife died age 43, 31 May 1953; [ch.]

Five - 3 Boys, 2 Girls; [ed.] Sec-Mod Minehead Somerset, (School Dunce); [occ.] Med-Retired (Angina); [oth. writ.] Other than poems If Hurt, Or Sad, Or In Any Way At Odds With The World, Or In Love, Express My Feelings This Way; [a.] Peterborough, Cambridgeshire, UK

HOWITT, ALEXANDER
[b.] 18 June 1927, Scotland; [m.] Isobel Barber, 28 October 1950; [ch.] 2 boys and 1 girl; [ed.] Drumblade Primary; [occ.] I was an Agricultural Engineer but now retired; [oth. writ.] Quite a number of poems for my own pleasure but never tried to get them published.; [pers.] Interested in the works of that Great Scottish poet Robert Burns also interested in the Doric of Aberdeenshire.

HOYAL, MARY
[pen.] Mary Hoyal; [b.] 1 August 1915, London; [p.] Henry and Ethel Munn; [m.] Charles Hoyal, 3 October 1939; [ch.] Six; [ed.] Girls Private Boarding, School Malvern House Lewisham Park Field and Morns School of Physiotherapy and Waterloo Hospital; [occ.] Retired; [memb.] Chartered Physiotherapist, Licensed Reader C. of E.; [hon.] Deputy Superintendant, Physiotherapist, Ashford Hospital I passed an O.V. Course on the Reformation, Cambridge Mahtc Exemption; [oth. writ.] Articles in Diocesan Magazines poems for use as hymns and poems read out on BBC Wales, poems on various subjects.; [pers.] I have always enjoyed poetry and literature and from time to time when I am not busy I love endeavowing to write poetry I am a Christian who considers Ecumanism very important.; [a.] Addustone, Surrey, UK

HUDDLESS, TARA-LOUISE
[pen.] Tara L. Huddless; [b.] 21 May 1979, Chesterfield; [p.] Helen and Norman Huddless; [ed.] Hasland Hall Community School, Chesterfield College I hope to do a BA (Hons) degree in Music Industry Management; [occ.] A level student law, Psychology, English; [memb.] Student of Maureen Swift School of dance for 11 years; [hon.] Numerous Dancing Awards; [oth. writ.] Poem "Friends Forever" published in "Absent Friends" July 1996; [pers.] I write my poems and songs about my feelings. It's an honour if they are chosen for publication. If people are touched or influenced by my poetry, that is a greater honour; [a.] Chesterfield, Derbyshire, UK

HUDDY, MRS. BESSIE OLIVE
[b.] 9 September 1912, N. London; [p.] William Watts and Harriet Watts; [m.] Gilbert Huddy (Deceased), February 1960; [ch.] Three sons 1 deceased; [ed.] Grammar School North Harringay London; [occ.] Retired Civil Servant now voluntary W.R.Y.S. worker; [memb.] In the 1980's I was the county clothing organizers for W.R.V.S. for the whole of Somerset for 12 years issuing clothing also when Asians came to British Isles for all Somerset.; [oth. writ.] Several poems not shown before.; [pers.] I love working for the elderly i.e. age concern (voluntary) driving to shops hospitals docs etc. and socially visiting.; [a.] Chard, Somerset, UK

HUGHES, COLIN
[b.] 22 May 1968, Glasgow; [p.] Patrick Hughes, Lillian Hughes; [m.] Lorraine Beattie; [ch.] Nicole, Natasha; [ed.] Bellarmine Secondary; [occ.] Warehouse Operative; [pers.] Inspired by many, influenced by none. My daughters guide my pen.; [a.] Glasgow, UK

HUGHES, LOUISE
[b.] 31 May 1972, Derby; [p.] Mary and John Broadhurst; [m.] Timothy Hughes, 15 May 1993; [ch.] Melissa, Aimee and Jamie; [ed.] De Ferrers High School; [occ.] Housewife, Full-Time mother; [oth. writ.] I've done many poems yet this is my first published piece.; [pers.] My words are my heritage which are reflected by love, hate, peace and war.; [a.] Burton, Staffs, UK

HUGHES, MISS NICOLA
[b.] 27 June 1975, Harold, Wood; [p.] Joyce Hughes; [ed.] Redden Court Senior Comprehensive; [occ.] Head Dental Nurse; [oth. writ.] No other work published never attempted to get any other work published.; [pers.] My work comes from my imagination, to keep it active I expand it by having a love for life. I hope my poems and stories bring a smile to people's faces and a thought to their minds.; [a.] Romford, Essex, UK

HUGHES, RHIANNAN
[b.] 24 October 1984, Bridgend; [p.] David and Lorna Hughes; [ed.] Aber Infants School, Tynewydd Junior School, Due to attend Ogmore comprehensive School; [memb.] Pocket Dragon Club; [hon.] Ballet - Primary, Grade 1, 2, 3, and 4 violin grade 2, classification a best pupil award at junior school; [a.] Bridgend, Mid-Glamorgan, UK

HUGHES, RICHARD
[b.] 7 February 1967, Stoke-on-Trent; [p.] Raymond and Mary Hughes; [ed.] Westwood High School, Leek, Staffordshire; [occ.] Building Society Mortgage Services Clerk; [hon.] G.C.E. 'A' Levels Design and Classical Studies, Certificate in Building Society Practice (C.B.S.I.); [oth. writ.] "Peace In Bosnia" published in 'A Passage In Time' - Spring, 1996.; [pers.] Poetry is the way in which I express my true feelings about things observed in everyday life.; [a.] Leek, Staffordshire, UK

HUGHES, WALTER EDWARD
[pen.] Walt; [b.] 1/12/31, London; [m.] Dorothy Margaret, Condie Hughes; [ch.] Matthew James, Charity Abigail, Sharon Kathryn; [ed.] Disrupted in war years culminated at St Mary's Secondary Modern School Hornsey London; [occ.] Lettering Artist Cartoonist - Jazz Musician Broadcaster Hosp. Radio; [memb.] Founder Member of Clarinet and Saxophone Society St. Britain - Founder of Wight Jazz Society; [hon.] Associate Imperial Society Teachers of Dancing; [oth. writ.] Unpublished poems, Interviewer-writer Jazz Times Magazine; [pers.] I savour the delight of expression in the perfect note it's tonality suspended fleeting in its harmonic place in a melody sheer poetry.; [a.] Saint Helens, I.O.W., UK

HULL, WANITA
[pen.] Wanita Hull; [b.] 21 March 1944, Jamaica; [p.] Deceased; [m.] 21 December 1968; [ch.] One and a grandson; [ed.] Modular Degree, Guild Hall University; [occ.] Unemployed; [oth. writ.] One poem, 'Destiny'.; [pers.] I strive to reflect love and good will among my fellow human beings.

HUMPHRIES, IRMA
[b.] 12 April 1920, Brynmawr; [oth. writ.] An anthology of 16 poems titled The Souls Mirror, already edited and prepared for publication at a future date. Many other poems 15 for each birthday of The Queen Mother. Received and appreciated by her majesty.; [pers.] My first inspiration to write poetry came just days after the death of my brother. It seemed that out of my grief was born a gift to express emotions that would otherwise have remained dormant locked within my own personality. Poetry is a means of opening the eyes of others.; [a.] Gilwern, Gwent, UK

HUNTER, EURING MARK
[b.] 18 December 1959, Bedford; [ed.] Wellingborough Grammar, Mander College, Bedford CCAT, Cambridge; [occ.] Engineer; [memb.] Institution of Electrical Engineers, Royal Aeronautical Society, Feani, East of England Agricultural Society, School Governor - Ruskin Infants Wellingborough.; [oth. writ.] Technical Reports; [pers.] This poem was written after visiting Belsen whilst taking part in a youth and community project in 1983.; [a.] Irthlingborough, Northants, UK

HURST, STUART
[b.] 1 September 1976, Wigan; [p.] David Hurst, Jean Hurst; [ed.] Abraham Guest High School; [occ.] Factory Worker, I.M.I. Patrol; [oth. writ.] "Who Cares?" in The International Library of Poetry's Anthology "Quiet Moments"; [pers.] Poetry is what you want it to be, its what you want it to mean, there's no rules, no do's and don't's, it is a way in which we can express how we really feel. Dedicated to Jim Morrison.; [a.] Wigan, Greater Manchester, UK 0DT

HUSSAIN, WAJID
[b.] 22 December 1976, Kashmir; [p.] Karamat Hussain, Zainab Bibi; [ed.] Kenton Comprehensive, University of Bradford; [oth. writ.] Watch this space!; [pers.] All praise be to the almighty creator, whose warning if I rejected, how terrible it would be if he rejected me.

HUTCHINSON, CATHERINE ARNOLD
[b.] 15 November 1919, Manchester; [p.] John Arnold Jones, Jessie Edith Jones; [m.] William John Hutchinson (Deceased), April 1954; [ch.] Caroline Van Howe, Christine Hutchinson; [ed.] Withington Girls School, MIC Uplands School (1929-1936) (School Certificate), Thames Polytechnic (now Univ. of Greenwich) 1984-1990 BA, and MA; [occ.] Retired State Registered Nurse, (formerly shorthand - typist); [memb.] Royal College of Nursing, Royal Brit. Legion, Burma Star Assoc., QA Assoc. Carmy Nursing Corps., Green Party, Amnesty International, Victory Club, Women's History Network, Prisoners Abroad, U. of Greenwich Alumni, Saga, Over - 50 Assoc. Retired, International Alglaucoma Assoc. RCN's History of Nursing Assoc.; [hon.] B.A. (Hons.) in Humanities (1987), M.A. in Historical Studies (1990) at Thames Poly. State Registered Nurse 1943 (Bristol Royal Infirmary); [oth. writ.] Poems in: To Stop a Rising Sun (reminiscences of wartime India and Burma), A Nurse's War by Brenda McBridge, poems of World War II, Oasis. Also Edith Cavill, The Nurse as Heroine (RCN's History of Nursing Journal).; [pers.] Exercise of mind and body staves off aging. Do as you would be done by.; [a.] East Grinstead, West Sussex, UK

HUTCHINSON, JOE
[b.] Heckmondwike; [ed.] Compared with today's standards - None; [occ.] Retired; [oth. writ.] None read, none published, written as a hobby.; [a.] Liversedge, West Yorks, UK

HYLAND, GERALDINE
[b.] 19 August 1976, Ireland; [p.] William (Bill) and Carmel Hyland; [ed.] Irish Leaving Certificate, Presentation College, Headford, Co. Galway, Ireland; [oth. writ.] Several poems, this is thus first I love what I have tried to publish as I have just left school. Poets that have influenced one are W. B. Yeats and W. Shakespeare, and my grandfather Patrick Hyland whose grant love of poetry was my greatest influence, whose appreciation and awareness of as the mutters never ceased to amaze me, oft when I dedicate this poem at his demise in February 1996.; [pers.] God gave us a wonderful world, to live in, we should stop to see, hear and taste it once in a while, from our mad-letter-shelter-dash of avarice and greed which will destroy our sense of beauty, our humanness and eventually our world, pause, my friend, be quiet-listen.; [a.] Plymouth, Devon, UK

IBBOTSON, FRANCIS N.
[pen.] "Mungo"; [b.] 12 April 1922, Cornwall; [p.] Percival Needham and Eileen Ibbotson; [m.] Joyce Knowles, 22 December 1949; [ch.] Stephen John Ibbotson; [ed.] Elementary only at St. Wilfrids RC and St. Marie RC School in Sheffield; [occ.] Retired H.M. Forces and Local Government in Harrogate, N York's; [memb.] Life membership of The Royal Army Pay Corps Association and Ex-member of Association of Cricket Umpires; [hon.] (Royal Navy) 1939-45 War-Ribbon, (Royal Navy) 1939-45 North Atlantic Star, (Army) 1956-59 Cyprus Medal, (Army) and Army L.S and G. C. Medal; [oth. writ.] "Do Not Weep At The Grave" under pen name "Mungo" published by "Poetry Now" (1-2 Wainman Road - Woodston) (1996) in "Absent Friends" publication; [pers.] Now aged 74 1/2, I tend to reminisce often. I have endeavoured in this short poem (joyce knowles) to pay a small tribute to my wife of almost 47 years. All the memories are factual.; [a.] Chesterfield, Derbyshire, UK

IBEKWE, NGOZI CLAIRE
[pen.] Ngozi; [b.] December 30, 1947, Amaba, Abia State; [p.] Alfred and Margaret Ibekwe; [ch.] 1 boy aged 4; [ed.] Government Trade (Comprehensive) Centre, Aba, University of Lausanne Fac. of Letters: (2 semesters) French Lang. and Literature, English and Lit., European History, History of Arts, Academie des Langues, Geneva, Higher Secretarial Dipl., French, English, Economics.; [occ.] A staff member of the United Nations (international civil servant); [memb.] "Extempore" UN Social Cultural Commission - Society of Writers; [oth. writ.] Over 80 poems some on Biafra war. The Oil Crisis and My Ancestors published by the Department of English, University of Nigeria, Nsukka (1983) in their "OMABE" poetry journal.; [pers.] My poems reflect my many pensive, even morose, enthusiastic and stentorian moods. Subjects span the spectrum from micro to macrocosmic, from pastoral bliss to polemic outrage over social injustice, discrimination and human sufferings in its many manifestations. I admire Rimbeaud, Johnson, Pope, Hugo, Poe, Hopkins, Tennyson and Coleridge.; [a.] Geneva, Switzerland

IGUANRE, SOLOMON ODIASE
[pen.] Paddy Sol; [b.] 26 November 1963; [p.] Mr. and Mrs. V. A. A. Iguanre; [ed.] B.A. (Hons) Theatre Arts, M.A. Theatre Art, University of Ibadan; [occ.] Post-Graduate Student; [memb.] (Member) National Association of Nigerian The-

atre Arts Practitioners (NANTAP); [oth. writ.] Several poems, drama sketches and full-length comedies, namely oh-obedeki I and II, Suzzie and Greg, the visit and others.; [pers.] I use my pen to remind mankind the need to affect the world positively. Basically, I use comedy to address a seemingly tragic situations.

IKHISEMOJIE, KIKI
[b.] 1 April 1968, Nigeria; [p.] Lawrence and Mary Ikhisemojie; [ed.] Federal Government Girls' College Owerri, Nigeria, University of Ibadan, Nigeria, (M.A. English, Ph.D.); [occ.] Researcher; [hon.] Contemporary Literary Theory, Creative Writing; [oth. writ.] Poems and academic articles published in departmental journals.; [pers.] Art, and especially poetry I believe is truth. Therefore, in my writing, I strive to portray this truth in words which I believe elevate the wealth of artistic experience, the beauty of which in turn transcends the decadence of our increasingly philistine times.; [a.] London, UK

ILSLEY, PAULINE
[b.] 11 March 1950, Liverpool; [p.] James Ilsley, Hilda Ilsley; [ed.] St. George's Secondary Modern Wallasey, Merseyside, Chester College of Further Education; [occ.] Houseperson/poet (ex-medical secretary); [memb.] Fellowship of the Holy name, Derby Anne Murray International Fan Club, Canada; [oth. writ.] Over 20 poems published in anthologies since 1992: Forward Press (Triumph House, Anchor Books, Poetry now) Peterborough. Poem in your cat magazine.; [pers.] I was initially influenced by John Lennon and Paul McCartney in the early 1960's. However not possessing the gift of music, lyrics became my passionate hobby. What are lyrics without music but poetry.; [a.] Birkenhead, Merseyside, UK

INGE, CHRISTOPHER
[pen.] Christopher Churton Inge; [b.] 31 January 1946, United Kingdom; [p.] Edward and Diana Inge; [m.] Rosemary Muriel Inge, 22 July 1971; [ch.] Alexia and Olivia; [ed.] Radley College and Hertford College, Oxford; [occ.] Creative Partner Churton Inge Assoc. (Advtg. and Pr); [memb.] IPA The Oxford Society RNLI; [hon.] 10 International Awards and Citations for copywriting, including Cannes, Clio Hollywood Radio and Television Society 1 LR, Intl. Film and TV Society of New York and London Intl. Advtg. Awards; [oth. writ.] A former journalist consistently published in the Johannesburg Star and other South African title between 1970 and 1976. Subsequently an award winning copywriter in London and the West Country.; [pers.] I have distrusted philosophers ever since reading socrates, and dislike mission statements and rule-books on the principle that they stifle originality. In the next life I small come back as a client.; [a.] Wells, Somerset, UK

INGLIS, HENRY G.
[pen.] Hifi; [b.] 9 March 1925, Shotts; [p.] Francis Inglis and Mary Jack; [m.] Jamesina Inglis, 31 February 1948; [ch.] Moira, Linda; [ed.] Secondary School (Calderhead); [occ.] Retired; [a.] Shotts, Lanarkshire, UK

IRELAND, LIZ
[b.] 23 September 1981, Winchester; [p.] Gill and Neil Ireland; [ed.] Bishops Waltham Infants Ridgemede Junior/Swanmore, Secondary School transfered to Kings School Winchester; [a.] Winchester, Hampshire, UK

IRVING, GERAINT ALAN
[b.] 8 December 1982, Glasfryn; [p.] Kirkland B. (Deceased) and Catherine L. Irving; [ed.] Tynefelin Primary, St. Winefrides RC primary, St. Mary's RC primary, St. Joseph's RC High; [occ.] School Student; [pers.] I composed this poem when I was twelve, a few months after a few months after my father died from Leukaemia.; [a.] Corwen, Clwyd, UK

IRVING, LEE ROBERT
[pen.] Lee R. Irving; [b.] June 6, 1972, Yarm, Cleveland; [p.] William and Sandra Irving; [ed.] Conyers School, Yarm, Keble College, Oxford University, York University; [occ.] History Teacher, Isle of Man; [memb.] Oxford Union Society, Raleigh International; [hon.] B.A. Hons. Modern History, Class 2=1 (Oxon), P.G.C.E. History, York University, Gold Duke of Edinburgh's Award.; [oth. writ.] Articles published in Oxford Student Newspaper 'Cherwell'. Currently working on a fictional travelogue influenced by my own experiences in South America; [pers.] My writing is inspired by a fascination with man's interaction with fellow man in political society, and the wondrous forces of nature.; [a.] Yarm, Cleveland, UK

ISHERWOOD, LUKA
[pen.] Luka Vincent Broden; [b.] 4 July 1975, Liverpool; [p.] Linda Frost; [m.] Michael Isherwood, 22 March 1996; [ed.] St. Damians, High School, Ashton-u-Lyne GCSE English Literature, Art, English Language; [occ.] Housewife, Student; [oth. writ.] I have gathered some of my other poetry together and called the "Bookette" - "Wild Moons"!; [pers.] If my writing makes you laugh, cry or any emotion, then its working! All I want is for people to remember how to use their imagination.; [a.] Oldham, Lancashire, UK

ISLAM, RUMA
[b.] 20 November 1982, Chatham; [p.] Mr. Nurul Islam, Mrs. Kushnahar Begum; [ed.] At the present moment I am in year 9 at Chatham Grammar School for Girls; [occ.] Student; [oth. writ.] Unpublished poems and stories e.g. "The Interview" and "Crazy".; [pers.] I have always enjoyed writing poetry. I like to write my inner thoughts and feelings in my poems and sometimes exaggerate incidents. I have not really been incidents. I have not really been influenced, but really enjoy a wide range of different poets work.; [a.] Gillingham, Kent, UK

ISMAIL, TAGREED M.
[b.] 22 March 1980, Farnborough, Kent; [p.] Ganiah and Mohammed Ismail; [ed.] Stratford House School, Bickley for 9 years, then Farringtons, Chislehurst for 1 year. Currently at Amman Baccalaureate School, Jordan; [occ.] International Baccalaureate Student; [hon.] Middleschool Scholarship; [oth. writ.] Several short stories and poems published in school magazines.; [a.] Chislehurst, Kent, UK

JACKSON, AMANDA ROSE
[b.] 21 October 1960, Leek, Staffordshire; [p.] Janet Ellen Masser and James Masser; [m.] Harvey Jackson; [ch.] Tracey Ellen and Jonathan James (JJ); [occ.] Lecturer, Wigan and Leigh College; [hon.] City and Guilds 7307 Teaching, Certificate; [oth. writ.] "Operations" and "Abused" many others written for friends in their time of need and on special occasions.; [pers.] Writing poems helped me through a very traumatic childhood, through

illness and bereavement, my only regret is that I discarded so many of my poems which may have been a great comfort to others.; [a.] Wigan, Lancashire, UK

JACKSON, MISS ANDREA
[b.] 17 January 1962, Bristol; [p.] Mary Jackson; [m.] Andrew James Clarke (Fiance); [ed.] St. Bernadettes R. C. Comprehensive School; [occ.] Qualified Nurse for people with Learning difficulties/special needs; [memb.] Until recently a member of St. Mary's Amateur Dramatic Group Concentrating mainly on musicals; [oth. writ.] For my own pleasure.; [pers.] Live life for the full and be happy! Endeavour in your pursuit and you will achieve!; [a.] Bristol, East Gloucestershire, UK

JACKSON, DORIS MURIEL
[b.] 13 November 1923, Wandsworth; [p.] Alice Muriel and Francis Edward Glasspool; [m.] Thomas Edward Jackson, 21 December 1946; [ch.] Susan Anne and Ian Francis; [ed.] Left school for course of Business Studies at Pitmans College, Wimbledon; [occ.] Housewife; [hon.] Certificates/Music; [oth. writ.] "Div. On The National Health" from: Prize-winning poetry by C. John Taylor, Oban, Scotland.; [pers.] Life's full of harvests and tares. If only we could "awaken to a dream" as this book suggest's.; [a.] Crawley, W. Sussex, UK

JACKSON, JOSEPHINE
[b.] 10 September 1967, Blackpool; [p.] Vaughan Trembath, Janine Trembath; [m.] Lee Readman; [ch.] Jason Mark, Georgina Anne; [ed.] John Hanson Grammer School; [occ.] Housewife; [oth. writ.] Personal poems for family and friends.; [pers.] My children have been my greatest influence as their vivid imaginations have helped me to keep my own imagination alive.; [a.] Andover, Hampshire, UK

JACOB, TERENCE
[b.] 30 January 1932, Warrington; [ed.] Bangor Grammar School, (N. Ireland) Brighton Grammar School. Brighton Technical College (Mech. Eng.); [occ.] Retired; [oth. writ.] Selected poems 1994 published by cross publishing, lyrical poems 1996 (10 Sonnets 25 Villanelles) Cross publishing.; [pers.] I am a natural poet heavily influenced by the French poets Baudelaire and Verlaine. I have no time for academic poetry, workshop wonders and new age publications.; [a.] Ryde, Isle of Wight, UK

JACOBS, RONALD
[pen.] Alexander Kovell; [b.] 18 November 1945, Woking, Surrey; [occ.] Ambulance Man; [pers.] I have a small voice but whether I write one or a thousand words I want everyone to hear what I have to say; [a.] Lancing, West Sussex, UK

JAMES, JOANNE
[b.] 19 October 1980; [occ.] Student; [pers.] I believe everybody had a special song and dance, mine happens to be writing. My unconventional views power my mind though where that power comes from I have yet to find out I have been greatly influenced by a wise friend.; [a.] Cwmbran, Torfean, UK

JAMES, JOSEPH N.
[b.] 18 January 1916, Pewzance, Cwll; [p.] Joseph T. James; [m.] Mabel James, 11 November 1938; [ch.] Five, 2 sons, 3 daughters; [ed.] St Tudy Church of England School served 27 years in RN retired 1960; [occ.] Retired; [memb.] Local con-

servative Branch Pres.. P.h pobey ORG, PR for S.G.A.F.A., R.B.L. have been Parish local District Counselor 3 years Chairman; [hon.] 2 War medals R.N. Blue Peter. R.E.L. 36 years Poppy Organizer. Missions to seaman supporter. Church of England children society Church warden 10 years; [oth. writ.] Book published 1993 "A Piece of Gin" autobiography of Navy IERS poems. To the people of London, the battle of the plate. Elegy in the North Atlantic outer space - Peace; [pers.] I served all the war years. Sunk in the South China Sea. For four hours, 2 years in the Atlantic Submarine War, have worked since I left the navy in 1960 to help all service men and their families; [a.] Trubo, Cornwall, UK

JANION, PAUL TERENCE
[b.] 10 February 1948, Totnes; [p.] Terence Janion and Patricia Janion; [m.] Catherine Janion, 17 September 1973; [ch.] Joanna Catherine, James Paul; [ed.] Plymouth College; [occ.] Businessman; [memb.] MENSA; [a.] Crediton, Devon, UK

JANSEN, CHRIS
[b.] 29 August 1982, Aylesbury; [p.] Ever Richard Jansen; [ed.] Aylesbury Grammar School; [occ.] Student; [memb.] British Sub Aqua Club Bicester Aylesburn Gym; [hon.] Musical Award Guildhall School of Music; [pers.] Think what you write, write what you think.; [a.] Aylesbury, Buckinghamshire, UK

JAUNZEMS, LYNDA E.
[b.] 6 March 1945, Canterbury, Kent; [p.] Walter and Elsie Bastable; [m.] Colin Jaunzems, 25 July 1981; [ch.] Gavin (28) son, Penelope (27) daughter; [ed.] Warren Wood C. S. Rochester Kent; [occ.] Care Assistant Local Nursing Home; [hon.] I'm sorry I sound very boring. I am just an Ordinary Housewife who likes Poetry Reading, Gardening. I'm not Academic although I have a good Command of English; [oth. writ.] Nothing published.; [pers.] I have always loved poetry, especially, browning and wordsworth, I get inspiration from every day life, and family happenings. I find writing therapeutic.; [a.] Gainsborough, Lincolnshire, UK

JAYAVANTH, DEEPAK
[b.] 6th July 1976, Madras, India; [p.] Pratap & Vedha Jayavanth; [ed.] Alpha Higher Secondary School, Madras Christian College, Currently studying mechanical engineering; [hon.] English literature; [oth. writ.] Several poems in college magazines, but "Paradise at Sunrise" is the first one to be published in this anthology.; [pers.] I have a vivid imagination and wish to paint the beauty of nature in poetic form, and also my inner feelings concerning love, relationships and people in general.; [a.] Madras, India

JEBARATNARAJAH, MRS. AMIRTHAVALLI
[pen.] Padmini, P.A.R.; [b.] Sri Lanka; [p.] Mr. and Mrs. P. Ramalingam; [m.] M. Jebaratnarajah; [ch.] J.J. Ramalingam and Meera Jeyakumar; [ed.] B.A. Dip. Ed. (Universities of Madras and Peradeniya, Sri Lanka), Cambridge Senior and Junior - Sacred Heart Convent, Yercaud, S. India; [occ.] Retd Teacher, School Administrator and Community worker; [hon.] Prize winner throughout school and university; [oth. writ.] Poems, articles and short stories published in various magazines in Madras, Nigeria and Montreal, Canada. Student and Staff Editor of college magazines in Madras and Sri Lanka; [pers.] I was

born in Sri Lanka but grew up in India, where my father served in the I.C.S. I taught English and History in Sri Lanka and Nigeria before moving to Canada. I have now joined my children here. I'm intensely moved by nature and music. I write for pleasure.; [a.] Ilford, Essex, UK

JEFFERIES, JODIE
[pen.] Jodie Jefferies; [b.] 5 January 1990, London; [p.] Maria and David Jefferies; [ed.] St. James School, C.E. London

JEFFERIES, KEITH
[b.] 23 October 1927, Hackmey, London; [p.] Alfred, Elsie Jefferies; [m.] Pamela, 30 May 1953; [ch.] Jane, Karen, Nicholas, Sarah; [ed.] Sir George Monoux Grammar School, Waltham Stow; [occ.] Retired; [memb.] Burgess Hill Theatre Club, Hassocks Theatre Guild; [oth. writ.] None published; [a.] Burgess Hill, West Sussex, UK

JELKS, PERCIVAL E.
[pen.] The Honourable Percival E. Pyke; [b.] 26 May, Yatton-Som-England; [p.] Archie and Madona Jelks; [m.] Pamela Joan Jelk, 1958; [ch.] Sharon Ann and Dean Edward Archie Jelks; [ed.] Technical - Electronics; [occ.] Electronics Distributor; [memb.] Managers Round Table of the Motion Picture Herald, 1270 Sixty Ave, New York, 20 N.Y. U.S.A., Royal Proclamation by the Prince Regent of Royal Patronage Honourable Status and Title - "The Honourable Percival E. Pyke" (Family Name) of the Principality of the Hutt River Province, Prince Kevin; [hon.] The 1939-45 Star, The Atlantic Star, The France and Germany Star, The 1939-45 Medal, The Defence Medal, Hutt River Province `Royal Ceremonial Jewel'; [oth. writ.] Joy, Joy, Joy: Tears remorse swept down and flooded o'er his shoulder round her face a golden brown, stared down upon the ground. Blue eyes did cry, and he did sigh, for one so young did try to shed her sorrow for the morrow. Shudders did her shoulders shake and ever still she made the break with years gone by not to return, shall they ever learn when happiness abounds so good to have around. That faded shirt will be a memory for them to see recorded yet for years untold even now as they grow old and greener grows life's tree. But years that go bring years not told, and happiness will yet unfold can still we see upon life's trees, a branch still free. But stay, the stains sincere and need you not to fear, ever be you always so or do'est thou want me just to go.; [pers.] In the beginning before you were, I was - we had the Grand Old Penny, it use to keep me in Dolly Mixtures all week and sometimes I even had a Farthing in change!; [a.] Southampton, Hampshire, UK

JEWITT, KATHERINE
[b.] 3 November 1940, Inverness; [p.] Rev. and Mrs. Higgins; [m.] Bruce Leonard Jewitt, 1 December 1973; [ch.] Jonathan and Victoria; [ed.] Hutcheson's Girls Grammar School, Glasgow Aberdeen University; [occ.] Teacher of Mathematics Kingston Adult Education; [memb.] Holmes Place Health Club; [oth. writ.] Lyrics for music composed by myself.; [pers.] I feel that people should try to do the things they want to do even if they not sure of success.; [a.] Esher, Surrey, UK

JOHNS, CHARLES
[b.] 30 June 1923, Greenwich; [p.] Beth (Deceased); [m.] Nil (Divorced); [ch.] Jennifer Quaife, Christopher, Richard Johns, Kasia Johns; [ed.] John Ruskin School, Croydon London University;

[occ.] Retired; [oth. writ.] Nothing published have written humorous poems for my friends and special cards for anniversaries etc. (Also accompanied by pen sketches - faces events!); [pers.] Appear to have any middle course of thought: My works swing from direct drama to direct humour and unless I can focus on either of these, nothing of merit is forth coming!; [a.] Worthing, West Sussex, UK

JOHNSON, LYNN
[b.] 16 March 1950, Lincoln; [p.] Len Coy and Olive Coy; [m.] Trevor Johnson, 13 July 1968; [ch.] Mark, Alistair, Victoria, Peter; [ed.] Spring Hill Girls Secondary Modern School, Lincoln Technical College; [oth. writ.] Various poems none entered in anything; [pers.] I keep my life in my mind to put on paper when the moon is right and the inspiration; [a.] Newark, Notts, UK

JOHNSTON, LICIA
[pen.] Carlotta Ottanelli; [b.] 5/6/1926; [p.] Deceased (Italian); [m.] Robert John Johnston, 29/06/1957; [ch.] Marco, Roberto (1959); [ed.] Italian Primary School plus various adult education courses, 1948 worked in Switzerland ENGLAND, 1957 Intermedial O/A' level in English Literature; [occ.] Nurse (Pediatric), retired (trained 1954/57 - England); [hon.] Poems published in various anthologies up to date - ten (1994/96), published by Anchor Books, Arrival Press and Triumph House, Woodston - Peterborough; [oth. writ.] Children's poems and stories, romantic short stories, so far unpublished.; [pers.] To me writing a poem about life or nature is like painting a picture with words instead of colours. I have been influenced by Dante, Wordsworth and Browning; [a.] Ashford, Kent

JONES, ALAN WILFRED MARK
[pen.] Wilf Jones; [b.] 28 May 1960; [p.] Doris Jones and Wilfred Jones; [ed.] Corby Boys School, Samuel Lloyds Comprehensive; [occ.] Account Co-ordinator; [a.] Corby, Northants, UK

JONES, EVELYN ROSEMARY
[b.] 2 October 1946, Penzance, Cornwall; [p.] Iris Clemens, Charles Clemens; [m.] Michael John Jones, 22 December 1984; [ch.] Lindsey, Treena, Simon-Peter; [ed.] Hayle Comprehensive School; [occ.] Housewife; [pers.] I like to think that my writing has been inspired by a greater force than' myself, and that it will bring joy to many.; [a.] Helston, Cornwal, UK

JONES, MAGGIE PRYCE
[pen.] Maggie Pryce Jones; [b.] 1920's, Trelewis; [p.] Martha and Lewis Price; [m.] Fred (Deceased), 14 August 1946; [ch.] Tanya, Brent, Cheryl, Leigh; [ed.] Hengoed County Grammar School, Merthyr Technical College; [occ.] Retired Civil Servant; [memb.] Church Choir; [oth. writ.] Several poems published. Book "Kingfisher Of Hope" published Various Articles published.; [pers.] I am a "Moods Writer" and write poetry and articles about things which move me - and depict my moods.; [a.] Treharris, Mid-Glam, UK

JONES, MARIA LOUISE
[pen.] Maria; [b.] 5 June 1979, Chuch Village; [p.] Jacqueline Jones; [occ.] College Student; [pers.] I am pleased to hear that my poem is to be published. Bullying is a serious problem for today's society, and should be recognized there is much to be done to to prevent bullying, not only in school but other aspects of life.; [a.] Pontypridd, Mid-Glam, UK

JONES, MICHAEL
[b.] 1 September 1961, Liverpool; [p.] Brian and Veronica Jones; [ed.] Penkith High School, Warrington, Warrington Technical College; [occ.] Bank Employee in the City of London; [memb.] Old Buckwellians Football Club, Highams Park Fencing Club; [hon.] Awarded the South Atlantic Medal for the Falklands War, Whilst in the Royal Navy.; [oth. writ.] Numerous poems and philosophical comments, mostly for personal satisfaction. However I have written for and about family and friends.; [pers.] First world was poetry is my preferred reading, although I enjoy anything about the great war.; [a.] Walthamstow, London, UK

JONES, MR. NEIL
[pen.] Nek Jones; [b.] 5 March 1961, Aberdare; [p.] Trevor Haydn and Gwenda; [m.] Catherine Jones, 29 June 1995; [ch.] Sarah Elizabeth Jones; [ed.] Gadlys Secondary School, Aberdare; [occ.] Father and Musician; [pers.] My poems personally portray the constant conflict between the blind madness and human kindness that we find in all our lives.; [a.] Aberdare, Mid-Glamorgan, UK

JONES, SHIRLEY
[b.] 24 August 1955, Salisbury; [p.] Catherine Bullen, Harry Bullen; [m.] Keith B. R. Jones; [ch.] Paul Michael; [ed.] Lochend Comprehensive Glasgow, Skelmersdale College; [occ.] Senior Supervisor Elderly Mentally Disordered Home; [hon.] City and Guilds N.V.Q. 3 in Caring, City and Guilds T.D.L.B. Assessor in Caring; [pers.] My poems are inspirations from friends and family. Without them, there would be no writings.; [a.] Skelmersdale, Lancashire, UK

JONES, STEVEN BRIAN
[b.] 21 December 1972, Stoke-on-Trent; [p.] Brian Reginald Jones, Ann Jones; [m.] Dawn Jones, 10 September 1994; [pers.] I find accomplishment in poetry by literally recording my thoughts and emotions of every day observations.; [a.] Staffordshire, UK

JOSEPH, JACK
[b.] 2 May 1925, London; [occ.] Writing and Hypnotherapy also qualified Yoga Teacher; [memb.] National Council for Hypnotherapists British Wheel of Yoga (Teachers Diploma) Member of Association of Ethical and Professional Hypnotherapists; [hon.] (Acc) MNCH and Maeph British wheel of Yoga Teachers Diploma all India Board Teacher Diploma (Honours); [oth. writ.] Omano oracle ISBN 0907322 638 Poems published in local magazines; [pers.] My writings are a blend of prose and poetry. Containing extracts from inspired/channelled work that have enabled many people to discover their own inner values as they awaken to true reality; [a.] Worthing, W. Sussex, UK

JOSHUA, OLUWOLE AYODELT
[pen.] Wole Joshua, Woljosh; [b.] 26 August 1966, Lagos, Nigeria; [p.] Mr. and Mrs. Olusola, Joshua Pelinah M. Joshua; [ed.] C.M.S. Grammar School Lagos Federal School of Arts and Science, Lagos, Obafemi Awoland University, Ile-Ile, Nigeria; [occ.] Literature Teacher, Holy Martrs of Uganda Seminary Effurun, Delta - State; [memb.] Man O' War Club, Nigeria, Dramatic Arts Students Association, (Data) IFE, Association of Nigeria Authors (Ana) C.R.M. Theatre, Lagos; [hon.] English Literature, Poetry and Film titled "The Zumma Quten" as a wrier and director.;

[oth. writ.] Poems short stories articles published in local magazine, short story, the joker read on B.B.C. Published a play tittle, "Double Six and Six" written several film poetry and stage scripts awaiting publication and sponsorship.; [pers.] My goal in my writing is to make people know and came closer to God, through the arts as I feel the sciences have appointed Him.

JUMBO, ANTONIO
[b.] 3 January 1965, Ecuador; [p.] Jose Jumbo and Maria Guarnizo; [ch.] Jessica Jacobsen; [ed.] "Laconcordia" School, Central University of Ecuador, University of London; [occ.] Spanish Lecturer, Wandsworth Adult College; [memb.] Nicaraguan Solidarity Campaign; [hon.] Spanish Language and Literature, MA. Linguistics; [oth. writ.] Several poems, essays on Linguistics.; [pers.] I would like to see the world free of homeless, and full of bicycles.; [a.] London, UK

KAISER, STAN
[b.] 22 August 1930, Hartlepool; [m.] Joyce; [ch.] Three daughters; [ed.] BSE (Hon) Physics/Maths Bristol University Dip. Ed. Durham University; [occ.] Management Consultant; [memb.] Commissioned Royal Air Formation Signals 1953, District Counselor for 27 years Harterpool; [a.] Hartlepool, UK

KAUR, JASPAL
[b.] 31 March 1962, London; [m.] Divorce; [ch.] Two Girls, ages 11 and 14; [ed.] English, Art, History; [occ.] Team Assistant; [oth. writ.] I am a great love of romantic poems I think what really made me write this poem was that I been threw Similar situation pain and heartache.

KEAN, VICTORIA
[b.] 24 March 1980, Banbury; [p.] W. V. and M. Kean; [ed.] Primary education at the Windrush Valley preparatory school. Secondary at Burford Secondary School (still attending.); [occ.] Student; [hon.] Duke of Edinburgh's Bronze Award. Merit Award for work on school year book.; [oth. writ.] Poem published in school year book (Burfordian); [pers.] I write my poems to reflect personal emotions and experiences. I am still only 16 years old, and I wrote "The Girl" two years ago.; [a.] Witney, Oxfordshire, UK

KEAR, REG
[b.] 24 August 1932, Bristol, England; [m.] Sylvia B., 15 February 1957; [ch.] Lee, Jason, Rachel; [occ.] N.L.P. Practitioner and Counsellor; [memb.] Wado-Ryu International Federation, Wado-Ryu. San No Ya. Australia; [oth. writ.] Several articles in Martial Arts, Publications. "Swinging The Lamp" a book of selected poetry.; [pers.] "Man's destiny, is but collective thought...."; [a.] Bristol, UK

KEAVENEY, MARY
[b.] 3 October 1951, Ireland; [p.] Sabina, Andrew Mannion; [ch.] David, Jim Keaveney; [ed.] National School - Kilkerrin, Sec. - Glenamaddy The Haven Centre - for Counseling Psychotherapy - Ealing, London; [occ.] Hotel work (part-time), Action Homeless concern - Emmans House (Vol. work), Studying at Central School of Counseling, Therapy (London); [pers.] I listen to the non-verbal expression of deep feelings and try to put them into words, there by give the comport that comes from being understood and valued.; [a.] Brentford, London, UK

KEEGAN, MARIE
[b.] 27 June 1973, Dublin; [p.] Con Keegan (Deceased) and Theresa Keegan; [ed.] Colehill National School, Ballymahon Vocational School; [occ.] Childminder/Nanny; [pers.] To dismiss and hide away from the dark tenements of the human mind, shows our ignorance and fear. Worldly knowledge and self-renewal only comes from picking at the mattered minds among us.; [a.] Killendowd, Longford, UK

KELLARD, DAVID A.
[b.] November 16, 1937, Finsbury, London; [p.] Alfred, Mary; [m.] Pauline, March 30, 1968; [ch.] Keith, Gaynor, Hazel; [ed.] Hornsey County, Trinity County Grammar; [occ.] Surgical Instrument Maker; [a.] Hoddesdon, Herts, UK

KELLY, PATRICIA ANNE
[pen.] Stiles - Kelly; [occ.] Company Manager; [oth. writ.] I was Hongkong's first commercial poet and also have poems published; [pers.] Waking briefly in the night with words upon my mind I gently pluck them out to record at break of day; [a.] Tywyn, Gwynedd, UK

KEMNA, INGRID
[b.] 4 May 1933, Wuppertal, Germany; [p.] Rolf and Hilde Kemna; [ed.] Municipal Grammar School for Girls Wuppertal-Barmen, Germany. Came to England in 1956 to learn English, private education.; [occ.] Freelance translator and PA to Continental Law Consultant; [memb.] Fellow Institute of Linguists, Member Federal German Translators' Guild, Member British-German Association; [pers.] I believe in "Life is what you make it" meaning that I take an active hand in shaping my life and try not to miss any more opportunities. Expressing negative feelings in the succinct way of a poem puts them in perspective and allows me to put them behind me. I write poetry in German and English, sometimes mixing the two for fun.; [a.] London, UK

KEMP, MARION MARGARET
[b.] 11 March 1948, Crowthorne, Berks; [p.] Leonard and Margaret Shadbolt; [m.] Divorced; [ch.] Matthew Lee Kemp, Nathan Stewart Kemp, Jacqueline Margaret Kemp, Lorraine Marion Kemp, Richard Raymond Brian Kemp, Robert Charles Kemp; [ed.] Secondary at Cove Country sec school access Pre-Degree at Faruborough Tech B.A. Degree in Geography and Development Studies at Reading University; [occ.] Just odd jobs, housewife and Mother; [pers.] My husband, Brian died in 1975 leaving me with 2 very young daughters. I re-married in 1979 and took or Matthew and Nathan as well as a new husband. It was very hard work, Richard and Robert made our children up to 6 Sadly my Ex-husband did not share my love of the family and was rarely at home. He ran up terrible debts and finally became violent. I had to ask him to leave. The sadness I felt over the years since loosing my husband Brian is reflected in almost every poem I've written none of which I've submitted for publication, almost every line of my verse is manic reflecting my sadness that nothing lasts forever.; [a.] Farnborough, Hants, UK

KENDALL, A. W.
[pen.] Lucky; [b.] 26 February 1917, Hendon; [p.] Mr. and Mrs. J. H. Kendall; [m.] 18 July 1938; [ch.] Three; [ed.] Secondary; [occ.] Retired; [hon.] National Life Story Awards 1994, Certify Accepted and Added to the British Library Collections; [oth. writ.] Memories, From the People of Kvam, Life on the Buses

KENDALL, CAROL ANN
[b.] 13 November 1948, Middlesbrough; [p.] Arthur and Doris Kendall; [ed.] Secondary Modern; [occ.] Secretary - Car Sales; [memb.] Egg Crafters Guild; [oth. writ.] Nothing published; [pers.] I have been greatly influenced by both parents, but lately by my Mother, my Father having died a few years ago.; [a.] Redcar, Cleveland, UK

KENNEDY, JEAN
[pen.] Jean Kennedy; [b.] 27 October 1938, West Hartlepool; [p.] Thomas Charles and Margaret Rorks; [m.] David Brian Kennedy, 23 July 1960; [ch.] Michelle, Anne; [ed.] Sacred Heart, Hartlepool, Kidbrooke Comprehensive, Woolwich Polytechnic, London; [occ.] House Wife; [oth. writ.] Poem 'Possession' printed in Northern voices, anchor books.; [pers.] I try to be realistic about life but sometimes the sheer enormity of my emotions engulf and consume me, my poetry then becomes a reflection of my heart and soul.; [a.] Hartlepool, Hartlepool, UK

KENNY, ROBERT
[pen.] Robert G. D'Cianaigh; [b.] 3 July 1939, Perthshire; [p.] John Kenny, Helen Kenny; [m.] June Kenny, 22 March 1966; [ch.] David and Michael; [occ.] Civil Servant; [memb.] The Caravan Club; [hon.] Royal Society of Arts C.P.C.'s National and International Passenger Transport Operations; [pers.] As a creationist, my heart bleeds in the sight of adversity. The creative writer pens untold energies in the mind of the beholder.; [a.] Blackpool, Lancs, UK

KENT, F. W.
[pen.] Reflection; [b.] 7 February 1940, Warrington; [p.] Fredrick and Dorothy; [m.] Ruth, 12 December 1940; [ch.] Frederick, Julie Dorothy; [ed.] St. Patrick, Manchester, St Agnes, Kennington, London; [occ.] Retired; [memb.] Labour Party; [oth. writ.] Book - Concern; [pers.] The poem I have written, was dedicated, to my mother. Who died in a fire when I was eleven. Poetry broadens the mind and is a beautiful creation.; [a.] Altrincham, Cheshire, UK

KENT, JAMES LESLIE GORDON
[pen.] Budro; [b.] 24 May 1941, Launceston; [p.] James and Kathleen Kent; [m.] Victoria Violet Kent, 30 September 1965; [ch.] Melanie, James, Cherrey, Trude; [ed.] Bude and Straton, Secondary Mondern School; [occ.] M/A and Stoker Princess Royal Hospital, Telford, Salop; [hon.] C.C.S.S.A.A., Merchant Navy, Powder Monkey, Gold Mining, Telephone Engineer, Postman, Refuse Collector Printer Sheep Hearder, Making Roads in the outback Ectect all had there awards.; [oth. writ.] My own works; [pers.] My wife's love mum and dad for all your love the love of the children and grandchildren and Rusty, Gabel thunder thanks.; [a.] Telford, Shropshire, UK

KERFOOT, LINDA KATHRYN
[pen.] Brenda Michaels; [b.] 23 December 1978, Liverpool; [p.] Dorothy Kerfoot, Alan Kerfoot; [ed.] St. Chads R. C. Comprehensive School Halton College of further Education; [occ.] Student; [pers.] I like my poetry to be happy, cheerful and easy to understand without being boring.; [a.] Runcorn, Cheshire, UK

KERR, LYNN
[b.] 16 February 1961, Glasgow; [p.] Mary and James Roberts; [m.] Neil Kerr, 28 June 1986; [ch.]

Emma and Christopher; [ed.] St. Patricks High School Coatbridge, University of Glasgow, M.A. Degree in French/Spanish; [occ.] Modern Languages Teacher - St. Aidans High, Wishaw.; [memb.]; [hon.] M.A. Degree French/Hispanic Studies; [oth. writ.] Many other poems as yet unpublished.; [pers.] I enjoy writing poems about life and creation. I have been greatly influenced by my own experiences and people I have met.; [a.] Glasgow, UK

KERRY, ELIZABETH
[b.] 18 April 1968, Derby; [p.] Eric and Joyce Kerry; [ch.] 1 daughter - Emma Louise Kerry; [ed.] Friesland Secondary School Sandiacre, Notts; [occ.] Full-time Mum; [hon.] Voted International Poet of the Year 1995, in America, and have had several poems published in local newspapers; [pers.] In all my poetry I try to bring out the spiritual being which is inside all of us.; [a.] Sandiacre, Nottinghamshire, UK

KETTLEWELL, STEVE
[b.] 18 July 1955, Bradford; [p.] Winifred Kettlewell, Roland K. (Both Deceased); [ed.] Secondary Holmewood Holmewood Junior School, Tong Comprehensive School; [occ.] Fork Lift Truck driver; [memb.] Anchors Aweigh poetry magazine, Triumph house poetry magazine for Christian Poetry.; [hon.] 30 poems published in various books, on various themes. E. G. religion, nature, Love and marriage, war and peace.; [oth. writ.] A total of 500 poems written in a 2 year period since my initial interest in poetry emerged. In May 1994 (until my mothers death, I had non prior interest in writing or poetry); [pers.] When my dear mother away 5th December 1993, we could not afford a headstone, so I wrote an epitaph. The outcome was words from out of the blue. I place on paper my emotions of life in general; [a.] Bradford, W. Yorkshire, UK

KIND, EVELYN MARY
[pen.] Eve Kind; [b.] 1 February 1913, Plymouth; [p.] Henry Styring and Elsie Styring; [m.] John Kind (Deceased), 23 July 1938; [ch.] Two; [ed.] Sheffield Pupil Teacher Centre; [occ.] Retired; [memb.] Liberal Democrats; [oth. writ.] Memoirs and Poetry at Sheffield University since 1984. My first poem appeared in my school magazine when I was 11 years old.; [pers.] At the age of 81 I "Awakened To A Dream" and joined a writing class or Sheffield University, writing my memoirs and poetry. Now at 83 I am still writing and feel I have proved to myself to the that it is never too lares to make a dreams come true.; [a.] Sheffield, South Yorkshire, UK

KIND, SARAH
[b.] 7 September 1981, Roughton; [p.] Anthony Kind, Susan Kind; [ed.] Kirkby-on-Bain Primary School, Gartree Secondary School; [occ.] A student; [memb.] Friskney and District Harriers Athletic Club, Horncastle Young Farmers Club; [oth. writ.] Two other poems published in hard back books and one in a poetry magazine; [pers.] I'm 14 years old and to see my poetry work published is an honour.; [a.] Woodhall Spa., Lincolnshire, UK

KING, ELIZABETH F. C.
[b.] 2 October 1942, Beith, Ayrshire; [p.] Matthew and Agnes Denholm; [m.] Robert Harvey King, 31 July 1964; [ch.] Robert-Derek, Gordon, Ian; [ed.] Beith Primary School, Speirs Secondary School, Garnock Academy (further education); [occ.] Computer Operator in Export Shipping;

[memb.] Beith Bowling Club, Book Clubs; [oth. writ.] Poems published in local magazines. Poems read at Burn's Suppers. Religious poems published in Beith Church and Largs Church Magazines. At present writing short stories.; [pers.] Most of my poems result from my own or friends experiences and also from events that affect me whether personal or worldwide.; [a.] Beith, Ayrshire, UK

KIRBY, MICHAEL FREDERICK
[b.] 17 September 1926, Preston, Lancs; [p.] Fred and Lucy Kirby; [ed.] Quarry Bank High School, Liverpool Keswick Hall College of Education Norwich; [occ.] Retired Teacher; [memb.] Grantham Music Club; [oth. writ.] Not worth Mentioning - Minor for local church magazine.; [pers.] I consider myself a 'Versifier' rather than a 'poet', 'Reverie' is a 'one-off', regarding its generation time (about a year).; [a.] South Witham, Nr. Grantham, Lincs, UK

KIRKLAND, MOIRA
[b.] 12 June 1921, Palmerston North; [occ.] Senior Citizen - Painting - Gardening - Short-stories; [hon.] "Trinity College of Music" Senior Division - London Elocution - 1935 - I couldn't finish my studies because I joined the Airforce; [oth. writ.] I have been writing poetry since I was at school and had a poem put in the school magazine but I have never before submitted one for publication; [pers.] I enjoy writing but I have only written short stories. I wrote this poem for my son - who had reasons for valuing his friend!; [a.] London, UK

KIRKPATRICK, DAPHNE
[b.] 8 March 1935, Jersey, Cayman Islands; [p.] Living in Jersey; [ch.] Juliette and Anton; [ed.] Jersey College for Girls (by scholarship) Furzedown College - London University; [occ.] Head teacher - Scotland and Abu Dhabi (retired) now writing; [memb.] Bennetts Bridge Writers Group, Ireland, Riposte - Ireland (recently re-located-writing solo); [hon.] Diving and swimming honours to British Universities level (early life) Awards - Scottish Open Poetry Comp. (2) Inclusions in Anthologies (Scotland and Ireland) - recent years. Led busy academic/Arts oriented life until recently; [oth. writ.] Title poem and others "Daughters Of The Wind" - Ireland. Two poems - "Tangerine Skies" - Ireland. Poem published in "Gulf News" 1993. Some poetry - Radio Scotland - Radio Kilkenny. Readings in several venues - Ireland.; [pers.] To survive the slings and arrows of life - to continue to love and care for those dear to me - to write with total honesty.; [a.] St. Levan, Cornwall, UK

KISTNAMAH, KUNDASAMY
[pen.] Appasawmy Kistnamah; [b.] 5 May 1929, Mauritius; [p.] Raj Gopalsamy Naidoo, Velamah Appasawmy; [m.] Moonsamy Kundasamy, 5 December 1952; [ch.] Devendren, Poonsamy, Dharmarajen, Indren and Abhimanu; [ed.] R.C. School and College Mauritius, School of Nursing at Leavesden Hospital Watford, R.C. of T. 1995-1996 DIP in I.I.H.H.T.; [occ.] Retired nurse since 1994 after 29 years nursing caring and teaching the people of learning disabilities; [memb.] N.H.S. and Alzheimer's Disease Society, Federation of Holistic Therapists; [hon.] Long service in N.H.S. 1st award in U.K.C.C. "Project for Elderly Care". Reading College of Technology, 1995-1996 Diploma received 1996, International Institute of Health and Holistic Therapists "Body Massage"; [oth. writ.] Project was published in the Hosp. magazine. My Diary, Letters, to my children and

grand children. And to write my autobiography; [pers.] True education is not pumped and crammed in from outward sources, but AIDS in bring to the surface the infinite hoard of wisdom within. I have been influenced by the great poet a. Rabindranath Tagore; [a.] Reading, Caversham, UK

KITCHENER, GLORIA
[pen.] Gloria Kitchener; [b.] 6 February 1970, Southend; [p.] Jean Kitchener, Barry Kitchener; [ed.] Southend Grammar School for Girls, Thurrock College of Technology, University of East London; [occ.] Student (teaching) P/T Youth Worker; [memb.] English Heritage, Local Gym/Fitness Centre Student Union; [hon.] Certificate in Playwork, HND Playwork, BA (hons) Education and Community Studies (upper 2nd); [oth. writ.] Several unpublished poems. I also write my own songs, 2 of which have been professionally recorded and I hope to send them to record companies in due course.; [pers.] I like to think that my work accurately reflects my own personal thoughts and experiences as well as those of my closest friends and family. I'd like people read my poetry and think: "Yes, I can relate to that."; [a.] Southend, Essex, UK

KITSON, VIKKI
[b.] 30 July 1979, Pontefract; [p.] John Kitson, Diane Kitson; [ed.] Brigshaw High School, Thomas Danby College, Leeds; [occ.] Student; [oth. writ.] Article published in local paper, co-wrote an article in regional paper. Several stories and mini poems, as yet unpublished.; [pers.] My poetry reflects my mood and the harshness of life the majority of times. My novels show both the good and bad of youths today. I am trying to get my message of experience over to people younger than me.; [a.] Leeds, West Yorkshire, UK

KLEANTHIDIS, IOANNIS
[b.] 1 December 1975, Chrisoupoli; [p.] Alexandros Kleanthidis (father), Stavroula (mother); [ed.] Greek General Lyceum; [occ.] Student in Aberdeen University 3rd year in MA Arts English with honors; [oth. writ.] Nothing published yet; [a.] Chrisoupoli, Macedonia, Greece

KNIGHT, JENNIFER TERESA
[b.] 9 December 1978, Hull; [p.] Glynis Knight; [ed.] Andrew Marvell Comprehensive Hull, J.H.P. Training, Hull; [hon.] English Literature G.C.S.E. NVQ level 2 Business Administration; [oth. writ.] Poetry; [pers.] I am inspired by natural settings and the many human emotion. Each and everything appeals to me as expressions of individual beautty.; [a.] Hull, East Yorkshire, UK

KNIGHT, WINIFRED
[b.] 24 March 1921, Swansea; [p.] Edwin Thornton, May Thornton; [m.] Walter Knight, 5 June 1943; [ch.] Robert, Jane, David (killed on road); [ed.] St. Winifred's Convent, Croydon Art School, Land Girl During War; [occ.] Commission Artist in oils; [memb.] Swansea Art Society, Llanelli Art Society, Liwchwr Art Group, Penclawdd Brass Band Life Member, Dunvant Choir Patron; [hon.] Emlyn Roberts Memorial Award 1991 Llanelli Art Society. Life Membership Penclawdd Brass Band.; [oth. writ.] "And Must I Leave This Place...." Last chapter heading in a book by Naturalist Ronald Lockley called "Orielton". "And After Rain The Gower Roads..." published in Anthology "Wish You Were Here" edited Michelle Abbot.; [pers.] Jesus said it all in the Sermon on the Mount.; [a.] Swansea, West Glamorgan, UK

KNOWELDEN, HOWARD
[b.] 8 October 1970, Cuckfield; [p.] Robert and Norma Knowelden; [ed.] Downlands Comprehensive Hassocks, Haywards Heath 6th Form; [occ.] Network Support Officer for Mid Sussex District Council; [memb.] Several Jean-Michael Jarre Fanzines. The Official Babylon 5 Fan Club; [oth. writ.] Poem published in a 1994 Anthology, Many articles published in Revolution - The Jean-Michel Jarre Magazine; [pers.] As a dyslexic I am indebted to technology and I am always in awe of the beauty in science; [a.] Hurstpierpoint, West Sussex, UK

KOEHLER, HELMUT
[pen.] James D'Havilland; [b.] 17 January 1949, Bochum; [p.] Helmut Koehler, Luise Koehler; [m.] Ethel Agnes Johnson Koehler, 28 April 1990; [ch.] Melissa, Samantha, Joanne; [ed.] Bochum Grammar, University Bochum, Queens University Belfast; [occ.] Clerical officer Doncaster Royal Infirmary; [memb.] Chamber of Commerce Bochum Germany; [oth. writ.] Non fictional book "Brainpower" not yet published various poems; [pers.] My poems reflect real life experiences. Non-fictional writing investigates matters of general interest, showing the way to new possibilities; [a.] Doncaster, S. Yorks, UK

KOPS, JACK
[b.] 3 April 1918, London; [p.] Deceased; [m.] Deceased, 5 November 1939; [ch.] One son; [ed.] Secondary School; [occ.] Retired Civil Servant; [memb.] Readers Digest; [hon.] Have written and typed 2 adventure books as yet unpublished. Although one book entry has been accepted for the National life story awards and added to the british library collections.; [pers.] All my writing is my own work, and does not coincide with other poems or authors J. Kops, Mr. 11 Yantlet House London Road. Leigh-on-Sea.; [a.] Southend, Essex, UK

KUSI, BENJAMIN
[b.] 29 October 1980, Britain; [p.] Ben and Florence Kusi; [ch.] Two daughters and a son; [ed.] I am studying for my GCSES a school; [memb.] I am currently a member of a leading ball team; [oth. writ.] I have just previously written a manuscript for a book.; [a.] London, UK

LA ROCHE, MS. COLLEEN
[pen.] Colleen La Roche; [b.] 23 May 1943, Hampshire, United Kingdom; [p.] Laurence and Mary Roche; [ch.] Cherie Mary, and Shane La Roche Laurence; [ed.] Secondary Pelham St. Brighton; [occ.] Single Parent!; [hon.] GCSE in a level, Fine Art; [pers.] This is the first time I've entered a poetry competition, I am only an amateur, I write poetry for the fun of it and special requests.; [a.] Brighton, Sussex, UK

LADZRIE, GWENDOLINE MARY
[pen.] Gwen; [b.] 26 April 1912, Windsor; [m.] Deceased, September 1939; [ed.] Church of England (day), followed by evening school; [occ.] Retired; [memb.] Town Counsellor 1977-1983, still a working member of my party.; [hon.] Defence Medal for service in last war, also Red Cross, V.A.D., attached to the East Anglian Regiment; [oth. writ.] "Ode of Life", published in a private residential homes book of verse 1996.; [pers.] I was directed to work on a mobile operating theatre on call to bomb casualties in the last war! And I would like to feel I have achieved something during my life, much has gone unnoticed.; [a.] Hove, East Sussex, UK

LAFFERTY, MICHAEL JOSEPH
[pen.] Micky Michael Murch; [b.] 12 September 1961, Donegal, Eire; [p.] Patrick Lafferty, Diana Lafferty; [ch.] Frances Hannah Murch; [ed.] Wells Alderman Peel School Norfolk, Norwich City College, Ipswitch Road Norwich; [occ.] Patient Care Assistant Kelling Hospital; [memb.] Norfolk National Trust; [oth. writ.] Halcyons Summer Days; [pers.] Would love to be a top rated Irish poet with poetry that flows from the heart and touches the soul.; [a.] Cley, Norfolk, UK

LAILEY, ANDREA J.
[b.] 12 September 1940, Salisbury; [p.] Arthur J. Willis O.B.E., Renee Willis; [m.] Gerald William Lailey, 2 December 1961; [ch.] Katrina (1963), Richard Cameron (1964), Jesse-John (1970), granddaughter Antonia May (1994); [ed.] 1st School (age 3) St. Andrews, Laverstock, too many to mention after that as father in bomb disposal, later met-man.; [occ.] Amateur Artist (Very); [memb.] Salisbury Bowling Club (Social Member, Gerald is the Cup-winner!); [hon.] Mostly Art Prizes; [oth. writ.] A few odd poems and Tales, nothing much have just illustrated a book for a local photographer (Fairy Tale); [pers.] Interests-Sci-Fi, Ecology, Tap-Dancing I seek the ability to recognize the Chameleon. (Or even how to spot the beef in a Lamburger...); [a.] Salisbury, Wiltshire, UK

LAIRD, PETER
[pen.] Peter Laird; [b.] 25 November 1940, Edinburgh; [p.] Alex Laird and Amy Fyffe; [m.] Dorothy Laird, 4 August 1962; [ch.] Two daughters, Sandra and Joanne; [ed.] Dunnotter Primary, Stonehaven, Castlehill Primary Edinburgh, Southbridge Primary, Edinburgh, James Clark Secondary, and R.A.F. Education; [occ.] Council Employee (Public Services) Glasgow City Council; [memb.] Royal are force Association, attends the Local Baptist Church, Social Secretary, Arthritis Care Wisham; [oth. writ.] Poems and early stories of childhood and earlier years, poems of Spain and Canada, England.; [pers.] Vivaldi's four seasons relates the feeling of the landscapes: Distance and the wild scenery of Canadian, vast trackland and natural beauty in this great world, as dues the Scottish borders, and the beauty's of rural England counties in great lover of burns and Sir Walter Scott and John Buchan, relate and witness in their time.; [a.] Wishaw, North Lanarkshire, UK

LAMB, CAROLINE M.
[b.] 30 October 1981, Barnsley; [p.] Dylan Lamb, Dawn Lamb; [ed.] Attending Sir John Nelthorpe School at Brigg in North Lincolnshire where I am a year 10 student.; [memb.] Girl Guide's Association; [pers.] This is my first attempt and I wrote it for fun.; [a.] Brigg, North Linconshire, UK

LAMB, CEDRIC
[pen.] Beau Bell - Wood; [b.] 8 August 1930, Huddersfield; [p.] Robert Lamb and Annie E. Steele; [m.] Marjorie Cooper (Deceased), 30 March 1964; [ed.] Dowdales Sec. School Dalton-in-Furness; [occ.] Retired; [pers.] Poetry is a favourite subject of mine, my Uncle was also good at poetry. So I take after Him.; [a.] Barron, Cumbria, UK

LAMB, KATIE
[b.] 23 August 1980, Aldershot; [p.] Jill Lamb (Healer), Jim Lamb (Builder); [ed.] Newport infant and Junior school from 4-10 the Connaught school from 11-15; [occ.] School leaver; [memb.] Albany, Dancing Centre Where I received 6 med-

als for dancing.; [hon.] I was made a prefect at school. I won a short story competition when I was 11. I received the award for personal, achievement in my tutor group when I was 14.; [oth. writ.] Winning a short story competition at school when I was 11.; [pers.] The poem, 'Faith' was influenced by Michael Jackson's heal the work] foundation and I wrote it when I was 11. My ambition is to become a t.v. presenter.; [a.] Aldershot, Hampshire, UK

LAMPE, DEBBIE
[b.] 20 January 1962, Dagenham; [p.] Derek Brockwell, Barbara Brockwell; [m.] Brian Lampe, 18 July 1986; [ch.] Sarah-Jane and Daryl Lampe; [ed.] McKentye Comprehensive Walthamstow; [occ.] Housewife; [memb.] I attend a Spiritual Circle; [oth. writ.] I have written a prayer and a poem for my friends in the circle I attend.; [pers.] I always write what I feel, and I dedicate this poem to my daughter Sarah-Jane.; [a.] Hoddesdon, Herts, UK

LANE, ELIZABETH
[b.] 24 November 1967, Youghal; [p.] Patrick Lane, Sheila Lane; [m.] Peter Goodwin, 4 October 1996; [ed.] Loreto Secondary School, Youghal, Co. Cork., Ireland; [occ.] Housekeeper; [pers.] When you find yourself between the tides of life, and the cold fear of nothingness drags you down, keep a grip on your self respect and you will swim the worlds oceans keeping your head above water.; [a.] Youghal, Cork, UK

LANNIGAN, WILLIAM
[b.] 30 March 1961, Coltness; [p.] John Lannigan and Jessie Lannigan; [m.] Mary Lannigan, 30 July 1983; [ch.] Vhari and Alistair; [ed.] Coltness High School; [occ.] Registered General Nurse; [memb.] Boy's Brigade; [oth. writ.] Several Poems for friends on special occasions (Leaving-Birthdays etc.); [pers.] Poem was originally written for my daughter.; [a.] Wisham, Strathclyde, UK

LATTIMORE, TOBY
[pen.] T. V. Lattimore; [b.] May 31, 1975, Luton; [p.] Philip and Susan Lattimore; [m.] Engaged to Joanna Brassington, coming up on June 30, 1997; [ed.] Beaumont School to Hertfordshire University to St. Helens College; [occ.] Student - studying a H.N.D. in Design TV and Video; [memb.] I'm a member of the R.S.P.B.; [oth. writ.] I have written many other poems which I have yet to send for publication; [pers.] My poetry is greatly influenced by Gustav Holst's 'The planets' and Ludwig Van Beethoven's Piano Concertos especially a Dagio Cantabile. I'm also very interested in environmental issues.; [a.] St. Albans, Herts, UK

LAWMAN, JUNE
[b.] 20 June 1942, Matlock, Derbyshire; [p.] William Len, Betty Len; [m.] Widowed; [ch.] Susan Kathleen, John Victor, Ian William; [ed.] Upper Clapton Comprehensive School; [occ.] Housewife (Spiritual Medium); [oth. writ.] Poetry published in "A Channel of Peace" 1994.; [pers.] Over the past 5 years I have written through spiritual inspiration approximately 40 poems, of love, hope and faith.; [a.] Braintree, Essex, UK

LAWRENCE, PATRICIA ELVIRA
[b.] 22 February 1920, Ealing; [p.] John James Wells and Elvira Maud Wells; [occ.] Retired; [hon.] President of the General Association of Ladies Hairdresser 1964-1966, Master Crafts-

man, Companion of Honour G.A.L.H.; [oth. writ.] Four poems published in "Poets of the Year" Book 1976. Newbury Gazette 1980 reading pensioners voice 1990's.; [pers.] As a child I started writing poetry. Still wake up at night. Thinking in Rhyme. I like to `Paint a Poem' so that readers. Can enjoy the picture. My poems take many different forms, as I write, not only from personal experience, but also from observation of people and things around me.; [a.] Caversham, Berkshire, UK

LAWS, GRAEME
[pen.] Grae Laws, Grae Storm; [b.] 9 November 1970, Northallerton; [p.] Charles Christopher and Catherine Shirley; [ed.] Wensleydale School; [occ.] Lithographic Printer; [memb.] National Anti Vivisection Soc.; [oth. writ.] See the sea scene, seen in a dream - poetry now book of art poetry Brigantia Metcalf, The Iron Age Antihero a self published illustrated poetic novel.; [pers.] My creative work is always a dedication to the following. Friends at home and those overseas. To friends of the past and those I have yet to meet.; [a.] Leyburn, North Yorkshire, UK

LE-VALLOIS, RUTH
[b.] Paisley; [m.] Maurice; [occ.] Doctors' Receptionist; [memb.] Local Writers' Group; [oth. writ.] Some poems published in anthologies; [pers.] I would like to be a successful comedy writer for T.V. or Radio - and have my book published. Forever hopeful!; [a.] Paisley, Renfrewshire, UK

LEADBITTER, DAVID WILLIAM
[pen.] David William Leadbitter; [b.] 14 February 1970, Cockermouth; [p.] Mr. and Mrs. William Thomas Leadbitter; [m.] Mrs. Karen Denise Leadbitter, 9 August 1996; [ed.] BSC (Hons) Microbiology at Newcastle Upon Tyne Uni., School - St. Bees School, Cumbria; [occ.] Pharmaceutical Sales Rep.; [pers.] If we are honest with ourselves about everything, then we honestly don't know anything.; [a.] Cockermouth, Cumbria, UK

LEAHY, GWEN
[pen.] Alexina Showe; [b.] Walworth, London; [p.] Mr. and Mrs. W. Howes (Deceased); [m.] Mr. M. Leahy, 8 April 1985; [ch.] 5 Boys; [ed.] 6 different schools including Upton Dorset was 8th when left school at Rorset out class of 40; [occ.] Housewife/Carer; [memb.] Attended Journalist/Writing Course in Finsbury/for short spell, writing poetry; [hon.] Nil, except for newspaper comp - prizes from mag.; [oth. writ.] Book poetry published 1981- have short stories poems accepted for publication in Welsh magazine. 1 poem for English mag., poem for royals in newspaper. In school play/2 parts. School Choir.; [pers.] As a very young child was interested in poetry and writing. Began writing again seriously after writing my biography for family.; [a.] London, Walthamstow, UK

LEAVY, BERNADETTE
[b.] 1934, Leeson St; [p.] Dermot Farrell McDonnell, Catrene Power; [m.] 1955; [ed.] Banaher's Bording School The School of Art; [occ.] Catering; [oth. writ.] In the middle of writing about my school days and score's of poems.; [pers.] Their's a price for everything and everything has its price so think twice. Other interests cooking, drawing and as astrolity.; [a.] Dublin, Ireland

LEDGER, THOMAS HENRY
[pen.] Tom Ledger; [b.] 17 September 1960, Bishops Cleeve; [p.] Joseph Richard, Marie Elizabeth; [m.] Vera, 12 February 1994; [ch.] Michael Samuel; [ed.] New Zealand; [occ.] Missionary; [memb.] Sulam Yaakov Messianic Fellowship; [oth. writ.] Poetry Volume - Emotions in time (NZ) articles for church magazines.; [pers.] My earlier poems came out of passion and pain to repentance and faith. Now I write of praise, revelation and love and devotion.; [a.] Manchester, Lancashire, UK

LEE, CHRISTOPHER ANDREW
[b.] 26 July 1956, Nottingham; [p.] Cyril Lee and Marion Lee; [m.] Valerie (Fletcher) Lee, 5 August 1978; [ch.] Mark Andrew; [ed.] Ripon Grammar; [occ.] Service Man; [oth. writ.] Several poems published in Arrival press anthologies and Service magazines; [pers.] Influenced by Owen, Ann Evans, Sassoon, Graves, Enjoy writing poetry/ song lyrics.; [a.] Innsworth, Gloucester, UK

LENK, R. S.
[b.] 9 June 1921, Vienna; [ed.] RG VII (Vienna), Birkbeck College (Univ. of London); [occ.] Retired Senior Lecturer Self-publishing author and Un-expert in Plastic Technology; [hon.] B. Sc. Chem., B. Sc. Zool., Ph.D., F.R.I.C., F.P.I.; [oth. writ.] The Mauritius Affair, The Greenbook of Animal Verse, The Adventure of a Bear Called Rancid, Extra-Terrestrial Creatures (Almanac of Millennium Blues, Bilingual Poetry (in print); [pers.] In my writings I have concerned myself with matters Jewish, with animals, children's poetry cosmology and contemporary philosophical issues.; [a.] Woodingdean-Brighton, Sussex, UK

LETHBRIDGE, ANN
[b.] 6 February 1943, Devon; [occ.] Early retired School Teacher, now running a business; [oth. writ.] Nothing published so far! Poems, stories for children as well as part of a novel - hidden in my desk.; [pers.] I love so many people and I write for them, although usually they are not aware of it.; [a.] Plymouth, Devon, UK

LETHBRIDGE, KATHARINE
[b.] 1 December 1904, Simla, India; [p.] John Maynard, Alfreda Eppes; [m.] John Lethbridge, 15 August 1925; [ch.] Nemone, Peter, Katharine; [ed.] Sherborne Girls; [occ.] Coping with age; [oth. writ.] Rout of the Ollaf UBS in search of Thunder, children's stories P. Faber, forthright and Meanders Faber, letters from East and West P. Merlin Press, Braunton.; [pers.] A love of english poetry ever since learning to recite "Over the Hills and Far Away," and "Hey diddle diddle, The Cat and The Fiddle.".; [a.] Morthoe, Devon, UK

LEVETT-DARLING, WENDY
[b.] 28/04/47, Sevenoaks; [p.] Bunny and Pat; [ed] Hatton Secondary Modern, Sevenoaks; Tunbridge Wells Technical College; Harrogate College of Arts and Technology; [memb.] Society for Psychical Research (SPR); Also, intended membership of Association of Speakers Clubs (ASC); [hon.] Honours and Awards as endowed by my peers at the University of life; [oth. writ.] Poems published in other anthologies as a new author; [pers.] I write in the modern vernacular whilst wearing an 'L' plate. The realms of ESP, fantasy and the unknown are my sources of inspiration intermingled with a personal belief in God for good measure.; [a.] Harrogate, N. Yorks

LEWIECKI, MARIE
[b.] 27 November 1981, Wrexham; [p.] Pauline and Andrew; [ed.] St. Mary's RC Primary, St. Josephs High Wrexham; [occ.] Full time student; [memb.] Wrexham Seals (Sub Aqua), Wrexham Police Judo Club, Duke of Edinburgh; [hon.] St. Johns certificate of First Aid. London College of Music Piano Honours grade one, two and three; [pers.] I would like to thank my poem moves you and makes you more aware of what is happening to the world and its creatures. Thanks Mum and Dad.; [a.] Wrexham, Wrexham County, UK

LEWIS, IRMA
[b.] 3 December 1941, Saint Kitts; [m.] 14 December 1959; [ch.] Five children all grown up; [ed.] YCE 'O' level in Sociology in 1980; [occ.] Cartering Ass at the local hospital; [memb.] Of two womens groups; [oth. writ.] Memories Of Back Home, Living Is A Strange Land, The Many Joys Of Life, Missing You.; [pers.] I came to this county age fifteen in 1956. I am married and has five grown up children. I write poem's in my spear time. I am on the committee of the West Indian Womens Class, also Spring Board Women's Groups.; [a.] Leeds, Yorkshire, UK

LEWIS, JOHN
[b.] 7 July 1936, Abertillery; [p.] Cliff Lewis, Lilian Lewis; [m.] Glynys Lewis, 25 March 1961; [ch.] Heidi, Peter; [ed.] Bryngwyn Sec Mod; [occ.] School Cartaker Ex-Mineworker; [memb.] Chairman Cwmtillery R.F.C.; [oth. writ.] Several poems published by arrival press and local newspaper.; [a.] Abertillery, Gwent, UK

LEWIS, MARY ISIDORA
[pen.] Dora Lewis; [b.] 25 January 1906, Bilbad, Spain; [p.] David and Edith Lewis; [ed.] Wellington High School, Salop, University of Birmingham, Whitelands College, London; [occ.] Retired Teacher; [hon.] B.A. (Hons in English Certificate in Education (University of London); [oth. writ.] Accounts of touch comic verse, a few poems a history of my family and ancestors some essays. All unpublished); [pers.] I look forward to achieving more in my next life!; [a.] Broadway, Worcs, UK

LEWIS, SIMON P.
[b.] 6 December 1980, Upton, Wirral; [p.] John Lewis, Janet Lewis; [ed.] Solar Campus, Year 11; [pers.] I think that love is the most powerful force mankind has. The happiness it can bring to people is never ending. This poem is dedicated to lovers that are yet to meet.; [a.] Hoylake, Wirral, UK

LILES, GARY
[b.] 1 November 1961, Watford; [p.] Clifford and Christine Ann Liles; [ed.] Bushey Meads (Before George Michael), Secondary Modern School and Royal Air Force Education Centre; [memb.] Royal British Legion; [hon.] Most Improved Athlete RAF 1990, RAF Champion Athletics Cyprus, 1991 Raf Sports Colours Cyrus, 1990 and 1991 Certificate of Accomplishment 70 Mile Walk for Charity, and Gulf War Medal; [oth. writ.] I have many other writings however none have ever been submitted to any one.; [pers.] To learn you must first observe, my only tool is the observation of other people and life around me.; [a.] Watford, Hertfordshire, UK

LINDEN, PETER
[b.] 4 April 1921, N.W. London; [p.] Ethel Linden, Percy Linden; [m.] Divorced; [ch.] Andrew Linden, Jeremy Linden; [ed.] Formal Boys' Boarding Schools - Tyttenhanger Lodge, Seaford, Sussex, Haileybury College, Hertford; [occ.] Retired after being M.D. (3rd Generation) of family, Advertising Display Designers and Manufacturers; [memb.] Royal Institute of Philosophy, London; [oth. writ.] A privately published paperback of my own (selected) poems titled "Slimmer Than Most"; [pers.] My business career was not to my like but it was a family `commitment.' Whenever possible, mostly evening and weekends, I used all available time writing verse and sculpture in abstract with metals and stone or rock. With exhibitions in England and Denmark. My extensive reading of philosophical work and of my best-loved poet, Dylan Thomas, is obvious in my work.; [a.] London, UK

LINFIELD, NICOLA
[pen.] Nicky; [b.] 10 October 1969, Rustington; [ed.] Washington Cote Primary School 1977, Sion School Worthing - 1987 1987-1991 Homerton College Cambridge University; [occ.] Primary Teacher and Youth Worker; [hon.] B. Ed.; [oth. writ.] Two books of personal history, one short, one of 360 and poem of my search for recovery in my eating disorder tempting to reach other sufferers cared and interested people - poems also; [pers.] Printed by proprint of Peterborough. PE2 7BU I find my writing a powerful tool for emotional release and celebration and enjoy writing.; [a.] Weston-super-Mare, North Somerset, UK

LINNEY, MISS BARBARA ANN
[pen.] Barbara Ella; [b.] 29 August 1937, London; [p.] Deceased; [ch.] Three: 35, 33, 30; [ed.] College A Level in Art Design; [occ.] Public School want to college; [oth. writ.] Book of my life sent off for publication; [pers.] I am pleased that you are publishing my poems its all my own work thank you; [a.] Kiddermenster, Worcs, UK

LITTEN, CLIVE HOWARD
[b.] 16 January 1947, Redding; [p.] Wallace Litten, Veronica Litten; [m.] Jean Eileen Litten, 2 May 1970; [ch.] Brett Andrew Litten; [ed.] The Grove Secondary Modern Reading College and Technology; [occ.] Managing Director, Building Firm; [memb.] Berkshire Masonry the Caravan Club; [oth. writ.] Many other poems composed, concerning all walks of life as yet unpublished.; [pers.] My poems reflects human nature and invariably based on life as it is. My Interest in poetry started at 14 after in death study of "The Listening" By Walter De La More..; [a.] Reading, Berkshire, UK

LLOYD, EMMA ELIZABETH JANE
[b.] 3 October 1979, Devon; [p.] Simon and Christine Lloyd; [ed.] Liskeard School and Community College; [occ.] 'A' Level Student; [a.] Liskeard, Cornwall, UK

LOBO, SUSAN READ
[pen.] Susan Read-Lobo; [b.] 25 May 1953, Guildford; [p.] Enid Read and Brian Read; [m.] Carlos Lobo-Abad, 10 November 1977; [ch.] Ivan (age 19), Xavier (age 16); [ed.] In various schools in Africa (Botwana and South Africa); [occ.] Left the hotel Business to bring up my sons 20 years ago.; [hon.] Spanish poetry competition - Participation honour. Poems read over radio Gibraltar X2 1st prizes in Gibraltar Poetry Competitions.; [oth. writ.] Book of African Poetry called "Africa My Africa". Book of poems called "The Housewife". A variety of poetry on various topics. Several children's stories. all yet unpublished.; [pers.] Life is a journey we have to go through and my poetry tries to see me through the bad patches. It is a dance of reality and fantasy intermingling, reflecting beauty fear love hate and humour - like looking into a mirror.; [a.] Los Barrios, Cadiz, Spain

LOCKER, ANNA LILLIAN
[pen.] Lily Locker; [b.] 22 November 1914, Ashington; [p.] Kate and Will White; [m.] Clarence Osterly Locker, 1 January 1940; [ed.] Comprehensive; [occ.] Housewife; [memb.] R.S.P.C.A., Mothers Union, St. Andrews Church, Wand WCVS, Victon Support; [hon.] RSPCA Medal and Certificate long service, Voluntary work 1954-1988; [oth. writ.] Lots of poems only two published - plus two with twins by our International Library - A small story Jackle Jackdaw; [pers.] The poem 'twins' I was a twin. But twin sister Delep in Jan. 1992. We were known as the white's Lily and Jean we were very close I miss her.; [a.] Ashington, Northumerland, UK

LOCKWOOD, MRS. DEBORAH GRACE
[pen.] Deborah Lockwood; [b.] 31 October 1944, Aldershot; [p.] Mildred Blandamer and Sidney-Constant Taylor; [m.] Rodney Lockwood, 28 March 1964; [ch.] Michaela and Mark; [ed.] St. Michael's Sec. Mod. Aldershot Farnham School of Art/Manor Park Adult - Typing and Shorthand/Farnborough Tec. College - Aromatherapy; [occ.] Cashier and Stock Holder at Aldershot Benefits Agency; [memb.] All England Netball - Umpire Approved, Genealogical Research Membership No. 12143; [hon.] N.V.Q. Level 2 in Administration; [oth. writ.] The rising sun (short story). Holy orders - (poem) letters in Bella and Prima Mags.; [pers.] I dedicate my poems, 'Cattle Branding,' 'Pow Wow' and 'Missouri River' to my brother Lawrence Taylor who opened my eyes to North America. I left my heart in the Black Hills.; [a.] Aldershot, Hants, UK

LODGE, EILEEN
[b.] 20 January 1927, Poona; [p.] Frederick and Doris Moore; [m.] James Alec Lodge, 27 June 1953; [ch.] Penelope Anne, Alexander John; [occ.] Retired; [memb.] Ex-Wartime W.A.A.F. Met. Office Cookham arts Club; [oth. writ.] Haiku etc. Published in small anthologies; [pers.] I write to amuse and entertain and hopefully to encourage others; [a.] Maidenhead, Berks, UK

LOMAS, ANTHONY CHARLES
[pen.] Tony Lomas; [b.] 15 May 1916, Barbados, West Indies; [p.] Lesley and Ruth Lomas; [m.] Joan Winifred Lomas, 9 March 1942; [ch.] Timothy and Judith; [ed.] Roborough School, Eastbourne Sussex; [occ.] Retired Architect; [memb.] Royal Institute of British Architects; [oth. writ.] "Ten O'Clock News" published in the poetry garden by "Poetry Now" other poems in Church Magazines.; [pers.] Aim: To write poems and word pictures on all subjects from the sad to the humorous.; [a.] Eastbourne, East Sussex, UK

LONG, BRUCE MARTIN
[b.] 11 October 1963, Bridgewater; [p.] Gordon and Judith Long; [ed.] Hele's School, Exeter, R.N.A.S. Deadalus, S.C.A.T. Taunton, Plymouth University; [occ.] Unemployed; [memb.] British Legion; [hon.] South Atlantic Medal; [pers.] I write poetry as a release from the stress and anxieties of everyday life.; [a.] Truro, Cornwall, UK

LONG, CHRIS
[b.] 2 September 1958, Worcester; [p.] Graham, Beryl Long; [m.] Rosemarie Long, 12 April 1986; [ch.] Stacey-Mae Long; [ed.] Christopher Whitehead Secondary School, Worcester College of Further Education; [pers.] I write to reflect the events in one's life, if the reader relates to it I have accomplished something.; [a.] Warley, West Midlands, UK

LONG, MILDRED FLORENCIA
[pen.] Millie Stone; [b.] Buenos Aires; [p.] Joseph Henry Stone and Martha N. Stone; [m.] Philip James Long (Deceased), 1956; [ch.] Step-daughter - Rita Mason; [ed.] Salvation Army Officer (Retired), State Registered Nurse, State Certified Midwife (Retired); [occ.] Retired; [memb.] NHS Retirement Fellowship - Chelmsford and District Branch, S.E. Essex Retired Salvation Army Officer's Fellowship; [oth. writ.] None published, except in S.A. Periodicals and occasional ones in NHS Retirement Fellowship Magazines (BL Monthly); [pers.] I give thanks for the influence of Godly parents, and by them encouragement to read good books. Early poetical works have always had charm and in later years - John Masefield, John Betjeman and Pam Ayres.; [a.] Rettenoon, Chelmsford, Essex, UK

LONG, MURIEL
[pen.] Muriel Long; [b.] 30 January 1913, Hartlepool; [p.] Ethel Balsdon and Harry Noble; [m.] Robert A. Long, July 1942; [ch.] Two daughters; [ed.] Grammar School then St. Peters College, Peterborough; [occ.] Retired but still writing.; [memb.] 1. National Trust, 2. NAGFAS (Nat. Associating of Graphical and Fine Arts, 3. Reaconsfield Historic Association; [oth. writ.] Several poems published in National Magazines, some poems broadcast from reading, various articles; [a.] Beaconsfield, Bucks, UK

LOWY, JACKIE
[b.] 3 May 1957, Canterbury, Kent; [p.] Philip E. High, Pamela High; [m.] Matthew Lowy, 20 November 1993; [ed.] Frank Hooker Secondary Modern, Canterbury Open University. University of Leicester. Coughborough University of Technology.; [occ.] Unemployed Nurse: Beginning Counsellor Training, November 1996; [memb.] Various Science Fiction Fan Clubs and Music Societies; [hon.] BA (hon) History of Art 1990. MA Information and Library Studies 1992.; [oth. writ.] Several poems published on local magazines Articles on 'Local Colour' for Music Society reviews of books, films, conventions for Science Fiction Clubs, belong to.; [pers.] To live life to the full, Learning from experience. Because if I can, anyone can. I use poetry as a form of catharsis, writing out my feelings helps me come to terms with them. Helping others do the sam. Early influences: Tennyson, Blake W. Owen S. Sasson Victorian Women Poets.; [a.] Benson, Oxfordshire, UK

LOXTON, JAMES
[b.] 18 April 1977, London; [p.] Peter Loxton, Heather Loxton Nee Forbes; [ed.] Milton Abbey School, Edinburgh University; [occ.] Student; [oth. writ.] Several articles published in school magazine; [pers.] I believe that self-expression is a gift to be shared with all.; [a.] Bere Regis, Dorset, UK

LUCAS, JUNE
[b.] 22 June 1932, Colnbrook; [m.] Frank, 28 August 1954; [ch.] Kevin and Jocelyn and 6 granddaughter; [ed.] Church of England School; [occ.] Supermarket Cashier; [memb.] Bowls, 30 years a brown owl of my local pack; [hon.] 30 year award for brownies top of the Windsor and Maidhead league for Bowls; [oth. writ.] Write children's short stories (as yet none published); [pers.] Like to write plays for my Brownie Pack; [a.] Horton, Berkshire, UK

LUCAS, MAURICE
[b.] 23 October 1958, England; [p.] Olga and Percy Lucas; [m.] Divorced; [ch.] One; [ed.] Highstorrs Comprehensive 1970-75, Sheffield Polytechnic 1988-89 Art and Design, Parkwood College, Architecture 1989-91.; [occ.] Artist; [hon.] Certificate in art and design. One man art Exhibitions and numerous Paintings in Private Collections. Currently working on paintings and photographs for major exhibition in Sheffield.; [a.] Sheffield, Yorkshire, UK

LUDGROVE, PENELOPE
[pen.] Penny Ludgrove; [b.] 7 February 1947, Brighton, Sx.; [p.] William and Daisy Baker; [m.] Les Ludgrove, 26 June 1965; [ch.] Phillip John, Leslie William; [ed.] Margaret Hardy Girls School, Brighton, Sussex; [occ.] Housewife; [pers.] I tend, not to take life too seriously, and hopefully through my poetry, make people smile.; [a.] Crawley, West Sussex, UK

LUNN, SADIE
[b.] 26 April 1978, Pembury, Kent; [p.] Sylvia Lunn, Stephen Lunn; [ed.] St. Gregory's School, and West Kent College; [occ.] A-Level Student; [memb.] Raleigh International; [pers.] The downfall in today's society is failing to recognize one's own prejudices but those of another.; [a.] Royal Tunbridge Wells, Kent, UK

LUSTY, JOANNE
[pen.] Issabelle Lacey; [b.] 4 March 1982, Birmingham; [p.] Kieth Lusty, Irene Leacy; [occ.] Student; [oth. writ.] "Our Faded Love" is my first piece.; [pers.] In my work I attempt to express my concerns for broken mankind. I wish to dedicate my poem to my mother.; [a.] Birmingham, West Midlands, UK

LYNCH, HELEN
[pen.] Justine Woodfine; [b.] 26 June 1980, Bedford; [p.] Matthew Lynch, Barbara Orchard; [ed.] Hastingbury Upper, currently studying 'A' levels at Bedford College; [occ.] Student of English, History Theatre Studies, Government and Politics; [oth. writ.] "Dad" is my first published poem.; [pers.] In my poems I strive to capture the essence of what it is to be young the turbulence of teenage years, embrace emotions involved and defining the triumph of breaking free from peer pressure. In "Dad" write of the heartache involved in the realisation that parents are barely worthy of the pedestal of perfection we put them on.; [a.] Bedford, Bedfordshire, UK

LYONS, GEORGE CLARK
[b.] 4 July 1961, Glasgow; [p.] John, Mary; [m.] Catherine, 1986; [ch.] Jonathan, Ashleigh; [occ.] Chef De Cuisine (Head-Chef); [oth. writ.] Poems - (Why, What if, Maybe, and Buts), (Forgotten Dreams), (Come What May), Short Stories - (Summer's Swing), (Loss of Innocence), (Lost in A Maze of Haze), Novel's - (Foresight and Vision

of Harsh-Realities).; [pers.] A contradiction is nothing more than a cell of the mind overshadowed in doubt. As you live for the day and fear for the morrow not quite. Knowing what to expect on the dawn of a new day in a world full of Human Sorrow.; [a.] Oban, Argyllshire, UK

MACARTHUR, NORMA A.
[pen.] Norma Anne; [b.] 8 March 1940, Edinburgh; [p.] Both parents deceased; [m.] Divorced, 20 March 1963; [ed.] Higher Leaving Certificate Scotland, McLaren High School, Callendar, Perthshire; [occ.] Nursing, Registered General Nurse; [memb.] Church of Scotland; [hon.] Several nursing prizes won during training at the Royal Infirmary of Edinburgh and Princess Margaret Rose Hospital, Edinburgh; [oth. writ.] A School Boy's Prayer, Hurry Scurry Up The Stairs, Railway Echoes, In The Park, Autumn Leaves, The Expert; [pers.] I became poetic when my marriage was dissolved some time ago. Over the years it has become a creative expressive outlet for my deepest joys and sorrows I regard it as a gift from God.; [a.] Edinburgh, Mid Lothian, UK

MACDONELL, DOUGLAS
[b.] 15 April 1920, Nairn, Scotland; [p.] Kenneth and Charlotte MacDonell; [m.] Bernice Alwyne MacDonell, 16 September 1944; [ch.] Two daughters; [ed.] Primary in Scotland, Canada and U.S.A., Secondary in U.S.A., Technical in England; [occ.] Retired Engineer; [memb.] Chartered Engineer, Fellow-Inst. Mech. Eng. (F.I. Mech. E.), Fellor-Inst. Elec. Eng. (F.I.E.E.), Aircrew Association R.A.F., Black Isle Writers' Group; [hon.] Mentioned in Dispatches (1943); [oth. writ.] Thesis "Production Management in Agricultural Implement Industry", published in Inst. Journal, 1958, 2 articles in production methods and 1966 machines short story in "Paperclifs - North Scotland" 1993, Various in Blackside Writers' Group Annual Anthology 1988.; [pers.] The poetry "Remembrance Parade" was written following a mass and parade in Sept. 89 in memory of F/lt David Lord, V. C., D.F.C. with whom I flew as navigator in 1944. He was shot down and killed at Arnhem while I was on marriage leave.; [a.] Dingwall, Ross-Shire, UK

MACHIN, THOMAS H.
[b.] 2 April 1970, Nottingham; [p.] Graham and Judith Machin; [ed.] Rudolph Steiner Education; [occ.] Unemployed - suffer from Schizophrenia- Do Voluntary work; [memb.] N.S.F.; [oth. writ.] Poem published in local paper in above called "Eye Of The Be Holder" compiled own anthology for an exhibition of creative art.; [pers.] I enjoy writing poetry because it gives me satisfaction hopefully people will begin to understand that people suffering from schrophrenia have creative ability.; [a.] Nottingham, Nottinghamshire, UK

MACMILLAN, MOUREEN KAY
[b.] 2 March 1959, Muir-of-Ord; [p.] Helen and Thomas McAteer; [m.] Colin John McMillan, 15 September 1979; [ch.] Colin - 15, Jonathan - 13, Michael - 9, Julie - 1; [ed.] Dingwall Academy, Ross-Shire; [occ.] Mother and Housewife; [memb.] Black Isle Writers Group, Fortrose; [hon.] The "Robert Burns" award for Literature; [oth. writ.] Two short stories in the Black Isle Writers Group Anthology "The Cuckoo's Egg" and The "Colour of Autumn"; [pers.] Thank you for allowing me to shake this poem with you.; [a.] Kirkhill, Inverness-shire, Scotland

MACPHERSON, FERGUS
[b.] 9 August 1921, Newmilns, Ayrshire; [p.] Hector and Catherine MacPherson; [m.] Myra, 8 November 1948; [ch.] Catherine, James, Myra, Alison, Elspeth, Fergus; [ed.] Daniel Stewart's College, Edinburgh, Edinburgh University (M.A. Hons), New College (Theol.) Ed. Univ. (Ph.D); [occ.] Retired (Minister and Missionary Educationist, Central Africa 1946-1976; [memb.] Dalgarno Singers, Thornhill, Baracuda Gymnasium, Dumfries; [oth. writ.] Approx 180 poems short and long, lyrical and narrative, rhyming and blank verse, two novels on African themes: One Blood and One Finger, published. Three academic published works on African History (O.U.P. and Longman).; [pers.] Though it seems that everywhere in Chinva Acher's Words' things fall apart, I am sure, viscerally, that the blueprint of the universe requires wholeness as personified in Jesus Christ.; [a.] Penpont, Dumfries-Shire, UK

MAHER, ANNA
[b.] 17 December 1979, Hertfordshire; [p.] Shirley and Philip Maher; [ed.] Cherwell School, Oxford; [occ.] A poet and still a student at school; [pers.] Live very moment like it's your last.; [a.] Oxford, Oxfordshire, UK

MAINWARING, ANNE-MARIE
[b.] 24 July 1979, Chipping, Sudbury; [p.] Malcolm Mainwaring, Valerie Mainwaring; [ed.] King Edmund Community School - Yate; [occ.] 'A' Level Student; [pers.] I am really pleased to have my first poem published and I would like to thank my sisters Susan and Claire as without them the poem would not be possible.; [a.] Bristol, South Gloucestershire, UK

MALKIN, MRS. M. E. Y.
[b.] 30 May 1925, Wootton, Bassett; [p.] Ernest Iles and Winifred Iles; [m.] Edmund Malkin (Deceased), 30 August 1945; [ch.] 2 adult sons; [ed.] Secondary Modern; [occ.] Retired; [oth. writ.] Church Magazine Entries; [pers.] On the death of my beloved husband I found a need to talk to someone who understood so I started to talk to God in my verses and found comfort in his nearness.; [a.] Wootton Bassett Swindon, Wilts, UK

MALLOCH, HEATHER
[pen.] Jenna Stephens; [b.] 3 July 1966, Dundee; [p.] David McFarlane, Catherine McFarlane; [m.] Stephen Malloch, 17 September 1988; [ch.] Lauren Jenna Malloch, Stephen David Malloch; [ed.] Kiriston High School; [occ.] Customer Link Manager, Tesco; [oth. writ.] Poem ('Brookside') - Book Soap Wars by Trudi Ram; [pers.] I enjoy writing short stories and poems. 'My Life' was especially interesting to write as it was a true account of my life.; [a.] Dundee, Tayside, UK

MANAGH, JOANNE
[pen.] Joanne Caseley; [b.] 11 March 1964, Solihull; [p.] Roy Henry Caseley, Ursula Mary Caseley; [ed.] Tauranga Girls College, Tauranga, New Zealand; [occ.] Communications officer, Metropolitan Police; [oth. writ.] Nearly 200 other poems. Maybe one day I will be fortunate enough to have them published.; [pers.] Inspired entirely by the joy of life and pursuit of personal happiness.; [a.] Greenford, Middlesex, UK

MANN, MR. MAURICE
[pen.] The Bard Ox (331) (162) (T.A. Units); [b.] 15 November 1939, Cheddington, Bucks; [p.] Deceased; [m.] Divorced, Engaged; [ed.] Sec.

Med., HM Forces Ace II III; [occ.] Forklift Truck Driver; [memb.] Ex Regular Soldier 7 yrs., Ex Territorial Army 25 yrs.; [hon.] Regular Army GSM, Clasp Borneo, Clasp South Arabia, Territorial Army LS and GCM with 2 Silver Rose Clasps; [oth. writ.] Poems published in various mags., article in USA newspaper events in Territorial Army Calendar, odes to various members TA.; [pers.] Inspiration gained by time, place, events, write as I see, usually in rhyme.; [a.] Bedford, Beds, UK

MANN, RACHEL
[b.] 22 April 1976, Pontypridd; [p.] Roger Mann, Avril Mann; [ed.] Coedylan Comprehensive; [occ.] Music and Drama Teacher on Penrhys Community Project; [oth. writ.] In the process of writing: 2 novels and the modern musical version of "Pride and Prejudice" for the stage.; [pers.] It has always been my life's ambition to see my work in print - now I shall have to set myself another goal!; [a.] Pontypridd, Mid-Glamorgan, UK

MANNERING, MELANIE
[pen.] Melanie Mannering; [b.] June 14, 1967, Margate, Kent; [p.] Monica and David Mannering; [m.] Stuart Taylor; [ch.] Jessica Lucy Taylor; [ed.] The King Ethelbert School, Birchington, Kent, West Kent College of F.E. Tonbridge, Kent; [occ.] Domestic; [memb.] Trainer and Youth Leader for British Red Cross, Margate, Birchington Silver Band; [oth. writ.] 'Little Sea Haven' was included in an anthology, 'Poetry in motion, Southeast'.; [pers.] I write poetry to express my inner thoughts and feelings as a relief.; [a.] Margate, Kent, UK

MANNION, BRIDIE
[b.] 10 March 1936, Tooreen, Co Galway; [p.] Peter Donohue, Bridget Curley; [m.] John Mannion, 28 September 1960; [ch.] Colette; [ed.] Convent of Mercy Ball in as Loe (ALCMLLCMTD) London College of Music (Speech and Drama), (D.H.H.S.A.) Institute of Hospital Administrators (Extra-Mural), University College Galway (Information Technology) Regional College Galway; [occ.] Health Board Official; [memb.] K.S.T. Bridge Club, Claddagh Bridge Club, Grattan Bridge Club; [hon.] Irish Literature; [oth. writ.] I compile crosswords for magazines - several published.; [pers.] Nature is wonderful, go out, look, listen, think and relax.; [a.] Galway, Galway, UK

MARKANDYA, SARLA
[b.] 22 December 1920, Campbellpur, India; [m.] Dr. O. P. Markandya, 16 April 1944; [ch.] Dr. Anil Markandya, Mr. Vinay Markandya; [ed.] M.A. Philosophy, Punjab University - Post Graduate Certificate in Teaching, Edinburgh Scotland. Retired as a teacher from Surrey in 1981, Taught in Uganda from 1949-1965, in England 1965-1981.; [occ.] Retired, Freelance Painter and Writer; [memb.] Friend of Royal Academy of Arts, Piccadilly, London, Member of a local Hard of Healing Club, served on several committees in Uganda like Uganda Association of University Women, Uganda Association of Women; [hon.] Status of Women and many more, Uganda Council, achieved Uganda Independence Medal in Eecognition of Voluntary Services; [oth. writ.] I have written a book, "Thoughts for the Day", which is widely distributed amongst friends. 2. Book of "Garland of Vverses", some poems published in Magazine.; [pers.] I have become profoundly hard of healing after my retirement. This loss has triggered my sensitivity towards other

intellectual pursuits. I try to portray goodness of mankind in all my paintings and writings. Communication is a problem but I have learnt to live with this loss.; [a.] Totteridge, Barnet, UK

MARRABLE, JOYCE
[b.] 14 December 1924, Dundee; [p.] Deceased; [ed.] Home Teacher for the Blind Qualified, 2 Certificate of Qualification for Social Work (CQSW); [occ.] Retired from Senior Case Worker - Social Services Dept.; [memb.] Toc.H.; [oth. writ.] Apart from church magazine, this is my first attempt; [pers.] I am physically handicapped with Arthritis in base of spine, so am now looking to a new way of life in poetry and crafts. I like to express the goodness of God and magnificence of creation.; [a.] Hatfield, Hertfordshire, UK

MARSHALL, JILL
[pen.] Jill Howard; [b.] 31 March 1933, Harrow on Hill, Middx; [p.] Arthur and Edith Howard; [m.] John Marshall (Second Marriage), 28 March 1980; [ch.] 3 - Mark, Sarah, Joanna Pashley; [ed.] Sacred Heart High School; [occ.] Housewife; [memb.] In the nos. I was a member of "Geoids" a Gilbert a Sullivan Amateur Operatic Society; [hon.] Scholarship to Trinity College of Music; [oth. writ.] I have several unpublished poems.; [pers.] Writing poetry is my greatest pleasure. It is the only time I feel I am really myself. Neither wife daughter or mother!; [a.] Granthar, Lincs, UK

MARTIN, AMANDA-JANE
[b.] 13 July 1964, Cardiff; [p.] John Martin, Gloria Martin; [ed.] Heathfield House, High School in Cardiff, (now known as a College); [occ.] Despatch operative in Memory Lane Cakes Cardiff; [memb.] The Library of studies, Newport RD Cardiff, The London's Burning Club, of the I.T.V. serial that is televised); [hon.] A level in both English Literature and English Language I have been nominated for written poetry by the British Poetry Institute of the British Isles; [oth. writ.] 'In Remembrance of a Friend' published by Andy Head, Peterborough poetry published by 'London's Burning' in newsletters Middlesex, shortly going into publication 'The Dying Rose' by Poetry Institute British Isles Ltd.; [pers.] I believe that meaningful and inspiring poetry can only come from the heart. I would dearly love to have a full time career into writing, and feel that I can accomplish this. I have great admiration for 17th and 18th century writers, of their time.; [a.] Cardiff, UK

MARTIN, BLANCHE SUSAN
[b.] 12 August 1923, London; [p.] Blanche and Thomas Abbott; [m.] Widowed Twice, 1 June 1942, 2 May 1984; [ch.] Patricia Ann, Kevin John; [ed.] St. John The Divine Kennington, Church School; [occ.] Retired, Motoring, Gardening, Craftwork; [memb.] Too busy with grandchildren and great grandchildren; [hon.] Oh when at school I won the honour for my school by winning a South London competition on road safety. All those years ago they were worried about accidents; [oth. writ.] What I call my scribblings. I found writing therapeutic, after my sadness's.; [pers.] I've always loved words, so I like writing. We have made a mess of this world and we are waking up to the fact and trying to right mistakes. Optimist am I. I think we'll make it.; [a.] Wellingborough, Northants, UK

MARTIN, MS. EILEEN D.
[b.] April 12, 1917, London; [p.] David Government Insp., Susan; [ed.] Was taught by very good teachers who encouraged me to go on learning, told by one I could become a writer, am still learning; [occ.] Retired; [hon.] Several prizes from school, one the British prize for character; [oth. writ.] Nothing published before, have written a short story and have started a book and have written several poems; [pers.] Have always loved writing, play piano, very interested in American Wild West days also red Indian tribes. Doing crosswords and competitions and gardening; [a.] Folkstone, Kent, UK

MARTIN, LEO J.
[b.] 24 June 1918, Massachusetts, USA; [p.] Deceased; [m.] Deceased; [ch.] Four children - two male - two female; [ed.] 8 years of Elementary Schooling 4 years of High School and 1 year of College; [occ.] Retired; [oth. writ.] Poems; [a.] Chelmsford, Essex, UK

MARTLAND, CATHERINE ANNE
[pen.] Catherine Anne Martland and Catherine Anne Cusack; [b.] 24 August 1962, Blackpool; [p.] Stanislaus and Ellen Bickerstaffe; [m.] Paul Martland, 28 July 1983; [ch.] Kerry-Anne and Glen Joseph; [ed.] St. Bedes High, Woodlands Private Brownedge St. Mary's High; [occ.] Housewife, Mum, Dog Breeder; [memb.] Local Canine Clubs; [hon.] Judge (Local Canine Club Terrier Dog Show) Finalist in numerous Poetry Comps.; [oth. writ.] 9 Poems, (to date) Grandma's Prayer, An Angel May, Yesterday Once More, My Homeland, Oh Folly, This Mums Mine, Best Friends, The Little Shepherdess. Published by Anchor Books and P.I.B.I. and International Society of Poets.; [pers.] The healthy mind is an active one. Use it always, look around and see, what goes on about you and you too can be free.; [a.] Preston, Lancashire, UK

MASSEY, JAYNE
[b.] 20 August 1969, Barnsley; [p.] Martin and June Doherty; [m.] Ian Massey, 3 October 1994; [ch.] Shannon, Laura; [ed.] Darton High School; [occ.] Freelance Writer; [hon.] Qualified Aromatherapist; [oth. writ.] Several articles published in weekly magazines.; [pers.] Believe in yourself.; [a.] Barnsley, South Yorkshire, UK

MATKIN, EDNA
[b.] 22 July 1938, Stretton Nr Burton-on-Trent, Staffs; [m.] Joseph Matkin, 22 December 1956; [ch.] Gillian Ann, Wendy Elizabeth; [ed.] Secondary Modern ("For Girls") School, Staffordshire; [occ.] Care Assistant; [memb.] St. Peter's Methodist Church Mablethorpe, Lincolnshire, Disability Lincs, Mablethorpe, W.I. Sutton-on-Sea Lincs, Red Cross, Salvation Army Lincs; [oth. writ.] Poems published in the church magazine.; [pers.] I write down what I feel in my heart to give comfort and pleasure.; [a.] Mablethorpe, Lincs, UK

MATTHEWS, JOAN Y.
[b.] 3 November 1940, Birmingham; [p.] Edward and Violet Crook; [m.] Derek George Matthews, 29 March 1958; [ch.] Jacqueline, Annette and Philip, grandchildren Katie, Lauren, Jay and Liam Joseph and Jessica; [ed.] Secondary Modern School; [occ.] Retired Sales Consultant; [memb.] Local W.I Institute and Patron of Local Operatic Society; [hon.] School Diplomas in Art and Design. Elocution and Handwriting won a diploma for painting displayed at the Glyn Vivian Art Galbry in

1952. Swansea; [oth. writ.] Other poems being published in Anthologies and also one of my poems are to be recorded on cassette tape; [pers.] Most of my poems are about the trials of life and experiences. I hope they will bring meaning to the reader.; [a.] Swansea, Glamorgan, UK

MATTHEWS, PETER ROBERT
[pen.] Schpeedle Bumpkin; [b.] 20th Century, Hereford; [p.] Oliver and Anne; [m.] Ursula, 7 October 1964; [ch.] Richard, David, Mark and Jane; [ed.] Deacon's Grammar School, Peterborough; [occ.] Director of Advertising Co.; [memb.] Barnet Copthall Swim Club, N. London Squash Club, Ronnie Scotts Jazz Club; [oth. writ.] Numerous songs, winner of LBC competition on Pete Murray Programme, other poems; [pers.] If life is just a bowl of cherries then give me the tree.; [a.] Halstead, Essex, UK

MAULKERSON, MARK
[b.] March 21, 1976, London; [p.] Ken Maulkerson and Pat Maulkerson; [m.] Engaged to Elle Forecast; [ed.] Morpeth Secondary School, Barking College of Technology; [occ.] Printer, Jet Press Operator; [hon.] City and Guilds, Print and Technology Sporting Achievements, e.g., Football, Swimming; [oth. writ.] Other Poems - Holiday, Winter Weather, Future, Contrast.; [a.] Dagenham, Essex, UK

MAUREE, ANDEEA
[pen.] Venn; [b.] 11 September 1958, Mauritius; [p.] Canda Mauree (F), Veda Mauree (M); [m.] Joan-Marie Mauree, 24 December 1986; [ch.] Keshini Anjushree, Anshula Priyanka; [ed.] Primary and Secondary Edu. in Mauritius, South Bank University, University of Hertfordshire; [occ.] Design/Estimate Co-ordinator Thames Water Utilities; [memb.] Institute of Plumbing Engineering Council; [oth. writ.] Written several unpublished poems; [pers.] The beauty of this complete universe fascinate my imagination. In my own little world, I try to reach this beauty through my writing.; [a.] Saint Albans, Hertfordshire, UK

MAY, SINDY-LOU
[b.] 9 August 1971, Lyndhurst, Hants; [p.] Ray and Sue Ward; [occ.] Work for Micron Clean as a team leader. We specialise in garment care, for pharmaceutical industries and computer/salilite industries; [pers.] Poetry is my hobby, and I write occasionally, when the mood takes me. I hope you enjoy reading it as I did writing it.; [a.] Thatcham, Berkshire, UK

MAYO, E. W.
[pen.] Tebil Malou (Music); [m.] Joan, 1952; [ch.] Two boys; [ed.] Secondary, College of Music 1950, Liverpool, Open University, Music, Art 1988; [occ.] Retired - Contract Management (self-employed), Past Teacher Music, Art (Private); [memb.] Past-Chairman, I.O.M. Art Society; [oth. writ.] Non published, T.V. play 'Silent Witness' poems, scenario for ballets (own music), anecdotes, philosophical quotes, short verses (to own paintings), songs.; [pers.] I firmly believe that I am a mere channel through which past souls continue their artistic endeavors.; [a.] Hope, Flintshire, UK

MCALLISTER, STUART JAMES
[pen.] M. Y. Connor; [b.] 10 January 1969, Biggar; [p.] Bill McAllister, Wilma Cook; [m.] Claire Johnston; [ch.] One on the way; [ed.] Loudon Academy; [occ.] Painter and decorator; [hon.] Northern Ireland Medal, Gulf War Medal;

[pers.] It matters not, what happens in our life time. As long as our son's and daughter's are free to do as they wish.; [a.] Coulter, Lanarkshire, UK

MCALPINE, MARGARET S.
[b.] 24 December 1943, Glasgow; [p.] William and Robina McAlpine; [ed.] Govan Senior Secondary School, Jordanhill College of Education Glasgow; [occ.] Primary Teacher for 29 yrs. Early retirement (aged 50) on health grounds; [memb.] Active member of New Govan Church of Scotland - editor of church magazine and teacher of Scottish country dancing; [hon.] Higher in English and French, O levels in Russian and Math, D.C.E. - Diploma of College of Education, R.S.C.D.S. - Royal Scottish Country Dance Society; [oth. writ.] I have written just 9 poems but never before offered any for possible publication.; [pers.] I am now middle-aged and have experience some of the trials of life. This has strengthened my faith and my poems reflect the importance of my faith in my life.; [a.] Glasgow, UK

MCCLELLAN, MARY D.
[pen.] Molly Helmrich; [b.] 13 December 1926, Aberdeen; [p.] Deceased; [m.] Deceased, 14 October 1974; [ed.] Limited; [occ.] Retired civil servant; [pers.] I first wrote poems when I was hospitalized for six months many years ago - since then I write as I am compelled to write.; [a.] Aberdeen, Grampian, UK

MCCONNACHIE, TOM
[pen.] Tammy Troot; [b.] 4 August 1936, Dundee; [p.] John and Mary; [m.] Frances Stone Ogilvie, 26 August 1958; [ch.] Five (one deceased); [ed.] Logie Secondary School, Dundee; [occ.] Night Duty Caretaker, Dundee City Council Housing Division; [memb.] Kiethick Angling Club; [hon.] Secondary School Dux for Art, Former Tutor Practical Fishing and Fly Tying Dundee, Education Committee (self taught); [oth. writ.] Published poems: 'Oor Heilan, Coo' in Poets Choice Book, 'Our Wild Primrose' in Anthology Quiet Moments.; [pers.] My poetry like My Fishing, Lets Me Get Away From It All, Hard As I Angle For Fish, Same Goes In Searching For Words, Comes Stages When The Quarry Is Hard To Identify, Lost In An Advanced Stage Of My Beloved Hobbies.; [a.] Dundee, Tayside, UK

MCCONNELL, ALICE
[b.] 19 March 1982, Saint Albans; [p.] Mrs. Hannah McConnell and Mr. Antony McConnell; [ed.] Attending Secondary School, year 9, (St. Anne's Convent School, Southampton); [memb.] St. Anne's Singers; [hon.] Haven't get any yet.; [oth. writ.] The poems not published; [pers.] Peace to all mankind and tranquility to sheep everywhere. Baaaa. - sense of humour! Seriously - Capo Derum; [a.] Hursley, Winchester, Hampshire, UK

MCCORMICK, ROBERT JENNINGS
[b.] 4 May 1932, Durham; [p.] William McCormick - Mary McCormick; [m.] Divorced; [ch.] Christopher and Samantha; [ed.] St. Bedes RC Sacriston Co Durham, Stroud Tech. College, Stroud Gloucestershire; [occ.] Medically Retired; [hon.] English/English Lit.; [oth. writ.] Many poems and short stories. I have had two other poems to be published by January 1997, they are 'No More The Darkness' and 'The Lion's Roar-Beware!'; [pers.] Try and listen to those who wish to be heard. I am greatly influenced by William Blake's work and Rudyard Kipling.; [a.] Stanley, Durham, UK

MCDERMOTT, DENIS
[b.] 10 May 1973, Galway; [occ.] Plasterer; [pers.] I wrote this poem to express the true feelings I have for my one true love Bernie Kenny; [a.] Castlerea, Roscommon, UK

MCGEEVER, SHARON
[pen.] Sharon McGeever; [b.] 1 April 1967, Paisley; [p.] Ann Boyle, Shaun Boyle; [m.] Patrick McGeever, 29 June 1988; [ch.] Louise, Anna, Patrick, Ryan; [ed.] Holyrood Secondary School, Glasgow; [occ.] Looking after my four children; [oth. writ.] Poems published in Local Poetry Competitions. Children's poems for enjoyment of my own children.; [a.] Glasgow, UK

MCGONIGLE, GEMMA JANE
[b.] 13 March 1983, Peterborough; [p.] Peter and Jane McGonigle; [occ.] School; [hon.] Piano grade 1; [oth. writ.] None as yet; [pers.] I express my feelings in my poems.; [a.] Whittlesey, Cambridgeshire, UK

MCGOWAN, HEATHER
[b.] 8 April 1969, Bournemouth; [p.] Susan and Rennick; [ch.] Two twins girls; [ed.] O' Level French studies, English Lan Lit grade 2; [occ.] Mother - Fulfilling dance, singing, lyrics — soon; [memb.] Past 2 entries turning down - typewriter didn't print (new ribbon) 2nd handed in 2 days late; [hon.] NIL; [oth. writ.] This is the third time entry the competition, kept the same (daily mail title) Changing Verses - Very Keen Lyricist.

MCINTYRE, DEBBIE
[pen.] Debbie McIntyre; [b.] 10 June 1984, Kirkcaldy; [p.] Kenneth McIntyre, Jane McIntyre; [ed.] Warout Primary School, Glenrothes Fife, Auchmuty High School, Glenrothes Fife; [hon.] Burn's Federation Certificates (three) presented Warout Primary, End of term awards for Reading, writing; [oth. writ.] "The Seashore" published in the book voices of Scotland; [pers.] I enjoy poetry very much. I was influenced for "The Rivers Life" by a previous project at school on which I studied rivers. I am very pleased and surprised that my poem has been chosen to be published.; [a.] Glenrothes, Fife, UK

MCKENNA, MRS. SHEILA
[pen.] Josephine Carey; [b.] 25 September 1938, Dublin, Ireland; [p.] Mary and Cyril Baker; [m.] Joseph McKenna (Deceased 28 June 1996), 6 September 1978; [ed.] Intermediate; [occ.] Home Lover; [memb.] Irish Hard of Hearing Association, Lifelines Amnesty International; [oth. writ.] Won Cup for School Awarded by Trinity College, Dublin for an Essay Entitled. "The Life Story of a Seagull"; [pers.] I follow The Philosophy of Rudyard Kipling's Poem - "If". Particularly the verse - "If you can dream - and not make dreams your master, if you can think and not make thoughts your aim.; [a.] Templeogue, Dublin, UK

MCLEAN, MRS. JANICE M.
[pen.] 'Rara Avis'; [b.] 15 January 1947, Motherwell; [p.] Agnes (Deceased) and Adam Crawford; [m.] George McLean, 14 September 1973; [ch.] Scott - 20 and Kirsty - 14; [ed.] Dalziel High School, Dalziel High Night School; [occ.] Receptionist/Telephonist Bell College of Technology Hamilton; [memb.] St Andrews Amb. Assoc.; [hon.] Scottish Ladies Champions F. AID (with BT) Team Leader; [oth. writ.] I have written various poems and am at present write a book.;

[pers.] I love romance and my writings reflect this aspect. I would like the whole world to be happy.; [a.] Carluke, Lanarkshire, UK

MCLEISH, ALEX
[b.] 23 November 1919, Edinburgh; [p.] Alexander McLeish and Elizabeth McLeish; [m.] Hilda Jane Wilding, 8 May 1945; [ch.] Ian; [ed.] North Merchiston School (Dux, 1932) Borughmuir School, Edinburgh; [occ.] Retired RAF Pilot; [memb.] Horticultural and Art Societies; [oth. writ.] Several poems accepted for publication this year E. G. The Master of Wine, Anyone for Tennis? The Old Privy, First Solo In A Tiger Moth. (I have just abandoned painting for poetry at the age of 75.); [pers.] My only aim is to perhaps make readers smile before passing on to more intellectual works. Any Anthology of my own might well be entitled "From Verse To Worse!"; [a.] Framlingham, Suffolk, UK

MCLEOD, SUE
[b.] 23 September 1945, Egham; [p.] Mr. and Mrs. W. Neil; [m.] Mr. Stewart McLeod, 30 July 1966; [ch.] 2; [ed.] Secondary, Egham; [occ.] Housewife; [hon.] Creative Writing Certificate; [oth. writ.] Some poetry local story in magazine.; [a.] Kirkwall, Orkney, UK

MCLOONE, THOMAS
[b.] 30 July 1960, Greenock; [p.] Thomas and Marion McLoone; [ed.] University of Strathclyde, University of Sheffield; [occ.] Unemployed; [hon.] First Class Honors in Mathematics, un-submitted Doctorate in Control Theory; [pers.] My poems have been published in local magazines. I have been influenced by my parents whom I greatly love and some skinheads.; [a.] Sheffield, Yorkshire, UK

MCMILLEN, JORDAN
[b.] 3 November 1987, Sheffield; [p.] Judie and Patrick; [ed.] Montessori Nursery School and Norton Free School, Sheffield; [occ.] School boy; [memb.] Cubs - 280th St James, Norton, Sheffield; [hon.] 500 m. swimming badge; [oth. writ.] Now working on a book of flower poems to be called "Jordan's Bloomers"; [pers.] Hobbies and interests: wrestling, swimming, art and canal boats.; [a.] Sheffield, South Yorkshire, UK

MCNEILL, DUNCAN L.
[b.] 16 December 1968, Singapore; [p.] John, Pauline McNeill; [m.] Divorced; [ch.] Dale, Bethany Hanna; [ed.] Carleton High School, Pontefract, Wakefield Technical College; [occ.] Chef; [memb.] I.A.K.S.A. International Amateur Kick boxing Sport Association; [hon.] Various Kick boxing Awards, Trophy's and Titles. Two Beautiful Children.; [pers.] I hope to prove dyslexics can write with confidence.; [a.] Carlisle, Cumbria, UK

MCOWAT, ELIZABETH
[b.] 8 December 1934, Malmesbury, Wilts; [p.] Estelle and Patrick Craig; [m.] W. John H. McOwat, 21 June 1958; [ch.] Andrew, Susan, Ian; [ed.] Fulneck Girls School in Yorkshire; [occ.] Semi-retired Teacher; [memb.] Amnesty International, Lifelines, Moravian Church; [oth. writ.] Poem published in 'Out of the Night' writings from death row.; [pers.] I believe absolutely in the equality of all people - which in turn explains my commitment to human rights and my stance as an abortionist of the death penalty - which in turn has influenced my writing.; [a.] London, UK

MCRAE, AGNES
[pen.] Chrissie Lorimer; [b.] 6 December 1948; [p.] Chrissie McRae; [ed.] Higher Standard; [occ.] Music Teaching; [pers.] Writing poetry is a completely new field ot me, I have always felt I had an affinity with the written word but it's establishing where. I have been given much encouragement by a friend.; [a.] Huntly, Aberdeenshire, UK

MCROBB, ADRIAN GERALD
[b.] 20 April 1955, Isleworth; [p.] Kieth and Beryl; [m.] Carole, 17 April 1976; [ch.] Kristina and James; [ed.] Flying Hall School, Robin Hoods Bay, Nr Whitby, N. Yorks; [occ.] Brewery Engineer for Scottish and Newcastle Plc.; [memb.] Not a joiner; Ex R.N. last time I signed to join something I ended up doing 10 years. But thoroughly enjoyed it.; [hon.] Always surprised and honoured when someone likes my stuff (ie) - yourselves, "Constantly surprisen by - Life's Banality"; [oth. writ.] "The Pipes Shrill Out.....", in Echoes Of Yesteryear, "A Nation That Went To War....", "The Oldman Dying In Hospital.....", in A Passage in Time, "The Thought That Died" and "Mother", in First Time Magazine, various others; [pers.] Always seem to see the humanity of people for good, but mostly bad. "Man's inhumanity to everything." Influenced by Michael Mackmin (The Play of The Rainbow).; [a.] Cramlington, Northumberland, UK

MEADE, MAJELLA MARGARET
[b.] 10 August 1978, Galway Hospital, Eire; [p.] Christopher and Mary-Jane; [ed.] Whitehall National School Tarmow Barry, Co. Roscommon, Scoil Mhuire, Co Longford; [occ.] Student; [memb.] Canteen (Teenage Cancer Society of Ireland); [hon.] Certificate of Merit (1996), Young Playwrights Programme, Certificate of Participation (1994); [oth. writ.] Articles for school and canteen magazines.; [pers.] My inspiration and love of writing has come from a recent sickness in my life. During that time I met people whom I care for clearly. With their encouragement and love, I learnt to accept my illness, and express my pain and love through my writing.; [a.] Longford, Longford, UK

MEAH, SAFIK JOHN
[pen.] Says; [b.] 7 March 1955, Bradford; [occ.] Cemetery Superintendent; [oth. writ.] Short Stories and other poems - never published.; [pers.] My poems are inspired by events in my life and my partner.; [a.] London, UK

MEAR, DOREEN
[pen.] Doreen Mear; [b.] 9 December 1942, Sutton-in-Ashfield; [p.] Deceased; [m.] Deceased; [ch.] Elizabeth; [ed.] Stoneyford Road School, Sutton-in-Ashfield Notts; [pers.] My married name is Fisher, but I want my poem under my maiden name of Mear; [a.] Sutton-in-Ashfield, Notts, UK

MEHRABIAN, VANESSA
[b.] 5 January 1980, Berlin; [p.] Monika and Garry Mehrabian; [ed.] Various secondary schools in Germany, New Zealand and Britain; [hon.] Several School merit awards, for all over good work and first equal in French; [pers.] Whenever I write poems I look upon them as lyrics which express a certain mood and could be used in my own song writing.; [a.] Uxbridge, Middlesex, UK

MELI, LYDIA
[pen.] Liddy; [b.] 8 December 1962, London; [p.] Phanos and Gerlinde Meli; [ed.] Mountview High Harrow; [occ.] Part Time Song Writer, Lyricist; [memb.] PRS; [oth. writ.] A catalogue of published and yet to be published songs and poems; [pers.] Dreams are the pathway to reality and we should give credence to the power of our imagination; [a.] Harrow, Middlesex, UK

MENTESH, YILDIZ
[pen.] Yildiz; [b.] 9 April 1978, London; [p.] Gunesh Mentesh and Sukran Mentesh; [ed.] Studied in North Cyprus/at the age of 14 came Kent at Ursuline College did 11 GCSE A-C grades, studying A levels English Lit., German, Classics; [memb.] Member of Cyprus Diving Centre - Open Water Diver; [hon.] Came 1st and 3rd in writing poems and short stories whilst living in Cyrpus; [oth. writ.] Currently published in school magazines and in newspapers daily reader's column. I write in 3 languages English, German, Turkish... however I have not tried writing in Latin yet!; [pers.] I am a person who is in love with nature, especially the sea and its mysterious tones, though "an old lie" indicates my very feelings after a broken relationship! I also like being quite imaginative in my writings and I write wherever I got the right inspiration.; [a.] Margate, UK

MERCER, SALLYANNE
[b.] 15 May 1970, Leicester; [p.] Mr. and Mrs. E. Mercer; [ed.] Gained 9 GCSE's, currently in second year of a-levels-theatre studies, English UT., and 16th century history.; [occ.] Student; [memb.] A member of South West Youth Theatre based at the London Academy of Performing Arts.; [hon.] Numerous school awards for Drama and English.; [oth. writ.] Various poems and short stories, covering a wide range of topics, currently unpublished.; [pers.] I find it very difficult to imagine the world devoid of the freedom of expression which I have found through my poetry. I have been influenced by many of the great writers of our time.; [a.] London, UK

MICHAEL, TONY
[b.] 15 March 1977; [pers.] The poems finale is love's silent voice in despair of man's blatant disregard for true love. This is due to us all depriving each other of what God has made sacred to us alone.; [a.] Coventry, UK

MICHANICOU, CHRIS
[b.] 21 September 1960, London; [p.] Demetrios Michanicou, Dora Michanicou; [ed.] Minchenden Comprehensive School; [occ.] Stock Credit Controller; [oth. writ.] Several poems published in local magazines also one published in an anthology; [pers.] Each poem paints it picture of every aspect of life, dealing with mankind and his relationship with the creator, and also about His love of man.; [a.] London, UK

MICKLESFIELD, CATHARINE
[b.] 6 March 1911, Liverpool; [p.] John and Elizabeth Green; [m.] Fred Micklesfield, 24 December 1964; [ed.] First Girls' Grammar School in U.K. Blackburne House, L'Pool. Now High Tec. College For Women. Opened 1844 in the presence of Charles Dicken; [occ.] Retired Teacher Plus Catering Officer in War time in a lange N.W. Engineering works; [memb.] At one period of 10 years a member of Oldham Soroptimists (Not now); [hon.] Certificate for Catering and Manage-ment in Hotels etc., a Certificate of Education which gave me Profesional Status to teach; [oth. writ.] Recently 1985-1991 I wrote a monthly page of verse in dialect for "Lancashire Life." Have been published in "The Country Man" and in the past. "Chamber's Journal" "Psychology" have been hear on radio.; [pers.] "Cast your bread upon the waters and it will return to you" a well known saying to which I add - buttered and sometimes with Jam on too! You get out of life what you put into it.; [a.] Liverpool, Merseyside, UK

MILES, GEOFFREY NOEL
[b.] 8 December 1951, Gosport; [m.] Elaine Noelle, 27 July 1974; [ch.] Hannah Louise, Graeme Marcus; [ed.] Bishopfield, Fareham; [occ.] Surveyor with Ordnance Survey; [memb.] ACU (Cricket Umpire); [hon.] NIL Worthy of note!; [oth. writ.] Several poems, some have been published in local papers. "Stuck" for many years on a book about Isle of Wight Railways, with so little time available.; [pers.] My `A' Level English brought me Wilfred Owen, and I was drawn to the sadness of life and the slender thread it hangs by. Betjamen haunts me now, as I "spy" on the life daily.; [a.] Fareham, Hants, UK

MILES, MARIELIA M. GONZALEZ JOBO
[pen.] Mariel Jobo-Miles; [b.] Venezuela, SA; [p.] Maria Teresa Jobo De Gonzalez, Jose Gonzalez; [m.] Peter Miles, 27 December 1995; [ed.] Andres Bello Catholic University, Cadacas, Venezuela; [occ.] Journalist; [memb.] Association of Stress Consultants, Aubudon Conservationist Society; [hon.] International Poetry Prize "Platero 1993" organized by Club Del Libro En Espanol De La Organizacion De Las Naciones Unidas (UN - Geneva - 1993); [pers.] Life is a challenge, but a celebration too and what I want to reflect in my compositions is that mysterious web of joy and pain that keep us alive.; [a.] North Finchley, London, UK

MILLER, FLORA
[b.] December 16, 1936, Argyllshire, Scotland; [p.] Deceased; [m.] Robert Miller, July 1, 1955; [ch.] 3, twins (boy and a girl) 1, daughter; [ed.] Tarbert School Argyllshire Scotland; [occ.] Housewife 'Amature' Watercolorist; [memb.] Used to be a member of cinque Ports Poets (Kent) But it no longer exists, it was through the 'Society' I was published in India.; [hon.] 2nd Prize Highland Arts poetry song writing competition 1980. Poem included in Anthology title - Island's Of Beauty; [oth. writ.] Various poems published in magazines, and anthologies. Two poems - 'Daughter of Scotland' and 'Thought Of Home', were published in 'The Bloom', A special compilation, and the 'Ocarina', in India, 'July 83'; [pers.] I also had a song (in the late 50's) of the (opportunity knocks) contest programme, way back in the days of television comp. Enjoy writing humorous Scottish stories; [a.] Crawley Witney, Oxon, UK

MILLER, LINDA
[b.] 7 October 1956, Dartford, Kent; [p.] Robert and Florence Wickham; [m.] Leslie Keith, 1 February 1975; [ch.] Daniel and David; [ed.] Normal Secondary Modern School. Dropped out at 16 with no formal qualifications.; [occ.] Housewife; [memb.] I support Animal Charities; [oth. writ.] Have contributed to many and various anthologies; [pers.] I feel that poetry both illuminates and empowers the soul.; [a.] Dartford, Kent, UK

MILNE, JESSICA
[pen.] Jessica Milne Davies; [b.] 26 June 1976, Truro; [p.] Marta Milne, David Milne; [ed.] Kimbolton School, University of Teesside (3rd year); [occ.] Student - 3rd year; [hon.] Currently studying for a BA (Hons) Eng. Literature; [oth. writ.] Published in Book 'Eastern Chorus' poem called 'The Last Warrior' 1992 aged 16 few publications in 6th form magazines offer of publication from Minerva Press.; [pers.] My poetry reflects life as I knew it. With influences from Slyvia Plath, Christ, in a Rossetti and W. B. Yeats 'Personal and from the soul'.; [a.] Huntingdon, Cambridgeshire, UK

MITCHELL, MANDY
[b.] 1 September 1963, Shepton, Mallet, Somerset; [p.] Brian Parfitt, Roona Moores; [m.] Divorced; [ch.] Kelly Marie; [ed.] St. Louis Convent, Glastonbury, St. Dunstans Comp. Glastonbury; [occ.] Bank Officer, Llouds Band, Langport Somerset; [pers.] My poems are influenced by my own personal experiences in life.; [a.] Somerton, Somerset, UK

MITCHELL, SUSAN
[b.] 7 March 1953, Chatham; [p.] Grace and Sid Merrick; [ch.] Corinne and Sharon Mitchell; [ed.] Walderslade Girls School; [occ.] Emergency Control Operator; [oth. writ.] Several short stories and poems not yet published. My tutor has encouraged me to write more and start sending my work to publishers; [pers.] I look at peoples lives today. At the sadness and hardship caused by the pressure of life in the 90's.; [a.] Minster, Sheerness, Kent, UK

MITCHELL-CRINKLEY, BILL
[pen.] Priory Bill; [b.] 27 November 1929, Morpeth; [p.] T. N. (Norman) Mitchell, Mary Jane (May) Crinkley; [m.] 27 December 1952 and 17 August 1960; [ch.] Carole Christine, Stuart, Kent, Melvyn Clarke; [ed.] Red Bow County Primary, Morpeth Forest of Dean Technical College, Gloucs.; [occ.] Retired; [oth. writ.] Poems in Local/Regional Press. Four in "Border Lines", published by: Blyth Borough Council, Northn'd. Also, "By Druridge (Druids) Bay" in poetry motion N. E., "Chills 'n Thrills", Hallowe'en, and "Cheviots' Lambs of God", poets in heart of England published by Arrival Press, Peterborough.; [pers.] If in doubt... Pen it out! Why keep it all in to yourself? Writing influenced by environment delay and local historical disregard, particularly: Chibburn Preceptory/Priory.; [a.] Choppington, Northumberland, UK

MITCHINSON, WALTER
[b.] 26 June 1957, Fleetwood; [p.] Walter and Kathleen Mitchinson; [m.] Deborah Mitchinson, 26 August 1989; [ch.] Dion and Dane Mitchinson; [ed.] Bailey Secondary Boy's School Fleetwood Lancs; [occ.] Highway Technician; [memb.] Fleetwood Conservative Club (CTTEE); [oth. writ.] Many poems which I keep for my own enjoyment.; [pers.] I love to write the beauty of nature, and surroundings in which we live.; [a.] Fleetwood, Lancashire, UK

MOMEN, SARAFAT IBN
[pen.] Shumon; [b.] 20 December 1979, England; [p.] (Father) M. A. Momen and (Mother) Nilufar Momen, of Banlades Origin, Elder brother Sakhawat Ibn Momen; [ed.] Ilford County High School (Grammar), Ilford, Essex, England, First Year (1991-92) he died on 24 February 1992;

[memb.] Former scout with The Drive cub-scouts in Ilford; [hon.] Accolades: The winner of first prizes for two poems Summer (1988) and Birds (1989) at Wanstead Library Branch Redbridge Library Services, Ilford; [oth. writ.] The book published posthumously called Shumon Momen - 95. Two more volumes to be published.; [pers.] Thomas Buxton School organises benefit charity called Shumon Momen Concert for financing Shumon Momen School. "School Under The Sky run by TOC at Sylhet in Bangladesh".; [a.] Ilford, Essex, UK

MONK, ARNOLD
[b.] 14 February 1928, Preston; [p.] Albert and Esther Monk; [ed.] Harris Institute Preston, Now University of Central Lancashire; [occ.] Retired Clinical Manager; [memb.] Preston Art Society, University of Central Lancs, Ex Chairman Probus 6 Chorley.; [hon.] R.G.N., B.T.A. Cert.; [oth. writ.] Articles for Nursing Press. Articles for University Association. Book reviews for medical papers. Essay competition winner B.M.A. 1960; [pers.] Greatly influence by John Betjeman. I write about the things I see about me. Present poem dedicated to Rosamund and Robin Dowling; [a.] Chorley, Lancashire, UK

MOODEY, DONNA MARIE
[b.] 24 June 1965, Manchester, England; [p.] Derek Moodey, Joan Moodey; [m.] Partner: Dustin Burton; [ch.] Daniel, Sharlene, Kristy; [ed.] Lived abroad most of my life, 13 years in Saudi Arabia, 5 years in the Philippines. Had an American Education - obtain a High School Diploma and also completed 3 years of Psychology at University; [occ.] Housewife and Full-time Mother; [hon.] With regards to my poems, "Autumn leaves, a winter breeze" was the first of my poems to be submitted into a competition and was life first offered to be published.; [oth. writ.] My poetry was mainly a hobby and an outlet for my personal experiences, thoughts, emotions and dreams. Family and close friends encouraged me to take my writing further. "Autumn leaves, a winter breeze" is my first achievement.; [pers.] Life itself and all that is encountered, the good times as well as the hardships, has been my greatest teacher and inspiration in my poetry.; [a.] Maidstone, Kent, UK

MOONE, MAGGIE
[b.] Birmingham; [p.] Patricia and Leslie Lippitt; [m.] Divorced; [ed.] British School of Commerce, Edgbaston, Birmingham; [occ.] Singer/Actress; [memb.] Playing Member of Edgeworth Polo Club, Cirencester, British Actor's Equity Association; [hon.] Recording Artiste and TV Personality. Resident singer on ITV series "Name That Tune" 1985-1989, Actress BBC's "Russ Abbot" series 1986-1990, Albums released "Dear Anyone", "The Thrill Of Love."; [pers.] This poem came from the heart. Writing is one of the most satisfying ways of expressing one's outlook on life.; [a.] London, UK

MOORE, MAGGIE
[b.] 2 May 1950, Douglas; [p.] Florence and William Christian; [m.] Divorced, 28 November 1970; [ch.] David James, Gary Steven; [ed.] Ballakermeen High School, Park Road Girls School; [memb.] Isle of Man Dog Obedience Club and the Weimaraner Club of Great Britain also canine Concern Scotland Trust; [hon.] Grade 'A' G.C.S.E. English which I gained aged 45; [oth. writ.] Several poems published in various anthologies,

magazines and newsletters.; [pers.] The majority of my poems are dog orientated, and I try to promote the cause of our canine companions in my writings. My own dog is a great inspiration.; [a.] Douglas, Isle of Man, UK

MOORE, PEGGY
[b.] Silverton; [p.] Ralph Bowerman and Edith Ellen Bowerman; [m.] Thomas Moore, 13 December 1947; [ch.] Maria Rose Moore; [ed.] C of E Girls School Silverton, Devon; [occ.] Retired; [memb.] The Royal British Legion; [pers.] This is my first poem, I hope it conveys my very deep love of nature and animals.; [a.] Silverton, Exeter, Devon, UK

MOORING, JEAN
[b.] 20 October 1928, Burnley, Lancs; [p.] Richard and Anne Stansfield; [m.] Sydney Mooring (Deceased), 9 February 1952; [ch.] Miss Pauline, Mr. Lionel Mooring, Mrs. Veronica Birbeck; [ed.] St. Mary's Girls' School, Burnley, Lancs, School of Art, Burnley, Lancs; [occ.] Retired widow; [memb.] Bleakholt Animal, Sanctuary, Edenfield, Lancs, St. Francis Animal Rescue, Burnley and Padiham, Lancs; [hon.] Certificate in Arts and Crafts, Board of Education, London 1948; [oth. writ.] One novel, three short stories, several articles and essays, thirty poems; [pers.] It is a joy for me to write verse and to be able to put into words aspects of life which I care about. Verse, like all art should seek the truth, and I have always tried to do so in my poems. I consider it a privilege.; [a.] Burnley, Lancashire, UK

MORANT, TANYA
[b.] 26 April 1967, Norwich; [p.] Gerald (Joe), Eileen Freestone; [ch.] Thomas Gerald Morant; [ed.] Litcham High School; [occ.] Single Mum; [oth. writ.] Unseen material over several years.; [pers.] Personal situations and events influences my poetry.; [a.] Dereham, Norfolk, UK

MORGAN, IAN JOHN
[b.] 5 February 1975, Ipswich; [p.] Shirley Morgan; [ed.] The Manningtree School, Colchester VIth Form College; [occ.] Quality Inspector, Warehouse Manager for Local Plastic Company; [oth. writ.] Many short stories and poems of various styles and subjects, that are currently unpublished.; [pers.] I love to write, regardless of the subject matter, though generally focusing on birth, death and the part in between. The influences in my writing range from Shakespeare to Ted Hughes.; [a.] Manningtree, Essex, UK

MORGAN, MRS. JANET
[b.] 7 April 1945, Norwich, Norfolk; [p.] Frederick and Florence Bean; [m.] Leslie, 13 January 1964; [ch.] David and Stephen; [ed.] Gurney Secondary Modern School, Bowthorpe Road Norwich, Norfolk, Norwich City Technical College; [occ.] Converting our old barge into a comfortable travelling home; [memb.] D.B.A. 'Dutch Barge Owner Abroad', Writers weekly and Writers News; [oth. writ.] Feature for weekly telegraph, 'Of Dreams And Dutch Courage', feature for D.B.A. 'A Trip To The Yard', poem for DBA 'Visitors', autobiographical story for BBC Radio Norfolk, 'Mums Monday' also a poem 'A Norfolk Monday'; [pers.] I want to show that even the most Mundane things in life have a little magic in them. I would like also to thank my husband for his unceasing support in all interests.; [a.] Gorinchem, The Netherlands

MORGAN, JEANETTE
[b.] 2 September 1946, Glasgow; [p.] Helen and Duncan McQuarrie; [m.] David Morgan (Deceased), 28 September 1968 (re-married 31 March 1973, Divorced); [ch.] Michelle and Nicole; [ed.] St. Joseph's Convent, Hendon Undergraduate, open university; [occ.] Headmaster's Secretary; [memb.] Society of Freelance, Editors and Proof Readers; [a.] London

MORGAN, LOUISE
[b.] 25 March 1982, Yeovil; [p.] Christopher Morgan, Kim Perry; [ed.] Wadham Community School, Crewkerne; [pers.] My poem reflects my uncertainty of life and the world with all it's prejudicial opinion and suffering.; [a.] Crewkerne, Somerset, UK

MORGAN, PAT
[b.] 7 October 1947, Merthyr Tydfil; [p.] Patrick and Edith Mulcahy; [m.] Elfed Morgan, 23 October 1967; [ch.] Simon, Barry and Nicholas; [ed.] Cyfarthfa Castle, Grammar School Merthyr Tydfil.; [occ.] State Enrolled Nurse (general); [memb.] I have recently joined the writers circle in Merthyr Tydfil, where they meet fortnightly. They have a full and varied programme for poets and short story writers. They are currently involved in reading some of their work in Merthyr's 1st Arts festival in various venues in the borough as per programme. As one of their newest members I am privileged to be asked to take part.; [pers.] It's never too late for achievement, with each new day come fresh opportunities; [a.] Merthyr, Mid-Glam, UK

MORRIS, CHRISTINE ANN
[pen.] Christina Angelique; [b.] July 24, 1942, Newport, Monmouthshire; [p.] Grace Ilunster and William Ilunster; [m.] Roger Morris, November 3, 1962; [ch.] Christopher James, Julie Ann, Michael and Richard David; granddaughter Emma Lucy; [ed.] Hatherleigh Secondary School, Nash Campus, Lliswerry, Newport Gwent; [occ.] Poet/Christian Houseperson; [memb.] International Interculture Exchange Cardiff; [hon.] English Language and Literature; [oth. writ.] Several poems published in anthologies, several poems published in 'Stepping Out' agoraphobic Magazine: Also poems published in Church Magazine; [pers.] Poetry affords the inspired spirits of the poet, a deeper awareness, expression, appreciation of life, love, the Creator and the beauty of Creation.; [a.] Newport, Gwent, UK

MORRIS, HAYLEY CHARLOTTE
[b.] 14 January 1982, Liverpool; [p.] Muriel Morris, Peter Morris; [ed.] St. Edward's College, Liverpool; [occ.] Student; [memb.] Horse Riding School; [hon.] Award for playing Clarinet from The Associated Board of The Royal Schools of Music.; [pers.] Experience is the key to a good poem.; [a.] Liverpool, Merseyside, UK

MORRIS, IAN MACGREGOR
[b.] 6 October 1971; [ed.] Rugby School, University College London; [occ.] Researching for a Ph.D. in history at the University of Manchester; [pers.] Influenced by Homer, Richard Glover, A. E. Housman, The Pre-Raphealites, if such combination is possible, and many other greats of Greek, Dutch and English art and literature

MORRIS, MRS. PAULA
[pen.] R. S.; [b.] 23 January 1950, South Heath; [p.] Dora and Gustav Breith; [m.] Mr. Richard Henry Morris, 5 September 1987; [ch.] Tara-Leigh-Emma Morris; [ed.] Great Missenden Secondary Modern School; [occ.] Helping the Elderly in their homes, helping children; [memb.] The Poetry Library London South Bank 5 Festival Hall; [hon.] English Literature Geography, Art, Graphics; [oth. writ.] 15 poems published in local mag. now two poems in anthologies I have 100 poems waiting to be discovered.. Italian and Romanian Blood.; [pers.] I have been writing poems in my sheep for 3 yrs 5 months, my poems are a tribute to my mom and dad who would have been proud of me; [a.] Wooborn Green, Bucks, UK

MORRIS, ROY
[b.] 30 May 1939, Llanfaelog, North Wales; [p.] William Morris, Matilda Morris; [m.] Marilyn Morris, 10 August 1963; [ch.] Karen, Andrea; [ed.] Holyhead County School, North Wales and Hinckley Grammar School, Leicestershire; [occ.] Domestic Electrical Retailer; [memb.] Dyke Golf Club Sussex; [pers.] I think that life is like poetry. Some of it is pleasant and some of it is not so pleasant.; [a.] Lancing, West Sussex, UK

MORRIS, SARAH
[b.] 25 August 1974, Basildon; [p.] Elizabeth Morris, Edward Morris; [ed.] Southend College of Art and Technology; [occ.] Model Maker, (Freelance); [oth. writ.] Several poems so far unseen.; [pers.] My poems reflect the harsh realities of life.; [a.] Basildon, Essex, UK

MORRIS, STEPHEN NORMAN
[b.] 17 November 1957, Cleator Moor, Cumbria; [p.] A. Morris, father G. Morris (Deceased); [ed.] Richmond Secondary Whitehaven; [occ.] (7 years ago) Retired due to deteriorating sight (registered blind); [memb.] The Planetary Society Amnesty International; [hon.] Gained diploma in astronomy, gained diploma in anatomy; [oth. writ.] Have written several poems not submitted any for publishment.; [a.] Saint Bees, Cumbria, UK

MORRIS, WILFRED
[ed.] Oldham High School, Goldsmiths' College, University of London; [occ.] Retired; [memb.] Rotary Club of Windsor and Eton; [oth. writ.] Religious Drama "All Mye I" (collected poems), teacher, musician, choral, conductor, headmaster, adviser in education; [pers.] Christian, three years in Palestine, many Jewish and Arabic interests.; [a.] Datchet, Berkshire, UK

MOSS, BARBARA
[b.] 3 February 1963, Manchester; [p.] George, Barbara Pearson; [m.] Antony Moss, 6 August 1982; [ch.] Jamie Kizzy Josephine; [occ.] House wife; [memb.] Springfields Tenants Association Fundraiser; [hon.] Thank you letter from Fred Talbot Granada tv for collecting monies for their christmas appeal December 1986; [pers.] I was inspired to write this poem by my fathers terminal illness, he has since passed away on 20-October 95, he was a very brave husband and father, and a special grandfather.; [a.] Cheltenham, Gloucestershire, UK

MOSS, LYNNE E. V.
[b.] 14 March 1930, London; [p.] Daisy and Eric Roffey; [m.] Divorced; [ch.] Two, 7 grandchildren, 1 great grandchildren; [occ.] Secretary; [memb.] Potters Bar Royal Births Legion; [hon.]

Long Service Medal Auxiliary Fire Service. 25 yrs. 'Silver Salva' Manager Avon Cosmetics Lid.; [oth. writ.] Poems are retirement, weddings other special occasions.; [pers.] I have always believed in "The Truth" and all my poems reflect this; [a.] Barnet, Hertfordshire, UK

MOULTON, ROBERT JOHN
[b.] 17 December 1932, Winterbourne; [p.] A. L. Moulton and L. J. Moulton; [m.] S. M. Moulton, 5 April 1958; [ch.] Pauline and Paula and Grandchildren Gemma Michael, John; [ed.] Chipping Sodbury Grammar School; [occ.] Farmer OOH ARR; [oth. writ.] Trudy, Tim, Meadow Sweet, The Changes in Farming, Calne Road Chaos, Dunmilkin; [pers.] Started writing poems in 1987 and have brought laughs and tears to many people since.; [a.] Corsham, Wilts, UK

MOUSSA, MOHAMED AKL
[pen.] Mohamed Akl; [b.] 16 March 1978, Cairo, Egypt; [p.] Abdel Rahman - Assistant Editor of Al-Ahram Newspaper, Youseria - Managing Director of Planning, A.K.I. Bank; [ed.] I.G.C.S.E., currently student of Political Science and Philosophy at the American University in Cairo; [occ.] Out of work Psuedo-intellectual, Old Guard Humanist Revolutionary; [oth. writ.] "The Other One", "Frozen Mountaintops", Theatre: "The Ticking Does Not Stop", and "One Lake Too Many"; [pers.] I have been influenced by 20th century existentialists namely "Camus" and Sartre". I have also ben influenced by the sixties hippie movement. My writing present the moment of confusion when man stands alone facing society and all his predetermined choices. As an internationalist liberal-humanist. I'm strongly opposed to: Racism, classicism, sexism, capitalism, socialism and nationalism. My interests are: 1.) Fighting the apathy and ignorance of my generation. 2.) Proving that Islam is a religion of peace that, like Christianity, has been manipulated by power animals.; [a.] Zamulem, Cairo, Egypt

MOYNIHAN, MABEL DOROTHY
[pen.] Katie Adams; [b.] 6 November 1908, Somerset; [p.] Ernest and Kate Knight; [m.] Christopher Moynihan, 12 September 1970; [ed.] Church of England School; [occ.] Retired but worked most of my day in private service; [memb.] Deering the 2nd war I was Air Raid Warden in Bristol; [hon.] Medal from the "Pope" for nearly 20 years working in the church.; [oth. writ.] None published but lots of tried

MULLAN, MADELINE
[b.] 17 January 1974, Derry; [p.] Kathleen and Patrick Mullan; [ed.] St. Patrick's and St. Brigio's High School, Claudy, N. Ireland, North West College of Technology, Derry, N. Ireland; [occ.] Nursery Nurse; [pers.] This poem was written for James 1913-1996.; [a.] Park, Derry, N. Ireland

MULLAN, THERESE M. T.
[pen.] Theresa Mullan; [b.] 26 April 1987, Dublin; [p.] Don Mullan and Margaret Beatty; [ed.] Sister of Carl and Emma.; [occ.] Pupil at presentation convent - Dublin; [oth. writ.] Peace Poem, "Up the Dubs", "To a very nice teacher", "Go away"; [pers.] I dream of peace in Ireland and for all hungry people to have food.

MULROY, ANNA R.
[pen.] Anna; [b.] Buckinghamshire; [p.] J. Patrick and Marie Fitzpatrick; [m.] Ralph William Mulroy, 27 September 1952; [ch.] Anne Lorraine and

grandchildren Saul Patrick York and Charlotte Sophia York; [ed.] Convent Grammar and McUniversity; [occ.] Retired; [memb.] C.N.D. Amnesty Int. B.H.F.; [hon.] Philosophy; [pers.] Dispel what offends you troubles your soul honest with one's self.; [a.] Cheadle Hulme, Cheshire, UK

MUNT, JOAN
[b.] 25 March 1916, Bournemouth; [p.] Harold Evart, Dicker Mabedickler; [m.] Riggie Samuell (Deceased), 18 May 1945; [ch.] Five sons; [ed.] Brighton Dyke School, Southall Girl's School; [occ.] Retired; [hon.] School learning Certificate space's Art prize, English prize, Cookery prize, medal for British Empire Essay for Memorizing, Resisting by General William Booth's Speech Large Certificate; [oth. writ.] Poetry, Blank verse, Children's Stories; [pers.] I have always loved poetry and reading poetry and started writing poetry who give young.; [a.] Portsmouth, Hampshire, UK

MURPHY, CARA JANE
[pen.] C. J. Murphy; [b.] 2 April 1979, Hitchin; [p.] John and Lorraine; [ed.] Attended Pingreen, Primary School, then Bedwell Senior School (both in Stevenage), passed English with a B at GCSE; [occ.] College student at Hitchin College, studying drama, dance, singing and A-level English; [hon.] Achieved an arts award in 1990, for a painting based on nature, which was sponsored by Co-op; [pers.] Being able to write poetry is a great escape, for me. I like to put my thoughts down on paper, because it's better on paper, than all clogged up in my mind.; [a.] Stevenage, Hertfordshire, UK

MURPHY, ELVA
[pen.] Elva Murphy; [b.] 11 June, Limerick; [p.] Michael and May Hayes; [m.] Aidan, 1973; [ch.] Robert, Louisa, Gareth, Michael; [ed.] Laurel Hill Convant School; [occ.] Mother; [memb.] Human Race, Westwood Health Club, Killiney Writers; [hon.] Highly Commended - Gerald Manley Hopkins International Poetry Competition 1994, Considered for Short List, Ian St. James Competition 1994 (short stories); [oth. writ.] Short Stories - presently working on my first novel; [pers.] I am delighted my entry to The International Library of Poetry has appealed to someone! I write for pleasure although sometimes I think there is a trace of masochism about it all.; [a.] Dublin, Dublin, UK

MURPHY, SADAYO TAKIZAWA
[pen.] Sadayo Takizawa; [b.] 6 August 1948, Saitama, Japan; [p.] Katsuji Takizawa, Mitsuko Takizawa; [m.] Kevin Murphy, 14 December 1988; [ed.] Fudogaoka High School, Kokugakuin University (Tokyo), University of Wales, Aberystwyth; [occ.] Student of Post Graduate at the department of Inter-pol, VCW; [hon.] BA in history, MLL in law and politics; [oth. writ.] One poem published in poetry magazine at the age 17 under the pen name Midori Taki. Two small poetry booklets published with self finance in early 20's of my age.; [pers.] I am currently doing a research on Francis Bacon (1561-1626). And am interested in how our minds work and how they create images.; [a.] Machynileth, Powyse, UK

MURRAY, MURIEL
[b.] 9 September 1947, Harrogate; [m.] Allan J. Murray, 11 February 1995; [ch.] Sharen-Louise Bosnier; [ed.] Hallcroft Secondary, Retford Workshop College; [occ.] Quality Manager; [oth. writ.]

2 poems in anthologies by Arrival Press. 1 poem in a poetry now anthology.; [pers.] Through the love of country side and my compilation of waterfalls in S. W. Scotland, hopefully one day I will have it published, I have found a source of never ending joy and amazement which I wish to share with the public as a whole.; [a.] Dalbeattle, Dumfries, Galloway, UK

MURRAY, PETER
[b.] 2 May 1951, Sunderland; [p.] Kenneth Goderey and Mildred Anne; [m.] Zoe Murray (Nee Robinson), 26 May 1990; [ch.] Laura Jane; [ed.] Bede Collegiate Grammar School for boys Langham Towers Training College; [occ.] Teacher of History; [a.] Hartlepool, UK

MUSSELWHITE, CHARLENE
[b.] 11 April 1981, Portsmouth; [p.] Mark and Sharon Musselwhite; [ed.] Brune Park Secondary School, Gosport Hants; [a.] Gosport, Hampshire, UK

MUSTO, ELSIE
[pen.] The Quiet One; [b.] 25 February 1916, Paddington; [p.] Mr. and Mrs. David Musto; [ed.] Elementary, free lance self taught; [occ.] Retired; [hon.] Oscar Award; [oth. writ.] Those Were The Days, The Walking Stick Brigade, The Learner, If Only, I Can't Think Why, Is The Lord In Control Of Your Car?; [pers.] All about me!! This is me Elsie calling to you out there, so you wish to know about me and in my thoughts share, I'd never heard of your library and would clearly like to know how you acquired retirement written long ago. I used to spend my holidays in a guest house by the sea out to enjoy myself and free, that I was free, the hotel was a Christian one, certainly not my score, but I enjoyed the company - entertaining not so keen. Friday nights was guests to do the entertaining, I just used to go out even if it was raining, I made many friends with my humour and writ, this I got involve in poetry and that my friends was it. Later in life I joined a Church night next door to me, I showed the priest, my poems which he was pleased to see, Elsie, my dear, you have a talent which could help you pass the line, for I was in a wheelchair, household, publishing not in mind. I like to act out my poems for that helps me be, until you have ago you don't know what you can do, how you know about me full of kindly humorous and this remarks are not just a rumors.; [a.] London, Westminster, UK

MYALL, MARTIN H.
[b.] 11 July 1957, Salisbury; [ed.] Hurn Court Boarding School; [occ.] Teaches English in Spain; [pers.] I am a poet. My ambition is that you find in my words, your feelings, and on doing so think, "Yes, that's exactly it!"; [a.] Andover, Hants, UK

MYERS, AUDREY
[b.] 24 March 1928, Cubbington; [p.] Frank Tarver and Jane Tarver; [m.] Kenneth Myers, 26 March 1949; [ch.] John, Colin, Susan, Michael; [ed.] Church of England School Cubbington, Leamington Spa; [oth. writ.] Two poems published in local magazine; [pers.] I try to put my thoughts and beliefs on paper especially through poetry.; [a.] Leamington Spa, Warwickshire, UK

NATHAN, VATHANI
[b.] 31 March 1976, London; [p.] Eur. Ing. Ponniah Swami and Thevi Nathan; [ed.] Boarding School and Day Schools Both in England and Africa (Zimbabwe). Presently at University.; [occ.] Student at University studying English and Drama

BA Hons.; [memb.] Amateur Theatre Group, Lorraine Dior Casting Agency; [hon.] 9 G.C.S.E.'s 3A - levels (speech and drama exams); [oth. writ.] Freelance scrip writing, (Freelance song writing), several poems including one published in 'The Space Between' anthology.; [pers.] There's nothing like personal experience! Appamma, Mum, Dad, Rohini, Dinesh, Angus, Tina, Rouji etc. if a person is reflected solely through those close to them...only then am I the best person ever!; [a.] Wallington, Surrey, UK

NEAL, JOE
[b.] 4 August 1946, Morfa Bychan, N. Wales; [m.] Divorced; [ch.] One son; [ed.] Bishop's Stortford College, University of Nottingham, Guildhall School of Music and Drama; [occ.] Divided working life between acting and journalism; [memb.] Equity, Nat. Union of Journalists, Actors Centre, Ronnie Scot's Jazz Club, Sky Club of Great Britain; [hon.] BA (Hons), Licenciate of Guildhall School of Music and Drama (LGSMD), TV, Film and Radio Work in UK, Eire, U.S. and France. Performed in Most Repertory Companies. Worked as Journalist for the Times. Guardian, Sunday Times, Daily Telegraph and Daily and Sunday Express; [oth. writ.] Maggott Moon, The Reluctant Trombonist, Culture Of Alienation; [pers.] Carpe Diem; [a.] Wexford, Eire, UK

NEEVES, JOAN
[b.] Swansea; [ch.] Three; [ed.] Pontardawe Grammar School, (NR. Swansea S. Wales) Secretarial College Swansea; [occ.] Housewife; [memb.] Business and Professional Women (BPW); [hon.] Awards for Poetry as a Young Woman; [oth. writ.] Short stories and poems (English and Welsh); [pers.] Have enjoyed writing and reciting in Welsh and English since a child. Nothing previously printed as I wrote only for my own pleasure.; [a.] Oakham, Leics, UK

NEIMAN, KATIE JANE
[b.] 29 March 1984, London; [p.] Caroline Neiman, Stephen Neiman; [ed.] Brighton and Hove High School (1989); [occ.] Scholar; [memb.] Starlite Theatre Group; [hon.] Grade 6 Verse and Prose, Grade 7 Acting (Lamda), Grade 4 Spoken English, Grade 4 Mine, Grade 3 Saxophone (Associated Board), Grade 3 Piano.; [a.] Hove, East Sussex, UK

NELDER, DEE
[b.] 17 May 1920, Bristol; [p.] British; [m.] British; [ed.] Elementary; [oth. writ.] Poem "Pretending" published, `Winter Chorus 1991. Poem to "Fergie" Duchess Of York on Birth Of Her Daughter Bea', Buckingham palace, Acknowledge! The poem, "Setting The Scene."; [pers.] I started writing in 1963 have thirty two poems. I wrote for my personal pleasure, two poems of my beloved dogs, and others I would love to see published, one day!!; [a.] Bristol, Avon, UK

NELLIST, KATHERINE L.
[b.] 25 August 1978, Yeovil; [p.] Peter and Elizabeth Nellist; [ed.] Queens College, Taunton; [occ.] Studying A-levels in French, Politics and English Literature; [a.] Corfe, Somerset, UK

NEVILLE, FRED
[b.] 10 October 1942, Derby; [m.] Margaret Neville, 30 September 1967; [ch.] One son, Matthew; [ed.] Secondary Modern School; [occ.] Fitter (Recently Made unemployed); [hon.] Won a puzzle competition in works own newspapers, for

which I received a framed award.; [oth. writ.] A juvenile story, many poems, and hundreds of puzzles, but nothing published so far except for the poem in this book.; [pers.] I regard every publishers refusal as a set-back, never a failure.; [a.] Derby, Derbyshire, UK

NEWBURY, INGRID
[b.] 7 August 1953, Orsett, Essex; [p.] Tony and Leny Cunningham; [m.] Michael J. Newbury, 17 August 1974; [ch.] Daniel M. Newbury; [ed.] Aveley Secondary School; [pers.] My inspiration comes from my family and friends.; [a.] Aveley, Essex, UK

NEWELL, PETER
[b.] 28 December 1925, Wakefield, Yorks; [p.] Harry and Francis Newell; [m.] Mary Newell, 30 July 1949; [ch.] David, Anthony, Christine; [ed.] Thornes House School, University of Leeds, University of Singapore; [occ.] Retired International School Headmaster; [hon.] BSC, Dip Ed (Leed), MED Singapore; [oth. writ.] Story read and several local BBC stations. Articles, stories, plays, poetry; [pers.] I write for the pleasure of it and have attempted a variety of media.; [a.] Torquay, Devon, UK

NEWLANDS, MARGARET S.
[b.] 22 June 1913, Edinburgh; [p.] George and Williamina Scott; [m.] George William Newlands, 30 December 1939; [ch.] Irene and Phily; [ed.] Boroughmuir High School, Viewforth, Edinburgh evening classes there in English; [occ.] Housewife (Retired); [oth. writ.] Edinburgh evening news, series of articles, mostly on the old days.; [pers.] Interested in painting, beauty culture collecting chiva headed dolls. Reading and television; [a.] Edinburgh, Midlothian, UK

NEWMAN, JOYCE
[b.] 24 February 1927, Hackney; [p.] Sidney C. Allen, Theresa M. Allen; [m.] Christopher W. Newman, 22 December 1951; [ch.] Wendy Theresa, Deborah, Lilian; [ed.] Wolverly Girls School Elementary Bethnal Green London E2; [occ.] Retired; [oth. writ.] Unpublished poems, 1 poem printed in local paper. Entitled "Awaken Britons".; [pers.] I am often inspired to write poetry through political issues, or everyday events which affect me or people in my life.; [a.] Thetford, Norfolk, UK

NEWMAN, KAREN ANNE
[b.] 27 March 1965, Kend L; [p.] Helen and George Newman; [ed.] Hulme Hall School Cheadle Hulme, Cheshire; [occ.] Auxiliary Nurse; [memb.] I am a member of South Trafford Operatic Society; [oth. writ.] I have written a number of poems but this is the first one I have had published.; [pers.] I would like to say a big thank you to Alan Millward, without him none of this would be possible. Also thanks to Mum and Dad for all their support over the last 31 yrs.; [a.] Chorlton, Manchester, UK

NEWMAN, PAM
[b.] July 16, 1937, Essex; [p.] Edward and Jessie Spence; [m.] Charles Newman, September 5, 1956; [ch.] 4 boys and 1 girl; [ed.] Secondary School; [occ.] Kennel Owner (Boarding); [oth. writ.] 2 poems with Anchor Books; [pers.] I am always writing poems and short children stories and find it very relaxing and enjoyable. I am influenced by flowers and seasons.; [a.] Brixham, Devon, UK

NEYLAND, JOAN
[ed.] Lausanne High School; [occ.] Co/Director, Co/Secretary to group of companies in the motor trade; [oth. writ.] None. Offered for publication; [pers.] When affected by some momentous happening. I am always moved to write; [a.] Swansea, West Glamorgan, UK

NICHOLLS, DELLA
[b.] 13 February 1970, Canterbury; [p.] Neville Nicholls, Pamela Nicholls; [ed.] Teynham Primary School, Rowena High School for Girls; [occ.] Writer; [oth. writ.] I have had my first novel published entitled The Grays of Nettlestead Hall.; [pers.] I have always enjoyed writing and if people like my work, then it has made it all worthwhile.; [a.] Teynham Nr Sittingbourne, Kent, UK

NICHOLLS, EILEEN
[b.] 2 September 1946, Sutton Coldfield, West Midlands; [p.] Mary (Assie) and Eric Squires; [m.] David Nicholls, 5 December 1985; [ed.] Riland Bedford SM Sutton Coldfield West Midlands; [occ.] Legal Secretary; [pers.] I just couldn't imagine life without my dogs previous and current (2 labs) who are my best friends; [a.] Sutton Coldfield, West Midlands, UK

NICHOLSON, JOHN A.
[b.] 7 July 1934, Coatbridge; [p.] Florence and Thomas Nicholson; [ed.] Clifton High School - Coatbridge Glasgow School of Art; [occ.] Town Artist/Sculptor East Kilbride Dev. Corporation; [memb.] I am a member of a recently formed concert party performing Soley for charity.; [hon.] Commended certificates and medal in Glasgow Art Gallery Drawing Competition. Diploma in Graphic Design Glasgow School of Art.; [oth. writ.] I regret that 'other writings' were done for my own personal satisfaction and have never been submitted for publication. I am, therefore, delighted to have a poem favourably received by the I.L.P.; [pers.] Being a romantic at heart I tend to try and express the finer and gentler side of human emotion.; [a.] Coatbridge, Lanarkshire, UK

NICOLLE, DENNIS PETER
[b.] 11 February 1962, Jersey; [m.] Separated; [ch.] Two; [occ.] Dog walker; [memb.] Jersey Pedigree Whippet Racing Club; [oth. writ.] Horace the Welterweight in Between A Laugh and A Tear; [pers.] We all have choices. The decision to choose is of our own; [a.] Saint John, Jersey, UK

NICOLSON, PENNILUCK
[pen.] Penni - Luck; [b.] 16 February 1946, Dundee; [p.] Margaret Lawrence, James McGinnis; [m.] John Nicolson, 31 August 1985; [ch.] Angela, John Paul, Stanley, William, Clen, Clint, Tammy, Donald, Cindy, Anna; [ed.] Studying for BSC; [occ.] Housewife; [oth. writ.] 'To Someone Not Yet Born' and unpublished poems, children's stories etc.; [pers.] Dignity and awareness of it, is what separates us from the lower animals. I dedicate this poem to my mother.; [a.] Redhill, Surrey, UK

NIH-OGAIN, SROLOSIN
[b.] 14 March 1926, Co Kerry; [p.] Irish; [m.] 1947; [ed.] National; [occ.] House wife; [oth. writ.] Short stories etc.; [pers.] Drawn from life; [a.] Wolverhampton, UK

NISBET, KENNETH
[pen.] Nizzi; [b.] 20 January 1973, Glasgow; [p.] Kenny Nisbet, Jean Nisbet; [m.] (To be) Deborah Elizabeth Tindal, 17 May 1997; [ed.] Chirnsyde Primary School, Colston Secondary School; [occ.] Electrician; [oth. writ.] Numerous poems, written for personal enjoyment, as yet unpublished.; [pers.] Writing is my own form of escapism, influenced by no one particular poet, but by the people I love and my own interest in the unusual.; [a.] Glasgow, Scotland

NISBET, LAURA
[pen.] Laura-Leigh Nisbet; [b.] 21 May 1983, Rutherglen; [p.] Myra and Anthony Nisbet; [ed.] Stonelaw High School; [occ.] 2nd year pupil at Stonelaw High School; [pers.] Hobbies include reading, creative writing, fashion, cinema and meeting new people, ambition is to become an actress or an author, writing gives me the freedom to express personal ideas. I have been influenced by the works of Stephen King and would like to write a blockbuster horror novel and have it filmed. Also, I have been influenced by my brother, who is a poet, and my English teacher Mr. Ali.; [a.] Toryglen, Glasgow, UK

NIXON, MR. KEITH
[b.] 8 November 1935, Rotherham, S Yorks; [p.] Deceased; [m.] Janet, 7 April 1958; [ch.] Two children; [ed.] Secondary Modern, Spurley Hey, St. Anne - Junior School; [occ.] 22 years Royal Marines, 20 years Social Worker now retired; [hon.] RFM for services to Royal Marines Welfare; [pers.] Very concerned about man's treatment to humanity and to the planet we live on.; [a.] Waterhooville, Hants, UK

NOBLE, STEPHANIE ANN
[pen.] Alexandra Katerina Anonomakova; [b.] 28 July 1946, Londonderry; [m.] Divorced; [ed.] Londonderry High School, Rhode Island School of Design; [occ.] Equine Consultant, Floral Designer; [memb.] British Horse Society, United States Combined Training Association; [oth. writ.] Poem published in "The Chronicle of the Horse" (U.S.A.), Several letters, comments and reports in local and national (American) magazines and newspapers.; [pers.] Currently preparing MS for Anthology of my own Poems, Prose and Letters with line-drawings, Central Theme being to share with readers that we are none of us alone with our emotions and experiences.; [a.] Litton, Derbyshire, UK

NOMAN, SERRY
[pen.] Shereen; [b.] 17 March, Alex, Egypt; [p.] Turkish Father, Greek Mother, born both in Egypt; [m.] Deceased; [ed.] BA Philosophy, also Linguist, French, English and Arabic literature, classic, modern and contemporary; [occ.] Hotelier; [oth. writ.] Novel (unpublished), The Conjuction Hinges of Life, Autobiography "The Paradox", Lyrics one of which is already recorded (performed by me, Named Autumn Sunshine), two plays and over 200 poems; [pers.] We as human being are given the power of art and insight to improve with it use it progressively, share it and enjoy it.; [a.] Croydon, Surrey, UK

NORMAN, MAUREEN ANNETTE
[b.] May 23, 1945, Derbyshire; [p.] Gordon and Margery Wardale; [ch.] Rachel Annette; [ed.] Ripley Girls School, Heanor College, Readers Business College; [memb.] National Federation of Spiritual Healers - Healer Member, Healer Member at Loughborough Self Help Cancer Group; [hon.] NFSH Certificate of Healing; [oth. writ.] Church Literature in Belize also: Other poems: "Shades of Green", "The Old Knotted Tree", One of Many", "Eyes of Deep Blue", "If this Can Happen to the Best", "Through the Eighties", etc.; [pers.] I write on my impressions and experience of life. "Music" is dedicated to Beatriz Brown Venezuelan - Music Teacher and Friend; [a.] Moira, Derbyshire, UK

NORRIS, ALLENE
[b.] Darlington; [m.] Widow; [ch.] Kerry-Susan and Richard James; [occ.] PR Consultant and Public Speaker; [hon.] Two Civic Receptions following journalism career in the North-East, mainly in broadcasting field.; [oth. writ.] "The Market" - a book which went round the world and resulted in National TV coverage. Features, articles and song lyrics.; [pers.] I have always loved reading, so writing was a national progression. Expression and experience of life is the key in poetry. I adore Dylan Thomas.; [a.] Darlington, Durham, UK

NORTON, ANGELA
[b.] 4 December 1979, Middlesbrough; [p.] Christine and Robert William Norton; [ed.] Awaiting Results of GCSE's. Eston Park Secondary School; [occ.] Student; [memb.] Runner up in Snicker's young sports writer of the year competition; [hon.] Several letters printed in local newspaper. Entry for young Sports writer competition.; [oth. writ.] The poem reflects how I feel about people who pollute the planet and don't realize how it can affect innocent people.; [a.] Middlesbrough, Cleveland, UK

NOTTAGE, KENIA M.
[b.] 17 April 1972, Freeport, Bahamas; [p.] Kendal Nottage and Rubie Nottage; [ed.] St. Elphin's School, University of Kent, BPP Law School, London; [occ.] Student; [hon.] Lord Snowdon Award - 1996, Various Acting, Music Awards; [oth. writ.] Several poems published in the University's Magazine; [pers.] To my brother Kelly Nottage and my sister Krista Nottage - I dedicate this poem to you both. Thanks for just being you!; [a.] London, UK

O'BRIEN, WINIFRED
[b.] 20 April 1969, Glasgow; [p.] William C. O'Brien, Winifred O'Brien; [ed.] Our Lady's High, Cumbernauld University of Paisley; [occ.] Engineer; [hon.] Beng in Electrical and Electronic Engineering, MSC in Information Technology; [oth. writ.] Several short stories and numerous poems in private collection.; [pers.] The stars shine only on darkness.; [a.] Cumbernauld, Lanarkshire, UK

O'CONNOR, CAROL
[b.] 27 May 1951, Dartford; [p.] William and Anna Vera Wright; [m.] John O'Connor, 18 August 1989; [ch.] Damian and Cavan; [ed.] Bexley Tech. High for Girls, New College of Speech and Drama, London N.W. II; [occ.] Home and individual Tuition for Bexley Borough; [memb.] English Speaking Board, Middlesex University Alumni, British Assoc. of Electrolysis, North Heath Baptist Church; [hon.] New College Diploma In SP/Drama (Distinction, University of London Diploma in Drama (Credit in Diction), International Phonetic Assoc. Cert., Kree Diploma in Electrolysis; [oth. writ.] Poems and play scripts (unpublished) occ. articles in church magazine.; [pers.] Life can be filled with painful experiences, but the pain we sometimes suffer makes our times of pleasure even more wonderful!; [a.] Erith, Kent, UK

O'DAY, PHILIP
[b.] 26 May 1972, Farnham, Surrey; [p.] Michael O'Day and Rosemary O'Day; [ed.] Oxted County, East Surrey College, Redhill; [occ.] Bank Clerk, Author to be; [oth. writ.] This is my first published work. A comedy and horror novel being written.; [a.] Oxted, Surrey, UK

O'DONOVAN, MARY
[b.] 11 October 1966, Mullingar, Co. Westmeath, Ireland; [p.] Mary O'Donovan and The Late Tom O'Donovan; [ed.] Presentation Convent - Mullingar, Loreto College - Mullingar; [occ.] Producer of Ornamental Bronze Sculptures; [memb.] Mullingar Tennis and Badminton Club; [hon.] Elected 'Lady Captain' of the Mullingar Tennis and Badminton Club '95-'96, Certificate for the completion of a 'Child Care Course'; [oth. writ.] Always writing poems for any occasion - such as birthdays/weddings/good luck, etc., for family, friends or anyone. (The only other were the ten lines when misbehaving at school!); [pers.] I get total enjoyment in writing either comical or serious poems. I like to achieve getting the personal touch across, in order to make people say - "Yes that's how I feel."; [a.] Mullingar, Co. Westmeath, Ireland

O'DONOVAN, SHEILA
[b.] 3 June 1962, Wigan; [p.] Ronald Cawley, Lilian Cawley; [ch.] 12 yr. old son, Shaun; [ed.] St. John Fisher High School, Baytree Road, Beechill, Wigan; [occ.] Unemployed; [memb.] I have no membership anywhere but my son is a member of a Horse Riding Centre which I enjoy just as much as he does.; [oth. writ.] I haven't had anything published in the past but now that this poem is I hope that appearing in "Awaken To A Dream", it will open new doors for me.; [pers.] If all mankind could write a poem and recite it at the same time, what a beautiful song would come from the earth and out to the heavens' above.; [a.] Wigan, Lancashire, UK

O'GARA, ROSSLINE
[b.] 25 September 1955, Warwick; [p.] Jack Groves, Frances Groves; [m.] Garry O'Gara, 30 August 1980; [ch.] Three Boys, ages 12, 7 and 4 Clarke, Glen and Lewis; [ed.] Leamington College for girls, Mid-Warwickshire College of further education, Lanchester Polytechnic; [occ.] Housewife and mother. Studying at home - Editorial skills.; [memb.] Mensa; [pers.] Expressing my thoughts in verse has been a constant source of pleasure for me, since childhood. To be acknowledged for this is a bonus.; [a.] Brighouse, West Yorkshire, UK

O'GORMAN, DONAL
[pen.] Daniel Martin; [b.] 7 July 1963, Ireland; [p.] Michael and Catherine O'Gorman; [m.] Susan Frawley, 21 July 1994; [ch.] One on the way (31 December); [ed.] Mary Immaculate College of Teacher Training, B. Ed. Degree (English); [occ.] Primary School Teacher - in Corpus Curisti School Mayross; [oth. writ.] Unpublished; [pers.] Listen before you speak.; [a.] Limerick, Limerick, UK

O'LEARY, JUDITH
[pen.] Yude the Star; [b.] 4 July 1980, Cork; [p.] Ann and Patrick O'Leary; [ed.] Primary Scoil Aiseirt Chriosti Farrankee, Cork., Sec. - North Presentation, Farrankee, Cork.; [occ.] Student; [pers.] I get my inspiration from my more than gorgeous and intelligent boyfriend Philip Meaphy.; [a.] Cork, Cork, UK

O'NEILL, CAROLINE
[pen.] Roberta Shore (Romantic Fiction); [b.] 21 April 1955, Dingle Peninsula, Western Ireland; [p.] Tom and Nora O'Neill; [ed.] Cloghane Secondary School (Ireland) various colleges of further education (London); [oth. writ.] New writer, presently working on a novel, a play, several short stories and more poetry. The Rogue is a first poem.; [pers.] Writing is just painting with words. A novel describes the painting. But a poem is the painting itself.; [a.] Twickenham, Middlesex, UK

O'NEILL, DENIS
[b.] September 27, 1935, Edinburgh; [p.] Mary MacDonald and James O'Neill; [ed.] Holy Cross Academy School, Secondary Modern; [occ.] Ex. Royal Navy Regular, Ex. Merchant Seaman. (Retired)

O'NEILL, ELEANOR
[b.] Cork City; [p.] Margaret, Sean Murphy; [ch.] Gregory, Jason, Lorraine; [ed.] Intermediate Certificate, South Presentation Convent, Cork Eire; [occ.] Teacher's Assistant, Beaumont School; [memb.] The Reiki Association, Usui System of Natural Healing; [oth. writ.] Fiction, including short stories, poetry; [pers.] He who underestimates himself shall never develop his true potential in life.; [a.] Cork, Cork, UK

O'NEILL, LUCY
[pen.] Lucy O'Neill; [b.] 23 March 1981, Cork; [p.] Anne O'Neill, Barry O'Neill; [ed.] St. Fergal's National School, Killeagh, Currently attending St. Aloysius College, Carrigtwohill; [occ.] Student; [oth. writ.] Several other poems - still unpublished; [pers.] My decisions in life are often expressed in my poetry and I would like to think my poetry may help others make their decisions.; [a.] Killeagh, Cork, UK

O'NEILL, MICHAEL FRANCES
[pen.] Niall; [b.] 27 August 1942, Glasgow; [p.] Joseph and Anne O'Neill; [m.] Margaret Ann O'Neill, 14 September 1968; [ch.] Colette, Angela and Clare; [ed.] St. Mary's College, Blairs, St. Peter's College, Darleith; [occ.] Quantity Surveyors, Clerk; [memb.] St. Helen's Parish Folkgroup; [hon.] Certificates and Medals for Folk singing and playing; [oth. writ.] Poems and songs published in Derry Journal; [pers.] Largely influenced by the classics and write to express rather than to impress.; [a.] Glasgow, Strathclyde, UK

O'SELLE, ANGELENA R.
[b.] 1 December 1984, London; [p.] Angela and Roger O'Selle; [ed.] The Broxbourne School; [memb.] Turnford Netball Club; [hon.] Received Honor at my Drama Class for my solo song. I received an Award for 1st prize. Presented to my by Mr. Robert Leeson; [a.] Turnford, Hertfordshire, UK

OAKES, DEREK K.
[b.] 10 February 1950, Coventry; [p.] Eric and Ann Oakes; [ed.] Whitley Abbey Comp. Polytechnic of Central London, Degree Modern Languages; [occ.] Bank Director Zambia; [oth. writ.] Several Unpublished; [pers.] My writings are all based on personal experience. Nothing is more reliable than life itself for material.; [a.] Coventry, Warks, UK

ODAM, PAMELA
[b.] 27 December 1949, Aldershot, Hants; [p.] Robert and Phyllis Evans; [m.] Gerald Odam, 22 November 1980; [ch.] Nathan David, Mark Royston; [ed.] Aldershot County High School; [occ.] Florist Shop Owner, Barmouth; [memb.] Church Organist, Conductor Chaunt singers, Bermo Arts Club; [hon.] Ass. Victoria College Music; [oth. writ.] Church Magazine Articles, Choir Newsletter; [pers.] My poetry is always the result of something that moves me, music, anger, laughter and this one despair, until now it has always been a very private way of expressing my feelings; [a.] Barmouth, Gwynedd, UK

OLDFIELD, ELLEN
[b.] 23 February 1941, Dublin, Eire; [p.] Mrs. Mary King, Joseph King (Deceased); [ch.] Catherine 30, Ernest 32, Caroline 34; [ed.] St. Bernard's School, Presentation Convent, Dundrum, Co. Tipperary, Eire; [occ.] Child Care Worker; [memb.] Charter 88, Lib-Dems Secretary Open University SE Region for Open University Graduates (Title Adue) Drama Groups Sackville Players, Brighton and Hove Singers and Musicians Club; [hon.] Bachelor of Arts from Open University 88 passed singing audition for Brighton Theatre Group Silver Medal Irish Dance, Brighton and Hove Drama Festival Award Sackville Players; [oth. writ.] Unpublished poems include Fate Of Two Innocents, Monument To A Life Deserving, Indispensability (written for radio), Absent Love; [pers.] My personal motto has always been "Carry On Regardless" no matter how many times life knocks you down. To brush yourself down and start all over again. To believe in yourself and your own personal worth.; [a.] Brighton, East Sussex, UK

OLDHAM, RAY
[b.] 1 October 1928, Salford, Lancs; [p.] Ellis and Annie Oldham, (Deceased); [m.] Joyce (Deceased); [ed.] Secondary School, Thornton, B'Pool, plus further education in Engineering, Illustration and Authorship; [occ.] Retired Civil Servant; [memb.] R.S.P.B. - National Trust - English Heritage - Civil Service Retirement Fellowship; [oth. writ.] Several poems published in anthologies by Triumph House and Anchor Press, Peterborough; [pers.] In both Christian and secular verse I try to write in the idiom and language of today in a conversational style people can relate to and with wherever possible, humour or an off-beat or appropriate punchline.; [a.] Otley, West Yorkshire, UK

OLDS, ANNE
[b.] 26 November 1944, Coventry; [p.] Eileen and Hubert Hughes; [m.] Clifford John Olds, 27 March 1965; [ch.] David and Christopher; [ed.] Banbury Grammar School; [occ.] A 'Team Member' within a Company; [memb.] Various Local Clubs; [hon.] Art, English Lit., Sciences and History; [oth. writ.] Unpublished poems.; [pers.] My writing is based very much on events and circumstances, both sad and funny, which affect our everyday lives.; [a.] Northend, Warwickshire, UK

OLIVER, JOHN H.
[b.] Willenhall, Staffs; [p.] Albert and Nellie; [m.] Audrey; [ch.] Mark and Paul; [occ.] Freelance Writer; [oth. writ.] Articles in Daily Telegram Magazine, The Lady and many Leading Health and Fitness Magazines both here and in America.; [pers.] 'Disillusions' was written after watching my mother die - and it is dedicated to her memory.; [a.] Newport, Shropshire, UK

OLIVER, MALCOLM
[b.] 19 December 1935, Portsmouth, Hampshire; [p.] Percival and Alexandra Oliver; [m.] Jennifer, 4 August 1956; [ch.] Paul, Martin, Susan, Philip, Andrew; [ed.] 1) St John's College, Portsmouth 2) Royal Dockyard School, Portsmouth 3) Royal Naval College, Greenwhich; [occ.] Retired Civil Servant (Ministry of Defence Naval Architect); [memb.] Royal Corps of Naval Constructors Chartered Engineer, Engineering Council; [pers.] Though you may choose your friends but not relations, at the end of the day it is family which counts.; [a.] Trowbridge, Wiltshire, UK

OLLEY, MARION
[m.] Ray Olley; [ed.] West Bridgford Grammar School, Nottingham. Anglia Polytechnic University. B.A. Combined studies degree - English and history; [occ.] Teacher of English to foreign students; [pers.] My writing influenced by, and dedicated to, my family and grandchildren; [a.] Colchester, Essex, UK

ORAM, KATHARINE ANNE
[b.] 14 February 1981, Swindon; [p.] Carole Oram, Richard Oram; [ed.] St. Johns School, Marlborough; [occ.] Student; [pers.] My poetry is an expression of my inner self without my poetry I would not be relieved of the struggle of life.; [a.] Baydon, Wiltshire, UK

ORRIDGE, ROLAND
[b.] 4 December 1919, Shirebrook, Derbyshire; [p.] Rose Edith Orridge, John Orridge; [m.] Constance Orridge (nee Croucher), 7 February 1944; [ch.] Patricia Ann; [ed.] Dunscroft Elementary, S. Yoks; [occ.] Retired; [pers.] I have been influenced in my writing by John Masefield and Lord Tennyson.; [a.] Burnham-on-Crouch, Essex, UK

OSBORNE, CYNTHIA YVONNE
[b.] 28 November 1937, England; [p.] Gladys and Albert Wagener; [m.] Divorced, 29 December 1969; [ch.] Two daughters; [ed.] Art College (Ealing Tech.) and Derwentwater, and Central Sec Mod.; [occ.] Clairvoyant; [oth. writ.] Poems from a Sleepless Night and Reflection in Still Waters.; [pers.] I believe in helping others as we pass through this present existence and trying most things at least once just for the laughter involved!; [a.] Ryde, UK

OSBORNE, JOHN
[pen.] John Osborne; [b.] 11 October 1930, Bath; [p.] Gerald and Kathleen Osborne; [m.] Rosemary, 19 October 1957; [ch.] Philip and Michael; [ed.] Bath Technical College; [occ.] Farmer; [memb.] N.F.U. The Anglican Church; [hon.] Craft Awards, Hedging, Thatching, Cattle Judging, Singing; [oth. writ.] "A Collection Of Poems", "The Flowers In Lifes Garden", and eighteen editions of "Poems Of A Farmer".; [pers.] My poems are my philosophy of life. A lifetime of farming and working with nature has given me an opportunity to think a great deal about life and I have tried to write about every aspect of it, some humorous, some serious and some in Somerset Dialect.; [a.] Bath, Somerset, UK

OSOBA, MARGARET M.
[ch.] Three, grandchildren Five; [ed.] Leadhills Public School, Biggar High School; [occ.] Free Lance Writer; [oth. writ.] Short stories, articles, poems published in magazines, newspapers and broadcast in several BBC radio programmers, also in record and cassette (Lismor Recordings).; [pers.]

Now retired, but formerly Assistant Editor - W. Collins, Publishers, Glasgow and Latterly Research Interviewer - B.B.C.; [a.] Thornliebank, Renfrewshire, UK

OTTER, ANNETTE
[b.] 5 April 1948, Hull; [p.] Mr. and Mrs. Shillito; [m.] Mr. David Otter, 13 July 1919; [ch.] Three daughters; [ed.] Secondary Education Hull, Hull College of Technology, Delapole Hospital Willberby Hull; [occ.] Nurse; [memb.] Life Long Membership Institute of Nursing; [hon.] SENM Delapole Hospital Willberby, Nurse of the year 1969; [a.] Scunthorpe, UK

OVELL, ROBERT JAMES
[b.] 25 January 1932, Four Marks, Nr. Alton; [p.] James Ovell and Ethel Ovell; [m.] Amy Eva, 17 September 1955; [ch.] Susan, Tina, Danny, Steve; [ed.] Perins School Alfresford; [occ.] Builder (Ex. Merchant Navy); [oth. writ.] Several poems in local magazine.; [pers.] I have a deeply rooted love of the countryside, and a greatest admiration for the sincerity of early romantic poets, esp. Thomas Moore.; [a.] Alton, Hampshire, UK

OWEN, ABIGAIL MAY
[b.] 22 May 1975; [p.] Rosemary and Robert Owen; [ed.] Nine Acres Primary School, Church of England Middle School, Carisbrooke High School; [occ.] Shop Assistant Shutlers Mace Convenience Store; [memb.] For the last six years have been a disc Jockey at St. Mary Hospital Radio.; [a.] Newport, Isle of Wight, UK

OWEN, GAVIN RUSSELL
[b.] 24 March 1971, Portsmouth; [p.] Eiron Owen (Deceased) and Fay Owen; [ed.] Brune Park Secondary; [occ.] Naval Writer; [oth. writ.] 8 anthologies entitled: Carbon Paper Promises, Red Rape Reasoning, Fridge Magnet Future, China Teapot Texture, Hostile Humour Liability, Candid Cynical Grudges, Flat Eleven Fixtures, Black Market Basics, unpublished.; [pers.] For dad the future is the past.; [a.] Gosport, Hants, UK

PAIGE, MRS. EVE
[b.] 20 November 1948, Leicester; [p.] Sam Phillips, Joan Phillips; [m.] Rupert Paige, 13 November 1967; [ch.] Brenda Paige, Lauren Paige; [ed.] Moat Girl School; [occ.] Artist; [memb.] Rosicrucion Organization; [hon.] I receive a prize at school for hard work in English and Art; [pers.] I am a member of the Rosicrucion Organization, that teach understanding of the inner body, and I get a lot of inspiration from that.; [a.] Flate, Ealing, UK

PANAYIOTON, CHRIS
[b.] 5 March 1976, Chelsea; [p.] Amin Badr and Mary Badr; [ed.] Hurlingham and Chelsea Secondary School, Westminster College; [occ.] Full time Student, studying Accounting at London Guildhall University; [hon.] I have attained various awards in arts and crafts, drama, first aid, swimming and sprinting. I have also achieved a BTEC (GNVQ) National Diploma in Business at Distinction Level.; [oth. writ.] None, although I am currently writing a series of poems which I hope to have published in the near future.; [pers.] My parents have always encouraged me to expand my creativity and it has always been in ambition to further my poetry by having some of my work published. My poems portray ideas, emotions and situations of love, life, hopes, and dreams.; [a.] Battersea, London, UK

PANNU, GURIQUBAL
[b.] 25 December 1980, Feroze Pur; [p.] Amarjit Kaur M. A., Gurmail Singh B.Sc.Engg.; [ed.] Downshall Juniors and Seven Kings High School; [occ.] Student; [memb.] Drama Club, Singing Lessons and School Choir; [hon.] Bronze Math's Award; [oth. writ.] A book called 'Back To Reality,' looking for a publisher.; [pers.] 'Nobody made a great mistake, than the man who did nothing, simply because he could only do a little' - something which I think everyone needs to remember throughout their lives.; [a.] Ilford, Essex, UK

PARGETER, RONALD ALBERT
[b.] 3 October 1919, London; [p.] Albert Pargeter, Lily Pargeter; [m.] Iva Patricia, 15 September 1978; [ch.] Julia, Lindsay, Simon, Deborah; [ed.] Archbishop Tenisons Grammar School; [occ.] Retired; [memb.] RAF Club, Guild of Freeman of City of London, Hove Club, Institute of Directors; [hon.] Diamond Star Award Bedia Ltd; [pers.] My candle burns at both ends it will not last the night but on my foes and on my friends it gives a lovely light!; [a.] Lewes, East Sussex, UK

PARISH, CHRISTINA
[pen.] Tina Parish; [b.] 17 January 1957, Tadworth, Surrey; [p.] Yvonne Zelia and Peter John Watson; [m.] Clive Frederick Parish, 4 May 1974; [ch.] Louise, Justin, Kellyanne, Luke and Zarah Parish; [ed.] De Burgh Secondary Grammar, School, now sadly closed down; [occ.] No longer working due to having Encephalitis, which left me disabled; [memb.] A member of the Encephalitis support group also of the Methodist church in Merland Rise Tadworth Surrey; [hon.] Duke of Edingborough award Bronze giver at school in my last year their. No other honours or awards.; [oth. writ.] I have a private collection or poems of which in a reflection on life, but I've never sent them to any one before now.; [pers.] I love poetry I always have since a little girl I like my poems to have meanings and to reflect on life and its situations many a time I've woken in the early hours unable to sleep and yet found the words for a new poem to write.; [a.] Tadworth, Surrey, UK

PARISH, LUCY JAYNE
[b.] 22 August 1973, Manchester; [p.] Gillian and Patrick Parish; [ed.] Manchester Metropolitan University; [occ.] Consultant; [pers.] My work reflects the enlightenment, distress and general depiction of emotional experience. To create verse gives me such a sense of strength and satisfaction, one hopes that the reader gains the same fulfillment.; [a.] Manchester, Lancashire, UK

PARK, VALERIE
[b.] 22 July 1942, Northwich, Cheshire; [m.] Divorced; [ed.] After leaving Wellington School in Ayr at Sixteen I had careers mostly to do with Jewellery and Cosmetics.; [occ.] Office Worker, Fulltime; [oth. writ.] At the moment a short story with a Christmas Theme and mostly suitable for children, is almost completed. Should it be a success I will write further stories with the same characters. It is my wish that Disney maybe interested in making it into an animated film.; [a.] Saint Helier, Jersey, UK

PARKER, LOUIS
[b.] 30 July 1970, Portsmouth; [p.] Susan Margaret; [ed.] Complain Comprehensive Southdowns College; [occ.] Computer Programmer, IBM; [oth.

writ.] Several pieces of work in local magazine, numerous unpublished poems, songs and short stories; [pers.] An open mind can be the door between dreams and reality.; [a.] East Harting, Hants, UK

PARKS, ANDREA M.
[pen.] Andrea Parks; [b.] 3 November 1979, Pontefract; [p.] John Parks, Linda Parks; [ed.] Carleton High School, Pontefract, New College Pontefract; [occ.] Student; [pers.] "Englands Pride" influenced by Rupert Brooke's "The Soldiers" and the reflection of man's inhumanity to man.; [a.] Pontefract, West Yorkshire, UK

PARRY, J. C.
[pen.] Jonathan Gabriel; [b.] 18 May 1947, Bolton; [p.] George and Mary Parry; [m.] Christine Marie Parry (Deceased), 30 June 1984; [ch.] Four boys and 1 girl; [ed.] The School of Life, and various human establishments; [occ.] Still learning; [hon.] The greatest honor of all consciousness; [oth. writ.] Handbook semi fiction scifi "2084 The Philosophy at Oneness", Vantage Press NY, Praised Upon by Prince Charles in the Daily Mail Tabloid various poems (published) and magazine and articles in the papers.; [pers.] If only the in-growing toenail could speak for it lays down its life to impart a message... The Hidden Destiny of Us All.; [a.] Worsley, Manchester, UK

PARSLOW, JOHN
[pen.] John E. Parslow; [b.] 26 June 1945, Aylesbury; [p.] Jack Parslow, Mary Parslow; [m.] Carol Parslow, 10 October 1980; [ch.] Louise, Richard; [ed.] Grange Secondary Modern Aylesbury, Bucks; [occ.] Self-employed Printed Circuit Board Designer; [memb.] Musicians Union Mensa; [oth. writ.] Currently working on a period novel in the Thomas Hardy Genre; [pers.] I have a ceaseless melancholy about man's in humanity to man. My writing tends towards a desire for global equality and justice for all. Influences: Hardy, Dickens, G. Elliot, Fav. Modern: Umberto Eco.; [a.] Aylesbury, Buckinghamshire, UK

PARSONS, PATRICIA
[b.] 17 March 1938, Isleworth; [p.] W. H. Dempster and Daisy Dempster; [m.] Deceased, 8 June 1970 (second); [ch.] Janice, James, Arnie; [ed.] Marlborough Secondary Modern School for Girls; [occ.] Retired; [hon.] Religious Studies (School); [oth. writ.] Poem in British Legion Magazine.; [pers.] To bring kindness into the world as taught to me my my father and a childhood friend - Honing.; [a.] Isleworth, Middlesex, UK

PARSONSON, JO
[b.] 9 November 1927, Warwick; [p.] Harry and Marjorie Pearson (Deceased); [m.] Roy Parsonson, 20 March 1954; [ch.] Three grown up sons; [ed.] Leamington Central School for girls; [occ.] (Retired/now just a Housewife), (Licensee's wife 20 yrs); [memb.] I am a member of my local Parish Church and member of the mothers union; [oth. writ.] "Latchkey Kid" published in poetry now 1994 also "Our New Grandchild" published in `Rhyme Arrival' 1995 yearbook; [pers.] I just fell a desire to put into verse some of my thoughts on topical events, and to my amazement ideas seemed to flow with the pen; [a.] Walton-on-Thames, Surrey, UK

PARTRIDGE, JODY
[b.] 22 April 1980, Faversham; [ed.] Canterbury College; [occ.] Student; [oth. writ.] Personal book

of over 100 unpublished poems.; [pers.] I like to base my poems on the personal experiences of myself and others then extend them to the limits of my imagination.; [a.] Faversham, Kent, UK

PASS, DORIS MARY
[pen.] Doris Mary; [b.] Hardsworth; [p.] Ada and Thomas; [ch.] Five; [ed.] Government and Private Queens College (5 years) Weybridge; [occ.] Retired Nurse Diploma Teacher; [hon.] NSCN Certificates British Red Cross Teaching Diploma; [oth. writ.] B School Beeches High School Aylsham - Norfolk. "Londsdale" (sch) Norwich St. Augustines Norwich (Nursery), "Ashridge" Herts.; [pers.] Certificate N.S.C.N. Nursery College Norwich Norfolk.; [a.] B'mouth, Dorset, UK

PATEL, DAKSHA
[b.] 18 October 1975, England; [memb.] The 'Karate Union of Great Britain - Shotokan'; [oth. writ.] Published: 'Survival' in the anthology 'Aspects Of Life' August, 1995, ISBN (SoftBack), 1 857316959. 'Under The Stars' in the Anthology 'Point Of No Return' August, 1996, ISBN (Soft back) 186188401X, ISBN (Hard back) 1861884060. 'An Alcoholic's Poem' in the anthology 'Quiet Moments', winter of 1996-97, ISBN (hard back) 1-57553-180, and also on the Recording (cassette tape) 'The Sound of Poetry' released by the International of poetry.; [pers.] Love is the peace within yourself, the part that hurts nothing.; [a.] London, Greater London, UK

PATERSON, N. D.
[b.] 17 March 1930, Manchester; [m.] 22 September 1956; [ch.] One Daughter; [ed.] Manchester School of Art 1934-1940; [occ.] Retired, Co Director; [hon.] D.A. (M/C) Primrose Medal 1939; [oth. writ.] Several other poems.; [pers.] Poems written during 2nd World War in India, with a longing for home!; [a.] Manchester, Cheshire, UK

PATON, SOFIE
[b.] 13 April 1978, Liverpool; [p.] Donna Taylor, Christopher Paton; [m.] Peter Townsley (Engaged); [ch.] First child due January '97; [ed.] Carnoustie High School; [occ.] Housewife; [oth. writ.] A couple of poems published in high school magazines.; [pers.] Born with a heart defect I have had to fight all my life. I want to show my generation that there is more to life than drugs and violence, before it is too late for them to learn from my writing.; [a.] Carnoustie, Angus, UK

PATRICK, WENDY
[b.] 16 December 1939, Fareham; [p.] Deceased; [m.] David Patrick, 16 August 1983; [ed.] Secondary School; [occ.] Housewife; [pers.] My desire and dream is for future generations of children to be able to grow up in a world that is peaceful and loving to all; [a.] Fareham, Hants, UK

PATTERSON, AVRIL
[b.] 23 April 1967, Belfast; [p.] Herby Patterson and Emily Patterson; [ed.] Glenlola Colleigate School, Bangor, N. Ireland, Belfast Southern College of Nursing, Belfast City Hospital; [occ.] Staff Nurse, Intensive Care Unit, Aberdeen Royal Infirmary; [pers.] My poetry tells, how I feel it, or is life, as I see it. It is simply, thoughts on paper. I greatly admire the works of Seamus Heaney, he paints such vivid pictures with his poems.; [a.] Aberdeen, Scotland

PATTERSON, GILLIAN
[pen.] Gillian Patterson; [b.] 3 December 1941; [p.] Joan, Jack Hill; [m.] David Patterson, 16 November 1963; [ch.] Suzanne, Sarah; [occ.] Counsellor and Psychotherapist; [oth. writ.] As yet unpublished, 2 poetry anthologies.; [pers.] I write to express the soul and beauty in the world through the human heart and imagination.; [a.] Camden Town, London, UK

PATTERSON, LINDA
[pen.] Linda Patterson; [b.] 20 September 1954, Wembley; [p.] William and Norah Stephenson; [m.] Separated; [ch.] Phillip, Claire, Stephen, Dean; [ed.] Grosvenor High School, Belfast Adult Training in Business Admin with "Subskills"; [occ.] Administration Assistant in Computer Software Company; [oth. writ.] A poem published in local newspaper; [pers.] During a time of personal heartbreak and grief, I wrote some poems which reflected how I felt. Every one ended in a hope for a brighter day. I would like now to pass that hope and optimism on to a world I think needs it.; [a.] Hillsborough, Down, UK

PAUL, DERRYAN
[b.] 18 August 1938, Radwinter, Essex; [p.] Andrew Paul, Elizabeth Paul; [ed.] Oakdene School, Beaconsfield, Bucks, Cambridge University, University College, London Leicester University; [occ.] Research Associate, Dept. of Information and Library Studies, Univ. of Wales, Aberystwyth; [oth. writ.] Articles on local history and archive administration; [a.] Aberystwyth, Ceredigion, UK

PAUL, WILLIAM GORDON
[b.] 27 March 1922, Broxburn; [p.] David Fordyce Paul (Founder Member of College of Opticians); [m.] Elizabeth Mary Urguhart, 1920; [ch.] William James Nancy; [ed.] Kirkcaldy High School, Skerrys College; [occ.] Retired; [hon.] Honours in Chiropidy honoured for saving life by "Royal Humane Society". 1947 "Five Army Medals" plus army pension which is an honour.; [oth. writ.] As `Monty' knew me chief scout of B.A. never had time to write my memoirs, of how I ordered the date of the normandy landings.; [pers.] Trust in God, trust in her majesty you'll win! Then go and buy yourself a medal out of Woolworths! I told her that too when she never let me down! - Spy; [a.] Bilston, Midlothian, UK

PEAKE, FABIAN
[b.] 2 April 1942, Sussex, England; [p.] Mervyn Peake and Maeve Gilmore; [m.] Phyllida Barlow (Sculptor), 23 July 1966; [ch.] Five children (3 girls and 2 boys); [ed.] St. John Fisher School Purley, Surrey, England Chelsea School of Art 1958-63, Royal College of Art 1963-1966; [occ.] Practising Painter and poet Senior Lecturer at Manchester Metropolitan University (Painting School); [hon.] Greater London Arts Association Major Bursary Arts Council of England Award in the Emotional Computing Scheme to put a poem of mine on to the Internet. Poem 'The Field'; [oth. writ.] Two pamphlets of my poems and mine and others - financially assisted by Manchester Metropolitan University. Also poems in several magazines, including two magazines in the USA 'Carnage Hall Magazine Eopus N.Y. and 'Silver Web', Tallahassee Florida.; [pers.] My work a both painter and poet involves using the two very different art forms, for rather similar ends. The image (in the work) is of prime importance - also conflict; [a.] Finsbury Park, London, UK

PEAKE, MARGARET ANNE
[b.] 24 May 1964, Belfast; [p.] David Beck, Annie Mills; [m.] Robert James Peake, 17 May 1990; [ed.] Elmgrove Primary School, Orangefield Girls Secondary School; [occ.] Housewife; [memb.] R.S.P.B., B.A.S.C., Royal Society Protection of Birds, British Association for Shooting and Conservation, Royal Signals Association; [oth. writ.] Poems printed in several school magazines.; [pers.] Life is the gift of God, and we must choose what we will make of it, for in the end it is God we answer to.; [a.] Belfast, Down, UK

PEARCE, DANIEL
[b.] 14 April 1977, Ware, Herts; [p.] Charles Pearce, Linda Pearce; [ed.] Torquay Grammar, Knowles Hill Sixth Form; [occ.] Dreamer; [memb.] Lead singer of locally popular progressive band 'Kudos'; [hon.] Received various awards for music including singing and piano playing; [pers.] Life without love is as pointless as Jeremy Beadle.; [a.] Newton Abbot, Devon, UK

PEARSON, MARK
[b.] 27 January 1969, Cumbria; [p.] Christine and Billy Dickinson; [ch.] Callum, age 4 years; [ed.] High School; [occ.] Care Officer; [pers.] There are many branches to a tree, just like there are to you and me, but ours are not for others to see, when withered away, just like a tree.; [a.] Huddersfield, West Yorkshire, UK

PEERLESS, BOB
[b.] 4 February 1946, Redhill; [p.] William Janet, Ethel Rose; [m.] Divorced; [ch.] Gary, Dean, Mandy; [ed.] Sec Modern; [occ.] Retired; [memb.] Sec-Croysow Social Clubs; [hon.] GSM (Borneo); [oth. writ.] Many poems as yet unpublished.; [pers.] I write mainly from personal experience and observation.; [a.] Croydon, Surrey, UK

PERCIVAL, MARJORIE
[pen.] Marny; [b.] 23 September 1929, Derby; [p.] Richard and Mary Francis Broughton; [m.] Thomas Douglas, 17 December 1964; [ch.] Richard, Mark, David, Nicholas; [ed.] Ashby School for Girls, Ashby, Scunthorpe; [occ.] Housewife; [oth. writ.] Local Newspapers, poems in several anthologies; [pers.] The love of poetry as been with me since school days. You are too young or too old to enjoy reading.; [a.] Scunthorpe, N Lincs, UK

PERRY, MARIE
[m.] Married; [oth. writ.] Shorts Stories, Novels, Libretto, Letters, Essays, Playlets; [pers.] I enjoy all the arts and have many interest. I believe language is the breath of life. The writer of Genesis understood the creative power of the Logos. Learning is the food of life. When we cease to enquire - we cease to live.

PETERS, STEPHEN
[b.] 30 September 1952, Doncaster; [p.] Ronald Peters and Eleanor Peters; [m.] Susan Peters, 14 April 1973; [ch.] Mark Wayne, Sarah Louise; [ed.] Bentley High St, Secondary; [occ.] Local Government Housing Officer; [oth. writ.] Several poems unpublished; [pers.] Live for today, in case tomorrow is cancelled. Do not be too arrogant, nor too humble and have consideration for others in case tomorrow isn't cancelled after all.; [a.] Doncaster, South Yorkshire, UK

PETRIE, RODERICK
[b.] December 25, 1970, Paisley; [p.] Alexander Petrie and Irene Petrie; [m.] Susan Byrne, engaged August 5, 1995; [ed.] Kelvinside Academy, Glasgow and Glasgow University - Hons Degree in Statistics; [occ.] Deputy Manager (Coral); [pers.] I want my poems to capture the reader, and then set them free also I'm glad others have the chance to read my poem, because 4 poem is nothing, if its not shared.; [a.] Romford, Essex, UK

PETTY, JEAN LEONORA
[b.] 10 June 1925, Sunderland; [p.] Deceased; [m.] Kenneth, 2 March 1946; [ch.] Kenneth (Deceased), Alan, Martyn; [ed.] Hendon Board Secondary School, Sunderland; [occ.] Retired; [memb.] Church Warden, St. Cuthberts Church Redhouse Est, Sunderland; [oth. writ.] Other poems; [pers.] Member of St. Cuthberts Ladies Choir.; [a.] Sunderland, Tyne and Wear, UK

PHELPS-GARDINER, ALEXA
[b.] 29 May 1985, Surrey; [p.] Alyia Phelps-Gardiner; [ed.] Foresters Primary School/Thomas More High School; [occ.] School Pupil; [memb.] Y.K.A. Amateur Martial Association, Westway School of Dance Stagecoach Performing Arts; [hon.] TA/Primary Grade 1/2, Bauer primary grade 1/2, Modern, primary grade 1/2; [pers.] I write for my grandfather Gordon Phelps-Gardiner (fa-fa) "Every day I feel you in my heart and hear you in my soul".; [a.] Beddington, Surrey, UK

PHILLIPS, FLORENCE ROSE JEANETTE
[b.] 7 April 1933, London; [p.] Caroline and John McDonald; [m.] Ernest Robert Phillips, 7 April 1978; [ch.] David Glandvill and Denise Webb; [ed.] Secondary School; [occ.] Retired; [hon.] Freedom of the City of London; [oth. writ.] "A Winters Morning"; [pers.] Always smile in the face of adversity.; [a.] Nr Hailsham, Sussex, UK

PHILLIPS, KEVIN JOHN
[pen.] Kevin Phillips; [b.] 15 October 1965, Llanelli; [p.] Allan Phillips and Joan Phillips; [ed.] Coedcae Comprehensive Camatheshire Technical College Music Teacher (Piano); [occ.] Supervisor (Catering); [memb.] R.Y.A. Sailing Club, British Red Cross; [hon.] Diploma in Health and Safety; [oth. writ.] First time published in this Anthology - Awaken To A Dream; [pers.] The poetry that I write is a portion of my heart. What I share with other I hope it will touch their hearts.; [a.] Llanelli, Dyfed, South Wales, UK

PHILLIPS, PATRICK RUSSEL
[b.] 8 September 1967, Manchester; [p.] Harry and Patricia Phillips; [ed.] Bramhall High School, Sunderland Polytechnic; [occ.] Manufacturing Consultants, Computers Sciences Corporation; [a.] Stockport, Cheshire, UK

PHILLIPS, SHANNA
[b.] 21 August 1939, London; [p.] Nathan and Dorothy Cashman; [m.] Norman Phillips, 8 June 1959; [ch.] Mark, Karen, David, Eli; [ed.] Henrietta Bamett School; [occ.] Company Director (Hairdressing Company); [memb.] Fine Arts NADFAS, MEA (Hairdressing Employees Association) WWF, RSPB; [oth. writ.] I have written only for family and friends to celebrate and comfort.; [pers.] I try to give comfort and pleasure to others, to share their Joys and sorrows and to always give hope for tomorrow.; [a.] Beaconsfield, Bucks, UK

PHILPOTT, LISA
[b.] June 23, 1972, Miroster; [p.] Martyn and Iris Philpott; [ed.] Rowena Girls School, Sittingbourne; Thanet Tech. College, Broadstairs; [occ.] Statistical Information Assistant, Police Maidstone Headquarters; [memb.] Senacre Dance Club Maidstone friend of the Marlowe Theatre Canterbury; [hon.] Rowena Girls School Drama Award; [pers.] My poems are my way of expressing myself. I find it easier to express on paper of what I feel in my heart and mind than to speak aloud.; [a.] Sittingbourne, Kent, UK

PIDSLEY, E. VESEY
[pen.] Evelyn; [b.] 5 October 1934, Eire; [m.] Richard Henery, 5 January 1975; [ch.] One; [occ.] Own Business; [hon.] Beauty Queen, Dancing Queen, Civil Servant; [oth. writ.] Fantasy and doctor of Divinity Synplonie Thunder, "The Hero," lyrics - I met a opera singer in a Honky Toe Bar, "The Bearded Pope."; [pers.] Truth is so much stranger than fiction, I thought "The House of Correction" was the worst I have written influenced by Oscot Wilde and Shaw.; [a.] Southend, Essex, UK

PIRIE, IAN
[b.] 16 September 1943, London; [ed.] University of Leeds; [occ.] Lecturer, University of East London; [a.] Upminster, Essex, UK

PLANT, MARGARET
[pen.] Emma Chapman; [b.] 1 October 1949, Hale, Cheshire; [p.] Harol Chapman, Doris Chapman; [m.] Alexander Plant, 16 January 1989; [ch.] Deborah, Anthony, Stephen; [ed.] Bradbury Secondary Modern; [occ.] Housekeeper; [oth. writ.] Several poems written wedding speeches and birthday greetings in verse for friends, none published as yet.; [pers.] I enjoy writing poetry, and to express feelings in words that way I find refreshing and very relaxing. I would like to write a book one day.; [a.] Altrincham, Cheshire, UK

PLATT, JONATHAN PHILIP
[pen.] Jake Platt; [b.] 11 September 1955, Bury, Lancs; [p.] Joan and Stanley; [m.] Glenn; [ch.] Gemma and Jordan; [a.] Stevenage, Herts, UK

PLATTS, CLAIRE LOUISE
[b.] 29 November 1985, Leicester; [p.] Michael J. Platts; [m.] Yvonne Platts; [ed.] Marshland Primary School, Moorend; [a.] Moorend, Doncaster, UK

PLEDGE, MARY
[pen.] Dirro; [b.] N London; [p.] Harvey and Hannah Abbott; [m.] Peter John, 1953; [ch.] Two and four grandchildren; [occ.] Retired nursing sister; [memb.] Keep Fit Association (past) St. Pauls Church Centre, Chean. (Mem.) R. College of Nursing (Past); [oth. writ.] Several poems published I'm Anthologies; [pers.] I have always loved word poems like heats, Shelley Eac. recently become more spiritually aware and wish to share my experience with others in some of my poems.; [a.] Ewell, Epsom, Surrey, UK

POMEROY, JAMES
[b.] 6 January 1962, New Malden; [p.] K. A. Pomeroy, S. D. Pomeroy; [m.] Sadie Pomeroy, 29 July 1989; [ch.] Emily Jane Pomeroy; [ed.] B.A. (Hons) History and Government, University of Essex; [occ.] Nursing Assistant; [a.] Harlow, Essex, UK

POOLE, DIANE R.
[b.] 7 July 1958, Rochdale, Lancashire; [m.] Gary, 10 September 1988; [ch.] Stuart - 7 and Christopher - 4; [ed.] Whitworth High School; [occ.] Qualified Nurse part time night duty; [oth. writ.] None published compiling my own work in a book. Have written many poems on particular subjects requested by family or friends.; [pers.] I was so overwhelmed by feelings of anger and helplessness when the Dunblane tragedy occurred I felt compelled to write the poem as my own personal memorial to those children, a constant reminder of how very precious my time with my children is.; [a.] Guernsey, Channel Islands, UK

POOLE, JEAN
[pen.] Jean Poole; [b.] 20 August 1936, London; [ed.] Hornsey County High N8; [occ.] Retired, worked for the Spastic Society in Essex; [memb.] Keep Fit and Indoor Bowls Wickford Community Centre Essex, Poems Published in Local Magazines; [pers.] I get great pleasure in writing poems and in my fellow writers I sense a great thrill when their poems are acknowledge.; [a.] Wickford, Essex, UK

POOLEY, RICHARD
[b.] 21 March 1928, Deptford; [p.] Patrick Pooley and Phylis Pooley; [m.] Elaine Pooley, 6 December 1973; [ch.] Richard Tim and Simon Pooley; [ed.] Mayford Approved School, Woking, Surrey; [occ.] Retired; [hon.] Arthur Koestler Award for Literature 1968; [oth. writ.] "The Evacuee", "The Exploding Prison".; [pers.] Having spent, between 1940-1972, twenty years of my adult life locked up in her majesty's prisons I came to the conclusion prisons I came to the conclusion that you don't have to be a bad person to spend time in prison.; [a.] Hull, East Yorkshire, UK

PORTEOUS, ALICE
[b.] 5 December 1918, Penarth, S. Wales; [p.] William and Lilian Wheeler; [m.] Sydney Porteous-Hall, 21 December 1941; [ch.] 5 Sons; [ed.] Penarth Country School; [occ.] Retired; [hon.] Silver Medalist Crystal Palace London. Soprano Soloist 1929. (Under 13 yrs) Chosen as Soloist - Queens Hall (London) 1931 by Carey Bonner in Large Temperance 'Cantata'; [oth. writ.] Short story writer - one published. Letters written and published in press.; [pers.] Most of my achievements were at a young age - now after bringing up 5 sons and a widow of many years - my poetry brings out Hidden Feelings and begins to make feel "Life is Worthwhile!"; [a.] Hull, E. Yorks, UK

PORTER, M.
[b.] 18 December 1926, Chichester, Sussex; [p.] Percy and Elsie Porter; [m.] Barbara Alison, 21 May 1949; [ed.] Alton Boys School, Alton Hampshire, Langastrian Boys School, Chichester Sussex; [occ.] Retired (after 34 yrs in the prison service); [memb.] I am CSMA; [hon.] BEM, ISM; [oth. writ.] Two hundred plus poems and verses (none published).; [pers.] At 19 yrs of age reached the rank of staff Sgt. in Signals Intelligence.; [a.] Chandlers Ford, Hampshire, UK

PORTER, REBECCA
[b.] 27 July 1981, Wordsley; [p.] Ann Porter and Michael Porter; [ed.] Greenfield Primary Stourbridge, Redhill Comprehensive Stourbridge; [occ.] Student; [memb.] Scott-Ward Dance Studio; [oth. writ.] I have had several articles printed in the Express and Star Wolverhampton during my

work experience.; [pers.] Most of my writing has been inspired by peoples response and reaction to those less fortunate in life than the majority. I have been greatly helped and influenced by Mr. Malcolm Thirlby of Redhill School.; [a.] Stourbridge, West Mildlands, UK

PORTER, SHIRLEY
[b.] 29 January 1960, Alyth, Scotland; [p.] David and Elspeth Marshall; [m.] Leslie Porter, 22 April 1994; [ch.] Heidi and Jai Stewart, stepson: Kevin Porter; [ed.] Bailey High School Fleetwood Lancashire; [memb.] Academy of Children's Writers; [oth. writ.] Poetry Printed by poetry now; [pers.] I would like to become a successful children's writer; [a.] Stirling, Central Scotland

PORTER-BRYANT, SEYMOUR
[b.] 1921, Bristol; [m.] Esme Beatrice Maud Porter-Bryant, 1947; [ch.] Brian Seymour Porter-Bryant and Antony Seymour Porter-Bryant; [ed.] Various schools and colleges and privately; [occ.] Retired Law Practitioner; [oth. writ.] One-time writer of travel articles for Chambers's Journal, The Traveller and Tourist and various newspapers.; [pers.] His personal philosophy can perhaps best the expressed by the couplet "No star is lost that once we may have seen, we may be yet what once we might have been".; [a.] Pill, North Somerset, UK

POTTS, NADINE M. B.
[pen.] Nadine Cope; [b.] 1 January 1939, Lichfield; [p.] Phyllis Edith and Sidney George Cope; [m.] Christopher Potts, January 1965; [ch.] Julia, Christopher, George; [ed.] Privately educated at Lichfield and Cannock Staffordshire; [occ.] Housewife; [oth. writ.] Poetry and short stories for children during my teenage years; [pers.] I need to "Feel" what I write; [a.] Forest Row, Sussex, UK

POTURICICH, NICK
[b.] 25/01/78, London; [p.] Dana & Pauline Poturicich; [ed.] American Academy, Larnaca, Cyprus; Coulsdon College, Surrey; [occ.] student; [oth. writ.] Poems published in Cypriot National Newspaper and other personal collections.; [pers.] I would like to dedicate this poem to someone who is very special in my life. her name is Vanja Radivoyevic, and she is a great inspiration to all my work. Thank you Vanja. I love you.; [a.] Sanderstead, Surrey

POUNDS, BARBARA
[b.] 20 January 1922, Plymstock; [p.] William Evans and Frances Evans; [m.] General Derek Pounds, 30 October 1944; [ch.] Vivian Barbara, Simon Francis; [ed.] State and Private; [occ.] Retired; [pers.] Served as W.R.N.S. officer during war, having graduated from the Naval College Greenwich.; [a.] Exton, Devon, UK

POUSSON, NATALIE
[b.] 8 October 1981, Empangeni, South Africa; [p.] Jean-Alain Pousson, Valerie Pousson; [ed.] Secondary School Tudor Grange (year 9); [occ.] Student; [memb.] National Ice-Skating Assoc. Ice Dance and Figure Skating Club. Member of Press Pack Writing Club. Member of "Starlets" - Precision Ice Skating Club; [hon.] Won Best Student Award 1996 (Prize day - Tudor Grange) numerous commendations obtained from Tudor Grange School; [oth. writ.] None published; [pers.] Writing poetry is a pleasure to me. It is so relaxing

to lose myself in new thoughts, ideas and imagenary. It is also a happy way to reflection on pleasant moments. Past and present.; [a.] Solihull, West Midlands, UK

POWERS, J. J.
[b.] 29 November 1972, Yeovil; [ed.] St. Martin's School, Crewkerne Yeovil College, Yeovil, University of Bath, University of Reading; [occ.] Student; [hon.] B. Sc. Mathematics, M. Sc. Biometry; [pers.] Inspiration for my poem came from Joseph Conrad's "The End Of The Tether" and the prospect of going to heaven.; [a.] South Petherton, Somerset, UK

PRINCE, CAROLINE MARIA GRUBER
[pen.] Florence May Richardson; [b.] 19 June 1961, Bournemouth; [p.] Michael Gruber, Patricia Gruber (Nee Dominey); [m.] Mark Prince, 8 April 1989; [ch.] Luke Daniel, Rose Bernadette; [occ.] Training Consultant, Writer and Photographer; [memb.] Home Business Alliance, FAW (International Fund for Animal Welfare), Edwings Horse Sanctuary, Hillside Animal Sanctuary; [oth. writ.] Co-Author with Teresita Heavens of the Home Business Management Correspond Course, compiled for the Home Business Alliance, currently being published as a book, children's books (unpublished) and other poems (unpublished); [pers.] I write from the heart hoping to show the need for peace and love for all Gods living things in a much troubled world. Florence May Richardson was my grandmother's name who due to an early death I was unable to meet. I would like to dedicate this poem to her memory, with my love.; [a.] Bournemouth, Dorset, UK

PRINGLE, MARIA
[b.] 18 November 1977, Birmingham; [p.] Elizabeth and Stephen Pringle; [ed.] Sir Wilfrid Martineao, Secondary School; [oth. writ.] Further poems of mine can be found in the books, "Live and Let Live" and "Moving Picture" published by the company "Poetry Now"; [pers.] I am very grateful to my family for encouraging and inspiring me to write and for giving me the confidence to enter my poems into competitions.; [a.] Birmingham, Warwickshire, UK

PRUDEN, TINA
[b.] 16 October 1973, Manchester; [p.] Christina Davison, Kevan Davison; [memb.] Collectable Doll Club Elefriends; [oth. writ.] Do you know soon to be published in anthology The Other Side of the Mirror other poems unpublished 12 months, Glorious Day, Mothers Poem; [pers.] My poems are written from the heart they are about feelings they were inspired by the person I wrote them for. And I know people everywhere will be able to relate to them in one form or another.; [a.] Catterick, North Yorkshire, UK

PUGH, GEMMA
[pen.] Lei; [b.] 12 August 1981, Chichester; [p.] Barbara Brownell, Dave Pugh; [pers.] In my writing I try to show what is happening in the world around me.; [a.] Billingshurst, West Sussex, UK

PUGH, PETER
[b.] 20 September 1948, Bangor, Cymru; [m.] Gloria, The light of my life; [ch.] Kenneth, David, My best friends; [pers.] A lost dreamer under the hill.; [a.] Bembridge, Isle of Wight, UK

QUARTERMAN, ERICA ANN
[b.] 17 June 1938, London; [m.] Maxwell Quarterman, 7 September 1957; [ch.] Karen and Quentin; [ed.] Secretarial, Art and Sculpture, B.A. (O.U), Post Grad. Cert. of Education, Reading University; [memb.] East Portlemouth Art Club, National Trust; [hon.] RYA Competent Crew and Day Skipper/Watch Leader, First Aid Certificate; [oth. writ.] Local newspaper - articles and photos. Article Irish Tourist Bureau, Dublin. I have written for my children always and now for my grandchildren. It is only recently that I have submitted work for possible publication.; [pers.] In my writing I attempt to create for the reader an atmosphere of interest and pleasure which I have gained from observations of people, life and nature, and hope to encourage a broader and more tolerant perspective of "man's attitude to man."; [a.] Salcombe, South Devon, UK

QUEMARD, JANET ROSE
[pen.] Rosemarie Dymond; [b.] 1 June 1956, Jersey; [ed.] Secondary School, St. Helier Girls, Jersey; [memb.] The Jersey Epilepsy Society; [oth. writ.] I have written many poems, unpublished I feel honoured to be recognized; [pers.] With unhappy events in life and ill health I was persuaded back in 1995 to write feelings down and before long there was a catalogue to work on and with others themes too. It's amazing it keep son growing. It's an achievement.; [a.] Jersey, Channel Islands, UK

QUINN, CAROL
[b.] 14 September 1977, Glasgow; [p.] Sandra and Thomas Quinn; [ed.] Bellarmine Secondary; [occ.] Retail Ass.; [oth. writ.] I have written many poems over the years though this is the first competition I've entered.; [pers.] I try to relate through poetry my out look as a whole, but also I try to reach people with feelings that they could recognize in themselves, reviving memories from long ago.; [a.] Glasgow, Lanarkshire, UK

QUINN, MRS. SHIRLEY ANN
[pen.] Shirley Ann Quinn; [b.] 28 November 1936, Thorne, Nr Doncaster; [p.] Herbert Holt, Annie Holt; [m.] Derek Quinn, 3 May 1958; [ch.] Derek Anthony; [ed.] Mooreno's Secondary Modern School for Girls; [occ.] Housewife; [oth. writ.] Local courier, several in books, of different types. One children's some with a christian point of view, and about anything I can write about. Really, and one British Iles.; [pers.] I have always loved to Rhyme. But never done anything with my poems till 1994, I was so thrilled when people said that was a good one Shirl that did it. I was trying for publication. I work alone, mostly in my kitchen, and I made it. At age 59. As I was in a low form at school and never did poetry. But will always remember as a child, my favorite one (Goosey Goosey Gander); [a.] Thorne, South Yorkshire, UK

QUINN-BURROWS, MRS. K. A.
[b.] 7 May 1931, Leicester; [p.] Edward Aubrey Ellis and Patricia Nellie Ellis; [ch.] J. D. Quinn and J. P. Davis; [occ.] State Registered Nurse trained at The Royal Tunbridge Wells School of Nursing; [oth. writ.] Our World - published in Poetry To-Day; [pers.] Anger at the injustices in the world today. It makes me very sad for importance people, I thope that the pen is mightier than the sword.; [a.] Sevenoaks, Kent, UK

RAE, FIONA ELIZABETH
[b.] 8 October 1969, Inverurie; [p.] George Rae, Anne Rae; [ed.] Speyside High School, Aberlour Dumfries Galloway College of Technology; [occ.] Assistant Catering Manager at Gordonstoun School, Duffus; [memb.] Hopeman Golf Club Hotel - Catering International Management Association, Royal Environmental Health Institute of Scotland; [pers.] My writings are inspired by the sea, friendships and personal experience.; [a.] Elgin, Morayshire, UK

RAHILA
[pen.] Raahilat Al-Baydaa'u; [ed.] She has MA in social history from Essex University; [oth. writ.] Rahila is a born writer, but "Dear Sahara" is her first ever poem written in English, and her first ever publication.; [pers.] Rahila was of Japanese origin, which she has recently, finally, rejected. New she is a rootless anarchist, and nature worshipper.

RAMCHURN, UFAM
[b.] 14 February 1968, Quatre Bornes, Mauritius; [p.] Rita Ramchurn, Devlall Ramchurn; [ed.] College du Saint Esprit - (Grammar School); [occ.] Student, College du Saint Esprit - taking G.C.E. 'A' Levels; [memb.] College du Saint Esprit Astronomy Club, English Speaking Union; [hon.] No Literary Awards, Best Actor under 15 at the National Drama Festival, 1992, Best Actor in 1993; [oth. writ.] Nothing published; [pers.] I have been probing a lot into the latent genius of childhood lately. But I have no fixed axioms, though in terms of form. I like to make my poems like like the visible part of an iceberg - a part of some bigger hidden thing.; [a.] Quatre Bornes, Mauritius

RAMM, YVONNE
[b.] 8th July 1943, Newcastle upon Tyne; [p.] John Oliphant and Isabella Oliphant; [m.] Robert Ramm, December 16, 1961; [ch.] Stephen and Jonathan, Martin and Sonja; [ed.] Newbiggin-By-The-Sea County Modern School; [occ.] Housewife; [oth. writ.] Several poems published in anthologies by (Arrival Press) of Peterborough; [pers.] Greatly encouraged by my husband who is my greatest advocate and soul mate but I am also greatly influenced from my past memories of the stalwart qualities and goodness I associate with both my grandparents and parents trying to reflect in my writing my thoughts to my own grandchildren.; [a.] Morpeth, Northumberland, UK

RAND, PAUL FREDERICK
[b.] 1 December 1958, Hounslow; [p.] Frederick Rand and Rita Rand; [ed.] Sunderland University; [occ.] Tutor; [memb.] London Library - Life Member; [hon.] History, Politics, Sword Fencing - Bronze Medal; [oth. writ.] Limericks in four Anthologies, a fifth to appear later this year. Compiled notes for church patronal festival various articles on charities and the voluntary sector. Complied local election manifesto for environment group.; [pers.] I believe the most important things in art and in life generally are style and a sense of enjoyment.; [a.] Feltham, Middlesex, UK

RANKIN, NAOMI TURNER
[b.] 30 June 1976, Luton, Beds; [p.] Joseph T. Rankin, Sylvia I. Rankin; [ed.] Challney Girls High School, Luton, Luton Sixth Form College; [occ.] Medical Administration Clerk; [pers.] There is a poet inside everyone who stops to see the creation around them. Most of my poems are about real things that happen to real people, namely my beloved friends and family who without I would be nothing.; [a.] Luton, Bedfordshire, UK

RAO, NAGY
[b.] 10 November 1926, Nellore, India; [p.] Subbarayudu and Mahalakshmi; [m.] Sobha, 8 December 1949; [ch.] Suresh, Ramesh, Naresh, and Subha; [ed.] B.E. - Annamalai University, India, M.B.A. Columbia University, New York; [occ.] Retired - Financial Consultant and Training Officer; [memb.] Institute of Management; [oth. writ.] "Anxious Moments" article on awaiting High School exam results "Traveler's Tale" poem, "Glimpses From Early Years" Auto Biography up to marriage (Arranged marriage). All above not submitted for publication.; [pers.] I see our lives as journeys through ages to provide our souls exposure to changes in human values and express these aspects now and then as an activity in retirement.; [a.] Croydon, Surrey, UK

RAWLINS, MR. LEIGH COLIN
[b.] 11 June 1971, Portsmouth; [p.] Vivienne Milne and David Rawlins; [m.] Vickie Christina Rawlins, 9 December 1995; [ch.] Rea Marie Rawlins and Samantha-Christina Rawlins; [ed.] Corpus Christi and Oaklands RC Comprehensive; [occ.] Deputy Computer Operations Manager; [memb.] Institute of Management; [hon.] YTS "Outstanding Student of the Week"; [oth. writ.] Millions of unpublished poems; [pers.] I write poems lest I forget how I felt when I'm old, and to release my emotions; [a.] Portsmouth, Hampshire, UK

RAYNER, LEONARD J.
[b.] 12 September 1926, Ipswich; [p.] Lily Ruth, Frederick William; [ed.] Westbourne Comprehensive; [occ.] Insurance Rep. (Retired); [pers.] I try to base my poems on the factual side of life, as I find that facts are often stranger than fiction.; [a.] Ipswich, Suffolk, UK

REA, MRS. R.
[pen.] Rita Rose; [b.] 16 March 1931, Redditch; [p.] Mr. and Mrs. N. Smith; [m.] Mr. G. Rea, 28 October 1950; [ch.] Pamela - 44 and Susan - 42; [ed.] St Stephens Girls School, Day Course Art; [occ.] Worked at Hymatic Engineering Co. Ltd (10 years) Clerk/Typist Computer. Retired; [pers.] My favourite poem is by Rudyard Kipling (If) for it reflects so much of life itself.; [a.] Bromsgrove, Worcs, UK

READ, EMMA
[b.] 15 June 1981, Basingstoke; [p.] Alan and Pat Read; [ed.] Old Basing Infant School, St. Mary's C. of E. Junior School, Harriet Costello Secondary School; [memb.] RSPCA, The Blue Cross, The Cats Protection League, Wocs, Care for the Wild, Redwings Horse Sanctuary, The Centre Gym Gymnasium, Inbasingstoke; [hon.] Certificate for 1st place clarinet trio in Basingstoke music festival with honour, Certificate for 3rd place (as above but with merit), Certificate for grades 3 and 4 Clarinet, Certificate for Competence in Information Technology, P.T.O.; [pers.] I hope that my poems create more awareness amongst people, and from this awareness positive action take place, to help make this a better world.; [a.] Basingstoke, Hampshire, UK

READ, NIKKI
[b.] 14 July 1968, Kingston; [p.] Alfred and Diane Weston; [m.] Tim Read, 1 June 1991; [ed.] Easthampstead Park School, Wokingham, Berkshire; [occ.] Clerk, Hallway Catering Services Ltd; [a.] Bracknell, Berkshire, UK

REES, VINCENT
[b.] 15 October 1964, Swansea; [p.] Colin Rees, Fay Thomas; [ed.] Cefn Hengoed Comprehensive; [occ.] Unemployed, Singer/Songwriter/Poet; [memb.] Two local pop outfits; [hon.] Degree in life; [oth. writ.] Just finished a book of poetry, in process of having it put into book form, hope to publish when totally finished; [pers.] We need you like you need us, everythings one so what's the fuss. Live and love, love and learn, turn the page, if you don't want to burn, we gotta love and learn!; [a.] Swansea, West Glamorgan, UK

REEVE, CHARLOTTE CAROLINE
[b.] 12 March 1980, Norwich; [p.] Terry and Carole Reeve; [ed.] Bungay High School; [occ.] Student ('A' Levels), English Literature; [hon.] Bronze Duke of Edinburgh Award, gained nine G.C.S.E.'s in the 1996 Summer Examinations; [oth. writ.] Written several poems but none published as yet.; [pers.] Inspired by earlier romantic poets such as Rupert Broke and William Butler Yeats. The beautiful Suffolk countryside also inspires some good ideas.; [a.] Bungay, Suffolk, UK

REEVE, TREVOR
[b.] 7 July 1947, Cambridge; [p.] Claude Reeve, Miriam Reeve; [m.] Christine Reeve, 16 October 1971; [ch.] Karen, Paul, Claire; [ed.] Keysoe Comprehensive; [occ.] Sales and Purchasing Clerk; [oth. writ.] Poem published in The Other Side Of The Mirror.; [pers.] Prepare to listen, never shout. And you will find out what life is all about.; [a.] Kempston, Bedforshire, UK

REEVES, ANNA
[b.] 15 November 1969, Clapton; [m.] Alex Reeves, 3 December 1988; [ch.] Jessica and Marc; [ed.] Bonner Primary, Forest Girls School; [occ.] Housewife and Mother; [memb.] Animal Lifeline; [pers.] My poetry is the key to my innermost thoughts allowing me total freedom to express everything I feel. I am influenced by everything.; [a.] West Molesey, Surrey, UK

REID, HELEN
[b.] 13 August 1902, Darwen; [p.] William and Jane Grant; [m.] Dr. James Baird Reid, 15 July 1931; [ch.] 2 sons, Peter, Alastair Grant; [ed.] Ayr Grammar School Ayr Academy, Glasgow University; [occ.] Retired; [hon.] M. A. Hons. Glasgow University

REID, VALERIE JOHNSTON
[b.] 28 July 1954, Kilmarnock; [p.] Alastair Irving and Patricia McCrone; [m.] William Reid (Deceased), 21 April 1976; [ch.] Alastair William and Lorna Patricia; [ed.] Grammar Primary, Kilmarnock Academy, Langside College, Glasgow; [occ.] Domestic Engineer; [pers.] 'Moving on' is dedicated to my family and friends who helped me during my late husbands illness and in my bereavement.; [a.] Kilmarnock, East Ayrshire, UK

REILLY, JOSEPH JOHN
[pen.] Joe-John; [b.] 3 September 1980, Glasgow; [p.] James and Yvonne Reilly; [ed.] Pupil at Our Lady's High School, Cumbernauld; [oth. writ.] This is my first poem ever, sent to International Library of Poetry.; [pers.] I'd love to be a poet someday.; [a.] Cumbernauld, North Lanarkshire, UK

REMPEL, ANTHONY PETER
[pen.] Tony and the Remp, plus (The Major of Ensbury Park); [b.] 29 November 1944, Bournemouth; [p.] George Jacob Rempel, Florence Mabel Clark; [m.] Ann Patricia Rempel, 1 April 1967; [ch.] Lon Rempel; [ed.] Secondary School only, no formal Education; [occ.] Master Builder; [memb.] Norton Owner's Club, Winton Conservative Club, The Church of Jesus Christ of Latter Day Saint's. Inactive at present, but working on this. The CBB Social Club; [hon.] An Aprentishship in Life, and the Love of my Family! And the Trust of my Friends, for the English man, that I am! Other than this, one certificate in Building and Construction Proficiency for Bricklaying; [oth. writ.] The Dove Of Peace, (Cyclop's) and (Man Not Needed), Can We Stay The Hand Of Time, (Possibilities) and (The Garden), (The Old Woman) and (Hope Lost), Free Human's Be and many other's yet to be published.; [pers.] We are all born with a conscience, so if in doubt, leave it out. For none of us can afford the luxury of even one negative thought. If we are to return to whence we came!; [a.] Bournemouth, Dorset, UK

RENDALL, MR. J. H. E.
[pen.] "The Bard of Umberleigh"; [b.] 10 May 1922, Twickenham, Middx; [p.] Both Deceased; [ed.] Hampton Grammar School, Kingston Technical School; [occ.] Retired Civil Servant; [oth. writ.] "The collected poems of John H. E. Rendall" and "The Collected poems of the Bard of Umberleigh."; [pers.] I began writing poems in 1943 and have written nearly 500 change few (I few) have been published. I do this for the pleasure it gives me and Roaches I entertain which examples of my work.; [a.] Umberleigh, Devon, UK

RENNIE, WINSTON JOSEPH
[b.] 22 December 1970, Madras, India; [p.] Dr. R. T. Joseph and Dr. V. M. Rennie; [ed.] Don Bosco H.S.S., Madras, Loyola College Madras, PSG Institute of medical sciences; [occ.] Doctor of Medicine; [memb.] Editor of "Panacea", Former Editor of College Magazine, former Member of "Quiz Club", Keen debater, Member of "PSG music Club"; [hon.] Best Debater Award South Zone Intermedicals; [oth. writ.] Several poems published in College magazine, short story "The Gift" published in College magazine; [pers.] Life is too short and the beauty of living it fully, too large, for one to waste time on petty battles over race, religion and political differences.; [a.] London, UK

RESZCZYNSKI, VANDA
[b.] 10 November 1958, Wirral; [p.] Doreen R. and Henryk Reszczynski; [ch.] Lisa Marie, Christopher, Paul, Liam; [occ.] Assistant to the Co-Ordinators, Crossroads in Wirral; [oth. writ.] Have written for pure pleasure since childhood.; [pers.] I hope my poetry has meaning to others as each verse I have written holds a personal part of me.; [a.] Birkenhead, Merseyside, UK

REVILL-POTT, KAREN A.
[pen.] Karen; [b.] 31 October 1964, Chichester, West Sussex; [pers.] Life - They didn't tell me it was gonna be like this...; [a.] Crans-Montana, Switzerland

RHODES, LINDA
[b.] 24 February 1949, Ramsgate, Kent; [occ.] Adult Education Teacher; [pers.] Once we stop believing on or blaming other people in our lives, we find happiness and contentment; [a.] Broadstairs, Kent, UK

RHYDER, JULIE
[b.] 12 April 1956, West Ham; [p.] Harold Hall, Audrey Hall; [ch.] Rebecca, Cleran, Ken, Stuey; [ed.] Heathcote Secondary Stevenage, Bognor Regis Comprehensive; [occ.] Horticultural Despatch Supervisor; [oth. writ.] Poems for my family not published.; [pers.] My love for nature, along with deep emotions are my inspiration.; [a.] Bognor Regis, West Sussex, UK

RICH, ANDREW
[b.] 30 September 1972; [occ.] Student; [pers.] The poem is about man's everyday relationship with death and God, and how death can lead to fears. But death may also be a liberation.; [a.] Kent, UK

RICHARDS, ALECIA
[b.] 30 September 1984, Birmingham; [p.] Pauline Richards and Dorrell Richards; [ed.] King Edwards Grammar School for Girls; [occ.] School Girl; [memb.] School Drama Club, School Hockey Team; [hon.] Junior essay writing competition (twice); [oth. writ.] Ghost and Ghouls - published in "All Aboard For The West Midlands" 1995; [pers.] In my writing I like to express my most in depth thoughts and loose myself in it hence creating interesting and hopefully very good stories or poems.; [a.] Birmingham, West Midlands, UK

RICHARDS, CHRISTOPHER PHILLIP SHELDON
[b.] 4 October 1934, Wolverhampton; [p.] Philip and Phyllis; [m.] Margarey Anne Thornley, 23 May 1959; [ch.] Mark Charles Oliver and Ian David; [ed.] Rossall School Fleetwood, Lancs, Joint Service School for Linguists, Bodmin Cornwall, Wolverhampton University; [occ.] Retired; [oth. writ.] Reporting on papers; [pers.] The standard of reporting is very poor in my opinion. There are a number of puerile puns and abysmal alliterations. We have a losing- Fare culture so next to no others. I had a hard life which undermined my health. It was my belief in Christ's Crucifixion which helped. [a.] Wolverhampton, West Midlands, UK

RICHARDS, GLADYS MURIEL SEYMOUR
[b.] 6 November 1914, Edmonton; [p.] Ethel and Philip Bowes British; [m.] Deceased, 2 January 1932; [ch.] One; [ed.] Secondary, Edmonton County School; [occ.] Retired; [oth. writ.] Tabanacles

RICHARDSON, TANYA DAWN
[pen.] Tarn Morgan; [b.] 24 June 1968, Eastbourne, E. Sussex; [p.] Terence and Pamela Richardson; [ch.] Two cats Wobbly and Scolly; [ed.] Hampden Park Comprehensive School, Eastborne College of Arts and Technology; [memb.] Anderida Writers, Green Peace, Amnesty International; [hon.] B/TEC Diploma; [oth. writ.] BBC, local newspapers, local magazines. In the book, 'One Small Step.'; [pers.] Having been quite ill for the last few years, I try to share my joys with others. It's nice to be important, but even more important to be mine.; [a.] Eastbourne, East Sussex, UK

RICHEY, ANNA
[pen.] Anna Richey; [b.] 28 January 1979, London; [p.] Christine Fox, Simen Richey; [ed.] Camden School for Girls (London); [occ.] Studying for my 'A' levels; [memb.] Highgate Literature Society. Hampstead Athletics Club; [oth. writ.] This is the first competition I have entered and it is my first publication.; [pers.] My poetry reflects my inner most feelings which I can express in no other way.; [a.] London, UK

RICHMOND, PATRICIA J.
[b.] 3 December 1942, South London; [p.] William and Elsie Bourne; [m.] David Richmond, 30 June 1962; [ch.] Julie Ginger and Ian Richmond; [ed.] Balham and Tooting College of Commerce; [occ.] Housewife; [pers.] I am just starting out, on trying to fulfill an ambition to have my name in print, but at the same trying time to bring pleasure to others.; [a.] Bordon, Hampshire, UK

RIDGE, AUDREY E.
[b.] 29 January 1932, Kingston, Surrey; [p.] W. J. Howe and L. M. A. Howe; [m.] E. P. Ridge, 16 June 1956; [ch.] Janice A. Mussard; [ed.] Former Pupil of the Lady Eleanor Holles School 1938 - 1949 Hampton Middx.; [occ.] Retired; [a.] Horsham, West Sussex, UK

RIDGLEY, CAROL SHEILA
[b.] 4 July 1955, Wolverhampton; [p.] Roy and Sheila Ridgley; [m.] Stephen Michael Ridgley, 29 June 1984; [ch.] Craig Andrew and Emma Jane Ridgley; [ed.] Bilston Girls High School, Liverpool University; [occ.] Housewife; [oth. writ.] One previous poem published in anthology.; [pers.] I strive to raise a smile through my poetry.; [a.] Rugby, Warwickshire, UK

RILEY, JOSEPH
[pen.] Joseph Riley; [b.] September 29, 1938, Manchester; [p.] John and Winifred Riley (Deceased); [ed.] St. Gregory's High School, Ardwick, Manchester; [occ.] I am a patient in a Mental Hospital; [memb.] Ex-Athlete for Salford Harriers Running Club; [hon.] 9 poems published by New Horizon, Now Bankrupt, Title of Book New British Poems, Vol. 1 Date 1982; [oth. writ.] Science Fiction Short Story, "The Andrumeda Gods" published in National Sunday Newspaper, (Sunday News and Echo) Now Bankrupt Oct 93!; [pers.] Surprisingly in view of my poem, I am a 100% Atheist, and believe space is completely endless and the universe is a "Vast Eternal Night."; [a.] Manchester, Lancashire, UK

RIMMER, JOHN S.
[pen.] Johnny Kittelsen; [b.] 23 December 1986, Merseyside; [p.] John Kittelsen, Kathleen M. Rimmer; [occ.] 3rd Year Pupil, St. Marks R. C. School, Halewood Merseyside; [oth. writ.] I want the world to stop fighting and taking drugs.; [a.] Halewood, Merseyside, UK

RIPPON, JENNIE
[b.] 9 October 1944, Bracknell, Berkshire; [p.] Rene and Bert Clover; [m.] William, 7 June 1969; [ch.] Melanie, Clare and Fleur; [ed.] Wick Hill School, Bracknell, Reading, Windsor and Solihull Colleges; [occ.] Lecturer in information Technology; [memb.] Society of Business Teachers in Education; [oth. writ.] I have had 24 other poems published in various books and I have just started a postal course in creative writing.; [a.] Solihull, West Midlands, UK

ROBBINS, ANNE C. M. H.
[pen.] Anne Robbins; [b.] 16 July 1947, Huddersfield; [p.] The Late Harry and Marjorie Hepworth; [m.] Divorced; [ch.] Christopher - 24; [ed.] Victoria County Secondary School, Percival Whitley College, Open University; [occ.] Secretary/P.A (Daytime) and Clairvoyant - Medium - Healer (Evenings); [memb.] Member of the British Council of Hypnotist Examiners; [hon.] C.M.H. (Certified Master Hypnotist); [oth. writ.] Poems in "A Taste Of The North" - Arrival press, Anne Diamond's book - "A Gift From Sebastian", and "A Passage In Time" International Society of Poets. "The Robbins Collection" - Awaiting publication.; [pers.] If my words can touch just one life and make a difference then I shall know the value of my gift.; [a.] Brighouse, West Yorkshire, UK

ROBERTS, CAROL
[b.] January 7, 1948, Birmingham; [p.] Eva; [m.] Bryan, April 6, 1968; [ch.] Tabitha, Simon, Samantha, Kristopher; [ed.] St. Albans C. of E School Birmingham; [occ.] Supervisor; [oth. writ.] Had poem published by local newspaper in response to the closure of local hospital where my son (an asthmatic) made frequent visits. (Hospital was saved.); [pers.] I love writing poetry. Hated reading it at school, until my eyes were opened by my children at a very young age. Never knew where to send any though.; [a.] Aylesbury, Bucks, UK

ROBERTS, LUCY
[b.] 14 December 1980, Bristol; [p.] David and Corinne Roberts; [ed.] Present School St. Bedes Roman Catholic Comprehensive School; [oth. writ.] Credited for poem sent to local magazine/catalogue poem published during autumn.; [pers.] In the majority of my work I have tried to reflect how I feel about, the past, the present and the future. I am influenced by all concepts of life but also by my parents for all the love and encouragement they have given me.; [a.] Clevedon, North Somerset, UK

ROBERTS, SYLVIA ANN
[b.] 22 January 1945, S Wales; [ch.] Rowena, Peter, Nicholas; [ed.] Secondary School; [oth. writ.] None published; [pers.] I write what I feel at the time of writing. Sometimes a particular event will pull at me. And I have to write it down on paper. And capture the feeling.; [a.] Swansea, West Glamorgan, UK

ROBERTS, TERRY
[b.] 15 January 1945, Bournemouth; [p.] Douglas and Elsie Roberts; [m.] Stella Roberts, 25 January 1969; [ch.] Anna, Rebecca and Sally; [ed.] Grammar School, Barrow-on-Soar, Leicestershire N.E. School of Wireless, Bridlington: Bournemouth College of Technology, Salisbury and Wells Theological College; [occ.] Priest, Church of England; [oth. writ.] Have always written poetry for personal pleasure; [pers.] I am continuously amazed by the wonders of the world and at the bounty of the creator.; [a.] Basingstoke, Hampshire, UK

ROBERTS, TONY
[b.] 22 August 1973, Martham, Norfolk; [p.] Ian and Joyce Roberts; [ed.] Hreod Parkway, Comprehensive, Swindon; [occ.] God Job man, also a factory worker; [memb.] Heaven; [hon.] Honours being part of God; [pers.] Everyday my God shows me the pure magic of his essence. We must all work towards a collective destiny. Heaven on Earth. Open yourself to God, love and repeat, and you will have nothing to tear when judged. God bless those who believe.; [a.] Swindon, Wiltshire, UK

ROBERTSON, MISS SUSAN MARY
[b.] 1 October 1952, Cardiff, Wales, UK; [p.] Mr. and Mrs. Robert Robertson; [ed.] Birkbeck College London 1995-96, Hammersmith and West London College 1993-95, King's College London B.S. (hons) Biochemistry 1976-77, Howell's School Llandaff Cardiff 1964-71; [occ.] Library Assistant at Chelsea and Westminster Hospital; [memb.] British Labour Party, Institure of Medical Laboratory Sciences, International Voluntary Service; [hon.] Certificate in Media Practice 1996, B.T.E.C. Management Studes 1995, B.Sc. (hons) Biochemistry 1977; [oth. writ.] "Health for Humanity" (1982), "The Dawn of the Space Age" (1990), "Dreaming in London" (1996), "Working Holidays" (1995).; [pers.] My interests include books, music, art, theatre, films, travel and cookey. I am concerned about peace for Progress, Prosperity and the Environment, and the Development of World Culture. And world civilisaiton.; [a.] London, Middlesex, UK

ROBERTSON, MR. SID
[pen.] Mr. Sid Robertson; [b.] 19 February 1924, Dundee; [p.] William Donald R., Mary Thompson Ross; [m.] Emily Hardwick R., 1 March 1947; [ch.] 3 and 6 Grandchildren; [ed.] I won a Borsary to attend Morgan Academy, Dundee - but I left a 14 years - to become a Gardener's apprentice - no regrets!; [occ.] (Apparently) retired but I still garden - happily!; [memb.] Hon. President of Cumberland Gardening Club (27 years); [hon.] 'The Scottish Horticultural Medal' - for outstanding service to Scottish Horticulture; [oth. writ.] Many intercultural articles for national, and provincial newspapers, plus gardening magazines. Guest presenter on "BBC Gardeners Question Time" 4 years presenter on BBC Scot Winds TV "The Beechgrove Garden" now non horticultural prose and poetry was reached the senior number 340!; [pers.] This gardener likes "plants and people" I find them so much alike - 'Tall/dwarf' "Hardy/ Non hardy!", "Quick/slow" or even "easy/or Awkward!" verse dominates my pen now a days. I think, then write, thus I will leave my thoughts behind.; [a.] Cumberland, Glasgow, N. Lanarskshire, UK

ROBERTSON, STUART DAVID
[pen.] Stuart David; [b.] 1 January 1946, Aldershot; [p.] Paul and Jack Robertson; [m.] Carol Ann, 14 June 1984; [ch.] Daughters - Hollie and Sophie; [ed.] Scorton Grammar School, Saltburn Manor Public School; [occ.] Sales and Marketing, EOC Advertisement Manager; [memb.] For Target Gun and Guns and Shooting Magazine, Present: Marketing Development Manager La Hu Idoson Group; [hon.] Various Awards for Drama (Festival Plays), Sports Shooting Trophies, One Act Play Written for me and published "Answers on a postcard, War Maja Drama Award; [oth. writ.] In the process of writing a children's book about a teddy bear called "One Eye"; [pers.] As an ex target shooter my spirit died for a short time on hearing, the news about "Dunblane", my daughters Hollne and Sophie gave it back to me.; [a.] Ludlow, Shorpshire, UK

ROBINSON, MRS. ANGELA
[b.] 7 October 1940, Cardiff; [p.] Basil Colls, Betty Colls; [m.] Alan G. Robinson, 11 April 1992; [ed.] Howell's school Llandaff open Uni-

versity; [occ.] Retired District Nursery Midwife/ Health Visitor; [memb.] RSPB, National Trust; [hon.] Balandpen University SRN, SCM, Hucert DN/QN; [oth. writ.] Article in midwifery magazine re small midwifery units - local paper article re local amenities - poems in church magazine - article in local RSPB news letter.; [pers.] It is never too late to learn. Life can be enjoyed to the full whatever your age. (I wish I'd know that when I was younger!; [a.] Carlisle, Cumbria, UK

ROBINSON, CRAIG
[b.] 25 December 1962, RAF, Halton; [p.] Peter and Janet Robinson; [m.] Penny Robinson (Nee Minall), 27 May 1989; [ch.] Georgina Claire, Conor James; [ed.] Aylesbury Grammar, University of Oxford; [occ.] Chartered Accountant; [memb.] Institute of Mathematics and its applications, The Oxford Society; [oth. writ.] Articles for various accountancy publications, poems for me patient organization magazine and newsletters.; [pers.] The inspiration for my poems derives from my love for my family, my battle with me and my feelings on what is right and wrong in modern society.; [a.] Princes Risborough, Bucks, UK

ROBINSON, DOREEN
[b.] 26 February 1945, Bristol; [p.] Lilian White and Albert White; [m.] Divorced; [ch.] Nathan, Rebecca, Matthew and Teresa; [ed.] St. Thomas More Secondary Modern School, Bristol; [occ.] Housewife and Volunteer A.B.E. tutor; [pers.] It is well to give when asked, but it is better to give unasked, through understanding. - Kahlil Gibran; [a.] Bristol, UK

ROBINSON, JAMES REGINALD
[b.] 5 April 1920; [p.] Henry Austin Robinson and Alice Emma; [m.] Phyllis Dorothy, 18 July 1942; [ch.] Barry, Austin, Robinson, Carol, June, Robert Peter and David James; [ed.] Began on leaving school, safe from the Newale of Cane Happy Teachers; [occ.] Retired; [memb.] Towarland Golf Club and Finchingfield Carpet, Bawks Club; [hon.] Once won a nepal as a pick nose champion from a school teacher who instead of resorting to pain for tears used humiliation; [oth. writ.] First time entry was included in the Anthology "Voices on the Wind".; [pers.] An inferiority complex should have denied me any recognition. But thanks to my daughter, my ego is now inflated; [a.] Finchingfield, Essex, UK

ROBINSON, JULIE A.
[pen.] Jewels, Ju; [b.] 30 July 1968, Lewisham; [p.] Marie Bell; [m.] Michael Dawkins; [ed.] Deptford Park Juniors School, Deptford Green Secondary School; [occ.] Nursery Officer; [pers.] My poems reflect me and my life based around love. Its what I am made from and also what I enjoy expressing physically as well as emotionally.; [a.] London, UK

ROBINSON, W.
[pen.] William; [b.] 14 December 1921, Widdrington; [p.] William, Jane Robinson; [m.] Georgina, 23 March 1946; [ch.] Christopher, Lorelei, Penelope; [ed.] Widdrington School; [occ.] Retired; [oth. writ.] Just the odd poem I used to write letters to a female cousin in verse it could be very hard. I have just finished a poem called (Memories) its not bad.; [pers.] Childhood in the country 45 years in the coal mines quiet an experience.; [a.] Morpeth, Northumberland, UK

ROBSON, CLIVE ALFRED
[b.] 13 March 1928, Croydon; [m.] Wendy, 1965; [ch.] Simon and Beth; [ed.] Clark's College Croydon, Trinity College of Music, Ex Gunner-Musician, Royal Artillery Band (Woolwich) 1945/ 1952; [occ.] Retired Teacher of violin and Viola, Ex Surrey Youth Music and Performing Arts; [memb.] Musicians Union Schools Music Association; [hon.] Editor's Choice Awards International Society of Poetry 1996, Leader and Soloist. East Grinstead Sinfonia (Misprinted in a "Passage In Time"); [oth. writ.] Short stories, Instrument music, Hymns and carols with musics.; [pers.] I am especially keen to see life simplified for everyone especially, politically and economically - with money made more equitable or indeed dropped from life altogether - seemingly impossible thoughts!; [a.] Horley, Surrey, UK

RODWAY, ANTHONY
[b.] 17 April 1929, London; [occ.] Voluntary Counselor, Monograph Editor for the AWCEBD Writing; [memb.] National Association of Head Teachers, Association of Workers for Children with Emotional and Behavioral Difficulties, Royal Philanthropic Society; [hon.] B. A. (Hons.); [a.] Redhill, Surrey, UK

ROGERS, GUY SCOTT
[b.] 28 July 1972, Taplow; [p.] David and Shirley Rogers; [ed.] Windsor Boy's School; [occ.] Fireman, Windsor Castle Fire Bridge; [memb.] Royal Household Golf Club, Bracknell Hurricanes Ice, Hockey Club, Cox Green Climbing Club; [oth. writ.] Songs from rap to folk, plus other poetry; [pers.] I gain my inspiration from close friends, popular artists such as Bob Dylan, and my inner self. And my driving force from the lack of Academic Achievement at School, which I deeply regret.; [a.] Windsor, Berks, UK

ROGERS, TRACEY KIM
[b.] 5 August 1976, Wakefield; [p.] Mr Tony Rogers and Wendy Anne Rogers; [ed.] Sheffield Hallam University, Wakefield College; [occ.] Student, part time at Warburtons in Accounts Dept.; [hon.] Higher national diploma in Home Economics. Currently studying for BA (hons) Home Economics; [a.] Wakefield, West Yorkshire, UK

ROSE, BRIDGET TANIA
[b.] 11 March 1972, Mutare, Zimbabwe; [p.] Reginald Rose and June Rose; [ch.] Aimee and Kimberly Leher; [ed.] A'Levels Cambridge, English Literature, Art History; [occ.] Bank Clerk; [pers.] The poem "A Probing Curiosity" was written at the age of sixteen. Since then I have come a long way in discovering myself, but the journey is endless...; [a.] Harare, Zimbabwe

ROSE, LIS
[b.] 31 May 1943, Denmark; [m.] Widowed, 17 September 1963; [ch.] Two sons; [ed.] In Denmark; [oth. writ.] "King Toad and Other Stories", Book of 9 short stories for children aged 4-8; [pers.] To quote Mabel Lucie Attwell, "The Greatest Treasure - The World Can Hold - Search as you will - end to end - it is not power - or fame - or gold - But Just The Love Of A Friend."; [a.] Nottingham, Notts, UK

ROSKILLY, NITA
[b.] 13 October 1942, Barnet, Herts; [p.] William and Juanita Dymott; [m.] George Roskilly, September 1969; [ch.] Karen Roskilly and Amanda Roskilly; [occ.] Paging Bureau Operator; [memb.]

Members of P.C.C. of Local C of E Church; [oth. writ.] None published, as yet. But have several ready to submit.; [pers.] My poems have helped me to express the ups and downs of life. The joy and pain of human love. They are inspired and mad possible by my savior's sacrificial love for me. My wish and prayer is that others will be helped by reading them.; [a.] Tottenham, London, UK

ROSS, EVELYN
[b.] Glasgow; [ed.] Newton-le-Willows (Merseyside) Grammar, University of Wales (English) Manchester Library School; [occ.] Bereavement Counsellor; [memb.] Museums Galleries on Merseyside Wea: RSPCA: Liberty 3C Folio poetry Soc. Friends of Liverpool Philharmonic; [oth. writ.] Poems in 3c Folio and Portfolio mag. (new). Article on alcohol and Bereavement (Bereavement Care' Mag). Material on Addiction and Bereavement for groups/centres; [pers.] I am immersed in the life of this aggravating and fascinating city with all its contrast.; [a.] Liverpool, Merseyside, UK

ROTHERY, DOREEN M.
[m.] Raymond E. F. Rothery, 22 May 1954; [ch.] Stephen Philip, Stuart Alan; [ed.] "University of Life"; [occ.] Wife, Mother, Grandmother, Retired; [oth. writ.] Numerous poems, verses for family friends and special occasions. Both humerous and inspirational nothing published.; [pers.] I reflect on things I see and hear. Love and laughter - joy and fear natures ever changing scenes - mankinds worries - childhood dreads.; [a.] Middleton, Manchester, UK

ROWLANDS, CHRISTINE
[b.] 22 July 1958, Aberystwyth; [m.] Barrie James; [ch.] Andrew Rowlands; [ed.] Aberaeron Comprehensive, Aberystwyth Further Education College, University of Wales Lampeter; [occ.] Mature Student; [hon.] Final year of a B.A. Course, History and Welsh joint; [pers.] Emotion spurns me to write.; [a.] Lampeter, Cardiganshire, UK

ROWLEY, JOHN STANDFORD
[b.] 29 January 1933, Bradford; [p.] Francis E. Rowley, Daisy Rowley; [m.] Shirley Rowley (Nee Wilkinson), 11 May 1974; [ch.] Tracy; [ed.] Belle Vue Boy's Grammar School (Bradford) Bradford Technical College; [occ.] Retired Chemical Maintenance Engr.; [memb.] Scout Association S.J.A.B. (Late Superintendent); [hon.] Lay Instructor S.J.A.B.; [oth. writ.] Scout sketches for gang shows - Personal poems for friends - poems for 1996 Christian poetry anthologies.; [pers.] When the writing school fails to honour your course: Carry on writing!; [a.] Filey, North Yorks, UK

ROZE, JANE RADCLIFFE
[b.] 26 October 1956, Blackpool; [p.] Wendy and Arthur Ashton; [m.] Claude Paul Roze; [ch.] Kirk, Abbie, Joseph, Zachary, Gregory; [ed.] Convent and High School "Charles Dickens"; [occ.] Mother Housewife and Poetess; [oth. writ.] "Poems of Paradox" published by Janus of London - "not I Lord but we" published in Anthology titled "Between a laugh and a tear"; [pers.] Poetry is the breath of the soul. It unlocks the hidden mysteries in all creation. It teaches and re-teaches us that nothing is ordinary everything has a depth beyond what is first seen...what hidden wonders and horrors are to unfold...; [a.] Cliftonville, Kent, UK

RUDGWICK, STEPHEN
[pen.] Stephen Rudgwick; [b.] 16 December 1957, London; [ed.] Epsom College, King's College, London; [memb.] Society of Sussex Downsmen; [oth. writ.] 'Thoughts of a worthing metal detective' (published by anchor books); [pers.] I don't consider myself a poet as much as a humorous rhymester, but it's the style in which I most enjoy writing.; [a.] Worthing, West Sussex, UK

RUDOLPH, K. H.
[b.] 17 February 1915, Battersea, London; [p.] Edgar Rudolph, Laura Rudolph; [ed.] Sir Walter St. John's School, Buttersea, St. Mark's St. John's Collage, Chelsea; [occ.] Retired school teacher of French, German, and religious Ins.; [memb.] Rambler Association, Society of Sussex Downsmen - Angelican Society Youth Hotels Association Queens English Society. London Omnibus Traction Society, Southdown Euthusiast's Society; [hon.] Teacher's Certificate M.R.S.T. (Member of Royal Society of Teacher); [oth. writ.] "A Year In Her Zealand", (Rhurchman Publication -ran out of print), many short poems in Parish magazines, "Ramblevider" for "Southdawns" But Cox (out of print); [pers.] I served in the intelligence corps during the Second World War, poetry is to prose what painting is to photography. It expresses the author real feelings. "Rusacts", The Holty; [a.] Washington, Sussex, UK

RUMBLE, PETER JOHN
[b.] 17 July 1925, London; [p.] William and Martha Rumble; [ed.] Secondary Grammar School and Ealing Art School; [occ.] Retired, my Conscience mainly in Commerce; [memb.] Have been a member of various choral societies and an operalic society over the years.; [oth. writ.] I plays (Underformed)! A few short stories and one or two poems.; [pers.] I always endeavor to be helpful and kind to my fellow men, and adhere to my Christian principles: I attend church regularly.; [a.] London, UK

RUSSELL, DAVID A.
[pen.] Braxton Sherman; [b.] 27 May 1969, Stourbridge; [ed.] King Edward Grammar; [hon.] English Literature; [oth. writ.] Poems published in City Limits Magazine. Five feature-length motion picture screenplays, currently being marketed.; [pers.] I endeavour to interpret the world in an original, creative way. I am influenced by the epic and romantic poets.; [a.] Hackney, London, UK

RUSSELL, GEMMA
[b.] 12 May 1983; [p.] Mr. Paul Russell and Miss Shannon Russell; [occ.] School girl/Secondary School; [hon.] 100% effort prize; [pers.] I enjoy writing poetry and stories. I hope this is one of many proud poems to have been published. It has influenced me very much and I shall continue to write more poems; [a.] Caterham, UK

RUSSELL, JULIE CHRISTINE
[b.] 20 April 1966, Worcester; [p.] Peter, Avril Badham; [ch.] Tracey, Neil Russell; [ed.] Ysgol Arudwy Harlech Gwynedd, Coleg Meirion Dwyfor, Dolgellau, Gwynedd; [a.] Harlech, Gwynedd, UK

RYAN, CATHERINE
[pen.] Catherine Ryan; [b.] 18 February 1978, Limerick City; [p.] Patricia O'Connor, Patrick Ryan; [ed.] Secondary School: Scoil Pol, Kilfinane, I am entering University College Cork in October 1996 to study for 3 years for a Bachelor of Arts Degree in early childhood education; [occ.] Student; [hon.] 2 Certificates from the Irish Board of Speech and Drama in which I received a merit in the Intermediate Four Exam and Honours in the Senior Four Exam.; [a.] Kilfinane, Limerick, Ireland

RYAN, CRISPIN
[pen.] Cris Ryan; [b.] 11 September 1970, Hastings; [p.] Pamela Ward, Allen Ward; [ed.] Torpoint Comprehensive Cornwall, Plymouth College of further education; [occ.] Patrol Officer, Blackburn Royal Infirmary; [memb.] Plymouth special constabulary police reserve. Western College players drama group, Plymouth; [oth. writ.] A film review for a local science fiction club magazine.; [pers.] The simple phrase 'I am a victim' going through my head one morning led me to write 'victims' and it is based on my experiences a special constable. We are all victims at one time or another.; [a.] Blackburn, Lancashire, UK

RYAN, ERIN
[pen.] 13 May 1977, Limerick, Ireland; [ed.] Crescent College Comprehensive, I'm currently studying Social Science at University College Cork; [occ.] Student; [memb.] I'm the Public Relation Officer and the UCC branch and the St. Vincent de Paul Society.; [pers.] Although I'm relatively new to the literary world, I would like to become a successful poet and/or songwriter. I would greatly appreciate any comments on my work.

RYAN, JASON
[b.] 18 August 1975, Aberdare; [p.] Marion Ryan, Steve Ryan; [ed.] Rhydfelen Welsh Comprehensive (Welsh speaking); [oth. writ.] Poem published in local newspaper; [pers.] This is the first poem I had ever written. And definitely not the last. I am extremely pleased that it will be printed in this anthology.; [a.] Aberdare, Mid-Glamorgan, UK

RYE, DAVID
[b.] 13 September 1944, Dunstable; [p.] George Rye, Margaret Rye; [m.] Anita Rye, 29 March 1975; [ch.] Nigel and Sharon; [ed.] Northfields Comprehensive School; [occ.] C.T.N. Proprietor; [memb.] Dunstable Conservative Club; [pers.] My endeavour is to achieve writings, so people from all walks of life can understand and enjoy them.; [a.] Leighton Buzzard, Beds, UK

RYEBURN-GILCHRIST, ELIZABETH JEAN
[b.] August 27, 1930, Greenock, Scotland; [p.] Robert Gilchrist, Mabel Gilchrist (Nee Galleway); [ed.] Privately educated at a Girl's Boarding - School 1941/44, then Day School 1944/48 in Scotland Secretarial College, London 1948/49; [occ.] Retired (since 1990) Interests - Music, Literature; [hon.] Certificate from the Associated Board of the Royal Schools of Music, London for passing an examination in Piano Forte (1943); [oth. writ.] Several poems published in magazines and in one newspaper. The story of my life and work in Europe published in my College magazine.; [pers.] The turning point in my life was working as an English Language Secretary for United Nations in France, Denmark and Germany (1957-1962) "The true poem is the poet's mind."; [a.] London, UK

RYRIE, LOUISE A.
[pen.] Louise A. Ryrie; [b.] 29 November 1977, Crawley; [p.] Mr. and Mrs. Alan and Anne Ryrie; [ed.] The Holy Trinity School, Crawley, 10 ACSE's, 1994, 3 A Levels - Theatre Studies, Religious Studies and Music, 1996; [hon.] Dancer in Ballet, Modern and Tap Dancing to Intermediate Standard, grade 8 Pianist, studying for Associ-

ate in I.S.T.D. Ballet and Diploma in Piano; [oth. writ.] Two poems published in anthologies by 'Poetry Now'. Articles for local newspaper.; [pers.] I work for my writing to have an individual message or meaning to the reader and to show the triumph and good over evil. I aim for my writing to reveal a new thought for each time read.; [a.] Crawley, West Sussex, UK

SADLER, MAGGIE
[b.] 13 September 1921, Scotland; [p.] Deceased; [m.] Allen Sadler, 20 August 1945; [ch.] One son, one daughter; [ed.] Portobello Higher Grade School, Civil Service College; [occ.] Retired/ Clerical Officer Government/Central Local Authority; [oth. writ.] Various Newspaper Letters Local/History Magazines etc.; [pers.] Schooled at Portobello higher grade till age 14. Taught English and Latin by Norman McCaig who prove an inspiration/humanist; [a.] Edinburgh, UK

SADLER, MARK ANDREW
[pen.] Marc; [b.] 3 March 1967, Bishop's Stortford; [p.] Tony Sadler, Jean Sadler; [ed.] Newport Free Grammar School, Newport Essex; [occ.] Duty Service Manager, Scheduled Airline in Amsterdam; [oth. writ.] In the process of writing a novel for publication; [pers.] Dedicated to my family who in my later year's have come to mean so much to me.

SANDAL, REKHA
[b.] 4 December 1979, Ashford; [p.] Satish Sandal, Sureshta Sandal; [ed.] Longford Community School (10 G.C.S.E's); [occ.] Student; [oth. writ.] A news story published in 'BT Today' (BT's Newspaper for it's employees); [pers.] There was a young girl whose main aim, in the world was to entertain. She wrote a silly rhyme, and although it did shine the meaning of it was lost in her brain!; [a.] Bedfont, Middlesex, UK

SANDERSON, JOHN
[b.] 3 November 1938, Blackpool; [p.] Deceased; [m.] Joan Sanderson, 3 June 1994; [ch.] Jonathan, Abigail and Naomi; [ed.] Blackpool Grammar School and Pembroke Coll. Camb. Univ.; [occ.] Retired Inland Rev., Adjudication Officer and Ret. Freelance Journalist; [memb.] Retired Member of what was known as The Chartered Institute of Secretaries; [hon.] Proficiency Awards from Inland Revenue and various scholarships; [oth. writ.] Various press articles and other poems published; [pers.] I enjoy others being able to identify with my human emotions and questions.; [a.] Blackpool, Lancs, UK

SANDERSON, OLWYN
[pen.] Lucinda Hayes-Rowe; [b.] 30 May 1949, Dorset; [m.] 20 September 1983; [ch.] Clare, Amy; [ed.] Campion High School for Girls, University of Warwick; [occ.] Marketing; [memb.] Leamington SPA Rambling Club, Malvern Hills District Footpath Society; [hon.] B.A. Degree in Classics University of Warwick; [oth. writ.] 'Reflections' published 'Up-Running', Andrew Head 1996, Artilles for Parish Magazine and for Pleasure 'Playroom Fun Times' latest work hoping to get published.; [pers.] I simply live for writing and would love to become professionally recognized. Primarily interested in fact and countryside/nature issues and topics.; [a.] Worcester, UK

SARKIS, ROSIE
[pen.] Rosie; [b.] 9 March 1982, Nicosia; [p.] Katerina Sarkis; [ed.] Falcon School; [occ.] Student; [oth. writ.] Several poems published in my school newspaper.

SAUNDERS, JUNE
[pen.] June Saunders; [b.] 5 February 1940, Edmonton, London; [p.] Violet Grace Barrett and Dennis William Barrett; [m.] Eric and Terry Saunders; [ch.] Two, four grandchildren; [ed.] Tottenham County Grammar, took opportunity to take exams and passed for Edmonton Technical School for fashion trades; [occ.] Proprietor of antique and period fireplace shop; [memb.] Middlesex University, retired members association, (I was secretary there for 18 years before taking an early retirement opportunity); [hon.] None, left school at 15 instead of the 16 agreed when passing entry exams, much to the disappointment of my parents at the time; [oth. writ.] As and when something inspires me I write down my thoughts and put them in a drawer. Have never thought any would be good enough to get published.; [pers.] I feel very fortunate to have grown up in a house where books played a large part of our leisure time. I believe the written word is an important way of teaching us compassion and understanding as the words are someone's thoughts and feelings; [a.] Edmonton, UK

SAVAGE, SHAUN
[b.] June 1963, Norwich; [p.] Bryan Savage, Patricia Savage; [ed.] Hewett School, Norwich City College; [occ.] Printer/Technician Hewett School, Norwich; [oth. writ.] One previous poem in the anthology "A Passage in Time"; [pers.] But an `alien' insect, with the mind of a fly, that talks in rhymes, and can never die, doesn't know the meaning of rebel, doesn't know the place we call hell, doesn't know the meaning of restrain, or that it's a subsystem of your brain.; [a.] Norwich, Norfolk, UK

SAYE, DAVID
[pen.] David Hayward Saye; [b.] 27 May 1931, Cheddar, Somerset; [p.] Winifred and Harold Saye; [m.] Winifred Marion Saye, 22 December 1956; [ch.] Caroline, Pamela and Joanne; [ed.] Grammar School, Bristol University; [occ.] Retired Administrator; [oth. writ.] One previous poem published in 1994 by Anchor Books dedicated to my youngest daughter who left this life in 1994.; [pers.] The sadness of losing someone more precious than life itself, does not diminish with time. My daughter lives on in my head - Christina Rossetti was our common band.; [a.] Cheddar, Somerset, UK

SAYERS, MARCIA
[b.] 6 March 1939, Croydon, Surrey; [p.] Jack Thomason, Mary Thomason Nee Hartfied; [m.] Divorced, 31 December 1960; [ch.] Honor and Lindsey; [ed.] Selhurst Grammar School for Girls, currently Studying with open University for BA Degree; [occ.] Retired Disabled, ex Accountant; [memb.] F.A.A.I. Ltd. (Retired); [pers.] Immediacy of the moment seem to inspire but I have only just started to write. I am enjoying the "discovery" process-still-may poets works influence me - and I do not have one particular style as yet.; [a.] Norwich, Norfolk, UK

SCALLAN, AURIL
[b.] 1 April 1936, Barking, Essex; [p.] Sidney and Minnie Hunt; [m.] James Peter, 6 July 1957; [ch.] Stephen James and Monica Anne; [ed.] South East Essex Technical College Dagenham; [occ.] Retired; [memb.] Woodbridge Golf Club and Orford Sailing, Club the Deben Decorative and Fine Arts Society worked in a voluntary capacity for S.C.F. for over 20 years; [hon.] Freedom of City of London; [pers.] After living school worked as a Secretary. While our children were growing up qualified as a craft teacher and worked in this capacity for several years. My poetry is just a reflection of life as I see it.; [a.] Woodbridge, Suffolk, UK

SCARODIMOS, SARAH
[b.] 17 July 1979, Hull; [p.] Tom Scarodimos, Maggie Scarodimos; [ed.] Constable Primary School, Amy Johnson High School, Hull College; [pers.] I feel that my poetry was surfacing at school when we used to read poetry in English.; [a.] Hull, East Yorkshire, UK

SCARRATT, DORIS
[b.] 29 July 1923, Staffs; [p.] Deceased; [m.] Deceased, 14 April 1947; [ch.] One son; [ed.] Elementary left at the age of 14 yrs; [occ.] House wife; [oth. writ.] Many but never sent any of before.; [pers.] The written word gives me great pleasure. Enabling me to voice my inner thoughts my pen and paper have become my friend and confident since the loss of my husbands.; [a.] Stoke-on-Trent, Staffs, UK

SCLATER, YVONNE NICOLE
[b.] 15 February 1977, Rockingham, Australia; [p.] Lyn and Eric Sclater; [occ.] Backpacker; [pers.] I believe that everyone is on a quest searching for an answer, a person or an object my poetry reflects that search and the emotions and experience we stumble across while we search for the unfindable.; [a.] Portree, Isle of Skye, UK

SCOTT, MASTER BEN
[b.] 9 July 1985, England; [p.] Mrs. Christine Scott and Mr. Allan Scott; [ed.] Prior Heath County First School, Ravenscote County Middle School; [memb.] National Geographic Society Royal Yachting Association, British Cande Union, Harley Lake Sail Training Centre, Army Sailing Association; [hon.] W.H. Smith Young Writers Awards - Commendation 1993 Joint Winner of Surrey Schools Writing Competition 1995; [oth. writ.] 3 Poems published in "Lending Our Minds Out" Anthology published by Pearce House Creative Writing Course; [pers.] I dedicate this published work to my teachers - Mrs. McKintosh and Mrs. B. Sinclair (of Prior Heath School) and Mrs. J. Bruce and Mrs. J. Merry (of Ravenscote School) for their enthusiasm and encouragement has fuelled my ambition and desire to become an author.; [a.] Camberley, Surrey, UK

SCOTT, FRED
[b.] 26 April 1908, Fatfield; [p.] J. J. Scott; [m.] M. J. Scott; [ch.] Five; [occ.] Retired; [hon.] Captian of the Rescue Team

SCOTT, IAN ANDREW
[oth. writ.] The as yet unpublished but under negotiation, book of humorous verse, "The Useful Hedgehog, and the soon to be finished novel "Perditions Flame".; [pers.] To my sister Ann Elizabeth Scott, Happy Birthday, September 3rd.

SCOTT, MARGARET
[b.] 11 December 1941, Glasgow; [p.] John Cumming and Lillias Cumming; [m.] Robert Scott, 5 March 1966; [ch.] Karen and John (Deceased); [ed.] Strathclyde Primary Riverside Senior Secondary; [occ.] Senior Medical Receptionist; [oth. writ.] Other Poetry not yet published; [pers.] If I can open eyes to beauty, hearts to emotion and give a message of hope, my poems have been understood.; [a.] Cumberland, North Lanarkshire, UK

SEAGULL, AMY
[pen.] Maud Carter; [b.] 2 August 1927, Radcliffe; [p.] Robert and Maud Tootill; [m.] Terence Seagull, 13 August 1966; [ch.] Angela, Kathryn, Deborah, Robert, Edward and Rebekah; [ed.] Secondary and Commercial; [occ.] Housewife; [oth. writ.] Four Children's stories and a 11,000 word novel, as Anglo Irish Historic Romance "Green Grow the Shamrock". Looking for a Publisher!; [pers.] I have been blessed by a mother who was very gifted in literary art and by my daughter Rebekah who is also a writer.; [a.] Lancaster, Lancashire, UK

SEARLE, FRANCES MARGERY
[b.] 2 March 1940, Helston, Cornwall; [p.] Edward Searle, Clara Searle (Both Deceased); [ed.] Helston Grammar School; [occ.] Retired; [memb.] Mullion Creative Arts Society, Helston Camera Club, Helston old Cornwall Society, Friends of Helston Folk Museum; [hon.] Sixteen Awards since 1976, in the poetry competitions of the Gorseth Kernow (Cornish Gorsedd) includes 4 first prizes/trophy cups; [oth. writ.] Published in the quarterly magazine "This England" published in an anthology `The Open Door By Triumph House' in 1995 also to be published in their next anthology October 1996 called `Faith Poets'; [pers.] To communicate a devotional or inspiration message to the reader.; [a.] Helston, Cornwall, UK

SELFE, ALBERT EDWARD JOHN
[pen.] A. E. J. Selfe; [b.] February 23, 1934, Canning Town, London; [p.] Albert Selfe and Rose Selfe; [m.] Gwendoline Patricia Selfe, March 28, 1959; [ch.] Kim, Roy, Glenn and Dawn Selfe; [ed.] Eastbrook Secondary - Dagenham returned to education 59 years old at Manor College, and passed 'City of Guilds' one, two and three in 'Business Administration'.; [occ.] Un-employed; [memb.] Latchington Bowls Club Hadleigh Conservative Club Essex Snooker Centre; [hon.] None on paper, but I did Co-Design and build the 'Hush Piling Rig' which reduces piling noise from 110dBA down to 70dBA.; [oth. writ.] I am currently attempting to write a fiction story based on some of my life's experiences; [pers.] There are no such words as it cannot be achieved if you keep an open mind.; [a.] Benfleet, Essex, UK

SELLEN, MARY BRIDGET
[b.] 15 May 1947, Ireland; [p.] Francis and Rose Rogers; [m.] Reginald Sellen, 3 April 1965; [ch.] Shirley, Christopher and Edward; [occ.] Martin Arts Instructor and Writer; [oth. writ.] Poems published in Several Anthologies and Martial Art Magazines.; [a.] London, Middlesex, UK

SENIOR, CHRIS
[pen.] Miriam Raymond; [b.] 16 February 1946, East Yorkshire; [p.] Beatrice Coates, Robert Coates; [m.] Alan Senior, 13 February 1965; [ch.] Karl, Jeremy, Claire, Louise; [ed.] Wyke Grammar/ College of Ripon and York St. John; [occ.] Head IV Drama Therapist; [memb.] Ass. of D/Therapy Family, Therapy Ass.; [hon.] Post Graduate Degree in Drama Therapy; [oth. writ.] 15 poems published in various anthologies/two anthologies of my own floating the moon and the gingerbread man published by Minerva Press. children's stories and short stories (unpublished).; [pers.] My work as a Drama therapist influences my writing: Very much as I try to help clients make sense of their emotional responses. I have always written from being a child and am delighted to be able to share my love of words with others.; [a.] Cottingham, East Yorks, UK

SETIAWAN, AGATHA
[pen.] Janis Casparindina; [b.] 31 March 1980, Kediri; [p.] Yohanes Bing Wahyudi and Candra Rahayu; [ed.] 3rd grade "Petra" Christian Senior High School, Kederi, Indonesia; [memb.] IYS: International Youth Service; [oth. writ.] Several poems published in school magazine, short stories and novels for personal collection.; [pers.] Reflect your feelings and minds through your poems! Cause through them, everyone could see who you really are.; [a.] Kediri, Jawa Timur

SEWELL, BETTY R.
[b.] 18 March 1938, Hull; [p.] Grace and Harry Huggins; [m.] Peter, 18 June 1955; [ch.] Paul, Elaine, Pat, Julie, Mark; [occ.] Housewife; [oth. writ.] Some more poems; [a.] Hull, East Yorkshire, UK

SHANBHAG, LILIANA ASSELLE
[b.] 8 April 1986, London; [p.] Suhas Shanbhag, Giovanna Asselle; [ed.] Moss Hall Infant and Junior School, Finchley, London; [occ.] Student; [pers.] I get an inspiration to write poetry when I visit new places.; [a.] London, UK

SHARP, BRENDA
[b.] 8 February 1929, Wolverhampton; [ed.] Handsworth Grammar School for Girls, Birmingham, Furzedown Training College, London 1946-48; [occ.] Retired primary peripatetic Head teacher for Gloucestershire; [pers.] I am a truth seeker, I have sought the meaning of life for many years. To observe and see life objectively is very difficult.; [a.] Weston-super-Mare, Somerset, UK

SHARPE, MRS. MARIA THERESE
[pen.] Maria T. Sharpe; [b.] 11 April 1962, Cardiff, S. Wales; [p.] Dennis Mark Green (Deceased), Jeanette Patricia Green; [m.] Mr. Errol John Sharpe, 3 April 1990; [ch.] Two step-daughters (5 grandsons); [ed.] 6 'O' Levels-Bayn Hafren Comprehensive English Literature, English Language, Biology, History, Art, Embroidery; [occ.] Housewife; [oth. writ.] Two Christmas poems published in local newspapers "The Barry Gem" 1991; [pers.] I try to express the wonderful kaleidoscope we are all part of as potential field individuals.; [a.] Barry, South Glamorgan, UK

SHARPE, ROBERT DANNATT
[b.] 6 April 1943, Portsmouth; [p.] Robert Sharpe, Winifred Sharpe; [m.] Jennifer Ursula, 28 December 1978; [ch.] Christopher James and Nadine Ursula; [ed.] St. John's College Southsea, Leicester University Southampton University Oxford University; [occ.] Retired teacher, now Tesco Stock controller part time; [memb.] Royal Observer Corps Association, Royal Naval Amateur Radio Society, Royal Airforce Amateur Radio Society, Fellow Zoological Society, Member Institute of Biology; [hon.] Land Lieutenants Meriturious Service Certificate for East Sussex 1989 Long service, Medal Royal Observer Corps. 1988; [oth. writ.] Several Scientific and Educational Publication. Interest in poetry of amusing nature especially relating to animals.; [pers.] I have been influenced by such writers as Gerald Darrel and like to Shaire in being able to see poetry from others with a like minded interest.; [a.] Uckfield, East Sussex, UK

SHARROD, ERIC JOHON
[b.] 3 February 1927, Overseal; [p.] Thomas and Marjory; [m.] Margaret Nee Proctor, March 1953; [ch.] Clive Thomas, Paul John and Helen; [ed.] Overseal Council School, Qualified Coal Mine Electrical Engineer. Fully trained in Coal Mine Rescue Service; [occ.] Retired; [oth. writ.] Duty is ours (Events Are God's) ISBN 1872479162 two true coal mine rescue stories married into one to make interest reading for the ordinary book worm.; [pers.] I gain pleasure writing to use words extracting their full meaning, I generated a hidden culture for verse from my hymn book during many years as church of England Choir Boy.; [a.] Burton, Derbyshire, UK

SHAW, SHEILA P.
[b.] 2 October 1935, London; [p.] Mitchelle Lily Goodall; [m.] Edwin Thomas Shaw, 19 August 1957; [ch.] Amanda Robert Jane - Alex; [ed.] St. Marks Rd Secondary St. Marks Rd Nth Kensington W10; [occ.] Housewife; [oth. writ.] War Poetry 1939-1945 a child war. (Unpublished); [pers.] And now abideth faith hope and love, these three: But the greatest of these is love.; [a.] Corshalton, Surrey, UK

SHAW-TAYLOR, MRS. MARY
[pen.] Donna Marie; [b.] 16 September 1938, Heaton; [p.] David Bottomley and Ada Bottomley; [m.] Divorced, 24 December 1988; [ch.] Pamela Eva, Karen Holden, Anne Taylor and Kenneth Taylor; [ed.] Secondary School; [occ.] Retired - disabled housewife; [memb.] 'The Bradford Players' Amateur Dramatics and 'Drama Unlimited' Amateur Dramatics; [hon.] For poetry and writing music, in my school days; [oth. writ.] Poems and short stories in local magazines, a good, many few years ago. Writing words and music for artists and myself.; [pers.] I long to be a success, in my writing and world wide known for my poems and music. I had very deep respect, for all kinds of poetry, and words and music from good, and great tenors and soprano's in my early days.; [a.] Bradford, West Yorkshire

SHEARD, MRS. MARY JOAN
[pen.] Mary Physick; [b.] 15 September 1916, Congleton; [p.] John Sunley and Mabel Emily Physick; [m.] William Charles Sheard, 12 February 1947; [ch.] 3 sons and 1 daughter; [ed.] Left School 14 yrs., Eventually guided place Nursing train-school did 2 yrs. Plastic Surgery. Joined 2 Arane served in England and India.; [occ.] Now retired as Director Building Firm (with husband); [memb.] Queen Alexander's Royal Army Nursing Corps Ass. Chester Branch; [oth. writ.] A few jottings over the year. Main hobby - art - oil and watercolor painting.; [pers.] Not for publishing at this stage please.; [a.] Congleton, Cheshire, UK

SHEEN, HANNAH
[pen.] Hannah Sheen; [b.] 2 November 1978, Southampton; [p.] Christine Sheen; [ed.] Cecil Jones High School, South End-on-Sea, North Lindsey College Scunthorpe; [occ.] Student; [hon.] Currently taking my 'A Levels' at college, in English literature and language, also in sociology; [pers.] I hope through my poem, that people will see the problems today with homelessness and prejudices.; [a.] Scunthorpe, North Lincolnshire, UK

SHELTON, MARTNE LOUISE
[pen.] Martine L. Shelton; [b.] 10 November 1969, Kettering; [p.] Carlene Shelton, Michael Shelton; [ed.] Samuel Lloyo Comprehensive School, Corby Tresham College; [occ.] Sales Secretary; [memb.] Member and Deacon with Gretton Baptist Church; [oth. writ.] Several poems published in various competitions, articles for local Baptist Fellowship Magazine.; [pers.] We are gifted by God in Different ways and should therefore use our gifts wisely, to the good and to the glory of God. My intention, therefore, is always to write and sing Prayerfully guided by - and with an effort hopefully worthy o f- my Lord and Saviour Jesus Christ.; [a.] Gretton, Northamptonshire, UK

SHEPHERD, MRS. HAZEL A.
[b.] 9 April 1930, Chesham, Bucks; [p.] Ellen, Ashley Pearce; [m.] Frederick Shepherd, 1 August 1953; [ch.] One boy, one girl; [ed.] Ordinary School; [occ.] House wife; [oth. writ.] Quite a lot of poems but nearly all of them have more than 20 lines, UK most of which are of a spiritual nature they are just my thought put into verse.; [pers.] "A dogs life" is about my own dog. called spike and is all true.; [a.] Dumfries, Dumfrieshire, UK

SHEPPARD, LINDA
[b.] April 2, 1957, Rhondda; [p.] Maureen and John; [m.] Partner George Lightfoot; [ch.] Michelle Gareth, Martin Jonathan; [ed.] Craig Er Eyos School, Penygraig, Tai School Penygraig; [occ.] Not working; [hon.] Have no honour or awards; [oth. writ.] I have a poem before published in a book called The Touch of Love, title of poem, Valentine's Day; [pers.] I want to say that my poems have been inspired by my partner whom I am living with Mr. George Lightfoot, he give me a lot of inspiration to write poems; [a.] Tonyrefail, Mid-Glam, UK

SHOTTER, EDNA
[b.] 9 April 30, Penge; [p.] James Shotter, Elsie Shotter; [ed.] Bromley Road School Beckenham, Eden Park School Beckenham; [occ.] Retired Clerical Assistant (1 worked at London University); [memb.] Beckenham Mind, Wings Club (Speaking); [oth. writ.] Poems stories and articles for Beckenham mind poem for works magazine of firm worked for prior to going to work at the University.; [pers.] I feel that poetry should express clearly the thoughts of the poets.; [a.] Upper Norwood, Kent, UK

SIMM, VERA
[pen.] "Velora"; [b.] 25 June 1921, Levenshulme; [p.] Robert and Lizzie Lowe; [m.] Alfred Simm (Deceased), 12 February 1944; [ch.] Robert, Pamela; [ed.] Church of England public school, (Robert) Lancaster University, (Pamela) St Johns College M/Cr School of Art; [occ.] Housewife (retired); [oth. writ.] "For You To Keep" (small family booklet) of poetry... several short stories inc. one for radio, children's bed-time series, in Hull during 1960's... I have loved writing from early years, (specially poetry).; [a.] Stockport, Cheshire, UK

SIMMONDS, MICHAEL
[b.] 21 July 1936, Bedford; [p.] Nathaniel and Violet Simmonds; [m.] Anne Theresa (Nee Taylor), 3 August 1964; [ch.] Bernadette, Clare, Francis, Dominic, Maria, Catherine; [ed.] Ratcliffe College Leicester, Two years National Service Bedford College of Higher Education, Taught General Subjects (1971-85), Remedial Specialist (Mainly At) St. Gregory's Middle School, Bedford; [occ.] Shop Assistant in Tobacconist-Quality Fancy Goods Shop; [memb.] Secular Franciscan Order, have been in Church Choir, Amateur Drama and operatic societies; [hon.] Teacher's Certificate, Certificate of Religious Education; [oth. writ.]

Children's handwriting book, Illustrated child's christmas story (unpublished), story dramatization several poems (limited local publication): Diary Of My First Home, Diary Of A Boy (and girl) Growing Up The Caterpillar And The Butterfly, John Bunyan of Bedford, Waiting, Life's Span, Love, Father's Day, Remember Me, The Wasp.; [pers.] Ecumenical christian I write when inspiration drives me. I often mention God in my life and so, also, in my writings.; [a.] Bedford, Beds, UK

SIMMONS, FREDERICK RONALD SEYMOUR
[pen.] Frederick Seymour; [b.] 24 August 1932, London; [p.] William Florelice Simmons; [m.] Rita, 9 August 1958; [ch.] Stewart Lisa; [ed.] Grove Lane Technical, Camberwell, London; [occ.] Semi-Retired; [memb.] St. Mary's Anglican Church, Green St., Green Orpington, Kent; [hon.] School Certificates, Poetry, English, Art, History; [oth. writ.] Several poems published in anthologies, researching for a book on Hafton garden and security; [pers.] I was influenced by my teacher at eleven years old. I have been writing poetry since then poetry to me is like a painting with beautiful lives and a picture of life.; [a.] Bromley, Kent, UK

SIMMS, DAVID
[b.] 28 June 1943, Essex; [m.] Lorraine Mary, 15 May 1971; [ch.] Diana, Alison, Lauren; [ed.] Grammar School; [occ.] Telecommunications Engineer; [pers.] Dedicated to the Inner Child of JRW and all Ancient Wisdom from The Tao to Turtle Island.; [a.] Southampton, Hants, UK

SIMPSON, IAIN
[b.] 7 May 1976; [memb.] Poetry Society; [pers.] Eyes drifting over the surface with only words reaching the blind shoals at the bottom of my thought.; [a.] Dundee, Tayside, UK

SIMPSON, JOAN
[b.] 6 December 1927, Bradford; [p.] Francis Charles and Doris Dixon; [m.] Eric Simpson (Deceased 19 May 1990), 6 August 1949; [ch.] Judith Ann Ibboisono (Nee Simpson); [ed.] Gregory Selective Central School for Girls, Bradford; [occ.] Enjoying Retirement; [memb.] St. Augustine's Church Mother's Union, Bradford, Baildon (W. Yorks) Flower Club National Canine Defence League; [oth. writ.] A potted history (on the reforpishment and re-opening after many years,) of a semi-derelict property known as "North Wing Mission" an outreach project of S. Augustine's Church. Various poems (for my own pleasure, none published), "Is Your Journey Really Necessary?" A light hearted account of 25 years of dogs, holidays and mishaps with family (have tried to publish, but no-one appears interested.; [pers.] I am an optimist and hope this comes through in the things I write. A sense of humour and the gift of laughter are of great importance to me and I try not to take myself too seriously.; [a.] Bradford, West Yorkshire, UK

SIMPSON, MR. FRED
[pen.] Fred; [b.] 10 September 1914, Colorado, Durham; [p.] Deceased; [m.] Deceased, 3 September 1948; [ed.] Elementary; [occ.] Retired; [pers.] A poets mind can't be measured, it stretches from ocean depths to outer space, so there are millions of themes to word will rhyme especially that of the human race.; [a.] Oxford, Oxfordshire, UK

SIMPSON, ROBERT J.
[pen.] Robert J. Simpson; [b.] 16 August 1950, Coventry; [p.] Raymond Martin and Patricia Rose Mary; [m.] Sheila Mary, 9 March 1973; [ch.] Martin James, Stephen John; [ed.] King Henry VIII Grammar, University of Plymouth, Open University; [occ.] International Customer Support Manager; [memb.] GPT (Coventry), Spartans Running Club (Chairman); [hon.] MBA, (currently in progress); [oth. writ.] Several poems published in various books, also by the open University, articles for running magazines.; [pers.] Writing can reflect the very essence of life and this is the basis of my poems. A sense of humour is always striving to rise to the surface.; [a.] Coventry, Warwickshire, UK

SINCLAIR, PATRICIA
[pen.] Tricia Sinclair; [b.] 19 March 1936, Clarkston, Near Glasgow; [p.] John and Dorothy Stewart; [m.] A. Birrell Sinclair, 30 September 1958; [ch.] Alan Grant and Lynn Karen; [ed.] The Park School, Glasgow; [occ.] Open university undergraduate studying Religion and English language for a B.A. degree; [memb.] Church of Scotland; [oth. writ.] First publication; [pers.] My poem is simply my own reflection on loss in life and my personal spiritual conclusion; [a.] Giffnock, Glasgow, UK

SINGH, AMARJIT
[b.] 28 February 1969, Coventry; [ed.] President Kennedy Comprehensive School; [oth. writ.] Poems on God and Manchester United, love songs; [pers.] Writing poetry is one of my main hobbies; [a.] Coventry, West Midlands, UK

SIRA, RAVINDER
[b.] 2 July 1964, Leeds, United Kingdom; [p.] Mr. and Mrs. C. S. Sagu; [m.] Mr. Manmohan S. Sira, 18 April 1987; [ch.] Darram S. Sira, San Saar M. S. Sira; [pers.] "If you can imagine it, you can achieve it, if you can dream it, you can become it." William Arthur Ward.; [a.] Birmingham, UK

SKELTON, DR. ROY ANTHONY
[b.] 6 October 1939, Farnsfield, Notts; [p.] Claude Henry and Betty Evelyn; [m.] Margaret Ann, 15 July 1969; [ch.] Elisabeth and Richard; [ed.] Rainworth Primary, Mansfield Secondary Technical, Leeds University; [occ.] Retired Fuel/Glass Technologist; [hon.] BSC (Hons) Fuels Science Ph.D. Combustion Engineering (Both at Leeds Univ.); [oth. writ.] Poem (A sylvan glade in troutbeck) in "North West Voices" (Anchor Books); [pers.] Inspired by the writings of the great nature essayists, especially Richard Jefferies, Edward Thomas and W. H. Hudson. Also J. H. B. Peel whose "country talk" essays first introduced me to the other great writers.; [a.] Standish, Greater Manchester, UK

SMIT, JUDINA G.
[b.] 18 May 1974, Amsterdam; [p.] Olfert Smit, Greetje de Vries; [ed.] Graduated from St. Mary's University, College with a BA. Hons in English with Classical Studies; [occ.] Presently Embarking on a Post Graduate Certificate in Secondary Education at Oxford University; [pers.] Poetry supplies a freedom that cannot be expressed otherwise. I wish to fuse the actual and the mystical.

SMITH, MR. CHARLIE
[pen.] Charlie Boy Smith; [b.] April 22, 1924, Wymondham; [p.] John Henry Smith, Alice Smith; [m.] Jean Smith, December 23, 1944; [ch.] Glenys Elaine Cavill; [ed.] Wymondham Elementary School plus self education whilst in the royal air force; [occ.] Retired; [memb.] Full member of the performing rights society full mechanical copyright protection society lid. British Academy of Songwriters Composers and Authors; [oth. writ.] About 1500 songs and poems, 250 of which were my repertoire, 30 songs published (1 album, 1 single) 3 cassettes. 8 poems published on record in local and National Magazines, 3 novels and 8 short stories; [pers.] I have always performed my best to make people laugh or cry and my poems and songs are always descriptive of my subject. I also have the ability to write a song in less than 1 hour, usually only minutes; [a.] Wymondham, Norfolk, UK

SMITH, CHRISTINE ELVERA
[pen.] Leanne Meadows; [b.] 16 November 1949, Staindrop; [m.] Allan Smith, 4 February 1978; [ch.] Sarah Jane; [ed.] Staindrop Secondary Modern; [pers.] Poetry comes from within; [a.] Thirsk, North Yorkshire, UK

SMITH, CLAIRE LOUISE
[pen.] Claire Smith; [b.] 23 October 1979, Pontefract; [p.] Graham Haigh, Valerie Smith; [ed.] Minsthorpe High School; [occ.] 'A' Level Student; [memb.] Yorkshire North and West Army Cadet Force; [hon.] Corporal in Army Cadet Force; [oth. writ.] Several poems unpublished; [pers.] Life is what you make it. Make the most of what you have.; [a.] Pontefract, West Yorkshire, UK

SMITH, EDNA
[b.] 13 January 1915, Birmingham; [p.] Joseph and Ethel Turner; [m.] Kenneth Raymond Smith, 25 July 1942; [ch.] Three; [ed.] Elementary Village School; [occ.] Retired Medical Secretary; [oth. writ.] Wartime magazines "Prospect". "Heart of England" booklet 1994, Original poems of wartime in archives of Imperial War Museum London from Salamander Oasis Trust. Just Published in "Joyous Just Published in Harvest anthology"; [pers.] If I am emotionally moved by any circumstances I have to write - at the age of 81 I am very concerned for his planet earth.; [a.] Heathfield, East Sussex, UK

SMITH, ELLA
[b.] 1 September 1969, Manchester; [p.] Inge and Phill Morgan; [m.] Andrew, 20 August 1994; [ed.] Greenhill Middle School (Birmingham), Culham European School, Larkmead School (Abingdon), Guy's Dental Hospital (London); [occ.] Dental Hygienist; [memb.] British Dental Hygienist Association; [hon.] 'Hu-Freidy' Best Student Hygienist '90-91'; [oth. writ.] Currently researching for biography about mother; [pers.] "Build lots of memories"!; [a.] Oxfordshire, UK

SMITH, RONALD JAMES
[b.] 18 August 1918, Cradley, Staffs; [p.] Deceased; [m.] Rachel Olwyn Smith, 30 December 1939; [ch.] Anthony smith - 50, Graham Smith - 46, Richard Smith - 37 and Jane Saotome - 47; [ed.] Local entered family mnfctg. business on finishing school, and apart from war years, mostly in the Indian Army, worked until recently.; [occ.] Retired, (Manufacturing Engineer) now fully involved in writing, mainly for pleasure.; [oth. writ.] Research life of Mid 19th century to mid 20th century Herefordshire family. Ongoing. Variety of philosophical poems. Humours, all ongoing.; [pers.] Interested in family values and humanity, and integrity of the family.; [a.] Stourbridge, West Midlands, UK

SMITHERS, GERALDINE
[b.] 27 October 1940, London; [p.] Gerry Fahey, Marie Fahey; [m.] William Harvey Smithers, 1 May 1966; [ch.] Matthew, Rebecca, Natasha; [ed.] Our Lady of Sion convent, Bayswater, RGN, Training University College Hospital and Knoston, Surrey; [occ.] Private Community Nurse, Caring for Elderly and Housebound; [memb.] Cobham Drama Group, Royal College of Nursing, Tansent (Ladies Excircle), Colet's Health Club, Writing Bureau course; [hon.] Registered Gen. Nurse; [oth. writ.] None except for fun - have had little time for the writing course so still pursuing this!; [pers.] Have always loved reading all types of poetry, trad, pop and modern - this was my first ever attempt really, but I love the feel for things and people as they are - I now feel greatly encouraged.; [a.] Cobham, Surrey, UK

SMYTH, B. FRANCES
[pen.] Graham Valette; [b.] 17 February 1900, Hackney, North London; [p.] Walter W. Winslade and Bertha M. Hebbearo; [m.] Hugh Fitzwalter Smyth R.N., 3 December 1927; [ch.] Four - 3 daughters, one son; [ed.] From Oct. 1904 until Det 1908, attended a Hackney Church School from Oct 1908 to Easter 1914, attended London County Council Sch. then went onto Business Training College at Clapham, S. London, until Oct. 1915. Started office-work 5 weeks - gave notice. Obtained a better but very strenuous job with Govt. Naval Architects staying there for 12 years until married in Dec. 1927.; [occ.] Retired Pensioner did temporary work as Typist/Secretary from March 1955 to Oct. 1974 - all for one Insurance Company; [memb.] No time to join anything, about 1919/20 became a member of a Sunday School Teachers' Society or Association in London. Do not recall name of such at the moment.; [hon.] Had won scripture prize and certificates at school and 7 attendance and excellent conduct medals. Never went in for anything spectacular. Too busy in spare time always writing letters or verses of some sort - for friends colleagues, etc. started doing this at age 7 (just before my 7th birthday); [oth. writ.] Mainly 'Bits and Pieces' for individual friends. In the eighties had several verses (and sketches) accepted by one of the big banks pensioners' magazines. Last year (1995) I had a hymn accepted and printed in Thora Hird's sing with praise no payment for any the above.; [pers.] I do not claim to be religious - but I firmly believe in the Bible, though it is not easy to read and understand. So much is told in "pieces as Isaiah says, "here a little, there a little", anyway, it is better to try to do good than otherwise or to be self-seeking all the time.; [a.] Harrow, Middlesex, UK

SMYTH, I. P.
[b.] 30 December 1975, Bristol; [p.] David Smyth, Kathleen Smyth; [ed.] Lockleaze Comprehensive School, ITEC College; [oth. writ.] Several poems published in magazines and one in a book.; [pers.] In my poetry I try to reflect upon real life and my dreams, and have been greatly influenced by Michael Jackson.; [a.] Bristol, UK

SNEAD, MS. CLARE
[b.] 16 November 1935, Liverpool; [p.] Harold Snead D. S. C. and Irene Snead; [ed.] Highfield Comp., Oxford College of Further Education (A Levels) Oxford Polytech (Certificate of Qualification in Social Work); [occ.] Retired, (Former Social Worker), now do voluntary work in cattery; [memb.] North of England Zoological Society, Phoenix Catroscue - (Founder Member and Trustee) Bornface Foundation Greenpeace C.S.A.N.

R.S.P.B. Cafod. Cats Protection League; [hon.] Certificate of Qualification in social work; [oth. writ.] A few short stories, have had 1 published. Have had a few poems published in The Ark (magazine of the Catholic Study Circle for Animal Welfare) and in "The Cat"; [pers.] I am a Christian (Catholic) and I believe in the basic rules of Christianity particularly that we should love and care about each other and the world we live in. Some of my poems reflect this others don't. I also do quite a lot of humorous poetry.; [a.] Liverpool, Merseyside, UK

SNEDDON, JOHN
[pen.] Johnnie Rocco; [b.] 23 March 1944, Bainsford, Sneddon; [p.] Margaret Giffen George; [ed.] Bainsford Primary, Graeme High School; [pers.] Unemployed in invalidity; [oth. writ.] I am a providing lyricist write hundreds of lyrics poetry love bulletin, science fiction in poetry future songs.; [a.] Enkirk, UK

SOWUNMI, SOKUNBI A.
[pen.] Sokunbi; [b.] 28 March 1969, Hammersmith, London; [p.] Olabisi Korashy and Sokunle Sowunmi; [ed.] St. Gregory's College Lagos, Nigeria (1979-84), LA City East London College (1986-1988), Inolverhamton University (1988-1991), University of Akron, Ohio (USA) (1989-1990), College of Law, Guildford Surrey (1991-1992), London, School of Economics (1992-1993); [occ.] Shipping Litigator (Solicitor); [hon.] Award for Academic Achievement. University of Akron. School of Law Akron, Ohio; [oth. writ.] Numerous unpublished works; [pers.] I write about my life and the lives of those around me, lives which touch me constantly which stir my soul.; [a.] London, UK

SPEAKE, WILLIAM EDWARD
[pen.] Gogia; [b.] 18 June 1925, Talgarth; [p.] Francis and Emily; [m.] Pearl Mary Towersey, 1 March 1952; [ch.] Carol, Vivienne, Russell, Paul; [occ.] Retired; [memb.] Royal College of Nursing British Horological Institute. Clacton-on-Sea British Legion Branch. Royal Regt of Wales Assoc.; [hon.] R.G.N. M.B.H.I.; [pers.] I have been greatly influenced by early romantic poets from my school days.; [a.] Little Clacton, Essex, UK

SPEIGHT, ALAN R.
[b.] 30 March 1947, Newport; [p.] Albert and Dorothy Speight; [m.] Divorced, 24 December 1970; [ed.] St. Andrews Secondary, Tynside Nautica College Presently Studying with O. U.; [occ.] Chief Marine Engineer; [memb.] Institute's of Marine Engineers and Diagnostic Engineers A Political Party; [oth. writ.] Many poems (None Before Entered Into Anything). Started On A Book.; [pers.] Unfortunately a lot of my poems are quite sad. Of war, death and the break up or Romance Ironically I am a very light hearted person.; [a.] Newport, S. Wales, UK

SPEIGHT, HEATHER
[pen.] Heather Speight; [b.] 25 June 1961, Wakefield; [p.] Annie Elizabeth Batty; [m.] Stephen Batty, separated; [ch.] 1 son Christopher; [ed.] Cathedral Middle School, Eastmoor High School, Wakefield, also Wakefield College; [occ.] Domestic Engineer; [hon.] Honours in Dance Modern, Ballroom. Later American P.D.S.A. Award for Charity Work, R.S.A. Stage I Word Processing R.S.A. Stage I and I Typing; [oth. writ.] Poems, Insomnia; [pers.] I have recently stayed in a mental hospital my 15th time in 14 years. the only way now is up.; [a.] Wakefield, West Yorkshire, UK

SPEY, C. M.
[pen.] Mhairi Ormsby, Hini Martin; [b.] Sydney; [p.] R. N. Officer, Mother - (Deceased); [m.] Deceased; [ch.] Three; [ed.] Royal Naval School, French Finishing School, Switzerland; [occ.] Language teacher, writer; [memb.] Variously: Poetry Society, Writers' Circle, Historical Society, Choir, Choral Society, Drama Club Bush Walkers' etc.; [hon.] Short Story winner, New Zealand, Poems, stories and travel articles in various magazines, Denman Silver Cup 1st Prize for "A Word picture in Prose", a film on HTV with my poems read voice over, winner of "Life Story" now kept in National Archives, London, Poems in 4 Archives, Silver Cup 1st prize Writers West Open Poetry Comp.; [oth. writ.] Poem and cash prize in International Library of Poetry, America anthology also in The International Library of Poetry, UK.; [pers.] Who wouldn't want to do it all again, some of it differently?; [a.] Portishead, North Somerset, UK

SPICER, MRS. SYLVIA
[pen.] Sylvia Spicer; [b.] 23 April 1922, Hull; [p.] Theodor and Annie; [m.] Percy, 16 November 1940; [ch.] Percy (one son); [ed.] Ordinary School leaving at age 14 years; [occ.] Widow Housewife; [pers.] After my husband died ten years ago, a small grey cat walked through my door. She is still with me and has provided all the love and affection I needed. I love my son and his family, they love me and it was my daughter in law who inspired me to write.; [a.] Hull, East Yorkshire, UK

SPICKERMANN, MRS. JOY
[pen.] Joy; [b.] 11 August 1927, Leicester; [p.] Mary Start, William Start (Deceased); [m.] William Spickermann, 27 January 1951; [ch.] 1 Karin Spickermann; [ed.] Mundella School, Community College, Wycombe Rd, Leicester; [occ.] Poet; [memb.] Triumph House, Aspec Bleeding Heart Yard London, Poetry Boon Society 22, Betterton Street London, British Legion Poetry, now Hastings National Poetry, Stand Magazine Newcastle; [hon.] 8 poems published, Assistant Plant Breeder and Land Clomy Yiel Retired; [oth. writ.] A Smile To Light The Day, Why Wars, Jims Dog Judy, My Faith, Being A Father, I Couldn't Live Without Love and My Faith and The Friendly Touch; [pers.] Do unto others as you would have them do to you. Be a good neighbour, A smile to light the day, give thanks, be a poet; [a.] Leicester, Leicestershire, UK

SQUIRE, DAVID
[pen.] David Squire; [b.] 25 September 1905, Jersey, CI; [p.] David and Florence; [m.] Violet Rachel, 9 August 1930; [ch.] Colin and Janet; [ed.] St. Pauls School, Chippenham, Wilts. Left school at 12 years of age, mother being a widow; [occ.] Founder and President of D.J. Squire & Co. Ltd. - Squire's Garden Centres; [memb.] Fellow R.H.S. over 60 years, Patron and Vice President Thomas Valley Harriers; [hon.] Hon. Freeman of the Borough of Spelthorne, Middlesex County Honours Athletics 1928, Ten mile cross country, Champion, Thomas Valley Harries 1928; [oth. writ.] Books, Harvest Home - autobiography, The Good Earth - autobiography, The Love of Roses - published 1991-2, All in a Lifetime - printed 1993; [pers.] Formed in 1990-1 the D.J. Squire 'Love of Roses' Charity Trust. Objects, the aged, sick and terminally ill. In four years raised approx. 100,000 pounds and formed five Bursaries for training nurses for cancer relief.; [a.] Laleham, Staines, Middlesex, UK

STAINER, MISS MARJORIE MAY V.
[b.] 9 December 1933, Farnborough; [p.] Victor and Lilian Stainer; [ed.] Cove Secondary Modern; [occ.] Retired; [memb.] Friends of St. Columba's Retreat House Woking R.N.I.B Partially Sighted by Glycoma Registered Blind; [hon.] 20 years Service Pin Schlymberger "Instrument" Electronics Print Room; [oth. writ.] Powerfully Held By His Love Women Priests, Concentration; [pers.] Practising Christian several poems in Cove Parish Magazine, my heart is in Religious Verse, although I have written other subjects.; [a.] Farnborough, Hampshire, UK

STALKER, MICHAEL DENHOLME HORTUS
[b.] 6 March 1955, Parkside, Middlesbrough; [p.] Francis David, Sybil Merna; [ed.] Secondary Modern School, further Education College, several major comprehensive correspondence courses.; [occ.] Leaflet Distributor, Travelling Salesman; [hon.] Successful completion of "Radio Teesside", Professional DJ Course.; [oth. writ.] Several published and broadcast poems. Working on various major scripts.; [pers.] "Continuously strive towards true self-advancement, via personally meaningful corresponden and conversation".; [a.] Cleveland, UK

STALKER, RICHARD
[b.] 27 October 1945, London; [p.] Alexander Bruce and Eileen Stalker; [m.] Patricia Stalker Nee Sadler, 29 January 1969; [ch.] Nicolas and Christopher; [ed.] Sedgehill Comprehensive School, then London College of Music, Post Graduate work with Peter Element of The Royal College of Music; [occ.] Concert Pianist, Composer and Teacher of Piano; [oth. writ.] Articles on Piano Technique for Piano Times, Lyrics for twenty songs for a musical on R.L. Stevenson's kidnapped, Lyrics for songs for "Night Porter", a one act operatta, Lyrics for various other songs, various unpublished poems and writings on philosophy.; [pers.] I tend to follow the romantic in all art forms. As I believe this raises the human spirit, and makes us search for the ideal. At the same time I believe we should raise our thoughts above, the day to day things, and question our reason for being.; [a.] Catford, London, UK

STANDEN, GWENDOLINE QUEENIE
[b.] 22 July 1939, Chelmsford; [memb.] Friend of the Royal Opera House Amici Di Verdi, ABWAK (ie. Association of British Wild Animal Keepers); [pers.] I enjoy trying to create poetry.

STANLEY, ALAN
[b.] 15 December 1914, Loughborough; [m.] Marjorie, 16 October 1937; [ch.] April Marjorie and Roger Andrew; [ed.] Elementary Firs Estate Derby; [occ.] Retired; [oth. writ.] Some in local magazines. A few published in Peterborough.; [pers.] I always strive for what is beautiful in my writings. The earth is already full of nastyness. May God be praised.; [a.] Derby, Derbyshire, UK

STAPLES, MICHAEL
[b.] 12 March 1961, Tonbridge, Kent; [p.] Richard and Edna Staples; [m.] Jackie Staples, 18 August 1990; [ch.] Sam and Jack; [ed.] Vinters Boys, Maidstone, Kent, Portsmouth College of Art and Design; [occ.] Technical Author; [oth. writ.] Various poems on my family, personal experiences and life as I see it.; [a.] Tetbury, Glos, UK

STAPLETON, MARGARET J.
[b.] 24 August 1931, Aldershot; [p.] Basil W. Matthews, Bertha Matthews; [m.] Alfred George Stapleton; [ch.] Paul, June, Pamela; [ed.] Convent of the assumption Richmond Yorkshire; [pers.] As a wife, mother, and senior citizen my feelings are in my poem; [a.] Salisbury, Wiltshire, UK

STARCK, MARGARET
[b.] 1923, West Yorkshire; [p.] Harry and Greta Midgley; [ch.] One son; [ed.] Newmillerdam Council School, Wakefield Girls High School, Bingley Training College; [oth. writ.] Poem printed in "The Other Side Of The Mirror", 1996.; [pers.] To be true to oneself and accept the individuality of others.; [a.] Krefeld, Germany

STARK, JOYCE
[b.] 29 June 1946, Montrose; [m.] Eric Stark, 11 March 1972; [ed.] Montrose Academy; [occ.] Administration Mngr.; [oth. writ.] Various poems in anthologies, local articles, company newspaper.; [pers.] My writing and I, are not the same thing.; [a.] Montrose, Angus, UK

STARKEY, JACQUI S.
[b.] 2 December 1962, Staffordshire; [p.] John Banks and Sarah Banks; [m.] Neil Starkey, 4 March 1987; [ch.] Gemma, Nikki-Anne and Amy-Leigh; [occ.] Housewife; [pers.] A photograph revives the memory, but the poetry revives the soul... for a family who never cease to inspire, and for my sister, who inspired me on this occasion.!; [a.] Meir, Stoke-on-Trent, UK

STEELE, JUNE LEONORA FRANCES
[pen.] Leonora Steele; [b.] 10 June 1932, Southampton; [p.] William Vallis, Ivy Vallis; [m.] 1st Brian Harrison, 1 December 1951, 2nd Ronald Steele, 12 December 1985; [ch.] Jennifer Lynn, Gillian Anne, Raymond Brian; [ed.] Gregg School (private grammar) Further Education - Day Release with Civil Service-RSA III Eng.; [occ.] Retired; [oth. writ.] Poem - 'Dawn Chorus' published in 1994.; [pers.] I started writing in 1989. We were living in a 'Bothy' Built into a Victorian Walled Garden. The beauty of the surrounding woods, the Fauna and flowers inspired me and I wanted to share it with others now working, I have written 70 poems and songs, on fairy stories in Rhymnne.; [a.] Wickham, Hampshire, UK

STENNING, CLAIRE
[pen.] Claire Stenning; [b.] 23 June 1962, Swindon; [p.] Dennis Deacon and Jean Kenyon (Re-married); [m.] Darren Stenning, 22 April 1995; [ed.] Commonwealth Grammar School, The Mall, Old Town, Swindon; [occ.] Sales Co-ordinator for Camas Building Materials South Cerney, Gloucestershire; [oth. writ.] I have a large portfolio of poems, and have started a novel.; [pers.] Most of my poems are drawn from my own experiences, good and bad. I find that this way they came from the heart.; [a.] Swindon, Wiltshire, UK

STEVENS, MRS. DOROTHY
[b.] 27 December 1927, Normandy, Surrey; [p.] James Crooke, Eleanor Crooke; [m.] Geoffrey Stevens, 28 May 1949; [ch.] James Paul, Charles John; [ed.] Church of England, Secondary School; [occ.] Retired Civil Servant; [memb.] Arthritis Club, Western Line Dancing; [oth. writ.] One poem published. It is the only one I have submitted for publication.; [pers.] I love people and my poems often reflect their comical side of nature.; [a.] Farnborough, Hants, UK

STEVENSON, JEAN
[b.] 11 May 1933, Ruddington; [p.] Horace Higgs, Nellie Higgs; [m.] David Stevenson, 21 July 1956; [ch.] Adrian; [ed.] Ruddington Church of England School; [occ.] Housewife; [memb.] (Committee member of) Women's Church Fellowship, Neighborhood Watch Co-ordinator; [oth. writ.] Poems in local paper article in imperial was museum archives - (growing up in the war years); [pers.] In addition to writing poetry my other interests are cookery and handicraft work.; [a.] Nottinghamshire, UK

STEWART, HARRY S.
[b.] 14 Sept. 1917; [p.] G. W. Stewart and Sarah Irene; [m.] Anne Stewart, 1951; [ed.] Anerley Residential School; [occ.] Retired; [hon.] M.I.D. Auth. London Gazette Dec. 1940; [oth. writ.] Freelance Journalist (ret) prospective book blessing of HM.Q. Mother numerous letters to the press copies retained.; [pers.] Lifetime lover of children, dogs and a few humans.; [a.] Staines, Middx, UK

STEWART, JOSEPHINE
[pen.] "My Pseudonym", I use often as it has great meaning; [p.] "Of Good Stock"; [m.] Retired Professional Design Eng., 4 September 1961; [ch.] One; [ed.] Colleges in Gloucester area; [occ.] House Manager. Gardener. Hobbies are painting, music, poetry, photography, pictures, observing textiles; [memb.] Honorary mem: International Adoption Whale Soc, was frontline Greenpeace (supporter still) "Nature Conservation" RSPCA supporter, badger group, "Compassion World Farming", supporter painswich shows men.; [hon.] "Merit" in photography. A remark at college was - we have a budding Shakespeare!! I was amused, flattered.; [oth. writ.] Poem's of mine have been sent to important people around this planet. "Regency Press" have published my poems (in 1974). I call all men to respect the "Jewel", "Mother Nature" the Children's "Noah's Ark of Compassion".; [pers.] My poetry comes naturally for planet and all animals. "I try to make a point of great importance". Hoping people will see. I read a few at St. Andrews "Scotland". (All understood) and here sometime ago. "I want respect, dignity, protection.".; [a.] Dursley, Gloucester, UK

STEWART, WALTER P.
[b.] 31 July 1924, Melfort, SK, Canada; [p.] James Mitchell Stewart; [m.] Sarah Stewart, 24 August 1914; [ch.] Eva Mae, Catherine Anne, Walter Pendlebury; [ed.] M.A. (U/Minnesota) History, M. Phil (U/Cambridge) History, M. Litt (U/Aberdeen) Scottish Lit.; [occ.] Academic Researcher; [memb.] Royal Nova Scotia Yacht Squadron, Halifax, Canada; [oth. writ.] Eagle Feathers In The Dust, My Name Is Piapot, G—S, A Time To Weep, etc.; [a.] Cambridge, UK

STOCK, DAPHNE MARY
[pen.] Daphne Duipont; [b.] 25 May 1937, Earling; [p.] Mr. and Mrs. Dallabar, (Adopted 1944) Mr. and Mrs. Andrews; [m.] Divorced; [ch.] Three; [ed.] Private Education Miss Shanney, Winthrope Wilton Gardens, Miss Cousins; [occ.] Looking after the elderly; [memb.] League of Friends, Cats Adoption Society; [hon.] Certificate in Community Care sitting for Citing Guild English Creative Writing Course; [oth. writ.] Several short stories one for Bella Magazine (true story) high recommended but turned down to many stories similar 3 poems accepted for publication in west country voices.; [pers.] Have always enjoyed writing told at school had a flair for it and flow concentrate on writing when leaving school cre-

ative writing tutor at W-SM college (Tec) keep good work of natural flow and talent.; [a.] Weston-super-Mare, Somerset, UK

STOCKTON, GEMMA
[b.] 3 August 1979, Middleton; [p.] Susan and Mike Stockton; [ed.] Siddal Moor High School then Hopwood Hall College; [occ.] Student; [oth. writ.] None as yet but hopefully there will be in the future.; [pers.] I would like to dedicate this poem to my Nan, Doris Burton, who always had faith in me and whom shall always have a special place in my heart.; [a.] Manchester, Lancashire, UK

STONE, MRS. BERYL J.
[b.] 1 November 1933, Hillingdon, Middlesex; [p.] Douglas and Jessie Stewart; [m.] Terence R. Stone, 23 August 1952; [ch.] (6) - Teresa, Janet, Russell, Graham, Nigel and Clifford; [ed.] Bishopshalt Grammar; [occ.] Director and Co. Secretary; [memb.] Secretary and Newsletter Scribbe of Rolls-Royce Enthusiats' Club (South West Section); [hon.] Matriculation, Trophy for work of R-Rec; [oth. writ.] Articles for Rolls-Royce Enthusiasts' Club, "Tailor Made" comical poems, for weddings and speeches.; [pers.] I enjoy putting my thoughts on feelings or situations in verse.; [a.] Dawlish, Devon, UK

STONE, EDNA
[b.] 25 September 1949, North Walsham; [p.] Eddie Gee, Marion Gee; [m.] David Stone, 15 September 1973; [ch.] Stephen James, Philip Andrew; [ed.] North Walsham Girls High; [occ.] Housewife; [oth. writ.] Religious words to music composed by my brother Leonard, published by Salvation Army in 'Songs For Young People.'; [pers.] I hope that my poems might be of help to other people. I try to keep them simple, but perhaps with a slight religious flavor or sometimes slightly humorous. My two favorite poets are patience strong and Helen Steiner Rice.; [a.] North Walsham, Norfolk, UK

STONER, BARRY Y.
[pen.] Poet Stoner; [b.] 2 October 1944, Wakefield; [p.] Patience Thomas; [ch.] Mark Stoner and Joanne Stoner; [ed.] Wakefield/Preston Polytechnic; [occ.] Marketing/Sales of Greeting Cards; [memb.] Corporate Member I.E.E.I.E. (Engineering) Technical Engineering. (C.E.I.) Chartered Institutes; [hon.] Works Manager Ministry of Defense (1980); [oth. writ.] Several poems published in Anthologies, as follows: Winter Bouquet, Christian Poetry North - West, Poetry North - West, At Day's End; [pers.] I write spiritual poetry, which people tend to identify with Christian values and morals. Inspiration verse, by Wesley and Steiner Rice, comes close to my verse.; [a.] Chorley, Lancashire, UK

STORIE, PATRICIA A.
[b.] 20 January 1937, Grantown-on-Spey; [p.] John and Gertrude Grant; [m.] John Muir Storie, 21 March 1992 (2nd Marriage); [ch.] 3 - Gavin, Fiona, Mhairi; [ed.] 3 years in teacher training college - Edinburgh, plus 1 year special education diploma (Handicapped, special needs children); [occ.] Retired (Medical grounds), Assistant Head Teacher of Special School

STOTT, NICOLA M.
[pen.] Nicola M. Stott; [b.] 14 May 1967, Oxford; [p.] Katharine Gardner, John Stott; [ed.] St. Hilarys School, Kent. University of Westminster, London; [occ.] Naval Fleet Manager; [memb.] IPD

(Part Qualified) Completing final year; [oth. writ.] Poem "Acceptance Amidst Confusion" published in "Voices From The Heart" (1995); [pers.] I write for relief, reflection and pure pleasure I have learnt that poetry can mirror the heart and therefore to be select.; [a.] London, UK

STRACHAN, MARGARET-ELIZABETH G.
[b.] 5 November 1978, Peterhead; [p.] George Strachan, Margaret Anderson; [ed.] Peterhead Central School, Peterhead Academy, The University of Aberdeen; [occ.] A Second Year Master of Arts Student at Aberdeen University; [memb.] Peterhead Arthritis Care Group, 'Biomorphic' - live P.A. (They have asked me to write songs for their band); [hon.] Dancing Awards in Highland Dancing, Ballet, Tap and Disco. Acting roles in over five Peterhead Panto Group Productions. 1996 Buchan Beauty Princess; [oth. writ.] I have been writing poetry and short stories since I was ten years old but I have never attempted to get any of them published. Most of them have only ever been read by me!; [pers.] I would like to thank my parents for the financial sacrifices they have made for me over the years. I hope I am an inspiration to any young poet because everything I have achieved comes from sheer determination and hard work. My aim to every reader is to inspire and give them hope in their lives.; [a.] Peterhead, Aberdeenshire, UK

STRATTON, STUART PAUL
[b.] 6 June 1969, Southampton; [p.] Sonia Fleming and Alan Fleming; [ed.] Wyvern Comprehensive Secondary School, Fair Oak, Eastleigh, Hants; [occ.] Driver/Care Assistant Bishopstoke Day Services; [hon.] City and Guilds in Heating and Ventilating (Crafts); [oth. writ.] This is my first piece of work I have ever submitted, and also, to be published. Yes, in my spare time, I am devoted to writing poetry, song lyrics and I am currently in the pieces of writing my first book (A Psychological Thriller); [pers.] I perceive, the path of life and the multiple personalities within human nature, to be, an abstract painting hung within the gallery of nature itself. For, as the elements and the emotions are its principal artist, we are just one aspect of their portraits. I am inspired by happiness and sadness, love and hatred, and, life and death.; [a.] Fareham, Hampshire, UK

STRAY, EDWIN
[pen.] Uncle Ted; [b.] 6 May 1930, Southampton; [p.] Mary Haimes, Edwin Stray; [ed.] Comprehensive School; [occ.] Carer; [oth. writ.] 2 poems published Modern Poets 81. Under the pen name Uncle Ted; [pers.] I have always been interested in poetry I have written many which have not been published as yet. I write poems about life as it happens; [a.] Portsmouth, Hampshire, UK

STUART, HILDA R.
[pen.] Hilda R. Stuart; [b.] 17 February 1917, Watford, Herts; [p.] Stanley and Sarah Jane Hall; [m.] Donald Charles Stuart, 16 September 1950; [ch.] Ian Stanely and Jennifer Mary Stuart; [ed.] Alexandra Mixed School Watford until I was 11 years. Won Scholarship to watford Grammar School for girls I'm 1908 - 1934 Eleventh in County; [occ.] Physiotherapist; [memb.] Chartered Society of Physiotherapy - with training 62 years of Physiotherapy completed; [hon.] No special honours or awards - just hard work!; [oth. writ.] Book title "People I Have Seem From Behind". Autobiographical and an account of my Job - Not technical - 1995 - but light hearted and

true to life much enjoyed by me; [pers.] I have enjoyed my profession, I like people and have tried to do some good in life. I am a methodist and enjoy my choir and church. I was very happy bringing up my family.; [a.] King's Langley, Herts, UK

STUART, KATE
[b.] 3 April 1970, Sheffield; [p.] Jonathan Stuart; [m.] Guy Hamilton; [a.] Oxford, UK

STUBBERFIELD, MARTIN R.
[b.] 17 April 1953, Trowbridge; [p.] Frederick and Joan; [ed.] Bath School of Art, The University of Wales College of Cardiff; [occ.] Yoga Teacher; [memb.] The British Wheel of Yoga; [hon.] Honours English Literature; [oth. writ.] Poems and short stories.; [pers.] Happiness is to be found only in what moves and develops.; [a.] Bath, Banes, UK

STUBBS, MARGARET
[b.] 3 May 1925, Yorkshire; [oth. writ.] "Poems for my grandchildren," and others.; [pers.] Buddhist.; [a.] Ilkley, Yorkshire, UK

SUTTON, KAYE MARY
[pen.] Kaye Sutton; [b.] 18 November 1946, Workington, Cumbria; [p.] The Late Phyll Sockett and Mr. Sydney Sockett; [m.] Mr. Michael Sutton, 18 September 1993; [ch.] Lorna-Kaye, Duncan-John, Simon Andrew Walker; [ed.] St. George's College of Technology Sleaford Lincolnshire; [occ.] Nursing - Staff Nurse in Ashdene private Nursing home; [memb.] Station Aerobic Club, Amateur Dramatics Society, Trainee Faith Healer at Local Spiritualist Church in Sleaford in my spare moments; [hon.] R.M.N.; [oth. writ.] Poem - Called, Spiritual Awareness; [pers.] In later life I seem to be developing a flair for writing poetry and hope to be able to write more in the near future.; [a.] Sleaford, Lincolnshire, UK

SWAILE, ELIZABETH
[m.] Deceased, 8 December 1962; [ch.] Boys 2 (adults); [ed.] Pomeroy No. 2 P.E. School, Dungannon Technical School; [occ.] Retired Nursing Sister South Tyrone Hospital Dungannon; [oth. writ.] A Part to Play, The Guided Hand, Spring Time, Woman of Faith, Leisure Approach, County Tyrone; [pers.] Commenced Writing Poetry October 1995 has been published in a few anthologies.; [a.] Dungannon, Tyrone, UK

SWINDELLS, FRED
[b.] 14 October 1918, Mexborough; [p.] Fred and Sarah Swindells; [m.] Evelyn Swindells (Nee Smith), 23 March 1940; [ch.] Ralph, Peter and Douglas; [ed.] Dolcliffe Elementary, N.C.L.C. Reading, Article Writing; [occ.] Retired Locomotive Driver, British Rail 43 years service; [memb.] Rounded Golf Club; [oth. writ.] This is my first and only effort to write a serious poem. Other writings are a comical nature, the outcome of which I have not considered yet. My poem Re: "It Made A Difference" - under "Personal Note".; [pers.] I believe the inability of partners, to communicate with each other in a caring and loving way, is the main cause of failure in marriage today, even though they may still love other, many remain silent, then, either spouse could be influenced by another, who was perfected this ability.; [a.] Swinton, Mexborough, South Yorks, UK

SWINN, SHIRLEY
[b.] 11 June 1996, Knutsford; [p.] Hilda and George Burman Watmough; [m.] Graham Rowland Swinn, 1957; [ch.] 3 boys and 1 girl; [ed.] Mottram

and Andrew Primary and Hilary's Alderley Edge, College of Commerce M/cr, Medical Technology Student (Christie Hosp M/cr); [occ.] Retired; [memb.] British Horticultural Society, Literary Club; [hon.] Mensa Challange Certificate, Diploma in Commerce, Merit from Alderley Edge, Urban District Council (Essay) 1949; [pers.] The dawn will break and in the wake will conquer strife and life will be anew!; [a.] Haslingden, Lancs, UK

SYLVESTER, LINDA
[b.] 25 November 1980, Athlone; [p.] Hamilton and Carol Sylvester; [ed.] "Our Lady's Bawer" Secondary school, Athlone; [occ.] Student; [memb.] "Greenpeace" Dublin; [oth. writ.] Poems and articles published in annual school magazine; [pers.] Through my involvement, with "Greenpeace" I hope to develop a healthier environment for future generations by projecting such images in my writings.; [a.] Athlone, Westmeath, UK

TAIT, NICOLA JANE
[b.] 6 October 1977, Manchester; [p.] Brenda, Allan Tait; [ed.] Schools in India and Singapore, Argoed School in North Wales - GCSE's Deeside College-'A' Levels; [occ.] Student; [oth. writ.] I am an avid writer of poems and short stories - all as yet undiscovered.; [pers.] My main concentrations are in the negative emotions of life, death and loneliness one of my influences is William Wordsworth.; [a.] Bryn-y-Baal, Flintshire, UK

TALBOT, DAVID
[b.] 1 May 1936, Clayton-le-Moors; [p.] William and Annie Talbot; [m.] Kathleen, 1 August 1981; [ed.] Clitheroe Royal Grammar, Accrington College of further Education; [occ.] Retired; [oth. writ.] Poems and articles local newspapers and church magazines.; [pers.] Seek and ye shall find. Probably what you're looking for lets hope it's fun.; [a.] Saint Clement, Jersey, CI, UK

TARLING, JOSEPH DONALD
[b.] 21 October 1929, Wembley; [p.] Florence and Ernest; [m.] Kathleen Ann Tarling, 1 March 1958; [ed.] Secondary School; [occ.] Retired; [memb.] Former member of Portsmouth and Hampshire Art Soc., Cowes Corinthian Yacht Club, Two Bowls Clubs, Havant and Southbourne; [oth. writ.] Two western ballads, other poetry.; [pers.] My poetry strives to reflect of war particularly the first world war which is one of my interests. Also other works I have written shows the wonders of life and nature.; [a.] Hayling Island, Hampshire, UK

TAYLOR, CHRISTINA
[b.] 25 December 1965, Birmingham; [p.] Maureen Baldwin; [m.] Clive Taylor, 25 June 1983; [ch.] Keith 12, Zoe 11, Victoria 9; [ed.] Colmers Farm Comprehensive; [occ.] Filling Machine Operator At N.P. Foods; [pers.] Writing poetry is a way of stating how I feel. In the midst of madness it is my form of sanity, my escape from a turbulent world.; [a.] Northfield, Birmingham, UK

TAYLOR, DONNA
[b.] 1 September 1958, USA; [p.] Paul and Wendy Grimwood; [m.] Roger Taylor, 20 December 1975; [ch.] Paul, Mark, Sarah, Darren and Thomas; [ed.] St. Ivo Comp.; [occ.] Housewife and Mother; [oth. writ.] Our Kids, published in Quiet Moments.; [pers.] Most of my poems family based but some of them are just everyday things you may see as you walk along.; [a.] Hemingford Grey, Cambs, UK

TAYLOR, GLYNN
[b.] 4 November 1955, Oldham; [p.] William and Jean; [m.] Lyn, 7 August 1985; [ch.] Joseph; [ed.] St. Anselm's R.C. Comprehensive School; [occ.] (Stonemason) Retired due to accident; [memb.] Lancashire C.C.C., Oldham Athletic A.F.C.; [hon.] English Language, G.L.S.E. grade 'A' 95/96; [oth. writ.] Several poems printed local newspapers; [pers.] Writing poetry both relaxes and stimulates me. Inspiration fills me with energy, a completed poem relaxes me.; [a.] Oldham, Lancashire, UK

TAYLOR, KERRY
[b.] 11 December 1977, Harlow; [p.] Alex Taylor and Pat Taylor; [ed.] Brays Grove Comprehensive, Harlow, and Harlow College; [occ.] Student; [pers.] As a new writer, I am enjoying my current success and strive to use everyday values as my inspiration for my work.; [a.] Harlow, Essex, UK

TAYLOR, MR. LACHLAN
[pen.] Mr. Lachlan Taylor; [b.] 26 June 1922, Falkirk; [p.] Mr. and Mrs. William Taylor (Deceased); [m.] Anne McFarlane Henry (Deceased), 3 March 1967; [ed.] Comprehensive School, left at 14 years. Received Day School Lower Certificate; [occ.] O.A.P. (74 years), was an Iron Moulder Originally; [memb.] Was a member of AYR, Auld Kirk in the Sixties. Was a member of British Legion; [hon.] Was medal from the 19-39/45 war, for the actions I was in.; [oth. writ.] Various poems selected for publication from triumph house publishers, Peterborough. (Religious and otherwise) and two published in Monthly Magazines.; [pers.] Wordsworth Burns and Shakespeare I loved as a boy. I have not much education, but am an avid reader, and I do like poetry. My work is not for intellectuals, just simple verse, illustrating my thoughts.; [a.] Falkirk, Stirlingshire, UK

TAYLOR, MISS MARY WINIFRID
[b.] 15 July 1941, St. Asaph, North Wales; [p.] John Taylor, Helen Taylor; [occ.] Home Help; [pers.] I am influenced by nature, and the world around me.; [a.] Crook, Durham, UK

TAYLOR, MURIEL M.
[pen.] Eve Lander; [b.] Huddersfield; [ed.] Private Education

TAYLOR, ROSEMARY
[b.] 13 June 1955, Pembury; [p.] Gwendolene and John Beaver Smith; [ed.] South Bourne School, Hampshire, University of Brighton; [occ.] Accounting Manager, in the Marine Engineering Industry; [oth. writ.] "Sarah's Home" published in `Help The Aged' magazine and "The Visitor" published in the 1996 anthology of poems - (`Feeling's pub. by M. Abbott.); [pers.] Poetry is an outing for your emotion.; [a.] Pulborough, West Sussex, UK

TAYLOR, SARAH
[b.] 11 September 1983, Beverly; [p.] Tina and Paul Taylor; [ed.] William Levick Primary, The Dronfield School; [occ.] Student; [memb.] The Boyzone Fan Club; [hon.] Football - 5A side girls winners; [oth. writ.] Red Friday, Dead, If; [pers.] I write poetry mostly expressing my feelings I don't feel I've been influenced by anybody.; [a.] Dronfield, Derbyshire, UK

TAYLOR, SHEILA
[b.] 28 June 1938, Marylebone; [p.] William Wilson, Annie Wilson; [m.] Maurice Taylor, 18 July 1959; [ch.] Ian, Steven, Heather; [ed.] Aida Fosters School of Dancing, Golders Green; [memb.] National Trust, RSPB; [pers.] Buttercups is in memory of my father William Lindsay Wilson; [a.] Bushey, Hertfordshire, UK

TAYLOR, SUE
[b.] 15 June 1964, Nottingham; [occ.] Housewife and Mother of two children; [oth. writ.] Several other poems published in anthologies; [pers.] I wish to become a recognized poet, producing fact and fictional poetry for everyone to enjoy and talk about for years to come. Poetry is the food for communication and the wealth for understanding.; [a.] Nottingham, Nottinghamshire, UK

TEAGUE, NOEL
[b.] Donegal; [p.] John Teague and Mary Teague; [m.] Ann O'Reilly, 17 October 1987; [ch.] Mary-Lea, Richard; [ed.] Lettercrann NS, De La Salle Secondary, Ballyshannon, Avondale School of Forestry, Art and Design plus Creative Writing from the open College of Art in Barnsley; [occ.] Forester "Runs a Private Woodland Development Business"; [memb.] Lettercanny "Errigal writers group" founder member; [pers.] I believe that man's obsession with materialistic well being has closed his eyes to the mystical beauty that is life itself.; [a.] Lettercanny, Donegal, Ireland

TEBBUTT, DORA
[b.] 15 July 1920, Clipston; [p.] Thomas Mutton, Clara Mutton; [m.] Reginald James Tebbutt, 3 April 1943; [ch.] Dorothy Jean; [ed.] Elementary only at Clipston Grammar School, leaving at the age of 15 years.; [occ.] Housewife, widowed since 1993; [memb.] Clipston Women's Institute, Clipston Baptist Church, former member of The John Clare Society; [hon.] Won a Hymn-Writing Competition in the Christian Herald in 1940; [oth. writ.] Poems printed in the Works Magazine of the firm by whom I was employed. Poem printed in the Northants County W.I. magazine in 1978.; [pers.] I owe much to my excellent English teacher, who, in my schooldays. Inspired in me a love of Words and who encouraged me to write, both in prose and verse. A lover of Nature, I write of the things I see around me in my Village, from the loss of the Elm trees, to the village Jumble Sale. There is interest all around us if we but open our eyes. I am an admirer of the works of John Clare, who, in spite of poverty and adversity, poured out his soul in most beautiful verse about the countryside in which he lived.; [a.] Clipston, Northamptonshire, UK

TEICHMANN, IRIS
[b.] 10 July 1966, Heilbronn, Germany; [ed.] Wirzburg University, Leeds University, School of Oriental and African Studies; [occ.] Administrator/Interpreter, Refugee Council London; [hon.] Chinese Studies; [pers.] Art is never about mind, but it originates in awareness of life and in the activities of the mind. The wind helps to express life it can never replace it, just of a work of out helps to express out - but ca never be out itself.; [a.] North London, UK

TELFORD, MAUREEN
[pen.] Marrianne Rydell; [b.] 19 Sept. 1941, Hebburn; [p.] George Washington Plews, Margaret Plews; [m.] Auguste Edward Telford, 31 December 1964; [ch.] Malcolm and Karen; [ed.] Jarrow Central School, South Shields Coll. Marine and Technology, Newcastle Coll. Arts and Technology.; [occ.] Housewife; [memb.] Local Education Appeals Committee; [oth. writ.] Short Stories under my pen name, (Romance) verses in local newspapers.; [pers.] I would like to see peace (world) in my lifetime; [a.] Hebburn, Tyne and Wear, UK

TERRY, DORA K.
[b.] 12 May 1924, Walthamstow; [p.] Ellen Vinsen and Charles Vinsen; [m.] Bob Terry, 25 May 1988; [ed.] William Morris Central School; [occ.] Retired; [memb.] Woodford Historical Society, Redbridge Art Group; [oth. writ.] Personalized verses for hand painted birthday cards; [pers.] To be able to put beauty onto a canvas and to express in verse the guys of life has been a very special gift for me.; [a.] Woodford, Essex, UK

TESTER, SHAUN
[pen.] "Arnie"; [b.] December 20, 1967, Guildford; [p.] Ros Tester, Colin Tester, (Andy Beck stepdad); [ed.] Sprowston High School; [occ.] Freelance Chef/Fitness Instructor; [oth. writ.] Other personal poetry writing, hoping to write a book of poetry.; [pers.] "To write with my heart where all are feelings to life are."; [a.] Norwich, Norfolk, UK

THOMAS, DEBBIE
[b.] 5 December 1963, Peterborough; [p.] Bryan Thomas, Pamela Newman; [ch.] Adam James (11); [ed.] Jack Hunt Secondary School Peterborough; [occ.] Departmental Accounts Payable Supervisor for 'Thomas Cook Ltd.'; [oth. writ.] "Contemplation of Desire" is the only one submitted.; [pers.] I write how I feel, I live what is written. I am motivated by heart, mind and simply life itself.; [a.] Peterborough, Cambridgeshire, UK

THOMAS, JUDY
[b.] September 28, 1941, Aylesbury; [p.] Daisy Collett and William Collett (Guardians); [m.] David Thomas, September 9, 1967; [ch.] Stephen John; [ed.] Swansea Secondary Technical School; [occ.] Shop Assist. Part Time; [memb.] Information of suitable Mothers Union - Church in Wales (of which I am enrolling member on Gowertor Parish); [oth. writ.] Poems published recently have included items for Christian anthologies. Published by Anchor Books, Arrival Press, Triumph Hse.; [pers.] I believe that poetry can help us to express our inner feelings and beliefs. Due to the vast styles of writing it is an art that can appeal to all people.; [a.] Gowerton Swansea, West Glam,

THOMAS, WILLIAM G.
[b.] 17 October 1938, Llanfyllin; [p.] William H. Thomas, Bessie Thomas; [m.] Marian Thomas, 20 August 1959; [ch.] Andrew, David, Christopher, Sarah, Melita; [ed.] Adams Grammar School Wem, H.M.S. Caledonia, Rosyth, H.M.S. Collingwood, fareham; [occ.] Industrial Elect/Mech Technician Supt. Elect Power Production Tech, Saudia Arabia. But awaiting hip replacement at this time; [pers.] Today has become the first day of the rest of my life, and/or my to wire let me thank you dear for the patience of your ear at times so surely tested til the right word was arrested.; [a.] Prees, Salop, UK

THOMPSON, ANN
[b.] 11 March 1944, London; [p.] Raymond and Gladys Stephenson; [m.] John Thompson, 13 June 1964; [ch.] Gavin Stephen and Simon Paul; [ed.] Doncaster; [occ.] Secretary and Adult Education Tutor (P/Time); [oth. writ.] Poem read out on radio, Sheffield. Writing poems in relation to life experience to photographs.; [pers.] To leave memories of the past ot future generations - so they can "Feel" if not see.; [a.] Goole, East Riding of Yorks, UK

THOMPSON, CHARLES
[b.] 14 October 1914, Tredegarmon; [p.] Charlie and Helen Thompson; [m.] Lydia (Deceased), 14 June 1958; [ch.] Josephine and Elizabeth (Deceased); [ed.] (Post Primary), Tredegar County School, Bablake School, Coventry University of Birmingham; [occ.] Retired Principal; [memb.] Hon. Member British Dyslexia Association (was foundation chairman), Hon. Member Association of Principal of College, Hon. Member Association Teachers in Technical Institutions, members of Antie Association; [hon.] Fellow of Further Education Staff College, B.Sc. Hon. Maths M.B.E; [oth. writ.] Various educational papers.; [a.] Box, Corsham, Wilts, UK

THOMPSON, NICOLA
[b.] 15 June 1978, Grantham; [p.] Celia Barnes and Jim Thompson; [ed.] The Earl of Scarbrough High School, Skegness; [occ.] Day time I work on a Barmy Bottle Stall, Morning and night a cashier; [oth. writ.] I wrote a poem to Reggie Kray and I write others poems in a book which I have in my bed room; [pers.] My poem was about a lad called Kelvin who I really did like a lot, I will never forget him, even though that he and a friend did was wrong and got us both in trouble with the police I still like him and wish to see him again.; [a.] Skegness, Lincolnshire, UK

THOMSON, ALISTER H.
[b.] 9 July 1928, Rogart, Sutherland; [p.] Angus and Jenny Thomson (Deceased); [m.] Liz Thomson (Died 27 April 1996), 14 December 1968; [ed.] Rogart Public School, Sutherland Technical School, Golspie, Sutherland; [occ.] Retired, 41 1/2 Years British Telecom (Post Office Prior to Bit); [memb.] Fraser Park Bowling Club, Westhill Indoor Bowling Club, Inverness, British Legion - Inverness, Local Horticultural Club; [oth. writ.] Several poems, published. One short story published.; [pers.] Attempt to write on what I feel and on life as I see it. 10 wishes view.; [a.] Inverness, Inverness-shire, UK

THOMSON, BETTY
[b.] East Sheen; [ch.] Three; [ed.] Twickenham Grammer; [occ.] Housewife; [memb.] Sidmouth Bowl's Club; [hon.] County Player; [oth. writ.] Two poems published; [pers.] My great Aunt was an artist and poet. Mary Brotherton Nee Rees. She was a great friend of a Tennison and the Brownings. She moved to Sidmouth in 1830 from India; [a.] Sidmouth, Devon, UK

THOMSON, DENISE
[pen.] Denise Fuggle; [b.] 23 February 1952, Sunderland; [p.] Wallace - Martha Fuggle; [m.] Peter; [ch.] Debra, Donna, twins Peter and Patrick; [occ.] Housewife, a volunteer for N.S.P.C.C.; [pers.] My daughter Donna for her inspiration. If you are told the wrong route on a journey you will stop. If you are told the right route you will see the light at the end of the tunnel."; [a.] City of Sunderland, UK

THOMSON, JOHN WYLIE
[pen.] Jonathan Wales; [b.] 6 February 1968, Blantyre; [p.] Annie and Edward (Deceased); [ed.] Blantyre High School Motherwell College of Technology Bell College of Technology; [occ.] Chef/Student of Accountancy; [hon.] Higher National Diploma in Accountancy; [oth. writ.] Poem published in Local magazine. Several poems unreleased. Several song lyrics.; [pers.] I have

been blessed with enough intelligence to see the problems of this world, but have been cursed with not enough intelligence to find the solutions.; [a.] Burnbank, Lanarkshire, UK

THOMSON, LYNNE HUNTER
[b.] 18 March 1955, Kilsyth; [p.] David and Irene Morrison; [m.] Jim Thomson; [ch.] Samantha, Gavin, Yvonne, John, Karyn, Heather; [pers.] Dedicated to Jim on our 10th Anniversary. Midge is the best for musicianship.; [a.] Dundee, UK

THOMSON, MELANIE-LEE
[b.] 14 May 1970; [m.] William Thomson, 10 October 1991; [ch.] Ashley Aird, Lauren Alexandra; [pers.] "The North Sea Tiger" is dedicated to my husband Bill Thomson.; [a.] Newtonmore, Inverness-shire, UK

THORPE, DAVID
[b.] 10 October 1967, Washington, DC, USA; [p.] Michael Thorpe, Gloria Thorpe; [ed.] Tonbridge School, Brown University U.S.A., Institute of Archaeology University College London; [occ.] Archaeologist/PhD student; [memb.] American Center for Oriental Research, Amman, Jordan, Amnesty International; [hon.] Ancient History (B.A.), Archaeology (M.A.); [pers.] My writing is mainly a product of two influences: severe, recurrent migraine, and the beauty, and often tragedy, of the many countries I have visited.; [a.] T. Wells, Kent, UK

TILZEY, MISS PENELOPE
[b.] 12 September 1962, Bromley; [p.] Gilbert and Eileen; [ed.] Southampton and Reigate and further Education at Bournemouth; [oth. writ.] Poems published or awaiting Publication by poetry now, Triumph House, The Poetry Guild, The Poetry Institute of the British Isles, Poetry in the British Isles and the International Library of Poetry in 'Quiet Moments.'; [pers.] My poetry stems from the need for and evidence of God, the consideration of situations in life both tragic and comic, and the beauty and power of nature.; [a.] Woolpit, Suffolk, UK

TINKLER, MRS. JANET
[b.] 29 October 1943, Low Fell; [p.] Leslie and Anne Armitage; [m.] Derek Tinkler, 8 October 1966; [ch.] Cheryl and Ian; [ed.] Stainsby Secondary School Acklam, Middlesbrough; [occ.] Housewife; [memb.] North East Disabled Writers Project - Cleveland; [oth. writ.] Two poems published in magazine and newspaper; [pers.] Only been writing for one year. Enjoy writing about my love for nature but don't mind turning my hand to other subjects as required for the writers project.; [a.] Middlesbrough, Cleveland, UK

TISSINGTON, KEITH
[b.] 9 September 1961, Doncaster; [p.] Ronald (Deceased) and Eileen; [ed.] Wilby Carr High School; [occ.] Postal Worker; [pers.] If at least one person finds pleasure in the words I write, then the time and effort will have not been wasted.; [a.] Doncaster, South Yorkshire, UK

TOBERT, GERALD
[b.] 10 March 1910, London; [m.] Dr. Alexandra Tobert, March 1945; [ch.] Four; [ed.] Robert Monte Flore School, White Chapel, London; [occ.] Retired, Managing Director; [memb.] Past M. Inst. P.I. (Member of the Institute of Patentees and Inventors); [oth. writ.] Loves and Hates, I love the

links that binds man together and helps the unity of humanity. I love the warmth of friendly greeting. The deference to differences and the joy of living and let living.; [pers.] I hate the use of envy, the despair of disadvantage, the domination of pleasant personalities, the shallowness of bumptious wealth, and the arrogance of the ignorant.; [a.] Southwell, Notts, UK

TOBIN, CLIFTON
[b.] 20 May 1945, Jamaica; [ch.] Two boys, girl; [ed.] Elementary; [occ.] Huffman Presser; [oth. writ.] I have been greatly influenced and inspired by the early poets such as king soloman from the Holy Bible.

TODD, WILLIAM NOBLE
[pen.] Bill Todd, William Noble; [b.] 4 April 1929, Northwich, Cheshire; [p.] Lawrence Todd, Vera Todd (Nee Noble); [m.] Joan (Nee Dormand) (Deceased, 1988), 17 December 1960; [ch.] Joanna, Patricia; [ed.] Lancaster Royal Grammar School 1940-1947; [occ.] Retired Accountant; [memb.] Yorkshire Mountaineering Club, Yorkshire Ramblers Club, John Buchan Society; [oth. writ.] Articles on mountaineering in "Dales Man", "Choice" magazine with photographs, photographs in "Climber" and in "Tight Rope" book by Denno Gray poem about climbing in anthology "Simple Pleasures"; [pers.] Also amateur violinist classical and folk I strive to emphasize that retirement and bereavement need not signify the end of fun. I most admire those who live happy and useful lives in spite of illness and disability; [a.] Leeds, West Yorks, UK

TOHILL, MISS FIONNUALA
[b.] 19 August 1981, Derry; [p.] Terence and Mary; [ed.] St. Canices Primary School, Dungiven Co. Derry, and Oakgrove Integrated College Clooney Road Derry, 3rd year; [occ.] Student; [memb.] "Clay Kids" Drama Club Dungiven (Camera, Lights Action for Youth); [hon.] Duke of Ed Bronze; [oth. writ.] Other poems not presented for evaluation or publishing or topics such as Peace, Theatre, Personal Moments etc.; [a.] Dungiven, Derry, UK

TOLLEY, CONSTANCE MAY
[pen.] Constance May Tolley; [b.] 21 April 1936, Corley, West Mids; [ed.] Secondary Modern School; [occ.] Retired; [hon.] Commended Ballerina in my early life, Certificates for classical guitar playing, 6th grade (Exam Material only); [oth. writ.] Essays "The Tramp", "The Old Oak Tree". Not published but received good marks from english teacher (mature student classes); [pers.] For me to have written this poem immortalizes forever - my partner of 19 yrs. It makes a statement to the whole world - I am alive - I exist. I was very much apart of Lorenzos's life. I loved. I cared. I hurt. Just like anyone else.; [a.] Birmingham, West Midlands, UK

TOMPKINS, MADGE
[b.] 9 November 1932, West Ireland; [p.] Ellen Coyle, William Meenaghan; [m.] Ronald, June 1957; [ch.] Two daughters; [ed.] National and Commercial Schools, Ireland; [occ.] Housewife; [memb.] Cayman Drama Society (Cayman Islands), Visual Arts Society (Cayman Islands), Co-Founder and Member Ladies International Club (Cayman), Astronomical Society, Various Golf Clubs; [oth. writ.] Items of topical interest as well as a number of poems published in local press; [pers.] Man commits so many atrocities against

fellowman and nature that subtle reminders are not enough. My first effort at poetry was inspired by Man's unkindness to animals, a few years ago.; [a.] Bournemouth, Dorset, UK

TOVELL, JANET
[b.] 17 January 1939, Bradwell, Gt. Yarmouth; [p.] Deceased, David; [m.] 1 March 1958; [ch.] Neil and Sally; [ed.] Gorleston High; [occ.] Home Carer, Norfolk County Council; [oth. writ.] Two poems published by Anchor Books Peterborough; [pers.] I enjoy writing poems of everyday life on the humours side.; [a.] Gorleston, Gt. Yarmouth, Norfolk, UK

TOWRIE, DAVID DREVER
[b.] 2 December 1922, Orkney; [p.] John Towrie, Catherine Towrie; [ed.] Scottish Certificate of Education O'Levels Certificates in Orcadian Studies from Aberdeen University Centre for Continuing Education.; [occ.] Retired; [hon.] Fellow of the Society of Antiquaries of Scotland; [oth. writ.] Book review, article, dialect short story to Orkney View Magazine dialect contributions to the Orkney wordbook.; [pers.] To observed the natural environment and protect its values at all times. To see its wild and wonderful sights and scenes and to reflect on them from other times I dearly love the works of the Scottish poet Robert Burns.; [a.] Orkney, UK

TOWRIE, DAVID
[ed.] Burness Parish School Sanday Orkney; [a.] Orkney, Scotland

TRIMBLE, FREDA BEATRICE
[b.] 22 April 1939, Stewartstown; [p.] Edward and Caroline Cromie; [m.] James Hugh Trimble, 28 July 1961; [ch.] Matthew George, Freda Sarah, Elizabeth, Edward James, Philip Thomas, Karen Debra; [ed.] Primary Y Class, Moy Regional Primary; [occ.] Housewife; [memb.] St. Columbus P.W.A. (President), St. Columbas Afternoon Club, St. Columba's Presbyterian and Methodist Church Member; [oth. writ.] Several poems published in other Christian poetry books, local newspapers and church magazines also many poems recited on local radio station.; [pers.] I feel my poetry is a gift from God, which helps me witness to others. This particular poem has helped many people.; [a.] Lisburn, Antrim, UK

TRODD, MRS. VIOLET DOROTHY BOSEIR
[b.] 13 February 1915, Southampton; [p.] Lilian and Frederick Bosier; [m.] Divorced; [ed.] Regents Park Elementary Richville Road Shirley Southampton; [occ.] Retired; [oth. writ.] I stopped writing poetry when I started to knit and embroider babies ankles strap shoes for charity, I stopped doing this after the 2000 pair and started again on my poetry, I was thrilled by your letter I feel at 81 years of age, it is quiet an achievement.; [a.] Southampton, Hampshire, UK

TRUBSHAW, ALWYN
[ed.] Queen Mary's School, Walsall, Emmanuel College, Cambridge; [occ.] Retired Schoolmaster; [memb.] Probus Club; [hon.] M.A. (Cantab); [oth. writ.] Articles on James Farrar for local Press and School Magazine; [pers.] My poems kept secret till recently when photo-copied for a few relatives and friends and some included in "Poetry Now" Peterborough. Age makes furtive inspiration unlikely.; [a.] Banstead, Surrey, UK

TSANIKIDOU, HELEN
[b.] 30 August 1947, Katerini; [p.] Costas Tsilikis, Chrisoula Tsiliki; [m.] Kyriakos Tsanikidis, 3 October 1976; [ch.] John Tsanikidis; [ed.] Aristotle University (Dept. of English Language and Literature), Post Graduate Studies of E.S.P. in University of Lancaster (1982) and UMIST (1983-84); [occ.] English Teacher; [oth. writ.] Several poems published in school magazine and E.S.P. Teaching Material for the Department of Food Technology and Nutrition of Thessaloniki T.E.I.; [pers.] I believe that in the magic world of poetry, the words acquire new dimensions, through which, both the poet and the reader can escape from triviality and be transferred to paths leading to eternity.; [a.] Thessaloniki, Thessaloniki

TUCKER, KAY GILLIAN
[b.] 2 July 1941, Caterham; [p.] Mr. and Mrs. W. Ponton (Both Deceased); [m.] Mr. Paul Tucker, 14 December 1988; [ch.] Robyn, Marcus, two step-children: Sarah and James; [ed.] State Junior School, Scholarship to Sydenham High, School for girls G.P.D.S.T.; [occ.] Psychiatric Nurse; [hon.] Qualified as a nurse at the age of 49; [oth. writ.] None published. I have always enjoyed writing poetry for friends and relatives; [pers.] I have always enjoyed the romantic poets. I find it easier to express strong emotions and deep feelings through poetry than by an other form of communication.; [a.] Shrewsbury, Shropshire, UK

TUNLEY, MARTYN
[b.] 30 October 1975, Solihull; [ed.] Arrow Vale High School, currently studying English Literature at Worcester College of Higher Education; [pers.] Through my poetry I am attempting to understand myself and life in a new perspective. I enjoy the poetry of Philip Larkin and John Keats.; [a.] Redditch, Worcs, UK

TUPPER, KATHLEEN M.
[pen.] Kathy M. Tupper; [b.] 18 August 1934, Haslemere, Surrey; [p.] Mr. and Mrs. Robert and Kathleen Toovey; [ch.] Live abroad in Australia; [ed.] Normal Leaving Standard; [occ.] Artist (Watercolorist); [memb.] W colour Society of W.A. founder Member of Wanneroo Art Society, W. Aust. Alton Art Society; [hon.] Nominated for BHP Award for Art and Writing Accomplishments 1984. Royal Show Peritwa 1991, Many countries have my Art work, from my artist in residency in W. Aust.; [oth. writ.] Poem's to be published Sep 1996 in "Home Counties Christian Messenger." Other's have been printed in Victoria, Australia. I also write, children's books.; [pers.] That which you share will multiply, that which you withhold will diminish; [a.] Ropley, Hants, UK

TURAY, MOHAMMAD S.
[b.] 21 April 1963, Sierra Leone; [p.] Bassie A. Turay and Mary F. Turay; [ch.] Bassie M. Turay, Monah K. Turay; [ed.] Fourah Bay College, Albert Academy, London School of Economics/Accountancy, City College London; [occ.] Information Technology Assessor; [hon.] Commonwealth Institute Award (Art), Assessor Award (IT) - Information Technology), Diamond Corporation of West Africa Award (Art); [oth. writ.] Several poems (have not yet presented them for publishing or to the local magazines or otherwise). Music lyrics, also in the process of writing a novel.; [pers.] I want to bring awareness and consciousness to mankind of all their actions and the effect it has on one another and the world as a whole be it good or detrimental.; [a.] Cambewell, London, UK

TURNER, FLORENCE
[pen.] Florrence; [b.] 1 August 1909, Blackburn; [p.] Mary Alice and Robert Richardson; [m.] John Turner, 20 July 1940; [ed.] Church School (Primary) and Secondary Modern Education; [occ.] Retired; [memb.] St. Gabriel's Mother's Union Preseden (Friendship Club); [oth. writ.] 1. The angle of Brownhill publisher - Cremer press book title: The Pied Piper of Words an Anthology of Poetry by Nothern Writers; [pers.] Education period I was always top girl in all subject, other hobby painting China, plates etc.; [a.] Blackburn, Lancashire, UK

TURNER, GILES
[b.] 22 October 1973, Hereford; [p.] Mike Turner and Janet Turner; [ed.] White Cross High School, Hereford Technical Collage Day Release and Work; [occ.] Machine Operator; [oth. writ.] Poems published in a 1995 collected poems. Forth coming poems in Martin Halroyds Poetry Monthly; [pers.] Water's wet, the sky's, blue and no matter what we do the sun will always rise on the other end of the night, so enjoy. Hugs and kisses on all your pink bits.; [a.] Hereford, Herefordshire, UK

TWEDDLE, NORMA A.
[b.] 1 November 1930, Wardle; [p.] Norman and Ellenor Potts; [m.] William H. Tweddle, 27 September 1952; [ch.] Mark Tweddle and Margaret Ripley; [ed.] Local Board School; [occ.] Retired; [memb.] PCC Dearley Church Littleborough. Local Home Watch Friends of Smithy Bridge School; [hon.] City and Guilds Fashion Grandma to five lovely grandsons, who are worth more than any awards that could be given to me.; [oth. writ.] "My Brother and I" published May 1996. Other writings not published as yet.; [pers.] Have only been writing poems for about 12 months. I enjoy writing and I am very surprised that my work is acceptable.; [a.] Littleborough, Lancs, UK

TYNAN, JOHN
[b.] April 23, 1945, Waterford, Ireland; [p.] Robert (Deceased) and Isabel (Nee Gamble); [m.] Divorced; [ch.] Sheila Kathleen and James Paul; [ed.] Royal Belfast Academical Institution, Queens University Belfast (Economics), Chartered Accountant; [occ.] Business Consultant in Finance in Paris; [memb.] American Interdenominational Church of Paris, Golf Club, Franco-Irish Chamber of Commerce; [oth. writ.] Articles on French business for UK magazines.; [pers.] Stimulated to write poems by personal emotion, reaction to social injustice and by frustration at institutional inaction.; [a.] Donaghadee, Down, UK

TYSON, WILLIAM L.
[b.] 1925; [m.] Barbara, 1956; [ch.] 2 daughters; [ed.] Grammar School, Colleges of F.E., University P/T; [occ.] Retired Personnel Manager; [memb.] The Methodist Church, Charitable and Voluntary Bodies; [hon.] C.I.P.D., Vice-President of The National Association of Choirs; [oth. writ.] A large pile of unpublished verse, short stories and plays.; [pers.] My object in writing is to entertain.; [a.] Cheadle Hulme, Gtr. Manchester, UK

UCHE, IFEDMA C.
[b.] 17 June 1970, Nigeria; [p.] Engr. and Mrs. O. Alexander Uche; [ed.] IMD State University Nig. Times Journalism Institute; [occ.] Client Services Manager Weight Watches Nig. Ltd.; [memb.] London Flower Lovers, Nigerian Union of Journalists; [hon.] English/English Literature; [oth. writ.] Several articles published in NNPC news letter (Nig.), articles for the daily times newspaper of Nigeria Plc.; [pers.] I strive through my writing to reach out tot he inner man. To also express reality. I have been influenced by my experiences past and present, it affects my writing and strives to reflect the goodness in man and his life.

ULLYATT, WAYNE ROBERT
[b.] 21 March 1966, Sheffield; [p.] Wilfred Ullyatt, Pauline Ullyatt; [m.] Fionna Ullyatt, 20 June 1992; [ed.] Hatfield House Lane Primary School, Firth Park Comprehensive; [occ.] Civil Servant; [memb.] Member of Local Preachers Methodist Association, Member of Hatfield House Lane Methodist Church; [hon.] I am a fully accredited Local Preacher in the Methodist Church (accredited May 1993); [oth. writ.] None as yet!; [pers.] To love and serve another and to love and serve God.; [a.] Sheffield, South Yorkshire, UK

UNSWORTH, LILIAN
[pen.] Sara Hylton; [occ.] Author; [memb.] Society of Authors; [oth. writ.] I have published eighteen novels under my pen name Sara Hylton. My publisher is Judy Piatkus.; [pers.] I have been influenced by favorite poets like Browning and Byron.; [a.] Bury, Lancs, UK

VALENCIA-RAMOS, HAZEL
[pen.] Avellana Coll; [b.] 12 August 1945, Leamington Spa; [p.] D. J. Love and V. M. Love; [m.] Juan Valencia-Ramos, 26 March 1976; [occ.] Caterer; [memb.] Friends of the Earth Greenpeace; [oth. writ.] At present in process of preparing book of poems for publication.; [pers.] My poems are armed at making the readers question who we are and our direction and to bring attention to the beauty of our natural surroundings and to enjoy them hence the simple form.; [a.] Leamington, Warwickshire, UK

VALENTINE JR., ALEX
[b.] 22 February 1956, Dumbarton; [occ.] Civil Servant; [a.] Alexandria, Dunbartonshire, UK

VALLOW, BRENDA
[b.] 20 July 1948, Brighouse; [p.] Harold and Gladys Saunders; [m.] Peter Vallow, 28 October 1967; [ch.] Craig Vallow; [ed.] Brighouse Girls Grammar School; [occ.] Part time Clerical Worker in Husband's Business a pit student; [memb.] Horton House Creative Writing Group Halifax; [hon.] City and Guilds Diploma in Information Technology; [oth. writ.] Magazine and Newspaper items; [pers.] I strive to think positively and hope that this reflects in my writing; [a.] Brighouse, West Yorkshire, UK

VAN BARNEVELD, SASKIA
[b.] 7 June 1979, Edinburgh; [p.] Jan and Sylvia Van Barneveld; [ed.] Ross High School, Tranent; [occ.] Student; [hon.] Catherine Marshall Prize for English (awarded in 5th year at school); [oth. writ.] Articles for 'Rewynd' magazine.; [pers.] The poetry I write mostly reflects what I experience in life. I am often inspired by a love of music, (many of my 'poems' may work well as songs.); [a.] Tranent, East Lothian, UK

VAN DER VEEN, ANTHONY
[pen.] Tone Bone; [b.] 18 October 1947, Durban, S. Africa; [p.] Sal and Lucy Van Der Veen; [m.] Chris Hirney, 9 December 1981; [ed.] Matriculation (S. Africa); [occ.] Hotel Director; [oth. writ.] "Love To Be One" self published booklet of poems (1991); [pers.] I love all kinds of music and am influenced by Tibetan Buddhism and the struggle for liberation and advancement of all sentiment beings.; [a.] Amsterdam, Netherlands

VAN RHEE, MARIANNE
[b.] 25 April 1947, Holland; [p.] Peter Nicolas Van Rhee, Adriana Maria; [ch.] Selina Yvonne Amanda Rose Graham, Paul Michael Douglas; [ed.] First Normal R.C. School then myself (Australian High School Moe Victoria then managers in Holland then 1969 here in England Warwick also capsten setter in engineering; [occ.] At the moment just Art (oils) and writing music; [memb.] Achievements in Sociology and drug abuse also Art plus helping the elderly; [hon.] Achievements in Sociology and drug abuse also Art plus helping the elderly, Language 4 altogether; [oth. writ.] None so far will do some more that was my first effect now I will definitely have the will to write more.; [pers.] No matter how ill or unfortunate you may feel in yourself there is always some one else worse of then you, so keep heart and love.; [a.] Coventry, Warwickshire, UK

VENABLE, MRS. SHEILA P.
[b.] Norfolk; [ch.] One Daughter; [ed.] Diss Grammar School and Norwich Teachers Training College; [occ.] Retired Head Teachers; [hon.] Share Your Memories Competition 1994 - "Once Upon a Time" highly commended - (Certificate); [oth. writ.] Have written short stories and poems over the years - but have not tried to have them published.

VERNEY, NORMA BERYL
[b.] 24 January 1923, Dulwich, London; [p.] Deceased; [m.] Died at 50 served as navigator on Lancaster Bombers in war, 4 November 1944; [ch.] Two boys and one girl; [ed.] Educated at Southend-on-Sea, Scholarship to High School, School Certificate at 16 War Closed School; [occ.] Retired from Local County Council; [memb.] 2 Pensions Groups, NALGO Retirement Section Raw, UNISGP One Ladies Group have been Secretary of 3 groups including Mothers Union, Choral Society Warwick and Revolution, but have left now.; [hon.] Won a cup once for Drama, have served on PCE of St. Marys, Collegiate Church Warwick, husband was Church Warden, sons sung in choir of eldest still does; [oth. writ.] I have many poems one sent to MU for publication in their monthly issue. I have sent one to a group who is publishing a book of prayers but here not heard from them.; [pers.] I served in the WRNS during the war in London. My children born in Westcliff on Sea. Come to Warwick early 60's as husband sent by Motor Insurance to Birmingham joined Country Council when sons at College.; [a.] Warwick, Warwickshire, UK

VINCENT, ROSEMARY FRANCES
[pen.] Fran Vincent; [b.] 9 July 1926, York; [p.] Rose and Harold Sparling; [m.] Frank (Deceased), 25 July 1954; [ch.] Christopher; [ed.] Girls higher grade shipton St. York; [occ.] Retired; [memb.] Richmonoshire Choir; [oth. writ.] Several published in anthologies during the last two years. Northern echo; [pers.] I have been writing for over forty years but only now sent for publication. I reflect all my deepest emotions in my work and try to show the worth of beauty and for beabrance in this age of troubles; [a.] Richmond, North Yorks, UK

VOLANTE, PAUL
[pen.] Poet Paul; [b.] 18 December 1932, London; [p.] Oregen F., Italen M. German; [m.] 2nd wife Deceased; [ch.] Six; [ed.] War Time Schooling London School Diploma Null Self Educated Bylingo, German, Italian, English; [occ.] At 63 years old unemployment prospects null, Ex Navy Engineer, Ex 250cc KART racing champion, Exm.o.t driving instructor; [hon.] MOT Approved Instructor, C.A.M.D.A. silver star, advanced Driving Examiner NADA Executive Committee, many silver pots of 1st place motor racing; [oth. writ.] 11 Poems publish in England and 4 in West Germany 1 in the USA short stories unpublished art work Sketch Work was on display in Delmenhorst West Germany Art Gallery.; [pers.] My poems and art work I hope to reflect the truth of the world to day.; [a.] Lavenham, Suffolk, UK

WAKEFORD, DOREEN
[pen.] Lily Rodgers; [b.] 6 February 1931, Finchley; [oth. writ.] "Gypsy Lover." "The Poppy Field" unpublished.; [pers.] With my writing I can have my flights of fancy and freedom of spirit.; [a.] Hitchin, Hertfordshire, UK

WALDRON, CARMEN
[pen.] Carmen Lamas Waldron; [b.] 27 April 1945, Lima, Peru; [p.] Carlos Lamas and Dora Crespo; [m.] Luke Waldron, 18 December 1971; [ch.] Kathleen, William and Anthony; [ed.] Social Studies, Public Relations and Literature; [occ.] Social Worker, Poet; [hon.] 1st prize Women's Festival Poetry Competition, Tallaght, Ireland Co. Dublin; [oth. writ.] Book of poems: "Coniemeandous" in Spanish.; [a.] Maywooth, Co. Kildare, Ireland

WALKER, BRIGITTE
[b.] 20 July 1921, Dublin; [p.] Patrick and Mary Byrne; [m.] Richard Walker (Deceased), 26 October 1974; [ed.] Convent Educated; [occ.] Retired; [pers.] I write poetry simply for pleasure and writing. Special poems for special people on special occasions makes writing poetry worth while.; [a.] Oxford City, Oxfordshire, UK

WALKER, DORA EMMA LAVINIA
[b.] December 29, 1904, London; [p.] Dr. Edward Jones, Mrs. Lavina Jones; [m.] Herbert John Walker, February 27, 1926; [ch.] Jill Gray, Doreen Dunbar; [a.] Welling, Kent, UK

WALKER, MRS. JEAN MARGARET
[pen.] "Rose Petal"; [b.] October 22, 1921, London; [p.] Roosina and Walter Bradstock; [m.] Thomas Leslie Walker, (Deceased) May 10, 1943; [ch.] Jill, Poosina and Peter Graham Walker; [ed.] Carlton House School Brighton Regretfully closed as a school many years ago, and Evening Classes Brighton Technical College; [occ.] Retired Fully trained ABTA Travel Agent Manager.; [memb.] Was a member of travel agent's club, and was on the committee. And various connections with travel; [hon.] Received several certificates connected with travel; [oth. writ.] Just one small article in national magazine, not a poem; [pers.] I want to dedicate this poem in everlasting memory of my beloved son and also with fondest love and deep gratitude to my dearest daughter who has helped me so much, and her family, and my beloved husband, without whom none of this poem would have been possible; [a.] Brighton, East Sussex, UK

WALKER, MAY
[b.] 30 May 1921, Glasgow; [p.] William and Jenny Wakes; [m.] A. S. Walker, 8 January 1948; [ch.] Two; [ed.] Senior Secondary School; [occ.] Housewife; [memb.] Williamwood Golf Club, John Bell School of Painting; [pers.] Have always been interested in English, watercolour artist, specialises in flower, bedhill take up this outlet till take in life. Have exhibited and sold all over Scotland.; [a.] Glasgow, Strathclyde, UK

WALKER, RAYMOND
[b.] 6 September 1953, Edgware; [p.] Wallace and Jean Walker; [m.] Sheila Walker, 8 April 1972; [ch.] Victor, Justin, Michelle, Dee; [ed.] Spur Rd. Comprehensive School Edgware; [occ.] Disabled; [oth. writ.] Anniversary published in the other side of the Mirror; [pers.] Idle thoughts pass slowly by of insignificance. Thoughts that travel through my mind in slow but Merry Dance. Just every now and then one opens my minds eye. Then it goes it slowly goes, as another passes by.; [a.] Frinton-on-Sea, Essex, UK

WALL, MABEL
[b.] 18 September 1921, Chesterfield; [oth. writ.] Publication of poem: "Living In Derbyshire" 1994 Arrival Press, "Midlands" Anthology; [pers.] I find writing poetry both relaxing and exciting. Condensing a wealth of information on to limited lines, with interesting rhythmical phrasing, creating stimulating verse.; [a.] Chesterfield, Derbyshire, UK

WALLEY, RUTH
[b.] 26 December 1975, Thornbury, Nr Bristol; [p.] John Walley, Shirley Barnes; [ed.] Stella Maris School, Bideford and St. Mary's University College, Strawberry Hill; [occ.] (Student)/Third year Undergraduate BA Hons. English and Drama; [a.] Lynton, Devon, UK

WALLIS, JOAN
[b.] 14 August 1932, Kensington; [p.] Mabel and Charles Gray; [m.] Gordon Wallis, 16 August 1952; [ch.] Linda and Martin; [ed.] St. Pauls School, Hammersmith, London; [occ.] Playground Leader; [memb.] Toga and Keep fit Classes; [hon.] Diploma for playground; [oth. writ.] Children's Poetry.

WALTON, JIM
[oth. writ.] Many-all unpublished; [pers.] I had biographical detail of the author irrelevant. The reader will find whatever be needs to know in the worth. I have dedicated my life to crusading against and hypocrasy and never let up an opportunity to print the balloon of pomposity of certain individuals, particularly politicians. I am a politically incorrect veillard terrible very ambitious! I wouldn't mind a penny of this length, let alone a portrade!; [a.] Castle Donington, Leics, UK

WALTRAUT-WANDSCHER, PAULA
[pen.] Paula Waltraut-Wandscher; [b.] 20 September 1929, Oldenburg; [p.] Norman; [m.] Deceased, 7 July 1959; [ch.] Two sons; [ed.] Educated in Germany Higher (A Britain); [occ.] Retired; [memb.] Chorester in Scottish Society od Choral Music with Glasgow Lyric Choir alo Church Choir and other Choirs of times; [hon.] RGN, SCM, Tropical Disease; [oth. writ.] At the moment a Hempling?!? To write a book about my midwifery days in the Gorbals Glasgow between 1955-57. (Hardwork!); [pers.] "Each day in my life is like a leaf falling off it's tree in Autumn and each one is move colorful than the one before."; [a.] Edinburgh, Leith, Lothian, UK

WANN, IRVINE SHEILA
[pen.] Sheila Irvine Fraser Wann; [b.] 5 September 1946, Perth; [p.] Constance and Irvine Fraser; [m.] John Wann, 8 April 1969; [ch.] Irvine, Fraser and Donald Wann; [ed.] Perth High School, Robert Gordons Domestic Science College, Aberdeen. Qualified in Institutional Management; [occ.] Catering Supervisor, Inchture Primary School; [memb.] Scottish Womans Rural Institute, Guild in Church of Scotland; [hon.] Institutional Management Association Certificate. For Matron Housekeepers; [oth. writ.] "The Countryside" in high Spots by Anchor books. "Country Freedom" Poets in Scotland by arrival press, and "The Old Lady" in inspirations from Scotland by Anchor Books.; [pers.] I win many prizes in the womans rural for art and crafts, cooking and baking, I won the trophy of Perth Agricultural Show 3 years in succession also win the trophy at Weal Rural.; [a.] Glencarse, Perth, UK

WARD, ANNIE
[b.] 24 July 1955, London; [p.] Arthur Ward, Iona Ward; [ed.] Walpole Grammar, Rose Bruford College of Speech and Drama; [occ.] Personnel and Administration Manager; [memb.] Association of Natural Medicine; [hon.] Cert. Ed. English and Drama, Diploma Counselling, Naturopathy, Massage, Cert. Management Studies.; [a.] London, UK

WARD, HILARY ANN
[pen.] Hilary Ann Torrens; [b.] 13 September 1947, Manchester; [p.] Eric Dawson and Irene May Dawson; [m.] Divorced; [ch.] Dawn, Julian, Gail and Jane, (Grandchildren) Jade and Daniel; [ed.] Fairfield Grammar School for Girls - Droylsden, Manchester, Audenshaw Night School; [occ.] Medically retired from Press Operator - Car Industry; [memb.] Stirchley Village, Spiritualist Church; [hon.] English and Typing (advance level) several Music Distinctions with Royal College of Music and Victoria College of Music; [oth. writ.] Church Parish Magazine (Manchester) short story. Several poems recently submitted to Anchor Books - Peterborough under review, who are also publishing a longer version of the Soldier Christmas in their new book inspirations from the West Country this September.; [pers.] I am to write on subjects which are meaningful and will give readers fond for thought and hope my words will help somebody. I am influenced by my religious belief, and inspired by events in my own life. Soldiers Christmas was influenced by my own War Hero - my father and his childhood stories to me. Patience Strong and Helena Ruberstein my favorite poets.; [a.] Telford, Shropshire, UK

WARD, JONATHAN MARK
[pen.] Jon Moon; [b.] 12 December 1971, York; [p.] Jack and Audrey Ward; [ed.] Joseph Rowntree School, Hayby Road New Earswick York; [occ.] Administration Funding Agency for Schools; [oth. writ.] Poetry published several times in York Magazine 'Subtext' lyrics for songs for York Band 'Frankly My Dear'.; [pers.] I dedicate my poetry to Jane Stockdale, who showed me the way and who I love with all my heart.; [a.] York, North Yorkshire, UK

WARD, MR. TERENCE FITZGERALD
[pen.] Terry; [b.] 7 February 1922, London; [p.] Deceased; [m.] Margaret Ward, 5 January 1946; [ch.] Two (Male); [ed.] 2nd Class Central School. N.C.O. Regular Army 1939-1946; [occ.] Retired, Coach, Driver (National Co.); [oth. writ.] Many short Stories published in the past in evening papers. 1 other poem published in "Anchor Press Anth".; [pers.] A firm belief in the spirit of mankind, and all creatures great and small. A firm belief in re-incarnation. An inner tranquility when writing.; [a.] Hemel Hempstead, Herts, UK

WARD, ROSEMARY CONSTANCE
[b.] 17 July 1939, Woodford Green; [occ.] Customer Service Assistant; [hon.] My poem being selected for publication in awaken to a dream; [oth. writ.] Several poems but none have been published; [pers.] An expression of my feelings of places and people closest to my heart.; [a.] Dagenham, Essex, UK

WARING, DARYL P.
[pen.] Knight Dallison; [b.] 2 November 1970, Sutton-in-Ashfield; [p.] Brenda and Jack Waring; [ed.] Sutton Centre Comprehensive, West Notts College; [occ.] European Planner; [hon.] Diploma in Social Care; [oth. writ.] None published at present. But I write poetry, songs, short stories and sketches.; [pers.] Diversity, kindness, the ability to laugh and to be thoughtful are great attributes. I am inspired by Roger McGough, Emily Dickinson, love and the repressed.; [a.] Sutton-in-Ashfield, Nottinghamshire, UK

WARLOW, DARREN
[b.] 14 July 1968, Warrington; [p.] Peter and June Warlow; [ed.] Padgate County High School; [occ.] Sales Assistant, Ikea Ltd.; [oth. writ.] Self-published book of poetry titled "Confessions From The Back Row". Articles and illustrations for work magazine; [pers.] I try to maintain a contemporary feel in my writing. By using observations of my surroundings. I am influenced by the contemporary and war poets such as Steve Turner, Stewart, Henderson and Wilfred Owens.; [a.] Warrington, Cheshire, UK

WARMAN, ANDREW
[b.] 26 April 1974, Deal; [p.] Allan Warman, June Warman; [m.] Janice Rubins; [ed.] Gemma, Kimberley, Sam, Jack; [occ.] Castle High Community School; [memb.] Unemployed; [oth. writ.] Written other poems ode to the moon is the first one published; [pers.] I've always loved reading poetry especially blake. I feel very proud to have one of my poems published; [a.] Deal, Kent, UK

WARREN, ROSINA D.
[b.] 22 February 1928, SE London; [p.] Charles Pearce, Annie Pearce; [m.] James Warren, 16 December 1944; [ch.] Patricia, Terence, James, Janice, Robert; [ed.] State Elementary Education; [occ.] Housewife; [oth. writ.] Several poems to include: "Where's the Boy?", "I Love To...", "From Morning Till Night" etc. None of which have been submitted anywhere for publication.; [pers.] As elderly and partially disabled, occasionally writing poetry is a comfort to me and a hobby - I write as I feel.; [a.] Nr Rye, East Sussex, UK

WARWICK, URSULA
[pen.] Ursula Warwick; [b.] 21 October 1926, Brentwood; [p.] Vincent and Cecilia Ffrench; [m.] Widowed, January 1951; [ch.] Three; [ed.] Convent 1930-37, Grammar School, Eye, Suffolk Commercial College, Carlisle; [occ.] Stress Mgt. Counselor, Medical Centre; [oth. writ.] A few other poems. 9 short stories, one "Somewhere Else", pub. 1993, new fiction ("Down The Middle"). One-time Agony Aunt Local Press.; [pers.] Inspired particularly by Shakespeare's Prose. Interested in after-line, "Otherness" - my stories reflect this. Love people but wry view of worldly values. Philosophy: Nothing is for ever.; [a.] Borehamwood, Herts, UK

WATKINS, EMMA WAY
[b.] 7 July 1983, Newport, Gwent; [p.] Catherine Watkins; [ed.] Caerleon Comprehensive School, Cold Bath Road, Caerleon Mamouthshire; [occ.] Student (at the above address); [pers.] I dedicate this poem to Violet Bibby.; [a.] Newport, Momouthshire, UK

WATKINS, JADE
[b.] 1 December 1952, Newport, Gwent; [p.] Lilian Pope, Trevor Pope (Deceased); [m.] Daniel Keith Watkins, 24 December 1994 (Second marriage); [ch.] 3 children Christopher Paul Catley, Lucy Catley and Grace Francine Catley; [ed.] Abersychan Secondary Modern School (British) Blandare College of Further Education, Ponty Pod, Gwent; [occ.] Poet/Writer; [memb.] Formally member of the Ponty Pool and district writers group, Brynteg, Abersychan Gwent, S. Wales; [hon.] English Literature Typing and music; [oth. writ.] Several anthologies: Lovers and Others, A New Frontier, poets in Wales, Life After Life, Heart and Soul. Magazine my weekly. And Ponty Pool Market Centenary; [pers.] I write mostly love poems, rhymed or free verse. My ambition is to have a collection of love poems published in the hole that others will derive as much pleasure in reading than as I have had writing them I have been inspired by: The Bronte's, Christina Rossetti and Dylan Thomas; [a.] Laugharne, Dyfed, UK

WATKIS, ADLIN
[pen.] Shirley May; [b.] 26 May 1938, Jamaica; [p.] Osborne Williams, Florence Williams; [ed.] Comprehensive School, St Ann Jamaica; [occ.] Catering Assistant; [memb.] Watchtower Bible Society, U.S.A. Pennsylvania, USA; [oth. writ.] Poem in Anthology "The Other Side of The Mirror", Other un-published works.; [pers.] I have been touched by the feelings of the Poets of Antiquity, in their Writings I see their hope for a better future for Mankind. I strive to show these feelings in my poems.; [a.] Ealing, UK

WATSON, CHRISTEL
[b.] 11 November 1987, Irvine; [p.] James and Kaef Watson; [ed.] Hurlford Primary School, Fenwick Primary School; [occ.] Primary School Pupil; [memb.] School Recorder Group; [oth. writ.] Battle of Britain, Scotland's Mists, The Polar Bear, Colours, The Picts, Gerbils, Rain, and other poems.; [pers.] This is the first poem I have shown to anyone other than at home or school, and I am very excited about getting it published. I wrote it when I was 7 but now I am 8 3/4.; [a.] Fenwick, Kilmarnock, E. Ayshire, UK

WATSON, FLORENCE
[pen.] Laurie; [b.] 1912, York; [p.] J. and A. Ellis; [m.] Tom Watson, 10 June 1989, widowed 2nd marriage; [ch.] Two; [ed.] Private school - Cheltenham; [occ.] Housewife; [memb.] Various farming societies and cookery. Luncheon club, oil painting. Cooking recipe adviser Farm Women's Club.; [oth. writ.] Short Poems, and short Prose, etc., have had poems published in magazines.; [pers.] Interested in gardening and country life. Enjoy reading biographies and walking. The theatre.; [a.] York, Yorkshire, UK

WATTS, ERIC GEORGE
[b.] 6 October 1915, London; [p.] Esther Watts, Hector Watts; [m.] Vera May, 4 September 1996; [ch.] Peter Bernard; [ed.] Hanwell Residential "Cuckoo Farm" Charlie Chaplin ran away from then Ashford W. London Residential; [occ.] Retired, Compositor/Musician; [memb.] Only liverpool, Os-re-o-por-o-sis Society, Porton Down, Veterans Association, the "Brethren"; [hon.] None except cycling medals. Had some medal for schools essay on British Empire from Prince of Wales in 1920's; [oth. writ.] Poems accepted by queen and letters by which her majesty got the ministry of defense acting to help Porton Down Sufferess, Letters to Papers; [pers.] Since Ex Bomb Disposer Landed on Head find thoughts come not in prose but Rhyme instead; [a.] Southport, Merseyside, UK

WAWMAN, YVONNE
[b.] 14 December 1936, Luton, Beds; [p.] Kenneth Bloomfield, Irene Bloomfield; [m.] John Wawman, 28 October 1961; [ch.] Roxana, George, Stephen; [ed.] St. Dominics Convent School Harpenden Herts; [occ.] Housewife; [memb.] The National Trust; [hon.] The British Federation of Music Festival. Diploma for Verse Speaking with Honours St. Albans Competitive Music Festival Certificate of Merit for Elocution. The Royal Drawing, Society Group III stage 1 and 2 honours standard stage 3 honours.; [per.] I was inspired to write poetry while on my travels abroad to describe the many wonders that I saw.; [a.] Norwich, Norfolk, UK

WAY, MRS. IRENE
[b.] 18 May 1924, East Ham, E.G.; [p.] Christopher and Rose Stothard; [m.] Norman D. Way, 8 August 1959; [ch.] Peter and Eleanor; [ed.] Romford County High School for Girls South Devon Technical College; [occ.] Retired; [oth. writ.] Several poems in religious magazines. Two children's book.; [pers.] Particularly interested in animal welfare and conservation. I try to reflect my love of nature in my work.; [a.] Chelmsford, Essex, UK

WEBBER, DEBORAH
[b.] 11 July 1962, Epsom; [occ.] Administration Manager; [memb.] Duffield Tennis Club; [hon.] Grade 7 piano - Merit; [oth. writ.] This is my first publication; [a.] Matlock, Derbyshire, UK

WEEDEN, A. E.
[b.] 14 May 1942, Kenley, Surrey; [p.] Joyce and Eric Godwin; [m.] D. F. Weeden, 23 February 1976; [ch.] Charlotte; [ed.] Hayes, Kent - Junior, Bromley, Kent. Girls Grammar, rich family life and extensive travel. 2 brothers and 2 sisters; [occ.] Access to Art course - Dartford; [memb.] 'White Rose' - Dartford Poetry Group - Dartford Art Group, Adult Education Courses - varied; [hon.] Scholarship - Royal Academy of Dancing 1956, Divali Dance Festival 1993, Italian Dance Festival 1974; [oth. writ.] Published 'White Rose' magazine. Writing poetry since 1952 - Canvey Isle flooding through the present day. Poets day - LBC Radio Reading.; [pers.] My passion for life has always impelled me to write poetry, and retain my free spirit.; [a.] Dartford, Kent, UK

WEGG, MAVIS P.
[b.] 30 May 1943, Hull; [p.] Evelyn, Herbert E.; [m.] Roy Wegg, 16 June 1962; [ch.] Four sons: Darrell, Lesley, Peter and Steven; [ed.] The Best Education Somerset Street, Westbourne St., County Council Schools, ON Hessle Rd., Hull; [occ.] Domestic Engineer Plus, Deputy Chair Lady of "Stand" and lots more!; [memb.] Just local young wife's a Methodist Church, and anything at all to do with my Church!; [hon.] None I can think! Except all medals, Bronze, Silver for Swimming, Running!; [oth. writ.] Just poetry and letters; [pers.] Just an ordinary person who loves gardening, keep fit, meeting people, remembering my family and home, and reading almost anything, of interest and beauty (Lakes Mountains) Homes et lovely stories, true life and autobiography.; [a.] Hull, East Yorkshire, UK

WELLS, FLORENCE MARY
[b.] 20 August 1934, Leicester; [p.] John H. Oldershaw and Ethel Oldershaw; [m.] Ernest H. H. Wells, 16 May 1953; [ch.] Julie Irene; [ed.] Secondary Modern at Melbourne Road School for Girls in Leicester; [occ.] Senior Citizen, Housewife and Grandmother; [memb.] I am a member of the International Fund for animal welfare.; [pers.] I have done the courses of art and painting at contest Harper College, and have bern influenced by my there grandchildren to write poetry and short stories. I have travelled greatly, when my husband was in the Royal Navy.; [a.] Wigston, Leicestershire, UK

WEST, AUDREY
[b.] 8 May 1956, Jamaica; [p.] Alvin West, Mary West; [ch.] Yola West - Dennis; [ed.] North Paddington School London, Southampton University 75-79 Iberian and Latin American Studies, Institute of Education Lond, PGCE Spanish/French; [occ.] Trainee in Psychosynthesis Counselling and Therapy; [hon.] B.A. Hons., Berian and Latin American Studies; [oth. writ.] Unpublished work.; [a.] London, UK

WESTALL, WENDY
[b.] 14 May 1969, London; [p.] William Howlett, Daisy Howlett; [m.] Guy Westall, 14 November 1987; [ch.] Janine Clare, Jenifer Suzanne; [occ.] Housewife; [pers.] Many thanks to my parents for their love and guidance and to my husband and daughters for their support and inspiration.; [a.] Gillingham, Kent, UK

WESTING, GLADYS WINIFRED
[pen.] Jackie Westing; [b.] 2 March 1915, Nottingham; [p.] Ellen Jackson, Harold Jackson; [m.] William Clifford Westing, 5 November 1938; [ch.] Margaret; [ed.] Nottinghamshire County Council Peoples College; [occ.] Retired; [memb.] Hollyfield Writer's Club, currently being considered for membership of Society of Women Writers and Journalism S.W.W.J; [oth. writ.] Cornucopia, A Collection by Hollyfield writer's club published 1993 ISBN No. 0952262606, Moods and Memories, a collection of poems by Surrey W.I. members also small articles on different subjects; [pers.] I have always been interested in poetry since I wrote and recited my first poem at 8 1/2 yrs.; [a.] Surbiton, Surrey, UK

WESTLEY, JEREMY
[b.] 13 April 1957, Wolverhampton; [p.] William Westley, Hilda Westley; [m.] Frances, 2 April 1988; [ch.] Richard, Emily and Michael; [ed.] Sir Gilbert Claughton Grammer/Technical School; [occ.] Registered General Nurse Guest Hospital Dudley; [oth. writ.] No other works published; [pers.] I have been greatly influenced by the pop stars/folk singers, Marc Bolan, Donovan and Bob Dylan; [a.] Dudley, West Midlands, UK

WESTWOOD, RAYMOND
[b.] 7 March 1934, Brierley Hill; [p.] Thomas Frederick, Ida Westwood; [m.] June Pauline Westwood, 31 May 1958; [ch.] Kim, Garwyn, Alun, Andrew, Anthony (Deceased); [ed.] Penswett Secondary School Brierley Hills States, Bourneville College, Birmingham, Bilston College, Wolverhampton.; [occ.] Care Assistant, Elderly Persons, Dudley, Social Services.; [hon.] Certificate - Social and Community Care. Certificate - in Social Care. 'O' Level Sociology, 'O' Level Psychology; [oth. writ.] Several articles and stories and articles for our in house magazine. Eventually took over the production and editoring this magazine.; [pers.] My articles the way of life and interests of my old people. Mainly of the pre-world war two period. Also local wildlife. "Why - One So Young" was some of my feelings, due to the death of my son.; [a.] Dudley, West Midlands, UK

WHALE, MRS. MARGARET R.
[b.] 21 September 1941, Micheldever; [p.] Arthur Hendy, Dorothy Hendy; [m.] Edward R. Whale, 29 July 1961; [ch.] Edward Kevin and Kim Rosemary; [ed.] Dane Mark County Secondary Girls School, Winchester; [occ.] Housewife; [hon.] 5 G.C.E. 'O' Levels-English Literature, History, Human Biology, Religious Instruction Cookery; [pers.] This is the first poem I have ever written, and I hope to be able to write more.; [a.] Aylesbury, Bucks, UK

WHEELER, ANNE CATHERINE
[pen.] Ditto; [b.] 3 September 1933, Thatcham, Berks; [p.] Clarice and Wilfred Street; [m.] Douglas J. C. Wheeler, 3 September 1955; [ch.] David, Robert, Caroline, Jaqueline; [ed.] Newbury Grammar School For Girls: Age 5-17 1/2 yrs. Miss Sprules Secretarial College Oxford: 18-19 years (1 year); [occ.] Wife/Secretary; [hon.] School certificate, 6 credits, 2 passes. (School) 1 'A' level (English Literature) Crammer Course - grade D (Newbury College Further Education), (Spanish Classes, 2 Extra Rural courses in Criminology at Reading, University, Life Through Literature Classes. Juvenile Deliquency Classes. (Reading University); [oth. writ.] 'Sea Verge' poem; [pers.] I like to write about personal experience and that which I observed or a mother of four children and to combine this with the rhythms and the beauty of Nature.; [a.] Thatcham, Berkshire, UK

WHEELER, MARJORIE MAUDE
[b.] 30 March 1905, Islington; [p.] English; [ed.] Croydon High School, Croydon Art School, Heatherly's Pierce Fe Ar School, London; [occ.] Artist when eye sight allows and odd writing work hung in work in Paris Saton and Royal Academy; [memb.] Certificate one of the Paris Salon Pictures; [oth. writ.] If I feel like in a may write some more poems; [pers.] Precious good health - a belief in the continuating life - also for animals and birdstrife. I am psychic and can see people and animals when they feel like showy themselves.; [a.] New Malden, Surrey, UK

WHEELER, THOMAS PATRICK WILLIAM
[pen.] William Crisp; [b.] 12 September 1952, London; [p.] Thomas and Rosehan Wheeler; [m.] Irene Wheeler, 19 August 1972; [ch.] Paul, Julie, Claire, Jean; [ed.] Longford Sec Mod - Feltham Middle; [occ.] General Foreman Construction Industry; [memb.] Chartered Institute of Building; [oth. writ.] First publication; [pers.] I write for the pleasure of myself and others. I draw my inspiration from every day life.; [a.] Bracknell, Berkshire, UK

WHELAN, E. N.
[b.] 1 May 1927, Charlton; [p.] Deceased; [ed.] Normal; [occ.] Retired; [pers.] Can't think of any.; [a.] London, Kent, UK

WHITCROFT, WILLIAM
[pen.] Williams Thoughts; [b.] 4 January 1927, Bowness; [p.] Both Deceased; [m.] Agnes Whitcroft, 1954; [ch.] Three boys all married; [ed.] Elementary school, Edenderry Tenant Street Belfast left school age 14 to start work, was made at school to learn poems; [oth. writ.] Many poems written none published at present enjoy writing every day. About every day things and read many years later.; [a.] Belfast, Antrim Belfast, UK

WHITE, EDNA
[pen.] Edna White; [b.] 25 August 1923, Birmingham; [m.] Colin White, 2 April 1949; [ch.] Angela; [ed.] Commercial College; [occ.] Retired; [memb.] Women's Institute, Over 60's Club, Methodist Church, Spiritual Healer; [oth. writ.] Poems have been in church magazines - also works (Kay's) magazine.; [pers.] I have been writing poetry for over 35 years. My friends have all suggested I put them in book form. 'To Bare' was written in about 20 minutes and was intended to be recited at 'Stroke Club'. Somehow the chance never arose.; [a.] Worcester, Worcs, UK

WHITE, MRS. PHYLLIS
[b.] 1 November 1937, Huddersfield; [p.] Mr. and Mrs. E. Marsh; [m.] Mr. Thomas Wetten White, 30 March 1973; [ed.] Holmfirth Secondary School, Huddersfield College, for Maths and English Course. Royds Hall Grammar School for Book-Keeping, English, Accountancy; [occ.] Cashier/Wages Clerk also Accounts Clerk; [memb.] None at the moment except the National Osteoporosis Society as I am an Osteoporosis Sufferer; [hon.] Various passes in Maths and English. Also award of merit for hand-writing; [oth. writ.] Four poems published by the Regency Press. Ltd., London, WCIA IBH, not the poem I sent to you. I have written around 35 poems altogether - including Mr. and Mrs. Gladstone - 27 verses.; [pers.] I base my poetry on reality in every day life, and try to make it as interesting as possible for people of all walks of life.; [a.] Bridlington, East Yorkshire, UK

WHITE, RONALD C.
[b.] 15 October 1938, Birmingham; [p.] Sidney Carl White, Enwice Victoria White; [m.] Jane Ellis-Francee; [ch.] James, Darron, Sandra, Debbie; [ed.] 'Kings Rise Boys School', Birmingham, Student of Spanish 'Culture and Language'; [occ.] Surgical Chiropody Student; [hon.] School prize for Best Short Story; [oth. writ.] Several other poems, not yet sent for publication.; [pers.] "Their is so much more to see, if you open your mind, as well as your eyes".; [a.] Tamworth, Staffordshire, UK

WHITE, WILLIAM
[b.] 29 June 1912, Wandsworth; [p.] Samual and Emily White; [m.] Lilian (Deceased 1993), 15 November 1941; [ch.] Philip, Yvonne; [ed.] Links Road Elementary School Tooting, London SW17; [occ.] Retired after Lithographer 1977; [hon.] Badge Good Conduct Award in Royal Navy. 1940-1945, 3 Medals, Two First Award Illuminated Pictures At Exhibitions; [oth. writ.] Fairy Tale, not published. Illuminated my book not published. Poetry many pictures of illuminated scripts original.; [pers.] At 84 I live alone yet not alone with memories and ability and still scribe for pictures.; [a.] Brentwood, Essex, UK

WHITEHALL, IRENE
[b.] 12 May 1949, Scotland; [p.] Leiselotte and John Doyle; [m.] A. R. Whitehall (Tony), 7 February 1970; [ch.] Dale, Stephanie, Suzie; [ed.] General; [occ.] Theatrical Costumers, Seamstress; [hon.] Certificate in Scottish Lit.; [oth. writ.] Several small poems printed in local anthology, poems also written for friends for occasions.; [pers.] I write poems which reflect how life is on a day to day basis.; [a.] Ventnor, Isle of Wight, UK

WHITEHEAD, ANNIE
[b.] 18 February 1912, Burnley, Lancashire; [p.] May M. Youngs, William J. Youngs; [m.] James Whitehead (Deceased), 7 August 1939; [ch.] Two sons and two daughters; [oth. writ.] Poetry, when I have the time, usually for my friends. Last year I entered one poem for the R.N.M.D.S.F. for which I had a mention.; [a.] Collingham, Newark, Nottinghamshire, UK

WHITEHEAD, ANTHONY CHARLES
[b.] 7 May 1962, Great Yarmouth; [p.] Henry Walter Whitehead, Joy P. F. Whitehead; [m.] Lynn Arnold; [ch.] Wesley Churchill, Shelley Churchill, Claire Arnold, Jason Arnold; [ed.] St Lukes, Roger Ashcham; [occ.] Unemployed (Scaffolder); [hon.] For my poem to be published in Awaken to a Dream; [pers.] I am from a Romany family with little Education, never under estimate the talent of the under privileged.; [a.] Cambridge, Cambridgeshire, UK

WHITEHURST, G. B.
[b.] 1 November 1930, Kirkintilloch; [p.] John and Sarah Docherty; [m.] Michael Whitehurst, 23 August 1977; [ed.] Higher Leaving Certificate Scotland; [occ.] Retired was SRN Sch trained with this late Madame Lily; [memb.] Paylingasa Singer (Scholarship); [oth. writ.] Many, but thrown out; [pers.] My favorite poet is Francis Thompson. I have now become a semi-professional landscape painter. I strongly believe that God is present in his beautiful works.; [a.] Kirkintilloch, Dunbartonshire, UK

WHITFIELD, CLARE
[b.] 17 May 1962, Newcastle, Staffs; [p.] Roger E. Whitfield, Janet Whitfield; [ed.] Edenhurst Howell's School, Marlborough Secretarial College; [a.] London, UK

WHITTAKER, HANNAH
[b.] 1 September 1986, Macclesfield; [p.] Mr. and Mrs. A. S. Whittaker; [occ.] At school; [pers.] This poem was written in memory of my beloved pop-pop. (Granddad - Died April '96) Trevor Whittaker.; [a.] Macclesfield, Cheshire, UK

WICKHAM, GERALD PETER
[b.] 29 May 1974, Wexford, Ireland; [p.] Gerry Wickham, Helen Green; [ed.] Christian Brothers School, Wexford, Carlow Regional Technical College, University of Ulster, at Jordanstown; [occ.] Physical Education Student; [memb.] St. Mary's (Rosslare) G.A.A. Club; [pers.] Endeavour is the most powerful word I know. Help is due to those who are incapable of trying yet poorer are those who avoid endeavour. May God help us all.; [a.] Rosslare Harbour, Ireland

WILCOX, ENID
[pen.] Enid; [b.] 7 October 1919, Monmouth; [p.] Oliver and Martha Young; [ch.] Colin John Wilcox; [ed.] Mitchel Troy School; [occ.] Retired; [oth. writ.] The Shrubs, The Trees, The Weeping Willows. (The Park at Dawlish); [pers.] I write what I see.; [a.] Monmouth, Monmouthshire, UK

WILKINS, EVELYN J.
[b.] 2 April 1924, London; [p.] Deceased; [m.] Brian Quiggin, 1956; [ch.] Two sons; [ed.] Edgbaston High School Cert 1940, Birmingham Chartered Physiotherapist 1921-1984. Shropshire Col. of Domestic Science 1941-1942 Qualified; [occ.] Retired Writing, Singing, Bird Watching, Walking; [memb.] NIL now was chair: Good Bears of the World, Sutton Writers, Vesey Residents Asso.; [oth. writ.] Nine different songs and music two love stories (not published) very long letters. Autobiography accepted by British Library in Competition certificate won.; [pers.] Since 1933 I have tried to help people, use much analysis. Never had much to live on, not worried by that. Never been in Debt. Gardener sister was writer - Eithne Kaiser, Dec. brother is Prof. Maurice Wilkins - Nobel prize for D.N.A., Dec. 10, 1962.; [a.] Birmingham, West Midlands, UK

WILLIAMS, CARRIE
[b.] 26 May 1980, Taunton; [p.] David and Sheila Williams; [ed.] Heathfield School, currently attending Richard Huish College; [occ.] Student - studying A levels including English Literature; [oth. writ.] Several articles for a local magazine in addition to poetry and numerous short stories written mainly for pleasure.; [pers.] All of my work, especially my poetry, is inspired by issues which I feel strongly about and is intended to provoke thought and awareness.; [a.] Taunton, Somerset, UK

WILLIAMS, CORINA
[b.] 6 July 1974, Tamworth; [p.] Ron Williams - Valarie Grove; [ed.] Tony Williams - Jake Williams; [occ.] Cockshut Hill Secondary; [hon.] Unemployed; [pers.] I just want to say thank you to the friends and family who have supported and encouraged me.

WILLIAMS, DELROY
[b.] 9 March 1965, London; [p.] Cornelius, Inajem Williams; [ch.] Ryan Marcon; [ed.] Bradford University, Birkbeck College; [occ.] Arts Admin-Freelance, Performer, Writer; [memb.] MNCMNT CTEE, Working Group Against Racism in Children's Resources, Black and Alliance, Black Theatre Forum, New Playrich Trust, Hammsey Arts Council; [hon.] Commendation in Art Rage, Remathan, Hammsey and Council Poetry Competition; [oth. writ.] Reviews, songs published in two Anthologies Performance/Life Arts' Piece(s).; [pers.] Committed to producing challenging work which leads to personal, social and spiritual enlightenment and unity, influenced by various "Urban Poets" of London.; [a.] London, UK

WILLIAMS, ELWYN
[b.] 21 June 1929, Bangor, North Wales; [p.] John Williams, Elizabeth Williams; [m.] Mary Williams, 21 March 1959; [ch.] Clive Williams, Peter Williams; [ed.] Friars Grammar School, North Wales, Liverpool College of Art; [occ.] Retired Head of Education Services, Manchester Art Galleries; [memb.] Founder Member, Mountaineering Club of North Wales; [hon.] During my appointment as head of Art Studies at the David Hughes School, Anglesey, my Art Department was visited by H.R.H. Princess Margaret and Lord Snowdon. C. 1963, Appointed the initial Chairman of Moderators to supervise Art Examinations in Secondary schools throughout Northern England. Responsible for 90,000 candidates in 1987. I was sent, several times, to Northern Ireland to help to develop art examinations in the province.; [oth. writ.] Practising artist. Many works held in private collections throughout England, and some held in private collections in Ireland, The United States of America and Australia. I have lectured at several universities and art galleries in the United Kingdom including the National Gallery, London.; [pers.] My intention is to record, as truthfully as I can, the world in which I live and to pass on ideas that I have found helpful.; [a.] Tarleton, Lancashire, UK

WILLIAMS, HAYLEY
[pen.] Hayley Williams; [b.] 11 May 1982, Bournemouth; [p.] Julia Williams, David Williams; [ed.] Still in full time education at St. Peters School, Bournemouth; [occ.] Waitress at the Cliffend Hotel (Part-time); [oth. writ.] I have written other poems including, 'Thoughts,' 'Words From the Dead', 'Now You've Gone' and 'They Watched'; [pers.] I wrote the poem. "You Helped Me Remember How To Smile" for my grandma and granddad as they helped me cope when my dad left the family. I have always liked reading and writing poetry and am just pleased to have one published.; [a.] Bournemouth, Dorset, UK

WILLIAMS, HAZEL
[pen.] Hazel Bowyer Williams; [b.] 1 October 1930, Shaw, Lancs; [p.] Albert and Alice Bowyer; [m.] Denis Vivian Williams, 1 August 1953; [ch.] Denis Albert and Hazel Jan; [ed.] Wirral County Grammar School for girls; [occ.] Retired; [memb.] WI Entertainments Group Choirs, Drama, Methodist Church Choir; [oth. writ.] One poem published in "Enter My World." By anchor books. One published by Arrival Press in "Poets of the West Country."; [pers.] Usually write personal verses for friends and relatives, i.e. Births, weddings, anniversaries, in fact, any special function. Have only tried for publication during the last two years. Have been pleasantly surprised.; [a.] Cheddar, Somerset, UK

WILLIAMS, IRIS D.
[pen.] Iris D.; [b.] 14 August 1939, South Africa; [p.] Mr. and Mrs. Grieve; [m.] George Williams, 3 June 1977; [ch.] Four: Charles, Helen, Shirley, Gordon; [ed.] South African Standard 8 certificate; [occ.] Housewife; [hon.] City Guilds Photography; [oth. writ.] None - My first attempt at poetry; [pers.] What is happening to the beauty of the world and all its people.; [a.] Catford, London, UK

WILLIAMS, LOUISA
[pen.] Louisa Soto, Louisa Williams; [b.] 2 January 1965, London; [p.] Bungy Williams, Valerie Edwards; [ed.] Nicholas Hawksmoor School

(Herts), Demontfort University (Leics); [occ.] Marketing/Sponsorship Consultant; [hon.] BA (Hons) Performing Arts 1987; [oth. writ.] Poems, plays, writing a novel (The Club 1996), songwriting several performed/recorded (1993 to present); [pers.] "At the seat of your soul is where your true creative vision lies". I strive to achieve this clarity in my writing.; [a.] Borehamwood, Herts, UK

WILLIAMS, MARK

[b.] 31 August 1972, Birmingham; [p.] Marilyn and David; [ed.] Exhall Grange School, Coventry, Queen Alexandra College for the blind, Birmingham, Solihull College, Coventry University; [occ.] Student; [memb.] Guide Dogs for the Blind, Royal National Institute for the Blind; [hon.] 2nd prize - National Poetry Competition (partially sighted society) and in Business and Finance, Assorted Business and Admin. Qualifications and GCSE's; [oth. writ.] Age, The Christmas Tree, City Orphan, Darkness, Ever on Wars, Figure of A..., Ghost Town, Greed, Infantry Man, The Lighthouse, Night Flight, Redundant, assorted limericks; [pers.] Partially blind since age of 10, often inspired by current affairs, etc. Currently studying degree in Business Admin. at Coventry Uni., other hobbies - computing, swimming, walking, listening to audio books.; [a.] Coventry, Warwickshire, UK

WILLIAMS, MELVIN

[pen.] Melvin Williams; [b.] 24 May 1967, Croydon; [ed.] Stanley Technical Boys High School, Ingram High School for boys, Oval Primary School; [occ.] Psychic Vigilante, Freelance Spy Freelance Journalist; [oth. writ.] I had several article published in the sun newspaper and in my local newspaper. And I secretly create two programme for the B.B.C. and I begged the B.B.C. to buy two other programme from I.T.V.; [pers.] Quotation: When a man's education is finished, He is finished us financier E.A. Felene.; [a.] Croydon, Surrey, UK

WILLIAMS, MOLLIE

[pen.] Mary Vanes; [b.] 1 September 1919, Shrewsbury; [p.] Edward Evans, Ethel Evans; [m.] John Wesley Williams, 8 July 1940; [ch.] John, Clive, Sheila, Judith, Anne-Marie; [ed.] Priory grammer School, Shrewsbury; [occ.] Retired; [oth. writ.] Poems published in women's magazines, age concern poetry comp., winner epic poem published in Shropshire magazine; [pers.] Have enjoyed poetry reading all my life, but only started writing in middle age - mostly about, life as I see it.; [a.] Shrewsbury, Shropshire, UK

WILLIAMS, NORAH

[pen.] Mary Willsalt; [b.] 22 February 1946, Liverpool; [p.] Bridget and George Salters; [m.] David Williams, 10 December 1966; [ch.] 1 daughter - Marie; [ed.] Comprehensive; [oth. writ.] Short stories for children short stories for woman.; [a.] Liverpool, Lancashire, UK

WILLIAMS, PETER VAUGHAN

[pen.] Peter Vaughan and "Dragonfly"; [b.] 7 June 1944, Bolton; [p.] Mrs. Anne Williams; [m.] Frances Lean, 28 May 1966; [ch.] Gareth Andrew, Theo Jason; [ed.] Smithills Moor Grammar, Bolton College of Art, Leeds University Institute of Education, Lancaster University (Post-Graduate Studies); [occ.] Retired educationalist (writer, artist, musician, composer and poet); [memb.] British Association of Songwriters Composers and Authors (B.A.S.C.A.), Member of Society of Industrial Artists and Designers (M.S.I.A.D.); [hon.] Intermediate in Art and Crafts, Licenciate of the Society of Industrial Artists and Designers (L.S.I.A.D.), National Diploma in Design (N.D.D.) (Leeds University) Art Teaching Degree (A.T.D.) Bachelor of Education (Hons.) at Lancaster University; [oth. writ.] Short Stories and Novels, ("As A Child...", "Correlation", "Brom - A Fairytale for Adults") Poems ("Listen To The Children Of Lancashire" - Published Nov. 1994) ("Model" published Sept. 1996) ("Body Music" published in this edition) over 800 songs (Music and Lyrics) 8 albums produced; [pers.] I continue to find occasionally the words to sing out the truth, that is the real beauty of life! My heroes range from Kingsley to Dylan Thomas and beyond to J. P. Don Leavy.; [a.] Bolton, Lancashire, UK

WILLIAMSON, PATRICK ANTHONY

[b.] 12 June 1961, Thornley; [p.] Thomas William - Ann; [m.] Jacqueline Williamson, 19 July 1986; [ed.] St. Bedes Comprehensive School Peterlee; [occ.] Occupational Therapy Assistant; [memb.] Hartlepool General Hospitals; [oth. writ.] An affair of conscience was published in my Hospital Magazine Comment November 1994 and was part or my English literature course work - summer 1994.; [pers.] My thoughts are expressed enabling everyone to relate - I dedicate this poem to my belated father who encourage me to further my education after leaving the mining industry.; [a.] Durham, UK

WILLIAMSON, PETER

[b.] 24 May 1937, Gutcher; [p.] John and Bella; [m.] Greta, 18 July 1968, (Deceased, 14 November 1985); [ch.] Ian Avril and Norman; [ed.] Mid Yell Jun High; [occ.] Ferry-Man; [pers.] The healing power of "Spring" after illness, or loss of a loved one; [a.] Shetland Isles, UK

WILLIS, JOYCE

[b.] 20 October 1921, Scarborough; [p.] Clarence John Pickering, Hilda Pickering; [m.] Charles Frederick Willis, 18 October 1952; [ch.] David Charles, Susan Mary, Jacqueline Elizabeth; [ed.] Ordinary Schooling two years Secondary Education at Worksop Central School, Notthinghamshire; [occ.] Housewife; [oth. writ.] I have written 38 poems altogether some about my childhood, others with a religious meaning, and life in general; [pers.] It is just 12 years ago since I started writing. My father was a clergyman and we tended to move about a bit, thus my education rather suffered, I was always good at English, really enjoyed writing. I am often asked to recite my poems at the local churches; [a.] Ebbw Vale, Gwent, UK

WILLMOTT, HAROLD

[pen.] Harold Willmott; [b.] 25 February 1910, Harborne Lane, Selly Oak; [p.] Thomas and Loly Willmott; [m.] Alice Willmott - formally Alice Hunt, 10 September 1932; [ch.] Cynthia, Keith and Valerie; [ed.] St. Wulstans School bournbrooke, Bournville College the Green and Ruskin Hall — Bournville; [occ.] Chocolate and Chemical Plant Supervisor; [memb.] St. John Ambulance Brigade Bournville Word's Division 1939-1986; [hon.] Serving Brother in Order of St. John Honoured by the Queen Award for Service 46 years in the valuable service to mankind; [oth. writ.] Many poems written. Also formulated and prayer for St. John Ambulance Brigade.; [pers.] Have always been able to put words into rhyme. Living alone after it has been my savior.; [a.] Birmingham, Warwickshire, UK

WILSON, BRENDA JEAN

[b.] 21 April 1922, Solihull; [p.] Frank and Frida Chatterley; [m.] Alexander Wilson, 11 August 1945; [ch.] Four daughters, one son (Deceased), nine grandchildren; [ed.] Church of England Boarding School Parkestone, Dorset, University of B'ham, Education Dept, Teacher's Training; [occ.] Retired - infant and Junior Teacher; [memb.] University of B'ham 'Alumni', Church Membership, Amateur Dramatics; [hon.] Various Verse-Speaking Competitions also - Elocution Medals and Award; [oth. writ.] Personal Collection of fair number of poems and some prose I publication recently appeared in 'Poets of the South'; [pers.] I write poetry and prose to express strong emotional feelings on many subjects gathered from personal experience, with a desire to helpfully uplift the thoughts of others.; [a.] Winchester, Hampshire, UK

WILSON, EMMA

[b.] Coventry; [p.] Neil Wilson, Annette Wilson; [ed.] Norwich High School for Girls; [occ.] Studet and Writer; [oth. writ.] A poem published in an anthology, eight unpublished poetry books, seven unpublished novels, one unpublished play.; [pers.] Through my writing I have learnt that: Life is limitless, as if freedom: Take the chances warmly, but let memories make you smile.; [a.] Norwich, Norfolk, UK

WILSON, ESME E.

[b.] 22 June 1942, Northampton; [p.] Irene and Harold Wilson; [ed.] Holy Cross Convent Chalfont St. Peter; [occ.] Retired P.E. Teacher now Aromatherapy and Massage Therapist; [memb.] Barnardos, Royal Life Saving Society, Pinewood Bowling Club, Member Independent Professional Therapists International; [hon.] Service Cross RLSS, Hon. Life Member RLSS; [oth. writ.] Four poems published this year with Arrival Press and Triumph House (Only started to write 18 month, ago).; [pers.] After leaving teaching, I felt the need to write and express. It has now developed into a passion. After 54 years I am allowing my 'creative' side some freedom! Very exciting and great fun.; [a.] Hindolveston, Norfolk, UK

WILSON, MS. FIONA

[b.] 19 May 1974, Bedford; [p.] Mr. S. D. Wilson (Deceased) and Mrs. E. Wilson; [ed.] Ursula Taylor Lower, Lincroft Middle, Sharn Brook Upper; [occ.] Aestiatition; [memb.] International Federation of Holistic Therapists; [hon.] City and Guilds Beauty Therapy, IFHB International Therapist; [a.] Bedford, Bedfordshire, UK

WILSON, HAZEL

[b.] October 27, 1935, Belfast; [p.] Mother - Martina Harriette; [ch.] Graeme - Nephew, Gillian - Niece; [ed.] A3 Level Standard, 1. Religious Education, 2. Sociology, 3. English Literature, RFN, SRM, SLM, O.N.D.; [occ.] Early Retirement Nursing (Ophthalmics) Sister; [memb.] "International Ophthalmology Nursing Association", Iowa Bloomfield Baptist Church, Choir; [hon.] "Ophthalmology Nursing Diploma"; [oth. writ.] "Snippets in Hospital Magazine", "Hospital Leaflets", "Creative Writing for Patients", wrote short appraisal of its therapy. 15 poems, variety of subjects e.g. childhood years. First Love, Sunshine Hope, Christmas Bells, Sunshine Fear.; [pers.] From an early age I have always enjoyed reading poetry. Now I love expressing my thoughts in poetic form and just write for pleasure. I hope to publish a book of poems in the future; [a.] Dundonald, Down, UK

WILSON, HERBERT
[b.] 24 April 1936, Wymondham; [p.] Charles Wilson, Ada Wilson; [m.] Divorced; [ch.] Glena Wilson; [ed.] Secondary/various correspondence courses with Trade Union; [occ.] Registered disabled unemployed, mainly paralysis; [memb.] Labour Party, Transport and General Workers Union, former: County/Urban District and Town Councilor; [hon.] Silver Badge LP; [oth. writ.] Published poetry in over eight anthologies/county mag. and smaller mags., articles in newspaper and mag.; [pers.] The human race must mature, to solve the problems of the world.; [a.] Wymondham, Norfolk, UK

WILSON, NORMA
[b.] 12 February 1937, Portland Bill, Dorset; [p.] Stanley and Elsie Jarrett; [m.] Norman Wilson, 22 October 1955; [ch.] Cathryn Georgia; [ed.] Copnor Secondary, Modern School Portsmouth Hants; [occ.] Health Care Assistant; [memb.] I am not a Member of any Society but my Hobbies are Sewing Salt Dough Craft, Playing the Piano and Gardening; [oth. writ.] Although I have written poetry for many years, this is the first time I have ever sent one to a publisher. I have never entered a competition before either, so I am very pleased to have a poem published.; [pers.] I find I can express myself in poetry much easier than in any other way. My father also wrote poetry so I think I have inherited this from him.; [a.] Polesworth, North Warks, UK

WILSON, PATRICIA
[b.] Scotland; [p.] John and Agnes McGarry; [ch.] Three; [ed.] G.C.S.E. English Language; [occ.] Housewife; [pers.] I have always been drawn to poetry - it has been therapeutic for me and gave me great strength to cope with the harsh realities of life. My true survival kit!; [a.] Rochdale, UK

WILSON, ROBERT
[pen.] Robert; [b.] 30 May 1919, Saltcoats; [p.] Deceased; [m.] Margt. McLardy (Deceased), 1 November 1944; [ch.] Sandra (Daughter); [ed.] Adrossan Academy; [occ.] Retired Ex Royal Navy; [memb.] West Kilbride Bowling Club; [oth. writ.] Made several poem's for my own amusement but never entered any competitions.; [pers.] I strive to follow the works of Robert Burn's bringing comedy and the behaviour of children into my poems. Writing one at the moment. Title (Jill's Devotion).; [a.] West Kilbride, Ayrshire, Scotland

WILSON, SUSAN
[pen.] T. E. Darwin (Sometimes/novels); [b.] 20 May 1936, Alton, Hants, UK; [p.] Mary and Joseph Phillips; [m.] Divorced, 26 December 1957; [ch.] Chris and Carol; [ed.] Eggars Grammar School Alton, Hants; [occ.] Retired but writing daily; [memb.] Newswriters Club, Trollope Society, Poetry Society; [hon.] Finalist in first Lichfield prize, 1989, successful participant in world one day novel cup contest 1995; [oth. writ.] Poetry in other anthologies, Musings, The West In Her Eyes, A Passage In Time. Poetry collection - 'Living With It' poetic account of survival after three strokes and permanent half paralysis. Seven unpublished novels.; [pers.] I continue to write against the odds with God's good grace and travel the world with determination, stick and trolley hence the villanelle; [a.] Burgess Hill, W. Sussex, UK

WILSON, YVONNE
[pen.] Yvonne Wilson-Hall; [b.] 7 June 1958, Hurley, Staffs; [p.] Beryl and Tom Wagstaff; [m.] Victor Harry Wilson, 25 February 1922; [ch.] 1. Stewart Harry and 2. Dean Victor; [ed.] Wilnecote High School, Nr Tamworth Staffs and Atherstone High School, Atherstone, Warks); [occ.] Telephonist-Receptionist; [oth. writ.] Small private collection of poems and children's stories written for and about my boys. None published.; [pers.] I write. About life as I see it influenced by the emotions and thoughts that situations provoke.; [a.] Northfield, West Midlands, UK

WILTON, LINDA R.
[b.] 12 March 1944, Worthing; [p.] Edgar and Doris Wilton; [ed.] Sandhurst Private Junior School and Worthing Technical High School; [occ.] Local Government Officer; [memb.] Founder Ex-Member of Brighton Festival Chorus, Choir member at St. Columba's Church; [oth. writ.] Purely personal poems as a Hobby.; [pers.] Experiencing the finest emotions, and holding the simplest yet deepest faith, can inspire the greatest work in all of us.; [a.] Worthing, West Sussex, UK

WINDLE, WENDY PATRICIA PENELOPE
[pen.] Wendy Windle; [b.] 12 October 1941, Salford; [p.] Marjorie and Harrold Sheppard; [m.] Stanley Windle MBE MIMF, 2 September 1961; [ed.] Cheetah Hill Methodist Primary School 1946-1952 Broughton High School for girls 1952-1957; [occ.] Retired Executive Officer; [oth. writ.] Many other poems all unpublished.; [pers.] Most of my poems have been written at times of crisis in my life. All have been written in the wee small hours of the morning when my mind seems to be at it's most productive.; [a.] Stockport, Cheshire, UK

WINGROVE, JOY
[b.] 10 February 1936, Sheffield; [p.] Percy Moor and Ethel Leech; [m.] Charles Wingrove, 2 October 1982; [ch.] Robert, Lorraine; [ed.] Dronfield Grammar School Derbyshire; [occ.] Nurse (Retired); [memb.] Royal College of Nursing, Motor Carvan Club; [hon.] Registered General Nurse, Registered Mental Nurse, Occupational Health Nurse (RGN), (RMN), (OHNC); [oth. writ.] Other poems and short stories (un-published as yet) this is my first published work.; [pers.] I wrote this poem a long time ago to my boyfriend, Brian, who was with the cold stream guards in Egypt. We were sweethearts from school days. Due to a misunderstanding we both married other partners but kept in touch until he died, a few years ago.; [a.] Lincoln, Lincs, UK

WINTERLUM, MOE
[b.] 28 May 1904, Quinton, Birmingham; [ed.] Tenter Street School Halerowen West Midlands; [occ.] Hairdresser for 57 years

WITNEY, KENNETH P.
[b.] 19 March 1916, Madanapalle, South India; [p.] Rev. T. C. and Dr. Myfanwy Witney; [m.] Joan Tait (Deceased), 5 April 1947; [ch.] Jane Witney-Smith, Nicholas Witney; [ed.] Hebron School, Coonor, India, Eltham College, Wadham College, Oxford (Scholar); [occ.] Retired Civil Servant (Home Office); [memb.] Kent Historical Society, Kent Archaeological Society; [hon.] M.A. (Oxon), C.V.O. DIP Arch. (Kent); [oth. writ.] The Jutish Forest (Athlone, 1976), The Kingdom of Kent (Phillimore, 1982); [pers.] This is one of a few, sporadic, poetical gleanings over a long life otherwise engaged - with early Kentish history a particular interest.; [a.] Tonbridge, Kent, UK

WOBO, AUSTIN
[pen.] Stino Tingle; [b.] 25 May 1970, Port Harcourt; [p.] Chief Ben I. Wobo (Late), Betty Wobo; [ed.] Bachelor of Science (BSC. Hons. Biochemistry) University of Port Harcourt, Rivers State, (1992), Nigeria; [occ.] Operations and Field Officer Bon Engineering Nig. Ltd.; [memb.] Nigerian Environmental Society, Friends of the Pen Society of Nigeria; [hon.] Nigerian Guinea Worm Eradication Programme (Niger) "Merit Award" (Under the Global 2000) 1993. National Youth Service Corps (NYSC) "Commendation Award" 1993; [oth. writ.] Most of my writings are unpublished, this includes: "Manna for Dead", "Bent Waist of Sustenance, "Storm of the Heart", "Fountain Head of Creation", "Hour Before Dawn", etc.; [pers.] The fetus of our dream world is our unseen tomorrow, it must be nurtured and feed with positive potentials, so we can be awaken to the realities we so deserve.; [a.] Port Harcourt, Nigeria

WOOD, BARBARA
[b.] 5 May 1937, Hull; [p.] Lily Sydney, Robert Hawkins; [m.] Bernard, 31 March 1956; [ch.] Tracy, Gillian Teresa, Kerry, Louise, Granddaughter Kodie Lily Wood; [ed.] Standard Education; [occ.] Teacher's Aide; [oth. writ.] One other poem "My 58th Birthday"; [pers.] I wrote this poem after working in a geography lesson at greatfield school it is now known as Isaac Newton school erosion is inevitable but sad; [a.] Hull, Yorkshire, UK

WOOD, DENISE
[pen.] Denise King; [b.] 25 September 1953, Dublin; [p.] Christopher and Eileen King; [ch.] Three; [ed.] Dominican Convent Primary Dominican Convent Secondary; [hon.] 1st Prize Cookery Award RSA Typing; [oth. writ.] I was inspired by Frank O'Connor and William Wordsworth among others.; [pers.] To live without hopes and dreams, is like the universe without the earth.; [a.] Rotherham, South Yorks, UK

WOOD, JAMES
[pen.] James Wood, James Lakeland; [b.] 30 January 1969, Kirkcaldy; [p.] Jim Wood, Katrina Wood; [m.] Charlotte Hellen Jean Wood, 28 July 1994; [ch.] One baby boy Wesley James; [ed.] Kirkcaldy High School, (Associated Board Of The) Royal School of Music, London; [occ.] Music Teacher, Composer; [hon.] LTCL Diploma (Music Award); [oth. writ.] A forever growing catalogue of songs and jingles recorded and published both home and abroad.; [pers.] I aspire to write lyrics that are meaningful and interesting, a poem in their own write, so music an only further enhance the power of the message I want to convey.; [a.] Kirkcaldy, Fife, UK

WOOD, LORNA ELIZABETH
[b.] 25 September 1981, Sheffield; [p.] Alan Wood, Elizabeth Wood; [ed.] Stocksbridge High School; [occ.] Student; [pers.] Let there always be open spaces to where we can all escape.; [a.] Sheffield, South Yorkshire, UK

WOOD, NICOLA
[pen.] Ryma John Lanark; [b.] 5 July 1979, Glasgow; [p.] Peter Wood, Elizabeth Wood; [ed.] Westhill Academy, Aberdeenshire; [occ.] School pupil at Westhill Academy; [memb.] Youth Theatre, Episcopal Church; [hon.] Nine Scotvec's, seven standard grades, two highers; [oth. writ.] A play called "Jeely Piece" plus several unpublished

short stories and poems; [pers.] We don't read and write poetry because it is fun or educated, we, read and write poetry because it is a way a crying heart and a screaming soul can be noticed and heard.; [a.] Westhill, Aberdeenshire, UK

WOOD, ROD
[pen.] Rod Wood; [b.] 24 September 1944, Newbury; [p.] Father disappeared 1957 (Mother still alive); [m.] Divorced, 1st 1966 - 2nd 1983; [ch.] Three daughters and one granddaughter; [ed.] Wandsworth School, Hammersmith College of Art and Croydon College of Theatre Design, Royal Court Theatre - National Theatre, Royal Opera - House - Old Vic etc.; [occ.] Scenic Artist; [memb.] BECTV and Equity; [hon.] Scenic Artist for British Theatre, Designer and Scenic Artist for Pantomine, Scenic Artist for British and International Businesses. Conferences - Trade Shows - Seminars.; [oth. writ.] A serious account of hell and a speculation of heaven 1964-1980. (Avon Books - first published 1995), ISBN 1-86033-038X.; [pers.] There seems to be much knowledge around but very little originality - if any. But it lurks and only just out f reach. Maybe knowledge could persuade.; [a.] Putney, London, UK

WOODFIELD, MRS. IDRIS
[b.] Birmigham; [memb.] Edgbaston Old Church Choir; [oth. writ.] Poems broadcast in the Midland home service 'Midland Poets. Also published in prospect, and anthologies the heart of England, South East voices, messengers for God, journeys to God, and our hopes for the future.; [pers.] I strive to reflect the beauty of nature in my poetry.; [a.] Chichester, West Sussex, UK

WOODHEAD, DUNCAN
[b.] 27 November 1975, Bristol; [p.] David Peter, Jane Woodhead; [m.] Elizabeth Derrick (Fiancee); [ed.] Currently Studying for a BA Hons in Politics/Economic and Social History at Strathclyde University; [occ.] Student; [memb.] Campaign for Real Ale (Camra), University Debates Society, University Christian Union; [pers.] I write poetry purely for pleasure, and generally when an event impresses upon me to do so. I would claim to have no great influences though Elizabeth inspires me often enough.; [a.] Glasgow, Strathclyde, UK

WOODROW, SYLVIA M.
[b.] 25 December 1981; [ch.] Three; [oth. writ.] Poems in my own book. One poems in "Poetry now 1994" (The Cottage Garden) 1 short story written last year. My First and Only and I was 76 at the time.; [pers.] I did not start to write until in my late 50's I am now a widow, spring was my first attempt and we really did see the blackbird and the daffodils etc. So it was for my husband. I seem to write with a sense of humor, sometimes, with a moral at the end.; [a.] Scunthorpe, Lincs, UK

WOOLLEY, DONNA
[pen.] Megan Rose; [b.] 4 March 1963, Trowbridge; [p.] Trevor and Irene Burbidge; [m.] Peter John Woolley, 10 September 1983; [ch.] Foster two children: Kerry and Daniel; [ed.] Forest and Sandridge Primary School then George Ward School Melksham, Wiltshire; [occ.] Lady Remington Jewelry Consultant; [memb.] Trowbridge Evangelical Church; [hon.] City and Guilds - Desk Top Publishing RSA Word Processing o Level Art; [oth. writ.] "Holiday's" published in 'Wiltshire Times' When I was Twelve Years Old. "The Queen Who's Known As Lilibet" Sent

To The Queen for her Jubilee, which was acknowledge.; [pers.] I try to draw people back to the wonders of creation, my love is laughter a necessity in todays world.; [a.] Trowbridge, Wiltshire, UK

WORRALL, NANCY
[pen.] Rebecca Barnett, Nancy Worrall; [b.] 9 April 1923, Newcastle-upon-Tyne; [p.] George Barnett, Ann Barnett (Nee Buchanan); [m.] Gordon, 20 July 1945; [ch.] Janice and Barry; [ed.] Whitehall Rd Central girls, Gateshead; [occ.] Retired; [memb.] RAF Association; [hon.] Publishers best year book for novel "Mellie" 1978; [oth. writ.] Two novels, `WAAF' autobiography, competitions book, odd articles.; [pers.] It doesn't take a reader to become a writer, just good observation and much imagination.!; [a.] Newcastle-upon-Tyne, UK

WRAY, JAMES T.
[b.] 3 July 1938, Caledon; [p.] James and Mary Wray; [m.] Kathleen Teresa, 10 September 1962; [ch.] James Thomas and John Patrick; [ed.] Caledon National Primary School, Dungannon Technical College; [occ.] Early retirement due to ill health; [memb.] Dungannon Golf Club, I also visit schools when invited, to talk to the children about me, and poetry in general; [hon.] Having a few of my works published this meant a lot to me as I missed out on my early education for various reasons; [oth. writ.] The Gift of Peace (pub.), Thanking God (published), My Wife is My Life (published), Let's (published), Reminder to a Human Race (published), Sweet Tyrone (published); [pers.] Poetry is my way of expressing myself. It helps me to see as other poets see life. It is a wonderful way to catalogue life and events for future generations. I owe great thanks to my dear old primary teacher Miss Mary O'Neill and to my wife Kathleen for encouragement.; [a.] Caledon, Tyrone, UK

WRIGHT, BEVERLEY JANE
[pen.] Beverley Wright, Beverley Belding; [b.] 3 April 1958, Westcliff-on-Sea, Essex; [p.] Thomas Wright, Ann Wright; [ch.] Serena Janeann Wright; [ed.] Comprehensive and High School, Private, Vocational and Community Colleges; [occ.] Mother and student; [memb.] U.S. Trotting Association, British Horse Society and affiliations. Woodford County Riding Club, Rospa and Southend Advanced Driving Associations, Salle Volte Dancing Club; [hon.] Numerous in several areas of work and activities; [oth. writ.] Poems, Stories, Screenplays artwork, articles in magazines, children's books; [pers.] God, give us grace to accept with serenity the things that cannot be changed, courage to change the things which should be changed, and the wisdom to distinguish the one from the other. (Reinhold Niebuhr, The Serenity Prayer); [a.] Southend-on-Sea, Essex, UK

WRIGHT, CLAIRE EMILY
[b.] 14 May 1979, Pontefract; [p.] Colin and Brenda Wright; [ed.] Hemsworth High School Pontefract, West Yorkshire; [occ.] Student taking GNVQ advanced business; [memb.] Former member of Minsthorpe Music Centre; [hon.] Passed 3 GCSE's (French, Drama, Design) and passed with merit three grades for flute; [oth. writ.] Other small poems within a note book; [pers.] I only write about what I feel and see, so all my work either comes from the heart or what catches my eyes.; [a.] Pontefract, West Yorkshire, UK

WRIGHT, FRANK
[b.] 30 January 1921, Sheffield; [p.] Deceased; [m.] Doris, 1 September 1990; [ed.] Elementary Crookesmoor Council Boys School Sheffield; [occ.] Senior Citizen; [oth. writ.] Trying to get publication of poems for donations to leukaemia.; [pers.] All my life I have had a flair for english language and enjoy writing of the satirical kind.; [a.] Sheffield, Yorkshire, UK

WRIGHT, HELEN ANNA
[pen.] Anna Zurlinden; [b.] Canton Aargau, Switzerland; [p.] Fritz Wespi, Helen Gertrude Wespi; [m.] Widowed in 1992; [ch.] Merryl, Shirley, Brenda, Brian; [ed.] Ursuline Convent in London Finishing School in Switzerland; [occ.] Retired. Attend Higher Education Colleges and Summer Schools; [memb.] Association of Historians, Welsh Academy, London Region Arts club connected with Open university.; [hon.] BA (Hons) Art History and Literature (English and European) Honours Art Certificate - Royal Drawing Society.; [oth. writ.] Articles in Parish magazine of Benedictine Church and Monastery of Christ the King, London N14 4HE Have submitted poems to Welsh Academy.; [pers.] I strive to reflect in my writing my country of origin, Switzerland, and the attitude of people to care about and protect the land and flora and fauna. These characteristics are inherent in the Swiss. However I am content to live in London which offers so much. Poets with whom I feel a special affinity are Blake, Byron, Keats, Tynnyson and Gerald Manley.; [a.] London, Hopkins, UK

WRIGHT, LINDA JAYNE
[pen.] Linda Handley-Wright; [b.] 2 March 1963, Derby; [p.] Mr. Peter and Mrs. Patricia Handley; [m.] Mr. Peter Richard Wright, 3 October 1987; [ch.] Charlotte Lynette Wright; [ed.] Littleover School, Pastures Hill, Littleover, Derby; [occ.] Writer; [memb.] Arab Horse Society, The Midland Railway Trust; [oth. writ.] Several articles for magazines which specialist in horses. Current projects include the writing of a period novel, research for a further book, various poetry competitions.; [pers.] My greatest virtue has to be that of endless determination.; [a.] Derby, Derbyshire, UK

WYLDE, LEANNE
[b.] 11 July 1981, Wallasey; [p.] Moira and Jimmy Wylde; [ed.] Oldershaw, Secondary School; [a.] Wallasey, Merseyside, UK

YARWOOD, DAVID A.
[b.] 16 March 1947, Essex; [p.] William Yarwood; [m.] Grace McAllister, 3 September 1966 - 3 January 1992; [ch.] Dale Spencer, Gaynor Elizabeth; [ed.] Lyndhurst Secondary Modern; [occ.] Team Leader; [pers.] My poems reflect some of my feelings through the different events in my life, also memories and imagination of the past.; [a.] Luton, Bedfordshire, UK

YOUNG, JAMES ROBERT
[pen.] James Robert Young; [b.] 25 August 1928, Hertforyshire; [p.] James and Edith Young (Deceased); [m.] Audrey Young (Deceased), 2 June 1951; [ch.] Diane Lydia and John Anthony; [ed.] Gladstone Street Technical School - Darlington; [occ.] Retired; [memb.] "Barbican Centre", Corporation of London; [oth. writ.] "Numerous poems", in book form.; [pers.] Poems: Lighthouses Erected in the Sea of Time.; [a.] Heighington Village, Durham, UK

YOUNG, RUTH MARGARET
[pen.] Ruth Margaret Young; [b.] 19 May 1947, Croydon, Surrey; [m.] Derek Young, 24 December 1992; [ch.] Kim Eileen (Born 19 February 67) and 3 grand children; [ed.] Secondary Modern, Wallington, Surrey - failed all exams!; [occ.] Post - 16 Tutor - Teaching Business Admin and it (computers); [memb.] Own animal sanctuary for beaten and starved animals - hence poo corner - house name; [hon.] Post - 16 teacher's certificate, certificate in education, D32/D33 Assessors award, Now in 2nd year of BA (hons) Education and Training Degree Course. (Uni of greenwich) Distance Learning; [oth. writ.] "Tomorrow" in faith in verse, published in 1994 by anchor books, ed. michelle abbott, ISBN I 85930 1681; [pers.] After 31 years professional Business Women and surviving cancer I decided to become a teacher. I have proved that all things are possible if you have the will and motivations to succeed.; [a.] Canterbury, Kent, UK

YOUNGMAN, CHERYL
[b.] 4 July 1955, South Lopham, Norfolk; [p.] Sydney Garnham, Joan Garnham; [m.] Bernard Youngman, 8 May 1976; [ch.] James Barnaby, Kristopher Jon; [ed.] Diss Secondary Modern; [memb.] Jehovah's Witness; [pers.] In search of love and truth.; [a.] Fersfield, Norfolk, UK

YUSOF, AMIR ALFATAKH
[pen.] Yoep; [b.] 1 October 1971, Kuala Lumpur, Malaysia; [p.] Yusof Yatim, Zawiyah Mohd; [ed.] University of Hull; [occ.] Student and worldwide traveller; [oth. writ.] Articles published in magazines and local newspaper; [pers.] It is amazing what you can see if you pay a bit more attention to life. But although living in a beautiful country do inspire, there is still no place like home.

ZAMMIT, ALDO
[b.] 4 June 1979; [p.] Joseph and Monica; [pers.] The Poem is a symphony of the Self. I especially criticize mass production and whatever corrupts individuality. I'm allured and influenced by the mystic and abstruse. In each work of mine are the notes which will ultimately compose the symphony.; [a.] Paola, Malta

ZAMMIT, SYLVIA
[b.] 23 June 1955, Malta; [p.] Joe Zammit, Stella Zammit; [occ.] Teacher in a Local State School - 1 year; [hon.] Last year I won first and second prize in a local competition.; [oth. writ.] Several poems (in Maltese) published in local papers, and in 2 anthologies. Some poems have also been broadcast on a local radio station.; [pers.] I believe life is a precious gift of God. In my poems I try to focus on the beauty that surrounds us - but that we tend to overlook. Working with little children helps!; [a.] Zabbar, Malta

ZHI-JUN, WANG
[occ.] Professor of English, Changchun University, People's Republic of China; [memb.] Visiting Scholar to Faculty of English, University of Cambridge; [oth. writ.] Some of the books: English-Chinese Dictionary of Banking, A Guide to the Correct English Grammar, A Guide to the English Language Learning; [pers.] Life is a poem of Nature, which I try to write better. Into it I put my heart, and it is stirring my blood.; [a.] Cambridge, UK

ZOBOKI, MYRA
[pen.] Myra Jones; [b.] 28 August 1940, Bridgend; [p.] Olwen Jones and Alfred Jones; [m.] Denes Pal Zoboki, 26 September 1959; [ch.] Gary Denes and Floyd Paul; [ed.] Park Street Sec-Modern, Wellingborough, Northants; [occ.] P/T Shop Assistant; [hon.] School prize for English, on leaving school; [oth. writ.] Recently finished a romantic novel titled - shadows of guilt, but I have not yet tried to get it published; [pers.] I am a very private person and find that writing helps to release some tension and helps to build my confidence, I write what I feel, and feel what I write.; [a.] Wellingbord, Northants, UK

ZULFEQUER, UMBREEN
[b.] 25 July 1983, Bury; [p.] (Dad) Zulfequer Khan, (Mum) Zahida Khan; [ed.] Broad Oak High School, Bury; [occ.] Full time high school pupil; [memb.] The Local Newspaper Writing Club, Art Club at School, Member of the Youth Forum Police Committee, and a member of The Urdu Language Club at School; [hon.] I have had one of my stories published in a schools a journal. Have received 5 achievements awards including for Art, religious studies and technology in school. I have won a number of competitions in newspapers.; [oth. writ.] A personal incident which I wrote as a story was published in an associated primary schools journal story's name was "A Broken Jug".; [pers.] Life is a journey, and we are all travelers so let's make it a pleasant trip - not just for ourselves but for everybody.; [a.] Bury, Lancashire, UK

Index
of
Poets